To AND

1988

# THE
# OXFORD
# HANDY
# DICTIONARY

# THE
# OXFORD
# HANDY
# DICTIONARY

First edited by
F. G. and H.W. Fowler

CHANCELLOR
PRESS

*Oxford University Press, Walton Street, Oxford* OX2 6DP

*London Glasgow New York Toronto*
*Delhi Bombay Calcutta Madras Karachi*
*Kuala Lumpur Singapore Hong Kong Tokyo*
*Nairobi Dar es Salaam Cape Town*
*Melbourne Auckland*
*and associates in*
*Beirut Berlin Ibadan Mexico City Nicosia*

**British Library Cataloguing in Publication Data**
The pocket Oxford dictionary of current
English. – 6th ed.
1. English language – Dictionaries
I. Sykes, John Bradbury
423      PE1625    77-30724
ISBN 0-19-861129-3

First published
in Great Britain in 1978 by
Oxford University Press under the title
*The Pocket Oxford Dictionary (Sixth Edition)*

This edition published in 1986 by
Chancellor Press
59 Grosvenor Street
London W1

Reprinted 1987

ISBN 1 85152 032 5

Printed in Austria

# PREFACE TO THE SIXTH EDITION

This sixth edition of the *Pocket Oxford Dictionary* represents a thorough revision, based largely on the latest (1976) edition of the *Concise Oxford Dictionary* and on the most recent materials available from the work still in progress on the new *Supplement to the Oxford English Dictionary*. The typography has also been modified in the same way as in the new *Concise*, with the same aim of greater ease of use.

American spellings are systematically included, and the symbol * now denotes 'chiefly American'; the symbol ‖ is used for 'chiefly British'. The appendices of abbreviations and foreign-word pronunciations have been incorporated into the main text. The publication of the late Professor Grahame Johnston's *Australian Pocket Oxford Dictionary* (1976) has made it unnecessary to retain the supplement of Australian and New Zealand words that appeared at the end of the previous edition.

Many hands besides my own have helped towards the creation of the new edition. The lexicographical skill of F. G. Fowler laid the foundations, before his untimely death left his brother H. W. Fowler to finish the compilation of the original *Pocket Oxford Dictionary* (1924). The task of keeping abreast of the continually evolving English language was successively undertaken by H. G. Le Mesurier and E. McIntosh before being entrusted to me. I could not have completed the revision so soon without the aid of valued colleagues. Mr. Robert W. Burchfield, C.B.E., Chief Editor of the Oxford English Dictionaries, has provided much helpful guidance. The initial revision of the entries has been largely done by three editorial assistants: Mr. Tony Augarde, Miss Jean Buchanan (Mrs. Harker), and Miss Julia Swannell; the late Dr. Rashid Ball, Miss Joyce Hawkins, and Mr. Lister Matheson also contributed. Mr. David Edmonds has read all the proofs, and Mr. Augarde many of them; substantial critical comments on the proofs have come from Mrs. W. K. Davin, Mr. M. W. Grose, Mr. T. F. Hoad, Mrs. E. J. Pusey, and Professor E. G. Stanley. Mrs. Anne Whear has given help with typing and in other ways. To all these, and to the many others who have drawn my attention in personal discussion or by correspondence to possible improvements, is due a share of whatever credit this new version of the *Pocket Oxford Dictionary* may be found to justify.

J.B.S.

*June* 1977

*From the*

# PREFACE TO THE FIRST EDITION

This book is nominally an abridgement of the *Concise Oxford Dictionary*, but has in fact cost its compilers more labour, partly because the larger book was found not to be easily squeezable, and partly owing to changes in method unconnected with mere reduction of quantity. The one merit, however, that they feel entitled to claim for the *C.O.D.* has been preserved to the best of their power in the abridgement—that is, they have kept to the principle that a dictionary is a book of diction, concerned primarily with words or phrases as such, and not, except so far as is needed to ensure their right treatment in speech, with the things those words and phrases stand for. This principle, while it absolves the dictionary-maker from cumbering his pages with cyclopaedic information, demands on the other hand that he should devote much more space than that so saved to the task of making clear the idiomatic usage of words. The bad dictionary, on a word that has half a dozen distinct meanings, parades by way of definition half a dozen synonyms, each of them probably possessed of several senses besides the one desired, and fails to add the qualifications and illustrations that would show the presumably ignorant reader how far each synonym is coextensive with his word, and what is the context to which one or the other is the more appropriate. To avoid this vice has been the chief aim of the *C.O.D.* and of this abridgement alike; but the smaller the scale of the book, the more difficult becomes the task.

F.G.F.
H.W.F.

1917

# INTRODUCTION

In this dictionary, the compilers have tried to present the maximum amount of useful information on present-day English that can be got into an easily portable volume. The reader is urged to study the following explanations in order to gain as much benefit as possible from what is in the book.

Although many examples of words in phrases or sentences are given, they can only be *examples*, and many similar expressions are necessarily omitted. The addition of 'etc.' sometimes hints at this, but is avoided where it would not clearly convey anything about the nature of other equally usual expressions.

There are numerous cross-references, shown by words in SMALL CAPITALS; for example, '**ā′blў**. See ABLE.' These always mean that further information will be found by consulting the entry so indicated.

The entry word (headword) is in **bold type,** or in ***bold italic*** if it is not yet naturalized in English and is usually found in italics in printed matter (for example, ***ab initio***). Raised figures (as in **bail**[1]) are used to distinguish two or more headwords having the same spelling. Derivatives are in bold type (**ă′bbėss** under **ă′bbot**), compounds and phrases in **semi-bold** (**~-bodied** and **~ seaman** under **ā′ble, out of ~** under **ă′ction**). The swung dash ~ is used to save space by standing for either the headword (*able, action*) or the part of the headword that is to the left of a vertical line (*abdic* at **ă′bdĭc|āte**, where **~ā′tion** = **ăbdĭcā′tion**).

A hyphen that happens to fall at the end of a line (for example, in 'sun-dried' at *adobe*) is repeated at the start of the next line to make clear that it does not arise simply from the usual practice of hyphenating a word divided between lines.

Where a word can function as three or more parts of speech, they are listed at the start of the entry.

Round brackets ( ) enclose letters or words that are explanatory or optional, for example, the labels of subject or usage such as (Law) or (literary), and the typical objects 'pain' and 'evil' for the verb *alleviate*; at *Aberdeen*, they show that 'Aberdeen Angus' can mean either the breed or an animal of that breed, and that an Aberdeen terrier may also be called just an Aberdeen. Subject or usage labels followed by a definition that begins with a capital letter apply as far as the next full stop.

Italic words in definitions are those normally used with the headword, for example *to* with *able* (I am able to go); ordinary (roman) type occurs within italics or semi-bold to show the possibility of replacement by other words, for example 'one' in *abandon* one*self*, which may be replaced by *my*, *him*, and so on.

There are bound to be occasions when a word or meaning or expression is sought in vain, probably because it was judged too uncommon or too specialized to deserve inclusion. The *Concise Oxford Dictionary* and the larger dictionaries in the Oxford series are available to fill such gaps.

## PREFIXES AND SUFFIXES

Many English words are formed by adding prefixes or suffixes to existing words (as when *taste* becomes *distaste* or *tasteful* or *tasteless*), and this should always be kept in mind if a word is not found in the dictionary.

In particular, in order not to waste space, words formed by nine suffixes are not given unless they present some special feature of spelling, pronunciation, or meaning, beyond what is stated in the respective entries for the suffixes (which should be consulted for further information). These nine are:

*-able* added to transitive verbs (although *-ible* forms such as *expressible* are sometimes more usual)                                   as in      *findable*

*-er* denoting one who does an action, added to verbs (although *-or* forms such as *collector* are sometimes more usual)                                    *feaster*

*-er* and *-est* denoting comparative and superlative, added (where comparison is possible) to adjectives or adverbs of one syllable, and to adjectives of two syllables ending in a consonant + *y*                                        *fresher, furriest*

*-ish* added to nouns and adjectives                   *frumpish, firmish*

*-less* added to nouns                                        *finless*

| | | |
|---|---|---|
| *-like* added to nouns | as in | *froglike* |
| *-ly* forming an adverb, added to adjectives (though rarely to those which themselves end in *-ly*, as *holy*) | | *fearsomely* |
| *-ness* added to adjectives | | *forcefulness* |

They can be attached to *any* word of the corresponding kind. See under -ABLE, -ER[2], -ISH, and 'Inflexion' below (paragraphs 3 and 5) for further information about spelling-rules.

Words formed by other suffixes are given if they are in current use, but are not defined if their meaning can be deduced from those of the original word and the suffix.

For example, *addable* from *add*, *adder-like* from *adder*, *adroitly* and *adroitness* from *adroit*, are not given at all; *addiction* from *addict*, *adequacy* from *adequate*, *adjectival* from *adjective*, are given but not defined.

The prefixes explained in their dictionary places are:

*a-, ab-, abs-, ac-, ad-, af-, ag-, al-, an-, ana-, ante-, anti-, ap-, apo-, ar-, arch-, as-, at-, auto-, be-, bi-, cata-, circum-, cis-, co-, col-, com-, con-, contra-, cor-, counter-, de-, demi-, di-, dia-, dif-, dis-, dys-, e-, ef-, em-, en-, epi-, eu-, ex-*[1, 2]*, extra-, for-, fore-, hemi-, hyper-, hypo-, il-*[1, 2]*, im-*[1, 2]*, in-*[1, 2]*, infra-, inter-, intra-, ir-*[1, 2]*, mal-, meta-, micro-, mini-, mis-, multi-, neo-, non-, ob-, oc-, of-, off-, omni-, on-, op-, out-, over-, pan-, para-*[1, 2]*, per-, peri-, poly-, post-, pre-, pro-*[1, 2]*, quasi-, re-*[1, 2]*, retro-, self-, semi-, step-, sub-, suc-, suf-, sug-, sup-, super-, supra-, sur-*[1, 2]*, sus-, syl-, sym-, syn-, trans-, tri-, ultra-, un-, under-, up-, vice-*.

The suffixes explained in their dictionary places are:

*-able, -ac, -aceous, -acy, -al, -an, -ana, -ance, -ancy, -ant, -ar, -ary, -ate, -ation, -bility, -cle, -cracy, -crat, -cratic(al), -cule, -cy, -cyte, -dom, -ectomy, -ed*[1, 2]*, -ee, -eer, -en, -ence, -ency, -ent, -er*[1] (agent), *-er*[2] *and -est, -ery, -esque, -ess, -eth, -ette, -ey, -faction, -ferous, -fic, -fication, -fold, -form, -ful, -fy, -gon, -gram, -graph, -grapher, -graphic(al), -graphy, -hood, -ial, -ian, -ible, -ic, -ical, -ician, -ics, -ide, -ie, -ine, -ing*[1, 2]*, -ion, -ise, -ish, -ism, -ist, -ite, -itic, -itis, -ity, -ive, -ization, -ize, -kin, -less, -let, -like, -ling, -logic(al), -logist, -logy, -ly*[1, 2]*, -mania(c), -ment, -meter, -metric(al), -metry, -mo, -most, -nce, -ncy, -ness, -nik, -nt, -o, -oid, -ol, -or, -ory, -ose, -osis, -osity, -ous, -phil(e), -phobe, -phobia, -phobic, -proof, -ry, -scope, -scopic, -ship, -shire, -so(ever), -some, -ster, -teen, -th, -tron, -tude, -ty*[1, 2]*, -ule, -ure, -ward(s), -ways, -wise, -worthy, -y*[1, 2]*.

# PRONUNCIATION

Only the pronunciation standard in Southern England is given. Where possible, the pronunciation is shown in the bold type; if not, part or all of the word is respelt in round brackets ( ). See 4 below for the use of the stress-mark ′.

## 1. With respelling

*Consonants*: b; ch (chin); d; dh (dhĕn = then); f; g (got); h; j; k; l; m; n; ṅ (French nasal; grahṅd = *grande*); ng (sing); ngg (finger); p; r; s; sh (ship); t; th (thin); v; w; y; z; zh (vĭ′zhon = vision); χ (Scots etc.; lŏχ = loch).

*Vowels*: ā ē ī ō ōō ū (fate meet bite goat boot due)
ă ĕ ĭ ŏ ŏŏ ŭ (fat met bit got book dug)
ār ēr īr ūr (fare fear fire pure)
âr êr ôr (far fur port)
ah aw oi oor ow owr (bah paw boil poor brow sour)
*a e i o u* (ago token basin flagon bonus)
*er* (baker)

Vowels such as ĕ may be pronounced in either way, for example as ē or ĕ (zĕ′brа).

Vowel combinations with -r include the consonantal value of r when followed by another vowel (*fearing, far away*).

## 2. Without respelling

The same symbols as above are used, and the following additional rules apply unless shown otherwise in the round brackets, for example at **break** (-āk), **gĕt** (g-), **grā′teful** (-tf-), **lōō′phōle** (-p-h-); in the last of these, the hyphen is used to show that ph is not to be pronounced as in *photo*.

Additional symbols: ė, y̆ = ĭ (nā′kėd, dū′ty̆), îr, ûr = êr (bîrth, bûrn), ȳ = ī (rėlȳ′), ȳr = īr (tȳre).

Final **e** is silent (**āpe**).

Other unmarked vowels correspond to *a* etc. above (**agō′**).

A doubled consonant is pronounced as single (**sĭ′lly̆**). This applies also in such combinations as **ck, dge, ûrr** (**băck, bădge, bûrr**).

Some letters and combinations have special values:
**ae** = ē (**ae′gĭs**), **ai** = ā (**pain**), **air** = ār (**fair**), **au** = aw (**maul**), **aur** = ôr (**dī′nosaur**), **ay** = ā (**say**), **c** before **e**

or **i** or **y** = s (ĭce, cĭ′tў, ĭ′cў, cў′prėss), **c** elsewhere is
'hard' and = k (cŏb, crў, ârc), **ea** = ē (mean), **ear** = ēr
(fear), **ee** = ē (meet), **eer** = ēr (beer), **eu** and **ew** = ū
(feud, few), **g** before **e** or **i** or **y** = j (āge, gĭn, ôr′gў,
gўbe), **g** elsewhere = g (gāme, băg, ôr′gan), **ie** = ē
(thief), **ier** = ēr (pier), **n** before 'hard' **c, k, q, x** = ng
(zĭnc, tănk, bă′nquėt, mĭnx), **oa** = ō (boat), **oar** = ôr
(boar), **ou** = ow (hound), **our** = owr (scour), **oy** = oi
(boy), **ph** = f (phō′tō), **qu** = kw (quĭt), **tion** = shon
(nā′tion, nă′tional), **wh** = w (whĭch), **x** = ks (fŏx);

(beginning a word) **kn-** = n (knŏt); **rh-** and **wr-** = r
(rhўme, wrĭst);

(ending a word) **-age** = ĭj (vĭ′llage), **-ey** = ĭ (dŏ′nkey),
**-le** after a consonant = el (cā′ble), **-ous** = us (fūr′ĭous),
**-sm** = zem (spă′sm), **-ture** = cher (nā′ture).

### 3. *Alternatives*

Alternative accepted pronunciations are shown, separated
by commas or introduced by *or*, but are not necessarily in
order of decreasing frequency of use.

### 4. *Stress*

The main stress or accent is shown by a mark ′ after the
stressed vowel. The stress on a hyphenated compound is
on the first part, and that on a compound written as two
words is on the second part, unless otherwise shown. The
swung dash carries with it the pronunciation and stress of
the word or letters it represents, unless something else is
shown for the derivative where the swung dash is used.

# INFLEXION

The following are the rules for the normal inflected forms of
words, and apply unless something else is shown in semi-bold
in round brackets ( ) after *n., a., adv., v.t.,* or *v.i.* in the
dictionary entry. The term 'sibilants' stands for words
ending in *s, x, z, sh,* or soft *ch,* '-o wds' for all words ending in
*o* but not in *oo,* '-e wds' for all ending in silent *e,* and '-y wds'
for all ending in *y* preceded by a consonant or *qu.*

   1. *Plural of nouns.* Sibilants add *es* (*boxes*); -y wds change *y*

into *ies* (*puppies*); for -o wds the plural is always stated (*photos*, *potatoes*); others add *s* (*books*, *cases*, *ways*).

2. *Possessive of nouns.* Singular nouns add *'s* (*cat's*); plurals ending in the sound of s or z add an apostrophe (*boys'*); other plurals add *'s* (*men's*).

3. *Comparative and superlative of adjectives and adverbs.* Those of one syllable, and -y adjectives of two syllables, add *er*, *est* (*faster*, *quickest*), -e wds dropping the *e* (*braver*) and -y wds changing *y* into *i* (*happiest*). Other adjectives and adverbs use *more* and *most* (*more beautiful*, *most nobly*). Where a doubled consonant is shown, e.g. (-**tt**-) for *fatter*, *fattest*, it occurs also in the derived adjective in -*ish* (*fattish*).

4. *Third person singular present of verbs.* Sibilants and -o wds add *es* (*pushes*, *goes*); -y wds change *y* into *ies* (*carries*); others add *s* (*cuts*, *stays*).

5. *Past tense and past participle of verbs.* -e wds add *d* (*moved*); -y wds change *y* into *ied* (*cried*); others add *ed* (*ended*, *seemed*). If the past tense and past participle are shown as irregular and are different, they are separated by a semicolon (**ran; run**). A single form stands for both (**brought**). Where a doubled consonant is shown, e.g. (-**nn**-) for *pin*, it occurs also in the derived forms in -*able*, -*er*, and -*ing* (*fittable*, *slogger*, *admitting*).

6. *Present participle and gerund of verbs.* All add *ing* (*fishing*, *studying*), -e wds (except those in -*ee*, -*ie*, -*oe*) dropping the *e* (*dancing*, *seeing*).

7. *Archaic second and third person singular of verbs* are formed in -(*e*)*st* for the second and -(*e*)*th* for the third person (*playest*, *canst*, *sangest*, *hadst*, *goeth*, *seeth*).

## ETYMOLOGY

The etymology is at the end of the entry, in square brackets [ ]. It shows only the direct line of derivation of the word. Forms in other languages are not given if they are exactly or almost identical with the English, e.g. the French *ablution*, or the Latin *abjectus* at *abject*.

Where an entry includes more than one word, the etymology applies only to the headword, but the derivation of the other words in the entry can be taken as being related to that of the headword, e.g. *acquisition* under *acquire* comes from the same Latin word, but not through French.

If no square brackets are shown, as at *absolve*, the etymological description is the same as for the last preceding entry for which one is given.

Round brackets ( ) indicate what supplements or explains the information before them, e.g. at *abduct*, where the primary Latin verb is shown, and at *abrupt*, referring to the derivation of *rupture* for further information on the history of *abrupt*.

For compound words (such as *besiege*) containing a prefix (*be-*) that has its own entry together with a complete word (*siege*), reference is often made to only the prefix or only the main element.

[E] is given for words that are known to have been used in Old English (before A.D. 1150). Where such words have come from other than Germanic sources, the further history is outlined, as at *church*, and where the Old English form has been reinforced by a further borrowing this is shown as at *psalm*. Other language names (F, L, Gk, Du., and so on) apply to all periods, without distinction between old and modern French, classical, late, medieval, and modern Latin, etc. (except that [N] stands only for Old Norse). The forms mentioned are therefore not necessarily those current in the modern language.

The names of language families (Gmc, Scand., and so on) are used when a word has certainly come from one or other branch of the family but it is impossible to say definitely which branch.

AF (Anglo-French) denotes the variety of French current in England in the Middle Ages after the Norman Conquest; the term Low Dutch (LDu.) as used in this dictionary comprises Dutch and Low German. Names of the rarer languages that have contributed to English (such as Balti at *polo*, and Cree at *wapiti*) are given in full without explanation; they may be found explained in larger dictionaries or in encyclopaedias.

The terms 'person' and 'place' mean that the word was originally the name of a person or place (shown in italics in the etymology or the definition, if not identical with the headword); 'imit.' means that the word was made to imitate the sound of the thing named, or otherwise to be suggestive of it.

Where the origin of a word cannot be reliably ascertained, the form [orig. uncert.] or [orig. unkn.] is used.

# ABBREVIATIONS AND SYMBOLS
## USED IN THE DICTIONARY

Abbreviations that are in general use appear in the dictionary itself.

a. adjective
abbr./eviation
abbrs. abbrevia-
    tions
abl./ative (case)
abs./olute
acc./usative (case)
act./ive
adj./ective
adjs. adjectives
adv./erb
advs. adverbs
Aeron./autics
AF Anglo-French
Afr./ican
Afrik./aans
AL Anglo-Latin
Alg./ebra
alt./eration (of)
Amer./ica(n)
Amh./aric
anal./ogy
Anat./omy
Ant./iquities
app./arently
approx./imate(ly)
Arab./ic
Aram./aic
arbitr./ary
arch./aic
Archaeol./ogy
Archit./ecture
Arith./metic
assim./ilated
assoc./iated
Assyr./ian
Astrol./ogy
Astron./omy
attrib./utive(ly)

Austral./ian
aux./iliary

bef./ore
Bibl./ical
Bill./iards
Biol./ogy
Bot./any

Can./adian
cc. centuries
Celt./ic
Chem./istry
Chin./ese
Cinemat./ography
cogn./ate
collect./ive
colloq./uial
comb. combination,
    combining
Commerc./ial
compar./ative
compd. compound
compl./ement
conj./unction
constr./uction
contr./action
Corn./ish
corresp./onding
corrupt./ion (of)
Crick./et

Da./nish
dat./ive (case)
dem./onstrative
Dent./istry
deriv./ative
derog./atory
dial./ect
diff./erent

dim./inutive
Diplom./acy
dist./inguished
Du./tch

E English (see
    Etymology above)
Eccl./esiastical
Ecol./ogy
Econ./omics
Egypt./ian
Electr./icity
ellipt./ically
emphat./ic
Engl./and
erron./eously
esp./ecially
etym./ology
euphem./ism
Eur./ope(an)
exc./ept
excl./amation
expr./essing

F French
f. from
fam./iliar
fem./inine
fig./urative
Finn./ish
Flem./ish
foll./owing (entry)
Footb./all
form./ation
Fortif./ication
freq./uently
frequent./ative
Fris./ian
fut./ure (tense)

G German
Gael./ic
gen./itive (case)
Geog./raphy
Geol./ogy
Geom./etry
Gk Greek
Gmc Germanic
Gram./mar

Heb./rew
Her./aldry
Hind./ustani
Hist./ory
Hort./iculture

i. intransitive
Icel./andic
imit./ative
imper./ative
impers./onal
incl./uding
Ind./ian (2nd sense)
ind./irect
indic./ative
inf./initive
infl./uenced
int./erjection
interrog./ative
intr./ansitive
Ir./ish
iron./ical
It./alian

Jap./anese
Jav./anese
joc./ular
Journ./alism

L Latin
lang./uage
LDu. Low Dutch
LG Low German
Ling./uistics
lit./eral

Math./ematics
Mech./anics

Med./icine
Metaphys./ics
metath./esis
Meteor./ology
Mex./ican
Mil./itary
Min./eralogy
mod./ern
Mount./aineering
Mus./ic
Myth./ology

N Old Norse
n. noun
Naut./ical
neg./ative
Norw./egian
ns. nouns

O Old
obj./ective (case)
obs./olete
occas./ionally
opp./osed to
Opt./ics
orig. origin,
    originally

P (see note below)
Paint./ing
parenth./etically
Parl./iament(ary)
part. (esp. present)
    participle
pass./ive
Path./ology
pedant./ic
perh./aps
Pers./ian
pers. person,
    personal
Peruv./ian
Philol./ogy
Philos./ophy
Phon./etics
Photog./raphy
phr./ase

phrs. phrases
Phys./ics
Physiol./ogy
pl./ural
poet./ical
Pol./ish
Polit./ics
pop./ularly, not
    technically
Port./uguese
poss./essive (case)
p.p. past participle
pr./onounced
prec./eding (entry)
pred./icative
pref./ix
prep./osition
pres./ent (tense)
Print./ing
prob./ably
pron./oun
prons. pronouns
pronunc./iation
prop./erly
Pros./ody
Prov./ençal
prov. proverb,
    provincial
Psych./ology

redupl./ication (of)
ref./erence
refl./exive
rel./ative
repr./esent(ing)
Rhet./oric
rhet./orical
Rom. Romanic,
    Roman
Russ./ian

Sc./ottish
Scand./inavian
sent./ence
Shak./espeare
sim./ilarly

sing./ular
Sinh./alese
Skr. Sanskrit
sl./ang
Slav./onic
Sp./anish
sp./elling
St. Exch. Stock
  Exchange
subj. subject,
  subjunctive
subord./inate
suf./fix
sufs. suffixes
superl./ative
Surg./ery
Surv./eying

Sw./edish
syll./able
symb./ol

t. transitive
tech./nically
Teut./onic
Theatr./e
Theol./ogy
thr./ough
trans./itive
transf. by trans-
  ference
transl./ation (of)
Turk./ish
Typ./ography

ult./imately

uncert./ain
unemphat./ic
univ./ersity
unkn./own
usu./ally

v. verb
var./iant (of)
vb. verb
vbl verbal
vbs. verbs
voc./ative
vulg./ar

W Welsh
w. with
wd(s) word(s)

Zool./ogy

**P** Proprietary name. See below.
\* chiefly U.S.
‖ chiefly Britain and Commonwealth
~ (swung dash; see p. vii)
¹ ² ³ etc. used to distinguish headwords spelt identically
**1 2 3** etc. used to separate parts of speech, and derivatives,
  within an entry
1 2 3 1st, 2nd, 3rd person of verb

*Note on proprietary terms*
This dictionary includes some words which are, or are
asserted to be, proprietary names or trade marks. Their
inclusion does not imply that they have acquired for legal
purposes a non-proprietary or general significance, nor is any
other judgment implied concerning their legal status. In
cases where the editor has some evidence that a word is used
as a proprietary name or trade mark this is indicated by the
letter **P**, but no judgement concerning the legal status of such
words is made or implied thereby.

*The power notation*
$10^2$ or ten squared $= 10 \times 10 = 100$
$10^3$ or ten cubed $= 10^2 \times 10 = 1,000$
$10^4 = 10,000$
$10^{10} = 1$ followed by ten noughts $= 10,000,000,000.$
$10^{-2} = 1/100; \ 10^{-10} = 1/10^{10} = 1/10,000,000,000.$

# A

**A, a¹,** (ā) *n.* (*pl.* **As, A's**). First letter; (Mus.) sixth note in diatonic scale of C major; (Alg.; *a*) first known quantity; (*A*) first hypothetical person or example; **A1** (āwŭ'n), (in Lloyd's Register, of ship) first-class, (colloq.) first-rate.

**a², an¹,** (*a, an; emphat.* ā, ăn) *a.* (For usage see AN¹.) One, some, any; one like (*a Daniel*); one single (*could not see a thing*); the same (*they are all of a size*); to or for each (*£40 a year, twice a day*; orig. f. foll.). [ONE]

**a³** *prep.* On, to, in, (now chiefly as pref. in *abed, afoot,* etc., or w. vbl n. as *go a-hunting, house is a-building,* or w. vbs. as *aflutter*). [ON]

**a-** *pref.* **1.** See AB-, AD-. **2.** (an- bef. vowel or *h*). Not, without [f. Gk].

**A.** *abbr.* ampere(s); ångström(s); answer; Associate of; ‖**A level,**= ADVANCED *level.*

**A.A.** *abbr.* anti-aircraft; ‖Automobile Association.

**Aar'on** (ăr'-) *n.* **~'s beard, rod,** pop. names of plants. [Bibl. person]

**ab-** *pref.* (**abs-** bef. *c, t*; **a-** bef. *m, p, v*). Away, from. [F or L]

**A.B.** *abbr.* Able rating or seaman. [*able-bodied*]

**abă'ck** *adv.* Backwards, behind; **take ~,** surprise. [A³]

**ă'bac|us** *n.* (*pl.* **~uses, ~i** *pr.* -sī). Frame with balls sliding on wires, used for calculating; (Archit.) upper member of capital, supporting architrave. [L f. Gk f. Heb.]

**aba'ft** (-ah'-; Naut.) **1.** *adv.* In stern half of ship. **2.** *prep.* Behind. [A³, BY, AFT]

**abă'ndon. 1.** *v.t.* Give up, yield oneself completely, forsake; (in *p.p.*) profligate; **~ment** *n.,* (esp.) = sense 2. **2.** (*or* ăbah'ńdawṅ) *n.* Careless freedom of manner. [F (AD-, BAN)]

**abā'se** *v.t.* Humiliate, lower, (person, one*self*); **~ment** (-sm-) *n.* [F (AD-, BASE)]

**abā'sh** *v.t.* (usu. in *pass.*) Embarrass, disconcert; **~ment** *n.* [F *es-* EX-¹, *baïr* astound]

**abā'te** *v.t. & i.* Diminish, make or become less; weaken; do away with

(nuisance); **~ment** (-tm-) *n.* [F *abatre* f. L *battuo* beat]

**ă'battoir** (-twăr) *n.* Slaughterhouse. [F (*abatre* fell, as prec.)]

**ă'bbey** *n.* (Buildings occupied by) body of monks or nuns under abbot or abbess; church or house that was formerly abbey; **the A~,** (esp.) Westminster Abbey. [F f. L (foll.)]

**ă'bbot** *n.* Head of an abbey of monks; **ă'bbacy** *n.,* office or jurisdiction of abbot or abbess; **abbā'tial** (-shal) *a.*; **abbé** (ă'bā) *n.,* Frenchman entitled to wear ecclesiastical dress, esp. without official duties; **ă'bbèss** *n.,* female head of abbey of nuns. [E f. L *abbas* f. Gk f. Aram.]

**abbrē'vi|āte** *v.t.* Represent (word) by a part; shorten; **~ā'tion** *n.* [L (BRIEF)]

**ABC** (ābēsē') *n.* The alphabet; rudiments (*of* subject); alphabetical guide. [*A, B, C*]

**ă'bdic|āte** *v.t.* Renounce (throne, right, etc., or abs.) formally or by default; **~ā'tion** *n.* [L (*dico* declare)]

**ă'bdomĕn** (*or* ăbdō'-) *n.* Belly, including stomach, bowels, etc.; hinder part of insect etc.; **ăbdŏ'minal** *a.* (-lly). [L]

**abdŭ'ct** *v.t.* Carry off (esp. woman, child) illegally by force or fraud; **~ion, ~or,** *ns.* [L (*duco* draw)]

**abea'm** *adv.* On line at right angles to ship's or aircraft's length. [A³]

**abē'd** *adv.* (arch.) In bed. [A³]

**abē'le** (*or* ā'bel) *n.* White poplar. [Du. *abeel* ult. f. L *albus* white]

**Aberdee'n** (ă-) *n.* **~ Angus,** (animal of) Scottish breed of black polled cattle; **~ (terrier),** Scotch terrier; **Aberdō'nian** (ă-) *a. & n.* [place]

**ăberrā'tion** *n.* Straying from the path; moral or mental slip or error; deviation from biological type; failure of rays to converge to one focus; apparent displacement of celestial body; **abĕ'rrant** *a.*; **abĕ'rrance, -cў,** *ns.* [L (ERR)]

**abĕ't** *v.t.* (-tt-). Encourage or assist (offender, offence; esp. *aid and abet*);

~ment, ~ter, ~tor, *ns.* [F (AD-, BAIT)]

**abey′ance** (-bā′-) *n.* Suspension, temporary disuse (*the rights fell into abeyance*). [F (AD-, *beer* gape)]

**abhor′** *v.t.* (-rr-). Regard with disgust and hatred; **abho′rrence** *n.*, detestation; **abho′rrent** *a.*, disgusting, hateful, *to* (person), not according *to*. [L (HORROR)]

**abi′de** *v.i.* & *t.* (abo′de *pr.* -ō′d, ~d). Remain, continue; (arch.) dwell; ~ **by**, remain faithful to, act upon (terms, promise); sustain, face, (*abide the storm, the issue, his anger*); submit to (doom etc.); (w. neg. or interrog.) tolerate (*cannot abide wasps*); **abi′dance** *n.*; **abi′ding** *a.*, permanent. [E (*a-* intensive, BIDE)]

**abi′lity** *n.* Sufficient power, being able, (*to* do something); cleverness, talent. [F (ABLE)]

**ab initio** (ăbĭnĭ′shĭō) *adv.* From the beginning. [L]

**ă′bject** *a.* Miserable, craven, degraded, (*abject slave, coward, fear*); **abje′ction** *n.*, abject state. [L (*jacio -ject-* throw)]

**abjur′e** (-joor′) *v.t.* Renounce on oath (opinion, claim, etc.); swear perpetual absence from (one's country etc.); **abjura′tion** (-joor-) *n.* [L (*juro* swear)]

**ă′blative** *a.* & *n.* ~ (**case**), case of Latin nouns expressing source, agent, cause, or instrument, of action; ~ ABSOLUTE, construction of noun and participle used as adverbial clause. [F or L (*ablatus* taken away)]

**ă′blaut** (-owt) *n.* Vowel change in related words (*sing, song, sung*). [G]

**ablā′ze** *adv.* & *pred. a.* On fire; glittering; excited. [A³]

**ā′ble** *a.* (~r, ~st). Having the power (*to*; esp. *is able, was able, shall be able*, etc., as pres., past, fut., etc., of *can*); talented, clever; ~**bodied**, robust; ~(**-bodied**) **rating, seaman**, (able to perform all duties); **ā′bly** *adv.*, capably, cleverly. [F f. L *habilis*]

**-able** *suf.* forming *adjs.*, esp. from trans. *vbs.*, w. sense *that may be* —*d*; *vbs.* drop silent final *e* except after *c* and *g* (*movable*; but *manageable pr.* -sa-; *placeable pr.* -sa-), change final *y* after a consonant into *i* (*reliable*), and double a final consonant as in inflexion (*gettable*); see note on Suffixes, p. viii. [F f. L *-abilis*]

**ablu′tion** (-loo′-) *n.* (usu. in *pl.*). Ceremonial washing of hands, vessels, etc.; water after use for this; (joc.) washing oneself. [F, or L *ablutio* (*luo* wash)]

**ā′bly.** See ABLE.

**ă′bnega|āte** *v.t.* Deny oneself (thing); renounce (a right etc.); ~**ā′tion** *n.* [L (*nego* deny)]

**abnor′mal** *a.* (~ly). Exceptional; deviating from its type; **ăbnormă′lity** *n.* [F (ANOMALOUS)]

**A′bō** (ă-), *n.* (*pl.* ~s) & *a.* (Austral. sl.) Aboriginal. [abbr.]

**aboar′d** *adv.* & *prep.* On BOARD; alongside. [A³]

**abō′de¹** *n.* Dwelling-place; **make** one's ~, dwell. [ABIDE]

**abō′de².** See ABIDE.

**abō′lish** *v.t.* End existence of (custom, institution); ~**ment, ăboli′tion**, *ns.*; **ăboli′tionist** *n.*, supporter of movement against capital punishment or (Hist.) Negro slavery. [F f. L *aboleo* destroy]

**A-bomb** (ā′bŏm) *n.* Atomic bomb. [A for ATOMIC]

**abō′min|able** *a.* (~ably). Detestable, loathsome, (*abominable cruelty*; colloq. of unpleasant weather etc.); **A~able Snowman**, unidentified anthropoid or ursine animal in Himalayas; ~**āte** *v.t.*, detest, loathe; ~**ā′tion** *n.*, (esp.) object of disgust. [F f. L, = to be deprecated (OMEN)]

**ăbori′ginal. 1.** *a.* (~ly). (Of race, animal, plant) indigenous, existing in a land from an early period; directly descended from these. **2.** *n.* Aboriginal inhabitant. **3.** **ăbori′ginē** *n.*, aboriginal inhabitant, plant, etc. [L (ORIGIN)]

**abor′t. 1.** *v.i.* & *t.* Suffer or cause abortion; (Biol., or fig.) (cause to) remain undeveloped, shrink away; (Aeron. etc.) terminate (flight) prematurely. **2.** *n.* (Aeron. etc.) (Termination of) unsuccessful flight. **3.** ~**ion** *n.*, (esp.) expulsion (spontaneous or induced) of foetus from uterus, (Med.) this in first 28 weeks of pregnancy, dwarfed or misshapen creature; ~**ionist** *n.*, one who performs abortions esp. illegally; ~**ive** *a.*, producing abortion, rudimentary, unsuccessful. [L (*orior* be born)]

**abou′nd** *v.i.* Be plentiful, be rich (*in*); teem (*with*). [F f. L (*unda* wave)]

**abou′t. 1.** *adv.* Around from outside or centre (*compass it about*; *look about*); somewhere near; here and there (*influenza is about*; *throwing litter about*); on the move, astir, in action (*will soon be about again*; **be ~ to do**, be on the point of doing, and sim. for all vbs. as fut. part.); facing in opposite direction (*wrong way about*; *turn about*; *put the ship about*); in rotation (*on duty week about*, *week and week about*); in the course of events (*it came about*; BRING *about*); approximately (*weighs about a pound*; *is (of) about my size*; *went at about four o'clock*; *is about right*; colloq., in iron. understatement, as *I'm about tired of this*). **2.** *prep.* Around, in, (*somewhere about the place*); somewhere near (*have one's* WITS *about one*); here and there in (*dotted about the place*); at a time near to (*went about four*, *about midnight*); in connection with, on the subject of, (*busy about his packing*; *what is he talking about?*; HOW or WHAT *about it?*). [E (ON, BY, OUT)]

**abo've** (-ŭ'v) *adv.*, *prep.*, *a.*, & *n.* **1.** *adv.* At or to a higher point, overhead, (*clear sky above*; **in the room ~**, upstairs); upstream; (rhet.) in heaven; on the upper side; in preceding part of book etc.; in addition (*over and above*). **2.** *prep.* Over, on the top of, higher than, (*heard above the din*; *head above water*); upstream from; north of; more than (*above fifty*); earlier in history than (*not traced above the third century*); of higher rank, position, importance, etc., than (*above all*); out of reach of (*above* SUSPICION); too good etc. for (*is above meanness*; *above one's station*; **~ one-self**, carried away by high spirits or conceit); **~-boar'd**, without concealment, open(ly). **3.** *a.* & *n.* (That which is) said, mentioned, or written above (*the above statement*; *the above proves*). [E (ON, BY, UP)]

**Abp.** *abbr.* Archbishop.

**ăbracadä'bra** *n.* Magic formula, spell; gibberish. [L f. Gk]

**abrā'|de** *v.t.* Scrape off, injure by rubbing, (skin, rock, etc.); **~sion** (-zhon) *n.*; **~sive** *a.* & *n.*, (substance) capable of rubbing or grinding down, (fig.) tending to hurt person's feelings. [L (*rado* scrape)]

**ăbrĕă'ction** *n.* (Psych.) Free expression and consequent release of previously repressed emotion. [AB-]

**abrea'st** (-ĕ'st) *adv.* Side by side and facing same way; not behind (*abreast of* or *with the times*). [A³]

**abri'dg|e** *v.t.* Condense, shorten,

(book etc., interview); curtail (liberty); **~(e)ment** (-jm-) *n.* [F (ABBREVIATE)]

**abroa'd** (-aw'd) *adv.* In or to foreign lands (**from ~**, from another country); broadly, in different directions, (*scatter abroad*); in circulation (*rumour is abroad*); (arch.) out of doors. [A³]

**ă'brog|āte** *v.t.* Repeal, cancel, (law, custom); **~ā'tion** *n.* [L (*rogo* propose law)]

**abrŭ'pt** *a.* Sudden, hasty, (*abrupt departure*); disconnected, not smooth, (*an abrupt manner of speaking*); steep, precipitous. [L (RUPTURE)]

**abs-.** See AB-.

**ă'bscèss** *n.* Collection of pus formed in the body. [L (AB-, CEDE)]

**absci'ssa** *n.* (*pl.* **~s**, **~e**). (Math.) Coordinate measured usu. horizontally. [L (*abscindo* cut off)]

**abscŏ'nd** *v.i.* Depart secretly; flee from the law. [L *abscondo* secrete]

**ă'bsence** *n.* Being away; time of this; non-existence or lack *of*; inattentiveness (*absence of mind*). [F f. L (foll.)]

**absent. 1.** (ă'bsent) *a.* Not present; not existing; **~(-mi'nded)**, forgetful, inattentive; **~lў** *adv.*, in absent-minded way. **2.** (absĕ'nt) *v. refl.* Keep one*self* away. **3. ăbsentee'** *n.*, person not present, landlord habitually living away from property he leases to others; **absentee'ism** *n.*, (esp.) practice of absenting oneself from work etc. esp. frequently or illicitly. [F f. L]

**ă'bsinth** *n.* Wormwood; **~(e)**, liqueur made (orig.) from this. [F f. L]

**absit omen** (ăbsĭt ō'mĕn) *int.* May suggested foreboding not become fact. [L]

**ă'bsolūte** (or -ōōt) *a.* Complete, perfect, (*absolute ignorance, impossibility, exhaustion, bliss*; *an absolute fool*; **~ alcohol**, free from water); unrestricted, independent, despotic, (*absolute submission, denial, ruler*; **~ majority**, majority over all rivals combined); out of (ordinary) grammatical relation (**~ construction**, e.g. in *dinner being over, we left the table*; *let us toss for it*, *loser to pay*, phr. used as adv. clause, similarly ablative **~** in L, genitive **~** in Gk); (of *adj.*, or *v.t.*) with its noun, object, understood but not expressed; not relative; (Philos.) self-existent (also as *n.*, the ~); ~ **pitch** (Mus., fixed standard, or ability to recognize pitch of note); ~ **temperature** (measured from *absolute* ZERO); ~**lȳ** (-tlĭ) *adv.*, in an absolute manner or sense, actually (*it absolutely exploded*), (w. neg.) at all, (colloq., *pr.* -ōō'-) quite so, yes; **ă'bsolŭtism** (*or* -ōōt-) *n.*, principle of absolute government; **ă'bsolūtĭst** (*or* -ōōt-) *n.* [L (SOLVE)]

**absŏ'lve** (*or* -z-) *v.t.* Set or pronounce free (*from* blame, obligation, etc., *of* sin, or abs.); acquit; **ăbsolū'tion** (*or* -ōō'-) *n.*

**absŏr'b** (*or* -z-) *v.t.* Swallow up, incorporate; take in, suck up, (heat etc., liquids); reduce intensity of (light, impact, etc.); consume (strength etc.); engross the attention of (~**ing** *a.*, deeply interesting); ~**abĭ'lity**, ~**ency**, *ns.*; ~**ent** *a.* & *n.*, (substance or organ) having tendency to absorb; **absŏr'ption** *n.*, **absŏr'ptive** *a.*, (*or* -z-). [L (*sorbeo* suck in)]

**abstai'n** *v.i.* Restrain oneself (*from* food etc., remark etc., doing); drink no alcohol; decline to use vote. [F f. L (*teneo tent-* hold)]

**abstē'mious** *a.* Sparing or not self-indulgent esp. in taking food and drink (*abstemious person, habits, meal*). [L (ABS-, *temetum* strong drink)]

**abstě'ntion** *n.* Abstaining. [F or L (ABSTAIN)]

**ă'bstĭnen|ce** *n.* Abstaining (*from* food, pleasure, etc.; total ~ce, i.e. from alcohol); ~**t** *a.*

**ă'bstrăct** *a.*, *n.*, & *v.* **1.** (ă'b-) *a.* Separated from matter or practice or particular examples, not concrete, (*abstract ideas*) ~ **art**, not representational; ~ **noun**, noun denoting quality or state); ideal, theoretical, (*the abstract citizen*; **in the** ~, existing only as an idea, in theory); abstruse. **2.** (ă'b-) *n.* Summary (of book etc.); abstract term; abstract painting etc. **3.** (-tră'-) *v.t.* Deduct, remove; (euphem.) steal; disengage (attention *from*; ~**ed**, inattentive); consider abstractly; summarize; ~**ion** *n.*, abstracting, abstract idea. [F or L (TRACT)]

**abstru'se** (-ōō's) *a.* Hard to understand, profound, (*abstruse problem, studies*). [F or L (*abstrudo -trus-* conceal)]

**absŭr'd** *a.* (~**est**). Inappropriate; unreasonable; ridiculous; ~**ĭtȳ** *n.* [F or L (SURD)]

**abŭ'ndan|ce** *n.* Quantity more

than enough, plenty, (*food in abundance*; *(an) abundance of instances*); overflowing emotion (*of the heart*); wealth; ~**t** *a.*, plentiful, rich *in.* [ABOUND]

**abū's|e. 1.** (-z) *v.t.* Make bad use of (talents, position, person's good nature); revile. **2.** (-s) *n.* Misuse (*of*); unjust or corrupt practice; reviling; ~**ĭve** *a.*, reviling, using bad language. [F f. L (USE)]

**abŭt** *v.t.* & *i.* (-tt-). (Of estates or countries) border on or *on* (another); (of building) touch, lean, (*on*, *against* another); ~**ment** *n.*, lateral support, point where this joins thing supported. [F, L (BUTT⁴)]

**abȳ'ss** (arch., poet.) ~**sm** *n.* Bottomless or deep chasm; primal chaos; **abȳ'smal** (-z-) *a.*, bottomless (esp. fig., *abysmal ignorance*), (colloq.) extremely bad (*his taste is abysmal*); **abȳ'ssal** *a.*, at or of ocean depths or floor. [L f. Gk,=bottomless]

**ac-.** See AD-.

**-ac** *suf.* forming *adjs.* (cf. *cardiac, maniac*) often also (or only) used as *ns.* [F or L or Gk]

**A.C.** *abbr.* ‖Aircraftman; alternating current; before Christ [L *ante Christum*].

**a/c** *abbr.* account. [*account current*]

**acā'cia** (-sha) *n.* Kind of leguminous tree esp. yielding gum arabic (false) ~, plant with sweet-scented white flowers. [L f. Gk]

**acā'demȳ** *n.* Place of study; secondary school, esp. (Sc.) grammar school; place for special training (*Royal Military Academy*); society for cultivating art etc. (**the** A~, the Royal Academy of Arts, its annual exhibition); (*A*~) garden near Athens where Plato taught, his followers, his philosophy; **ă'cadēme** *n.*, university (environment); **ăcadě'mĭc**, (*a.*) -ically) scholarly, of a university etc., abstract, unpractical, (*n.*) member of university etc.; **ăcadě'mĭcal**, (*a.*; -lly) of university etc., (*n. in pl.*) university costume; **ăcadēmĭ'cian** (-shan) *n.*, member of an Academy, esp. the Royal Academy of Arts. [F or L, f. Gk *Akadēmos*, after whom Plato's garden was named]

**acă'nthus** *n.* Kind of herbaceous plant with prickly leaves; (Gk Archit.) representation of its leaf. [L f. Gk]

**accē'de** (ăks-) *v.i.* Enter upon an office; join a party; assent (*to* request, proposal, opinion); ~ **to**, enter upon (office), join (party). [L (CEDE)]

**accělěrà'nd|ō** (aks-, ăch-) *adv.*, *a.*, & *n.* (*pl.* ~**os**, ~**i**). (Mus.) (Passage performed) with gradually increasing speed. [It. (foll.)]

**accě'ler|āte** (aks-) *v.t.* & *i.* Make or become quicker; (cause to) happen earlier; ~**ā'tion** *n.*; ~**ative** *a.*; ~**ātor** *n.*, (esp.) pedal for increasing speed of motor engine etc., (Phys.) apparatus to produce fast charged particles. [L (CELERITY)]

**accent. 1.** (ă'ks-) *n.* Prominence given to syllable by stress or pitch; mark used with letter to indicate pitch, stress, quality of vowel, etc. (as acute ~ ´, GRAVE⁵ accent, CIRCUMFLEX accent); individual, local, or national mode of pronunciation (*a cockney accent*); modulation to express feeling; (in *pl.*) speech; rhythmical stress; distinctive character or detail; **accě'ntŭal** (aks-) *a.* (-lly). **2.** (akse'nt) *v.t.* Pronounce with accent; write accents on; accentuate. **3.** ~**ŭāte** (ăksě'-) *v.t.*, emphasize, make conspicuous; ~**ŭā'tion** (ăksě-) *n.* [F or L (*cantus* song)]

**accě'pt** (aks-) *v.t.* Consent to receive (thing or service offered, thanks, etc., or abs.); answer affirmatively (invitation, suitor); regard with favour; receive as adequate or true (*will accept your explanation*); take thing inserted (*slot machine accepts only tokens*); undertake (office); agree to meet (bill of exchange); ~**able** *a.* (~**ably**), worth accepting, welcome; ~**abi'litў**, ~**ance**, *ns.*; ~**ā'tion** (ăks-) *n.*, sense in which word is used; ~**or** *n.* [F or L (*capio* take)]

**ă'ccěss** (ă'ks-) *n.* Approach; right or means of approaching or reaching (*gain access to*; *easy of* ~, easily approached); ~ **time**, time needed to retrieve information stored in computer); passage, doorway; attack, outburst, (*of* illness or emotion); ~**arў** (ăksě'-) *n.*, one that helps in or is privy to an act; ~**ible** (ăksě'-) *a.* (~**ibly**), able to be reached (*accessible to all*); ~**ibi'litў** (aks-) *n.*; ~**ion** (ăksě'shon), (*n.*) acceding or attaining (*to* throne, status), thing added, (*v.t.*) record addition of (book etc.) to library; ~**orў** (ăksě'-) *a.* & *n.*, additional, adventitious, (thing, minor attachment, esp. in *pl.*), accessary. [F or L (ACCEDE)]

**ă'ccǐděn|t** (ă'ks-) *n.* Event without apparent cause, unexpected event; unintentional act, chance, (*did it by accident*); unfortunate esp. harmful event (*killed in a car accident*); irregularity in structure; non-essential quality etc.; mere accessory; ~**ce** *n.*, the part of grammar dealing with variable forms of words; ~**tal** (-ě'-), (*a.*; -lly) happening or done by accident, occasional, non-essential (~**tal sharp, flat, natural,** Mus. sign attached to single note and not in signature), (*n.*) non-essential quality etc., (Mus.) accidental sign. [F f. L (*cado* fall)]

**acclai'm. 1.** *v.t.* Welcome or applaud enthusiastically; hail (as) (*acclaim him king*); **ăcclamā'tion** *n.*, loud and eager assent (*voted by acclamation*), (usu. in *pl.*) shouting in person's honour. **2.** *n.* Shout of applause, welcome. [L *acclamo* (CLAIM)]

**accli'matize, \*ă'cclĭmāte** (or-ī'-), *v.t.* & *i.* Habituate (animal, plant, oneself), become habituated, to new climate; **acclimatizā'tion, ăcclimā'tion,** *ns.* [F *acclimater* (CLIMATE)]

**accli'vitў** *n.* Upward slope. [L (DECLIVITY)]

**ă'ccolāde** (or -ā'd) *n.* Sign (now usu. stroke on shoulder with flat of sword) at bestowal of knighthood; bestowal of praise. [F f. Prov., f. L *collum* neck]

**accŏ'mmodāt|e** *v.t.* Adapt (thing, person, oneself, *to*); harmonize (two things, one *to* another); reconcile; supply (person *with*); do favour to (~**ing** *a.*, obliging, compliant); provide lodging for; ~**ion** (-dā'-) *n.*, adaptation, adjustment, convenient arrangement (~**ion address,** for person without permanent address for letters etc.; ~**ion ladder,** up ship's side), lodging, loan; ~**or** *n.* [L (COMMODE)]

**accŏ'mpanў** (-ŭ'm-) *v.t.* Go with, escort, attend, be put or found with, (*accompanied by a friend*; *speech accompanied with gestures*); supplement (e.g. word *with* blow); (Mus.) support (singer, player, chorus) by performing subsidiary part; ~**iment** *n.*, accompanying thing, (Mus.) subsidiary esp. instrumental part; ~**ist** *n.* (Mus.) [F (COMPANION)]

**accŏ'mplĭce** (or -ŭ'm-) *n.* Partner in crime. [F f. L (COMPLICE)]

**accŏ'mplĭsh** (or -ŭ'm-) *v.t.* Perform, complete, succeed in doing, (design, wish, task, etc.); **~ed** (-sht) *a.*, skilled, having social accomplishments; **~ment** *n.*, (esp.) skill, acquired socially-useful ability. [F f. L (COMPLETE)]

**accor'd. 1.** *v.i.* & *t.* Be consistent (*this does not accord with the evidence*); grant (permission, request), give (welcome etc.). **2.** *n.* Consent (*all with one accord replied*; **of** one's own **~**, spontaneously); harmony or agreement in colour, tone, etc. **3.** **~ance** *n.*, harmony, agreement, (*in accordance with*); **~ant** *a.* [F, f. L *cor cord-* heart]

**accor'ding** *adv.* In a manner or degree that varies *as* or corresponds to (*pays according as he is able, according to his ability*); **~ to**, as stated by; **~ly** *adv.*, as the (stated) circumstances suggest (*I accordingly sent for the manager*; *will you arrange accordingly?*); **~ly as**, according as.

**accor'dion** *n.* Portable musical instrument with bellows, metal reeds, and keyboard and/or buttons; **~ pleat, wall,** (folding like bellows); **~ist** *n.* [G, f. It. *accordare* to tune]

**acco'st** *v.t.* Approach and address, esp. boldly; (of prostitute) solicit. [F, f. L *costa* rib]

**accouch|ement** (ăkōō'shmahn̄) *n.* Childbirth, lying-in; **~eur** (-ēr') *n.* (*fem.* **~euse** *pr.* -ēr'z), (man) midwife. [F]

**accou'nt. 1.** *'v.t.* & *i.* Consider, regard as, (*account him a fool, wise*); **~ for**, give reckoning of (money entrusted), answer for (conduct), explain cause of (*can you account for it?*; *this accounts for his reluctance*), kill (game), defeat (player, side), take (wickets). **2.** *n.* Counting, reckoning, (**money of ~**, not current as coin or note); statement of money, goods, or services received and expended, or of debit and credit (*open an account with*; **keep ~s**, enter expenditure for comparison with income; *£5 on ~*, in part payment; *goods on ~*, to be paid for at later time; **on one's own ~**, for one's own purposes; **on ~ of**, because of; **on no ~**, certainly not); profit (**turn to ~ or good ~,** make useful); business relationship esp. with bank or with firm granting credit (**current ~**, at bank, from which money can be drawn on demand); statement of administration as required by creditor (*demand,

RENDER, an account*; **call** person **to** account; **gone to his ~**, dead; **give a good ~ of** oneself, be successful or impressive); estimation (*take account of*; *take into account*); importance (*of some, no, account*); narration, description, (*give account of*; *accounts differ*; **by all ~s**, in the opinion of all). **3.** **~able** *a.* (-bly), responsible (*for* thing, *to* person), explicable; **~abi'lity** *n.*; **~ant** *n.*, keeper and inspector of accounts; **~ancy** *n.*, his profession. [F (COUNT[1])]

**accou't|rements, \*~|erments,** (-ōō't-) *n.pl.* Equipment, trappings; soldier's outfit other than arms and garments; **~red, \*~ered,** (-tèrd) *a.*, equipped, attired. [F]

**accre'dit** *v.t.* Gain belief or influence for (adviser, advice, statement); send (ambassador etc.) with credentials *to* person, *to* or *at* a court or government; attribute (saying etc. *to* person), credit (person *with* saying etc.); **~èd** *a.*, (esp., of beliefs) accepted. [F (CREDIT)]

**accre'tion** *n.* Growth by organic enlargement; growing of separate things into one, the resulting whole; (adhesion of) extraneous matter added. [L (*cresco cret-* grow)]

**accru'|e** (-ōō') *v.i.* Come (*to* person, *from* thing) as natural increase or advantage (esp. of interest on invested money); **~al** *n.* [F f. L (as prec.)]

**accu'mulāt|e** *v.t.* & *i.* Heap up, get together, get more and more of, (*accumulate rubbish, papers on table, examples, ill-will*); produce or acquire (heap, fortune) thus; grow numerous, form an increasing mass or quantity; **~ion** (-lā'-) *n.*, accumulating, being accumulated, growth of capital by continued interest, accumulated mass; **~ive** (-at-) *a.*, acquisitive, given to hoarding, cumulative (proof, evidence); **~or** *n.*, (esp.) ||rechargeable electric cell, bet placed on sequence of events with winnings on each staked on next. [L (CUMULUS)]

**a'ccūra|te** *a.* Precise, conforming exactly with truth or a standard, (*accurate reckoning, statement, historian, weights*); **~cy** *n.* [L (*cura* care)]

**accūr'sèd** *a.* Lying under a curse; (colloq.) detestable, annoying. [E; *a*-intensive, CURSE]

**accu's|e** (-z) *v.t.* Indict, charge

with fault, (*accuse* person *of* offence, *of* do*ing*, *as* offender etc.); lay the blame on; ~**a'tion** (ă-) *n*.; ~**ative** *a*. & *n*., (Gram.) (case) expressing object of action; ~**ati'val** *a*. (-lly); ~**ator'ial** *a*. (-lly), (of procedure) in which prosecutor is distinct from judge; ~**atory** *a*., of or conveying accusation. [F f. L (CAUSE)]

**accu'stom** *v.t.* Make (one*self*, person or thing) used *to* (thing) (esp. in pass., *am accustomed to*); ~**ed** (-md) *a*., (esp.) customary. [F (CUSTOM)]

**ace** *n*. The 'one' on cards or dominoes or dice; (Lawn Tennis) stroke esp. service that opponent cannot return; smallest possible amount (*within an ace of*); pilot who has brought down many enemy aircraft, (transf.) expert performer. [F f. L *as* unity]

**-a'ceous** (-shŭs) *suf.* forming *adjs.* w. sense 'of the nature of', esp. in natural sciences (*herbaceous, rosaceous, farinaceous*). [L]

**acer'bity** *n*. Bitterness of speech, temper, etc.; sourness, harsh taste. [F or L (*acerbus* sour)]

**ace'tic** *a*. Of vinegar (~ **acid**, contained in vinegar); **ă'cetate** *n*., salt or ester of acetic acid, esp. its cellulose ester used for textile fibre etc.; **ă'cetone** *n*., a colourless volatile solvent of organic compounds; **ace'tylene** *n*., a colourless gas burning with bright flame used for welding. [F, f. L *acetum* vinegar]

**ache** (āk) *v.i.*, & *n*. (Suffer, be source of) continuous or prolonged dull pain or mental distress; ~'**y** *a*. [E]

**achie've** *v.t.* Accomplish, perform, (feat, task); acquire; reach (success, glory, objective); ~**ment** (-vm-) *n*., achieving, feat achieved, escutcheon with adjuncts. [F *achever* (CHIEF)]

**Achi'lles** (akĭ'lēz) *n*. ~' heel, heel of ~, vulnerable spot; ~ **tendon** (attaching calf muscles to heel). [person in *Iliad*]

**achroma'tic** (ăk-) *a*. (~ically). Free from colour; transmitting light without separating it into constituent colours. [F (A- 2)]

**achy.** See ACHE.

**ă'cid. 1.** *a*. Sour (*acid taste*; ∥~ **drop,** sharp-tasting sweetmeat; *acid look, speech, temper*); (Chem.) having properties of an acid. **2.** *n*., Sour substance; (Chem.) any of a class of substances that ..contain hydrogen

and neutralize alkalis, and of which most are sour (~ **test**, in which acid is applied to test for gold etc.; often fig.); (sl.) drug LSD. **3. aci'dic** *a*. (Chem.). **aci'dify** *v.t.*; **aci'dity** *n*.; ~**ō'sis** *n*., over-acidity of blood or tissue; **aci'dulate** *v.t.*, make (thing) somewhat acid; **aci'dulous** *a*., somewhat acid. [F or L]

**ăck-ă'ck** *a*. & *n*. (colloq.) Anti-aircraft (gun etc.). [formerly signallers' name for letters *A.A.*]

∥**ăck ĕ'mma** *adv*. & *n*. (colloq.) =A.M. [formerly signallers' name for letters *A.M.*]

**acknow'ledge** (aknŏ'l-) *v.t.* Agree to the truth of, admit, (*I acknowledge it, the truth of it, it as true, it to be true, that it is true*); own, recognize the claims of, (*do you acknowledge this signature?*; *the acknowledged king*); show that one has noticed (*acknowledged my presence with a sniff*); express appreciation of, reward, (service etc.); announce receipt of (*acknowledged my letter*); ~**(e)ment** (-jm-) *n*., (esp.) thing given or done in return for service etc. [A³, KNOWLEDGE]

**ă'cmē** *n*. Highest point; point of perfection. [Gk]

**ă'cnē** *n*. Skin eruption with red pimples. [L]

**ă'colyte** *n*. Church officer attending priest; assistant; beginner. [F or L (Gk *akolouthos* follower)]

**ă'conite** *n*. (Drug from) a poisonous plant, esp. monkshood. [F, or L *aconitum* f. Gk]

**ă'corn** *n*. Fruit of oak; ~ **shell**, cirriped living on rocks. [E]

**acou'stic** (-ōō'-) *a*. (~ally). Of sound, of sense of hearing; (of mine) exploded by sound vibrations; (Mus.) not electr(on)ic; ~**al** *a*.; ~**s** *n.pl.*, acoustic properties, (as *sing.*) science of sound. [Gk *akouō* hear]

**acquai'nt** *v.t.* Make aware or familiar (*acquaint him with the facts*, one*self with* one's *duties, the country*, etc.); **be** ~**ed** (**with** person), have slight personal knowledge of (of him). [F f. L (AD-, COGNIZANCE)]

**acquai'ntance** *n*. Being acquainted (*with* person, thing; **make the** ~ **of**, come to know); person(s) one knows slightly (*friends and acquaintances*); ~**ship** (-s-sh-) *n*.

**ăcquie'sce** *v.i.* Agree esp. tacitly; .not object; ~ **in**, accept (arrangement etc.); ~**nce** *n*.; ~**nt** *a*. [L (AD-, QUIET)]

**acquir′e** v.t. Gain for oneself, come into possession of, (*acquire property, rights, abilities*; *had acquired a bad reputation*); ~**d taste**, gained by experience, not innate); ~**ment** (-ir′m-) n., (esp.) mental attainment; **acquisi′tion** (-zi′-) n., (esp.) useful thing acquired; **acqui′sitive** (-zi-) a., keen to acquire things. [F f. L (AD-, *quaero* -quisit- seek)]

**acqui′t** v.t. (-tt-). Declare (person) not guilty (*of* offence); free or clear (person of blame or responsibility etc.); ~ **oneself**, perform one's part *well, ill*, etc.; ~**tal** n., deliverance from a charge by verdict etc., performance (*of* duty); ~**tance** n., payment of or release from debt, receipt in full. [F f. L (AD-, QUIT)]

**a′cre** (-ker) n. Measure of land, 4840 sq. yds., 0·405 ha.; piece of land, field, (*broad acres*); ~**age** n., number of acres, extent of land. [E]

**a′crid** a. (~**er**, ~**est**). Bitterly pungent; bitter in temper etc.; ~**ity** (-i′d-) n.; **a′crimony** n., bitterness of temper etc.; **acrimo′nious** a. [L *acer* keen, pungent]

**a′crobat** n. Performer of spectacular gymnastic feats, (fig.) one who changes position nimbly in argument; ~**ic** (-ba′-) a. (~**ically**); ~**ics** n.pl., acrobatic feats, (as *sing.*) performance of these. [F f. Gk *akrobatēs* (*akron* summit, *bainō* walk)]

**acrome′galy** n. Excessive growth of hands etc. from over-active pituitary gland. [F f. Gk (*akron* extremity, *megal-* great)]

**a′cronym** n. Word formed from initial letters of other words (e.g. *Ernie, Nato, radar*). [Gk *akron* end, *onoma* name]

**acro′polis** n. Citadel or upper fortified part of Gk city, esp. of Athens. [Gk (*akron* summit, *polis* city)]

**acro′ss** (or -aw′s). **1.** *prep.* Forming a cross with (*laid across each other*; fig., COME *across*); from side to side of (*stretched across the harbour*; ~ **the board**, general(ly), applying to all); to or on the other side of (*ran, lives, across the road*). **2.** *adv.* From side to side, to or on the other side, (*stretched, ran, across*; *shall soon be across*). [F à, en, *croix* (CROSS)]

**acro′stic** n. Poem etc. in which the first (**single** ~) or first and last (**double** ~) or first, middle, and last (**triple** ~) letters of lines form

word(s); word-puzzle so made. [F or Gk (*akron* end, *stikhos* row)]

**acry′lic** a. & n. Synthetic (fibre etc.) made by polymerizing ~ **acid**, an organic substance. [L *acer* pungent]

**act. 1.** n. Thing done, deed, (~ **of God**, operation of uncontrollable natural forces; **Acts of the Apostles**, N.T. book); process of doing, operation, (*caught in the act*); decree of legislative body etc.; ~ (**and deed**), document of legal transaction (*I deliver this as my act and deed*, said at time of signing); main division of play; one of series of short performances in circus or variety programme (*get into the* ~, sl., become participant; **put on an** ~, colloq., pretend). **2.** v.t. & i. Portray (incident, story) by actions (~**′ing copy**, of play for actors' use); personate (character in play or life; *act Othello, the fool*); perform actions, behave, (*you acted wisely*); ~ (**up**)**on**, carry out (suggestion), influence; ~ **up to** a principle, put it into practice); perform functions (*act as umpire*; *brake did not act*; *policeman declined to act*; ~ **for**, be the representative of); be actor or actress; ~**ing manager** etc., doing duties nominally shared with others; **Acting Captain** etc., doing duty temporarily. [F & L (*ago* act- do)]

**A.C.T.** abbr. Australian Capital Territory.

**a′ctinism** n. Property of short-wave radiation that produces chemical changes, as in photography; **acti′nic** a. [Gk *aktis* ray]

**a′ction. 1.** n. Process of acting, exertion of energy or influence, (*put into action*; *action of acid on metal*; **man of** ~, energetically active, opp. one in studious or sedentary occupation; **out of** ~, not working; **take** ~, begin to act; ~ **committee, group**, formed to take active steps); thing done (*generous actions*); series of events in drama; mode or style of movement of horse, player, etc.; mechanism of instrument; legal process (*bring an action*; *an action would lie*); battle (*killed in action*; ~ **stations**, positions taken up by troops etc. before battle). **2.** v.t. Bring a legal action against (person *for* offence); ~**able** a. (-bly), affording ground for action at law. [F f. L (ACT)]

**ă'ctǐve** *a.* Working, operative, (~ **list,** of officers liable to be called up; *active* SERVICE; ~ **volcano,** not extinct); consisting in or marked by action (*active life, measures*; **market is ~,** much business is transacted); originating action, not merely passive or receptive or inert, (*active reformers, resistance, ingredients*); energetic, diligent, (*active helpers, co-operation*); radioactive; (Gram.) attributing action of verb to person or thing whence it proceeds (as *we saw him*; ~ **voice,** comprising active forms of transitive and all forms of intr. vbs.; cf. PASSIVE); **ă'ctǐvāte** *v.t.,* make active; **ăctǐvā'tǐon** *n.*; **ă'ctǐvǐst** *n.,* one who follows policy of vigorous action in politics etc.; **ăctǐ'vǐtў** *n.,* being active, sphere or kind of action. [F or L (ACT)]

**ă'ctor** *n.* Performer in stage play, film, etc.; **ă'ctrĕss** *n.* [L (ACT)]

**ă'ctūal** *a.* Existing in fact, real; present, current; **ăctūă'lǐtў** *n.,* reality, (in *pl.*) existing conditions; **~lў** *adv.,* really, for the time being, strange as it seems (*he actually refused!*). [F f. L (ACT)]

**ă'ctūarў** *n.* Expert in statistics, esp. one who calculates insurance risks and premiums; **~ār'ǐal** *a.* (-lly). [L *actuarius* bookkeeper]

**ă'ctūāte** *v.t.* Communicate motion to (machine etc.); be motive for action of (person); **~ā'tǐon** *n.* [L]

**acū'ǐtў.** See ACUTE.

**acū'mĕn** *n.* Keen insight or discernment. [L,=ACUTE thing]

**ă'cūpŭncture** *n.* (Med.) Pricking of tissues with needles as treatment. [L *acu* with needle]

**acū'te** *a.* (~r, ~st). Sharp, pointed, (~ *angle,* less than 90°); shrewd, clever, (*an acute critic*); keen, penetrating, (*acute pain, hearing*); (of sound) high, shrill, (*acute* ACCENT); (of disease) coming sharply to crisis, not chronic; (of difficulty etc.) sharp in effect, serious, (*an acute shortage*); **acū'ǐtў** *n.,* sharpness, acuteness. [L *acutus* pointed]

**-acў** *suf.* forming *ns.* esp. (1) of quality, f. *adjs.* (*accuracy, obstinacy*), (2) of state, condition, office, etc., f. *ns.* (*lunacy, magistracy, piracy*). [F -*acie,* L -*acia,* -*atia,* Gk -*ateia*]

**ăd** *n.* (colloq.) Advertisement. [abbr.]

**ad-** *pref.* (**ac-** bef. *c, k, q;* **af-, ag-, al-, an-, ap-, ar-, as-, at-,** bef. *f, g,*

*l, n, p, r, s, t;* **a-** bef. *sc, sp, st*) w. senses: motion or direction to; change into; addition, adherence, increase, or mere intensification. [F or L]

**A.D.** *abbr.* of the Christian era. [ANNO DOMINI]

**ă'dage** *n.* Traditional maxim, proverb. [F f. L]

**ada'giō** (*adah'jyō*) *adv., a.,* & *n.* (*pl.* **~s**). (Mus.) (Movement) in slow time. [It.]

**A'dam** (ă'-) *n.* The first man; **the old ~,** sinful nature innate in person; **not know person from ~,** have no knowledge of his looks; **~'s apple,** cartilaginous projection in front of (esp. man's) neck. [Heb.,= man]

**ă'dam|ant. 1.** *n.* (arch.) Hard substance; **~ă'ntǐne** *a.* **2.** *a.* Unyielding to requests. [F f. L f. Gk *adamas -ant-* untameable]

**ada'pt** *v.t.* Fit, adjust, make suitable, (thing to another, *to* or *for* a purpose, *to do, for doing*; *adapt oneself to circumstances*); modify, alter, (*adapted from the Bible story*); **~able** *a.,* (esp.) able to adapt oneself to new surroundings; **~abǐ'lǐtў, ădaptā'tǐon,** *ns.*; **~ǐve** *a.*; **~or** *n.* (esp. to connect equipment). [F f. L (APT)]

**A.D.C.** *abbr.* aide-de-camp.

**ădd** *v.t.* & *i.* Join as increase or supplement (*add insult to injury; add a spoonful of gin; this* **~s** *to the expense,* increases it; ~ **in,** include); say further (*'the key', he added, 'is in the lock'*); unite numbers to get total (~ **up, together,** find sum of); **addĕ'ndum** *n.* (*pl.* -**da**), thing to be added, (in *pl.*) additional matter at end of book. [L *addo*]

**ă'dder** *n.* Small venomous snake, esp. common viper. [E, orig. *nadder, a nadder* being divided as *an adder*]

**ă'ddǐct** *n.* Person addicted to drug etc. (*a heroin addict*); enthusiastic devotee of sport etc. (*a golf addict*); **addǐ'cted** *a.,* (with *to*) having formed (a habit; *addicted to swearing*) or become dependent on (harmful drug etc.), devoted *to* (sport etc.); **addǐ'ctǐon** *n.*; **addǐ'ctǐve** *a.,* causing addiction. [L (*dico* say)]

**addǐ'tǐon** *n.* Adding; thing added (*a useful addition*); **in ~,** as an added thing etc. (*to*); **~al** *a.* (-lly), added, supplementary. [F or L (ADD)]

**ă'ddǐtǐve. 1.** *a.* To be added; characterized by addition (*additive* *process*). **2.** *n.* Thing (esp. substance) added. [L (ADD)]

**ǎ'ddle. 1.** *a.* Muddled, crazy, (*addle-brained*); (of egg) addled. **2.** *v.t. & i.* Muddle, confuse; become addled; ∼d, (of egg) rotten and producing no chick. [E,= filth]

**addrĕ'ss. 1.** *v.t.* Direct in speech or writing (*address remarks, petition,* etc., *to* person; ∼ oneself *to,* speak or write to); write directions for delivery on (envelope, parcel, etc.); speak or write to, esp. make a speech to, (person, audience); apply (one-*self to* task); take aim at (golf ball); **ǎddrĕssee'** *n.,* person to whom letter etc. is addressed. **2.** *n.* Superscription of letter usu. not including person's name; particulars of place where person lives or where firm etc. is situated; place of residence; speech delivered to audience; skill, dexterity; (in *pl.*) courtship (*pay* one's *addresses to*); **A∼ograph** (-ahf) *n.,* (P) machine for printing addresses on envelopes. [F (AD-, DIRECT)]

**addŭ'ce** *v.t.* (-cible). Cite as proof or instance; **addŭ'ction** *n.* [L (*duco* lead)]

**ǎ'dĕnoids** (-z) *n.pl.* (Path.) Enlarged lymphatic tissue between back of nose and throat, often hindering breathing. [Gk *adēn* gland]

**ǎ'dĕpt** *a.* (or adĕ'-) & *n.* (Person who is) thoroughly proficient (*at, in*). [L *adipiscor -ept-* attain]

**ǎ'dĕqua|te** *a.* Sufficient, proportionate *to* needs; satisfactory; barely sufficient; ∼cy̆ *n.* [L (EQUATE)]

**à deux** (ahdĕr') *adv. & a.* For or between two. [F]

**adhĕr'e** (-h-) *v.i.* Stick fast (*to* substance); give support or allegiance (*to* person, party, opinion); behave according *to* (rule); ∼nce *n.,* ∼nt, (*a.*) sticking *to* substance, adhering to rule etc., (*n.*) supporter (*of* party etc.); **adhĕ'sion** (-hē'zhon) *n.,* adhering (lit. or fig.), (Path.) unnatural union of surfaces due to inflammation; **adhĕ'sive** (-h-) *a. & n.,* sticking, sticky (substance); *adhesive* TAPE. [F or L (*haereo* stick)]

**ad hoc** (ǎd hŏ'k) *adv. & a.* For this purpose, special(ly); **ad hominem** (ǎd hŏ'mĭnĕm) *adv. & a.,* to a particular person. [L]

**adieu'** (adū') *int. & n. (pl.* ∼s, ∼x, *pr.* -z). Goodbye. [F,= to God]

**ad infinitum** (ǎd ĭnfĭnī'tum) *adv.* Without limit, for ever. [L]

**ǎ'dĭp|ōse** *a.* Of fat, fatty, (*adipose tissue*); ∼ŏ'sĭty̆ *n.* [L (*adeps* fat)]

**adjā'cen|t** *a.* Lying near, contiguous, (*to*); ∼cy̆ *n.* [L (*jaceo* lie)]

**ǎ'djĕct|ĭve** *n.* Word indicating an attribute, added to noun to describe it (*old, tall, Swedish, my, this*); ∼ĭ'val *a.* (-lly). [F f. L (*jacio -ject-* throw)]

**adjoi'n** *v.t.* Be contiguous with. [F f. L (*jungo* JOIN)]

**adjour'n** (ajĕr'n) *v.t. & i.* Put off, postpone, (*meeting, discussion, matter,* often *until* or *to* fixed time, *for* a week); break off for later resumption; (of assembled persons) suspend proceedings and separate, transfer meeting *to* another place; ∼ment *n.* [F f. L (AD-, *diurnum* day)]

**adjŭ'dg|e** *v.t.* Pronounce judgement on (matter); pronounce judicially (*that* thing is, thing *to* be); award judicially; ∼(e)ment (-jm-) *n.* [F f. L (*judex* judge)]

**adju'dĭc|āte** (ajōō'-) *v.t. & i.* Adjudge (claim etc., thing etc. *to* be); act as judge in court, tribunal, competition, etc., and give decision etc. (*upon*); ∼ā'tion, ∼ātor, *ns.*; ∼ātĭve *a.* [L]

**ǎ'djŭnct** *n.* Thing subordinate or incidental (*to, of,* another); (Gram.) amplification of predicate, subject, etc. [L (ADJOIN)]

**adjur'e** (ajoor') *v.t.* Charge or request solemnly or earnestly (*to* do); **ǎdjurā'tion** (ǎjoor-) *n.* [L *adjuro* put to oath (JURY)]

**adjŭ'st** *v.t. & i.* Arrange, put in order; regulate; assess (loss etc.); harmonize (discrepancies); adapt (thing *to* needs etc.); adapt oneself (*to* environment etc.); ∼ment *n.* [F f. L (*juxta* near)]

**ǎ'djutan|t** (ǎ'jōō-) *n.* Assistant; (Mil.) officer assisting superior by communicating orders, conducting correspondence, etc.; ∼t (**bird**), large Indian stork; ∼cy̆ *n.* [L (*juvo* help)]

**ǎd lĭ'b** *adv., a., & v.* **1.** *adv.* (or *ad li'bitum*). To any desired extent. **2.** (*ad-lib*). *a., & v.i.* (-bb-). (colloq.) (Speak) without preparation, improvise(d). [abbr. L *ad libitum* according to pleasure]

**Adm.** *abbr.* Admiral.

**ǎ'dmĭn** *n.* (colloq.) Administration. [abbr.]

**admĭ'nĭst|er** *v.t. & i.* (∼rable). Manage (affairs, person's estate, etc.); formally give out (sacrament, justice) or present (oath *to*); furnish, give, (*administer a dose, a rebuke*); apply (remedy *to*); act as administrator; ∼**rāte** *v.t.* & *i.*, administer, esp. act as administrator, manage; ∼**rā'tion** *n.*, administering (esp. of public affairs; cf. LETTER), the Government; ∼**rative** *a.*; ∼**rātor** *n.*; ∼**rātrix** *n.* (*pl.* **-trices** *pr.* -isēz). [F f. L (MINISTER)]

**a'dmirab|le** *a.* (∼**ly**). Worthy of admiration; excellent. [F f. L (ADMIRE)]

**a'dmiral** *n.* Commander-in-chief of navy; naval officer of high rank, commander of fleet or squadron (A∼ **of the Fleet** or \*Fleet A∼, A∼, Vice-A∼, Rear-A∼, four grades); **red, white,** ∼, species of butterfly; ∼**ty** *n.*, (Law) trial of maritime questions; ‖A∼ (**Board**), Department administering the Navy. [F f. L f. Arab. (AMIR)]

**admīr'|e** *v.t.* Regard with pleased surprise, respect, or approval; (colloq.) express admiration of; **ǎd-mirā'tion** *n.*; ∼**er** *n.*, (woman's) suitor; ∼**ing** *a.*, (esp.) showing or feeling admiration for). [F or L (*miror* wonder at)]

**admi'|t** *v.t.* & *i.* (**-tt-**). Let in, allow entrance of, (person etc. *to* place, category, privilege, etc.); accept (proof, plea, statement) as valid; acknowledge (*admit this to be so, that it is so, that I, I admit, is true*); confess *to*; (of enclosed space) have room for; ∼**t of**, leave room for (doubt, improvement, etc.); ∼**ssible** *a.* (**-bly**); ∼**ssibi'lity** *n.*; ∼**ssion** (**-shon**) *n.*, admitting or being admitted (*to*), fee for this, acknowledgement (*of* fact, error); ∼**ssive** *a.*; ∼**ttance** *n.*, admitting, being admitted, esp. to place; ∼**ttědly** *adv.*, confessedly, as acknowledged fact. [L (*mitto miss-* send)]

**admi'x** *v.t.* & *i.* Add as ingredient; mix (*with*); ∼**ture** *n.* [MIX]

**admo'nish** *v.t.* Urge, give advice, remind, (person *to do*, *that*); warn (*of* thing); reprove; ∼**ment**, **ǎd-moni'tion**, *ns.*; **admo'nitory** *a.* (**-ily**). [F f. L (*moneo* warn)]

**ad nauseam** (ǎd naw'siǎm, -z-) *adv.* To a disgusting extent. [L, = to sickness]

**ado'** (adoō') *n.* Busy activity, fuss; difficulty. [AT, DO⁴; orig. in *much* ∼ = much to do]

**adō'be** (or -ō'b) *n.* Unburnt sun-dried brick. [Sp.]

**ǎdolě'scen|t** *n.* & *a.* (Person) between childhood and adulthood; ∼**ce** *n.* [F f. L (ADULT)]

**adō'pt** *v.t.* Take (person) into a relationship (*as* heir, son, etc., or ‖*as* candidate for office); take over (another's idea etc.); choose (course etc.); ‖accept responsibility for maintenance of (road etc.); accept (report etc.); ∼**ion** *n.*; ∼**ive** *a.*, by adoption (*adoptive son*). [F, or L (*opto* choose)]

**adōr'|e** *v.t.* Regard with deep respect and affection; worship; (R.C. Ch.) reverence (HOST³ etc.); (colloq.) like greatly; ∼**able** *a.* (**-bly**), (esp., colloq.) charming, delightful; **ǎdorā'tion** *n.*; ∼**er** *n.*, (esp.) ardent admirer. [F f. L *adoro* worship]

**adōr'n** *v.t.* Add beauty to, be an ornament to; deck with ornament(s); ∼**ment** *n.* [F f. L (*orno* deck)]

**adrē'nal** *a.* Close to the kidneys; **adrē'nalin(e)** *n.*, hormone secreted by adrenal glands, affecting circulation and muscular activity, this extracted or synthesized for medicinal use. [RENAL]

**adri'ft** *adv.* & *pred. a.* Drifting; (fig.) at the mercy of circumstances; (colloq.) unfastened. [A³]

**adroi't** *a.* Dextrous, skilful. [F (AD-, DIRECT)]

**ǎdsŏr'|b** *v.t.* (Of solid) hold (particles of another substance) to its surface; ∼**ption** *n.* [AD-, ABSORB]

**a'dŭl|āte** *v.t.* Flatter obsequiously; ∼**ā'tion**, ∼**ātor**, *ns.*; ∼**ātory** *a.* [L *adulor* fawn on]

**a'dŭlt** (or adŭ'-) *a.* & *n.* Grown-up, mature, (person etc.); ∼**hŏŏd** (-h-) *n.* [L *adolesco adultus* grow up]

**adŭ'lter|ate. 1.** (-āt) *v.t.* (∼**able**). Debase (esp. foods) by admixture of other substances (also fig.); ∼**ant** *a.* & *n.*, (substance) used thus; ∼**ā'tion**, ∼**ātor**, *ns.* **2.** (-at) *a.* Adulterous; adulterated. [foll.]

**adŭ'lter|y** *n.* Voluntary sexual intercourse of married person other than with spouse; ∼**er**, ∼**ess**, *ns.*, one guilty of adultery; ∼**ine** *a.*, (born) of adultery; spurious; ∼**ous** *a.*, (guilty) of adultery. [F f. L *adulter* adulterer]

**a'dumbr|āte** *v.t.* Represent in outline; faintly indicate; foreshadow; overshadow; ∼**ā'tion** *n.*; **adŭ'mbrative** *a.* [L (*umbra* shade)]

**ad valo′rem** (ăd valŏr′ĕm) adv. & a. (Of taxes) proportionate to estimated value of goods. [L]

**adva′nce** (-vah′-). 1. *v.t. & i.* Move or put forward (*advance the left foot, the hour hand*); help on, promote, (plan, person); make (claim, suggestion); bring (event) to earlier date; pay (money) beforehand; lend (money); raise (price), (of price) rise; come or go forward; progress (~d *ideas*, ahead of the times; ‖~d *level*, G.C.E. examination; ~d *student*, *studies*, not elementary); ~**ment** (-sm-) *n.* 2. *n.* Going forward; progress; friendly or amorous approach (*make advances to*); rise in price; payment beforehand; loan; (*attrib.*) done etc. beforehand (~ *copy*, supplied before date of publication); **in** ~, ahead in place or time. [F f. L *ab-*, *ante* before]

**adva′ntage** (-vah′-). 1. *n.* Better position, superiority, (*gain an advantage over* person; **you have the** ~ **of** me, esp., you know me but I do not know you; **take** ~ **of**, utilize (circumstance), outwit (person), seduce (woman)); favourable circumstance (*has the advantage of cheapness*; *seen*, *heard*, etc., **to** ~, in a way that exhibits merits); (Tennis) next point won after deuce; **ăd-vantā′geous** (-jus) *a.* (to). 2. *v.t.* Be an advantage to, help, (person, plan). [F (prec.)]

**ă′dvent** *n.* Arrival of important person or event; (*A*~) season before Christmas; coming of Christ; **A~ĭst** *n.*, member of sect believing in imminent second coming of Christ. [E f. F f. L *adventus* (*venio* come)]

**ădventi′tious** (-shus) *a.* Coming from outside; accidental, casual; (Biol.) in unusual place. [L (prec.)]

**advě′ntur|e**. 1. *n.* Daring enterprise; unexpected or exciting experience; ~**ous** (-cher-) *a.*, venturesome, enterprising. 2. *v.i.* Incur risk; venture (*into* place, (*up*)*on* undertaking); ~**er** (-cher-) *n.*, one who seeks adventures, mercenary soldier, speculator, one who lives by his wits; ~**ĕss** (-cher-) *n.*, (esp.) woman who lives by her wits. [F f. L (ADVENT)]

**ă′dvĕrb** *n.* Word modifying *adj.*, *v.*, or *adv.*, and expressing manner, degree, circumstance, etc. (*gently*, *quite*, *here*, *why*); **advě′rbial** *a.* (-lly). [F or L (*verbum* word, VERB)]

**ă′dvĕrs|e** *a.* Contrary, hostile, injurious, (*an adverse opinion*; *adverse to our interests*); **ă′dversary** *n.*, opponent, enemy; **the A~ary**, the Devil; **advě′rsĭty** *n.*, adverse fortune, misfortune. [F f. L (*verto vers-* turn)]

**‖ă′dvĕrt**[1] *n.* (colloq.) Advertisement. [abbr.]

**advě′rt**[2] *v.i.* Refer *to* (in speech or writing). [ADVERSE]

**ă′dvĕrtise** (-z) *v.t. & i.* Make generally or publicly known, describe merits of (goods etc.) esp. to encourage sales; ~ **for**, ask for by public notice; **advě′rtisement** (-sm-) *n.*

**advī′c|e** *n.* Opinion given as to future action (*my advice to you is to go*); **take** ~**ce**, seek it esp. from expert, act according to it); information, news; formal notice of transaction; ~**se** (-z) *v.t. & i.*, give advice (to), recommend (*he advised caution*, *me to rest*), inform (*of* thing, *that*), *con*-sult *with*; ~**sable** (-z-) *a.* (-bly), to be recommended, expedient; ~**sabĭ′lĭty** (-z-) *n.*; ~**sed** (-zd) *a.* (esp. in *comb.*, as ILL-*advised*); ~**sĕdly** (-z-) *adv.*, deliberately; ~**ser**, ~**sor**, (-z-) *ns.*; ~**sŏry** (-z-) *a.*, giving advice (*advisory committee*). [F f. L (*video* see)]

**ă′dvoc|ate**. 1. *n.* One who pleads for another; professional pleader in lawcourts (LORD *Advocate*); one who speaks in favour *of* (policy etc.); ~**acў** *n.*, function of advocate, pleading in support of. 2. (-āt) *v.t.* (~**able**). Plead for, support (policy etc.). [F f. L (*voco* call)]

**‖advow′son** (-z-) *n.* Right to present to benefice. [F f. L (prec.)]

**advt.** *abbr.* advertisement.

**ădze**, *ădz* *n.*, & *v.t.* (Cut with) kind of axe with arched blade at right angles to handle. [E]

**ae′gĭs** *n.* Protection; **under the** ~ (sponsorship) **of.** [L f. Gk *aigis* shield of Zeus or Athene]

**aeō′lian**, *ēō′lian*, *a.* Wind-borne; ~ **harp**, stringed instrument giving musical sounds on exposure to wind. [L (*Aeolus* wind-god, f. Gk)]

**ae′on**, **ē′on**, *n.* Immense period, an age. [L f. Gk]

**ā′er|āte** (or ār′-) *v.t.* Expose to action of air; charge with carbon dioxide (‖*aerated water*); ~**ā′tion** *n.* [L *aer* AIR]

**aer′|ial** (ār′-). 1. *a.* (~lly). Of or like air, gaseous; existing etc. in the air; imaginary; by or from aircraft (*aerial attack, photography*). **2.** *n.* Wire or rod for transmitting or receiving radio waves. [L f. Gk (AIR)]

**aerie.** See EYRIE.

**aer′o-** (ār′ō) *in comb.* Air; aircraft; **~bǎ′tǐcs** *n.* (as *sing.* or *pl.*), feats of expert and usu. spectacular flying of aircraft [(ACRO)BATICS]; ‖**~drōme** *n.,* airfield [(HIPPO)DROME]; **~dynǎ′mǐc** *a.,* of **~dynǎ′mǐcs** *n.,* dynamics of solid bodies moving through air [DYNAMICS]; **~nau′tǐc(al)** *adjs.* (-ically), of **~nau′tǐcs** *n.,* science, art, or practice of aerial navigation [NAUTICAL]; ‖**~plāne** *n.,* mechanically driven heavier-than-air aircraft with wings [F (PLANE²)]; **~sŏl** *n.,* system of minute particles suspended in gas, device for producing fine spray of substance packed under pressure [SOL]; **~space** *n.,* (aviation in) earth's atmosphere and outer space [SPACE]. [Gk (AIR)]

**aesthē′tǐc. 1.** *a.* (**~ally**). Concerned with or capable of appreciation of the beautiful; in good taste; **~ǐsm** *n.* **2.** *n.* Set of principles of good taste; (in *pl.*) philosophy of the beautiful in art etc. **3. ae′sthēte** *n.,* appreciator of beauty in art etc. [Gk (*aisthanomai* perceive)]

**aetǐ|ŏ′logȳ, *ēt-,** *n.* Assignment of a cause; study of causation or of causes of disease; **~ŏlŏ′gǐc(al)** *adjs.* (-ically). [L f. Gk (*aitia* cause)]

**af-.** See AD-.

**A.F.** *abbr.* audio frequency.

**afar′** *adv.* At or to a distance (esp. *afar off*; **from ~,** from a distance). [A³]

‖**A.F.C.** *abbr.* Association Football Club.

**ǎ′ffab|le** *a.* (**~ly**). Easy to approach and talk to; courteous and not arrogant; **~ǐ′lǐtȳ** *n.* [F f. L *affabilis*]

**affair′** *n.* Thing to be done, matter, concern, (*that is my affair*; *the Dreyfus affair*); love affair; (colloq.) thing, happening, (*his tie was a gorgeous affair*); (in *pl.*) public or private business (*current affairs*; *put your affairs in order*); **~ of honour,** duel; **affaire** (*de cœur*) (ăf′ārdekĕr′) *n.,* love affair. [F *à faire* to do]

**affĕ′ct** *v.t.* Use (a costume, style, etc.) by preference; pose as (*affect the aesthete*); pretend (*affect ignorance, to do*); produce effect on (*does not affect metals*; *how does it affect me, my plans?*); move, touch the feelings of, (*an affecting sermon*); (of disease) attack (*his lungs are affected*); **ǎffĕc-tā′tion** *n.,* studied display (*of modesty etc.*), artificial manner, pretence; **~èd** *a.,* (esp.) full of affectation, (w. *adv.*) disposed (*towards* person); **~ion** *n.,* goodwill, love, (*for, towards*), malady, disease; **~ionate** *a.,* loving; **~ǐve** *a.,* of the emotions. [F, or L *affecto*]

**affǐ′ance** *v.t.* (usu. in *pass.*) Promise in marriage (*affianced to; his affianced bride*). [f f. L (*fidus* trusty)]

**ǎffǐdā′vǐt** *n.* Written statement, confirmed by oath, for use as judicial evidence (*deponent made, swore, took, an affidavit*). [L, = he has stated on oath]

**affǐ′lǐ|āte. 1.** *v.t.* (**~able**). Adopt, attach, connect, as member or branch (*I, the society, was affiliated to* or *with* an organization); **~ā′tion** *n.* (‖**~ation order,** compelling putative father of illegitimate child to help support it). **2.** *n.* Affiliated person or society etc. [L (FILIAL)]

**affǐ′nǐtȳ** *n.* Relationship esp. by marriage; structural resemblance (*with, between,* animals, plants, languages; also fig.) due to or suggesting relationship; liking, attraction, (**has an ~ for,** attracts, is attracted by); (Chem.) tendency of substances to combine with others. [F f. L (*finis* border)]

**affǐr′m** *v.t.* & *i.* Assert, state as fact; make affirmation; **ǎffǐrmā′-tion** *n.,* (esp.) solemn declaration by one who conscientiously declines oath; **~ative,** (*a.*) affirming, (*n.*) affirmative statement or word (**answer in the ~,** say yes, say thing is so); **~atorȳ** *a.* [F f. L (FIRM)]

**affǐx. 1.** (-ǐ′-) *v.t.* Attach (label, stamp, *to* parcel etc.); add (element *to* word, signature *to* document); impress (seal). **2.** (ǎ′-) *n.* Thing affixed; (Gram.) prefix or suffix. [F or L (FIX)]

**afflǐ′ct** *v.t.* Distress physically or mentally (**~ed with,** suffering from); **~ion** *n.,* distress, (cause of) pain or calamity. [L (*fligo flict-* strike down)]

**ǎ′ffluen|t** (-lōō-). **1.** *a.* Rich (**~t society,** with wide distribution of wealth); abundant; **~ce** *n.* **2.** *n.* Tributary stream. [F f. L (FLUENT)]

**affōr′d** *v.t.* Provide (*records afford an explanation; farm affords fresh food*); **can ~,** have enough money, means, time, etc., be able to spare, (*can* afford £50, to lose £50; cannot afford a holiday), be in a position to do (can afford to be critical). [E (ge- pref. implying completeness, FORTH)]

**affo′rest** v.t. Convert into forest; plant with trees; **~a′tion** n. [L (FOREST)]

**affray′** n. Breach of the peace by fighting or rioting in public. [AF (EX-[1], Gmc = peace)]

**affro′nt** (-ŭ′-). **1.** v.t. Insult openly; offend, embarrass; face, confront. **2.** n. Open insult. [F f. L (FRONT)]

**A′fghăn** (ă′fgăn) n. & a. (Native, language) of Afghanistan; **~ hound**, dog with long silky hair. [Pushtu]

**afie′ld** adv. Away from home, to or at a distance, (far afield). [E (A[3])]

**afir′e** adv. & pred. a. On fire (lit. or fig.); **afla′me** adv. & pred. a., in flames (lit. or fig.). [A[3]]

**afloa′t** adv. & pred. a. Floating in water or air; at sea; out of debt; in circulation, current. [E (A[3])]

**à fond** (ahfaw′n) adv. Thoroughly. [F, = to bottom]

**afoo′t** adv. & pred. a. Progressing, in operation, (a plot is afoot). [A[3]]

**afor′e** adv. & prep. (Naut.) In front (of); (arch.) before, previously; **~mentioned, ~said**, etc., previously mentioned etc.; **~thought**, premeditated (malice aforethought). [E (A[3])]

**a fortiori** (ā fōrtiōr′ī) adv. & a. With stronger reason, more conclusively. [L]

**afrai′d** pred. a. Alarmed, frightened, (afraid of ghosts, of being late, that we shall or lest we should be late); **be ~** to do something, dare not do it); **I′m ~**, (colloq.) I admit with regret (I'm afraid I'm late, there's none left). [AFFRAY]

**afre′sh** adv. Anew, with fresh beginning. [OF, FRESH]

**A′frĭcan** (ă′-) a. & n. (Native, esp. dark-skinned, or inhabitant) of Africa; **~ize** v.t. [L]

**Afrĭk|aa′ns** (ăfrĭkah′ns) n. S. Afr. Dutch language; **~a′ner** (-ah′-) n., Afrikaans-speaking white person in S. Africa, esp. of Dutch descent. [Du., = African]

**A′frŏ** (ă′-) a. (Of hair) long and bushy, like that of some Blacks; (in comb.) African (**~-American**, esp. of Amer. Blacks). [L, or abbr.]

**aft** (ahft) adv. (Naut., Aeron.) In, near, to, or towards stern or tail. [E]

**a′fter** (ah′-) adv., prep., conj., & a.

**1.** adv. Behind in place (follow after; look before and after); later (soon after; a week after). **2.** prep. In pursuit or quest of (run after him; he is after a job; hanker after); behind (shut the door after you); about, concerning, (ask after her, her health); following in time, later than, (arrived after me, after his death; returned **~ six months**, when that interval had elapsed; **time ~ time**, many times in succession); in view of, because of, (after such behaviour); next in importance to; according to; in imitation of, in allusion to, (after the same pattern; a picture after Rubens; named after Nelson); **~ all**, in spite of what has been said or done or expected; **~noo′n** n., time from noon to evening (tomorrow afternoon, this afternoon; in or during the afternoon; every Monday afternoon, on Monday afternoons; afternoon TEA), (colloq.) = GOOD afternoon; **~ one's own heart**, such as one delights in. **3.** conj. After the time when (arrived after I did; this was after he died). **4.** a. Later, following, (in after years); (Naut.) nearer stern (after cabin; **~most** a., farthest aft); **~birth**, placenta etc. discharged after childbirth; **~-care**, attention after leaving hospital etc.; **~-effect**, delayed effect following interval or primary effect; **~life** (later, or after death); **~math** (-mă-, -mah-), grass growing after mowing, (fig.) consequences (the aftermath of war), [math mowing]; **~shave**, (lotion) used after shaving, **~taste** (remaining after eating or drinking); **~thought**, thing thought of or added later. **5.** ‖**~s** (-z) n.pl., (colloq.) course following main course at meal. [E]

**a′fterwards** (-z), **\*a′fterward**, (ah′-) adv. Later, subsequently. [E (AFT, -WARD(s))]

**ag-.** See AD-.

**agai′n** (or agĕ′n) adv. Another time, once more, (try again; COME again; **~ and ~, time and (time) ~**, repeatedly; **as much ~**, twice as much; cf. HALF); further, besides, likewise, (then, again, why did he write?); on the other hand (I might, and again I might not). [E, = opposite]

**agai′nst** (or agĕ′-) prep. In opposition to (fight against; arson is against the law); to the disadvantage of (his age is against him); in contrast to (against a dark background); in anticipation of (*against his coming*; *warned against pickpockets*); in return for (*is provided against payment of a fee*); into collision or in contact with (*ran against a rock*; *lean against the wall*).

**aga'pe**[1] *pred. a.* Gaping, open-mouthed. [A[3]]

**agape**[2] (ă'găpē) *n.* Love-feast of early Christians in connection with Lord's Supper; Christian love. [Gk, = brotherly love]

**a'garic** *n.* Fungus with cap and stalk, e.g. common mushroom. [L f. Gk]

**a'gate** *n.* Kind of chalcedony. [F f. L f. Gk]

**aga've** *n.* Kind of spiny-leaved plant flowering only once. [person in Gk myth]

**age.** **1.** *n.* Length of past life or existence (*what is his age?*; *died at a great age*; **middle, old, ~,** middle, later, part of normal life; **moon's ~,** since new moon; **of full ~,** of adult status (18 years, formerly 21), so **under ~,** below this, **come of ~,** reach this); old age (*the peevishness of age*); historical or other period (ICE-*age*; BRONZE, IRON, STONE, *age*; **golden, silver, ~,** best, second-best, as regards prosperity or in Latin or other literature etc.); (colloq., esp. in *pl.*) long time (*waiting for ages*); **~-long, ~-old,** having existed for a very long time; **~less** (-jl-) *a.*, never growing or appearing old. **2.** *v.t. & i.* (~'ing, a'ging). (Cause to) grow old or show signs of age. [F f. L *aetas*]

**aged** *a.,* (ājd) of the age of, (ā'jĭd) old (esp. of person). [F f. L *aetas*]

**a'gency** *n.* Active operation, action, (*moral, free, agency*); intervening action (*fertilized by the agency of bees*); function of agent; business establishment of agent (*travel agency*). [L (ACT)]

**age'nda** *n.* (List of) items of business to be considered at meeting etc.

**a'gent** *n.* One who or that which exerts power or produces effect (*soda is the active agent*); one who acts for another in business, politics, etc., (*insurance* agent); (**secret**) **~,** spy; **age'ntial** (-shal) *a.*

**agent provocateur** (ahzhahn prŏvŏkatĕr') *n.* (*pl.* **-ts -rs** *pr.* same). Person employed to detect suspected offenders by tempting them to overt action. [F, = provocative agent]

**agglo'mer|ate** *v., a., & n.* **1.** (-āt) *v.t. & i.* Collect into a mass; **~ā'tion**

*n.*; **~ative** *a.* **2.** (-at) *a. & n.* (Collected into) a mass (esp. Geol., of volcanic fragments). [L (*glomus -eris* ball)]

**agglu'tin|ate** (-lōō'-) *v.t. & i.* Unite as with glue, coalesce; form (words) into compounds; **~ā'tion** *n.*; **~ative** *a.* [L (GLUTEN)]

**aggra'nd|ize** *v.t.* Increase power, rank, or wealth of (person, State); make seem greater; **~izement** (-zm-) *n.* [F (GRAND[1])]

**a'ggrav|ate** *v.t.* Increase gravity of (illness, offence, etc.); (colloq.) annoy; **~ā'tion** *n.* [L (*gravis* heavy)]

**a'ggreg|ate** *a., n., & v.* **1.** *a.* Collected; collective, total, (*the aggregate amount spent*). **2.** *n.* Sum total; assemblage (**in the ~ate,** as a whole); broken stone etc. used in making concrete; mass of particles or minerals. **3.** (-āt) *v.t. & i.* (~able). Collect, form into an aggregate; unite (individual to company); (colloq.) amount to; **~ā'tion** *n.*; **~ative** *a.* [L (*grex greg-* flock)]

**aggre'ss|ion** (-shon) *n.* Unprovoked attack; hostile act or feeling; **~ive** *a.,* apt to make attacks, self-assertive; **~or** *n.* [F or L (*gradior gress-* walk)]

**aggrie'ved** (-vd) *a.* Having a grievance. [F (GRIEF)]

**a'ggro** *n.* (sl.) Deliberate trouble-making. [abbr. *aggravation* or *aggression*]

**agha'st** (agah'-) *a.* Terrified, amazed, (*stand aghast at*). [E, p.p. of obs. (*a*)*gast* terrify]

**a'gile** *a.* Quick-moving, nimble; **agi'lity** *n.* [F f. L *agilis* (ACT)]

**a'git|ate** *v.t. & i.* Shake (liquid etc.); disturb, excite, (feelings, person); turn over in one's mind, discuss, (plan etc.); stir up (public) interest or disquiet (*for, against*); **~ā'tion** *n.,* (esp.) disturbed state of mind; **~ātor** *n.,* (esp.) one who agitates politically. [L *agito* (ACT)]

**agley'** (-ā', -ē') *adv.* (Sc.) Askew, awry (GANG[2] *agley*). [Sc. *gley* squint]

**A.G.M.** *abbr.* annual general meeting.

**a'gnail** *n.* Torn skin at root of finger-nail, the resulting soreness. [E, = tight (metal) nail, painful lump]

**a'gn|ate** *n. & a.* (One who is) descended esp. by male line from same male ancestor; (person) of same clan or nation; **~a'tic** *a.* [L (AD-, *nascor* be born)]

**agnŏs'tĭc** n. & a. (~**ally**). (Adherent) of the view that nothing is or can be known of the existence of God or of anything but material phenomena; ~**ism** n. [A- 2, GNOSTIC]

**agō'** adv. In the past (ten years ago; long ~, long since). [agone p.p. = gone away, past]

**agŏ'g** adv. & pred. a. Eager, expectant, (all agog for mischief). [F]

**ă'gon|y** n. Extreme physical or mental suffering (||~**y column**, colloq., PERSONAL column; **death** ~**y**, pangs of death); severe struggle; ~**ize** v.t. & i., cause agony to (agonizing suspense, in p.p.) showing agony (agonized look), suffer agony, make desperate efforts. [F or L f. Gk (agōn contest)]

**ăgoraphō'bĭ|a** n. Morbid dread of open spaces; ~**c** a. & n. [Gk agora market-place, -PHOBIA]

**agrā'r'ian. 1.** a. Relating to landed property or cultivated land. **2.** n. Advocate of redistribution of landed property. [L agrarius (ager field)]

**agree'** v.i. & t. Consent (to proposal or statement, to do; ~ to **differ**, cease to try to convince each other); consent to or approve of (proposal, terms, etc.); hold similar opinion (I agree with you about this, agree that it is too late; **be ~d**, have reached similar opinion); ||**reach agreement** about; become or be in harmony (with person; ~ **on**, decide by mutual consent; ~ **with**, suit constitution of; climate does not agree with me); (Gram.) be of same number, gender, case, or person (with); ~**able** (-rĭ'a-) a. (-**bly**), pleasing, conformable to, (colloq.) willing to agree (to thing, to do); ~**ment** n., (esp.) mutual understanding, contract or promise. [F f. L (AG-, gratus pleasing)]

**agrĕ'stĭc** a. Rural, rustic. [L agrestis (ager field)]

**ă'grĭc|ŭlture** n. Cultivation of soil and rearing of animals; ~**ŭ'ltural** (-cher-) a. (-**lly**); ~**ŭ'ltur(al)ĭst** (-cher-) ns. [F or L (ager field)]

**ă'grĭmony** n. Yellow-flowered perennial plant. [F f. L f. Gk]

**agrŏ'nomy** n. Science of soil management and crop production. [F f. Gk (agros land)]

**agrou'nd** adv. Upon the bottom of shallow water (ship ran, is, aground). [A³]

**ā'gūe** n. Malarial fever with cold,

hot, and sweating stages; fit of shivering. [F f. L (ACUTE)]

**ah** int. expr. joy, sorrow, surprise, boredom, admiration, ⊙ contempt, entreaty, etc. [F, imit.]

**A.H.** abbr. Of the Muslim era. [L anno Hegirae in the year of the Hegira]

**aha** (ahhah', a-hah') int. expr. surprise, triumph, or mockery. [AH, HA]

**ahea'd** (a-hĕ'd) adv. Farther forward in space or time (went on ahead; ahead of his times; breakers ahead!); straight forwards (GO¹ ahead). [A³]

**ahĕ'm** (a-h-) int. used to call attention or gain time. [HEM²]

**ahoy'** (a-h-) int. (Naut.) used in hailing. [AH, HOY²]

**aid. 1.** v.t. Help (person to do, in doing); promote (recovery etc.). **2.** n. Help; helper; helpful thing (HEARing aid); **what's (all) this in ~ of?**, (colloq.) what is the purpose of this? [F f. L (ADJUTANT)]

**A.I.D.** abbr. artificial insemination by donor.

**aide** n. Aide-de-camp; *assistant; ~**-de-camp** (ād-dekah'n) n. (pl. ~**s-de-camp** pr. same), officer assisting senior officer; ~**-mémoire** (ā'dmĕmwār) n., (book or document serving as) aid to memory (esp. Diplom.). [F]

**ail** v.t. & i. Trouble, afflict, in body or mind (what ails him?; not in pass. nor with n. as subj.); be ill; ~**ing** a., (frequently), ill, in poor condition; ~**ment** n., illness esp. slight one. [E]

**ai'lerŏn** n. Hinged flap on aeroplane wing, controlling lateral balance. [F (aile wing)]

**aim. 1.** v.t. & i. Direct (blow or missile at); intend (remark, law, etc.) as attack on; take aim (~ **high**, show ambition); intend or try (to do, at doing); ~ **at**, point (gun etc.) towards, seek to attain. **2.** n. Aiming, directing of weapon, missile, etc., at object (**take ~**, direct weapon thus); object aimed at, purpose (what are his aims?); ~**less** a., purposeless. [F f. L (ESTIMATE)]

**ain't.** See BE, HAVE.

**air. 1.** n. Gaseous mixture mainly of oxygen and nitrogen enveloping earth and breathed by all land animals and plants; atmosphere; open space in atmosphere (in the open air; **in the ~**, (of feelings etc.) prevalent, (of plan) uncertain; **on the ~**, broadcast(ing); **take the ~**, go out of doors); atmosphere as place where aircraft operate (by ~, in or by aircraft); appearance (*it, he, has an air of mystery*); confident manner (*does things with an air; in pl.*, affected manner, haughtiness; *give one*self *airs*); melody, tune; **~-bed**, inflated mattress; **~-bladder** (filled with air, in plants or animals); **~borne**, transported by air, (of aircraft) in the air after taking off; **~-brick** (perforated, for ventilation); ||*air* COMMODORE; **~-conditioned**, furnished with **~-conditioning**, (apparatus for) bringing air in building etc. to required humidity and temperature; **~-cooled** (by current of cold air); **~craft**, aeroplane(s), helicopter(s); **~craft-carrier**, ship that carries, and acts as base for, aeroplanes; **~craftman**, lowest rank in R.A.F. (**~craftwoman**, in W.R.A.F.); **~-cushion**, cushion inflated with air, layer of air supporting hovercraft; **~field**, area equipped with hangars and runways for aircraft; **~ force**, branch of armed forces fighting in the air (||*Royal Air Force*); **~gun** (using compressed air as propelling force); **~ hostess**, stewardess in passenger aircraft; ||**~letter**, light sheet for letter to go by cheap air mail; **~lift**, (*n.*) transport of supplies etc. by air esp. in emergency, (*v.t.*) transport thus; **~line**, public air transport system or company; **~lock**, stoppage of flow by air-bubble in pump or pipe, compartment providing access to pressurized chamber; **~ mail** (carried by air); **~man**, **~woman**, pilot or member of crew of aircraft; **Air (Chief, Vice-) Marshal**, high ranks in R.A.F.; *~**plane**, aeroplane; **~ pocket**, apparent vacuum in air causing aircraft in flight to drop suddenly; **~port**, airfield with facilities for passengers and goods; **~ pump** (for pumping air into or out of vessel); **~ raid**, attack by aircraft; ||**~screw**, propeller of aircraft; **~ship**, flying machine lighter than air; **~sick(ness)**, (affected with) nausea due to motion of aircraft; **~space**, air above country and subject to its jurisdiction; **~ speed**, aircraft's speed relative to air through which it moves; **~strip**, strip of ground for take-off and landing of aircraft; **~ terminal**, place in town with transport to and from airport;

**~tight**, impermeable to air; **~-way**, regular route of aircraft; **~woman** (see **airman**); **~worthy**, (of aircraft) fit to fly. **2.** *v.t.* Expose to air, ventilate; dry off (clothes etc.); show off (clothes, qualities); make known (grievance, theory). [F f. L f. Gk *aër*; sense 'appearance' F f. L. *area*, 'melody' f. It. *aria* air]

**Air'edāle** (ār'd-) *n.* Large rough-coated terrier. [place]

**air'less** *a.* Stuffy; still, calm. [AIR]

**air'|y̆** *a.* (~ily, ~iness). Breezy; well-ventilated; light as air, unsubstantial; flippant.

**aisle** (īl) *n.* Division of church, esp. parallel to and divided by pillars from main nave, choir, or transept; passage between rows of pews or seats. [F f. L *ala* wing]

||**ait**, ||**eyot**, (āt) *n.* Small isle esp. in river. [E]

**aitch** *n.* Letter H. [phon. sp.]

||**ai'tchbōne** *n.* Rump-bone; cut of beef lying over this. [F f. L *natis* buttock (for loss of *n*- cf. ADDER)]

**ajar'** *adv.* & *pred. a.* (Of door) slightly open. [A³, obs. CHAR¹ turn]

**aki'mbō** *adv.* (Of the arms) with hands on hips and elbows turned outwards. [E, prob. f. N]

**aki'n** *pred. a.* Related by blood (*are near akin to him*; *are they akin?*); similar (*a feeling akin to envy*). [A³]

**al-.** See AD-.

**-al** *suf.* forming (1) *adjs.* w. sense 'of, of the nature of, characteristic of' (*postal, sensational, terrestrial, tropical*), (2) *ns.* esp. of verbal action (*acquittal, removal*). [F or L]

**Ala.** *abbr.* Alabama.

**ă'labaster** (-bah-). **1.** *n.* Translucent usu. white form of gypsum, freq. carved into ornaments. **2.** *a.* Of, white or smooth as, alabaster. [F f. L f. Gk]

**à la carte** (ah lah kār't) *adv.* & *a.* (Of meal etc.) ordered as separate items from the menu. [F]

**ală'ck** *int.* (arch.) expr. sorrow (esp. *alack-a-day!*). [*ah lack*]

**ală'crity̆** *n.* Briskness, cheerful readiness. [L (*alacer* brisk)]

**Ală'ddĭn** (a-) *n.* **~'s lamp**, talisman enabling holder to gratify any wish. [character in *Arabian Nights*]

**à la** (ah lah) *prep.* In the manner of; **~ mōde** *adv.* & *a.*, in the fashion, fashionable. [F]

**alăr'm. 1.** *n.* (Apparatus giving) warning sound (**~ (clock)**, with device that rings at set time); warning of danger (*give, raise, the alarm*); frightened anticipation of danger; ∼**ist** *n.*, person rousing needless or excessive alarm. **2.** *v.t.* Arouse to sense of danger; disturb, frighten. **3. alăr'um** *n.* (arch.)= ALARM; see EXCURSION. [F f. It. *all' arme!* to arms!]

**ală's** (*or* -ah's) *int.* expr. grief. [F (AH, L *lassus* weary)]

**Alas.** *abbr.* Alaska.

**ălb** *n.* White vestment reaching to feet, worn by priests etc. [E f. L *albus* white]

**ă'lbacŏre** *n.* Large kind of tunny, or related fish. [Port. f. Arab., = the young camel]

**ă'lbatrŏss** *n.* Long-winged bird allied to petrel. [Sp., Port. *alcatraz* f. Arab., = the jug]

**albē'it** (awl-) *conj.* (literary). Although. [*all be it*]

**ălbi'nō** (-bē'-) *n.* (*pl.* ∼**s**). Person or animal with congenital lack of colouring pigment in skin and hair; plant lacking normal colouring; **ă'lbinĭsm** *n.* [Sp., Port., (ALB)]

**ă'lbum** *n.* Book for autographs, photographs, stamps, etc.; (holder for) set of gramophone records; record comprising several items. [L (ALB)]

**ă'lbūm**|**ĕn** *n.* White of egg; (esp. eatable) constituent of many seeds; ∼**ĭn** *n.*, water-soluble protein found in egg-white, milk, blood, etc.; ∼**ĭnous** (-ū'-) *a.*

**ă'lchem**|**y̆** (-k-) *n.* Medieval chemistry, esp. pursuit of transmutation of baser metals into gold; **ălchĕ'mĭc(al)** (-k-) *adjs.* (-ically); ∼**ĭst** *n.* [F f. L f. Arab.]

**ă'lcohŏl** *n.* Colourless volatile liquid, intoxicant present in wine, beer, whisky, etc., also used as solvent and fuel; liquor containing this; (Chem.) compound of same type as alcohol; ∼**ĭc** (-hŏ'-), (*a.*) of, like, containing, due to, alcohol, (*n.*) person suffering from alcoholism; ∼**ĭsm** *n.*, (diseased condition resulting from) continual heavy drinking of alcohol. [F or L f. Arab., = the staining powder (KOHL)]

**ă'lcŏve** *n.* Vaulted recess in room-wall; recess in garden wall etc. [F f. Sp. f. Arab., = the vault]

**ă'ldéhy̆de** *n.* Volatile fluid with suffocating smell, got by oxidation of alcohol; (Chem.) compound of

same type as this. [ALCOHOL, DE-, HYDROGEN]

**a'lder** (awl-) *n.* Tree related to birch (**black, red, white, ∼**, other trees not related). [E]

**a'lderman** (awl-) *n.* (*pl.* -**men**). (esp. Hist.) Co-opted member of English county or borough council, next below Mayor; ∼**ĭc** (-mă'-) *a.*; ∼**shĭp** *n.* [E (OLD, MAN)]

**A'lderney** (awl-) *a.* & *n.* (Animal) of breed of cattle from *Alderney* or elsewhere in Channel Islands. [place]

**ā'le** *n.* (arch., exc. as trade wd.) Beer. [E]

**ā'leătŏry** *a.* Depending on chance; involving performer's random choice. [L (*alea* DIE[1])]

**alĕ'mbĭc** *n.* Apparatus formerly used in distilling (also fig. *the alembic of fancy* etc.). [F f. L f. Arab. f. Gk *ambix -ikos* cap of still]

**alĕr't** *a.*, *n.*, & *v.* **1.** *a.* Watchful, vigilant; nimble. **2.** *n.* Alarm-call; (period of) air-raid warning; **on the ∼**, on the look-out. **3.** *v.t.* Make alert, warn. [F f. It. *all' erta* to the watch-tower]

**Alĕxa'ndrĭan** (ălĭgzah'-) *a.* Relating to the Hellenistic civilization of *Alexandria* in Egypt, 3rd–2nd c. B.C. [place]

**ălĕxă'ndrĭne** (-ĭgz-) *a.* & *n.* (Verse) of six iambic feet. [F (*Alexandre* Alexander the Great)]

**ălfă'lfa** *n.* Lucerne. [Sp. f. Arab., = a green fodder]

**ălfrĕ'scō** *adv.* & *a.* In the open air. [It., = in the fresh (air)]

**ă'lg**|**a** *n.* (*pl.* ∼**ae** *pr.* -jē, -gē). Primitive cryptogam, e.g. plankton, some seaweeds; ∼**al** *a.* [L]

**ă'lgĕbr**|**a** *n.* Investigation of properties of numbers, using letters etc. as general symbols; ∼**ā'ĭc(al)** *adjs.* (-ically); ∼**(ā)ĭst** *ns.* [It., Sp., L f. Arab., = reunion of broken parts]

**ă'lgorĭthm** (-dhem) *n.* Process or rules for (esp. machine) calculation etc. [F f. L f. Pers. (name of 9th-c. mathematician)]

**ā'lĭas** *adv.* & *n.* (Name by which one is or was) called on other occasions. [L, = at another time]

**ă'libī** *n.* Plea that when alleged act took place one was elsewhere; (colloq.) excuse. [L, = elsewhere]

**ā'lien. 1.** *a.* Not one's own; foreign; differing in nature (*from, to*); out of harmony; repugnant (*to*). **2.** *n.* Non-naturalized foreigner; a being from another world. **3. ~āte** *v.t.* (~**able**), estrange, transfer ownership of, divert (thing *from intended use*); **~abi'litў, ~ā'tion**, *ns.* [F f. L *alienus* (*alius* other)]

**ali'ght¹** (-ī't) *v.i.* Get down (*from horse, vehicle*); settle, come to earth, from the air. [E]

**ali'ght²** (-ī't) *pred. a.* On fire; lighted up. [*on a light* (lighted) *fire*]

**ali'gn** (-ī'n), **ali'ne**, *v.t.* Place in line; bring into line; bring three or more points into straight line, e.g. in taking aim; ally (one*self*) *with* party or cause; **~ment** (-ī'nm-) *n.* [F (*à ligne* into line)]

**ali'ke. 1.** *adv.* In like manner (*we think alike; all alike are inadequate*). **2.** *pred. a.* Similar, like. [A³]

**ă'liment** *n.* Food; (fig.) **~al** (-ĕ'-) *a.*; **~arў** (-ĕ'-) *a.*, nourishing, nutritive, (**~ary canal**, channel through which food passes from mouth to anus); **~ā'tion** *n.*, nourishment; **ă'limonў** *n.*, allowance due to woman from (ex-)husband after or pending divorce or legal separation. [F or L (*alo* nourish)]

**ali'ne** etc. See ALIGN.

**ălipha'tic** *a.* (Chem.) (Of certain organic compounds) related to fats; in which carbon atoms form open chains. [Gk *aleiphar* -*at*- fat]

**ă'liquŏt** *a.* & *n.* (Part) contained by the integral number of times (*4 is an aliquot part of 12, 5 is not*). [F f. L, = some]

**ali've** *pred. a.* Living (*am still alive; the worst scoundrel alive;* **man ~!**, colloq. expletive); (Electr.) live; alert, responsive, *to* (idea); active, brisk, (LOOK *alive!*); swarming *with* (*river is alive with boats*). [A³, LIFE]

**ă'lkal|ī** *n.* (*pl.* **~is, ~ies**) Any of a class of substances that neutralize acids and form caustic or corrosive solutions in water, e.g. caustic soda; **~īne** *a.*; **~oïd** *n.*, nitrogenous vegetable base, e.g. quinine. [L f. Arab.,= the calcined ashes]

**all** (awl) *a., n.,* & *adv.* **1.** *a.* Whole amount, quantity, or extent of (*waited all day; all his life; all London knew it; we all know why; all hares are timid; hares are all timid; take it all;* **~ kind(s) of, ~ manner of**, many different kinds of; *stop* **~ this** (this excessive) *noise;* **in ~ honesty, with ~ speed**, greatest possible); any whatever (*beyond all doubt; disclaim all knowledge of it*). **2.** *n.* All persons concerned, everything, (*all and* SUNDRY; *all is lost; that is all*); one's whole property (*lost his all*); (in games) for both sides (*four goals all*); **and ~** (the rest); AT *all;* **in ~**, in total number. **3.** *adv.* Entirely, quite, (*dressed all in white; all covered with mud; all the better* etc.; *all* ALONG; *all at once; all too soon; an all-powerful dictator; the all-important thing*); (colloq.) very (*went all coy*); **~ for**, (colloq.) much in favour of. **4. All Blacks**, (colloq.) N.Z. international Rugby Union football team; **~ but**, very little short of (*all but impossible*); **~-clear**, signal that danger or difficulty is over; **All Fools' Day**, 1 Apr.; *all* FOURS; **~ hail**, int. of greeting; **All** HALLOWS; **~ in**, exhausted; **~-in**, (*attrib.*) inclusive of all, (of style of wrestling) with few or no restrictions; **~ in ~**, taken as a whole, of supreme importance; **~ of**, the whole of, every one of, (*all of it; all of us; walked all of 7 miles*); **~ of a dither**, dithering; *it is* **~ one** (a matter of indifference *to*); **~ out**, involving all one's extreme strength. (*going* **~ out**, at full speed); *all* OVER; **~ right**, (*adv.*) as desired, satisfactorily, (*int.*) I consent, also iron. in threats (*all right! you shall repent this*), (*pred. a.*) safe and sound, in good condition, satisfactory; **~ round**, in all respects, for each person; **~-round('er)**, (person) able to perform tasks etc. of many kinds; **All Saints' Day**, 1 Nov.; **All Souls' Day**, 2 Nov.; **~ there**, (colloq.) not deficient in intellect etc.; **~ the same**, (*adv.*) in spite of this, (*pred. a.*) just the same, making no difference, (*if it's* **~ the same to** *you*, if you don't mind); **~ the time**, during the whole of the time referred to, at all times; **~-time**, (of record) hitherto unsurpassed; *all* UP; **~ very fine** or **well**, colloq. formula of dissatisfaction. [E]

**A'llah** (ă'la) *n.* Muslim name of God. [Arab.]

**allay'** *v.t.* Alleviate (pain); diminish (fears, pleasure). [E (*a*- intensive, LAY⁴)]

**allē'ge** *v.t.* Affirm, **esp.** without proof, (thing, *that*); advance as argument or excuse; **allēgā'tion** *n.*; **allē'gĕdlў** *adv.* (in statement which author does not vouch for). [F f. L (*lis lit-* lawsuit)]

**allē'giance** (-jans) *n.* Duty of

subject to sovereign or government; loyalty. [F (LIEGE)]

**ă'llegor|ў** *n.* Narrative describing one subject under the guise of another; **ăllĕgŏ'rĭc(al)** *adjs.* (**-ically**) ~**ĭst** *n.*; ~**ĭze** *v.t.*, treat as allegory. [F f. L f. Gk]

**ălle'grō** (-lā'-), **ăllĕgrĕ'ttō**, *advs.*, *adjs.*, & *ns.* (*pl.* **-os**). (Mus.) (Movement) in brisk, (-*etto*) fairly brisk, time. [It., = lively, gay; -*etto* dim.]

**ăllĕlu'ia**, **hăllĕlu'jah**, (-lōō'ya) *n.* (Song of) praise to God. [L f. Gk f. Heb., = praise the Lord]

**ă'llergў** *n.* Condition of reacting adversely to certain foods, pollens, etc.; (colloq.) antipathy; **allẽr'gĭc** *a.*, having allergy, (colloq.) antipathetic, *to.* [G, f. Gk *allos* other, ENERGY]

**ălle'vĭ|āte** *v.t.* Lessen, make less severe, (pain, evil); ~**ā'tion**, ~**ātor**, *ns.*; ~**ātorў** *a.* [L (*levo* raise)]

**ă'lley** *n.* Narrow street (BLIND *alley*); walk or passage in garden etc.; enclosure for game of skittles etc. [F (*aller* go)]

**ăllĭä'ceous** (-shŭs) *a.* Of or like garlic. [L *allium* garlic]

**alli'ance** *n.* Union esp. of States by treaty or families by marriage (*form an alliance*; *enter into alliance with*); community in qualities etc. (*a close alliance between*). [F (ALLY)]

**ă'llĭgātor** *n.* Amer. or Chin. reptile of crocodile family. [Sp. *el lagarto* the lizard]

**allĭterä'tion** *n.* Beginning of several words in same sentence etc. with same letter or sound (*sing a song of sixpence*); **alli'terāte** *v.i.*, use alliteration; **alli'terătĭve** *a.* [L (LETTER)]

**ă'llŏc|āte** *v.t.* (~**able**). Assign (to person, purpose, place); ~**ā'tion**, ~**ātor**, *ns.* [L (LOCAL)]

**ăllocū'tion** *n.* Formal or hortatory address. [L (*alloquor* exhort)]

**allŏ't** *v.t.* (**-tt-**). Distribute by lot or with authority; apportion (*to*); ~**ment** *n.*, ∥(esp.) small portion of usu. public land let out for cultivation; **ăllŏttee'** *n.*, one to whom thing is allotted. [F (AL-, LOT)]

**ăllŏ'tropў** *n.* Existence of several forms of a chemical element in same state but with different properties; **ăllotrŏ'pĭc(al)** *adjs.* (**-ically**). [Gk *allos* other, *tropos* manner]

**ăllŏttee'.** See ALLOT.

**allow'** *v.t.* & *i.* Admit (thing *to be*,

*that*; *of* alteration etc.); permit (*smoking is allowed*); *consider, assert, (that)*; give periodically (*I allow him £200 a year*); add or deduct in estimating (*allow 10% for inflation*); ~ **for**, take into consideration, provide for, (*allow for shrinkage, human weakness*); ~'**ance**, (*n.*) limited quantity or sum esp. of money or food, money paid to cover special expenses (*entertainment, family, allowance*), deduction from account etc., allowing or amount allowed in reckoning (*make some allowance for*; **make** ~**ances for** person, judge him leniently), (*v.t.*) make an allowance to. [F (AL-, L *laudo* praise & *loco* place)]

**ă'lloy** (or aloi'). **1.** *n.* Mixture of metals; inferior metal mixed esp. with gold or silver. **2.** *v.t.* Mix (metals); debase by admixture; moderate (pleasure etc. *with*). [F (ALLY)]

**a'llspīce** (aw'l-) *n.* (Aromatic spice obtained from) dried ground berry of a W. Ind. tree. [ALL, SPICE]

**allū'|de** (or -ōō'd) *v.i.* Refer transiently or indirectly *to* (thing presumed known); ~**sion** (-zhŏn) *n.*; ~**sĭve** *a.* [L (*ludo* play)]

**allūr'e** *v.t.* Entice, tempt, (person etc. *to, into, from*); charm; ~**ment** (-ūr'm-) *n.* [F (AL-, LURE)]

**allusion, -sive.** See ALLUDE.

**allū'vĭ|um** (or -ōō'-) *n.* (*pl.* ~**a**, ~**ums**). Deposit left by flood; ~**al** *a.* (-**lly**). [F f. L (*luo* wash)]

**ă'llў. 1.** (or ali') *v.t.* Combine or unite for special purpose *to* or *with* (esp. of States by treaty or families by marriage); **allied to**, connected in origin or character *with*. **2.** *n.* State or person allied with another. [F f. L *alligo* bind]

**Alma Mā'ter** (ă-; or -mah'-) *n.* One's university or school. [L, = bounteous mother]

**a'lmanăc**, (rare) **-ăck**, (aw'l-, ŏ'l-) *n.* Calendar of months and days, usu. with astronomical data etc. [L f. Gk]

**almi'ghtў** (awlmi'tĭ). **1.** *a.* (-**iness**). All-powerful (*Almighty God*; **the A~**, God); (sl.) very great (*an almighty nuisance*). **2.** *adv.* (sl.) Very (*almighty glad*). [E (ALL, MIGHT²)]

**a'lmond** (ah'm-) *n.* Kernel of, tree bearing, fruit allied to plum and peach; ~ **eyes** (almond-shaped). [F f. L f. Gk *amugdalē*]

**ǎ'lmoner** (*or* ah'm-) *n.* Official distributor of alms; ‖social worker attached to hospital. [F (ALMS)]

**a'lmōst** (awl-) *adv.* All but, as the nearest thing to. [E (ALL, MOST)]

**alms** (ahmz) *n.* Donation of money or food given to the poor; **∼'house** (founded by charity for the poor). [E f. L f. Gk *eleēmosunē* compassion]

**ǎ'lōe** *n.* Plant with erect spikes of flowers and bitter juice; (in *pl.*) purgative drug from aloe juice. [E f. L f. Gk]

**alǒ'ft** (*or* -aw'ft) *adv.* High up, overhead; upward. [E]

**alō'ne.** **1.** *pred. a.* Not with others (*found him all alone*; **am not ∼ in** *this opinion*, others share it; *this fact* ∼ *would discredit him*, nothing else would, *or* even if nothing else did; **go it ∼**, act by oneself without assistance; **LEAVE** *alone*; **LET** *alone*). **2.** *adv.* Only, exclusively, (*you alone can help me*). [all one]

**alǒ'ng.** **1.** *adv.* Through part or whole of thing's length (*along by the hedge*; *knew it all* ∼, from the beginning); in company with one, in conjunction with, (*have brought a gun along*; *I'll be along soon*; *along with other advantages*); onward, into more advanced state, (*push it along*; **GET** *along*; *is coming along nicely*); **∼shore**, along the shore; **∼side**, close to side of ship; **∼side of**, side by side with. **2.** *prep.* Through (any part of) length of (*arranged along the wall*). [E, orig. adj. = facing against]

**alōo'f.** **1.** *adv.* Away, apart, (*stand aloof from*). **2.** *a.* Unconcerned, lacking in sympathy. [A³, LUFF]

**alou'd** *adv.* In the normal voice, not silently or in a whisper, (*say it aloud*; **read** ∼, read and reproduce with the voice). [A³]

**ǎlp** *n.* Mountain-peak; green pasture-land on Swiss mountainside; **the Alps**, mountains between Switzerland etc. and Italy. [F f. L]

**ǎlpǎ'ca** *n.* Kind of llama with long wool; its wool; fabric made from this. [Sp. f. Quechua]

**ǎ'lpenstock** *n.* Iron-tipped staff used in climbing. [G, = Alps-stick]

**ǎ'lpha** *n.* First Gk letter (A, α) = a (**A∼ and Omega**, beginning and end); first-class mark in examination (∼ **plus**, superlatively good); ∼ **particles**, **rays**, helium nuclei

emitted by radioactive substances, orig. regarded as rays. [L f. Gk]

**ǎ'lphabět** *n.* Set of letters used in a language; symbols or signs for these (*Morse alphabet*); **ǎlphabě't-ǐc(al)** *adjs.* (**-ically**), of the alphabet (∼**ical order**, that in which the alphabet is arranged); **ǎlpha-nūmě'rǐc(al)** *adjs.*, containing both alphabetic and numerical symbols. [L f. Gk ALPHA, BETA]

**A'lp|ine** (ǎ'-). **1.** *a.* Of the Alps or other high mountains. **2.** *n.* Plant suited to mountain regions. **3.** **∼inǐst** *n.*, Alpine climber. [L (ALP)]

**alrea'dy** (awlrě'dǐ) *adv.* Before this or that time (*have already seen him*; *had already gone*); as early as this (*is he back already?*). [ALL, READY]

‖**Alsa'tian** (ǎlsā'shan) *n.* (Dog of) a wolfhound breed. [L *Alsatia* Alsace]

**a'lsō** (aw'l-) *adv.* In addition, besides; **∼-ran** *n.*, horse or dog not in first three in race, person failing to win distinction. [E (ALL, SO)]

**ǎlt** *n.* (Mus.) High note (**in ∼**, in octave above treble staff beginning with G). [It. f. L *altus* high]

**Alta.** *abbr.* Alberta.

**a'ltar** (aw'l-, ŏ'l-) *n.* Flat-topped block for offerings to deity; Communion table; **lead to the ∼**, marry (woman); **∼-piece**, reredos, esp. a painting. [E f. L *altus* high]

**a'lter** (aw'l-, ŏ'l-) *v.t. & i.* Change in character, position, etc.; **∼ā'tion** *n.* [F f. L (*alter* other)]

**a'lterc|āte** (aw'l-, ŏ'l-) *v.i.* Dispute, wrangle, (*with*); **∼ā'tion** *n.* [L]

*alter ego* (ǎlter ě'gō) *n.* (*pl.* ∼**s**). Intimate friend. [L, = other self]

**altern|ate** *a.,n., & v.* **1.** (awltěr'nat, ŏl-) *a.* (Of things of two kinds) coming each after one of the other kind (*alternate failure and success*; **∼ate leaves**, **angles**, placed alternately on two sides of stem, line); (of sequence etc.) consisting of alternate things; (w. *pl.*, of one class of things) every second one (*comes on alternate days*). **2.** (awltěr'nat, ŏl-) *n.* Deputy, substitute. **3.** (aw'lternāt, ŏ'l-) *v.t. & i.* Arrange or perform, occur, alternately, (*alternate the red and blue lines*, *red lines with blue*; *red and blue lines alternate*; *red lines alternate with blue*); consist of alternate things (∼**ating current**, Electr., reversing its direction at regular intervals); **∼ā'tion** (awl-, ŏl-) *n.* (∼**ation**

**of generations**, reproduction by alternate processes, e.g. sexual and asexual); **~ātor** (aw'l-, ŏ'l-) n., dynamo giving alternating current. [L alterno do by turns (ALTER)]

**altĕr'native** (awl-, ŏl-). **1.** a. Available in place of something else; (of two or more things) available in such a way that when one is accepted the other(s) must be rejected. **2.** n. Liberty of choice (you have no alternative but to go); one of two or more possibilities.

**althou'gh** (awldhō') conj. Though. [ALL, THOUGH]

**a'ltimĕter** n. Instrument showing height above sea-level. [foll.]

**a'ltitūde** n. Height (of object, esp. above sea-level; **~ of triangle**, perpendicular distance from vertex to base); depth; (fig.) eminence. [L (altus high)]

**a'lto** n. (pl. **~s**). (Mus.) Highest adult male voice; female voice of similar range; singer with, part written for, alto voice; **~ clef** (with middle C on middle line of staff). [It. (prec.)]

**altoge'ther** (awl-, ŏl-; -gĕ'dh-). **1.** adv. Totally (altogether absurd); on the whole. **2.** n. **In the ~**, (colloq.) nude. [ALL, TOGETHER]

**a'ltruǀism** (-roo-) n. Regard for others as a principle of action; **~ist** n.; **~i'stǐc** a. (-ically). [F f. It. altrui somebody else]

**a'lum** n. Double sulphate of aluminium and potassium; any of several similar compounds; **alu'mǀina** (-loo'-) n., aluminium oxide; ||**alūmǐ'nǐum**, *alū'mǐnum, n., silvery light ductile and malleable metallic element, not tarnished by air; **alū'mǐnize** v.t., coat with aluminium. [F f. L alumen -min-]

*alū'mnǀus n. (pl. **~i** pr. -i; fem. **~a**, pl. **~ae**). (Former) pupil or student. [L, = nursling, pupil]

**a'lways** (aw'lwāz, -ĭz) adv. At all times, on all occasions; whatever the circumstances (I can always sleep on the floor); repeatedly (is always complaining). [ALL, WAY]

**a'lyssum** n. Plant with small usu. yellow or white flowers. [L f. Gk]

**am.** See BE.

**A.M.** abbr. amplitude modulation; in the year of the world [L Anno Mundi].

**a.m.** abbr. before noon. [L ante meridiem]

**amai'n** adv. (arch., poet.) With force; in haste. [A³, MAIN¹ = force]

**ama'lgam** n. Mixture of a metal with mercury (gold amalgam); any mouldable mixture; **~āte** v.t. & i., mix, unite (classes, societies, ideas), (of metals) alloy with mercury; **~ā'tion**, **~ātor**, ns. [F or L]

**amănuĕ'nsǀis** n. (pl. **~es** pr. -ēz). One who writes from dictation; literary assistant. [L, = secretary]

**a'marǀanth** n. Kind of plant with coloured foliage, esp. prince's feather and love-lies-bleeding; imaginary unfading flower (**~ǎ'nthine** a.); purple. [F or L f. Gk amarantos fadeless]

**amarў'llǐs** n. Bulbous plant with lily-like flowers. [L f. Gk girl's name]

**amā'ss** v.t. Heap together; accumulate (esp. riches). [F (AD-, MASS²)]

**a'mateur** (-tūr, -tĕr) n. One who practises a thing only as a pastime (often attrib.: amateur gardener, theatricals), esp. unpaid player etc., opp. PROFESSIONAL; **~ish** a., of or suggesting an (unskilful) amateur. [F f. It. f. L amator lover (foll.)]

**a'matory** a. Of lovers or sexual love. [L (amo to love)]

**amā'ze** v.t. Overwhelm with wonder; **~ment** (-zm-) n. [E]

**A'mazǀon** (ă'-) n. Female warrior, esp. of mythical race in Scythia; strong or athletic woman; **~ō'nǐan** a. [L f. Gk]

**ămbă'ssadǀor** n. Diplomat sent by sovereign or State as permanent representative or on mission to another; official messenger; **~ōr'ǐal** a. (-lly); **~rĕss** n., female ambassador, ambassador's wife. [F f. It. f. Rom. f. L f. Gmc (L ambactus servant)]

**a'mber. 1.** n. A yellow translucent fossil resin used for ornaments etc.; yellow traffic-light shown as caution between red (=stop) and green (=go). **2.** a. Made of or coloured like amber. [F f. Arab., = amber-(gris)]

**a'mbergrǐs** (or -ēs) n. Waxlike substance found floating in tropical seas, and in intestines of sperm whale, used in perfumery etc. [F, = grey amber]

**ămbi-** in comb. On both sides. [L]

**ambiance** (ahnbǐah'ns) n. Surroundings. [F (AMBIENT)]

**ămbidĕ'xtǀ(e)rous** a. Able to use either hand equally well; deceitful; **~ĕ'rǐtў** n. [L (AMBI-, DEXTER)]

**ă'mbĭen|t** *a.* Surrounding (*the ambient air*); **~ce** *n.*, (esp.) surroundings. [F, or L *ambio* go round]

**ămbĭg'g|ūous** *a.* Of double or doubtful meaning; of uncertain character, tendency, etc.; **~ū'ĭtў** *n.* [L (AMBI-, *ago* drive)]

**ă'mbĭt** *n.* (literary). Precincts, bounds; scope. [L (AMBIENT)]

**ămbĭ'|tion** *n.* Desire for distinction; desire for specified attainment (*my ambition is to be a doctor, to practise medicine*); object of such desire; **~tious** (-shŭs) *a.*, full of ambition, strongly desirous (*of* thing, *to* do), showing ambition (*an ambitious attempt*). [F f. L, = canvassing (AMBIENT)]

**ămbi'valen|ce** *n.* Coexistence in one person of opposite feelings towards the same object etc.; **~t** *a.* [G (AMBI-, EQUIVALENCE)]

**ă'mble. 1.** *v.i.* (Of horse etc.) move by lifting two feet on one side together; ride ambling horse; ride or move at easy pace. **2.** *n.* Ambling or easy pace. [F f. L *ambulo* walk]

**ămbrō'sia** (-zĭa, -zhуa) *n.* (Gk Myth.) food of the gods; thing delightful to taste or smell; **~l** *a.* (-lly). [L f. Gk, = elixir of life]

**ă'mbŭlan|ce** *n.* Conveyance for sick or injured persons; mobile hospital following army; **~t** *a.*, (of treatment) not confining patient to bed, (of patient) able to walk about. [F f. L (AMBLE)]

**ă'mbŭlatorў. 1.** *a.* Of or for walking; movable. **2.** *n.* Arcade esp. in apse; cloister. [L (prec.)]

**ă'mbush** (-ŏŏsh). **1.** *n.* Concealment of troops etc., act of lying concealed, for surprise attack; person(s) thus concealed; attack thus made. **2.** *v.t.* Attack from ambush; lie in wait for. **3. ămbuscă'de,** (*n.*) ambush, (*v.t. & i.*) attack from ambush, lie in wait. [F (IN-¹, BUSH¹)]

**amē'lĭor|āte** *v.t. & i.* (**~able**). Make or become better; **~ā'tion, ~ātor,** *ns.*; **~ative** *a.* [AD-, L *melior* better]

**āmē'n** (or ah-) *int.* So be it (esp. at end of prayer etc.); **say ~,** assent *to* opinion etc. [L f. Gk f. Heb., = certainly]

**amē'nab|le** *a.* (**~ly**). Responsible (*to* law etc.); that may be subjected (*to* a test etc.); tractable (*amenable to discipline*); **~i'lĭtў** *n.* [F (AD-, L *mino* drive animals)]

**amĕ'nd** *v.t.* Correct error in (document etc.); make or propose minor alterations in (motion etc. under discussion); **amende honorable** (amahṅd ŏnŏrah'bl) *n.* (*pl.* **-es -es** *pr.* same), public apology and reparation; **~ment** *n.*, addition or alteration in document etc.; **~s** (-z) *n.*, reparation, compensation, (*make amends for*). [F f. L (EMEND)]

**amĕ'nĭtў** *n.* Pleasantness (of place, mode of life, etc.; ‖**~ bed,** in hospital, giving privacy for small payment); (in *pl.*) pleasant features of place. [F, or L (*amoenus* pleasant)]

**Amĕ'rĭcan** (a-). **1.** *a.* Of the continent of *America*; of the United States; **~ĭsm** *n.*, word or sense or phrase peculiar to or originating from U.S., attachment to or sympathy with U.S.; **~īze** *v.t. & i.*, naturalize as an American, make or become American in character. **2.** *n.* Native of America of Old-World descent; citizen of U.S.; English language as spoken in U.S. [place]

**ă'mĕthўst** *n.* A precious stone, purple or violet quartz; **~ў'stĭne** *a.* [F f. L f. Gk]

**Amhă'rĭc** (ă-) *n. & a.* (Of the) official language of Ethiopia. [*Amhara*, place]

**ă'mĭab|le** *a.* (**~ly**). Feeling and inspiring friendliness, lovable; **~i'lĭtў** *n.* [F f. L (foll.)]

**ă'mĭcab|le** *a.* (**~ly**). Friendly; **~i'lĭtў** *n.* [L (*amicus* friend)]

**ami'd(st)** *prep.* In the middle of (*amid(st) the corn*; *amid shouts of dissent*); **ami'dshĭps** *adv.*, in middle of ship. [A³]

**ă'mĭde, ă'mĭne** (-ēn), *ns.* (Chem.) Kinds of compound formed from ammonia; **amīnō-ă'cĭd** (-ēn-) *n.*, organic acid derived from ammonia and found in proteins. [AMMONIA]

**amir'** (-ēr') *n.* Title of various Muslim rulers; **~ate** *n.*, position, reign, or domain, of amir. [Arab.]

**ami'ss** *adv.* Out of order (*what's amiss with it?*); wrongly, inappropriately, (*turned out amiss*; **take remark** etc. **~,** be offended at it). [A³]

**ă'mĭtў** *n.* Friendly relationship. [F f. L (*amicus* friend)]

**ă'mmĕter** *n.* Instrument measuring electric current, esp. in amperes. [AMPERE, -METER]

**ammō'nĭ|a** *n.* Colourless pungent gas with strong alkaline reaction; (liquid) **~a,** solution of ammonia in water; **ămmoni'acal** *a.*, of ammonia or sal ammoniac; **~ăted** *a.*; **~um** *n.*, radical of ammonia salts. [L (SAL AMMONIAC)]

**ă'mmonite** *n.* Coil-shaped fossil shell. [L, = horn of Jupiter Ammon]

**ămmuni'tion** *n.* Military projectiles (bullets, shells, grenades, etc.) and propellants; (fig.) facts etc. used in argument. [F *la* MUNITION taken as *l'ammu-*]

**ămne'si|a** (-z-) *n.* Loss of memory; **~ăc** *n.*; **~c** *a.* & *n.* [L f. Gk]

**ă'mnĕsty. 1.** *n.* General pardon, esp. for political offence. **2.** *v.t.* Give amnesty to. [F or L f. Gk *amnēstia* oblivion]

**ă'mni|on** *n.* Innermost foetal membrane; **~ŏ'tĭc** *a.* [Gk, = caul]

**amoe'ba** (-mē'-) *n.* (*pl.* **~s, ~e**). Single-celled aquatic protozoan perpetually changing shape. [L f. Gk, = change]

**amŏ'k, amŭ'ck,** *adv.* Run ~, run about in murderous frenzy. [Malay]

**amo'ng(st)** (-ŭ'-) *prep.* In assemblage of, surrounded by; in the principles of (group etc.; *there is honour among thieves*); in the number of (*reckoned among his best works*); within the limits of, between, (*have not £5 among us; divided among us*); quarrelled **~ themselves,** with one another. [E, = in assemblage]

**āmŏ'ral** *a.* Outside the scope of morality; having no moral restraints. [A- 2]

**ă'morous** *a.* Of or inclined to (esp. sexual) love; in love. [F f. L (*amor* love)]

**amŏr'phous** *a.* Shapeless; (Min., Chem.) uncrystallized; unorganized. [Gk *a-* not, *morphē* form]

**amŏr'tiz|e** *v.t.* Extinguish (debt) esp. by means of a sinking fund; gradually write off (assets); **~ā'tion** *n.* [F f. L *ad mortem* to death]

**amou'nt. 1.** *v.i.* Be equivalent (in total value, quantity, significance, etc.) *to.* **2.** *n.* Total to which thing amounts; quantity; ANY *amount of*; **no ~ of,** not even a large amount of. [F f. L (*ad montem* up the hill)]

**amour'** (-oor') *n.* Love affair; **~ propre** (ămoor prŏ'pr) *n.*, self--esteem. [F, = love]

**ămp** *n.* (colloq.) Ampere; amplifier. [abbr.]

**ămpĕlŏ'psĭs** *n.* Climbing plant allied to vine. [L, f. Gk *ampelos* vine, *opsis* appearance]

**ă'mpēr|e** (*or* -ār) *n.* (Electr.) Fundamental unit of current; **~age** *n.*, strength of current in amperes. [*Ampère,* person]

**ă'mpersănd** *n.* The sign & (= *and*). ['and PER SE and']

**ămphe'tamīne** (*or* -ēn) *n.* Synthetic drug used as stimulant etc. [abbr. of chem. name]

**ămphĭ-** *in comb.* Both; of both kinds; around. [Gk]

**ămphi'bĭ|an** *a.* & *n.* (Member) of the Amphibia class of vertebrates incl. frogs, newts, etc., able to live both on land and in water; (tank, aircraft, etc.) adapted to operate both on land and in water; **~ous** *a.*, living or operating both on land and in water, involving both sea and land forces. [Gk (AMPHI-, *bios* life)]

‖**ă'mphĭtheatre, *-ter,** (-ĭater) *n.* Round building with tiers of seats surrounding central space; semicircular gallery for spectators in theatre; scene of contest. [L f. Gk (AMPHI-)]

**ă'mphora** *n.* (*pl.* **~e, ~s**). Greek or Roman two-handled vessel. [L, f. Gk *amphoreus*]

**ă'mpl|e** *a.* (**~er, ~est; ~y**). Spacious; extensive; abundant; quite enough (*ample evidence; two metres will be ample*); (euphem.) stout; **~ify** *v.t.* & *i.*, enhance, increase loudness of (sound) or strength of (electrical signal), add detail to (story etc.), expatiate; **~ifĭcā'tion** *n.*; **~ifĭer** *n.*, (esp.) apparatus for amplifying sounds or electrical signals; **~ĭtūde** *n.*, spaciousness, abundance, (Phys.) extent of vibration or oscillation, (Electr.) maximum departure from average of alternating current or wave (**~ modulation,** varying carrier-wave amplitude). [F f. L]

**ă'mpoule** (-ool) *n.* Small sealed vessel holding solution for injection. [F, as foll.]

**ămpu'lla** *n.* (*pl.* **~e**). Roman globular two-handled flask; vessel for sacred uses. [L]

**ă'mpŭt|āte** *v.t.* Cut off (limb etc.); **~ā'tion** *n.*; **~ee'** *n.*, one who has lost limb etc. by amputation. [L (*amb-* about, *puto* prune)]

**amŭ'ck.** See AMOK.

**ă'mŭlĕt** *n.* Thing worn as charm against evil. [L]

**amū'se** (-z) *v.t.* Make (person) laugh or smile (*be amused with, at,* *by*); interest *with* pleasant trifling matters (~ oneself, pass time in small diversions[1]); **~ment** (-zm-) *n.* [F (AD-, MUSE[1])]

**an**[1] (an, *emphat.* ăn) *a.* See A[2]; *an* is used before vowel sounds (except ū) and sometimes before h in unstressed syllable (*an egg, an hour, an hypothesis*; but *a unit*).

**ăn**[2] *conj.* (arch.) If. [AND]

**an-. 1.** See AD-. **2.** = A- 2.

**-an** *suf.* forming *adjs.* (often used as *ns.*) meaning *of, of the nature of*; **-a'na** (-ah'-) *suf.* forming *pl. ns.* w. sense 'anecdotes, materials, etc. concerning'. [F *-ain*, L *-anus*]

**ăna-** *pref.* Up; back; again. [Gk]

**Anaba'ptĭst** (ă-) *n.* (Hist.) Member of sect (re)baptizing adult believers. [L f. Gk (ANA-)]

**ană'bolĭsm** *n.* (Biol.) Constructive METABOLISM (opp. *catabolism*). [ANA-, Gk *ballō* throw]

**ană'chron|ĭsm** (-k-) *n.* Chronological error; person or thing out of harmony with period; relating to an event, custom, etc., to a wrong period; **~ĭ'stĭc** *a.* [F or Gk (ANA-, CHRONIC)]

**ănacŏ'nda** *n.* Large tropical S. Amer. snake. [ult. f. Sinh.]

**‖anae'mĭ|a, *anē'mĭ|a**, *n.* Deficiency of red blood-corpuscles or their haemoglobin, often causing pallor; **~c** *a.* (~cally), (lit., or fig. lacking vigour etc.). [L f. Gk (A- 2, *haima* blood)]

**‖ănaesth|ē'sĭa** (ănĭs-), *ănĕsth-**, (-zĭa) *n.* Absence of sensation, esp. artificially induced insensibility to pain; **~ĕ'tĭc** *a.* & *n.*, (substance etc.) producing anaesthesia; **~etĭst** (-ē's-) *n.*, one who administers anaesthetics; **~etize** (-ē's-) *v.t.*, (esp.) administer anaesthetic to. [L f. Gk (A- 2, AESTHETIC)]

**ă'nagrăm** *n.* Word or phrase formed from transposed letters of another; **ănagrammă'tĭc(al)** *adjs.* (-ically); **~matize** (-ă'm-) *v.t.*, form into an anagram. [F or L, f. Gk (ANA-)]

**ā'nal** *a.* Of the anus. [ANUS]

**ă'nalĕcts, ănalĕ'cta**, *n.pl.* Literary gleanings. [L f. Gk (*legō* pick)]

**ănalgē'sĭ|a** *n.* Absence or relief of pain; **~c** *a.* & *n.*, (drug) producing analgesia. [L f. Gk (A- 2, *algos* pain)]

**ană'log|ў** *n.* Agreement or similarity (*to, with, between*); analogue; reasoning from parallel cases; inflexion or construction of words in imitation of others; **false ~y** (where the parallel is only apparent); **ănaló'gĭcal** *a.* (-lly), according to analogy, expressing an analogy; **~ize** *v.t.* & *i.*, represent by analogy, show to be analogous, have analogy (*with*); **~ĭst** *n.*; **~ous** *a.*, similar or parallel (*to*); **ă'nalŏgue** (-g), *ă'nalŏg**, *n.*, analogous thing (**~ue computer**, using physical quantities, e.g. voltage, length, etc., to represent numbers). [F or L f. Gk *analogia* (*logos* proportion)]

**ă'nalŷse** (-z), *-ŷze**, *v.t.* Ascertain the elements or structure of (substance, sentence, etc.); examine minutely the constitution of; psycho-analyse. [foll.]

**ană'lŷs|ĭs** *n.* (*pl.* **~es** *pr.* -ēz). Resolution into simpler elements by analysing (opp. *synthesis*); psycho-analysis; **ă'nalŷst** *n.*, one skilled in (esp. chemical) analysis, psycho-analyst; **ănalŷ'tĭc(al)** *adjs.* (-ically), of or employing analysis, (of language) using separate words and not inflexions. [L f. Gk (*luō* set free)]

**ā'napaest** *n.* A metrical foot (~ ~ -); **~ĭc** (-pē'-) *a.* [L f. Gk *anapaistos* reversed (dactyl)]

**ă'narch|ў** *n.* (-kĭ) Absence of government; disorder, confusion; **ănăr'chĭc(al)** (-k-) *adjs.* (-ically); **~ĭsm**, **~ĭst**, *ns.*, (adherent of) doctrine that all governments should be abolished; **~ĭ'stĭc** *a.* [L f. Gk (A- 2, *arkhē* rule)]

**ană'thēma** *n.* Curse, esp. of God or of the Church; accursed or detested thing; **~tize** *v.t.*, curse. [L f. Gk, = devoted or accursed thing]

**ană'tom|ў** *n.* (Science of) bodily structure; (joc.) human body; analysis; **ănatŏ'mĭcal** *a.* (-lly); **~ize** *v.t.* & *i.*, dissect, analyse; **~ĭst** *n.* [F or L f. Gk (-*tomia* cutting)]

**-ance.** See -NCE.

**ă'ncĕst|or** *n.* Any person from whom one's father or mother is descended; **ăncĕ'stral** *a.* (-lly), (esp.) inherited from ancestors; **~rў** *n.*, one's ancestors, ancient descent. [F f. L (ANTECEDENT)]

**ă'nchor** (-k-). **1.** *n.* Heavy metal structure used to moor ship to sea-bottom etc. or balloon etc. to ground (**at ~**, thus moored; **cast, come to, ~**, let it down; **weigh ~**, take it up; **~man**, one playing vital part in sports team, compère in broadcast, etc.); **~age** *n.*, (place for) anchoring, lying at anchor, dependable thing. **2.** *v.t. & i.* Secure (ship) with anchor; cast anchor; be moored by anchor; fix firmly (lit. or fig.). [E & F f. L f. Gk *agkura*]

**ă'nchor|ite**, **~|ĕt**, (-k-) *n.* Hermit, recluse; **~ĕss** *n.*; **~ĕ'tĭc**, **~ĭ'tĭc**, *adjs.* [L f. Gk (ANA-, *khōreō* go)]

**ă'nchovy** (or -ō'-) *n.* Small rich-flavoured fish of herring family; **~ toast** (spread with paste made from anchovies). [Sp., Port.]

**ănchū'sa** (-k-; *or* -choō'-) *n.* Kind of hairy-stemmed plant. [L f. Gk]

*ancien régime* (ahǹsyǎǹ rāzhě'm) *n.* (*pl.* -ns -es *pr.* same). System of government in France before the Revolution of 1789; (transf.) superseded regime. [F]

**ā'ncient** (-shĕnt). **1.** *a.* Of times long past (**~ history**, esp. before fall of Western Roman Empire); having lived or existed long (**~ lights**, window that neighbour may not deprive of light by building; **||~ monument**, old building etc. preserved usu. under Government control). **2.** *n.* **The A~ of Days**, God; **the ~s**, civilized nations of antiquity. [F f. L *ante* before]

**ănci'llary** (*or* ǎ'-) *a.* Subservient, subordinate, (to). [L (*ancilla* handmaid)]

**-ancy.** See -NCE.

**and** (*or emphat.* ă-) *conj.* connecting words, clauses, or sentences (*cakes and buns; he brews and his wife bakes; better ~* (steadily) *better; she cried ~ cried*, for a long time; *miles ~ miles*, very many; NICE *and*; TRY *and*; *there are books ~ books*, good and bad etc.; *two ~ two*, two added to two, by twos; *move ~* (if you move) *I shoot*); *A* and/or *B*, A or B or both. [E]

**ăndā'ntĕ** (*or* -ā) *adv.*, *a.*, & *n.* (Mus.) (Movement) in moderately slow time; **ăndanti'nō** (-tē'-) *adv.*, *a.*, & *n.* (*pl.* -os), (movement) rather quicker (orig. slower) than andante. [It., = going; -*ino* dim.]

**ă'ndiron** (-ïern) *n.* Metal log-support on hearth. [F *andier*]

**ă'nĕcdŏt|e** *n.* Narrative of amusing or interesting incident; **~al** (-lly), **~ĭc**, (*or* -ō'-) *adjs.*; **~(al)ĭst** *ns.* [F *or* L f. Gk (AN- 2, *ekdidōmi* publish)]

**\*anē'mĭa** etc. See ANAEMIA etc.

**ănĕmŏ'mĕt|er** *n.* Instrument for measuring force of wind; **ănĕmomĕ'trĭc** *a.*; **~ry̆** *n.* [Gk *anemos* wind]

**anĕ'monĕ** *n.* Plant akin to buttercup (**wood ~, wild kind**); **sea ~**, large polyp with petal-like tentacles. [L f. Gk (*anemos* wind)]

**anĕ'nt** *prep.* (arch., joc., or Sc.) Concerning. [E, = on a level with]

**ā'neroid** *a. & n.* (Barometer) that measures air-pressure by its action on lid of box containing vacuum, not by height of fluid column. [F (A- 2, Gk *nēros* wet)]

**\*anesthesia.** See ANAESTHESIA.

**ā'neury̆sm**, **-ĭsm**, (-nūr-) *n.* Morbid dilatation of artery; **~al** (-ĭ'z-) *a.* [ANA-, Gk *eurus* wide]

**anew'** *adv.* Again; in a different way. [OF, NEW]

**ā'ngel** (-nj-) *n.* Divine attendant or messenger (one's **evil, good,** GUARDIAN, **~**, attendant spirit); lovely or innocent being; obliging or loving person (*be an angel and help me with this*); (sl.) financial backer of enterprise; old English coin with archangel Michael and dragon; **~ cake**, very light sponge-cake; **~-fish** (with winglike fins); **ăngĕ'lĭc** (-nj-) *a.* (-ically), of, like, worthy of, an angel. [F f. L f. Gk *aggelos* messenger]

**ăngĕ'lĭca** (-nj-) *n.* Aromatic plant used in cookery etc.; its candied stalks.

**ă'ngĕlus** (-nj-) *n.* (R.C. Ch.) Devotional exercise commemorating the Incarnation, said at morning, noon, and sunset, at sound of **~** (**bell**). [L *Angelus Domini* (= the ANGEL of the Lord), opening wds]

**ă'nger** (-ngg-). **1.** *n.* Extreme displeasure. **2.** *v.t.* Make angry. [N, = grief]

**A'ngĕvĭn** (ă'nj-) *a. & n.* (One) of the PLANTAGENETS. [F, = of Anjou]

**ăngī'na** (pĕ'ctorĭs) (-nj-) *n.* Pain in chest due to over-exertion when heart is diseased. [L, f. Gk *agkhonē* strangling]

**ă'ngle¹** (-nggel). **1.** *n.* Space between two meeting lines or planes; inclination of two lines etc. to each other; corner; point of view (lit. or fig.). **2.** *v.t. & i.* Move or place obliquely; (colloq.) present (news etc.) from particular point of view. [F, *or* L *angulus*]

**ă'ngle²** (-nggel) *v.i.* Fish with hook and bait (*for*, or abs.; lit. or fig.); **ă'ngler** (-ngg-) *n.* [E]

**A'ngle³** (ă'nggel) *n.* Member of

tribe from Schleswig that settled in E. Britain in 5th c. [L *Anglus* f. Gmc]

**A'nglican** (ă'ngg-) *a.* & *n.* (Adherent) of the reformed Church of England; **~ïsm** *n.* [L *Anglicanus* (foll.)]

**A'nglïc|ize** (ă'ngg-) *v.t.* Make English in form or character; **ă~ē** *adv.*, in English; **~ïsm** *n.*, English idiom. [L *Anglicus* (ANGLE³)]

**Anglō-** (ăngg-) *in comb.* English; of English origin; English or British and (*an Anglo-American agreement*); **~-Că'tholïc** *a.* & *n.*, (adherent) of section of Church of England that insists on its accordance with Catholic Church doctrine; **~-I'ndïan** (-ĭ'n-) *a.* & *n.*, (person) of British birth but having lived long in India, (of word) adopted from an Indian language into English; **A'nglophïle, -phōbe, -phō'bĭa,** (ă'ngg-) *ns.*; **~-Să'xon** *n.* & *a.*, Old English (person, language) before Norman Conquest, (person) of English descent. [L (ANGLE³)]

**ăngŏr'a** (-ngg-) *n.* Fabric made from wool of angora goat; **~ cat, goat, rabbit,** (long-haired varieties); **~ (wool)**, mixture of sheep's wool and angora rabbit hair. [place (= Ankara)]

**ăngostūr'a** (-ngg-) *n.* Aromatic bitter bark of S. Amer. tree. [place]

**ă'ngr|ў** (-ngg-) *a.* (**~ily**) Feeling or showing anger; (of sore etc.) inflamed, painful. [ANGER]

**Angst** (ă-) *n.* Feeling of guilt. [G]

**ă'ngström** (ă'ngstrēm; *or* ŏ'-) *n.* Unit of wavelength-measurement, $10^{-10}$ metre. [person]

**ă'nguïsh** (-nggw-) *n.* Severe bodily or mental pain; **~ed** (-sht) *a.* [F f. L *angustia* tightness]

**ă'ngūl|ar** (-ngg-) *a.* Having angles; sharp-cornered; lacking plumpness or smoothness; placed in or at an angle; measured by angle (*angular distance*); **~ă'rĭtў** *n.* [L (ANGLE¹)]

**ănhÿ'drous** *a.* (Chem.) Lacking water of crystallization. [Gk *anudros* lacking water]

**ă'nïlïne** (*or* -ēn, -ĭn) *n.* Oily liquid got from coal tar; **~ dye,** dye made from this, any synthetic dye. [G (*anil* indigo)]

**ănimadver'|t** *v.i.* Pass criticism or censure (*on*); **~sion** (-shon) *n.* [L (*animus* mind, ADVERT²)]

**ă'nïmal. 1.** *n.* Organized being endowed with life, sensation, and voluntary motion, (esp.) such a being other than man; quadruped; brutish man. **2.** *a.* Of (the nature of) animals; carnal, sensual; *animal* KINGDOM; **~ spirits,** natural exuberance. **3. ănïmă'lcūle** *n.*, microscopic animal; **~ïsm** *n.*, (mere) animal activity or enjoyment; **ănïmă'lĭtў** *n.*, (merely) animal nature; **~īze** *v.t.*, convert to animal substance, sensualize. [L (*anima* breath)]

**ă'nïm|ate. 1.** *a.* Living; lively. **2.** (-āt) *v.t.* Breathe life into; enliven (*an animated discussion*); **~ated cartoon,** film made from gradually varying sequence of drawings; **~ā'tion** *n.*, (esp.) ardour, vivacity.

**ă'nïm|ïsm** *n.* Attribution of living soul to inanimate objects and natural phenomena; **~ïst** *n.*; **~ĭ'stïc** *a.*

**ănïmŏ'sĭtў** *n.* Spirit of enmity; **ă'nïmus** *n.*, animosity shown in speech or action. [F or L (*animus* spirit)]

**ă'nïon** *n.* Negatively charged ion; **ănĭŏ'nïc** *a.* [ANA-, ION]

**ă'nïs|e** *n.* A plant with aromatic seeds; **~eed** *n.*, seed of anise, used for flavouring. [F f. L Gk *anison*]

**ă'nkl|e** *n.* Joint connecting foot with leg; part between this and calf; **~et** *n.*, ornament or fetter for ankle. [N]

**ănkÿlō'sïs** *n.* Stiffening of joint by uniting of bones; **ă'nkÿlōse** (-z) *v.t.*, affect with ankylosis. [L f. Gk (*agkulos* crooked)]

**ă'nnal|s** (-z) *n.pl.* Narrative of events year by year; records; **~ïst** *n.*, writer of annals; **~ĭ'stïc** *a.* [F or L (*annus* year)]

**annea'l** *v.t.* Toughen by heating and usu. slow cooling; (fig.) toughen. [E, = bake]

**ă'nnelïd** *n.* Segmented worm, e.g. earthworm, leech; **annē'lïdan** *a.* [F or L (*anulus* ring)]

**ănnĕx. 1.** (-ĕ'-) *v.t.* Add or append (thing *to* another) as subordinate part; take possession of (territory etc.), (colloq.) take without right; attach as attribute, condition, etc.; **ănnĕxā'tion** *n.* **2. ă'nnĕx(e)** *n.* Addition to document; (‖usu. *-exe*) supplementary building. [F f. L (*necto* bind)]

**anni'hĭl|āte** (-nī'ĭ-) *v.t.* Destroy utterly; **~ā'tion, ~ātor,** *ns.* [F f. L (*nihil* nothing)]

**ănnĭver'sarў** *n.* Yearly return of a

date; celebration of this. [L (*annus* year, *verto vers-* turn)]

**Annŏ Dŏ'mĭnī** (ă-). **1.** *adv.* (usu. abbr. A.D.). In the year of the Christian era (A.D. *1900*). **2.** *n.* (colloq.) Advancing age. [L, = in the year of the Lord]

**ă'nnot|āte** *v.t.* Add notes to (book etc.); ~**ā'tion**, ~**ātor**, *ns.* [L (AN-1, NOTE)]

**annou'nce** *v.t.* Make publicly known (*announce one's intention, that one intends; a new edition is announced*); make known the approach etc. of (*a visitor, dinner, was announced*); be sign of; ~**ment** (-sm-) *n.*; ~**r** *n.* (esp. in broadcasting). [F f. L (*nuntius* messenger)]

**annoy'** *v.t.* Cause slight anger or mental distress to; (in *p.p.*) somewhat angry *with* person, *at* thing, *to* discover etc.; molest; ~**ance** *n.* [F f. L *in odio* hateful]

**ă'nnūal. 1.** *a.* (~**ly**). Reckoned by the year (*annual income, output*); recurring yearly (*his annual visit*); living or lasting (only) a year. **2.** *n.* Plant living only a year; book etc. published in yearly numbers. [F f. L (*annus* year)]

**annŭ'ĭt|y̆** *n.* Yearly grant or allowance; investment entitling one to a fixed annual sum; ~**ant** *n.*, holder of annuity.

**annŭ'l** *v.t.* (-ll-). Abolish, cancel; declare invalid; ~**ment** *n.* [F f. L (AN-1, NULL)]

**ă'nnūl|ar** *a.* Ring-shaped (~**ar eclipse** of sun, when ring of light remains visible); ~**ate** *a.*, marked with or formed of rings. [F or L (*anulus* ring)]

**annŭ'ncī|āte** (-shī-) *v.t.* (~**able**). Proclaim; ~**ā'tion** (-sĭ-) *n.* (esp., A-) announcement of the Incarnation made by Gabriel to Mary, festival of this = Lady Day; ~**ātor** *n.*, (esp.) device showing from which room etc. a bell has been rung. [L (ANNOUNCE)]

**ă'nŏd|e** *n.* Positive electrode or terminal (opp. CATHODE); **ă'nŏdize** *v.t.*, coat (metal) with protective layer by electrolysis. [Gk (ANA-, *hodos* way)]

**ă'nŏdȳne. 1.** *a.* Pain-killing, soothing. **2.** *n.* Anodyne drug or circumstance. [L f. Gk (A- 2, *odunē* pain)]

**anoi'nt** *v.t.* Apply ointment or oil to, esp. as religious ceremony on consecration as king etc. (the Lord's Anointed, Christ, or king by divine right); smear, rub, (thing *with* grease etc.). [F f. L *inungo* (UNCTION)]

**anŏ'mal|ous** *a.* Irregular, abnormal; ~**y̆** *n.*, anomalous thing, irregularity. [L f. Gk (A- 2, *homalos* even)]

**ă'nomy̆, ă'nomĭe,** *n.* Absence of usual social standards; **anŏ'mĭc** *a.* [Gk (A- 2, *nomos* law)]

**anŏ'n** *adv.* (arch.). Soon, presently; EVER *and* anon. [E (ON, ONE)]

**anŏ'ny̆mous** *a.* (abbr. anon.) Of unknown name (*anonymous author*); of unknown authorship (*anonymous letter*); **ănony̆'mĭty̆** *n.* [L f. Gk (A- 2, *onoma* name)]

**ă'norăk** *n.* Skin or cloth jacket with attached hood. [Eskimo]

**ănorĕ'xĭa** *n.* Absence of appetite or desire. [L f. Gk (A- 2, *orexis* appetite)]

**ano'ther** (-ŭ'dh-) *pron.* (*pl.* others) & *a.* (*pl.* other). An additional (one) (*have another pear*; *is just* such ~, one of the same sort; ~ *Solomon*, one like); a different (one) (*that is quite another thing*; *this pipe leaks, fit another*); some or any other (one) (*will not do another man's work*); ONE *another*; ||unnamed additional participant, esp. in legal action (A. N. Other, player unnamed or not yet selected). [*an other*]

**ă'nserine** *a.* Of or like a goose; silly. [L (*anser* goose)]

**a'nswer** (ah'nser). **1.** *n.* Thing said or written or done to deal with question, accusation, etc., (*I had no answer to my letter; his answer was to slam the door*); solution to problem. **2.** *v.t.* & *i.* Make an answer (to) (*answer me, my question; answered that it was impossible*; ~ **back**, colloq., answer rebuke impudently); act in response to (~ (summons to) the *door, the telephone, etc.*; ~ **to the name of**, be called); be satisfactory for (purpose etc.); be responsible (*for* person, performance of task, etc.); correspond *to* description; ~**able** *a.*, that can be answered, responsible (*to* person, *for* person or thing). [E, = swear against (charge)]

**ănt** *n.* Small social hymenopterous insect proverbial for industry; ~**-eater**, mammal living on ants; ~**'hill**, mound over ants' nest. [E]

**-ant.** See -NT.

**ăntă′cĭd** n. & a. Preventive or corrective of acidity. [ANTI-]

**ăntă′gon|ĭsm** n. Active opposition (to, against; the antagonism between them); ~**ĭst** n., opponent; ~**ĭ′stĭc** a. (-ically); ~**īze** v.t., evoke hostility or opposition in. [F (AGONY)]

**ăntăr′ctĭc. 1.** a. Of south polar regions (A~ **Circle**, parallel of 66° 33′ S.). **2.** n. (A~). Regions round S. Pole. **3.** A~a (ă-) n., continent mainly within Antarctic Circle. [F or L f. Gk (ARCTIC)]

**ă′ntĕ. 1.** n. Stake put up by poker-player before drawing new cards. **2.** v.t. Put up (an ante); *stake, pay up. [L, = before]

**ănte-** pref. w. sense 'before, preceding' forming ns. (ante-room), and adjs. with or without adj. suf. (ante-natal, ante-post).

**ăntĕce′den|t. 1.** a. Previous (to); presumptive, a priori, (the antecedent probability)); ~**ce** n. **2.** n. Preceding thing or circumstance; (in pl.) person's past history; (Gram.) noun or pronoun, clause, sentence, to which a following (esp. relative) pronoun or adverb refers. [F or L (cedo go)]

**ă′ntĕchămber** n. Room leading to more important one. [ANTE-]

**ăntĕdā′te** v.t. Affix or assign an earlier (esp. than the true) date to (document, event); precede in time. [ANTE-]

**ăntĕdĭlū′vĭan** (or -loo′-) a. Of the time before the Flood; (colloq.) very antiquated. [ANTE-, DELUGE]

**ă′ntĕlōpe** n. (pl. same, ~s). Deer-like ruminant esp. in Africa (e.g. gazelle, chamois); leather from its skin. [F or L f. Gk antholops]

**ăntĕnā′tal** a. Before birth; relating to pregnancy. [ANTE-]

**ăntĕ′nn|a** n. (pl. ~ae). Sensory organ found in pairs on heads of insects and crustaceans, feeler; *(pl. ~as) = AERIAL; ~**al**, ~**arỹ**, adjs. [L, = sail-yard]

**ăntĕpĕnŭ′lt(ĭmate)** adjs. & ns. Last but two (esp. syllable). [ANTE-]

**‖ăntĕ-pō′st** a. (Of racing bet) made before runners' numbers are displayed. [POST¹]

**ănter′ĭ|or** a. More to the front; prior (to); ~**ŏ′rĭtỹ** n. [F or L (ANTE)]

**ă′ntĕ-rōōm** (or -ōōm) n. Antechamber. [ANTE-]

**ă′nthem** n. Composition for church use sung antiphonally; scriptural words set to music; song of praise. [E f. L (ANTIPHON)]

**ă′nther** n. Part of stamen containing pollen; ~**al** a. [F or L f. Gk (anthos flower)]

**ănthŏ′log|ỹ** n. A collection of passages from literature (esp. poems), songs, paintings, etc.; ~**ĭst** n. [F or L f. Gk (as prec.)]

**ă′nthrac|īte** n. Non-bituminous hard kind of coal; ~**ĭ′tĭc** a. [Gk (foll.)]

**ă′nthrăx** n. Disease of sheep and cattle, transmissible to man. [L f. Gk, = coal, carbuncle]

**ănthropo-** in comb. Human. [Gk]

**ă′nthropoid. 1.** a. Manlike in form. **2.** n. Anthropoid ape.

**ănthropŏ′log|ỹ** n. Study of mankind, esp. of its societies and customs; study of man as an animal; **ănthropolŏ′gĭcal** a. (-lly); ~**ĭst** n.

**ănthropomŏr′ph|ĭsm** n. Attribution of human form or personality to god, animal, etc.; ~**ĭc** a. (-ically); ~**īze** v.t.; ~**ous** a., of human form. [Gk morphē form]

**ănthropŏ′phag|ỹ** n. Cannibalism; ~**ous** a. [Gk -phagos -eating]

**ă′ntĭ** n. & prep. (Person) opposed to (a certain policy etc.). [ANTI-]

**ăntĭ-** pref. freely used to form (1) adjs., w. senses 'opposed to' (ANTI-SEMITIC; anti-slavery society), 'retarding or preventing' (ANTISCORBUTIC), (2) ns., w. senses 'of opposing kind' (antipope), 'opponent of, opposition to' (opp. PRO-¹; anti-imperialist, -ism), 'unlike the conventional form' (anti-hero, anti-novel). [Gk]

**ăntĭ-air′craft** (-ahft) a. (Of gun etc.) for shooting down hostile aircraft. [ANTI-]

**ăntĭbĭŏ′tĭc** a. & n. (Substance) capable of destroying or injuring living organisms, esp. bacteria. [F (BIOTIC)]

**ă′ntĭbŏdỹ** n. Protein in the human body, produced by and counteracting antigens. [transl. f. G (ANTI-)]

**ă′ntĭc. 1.** n. (usu. in pl.). Grotesque or absurd posture or action. **2.** a. (arch.) Grotesque; bizarre. [It. antico ANTIQUE]

**A′ntĭchrĭst** (ă′-; -k-) n. Enemy of Christ, esp. one expected by early Church to appear before end of world; **ăntĭchrĭ′stian** (-k-; -tyan) a., of Antichrist, opposed to Christianity. [F f. L f. Gk ANTIkhristos]

**ăntĭ′cĭp|āte** v.t. Look forward to, expect, (I anticipate trouble, that there will be trouble); discuss or deal with or use etc. before due or natural time (*need not anticipate this problem*; *has been anticipating his income*); forestall (person or thing); ~**ā′tion** *n.* (**thanking you in** ~**ation**, closing formula in letter of inquiry or request); ~**ātĭve**, ~**ātŏrȳ**, *adjs.*; ~**ātor** *n.* [L (ANTE-, *capio* take)]

**anticli′max** *n.* Lame or trivial conclusion to a sentence or passage, or to a course of events, that promised a climax. [ANTI-]

**anticlŏ′ckwise** (-z). See CLOCK¹.

**anticy′clone** *n.* System of winds rotating outwards from area of high barometric pressure.

**a′ntidōt|e** *n.* Medicine used to counteract poison (*against*, *for*, *to*); (fig.) thing that counteracts an evil; ~**al** *a.* [F or L f. Gk (*didōmi* give)]

**a′ntifreeze** *n.* Substance added to water (esp. in radiator of motor vehicle) to lower its freezing-point. [ANTI-]

**a′ntig|ĕn** *n.* Substance that stimulates production of antibodies; ~**ĕ′nic** *a.* [G (ANTI-, Gk -*genēs* of a kind)]

**antihi′stamīne** (*or* -ēn) *n.* & *a.* (Substance) that counteracts effects of histamine, used esp. in cases of allergy; **antimacá′ssar** *n.*, (esp. Hist.) protective or ornamental covering for chair-back. [ANTI-]

**a′ntimony** *n.* Brittle metallic element used esp. in alloys. [L]

**antinō′mian.** **1.** *n.* (*A*~). One who holds that the moral law is not binding on Christians. **2.** *a.* Of this theory or its supporters. [L (ANTI-, Gk *nomos* law)]

**anti′nomȳ** *n.* Contradiction in a law, or between laws, authorities, or conclusions.

**anti′path|ȳ** *n.* Constitutional or settled aversion (*to*, *for*, person or thing, *between* two); ~**ĕ′tic** *a.* (**-ically**), opposed in nature or disposition (*to*). [F or L f. Gk (ANTI-, PATHOS)]

**antipe′rspirant** *a.* & *n.* (Substance) inhibiting sweating. [ANTI-]

**a′ntiphon** *n.* Verse, sentence, sung by one choir in response to another; **anti′phonal**, (*a.*; -lly) sung alternately, (*n.*; also **anti′phonarȳ** book of antiphons; **anti′phonȳ** *n.*, antiphonal singing. [L f. Gk (ANTI-, *phōnē* sound)]

**anti′pod|ēs** (-z) *n.pl.* Places diametrically opposite (to each other), esp. Australasia as region on opposite side of earth to Europe; (also

**a′ntipōde** *sing.*) exact opposite (*of*, *to*); ~**al** *a.* (-lly), directly opposite (*to*); ~**ē′an** *a.*, of the antipodes. [F or L f. Gk (ANTI-, *pous pod-* foot)]

**a′ntipōpe** *n.* Person set up as pope in opposition to one (held by others to be) canonically chosen. [ANTI-]

**antipyrē′tic** *a.* & *n.* (Drug) counteracting fever.

**antĭque** (-ē′k). **1.** *a.* Of, existing since, old times; old-fashioned. **2.** *n.* Antique object, esp. piece of furniture etc. **3.** **a′ntĭquary** *n.*, student or collector of antiques or antiquities; **antiquār′ian** *a.* & *n.*; **antiquār′ianĭsm** *n.*; **a′ntĭquātĕd** *a.*, old-fashioned, out of date; **antī′quitȳ** *n.*, ancientness, old times (esp. before Middle Ages), (in *pl.*) customs, events, relics, of ancient times. [F, or L *antiquus*]

**antĭrrhī′num** (-rī′-) *n.* (Bot.) Snapdragon. [L f. Gk (*rhis* nose), as resembling animal's snout]

**antiscŏrbū′tic** *a.* & *n.* (Medicine) preventing or curing scurvy. [ANTI-]

**anti-Sĕmī′tic** *a.* Hostile to Jews; **antĭ-Sĕ′mĭte** *n.*, anti-Semitic person; **antĭ-Sĕ′mĭtĭsm** *n.* [SEMITE]

**antĭsĕ′ptic** *a.* (~**ally**) & *n.* (Drug etc.) counteracting sepsis, esp. by destroying bacteria. [ANTI-]

**antĭsō′cial** (-shal) *a.* Opposed to the existing social order or practices; not sociable; **antĭstă′tic** *a.*, counteracting effects of static electricity.

**anti′strophē** *n.* Section of choral ode corresponding in metre to STROPHE. [L f. Gk]

**antĭ′th|esĭs** *n.* (*pl.* ~**eses** *pr.* -ēz) Contrast of ideas marked by parallelism of contrasted words; contrast (*of*, *between*); direct opposite (*of*, *to*); ~**ĕ′tic(al)** *adjs.* (**-ically**). [L f. Gk (ANTI-, *tithēmi* place)]

**antĭtŏ′xi|c** *a.* Serving to neutralize a toxin; ~**n** *n.*, antitoxic substance. [ANTI-]

**a′ntitrāde** *a.* & *n.* (Wind) blowing in opposite direction to trade wind.

**a′ntitype** *n.* That which a type or symbol represents; one of the opposite type. [Gk (ANTI-, TYPE)]

**a′ntler** *n.* (Branch of) horn of (usu. male) deer. [F]

**a′ntonym** *n.* Word of contrary meaning to another, as *bad* to *good*. [F (ANTI-, Gk *onoma* name)]

**a′ntr|um** *n.* (*pl.* ~**a**). Cavity in the body (esp. one in the upper jaw-bone). [L f. Gk]

**ā′nus** n. Excretory opening at end of alimentary canal. [L]

**ǎ′nvil** n. Block (usu. iron) on which smith works metal. [E]

**ǎ′nxious** (ǎ′ngkshŭs) a. Troubled, uneasy in mind, (about etc.); causing, marked by, anxiety (an anxious business, moment); earnestly desirous (for thing, to do); **ǎnxī′etў** (ǎngz-) n. [L anxius]

**a′nў** (ě′-) a., pron., & ǎdv. **1.** a. & pron. (With neg., interrog., if, etc.) one or some but no matter which (cannot find any of them; have you ~ wool, sheep?, unspecified quantity or number; hardly any difference; **not having** ~, colloq., unwilling to participate or agree); whichever is chosen (any fool knows that; at any RATE[1]; has ~ **amount** of money, a great deal; an appreciable or significant (did not stay for any length of time). **2.** adv. (Usu. w. compar., and neg. or interrog.) at all, in some degree, (is that any better?; is not any the wiser). **3.** ~**bǒdў** n. & pron., any person (~**body's guess**, an unpredictable matter), person of importance; ~**how** adv., anyway, haphazardly (things are all anyhow); ~**one** (-wŭn) n. & pron., anybody; *~**plǎce** adv.*, anywhere; ~**thing** n. & pron., any thing (anything will do; have you lost anything?; ~**thing but**, far from; LIKE[1] anything); ~**way** adv., in any way, at any rate; ~**where** (-wār) adv. & pron., (in or to) any place. [E (ONE, -Y[1])]

**A′nzǎc** (ǎ′-) n. & a. (Member) of the Australian and New Zealand Army Corps (1914–18); Australian or New Zealand(er); ~ **Day**, 25 Apr. [initials]

**ā′orist** n. (Gk Gram.) Tense merely denoting occurrence without ref. to continuance, completion, etc. [Gk, = indefinite]

**āŏr′t|a** n. Great artery issuing from left ventricle of heart; ~**ic** a. [Gk]

**ap-.** See AD-.

**apā′ce** adv. Swiftly. [F, = at PACE[1]]

**ǎ′panage, ǎ′pp-,** n. Perquisite; natural adjunct. [F (AD-, L panis bread)]

**apâr′t** adv. Aside, separately, (SET[1], TELL, apart; ~ **from**, not considering; joking ~, seriously); to or at a distance; into pieces (come apart). [F, = to one side]

**apâr′theid** (-t-hāt) n. Racial segregation, esp. in S. Afr. [Afrik.]

**apâr′tment** n. Single room; *flat; (in pl.) set of rooms. [F f. It (a parte apart)]

**ǎ′path|ў** n. Insensibility, indifference; mental indolence; ~**ě′tic** a. (-ically). [F f. L f. Gk (A- 2, PATHOS)]

**āpe. 1.** n. Tailless monkey; imitator; **ā′perў** n., mimicry, apehouse. **2.** v.t. Imitate, mimic. [E]

**apercu** (ǎpẽrsū′) n. Summary, conspectus; insight. [F, = perceived]

**apē′rient** a. & n. Laxative (medicine). [L aperio open]

**apě′ritif** (-ēf) n. Alcoholic drink as appetizer. [F f. L (prec.)]

**ǎ′perture** n. Opening, gap. [L (APERIENT)]

**ā′perў.** See APE.

**ā′pěx** n. (pl. ~**es, apices** pr. -ĭsēz). Tip, topmost point, pointed end, (apex of triangle, cone, leaf). [L]

**aphā′sia** (-z-) n. Loss of (understanding) of speech, due to brain damage. [L f. Gk (aphatos speechless)]

**aphē′li|on** n. (or -lyon) n. (pl. ~**a**). Point of orbit farthest from sun. [L f. Gk apo from, hēlios sun]

**ǎ′phid** n. Plant-louse. [foll.]

**ǎ′phi|s** n. (pl. ~**des** pr. -dēz). Aphid. [L, made by Linnaeus]

**ǎ′phor|ism** n. Short pithy statement or maxim; ~**i′stic** a. (-ically). [F or L f. Gk aphorismos definition]

**ǎphrodī′siǎc** (-z-) a. & n. (Drug etc.) arousing sexual desire. [Gk (Aphroditē goddess of love)]

**ā′piar|ў** n. Place where bees are kept; ~**ist** n. [L (apis bee)]

**ā′pical** a. Of or at an apex. [APEX]

**ā′picultur|e** n. Bee-keeping; ~**ist** n. [L apis bee, CULTURE]

**apie′ce** adv. Severally, each, (gave them, they had, £5 apiece). [A[2]]

**ā′pish** a. Of or like an ape; affected, silly. [APE]

**aplǒ′mb** (-m) n. Self-possession. [F, lit. (perpendicularity) by plummet]

**ǎpo-** pref. Away from, separate. [Gk]

**apǒ′calypse** n. Revelation, esp. that made to St. John (the A~), N.T. book, = REVELATION); grand or violent event; **apǒcalў′ptic(al)** adjs. (-ically). [F f. L f. Gk (kaluptō cover)]

**Apocr.** abbr. Apocrypha.

**Apǒ′crўph|a** (a-) n. O.T. books included in Septuagint and Vulgate but not in Hebrew Bible; **a~al** a. (-lly), of the Apocrypha, of doubtful authenticity, sham. [L f. Gk (*kruptō* hide)]

**ă′pogee** *n*. Point (in orbit of moon etc.) that is farthest from earth; (fig.) highest point, climax; **ăpogē′an** *a*. [F or L f. Gk (*gē* earth)]

**ăpoli′tĭcal** *a*. (~ly). Unconcerned with politics. [A- 2]

**Apŏllĭnā̆r′ĭs** (*a*-) *n*. A mineral water. [place]

**Apŏ′llyon** (*a*-) *n*. The Devil. [L f. Gk, = destroyer]

**ăpolŏ′gĭa** *n*. Written defence of one's conduct or opinions. [L f. Gk (foll.)]

**apŏ′log|ў** *n*. Regretful acknowledgement of fault or failure, assurance that no offence was intended, (make or offer an one's *apology* or *apologies*); explanation; ~ **for**, poor or scanty specimen of (*this apology for a letter*); ~**ĕ′tĭc**, (*a*.; -**ically**) making an apology, expressing regret, of the nature of an apology, (*n*., usu. in *pl.*) reasoned defence esp. of Christianity; ~**ĭst**, one who defends by argument; ~**ĭze** *v.i*., make an apology (to person, for thing etc.). [F or L f. Gk (APO-, -LOGY)]

**ă′pophthĕgm** (-ŏfthĕm, -ŏthĕm) *n*. Terse or pithy saying; ~**ă′tĭc** (-ĕgm-) *a*. (-**ically**). [F or L f. Gk]

**ă′popl|ĕxў** *n*. Sudden inability to feel and move, caused by blockage or rupture of brain artery; ~**ĕ′ctĭc** *a*. (-**ically**), of, causing, suffering from, liable to, apoplexy. [F f. L f. Gk (APO- completely, *plēssō* strike)]

**apŏ′st|asў** *n*. Abandonment of one's religion, party, etc.; ~**ate** *n*. & *a*., (person) guilty of apostasy; ~**atize** *v.i*., become an apostate (*from* one *to* another). [F or L f. Gk, = defection]

**ā̆ pŏstēriŏ̆r′ĭ** (*or* -ĕr-) *adv*. & *a*. (Reasoning) from effects to causes, inductive(ly). [L, = from what is after]

**apŏ′stle** (-sel) *n*. (A~) any of the twelve sent forth by Christ to preach Gospel (~ **spoon**, with figure of Apostle on handle); leader of reform (*apostle of temperance*); **apŏ′stolate** *n*., apostleship, leadership in reform; **ăpostŏ′lĭc** *a*. (-**ically**), of the Apostles, of the character of an apostle, of the Pope (*apostolic* SUCCESSION). [E f. L f. Gk *apostolos* messenger]

**apŏ′stroph|ē** *n*. Exclamatory passage by orator or poet, addressed to a person (often dead or absent);

sign of omission of letter (*can't*) or numbers ('78, i.e. 1978); sign of possessive case (*boy's*, *boys'*); **ăpostrŏ′phĭc** *a*. (-**ically**); ~**ĭze** *v.t*., address in apostrophe. [L f. Gk, lit. turning away]

**apŏ′thĕcar|ў** *n*. (arch.) Druggist, pharmaceutical chemist; ~**ies′ measure, weight**, units used in pharmacy. [F f. L (Gk *apothēkē* storehouse)]

**apŏthĕŏ′s|ĭs** *n*. (*pl*. ~**es** *pr*. -ēz). Deification; canonization; deified ideal; **apŏ′thĕosize** *v.t*. [L f. Gk (*theos* god)]

**appa′l** (-aw′l) *v.t*. (-**ll**-). Dismay, terrify; ~**ling** *a*., (colloq.) shocking, unpleasant. [F (AP-, PALE²)]

**ă′ppanage**. See APANAGE.

**ăpparā̆′tus** *n*. Equipment for scientific or other work. [L (*paro* prepare)]

**appă′rel.** (arch.) **1.** *v.t*. (‖-**ll**-). Clothe. **2.** *n*. Clothing. [F (L *par* equal)]

**appă′rent** *a*. Manifest, palpable, (HEIR *apparent*); seeming (*his reluctance was only apparent*). [F f. L (APPEAR)]

**ăpparĭ′tion** *n*. Appearance, esp. of startling or remarkable kind; ghost.

**appea′l. 1.** *v.i*. & *t*. Make request (to higher tribunal, or abs.) for alteration of decision of lower one (‖*appeal to the* COUNTRY); remove (case) to higher court etc.; call attention to (evidence); make earnest request (to person, for thing or to do); be attractive to (*puns do not appeal to me*); (Crick.) ask umpire whether batsman is out. **2.** *n*. Act or right of appealing; quality etc. that appeals (*has snob appeal*). **3. appĕ′llant** *a*. & *n*., (person) appealing to higher court, appellate; **appĕ′llate** *a*., (Law) concerned with appeals. [F f. L *appello* address]

**appear′** *v.i*. Become or be visible; present oneself formally or publicly; act as counsel in court; be published (*it appeared in the papers*; *new edition will appear*); be manifest; give a certain impression, seem, (*you appear to forget*; *strange as it may appear*; *it appears that*); ~**ance** *n*., appearing (**put in an ~ance**, present oneself), semblance (*has an appearance of meanness*; **to all ~ance(s)**, so far as can be seen), outward aspect, (in *pl*.) outward show of prosperity or good behaviour etc. (*keep up appearances*). [F f. L *appareo*]

**appea'se** (-z) *v.t.* Make calm or quiet; try to conciliate or bribe (potential aggressor) by making concessions; satisfy (appetite, scruple); **~ment** (-zm-) *n.* [F (AP-, PEACE)]

**appe'llant, -ate.** See APPEAL.

**äppellā'tion** *n.* Name, title; nomenclature; **appe'llative** *a.,* (of noun) designating a class, common (opp. *proper*). [F f. L (APPEAL)]

**appe'nd** *v.t.* Attach (thing *to* another) as pendant or accessory; add esp. in writing; **~age** *n.,* thing appended (*to*), accompaniment; **~ix** *n.* (*pl.* **~ices** *pr.* -isēz, **~ixes**), subsidiary addition (*to* book etc.), small process developed from surface of any organ; **~ici'tis** *n.,* inflammation of vermiform appendix of intestine. [L *appendo*]

**äppertai'n** *v.i.* Belong naturally or as a possession or right (*to*); relate (*to* a subject). [F f. L (PERTAIN)]

**a'ppetite** *n.* Desire, inclination, natural craving, (*for* food, pleasure, etc.); one's relish for food (*has a good, no, appetite*); **~ence, -cȳ,** *ns.,* desire, craving, (*for*); **~ent** *a.,* eagerly desirous (*of*); **appe'titive** *a.,* of the nature of appetite; **~izer** *n.,* thing eaten or drunk to stimulate appetite; **~izing** *a.,* (of food) giving appetite. [F f. L (*peto* seek)]

**applau'|d** *v.t.* & *i.* Express approval (of), esp. by clapping; commend (*I applaud your decision*); **~se** (-z) *n.,* clapping, loud approbation, warm approval. [L (PLAUDIT)]

**a'pple** *n.* Round firm fleshy fruit of a rosaceous tree; **upset** person's **~cart,** spoil his plans; **~ of the,** one's, **eye,** cherished object; **~pie bed** (with sheets so folded that one's legs cannot get down); **~pie order,** perfect order; **~ sauce,** apples stewed to pulp, *(sl.)* nonsense. [E]

**appli'ance** *n.* Thing applied as a means; device, equipment; fire-engine. [APPLY]

**a'pplic|able** *a.* (-bly). That may be applied (*to*); **~abi'litȳ** *n.;* **~ant** *n.,* one who applies (*for* job etc.); **~ā'tion** *n.,* applying, thing applied, relevance, diligence, request; **~ātor** *n.,* device for applying thing esp. to the body. [F or L (APPLY)]

**äppli'qué** (-lē'kā) *n., a., & v.* **1.** *n.* & *a.* (Cut-out ornamental fabric etc.) sewn or fixed to surface of another fabric. **2.** *v.t.* Ornament thus. [F (foll.)]

**apply'** *v.t.* & *i.* Put close (*to*) or in contact, spread on surface, (*apply a match to gunpowder; apply paint evenly*); administer (remedy etc. *to*); devote, direct, (instrument, faculty, knowledge, one*self, to* task, *to* doing); put to practical use (*applied* MATHEMATICS, SCIENCE); have relevance, use as relevant, (*to*); make formal request (*for* help, a job, etc., *to* person). [F f. L *applico*]

**appo'ggiatu're** (-ŏjatoo'rǎ) *n.* Prefixed grace-note. [It.]

**appoi'nt** *v.t.* Fix (time, place, etc., *for* purpose); prescribe, ordain, (*our appointed lot*); assign to office (*appoint an agent; appoint him agent; appoint him to act; appoint him to the post*) (in *p.p.*) equipped (*a well-appointed fleet*); **~ee** *n.;* **~ment** *n.,* appointing, esp. of time and place for meeting (*can you give me an appointment for tomorrow?; kept, broke, his appointment*), assigned office (*a lucrative appointment*), (in *pl.*) equipment, fittings. [F (POINT)]

**appo'rtion** *v.t.* Portion out; assign as share (*to*); **~ment** *n.* [F or L (PORTION)]

**a'pposite** (-z-) *a.* Well expressed, appropriate (*to*); **~i'tion** *n.,* placing of word, esp. noun, in syntactic parallelism with another (e.g. in *William the Conqueror*), juxtaposition; **~i'tional** *a.* (-lly). [L (*appono* apply)]

**apprai's|e** (-z) *v.t.* (Esp. of valuer) fix price of; estimate; **~al, ~ement** (-zm-), *ns.;* **~ive** *a.* [APPRAISE, assim. to PRAISE]

**appre'ci|ate** (-shi-) *v.t.* & *i.* Set high value on, esteem, (*I appreciate your kindness; gift was much appreciated*); estimate rightly; recognize *that*; estimate; raise, rise, in value; **~able** (-sha-) *a.* (-bly), perceptible, capable of being estimated, considerable; **~ā'tion, ~ātor,** *ns.;* **~ātive, ~atorȳ,** *adjs.,* (esp.) expressing esteem. [L (*pretium* price)]

**äpprehě'n|d** *v.t.* Seize, arrest; perceive, understand, (*I do not apprehend your meaning*); anticipate with fear (*I apprehend violence*); **~sible** *a.* (-bly), perceptible to senses or intellect; **~sibi'litȳ** *n.;* **~sion** (-shon) *n.,* arrest, understanding, uneasiness; **~sive** *a.,* (esp.) uneasy in mind, fearful, (*of* thing, *that*). [F or L (*prehendo* grasp)]

**appre'ntice.** **1.** *n.* Learner of a

craft, bound to employer for specified term; novice (jockey etc.); **~shĭp** (-s-sh-) *n*. **2.** *v.t.* Bind (person *to* another) as apprentice. [F (*apprendre* learn)]

**apprī'se** (-z) *v.t.* Inform (*of*). [F (APPREHEND)]

**apprī'ze** *v.t.* (arch.) Appraise; esteem highly. [F (PRICE)]

‖**ă'pprŏ** *n*. (colloq.) **On ~**, on APPROVAL. [abbr.]

**approa'ch. 1.** *v.t.* & *i.* Come near(er) (to) in space or time (*castle is approached by a path; the time approaches*); set about (task); make tentative proposal to; be similar to, approximate to, (esp.) **~able** *a.*, (esp.) easy to talk to; **~abi'lĭty** *n.* **2.** *n.* Act or means of approaching; approximation (*his nearest approach to a smile*); final part of aircraft's flight before landing; (Golf) stroke, not from tee, intended to reach green. [F f. L (*prope* near)]

**ăpprŏbā'tion** *n.* Sanction, approval. **ă'pprŏbātŏry** *a.* [F f. L (APPROVE)]

**apprŏ'prĭ|ate. 1.** *a.* Proper, suitable (*to, for,* occasion etc.); belonging or peculiar (*to*). **2.** (-āt) *v.t.* (~able). Take possession of; devote (fund etc. *to* purpose); **~ā'tion, ~ātor,** *ns.*; **~ative** *a.* [L (PROPER)]

**apprŏ'v|e** (-ōō'v) *v.t.* & *i.* Confirm, sanction, (*parliament approved the bill*); **~e** (*of*), pronounce or consider good; **~al** *n.*, approving (**on ~al,** returnable to supplier if not satisfactory). [F f. L (PROVE)]

**apprŏ'xĭm|ate. 1.** *a.* Fairly correct, near to the actual, (*approximate total, price, result*). **2.** (-āt) *v.i.* & *t.* Be or make approximate or near (*to*); **~ā'tion** *n.* [L (PROXIMATE)]

**appŭr'tĕnance** *n.* (usu. in *pl.*) Belonging(s), appendage(s), (*of*). [F (PERTAIN)]

**Apr.** *abbr.* April.

**après-ski** (ăpräskē') *a.* & *n.* (Worn or done at) time after day's skiing at resort. [F]

**ā'prĭcŏt** *n.* Juicy stone-fruit allied to plum and peach; its orange-pink colour. [Port. or Sp. f. Arab. f. Gk (L *praecox* early-ripe)]

**A'prĭl** (ā-; *or* -il) *n.* Fourth month, noted for alternations of sunshine and showers; **~ fool,** person hoaxed on 1 Apr. (**~ Fool's Day**). [L]

**ā prĭŏr'ĭ** *adv.* & *a.* (Reasoning) from causes to effects, deductive(ly);

presumptive(ly), without investigation; (of knowledge) existing in the mind independently of sensory experience. [L, = from what is before]

**ā'pron** *n.* Garment worn in front of body to protect clothes (**tied to** *mother's, wife's,* **~-strings,** unduly controlled by); official dress of this kind for bishop etc.; hard-surfaced area on airfield where aircraft are moved, (un)loaded, etc.; (Theatr.) advanced strip of stage for playing scenes in front of curtain. [orig. *naperon,* f. F; for loss of *n*- cf. ADDER]

**ăpropo's** (-pō; *or* ă'-) *adv.* & *a.* To the point or purpose; appropriate(ly); (abs.) incidentally; **~ of,** in connection with. [F *à propos*]

**ăpse** *n.* Arched or domed recess esp. at end of church; **ă'psĭdal** *a.*, of the form of an apse, of apsides; **ă'psĭs** *n.* (*pl.* apsides *pr.* -dēz), aphelion or perihelion of planet, apogee or perigee of satellite. [L, f. Gk *apsis*]

**ăpt** *a.* Suitable, appropriate, (*an apt quotation*); having a tendency (*to* do or be); quick-witted (*at*; *an apt pupil*); **~ĭtŭde** *n.*, (esp.) talent (*for*). [L *aptus*]

**ă'pteryx** *n.* Flightless N.Z. bird with rudimentary wings and no tail, kiwi. [L (Gk *a-* not, *pterux* wing)]

**ă'ptĭtŭde.** See APT.

**ă'qua** *n.* The colour aquamarine. [abbr.]

**ăqua fŏr'tĭs** *n.* Nitric acid [L *fortis* strong]; **ă'qualŭng** *n.*, & *v.i.*, (use) diver's portable breathing--apparatus; **ăquamarī'ne** (-ē'n) *n.*, bluish-green (beryl); **ă'quaplāne,** (*n.*) board for riding on, towed by speedboat, (*v.i.*) ride on this, (of vehicle) glide uncontrollably on wet surface of road, [PLANE[2]]; **ăqua rē'gĭa** *n.*, mixture of acids, able to dissolve gold [REGIUS]; **ăquarĕ'lle** *n.*, painting in thin usu. transparent water-colours [F f. It.]; **aquār'ĭum** *n.* (*pl.* **-iums, -ia**), tank for live aquatic animals and plants, place containing such tanks; **Aquār'ĭus** (*a-*) *n.*, sign of ZODIAC; **aquā'tĭc,** (*a.*) living in or near water, conducted in or on water, (*n.*) aquatic plant or animal, (in *pl.*) aquatic sports; **ă'quatint** *n.*, engraving on copper with nitric acid; **ăqua vī'tae** *n.*, alcoholic spirits, esp. of first distillation [VITAL]; **ă'quĕdŭct** *n.*, artificial channel, esp. raised structure of masonry, to convey water; **ā′quéous** *a.*, of water, watery (*aqueous* HUMOUR), produced by water (*aqueous rocks*). [L *aqua* water]

**áquilē′gia** *n.* Columbine, usu. blue-flowered. [L]

**ă′quilīne** *a.* Of or like an eagle; ~ **nose** (hooked like eagle's beak). [L (*aquila* eagle)]

**ar-.** See AD-.

**-ar** *suf.* forming *adjs.* w. sense 'of, of the nature of'. [L -*aris*]

**A.R.A.** *abbr.* Associate of the Royal Academy.

**A′rab** (ă′-) *n.* & *a.* (Member) of a Semitic people inhabiting the Middle East (orig., Saudi Arabia and neighbouring countries; STREET *arab*); Arabian horse; **ărăbe′sque** (-k) *n.*, decoration with intertwined leaves, scrollwork, etc., ballet-dancer's posture in which body is bent forward and supported on one leg with other leg extended horizontally backwards; **Arā′bian** (*a*-) *a.* & *n.*, (native) of Arabia; **A′rabic** (ă′-) *a.* & *n.*, of Arabia (**gum arabic**, exuded by some acacias; **arabic numerals**, 1, 2, etc., opp. *Roman*), (of) the Arabs' language or literature. [F f. L f. Gk f. Arab.]

**ă′rable** *a.* & *n.* (Land) ploughed or fit for ploughing; ‖(of crop) that can be grown on arable. [F or L (*aro* to plough)]

**ară′chnid** (-k-) *n.* Any of a class comprising spiders, scorpions, etc. [F or L (Gk *arakhnē* spider)]

**ară′k.** See ARRACK.

**Aramā′ic** (ă-) *a.* & *n.* (Of) language of Syria in time of Christ; (of) the northern Semitic group of languages including Syriac. [Gk *Aramaios* of Aram (= Syria)]

**ăr′bĭt|er** *n.* Judge, arbitrator; one with entire control (*of*); ~**rage** (-ahzh) *n.*, traffic in stocks etc. to take advantage of prices in other markets; ~**ral** *a.* (-lly), of arbitration; **ărbĭ′trament** *n.*, arbitration, decision by arbiter, authoritative decision; ~**rary** *a.* (-ily, -iness), derived from mere opinion or random choice, capricious, despotic; ~**rāte** *v.t.* & *i.*, decide by arbitration; ~**rā′tion** *n.*, settlement of dispute by arbitrator; ~**rātor** *n.*, one appointed to settle dispute. [L]

**ăr′bor**[1] *n.* Axle or spindle on which thing revolves; **A~ Day**, day set apart annually in some countries for public tree-planting; ~**ā′ceous** (-shŭs) *a.*, treelike, wooded; **ăr-bŏr′ēal** *a.* (-lly), of, living in, trees; ~**ě′scent** *a.*, treelike in growth or form; ~**ě′scence** *n.*; ~**ě′tum** *n.* (*pl.* -a, *-ums*), botanical tree-garden; ~**ĭcŭlture** *n.*, cultivation of trees and shrubs; ~**ĭcŭ′ltural** *a.*, ~**ĭcŭ′lturist** *n.*, (-cher-); ~ **vī′tae**, kind of evergreen conifer. [F f. L, = tree]

**ăr′bour**, *\****ăr′bor**[2], (-er) *n.* Shady retreat with sides and roof formed mainly by trees or climbing plants. [F (HERB)]

**ărbū′tus** *n.* Kind of evergreen, esp. strawberry-tree. [L]

**ărc.** **1.** *n.* Part of circumference of circle or other curve; luminous discharge between electrodes in gas; ~ **lamp, light, welding,** (using this). **2.** *v.i.* (~**ing,** ~**ed,** *pr.* -k-). Form arc. [F f. L *arcus* bow]

**ărcā′d|e** *n.* Covered walk esp. lined with shops; series of arches supporting or along wall; ~**ěd** *a.*

**Arcā′dian** (är-) *a.* & *n.* Ideal(ly) rustic; **Ar′cadў** (är-) *n.*, (poet.) rustic paradise. [L f. Gk *Arkadia*]

**ărcā′n|e** *a.* Mysterious, secret; ~**um** *n.* (usu. in *pl.* ~a), mystery, secret. [F, or L (*arca* chest)]

**ărch**[1]. **1.** *n.* Curved structure supporting bridge, floor, etc., or as ornament; archlike curvature; vault; ~**′way**, vaulted passage, arched entrance; ~**′wise** (-z) *adv.*, like an arch. **2.** *v.t.* & *i.* Furnish with or form into arch; span like arch; (of branches etc.) form arch. [F f. L *arcus* arc]

**ărch**[2] *a.* Consciously or affectedly playful (*an arch look, smile, girl*). [foll., orig. in *arch rogue* etc.]

**ărch-** *pref.* Chief, superior, (*archbishop*); pre-eminent, esp. extremely bad (*arch-fiend*). [E or F f. L f. Gk (*arkhos* chief)]

**Archae′an,** *\****Arch′ean,** (ärk-) *a.* & *n.* (Of) the earliest geological period. [Gk (ARCHAIC)]

**ărchae|ŏ′logў,** *\****ărchě|ŏ′logў,** (-kĭ-) *n.* Study of antiquities, esp. of prehistoric period, usu. by excavation; ~**olŏ′gical** *a.* (-lly); ~**ŏ′logĭst** *n.* [L f. Gk (foll.)]

**ărchā′ic** (-k-) *a.* (~**ally**). Primitive, antiquated; (of word etc.) no longer in ordinary use; **ăr′chāism** (-k-) *n.*, use of the archaic esp. in language and art, archaic word; **ăr′chāĭst** *n.*, **ărchāĭ′stic** *a.*, (-k-); **ăr′chāīze** (-k-)

*v.t. & i.*, make archaic, imitate the archaic. [F f. Gk (*archaios* ancient)]

**ar'changel** (-kānj-) *n.* Angel of highest rank; **archangĕ'lic** (-kānj-) *a.* [F f. L f. Gk (ARCH-)]

**archbi'shop** *n.* Chief bishop; ~**rĭc** *n.*, office or diocese of archbishop. [E (ARCH-)]

**archdea'con** *n.* Church dignitary, next below bishop; ~**rў** *n.*, jurisdiction, rank, or residence of archdeacon. [E f. L f. Gk (ARCH-)]

**archdī'ocèse** *n.* Archbishop's diocese. [ARCH-]

**ar'chdūke** *n.* (*fem.* ~**duchess;** *Hist.*) Chief duke, esp. as title of son of Emperor of Austria; ~**dū'cal** *a.*; ~**dŭchў** *n.*, archduke's territory. [F f. L (ARCH-)]

***Archean, *archeology,** etc. See ARCHAEAN etc.

**ar'cher** *n.* One who shoots with bow and arrows; (*A*~) sign of ZODIAC; ~**ў** *n.*, use of bow and arrows. [F f. L *arcus* bow]

**ar'chetyp|e** (-k-) *n.* Original model, prototype; typical specimen; ~**al, archetў'pĭcal** (-k-), *adjs.* (-lly). [L f. Gk (ARCH-, TYPE)]

**arch-fie'nd** *n.* The Devil. [ARCH-]

**archĭdiă'conal** (-kĭ-) *a.* Of an archdeacon. [L (ARCH-)]

**archĭépĭ'scopal** (-kĭĭ-) *a.* Of an archbishop. [L f. Gk (ARCH-)]

**archĭmă'ndrīte** (-k-) *n.* Superior of monastery in Orthodox Church (also as honorific title). [F or L f. Gk (ARCH-, *mandra* monastery)]

**Archĭmē'dēs** (ārk-; -z) *n.* ~' **principle** (that body in fluid is subject to upward force equal to weight of displaced fluid). [person]

**archĭpĕ'lagō** (-k-) *n.* (*pl.* ~**s,** ~**es**). Sea with many islands; group of islands. [It. f. Gk *arkhi-* chief, *pelagos* sea]

**ar'chĭtĕct** (-kĭ-) *n.* Designer of buildings (**naval** ~, of ships) who prepares plans and superintends construction; designer of complex structure; maker, constructor, (*architect of his own fortunes*); ~**ure** *n.*, art or science of building, style of building, construction; **archĭtĕ'ctural** (-kĭtĕ'kcher-) *a.* (-lly); ~**ŏ'nĭc** *a.* (-ically), of architecture, constructive, of the systematization of knowledge. [F f. It. or L, f. Gk (ARCH-, *tektōn* builder)]

**ar'chĭtrāve** (-k-) *n.* Beam resting on abacus of column; moulded frame round doorway, window, or exterior of arch. [F f. It. (ARCH-, L *trabs* beam)]

**ar'chīves** (-kĭvz) *n.pl.* Public records or documents; place where these are kept; **ar'chĭvĭst** (-k-) *n.*, keeper of archives. [F f. L f. Gk (*arkhē* government)]

**ar'ctĭc. 1.** *a.* Of north polar regions (A~ **Circle,** parallel of 66° 33′ N.); (colloq., of weather) very cold. **2.** *n.* (*A*~). Regions round N. Pole. [F f. L f. Gk (*arktos* Great Bear)]

**ar'den|t** *a.* Eager, zealous, fervent; burning (~**t spirits,** alcoholic); ~**cў** *n.*; **ar'dour, *ar'dor,** (-er) *n.*, zeal, enthusiasm, (*for*). [F f. L (*ardeo* burn)]

**ar'dūous** *a.* Hard, laborious, (*arduous task*); strenuous, energetic, (*arduous life, workers*). [L, =steep]

**are.** See BE.

**ar'ėa** *n.* Extent or measure of surface (*over a vast area*; *the area of a triangle*); region (*a mountainous area*; *picnic* etc. ~, for such use); scope or range of activity etc.; sunk court in front of house basement. [L, = vacant space]

**ă'rėca** (or arē'-) *n.* Kind of palm-tree; ~ **nut,** its astringent seed. [Port. f. Malayalam]

**arē'na** *n.* Centre of amphitheatre; scene of conflict, sphere of action; **ărėnă'ceous** (-shus) *a.*, sandy. [L, =sand]

**aren't.** See BE.

**arē'ol|a** *n.* (*pl.* ~**ae**). Circular pigmented area e.g. around nipple; ~**ar** *a.* [L dim. of AREA]

**arête** (ără't) *n.* Sharp mountain ridge. [F f. L *arista* spine]

**ar'gent** *n. & a.* (esp. Her.) Silver (colour); ~**i'ferous** *a.*, yielding silver; ~**īne** *a.*, of silver, silvery (**the** A~**ine,** Argentina). [F f. L *argentum*]

**ar'gosў** *n.* (Hist., poet.) Large merchant-ship. [It. *Ragusa,* place]

**ar'gŏt** (-ō) *n.* Jargon, formerly esp. of thieves. [F]

**ar'gū|e** *v.t. & i.* Maintain by reasoning (*that*); treat (matter) by reasoning (~**e away,** get rid of by reasoning); persuade (person) *into, out of*; reason esp. contentiously (*with, against,* person; *for, against, about,* thing); prove, indicate; ~**ment** *n.*, reason advanced (*for, against*), reasoning, (heated) debate, summary in book etc.; ~**mĕntā'tion** *n.*, reasoning, arguing; ~**mĕ'ntative** *a.*, fond of arguing. [F f. L (*arguo* make clear, prove)]

**Ar′gus** (är′-) *n.* Watchful guardian; ~**eyed**, vigilant. [L, f. Gk *Argos* mythical person w. 100 eyes]

**ar′ia** *n.* Long accompanied song for one voice in opera etc. [It.]

**Ar′ian** (är′-) *a.* & *n.* (Holder) of the doctrine of *Arius* (4th c.), who denied full divinity of Christ; ~**ism** *n.* [person]

**a′rid** *a.* Dry, parched, (*arid desert, region*); (of subject etc.) dry, dull; **arī′dĭty** *n.* [F or L (*areo* be dry)]

**Ar′ies** (är′ēz). Sign of ZODIAC. [L, = ram]

**arī′ght** (-ī′t) *adv.* Rightly. [A³]

**arī′s|e** (-z) *v.i.* (**arose; arisen;** *pr.* -ō′z, -ī′zen). Originate, come into notice, (*a prophet arose*); result (*from, out of*), present itself, (*questions, difficulties, arose*); rise, esp. from the dead; ~**ings** (-z) *n.pl.*, secondary or waste products. [E (*a-* intensive)]

**ărĭsto′cracy** *n.* Government by the best citizens; State so governed; ruling body of nobles; *the* nobles; best representatives (*of* intellect etc.); **ă′ristocrăt** *n.*, member of aristocracy, noble; **ărĭstocră′tic** *a.* (**-ically**) of (the) aristocracy, grand, stylish. [F f. Gk (*aristos* best)]

**Aristotē′lian** (ä-) *a.* & *n.* (Disciple, student) of the Gk philosopher *Aristotle*. [L f. Gk]

**arĭ′thmetic¹** *n.* Science of numbers; computation, use of figures, (*a mere matter of arithmetic*); *I challenge your arithmetic*); **ărĭthmĕ′tic²(al)** *adjs.* (**-ically**), of arithmetic; *arithmetic* MEAN³; ~**al progression**, (series of numbers showing) increase or decrease by a constant quantity (e.g. 1, 3, 5, 7); **arĭthmetĭ′cian** (-shǎn) *n.* [F f. L f. Gk (*arithmos* number)]

**Ariz.** *abbr.* Arizona.

**ărk** *n.* Ark (of the Covenant), wooden chest or cupboard containing tables of Jewish Law; NOAH′s *ark*. [E, f. L *arca*]

**Ark.** *abbr.* Arkansas.

**ărm¹** *n.* Upper limb of human body from shoulder to hand (~**pit**, hollow under arm at shoulder; ~ **in** ~, of two persons with arm of one linked in arm of the other; **at** ~**'s length**, esp., aloof; *baby* **in** ~, too young to walk; **under** one's ~, between it and body; **with open** ~**s**, cordially); forelimb of animal;

sleeve; raised side part of chair to support sitter's arm (~′**chair**, with such supports); branch; armlike thing (*arm of the sea*); ~′**ful** (-ŏol) *n.*, quantity held by arm(s). [E]

**ărm².** **1.** *n.* (usu. in *pl.*) Weapon (**small** ~**s**, portable firearms; **lay down, take up,** ~**s**, cease, begin, war; **under** ~**s**, equipped for war; **up in** ~**s**, actively rebelling, lit. or fig.); branch of military forces, e.g. infantry, artillery; (in *pl.*) heraldic devices. **2.** *v.t.* Furnish (person, one*self*, or abs.) with weapons (~**ed neutrality**, of nation prepared for war); furnish with tools or other requisites (also fig.); make (bomb etc.) ready to explode. **3.** ~**a′da** (-ah′-) *n.*, fleet of warships, esp. the *Spanish Armada* sent against England in 1588; ~**adĭ′llō** *n.* (*pl.* ~**s**), S. Amer. burrowing mammal with body encased in bony plates, able to roll itself into ball; ~**ament** *n.*, equipping, force equipped, for war, military weapons etc. esp. guns on warship; ~**ature** *n.*, protective covering of animals or plants, wire-wound core of dynamo or electric motor. [F f. L *arma* pl.]

**Armagĕ′ddon** (ärmag-) *n.* Supreme conflict of the nations. [Rev. 16: 16]

**är′mĭstice** *n.* Cessation from hostilities; short truce. [F or L (*arma* arms, *-stitium* stoppage)]

**är′mlet** *n.* Band worn round arm. [ARM¹]

**är′mory** *n.* Heraldry; **ärmór′ial** *a.* [foll.]

**är′mour, *är′mor,** (-er). **1.** *n.* Defensive covering formerly worn in fighting; metal plates etc. protecting warship, car, tank, etc., armoured fighting vehicles collectively; diver's suit; plant's or animal's armature; heraldic devices; ~**y** *n.*, arsenal. **2.** *v.t.* Furnish with armour (~**ed car** etc., with protective steel plates and usu. guns; ~**ed division** etc., one equipped with armoured cars, tanks, etc.); ~**er** *n.*, maker of arms or armour, official in charge of arms. [F f. L (ARM², -URE)]

**är′my** *n.* Organized force armed for fighting on land (||A~ **List**, of commissioned officers); *the* military profession; vast host or number (*an army of locusts*); organized body for a cause (*Salvation Army*). [F (ARM²)]

**ar'nica** n. Kind of composite plant; medicine made from it. [L]

**arō'ma** n. Fragrance, sweet smell; subtle pervasive quality; **ăromă'tic** a. (-ically). [L f. Gk, = spice]

**arose.** See ARISE.

**arou'nd. 1.** adv. On every side, all round; (colloq.) near at hand; here and there (shop around; fool around). **2.** prep. On or along the circuit of; on every side of; \*approximately at, about. [A³]

**arou'se** (-z) v.t. Rouse. [a- intensive pref.]

**A.R.P.** abbr. air-raid precautions.

**ărpĕ'ggiŏ** (or -ĕ'jŏ) n. (pl. ~s). Sounding of notes of chord in rapid succession; chord so sounded. [It. (arpa harp)]

**ăr'quĕbus.** See HARQUEBUS.

**arr.** abbr. arranged by; arrives.

**ă'rrack, ară'k,** n. Alcoholic spirit, esp. made from coco sap or rice. [Arab.]

**arrai'gn** (-ā'n) v.t. Indict, accuse; find fault with (action, statement); ~ment n. [F f. L (REASON)]

**arra'nge** (-nj) v.t. & i. Put into order; settle (dispute); settle procedure etc. beforehand, form plans, give instructions, (arrange to be there, for the car to be there; it is all arranged); come to agreement (with person about thing); (Mus.) adapt (composition) for different medium; adapt (play etc.) for broadcasting; ~ment (-njm-) n., arranging, thing arranged, settlement of dispute, (in pl.) plans, measures, (cannot alter my arrangements). [F (RANGE)]

**ă'rrant** a. Downright, unmitigated, (arrant liar, nonsense). [ = errant, orig. in arrant (=outlawed roving) thief etc.]

**ă'rras** n. Tapestry; (Hist.) screen of this hung loosely round walls of room. [place]

**array'. 1.** v.t. Marshal or dispose (forces); dress, esp. with display. **2.** n. Imposing series (what an array of umbrellas!); (Hist.) martial order (battle array). [F (AD-, READY)]

**arrear'** n. (in pl.) Outstanding debts, what remains not done (arrears of work); **in** ~(s), behindhand (with payment, work, etc.). [F f. L (AD-, retro backwards)]

**arrĕ'st. 1.** v.t. Stop (a moving person or thing, motion, growth, process); ~ **judgement,** stay legal proceedings after verdict, on ground

of error); seize by authority; catch (person's attention, eye, glance); catch attention of; ~able a., (of offence) such that offender may be arrested without a warrant; ~er, ~or, ns., device for retarding aircraft by hook and cable when it lands; ~ment n., (esp., Sc.) attachment of earnings. **2.** n. Stoppage; seizure; legal arresting of offender; cardiac ~, heart failure. [F, f. L resto remain]

**arrière-pensée** (ăriărpah'nsā) n. Ulterior motive; mental reservation. [F]

**ă'rris** n. Sharp edge where two plane or curved surfaces meet. [F areste, = ARÊTE]

**arri've** v.i. Come to destination or end of journey (arrive at Bath, in Paris; arrive on the scene; train arrives at 4.10; goods did not arrive); ~e at a conclusion, reach it); establish one's reputation or position; (colloq., of child) be born; (of time) come; ~al n., arriving, appearance on scene, person or thing that has arrived, (colloq.) new-born child. [F, f. L ripa shore]

**ă'rrogant** a. Aggressively haughty; presumptuous; ~ance n.; ~ate v.t., claim unduly (thing to oneself), attribute unjustly (to another); ~a'tion n. [L (rogo ask)]

**ă'rrow** (-ō) n. Pointed slender missile shot from bow; representation of arrow, esp. (broad) ~, mark on British Government stores; ~root, plant from which a nutritious starch is prepared; ~ў a. [E]

‖**arse, \*ass²,** n. (vulg.) Buttocks, rump. [E]

**ăr'senal** n. Government establishment for storage or manufacture of weapons and ammunition. [F or It. f. Arab., = workshop]

**ăr'senic¹** n. A semi-metallic element; trioxide of this, a violent poison; **ărsĕ'nic², ărsĕ'nious,** adjs.; **ărsĕ'nical** a. & n., (drug) containing arsenic. [F f. L f. Gk f. Arab. f. Pers.]

**ăr'son** n. Malicious setting on fire of house or other property; ~ist n., person guilty of arson. [F f. L (ardeo ars- burn)]

**art¹.** See BE.

**ărt²** n. Skill, esp. human skill as opp. to nature; imitative or imaginative skill in design, e.g. in paintings etc., (attrib., ~ needlework etc.) of artistic design, (in pl.) = FINE² arts;

thing in which skill may be exercised, (in *pl.*) certain branches of learning (esp. languages, literature, history, etc.) as dist. from sciences (BACHELOR, MASTER, *of Arts*); knack; cunning, artfulness, (~ **and part**, accessory, participant); stratagem; ~ *nouveau* (ärnōōvō') [F, = new art], late-19th-c. style of art with ornamental and flowing designs. [F f. L *ars* art-]

**ar'tĕfăct, ar'tĭ-**, *n.* (esp. Archaeol.) Man-made object. [L *arte* by art, *facio* make]

**ar'tery** *n.* Any of the tubes by which blood is conveyed from heart (cf. VEIN) to all parts of the body; (fig.) important channel of transport, e.g. main road or railway; ~ **ar-ter'ial** *a.* (-lly), of (the nature of) an artery (**arterial road**, important main road); **ar-tēri-ōsclĕro'sis** *n.*, hardening of walls of arteries. [L f. Gk (*airō* raise)]

**artē'sian** (-zhạn) *a.* ~ **well** (in which water rises spontaneously to surface when hole is bored vertically through oblique strata. [F (*Artois*, place)]

**ar'tful** *a.* (~ly). Crafty, sly. [ART²]

**ar-thri'tis** *n.* Inflammation of joint(s); ~**i'tic** *a.* [L f. Gk (*arthron* joint)]

**ar'thropŏd** *n.* Animal with segmented body and jointed limbs, e.g. insect, spider, crustacean. [Gk *arthron* joint, *pous* foot]

**Arthū'rian** (är-) *a.* Relating to King *Arthur* or his knights. [person in legend]

**ar'tichōke** *n.* Plant allied to thistle, with partly edible flower (**globe** ~); **Jerusalem** ~, kind of sunflower with edible root. [It. f. Arab. *Jerusalem*, corrupt. of It. *girasole* sunflower]

**ar'ticle. 1.** *n.* Distinct portion of anything written; clause of agreement etc. (THIRTY-*nine Articles*; *articles of apprenticeship*); independent prose composition in newspaper etc.; particular thing; (Gram.) **definite** ~, 'the', **indefinite** ~, 'a, an', or corresp. adj. in other languages. **2.** *v.t.* Bind by articles of apprenticeship. [F f. L *articulus* (*artus* joint)]

**arti'cūlate. 1.** *a.* Having joints; (of speech) in which the separate sounds and words are clear; expressing oneself fluently and coherently. **2.** (-āt) *v.t. & i.* (~**able**). Pronounce

distinctly, speak; (usu. in *pass.*) connect by or divide with joints (~**ated lorry**, with flexibly connected sections); form joint *with*. **3.** ~**ar** *a.*, of the joints; ~**ā'tion** *n.*, articulate utterance, jointing, joint; ~**ātory** *a.* [L (prec.)]

**ar'tĭfăct.** See ARTEFACT.

**ar'tifice** *n.* Device, contrivance; (piece of) cunning; skill; **arti'ficer** *n.*, craftsman, skilled mechanic in army or navy. [F f. L (ART², *facio* make)]

**artifi'cial** (-shạl) *a.* (~ly). Produced by art (opp. *natural*), not originating naturally; made or done in imitation of the natural (*artificial flowers*, KIDNEY, SILK, *teeth*; ~ **insemination**, injection of semen into uterus artificially; ~ **respiration**, manual or mechanical stimulation of breathing); affected, insincere; ~**ity** (-shiạ'-) *n.*; ~**ize** *v.t.* [F or L (prec.)]

**arti'llery** *n.* Large guns used in fighting on land; branch of army that uses these; ~**ist**, ~**yman**, *ns.* [F (*artiller* equip)]

**artisă'n** (-z-) *n.* Mechanic, skilled (esp. manual) worker. [F f. It. (L *artio* instruct in arts)]

**ar'tist** *n.* One who practises one of the fine arts, esp. painting; one who makes his craft a fine art; **arti'ste** (-ē'-) *n.*, professional singer, dancer, etc.; **arti'stic** *a.* (-ically), of or befitting an artist, of art; ~**ry** *n.*, occupation or skill of an artist. [F f. It. (ART²)]

**ar'tless** *a.* Guileless, ingenuous; not resulting from art; crude, clumsy. [ART²]

**ar'tȳ** *a.* (colloq.; ~**iness**). Pretentiously or quaintly artistic.

**ar'um** *n.* Kind of plant including cuckoo-pint, usu. with large spathe; ~ **lily**, cultivated white arum. [L f. Gk *aron*]

**-ary** *suf.* forming *adjs.* w. sense 'of, connected with'. [F -*aire* or L -*ari(u)s*]

**Ar'yạn** (är'-) *a. & n.* (Speaker) of the parent language of (esp. Eastern) Indo-European family; (improp., esp. in Nazi Germany) non-Jewish German. [Skr.]

**as¹** (ạz, *emphat.* ăz) *adv., conj., & rel. pron.* **1.** *adv. & conj.* (*adv.* in main sentence, foll. by *conj.* in expressed or understood subord. clause) In the degree..in which (*I am as tall as he is* or *as he* or colloq. *as him*; *they are as like as two peas*; *am not as*, or *not so*, *young as I was*; *as sure as* FATE; also w. rel. clause omitted, *this is just as easy*; *I thought as much*, i.e. as you tell me, = I thought so; w. antecedent *so*, expr. result or purpose, *so distinct as to preclude all doubt*; *came early so as to meet her*; w. antecedent adv. omitted, *fair as she is, though she is so fair*); in the manner in which (*do as you like*; *was regarded as a mistake, as monstrous*, held to be so; *they rose as one man*); in the form or function of (*speaking as your legal representative*; *Olivier as Hamlet*; *as a matter of fact*); for instance (*cathedral cities, as Norwich*); while, when, (*came up as I was speaking*; *just as I reached the door*); for the reason that, seeing that, (*as he refuses, we can do nothing*). **2.** rel. pron. That, who, which, (*I had the same trouble as you*; *such towns as York*; vulg., *it was him as did it*; w. sentence as antecedent, *he was a foreigner, as I knew from his accent*). **3.** *as* FAR *as*; **as for**, with regard to (*as for you, I despise you*); **as from** (in formal dating, introducing date from which thing becomes or became operative); *as* GOOD *as*; *as* IF; **as it is** or **was**, in the actual circumstances; **as it were**, to some extent, as if it were actually so (*he became, as it were, a man without a country*); *as* LONG[1] *as*; **as of**, \*as from, as at (date); *as* PER; *as* REGARDS; *as* SOON *as*; *as* THOUGH; = *as* IF; **as to**, concerning, with respect to, (*said nothing as to hours*; *as to you, I despise you*); **as well**, advisable, desirable, -bly, with equal reason, (*it might be as well to go, we may as well go*; *you might as well!*, ellipt. = do so); **as well (as)**, in addition (to), besides; **as yet**, hitherto (with implied reserve about the future). [E, = ALSO]

**as**[2] *n.* (*pl.* **a′sses**). (Rom. Ant.) A copper coin. [L]

**as-.** See AD-.

**A.S.** *abbr.* Anglo-Saxon.

**ăsafoe′tĭda** (-fē′t-), **\*-fē′t-**, *n.* Resinous plant gum with strong smell. [L f. Pers. *azā* mastic; FETID]

**ăsbĕ′st|ŏs** (*or* ăz-) *n.* A fibrous silicate mineral; incombustible fabric woven from this; **~ŏ′sĭs** *n.*, lung disease from inhaling asbestos particles. [F f. L f. Gk, = unquenchable]

**ascĕ′nd** *v.t. & i.* Go or come up, mount, climb, (*ascend to a height*; *ascend hill, stairs*; **~ a river**, go along it towards its source; **~ the throne**, become king or queen); rise (*ascend to the highest rank*); **~ing scale** (Mus.), with notes rising in pitch). [L *scando* climb)]

**ascĕ′ndan|t. 1.** *a.* Rising; (Astron.) rising towards zenith; (Astrol.) just above eastern horizon; predominant. **2.** *n.* Point of ecliptic that is ascendant at a given time; **in the ~t**, supreme, dominating, (pop.) rising; **~cў, ascĕ′ndencў**, *n.*, dominant control (over).

**ascĕ′nsion** (-shon) *n.* Ascent, esp. (A~) of Christ to Heaven on 40th day after Resurrection; **A~ Day**, Thursday on which this is commemorated. [F f. L (ASCEND)]

**ascĕ′nt** *n.* Ascending, rising; upward path or slope; flight of steps. [ASCEND]

**ăscertai′n** *v.t.* Find out for certain; **~ment** *n.* [F (CERTAIN)]

**ascĕ′tĭc** (**~ally**) & *n.* (Person who is) severely abstinent or severe in self-discipline; **~ĭsm** *n.* [L or Gk (*askeō* exercise)]

**ascŏ′rbĭc** *a.* **~ acid**, vitamin C. [A- 2, SCORBUTIC]

**ascrī′be** *v.t.* **~ thing to** (event, person, etc.), consider (event, person, etc.) to be its cause, origin, or author (*poems ascribed to Homer*), regard (quality, conduct) as belonging to (person etc.); **ascrī′ption** *n.*, (esp.) preacher's words ascribing praise to God at end of sermon (cf. INVOCATION). [L (*scribo* write)]

**a′sdĭc** (ă′z-) *n.* Earlier form of sonar. [*Anti-Submarine Detection Investigation Committee*]

**ăsĕ′p|sĭs** *n.* Absence of sepsis or putrefactive bacteria; aseptic method in surgery; **~tĭc** *a.*, free from sepsis, surgically sterile, securing absence of septic matter. [A- 2]

**ăsĕ′xŭal** (*or* -kshŏo-) *a.* (**~ly**). Without sex(uality); **~ reproduction** (not involving fusion of gametes).

**ăsh**[1] *n.* A tree with silver-grey bark and pinnate foliage; its close-grained wood; **~-key**, winged fruit of ash; **~-plant**, sapling of ash. [E]

**ăsh**[2] *n.* Powdery residue left after combustion of a substance (freq. in *pl.*; *heap of cigar ash* or *ashes*; **in ~es**, destroyed by fire); (in *pl.*) remains of human body after cremation, ‖symbol of victory in Anglo-Australian test cricket; ‖**~-bin**, \***~-can**, dustbin; **~-tray**, receptacle for tobacco ash; **Ash Wednesday**, first day of Lent; **~'en** *a.*, of ashes, pale as ashes. [E]

**asha'med** (-md) *a.* (usu. *pred.*) Embarrassed by shame (*ought to be ashamed of yourself*, *of having lied, that you lied*); **~ for** *you* (on account of); *to say*, reluctant but not necessarily refusing. [E (*a-* intensive pref.)]

**a'shen.** See ASH[2].

**Ashkĕna'z|ĭ** (ă-; -ah'-) *n.* (*pl.* **~im**). Eastern European Jew (cf. SEPHARDI); **~ĭc** *a.* [Heb.]

**a'shlar** *n.* Square-hewn stone(s); masonry of this, or of thin slabs as facing to rubble or brick wall; **~ĭng** *n.*, short upright wall in garret cutting off angle of roof, ashlar masonry. [F f. L (*axis* board)]

**ashŏ're** *adv.* To or on shore. [A[3]]

**a'shў** *a.* Ashen; covered with ashes. [ASH[2]]

**A'sian** (ā'shan), (less usu. **Asiă'-tĭc** (āshĭ-), *a. & n.* (Native, inhabitant) of *Asia*. [place]

**asi'de** *adv.* **1.** To or on one side, away, apart, (\*~ **from**, apart from; **set** or **put ~**, esp. for future or special use; **set verdict ~**, quash it; **take** person **~**, esp. to converse privately). **2.** *n.* Words spoken aside, esp. by actor and supposed not to be heard by other actors. [A[3]]

**a'sin|ine** *a.* Of asses; stupid; **~i'nĭtў** *n.* [L (*asinus* ass)]

**ask** (ah-) *v.t. & i.* Call for an answer to or about (*ask* (*him*) *a question* or *this*; *ask* (*him*) *who he is* or *his name*; *no questions were asked of us*; **I ~ you**, excl. of disgust etc.; **if you ~ me**, colloq., in my opinion); seek to obtain from another person (*ask a favour of him*; *ask* (*him*) *a favour*; *asked £5 for the book*; *ask him to do it*; *ask that it may be done*; *can have it for the* (mere) **~ing**; **~ for**, seek to obtain (*ask for the book*) or speak with (*ask for his secretary*) or be directed to (*ask for the sports ground*); **~ for it**, sl., = *ask for* TROUBLE); invite (*to dinner, out, in*, etc.). [E]

**askă'nce, -ă'nt,** (or -ah'-) *adv.* Sideways (**look ~ at**, view suspiciously). [orig. unkn.]

**askew'** *adv. & pred. a.* Oblique(ly), awry, (*hanging askew*). [A[3]]

**asla'nt** (-ah'-) *adv. & prep.* Obliquely (across). [A[3]]

**aslee'p** *adv. & pred. a.* In or into a state of sleep (*is asleep*; *fell asleep*); (of limbs) benumbed; (of top) spinning without apparent motion.

**‖A.S.L.E.F.** (ă'zlĕf) *abbr.* Associated Society of Locomotive Engineers and Firemen.

**aslŏ'pe** *adv.* Sloping, crosswise. [orig. uncert.]

**āsŏ'cial** (-shal) *a.* Not social; antisocial; (colloq.) inconsiderate. [A- 2]

**ăsp** *n.* Small viper of S. Europe; viper of N. Africa and Arabia. [F or L f. Gk *aspis*]

**aspă'ragus** *n.* Plant whose young shoots are cooked and eaten as vegetable; these shoots. [L f. Gk]

**a'spĕct** *n.* Way a thing presents itself to eye or mind (*of pleasing aspect*; *view the matter in, under, this aspect*); look, expression; direction in which a thing fronts (*southern* etc. *aspect*, such side of building); one part of a complicated matter; (Astrol.) relative position of planets. [L ⟨AD-, *specio* look)]

**a'spen** *n.* Kind of poplar with tremulous leaves. [E; orig. adj.]

**aspĕ'rĭtў** *n.* Harshness of temper or tone (*spoke with asperity*); roughness of surface (*the asperities of the ground*). [F or L (*asper* rough)]

**aspĕr's|e** *v.t.* Attack the reputation of (person, his name, *with* reports), calumniate; besprinkle; **~ion** (-shon) *n.* (*casting aspersions on his rivals*). [L *aspergo* (SPARSE)]

**a'sph|ălt. 1.** *n.* Bituminous pitch from petroleum; mixture of this with sand etc. used for paving etc.; **~ă'ltĭc** *a.* **2.** *v.t.* Surface with asphalt. [L f. Gk]

**a'sphodĕl** *n.* Kind of lily; (poet.) immortal flower in Elysium. [L f. Gk]

**ăsphў'xĭ|a** *n.* Condition caused by lack of air in lungs; suffocation; **~ant** *a. & n.*; **~āte** *v.t.*, suffocate; **~ā'tion** *n.* [L f. Gk (A- 2, *sphuxis* pulse)]

**a'spĭc** *n.* Savoury jelly with cold game, eggs, etc., in it. [F, = ASP, suggested by various colours of jelly]

**ăspĭdi'stra** *n.* Plant with broad tapering leaves. [L f. Gk *aspis* shield]

**aspīr'e** *v.i.* Feel earnest desire or ambition (*to* or *after* thing, *to do*); rise high, tower; **a'spirant** (or aspīr'-) *a. & n.*, (one) who aspires; **a'spirate**, (*a. & n.*) sound of *h*, (consonant) blended with this, (-āt; *v.t.*), pronounce with *h*, draw (fluid) by suction from cavity etc.; **ăspirā'tion** *n.*, drawing of breath, desire (*for, to, after*), aspirating;

**ă′spĭrător** n., apparatus for aspirating fluid. [F, or L *aspiro* breathe upon]

**ă′spĭrĭn** n. Kind of analgesic and febrifuge; tablet of this. [G]

**ăss¹** (*or* ahs) n. Long-eared quadruped of horse genus, proverbial for stupidity; stupid person (**make an ~ of**, make look foolish). [E f. L]

**\*ăss².** See ARSE.

**assagai.** See ASSEGAI.

**assai** (*asah′ē*) adv. (Mus.) Very (*adagio assai*). [It.]

**assai′l** v.t. Attack physically or otherwise (*he, the place, was assailed on all sides*; *assailed with questions, by doubts*; *shouts assail my ears*); begin (task) resolutely; **~ant** n. [F f. L (*salio* leap)]

**assă′ssĭn** n. One who undertakes to kill treacherously; **~ăte** v.t., kill (esp. political or religious leader) by treacherous violence; **~ā′tion, ~ător,** ns. [F or L f. Arab., = hashish-eater]

**assau′lt** (*or* -ŏ′-). **1.** n. Attack (lit. or fig.; **carry** fortress etc. **by ~**, by sudden rush); unlawful personal attack on another even if only with menacing words (**~ and battery**, with blow or touch); (euphem.) rape (of woman). **2.** v.t. Make assault upon (person, fortress); (euphem.) rape (woman). [F f. L (ASSAIL)]

**assay′. 1.** n. Trial of metal or ore for quality. **2.** v.t. & i. Make assay of (metal); (arch.) attempt (task, *to* do). [F, var. of ESSAY]

**ă′ssĕgai, ă′ssag-,** (-gī) n. Spear of S. Afr. peoples. [F or Port. f. Arab.]

**assĕ′mbl|e** v.t. & i. Bring or come together; fit together (parts of machine etc.); **~age** n., collection, concourse, group; **~y̆** n., assembling, concourse of persons, esp. of deliberative body; **~y̆ line**, group of machines and workers progressively assembling some product. [F f. L *ad* to, *simul* together]

**assĕ′nt. 1.** v.i. Consent (*to* proposal, request); express agreement (*to* statement or opinion, or abs.); **~ĭent** (-shĭ-, -shĕnt) a. & n., (person) that assents; **~or** n. **2.** n. (Official) consent or sanction. [F f. L (*sentio* think)]

**assĕ′rt** v.t. Vindicate claim to (rights; **~ oneself**, insist on one's rights); declare, state; **~ion** n., (esp.) thing asserted; **~ĭve** a., assert-

ing (oneself), dogmatic; **~or** n. [L *assero -sert-*]

**assĕ′ss** v.t. Fix amount of (tax, fine); fix and impose (tax etc. *on*); fine, tax, (person etc. *in, at,* so much); value (property) for taxation; **~ment** n.; **~or** n., one who assesses, adviser to judge etc. [F f. L *assideo -sess-* sit by]

**ă′ssĕt** n. Property available to meet debts (freq. in *pl.*); any possession; (person or thing having) any useful quality. [F *asez* f. L *ad satis* enough]

**assĕ′ver|ăte** v.t. (**~able**). Declare solemnly; **~ā′tion** n. [L (SEVERE)]

**assĭ′duous** a. Persevering, diligent; attending closely; **ăssĭdū′ĭty** n. [L (ASSESS)]

**assĭ′gn** (-ī′n). **1.** v.t. Allot as share (*to*); transfer formally (esp. personal property, *to*); appoint (time, place, function, etc., *to*); ascribe (event *to* date, reason *for* thing, motive *to* conduct); **assĭgnā′tion** n., (esp.) appointment (of time and place), illicit lovers' meeting; **~ee′** n., one appointed to act for another, assign; **~ment** n., (esp.) task assigned; **~or** (*or* asĭnŏr′) n., one who assigns property. **2.** n. One to whom property or right is legally transferred. [F f. L *assigno* (SIGN)]

**assĭ′mil|ăte** v.t. & i. (**~able**). Make or become like (*to, with*); make (phonetic sound) become similar to contiguous sound or word; absorb, be absorbed, into the system; **~ā′tion, ~ător,** ns.; **~ătĭve, ~ător̆y̆,** adjs. [L (SIMILAR)]

**assĭ′st.** **1.** v.t. & i. Help; be present (*at* ceremony etc.); **~ance** n.; **~ant,** (a.) helping, (n.) helper, subordinate worker. **2.** n. \*Help(ing), action in helping to score goal etc. [F f. L *assisto* stand by]

**assĭ′ze** n. (Hist., usu. in *pl.*) Periodical county session for administration of civil and criminal justice. [F (ASSESS)]

**Assoc.** abbr. Association.

**assŏ′cĭ|ate¹** (*or* -shĭ-) a. & n. Joined or allied (partner, colleague, subordinate member of institute etc.); **~ăte²** v.t. & i. (**~able**). join (persons, things, one or one*self with* another), combine (v.i.) for common purpose, have frequent dealings (*with*), connect as idea, declare oneself in agreement *with*; **~ā′tion** n., (esp.) body of persons organized for common purpose (‖A**~ation football**, played with round ball not handled during play exc. by goalkeeper), mental connection between ideas, fellowship; **~atĭve** a. [L (socius allied)]

**ă'ssonan|ce** n. Resemblance of sound between two syllables; rhyme depending on identity in vowels only (rabid, malice), or in consonants only (killed, cold); **~t** a. [F f. L (sonus a sound)]

**assŏr't** v.t. & i. Arrange in sorts (**~ed** chocolates, of various sorts); suit, harmonize (ill-assorted pairs); **~ment** n., (esp.) set composed of several sorts. [F (SORT)]

**Asst.** abbr. Assistant.

**assuā'ge** (asw-) v.t. Soothe, appease, (pain, appetite, person); **~ment** (-jm-) n. [F, f. L suavis sweet]

**assŭ'm|e** v.t. Take or put on oneself (assumed a serious expression, the office of treasurer, the mantle of Elijah; **~ing**, arrogant); simulate (ignorance etc.); arrogate (credit etc.) to oneself; take as being true; **assŭ'mption** n., assuming, thing assumed, arrogance, (A-; feast, 15 Aug., in honour of) reception of Virgin Mary bodily into Heaven. [L (sumo take)]

**assŭr'|e** (ashoor') v.t. Make safe; ‖insure (esp. life); ensure the happening etc. of; make (person) sure (of fact); tell (person) confidently (assured me of his innocence, that he was innocent); **~ance** n., formal guarantee, positive declaration, certainty (make assurance double sure), self-confidence, impudence, ‖insurance esp. of life; **~ĕdlў** adv., certainly. [F f. L (SECURE)]

**Assўrĭŏ'log|ў** (a-) n. Study of language, history, etc., of Assyria; **~ĭst** n. [Assyria, -LOGY]

**ă'ster** n. Composite plant with showy radiate flowers. [L f. Gk, = star]

**ă'sterĭsk** n., & v.t. (Mark with) star-shaped symbol (*) put beside words etc. for reference or distinction. [L f. Gk, = little star]

**astĕr'n** adv. In, at, towards, ship's stern or aircraft's tail; behind. [A3]

**ă'sterǀoid** n. Any of the small planets revolving round sun esp. between orbits of Mars and Jupiter; **~oi'dal** a. [Gk (ASTER)]

**ă'sthm|a** (-sm-) n. Disease marked by difficulty in breathing; **~ă'tĭc**, (a.; -ically) of, caused by, suffering

from, asthma, (n.) person suffering from asthma. [L f. Gk azō breathe hard]

**astĭ'gmatĭsm** n. Defect in eye or lens, preventing proper focusing; **ăstĭgmă'tĭc** a. [A- 2, STIGMA]

**astĭr'** adv. & pred. a. In motion; out of bed. [A3]

‖**A.S.T.M.S.** abbr. Association of Scientific, Technical, and Managerial Staffs.

**astŏ'nĭsh** v.t. Amaze, shock with surprise; **~ment** n.; **astou'nd** v.t., astonish greatly. [F (EX-1, L tono thunder)]

**ăstrakha'n** (-kă'n) n. Dark curly fleece of Astrakhan lamb; imitation of this. [place]

**ă'stral** a. (**~ly**). Of stars; **~ body**, spiritual counterpart of body, supposed to survive death. [L (astrum star)]

**astray'** adv. & pred. a. Out of the right way; **go ~**, fall into error or sin, (fig.) be mislaid. [F f. L (EX-TRAVAGANT)]

**astrī'de. 1.** adv. With legs wide apart; with one leg on either side (of). **2.** prep. Astride of; extending across. [A3]

**astrĭ'ngen|t** (-nj-) a. & n. (Substance) causing contraction of body tissue; severe; austere; **~cў** n. [F f. L astringo draw tight]

**ă'strolābe** n. Instrument for measuring altitudes of stars etc. [F f. L f. Gk, = star-taking]

**astrŏ'log|ў** n. Study of reputed occult influence of stars on human affairs; **~er** n., one who practises astrology; **astrolŏ'gĭcal** a. (-lly). [F f. L f. Gk (astron star)]

**ă'stronǀaut** n. Space traveller; **~au'tical** a. (-lly); **~au'tĭcs** n., science of space travel. [Gk astron star, nautēs sailor]

**astrŏ'nom|ў** n. Science of the heavenly bodies; **~er** n., one who practises astronomy; **ăstronŏ'mĭc(al)** adjs. (-ically); **~ical** amount etc., enormous. [F f. L f. Gk (astron star, nemō arrange)]

**ăstrophŷ'sĭc|s** (-zĭ-) n. Study of physics and chemistry of heavenly bodies; **~al** a. (-lly); **~ĭst** n. [Gk astron star]

**astū'te** a. Shrewd; crafty. [F, or L astutus]

**asŭ'nder** adv. (formal). Apart, in pieces, (torn asunder). [A3]

**asŷ'lum** n. Sanctuary, place of

refuge and safety, esp. formerly for criminals, (**political** ∼, for refugees from political persecution); (Hist.) institution for shelter and support of afflicted or destitute persons, esp. the insane. [L f. Gk]

**asy̆'mmĕtry̆** (or ă-) *n.* Lack of symmetry; **ă̆sy̆mmĕ'trĭc(al)** *adjs.* (-ically). [Gk (A- 2)]

**at** (or *emphat.* ă̆t) *prep.* **1.** Expr. exact or approximate position, lit. or fig. of condition, occasion, price, time, etc., (*wait at the corner, at the top; at Bath,* cf. IN; at SCHOOL[2], at SEA; *at a* DISTANCE; SICK[2] *at heart, out at* ELBOWS; *at dinner, at WAR, at a* STANDstill, *at* VARIANCE; *at boiling--point, seen at his best, at a disadvantage; annoyed at failing; play at fighting; good at repartee; came at a run; sold at £1 each; at* ONCE, *at midday, at short notice; at (the age of) 70; at* BEST; *at all* EVENTS; *at* FIRST; *at* HOME; *at* LAST[3]; *at* LEAST; *at* MOST; *at* ONE; *at* TIMES; *at* (*the*) WORST); **at all,** (w. neg. or interrog.) in any way, to any extent, (*not at all; did you see him at all?*); **at it,** at work or other activity; **at that,** at that point (LEAVE[2] *it at that*), moreover (*lost an arm. and the right arm at that*), nevertheless. **2.** Expr. motion or aim towards, lit. or fig. (*arrive at a place; aim, hit, rush, at; grumble, guess, hint, laugh, at*). [E]

**at-.** See AD-.

**ă̆'tav|ĭsm** *n.* Resemblance to remote ancestors rather than parents; reversion to earlier type; ∼**ĭ'stĭc** *a.* (-ically). [F f. L *atavus* ancestor]

**ată̆'x|y̆, ∼ĭa,** *n.* Imperfect control of one's bodily movements (**loco-motor** ∼**y,** affecting use of limbs); ∼**ĭc** *a.* [L f. Gk (A- 2, *taxis* order)]

**ate.** See EAT.

**-ate** *suf.* forming *adjs.* equivalent to past participles of verbs in -ate (*associate*) or to words in -ed w. sense 'having, furnished with', (*-foliate* -leaved), occas. w. **-ātĕd** as alternative form. [L *p.p.*]

**atĕ'lier** (-lyā) *n.* Workshop, studio, of artist etc. [F]

*a* **tempo** (ăhtĕ'mpō) *adv.* (Mus.) In the previous tempo. [It.]

**Athanā'sian** (ă̆-; -shən) *a.* ∼ **Creed,** that beginning *Whosoever will.* [*Athanasius,* person]

**ā'thĕ|ĭsm** *n.* Disbelief in the existence of a deity; ∼**ĭst** *n.*; ∼**ĭ'stĭc** *a.* (-ically). [F f. Gk (A- 2, *theos* god)]

**ă̆thĕrŏsclĕrō'sĭs** *n.* Arteriosclerosis with fatty degeneration. [G f. Gk *athērē* groats]

**athĭr'st** *pred. a.* Thirsty; eager (*for*). [A[3]]

**ă̆'thl|ēte** *n.* One who competes or excels in physical exercises (∼**ete's foot,** ringworm of feet); ∼**ĕ'tĭc** *a.* (-ically), of athletes, physically powerful; ∼**ĕ'tĭcĭsm** *n.*; ∼**ĕ'tĭcs** *n.pl.* (occas. *sing.*), athletic sports. [F or L f. Gk (*athlon* prize)]

**athwar't** (-ôr't) *adv. & prep.* Across esp. obliquely; in opposition (to). [A[3]]

**-ā'tion** *suf.* forming *ns.* denoting verbal action (*creation, hesitation*), instance of this (*flirtations*), resulting condition (*in perfect preservation*), or resulting product (*plantation*). [F, or L (a form of -ION]

**Atlă̆'ntĭc** (a-) *a.* & *n.* (Of, adjoining) the ocean between Europe and Africa on east and America on west; **ă̆'tlas** *n.,* book of maps. [L, f. Gk *Atlas -antos,* giant who held up the sky, mountain(s) in N. Africa]

**atm.** *abbr.* (Phys.) atmosphere(s).

**ă̆'tmosph|ēre** *n.* Gaseous envelope surrounding heavenly body esp. earth; mental or moral environment, tone or mood pervading book, work of art, etc.; air (in room etc., esp. w. reference to temperature or purity); pressure of about 1 kg weight per sq. cm, being that exerted by atmosphere on earth's surface; ∼**ĕ'rĭc(al)** *a.* (-ically), ∼**ĕ'rĭcs** *n.pl.,* (interference with telecommunications, due to) electrical disturbances in atmosphere. [L f. Gk *atmos* vapour, SPHERE]

**ă̆'toll** (or ătŏ'l) *n.* Ring-shaped coral reef enclosing lagoon. [Maldive]

**ă̆'tom** *n.* Smallest particle of chemical element; this as source of atomic energy; minute portion or thing (*not an atom of truth in it*); (*attrib.*) atomic (*atom bomb*); ∼**ic** *a.* (∼ically), of atoms; ∼**ic bomb,** deriving its destructive power from ∼**ic energy** (= nuclear energy); ∼**ic mass,** = atomic weight; ∼**ic number,** number of unit positive charges carried by nucleus of atom; ∼**ic philosophy,** atomism; ∼**ic** (= nuclear) **power;** ∼**ic theory,** that chemical elements consist of atoms of definite relative weight uniting with those of other elements in fixed proportions; ∼**ic warfare**

(in which atomic bombs are used); ~**ic weight,** ratio between mass of one atom of an element or isotope and 1/12 weight of atom of the isotope carbon 12; ~**ism** *n.,* theory that all matter consists of minute individual particles; ~**ĭst** *n.;* ~**ĭ'stĭc** *a.* (-ically); ~**ize** *v.t.,* reduce to atoms or fine particles; ~**izā'tion** *n.;* ~**izer** *n.,* instrument for reducing liquids to fine spray. [F f. L f. Gk, = indivisible]

**atō'ne** *v.i.* Make amends; ~ **for,** expiate (*you cannot, nothing can, atone for your negligence*); ~**ment** (-nm-) *n.* (the A~ment, expiation of mankind's sin by Christ; Day of A~ment, most solemn religious fast day of Jewish year). [*atonement* (AT, ONE, -MENT)]

**atō'nĭc** *a.* Unaccented. [A- 2]

**atō'p** *adv. & prep.* On the top (*of* or *of*). [A³]

**ătrabĭ'lious** (-lyus) *a.* Melancholy, ill-tempered. [L *atra bilis* black bile; cf. MELANCHOLY]

**ā'trĭ|um** *n.* (*pl.* ~**a,** ~**ums**). Central court of Roman house; (Anat.) either of two upper cavities in heart. [L]

**atrō'cious** (-shus) *a.* Extremely wicked, very bad, (*atrocious crimes, puns*); **atrō'cĭty** *n.,* (esp.) atrocious deed, repellent thing. [L *atrox* cruel]

**ă'trophў.** 1. *n.* Wasting away through under-nourishment or lack of use; emaciation. 2. *v.t. & i.* Cause atrophy in; suffer atrophy. [F or L f. Gk (A- 2, *trophē* food)]

**ă'tropine** (*or* -ēn) *n.* Poison of deadly nightshade. [L f. Gk (*Atropos* a Fate)]

**attă'ch** *v.t. & i.* Fasten, join, affix, (*attach label to parcel*); person, oneself, *to,* a company, undertaking, etc.; *a gift with no conditions attached*); attribute (importance, meaning, name, etc., *to*); be attributable (*no blame attaches to the firm*); (usu. in *pass.*) bind in friendship, make devoted, (*is deeply attached to her*); seize (person, property) by legal authority; **attă'ché** (-shā) *n.,* person attached to ambassador's staff (*military attaché*; ~**é case,** small rectangular case for carrying documents etc.); ~**ment** *n.,* (esp.) affection, devotion, legal seizure (*attachment of earnings*). [F f. Gmc (STAKE)]

**attă'ck.** 1. *v.t. & i.* Act against with (esp. armed) force; make an attack;

criticize adversely; act harmfully on (*rust attacks metals*); begin vigorous work on. 2. *n.* Act of attacking; sudden start of illness etc. (*an attack of gout*); player(s) seeking to score goals etc. [F f. It. (as prec.)]

**attai'n** *v.t. & i.* Arrive at, reach, gain, accomplish, (*attain distinction, one's object; the height to which he attained; attain to years of discretion*); ~**ment** *n.,* (esp., in *pl.*) personal achievements. [F f. L *attingo* reach]

**ă'ttar** *n.* Fragrant oil from rose-petals. [Pers.]

**attĕ'mpt.** 1. *v.t.* Try (*attempt to conceal; attempt concealment*); try to conquer (mountain, fortress, etc.; ~ **the life of,** arch., try to kill); try to accomplish (*attempt the impossible*). 2. *n.* Attempting, endeavour, (*to do, at* thing, *on* person's *life*); (unsuccessful) result of attempting. [F f. L (TEMPT)]

**attĕ'nd** *v.i. & t.* Turn or apply one's mind (*attend to me, to what I say; are you attending?;* ~ **to,** deal with); be present (at), go regularly to, (*attend at or attend the ceremony; attend school*); accompany (*queen was attended by a lady-in-waiting*); ~**ance** *n.,* attending (*on* person, *at* lecture etc.); ‖~**ance centre,** where young delinquents must regularly attend), persons present (*a small attendance*); ~**ant,** (*a.*) waiting (*on*), accompanying, (*n.*) person attending esp. to provide service (*cloakroom attendant*). [F f. L (TEND¹)]

**attĕ'ntion.** 1. *n.* Act or faculty of applying one's mind (*pay attention to him; called my attention to the fact; attracts attention*); consideration, care, (*matter shall have attention*); (in *pl.*) ceremonious politeness; (Mil.) erect attitude of readiness (*come to, stand at, attention*). 2. *int.* (A~!) used to call persons to take notice or (Mil.) assume attitude of attention. 3. **attĕ'ntĭve** *a.,* paying attention, assiduous. [L (prec.)]

**attĕ'nŭāte.** 1. *v.t.* Make slender or thin; reduce in force or value; ~**ā'tion** *n.,* ~**ātor,** *ns.* 2. (-at) *a.* Slender, tapering; rarefied. [L (TENUOUS)]

**attĕ'st** *v.i. & t.* Bear witness *to,* certify validity of, (thing, *that,* etc.); **ăttĕstā'tion** *n.,* act of attesting, testimony. [F f. L (*testis* witness)]

**ă'ttĭc.** 1. *n.* Room in top storey of house; (A~) Attic dialect. 2.

(A∼). Of Athens or Attica (A∼
order, Archit., square column of
any of the five orders); ∼ism n.,
Attic idiom, elegance of speech. [F
f. L f. Gk]

attir′e v.t., & n. Dress, esp. fine(ly)
or formal(ly). [F (à tire in order)]

ă′ttĭtūde n. Posture of body;
(settled behaviour as showing)
opinion (his attitude towards Communists; ∼ of mind, settled way of thinking); ăttĭtū′dĭnīze v.i. adopt (esp.
affected) attitudes, show affectation.
[F f. It. f. L (APTITUDE)]

attor′ney (-tẽr′-) n. One appointed
to act for another in business or legal
matter(s) (power of ∼, authority to
act thus); *qualified lawyer (district
∼, prosecuting officer of district);
A∼-General, chief legal officer in
some countries and States. [F (TURN)]

attră′ct v.t. Draw to itself or oneself (magnet attracts iron; accident
attracted a crowd; try to attract his
attention); arouse interest or pleasure
in (such a style does not attract me);
∼ant a. & n. (esp. substance attracting insects); ∼ion n., act or faculty
of attracting, thing that attracts by
pleasing etc.; ∼ĭve a., capable of
attracting (esp. fig.). [L (traho draw)]

ă′ttrĭb|ūte[1] n. Quality ascribed to
person or thing; characteristic
quality; object regularly associated
with person etc. (e.g. St. Peter's keys,
Hercules' club); attrĭ′būte[2] v.t.,
regard as belonging or appropriate
(attribute such a motive to him; attributes
this pottery to the Bronze Age); ∼ute
to, consider to be caused by (attributes his stiffness to rheumatism);
∼ū′tion n.; attrĭ′būtive a., expressing an attribute (e.g. old in the old
dog but not in the dog is old; cf.
PREDICATIVE). [F or L (TRIBUTE)]

attri′tion n. Friction; abrasion;
gradual exhaustion (a war of attrition). [L (TRITE)]

attū′ne v.t. Bring into musical
accord (to); adapt (one's mind,
words, etc., to subject etc.); tune.
[TUNE]

ă′tў′pĭcal a. (∼ly). Not conforming
to type. [A- 2]

au′bergine (ō′berzhēn) n. (Edible
purple fruit of) plant of potato genus.
[F f. Catalan f. Arab. f. Pers. f. Skr.]

aubrie′tia, (erron.) -rē′tia, (-sha)
n. Spring-flowering dwarf perennial
rock-plant. [Aubriet, person]

au′burn a. Reddish-brown (auburn

hair). [orig. = yellowish white, F f
L (albus white)]

au courant (ōkoō′rahn) pred. a
Acquainted with or of what is going
on. [F, = in the course]

au′ction. 1. n. Public sale in which
articles are sold to highest bidder
∼ bridge, form of BRIDGE[2] with
bidding for contract. 2. v.t. Sell by
auction; ∼eer′ n., holder of auctions
∼eer′ing n., his work. [L (augeo
auct- increase)]

audā′cious (-shus) a. Daring, bold
impudent; audā′cĭtў n. [L (audax
bold)]

au′dĭb|le a. (∼ly). That can be
(esp. distinctly) heard; ∼ĭ′lĭtў n. [L
(audio hear)]

au′dĭence n. Group of listeners or
spectators; hearer's attention (give
∼, listen); formal interview (had ∼
of, had an ∼ with, admission to
speak to).

au′dĭō n. (Reproduction of) sound
∼ frequency (comparable to that
of audible sound); ∼ typist typing
direct from a recording); ∼-vi′sual,
using both sight and sound.

au′dĭt. 1. n. Official examination
of accounts. 2. v.t. Conduct audit of
3. audĭ′tion, (n.) faculty of hearing,
trial hearing or seeing of actor etc.
(v.t. & i.) give trial hearing etc. (to)
∼or n., hearer, one who audits
∼ōr′ĭum n. (pl. -iums, -ia), part of
building occupied by audience;
∼orў a., of hearing.

‖A.U.E.W. abbr. Amalgamated
Union of Engineering Workers.

au fait (ōfā′) pred. a. Well acquainted with subject; au fond (ōfawn′)
adv., at bottom, basically. [F]

Aug. abbr. August.

Augē′an a. Filthy, like the stables
of Augeas, which Hercules cleansed
by turning river Alpheus through
them. [person in legend]

au′ger (-g-) n. Boring-tool with
long shank ending in screw point, and
handle at right angles. [E (NAVE[2]
gār piercer; for loss of n- cf. ADDER]

aught (awt) n. (arch., poet.). Anything (for aught I know; if aught there
be). [E]

au′gment[1] n. Vowel prefixed to
past tenses in Greek and Sanskrit;
augmě′nt[2] v.t. & i., increase, make
or become greater, (in p.p., Mus.)
increased by a semitone; ∼ā′tion n.,
enlargement, increase; augmě′nta-
tĭve a., (esp., Gram., of affix etc.)

increasing in force the idea of the original word. [F or L (AUCTION)]

*au gratin.* See GRATIN.

**au′gur. 1.** *n.* Roman religious official who foretold events by observing movements of birds etc.; soothsayer; **au′gural** *a.*, of augurs or omens; **au′gŭrў** *n.*, divination, omen. **2.** *v.t.* & *i.* Foresee, portend; indicate (~ *well, ill*, have good, bad, implications *for*). [L]

**augŭst¹** *a.* Venerable, imposing. [F or L]

**Au′gust²** *n.* Eighth month; **Augŭ′stan** *a.*, of the reign of *Augustus* Caesar esp. as best period of Latin literature, (of any national literature) classical. [E (person)]

**auk** *n.* Northern sea-bird with small narrow wings. [N]

**auld** *a.* (Sc.) Old; ~ *lang syne*, days of long ago. [E, = OLD]

**au naturel** (ōnătūrĕ′l) *adv.* & *pred. a.* Uncooked; (cooked) in the simplest way. [F]

**aunt** (ahnt) *n.* Parent's sister(-in--law); (children's colloq.) unrelated woman friend; A~ *Sally*, figure used as target in throwing-game, (fig.) target of general abuse; ~′ie *n.* [F f. L *amita*]

‖**au pair′** (ōp-) *a.* & *n.* ~ (girl), young woman usu. from overseas, helping with housework and receiving board and lodging. [F]

**aur′a** *n.* (*pl.* ~e, ~s). Subtle emanation from anything; atmosphere diffused by or attending a person etc. (esp. in mystical use); premonitory symptom of epileptic fit; **aur′al¹** *a.* [L f. Gk, = breeze]

**aur′al²** *a.* (~ly). Of the ear. [L (*auris* ear)]

**aur′eate** *a.* Golden; resplendent. [L (*aurum* gold)]

**aure′ola, aur′eŏle,** *n.* Celestial crown of martyr etc.; glory round head or body of pictured divine figure; halo round sun or moon. [L, = golden (crown)]

**au revoir** (ōrevwār′) *int.* & *n.* (Goodbye) till we meet again. [F]

**aur′icle** *n.* External ear; (appendage to) atrium of heart. [foll.]

**auri′cŭla** *n.* Species of primula. [L dim. (AURAL²)]

**auri′cŭlar** *a.* Of the ear; shaped like an auricle; told privately in the ear (*auricular confession*).

**auri′ferous** *a.* Yielding gold. [L (*aurum* gold, -FEROUS)]

**aur′ŏchs** (owr′ŏks, ōr′-) *n.* Extinct wild ox; European bison. [G]

**aurŏr′a** *n.* A luminous electrical radiation from northern (~ **bŏre′ā′lĭs**) or southern (~ **austrā′lĭs**) magnetic pole. [L, = (goddess of) dawn]

**auscultā′tion** *n.* (Med.) Listening to sounds of heart etc.; **auscŭ′l-tatorў** *a.* [L *ausculto* listen]

**au′spice** *n.* Omen, orig. one drawn from flight etc. of birds (*take the auspices*; *a favourable auspice*); (in *pl.*) patronage (*under the auspices of*); **auspi′cious** (-shŭs) *a.*, of good omen, favourable. [F, or L *auspicium* (*avis* bird)]

**Au′ssie** (ŏ′zĭ, ŏ′sĭ) *n.* & *a.* (colloq.) Australia(n). [abbr.]

**austēr′e** (or ŏ-) *a.* (~r, ~st). Morally strict; severely simple; stern; **austē′rĭtў** (or ŏ-) *n.* [F f. L f. Gk *austēros*]

**au′stral** (or ŏ-) *a.* Southern; (A~) of Austral(as)ia. [L (*Auster* S. wind)]

**Australā′sian** (-shan; or ŏ-), **Austrā′lian** (or ŏ-), *adjs.* & *ns.* (Native, inhabitant) of *Australasia* or *Australia*; **Australian bear,** koala; **Australian Rules,** football with Rugby ball and teams of 18. [places]

**au′tarchў** (-kĭ) *n.* Absolute sovereignty. [L f. Gk (AUTO-, *arkhō* rule)]

**au′tarkў** *n.* Self-sufficiency. [Gk (AUTO-, *arkeō* suffice)]

**authĕ′ntĭc** *a.* (~ally). Trustworthy, entitled to acceptance, (*authentic statement*); of undisputed origin, not forged etc., (*authentic documents, pictures*); ~**āte** *v.t.* (~**able**), establish truth or authorship or validity of (statement, document, claim); ~**ā′tion,** ~**ātor,** **authĕn-tĭ′cĭtў,** *ns.* [F f. L f. Gk *authentikos* genuine]

**au′thor** *n.* Writer of book etc.; originator (*of* event, policy, state of affairs); ~**ĕss** *n.*; **authŏr′ĭal** *a.*; ~**shĭp** *n.*, occupation as author, origin of book. [F f. L *auctor*]

**authŏ′rĭt|ў** *n.* Power or right to enforce obedience; delegated power (*to do, for* an act); person or (esp. in *pl.*) body having authority (*apply to the authorities*); personal influence (*has no authority over his children*); book etc. that supplies authentic information or evidence; declaration etc. that may be cited in support of statement (*on the authority of Plato*); person thought qualified to pronounce (*on* subject etc.); ~**ār′ĭan**, (*a.*) favouring obedience to authority, (of State etc.) that is a dictatorship, (*n.*) supporter of authoritarian principles; ~**atĭve** *a.*, possessing, claiming, or entitled to, authority; **au′thorĭze** *v.t.*, sanction (**Authorized Version**, English transl. of Bible, 1611), give authority to (person *to* do); **authorizā′tion** *n.*

**au′tĭsm** *n.* Severe form of mental illness in children, preventing proper response to environment; **autĭ′stĭc** *a.* [L (AUTO-)]

***au′tō** *n.* (*pl.* ~**s**). (colloq.) Motor car. [abbr. AUTOMOBILE]

**auto-** in comb. Self, own, of or by oneself or itself. [Gk *autos*]

**autobahn** (aw′tŏbahn) *n.* (*pl.* ~**s**, ~**en**). German motorway. [G]

**autobiō′graph|ў** *n.* Story of one's life written by oneself; the writing of it; ~**er** *n.*, writer of autobiography; **autobiogrā′phĭc(al)** *adjs.* (**-ically**). [AUTO-]

**au′tocār** *n.* (arch.) Motor vehicle. [abbr.]

**autŏ′chthonous** (-k-) *a.* Indigenous, aboriginal. [Gk (AUTO-, *khthōn* land)]

**au′toclāve** *n.* Strong vessel used esp. as sterilizer with high-pressure steam. [L *clavus* nail or *clavis* key]

**au′tocrăt** *n.* Absolute ruler; **autŏ′cracў** *n.*, absolute government by one person; **autocrā′tĭc** *a.* (**-ically**). [F f. Gk (AUTO-, *kratos* power)]

**au′tocrŏss** *n.* Motor-racing across country or on unmade roads. [AUTO(MOBILE)]

*auto-da-fé* (awtŏdahfā′) *n.* (*pl.* -**tos**-). Sentence of the Inquisition; execution of this, esp. burning of heretic. [Port., = act of the faith]

**au′todĭdăct** *n.* Self-taught person. [DIDACTIC]

**au′togr|aph** (-ahf) **1.** *n.* Person's own handwriting esp. signature; manuscript in author's handwriting; ~**ă′phĭc** *a.* (**-ically**). **2.** *v.t.* Write with one's own hand; sign. [F or L f. Gk (AUTO-, -GRAPH)]

*au′tomăt** *n.* Cafeteria providing meals from slot-machines; slot-machine. [G f. F (AUTOMATON)]

**au′tomāte** *v.t.* Subject to or operate by automation. [AUTOMATION]

**automā′tĭc. 1.** *a.* (~**ally**). Working of itself, without direct human actuation; (of motor vehicle's transmission system) with correct gear

selected automatically acc. to vehicle speed and acceleration; (of firearm) having mechanism for continuous loading and firing; done without thought, done from habit; as a necessary consequence (*incurs automatic disqualification*); ~ **pilot**, device to keep aircraft or ship on set course. **2.** *n.* Automatic tool, firearm, etc.; (colloq.) vehicle with automatic transmission system. **3.** **automā′tion** *n.*, use of automatic equipment to save mental and manual labour; **autŏ′matĭsm** *n.*, involuntary action, unthinking routine; **autŏ′maton** *n.* (*pl.* -**ta**, -**tons**), mechanism with concealed motive power, a living being whose actions are purely mechanical. [Gk *automatos* (AUTO-)]

*au′tomobile** (-ēl) *n.* Motor car. [F]

**autŏ′nom|ў** *n.* Right of self-government; personal freedom; ~**ous** *a.* [Gk (AUTO-, *nomos* law)]

**au′tōpĭlot** *n.* Automatic pilot. [abbr.]

**au′tŏpsў** (*or* -ŏ′-) *n.* Post-mortem. [F or L f. Gk (AUTO-, OPTIC)]

**auto-suggĕ′stion** *n.* Hypnotic or subconscious suggestion proceeding from the subject himself. [AUTO-]

**au′tumn** (-m) *n.* Third season of year; season of incipient decay; ~ **crocus**, colchicum plant; **autŭ′mnal** *a.* (**-lly**). [F f. L *autumnus*]

**auxi′liarў** (-gzi′lyerĭ) *a.* & *n.* (Person, thing) giving help, subsidiary, *to*; (in *pl.*, or ~ **troops**) foreign or allied troops in service of nation at war; (verb that is) used in forming tenses, moods, or voices of other verbs. [L (*auxilium* help)]

**A.V.** *abbr.* Authorized Version.

**avai′l. 1.** *v.t.* & *i.* Be of use or help (to), serve, (*his words availed very little*; *will not avail you*); ~ oneself **of**, profit by, utilize); ~**able** *a.* (**-bly**), capable of being used, at one's disposal, (*available for my purpose*; *all available funds*); ~**abĭ′litў** *n.* **2.** *n.* Use, profit, (*of no avail*; *without avail*). [obs. *vail* f. F f. L *valeo* be strong]

**ă′valanche** (-ahnsh) *n.* Mass of snow, rock, and ice, descending mountain rapidly; sudden onrush. [F]

**avant-gắr′de** (ăvahṅ-) *n.* & *a.* (Of) innovators in art, literature, etc. [F, = vanguard]

**ă′var|ĭce** *n.* Greed for gain;

**~i′cious** (-shŭs) *a.* [F f. L (*avarus* greedy)]

**ava′st** (-ah′st) *int.* (Naut.) Stop, cease. [Du. *houd vast* hold fast]

**a′vatàr** *n.* (Hindu Myth.) descent of deity to earth in incarnate form; incarnation. [Skr., = descent]

**a′ve** (ah′vi̇̄, -vā). **1.** *int.* Hail; farewell. **2.** *n.* The cry *ave*; Ave (**Maria**), devotional recitation and prayer to Virgin Mary (Luke 1: 28, 42). [L]

**Ave.** *abbr.* Avenue.

**ave′nge** (-nj) *v.t.* Inflict retribution on behalf of (person etc.; **be ~d**, avenge oneself); take vengeance for (injury). [F f. L *vindico*]

**a′venue** *n.* Roadway bordered by trees etc.; ‖tree-lined approach to country house; way of approach (usu. fig.; *avenues to fame*); broad street. [F (VENUE)]

**aver′** *v.t.* (-rr-). Assert, affirm; **~ment** *n.*, positive statement. [F f. AD-, L *verus* true]

**a′verage** *n.*, *a.*, & *v.* **1.** *n.* Generally prevailing rate, degree, or amount (*below the average*; *a high average*; **on** (**an**) **~**, at a middle estimate); arithmetic mean; damage to or loss of insured ship or cargo; **law of ~s** (that both extremes will occur if either does). **2.** *a.* Estimated by average, of the ordinary standard or kind, (*the average output, man*). **3.** *v.t.* & *i.* Estimate average of; **~** (**out at**), amount on average to; do etc. on average (*he averages six hours' work a day*). [F f. It. f. Arab., = damaged goods]

**aver′ment.** See AVER.

**aver′|se** *pred. a.* Opposed, disinclined, unwilling, (*to or from* thing esp. action); **~sion** (-shon) *n.*, dislike, unwillingness, (*to, from, for*), object of dislike (*my pet aversion*); **~t** *v.t.* (**~tible**, **~table**), turn away (eyes, thoughts, *from*), ward off (danger etc.). [L (*verto vers-* turn)]

**Avesta.** See ZEND.

**a′viary** *n.* Large cage or building for keeping birds. [L (*avis* bird)]

**avia′tion** *n.* Flying of aircraft; **a′viàte** *v.i.*, fly in aircraft; **a′viàtor** *n.*, airman. [F f. L (prec.)]

**a′vid** *a.* Eager, greedy, (*of, for*); **avi′dity** *n.* [F, or L *avidus*]

**ăvoca′dō** (-ah′-) *n.* (*pl.* **~s**). **~** (**pear**), rough-skinned pear-shaped tropical fruit. [Sp. f. Aztec]

**ăvoca′tion** *n.* Minor occupation;

(colloq.) vocation, calling. [L (*avoco* call away)]

**ă′vocĕt** *n.* Wading bird with upturned bill. [F f. It.]

**avoi′d** *v.t.* Keep away or refrain from, (*avoid the ditch, his company, making any promises*); escape from (*hope to avoid collision*; *cannot avoid seeing him*); (Law) annul, quash; **~ance** *n.* [F (VOID)]

**ăvoirdüpoi′s** (ăver-; -z) *n.* System of weights based on pound of 16 ounces or 7,000 grains. [F, = goods of weight]

**avou′ch** *v.t.* & *i.* (arch., rhet.) Guarantee; affirm; confess; **~ment** *n.* [F f. L (ADVOCATE)]

**avow′** *v.t.* Admit, confess, (*his avowed negligence*; *I avow myself the culprit*); **~al** *n.*; **~ĕdly̆** *adv.* [F (VOW)]

**avŭ′ncular** *a.* Of or resembling an uncle. [L *avunculus* uncle]

**awai′t** (a-) *v.t.* Wait for (*I await your reply*); be in store for (*a surprise awaits you*). [F (WAIT)]

**awā′ke** (a-). **1.** *v.i.* & *t.* (*past* awo′ke *pr.* -ō′k; *p.p.* awo′ken, **~d**). Cease to sleep; (fig.) become active (**~ to** fact etc., become conscious of it); rouse from sleep. **2.** *pred. a.* No longer or not yet asleep; vigilant (**~ to**, aware of). **3.** **awā′ken** (a-) *v.t.* & *i.*, awake, arouse consciousness of (person *to* fact etc.). [E (A³)]

**awar′d** (awor′d). **1.** *v.t.* Order to be given as payment, penalty, or prize. **2.** *n.* Judicial decision; what is awarded. [F (WARD)]

**awar′e** (a-) *pred. a.* Conscious, having knowledge, (*of* thing, *that*). [E (ge- pref. implying completeness, WARE²)]

**awa′sh** (awŏ′-) *pred. a.* Level with surface of water; washed (over) or tossed by waves about. [A³]

**away′** (a-) *adv.*, *a.*, & *n.* **1.** *adv.* To or at a distance from the place, person, etc., in question (*go away*; *throw it away*; *is away from home*; *dwindle away*; *explain it, sound dies, ~*, into non-existence; FAR *and away*; **out and ~**, by far; **~ with it!**, take it away; DO³, GET, MAKE, *away with*); constantly, persistently, (*work away*); without delay (FIRE *away*). **2.** *a.* Played on opponent's ground etc. (*away match, win*). **3.** *n.* Away match or win. [E (A³, WAY)]

**awe. 1.** *n.* Reverential fear or wonder; **~′stricken**, **~′struck**, (aw′s-) struck with awe; **~′some**

(aw's-) *a.*, dreaded; **aw′ful** *a.*, inspiring or worthy of awe, (colloq.) notable (esp. bad) in its kind (*an awful bore*); **aw′fullȳ** *adv.*, (esp., colloq. *pr.* aw′flī) very (*awfully good of you*). **2.** *v.t.* Inspire with awe. [N]

**aweigh** (awā′) *adv.* (Of anchor) just lifted from the bottom in weighing. [A³]

**awhīle** (awī′l) *adv.* For a short time. [A²]

**aw′kward** *a.* Ill-adapted for use (*an awkward tool, system*); clumsy, ungainly; embarrassing, inconvenient (*came at an awkward time*); embarrassed (*felt awkward about it*); hard or dangerous to deal with (*an awkward situation, corner*). [obs. awk backhanded, -WARD]

**awl** *n.* Small pricking-tool, esp. shoemaker's. [E]

**awn** *n.* Stiff bristle at top of grain-sheath of barley etc. [E]

**aw′ning** *n.* Rooflike shelter of canvas etc. esp. over ship's deck. [orig. uncert.]

**awoke(n).** See AWAKE.

**A.W.O.L.** (ā′wŏl) *abbr.* absent without leave.

**awrȳ′** (arī′) *adv. & pred. a.* Crooked(ly) (*hang awry*); wrong, amiss, (*things went awry*). [A³]

**axe, *ax. 1.** *n.* Chopping-tool usu. with steel edge and wooden handle (*has an ~ to grind*, private ends to serve). **2.** *v.t.* Cut down (costs, services) drastically; remove, dismiss. [E]

**a′xial** *a.* (~ly). Of, forming, placed round, an axis. [AXIS]

**a′xiom** *n.* Self-evident truth; established principle; ~a′tic *a.* (-ically). [F or L f. Gk]

**a′xis** *n.* (*pl.* a′xes *pr.* -ēz). Imaginary line about which a body rotates; line dividing a regular figure symmetrically; straight line between poles or ends; reference line for measurement of coordinates etc.; **the A~**, (Hist.) (pact between) Germany and Italy (and later Japan) in the 1939–45 war. [L, = axle]

**a′xle** *n.* Spindle on or with which wheel revolves; ~(-tree), bar connecting pair of wheels of vehicle. [N]

**a′xolotl** *n.* Newtlike amphibian in Mexican lakes. [Nahuatl, = water-servant]

**ay, aye¹,** (i). **1.** *adv.* (esp. arch. or Naut.) Yes. **2.** *n.* (*pl.* ayes). Affirmative answer or vote (**the ayes have it,** are in the majority). [orig. uncert.]

**aye²** (ā) *adv.* (arch.) Always (*for aye*). [N]

**azā′lea** *n.* Kind of flowering shrubby plant. [L f. Gk]

**a′zimuth** *n.* Arc of sky from zenith to horizon; angular distance of this along horizon from meridian; **ăzĭ-mū′thal** *a.* (-lly). [F f. Arab.]

**A′ztĕc** (ă′-) *a. & n.* (One) of the native Mexican people dominant till conquest by Cortes (1519); (of) their language. [F or Sp. f. Nahuatl, = men of the north]

**a′zure** (or -zher, -zhyer) *n. & a.* Sky-blue (colour); (Her.) blue; unclouded (sky). [F f. L f. Arab.]

# B

**B, b,** (bē) *n.* (*pl.* Bs, B's). Second letter; (Mus.) seventh note in diatonic scale of C major; (Alg.; *b*) second known quantity; (*B*) second hypothetical person or example.

**B.** *abbr.* Bachelor; bel(s); black (pencil-lead); Blessed.

**b.** *abbr.* born; bowled by; bye.

**B.A.** *abbr.* Bachelor of Arts; British Academy; British Association.

**baa** (bah) *n. & v.* (~ed, ~'d, *pr.* bahd). Bleat; ~-**lamb,** childish name for lamb. [imit.]

**ba′ba** (bah′bah) *n.* Sponge-cake soaked in rum syrup. [F]

**bă′bble. 1.** *v.i. & t.* Talk half-articulately, incoherently, or excessively; repeat or divulge foolishly; (of stream etc.) murmur. **2.** *n.* Babbled speech; idle talk; murmur of water etc. **3.** ~**r** *n.*, teller of secrets, loud-voiced passerine bird. [imit.]

**bābe** *n.* Innocent person (~**s and sucklings,** the utterly inexperienced); (poet.) baby; *(sl.) young woman. [imit. of child's *ba, ba*]

**bā'bel** n. Scene of confusion; confused noise of talk; confused mixture of languages. [Heb., = Babylon (Gen. 11)]

**baboo͞n** n. Large African and Arabian monkey. [F or L]

**ba'bu** (bah'bo͞o) n. (Ind.) Title of respect, given to Hindus; (Hist., derog.) English-writing Indian clerk. [Hindi]

**bā'by̆** n. Very young child; childish person; young or small animal, thing small of its kind, (*baby elephant*; ~ **grand**, small grand piano); (sl.) sweetheart; ~**farmer**, (derog.) person who looks after babies for payment; ~**sit** *v.i.*, act as ~**sitter**, person looking after child while its parents are out; ~**hoo͞d** n. [BABE]

**bă'ccarat** (-rah) n. A gambling card-game. [F]

**Bă'cchan|al** (-ka-) a. & n. (Priest, priestess, votary) of Bacchus or his rites; riotous (reveller, revelry); ~**ā'lia** n.pl., festival of Bacchus, drunken revelry; ~**t** n. (pl. ~**ts**, ~**tes** pr. bakă'ntĕz) & a., ~**te** (or bakă'-, bakă'ntĭ) n. fem., Bacchanal; **Bă'cchic** (-kĭk) a., Bacchanal. [L (*Bacchus* f. Gk, god of wine)]

‖**bă'ccy̆** (-kĭ) n. colloq.) Tobacco. [abbr.]

**bă'chelor** n. Unmarried man; person who has taken university degree below that of Master (*Bachelor of Arts*); ~'s **button**, kind of button-like flower; **knight** ~ (of no special order); ~**hoo͞d** n., man's unmarried life. [F f. L baccalaureus]

**bacĭ'll|us** n. (pl. ~**i** pr. -ī). Rodlike bacterium, esp. one causing disease by entering and multiplying in animal and other tissues; ~**ary̆** a. [L dim. of baculus stick]

**băck** n., a., adv., & v. **1.** n. Hinder surface of human body from shoulder to hip (**at the** ~ **of**, behind in support, pursuit, or concealment; **get, put**, person's ~ **up**, make him angry or stubborn; **on** one's ~, in bed; SEE[1] *the back of*; **turn** one's ~ **on**, abandon, ignore); upper surface of animal's back, similar ridge-shaped surface (*ship broke her* ~, keel); surface corresp. to human back (*back of head*), less active or important or visible part (~ **of book**, spine or final pages; ~ **of knife**, non-cutting edge); side or part normally away from spectator or direction of motion (*back of house,*

*chair, bus*); part of garment covering back esp. above waist; (position of) defensive player in football etc.; **the B~s**, grounds of Cambridge colleges on the Cam, of noted beauty; *\*in* ~ (**of**), behind; ~**lĕss** a., (of dress) low-cut at back. **2.** a. (superl. ~'**most**). Situated behind, esp. as remote or inferior, (*back teeth*; *back street*); overdue (*back pay*); reversed (*back flow*). **3.** adv. To the rear (*back and* FORTH); away from the front (*sit back in your chair*); in(to) the past or an earlier or normal position or condition (*look back on one's life*; *three years* ~, ago; *go back to one's home*; *back home*; *it happened back in April*; **will be** ~ *at six*, will return then); in return (*pay back*); at a distance (*stands back from the road*); in check (*keep back*); *\**~ **of**, behind. **4.** v.t. & i. Put or be a back or background to; assist with money or argument; bet on success of; lie at back of; endorse (cheque etc.); cause (horse, car, etc.) to move backwards; go backwards; (of wind) change direction counter-clockwise (cf. VEER); ~ **down**, abandon claim etc.; ~ **out**, (fig.) withdraw (from undertaking etc.); ~ **up**, help by subordinate action, *\*reverse (vehicle); ~**er** n., (esp.) one who bets on horses etc.; ~**ing** n., (esp.) body of supporters, material used to form thing's back or support. **5.** ~**ache**, pain in one's back; ‖~-**be'nch**(**er**), (occupant of) seat in House of Commons etc. used by member not entitled to sit on front bench; ~**bite** v.t., speak ill of; ~**blocks**, (Austral. & N.Z.) land in remote interior; ‖~-**boiler** (behind domestic fire etc.); ~**bone**, spine, main support, firmness of character; ~**chat**, (colloq.) impudent repartee; ‖~**cloth**, (Theatr.) painted cloth at back of stage as main part of scenery; ~**date** v.t., put earlier date to, make retrospectively valid; ~ **door**, (fig.) secret means of approach; ~**drop**, backcloth; ~**fire** n., explosion prematurely in cylinder or in exhaust-pipe of vehicle engine; ~**fir'e** v.i., undergo backfire, (of plan etc.) have opposite of intended effect; ~**formation**, (word got by) making from a supposed derivative (as *automation*, *lazy*) a previously non-existent word (*automate*, *laze*) from which it might have come; ~'**ground**, back part of scene etc. esp. as setting for chief part, inconspicuous accompaniment, obscurity or retirement (*in the background*), explanatory information, person's cultural knowledge, education, etc.; ~'**hand(ed)**, (stroke, blow) with back of hand turned outwards, (fig.) indirect, ambiguous; ~**ha'nder**, such blow etc., indirect attack; ~'**lash**, irregular recoil in machinery, excessive or violent reaction; ~'**log**, arrears of uncompleted work etc.; ~ **number**, old issue of magazine etc., (sl.) out-of-date method or person; \*~'**pack** *n.*, & *v.i.*, (travel with) rucksack etc.; *back* PASSAGE; ~'**pedal**, work pedal backwards, (fig.) reverse one's previous action; ~ **room**, place where secret research is done; ~ **seat**, (fig., colloq.) inferior or unimportant position; ~**seat driver**, one who has no responsibility but is eager to advise; ~'**side**, buttocks; ~ **slang** (using words spelt and pronounced backwards); ~'**slide** *v.i.*, relapse into sin or error; ~'**stage**, (Theatr. or fig.) behind the scenes; ~ **stairs**, (fig.) = *back door*; ~'**stitch**, sew(ing) with overlapping stitches; ~'**stroke** (by swimmer lying on back); ~'**track**, (fig.) = *back-pedal*; ~'**wash**, motion of receding wave, repercussions; ~'**water**, still water beside stream and fed by its back flow, (place of) intellectual stagnation; ~'**woods**, remote uncleared forest land; ~'**woodsman**, inhabitant of this, ‖(fig.) peer who seldom or never attends House of Lords. [E]

**ba'ckga'mmon** *n.* Game on double board with draughts and dice; completest victory in this. [prec. + obs. form of GAME[1]]

**ba'ckward(s)** (-dz) *adv.*, **ba'ckward** *a.* **1.** *adv.* Away from one's front (*lean backwards*); back foremost (*walk backwards*); (of thing's motion) back to starting-point (*flow backwards*); in the reverse of the usual way (*count backwards*; *spell backwards*); bend, fall, lean, over ~s, go to opposite extreme, do one's utmost. **2.** *a.* Directed to rear or starting-point; reversed; reluctant, slow, behindhand, (*in* action etc.); shy. **3.** ‖~**ā'tion** *n.*, percentage paid by seller of stock for right of delaying delivery. [-WARD(s)]

**ba'con** *n.* (Piece of) cured back or side of pig (**bring home the ~**, colloq., be successful; **save one's ~**, escape death or injury). [F f. Gmc]

**bactēr'ĭ|um** *n.* (*pl.* ~a). Single-celled microscopic organism of widely distributed class; ~**al**, ~**olŏ'gĭcal**, *adjs.*; ~**o'logў**, ~**o'logĭst**, *ns.* [L f. Gk.= little stick]

**băd** *a.* & *adv.* (WORSE, WORST) & *n.* **1.** *a.* Worthless, inferior, defective, not valid, incorrect, (*bad cheque*; *bad light*; ~ **coin**, counterfeit, debased; ~ **debt**, not recoverable; ~ **egg**, ‖~ **hat**, person of bad character; **not** ~, colloq., fairly good; **too** ~, colloq., regrettable) unpleasant (*bad breath, news, weather*); noxious, harmful, (*sweets are bad for your teeth*); wicked (*bad* BLOOD, LANGUAGE); putrid, decayed, (*meat has gone bad*); ill, injured, (*is very bad today*; *a bad leg*); (colloq., of things in no case good) notable, serious, (*a bad blunder, headache*); ~'**dĭsh** *a.*; ~'**dў** *n.*, (colloq.) criminal, villain; ~'**lў** *adv.* (WORSE, WORST), (esp.) faultily (*behave badly*), by much (*badly defeated*), very much (*needs it badly*). **2.** *adv.* \*(colloq.) Badly. **3.** *n.* Ill fortune; debit side of account (£*500 to the bad*); ruin (*go to the bad*). [E]

**băde.** See BID.

**bădge** *n.* Thing worn as mark of office, membership, etc.; thing that reveals a quality or condition (*badge of servitude*). [orig. unkn.]

**bă'dger.** **1.** *n.* Burrowing mammal of weasel family, noted for fierce defence of its burrow. **2.** *v.t.* Pester, torment, (person etc.). [orig. uncert.]

**badinage** (ba'dĭnahzh) *n.* Banter. [F]

**ba'dmĭnton** *n.* Game with net, rackets, and shuttlecock. [place]

**bă'ffle.** **1.** *v.t.* Frustrate, perplex, stop progress of, (person, attempt, etc.); ~**ment** (-fĕlm-) *n.* **2.** *n.* Plate, board, etc., hindering or regulating passage of fluid etc. [orig. uncert.]

**băg.** **1.** *n.* Receptacle of flexible material with opening at top (**in the** ~, colloq., in one's possession or power; ~ **and baggage**, with all one's belongings; ~ **of bones**, lean creature; ~'**pipe(s)**, reed-pipe wind instrument with air-bag); sac in animal body for honey, poison, etc.; amount of game shot by sportsman; (in *pl.*, sl.) large amount, ‖trousers; ~'**ful** (-ōŏl) *n.*; ~'**gage** *n.*, luggage, portable equipment of army, (joc.)

saucy girl; **~'gў** (-gĭ) *a.* (**-ily, -iness**), puffed out, hanging loosely. **2.** *v.t.* (**-gg-**). Put in bag; secure, take possession of, ‖(school sl.) lay claim to (*bags first innings*). [orig. unkn.]

**băgàtě'lle** *n.* A mere trifle; game like billiards played with small balls on board with holes. [F f. It.]

**bă'ggage, baggy.** See BAG.

**bah** *int.* of contempt. [F]

**bail**[1]. **1.** *n.* Security given for released prisoner's return for trial, person(s) pledging this, (**on ~**, released on such security); **go ~ for**, act as bail for, guarantee truth of; **surrender to, forfeit**, one's **~**, duly appear, fail to appear, for trial). **2.** *v.t.* Deliver (goods) in trust; become bail for and secure liberation of (**~ out**, esp. person already in prison); (of magistrate etc.) release on bail; **~'able** *a.*, (of offence) admitting of bail; **~ee'** *n.*, one to whom goods are entrusted; **~'ment** *n.* (of goods or prisoner); **~'or** *n.*, one who entrusts goods. [F f. L (*bajulus* carrier)]

**bail**[2] *n.* Bar separating horses in open stable; (Cricket) either of 2 cross pieces over stumps; bar holding paper against typewriter platen. [F]

**bail**[3], **bāle**[3], *v.t. & i.* Scoop water out of (boat etc.); **~ out**, make emergency parachute descent from aircraft. [F (BAIL[1])]

**bai'lable, bailee'.** See BAIL[1].

**bai'ley**[1] *n.* Defensive wall of castle; court enclosed by this. [BAIL[2]]

**Bai'ley**[2] *n.* **~ bridge**, prefabricated bridge designed for rapid construction. [person]

**bai'liff** *n.* Officer under sheriff for writs, processes, and arrests; landlord's agent or steward; first civil officer in Channel Islands; **bai'lie** *n.*, Scots municipal officer and magistrate; **bai'liwĭck** *n.* [obs. *wick* district], district of bailie or (C.I.) bailiff, (joc.) person's sphere. [F f. L (BAIL[1])]

**bai'lment, bai'lor.** See BAIL[1].

**bain-marie'** (băn-) *n.* Vessel of hot water for slow heating of cooking-pans. [F f. L f. Gk (*Mary*, supposed person)]

**bairn** *n.* (Sc.) Child. [BEAR[2]]

**bait. 1.** *v.t.* Torment (chained animal) by setting dogs at it, (person) with jeers etc.; put bait on or in (hook, trap, fishing-place). **2.** *n.*

Food, real or sham, to entice prey; an allurement. [N (BITE)]

**baize** *n.* Coarse usu. green woollen stuff used for coverings. [F (BAY[5])]

**bāke** *v.t. & i.* Cook by dry heat in closed place or on hot surface; harden by heat; be or become baked; **~'house**, house or room for baking bread; **~d Alaska**, sponge-cake and ice cream in meringue; **~d beans**, haricot beans baked and usu. tinned with tomato sauce; **baking-powder**, mixture of sodium bicarbonate, cream of tartar, etc., as raising-agent for cakes etc.; *baking-*SODA; **bā'ker** *n.*, one who bakes and sells bread (**~r's dozen**, 13, extra loaf being retailer's profit); **bā'kerў** *n.* [E]

**bā'kelīte** *n.* Plastic made from formaldehyde and phenol etc. [P; G f. *Baekeland*, inventor]

**bă'ksheesh** *n.* Gratuity, tip. [Pers.]

**Bălacla'va** (-ah'-) *n.* **~ (helmet)**, woollen covering for head and neck. [place]

**bălalai'ka** (-lī'-) *n.* Triangular musical instrument like guitar. [Russ.]

**bă'lance. 1.** *n.* Weighing-apparatus esp. with central pivot, beam, and two scales (**B~**, sign of ZODIAC; *question is in the* **~**, remains uncertain); regulating-gear of clock etc.; counterpoise; even distribution of weight or amount (**~ of mind**, sanity; **~ of power**, with no State greatly preponderant); steady position (**lose, keep**, one's **~**, *fall, not fall*); preponderating weight or amount (*the balance of opinion is on our side*); difference between credits and debits (**~ sheet**, statement of assets and liabilities; STRIKE *a balance*; **~ of payments** or **trade**, difference of value between payments into and out of a country, between exports and imports; **on ~**, taking everything into consideration); excess of amount offered over amount due (*you may keep the balance*); (colloq.) remainder. **2.** *v.t. & i.* Weigh (question, opposed arguments); match (thing *with*, *by*, *against*, another); bring or come into, keep in, equilibrium (*balance a cup on* one's *head*); equal or neutralize weight or importance of; compare (debits and credits of account), equalize these by an entry, (of account) have these equal. [F f. L *bilanx* scale]

**bă'lconў** *n.* External balustraded

platform with access from upper-
-floor window; theatre seats above
dress-circle, usu. = gallery; upstairs
seats in cinema. [It. (BALK)]

**bald** (bawld) *a.* With scalp wholly
or partly hairless; without the usual
covering, hairless, featherless, leafless,
etc.; (of tyre, colloq.) with tread
worn away; (of style) meagre, dull;
(of bad qualities) undisguised;
∼'**head**, ∼'**pate**, bald person; ∼-
-**headed** *a.* (go bald-headed, sl., proceed regardless of consequences);
∼'**ing** *a.*, becoming bald. [E]

**bă'ldăchĭn, -quĭn,** (-kĭn; *or* baw'-)
*n.* Canopy over throne etc. [f. It.
name of Baghdad]

**ba'lderdăsh** (-aw'l-) *n.* Jumble of
words, nonsense. [orig. unkn.]

**ba'ldrĭc** (-aw'l-) *n.* (Hist.) Belt for
sword, bugle, etc., hung from
shoulder to opposite hip. [F]

**bāle**[1] *n.* (poet., arch.) Evil,
destruction, woe. [E]

**bāle**[2] *n.*, & *v.t.* (Make up into)
package of merchandise usu.
wrapped in canvas and corded or
hooped. [Du. (BALL[1])]

**bāle**[3]. See BAIL[3].

**balee'n** *n.* Whalebone. [F f. L
*balaena* whale]

**bā'leful** (-lf-) *a.* (∼ly). Pernicious,
destructive; malignant. [BALE[1]]

**ba(u)lk** (bawk, -lk). **1.** *n.* Ridge
left unploughed between furrows;
stumbling-block, hindrance; (*baulk*)
area on billiard-table where ball may
be exempt from direct stroke;
roughly squared timber beam. **2.**
*v.t.* & *i.* Shirk, miss, (topic, chance);
thwart, hinder, disappoint, (*baulked
of his prey*); jib, shy. [E]

**Ba'lkan** (-aw'l-) *a.* Of the penin-
sula bounded by the Adriatic,
Aegean, and Black Seas, or of its
peoples and countries; ∼**s** (-z) *n.pl.*,
*the* Balkan countries. [place]

**ball**[1] (bawl). **1.** *n.* Solid or hollow
sphere (∼ **and socket joint**, kind
having great freedom of movement;
∼-**bear'ing**, Mech., using small balls
to avoid friction, one such ball; ∼'-
**cock**, device with floating ball to
control cistern water-level; ∼ **lightning**, of rare globular form; ∼-**pen,
-point**, pen with tiny ball as writing-
-point); such sphere used in games
(**have the ∼ at one's feet,** have
one's opportunity; **keep the ∼-
rolling,** do one's part in talk etc.;
**on the ∼,** colloq., alert; **play ∼,**

colloq., co-operate; **start the ∼ rolling,** begin); single delivery of ball
by bowler in cricket (**no-∼,** disquali-
fied and penalized), or by pitcher
in baseball; material gathered or
wound in round mass (*ball of snow,
wool, string*); solid missile for cannon,
rifle, etc.; rounded part (EYE*ball*; ∼
**of foot, of thumb,** at base of big toe,
of thumb); (in *pl.,* vulg.) testicles,
(fig.) nonsense, muddle (*make a balls
of;* ∼**s-up,** confusion). **2.** *v.t.* & *i.*
Form into ball. [N]

**ball**[2] (bawl) *n.* Social assembly for
dancing (**have a ∼,** sl., enjoy oneself; **open the ∼,** lead first dance,
fig. commence operations); ∼'**room**
(used for ball). [F f. L f. Gk *ballō*
dance]

**bă'llad** *n.* Simple song; sentimental
song of several verses sung to same
melody; poem in short stanzas narrating popular story; **balla'de** (-ah'd)
*n.,* poem of one or more triplets
of 7-, 8-, or 10-lined stanzas each ending with refrain, and envoy; ∼**rў** *n.,*
ballad poetry. [F f. Prov. (prec.)]

**bă'llast. 1.** *n.* Heavy material
placed in ship's hold for stability
(*ship is in* ∼, laden with ballast
only); experience etc. as steadying
character; coarse stone etc. as bed
of railway or road. **2.** *v.t.* Furnish
with ballast. [LG or Scand.]

**balleri'na** (-ē'na) *n.* Female ballet-
-dancer, esp. taking one of the leading
classical roles in ballet. [It. (BALL[2])]

**bă'llet** (-lā) *n.* Dramatic performance of dancing and mime to
music; **bă'llĕtomāne, băllĕtomā'-
nĭa,** *ns.,* enthusiast, enthusiasm, for
ballet performances. [F (BALL[2])]

**balli'st|a** *n.* (*pl.* ∼ae). Ancient
military engine for hurling stones;
∼**ic** *a.,* of projectiles (∼**ic missile,**
moving under gravity after being
initially powered and guided); ∼**ics**
*n.pl.,* science of projectiles or of
firearms. [L, f. Gk *ballō* throw]

**balloo'n. 1.** *n.* Round or pear-
-shaped airtight envelope inflated
with gas so as to rise in air, esp. one
with car for carrying persons; small
inflated rubber bag as child's toy;
hollow inflated thing; (colloq.)
balloon-shaped line enclosing words
or thoughts of characters in comic
strip; ∼ **tyre,** low-pressure tyre of
large cross-section. **2.** *v.i.* Travel
in balloon; swell out like balloon;
∼**er,** ∼**ĭst,** *ns.* [F or It. (BALL[1])]

**bă'llot. 1.** *n.* Secret voting; ball, paper, used in ballot; votes recorded in ballot; lot-drawing; **~-box** (used to hold marked ballot-papers). **2.** *v.i.* Vote by ballot; draw lots (*for* precedence). [It. *ballotta* (BALL¹)]

‖**bă'lly** *a.* & *adv.* (sl.) euphem. for BLOODY as vague intensive (*took the bally lot*). [= *bl—y* (*bloody*)]

**bă'llyhoo'** *n.* (sl.) Vulgar or misleading publicity. [orig. unkn.]

**bă'llyrăg** *v.t.* & *i.* (-**gg**-). Maltreat by jeering, play practical jokes on; indulge in horseplay.

**balm** (bahm) *n.* Fragrant and medicinal exudation from some trees; ointment; fragrance; healing or soothing influence; tree yielding balm; kind of aromatic herb; **~ў** *a.* (**-ily, -iness**), of or like balm, fragrant, mild, soothing, healing, (sl.) crazy. [F f. L (BALSAM)]

**balo'ney.** See BOLONEY.

**ba'lsa** (baw'l-, bŏ'l-) *n.* (Amer. tropical tree yielding) light strong wood; raft or float. [Sp.]

**ba'lsam** (baw'l-, bŏ'l-) *n.* Balm from trees; ointment esp. of substance dissolved in oil or turpentine; tree yielding balsam; a flowering plant; **bălsă'mic** (*or* bawl-, bŏl-) *a.* [E f. L *balsamum*]

**bă'lust|er** *n.* Short pillar with curving outline; post supporting rail; **~ra'de** *n.*, row of balusters with rail or coping as parapet to balcony etc. [F f. It. f. Gk]

**bămboo'** *n.* Tropical giant grass; its stem as stick or material for food. [Du. f. Port. f. Malay]

**bămboo'zle** *v.t.* (sl.) Hoax, mystify; cheat (person *into* doing, *out of* property etc.); **~ment** (-zelm-) *n.* [orig. unkn.]

**băn. 1.** *v.t.* (-**nn**-). Forbid, prohibit, esp. formally. **2.** *n.* Formal or authoritative prohibition (*a ban on advertising*). [E, = summon]

**bănă'l** (*or* banah'l, bā'nal) *a.* (**~ly**). Commonplace, trite; **banā'lĭtў** *n.* [F (BAN); orig. = compulsory, hence = common]

**bana'na** (-nah'-) *n.* Tropical fruit-tree; its finger-shaped fruit. [Sp. or Port., f. Afr. name]

**Bă'nburў** *n.* **~ cake**, pastry filled with currant mixture. [place]

**bănd. 1.** *n.* Flat strip of thin material; hoop or loop of iron, rubber, etc., round a thing; strip forming part of garment (**wai'st~,** on skirt etc.); paper strip serving as label etc.; (in *pl.*) pair of strips hanging below collar as part of clerical etc. dress; belt connecting wheels or pulleys; stripe of colour etc.; range of values, wavelengths, etc., within a series; organized group of persons; body of musicians; **~'box**, box for millinery (*look as if one came out of a ~-box*, extremely neat); **~'master**, conductor of musical band; **~-saw**, endless saw running over wheels; **~'sman, ~'stand**, member of, platform for, musical band; **~'-wagon**, wagon for musical band esp. in circus parade (*climb on the ~-wagon*, fig., seek to join cause or political party etc. that seems likely to succeed). **2.** *v.t.* Put a band on; mark with stripes; form into a league (*banded together*). **3. ~'age**, (*n.*) strip of material for binding up wound etc., (*v.t.*) bind up with this. [N (BIND) & F]

**bă'ndă'nna** *n.* Coloured handkerchief with yellow or white spots. [Port. f. Hindi]

**b. & b.** *abbr.* bed and breakfast.

**bă'ndeau** (-dō, -dō') *n.* (*pl.* **-x** *pr.* -z). Band worn round head. [F]

**bănderŏ'l(e)** *n.* Long narrow flag with cleft end; ribbon-like scroll with inscription. [F f. It. (BANNER)]

**bă'ndicōōt** *n.* (Ind.) very large kind of rat; (Austral.) insectivorous and herbivorous marsupial. [Telugu, = pig-rat]

**bă'ndĭt** *n.* (*pl.* **~s**, **-i'tti**). Outlaw; brigand; **~rў** *n.* [It. (BAN)]

**băndoleer', -ier',** *n.* Shoulder-belt with cartridge-loops. [Du. or F (BANDEROLE)]

**bă'ndў¹** *v.t.* Throw or pass to and fro (*ball, story, was bandied about*); discuss; exchange, give and take, (blows, compliments; *with* person). [F (BAND)]

**bă'ndў²** *a.* (**-iness**). (Of legs) curved wide apart at the knees; **~-legged**, having bandy legs. [obs. *bandy* curved stick]

**bāne** *n.* Cause of ruin or trouble; (poet.) ruin; (arch.) poison (RATS-*bane*); **~'ful** (-nf-) *a.* (**-lly**). [E]

**băng** *v., n.,* & *adv.* **1.** *v.t.* & *i.* Strike or shut noisily (*bang the drum, the door; door bangs*); (cause to) make sound as of blow or explosion; cut (hair) straight across forehead; **~'er** *n.*, (esp., sl.) sausage, noisy old car. **2.** *n.* Sharp blow; sound of blow or explosion; fringe of hair across forehead. **3.** *adv.* With a bang, abruptly, explosively, (go ~ explode or shut with bang; ~ **go** *my hopes* etc., are suddenly dashed); (colloq.) exactly (*bang in the middle*); ~ **on**, (sl.) exactly right. [imit.]

**bă′ngle** (-nggel) *n.* Rigid ring as bracelet or anklet. [Hindi *bangri*]

**bă′nĭan, bă′nyan,** *n.* Hindu trader; Indian fig-tree with branches that root themselves over large area. [Port. f. Skr., = merchant]

**bă′nĭsh** *v.t.* Condemn (person) to exile (*from* place); dismiss from one's presence or mind; ~**ment** *n.* [F (BAN)]

**bă′n(n)ĭster** *n.* (usu. in *pl.*) Upright(s) supporting stair handrail; (in *pl.*) these uprights and rail together. [BALUSTER]

**bă′njō** *n.* (*pl.* ~s, ~es). Instrument like guitar with tambourine-shaped body; ~**ĭst** *n.* [Negro corrupt. of *bandore* (Gk *pandoura* lute)]

**bănk¹. 1.** *n.* Raised shelf of ground e.g. in sea or river bed, slope; flat-topped mass of cloud etc.; sloping margin of river, ground near river, (**left, right,** ~, to one looking down stream). **2.** *v.t. & i.* Contain or confine with bank(s); incline (car or aeroplane) laterally in rounding a curve, (of car etc.) incline thus; build (road etc.) higher at outer edge of bend; ~ (**up**), heap or rise in banks, pack (fire) close for slow burning. [N (BENCH)]

**bănk². 1.** *n.* Establishment for custody of money, which it pays out on customer's order (‖**the B**~, Bank of England); domestic receptacle for money; money held by keeper of gaming-table; storage place (*blood bank*); ~ **card**, = CHEQUE *card*; ~ **holiday,** day on which banks are officially closed, ‖usu. kept as public holiday; ~′**note,** banker's promissory note payable to bearer on demand, serving as money; \*~′**roll,** roll of banknotes etc. **2.** *v.t. & t.* Keep a bank; deposit (money) in bank; keep money *at* or *with* bank; ~ **on,** base one's hopes on, reckon reliable; ~′**able** *a.,* acceptable to a bank; ~′**er** *n.,* manager of bank, keeper of gaming bank, result forecast identically in series of football-pool entries. [F *banque* or It. *banco* (prec.)]

**bănk³** *n.* Row of lights, switches,

keys, etc.; tier *of oars.* [F f. Gmc (BANK¹)]

**bă′nkable, bă′nker.** See BANK².

**bă′nkrŭpt** *n., a., & v.* **1.** *n.* Insolvent person, esp. one whose estate is administered and distributed for benefit of creditors. **2.** *a.* Insolvent, undergoing legal process because of insolvency; bereft (*of* a quality etc.); ~**cў** *n.* **3.** *v.t.* Make bankrupt. [It. *banca rotta* broken bench (BANK²)]

**bă′nksĭa** *n.* A flowering shrub, orig. Australian. [*Banks,* person]

**bă′nner** *n.* Flag of a country, army, etc. (*follow the banner of,* usu. fig.); ensign usu. on crossbar or between two poles borne in political etc. demonstrations; ~ **headline** etc. (extending across newspaper page). [F f. L *bandum* standard (BAND)]

**bă′nnĭster.** See BANISTER.

**bă′nnock** *n.* (Sc., N. Engl.) Round flat loaf, usu. unleavened. [E]

**bănns** (-z) *n.pl.* Notice in church of intended marriage, read on three Sundays to give opportunity of objection (ask, publish, put up, the banns; **forbid the** ~, raise such objection). [BAN]

**bă′nquĕt. 1.** *n.* Sumptuous feast; dinner with speeches in celebration or to further a cause. **2.** *v.t. & i.* Regale (person); take part in banquet. [F dim. (BANK²)]

**bănquĕ′tte** (-ngk-) *n.* Upholstered seat along wall. [F f. It. dim. (BANK²)]

**bă′nshee** *n.* (Ir., Sc.) Female spirit whose wail portends death in a house. [Ir., = woman of the fairies]

**bă′ntam** *n.* Small kind of fowl, of which the cock is pugnacious; small but spirited person; ~**weight** (see BOX). [place]

**bă′nter. 1.** *n.* Humorous gentle ridicule. **2.** *v.t. & i.* Make fun of; jest. [orig. unkn.]

**bă′ntlĭng** *n.* Brat, child.

**Bă′ntu** (-ōō, -ōō′) *n.* (*pl.* same, ~s) & *a.* (One) of a group of African Negroid peoples or their languages; ~**sta′n** (-ōōstah′n) *n.,* area in S. Afr. reserved for Bantu. [Bantu, = people]

**bă′nyan.** See BANIAN.

**bā′obăb** *n.* Afr. tree with huge trunk and edible fruit. [L f. Afr.]

**B.A.O.R.** *abbr.* British Army of the Rhine.

**băp** *n.* (esp. Sc.) Large soft bread roll. [orig. unkn.]

**bă′pt│ism** *n.* Religious rite of immersing in or sprinkling with water in sign of purification and (with Christians) admission to the Church, usu. with name-giving; naming of ship etc.; ~**i′smal** (-z-) *a.* (**-lly**); ~**ist** *n.*, one who baptizes, esp. John the Baptist, (**B**~) one of a sect objecting to infant baptism and practising immersion; ~**ist(e)rў** *n.*, part of church (or, formerly, separate building) used for baptism, immersion receptacle in Baptist chapel; ~**i′ze** *v.t.*, administer baptism to, christen, name or nickname. [F f. L f. Gk]

**bar**[1]. **1.** *n.* Long piece of rigid material, esp. used to confine or obstruct (*bar of metal, wood*; *bars of gate, grate*; **behind ~s**, in prison; ~**bell**, weight-lifter's bar with heavy ball at each end); oblong piece of (chocolate, soap, etc.); strip of silver below clasp of medal as extra distinction; band of colour etc., esp. Her. (~ **sinister**, erron. = BATON, BEND, *sinister*); sandbank or shoal at mouth of harbour or estuary; (Mus.) vertical line dividing piece into sections of equal time value, such section; (fig.) obstacle or barrier, restriction; place where prisoner stands in lawcourt; a particular lawcourt (**be called to the ~** separating benchers from others in Inns of Court, be admitted as barrister; **be called within the ~**, be appointed Q.C.; **the ~**, barristers, their profession); counter across which refreshments are served, space behind this or room etc. containing it, (*drinks are served at the bar*; *coffee bar*; *snack bar*; ‖also BILLIARDS; ‖~**maid**, ~**man**, ~**tender**, attendant at bar in inn etc.); specialized department in large shop (*heel bar*). **2.** *v.t.* (**-rr-**). Fasten (door etc.) with bar(s); keep (person) **in**, **out**; obstruct or prevent (action); exclude from consideration (*barring accidents*; in *imper.* as *prep.*, except); ‖(sl.) dislike; mark with stripe(s). [F]

**bar**[2] *n.* (esp. Meteor.) Unit of pressure, $10^5$ newton per sq. metre, approx. one atmosphere. [Gk *baros* weight]

**bărăthe′a** *n.* Fine wool cloth. [orig. unkn.]

**barb**[1]. **1.** *n.* Secondary recurved point of arrow, fish-hook, etc., (fig.) wounding remark; lateral filament branching from shaft of feather; fleshy appendage from mouth of barbel etc. **2.** *v.t.* Furnish (arrow, hook) with barb; ~**ed wire** (with wire spikes at intervals, used in fences, and esp. as obstruction in war). [F f. L *barba* beard]

**barb**[2] *n.* Horse, pigeon, of Barbary breed; (Austral.) black kelpie. [F f. It. *barbero*]

**barbār′ian** *n.* & *a.* Wild or uncultured (person); **barbă′ric** *a.* (**-ically**), of, suitable to the taste of, barbarians; **bar′barism** *n.*, rude or uncultured state or act, (use of) undesirable form or expression in language; **barbă′rity** *n.*, savage cruelty; **bar′barize** *v.t.* & *i.*, make or become barbarous; **bar′barous** *a.*, uncivilized, cruel, coarse. [F f. L f. Gk, = foreign]

**bar′becue. 1.** *n.* Metal frame for cooking meat esp. above open fire; meat thus cooked; open-air party at which such food is served. **2.** *v.t.* Cook on barbecue. [Sp. f. Haitian]

**bar′bel** *n.* A freshwater fish with fleshy filaments hanging from mouth; such filament in any fish. [F f. L (BARB[1])]

**bar′ber** *n.* One who cuts men's hair and shaves beards; ~**'s pole** (spirally painted and used as sign).

**bar′berry** *n.* A yellow-flowered prickly-stemmed shrub; its oblong red berry. [F BERBERIS]

**bar′bican** *n.* Outer defence to city or castle, esp. double tower over gate etc. [F]

**barbi′t|urate** *n.* Soporific or sedative drug derived from an organic (~**ur′ic**) acid. [G, f. name *Barbara*]

**bar′carōle, -ōlle,** *n.* Gondolier's song. [F f. It. (BARK[2])]

**bard** *n.* Celtic minstrel; poet honoured at Eisteddfod; poet; ~**′ic** *a.*, of Celtic bards. [Celt.]

**bāre. 1.** *a.* Unclothed, uncovered, (*bare arms*); ~**back**, on unsaddled horse; ~**faced**, shameless, impudent; ~**foot(ed)**, without shoes or stockings; **with one's ~ hands**, not using tool or weapon; ~**hea′ded**, hatless; (of tree) leafless; (of floor) without carpet; exposed, undisguised, (*lay bare the truth*); unadorned (*bare facts, walls*); empty (*cupboard was bare*); scanty, only just sufficient, (*a bare majority*; *bare necessities of life*); ~**lў** (bar′li) *adv.*, (esp.) scarcely, only just, scantily. **2.** *v.t.* Uncover, reveal, (*bared its teeth in a snarl*). [E]

**bar′gain** (-gĭn). **1.** *n.* Agreement

on terms of a transaction (**into**, *__in__, **the** ~, moreover; **make, strike, a** ~, come to terms); thing acquired by such agreement (**a** ~, **a good** ~, thing got cheaply, **a bad** ~, dearly). **2.** *v.t.* & *i.* Discuss terms of transaction (*with* person, *for* thing); ~ **away**, part with for a consideration; ~ **for, on**, be prepared for, expect; ~ **on**, rely on. [F f. Gmc]

**barge. 1.** *n.* Flat-bottomed freight-boat for canal or river; ornamental vessel for state occasions; house-boat; ~**-pole** for fending; *would not touch with a* ~*-pole*, refuse to associate etc. with); ‖**bargee'** *n.*, person in charge of barge. **2.** *v.i.* Lurch, come heavily, (*into* person etc.); ~ **in**, intrude. [F (cf. BARK²)]

**bar'ge-board** *n.* Board or ornamental screen along gable-edge. [orig. uncert.]

**ba'ritone** *n.* Male voice between tenor and bass; singer with, part written for, this. [It. f. Gk (*barus* heavy, TONE)]

**bar'ium** *n.* White metallic element (~ **meal**, mixture used in radiography of alimentary canal). [BARYTA]

**bark¹. 1.** *n.* Outer sheath of tree trunks and branches; tan. **2.** *v.t.* Strip (tree) of bark; abrade (knuckles etc.). [Scand.]

**bark²** *n.* (poet.) Ship, boat. [= BARQUE]

**bark³. 1.** *v.i.* & *t.* (Of dog, fox, etc.) utter sharp explosive cry; speak or utter petulantly or imperiously; ~ **up the wrong tree**, make effort in wrong direction; ~**'er** *n.*, (esp.) tout at auction, sideshow, etc. **2.** *n.* Barking cry (**his** ~ **is worse than his bite**, he is irritable but harmless); (colloq.) cough. [E]

**bar'ley** *n.* Awned cereal used as food and in malt liquors and spirits; ~**(corn)**, its grain; ~ **sugar**, (freq. twisted) sweetmeat of boiled sugar; ~**-water**, soothing decoction for invalids. [E]

**barm** *n.* Froth on fermenting malt liquor; yeast. [E]

**bar mi'tzvah** (-tsvá) *n.* (Religious initiation for) Jewish boy of 13. [Heb., = son of commandment]

**bar'm|y̆** *a.* (~**ily**, ~**iness**). Frothy; (sl.) crazy. [BARM]

**barn** *n.* Roofed building for storing grain etc.; ~ **dance**, kind of schottische; ~**-door**, (fig.) target too large to be missed; ~ **owl** (kind frequenting barns); ~**-stormer**, itinerant or ranting actor; ~**'yard**, farmyard. [E, = barley house]

**bar'nacle** *n.* Arctic goose visiting Britain in winter; cirriped clinging by fleshy foot-stalk to ship's bottom; (fig.) follower hard to shake off. [L]

**ba'rograph** (-ahf) *n.* Self-recording barometer; **baro'meter** *n.*, instrument measuring atmospheric pressure and used to forecast weather and find height above sea-level; **barome'tric(al)** *adjs.* (**-ically**). [Gk *baros* weight]

**ba'ron** *n.* Member of lowest order of British or foreign nobility; great merchant in specified commodity; influential person; (Hist.) holder of lands etc. from king; ~ **of beef**, double sirloin; ~**ess** *n.*, baron's wife or widow, woman with own rank of baron; ~**et** *n.*, member of lowest hereditary titled British order; ~**etcy̆** *n.*; **baro'nial** *a.*, of or befitting baron(s); ~**y̆** *n.*, baron's domain or rank. [F f. L, = man]

**baro'que** (-k). **1.** *a.* Grotesque, whimsical; of exuberant extravagant style in 17th–18th-c. arts. **2.** *n.* Baroque style or ornamentation. [F, orig. 'misshapen pearl']

**barqu|e** (-k) *n.* Vessel with aftermost mast fore-and-aft rigged, remaining masts square-rigged; ~**'entine, bar'k-**, (-kentēn) *n.*, three-masted vessel with only the foremast square-rigged. [F f. Prov. f. L *barca*]

**ba'rrack. 1.** *n.* (usu. in *pl.*) Permanent building for lodging soldiers; large building of barrack-like appearance. **2.** *v.t.* (sl.) Shout or jeer at (performers at cricket etc.) [perh. f. Austral. sl. *borak* banter]. [F f. It. or Sp.]

**barracou'ta** (-oo't-) *n.* Long slender Pacific food-fish; **barra-cu'da** (-oo'd-) *n.*, large W. Ind. sea-fish. [Sp.]

**ba'rrage** (-ahzh) *n.* Artificial barrier in river (esp. in Nile); barrier to military action, e.g. by bombardment; (fig.) rapid succession (*of* questions etc.); heat or deciding event in fencing etc.; ~ **balloon**, large captive balloon supporting steel cable as part of barrier against aircraft. [BAR¹]

**ba'rrat|or** *n.* Vexatious litigant; malicious raiser of discord; ~**rous** *a.*; ~**ry̆** *n.*, (incitement to) vexatious

**barre** *n.* Waist-level horizontal bar for dancers' exercises. [F, = BAR[1]]

**bă′rrel. 1.** *n.* Wooden vessel of hooped staves, with flat ends and usu. bulging out at middle (**over a ~**, helpless; **scrape the ~**, use one's last resources); contents or capacity of this; revolving cylinder in machinery (**~organ**, in which pin-studded barrel acting on pipes); metal tube of gun. **2.** *v.t.* (||-ll-). Put in barrels. [F]

**bă′rren** *a.* (**~er**, **~est**; **~ness** *pr.* -n-n-). Not bearing, incapable of bearing, children, young, fruit, or vegetation (*barren woman, cow, tree, region*); unprofitable, dull. [F]

**bărrică′de. 1.** *n.* Barrier, esp. hastily erected one of barrels, carts, etc., across street. **2.** *v.t.* Block (street etc.), defend (place, person), with barricade. [F (Sp. *barrica* cask)]

**bă′rrier** *n.* Fence, rail, etc., barring advance or access; gate at which tickets must be shown; obstacle, circumstance, etc., that keeps apart; **~ cream** (to protect skin from damage or infection); **~ reef,** coral reef separated from land by channel. [F (BAR[1])]

**bă′rring.** See BAR[1].

**bă′rrister** *n.* ||Person called to bar and entitled to practise as advocate in higher courts; *lawyer. [BAR[1]]

**bă′rrow[1]** (-ō) *n.* (Archaeol.) Grave-mound, tumulus. [E]

**bă′rrow[2]** (-ō) *n.* (Hand-)**~,** frame for two persons to carry loads etc.; (wheel)**~,** shallow box with shafts and wheel similarly used by one person; ||two-wheeled hand-cart; metal frame with two wheels for moving luggage etc.; **~-boy,** coster. [E (BEAR[2])]

**Bart.** *abbr.* Baronet.

**bă′rter. 1.** *v.t.* & *i.* Exchange (goods, rights, etc., *for* something other than money or *away*); **~ away,** part with for usu. unworthy consideration); trade by exchange. **2.** *n.* Trade by exchange. [BARRATOR]

**bărtiză′n** *n.* Battlemented parapet; projecting corner turret at top of tower. [Sc. var. of *bratticing* parapet]

**bary′t|a** *n.* Barium (hydr)oxide;

**~ēs** (-z) *n.*, barium sulphate, used in some white paints. [Gk *barus* heavy]

**bă′sal.** See BASE[2].

**basalt** (bă′sawlt, basaw′lt) *n.* A dark igneous rock often in columnar strata; **basa′ltic** (-saw′l-) *a.* [L *basaltes* f. Gk]

**bă′scule** *n.* **~ bridge,** kind of drawbridge worked by counterpoise. [F, = see-saw etc.]

**bāse[1]** *a.* Morally low, cowardly, despicable; menial; debased, not pure, (*base coin*); of inferior value (*base metals*); **~′born,** of low birth, illegitimate. [F f. L *bassus*]

**bāse[2]. 1.** *n.* What a thing rests or depends on; support, foundation, principle, starting-point; main ingredient of mixture; part of column between shaft and pedestal or pavement; end at which organ is attached to trunk; (Geom.) line or surface on which figure is regarded as standing; (Chem.) substance (e.g. alkali) capable of combining with acid to form a salt; (Mil.) town etc. in rear of army where drafts, stores, and hospitals are concentrated; operational headquarters; known line as geometrical base in surveying; number in terms of which other numbers or logarithms are given; one of four stations to be reached in turn by runner in baseball (**get to first ~,** fig., achieve first step to objective); **~′ball** (ball used in) U.S. national game in which players seek to strike ball thrown by opponent and traverse circuit of four bases; **~′-line,** starting-point, (Tennis) line at each end of court. **2.** *v.t.* Found, rest, (thing) *on*; establish (*family* etc.); **~** oneself on, rely upon (in argument etc.); **~d,** **~d on,** using as fundamental station or means. **3.** **bă′sal** *a.*, of, at, forming, the base; **bā′sic** *a.* (-ically), basal, (Chem., e.g. of salt) having properties of a base; **basic slag,** fertilizer containing phosphates that is by-product in steel manufacture; **~′less** (-sl-) *a.*, groundless, unfounded; **~′ment** (-sm-) *n.*, lowest part of structure, inhabited storey below ground level. [F, or L f. Gk *basis* stepping]

**basĕ′nji** *n.* Small rarely-barking Afr. hunting-dog. [Bantu]

**băsh. 1.** *v.t.* Strike so as to smash in; attack violently. **2.** *n.* Heavy blow; (sl.) attempt. [imit.]

**bă′shful** *a.* (**~ly**) Shy; sheepish. [ABASH]

**bă′sĭc.** See BASE[2].

**bă′sĭl** (-z-) *n.* An aromatic herb. [F f. L f. Gk (foll.)]

**basĭl′ica** *n.* Oblong hall with double colonnade and apse used as lawcourt etc. or as church; church with special privileges from Pope. [L f. Gk, = royal]

**bă′sĭlĭsk** (-zĭ-) *n.* Mythical reptile with lethal breath and look; lizard with crest inflated at will. [L f. Gk, dim. of *basileus* king]

**bā′sĭn** *n.* Round vessel, less deep than wide and narrowing downwards, for holding water etc.; hollow depression, round valley, tract drained by river; (coal etc. in) group of strata dipping to centre; dock with floodgates; land-locked harbour; **~ful** (-ŏŏl) *n.* [F f. L *bacinus*]

**bā′sĭs** *n.* (*pl.* ~es *pr.* -ēz). Foundation, main principle or ingredient, thing to work upon. [L f. Gk (BASE[2])]

**bask** (-ah-) *v.i.* Lie, sit, etc., comfortably warming oneself (*in* sun, firelight, popularity); **~′ing shark** (large species lying near water surface). [N (BATHE)]

**ba′skĕt** (-ah′-) *n.* Container of plaited or woven cane, wire, etc., contents of, amount held by, basket; basket-like structure; (euphem., colloq.) bastard; **~ball,** (large inflated ball used in) game in which goal is scored when ball is thrown into net fixed 10 ft. above ground; **~weave** (like basket material); **~work** (of basket material or style); **~ful** (-ŏŏl) *n.*; **~ry** *n.*, basketwork, baskets. [F]

**basque** (bahsk). *n.* Continuation of bodice below waist; (B~) native or language of W. Pyrenees. [F f. L *Vasco*]

**bă′s-relief** *n.* (Carving or sculpture in) low RELIEF. [F, & It. *basso rilievo*, = low relief]

**băss[1]** *n.* (*pl.* ~, ~′es). Common perch; other fish of perch family. [E]

**băss[2], băst,** *ns.* Inner bark of lime tree, other similar fibre, used for mats etc.; **~′wood,** Amer. lime. [E]

**băss[3]. 1.** *a.* Deep-sounding; of, suited to, lowest part in music; ~ **clef** (with F below middle C on second highest line of staff). **2.** *n.* Bass voice or singer or part; (colloq.) double-bass; **figured ~,** bass part with numerals etc. to indicate proper harmony. [BASE[1]]

**bă′ssĕt** *n.* Short-legged hound used for hunting hares etc. [F dim. (BASE[1])]

**bă′ssĕt-horn** *n.* Tenor clarinet with extended range. [G f. F f. It. *corno di bassetto* (*basso* BASE[1])]

**băssĭnĕt** *n.* Hooded wicker cradle or pram. [F dim. (BASIN)]

**bă′ss|ō** *n.* (*pl.* ~os, ~i). Man, esp. singer, with deep bass voice. [It., = BASS[3]]

**bassŏŏ′n** *n.* Bass instrument of oboe family; its player; **~ĭst** *n.* [F f. It. (BASE[1])]

**băst.** See BASS[2].

**bă′stard** (*or* bah′-). **1.** *a.* Born out of wedlock, illegitimate; unauthorized, hybrid, counterfeit. **2.** *n.* Bastard person or thing; (colloq.) disliked or unfortunate person or thing. **3.** **~ĭze** *v.t.*, declare bastard; **~y** *n.*, illegitimacy. [F f. L, = pack-saddle child]

**bāste[1]** *v.t.* Sew together loosely with temporary stitches. [F f. Gmc]

**bāste[2]** *v.t.* Moisten (roasting meat) with gravy or fat; thrash, cudgel. [orig. unkn.]

**băstĭnā′dō. 1.** *n.* (*pl.* ~s, ~es). Caning on soles of feet. **2.** *v.t.* Cane thus as punishment or torture. [Sp. (*baston* stick)]

**bă′stĭon** *n.* Pentagonal projection from a fortification; (fig.) institution serving as defence (*bastion of freedom*). [F f. It. (*bastire* build)]

**băt[1]** *n.* Nocturnal mouselike mammal flying by means of winglike membrane on forelimbs; **blind as a ~,** completely blind; **have ~s in the belfry,** (colloq.) be crazy or eccentric. [Scand.]

**băt[2]. 1.** *n.* Implement with handle, for striking ball in cricket, baseball, table tennis, etc., (**carry one's ~,** Crick., be not out at end of side's completed innings; ‖**off** one's **own ~,** fig., unaided); act of using this; batsman (*a good* etc. *bat*). **2.** *v.i.* & *t.* (-tt-). Use bat, strike (as) with bat; (sl.) move (*around* etc.). **3.** **~′sman,** user of cricket etc. bat. [E f. F]

‖**băt[3]** *n.* (sl.) Pace (*going at a rare bat*). [orig. uncert.]

**băt[4]** *v.t.* (-tt-). Wink (**never ~ted an eyelid,** betrayed no emotion). [var. of obs. *bate* flutter]

**bătch. 1.** *n.* Loaves baked at a time; number of things or persons coming or dealt with together (*batch of letters*) **2.** *v.t.* Arrange in batches. [E (BAKE)]

**băte**[1] *v.t. & i.* Restrain (with ~d breath, anxiously). [ABATE]

||**băte**[2] *n.* (sl.) Rage (*was in an awful bate*). [BAIT]

**bath** (-ah-). **1.** *n.* (*pl. pr.* -dhz). Immersion in liquid etc. for cleansing or therapy (*have, take, a bath*); water etc. for bathing in; surrounding medium for developing films, etc.; ~(-tub), vessel for bathing in; (usu. in *pl.*) building for bathing or swimming in; ||order of knighthood [named from ceremonial bath preceding installation]; ~ cube, salts, etc., (for softening or scenting bath-water); *~robe, dressing-gown; ~room, room containing bath, (euphem.) lavatory. **2.** (*B~*). Town in Avon named from hot springs; B~ brick, a preparation for cleaning metal; B~ bun, round spiced kind with currants and icing; B~ chair (wheeled, for invalid); B~ Oliver, unsweetened biscuit [invented by Dr. Oliver of Bath]. **3.** *v.t. & i.* ||Wash in, take, a bath. [E]

**băth|e** (-dh). **1.** *v.t. & i.* Immerse (oneself) in liquid etc.; (of sunlight etc.) envelop; moisten all over (*bathe* one's *eyes*); ~'ing beauty, attractive woman in bathing-suit; ~'ing-machine, (Hist.) wheeled box drawn into sea for bathing from; ~'ing-suit, garment worn when bathing. **2.** *n.* ||Immersion in sea, river, or swimming-bath. [E]

**bă'thŏs** *n.* Fall from sublime to commonplace, anticlimax; performance absurdly unequal to occasion; bathĕ'tic, bathŏ'tic, *adjs.* (-ically). [Gk, = depth]

**bă'thӯscăphe, bă'thӯsphēre**, *ns.* Kinds of vessel for deep-sea diving and observation. [Gk *bathus* deep, *skaphos* ship, SPHERE]

**bă'tĭk** (*or* batĕ'k) *n.* Method (orig. Javanese) of printing coloured designs on textiles by waxing parts not to be dyed; material so treated. [Jav., = painted]

**bati'ste** (-ē'st) *n.* A fine fabric like cambric. [F; person]

**bă't|man** *n.* (*pl.* ~men). (Mil.) Officer's servant. [*bat* pack-saddle f. F f. Prov. f. L *bastum*]

**bă'ton** *n.* Staff of office; constable's truncheon; conductor's stick for beating time; drum major's stick; short tube or stick carried in relay race; ~ sinister, (Her.) badge of bastardy. [F f. L]

**batrā'chian** (-k-). **1.** *a.* Of frogs or toads, animals that discard gills and tail. **2.** *n.* Such animal. [Gk *batrakhos* frog]

**băts** *a.* (sl.) Crazy. [BAT[1]]

**bă'tsman**. See BAT[2].

**battă'lion** (-yon) *n.* Large body of men in battle array; unit of infantry composed of several companies and forming part of brigade; large group of persons with similar tasks etc. [F f. It. (BATTLE)]

||**bă'ttels** (-z) *n.pl.* (Oxf. Univ.) College accounts esp. for provisions. [orig. uncert.]

**bă'tten**[1]. **1.** *n.* Long narrow piece of squared timber; cross board or strip; strip of wood esp. for electric lamps or to secure hatchway tarpaulin. **2.** *v.t.* Strengthen with battens; ~ down, close (hatches) with battens. [F (BATTER)]

**bă'tten**[2] *v.i.* Feed greedily (*on*); grow fat, esp. at another's expense. [N]

**bă'tter**. **1.** *v.t. & i.* Strike repeatedly so as to bruise or break, knock about, beat out of shape, (*face was battered*; *battered about*; *batter the door down, in*; *batter at the door*; ~ed **baby**, with symptoms of repeated violence by adults); criticize etc. severely; ~ing-ram, (Hist.) swinging beam with ram's-head end for breaching walls. **2.** *n.* Mixture of flour and egg beaten up with milk or water for cooking. [F *battre* (BATTLE)]

**bă'ttery** *n.* Set of connected similar units of equipment; portable cell(s) supplying electricity; series of cages etc. for poultry or cattle; emplacement for gun(s); artillery unit; (Law) infliction of blows or menacing touch to clothes or person.

**bă'ttle**. **1.** *n.* Fight, esp. between large organized forces (do, join, ~, begin it; ~ royal, involving several combatants or all available forces); victory in fight (*is* half the ~, a great help); (fig.) contest (*battle of wits*). **2.** ~axe, medieval or prehistoric weapon, (colloq.) domineering middle-aged woman; ~cruiser, heavy-gunned ship of higher speed and lighter armour than battleship; ~cry, war-cry, slogan; ~dress, soldier's etc. everyday uniform of blouse and trousers; ~field, ~ground, scene of battle; ~ship, most heavily armed and armoured warship. **3.** *v.i.* Struggle (*with, against,* difficulties, person, etc., *for* one's rights etc.). [F f. L (*battuo* beat).]

**băˊttledŏre** (-teld-) *n.* Small racket for striking shuttlecock in game of ~ **and shuttlecock.** [Prov. *batedor* (BATTLE)]

**băˊttlement** (-telm-) *n.* (usu. in *pl.*) Indented defensive parapet at top of wall; this and roof. [F *batailler* furnish with ramparts]

*battue* (bătūˊ, -ōōˊ) *n.* Driving of game by beaters to sportsmen; shooting-party with this; wholesale slaughter. [F, = beating (BATTER)]

**băˊtt| y̆** *a.* (~iness). (sl.) Crazy. [BAT¹]

**bauˊble** *n.* Showy trinket; mere toy. [F *ba(u)bel* child's toy]

**baulk.** See BALK.

**bauˊxite** *n.* Earthy mineral, the chief source of aluminium. [F (*Les Baux*, place)]

**bawd** *n.* Procuress; ~ˊy̆, (*a.*; ~ily, ~iness) humorously indecent, (*n.*) such talk; ~y-house, brothel. [F *baudetrot*]

**bawl** *v.t.* & *i.* Say or speak or weep noisily; ~ **out**, (colloq.) reprimand severely. [imit.]

**bay¹** *n.* Kind of laurel with deep-green leaves and purple berries; (in *pl.*) conqueror's or poet's bay wreath; ~**berry**, a fragrant W. Ind. tree; ~**leaf** (usu. dried, used as flavouring); ~ **rum**, perfume of bayberry leaves in rum. [F f. L *baca* berry]

**bay²** *n.* Part of sea filling wide-mouthed opening of land. [F f. Sp. *bahia*]

**bay³** *n.* Division of wall between buttresses etc.; projecting window-space (~ **window**, filling bay); recess, compartment; marked-off area for parking etc. [F (*baer* gape f. L)]

**bay⁴. 1.** *n.* Deep bark of large dog, esp. chorus of pursuing hounds as they draw close (hunted animal **stands** or **is at** ~, holds hounds **at** ~, turns to defend itself; hounds **bring** quarry **to** ~, come to close quarters; often fig. of desperate persons). **2.** *v.i.* & *t.* (Of large dog) bark, bark at, (*bay the moon*) bark. [F *bayer* to bark]

**bay⁵. 1.** *a.* (Of horse) reddish-brown, with black mane and tail. **2.** *n.* Bay horse. [F f. L *badius*]

**bayˊonĕt. 1.** *n.* Stabbing blade attachable to rifle-muzzle; ~ **plug** etc. (engaging by pushing and

twisting). **2.** *v.t.* Stab with bayonet. [F (*Bayonne*, place)]

**bazaarˊ** (-zärˊ) *n.* Oriental market; large shop selling fancy goods; sale to raise funds for charities. [Pers.]

**\*bazōōˊka** *n.* Anti-tank rocket-gun; crude trombone-like musical instrument. [orig. unkn.]

**BB** *abbr.* double-black (pencil-lead).

**B.B.C.** *abbr.* British Broadcasting Corporation.

**B.C.** *abbr.* Before Christ; British Columbia; British Council.

**B.D.** *abbr.* Bachelor of Divinity.

**Bde.** *abbr.* (esp. Mil.) Brigade.

**bdĕˊllĭum** (d-) *n.* (Tree yielding) a resin used as perfume etc. [L f. Gk]

**bē** (or bĭ) *v.* (*pres. indic.*: 1 **am** *pr.* ăm, am; 2 **art** (arch.) *pr.* ärt, ert; 3 **is** *pr.* ĭz; *pl.* & 2 *sing.* **are** *pr.* är, er, *pl.* arch. **be**; *past indic.*: 1 & 3 **was** *pr.* wŏz, woz; 2 **wast** (arch.) *pr.* wŏst, wost; *pl.* & 2 *sing.* **were** *pr.* wêr, wār, wer; *pres. subj.* **be**; *past subj.* **were**, exc. 2 *sing.* **wert** (arch.) *pr.* wêrt, wert; *imper.* **be**; *part.* **being** *pr.* bēˊĭng; *p.p.* **been** *pr.* bēn, bĭn; colloq. abbr. forms **'m** = am, **'s** = is, **'re** = are; **aren't** (ärnt) = am not (interrog.), are not; **isn't** (ĭˊzent) = is not; **wasn't** (wŏˊzent) = was not; **weren't** (wêrnt, wārnt) = were not; **ain't** colloq. = am not, vulg. = is not, are not). Exist, occur, live, (often with *there*; *there is a green hill far away*; *I think, therefore I am*; *can such things be?*; the POWERS *that be*; *when is the wedding to be?*; **for the time being**, for the PRESENT¹; **be that as it may**, no matter what is the fact concerning that); remain, continue, (**let it be**, do not disturb it); occupy position in space or time (*is in the garden*); take or direct oneself (*be off!*; **is from** *Canada*, has come from there; **have been to**, have visited); experience condition (*he is better today*); occupy oneself (*mice have been at the food*); hold view (*I am against abortion*); have state or quality (*he is a stranger, is ill; be quick about it*); coincide in identity with (*you are the man I want; today is Monday*); amount to (*twice two is four*); cost (*how much are these pears?*); signify (*it is nothing to me*); as aux. v. with *p.p.* of *v.t* forming passive (*this was done*), with *pres. part.* forming progressive tenses (*it is rising, he is raising it, it is being raised*), with *inf.* expr. duty (*I am to* *inform you*), intention (*he is to be there*), possibility (*house is to let; it was not to be found*), destiny (*they were never to meet again*), hypothesis (*if I were to die*); **be-all (and end-all)**, whole being or essence (*of*); **-to-be**, future (*his bride-to-be*). [E]

**bē-** *pref.* forming *vbs.* w. added notion of: all over (*besmear*), transitive action (*bemoan, befool*), thoroughly (*belabour*), surrounding with or treating as (*befog, befriend*), having (*n.* with suffix *-ed* to form *adjs.*: *bewigged*). [E, = BY]

**beach. 1.** *n.* Shore esp. of sea between high and low water mark; (shore with) water-worn pebbles or sand; **~'comber**, Pacific-island settler (usu. wastrel etc.), long rolling wave; **~head**, fortified position set up on beach by landing forces [after *bridgehead*]. **2.** *v.t.* Run or haul up (boat, whale) on shore. [orig. unkn.]

**bea'con** *n.* Signal-fire on hill or pole; signal; signal station; far-seen hill; lighthouse; ‖amber globe on pole marking pedestrian crossing. [E]

**bead. 1.** *n.* Small rounded usu. pierced object for threading with others on string or wire (TELL one's *beads*); drop of liquid, bubble, small knob in foresight of gun (draw a **~ on**, take aim at); inner edge of pneumatic tyre gripping rim of wheel; moulding like series of beads or with semicircular section; **~'y** *a.* (**~ily, ~iness**), (esp., of eyes) small and bright. **2.** *v.t.* Furnish with beads; string together. [E, = *prayer*]

‖**bea'dle** *n.* Ceremonial officer of church, college, etc.; (Hist.) parish officer appointed by vestry to punish petty offenders etc.; (Sc.) church officer attending upon minister. [F f. Gmc]

**bea'dy.** See BEAD.

**bea'gle** *n.* Small hound used for hunting hares; spy, informer. [F]

**beak** *n.* Bird's horny projecting jaws; mandibles of turtle etc.; hooked nose; (Hist.) pointed prow of warship; spout; ‖(sl.) magistrate, schoolmaster. [F f. Celt.]

**bea'ker** *n.* Lipped glass for scientific experiments; small drinking-vessel. [E]

**beam. 1.** *n.* Long piece of squared timber or of metal supported at both ends in house etc. (**~ in one's eye**, fault great compared to another's, cf. MOTE); chief timber of plough;

bar of balance; (in *pl.*) horizontal cross timbers of ship; side of ship; ship's breadth; ray of radiation; this as guide to aircraft or missile (**off ~**, colloq., mistaken; **on the ~**, colloq., on the right track); directional flow of particles; radiance; bright look, smile; **~ends**, side of ship (*on one's ~-ends*, near end of resources). **2.** *v.t. & i.* Emit (light, affection); shine; look radiantly, smile. [E, = *tree*]

**bean** *n.* Kind of leguminous plant with kidney-shaped seeds in long pods; such seed, used as food, (**full of ~s**, colloq., in high spirits; **give** person **~s**, sl., punish or scold him; **not a ~**, sl., no money; SPILL[2] *the beans*); similar seed of coffee or other plant; ‖**~'feast**, ‖**~'ō** *n.* (sl.; *pl.* **~s**), workers' annual dinner, (colloq.) celebration. [E]

**bear**[1] (bār) *n.* Thick-furred usu. heavy mammal (**Great B~, Little B~**, constellations near north pole; **like a ~ with a sore head**, colloq., ill-tempered); child's toy like it; rough or uncouth person; (St. Exch.) one who sells for future delivery and hopes to buy cheaper before then; **~-baiting**, (Hist.) setting dogs to attack captive bear; **~'garden**, (fig.) scene of tumult; **~hug**, powerful embrace; **~'skin**, (wrap etc.) of bear's skin, Guards' tall furry cap. [E]

**bear**[2] (bār) *v.t. & i.* (**bore, borne, BORN**; in pass. *born* w. ref. to birth, but *borne by* with mother's name). **1.** Carry visibly, show, have habitually, be known by, (banner, marks *of*, relation *to*, name); **~** (away, off), win (prize etc.); (poet. or formal) carry; bring needed thing (**~ a hand**, help; *bear* WITNESS); exercise (office); carry in mind (*bear a grudge*; **~ in mind**, not forget); wear (**~ arms**, be soldier, have heraldic arms); sustain (weight, responsibility, cost; **~ a part in**, share); stand (test etc.), endure; (usu. neg. or interrog.) tolerate, admit of; be fit for; give birth to; produce, yield (*land bears crops*; **~ fruit**, fig., have results); make a thrust, strive, apply weight, (**bring to ~**, apply, aim (gun)); **~ down**, exert downward pressure; **~ down on**, move rapidly or purposefully towards; **~ hard on**, oppress; **~ on**, = *bear upon*; **~ out**, confirm (story), confirm account given by (person); **~**

oneself, behave (*well* etc.); ~ **up**, uphold, not despair; ~ **upon**, be relevant to; ~ **with**, tolerate patiently; (in *p.p.*:) **-borne**, carried or transported by (*airborne*); **is borne in upon** one, becomes one's conviction *that*. 2. ~'**able** *a*. (**-bly**), (esp.) endurable; ~'**er** *n*., (esp.) carrier of message, cheque, or equipment on safari; ~'**ing** *n*., (esp.) outward behaviour, being endurable, heraldic charge or device, relation, aspect (*in all its bearings*), friction-bearing part of machine (BALL[1]-*bearing*), direction to a place, (in *pl.*) relative position; **have lost my** ~**ings**, do not know where I am. [E]

**beard. 1.** *n*. Hair of lower face (excluding moustache and whiskers); chin tuft of goat etc.; gills of oyster; awn. 2. *v.t.* Oppose openly, defy, (esp. ~ **the lion in his den**, fig.). [E]

**bearer, bearing.** See BEAR[2].

**beast** *n*. (Esp. wild) animal; quadruped; domesticated bovine animal; brutal man; disliked person or thing; **the** ~, animal nature in man; ~'**lÿ**, (*a.*; ~**liness**) like a beast, sensual, unfit for human use, (colloq.) unpleasant, (*adv.*) very, regrettably (*beastly drunk, wet*). [F f. L *bestia*]

**beat. 1.** *v.t.* & *i*. (**beat**; ~'**en**, or **beat** as below). Strike repeatedly or persistently (~ **the air**, strive in vain; ~ **one's breast**, in mourning or woe); remove dust from (carpet) by beating; knock loudly *at door* etc.; make (path) by trampling (~**en track**, well-trodden way, lit. or fig.); inflict blows on; (*p.p.* also **beat**) overcome, surpass, (~ **person to it**, get there first, lit. or fig.; **take some** ~**ing**, be difficult to surpass), exhaust, perplex; (of wings) move up and down; (of heart etc.) move rhythmically; mark or follow (time of music) with baton, foot, etc.; shift, drive, alter, shape, by blows; strike (bushes etc.) to rouse game; make (eggs etc.) into frothy smooth mixture by vigorous stirring; play on drum; ~ **about**, search (*for excuse* etc.); ~ **about the bush**, approach subject indirectly; ~ **down**, bargain with (seller), cause seller to lower (price); ~ **in**, crush; ~ **it**, (sl.) go away; ~ **off**, drive back (attack etc.); ~ **out**, forge (metal); ~ **up**, beat (person) severely, collect (recruits etc.). **2.** *n*. Stroke on drum; movement of conductor's baton;

principal recurring accent in music or verse; measured sequence of strokes; strongly marked rhythm of popular music; throbbing; pulsation due to mixing of sounds at different frequencies; sentinel's or policeman's appointed course, area covered by this; one's habitual round; ~('**nik** *n*.), member of ~ **generation**, young people with unconventional dress and behaviour as expression of social philosophy. **3.** ~'**er** *n*., (esp.) man employed to rouse game, implement for beating carpets or eggs. [E]

**bēati'fic** *a*. (~**ally**). Making blessed, (colloq.) blissful (*beatific smile*); **běǎ'tǐfy** *v.t.*, make happy, (of Pope) declare (person) to be in bliss, as first step to canonization; **běǎtǐfǐcā'tion** *n*.; **běǎ'tǐtūde** *n*., blessedness, (in *pl.*) *the* blessings in Matt. 5: 3–11. [F or L (*beatus* blessed)]

**bea'tnik.** See BEAT.

**beau** (bō) *n*. (*pl.* ~**x**, ~**s**, *pr.* -z). Fop, dandy; ladies' man, admirer. [F f. L *bellus* pretty]

**Beau'fort** (bō'f-) *n*. ~ **scale**, of wind velocity ranging from 0 (calm) to 12 (hurricane). [person]

**beau idē'al** (bō-) *n*. One's highest type of excellence. [F, = the ideal beautiful]

**Beau'jolais** (bō'zholā) *n*. Red or white burgundy wine from Beaujolais district. [place]

**Beaune** (bōn) *n*. Red burgundy wine from Beaune district. [place]

**beau't|ÿ** (bū'-) *n*. Combination of qualities that delights the sight or other senses or the mind; person or thing having this; fine specimen (*here's a beauty*); beautiful feature (**the** ~**y of it**, the particular point that gives satisfaction); ~**y parlour**, place where women receive beautifying treatment; ~**y queen**, woman judged most beautiful in a competition; ~**y spot**, beautiful locality; **beaut** (būt) *n*. & *a*., (Austral., N.Z., & U.S.: sl.) beautiful (person or thing) [abbr.]; ~**éous** *a*., (rhet.) beautiful; ~**ïful** *a*. (**-lly**), having beauty, delighting eye or ear, gratifying any taste (*beautiful picture, pizza, play*), impressive, charming, satisfactory; ~**ïfÿ** *v.t.*, make beautiful, adorn; ~**ïficā'tion** *n*. [F f. L (*bellus* pretty)]

**beaux.** See BEAU.

**bea'ver**[1]. **1.** *n*. Amphibious broad-tailed soft-furred rodent that cuts down trees and builds dams; its brown fur; hat of this; **eager ~,** (colloq.) (over-)zealous person. 2. *v.i.* **~ away,** work hard *at.* [E]

**bea'ver²** *n.* Lower face-guard of helmet. [F, = bib]

**bě'bŏp** *n.* Kind of jazz music. [imit.]

**běca'lm** (-ah'm) *v.t.* (usu. in *pass.*) Deprive (ship) of wind. [BE-]

**'běcá'me.** See BECOME.

**běcau'se** (-kŏz'). **1.** *adv.* By reason (*because of his age*). **2.** *conj.* For the reason that, since. [BY, CAUSE]

**běck¹** *n.* (literary). Significant nod or gesture (**at the ~ and call of,** wholly dominated by). [BECKON]

**běck²** *n.* (N. Engl.) Brook, mountain stream. [N]

**bě'ckon** *v.i.* & *t.* Make mute signal (*to*) esp. to approach; summon thus. [E]

**běco'm|e** (-ŭm') *v.i.* & *t.* (**-ca'me, -co'me**). Come to be, begin to be, (*become Prime Minister, known, morose, an invalid*); **what has ~e** of person or thing?, what has happened to him?, where can it be?); suit, befit, look well on, (*it ill becomes you to complain; a becoming hat, modesty*); **~ingly** *adv.,* suitably, gracefully, elegantly. [E (BE-)]

**běd. 1.** *n.* Thing to sleep or rest on; framework with mattress and coverings; animal's resting-place; flat base on which thing rests; garden plot for plants; bottom of sea, river, etc.; foundation of road or railway; layer. **2. ~ and board,** lodging and food; **~ and breakfast,** sleeping accommodation and food next morning; **~ of roses,** easy position; **brought to ~,** in childbirth; DIE² *in* one's *bed*; GET *out of bed on wrong side*; **go to ~,** retire for the night, (fig.) have sexual intercourse *with*; **lie in, on, the ~ one has made,** accept consequences of one's acts; **make the ~,** arrange its coverings for further use; **put to ~,** cause (child etc.) to go to bed. **3. ~chamber,** (arch.) **~clothes,** sheets, pillows, blankets, etc.; **~fellow,** sharer of bed, (fig.) associate; **~pan,** invalid's utensil for urination or defecation when in bed; **~post,** upright support of bed; **~ridden,** confined to bed by infirmity [E, = bed--rider]; **~rock,** solid rock under alluvial deposits etc., (fig.) ultimate principles; **~room** (for sleeping in); **~side,** side of esp. invalid's bed; **||~sitting-room,** (colloq.) **~sitter,** combined bedroom and sitting-room; **~sock,** warm sock worn in bed; **~sore** (developed by lying in bed); **~spread,** cloth or sheet over bed esp. when not in use; **~stead,** framework of bed; **~straw,** a herbaceous plant; **~time,** hour for going to bed; **~wetting,** involuntary urination while asleep. **4.** *v.t.* & *i.* (**-dd-**). **~ (down),** put or go to bed; (fig.) have sexual intercourse with; **~ (out),** plant in a garden bed; cover or fix firmly in something; arrange in layer. **5. ~ding** *n.,* (esp.) mattress and bedclothes, litter for cattle etc., (visible) strata. [E]

**bědă'bble** *v.t.* Stain, splash, with liquid; **bědau'b** *v.t.,* smear with paint etc.; **bědă'zzle** *v.t.,* completely dazzle, confuse. [BE-]

**bědě'ck** *v.t.* Adorn. [BE-]

**||bě'del(l)** *n.* University official with chiefly processional duties. [= BEADLE]

**bědě'vil** *v.t.* (**||-ll-**). Treat diabolically; bewitch; afflict; impair; **~ment** *n.,* (esp.) maddening trouble or confusion; **bědew'** *v.t.,* cover with dew; **bědi'zen** *v.t.,* deck out gaudily. [BE-]

**bě'dlam** *n.* Madhouse; scene of uproar. [*Bethlehem* in name of London hospital]

**Bě'dlington** *n.* **~ (terrier),** long--legged grey-haired narrow-headed sporting terrier. [place]

**bě'd(o)uin** (-ōō-) *n.* (*pl.* same). Arab of the desert; wandering person. [F, f. Arab., = dwellers in desert]

**bědrǎ'ggle** *v.t.* Wet (dress etc.) by trailing it; (in *p.p.*) untidy, dishevelled. [BE-]

**Beds.** *abbr.* Bedfordshire.

**bee** *n.* Four-winged stinging social insect collecting nectar and pollen and producing wax and honey (**have a ~ in** one's **bonnet,** be obsessed on some point); busy worker; *meeting for combined work or amusement;* SPELL¹*ing-bee;* beeHIVE; **~line,** straight line between two places; **bee'swax** (-z-), wax secreted by bees for comb; **bee'swing** (-z-), filmy second crust on old port wine. [E]

**||Beeb** *n.* (sl.) *The* B.B.C. [abbr.]

**beech** *n.* A smooth-barked glossy--leaved forest tree; its wood; **~-mast,** fruit of beech, beech-nuts; **~en** *a.,* of beech. [E]

**beef. 1.** *n.* Flesh of ox, bull, or cow; (*pl.* **beeves**) oxen, esp. fattened oxen; (of men) size, muscle; (sl.) protest. **2.** *v.i.* & *t.* (sl.) Complain; ~ **up**, reinforce. **3.** ~'**burger**, hamburger; ||~'**eater**, (colloq.) warder in Tower of London; *beef*-STEAK; ~ **tea**, stewed beef juice for invalid; ~'**y̆** *a.* (~ily, ~iness), like beef, solid, muscular. [F, f. L *bos bovis* OX]

**Bĕĕ'lzĕbŭb** *n.* The Devil. [E f. L f. Gk f. Heb., = lord of flies]

**been.** See BE.

**beer** *n.* Alcoholic liquor made from fermented malt etc. flavoured with hops etc.; glass of this; ~ **and skittles**, amusement, fun; GINGER-*beer*; **small ~**, (fig.) trifling matter; ~'**y̆** *a.* (~ily, ~iness), (esp.) betraying influence of beer. [E]

**beeswax, beeswing.** See BEE.

**beet** *n.* Kind of plant with succulent root used for salad etc. and sugar-making; *beetroot; ||~'root, root of beet esp. as vegetable. [E]

**bee'tle**[1] *n.* Heavy-headed tool for ramming, crushing, etc. [E]

**bee'tle**[2] *n.* Coleopterous insect (pop. of large black kinds, and of similar insects). [E (BITE)]

**bee'tle**[3]. **1.** *a.* Projecting, shaggy, scowling, (*beetle brows*). **2.** *v.i.* Overhang (*beetling cliff*). [orig. unkn.]

**bee'trŏŏt.** See BEET.

**beeves.** See BEEF.

**befa'll** (-awl) *v.t.* & *i.* (-fe'll; -fa'llen). Happen, happen to, (*what befell?; evil befell him*). [E (BE-)]

**befi't** *v.t.* (-tt-). Be suited to; be incumbent on; **befŏ'g** *v.t.* (-gg-), envelop in fog, confuse, obscure; **befŏŏ'l** *v.t.*, make a fool of. [BE-]

**befŏr'e** *adv., prep.,* & *conj.* **1.** *adv.* Ahead (*go before*); on the front (*before and behind*); previously, already, (*have heard this before*); in the past (*long before*). **2.** *prep.* In front of, ahead of, (*a lamp before the door; look before you*); under the impulse of (*before the wind; recoil before the attack; carry all before you*); in presence of (*appear before judge*; ~ **God**, as God sees me, used as solemn asseveration); earlier than (*arrived before me; before his arrival*); ~ **Christ**, of date reckoned backwards from birth of Christ); rather than (*would starve before stealing*). **3.** *conj.* Earlier than (*arrived before I did, before I expected*

*him*); rather than (*would starve before he stole*). **4.** ~**hand,** in anticipation, advance, or readiness. [E (BY, FORE)]

**befou'l** *v.t.* Make foul; **befrie'nd** (-rĕ'nd) *v.t.*, act as a friend to, help; **befŭ'ddle** *v.t.*, make drunk, confuse. [BE-]

**bĕg** *v.t.* & *i.* (-gg-). Ask for or *for* (food, money, etc.) as gift, live by begging; (of dog) sit up with fore-paws raised; ask earnestly or humbly (thing, *for* thing, *of* person, person *to* do, *that*); ask formally (*beg leave*, PARDON); take or ask leave *to* do (*I beg to differ; begged to see me*); ~ **off,** get (person) excused, decline to take part; ~ **one's bread,** live by begging; ~ **the question,** assume truth of thing to be proved; **go** (a-)~**ging,** (fig.) find no accepter, (of thing) be unwanted. [E (BID)]

**bĕga'n.** See BEGIN.

**bĕgĕ't** (-g-) *v.t.* (-tt-; -go't, arch. -ga't; -go'tten). (Of father, rarely of both parents) procreate; give rise to (*beget strife, doubt*). [E (BE-)]

**bĕ'ggar. 1.** *n.* One who begs, esp. who lives by begging; poor person (~**s must not be choosers,** must take what is offered); (colloq.) person, fellow, (*insolent beggar; poor little beggar!*). **2.** *v.t.* Reduce to poverty; exhaust resources of (*beggar description*). **3.** ~**ly̆** *a.* (-iness), needy, wretched, mean; ~**y̆** *n.*, extreme poverty. [BEG]

**bĕgi'n** (-g-) *v.t.* & *i.* (-nn-; -ga'n; -gu'n). Perform first part of (*begin work, crying, to cry*); come to do at certain time (*begin to feel ill; I began to wish*); (colloq.) show any attempt or likelihood *to*; be first to do a thing, take first step; start speaking; be begun (*meeting begins at 7*); come into being, arise, have commencement or nearest boundary (*at*); ~ (**up)on,** set to work at; ~ **with,** take as starting-point; **to ~ with,** as the first thing; ~**ner** *n.*, one who is just beginning to learn a skill etc. (~**ner's luck,** good luck supposed to attend beginner at games etc.); ~**ning** *n.*, (esp.) time or place at which thing begins, source, origin, first part; ~**ning of the end,** first clear sign of final result. [E]

**bĕgŏ'ne** (or -aw'n) *int.* Go away at once! [*be gone*]

**bĕgŏ'nia** *n.* Kind of plant with petal-less flowers and often with brilliant foliage. [*Bégon,* person]

**begŏ′rra** int. (Ir. colloq.) By God! [corrupt.]

**begŏ′t(ten).** See BEGET.

**begri′me** v.t. Make grimy; **begrŭ′dge** v.t., be dissatisfied at, envy (person) the possession of; **begui′le** (-gī′l) v.t., delude, cheat (person *of*, *out of*, thing, *into* doing etc.), charm, amuse, cause (time, toil) to pass by easily; **begui′lement** (-gī′lm-) n. [BE-]

**begui′ne** (-gē′n) n. (Rhythm of) a W. Ind. dance. [F *béguin* infatuation)]

**be′gum** (or bā′-) n. Indian Muslim lady of high rank. [Urdu f. Turk. (BEY)]

**begŭ′n.** See BEGIN.

**behä′lf** (-ah′f) n. On or *in* ~ of, in the interest of, as representative of, (done on my behalf; writing on behalf of his employers). [BY, HALF in sense *part, side*]

**behä′v|e** v.i. & refl. Act or react (in specified way; ~e **towards**, treat *well* etc.; ILL-, WELL²-, *behaved*); (of machine etc.) work (well etc.); ~e (oneself), (esp. to or of child) conduct oneself properly, show good manners; ~**iour**, *~**ior**, (-vyer) n., manners, way of behaving (be on one's **good** or **best** ~iour, take care to behave well during observation or test); ~**iourism**, *-**ior**-, (-vyer-) n., study of human actions by analysis into stimulus and response, doctrine that this is the only valid method in psychology. [BE-, HAVE]

**behea′d** (-hĕ′d) v.t. Cut the head from; kill, execute, thus. [E (BE-)]

**behē′ld.** See BEHOLD.

**behē′moth** (or bē′ĭ-) n. Huge creature. [Heb.]

**behē′st** n. (literary). Command. [E]

**behĭ′nd** adv., prep., & n. **1.** adv. In or to the rear (fall, lag, ~, not keep up); on farther side; farther back in space or time (come from ~, win after lagging); in support; in an inferior position; remaining after others' departure; in arrear (with payments etc.). **2.** prep. In any of these relations to (look behind you; all that trouble is behind me; the man behind the project); hidden by (lit. or fig.; what is behind all this?); put ~ one, refuse to consider; ~ person's **back**, without his knowledge; ~ **the times**, antiquated; ~ **time**, unpunctual; ~**hand**, in arrear, out of date, behind time. **3.** n. Buttocks. [E]

**behō′ld** v.t. (behe′ld). (arch. or literary). See with the eyes; (in *imper.*) take notice, observe; ~**en** a., under obligation (to). [E (BE-); ~en p.p., obs. in other senses]

**behoo′f** n. (arch.) Benefit, advantage, (for, to, on, whose behoof?); **behō′ve**, -hoo′ve, v.t. impers., be incumbent on, (with neg.) befit, (usu. it behoves person to do). [E (HEAVE)]

**beige** (bāzh) n. Yellow-grey colour of undyed unbleached wool. [F]

**be′ing** n. Existence (**in** ~, existing); constitution, nature, essence; existing person (human being). [BE]

**bejew′elled,** *-eled, (-joo′eld). a. Adorned with jewels. [BE-]

**bĕl** n. Unit of relative power level, corresponding to intensity ratio 10:1; cf. DECIBEL. [Bell, person]

**belä′bour,** *-or, (-er) v.t. Thrash (lit. or fig.); labour (a subject). [BE-]

**belä′ted** a., coming too late. [BE-]

**belay′. 1.** v.t. Fix (running rope) round cleat etc. to secure it; ~ (there)!, (Naut. sl.) stop!; ~ing--**pin**, fixed pin for belaying on. **2.** n. (Spike of rock for) act of belaying. [Du. *beleggen*]

**bĕl cǎ′ntō** n. Singing marked by full rich broad tone and accomplished technique. [It., = fine song]

**bĕlch. 1.** v.i. & t. Emit wind noisily from stomach through mouth; (of volcano, gun, etc.) send out or up (fire, smoke, etc.). **2.** n. Act of belching. [E]

**bĕ′ldam(e)** n. (arch.) Hag; virago. [BELLE, DAME]

**belea′guer** (-ger) v.t. Besiege. [Du. (BE-, *leger* camp)]

**bĕ′lemnīte** n. Common fossil of sharp-pointed tapering shape. [L, f. Gk *belemnon* dart]

**bĕ′lfrў** n. Bell tower; bell space in church tower. [F f. Gmc, prob.= peace-protector, assim. to BELL¹]

**Bē′lial** n. The Devil. [Heb., = worthless]

**belī′e** v.t. (-ly′ing). Fail to confirm (his looks belie his words); fail to fulfil or justify (promise, hope); give false notion of (report belies him). [E (BE-)]

**belie′f** n. Trust, confidence, (in); acceptance of received theology; acceptance of thing as true or existing (belief in, that, of; **beyond** ~, incre.ible); what one firmly believes (*my belief is that he forgot*; **to the best of my** ~, so far as I know); a religion. [E (foll.)]

**belie've** *v.t. & i.* Accept as true or as speaking or conveying truth (*I believe you, what he says, that he means well, him to be honest*; *could not believe my ears*); think, suppose, (*has, I believe, no children*; *is believed to be in Rome*); ~ **in**, have faith in the existence, efficacy, advisability, etc., of (*believe in God, in ghosts*); MAKE believe; ~**r** *n.*, (esp.) adherent of specified religion. [E]

**beli'ke** *adv.* (arch., often iron.) Probably; perhaps. [BY, LIKE]

||**Beli'sha** (-ē´-) *n.* ~ **beacon** (marking pedestrian crossing). [Hore--*Belisha*, person]

**beli'ttle** *v.t.* Disparage; make seem small, dwarf; ~**ment** (-tĕlm-) *n.* [BE-]

**bell**[1]. **1.** *n.* Cup-shaped metal instrument made to emit musical sound when struck; stroke of bell (**one to eight** ~**s**, half-hours of nautical watch); signal for start or end of boxing round; bell-shaped thing, e.g. flower corolla; thing designed to attract attention by bell--like sound (*electric bell*); **sound as a** ~, quite SOUND[2]; ~**bird** (with bell-like note); ~**-bottomed** (of trousers) bell-shaped below knee; *\*~'boy**, page in hotel or club; ~**-glass** (bell-shaped, as cover for plants); ~**jar**, bell-shaped glass to cover instruments; ~'**man**, (Hist.) town crier; ~**-pull**, cord, handle, attached to wire to sound a bell; ~**-push**, button to operate electric bell; ~**-ringing** (esp. of church bells); ~**-tent** (conical, with central pole); ~**-wether**, leading sheep of flock, ringleader. **2.** *v.t.* Furnish with bell(s); ~ **the cat**, undertake danger in a shared enterprise. [E]

**bell**[2]. **1.** *n.* Stag's cry. **2.** *v.i.* Utter bell. [E]

**belladŏ'nna** *n.* Deadly nightshade; drug obtained from this; ~ **lily**, a S. Afr. amaryllis. [L f. It., = fair lady]

**belle** *n.* Handsome woman; reigning beauty. [F fem. of BEAU]

**belles-lettres** (bĕl-lĕ'tr) *n.pl.* Studies, writings, of purely literary kind; **bĕlle'trist** (-l-l-) *n.*; **bĕlletri'stic** (-l-l-) *a.* [F, = fine letters]

**belli'cose** *a.* Inclined to fight; ~o'sity *n.* [L (*bellum* war)]

**belli'geren|t. 1.** *a.* Waging regular war; engaged in conflict; pugnacious; ~**cy** *n.*, status of a belligerent. **2.** *n.* Belligerent nation, party, or person. [L *belligero* wage war]

**bě'llow** (-ō). **1.** *v.i. & t.* Roar like bull (~ **out, forth**, utter loudly); roar with pain. **2.** *n.* Bellowing sound. [orig. uncert.]

**bě'llows** (-ōz) *n.pl.* Contrivance for driving air into fire, organ, etc.; expansible part of camera etc.; **pair of** ~, two-handled bellows for fire. [foll.]

**bě'lly. 1.** *n.* Cavity of the body with stomach, bowels, and other contents, abdomen; stomach; body as needing food; womb; front of body from waist to groin; cavity or bulging part of anything. **2.** *v.t. & i.* Swell out (*sails belly out, are bellied out by wind*). **3.** ~**ache**, (*n.*) colic, (*v.i.*) complain whiningly; ~**button**, (colloq.) navel; ~**-dance**, oriental dance by woman with movements of belly; ~**-laugh** (deep, unrestrained); ~**ful** (-ŏol) *n.*, as much as or more than one wants esp. of fighting. [E, = bag]

**belŏ'ng** *v.i.* Be rightly assigned *to* (as duty, right, possession, accompaniment, example, part, inhabitant, etc.); ~ **to**, be member of (club, family, social class, etc.); be rightly placed or classified (*in, under*); fit a specified environment etc.; ~**ings** (-z) *n.pl.*, person's movable property or luggage. [BE-, obs. *long* belong]

**belŏ'ved. 1.** *a.* (-ŭ'vĭd) & *p.p.* (-ŭ'vd). Much loved (*my beloved son*; *was beloved by or of all*). **2.** *n.* (-ŭ'vĭd). Beloved person, darling. [BE-]

**below'** (-ō). **1.** *adv.* At, to, a lower point; downstream; downstairs; under deck (*go below*); (rhet.) on earth, in hell; at foot of page, farther on in book etc. **2.** *prep.* Lower in position, amount, degree, rank, etc., than (*below* STAIRS, *the surface*; *sums below £5*); covered by; downstream from; at or to greater depth than; unworthy of. [BY, LOW[2]]

**belt. 1.** *n.* Strip of leather etc. worn round waist or like baldric (HIT *below the belt*; **under** one's ~, eaten, or otherwise secured); mark of rank of earl or knight or boxing etc. champion; encircling strip of colour etc.; region; endless strap connecting pulleys; (sl.) heavy blow. **2.** *v.t. & i.* Put belt round; fasten *on* with belt; mark with belt of colour etc.;

thrash with belt; (sl.) move rapidly; ~ **out**, (sl.) utter forcibly; ~ **up**, (colloq.) wear seat-belt, (sl.) be quiet. [E]

**belu'ga** (-ōō'-) n. (Caviare from) a large sturgeon; white whale. [Russ.]

**bě'lvédère** n. Raised turret to view scenery from. [It., = beautiful view]

**běly'ing.** See BELIE.

**B.E.M.** abbr. British Empire Medal.

**běmoa'n** v.t. Lament. [BE-]

**běmū'se** (-z) v.t. Stupefy; make (person) confused. [BE-, MUSE¹]

**běnch** n. Long seat of wood or stone; seat across boat; judge's seat; lawcourt (‖**King's, Queen's, B~**, a division of the High Court of Justice; **be on the ~**, be a judge or magistrate); working-table of carpenter etc. or in laboratory; ~**-mark**, surveyor's mark at point in line of levels, (fig.) criterion, point of reference; ‖~**er** n., senior member of one of the Inns of Court. [E]

**běnd¹. 1.** v.t. & i. (bent, exc. in bended KNEE). Force (thing that was straight) into curve or angle; modify (rules etc.) to suit oneself; receive curved or angular shape; bring to bear (energies, efforts, oneself, etc., on, to), (in pass.) be determined (on thing or doing); (sl.) make illicit or dishonest; attach (cable etc.) with knot; turn (steps) in new direction; incline from vertical (bend over BACKWARDS); submit, bow, (to, before); force to submit; **catch** person ~**ing**, (colloq.) take him at disadvantage; **be'ntwood** (artificially curved for chairs etc.). **2.** n. Bending, curve (**round the ~**, colloq., crazy); bent part of thing; ~**('er)**, (sl.) spree (in pl., colloq.) (symptoms of) caisson disease. [E]

**běnd²** n. (Naut.) kind of knot; (Her.) diagonal stripe (~ **sinister**, sign of bastardy). [E (BIND)]

**běnea'th** adv. & prep. Below, under, (now arch. or literary, exc. as foll.): ~ **contempt**, one's **notice**, etc., not worth despising etc.; **marry ~ one**, marry person of lower status; **conduct** etc. **is ~** person, is unworthy of). [E (BE-, NETHER)]

**běnědi'ct|ion** n. Utterance of blessing esp. at table or at end of church service; a blessing; ~**ory** a., of or expressing benediction; **B~ine¹** n., monk or nun of order founded by St. Benedict; ~**ine²** (-ēn) n., herb-flavoured brandy liqueur made orig. by such monks. [F f. L (benedico bless)]

**běně|fǎ'ction** n. Doing good; charitable gift; **bě'néfàctor** n., one who has given friendly aid, patron or donor; **bě'néfàctrèss** n.; **běně'-fĭc** a. (-ically), having favourable influence; **bě'néfĭce** n., church living; **běné'fĭcent** a., doing good, actively kind; **běné'fĭcence** n.; ~**fĭ'cial** (-shǎl) a. (-lly), advantageous, (Law) of, having use or benefit of property etc.; ~**fĭ'ciarў** (-sherĭ) n., holder of church living, receiver of benefits as heir etc. [L (bene well, facio do)]

**bě'néfĭt. 1.** n. Advantage (**for the ~ of**, on behalf of, iron. for the instruction or disadvantage of; **the ~ of the doubt**, assumption of innocence rather than guilt); allowance under insurance or social security; game, theatre-performance, etc., of which proceeds go to particular player; ~**club**, ~**society**, (for mutual insurance against illness or effects of old age). **2.** v.t. (*or -tt-). Do good to; receive benefit (by, from). [F f. L benefactum (prec.)]

**Bě'nélŭx** n. Belgium, the Netherlands, and Luxemburg as regional economic group. [Belgium, Netherlands, Luxemburg]

**běně'volen|t** a. Desirous of doing good; charitable (benevolent fund); kind and helpful; ~**ce** n. [F f. L bene volens well wishing]

**Běnga'lĭ** (-nggaw'lĭ). a. & n. (Native, language) of Bengal. [place]

**běnī'ghtéd** (-nī't-) a. Overtaken by night; involved in intellectual or moral darkness. [BE-]

**běnī'gn** (-ī'n) a. Gracious, mild, gentle; fortunate, salutary; (of disease) mild, not malignant; **bě-nī'gnant** a., kindly esp. to inferiors, gracious, salutary, beneficial, (of disease) benign; **běnī'gnancў** n.; **běnī'gnitў** n., (esp.) kindliness. [F f. L benignus]

**bě'nĭson** (-z-) n. (arch.) A blessing. [F f. L benedictio BENEDICTION]

**běnt¹** n. Stiff-stemmed grass; (also **be'nnet**) stiff flower-stalk of grass, old stalk of grass; unenclosed pasture. [E]

**běnt²** n. Inclination, bias, (**to the top of one's ~**, to heart's content); **běnt³**, see BEND¹. [BEND¹]

**Bě'nthamĭsm** (-ta-) n. (Philosophy with) greatest happiness of greatest number as guiding principle of ethics. [*Bentham*, person]

**bĕ′nth|ŏs** *n.* Flora and fauna found at sea- or lake-bottom; **~ĭc** *a.* [Gk, = depth of sea]

*ben trovato* (bĕn trovah′tō) *a.* (Of anecdote) well invented, plausible. [It., = well found]

**bĕ′ntwŏŏd.** See BEND[1].

**bĕnŭ′mb** (-m) *v.t.* Make numb or torpid; paralyse (mind, action). [BE-]

**Bĕ′nzĕdrĭne** (*or* -ēn) *n.* Amphetamine. [P]

**bĕ′nzēne** *n.* Aromatic liquid hydrocarbon used as solvent etc.; **bĕ′nzine** (-ēn) *n.,* mixture of liquid hydrocarbons got from petroleum and used as cleansing agent; **bĕ′nzŏĭn** *n.,* aromatic resin of an E. Asian tree; **bĕnzŏ′ĭc** *a.*; **bĕ′nzŏle** *n.,* (unrefined) benzene. [*benzoin* F f. Arab. *lubān jāwī* incense of Java]

**bĕquea′th** (-dh) *v.t.* Leave by will (personal estate *to* person; cf. DEVISE); transmit to posterity; **bĕquĕ′st** *n.,* bequeathing, thing bequeathed. [E (BE-, QUOTH)]

**bĕrā′te** *v.t.* Scold. [BE-]

**Bĕr′ber** *n. & a.* (Member, language) of N. Afr. races including aboriginal races of Barbary. [Arab.]

**bĕr′berĭs** *n.* Barberry shrub. [L]

**berceuse** (bārsĕr′z) *n.* Cradle-song; piece of music in this style. [F]

**bĕrea′ve** *v.t.* **1.** (bere′ft). Rob, deprive, (*of* life, hope, etc.). **2.** (~d). Leave desolate; (of death etc.) deprive *of* child, wife, etc.; **~ment** (-vm-) *n.* [E (REAVE)]

**bĕ′ret** (-rā, -rĭ) *n.* Round flat felt or cloth cap. [F; cf. BIRETTA]

**bĕrg** *n.* Iceberg. [abbr.]

**bĕr′gamŏt** *n.* A citrus tree; perfume got from its fruit; an aromatic herb. [*Bergamo,* place]

**bĕrĭbĕ′rĭ** *n.* A deficiency disease (esp. in the tropics). [Sinh.]

**Berks.** *abbr.* Berkshire.

**Bermū′da** *n.* ~ **shorts,** ~**s,** knee-length shorts. [place]

**bĕ′rrў** *n.* Small roundish juicy stoneless fruit; (Bot.) fruit with seeds enclosed in pulp (e.g. tomato, banana). [E]

**bĕr′sĕrk. 1.** *n.* Norse warrior fighting with mad frenzy. **2.** *a.* (or bersĕr′k, -z-). Wild, frenzied; **go berserk,** act wildly. [Icel., = bear-coat]

**bĕrth. 1.** *n.* Sea-room (give a **wide** ~ **to,** avoid); room for ship to swing at anchor; ship's place at wharf; sleeping-place in ship, train, etc.; situation, appointment. **2.** *v.t. & i.* Moor (ship) in berth; (of ship) come to mooring; provide sleeping-berth for. [BEAR[2]]

**bĕ′rўl** *n.* Kind of (esp. pale-green) transparent precious stone; mineral species including this and emerald; **bĕrў′llĭum** *n.,* very light hard white metallic element. [F f. L f. Gk]

**bĕsee′ch** *v.t.* (-sought *pr.* -saw′t). Entreat (person *to* do, *for* thing); ask earnestly for. [BE-, SEEK]

**bĕsĕ′t** *v.t.* (-tt-; beset). Hem in, assail, (person); (of temptation, difficulties, etc.) assail persistently (*his besetting sin*). [E (BE-)]

**bĕsĭ′de** *prep.* At the side of, close to; compared with; wide of (*is beside the* POINT, *the question*); ~ oneself, out of one's wits); **bĕsĭ′des** (-dz), (*prep.*) in addition to, else than, otherwise than; (*adv.*) also, as well, else. [BY, SIDE)]

**bĕsĭe′ge** *v.t.* Lay siege to; crowd round; assail with requests. [BE-]

**bĕsmear′** *v.t.* Smear with greasy or sticky stuff; **bĕsmĭr′ch** *v.t.,* soil, discolour, (fig.) sully. [BE-]

**bĕ′som** (-z-) *n.* Broom made up of twigs tied round stick. [E]

**bĕsŏ′t** *v.t.* (-tt-) (usu. in *p.p.*) Stupefy mentally or morally; infatuate; **besought,** see BESEECH; **bĕspă′ngle** (-nggel) *v.t.,* cover with spangles; **bĕspă′tter** *v.t.,* spatter all over, cover with abuse etc. [BE-]

**bĕspea′k** *v.t.* (-spo′ke; -spo′ke as *adj.,* otherwise -spo′ken). Engage beforehand; order (goods); suggest, be evidence of; bespoke tailor, coat, etc., (seller of) clothes made to order. [E (BE-)]

**bĕspĕ′ctacled** (-kld) *a.* Wearing spectacles; **bĕspo′ke(n),** see BESPEAK; **bĕsprĭ′nkle** *v.t.,* sprinkle (*with, over*). [BE-]

**bĕst** *a., adv., n.,* & *v.* **1.** *a.* (superl. of GOOD). Of most excellent or desirable kind (*the best friend I have*; *the best bedroom; the best thing would be to leave*); ~ **end,** rib end of lamb's neck for cooking; **put one's** ~ **foot forward,** go at full pace, exert all one's efforts; ~ **man,** bridegroom's chief attendant at wedding; ~ **part,** most *of*; ~ **seller,** (author of) book with large sale. **2.** *adv.* (superl. of WELL[2]). In best manner; to greatest degree; most usefully (*is best ignored*); **as** ~ **one can,** as well as one is able to under the circumstances; **had ~**, would find it wisest to. **3.** *n.* That which is best; chief merit or advantage (*bring out the best in him*); victory in fight or argument (*get the best of it*; *give person best*; **~ of three games**, winning 2); **all the ~** (expr. goodwill); **at ~**, in the most hopeful view; **at its**, one's, **~**, in the best state; **do one's ~** (to win etc.), do all one can; **make the ~ of**, be as effective or contented as possible with (**Sunday**) **~**, best clothes; **to the ~ of** one's ability, as well as one can do; **with the ~** (of them), as well as anyone. **4.** *v.t.* (colloq.) Defeat, outwit. [E]

**be'stial** *a.* (**~ly**). Of or like beast(s); brutish (*bestial ferocity, lust*); **běstiă'lĭtў** *n.*, (esp.) copulation of person and animal; **~īze** *v.t.*; **be'stiarў** *n.*, medieval treatise on beasts. [F f. L (BEAST)]

**běstir'** *v. refl.* (**-rr-**). Exert, rouse, one*self*; **běstow'** (-ō') *v.t.*, confer (thing *on, upon*, person) as gift, lodge, deposit; **běstow'al** (-ō'ạl) *n.*; **bestrew'** (-rōō') *v.t.* (*p.p.* **-ew'ed, -ew'n**), strew (surface *with*), lie scattered over; **běstri'de** *v.t.* (-o'de; -i'dden), sit astride on, stand astride over. [BE-]

**bět. 1.** *v.i.* & *t.* (**-tt-**; **bet, be'tted**). Risk one's money etc. against another's, risk (amount) thus, on result of doubtful event, (*on, against*, result or competitor, *that* thing will happen); **I ~**, (colloq.) I feel sure; **you ~**, (colloq.) you may be sure; **~'ting-shop**, bookmaker's shop or office. **2.** *n.* Such engagement (*make a bet*); sum of money bet; (colloq.) opinion (*my bet is that*); **good ~**, person or course of action likely to succeed. [orig. uncert.]

**bē'ta** *n.* Second Gk letter (B, β) = b; second-class mark; **~ particles, rays**, fast-moving electrons emitted by radioactive substances (orig. regarded as rays). [L f. Gk]

**bětā'ke** *v. refl.* (**-too'k; -ta'ken**). **~** oneself to, go to (place, person). [BE-]

**bě'tatrŏn** *n.* (Phys.) Apparatus for accelerating electrons in circular path. [BETA, (ELEC)TRON]

**bě'tel** *n.* Leaf of a plant, chewed by Indians with areca nut; **~-nut**, areca nut. [Port. f. Malayalam]

**bête noire** (bāt nwär) *n.* Particularly disliked person or thing [F, lit. black beast]

**běthi'nk** *v. refl.* (**-thou'ght** *pr.* -thaw't). **~ oneself**, reflect, stop to think, be reminded by reflection (*of, that, how*). [BE-] (E)

**běti'de** *v.i.* & *t.* (*inf.* or 3 *sing. pres. subj.*) Happen (*whatever betide* or *may betide*); happen to (*woe betide him who* etc., orig. a curse, now usu. as warning etc.). [BE-, *tide* befall]

**běti'mes** (-mz) *adv.* (literary). In good time, early. [BY]

**bêtise** (bātē'z) *n.* Foolish, ill-timed, remark or action. [F]

**bětō'ken** *v.t.* Be a sign of, indicate. [E (BE-)]

**bě'tonў** *n.* A purple-flowered plant. [F f. L]

**bětoo'k.** See BETAKE.

**bětray'** *v.t.* Give up (person etc. *to* enemy), reveal, treacherously; be disloyal to; lead astray; reveal involuntarily; be evidence of; **~al** *n.* [BE-, obs. *tray* f. F f. L (*trado* hand over)]

**bětrō'th** (-dh) *v.t.* Bind with promise to marry; **~al** *n.*; **~ed** (-dhd) *a.* & *n.* [BE-, TRUTH]

**bě'tter¹** *a., adv., n.,* & *v.* **1.** *a.* (*compar.* of GOOD). Of more excellent or desirable kind; partly or fully recovered from illness; **~ feelings, conscience**; **~ half**, (joc.) wife; **~ part**, most *of*; **no ~ than**, practically, merely. **2.** *adv.* (*compar.* of WELL²). In better manner; to greater degree; more usefully (*is better ignored*); GO¹ *one better*; **had ~**, would find it wiser to; *better* OFF; **know ~** (than), not be so foolish or ill-mannered (as); THINK *better of.* **3.** *n.* That which is better (*change for the better*); **get the ~ of**, defeat, outwit; person more skilful etc. than oneself; (in *pl.*) persons of higher rank than oneself. **4.** *v.t.* Improve; surpass (feat); **~ oneself**, get better situation etc.; **~ment** *n.* (esp. of property-value). [E]

**bě'tter²** *n.* One who bets. [BET]

**bětwee'n. 1.** *prep.* In, into, along, or across, a space, line, interval, or route, bounded by two or more points, lines, dates, etc., (*between York and Leeds, Monday and Friday*; READ *between the lines*); separating (*difference between right and wrong*); to and from (*runs between London and Oxford*); owing to each of, shared by, confined to (**~ you and me, ~ ourselves**, in confidence); taking one and rejecting the other of (*choose between*); ~ **times, whiles,** in the intervals. **2.** *adv.* Between two or more points etc.; (in) ~, intermediately in place, time, amount, or order; separated (FAR *between*). [E (BY, TWO)]

**bĕtwĭ'xt** *prep.* & *adv.* (arch.) = BETWEEN; ~ **and between,** (colloq.) intermediate(ly).

**bĕ'vel. 1.** *n.* Joiner's, mason's, tool for adjusting angles; slope from horizontal or vertical; sloping edge or surface. **2.** *v.t.* & *i.* (‖-ll-). Reduce (square edge) to a bevel; not be at right angle; ~ **wheel** (with cogs oblique to axis). [F]

**bĕ'verage** *n.* (formal, joc.) Liquid meant for drinking. [F f. L (*bibo* drink)]

**bĕ'vy** *n.* A company (*of ladies, roes, quails, larks*). [orig. unkn.]

**bĕwai'l** *v.t.* Wail over, mourn for. [BE-]

**bĕwā're** *v.i.* & *t.* (*imper.* or *inf.*). Take heed, be cautious, (*beware of pickpockets!*; *I will, let him, beware*; *beware lest* or *how you provoke him*); be cautious of. [BE, *ware* cautious]

**bĕwi'lder** *v.t.* Perplex, confuse; ~**ment** *n.* [BE-, obs. *wilder* lose one's way]

**bĕwi'tch** *v.t.* Cast magic spell on; enchant, delight exceedingly. [BE-]

**bey** (bā) *n.* (Hist.) Turkish governor. [Turk.]

**bĕyŏ'nd** *adv.*, *prep.*, & *n.* **1.** *adv.* At or to the farther side, farther on, outside. **2.** *prep.* At or to the farther side of; outside the range of (*beyond dispute, repair*); ~ **measure,** exceedingly; **it is ~ me,** I cannot understand it); more than. **3.** *n.* The ~, the future life, the unknown; **the back of ~,** very remote place. [E (YON)]

**bĕ'zel** *n.* Groove for watch-glass etc.; rim holding glass etc. cover. [F]

**bĕzi'que** (–ē'k) *n.* A card-game for two players. [F]

**b.f.** *abbr.* ‖Bloody fool; bold face; brought forward.

‖**B'ham** *abbr.* Birmingham.

**bhăng** (bă-) *n.* Indian hemp; its leaves smoked, chewed, etc., as narcotic and intoxicant. [Port. f. Skr.]

**b.h.p.** *abbr.* brake horsepower.

**bi-** *pref.* (Thing) having 2 (*bilateral, biplane*); doubly (*biconcave*); (Bot., Zool., of division and subdivision) twice over (*bipinnate*); (Chem.) substance having a double proportion of the acid etc. indicated by the

simple word (*bicarbonate*); appearing twice in or once in two (*biannual, half-yearly,* cf. BIENNIAL; *bi-weekly*). [L]

**bī'as. 1.** *n.* (In game of bowls) bowl's oblique course due to its lopsided form; such form; predisposition, prejudice, (*have a bias towards*); distortion of result by neglected factor; (Dressmaking etc.) oblique direction (*cloth is cut on the bias*; ~ **binding,** strip so cut). **2.** *v.t.* (-s-, -ss-). Give a bias to; prejudice. [F]

**bĭb. 1.** *v.i.* & *t.* (-bb-). (arch.) Drink much or often, tipple. **2.** *n.* Cloth etc. put under child's chin to keep clothes clean; apron-top (one's **best ~ and tucker,** best clothes); ~**cock,** tap with bent nozzle. [orig. uncert.]

**Bī'ble** *n.* (Copy of) Christian scriptures of Old and New Testament; scriptures of other religion; authoritative book; ~ **oath** (taken on Bible); **bĭ'blĭcal** *a.* (-lly), of or in the Bible, resembling Bible language. [F f. L f. Gk *biblia* books]

**bĭbliŏ'graph|y** *n.* History or description of books, their editions, etc., list of books of any author, printer, country, or subject; ~**er** *n.,* writer of bibliography; **bĭbliŏgră'phĭc(al)** *adjs.* (-ically); ~**b'liophĭle** *n.,* lover of books, collector of books. [F f. L f. Gk (prec.)]

**bī'bŭlous** *a.* Addicted to alcoholic drink. [L (*bibo* drink)]

**bica'meral** *a.* With 2 (legislative) chambers. [BI-, L CAMERA chamber]

**bicĕntĕ'nary** (or -sĕ'nti-), **bicĕntĕ'nnial,** *ns.* (Festival of) 200th anniversary. [BI-]

**bi'cĕps** *n.* Muscle with double head or attachment, esp. that which bends elbow; muscularity. [L (*caput* head)]

**bĭ'cker** *v.i.* Quarrel, wrangle; (of stream, rain, etc.) brawl, patter. [orig. unkn.]

**bicŭ'spĭd. 1.** *a.* Two-cusped. **2.** *n.* Any of the 8 bicuspid teeth (between molars and canines). [CUSP]

**bī'cycl|e. 1.** *n.* Two-wheeled pedal--driven vehicle; ~ **clip** (to confine trousers at ankle). **2.** *v.i.* Ride on bicycle; ~**ĭst** *n.* [CYCLE]

**bĭd. 1.** *v.t.* & *i.* (-dd-; bid). (Esp. at auction) offer price, offer (a certain price) *for*; offer to do work etc. for stated price; (Cards) make bid (of or in); **~ fair to** do, show promise of doing. **2.** *v.t.* (arch., poet.; **-dd-**; **bade** *pr.* băd, bid; bid, bi'dden). Command to, tell to, (*do as you are bid*); proclaim (defiance); invite; salute (person) with *welcome* etc.; **~'ding-prayer** (inviting congregation to join in); **~'dable** *a.*, obedient. **3.** *n.* Offer of price, esp. at auction (**make a ~ for**, fig., attempt to secure); (Cards) statement of number of tricks player proposes to win; attempt, effort. **4.** **~'ding** *n.*, (esp.) offers at auction, bids made, a command. [E]

**bide** *v.t.* **~ one's time**, await best opportunity. [E]

**bi'det** (bē'dā) *n.* Low washing-basin that one can sit astride on. [F, = pony]

**biě'nnïal. 1.** *a.* (**~ly**). Lasting, recurring every, 2 years. **2.** *n.* Plant that springs one year and flowers and dies the next. [L (*annus* year)]

**bier** *n.* Movable stand on which coffin or corpse rests. [E]

**biff.** (sl.) **1.** *n.* Smart blow. **2.** *v.t.* Strike (person). [imit.]

**bi'fïd** *a.* Divided by deep cleft into 2 parts. [L (*findo* cleave)]

**bifō'cal. 1.** *a.* Having 2 foci (esp. of combined distant and near vision spectacles). **2.** *n.* (in *pl.*) Bifocal spectacles. [FOCUS]

**bi'furcāte** *v.t.* & *i.* Divide into 2 branches, fork; **bifurcā'tion** *n.*, fork of branch etc., forking(-point), either member of fork. [L (FORK)]

**big. 1.** *a.* (-gg-). Of considerable size, amount, intensity, etc.; of large(st) size (*big drum, game, toe*); (more) grown up (*big sister*); advanced in pregnancy (esp. of animals, or fig.); important (*the Big Four; the big race*); boastful (*big words*); (colloq.) generous, ambitious (*have big ideas*), outstanding (*my big moment*). **2.** *adv.* (-gg-). In a big manner. **3.** ‖**Big Ben**, great bell, clock, and tower, of Houses of Parliament; **too ~ for one's boots,** (sl.) conceited; **Big Brother,** all-powerful seemingly benevolent dictator; **~ bug, cheese, name, noise, pot, shot, \*wheel,** (sl.) bigwig; **~ business,** commerce on grand scale; **~ end** (of connecting-rod, encircling crankpin); **~ head,** (colloq.) conceit(ed person); **~-hearted,** generous, **~ money,** large amounts, high profit or pay; **~ time,** (sl.) highest rank among

entertainers etc.; **~ top,** main tent at circus; **in a ~ way,** with great enthusiasm, display, etc.; **~'wig,** important person. [orig. unkn.]

**bi'gam|ў** *n.* Crime of making second marriage while first is still valid; **~ous** *a.*, guilty of or involving bigamy; **~ist** *n.*, such person. [F f. L f. Gk (*gamos* marriage)]

**bight** (bīt) *n.* Loop of rope; recess of coast, bay. [E]

**bi'got** *n.* Obstinate and intolerant adherent of a creed or view; **~ěd** *a.*, that is (typical of) a bigot; **~rў** *n.*, conduct, state, of a bigot. [F]

*bijou* (bē'zhōō). **1.** *n.* (*pl.* **~x** *pr.* same). Jewel, trinket. **2.** *a.* Small and elegant. [F]

**bike** *n.*, & *v.i.* (colloq.) (Ride on) bicycle or motor cycle. [abbr.]

**biki'nï** (-kē'-) *n.* Woman's scanty two-piece beach garment. [place]

**bilā'teral** *a.* (**~ly**). Of, on, with, 2 sides; existing etc. between 2 parties. [BI-]

**bi'lberrў** *n.* (Small blue fruit of) a N. European shrub, growing on heaths etc. [Scand.]

**bile** *n.* Bitter fluid secreted by liver to aid digestion; derangement of bile; peevishness. [F f. L *bilis*]

**bilge. 1.** *n.* Nearly horizontal part of ship's bottom, inside or out; **~-(-water),** foul water in bilge; (sl.) nonsense, rubbish. **2.** *v.t.* & *i.* Stave-in the bilge of; spring leak in the bilge. [BULGE]

**bilhăr'z|ïa** *n.* Tropical flatworm parasitic in human pelvis; **~ï'asïs** *n.*, chronic disease caused by this. [*Bilharz,* person]

**bi'liarў** (-lyerï) *a.* Of the bile. [F (BILE)]

**bili'ngual** (-nggw-) *a.* (**~ly**). Of, in, speaking, 2 languages. [L (*lingua* tongue)]

**bi'lious** (-lyŭs) *a.* Liable to, affected by, due to, derangement of the bile; peevish. [F f. L (BILE)]

**-bi'litў** *suf.* forming *ns.* of quality corresp. to *adjs.* in *-ble*. [L]

**bilk** *v.t.* Evade payment of (creditor, bill); cheat. [orig. uncert.]

**bill**[1] *n.* Halberd with hook instead of blade; **~('hook),** concave-edged pruning-instrument. [E]

**bill**[2]**. 1.** *n.* Beak (esp. if slender, flat, or weak, and of pigeons and web-footed birds); narrow promontory; point of anchor-fluke. **2.** *v.i.* (Of doves) stroke bill with bill (persons ~ **and coo**, exchange caresses). [E]

**bill**[3]. **1.** *n.* Draft of proposed law; (Law) written statement of case (TRUE *bill*); note of charges for goods supplied or services rendered; poster, placard; (programme (of) entertainment; *banknote; ~ **(of exchange)**, written order to pay sum on given date; ~ **of fare**, menu; **clean ~ of health**, certificate of no disease on ship or in port at time of sailing, (fig.) of no defect on examination; ~'**board**, large outdoor board for advertisements; ~'**poster**, ~'**sticker**, one who pastes up placards. **2.** *v.t.* Announce, put in programme; advertise *as*; send note of charges to. [AF f. L *bulla* seal]

**bi'llabŏng** *n.* (Austral.) River branch forming backwater. [Aboriginal]

**bi'llĕt**[1]. **1.** *n.* Order requiring person to board and lodge soldier etc.; place where troops etc. are lodged; destination; appointment, job. **2.** *v.t.* Quarter (soldiers etc. *on* town or householder, *in, at*). [AF dim. of BILL[3]]

**bi'llĕt**[2] *n.* Thick piece of firewood; small metal bar; (Archit.) short roll at intervals in hollow moulding. [F dim. of *bille* tree-trunk]

**billet-doux** (bilĭdōō′) *n.* (joc.) Love-letter. [F, = sweet note]

**bi'lliard|s** (-lyerdz) *n.* Game with cues and 3 balls on cloth-covered table; ‖**bar ~s**, variant in which balls are struck into holes on table; ~**-table**, on which billiards is played. [F (BILLET[2])]

**bi'llingsgāte** (-z-) *n.* Violent abuse. [ref. to language (for which the market was once notorious) in B~ fish-market]

**bi'llion** (-lyon) *a. & n. (pl. ~, ~s*; for pl. usage see HUNDRED). ‖Million millions; thousand millions; ~**th** *a. & n.* [F (BI-, MILLION)]

**bi'llow** (-ō). **1.** *n.* Great wave; **the ~(s)**, (poet.) the sea; ~**y** *a.* **2.** *v.i.* Rise, move, in billows. [N]

**bi'lly** *n.* ~**(can)**, tin or enamelled container serving as kettle etc., orig. in Austral. and N.Z. [orig. uncert.]

**bi'lly-goat** *n.* Male goat. [*Billy*, pet-form of *William*]

**bi'lly-ō** *n.* (colloq.) *Fighting, raining, like ~* (fiercely, very hard). [orig. unkn.]

**bimĕtǎ'llic** *a.* Of two metals. [F

**bĭn** *n.* Receptacle for corn, coal, rubbish, litter, bottled wine, etc.; canvas receptacle used in hop-picking. [E]

**bī'narў** *a.* Dual, of or involving two(s); ~ **compound** (Chem., of two elements or radicals); ~ **digit**, one of two used in binary scale; ~ **measure** (Mus., of 2 beats to bar); *binary* SCALE[3] of notation; ~ **star**, system of two stars revolving round each other. [L (*bini* two together)]

**bĭnd. 1.** *v.t. & i.* (**bound**). Tie, fasten, attach (*to, on*; things together); put in bonds; obstruct (*snow-bound*); hold together, (cause to) cohere; constipate; be obligatory, impose constraint or duty, on; ~ **(over)**, subject to promise or legal obligation; indenture as apprentice; ~ **(up)**, bandage; encircle (head etc.) *with*, wreathe (material) *round, on*; edge with braid, iron, etc.; fasten sheets of (book) into cover; (sl.) complain; ~'**weed**, convolvulus, honeysuckle; **bound**, required by duty, certain, *to* do; **I'll be bound**, I guarantee truth of (statement); **I feel certain; bound up**, closely associated *with*; **bou'nden** [arch. *p.p.*], obligatory (duty). **2.** *n.* (Mus.) tie; bine; (sl.) nuisance. **3.** ~'**er** *n.*, (esp.) bookbinder, cementing substance, machine for reaping and binding grain into sheaves, loose cover for papers; ~'**erў** *n.*, bookbinder's workshop; ~'**ing**, (*a.*) obligatory (*on*), (*n.*, esp.) book-cover, braid etc. for edging. [E]

**bīne** *n.* Flexible shoot; stem of climbing plant esp. hop.

**binge** (-nj) *n.* (sl.) Drinking-bout, spree. [dial. *binge* to soak]

**bĭ'ngō** (-ngg-) *n.* Game in which numbers are drawn at random and corresponding numbered squares on cards are to be marked off. [perh. f. winner's excl.]

**bi'nnacle** *n.* Box of ship's compass. [Sp. or Port. f. L *habitaculum* lodge]

**bĭnŏ'cūlar. 1.** *a.* For two eyes. *n.* (usu. in *pl.*) Binocular field- or opera-glasses. [as BINARY, OCULAR]

**bīnō'mial** *a.* (~**ly**) *& n.* Algebraic sum or difference) of 2 terms (~ **theorem**, formula giving any power of binomial); (also **bīnō'minal** *a.*) (name) composed of 2 names (esp. in scientific nomenclature by genus and species). [F or L (Gk *nomos* part; NOMINAL)]

**bio-** *in comb.* Life (biography); biological; of living beings. [Gk *bios* course of life]

**bĭochĕ'mĭstrỹ** (-k-) *n.* Chemistry of living organisms; **~ical** *a.*; **~ist** *n.*; **bĭŏdĕgrā'dable** *a.,* capable of being decomposed by bacteria; **bĭŏfee'dbàck** *n.,* use of feedback of normally automatic body functions to gain voluntary control of them; **bĭogĕ'nèsis** *n.,* hypothesis that living matter arises only from living matter, synthesis of substances by living matter, hypothetical development of living matter from complex inanimate substances.

**bĭŏ'graph|ỹ** *n.* Written life of a person; such lives as branch of literature; **~er** *n.*; **bĭogrà'phĭcal** *a.* (-lly). [F or L f. Gk (BIO-)]

**bĭŏ'log|ỹ** *n.* Science of physical life of animals and plants; **bĭolŏ'gĭcal** *a.* (-lly); **~ical clock,** innate mechanism controlling rhythmic activities of an organism; **~ical warfare,** involving use of living organisms esp. disease germs; **~ist** *n.* [F f. G (BIO-)]

**bi'ŏpsỹ** *n.* Examination of tissue cut from living body. [F (BIO-, OPTIC)]

**bĭŏ'sphēre** *n.* Regions of earth's crust and atmosphere occupied by living matter. [G (BIO-)]

**bĭŏ'tĭc** *a.* (~ally). Relating to life or living things. [F or L f. Gk (*bios* life)]

**bipàrtĭsà'n** (-z-; *or* -ăr'-) *a.* Of or involving 2 (political) parties. [PARTISAN]

**bipàr'tĭte** *a.* Consisting of 2 parts; in which 2 parties are concerned (*bipartite treaty*). [L *bipartio* divide into two parts]

**bi'pĕd** *a. & n.* Two-footed (animal); **bi'pĕdal** *a.* [L (PEDAL)]

**bi'plāne** *n.* Aeroplane with 2 sets of wings; **bipō'lar** *a.,* having 2 poles or extremities. [BI-]

**bĭrch. 1.** *n.* A smooth-barked northern forest tree; its wood; **~(-rod),** bundle of birch twigs for flogging; **~'en** *a.,* of birch. **2.** *v.t.* Flog with birch. [E]

**bĭrd** *n.* Feathered vertebrate with two wings and two feet; game-bird; (sl.) young woman; (colloq.) person; **~ in the hand,** something certain; **~ is, has, flown,** prisoner etc. has

escaped; **~ of paradise** (with brilliant plumage); **~ of passage,** migrant, (fig.) transient visitor; **~s of a feather,** people of like character; **for the ~s,** (sl.) uninteresting; **get the ~,** (sl.) be dismissed or derided; **kill two ~s with one stone,** achieve two aims at once; **like a ~,** without difficulty; **little ~,** unnamed informant; **~-bath,** basin with water for birds to bathe in; **~'lime,** sticky substance spread to catch birds; **~'seed,** special seeds for caged birds; **~'s-eye view,** general view from above *of* town etc. or (fig.) *of* subject; **~-table,** platform on which food for birds is placed; **~-watcher,** observer of birds in natural surroundings; **~'ie** *n.,* little bird, (Golf) hole played in one under par or bogey. [E]

**bĭrĕ'tta** *n.* Square cap of R.C. and other clergymen. [It. or Sp. dim. f. L *birrus* cape]

**Bī'rŏ** *n.* (*pl.* **~s**). (Make of) ball-point pen. [P (person)]

**bĭrth** *n.* Emergence of young from mother's body (**give ~ to,** produce (young) thus, lit. or fig.); origin, beginning; parentage, descent, inherited position; noble lineage; **~ certificate,** official document with date and place of person's birth; **~-control,** (practice of) methods of preventing undesired pregnancy; **~'day,** (anniversary of) day of one's birth (**||~day honours,** titles etc. given on sovereign's official birthday; **~day suit,** joc., state of nakedness); **~'mark,** unusual (esp. brown or red) mark on one's body at or from birth; **~'place** (where one was born); **~ rate,** number of births per thousand of population per year; **~'right,** rights belonging to one by birth esp. as eldest son. [N]

**bĭ'scuit** (-kĭt) *n.* ||(Flat thin piece of) unleavened cake or bread, usu. dry and crisp, and often sweetened etc. (TAKE *the biscuit*); porcelain after firing but before glazing and painting; light-brown colour. [F f. L (*bis* twice, *coquo* to cook)]

**bĭsĕ'ct** *v.t.* Divide into 2 (prop. equal) parts; **~ion** *n.*; **~or** *n.,* bisecting line. [L *seco sect-* cut]

**bĭsĕ'xūal** (*or* -kshŏŏ-) *a.* Of 2 sexes; having both sexes in one individual; sexually attracted by members of both sexes; **~itỹ** (-ă'l-) *n.* [BI-]

**bĭ'shop** *n.* Clergyman consecrated

as governor of diocese and possessing powers of confirming, instituting, and ordaining; mitre-shaped chess piece; mulled and spiced wine; ~ **sleeve** (full, gathered at wrist); **~ric** n., office or diocese of bishop. [E f. L f. Gk *episkopos* overseer]

**bi'smuth** (-z-) n. Reddish-white metal used in alloys etc.; compound of it used medicinally. [L f. G]

**bi'son** n. (*pl.* same). Wild ox of Europe or America. [L f. Gmc]

**bisque**[1] (-k) n. Right of scoring unearned point at any stage of tennis or deducting a stroke at a hole in golf, or playing extra turn at croquet, etc. [F]

**bisque**[2] (-k) n. Unglazed white china for statuettes. [BISCUIT]

**bisque**[3] (-k) n. Rich soup made from shellfish etc. [F]

**bi'stort** n. Herb with spike of flesh--coloured flowers and twisted root. [F f. L (*tortus* twisted)]

**bi'stre** (-ter), **\*bi'ster**, n. Brown pigment from soot; its colour. [F]

**bi'strō** (or bē'-) n. (*pl.* ~s). Small bar or restaurant. [F]

**bit**[1] n. (Small) piece or quantity or portion (~ **by** ~, gradually; **~s and pieces**, odds and ends; **a** ~, colloq., somewhat; **a** ~ **of**, colloq., rather, a fair quantity of; **do** one's ~, colloq., contribute service or money; EVERY **bit** *as*; **not a** ~, colloq., not at all); short time or distance; small coin; small part in play or film; boring-piece of drill, cutting or gripping part of plane, pincers, etc.; mouthpiece of bridle (**take the** ~ **between** one's **teeth**, fig., escape from control). [E (BITE)]

**bit**[2] n. Unit of information expressed as choice between two possibilities. [*binary digit*]

**bit**[3]. See BITE.

**bitch. 1.** n. Female dog; female fox, otter, or wolf; (derog.) sly or spiteful woman or girl; (colloq.) unpleasant or difficult thing; **~y** a. (-iness), spiteful, ill-tempered. **2.** v.i. & t. Be spiteful or unfair (to); grumble; (colloq.) muddle. [E]

**bite. 1.** v.t. & i. (bit; **bi'tten**). Cut into, nip, with teeth; (of snake) sting; (of insect) sting and suck blood from; detach (*off, out*) with teeth; snap *at*; accept bait; penetrate, grip, have (desired) adverse effect; cause smarting pain, be pungent, (*biting wind, sarcasm*); (usu.

in *pass.*) swindle; (in *p.p.*) infected *with* enthusiasm etc.; ~ **back**, restrain (speech) by biting the lips; ~ person's **head off**, respond curtly or angrily; *bite* one's LIP, NAILS; ~ **off more than one can chew**, be too ambitious in attempting task; ~ **the dust**, (rhet.) fall and die; **something to ~ on**, enough to get grip or understanding; **what's biting** (colloq., worrying) **you? 2.** n. Act of, wound made by, piece detached by, biting; food to eat, small meal; taking of bait by fish; (fig.) incisiveness, pungency. [E]

**bi'tter. 1.** a. Tasting like wormwood or quinine, not sweet; (of beer) much flavoured with hops; causing or caused by or showing or feeling mental pain or resentment; virulent, relentless; biting, harsh; piercingly cold; **to the ~ end**, to last extremity [perh. orig. w. ref. to last part of cable round bitts; *bitter* PILL]; **~-sweet**, sweet with bitter after-taste or element, woody nightshade. **2.** n. ||Bitter beer; (in *pl.*) liquors containing wormwood etc. to promote appetite or digestion. [E]

**bi'ttern** n. Kind of marsh bird allied to heron, esp. one with booming note from male. [F *butor* f. L]

**bitts** n.*pl.* (Naut.) Pair of posts on deck for fastening cables. [LDu.]

**bi'tt| y** a. (~iness). Made up of unrelated bits, scrappy. [BIT[1]]

**bi'tum|en** n. Brown or black mixture of tarlike substances got from petroleum; **bitū'minous** a. (~**inous coal**, burning with smoky flame). [L]

**bi'valve. 1.** a. Two-valved; (of shellfish) with hinged double shell. **2.** n. Bivalve shellfish; oyster. [BI-]

**bi'vouac** (-vŏŏ-). **1.** n. Temporary encampment without tents etc. **2.** v.i. (-ck-). Remain (esp. overnight) in bivouac. [F f. G (BY, WATCH)]

**biz** n. (colloq.) Business. [abbr.]

**biză'rre** a. Of fantastic appearance or effect, eccentric, grotesque; **~rie** (-rerē) n., bizarre quality. [F]

**bk.** *abbr.* book.

**blăb** v.i. & t. (-bb-). Be indiscreet in talk, let things out; let out (secret). [imit.]

**blăck** a., n., & v. **1.** a. Opposite to white, colourless from absence or total absorption of light (like coal or soot); dark with no distinguishable colour (~ **in the face**, purple with exertion etc.); dark-skinned; (B~) of Negroes; (of sky etc.) dusky, gloomy; deadly, sinister, wicked; dismal, sulky (*black looks*); threatening (*things look black*); presenting tragedy in comic terms (*black humour*); (of goods etc.) not to be handled by workers on strike. **2.** *n.* Black colour or pigment; black clothes or material (*dressed in black*); black ball in snooker etc.; (player of) black men in chess etc.; credit side of account (*in the ~, solvent*); Negro. **3.** *v.t.* Make black; polish with blacking; declare (goods etc.) 'black'. **4.** ~**amoor**, Negro, dark-skinned person; ~ **and blue**, discoloured by bruises; ~ **and white**, (of film etc.) not in colour, (fig.) comprising only opposite extremes; *in ~ and white*, written or printed; ~ **art**, magic; ~ **ball** (used to reject candidate in ballot); ~**ball** *v.t.*, reject (candidate); ~**beetle**, common cockroach; ~**berry**, (dark fruit of) bramble; ~**bird**, a European song-bird; ~**board** (for writing etc. with chalk in schools etc.); *in black* BOOKS *of*; ~ **box**, flight-recorder in aircraft; ~ **bread**, coarse rye bread; ‖~ **cap** (Hist.), worn by judge in sentencing to death); ~'**cap**, bird with black-topped head; ‖~-**coat worker**, clerk etc. (opp. industrial worker); ~'**cock**, male black grouse; ~ **coffee** (without milk or cream); ‖**B~ Country**, smoky grimy district in Midlands; *black* CURRANT; *Black* DEATH; *black* DIAMONDS; ~ **dog**, sulks; ~ **eye** (with dark iris, or with bruise round it); ~'**fellow**, Austral. aboriginal; *black* FLAG[3]; ~'**fly**, aphid etc. infesting plants; *black* FRIAR; ~ **frost** (without hoar-frost); ~ **game**, **grouse**, a European GROUSE[1]; ~'**guard** (blǎ'gǎrd), (*n.* & *a.*) scoundrel(ly), foul-mouthed (person), (*v.t.*) abuse scurrilously, [orig. of household menials]; ~**guardly** (blǎ'gǎrdlǐ) *a.*; ~'**head**, bird with black head, black-topped pimple; ~ **hole**, (Astron.) region from which matter and radiation cannot escape, (Mil.) place of confinement for punishment); ~'**ice** (thin hard transparent); ~'**jack**, \*bludgeon, tarred-leather liquor-vessel, pirates' black flag; ~'**lead**, (polish with) graphite; ~'**leg**, (*n.*) person who refuses to join strike or trade-union, (*v.i.* & *t.*) act or injure thus; *black*

LEOPARD; ~ **letter**, old heavy style of type; ~ **list** (of persons in disfavour); ~'**list** *v.t.*, enter name of (person) on black list; *black* MAGIC; ~'**mail** *v.t.*, & *n.*, compel, compulsion, to make payment or action in return for concealment of discreditable secret, (fig.) use (of) threats or moral pressure [obs. *mail* rent]; B~ **Maria**, police vehicle for conveying prisoners; ~ **mark** (of discredit); ~ **market**, (place of) illegitimate traffic in officially controlled or scarce commodities; ~ **mass**, Requiem Mass, travesty of the Mass in worship of Satan; B~ **Monk**, Benedictine; ~ **out**, obliterate, obscure (windows etc.) so that no light is seen outside, undergo black-out; ~**out**, being blacked out, period when lights must be obscured, sudden darkening of theatre stage, loss of radio reception by fading or jamming, temporary loss of consciousness or failure of memory, aviator's temporary blindness esp. after sudden turn; *black* PEPPER; ~ **pudding**, sausage of blood, suet, etc.; ‖B~ **Rod**, gentleman usher of Lord Chamberlain's Department, House of Lords, etc.; ~ **sheep**, scoundrel, unsatisfactory member *of* family etc.; ~'**smith** (working in iron); ~ **spot**, place of danger or difficulty; ~ **tea** (fully fermented before drying); ~'**thorn**, thorny shrub bearing white flowers and sloes; ~ **tie**, man's black bow-tie worn with dinner-jacket; ‖B~ **Watch**, Royal Highland Regiment [f. dark tartan]; ~ **widow**, Amer. spider of which female devours mate. **5.** ~**en** *v.t.* & *i.*, make or become black, defame; ~'**ing** *n.*, (esp.) polish for boots. [E]

**blǎ´dder** *n.* Membranous (esp. urinary) bag in human or other animal's body; animal's bladder or part of it inflated etc. for various uses; inflated thing; wordy person; inflated vesicle in seaweed etc. [E]

**blāde** *n.* Flat narrow leaf esp. of grass and cereals; whole of such plants before ear comes; (Bot.) flat part of leaf apart from petiole; flat part of oar, spade, paddle-wheel, propeller, etc.; cutting-piece of sword, knife, etc., opp. to handle; razor-blade; flat bone esp. of shoulder; gay, jovial, or dashing fellow. [E]

**blah(-blah)** n. (colloq.) Pretentious nonsense. [imit.]

**blain** n. Inflamed sore. [E]

**blame. 1.** v.t. Find fault with (**be to ~**, deserve censure); fix responsibility on; **~ thing on** person, (colloq.) hold him responsible for it. **2.** n. Censure; responsibility for bad result; **~'worthy** a. (-iness), deserving blame; **~'less** (-ml-) a., innocent. [F (BLASPHEME)]

**blanch** (-ah-) v.t. & i. Make white by withdrawing colour, peeling (almonds), or depriving (plants) of light; make, grow, pale with fear, cold, etc. [F (BLANK)]

**blancma'nge** (blamŏ'nzh) n. Opaque jelly of cornflour etc. and milk. [F blancmanger, = white food]

**blä'ncō** n. (Mil.) White substance for whitening belts etc. [P]

**bländ** a. Polite, suave, mild, in manner; not irritating or stimulating; **~'ĭsh** v.t., flatter, cajole; **~'ĭshment** n. (usu. in pl.), flattering attentions, cajolery. [L blandus smooth]

**blänk** a., n., & v. **1.** a. Not written or printed on (blank sheet); with spaces left for signature or details (blank form); not filled (blank space); without interest, result, or expression (**look ~**, appear puzzled); unrelieved (blank wall); **~ cartridge** (without bullet, to make sound only); **~ cheque** (with amount entered by payee, hence = carte blanche); **~ test** (without specimen, to verify that reagents etc. have no independent effects); **~ verse** (unrhymed, esp. iambic pentameters). **2.** n. Lottery ticket winning no prize; space to be filled up in document; empty surface (one's mind **is a ~**, has no impressions etc.); document with blanks; = blank cartridge; dash written for word or letter, e.g. as euphem. substitute for profanity or abuse; **draw (a) ~**, elicit no response, fail. **3.** v.t. Screen off or out. [F blanc white f. Gmc]

**blä'nkėt** n., a., & v. **1.** n. Large woollen sheet for warmth esp. as bed-covering (ELECTRIC blanket; wet **~**, gloomy person preventing others' pleasure; **born on the wrong side of the ~**, illegitimate); thick covering mass or layer (of fog etc.). **2.** a. General, covering all cases or classes. **3.** v.t. Cover with blanket; keep quiet (scandal etc.). [F (prec.)]

**blāre. 1.** v.i. & t. Make sound of trumpet; utter or sound loudly. **2.** n. Blaring sound. [LDu., imit.]

**blā'rney. 1.** n. Cajoling talk; nonsense. **2.** v.t. & i. Cajole, use blarney. [place]

**blasé** (blä'zā) a. Tired of pleasure; bored through familiarity. [F]

**bläsphē'me** v.i. & t. Talk impiously; profane in words, revile; **blä'sphemy** n., impious speech, profanity; **blä'sphemous** a. [F f. L f. Gk blasphēmeō]

**blast** (-ah-). **1.** n. Strong gust; sound of wind-instrument, car horn, whistle, etc.; destructive wave of air from explosion; (colloq.) severe reprimand; **at full ~**, (colloq.) working at maximum speed etc.; **~-furnace** (for smelting, with compressed hot air driven in). **2.** v.t. & i. Blow up (rocks etc.) with explosives; wither, blight, (plant, animal, prosperity, etc., esp. w. subj. God expr. or understood in curses, also abs. as int.; **~'ėd** a. & adv., damned); **~ off**, (of rocket etc.) take off from launching site; **~-off** n. [E]

**blä'tan|t** a. Loudly obtrusive; flagrant; unashamed; **~cy** n. [made by Spenser]

**blather.** See BLETHER.

**blāze¹. 1.** n. Bright flame or fire (**in a ~**, on fire); (in pl., sl.) hell (**go to blazes; LIKE¹** blazes); violent outburst of passion etc.; bright display; full light (blaze of publicity). **2.** v.i. Flame, burn with excitement etc., (**~ up**, show sudden flame or anger); **~ away**, fire continuously with rifles etc., work vigorously (at). [E, = torch]

**blāze². 1.** n. White mark on animal's face; mark chipped in bark of tree to mark route. **2.** v.t. Mark (tree, path) with blazes; **~ a trail**, show the way for others, lit. or fig. [orig. uncert.]

**blāze³** v.t. Proclaim (blaze the news abroad). [LDu. (BLOW¹)]

**blā'zer** n. Coloured light jacket for sport or as part of school uniform etc.; man's plain jacket. [BLAZE¹]

**blā'zon. 1.** n. Heraldic shield, coat of arms, or banner; correct description of these. **2.** v.t. Describe or paint (arms) heraldically; inscribe with arms, names, etc., in colours or ornamentally; proclaim; **~ment** n.; **~ry** n., heraldic devices, bearings, art of blazoning. [F, orig. = shield]

**bleach. 1.** *v.t.* & *i.* Whiten in sunlight or by chemical process; ~'ing-powder, chloride of lime esp. to remove colour from materials. **2.** *n.* Bleaching substance or process. [E]

**bleak**[1] *n.* Small European river-fish. [N]

**bleak**[2] *a.* Dreary; bare, wind-swept; chilly. [N]

**blear. 1.** *a.* (or ~'y̆). Dim-sighted, filmy, (*blear eyes*); indistinct in outline; ~(y)-eyed, with blear eyes. **2.** *v.t.* Make blear. [LG]

**bleat. 1.** *v.i.* & *t.* Utter cry of sheep, goat, or calf; speak, utter, feebly or foolishly or plaintively. **2.** *n.* Cry of sheep, goat, or calf. [E]

**bléb** *n.* Blister, bubble. [BLOB]

**bleed. 1.** *v.i.* & *t.* (bled). Emit blood (one's **heart** ~**s**, one is very sorrowful); ~ **for** a cause etc., suffer wounds or death); draw blood surgically from; (of plant) emit sap; (of dye) come out in water; allow (fluid) to escape from closed system, treat (system) thus; extort money from, suffer extortion; ~'**er** *n.*, (esp.) haemophiliac, (vulg.) person (esp. unpleasant); ||~'**ing** *a.* & *adv.*, (esp., vulg.) bloody= damned. **2.** *n.* Act of bleeding. [E (BLOOD)]

**bleep** *n.*, & *v.i.* (Emit) intermittent high-pitched sound. [imit.]

**blĕ'mĭsh. 1.** *v.t.* Spoil the beauty or perfection of, mar. **2.** *n.* Flaw, defect, stain. [F]

**blĕnch** *v.i.* & *t.* Flinch, quail. [E]

**blĕnd. 1.** *v.t.* & *i.* Mix (esp. sorts of tea, spirit, etc., to get certain quality); mingle intimately *with*; become one; (of colours etc.) pass imperceptibly into each other. **2.** *n.* Mixture made of various sorts. [N]

**blĕnde** *n.* Native zinc sulphide. [G]

**blĕ'nny̆** *n.* Spiny-finned sea-fish. [L f. Gk *blennos* mucus (from its slimy scales)]

**blĕss** *v.t.* (*p.p.* usu. *pr.* -sĭd *attrib.*, -st *pred.*). Consecrate (food etc.); sanctify by sign of cross; call holy, praise, (God); attribute one's good luck to (one's stars etc.); pronounce invocation of divine or supernatural favour upon; make happy or successful (*with*); (God) ~ **me** etc., excl. of surprise or pleasure or indignation; *bless my* **HEART**; ~'**ed** *a.*, in paradise, (R.C. Ch.) beatified; ~'**ing** *n.*, (esp.) declaration or invocation of (divine) favour, grace before or after food, gift of God etc., thing one is glad of (~**ing in disguise**, unwelcome but eventually beneficial experience). [E]

**blĕ'ther, blă'ther,** (-dh-) *v.i.*, & *n.* (Talk) loquacious nonsense. [N]

**blew.** See BLOW[1,2].

**blight** (-īt). **1.** *n.* Plant disease due to fungoid parasite etc.; ||species of aphid; obscure malignant influence; unsightly urban area. **2.** *v.t.* Exert baleful influence on, wither, mar; affect with blight; ~'**er** *n.*, (esp., sl.) contemptible or annoying person or thing. [orig. unkn.]

||**Bli'ghty̆** (-ī'tĭ) *n.* (Army sl.) England, home, after foreign service. [Hind., = foreign]

||**bli'mey** *int.* (vulg.) expr. astonishment or contempt. [(*God*) *blind me*]

**blĭmp** *n.* Small non-rigid airship; ||(*B*~), diehard, reactionary. [orig. uncert.]

**blind** *a., adv., v.*, & *n.* **1.** *a.* Without sight; without direct observation; without foresight, discernment, or adequate information, (**is** ~ **to**, cannot appreciate); reckless (*blind hitting*); not ruled by purpose (*blind forces*); concealed; closed at one end; (sl.) drunk(en). **2.** *adv.* Blindly (*flying blind*). **3.** *v.t.* & *i.* Make unable to see, permanently or temporarily; rob of judgement, deceive, (~ **with science**, overawe by display of knowledge); ||(sl.) go blindly or heedlessly. **4.** *n.* Obstruction to sight or light; screen (esp. on roller) for window; ||awning of shop-window; pretext; ||(sl.) heavy drinking-bout. **5.** ~ **alley** (closed at one end, often fig. of prospectless or unprofitable course of action); ~ **corner** (round which motorist etc. cannot see); ~ **date**, social engagement between man and woman who have not met before; **turn a** ~ **eye to**, pretend not to notice; ~'**fold**, (*a.* & *adv.*) with eyes bandaged, without circumspection, (*v.t.*) deprive of sight with bandage, (*n.*) bandage to prevent person from seeing [orig. *blindfelled* = struck blind]; ~**man's buff**, game in which blindfold player tries to catch others who push him about [obs. *buff* = buffet]; ~ **side**, direction in which one cannot see danger; ~ **spot**, (Anat.) insensitive point on retina, (fig.) area where vision or understanding is lacking; ~ **stamping, tooling,** (in bookbinding without colour or gilt); ~'**worm**, slow-worm. [E]

**blink.** 1. *v.i.* & *t.* Move the eyelids; look with eyes opening and shutting; shut the eyes for a moment; shine with unsteady light, cast transient gleam; ignore, shirk, (facts). 2. *n.* Blinking movement; momentary gleam; **on the** ~, (sl.) out of order. 3. ~'**er** *n.*, (esp., usu. in *pl.*) horse's eye-screen(s); ‖~'**ing** *a.* & *adv.*, (euphem.) bloody = damned. [Du., var. of BLENCH]

**blip.** 1. *v.t.* (-pp-). Strike briskly. 2. *n.* Act or sound of blipping; small image on radar screen. [imit.]

**bliss** *n.* Gladness; perfect joy; being in heaven; ~'**ful** *a.* (-lly). [E (BLITHE)]

**bli'ster.** 1. *n.* Vesicle on skin filled with serum, caused by friction etc.; similar swelling on painted wood etc.; (Med.) thing applied to raise blister. 2. *v.t.* & *i.* Raise blister on; become covered with blisters; (fig.) attack sharply. [orig. uncert.]

**blithe** (-dh) *a.* Careless, casual; (poet.) gay, joyous; ~'**some** (-dhs-) *a.*, (poet.) cheerful. [E]

**bli'thering** (-dh-) *a.* (colloq.) Senselessly talkative; contemptible; utter, complete, (*blithering idiot*). [BLETHER]

**B. Litt.** *abbr.* Bachelor of Letters. [L *Baccalaureus Litterarum*]

**blitz** (-ts; colloq.). 1. *n.* Intensive or sudden (esp. aerial) attack (lit. or fig.). 2. *v.t.* Damage, destroy, in blitz. [abbr. of foll.]

**bli'tzkrieg** (-tsk-) *n.* Violent campaign intended to bring about swift victory. [G, = lightning war]

**bli'zzard** *n.* Severe snowstorm. [orig. uncert.]

**bloat** *v.t.* & *i.* Cure (herring) by salting and smoking slightly; inflate, become inflated, (esp. ~'**ed** *a.*, puffed up, overfed, pampered); ~'**er** *n.*, bloated herring. [N]

**blob** *n.* Drop of liquid; small round mass or spot; (Crick. sl.) score of 0. [imit.]

**bloc** *n.* Combination of countries, parties, or groups to effect some common purpose. [F, = foll.]

**block.** 1. *n.* Log, tree-stump, (CHIP *off the old block*); large piece of wood for chopping, beheading, or hammering on, or mounting horse from; pulley(s) mounted in case (*block and* TACKLE); piece of wood or metal

engraved for printing; bulky or shaped piece of anything; (sl.) head; mass of buildings between streets; *(length of)* area between streets; large building (*block of flats*); = STARTING-*block*; obstruction; (mental) ~, mental inability due to subconscious factors; spot where batsman rests bat before playing; large quantity as unit; set of sheets of paper fastened at edge, for writing or drawing on; (*attrib.*) made or treated as a large unit (*block booking*). 2. *v.t.* Obstruct (passage etc., progress); restrict use of (currency or other asset); stop (cricket ball) with bat; emboss or impress design on (book cover); ~ **out, in,** sketch roughly; ~ **up, in,** confine. 3. ~-**buster,** (sl.) bomb able to destroy whole block of buildings, (fig.) thing of great power; ~ **diagram** (showing general arrangement of parts); ~'**head,** stupid person; ~'**house,** house of squared logs, reinforced concrete shelter; ~ **letters** (each separate as in print, usu. in capitals); ~ **vote** (in which voter has influence according to number of persons he represents). 4. ~'**age** *n.*, blocked(-up) state. [F f. LDu.]

**blockä'de.** 1. *n.* Surrounding or blocking of a place by hostile forces esp. in order to prevent entry of goods etc. (**run** ~, evade blockading force). 2. *v.t.* Subject to blockade. ‖**bloke** *n.* (colloq.) Man, fellow. [Shelta]

**blond,** (of woman or her hair) **blonde.** 1. *a.* Light-coloured, flaxen, (*blond(e)* hair); (of complexion or person) fair. 2. *n.* Blond(e) person. [F f. L *blondus* yellow]

**blood** (-ŭd). 1. *n.* Liquid (usu. red) circulating in arteries and veins of animals (*blood* BOIL²*s*); one's ~ **runs cold,** one is horrified; **first** ~, first shedding of blood in fight, lit. or fig.; **out for** person's ~, determined to defeat him; **taste** ~, fig., be stimulated by early success); taking of life; passion, temperament, (**bad** ~, ill feeling; ~ **from a stone,** pity from the pitiless or money from the miserly; **in cold** ~, without passion; one's ~ **is up,** one is in fighting mood); race, descent, parentage, (BLUE *blood*; **fresh** or **new** ~, new members etc.; **in** one's ~, fundamental in one's character; *prince* etc. **of the** ~, royal); relationship;

relations, kindred; man of fashion.
**2.** *v.t.* Give first taste of blood to
(hound), initiate (person). **3.** ~-
**-and-thunder,** melodrama(tic); ~
**bank,** place where supply of blood
for transfusion is stored; ~-**bath,**
massacre; ~ **count** (of number of
corpuscles in quantity of person's
blood); ~-**curdling,** horrifying; ~
**donor,** one who gives blood for transfusion; ~ **feud** (between families,
one of which has caused death·or
injury to the other); ~ **group,** one
of types of human blood as regards
compatibility in transfusion; ~-**guilt,**
responsibility for murder; ~-**heat,**
ordinary temperature of healthy
human blood, about 98°F. or 37°C.;
~ **horse,** thoroughbred; ~'**hound,**
large keen-scented dog formerly
used to track cattle etc.; ~-**letting,**
surgical removal of blood; ~-**money,**
fine paid to next of kin of slain person; ~ **orange** (with red-streaked
pulp); ~-**poisoning** (due to harmful bacteria in blood); ~ **pressure,**
varying pressure of blood in vessels,
measured for diagnosis; ~-**red,** red
as blood; ~-**relation** (related by
blood, not by marriage); ~ **royal,**
royal family; ~'**shed,** spilling of
blood, slaughter; ~'**shot,** (of eyeball) tinged with blood; ~ **sports**
(involving bloodshed or animal-
-killing); ~-**stained,** stained with
blood, disgraced by bloodshed;
~'**stock,** thoroughbred horses; ~'-
**stream,** circulating blood; ~'-
**sucker,** leech, extortioner; ~ **test,**
examination of blood for diagnosis
etc.; ~'**thirsty,** eager for bloodshed;
~-**vessel,** vein, artery, or capillary,
conveying blood. **4.** ~'**less** *a.*, without blood(shed), unemotional, pale.
[E]

**bloo'dy** (-ŭ'-) *a., adv.,* & *v.* **1.** *a.*
(-**ily, -iness**) Of, like, running or
smeared with, blood; involving,
loving, due to, bloodshed; cruel; ‖(in
strong language) damned (*a bloody
shame, nuisance*), or as mere intensive
(*not a bloody one*), also as *adv.* (*bloody
awful*). **2.** *v.t.* Stain with blood. **3.**
B~ **Mary,** drink of vodka and
tomato juice; ~-**minded,** (colloq.)
deliberately unco-operative. [E
(prec.)]

**bloom.** **1.** *n.* Flower, esp. of plant
valued chiefly for this; flowering state
(*in bloom*); prime; flush, glow;
powdery deposit on grapes etc.;

freshness. **2.** *v.i.* & *t.* Bear blooms, be
in bloom; be in the prime; flourish;
‖~'**er** *n.*, (sl.) blunder; ~'**ing** *a.* &
*adv.*, ‖(esp., sl. euphem.; also -ōō'-)
bloody = damned. [N]

**bloo'mers** (-z) *n.pl.* (Hist.)
woman's loose knee-length trouser
costume or similar undergarment;
(colloq.) knickers. [*Bloomer,* person]

**blo'ssom.** **1.** *n.* Flower, esp. as
promising fruit; mass of flowers on
fruit-tree etc.; early stage of growth.
**2.** *v.i.* Open into flower (lit. or fig.;
*blossom out into a statesman* etc.). [E]

**blot.** **1.** *n.* Spot of ink etc.; blemish;
disgraceful act or quality. **2.** *v.t.*
(-**tt**-). Make blot on; stain (character; ~ one's *copy-book,* colloq.,
spoil one's character, be indiscreet);
dry with blotting-paper; ~ **out,**
obliterate (writing), obscure (view),
destroy; ~'**ting-paper** (absorbent,
for drying wet ink); ~'**ter** *n.*, pad of
blotting-paper. [prob. Scand.]

**blotch** *n.* Inflamed or discoloured
patch on skin; dab of ink etc.; ~**ed**
(-cht), ~'**y,** *adjs.* [obs. *plotch,* BLOT]

**blo'tto** *a.* (sl.) Very drunk. [orig.
uncert.]

**blouse** (-owz) *n.* Workman's or
peasant's loose upper garment, usu.
belted at waist (chiefly French);
woman's loose upper garment tucked
into skirt or trousers at waist; upper
part of soldier's or airman's battle-
dress. [F]

**blow**[1] (-ō). **1.** *v.i.* & *t.* (**blew** *pr.*
-ōō; ~**n** exc. in sense 'cursed').
Move as wind does (*it, the wind, blew*);
send directed air-current (at) e.g.
from mouth; puff, pant; (of whale)
eject air and water; (of fuse etc.)
melt when overloaded, cause to melt
thus; (in *pass.*) exhaust of breath;
send out by breathing; drive by
blowing; shape (glass, bubble) by
blowing air in; sound (wind instrument, note or signal *on* or *with* it);
clear (nose etc.) by air-current; send
flying (*off* etc.) by explosion; break
into (safe etc.) with explosives; (sl.)
reveal (secret etc.); (of flies) deposit
eggs in; (sl.) curse, confound, (*I'll be
blowed if; blow you, Jack, I'm all right*);
(sl.) squander. **2.** *v.i.* Blowing; exposure to fresh air. **3.** ~ **a kiss,** kiss
one's hand and wave it to distant
person; ~'**fly,** meat-fly, bluebottle;
~-**hole** (for blowing or breathing
through, or venting tunnel); *blow*

HOT *and cold*; ~ **in**, break inwards by explosion, colloq.) come in unexpectedly; ~'**lamp** (for directing very hot flame on selected spot); ~ one's **mind**, (sl.) indulge in hallucinations; ~ **out**, extinguish by blowing, send outwards by explosion, (of tyre) burst; ~-**out** n., (also, colloq.) large meal; ~ **over**, (of crisis etc.) pass off; ~ one's **own trumpet**, praise oneself; ~'**pipe**, tube for heating flame by blowing air etc. into it or for propelling darts by blowing; ~ one's **top**, (colloq.) become very angry; ~ **up**, send upwards or shatter or be shattered by explosion, inflate, exaggerate, (colloq.) reprove, (colloq.) enlarge (photograph), come to notice, lose one's temper. **4.** ~'**er** n., (also, colloq.) telephone; ~'**y** a., windy. [E]

**blow**² (-ō). (arch.) **1.** v.i. (**blew** pr. -ōō; ~**n**). Come into, be in, flower. **2.** n. Flowering condition. [E]

**blow**³ (-ō) n. Hard stroke with fist, hammer, etc., (**at one or a** ~, by a single stroke, in one operation); ~-**by**--~, describing all details in sequence; **come to** ~**s**, begin fighting); disaster, shock. [orig. unkn.]

**blow'z**|**y** a. (~**ily**, ~**iness**). Red--faced, coarse-looking, slatternly, dishevelled. [obs. *blowze* beggar's wench]

**blŭb** v.i. (sl.; -**bb**-). Weep. [foll.]

**blŭb'ber** n., a., & v. **1.** n. Whale fat. **2.** a. (Of lips) swollen, protruding. **3.** v.t. & i. Sob out (words), sob noisily. [imit.]

**blŭ'dgeon** (-ŭ'jon). **1.** n. Heavy--headed stick. **2.** v.t. Strike repeatedly with bludgeon; coerce. [orig. unkn.]

**blue** (-ōō) a., n., & v. **1.** a. Of colour between green and violet, coloured like clear sky or deep sea; livid with cold, anger, etc.; sad, depressed, (*look, feel, blue*); (of state of affairs etc.) dismal; belonging to Conservative party; indecent (*blue films*). **2.** n. Blue colour or pigment; blue powder used to whiten laundry; blue clothes or material (*dressed in blue*); blue ball in snooker etc.; **the** ~, the clear sky (*out of the blue*), the sea; one who has represented his university in a sport (*dark* ~, Oxford; *light* ~, Cambridge; get one's ~, be chosen as representative; (in *pl.*) melancholy, (type of) melancholy song of Amer. Negro origin.

**3.** v.t. (~**ing**, **bluing**). Make blue; treat with laundering blue; (sl.) squander (money). **4.** ~ **baby** (with congenital blueness of skin from heart defect); ~'**bell**, plant with blue bell-shaped flowers, wild hyacinth or harebell; ~ **blood**, noble birth; ~ **book**, Parl. or Privy-Council report; ~'**bottle**, large buzzing fly with blue body; ~ **cheese** (with veins of blue fungus); ~-**chip**, of highest quality, (of shares) constituting fairly safe investment, [f. high-valued blue chips in Poker); ||~-**coat boy**, scholar in charity school, esp. Christ's Hospital; ~ -**collar worker**, manual or industrial (opp. office) worker; *blue* ENSIGN; ~ **eye** (with blue iris); ~-**eyed boy**, (colloq.) favourite; ~ **funk**, (sl.) acute fear; ~ **gum**, kind of eucalyptus; ~'**jacket**, seaman in Navy; **once in a** ~ **moon**, very rarely; *blue* MURDER; ~ **pencil** (for marking deletions, corrections, etc.); B~ · **Peter**, blue flag with white square hoisted before sailing; ~'**print**, blue photographic print of final plans, (fig.) detailed plan of work etc.; ~ **ribbon** (of Garter; fig., highest honour in any sphere); ~'**stocking**, woman having or affecting literary tastes and learning [f. name of 18th-c. society where some men wore ordinary blue stockings]; *blue* TIT¹; ~ **water**, open sea; ~ **whale**, rorqual. **5.** blu'**ish** (-ōō'-). [f F. Gmc]

**blŭff**¹. **1.** a. (Of ship's bows, cliffs) with perpendicular broad front; (of person, manner) abrupt, frank, hearty. **2.** n. Bluff headland or cliff. [orig. unkn.]

**blŭff**². **1.** v.i. & t. Make pretence of strength to gain advantage; deceive thus. **2.** n. Act of bluffing (**call** person's ~, challenge his attempt to deceive by bluffing); threat designed to operate without action. [Du. *bluffen* brag]

**bluish.** See BLUE 5.

**blŭ'nder. 1.** v.i. & t. Move blindly, stumble, (*along* etc.; ~ **upon**, find by chance); make gross mistake; mismanage; ~ **away** one's *chances* etc., waste them thus. **2.** n. Stupid or careless mistake. [prob. Scand.]

**blŭ'nderbŭss** n. (Hist.) Short gun with large bore firing many balls. [Du. *donderbus* thunder gun]

**blŭnt. 1.** *a.* Dull, not sensitive; without sharp edge or point, not sharp; outspoken, uncompromising. **2.** *v.t.* Make blunt(er). [prob. Scand.]

**blŭr. 1.** *n.* Smear of ink etc.; dimness. **2.** *v.t.* (**-rr-**). Smear (writing etc.) with ink etc.; make indistinct; dim (perception). [BLEAR]

**blŭrb** *n.* Publisher's (usu. eulogistic) description of book. [made by G. Burgess 1907]

**blŭrt** *v.t.* Utter abruptly or tactlessly (usu. *blurt out*). [imit.]

**blŭsh. 1.** *v.i.* Become red in the face, (of face) redden, with emotion esp. shame (*at* thing); be ashamed (*I blush to own*; *I blush for you*); be red or pink. **2.** *n.* Glance, glimpse, (**at** (**the**) **first** ∼, at first sight); blushing (*put to the blush*; **spare** person's ∼**es**, not embarrass him by praise); rosy glow. [E]

**blŭ'ster. 1.** *v.i.* (Of wind, waves, person) storm boisterously. **2.** *n.* Blustering; self-assertive talk, threats; ∼**y̆** *a.* [imit.]

**B.M.** *abbr.* Bachelor of Medicine; British Museum.

**B.M.A.** *abbr.* British Medical Association.

**B.Mus.** *abbr.* Bachelor of Music.

**Bn.** *abbr.* (esp. Mil.) Battalion.

**B.O.** *abbr.* (colloq.) body odour.

**bō** *int.* = BOO. [imit.]

**bō'a** *n.* Large S. Amer. non-poisonous snake killing by compression; python; woman's long throat-wrap of fur or feathers; ∼ **constrictor**, a Brazilian boa, any boa or python. [L]

**boar** *n.* Uncastrated male pig; its flesh; male guinea-pig etc. [E]

**board. 1.** *n.* Long thin usu. narrow piece of sawn timber; slab of one or more such pieces of wood etc. used in games, for posting notices, etc.; (in *pl.*) theatre stage, actor's profession; stiff material of sheets of compressed fibres; table (spread for meals), food served, daily meals at contract price or in return for services (*board and lodging*); council-table, councillors, committee, body of examiners or interviewers, directors of company (∼**'room**, their meeting-place); side of ship (**by the** ∼, overboard, fig. neglected); **on** ∼, on or into ship, aircraft, train, bus, etc. **2.** *v.t. & i.* Cover or close (*up*) with boards; provide, be provided with stated meals at fixed rate; bring (candidate etc.) before board of interviewers; come alongside (ship, usu. to attack); force one's way on board (ship); go on board (ship etc.); ∼ **out**, place (destitute etc. child) in a family; ∼**'er** *n.*, (esp.) pupil at boarding-school, one who boards enemy ship; ∼**'ing** *n.* (∼**ing-house**, **-school**, in which persons, schoolchildren, board). [E]

**boast. 1.** *n.* Excessively proud statement; fact, thing, one is proud of; ∼**'ful** *a.* (**-lly**), apt to boast. **2.** *v.i. & t.* Brag, make boast (*of*, *about*, *that*); be the proud possessor of. [AF]

**boat. 1.** *n.* Small open oared or engined or sailing vessel; small steamer; boat-shaped utensil for sauce etc.; **in the same** ∼, in same predicament; MISS[1] *the boat*. **2.** *v.i.* Go in boat, esp. for amusement; ∼**'er** *n.*, hard flat straw hat. **3.** ∼**-hook**, long pole with hook and spike; ∼**-house**, shed at water's edge for boat(s); ∼**'load**, as much or many as boat can hold; ∼**'man**, one who hires out, or provides transport by, boat; ∼ **race** (between rowing crews); ∼**'swain**, **bo'sun**, (bō'sun), ship's officer in charge of sails etc., summoning men to duty; ∼**-train** (timed to catch or meet boat). [E]

**bŏb[1]. 1.** *n.* Weight on pendulum etc.; knot of hair, curl; horse's docked tail; bobbed hair; jerk, bouncing movement; one of several kinds of change in bell-ringing. **2.** *v.i. & t.* (**-bb-**). Move up and down, rebound; curtsy; cut (hair) to hang short of shoulders. **3.** ∼(**-sled**), **-sleigh**, (one of) two short sledges coupled; ∼**'stay**, rope holding bowsprit down; ∼**'tail**, (horse or dog with) docked tail; ∼ **up**, become active or conspicuous again. [imit.]

**bŏb[2]** *n.* Dry, wet, -∼, cricketing, boating, Etonian; ∼**'s your uncle**, (sl.) all is well. [pet-form of *Robert*]

‖**bŏb[3]** *n.* (sl.; *pl.* same). Shilling; 5p. [orig. unkn.]

**bŏ'bbin** *n.* Cylinder for holding thread etc.; small bar and string for raising door-latch; ∼**ĕt** *n.*, machine-made cotton net imitating ∼**-lace** (made with bobbins). [F]

‖**bŏ'bbish** *a.* (sl.) Brisk, well. [BOB[1]]

**bŏ′bble** n. Small woolly ball as ornament. [dim. of BOB¹]

‖**bŏ′bbў** n. (colloq.) Policeman. [Sir *Robert* Peel]

**bŏ′bbў-sŏ|cks** n.pl. Short socks over ankle; ~**xer** n., (usu. derog.) adolescent girl wearing these. [BOB¹]

**bo′blĕt** n. Bob-sleigh for two. [BOB¹]

**Bŏche** (-sh) n. & a. (sl., derog.) German. [F]

‖**bŏd** n. (sl.) Person. [BODY]

**bōde** v.t. & i. Foresee, foretell, (evil); portend (~ **well, ill,** be good, bad, sign). [E]

**bodē′ga** n. Cellar, shop, for sale of wine. [Sp. (APOTHECARY)]

**bŏ′dĭce** n. Upper part of woman's dress down to waist; woman's undergarment for same part of body. [orig. *pair of bodies*]

**bŏ′dĭless, bŏ′dĭlў.** See BODY.

**bŏ′dkĭn** n. Blunt thick needle for drawing tape etc. through hem; long pin for fastening hair. [orig. uncert.]

**bŏ′dў. 1.** n. Man or animal dead or alive (**keep ~ and soul together,** manage to remain alive); trunk apart from head and limbs; main part of thing; majority; person (*anybody*); aggregate of persons (*governing body*), things, or substance (*body of water*; **in a ~,** all together); piece of matter (HEAVENLY *bodies*); bulk, quantity; solidity, substantial character or flavour; thing perceptible to senses. **2.** v.t. ~ **forth,** give mental shape to, exhibit in outward shape, typify. **3.** ~**-blow,** (fig.) severe set-back; ~**-building,** strengthening the body esp. by exercise; ~**-colour,** opaque pigment; ~**guard,** escort or personal guard of dignitary; ~**line bowling** (persistently threatening batsman's body); ~ **odour,** (esp. unpleasant) smell of the body; *body* POLITIC; ~ **stocking,** woman's undergarment covering trunk and legs; ~**work,** structure of vehicle body. **4. bŏ′dĭless** a.; **bŏ′dĭlў,** (a.) of or affecting human body or physical nature, (adv.) as a whole, in the body. [E]

**Bō′er** (or boor) n. & a. (Of) Dutch or Dutch-descended S. African(s). [Du. = farmer]

**bŏ′ffĭn** n. (sl.) Person engaged in (technical) research. [orig. unkn.]

**bŏg.** 1. n. Wet spongy ground, morass; ‖(sl.) lavatory; ~ **myrtle,** fragrant-leaved shrub found in bogs; ~**-trotter,** (derog.) Irishman; ~**gў**

(-gĭ) a. (-iness). **2.** v.t. (-gg-; usu. in *pass.*) Submerge in bog, lit. or fig. [Ir. or Gael. *bogach*]

**bō′gey¹** (-gĭ) n. Score that good golfer should do hole or course in. [perh. BOGY, imaginary person]

**bogey².** See BOGY.

**bŏ′ggle** v.i. Hesitate, demur, (*about*, *at*); be startled or baffled. [BOGY]

**boggy.** See BOG.

‖**bō′gie** (-gĭ) n. Undercarriage pivoted below end of locomotive etc. [orig. unkn.]

**bō′gus** a. Spurious, sham. [orig. unkn.]

**bō′gў, -gey²,** (-gĭ) n. The Devil; ~**(man),** evil spirit, goblin; bugbear. [orig. (*Old*) *Bogey* the Devil]

**Bōhē′mian. 1.** a. Of *Bohemia*, Czech; socially unconventional; of free-and-easy habits. **2.** n. Such person, esp. artist; **b~ĭsm** n. [place]

**boil¹** n. Inflamed suppurating swelling. [E]

**boil².** **1.** v.i. & t. (Of liquid at temperature at which it becomes vapour, or of containing vessel) bubble up; (of sea etc., feelings, person) be agitated like boiling water or its vessel; bring (liquid, vessel) to temperature at which it boils; subject to heat of boiling liquid, cook or be cooked by boiling; manufacture (soap etc.) by boiling; **blood** ~**s** (with indignation); ~ **down,** reduce by boiling, amount basically *to*; ~**ed shirt** (with starched front); ‖~**ed sweet** (made of boiled sugar); ~ **over,** overflow by boiling; ~**′er** n., (esp.) vessel for boiling, esp. for making steam under pressure, water-tank attached to fire etc. in house, metal tub for boiling laundry; ~**′ing,** (a., esp.) ~ (**hot**), (colloq.) very hot, (n.) **the whole ~,** (sl.) the whole lot; ~**ing-point,** temperature at which liquid boils, (fig.) high excitement. **2.** n. Boiling(-point) (*on*, *at*, *to*, the *boil*). [F f. L *bullio* to bubble]

**boi′sterous** a. Violent, rough, (*boisterous wind, sea, behaviour*); noisily cheerful. [orig. unkn.]

**bōld** a. Courageous, enterprising, confident, (**make ~ to, make so ~ as to,** venture, presume); impudent, immodest; vigorous, well-marked, prominent, (*bold handwriting, headland, relief*); ~ **type** (with heavy or conspicuous face, as **bōld** above). [E]

**bōle** n. Stem, trunk, of tree. [N]

**bolēr′ō** (-ār′-) n. (pl. ~s). Spanish

dance; music for this; (or bŏ′lerō) woman's short open jacket. [Sp.]

**bŏll** n. Round seed-vessel of flax, cotton, etc. [Du.]

**bŏ′llard** n. Post on ship or quay for securing rope; short post on traffic island. [BOLE]

**bolo′ney, bal-,** n. (sl.) Nonsense. [orig. uncert.]

**Bŏ′lshĕv|ĭk** n. (Hist.) advocate of proletarian dictatorship in Russia by soviets; (pop.) socialist revolutionary; ~**ĭsm,** ~**ĭst,** ns.; ~**ĭze** v.t. [Russ., = member of majority]

**Bŏ′lshĭe, -shў,** (sl.) **1.** n. Bolshevik. **2.** Of Bolsheviks; left-wing; un-co-operative. [abbr.]

**bŏ′lster. 1.** n. Long (esp. under-) pillow across bed. **2.** v.t. & i. ~ (up), support (as) with bolster. [E]

**bŏlt**¹ n., v., & adv. **1.** n. Door-fastening of sliding bar and socket; sliding piece of lock or rifle-breech; metal pin with head for holding things together; short heavy crossbow-arrow (one's ~ **is shot,** he has done all he can); discharge of lightning (~ **from the blue,** complete surprise); act of bolting. **2.** v.i. & t. Dart off or away; (of horse) escape from control; run to seed; gulp down unchewed; fasten with bolt, keep in or out by bolting door; fasten together with bolts; ~**hole,** (fig.) means of escape. **3.** adv. ~ **upright,** rigidly erect. [E]

**bŏlt**², **boult,** (bōlt) v.t. Sift. [F]

**bŏmb** (-m). **1.** n. High-explosive or incendiary material or smoke etc. in container for explosion on impact or by time mechanism; **the** ~, atomic or hydrogen bomb as supreme weapon; **like a** ~, (colloq.) very successfully; ~**′shell,** bomb fired from gun, (fig.) cause of great surprise or excitement. **2.** v.t. & i. Attack with bombs, drive out by bombs; throw or drop bombs; ~**′er** n., (esp.) aircraft used for bombing. [F f. It. f. L f. Gk bombos hum]

**bŏmbăr′d** v.t. Attack with heavy guns; (Phys.) subject to stream of high-speed particles; (fig.) assail persistently with abuse etc.; **bŏm-bardier′** n., ‖artillery N.C.O., *airman who aims and releases bombs; ~**ment** n. [F f. L (prec.)]

**bŏ′mb|ast** n. Pompous or extravagant language; ~**ă′stĭc** a. (-ically). [earlier = 'cotton wool' f. F f. L (BOMBAZINE)]

**Bŏmbay dŭ′ck** n. Bummalo, esp. as relish. [corrupt. of bombil, native name of fish]

**bŏ′mbazine** (-ēn) n. Twilled dress-material of worsted, esp. black kind formerly much used for mourning. [F f. L f. Gk (bombux silk)]

**bōna fī′dé** a. & adv. Genuine(ly), sincere(ly); **bōna fī′dēs** (-z) n., honest intention, sincerity. [L, = in good faith]

**bonă′nza. 1.** n. Prosperity; large output of mine etc.; run of luck. **2.** a. Prosperous, productive. [Sp., = fair weather]

**bŏ′n-bŏn** n. Sweetmeat. [F (bon good)]

**bŏnd**¹. **1.** n. Thing or force that unites or (usu. in pl.) restrains; adhesion; (Chem.) linkage of atoms in molecule; binding agreement (his word is as good as his bond); deed binding person to pay money; government's or company's documentary promise to repay borrowed money usu. with interest; ~ (**paper**), high-quality writing-paper; **in** ~, stored by Customs until duty is paid. **2.** v.t. Bind together; connect or reinforce with bond; place (goods) in bond; ~**ed warehouse** (for goods in bond). [BAND]

**bŏnd**² a. (arch.) In slavery, not free; ~**′maid,** ~**′man,** ~**′slave,** ~**′sman,** ~**′woman,** serf or slave; ~**′age** n., serfdom or slavery or confinement, subjection to constraint or influence. [E f. N, = husbandman]

**bōne. 1.** n. One of hard pieces making up vertebrate skeleton, (in pl.) the body (**feel in one's** ~**s,** feel sure; **make old** ~**s,** live to old age) or its remains; hard, solid, or essential part of the body (**bare** ~**s,** mere essentials; MAKE no bones; **near the** ~, destitute, indecent; **to the** ~, penetratingly, to the bare minimum); material of bones; similar substance, e.g. ivory; thing made of bone; ~ (**of contention**), subject of dispute (bone to pick with someone); ~ **china** (made of clay mixed with bone ash); ~**dry,** quite dry; ~**′head,** (sl.) stupid person; ~ (utterly) **idle, lazy, weary;** ~**-meal,** crushed bones as fertilizer; ~**-setter,** one who treats fractures etc., esp. one not qualified as surgeon; ~**-shaker,** jolting vehicle. **2.** v.t. & i. Remove bones from; stiffen with bone; (sl.) steal; *~ **up on,** (sl.)

study intensively. **3. bō′ner** *n.*, (sl.) stupid mistake. [E]

**bŏ′nfīre** *n.* Open-air fire to celebrate event, give signal, or consume rubbish (**make a ~ of**, destroy by burning); **B~ Night**, 5 Nov. [BONE, FIRE]

**bŏ′ngō** (-nggō) *n.* (*pl.* ~**s**, ~**es**). One of pair of small drums usu. held between knees and played with fingers. [Amer. Sp.]

*bonhomie* (bŏ′nomē) *n.* Geniality. [F]

||**bŏ′nkers** (-z) *a.* (sl.) Crazy. [orig. unkn.]

*bon mot* (bawṅ mō′, bŏn-) *n.* (*pl. bons mots* pr. same *or* -mō′z). Witty saying; *bonne bouche* (bŏn boō′sh) *n.*, titbit. [F (*bon* good, *mot* saying, *bouche* mouth)]

**bŏ′nnĕt** *n.* Woman's or child's outdoor head-dress tied with strings below chin; man's round brimless Scots cap; bonnet-like structure; ||hinged cover over engine of motor vehicle. [F]

**bŏ′nn|ў** *a.* (chiefly Sc.; ~**ily**, ~**iness**). Comely, healthy-looking, pleasing. [orig. uncert.]

**bŏ′nsai** (-sī) *n.* (Method of growing) artificially dwarfed plant. [Jap.]

**bŏ′nus** *n.* Something extra, esp. dividend to shareholders, gratuity added to normal pay. [L, = good]

*bon vivant* (bawṅ vē′vahṅ) *n.* Gourmand. [F, lit. good liver (*vivre* live)]

**bŏ′n|ў** *a.* (~**ily**, ~**iness**). Like or of bone; having big bones with little flesh. [BONE]

**bŏnze** *n.* Buddhist priest esp. in Japan. [F or Port. f. Jap. f. Chin.]

**boō** *int.*, *n.*, & *v.* **1.** *int.* expr. disapproval or contempt; **can't say ~ to a goose**, is very shy or timid. **2.** *n.* The sound boo. **3.** *v.i.* & *t.* Emit boos, jeer at (speaker, announcement, etc.). [imit.]

**boŏb.** (sl.) **1.** *n.* Simpleton; (also ~**′oō**) mistake. **2.** *v.i.* Make mistake. [foll.]

**boō′bў** *n.* Silly or stupid or childish person; ~ **prize** (awarded to last competitor in a contest); ~ **trap**, thing balanced on door ajar to fall on head of first comer, apparently harmless object designed to explode when touched. [Sp. *bobo*]

**boō′dle** *n.* (sl.) Money for political bribery. [Du. *boedel* possessions]

**boŏk. 1.** *n.* Portable written or printed work on sheets fastened together usu. hingewise in cover; literary composition that would fill such sheets; telephone directory; (colloq.) magazine; thing one may learn from; imaginary record or list; **the** (**good**) **B~**, the Bible; main division of literary work or Bible; libretto; script of play; booklike set of blank sheets for accounts, notes, exercises, etc.; (in *pl.*) society's records, trader's accounts; bets on horse-race book (**make a book**) set of tickets, stamps, matches, cheques, etc., bound up together; **bring to ~**, call to account; **in** person's **bad** *or* **black**, **good**, ~**s**, in disfavour, favour, with him; **in my ~**, as I see the matter; **not in the ~**, disallowed; **read** person **like a ~**, fully understand his motives; **speak like a ~** (in formal phrases); **suit** person's *book*; **take a leaf out of** person's ~, imitate him; **throw the ~ at**, make all possible charges against. **2.** *v.t.* & *i.* Enter in book or list; engage beforehand; enter name of (person engaging seat etc.); issue railway etc. ticket (to); obtain ticket for journey etc.; ~ **in**, register at hotel etc. **3.** ~**′binder**, one who binds books; ~**′binding**, binding of books; ~**′-case** (containing shelves for books); ~ **club**, society whose members can buy certain books on special terms; ~**-ends**, pair of props to support row of books; ~**′keeper**, ~**′keeping**, one who keeps, keeping, accounts of business etc.; ~**′maker**, ~**′making**, compiler, compiling, of books, professional betting (man); ~**′man**, literary man; ~**′mark**, strip of leather etc. to mark place in book; ~**-plate**, label in book with owner's name; ~**′seller**, dealer in books; ~**′shop**, ||~**′stall**, ~**′store**, (where books are sold); ||~ **token**, voucher for sum of money to buy book(s); ~**-trough**, V-shaped rack for display of books to show titles; ~**′work**, study of books; ~**′worm**, larva that eats through books, (fig.) person devoted to reading. **4.** ~**′ie** *n.*, (colloq.) betting bookmaker; ~**′ish** *a.*, fond of reading, getting or showing knowledge from books only; ~**′lĕt** *n.* small usu. paper-covered book. [E]

**boōm**[1] *n.* Long pole with fixed end; floating timber barrier across harbour etc. [Du. (BEAM)]

**bo͞om²**. **1.** *n.* Deep resonant sound; sudden activity in commerce, concentration of attention on a commodity etc.; ~ **town** (undergoing sudden growth due to boom). **2.** *v.i.* Emit boom; (of commodity etc.) be in great demand. [imit.]

**bo͞o'meräng. 1.** *n.* Australian missile of thin curved wood that can be so thrown as to return to thrower; (fig.) argument or proposal that recoils on author. **2.** *v.i.* (Of scheme etc.) recoil on originator. [Aboriginal]

**bo͞on¹** *n.* Request (*ask, grant, a boon*); a favour or blessing. [N]

**bo͞on²** *a.* ~ **companion** (congenial, jolly). [F *bon* f. L *bonus* good]

**boor** *n.* Ill-mannered person. [LDu.]

**bo͞ost. 1.** *v.t.* Increase reputation of (person, scheme, goods) by praise; (colloq.) push from below, assist; ~'**er** *n.*, (Electr.) device for increasing voltage or signal, auxiliary engine or rocket for initial acceleration, dose increasing effect of earlier one. **2.** *n.* Act or effect of boosting. [orig. unkn.]

**bo͞ot¹.** (arch.) **1.** *n.* Advantage (now only in **to** ~, as well, additionally). **2.** *v.t. impers.* Be of avail. [E]

**bo͞ot². 1.** *n.* Outer foot-covering of leather etc. reaching above ankle (**get, give, the** ~, sl., be dismissed, dismiss, from employment; **put the** ~ **in**, sl. brutally, take decisive action; **the** ~ **is on the other leg** or **foot**, truth is just the other way round); (Hist.) torture-instrument encasing foot; ‖luggage-receptacle of motor car; \*~'**black**, shoeblack; ~'**faced**, grim or expressionless; ~'**lace**, cord or strip for lacing boots; ~'**leg**, smuggle(d) (esp. of liquor); ~'**licker**, toady; ~'**straps**, (fig.) unaided effort (*raise oneself by one's own bootstraps*); ~-**tree**, mould for keeping boot in shape. **2.** *v.t.* Kick; (sl.) kick or drive (person) *out*. **3.** ~**ee'** *n.*, infant's woollen etc. boot; ‖~**s** *n.*, boot-cleaner and messenger at hotel. [N]

**bo͞oth** (-dh) *n.* Structure of canvas or wood esp. as market stall or tent at fair; enclosure for telephoning, voting, etc. [N]

**bo͞o'tless** *a.* Unavailing; without boots. [BOOT¹·²]

**bo͞o'ty** *n.* Plunder or profit acquired in common; gain, prize. [G]

**bo͞oz|e. 1.** *v.i.* Drink (liquor) habitually or excessively. **2.** *n.* Drinking-bout, deep drinking (*on the booze*); (alcoholic) drink; ~'**y** *a.* (~**ily**, ~**iness**), drunk, addicted to drink. [Du.]

**bŏp** *n.* = BEBOP. [abbr.]

**bora'cĭc** *a.* Of borax; ~ **acid**, boric acid. [BORAX]

**bŏ'rage** (*or* bŭ'-) *n.* Blue-flowered plant used in salads etc. [F f. L f. Arab.]

**bor'äx** *n.* A salt used as antiseptic and in glass and china.

**Bordeau'x** (-dō') *n.* Claret or white wine from Bordeaux district. [place]

**bor'der. 1.** *n.* Side, edge, boundary or part near it; frontier district (**the B**~, between England and Scotland, N. Ireland and Irish Republic, etc.); continuous bed round garden; edging for strength or ornament or definition; ~**land**, district near border, intermediate condition, debatable ground; ~**line**, (*n.*) line of demarcation, (*a.*) on the borderline; ~**er** *n.*, dweller on border. **2.** *v.t.* & *i.* Put or be border to; ~ (**on**), adjoin, be like, come close to being. [F f. Gmc (BOARD)]

**bore¹.** See BEAR².

**bore². 1.** *v.t.* & *i.* Make (hole), make hole(s), make hole in, esp. with revolving tool; hollow out (tube); drill well (for oil etc.); (of racehorse) push another horse out of the way. **2.** *n.* Hollow of firearm barrel or of cylinder in internal combustion engine; diameter of this; ~('**hole**), deep narrow hole made to find water etc. [E]

**bore³** *n.* Tide-wave of exceptional height rushing up estuary. [Scand.]

**bore⁴. 1.** *n.* Nuisance; tiresome or dull person. **2.** *v.t.* Weary by tedious talk or dullness. **3.** ~'**dom** (-ŏr'd-) *n.*, bored state. [orig. unkn.]

**bor'ĭc** *a.* ~ **acid** (derived from borax, used as antiseptic). [BORAX]

**born** *a.* Having come into existence by birth; destined to be (*born rich*; *a born orator*); ~ **of**, owing origin to; **not** ~ **yesterday**, (fig.) far from stupid; **in all my** ~ **days**, (colloq.) in my life hitherto. [p.p. of BEAR²]

**borne.** See BEAR².

**borné** (bor'nā) *a.* Of limited ideas, narrow-minded. [F]

**bo'rough** (bŭ'ro) *n.* (esp. Hist.) town with municipal corporation etc.

conferred by royal charter, town represented in House of Commons (**pocket, rotten, ~s,** constituencies that had lost independence, abolished 1832). [E]

**bŏ′rrow** (-ō) *v.t.* & *i.* Get temporary use of with promise or intention of returning, borrow money, (*of, from*); use without being the true or original owner or inventor, use passages or ideas thus, plagiarize, (*from*; **in ~ed plumes,** taking the credit etc. that belongs to another); (Golf) allow for wind or slope. [E]

‖**Bŏr′stal** *n.* Institution for reformative training of young offenders. [place]

**bŏr′zoi** *n.* Russian wolfhound. [Russ.]

**bŏsh.** (sl.) **1.** *n.* Foolish talk, nonsense. **2.** *int.* ridiculing what has been said. [Turk., = empty]

**bo′som** (boŏ′zom) *n.* Breast of person or dress; enclosure of breast and arms in embracing, space between breast and dress; enfolding relationship (*in the bosom of* one's *family*); **~ friend,** intimate. [E]

**bŏss[1]. 1.** *n.* (colloq.) Master or manager or overseer; **~′y** *a.* (**-iness**); domineering. **2.** *v.t.* (sl.) Be boss of, control; **~ about,** continually give peremptory orders to. [Du. *baas*]

**bŏss[2]** *n.* Protuberance, round knob or stud esp. on centre of shield; (Archit.) carved or sculptured projection at crossing of vault-ribs. [F]

‖**bŏss[3]** *n.* (sl.) Bad shot or guess, blunder; **~-eyed,** blind in one eye, cross-eyed, crooked. [orig. unkn.]

**bō′sun.** See BOATS*wain.*

**bŏ′tan′**|**y̆** *n.* Science of plants; **botă′nic** (arch.), **botă′nical,** *adjs.* (**-ically**); **~ĭst** *n.*; **~ize** *v.i.,* study plants esp. where they grow. [F or L f. Gk *botanē* plant]

**bŏtch. 1.** *v.t.* Patch clumsily, spoil, bungle. **2.** *n.* Clumsy patch; spoilt or bungled work. [orig. unkn.]

**bŏth** *a.,* *pron.,* & *adv.* **1.** *a.* & *pron.* The two, not only one, (*both brothers, both the brothers, both of the brothers, both, are dead; the brothers are both dead*); **have it ~ ways,** choose now one now the other alternative to suit one's argument etc. **2.** *adv.* With equal truth in two cases (*both brother and sister are dead*; *is both dead and buried*). [N]

**bŏ′ther** (-dh-) *v.,* *n.,* & *int.* **1.** *v.t.* & *i.* Give trouble to, worry (**~ it, you,**

etc., colloq. expr. of impatience); take trouble (*to do, about*); be concerned *with;* **can't be ~ed,** will not make the effort needed. **2.** *n.* Worried state, (cause of) minor trouble. **3.** *int.* of impatience. **4. ~ā′tion** *n.* & *int.,* bother; **~some** *a.,* troublesome. [orig. unkn.]

**bō′-tree** *n.* Sacred pipal tree of India. [Sinh.]

**bŏ′ttle. 1.** *n.* Narrow-necked usu. glass or plastic vessel for storing liquid; amount of liquid in it; act or habit of drinking alcoholic liquor; feeding-bottle; **~-glass** (coarse dark-green); **~-green** (dark); **~-neck,** (fig.) narrow place, obstruction to an even flow of production etc.; **~-opener,** device for opening bottles of beer etc.; **~-party** (to which each guest brings bottle of liquor). **2.** *v.t.* Store in bottle(s) or jars; **~ up,** conceal, restrain for a time, entrap (enemy forces). [F f. L BUTT[1]]

**bŏ′ttom** *n.,* *a.,* & *v.* **1.** *n.* Lowest point or part, part on which thing rests; buttocks; seat (of chair); ground under water of sea etc.; less honourable end of table, class, etc.; farthest point (*fairies at the bottom of my garden; bottom of* one's HEART; keel, hull, ship; basis, origin; essential nature; **~ falls out,** collapse occurs; **~s up!,** call to drain one's glass; **at ~,** basically; **be at the ~ of,** cause; **get to the ~ of,** fully investigate and explain; **go, send, to the ~,** sink; **knock the ~ out of,** prove worthless; **touch ~,** reach lowest or worst point or firm facts. **2.** *a.* Lowest, last; **~ dog,** underdog; **bet** one's **~ dollar,** stake all; **~ drawer,** ‖(fig.) woman's clothes etc. stored in preparation for marriage. **3.** *v.t.* & *i.* Provide with bottom; touch bottom (of), find extent of; **~ (out),** reach lowest level. **4. ~less** *a.,* without bottom, inexhaustible; **~mŏst** (-m-m-) *a.,* lowest. [E]

**bŏ′tŭlĭsm** *n.* Poisoning by bacillus in infected sausages or tinned food. [G f. L *botulus* sausage]

**bou′clé** (boō′klā) *n.* (Fabric of) yarn with looped or curled ply. [F, = buckled]

**bou′doir** (boō′dwār) *n.* (Woman's) small private room. [F (*bouder* sulk)]

**bougainvi′llaea** (boōgən-) *n.* Tropical plant with large coloured bracts. [*Bougainville,* person]

**bough** (-ow) *n.* Main branch on or of tree. [E]

**bought.** See BUY.

*bougie* (bōō'zhē) *n.* (Surg.) Thin flexible instrument for exploring passages of the body. [F]

**bouillabai'sse** (bōōyabā's) *n.* Rich fish-stew orig. of Marseilles; *bouillon* (bōō'yawn) *n.*, broth.

**bou'lder** (bō'l-) *n.* Large weather- or water-worn stone. [Scand.]

**bou'leva̅rd** (bōō'-) *n.* Broad tree--lined street; *broad main road. [F. G (BULWARK)]

**boult.** See BOLT².

**bounc|e** *v.i.* & *t.* (Cause to) rebound; (sl., of cheque) be returned by bank when there are no funds to meet it; throw oneself *about*, rush (noisily etc.) *into* or *out of* (room), *in* or *out*. 2. *n.* Rebound(ing power); boast, swagger. 3. ~'er *n.*, (Crick.) bumper, (sl.) chucker-out; ~'ing *a.*, big and healthy; ~'y̆ *a.* (-iness). [imit.]

**bound¹.** 1. *n.* Limit of territory (‖beat the ~s, mark parish boundaries by striking certain points with rods); (usu. in *pl.*) limitation, restriction, (‖out of ~s, beyond permitted area). 2. *v.t.* Set bounds to; be boundary of. 3. ~'ary̆ *n.*, limit--line of land etc., (Cricket) hit to limit of field scoring 4 or 6 runs; ~'less *a.*, unlimited. [F f. L]

**bound².** 1. *v.i.* (Of ball etc.) recoil from wall or ground; spring or leap, advance with such motions. 2. *n.* Recoil of ball etc.; springy upward or forward movement; ~'er *n.*, (esp., sl.) (ill-bred) person. [F *bondir* f. L (*bombus* hum)]

**bound³** *a.* Ready to start or having started (*for* place); moving in specified direction (*northbound*). [N, = ready]

**bound⁴.** See BIND; **bou'ndary̆**, BOUND¹; **bou'nden**, BIND; **bou'nder**, BOUND²; **bou'ndless**, BOUND¹.

**bou'nt|y̆** *n.* Liberality in giving; gift; sum paid to encourage trade or for killing dangerous animal etc.; gratuity on enlistment; ~eous *a.*, (rhet.) beneficent, freely bestowed; ~iful *a.* (-lly), generous, profuse in giving. [F f. L (*bonus* good)]

**bouque't** (bōōkā', bō-) *n.* Bunch of flowers esp. for carrying at ceremony; (fig.) praise; perfume of wine; ~ **garni**, bunch of herbs for flavouring. [F (*bois* wood)]

**bour'geois** (boor'zhwah). 1. *a.* Of the middle class; humdrum, conventional; materialist; capitalist. 2. *n.* Bourgeois person. 3. ~ie (boorzh-wahzē') *n.*, the bourgeois class. [F (BURGESS)]

**bourn¹** (-oor-, -ôr-) *n.* Small stream. [BURN¹]

**bourn²(e)** (-oor-, -ôr-) *n.* (arch.) Goal; limit. [BOUND¹]

**bourse** (-oor-) *n.* Foreign money--market. [F (PURSE)]

**bout** *n.* Spell or turn or fit (*of, at*); trial of strength, match at wrestling or boxing. [LG (BIGHT)]

**bouti'que** (bōōtē'k) *n.* Small shop or department selling (esp. fashionable) clothes etc. [F]

**bō'vine** *a.* Of oxen; dull, inert. [L (*bos* ox)]

**bow¹** (bō). 1. *n.* Weapon for shooting arrows with string joining ends of curved piece of wood etc. (*two* STRINGS *to* one's *bow*); rod with stretched horsehair for playing violin etc.; slip-knot with single or double loop; ribbon etc. so tied; curve, rainbow, saddle-bow; ~-legged, having bandy legs; ~'man, archer; ~-saw, narrow saw stretched on light frame; ~-tie, necktie to- be) tied in shape of double loop; ~--wi'ndow, curved bay window. 2. *v.t.* Use bow on (violin etc., or abs.). [E]

**bow².** 1. *v.i.* & *t.* Bend *down* or kneel (*to, before,* person or fig. destiny etc.) in sign of submission or reverence; incline head or body in salutation, assent, etc., (*to* person), express (thanks etc.) thus, usher *in* or *out* thus (~ **out**, make esp. formal exit); cause to bend (lit. or fig.); *bow and* SCRAPE; ~ **down**, crush, make stoop (*bowed down with* care etc.). 2. *n.* Bowing of head or body; **make** one's ~, make formal entry or exit; **take a** ~, acknowledge applause. [E]

**bow³** *n.* (often in *pl.*) Fore-end of boat or ship; rower nearest bow. [LDu. (BOUGH)]

**bow'dler|ize** *v.t.* Expurgate (book, author); ~ism, ~iza̅'tion, *ns.* [*Bowdler*, person]

**bow'el** *n.* Division of alimentary canal below stomach, intestine; (in *pl.*) innermost parts, (arch.) feelings of compassion (*bowels of mercy*). [F f. L *botulus* sausage]

**bow′er**[1] *n.* Anchor at ship's bow. [BOW[3]]

**bow′er**[2] *n.* **Right, left, ~,** jack of trumps, other jack of same colour, at euchre etc. [G *bauer* peasant, jack at cards]

**bow′er**[3] *n.* Arbour or summer--house or leafy nook; (poet.) inner room; **~-bird,** kind of bird of paradise adorning its run with shells etc.; **~y** *a.* [E, = dwelling]

**bow′ie** (bō′ĭ) *n.* **~ (knife),** kind of long hunting-knife. [person]

**bowl**[1] (bōl) *n.* Basin esp. deep or for food or liquid (e.g. punch, milk, salad); contents of bowl; hollow of tobacco-pipe, spoon, etc. [E]

**bowl**[2] (bōl). **1.** *n.* Wooden ball made slightly non-spherical to run in curve, (in *pl.*) game with these on grass; flattened or spherical wooden ball at skittles. **2.** *v.t.* & *i.* Play bowls or skittles; roll (hoop etc.) along ground; go along by revolving or on wheels; (Crick.) deliver (ball etc.), knock *down* (wicket), put (batsman) *out* by knocking down wicket with delivered ball; **~ out,** dismiss (batsman thus, or side by any means); **~ over,** knock down, (fig.) disconcert or make helpless; **~′er**[1] *n.,* player at bowls, (Crick.) fieldsman who bowls; **~′ing-alley,** long enclosure for playing skittles; **~′ing--crease,** line from behind which bowler delivers ball; **~′ing-green,** lawn for playing bowls. [F f. L *bulla* bubble]

**bow′ler**[2] (bō′-) *n.* Round-crowned hard felt hat. [person]

**bow′line** (bō′-) *n.* Knot used in making fixed end-loop; **bow′sprit** (bō′-) *n.,* spar running forward from ship's bow. [BOW[3]]

**bow′-wow** *n.* & *int.* Dog's bark; childish name for dog. [imit.]

**box. 1.** *n.* Kind of evergreen shrub esp. with small dark leaves for garden borders; **~(′wood),** its wood; container (usu. with lid, for solids) of wood, metal, cardboard, etc.; quantity contained in this; coachman's seat; receptacle at newspaper office for replies to advertisement; separate compartment in theatre etc.; compartment for horse in stable or vehicle; = ‖telephone-box, witness-box, etc.; small country house for fishing, shooting, etc.; confined area; space enclosed by printed lines; slap with hand on ear(s); **the ~,** (colloq.) television (set). **2.** *v.t.* & *i.* Put in or provide with box; slap (person's ears); fight with fists usu. in padded gloves as sport. **3. ~ girder** (made of plates fastened in box shape); **~ in,** confine and restrict movement of; ‖**~ junction,** yellow-striped road area which vehicle must not enter if it cannot leave immediately; **~-kite** (tailless, with light rectangular frame at each end); **~-office** (for booking seats in theatre etc.); **~-pleat** (of two parallel pleats forming raised band); ‖**~-room** (where boxes etc. are stored); **~-spring,** one of set of vertical springs in mattress; **~ the compass,** (Naut.) state the points in correct order, (fig.) make complete revolution and end where one began (in argument etc.); **~ up,** confine uncomfortably, muddle. **4. ~′er** *n.,* fighter with fists (**~ shorts,** men's loose underpants), medium-sized smooth-haired kind of dog; **~′ful** (-ool) *n.;* **~′ing** *n.,* fighting with fists (**~ing-glove,** padded kind worn in this; **~ing-weight,** at which boxers, wrestlers, weight--lifters, are matched, with approx. upper limits light flyweight 48 kg, flyweight 51 kg, bantamweight 54 kg, featherweight 57 kg, lightweight 60 kg, light welterweight 63¼ kg, welterweight 67 kg, light middleweight 71 kg, middleweight 75 kg, light heavyweight or cruiserweight 81 kg, heavyweight no limit); ‖**Boxing Day,** first weekday after Christmas [on which Christmas--boxes were traditionally given]; **~′y** *a.,* like a box. [E f. L *buxus, buxis*]

**Box and Cox** *n.* Two persons who are never together, never at home at the same time. [play]

**box′calf** (-kahf) *n.* Chrome-tanned calfskin with hatched grain. [*Box,* person]

**boy** *n.* Male child; young man; male native servant; **~-friend,** girl's, woman's, usual or preferred male companion; **~ scout,** Scout; **my ~** (as familiar voc.); **the ~s,** group of men esp. with similar interests, (grown-up) sons in family; **~s will be ~s,** juvenile behaviour must be tolerated; **jobs for the ~s,** assurance of gain for one's friends; **(oh) ~** (expr. surprise, excitement, etc.); **~′hood** *n.;* **~′ish** *a.,* (esp.) high-spirited. [orig. uncert.]

**boy′cott. 1.** *v.t.* Refuse social or commercial relations with (person, class, nation) by common consent, combine thus in refusing to handle (goods). **2.** *n.* Such refusal. [person]

**B.P.** *abbr.* boiling-point; British Petroleum; British Pharmacopoeia.

**Bp.** *abbr.* Bishop.

**B.R.** *abbr.* British Rail.

**Br.** *abbr.* British; Brother.

**bra** (-ah) *n.* Brassière. [abbr.]

**brace. 1.** *v.t.* Give firmness to, make steady by supporting, stretch, string up, invigorate; ~ oneself (for an effort). **2.** *n.* Thing that braces (e.g. strengthening-iron or timber in building, rope attached to ship's yard); ‖(in *pl.*) straps supporting trousers from shoulders; wire device for straightening teeth; connecting mark { }, in printing; (*pl.* same) pair (*of* dogs, game, etc.); ~ **and bit**, revolving tool for boring; ~′let (-sl-) *n.*, ornamental band, chain, etc., for wrist or arm, (sl.) handcuff. [F f. L *bracchia* arms]

**brack′en** *n.* Large fern abundant on heaths; mass of these. [N]

**brack′et. 1.** *n.* Flat-topped projection from wall as support for arch etc.; shelf with slanting prop hung against wall; wooden or metal angular support; lamp-support projecting from wall; mark used in pairs ( ) [ ] { } for enclosing words or figures; group bracketed together as similar or falling between limits (*income bracket*). **2.** *v.t.* Enclose in brackets, couple (names etc.) with brace, imply connection or equality of; place shots short of and beyond (target) in range-finding. [F or Sp. f. L *bracae* breeches]

**brack′ish** *a.* (Of water) slightly salt. [LDu.]

**bract** *n.* (Usu. small) leaf or scale below calyx. [L *bractea* thin sheet]

**brad** *n.* Thin flat nail with slight projection on one side as head; ~′awl *n.*, small non-spiral boring-tool. [N]

**brae** (-ā) *n.* (Sc.) Hillside. [N]

**brag. 1.** *v.i.* & *t.* (-gg-). Talk boastfully, boast of or *of* or *that.* **2.** *n.* Boastful statement or talk; card-game like poker. **3.** ~**gadǒ′ciǒ** (-shǐ-) *n.*, bragging talk; ~′gart *n.* & *a.*, (person) given to bragging. [orig. unkn.]

**Brah′ma¹** *n.* Supreme Hindu deity; divine reality of which world is manifestation; **brah′ma²** = foll.; **brah′man** etc., see BRAHMIN. [Skr., = creator]

**brahmapu′tra** (-ōō′t-) *n.* Large Asian breed of domestic fowl. [place]

**brah′min, -man,** *n.* Member of Hindu priestly caste; **brahmǐ′nic(al)** *adjs.*; ~**ism** *n.* [Skr.]

**braid. 1.** *n.* Plaited tress of hair; silk or thread or wire woven into a band esp. as edging or trimming. **2.** *v.t.* Form into braid, interweave; trim with braid. [E]

**brail.** (Naut.) **1.** *n.* ~**s**, trussing-cords along sail-edge. **2.** *v.t.* ~ (**up**), truss (sail). [F f. L *bracale* girdle (BRACKET)]

**Braille. 1.** *n.* Printing or writing for the blind with embossed letters consisting of 6 points variously disposed in an oblong. **2.** *v.t.* Transcribe in Braille characters. [person]

**brain. 1.** *n.* Convoluted nervous tissue in skull of vertebrates; (in *pl.*) substance of this esp. as food; centre of sensation or thought; (source of) intellectual power; electronic device comparable to brain; **get, have, on the ~**, be constantly thinking of; **pick** person's ~s, extract and use his ideas or information; ~**child**, (colloq.) product of thought; ~**drain**, (colloq.) loss of intellectual or highly trained workers by emigration; ~**fag**, mental exhaustion; ~′**power**, mental ability or intelligence; ~′**storm**, violent mental disturbance; ~**s trust**, group of experts giving impromptu answers to questions; ~′**washing**, systematic replacement of established ideas in person's mind by others; ~′**wave**, electrical impulse in brain, (colloq.) sudden bright idea; ~′**work**, mental activity. **2.** *v.t.* Dash out brains of. **3.** ~′**less** *a.*, lacking intelligence; ~′ÿ *a.* (~**ily**, ~**iness**), intellectually clever or active. [E]

**braise** (-z) *v.t.* Stew (esp. meat) slowly in closed container. [F (*braise* live coals)]

**brake¹** *n.* Bracken. [BRACKEN]

**brake²** *n.* Thicket, brushwood. [E]

**brake³. 1.** *v.t.* Crush (hemp, flax) by beating. **2.** *n.* Toothed braking-instrument; heavy harrow. [LDu. (BREAK)]

**brake⁴. 1.** *n.* Apparatus for checking motion of wheel, vehicle, train, etc.; ~**drum**, cylinder in wheel on which brake-shoe presses; ~

**horsepower** (of engine, measured by force needed to brake it); ~-**shoe**, part of brake that touches wheel etc. **2.** *v.i.* & *t.* Apply brake; retard with brake. [orig. uncert.]

**brake**[5] *n.* Large wagonette; estate car. [BREAK]

**brä'mbl**|**e** *n.* Wild prickly shrub, esp. blackberry bush; blackberry; ~**ing** *n.*, the mountain finch. [E]

**brän** *n.* Husks separated from flour; ‖~-**tub** (filled with bran in which toys etc. are hidden). [F]

**branch** (-ah-). **1.** *n.* Limb springing from tree or bough; lateral extension or subdivision of something (e.g. road, railway, family, knowledge, legislature); local establishment of business (e.g. library, bank). **2.** *v.i.* Send branches forth or *forth* or *out*; (of road etc.) split into two or more; spring *out*, spread *forth*, tend *away* or *off*, diverge *into*. **3.** ~'**y** *a.*, with many branches. [F f. L *branca* paw]

**bränd. 1.** *n.* Piece of burning or charred wood, (poet.) torch; permanent mark deliberately made by hot iron, iron stamp for this; stigma; trade mark, goods of particular make or trade mark (lit. or fig.); (poet.) sword; ~ **from the burning**, a convert; ~ **of Cain**, blood-guilt; ~-**new'**, obviously or wholly new. **2.** *v.t.* Stamp with hot iron (as punishment or mark of ownership); label with trade mark; impress indelibly; stigmatize. [E]

**brä'ndish** *v.t.* Wave, flourish, (weapon etc.) in display or threat. [F f. Gmc]

**brä'ndy** *n.* Strong spirit distilled from wine or fruit-juice; ~-**snap**, rolled gingerbread wafer. [Du. *brandewijn*]

**bräsh** *a.* (colloq.) Cheeky, saucy; self-assertive. [dial.]

**brass** (-ah-) *n., a.,* & *v.* **1.** *n.* Yellow alloy of copper and zinc; inscribed sepulchral tablet of brass; brass ornament worn by horse; (Mus.) brass instruments; effrontery; ‖(sl.) money; **as bold as** ~, excessively bold or self-assured. **2.** *a.* Made of brass. **3.** *v.i.* & *t.* (sl.) ~ **up**, pay up; ~**ed off**, fed up. **4.** ~ **band** of musicians with brass instruments; ~ **farthing**, least possible amount; ‖~ **hat**, (sl.) high-ranking officer; **part** ~ **rags**, (sl.) cease friendship; ~-**rubbing**, reproducing design of

sepulchral brass by rubbing paper laid on it with chalk etc.; ~ **tacks**, (sl.) actual details; ~'**ware**, utensils etc. of brass. [E]

**brä'sserie** *n.* Establishment serving beer (with food). [F (*brasser* brew)]

**brä'ssica** *n.* Plant of genus including cabbage, turnip, etc. [L]

**brä'ssière** (-syār) *n.* Woman's undergarment worn to support breasts. [F]

**bra'ss**|**ÿ** (-ah'-) *a.* (~**ily**, ~**iness**). Like brass in colour or sound or taste; simulating gold, pretentious; impudent. [BRASS]

**brät** *n.* (derog.) Child. [orig. unkn.]

**bräve** *a., n.,* & *v.* **1.** *a.* Able to face and steadily endure danger or pain; (literary) splendid, admirable. **2.** *n.* Amer. Indian warrior. **3.** *v.t.* Defy, encounter bravely; ~ **it out**, behave defiantly under suspicion etc. **4.** **brava'dō** (-ah'-) *n.*, show of boldness; **brä'very** *n.*, brave conduct or nature, (literary) splendour; **bra'vō** (-ah'-), (*n., pl.* ~**es**, ~**s**) hired ruffian, (*int.,* & *n., pl.* ~**s**) cry of approval to actor etc.; **bravūr'a** (or -oor'*a*) *n.*, brilliant or ambitious performance, (esp. vocal) music needing exceptional powers. [F f. It. or Sp. f. L (BARBARIAN)]

**brawl. 1.** *n.* Noisy quarrel. **2.** *v.i.* Engage in brawl; (of stream) be noisy. [Prov.]

**brawn** *n.* Muscle, lean flesh; cold dish made chiefly of meat of pig's head boiled, chopped, and pressed in a mould; ~'**ÿ** *a.* (~**ily**, ~**iness**), muscularly strong. [F f. Gmc]

**bray**[1]**. 1.** *n.* Ass's cry; blare of trumpet(s) etc. **2.** *v.i.* & *t.* Emit bray; utter in braying tone. [F *braire*]

**bray**[2] *v.t.* Pound in mortar. [F]

**brä'zen. 1.** *a.* Of brass; strong or yellow or harsh-toned as brass; ~(-**faced**), shameless. **2.** *v.t.* Make shameless; ~ (**affair, it**) **out**, face or undergo impudently. **3.** **bräze** *v.t.*, solder with alloy of brass and zinc; **brä'zier**[1] (or -zher) *n.*, brass-worker. [E (BRASS)]

**brä'zier**[2] (or -zher) *n.* Pan or stand with lighted coal etc. as portable heater. [F (BRAISE)]

**Brazi'l** *n.* ~(-**nut**), large three-sided nut. [place]

**breach. 1.** *n.* Breaking or neglect (*of* rule, duty, contract; ~ **of the peace**, riot or affray; ~ **of promise** esp. to marry); breaking of relations, quarrel; broken state, gap lit. or fig. (**stand in the** ~, bear brunt of attack; **step into the** ~, give help in crisis). 2. *v.t.* Break through, make gap in. [F f. Gmc (BREAK)]

**bread** (-ĕd-). 1. *n.* Flour moistened, kneaded, usu. leavened, and baked; ~ (**and butter**), necessary food, livelihood; (sl.) money; ~ **and butter**, bread slices spread with butter; ~ **and milk**, broken bread in hot boiled milk; ~ **and water**, plainest possible diet; ~-**basket**, (sl.) stomach; ~-**bin**, container for loaves; ~'**board** (for cutting bread on); *~'**line**, queue of poor people waiting for food; ~ **sauce**, milk sauce thickened with bread crumbs; ~-**winner**, person whose work supports a family. 2. *v.t.* Coat with bread crumbs for cooking. [E]

**breadth** (-ĕd-) *n.* Broadness, distance or measure from side to side; extent, distance; freedom from mental limitations or prejudices or intolerance (often *of mind* or *view*); ~'**ways**, ~'**wise**, (-z) *advs.* [BROAD]

**break** (-āk). 1. *v.i.* & *t.* (broke *pr.* -ōk; BROKEN, BROKE). (Cause to) go into two or more pieces under blow or strain, make or become discontinuous, divide or disperse into two or more parts; shatter (*break a window*); penetrate by breaking; have interval between spells of work (*break for coffee*); make way with effort, suddenness, or violence; make or become weak, discourage, destroy; make or become bankrupt; tame, subdue, (HEART, horse, resistance, spirit); (of waves) curl over and be dashed into foam; (of weather) change suddenly esp. after settled period; (of troops) disperse in confusion; (of clouds) show gap; (of voice) change tone with emotion or at manhood; (Crick., of bowled ball) deviate from original direction on pitching; (of day) dawn; (of storm) begin violently; disconnect (electric circuit); break bone in (limb, back, nose) or dislocate (back, NECK); break skin of (head, crown); make (way) by separating obstacles; cause (spell, silence, journey) to cease or be interrupted; unfurl (flag etc.); solve (cipher etc.); win game at tennis against (opponent's service); escape, emerge from, (prison, cover; *break free* or *loose*); reveal (news), be revealed; weaken effect

of (blow, fall); be no longer subject to (habit); act contrary to (law, promise, etc.). 2. ~ **away**, make or become free or separate; ~'**away**, breaking away, secession; ~ **down**, demolish, collapse, fail, cease to function, suppress (resistance), analyse into components, lose self-control; ~'**down**, collapse, disintegration, failure of health or mechanical action or (esp. mental) power, analysis; ~ **even**, emerge from transaction etc. with neither gain nor loss; ~ one's **fast**, (arch.) eat after fasting esp. overnight; ~'**fast** (-ĕ'kfa-) *n.*, & *v.i.*, (take) first meal of day; ~ **in**, intrude forcibly esp. as thief (so ~-*in n.*), interrupt, accustom to habit, wear etc. until comfortable; ~ **in on**, disturb, interrupt; ~ **into**, enter abruptly or as thief, interrupt (talk etc.), suddenly begin to utter, perform, etc., (*laughter*, *a run*, *tears*), establish oneself in (profession); ~'**neck**, (of pace) dangerous; ~ **person of**, make him no longer subject to (habit); ~ **off**, detach by breaking, bring to an end, cease talking etc.; ~ **open**, open by breaking; ~ **out**, escape from prison etc. (so ~-*out n.*), burst from restraint or concealment, release (flag run up), become covered in (rash etc.), exclaim; ~ **the back of**, do hardest or greatest part of, overburden; ~ **the bank**, exhaust its resources or limit of payment; *break the* ICE; ~'**through**, act of breaking through obstacle, major advance in knowledge etc.; ~ **up**, break into small pieces, disband, depart, disconcert, become feeble; ~'**up**, disintegration, collapse, dispersal; ~'**water**, object breaking force of waves; ~ **wind**, release wind from bowels by anus; ~ **with**, quarrel or cease relations with. 3. *n.* Breaking; gap, broken place, interruption, pause in work (COFFEE, TEA, -*break*); points scored continuously at billiards etc.; (colloq.) piece of good luck; (bad) ~, (colloq.) piece of ill luck; = BRAKE[5]. 4. ~'**able** *a.* (-bly) & *n.* in *pl.*, (things) easily broken; ~'**age** *n.*, (damage caused by) breaking; ~'**er** *n.*, (esp.) heavy wave breaking on coast or over reef; ~'**ing** *n.* (~**ing-point**, at which thing or person gives way; ~**ing-strength**, maximum stress a body can endure without breaking). [E]

**bream** *n.* (*pl.* same). Yellow arch-backed freshwater fish; similarly shaped sea-fish. [F f. Gmc]

**breast** (-ĕst). **1.** *n.* Either milk-secreting organ on upper front of woman's body, corresponding usu. rudimentary part of man's body; (fig.) source of nourishment; upper front of human body or of coat etc., corresponding part of animals; heart, emotions; **~'bone,** thin flat vertical bone in chest between ribs; **~-feeding** (at mother's breast, not from bottle); **~-high,** up to the breast; **~-pin** (jewelled etc., worn in tie); **~'plate,** vestment or armour covering breast; **~-stroke** (made while swimming on breast by extending arms forward and sweeping them back); **~'work,** temporary breast-high defence or parapet. **2.** *v.t.* Oppose breast to, contend with (waves, hill); climb (hill); **~ the tape,** win race. [E]

**breath** (-ĕth) *n.* Air as used in the lungs to supply oxygen to blood, breathing or ability to breathe; one respiration; breath as perceptible to sight, smell, hearing, or touch; slight movement of air; whiff of perfume etc.; **a ~ of** (brief time in or small amount of) **fresh air; below, under,** one's ~, in a whisper; **~ of life,** a necessity; **~ test** (given with **~'alȳser** (-z-) *n.*, instrument measuring amount of alcohol in breath); **catch, hold,** one's ~, cease breathing for a moment in fear or absorbing emotion; **draw ~,** breathe, live; **out of ~,** not able to breathe quick enough after exertion; SAVE one's *breath*; **say** (inconsistent things) **in the same ~; take** person's **~ away,** make him breathless with delight, surprise, etc.; **~'lèss** *a.*, panting, holding the breath through excitement etc., unstirred by wind. [E]

**breathe** (-dh) *v.i.* & *t.* Take air into and expel it from lungs; be or seem alive; take breath, pause; sound, speak, (of wind) blow, softly; send out or take in (as) with breathed air; utter; exhibit (defiance etc.); **~ again, freely,** recover from fear etc.; **not ~ a word of,** keep quite secret; **~ down** person's **neck,** be close behind him in pursuit or from mistrust; **~** one's **last,** die; **~ upon,** taint; **brea'ther** (-dh-) *n.*, (esp.) short spell of exercise, brief pause for rest, safety-vent; **brea'thĭng** (-dh-) *n.*, (esp.) sign indicating whether Gk vowel is aspirated; **breathing-space,** time to breathe.

**brĕd.** See BREED.

**breech** *n.* Back part of gun or rifle or gun barrel; (arch. exc. w. ref. to baby's position at or before birth) buttocks; (in *pl.*, *pr.* brĭ'chĭz) short trousers fastened below knee for riding or in court costume; **~-loader,** gun loaded at breech, not through muzzle; **wear the ~es,** (of wife) dominate husband; **~'es-buoy,** lifebuoy on rope with canvas breeches for user's legs. [E]

**breed. 1.** *v.t.* & *i.* (**bred**). Bear, generate, (offspring); propagate (**~ in and in,** always mate with near relations); yield, result in; cause to propagate, raise, (cattle etc.); train up, bring up; arise, spread; create (fissile material) by nuclear reaction in **~er reactor; bred and born,** by birth and upbringing; **bred in the bone,** hereditary. **2.** *n.* Stock of animals etc. within species, having similar appearance and usu. developed by deliberate selection; race, lineage; sort, kind. **3. ~'ĭng** *n.*, (esp.) result of training; **(good) ~ing,** good manners. [E]

**breeze**[1] *n.* Gadfly. [E]

**breez|e**[2]. **1.** *n.* Gentle wind; (sl.) easy task, quarrel; **~'ȳ** *a.* (**~ily, ~iness**), pleasantly windy, (of manner) lively, jovial. **2.** *v.i.* (colloq.) Move like breeze or in lively or offhand manner. [Sp. & Port. *briza*]

**breeze**[3] *n.* Small cinders, used with sand and cement in making **~ blocks** (lightweight building-blocks). [F (BRAISE)]

**Brĕn** *n.* Light-weight quick-firing machine-gun. [*Br*no, *En*field, places]

**brĕnt** *n.* **~(-goose**), smallest kind of wild goose. [orig. unkn.]

**brethren.** See BROTHER.

**Brĕ'ton** *a.* & *n.* (Native, language) of Brittany. [F (BRITON)]

**brēve** *n.* (Mus.) note = two semibreves, now rarely used; written or printed mark ˘ of short or unstressed vowel. [BRIEF]

**brĕ'vėt. 1.** *n.* Document conferring army rank without corresponding pay. **2.** *v.t.* Confer rank by brevet. [F (BRIEF)]

**brē'vĭarȳ** *n.* Book containing R.C. Ch. daily office. [L (ABBREVIATE)]

**bre̅′vitў** n. Compactness of written or spoken expression; shortness of life etc. [AF (BRIEF)]

**brew** (-ōō). **1.** v.t. & i. Make (beer etc.) by infusion, boiling, and fermentation; make (tea etc.) by infusion or mixture; undergo these processes; concoct, threaten, (*mischief is brewing*). **2.** n. Process of brewing; amount brewed at once; (quality of) what is brewed. **3.** ~′erў n., place where beer is brewed commercially. [E]

**bri′ar**¹, ². See BRIER¹, ².

**brib|e. 1.** n. Money etc. offered to procure (often) dishonest or illegal action or decision in favour of giver. **2.** v.t. & i. Give bribe to (person *to* do), give bribes; ~′erў n., offering or accepting bribes. [F *briber* beg]

**bri′c-à-bräc** n. Miscellaneous old ornaments, furniture, etc. [F]

**brick. 1.** n. Building-material of baked or sun-dried clay; small usu. rectangular block of this (**drop a** ~, sl., say indiscreet thing; MAKE *bricks without straw*); similarly shaped piece of concrete, ice cream, etc.; child's toy building-block; (sl.) generous or loyal person; ~′bat, piece of brick esp. as missile, uncomplimentary remark; ~′layer, workman building with bricks; ~-red, of red colour of bricks; *bricks and* MORTAR; ~′work, building in brick. **2.** v.t. Block *up*, close in, with bricks. [LDu.]

**bride** n. Woman on wedding-day and for some time before and after; ~′groom, man on wedding-day etc.; ~′smaid, unmarried woman or girl attending bride at wedding. **bri′dal** a., of bride or wedding. [E]

**bridge**¹. **1.** n. Structure carrying road, railway, etc., across stream, road, etc.; raised platform from which ship is directed; upper bony part of nose; piece of wood etc. over which violin strings are stretched; ~′head, post held on far side of river etc. facing enemy; ~ **of asses**, *pons asinorum*; ~ **of boats** (over boats moored abreast); ~′work, partial denture supported by teeth on each side. **2.** v.t. Be or make bridge over; span as with bridge. [E]

**bridge**² n. Card-game developed from whist, in which one player's cards are exposed and played by his partner. [orig. unkn.]

**bri′dle. 1.** n. Gear to control (esp. riding-)horse etc.; restraint; ~-**path**, **-road**, (fit for riders but not vehicles). **2.** v.t. & i. Put bridle on; curb, bring under control; ~ (**up**), express resentment etc. (as if) by throwing up head and drawing in chin. [E]

**Brie** (brē) n. Kind of soft French cheese. [place]

**brief** a., n., & v. **1.** a. Of short duration; concise in expression; **be** ~, speak in few words; **in** ~, in short. **2.** n. Pope's letter on discipline; summary of facts etc. in case drawn up for counsel (**hold a** ~ **for**, be retained as counsel for, be obliged to argue in favour of); ‖piece of employment for barrister; (in *pl.*) men's very short underpants, women's very short knickers; ~-**case**, rectangular case for documents etc. **3.** v.t. ‖Instruct by brief; instruct with regard to planned operation. [F f. L *brevis* short]

**bri′er**¹, -**ar**¹, n. Wild rose or other prickly bush. [E]

**bri′er**², -**ar**², n. Heath with root used for tobacco-pipes; brier pipe. [F *bruyère*]

**brig**¹ n. (Sc. & N. Engl.) Bridge. [BRIDGE¹]

**brig**² n. Two-masted square-rigged vessel with additional fore-and-aft sail on mainmast. [abbr. BRIGANTINE]

**Brig.** abbr. Brigadier.

**bri̅ga̅′de. 1.** n. ‖Military unit forming part of division; organized or uniformed band of workers. **2.** v.t. Form into brigade. **3. brigadier′** n., officer commanding brigade, staff officer of similar standing; **bri′gand** n., member of robber band living by pillage and ransom; **bri′gandage** n., conduct of brigands; **bri′gandry**, ns., conduct of brigands; **bri′gantine** (-ēn) n., two-masted vessel with square-rigged foremast and fore-and-aft-rigged mainmast. [F f. It. (*briga* strife)]

**bright** (-it). **1.** a. Emitting or reflecting much light, shining, brilliant, vivid, conspicuous, cheering or cheerful, vivacious, quick-witted, talented, (*bright flash, steel, complexion, red, example, side of things, face, manner, child, idea*); ~′en v.t. & i. **2.** adv. Brightly; ~ **and early**, very early in the morning. [E]

**Bri′ght's di̅se̅ase** (-i′ts; -zēz) n. A kidney disease. [*Bright*, person]

**brill** n. A European flat-fish. [orig. unkn.]

**bri'llian|t** (-lya-). **1.** a. Bright, sparkling, distinguished, talented, showy. **2.** n. Diamond of finest quality cut in two flat faces joined by facets. **3.** ~**ce**, ~**cÿ**, ns.; ~**tine** (-ēn) n., cosmetic for making hair glossy. [F (*briller* shine f. It.)]

**brim. 1.** n. Edge of cup, hollow, channel, etc., (*full to the brim*); projecting edge of hat; ~**-full** (to the brim). **2.** v.i. & t. (-**mm**-). Fill or be full to the brim (esp. in *part.*, often *over*). [orig. unkn.]

**bri'mston|e** n. Sulphur (arch.); fuel of hell-fire; ~**e butterfly, moth**, sulphur-coloured varieties; ~**ÿ** a., (esp.) suggestive of hell or the Devil. [BURN², STONE]

**bri'ndled** (-dəld) a. Brown with streaks of other colour (esp. of dogs and cattle). [Scand.]

**brine. 1.** n. Salt water; sea-water. **2.** v.t. Treat with brine. [E]

**bring** v.t. (**brought** *pr.* -awt). Cause to come, come with or convey by carrying, leading, impelling, attracting; be sold for (price); cause, result in; prefer (charge), initiate (legal action), adduce (argument); cause to become (*bring* LOW²); cause despite reluctance (*cannot bring myself to*); ~ **about**, cause to happen; ~**-and-buy** *sale* etc. (at which customers bring things for sale and buy what is brought by others); ~ **back**, call to mind; ~ **down**, (esp.) cause to fall, abase, lower (price); ~ *down the house*, (Theatr.) get loud applause; ~ **forth**, give birth to, cause; ~ **forward**, draw attention to, move to earlier time, transfer from previous page; ~ **home to** person, convict or convince him of; ~ **in**, introduce (custom, commodity, fashion, topic), produce as profit, pronounce (verdict; person *guilty, not guilty*); ~ **into being**, cause to exist; ~ **off**, conduct (attempt) successfully; ~ **on**, cause, advance progress of; ~ **out**, express, exhibit clearly, introduce (girl) to society, publish; ~ **over**, convert to one's own side; ~ **round**, restore to consciousness, bring informally, win over (*to* opinion); ~ **through**, save (sick person); ~ **to**, check motion of (ship), restore to consciousness; *bring to* LIGHT¹, *to* MIND, *to* PASS¹; ~ **under**, subdue; ~ **up**, supervise

training of (child) in habits, manners, etc., cause to appear in court, anchor (ship), draw attention to, vomit. [E]

**brink** n. Extreme edge of precipice, river, etc., esp. when steep; **on the** ~ **of**, about or likely to plunge or fall or pass into *destruction, ruin, eternity, death*, etc., in imminent danger of doing; ~**'manship**, art of advancing to the very brink of war but not engaging in it. [N]

**bri'nÿ** a. (-iness). Of brine or sea, salt; **the** ~, (sl.) the sea. [BRINE]

**brio** (brē'ō) n. Vivacity. [It.]

**briqué'tte** (-k-) n. Block of compressed coal-dust. [F dim. (BRICK)]

**brisk. 1.** a. Active, lively, enlivening, (*brisk pace, trade, air*). **2.** v.t. & i. ~ (**up**), make or grow brisk. [prob. F BRUSQUE]

**bri'skėt** n. Animal's breast esp. as joint of beef or other meat. [F]

**bri'sling** (*or* -z-) n. Small herring or sprat. [Norw. & Da.]

**bri'stle** (-sel). **1.** n. A short stiff hair, esp. one of those on pig's back etc. used in brushes etc.; **bri'stlÿ** (-slī) a. (-iness). **2.** v.i. & t. (Of hair, feathers) stand up, (of dog, bird, person) make (hair etc.) bristle, bristle the hair, prepare for fight or show temper, (usu. *up*); be thickly set *with* guns, difficulties, etc. [E]

**Brit.** *abbr.* Britain; British.

**Britǎ'nn|ia** (-nya) n. Britain personified (~**ia metal**, a silvery alloy); ~**ic** a., of Britain (chiefly in **Her, His,** ~**ic Majesty**). [L]

**Bri'tish** a. Of (Great) Britain; **the** ~, (*pl.*) British people; \*~**er** n., British subject; ~**ism, Bri'tĭcĭsm,** n., idiom used in Britain but not U.S. etc.; **Bri'ton** n., one of people in S. Britain before Roman conquest, native or inhabitant of Great Britain. [E]

**bri'tt|le** a. (~**ler,** ~**lest;** ~**ly,** ~**lely,** ~**leness**). Apt to break, fragile. [E]

**broach. 1.** n. Roasting-spit; spire continuing tower-top without parapet; boring-bit. **2.** v.t. Pierce and begin drawing liquor from (cask); open and start using; bring up (subject) for discussion. [F BROOCH]

**broad** (-awd) a., n., & adv. **1.** a. Large across, wide, not narrow, extensive, tolerant, (after measurement) in breadth, (*broad river, acres, views; is 6 ft. broad; as* ~ *as it is*

**long**, without preference either way); full, main, explicit, somewhat coarse, strongly dialectal, generalized, bold in artistic style, (*broad daylight*, *facts*, HINT, *comedy*, *accent*, *rule*, *effect*); ~**ly speaking**, neglecting minor exceptions. **2.** *n.* Broad part; ‖large piece of fresh water in Norfolk etc. formed by widening of river; *(sl.)* (immoral) woman. **3.** *adv.* Broadly, fully. **4.** *broad* ARROW; ~ **bean**, (large flat seed of) an edible bean; ~**cast**, (*a.* & *adv.*) (of seed) scattered freely, widely disseminated, (*v.t.* & *i.*, *past* ~**cast**, ~**casted**) sow thus, disseminate widely, esp. (news, music, etc.) by radio or television, speak etc. on radio or television, (*n.*) transmission by radio or television; B~ **Church** (Anglican, favouring toleration); ~**cloth**, fine twilled woollen etc. or plain-woven cotton cloth; *~***jump**, long jump; ~**loom**, (carpet) woven in broad width; ~**mi'nded**, tolerant or liberal in thought or opinion; ~**sheet**, large sheet of paper printed on one side only; ~**side**, broadsheet, side of ship between bow and quarter, (discharge of) all guns on one side of ship, (fig.) powerful verbal attack; ~**side on**, transversely; ~**sword**, broad-bladed cutting-sword. **5.** ~**en** *v.t.* & *i.*; ~**ways**, ~**wise**, (-z) *advs.* [E]

**broca'de. 1.** *n.* Fabric woven with raised pattern. **2.** *v.t.* Weave thus. [Sp. & Port. *brocado* f. It. (*brocco* twisted thread)]

**bro'ccoli** *n.* Hardy variety of cauliflower. [It.]

**bro'chure** (-sh-) *n.* Booklet, pamphlet, esp. with information about place etc. [F (*brocher* stitch)]

**brock** *n.* Badger. [E f. Celt.]

**broderie anglaise** (brōdrǐ ahn-glā'z) *n.* Open embroidery on white linen or cambric. [F, = English embroidery]

**brogue** (-g) *n.* Rough shoe of untanned leather; strong shoe for golf etc.; marked Irish or other accent. [Celt.]

**broil**[1] *n.* (arch.) Quarrel, tumult. [F *brouiller* mix]

**broil**[2] *v.t.* & *i.* Cook on fire or gridiron; make or be very hot (of or with sun etc.); ~**er** *n.*, (esp.) young chicken reared for broiling. [F *bruler* burn]

**broke** *past* of BREAK, & *p.p.* arch. exc. in colloq. sense 'destitute of money'. [BREAK]

**bro'ken** *a.* ~ **chord** (Mus., with notes not performed simultaneously); ~**-down**, used or worn and hence (almost) broken; ~ **English** etc. (imperfect); ~ **ground** (uneven); ~**-hearted**, crushed by grief; ~ **home** (of family lacking one parent); ~ **line** (made up of dashes); ~ **man** (reduced to despair); broken REED; ~ **sleep** (disturbed and intermittent); ~ **time** (reduced by interruptions); ~ **water** (choppy).

**bro'ker** *n.* Middleman between buyer and seller, agent; pawnbroker; stockbroker; ‖appraiser and seller of distrained goods; ~**age** *n.*, broker's fee or commission; **bro'king** *n.*, broker's trade. [AF]

‖**bro'lly** *n.* (colloq.) Umbrella. [abbr.]

**bro'm|ine** (-ēn) *n.* (Chem.) A liquid element with rank smell; ~**ic** *a.*, containing bromine; ~**ide** *n.*, binary compound of bromine, such compound as sedative, commonplace bore, trite remark. [Gk *brōmos* stink]

**bro'nch|ial** (-k-) *a.* (**-lly**). Of the ramifications of the windpipe; ~**i'tis** *n.*, inflammation of bronchial mucous membrane. [L f. Gk]

**bro'nco** *n.* (*pl.* ~s). Wild or half-tamed horse of western U.S.; *~***-buster**, (sl.) breaker-in of broncos. [Sp., = rough]

**bronze** *n.*, *a.*, & *v.* **1.** *n.* Brown alloy of copper and tin, its colour, work of art or medal in it; B~ **Age**, when weapons and tools were made of bronze; **bro'nzy** *a.* **2.** *a.* Made of or coloured like bronze; ~ **medal** (usu. as 3rd prize). **3.** *v.t.* & *i.* Give bronze surface to, make or grow brown, tan, (esp. of sunburn). [F f. It.]

**brooch** (-ō-) *n.* Ornamental hinged pin worn as part of woman's dress or as badge. [F *broche* BROACH f. L]

**brood. 1.** *n.* Bird's or other animal's young produced at a hatch or birth; (derog.) children of a family; bee or wasp larvae; group of related things; ~ **mare** etc. (for breeding). **2.** *v.i.* Sit as hen on eggs, (of night etc.) hang close *over* or *on* place etc.; meditate deeply, ponder resentfully (*up*)*on* or *over*; ~**y** *a.* (**-iness**), (of hen) wishing to incubate eggs, (fig.) depressed. [E]

**brook**[1] *v.t.* (literary; usu. w. neg.) Tolerate (insult etc.); (of affairs) admit of (delay etc.). [E]

**brook**[2] *n.* Small stream; ~**let** *n.* [E]

**broo'klime** *n.* Kind of speedwell common in ditches. [E (prec.)]

**broom** *n.* Yellow-flowered shrub growing on sandy soil; long-handled sweeping-brush (**new** ~, newly appointed person eager to make changes); ~**'stick**, broom-handle (allegedly ridden on through air by witches and jumped over by parties to sham marriage). [E]

**Bros.** *abbr.* Brothers (esp. in name of firm).

**broth** (*or* -aw-) *n.* Thin meat or fish soup; ~ **of a boy**, (Ir.) good fellow. [E]

**bro'thel** *n.* House of prostitution. [E, = worthless man]

**bro'ther** (-ŭ'dh-) *n.* Son of same parent(s) (HALF-*brother*); close man friend, associate, equal; (*pl.* **brethren** *pr.* brĕ'dhrĭn) man who is fellow member of class or sect or human race, (as title) member of religious order; ~**-in-law**, one's husband's or wife's brother, one's sister's husband; ~**hood** *n.*, relationship or group of brothers, comradeship; ~**ly** *a.* (~**liness**). [E]

**brought.** See BRING.

**brou'haha** (broō'hah-hah) *n.* Commotion, uproar. [F]

**brow** *n.* Eyebrow (usu. in *pl.*); forehead; (colloq.) level of intellect; edge of cliff etc., summit of pass or hill in road; ~**'beat**, intimidate with looks and words. [E]

**brown** *a., n.,* & *v.* **1.** *a.* (~**'ness** *pr.* -n-n-). Of colour made by mixing red, yellow, and black, toast-coloured; dark-skinned, sun-tanned. **2.** *n.* Brown colour or pigment; brown clothes or material (*dressed in brown*); brown ball in snooker etc. **3.** *v.t.* & *i.* Make or become brown; ||~**ed off** (sl.) bored, fed up. **4.** ~ **bread** (of unbolted flour); ~ **coal**, lignite; ~ **eye** (with brown iris); ~ **paper** (unbleached, for packing etc.); *~**'stone**, red-brown sandstone for building; ~ **study**, absorption in own thoughts; ~ **sugar** (partly refined); **do** ~, (sl.) cheat; ~**'ie** *n.*, benevolent domestic goblin, (B-) junior Guide; ~**'ing** *n.*, browned sugar or flour to colour gravy. [E]

**browse** (-z). **1.** *v.i.* & *t.* Feed on or on leaves and young shoots, crop *down* or *away*; (fig.) read desultorily. **2.** *n.* Browsing or material for it. [F *brost* bud]

**Bru'in** (-ōō'-) *n.* (Personal name for) bear. [Du. (BROWN)]

**bruis|e** (-ōōz). **1.** *n.* Injury to flesh of person or animal or plant caused by blow or pressure and discolouring without breaking the skin. **2.** *v.t.* & *i.* Pound, grind small, batter; inflict bruise on, be susceptible to bruises; (fig.) hurt mentally; ~**er** *n.*, (esp.) prize-fighter. [E]

**bruit** (-ōōt) *v.t.* (arch.) Spread (report, fame, *that*) *about* or *abroad*. [F, = noise]

||**Brŭm** *n.* (colloq.) Birmingham; **Brŭ'mmagem** *a.*, counterfeit, cheap and showy; ||~**'mie** *n.*, (colloq.) person from Birmingham. [place]

**brŭnch** *n.* (colloq.) Single meal instead of breakfast and lunch. [portmanteau wd]

**brunĕ'tte** (-ōō-) *n.* Dark-skinned and/or brown-haired white woman. [F (BROWN)]

**brŭnt** *n.* Chief stress *of* attack (esp. *bear the brunt of*). [orig. unkn.]

**brush. 1.** *n.* Cleaning or hairdressing or painting implement of bristles or feathers or hair or wires set in wood etc.; thin stick with wire bristles for striking a cymbal etc.; brushlike carbon or metal piece for good electrical connection; fox's bushy tail; application of brush; short sharp encounter. **2.** *v.t.* & *i.* Move briskly (*through* etc.); sweep or scrub or put in order with brush; graze or touch in passing; remove with brush. **3.** ~ **against**, graze; ~ **aside**, dismiss curtly or lightly; ~ **off** *v.t.*, ~**-off** *n.*, dismiss(al), rebuff; ~ **up**, furbish, renew acquaintance with (subject); ~**'wood**, undergrowth, thicket, cut or broken twigs etc.; ~**'work**, painter's (style of) manipulation of brush; ~**'less** *a.*, not requiring use of brush. [F]

**brŭsque** (-k; *or* -ōōsk) *a.* Blunt, offhand, in manner; ~**'rie** (-skerē) *n.*, brusque behaviour or tone. [F f. It. (*brusco* sour)]

**Brŭ'ssels** (-z) *n.* ~ **carpet, lace,** (kinds made at Brussels); ~ **sprouts,** edible buds of kind of cabbage. [place]

**brut|e** (-ōōt). **1.** *a.* Unable to reason; stupid, sensual, animal-like;

cruel; merely material (*brute force*). **2.** *n.* Brute person or animal; (colloq.) disliked person. **3.** ~**al** *a.* (-**lly**), coarse, savagely cruel, mercilessly frank; ~**ă'lĭtў** *n.*; ~**'alize** *v.t.* [F f. L *brutus* stupid]

**brў'onў** *n.* One of two kinds of climbing hedge plant. [L f. Gk]

**B.S.** *abbr.* Bachelor of *Science, of Surgery; British Standard.

**B.Sc.** *abbr.* Bachelor of Science.

**B.S.I.** *abbr.* British Standards Institution.

**B.S.T.** *abbr.* British Summer Time.

**Bt.** *abbr.* Baronet.

**bu.** *abbr.* bushel.

**bŭ'bble. 1.** *n.* Globe or half-globe of liquid enclosing air or gas; air--filled cavity in glass or amber; transparent domed canopy; visionary project; **prick the ~,** (fig.) unmask pretentiousness etc. **2.** *v.i.* Send up, rise in, make sound of, bubbles; ~ **(over),** be exuberant. **3.** ~ **and squeak,** cold meat or potatoes fried with chopped vegetables; ~ **bath** (in which water is foamed by perfumed substance); ~ **car,** small car with transparent dome; ~ **gum,** chewing-gum that can be blown into large bubbles; ~ **pack,** small package enclosing goods in transparent material on backing; **bŭ'bblў,** (*a.*) full of bubbles, (*n.*, ǁsl.) champagne. [imit.]

**bŭ'bō** *n.* (*pl.* ~**es**). Inflamed swelling in groin or armpit esp. as symptom of plague; **būbŏ'nĭc** *a.* (of plague). [L f. Gk *boubōn* groin]

**bŭccaneer'** *n.* Pirate orig. of Spanish Main; adventurer; ~**ĭng,** (*a.*) piratical, (*n.*) piratical roving. [F]

**bŭck¹. 1.** *n.* Male fallow-deer, roe--deer, reindeer, chamois, antelope, hare, rabbit, ferret, or rat; (arch.) dandy; (*attrib.*, sl.) male. **2.** *v.i.* & *t.* (Of horse) jump vertically with back arched, throw (rider) thus; *oppose, resist; ~ (up), make haste, become or make vigorous or cheerful; (in *p.p.*) elated. **3.** ~**-hound,** small kind of staghound; ~**'shot,** coarse shot; ~**'skin,** (leather of) buck's skin, thick smooth cotton or woollen cloth; ~**'thorn,** thorny shrub with purgative berries; ~**-tooth** (projecting). [E]

***bŭck²** *n.* (sl.) A dollar; FAST² *buck*. [orig. unkn.]

**bŭck³** *n.* (sl.) Object indicating

dealer at poker; **pass the ~,** (colloq.) shift responsibility (*to*).

**bŭ'ckĕt. 1.** *n.* Round open vessel for carrying or holding water; amount contained in this; (in *pl.*) large quantities (of rain etc.); compartment in water-wheel, dredger, or grain-elevator; **kick the ~,** (sl.) die; ~**-shop,** office for gambling in stocks. **2.** *v.i.* & *t.* Move or drive bumpily; (of rain etc.) pour down heavily. [AF]

**bŭ'ckle. 1.** *n.* Metal rim with hinged pin for securing a strap, belt, etc. **2.** *v.t.* & *i.* Fasten (*up, on,* etc.) with buckle(s); ~ **(down) to,** set about (work); ~ **(up),** (cause to) crumple under longitudinal pressure; ~**r** *n.,* (Hist.) small round shield with handle. [F f. L *buccula* cheek-strap]

**bŭ'ckram** *n.* Coarse linen or cloth stiffened with paste etc. [F *boquerant*]

**Bŭcks.** *abbr.* Buckinghamshire.

ǁ**bŭ'ckshee** *n., a.,* & *adv.* (sl.) **1.** *n.* Something extra, free, or additional to usual allowance. **2.** *a.* & *adv.* Gratuitous(ly). [corrupt. BAKSHEESH]

**bŭ'ckwheat** *n.* Cereal with seeds shaped like beechmast. [Du., = beech-wheat]

**būcŏ'lĭc. 1.** *a.* (~**ally**). Of shepherds, rustic, pastoral. **2.** *n.* Pastoral poem(s). [L f. Gk (*boukolos* herdsman)]

**bŭd. 1.** *n.* Projection from which branch or leaf-cluster or flower develops, flower or leaf not fully open, (in ~, putting forth buds; **nip in the ~,** destroy at early stage); (Zool.) asexual growth separating as new animal. **2.** *v.i.* & *t.* (-**dd**-). Put forth buds, sprout as bud, begin to grow or develop (*budding lawyer, cricketer*); (Gardening) graft bud of; (Zool.) form (as) bud. [orig. unkn.]

**Bu'ddh|a** (bōō'da) *n.* The Enlightened (as title esp. of the founder of Buddhism); ~**ĭsm** *n.,* Asian religion founded by Gautama Buddha in 5th c. B.C.; ~**ĭst** *n.* & *a.;* ~**ĭ'stĭc(al)** *adjs.* (-**ically**). [Skr.]

**bŭ'ddleia** (-lĭa) *n.* Shrub or tree with lilac or yellow flowers of various forms. [*Buddle,* person]

**bŭ'ddў** *n.* (colloq., often as form of address). Brother, chum, mate. [perh. f. BROTHER]

**bŭ'dge** *v.i.* & *t.* Move in the least degree (in neg. context; *cannot budge it*). [F *bouger*]

**bŭ′dgerĭgăr** n. Australian grass parakeet. [Aboriginal]

**bŭ′dgĕt. 1.** n. Annual estimate of country's revenue and expenditure with statement of intentions; similar estimate of body or person; money needed or available; **on a ~**, avoiding undue expense; **~arỹ** a. **2.** v.t. & i. Allow or arrange for or *for* in budget. [F f. L *bulga* bag]

**bŭ′dgie** n. (colloq.) Budgerigar. [abbr.]

**bŭff. 1.** n. Velvety dull-yellow leather; colour of this; the skin (**in the ~**, naked; *stripped to the buff*); *(colloq.) enthusiast. **2.** v.t. Polish (metal etc.); make velvety like buff. **3. ~alō** n. (*pl.* -oes, same), one of three kinds of ox. [F *buffle* & Port. *bufalo* buffalo]

**bŭ′ffer** n. Apparatus for deadening impact esp. ‖of railway vehicles (**~ State**, small one between two great ones, regarded as diminishing danger of quarrels); **old ~**, (sl.) old-fashioned or incompetent man. [imit.]

**bŭ′ffĕt**[1]. **1.** n. Blow (as) of hand; blow of fate or fortune. **2.** v.t. Deal blows to; contend with (waves etc.). [F dim. (*bufe* blow)]

**bŭ′ffet**[2] (bŏŏ′fā) n. Sideboard or recessed cupboard; (place offering) self-service of food from sideboard or counter; **~ car**, railway coach serving light meals. [F, = stool]

**buffoo′n. 1.** n. Facetious person, (clumsy or coarse) jester; **~erỹ** n. **2.** v.i. Play the buffoon. [F f. It. f. L *buffo* clown]

**bŭg. 1.** n. Flat evil-smelling blood-sucking insect infesting beds; *any small insect; (sl.) (disease caused by) virus, (person having) obsession, concealed microphone, defect in machine etc.; **~-eyed**, with bulging eyes; **~-hunter**, (colloq.) entomologist. **2.** v.t. (sl.; **-gg-**). Install concealed microphone in; listen to thus; *annoy. [orig. unkn.]

**bŭ′gabōō, bŭ′gbear** (-bār), ns. Object of baseless terror, mental bogy; cause of annoyance. [*bug* = bogy]

**bŭ′gger** (-g-). **1.** n. Sodomite; so **~ỹ** n. **2.** (vulg.) (Unpleasant) person or thing; **~-all**, nothing. **3.** v.t. & i. Commit buggery with. **4.** (vulg.) = DAMN; mess *about* (*with*), *up*; make *off*. [Du. f. F f. L *Bulgarus* Bulgarian heretic]

**bŭ′ggỹ** (-gĭ) n. Light horse-drawn vehicle for one or two; small sturdy motor vehicle. [orig. unkn.]

**bū′gle**[1] n. Creeping plant with usu. blue flowers. [L *bugula*]

**bū′gle**[2] n. Long glass bead sewn on dress etc. for ornament. [orig. unkn.]

**bū′gle**[3]. **1.** n. Brass instrument like small trumpet, used for giving signal-calls. **2.** v.i. & t. Sound bugle, sound (call) on bugle; **bū′gler** n., bugle-signaller; **bū′glĕt** n., small bugle. [F f. L *buculus* young bull]

**bū′glŏss** n. One of several kinds of rough-leaved plant. [For L f. Gk, = ox-tongued]

**buhl** (bool) n. Inlaid work of brass and tortoise-shell. [*Boule*, person]

**build** (bĭ-). **1.** v.t. & i. (**built** *pr.* bĭ-). Construct by putting parts or material together (house, nest, fire, vehicle, fire, road, fortune, reputation); (in *p.p.*) having specified build (*sturdily built*); **~ in**, surround with houses etc., insert as part of structure; **built-in**, forming integral part of structure, (fig.) personality, etc.; **~ on**, rely on; **~ up**, block by building, praise, gradually establish itself; **~′up** n., favourable description in advance, gradual approach to climax; **built-up**, increased in height etc. by additions, composed of separately made parts, (of locality) fully occupied by houses. **2.** n. Style of construction; proportions of human body (*sturdy build*). **3. ~′er** n., (esp.) contractor for building houses; **~′ing** n., (esp.) house, school, factory, etc.; ‖**~ing society** (of investors in fund for loan to persons buying houses etc.). [E]

**bŭlb** n. Globular base of stem of some plants (onion, lily, etc.) sending roots down and leaves up; roundish swelling in cylindrical organ; compressible globular rubber part of syringe etc.; (glass container of) electric lamp-filament; dilated part of thermometer etc.; **~′ous** a., bulb-shaped, having bulb(s), (of plant) growing from bulb. [L *bulbus* f. Gk, = onion]

**bŭlge. 1.** n. Irregular swelling-out of a surface or line; (colloq.) temporary increase in volume or numbers; **~iness** (-ji-). **2.** v.i. Form bulge. [F f. L *bulga* bag]

**bŭlk. 1.** n. Cargo; large quantity (*transported in bulk*); large shape, person, or body; size, magnitude; great size or mass; roughage; *the greater part or number of*; ~ **buying** (in large amounts, or by one buyer of much of one producer's output). **2.** *v.i. & t.* Seem in respect of size or importance (*bulk large*); make (textile yarn etc.) seem thicker by suitable treatment. **3.** ~**'head,** upright partition between compartments in ship etc.; ~**'y̆** *a.* (~**ily,** ~**iness**), of (too) great size, unwieldy. [N]

**bull**[1] (-ŏŏ-) *n.* Papal edict. [F f. L *bulla* seal]

**bull**[2] (-ŏŏ-) *n.* **(Irish)** ~, statement so made as to imply an absurdity (e.g. *It is impossible that I could have been in two places at once, unless I were a bird*); (sl.) unnecessary routine tasks. [orig. unkn.]

**bull**[3] (-ŏŏ-). **1.** *n.* Uncastrated male ox; male whale, elephant, etc.; (*B*~) sign of ZODIAC; (St. Exch.) one who buys hoping to sell at higher price later; bull's-eye of target. **2.** *a.* Like that of bull (~ *neck*, short and thick). **3.** ~**-at-a-gate,** directly attacking; **take the ~ by the horns,** meet difficulty boldly; ~**'dog,** dog of powerful courageous large-headed breed, tenacious and courageous (person), (Oxf. & Camb.) University proctor's attendant; ~*dog clip,* fastener with strong closure; ~**'doze** *v.t.,* (colloq.) clear with bulldozer, make one's *way* forcibly, intimidate; ~**'dozer,** powerful tractor with broad vertical blade for clearing ground; ~**'fight(ing),** Spanish etc. sport of baiting bulls; ~**'finch,** strong-beaked fine-plumaged song-bird; ~**'frog,** large Amer. frog with bellowing cry; ~**'head,** small large-headed fish; ~**-headed,** obstinate, blundering; ~ **in a china shop,** reckless or clumsy destroyer; ~**-market** (with rising prices); ~**-nosed,** with rounded end; ~ **point,** (colloq.) point of superiority; ~**'ring,** arena for bullfight; ~**'roarer,** Australian Aboriginals' noise-making whirled strip of wood on string; ~**'s-eye,** boss of glass at centre of blown glass sheet, hemisphere or thick disc of glass as window in ship, small circular window, (lantern with) hemispherical lens, centre of target, kind of round sweetmeat; ~**-terrier,** cross between bulldog and terrier; ~**'trout,** salmon trout. [N]

**bu'llace** (bŏŏ'lĭs) *n.* Small (half-) wild plum(-tree). [F]

**bu'llet** (-ŏŏ-) *n.* Missile usu. round, or cylindrical with pointed end, for rifle, revolver, etc.; ~**-head(ed),** (with) round head. [F dim. (*boule* ball)]

**bu'llĕtĭn** (-ŏŏ-) *n.* Short official statement or broadcast report of public event or news or of invalid's condition. [F f. It. dim. (BULL[1])]

**bu'llion** (bŏŏ'lyon) *n.* Gold or silver in the lump or valued by weight. [F (BOIL[2])]

**bu'llock** (-ŏŏ-) *n.* Castrated bull. [E (BULL[3])]

**bu'llў** (-ŏŏ-) *n., v., a., & int.* **1.** *n.* Person using strength or power to coerce others by fear; ~(-**boy**), hired ruffian. **2.** *v.t.* Persecute or oppress by (threat of) superior force (*into, out of*). **3.** *a. & int.* (sl.) Very good; ~ **for you,** bravo. [Du.]

**bu'llў**[2] (-ŏŏ-) *n.* ~ (**beef**), corned beef. [F (BOIL[2])]

**bu'llў**[3] (-ŏŏ-; Hockey). **1.** *n.* Putting ball in play after threefold striking of two opponents' sticks. **2.** *v.i.* ~ **off,** start play thus. [orig. unkn.]

**bu'lrush** (-ŏŏ-) *n.* Tall rush, esp. reed-mace; (Bibl.) papyrus. [perh. BULL[3] + RUSH[1]]

**bu'lwark** (-ŏŏ-) *n.* Earthwork or other material defence; person or principle that protects; ship's side above deck. [BOLE, WORK]

**bŭm**[1] *n.* ‖(sl.) Buttocks; ~(-**bailiff**), (Hist.) sheriff's officer for arrests etc.; ~**-boat** (plying with fresh provisions etc. for ships). [orig. uncert.]

***bŭm**[2] *n., a., & v.* (colloq.) **1.** *n.* Habitual loafer; lazy dissolute person; **on the ~,** vagrant, begging. **2.** *a.* Of poor quality. **3.** *v.i. & t.* (-mm-). Loaf, wander *around*; cadge. [*bummer* f. G *bummler* loafer]

**bŭ'mble** *v.i.* Make buzz; ramble *on* in speech; act ineptly; ~**-bee,** large loud-humming bee. [BOOM[2]]

**bŭ'mbledom** (-beld-) *n.* Self-important minor officials and their ways. [*Bumble* in *Oliver Twist*]

‖**bŭmf** *n.* (sl.) Toilet-paper; papers, documents. [abbr. of BUM[1]-*fodder*]

**bŭ'mmalō** *n.* (*pl.* same). Small S. Asian fish. [Marathi]

**bŭmp** *n., adv., & v.* **1.** *n.* Dull-sounding blow, knock, collision; swelling caused by it; uneven patch on road, cricket-pitch, etc.; prominence on skull, faculty thought to be indicated by it (~ **of locality**, ability to find one's way); touching of boat in bumping-race; ~'**y** *a.* (~**ily**, ~**iness**). **2.** *adv.* With a bump. **3.** *v.t.* & *i.* Come or strike with a bump against or *against* (one's head, boat in front), hurt thus; move *along* etc. with bumps. **4.** ~'**ing-race** (where boats start successively at fixed intervals and each seeks to overtake the next); ~ **into**, (colloq.) meet by chance; ~ **off**, (sl.) murder; ~**-supper** (celebrating success in bumping-races); ~ **up**, (colloq.) increase (prices etc.). [imit.]

**bŭ'mper** *n.* Brim-full glass; unusually large or abundant or excellent example; metal etc. bar on motor vehicle to reduce damage in collisions (~**to-~**, travelling very close together; (Crick.) ball rising high after pitching.

**bŭ'mpkĭn** *n.* Rustic or awkward fellow. [Du.]

**bŭ'mptious** (-pshŭs) *a.* Self-assertive, offensively conceited. [BUMP, after *fractious*]

**bŭn** *n.* Small soft round sweet cake with currants etc.; hair dressed in bun shape; ‖~**-fight**, (sl.) tea-party. [orig. unkn.]

**bŭnch. 1.** *n.* Set of things growing or fastened together (*bunch of flowers, grapes, keys*); lot, collection, (*best of the bunch*); (sl.) gang, group; ~'**y** *a.* (~**ily**, ~**iness**). **2.** *v.t.* & *i.* Make into bunch(es); gather into close folds; form group or crowd.

**bŭ'ndle. 1.** *n.* Odds and ends tied up in cloth etc.; set of sticks etc. bound up or of parallel fibres or NERVES. **2.** *v.t.* & *i.* Do *up* or tie in bundle(s); throw confusedly *into* receptacle; go or send (person) hurriedly or unceremoniously *out, off, away*, etc. [LDu.]

**bŭng. 1.** *n.* Stopper of cork or other material for hole in cask; ~**-ho'** (excl. at parting or as toast). **2.** *v.t.* Stop with bung (~**ed up**, closed, blocked); (sl.) throw (stone etc.). [Du.]

**bŭ'ngalow** (-nggalō) *n.* One-storeyed house. [orig. in India; Gujarati f. Hindi, = of Bengal]

**bŭ'ngle** (-nggel). **1.** *v.i.* & *t.* Work clumsily, blunder over or mismanage or fail at (task). **2.** *n.* Piece of bungling. [imit.]

**bŭ'nion** (-yon) *n.* Inflamed swelling on foot, esp. on big toe. [F]

**bŭnk**[1] *n.* Sleeping-berth; ~**-bed**, piece of furniture with one bunk above another. [orig. unkn.]

**bŭnk**[2] *v.i.*, & *n.* (sl.) (**Do a**) ~, make off, vanish.

**bŭnk**[3] *n.* (sl.) Humbug, nonsense. [BUNKUM]

**bŭ'nker. 1.** *n.* Fuel-container; (Golf) pit containing sand etc. as obstacle; (Mil.) reinforced underground shelter. **2.** *v.t.* Fill fuel bunkers of (ship etc.); (usu. in *p.p.*) trap in bunker, bring into difficulties. [orig. unkn.]

**bŭ'nkum** *n.* Insincere talk, claptrap; nonsense. [*Buncombe*, place]

**bŭ'nny** *n.* (Child's name for) rabbit; ~ (**girl**), club hostess wearing costume suggesting rabbit. [*bun* rabbit]

**Bŭ'nsen** *n.* ~ **burner** (burning mixed air and gas, giving great heat). [person]

**bŭnt** *n.* (Naut.) Baggy middle of sail; ~'**line**, rope confining bunt in furling. [orig. unkn.]

**bŭ'nting**[1] *n.* Small bird of group allied to finches; **bŭ'nting**[2] *n.*, flags or their usual material.

**buoy** (boi). **1.** *n.* Anchored float as navigation mark etc.; = LIFE*buoy.* **2.** *v.t.* Bring to surface of, keep up in, water; sustain (*him* etc., courage etc., often *up*); mark (course, rocks, etc., *out*) with buoys. **3.** ~'**ant** *a.*, apt to float, rise, keep up, or recover spirits, light-hearted, (of liquid) keeping things afloat; ~'**ancy** *n.* [Du.]

**bŭr** *n.* Clinging seed-vessel or flower-head of plant, plant producing burs; person hard to shake off; ~'**dock**, plant with prickly flowers and docklike leaves. [Scand.]

**bŭ'rble** *v.i.* Make murmuring noise; speak ramblingly. [imit.]

**bŭr'bot** *n.* Eel-like freshwater fish. [F]

**bŭr'den. 1.** *n.* Load (lit., or fig. of duty, sorrow), obligation; obligatory expense; ship's carrying-capacity; bearing or drawing of loads (*beast of burden*); refrain of song, theme or gist of speech etc.; ~ **of proof**, obligation to prove one's assertions; ~**some** *a.*, imposing a burden. **2.** *v.t.* Load (lit. or fig.), encumber, oppress. [E (BIRTH)]

**bŭr'dock.** See BUR.

**bŭr'eau** (-ō) n. (pl. **~x**, **~s**, pr. -ōz). ‖Writing-desk with drawers; *chest of drawers; office or department for transacting specific business; Government department; **~cracy** (-ŏ'-) n., government by centralization, officialism, *a or the* set of dominant officials; **~crăt** n., official in bureaucracy; **~crä'tic** a. (-ically). [F, orig. = baize]

**bŭrĕ'tte**, *bŭrĕ't, n. Graduated glass tube with tap at end for measurement of liquid in chemical analysis. [F]

*bŭrg n. (colloq.) Town, city. [BOROUGH]

**bŭrgee'** n. Triangular pennant of yacht etc. [F]

**bŭr'geon** (-jon) n., & v.i. (literary). Bud, shoot; begin to grow rapidly. [F f. L burra wool]

**bŭr'gĕss** n. ‖Citizen of borough; ‖(Hist.) M.P. for borough or corporate town or university; *borough magistrate; **burgh** (bŭ'ro) n., Scottish borough; **bŭr'gher** (-ger) n., citizen of foreign town. [F f. L (burgus BOROUGH)]

**bŭr'glary** n. Entering building illegally (formerly only by night) with felonious intent; **bŭr'glar** n., person committing burglary; **bŭrglär'ious** a.; **bŭr'gle** v.t. & i., commit burglary on (house, person), commit burglary. [AF]

**bŭr'gomaster** (-ah-) n. Dutch or Flemish mayor. [Du. (BOROUGH)]

**bŭr'gundy** n. Red (or white) wine (as) of Burgundy. [place]

**bu'rial** (bĕ'-) n. Burying esp. of dead body, funeral; **~-ground**, cemetery; **~-service**, religious ceremony at funeral. [BURY]

**bŭr'in** n. Tool for engraving on copper. [F]

**bûrke** v.t. Avoid, stifle, (inquiry, discussion, rumour, etc.). [person who smothered victims]

**bûrlĕ'sque** (-k) a., n., & v. **1.** a. Of derisively imitative kind. **2.** n. Burlesque presentation of something, dramatic or literary parody, this branch of art; *variety show esp. with strip-tease. **3.** v.t. Make or give burlesque of. [F f. It. (burla mockery)]

**bûr'l|y** a. (**~iness**). Of stout sturdy build. [E]

**Bûrme'se** (-z) a. & n. (pl. same). (Native, language) of *Burma*; **Bûr'man** a. & n., Burmese. [place]

**burn¹** n. (Sc.) Brook. [E]

**burn². 1.** v.i. & t. (**~t**, **~ed**). (Cause to) be consumed or destroyed by fire, blaze or glow with fire, (money to **~**, in great abundance); (cause to) give light from fuel; (cause to) die by fire; subject to heat, make, harden (bricks), by heating (money **~s a hole in** one's pocket, one is eager to spend it); (cause to) be injured or damaged by fire or sun or great heat; char or scorch in cooking; cauterize, brand; colour *brown* etc. with heat or light; use energy of (propellant, nuclear fuel); give or feel sensation or pain (as) of heat (ears **~**, esp. allegedly when one is talked of); make or be hot or passionate; **~ away**, diminish to nothing by burning; **~** one's **boats** or **bridges**, commit oneself irrevocably; **~ down**, burn less vigorously, destroy (building) by burning; **~** one's **fingers**, suffer for meddling or rashness; **~ in**, imprint by burning (lit. or fig.); **~'ing-glass**, lens to concentrate sun's rays and burn an object; **~ out**, (make) fail by burning, make homeless by burning of house; **~t cork** (used to blacken face); burn the CANDLE at both ends; burn the midnight OIL; **~t ochre** (calcined to deeper colour); **~t offering**, sacrifice offered by burning; **~ up**, get rid of by fire, flash into blaze, *(sl.) be or make furious. **2.** n. Sore or mark made by burning. **3.** **~'er** n., (esp.) part of lamp or cooker that shapes the flame; **~'ing** a., (esp.) ardent (burning desire), flagrant (burning shame), hotly discussed (burning question). [E]

**bûr'nĕt** n. Kind of brown-flowered plant; kind of greenish moth. [F (BRUNETTE)]

‖**Bûr'nham** (-nam) n. **~ scale**, national salary scale for schoolteachers. [person]

**bûr'nish** v.t. Polish by rubbing. [F (BROWN)]

**bûrnou's** (-ōō's) n. Arab or Moorish hooded cloak. [F f. Arab. f. Gk]

**bûrnt.** See BURN².

**bûrp** n., & v.i. (sl.) Belch. [imit.]

**bûrr. 1.** n. Whirring sound; rough sound of letter *r*; rough edge on metal or paper; small drill; = BUR. **2.** v.i. Make burr. [imit.]

**bu'rrow. 1.** n. Hole excavated by fox or rabbit or other animal as dwelling. **2.** v.i. & t. Make or live in burrow; make (hole, one's *way*) by excavation; hide oneself; ~ **into**, (fig.) investigate. [BOROUGH]

**bŭr'sar** n. Treasurer of college etc.; holder of bursary; **bŭrsār'ial** a.; ~ў̆ n., bursar's office, allowance to student. [F or L (*bursa* PURSE)]

**bŭrst. 1.** v.i. & t. (burst). Fly violently apart or open forcibly by expansion of contents or internal pressure, send (containing case) violently apart; make way *out* or *in*, get away from or through, or express one's feelings, forcibly or suddenly; be full to overflowing; appear or come suddenly (*burst into flame*); be as if about to burst because of excitement etc.; ~ **into**, suddenly begin to utter (song, laughter, tears); ~ **out**, suddenly begin (laughing etc.). **2.** n. Bursting; sudden issuing forth (*burst of flame*); outbreak; spurt, gallop. [E]

‖**bŭr'ton** n. (sl.) **Go for a** ~, be lost or destroyed or killed. [orig. uncert.]

**bu'rў** (bĕ'-) v.t. Deposit (corpse etc.) in earth, tomb, or sea; lose by death (*has buried 3 husbands*); put under ground, hide in earth, cover up; consign to obscurity, put out of sight; involve one*self* deeply in (work etc.); ~ **the hatchet** or ***toma-hawk**, cease to quarrel. [E]

**bŭs. 1.** n. (*pl.* ~ **es**). Large passenger vehicle with fixed route; (colloq.) motor car, aeroplane; ‖~ **lane**, strip of road for use by buses only; ~**'man**, driver of bus; ~*man's holiday*, leisure time spent in work similar to one's regular work; ~**-shelter**, roadside shelter for persons awaiting bus; ~**-stop**, regular stopping-place of bus. **2.** v.i. & t. (***-ss-**). Go by bus; *transport by bus (esp. to counteract racial segregation). [abbr. of OMNIBUS]

‖**bŭ'sbў** (-z-) n. Tall fur cap of hussars and guardsmen. [orig. unkn.]

**bush¹** (-ŏŏ-) n. Shrub, clump of shrubs, (BEAT *about the bush*); bunch of ivy as ancient sign of vintner (**good wine needs no** ~, only inferior things need advertisement); luxuriant growth of hair; (Austral. etc.) woodland, forest, untilled district; ~**-baby**, small Afr. tree--climbing lemur; B~**'man**, aboriginal or language of a S. Afr. people; ~**'man**, dweller, farmer, or traveller in Austral. bush; ~ **tele-graph**, rapid spreading of informa-

tion, rumour, etc.; ~**ed** (-sht) a., (Austral. & N.Z. colloq.) lost in the bush, bewildered, *(colloq.) tired out; ~**'ў** a. (~**ily**, ~**iness**), having many bushes, growing thickly. [E & N]

**bush²** (-ŏŏ-) n. Perforated plug, metal lining of orifice, box in which shaft revolves. [Du. (BOX)]

**bu'shel** (-ŏŏ'-) n. Measure of capacity (‖8 gal., *32 qt.) for corn, fruit, etc. (**hide one's light under a** ~, conceal one's merits). [F]

**bushy.** See BUSH¹.

**bu'siness** (bĭz'zn-) n. Task, duty; thing that is one's concern; habitual occupation; serious work; thing(s) needing dealing with; difficult matter; (derog.) process, affair, structure, (*sick of the whole business*; *a lath-and-plaster business*); action on theatre stage; buying and selling, trade; commercial house, firm; **bad** ~, an unfortunate matter; ~ **as usual**, things will proceed normally despite disturbances; ~ **end**, (colloq.) working end of tool etc.; ~ **is** ~, commercial considerations have priority; ~**-like**, practical, systematic; ~ **man** (engaged in trade or commerce); **get down to** ~, begin in earnest; **has no** ~ **to** *interfere* etc. (no right); **in** ~, trading, (fig.) able to begin operations; **like nobody's** ~, (colloq.) extraordinarily; **make it** one's ~, undertake *to*; **mean** ~, be in earnest; **mind** one's **own** ~, not meddle; **on** ~, with definite purpose. [BUSY]

**bu'sker** n. Itinerant (esp. street) musician or actor. [obs. *busk* peddle]

**bŭss** n., & v.t. (arch.) Kiss. [cf. F *baiser* f. L]

**bŭst¹** n. Sculptured head, shoulders, and chest; upper front, circumference of upper part, of (esp. woman's) body; ~**'ў** a., (of woman) having prominent bust. [F f. It.]

**bŭst².** (colloq.) **1.** n. Sudden failure; worthless thing; drinking--bout. **2.** v.t. & i. (~**ed**, ~). Burst, break; ~**-up**, explosion, quarrel, collapse. **3.** a. Burst, broken; bankrupt. [BURST]

**bŭ'stard** n. Kind of large swift--running bird. [AF f. L *avis tarda* slow bird]

**bŭ'stle** (-sel) **1.** v.t. & i. Make show of activity, hurry *about*; make (person) hurry or work hard. **2.** n.

Excited activity; (Hist.) padding inside top of woman's skirt at back. [orig. uncert.]

**bu'sy** (bi'zi) *a. & v.* **1.** *a.* (-ily; ~ness, cf. BUSINESS). Occupied, working, with attention concentrated, (*busy doing, at, in, with*); unresting, always employed; fussy, meddlesome; ~**body**, meddlesome person, mischief-maker. **2.** *v.t.* Occupy or keep busy (esp. one*self*, one's hands etc., *doing, with, in, at, about*). [E]

**but** (or *emphat.* bŭt) *adv., prep., conj., pron., n., & v.* **1.** *adv.* Only, no more than, (*she is but a child*; *I can but do it*). **2.** *prep.* Except, apart from, short of the condition that, (*they are all wrong but he or him*; *nothing would content him but I must come*; *but that I saw it I could have not believed it*). **3.** *conj.* (before words of contrary tendency) Nevertheless, however, (*tried hard but did not succeed, but without success*); that not (*not such a fool but he can see the reason*); other(wise) than (*cannot choose but do it*); without the result that (*justice was never done but someone complained*). **4.** *pron.* Who not (*there is no one but knows*). **5.** *adv.* (Introducing emphasized wd) it *must be used always, but always*. **6.** ~ **for**, if . . . were or had been absent (*but for you I should have drowned*); *last, next,* etc., *one, two*, etc., if one, two, etc., were excluded from the count; ~ **that**, (colloq.) ~ **what**, (to say) that not (*who knows but that, but what, it is true?*); ~ **that**, (after neg.) that (*I do not doubt but that he will come*). **7.** *n.* An objection (*ifs and buts*). **8.** *v.t.* ~ **me no** ~**s**, do not raise objections. [E (BY, OUT)]

**bū'tāne** *n.* A hydrocarbon of the paraffin series, used in liquefied form as fuel. [ult. f. L *butyrum* BUTTER]

**bu'tcher** (-ŏŏ'-). **1.** *n.* One who slaughters animals for food; dealer in meat; one who has people killed needlessly or brutally; ~**bird**, kind of shrike; ~**'s meat** (excluding poultry, game, and bacon etc.). **2.** *v.t.* Slaughter or cut up (animal); kill wantonly or cruelly; ruin by bad performance etc. **3.** ~**y** *n.*, butcher's trade, needless or cruel killing. [F (BUCK[1])]

**bu'tler** *n.* Manservant in charge of wine-cellar and plate; principal manservant. [F (BOTTLE[1])]

**bŭtt**[1] *n.* Large cask. [F f. L *buttis*]

**bŭtt**[2] *n.* Mound behind target, in (*pl.*) shooting-range; object *of* ridicule etc., person habitually ridiculed or teased. [F *but* goal]

**bŭtt**[3] *n.* Thicker end of tool or weapon; ~(**-end**), remnant, stub of cigarette; ~ **weld** (without overlap). [Du.]

**bŭtt**[4]. **1.** *v.i. & t.* Push with head like ram or goat, run (one's head) *into* or *against*, go headlong or meddlesomely *into* affair etc. or *in*. **2.** *n.* Act of butting. [F f. Gmc]

**\*bŭtte** *n.* Conspicuous isolated hill, esp. one with steep or clifflike sides. [F, = mound]

**bŭ'tter. 1.** *n.* Edible yellow fatty substance into which cream solidifies on churning, used on bread and in cookery (*look as if ~ would not melt in* one's *mouth*, seem demure); substance of similar form (COCOA, PEAnut, *butter*); ~**bean** (with yellow pods, or flat white dried kind); ~**cup**, a yellow-flowered plant; ~**fingers**, person likely to drop things; ~**fly**, diurnal insect with large often showy wings (*break ~fly on wheel*, use needless destructive force; ~*fly-nut*, with projections turned by thumb and finger; ~*fly stroke*, method of swimming with both arms lifted at same time); ~**milk**, somewhat acid liquid left after churning butter; ~ **muslin**, thin loosely woven cloth orig. for wrapping butter; ~**scotch**, kind of toffee; ~**y**[1] *a.* (~**iness**). **2.** *v.t.* Spread, cook, serve, with butter (*fine words ~ no parsnips*, do not alter facts); ~ **up**, flatter. [E f. L f. Gk *bouturon*]

**bŭ'ttery**[2] *n.* Place in college etc. where provisions are kept and supplied. [BUTT[1]]

**bŭ'ttock** *n.* Either protuberance of the seat of the body; corresponding part of animal. [*butt* ridge]

**bŭ'tton. 1.** *n.* Knob or disc sewn to garment to fasten it by passing through buttonhole or as ornament or badge; (in *pl.*) liveried page-boy; thing of little value; small rounded object; bud; mushroom not yet open; knob etc. pressed to operate electrical device. **2.** *v.t. & i.* ~ (**up**), fasten with buttons, (fig.) complete satisfactorily. **3.** ~**hole**, (*n.*) slit to receive fastening button, ||flower(s) worn in coat-lapel buttonhole, (*v.t.*) make buttonholes in, hold by coat-button, detain (reluctant listener);

**~-through,** (of dress) fastening by buttons over its whole length. [F f. Gmc]

**bŭ′ttrĕss. 1.** *n.* Support built against wall etc.; buttress-like projection of hill; prop, person, etc., that strengthens a cause etc. **2.** *v.t.* Support or strengthen (as) with buttress(es). [F (BUTT⁴)]

**bŭ′xom** *a.* Plump, comely, (esp. of women). [E (BOW²)]

**buy** (bī). **1.** *v.t.* (**bought** *pr.* -awt). Obtain in exchange for money etc. or by some sacrifice (*dearly bought victory*); secure compliance of (person) by bribery; (sl.) accept, believe, suffer; **~ in,** buy a stock of, withdraw at auction by naming higher price than highest offered; **~ it,** (sl.) be killed; **~ off,** pay to get rid of; **~ out,** pay (person) to give up ownership etc.; **~ over,** bribe; **~ up,** buy as much as possible of, absorb (firm) by purchase. **2.** *n.* Purchase; **best ~** (giving best value for money paid); **good ~,** favourable bargain, thing cheaply bought. **3.** **~′er** *n.,* (esp.) agent selecting and purchasing stock for large shop; **~er′s market** (where goods are plentiful and cheap). [E]

**bŭzz. 1.** *n.* Humming (as) of bee; sound of buzzer; sound of people talking or moving; confused low sound; (sl.) telephone call; **\*~-saw,** circular saw. **2.** *v.i. & t.* Make buzz; move *about* busily; (sl.) go *off* quickly; threaten (aircraft) by flying very close to it; **~′er** *n.,* buzzing thing, esp. electrical signalling-device. [imit.]

**bŭ′zzard** *n.* Kind of raptorial bird. [F f. L *buteo*]

**B.V.M.** *abbr.* Blessed Virgin Mary.

**bwa′na** (-ah′-) *n.* (Afr.) Master, sir. [Swahili]

**by** *adv., prep., a., & n.* **1.** (bī) *adv.* Near (STAND *by*); aside, in reserve, (*lay,* PUT, *by*); past (*go, march, by*). **2.** (bī, *occas.* bī) *prep.* Near, beside, in possession or company or region of (*a house by the church; come and sit by me;* STAND *by; have not got it by me;* **north by east,** between N. and N.N.E.); along, passing through or beside, avoiding, (*path by the river; travel by Paris, by sea; pass, go, by him*); in circumstances of (*by day, daylight*); through agency, means, instrumèntally, or causation, of (*by proxy, skill, rail, chance, nature; lead by the hand; go by the name of; what do you mean by that?; approved, written, made, by me; novels by Scott*); as soon as, not later than, (*by now, next week*); according to, using as standard, (*by your* LEAVE¹; *judge by appearances; sell by retail, by the yard; paid by the hour*); with succession of (*by degrees;* \**getting worse by the minute; day by day;* LITTLE *by little*); to the extent of (*missed by a foot; better by far*); in respect of (*Jones by name; pull up by the roots; do as you would be done by*); as surely as one believes in (*by God;* SWEAR *by*). **3.** (bī) *a.* Subordinate, incidental, secondary, side. **4.** (bī) *n.* = BYE². **5. by and by,** (*adv.*) before long, (*n.*) the future; **by and large,** on the whole, everything considered; **by--ELECTION; by′gone,** (*a.*) past, antiquated, (*n.,* in *pl.*) past offences (*let bygones be bygones,* forgive and forget); **by′line,** line in newspaper etc. naming writer of article, secondary line of work; **by′pass,** (*n.*) secondary channel for gas etc. when main channel is closed, road round town or its centre (as alternative route·for through traffic), (*v.t.*) provide with bypass, avoid; **by′path,** secluded path, minor branch of subject; **by--play,** subsidiary action in play (lit. or fig.); **by-product,** incidental or secondary product of manufacture etc.; **by-road,** minor road; **by** oneself, alone, without help or prompting; **by′stander,** spectator; **by-street,** side-street; **by the dozen** etc., in at least that quantity; **by the head, stern,** (of ship) deeper in water there; *by the* WAY; **by′way,** by-road or bypath; **by′-word,** proverb, person notorious *for.* [E]

**bȳe¹** *a.* = BY *a.*

**bȳe²** *n.* Run made at cricket for ball that passes batsman or (**leg-~**) touches his body but not bat or hand; (being) unpaired competitor; **by the by(e),** incidentally, parenthetically. [BY]

**bȳe³** *int.* (colloq.) = GOODBYE. [abbr.]

**bȳ′e-bȳe¹, bȳ′e-bȳes** (bī′bīz), *n.* (Child's word for) sleep, bed. [imit. of lullaby]

**bȳe-bȳ′e²** *int.* (colloq.) = GOODBYE. [childish corrupt.]

**by(e)-law** (bī′l-) *n.* Regulation made by local authority or corporation. [obs. *by* town, *law*]

**bȳre** n. Cow-shed. [E]

**Bȳză'nt|ine. 1.** a. Of Byzantium or E. Roman Empire; of the architectural style of the Eastern Empire; complicated; inflexible; underhand. **2.** n. Inhabitant of Byzantium; Byzantine architect, artist, etc. **3.** **~ĭnĭsm** n. [F or L (place)]

# C

**C, c,** (sē) n. (pl. **Cs, C's**). Third letter; (Mus.) first note of natural major scale; (as Roman numeral) 100; (Alg.; c) third known quantity; (C) third hypothetical person or example.

**C.** abbr. Cape; Celsius; Centigrade; Conservative; coulomb(s).

**c.** abbr. caught by; cent(s); centi-; century; chapter; circa; cold.

**C** symb. carbon; copyright.

**ca.** abbr. circa.

**căb** n. Taxi or (Hist.) hackney carriage; shelter or compartment for driver of train, lorry, or crane; **~'man**, driver of cab; **~-rank**, place where cabs may wait for hire. [abbr. CABRIOLET]

**căbă'l** n. Secret intrigue; political clique; **cabala**, see CABBALA. [F f. L (CABBALA)]

**că'baret** (-rā) n. Entertainment in restaurant etc. while customers are at table; such restaurant or night-club. [F, = tavern]

**că'bbage** n. Green culinary vegetable with leaves in round heart or head; **~ butterfly, white**, white butterfly feeding on cabbage leaves; **~-rose** (with large round compact flower). [F caboche head]

**că'b(b)al|a** (or kabah'la) n. Jewish oral tradition; occult lore; **~ĭsm, ~ĭst,** ns.; **~ĭ'stĭc** a. (-ically). [L f. Heb., = tradition]

**că'bby** n. (colloq.) Cabman. [CAB]

**că'ber** n. Tree-trunk used in Sc. sport of **tossing the ~.** [Gael.]

**că'bĭn** n. Small dwelling or shelter esp. of wood; room or compartment in ship, aircraft, etc., for passengers or crew, or in aircraft for cargo; driver's cab; signal-box; **~-boy**, ship's waiter; **~ cruiser**, power-driven vessel with cabin; **~ed** (-nd) a., cramped in small space. [F f. L]

**că'bĭnĕt** n. Cupboard or case with drawers, shelves, etc., for storing or displaying articles (**~-maker**, skilled joiner); piece of furniture containing radio or television set etc.; (Polit.; C~) group of ministers controlling Government policy (||C~ **Minister**, member of Cabinet); **~ pudding**, steamed pudding with dried fruit. [dim. prec.]

**că'ble. 1.** n. Thick rope of wire or hemp; anchor chain; (as measure) 200 yds.; (esp. submarine or underground telegraph) line containing insulated wire; **~(gram)**, message sent by submarine cable; **~-car, ~ railway**, (with movement by endless cable); **~ stitch**, knitted stitch resembling twisted rope. **2.** v.i. & t. Transmit (message), send message to (person), by submarine cable. [F f. L caplum halter f. Arab.]

**că'bŏchŏn** (-sh-) n. Gem polished but not faceted. [F (CABBAGE)]

**cabōō'dle** n. (sl.) The whole lot. [orig. uncert.]

**cabōō'se** n. Cooking-room on ship's deck; *guard's van. [Du.]

**că'brĭole't** (-lā') n. (Hist.) Light two-wheeled hooded one-horse carriage. [F (CAPRIOLE)]

**ca'canny.** See CANNY.

**cacă'ŏ** (or -kah'ō) n. (pl. **~s**). (Tree producing) seed from which cocoa and chocolate are made. [Sp. f. Nahuatl]

**că'chalŏt** (-sh-; or -lō) n. Sperm whale. [F f. Sp. & Port.]

**cache** (-sh). **1.** n. (Things in) hiding-place for treasure etc. **2.** v.t. Place in cache. [F (cacher hide)]

**că'chet** (-shā) n. Distinguishing mark; internal evidence of authenticity; prestige; small capsule of medicine. [F (cacher press)]

**că'ckle. 1.** n. Clucking of hen; noisy inconsequential talk; loud silly laugh; **cut the ~,** (colloq.) come to the point. 2. *v.i.* & *t.* Emit cackle; utter or express with cackle. [imit.]

**cacŏ'phon|y̆** *n.* Discordant sound; **~ous** *a.* [F f. Gk (*kakos* bad, *phōnē* sound)]

**că'ct|us** *n.* (*pl.* ~i *pr.* -ī, ~uses). Plant with thick fleshy stem, usu. with spines but no leaves. [L f. Gk]

**căd** *n.* Man guilty or capable of ungentlemanly conduct; ill-bred man; **~'dish** *a.* (abbr. of CADDIE.)

**cadā'ver** *n.* (esp. Med.) Corpse; **cadā'verous** *a.*, corpselike, deathly pale. [L (*cado* fall)]

**că'ddĭe, că'ddy̆²**. **1.** *n.* Golfer's attendant carrying clubs etc. **2.** *v.i.* Act as caddie. [F CADET]

**că'ddĭs** *n.* **~-fly**, a four-winged insect living near water; **~(-worm)**, larva of caddis-fly. [orig. unkn.]

**că'ddy̆¹** *n.* Small box for holding tea. [Malay]

**că'ddy̆²**. See CADDIE.

**cā'dence** *n.* Movement of sound; fall of voice, esp. at end of sentence etc.; close of musical phrase; **cadē'nza** *n.*, passage for solo instrument or voice, usu. near close of movement. [F f. It. f. L (*cado* fall)]

**cadě't** *n.* Young person receiving (usu. elementary) military, naval, police, etc., training; younger son. [F f. dim. of L *caput* head]

**cădge** *v.t.* & *i.* (Try to) get by begging; be beggar. [orig. unkn.]

**că'dĭ** (*or* kah'-) *n.* Judge in Muslim country. [Arab.]

**cadre** (kah'der, kahdr, kă'drĭ) *n.* (Mil. etc.) permanent unit forming nucleus for expansion at need; (member of) group promoting interests of Communist Party. [F f. It. f. L *quadrus* square]

**cae'c|um** (sē'-), *\*cē'c|um, n.* (*pl.* ~a). Blind end of first part of large intestine; **~al** *a.* [L (*caecus* blind)]

**Caenozoic.** See CAINOZOIC.

**Caerphi'lly̆** (kār-, kâr-, ker-) *n.* Kind of mild white cheese. [place]

**Cae'sar** (sē'z-) *n.* Any of the Roman emperors, esp. from Augustus to Hadrian; autocrat; **Caesār'èan, -ĭan**, (sĭz-) *a.*, of Caesar(s), imperial, autocratic, (of birth) effected by cutting wall of abdomen. [person]

**caesūr'a** (sĭz-) *n.* Pause in verse line. [L (*caedo* cut)]

**café** (kă'fā) *n.* Coffee-house, tea-shop, restaurant, \*bar; **~ au lait**

(-ōlā), coffee with milk, colour of this. [F]

**căfetēr'ĭa** *n.* Restaurant in which customers serve themselves with food. [Amer. Sp., = coffee-shop]

**‖căff** *n.* (sl.) Café. [abbr.]

**că'ffeine** (-fēn) *n.* Alkaloid stimulant found in tea leaves and coffee beans. [F (COFFEE)]

**că'ftăn, k-,** *n.* Eastern man's long girdled tunic; woman's long loose dress; loose shirt. [Turk.]

**cāge. 1.** *n.* Prison of wire or with bars, esp. for animals; open framework, mine-shaft lift-frame, etc.; **~-bird**, bird (of kind) kept in cage. **2.** *v.t.* Confine in cage. [F f. L *cavea*]

**cā'g|ey** *a.* (~ier, ~iest; ~ily, ~iness). (colloq.) Shrewd; wary; uncommunicative. [orig. unkn.]

**\*cahōo't** (ka-h-) *n.* (sl., usu. in *pl.*) Partnership; collusion; **in ~s**, in league *with*. [orig. uncert.]

**cai'man.** See CAYMAN.

**Cain** *n.* Raise **~**, (colloq.) make a disturbance. [person (Gen. 4)]

**Cainozō'ĭc** (kīn-), **Caen-** (sēn-), **\*Cēn-**, *a.* & *n.* (Of) third geological era. [Gk *kainos* new, *zōion* animal]

**cairn** *n.* Pyramid of rough stones as memorial, landmark, etc.; **~-gorm**, yellow or wine-coloured gem-stone (found on mountain so named); **~ (terrier)**, small short-legged shaggy-haired terrier. [Gael.]

**cai'sson** *n.* Watertight structure used in laying foundations under water; **~ disease** (caused by too rapid decompression of workers in compressed air). [F (CASE²)]

**cai'tiff** *n.* & *a.* (arch., poet.) Cowardly or despicable (person). [F (CAPTIVE)]

**cajō'l|e** *v.t.* Persuade or soothe by flattery, deceit, etc.; **~ement** (-lm-), **~ery̆**, *ns.* [F]

**cāke. 1.** *n.* Mixture of flour, butter, eggs, sugar, etc., baked in oven (piece of **~**, colloq., something easy or pleasant); quantity of this baked in thick disc or ornamental shape (**have one's ~ and eat it**, **eat one's ~ and have it**, enjoy both alternatives; *sell* etc. **like hot ~s**, very rapidly; TAKE *the cake*); flattish compact mass of food (*fish cake*), soap, tobacco, etc. **2.** *v.i.* & *t.* Form into compact mass; cover with hardened mass (*caked with dirt*). [N]

**Cal.** *abbr.* California.

**cal.** *abbr.* calorie(s).

**că'labăsh** *n.* Gourd whose shell serves for holding liquid etc.; (fruit of) tropical Amer. tree whose fruit is so used. [F f. Sp.]

**că'lamine** *n.* (Pink powder of) zinc carbonate or oxide etc., used esp. in lotion. [F f. L]

**cală'mĭt|ÿ** *n.* Grievous disaster; deep distress; ~ous *a.*, causing or marked by calamity. [F f. L]

**calando** (kălă'ndō) *adv.* (Mus.) Gradually decreasing in speed and volume. [It.]

**călcăr'e̅ous, -ĭous,** *a.* Of or containing calcium carbonate. [CALX]

**călceolăr'ĭa** *n.* Plant with slipper--shaped flower. [L (*calceus* shoe)]

**calces.** See CALX.

**că'lcĭf|ÿ** *v.t. & i.* Convert into, harden by deposit of, calcium carbonate etc.; undergo such change; ~ĭcă'tion *n.* [CALX]

**că'lcĭne** *v.t. & i.* Reduce to quicklime or powder by burning or roasting; undergo such process; **călcĭnă'tion** *n.* [F or L (CALX)]

**că'lcĭte** *n.* Crystalline calcium carbonate. [G (CALX)]

**că'lcĭum** *n.* Metallic element whose oxide is quicklime and which occurs widely as calcium carbonate. [L (CALX)]

**că'lcŭl|āte** *v.t. & i.* (~able). Ascertain or forecast, esp. by mathematics or by reckoning; plan deliberately; rely (*up*)on; *(colloq.)* suppose, believe; (in *part.* and *p.p.*) shrewd, cold-blooded; (in *p.p.*) designed or suitable to *do* etc.; ~ā'tion, ~ātor, *ns.* [L (foll.)]

**că'lcŭl|us** *n.* (*pl.* ~i *pr.* -ī, ~uses). (Math.) particular method of calculation, esp. = INFINITESIMAL *calculus*; (Med.) stone, concretion in some part of body. [L, = small stone, abacus-ball]

**caldron.** See CAULDRON.

**Călēdō'nian** *a. & n.* (usu. joc. or Hist. exc. in titles of institutions) Scots(man). [L *Caledonia* N. Britain]

**că'lendar. 1.** *n.* System fixing year's beginning, length, and subdivision (*calendar* MONTH, YEAR); table(s) exhibiting (important) dates of year etc.; adjustable device showing the day's date etc.; register or list, esp. of canonized saints, cases for trial, series of documents, or *matters for debate; calĕ'ndrĭc(al) adjs.* (-ically). **2.** *v.t.* Enter in list; arrange, analyse, and index (documents). [F f. L (CALENDS)]

**că'lender. 1.** *n.* Machine for rolling cloth, paper, etc., to glaze or smooth it. **2.** *v.t.* Press in calender. [F]

**că'lĕnds** (-z) *n.pl.* First of month in ancient Roman calendar (**on, till, the Greek ~,** never, for ever). [F f. L *calendae*]

**calf¹** (kahf) *n.* (*pl.* **calves** *pr.* kahvz). Young of ox, or of elephant, whale, deer, etc., (*cow* in *or* with ~, pregnant; **golden ~,** wealth as object of worship; *kill the* FATted *calf*); ~('skin), calf-leather, esp. in bookbinding and shoemaking; ~-love, childish love-affair. [E]

**calf²** (kahf) *n.* (*pl.* **calves** *pr.* kahvz). Fleshy hind part of human leg below knee. [N]

**că'lib|re** (-ber), *-b|er, n.* Internal diameter of gun or tube; diameter of bullet or shell; weight of character, importance, ability; ~rāte *v.t.,* find calibre of, graduate (gauge) with allowance for irregularities, correlate readings of (instrument etc.) with a standard; ~rā'tion *n.* [F f. It. f. Arab., = mould]

**calices.** See CALIX.

**că'licō. 1.** *n.* (*pl.* ~es, *~*s). (Esp. plain white) cotton cloth; *printed cotton fabric. **2.** *a.* Of calico; *multicoloured, piebald. [*Calicut,* place]

**că'liph** *n.* Muslim chief civil and religious ruler; ~ate *n.,* caliph's (term of) office or domain. [F f. Arab., = successor (of Muhammad)]

**că'li|x** *n.* (*pl.* ~ces *pr.* -sēz). Cup-like cavity or organ. [L, = cup]

*****calk.** See CAULK.

**call** (kawl). **1.** *v.i. & t.* Cry, shout, speak loudly, (*out, to* person); (of bird etc.) utter characteristic sound; summon; order; invite (*call* attention *to*); rouse from sleep (*call me at 7*); communicate (with) by radio or telephone; name, describe, or regard as, (*call him John; I call that silly; call it a* DAY); (Cards) name (suit) in bidding; predict result of tossing coin etc.; make brief visit (*at* place, (*up*)*on* person); ~ **a halt,** decide to stop; *call* person's BLUFF²; ~ **for,** demand, require, go and fetch; ~ **forth,** elicit; ~ **in,** withdraw from circulation, seek advice from, make brief visit; ~ **in question,** dispute (statement etc.); ~ **into being,** create; ~ **into play,** bring into action; *call* person NAMES; ~ **off,** cancel (engagement etc.), order (dog etc.) to stop attacking etc.; ~ **on,** = *call upon*; ~ **out,** elicit, summon to action, order (workers) to strike; ~ **over,** call (names) in sequence; *call the* TUNE; ~ **to order,** request to be orderly, declare (meeting) open; *call to the* BAR[1]; ~ **up,** imagine, recollect, telephone to, summon (esp. to do military service); ~ **upon,** invoke, appeal to, request or require (person *to* act, speak, etc.). **2.** *n.* Shout; bird's cry, instrument imitating it; signal on bugle etc.; act of telephoning, conversation over telephone; invitation, summons, demand, (*the call of the sea*; *I have many calls on my time*; **at, on,** ~, ready or available when wanted; **within** ~, near enough to be summoned by calling); vocation; need, occasion, (*there's no call to blush*); short esp. formal visit (**pay a** ~, make such a visit, colloq. go to lavatory); (St. Exch.) option of buying stock at given date; (Cards) player's right or turn to bid, bid thus made; ~**box,** telephone-box; ~**boy** (summoning actors to go on stage); ~**girl,** prostitute who accepts appointments by telephone; ~ **of nature,** need to urinate or defecate; ~**sign(al)** (indicating identity of radio transmitter); ~**up,** summons to serve in army etc. **3.** ~'**er** *n.,* (esp.) person who pays visit, makes telephone call, announces numbers in bingo etc., or gives directions in square dance; ~'**ing** *n.,* (esp.) profession or trade. [E f. N]

**calli'graph|y** *n.* (Beautiful) handwriting; ~**er** *n.;* **cǎllĭgrǎ'phĭc** *a.* [Gk *(kallos* beauty)]

**cǎ'lliper** *n.* Metal support for weak or injured leg; (in *pl.*) compasses for measuring diameter of bullets, tubes, etc. [var. CALIBRE]

**cǎllǐsthě'nǐcs** *n.pl.* Exercises to develop strength and grace. [Gk *kallos* beauty, *sthenos* strength]

**cǎ'llous. 1.** *a.* (Of skin) hardened, horny; (of person, heart, etc.) unfeeling, insensitive. **2.** *n.* Callus. **3. callo'sǐtў** *n.,* hardness of skin, callus. [L (CALLUS)]

**cǎ'llow** (-ō) *a.* (~**er,** ~**est**). Unfledged; raw, inexperienced. [E]

**cǎ'llus** *n.* Thickened part of skin or soft tissue; bony material formed while bone-fracture heals. [L]

**calm** (kahm) *a., v.,* &~ *n.* **1.** *a.* Tranquil, quiet, windless, not agitated, (lit. or fig.); (colloq.) self--confident, impudent. **2.** *v.t.* & *i.* Make calm, pacify; ~ **down,** become or make calm. **3.** *n.* Calm condition or period. [L f. Gk *kauma* heat]

**cǎ'lomĕl** *n.* A purgative compound of mercury. [L f. Gk]

**Cǎ'lor** *n.* ~ **gas,** liquefied butane etc. under pressure in containers for domestic use. [P; L *calor* heat]

**cǎ'lorǐc** *a.* & *n.* (Of) heat; of calories; **cǎ'lorǐe** *n.,* unit of quantity of heat, the amount needed to raise one gram (**small** ~) or one kilogram (**large** ~) of water 1°C, large calorie as unit of energy value of foods; **cǎlorǐ'fǐc** *a.,* producing heat; **cǎlorǐ'mĕter** *n.,* apparatus for measuring heat. [F f. L (prec.)]

**cǎ'lumnў. 1.** *n.* Malicious misrepresentation; slander. **2.** *v.t.* Slander. **3. calu'mnǐăte** *v.t.,* slander; **calu'mnǐător** *n.;* **calu'mnǐous** *a.,* slanderous. [L]

**Cǎ'lvarў** *n.* Place or representation of the Crucifixion. [L *calvaria* skull]

**calve** (kahv) *v.i.* Give birth to calf; **calves,** see CALF[1,2]. [E (CALF[1])]

**Cǎ'lvǐn|ǐsm** *n.* Theology of *Calvin* or his followers; adherence to this; ~**ǐst** *n.;* ~**ǐstǐc(al)** *adjs.* [person]

**cǎlx** *n.* (*pl.* **ca'lces** *pr.* -sēz). Powdery or friable substance left after burning of metal or mineral. [L *calx calc-* lime]

**calў'psō** *n.* (*pl.* ~**s**). Topical usu. spontaneous W. Ind. song in Afr. rhythm. [orig. unkn.]

**cǎ'lў|x** *n.* (*pl.* ~**yces** *pr.* -Isēz, ~**yxes**). Whorl of leaves forming outer case of bud or envelope of flower. [L f. Gk, = husk]

**cǎm** *n.* Projecting part of wheel etc. in machinery, shaped to convert circular into reciprocal or variable motion; ~'**shaft,** shaft carrying cam(s). [Du. *kam* comb]

**cǎmara'derie** (-ah'd-) *n.* Mutual trust and sociability of comrades. [F]

**Camb.** *abbr.* Cambridge.

**cǎ'mber. 1.** *n.* Convex or arched shape of road, deck, etc. **2.** *v.t.* Construct (road etc.) with camber. [F f. L *camurus* curved]

**Cǎ'mbrǐan** *a.* & *n.* Welsh(man); (of) earliest Palaeozoic period or system. [L f. W (CYMRIC)]

**că'mbrĭc** n. Fine linen or cotton cloth. [*Kamerijk = Cambrai*, place]

**Că'mbrĭdge** n. ~ blue, light blue. [place]

**Cambs.** *abbr.* Cambridgeshire.

**cāme.** See COME.

**că'mel** n. Large long-necked ruminant quadruped with (**Arabian** ~) one hump or (**Bactrian** ~) two; shade of fawn colour; ~('s)-**hair**, made of camel's hair or (paint-brushes) of squirrel's tail hairs. [E f. L f. Gk]

**camĕ'llĭa** n. Flowering evergreen shrub. [*Camellus*, person]

**Că'membert** (-bār) n. Kind of soft rich cheese. [place]

**că'mĕŏ** n. (*pl.* ~s). Onyx or similar material so carved in relief that design and background are in different-coloured layers; short literary sketch or acted scene. [F & L]

**că'mera** n. Apparatus for taking photographs or television pictures; ~**man**, one who operates camera professionally, esp. in cinema or television; **in** ~, in judge's private room, not in public, secretly. [L (CHAMBER)]

**că'momile, ch-** (k-), n. Aromatic herb used as tonic; ~ **tea**, infusion of its flowers. [F f. L f. Gk, = earth-apple]

**că'mouflage** (-*o*flahzh). **1.** n. Disguise of guns, ships, etc., by obscuring with splashes of various colours, smoke-screens, foliage, etc.; means of disguise or evasion. **2.** v.t. Hide by camouflage. [F (*camoufler* to disguise, f. It.)]

**cămp¹. 1.** n. Place where troops are lodged or trained; fortified site; temporary quarters of holiday-makers, explorers, nomads, detainees, etc.; ~-**bed**, -**chair**, etc., (folding and portable); ~-**fire** (made in the open air at camp etc.); ~-**follower**, non-military worker or hanger-on in or around camp, disciple of group or theory; ~'**site**, place for camping. **2.** v.i. Encamp, be in camp; ~ **out**, lodge in open air or in temporary quarters. [F f. It. f. L *campus* level ground]

**cămp².** a., n., & v. **1.** a. Affected, effeminate; homosexual; exaggerated, bizarre. **2.** n. Camp behaviour. **3.** v.i. & t. Behave or do in camp way; ~ **it up**, overact. [orig. uncert.]

**cămpai'gn** (-ā'n). **1.** n. Series of military operations in a definite area

or with one objective or forming the whole or a distinct part of a war; military service in the field (on *campaign*); organized course of action, esp. attempt to arouse public interest. **2.** v.i. Serve in or conduct campaign; old ~**er**, veteran, person skilled in adapting himself to circumstances. [F f. It. f. L (CHAMPAGNE)]

**cămpan|i'lĕ** (-nē'-) n. Bell-tower, usu. detached, esp. in Italy; ~**ŏ'logў** n., study of bells, bell-ringing.

**cămpă'nŭla** n., plant with bell-shaped flowers, usu. blue, pink, or white. [It. (*campana* bell f. L)]

**că'mphor** n. Crystalline aromatic bitter substance used in medicine and to repel insects; ~**āte** v.t., impregnate with camphor. [F or L f. Arab. f. Skr.]

**că'mpĭon** n. Wild plant usu. with white or red notched flowers. [orig. uncert.]

**că'mpus** n. University or college grounds; university as teaching etc. institution. [L, = field]

**căn¹. 1.** n. Metal vessel for liquid (carry the ~, sl., bear responsibility or blame); tin-plate container in which food or drink is hermetically sealed; (sl.) prison, *lavatory. **2.** v.t. (-**nn**-). Put or preserve in can; (in *p.p.*, sl.) drunk; ~**ned music** (recorded for reproduction). [E]

**căn²** (or *emphat.* **kăn**) v. aux. (*pres.* **can** exc. 2 *sing.* arch. ~**st**; *neg.* ~'**not**, colloq. ~'**t** *pr.* kahnt; *past* **could** *pr.* kud, kŏŏd, exc. 2 *sing.* arch. **couldst, couldest,** *neg.* **could not,** colloq. **couldn't** *pr.* kŏŏ'dent; no other parts used). Be able to; have right to (do); be permitted to (*you can go*); could, feel inclined to (*could eat a chop*; *couldn't think of allowing it*); could be, (colloq.) that may be true. [E, = know]

**Can.** *abbr.* Canada; Canadian.

**Canā'dĭan** a. & n. (Native, inhabitant) of *Canada*. [place]

**cană'l** n. Artificial watercourse for inland navigation or irrigation; duct; (on planet Mars) narrow seasonal marking observable from the Earth; **că'nalize** v.t., make canal through, convert (river) into canal, (fig.) give desired direction to. [F or It. f. L *canalis*]

**că'napé** (-pī) n. Piece of bread, toast, etc., with small savoury on top; sofa. [F]

**canār′d** (*or* kă′nȧrd) *n.* Unfounded rumour or story. [F, = duck]

**canār′ÿ** *n.* Yellow-feathered song-bird; ~(-coloured, yellow), bright yellow; ~ **creeper**, yellow-flowered climbing plant. [place]

**canā′sta** *n.* Card-game resembling rummy, using two packs and four jokers. [Sp., = basket]

**că′ncăn** (-n-k-) *n.* High-kicking dance by woman. [F]

**că′ncel** *v.t. & i.* (‖-ll-). Obliterate, delete; annul; countermand, neutralize; counterbalance; deface (postage stamp etc.) to prevent further use; (Math.) strike out (equal factor) on each side of equation etc.; ~ **out**, neutralize (each other); ~lā′tion *n.* [F f. L (CHANCEL)]

**că′ncer** *n.* (C~) sign of ZODIAC (TROPIC *of Cancer*); (disease in which there is) malignant tumour tending to spread and to recur when removed; (fig.) evil, corruption, etc., acting similarly; ~ous, **că′ncroid** *adjs.* [L, = crab]

**că′ndēla** (*or* -ē′la) *n.* Unit of luminous intensity; **că′ndělā′brum** (*or* -ah′-) *n.* (*pl.* ~**bra**, ‖~**brums**), large usu. branched candlestick or lampstand. [L, = candle]

**că′ndĭd** *a.* Frank, not hiding one's thoughts; ~ **camera**, camera for taking informal pictures of people freq. without their knowledge. [F, or L *candidus* white]

**că′ndĭd|āte** *n.* Person who seeks, or is nominated for, an office, honour, etc.; person or thing likely to gain any position; examinee; ~**acÿ**, ‖~**ature**, *ns.*, standing for election, being candidate. [F or L, = white-robed]

**că′ndle** *n.* Cylinder of wax, tallow, etc., enclosing wick for giving light (burn the ~ at both ends, exhaust one's strength or resources by undertaking too much; can't, is not fit to, hold a ~ to, is not comparable with, is much inferior to; GAME[1] *not worth the candle*); ~(-power), unit of luminous intensity; C~mas, feast-day (2 Feb.) when candles are blessed [MASS[1]]; ~stick, holder for candle(s); ~wick, (material with raised pattern in) thick soft yarn. [E f. L *candela*]

**că′ndour**, *\*ca′ndor, (-er) n.* Candid behaviour or quality. [F, or L *candor*]

**că′ndÿ. 1.** *n.* (Sugar-)~, sugar crystallized by repeated boiling and slow evaporation; \*sweetmeat; ~-floss, mass of fluffy spun sugar; ~-stripe(d), pattern(ed) in alternate white and coloured stripes. **2.** *v.t.* Preserve (fruit etc.) by coating or impregnating with candy; **candied** PEEL. [F f. Arab.]

**că′ndÿtŭft** *n.* Garden plant with white, pink, or purple flowers. [*Candia*, place; TUFT]

**cāne. 1.** *n.* Stem of giant reed or grass (*bamboo* cane) or of slender palm; SUGAR-*cane*; such stem for wickerwork etc.; this stem etc. used as instrument of punishment or walking-stick or to support plant; ~**chair** (with seat of woven canes); ~**sugar** (obtained from sugar-cane). **2.** *v.t.* Beat with cane; weave cane into (chair etc.). [F f. L f. Gk *kanna* reed]

**că′nine. 1.** *a.* Of a dog or dogs; **tooth** (between incisors and molars). **2.** *n.* A dog; canine tooth. [F or L (*canis* dog)]

**că′nĭster** *n.* Small container usu. of metal for tea, shot, etc. [L f. Gk *canastron* wicker basket]

**că′nker. 1.** *n.* Ulcerous disease of animals; necrotic disease of plants; (fig.) corrupting influence; ~ous *a.* **2.** *v.t.* Consume with canker; corrupt; (in *p.p.*) soured, malignant. [E & F f. L (CANCER)]

**că′nna** *n.* Bright-flowered ornamental-leaved plant. [L (CANE)]

**că′nnabĭs** *n.* Hemp plant; preparation of parts of it used as intoxicant or hallucinogen. [L f. Gk]

**că′nnerÿ** *n.* Canning-factory. [CAN[1]]

**că′nnĭbal. 1.** *n.* Person or animal that eats own species. **2.** *a.* Of or having this habit. **3.** ~**ĭsm** *n.*; ~**ĭ′stĭc** *a.* (-ically); ~**ĭze** *v.t.*, use (machine etc.) as source of spare parts for others. [Sp. f. Carib]

**că′nnon. 1.** *n.* (Hist.) large gun (*pl.* usu. same); ‖(Bill.) hitting of two balls successively by player's ball; ~**ball**, round projectile fired by cannon; ~**fodder**, men regarded merely as material to be consumed in war. **2.** *v.i.* Come into collision, strike obliquely, *against*, *into*. **3.** ~**ā′de** *n.*, continuous gunfire. [F f. It. (CANE); in Bill. sense, corrupt. CAROM]

**că′nnot.** See CAN[2].

**că′nnÿ** *a.* (-ily, -iness). Shrewd,

(esp. of Scots) thrifty; circumspect; **ca'~** (kah-), [Sc., = proceed warily] caution, go-slow esp. by workers. [CAN²]

**canoe'** (-ōō') *n.*, & *v.i.* (~ing). (Go in) keelless boat propelled by paddle(s) (PADDLE¹ *one's own canoe*); ~'**ist** *n.* [Sp. & Haitian]

**ca'non** *n.* Church decree (~ **law**, ecclesiastical law); general law, rule, or principle; criterion; list of (esp. sacred) writings etc. accepted as genuine; (Mus.) piece with different parts taking up same theme successively; member of cathedral chapter; **canō'nic(al)**, (*a.*; **-ically**) appointed by canon law, included in canon of Scripture, authoritative or accepted, of cathedral canon or chapter, (*n.*, in *pl.*) canonical dress of clergy; ~**i'city** *n.*, canonical status of book; ~**ist** *n.*, expert in canon law; ~**ize** *v.t.*, admit to list of saints, regard as saint, authorize; ~**izā'tion** *n.*; ~**ry** *n.*, office of cathedral canon. [L f. Gk *kanōn* rule]

**cañon.** See CANYON.

**ca'nopy. 1.** *n.* Covering hung or held up over throne, bed, person, etc.; (fig.) sky, overhanging shelter; (Archit.) roof of niche etc.; expanding part of parachute; cover of aircraft's cockpit. **2.** *v.t.* Supply or be canopy to. [L f. Gk, = mosquito-net]

**canst.** See CAN².

**cant¹. 1.** *n.* Bevel, slanting surface; tilted position; oblique push or jerk. **2.** *v.t.* & *i.* Push, jerk, or hold out of level; take, be in, tilted position. [LDu., = edge]

**cant². 1.** *n.* Language peculiar to one class of people; jargon; ephemeral catchwords; insincere pious or moral talk; hypocrisy. **2.** *v.i.* Use cant. [prob. CHANT]

**can't.** See CAN².

**Cant.** *abbr.* Canticles (O.T.).

**Ca'ntab.** *abbr.* of Cambridge Univ.

**canta'bile** (kăntah'bĭlĭ) *n.* & *adv.* (Mus.) (Piece) in smooth flowing style. [It., = singable]

**Cantabri'gian** *n.* & *a.* (Member) of Cambridge Univ.; (citizen) of Cambridge. [*Cantabrigia* Latinized name of Cambridge]

**ca'ntaloup(e)** (-ōōp) *n.* Small ribbed melon. [F f. *Cantaluppi*, place]

**cantā'nkerous** *a.* Bad-tempered, quarrelsome. [orig. uncert.]

**cantā'ta** (-tah'-) *n.* (Mus.) Choral work like oratorio but usu. shorter and often secular in subject. [It. (CHANT)]

**cantee'n** *n.* Shop for provisions or liquor in barracks or camp; ‖restaurant in factory, office, barracks, etc.; case or chest containing set of cutlery; soldier's or camper's water-flask or set of eating and drinking utensils. [F f. It., = cellar]

**ca'nter** *n.*, & *v.i.* (Go at) easy gallop; **C~bury bell**, kind of campanula. [*Canterbury*, place]

**ca'nticle** *n.* Anglican Prayer-Book hymn; (C~ **of**) C~**s**, SONG of Solomon. [F or L (*canticum* CHANT]

**ca'ntilēver** *n.* Beam, bracket, etc., projecting from wall to support balcony etc.; beam or girder fixed at only one end; ~ **bridge** (in which cantilevers connected by girders project from piers). [orig. unkn.]

**ca'ntō** *n.* (*pl.* ~**s**). Division of long poem. [It. f. L *cantus* (CHANT]

**canton. 1.** *n.* (kǎ'nton, kăntō'n). Subdivision of country, esp. of Switzerland. **2.** *v.t.* (kăntō'n) divide into cantons; (kantōō'n) put (troops) in their quarters; **cantō'nment** (or -ōō'n-) *n.*, lodgings of troops, (Ind.) military station. [F (CANT¹]

**ca'ntor** *n.* Precentor, esp. in synagogue; **cantōr'ial** *a.*, of precentor's or N. side of choir. [L, = singer]

**ca'nvas. 1.** *n.* Strong coarse cloth used for sails, tents, oil-paintings, etc., (**under** ~, in tent(s), with sails spread); a painting on canvas, esp. in oils; racing-boat's covered end; ~**-back**, N. Amer. wild duck. **2.** *v.t.* (‖-ss-). Cover with canvas. **3. ca'nvass**, (*v.i.* & *t.*). solicit votes, solicit votes from (electors in constituency), ascertain opinions of, ask custom from, discuss, ‖propose (plan etc.), (*n.*) canvassing of constituency. [F f. L (CANNABIS]

**ca'nyon, cañon**, (kǎ'nyon) *n.* Deep gorge. [Sp. *cañón* tube]

**caou'tchouc** (kow'chŏŏk) *n.* Unvulcanized rubber. [F f. Carib]

**cap. 1.** *n.* Soft brimless head-covering, usu. with peak (~ **in hand**, fig., humbly; **the ~ fits**, the general remark is true of the particular person; **set one's ~ at**, try to attract as suitor); nurse's or woman servant's indoor head-dress; cap awarded as sign of membership of sports team; academic mortar-board; cover resembling cap or designed for specific purpose; = DUTCH[1] *cap*, PERCUSSION *cap*; ~ **and bells,** cap trimmed with bells, worn by professional jester. **2.** *v.t.* (**-pp-**). Put cap on; cover top or end of; award cap to (player); lie on top of; form top of; follow (anecdote, quotation, etc.) with another, usu. better. [E f. L *cappa*]

**cap.** *abbr.* capital (letter); chapter [L *caput*].

**că'pab|le** *a.* (**~ly**). Gifted, able, competent; **~le of,** having the ability, fitness, or necessary wickedness for, susceptible or admitting of (explanation, improvement, etc.); **~i'lĭty** *n.*, ability, power, undeveloped or unused faculty. [F f. L (*capio* hold)]

**capā'cious** (-shŭs) *a.* Roomy, able to hold much. [L *capax* (prec.)]

**capă'cĭt|y** *n.* Power of containing, receiving, experiencing, or producing; maximum amount that can be contained, produced, etc., (**to ~y,** fully); mental power; function or character (*in my capacity as a critic*); legal competency; **~ance** *n.*, (Electr.) ability to store a charge of electricity; **~āte** *v.t.*, make capable or competent; **~or** *n.*, device having capacitance. [F f. L (prec.)]

**capă'rison. 1.** *n.* (usu. in *pl.*) Horses' trappings. **2.** *v.t.* Put caparisons on. [F f. Sp. (foll.)]

**cāpe**[1] *n.* Short sleeveless cloak, separate or as attached part of long coat. [F f. L *cappa* CAP]

**cāpe**[2] *n.* Headland, promontory; **the C~** (of Good Hope); **C~ Coloured,** (member) of COLOURED population of Cape Province; **C~ Dutch,** (arch.) Afrikaans. [F f. Prov. f. L *caput* head]

**că'per**[1] *n.* Bramble-like shrub; (in *pl.*) its buds pickled (esp. for ~ sauce). [L f. Gk *kapparis*]

**că'per**[2]. **1.** *n.* Frisky movement, leap (**cut a ~, ~s,** dance or act friskily); (sl.) an activity. **2.** *v.i.* Move friskily. [abbr. CAPRIOLE]

**căpercai'llie, -lzie** (-lyĭ, -lzĭ) *n.* Largest kind of grouse. [Gael., = horse of the wood]

**capi'llary. 1.** *a.* Of hair; (of tube, blood-vessel, etc.) of hairlike diameter; **~ attraction, repulsion,** (by which liquid is drawn up, down, in capillary tube). **2.** *n.* Capillary tube etc. **3.** **căpĭllă'rĭty** *n.*, (power

of) capillary attraction or repulsion. [L (*capillus* hair)]

**că'pital. 1.** *a.* (**~ly**). Principal, most important, (**~ city, town,** chief city or town of country, county, etc.); (colloq.) excellent; (of offence, punishment, sentence) involving death penalty; (of error etc.) vitally injurious, fatal; (of letter of alphabet) of large size, usu. used to begin sentence, name, etc. **2.** *n.* Capital city or town; capital letter; head of column or pillar; stock with which company etc. starts business; accumulated wealth, esp. as used in further production (**make ~ out of,** use to one's advantage; capitalists collectively. **3.** **~ gain,** profit from sale of investments or property; **~ goods,** goods (to be) used in producing commodities; **~ levy,** general tax on wealth or property; **~ ship,** battleship or similar warship; **~ sum,** lump sum of money, esp. payable to insured person. **4.** **~ism** *n.*, system in which private capital and wealth is used in production and distribution of goods, (Polit.) dominance of private owners of capital and production for profit; **~ist,** (*n.*, freq. derog.) person using or possessing capital, rich person, (*a.*) of capitalism or capitalists; **~i'stĭc** *a.* (**-ically**); **~ize** *v.t.* & *i.*, convert into or provide with capital, write (letter of alphabet) as capital, begin (word) with capital letter; **~ize** (**on**), use to one's advantage; **~izā'tion** *n.*; **căpĭtā'tion** *n.*, (reckoning or levying of) tax or payment of a fixed amount per person; **Că'pĭtol** *n.*, Roman temple of Jupiter, *Congress or State legislature's building; **capi'tŭlar** *a.*, of a cathedral chapter; **capi'tŭlāte** *v.i.*, surrender esp. on stated conditions; **capĭtŭlā'tion** *n.* [F f. L (*caput* head)]

**că'pon** *n.* Domestic cock castrated and fattened for eating. [E f. F f. L *capo*]

**capri'cciŏ** (-i'chĭō) *n.* (*pl.* **~s**). Lively (usu. short) musical composition. [It. (foll.)]

**capri'ce** (-ē's) *n.* Unaccountable change of mind or conduct; tendency to this; work of lively fancy in art etc.; **capri'cious** (-shŭs) *a.*, liable to caprice, unpredictable. [F f. It. *capriccio* sudden start]

**Că'pricŏrn** *n.* Sign of ZODIAC

(TROPIC *of Capricorn*); **ca'prine** *a.*, of or like a goat; **ca'priole** *n.*, & *v.i.* (make) leap or caper, esp. of trained horse. [F f. L (*caper* goat, *cornu* horn)]

**ca'psicum** *n.* (Fruit of) tropical plant with pungent capsules. [L (CASE²)]

**capsi'ze** *v.t.* & *i.* Overturn (boat etc.); be capsized. [Sp. *capuzar* sink]

**ca'pstan** *n.* Revolving cylinder with vertical axis, turned by men pushing against horizontal bars inserted in its top or by steam etc., for winding cable, halyard, etc.; revolving spindle on tape-recorder etc.; ~ **lathe** (with tools mounted on a capstan-like holder). [Prov.]

**ca'psul|e. 1.** *n.* Enclosing membrane; plant's seed-case opening when ripe; (Med.) small case of gelatine enclosing dose; detachable nose-cone of rocket etc. or cabin of spacecraft. **2.** *a.* Highly condensed (description etc.). **3.** ~**ize** *v.t.*, put (information etc.) in capsule form. [F f. L (CASE²)]

**Capt.** *abbr.* Captain.

**ca'ptain** (-tĭn). **1.** *n.* Chief, leader, (~ **of industry,** industrial magnate); Army officer of rank next below major; (Navy) commander of ship, officer of rank next below commodore; master of merchant ship; pilot of civil aircraft; ‖head pupil at school; leader of side in games; ~**cy** *n.*, position of captain. **2.** *v.t.* Be captain of. [F f. L (*caput* head)]

**ca'ption. 1.** *n.* Heading of chapter, article, etc.; wording on cinema or television screen, appended to illustration or cartoon, etc. **2.** *v.t.* Provide with caption. [L (*capio* take)]

**ca'ptious** (-shŭs) *a.* Fond of finding fault, raising objections, etc. [F or L (prec.)]

**ca'ptive. 1.** *a.* Taken prisoner, in confinement, unable to escape; ~ **audience** (unable to avoid being addressed etc.); ~ **balloon** (held to ground by rope etc.). **2.** *n.* Captive person or animal. **3.** **ca'ptivate** *v.t.*, fascinate, charm; **captiva'tion** *n.*; **capti'vity** *n.*; **ca'ptor** *n.*, taker of captive; **ca'pture,** (*v.t.*) take prisoner, seize, (*n.*) act of capturing, thing or person captured.

**Ca'puchin** *n.* Kind of Franciscan friar; ~ **monkey, pigeon,** (with hair, feathers, like cowl). [F f. It. (CAPE¹)]

**capy̆bar'a** *n.* Large S. Amer. rodent. [Tupi]

**car** *n.* Wheeled vehicle; = MOTOR car; *railway carriage or van; passenger compartment of airship, balloon, or cableway; *lift-cage; ~'- **man,** van-driver, carrier; ~**park,** place for parking cars; ~**port,** roofed open-sided shelter for car; ~**-sick(ness),** travel-sick(ness) through motion of car. [F f. L]

**caracul.** See KARAKUL.

**cara'fe** (*or* -ahˈf) *n.* Glass bottle for water or wine. [F f. It. f. Sp. f. Arab.]

**ca'ramel** *n.* Burnt sugar or syrup as colouring; kind of toffee; light-brown colour; ~**ize** *v.t.* [F f. Sp.]

**ca'rapace** *n.* Tortoise's or crustacean's upper shell. [F f. Sp.]

**ca'rat** *n.* Unit of weight for precious stones (200 mg) or of purity of gold (pure gold = 24 carats). [F f. It. f. Arab. f. Gk]

**ca'ravan. 1.** *n.* Company travelling together, esp. across desert; ‖house on wheels, usu. designed to be towed by car or horse; ~ **park, site,** place where caravans are parked as dwellings. **2.** *v.i.* (‖-nn-). Travel or live in caravan. **3.** ~**serai** (-ă'nserĭ) *n.*, Eastern inn with inner court. [F f. Pers.]

**ca'ravel, car'vel,** *n.* (Hist.) Small light fast ship. [F f. Port. f. Gk]

**ca'raway** (-a-w-) *n.* Umbelliferous plant; ~ **seed,** its fruit, used in cakes. [Sp. f. Arab.]

**car'bide** *n.* Binary compound of carbon, esp. (**calcium**) ~ (used in making acetylene gas). [CARBON]

**car'bine** *n.* Short rifle orig. for cavalry use. [F]

**car'bon** *n.* Non-metallic element occurring as diamond, graphite, and charcoal, and in all organic compounds; = *carbon copy, carbon paper*; rod of carbon used in arc lamp; ~ **copy,** copy made with carbon paper, (fig.) exact copy; ~ **dating,** determination of age from decay of radio-carbon; ~ **dioxide,** gas formed by burning carbon or by breathing; ~ **monoxide,** poisonous gas formed by burning carbon incompletely; ~ **paper** (coated with carbon etc. for making copy of words typed or written); **carbohy̆'drate** *n.*, energy-producing compound of carbon with oxygen and hydrogen (e.g. starch, sugar, glucose); **carbo'lic** *a.* (**carbolic acid,** phenol; **carbolic**

soap, soap containing this); ~**ā′-
ceous** (-sh*u*s) *a*.; ~**āte,** (*n*.) salt of carbonic acid, (*v.t.*) impregnate with carbon dioxide, aerate, convert into carbonate; **carbŏ′nic** *a*., of carbon (~**ic acid,** weak acid formed from carbon dioxide and water); **C~ĭ′fer-
ous** *a*. & *n*., (of) Palaeozoic period or system above Devonian and below Permian, often with coal; ~**ize** *v.t.*, convert into carbon, reduce to charcoal or coke, coat with carbon; ~**izā′tion** *n*.; **carborŭ′ndum** *n*. [\*P], compound of carbon and silicon used as abrasive etc. [F f. L *carbo* charcoal]

**car′boy** *n*. Large globular glass bottle protected by frame. [Pers.]

**car′buncle** *n*. Red jewel, esp. cabochon garnet; severe abscess; **carbŭ′ncular** *a*. [F f. L (CARBON)]

**carburā′tion** *n*. Process of charging air with spray of liquid hydrocarbon fuel; **carbŭrĕ′ttor, -tter, \*-ĕ′tor,** *n*., apparatus for carburation in petrol engine. [CARBON]

**car′cass,** ‖**-ase,** *n*. Dead body of animal or bird; human body, (joc. or derog.) alive or (derog.) dead; trunk of slaughtered animal; framework, worthless remains (*of*). [F]

**carci′nog|en** *n*. Cancer-producing substance; ~**ĕ′nic** *a*.; **carcinō′ma** *n*. (*pl*. **-mata, -mas**), cancer. [L *carcinoma* f. Gk]

**card**[1]**. 1.** *n*. Toothed instrument or wire-brush for raising nap on cloth or for disentangling fibres before spinning. **2.** *v.t.* Brush or comb with card. [F f. Prov. f. L *caro* to card]

**card**[2] *n*. = PLAYING-*card* (COURT-
-*card*; **on the ~s,** likely, possible; PLAY one's *cards*; **put** or **lay one's ~s
on the table,** disclose one's resources, plans, etc.); (in *pl*.) card-playing; (*sure, safe, doubtful,* etc.) plan, move; (colloq.) (eccentric) person; piece of thick paper or thin pasteboard for various purposes (CHRISTMAS *card*, POST[2]*card*); programme of events at race-meeting etc., or for recording cricket-scores; (*visiting-*)~ (with name etc., esp. sent or left in lieu of formal visit); (in *pl*., colloq.) employee's documents (**ask for, get,**
one's ~**s,** ask, be told, to leave one's employment); ~**′board,** pasteboard, (*attrib.*, fig.) insubstantial; ~**-carry-
ing,** having valid membership (esp. of political party); ~**-game,** game using playing-cards; ~ **index** (in

which each item is entered on a separate card); ~**-sharp(er),** swindler at card-games; ~**-table,** (esp. folding) table for card-playing; ~
**up one's sleeve,** plan in reserve; ~
**vote,** = BLOCK *vote*. [F f. L *charta* f. Gk, = papyrus-leaf]

**car′damom** *n*. An E. Ind. spice. [F or L f. Gk]

**car′diäc** *a*. Of the heart (*cardiac*
ARREST). [F or L f. Gk (CARDIO-)]

**car′digan** *n*. Knitted jacket. [person]

**car′dinal. 1.** *a*. (~**ly**). On which something hinges, fundamental, central; of deep scarlet; ~ **numbers,**
1, 2, etc. (opp. *ordinal numbers*; cf. NUMERAL); ~ **points** (of compass), N., S., E., W.; *cardinal* VIRTUES. **2.** *n*. One of leading dignitaries of R.C. Church, electing Pope and wearing red robes; small scarlet Amer. bird; ~**āte, ~shǐp,** *n*s., cardinal's position. [F f. L (*cardo -din-* hinge)]

**car′dio-** *in comb*. Heart; ~**grăm**
*n*., record of heart movements; ~**graph** (-ahf) *n*., instrument for taking such records; **cardiŏ′logy̆** *n*., study of the heart; ~**-vascular,** *a*., of heart and blood-vessels. [Gk *kardia* heart]

**care. 1.** *n*. Trouble, anxiety; occasion for these; matter of concern; task; serious attention, caution, (**have a, take, ~,** be cautious or neglect or fail *to* do); charge, protection, (~ **of,** at the address of; **take ~ of,** ensure safety of, deal with, dispose of); = CHILD *care*; ~**′free,** free from anxiety or responsibility; ~**′taker,** person in charge of house, ‖building, etc., (*attrib.*) exercising temporary control (*caretaker government*); ~**-worn,** fatigued by care(s). **2.** *v.i.* & *t.* Feel concern, interest, regard, or liking, (*about, for, whether*; freq. in neg. contexts; with expletive: *not care a damn* etc.; **for all I ~, I couldn't ~ less,
who ~s?,** colloq., I don't care at all); wish or be willing *to* (*don't care to be seen with him*); ~ **for,** provide for, look after. **3.** ~**′ful** (-ār′f-) *a*. (**-lly**), painstaking, watchful, cautious (*that,* or *to* do), done with care, concerned *for,* taking care *of*; ~**′lĕss** (-ār′l-) *a*., unconcerned, lighthearted, thoughtless, negligent *of,* inaccurate. [E, = sorrow]

**caree′n** *v.t.* & *i.* Turn (ship) on side for repair etc.; heel over; \*(of vehicle etc.) career. [F f. It. f. L *carina* keel]

**career'. 1.** *n.* Swift course (*in full career*); course through life; way of making one's living, profession; ~ **diplomat**, professional diplomat; ~ **girl, woman**, one who works permanently in a profession; ~**s master, mistress**, teacher advising pupils on choice of career. **2.** *v.i.* Go swiftly or wildly. **3.** ~**ïst** *n.*, one intent mainly on personal advancement. [F f. It. f. Prov. f. L (CAR)]

**careful, careless.** See CARE.

**care'ss. 1.** *n.* Fondling touch, kiss. **2.** *v.t.* Give caress to. [F f. L (*carus* dear)]

**că'rět** *n.* Mark ∧ showing where something is to be inserted in printing or writing. [L, = is lacking]

**car'gō** *n.* (*pl.* ~**es**, *~**s**). Goods carried by ship, aircraft, or *motor vehicle. [Sp. (CHARGE)]

**Că'rïb** *n.* Aboriginal inhabitant of southern W. Ind. islands and adjacent coasts; their language; ~**bē'an** *a.*, of these people or W. Indies generally. [Sp.]

**că'ribou** (-bōō) *n.* (*pl.* same). N. Amer. reindeer. [F f. Amer. Ind.]

**că'ricatūr|e. 1.** *n.* Grotesque representation of person etc. by exaggeration of characteristics; ridiculously poor imitation or version; ~**ïst** *n.* **2.** *v.t.* Make or give caricature of. [F f. It. (CHARGE)]

**car'ïes** (-z; *or* -rēz) *n.* (*pl.* same). Decay of tooth or bone. [L]

**cari'llon** (-lyon, kă'rĭl(y)on) *n.* Set of bells sounded either from keyboard or mechanically; tune played on bells. [F]

**car'ïous** *a.* Decayed (esp. of bones or teeth). [L (CARIES)]

**Carlovingian.** See CAROLINGIAN.

**Căr'mélite** *n.* & *a.* (Member) of mendicant order of white-cloaked friars or of similar order of nuns. [F or L (*Carmel*, place)]

**căr'mïnative** *a.* & *n.* (Drug) curing flatulence. [F or L (*carmino* heal by CHARM)]

**căr'mïne** *n.* & *a.* (Of or like) vivid crimson colour or pigment from cochineal. [F or L (CRIMSON)]

**căr'n|age** *n.* Great slaughter, esp. in battle; ~**al** *a.* (~**ally**), sensual, sexual, worldly; ~**ă'lĭtў** *n.*; ~**ă'tion** *n.* & *a.*, (of) rosy-pink colour, cultivated clove pink; ~**ě'lïan**, see CORNELIAN[2]; ~**ïval** *n.*, festival or

festivities, esp. preceding Lent, riotous revelry, *fun-fair or circus, [L *carnem levo* put away meat]; **C~ï'vora** *n.pl.*, carnivorous order of mammals (cats, dogs, foxes, bears, etc.) [L *voro* devour]; ~**ïvŏre** *n.*, carnivorous animal or plant; ~**ï'vorous** *a.*, flesh-eating. [F f. L (*caro carn-* flesh)]

**că'rol. 1.** *n.* Joyous song, esp. Christmas hymn. **2.** *v.i.* & *t.* (‖-ll-). Sing (as) carol; sing joyfully. [F]

**Cărolē'an, Că'roline**, *adjs.* Of the time of Charles I or II of England. [L *Carolus* Charles]

**Căroli'ngïan, Căr̆lovi'ngïan**, (-nj-) *n.* & *a.* (Member) of second French dynasty, founded by Charlemagne. [F (prec., MEROVINGIAN)]

***că'rom. 1.** *n.* Cannon at billiards. **2.** *v.i.* Make carom; strike and rebound *off*. [abbr. of *carambole* f. Sp.]

**carō'tïd** *a.* & *n.* ~ (*artery*), one of two main arteries carrying blood to head. [F or L f. Gk]

**carou'se. 1.** (-z) *v.i.*, *n.* & *n.* (Have or engage in) drinking-bout or drunken revelry; ~**al** *n.* [G *gar aus* (drink) right out]

**cărouse'l, *cărr-**, (-ōō-; *or* -z-) *n.* Rotating delivery or conveyor system; *merry-go-round, roundabout. [F f. It.]

**cărp[1]** *n.* (*pl.* same). A freshwater fish freq. bred in ponds. [F f. Prov. or L]

**cărp[2]** *v.i.* Talk querulously, find fault, (usu. *at*). [N, = brag]

**căr'pal.** See CARPUS.

**căr'pel** *n.* (Bot.) One of the constituent units of a compound ovary. [F or L f. Gk *karpos* fruit]

**căr'pĕnt|er. 1.** *n.* Craftsman in woodwork, esp. of rough solid kinds; ~**rў** *n.* **2.** *v.i.* & *t.* Do, make by, carpenter's work. [AF f. L (*carpentum* wagon)]

**căr'pĕt. 1.** *n.* Thick fabric for covering floor or stairs (**on the ~**, being reprimanded, under discussion; **sweep under the ~**, conceal (problem etc.), ignore); expanse of grass, flowers, etc.; ~**-bag**, travelling-bag, orig. made of carpet-like material; ~**-bagger**, political candidate etc. without local connections; ~ **slipper** (of kind with uppers made orig. of carpet-like material); ~**-sweeper**, household implement for sweeping carpets. **2.** *v.t.* Cover (as) with carpet; (colloq.) reprimand. [F or L f. It.]

**căr′p|us** n. (pl. ∼i pr. -ī). The small bones connecting hand and forearm (wrist, horse's knee, etc.); ∼al a. [L f. Gk]

**căr′rel** n. Small cubicle for reader in library. [var. of CAROL = cloister--room]

**căr′riage** (-rĭj) n. Conveying of goods etc.; cost of this (∼ **forward**, to be paid by recipient; ∼ **paid**, by sender); manner of carrying oneself, deportment; wheeled vehicle for persons; four-wheeled vehicle with two (∼ **and pair**) or more horses; ‖railway passenger vehicle; part of machine that carries other parts into desired position; (**gun-**)∼, wheeled support of gun; ∼**way**, part of road for vehicular traffic. [F (CARRY)]

**căr′rier** n. Person or thing that carries; person or company conveying goods or passengers for payment; part of bicycle etc. for carrying luggage or passenger; person or animal that without suffering from a disease or showing a characteristic transmits it to others; = AIR*craft-carrier*; ∼(-**bag**), paper or plastic bag for shopping etc.; *carrier* PIGEON[1]; ∼ **wave**, (Telecommunications) high-frequency electromagnetic wave modulated in amplitude or frequency to convey signal. [CARRY]

**căr′rion** n. Dead putrefying flesh; something vile or filthy; ∼ **crow**, black crow. [F f. L *caro* flesh]

**căr′rot** n. Plant or its tapering orange-coloured root used as vegetable; (fig.) means of enticement; (in *pl.*, sl.) red hair, red-haired person; ∼y̆ a. [F f. L f. Gk]

**căr′ry̆. 1.** v.t. & i. Transport, convey, (∼ **all before** one, overcome all opposition); cause or enable to go to; conduct (*pipes carry water*; *wires carry electric current*); take (process etc.) to specified point (*carry into effect*; *carry joke too far*); continue or prolong to (*carry modesty to excess*); transfer (figure) to column of higher value; (of gun etc.) propel to specified distance; (of sound, voice, etc.) be heard at a distance; win, capture (prize, fortress, etc.; ∼ **the day**, be victorious); win victory or acceptance for (motion, bill, etc.); have with one, possess, (*a stick*,

*a watch*, one's BAT[2]; ∼ **conviction**, be persuasive); involve, imply, (*loans carry interest*; *principles carry consequences*); stock (goods for sale); (of newspaper, radio station, etc.) publish, broadcast, esp. regularly; hold in a certain way (*carry* one's *head* or *body*, *oneself*, *erect*, etc.); endure weight of, support, (*ships carry sail*; *columns carry dome*; ∼ **weight**, be important or influential); be pregnant with (*she was carrying twins*). **2.** ∼ **away**, remove, inspire, deprive of self-control; ∼ **back**, remind (person) of former time; ∼--**cot**, portable cot for baby; ∼ **forward**, transfer to new page or account; ∼ **off**, remove by force, win, render acceptable or passable, manage; ∼ **on**, advance (process) by a stage, take part in (conversation etc.), manage (business), continue, go on with one's job, (colloq.) behave strangely or excitedly, flirt or have an affair (*with*); ∼ **out**, put (principles, orders, etc.) into practice; ∼ **over**, carry forward, postpone; ∼ **through**, bring safely out of difficulties, complete; ∼ **with** one, remember, persuade or get support of (audience etc.). **3.** n. Act of carrying; (Golf) ball's flight before pitching. [AF (CAR)]

**cărt. 1.** n. Strong two- or four--wheeled vehicle used for carrying heavy goods etc. (HAND*cart*; ‖**in the** ∼, sl., in an awkward or losing position; **put the** ∼ **before the horse**, reverse proper order); light two-wheeled one-horse vehicle for driving in; ∼-**horse** (of heavy build); ∼-**load**, cartful, large quantity; ∼-**road**, -**track**, (too rough for carriages); ∼-**wheel**, wheel of cart, sideways somersault with arms and legs extended, large circular hat. **2.** v.t. Convey (as) in cart; (sl.) carry (esp. cumbersome thing) with difficulty, over long distance, etc. **3.** ∼′**age** n., carting or its cost; ∼′**ful** (-ŏŏl) n. [E & N]

**carte blanche** (kărt blah′nsh) n. Full discretionary power given to person. [F, = blank paper]

**cărtĕl′** n. Manufacturers' union to control prices etc.; political combination between parties. [G f. F f. It. dim. (CARD[2])]

**Cărtē′sĭan** (-zyan) a. & n. (Follower) of Descartes or his thinking; ∼ **coordinates** (Math., measured from straight axes). [L (*Cartesius* Descartes)]

**Cārthū′sian** (-zyan) *a.* & *n.* (Member) of order of monks founded by St. Bruno; ||(member) of Charterhouse School. [L (CHARTREUSE)]

**cār′til|age** *n.* Firm elastic tissue in vertebrates; structure of this; ~**ă′ginous** *a.*, of, like, with skeleton of, cartilage. [F f. L]

**cārtŏ′graph|y̆** *n.* Map-drawing; ~**er** *n.*; **cārtŏgră′phĭc(al)** *adjs.* (**-ically**). [F (CARD²)]

**cār′ton** *n.* Light cardboard etc. box for goods. [F, as foll.]

**cārtōō′n. 1.** *n.* Full-size drawing as sketch for work of art; humorous (esp. topical) drawing in newspaper etc., sequence of these (STRIP *cartoon*); = ANIMATE*d* cartoon; ~**′ist** *n.*, one who draws cartoons. **2.** *v.t.* Draw cartoon of. [It. (CARD²)]

**cārtou′che** (-ōō′sh) *n.* Scroll ornament; oval frame enclosing name and title of Egyptian king. [F, as prec.]

**cār′tridge** *n.* Case containing charge of propellant explosive for firearms or blasting, with bullet or shot if for small arms (BLANK *cartridge*); spool of film, magnetic tape, in, in container; removable pick-up head of record-player; ink-container for insertion in pen; ~**paper** (thick and rough, for drawing, large envelopes, etc.).

**cārve** *v.t.* & *i.* Cut up (meat etc.) at or for table; cut patterns, designs, etc., in (wood etc.); produce by cutting (statue, one's name, etc.; ~ one's **way**, lit. or fig.); make (material) *into* object thus; ~ **out**, take from larger whole, make (career, name, etc., *for* one*self*); ~ **up**, subdivide; ~**up** *n.*, (sl.) sharing-out, esp. of spoils; **cār′ver** *n.*, (esp.) carving-knife, (in *pl.*) carving-knife and fork; **cār′ving** *n.*, (esp.) carved wood etc.; **carving-knife** (for carving meat). [E]

**cār′vel** *n.* See CARAVEL; ~**-built**, with planks flush (cf. CLINKER²-*built*).

**Căsanō′va** (or -z-) *n.* Man noted for his love affairs. [person]

**căscā′de. 1.** *n.* Waterfall; section of large broken waterfall. **2.** *v.i.* Fall in or like cascade. [F f. It. (CASE¹)]

**căscā′ra** *n.* ~ (**sagrada** *pr.* -ah′da), a purgative bark. [Sp.]

**căse¹** *n.* Instance of thing's occurring; actual or hypothetical situation (**as the ~ may be,** according to the situation; **in any ~,** whatever the fact is; **in ~,** if, in the event that, lest, because of a possibility; **in ~ of,** in the event of; **in no ~,** under no circumstances; **in that ~,** if that is true, if that should happen; **in the ~ of,** as regards; **is, is not, the ~,** is true, false); (instance of) diseased condition of person, person suffering from this; crime etc. investigated by detective or police; (Law) cause or suit for trial, facts presented for reference to higher court, sum of arguments presented on one side; valid set of arguments; (Gram.) (form of noun, adjective, or pronoun expressing) relation to other word(s) in sentence; ~**book** (recording legal or medical cases, also fig.); ~ **history,** record of person's ancestry, personal history, etc., for use in deciding treatment etc.; ~**law,** law as settled by decided cases; ~**study,** (record of) study of person etc. from relevant information; ~**′work(er),** social work(er) concerned with individuals or groups. [F f. L *casus* (*cado* fall)]

**căse². 1.** *n.* Box, crate, cabinet, covering, etc., designed or serving to enclose or contain something (BOOK-, BRIEF-, GLASS, PILLOW-, SUIT*case*); box with appropriate contents (DRESSING-*case*); (Print.) partitioned receptacle for type (**lower ~,** small letters; **upper ~,** capitals); ~**harden,** harden surface of, (fig.) render callous. **2.** *v.t.* Enclose in a case; surround *with*; (sl.) examine (house etc., esp. in preparation for robbery). [F f. L *capsa* box]

**că′semāte** (-sm-) *n.* Embrasured room in thickness of fortress wall; armoured enclosure for warship's guns. [F & It.]

**că′sement** (-sm-) *n.* Hinged window or part of window; (poet. etc.) window. [AL (CASE²)]

**căsh. 1.** *n.* Money in form of coins or banknotes; ~ **and carry,** (of) store selling goods which are paid for in cash and removed by buyer, (of) this method of trading; ~ **crop** (to be sold, not used as food etc.); ~ **desk** (where cash is taken in shop etc.); *cash* DOWN³; ~ **on delivery,** system of paying carrier for goods when they are delivered; ~ **price** (lowest, for immediate payment); ~ **register,** TILL² recording amount of each purchase. **2.** *v.t.* & *i.* Give or obtain cash for (cheque etc.); ~ **in (on)**, make profit (out of), get advantage (from). [F or It. f. L (CASE²)]

**ca'shew** (-ōō) *n.* A tropical tree; ~(-**nut**), its edible kidney-shaped nut. [Port. f. Tupi]

**cashier'¹** *n.* Person in charge of cash. [CASH]

**cashier'²** *v.t.* Dismiss from service, esp. in disgrace. [Flem. f. F (QUASH)]

**ca'shmere** *n.* Fine soft wool (as) of *Kashmir* goat. [place]

**ca'sǐng** *n.* Enclosing material. [CASE²]

**casi'nŏ** (-sē'-) *n.* (*pl.* ~**s**). Public building or room for amusements, esp. gambling. [It. dim. (*casa* house)]

**cask** (-ah-) *n.* Barrel, esp. for alcoholic drinks; its contents. [F or Sp. (*casco* helmet)]

**ca'skėt** (-ah'-) *n.* Small box, freq. ornamental, for valuables; *oblong coffin. [AF f. It. dim. f. L (CASE²)]

**Cassă'ndra** *n.* Prophet of disaster, esp. if disregarded. [person]

**cassa'va** (-ah'-) *n.* Tropical plant; its starch or flour; bread from these. [Taino]

**ca'sserōle. 1.** *n.* Covered heat-·proof vessel in which food is cooked and served; food thus prepared. **2.** *v.t.* Cook in casserole. [F f. Prov. f. L f. Gk *kuathion* little cup]

**cassĕ'tte** *n.* Container of film, magnetic tape, etc., for insertion into camera, tape-recorder, etc. [F dim. (CASE²)]

**ca'ssǐa** (or -sha) *n.* Kind of cinnamon; plant yielding senna-leaves. [L f. Gk f. Heb.]

**ca'ssock** *n.* Long close garment worn esp. by clergy and choristers. [F f. It.]

**ca'ssowarў** (-o-) *n.* Large flightless bird related to emu. [Malay]

**cast** (-ah-). **1.** *v.t.* & *i.* (**cast**). Move by throwing (STONE, dice on table, etc.); shed or lose (horns, skin, horseshoe, etc.); throw out (fishing-·line, net, etc., into water etc.); give or register (vote); let down (anchor etc.); cause to fall, direct, (eye, glance, light, shadow, spell, etc., *on, upon*, etc.); utter (aspersions etc. *on*); arrange (facts etc.) *into* specified form; reckon or add up (accounts, figures); calculate (horoscope); shape (molten metal or plastic material)

in mould, make (product) thus; assign (actor) *as* character; allocate roles in (play, film, etc.). **2.** ~ **about or (a)round for**, try to find or think of; ~ **adrift**, leave to drift; ~ **aside**, discard, abandon; ~ **away**, reject, (in *pass.*) be shipwrecked; ~'**away**, shipwrecked person; ~ **down**, depress; ~**ing vote** (that decides between two equal parties); ~ **in** one's **lot with**, decide to share fortunes of; ~ **iron**, hard alloy of iron, carbon, and silicon cast in mould; ~-**iron** *a.*, of cast iron, (fig.) hard, unchangeable, impregnable; ~ **off**, abandon, detach (oneself); (Knitting) take (stitches) off needle and finish edge, (Naut.) loosen and throw off (rope etc.), (Print.) estimate space taken in print by MS. copy; ~-**off** *a.* & *n.*, abandoned or discarded (thing, esp. garment); ~ **on**, (Knitting) make first row of loops on needle; *cast to the* WIND¹*s*; ~ **up**, throw on to shore etc., add up (figures etc.); ~'**ing** *n.*, (esp.) object made by casting molten metal etc. **3.** *n.* Throwing of missile, dice, line, net, etc.; earth excreted by worm; thing made in mould for molten metal, clay, etc.; moulded mass of solidified material (*leg in a plaster cast*); set of actors taking parts in play, film, etc.; form, type, or quality (*of* features, mind, etc.); slight squint; tinge of colour. [N]

**castanĕ't** *n.* (usu. in *pl.*). Small concave piece of hardwood, ivory, etc., clicked or rattled in pairs as rhythmic accompaniment to dance etc. [Sp. (CHESTNUT)]

**caste** (-ah-) *n.* Hindu hereditary class, with members practising certain rites and trades and having no social intercourse with other castes; exclusive social class; system of such classes; position given by class (**lose ~**, descend in social scale). [Sp. & Port. (CHASTE)]

**ca'stellātėd** *a.* Castle-like, battlemented. [CASTLE]

**caster.** See CASTOR².

**ca'stĭgāte** *v.t.* (~**able**). Chastise with blows or words; ~**ā'tion**, ~**ātor**, *ns.* [L (CHASTE)]

**ca'stle** (kah'sel). **1.** *n.* Building(s) designed to serve as both residence and fortress, usu. with towers, battlements, etc.; = ROOK¹; ~ **in Spain**, ~ **in the air**, visionary project, day-dream. **2.** *v.i.* Make special move with chess king and rook. [AF f. L *castellum*]

**ca'stor**[1] (-ah'-) *n.* Substance got from beaver and used in medicine and perfumery. [F or L f. Gk]

**ca'stor**[2], **-er,** (-ah'-) *n.* Small bottle etc. with holes in top for sprinkling contents; small swivelled wheel on table-leg etc.; ~ **sugar** (white, finely granulated). [CAST]

**ca'stor**[3] (-ah'-) *n.* ~ **oil,** purgative and lubricant vegetable oil. [orig. uncert.]

**ca̅str|a̅'te** *v.t.* Remove testicles of, geld; ~**a̅'tion** *n.*; ~**a̅'to̅** (-ah'-) *n.* (*pl.* ~**ati** *pr.* -ah'te̅), (Hist.) male singer castrated in boyhood to retain soprano or alto voice. [L *castro*]

**ca'sual** (-zho͞oăl, -zyo͞oăl). **1.** *a.* (~**ly**). Accidental, due to chance; not regular or permanent (*casual labourer*); (colloq.) careless, unconcerned, unceremonious; (of clothes) informal; ‖~ **ward,** place for temporary accommodation of vagrants. **2.** *n.* Casual labourer; (usu. in *pl.*) casual clothes, esp. low-heeled shoes. **3.** ~**ty** *n.*, accident, person killed or injured in war or accident, thing lost or destroyed; ~**ty department, ward,** (colloq.) ~**ty,** part of hospital where casualties are attended to. [F & L (CASE[1])]

**ca'su|ist** (-zho͞o-, -zū-) *n.* Person who resolves cases of conscience, duty, etc., often with false but clever arguments; sophist, quibbler; ~**i'stic(al)** *adjs.* (**-ically**); ~**istry** *n.* [F f. Sp. f. L (CASE[1])]

**cat** *n.* Small furry domesticated carnivorous quadruped (**a ~ may look at a king,** even inferiors must be allowed some privileges; ~ **among the pigeons,** violent intruder; ~**-and-dog** *life* etc., full of quarrels; **enough to make a ~ laugh,** extremely amusing; **fight like Kilkenny ~s** (to mutual destruction); **let the ~ out of the bag,** reveal secret, esp. involuntarily; **like a ~ on hot bricks,** uneas(il)y; **not a ~ in hell's chance,** no chance whatever; **not room to swing a ~,** very confined space; RAIN **cats and dogs; see which way the ~ jumps,** wait for opinion or result to be revealed); any feline animal (e.g. lion, tiger) or catlike animal (*polecat*); (colloq., derog.) spiteful or malicious woman; (sl.) person, esp. jazz enthusiast; = *cathead, cat-o'-nine-tails;* ‖~ **burglar** (who enters by climbing wall to upper storey); ~**'call** *n.,* & *v.i.,* (make) shrill whistle etc. of disapproval; ~**'fish,** fish with barbels like cat's whiskers round mouth; ~**'gut,** twisted intestines of sheep, horse, or ass, used for strings of musical instruments and surgical sutures; ~**'head,** (Naut.) projection from each side of bow for raising and carrying anchor; ~**'mint,** ~**'nip,** blue-flowered aromatic plant; ~**'nap** *n.,* & *v.i.,* (have) brief sleep; ~**-o'-nine-tails,** (Hist.) nine-lashed rope whip for flogging; ~**'s-cradle,** child's game with string forming patterns between fingers; ~**'s-eye,** reflector stud on road, a precious stone; ‖~**'s-meat,** flesh of horse etc. sold as food for cats; ~**'s-paw,** person used as tool by another, slight breeze; ~**'suit,** close-fitting garment with trouser legs, covering body from neck to feet; ~**'s whiskers,** (sl.) excellent person or thing; ~**'walk,** narrow footway; ~**'tish,** ~**'ty** (**-ily, -iness**), *adjs.,* catlike, (fig.) sly or spiteful. [E & AF f. L *cattus*]

**cata-** *pref.* Down; wrongly. [Gk]

**cata'bolism** *n.* (Biol.) Destructive METABOLISM (opp. *anabolism*). [CATA-, Gk *ballō* throw]

**catachr|e̅'sis** (-k-) *n.* (*pl.* ~**eses** *pr.* -e̅z). Incorrect use of words; ~**e̅'stic** *a.* (**-ically**). [L f. Gk (*khraomai* use)]

**ca'tacl|ysm** *n.* Violent event; political or social upheaval; ~**y'smic** (-z-) *a.* (**-ically**). [F f. L f. Gk (*kluzō* wash)]

**ca'tacomb** (-o͞om, -o̅m) *n.* Subterranean gallery with side recesses for tombs. [F f. L]

**ca'tafalque** (-k) *n.* Structure for display or conveyance of coffin at important funeral. [F f. It.]

**Ca'talan** *a.* & *n.* (Native, language) of *Catalonia* in Spain. [F f. Sp.]

**ca'tal|epsy** *n.* Seizure or trance with rigidity of body; ~**e'ptic** (*a.*; **-ically**) of or having catalepsy, (*n.*) person with catalepsy. [F or L f. Gk (*lēpsis* seizure)]

**ca'talo̅gue** (-g), **\*-lŏg. 1.** *n.* Complete list usu. in alphabetical or other systematic order and often with particulars added to items. **2.** *v.t.* Make catalogue (entry) of. [F f. L f. Gk (*legō* choose)]

**cata'lpa** *n.* Flowering tree with long pods. [N. Amer. Ind.]

**cată'lȳs|ĭs** n. (*pl.* ∼es *pr.* -ēz). (Chem.) Effect produced by substance that, without itself undergoing change, aids chemical change in other substances; **că'talȳse, *-ze,** *v.t.,* accelerate (process) by catalysis; **că'talȳst** n., substance causing catalysis, (fig.) person or thing that facilitates change; **cătalȳ'tic** a. (-ically). [Gk (*luō* set free)]

**cătamară'n** n. Raft of yoked logs or boats; twin-hulled boat. [Tamil]

**că'tamite** n. (Boy as) passive partner in sodomy. [L f. Gk,= Ganymede, servant of Zeus]

**că'tapŭlt. 1.** n. ‖Boy's shooting contrivance of forked stick and elastic; (Hist.) military machine for hurling stones etc.; mechanical device for launching glider, aircraft from deck of ship, etc. **2.** *v.t. & i.* Launch with catapult; fling forcibly (lit. or fig.); move (as if) from catapult. [F or L f. Gk]

**că'tarăct** n. Waterfall (esp. large and sheer); downpour; progressive opacity of eye-lens. [L *cataracta* f. Gk,= down-rushing]

**catăr'rh** (-är') n. Inflammation of mucous membrane; watery discharge in nose or throat due to this; ∼al a. [F f. L f. Gk (*rheō* flow)]

**cată'strophē** n. Great, usu. sudden, disaster; disastrous end; dénouement of drama; **cătastrŏ'phic** a. (-ically). [L f. Gk (*strephō* turn)]

**cătat|ō'nĭa** n. Schizophrenia with intervals of catalepsy and occas. violence; ∼ō'nĭc, (a.; -ically) of or having catatonia, (n.) person with catatonia. [Gk (TONE)]

**cătch. 1.** *v.t. & i.* (**caught** *pr.* kawt). Capture in net, hands, etc.; trap into revelation, contradiction, etc.; detect or surprise (do*ing*; *at* or *in*; *catch* BEND[1]*ing*, NAP[1]*ping*); (of storm etc.) come down upon; overtake; be in time for (train, person about to depart, etc.); grasp; check suddenly, by adhesion etc. (*catch* one's BREATH); become fixed or entangled, be checked, (*foot catches in wire*; *bolt does not catch*); suffer check or entanglement of (∼ one's **foot**, stumble); receive and hold (moving thing) in hands etc.; (Crick.) dismiss (batsman) by catching ball direct from bat; get or contract by infection, contagion, or example, (disease, person's manner, enthusiasm, etc.; ∼ **cold**, contract a

cold; *catch* one's DEATH); draw attention of, captivate, (eye, fancy); apprehend (meaning, sight, sound, etc.) with senses or mind; hit (*he, a stone, caught me on the nose*; *caught him a blow* or *one*); begin to burn. **2.** ∼**-all**, (thing) designed to catch or include various items; ∼**-as-**∼**-can**, wrestling in which all holds are permissible; ∼ **at**, try to grasp (*catch at a* STRAW); ∼ **crop** (grown between two staple crops in position or time); ∼ **fire**, ignite, start to burn; ∼ **hold of**, grasp, seize; ∼ **it**, (sl.) be punished; ∼ **on**, (colloq.) become popular, understand what is meant; ∼ **out**, detect in mistake etc., take unawares, (Crick.) get (batsman) out by catching; ∼**'penny**, intended merely to sell quickly, superficially attractive; ∼**-phrase** (in frequent current use); ∼ **up**, overtake, make up arrears, pick up hurriedly; ∼**'-weight** a. & n., (Sports) unrestricted (as regards) weight; ∼**'word**, word so placed as to draw attention, word or phrase in frequent use, slogan. **3.** n. Act of catching; amount of fish etc. caught; thing or person caught or worth catching, esp. in matrimony; question, trick, etc., intended to deceive, incriminate, etc.; unexpected difficulty or disadvantage; contrivance for fastening door, window, etc.; (Crick. etc.) chance or act of catching the ball; (Mus.) round, esp. with words arranged to produce humorous effect; ∼**-22**, (sl.) dilemma where victim cannot win [title of novel]. **4.** ∼**'er** n., (esp., Baseball) fielder behind batter; ∼**'ing** a., (esp.) infectious; ∼**'ment** n. (∼**ment area,** area from which rainfall flows into river etc., fig. area from which school's pupils, hospital's patients, etc., are drawn); ∼**'ȳ** a. (∼**ily,** ∼**iness**), (of tune) attractive, easily remembered. [AF f. L *capto* try to catch (*capio* take)]

**că'tĕch|ĭsm** (-k-) n. Instruction by question and answer; published example of this, esp. (**the C**∼) Prayer Book form for instruction before Confirmation; series of questions; ∼**ĕ'tic(al)** a. (-ically), catechizing, of catechism; ∼**ĭst** n., religious teacher, esp. using catechism; ∼**īze** *v.t.,* instruct, examine, by or in catechism or the Catechism; ∼**ū'mĕn** n., person being instructed before baptism. [L f. Gk]

**că′teg|orў** *n.* Class or division (of things, ideas, etc.); **~ŏ′rĭcal** *a.* (**-lly**), unconditional, absolute, explicit; **~orical imperative**, moral obligation from pure reason or conscience. [F or L f. Gk, = statement]

**că′ter**[1] *v.i.* Purvey food; provide meals, amusements, etc., *for;* pander *to* (evil inclinations); **~er** *n.,* (esp.) one who supplies food for social events. [AF *acatour* buyer f. L *capto* (CATCH)]

**că′ter**[2] *n.* 'Four' on dice. [F *quatre* f. L *quattuor* four]

**că′terpĭllar** *n.* Larva of butterfly or moth; (*C~*; P) vehicle with endless articulated steel band (~ **track, tread**) passing round two wheels, to travel on rough ground. [AF (CAT, PILE[3])]

**că′terwaul** *v.i.* Stream like cat. [CAT; -*waul* imit.]

**Cath.** *abbr.* Cathedral; Catholic.

**cathăr′|sis** *n.* (*pl.* **~ses** *pr.* **-ēz**) (Med.) purgation; outlet to emotion afforded by drama etc.; **~′tĭc,** (*a.*; **-ically**) effecting catharsis, purgative, (*n.*) such drug. [L f. Gk (*katharos* clean)]

**cathe′dral** *n.* & *a.* ~ (**church**), principal church of diocese. [F or L f. Gk *kathedra* seat]

**Că′therine** *n.* ~ **wheel**, rotating firework. [person]

**că′theter** *n.* (Med.) Tube inserted into body-cavity to allow movement of fluid; **~ize** *v.t.,* insert catheter into. [L f. Gk]

**că′thŏde** *n.* Negative electrode or terminal (opp. ANODE); ~ **ray**, beam of electrons from cathode of high-vacuum tube; **~-ray tube**, vacuum tube in which cathode rays produce luminous image on fluorescent screen. [Gk (CATA-, *hodos* way)]

**că′tholĭc.** 1. *a.* Universal, of interest or use to all, all-embracing, of wide sympathies or interests (*has catholic tastes*); (of Church; *C~*) including all Christians, or all of the Western Church (cf. ORTHODOX), or all of the Roman Church. 2. *n.* Member of Catholic Church, esp. (*C~*) Roman Catholic Church. 3. **cathŏ′licĭsm** (Eccl.), **cătholi′cĭtў,** *ns.;* **cathŏ′licize** *v.t.;* **~lў, cathŏ′licallў,** *advs.* [F or L f. Gk (CATA-, *holos* whole)]

**că′tion** *n.* Positively charged ion; **cătĭŏ′nĭc** *a.* [CATA-, ION]

**că′tkĭn** *n.* Downy hanging flower of willow, hazel, etc. [Du. (CAT)]

**că′ttĭsh.** See CAT.

**că′ttle** *n.pl.* Oxen; **black ~** (orig. black, of Sc. & Welsh highland breeds); ||**~-grid,** \***~-guard,** ditch covered by spaced bars to allow passage of vehicles and pedestrians but not of cattle etc.; \***~-man,** one who tends or rears cattle; **~-plague,** rinderpest. [AF *catel* (CAPITAL)]

**că′ttў.** See CAT.

**Caucā′sĭan** (-z-; or -zhan) *a.* & *n.* (Member) of the 'white' or light-skinned division of mankind; (native) of the *Caucasus.* [place]

**cau′cus** *n.* (||usu. derog.) Local committee for political party organization; party meeting. [perh. f. Algonquin]

**cau′d|al** *a.* (**-lly**). Of or like tail; of posterior part of body; **~āte** *a.,* tailed. [L (*cauda* tail)]

**caught.** See CATCH.

**caul** *n.* Membrane enclosing foetus; part of this sometimes found on child's head at birth. [F]

**cau′ldron, ca′l-** (kaw′l-), *n.* Large usu. basin-shaped boiling-vessel. [AF f. L *caldarium* hot bath]

**cau′liflower** (kŏ′l-) *n.* Cabbage with large white flower-head; ~ **cheese,** savoury dish of cauliflower and cheese (sauce); ~ **ear** (thickened by repeated blows). [F *chou fleuri* flowered cabbage]

**caulk,** \***calk,** (kawk) *v.t.* Stop up (seam), stop up seams of (ship), with oakum etc. and waterproofing material or by driving plate-joins together. [F f. L *calco* tread]

**caus|e** (-z). 1. *n.* What produces an effect (**First C~,** the Creator of the universe); person or thing that occasions or produces something; reason or motive; justification (esp. *show cause*); matter about which person goes to law; his case (*plead a cause*); lawsuit; principle, belief, advocated or upheld, esp. zealously, (**lost ~,** hopeless undertaking; **make common ~,** unite efforts for a purpose *with*); subject of interest (**good ~,** movement, charity, etc., deserving support); ~ **célèbre** (kōz sělě′br; *pl.* ~s **célèbres** *pr.* same), lawsuit that attracts much interest. 2. *v.t.* Be the cause of, produce; induce, make, (person or thing *to* do, thing *to be* done). 3. **~′al** *a.* (**~ally**), (esp.) of the nature of cause and effect; ~**ă′lĭtў** *n.*, (esp.) relation of cause and effect, principle that everything has a cause; ~**ā′tion** *n.*, causing, causality; ~**ative** *a.*, acting as or expressing cause. [F f. L *causa*]

**causerie** (kō′zerĭ) *n.* (*pl. pr.* same). Informal article or talk, esp. on literary subject. [F]

**cau′seway** (-zw-) *n.* Raised road across low or wet ground; raised way by road. [AF *caucee* f. L. CALX]

**cau′stic. 1.** *a.* (~ally). That burns or corrodes organic tissue (*caustic* POTASH, SODA); sarcastic, biting. **2.** *n.* Caustic substance. **3. causti′cĭtў** *n.*; **cau′terize** *v.t.*, sear with caustic or cautery; **cauterizā′tion** *n.*; **cau′terў** *n.*, (device for) surgical searing. [L f. Gk (*kaiō* burn)]

**cau′tion. 1.** *n.* Taking care, attention to safety, avoidance of rashness, (||~ **money**, sum deposited as security for good conduct); warning, esp. by police, magistrate, etc.; (colloq.) surprising or amusing person or thing. **2.** *v.t.* Warn (*against, to* or *not to do*); admonish not to repeat offence. **3.** ~**arў** *a.*, that warns; **cau′tious** (-shŭs) *a.*, having or showing caution. [F f. L *cautio* (*caveo* take heed)]

**căvalcā′de** *n.* Procession or company of riders, motor cars, etc. [F f. It. (foll.)]

**căvalier′. 1.** *n.* Courtly gentleman or soldier; (arch.) horseman; (Hist.) *C*~) supporter of Charles I in Civil War. **2.** *a.* Offhand, curt, supercilious. **3. că′valrў** *n.* (usu. treated as *pl.*), soldiers on horseback or in motor vehicles; **cavalry twill**, strong cloth in double twill. [F f. It. (CHEVALIER)]

**cāve[1]. 1.** Large hollow in side of hill, cliff, etc., or underground; ~**-dweller**, (prehistoric) man living in cave; ~**′man**, cave-dweller, (fig.) man of primitive or violent passions, behaviour, etc.; ~**-painting**, (esp. prehistoric) pictures of animals etc. on interior of cave. **2.** *v.t.* & *i.* Explore caves; ~ **in**, (cause to) subside or fall in, (fig.) yield to pressure, submit, withdraw opposition. [F f. L (*cavus* hollow)]

||**cā′vē[2]** *int.* (school sl.) Look out!; **că′vĕat** *n.*, warning, proviso, (Law) process to suspend court proceedings; *caveat emptor* (-ĕ′mptŏr), let the buyer beware (he alone is

responsible if he is disappointed). [L *caveo* beware]

**că′vern** *n.* Cave, esp. large or dark one; ~**ous** *a.*, like a cavern, full of caverns. [F, or L *caverna* (CAVE[1])]

||**că′viăre, *-ăr**, (*or -ăr′*) *n.* Pickled roe of sturgeon etc. (~ **to the general**, good thing unappreciated by the ignorant). [It. f. Turk.]

**că′vĭl. 1.** *v.i.* (||-ll-). Take exception (*at*), carp, find fault. **2.** *n.* (Captious or frivolous) objection. [F f. L *cavillor*]

**că′vĭtў** *n.* Hollow within solid body; ~ **wall**, double wall with internal cavity; **căvĭtā′tion** *n.*, formation of cavity within a body. [F or L (CAVE[1])]

**cavŏr′t** *v.i.* (colloq.) Prance, caper. [orig. uncert.]

**caw** *n.*, & *v.i.* (Make) cry of rook, crow, etc. [imit.]

**caye′nne** *n.* ~ (**pepper**), pungent red pepper from capsicum. [Tupi]

**cay′man, cai′man**, *n.* S. Amer. alligator. [Sp. & Port. f. Carib]

**C.B.** *abbr.* ||Companion (of the Order) of the Bath; confined, confinement, to barracks.

||**C.B.E.** *abbr.* Commander (of the Order) of the British Empire.

||**C.B.I.** *abbr.* Confederation of British Industry.

||**C.C.** *abbr.* County Council(lor); Cricket Club.

**c.c.** *abbr.* cubic centimetre.

**C.D.** *abbr.* civil defence; *Corps Diplomatique*.

**cd** *abbr.* candela.

**Cdr.** *abbr.* Commander.

**Cdre.** *abbr.* Commodore.

**C.E.** *abbr.* Church of England; civil engineer; Common Era.

**cease. 1.** *v.i.* & *t.* (usu. literary). Desist *from*; stop doing, being, etc. (or *to do*, be, etc.); bring or come to an end; ~ **fire**, (Mil.) stop firing; ~**-fire** *n.*, (Mil.) signal to do this, time when hostilities are stopped. **2.** *n.* (literary): without ~, not ceasing; ~**lĕss** (-sl-) *a.*, never-ending. [F f. L *cesso*]

*****cē′cum.** See CAECUM.

**cē′dar** *n.* Evergreen coniferous tree with hard fragrant wood; its wood. [F f. L f. Gk]

**cēde** *v.t.* Surrender (territory etc. *to* person etc.). [F, or L *cedo cess-* yield]

**cēdĭ′lla** *n.* Mark written under *c* (ç) to show that it is sibilant; similar mark under *s* in Turkish etc. [Sp. dim. of *zeda* letter Z]

‖**ceilidh** (kā'lǐ) *n.* (Sc., Ir.) Informal gathering for music, story-telling, dancing, etc. [Gael.]

**cei'ling** (sē'-) *n.* Upper interior surface of room or other compartment; material forming this; maximum altitude a given aircraft can attain under specified conditions; upper limit of prices, wages, performance, etc. [orig. uncert.]

**cě'landine** *n.* One of two yellow-flowered plants. [F f. L f. Gk (*khelidōn* the swallow)]

**cě'lěbr|āte** *v.t.* & *i.* Perform (rite, ceremony, esp. Eucharist); (of priest) officiate at Eucharist; observe (festival) or honour (event) with rites, festive behaviour, etc.; make widely known, praise; (in *p.p.*) widely known; ∼**ant** *n.*, (esp.) priest celebrating Eucharist; ∼**ā'tion**, ∼**ātor**, *ns.*; ∼**ātory** *a.*; **cělě'brǐtý** *n.*, well-known person, fame. [L (*celeber* renowned)]

**cělě'rǐtý** *n.* (arch., literary). Swiftness. [F f. L (*celer* swift)]

**cě'lerý** *n.* (Blanched stems of) plant used as salad and vegetable. [F *céleri* f. It. f. L f. Gk *selinon* parsley]

**cělě'sta, cělě'ste,** *n.* Keyboard instrument with hammers striking metal bars. [F f. L (foll.)]

**cělě'stĭal** *a.* (∼ly). Of the sky or heavenly bodies (*celestial globe*); heavenly, divinely good, beautiful, etc. [F f. L (*caelum* sky)]

**cě'lĭb|acý** *n.* Unmarried state; ∼**ate** *a.* & *n.*, unmarried (person). [F or L (*caelebs* unmarried)]

**cěll** *n.* Small room usu. for one person, esp. in monastery or prison (**condemned** ∼, for person condemned to death); hermit's one-roomed dwelling; vessel containing electrodes for current-generation or electrolysis; cavity or interstice in natural structure; (Biol.) unit of structure of organic matter, portion of protoplasm usu. enclosed in membrane; (fig.) group as nucleus of political (esp. revolutionary or subversive) activity. [F, or L *cella*]

**cě'llar. 1.** *n.* Underground room, esp. for storing wine etc.; (person's) stock of wine. **2.** *v.t.* Store in cellar. **3.** ∼**er** *n.*, keeper of monastery's wine and food. [AF f. L *cellarium* (CELL)]

**cě'll|ō** (ch-) *n.* (*pl.* ∼**os**). Violon-

cello; its player (also ∼**ĭst** *n.*). [abbr.]

**cě'llophāne, C-,** *n.* Transparent wrapping material made from viscose. [P]

**cě'llūl|ar** *a.* Consisting of cells, of open texture, porous; ∼**ā'rǐtý** *n.*; ∼**e** *n.*, small cell or cavity; ∼**oid** *n.*, plastic made from camphor and cellulose nitrate [*P], (fig.) cinema films; ∼**ōse** (or -z) *n.*, main constituent of plant-cell walls and textile fibres, (pop.) paint or lacquer consisting of esp. cellulose acetate or nitrate in solution. [F or L (CELL)]

**Cě'lsĭus** *a.* Pertaining to ∼ scale of temperature, on which water freezes at 0° and boils at 100°. [person]

**Cělt**[1] (k-), **Kělt**[1], *n.* Member of a group of W. Eur. peoples (incl. ancient Gauls and Britons; modern Bretons, Cornish, Gaels, Irish, Manx, Welsh); ∼**ǐc** (or s-), (*a.*) of the Celts (∼**ǐc cross**, Latin cross with circle round centre; ∼**ǐc Sea**, S. of Ireland and W. of Cornwall), (*n.*) language of the Celts. [L f. Gk]

**cělt**[2] *n.* Chisel-edged prehistoric tool. [L]

**cěmě'nt. 1.** *n.* Substance made by calcining lime and clay, applied as paste and hardening to stony consistency, used as mortar or as material for floors, walls, etc., (∼-**mixer**, revolving drum in which cement or concrete is mixed); type of glue; substance for filling teeth. **2.** *v.t.* Unite (as) with cement; apply cement to; line or cover with cement; **cěměntā'tion** *n.* [F f. L (*caedo* cut)]

**cě'měterý** (-trǐ) *n.* Burial-ground other than churchyard. [L f. Gk, = dormitory]

‖**C. Eng.** *abbr.* chartered engineer.

\*cě'nobite. See COENOBITE.

**cě'notaph** (-ahf) *n.* Sepulchral monument to one whose body is elsewhere. [F f. L f. Gk (*kenos* empty, *taphos* tomb)]

\*Cěnozō'ǐc. See CAINOZOIC.

**cě'nser** *n.* Vessel in which incense is burnt; **cěnse** *v.t.*, worship or perfume with incense. [AF (INCENSE[2])]

**cě'nsor. 1.** *n.* Official with power to suppress whole or parts of books, plays, films, letters, news, etc., on grounds of obscenity, seditiousness, etc. **2.** *v.t.* Act as censor of; make deletions or changes in. **3. cěn-sŏr'ial** a. (-lly), of censor; **cěn-sŏr'ious** a., fault-finding, severely critical; ~**shĭp** n.; **cě'nsure** (-sher), (n.) expression of disapproval, reprimand, (v.t.) criticize harshly or unfavourably, reprove; **cě'nsus** n., official counting of population or of a class of things. [L (censeo assess)]

**cěnt** n. See PER CENT; (coin of value of) hundredth of U.S. etc. dollar; (colloq.) smallest amount (don't care a cent; never paid a cent). [F or It. or L (centum 100)]

**cent.** abbr. century.

**cě'ntaur** n. (Gk Myth.) Creature with head, arms, and trunk of man joined to body and legs of horse; ~**ў** n., plant formerly used in medicine. [L f. Gk]

**cěntěnār'ian** a. & n. (Person) a hundred or more years old; **cěn-tě'narў** (or sě'ntĭ-) a. & n., (festival) of hundredth anniversary. [L (centeni 100 each)]

**cěntě'nnial. 1.** a. Lasting, occurring every, hundred years. **2.** a. & n. Centenary. [L centum 100, BIENNIAL]

**\*cě'nter.** See CENTRE.

**cěntě'sĭmal** a. (~ly). Reckoning or reckoned by hundredths. [L (centum 100)]

**cě'ntĭ-** in comb. Hundred; one-hundredth (esp. of unit in METRIC system, as: centigram(me), centilitre); ~**grāde** a., having 100 degrees, esp. = CELSIUS, [L gradus step]; ~**mètre** (-ter), \*-ter, n., one-hundredth of a METRE, about 0·4 inch. [L centum 100]

**cě'ntĭpēde** n. Small many-legged wingless crawling animal. [F or L (prec., PEDAL)]

**cě'ntō** n. (pl. ~s). Work composed of quotations. [L, = patchwork garment]

**cě'ntral. 1.** a. (~ly). Of, in, at, or from the centre (~ **bank**, national, not commercial; ~ **heating**, method of warming a building by hot water or hot air or steam conveyed by pipes from central source, or by system of radiators etc.; ~ **nervous system**, brain and spinal cord); leading, principal, dominant, essential. **2.** n. \*Telephone exchange. **3.** ~**ism** n., centralizing system; ~**ĭst** n., advocate of this; **cěntrǎ'l-ĭtў** n.; ~**ĭze** v.t. & i., concentrate (administration etc.) at single centre, subject (State etc.) to this system; ~**ĭzā'tion** n. [F or L (foll.)]

**cě'ntre** (-ter), **\*cě'nter,** n., a., & v. **1.** n. Middle point or part, esp. of line, circle, or sphere; pivot or axis of revolution; point of concentration (likes to be the centre of attention) or dispersion, nucleus, source; place or group of buildings forming central point in district etc. or main area for an activity (city, DETENTION, SHOP-PING, centre); (Polit.) party holding moderate opinions; (Footb., Hockey) middle player in line, kick or hit from side to centre of pitch; ~**-bit,** kind of boring-tool; ~**-board** (for lowering through boat's keel to prevent leeway); ~**-forward, -half,** (Footb. etc.) middle player in forward, half-back, line; centre of GRAVITY, of MASS[2]; ~**-piece,** ornament for middle of table, principal item. **2.** a. At or of the centre. **3.** v.i. & t. Concentrate or be concentrated in, on, round, upon, etc.; place in centre. **4.** ~**mŏst** a., most central; **cě'ntrĭc(al)** adjs. (-ically), at or near the, from a, centre; **cěntrĭ'-fūgal** (or sě'-) a. (-lly), moving or tending to move from centre (esp. of force with which body revolving round centre seems to tend from it), (of machine etc.) in which rotation causes such motion [L fugio flee]; **cě'ntrĭfūge** n., centrifugal machine rotating at very high speed, for separating solids from liquids, or liquids from other liquids (e.g. cream from milk); **cěntrĭ'pětal** a. (-lly), moving or tending to move towards centre [L peto seek]; **cě'n-trĭsm, -ĭst,** ns., (holder of) moderate views. [F, or L centrum f. Gk kentron sharp point]

**cě'ntūrў** (or -cherĭ) n. (Period of) 100 years, esp. reckoned from birth of Christ (**twentieth** ~, the years 1901–2000 inclusive); 100 runs in one batsman's innings at cricket; company in ancient Roman army, orig. of 100 men; **cěntūr'ĭon** n., commander of century in ancient Roman army. [L centuria (CENT)]

**cěphǎ'lĭc** a. Of or in the head; **cě'phalopŏd** n., mollusc with distinct tentacled head, e.g. octopus [Gk pous pod- foot]. [F f. L f. Gk (kephalē head)]

**cěrǎ'mĭc. 1.** a. Of (the art of) pottery; of (substances produced by) process of strong heating of clay etc. minerals. **2.** n. Article made of pottery; ceramic substance. **3.** ~s, **ce′ramĭst,** ns. [Gk]

**cer′·eal. 1.** a. Of edible grain. **2.** n. (usu. in pl.) Kind(s) of edible grain; breakfast food made from a cereal. [L (*Ceres* goddess of agriculture)]

**ce′rĕbr|um** n. Principal part of brain; **cĕrĕbĕ′llum** n., smaller part of brain; **~al** a. (-lly), of the brain, intellectual, (**~al palsy,** spastic paralysis from brain damage before or at birth); **~ā′tion** n., working of the brain; **~ō-spī′nal** a., of brain and spine. [L]

**ce′rĕmŏny** n. Rite or observance; formalities, punctilious behaviour, (MASTER of Ceremonies; **stand on ~,** insist on observance of formalities; **without ~,** informally, casually); **cĕrĕmō′nial,** (a.; -lly) with or of ceremony, (n.) system of rites, ceremonies proper to an occasion; **cĕrĕmō′nious** a., addicted or showing addiction to ceremony. [F, or L *caerimonia* worship]

**ceri′se** (-ē′z, -ē′s) a. & n. Light clear red. [F (CHERRY)]

**cert.** abbr. certificate.

**cer′tain** (-tan) a. Settled, unfailing; unerring, reliable; that may be relied on to happen (**for ~,** as a certainty; **make ~,** ensure (*that*); **make ~ of,** verify, ensure that one will obtain); indisputable, convinced (*of, that*); destined, undoubtedly going, *to do*; that might but need not or should not be specified (*a certain person; lady of a certain age*); some though not much (*felt a certain reluctance*); existing but probably unknown to reader or hearer (*a certain John Smith*); ‖**cĕrt** n., (sl.) a certainty, esp. horse considered certain to win race; **~lў** adv., (also, in answers) I admit it, no doubt, yes; **~tў** n., undoubted fact (**for a ~ty,** undoubtedly), indubitable prospect, absolute conviction (*of, that*). [F f. L *certus*]

**certi′ficate. 1.** n. Document formally attesting a fact, esp. birth, marriage, death, health, abilities, etc.; **C~ of Secondary Education,** examination set for secondary-school pupils in England and Wales. **2.** (-āt) v.t. (esp. in p.p.) Provide with certificate. **3.** **cĕrtĭfĭcā′tion** n.; **cĕr′tĭfy** v.t., declare by certificate, make formal statement of, officially declare (person) insane; **certified**

**cheque** (with value guaranteed by bank). [F f. L (as prec.)]

**cer′tĭtūde** n. Feeling certain or convinced. [L (CERTAIN)]

**ceru′lean** (-ōō′-) a. Sky-blue. [L *caeruleus*]

**cer′vĭ|x** n. (pl. **~ces** pr. -sēz). (Anat.) Neck; necklike structure, esp. that of womb; **~cal** a. [L]

**cĕssā′tion** n. Ceasing. [L (CEASE)]

**ce′ssion** (-shŏn) n. Ceding. [F or L (CEDE)]

**ce′sspool** n. Underground chamber for temporary storage of liquid waste or sewage; **ce′sspĭt** n., pit for sewage or refuse. [orig. uncert.]

**cētā′cean** (-shn) a. & n. (One) of the Cetacea or marine mammals (whales etc.); **cētā′ceous** (-shŭs) a. [L f. Gk *kētos* whale]

*ceteris paribus* (kāterēs pā′rĭbŭs; *or* sĕt-) adv. Other things being equal or unchanged. [L]

**cf.** abbr. compare. [L *confer*]

**c.f.** abbr. carried forward.

**C.G.S.** abbr. Chief of General Staff.

‖**C.H.** abbr. Companion of Honour.

**ch.** abbr. chapter; church.

**Chă′blis** (shä′blē) n. A white burgundy wine. [place]

**chaco′nne** (sh-) n. (Dance to) music on ground bass. [F f. Sp.]

**chāfe. 1.** v.t. & i. Rub (skin etc.) to restore warmth or sensation; make or become sore or damaged by rubbing; irritate; become annoyed, fret; **cha′fing-dish,** vessel in which food is cooked or kept warm at table. **2.** n. (Sore made by) chafing; state of annoyance. [F f. L *calefacio* make warm]

**chā′fer** n. Large slow-moving beetle, esp. COCK[1]*chafer*. [E]

**chaff** (-ahf). **1.** n. Separated husks of corn etc. (**separate wheat from ~,** fig., distinguish good from bad); chopped hay or straw; worthless stuff; banter. **2.** v.t. & i. Banter, tease. [E]

**chă′ffer. 1.** v.i. Bargain, haggle. **2.** n. Chaffering. [E]

‖**chă′ffĭnch** n. Common European finch. [E (CHAFF, FINCH)]

**chagrin** (shă′grĭn, shagrē′n) n., & v.t. (Affect with) acute vexation or mortification. [F]

**chain. 1.** n. Connected flexible series of links or rings usu. of metal; length or loop of this for specific purpose (as badge of office; for transmitting power from bicycle pedals to wheel); (in *pl.*) fetters, confinement, restraining force; sequence, series, or set of mountains, posts, facts, events, etc.; line of people; group of associated shops, hotels, newspapers, etc.; measuring-line of linked metal rods, its length (66 ft.); ~-**armour** (of interlaced rings); ~-**gang** (of convicts, chained together, or forced to work in chains); ~-**letter**, letter of which recipient is asked to make copies to be sent to a (named) number of others (these being asked to do the like); ~-**link**, of wire mesh; ~-**mail**, = *chain--armour*; ~ **reaction**, (Chem.) reaction forming intermediate products which react with the original substance and are repeatedly renewed, (Phys.) series of fission reactions each initiated by neutrons from previous one, (fig.) series of events each due to previous one; ~-**smoker**, one who lights another cigarette etc. from the end of that last smoked; ~ **store**, one of series of shops owned by one firm and selling same class of goods. **2.** *v.t.* ~ (**up**), secure with chain. [F f. L *catena*]

**chair. 1.** *n.* Separate usu. movable seat for one (**take a** ~, sit down); seat of authority; professorship; seat, office, or authority of chairman (**be in, take, the** ~, be chairman); chairman (*address, appeal to, the chair*); (Hist.) sedan; *\* =*ELECTRIC *chair*; ~-**borne**, (colloq.) administrative, not active; ~-**lift**, series of chairs on endless cable for carrying passengers up mountain etc.; ~′**man**, ~′**person**, ~′**woman**, person who presides over meeting, permanent president of committee, board of directors, country, etc., master of ceremonies at entertainment. **2.** *v.t.* Install in chair of authority; ‖carry (winner of contest etc.) aloft; conduct (meeting) as chairman. **3. chaise** (shāz) *n.*, (esp. Hist.) pleasure or travelling carriage, esp. light open carriage for one or two persons; *chaise longue* (-lŏng) [F, = long chair] low chair long enough to support user's legs. [F f. L (CATHEDRAL)]

**chălcě′dǒnў** (k-) *n.* Precious or semi-precious stone, a variety of quartz, e.g. agate, onyx, cornelian. [L f. Gk]

**Chăldě′an, Chăldee′,** (k-) *a. & n.* (Native, language) of Chaldea or Babylonia. [L f. Gk f. Assyr.]

**chă′let** (shă′lā) *n.* Swiss hut or cottage; small villa; small house in holiday camp etc. [Swiss F]

**chă′lice** *n.* Goblet; Eucharist-cup. [F f. L CALIX]

**chalk** (-awk). **1.** *n.* White soft limestone used esp. for burning to make lime and for writing and drawing (**as different as** ~ **and,** or **from, cheese,** unlike in essentials; **by a long** ~, by far); (piece of) coloured substance of like texture used for crayons; FRENCH *chalk*; ~-**stone,** chalklike concretion in hands, feet, etc.; ~-**stripe(d),** (having) pattern of thin white stripes on dark background; ~-ў *a.* (-iness). **2.** *v.t.* Mark, draw, write, rub, with chalk; ~ **out,** mark out (as) with chalk; ~ **up,** register or gain (success etc.). [E f. L CALX]

**chă′llěnge** (-nj). **1.** *n.* Calling to respond, esp. sentry's call for password etc.; summons to take part in duel or other contest; demanding or difficult task. **2.** *v.t.* (Of sentry etc.) call to respond; take exception to (juryman, evidence, etc.); dispute, deny, (statement etc.); summon to contest etc.; (in *part.*) interestingly difficult. [F f. L (CALUMNY)]

**chalў′beate** (ka-) *a.* (Of water etc.) impregnated with iron salts. [L (*chalybs* steel f. Gk)]

**chă′mber** *n.* Room, esp. bedroom; (arch.); (in *pl.*) set of rooms let separately from rest of building (esp. in Inns of Court), judge's room for hearing cases not needing to be taken in court; (hall used by) deliberative or judicial body; one of the houses (*upper, lower, chamber*) of a parliament; cavity or compartment in body, machinery, etc., esp. part of gun-bore that contains charge; = *chamber-pot*; **C~ of Commerce,** association to promote local commercial interests; ~**maid,** housemaid at hotel etc., \*housemaid; ~ **music** (for small group of instruments); ~-**pot,** receptacle for urine etc., used in bedroom; ~**lain** (-lĭn) *n.*, officer managing royal or noble household (LORD *Chamberlain*), treasurer of corporation etc. [F f. L *camera* f. Gk *kamara* vault]

**chamē′lě|on** (k-) *n.* Small lizard with power of changing colour; variable or inconstant person; ~ŏ′nic *a.* [L f. Gk, = ground-lion]

**chă′mfer. 1.** *v.t.* Bevel symmetric-

ally (right-angled edge or corner).
**2.** *n.* Surface so made. [F (CANT¹, *fraint* broken)]

**chă′mois** (shă′mwah) *n.* (*pl.* same *pr.* -z). Small European and Asian mountain antelope; (*or* shă′mǐ) **~(-leather)**, (piece of) soft leather from sheep, goats, deer, etc. [F]

**chamomile.** See CAMOMILE.

**chămp¹. 1.** *v.t.* & *i.* (Of horse etc.) munch or bite noisily or vigorously; **~ (at the bit)**, (fig.) show impatience. **2.** *n.* Sound of champing. [imit.]

**chămp²** *n.* (sl.) Champion. [abbr.]

**chămpā′gne** (shămpā′n) *n.* White (esp. sparkling) wine from *Champagne* in France, or elsewhere; pale straw colour; **chă′mpaign** (-ān) *n.*, (expanse of) open country; ||**chă′mpers** (sh-; -z) *n.*, (sl.) champagne. [F f. L *campania* (CAMP¹)]

**chă′mpion** *n.*, *a.*, *adv.*, & *v.* **1.** *n.* Person who fights, argues, etc. for another or for a cause; athlete, boxer, etc., animal, plant, etc., that has defeated all competitors (often attrib.: *champion boxer, horse*). **2.** *a.* & *adv.* (colloq. or dial.) First-class, splendid(ly). **3.** *v.t.* Support the cause of, defend. **4. ~ship** *n.*, (esp.) position of having defeated all rivals in a sport, contest to decide this. [F f. L *campio* (CAMP¹)]

**chance** (-ah-) *n.*, *a.*, & *v.* **1.** *n.* Way things happen, fortune, absence of design or discoverable cause, course of events regarded as a power, fate, (**by ~**, as it happens or happened, without design; **game of ~**, decided by luck not skill; **take one′s ~**, consent to take what comes); undesigned occurrence, opportunity, e.g. of success, or of dismissing batsman at cricket, possibility, probability, prospect, (MAIN¹, OFF, *chance*); **stand a ~**, have a prospect of success; **take a ~, take ~s**, behave riskily). **2.** *a.* Fortuitous, accidental, (*a chance meeting, occurrence*). **3.** *v.i.* & *t.* Happen (*it chanced that; I chanced to see*); (colloq.) risk, take no thought for; **~ one′s arm, ~ it**, (colloq.) take one′s chance (possibly slight) of achieving something; **~ (up)on**, happen to find, meet, etc. [F f. L *cado* fall]

**chă′ncel** (-ah′-) *n.* (Enclosed) part of church near altar. [F f. L *cancelli* grating]

**chă′ncellor** (-ah′-) *n.* State or law official; ||C**~** (**of the Exchequer**),

U.K. finance minister; ||**Lord (High) C~** (presiding in House of Lords, Chancery Division, and Court of Appeal); non-resident head of university; (Germany etc.) chief minister of State; **cha′ncellery** (-ah′-) *n.*, chancellor′s department, staff, or residence, office attached to embassy; **cha′ncery** (-ah′-) *n.*, records office, chancellry, \*court of equity, ||(C**~**) Lord Chancellor′s division of High Court of Justice (**in chancery**, of boxer with head held under opponent′s arm to be pummelled). [AF f. L *cancellarius* porter (prec.)]

**cha′nc|y** (-ah′-) *a.* (**~ily, ~iness**). Risky, uncertain. [CHANCE]

**chăndelier′** (sh-) *n.* Branched hanging support for lights. [F (CANDLE)]

**cha′ndler** (-ah′-) *n.* Dealer in candles, oil, soap, groceries, corn, etc. (arch.); **ship′s ~**, dealer in ropes, canvas, etc.; **~y** *n.*

**chānge** (-nj). **1.** *n.* Making or becoming different, difference from previous state, substitution of one for another, (**~ of air**, different climate; **~ (of clothes)**, second outfit in reserve; **~ (of life)**, menopause); variety, variation, (*for a change*); money exchanged for coins of larger value or for different currency, money returned as balance of that tendered in payment, (**get no ~ out of**, sl., get no satisfaction, help, etc., from; **give, \*make, ~**, give money to customer as change); = SMALL *change*; one of different orders in which peal of bells can be rung (**ring the ~s**, fig., vary ways of doing thing). **2.** *v.i.* & *t.* Undergo, show, or subject to change; make or become different (*from* previous, (*in*)*to* or *for* new, state); take or use another instead of (*change* one′s *coat, bank*); put fresh clothes, coverings, etc., on (child, bed, etc.); put on other clothes; go from one to another of (houses, sides, trains, etc.); (of moon) arrive at fresh phase; change trains etc.; interchange, exchange, (places, seats, often *with* person); get or give money change for (*must change, if you can change, a £5 note*); **~ colour**, alter in colour, turn pale, blush; **~ down**, engage lower gear in vehicle; **~ gear**, engage different gear in vehicle; *change* HAND¹*s*; *change* one′s MIND; **~ over** *v.t.* & *i.*, **~-over** *n.*, change from one system or situation to another; *change* one's TUNE; ~ **up**, engage higher gear in vehicle. **3.** ~**able** (-nja-) *a.* (-bly), (esp.) inconstant, liable to change; ~**ful** (-jf-; -lly), ~**'less** (-jl-), *adjs.*; ~**'ling** (-jl-) *n.*, (elf-)child believed to have been substituted for another child. [F f. L *cambio* barter]

**chă'nnel. 1.** *n.* Bed in which water runs; navigable part of waterway; piece of water (wider than strait) connecting two seas (||the C~, English Channel); passage for liquid; groove; course or line of motion; medium of communication, agency, (*through the usual channels*); (Broadcasting) narrow band of frequencies used for transmission, esp. of a particular programme. **2.** *v.t.* (||-ll-). Form channel(s) in, groove; (fig.) guide, direct. [F f. L (CANAL)]

**chant** (-ah-). **1.** *n.* Song; short melody with long reciting-note(s) for psalms etc. **2.** *v.i.* & *t.* Sing; intone, sing to a chant. **3.** ~**'er** *n.*, (esp.) melody-pipe of bagpipe; ~**'icleer** *n.*, (personal name for) domestic cock [CLEAR]; ~**'rỹ** *n.*, endowment for singing of masses, chapel or priests so endowed; ~**'ỹ** *n.*, = SHANTY[2]. [F f. L *canto* (*cano* sing)]

**chă'ŏs** (k-) *n.* Formless primordial matter; utter confusion; **chaŏ'tic** (k-) *a.* (-ically), utterly without order or arrangement. [F or L f. Gk]

**chăp**[1] *n.* (colloq.) Man, boy, fellow. [abbr. of CHAPMAN]

**chăp**[2]. **1.** *v.i.* & *t.* (-pp-). (Of skin, hands, etc.) develop cracks or soreness; (of wind, cold, etc.) cause to chap. **2.** *n.* (usu. in *pl.*) Crack in skin etc. **3.** ~**'pỹ** *a.*, chapped. [orig. uncert.]

**chăp**[3] *n.* Lower jaw or half of cheek, esp. of pig as food; ~**fallen**, with jaw hanging down, dejected; see also CHOP[2]. [var. of CHOP[2]]

**chap.** *abbr.* chapter.

**\*chăparrā'l** (*or* sh-) *n.* Dense tangled brushwood. [Sp.]

**chapat(t)i.** See CHUPATTY.

**chă'pel** *n.* Place of Christian worship other than cathedral or parish church, esp. attached to or part of institution or private house (~ **of ease**, for parishioners living far from their parish church); separate part of cathedral or church, with its own altar (LADY *chapel*); ||place of worship of Nonconformist bodies; service in, attendance at, chapel;

association or meeting of workers in printing-office (**father of the** ~, its president). [F f. L (*cappa* cloak; St. Martin's cloak was kept by *cappellani* or chaplains in a sanctuary)]

**chă'perŏn** (sh-). **1.** *n.* Married or elderly woman accompanying young unmarried woman for sake of propriety on social occasions; ~**age** *n.*, chaperon's care. **2.** *v.t.* Act as chaperon to. [F (*chape* cope, as CAPE[1])]

**chă'plain** (-lĭn) *n.* Clergyman of institution, private chapel, ship, regiment, etc.; ~**cỹ** *n.* [F f. L (CHAPEL)]

**chă'plĕt** *n.* Wreath or circlet for head; string of beads, minor rosary. [F f. L (CAP)]

||**chă'pman** *n.* (*pl.* -men). (Hist.) Pedlar. [E (CHEAP, MAN)]

**chă'ppïe** *n.* (colloq.) = CHAP[1]. [-IE]

**chă'pter** *n.* Main division of book (~ **and verse**, exact reference or authority); (fig.) period, epoch, (~ **of accidents**, series of misfortunes); (meeting of) canons of cathedral or collegiate church or members of monastic or knightly order (~ **house**, building used for such meetings); \*local branch of a society. [F f. L (CAPITAL)]

**chār**[1]. **1.** *n.* ||(colloq.) = *charwoman*; ||~**lady**, ~**'woman**, woman employed to clean rooms in ||houses or offices. **2.** *v.i.* (-rr-). Work as charwoman. [orig. = CHORE; E, = turn]

**chār**[2] *n.* (*pl.* same). Small trout. [orig. unkn.]

**chār**[3] *v.t.* & *i.* (-rr-). Burn to charcoal; scorch, blacken with fire. [CHARCOAL]

||**chār**[4] *n.* (sl.) Tea. [Chin. *ch'a*]

**chă'rabănc** (sh-; -ăng) *n.* (arch.) Motor coach. [F *char à bancs* carriage with seats]

**chă'racter** (kă'rĭk-) *n.* Distinctive mark; (in *pl.*) inscribed letters etc.; graphic symbol; characteristic (esp. Biol., of species etc.); collective peculiarities, sort, style; idiosyncrasy, individuality, mental or moral qualities; moral strength; reputation, good reputation, (~ **assassination**, deliberate destruction of person's reputation); written description of person's qualities, testimonial; personage, personality; person in novel, play, etc.; part played by actor; person's role or ways (**in, out of**, ~, consistent, inconsistent, with these); eccentric or noticeable person

(~ **actor,** who plays such parts); **~ĭ′stĭc** *a.* (-ically) & *n.*, typical or distinctive (trait, mark, or quality); **~ize** *v.t.*, describe character of, describe *as*, give character to, be characteristic of; **~izā′tion** *n.* [F f. L f. Gk]

**chara′de** (sharahd′) *n.* Game of guessing a word from written or acted clue given for each syllable and for the whole; (fig.) absurd pretence. [F f. Prov. (*charra* chatter)]

**char′coal** *n.* Black porous residue of burnt wood etc., a form of carbon; ~ (grey), dark grey. [orig. unkn.]

**charge. 1.** *n.* Appropriate quantity of material to put into receptacle, mechanism, etc., at one time, esp. of explosive for gun; quantity of electricity carried by a body; energy stored chemically for conversion into electricity; (Her.) device, bearing; expense or cause of expenditure, price demanded; task, duty, commission; directions, exhortation; care, custody, responsible possession, (*I am in charge of him*; *he is in my charge*; ||give person **in** ~, hand him over to police; **take** ~, assume control *of*); thing or person entrusted; accusation or discredit (**lay to** person's ~, accuse him of); impetuous attack or rush esp. in battle, signal for this, (**return to the** ~, renew argument etc.); *\** ~ **account,** credit account at shop etc.; ||~-**hand,** workman in charge of a job; ||~- **-nurse,** nurse in charge of a ward etc.; ~-**sheet,** record of cases at police station. **2.** *v.t.* & *i.* Load or fill with charge of explosive etc.; fill *with*; saturate with liquid, vapour, or chemical; give electric charge to; store energy in (battery etc.); entrust *with* task; command, instruct, or urge (*to* do); ask (price) *for*, demand (price) from (person); debit cost of (*up*) *to* person or account; attack or rush impetuously; throw oneself (against); make accusation *that*; ~ **with,** accuse (person) of (crime etc.). **3.** ~′**able** (-ja-) *a.*, (esp.) capable of being charged *to* a particular account; **chargé d′affaires** (shārzhādáfār′) *n.* (*pl.* **-gés** *pr.* same), ambassador's deputy, ambassador to minor government; **char′ger** *n.*, (Mil.) cavalry horse, (arch.) large flat dish. [F f. L (*carrus* car)]

**chă′riot** *n.* (Hist.) two-wheeled vehicle used in ancient fighting and racing; (poet.) stately or triumphal vehicle; ~**eer** *n.*, chariot-driver.

**chari′sma** (k-; -z-) *n.* (*pl.* ~**ta**). Divinely conferred power or talent; capacity to inspire followers with devotion and enthusiasm; **chărĭs-mă′tĭc** (k-; -z-) *a.* (-ically). [L f. Gk (*kharis* grace)]

**chă′rĭty** *n.* Love of fellow men; kindness; leniency in judging others; liberality to those in need or distress, alms-giving, alms; institution or organization for helping those in need, help so given, (~ **begins at home,** charity is due first to one's own family etc.); **chă′rĭtable** *a.* (-bly), having or marked by charity, connected with charities or a charity. [F f. L *caritas* (*carus* dear)]

**chăr′latan** (sh-) *n.* False pretender to knowledge or skill, esp. in medicine; ~**ĭsm,** ~**rў,** *ns.* [F f. It., = babbler]

**chăr′lock** *n.* Wild mustard, a yellow-flowered weed. [E]

**chăr′lotte** (sh-) *n.* Pudding of stewed fruit, esp. apples, with covering or casing of bread-crumbs etc.; ~ **russe** (-rōō′), cream, custard, etc., enclosed in sponge-cake or sponge-biscuits. [F]

**chărm. 1.** *n.* Word(s), act(s), or object supposedly having occult or magic power (*work like a* ~, perfectly); trinket on bracelet etc.; fascination, attractiveness, power of giving delight; (usu. in *pl.*) quality or feature that arouses love or admiration. **2.** *v.t.* Bewitch; influence or bring (as) by magic; protect by magic; endow with seemingly magic power, (*he bears a charmed life*); captivate, delight; ~′**er** *n.*, (esp.) delightful person; ~′**ing** *a.*, (esp.) delightful. [F f. L *carmen* song]

**chăr′nel-house** *n.* Repository of corpses or bones. [F f. L (CARNAGE)]

**chărt. 1.** *n.* Navigator's sea map showing rocks, depths, etc.; sheet of tabulated or diagrammatic information, esp. (in *sing.* or *pl.*) listing gramophone records that are currently most popular. **2.** *v.t.* Make chart of, map. [F f. L *charta* (CARD²)]

**chăr′ter. 1.** *n.* Written grant of rights, esp. by sovereign or legislature; privilege, admitted right(s); ~(-**party**), agreement between ship-owner and merchant for hire of ship [F *partie* divided]; ~ **flight** (by chartered aircraft). **2.** *v.t.* Grant charter to; hire (aircraft, vehicle, etc.); ‖~ed **accountant, engineer, librarian,** etc., member of professional body that has royal charter. [F f. L *chartula* dim. (prec.)]

**Chăr′t|ĭsm** *n.* (Hist.) Principles of U.K. democratic reform movement *c.* 1840; ~**ĭst** *n.* [prec.; name taken from 'People's Charter']

**chártreu′se** (shärtrē′z) *n.* Green or yellow liqueur. [place]

**chăr′|ў** *a.* (~ily, ~iness). Shy *of* or sparing *in doing*; sparing *of* praise etc.; wary (*of*). [E (CARE)]

**Chary′bdĭs** (k-) *n.* See SCYLLA.

**chāse¹. 1.** *v.t.* Pursue; drive *from, out of, to,* etc.; hurry (*after* etc.); (colloq.) try to attain; ~ **up,** (colloq.) pursue with specific purpose. **2.** *n.* Pursuit (**give** ~, **go in pursuit**; **the** ~, hunting, esp. as sport); unenclosed hunting-land. **3. chā′ser** *n.,* (esp.) horse for steeplechasing, (colloq.) drink taken after another of different kind. [F f. L *capto* (CATCH)]

**chāse²** *v.t.* Emboss or engrave (metal). [F (CASE²)]

**chāse³** *n.* (Print.) Metal frame holding composed type. [F f. L *capsa* CASE²]

**chă′sm** (kă′zem) *n.* Deep fissure or opening in earth, rock, etc.; (fig.) wide difference of feeling, interests, etc. [L f. Gk]

**chă′ssis** (shă′sĭ, -sē) *n.* (*pl.* same *pr.* -z). Base-frame of motor vehicle, carriage, etc.; frame to carry radio etc. equipment. [F f. L (CASE²)]

**chāste** *a.* Abstaining from unlawful or immoral, or from all, sexual intercourse; pure, virtuous, virgin; pure in taste or style, unadorned, simple; **chă′sten** (-sen) *v.t.,* punish, discipline by inflicting suffering, restrain, moderate; **chăstı̆′se** (-z) *v.t.,* punish, thrash; **chăstı̆′sement** (-zm-) *n.*; **chă′stı̆tў** *n.,* chasteness (**chastity belt,** garment designed to prevent woman from having sexual intercourse). [F f. L *castus*]

**chă′sŭble** (-z-) *n.* Sleeveless mantle worn by celebrant of Mass or Eucharist. [F f. L *casubla*]

**chăt. 1.** *v.i.* & *t.* (-tt-). Talk in light and familiar manner; ~ (**up**), (sl.) chat to, esp. flirtatiously or with ulterior motive. **2.** *n.* Such talk; song-bird, esp. STONE*chat,* WHIN*chat.* [CHATTER]

**château** (shă′tō) *n.* (*pl.* -x *pr.* -z).

Large French country-house; **chă′te-laine** (sh-) *n.,* mistress of large house, (Hist.) appendage to woman's belt for carrying keys etc. [F (CASTLE)]

**chă′ttel** *n.* (usu. in *pl.*) Movable possession. [F (CATTLE)]

**chă′tter. 1.** *v.i.* Talk quickly, incessantly, trivially, or indiscreetly; (of bird) emit short quick notes; (of teeth etc.) rattle together. **2.** *n.* Chattering; ~**box,** talkative person. **3. chă′ttў** *a.* (-ily, -iness), fond of or resembling chat. [imit.]

**chauffeu|r** (shō′fer, shōfer′). **1.** *n.* (*fem.* ~**se** *pr.* -ẽrz). Person employed to drive a private or hired motor car. **2.** *v.t.* Drive (car) as chauffeur; convey (person) by car. [F, = stoker]

**chau′vĭn|ĭsm** (shō′-) *n.* Bellicose patriotism; fervent support for a cause; excessive pride in or loyalty to something (**male** ~**ism,** men's excessive loyalty to other men and prejudice against women); ~**ĭst** *n.*; ~**ĭ′stĭc** *a.* (-ically). [*Chauvin,* character in F play]

**cheap. 1.** *a.* Low in price, value, or charge made (~ **and nasty,** of low cost and bad quality; ~**jack** *a.,* inferior, shoddy; *cheap* SKATE³; **on the** ~, cheaply); worth more than its cost; easily got or made; worthless, of little account, (**feel** ~, sl., feel ashamed; **hold** ~, despise). **2.** *adv.* Cheaply (*going cheap; got it cheap*). **3.** ~**′en** *v.t.* & *i.,* make or become cheap, depreciate, degrade. [E, = price, bargain]

**cheat. 1.** *v.t.* & *i.* Trick, deceive, (person *into, out of,* thing); deprive *of* by deceit; act fraudulently. **2.** *n.* Deception, trick; swindler, impostor, unfair player. [ESCHEAT]

**chĕck. 1.** *n.* (Announcement of) exposure of chess king to attack (also as *int.*); sudden stopping or slowing of motion; pause; rebuff; (Hunting) loss of the scent; restraint (**keep in** ~, control); person or thing that restrains; means or act of testing or ensuring accuracy; token of identification; \*bill in restaurant; \* = CHEQUE; \*counter used in games (**hand in, pass in,** one's ~**s,** colloq., die); cross-lined pattern of small squares, fabric so patterned; ~**-list,** (complete) list for reference and verification; ~**-point** (where vehicles, documents, etc., are checked or inspected). **2.** *v.t.* & *i.* Threaten (opponent's king) at chess; stop or slow the motion (of); restrain; (of hounds) stop on losing scent; test, examine, verify; *agree on comparison, mark with tick etc., deposit (luggage etc.); ~ **in**, arrive or register at hotel, airport, factory, etc., record arrival of (so ~ **out**); ~ **off**, mark on list etc. as having been found correct; ~ **on**, *out, test, verify, investigate; ~-**out**, act of checking out, pay-desk in supermarket etc.; ~ **up (on)**, = check on; ~-**up**, careful (esp. medical) examination. **3.** ~ed (-kt) a., (esp.) of check pattern; ~'**er**¹ n., one who checks; ~'**mäte**, (n.) inextricable check at chess (also as int.), final defeat or deadlock, (v.t.) put into checkmate, frustrate. [F f. L f. Arab. f. Pers., = king (mät is dead)]

**chĕ'cker**¹,². See prec., CHEQUER.

**Chĕ'ddar** n. Kind of cheese. [place]

**cheek. 1.** n. Side-wall of mouth, side of face below eye, (~ **by jowl**, close together, intimate; **turn the other** ~, accept attack etc. meekly, refuse to retaliate); impertinent speech; cool confidence, effrontery, (have the cheek to); (in pl.) jaws of vice, twin side-pieces in machine; ~-**bone** (below eye); ~'**ў** a. (~**ily**, ~**iness**), insolent, impudent. **2.** v.t. Address saucily. [E]

**cheep** v.i., & n. (Utter) shrill feeble note (as) of young bird; **not a** ~, (colloq.) no sound at all. [imit.]

**cheer. 1.** n. Shout of encouragement or applause (**three** ~**s**, three successive united hurrahs, often for person or thing honoured); disposition, mood, (**of good** ~, in good spirits; **what** ~?, how do you feel?); food, fare; ~-**leader**, one who leads applause etc. **2.** v.t. & i. Comfort, gladden; urge on, esp. by shouts; applaud; shout with joy; ~ **up**, make or become happier. **3.** ~'**ful** a. (-**lly**), contented, in good spirits, bright, pleasant, not reluctant; ||~**iŏ'** int., (colloq.) expr. good wishes on parting or before drinking, goodbye; ~'**lĕss** a., gloomy, dreary; ~'**ў** a. (~**ily**, ~**iness**), lively, genial. [F f. L cara face f. Gk]

**cheese**¹ (-z) n. Food made of pressed curds (**hard** ~, sl., bad luck); cake etc. of this within rind; round flat object; ~-**board** (from which cheese is served); ~'**burger**,

hamburger with cheese in or on it; ~'**cake**, tart(let) filled with sweetened curds, (colloq.) display of shapely female body in advertisement etc.; ~'**cloth**, BUTTER muslin; ~-**fly** (breeding in cheese); ~-**paring**, stingy, stinginess; ~ **straw**, thin cheese-flavoured pastry strip; **chee'sў** (-z-) a. [E f. L caseus]

**cheese**² (-z) v.t. (sl., esp. in imper.) Stop it, leave off; ||~**d (off)**, bored, exasperated. [orig. unkn.]

**chee'tah** (-a) n. Swift-running spotted feline like leopard. [Hindi]

**chĕf** (sh-) n. Man who is (usu. chief) cook in hotel etc. [F]

**Chĕ'lsea** (-ĭ) n. ~ **bun**, kind of rolled currant-bun; ~ **pensioner**, inmate of Chelsea Royal Hospital for old or disabled soldiers. [place]

**chĕ'mical** (k-). **1.** a. (~**ly**). Of, made by, or employing chemistry; (of lavatory) decomposing waste by chemical process; (of warfare) using poison gas or other chemicals; ~ **engineering**, industrial applications of chemistry. **2.** n. Substance obtained by or used in chemistry. [F or L (ALCHEMY)]

**chemi'se** (shĕmē'z) n. Woman's loose-fitting undergarment or dress. [F f. L camisia shirt]

**chĕ'mistrў** (k-) n. Science of the elements and compounds and their laws of combination and change under various conditions; (fig.) mysterious change or process; **chĕ'mist** (k-) n., expert in chemistry, ||dealer in medicinal drugs etc. [F f. L (ALCHEMY)]

**chenille** (shĕnē'l) n. (Fabric made of) tufted velvety cord or yarn. [F, = hairy caterpillar f. L (CANINE)]

||**chĕque** (-k), *check, n. Written order to bank(er) to pay sum from drawer's account; form on which such order is to be written; ~-**book** (of forms for writing cheques); ~ **card** (issued by bank to guarantee honouring of cheques up to stated value); **chĕ'quer** (-kĕr), **chĕ'cker**², (n., often in pl.) pattern of squares often alternately coloured, *(in pl.) game of draughts, (v.t.) mark with chequers, variegate, break uniformity of, (in p.p.) with varied fortunes (chequered career). [CHECK]

**chĕ'rish** v.t. Protect or tend (child, plant, etc.) lovingly; hold dear or cling to (hopes, feelings, etc.). [F (cher dear f. L carus)]

**cheroo't** (sh-) *n.* Cigar with both ends open. [F f. Tamil]

**che'rry. 1.** *n.* Small stone-fruit (**two bites at a ~**, unenterprising or hesitant action, a second chance); tree bearing this fruit or grown for its ornamental flowers, its wood; ~ **brandy**, liqueur of brandy and cherries. **2.** *a.* Red, esp. of colour of ripe cherries. [F f. L f. Gk *kerasos*]

**che'rub** *n.* (*pl.* ~**s**, ~**im**). Angelic being; one of the second order (cf. SERAPH) of the celestial hierarchy; (Art) winged (head of) child; beautiful or innocent child; **cheru'bic** (-ōō'-) *a.* [E & Heb.]

**cher'vil** *n.* Salad herb. [E f. L f. Gk]

**Ches.** *abbr.* Cheshire.

**Che'shire** (-er, -ĕr) *n.* ~ (**cheese**), cheese resembling Cheddar; **grin like a ~ cat** (broadly and fixedly). [place]

**chess** *n.* Game for two players with 32 ~**men** on chequered ~**board** of 64 squares. [F = CHECK]

**chest** *n.* Large box, esp. for storage or transport; coffer or treasury; part of body enclosed by ribs, front surface of body from neck to waist (**get thing off** one's ~, colloq., relieve one's anxiety by disclosing something); ~ **of drawers**, piece of furniture with set of drawers in frame; ~'**ў** *a.*, (colloq.; ~**ily**, ~**iness**) inclined to or symptomatic of chest disease. [E f. L *cista* f. Gk]

**che'sterfield** *n.* Sofa with padded seat, back, and ends. [person]

**che'stnut** (-sn-). **1.** *n.* (Tree with) glossy hard brown edible fruit (also **Spanish, sweet,** ~); = HORSE-*chestnut*; stale joke or anecdote; (horse of) reddish-brown colour. **2.** *a.* Reddish-brown. [F f. L f. Gk *kastanea*, NUT]

**cheva'lier'** (sh-) *n.* Member of certain orders of knighthood, or of French Legion of Honour etc.; **cheva'l-glass** (sh-; -ahs) *n.*, tall mirror on upright frame. [F f. L *caballarius* horseman (*caballus* horse)]

**che'viot** *n.* (Animal of) breed of sheep from Cheviot Hills; wool or cloth from such sheep. [place]

**che'vron** (sh-) *n.* (Her. & Archit.) bent bar of inverted V shape; badge in V shape (inverted or not) on sleeve of uniform indicating rank or length of service. [F f. L *caper* goat]

**chew** (-ōō). **1.** *v.t.* & *i.* Work (food etc.) between the teeth, crush or

indent thus, (**chew the CUD**; ~ **the fat, the rag**, sl., discuss or grumble about something); meditate *on*, *over*; discuss, talk *over*; ~'**ing-gum**, flavoured gum used for prolonged chewing. **2.** *n.* Act of chewing; sweetmeat or piece of tobacco for chewing. **3.** ~'**ў** *a.* (-**iness**), suitable for or requiring chewing. [E]

**chez** (shā) *prep.* At the house or home of. [F f. L *casa* cottage]

**chi** (kī) *n.* Twenty-second Gk letter (X, χ) = kh, ch. [Gk]

**Chiă'nti** (k-) *n.* Dry, usu. red, Italian wine. [place]

**chiăroscur'o** (kyărŏskoor'ō, -ūr'ō) *n.* (*pl.* ~**s**). Treatment of light and shade in painting; contrast in literature etc. [It. (CLEAR, OBSCURE)]

**chic** (shēk). **1.** *n.* Stylishness, elegance in dress. **2.** *a.* (~-**er**, ~-**est**). Stylish, elegant. [F]

**chica'ne** (sh-). **1.** *n.* Chicanery; artificial barrier or obstacle on motor-racing course. **2.** *v.i.* & *t.* Use chicanery; cheat (person *into* etc.). **3.** ~**rў** (sh-) *n.*, trickery or sophistry, esp. in legal argument. [F]

**chi'chi** (shē'shē) *a.* & *n.* Showy, pretentious, (thing); fussy or affected (person, behaviour). [F]

**chick** *n.* Young bird; (sl.) young woman; ~'**weed**, a small weed. [CHICKEN]

*****chi'ckadee** *n.* Amer. titmouse with dark-crowned head. [imit.]

**chi'cken** *n.*, *a.*, & *v.* **1.** *n.* (*pl.* ~**s**, ~). Young domestic fowl (**count** one's ~**s before they are hatched**, be over-optimistic or precipitate); (flesh of) domestic fowl as food; youthful person (esp. *is no chicken*); (sl.) a game testing courage; ~**feed**, food for poultry, (colloq.) unimportant amount of money etc.; ~**hearted**, ~**livered**, cowardly; ~**pox**, mild disease usu. causing eruptions on skin. **2.** *a.* (sl.) Cowardly. **3.** *v.i.* ~ **out**, (sl.) withdraw through cowardice. [E]

**chi'ckling** *n.* ~ (**vetch**), common cultivated vetchling; **chi'ck-pea** *n.*, dwarf pea. [F f. L *cicer*]

**chi'cle** (or -ĕ'-; or -ē) *n.* Milky juice of various trees. [Sp. f. Nahuatl]

**chi'corў** *n.* Blue-flowered plant used for salad; its root, roasted and ground, used with or instead of coffee. [F f. L f. Gk]

**chide** *v.t.* & *i.* (arch., literary; ~**d-**

chid; ~d, **chidden**). Scold, rebuke. [E]

**chief. 1.** n. Leader, ruler; head of tribe, clan, etc.; head of department, highest official, etc.; (Her.) upper third of shield; **-in-~**, supreme (*Commander-in-Chief*). **2.** a. First in position, importance, influence, etc.; prominent, leading. **3.** ~'ly adv., above all, mainly but not exclusively; ~'tain (-tan) n., chief of clan, tribe, robber-band, etc.; ~'taincy, ~'- tainship, (-tan-) ns. [F f. L *caput* head]

**chi'ff-chăff** n. European bird of warbler family. [imit.]

**chi'ffon** (sh-). **1.** n. Light dia- phanous fabric. **2.** a. (Of fabric) lightweight; (of pie etc.) light- -textured. [F (*chiffe* rag)]

**chi'gger** (-g-), **chi'gŏe**, n. Tropical flea, burrowing into skin. [Carib]

**chi'gnon** (shē'nyawn) n. Coil or mass of hair at back of woman's head. [F]

**chihua'hua** (chĭwah'wa) n. Very small breed of dog, originating in Mexico. [place]

**chi'lblain** n. Itching sore on hand, foot, etc., caused by exposure to cold. [CHILL, BLAIN]

**child** n. (pl. ~ren pr. chĭ'-). Young or unborn human being (**with ~**, pregnant); childish person; one's son or daughter; descendant (lit. or fig.), follower, product, *of*; ~ **benefit**, family allowance; ~'**birth**, par- turition; ~ **care**, care of children, esp. of those temporarily without normal home; ~ **guidance**, super- vision of children's welfare; ~'**s play**, easy task; ~'**hŏŏd** (-h-) n., state or period of being a child (SECOND *childhood*); ~'**ĭsh** a., of, like, or proper to a child, unsuitable for an adult; ~'**like** a., having good qualities of child, innocent, frank, etc. [E]

**chi'lĭ.** See CHILLI.

**chill** n., a., & v. **1.** n. Cold sensation, lowered body-temperature, feverish cold (*catch a chill*); unpleasant cold- ness of air, water, etc., (**take the ~ off**, warm slightly); depressing in- fluence (*cast a chill over*); coldness of manner. **2.** a. (literary). Lacking warmth; feeling cold; unemotional, austere. **3.** v.t. & i. Make or become cold; depress, dispirit; harden (mol- ten metal) by contact with cold material; preserve (meat etc.) at

low temperature without freezing. **4.** ~'y̆ a. (~iness), somewhat cold, sensitive to cold, unfriendly. [E]

**chi'l(l)ĭ** n. (pl. ~es). Dried capsi- cum pod; ~ **con carne**, stew of chilli-flavoured minced beef. [Sp. f. Aztec]

||**Chĭltern Hŭ'ndreds** (-z) n.pl. Crown manor, for administration of which M.P. applies as a way of resigning from Parliament. [place]

**chime. 1.** n. (Sounds made by) set of attuned bells; sound resembling this. **2.** v.i. & t. (Of bells) ring chimes; ring chimes on (bells); show (hour) by chiming; be in agreement (*to- gether, with*, etc.); ~ **in**, join in harmoniously, interject remark, fit or agree *with*. [E (CYMBAL)]

**chĭm|ēr'a** (k-) n. (Gk Myth.) goat with lion's head and serpent's tail; bogy; wild impossible scheme or unreal conception; ~ē'rĭcal a. (-lly). [L f. Gk]

**chi'mney** n. Structure by which smoke or steam is carried off from fire, furnace, engine, etc.; part of this above roof; glass tube protecting lamp-flame; narrow vertical cleft in rock-face; ~**breast**, projecting wall between chimney and room; ~- **-corner**, warm seat inside old- -fashioned wide fireplace; ~**piece**, mantelpiece; ~**pot**, earthenware or metal pipe at top of chimney; *chimney*-STACK; ~**sweep**, one who clears chimneys of soot. [F f. L (*caminus* from Gk)]

**chĭmpanzee'** n. Afr. ape re- sembling man (colloq. abbr. **chimp**). [F f. Kongo]

**chin** n. Front of lower jaw (**keep one's ~ up**, remain cheerful; **take on the ~**, suffer severe blow from, endure courageously); ~**wag** n., & v.i., (sl.) talk; ~'**less** a., (fig., of person) of weak character. [E]

**chi'na. 1.** n. Fine semi-transparent or white earthenware, porcelain; ~(**ware**), objects of this; ~ **clay**, kaolin. **2.** a. Made of china; (C~) from or of China (*China aster, tea*); **C~man** (pl. ~**men**), (arch.) a Chinese, (Crick.) left-handed bowler's off-break or googly. [place]

**chĭnchĭ'lla** n. (Grey fur of) small S. Amer. rodent. [Sp. (*chinche* bug)]

||**chĭn-chĭ'n** int. of greeting and farewell, or as toast. [Chin.]

||**chine**[1] n. Deep narrow ravine, esp. in Isle of Wight. [E]

**chine²** n. Backbone; joint of meat including (part of) this; hill-ridge. [F f. Gmc & L]

**Chinē′se** (-z). **1.** a. Of China; ~ **goose,** small domesticated goose; ~ **lantern,** collapsible paper lantern, plant with inflated orange calyx; ~ **puzzle** (intricate). **2.** n. (pl. same). Chinese native or language. [CHINA]

**chink¹** n. Narrow slit, peep-hole. [rel. to CHINE¹]

**chink².** **1.** n. Sound (as) of glasses or coins striking together. **2.** v.i. & t. Make this sound (with). [imit.]

**Chink³** n. (sl., derog.) A Chinese. [abbr.]

**Chino-** in comb. = SINO-. [CHINA]

**chintz** (-ts) n. Colour-printed, usu. glazed, cotton cloth; ~′ÿ a., (fig.) gaudy, cheap. [Hindi f. Skr.]

**chip.** **1.** v.t. & i. (-pp-). Break or cut edge or surface of (stone, crockery, wood), shape thus; cut or break (piece etc.) away, off; be apt to break at edge; cut (potato) into chips; ~ **in,** (colloq.) interrupt, contribute (money etc.). **2.** n. Piece chipped off (~ **off the old block,** child resembling parent, esp. in character; ~ **on** one's **shoulder,** grievance, inclination to fight or quarrel); chipped place on china etc.; wood or woody fibre split for making baskets, hats, etc.; long slender piece of potato fried (fish and chips); *(in pl.) potato crisps; counter used in game (**have had** one's ~**s,** sl., be beaten, killed, etc.; **when the** ~**s are down,** when it comes to the point); ~′**board,** board made of compressed wood chips. [E]

**chi′pmŭnk** n. N. Amer. ground--squirrel. [Algonquian]

**chipola′ta** (-lah′-) n. Small spicy sausage. [F f. It.]

**Chi′ppendāle** n. Elegant style of furniture. [person]

**chirŏ′pod**|ÿ (k-, sh-) n. Treatment of feet, esp. for corns, bunions, etc.; ~**ĭst** n. [Gk kheir hand, pous pod- foot]

**chīropră′ct**|**ic** (k-) n. & a. (Of) treatment of disease by manipulating the spinal column; ~**or** n. [prec., Gk pratto do]

**chĭrp.** **1.** n. Short sharp note as of sparrow. **2.** v.i. & t. Emit chirp(s); express or utter thus; talk merrily. **3.** ~′ÿ a. (colloq.; ~**ily,** ~**iness**), lively, cheerful; **chĭ′rrup** v.i., & n., (make) series of chirps. [imit.]

**chi′sel** (-z-). **1.** n. Tool with bevelled sharp end for shaping wood, stone, or metal; **cold** ~ (suitable for cutting cold metal). **2.** v.t. (||-ll-). Cut or shape with chisel (~**led** features etc., clear-cut); (sl.) defraud, treat unfairly. [F f. L (caedo cut)]

**chĭt¹** n. Short letter or note; note of order made, sum owed, etc. [Hindi f. Skr.]

**chĭt²** n. Young child; young, small, or slender woman (usu. derog.; chit of a girl). [orig. = whelp, cub]

**chĭ′t-chăt** n. Light conversation; gossip. [redupl. CHAT]

**chĭ′tterlĭng** n. (usu. in pl.) Smaller intestines of pig etc. as food. [orig. uncert.]

**chĭ′valr**|ÿ (sh-) n. Medieval knightly system with its religious, moral, and social code; ideal knight's characteristics, courage and courtesy; inclination to defend or help weaker party; ~**ĭc** a. (literary), of the age of chivalry, chivalrous; ~**ous** a., of, as of, marked by, chivalry. [F f. L (CHEVALIER)]

**chive** n. Small herb allied to onion and leek. [F f. L cepa onion]

**chĭ′vvÿ, chĭ′vÿ,** v.t. Pursue, harass; ~ **along, up,** etc., urge (person) to do something more quickly. [f. ballad of Chevy Chase]

**chlŏr**|**ine** (klŏr′ēn) n. Non-metallic element, a yellowish-green heavy gas; ~**al** n., a hypnotic and anaesthetic [al(cohol)]; ~**ide** n., binary compound of chlorine, bleaching agent containing this; ~**ĭnāte** v.t., impregnate or treat with chlorine (esp. to disinfect water); ~**ĭnā′tion** n.; ~**ofŏrm** (klŏ′r-), (n.) thin colourless liquid whose inhaled vapour produces unconsciousness, (v.t.) render (person) unconscious with this [FORMIC]; ~**ophyll** (klŏ′r-) n., colouring-matter of green parts of plants [Gk phullon leaf]; ~**ō′sĭs** n., anaemic disease causing greenish complexion. [Gk khlōros green]

||**chŏc** n. (colloq.) Chocolate; ~**-ice,** bar of ice cream enclosed in chocolate. [abbr.]

**chŏck.** **1.** n. Block of wood, esp. wedge for stopping motion of wheel, cask, etc.; ~**-a-block,** jammed together, crammed with; ~**-full,** crammed full (of). **2.** v.t. Make fast with chocks. [F]

**chŏ′colate** (or -kl-). **1.** n. Edible substance made as paste, powder, solid block, etc., from ground cacao seeds; sweetmeat made of or covered with this; drink of chocolate in hot milk or water; dark brown colour; ~ **biscuit** (coated with chocolate). **2.** *a.* Flavoured with chocolate; chocolate-coloured. [F or Sp. f. Aztec]

**choice. 1.** *n.* Act of choosing (**by, for, ~,** preferably; **make, take,** one's **~,** decide between alternatives; **of** one's **~,** that one chooses); power of choosing (**from ~,** willingly; **have no ~ but to,** must; HOBSON's *choice*); variety to choose from; thing or person chosen. **2.** *a.* Of special quality. [F f. Gmc (CHOOSE)]

**choir** (kwīr), (arch.) **quire²,** *n.* Organized band of singers, esp. in church; chancel of cathedral or large church; birds etc. singing; **~boy,** boy singer in choir; **~ school,** school maintained by cathedral etc. for choirboys and other pupils. [E]

**chōke. 1.** *v.t.* & *i.* Stop breathing of, suffocate; suffer such stoppage; make or become speechless from emotion; suppress (feelings); smother or kill (fire, plant, etc.) by depriving of air or light; fill chock-full; block up or narrow (channel, tube, etc.); **~ back,** suppress (emotion etc.); **~ down,** swallow with difficulty; **~ off,** dissuade or discourage (person, attempt), esp. forcibly; **~ up,** block (channel etc.). **2.** *n.* Valve in petrol engine controlling inflow of air; (Electr.) device for smoothing variations of current; **~-damp,** carbon dioxide in mines etc. **3. chō'ker** *n.,* (esp.) high collar, close-fitting necklace. [E]

**chŏ'lera** (k-) *n.* Infectious often fatal bacterial disease with severe intestinal symptoms; **chŏ'ler** *n.,* (Hist.) one of the four HUMOURS; (arch.) anger or irascibility; **chŏ'leric** (k-) *a.,* irascible. [L f. Gk (*kholē* bile)]

**cholĕ'sterŏl** (k-) *n.* Steroid alcohol in body cells and fluids, believed to promote arteriosclerosis.

**chōose** (-z) *v.t.* & *i.* (chose *pr.* chŏz; chosen *pr.* chō'zen). Select out of greater number; (w. compl.) select as (*was chosen king*); (Theol.) destine to salvation (**chosen people, race,** Jews); decide or think fit (*to do,* esp. one thing rather than another); make choice (**between,**

*from;* **cannot ~ but,** arch., must necessarily; **there is nothing** etc. **to ~ between them,** one is as good as another); **chōo'se(e)y** (-zĭ) *a.* (-iness), (colloq.) fastidious. [E]

**chŏp¹. 1.** *v.t.* & *i.* (-pp-). Cut with axe, heavy knife, etc. (*down, off, through,* etc.); make chopping blow (*at*); cut (meat etc.) into small pieces; strike (ball) with heavy edgewise blow; **~ up,** cut into small pieces. **2.** *n.* Chopping stroke (**the ~,** sl., action of killing or dismissing; *get the chop; he's for the chop*); thick slice of meat, esp. pork or lamb, usu. including rib; **~-house,** cheap restaurant; **~pў** *a.* (-ily, -iness), (of water) breaking in short waves. [rel. to CHOP²]

**chŏp²** *n.* (usu. in *pl.*) Jaw of animal or person. [var. of CHAP³]

**chŏp³** *v.i.* & *t.* (-pp-). **~ about,** (of wind, person) change direction suddenly, vacillate; **~ and change,** vacillate; **~ logic,** engage in pedantically logical arguments; **~ round,** = *chop about.* [perh. rel. to CHEAP]

**chŏ'pper** *n.* Large-bladed short axe; cleaver; (colloq.) helicopter. [CHOP¹]

**chŏ'pstĭck** *n.* (usu. in *pl.*) One of pair of sticks of wood, ivory, etc., held in one hand esp. by Chinese to lift food to mouth. [Chin. *chop* nimble, STICK²]

**chŏp-sū'ey** (or -sōō'-) *n.* Chinese dish of meat or fish fried with vegetables. [Chin., = mixed bits]

**chŏr'al¹** (k-) *a.* (**~**ly). Of, for, sung by, choir; of or with chorus; **chŏra'le, chŏra'l²,** (kŏrah'l) *n.,* simple tune or hymn usu. sung in unison, harmonized form of this, group of singers. [L (CHORUS)]

**chŏrd¹** (k-) *n.* String of harp etc. (poet. or fig.); strike a **~,** recall something to person's memory; **touch the right ~,** appeal skilfully to emotion); (Math., Aeron., etc.) straight line joining ends of arc, wing, etc. [var. of CORD]

**chŏrd²** (k-) *n.* (Mus.) Combination of several simultaneous notes. [orig. *cord* f. ACCORD]

**chōre** *n.* Small or odd job; recurrent or tedious task. [CHAR¹]

**chŏrĕŏ'graphў** (k-) *n.* (Art of) arranging ballet or stage-dance; **~er** *n.;* **chŏrĕogră'phĭc** (k-) *a.* [Gk *khoreia* choral dancing to music]

**chŏr′ĭc** (-k-) *a*. Of or like Greek chorus; **chŏ′rĭster** (-k-) *n*., member of choir, choirboy. [L f. Gk (CHORUS)]

**chŏr′tle** *v.i.*, & *n*. (Give) loud chuckle. [see PORTMANTEAU]

**chŏr′us** (-k-). **1.** *n*. Band of singers, choir; thing sung or said by several people at once (**in ~**, with all singing or speaking together); refrain or main part of popular song, jazz improvisation on this; (Gk Ant.) band of dancers and singers in plays and religious rites, any of its utterances; character speaking prologue etc. in play; group of singing dancers in musical comedy etc. (**~-girl**, young woman who sings or dances in this); **~-master**, conductor of chorus or choir. **2.** *v.t.* & *i.* Say or sing in chorus. [L f. Gk]

**chose(n).** See CHOOSE.

**chou** (shoo) *n*. (*pl*. **~x** *pr*. same). Small round cake of pastry filled with cream etc. [F, = cabbage]

**chough** (chŭf) *n*. Red-legged crow. [imit.]

**choux** (shoo) *n*. = CHOU (*sing*. or *pl*.); **~ pastry**, light pastry enriched with eggs. [CHOU]

**chow** *n*. Chinese breed of dog; (sl.) food. [Chin. *chow-chow*]

**\*chow′der** *n*. Stew or soup of fish or clams. [perh. F *chaudière* (CAULDRON)]

**chrĭ′sm** (krĭ′zem) *n*. Consecrated oil; anointing. [E f. L *chrisma* f. Gk]

**Chrĭst** (k-) *n*. Messiah or Lord's anointed in Jewish prophecy; (title, now treated as name, of) Jesus as fulfilling this prophecy; image or picture of Jesus; **~!**, (vulg.) excl. of surprise etc.; **the ~-child**, Jesus as a child. [E f. L f. Gk, = anointed]

**Christadĕl′phĭan** (k-) *a*. & *n*. (Member) of religious sect rejecting doctrine of Trinity and expecting second coming of Christ. [prec., Gk *adelphos* brother]

**chrĭ′sten** (krĭ′sen) *v.t.* Admit to Christian Church by baptism; give name or nickname to (person, ship, etc.); (colloq.) use etc. for first time; **C~dom** *n*., Christians, Christian countries. [E f. L (foll.)]

**Chrĭ′stian** (krĭ′styan) *a*. & *n*. Of Jesus or his teaching; (person) believing in, professing, belonging to, or in harmony with the Christian religion; **~ burial** (with the ceremonies of the Church); **~ era** (reckoned from birth of Christ); **~**

**name,** name given (as) at baptism, personal name, opp. SURNAME; **~ Science,** system by which Christian faith is alleged to overcome disease etc. without medical treatment (**~ Scientist,** adherent of this); *Christian* YEAR; **Christiă′nĭty** (k-) *n*., the Christian faith, being a Christian, Christian quality or character; **~ĭze** *v.t.* [L *Christianus* of CHRIST]

**Chrĭ′stmas** (krĭs′m-) *n*. Festival of Christ's birth celebrated on 25 Dec. (**~ Day**) and devoted esp. to family reunion and merry-making; **~(-tide),** period of some days beginning on **~ Eve** (24 Dec.); ‖**~-box,** small present or gratuity given at Christmas, esp. to employees of firms providing regular services; **~ card** (of greeting, sent for Christmas); **~ present,** gift at Christmas; ‖**~ pudding,** rich plum pudding; **~ rose,** white-flowered winter-blooming hellebore; **~ stocking** (hung up by children on Christmas Eve to be filled with presents); **~ tree,** evergreen tree hung with lights, presents, etc., at Christmas; **~sy** *a*., of festive appearance etc. [E (CHRIST, MASS[1])]

**chromă′tĭc** (k-) *a*. (**~ally**). Of colour, in colours; (Mus.) of or having notes not included in diatonic scale; **~ scale** (proceeding by semitones). [F or L f. Gk (foll.)]

**chrōme** (k-) *n*. **~ (yellow),** yellow pigment got from compound of chromium; **~-nickel,** stainless (steel) containing chromium and nickel; **~ steel,** hard steel containing much chromium; **chrō′mĭum** (k-) *n*., a metallic element with coloured compounds; **chrō′mosŏme** (k-) *n*., (Biol.) structure occurring in pairs in cell-nucleus, carrying genes [Gk *sōma* body]. [F f. Gk (*khrōma* colour)]

**Chron.** *abbr*. Chronicles (O.T.).

**chrŏ′nĭc** (k-) *a*. (**~ally**). (Of disease etc.) lingering, long-lasting; (of invalid) with chronic disease; ‖(colloq.) bad, intense, severe; **chroni′cĭty** (k-) *n*. [F f. L f. Gk (*khronos* time)]

**chrŏ′nĭcle** (k-). **1.** *n*. Record of events in order of their occurrence; **C~s,** two O.T. books. **2.** *v.t.* Enter or relate in a chronicle, report. **3.** **chrŏnolŏ′gĭcal** (k-) *a*. (**-lly**), of chronology, following sequence of time; **chronŏ′logÿ** (k-) *n*., science of computing dates, arrangement of events according to dates of occurrence; **chrono′meter** (k-) *n.*, time-measuring instrument, esp. one keeping accurate time at all temperatures etc. as used in navigation.

**chry′salis** (k-) *n.* (Case of) pupa, esp. quiescent one of butterfly or moth. [L f. Gk (*khrusos* gold)]

**chrysa′nthemum** (k-) *n.* Garden plant flowering in autumn. [L f. Gk, = gold flower]

**chrysobe′ryl, chry′solite, chry′soprase** (-z), (k-), *ns.* Yellowish-green, olive-green, apple-green, precious stones. [Gk *khrusos* gold, BERYL, *lithos* stone, *prason* leek]

**chub** *n.* (*pl.* same). Thick-bodied river fish; **∼′by** *a.* (-ily, -iness), plump(-faced). [orig. unkn.]

**chuck**[1]. (colloq.) **1.** *v.t.* Fling with carelessness, contempt, or ease, = THROW, (*away, in, out, up,* etc.); ∼ **it**, (sl.) stop, desist; ∼ **out**, expel (troublesome person) from meeting, public house, etc., (∼**er-ou′t**, person employed to do this); ∼ person **under the chin**, give playful or affectionate touch there. **2.** *n.* Act of chucking; **the ∼,** (sl.) dismissal. [perh. F *chuquer* knock]

**chuck**[2]. **1.** Contrivance in lathe etc. for holding workpiece; cut of beef from neck to ribs. **2.** *v.t.* Fix in chuck. [var. of CHOCK]

**chu′ckle** *v.i.,* & *n.* (Make) quiet or suppressed laugh. [*chuck* cluck]

**chu′ckle-head** (-hĕd) *n.* Stupid person; ∼**ĕd** *a.*, stupid. [CHUCK[2]]

**chuff** *v.i.* (Of engine etc.) work with regular puffing sound. [imit.]

**chuffed** (-ft) *a.* (sl.) Pleased; displeased. [dial. *chuff*]

**chug**, *n.,* & *v.i.* (-gg-). (Make or move with) muffled sound (as) of slowly-running engine. [imit.]

**chu′kker, -kka,** *n.* Period of play in game of polo. [Hindi, f. Skr. *chakra* wheel]

**chum.** (colloq.) **1.** *n.* Familiar friend; **new ∼,** (Austral. & N.Z.) recent immigrant; ∼′**my** *a.* (-ily, -iness). **2.** *v.i.* (-mm-). ∼ **up,** form friendship (*with*). [abbr. of *chamber-fellow* (Oxf. Univ.)]

**chump** *n.* Short thick lump of wood; ‖thick end of loin of mutton (esp. ∼ **chop**); ‖(colloq.) head (**off** one's ∼, crazy); (colloq.) foolish person. [foll., LUMP]

**chunk** *n.* Thick lump (*of* cheese, wood, etc.) cut or broken off; **∼′y** *a.* (-iness), consisting of or resembling chunks, small and sturdy. [var. of CHUCK[2]]

**chu′nter** *v.i.* (colloq.) Mutter; talk at length; grumble. [prob. imit.]

**chupă′tty, -ĭ, chapă′t(t)ĭ,** (*or* -ah′-) *n.* (Ind.) Small flat thin cake of coarse unleavened bread. [Hindi]

**church. 1.** *n.* Building for public Christian worship, ‖esp. according to established religion of country; public worship (*go to church; meet after church*); (C∼) body of all Christians, organized Christian society (**Established C∼,** Church recognized by State), clergy of such Church, the clerical profession (**go into, enter, the C∼,** take holy orders); ∼**goer, -going,** attender, attendance, at public worship; ∼′**man,** member of clergy or church; **C∼ militant,** Christians on earth regarded as warring against evil; ∼ **mouse,** proverbial type of poverty; **C∼ of England,** English branch of Western Church rejecting Pope's supremacy; **C∼ of Scotland,** Established Church (Presbyterian) in Scotland; ∼ **parade,** (Mil. etc.) attendance at worship; ∼ **school** (founded by or associated with Church of England etc.); ∼ **service,** public worship; **C∼ triumphant,** Christians at peace in heaven; ∼′**warden,** elected lay representative of parish (usu. one of two) assisting incumbent in organization, long clay pipe, *church administrator; ∼′**yard,** enclosed ground round church, esp. as used for burials. **2.** *v.t.* Perform church service of thanksgiving for (esp. woman after childbirth). ∼′**y** *a.* (∼iness), strictly or over-zealously devoted to or characteristic of the Church. [E f. Gmc f. Gk *kurikon* Lord's (house)]

**churl** *n.* Bad-mannered, surly, or stingy person (arch.); ∼′**ĭsh** *a.*, surly, niggardly. [E, = man]

**churn. 1.** *n.* Butter-making machine; ‖large milk-can. **2.** *v.t.* & *i.* Agitate (milk etc.) in churn; make (butter) in churn; ∼ (**up**), stir or agitate violently; ∼ **out,** produce in quantity without quality. [E]

**chute** (shōōt) *n.* Sloping channel or slide for conveying things to lower level; (colloq.) parachute. [F (L *cado* fall)]

**chu′tney** *n.* Pungent condiment made of fruits, spices, etc. [Hindi]

**chu′tzpah** (hŏŏ′tspa) *n.* (sl.) Shameless audacity. [Yiddish]

**chȳle** (k-) *n.* Milky fluid formed from chyme by pancreatic juice and bile; **chȳme** (k-) *n.*, pulp into which gastric secretion converts food. [L f. Gk]

‖**C.I.** *abbr.* Channel Islands.

\***C.I.A.** *abbr.* Central Intelligence Agency.

**ciao** (chow) *int.* (colloq.) Goodbye; hello. [It.]

**cica′da** (or -ä′-), **cica′la**, **ciga′la**, (-ah′-) *n.* Transparent-winged shrill--sounding insect. [L *cicada*, It. f. L *cicala*, It. *cigala*]

**ci′catr|ice** *n.* Scar of healed wound; ∼**ize** *v.i. & t.*, skin over, heal. [F or L]

**ci′cely** *n.* Flowering plant allied to parsley and chervil. [L f. Gk *seselis*]

**cicero′ne** (or chĭch-) *n.* (*pl.* -**ni** *pr.* -ē). Guide who understands and describes antiquities etc. [It. f. L *Cicero*, person]

‖**C.I.D.** *abbr.* Criminal Investigation Department.

**ci′der** *n.* Drink of fermented apple--juice; ∼-**press** (for squeezing juice out of apples). [F f. L f. Gk f. Heb., = strong drink]

**ci-devant** (sēdevah′ṅ) *a.* Former, that was formerly. [F]

**c.i.f.** *abbr.* cost, insurance, freight.

**cig** *n.* (colloq.) Cigar(ette). [abbr.]

**cigala.** See CICADA.

**cigar′** *n.* Roll of tobacco-leaf for smoking; ∼-**shaped**, cylindrical with pointed ends; **cigare′tte**, \*-**ě′t**, *n.*, cylinder of finely-cut tobacco etc. rolled in paper for smoking (**cigarette-end**, unsmoked remainder of cigarette; **cigarette--holder**, device for holding cigarette while it is being smoked); **cigari′llo** *n.* (*pl.* -os), small cigar. [F or Sp.]

**ci′li|um** *n.* (*pl.* ∼**a**). Eyelash; similar fringe on leaf, insect's wing, etc.; hairlike vibrating organ on animal or vegetable tissue; ∼**ary** (-lyerĭ), ∼**ate**, ∼**ātèd**, *adjs.* [L]

**C.-in-C.** *abbr.* Commander-in--Chief.

\***cinch** *n.* (sl.) Sure thing, certainty; easy task. [Sp. *cincha* saddle--girth]

**cinchō′na** (-ngkō′-) *n.* An evergreen tree or shrub, orig. S. Amer.; (drug made from) its bark, containing quinine. [*Chinchón*, person]

**ci′ncture** *n.*, & *v.t.* (literary). (Surround with) girdle, belt, or border. [L (*cingo* gird)]

**ci′nder** *n.* Residue of coal, wood, etc., that has ceased to flame; ∼-**path**, -**track**, footpath or running--track made with fine cinders; **C∼ě′lla** *n.*, person or thing of unrecognized or disregarded merit or beauty [character in fairy-tale]; ∼**ȳ** *a.* [E (orig. *sinder*), = slag]

**ci′nema** *n.* Moving pictures; theatre where these as shown; production of these as an art or industry; **ci′nè** *a.*, cinematographic (**cine camera**, **film**); **cĭnemă′tĭc** *a.*, of cinematographic film or the cinema; **cĭnemă′tograph**, **kĭ-**, (-ahf) *n.*, device for projecting long film with successive photographs on screen to give illusion of motion; **cĭnematŏ′grapher** *n.*, cinematographic film--maker; **cĭnematŏgrǎ′phĭc** *a.* (-ically); **cĭnematŏ′graphȳ** *n.* [abbr. f. Gk (KINEMATIC)]

**cinerā′ria** *n.* Flowering plant with ash-coloured down on leaves; **ci′nerarȳ** *a.*, of ashes (esp. of urn holding ashes of dead after cremation). [L (*cinis -ner-* ashes)]

**ci′nnabar** *n.* Red mercuric sulphide; vermilion; moth with reddish--marked wings. [L f. Gk]

**ci′nnamon** *n.* S.E. Asian tree; its aromatic inner bark used as spice; ∼-**coloured**, yellowish-brown; ∼ **toast**, buttered toast spread with cinnamon and sugar. [F f. L f. Gk]

**cinq(ue)** (-k) *n.* 'Five' on dice; **ci′nq(ue)foil** (-kf-) *n.*, plant with 5-lobed leaves, (Archit.) 5-cusped ornament in circle or arch [L *folium* leaf]; **Cinque Ports** (-nk-) *n.pl.*, group of ports (orig. 5) in S.E. England with ancient privileges. [F f. L *quinque* five]

**ci′pher**, **cȳ′pher**. **1.** *n.* Arithmetical symbol (0) of no value in itself but used to occupy vacant place in decimal etc. numeration; person or thing of no importance; secret or disguised writing (**in** ∼, so written), key to it; monogram. **2.** *v.t.* Work (sum, result) *out*; put into cipher writing. [F f. L f. Arab. (ZERO)]

**circa** (sẽr′ka) *prep.* About (a specified date); **cĭrcā′dian** *a.*, (Physiol.) occurring about once per day. [L (*dies* day)]

**cir′cle. 1.** *n.* (Line enclosing) perfectly round plane figure (**great** ∼, whose plane passes through centre of sphere on which circle lies; SQUARE *the circle*); roundish enclosure, structure, etc.; curved tier of seats at theatre etc. (DRESS-*circle*); persons grouped round centre of interest; set, coterie, or class, (*literary circles*; *not done in the best circles*); circular route (lit. or fig.; **come full ~**, return to starting-point; **go, run, round in ~s**, make no progress despite effort or fuss); (**vicious**) **~**, fallacy of proving by assuming proposition dependent on what is to be proved, unbroken sequence of reciprocal cause and effect or action and reaction. **2.** *v.i.* & *t.* Move in a circle (*about, around, round*); revolve round; form circle round. **3.** cir̄'clet *n.*, small circle, circular band esp. as ornament. [F f. L dim. (CIRCUS)]

cir̄'cuit (-kǐt) *n.* Closed or circuitous course; motor-racing track; sequence of sporting events or athletic exercises; judge's itinerary through district to hold courts, such a district, lawyers following a circuit; chain of theatres, cinemas, etc., under single management; group of Methodist churches forming minor administrative unit; (Electr.) path of current (SHORT *circuit*), apparatus through which current passes; circu̅'itous *a.*, indirect, going a long way round; **~rȳ** *n.*, (equipment forming) electrical circuits. [F f. L (CIRCUM-, *eo it-* go)]

cir̄'cular. **1.** *a.* Having form of circle; taking place along circle; of or depending on a vicious circle; (of letter, notice) addressed to a circle of persons, customers, etc.; **~ saw**, rotating toothed disc for sawing wood etc.; ‖**~ tour** (which brings traveller back to starting-place). **2.** *n.* Circular letter or notice. **3.** cir̄cula̅'rity *n.*; **~ize** *v.t.*, send circulars to. [F f. L (CIRCLE)]

cir̄'cul|āte *v.i.* & *t.* (**~able**). Be or put in circulation; send circulars to; **~ā'tion** *n.*, movement to and fro, or from and back to starting-point, esp. that of blood in body from and to heart, (**in, out of, ~ation**, circulating, or not, fig. participating, or not, in activities etc.); transmission or distribution (of news, books, etc.); number of copies sold, esp. of newspapers; **~ātor** *n.*; **~'tory** (or se̅r'-) *a.*, (esp.) of circulation of blood. [L (CIRCLE)]

cir̄cum- *pref.* Round, about. [L]

cir̄cumci'sion (-zhon) *n.* Religious rite or surgical operation of cutting off foreskin or clitoris; the C~, (Eccl.) feast of Christ's circumcision, 1 Jan.; cir̄'cumcise (-z) *v.t.*, subject to circumcision. [F f. L (*caedo* cut)]

cir̄cu̅'mference *n.* Line (esp. a circle) that encloses; distance round; cir̄cumfere̅'ntial (-shal) *a.* (-**lly**) [F f. L (*fero* carry)]

cir̄'cumflĕx *n.* & *a.* **~** (**accent**) mark placed over vowel in some languages (à) to indicate contraction, length, or special quality. [L (FLEX)]

cir̄cumja̅'cent *a.* Situated around. [L (*jaceo* lie)]

cir̄cumlocu̅'tion *n.* Roundabout expression; verbosity; evasive talk; cir̄cumlo̅'cutory *a.* [F or L (LOCUTION)]

cir̄cumna̅'vig|āte *v.t.* (**~able**). Sail round (esp. the world); **~ā'tion**, **~ātor**, *ns.* [L (NAVIGATE)]

cir̄cumpo̅'lar *a.* About or near one of the earth's poles. [POLAR]

cir̄'cum|scribe *v.t.* (Of line etc.) enclose or outline; mark or lay down limits of, confine, restrict; (Geom.) draw (figure) round another so as to touch it at points without cutting it; **~scri'ption** *n.*, (esp.) inscription round coin etc. [L (*scribo* write)]

cir̄'cumsp|ĕct *a.* Wary, taking everything into account; **~ĕ'ction** *n.*, (exercise of) caution. [L (*specio spect-* look)]

cir̄'cumstance *n.* Occurrence, fact, detail, (*an unforeseen circumstance*); ceremony, fuss, (*pomp and circumstance*); (arch.) full detail in narrative; (in *pl.*) conditions, facts, etc., connected with or affecting an event, act, etc., (**in, under, the ~s**, the state of affairs being what it is; **under no ~s**, never); (in *pl.*) financial condition (*in reduced, straitened, circumstances*); cir̄'cumstanced (-st) *a.*, in (specified) circumstances; cir̄cumsta̅'ntial (-shal) *a.* (-**lly**), (of account, story) detailed, (of evidence) tending to establish a conclusion by inference from known facts hard to explain otherwise; cir̄cumstānti̇ä'li̇ty (-shǐ-) *n.* [F or L (*sto* stand)]

cir̄cumvĕ'nt *v.t.* Outwit, baffle; evade (difficulty etc.); **~ion** *n.* [L (*venio vent-* come)]

**cir′cus** *n.* Travelling show of performing animals, acrobats, clowns, etc.; (colloq.) scene of lively action, group of persons performing in sports etc.; (Hist.) arena, usu. circular and surrounded by tiers of seats, for equestrian and other performances; ||open space in town with streets converging on it. [L, = ring]

**cirque** (-k) *n.* (Geog.) Bowl--shaped hollow. [F (CIRCUS)]

**cirrhō′s**|**is** (sǐrō′-) *n.* (*pl.* ~es *pr.* -ēz). Disease of liver, esp. suffered by alcoholics. [L f. Gk *kirrhos* tawny]

**cir′r**|**us** *n.* (*pl.* ~i *pr.* -ī). White wispy cloud, usu. at high altitude; ~**ipĕd** *n.*, marine crustacean in valved shell, e.g. barnacle, [PEDAL]; ~**ous** *a.* [L, = curl]

**cis-***pref.* On this side of; **cisa′lpine**, on south side of Alps; **cispo′ntine**, on north side of Thames. [L]

**ci′ssy.** See SISSY.

**Cister′cian** (-shan) *n.* & *a.* (Monk, nun) of order founded as stricter branch of Benedictines. [F (*Cîteaux*, place)]

**ci′stern** *n.* Reservoir or tank for water, esp. one in roof-space supplying taps, or above water-closet. [F f. L *cisterna* (*cista* box f. Gk)]

**ci′stus** *n.* Shrub with white or red flowers. [L f. Gk]

**ci′tadel** *n.* Fortress, usu. on high ground protecting or dominating city; meeting-hall of Salvation Army. [F or It. dim. (CITY)]

**cite** *v.t.* Summon at law; adduce as instance, quote (passage, book, author) in support; **cita′tion** *n.*, (esp.) description of reasons for award. [F f. L (*cieo* set in motion)]

**ci′tizen** *n.* Inhabitant or freeman of city; townsman; *civilian; native or inhabitant *of* State (~ **of the world**, cosmopolitan); ~**rў**, ~**ship**, *ns.* [AF (CITY)]

**ci′tron** *n.* (Tree bearing) fruit like lemon but larger; **ci′trate** *n.*, salt of citric acid; **ci′tric** *a.*, (Chem.) derived from citron (**citric acid**, sharp-tasting acid in lemon-juice etc.); **citronĕ′lla** *n.*, (grass yielding) a fragrant oil; **ci′trus** *n.*, (fruit of) tree of genus *Citrus*, including citron, lemon, orange, etc. [F f. L *citrus*]

**ci′tў** *n.* Large town (C~ **of God**, **Heavenly C~**, Paradise; C~ **of the Seven Hills**, **Eternal C~**, Rome); ||town created city by charter, esp. as containing cathedral; **the C~**,

part of London governed by Lord Mayor and Corporation, business quarter of this, commercial circles; ||C~ **Company**, corporation representing ancient trade guild; ~ **fathers**, persons responsible for administration of city; *~ **hall**, municipal offices or officers; ~ **slicker**, sophisticated city-dweller, plausible rogue; ~**state**, (Hist.) city that is also an independent state. [F f. L *civitas* (CIVIL)]

**ci′vet** *n.* Strong musky perfume got from the ~(**-cat**), a carnivorous quadruped. [F f. It. f. L f. Arab.]

**ci′vic** *a.* (~**ally**). Of citizens, citizenship, or a city (~ **centre**, area where municipal offices etc. are situated); ~**s** *n.pl.*, study of rights and duties of citizenship. [F or L (*civis* citizen)]

**ci′vil** (*or* -ǐl) *a.* (~**ly**). Of or proper to citizens; polite, obliging, not rude; non-military; (Law) concerning private rights and not criminal offences; (of length of day, year, etc.) fixed by custom or law, not natural or astronomical; ~ **defence**, organization for dealing with air raids etc.; ~ **disobedience**, refusal to obey laws, pay taxes, etc., as part of political campaign; *civil* ENGINEER, LIBERTY; ||~ **list**, annual allowance by Parliament for sovereign's household expenses etc.; ~ **marriage** (solemnized without religious ceremony); ~ **rights**, rights of citizens, *esp. of Blacks, to liberty, equality, etc.; ~ **servant**, member of Civil Service; C~ **Service**, all non-military branches of State administration; ~ **war** (between citizens of same country); **civi′lian** (-yan) *n.* & *a.*, (person) not in or of the armed forces; **civi′litў** *n.*, politeness, (in *pl.*) acts of politeness; ~**lǐzā′tion** *n.*, (esp.) advanced stage or system of social development, all civilized States; **ci′vilize** *v.t.*, bring out of barbarism, enlighten, refine and educate; **ci′v(v)ies** (-vǐz) *n.pl.*, (sl.) civilian clothes; ||**Ci′vvў Street** *n.*, (sl.) civilian life. [F f. L *civilis* (prec.)]

**Cl** *symb.* chlorine.

**clăck** *n.*, & *v.i.* (Make) sharp sound (as) of boards struck together; (make) noise of continual talking, chatter. [imit.]

**clăd**[1]. See CLOTHE.

**clăd**[2] *v.t.* (**-dd-**). Provide with cladding; **clă′dding** *n.*, coating or covering on structure, material, etc. [prec.]

**claim. 1.** *v.t.* Demand as one's due or property (payment, recognition, etc., *to* be or do, *that*); have as achievement or consequence (*the fire claimed many victims*); represent oneself as having (accuracy etc.); profess *to* (be, have done, know, etc.); assert; (of thing) deserve (attention etc.). **2.** *n.* Demand (*lay claim to*; *put in a claim*); right or title (*to* thing); assertion; (Mining etc.) piece of ground allotted or taken; **stake (out) a ~,** (fig.) make statement of one's rights or demands; **no--claim'm(s) bonus,** reduction of insurance premium when insured person has not made claim for payment. **3. ~'ant** *n.,* person making claim, esp. in lawsuit. [F f. L *clamo* call out]

**clairvoy'an|ce** *n.* Faculty of seeing mentally what is normally out of sight; exceptional insight; **~t** *a.* & *n.* [F (CLEAR, *voir* see)]

**clăm. 1.** *n.* Edible bivalve mollusc; (sl.) taciturn person; *\*~'bake,* (outdoor) social gathering for eating etc. **2.** *v.i.* (**-mm-**). Dig for clams; *\*~ up,* cease talking. [CLAMP[1]]

**clă'mant** *a.* (literary). Noisy, insistent. [L (CLAIM)]

**clă'mber** *v.i.,* & *n.* Climb with hands and feet; climb with difficulty. [CLIMB]

**clă'mmў** *a.* (**-ily, -iness**). Moist, usu. cold, and sticky or slimy; (of weather) cold and damp. [*clam* to daub]

**clă'mour, \*clă'mor,** (**-er**). **1.** *n.* Loud or vehement shouting, protest, demand, or noise; **clă'morous** *a.* **2.** *v.i.* & *t.* Make clamour; shout or assert (words etc.). [F f. L (CLAIM)]

**clămp[1]. 1.** *n.* Brace or band of iron etc. for strengthening or holding things together; appliance tightened by screw, for holding or compressing. **2.** *v.t.* & *i.* Strengthen or fasten (as) with clamp; **~ down on,** become stricter regarding, restrain, suppress, (**~down,** act of doing this). [LDu.]

**clămp[2]** *n.* Pile (of bricks for burning, ‖potatoes under straw or earth, etc.). [Du. (CLUMP)]

**clăn** *n.* Group of (esp. Highland) Scots with common ancestor, esp. while patriarchally controlled; family holding together; party, coterie; **~'nĭsh** *a.;* **~'sman** (-z-) *n.,* member of clan. [Gael.]

**clăndĕ'stīne** *a.* Surreptitious, secret. [F or L]

**clăng** *n.,* & *v.i.* (Make) loud resonant metallic sound (of bell, trumpet, hammer, etc.); **~'er** *n.,* (esp., sl.) blunder (**drop a ~er,** make a blunder); **~'our, \*~'or,** (-ngger) *n.,* continued clanging; **~'orous** (-ngg-) *a.* [L *clango* resound]

**clănk** *n.* & *v.* (Make, or cause to make) sound (as) of heavy pieces of metal meeting or chain rattling. [imit.]

**clăp[1]. 1.** *v.t.* & *i.* (**-pp-**). **~ (one's hands),** strike palms loudly together esp. as applause, applaud thus; put *in* or *on* quickly or energetically, impose (tax *on* goods etc.) thus; **~ eyes on,** (colloq., esp. w. neg.) see; **~ on the back,** strike (person) on back as encouragement or congratulation; **~ped out,** (sl.) exhausted, worn out. **2.** *n.* Explosive noise, esp. of thunder; act of applauding; slap, pat. **3. ~'per** *n.,* (esp.) tongue or striker of bell; **~per(--board),** (Cinemat.) device for making sharp noise for synchronization of picture and sound; **like the ~pers,** (sl.) very fast or very hard; **~'trăp** *n.,* insincere or pretentious language, nonsense. [E]

**clăp[2]** *n.* (vulg.) Venereal disease, esp. gonorrhoea. [F]

**\*clă'pboard** (*or* klă'berd) *n.* = WEATHER-*board.* [LG]

**clăque** (-k) *n.* Hired group of applauders in theatre etc. [F]

**clă'ret** *n.* Red wine esp. from Bordeaux; **~(-coloured)** a., reddish--violet; **clă'rĭfÿ** *v.t.* & *i.,* make or become clear, free (mind, sight, subject, etc.) from obscurity or dimness, free (liquid etc.) from impurities or opaqueness; **clărĭfĭcā'tion** *n.;* **clărĭnĕ't** *n.,* (player of) a wood-wind musical instrument; **clărĭnĕ'ttist, \*-ĕ'tĭst,** *n.;* **clă'rĭon** *n.,* rousing sound, call to action, (Hist.) shrill war-trumpet; **clă'rĭtÿ** *n.,* clearness (esp. fig.). [F f. L (CLEAR)]

**clăr'kĭa** *n.* Garden plant with showy flowers. [*Clark,* person]

**clăr'ÿ** *n.* An aromatic herb. [F f. L *sclarea*]

**clăsh. 1.** *n.* Loud jarring sound (as) of striking weapons, cymbals, bells rung together, etc.; collision, conflict; discord of colours etc. **2.** *v.i.* &

*t.* (Cause to) make clash; collide; come into conflict or be at variance (*with*). [imit.]

**clasp** (-ah-). **1.** *n.* Contrivance of interlocking parts for fastening; buckle; grip of arms or hand, embrace, handshake; silver bar on medal-ribbon with name of battle etc.; ~**-knife**, folding knife, esp. with catch fixing blade when open. **2.** *v.t.* & *i.* Fasten (clasp); fasten as or with clasp; encircle, embrace, hold closely; grasp (~ **hands**, shake hands warmly; ~ one's **hands**, interlace fingers). [E]

**class** (-ah-). **1.** *n.* Rank or order of society (*lower, middle, upper, working, professional*, etc., *class* or *classes*); existence of such classes as a social factor; any set of persons or things differentiated, esp. by quality, from others (FIRST, SECOND, THIRD, *class*; **in a ~ of** (*or* on) its (*or* one's) **own**, unequalled; **no ~,** colloq., quite inferior); set of students taught together, their time of meeting, their course of instruction; *all college students of same year (~ of 1970 etc., those graduating in that year); ||division of candidates by merit in examination; (Biol.) division of animals or plants next below phylum or division; ~**-conscious(ness)**, aware(ness) of the divisions between social classes; ~**-list**, list by classes of those successful in examination, esp. at university; ~**-room** (where school etc. class is taught); ~ **war(fare)**, conflict or enmity between social classes. **2.** *v.t.* Place in a class; ~ **with**, put in the same class as. [L *classis* assembly]

**clăs'sic. 1.** *a.* (~**ally**). Of acknowledged excellence; outstandingly important, remarkably typical, (*a classic case*); of ancient Greek and Latin literature, art, culture, etc.; resembling this, esp. in simplicity, harmony, and restraint (cf. ROMANTIC); having historic associations; ||**the ~ races,** One and Two Thousand Guineas, Derby, Oaks, St. Leger. **2.** *n.* Classic writer, artist, work, example, garment, race, etc.; (in *pl.*) study of ancient Greek and Latin. **3.** ~**al** *a.* (-**lly**) of ancient Greek and Latin literature etc. (cf. CLASSIC), (of language) having form used by ancient standard authors (*classical Hebrew,* LATIN), (of music) serious or conventional, opp. *roman-*

*tic,* or *modern, popular*, etc., (Phys.) relating to concepts preceding relativity, quantum theory, etc.; ~**ăl'ĭtў** *n.*; ~**ĭsm** *n.*, following of classic style, classical scholarship, ancient Greek or Latin idiom; ~**ĭst** *n.*; ~**ĭze** *v.t.* & *i.*, make classical, imitate the classics. [F, or L *classicus* (prec.)]

**clăss'ĭfў** *v.t.* Arrange in classes; class; designate as officially secret or not for general disclosure; ~**ĭfĭcā'tion** *n.*; ~**ĭfĭcā'torў** *a.*; ~**ў** (-ah'-) *a.* (~**ily**, ~**iness**), (colloq.) superior, stylish. [CLASS]

**clăt'ter. 1.** *n.* Sound (as) of plates or wood struck together or falling; noisy talk. **2.** *v.i.* Make clatter; fall, move, etc., with clatter. [E]

**claus|e** (-z) *n.* Single statement in treaty, law, contract, etc.; (Gram.) distinct part of sentence, including subject and predicate; ~**'al** *a.* [F f. L *clausula* (CLOSE[1])]

**clau'stral.** See CLOISTER.

**claustrophō'b|ia** *n.* Morbid dread of confined places; ~**ĭc** *a.* (~**ically**), suffering from or inducing claustrophobia. [L (CLOISTER, -PHOBIA)]

**clă'vĭchŏrd** (-k-) *n.* (Hist.) Keyboard instrument, predecessor of piano; **clă'vĭcle** *n.*, collar-bone; **clavī'cŭlar** *a.* [L (*clavis* key)]

**claw. 1.** *n.* Pointed nail of animal's or bird's foot; foot armed with claws; pincers of shellfish; contrivance for grappling, holding, etc.; ~**-hammer** (with one side of head forked for extracting nails). **2.** *v.t.* Scratch or maul or pull with claws; scratch with finger-nails; ~ **back,** regain laboriously or gradually. [E]

**clay** *n.* Stiff tenacious earth, esp. used for making bricks, pottery, etc.; substance of the body; *clay* PIGEON[1]; ~ **(pipe),** tobacco-pipe made of clay; ~**'ey** *a.* [E]

**clay'more** *n.* (Sc. Hist.) Two-edged broadsword. [Gael., = great sword] **-cle.** See -CULE.

**clean** *a., adv., v.,* & *n.* **1.** *a.* (~**ness** *pr.* -n-n-). Free from dirt or contaminating matter, unsoiled; not having what is regarded as making defective or destroying original state; free from ceremonial defilement or disease; = CLEANLY[2]; (of children and animals) trained to defecate in proper place; shapely or well-formed; adroit, not bungling; clear--cut, complete; (colloq.) free from obscenity or impropriety; **come ~,**

(colloq.) confess. **2.** *adv.* Completely, outright, simply; in a clean manner. **3.** *v.t. & i.* Make or become clean; ~ **out**, clean thoroughly, empty or strip (esp., sl., person of his money); ~ **up**, make (things, oneself) clean or tidy, clear (mess) away, (colloq.) acquire as or make profit, (fig.) deal with disorder, immorality, crime, etc., in (place) (~**up**, act of doing this). **4.** *n.* Process of cleaning (*give it a clean*). **5.** clean BILL³ *of health*; ~ **bowled**, (Crick.) bowled directly, not off bat etc.; ~ **break** (quick and complete); MAKE *a clean breast of*; ~**cut**, sharply outlined; ~ **hands**, absence of guilt; ~**limbed**, well--proportioned, lithe; ~**living**, living morally; *clean pair of* HEEL¹*s*; ~**-shaven**, without beard, whiskers, or moustache; ~ **sheet, slate**, freedom from commitments or imputations; MAKE *a clean sweep of*. **6.** ~'**er** *n.*, (esp.) device for cleaning, person who cleans rooms or clothes (**take** person to the ~**ers**, sl., defraud or rob him of his money, criticize him strongly); ~**ly**¹ *adv.*, in a clean manner; ~**ly**² (-ĕ'n-) *a.* (-**ily, -iness**), habitually clean, attentive to cleanness; **cleanse** (-ĕnz) *v.t.*, make clean, purify (*of* sin etc.), (Bibl.) heal (leper etc.), (formal or arch.) make clean. [E]

**clear** *a., adv., & v.* **1.** *a.* Transparent; not clouded or turbid or spotted; distinct, unambiguous, intelligible, manifest; (of sight, hearing, mind) discerning, distinguishing, not confused; (of conscience) free from guilt; confident or feeling sure (*about, that*); net, without deduction, complete, (*a clear £1000*; *three clear days*); (of road etc.) unobstructed, open, (*the* COAST *is clear*); unhampered, free (*of* debts, engagements, etc.); **in the ~**, free of suspicion or difficulty. **2.** *adv.* Clearly (*speak loud and clear*); completely (*he got clear away*); apart, out of contact, (*stand clear*; STEER¹ *clear of*); \*all the way *to*. **3.** *v.t. & i.* Make or become clear; show or declare to be innocent (*of*); free from or *of* obstruction, suspicion, etc.; declare (person) fit to have secret information etc.; pass over or by without touching (esp. by jumping); pass (cheque) through clearing--house; pass through (customs office etc.); make (amount of money) as net gain or to balance expenses. **4.**

~ **away**, remove, remove remains of meal from table, (of mist etc.) disappear; ~**cut**, sharply defined; ~ **off**, get rid of, complete payment of (debt etc.), go away; ~ **out**, empty, go away, remove; ~**sighted(ness)**, sagacious, sagacity; ~ **soup** (containing little solid matter); ~ **the air**, (fig.) remove suspicion, tension, etc.; ~ **the decks**, (fig.) prepare for action; ~ **one's throat** (by slight coughing); ~ **up**, tidy up, solve (mystery etc.), (of weather) become fine; ||~'**way**, road on which vehicles must not stop; ~ **thing with**, get approval or authorization of it from (person). **5.** ~'**ance** *n.*, removal of obstructions etc., clearing of cheques, clearing of ship etc. at customs or certificate showing it, permission (esp. for aircraft to take off or land, or for person to have secret information etc.), space allowed for the passing of two objects or parts in machinery etc.; ~**ance sale** (to dispose of superfluous stock); ~'**ing** *n.*, (esp.) piece of land in forest cleared for cultivation; ~**ing bank**, member of ~**ing-house**, bankers' institution where cheques etc. are exchanged, so that only the balances need be paid in cash, (fig.) agency for collecting and distributing information etc. [F f. L *clarus*]

**cleat** *n.* Projecting piece of metal, wood, etc., on which ropes are fastened; projecting piece on spar, gangway, etc., to prevent slipping etc. [E]

**cleave**¹ *v.t. & i.* (CLOVE³, **cleft**; clo'ven, cleft). Split; chop, break, or come apart, esp. along grain or line of cleavage (**cleft palate**, congenital split in roof of mouth; **in a cleft stick**, in difficult position; **cloven hoof**, of ruminant or of Satan); make way through (water, air); **clea'vage** *n.*, way in which thing tends to split, division, (colloq.) hollow between woman's breasts; **clea'ver** *n.*, (esp.) butcher's tool for chopping. [E]

**cleave**² *v.i.* (arch.) Stick fast or adhere *to*; **clea'vers** (-z) *n.*, plant with prickly stem catching in clothes etc. [E]

**clef** *n.* (Mus.) Symbol showing pitch of staff (ALTO, BASS³ or F, TREBLE or G, *clef*). [F f. L *clavis* key]

**cleft**¹ *n.* Split, fissure. [E (CLEAVE¹)]

**cleft**². See CLEAVE¹.

**cle′matis** (or klemā′-) n. A climbing or erect flowering plant. [Gk]

**cle′men|t** a. Mild, esp. of weather; merciful; **~cy** n. [L *clemens*]

**cle′mentine** (or -ēn) n. Kind of small orange. [F]

**clench. 1.** v.t. Close (teeth, fingers) tightly; grasp firmly; clinch (nail etc.). **2.** n. Clenching action; clenched state. [E]

**cle′psydra** (or -sĭ′-) n. Ancient water-clock. [L f. Gk, = water-thief]

**cler′estory** (-ēr′s-) n. Upper wall of cathedral or large church, with series of windows, above aisle roof. [*clear storey*]

**cler′gy** n. (usu. treated as *pl.*) All persons ordained for religious duties, clergymen; **~man**, ordained minister, ‖esp. of Church of England; **cle′ric** n., clergyman; **cle′rical** a. (-lly), of clergy(man), of or made by clerk(s), (**clerical collar**, upright white collar fastening at back; **clerical error**, error in copying or writing out); **cle′ricalism, -ist,** ns. [F f. L (foll.)]

**clerk** (-ärk). **1.** n. Person employed to keep records or accounts, attend to correspondence, etc.; secretary, record-keeper, agent, of local council, court, etc.; *assistant in shop or hotel; lay officer of parish church etc.; (arch.) clergyman; **~ of the course**, judges' secretary etc. in horse or motor racing; **~ of the weather**, imaginary person supposed to control weather; **~ of (the) works**, overseer of building works etc. **2.** v.i. Work as clerk. **3.** **~′ly** a. (**~liness**), of clerks, good in penmanship, (arch.) scholarly; **~′ship** n. [E & F f. L f. Gk *klērikos* clerical]

**cle′ver** a. (**~er**, **~est**). Skilful, talented, quick to learn and understand; ingenious; adroit, dextrous; **~-clever**, ostentatiously (trying to be) clever; **~ Dick**, (colloq.) (would-be) clever person. [E]

**clew** (-ōō). **1.** n. Ball of thread or yarn, this as used in myth to guide through labyrinth; = CLUE. (Naut.) (loop attached to) lower or after corner of sail, cords supporting hammock. **2.** v.t. (Naut.) Haul *up* or let *down* (sail) in furling or unfurling. [E]

**cliché** (klē′shā) n. Hackneyed phrase or opinion. [F, = stereotype]

**click. 1.** n. Slight sharp sound, as of latch being dropped or billiard-balls meeting; catch in machinery. **2.** v.i. & t. Make click; (sl.) be successful or understood, become friendly *with* person, esp. of opposite sex. [imit.]

**cli′ent** n. Person using services of lawyer, architect, social worker, etc.; customer; **clientè′le** (klēon-) n., clients collectively, patrons of theatre etc. [L *cliens*]

**cliff** n. Steep rock-face, esp. on coast; **~hanger**, **~hanging**, (story etc.) with outcome excitingly uncertain. [E]

**clima′cteric** (or -ĕr′r-). **1.** a. Constituting a turning-point, critical; (Med.) of period of life when vital force begins to decline. **2.** n. Critical point or period in life, esp. supposedly occurring every 7 years. **3.** **climā′ctic** a. (-ically), of or constituting a climax. [F or L f. Gk (CLIMAX)]

**cli′mate** n. (Region with certain) weather characteristics; (fig.) prevailing trend of opinion or feeling in community or period (*climate of opinion*; *the political climate*); **climā′tic** a. (-ically); **climató′logy** n. [F or L f. Gk *klima*]

**cli′max. 1.** n. Event or point of greatest intensity or interest, culmination; sexual orgasm. **2.** v.i. & t. Reach or bring to a climax. [L f. Gk, = ladder]

**climb** (-m). **1.** v.t. & i. Ascend, mount, go *up*, esp. with use of one's hands; (of plant) grow up wall or other support by clinging etc.; rise by effort in social rank, intellectual powers, etc.; **~ down**, descend with use of hands, retreat from position taken up, admit defeat (**~-down**, such admission); **~′ing-frame**, structure of pipes etc. for children to climb on; **~′ing-iron**, spikes attachable to boot. **2.** n. Action of climbing; place (to be) climbed. **3.** **~′er** n., (esp.) mountaineer, climbing plant, social aspirant. [E]

**clime** n. (literary) Region, tract; climate. [L (CLIMATE)]

**clinch. 1.** v.i. & t. (Of boxers) come too close together to punch properly; (colloq.) embrace; confirm or settle (argument, bargain, etc.) conclusively; secure (nail etc.) by driving point sideways when through. **2.** n. Clinching; clinched state. **3.** **~′er** n., (esp.) argument etc. that clinches a matter; **~er-built,** = CLINKER[2]-built. [var. of CLENCH]

**cling** *v.i.* (**clung**). Maintain grasp, keep hold, resist separation; **~ to,** adhere to, hold on to (support etc.), be reluctant to give up (friend, habit, belief, etc.); **~('stone),** peach in which flesh adheres to stone. [E]

**cli'nic** *n.* Place or occasion for giving medical treatment or advice; private or specialized hospital; (class for) teaching of medicine at hospital bedside; **~al** *a.* (**-lly**), of or at the sick-bed (*clinical teaching*); **~al death,** death judged by observation of person's condition; **~al thermometer,** thermometer for taking patient's temperature, (fig.) objective, coldly detached. [L f. Gk (*klinē* bed)]

**clink[1]** *n.,* & *v.i.* & *t.* (Make, cause to make) sharp ringing sound. [Du.; imit.]

**clink[2]** *n.* (sl.) Prison (*in clink*). [orig. unkn.]

**cli'nker[1]** *n.* Mass of slag or lava; stony residue from burnt coal. [Du. (CLINK[1])]

**cli'nker[2]** *n.* **~-built,** (of boat) with external planks overlapping downwards and secured with clinched nails. [CLINCH]

**clip[1]. 1.** *v.t.* (**-pp-**). Grip tightly; fix with clip (*on, to*); **~-on** *a.,* attached by a clip. **2.** *n.* Appliance for holding things together, usu. worked by spring; piece of jewellery fastened by a clip; receptacle containing several joined cartridges for firearm; **~'board,** small board with spring clip to hold papers etc. [E]

**clip[2]. 1.** *v.t.* (**-pp-**). Cut (hair, wool, etc.) short with shears etc.; **~** person's **wings,** prevent or hinder him from acting etc.); trim hair etc. of (person, sheep, etc.); pare edge of (coin); remove small piece from (railway, bus, etc., ticket) to show that it has been used; *cut from newspaper etc.; omit (letter etc.); omit letters or syllables of (words pronounced); (colloq.) hit sharply; (sl.) swindle, rob. **2.** *n.* Action of clipping; yield of wool; extract from motion picture; sharp blow; (colloq.) speed, esp. rapid; **~-joint,** (sl.) club etc. charging exorbitant prices. **3.** **~'per** *n.,* (esp.) fast sailing-ship, (usu. in *pl.*) instrument for clipping hair; **~'ping** *n.,* (esp.) piece clipped off, *newspaper cutting. [N]

**clique** (-ēk) *n.* Exclusive set of associates; **cli'qu(e)y** (-ē'kĭ) *a.* [F]

**cli'toris** *n.* Small erectile part of female genitals. [L f. Gk]

**cloak. 1.** *n.* Long usu. sleeveless outdoor upper garment (**~-and--dagger,** involving intrigue and espionage); covering (*cloak of snow*); pretext (*under the cloak of charity*); **~'room,** room for temporary deposit of clothes or luggage, ‖(euphem.) lavatory. **2.** *v.t.* Cover or hide (as) with cloak. [F f. L (CLOCK)]

**clo'bber.** (sl.) **1.** *n.* Clothing, equipment. **2.** *v.t.* Hit, thrash; defeat; criticize severely. [orig. unkn.]

**clôche** (-sh) *n.* **~** (**hat**), woman's bell-shaped hat; (orig. bell-shaped) small translucent cover for outdoor plants. [F, = bell f. L (foll.)]

**clock[1]. 1.** *n.* Instrument, worked by springs, weights, electricity, etc., for measuring time and indicating hours, minutes, etc., by hands on a dial or by displayed figures (**against the ~,** so as to finish by a certain time; **o'clock** = of the clock, appended to hour: *six o'clock*; **put the ~ back,** fig., go back to a past age or outmoded practice; **round the ~, the ~ round,** for all 12 or 24 hours); clocklike device showing readings on dial; (colloq.) taximeter, speedometer, odometer, stop-watch; seed-head of dandelion; (sl.) person's face; **~ golf,** game in which golf-ball is putted into hole from successive points in a circle; **~--watcher,** one who waits eagerly for the end of the day's work; **~'wise,** (moving) in a curve in same direction as that taken by hands of a clock (**anti-** or **counter--~'wise,** in the opposite direction); **~'work,** mechanism on clock principle (**like ~work,** smoothly, with mechanical precision; (*attrib.*) mechanical, regular, precise. **2.** *v.i.* & *t.* Time (race) with stop-watch; (sl.) hit; **~ in, on,** register one's arrival at work by means of automatic clock; **~ off, out,** register departure similarly; **~** (**up**), (colloq.) attain or register (stated time, distance, or speed). [LDu. f. L *clocca* bell]

**clock[2]** *n.* Ornamental pattern on side of stocking or sock. [orig. unkn.]

**clod** *n.* Lump of earth, clay, etc.; **~'hopper,** bumpkin, lout, (colloq.) large heavy shoe; **~'dish** *a.,* loutish, foolish, clumsy. [var. of CLOT]

**clŏg. 1.** *n.* Wooden-soled shoe; (arch.) encumbrance; ~-**dance** (performed in clogs). **2.** *v.t. & i.* (-**gg**-). Impede; (cause to) become obstructed; choke *up*. [orig. unkn.]

**cloi′ster. 1.** *n.* Covered walk, usu. walled on one side and open to quadrangle on the other, esp. in convent, college, or cathedral; monastic house, life, or seclusion. **2.** *v.t.* (esp. in *p.p.*) Place or enclose in convent etc.; seclude, shelter. **3. clau′stral, cloi′stral**, *adjs.* [F f. L *claustrum* (CLOSE¹)]

**clŏn|e. 1.** *n.* Group of plants produced vegetatively from one original seedling or stock; group of organisms formed asexually from one ancestor; ~**al** *a.* (-**lly**). **2.** *v.t.* Propagate as clone. [Gk *klōn* twig]

**clōse¹** *a.*, *adv.*, & *n.* **1.** *a.* Near; in near relation or connection (*close friend, relative*); in or nearly in contact (*close combat, proximity*; **at ~ quarters**, very close together); fitting almost exactly (*close resemblance*); in which competitors are nearly equal (*close contest, election*); dense, compact, with no or only slight intervals, (*close formation, texture, writing*); leaving no gaps or weaknesses, rigorous, (*close confinement, reasoning*); concentrated, searching, (*close attention, examination*); closed, shut; limited to certain persons etc. (*close corporation*); hidden, secret, secretive, (**keep, lie, ~**, be in hiding); niggardly; (of air etc.) stifling, oppressively warm or humid; **~ call**, = *close shave*; ~-**-fisted**, niggardly; ~-**grained**, without gaps between fibres etc.; ~ **harmony** (in which parts composing chords are close together); ~-**hauled**, with sails hauled aft to sail close to wind; ‖~ **season**, period when something, esp. killing or catching of certain birds, fish, etc., is illegal; ~ **shave, thing**, (fig.) narrow escape from accident etc.; ~-**up**, photograph or film taken at short range, (fig.) intimate description. **2.** *adv.* Closely; in near position (*close to the* WIND¹); ~ **by, on, to**, very near to. **3.** *n.* Enclosed place; street closed at one end; ‖precinct of cathedral; ‖school playground. [F f. L *clausus* (*claudo* shut)]

**clōse²** (-z). **1.** *v.t. & i.* Shut (~ *one's eyes*, die, pay no attention *to*); declare or be declared no longer open for business (**clo′sing-time**,

time when public houses, shops, etc., stop business); bring or come to an end; finish speech etc. (often *with* final remark or act); bring or come closer or into contact (*close the ranks*); make (electric circuit etc.) continuous; ~**d book**, thing one does not understand; ~**d-circuit**, (of television) for restricted number of receivers with wires, not waves, for transmission; ~ **down**, (of shop, factory, etc.) close, esp. permanently; ~**d shop**, workshop or other establishment where only members of a trade union may be employed; ~ **in**, enclose, approach, (of days) get successively shorter; ~ **up**, move closer (*to*), shut (esp. temporarily), block up, (of aperture) grow smaller; ~ **with**, make bargain with, join battle or start fighting with. **2.** *n.* Conclusion, end. **3. clō′sĕt** (-z-) *n.*, private or small room, esp. for study or interviews, cupboard for special purpose, *cupboard, water-closet; **clō′sĕtĕd** (-z-) *a.*, in private consultation (*with*); **clō′sure** (-zher), (*n.*) closing, closed state, (Parl. etc.) closing of debate and putting of question forthwith by vote to that effect, (*v.t.*) apply closure to. [F f. L (prec.)]

**clŏt. 1.** *n.* Mass of material stuck together; semi-solid lump of coagulated liquid, esp. of blood; (sl.) stupid person. **2.** *v.i. & t.* (-**tt**-). Form into clots; ~**ted cream** (made by scalding milk). [E]

**clŏth** (or -aw-) *n.* (Piece of) woven or felted material; = TABLE-*cloth*; fabric, esp. woollen, for clothes; clerical status as shown by clothes (*respect due to his cloth*; **the ~**, clergy); ~ **binding**, book-cover of linen etc. cloth over cardboard; ~ **of gold, of silver**, fabric with gold or silver threads interwoven. [E]

**clōthes** (-dhz, -ōz) *n.pl.* Things worn to cover the body and limbs; = BED*clothes*; ~-**bag, -basket**, (for laundry linen); *clothes*-HANGER¹; ~-**-horse**, -line, frame or line on which clothes etc. are hung for drying or airing; ~-**moth** (with larva destructive to clothes); ‖~-**peg**, *~-**pin**, clip or forked device to hold clothes on clothes-line; ~-**post, -prop**, (supporting clothes-line); **clōthe** (-dh) *v.t.* (-**d**; arch., tech., formal **clad**), provide with clothes, put clothes upon, cover as with clothes;

**clō'thier** (-dh-) *n.*, seller of men's clothes; **clō'thing** (-dh-) *n.*, (esp.) clothes collectively.

**cloud. 1.** *n.* (Mass of) visible condensed watery vapour floating high above the earth (**with one's head in the ~s**, absent-minded(ly), fanciful(ly)); mass *of* smoke, dust, etc., in the air; great number *of* birds, insects, etc., moving together; frowning or discontented look (*on* brow or face); general feeling of suspicion, doubt, grief, etc., (**under a ~**, under suspicion, out of favour); **~'berry**, small mountain bramble; **~'burst**, sudden violent rainstorm; **~(cuckoo-)land**, fanciful or ideal realm. **2.** *v.t. & i.* Overspread or darken (as) with a cloud or clouds; become overcast or gloomy (*cloud over, up*). **3.** **~'y** *a.* (**~ily**, **~iness**), containing or full of clouds, lacking clearness. [E (CLOD)]

**clout. 1.** *n.* Heavy blow; (colloq.) influence, power of effective action, esp. in politics; patch; piece of cloth or clothing. **2.** *v.t.* Hit, esp. with open hand; mend with patch. [E]

**clōve**[1] *n.* Nail-shaped dried bud of tropical myrtle, used as flavouring; **~ gillyflower, pink**, clove-scented pink. [F f. L *clavus* nail]

**clōve**[2] *n.* One sector of bulb of garlic etc.; **clove**[3](n), see CLEAVE[1]; **~ hitch** (securing cord round spar or rope that it crosses at right angles). [E (CLEAVE[1])]

**clō'ver** *n.* Trefoil plant, used as fodder; **in ~**, in ease and luxury. [E]

**clown. 1.** *n.* Comic entertainer, esp. in circus; jester, joker; ignorant or boorish man; (*arch.*) rustic. **2.** *v.i.* Behave like a clown. [orig. uncert.]

**cloy** *v.t.* Satiate, esp. *with* sweetness. [obs. *acloy* f. AF (ENCLAVE)]

**club. 1.** *n.* Heavy stick with one thick end used as weapon etc. (INDIAN *club*); stick with head used in golf etc.; (Bot. etc.) structure with knob at end; playing-card of suit (**~s**) denoted by black trefoil; association of people united by common interest, usu. meeting periodically for shared activity (**in the ~**, sl., pregnant); body of persons united for social etc. purposes and having premises for members' use, these premises; group of persons, nations, etc., having something in common; **~-foot**, congenitally distorted foot; **~'house**, premises used by club;

**~-man**, member of one or more clubs; **~-moss** (with club-shaped spore-cases). **2.** *v.t. & i.* (**-bb-**). Strike (as) with club; combine *together* or *with* for joint action, making up sum of money, etc.; **~'bable** *a.*, fit for club membership, sociable. [N]

**clŭck** *n.*, & *v.i.* (Make) guttural cry of hen or click with tongue; = DUMB *cluck*. [imit.]

**clue** (-ōō). **1.** *n.* Guiding or suggestive fact or principle in problem or investigation (**not have a ~**, colloq., be ignorant or incompetent); piece of evidence etc. in detection of crime; word(s) used to indicate word(s) for insertion in crossword. **2.** *v.t.* Provide clue to; **~ in, up**, (sl.) inform. **3.** **~'less** *a.*, (esp., colloq.) ignorant, stupid. [var. of CLEW]

**clŭmp. 1.** *n.* Cluster *of* trees etc. **2.** *v.i. & t.* Tread heavily; form into clump; (colloq.) hit. [LDu.]

**clŭm'sy** (-zǐ) *a.* (**-ily**, **-iness**). Awkward in movement or shape; ill-contrived; tactless. [obs. *clumse* be numb with cold]

**clŭng.** See CLING.

**clŭs'ter. 1.** *n.* Close group or bunch of similar people, animals, or things, esp. such as grow together. **2.** *v.i. & t.* Be in, form into, cluster(s); gather (*a*)*round*. [E]

**clŭtch**[1]. **1.** *v.t. & i.* Seize eagerly, grasp tightly; snatch *at*. **2.** *n.* Tight grasp; (in *pl.*) grasping hands, cruel or relentless grasp; (Mech.) device for connecting or disconnecting working parts, e.g. motor vehicle engine and transmission, pedal operating this. [E]

**clŭtch**[2] *n.* Set of eggs; brood of chickens. [N, = hatch]

**clŭt'ter. 1.** *n.* Confused mass, untidy state, litter. **2.** *v.t.* Litter *with*; **~ up**, crowd untidily (*with*). [CLOT]

**cm** *abbr.* centimetre(s).

‖**Cmd.** *abbr.* COMMAND Paper.

‖**C.M.G.** *abbr.* Companion (of the Order) of St. Michael & St. George.

‖**Cmnd.** *abbr.* COMMAND Paper.

‖**C.N.D.** *abbr.* Campaign for Nuclear Disarmament.

**cō-** *pref.* meaning: (with *n.*) joint, mutual, common, (*co-author, coequality*); (with *a.* or *adv.*) jointly, mutually, (*co-belligerent, coequal, coequally*); (with *v.*) together with another or others (*co-operate*). [COM-]

**C.O.** *abbr.* Commanding Officer; conscientious objector.

**Co.** *abbr.* company; county; **and Co.** (-kō′), and other partners unnamed, (colloq.) and the rest.

**c/o** *abbr.* care of.

**coach. 1.** *n.* State or privately owned carriage; = STAGE-*coach*; railway carriage; single-decker bus chartered, or used for long journeys or tours; private tutor; instructor of athletic team etc.; ~-**house** (for carriages); ~′**man,** driver of horse--carriage; ~′**work,** bodywork of road or rail vehicle. **2.** *v.t. & i.* Instruct or tutor (pupil), esp. intensively or individually; train (crew etc. *for* race etc.); travel by coach. [F f. Magyar]

**coă′gŭl|āte** *v.i. & t.* (~**able**). Change from fluid to more or less solid state; clot, curdle; ~**ant** *n.,* coagulating agent (e.g. rennet); ~**ā′tion** *n.* [L (*coagulum* rennet)]

**coal. 1.** *n.* Hard black mineral, mainly carbonized plant matter, found below ground and used as fuel and in making gas, tar, etc.; ‖piece of this ready for burning in fire (~**s to Newcastle,** thing brought where already plentiful, unnecessary action; **haul, call, over the ~s,** reprimand; **heap ~s of fire on** person's **head,** cause him remorse by returning good for evil. [Prov. 25: 22]); ~-**black,** absolutely black; ~-**cellar,** basement storage-place for coal; ~-**face,** exposed surface of coal in mine; ~′**field,** area yielding coal; ~ **gas,** mixed gases extracted from coal and used for lighting and heating; ‖~-**hole,** small coal-cellar; ~′**man,** man who carries or delivers coal; ~ **measures,** (Geol.) seams of coal with intervening strata; ~-**mine** (in which coal is dug); ~′**mouse,** = *coal-tit;* ~-**scuttle,** receptacle for coal to supply fireplace; ~ **tar** (extracted from bituminous coal and yielding paraffin, naphtha, benzene, etc.); ~-**tit,** small greyish bird with dark head; ~′**ỹ** *a.* **2.** *v.t. & i.* Put coal into (ship etc.); take in supply of coal. [E]

**coălě′sce** *v.i.* Come together and form one whole; ~**nce** *n.;* ~**nt** *a.;* **coăli′tion** *n.,* fusion into one whole, ‖(Polit.) temporary combination between parties retaining distinctive principles. [L *alo* nourish]

**coa′ming** *n.* Raised border round ship's hatches etc. to keep out water. [orig. unkn.]

**coars|e** *a.* Common, inferior, (~**e fish,** ‖freshwater fish other than salmon and trout); rough, loose, or large in texture or make; lacking delicacy of perception, manner, or taste, unrefined, vulgar; (of language) obscene; ~′**en** *v.t. & i.,* make or become coarse.

**coast. 1.** *n.* Border of land near sea, sea-shore, (**the ~ is clear,** there is no chance of being hindered or observed); travel, usu. downhill, on bicycle without pedalling or in motor vehicle without using engine; ~′**guard,** (one of a) body of men employed to keep watch on coasts, prevent smuggling, etc.; ~′**line,** line of sea-shore esp. with regard to its shape. **2.** *v.i.* Sail along coast; ride, usu. downhill, without use of power; (fig.) make progress without exertion. **3.** ~′**al** *a.* (-lly); ~′**er** *n.,* (esp.) coasting vessel, tray or mat for bottle or glass; ~′**wise** (-z) *a. & adv.,* along coast. [F f. L *costa* side]

**coat. 1.** *n.* Outer garment fitting upper part of body, with sleeves, and often extending below the hips, jacket, overcoat, (CUT *coat according to cloth;* on person's ~-**tails,** undeservedly benefiting from or depending on his success, wealth, etc.; **trail** one's ~, act provocatively or defiantly); covering comparable to garment (membrane, layer of bulb, etc.); animal's hair or fur; covering of paint etc. laid on a surface at one time; ~ **armour,** heraldic arms; ~ **dress,** tailored dress resembling coat; *coat*-HANGER[1]; ~ **of arms,** person's or corporation's heraldic bearings or shield, herald's tabard; *coat of* MAIL[1]. **2.** *v.t.* Cover *with* a coat or layer; (of paint etc.) form a covering to. **3.** ~**ee′** *n.,* woman's or infant's short coat; ~′**ing** *n.,* (esp.) layer of paint etc. [F f. Gmc]

**cō-au′thor** *n., & v.t.* (Be) joint author (of ). [CO-]

**coax** *v.t.* Persuade gradually or by flattery (*to do, into* doing or good temper etc., *out of* ); get (thing) *out of* person thus; manipulate (thing) carefully or slowly. [obs. *cokes* a fool]

**coă′xial** *a.* (~**ly**). Having common axis; ~ **cable,** electric cable with several coaxial lines, a coaxial line; ~ **line,** electrical transmission line with two concentric conductors separated by insulator. [CO-]

**cŏb** *n.* Stout short-legged riding-

-horse; male swan; roundish lump of coal etc.; ~(**-nut**), large hazel--nut; round-headed loaf; CORN[1]-*cob*. [orig. unkn.]

**cŏ'balt** (-awlt, -ŏlt) *n.* Silvery--white metallic element; deep-blue colour (of pigment made from it). [G, prob. = *kobold* spirit in mines]

**cŏ'bber** *n.* (Austral. & N.Z. colloq.) Companion, mate, friend. [orig. uncert.]

**cŏ'bble**[1]. **1.** *n.* ~(**-stone**), small rounded stone used for paving. **2.** *v.t.* Pave with cobbles. [COB]

**cŏ'bble**[2] *v.t.* Mend or patch up (esp. shoes); put together roughly; **cŏ'bbler** *n.*, mender of shoes, clumsy workman. [orig. unkn.]

**cŏ'bra** *n.* Venomous hooded snake. [Port., f. L *colubra* snake]

**cŏ'bwĕb** *n.* Spider's network or thread; **blow away the ~s**, remove fustiness; **~'bed** (-bd), **~bў**, *adjs.* [*coppe* spider]

**cŏ'ca** *n.* S. Amer. shrub; its leaves chewed as stimulant; **cocai'ne** *n.*, drug from coca, used as local anaesthetic and as stimulant. [Sp. f. Quechua]

**cŏ'chĭneal** *n.* (Dried insects yielding) a scarlet dye. [F or Sp. f. L *coccinus* scarlet f. Gk *kokkos* kermes]

**cŏck**[1]. **1.** *n.* Male bird, esp. of domestic fowl (that **~ won't fight**, that argument etc. will not work); woodcock; male lobster, crab, or salmon; (**old**) ~ (vulg. form of address to man); ||(sl.) nonsense; tap, valve controlling flow; (vulg.) penis; lever in gun-lock that is raised so as to be released by trigger, cocked position, (**at half-~**, when not fully ready). **2.** *v.t.* Put in noticeably or significantly upright position; turn or move (eye or ear) attentively, knowingly, etc.; set aslant, turn up brim of, (hat; **~ed hat**, brimless triangular hat pointed at front, back, and top; **knock into a ~ed hat**, defeat utterly); raise cock of (gun). **3.** **~-a-doodle-doo**, cock's crow, childish name for cock; **~-a-hoop**, exultant; **~-a-leekie**, Sc. soup of cock boiled with leeks; **~-and-bull story** (incredible or absurd); *cock a* SNOOK; **~'chafer**, pale-brown loud-humming nocturnal beetle; **~-crow**, dawn; **~-eyed**, (sl.) squinting, crooked, absurd, drunk; **~-fight(ing)**, setting game-cocks to fight as sport; **~ of the**

walk, dominant person; **~'pit**, cock-fighting arena, site of battle(s), place for pilot etc. in aircraft or spacecraft, driver's seat in racing car; **~-shy,** object set up to be thrown at, a throw at this, (fig.) object of ridicule or criticism; **~ sparrow,** male sparrow, small lively person; **~sure'**, self-confident, dogmatic, absolutely sure; **~'tail**, drink of spirits with bitters etc., appetizer containing shellfish etc.; FRUIT *cocktail*; **~-up**, (sl.) mistake, muddle. [E & F]

**cŏck**[2] *n.* Small conical heap of hay etc. in field. [perh. Scand.]

**cockā'de** *n.* Rosette etc. worn in hat as badge of office etc. [F (COCK[1])]

**cockatoo'** *n.* Crested parrot. [Du. f. Malay]

**cŏ'ckboat** *n.* Ship's small boat. [orig. *cock* f. F]

**cŏ'cker** *n.* ~ (**spaniel**), small spaniel, orig. used in hunting woodcock etc. [COCK[1]]

**cŏ'ckerel** *n.* Young cock.

**cŏ'ckle**. **1.** *n.* An edible bivalve; its shell; bulge or wrinkle in paper etc.; **~s** of one's **heart**, one's feelings (*it warms the cockles of my heart*). **2.** *v.i.* & *t.* Wrinkle, pucker, shrivel, (paper, leather, etc.). [F *coquille* f. L f. Gk (CONCH)]

**cŏ'ckney** *n.* & *a.* (Of, characteristic of) native of London, esp. of the East End or speaking its dialect; this dialect; [*cokeney* 'cock's egg']

**cŏ'ckroach** *n.* Voracious dark--brown insect. [Sp.]

**cŏ'ckscŏmb** (-m) *n.* Cock's crest; a garden plant; cf. COXCOMB. [COCK[1]]

**cŏ'ckў** *a.* (-ily, -iness). Conceited, saucy.

**cō'cō** *n.* (*pl.* **~s**). A tropical palm-tree. [Sp. & Port., = grimace]

**cō'coa** *n.* Powder of crushed cacao seeds, often with other ingredients; (usu. hot) drink made from this; ~ **bean**, cacao seed; ~ **butter**, fatty substance got from this; **~nut,** = COCONUT. [CACAO]

**cō'conŭt** *n.* Large brown egg--shaped seed of coco, with edible white lining enclosing whitish liquid (~ **milk**); coco; ~ **matting** (made from fibre of coconut husks); ~ **shy**, fairground sideshow where balls are thrown to dislodge coconuts. [COCO]

**cocoo'n**. **1.** *n.* Silky case spun by larva, esp. of silkworm, to protect it as chrysalis; protective covering, esp. to prevent corrosion of metal equipment. **2.** *v.t.* Wrap or coat (as) in cocoon. [F f. Prov. (*coca* shell)]

**cocŏ'tte** *n.* Small fireproof dish for cooking and serving food. [F]

**cŏd¹** *n.* (*pl.* same). ~('fish), a large sea fish; ~-liver oil (used as source of vitamins A and D). [orig. unkn.]

**cŏd²** *v.t.* & *i.* (-dd-), & *n.* (sl.) Hoax; parody. [orig. unkn.]

**cŏd³** *n.* (sl.) Nonsense. [abbr. of CODS(WALLOP)]

**C.O.D.** *abbr.* cash on delivery.

**cŏ'da** *n.* (Mus.) Final passage of piece of music, usu. elaborate or distinct. [It. f. L *cauda* tail]

**cŏ'ddle** *v.t.* Treat as an invalid, keep from cold and exertion, pamper; feed *up*; cook (egg) lightly. [*caudle* gruel f. F f. L (*calidus* warm)]

**code. 1.** *n.* Systematic set of laws etc.; prevalent morality of a society or class; person's standard of moral behaviour; system of signals, esp. used to ensure secrecy; system of letter, figure, or word groups or symbols for brevity or secrecy, or for machine processing of information; ~-book, list of symbols etc. used in code; ~-name, -number, word or symbol, number, used for secrecy etc. instead of ordinary name. **2.** *v.t.* Put (message etc.) into code. **3.**

**cŏ'dĭfy** *v.t.*, arrange (laws etc.) into a code; **cŏdĭfĭca'tion** *n.*; **cŏ'dĕx** *n.* (*pl. codices pr.* kŏ'dĭsēz), manuscript volume, esp. of ancient texts, collection of descriptions of medicines etc. [F f. L *codex* book]

**cŏ'deine** (-dēn, -dīen) *n.* Alkaloid got from opium, used as analgesic and hypnotic. [Gk *kōdeia* poppy-head]

**cŏ'dĕx.** See CODE.

**cŏ'dger** *n.* (colloq.) Fellow; strange person. [orig. uncert.]

**codices.** See CODE.

**cŏ'dĭcĭl** *n.* Supplement modifying, revoking, or explaining a will. [L (CODE)]

**cŏdĭfĭca'tion, cŏ'dĭfy.** See CODE.

**cŏ'dlĭn(g¹)** *n.* Cooking apple of tapering shape. [AF *quer de lion* lion-heart]

**cŏ'dlĭng²** *n.* Small codfish. [COD¹]

**cŏ'dpiece** *n.* (Hist.) Bagged appendage to front of man's breeches. [*cod* scrotum]

**cŏ'ds(wallop)** (-dzwŏ'-) *n.* (sl.) Nonsense. [orig. unkn.]

**cŏĕdūca'tion** *n.* Education of people of both sexes together; ~al *a.*; **cŏ'ĕd** *n.*, (colloq.) female student at coeducational institution. [CO-]

**cŏĕffĭ'cient** (-shent) *n.* (Alg.) quantity placed before and multiplying another quantity; (Phys.) multiplier or factor that measures some property (*coefficient of expansion, of friction*). [L (CO-)]

**coe'lacanth** (sē'l-) *n.* Kind of fish extinct but for one species. [L f. Gk *koilos* hollow, *akantha* spine]

**coe'nŏb|ite** (sē'n-), *\*cē'n-,* *n.* Member of monastic community; ~ĭ'tĭc(al) *adjs.* (-ically). [F or L f. Gk (*koinos bios* common life)]

**cŏē'qual** *a.* (~ly) & *n.* (arch., literary) Equal. [L (CO-)]

**cŏēr'|ce** *v.t.* (~cible). Constrain or force *into* obedience etc.; ~cion (-shon) *n.*, act of coercing, government by force; ~cĭve *a.* [L *coerceo* restrain]

**cŏē'val** *a.* (~ly) & *n.* (Person) of same age, existing at same epoch; **cŏēvă'lĭtў** *n.* [L *aevum* age]

**cŏĕxĭ'st** (-gz-) *v.i.* Exist together (*with*); ~ence *n.*, (esp.) mutual tolerance of nations professing different ideologies etc.; ~ent *a.* [CO-]

**cŏĕxtĕ'nsĭve** *a.* Extending over same space or time.

**C. of E.** *abbr.* Church of England.

**cŏ'ffee** (-fĭ) *n.* A shrub; its seeds or a powder made from them after roasting; (usu. hot) drink made from this; cupful of, light refreshments including, this drink; light brown colour; ~ bar, café serving coffee and light refreshments; ~-bean (seed); ~-break, interval from work when coffee is drunk; ~-mill (for grinding coffee-beans); ~ morning, morning gathering at which coffee is drunk; *\*~ shop*, small restaurant; ~-table, small low table (~-*table book*, large expensive illustrated book). [Turk. f. Arab.]

**cŏ'ffer** *n.* Box for valuables; (in *pl.*) funds, treasury; recessed panel in ceiling etc.; ~(-dam), caisson for bridge-building etc. [F f. L *cophinus* basket f. Gk]

**cŏ'ffĭn. 1.** *n.* Box in which corpse is buried or cremated. **2.** *v.t.* Put in coffin. [F f. L f. Gk (prec.)]

**cŏg** *n.* One of set of projections on edge of wheel or bar transferring motion by engaging with another set; (fig.) unimportant member of organization etc.; **~-wheel** (with cogs). [prob. Scand.]

**cō′gen|t** *a*. (Of reasoning etc.) convincing; **~cȳ** *n*. [L (*cogo* drive)]

**cŏ′git|āte** *v.i.* & *t*. Ponder, meditate; **~ā′tion, ~ātor,** *ns*.; **~ative** *a*.

**cŏ′gnac** (kŏ′nyăk) *n*. French brandy. [place]

**cŏ′gnāte. 1.** *a*. Descended from common ancestor (cf. AGNATE); akin (*with*), related (*to*); (Philol.) of same linguistic family or derivation; **~ object,** (Gram.) object whose meaning is not distinct from that of its verb (e.g. in *he lived the* life *and died the* death *of a Christian*). **2.** *n*. Relative; cognate word. [L *cognatus*]

**cŏgnī′tion** *n*. Knowing, perceiving, or conceiving as an act or faculty distinct from emotion and volition; result of this; **~al (-lly), cŏ′gnĭtive,** *adjs*. [L *cognitio* (foll.)]

**cŏ′gnizance** (or kŏ′n-) *n*. Being aware, notice, (**take ~ of,** notice, attend to); sphere of observation or concern or competence; distinctive device or mark; **cŏ′gnĭzant** (or kŏ′n-) *a*., having cognition. [F f. L *cognosco* get to know]

**cŏgnō′mĕn** *n*. Nickname; (Rom. Ant.) third name (Marcus Tullius *Cicero*), or fourth name as personal epithet (Publius Cornelius Scipio *Africanus*). [L]

**cognoscent|e** (kŏnyōshĕ′nti) *n*. (*pl.* **~i** *pr.* **-ē,** same). Connoisseur. [It.]

**cōhă′bit** *v.i.* Live together as husband and wife (usu. of unmarried couple); **~ā′tion** *n*. [L (*habito* dwell)]

**cōhēr′e** *v.i.* Stick together, remain united; (of reasoning, style, etc.) be consistent or well-knit; **~nt** *a*., sticking together, consistent, easily understood, (of radiation) able to interfere with other radiation because their phase difference is constant; **~nce** *n*.; **cōhē′sion** (-zhon) *n*., force with which parts cohere, tendency to cohere; **cō-hē′sive** *a*. [L (*haereo haes-* stick)]

**cŏ′hŏrt** *n*. Tenth part of Roman LEGION; (in *pl*., rhet.) troops; league or band *of*. [F or L]

**coif** *n*. (Hist.) Close-fitting cap; *coiffeur* (kwahfēr′) *n*. (*fem. coiffeuse pr.* **-ēr′z**), hairdresser; *coiffure* (kwahfūr′) *n*., arrangement of hair. [F]

**coign** (koin) *n*. **~ of vantage,** place affording good view. [COIN]

**coil. 1.** *v.t.* & *i*. Arrange (rope etc.) in concentric rings; twist (*up*) into circular or spiral shape; move sinuously. **2.** *n*. Coiled length of rope etc.; coiled arrangement; single turn of coil; flexible loop as contraceptive device in womb; (Electr.) coiled wire for passage of current. [F f. L (COLLECT²)]

**coin. 1.** *n*. Piece of stamped metal money (**other side of the ~,** fig., opposite view of a matter); metal money (**false ~,** counterfeit money, fig. anything spurious; **pay** person **in his own ~,** reciprocate his action); **~-box,** (receptacle for coins in) telephone operated by inserting coins. **2.** *v.t.* Make (money) by stamping metal (**~ money,** fig., get money quickly); make (metal) into money; invent (new word etc.). **3.** **~′age** *n*., coining, coins, system of coins in use, invention of new word, word so invented; **~′er** *n*., (esp.) ‖maker of counterfeit money. [F f. L *cuneus* wedge]

**cŏïnci′de** *v.i.* Fill same portion of space or time; agree or be identical (*with*); concur in opinion etc.; **cŏï′ncidence** *n*., coinciding, notable concurrence of events or circumstances without apparent causal connection; **cŏï′ncident** *a*., coinciding; **cŏïncidĕ′ntal** *a*. (-lly), of (nature of) coincidence. [L (INCIDENT)]

**coir** (koi′er) *n*. Coconut fibre, used for ropes, matting, etc. [Malayalam *kāyar* cord]

**cōï′tion, cō′ĭtus,** *n*. Sexual intercourse; **coitus interru′ptus** (in which penis is withdrawn before ejaculation); **cō′ĭtal** *a*. [L *coitio, coitus* (*eo* go)]

**cōke¹** *n*., & *v.t.* (Convert into) solid substance left after heating coal. [dial. *colk* core]

**cōke²** *n*. (sl.) Cocaine. [abbr.]

**cŏl** *n*. Depression in mountain-chain. [F f. L *collum* neck]

**col-.** See COM-.

**Col.** *abbr.* Colonel; Colossians (N.T.).

**col.** *abbr.* column.

**cō′la, kō′la,** *n*. W. Afr. tree; its seed as tonic etc.; carbonated drink flavoured with this. [W. Afr.]

**co′lander** (kŭ′-) *n*. Perforated vessel used as strainer in cookery. [L *colo* strain]

**cŏ′lchĭcum** (or -kĭ-) *n*. Meadow saffron or similar plant; dried part of it, used as medicine. [*Colchis*, place]

**cŏld. 1.** *a.* Of or at low temperature; not heated, having lost heat; feeling cold; dead; lacking ardour, affection, or geniality; undemonstrative, apathetic (LEAVE² person *cold*); depressing, dispiriting, uninteresting, (*cold facts, news*); (of colour) suggestive of cold sunless day; (of scent in hunting) grown faint; (colloq.) at one's mercy; (sl.) unconscious. **2.** *n.* Prevalence of low temperature (**leave** person **out in the** ~, ignore, neglect); cold condition; catarrh of nose or throat or both (esp. *common cold, cold in the head*). **3.** *cold* BLOOD; ~**-blooded,** (of fish etc.) having blood temperature varying with that of environment, (of person etc.) callous or sluggish; *cold* CHISEL; ~ **comfort,** poor consolation; *cold* CREAM; ~ **feet,** fear or cowardice; ~ **frame** (unheated for growing small plants); ~ **meat,** cooked meat allowed to become cold; ~ **shoulder,** (fig.) intentionally unfriendly treatment; *cold* SNAP, STEEL; ~ **storage,** storage in refrigerator, (fig.) state of abeyance; *cold* SWEAT, TURKEY¹; ~ **war,** unfriendly relations between nations (esp. U.S.S.R. and West after Second World War), with hostile propaganda but no fighting; ~ **water** *n.*, (fig.) depreciation or discouragement (*throw* etc. ~ *water on*, disparage, discourage). [E]

**cōle** *n.* Cabbage (usu. in *comb.*); ~**-seed,** rape, plant yielding oil; ~**-slaw** [Du.], salad of sliced raw cabbage. [N f. L *caulis* stem]

**cŏlĕŏ'pter|ous** *a.* Of the order Coleoptera (beetles, weevils), with front wings serving as sheaths; ~**ĭst** *n.,* one who studies beetles. [L f. Gk (*koleon* sheath, *pteron* wing)]

**cŏ'lic** *n.* Griping pain in belly; -**kў** *a.;* **coli'tĭs** *n.,* inflammation of lining of colon. [F f. L (COLON¹)]

**cŏllǎ'bor|āte** *v.i.* Work jointly (*with*), esp. at literary or artistic production; co-operate traitorously with enemy; ~**ā'tion,** ~**ātor,** *ns.* [L (LABOUR)]

**cŏlla'ge** (-ah'zh) *n.* Form or work of art in which objects are glued to a backing to form a picture. [F, = gluing]

**cŏ'llagėn** *n.* Protein found in bone, tendons, etc., yielding gelatin on boiling. [F f. Gk *kolla* glue]

**cŏlla'ps|e. 1.** *n.* Tumbling down or falling in of a structure; total failure of plan etc.; physical or mental breakdown. **2.** *v.i.* & *t.* Undergo collapse; cause to collapse; fold up; ~**ible** *a.,* (of boat, chair, etc.) folding. [L (*labor laps-* slip)]

**cŏ'llar. 1.** *n.* Neckband, upright or turned over, of coat, shirt, etc.; band round animal's (esp. dog's) neck; (**horse-**)~, roll round draught-horse's neck bearing stress; collar-shaped piece in machine etc.; ~**-bone** (joining breastbone and shoulder-blade); *\**~**-button,** ‖~**-stud,** device for fixing separate collar to shirt. **2.** *v.t.* Seize by collar, lay hold of, (person); (sl.) take, esp. illicitly. [AF f. L (*collum* neck)]

**cŏlla'te** *v.t.* Compare in detail (copies or texts, one copy etc. *with* another); put together (esp. information); gather and put in order; ~**or** *n.* [L (CONFER)]

**cŏlla'teral. 1.** *a.* (~**ly**). Side by side; subordinate but from same source; connected but aside from main subject, course, etc.; (of descent) from same stock but by different line; (of facts etc.) indirectly contributory to conclusion; ~ **security,** property pledged as guarantee for repayment of money. **2.** *n.* Collateral person or security. [L (LATERAL)]

**cŏlla'tion** *n.* Collating; light meal, esp. at unusual time (*cold collation*). [F f. L (CONFER)]

**cŏ'lleague** (-g) *n.* Fellow official or worker, esp. in a profession or business. [F f. L *collega* (LEGATE)]

**cŏ'llĕct¹** (*or* -ĭkt) *n.* Short prayer of Anglican or R.C. Church, esp. one assigned to particular day or season. [F f. L *collecta* (foll.)]

**cŏllĕ'ct².** *v.t.* & *i.* Assemble, accumulate, bring or come together; (colloq.) call for, fetch; get (contributions, tax, etc.) from a number of people; obtain (books, stamps, etc.) for addition to others, esp. as hobby; regain control of, concentrate, recover (one*self*, one's thoughts, courage, etc.); (in *p.p.*) not perturbed or distracted; ~**ion** *n.,* collecting, collecting of money at meeting or church service, sum so collected, regular emptying of letter-box, accumulation (*of*), a set of collected things. [F or L (*lego lect-* pick)]

**collĕ′ctĭve. 1.** *a.* Collecting many into one, compound; representing or including many; combined, aggregate, common; ~ **bargaining**, negotiation of wages etc. by organized body of employees; ~ **farm**, jointly-operated amalgamation of several smallholdings; ~ **noun**, singular noun denoting group of individuals, e.g. *bunch, family, flock*; ~ **ownership** (by all for common benefit). **2.** *n.* Collective enterprise or noun. **3. collĕ′ctĭvĭsm** *n.*, collective ownership of land, means of production, etc., as social theory; **collĕ′ctĭvĭst** *n.*; **collĕ′ctĭvĭze** *v.t.*; **collĕ′ctor** *n.*, (esp.) one who collects taxes, debts, etc., one who collects books, stamps, etc. (**collector's piece**, thing of interest to collectors for its beauty, rarity, etc.).

**collee′n** *n.* (Ir.) Girl. [Ir. *cailín*]

**cŏ′llège** *n.* Organized body of persons with shared functions and privileges (‖**Heralds' C~, C~ of Arms**, recording lineage and granting arms); ‖corporation of scholars in university; small university; place of higher or professional education; ‖public school; private school; buildings of college (*he lives in college*); ~ **pudding**, small plum pudding for one person; **collē′gian** *n.*, member of college; **collē′giate** *a.*, of or constituted as a college (**collegiate church**, church endowed for a chapter but without a see). [F or L (COLLEAGUE)]

**collī′de** *v.i.* Come into collision or conflict (*with*). [L *collido -lis-* clash]

**cŏ′llie** *n.* Sheep-dog orig. of Sc. breed. [perh. f. *coll* COAL]

**cŏ′llier** (-yer) *n.* Coal-miner; coal-ship, member of its crew; ~**y** *n.*, coal-mine and its buildings. [COAL]

**collī′sion** (-zhon) *n.* Violent striking of moving body against another, or against a fixed object; clashing of opposed interests etc.; ~ **course**, course or action bound to cause collision (lit. or fig.); **come into ~ with**, crash into, clash with; **in ~**, involved in collision. [L (COLLIDE)]

**cŏ′lloc|āte** *v.t.* Place (esp. words) together; arrange; set in particular place; ~**ā′tion** *n.* [L (LOCUS)]

**cŏ′llocūtor** *n.* One's partner in colloquy. [COLLOQUY]

**cŏ′lloid** *n.* Substance in non-crystalline state, with large molecules; **colloi′dal** *a.* [Gk *kolla* glue)]

**cŏ′llop** *n.* Slice of meat. [Scand.]

**collō′quial** *a.* (~**ly**). In or of talk, belonging or proper to ordinary or familiar conversation, not formal or literary; ~**ism** *n.*, colloquial word or phrase, use of these; **collō′quium** *n.* (*pl.* **-ia**), academic conference or seminar; **cŏ′lloquy** *n.*, talk, a conversation. [L (*loquor* speak)]

**collū′sion** (-zhon; *or* -lōō′-) *n.* Fraudulent secret understanding, esp. between ostensible opponents; **collu′sive** (-ōō′-) *a.* [F or L (*ludo lus-* play)]

**cŏ′llywŏbbles** (-belz) *n.pl.* (colloq.) Ache or rumbling in stomach; apprehensive feeling. [COLIC, WOBBLE]

**Colo.** *abbr.* Colorado.

**colō′gne** (-ō′n) *n.* Eau-de-Cologne; toilet water. [abbr.]

**cŏ′lon¹** (*or* -ŏn) *n.* (Anat.) Greater part of large intestine; **colō′nic** *a.* [F or L f. Gk]

**cŏ′lon²** *n.* Punctuation-mark (:). [L f. Gk, = clause]

**colonel** (ker′nel) *n.* Highest regimental officer; = *lieutenant-colonel*; ~**cy** *n.* [F f. It. *colonello* (COLUMN)]

**colō′nial** *a.* & *n.* (Native, inhabitant) of colony or colonies; ~**ism** *n.*, policy of having colonies, esp. (derog.) alleged policy of exploiting colonies; ~**ist** *n.*; **cŏ′lonist** *n.*, settler in or inhabitant of colony; **cŏ′lonize** *v.t.* & *i.*, establish colony (in); **cŏlonizā′tion** *n.* [COLONY]

**colonnā′de** *n.* Series of columns with entablature. [F (COLUMN)]

**cŏ′lony** *n.* Settlement or settlers in new country forming community fully or partly subject to the State from which they have emigrated; their territory; group of one nationality, occupation, etc., esp. living more or less in isolation; group of animals etc. that live close together. [L *colonia* farm]

**cŏ′lophon** *n.* Tailpiece in MS. or book, giving writer's or printer's name, date, etc.; publisher's emblem on title-page. [L f. Gk, = summit]

**\*color.** See COLOUR.

**Cŏlora′do** (-rah′-) *n.* ~ **beetle**, striped beetle or its larva destructive to potato plant. [place]

**colorā′tion** (kŭ-) *n.* Disposition of colour(s). [F or L (COLOUR)]

**cŏloratū′a** (*or* -toor′a) *n.* Florid passages in vocal music; singer of these, esp. soprano. [It. (COLOUR)]

**colori′mĕter** (kŭ-) n. Instrument for measuring intensity of colour. [COLOUR]

**colŏ′ss│us** n. (pl. ∼i pr. -ī, ∼uses). Statue of much more than life size; gigantic person or personified power, esp. conceived as standing astride over subjects etc.; ∼′al a. (-lly), of or like colossus, huge, (colloq.) splendid or glorious. [L f. Gk]

**colŏ′(s)tomў** n. (Surg.) Operation of making incision in colon (colostomy to give artificial anus). [COLON¹]

**co′lour**, *color, (kŭ′ler). 1. n. Sensation produced in eye by rays of light when resolved by prism etc.; a particular hue; one, or any mixture, of the constituents into which light can be separated as in spectrum or rainbow, sometimes including (loosely) white and black (primary ∼s, red, green, violet, or for pigments red, blue, yellow, giving all other colours by mixture; secondary ∼, mixture of two primary colours); (Photog. etc.) use of all colours, not just black and white; (dark) skin pigmentation, esp. as reason for discrimination, prejudice, etc.; ruddiness of face (a good colour; has no colour; OFF colour); (in pl.) appearance or aspect (see things in their true colours); (Art) colouring, pigment, paint; (in pl.) flag of regiment or ship (nail one's ∼s to the mast, refuse to give in; sail under false ∼s, be hypocrite or impostor; show one's (true) ∼s, reveal true character or intentions; TROOPING the colour; come through with flying ∼s, very successfully; with the ∼s, serving in the armed forces); (in pl.) coloured ribbon, rosette, dress, etc., worn as symbol of (membership of) school, club, team, party, etc.; show of reason, pretext, (lend colour to; under colour of); quality, mood, variety, etc., in music, literature, etc., (LOCAL colour); ∼ bar, distinction or discrimination between white and non-white persons; ∼-blind, unable to distinguish certain colours; ∼ code, use of colours as standard means of identification; ∼ scheme, arrangement of colours in room-decoration etc.; ∼-sergeant, senior sergeant of infantry company. 2. v.t. & i. Give colour to; paint, stain, dye; imbue with its own character (emotion colours your judgement); misrepresent, exaggerate, (he colours his

facts); take on colour; ∼ (up), blush. 3. ∼able a. (-bly), plausible, specious, counterfeit; ∼ed (-erd) a. & n., (person) wholly or partly of non-white descent, or (in S. Afr.) of mixed black or brown and white descent; ∼ful a., full of colour or interest, vivid; ∼ing n., (esp.) coloration, substance giving colour, artist's use of colour, facial complexion; ∼ist n., artist skilful in use of colour; ∼less a., (fig.) lacking character or vividness. [F f. L color]

**cŏlt¹** n. Young male horse; inexperienced person, esp. young cricketer etc. in junior team; ∼′sfoot, large-leaved yellow-flowered weed. [E]

**Cŏlt²** n. Type of automatic firearm, esp. repeating pistol. [P; person]

*cŏ′lter. See COULTER.

**cŏ′lumbine** n. Garden plant with flower like five clustered pigeons. [F f. L (columba pigeon)]

**cŏ′lumn** (-m) n. Pillar of circular section, esp. one with base and capital; column-shaped object; vertical cylindrical mass of liquid or vapour; vertical division of page in printed matter (our, these, etc., ∼s, contents of this newspaper); part of newspaper devoted to particular subject, by one regular writer, etc. (GOSSIP, PERSONAL, column); narrow-fronted deep arrangement of troops, vehicles, etc., in successive lines (dodge the ∼, colloq., shirk duty, avoid work; FIFTH column); ∼ar (-mn-) a.; ∼ist (or -mn-) n., journalist who contributes regularly to a newspaper. [F & L]

**com-, co-, col-** (bef. l), **con-, cor-** (bef. r), pref. = 'with', 'together', 'altogether'. [L com-, cum with]

**cŏ′ma** n. Unnatural heavy sleep, prolonged unconsciousness; ∼tōse a., in or like coma. [L f. Gk]

**cŏmb** (-m). 1. n. Toothed strip of rigid material for arranging, cleaning, or confining the hair; part of machine having similar shape or purpose; red fleshy crest of fowl esp. cock; honeycomb. 2. v.t. & i. Draw comb through (hair); curry (horse); dress (wool etc.) with comb; (of wave) curl over; (colloq.) search (place) thoroughly; ∼ out, disentangle or arrange (hair) with comb; ∼′ing n., (esp., in pl.) hairs combed off. [E]

**cŏ′mbăt.** 1. n. Battle or contest

(single ~, duel). **2.** *v.t.* & *i.* Engage in combat (with); oppose or strive against; **cŏ′mbatant** *a.* & *n.*, (person) that fights; **cŏ′mbative** *a.*, pugnacious. [F f. L (BATTLE)]

‖**combe**. See COOMB.

**cŏmbĭnā′tion** *n.* Combining; combined state; combined set of persons or things; small instrumental band; united action; (Chem.) union of substances in compound whose properties differ from theirs; ‖motor cycle with side-car attached; ‖(in *pl.*) single undergarment for body and legs; sequence of numbers etc. used to open ~ **lock** (locking arrangement used for safes, strong--rooms, etc.); ‖~**-room**, (Cambridge Univ.) common-room; **cŏ′mbinative** *a.* [F or L (*bini* pair)]

**combine. 1.** (-ī′n) *v.t.* & *i.* Unite for common purpose, join together; possess (qualities) in combination; form into chemical compound; co--operate; ~**d operation** (in which the fighting services, or others, combine); **combining form**, (Gram.) form of word used in combinations (e.g. *Anglo-* repr. *English*). **2.** (kŏ′m-) *n.* Combination of persons or firms to control prices etc.; **combine (harvester)**, combined reaping and threshing machine.

**combŭ′stible** *a.* & *n.* (Substance or thing) capable of or used for burning; **combŭstibi′lity** *n.*; **combŭ′stion** (-schon) *n.*, development of light and heat with chemical combination, consumption by fire. [F or L *comburo -ust-* burn up]

**come** (kŭm) *v.i.* (**came; come**). Move or be brought towards, or reach, a place, time, situation, or result, (*come and see me; it came to my attention; you'll come to no harm; have come to believe it; it comes expensive; time will come when you will regret it;* **not know whether** one is **coming or going**, be utterly confused); (colloq., in *subj.*) ~ **Friday** etc., when Friday etc. comes; be available (*this dress comes in three sizes;* **as tough** etc. **as they ~**, supremely); become perceptible (*church came into sight; news comes as a surprise*); reach or extend to specified point (*motorway comes within ten miles of us*); occur, happen, take or occupy specified position, (*how did you come to break your leg?; it comes on the third page;*

have it coming to one, colloq., deserve what one suffers; **how ~?**, colloq., how did that happen?; **to** ~ *pred. a.*, future: *in the years to come*); become (*the handle came loose*); traverse, accomplish, (*have come 5 miles, a long way*); (colloq.) play the part of, behave like, (*don't come the bully with me*); (vulg.) have sexual orgasm; (in *imper.*) excl. of mild protest or remonstrance (freq. *come, come* or *come, come, now*) or of encouragement; ~ **about,** happen; ~ **across,** meet or find by chance, (sl.) be received or effectively communicated, (sl.) hand over money etc.; ~ **again,** make second effort, (as *imper.*, colloq.) what did you say?; ~ **along,** move forward, arrive, (in *imper.*, colloq.) hurry; ~ **and go,** pass to and fro, be transitory; ~ **at,** reach, get access to, attack; ~ **away,** become detached, be left *with* (impression etc.); ~ **back,** return, recur to memory; ~-*back*, return to former position, (colloq.) retort or retaliation; ~ **before,** be dealt with by (judge etc.); ~ **between,** separate, interfere with relationship of; ~ **by,** pass by, obtain; ~ **clean,** (colloq.) confess; ~ **down,** come to lower place, fall, be handed down by tradition, decide (*in favour of* etc.), amount basically *to*, be humbled (esp. ~ *down in the world*, lose social status); ~-*down n.*, downfall, degradation; ~ **down on,** pounce on, rebuke, punish; ~ **down with,** begin to suffer from (disease); ~ **forward,** advance, offer oneself for task, post, etc.; ~-**hi′ther** *a.*, enticing, flirtatious; *come* HOME *to*; ~ **in,** enter (*this is where we came in,* we are back to where we started; (Crick.) begin innings, finish *first* etc. in race etc., be elected, be received esp. as income, begin speaking esp. in radio transmission, become seasonable or fashionable, have a place or function; ~ **in for,** receive, get *share of*; ~ **in handy, useful,** be useful; ~ **in on,** join (enterprise etc.); ~ **into,** enter, be brought into (collision, prominence, force.), receive esp. as heir; ~ **it over,** (sl.) attempt to dominate or get the better of (person); ~ **it strong,** (sl.) behave vigorously or excessively; ~ **of,** be the result of, be descended from; *come of* AGE; ~ **off,** be detached or detachable (from), fare (*badly, well,* etc.), succeed, occur; ~ **off it**, (colloq.) stop talking or behaving like that; ~ **on**, (prep.) = *come upon*, (adv.) continue coming, advance esp. to attack, progress, thrive, begin, be seen or heard on television, telephone, etc., appear on stage etc., arise to be discussed, (in *imper.*) hurry, follow me, please do what I ask, I defy you; ~*on* n., (sl.) lure; ~ **out**, emerge, appear, go on strike, emerge from examination etc. with specified result, declare oneself (*for, against*, etc.), be satisfactorily visible in photograph, be solved, (of stains etc.) be removed, become covered *in* (rash etc.), be published, make début on stage or in society; ~ **out with**, say; ~ **over**, come from distance or across obstacle, change sides or opinion, (of feeling etc.) overtake or affect (person), (colloq.) feel suddenly (*come over faint*); ~ **round**, pay informal visit, (of date) recur, recover normal state esp. consciousness, be converted to other person's opinion; *come SHORT of*; ~ **to**, (prep.) reach, approach, return to (one*self* or one's *senses*, from unconsciousness, folly, etc.), inherit, become, be assigned to, amount or be equivalent to (*come to* NOTHING; ~ or **if it** ~s **to that**, if that is the case, in fact), (adv.) cease moving, regain consciousness; ~ **to a head**, reach climax; (**if you**) ~ **to think of it**, (colloq.) on reflection; *come* TRUE; ~ **under**, be classed among, be subject to (influence etc.); ~ **up**, come to higher place, arise, come to university, present itself, be mentioned or discussed, come forward; ~ **up against**, be faced with or opposed by; ~ **upon**, attack by surprise, make demand on, be burden to, meet or find by chance; ~ **up to**, reach, be equal to (standard etc.); ~ **up with**, produce (idea etc.), draw level with; ~ **what may**, whatever happens. [E]

**cŏ′medy̆** n. Stage-play or film of light amusing character, usu. with happy ending (*comedy of* MANNERS; MUSICAL *comedy*); humorous genre of drama etc. (cf. TRAGEDY); humour; amusing or farcical incident(s) in life; **come′dian** n., humorous performer on stage, radio, etc., actor in comedy; **comĕdĭĕ′nne** n., woman comedian. [F f. L f. Gk (COMIC)]

**cŏ′mel̦y̆** (kŭ′mlĭ) a. (~**iness**).

Pleasant to look at (usu. of personal appearance). [E]

**co′mer** (kŭ′-) n. One who comes (**all** ~**s**, anybody who applies, takes up challenge, etc.). [COME]

**comĕ′stible** n. (formal or joc.; usu. in *pl.*) Thing to eat. [F f. L]

**cŏ′mĕt** n. (Astron.) Hazy object usu. with starlike nucleus and with tail pointing away from sun, moving in path about the sun; ~**ar̆y̆** a. [F f. L f. Gk]

**come-ŭ′ppance** (kŭm-) n. Deserved retribution etc. [*come up*]

**cŏ′mfĭt** (kŭ′-) n. Sweetmeat containing nut etc. in sugar. [F f. L (CONFECTION)]

**cŏ′mfort** (kŭ′-). **1.** n. (Person or thing that brings) relief or freedom from trouble or hardship; consolation (COLD *comfort*); physical or mental well-being; comfortable circumstances; (in *pl.*) things that make life easy. **2.** v.t. Bring comfort to; make comfortable. **3.** ~**able** a. (~**ably**), providing or enjoying comfort, having ample money for one's needs; ~**er** n., one who comforts (**the C**~**er**, Holy Spirit); ‖baby's dummy, ‖woollen scarf; ~**less** a., (esp.) dreary, cheerless. [F f. L (*fortis* strong)]

**cŏ′mfrey** (kŭ′-) n. Tall bell-flowered ditch-plant. [F f. L]

**cŏ′mf̆y̆** (kŭ′-) a. (colloq.; -**ily**, -**iness**). Comfortable. [abbr.]

**cŏ′mĭc. 1.** a. (~**ally**). Of or like comedy; designed to amuse, facetious, funny, (*comic paper, song*); *comic* OPERA[1]; ~ **strip**, sequence of drawings telling comic or serial story in newspaper etc. **2.** n. Comedian; comic paper, esp. periodical with narrative mainly in pictures. **3.** ~**al** a. (~**ally**), laughable; ~**ă′lĭt̆y̆** n. [L f. Gk (*kōmos* revel)]

**co′mĭng** (kŭ′-). **1.** n. Arrival (SECOND *coming*). **2.** a. Approaching, (next) future; ~ **man**, man likely to be important in future; ~ **up**, (colloq.) ready. [COME]

**cŏ′mĭt̆y̆** n. Courtesy (~ **of nations**, friendly recognition of each other's laws and usages); association of nations etc. for mutual benefit. [L (*comis* courteous)]

**cŏ′mma** n. Punctuation-mark (,), indicating slight pause or break between words, parts of sentence, etc. [L f. Gk, = clause]

**comma′nd** (-ah′-). **1.** v.t. &

Give command(s) to; order (person *to* do, thing *to be* done, *that*); have authority over or control of; have command; restrain or hold in check (one*self*, passions); have at disposal or within reach (money, skill, etc.); deserve and get (sympathy etc.); dominate (strategic position) from superior height, look down over. **2.** *n*. Order given (**at, by,** person's ~, in pursuance of his bidding); exercise or tenure of authority, esp. naval or military (**in** ~ **of,** commanding; **under (the)** ~ **of,** commanded by); control, mastery, possession (at ~, available); forces or district under commander (*Bomber Command*); ‖C~ **Paper,** paper laid before Parliament by royal command; ~ **performance** (given by royal command). **3. cŏmmandă′nt** *n*., commander of military force etc.; **cŏmmandeer′** *v.t.*, seize (men or goods) for military service or use, take arbitrary possession of; ~**er** *n.*, (esp.) naval officer next below captain, member of higher class in some orders of knighthood (*Knight Commander*); *Commander-in-*CHIEF; ~**ing** *a.*, that commands, (of ability, appearance, etc.) exalted or impressive, (of hill, position) giving wide view; ~′**ment** *n.*, divine command (**the Ten C~ments,** those given by God to Moses, Exod. 20: 1–17); ~**ō** *n*. (*pl.* ~os), (member of) unit of specially-trained shock troops. [F f. L (MANDATE)]

*comme il faut* (kŏm ēl fō′) *pred. a.*, & *adv.* Proper(ly), as it should be. [F, = as is necessary]

**commĕ′mor‖āte** *v.t.* Celebrate in speech or writing or by some ceremony; be a memorial of; ~**ā′tion** *n.*; ~**ative** *a.*; ~**ātor** *n.* [L (MEMORY)]

**commĕ′nce** *v.t.* Begin; ~′**ment** (-sm-) *n.*, beginning, ceremony of degree conferment. [F f. L (INITIATE)]

**commĕ′nd** *v.t.* Entrust (thing to person's care); praise (**highly** ~**ed,** of competitor just failing to win a prize); recommend (*I commend this method to you; method commends itself*); ~**able** *a.*, praiseworthy; **cŏmmendā′tion** *n.*, praise; ~**atory** *a.*, commending. [L (MANDATE)]

**commĕ′nsur‖able** (-sher-, -syer-) *a.* (~**ably**). Measurable by same standard (*with,* to); (of numbers) in ratio equal to ratio of integers; proportionate *to*; ~**abi′lity** *n.*; ~**ate** *a.*,

coextensive (*with*), proportionate (*to*). [L (MEASURE)]

**cŏ′mmĕnt. 1.** *n*. Explanatory note; remark, opinion, (**no** ~, colloq., I decline to answer your question). **2.** *v.i.* Make comment(s) (*on, that, upon*). **3. cŏ′mmentarў** *n.*, series of comments, description (esp. broadcast or accompanying film) of event, performance, etc. (*RUNNING commentary*); **cŏ′mmentāte** *v.i.*, act as commentator; **cŏ′mmentātor** *n.*, writer or speaker of commentary, one who comments on events. [L]

**cŏ′mmĕrce** *n.* Buying and selling; exchange, etc., of merchandise or services, esp. on large scale; trade. [F or L (MERCER)]

**commĕr′cial** (-shal). **1.** *a.* (~**ly**). Of, in, for, commerce; primarily interested in or done for financial profit; (of broadcasting) in which advertisements are included to gain revenue; (of chemicals) unpurified; ~ **college** etc. (giving instruction in commercial subjects); ‖~ **traveller,** firm's representative who visits shops etc. to show samples and get orders; ~ **vehicle** (used for transport of goods). **2.** *n*. An advertisement, esp. broadcast on radio or television. **3.** ~**ism** *n.*; ~**ize** *v.t.*, make commercial, (try to) derive financial profit from; ~**izā′tion** *n.* [L]

**Cŏ′mmie** *n.* (sl.) Communist. [abbr.]

**comminā′tion** *n.* Threatening of divine vengeance; **cŏ′mminatorў** *a.*, threatening vengeance. [L (MENACE)]

**commi′ngle** (-nggĕl) *v.t. & i.* (literary). Mix together. [COM-]

**cŏmmi′n‖ute** *v.t.* Reduce to small fragments or portions; ~**ū′tion** *n.* [L (MINUTE²)]

**commi′ser‖āte** (-z-) *v.i.* Have or express sympathy *with* (person); ~**ā′tion** *n.*, feeling or act of commiserating; ~**ative** *a.* [L (MISER)]

**cŏ′mmissār** *n.* Russian Communist Party official responsible for political organization and discipline. [Russ. (foll.)]

**cŏ′mmissarў** *n.* Deputy, delegate; (Mil.) officer responsible for, \*store for, supply of food etc.; \*restaurant in film studio etc.; **cŏmmissār′ial** *a.* (-lly); **cŏmmissār′ĭat** (*or* -āt-) *n.*, (department, esp. Mil., responsible for) supply of food. [L (COMMIT)]

**commi′ssion** (-shon). **1.** *n.* Committing (*of* authority or task *to* person; *of* crime); task given to person to perform, such person's authority or instructions (*I cannot go beyond my commission*); pay received by agent, percentage of amount involved, (**~-agent,** esp. bookmaker); body or board of persons constituted to perform certain duties (HIGH *Commission*; ||**Royal C~,** commission of inquiry appointed by Crown at the request of the Government); warrant conferring authority, esp. that of officer in armed forces above a certain rank; **in ~,** (of warship etc.) ready for active service; **out of ~,** not in service, not in working order. **2.** *v.t.* Empower by commission; employ (person *to* do piece of work); give (officer) command of ship; prepare (ship) for active service; bring (machine etc.) into operation. **3.** ||**~air′e** *n.,* uniformed door--attendant at theatre, office, etc.; **~er** *n.,* member of commission, one who has been commissioned, representative of supreme authority in a district, department, etc., (HIGH *Commissioner*); **co′mmissure** *n.,* (Anat.) junction or seam between two bones, lips, etc. [F f. L (foll.)]

**commi′t** *v.t.* (-tt-). Entrust or consign for treatment or safe keeping (*commit to writing*); put or throw in (*to* the earth, the flames, etc.); send (person) to prison; be doer of (blunder, crime, etc.); expose to risk, involve in course of action (*that will commit us*); pledge or dedicate one*self* (*to* a course of action etc.); **~ to memory,** learn by heart; **~tal** *n.,* action of committing; **~ted** *a.,* (esp.) dedicated *to* or involved with a particular doctrine, course of action, etc.; **~ment** *n.,* (esp.) undertaking or pledge that restricts freedom of action, dedication to or involvement with a particular doctrine, course of action, etc. [L *committo -miss-*]

**commi′ttee** (-tĭ) *n.* Group of persons appointed for special function by (and usu. out of) a (usu. larger) body (SELECT *committee*; **standing ~,** one that is permanent during existence of appointing body); **C~** (**of the whole House**), whole House of Commons when sitting as committee. [-EE]

**commo′de** *n.* Chest of drawers;

(night-)**~,** chamber-pot mounted in chair or box with cover; **commo′dious** *a.,* roomy and convenient; **commo′dity** *n.,* article of trade, esp. product as opp. to service. [F f. L]

**co′mmodore** *n.* Naval officer next below rear-admiral; commander of squadron or other division of fleet; president of yacht-club; ||**air ~,** R.A.F. officer next above group captain. [Du. f. F (COMMANDER)]

**co′mmon. 1.** *a.* (**~er, ~est; ~ness** *pr.* -n-n-). Shared by, coming from, or affecting all those concerned alike (*by common consent; our common humanity; make common* CAUSE); occurring often (*a common experience*); ordinary, of the most familiar or numerous kind, (common COLD, SALT, *snake,* SOLDIER); of inferior quality, low-class, vulgar, (Gram.) (of noun) applicable to any one of a class (opp. PROPER), (of gender) applicable to individuals of either sex. **2.** *n.* Land belonging to a community; (piece of) unenclosed waste land; (**right of**) **~,** right of using land not one's own; (sl.) common sense; **in ~,** in joint use, shared, equally; **out of the ~,** unusual. **3. ~ carrier** (legally obliged to serve public); **~ chord,** (Mus.) any note with its major or minor third and perfect fifth; common DENOMINATOR, FORM; **~ ground,** basis for argument etc. accepted by both sides; **~ knowledge,** thing known to many or all; **~ law,** unwritten law of England derived from ancient usage and decisions made by judges (*~-law husband, wife,* one recognized by common law, usu. after cohabitation without ceremony of marriage); *Common* MARKET; **~ or garden,** (colloq.) ordinary; **C~ Prayer,** the Anglican liturgy; ||**~-room,** room for use of teachers, students, etc., in college etc.; **~ sense,** normal understanding, good practical sense esp. in everyday matters; **~se′nsical,** having or marked by common sense; **~ time,** (Mus.) four crotchets in bar; **~ weal, ~weal,** (arch.) public welfare. **4. ~ă′lity** *n.,* sharing of an attribute, common occurrence; **~alty** *n.,* the common people, general body (of mankind etc.); **~er** *n.,* one of the common people (below rank of peer), student without financial support from college, person with right of common; **~ly**

*adv.*, (esp.) usually, frequently, (even) to an ordinary degree; ~**s** (-z) *n.pl.*, the common people, all commoners, provisions shared in common (**short ~s**, not enough food); **House of C~s, the C~s**, Lower House of Parliament or its buildings. [F f. L *communis*]

**cŏ'mmonplăce. 1.** *n.* Event, topic, etc. that is ordinary or usual; trite remark. **2.** *a.* Ordinary; lacking originality or individuality; trite. [transl. L *locus communis*]

**cŏ'mmonwealth** (-wĕl-) *n.* Independent State or group of federated States; community; **the C~**, republican government in Britain 1649–60; (**British**) **C~ (of Nations)**, association of U.K. with various independent States (previously subject to Britain) and dependencies; **C~ Day** (celebrated on Queen's official birthday); **[WEALTH]**

**commŏ'tion** *n.* Agitated stir, violent disturbance. [F or L (COM-)]

**cŏ'mmun|e. 1.** *n.* Communal settlement, esp. group of people (not all of one family) sharing living accommodation and goods; small territorial administrative district; **the C~e**, Paris revolutionary government of 1871. **2.** (*or* komū'n) *v.i.* Have intimate discussion or feel in close touch (*with* friend, Nature, etc.). **3.** **~al** *a.* (**~ally**), of or for the community, for the common use, of a commune; **~alĭsm** *n.*, principle of communal organization of society. [F (COMMON)]

**commū'nĭc|āte** *v.t.* &*i.* (**~able**). Impart or convey (news, heat, motion, feeling, etc., *to*); have communication (*with*); succeed in conveying information; receive Communion; administer Communion to; **~ant** *n.*, receiver of Communion, one who imparts information; **~ā'tion** *n.*, (esp.) imparting or exchange of information etc., such information etc., social dealings, connection or means of access between places or things (**~ation cord**, cord or chain for pulling by passenger to stop train in emergency), (in *pl.*) science and practice of transmitting information, (in *pl.*, Mil.) means of transport between base and front; **~ative** *a.*, ready to talk openly, not reserved; **~ātor** *n.* [L (prec.)]

**commū'nion** (-yon) *n.* Communing; fellowship, esp. on basis of religion; mutual relation between members of Church or between branches of Catholic Church; branch of Christian Church; social dealings; (**Holy**) **C~**, Eucharist; *communion of* SAINTS. [F or L (COMMON)]

**commū'nĭqué** (-kā) *n.* Official communication, esp. report. [F, = communicated]

**cŏ'mmun|ism** *n.* (Belief in) system of society in which property etc. is owned communally; (usu. *C-*) movement or political party advocating communism esp. as derived from Marxism, communistic form of society established in U.S.S.R. and elsewhere; **C~ĭst** *n.* & *a.*, (person) believing in or supporting Communism; **~i'stĭc** *a.* [F (COMMON)]

**commū'nĭtў** *n.* Group of people etc. living in same locality or having same religion, race, profession, interests, etc.; *the* public; communal settlement, COMMUNE; fellowship (*community of interest*); state of being shared or held in common; joint ownership or liability; **~ centre**, place providing social, recreational, and educational facilities for a neighbourhood; ||**~ home** (for housing young offenders); **~ singing** (in chorus by large gathering of people).

**commū'te** *v.t.* & *i.* Make payment etc. to change (one obligation) *for, into,* another; change (punishment *to* another less severe); change (payment) *for, into,* another; travel, esp. by train or car, to and from one's daily work in city etc.; **cŏmmūtā'tion** *n.* (*commutation ticket, season-ticket*); **commū'tative** (*or* kŏ'mūtāt-) *a.*; **cŏ'mmūtātor** *n.*; **commū'ter** *n.*, one who commutes to work. [L (MUTABLE)]

**cŏ'mpăct¹** *n.* Agreement or contract. [L (PACT)]

**compă'ct²** *a., v.,* & *n.* **1.** *a.* Closely or neatly packed together; occupying small space. **2.** *v.t.* Make compact. **3.** (kŏ'mp-) *n.* Small flat case for face-powder etc. [L (*pango* fasten)]

**compă'nion** (-yon) *n.* One who accompanies or associates with another; associate *in,* sharer *of;* woman paid to live with another; handbook or reference-book; thing that matches or accompanies another; ||member of lowest grade of some orders of knighthood (*Companion* *of the Bath*; *Knight Companion*; ‖C~ of **Honour, Literature**, member of orders founded 1917, 1961); ~ (-way), staircase from deck of ship to cabins etc.; ~**able** *a.* (-bly), sociable, agreeable as companion; ~**ship** *n.*, state of being companions. [F f. Rom. *companio* (L *panis* bread); Naut. sense thr. Du. *kompanje*]

**co'mpany** (kŭ'-) *n.* State of being companion or with other people (**in** ~, not alone; **in** ~ **with**, together with; **keep** person ~, accompany him, save him from feeling lonely; **keep** ~, associate habitually *with*; **part** ~, lit. or fig., cease connection or association); one's associate(s) (**good, bad,** ~, a pleasant, dull, companion); number of people assembled, guests; (*abbr.* Co.) body of persons combined for commercial or other end; group of actors etc.; (Mil.) subdivision of infantry battalion (~ **officer**, captain or lower commissioned officer; ~ **sergeant-major**, senior warrant-officer of company). [F (prec.)]

**cŏ'mparab|le** *a.* (~ly). That can be compared (*with, to*); ~**i'lĭty** *n.* [F f. L (COMPARE)]

**compa'rative. 1.** *a.* Of or involving comparison; perceptible (only) by comparison (*in comparative comfort*); ~ **adjective, adverb,** one in the ~ **degree**, expressing a higher degree of a quality (*braver, more speedily*). **2.** *n.* (Gram.) Comparative degree or form. [L (foll.)]

**compa're. 1.** *v.t.* & *i.* Liken, suggest as similar, *to*; estimate or check (dis)similarity of (two things, one thing *to* another in quality, *with* another in quality or quantity; ~ **notes**, exchange information or ideas); (Gram.) form comparative and superlative degrees of (adjective or adverb); bear comparison (*this compares favourably with previous results*); be on terms of equality *with*. **2.** *n.* (literary) Comparison (*beyond, without, compare*). [F f. L (*compar* equal)]

**compa'rison** *n.* Comparing (**bear, stand,** ~, be able to be compared favourably *with*; **beyond** ~, totally different; **in** ~ **with**, compared with); **degrees of** ~, (Gram.) positive, comparative, and superlative (of adjectives and adverbs).

**compa'rtment. 1.** *n.* Space partitioned off, e.g. in railway carriage; watertight division of ship. **2.** *v.t.* Put into compartments (lit. or fig.). **3.** **cŏmpartme'ntal** *a.* (-lly); **cŏmpartme'ntalize** *v.t.* [F f. It. f. L (PART)]

**co'mpass** (kŭ'-). **1.** *n.* Instrument showing direction of magnetic or true north and bearings from it (BOX *the compass*); (usu. in *pl.*) V-shaped hinged instrument for drawing circles and taking measurements; circumference, boundary; area, extent, scope, (lit. or fig.; *beyond, within, my compass*); range of voice or musical instrument; (arch.) detour (*fetch a compass*). **2.** *v.t.* (literary). Encompass; contrive; accomplish. [F f. L (*passus* pace)]

**compa'ssion** (-shon) *n.* Pity inclining one to be helpful or merciful; ~**ate** *a.*, feeling or showing compassion, granted out of compassion. [F f. L (PASSION)]

**compa'tĭb|le** *a.* (~ly). Consistent, able to coexist, (*with*); mutually tolerant; (of equipment etc.) able to be used in combination; ~**i'lĭty** *n.* [F f. L]

**compa'trĭot** *n.* Person from same country. [F f. L *compatriota*]

**compeer'** *n.* Person of same rank, standing, or qualities. [F (PEER²)]

**compe'l** *v.t.* (-ll-). Force or constrain; bring about (action) irresistibly; ~**ling** *a.*, rousing strong interest or feeling of admiration. [L (*pello puls-* drive)]

**compe'ndi|um** *n.* (*pl.* ~**ums**, ~**a**). Abridgement, summary; collection of table-games etc.; ~**ous** *a.*, brief but comprehensive. [L]

**cŏ'mpĕns|āte** *v.t.* & *i.* Counterbalance; recompense (person *for* thing); make amends (*for* thing, *to* person, or abs.); (Mech.) provide (pendulum etc.) with arrangement to neutralize effects of temperature etc.; (Psych.) offset deficiency or frustration by developing another characteristic; ~**ā'tion** *n.*, (esp.) thing (esp. money) that compensates; ~**ātor** *n.*; **compe'nsatŏry** *a.* [L (*pendo pens-* weigh)]

‖**cŏ'mpère** (-pār). **1.** *n.* Person who introduces artistes in variety entertainment etc. **2.** *v.t.* Act as compère to. [F, = godfather]

**compe'te** *v.i.* Take part in contest, race, etc.; strive (*with* or *against* another). [L (*peto* seek)]

**cŏ'mpĕt|ent** *a.* Having adequate ability, knowledge, power, qualifications, etc.; sufficient, effective; **~ence**, **~ency**, *ns.*, competent capacity, comfortably adequate income; **compěti'tion** *n.*, competing, event in which persons compete, those competing with one; **compě'titive** *a.*, of or involving competition, (of prices etc.) comparable with those of rival sellers etc.; **compě'titor** *n.*, one who competes, rival esp. in trade. [F or L (*prec.*)]

**compi'le** *v.t.* Collect (facts, quotations, etc.) to form a list, volume, etc.; make (book etc.) thus; accumulate; **compǐlā'tion** *n.*, (esp.) compiled book. [F, or L *compilo* plunder]

**complā'cen|t** *a.* Self-satisfied; calmly content; **~cý** *n.* [L (*placeo* please)]

**complai'n** *v.i.* Express dissatisfaction (*at*, *that*); emit mournful sound; **~ of**, express dissatisfaction at, say that one is suffering from (pain etc.), state grievance concerning; **~ant** *n.*, plaintiff; **~t** *n.*, action of complaining, formal accusation, reason for dissatisfaction, illness. [F f. L (*plango* lament)]

**complai'san|t** (-z-) *a.* Inclined to please or defer to others; acquiescent; **~ce** *n.* [F (COMPLACENT)]

**complea't.** See COMPLETE.

**co'mplement. 1.** *n.* Something which makes up a whole; number required to man ship, fill conveyance, etc.; (Gram.) word(s) added to verb to complete the predicate; angle making up 90°; **complemě'ntarý** *a.* (-ily). **2.** (-ěnt) *v.t.* Form complement to. [L (*compleo* fill up)]

**complē'te.** *a.* (**~r**, **~st**). Having all its parts, entire; finished; having the maximum extent, total, in every way, (*a complete stranger, surprise*); accomplished, skilful. **2.** *v.t.* Make complete; finish; fill in (form etc.); **complē'tion** *n.* [F or L (*prec.*)]

**co'mplěx. 1.** *a.* Consisting of several parts, composite, (*complex* SENTENCE); complicated, involved. **2.** *n.* A complex whole; (Psych.) group of usu. repressed ideas etc. causing abnormal behaviour or mental state; (pop.) obsession. **3. complē'xion** (-kshon) *n.*, colouring or texture of skin, esp. of face, (fig.) character or appearance (*that puts a different complexion on the matter*); **complē'xitý** *n.*, complex condition. [F, or L *complexus*]

**compli'ance** *n.* Complying (**in ~ with,** according to); **compli'ant** *a.*, disposed to comply, yielding. [COMPLY]

**co'mplǐcāte** *v.t.* (esp. in *p.p.*) Make complex, confused, or difficult; **complǐcā'tion** *n.*, complicated condition or situation, complicating circumstance, (Path.) secondary disease or condition aggravating an existing one; **compli'citý** *n.*, taking part in evil. [L (*plico* to fold)]

**co'mpliment. 1.** *n.* Expression or implication of praise (*pay a compliment to*; *your presence is a great compliment*); (in *pl.*) formal greetings, esp. as accompaniment to message, note, present, etc.; **the ~s of the season,** greetings appropriate to the (esp. Christmas) season. **2.** (-ěnt) *v.t.* Pay compliment to (person *on* achievement, quality, etc.). **3. complimě'ntarý** *a.* (-ily), laudatory, given free of charge. [F, f. It. f. L (as COMPLEMENT)]

**co'mpline** *n.* (Office of) last of the canonical hours of prayer. [F f. L (foll.)]

**comply'** *v.i.* Act in accordance (*with* request or command). [It. f. Sp. f. L *compleo* fill up]

**compō'nent. 1.** *a.* Contributing to the composition of a whole, constituent. **2.** *n.* Component part, esp. of vehicle. [L (COMPOUND[1])]

**compor't** *v.t.* & *i.* (literary). Behave or conduct one*self*; be in harmony *with*. [L (*porto* carry)]

**compō's|e** (-z) *v.t.* & *i.* Construct or put together (writing, music, etc.) in appropriate form; (of elements) form or constitute; (Print.) arrange (type), arrange (words etc.) in type; arrange artistically, neatly, or for specified purpose; calm or control (one*self*, feelings, etc.; esp. in *p.p.*); settle (dispute etc.); **~ědlý** *adv.*, calmly; **~er** *n.* (esp., of music) [F (POSE)]

**co'mposǐte** (-z-) *a.* & *n.*, (thing) made up of various parts or materials, (plant) of family in which so-called flower is a head of many flowers, (Archit.) combining Ionic and Corinthian orders. [F (COMPONE)]

**composǐ'tion** (-z-) *n.* Act, method, or style of composing; thing composed, esp. piece of music or writing; constitution of person or substance; compound artificial substance, esp. one serving the purpose of a natural one; (agreement for payment of) sum in lieu of larger sum or other obligation; **~al** *a.* (-lly); **compŏ′sĭtor** (-z-) *n.*, (Print.) one who sets up type; **cŏ′mpŏst** *n.*, & *v.t.* (treat with or make into) mixed organic manure; **compŏ′sure** (-zher) *n.*, calmness; **cŏ′mpŏte** *n.*, fruit in syrup. [F f. L (COMPOUND¹)]

**cŏ′mpound¹** *a.*, *n.*, & *v.* **1.** *a.* Made up of two or more parts or ingredients; combined, collective; **~ fracture** (complicated by wound); *compound* INTEREST, SENTENCE. **2.** *n.* Compound thing, esp. compound word; mixture of elements; (Chem.) substance consisting of two or more elements chemically united in fixed proportions. **3.** (kompow′nd) *v.t. & i.* Mix or combine (ingredients, verbal elements, etc.); make up (a composite whole); increase or complicate (difficulty, offence, etc.); settle (matter by mutual concession, commutation, etc.); come to terms (*with* person, *for* concession etc., *for* offence); condone (liability, offence) for money etc. [F f. L *compono -post-* put together]

**cŏ′mpound²** *n.* (In India, China, etc.) enclosure in which house or factory stands; large fenced-in space in prison etc. [Port. or Du., f. Malay]

**cŏmprĕh|ĕ′nd** *v.t.* Grasp mentally, understand; include, comprise; **~ĕ′nsĭble** *a.* (-bly), intelligible; **~ĕnsĭbi′lĭty** *n.*; **~ĕ′nsion** (-shon) *n.*, act or faculty of understanding, inclusion; **~ĕ′nsĭve**, (*a.*) including much or all, of wide scope, (of secondary school) catering for secondary education of all or most children in a district, (*n.*) comprehensive school. [F, or L *comprehendo* seize]

**comprĕss. 1.** (-ĕ′s) *v.t.* (**~ĭble**). Squeeze together; bring into smaller space, condense. **2.** (kŏ′-) *n.* Pad or cloth pressed on to part of body to stop bleeding, relieve inflammation, etc. **3.** **comprĕ′ssion** (-shon) *n.*, compressing, esp. (amount of) compressing of fuel mixture in internal combustion engine before ignition; **comprĕ′ssĭve** *a.*; **comprĕ′ssor** *n.*, machine for compressing air or other gases. [F or L (PRESS¹)]

**comprī′se** (-z) *v.t.* Have or include as constituent parts, consist of; (less usu.) compose, make up. [F (COMPREHEND)]

**cŏ′mpromise** (-z). **1.** *n.* Agreement reached by mutual concession;

(finding of) intermediate course *between* conflicting opinions etc. **2.** *v.t. & i.* Settle (dispute) or modify (principles etc.) by compromise; make a compromise; bring (person, one*self*, beliefs, etc.) under suspicion or into danger by indiscreet action. [F f. L (PROMISE)]

**comptrŏ′ller** (kont-) *n.* (In titles of some financial officers) controller. [var. of CONTROLLER]

**compŭ′ls|ion** (-shon) *n.* Act of compelling (**under ~ion**, because one is compelled); (Psych.) irresistible urge to a form of behaviour, esp. contrary to one's normal wishes; **~ĭve** *a.*, resulting or acting (as if) from compulsion, irresistible, tending to compel; **~orȳ** *a.* (-ily, -iness), enforced, that must be done or followed. [F f. L (COMPEL)]

**compŭ′nction** *n.* Pricking of conscience; scruple. [F f. L (POINT)]

**compŭ′te** *v.t. & i.* Reckon, calculate; use computer; **compŭtā′tion** *n.*; **~r** *n.*, calculator, esp. automatic electronic apparatus for making calculations or controlling operations; **~rīze** *v.t.*, equip with, perform by, produce by, computer; **~rizā′tion** *n.* [F or L (*puto* reckon)]

**cŏ′mrāde** (*or* -rĭd) *n.* Friend; friendly associate (usu. man) in some activity, esp. fellow soldier; fellow socialist, communist, etc.; **~lȳ** (-dlĭ) *a.*; **~shĭp** (-dsh-) *n.* [F f. Sp. (CHAMBER)]

**cŏn¹** *v.t.* (-nn-). (arch.) **~** (**over**), study or learn (lesson etc.). [CAN²]

**cŏn², *cŏnn**, *v.t.* (-nn-). Direct steering of (ship); **conning-tower**, superstructure of submarine from which steering, firing, etc., are directed when it is on or near the surface, warship's armoured pilot-house. [orig. *cond* f. F (CONDUCT)]

**cŏn³. 1.** *n.* Confidence (trick etc.; colloq.); (sl.) convict. **2.** *v.t.* (-nn-; colloq.) Persuade, swindle. [abbr.]

**cŏn⁴.** See PRO².

**con-.** See COM-.

**concă′tĕn|āte** (-n-k-) *v.t.* Link together (fig.); **~ā′tion** *n.*, (esp.) series of events. [F or L (*catena* chain)]

**cŏ′ncăve** (-n-k-) *a.* With outline or surface curved like interior of circle or sphere; **concă′vĭty** (-n-k-) *n.* [L (CAVE¹)]

**concea′l** *v.t.* Hide or keep secret (*from*); **~ment** *n.* [F f. L (*celo* hide)]

**concē′de** *v.t.* Admit to be true (*that*,

defeat, etc.); grant (privilege etc. *to* person); acknowledge as won by opponent etc. [F or L (CEDE)]

**concei't** (-sē't) *n.* Personal vanity; fanciful notion, comparison, etc., esp. as affectation of style; **~ed** *a.*, having too high an opinion of one's own beauty, ability, etc. [foll.]

**concei've** (-sē'v) *v.t. & i.* Form or have (idea, plan, etc.); think (*that*); become pregnant (with); **~** (of), imagine, think of. [F f. L *concipio -cept-*]

**co'ncentrat|e. 1.** *v.t. & i.* Bring together (troops, power, attention, etc.) at or on one point; employ one's full thoughts or efforts (*on, upon*), increase strength of (liquid etc.) by removing water etc. **2.** *n.* Concentrated substance, esp. food. **3. ~ed** *a.*, (esp., of hate etc.) intense; **concentra'tion** *n.*, (esp.) mental faculty of exclusive attention; **~ion camp** (for detention of political prisoners, internees, etc.); **~ter,** *-ter, v.t. & i.*, bring or come to a common centre; **conce'ntric** *a.* (*-ically*), sharing a common centre; **concentri'city** *n.* [F f. L (CENTRE)]

**co'ncept** *n.* Idea of a class of things; general notion (*the concept of evolution*); **conce'ption** *n.*, conceiving, idea; **conce'ptional** *a.* (*-lly*); **conce'ptive** *a.*, of (esp. mental) conception; **conce'ptual** *a.* (*-lly*), of concepts, of the nature of a concept; **conce'ptualize** *v.t.*, form a concept or idea of. [L (CONCEIVE)]

**conce'rn.** **1.** *v.t.* Relate to, affect, be relevant or important to; **~** oneself, feel an interest or anxiety (*in, about,* matter; *to* do), have desire to deal *with*. **2.** *n.* Related or interested condition or feeling, connection, (have a **~** in, have an interest or share in; have no **~** with, have nothing to do with); thing that affects or interests one (*it's no concern of mine*); (in *pl.*) one's affairs; (feeling of) anxiety or worry; business or firm (GOING concern); (colloq.) thing, contrivance; **~ed** (-nd) *a.*, involved or interested, anxious or troubled (*am concerned about, at; for* person; *to* hear); **be ~ed,** take part (*in*); **~ed̄ly** *adv.*; **~edness** *n.*; **~ing** *prep.*, about, regarding; **~ment** *n.* [F or L (*cerno* sift)]

**concert.** **1.** (kŏ'n-) *n.* Agreement, union, (in **~,** together, working in

combination *with*); combination of voices or sounds (*voices raised in concert*); a musical entertainment; **~ pitch,** (Mus.) pitch normally used for performances, (fig.) state of extreme efficiency or readiness. **2.** (-sē'rt) *v.t.* Arrange or plan with partners etc.; (Mus., in *p.p.*) arranged in parts for voices or instruments. **3. concerti'na** (-tē'-), (*n.*) portable musical instrument consisting of reeds sounded by bellows worked by the player's hands, with finger-studs at each end to control valves, (*v.t. & i.*) compress or collapse in folds like those of concertina; **concer'tō** (-nch-; *or* -ār'-) *n.* (*pl.* **~os, ~i** *pr.* -tē), musical piece for solo instrument(s) accompanied by orchestra. [F f. It.]

**conce'ssion** (-shon) *n.* Conceding; thing conceded; esp. right to use land etc. or sell goods; land or premises thus used; **concession(n)-air'e** (-shonār') *n.*, holder of concession; **conce'ssionary** (-shon-) *a.*; **conce'ssive** *a.*, (esp., Gram.) of conjs. such as *although* or *even if*, and clauses expressing an admission. [F or L (CONCEDE)]

**conch** (*or* -ngk) *n.* Shellfish, esp. large gastropod; its shell; **conchoi'dal** (-ngk-) *a.*, (Min., of crystal fracture etc.) like the surface of a bivalve shell; **concho'logy** (-ngk-) *n.*, study of shells and shellfish. [L *concha* f. Gk]

**co'ncierge** (kaw'nsiārzh, kŏ'n-) *n.* (In France etc.) door-keeper or porter, esp. of block of flats. [F]

**conci'li|ate** *v.t.* (**~able**). Pacify; reconcile (disagreeing parties etc.); **~ā'tion, ~ator,** *ns.*; **~atory** (-lya-) *a.* (*-ily, -iness*). [L (COUNCIL)]

**conci'se** *a.* (Of speech, writing, etc.) brief but comprehensive in expression; **conci'sion** (-zhon) *n.*, conciseness. [F or L (*caedo* cut)]

**co'nclāve** (-n-k-) *n.* Private meeting; meeting-place or assembly of cardinals for papal election. [F f. L (*clavis* key)]

**conclu'de** (kon-klŏō'd) *v.t. & i.* Bring or come to an end; draw conclusion *that*, infer; make (treaty, peace, bargain); decide (*to* do). [L *concludo* (CLOSE¹)]

**conclu'sion** (kon-klŏō'zhon) *n.* Ending (in **~,** lastly, as the final point); judgement reached by reasoning (*draw the conclusion that;* JUMP to *conclusions*); final opinion; (Logic) proposition reached from previous ones; concluding of peace etc.; **try ~s**, engage in contest (*with* person); **conclu'sive** (-n-klōō'-) *a.*, (of argument, fact, etc.) decisive, convincing.

**conco'ct** (-n-k-) *v.t.* Prepare, esp. by mixing (soup, drink, etc.); invent or devise (story, plot, etc.); **~ion** *n.*, concocting, concocted liquid, story, etc. [L (*coquo coct-* to cook)]

**conco'mitan|t** (-n-k-). **1.** *a.* (Of circumstances etc.) attendant, accompanying; **~ce** *n.*, coexistence. **2.** *n.* Accompanying thing. [L (*comes comit-* companion)]

**co'ncord** (*or* -n-k-) *n.* Agreement, harmony; (Mus.) chord pleasing or satisfactory in itself; (Gram.) agreement between words in gender, number, etc.; **concor'dance** (-n-k-) *n.*, agreement, alphabetical list of words used by author or in book (esp. Bible), usu. with quotations of passages concerned; **concor'dant** (-n-k-) *a.*, agreeing, harmonious; **concor'dat** (-n-k-) *n.*, agreement, esp. between Church and State. [F f. L (*cor cord-* heart)]

**co'ncourse** (-ôrs; *or* -n-k-) *n.* Crowd; coming together; open central area in large public building, railway station, etc. [F f. L (CONCUR)]

**co'ncrete** (*or* -n-k-) *a., n., & v.* **1.** *a.* Existing in material form, having objective reality, existing in a particular example, (**in the ~**, in the sphere of reality or practice); specific, definite, (*concrete evidence*, *proposals*); (Gram., of noun) denoting thing as opposed to quality, state, or action, not abstract; **~ music** (constructed by arrangement of recorded sounds); **~ poetry** (using typographical devices to enhance effect). **2.** *n.* Composition of cement, gravel, etc., for building; **~-mixer**, = CEMENT-*mixer*. **3.** *v.t. & i.* Cover with or embed in concrete; (kon--krē't) solidify, form into a mass. **4.** **concre'tion** (-n-k-) *n.*, (mass formed by) coalescence, stone or similar morbid formation in the body; **concre'tionary** (-n-k-) *a.* [F or L (*cresco cret-* grow)]

**co'ncubine** *n.* Woman who cohabits with a man, without being his wife; **concu'binage** (-n-k-) *n.*, such cohabitation. [F f. L (*cubo* lie)]

**concu'piscen|ce** (kon-k-) *n.* Sexual desire; **~t** *a.* [F f. L (*cupio* desire)]

**concur'** (-n-k-) *v.i.* (-**rr**-). Occur together, coincide; agree or express agreement in opinion (*with*); **concu'rrence** (-n-k-) *n.*; **concu'rrent** (-n-k-) *a.*, concurring, running in same direction, meeting at one point, existing together. [L (*curro* run)]

**concu'ssion** (-n-kŭ'shon) *n.* Violent shaking or shock; (Med.) injury to brain etc. caused by heavy blow etc.; **concu'ss** (-n-k-) *v.t.*, subject to concussion. [L (*quatio* shake)]

**conde'mn** (-m) *v.t.* **~able** *pr.* -mn-). Censure, blame; give judgement against; sentence *to* punishment; prove guilt of (*his looks condemn him*); pronounce forfeited, unfit for use, incurable, etc.; *condemned* CELL; **condemna'tion** (-n-k-) *n.*; **conde'mnatory** *a.* [F f. L (DAMN)]

**conde'ns|e** *v.t. & i.* Make denser or more compact (**~ed milk**, thickened by evaporation and sweetened); reduce or be reduced from gas or vapour to liquid; express in fewer words; **condensa'tion** *n.*; **~er** *n.*, (esp.) vessel or apparatus for converting steam to water, (Electr.) capacitor. [F or L (DENSE)]

**condesce'nd** *v.i.* Consent *to* do something less dignified than is fitting or customary, esp. while showing one's feeling of superiority; disregard one's superiority (*to* person); **~ing** *a.*, patronizing, kind to inferiors; **condesce'nsion** (-shon) *n.*, condescending manner or act. [F f. L (DESCEND)]

**condi'gn** (-ī'n) *a.* (Usu. of punishment) severe and well-deserved. [F f. L (*dignus* worthy)]

**co'ndiment** *n.* Relish or seasoning used with food. [L *condio* to pickle)]

**condi'tion. 1.** *n.* Stipulation, thing necessary for something else to be possible, (**on ~ that**, with the condition that, only if); (in *pl.*) circumstances, esp. those essential to a thing's existence (*favourable conditions*; *under existing conditions*); thing's or person's state of being (*eggs arrived*, *machine is still*, *in good condition*); social rank (*all sorts and conditions of men*); physical or mental abnormality or disease (*has a heart condition*); **in, out of, ~**, in good, bad, condition; **~ powder**, medicine to keep animal in good condition. **2.** *v.t*

Govern, determine, be essential to existence of, (*the two things condition each other*); bring into desired condition, teach, accustom, (*conditioned to respond to the stimulus*); ~ed reflex, habitual response, esp. to stimulus not naturally associated with it); bring into good condition (AIR--*conditioning*). 3. ~al a. (~ally), dependent (*on*), not absolute, (Gram., of clause etc.) expressing or containing a condition; ~ă'litў n. [F f. L (*dico* say)]

condǒ'le v.i. Express sympathy *with* (grieving person etc.); ~nce n. [L *condoleo* grieve with another]

cǒ'ndom n. Contraceptive sheath. [orig. unkn.]

condomi'nium n. Joint control of a State by other States; *set of rented or bought cottages, flats, etc. [L *dominium* lordship]

condo'ne v.t. Forgive, overlook, (offence); condonă'tion n. [L (*dono* give)]

cǒ'ndor n. Large S. Amer. vulture. [Sp. f. Quechua]

condū'ce v.i. Tend to lead or contribute *to* (result); condū'cive a. [L (foll.)]

conduct. 1. (kǒ'n-) n. Person's actions, behaviour (esp. in its moral aspect); (manner of) conducting business etc., SAFE *conduct*. 2. (-dǔ'kt) v.t. & i. Lead, guide, escort, (~ed tour, tour led by guide on fixed itinerary); direct or manage (business etc.); be conductor of (orchestra etc.); behave one*self* in specified way; (Phys.) transmit (heat, electricity, etc.) by contact. 3. condū'ction n., conducting of heat etc.; condū'ctive a.; cǒnducti'vitў n., (Phys.) conductive power; condū'ctor n., (esp.) one who directs playing of orchestra etc., official in charge of bus, tram, or *train, conducting substance or object; condū'ctrèss n. (esp. in bus etc.); cǒ'ndūit (or kǒ'ndǐt, kǔ'ndǐt) n., channel or pipe for liquid or wire. [L (*duco* duct-lead)]

cōne n. Solid figure with usu. circular base, tapering to a point; cone-shaped object; dry fruit of pine or fir; ice-cream cornet. [F f. L f. Gk]

cō'ney. See CONY.

confă'būlāte v.i. Talk together; ~ā'tion (colloq. abbr. cǒ'nfăb) ~ātor, ns. [L (FABLE)]

confě'ction n. Compounding; mixture; a delicacy, esp. made of sweet ingredients; fashionable dress etc.; ~er n., dealer in sweets, pastry, etc.; ~erў n. [F f. L (*conficio* prepare)]

confě'derate, a., n., & v. 1. a. Allied, esp. as members of a confederation; C~ States (seceding from U.S., 1861–5). 2. n. Ally, partner, usu. (in bad sense) accomplice; C~, supporter of the Confederate States. 3. (-āt) v.t. & i. Bring or come into alliance. 4. confě'deracў n., alliance, league, esp. of confederate States; confěderā'tion n., (esp.) permanent union of States. [L (FEDERAL)]

confer' v.t. & i. (-rr-). Bestow (title, favour, etc., *on* or *upon*); converse, meet for discussion; cǒ'nference n., consultation, meeting (esp. annual) for discussion etc., (in ~ence, engaged in discussion; PRESS *conference*); ~ment n., conferring of honour etc.; ~rable a. [L *confero collat-* bring together, take counsel]

confě'ss v.t. & i. Admit or acknowledge (sin, crime, etc.; *I confess my fault, that I did it, to doing it, to having done it, to a dread of spiders*); (Eccl.) declare one's sins, esp. to a priest, (of priest) hear confession of; ~ědlў adv., by personal or general admission. [F f. L *confiteor -fess-*]

confě'ssion (-shon) n. Confessing (of crime etc.; of sins to priest); thing(s) confessed; ~ . of faith, declaration of religious belief, statement of one's principles in any matter; ~al, (a.) of confession, denominational, (n.) enclosed place where priest hears confession, act or practice of confession; confě'ssor n., (esp.) priest who hears confession, person (honoured by Church for) avowing his religion in face of danger. [F f. L (prec.)]

confě'tti n.pl. Small bits of coloured paper, thrown by wedding guests at bride and bridegroom. [It.]

confī'de v.i. & t. Tell (secret) or entrust (task) *to*; ~ in, trust in, talk confidentially to; cǒnfidă'nt (or kǒ'-) n. (*fem.* -ante *pr.* same), person to whom one confides one's private affairs. [L *confido* to trust]

cǒ'nfidence n. Firm trust; state of mutual trust between people (in ~, as a secret; in person's ~, allowed to know his secrets; take into one's ~, confide in); thing told as a secret; freedom from apprehension; assured expectation; self-confident or enterprising disposition; \*~ **game**, ‖~ **trick**, swindle achieved by winning the trust of a credulous person; ~ **man**, such swindler; **cŏ'nfĭdent** *a.*, feeling or showing confidence; **cŏnfĭdĕ'ntĭal** (-shal) *a.* (-lly), imparted in confidence, entrusted with secrets or a secret task, inclined to confide; **cŏnfĭdĕntĭă'lĭtў** (-shĭ-) *n.*

**cŏnfĭgŭră'tion** *n.* (Arrangement producing) outline or shape; relative position. [L (FIGURE)]

**confine. 1.** (-ī'n) *v.t.* Limit or restrict (*in, to, within*, space, area, etc.); imprison, hold in custody; (in *pass.*) be in childbirth. **2.** (kŏ'n-) *n.* (usu. in *pl.*) Border or edge (lit. or fig.). **3.** ~**ment** (-nm-) *n.*, being confined, imprisonment, childbirth. [F f. L (*finis* limit)]

**confĭr'm** *v.t.* Make firmer or stronger (habit, opinion, person *in* these); establish more firmly (power, possession, person *in* these); ratify (treaty, title, etc.); certify, make definitely valid, (statement etc.); administer rite of confirmation to; **cŏnfĭrmă'tion** *n.*, (esp.) rite confirming baptized person as member of Christian Church, act or age of discretion; ~**atĭve**, ~**atorў** (-ily), *adjs.*, (esp.) corroborating; ~**ed** (-md) *a.*, (esp.) permanent, unlikely to change, (*confirmed bachelor, drunkard*). [F f. L (FIRM²)]

**cŏ'nfĭsc|ăte** *v.t.* (~**able**). Seize (property etc.) (as) by authority or summarily; ~**ā'tion**, ~**ā'tor**, *ns.*; **confĭ'scatorў** *a.* [L (FISCAL)]

**cŏnflagră'tion** *n.* Great and destructive fire. [L (FLAGRANT)]

**confl|ā'te** *v.t.* Fuse together, blend, esp. two variant texts into one; ~**ā'tion** *n.* [L (*flo flat-* blow)]

**conflĭct. 1.** (-ŏ'-) *n.* Fight, struggle, opposition, (lit. or fig.); clashing (*of* opposed principles etc.); **in ~**, inconsistent (*with*). **2.** (-ĭ'-) *v.i.* Struggle, clash, be incompatible, (*with*). [L (*fligo flict-* strike)]

**cŏ'nflu|ence** (-lōō-) *n.* Meeting- (-place) of two streams etc.; ~**ent**, (*a.*) flowing together, uniting, (*n.*) stream joining another. [L (*fluo* flow)]

**confo'rm** *v.i. & t.* (Cause to) fit or be suitable; comply with rules or general custom; ~ **to, with**, comply with, be in accordance with; ~**able** *a.* (~**ably**), (esp.) adapted or cor-

responding (*to*); **cŏnformā'tion** *n.*, (esp.) thing's structure; ~**ĭsm** *n.*, (practice of) conforming; ~**ĭst** *n.*, one who conforms, ‖esp. to Anglican doctrines; ~**ĭtў** *n.*, conforming, ‖esp. to Anglican doctrines, compliance *to* or agreement *with*. [F f. L (FORM)]

**confou'nd** *v.t.* Overthrow or defeat (plan, hopes, etc.); perplex, baffle, confuse (ideas etc.); cause or increase disorder in; (in *subj.*, as mild oath) damn (*confound it!*); ~**ĕd** *a.*, (colloq.) damned (*a confounded nuisance*); ~**ĕdlў** *adv.*, (colloq.) extremely, unpleasantly, (*confoundedly hot*). [F f. L *confundo -fus-* mix up]

**cŏnfrater'nĭtў** *n.* Guild or brotherhood. [F f. L (COM-)]

**cŏ'nfrère** (-rār) *n.* Fellow member of profession etc.

**confro'nt** (-ŭ'nt) *v.t.* Meet or stand facing, esp. in hostility or defiance (lit. or fig.); (of difficulty etc.) oppose, present itself to; ~ person **with**, bring him so as to face or be forced to consider (accusers, evidence, etc.); **cŏnfrontā'tion** *n.*, (esp.) (act of) defiant opposition. [F f. L (FRONT)]

**Confū'cian** (-shan) *a. & n.* (Follower) of *Confucius*; ~**ĭsm** *n.* [person]

**confū'se** (-z) *v.t.* Throw into disorder; make indistinct (*confuse the issue*); disconcert, perplex, bewilder; ~ person or thing **with**, mistake him or it for (another) in the mind; **confū'sedlў** (-z-) *adv.*; **confū'sion** (-zhon) *n.*, act or result of confusing. [CONFOUND]

**confū'te** *v.t.* Prove (person, contention) to be in error; **cŏnfŭtā'tion** *n.* [L]

**congé** (kaw'nzhā) *n.* Unceremonious dismissal (*give person his, get one's, congé*); leave-taking. [F f. L *commeatus* leave of absence]

**congea'l** (-nj-) *v.t. & i.* Solidify by freezing or otherwise; **cŏngelā'tion** (-nj-) *n.* [F f. L (*gelo* freeze)]

**cŏ'ngèner** (-nj-) *n.* Thing or person of the same kind or class (*the goldfinch is a congener of the canary*). [L (GENUS)]

**congē'nĭ|al** (-nj-) *a.* (-lly). Having an agreeable nature, similar interests, etc., (*to, with*); suited or agreeable (*to*); ~**ă'lĭtў** *n.* [COM-]

**congē'nĭtal** (-nj-) *a.* (-lў). Existing from birth (*congenital disease*); that is so from birth (*congenital idiot*).

**cŏ'nger** (-ngg-) n. ~ **(eel)**, large sea eel. [F f. L f. Gk *goggros*]

**congĕr'ies** (-njēr'ēz, -njē'rĭēz) n. (*pl.* same); **congĕ'st** (-nj-) *v.t.*, (usu. in *p.p.*) affect with congestion; **congĕ'stion** (-njě'schon) *n.*, abnormal accumulation or obstruction (of blood etc. in part of the body; of traffic etc.). [L (*congero* heap together)]

**conglŏ'merate** (-n-g-) a., n., & v. **1.** a. Gathered or cemented into a (round) mass (lit. or fig.). **2.** n. Conglomerate mass (esp. rock) or mixture; business etc. corporation formed by merging separate firms. **3.** (-āt) *v.t. & i.* Collect into a coherent mass (lit. or fig.); ~ā'tion n. [L (*glomus -eris* ball)]

**Cŏngolē'se** (-nggolē'z) a. & n. (Native) of Congo region or republic. [F (*Congo* river)]

**congrä'tŭl|āte** (-n-g-) *v.t.* (~able). Express pleasure at happiness or excellence or good fortune of (person, *on* event); ~ate oneself, consider oneself fortunate; ~ā'tion n., action or (usu. in *pl.*) expression of congratulating; ~ātor n.; ~ātorў a. [L (*gratus* pleasing)]

**cŏ'ngregāte** (-ngg-) *v.i. & t.* Come or bring together in a crowd; ~ant n., member of (esp. Jewish) congregation. [L (*grex greg-* flock)]

**cŏngregā'tion** (-ngg-) n. Action or result of congregating; assembly of people, esp. for religious worship; group of persons regularly attending a particular church etc.; ||(Oxford etc.) C~) assembly of resident senior members of university; ~al a. (~ally), of a congregation, (C-) of or adhering to Congregationalism; C~alĭsm n., system of ecclesiastical organization whereby individual churches are self-governing (in England and Wales largely merged in United Reformed Church since 1972); C~alĭst n. [F or L (prec.)]

**cŏ'ngress** (-ngg-) n. Meeting, esp. formal meeting of delegates for discussion; (C~) national legislative body, esp. of U.S.; C~ (**Party**), (Ind.) a political party; C~man, C~woman, member of Congress; **congrĕ'ssional** (-n-grě'sho-) a., of congress. [L (*gradior gress-* walk)]

**cŏ'ngru|ence** (-nggroŏens), ~encў, ns. Agreement, consistency; (Geom.) state of being congruent;

~ent a., suitable, agreeing (*with*), (Geom., of figures) coinciding exactly when superimposed; **cŏ'ngru'itў** (-nggroŏ'-) n.; ~ous a. [F, or L (*congruo* agree)]

**cō'nĭc** a. Of cone; ~ **section**, (Math.) figure formed by intersection of cone and plane; ~al (~ally), cone-shaped; **cŏ'nĭfer** n., cone-bearing tree; **conĭ'ferous** a. [L f. Gk (CONE)]

**conjĕ'cture. 1.** n. Formation of opinion on incomplete grounds; guessing; a guess, esp. proposed emendation of a text. **2.** *v.i. & t.* Guess; foretell or estimate by conjecture; propose as emendation. **3.** **conjĕ'ctural** (-kcher-) a. (-lly), involving conjecture. [F, or L *conjectura* (*jacio* throw)]

**conjoi'n** *v.t. & i.* Join, combine; ~t a., conjoined. [F f. L (JOIN)]

**cŏ'njugal** (-oŏ-) a. (~ly). Of marriage; between married persons; ~itў (-ă'l-) n. [L (*conjux* consort)]

**cŏ'njug|ate** (-oŏ-) v., a., & n. **1.** (-āt) *v.t. & i.* (~able). Inflect (verb); unite, become fused. **2.** (-at) a. Joined together, coupled, fused. **3.** (-at) n. Conjugate word or thing. **4.** ~ā'tion n., fusion, (Gram.) system of verbal inflexion. [L (*jugum* yoke)]

**conjŭ'nct** a. Joined together; combined; associated. [L (foll.)]

**conjŭ'nction** n. Joining, connection; (Gram.) uninflected word used to connect clauses, phrases, words, etc., (e.g. *and, but, if, unless*); (Astrol. & Astron.) apparent proximity of two heavenly bodies to each other; simultaneous occurrence; in ~, together (*with*); ~al a. (~ally); **cŏnjuncti'va** n., mucous membrane connecting eyeball and inner eyelid; **conjŭ'nctive** a., serving to join, (Gram.) of the nature of a conjunction; **conjunctivi'tĭs** n., inflammation of conjunctiva; **conjŭ'ncture** n., state of affairs. [F f. L (CONJOIN)]

**co'njure** (kŭ'njer) *v.i. & t.* Produce magical effects by secret but natural means; convey *away*, bring *out*, (as if) by magic; constrain (a spirit) to appear by invocation (**a name to ~ with**, a name of great importance); ~ **up**, make appear (as if) by magic, evoke (picture etc.) in the mind etc.); (konjoor') appeal solemnly to (person *to* do); **cŏnjurā'tion** n., solemn entreaty, incantation; **co'njurer, co'njuror,** (kŭ'njerer) n., (esp.)

expert at sleight of hand. [F f. L (*juro* swear)]

**cŏnk**[1] *n.*, & *v.t.* (sl.) (Hit esp. on) nose or head. [?CONCH]

**cŏnk**[2] *v.i.* (colloq.) ~ **(out)**, (of mechanism etc.) break down, (of person) faint or die. [orig. unkn.]

**cŏ'nker** *n.* Horse-chestnut fruit; (in *pl.*) children's game played with these threaded on strings, each player trying to break that held by opponent. [dial. *conker* snail-shell]

**\*cŏnn.** See CON[2].

**Conn.** *abbr.* Connecticut.

**conně'ct** *v.t.* & *i.* Join (two things, one *to*, *with*, another); be joined (*with*); associate mentally or practically (*with*); be meaningful or relevant; (usu. in *pass.*) unite or associate *with* others in relationship etc.; (colloq.) hit target with blow etc.; ~ **with**, (of train, boat, etc.) arrive at a place in time for passengers to catch (another conveyance); ~**ěd** *a.*, (esp.) coherent, having specified relationships (**well ~ed**, associated with persons of good social position); ~**ing-rod** (between piston and crankpin etc. in engine); ~**or** *n.*, thing that connects. [L (*necto nex-* bind)]

**conně'ction,**‖**conně'xion,**(-kshǒn) *n.* Act of connecting; state of being connected or related; relation of ideas (**in this, that,** ~ with reference to this, that); connecting part; connecting train, boat, etc. (*miss the* or *one's connection*); personal dealings; person or set of people connected with others by family relationship, marriage, church membership, etc.; body of customers etc. (*business with a good connection*); (sl.) supplier of narcotics; **conně'ctive** *a.*, serving to connect (esp. Anat., of tissue that connects and supports organs etc.).

**conni've** *v.i.* ~ **at**, disregard or tacitly consent to (misbehaviour etc.); **conni'vance** *n.* [F, or L *conniveo* shut the eyes]

**cŏnnoisseur'** (-nosěr') *n.* Person with good taste and judgement (*of*, *in*, pictures, wine, beauty, etc.). [F (*connaître* know)]

**connō'te** *v.t.* (Of word) imply in addition to the primary meaning; (of fact etc.) imply as consequence or condition; mean, signify; **cŏnnotā'tion** *n.*; **cŏ'nnotātive** (or konō'tātīv) *a.* [L (NOTE)]

**connū'bial** *a.* (~ly). Conjugal. [L (*nubo* marry)]

**cŏ'nquer** (-ngkₑr) *v.t.* & *i.* Overcome or defeat (opponent, difficulty, habit, etc.); be the victor; subjugate (country); climb (mountain) successfully; ~**or** *n.*, one who conquers (**the C**~**or**, William I of England); **cŏ'nquěst** *n.*, conquering (**the** (**Norman**) **Conquest,** conquest of England by Normans in 1066), conquered territory, person whose affections have been won, such winning. [F f. L *conquiro* win]

**cŏnsăngui'n**|**eous** (-nggw-) *a.* Descended from the same parent or ancestor; ~**ĭtў** *n.* [L (*sanguis* blood)]

**cŏ'nscience** (-shₑns) *n.* Moral sense of right and wrong (**good or clear, bad** or **guilty,** ~, consciousness that one's behaviour has been good, bad; **freedom, liberty, of** ~, free choice of religion to all citizens; **have on** one's ~, feel guilty about; **in all** ~, by any reasonable standard; **prisoner of** ~, person in prison for act of conscientious protest etc.); ~ **clause** (in a law, ensuring respect for the consciences of those affected); ~ **money** (paid to relieve one's conscience, esp. in settlement of evaded income-tax); ~~**-smitten,** **-stricken, -struck,** made guilty or uneasy by bad conscience; **cŏnsciě'ntious** (-shiě'nshus) *a.*, scrupulous, obedient to conscience; **conscientious objector,** one who objects to something, esp. conscription, which he considers morally wrong. [F f. L (SCIENCE)]

**cŏ'nscious** (-shus). **1.** *a.* Knowing, aware (*of* something; *that*); awake to one's surroundings and identity; (of actions, emotions, etc.) realized or recognized by the doer, intentional, (*a hardly conscious movement*; *with conscious superiority*); (as *suf.*) aware of or concerned with (*class- -conscious*). **2.** *n. The* conscious mind. **3.** ~**nèss** *n.*, (esp.) awareness, person's conscious thoughts and feelings as a whole. [L (*scio* know)]

**conscript. 1.** (-ī'-) *v.t.* Enlist compulsorily for State (esp. military) service; **conscri'ption** *n.* & (kŏ'n-) *n.* Conscripted person. [F f. L *scribo* write)]

**cŏ'nsĕcrāt**|**e** *v.t.* Set apart or dedicate as sacred (*to* God etc.); devote *to* purpose; render sacred; **cŏnsĕcrā'tion** *n.*, consecrating, ordination esp. of bishop; **~or** n.; **~orў** a. [L (SACRED)]

**conse′cutive** a. Following continuously; proceeding in logical sequence; (Gram., of clause etc.) expressing consequence. [L (*sequor secut*- follow)]

**conse′nsus** n. Agreement, unanimous opinion; majority view (*consensus politics*); **conse′nsūal** (or -shŏŏ-) a., of consensus or consent. [L (foll.)]

**conse′nt. 1.** v.i. Express willingness, give permission, agree, (*to* proposal or request, *to* do, *that*, or abs.). **2.** n. Voluntary agreement, compliance; permission; **age of ~** (at which consent, esp. of girl to sexual intercourse, is legally valid). [F f. L (*sentio* feel)]

**co′nsēqu|ence** n. What comes by causation or follows from logic (in **~ence**, as a result (*of*); **take the ~ences**, endure whatever results from one's choice or act); importance (*of great, no, consequence*); influential position or high rank (*persons of consequence*); **~ent**, (a.) following as a consequence (*on, upon*), logically consistent, (n.) thing that follows another; **~ĕ′ntial** (-shăl) a. (-lly), consequent, resulting indirectly, (of person, manner, etc.) self-important; **~ĕntiă′lĭtỹ** (-shĭ-) n.; **~ĕntlỹ** adv. & conj., as a result, therefore. [F f. L (CONSECUTIVE)]

**conse′rv|e. 1.** v.t. Keep from harm, change, or loss, esp. with view to later use. **2.** n. Fruit etc. preserved in sugar; jam. **3. ~ancỹ** n., conservation, body conserving natural resources, ||commission etc. controlling river, port, etc.; **cŏnservā′tion** n., preservation esp. of natural environment (**conservation of energy, momentum**, etc., Phys. principle that quantity of energy etc. of any system of bodies not subject to external action remains constant); **cŏnservā′tionĭst** n., supporter or advocate of conservation; **~atĭsm** n., conservative principles or policies; **~atĭve,** (a.) tending to conserve, averse to rapid changes, (of views, taste, etc.) avoiding extremes, (of estimate etc.) moderate or purposely low, ||(C-, Polit.) disposed to maintain existing institutions and promote individual enterprise, (n.) conservative person, (C-) member of Conservative Party; **conservatoire** (kon-

sĕr′vatwăr) n., (usu. Continental) school of music or other arts; **cŏ′nservātor** (or konsĕr′va-) n., preserver, member of conservancy, custodian of museum etc.; **~′atorỹ** n., greenhouse for tender plants, *= conservatoire. [F f. L (*servo* keep)]

**consi′der** v.t. Contemplate mentally; examine merits of (plan, claim, candidate, etc.); look attentively at; bring to one's mind (*that, whether*, etc., or abs.); reckon with, make allowance for, (**all things ~ed**, on the whole); be thoughtful for (others); have the opinion that or *that*; regard as (*I consider him a swindler; consider yourself under arrest*); (in p.p.) reached after careful thought (*considered opinion*); **~able** a. (**~ably**), not negligible, amounting to something, of some importance or size, great; **~ate** a., thoughtful for others, careful not to hurt feelings or cause inconvenience; **~ĭng** prep., in view of, (ellipt. colloq.) in view of the circumstances (*that's not so bad, considering*). [F f. L]

**considerā′tion** n. Act of considering (**in ~ of**, in return for, on account of; **leave out of ~**, fail to consider; **take into ~**, consider, make allowance for; **under ~**, being considered); thoughtfulness for others; fact or thing regarded as a reason (**on no ~**, not on any account); thing given or done as compensation or inducement (*for a consideration*). [F f. L]

**consi′gn** (-ī′n) v.t. Commit or deliver *to* (misery, person's care, etc.); send (goods) (*to* person etc.); **~ee′, ~or,** ns., person to whom, by whom, goods are sent; **~ment** n., consigning, goods consigned. [F f. L (SIGN)]

**consi′st** v.i. Be composed *of*; have its essential feature(s) *in*; be consistent *with*; **~ence, ~encỹ,** ns., consistent condition, degree of density esp. of thick liquids; **~ent** a., compatible, not contradictory, (*with*), (of person) constant to same principles; **~orỹ** (or kŏ′-) n., ecclesiastical court or council. [L (*sisto* stand)]

**cŏnsolā′tion** n. Act of consoling; consoling circumstance; **~ prize** (given to competitor who just fails to win main prize); **consŏ′latorỹ** a. (-ily), tending or intended to console. [F f. L (SOLACE)]

**consŏ'le**[1] *v.t.* Comfort, esp. in grief or disappointment. [F]

**cŏ'nsōle**[2] *n.* Bracket supporting a shelf etc.; (frame containing) keyboards, stops, etc., of an organ; panel for switches etc.; cabinet for television set etc. [F]

**consŏ'lid|āte** *v.t. & i.* Make or become strong or solid (lit. or fig.); combine (territories, companies, debts, etc.) into one whole; ‖~ated annuities, consols; ~ā'tion, ~ātor, *ns.*; ~ātorў *a.*; **consŏ'ls** (-z; *or* kŏ'-)[2] *n.pl.*, government etc. securities without maturity date. [L (SOLID)]

**consŏ'mmé** (-mā) *n.* Clear meat soup. [F]

**cŏ'nsonance** *n.* Agreement in sound, meaning, taste, etc.; (Mus.) concord; **cŏ'nsonant,** (*n.*) (letter representing) speech sound that forms a syllable only in combination with vowel, (*a.*) harmonious, agreeable *to*, consistent *with*; **cŏnsonā'ntal** *a.* (-lly). [F or L (*sono* to sound[1])]

**cŏnsort**[1]. **1.** (kŏ'n-) *n.* Spouse (PRINCE, QUEEN, *consort*); ship sailing with another. **2.** (-sŏ't) *v.i.* Associate or keep company (*with, together*); be in harmony (*with*). [F f. L (SORT)]

**cŏ'nsort**[2] *n.* (Mus.) Group of players or instruments. [var. CONCERT]

**consŏr'ti|um** *n.* (*pl.* ~a). Association esp. of several business companies. [L (CONSORT[1])]

**conspĕ'ctus** *n.* General view or survey; synopsis; **conspĭ'cŭous** *a.*, clearly visible, attracting attention, noteworthy. [L (*specio* look)]

**conspĭ'ra|cў** *n.* Plot(ting) for evil-doing (~cy of silence, agreement not to talk about something); ~tor *n.*, person taking part in conspiracy; ~tŏr'ial *a.* (-lly); **conspīr'e** *v.i.*, form or take part in conspiracy, combine or work together (*events conspired to thwart him*). [F f. L (*spiro* breathe)]

**cŏ'nstable** (*or* kŭ'n-) *n.* ‖Policeman (Chief C~, head of police force of county etc.; **police** ~, policeman or policewoman of lowest rank; SPECIAL *constable*); governor of royal castle; (Hist.) principal officer of royal household; **constă'bŭлару** *n.*, a police force. [F f. L *comes stabuli* count of the stable]

**cŏ'nstancў** *n.* Faithfulness (*to*); unchangingness; endurance. [L (*sto* stand)]

**cŏ'nstant. 1.** *a.* Continuous (*con-*

stant anxiety, attention); frequently occurring (*constant chatter, complaints*); having constancy. **2.** *n.* (Math.) unvarying quantity; (Phys.) number expressing relation, property, etc., and remaining same in all circumstances (*constant of gravitation*) or for same substance in same conditions (*dielectric constant*). **3.** ~lў *adv.*, (esp.) often.

**cŏnstellā'tion** *n.* Group of fixed stars; (fig.) group of associated people etc. [F f. L (*stella* star)]

**cŏnsternā'tion** *n.* Amazement or dismay that creates mental confusion. [F or L (*sterno* throw down)]

**cŏnstipā'tion** *n.* Infrequent or difficult defecation; (fig.) restrictedness; **cŏ'nstipāte** *v.t.*, affect with constipation. [F or L (*stipo* cram)]

**constĭ'tŭen|t. 1.** *a.* Composing or helping to make a whole (*constituent part*); able to make or change a constitution (*constituent assembly, power*); electing a representative (*constituent body*). **2.** *n.* Constituent part; member of a constituency. **3.** ~cў *n.*, body of voters who elect a representative, area so represented, clientele or supporters. [L (foll.)]

**cŏ'nstitūte** *v.t.* Appoint; form, establish, (*does not constitute a precedent*); give (legal) form to (assembly etc.); compose, be the essence or components of. [L *constituo* establish]

**cŏnstitū'tion** *n.* Act or method of constituting, composition; condition of person's body as regards health, strength, etc.; form in which State is organized; body of fundamental principles according to which a State etc. is governed; ~al, (*a.*; -lly) of or in harmony with or limited by the constitution, (*n.*) walk taken regularly as healthy exercise; ~alism, ~alist, ~ă'litў, *ns.*; **cŏ'nstitūtive** *a.*, constructive, constituent, essential. [F or L (prec.)]

**constrai'n** *v.t.* Urge irresistibly, force, (person *to do, to action*, etc.); confine forcibly, imprison (lit. or fig.); (in *p.p.*, of voice, manner, etc.) forced, embarrassed; ~t *n.*, act or result of constraining or being constrained, restriction. [F f. L (*stringo strict-* bind)]

**constrĭ'ct** *v.t.* Compress, make narrow or tight; ~ion *n.*; ~ive *a.*; ~or *n.*, muscle that constricts; BOA *constrictor*.

**construct. 1.** (-ŭ'-) *v.t.* Fit to-

gether, frame, build, (lit. or fig.);
(Geom.) delineate (figure). **2.** (kŏ'-)
*n.* Thing constructed, esp. by the
mind. **3. constrŭc'tion** *n.*, (esp.)
thing constructed, syntactical connection, interpretation or explanation of statement or action (*what
construction are we to put on that?*);
**constrŭc'tional** *a.* (**-lly**); **constrŭc'tive** *a.*, (esp.) tending to
construct, helpful (*constructive criticism*), derived by inference; **constrŭc'tor** *n.* [L (*struo struct-* build)]
**construe'** (-oo') *v.t.* Interpret
(words, actions); combine (words
*with* others) grammatically; analyse
(sentence); translate word for word.
**cŏnsubstă'ntial** (-shal) *a.* (**~ly**).
Of one substance; **cŏnsubstăn-
tiā'tion** (-shǐ-) *n.*, (doctrine of)
presence of Christ's body and blood
together with bread and wine in
Eucharist. [L (SUBSTANCE)]
**cŏ'nsul** *n.* State agent living in
foreign town to protect subjects there
and assist commerce; (Hist.) one of
two annually-elected magistrates
exercising supreme authority in
Roman Republic; **cŏ'nsŭlar** *a.*;
**cŏ'nsŭlate** *n.*, consul's position or
offices. [L]
**consŭ'lt** *v.t. & i.* Seek information
or advice from (person, book, etc.);
take counsel (*with*); take into consideration (feelings etc.); **~ing
engineer, physician,** etc., (who
gives advice about his speciality);
**~ing room** (in which doctor ex-
amines his patients); **~ancy** *n.*,
work or position of consultant,
department of consultants; **~ant** *n.*,
consulting physician etc.; **cŏnsul-
tā'tion** *n.*, (meeting for) consulting;
**~ative** *a.*, of or for consultation. [F
f. L *consulo* take counsel]
**consŭ'm|e** *v.t.* Eat or drink; use
up; destroy; (in *p.p.*) possessed by or
entirely preoccupied *with* (envy etc.);
**~able** *a.* & *n.* (usu. in *pl.*), (article)
intended for consumption; **~er** *n.*,
(esp.) user of product (opp. *producer*),
purchaser of goods or services (**~er
goods,** goods used domestically, not
in manufacturing etc.; **~er research,** investigation into needs and
opinions of consumers); **~erĭsm** *n.*,
protection or promotion of consumers' interests, (belief in) high
consumption of goods; **~erĭst** *n.* [L
*consumo -sumpt-*]
**consummate. 1.** (kŏnsŭ'mat) *a.*

Complete; perfect; supremely skilled.
**2.** (kŏ'nsŭmāt) *v.t.* Make perfect or
complete; complete (marriage) by
sexual intercourse; **cŏnsummā'-
tion** *n.*, completion, perfection, desired end or goal. [L (SUM)]
**consŭ'mpt|ion** *n.* Consuming;
purchase and use of goods etc.;
amount consumed; wasting disease,
esp. pulmonary tuberculosis; **~ive,**
(*a.*) of or tending to consumption,
affected with tuberculosis, (*n.*) con-
sumptive patient. [F f. L (CONSUME)]
**cŏ'ntăct. 1.** *n.* Condition or state of
touching, meeting, or communicating (**come in** or **into ~** (with),
touch, meet, come across; **in ~**
(with), touching, communicating);
person who is, or may be, contacted
for information, assistance, etc.;
(Med.) person likely to carry contagion through being near infected
person; (Electr.) connection for
passage of current (*make, break, contact*); **~ lens,** small lens placed
against eyeball to correct faulty
vision. **2.** (or kontă'kt) *v.t.* Get in
touch with (person); begin communication or personal dealings with.
[L (*tango tact-* touch)]
**contā'gion** (-jon) *n.* Communication of disease from body to body,
disease so transmitted, corrupting
moral influence; **contā'gious** (-jus)
*a.*
**contai'n** *v.t.* Hold, have within
itself; include, comprise, enclose,
prevent from moving or extending;
(of vessel) have capacity for
(amount); (of measure) be equal to
(so many units of lower denomination; *metre contains 100 centimetres*);
(of number etc.) be divisible by
(factor) without remainder; control
or restrain (*contain your anger; couldn't
contain himself for joy*); **~er** *n.*, (esp.)
vessel, box, etc., designed to contain
particular thing(s), esp. large boxlike
receptacle of standard design for
transport of goods (**~er ship** etc.,
ship etc. carrying goods packed in
these containers); **~erize** *v.t.*, pack
in or transport by container;
**~erizā'tion** *n.*; **~ment** *n.*, (esp.)
action or policy of preventing expansion of hostile nation etc. [F f. L
(*teneo* hold)]
**contă'min|āte** *v.t.* (**~able**). Pol-
lute, esp. with radioactivity; infect;
**~ant, ~ā'tion, ~ātor,** *ns.* [L]
‖**contā'ngo** (-ngg-) *n.* (*pl.* **~s**). (St.

Exch.) Percentage paid by buyer of stock for postponement of transfer. [orig. unkn.]

**conté'mn** (-m) *v.t.* (literary). Despise; disregard. [F or L]

**có'ntempl|āte** *v.t. & i.* Survey with eyes or in mind; regard (event) as possible; intend; meditate; ~**ā'-tion** *n.*, (esp.) meditative state; **in** ~**ation**, intended; **conté'mplable** *a.*; **conté'mplative**, (*a.*) of or given to (esp. religious) contemplation, meditative, (*n.*) contemplative person; ~**ātor** *n.* [L]

**conté'mpor|arў. 1.** *a.* (-ily, -iness). Belonging to same time or of same age, esp. as oneself; (ultra-) modern in style or design. **2.** *n.* Contemporary person, newspaper, etc. **3.** ~**ā'neous** *a.*, existing or occurring at the same time (*with*); ~**anē'itў** *n.* [L (COM-)]

**conté'mpt** *n.* Feeling that person or thing is inferior or worthless, condition of despising or being despised, (**have, hold, in** ~, have contempt for); disobedience or disrespect (~ **of court**, disobedience to court of law or interference with its administration of justice); ~**ible** *a.* (~**ibly**), deserving contempt; ~**ūous** *a.*, feeling or showing contempt. [L (CONTEMN)]

**conté'nd** *v.i. & t.* Struggle or compete (*for* thing, *with* person, difficulties, etc.); argue (*with*); maintain, assert, (*that*). [F or L (TEND[1])]

**có'ntĕnt[1]** *n.* Capacity (of vessel); volume (of solid); amount contained or yielded; substance (of book, speech, etc., as opposed to *form*); (in *pl.*) what is contained in vessel, house, book, mind, etc.; (**table of**) ~**s**, list of subject-matter of book etc. [L (CONTAIN)]

**conté'nt[2]** *a., v., & n.* **1.** *pred. a.* Satisfied; willing (*to* do). **2.** *v.t.* Make content, satisfy; ~ **oneself with**, be satisfied with, accept or do no more than. **3.** *n.* Contented state, satisfaction; **to one's heart's** ~, to the full extent of one's desires. **4.** ~**ĕd** *a.*, content (*with, to* do); ~**ment** *n.*, satisfaction with one's lot, tranquil happiness. [F f. L (CONTAIN)]

**conté'nt|ion** *n.* Contending; point contended for in argument; ~**ious** (-shus) *a.*, quarrelsome, involving contention. [F or L (CONTEND)]

**conté̄r'mǐnous** *a.* Having a common boundary (*with*). [L (TERM)]

**contĕst. 1.** (-ŏ'-) *n.* Contending; a competition. **2.** (-ĕ'-) *v.t. & i.* Dispute (point, statement, etc.); contend or compete for (prize, seat in Parliament, etc.) or in (||election); strive in argument (*with, against*); **conté'stant** *n.*, one who contests; **cŏntĕstā'tion** *n.* [L (*testis* witness)]

**có'ntĕxt** *n.* What precedes or follows a word or passage and fixes its meaning (**out of** ~, without this and hence misleading); circumstances (**in this** ~, in this connection); **conté'xtŭal** *a.* (-lly); **conté'xture** *n.*, structure, style of literary composition. [L (TEXT)]

**contǐ'gŭous** *a.* Adjacent, next, (*to*); **cŏntǐgū'itў** *n.* [L (CONTACT)]

**có'ntǐn|ent. 1.** *n.* One of the main continuous bodies of land (Europe, Asia, Africa, N. & S. America, Australia, Antarctica; **the C~ent**, mainland of Europe as dist. from British Isles). **2.** *a.* Exercising self-restraint; sexually chaste; able to control one's excretions. **3.** ~**ence** *n.*, being continent; ~**ĕ'ntal** *a.* (-lly), of or characteristic of a continent (~**ental shelf**, shallow sea-bed bordering continent), (*C*-) characteristic of the Continent (**C~ental breakfast**, light breakfast of coffee, rolls, etc.). [L (CONTAIN)]

**contǐ'ng|ent** (-nj-). **1.** *a.* That may or may not occur; incidental (*to* action); conditional or dependent (*on, upon*); (of statement etc.) true only under existing or specified conditions. **2.** *n.* Body of troops, ships, etc., forming part of larger group. **3.** ~**encў** *n.*, being contingent, contingent event. [L (CONTACT)]

**contǐ'nū|e** *v.t. & i.* Maintain, keep up, not cease, (action, *with* action, doing, *to* do, etc.); resume, prolong, (narrative, journey, etc., or abs.); remain (*at* or *in* place, *in* a state); not become other than (*weather continues fine*); ~**al** *a.* (~**ally**), frequently recurring, always happening; ~**ance** *n.*, continuing in existence or operation, duration; ~**ā'tion** *n.*, act of continuing, thing that continues something else; ~**ative** *a.*, serving to continue; **cŏntĭnū'itў** *n.*, (esp.) logical sequence, connecting announcements etc. between broadcast items, detailed scenario of film (~**ity girl** etc., person who ensures consistency in details of different parts of film); ~**ō** *n.*, (Mus.) *pl.* ~**os**

figured BASS³, (usu. keyboard) accompaniment improvised from this, instrument(s) playing this [It.]; ~**ous** a., connected throughout in space or time, without interval or break, uninterrupted, (~**ous creation,** creation of matter in the universe regarded as continuous process); ~**um** n. (pl. ~a), thing of continuous structure. [F f. L (CONTAIN)]

**contor′t** v.t. Twist or force out of normal shape; ~**ion** n.; ~**ionĭst** n., acrobat who contorts himself. [L (torqueo tort- twist)]

**co′ntour** (-oor) n. Outline; line separating differently-coloured parts of design; line on map joining points at same altitude; ~ **map** (with contours). [F f. It. (TURN)]

**cŏ′ntra.** See PRO². [L, = against]

**cŏntra-** pref. Against, counter-.

**cŏ′ntrabănd** n. & a. (Of) smuggling; smuggled (goods); ~ **of war,** munitions or other goods forbidden to be supplied by neutrals to belligerents. [Sp. f. It.]

**cŏntrace′p**|**tĭve** a. & n. Preventive of pregnancy; ~**tion** n. [CONCEIVE]

**contrăct. 1.** (-ŏ′-) n. Written or spoken arrangement or agreement made between two or more persons etc., usu. enforceable by law; (Cards) commitment to make stated number of tricks; ~ **(bridge),** type of auction bridge in which only tricks bid and won count towards game. **2.** (-ă′-) v.t. & i. Make a contract (with party, for work, to do, etc.); form or enter into (marriage, debt, etc.); arrange (work) to be done by contract; catch or develop (disease); draw together (muscles, brow, etc.); make or become smaller; shorten word by combination or elision (as do not to don′t); ~ **in, out,** enter, withdraw from, scheme etc.; ~ **out,** arrange (work) to be done by other workers, firms, etc. **3. contră′ctĭble, contră′ctĭle,** adjs., capable of or producing contraction; **cŏntrăcti′lĭty** n.; **contră′ction** n., act of contracting, shrinking, diminution, act or result of contracting word(s); **contră′ctor** n., one who makes a contract, esp. for building to specified plans; **contră′ctŭal** a. (-lly), of (the nature of) a contract. [F f. L contractus (TRACT)]

**cŏntradĭ′ct** v.t. & i. Deny (statement); deny statement made by (person); (of facts, statements, etc.) be at variance or conflict with (others); ~**ion** n., statement etc. contradicting another, inconsistency (~**ion in terms,** self-contradictory phrase etc., e.g. two-sided triangle); ~**ious** (-shʊs) a., inclined to contradict; ~**or** n./~**orў** a. (-ily, -iness), conveying denial, conflicting, inconsistent, inclined to contradict. [L (dico dict- say)]

**cŏntradĭst**|**i′nction** n. (Distinguishing one thing from another by) contrast; ~**i′nguĭsh** (-nggw-) v.t. [CONTRA-]

**contră′ltŏ** n. (pl. ~s). (Mus.) Lowest female voice; singer with, part written for, such voice. [It. (CONTRA-, ALTO)]

**contră′ption** n. (colloq.) Strange machine or device. [orig. unkn.]

**cŏntrapŭ′nt**|**al** a. (~ally). Of or in counterpoint; ~**ĭst** n., expert in counterpoint. [It.]

**cŏ′ntrar**|**ў** a., n., & adv. **1.** a. (~ily, ~iness). Opposed in nature, tendency, or direction (they hold contrary opinions); in opposition to (it is contrary to my wishes); (of wind) impeding, unfavourable; (kontrār′ĭ; colloq.) perverse, self-willed. **2.** n. The opposite of a person or thing; **by contraries,** with the opposite of what is expected or logically understood; **on the ~y** (introducing or emphasizing an implied or expressed denial or contrast); **to the ~y,** to the opposite effect (there is no evidence to the contrary). **3.** adv. In opposition to (act contrary to nature; contrary to my expectation, all went well). **4. cŏntrarī′etў** n., opposition, disagreement; **contrār′iwīse** (-z) adv., on the other hand, in the opposite way. [AF f. L contrarius (CONTRA)]

**contrăst. 1.** (kŏ′ntrahst) n. Juxtaposition or comparison showing striking differences (in ~ **with,** thus compared with, markedly different from); difference so revealed; thing or person having noticeably different qualities (to); degree of difference between tones in photograph or television picture. **2.** (kŏntrah′st) v.t. & i. Make or show contrast (between). **3. contra′stĭve** (-ah′-) a. [F f. It. f. L (sto stand)]

**cŏntravē′ne** v.t. Violate (law etc.); (of things) conflict with; ~**vē′ntion** n. [L (venio come)]

**co′ntretemps** (kaw′ṅtretahṅ) n.

Unexpected or unfortunate occurrence. [F]

**contri′bute** v.t. & i. Pay or give (*to* common fund, effort, etc.); supply (written work etc. for publication with others); ~ **to**, help to bring about; **cŏntribū′tion** n., thing contributed, act of contributing; **contri′butor** n.; **contri′butory** a., that contributes (*contributory* NEGLIGENCE), using contributions. [F or L (TRIBUTE)]

**cŏ′ntrite** a. Sorrowing or penitent for one's sin; **contri′tion** n. [F f. L (TRITE)]

**contri′v|e** v.t. & i. Devise, plan or make with skill; manage (*to* do); ~**ance** n., contriving, contrived object or appliance, inventive capacity. [F f. L]

**contrŏ′l. 1.** n. Power of directing or restraining (**in** ~, in charge (*of*); **out of** ~, no longer subject to guidance; **under** ~, fig. in proper order); means of restraining or regulating; standard of comparison for checking results of experiment, esp. patient, specimen, etc., like those being investigated but not specially treated etc.; place where something is controlled or verified; personality directing actions of spiritualist medium; (usu. in *pl.*) devices to operate machine, e.g. in aircraft or vehicle to control direction, speed, etc.; ~ **tower**, building at airport etc. from which air traffic is controlled by radio. **2.** v.t. (**-ll-**). Have control of; regulate; serve as control to; check, verify; ~**ler** n., (esp.) one who controls expenditure. [AF f. L (CONTRA-, ROLL; copy of accounts as check)]

**cŏntrover′sial** (-shal) a. (~**ly**). Of, open to, or fond of controversy; ~**ĭst** n.; **cŏ′ntroversў** (*or* kontrŏ′-) n., disputation, (prolonged) argument; **cŏ′ntrovert** (*or* -vēr′t) v.t. (-tible), dispute, deny. [L (*verto vers-* turn)]

**cŏ′ntumacў** n. (literary). Stubborn disobedience; **contumā′cious** (-shus) a.; **cŏ′ntumelў** (*or* kontū′mĭlĭ) n., (subjection to) insulting language or treatment; **cŏntumē′lious** a. [L (*tumeo* swell)]

**contū′se** (-z) v.t. Bruise; **contū′sion** (-zhon) n. [L (*tundo tus-* thump)]

**conu′ndrum** n. Riddle, esp. one with punning answer. [orig. unkn.]

**cŏnŭrbā′tion** n. An aggregation of urban areas. [L *urbs* city]

**cŏnval|ĕ′scent** a. & n. (Person) recovering from illness; ~**escent home** or **hospital** (for such persons); ~**ĕ′sce** v.i., be convalescent; ~**ĕ′scence** n., (period of) being convalescent. [L (*valeo* be well)]

**convĕ′ct|ion** n. Transport of heat by movement of heated substance; ~**or** n., heating appliance for circulating warm air. [L (*veho vect-* carry)]

**convē′n|e** v.t. & i. Summon or arrange (assembly, meeting, etc.); assemble; ~**er**, ~**or**, ns., (esp.) person who arranges meetings of committee etc. [L (*venio vent-* come)]

**convē′nience** n. Suitability, freedom from difficulty or trouble, (**at your** ~, at a time or in a way convenient to you; **at your earliest** ~, as soon as you can); material advantage (**marriage of** ~, marriage not made primarily for love); an advantage (*a great convenience*; **make a** ~ **of** person, utilize his services without considering his feelings); useful thing; water-closet; public lavatory; ~ **food** (needing little preparation); **convē′nient** a., providing or characterized by convenience, available or occurring at a suitable time or place, (colloq.) well situated for access.

**cŏ′nvent** n. Religious community, esp. of women, living together usu. under vows; building(s) occupied by this; ~ **school** (conducted by members of convent); ‖**convĕ′nticle** n., (Hist.) clandestine meeting or meeting-house, esp. of Dissenters; **convĕ′ntion** n., convening, assembly or conference, agreement, (practice established by) implicit consent of the majority, accepted social behaviour esp. artificial or formal, (Cards) accepted method of play (in leading, bidding, etc.) used to convey information; **convĕ′ntional** a. (-**lly**), of or depending on convention(s), not spontaneous or sincere or original, having an agreed meaning, (of bomb, power sources, etc.) other than nuclear; **convĕ′ntionalĭsm, convĕntionă′lĭtў**, ns.; **convĕ′ntionalize** v.t.; **convĕ′ntual** a. (-**lly**), of convent(s). [F f. L *conventus* (CONVENE)]

**conver′g|e** v.i. Come together (as if) to meet or join; ~**e** (**up**)**on**, approach from different directions;

~ent *a.*, converging; ~ence *n.* [L (*vergo* incline)]

**cŏnversā'tion** *n.* Informal exchange of ideas by spoken words; instance of this; ~ **piece**, thing that serves as topic of conversation, painting of group of people conversing etc.; **convĕr'sant** (*or* kŏ'nver-) *a.*, well acquainted (*with* subject etc.); ~**al** *a.* (~**ally**), of or in conversation, fond of conversation, colloquial; ~**alĭst** *n.*, person fond of or good in conversation; **cŏnversāziō'nĕ** (-ǎts-) *n.*, social gathering held by learned society etc. [F f. L (foll.)]

**convḗrse**[1]. 1. (-ĕ'r-) *v.i.* Hold conversation, talk (*with* person). 2. (-ō'-) *n.* (arch.) Conversation. [F f. L (foll.)]

**cŏ'nverse**[2]. 1. *a.* Opposite, contrary, reversed. 2. *n.* Converse statement, proposition, etc., esp. one produced from another statement by transposition of some words (*he had learning without wealth* is the converse of *he had wealth without learning*). 3. **convĕr'selÿ** (-slĭ) *adv.*, in converse manner, as the converse; **convĕr'sion** (-shon) *n.*, converting or being converted. [L (*verto vers-* turn)]

**convĕrt**. 1. (-ĕ'r-) *v.t. & i.* Change, esp. in function (*into*); cause (person) to change beliefs, opinion, party, etc.; make structural alterations in (building) for new purpose; (Footb.) complete (a try) by kicking a goal; ~ **to** one's **own use**, use or take (another's money) dishonestly. 2. (-ŏ'-) *n.* Converted person. 3. **convĕr'tĭble**, (*a.*; -bly) liable to or capable of conversion, (of currency etc.) that may be changed into gold, other currency, etc., (of motor car) with folding or detachable roof, (*n.*) convertible motor car; **convĕr'tĭbī'lĭtÿ** *n.*

**cŏ'nvĕx** *a.* With outline or surface curved like exterior of circle or sphere; **convĕ'xĭtÿ** *n.* [L]

**convey'** (-vā') *v.t.* Transport or carry (goods, passenger, etc.); transmit (sound etc.); (Law) transfer (property); communicate (idea, meaning, etc.); ~**ance** *n.*, conveying, means of transport, vehicle, (deed effecting) transfer of property; ~**ancer** *n.*, lawyer arranging conveyances; ~**ancing** *n.*, work of conveyancer; ~**er**, ~**or**, *ns.*, (esp.) endless belt for conveying articles or

materials, esp. during manufacture. [F f. L (*via* way)]

**convĭct**. 1. (-ĭ'-) *v.t.* Prove or find guilty (*of* crime etc.). 2. (-ŏ'-) *n.* Imprisoned criminal. 3. **convĭc'tion** *n.*, convicting, verdict of guilty, being convinced, convinced state, firm belief, (CARRY conviction); **convi'nce** *v.t.* (-cible), firmly persuade (*of*, *that*); **convi'ncement** *n.* [L (*vinco vict-* conquer)]

**convĭ'vĭal** *a.* (-lly). Of, for, or fond of feasting, good company, etc.; jovial; ~**ă'lĭtÿ** *n.*, convivial behaviour or character. [L (*vivo* live)]

**cŏnvocā'tion** *n.* Convoking; ‖provincial synod of Anglican clergy; ‖legislative assembly of university; ~**al** *a.*; **convō'ke** *v.t.*, summon to assemble. [L (*voco* call)]

**cŏnvolū'tion** (-ōō'-) *n.* Coiling; coil, twist, complexity; sinuous fold of brain surface; **cŏ'nvolutĕd** (-ōot-) *a.*, coiled, twisted, complex; **cŏnvŏ'lvŭlus** *n.*, twining plant, esp. bindweed. [L (*volvo volut-* roll)]

**cŏ'nvoy**. 1. *v.t.* Escort (ships etc.) to protect them. 2. *n.* Convoying; group of ships, vehicles, etc., travelling together or escorted. [F (CONVEY)]

**convŭ'lsion** (-shon) *n.* Violent irregular motion of limb(s) or body caused by involuntary contraction of muscles (usu. in *pl.*, esp. of infants); violent disturbance; (in *pl.*) uncontrollable laughter; **convŭ'lse** *v.t.* (usu. in *pass.*), affect with convulsion(s); **convŭ'lsĭve** *a.* [F or L (*vello vuls-* pull)]

**cŏ'nÿ, cŏ'ney**, *n.* Rabbit (fur). [F f. L *cuniculus*]

**cōō** *n., v., & int.* 1. *n.* Soft murmuring sound (as) of dove. 2. *v.i. & t.* Emit coo; talk or say in soft or amorous voice. 3. *int.* (sl.) expr. surprise or incredulity. [imit.]

**cōō'ee** *n., v., & int.*, (esp. Austral. & N.Z.) 1. *n.* Sound used to attract attention, esp. at a distance; **within** (a) ~ (*of*), (colloq.) very near (to). 2. *v.i.* Emit cooee. 3. *int.* (colloq.) used to attract attention. [imit.]

**cŏŏk**. 1. *v.t. & i.* Prepare (food) by heating (~ person's **goose**, ruin his chances); undergo cooking (**what's** ~**ing?**, colloq. what is happening or planned?); falsify (accounts etc.); ~ **up**, invent or concoct (excuse, tale, etc.). 2. *n.* One whose occupation is to cook food, or who can do so in specified way (*good cook*; *plain cook*); **too many ~s spoil the broth**, one organizer etc. is enough; \*~'**book**, cookery book; ~'**house**, outdoor or camp kitchen, ship's galley; ~'**out**, outdoor gathering at which food is cooked, barbecue. **3.** ~'**er** *n.*, appliance or vessel for cooking food, apple etc. suited for cooking; ~'**erў** *n.*, art or practice of cooking (~**erў book**, book containing recipes for preparing food); ~'**ing** *n.*, (esp., *attrib.*) suitable for or used in cooking (*cooking sherry*). [E f. L *coquus*]

**coō'kie** *n.* \*Small sweet biscuit; (Sc.) plain bun. [Du. *koekje*]

**coōl** *a., n.,* & *v.* **1.** *a.* (~**ly** *pr.* -l-lĭ). Of or at fairly low temperature, fairly cold; unexcited, calm; (colloq., esp. of jazz or its performers) restrained, unemotional, excellent; lacking zeal or cordiality; calmly audacious; **a ~**, (of large sum of money) no less than (*six thousand etc.*); ~**-headed**, not easily excited. **2.** *n.* Coolness; cool air or place; (sl.) composure (*keep, lose,* one's *cool*). **3.** *v.t.* & *i.* ~ (**down, off**), make or become cool; *cool* one's HEEL[1]s; ~ **it**, (sl.) relax, calm down; ~'**ing tower**, industrial structure for cooling hot water before reuse. **4.** ~'**ant** *n.*, cooling agent, esp. fluid used to lessen friction of cutting tool or to remove heat from machine; ~'**er** *n.*, (esp.) vessel in which a thing is cooled, \*refrigerator, (sl.) prison cell. [E]

**coō'lie** *n.* Unskilled native labourer in Eastern countries. [orig. uncert.]

‖**coōmb**, ‖**combe**, (koōm) *n.* Hollow on flank of hill; steep short valley. [E]

**coōn** *n.* \*Racoon; (sl., derog.) Black. [abbr.]

**coōp. 1.** *n.* Cage for confining poultry (\***fly the ~**, sl., depart abruptly). **2.** *v.t.* Put (fowl) in coop; ~ (**in, up**), confine (person). **3.** ~'**er** *n.*, maker or repairer of casks or similar vessels. [LDu.]

**coō-ŏp** *n.* (colloq.) Co-operative (society or store). [abbr.]

**coō-ŏ'per|āte** *v.i.* Work or act together (*with* person, *in* or on task, *for* purpose, etc.); ~**ā'tion** *n.*, co-operating, (Econ.) production and distribution by a group whose members share the profits or benefits; ~**ative**, (*a.*) of co-operation,

that does or will co-operate, (of farm, society, etc.) run on basis of economic co-operation, (*n.*) co--operative farm etc., \*dwelling jointly owned or leased by occupiers; ~**ātor** *n.* [CO-]

**coō-ŏ'pt** *v.t.* Elect (person) to committee etc. by votes of existing members; ~**ā'tion**, ~**ion**, *ns.*; ~(**at**)**ive** *a.* [L *co-opto* (*opto* choose)]

**coō-ŏr'din|ate** *a., n.,* & *v.* **1.** *a.* Equal in rank or importance, esp. (Gram.) of parts of compound sentence; consisting of co-ordinate things. **2.** *n.* Co-ordinate thing; (Math., usu. *coo-*) each of set of quantities used to fix position of point, line, or plane (e.g. place's latitude and longitude); (in *pl.*) women's outer clothes that can be worn together harmoniously. **3.** (-āt) *v.t.* Make co-ordinate; bring (parts, movements, etc.) into proper relation; cause (limbs, parts, etc.) to function together or in proper order; ~**ā'tion**, ~**ātor**, *ns.*; ~**ative** *a.* [L *ordino* (ORDER)]

**coōt** *n.* Aquatic bird with base of upper mandible extended to form white band on forehead (**bald as a ~**, entirely bald); (colloq.) stupid person. [prob. LG]

**cŏp.** (sl.) **1.** *v.t.* & *i.* (**-pp-**). Catch (offender); receive, obtain, take; ~ **it**, get into trouble, be punished, die; ~ **out**, escape, withdraw, cease work, commitment, etc.; ~**-out** *n.*, (way of) escape, cowardly evasion. **2.** *n.* Policeman; capture or arrest (*it's a fair cop*); **not much ~**, of little value or use. [F *caper* seize]

**cō'pal** *n.* Resin of tropical tree, used for varnish. [Sp. f. Aztec]

**cōpā'rtner** *n.* Partner, sharer, associate; ~**ship** *n.* [CO-]

**cōpe**[1]. **1.** *n.* (Eccl.) Long cloak worn in processions etc. **2.** *v.t.* Furnish with cope or coping. [E f. L *cappa* CAP]

**cōpe**[2] *v.i.* Deal effectively or contend *with*; (colloq.) manage successfully. [F (COUP)]

**cŏ'pĕck** *n.* Russian coin (₁₀₀ rouble). [Russ.]

**Copĕr'nican** *a.* Of or according to the theory of *Copernicus* that the planets, including the earth, move round the sun. [person]

**cŏ'pier** *n.* Person or machine that copies (esp. documents). [COPY]

**cŏ′-pĭlot, \*cŏ′p-,** n. Second pilot in aircraft. [co-]

**cŏ′pĭng** n. Top (usu. sloping) course of masonry; **~-stone** (used for coping). [cope¹]

**cŏ′pious** a. Consisting of, drawing upon, or producing an abundance of material. [F or L (copia plenty)]

**cŏ′pper¹. 1.** n. Reddish malleable ductile metallic element; bronze coin; large metal vessel for boiling esp. laundry; (attrib.) made of, coloured like, copper; **~ beech** (with copper-coloured leaves); **~-bottom** v.t., sheathe bottom of (ship, pan, etc.) with copper, (in p.p.) reliable or genuine; **~head,** venomous Amer. or Austral. snake; **~plate,** polished copper plate for engraving or etching, print from this, (a., of writing) careful and neat; **~ÿ** a., (esp.) copper-coloured. **2.** v.t Cover with copper. [E f. L cuprum]

||**cŏ′pper²** n. (sl.) Policeman. [cop]

**cŏ′ppĭce, cŏpse,** ns. Small area of undergrowth and small trees, grown for periodical cutting. [F f. L (coup)]

**cŏ′pra** n. Dried coconut-kernels. [Port. f. Malayalam]

**cŏpse.** See COPPICE.

**Cŏpt** n. Egyptian Christian; **Cŏ′ptĭc** a. & n., (language) of the Copts. [F or L f. Arab.]

**cŏ′pŭl|a** n. Part or word acting as a connecting link, esp. part of verb be connecting predicate with subject; **~āte** v.i., have copulation (with); **~ā′tion** n., sexual intercourse, similar act of lower animals; **~ative** a., serving to connect, (also **~atorÿ**) of copulation. [L]

**cŏ′pÿ. 1.** n. Thing, esp. piece of writing, made to be or look (exactly) like another (fair **~,** written matter transcribed after correction; ROUGH copy); specimen of book etc. (an edition of 5,000 copies); manuscript or matter to be printed; interesting material for a newspaper etc. (this will make good copy); text of advertisement. **2.** v.t. & i. Make copy (of); **~ out,** transcribe, copy carefully; imitate (person etc.); **~ist** n., person who makes copies, imitator. **3. ~-book,** book containing models of handwriting etc. for learners to imitate (BLOT one's copy-book), (a.) tritely conventional, exemplary; **~-cat,** (colloq.) slavish imitator; **~hold,** (Hist.) tenure in accordance with transcript of manorial records,

land so held; **~right,** (n.) exclusive right to print, publish, perform, etc., a work, (a.) protected by copyright, (v.t.) secure copyright for (book etc.); **~typist,** one who makes typewritten copies; **~writer,** writer of copy for publication, esp. of advertisements. [F f. L copia transcript]

**coquĕtt|e** (-kĕ′t) n., & v.i. (Behave as) woman who trifles with men's affections; flirt; **cŏ′quĕtrÿ** (-kĭt-) n., flirting, coquettish act; **~ish** a. [F dim. (COCK¹)]

||**cŏr** int. (vulg.) expr. astonishment, exasperation, etc.; esp. cor BLIMEY! [corrupt. of God]

**cor-.** See COM-.

**Cor.** abbr. Corinthians (N.T.).

||**cŏ′racle** n. Small boat of wickerwork covered with watertight material. [W]

**cŏ′ral** n. Hard red, pink, or white calcareous substance built up on sea-bed by marine polyps; unimpregnated roe of lobster; (attrib., of lips etc.) like coral in colour, red or pink; **~ island, reef,** (formed by growth of coral); **~line** a., of or like coral. [F f. L f. Gk]

**cŏr a′nglais** (kŏr ah′nglā, ŏ′ngglā) n. (Mus.) Woodwind instrument like low-pitched oboe; its player. [F]

**cŏr′bel** n. Stone or timber projection from a wall to support something; **~-table,** projecting course supported on corbels; **~led** (-ld) a.; **cŏr′bie** n., (Sc.) raven, black crow; **corbie-steps,** (Archit.) stepline ornament on gable. [F f. L corvus crow]

**cŏrd. 1.** n. (Piece of) thin rope or thick string; (Anat.) similar structure in body (SPINAL cord; VOCAL cords); \*electric flex; ribbed cloth, esp. corduroy; (in pl.) corduroy trousers; measure of cut wood (usu. 128 cubic ft.). **2.** v.t. Secure with cord; (in p.p., of cloth) ribbed. **3. ~′age** n., cords or ropes, esp. in rigging of ship. [F f. L f. Gk khordē string]

**cŏr′dial. 1.** a. (**~ly**). Heartfelt, sincere; warm, friendly; (arch., of medicine, drink, etc.) stimulating the heart; **cŏrdiă′lĭtÿ** n. **2.** n. Flavoured and sweetened drink made from fruit; invigorating drink. [L (cor cord- heart)]

**cŏr′dĭte** n. Cordlike smokeless explosive. [CORD]

**cŏr′don. 1.** n. Line or circle of police, soldiers, guards, etc., esp.

preventing access to or from an area; ornamental cord or braid; fruit-tree trained to grow as single stem; ~ **bleu** (kȯrdawn blĕr'), first-class cook; ~ **sanitaire** (kȯrdawn sănĭtār'), guarded line between infected and uninfected districts (lit. or fig.). **2.** *v.t.* ~ (**off**), enclose or separate with police etc. cordon. [It. & F (CORD)]

**cŏr'duroy** (*or* -ūr-) *n.* Thick ribbed cotton velvet; (in *pl.*) corduroy trousers. [CORD = ribbed fabric]

**cŏre. 1.** *n.* Horny capsule containing seeds of apple, pear, etc.; central or most important part (lit. or fig.; **to the** ~, thoroughly, completely); central region of the earth; piece of soft iron forming centre of magnet or induction coil; inner strand of electric cable; region of fissile material in nuclear reactor; unit of structure in computer, whose magnetization is reversible. **2.** *v.t.* Remove core from. [orig. unkn.]

**cŏrĕŏ'psĭs** *n.* Plant with rayed usu. yellow flowers. [L f. Gk *koris* bug, *opsis* appearance (w. ref. to seed)]

**cō-rĕspŏ'ndent,** *\*cŏre-, n.* Person (esp. man) charged with committing adultery with respondent in divorce case. [CO-]

**cŏr'gĭ** (-gĭ) *n.* (Welsh) ~, short-legged dog with foxlike head. [W]

**cŏrĭă'nder** *n.* Plant with aromatic fruit (~ **seed**) used as flavouring. [F f. L f. Gk]

**Corĭ'nthĭan** *a.* ~ **order,** (Archit.) the most ornate Greek order, with acanthus leaves decorating the capital. [L f. Gk (*Corinth*, place)]

**cŏrk. 1.** *n.* Bark of cork-oak, a buoyant light-brown substance; float of cork, bottle-stopper of cork or other material; ~**-oak,** a S. European oak; ~'**screw,** (*n.*) spiral steel device for extracting corks from bottles, (usu. *attrib.*) thing similarly shaped, (*v.t.* & *i.*) move spirally; ||~**-tipped,** (of cigarette) having filter of corklike material. **2.** *v.t.* Stop (*up*) (as) with cork; bottle *up* (feelings etc.); (in *p.p.*, of wine) impaired by a contaminated cork. **3.** ~'**age** *n.*, charge made by restaurant etc. for serving wine etc. (esp. that brought from elsewhere); ~'**er** *n.*, (sl.) astonishingly or surpassingly good thing or person; ~'**ing** *a.*, (sl.) unusually large or excellent; ~'**y** *a.*, (~**ily,**

~**iness;** esp., of wine) corked. [LDu. f. Sp. *alcorque* f. Arab.]

**cŏrm** *n.* (Bot.) Bulblike underground stem. [L f. Gk *kormos* lopped tree-trunk]

**cŏr'morant** *n.* Large voracious sea-bird. [F f. L *corvus marinus* sea-raven]

**cŏrn¹. 1.** *n.* Cereal(s) before or after harvesting, esp. wheat, oats, or maize; grain or seed, esp. of cereal plant; (colloq.) something corny; ~**-cob,** cylindrical centre of ear of maize, to which grains are attached (~ **on the cob,** maize cooked and eaten in this form); ~'**crake,** bird with harsh grating cry; ~ **dolly,** symbolic or decorative figure made of plaited straw; *corn* EXCHANGE; ~'**field** (in which corn is grown); ~'**flakes,** breakfast cereal of toasted flakes made from maize flour; ~'**flour,** fine-ground flour made from maize, rice, etc.; ~'**flower,** plant (esp. blue-flowered one) growing in cornfields; ~ **marigold,** cornfield weed like yellow daisy. **2.** *v.t.* Preserve with salt or brine; ~**ed beef** (thus preserved and tinned). **3.** ~'**y** *a.* (colloq.; ~**ily,** ~**iness**), out of date, old-fashioned, trite, sentimental. [E]

**cŏrn². 1.** *n.* Small tender horny place on skin, esp. on toe (TREAD *on* person's *corns*); ~'**ea** *n.,* transparent membrane covering iris and pupil of eyeball; ~'**eal** *a.* [AF f. L *cornu* horn]

**cŏr'nel** *n.* Hard-wooded tree, esp. **cŏrnē'lĭan¹ cherry,** European berry-bearing tree. [L *cornus*]

**cŏrnē'lĭan², car-,** *n.* Dull red chalcedony. [F]

**cŏr'ner. 1.** *n.* Place where converging sides or edges meet; projecting angle, esp. where two streets meet (cut off *or* cut a ~, take short cut, lit. or fig.); **just** (a) **round the** ~, colloq., very near, imminent; **turn the** ~, pass round corner into another street, fig. pass critical point in illness etc.); recess formed by the meeting of two internal sides of room, box, etc., (**drive into a** ~, force into position allowing no escape; TIGHT *corner*); (Boxing etc.) angle of ring, esp. one where contestant rests between rounds; region, quarter, esp. remote (*the* FOUR *corners*); secluded or remote place (HOLE-*and-corner*); action or result of buying the whole available stock of a commodity (*he made a corner in wheat*); ~(-hit, -kick), (Hockey, Assoc. Footb.) free hit or kick from corner of pitch after ball has been hit or kicked over his own goal-line by an opponent; ~-stone, stone in projecting angle of wall, foundation-stone, (fig.) indispensable part or basis. 2. *v.t. & i.* Drive into corner (esp. fig.); establish corner in (commodity etc.); (esp. of, or in, vehicle) go round corner. [AF f. L (CORN²)]

cŏr′nĕt n. (Player of) brass musical instrument resembling trumpet; ‖conical wafer containing ice cream; ~(t)ĭst (or -nĕ′t-) n., cornet-player. [F dim. f. L *cornu* (CORN²)]

cŏr′nice n. Horizontal projecting moulding on building etc., esp. topmost part of entablature; ornamental moulding round wall of room just below ceiling; overhanging mass of snow above precipice. [F f. It.]

Cŏr′nish. 1. *a.* Of Cornwall; ~ pasty, seasoned meat and vegetables baked in pastry. 2. *n.* Celtic language used in Cornwall. [place]

cŏrnŭcō′pĭa n. Symbol of plenty consisting of goat's horn overflowing with flowers, fruit, and corn. [L (CORN², COPIOUS)]

cŏr′nў. See CORN¹.

corŏ′lla n. Whorl of petals forming inner envelope of flower; ~rў n., proposition that follows from one already proved, natural consequence (*of* something). [L dim. (foll.)]

corŏ′na n. (*pl.* ~e, ~s). Ring of light round sun or moon, esp. during eclipse; cŏ′ronal *a.*; cŏ′ronarў, (*a.*) resembling or encircling like a crown (coronary artery, supplying heart with blood; coronary thrombosis, thrombosis in this artery), (*n.*) coronary artery or thrombosis; cŏronā′tion n., ceremony of crowning; cŏ′roner n., officer holding inquests on deaths thought to be violent or accidental; cŏ′ronĕt (or -ĕt) n., small crown, esp. as worn, or used as heraldic device, by peer or peeress. [L, = crown]

cŏ′ronăch (-χ, -k) n. (Sc.) Highland dirge. [Gael.]

Corp. *abbr.* *Corporation.

cŏr′pora. See CORPUS.

cŏr′poral¹ n. Non-commissioned army or R.A.F. officer next below sergeant. [F f. It.]

cŏr′poral² *a.* (~ly). Of the human body (~ punishment, esp. flogging); ~itў (-ă′l-) n., being or having a body. [F f. L (CORPUS)]

cŏr′porate *a.* Of, being, belonging to, a corporation or group; cŏr′porā′tion n., united body of persons, esp. civic authorities of borough, town, or city, or group constituted to act as individual in business, administration, etc., (colloq.) prominent abdomen; cŏr′porative *a.*, of a corporation, governed by or organized in corporations esp. of employers and employed; cŏr′pŏr′eal *a.* (-lly), bodily, physical, material; cŏrpŏrĕ′alitў, cŏrpŏrĕ′-itў, ns. [L (prec.)]

cŏr′posant (-z-) n. Luminous electrical discharge occas. seen on ship or aircraft in storm. [Sp., Port., It. *corpo santo* holy body]

cŏrps (kōr) n. (*pl.* same *pr.* kōrz). A military force or division; group of persons engaged in same activity; ~ de ballet (kôrdebă′lā), a company of ballet dancers; ~ d'élite (kôrdālē′t), select group; ~ diplomatique (kôrdĭplŏmătē′k) = DIPLOMATIC corps; cŏr′pse n., dead (usu. human) body; cŏr′pŭlent *a.*, bulky in body; cŏr′pŭlence n. [F (foll.)]

cŏr′pus n. (*pl.* cor′pora). Body or collection of writings etc.; C~ Christi (krī′stī), Feast of the Body of Christ, on Thursday after Trinity Sunday. [L, = body]

cŏr′puscle (-sel) n. Minute body or cell in organism, esp. (in *pl.*) those constituting large part of blood in vertebrates; cŏrpŭ′scular *a.* [L. dim. of prec.]

corra′l (-ah′l). 1. *n.* *Pen for horses, cattle, etc.; enclosure for capture of wild animals; defensive enclosure of wagons. 2. *v.t.* (-ll-). Put or keep in corral. [Sp. & Port. (KRAAL)]

corrĕ′ct. 1. *a.* True, accurate; (of conduct, manners, etc.) right, proper, complying with etiquette, good taste, etc. 2. *v.t.* Set right (error, omission, etc.); substitute right thing for (wrong one); mark errors in (proof-sheet etc.); admonish (person); punish (person, fault); counteract (harmful or divergent tendency etc.); bring into accordance with standard; eliminate aberration etc. from (lens etc.). 3. ~ion n., correcting (*speak under* ~ion, speak while recognizing that one may be wrong), thing substituted for what is wrong, (arch.) punishment; ~**ĭtŭde** *n.*, consciously correct behaviour; ~**ĭve**, (*a.*) serving to correct or counteract something harmful, (*n.*) corrective measure or thing; ~**or** *n.* [F f. L (*rego rect-* guide)]

**cŏrrĕl|āte. 1.** *v.t.* & *i.* Bring into, or be in, correlation (*with*). **2.** *n.* Either of two things or words which imply or complement one another. **3.** ~**ā'tion** *n.*, mutual relationship, (measure of extent of) interdependence of variable quantities, act of correlating; **cŏrrĕ'lative**, (*a.*) having correlation, being correlates, (*n.*) a correlate; **cŏrrĕlati'vĭty** *n.* [L]

**cŏrrĕspŏ'nd** *v.i.* Be analogous (*to*) or in agreement (*with*); communicate by interchange of letters (*with*); ~**ence** *n.*, agreement or similarity, (communication by) letters (~**ence course**, course of study conducted thus); ~**ent** *n.*, one who writes letter(s) to person, newspaper, etc., person employed by newspaper etc. to contribute matter for publication. [F f. L]

**cŏrri'da** (-ē'-) *n.* Bullfight. [Sp.]

**cŏ'rridor** *n.* Passage from which doors lead into rooms (~**s of power**, fig., places where covert influence is exerted in government) or railway carriage compartments (~ **train**, train of such carriages); strip of a State's territory running through that of another; route to which aircraft are restricted. [F f. It.]

**cŏ'rrie** *n.* (esp. Sc.) Circular hollow on mountainside. [Gael.]

**cŏrrĭgĕ'nd|um** *n.* (*pl.* ~**a**). Thing to be corrected, esp. error in book; **cŏ'rrĭgible** *a.* (-**bly**), that can be corrected, (of person) submissive. [L (*corrigo* to CORRECT)]

**corrŏ'bor|āte** *v.t.* (~**able**). Confirm or give support to (person, statement, belief); ~**ant** *a.* & *n.*, (arch.) corroborating (fact); ~**ā'tion**, ~**ātor**, *ns.*; ~**ātive**, ~**atŏry**, *adjs.* [L (*robur* strength)]

**corrŏ'boree** *n.* (Austral.) Festive or warlike dance of Aboriginals; noisy party. [Aboriginal]

**corrŏ'de** *v.t.* & *i.* (-**dible**). Wear away esp. by chemical action, destroy gradually, decay; **corrŏ'sion** (-zhon) *n.*, corroding; **corrŏ'sĭve** *a.* & *n.*, (substance) that causes corrosion. [F or L (*rodo ros-* gnaw)]

**cŏ'rrug|āte** (-ŏŏ-) *v.t.* & *i.* (esp. in *p.p.*) Bend or form into folds or ridges, esp. to produce stronger material (*corrugated iron, paper*); ~**ā'tion** *n.* [L (*ruga* wrinkle)]

**corrŭ'pt. 1.** *a.* Rotten; depraved, wicked; influenced by or using bribery; (of language, text, etc.) vitiated by errors or alterations. **2.** *v.t.* & *i.* (~**ible**). Make or become corrupt; ~**ĭbĭ'lĭty** *n.*; **corrŭ'ption** *n.*, corrupting, corrupt condition. [F or L (RUPTURE)]

**cŏrsage** (-ah'zh) *n.* (*Small bouquet worn on) bodice of woman's dress. [F (CORPS)]

**cŏr'sair** *n.* (Hist.) Pirate(-ship), esp. of Barbary. [F (COURSE)]

**cŏrse** *n.* (arch. or poet.) corpse; **cŏr'selĕtte** (*or* -sl-) *n.*, woman's foundation garment combining corset and brassière [*P]; **cŏr'sĕt** *n.*, woman's close-fitting undergarment supporting waist and hips, man's or woman's similar garment worn because of injury etc.; **cŏr'sĕtĕd** *a.*; **cŏr'sĕtière** (-tyār) *n.*, woman who makes or fits corsets; **cŏr'sĕtrў** *n.*; **cŏr'slĕt, -selĕt**, (-sl-) *n.*, (Hist.) coat of armour, garment (usu. tight-fitting) covering body. [var. of CORPSE]

**cŏrtège** (-tā'zh) *n.* Procession, esp. for funeral. [F]

**cŏr'tĕx** *n.* (*pl.* ~**ices** *pr.* -isēz). Outer part or covering (e.g. of kidney); outer grey matter of brain; ~**ical** *a.* (-**lly**); ~**icātĕd** *a.*, having cortex. [L, = bark]

**cŏr'tĭsōne** (-z-) *n.* Hormone used medicinally against inflammation and allergy. [abbr. of Chem. name]

**corŭ'ndum** *n.* Extremely hard crystallized alumina, used esp. as abrasive. [Tamil f. Skr.]

**cŏ'rusc|āte** *v.i.* Sparkle (lit., or fig. of wit etc.); ~**ā'tion** *n.* [L]

**cŏrvĕ'tte** *n.* Small naval escort-vessel; (Hist.) flush-decked warship with one tier of guns. [F f. Du.]

**cŏ'rўmb** *n.* (Bot.) Flat-topped raceme with lower flower-stalks proportionally longer. [F or L f. Gk]

**cŏ'rўphée** (-fā) *n.* Leading dancer of *corps de ballet*. [F]

**cŏs**[1] *n.* Crisp long-leaved lettuce. [place]

**cŏs**[2] (*or* -z) *abbr.* cosine.

**‖cŏsh** *n.*, & *v.t.* (colloq.) (Strike with) heavy stick or bludgeon. [orig. unkn.]

**cŏ′sher** v.t. Pamper. [orig. unkn.]

**cŏ′sĭne** n. (Math.) Sine of complement of given angle or quantity. [CO-]

**cŏsmĕ′tĭc** (-zm-) a. (~**ally**) & n. (Substance) designed to beautify skin, hair, etc.; (fig.) intended to improve appearances; (of surgery or prosthetic device) imitating or restoring normal appearance. [F f. Gk (COSMOS²)]

**cŏ′sm|ĭc** (-z-) a. (~**ically**). Of the cosmos, esp. as opp. to the earth; of or for space travel; ~**ic radiation, rays,** radiation from outer space etc. with high energy and penetrative power; ~**ŏ′gony** n., (theory of) the origin of the universe [Gk -gonia -begetting]; ~**ŏ′graphy** n., description or mapping of universe or earth; ~**ogră′phic(al)** adjs. (-ically); ~**ŏ′logy** n., science or theory of the universe; ~**olŏ′gical** a. (-lly); ~**ŏ′logist** n.; ~**onaut** n., (esp. Russian) astronaut; ~**opŏ′litan,** (a.) of or from all or many parts of the world, free from national limitations or prejudices, (n.) cosmopolite; ~**opŏ′litanism** n.; ~**ŏ′polite** n., cosmopolitan person. [foll.]

**cŏ′smŏs¹** (-z-) n. The universe as a well-ordered whole. [Gk]

**cŏ′smŏs²** (-z-) n. Plant bearing single dahlia-like flowers. [L f. Gk, = ornament]

**Cŏ′ssăck** n. Member of a people of S. Russia, esp. (Hist.) as horsemen in Russian army; ~ **hat,** brimless hat widening towards top. [F f. Russ. f. Turk.]

**cŏ′ssĕt** v.t. Pamper. [AF f. E (COT², SIT)]

**cŏst** (or kaw-). **1.** v.t. (**cost;** w. ind. obj.) Involve payment, sacrifice, or loss of, have as price, (what does it cost?; it cost him £5, his honour, his life, much effort); ~ **person dear,** involve him in much expense or loss); (~**ed**) fix or estimate cost of. **2.** n. What thing costs, price, (**at all ~s, at any ~,** no matter what it may cost; **at ~,** at cost price; **at the ~ of,** with the expense or loss of; **count the ~,** consider the risks before action; **to** one's ~, resulting in or as result of one's loss or disadvantage); (in pl.) legal expenses, esp. those allowed to successful litigant; ~**-benefit,** assessing relation of cost of operation to value of benefits resulting; ~**-effective,** effective

in relation to its cost; cost of LIVING¹; ~ **price,** price paid for thing by one who later sells it. [F f. L consto stand at a price]

**cŏ′stal** a. (~**ly**). Of the ribs; ‖**cŏ′stard** n., large ribbed apple; ‖**cŏ′ster(monger)** (-ŭngg-) n., man who sells fruit, vegetables, etc., from barrow in street. [F f. L (costa rib)]

**cŏ′-stär. 1.** n. Cinema or stage star appearing with other star(s) of equal importance. **2.** v.i. & t. (-rr-). Perform or include as co-star. [CO-]

**cŏ′stive** a. Constipated. [AF f. L (CONSTIPATION)]

**cŏ′stl|ў** (or kaw′-) a. (~**iness**). Costing much, expensive. [COST]

**cŏ′stūme. 1.** n. Style of dress; set of outer clothes; garment(s) for a particular activity (bathing-costume); woman's matching jacket and skirt; ~ **jewellery** (artificial); ~ **piece, play,** play in which actors wear historical costume. **2.** v.t. Provide with costume; **cŏstū′mier** n., maker of or dealer in costumes. [F f. It. f. L (CUSTOM)]

**cŏ′sў** (-zǐ), *****cŏ′zў,** a., n., & v. **1.** a. (-ily, -iness). Comfortable, snug; warm and friendly; (derog.) complacent. **2.** n. Cover to retain heat in teapot, boiled egg, etc. **3.** v.t. & i. (colloq.) ~ (**along**), reassure, delude; *****~ up to,** snuggle up to, ingratiate oneself with. [orig. unkn.]

**cŏt¹** n. Small or light bed; ‖small tall-sided bed for child; *****camp-bed; ~-death,** unexplained death of sleeping baby. [Hindi]

**cŏt²** n. Small house or hut; cote; (poet.) cottage. [E]

**cōte** n. Shelter or shed for animals or birds (DOVE¹cote). [E]

**cŏ′terĭe** n. Group of persons exclusively sharing interests etc. [F]

**cotŏnĕă′ster** n. Shrub or small tree bearing red or orange berries. [L (cotonium quince)]

**cŏ′ttage** n. Small house, esp. in the country; ~ **cheese,** soft white cheese; ~ **hospital** (without resident medical staff); ~ **industry** (partly or wholly carried on at home); ~ **loaf** (of two round masses, smaller on top of larger); ~ **pie,** shepherd's pie; **cŏ′ttager** (-tĭj-) n., one who lives in a cottage; **cŏ′ttar, cŏ′tter¹,** n., (Hist., Sc.) peasant occupying cottage and labouring as required. [AF (COT²)]

**cŏ'tter**[2] *n.* ~(-**pin**), bolt or wedge for securing parts of machinery etc. [orig. unkn.]

**cŏ'tton. 1.** *n.* (Plant with seeds covered by) white downy fibrous substance, used for making cloth, thread, etc.; thread or cloth made from this; GUN-cotton; ~ **waste**, refuse yarn for cleaning of machinery etc.; ~ **wool**, raw cotton, wadding made of it; ~y̆ *a.* **2.** *v.i.* ~ **on** (to), (sl.) understand, realize; ~ (**on**) **to**, form liking for (person, thing). [F f. Arab.]

**cŏtȳlē'don** *n.* (Bot.) Primary leaf of plant embryo. [L f. Gk (*kotulē* cup)]

**couch**[1]. **1.** *n.* Long bedlike seat, usu. with head-rest at one end, (esp.) place where psychiatrist's patient reclines; (arch., literary) bed, place where one sleeps. **2.** *v.t. & i.* Place (as) on couch; lower (spear) to position for attack; express (thought etc. *in* words); (of animal) lie, esp. in lair. [F f. L *colloco* lay in place]

**couch**[2] (*or* kŏō-) *n.* ~(-**grass**), weed with long creeping roots. [QUITCH]

*\***cou'gar** (kōō'-) *n.* Puma. [F f. Guarani]

**cough** (kŏf, kawf). **1.** *v.i. & t.* Expel air etc. from lungs violently and noisily; (of engine etc.) make similar noise; ~ **out**, **up**, eject or say with cough(s); ~ **up**, (sl.) bring out or provide (information, money, etc.) reluctantly. **2.** *n.* Act or sound of coughing; tendency to cough; affection of respiratory organs causing coughing; ~-**drop**, ~-**sweet**, medicated sweet to relieve cough; ~ **mixture**, medicine to relieve cough. [E, imit.]

**could.** See CAN[2].

**couli'sse** (kōōlē's) *n.* Corridor; the wings in a theatre; group of unofficial dealers on bourse; **cou'loir** (kōō'lwăr) *n.*, steep gully in mountainside. [F (*couler* glide)]

**cou'lŏmb** (kōō'lŏm) *n.* Unit of electric charge. [person]

**cou'lter** (kō'l-), *\***cō'l-, *n.* Vertical blade in front of ploughshare. [E f. L *culter* knife]

**cou'ncil** *n.* Advisory, deliberative, or administrative body, or one of its meetings (~ **of war**, assembly of officers called in special emergency, also fig.; ORDER *in* Council; PRIVY *Council*); local administrative body of county, city, town, etc.; ~-

-**chamber,** room in which council meets; ~ **estate, flat, house,** etc., dwelling(s) owned and let by local council; ~ **school** (supported by town or county council); ~**lor** *n.*, member of council. [AF f. L *concilium*]

**cou'nsel. 1.** *n.* Consultation (**take** ~, think or talk over *with* person what is to be done); advice (~ **of despair**, action taken when all else fails; ~ **of perfection**, advice that is ideal but impracticable; **keep** one's **own** ~, not confide in others); legal adviser(s); (*pl.* same) barrister(s) (**Queen's, King's, C~,** counsel to the Crown, taking precedence over other barristers). **2.** *v.t.* (||-ll-). Advise (person *to do, that,* action); ~**lor**, *\**~**or**, *n.*, adviser, *\**esp. of students. [F f. L *consilium*]

**count**[1]. **1.** *v.t. & i.* Find number of (things etc.), esp. by assigning successive numerals; repeat numerals in order; include or be included in reckoning or consideration; consider (thing, person) to be (lucky etc.); ~ **against**, be considered as factor against; ~ **down**, count numbers backwards to zero, esp. before launching rocket etc. (~-**down** n.); ~ **for**, be worth (*much, little,* etc.); ~ **in**, include; ~'**ing-house**, place where accounts are kept; ~ (**up**)**on**, rely on for help etc., expect; ~ **out**, count one by one from a stock, complete count of 10 seconds over (fallen boxer), (colloq.) not include; ||procure adjournment of (House of Commons) for lack of quorum; *count the* COST; ~ **up**, find total of. **2.** *n.* Counting, reckoning, (**keep, lose,** ~, be aware, fail to know, how many there have been); total; (Law) each charge in an indictment; **out for the** ~, defeated. [F f. L (COMPUTE)]

**count**[2] *n.* Foreign noble corresp. to earl (cf. COUNTESS; *Count* PALATINE[1]). [F f. L *comes* companion]

**cou'nténance. 1.** *n.* The face esp. with respect to its permanent or temporary expression, composure of face, (**change** ~, show emotion; **keep** one's ~, esp. refrain from laughing; **keep** person **in** ~, save him from embarrassment by show of support; **lose** ~, become embarrassed; **out of** ~, abashed); moral support, corroboration, (**find no** ~ **in**, be unsupported by). **2.** *v.t.*

Give approval to, look on with favour at, connive at, (practice, person in or *in* practice). [F (CONTAIN)]

**cou'nter**[1] *n.* Small disc etc. used in scoring at cards etc.; token representing coin; thing used in bargaining; banker's or shopkeeper's table between himself and customers (~-**jumper**, derog., shop assistant; **under the ~**, surreptitiously, esp. illegally); similar structure in cafeteria etc.; device for counting things. [COUNT[1]]

**cou'nter**[2] *n., a., adv.,* & *v.* **1.** *n.* Part between horse's shoulders and below its neck; curved part of ship's stern; part of shoe or boot round heel; return blow, countermove. **2.** *a.* Opposite. **3.** *adv.* In the opposite direction; **go, run, ~ to**, disobey (instructions etc.). **4.** *v.t. & i.* Oppose, contradict; meet or baffle (opponent, blow, move) by an answering move etc.; counter opponent or move; (Boxing) give return blow while parrying. [foll.]

**counter-** *pref.* of *vbs., ns., adjs.,* and *advs.,* meaning rival (*counter-attraction*), retaliatory (*counterstroke*), reversed (*counter-clockwise*), opposite (*counter-current*), or corresponding (*counterpart*). [F f. L CONTRA]

**counterâ'ct** *v.t.* Neutralize or hinder by contrary action; **~ion** *n.*; **~ïve** *a.*

**cou'nter|-attãck** *n.,* & *v.t. & i.* Attack (lit. or fig.) in reply to attack by enemy or opponent; **~-attrãction** *n.,* attraction of contrary tendency to another, rival attraction; **~bãlance,** (*n.*) weight (lit. or fig.) balancing another, (*v.t.*) neutralize by contrary power or influence; **~blast** (-ah-) *n.,* energetic declaration or action against (*to*) something; **~chãrge** *n.,* & *v.t.,* charge in opposition to another, charge against accuser; **~chĕck** *n.,* check that operates against a thing or against another check; **~-claim** *n.,* & *v.t.,* claim against another claim, claim as defendant in suit; **~-clŏ'ckwise** (-z), see CLOCK[1]; **~-ĕ'spionage** (*or* -ah'zh) *n.,* action against an enemy's spy system.

**cou'nterfeit** (-fĭt, -fēt) *a., n.,* & *v.* **1.** *a.* Made in imitation and usu. of inferior material; forged, not genuine, spurious. **2.** *n.* Counterfeit thing. **3.** *v.t.* Imitate with intent to deceive; forge (coin, signature, etc.); (literary) resemble closely. [F (FACT)]

**cou'nterfoil** *n.* Part of cheque, receipt, etc. retained as record by person issuing such document. [FOIL[1]]

**cou'nter-intĕlligence** *n.* Counter-espionage. [COUNTER-]

**counter-i'rritant** *n.* Thing used to produce surface irritation and so relieve symptoms of disease.

**counterma'nd** (-ah'-) *v.t.* Revoke (order); recall (person, forces) by contrary order; cancel order for (action, goods). [F f. L (MANDATE)]

**cou'nter|mãrch** *n.,* & *v.i.* & *t.* March in contrary direction; **~measure** (-ĕzher) *n.,* action against danger or threat; **~move** (-ōōv) *n.,* move or action in opposition to another. [COUNTER-]

**cou'nterpãne** *n.* Bedspread. [F f. L *culcita puncta* quilted mattress]

**cou'nterpãrt** *n.* Thing so like another as to be mistakable for it; person or thing that is the complement or correlative of another (e.g. male and female, night and day); opposite part of indenture. [COUNTER-]

**cou'nterplŏt. 1.** *n.* Plot contrived to defeat another. **2.** *v.i.* (-tt-). Make counterplot.

**cou'nterpoint. 1.** *n.* (Mus.) Melody added so as to supplement given melody; art or mode of adding counterpoints according to rule. **2.** *v.t.* Add counterpoint to; set in contrast. [F f. L (POINT)]

**cou'nterpoise** (-z). **1.** *n.* Balancing of each other by two weights or forces; counterbalancing weight or force. **2.** *v.t.* Counterbalance; compensate for. [F f. L *pensum* weight]

**counter-prodŭ'ctive** *a.* Having the opposite of the desired effect. [COUNTER-]

**counter-rĕvolu'tion** (-lōō'-) *n.* Revolution opposed to a former one or reversing its results.

**cou'nterscãrp** *n.* Outer wall or slope of ditch in fortification. [F f. It. (SCARP)]

**cou'ntersign** (-in). **1.** *n.* Word to be given in answer to sentry's challenge; mark used for identification etc. **2.** *v.t.* Add confirming signature to (document already signed by another); **countersi'gnature** *n.* [F f. It. (SIGN)]

**cou'ntersink** *v.t.* (-sunk). Shape

(screw-hole) to admit screw-head; provide (screws) with countersunk holes; **cou'nterstroke** n., stroke given in return. [COUNTER-]

**counter-tĕ'nor** n. (Mus.) Male voice above but like tenor; singer with, part written for, this voice. [F f. It. (CONTRA-)]

**cou'ntervail** v.t. Counterbalance; avail against. [AF f. L (valeo have worth)]

**cou'nterweight** (-wāt) n. Counterbalancing weight. [COUNTER-]

**cou'ntĕss** n. Earl's or count's wife or widow; woman with own rank of earl or count. [F f. L comitissa (COUNT²)]

**cou'ntlĕss** a. Too many to be counted. [COUNT¹]

**cou'ntrў** (kŭ'-) n. Land of a region with regard to its aspect or associations (in mountainous, the Hardy, country); nation's territory, State of which one is a member, ‖national population esp. as electors, (**appeal, go, to the ~**, dissolve Parliament and hold general election; **leave the ~**, go abroad); rural parts as opp. towns or the capital (**across ~**, not keeping to main roads etc.; **in the ~**, Crick. sl., far from the wickets); (attrib.) of the rural parts, of rural life; **~(-and-western)**, rural or cowboy songs to guitar etc.; **~ club**, sporting and social club in rural area; **~ cousin**, countrified visitor to town; **~ dance**, English rural, native, or traditional dance; **~ house**, (esp. gentleman's) rural residence; **~man**, member of same State or same district as another person, person of specified district (esp. north, south, west, -cou'ntryman), person living in rural parts; **~ seat**, country house with park; **~side**, any rural district; **~-wide** a., extending throughout a nation; **~-woman** (as countryman); **cou'ntrified, -rўf-**, (kŭ'ntrĭfid) a., rustic in appearance or manners. [F f. L contrata (CONTRA)]

**cou'ntў. 1.** n. ‖Territorial division forming administrative, judicial, and political unit; *political and administrative division next below State; people of a county, esp. county families; **~ borough**, (Hist.) large borough ranking as administrative county; **~ council**, elected governing body of administrative county; **~ court**, court for civil

(*and criminal) cases; **~ family** (with ancestral seat in a county); County PALATINE¹; *~ **seat**, ‖~ **town**, (in which business of county is transacted). **2.** a. Having social status or characteristics of county families. [F f. L comitatus (COUNT²)]

**coup** (kōō) n. Successful stroke or move; **~ de grâce** (-degrah's), finishing stroke; **~ d'état** (-dātah'), violent or illegal change of government; **~ d'œil** (-dü'ē), comprehensive glance, view as taken in by this; **coupé** (kōō'pā), *coupe (kōōp), n., enclosed motor car with sloping back. [F f. L colpus blow f. Gk]

**cou'ple** (kŭ'-) **1.** n. Married or engaged pair; pair of partners in dance etc.; (pl. same) pair of hounds; **a ~ of**, two, a few. **2.** v.t. & i. Link or fasten or associate together (dogs in pairs, two railway carriages or one to another, justice etc. and or with mercy etc., his name with hers, names together); copulate. **3. ~r** n., (esp., Mus.) device in organ for making two parts work together without separate handling; **cou'plĕt** (kŭ'-) n., pair of successive lines of verse, esp. when rhyming and of same length; **cou'plĭng** (kŭ'-) n., (esp.) link etc. connecting railway carriages or parts of a machine, arrangement of items on gramophone record(s). [F f. L COPULA]

**cou'pŏn** (kōō'-) n. Detachable ticket entitling holder to payment, goods, services, etc., or ration of food, clothes, etc.; form etc. to be completed and sent as application for information, gift, etc.; entry-form for football pool etc.; voucher given with retail purchase, a certain number of which entitle holder to a 'free gift'. [F (couper cut)]

**cou'rage** (kŭ'-) n. Readiness to face and capacity to endure danger, inherent freedom from fear or from its disturbing effects, (**have the ~ of** one's **convictions**, be ready to declare or act upon them; **take** one's **~ in both hands**, venture boldly); courageous mood (take courage, often to do); **coura'geous** (kŭrā'jus) a. [F f. L (cor heart)]

**courgĕ'tte** (koorzhĕ't) n. Small vegetable marrow. [F]

**cou'riĕr** (kōō'-) n. Special messenger; person employed to guide and assist group of tourists. [F f. It. f. L curro curs- run]

**course** (kōrs). **1.** *n.* Going on in space or time (**in the ~ of,** during, before the end of), run or career (*in mid course*); direction of going (*change* one's *course*; *ship's course*; *hold,* *take, a course*); direction followed by river etc.; intended direction of going (*off course*); successive development *of* events, ordinary sequence or order (*in the course of nature*); **in ~ of,** in the process of; **in due ~,** at about the expected time; **as a matter of ~,** as a thing to be expected; **of ~,** naturally, presumably, admittedly); line of conduct or action (*what course do you advise?*); series *of* lectures or lessons or exercises, book for or like such series; sequence of study, medical treatment, etc.; each successive part of a meal (esp. soup, fish, meat, etc.); continuous line of masonry at one level in a building; = GOLF-*course*, RACE¹*course*. **2.** *v.t. & i.* (Of hounds) pursue (game, esp. hares by sight), pursue game; use hounds in coursing; (of animals, liquids) run, career. **3. cour'ser** (kōr'-) *n.,* fast-running African or Asian bird, (poet.) swift horse. [F f. L *cursus* (prec.)]

**court** (kōrt). **1.** *n.* ~('yard), space enclosed by walls or buildings; quadrangle; number of houses enclosing a yard communicating with street by an entry; delimited part of building; area within walls or marked boundaries used for some games esp. tennis (**ball is in your ~,** you must act next); (or *C~*) sovereign's presence and normal surroundings (*go to, be presented at, Court*); reception at Court (*hold ~,* fig., preside over admirers etc.); sovereign and courtiers (*Court etiquette*; **pay ~ to,** treat with courtier-like or flattering or amorous attention), sovereign and his Government as representing a country (*C~ of St. James's,* British sovereign's court); ~ (**of law**), body with judicial powers, tribunal, *the* judge(s) of a law-court, place in which court sits, (*must be decided in Court*; *invite the Court's attention to*; *ordered the court to be cleared,* i.e. of spectators; **go to ~,** take legal action; **out of ~,** not entitled to be heard in court, (of settlement) before hearing or judgement, fig. not worth discussing; **put out of ~,** refuse to consider); qualified members of company,

university, etc., meeting of these; **~-card,** playing-card that is king, queen, or jack, [orig. *coat-card*]; **~-house,** building in which lawcourt is held, *building containing administrative offices of county; **~ martial** (*pl.* **~s martial**), judicial court of Service officers; **~-mar'tial** *v.t.* (‖-ll-), try by this; **~ of justice,** = *court of law*; **~ plaster,** sticking-plaster for cuts etc. [f. former use by Court ladies for face-patches]; **~ shoe,** woman's light shoe with low-cut upper. **2.** *v.t.* Pay court to; seek the favour or love of; seek to win, unwisely invite, (popularity, inquiry; **~ disaster,** do what is likely to bring it). [F f. L (COHORT)]

**cour'teous** (ker'-) *a.* Polite or considerate in behaviour or wording. [F (COURT)]

**courtesa'n** (kôrtǐzǎ'n) *n.* Refined or high-placed prostitute. [F f. It. (prec.)]

**cour'tesy** (ker'-) *n.* Courteous behaviour or act; **by ~ of,** with the kind permission of (person etc.); **~ light,** light in motor car switched on by opening door; **~ title** (held by favour, having no legal validity); **cour'tier** (kôr'-) *n.,* frequenter of royal Court; **cour'tly** (kôr'-) *a.* (-iness), polished or refined in manners (**courtly love,** conventional medieval tradition of knightly love and etiquette); **cour'tship** (kôr'-) *n.,* courting esp. of intended wife or mate. [F (COURTEOUS)]

**cou'sin** (kŭ'z-) *n.* Person related to another by descent from one person through two of his or her children (~, **first ~,** **~ german,** child of one's uncle or aunt; **second ~,** one's parent's first cousin's child; **~ once, twice,** etc., **removed,** when one of the cousins is one, two, etc., generations further from the common ancestor than the other); title used by sovereigns as polite designation to and of sovereign or noble; **~hŏŏd,** **~ship,** *ns.*; **~ly** *a.* (-iness). [F f. L *consobrinus*]

**coutur'|e** (kōō-) *n.* Dressmaking; design and making of fashionable garments; HAUTE *couture*; **~ier** (-yā) *n.* (*fem.* **~ière** *pr.* -yār), fashion designer. [F]

**cōve¹. 1.** *n.* Small bay or inlet of coast; sheltered nook; (Archit.) curve sometimes connecting ceiling and walls. **2.** *v.t.* (Archit.) Provide (room etc.) with cove; slope (sides of fireplace) inwards. [E]

**cōve²** *n.* (sl.) Fellow, man. [cant]

**co'ven** (kŭ'-) *n.* Assembly of witches. [CONVENT]

**co'venant** (kŭ'-). **1.** *n.* Agreement; (Law) sealed contract; (Bibl.) compact between God and Israelites. **2.** *v.i.* & *t.* Agree, esp. by legal covenant, (*with person for* thing, *to* do, *that*); ~**ĕd** *a.*, bound or secured by covenant; ~**er** *n.*, (esp., Sc. Hist.) subscriber to or adherent of National Covenant 1638 or Solemn League and Covenant 1643. [F (CONVENE)]

**Cŏ'ventry** *n.* Send to ~, refuse to associate with or speak to. [place]

**co'ver** (kŭ'-). **1.** *v.t.* Be over the (whole) top or front of (lit. or fig.); conceal by overlying or obstructing sight; enclose or include; investigate or describe as reporter; (of sum) be large enough to meet (expense); travel (specified distance etc.); (of fieldsman) stand behind (other fieldsman); (of stallion etc.) copulate with; (of person or animal) put something over, conceal *with* something thus, strew thoroughly *with*, provide with something that covers; aim gun at; (of fortress, gun) command (place etc.); (in *p.p.*) wearing hat, having roof; ~ **in**, provide with roof etc.; ~**ing letter** etc. (explaining purport of enclosure); ~ **up**, conceal (feelings, crime, etc.; so ~-*up* n.). **2.** *n.* Thing that covers, lid, wrapper, envelope (*under separate cover*), bookbinding or one of its boards, shelter, screen or pretence, covert for game, (**from ~ to ~**, from beginning to end of book; **under ~**, in secret, sheltered from weather; **under ~ of**, hidden by, with ostensible show of; **take ~**, use natural or prepared shelter against attack); funds (esp. to be obtained by insurance) to meet liability or contingent loss; place laid for one person at meal; = *cover--point*; ~ **charge**, service charge per person in restaurant; ~ **girl**, girl or woman whose picture illustrates cover of magazine etc.; ~ **note** (certifying existence of current insurance policy); ~**-point**, (Crick.) fieldsman covering point. **3.** ~**age** *n.*, area or amount covered, area reached by a particular broadcasting station or advertising medium, re-

porting of events etc. for newspaper etc.; ~**all** *n.*, thing covering entirely, (usu. in *pl.*) full-length outer garment; ~**lĕt** (kŭ'-), bedspread [F *lit* bed]; **co'vert** (kŭ'-), (*a.*) not open or explicit, veiled, (*covert glance, threat, insolence*), (*n.*) wood or thicket affording cover for game (~**t coat**, short light overcoat worn for shooting, riding, etc.), feather covering base of bird's wing feather or tail feather. [F f. L *cooperio*]

**co'vet** (kŭ'-) *v.t.* Envy another the possession of, long to possess; ~**ous** *a.*, avaricious, grasping, eagerly desirous *of*. [F f. L (CUPID)]

**co'vey** (kŭ'-) *n.* Brood of partridges esp. flying together; group *of* persons. [F f. L (*cubo* lie)]

**cow¹** *n.* (*pl.* ~**s**, arch. **kine**). Female of any bovine animal, esp. of the domestic species used as source of milk and beef; female elephant, rhinoceros, whale, seal, etc.; (vulg. derog.) woman; ~**bell** (worn round cow's neck); \*~**boy**, man in charge of grazing cattle on ranch; \*~**catcher**, fender of locomotive throwing off obstructions; ~**heel**, ox-foot stewed to jelly; ~**herd**, ~**man**, tender of cattle at pasture; ~**hide**, (leather or whip of) cow's hide; ~**lick**, projecting lock of hair; ~**pat**, roundish piece of cow-dung; ~**pox**, disease of cows, source of smallpox vaccine; \*~**puncher**, = cowboy; ~**shot**, (Crick., sl.) pull across ball to leg side; ~**slip**, yellow-flowered plant growing in pastures, \*marsh marigold, [obs. *slyppe* dung]. [E]

**cow²** *v.t.* Intimidate, dispirit. [N]

**cow'ard** *n.* Person having little or no bravery; (*attrib.*, poet.) cowardly; ~**ĭce** *n.*, cowardly feelings or conduct; ~**lў** *a.* (**-iness**), lacking bravery, of or like a coward, (of blow etc.) struck etc. at one who cannot retort. [F f. L *cauda* tail]

**cow'er** *v.i.* Crouch or shrink or huddle oneself up in fear or with cold. [LG]

**cowl** *n.* Monk's hooded cloak, its hood; hood-shaped top of chimney or shaft; ~**ing** *n.*, (esp.) removable cover of engine. [E f. L *cucullus*]

**cō'-worker** (-wêr'-) *n.* One who collaborates with another. [co-]

**cowr'ie** *n.* Small gastropod; its shell, used as money in Africa & S. Asia. [Urdu, Hindi]

**cŏx. 1.** *n.* Coxswain, esp. of racing boat. **2.** *v.t.* & *i.* Act as cox (of). [abbr.]

**cŏ′xcōmb** (-ōm) *n.* Conceited showy person; (Hist.) medieval jester's cap; ~**rȳ** *n.* [= *cock's comb*]

**cŏ′xswain** (-kswān, -ksǝn). **1.** *n.* Steersman of (esp. rowing-)boat. **2.** *v.t.* & *i.* Act as coxswain (of). [*cock* (COCKBOAT), SWAIN]

**coy** *a.* (Esp. of girl) modest, shy; affectedly modest; archly reticent. [F f. L QUIET]

**Coy.** *abbr.* (esp. Mil.) Company.

**coyŏ′tĕ** (kǝ-; *or* koi′ŏt) *n.* N. Amer. prairie-wolf. [Mex. Sp.]

**coy′pu** (-ōō) *n.* Aquatic beaver-like rodent, orig. from S. America. [Araucan]

**co′zen** (kŭ′-) *v.t.* & *i.* (literary). Cheat; ~**age** *n.*, cozening. [cant]

*****cō′zy.** See COSY.

**C.P.** *abbr.* Communist Party.

**c.p.** *abbr.* candle-power.

**cp.** *abbr.* compare.

**Cpl.** *abbr.* Corporal.

‖**C.P.R.E.** *abbr.* Council for the Protection of Rural England.

**c.p.s.** *abbr.* cycles per second.

**Cr.** *abbr.* Councillor; credit(or).

**crăb. 1.** *n.* Crustacean with ten legs, with front pair modified into pincers (**catch a ~**, get oar jammed under water by faulty stroke); flesh of this as food; (*C*~) sign of ZODIAC; ~**(-apple)**, fruit of crab-tree; ~**(-louse)**, parasite infecting hairy parts of body; ~**(-tree)**, wild (or similar cultivated) apple tree with fruit of harsh sour flavour. **2.** *v.t.* & *i.* (colloq.; **-bb-**). Criticize adversely or captiously; act so as to spoil. **3.** ~**′bĕd** (*or* -bd) *a.*, crabby, (of hand-writing) ill-formed and hard to decipher; ~**′bȳ** *a.* (**-ily, -iness**), perverse, morose, irritable; ~**′wise** (-z) *adv.*, (moving) sideways or backwards like a crab. [E]

**crăck** *n.*, *v.*, & *a.* **1.** *n.* Sudden sharp noise (crack of rifle, whip, china breaking; **fair ~ of the whip**, colloq., fair chance to participate); sharp blow (*a crack on the head*; **have a ~ at**, colloq., attempt); narrow opening; split or rift not extending far enough to break thing into fragments, mark caused by this; (colloq.) = WISE¹*crack*. **2.** *v.i.* & *t.* (Of whip, rifle, etc.) make crack; suffer a crack or partial break; (of voice) become dissonant as effect of emotion or old age

or at manhood; (of ground, skin, etc.) gape with crack(s); make (whip, china, skin, etc.) crack (**~ a joke**, tell it); break case of (nut; **get ~ing**, colloq., start working; **~ a bottle**, open it and drink its contents); break into (safe etc.); find solution to (problem etc.); give way, yield, (under torture etc.); (in *p.p.*, colloq.) crazy, infatuated. **3.** *a.* (colloq.) First-rate (*crack regiment, shot, player*). **4.** ~**-brained**, crazy; **~ down on**, (colloq.) take severe measures against; **~ of dawn**, (colloq.) daybreak; **~ of doom**, thunderclap announcing Day of Judgement; ~**′-pot**, (colloq.) eccentric or impractical (person); ~**′sman**, burglar; **~ up**, (colloq.) praise, collapse under strain. **5.** ~**′er** *n.*, (esp.) kind of firework, small paper toy containing paper hat etc. and made so as to explode when ends are pulled, thin crisp biscuit, *****biscuit; ~**′ers** (-z) *pred. a.*, (sl.) crazy, infatuated; **crä′ckle**, (*n.*) sound of repeated slight cracks (e.g. of distant rifle-fire or burning wood or stiff paper crumpled), (*v.i.*) emit this; ~**′ling** *n.*, (esp.) crisp skin of roast pork; ~**′nel** *n.*, light crisp kind of biscuit. [E]

**-cracȳ** *suf.* Rule, ruling body, of. [F f. L *-cratia* f. Gk (*kratos* power)]

**crä′dle. 1.** *n.* Infant's bed esp. on rockers (**from the ~ to the grave**, throughout life); earliest location of an art, nation, etc.; cradle-like frame for supporting or protecting or conveying something or someone, part of telephone supporting receiver when not in use. **2.** *v.t.* Place in cradle; contain or shelter as in cradle. [E]

**craft** (-ah-). **1.** *n.* Skill; cunning, guile; branch of skilled handiwork, people practising this, (*arts and crafts*; *the* GENTLE *craft*); (*pl.* same) boat, ship, aircraft, or spacecraft; ~**′s-man**, one who practises a craft, skilled person; ~**′smanship** *n.* **2.** *v.t.* *****Make in skilful manner (*hand-crafted jewelry*). **3.** ~**′ȳ** *a.* (~**ily,** ~**iness**), guileful, ingenious. [E]

**crăg** *n.* Steep rugged rock; ~**′s-man**, rock-climber; ~**′gȳ** (-gĭ) *a.* (**-ily, -iness;** esp., of person, face, etc.) rugged. [Celt.]

**crāke** *n.* Bird of the rail family, esp. CORN¹*crake*; corncrake's cry. [N, imit.]

**cram** *v.t.* & *i.* (**-mm-**). Fill (receptacle) to repletion, feed (poultry, child, etc.) to excess, (*with*); force (thing) *in, into*; prepare for examination by intensive study; eat greedily; ~**full**, as full as cramming can make it; ~'**mer** *n.*, (esp.) one who crams examinees. [E]

**cramp. 1.** *n.* Painful involuntary muscular contraction in limb, stomach, etc., caused by cold or over-exertion; ~(**-iron**), kind of clamp esp. for holding masonry or timbers together. **2.** *v.t.* Affect with cramp; ~ (**up**), restrict (energies, movement, person in these), confine narrowly; ~ person's **style**, prevent him from acting freely; (in *p.p.*, of handwriting) small and difficult to read, (of space) too narrow; **cra'mpons, *-oo'ns**, (**-z**) *n.pl.*, spiked appliances fixed to boots for ice-climbing. [F f. LDu.]

**cra'nberry** *n.* (Shrub with) acid red berry. [G *kranbeere* crane-berry]

**crane. 1.** *n.* Large wading bird with long legs, neck, and bill; machine of various forms to move heavy weights; ~**-fly**, long-legged two-winged fly; ~'**s-bill**, kind of wild geranium. **2.** *v.t.* & *i.* Stretch (neck, head) in order to see better; stretch neck (*out, over, down*, etc.). [E]

**cra'ni|um** *n.* (*pl.* ~**a**). Bones enclosing the brain; skull; ~**al** *a.*; ~**o'logy**, ~**o'metry**, *ns.* [L f. Gk]

**crank. 1.** *n.* Arm or shaft proceeding from an axis at a right angle and serving to turn the main shaft (as in common draw-well) or to convert reciprocal into rotary motion or vice versa (as in steam-engine etc.); eccentric person; ~'**case** (enclosing crankshaft); ~'**pin** (attaching connecting-rod to crank); ~'**shaft** (driven by crank). **2.** *v.t.* Turn with crank; ~ **up**, start (car engine) by turning a crank, (sl.) increase (speed etc.) by intensive effort. **3.** ~'**y** *a.* (~**ily**, ~**iness**), shaky or crazy, crotchety, eccentric, ill-tempered. [E]

**cra'nny** *n.* Small opening, chink, possible place of concealment (*search every cranny*); ~**ied** (**-id**) *a.* [F]

**crap**[1]. (vulg.) **1.** *n.* Faeces; nonsense, rubbish; ~'**py** *a.* **2.** *v.i.* (**-pp-**). Defecate; ~ **out**, be unsuccessful, withdraw from game etc. [Du.]

**\*crap**[2] *n.* Losing throw of 2, 3, or 12 in craps; ~ **game**, game of craps. [ CRAPS]

**crêp|e. 1.** *n.* Crêpe, usu. of black silk, esp. for mourning dress; ~'**y** *a.* **2.** *v.t.* Cover, clothe, drape, with crape. [CRÊPE]

**\*craps** *n.pl.* Game of chance played with dice; **shoot** ~, play this. [orig. uncert.]

**crä'pul|ence** *n.* State following excessive drinking or eating; ~**ent**, ~**ous**, *adjs.* [L *crapula*]

**crash**[1] *n., v.,* & *adv.* **1.** *n.* Violent fall or impact esp. with loud noise; sudden downfall or collapse (e.g. of Government, commercial firm); burst of mixed sound (e.g. of broken crockery, loud music or thunder); (*attrib.*) done rapidly or urgently (*crash course, programme*). **2.** *v.i.* & *t.* Fall with a crash (*through, down*, etc.), come with a crash (*into, against, together*, etc.); (of thunder etc.) make crash; (of airman or aircraft) fall violently to land or sea; throw or drive with a crash; cause (vehicle etc.) to crash; pass (red traffic-light etc.); (colloq.) enter without permission. **3.** *adv.* With a crash (*stone came crash through window*). **4.** ~ **barrier**, barrier against car leaving road etc.; ~**-dive** (of submarine) dive hastily and steeply in an emergency, (of aircraft) dive and crash (so ~**-dive** *n.*); ~**-halt**, sudden stop by vehicle; ~**-helmet** (worn to protect head in case of crash); ~**-land**, (of aircraft or airman) land hurriedly with a crash. **5.** ~'**ing** *a.* (esp., colloq.) overwhelming (*a crashing bore*). [imit.]

**crash**[2] *n.* Coarse linen for towels etc. [Russ.]

**crass** *a.* Grossly stupid, without sensitivity. [L *crassus* thick]

**-crat** *suf.* forming *ns.* meaning supporter or member of the -CRACY; **-cra'tic(al)**, *sufs.* forming *adjs.* f. *ns.* in *-crat*. [F (-CRACY)]

**crate. 1.** *n.* Open-work case for conveying fragile goods; (sl.) aeroplane or other vehicle. **2.** *v.t.* Pack in crate. [perh. Du.]

**cra'ter. 1.** *n.* Volcano-mouth, bowl-shaped cavity, esp. hole made by explosion of shell or bomb. **2.** *v.t.* Form crater in. [L f. Gk, = mixing-bowl]

**-cra'tic(al).** See -CRAT.

**cravä't** *n.* Scarf; neck-tie; ~**ted** *a.* [F f. Serbo-Croatian, = Croat]

**crä'v|e** *v.i.* & *t.* Have a craving or vehement desire *for* (stimulant particular food, person or his society, sleep, etc.); ask *pardon* or *leave* or *permission*; (literary) desire, ask, ask for; ~**ing** *n.*, strong desire (*for*). [E]

**crā'ven. 1.** *a.* Of abject spirit, consciously or confessedly cowardly. **2.** *n.* Craven person. [perh. F *f.* L (*crepo* burst)]

**craw** *n.* Bird's, insect's, crop; **stick in** one's ~, be unacceptable. [LDu.]

**craw'fish.** *n.* Marine spiny lobster. [var. of CRAYFISH]

**crawl. 1.** *v.i.* Advance on hands and knees or on the belly; walk or move or (of time) pass with extreme slowness; (colloq.) behave abjectly or ingratiatingly *to*; (of ground, bed, cheese, etc.) be covered *with* insects etc.; feel creepy. **2.** *n.* Crawling motion (*at a crawl*); ~ (**stroke**), high-speed swimming stroke. **3.** ~**er** *n.*, (esp., in *pl.*) baby's overall for crawling in; ~'**y** *a.*, causing creepy sensation. [orig. unkn.]

**cray'fish** *n.* Freshwater lobster-like crustacean; crawfish. [F *crevice* (CRAB); assim. to FISH¹]

**cray'on. 1.** *n.* Stick or pencil of coloured chalk etc. (**in** ~ or ~**s**, drawn with these); picture in crayons. **2.** *v.t.* Draw with crayons. [F (*craie* chalk)]

**crā'z|y** *a.* (~**ily**, ~**iness**). Insane, outrageously foolish; (colloq.) madly eager (*about*, *for*); (sl.) unrestrained, excellent; (of ship, building, etc.) unsound, shaky; (of paving etc.) made of irregular pieces fitted together; ~**e**, (*v.t.*) make crazy, (*n.*) general or individual mania, (object of) temporary enthusiasm. [F]

**creak. 1.** *n.* Strident noise as of unoiled hinge; ~'**y** *a.* (~**ily**, ~**iness**). **2.** *v.i.* Emit creak. [imit.]

**cream. 1.** *n.* Part of milk with high content of fat, gathering at the top and convertible into butter; *the* best part or pick *of*; = *cream-colour*, (*attrib.*) cream-coloured; creamlike preparation or ointment (**cold** ~, cooling skin-unguent); sweet dish like or made with cream; full-bodied mellow sherry; soup or sauce containing cream or milk; ~ **cake** (filled with cream); ~ **cheese**, soft rich kind made of cream and unskimmed milk; ~**-colour(ed)**, yellow-white; ~ **cracker**, crisp unsweetened biscuit; ~ **of tartar**, purified tartar used in medicine and cooking; ~ **puff**, puff pastry filled

with cream; ~ **tea**, afternoon tea with jam and clotted cream. **2.** *v.i.* & *t.* Send up cream or scum; take cream from (milk); treat (skin) with cosmetic cream; work (butter etc.) to creamy consistency; ~ (**off**), abstract best (or any specified) part of. **3.** *\*~'er* *n.*, jug for cream; ~'**er|y** *n.*, butter (and cheese) factory, shop where cream etc. is sold; ~'**y** *a.* (~**ily**, ~**iness**). [F, f. L *cramum* & *chrisma* CHRISM]

**crease. 1.** *n.* Line made by folding, wrinkle; = BOWL²*ing-crease*, POP¹*ping--crease*. **2.** *v.t.* & *i.* Make creases in (dress etc.); develop creases; (sl.) tire out, stun, kill. [orig. CREST = ridge in material]

**creā'te** *v.t.* & *i.* Bring into existence, give rise to; invest (person) with rank (*was created a baronet*); originate (*actor creates a part*); (sl.) make a fuss (*mustn't create about it*); **creā'tion** *n.*, creating, esp. (**the Creation**) of the world, all created things, product of (esp. designer's, actor's) mind; **creā'tive** *a.*, (esp.) inventive, imaginative; **creāti'vity** *n.*; **creā'tor** *n.*, (esp., **the Creator**, God). [L *creo*]

**crea'ture** *n.* Created thing (~ **comforts**, good food, clothes, etc.); person or animal (**dumb** ~**s**, animals, person (esp. in emotional use with epithet, as *dear*, *disgusting*, *creature*; *a*, *that*, *the*, *creature*, derog.); person's dependent and tool; person under control of (*is a creature of habit*). [F f. L (prec.)]

**crèche** (-āsh) *n.* Day nursery for infants. [F (CRIB)]

**crē'dal** *a.*, see CREED; **crē'dence** *n.*, belief (*give*, *refuse*, *credence to*; *letter of credence*, letter of introduction, esp. of ambassador), shelf, side-table, or niche for elements of Eucharist before consecration; **crē-dĕ'ntials** (-shalz) *n.pl.*, letter(s) of credence, evidence of achievement or trustworthiness; **crē'dible** *a.* (-bly), worthy of belief, sufficiently likely to be believable; **crēdibi'lity** *n.* (**credibility gap**, seeming difference between official statements and the facts). [CREED]

**crē'dit. 1.** *n.* Belief, confidence felt in the veracity or honour or honesty or in the ability and intention to pay of a person or body, (*tale*, *person*, *deserves no credit*; *his financial credit stands high*); good reputation or the power or influence it gives, thing that brings this *to* person etc., (*your son is a great, no, credit to you* or *your training*; *the offer does you credit*); acknowledgement of merit (*the wrong man got the credit for it*); (usu. in *pl.*) acknowledgement of contributor's services to film, book, etc., (~ *title*, this at beginning or end of cinema or television film); allowing customers to take goods and defer payment (*give* or *allow credit*; **on** ~, according to this system; ~ **card**, card authorizing obtaining of goods on credit); sum at person's disposal in bank (**letter of** ~, authorizing person to draw money at another place), entry in account of sum paid, (sum entered on) credit side of account (**give** person ~ **for**, fig., acknowledge that he may have; **to** one's ~, in one's favour); *certificate of completion of course by student. 2. *v.t.* Believe (tale, statement or its maker); enter on credit side of account (amount *to* person, person *with* amount); ~ **person with**, ascribe (quality, feeling) to him. 3. ~**able** *a.* (-**bly**), bringing honour *to* doer etc., praiseworthy; ~**or** *n.*, person or body to whom one owes money, one who gives credit for money or goods; **crē′dō** (or -ā′-) *n.* (*pl.* -os), creed; **crē′dulous** *a.*, (showing that one is) too ready to believe; **crēdū′litӯ** *n.* [F f. It. or L (foll.)]

**creed** *n.* System of religious belief, formal summary of Christian doctrine; person's or class's or nation's code of honour or ethical principles or set of opinions on any subject; ~**al**, **crē′dal**, *adjs.* [E f. L *credo* 'I believe']

**creek** *n.* ‖Inlet on sea-coast; arm of river; (U.S. etc.) tributary of river; **up the** ~, (sl.) in difficulties, crazy. [N & Du.]

**creel** *n.* Fisherman's wicker basket. [orig. unkn.]

**creep. 1.** *v.i.* (**crept**). Move with body prone and close to ground; (of plant) grow along ground, wall, etc.; go with stealthy movements *in, up*, etc.; (of mouse, cat, etc., or person) go about meekly or abjectly or (of the old or sick) with extreme slowness; develop gradually (*creeping inflation*); (of one's flesh, or of person in regard to it) experience nervous shivering sensation due to repugnance or fear (*makes my flesh creep, me creep all over*). **2.** *n.* Spell of creeping; gradual change in shape of metal under stress; (sl.) disliked person; **the** ~**s**, (colloq.) creeping sensation. **3.** ~**er** *n.*, (esp.) creeping or climbing plant (TREE-*creeper*), (sl.) soft-soled shoe; ~**′ӯ** *a.* (-**ily**, ~**iness**), feeling or causing or apt to cause the creeps; ~**′y-crawly** *a.* & *n.*, creeping and crawling (insect etc.). [E]

**creese.** See KRIS.

**crēmā′tion** *n.* Burning as method of disposing of corpses; instance of this; **crēmā′te** *v.t.*, consume by cremation; **crēmatŏr′ium** *n.* (*pl.* -**ia**, -**s**), place for cremating corpses; **crē′matorӯ**, (*a.*) of cremation, (*n.*) *crematorium. [L *cremo* burn]

**crème** (krām) *n.* ~ **brûlée** (broo′lā), cream or custard topped with caramelized sugar; ~ **de la** ~ (-dlah-), the very pick, the élite; ~ **de menthe** (demah′nt), peppermint liqueur. [F, = cream]

**crē′nellātēd** *a.* Having battlements; **crēnellā′tion** *n.*, crenellated state, (indentation of) battlements. [F *crenel* embrasure]

**Crē′ole. 1.** *n.* Descendant of European settlers in W. Indies, Central or S. Amer., or of French settlers in southern U.S.; person of mixed European and Black descent; creolized language. **2.** *a.* That is a Creole; (*c*~) of local origin. [F f. Sp.]

**crē′osōte. 1.** *n.* Oily antiseptic liquid distilled from wood tar; ~ (**oil**), oil distilled from coal tar, used as wood-preservative. **2.** *v.t.* Treat with creosote. [G f. Gk wds, = flesh-preserver]

**crêpe** (-āp) *n.* Gauzelike fabric with wrinkled surface; ~ **de Chine** (deshē′n), fine silk crêpe; ~ **paper**, thin crinkled paper; ~ (**rubber**), very durable rubber used for shoe-soles etc.; ~ **Suzette**, small dessert pancake served heated in sauce. [F f. L (CRISP)]

**crĕ′pitāte** *v.i.* Make crackling sound; ~**ā′tion** *n.* [L (*crepo* creak)]

**crĕpt.** See CREEP.

**crĕpŭ′scular** *a.* Of twilight; (of light or enlightenment) dim; (Zool.) active etc. at twilight. [L *crepusculum* twilight]

**crēscĕ′ndō** (krish-) *adv.*, *a.*, & *n.* (Mus.) **1.** *adv.* With gradual increase of loudness. **2.** *a.* So performed. **3.** *n.* (*pl.* ~**s**). Passage (to be) so performed; (fig.) progress towards a climax. [It. (foll.)]

**crĕ'scent. 1.** *n.* Moon as seen in first or last quarter; figure with this outline fig. as emblem of Turkey or Islam; ‖street of houses on curve of this shape. **2.** *a.* Increasing; crescent-shaped. [F f. L *cresco* grow]

**crĕss** *n.* Cruciferous plant with pungent edible leaves. [E]

**crĕst. 1.** *n.* Comb or tuft on bird's or animal's head; plume or tuft of feathers; top of mountain, roof, or ridge; curl of foam on wave; thing borne on coat of arms above helmet, or separately, as on seal, notepaper, plate, etc.; ~'**fallen**, dejected, abashed. **2.** *v.t.* & *i.* Serve as crest to, crown; reach top of (hill, wave); (of wave) form crest. [F f. L *crista*]

**crĕtā'ceous** (-shŭs). **1.** *a.* Chalky. **2.** *a.* & *n.* (*C*~). (Of) the latest Mesozoic period or system, containing chalk. [L (*creta* chalk)]

**crĕ'tĭn** *n.* Deformed idiot suffering from thyroid deficiency; (colloq.) stupid person; ~**ism** *n.*; ~**ous** *a.* [F *crétin* (CHRISTIAN)]

**crĕtŏ'nne** (*or* -ĕ'-) *n.* Colour-printed cotton cloth used for chair-covers etc. [F (*Creton*, place)]

**crevā'sse** *n.* Deep open split or chasm in glacier; **crĕ'vice** *n.*, narrow opening, fissure, esp. in rock, building, etc. [F f. L *crepo* crack]

**crew**[1] (-ōō). **1.** *n.* Ship's or boat's or aircraft's etc. company (excluding passengers); set or gang of people belonging together or having common characteristics (usu. derog.; *a dissolute crew*); ~ **cut**, man's hair cut short all over; ~ **neck**, round close-fitting neckline. **2.** *v.t.* & *i.* Supply, act as, (member of) crew (for). [F (L *cresco* increase)]

**crew**[2]. See CROW.

**crew'el** (-ōō'-) *n.* Thin worsted yarn for tapestry and embroidery. [orig. unkn.]

**crĭb. 1.** *n.* Barred receptacle for fodder etc.; child's bed with barred or latticed sides; dealer's cards at cribbage consisting of cards thrown out by each player; (colloq.) cribbage, piece of plagiarism (*from*), a translation. **2.** *v.t.* & *i.* **-bb-**). Confine in small space; plagiarize or copy unfairly or without acknowledgement. **3.** ~'**bage** *n.*, a card-game; ~**bage-board** (with peg-holes for scoring). [E]

**crick. 1.** *v.t.* Slight, sprain or strain (neck, back, etc.). **2.** *n.* Such injury. [orig. unkn.]

**crĭc'kĕt**[1] *n.* Jumping chirping insect. [F, imit.]

**crĭc'kĕt**[2]. **1.** *n.* Open-air game for two teams of 11 with ball, bats, and wickets (‖**not** ~, colloq. infringing code of fair play between honourable opponents). **2.** *v.i.* Play cricket. [orig. unkn.]

**cri de cœur** (krē de kếr') *n.* Passionate appeal, complaint, or protest. [F, = cry from heart]

**cried, cri'er.** See CRY.

**cri'key** *int.* (sl.) expr. astonishment. [CHRIST]

**crime. 1.** *n.* Act (usu. grave offence) punishable by law; prevalence of crimes (*a decrease in crime*); (colloq.) shameful act; ~**-sheet**, record of soldier's offences against regulations; ~**-writer** (who writes about fictional crimes). **2.** *v.t.* (Mil. etc.) Charge with or convict of offence. **3.** **crī'minal**, (*a.*; -**lly**) of, of the nature of, guilty of, crime (**criminal law**, concerned with punishment of offenders), (*n.*) person guilty of crime; **crimină'lity** *n.*; **criminali'stic** *a.*, pertaining to (the habits of) criminals; **crimino'logy** *n.*, scientific study of crime; **crimi-nŏ'logist** *n.* [F f. L *crimen*]

**crĭmp. 1.** *v.t.* Press (textile, the hair) into small folds or waves, frill, corrugate. **2.** *n.* Crimped thing or form; \***put a** ~ **in**, (sl.) thwart, interfere with. [LDu.]

**crĭm'son** (-z-) *a.*, *n.*, & *v.* **1.** *a.* Of rich deep red inclining to purple. **2.** *n.* Crimson colour. **3.** *v.t.* & *i.* Turn crimson. [ult. f. Arab. (KERMES)]

**crĭnge** (-nj) *v.i.* Cower; behave obsequiously (*to*). [E]

**crĭn'kle. 1.** *n.* Wrinkle or bend esp. as one of a series in a line or surface; **crĭn'klў** *a.* (**-iness**). **2.** *v.i.* & *t.* Form crinkles (in). [E]

**crĭn'olīne** (*or* -ēn) *n.* Stiff fabric of horsehair etc. for linings, hats, etc.; (Hist.) hooped petticoat used to expand skirt. [F f. L *crinis* hair, *linum* thread]

**crĭ'pes** (-ps) *int.* (vulg.) expr. astonishment. [CHRIST]

**crĭ'pple. 1.** *n.* (Permanently) lame person. **2.** *v.t.* Disable for walking or working; diminish effectiveness of. [E]

**crī′s|ĭs** n. (pl. ~es pr. -ēz). Turning-point or decisive moment, esp. in illness; time of acute danger or suspense. [L f.·Gk, = turning-point]

**crisp** a., n., & v. **1.** a. Hard but brittle; (of hair, waves) curly; (of air) enlivening, fresh; (of features, outline, edge) clear-cut; (of intonation, speech) staccato or decided; (of manner) brisk and decisive; (of style) lively or piquant; (of paper etc.) crackling; ~′**bread**, thin crisp biscuits of crushed rye etc. grains. **2.** n. ‖Thing overdone in roasting etc.; (usu. in pl.) ‖thin fried slice of potato, sold in packets. **3.** v.t. & i. Make or become crisp; crimp (hair). **4.** ~′**ў** a. (~ily, ~iness), curly, brittle, crisp. [E f. L crispus curled]

**crī′ss-crŏss** (or -aws) n., a., adv., & v. **1.** n. Crossing of lines, currents, etc.; network of crossing lines. **2.** a. Crossing, in cross lines, (criss-cross traffic, pattern). **3.** adv. Crosswise, at cross purposes (everything went criss--cross). **4.** v.i. & t. Go criss-cross; make criss-cross pattern; intersect repeatedly. [Christ's Cross]

**critēr′i|on** n. (pl. ~a). Principle or standard taken in judging. [Gk, = means of judging]

**crī′tĭcĭsm** n. Judging of merit of works of art and literature or of persons and things in general; expression and exposition of such judgement; any detail of such exposition esp. the pointing out of a fault; censure; **higher ~** (esp. that dealing with composition and status of Bible books); **lower, textual, ~** (dealing with readings and meaning of the text); **crī′tĭc** n., person who attempts or is skilled in criticism, one who censures; **crī′tĭcal** a. (-lly), of or skilled in or given to or providing criticism, of the nature of a crisis, decisive for good or ill, marking transition from one state to another, (of nuclear reactor) maintaining a self-sustaining chain reaction; **crī′tĭcĭze** v.t. & i., utter or write criticism of, find fault (with); **crĭtī′que** (-ē′k) n., critical essay or analysis, criticism. [L criticus f. Gk krĭtēs judge]

**croak. 1.** n. Deep hoarse sound esp. of raven or frog; ~′**ў** a. (~ily, ~iness). **2.** v.i. & t. Utter croak, be hoarse; talk or utter gloomily; (sl.) die, kill. [imit.]

**Crō′ăt** n. Native of Croatia in Yugoslavia; language of Croats; **Crōā′tian** (-shan) a. & n. [L f. Serbo-Croatian Hrvat]

**crŏc** n. (colloq.) Crocodile. [abbr.]

**crŏ′chet** (-shā, -shǐ). **1.** n. Knitting done with hooked needle; crochet-work. **2.** v.t. & i. Do crochet; make by crochet. [F (CROTCHET)]

**crŏck¹** n. Earthenware jar; broken piece of earthenware; ~′**erў** n., earthenware vessels, plates, etc. [E]

**crŏck². (colloq.) 1.** n. Worn-out or disabled or inefficient person or thing. **2.** v.t. & i. Disable, (cause to) collapse. [orig. Sc.]

**crŏ′ckĕt** n. (Archit.) One of the curled leaves or similar ornaments on sloping side of pinnacle etc. [var. of F crochet CROTCHET]

**crŏ′codīle** n. Large thick-skinned long-tailed amphibious tropical reptile; its skin; ‖(colloq.) line of school-children etc. walking in pairs; **~ tears,** hypocritical grief [f. belief that crocodile wept while devouring victim]; **crŏcodī′lian** (-yan) a. [F f. L f. Gk krokodīlos]

**crŏ′cus** n. Dwarf spring-flowering plant with usu. yellow or purple flowers; AUTUMN crocus. [L f. Gk]

**Croe′sus** (krē′s-) n. Person of great wealth. [person]

‖**crŏft** (or -aw-). **1.** n. Small piece of arable land close to house; crofter's holding. **2.** v.i. Farm croft; live as crofter; ~′**er** n., one who cultivates a croft, (Sc.) joint tenant of divided farm. [E]

**croi′ssant** (krwah′sahn̄) n. Crescent-shaped bread roll. [F (CRESCENT)]

**crŏ′mlĕch** (-k) n. Dolmen; circle of upright stones. [W]

**crōne** n. Withered old woman. [Du. croonje carcass f. F (CARRION)]

**crō′nў** n. Intimate friend. [Gk khronios long-lasting]

**crŏŏk. 1.** n. Hooked staff esp. of shepherd or bishop; hooked end or piece; bend or curve; sharp bend of road or stream; wry turn (has a crook in his back, nose, character); (colloq.) dishonest person, professional criminal; **on the ~,** dishonestly; ~--**back(ed),** humpback(ed). **2.** v.t. & i. Bend, curve; ~**ed** a., (-kt) having a crook, (-ĭd; -er, -est) not straight, bent, wry, deformed, bowed, not straightforward, dishonest. [N]

**crŏŏn. 1.** n. Low subdued voice. **2.** v.i. & t. Hum, sing, etc., with croon

~**'er** *n.*, singer of popular sentimental songs in low smooth voice. [LDu.]

**crŏp. 1.** *n.* Pouch in bird's gullet as preliminary digesting-place (NECK and *crop*); thick end of whip; close-shorn head, cutting of hair short, wearing of one's hair short; yield of any cultivated plant or of the portion of it in a country or farm or field (*the wheat, cotton, crop*; *has a fine crop of apples, roses*; *crop*-DUSTING), such portion during growth (*standing, growing, crop*); group or amount produced at one time (*a crop of disputes, questions*; *this year's crop of students*); (**hunting-**)~, whip-handle with loop for affixing lash; ~**-eared**, with ears (or hair) cut short. **2.** *v.t. & i.* (**-pp-**). Poll or clip (tree, twigs, hedge, ears, tail, hair); bite off ends of or eat down (grass etc.); raise crop on or occupy *with* specified crop (land); (of land) yield *well* etc.; turn *up* unexpectedly; ~ **up, out,** (Geol.) appear at surface; ~**'per** *n.*, (esp., sl.) heavy fall (**come a** ~**per,** fall heavily, fig. meet with disaster), (of plant, with *good* etc.) crop-producer. [E]

**crŏ'quet** (-kā, -kǐ). **1.** *n.* Lawn game with hoops and wooden balls and mallets; croqueting. **2.** *v.t. & i.* Drive away (player's ball) by striking one's own ball placed in contact with the other, do this, (cf. ROQUET). [as CROCKET]

**croquĕ'tte** (-kĕ't) *n.* Fried breaded ball or roll of potato, meat, etc. [F (*croquer* crunch)]

**crõre** *n.* (Ind.) A hundred lakhs (of rupees, persons, etc.). [Hindi]

**crŏ'sier, -zier** (-z-, -zher) *n.* Staff or crook borne by or before bishop etc. [F *croisier* cross-bearer & *crossier* crook-bearer]

**crŏss** (*or* -aws) *n., a., & v.* **1.** *n.* Stake used for crucifixion usu. with transverse bar (**the C~,** that on which Christ was crucified); (staff bearing) model of this esp. in Latin shape as emblem of Christianity (**the C~,** Christianity, Christendom); figure of similar shape (GREEK, LATIN, MALTESE, SAINT *Andrew's*, *Anthony's*, TAU, *cross*); = *Southern Cross*; monument in form of cross, esp. one in centre of town; decoration indicating rank in some orders of knighthood (**Grand C~,** highest degree of this) or awarded for personal valour (*Victoria, George, Cross*); cross-shaped figure or object; = SIGN *of the cross*; line that intersects another, point of intersection; affliction to be borne with Christian patience, a trial or annoyance; inter-mixture of breeds, a hybrid; mixture or compromise *between*; crosswise movement of actor, football, boxer's fist, etc., (**on the** ~, diagonally); (sl.) swindle. **2.** *a.* Transverse, reaching from side to side; intersecting; lying or tending athwart each other or the main direction or purpose; reciprocal (*cross accusations, effects*, etc.); (colloq.) out of temper, angry *with*. **3.** *v.t. & i.* Place so as to intersect or be across one another (*cross one's legs, hands, knife and fork*; ~ one's **fingers, have, keep,** one's **fingers** ~**ed,** crook one finger over another to bring good luck); make sign of cross on or over; draw line across (*cross one's* or *the t's*, see T); go across (road, river, sea, any area), cross road etc.; meet and pass (each other, another), cross each other (esp. of letters each sent before other's arrival); thwart or fail to comply with or anger by show of resistance (person, will, plan); (cause to) interbreed; cross-fertilize (plants). **4. as** ~ **as two sticks,** in bad temper; ~**'bar** (horizontal, esp. between uprights); ~ **bat** (in cricket, held aslant); ||~**-bench** (in Parliament for members not belonging to Government or official Opposition party); ~**'bill,** bird whose mandibles cross when bill is closed; ~**-bones,** figure of two thigh-bones (see SKULL); ~**'bow,** bow fixed across wooden stock, with mechanism working string; ~**-bred,** hybrid; ~**-breed,** hybrid animal or plant; ~**-buttock,** throw over hip in wrestling; ~**-check** *n. & v.*, check by alternative method of verification; ||~ **cheque,** draw two lines across it signifying that payment is to be through a bank; ~**-country,** (of run, course, walk) across fields etc., not along (main) roads; ~**-cut,** diagonal cut, path, etc.; ~**-cut saw** (for cutting across grain of wood); ~**-examine,** examine (esp. witness in lawcourt) minutely to check or extend previous testimony (so *cross-examination* n.); ~**-eyed,** having one or both eyes turned inwards; ~**-fertilize,** fertilize (animal or plant) from one of a different species, or fig.

of interchange of ideas etc.; ~-**fire**, converging gunfire, or questions assailing one from different quarters; ~-**grained**, (of wood) with grain running irregularly, (of person) perverse, intractable; ~ person's **hand** or **palm with**, give her (coin) for fortune-telling; ~-**hatch** *v.t.*, shade with intersecting parallel lines; ~-**head(ing)**, heading printed across column before section of article in newspaper etc.; ~ one's **heart**, make sign of cross over it as token of sincerity; ~-**legged** (esp. of person squatting); ~ person's **mind**, (of image, idea) occur to him; ~ **off**, **out**, cancel, expunge; ~-**over**, (having) point or place of crossing from one side to the other; ~-**patch**, ill-tempered person; ~ person's **path**, come in his way, esp. as obstacle; ~-**piece**, transverse component of structure etc.; ~-**ply**, (of tyre) having fabric layers with cords lying crosswise; ~ **purposes**, conflicting purposes (*be at ~ purposes*, misunderstand each other, be in pursuit of conflicting objects); ~-**question**, = *cross-examine*; ~-**reference** (to another passage in same book); ~'**road(s)**, intersection of two roads (*at the ~roads*, fig. at critical turning-point in life etc.); ~-**section**, transverse SECTION, (fig.) representative sample; ~ **oneself**, make sign of the cross on oneself; ~-**stitch**, one formed of two stitches that cross; *cross* SWORDS; ~-**talk**, unwanted transfer of signals between communication channels, repartee; ~ **the floor**, join opposing side in debate; ~-**trees**, horizontal timbers to support mast; ~-**voting**, voting for a party not one's own or for more than one party; ~-**wind** (blowing at right angles, or not parallel, to one's direction of travel); ~'**word**, puzzle in which words crossing each other vertically and horizontally according to given pattern have to be filled in from clues. **5.** ~'**ing** *n.*, (esp.) intersection of roads or railways or one of each, intersection of nave and transepts, part of street marked for pedestrians to cross by (*pedestrian crossing*); ~'-**ways**, ~'**wise**, (-z) *advs.*, in the manner of a cross, across, athwart. [E f. N f. Ir. f. L *crux*]

**crosse** *n.* Netted crook used in lacrosse. [F]

**crotch** *n.* Bifurcation, fork (esp. of human body or garment). [CROOK]

**crotchet** *n.* ‖(Mus.) black-headed note with stem, = two quavers, or half minim; whim, fad; ~**y** *a.* (~**iness**), whimsical, peevish. [F dim. of *croc* CROOK]

**crouch.** **1.** *v.i.* Stand or lie with legs bent close to body. **2.** *n.* Crouching. [F f. N (CROOK)]

**croup**[1] (-ōō-) *n.* Laryngitis of children, with hard cough; ~'**y** *a.* [imit.]

**croup**[2] (-ōō-) *n.* Animal's (esp. horse's) rump; **crou'pier** (-ōō'-; or -iā) *n.*, raker-in and payer-out of money at gaming table. [F (CROP)]

**croûton** (krōō'tawn) *n.* Small piece of fried etc. bread served with soup or used as garnish. [F (CRUST)]

**crow** (-ō). **1.** *v.i.* (‖*past* in first sense also **crew** *pr.* krōō). Utter cock's cry; (of infant) utter joyful sound; express exultation (*over beaten rival*). **2.** *n.* Cock's cry; infant's crowing; kind of bird (e.g. raven, rook, jackdaw, chough, and esp. carrion crow) with black or black and grey plumage (*white ~*, rarity; **as the ~ flies**, in a straight line; *\*eat ~*, submit to humiliation); ~('**bar**, bar of iron with bent end used as lever; ~'**berry**, black-berried heath shrub, \*cranberry; ~'**foot**, name of various plants; ~'**s-foot**, wrinkle at outer corner of eye; ~'**s-nest**, barrel at masthead as shelter for look-out man. [E]

**crowd.** **1.** *n.* Number of people or animals standing or moving close together without order, press or throng, (**follow the ~**, conform with the majority; **would pass in a ~**, is not conspicuously inferior); mass of spectators; *the* multitude; (colloq.) company, set, gang; large number *of* things. **2.** *v.i. & t.* Form a crowd, come in crowds, (*round*, *in*, *to* place, *to* see); fill (place) or incommode (person) thus; pack (people, space, things) too closely; force (people, things) *into* space etc.; come aggressively close to; thrust (person, object, task, idea) *out* by occupying space or time or thoughts; ~ (**on**) **sail**, hoist unusual spread of sail. [E]

**crown.** **1.** *n.* Wreath for the head esp. as emblem of victory, what rewards or consummates effort;

monarch's head-covering or circlet usu. of gold and jewels worn as symbol of power; (C~) regal power, *the* king or queen, *the* supreme governing power in a monarchy; thing like garland or crown about top of anything; figure of crown as mark; British coin worth 25p; foreign coin, esp. krona or krone; top of *of* head, hat, etc.; highest or central point *of* arch etc.; visible part of tooth (opp. *root*), artificial replacement for (part) of this; size of paper, 508×381 mm; C~ **Colony** (subject to British Government's control); C~ **Court**, court of criminal jurisdiction in England and Wales; C~ **Derby**, kind of china made at Derby and often marked with crown; ~ **glass** (without lead or iron, used formerly in windows); ~ **green**, bowling-green with raised middle part; ~ **jewels** (forming part of sovereign's regalia); C~ **prince**, male heir to sovereign throne (also fig. of likely successor in any office); C~ **princess**, Crown prince's wife, female heir to sovereign throne; ~ **wheel** (with teeth or cogs at right angles to its plane). **2.** *v.t.* Put crown on (head, person); invest with regal crown or office (*crown him, crown him king*; ~ed **heads**, kings and queens); (Draughts) mark (piece) as king by putting another on top of it; be a crown to, encircle or rest on the top of; be the consummation or reward or finishing touch to (**to ~ all,** at climax); (sl.) hit on the head; ~ **a tooth**, provide its stump with cap of gold etc. cemented on. **3.** ~'er *n.*, (arch., joc., dial.) coroner. [F f. L *corona*]

**crozier.** See CROSIER.

**CRT** *abbr.* cathode-ray tube.

**cruces.** See CRUX.

**cru'cial** (-ōō'shal) *a.* (~ly). Decisive between two hypotheses (*crucial instance, test*); (colloq.) very important; **cru'cible** (-ōō'-) *n.*, vessel in which metals can be melted, fig. severe trial; **cruci'ferous** (-ōō'-) *a.*, (Bot.) with four equal petals arranged crosswise; **cru'cifix** (-ōō'-) *n.*, model of (Christ on) the Cross [for FIX]; **crucifi'xion** (-ōō-; -kshon) *n.*, crucifying, esp. that of Christ or a picture of it; **cru'ciform** (-ōō'-) *a.*, cross-shaped (esp. of church with Latin cross as ground-plan); **cru'cify** (-ōō'-) *v.t.*, put to death on a cross,

mortify (one's passions, flesh, etc.), persecute, torment. [F f. L (CROSS)]

**crud|e** (-ōōd) *a.* In the natural or raw state; lacking finish, unpolished; (of action, manners, etc.) rude, blunt; ~**ïtÿ** *n.* [L *crudus* raw]

**cru'el** (-ōō'-) *a.* (~er, ~est, ‖-ll-; ~ly). Having or showing indifference to or pleasure in another's suffering; causing pain or suffering; ~**tÿ** *n.* [F f. L (prec.)]

**cru'et** (-ōō'-) *n.* Small stoppered bottle for condiments at table, or for Eucharistic wine or water; ~(-stand) (holding cruets and mustard and pepper pots). [AF dim. (CROCK[1])]

**cruise** (-ōōz). **1.** *v.i.* Sail about without precise destination, or calling at series of places; (of motor vehicle or aircraft) travel at **cruising speed** (economical travelling speed, less than top speed); (of vehicle or driver) travel at random, esp. slowly. **2.** *n.* Cruising voyage. [Du. (CROSS)]

**crui'ser** (-ōō'z-) *n.* Warship of high speed and medium armament; CABIN *cruiser*; ~-**weight**, see BOX.

**crumb** (-m). **1.** *n.* Small fragment of bread or *of* food etc.; soft inner part of loaves (*crust and crumb*); small particle, atom, (*of* comfort etc.); (sl.) objectionable person. **2.** *v.t.* Cover (cutlet etc.) with bread-crumbs, crumble (bread). **3.** **crü'mble**, (*v.t.* & *i.*) break or fall into crumbs or fragments, (of building, power, reputation, etc.) suffer decay, (*n.*) crumbly or crumbled substance, dish esp. of cooked fruit with crumbly topping; **crü'mblÿ** *a.* (-iness), apt to crumble; ~**ÿ** (-mi) *a.* (~ily, ~iness), strewn with crumbs, (of loaf) with much crumb. [E]

**crümbs** (-mz) *int.* expr. dismay. [CHRIST]

**crü'mm|ÿ** *a.* (sl.; ~iness). Dirty, unpleasant; inferior, worthless. [var. of CRUMBY]

**crü'mpet** *n.* Flat soft batter-cake eaten toasted with butter; (sl.) head, sexually attractive woman or women. [orig. uncert.]

**crü'mple** *v.t.* & *i.* Crush together or *up* into creased state; ruffle, wrinkle; become creased; ~ (**up**), collapse, give way. [obs. *crump* curl up]

**crünch. 1.** *n.* Sound made by chewing crisp food or treading etc.

on gravel or dry snow; act of crunching; decisive event (**when the ~ comes**, in a show-down). **2.** *v.t.* & *i.* Chew (food) or tread etc. on (gravel etc.) with crunch; go with a crunch. [imit.]

**crŭp'per** *n.* Strap holding harness back by passing under horse's tail; horse's croup. [F (CROUP²)]

**crusa'de** (-ōō-). **1.** *n.* Medieval Christian military expedition to recover Holy Land from Muslims; war instigated by Church for religious ends; campaign or movement against poverty etc. **2.** *v.i.* Go on or take part in crusade. [F (CROSS)]

**cruse** (-ōōs, -ōōz) *n.* (arch.) Earthenware jar; WIDOW'*s cruse.* [E]

**crush. 1.** *v.t.* Compress with violence so as to break or bruise or pulverize or crumple; defeat utterly, overwhelm, discomfit, (*crushing defeat, grief, retort*). **2.** *n.* Act of crushing; crowded mass of persons etc.; (colloq.) crowded social gathering; drink made from juice of crushed fruit; (sl.) (object of) infatuation (**have a ~ on**, be infatuated with); **~ bar**, place for theatre audience to buy drinks in the intervals; **~-barrier**, (temporary) barrier for restraining crowd. [F]

**crust. 1.** *n.* Hard outer part of bread (opp. *crumb*); *a* piece of it esp. as scanty food; similar casing over anything (e.g. hardened surface of snow, ice, shell, piecrust, scum, scab, earth's rocky outer part, deposit from wine); (sl.) impudence. **2.** *v.t.* & *i.* Be the crust of, cover with crust, become crusted; (in *p.p.*) having formed a crust, matured, (*crusted port*), inveterate or antiquated (*crusted prejudice, habit, theory*). **3.** **~ā'cean** (-shan) *a.* & *n.*, (member) of the Crustacea or hard-shelled mainly aquatic animals including crabs, lobsters, shrimps, etc.; **~'y̆** *a.* (**~ily, ~iness**), (of loaf) with much or hard or crisp crust, (of person or behaviour) irritable, surly. [F f. L *crusta* rind, shell]

**crutch** *n.* Lame person's walking-implement of stick from ground to armpit with cross-piece at top; support, prop, (lit. or fig.); fork of human body or garment. [E]

**crŭx** *n.* (*pl.* **~es**, **cruces** *pr.* krōō'sēz). Difficult point, puzzle; point at issue. [L, = cross]

**cry̆. 1.** *v.i.* & *t.* Utter call esp. of

shrill or loud or urgent tone, express pain or make appeal or give signal thus; weep or wail; (of crier, hawker) proclaim (notice, goods for sale, etc.) in streets; say or exclaim (specified words, *that*) excitedly; **~ down**, disparage; **~ (out) for**, demand, ask for, (**~ for the moon**, ask for what is unattainable); **~ one's heart** or **eyes out**, weep bitterly; **~ off**, abandon undertaking, decline to keep promise; *cry over spilt* MILK; *cry* QUARTER, QUITS; **~ stinking fish**, condemn one's own wares; **~ up**, extol; *cry* WOLF. **2.** *n.* Loud utterance of grief, pain, fear, joy, etc.; loud excited utterance of words; urgent appeal or entreaty; hawker's street-call; phrase etc. that serves to rally partisans; urgent movement of public opinion (*for* or *against* measure etc.); spell of weeping (*have a good cry*); yelping of hounds on scent (**in full ~**, hotly pursuing); **~-baby**, person who weeps easily or without good reason; **a far ~**, a long way. **3.** **cri'er** *n.*, (esp.) official making public announcements in law-court or streets; **~'ing** *a.*, (esp., of injustice etc.) flagrant, demanding redress. [F f. L *quirito*]

**cry̆ōgĕ'nĭc** *a.* (**~ally**). Relating to very low temperatures. [Gk *kruos* frost, *-genês* born]

**cry̆pt** *n.* Vault esp. below church, often used as chapel or burial-place; **~'ic** *a.* (**~ically**), of mysterious purport, veiled in obscurity; **~'ŏ** *n.* (*pl.* **~os**), (colloq.) person owing secret allegiance to a political creed etc., esp. Communism; **cry̆'ptogăm** *n.*, plant without stamens or pistils, non-flowering plant (ferns, mosses, algae, lichens, fungi), [Gk *gamos* marriage]; **~ogă'mic, ~ŏ'gamous,** *adjs.*; **~'ogrăm** *n.*, piece of cipher-writing; **~ŏ'grapher** *n.*; **~ogră'phic** *a.*; **~ŏ'graphy̆** *n.* [L *crypta* f. Gk (*kruptos* hidden)]

**cry̆'stal. 1.** *n.* Clear transparent icelike mineral (ROCK¹-*crystal*); piece of this; highly transparent glass, flint glass, vessel etc. of this; (Chem. etc.) aggregation of molecules with definite internal structure and external form of solid enclosed by symmetrically arranged plane faces; **~ ball**, globe-shaped crystal used for forecasting the future by **~-gazing**, concentrating one's gaze on a crystal to obtain a picture by hallucination etc.; ~ **set,** simple form of early radio using a crystal rectifier. **2.** *a.* Made of, like, clear as, crystal. **3.** ~**line** *a.,* of or like or clear as crystal, (Chem.) having structure of crystals; ~**li'nĭtў** *n.;* ~**lĭte** *n.,* small crystal; ~**lize** *v.t.* & *i.,* form into crystals or (fig.) into definite permanent shape (often *into*); ~**lized fruit** (preserved by impregnation with sugar); ~**lizā'tion** *n.;* ~**lŏ'grapher,** ~**lŏ'graphў,** *ns.,* student of, science of, crystal structure; ~**logră'phĭc** *a.* (-ically); ~**loid** *a.,* substance having or tending to crystalline structure (opp. COLLOID). [E f. F f. L f. Gk]

**c/s** *abbr.* cycles per second.

‖**C.S.E.** *abbr.* Certificate of Secondary Education.

‖**C.S.M.** *abbr.* Company Sergeant-Major.

**cu.** *abbr.* cubic.

**cŭb. 1.** *n.* Young of fox, bear, lion, etc.; young man lacking good manners etc.; \*apprentice; ~ (**reporter**), (colloq.) young or inexperienced newspaper reporter; C~ (**Scout**), member of junior branch of Scout Association. **2.** *v.t.* & *i.* (-**bb-**): Bring forth (cubs); hunt fox-cubs. [orig. unkn.]

**Cū'ban** *n.* & *a.* (Native) of *Cuba;* ~ **heel,** moderately high straight heel of shoe. [place]

**cŭ'bbў** *n.* ~**(-hole),** snug or confined place. [LG]

**cūbe. 1.** *n.* Solid figure contained by six equal squares; cube-shaped block (e.g. die); product of a number multiplied by its square (~ **root,** number which produces a given number when cubed). **2.** *v.t.* Find cube of (number); dice (food). **cū'bĭc** *a.* (-ically), of three dimensions (**cubic content,** volume expressed in cubic metres etc.; **cubic metre, foot,** etc., volume of cube whose edge is one metre etc., (of equation etc.) involving third power of unknown quantity or variable; **cū'bĭcal** *a.* (-lly), cube-shaped. [F, or L f. Gk]

**cŭ'bĭcle** *n.* Small separate sleeping-compartment; small partitioned space for dressing, private discussion, etc. [L (*cubo* lie)]

**cū'bĭs|m** *n.* Style in art of so presenting objects as to give the effect of an assemblage of geometrical figures; ~**t** *n.* [F (CUBE)]

**cū'bĭt** *n.* (Hist.) Measure of length, equal to length of forearm. [L *cubitum* elbow]

**cū'boid. 1.** *a.* Cubical, more or less cube-shaped. **2.** *n.* Rectangular parallelepiped; **cūboi'dal** *a.* [L f. Gk (CUBE)]

**cŭ'ckold. 1.** *n.* Husband of adulteress; ~**rў** *n.* **2.** *v.t.* Make cuckold of. [F]

**cu'ckoo** (koo'-). **1.** *n.* Migratory bird with characteristic cry, depositing eggs in nests of small birds; simpleton; ~ **clock** (striking with sound like cuckoo's note); ~ **flower,** meadow plant with lilac-white flower, lady-smock; ~ **in the nest,** unwanted intruder; ~**-pint,** wild arum; ~**-spit,** froth deposited on leaves by insects for larvae to lie in. **2.** *a.* (sl.) Crazy. [F, imit.]

**cū'cumber** *n.* Long fleshy green fruit of a creeping plant, usu. eaten raw as salad; the plant; **cool as a ~,** not flurried. [F f. L]

**cŭd** *n.* Ruminant's half-digested food (**chew the ~,** fig. reflect, ruminate); ~**weed,** woolly composite herb with scales round flower-heads. [E]

**cŭ'ddl|e. 1.** *v.t.* & *i.* Hug (child etc.); lie curled up; nestle together. **2.** *n.* Close embrace; ~**esome** (-dels-), ~**ў** (~**iness**), *adjs.,* fond of cuddling or tempting to cuddle. [orig. uncert.]

**cŭ'dgel. 1.** *n.* Thick stick as weapon (**take up the ~s for,** defend esp. in argument). **2.** *v.t.* (‖-**ll-**): Beat with cudgel (~ **one's brains,** think hard about a problem). [E]

**cūe¹. 1.** *n.* Actor's word(s) serving as signal for another to begin speaking or enter or do something; stimulus to perception etc.; signal for action; hint how to behave (**take one's ~ from,** be guided by). **2.** *v.t.* (~**'ing** *pr.* kū'ĭ-). Label so as to help recognition; give cue to; ~ **in,** insert cue for, (fig.) give information to. [orig. unkn.]

**cūe². 1.** *n.* Billiard-player's tapering rod for striking the ball. **2.** *v.i.* & *t.* Use cue (on). [var. of QUEUE]

**cŭff. 1.** *v.t.* Strike with open hand. **2.** *n.* Blow so given; end of coat or shirt sleeve, separate band of linen etc. worn at wrist (**off the ~,** extempore, without preparation); trouser turn-up; (in *pl.,* colloq.) handcuffs; ~**-link,** device of two joined buttons etc. to fasten sides of cuff together. [orig. unkn.]

**Cū′fĭc, Kū′fĭc,** n. & a. (Of) early form of Arabic alphabet esp. in inscriptions. [*Cufa*, place]

**cuĭră′ss** (kw-) n. Breast and back plate forming body armour; **~ier′** n., cavalryman esp. of French army with cuirass. [F f. L (*corium* leather)]

**cuisi′ne** (kwĭzē′n) n. Cooking methods of a country or establishment. [F]

**cŭ′l-de-săc** (or kŏŏ′-) n. (pl. culs-pr. same). Street, passage, etc., closed at one end. [F, = sack-bottom]

**-cŭle, -cle,** suf. forming (orig. dim.) ns. (*molecule, article, particle*). [F or L]

**cŭ′linărў** a. Of or for cooking. [L (*culina* kitchen)]

**cŭll. 1.** v.t. Pick (flowers); select; select and kill (surplus animals etc.). **2.** n. Culling; what is culled. [F (COLLECT[2])]

**cŭ′lmĭn|āte** v.i. Reach climax or highest point of development (*in*); (Astron.) be on the meridian; **~ā′tion** n. [L (*culmen* top)]

**cŭlŏ′tte** n. (usu. in pl., pr. same). Women's trousers cut to resemble skirt. [F, = knee-breeches]

**cŭ′lpab|le** a. (**~ly**). Blameworthy; **~ĭ′lĭtў** n.; **cŭ′lprĭt** n., person accused of or guilty of offence. [F f. L (*culpo* blame)]

**cŭlt** n. A religious worship esp. as expressed in ceremonies; study and pursuit or worship *of* (esp. derog. of transient fad). [F, or L (foll.)]

**cŭ′ltĭv|āte** v.t. (**~able**). Raise crops from (land) by clearing, ploughing, planting, sowing, etc.; grow (crops) thus; culture (bacteria etc.); develop (faculty, manner, habit) in oneself or others by practice or training, cultivate faculties etc. of (person; esp. in p.p.); **~āte** (**the acquaintance of**), make or take opportunities of associating with; **~ā′tion, ~ātor,** ns. [L (*colo cult-* till, worship)]

**cŭ′lture. 1.** n. Trained and refined state of the understanding and manners and tastes, or of the body; phase of this prevalent at a time or place; instilling of it by training; artificial rearing *of* bees, fish, bacteria, etc., set of bacteria so reared; cultivation (*of*); **cŭ′ltural** (-cher-) a. (**-lly**); **cŭ′ltured** (-cherd) a., exhibiting culture. **2.** v.t. Maintain

(bacteria etc.) in artificial conditions for growth; **~d pearl** (formed by oyster after insertion of suitable foreign body).

**cŭ′lvert** n. Tunnel-drain for water crossing road, canal, etc. [orig. unkn.]

**cŭm** prep. With (**~ dividend**, of stocks and shares, including dividend about to be paid); (indicating combined nature or function) *laboratory--cum-workshop*. [L]

**cŭ′mber** v.t. (literary). Block up, obstruct movement in or of, inconvenience. [ENCUMBER]

**cŭ′mbersome, cŭ′mbrous,** adjs. Hampering, inconvenient in size or weight or shape.

**cŭ′mĭn, cŭ′mmĭn,** n. Plant with aromatic seed. [F f. L f. Gk]

**cŭ′mmerbŭnd** n. Waist sash. [Hindi & Pers.]

**cŭ′mmĭn.** See CUMIN.

**cŭ′mquat, k-,** (-ŏt) n. Plum-size orange-like fruit used in preserves. [Chin. *kin kü* gold orange]

**cŭ′mŭlatĭve** a. Representing the sum of many items (*the cumulative effect of separately unimportant facts*); **~ evidence** (depending on many small indications); **~ vote**, system allowing voter as many votes as there are candidates with right of giving all to one; **cŭ′mŭlāte** v.t. & i., accumulate, combine (catalogue entries etc.); **cŭ′mŭlus** n. (pl. -li pr. -li), form of cloud consisting of rounded masses heaped on horizontal base. [L *cumulus* heap]

**cŭ′nĕĭfŏrm. 1.** a. Wedge-shaped. **2.** n. Writing in cuneiform impressed strokes in ancient Persian and Assyrian inscriptions. [F, or L (*cuneus* wedge)]

**cŭ′nnĭng. 1.** n. Selfish cleverness or insight, skill in deceit or evasion; (arch.) skill, dexterity, ingenuity. **2.** a. Artful, crafty; (arch.) skilful, ingenious. [E]

**cŭnt** n. (vulg.) Female genitals; (derog.) person, esp. woman. [E]

**cŭp. 1.** n. Drinking-vessel usu. with one side-handle (*teacup, coffee-cup, cup and saucer*; **in** one's **~s**, while (getting) drunk); amount that it holds (*cup of tea*); one's **~ of tea**, colloq. what one likes, what suits one best); (Eucharist) chalice or its contents; ornamental vessel as prize; wine, cider, etc., with various flavourings (*claret-cup*); (fig.) fate, experience, (*a bitter cup*; *drain the cup of life*, *humiliation*, etc.; *one's* or **the ~ is full,** one's happiness or misery is complete); part of brassière to contain or support one breast; rounded cavity, socket etc.; **~'bearer,** (Hist.) officer in great household pouring wine for company; **~-cake** (baked in paper cup or from ingredients measured in cupfuls); **C~ Final,** (Footb. etc.) final match in competition for cup; **~-tie,** match in such competition. **2.** *v.t.* Take or hold as in a cup; make cup-shaped; (Hist.) bleed (person) by applying suction with **~'ping-glass. 3. ~'ful** (-ŏŏl) *n.*, (\*esp.) half-pint measure in cookery. [E f. L *cuppa*]

**cŭ'pboard** (kŭ'berd) *n.* Shelved recess or cabinet esp. for crockery, provisions, etc.; **~ love** (simulated for what can be got by it). [CUP, BOARD]

**Cū'pĭd** *n.* Roman god of love pictured as winged boy with bow; **~'s bow,** upper edge of upper lip etc., shaped like Cupid's double-curved bow; **cūpĭ'dĭtў** *n.*, greed for gain. [L (*cupio* long for)]

**cū'pola** *n.* Small dome; kind of furnace; ship's or fort's revolving gun-turret. [It. f. L *cupa* cask]

**cŭ'ppa, cŭ'pper,** *n.* (colloq.) Cup of (tea). [corrupt.]

**cŭ'pr|eous** *a.* Of copper, coppery; **~ĭc, ~ous,** *adjs.*, (Chem.) containing bivalent, univalent, copper; **~ĭ'ferous** *a.*, copper-yielding; **~ō-nĭ'ckel** *n.*, copper–nickel alloy esp. as in British 'silver' coins. [L (COPPER[1])]

**cŭr** *n.* Worthless or snappish dog; ill-bred, surly, or cowardly fellow; **~'rĭsh** *a.* [E]

**cŭr'açao** (-sō) *n.* Orange-peel liqueur. [place]

**cūr'acў** *n.* Curate's office or tenure of it. [CURATE]

**cūrār'é** *n.* Vegetable poison paralysing motor nerves. [Carib]

**cŭr'assow** (-ō) *n.* S. Amer. bird like turkey. [CURAÇAO]

**cūr'ate** *n.* Parish priest's assistant; **~-in-charge** (with charge of parish during incumbent's incapacity or suspension); **~'s egg,** thing partly good and partly bad; **cūr'ative,** (*a.*) tending to cure disease etc., (*n.*) curative drug or measure; **cūrā'tor** *n.*, person in charge of something esp. of museum or library, ‖member of

managing board esp. in universities; **cūrātōr'ial** *a.* [L *curatus* (CURE)]

**cŭrb. 1.** *n.* Chain or strap passing under horse's lower jaw and giving powerful control; (fig.) means of constraint, check; enclosing framework or border or edging, kerb; **~ roof** (with faces having two slopes, the steeper below). **2.** *v.t.* Apply curb to (horse); restrain (subjects, passions, etc.). [F (CURVE)]

**cŭrd** *n.* Solid part of coagulated substance (**~s and whey**) formed by action of acids on milk and serving as material for cheese; (in *pl.*) broken up curd as food; LEMON[2] *curd*; **~'ў** *a.* (**~iness**); **cŭr'dle** *v.t.* & *i.*, form into curd, coagulate, (fig.) check flow of (blood) with horror. [orig. unkn.]

**cūre. 1.** *n.* Thing that cures; restoration to health; course of medicinal or healing treatment (REST[1]-*cure*); **~ of souls,** spiritual charge of parish or congregation. **2.** *v.t.* Restore to health; relieve (*of* disease); eliminate (evil); preserve (meat, fruit, tobacco) by various processes. **3.** *curé* (kūr'ā) *n.*, parish priest in France etc.; **cūrě'tte,** (*n.*) surgeon's scraping-instrument, (*v.t.*) scrape with this. [F f. L *cura* care]

**cŭr'few** *n.* Ringing of bell at fixed evening hour (orig. as notice to put out fires; Hist.); (under martial law etc.) signal or time after which persons must remain indoors. [F (COVER, L FOCUS)]

**Cūr'ia** *n.* Papal court, government departments of Vatican. [L]

**cūr'ie** *n.* Unit of radioactivity. [person]

**cūr'ĭ|ous** *a.* Eager to learn; inquisitive, prying; stirring curiosity, puzzling, inviting attention; strange, odd; **~ō'sĭtў** *n.*, eager receptiveness of mind, desire to know details of something, tendency to pry into others' concerns, *a* strange or rare thing; **~ō** *n.* (*pl.* **~os**), rare or unusual object. [F f. L (CURE)]

**cŭrl. 1.** *v.t.* & *i.* Bend or coil (*up*) into spiral or curved shape; (of smoke etc.) move in spiral or curve; play at curling; **~ up,** (fig.) writhe with horror, shame, etc., (colloq.) lie or sit with knees drawn up, (sl.) collapse. **2.** *n.* Coiled lock of hair; curled state (*keep one's hair in curl*); spiral or inward-curving form or motion; **~ of the lip,** scornful expression; ~**-paper** (for twisting hair into curls). **3.** ~'**er** n., (esp.) pin, clip, etc., for curling the hair; ~'**ing** n., (esp.) game like bowls played on ice with large flattish stones. [Du.]

**cur'lew** n. Long-billed wading bird. [F]

**cur'l|y** a. (~**iness**). Having or arranged in curls, moving in curves; *curly* KALE; **cur'licue** n., decorative curl or twist [CUE² (=pigtail) or Q]. [CURL]

**curmu'dgeon** (-ŭ'jon) n. Churl or miser; ~**ly** a. [orig. unkn.]

**cu'rrant** n. Dried fruit of small seedless Levantine grape used in cookery; (fruit of) kind of ribes (*black, red, white, currant*). [AF (*Corinth*, place)]

**cu'rrent. 1.** a. (Of money, opinion, word) in circulation or general use (*current* ACCOUNT); **pass** ~, be generally accepted); still going on, not yet superseded by another (*the current week, reign, issue or number of* periodical). **2.** n. Body of water or air moving in definite direction esp. through stiller surrounding body; tendency or course *of* opinion, events, etc.; movement of electrically charged particles. **3. cu'rrency** n., time during which thing is current, being current (**give currency to,** circulate), money current in a country; ~**ly** adv., (esp.) at the present time; **cu'rricle** n., (Hist.) light open two-wheeled two-horsed carriage; **curri'culum** n. (*pl.* **-la**), appointed course of study; *curriculum vitae* (-vē'tī), summary of one's previous career. [F f. L *curro curs-* run]

**cu'rrier** n. Leather-dresser. [F f. L (*corium* leather)]

**cu'rrish.** See CUR.

**cu'rry¹. 1.** n. Dish of meat, fish, eggs, vegetables, etc., cooked with crushed spices and usu. served with rice; ~**-powder,** preparation of turmeric, spices, etc. **2.** v.t. Make (meat etc.) into curry. [Tamil]

**cu'rry²** v.t. Comb (horse) with curry-comb; treat (leather, esp. after tanning); ~**-comb** (of metal for horses etc.); ~ **favour,** ingratiate oneself (*with* person). [F (READY)]

**curse. 1.** n. Divine decree or human invocation of destruction or punishment on person or thing (*curses come home to* ROOST; **under a** ~, feel-

ing or liable to its effects); profane oath (**not care** or **give a** ~ **for,** be indifferent to; **not worth a** ~, useless); thing whose effects are disastrous; bane or scourge (*the curse of drink*); **the** ~, (colloq.) menstruation. **2.** v.t. & i. Utter curse against; utter expletive curses (*curse and swear*); afflict *with*; be a curse to; **cur'sed** a. & adv., = DAMNED. [E]

**cur'sive** a. & n. (Writing) done with joined characters, opp. *block*; **cur'sor** n., transparent part with line on slide-rule; **cur'sory** a. (-ily, -iness), (of inspection, reading, etc.) without attention to details, rapid or general or desultory. [L, = running (CURRENT)]

**curt** a. (Of speech or speaker) noticeably or rudely brief; (of literary style) over-concise; ~**ail'** v.t., cut down, shorten, reduce, in length or extent or amount; deprive *of*; ~**ail'ment** n. [L *curtus* short; *curtail* corrupt. of obs. adj. *curtal*]

**cur'tain** (-tan). **1.** n. Cloth suspended as screen usu. with fittings enabling it to be moved sideways or upwards; (*C*~) =IRON *Curtain*; screen separating stage and auditorium in theatre, raised at start of action and lowered at the end; rise of curtain at start of play etc.; fall of curtain at end of scene; (in *pl.*, sl.) the end; (Fortif.) connecting wall between bastions etc.; ~**(-call),** audience's summons to actor(s) to take bow after fall of curtain; ~**-fire,** artillery barrage; ~ **lecture,** wife's private reproof to husband; ~**-raiser,** short opening theatre-piece, (fig.) preliminary event. **2.** v.t. Provide, shut *off,* with curtain(s). [F f. L *cortina*]

**cur'tilage** n. Area attached to dwelling-house as part of its enclosure. [F (COURT)]

**cur'tsy, -sey. 1.** n. Woman's or girl's act of salutation made by bending knees and lowering body (*drop a curtsy*). **2.** v.i. Drop curtsy (*to* person). [var. of COURTESY]

**curv|e. 1.** n. Line or surface or shape of which no part is straight; line showing diagrammatically a continuous variation of quantity, force, etc. **2.** v.i. & t. Bend or change direction so as to form curve. **3.** ~**a'ceous** (-shŭs) a., having many curves (esp. of shapely female figure); ~**'ature** n., curving, curved shape; **curve't, (n.)** horse's short trained leap, (v.i.; -tt-, -t-) perform this; **cŭrvili′near** a., of curved lines. [L *curvus* curved]

**cu′shion** (kŏŏ′shon). **1.** n. Bag filled with mass of soft material, air, etc., for sitting, kneeling, leaning, on; means of protection against shock; elastic lining of billiard- -table's sides; body of air supporting hovercraft etc. **2.** v.t. Furnish or protect with cushions (lit. or fig.); mitigate effects of (as) with cushion (*cushion the blow*). [F f. L *culcita* mattress]

**Cŭshi′tic** a. & n. (Of) group of E. Afr. languages of Hamitic type. [*Cush*, place]

**cu′shў** (kŏŏ′-) a. (colloq.) (Of job etc.) easy, comfortable. [Hindi *khush* pleasant]

**cŭsp** n. Point of meeting of two (usu. similar) curves (e.g. spear- -point, meeting of trefoil arcs, horn of moon); **cŭ′spate, cŭ′spidal** (-lly), adjs. [L *cuspis -id-* point]

**cŭss** n., & v.i. & t. (colloq.) Curse; (usu. derog.) creature, person; *\*∼- -word*, swear-word; *∼′ĕd* a., cursed, perverse. [CURSE]

**cŭ′stard** n. Baked usu. sweetened mixture of eggs and milk (also egg ∼); sauce made of sweetened mixture of milk and cornflour etc.; *∼- -apple*, W. Ind. fruit with custard- -like pulp; *∼-pie*, (fig.) slapstick comedy acting. [obs. *crustade* (CRUST)]

**cŭ′stodў** n. Keeping (*have, be in, the custody of*); imprisonment (**in ∼,** imprisoned; **take into ∼,** arrest); **custo′dian** n., curator, keeper, caretaker. [L (*custos -od-* guard)]

**cŭ′stom** n. Usual way of behaving or acting, established usage as a power or as having legal force (*it is the custom to; the custom of* doing); business patronage, regular dealings or customers; (in pl.) duty levied on imports, government department dealing with this; *\*∼ clothes* etc. (made to customer's order), so *∼-built, -made*; *∼-house*, office at seaport or frontier at which customs duties are collected; *∼arў* a. (-ily, -iness), according to custom, based on custom rather than law; *∼er* n., person entering shop to buy, person with whom one is concerned, (colloq.) *awkward* etc. person or animal to deal with; *∼ize* v.t., make to order or according to individual requirements. [F f. L *consuetudo*]

**cŭt. 1.** v.i. & t. (-tt-; cut). Make way, make (way), by parting something with pressure of an edge (of knife, ship, plough, etc.; *knife will not ∼,* is blunt); penetrate (substance) or wound (limb etc.) or divide (cloth etc.) by cutting; pain (as) by cutting (*cutting wind, irony*); detach or trim by cutting (corn, flowers, hedge, one's nails, hair); reduce (prices, rates, time, services, etc.); cease (services etc.); bring *away* or *down* or *off* or *out*, divide *in two* etc. or *in pieces* or *up*, set *adrift* or *loose*, lay *open*, make *short*, by cutting; carve (meat); (of line or lines) cut (another, each other) in two, cross, intersect; shape (garment, gem, record) by cutting; (Cards) divide (pack), cut pack, in two; sever oneself from person's *acquaintance* or from *the connection* with something, cut the acquaintance or ignore the presence of (person); cut the connection with or avoid or absent oneself from (affair, meeting, lecture, etc.); (Cinemat.) edit, stop the cameras, go quickly to another shot; hit (ball) with chopping motion, hit ball thus; switch off (engine etc.); *\*dilute, adulterate*; (sl.) go quickly, hurry along. **2.** n. Act of cutting; wound made by cutting; stroke with sword, whip, cane, etc.; (Crick., Lawn Tennis, etc.) stroke made by cutting; cutting of an acquaintance; excision of part of play, film, book, etc.; reduction (in prices, wages, service, etc.), cessation (of power supply etc.); way garment or hair is cut, style; joint or piece of meat regarded as yielding slices etc. (*prime cuts*), slice or helping of or of meat (*a cut of the joint*); (sl.) commission, share of profits etc.; SHORT *cut; =* WOODcut; **a ∼ above,** noticeably superior to. **3.** *cut a* CAPER[2], *a* CORNER; **∼ across,** go transversely over, not run parallel with; *cut a* DASH, *a poor* etc. FIGURE; **∼ a loss** or one's **losses,** abandon losing speculation etc. in good time; **∼-and-come-again,** abundance; **∼ and dried,** (of plans, method, etc.) ready-made, over-precise, lacking flexibility; **∼ and run,** (sl.) run away; **∼ and thrust,** sword-play with edge as well as point, (of argument etc.) lively interchange; **∼ a tooth,** have it appear through gum; **∼′away,** (of diagram etc.) showing some parts absent to reveal interior, (of coat) with skirt cut back from waist; **~ back**, reduce (expenditure etc.), prune, (Cinemat.) repeat part of previous scene; ~*back* n.; **~ both ways** (of factor, argument, etc., serving both sides); ~ one's **coat according to one's cloth**, limit ambition etc. to what is possible; **~ person dead**, completely refuse to recognize him; **~ down**, (fig.) reduce (expenses etc.); **~ in**, interpose in talk or action, obstruct path of vehicle one has just overtaken by returning to one's own side of the road too soon, give share of profits etc. to (person); *cut it* FINE²; *cut* LOOSE; **~ no ice**, (sl.) achieve little or nothing; **~ off**, bring to abrupt end or (esp. early) death, intercept (supplies, communications, troops), shut off (flow), exclude *from* access etc.; **~ off with a shilling**, disinherit (bequeathing only a shilling); ~*off* n., device for stopping flow; *cut of* one's JIB; **~ out**, (fig.) stop doing or using something, outdo or supplant, (Dressmaking, Tailoring) cut parts of (garment) for sewing (*have* one's WORK *cut out*), (usu. in *pass.*) make suitable for (*was not cut out to be a teacher*), (cause to) cease functioning; ~*out* n., device for automatic disconnection, release of exhaust gases, etc., figure cut out of paper etc.; **~-price, -rate**, selling or sold at reduced price; **~ short**, (fig.) hasten end of, interrupt; **~ one's teeth on**, (fig.) acquire experience from; **~ the knot**, dispose of difficulty in rough and ready way esp. by brushing aside accepted conditions; ~'**throat**, (n.) murderer, (a.) intense and merciless (*cutthroat competition*), (of card-game) three-handed, (of razor) having long blade set in handle; **~ through**, (esp.) pass through as shorter way; **~ to pieces**, (fig.) utterly defeat (army etc.), criticize damagingly; **~ to the heart**, keenly distress; **~ up**, = *cut to pieces*, (usu. in *pass.*) = *cut to the heart*; **~ up rough**, show resentment; ~'**water**, forward edge of ship's prow. **4.** ~'**ter** n., (esp.) tailor etc. who takes measurements and cuts cloth, warship's rowing and sailing boat, small sloop-rigged vessel with running bowsprit, *light sleigh; ~'**ting** n., (esp.) ‖excavation for railway or road or canal through

high ground, ‖piece cut from newspaper etc., piece cut from plant for propagation. [E]

**cūtā′néous** *a.* Of the skin. [L (CUTICLE)]

**cūt′e** *a.* (colloq.) Clever; ingenious; *attractive, quaint; ~′**ie** *n.*, (sl.) attractive young woman. [ACUTE]

**cū′ticle** *n.* Outer skin, epidermis; skin at base of finger-nail or toe-nail; **cū′tis** *n.*, true skin beneath cuticle. [L dim. (*cutis* skin)]

**cū′tlass** *n.* (Hist.) sailor's short broad-bladed sword; **cū′tler** *n.*, knife-maker or -dealer; **cū′tlery** *n.*, knives, forks, and spoons for domestic use. [F f. L *cultellus* dim. (COULTER)]

**cū′tlet** *n.* Neck-chop of mutton or lamb; small piece of veal etc. for frying; minced meat etc. in shape of cutlet. [F dim. f. L *costa* rib]

**cū′tter, cū′tting.** See CUT.

**cū′ttle** *n.* ~(**fish**), ten-armed sea mollusc ejecting black fluid when pursued. [E]

‖**C.V.O.** *abbr.* Commander of the Royal Victorian Order.

**Cwlth.** *abbr.* Commonwealth.

**cwm** (kōōm) *n.* Welsh var. of COOMB; cirque. [W]

**cwt.** *abbr.* hundredweight.

**-cy̆** *suf.* denoting status or condition (*bankruptcy, baronetcy*). [L -*cia*, Gk -*kia*]

**cyă′nic** *a.* Of or containing cyanogen; **cy̆′anide** *n.*, highly poisonous substance used in extraction of gold and silver; **cyă′nogèn** *n.*, colourless poisonous gas; **cyano′sis** *n.*, blue discoloration of skin. [Gk *kuanos* blue mineral]

**cy̆bernĕ′tics** *n.* Science of systems of control and communications in animals and machines. [Gk *kuber-nētēs* steersman]

**cy̆′clamāte** *n.* Artificial sweetening agent. [Chem. name]

**cy̆′clamen** *n.* Plant with pinkish-purple or white flowers with reflexed petals. [L f. Gk]

**cy̆′cle. 1.** *n.* Round of events proceeding in regular succession after and before similar rounds (e.g. complete day, century); duration of this; hertz; development following normal course (e.g. larva, pupa, imago); recurrent series; series of poems etc. centring on a person or incident or idea (*the Arthurian cycle*); bicycle or other wheeled riding-machine; **~-track, ~way**, road or path for cycles. **2.** *v.i.* Move in cycles; use bicycle etc. **3. cy′clĭc(al)** *adjs.* (**-ically**), recurring in cycles, belonging to a cycle or period; **cy′clĭst** *n.*, user of bicycle etc.; **cy′clŏne** *n.*, system of winds rotating inwards to area of low barometric pressure, hurricane of limited diameter, tornado, centrifugal machine for separating solids; **cyclŏ′nĭc** *a.* (**-ically**). [F or L f. Gk *kuklos* circle]

**cyclopae′d|ĭa, -pē′d|ĭa,** *n.* Encyclopaedia; **~ĭc** *a.* (**-ically**). [abbr.]

**Cy′clŏps** *n.* (*pl.* same, **~es**, Cyclopes *pr.* -ō′pēz). (Gk Myth.) One-eyed giant; **Cyclŏpē′an, Cyclō′pĭan,** *adjs.* [L f. Gk (CYCLE, *ōps* eye)]

**cy′clostȳle. 1.** *n.* Duplicating apparatus with stencil written on with pen tipped with small toothed wheel. **2.** *v.t.* Print or reproduce with this. [CYCLE, STYLE]

**cy′clotrŏn** *n.* (Phys.) Apparatus for acceleration of charged atomic particles revolving in magnetic field. [CYCLE, -TRON]

**cy′gnĕt** *n.* Young swan. [AF dim. f. F f. L *cygnus* swan f. Gk]

**cy′lĭnder** *n.* Solid or hollow roller-shaped body (e.g. shaft of round pillar of equal girth throughout); container for liquefied gas etc.; cylindrical part of machine etc., esp. piston-chamber in engine; **cylĭn′drĭcal** *a.* (**-lly**). [L *cylindrus* f. Gk]

**cy′mbal** *n.* Concave brass or bronze plate, struck with another or with stick etc. to make ringing sound. [L f. Gk]

**cym|e** *n.* (Bot.) Inflorescence in which each flower-stem, main or branch, ends in a flower; **~′ōse** *a.* [F f. L f. Gk]

**Cy′mrĭc** (k-) *a.* Welsh. [W *Cymru* Wales]

**cy′nĭc** *n.* (*C~*) ancient Greek philosopher of sect affecting contempt for sophistication and luxury; (*attrib.*) of the Cynics; one who sarcastically doubts human sincerity and merit; **~al** *a.* (**-lly**), sceptical of or sneering at goodness, in the habit of exposing human weaknesses; **~ĭsm** *n.* [L f. Gk (*kuōn* dog)]

**cy′nosūre** (-z-) *n.* Centre of attention (*cynosure of all eyes*). [F, or L f. Gk, = dog's tail, name of constellation containing pole-star]

**cy′pher.** See CIPHER.

**cy′prèss** *n.* Coniferous tree with dark foliage, taken as symbol of mourning. [F f. L f. Gk]

**Cy′prĭan, Cy′prĭot,** *adjs.* & *ns.* (Native) of Cyprus. [L f. Gk]

**Cyrĭ′llĭc** *a.* Of alphabet used in the languages of Slavs of the Orthodox Church. [St. *Cyril*, person]

**cyst** *n.* Bladder or sac containing liquid secretion or morbid matter or parasitic larva etc.; **~′ĭc** *a.*, (esp.) of the urinary bladder; **~i′tĭs** *n.*, inflammation of the urinary bladder; **~′oscōpe** *n.*, instrument for cystic examination. [Gk *kustis* bladder]

**-cȳte** *suf.* (Biol.) Mature cell (*leucocyte*). [foll.]

**cytŏ′logy** *n.* Study of biological cells; **cytoplăsm** *n.*, protoplasm in cell outside nucleus. [Gk *kutos* vessel]

**czar.** See TSAR.

**Czĕch** (chĕk) *n.* & *a.* (Native or language) of Bohemia; = foll. [Bohemian *Čech*]

**Czĕchōslŏ′văk, Czĕchōslová′kĭan,** (chĕk-) *adjs.* & *ns.* (Native) of Czechoslovakia. [prec., SLOVAK]

# D

**D, d,** (dē) *n.* (*pl.* **Ds, D's**). Fourth letter; (Mus.) second note in diatonic scale of C major; (as Roman numeral) 500; = DEE.

**d.** *abbr.* daughter; deci-; died; ‖(former) penny [L DENARIUS].

**'d** *v.* (colloq.; chiefly after *prons.*) = had, would. [abbr.]

**da** *abbr.* deca-.

**dăb**[1] *n.* & *a.* (colloq.) Adept (*at*): **~ hand,** expert. [orig. unkn.]

**dăb**[2] *n.* Kind of flat-fish.

**dăb**[3]. **1.** *v.t.* & *i.* (**-bb-**). Press briefly but not rub (surface) with sponge etc., press (sponge, brush; colour etc.) on surface thus, aim feeble blow (*at*), strike lightly. **2.** *n.* Dabbing; light blow; smear of paint etc.; (in *pl.*, sl.) fingerprints. **3.** dă′bble *v.i.* & *t.*, move feet, hands, bill, about in shallow water, stain with splashes of mud etc., engage (in subject) as desultory hobby. [imit.]

dă′bchick *n.* Small grebe. [E]

*da capo* (dahkah′pō) *adv.* (Mus.) Repeated from the beginning. [It.]

dāce *n.* (*pl.* same). Small fresh-water fish. [F *dars* (DART)]

dă′cha *n.* Small country villa in Russia. [Russ.]

dă′chshund (-ks-hŏŏ-) *n.* Short-legged long-bodied dog. [G, = badger-dog]

dă′ctyl *n.* A metrical foot (—∪∪); dăctў′lĭc, (*a.*) of dactyls, (*n.*, usu. in *pl.*) dactylic verse. [L f. Gk, = finger]

dăd *n.* (colloq.) Father. [imit. of child's *da*, *da*]

**Da′da** (dah′dah) *n.* 20th-c. international movement in art etc. repudiating conventions; ∼ism, ∼ist, *ns.* [F (*dada* hobby-horse)]

dă′ddy *n.* (colloq.) Father; oldest or most important person or thing; ∼-lo′ng-legs, crane-fly. [DAD]

dă′dō *n.* (*pl.* ∼s). Cube of pedestal; plinth of column; lower part of room-wall when visibly distinct from upper part. [It. (DIE[1])]

daemon(ic). See DEMON(IC).

dă′ffodĭl *n.* Yellow narcissus (colloq. abbr. daff); this as Welsh national emblem. [ASPHODEL]

daft (-ah-) *a.* Crazy, foolish. [E, = mild]

dă′gger (-g-) *n.* Short edged stabbing-weapon (at ∼s drawn, in bitter enmity; look ∼s, stare angrily); (Print.) = OBELUS. [orig. uncert.]

dā′gō *n.* (*pl.* ∼s, ∼es). (sl., derog.) Spaniard, Portuguese, Italian; any foreigner. [Sp. *Diego* = James]

daguĕ′rreotype (-gĕ′ro-) *n.* Early kind of photograph. [*Daguerre*, person]

dah′lia (dā′l-) *n.* Garden plant with large flowers. [*Dahl*, person]

**Dáil (Éireann)** (doil (ā′ran)) *n.* Lower house of Parliament in Republic of Ireland. [Ir., = assembly (of Ireland)]

dai′ly *adv.*, *a.*, & *n.* **1.** *adv.* Every (week)day, constantly. **2.** *a.* Produced, occurring, daily (∼ bread, one's necessary food or livelihood). **3.** *n.* Daily newspaper; ‖(colloq.) charwoman coming daily. [DAY]

dai′nty. **1.** *n.* Choice morsel,

delicacy. **2.** *a.* (-ily, -iness). (Of food) choice; of delicate beauty; fastidious; having delicate tastes and sensitivity. [F f. L (DIGNITY)]

dai′quiri (dī′k-, dă′k-) *n.* Cocktail of rum, lime-juice, etc. [place]

dair′y *n.* Place for dealing with milk and its products; ∼ cattle (kept for milk production); ∼ cream (real, not synthetic); ∼ farm (producing esp. dairy products); ∼maid, woman employed in dairy; ∼man, dealer in milk etc.; ∼ products, milk, cream, butter cheese, etc.; ∼ing *n.*, dairy operations. [E]

dā′ĭs (*or* dās) *n.* Low platform usu. at upper end of room or hall. [F f. L DISCUS table]

dai′sў (-zĭ) *n.* Small field and garden flower (pushing up the daisies, sl., dead and buried); ∼-chain, string of daisies threaded together. [E, = day's eye]

dāle *n.* Valley (esp. in N. Engl.); ∼′sman (-z-), inhabitant of dales in N. Engl. [E]

dă′lly *v.i.* Amuse oneself, flirt, (with); idle, loiter; dă′lliance *n.*, (poet.; esp.) amorous dallying. [F]

Dălmā′tian (-shan) *n.* Large white dog with dark spots; dălmă′tĭc *n.*, ecclesiastical and royal vestment. [*Dalmatia*, place]

*dal segno* (dălsā′nyō) *adv.* (Mus.) Repeated from point indicated. [It., = from the sign]

dăm[1]. **1.** *n.* Barrier checking flow of water to form reservoir, to prevent flooding, etc. **2.** *v.t.* (-mm-). Furnish or confine with dam; obstruct, block (*up*). [LDu.]

dăm[2] *n.* Mother (usu. of animal). [var. of DAME]

dă′mage. **1.** *n.* Injury impairing value or usefulness, loss of what is desirable, (the damage done by the storm; to my great damage); (in *pl.*) sum claimed or adjudged as compensation for damage; (sl.) cost (what's the damage?). **2.** *v.t.* (∼able *pr.* -ija-). Do harm to, injure, (goods damaged in transit; has a damaged finger; a damaging admission). [F f. L *damnum*]

dă′mask *n.*, *a.*, & *v.* **1.** *n.* Figured woven material, esp. white table-linen with designs shown by reflection of light; ∼ rose (grown esp. to make attar). **2.** *a.* Made of damask; coloured like damask rose, velvety pink. **3.** *v.t.* Weave with figured designs. **4. dămascë′ne** v.t., ornament (steel etc.) with inlaid gold or silver or with watered pattern produced in welding. [*Damascus*, place]

**dāme** n. Woman (arch., joc., *sl.*); ‖(title of) woman Commander or holder of Grand Cross in Orders of chivalry; comic middle-aged woman in modern pantomime, usu. played by man. [F f. L *domina* mistress]

**dămn** (-m) v., n., a., & adv. **1.** v.t. Doom to hell, cause damnation of, curse (person or thing, or abs.; often in subj.,= *may God damn* person or thing, or without object; ‖~ **all**, sl., nothing at all; **I'll be ~ed**, colloq., I am astonished; (**I'm, I'll be**) **~ed if** I know, will agree, etc., colloq., I certainly do not); condemn, censure, (~ **with faint praise**, commend so frigidly as to suggest disapproval); bring condemnation upon, be the ruin of, serve as proof of guilt of, (*that is enough to damn him*; *damning evidence*). **2.** n. Uttered curse; a negligible amount (*don't care or give, not worth, a damn*; TINKER's *damn*). **3.** a. & adv. (colloq.) Damned. **4. dă′mnable** a. (-bly), deserving damnation, hateful, annoying, **dămnā′tion**, (n.) eternal punishment in hell, (*int.*) = may damnation take person or thing; **dă′mnatory** a., conveying censure; **~ed** (-md), (a.) damnable (**do** one's **~edest**, one's utmost), (adv.) damnably, extremely, (*damned hot, funny*), **~ed well**, simply (*damned well do without*). [F f. L (*damnum* loss)]

**Dă′moclēs** (-z) n. **Sword of ~**, imminent danger esp. in midst of prosperity. [person]

**dămp** n., a., & v. **1.** n. Diffused moisture esp. as inconvenience or danger (*spoilt by damp*); = CHOKE-*damp*, FIRE*damp*; ~ **course**, layer of damp-proof felt etc. preventing rise of damp in wall; *damp*-PROOF, damp SQUIB. **2.** a. Slightly or fairly wet. **3.** v.t. & i. Make damp; take vigour or crispness out of, reduce vibration of, make flaccid or spiritless; ~ **down**, heap (fire etc.) with ashes to retard burning; ~′**er** n., (esp.) silencing-pad in piano mechanism, shock-absorber in vehicle, plate in flue controlling draught and combustion. [LG]

**dă′msel** (-z-) n. (arch., literary) Young woman. [F dim. (DAME)]

**dă′mson** (-z-) n. Small dark-purple plum; its colour; tree bearing it. [L DAMASCENE)]

**dăn** n. (Holder of) degree of proficiency in judo etc. [Jap.]

**Dan.** *abbr.* Daniel (O.T.).

**dance** (-ah-). **1.** v.i. & t. Move rhythmically, usu. to music, alone or with partner or set; move in lively way, skip; bob up and down; perform (specified dance); move up and down, dandle, (child); ~ **attendance** (*on* person), be kept waiting (by), follow obsequiously; ~ **to** person's **tune**, do as he demands. **2.** n. Piece of dancing, special form of this, single round or turn of one; dancing-party; tune for dancing to; **lead** person **a ~**, cause him much trouble; **D~ of Death**, medieval picture-subject of Death leading all to grave. **3. da′ncer** (-ah′-) n., (esp.) one who dances in public for pay. [F]

**dă′ndelion** n. Yellow-flowered wild plant with toothed leaves. [F f. L, = lion's tooth]

**dă′nder** n. (colloq.) Temper, indignation, (person's ~ **is up**, he is angry). [orig. uncert.]

**dă′ndle** v.t. Dance (child) on one's knees or in one's arms; pamper. [orig. unkn.]

**dă′ndruff** n. Dead skin in small scales among the hair; condition of having this. [orig. uncert.]

**dă′nd‖y. 1.** n. Man unduly devoted to smartness and fashion in dress etc.; (colloq.) excellent thing. **2.** a. (colloq.) Splendid, first-rate. **3.** **~ïf ied** (-id) a., like a dandy; **~ÿism** n. [perh. name *Andrew*]

**Dāne** n. Native of Denmark; (Hist.) Northman invader of England in 9th–11th c.; (**Great**) **~**, large breed of dog. [N]

**dă′nger** (-nj-) n. Liability or exposure to harm, thing that causes peril, (**in** ~ **of**, likely to incur etc.; *is a danger to peace, navigation, etc.*); **at ~**, (of railway signal) giving warning of danger; ~ **list** (of those dangerously ill); ~ **money**, payment above basic wages, for dangerous work; **~ous** a., involving danger (*dangerous* DRUG). [F f. L *dominus* lord]

**dă′ngle** (-nggel) v.i. & t. Be loosely suspended, hold in such suspension; hold out (bait, temptation); (arch.) linger as lover, follower, etc., (*about, round, after*). [imit.]

**Dā′nish. 1.** *a.* Of Denmark or the Danes; ~ **blue,** white cheese with blue veins; ~ **pastry,** yeast cake topped with icing, nuts, etc. **2.** *n.* Danish language. [F f. L (DANE)]

**dănk** *a.* Oozy, unwholesomely cold and damp. [prob. Scand.]

**danse macabre** (dahńs mǎkah′br) *n.* DANCE of Death. [F]

**dä′phnē** *n.* A flowering shrub. [Gk]

**dä′pper** *a.* (~est). Neat and precise esp. in dress; sprightly. [LDu.]

**dä′pple** *v.t.* Variegate with rounded spots of colour or shade; ~-**grey** *a.* & *n.,* (horse) of grey with darker spots. [orig. unkn.]

**Dar′by** *n.* ~ **and Joan,** devoted old married couple; ‖~ **and Joan club,** club for elderly people. [persons in poem]

**dāre. 1.** *v.t.* (3 *sing. pres.* usu. **dare** bef. expressed or implied inf. without *to; past* in this position arch. **durst**). Venture or have the courage or impudence to or *to* (*dare he do it?*; *he dares to insult me*; *I would if I dared*; *they dared not come, did not dare to come*; *how dare you?*); defy, challenge *to,* (*will do it if I am dared to*); ~**′devil** *a.* & *n.,* reckless (person); **I** ~ **say,** I am prepared to believe, do not deny. **2.** *n.* Act of daring, challenge. **3.** **dār′ing,** (*n.*) adventurous courage, (*a.*) bold. [E]

**dä′riole** *n.* Savoury or sweet dish cooked and served in small mould. [F]

**dark. 1.** *a.* With little or no light (*a dark night*); of deep or sombre colour (*dark* BLUE, *leaves,* etc.); with brown or black complexion or hair (opp. *blond, fair*); gloomy, dismal, obscure, mysterious, secret, (*scowling darkly*; *keep* thing *dark*; **keep** ~, remain in hiding; **the** ~ **side of things,** their worst aspect); cheerless, unenlightened (*the darkest ignorance*). **2.** *n.* Absence of light; lack of knowledge; dark area in painting; **after** ~, after nightfall; **in the** ~, with no light, lacking information. **3.** **D**~ **Ages,** Middle Ages, esp. 5th–10th c., (fig.) period of unenlightenment; *dark* BLUE; **D**~ **Continent,** Africa; ~ **days** (of adversity); ~**est Africa** (with ref. to its being little known, or unenlightened, hence joc. *in* ~*est Surrey* etc.); ~ **glasses,** spectacles with dark-tinted lenses;

~ **horse,** racehorse whose form is little known, person who is little known yet successful in contest; ~ **lantern** (with means for covering its light); ~**-room** (used in developing photographs); ~ **saying** (of dubious meaning). **4.** ~**′en** *v.t.* & *i.* (**never** ~**en** person's **door,** not visit him); ~**′ling** *adv.* & *a.,* in the dark; ~**′ness** *n.,* (esp.) wickedness (*the powers of darkness*; *Prince of Darkness*); ~**′y̆** *n.,* (colloq., derog.) Black. [E]

**dar′ling. 1.** *n.* Beloved or lovable person or thing. **2.** *a.* Beloved or prized, (colloq.) pretty. [E (DEAR)]

**darn**[1]**. 1.** *v.t.* Mend (knitted material) by interweaving yarn with needle across hole; ~**′ing** *n.,* (esp.) things to be darned. **2.** *n.* Place so mended. [orig. uncert.]

**darn**[2] *v., n., a.,* & *adv.,* **darned** (-nd) *a.* & *adv.,* (sl.) (Mild forms of) DAMN, DAMNED. [corrupt.]

**dar′nel** *n.* Kind of weed growing in corn. [orig. unkn.]

**dart. 1.** *n.* Small pointed missile, esp. used as weapon; insect's sting; (in *pl.*) indoor game with feathered darts and target (~**′board**); darting motion; tapering stitched tuck in garment. **2.** *v.t.* & *i.* Throw (missile); direct suddenly (glance, flash); go rapidly like missile (*out, in, past,* etc.). [F f. Gmc]

**Darwi′nian** *a.* & *n.* (Adherent) of *Darwin*'s doctrine of evolution of species; **Dar′winism** *n.* [person]

**dash. 1.** *v.t.* & *i.* Strike with violence so as to shatter (*dash to pieces*); fling (*against* etc.; *dashed water in her face*); knock, drive, throw, thrust, (*away, off, out,* etc.); frustrate (*his hopes were dashed*); daunt, dispirit; (sl.; mild form of) DAMN; go with haste or great force; ~ **against,** collide with; ~**′board,** board beneath motor-vehicle windscreen, in aircraft, etc., containing instruments; ~ **down, off,** write down, compose, rapidly (letter, verses, etc.); ~ **up,** arrive at full speed. **2.** *n.* Rush, onset, sudden advance, (**make a** ~ **for,** try to reach by quickness); impetuous vigour; showy appearance or behaviour (**cut a** ~, make brilliant show); *sprinting-race; horizontal stroke (—) in writing or printing to mark break in sense, omitted words, etc.; longer signal of two in Morse code; slight admixture (*dash of good *blood, of salt*); = *dashboard*. **3.** ~'**ing** *a.*, (esp.) spirited, showy. [imit.]

**da̵'stard** *n.* Mean, base, or despicable coward; ~**lў** *a.* (-iness). [orig. uncert.]

**dā'ta.** See DATUM.

**dāte¹** *n.* ~(-**palm**), W. Asian and N. Afr. tree; its oblong single-stoned fruit. [F f. L f. Gk (DACTYL; from leaf-shape)]

**dāte².** **1.** *n.* Statement in document etc. of the time (and often place) of composition etc., time of thing's occurrence, period to which work of art etc. belongs (*a tapestry of early date*; *out of* ~, obsolete; *to* ~, until now; *up to* ~, meeting, according to, latest requirements or knowledge); appointment; *(colloq.) person of opposite sex with whom one has social engagement; ~**line**, line partly along meridian 180° from Greenwich, east and west of which date differs, line in newspaper at head of dispatch or special article to show date and place of writing. **2.** *v.t. & i.* Mark with date; refer (event, thing) to a time (*pottery dated to 1500 B.C.*); be recognizable as of a past or particular period; (colloq.) be or become or make out of date; ~ (**up**), *(colloq.) make social engagement with; ~ **back to**, ~ **from**, have existed since. **3.** **dā'tive** *a. & n.*, (Gram.) (case) expressing indirect object or recipient; **dati'val** *a.* (-**lly**)

**dā'tum** (*or* dah'-) *n.* (*pl.* -**ta**, also treated as *sing.*), thing known or assumed as basis for inference or reckoning (*we have no data to go upon*; *sea-level to be the datum-line*), (in *pl.*) quantities or characters operated on by computers etc.; **data bank,** place where data are stored in large amounts; **data processing,** automatic performance of operations on data; **data sheet,** leaflet summarizing information on a subject. [F f. L *data* (*do* give)]

**datū'ra** *n.* Poisonous plant, e.g. stramonium. [Hindi]

**daub. 1.** *v.t. & i.* Coat (wall etc.) with clay etc.; smear (surface), lay on (greasy or sticky stuff); paint crudely and unskilfully; stain. **2.** *n.* Clay, plaster, etc., for surface-coating; smear; crude painting. **3.** ~'**er**, ~'**ster**, *ns.*, (esp.) bad painter. [F f. L (DE-, ALB)]

**dau'ghter** (daw't-) *n.* Female child in relation to her parents; female

descendant, female member *of* family etc.; woman who is the spiritual product *of*; product personified as female (*Fortune and its daughter Confidence*); ~-**in-law,** son's wife; ~**lў** *a.* (-iness). [E]

**daunt** *v.t.* Discourage, intimidate; ~'**less** *a.*, not to be daunted, intrepid. [F f. L *domito* (*domo* tame)]

**dau'phin** *n.* (Hist.) King of France's eldest son; ~**ėss** *n.*, dauphin's wife. [F f. L *delphinus* DOLPHIN, w. ref. to territorial name]

**da̵'venport** *n.* ‖Kind of writing-desk; *large sofa. [person]

**da̵'vĭt** *n.* Crane on board ship, esp. one of pair used for suspending or lowering boat. [F (dim. of name *David*)]

**Dā'vȳ** *n.* ~ (**lamp**), miner's safety lamp. [person]

**Dāvy Jō'nes** (-nz) *n.* (Naut. sl.) ~'s locker, sea regarded as a grave. [orig. unkn.]

**daw** *n.* = JACK*daw*. [E]

**daw'dle** *v.i.* Idle, waste time. [orig. unkn.]

**dawn. 1.** *v.i.* (Of day, intelligence, or thing becoming evident, etc.) begin to appear or grow light; ~ (**up**)**on,** begin to be perceptible to. **2.** *n.* First light, daybreak, incipient gleam of something; ~ **chorus,** early-morning bird-song. [E]

**day.** *n.* Time during which sun is above horizon, daylight (*was broad day*; *clear as day*; *all* (**the**) ~, as long as the sun is up; ~ **and night,** throughout these or in both alike; TIME *of* day); time during which work etc. is customarily done (*works an 8-hour day*; *all* ~, throughout the working day; *all in a or the* ~'s **work,** part of normal routine; **call it a** ~, cease working etc.; **at the end of the** ~, fig., in the final reckoning; ~ **off, out,** day away from work, home; **late in the** ~, fig., too late to be useful; **not one's** ~, one of those ~**s,** day when things go badly); period of 24 hours as unit of time (CIVIL, SIDEREAL, SOLAR, *day*; *any* ~, fig., under any conditions; *day* BY *day*; ~ **to** ~, ~ **in** ~ **out,** continuous(ly), routine(ly); FROM *day to* day; *days of* GRACE; *if* he's a ~, of age etc., at least); (in *sing. or pl.*) period (*in the days of old*; *seen, known, better days*; *to this day*; **the** ~, **this** ~ **and age,** the present time; **those were the** ~**s,** past times were better); (in *sing.* or *pl.*) lifetime, period of prosperity etc., (**end** one's ~**s**, die, pass last part of one's life; *in one's day*; **has had its** ~, is no longer useful; **in those** ~**s**, at that period; **on** one's ~, at time of best achievement); civil day as point of time (ONE *day*, **one of these (fine)** ~**s**, before long; *the* OTHER *day*; **some** ~, in the future; **that will be the** ~, that will be worth waiting for, iron. that will never happen); date of specific festival, day of notable eventfulness or of agreed event, (CHRISTMAS *Day*; *pay--day*); victory (CARRY, WIN, *save, lose, the day*); ~**bed** (for daytime sleep); ~**book** (in which sales etc. are noted for later transfer to ledger); ‖~**boy**, schoolboy living at home; ~'**break**, dawn, first light of day; ~**dream** *n*., & *v.i.*, (indulge in) fancy or reverie while awake; ‖~**girl**, schoolgirl living at home; ~**labourer** (hired by the day); ~**long** *a*. & *adv.*, (lasting) all day; ~ **nursery** (for children in daytime, at home or while mothers work); ~ **release**, system of allowing employees days off work for education; ~**return** *a*. & *n*., (ticket) at reduced rate for journey both ways in one day; ~**room** (used by day only, esp. common living-room in boarding-schools etc.); ~**school** (for day-pupils only); ~ **shift**, opp. *night shift*; ~'**time**, not night (*in the daytime*). [E]

**day'light** (-līt) *n*. Light of day, dawn, publicity, visible interval e.g. between boats in race, (in *pl.*, sl.) internal organs (*beat, scare, the (living) daylights out of*); **see** ~, understand what was previously puzzling; ~ **robbery**, unashamed swindling; ~ **saving**, obtaining longer evening daylight in summer by making clocks show later time.

**dāze. 1.** *v.t.* Stupefy, bewilder. **2.** *n.* State of being dazed. **3. dă'zzle,** (*v.t.*) blind temporarily or confuse sight of by excess of light, impress, delude, or surprise by brilliant display or prospect, (*n.*) bright confusing light. [N]

**dB** *abbr.* decibel(s).

‖**D.B.E.** *abbr.* Dame Commander (of the Order) of the British Empire.

**D.C.** *abbr. da capo*; direct current; District of Columbia.

**D.C.L.** *abbr.* Doctor of Civil Law.

**D.C.M.** *abbr.* Distinguished Conduct Medal.

‖**D.C.V.O.** *abbr.* Dame Commander of the Royal Victorian Order.

**D.D.** *abbr.* Doctor of Divinity.

**D-Day** (dē'dā) *n.* Day (6 June 1944) on which British and Amer. forces invaded N. France; day on which any operation is scheduled to begin. [*D* for *day*]

**D.D.T.** (dēdētē') *n.* White chlorinated hydrocarbon used as insecticide. [f. chem. name]

**de-** *pref.* Down, off, completely, (*descend, denude*); removal or reversal forming compd. *vbs.* (w. derivs.) f. *vbs.* (*decentralize, decentralization, desegregate*) and *ns.* (*defuse, de-ice, delouse*). [L]

**dea'con** *n.* (In Episcopal Ch.) minister of third order, below bishop and priest; (in Nonconformist Ch.) secular officer of congregation; (in early Ch.) minister of charity; ~**èss** *n.*, woman in early and some modern Churches, performing deacon's functions; **diă'conal** *a.* (-**lly**) **diă'conāte** (*or* -at) *n.*, deacon's office, body of deacons. [E f. L f. Gk *diakonos* servant]

**dead** (dĕd) *a.*, *adv.*, & *n.* **1.** *a.* (no *adv.* in ~**ly**) No longer alive (~ **as a doornail, as mutton**, quite dead; **the** ~, dead person(s), all who have died; **rise from the** ~, experience resurrection); having lost sensation (*my fingers are dead*; ~ **to**, unconscious, unappreciative, of; ~ **to the world**, unconscious, asleep); obsolete, not effective, (*dead as the* DODO); extinct (*dead volcano, match*); dull, lustreless, not resonant, without force, no longer effervescent; inactive (*the dead season*); inanimate, inert; (of microphone, telephone, etc.) not transmitting sounds; (of ball in games) out of play; abrupt, complete, exact, unqualified, (*dead stop, faint, calm, silence, certainty, earnest*); extremely tired or ill. **2.** *adv.* Profoundly, absolutely, completely, exactly, (*dead asleep, tired, drunk, on the target*); CUT person *dead*; ~ **against**, directly opposed or opposite to. **3.** *n.* Inactive or silent time (*the dead of night, winter*). **4.** ~**-(and-)alive**, dull, spiritless; ~**beat**, (person) completely exhausted or without money; ~ **centre**, exact centre, position of crank etc. in line with connecting-rod and not exerting torque; ~

**duck,** (sl.) unsuccessful or useless person or thing; ~ **end,** closed end of passage etc., (w. hyphen, fig., of job etc.) having no prospects; *~'fall,* trap with falling weight to kill animal (also fig.); ~ **hand,** oppressive posthumous control; ~'**head,** faded flower-head (*v.t.,* remove these from (plant)), non-paying member of audience, useless person; ~ **heat,** race in which two or more competitors finish exactly level; ~ **language,** one no longer ordinarily spoken, e.g. Latin; ~ **letter,** law no longer observed, unclaimed or undelivered letter; ~'**light,** (Naut.) shutter inside porthole; ~'**line,** time-limit; ~'**lock,** lock which opens and shuts only with key, state of affairs in which no progress can be made; ~ **loss,** complete loss, (colloq.) worthless person or thing; ~ **man's handle,** controlling-handle on electric train, disconnecting power supply if released; ~ **march,** march like funeral music; *dead men's* SHOES; ~ **nettle,** non-stinging nettle-like plant; ~**-pan,** expressionless (face); ~ **reckoning** (of ship's position by log, compass, etc., when observations are impossible); *dead* SET[3]; ~ **shot** (who never misses); ~ **weight,** inert mass, (fig.) debt not covered by assets, weight of cargo, fuel, crew, and passengers carried on ship; ~ **wood,** wood no longer alive, (fig.) useless person(s) or thing(s). **5.** ~'**en** *v.t.* & *i.,* deprive of or lose vitality, force, brightness, feeling, etc., make insensitive *to;* ~'**lȳ,** (*a.;* -**iness**) causing fatal injury or serious damage (*deadly* NIGHTshade, SIN), intense, extreme, as death (*deadly paleness, dullness*), accurate (*deadly aim*), (*adv.*) as if dead, extremely, (*deadly pale, serious*). [E]

**deaf** (děf) *a.* Wholly or partly without hearing (**the** ~, deaf people), not giving ear *to* (**turn a** ~ **ear,** be unresponsive); ~**-aid,** hearing aid; ~**-and-dumb alphabet,** manual signs for communication with the deaf; ~ **mute,** deaf and dumb person; ~'**en** *v.t.,* deprive of hearing by noise esp. temporarily. [E]

**deal**[1] *n.* Sawn fir or pine timber; deal board of standard size. [LG]

**deal**[2]. **1.** *v.t.* & *i.* (~**t** *pr.* dĕlt). Distribute in shares (*out, round*) to a number of people etc.; distribute (cards) to players; assign as share or deserts, administer, cause to be received (*has dealt me a heavy blow* lit. or fig.); behave in specified way (*deal honourably* etc., esp. *with* or *by* person); ~ **in,** be a seller of; ~ **with,** do business with, take measures regarding (question, situation, person), treat (subject). **2.** *n.* Dealing or turn to deal at cards, round of play following this; (colloq.) bargain, transaction, (*do a deal with;* NEW *deal*; **raw** or **rough** ~, harsh or unfair treatment; SQUARE *deal*); **a great, good,** ~, (colloq.) **a** ~, a large or considerable amount (as *n.* or *adv.*; *has lost a good deal; is a great deal better*). **3.** ~'**er** *n.,* (esp.) person dealing at cards, trader (in *comb.* or with *in; cattle-dealer, dealer in tobacco*); ~'**ings** (-z) *n.pl.,* (esp.) person's conduct or transactions. [E]

**dean**[1] *n.* Head of chapter of cathedral etc.; ‖(rural) ~, head of clergy in division of archdeaconry; fellow of college etc. with disciplinary and advisory functions; head of university faculty or department; ~'**erў** *n.,* dean's house or office, ‖rural dean's division of archdeaconry. [F f. L *decanus*]

‖**dean**[2]. See DENE.

**dear** *a., n., adv.,* & *int.* **1.** *a.* Beloved (often as ironical or merely polite form, and now part of polite formula at beginning of most letters); precious *to,* cherished, (*for dear* LIFE); earnest (*would dearly like to know*); high-priced, having high prices. **2.** *n.* (esp. in *voc.*; also ~'**est**). Dear person. **3.** *adv.* At high price (*buy,* COST *person, pay, sell, dear*). **4.** *int.* expr. surprise, distress, etc. (*dear, dear!; dear me!; oh dear!*). **5.** ~'**ie** *n.,* (usu. in *voc.*) dear one; **dearth** (dĕr-) *n.,* scarceness and dearness of food, deficiency *of.* [E]

**death** (dĕth) *n.* Dying, final cessation of vital functions, (**sure as** ~, quite certain); being killed or killing, event which ends life, (**be the** ~ **of,** cause to die; **Black D~,** 14th-c. plague epidemic in Europe; **catch** one's ~, colloq. catch fatal chill etc.; **do to** ~, kill, fig. overdo; **fate worse than** ~, joc., being raped; **be in at the** ~, see fox killed, or fig. any enterprise ended; **put to** ~, kill, cause to be killed; **bored, tired,** etc., **to** ~, to the utmost limit; **worked to** ~, hackneyed);

ceasing to be, annihilation (*death of one's hopes*); (*or* D~) personified power that annihilates (**at ~'s door**, close to death; **like ~ warmed up**, sl., very tired or ill; **like grim ~**, with all one's force); being dead; lack of spiritual life (**everlasting ~**, damnation); **~'bed**, bed on which one dies (*~bed repentance*, last--minute change of conduct or policy); **~-blow**, lethal blow (lit. or fig.); **~ cap**, poisonous toadstool; **~ cell** (for person condemned to death); **~ certificate**, official statement of cause and date and place of person's death; **~-dealing**, lethal; ||**~ duty**, tax levied on property after owner's death; **~-knell**, tolling of bell to mark person's death, (fig.) event that heralds the end of something; **~-mask**, cast taken of dead person's face; **~ penalty**, capital punishment; **~ rate**, number of deaths per 1,000 of population per year; **~--rattle**, sound in dying person's throat; **~-ray**, (imaginary) ray that causes death; **~-roll**, list or number of those killed; **~'s head**, skull as emblem of mortality; **\*~ tax**, = *death duty*; **~-trap**, unwholesome or dangerous place; **~-warrant** (for execution of criminal or fig. abolition of custom etc.); **~-watch** (beetle), small beetle whose larva bores in wood with ticking sound, once supposed to portend death; **~-wish**, (usu. unconscious) wish for death of oneself or another; **~'ly** *a*. & *adv*., suggestive(ly) of death (*deathly paleness*, *silence*; *deathly white face*). [E]

**dĕb** *n*. (colloq.) Débutante. [abbr.]

**débâcle** (dābah'kl) *n*. Sudden collapse; downfall; confused rush. [F]

**dĕbă'g** *v.t.* (sl.; **-gg-**). Remove trousers of, as punishment or joke. [BAG]

**débar'** *v.t.* (**-rr-**). Exclude *from* admission or right. [F (BAR[1])]

**débärkā'tion** *n*. Disembarkation. [F (BARQUE)]

**débā'se** *v.t.* Lower in quality, value, or character; depreciate (coin) by alloying etc.; **~'ment** (-sm-) *n*. [ABASE]

**débā't|e**. **1**. *v.t.* & *i*. Discuss (question); hold formal argument, esp. in legislature or public meeting; consider, ponder; **~ing society** (for practice in debate); **~'able** *a*. (**-bly**), subject to discussion or

dispute. **2**. *n*. Formal discussion; public argument. [F (BATTLE)]

**débau'ch**. (literary). **1**. *v.t.* Pervert from virtue; make intemperate or sensual; seduce (woman); vitiate (taste, judgement); (in *p.p.*) dissolute. **2**. *n*. Bout of sensual indulgence. **3**. **~ee'** *n*., excessively sensual person; **~erŷ** *n*., indulgence in or prevalence of sensual habits. [F]

**débě'nture** *n*. ||Sealed bond of corporation or company acknowledging sum on which interest is due, esp. as prior charge on assets; **\*~** (**bond**), fixed-interest bond of corporation or company. [L *debentur* are owed]

**débi'lit|āte** *v.t.* Enfeeble; **~ȳ** *n*., feebleness, esp. of health. [L (*debilis* weak)]

**dě'bĭt**. **1**. *n*. Record of sum owing by entry in account; (sum entered on) debit side of account. **2**. *v.t.* Enter on debit side of account (amount *against*, *to* person, person *with* amount). [F f. L *debitum* DEBT]

**débonair'** *a*. Having pleasant manners; gay, unembarrassed. [F]

**débou'ch** (*or* -ōō'sh) *v.i.* (Of troops, stream) issue from ravine, wood, etc., into open ground; (of river, road, etc.) merge into larger body or area (sea, square, etc.). [F (*bouche* mouth)]

**débrie'f** *v.t.* (colloq.) Interrogate (person) after completion of mission etc. [BRIEF]

**dě'bris** (-rē; *or* dā'-) *n*. Scattered fragments, wreckage. [F (*briser* break)]

**dĕbt** (dĕt) *n*. Money etc. owing, obligation, (*pay, incur, debts*; **floating ~**, repayable on demand or at stated time); **in** person's **~**, under obligation to him; **National D~**, money owed by State because of loans to it); state of owing something (*in, into, out of, debt*); **~-collector** (employed to collect debts for creditors); **~ of honour** (not legally recoverable, esp. of sum lost in gambling); **~ of nature**, (necessity of) death; **~'or** *n*., person in debt. [F f. L (*debeo* debit- owe)]

**débŭ'g** *v.t.* (**-gg-**). Remove bugs from; (sl.) rid of concealed microphones, remove defects from (machine, computer program, etc.). [BUG]

**débŭ'nk** *v.t.* (colloq.) Remove falsely good reputation from (person, institution, cult, etc.); expose false-ness of (claim etc.). [BUNK³]

**début**, \***debut**, (dā′bōō, -bū) n. First appearance (as performer, in society etc.); ∼**ante** (dĕ′būtahnt, dā′-) n., girl making social début, woman making début. [F]

**Dec.** abbr. December.

**dec.** abbr. deceased; declared.

**dĕ′ca-** in comb. Tenfold; ∼**gram(me)**, ∼**litre**, ∼**metre**, units in metric system. [Gk]

**dĕ′cāde** (or dĭkā′d) n. Ten-year period, set etc. of ten. [F f. L f. Gk (prec.)]

**dĕ′cad|ence** n. Deterioration, de-cline, (esp. of nation, art, or litera-ture after culmination); ∼**ent**, (a.) declining, of a period of decadence, self-indulgent, (n.) decadent person. [F f. L (DECAY)]

**dĕcă′ffeināte** (-fĭn-) v.t. Remove or reduce quantity of caffeine in (coffee). [CAFFEINE]

**dĕ′cagon** n. Plane figure with 10 sides and angles; **dĕcă′gonal** a. [L f. Gk (-GON)]

**dĕ′cal** n. Picture transferred to and permanently fixed on china etc. [abbr. of decalcomania f. F (décalquer transfer)]

**Dĕ′calŏgue** (-g) n. The Ten Commandments. [F or L f. Gk (DECA-, LOGOS)]

**dĕcă′mp** v.i. Break up or leave camp; take oneself off, abscond; ∼**ment** n. [F (CAMP¹)]

**dĕcă′nal** (or dĕ′ka-) a. Of dean; of dean's or S. side of choir. [L (DEAN¹)]

**dĕcă′nt** v.t. Pour off (wine, liquid, solution) leaving sediment behind; (fig.) transfer as if by pouring; ∼**er** n., stoppered bottle in which wine or spirit is brought to table. [L f. Gk (kanthos lip of beaker)]

**dĕcă′pĭt|āte** v.t. Behead; ∼**a′tion**, ∼**ātor**, ns. [L (CAPITAL)]

**dĕ′capŏd** n. Ten-footed crustacean, e.g. crab. [F f. L f. Gk (pous pod- foot)]

**dĕcă′rbonize** v.t. Remove carbon from (internal combustion engine etc.); ∼**a′tion** n. [DE-]

**dĕ′casyll|able** n. Metrical line of 10 syllables; ∼**ă′bic** a. [DECA-]

**dĕcă′thlon** n. Athletic contest comprising 10 different events for competitor. [Gk athlon contest]

**dĕcay′. 1.** v.i. & t. (Cause to) rot, decompose; (cause to) decline in quality, power, wealth, energy,

beauty, etc.; (of substance) undergo change by radioactivity. **2.** n. Decline in health, loss of quality; rotten or ruinous state; radioactive change. [F f. Rom. (L cado fall)]

**dĕcea′se** (esp. in legal use). **1.** n. Death. **2.** v.i. Die. **3.** ∼**d** (-st) a. & n. (with or without the), (person) who has died (esp. recently); \***dĕcĕ′dent** n., deceased person. [F f. L (cedo go)]

**dĕcei′ve** (-sē′v) v.t. & i. Persuade of what is false, mislead purposely; disappoint; use deceit; **dĕcei′t** (-sē′t) n., deceiving, trick, stratagem, deceitfulness; **dĕcei′tful** (-sē′t-) a. (-lly), given to, marked by, deceit. [F f. L (capio take)]

**dĕcĕ′ler|āte** v.t. & i. Cause or begin to move more slowly; ∼**a′tion** n. [DE-, (AC)CELERATE]

**Dĕcĕ′mber** n. Twelfth month. [F f. L (decem ten, orig. 10th month of Roman year)]

**dĕ′cency** n. Good behaviour; recognized code of propriety; avoid-ance of obscenity; (in pl.) require-ments of respectable behaviour. [L (DECENT)]

**dĕcĕ′nnial** a. (∼ly). Lasting, recurring every, 10 years. [L (decem ten, annus year)]

**dĕ′cent** a. Seemly, not immodest or obscene or indelicate; respectable; passable, good enough; ||(colloq.) kind, obliging. [F or L (decet is fitting)]

**dĕcĕ′ntraliz|e** v.t. Transfer from central to local authority; distribute among local centres; ∼**a′tion** n. [DE-]

**dĕcĕ′pt|ion** n. Deceiving, being deceived; thing that deceives; ∼**ive** a., apt to mislead, easily mistaken for something else. [F or L (DE-CEIVE)]

**dĕ′ci-** in comb. One-tenth; ∼**bel**, unit used in comparison of power levels in electrical communication or intensities of sound; ∼**gram(me)**, ∼**litre**, ∼**metre**, units in metric system. [L decimus tenth]

**dĕcī′d|e** v.t. & i. Settle (issue etc.) by giving victory to one side; give judgement (between, for, in favour of, against, that); bring, come, to a resolution (to do, on, for, or against doing, that); ∼**ed** a., (esp.) definite or unquestionable (a decided superior-ity), (of person) having clear views, not vacillating; ∼**edly** adv., (esp.)

undoubtedly, undeniably; ~'er n., game, race, etc., to decide between competitors with equal scores. [F or L (*caedo* cut)]

**dĕcĭ'dŭous** a. (Of leaves, horns, teeth, etc.) shed periodically or normally; (of tree) shedding its leaves annually. [L (*cado* fall)]

**dĕ'cĭmal. 1.** a. (~ly). Of tenths or ten, proceeding by tens; of decimal coinage (go ~, adopt decimal coinage). **2.** n. Decimal fraction. **3.** ~ **coinage, currency,** (in which units are decimal multiples or fractions of each other); ~ **fraction** (with a power of 10 as denominator, esp. when written as figures after decimal point); ~ **point,** dot placed after the unit figure in decimal notation; ~ **system** (in which each denomination, weight, measure, is 10 times the value of the preceding one). **4.** ~**ĭze** v.t., express as decimal, convert to decimal system; ~**ĭzā'-tion** n. [L (*decem* ten)]

**dĕ'cĭm|āte** v.t. (Of epidemic etc.) destroy tenth, large proportion, of; (Hist.) kill one in ten of (mutinous or cowardly soldiers); ~**ā'tion, ~ātor,** ns.

**dĕcī'pher** v.t. Turn into ordinary writing, make out (text written in cipher); make out meaning of (bad writing, anything puzzling); ~**ment** n. [CIPHER]

**dĕcī'sion** (-zhon) n. Act of deciding; settlement (of issue etc.); conclusion come to, resolve made; decidedness of mind; **dĕcī'sĭve** a., that decides an issue or contributes to a decision (*decisive battle*), (of person, preference, etc.) decided. [F or L (DECIDE)]

**dĕck. 1.** n. Platform in ship covering whole or part of hull's area at any level (**below** ~(s), in(to) space under main deck; CLEAR *the decks*; **on** ~, not below deck, fig. available for work etc.); floor or compartment of bus etc.; device for carrying and moving magnetic tape in recorder; *pack of cards; (sl.) ground; ~-**chair,** portable folding chair (orig. placed on deck in passenger ships); ~**hand,** man employed on vessel's deck in cleaning and odd jobs. **2.** v.t. Furnish with, cover as, deck; ~ (**out**), array, adorn. **3.** **-dĕcker** *in comb.,* having (specified) decks (*double-decker bus*). [Du., = cover]

**dĕclai'm** v.i. & t. Practise oratory; speak, utter rhetorically; deliver (passage), make speech thus; inveigh *against*; **dĕclamā'tion** n.; **dĕcla'matorў** a. (-ily, -iness). [F or L (CLAIM)]

**dĕclār'e** v.t. & i. Announce openly or formally (*declare war, a dividend*); pronounce (person etc.) to be something (*was declared invalid*); assert emphatically (*that*); acknowledge possession of (dutiable goods, income, etc.); (Cards) name trump suit, announce that one holds (certain combinations of cards etc.); (in p.p.) that is such by his own admission (*a declared atheist*); **Well, I (do)** ~**!** (excl. of surprise etc.); ~ one**self,** reveal one's intentions or identity; ~ **for, against,** come side with, against; ~ (**innings closed**), (Crick.) decide to cease batting before all wickets have fallen; **dĕclarā'tion** n., declaring, emphatic or deliberate statement, formal announcement; **dĕcla'ra-tĭve, dĕcla'ratorў** (-ily), *adjs.*; **dĕclār'er** n. (esp. Cards). [L (*clarus* clear)]

**dĕclī'ne. 1.** v.i. & t. Slope downwards; bend down, droop; (of day, life, etc.) draw to close (**declining years,** old age); deteriorate; decrease in price etc.; refuse (challenge, battle, invitation, offer; *to do, to be made use of* etc.); give or send refusal (~ **with thanks,** freq. iron., reject scornfully); (Gram.) inflect, state case-forms of. **2.** n. Gradual loss of vigour etc.; deterioration, decay; fall in price; latter part of day, life, etc.; (arch.) tuberculosis or similar disease. **3.** **dĕclē'nsion** (-shon) n., falling-off, deterioration, (Gram.) declining, class according to which noun etc. is declined; **dĕclinā'-tion** n., downward bend, *refusal, (Astron.) angular distance of star etc. N. or S. of celestial equator, (Phys.) deviation of compass needle from true north; **dĕclinā'tional** a. [F f. L (*clino* bend)]

**dĕclī'vĭtў** n. Downward slope. [L (*clivus* slope)]

**dĕclŭ'tch** v.i. Disengage clutch of motor vehicle; **double-~,** release and re-engage clutch twice when changing gear. [DE-]

**dĕcŏ'ction** n. Extraction of essence by boiling; liquor resulting from this. [F or L (CONCOCT)]

**dĕcō′de** v.t. Interpret (coded message). [DE-]

‖**dĕcō′ke.** (colloq.) **1.** v.t. = DE-CARBONIZE. **2.** n. This process. [COKE¹]

**décolletage** (dākŏ′ltahzh) n. (Exposure of neck and shoulders by) low-cut neck of woman's dress or blouse; **décolleté** (dākŏ′ltā) a. (fem. -ée pr. same), low-necked, wearing low-necked dress. [F (collet collar)]

**dĕcŏmpō′se** (-z) v.t. & i. Separate (substance etc.) into its elements; rot, decay; **dĕcŏmposi′tion** (-z-) n. [F (DE-)]

**dĕcŏmprĕ′ss** v.t. Relieve pressure on (underwater worker etc.) gradually; **~ion** (-shon) n. [DE-]

**dĕcŏntă′min|āte** v.t. (**~able**). Remove contamination from (esp. what is affected by poison gas or radioactivity); **~ā′tion** n. [DE-]

**décor** (dā′kŏr, dĕ′-) n. Furnishing and decoration of room or stage. [F (foll.)]

**dĕ′corāt|e** v.t. Furnish with adornments; paint, paper, etc., room or house; serve as adornment to; invest with order, medal, etc.; **D~ed style,** (Archit.) second stage of English Gothic (14th c.), with increasing decoration; **dĕcorā′tion** n., decorating, medal etc. conferred and worn as an honour, thing that decorates, (in pl.) flags etc. put up on festive occasion; **dĕ′corative** a.; **~or** n., (esp.) tradesman who paints, papers, etc., rooms or houses. [L (decus beauty)]

**dĕcō′rum** n. Seemliness; usage required by decency or politeness; **dĕ′corous** a., not offending against decorum. [L]

**dĕcoy′. 1.** (or dĕ′koi) n. Netted pond into which wild duck may be enticed; bird, person, animal, trained or used to entice others; bait, enticement. **2.** v.t. Entice by means of a decoy. [Du.]

**decrease. 1.** (dīkrē′s) v.t. & t. Diminish. **2.** (dĕ′krēs) n. Diminution. [F f. L (DE-, cresco grow)]

**decrē′e. 1.** n. Authoritative order having force of law; judgement in court of equity, admiralty, probate, or divorce (**~ nisi** pr. nisī, provisional order for divorce, made absolute unless cause to the contrary is shown within fixed period); will of God, Providence, or Nature as shown by events. **2.** v.t. Ordain by decree. [F f. L decretum (cerno sift)]

**dĕ′crĕment** n. (Amount of) decrease. [L (DECREASE)]

**dĕcrĕ′pi|t** a. Enfeebled with age and infirmities; dilapidated; **~tŭde** n. [L (crepo creak)]

**dĕcrē′tal** n. Papal decree. [L (DECREE)]

**dĕcrȳ′** v.t. Disparage, depreciate. [CRY]

**dĕ′cŭple** a. & n. Tenfold (amount). [L (decem ten)]

**dĕ′dĭcāt|e** v.t. (**~cable**). Devote with solemn rites (to God or saint, or to sacred use); devote, give up, (to special purpose); put words in (book etc.) as compliment to friend, patron, etc.; (in p.p.) devoted to vocation etc., having single-minded loyalty; **dĕdĭcā′tion** n., (esp.) words with which book is dedicated; **~ee′**, **~or**, ns.; **~ory** a. [L (dico declare)]

**dĕdū′c|e** v.t. (**~ible**). Infer, draw as logical conclusion, from; **dĕdŭ′ct** v.t., take away, put aside, withhold, (portion, amount, from); **dĕdŭ′ct-ible** a., (esp.) that may be deducted from one's tax or taxable income; **dĕdŭ′ction** n., deducting, amount deducted, deducing, inferring of particular instances from general law (cf. INDUCTION), conclusion deduced; **dĕdŭ′ctive** a., of, reasoning by, deduction. [L (duco lead)]

**dee** n. (Thing shaped like) letter D. [name of letter D]

**deed. 1.** n. Thing consciously done; brave, skilful, or conspicuous act; actual fact, performance, (kind in word and deed; in deed and not in name); document effecting legal disposition and bearing disposer's signature and seal; **~-box,** strong box for keeping deeds and other documents; **~ poll,** deed made and executed by one party only. **2.** v.t. *Convey, transfer, by legal deed. [E (DO³)]

**deem** v.t. Regard, consider, judge, to be (I deemed it my duty to go; was deemed sufficient or to be enough); **~′ster** n., Manx judge. [E]

**deep** a., n., & adv. **1.** a. Extending, going, far down or in from top, front, surface, edge, etc., (deep hole, water, plunge, border, shelf; go off the deep END; in deep WATERS); lying or situated far down, back, or inwards, or in (ship deep in the water; hands deep in pockets; fig., deep in thought, debt);

fully absorbed *in* (study, book); coming or brought from far down, far in, etc., (*deep breath, sigh*); extending to or lying at specified depth (*ankle-deep in mud; water 6 ft. deep; soldiers drawn up 6 deep*, in 6 ranks); heartfelt, intense, extreme, (*deep affection, interest, colour, sleep, disgrace*); low-pitched, full-toned, not shrill, (*deep voice, note, bell*); (fig.) profound, penetrating, difficult to understand, (*deep thinker, thought, insight*); ~-freeze [*P], refrigerator etc. in which foods can be quickly frozen and kept very cold for long periods, (fig.) suspension of activity; ~ mourning (expressed by wearing only black clothes); **a ~ one**, (sl.) cunning or secretive person; ~ **sea**, deeper parts of the ocean. **2.** *n.* Deep part(s) of the sea; abyss, pit; (poet.) *the sea*; (Crick.) position of fieldsman distant from batsman. **3.** *adv.* Deeply, far down or in, (*dig deep; read deep into the night*; **still waters run ~**, quiet manner covers depths of feeling, knowledge, or cunning); ~-**fried**, fried in fat etc. covering food; ~-**laid**, (of scheme) secret and elaborate; ~-**rooted** (of convictions etc.); ~-**seated** (of emotion, disease, etc.). **4.** ~**en** *v.t. & i.* [E]

**deer** *n.* (*pl.* same). Ruminant quadruped noted for speed, the male usu. with deciduous branching horns; ~'**skin**, (made of) deer's skin; ~'**stalker**, sportsman stalking deer, cloth cap with peak in front and behind. [E]

**defa´ce** *v.t.* Spoil appearance of; make illegible; ~**ment** (-sm-) *n.* [F (FACE)]

**de facto** (dēfă'ktō, dā-) *a. & adv.* (Existing) in fact, whether by right or not. [L]

**defalca´tion** *n.* Misappropriation of money; amount misappropriated; shortcoming; **dē'falcāte** *v.i.*, commit defalcation(s); **dē'falcātor** *n.* [L (*falx* sickle)]

**defā´me** *v.t.* Attack good reputation of; speak ill of; **dĕfămā´tion** *n.*; **dĕfă'matory** *a.* (-ily). [F f. L (FAME)]

**defau´lt** (or -ŏ'lt). **1.** *n.* Failure to act, appear, or pay (**go by ~**, be absent, be ignored because of absence; **judgement by ~**, given for plaintiff on defendant's failing to plead; **in ~ of**, if or since thing is lacking). **2.** *v.i.* Fail to meet pecuni-

ary or other obligation. **3.** ~**er** *n.* (esp., ||) soldier guilty of military offence. [F (FAIL)]

**defea´sible** (-z-) *a.* (~**ly**). Able to be annulled or forfeited; ~**i'lity** *n.* [F (*faire* make)]

**defea´t. 1.** *v.t.* Overcome in battle or other contest; frustrate, baffle. **2.** *n.* Defeating; being defeated. **3.** ~**ism** *n.*, conduct tending to bring about acceptance of defeat; ~**ist** *n.* [AF f. L (DIS-, FACT)]

**dĕ'fĕcāte** *v.i. & t.* (~**able**). Discharge faeces from body; clear of impurities, refine; ~**ā'tion**, ~**ātor**, *ns.* [L (*faex* dregs)]

**dĕfĕ'ct. 1.** (or dē'fĕkt) *n.* Lack of something essential to completeness; blemish; shortcoming, failing, (**the ~s of one's qualities**, those often found to go with the virtues one has). **2.** *v.i.* Desert, esp. to another country etc. **3.** ~**ion** *n.*, abandonment of one's leader, side, cause, country, etc., (*from*); ~**ive** *a.*, incomplete, faulty, lacking or deficient, esp. mentally, (Gram.) not having all the usual inflexions; ~**or** *n.*, person who defects. [L (*deficio -fect-* fail)]

**defĕ'nd** *v.t. & i.* Ward off attack made on, protect (*against, from*; *person, thing, oneself* or abs.); uphold by argument, speak or write in favour of; conduct defence in lawsuit; ||**defĕ'nce**, *defĕ'nse**, *n.*, defending, protection, means of resisting attack, justification, vindication, player's in defending position in game, (Law) defendant's case or its conduct, counsel for defendant, (in *pl.*) fortifications; *defence in* DEPTH; **defence mechanism**, body's reaction against disease organisms, (Psych.) mental process avoiding conscious conflict; **defĕ'ndant** *n.*, person etc. sued or accused in court of law; ~**er** *n.*, (esp., Sport) holder of championship etc. defending the title (opp. *challenger*); **D~er of the Faith** (title of English sovereigns); **defĕ'nsible** *a.* (-bly); **defĕnsibi'lity** *n.*; **defĕ'nsive**, (*a.*) serving, done, etc., for defence and not for aggression, (*n.*) state or position of defence (*be, stand, act, on the defensive*). [F f. L *defendo -fens-*]

**defĕ'r**[1] *v.t.* (-rr-). Put off to later time, postpone, (~**red payment**, by instalments; *deferred SHARES*); ~**ment**, ~**ral**, *ns.* [DIFFER]

**děfėr'²** *v.i.* (**-rr-**). Submit or make concessions in opinion or action (*to* person); **dě'ference** *n.*, respect, manifestation of desire to comply, respectful conduct, (**in ~ence to**, out of respect for); **deferě'ntial** (-shal) *a.*, (**-lly**), showing deference. [F f. L *defero delat-* carry away]

**defī'ance, defī'ant.** See DEFY.

**defī'cien|t** (-shent) *a.* Incomplete (*in*); insufficient in or in quantity, force, etc.; (**mentally**) **~t**, having imperfect mental development and so incapable of adequate behaviour; **~cy̆** *n.*, being deficient, lack or shortage (*of*), thing lacking, deficit; **~cy disease** (caused by lack of some essential element in diet); **dě'ficit** *n.*, amount by which sum of money is too small, excess of liabilities over assets. [L (DEFECT)]

**defī'le¹. 1.** *v.i.* March in file(s). **2.** (*or* dē'fīl) *n.* Gorge or pass through which troops must defile. [F (FILE²)]

**defī'le²** *v.t.* Make dirty, befoul; pollute, profane; deprive of virginity; **~ment** (-lm-) *n.* [*defoul* f. F *defouler* trample down (FOIL²)]

**defī'ne** *v.t.* Mark out (limits, boundary); make clear esp. as to outline, state exact meaning or scope of, (*a well-defined image*; **~ one's position**, state it precisely); frame definition of; **dě'fĭnīte** *a.*, having exact limits, determinate, precise, distinct, not vague; *definite* ARTICLE; **dě'fĭnītely** (-tli) *adv.*, & *int.* (colloq.) yes, certainly; **dĕfĭnĭ'tion** *n.*, defining, statement of precise meaning of a term, degree of distinctness in outline of object or image; **defī'nĭtive** *a.*, (of answer, treaty, verdict, etc.) final, decisive, unconditional, (of edition of book etc.) most authoritative. [F f. L (*finis* end)]

**deflā't|e** *v.t.* & *i.* Empty (tyre, balloon, etc.) of its air or gas; (Econ.) subject (currency) to deflation; reduce importance of; (cause to) lose conceit or confidence; pursue policy of deflation; **~ion** *n.*, deflating, reverse or reversal of INFLATION (Econ.); **~ionary** *a.* [DE-, INFLATE]

**deflě'ct** *v.t.* & *i.* Turn aside from straight course; (cause to) deviate (*from*); **deflě'xion** (-kshon), **~ion**, **~or**, *ns.* [L (*flecto* bend)]

**deflow'er** *v.t.* Deprive (woman) of virginity; ravage; strip of flowers. [F f. L (FLOWER)]

**defō'li|ate** *v.t.* Remove leaves

from, esp. as military tactic; **~ant**, **~ā'tion**, *ns.* [L (FOIL¹)]

**defōr'm** *v.t.* Spoil appearance or shape of; (in *p.p.*, of person or his limbs etc.) misshapen; **defōrmā'tion** *n.*, deforming, perverted or changed form of something; **~ĭty** *n.*, deformed state, malformation esp. of body or limb. [F f. L (FORM)]

**defrau'd** *v.t.* Cheat by fraud (person, person *of*, or abs.). [F or L (FRAUD)]

**defray'** *v.t.* Provide money to pay (cost, expense); **~al** *n.* [F (*frai* cost f. L *fredum* fine)]

**defrō'st** (*or* -aw'-) *v.t.* Remove frost from, unfreeze, (esp. frozen food, interior of refrigerator, or windscreen). [DE-]

**děft** *a.* Dextrous, (esp. manually) skilful, adroit. [var. of DAFT = 'mild']

**defu'nct** *a.* Dead; no longer existing or in use or fashion. [L (*fungor* perform)]

**defu'se** *v.t.* Remove fuse from (explosive); reduce likelihood of trouble from (crisis etc.). [DE-]

**defy'** *v.t.* Challenge *to* do or prove something; refuse to obey, resist openly; (of thing) present insuperable obstacles to (*defy solution, definition, comparison*, etc.); **defī'ance** *n.*, defying, open refusal to obey, bold resistance, (*in defiance of*; **bid defiance to**); **defī'ant** *a.*, showing defiance. [F f. Rom. (L *fides* faith)]

**deg.** *abbr.* degree.

**děgě'ner|ate** *a.*, *n.*, & *v.* **1.** *a.* Having lost the qualities that are normal and desirable or proper to its kind. **2.** *n.* Degenerate person or animal. **3.** (-āt) *v.i.* Become degenerate. **4.** **~acy̆** *n.*, degenerate state; **~ā'tion** *n.*, becoming degenerate. [L (*genus* race)]

**děgrā'd|e** *v.t.* & *i.* Reduce to lower rank or simpler structure; bring into dishonour or contempt; degenerate; **děgradā'tion** *n.*, degrading, degraded state, thing that degrades; **~ing** *a.*, (esp.) lowering one's self-respect. [F f. L (GRADE)]

**degree'** *n.* Stage in ascending or descending scale (**by ~s**, a little at a time); step in direct genealogical descent (**forbidden, prohibited, ~s**, number of these too few to allow of marriage between two related persons); social or official rank; relative condition (*each good in its degree*); stage in intensity or amount (*to* *a high, the last, degree*; **to a ~**, colloq., considerably; COMPARATIVE, SUPERLATIVE, *degree*; *degrees of* COMPARISON; **third ~**, \*severe and protracted interrogation by police); (Law) grade of crime, criminality, (*murder, principal, in the first* etc. *degree*); academic diploma of proficiency in specified subject(s) (**honorary ~**, given to distinguished person; **~ day**, when these are formally awarded); (Math.) unit of angular or circular-arc measurement (symbol °, as *45*°); (Phys.) unit in scale of temperature, hardness, etc., (symbol °, deg., or omitted where letter indicating scale used serves as symbol). [F f. Rom. (L *gradus* step)]

**dėgrĕ′ssive** *a.* Descending; (of taxation) at successively lower rates on low amounts. [L (*gradior* walk)]

*dégringolade* (dāgrăṅgōlah′d) *n.* Rapid fall or deterioration. [F]

*de haut en bas* (deōtahṅbah′) *adv.* In a condescending manner. [F, = from above to below]

**dėhī′scent** *a.* (Of seed-vessel) gaping, bursting open. [L (*hio* gape)]

**dėhū′manize** *v.t.* Divest of human characteristics, make impersonal. [DE-]

**dėhȳ′dr|āte** *v.t. & i.* Remove water from esp. foods for preservation and reduction of bulk; make dry (lit. or fig.); lose water; **~ā′tion** *n.* [Gk *hudōr* water]

**dė-ī′c|e** *v.t.* Remove, prevent formation of, ice on aircraft, windscreen, etc.; **~er** *n.* [DE-]

**dė′if|ȳ** *v.t.* Make a god of; treat as a god, worship; **~icā′tion** *n.* [F f. L (*deus* god)]

**deign** (dān) *v.t.* Condescend *to* do. [F f. L (*dignus* worthy)]

*Dei gratia* (dāigrah′tia, -shīa) *adv.* By God's grace. [L]

**dē′ism** *n.* Belief in the existence of a god without accepting revelation (cf. THEISM); natural religion; **dē′ist** *n.*; **dēī′stic** *a.* (-**ically**); **dē′itȳ** (or dā′-) *n.*, divine status or nature, god; **the Deity**, God. [L *deus* god]

*déjà vu* (dāzhahvū′) *n.* Illusory feeling of having already experienced a present situation; something tediously familiar. [F, = already seen]

**dėjĕ′ct** *v.t.* (esp. in *p.p.*). Make sad or gloomy; **dėjĕ′ction** *n.*, dejected mood. [L (*jacio* throw)]

*de jure* (dē joor′i, dā yoor′ā) *a. & adv.* Rightful(ly), by right. [L]

**dĕ′kkō** *n.* (sl.; *pl.* **~s**). A look (*let's have a dekko*). [Hindi]

**Del.** *abbr.* Delaware.

**dėlai′ne** *n.* Light dress-fabric. [F, = woollen]

**dėlā′tion** *n.* (arch.) Act of informing against a person. [L (DEFER[2])]

**dėlay′. 1.** *v.t. & i.* Postpone; make or be late; hinder; loiter; wait; **~ed-action** *a.*, operating after an interval of time. **2.** *n.* Act, process, of delaying; hindrance; time lost by inaction or inability to proceed. [F]

**dėlĕ′ctab|le** *a.* (literary or iron.; **~ly**). Delightful; **dėlĕctā′tion** *n.*, enjoyment (usu. *for* one's *delectation*). [F f. L (DELIGHT)]

**dė′légate. 1.** (-āt) *v.t.* Send as representative(s) to conference etc.; commit (authority, powers, etc.) to or *to* representative(s). **2.** (-at) *n.* Delegated representative; deputy; member of committee. **3. dė′légacȳ** *n.*, body of delegates; **dėlėgā′tion** *n.*, delegating, delegacy. [L (LEGATE)]

**dėlē′te** *v.t.* Cancel, remove, (letter, word, passage); **dėlē′tion** *n.* [L *deleo*]

**dėlētēr′ious** *a.* Harmful. [L f. Gk]

**dĕlf, dĕlft,** *n.* Kind of glazed earthenware. [place]

**dėlī′ber|ate. 1.** (-āt) *v.i. & t.* Take counsel, hold debate; think carefully; consider (*question, what to do*, etc.). **2.** (-at) *a.* Intentional, fully considered, (of movement etc.) unhurried. **3. ~ā′tion** *n.*, deliberating, being deliberate; **~ative** *a.*, for or of deliberating (*deliberative assembly, functions*). [L (*libra* balance)]

**dĕ′lica|te** *a.* Fine, slender, exquisite, intricate; (of food) dainty; subtle, hard to discern, (*delicate flavour, colour*); deft, sensitive, (*delicate touch, instrument*); tender, easily harmed, subject to illness, (*delicate skin, health, child*); requiring deftness or tact (*a delicate operation, subject, situation*); avoiding coarseness or impropriety; (esp. of actions) considerate; **~cȳ** *n.*, delicateness, consideration for others' feelings, choice food. [F or L]

**dĕlicatĕ′ssen** *n.* (Shop selling) table delicacies or relishes. [G f. F (prec.)]

**dėlī′cious** (-shᴜs) *a.* Highly delightful, esp. to taste, smell, or sense of humour. [F f. L (*deliciae* delight)]

**dėlī′ght** (-ī′t). **1.** *v.t. & i.* Please greatly (**~ed to**, very glad to); take great pleasure *in*; be highly pleased *to* do. **2.** *n.* Great pleasure; thing that gives it; ~**ful** *a.* (**-lly**), giving delight. [F f. L (*delecto*)]

**dēli'mĭt** *v.t.* Determine limits or territorial boundaries of; ~**ā'tion** *n.* [F f. L (LIMIT)]

**dēli'nė|āte** *v.t.* (~**able**). Portray by drawing or description; ~**ā'tion**, ~**ātor**, *ns.* [L (LINE)]

**dēli'nquen|t. 1.** *a.* Defaulting, guilty; \*in arrears. **2.** *n.* Offender (esp. *juvenile delinquent*). **3.** ~**cў** *n.*, neglect of duty, guilt. [L *delinquo* offend]

**dēlĭquĕ'sce** *v.i.* Become liquid, melt; ~**nce** *n.*; ~**nt** *a.* [L (LIQUID)]

**dēli'rĭum** *n.* Disordered state of mind with incoherent speech and hallucinations; wildly excited mood; ~ **tremens** (trē'mĕnz), form of delirium with tremors and terrifying delusions due to prolonged consumption of alcohol; **dēli'rĭous** *a.*, affected with delirium, raving, wildly excited, ecstatic. [L (DE-, *lira* ridge between furrows)]

**dēli'ver** *v.t.* Set free (*from*); transfer possession of, give *up* or hand *over* to another; convey (goods, letters, etc.) to destination; launch, aim, (blow, attack, ball); utter (speech, sermon); assist at birth of or in giving birth; **be** ~**ed of**, give birth to, (fig.) produce (poem, joke, etc.); ~ **oneself of**, solemnly announce (opinion etc.); ~ **the goods**, (fig.) carry out one's part of bargain; ~**ance** *n.*, rescue, setting free; ~**ў** *n.*, delivering, being delivered, periodical distribution of letters or goods by post office or firm, person's manner of delivering ball, speech, etc.; **take** ~**y of**, receive (thing purchased). [F f. L (*liber* free)]

**dĕll** *n.* Small wooded hollow. [E]

**dēlou'se** *v.t.* Rid of lice or (fig.) disagreeable things. [DE-]

**Dĕ'lphĭan, -phĭc**, *adjs.* Of or as of the ancient Greek oracle at *Delphi*; obscure, enigmatic. [place]

**dĕlphi'nĭum** *n.* Kind of usu. blue--flowered garden plant, e.g. larkspur. [L f. Gk (DOLPHIN)]

**dĕ'lta** *n.* Fourth Gk letter (Δ, δ) = d; fourth-class mark in examination; triangular alluvial tract at river's mouth enclosed or watered by diverging outlets; ~ **wing**, aircraft's triangular swept-back wing. [Gk]

**dēlŭ'de** (*or* -ōō'd) *v.t.* Fool, deceive. [L (*ludo* mock)]

**dĕ'lŭge** *n.*, & *v.t.* Flood, downpour, (**the D**~), Noah's flood; fig. *a deluge of, was deluged with, applications*. [F f. L *diluvium*]

**dēlu'sion** (-zhon; *or* -lōō'-) *n.* False belief or impression, (*was under the delusion that*); vain hope; hallucination; ~**s of grandeur**, false exaggeration of one's own personality or status; **dēlu'sĭve** (*or* -lōō'-) *a.*, raising vain hopes, deceptive. [DELUDE]

**de lŭ'xe** (*or* de1ōō'ks) *a.* Sumptuous; of superior kind. [F, = of luxury]

**dĕlve** *v.i.* & *t.* Make research in documents etc.; (poet.) dig. [E]

\***Dem.** *abbr.* Democrat.

**dĕ'mag|ŏgue** (-g), \*~**|ŏg**, *n.* Leader or agitator of the populace; ~**ŏ'gĭc** (-gǐ-) *a.* (**-ically**); ~**ŏguerў** (-gerǐ), ~**ŏgў** (-gǐ), *ns.*, practices of demagogues. [Gk, = people-leader]

**dėma'nd** (-ah'-). **1.** *n.* Request made as of right or peremptorily (*payable* etc. **on** ~, as soon as asked for); urgent claim (*many demands on my purse, time, attention*); desire of would-be purchasers or users for commodity (**in** ~, sought after; SUPPLY *and demand*). **2.** *v.t.* Make a demand for (*of, from*, person; *demand an answer, to know, that one be told*); insist on being told (*demand* person's *business*); require, call for, (*tasks that demand special knowledge*); ~**ing** *a.*, requiring skill or effort. [F f. L (MANDATE)]

**dēmārcā'tion** *n.* Marking of boundary or limits, esp. between work considered by trade unions to belong to different trades (*demarcation dispute*). [Sp. (MARK[2])]

**démarche** (dā'märsh) *n.* (Diplom.) Step or proceeding. [F]

**dēmatēr'ĭalĭz|e** *v.t.* & *i.* Make, become, non-material or spiritual; ~**ā'tion** *n.* [DE-]

**dēmea'n**[1] *v.t.* Lower the dignity of. [MEAN[1]]

**dēmea'n**[2] *v. refl.* (w. adv.). Behave, conduct one*self*; ~**our**, \*~**or**, (-er) *n.*, one's bearing. [F, f. L *mino* drive animals]

**dēmĕ'ntĕd** *a.* Driven mad, crazy. [F f. L (*mens* mind)]

**dēmĕ'ntĭa** (*or* -sha) *n.* (Med.) Insanity with loss of intellectual power due to brain disease or injury; ~ **praecox** (prē'kŏks), schizophrenia. [L (DEMENTED)]

**dēmerār'a** (*or* -ār'a) *n.* Yellowish--brown raw cane sugar. [place]

**děmě'rĭt** n. Fault, undesirable quality, in person or thing (*merits and demerits*). [F or L (MERIT)]

**děme'sne** (-ē'n, -ā'n) n. Possession (of land) as one's own (*estate held in* ~, occupied by owner, not by his tenants); land attached to mansion etc.; sovereign's or State's territory; landed estate; (fig.) sphere, province, or field of action. [F f. L *dominicus* (*dominus* lord)]

**dě'mĭ-** *pref*. Half-. [F f. L *dimidius* half]

**dě'mĭgŏd** n. Partly divine being; offspring of god(dess) and mortal; (fig.) worshipped person. [GOD]

**dě'mĭjŏhn** (-jŏn) n. Large wicker-cased bottle. [F]

**dēmĭ'lĭtarĭz|e** v.t. Remove military organization or forces from (zone etc.); ~ā'tion n. [DE-]

**demi-mond|e** (dě'mĭmawnd) n. Women of doubtful repute in society; group behaving with doubtful legality etc.; ~aine n., woman of the *demi-monde*. [F, = half-world]

**demi-pension** (dĕmĭpah'ñsyawñ) n. Accommodation at hotel etc. with bed, breakfast, and one main meal per day. [F]

**děmĭ'se** (-z). 1. v.t. Convey (estate) to another by will or lease; transmit (title etc.) by death or abdication. 2. n. Conveyance, transfer, by demising; death (lit. or fig.). [AF (DISMISS)]

‖**dĕmĭsě'mĭquāver** n. (Mus.) Note with 3-hooked symbol, = half semiquaver. [DEMI-]

**dēmĭ'st** v.t. Clear mist from (windscreen etc.). [DE-]

**dě'mĭtāsse** n. Small coffee-cup. [F, = half-cup]

**dě'mŏ** n. (colloq.; pl. ~s) = (political etc.) DEMONSTRATION. [abbr.]

**dēmŏ'bĭlĭz|e** v.t. Release (troops) from mobilized state (colloq. **děmŏ'b, -bb-**); ~ā'tion n. [F (DE-)]

**dēmŏ'cracy** n. (State having) government by all the people, direct or representative; form of society ignoring hereditary class distinctions and tolerating minority views; **dě'mocrăt** n., advocate of democracy, *(D-) member of Democratic Party; **děmocrǎ'tĭc** a. (-ically), of, according to, advocating, constituting, democracy (*Democratic Party*, party opposed to Republican Party); **děmŏ'cratize** v.t. [F f. L f. Gk (*dēmos* the people)]

**démodé** (dāmŏ'dā) a. Out of fashion. [F (MODE)]

**dēmŏ'graphy** n. Study of statistics of births, deaths, disease, etc., as illustrating conditions of life in communities; **děmŏgrǎ'phĭc** a. (-ically). [Gk *dēmos* the people]

**dēmŏ'lĭsh** v.t. Pull or throw down (building); destroy; overthrow (institution); refute (theory); **děmolĭ'-tion** n. [F f. L (*moles* mass)]

**dē'mon** n. Devil, evil spirit; personified evil passion; cruel, malignant, or energetic person (~ **bowler**, Crick., very fast bowler; *is a demon for work*); (Gk Myth.; *or* dae'-) supernatural being; **dēmŏ'-nĭăc,** (n.) person possessed by a devil, (a.) demoniacal; ~ĭ'acal a. (-lly), of or by a demon (*demoniacal possession*), like demons, cruel or malignant; **dēmŏ'nĭc, dae-,** a. (-ically), demoniac, having supernatural genius or power; ~ŏ'latry, ~ŏ'logy, ns., worship, study, of demons. [L f. Gk *daimōn* deity]

**dě'monstr|āte** v.t. & i. (~able). Show evidence of (feelings etc.); logically prove truth or existence of; act as demonstrator (of); make, take part in, a (political etc.) demonstration; ~ā'tion n., proving or proof, exhibition and explanation of specimens or experiments, show of feeling, expression of opinion on political or other question, meeting or procession for such purpose; ~ā'tional a. (-lly); **dēmŏ'nstra-tĭve,** (a.) (of evidence, proof, etc.) conclusive, given to or marked by open expression of feelings (*demonstrative person, behaviour*, etc.), (Gram.) indicating person or thing referred to (*demonstrative PRONOUN*), (n., Gram.) demonstrative word; ~ātor n., (esp.) one who teaches by demonstration, esp. in laboratory etc., person who explains working of machine etc. to prospective customers. [L (*monstro* show)]

**dēmŏ'raliz|e** v.t. Destroy morale of; ~ā'tion n. [F]

**dēmŏ'|te** v.t. Reduce to lower rank or class; ~tion n. [DE-, PROMOTE]

**dēmŏ'tĭc** a. Popular, vulgar; (of) the popular form of modern Greek; (of) the simplified form of ancient Egyptian writing. [Gk (*dēmos* the people)]

**dēmūr'. 1.** v.i. (-rr-). Raise objections, take exception *to* (inference, proposal); (Law) enter a demurrer. **2.** n. Raising of objection (usu. *without demur*). [F f. L (*moror* to delay)]

**dĕmūr′e** a. (~r, ~st). Sober, grave, composed; decorous; affectedly or artificially quiet and serious. [F (prec.)]

**dĕmū′rr|age** n. Rate or amount payable to shipowner by charterer for failure to load or discharge ship within time allowed; similar charge on railway trucks or goods; ~er n., legal objection to relevance of opponent's point. [DEMUR]

**dĕmў′** n. Size of paper, 216 × 138 mm; ‖scholar of Magdalen College, Oxford; ~′shĭp n. [var. of DEMI-]

**dĕn** n. Wild beast's lair; resort of criminals etc. (*opium den*; *den of vice*); person's small private room. [E]

**dēnā′r|ĭ|us** n. (*pl.* ~**ĭ** *pr.* -ĭ). Ancient Roman silver coin; **dē′narў** a., of ten, decimal (see SCALE⁹). [L (*deni* by tens, *decem* ten)]

**dēnā′tionaliz|e** v.t. Transfer (institution, industry, etc.) from national to private ownership; ~**ā′tion** n. [DE-]

**dēnā′tur|e** v.t. Change properties of; make (alcohol etc.) unfit for drinking; ~**ant** (-cher-) n., substance used in denaturing. [F]

**dĕndrŏchronŏ′logў** (-k-) n. Chronology by study of annual growth-rings in timber. [Gk *dendron* tree]

**‖dēne**, **‖dean²**, n. Deep wooded valley. [E]

**dĕ′nguĕ** (-nggĭ) n. Infectious eruptive fever causing acute pain in joints. [Sp. f. Swahili]

**dēnī′al.** See DENY.

**dē′nier** (-nyer) n. Unit of weight for estimating fineness of silk, rayon, or nylon yarn. [orig. name of small coin; F f. L (DENARIUS)]

**dĕ′nĭgr|āte** v.t. Blacken (fig.), defame; ~**ā′tion** n. [L (*niger* black)]

**dĕ′nĭm** n. Twilled cotton fabric for overalls, jeans, etc.; (in *pl.*) garment made of this. [F *de* of, *Nîmes* (place)]

**dĕ′nĭzen** n. Inhabitant, occupant (*of* place); foreigner admitted to residence and certain rights; naturalized foreign word, animal, or plant. [AF f. L *de intus* from within]

**dēnŏ′mĭn|āte** v.t. (~**able**). Give name to; describe (person or thing) as; ~**ā′tion** n., name, designation, esp. characteristic or class name, class of units in numbers or weights

or money (*reduce to the same denomination*; *money of small denominations*), Church, religious sect, rank of playing-card within suit; ~**ā′tional** a. (-lly); ~**ātor** n., number below line in vulgar fraction (cf. NUMERATOR), divisor; (**least**, **lowest**) **common** ~**ator**, (least) common multiple of denominators of several fractions, (fig.) common feature of members of a group. [F or L (*nomen* name)].

**dēnō′te** v.t. Stand for, be the name or sign of, signify, indicate, give to understand, (esp. *that*; *d.c.* denotes *direct current*; *an asterisk denotes that the word is American*); **dēnotā′tion** n.; **dēnō′tative** a., indicative *of*. [F or L (NOTE)]

**dénouement** (dānōō′mahṅ) n. Final resolution in play, novel, etc.; unravelling of plot etc. [F (NODE)]

**dēnou′nce** v.t. Inform or inveigh against, accuse publicly; give notice of intention to withdraw from (treaty etc.). [F f. L (*nuntius* messenger)]

**de nouveau** (denōōvō′), **de novo** (dēnō′vō, dā-), advs. Afresh, starting again. [F, L]

**dĕnse** a. Closely compacted in substance (*dense fog, forest*); crowded together (*dense population*); crass, stupid; **dĕ′nsĭtў** n., denseness, (Phys.) degree of consistency measured by quantity of mass in unit of volume, (Photog.) opaqueness of image. [F, or L *densus*]

**dĕnt. 1.** n. Depression in surface (as) from blow of blunt-edged instrument. **2.** v.t. Mark with dent; (fig.) have (esp. adverse) effect on. [INDENT]

**dĕ′ntal** a. (~ly). Of tooth, teeth, or dentistry; (Phon., of consonant) pronounced with tongue-tip against upper front teeth or ridge of teeth; ~ **floss**, threads of floss silk etc. used to clean between teeth; ~ **mechanic**, person who makes and repairs artificial teeth; ~ **surgeon**, dentist; **dĕ′ntāte** a. (Bot., Zool.), toothed, notched; **dĕ′ntĭfrĭce** n., powder, paste, etc., for tooth-cleaning; **dĕ′ntĭne** (-ēn), *dĕ′ntĭn*, n., substance of which teeth are mainly composed; **dĕ′ntĭst** n., one who treats diseases and malformations of the teeth; **dĕ′ntĭstrў** n., his work or profession; **dĕntĭ′tion** n., teething, characteristic arrangement of teeth in a species etc.; **dĕ′nture**

*n.*, set of (esp. artificial) teeth. [L (*dens dent-* tooth)]

**dēnū'de** *v.t.* Make naked or bare; strip *of* clothes, covering, property, etc.; (Geol.) lay (rock, formation) bare by removal of what lies above; **dēnūdā'tion** *n.* [L (*nudus* naked)]

**dēnŭncia'tion** *n.* Denouncing, invective; **dēnŭ'nciatorў** (-sha-) *a.* (**-ily**). [F or L (DENOUNCE)]

**dēn|ў'** *v.t.* Declare untrue or non-existent, disavow or repudiate, (*deny the report, having lied, that it was so, the possibility, God,* one's *signature* or *faith*); refuse (request, applicant, thing *to* person; *can you deny me this?*; *this was denied* (to) *me*; *I was denied satisfaction*); ~y oneself, be abstinent; ~i'al *n.*, denying, refusal of request or wish (SELF-*denial*), statement that thing is not true or existent, contradiction, disavowal of person as one's leader. [F f. L (NEGATE)]

**dē'odār** *n.* Himalayan cedar. [Hindi f. Skr., = divine tree]

**dēŏ'doriz|e** *v.t.* Destroy odour of; ~ā'tion *n.*; **dēŏ'dorant** *a.* & *n.*, (substance) that removes or conceals unwanted odours. [ODOUR]

***Deo gratias*** (dāŏ grah'tĭas, -shĭas) *int.* Thanks be to God. [L]

***Deo volente*** (dāŏ volĕ'ntā) *adv.* If nothing prevents it. [L, = God being willing]

**dēŏxўrībonūclē'ĭc** *a.* ~ **acid**, substance in chromosomes of higher organisms, storing genetic information. [DE-, OXYGEN, RIBONUCLEIC]

**dep.** *abbr.* departs; deputy.

**dēpā'rt** *v.i.* & *t.* (formal, literary). Go away (*from*); set out, leave, (*for* place; esp. of public transport); die, leave by death, (*depart from life*; *depart this life*); diverge, deviate, (*depart from accepted view, custom*); ~ĕd, (*a.*) bygone, deceased, (*departed glory, heroes*), (*n.*) *the dead*; ~ment *n.*, separate branch of complex whole, branch, esp. of municipal or State administration, university, or shop, administrative district of France etc., area of activity, (~ment store, large shop supplying many kinds of goods from various departments); **dēpārtmĕ'ntal** *a.* (**-lly**); **dēpārtmĕ'ntalize** *v.t.*, divide into departments; ~ure *n.*, going away, deviation *from* (truth etc.), starting of train, aircraft, etc., (*departure platform, lounge*), setting out on course of

action or thought (esp. *new departure*). [F f. L *dispertio* divide]

**dēpĕ'nd** *v.i.* Be contingent (**that** ~**s**, the question can only be answered conditionally); (Gram.) be dependent (*up*)*on*; (arch.) be suspended *from*; ~ (**up**)*on*, be controlled or determined by (*much depends on you*, i.e. on what you do), be obliged to use or unable to do without (*depend upon one's own efforts,* one's *parents*), rely on (~ **upon it,** you may be sure); ~able *a.* (**-bly**), reliable; ~abī'litў *n.*; ~ant *n.*, one who depends on another for support, supported member of a household or family; ~ence *n.*, depending, being dependent, reliance; ~encў *n.*, (esp.) country or province controlled by another; ~ent *a.*, depending or contingent (*up*)*on*, in the position of a dependant or subject, (Gram.) in subordinate relation to another word or sentence. [F f. L (*pendeo* hang)]

**dēpĭ'ct** *v.t.* Represent visually or in words; ~ion, ~or, *ns.* [L (PICTURE)]

**dē'pĭl|āte** *v.t.* Remove hair from; ~ā'tion *n.*; **dēpĭ'latorў** *a.* & *n.*, (ointment etc.) used in or effecting depilation. [L (*pilus* hair)]

**dēplā'ne** *v.i.* & *t.* Descend or remove from aeroplane. [PLANE²]

**dēplē't|e** *v.t.* Empty, exhaust; reduce numbers or quantity of (*depleted forces, stores*); ~ion *n.* [L (*pleo* fill)]

**dēplōr'able** *a.* (**-bly**). (Of event or action) lamentable, much to be regretted, very bad, blameworthy; **dēplōr'e** *v.t.*, find or call deplorable. [F or It. f. L (*ploro* wail)]

**dēploy'** *v.t.* & *i.* Bring (forces, arguments, etc.) into effective action; (Mil.) spread out from column into line; ~ment *n.* [F f. L (*plico* fold)]

**dēpō'nent. 1.** *n.* Person making deposition; (Gram.) deponent verb. **2.** *a.* (Of verb, esp. in Gk and L) of passive form but active meaning. [L. *depono* put down, lay aside]

**dēpŏ'pul|āte** *v.t.* Reduce population of; ~ā'tion *n.* [L (*populus* people)]

**dēpōr't** *v.t.* Convey into exile; behave or conduct one*self* in (specified way); **dēpōrtā'tion** *n.*, conveyance into exile; **dēpōrtee'** *n.*; ~ment *n.*, behaviour, bearing. [F f. L (*porto* carry)]

**dēpō'se** (-z) *v.t.* & *i.* Remove from

office, (esp.) dethrone; (of deponent) state *that*, testify *to*. [F f. L (*pono* put)]

**dĕpŏ´sĭt** (-z-). **1.** *n.* Thing stored or entrusted for safe keeping; sum placed in bank, ‖usu. to receive interest and to be drawn out without notice (**on ~**, so placed; *has a deposit and a current account*); sum required to be paid as pledge or first instalment; layer of precipitated matter, natural accumulation. **2.** *v.t.* Lay down in a place; (of water etc.) leave (matter) lying; store or entrust for keeping (*with* person; sum in bank etc.); pay as deposit. **3. ~arў** *n.*, person with whom thing is deposited; **dĕposĭ´tion** (-z-) *n.*, deposing, (giving of) sworn evidence, allegation, depositing; **~or** *n.*; **~orў** *n.*, storehouse (lit. or fig.), =*depositary*; **dĕ´pŏt** (-ō) *n.*, storehouse or emporium, (Mil.) place for stores, headquarters of regiment, bus or \*railway station. [L (*pono posit-* put)]

**dĕprā´ve** *v.t.* Corrupt morally (esp. in *p.p.* as *a.* = wicked, dissolute); **dĕprā´vĭtў** *n.*, wickedness, moral corruption. [F or L (*pravus* crooked)]

**dĕ´prĕc|āte** *v.t.* Express wish against or disapproval of (*deprecate war, panic*); try to avert (anger etc.) by entreaty; **~ā´tion**, **~ātor**, *ns.*; **~ātorў** *a.* (**-ily**). [L (PRAY)]

**dĕprē´cĭ|āte** (-shĭ-) *v.t.* & *i.* Disparage, belittle; diminish in value, price, or purchasing power; **~ā´tion** *n.*, (esp.) (allowance made in valuations etc. for) wear and tear; **~atorў** (-sha-) *a.* (**-ily**), (esp.) disparaging. [L (PRICE)]

**dĕprĕdā´tion** *n.* (usu. in *pl.*). Despoiling, ravages; **dĕ´prĕdātor** *n.*, despoiler. [F f. L (PREY)]

**dĕprĕ´ss** *v.t.* (**~ible**). Push down, lower, reduce activity of (esp. trade), affect with low spirits, (*depress the handle*; *has been depressed since his failure*); **~ant** *a.* & *n.*, (influence) that depresses, (Med.) sedative drug; **~ion** (-shon) *n.*, depressing, sunken place or hollow on surface, bad state of trade (**the D~ion**, the slump of 1929–), local lowering of barometric pressure, low spirits or vitality, (Psych.) morbidly excessive melancholy; **dĕprĕ´ssive**, (*a.*) tending to depress, (Psych.) involving depression, (*n.*) person with depression. [F f. L (PRESS¹)]

**dĕprī´v|e** *v.t.* Dispossess, strip,

debar from enjoyment *of*, (person or thing *of*, clergyman etc. of office; *am I depriving you of the chance?*; *the amendments deprive the Bill of all meaning*); (in *p.p.*, of child etc.) prevented from having normal home life; **~al** *n.*, depriving; **dĕprĭvā´tion** (or dēprī-) *n.*, (esp.) loss of desired thing (*that is a great deprivation*). [F f. L (PRIVATION)]

*de profundis* (dā prŏfŏo´ndĭs) *adv.* From the depths (of sorrow etc.). [L]

**Dept.** *abbr.* Department.

**dĕpth** *n.* Deepness or measure of it (*to a depth of 3 m*; *with great depth of feeling*; **in ~** *adv.* & *a.*, thorough(ly), profound(ly); **defence in ~**, system of defence with successive areas of resistance; **in the ~ of** *winter*, in the middle of; **out of** one's **~**, in water too deep to stand in, fig. engaged on subject beyond one's powers); (in *pl.*) deep water or place, abyss, low moral condition, inmost part (*from the depths*; *in the depths of the country*); **~-charge**, bomb exploding under water, for dropping on submerged submarine etc. [DEEP]

**dĕpū´te** *v.t.* Commit (task, authority) to or to substitute; appoint as deputy; **dĕpūtā´tion** *n.*, body of persons appointed to represent others; **dĕ´pūtize** *v.i.*, act as deputy (*for*); **dĕ´pūtў** *n.*, person acting or authorized to act as substitute for another (often *attrib.*: *Deputy Governor*, ‖LIEUTENANT, *Speaker*), parliamentary representative in some countries. [F f. L (*puto* consider)]

**dĕraī´l** *v.t.* Cause (train) to leave the rails; **~ment** *n.* [F (RAIL¹)]

**dĕrā´nge** (-nj) *v.t.* Put out of order, disorganize, cause to act irregularly, interrupt, (*derange* person's *thoughts*, *plan*, *working*); (esp. in *p.p.*) make insane; **~ment** (-jm-) *n.* [F (RANK¹)]

**Der´bў** (dā´-) *n.* Annual horse-race at Epsom; similar race elsewhere; important sporting contest (LOCAL *Derby*; (d~) \*bowler hat. [Earl of ~, person]

*de règle* (derā´gl) *pred. a.* Customary, proper. [F, = of rule]

**dĕ´rĕlĭct. 1.** *a.* Left ownerless (esp. of ship at sea or decrepit property); \*negligent. **2.** *n.* Derelict property, esp. ship; socially forsaken person. **3. dĕrĕlĭ´ction** *n.*, abandonment, neglect of *duty*, shortcoming. [L (RELINQUISH)]

**dĕrĕquĭsĭ´tion** (-z-) *v.t.* Return

(requisitioned property) to former owner; **dĕrĕstrī′ct** v.t., remove restrictions from, (esp.) remove or not impose speed limit on specified road etc. [DE-]

**dĕrī′de** v.t. Scoff at; **dĕrī′sion** (-zhon) n., ridicule, mockery; **dĕrī′sĭve** a., scoffing, ironical, (derisive laughter); **dĕrī′sory** (or -z-) a., derisive, so small or unimportant as to be ridiculous (derisory offer). [L (rideo laugh)]

**de rigueur** (derīgér′) pred. a. Required by custom or etiquette. [F, = of strictness]

**derision** etc. See DERIDE.

**dĕrī′ve** v.t. & i. Get or obtain (from a source), trace or assert descent or formation of (word etc.) from, have origin etc. from, be descended from, (I derive much pleasure, my income, from books; deride is derived from Latin rideo to laugh; morality is derived from fear; we all derive from Adam); **dĕrĭvā′tion** n., (esp.) formation of word from word or root, tracing or statement of this; **dĕrĭ′vative** n. & a., (thing, word, substance) derived from a source, not primitive or original, (Math.) quantity giving rate of change of another. [F or L (rivus stream)]

**dĕrmat|ī′tĭs** n. Inflammation of skin; **~ŏ′logy** n., study of skin and its diseases; **~ŏ′logĭst** n. [Gk derma skin]

**dernier cri** (dārnyākrē′) n. The very latest fashion. [F, = last cry]

**dĕ′rog|āte** v.i. Detract (from a right, merit, etc.); deviate (from correct behaviour etc.); **~ā′tion** n., (esp.) impairment or partial surrender of a right etc., debasement; **dĕrŏ′gatory** a. (-ily, -iness), involving impairment, disparagement, or discredit to, unsuited to one's dignity, depreciatory. [L (rogo ask)]

**dĕ′rrick** n. Kind of hoisting-machine; framework over oil-well etc. [person]

**derrière** (dĕriār′) n. (colloq.) Buttocks. [F]

**dĕrring-do′** (-dōō′) n. (literary). Heroic courage or action. [DARE, DO]

**dĕ′rrĭs** n. Tall woody tropical climbing plant; insecticide made from powdered root of some kinds of derris. [L f. Gk]

||**dĕrv** n. Fuel oil used in heavy road-vehicles. [diesel-engined road vehicle]

**dĕr′vish** n. Muslim religious man vowed to poverty and austerity; dancing or whirling ~, howling ~, (according to the practice of his order). [Turk. f. Pers., = poor]

**dĕsă′lin|āte** v.t. Remove salt from (esp. sea-water); **~ā′tion** n. [SALINE]

**descă′nt** v.i. Talk lengthily, dwell esp. with enthusiasm, upon; **dĕ′scant**[2] n., (poet.) song, melody, (Mus.) melodic independent treble part; ~ **recorder** (highest-pitched of standard kinds). [F f. L DIS-, cantus song (CHANT)]

**descĕ′nd** v.i. & t. Go or come down (descend to the valley; descend a hill, stairs; ~ **a river**, go along it towards the sea); sink, fall (in rank, quality, etc.); behave so unworthily as to do, stoop to (unworthy action); make sudden attack or (fig.) unexpected visit (on); be transmitted by inheritance (from, to); **~ant** n., person etc. descended from another; **~ĕd** a., sprung, having origin, from (ancestor or stock); **descĕ′nt** n., descending, falling, downward path or slope, sudden attack, being descended (from), lineage, transmission by inheritance. [F f. L (scando climb)]

**descrī′be** v.t. Set forth in words, recite the characteristics of, (~ **as**, assert to be, call); mark out, draw, (esp. figure in Geom.); move in (specified line or curve); **descrī′p-tion** n., describing, verbal portrait(ure) of person, object or event, (**answers** (**to**) or **fits the description**, has the qualities specified), sort, kind, class, (no food of any description; a tyrant of the worst description); **descrī′ptive** a., serving or seeking to describe (descriptive touches, writer), not expressing feelings or judgements (descriptive report. account). [F f. L (scribo write)]

**descrȳ′** v.t. Catch sight of, succeed in discerning. [F (CRY)]

**dĕ′secr|āte** v.t. (~able). Violate sanctity of; outrage, profane, (sacred thing); **~ā′tion**, **~ātor**, ns. [DE-, CONSECRATE]

**dĕsĕ′greg|āte** v.t. Abolish racial segregation in (schools etc.); **~ā′tion** n. [DE-]

**dĕsĕr′t**[1] (-z-) n. (usu. in pl.). Acts or qualities deserving good or bad recompense, such recompense, (reward him according to, he has got, his deserts, his just deserts). [F (DESERVE)]

**desert²** v., a., & n. **1.** (dĭzẽr't) v.t. & i. Abandon, cease to frequent, leave (place) empty, forsake (person or thing having claims on one; *desert the ship*, one's *wife*); fail (*his courage deserted him*); become a deserter (*from*). **2.** (dĕ'zert) a. (Of region) uninhabited, barren. **3.** (dĕ'zert) n. Waterless and treeless region; (fig.) uninteresting or unprofitable subject etc.; ~ **island**, remote and presumably uninhabited island. **4.** **dèsẽr'ter** (-z-) n., (esp.) one who has run away from service in the armed forces. **dèsẽr'tion** (-z-) n., deserting or being deserted. [F f. L (*desero -sert-* leave)]

**dèsẽr'v|e** (-z-) v.t. & i. Be entitled by conduct or qualities to (reward or punishment; *to* be or do), (of thing) be worth, (*deserves a medal, to be happy, mention*, etc.); have established a claim to be *well* or *ill* treated at the hands of (*deserves better of them*); ~**ĕdly̆** adv., as he etc. fully deserved or deserves; ~**ĭng** (-z-) a., meritorious, worthy (*of*). [F f. L (*servio* serve)]

**déshabillé** (dāzăbē'ā) n. (State of) being only partly or not carefully dressed. [F, = undressed]

**dě'sĭccat|e** v.t. Remove moisture from, dry up, (esp. foodstuffs for preservation); **dèsĭccā'tion** n.; ~**ĭve** a.; ~**or** n., (esp.) desiccating apparatus. [L (*siccus* dry)]

**dèsĭ'der|āte** v.t. (arch.) Feel to be missing, wish to have; ~**ative** a. & n., (Gram.) (verb, conjugation) formed from a verb and denoting desire to perform the action of that verb; ~**ā'tum** n. (*pl.* **-ta**), thing lacking but needed or desired. [L (DESIRE)]

**dèsĭ'gn** (-zī'n). **1.** n. Outline, sketch, plan, pattern, for future product (*design for a picture, dress, book, machine, building*, etc.); art of making these (*school of design*); general arrangement, layout, (*the garden has a formal design*); established form of a product; mental plan, scheme of attack (**have ~s on**, plan to harm or appropriate); intention, purpose, (**by ~**, on purpose; *whether by accident or design*), adaptation of means to end (**argument from ~**, deducing the existence of a God from evidence of such adaptation in the universe); arrangement of lines, drawing, etc., decorating a thing (*plates, curtains*, etc. *with a floral design*). **2.** v.t. & i. Make design for (picture); be a designer; set apart (person or thing *for* a service, thing *for* person); contrive, intend, plan, (action, *to do, doing, that*). **3.** **dě'sĭgnāte¹** (-z-) v.t. (**-nable**), serve as name or distinctive mark of, style, describe as, specify, particularize, appoint to office (*as, for, to*); **dě'sĭgnāte²** (-z-) a. (after n.), appointed to but not yet installed in office (*bishop designate*); **dèsĭgnā'tion** (-z-) n., designating, name or title; ~**ĕdly̆** adv., purposely; ~**er** n., (esp.) person who makes designs for manufacturers or prepares designs for clothing etc.; ~**ĭng** a., (esp.) crafty, scheming. [F f. L (*signum* mark)]

**dèsīr'|e** (-z-). **1.** n. Unsatisfied longing, earnest wish (*for, of, to* do or be); expression of this, request (*I did it at your desire*); thing desired; lust. **2.** v.t. Long for, want earnestly, (thing, *to* do or be, *that*); ask for (**leaves much to be ~ed**, is very imperfect); (arch.) wish, request, command, (*desire him to wait*). **3.** ~**able** a. (**-bly**), worth having or wishing for, causing desire; ~**abĭ'lĭty̆** n.; ~**ous** *pred.* a., having the desire of, to do, that. [F f. L *desidero* long for]

**dèsī'st** (or -zī'-) v.i. (literary). Abstain *from* continuing (action etc.). [F f. L *desisto*]

**dĕsk** n. Piece of furniture with flat or sloped surface serving as rest for writing or reading at; compartment for cashier, receptionist, etc.; music-stand; section of newspaper office etc. dealing with specified topics or *editorial work. [L (DISCUS table)]

**dě'sol|āte. 1.** a. Left alone; uninhabited, depopulated; ruinous, neglected; forlorn, wretched. **2.** (-āt) v.t. Depopulate; devastate; make (person) desolate; ~**ā'tion**, ~**ātor**, ns. [L (*solus* alone)]

**dèspair'. 1.** v.i. Lose hope (*of*); ~ **of**, lose hope that person or thing will succeed, be maintained, etc. (*his life is despaired of*). **2.** n. Loss or absence of hope; thing that causes this by badness, difficulty, or unapproachable excellence. [F f. L (*spero* hope)]

‖**dèspă'tch**. See DISPATCH.

**dě'sperate** a. Leaving little or no room for hope; extremely dangerous or serious (*desperate situation*); reckless from despair, violent, lawless, (*a desperate criminal*); staking all on a small chance (*desperate remedy*); extremely bad (*desperate night, storm*); **děspěraˈdō** (-ahˈdō) n. (*pl.* **-oes, \*-os**), desperate or reckless person, esp. criminal; **děsperaˈtion** n., despair, reckless state of mind, readiness to take any way out of a desperate situation. [L (DESPAIR)]

**děspĭˈcabǀle** (*or* dĕˈ-) a. (**~ly**). Vile, morally contemptible. [L (*specio spect-* look at)]

**děspīˈse** (-z) v.t. Regard with contempt. [F f. L (prec.)]

**děspīˈte. 1.** *prep.* In spite of. **2.** *n.* (arch.) Outrage, malice, hatred; (**in**) **~ of**, in spite of.

**děspoiˈl** v.t. (literary). Plunder, strip, (person or place; often *of*); **~ment, děspōliäˈtion**, ns. [F f. L (SPOIL)]

**děspoˈnd** v.i. Lose heart or hope; **~ent** a.; **~encÿ** n. [L *despondeo* (SPONSOR)]

**děˈspŏt** n. Tyrant, oppressor; absolute ruler; **děspŏˈtic** a. (**-ically**), (of power, ruler, etc.) subject to no constitutional checks, (of temper, action, etc.) tyrannous; **děˈspotism** n., tyrannical conduct, autocratic government or State subject to it. [F f. L f. Gk *despotēs* master]

**děˈsquamǀate** v.i. Come off in scales; **~āˈtion** n. [L *squama* scale]

**děssěrˈt** (-z-) n. Sweet course ending meal; ǁcourse of fruit, nuts, etc., ending dinner; *dessert-*SPOON; **~ wine** (for drinking with dessert or after meal). [F (DIS-, SERVE)]

**děˈstĭnǀe** v.t. Appoint, foreordain, devote, set apart, (person or thing *to do, to* or *for* a service, achievement, etc.); **~āˈtion** n., place to which person or thing is going; **~ÿ** n., power that foreordains, what is destined to happen to person etc., predetermined course of events. [F f. L]

**děˈstĭtǀute** a. In great need, esp. of food, shelter, etc.; devoid *of*; **~uˈtion** n. [L]

**děstroyˈ** v.t. Pull or break down, make useless, kill, neutralize effect of, (*enemy bombers destroyed a village*; *the dog had to be destroyed*; *destroy an argument*); **~ˈer** n., (esp.) fast warship designed to protect other ships by attacking submarines etc.; **\*děstrŭˈct**, (v.t.) bring about deliberate destruction of (rocket etc.), (n.)

action of destructing; **děstrŭˈctǀible** a. (**-bly**), destroyable; **děstrŭˈction** n., destroying or being destroyed, cause of this; **děstrŭˈctǀive** a., causing destruction (*of, to*), tending to destroy, merely negative or refuting without amending, (*destructive criticism*); ǁ**děstrŭˈctor** n., refuse-burning furnace. [F f. L (*struo struct-* build)]

**děsŭˈetǀude** (*or* dĕˈswĭ-) n. (Passing into) state of disuse. [F or L (*suesco* be accustomed)]

**dēˈsultorǀy** a. (**-ily, -iness**). Going constantly from one subject to another; unmethodical. [L *desultorius* superficial]

**dětăˈch** v.t. Unfasten and remove (*from*); send (part of force) on separate mission; **~ed** (-cht) a., standing apart, isolated from others, (fig.) unemotional, impartial, (*a detached mind, view*); **~ed house**, one not joined to another on either side); **~ment** n., detaching, detached party of soldiers etc., being aloof from or unaffected by surroundings, public opinion, etc. [F (as ATTACH)]

**dēˈtail. 1.** n. Item, small or subordinate particular, these collectively, a discussion of them, (*complete in every detail*; *the detail of the decoration*; **in ~**, item by item; **go into ~**, be minute or thorough); part of picture etc. shown alone; (Mil.) small detachment. **2.** v.t. Relate in detail or circumstantially; (Mil.) assign for special duty. **3. ~ed** (-ld) a., (of examination, narrative, list) (described) item by item, minute. [F (TAIL²)]

**dětaiˈn** v.t. Keep in confinement or under restraint; keep waiting, delay; **~eeˈ** n., person detained in custody, usu. on political grounds. [F f. L (*teneo* hold)]

**dětěˈct** v.t. Reveal guilt of, discover, (person, person *in* doing); discover existence or presence of; (Phys.) use instrument to observe (signal, radiation, etc.); **~ion** n., detecting, work of a detective; **~ĭve**, (a.) serving to detect, (n.) policeman or other person employed to investigate crimes (*private* **~ive**, person undertaking special enquiries for pay); **~ive story** etc. (describing crime and detection of criminals); **~or** n., (esp., Electr.) device for detecting signals. [L (*tego tect-* cover)]

**détente** (dātah'nt) *n.* End of strained relations. [F, = relaxation]

**detě'ntion** *n.* Detaining, being detained; military imprisonment; (at schools) keeping in as punishment; ‖~ **centre**, institution for brief detention of young offenders. [F or L (DETAIN)]

**deter'** *v.t.* (-rr-). Discourage or hinder (*from*) by fear, dislike of trouble, etc.; ~**ment** *n.*; **detě'rrent**, (*a.*) that deters, (*n.*) thing that deters, esp. nuclear weapon of a State or alliance as deterring attack by another. [L (*terreo* frighten)]

**deter'gent** *a.* & *n.* Cleansing (agent), esp. substance used with water for removing dirt etc. (usu. a synthetic substance other than soap). [L (*tergeo* wipe)]

**deter'ior|ate** *v.i.* & *t.* Make or become worse; ~**ā'tion** *n.* [L (*deterior* worse)]

**detěr'min|e** *v.t.* & *i.* Settle, decide, come to a conclusion, give decision, (*determine* person's *fate*, *what is to be done*, *that*, *whether*); be decisive factor in regard to (*demand determines supply*); decide (person) *to* do, resolve (*to* do, *that*, *on* a course of action); be ~**ed**, have resolved); ascertain, fix with precision, (*determine the facts*); (esp. Law) bring or come to an end; limit in scope, define; ~**ant** *a.* & *n.*, decisive (factor etc.); ~**ate** *a.*, limited, of definite scope or nature; ~**ā'tion** *n.*, (esp.) fixing of intention, resolute purpose or conduct, (Law) cessation of estate or interest, conclusion of debate, judicial decision or sentence; ~**ative** *a.* & *n.*, (thing) that serves to define, qualify, or direct; ~**ed** (-nd) *a.*, resolute; ~**ism** *n.*, doctrine that action is determined by motives regarded as external forces acting on the will; ~**ist** *n.*; ~**i'stic** *a.* (-ically). [F f. L (*terminus* boundary)]

**detě'rrent.** See DETER.

**detě'st** *v.t.* Hate, loathe; ~**able** *a.* (-bly), intensely hateful **detěstā'-tion** *n.*, abhorrence, intense dislike. [L *detestor* (*testis* witness)]

**dethrō'ne** *v.t.* Remove from throne (ruler, fig. dominant influence); ~**ment** (-nm-) *n.* [DE-]

**dě'tonat|e** *v.i.* & *t.* (Cause to) explode with loud report; **dětonā'-tion** *n.*, (esp.) premature combustion of fuel in internal combustion engine; ~**or** *n.*, (esp.) part of bomb etc. that

sets off explosive, railway fog signal that detonates. [L (*tono* to thunder)]

**dě'tour** (-oor; *or* dā'-). **1.** *n.* Roundabout way, digression, (*make a detour*). **2.** *v.t.* Cause to make a detour. [F (TURN)]

**detrǎ'ct** *v.t.* & *i.* Take away (*much*, *little*, etc.) *from* a whole; ~ **from**, reduce credit due to, depreciate; ~**ion**, ~**or**, *ns.* [L (*traho* tract-draw)]

**dě'triment** *n.* Harm (esp. *without detriment to*); thing that causes harm; **dětrimě'ntal** *a.* (-lly), harmful. [F or L (TRITE)]

**detrī'tus** *n.*, (Geol.) worn-down matter such as gravel or rock-debris. [F or L (TRITE)]

**de trop** (detrō') *pred. a.* Not wanted, unwelcome. [F, = excessive]

**deuce**[1] *n.* 'Two' on dice or (arch.) cards; (Tennis) state of score (40 all, or 5 or more games all) at which either side must gain two consecutive points or games to win. [F f. L *duos* two]

**deuce**[2] *n.* Misfortune; the Devil (*deuce take it!*; **what**, **where**, **why**, etc., **the** ~**?**, imprecations expr. annoyance or complete ignorance; **the** ~**!**, excl. of annoyance or surprise; **the** ~ **to pay**, trouble to be expected; **a** (or **the**) ~ **of a**, a very bad or remarkable (mess, fellow, etc.); **like the** ~, with great vigour); **deu'ced** (*or* dūst) *a.* & *adv.* (arch.) = DAMNED. [LG *duus* two (as worst throw at dice)]

**deus ex machina** (dāōs ěks mǎ'kǐna) *n.* Providential interposition, esp. in novel or play. [L transl. Gk, = god from the machinery (by which in Gk theatre gods were shown in the air)]

**Deut.** *abbr.* Deuteronomy (O.T.).

**deutěr'ium** *n.* Heavy isotope of hydrogen with mass about twice that of ordinary hydrogen; **Deuterǒ'-nomỹ** *n.*, O.T. book repeating Decalogue and laws. [L f. Gk *deuteros* second]

**Deu'tschmǎrk** (doi'ch-) *n.* Currency unit in Federal Republic of Germany. [G, = German MARK[1]]

**deu'tzia** (-ts-) *n.* White-flowered ornamental shrub. [*Deutz*, person]

**děvǎ'lū|e** *v.t.* Reduce value of; reduce value of (currency) relative to that of other currencies or gold; ~**ā'tion** *n.* [DE-]

**dě'vast|āte** *v.t.* Lay waste; ~**ātīng** *a.*, (esp., of criticism, handicap, etc.)

very effective, overwhelming; ~ā'-tion, ~ātor, ns. [L (*vasto* lay waste)]

dĕvĕ'lop *v.t.* & *i.* Bring or come to active or visible state, or to maturity, unfold, reveal or be revealed, make progress, make or become fuller or bigger or more elaborate or systematic, (develop character, muscles, *a scheme; a developing talent, shoot; a storm is developing*); ~ing country, poor or primitive country that is developing better economic and social conditions); begin to exhibit or suffer from (develop a habit, *a squeak, measles*); construct new buildings on (land), convert (land) to new use so as to realize its potentialities; treat (photographic material) to make picture visible; (Mus.) elaborate (theme) by modification of melody, harmony, rhythm, etc.; ~ment n., developing (~ment area, one where new industries are encouraged in order to counteract severe unemployment there), growth, evolution (of animal and plant races), full-grown state, stage of advancement, product, developed land; ~mĕ'ntal *a.*, incidental to growth (*developmental diseases*), evolutionary. [F]

dē'vǐate. 1. (-āt) *v.i.* Turn aside, diverge, (*from* course of action, truth, etc.); digress. 2. (-at) *n.* Deviant, esp. sexual pervert. 3. ~ant *a.* & *n.*, (thing or person) that deviates from normal behaviour; ~ā'tion *n.*, (esp.) deflexion of compass-needle by iron in ship etc., (Polit.) departure from (esp. Communist) party doctrine; ~ā'tionist, ~ātor, ns. [L (*via* way)]

dĕvī'ce *n.* Scheme, trick; invention, thing adapted for a purpose or designed for a particular function; (in *pl.*) fancy, will, (left to one's own ~s, allowed to do whatever one can or wishes by oneself); heraldic or emblematic design, motto. [F (DEVISE)]

dĕ'vǐl. 1. *n.* Evil spirit, demon; (the D~) supreme spirit of evil, Satan; one of Satan's followers, superhuman malignant being; personified evil quality (*the devil of greed*, etc.), fighting spirit, mischievousness (*the devil is in him tonight*); wicked or cruel person, mischievously energetic, clever, or self-willed person, luckless or wretched person (usu. *poor devil*); vicious animal; awkward problem

etc.; (or D~) = DEUCE (q.v. for phrases; the very ~, a great difficulty, nuisance; go to the ~, be damned, in *imper.* depart at once; junior legal counsel working for a principal, literary hack doing what his employer takes the credit and pay for, (printer's ~, Hist., errand-boy in printing-office); ~ a one, not even one; ~-may-care, reckless, rollicking; ~'s advocate, official who puts the case against beatification or canonization by R.C. Church, (transf.) one who indicates shortcomings so as to cause discussion; ~'s own, very difficult or unusual (*devil's own job, luck*, etc.); *devil's* TATTOO[1]; between the ~ and the deep blue sea, in a dilemma; *give the Devil his* DUE; play the ~ with, cause severe damage to; RAISE *the devil*; speak or talk of the ~ (and he is sure to appear) (said when person just mentioned is seen coming). 2. *v.t.* (||-ll-). Cook with peppery condiments; work (*for*) as lawyer's or author's devil; *(colloq.) worry, harass. 3. ~ish, *a.*) like, worthy of, the Devil, (*adv.*, also ~ishlȳ; colloq.) very; ~ment *n.*, mischief, wild spirits, devilish or strange phenomenon; ~rȳ *n.*, black magic, the Devil and his works, wickedness, cruelty, reckless mischief, daring, or hilarity. [E f. L f. Gk *diabolos* accuser, slanderer]

dē'vǐous *a.* Circuitous, erratic; unscrupulous, insincere. [L (*via* way)]

dĕvī's|e (-z) *v.t.* Plan, invent, scheme, (thing, *how*, or abs.); (Law) leave by will (realty *to* person; cf. BEQUEATH); ~ee', ~ōr, ns., person to whom, by whom, property is devised. [F f. L (DIVIDE)]

dĕvoi'd *a.* ~ *of*, quite lacking or free from. [F (VOID)]

dĕ'voir (-vwǎr) *n.* (arch.) Duty, one's best, (do one's *devoir*); pay one's ~s, show respect by visit (*to*). [F f. L *debeo* owe]

dĕvŏ'lve *v.t.* & *i.* Throw (work, duty), (of duties) be thrown, *upon* (deputy, or one who must act for want of others; *it devolves upon me to do it*); (of property etc.) descend, pass (*to, upon*); dĕvolu'tion (-lōō'-) *n.*, (esp.) delegation of power (esp. by House of Parliament to bodies appointed by and responsible to it, or by central government to local or regional administration). [L (*volvo volut*- roll)]

**Dĕvō′nĭan** *a.* & *n.* (Native) of *Devon*(shire); (of) Palaeozoic period or system, above Silurian and below Carboniferous; **Dĕ′vonshire** (*-er*, *-ēr*) *n.* (**Devonshire cream,** CLOTTED cream). [place]

**dĕvō′t|e** *v.t.* Consecrate, give up, (one*self*, thing, one's life, efforts, etc.) exclusively *to* (God, person, pursuit, pursuit); **~ĕd** *a.*, (esp.) zealously loyal or loving; **dĕvotee′** *n.*, votary *of*, one devoted *to*, zealously or fanatically pious person, enthusiast *of* sport etc.; **~ion** *n.*, devoutness, devotedness (*to*), divine worship, (in *pl.*) prayers, worship, (*was at his devotions*); **~ional** *a.* (*-lly*), of or assisting the devotions. [L (*voveo vot*- vow)]

**dĕvour′** *v.t.* (Of animal) eat; eat like an animal or ravenously; (of fire etc.) destroy, engulf; take in greedily with eyes or ears (*devour novel after novel, me with their eyes, every word*); (esp. in *pass.*) absorb attention of (*am devoured by anxiety*). [F f. L (*voro* swallow)]

**dĕvou′t** *a.* (Of person, act, etc.) reverential, earnestly religious, pious; heartfelt, genuine, (*devout wish*; *I devoutly hope*). [F f. L (DEVOTE)]

**dew.** **1.** *n.* Atmospheric vapour condensing in small drops on cool surfaces between nightfall and morning; beaded moisture resembling this. **2.** *v.t.* & *i.* Wet as with dew; (*impers.*) form or fall as dew (*it is beginning to dew*). **3.** **~′berry**, bluish fruit like blackberry; **~-claw**, rudimentary inner toe of some dogs, false hoof of deer etc.; **~-point**, temperature at which dew forms; ||**~-pond**, shallow, usu. artificial, pond once supposed fed by atmospheric condensation; **~′y̆** *a.* (**~ily**, **~iness**), wet with dew; **~y**(**-eyed**), innocently trusting, naïvely sentimental. [E]

**D.E.W.** *abbr.* distant early warning.

**dew′lăp** *n.* Fold of loose skin hanging from throat esp. in cattle. [DEW, LAP²]

**dew′y̆.** See DEW.

**dĕ′xter** *a.* (Her.) On right-hand side (i.e. to observer's left) of shield etc., opp. *sinister*; **dĕ′xt(e)rous** *a.*, handling things neatly, skilful, mentally adroit or clever; **dĕxtĕ′rĭty̆** *n.*, dextrousness; **dĕ′xtral** *a.* & *n.*, right-handed (person). [L, = on the right]

||**D.F.C.,** ||**D.F.M.,** *abbrs.* Distinguished Flying Cross, Medal.

**D.G.** *abbr.* Dei gratia; Deo gratias.

**dhar′ma** (dār′-, der′-) *n.* (Ind.) Social custom, right behaviour, virtue, justice; Buddhist truth; Hindu moral law. [Skr., = decree, custom]

**dhō′ti** (dō′-) *n.* Loincloth worn by male Hindus. [Hindi]

**dhow** (dow) *n.* Lateen-rigged Arabian-Sea ship. [orig. unkn.]

**di-¹** *pref.* = DIS-.

**di-²** *pref.* meaning two-, double-. [Gk (*dis* twice)]

**di-³, dia-,** *prefs.* meaning through (*diaphanous*), apart (*diacritical*), across (*diameter*). [Gk (*dia* through)]

||**D.I.** *abbr.* Defence Intelligence.

**dia.** *abbr.* diameter.

**diabē′tēs** (-z) *n.* **~ insipidus,** disease of pituitary; **~** (**mellitus**), disease in which sugar and starch are not properly absorbed; **diabĕ′tĭc,** (*a.*; **-ically**) of or having diabetes, for diabetics, (*n.*) diabetic person. [L f. Gk]

**diă′blerie** (-ah′-) *n.* Sorcery; wild recklessness. [F (*diable* DEVIL)]

**diabŏ′lĭc(al)** *adjs.* (**-ically**). Of, like, the Devil; devilish, inhumanly cruel or wicked; **diă′bolĭsm** *n.*, sorcery, diabolic conduct, devil-worship. [F or L (DEVIL)]

**diachrŏ′nĭc** (-k-) *a.* (Ling. etc.; **~ally**). Concerned with historical development of a subject (opp. *synchronic*). [f. f. Gk (*khronos* time)]

**diă′conal, -nāte.** See DEACON.

**diacri′tical.** **1.** *a.* (**~ly**). Distinguishing, distinctive; **~ mark, sign,** (used to indicate different sounds or values of a letter: accent, diaeresis, cedilla, etc.). **2.** *n.* Diacritical sign. [Gk (CRITICISM)]

**di′adĕm** *n.* Crown, or band round head, as badge of sovereignty; wreath of leaves or flowers worn round head; sovereignty; crowning distinction or glory. [F f. L f. Gk *deō* bind)]

**diaer′es|ĭs** (-er′-), **\*diĕr′es|ĭs,** *n.* (*pl.* **~es** *pr.* -ēz). Mark (as in *Brontë, naïve*) over vowel indicating that it is sounded separately. [L f. Gk, = separation]

**diagnō′s|ĭs** *n.* (*pl.* **~es** *pr.* -ēz). Identification of disease by means of patient's symptoms etc., formal statement of this; ascertainment of cause of mechanical fault etc.; **diagnō′se** (-z) *v.t.*, make diagnosis of (disease, mechanical fault, etc.), infer presence of (specified disease etc.) from symptoms; **diagnŏ′stic,** (*a.*; **-ically**) of or assisting diagnosis, (*n.*) symptom, (in *pl.*, usu. treated as *sing.*) diagnosis as an art; **diagnŏsti′cian** (-shan) *n.* [L f. Gk (*gignŏskō* know)]

**diă′gonal** *a.* (**-ly**) & *n.* (Straight line) joining two non-adjacent angles of a rectilinear figure or a solid contained by planes, or opposite corners of a thing; (line) obliquely placed, like the diagonal of a parallelogram; inclined at other than a right angle, having some part so inclined. [L f. Gk (*gōnia* angle)]

**di′agram. 1.** *n.* Sketch showing the features of an object needed for exposition; graphical or symbolic representation (by lines) of process, force, etc. **2.** *v.t.* (‖-mm-). Represent in diagram. **3. diagrammă′tic** *a.* (-ically). [L f. Gk (-GRAM)]

**di′al. 1.** *n.* Face of clock or watch marked in hours etc.; plate on which measurement (of pressure, consumption, speed, etc.) is registered usu. by means of a pointer; circular plate on telephone with numbers etc. and movable disc with finger-holes for making connection with other telephones; plate on radio or television set showing wavelength or channel selected; (sl.) face; = SUNdial. **2.** *v.t.* & *i.* (‖-ll-). Indicate (as) with dial; make telephone call by using dial; ring up (number etc.) thus; ~(**ling**) **tone,** sound given by automatic--exchange telephone to show that caller may start to dial; ~**ling code** (of numbers for telephone exchange to be dialled before number of person called). [L *diale* (*dies* day)]

**di′alĕct** *n.* Form of speech peculiar to a district or class; subordinate variety of a language with non--standard vocabulary, pronunciation, or idioms; **dialĕ′ctal** *a.* (-lly); **dialĕ′ctic**[1] *n.* (*or* ~**ics,** occas. treated as *sing.*), art of investigating the truth of opinions, testing the truth by discussion, logical disputation, existence or action of opposing social forces etc.; **dialĕ′ctic**[2], **-ical,** *adjs.* (-ically), concerned with dialectics (~**ical materialism,** theory of political events as due to conflict of social forces caused by man's material needs); **dialĕcti′cian** (-shan) *n.,* expert in dialectics; **di′alŏgue** (-g), *\*di′alŏg, n.,* con-

versation, piece of written work representing this, conversational part in a novel etc., discussion between representatives of two groups etc. [F or L f. Gk (*legō* speak)]

**diă′lysis** *n.* (*pl.* ~**es** *pr.* -ēz). Separation of particles by difference in rate of passage through membrane between liquids; purification of blood by this means. [L f. Gk (*luō* set free)]

**diă′mēter** *n.* Straight line passing from side to side of any figure or body through its centre; transverse measurement; unit of linear magnifying power (*magnifies 2,000 diameters*); **diă′mĕtral** *a.* (-lly), of or along a diameter; **diamĕ′trical** *a.* (-lly), diametral, (of opposition etc.) direct, complete, (*diametrically opposed views*). [F f. L f. Gk (-METER)]

**di′amond** *n.* Transparent usu. colourless brilliant precious stone noted for hardness and costliness (black ~s, fig., coal; rough ~, fig., person of intrinsic worth but rough manners); tool with small diamond for glass-cutting; rhombus, (*attrib.*) so shaped (*diamond panes, pattern*); playing-card of suit (~s) denoted by red rhombus; (Baseball) space enclosed by bases, entire field; ~ **jubilee, wedding,** 60th or 75th anniversary. [F f. L f. Gk (ADAMANT)]

**diă′nthus** *n.* Flowering plant of kind including carnation. [Gk, = flower of Zeus]

**diapā′son** (*or* -z-) *n.* Compass of instrument or voice; range, scope; organ-stop extending through the whole compass; combination of notes or parts in a harmonious whole; fixed standard of musical pitch. [L f. Gk, = through all (notes)]

**di′aper** *n.* Linen or cotton fabric with small diamond pattern; baby's nappy (orig. of this material); ornamental design for panels, walls, etc.; ~**ed** (-erd) *a.,* with diaper decoration. [F f. L f. Gk (*aspros* white)]

**diă′phanous** *a.* (Of fabric etc.) light and delicate, and so almost transparent. [L f. Gk (*phainō* show)]

**diaphorĕ′tic** *n.* & *a.* (~**ally**). (Drug) inducing perspiration. [L f. Gk (*phoreō* carry)]

**di′aphrăgm** (-ăm) *n.* Muscular partition between thorax and abdomen in mammals; thin sheet used as partition etc.; disc pierced by one or more holes in optical and acoustic systems etc.; device for varying lens aperture in camera etc.; contraceptive cap fitting over cervix of womb; **diaphrăgmă'tic** a. (-ically). [L f. Gk (*phragma* fence)]

**di'arist** n. Keeper of diary. [DIARY]

**diarrhœa', *diarrhē'a**, (-rē'a) n. Excessive evacuation of too fluid faeces. [L f. Gk (*rheō* flow)]

**di'ary** n. Daily record of events or thoughts, book prepared for keeping this in; book for noting future engagements etc. (often with daily memoranda esp. for persons of a particular profession). [L (*dies* day)]

**Diă'spora** n. The Dispersion (of the Jews); Jews so dispersed. [Gk]

**di'astāse** n. Enzyme converting starch to sugar, important in digestion. [F f. Gk, = separation]

**diă'stolĕ** n. Dilatation of heart alternating with systole to form pulse. [L f. Gk (*stellō* place)]

**di'atŏm** n. Microscopic one-cell water-plant found as plankton and forming fossil deposits; **diatomā'ceous** (-shus) a., (consisting) of diatoms. [L f. Gk, = cut in half]

**diato'mic** a. (Chem.) Of two atoms. [DI-²]

**diato'nic** a. (Mus.; ~ally). (Of scale or interval) involving only notes proper to key without chromatic alteration. [F or L f. Gk (TONIC)]

**di'atribe** n. Denunciatory harangue. [F f. L f. Gk (*tribō* rub)]

**di'bble. 1.** n. (Also **di'bber**) implement for making holes to receive bulbs or seeds or plants. **2.** v.t. Prepare (ground), sow, plant, with dibble. [orig. uncert.]

**dibs** (-z) n.pl. (sl.) Money.

**dice, di'cey.** See DIE¹.

**dĭchŏ'tomy** (-k-) n. Division (esp. sharply defined) into two; binary classification. [L f. Gk (*dikho-* apart, TOME)]

**dichromă'tic** (-k-) a. (~ally). Two-coloured; having vision sensitive to only two of three primary colours. [DI-²]

**||dĭck¹** n. (sl.) Take one's ~, swear (*that*). [abbr. of *declaration*]

**dĭck²** n. (sl.) Detective. [abbr.]

**di'ckens** (-z) n. (colloq., in imprecations etc.) Deuce, Devil. [prob. name *Dickens*]

**Dĭcke'nsian** (-z-) a. Of *Dickens* or his works; having similarities to situations described by him. [person]

**di'cker** v.i. Bargain, haggle. [orig. uncert.]

**di'cky. 1.** n. (colloq.) False shirt-front; ||driver's seat; ||extra folding seat at back of vehicle; ~**(-bird)**, small bird. **2.** a. (sl.) Shaky, unsound. [*Dicky* dim. of *Richard*]

**dicŏtylē'don** n. Flowering plant having two cotyledons (abbr. **di'cŏt**); ~**ous** a. [DI-²]

**di'cta.** See DICTUM.

**dĭctāte. 1.** (-ā'-) v.t. & i. (-atable). Say or read aloud (matter to be written down, *to* writer); (of person, motive, etc.) prescribe, lay down authoritatively, (terms, things to be done, etc.); give peremptory orders (*will not be dictated to*). **2.** (-ĭ'-) n. (usu. in *pl.*) Authoritative instruction (esp. of reason, conscience, nature, etc.). **3. Di'ctaphŏne** n., machine that records and later reproduces for transcription or rehearing what is spoken into it [P]; **dĭctā'tion** n. (dictation speed, rate of speech used by person dictating); **dĭctā'tor** n., (esp.) absolute ruler of a State, esp. one who suppresses or succeeds a democratic government, person with absolute authority in any sphere; **dĭctatŏr'ial** a. (-lly), of a dictator, imperious, overbearing; **dĭctā'torship** n., (esp.) State ruled by dictator. [L *dicto* (*dico* say)]

**di'ction** n. Choice of words and phrases in speech or writing; manner of enunciation in speaking or singing; ~**ary** n., book explaining, usu. in alphabetical order, the words of a language or words and topics of some special subject, author, etc., (French–English etc. ~ary, list of French etc. words with English etc. translation or explanation; *dictionary of Americanisms, of architecture, of the Bible, of proverbs, Dictionary of National Biography, Shakespeare Dictionary*, etc.); **Di'ctograph** (-ahf) n., loud-speaking telephone for use between rooms of a building [P]; **di'ctum** n. (*pl.* -ta), formal saying, pronouncement, maxim, (Law) = OBITER DICTUM. [F, or L *dictio* (*dico* dict- say)]

**dĭd.** See DO³.

**dĭdă'ctic** a. (~ally). Meant to instruct; having the manner of an authoritarian teacher; ~**ism** n. [Gk (*didaskō* teach)]

**di'dapper** n. Dabchick. [E (DIVE, DIP)]

**di'ddest.** See DO³.

**di'ddle** v.t. (sl.) Cheat, swindle. [prob. f. older *diddler* f. character in play]

**di'dn't, di'dst.** See DO[3].

**die**[1] n. **1.** (*pl.* **dice**, also colloq. as *sing.*) Small cube with faces bearing usu. 1–6 spots in games of chance, (in *pl.*) game played with these (*lost his fortune at dice*); (in *pl.*) small cubes of meat etc. for cooking; **the ~ is cast**, irrevocable step is taken; **no dice**, (colloq.) no success or prospect of it; **as straight, true, as a ~**, entirely honest or loyal. **2.** (*pl.* **~s**). Coining or embossing stamp; (Archit.) cube of pedestal, plinth of column; hollow mould for shaping extruded metal etc.; **~-casting**, process or product of casting from metal moulds; **~-sinker**, engraver of dies; **~-stamping**, embossing paper etc. with die. **3. dice** v.i. & t., play dice, gamble *away* at dice, take great risks (*dicing with death*), (Cookery) cut into small cubes; **di'cey** a., (sl.) risky, unreliable. [F f. L *datum* (*do* give, play)]

**die**[2] v.i. (**dying** *pr.* di'ĭ-). (Of person or animal) cease to live, expire, (*of* illness, hunger, etc., *by* violence, one's own hand, *from* wound etc., *through* neglect, *on* scaffold, *at* the stake, *in* battle, *for* friend, cause, etc., *in* poverty; *die a beggar, a martyr; die a glorious death*; **dying words**, uttered at time of death); (of plant etc.) lose vital force, decay (**~ back**, from tip towards root); come to an end, cease to exist or function; (of flame, fame, sound, etc.) go out, disappear, be forgotten, fade away, (*away, down, off*); **be dying** *for*, *to* do, have great desire; **~ of** *boredom* etc., find it exceedingly vexatious; **~ (of) laughing**, laugh to exhaustion; **~-away**, languishing; **~ the death**, (arch. or joc.) be put to death, (sl.) have one's performance ill received; **~ game** (fighting, not tamely); **~ hard** (not without struggle), **~-hard**, conservative or stubborn person; **~ in one's bed** (of age or illness); **~ in one's boots** or **shoes** (by violence); **~ in harness** (while still at work); **~ in the last ditch** (desperately defending something); **~ out**, become extinct; **never say ~**, not give in, keep up courage; *secret* etc. **~s with** person, he dies without revealing it. [N]

**dièlè'ctric** a. & n. (Electr.) Insulating (medium or substance). [DI-[3]]

**\*diær̄'ésĭs.** See DIAERESIS.

**die'sel** (-z-) n. **~** (**engine**), internal combustion engine in which fuel is ignited by heat of air highly compressed; vehicle driven by, fuel for, diesel engine; **~-electric**, driven by electric current from generator driven by diesel engine; **~ oil**, petroleum fraction used in diesel engines. [person]

**di'et**[1] n. Conference, congress (esp. as English name for some foreign parliaments etc.). [L *dieta*]

**di'et**[2]. **1.** n. One's habitual food; prescribed course of food. **2.** v.i. Restrict oneself to special food, esp. in order to control one's weight; **di'etarȳ, diĕtĕ'tĭc** (-ically), *adjs.*, of diet; **diĕtĕ'tĭcs** n.pl., science of diet; **diĕtī'tian, -ĭ'cian,** (-shan) n., one versed in or practising dietetics. [F f. L f. Gk *diaita* way of life]

**dif-** *pref.* = DIS-.

**di'ffer** v.i. Be unlike, be distinguishable *from*; disagree, be at variance (*with*, *from*); **~ence** n., non-identity, unlikeness, point in which things differ (*make a great, a slight, no, difference*); **make all the ~ence** be very important or significant; **make a ~ence between**, treat differently; **with a ~ence**, in a special way), quantity by which amounts differ, remainder after subtraction (**split the ~ence**, take average of two proposed amounts), disagreement in opinion, dispute, quarrel; **~ent** a., able to be distinguished, unlike, of other nature, form, or quality, (*from*, *to*, *than*), distinct, separate, (*several different people, colours*), unusual; **~ĕ'ntĭa** (-shĭa) n. (*pl.* -ae), distinguishing mark, esp. of species within a genus; **~ĕ'ntial** (-shăl), (*a.*; **-lly**) varying according to circumstances, constituting a specific difference, relating to specific differences (*differential diagnosis*), (Math.) relating to infinitesimal differences, (**~ential calculus**, for finding rates of change, maximum and minimum values, etc.; **~ential (gear)**, enabling motor vehicle's rear wheels to revolve at different speeds in rounding corners), (n.) difference between rates of interest etc., difference in wage between industries or between different classes of workers in same industry;

**~ĕ′ntiāte** (-shǐ-) v.t. & i. (-iable), constitute difference between, of, or in, discriminate (between things, one from another), (of organs, species, synonyms, etc.) make or become different in process of growth or development; **~ĕntiā′tion** (-shǐ-, -sǐ-) n. [F f. L differo dilat- bring apart]

**dĭ′fficult** a. Needing much labour to do or practise, obscure, perplexing, troublesome, unaccommodating, stubborn, (a difficult task, art, passage, question, person; difficult of access, to answer); **~y** n., being difficult, difficult thing or problem, hindrance, (often in pl.) trouble, esp. shortage of money (in difficulties); **make ~ies**, be unaccommodating; **with ~y**, not easily. [difficulty f. L difficultas (FACULTY)]

**dĭ′ffiden|t** a. Lacking self-confidence; **~ce** n. [L diffido distrust]

**diffrǎ′ct** v.t. (Phys.; of edge of opaque body, narrow slit, etc.) break up (beam of light) into series of dark and light bands or coloured spectra, or (beam of radiation or particles) into series of high and low intensities; **~ion** n.; **~ive** a. [L diffringo (FRACTION)]

**diffū′se. 1.** (-z) v.t. & i. Disperse, be dispersed, from a centre, (be) spread widely, (light, particles, warmth, knowledge, influence, etc.); cause (fluids) to intermingle. **2.** (-s) a. Spread out, diffused; (of style, discourse, etc.) verbose, not concise. **3.** **diffū′sible** a., **diffūsĭbi′litў** n., (-z-); **diffū′sion** (-zhon) n.; **diffū′sive** a. [F or L (FOUND[2])]

**dĭg. 1.** v.i. & t. (-gg-; dug). Use spade or pick, claws, hands, snout, etc., in excavating or turning over ground; excavate archaeologically; make search (for information, into book etc.); make way by digging into, through, under; excavate or turn up (ground) with spade etc. or for archaeological purposes; make (hole, grave, etc.) by digging; obtain by digging (potatoes etc.); (sl.) understand, experience, admire; thrust (one's nails, feet, point of weapon, etc.) into something or in (~ one's feet, heels, or toes in, be obstinate); poke (person in the ribs); **~** (oneself) **in**, prepare defensive trench or pit, establish one's position; **~ in, into,** mix (thing) with the soil by digging, (colloq.) begin eating; **~ out, up,** get or find by digging (lit. or fig.);

**~ up,** break soil of (fallow land). **2.** n. Piece of digging; archaeological excavation; thrust, poke, (esp. in the ribs; **~ at,** fig., remark directed against); ‖(in pl., colloq.) lodgings. **3.** **~′ger** (-g-) n., (esp., colloq.) Australian, New Zealander; **~′ging** (-g-) n., (esp. in pl.) goldfield, ‖lodgings. [E]

**digest. 1.** (dīˈjĕst) v.t. Reduce to convenient form, classify, summarize, (facts, laws, etc.); think over, arrange in the mind; assimilate (food) in stomach and bowels; treat (substance) with heat or solvent to decompose it, extract essence, etc.; endure (insults etc.); understand and assimilate mentally. **2.** (dīˈjĕst) n. Compendium, esp. of laws; periodical synopsis of current literature or news. **3.** **digĕ′stible** a., **digĕstĭbi′litў** n., (esp. of food); **digĕ′stion** (-schon) n., (esp.) person's power of digesting food; **digĕ′stive** a., assisting digestion, ‖kind of wholemeal (biscuit). [L digero -gest-]

**digger, digging.** See DIG.

**dĭ′git** n. Any numeral from 0 to 9; (Zool., Anat., or joc.) finger or toe; **~al** a.; **~al clock** (showing time by displayed digits, not by hands); **~al computer** (making calculations with data represented by digits etc.); **~ā′lis** n., drug made from foxglove leaves, used as heart-stimulant; **~(al)ize** v.t. [L, = finger, toe]

**dĭ′gni|fý** v.t. Confer dignity on, ennoble; give high-sounding name to (school dignified with the name of college); **~fied** (-id) a., self-respecting, stately; **~tarў** n., person holding high rank, esp. ecclesiastical; **~tў** n., true worth, excellence, (the dignity of labour), high rank or estimation (beneath one's **~tў**, unfitting for one to do), honourable office or rank or title, elevated manner, proper stateliness (stand on one's **~tў**, insist on respectful treatment). [F f. L (dignus worthy)]

**dī′graph** (-ahf) n. Two letters composing single sound (e.g. sh, oa, in ship, broad). [DI-[2], -GRAPH]

**digrĕ′ss** v.i. Diverge temporarily from the main track esp. in speech or writing; **~ion** (-shon) n.; **~ive** a. [L digredior -gress-]

**dike, dȳke. 1.** n. Ditch; embankment, long ridge of earth etc. raised as causeway or to keep out sea or floods; low wall esp. of turf. **2.** *v.t.* Protect with dikes. [N, = ditch]

**di′ktăt** *n.* Imposition of severe terms by victor; categorical statement. [G, = DICTATE]

**dĭlăpĭdā′tion** *n.* Bringing or coming into, being in, disrepair; **dĭlă′pĭdātĕd** *a.,* in disrepair or decay. [L (DI¹-, *lapis* stone)]

**dĭlā′t|e** *v.t.* & *i.* Make or become wider or larger, expand, (*with* dilated *or* dilating *eyes*); speak or write at length (*upon*); **dĭlātā′tion** *n.* (esp. Med.); **~ion, ~or,** *ns.* [F f. L (*latus* wide)]

**dĭ′lator|ў** *a.* (**~ily, ~iness**). Tending to, designed to cause, given to, delay. [L *dilatorius* (DIFFER)]

**dĭlě′mma** *n.* Logical or actual position presenting only a choice between equally unwelcome alternatives (horns of the dilemma). [L f. Gk (*lêmma* premiss)]

**dĭlĕttă′nt|ė. 1.** *n.* (*pl.* **~i** *pr.* -ē, **~es**). Lover of the fine arts; amateur, one who toys with subject or studies it lightly; **~ism** *n.* **2.** *a.* Trifling, not thorough; amateur. [It. (*dilettare* to DELIGHT)]

**dĭ′ligen|t** *a.* Steady in application, industrious; **~ce** *n.,* persistent effort or work, industrious character. [F f. L (*diligo* love)]

**dill** *n.* Herb with scented leaves and seeds; **~ pickle,** pickled cucumber etc. flavoured with dill. [E]

**dĭ′lly-dăllў** *v.i.* (colloq.) Vacillate; dawdle. [redupl. DALLY]

**dĭlū′te. 1.** *v.t.* Reduce strength of (fluid) by adding water etc.; diminish brilliance of (colour); make (doctrine, zeal) less strict or forceful; substitute a proportion of unskilled for skilled (workers). **2.** *a.* (*or* -ī′-) Diluted. **3.** **dĭlū′tion** (*or* -ōō′-) *n.* [L *diluo* -*lut*- wash away]

**dĭlū′vĭal** (*or* -ōō′-) *a.* (**~ly**). Of a flood, esp. of the Flood in Genesis. [L (DELUGE)]

**dim. 1.** *a.* (-mm-). Faintly luminous or visible; not bright, clear, or well-defined; (colloq.) stupid; perceiving or perceived indistinctly; **take a ~ view of,** (colloq.) regard with disfavour or pessimism; **~-wit(ted),** (colloq.) stupid (person). **2.** *v.i.* & *t.* (-mm-). Become or make dim; *dip (headlights). [E]

**dim.** *abbr.* diminuendo.

***dīme** *n.* Silver coin, 1/10 of dollar; **a ~ a dozen,** commonplace; **~ novel** (cheap and sensational). [F f. L *decima* tenth (part)]

**dĭmě′nsion** (-shǝn) *n.* Measurable extent of any kind, as length, breadth, thickness, etc., (often in *pl.*); **of great ~s,** very large; **the three ~s,** length, breadth, and thickness); extent in a particular aspect (*gave the problem a new dimension*); **~al** *a.* (-lly) (TWO-*dimensional* etc.). [F f. L (*metior mens*- measure)]

**dĭ′mĕter** *n.* (Pros.) Verse of two measures. [L f. Gk (DI-², -METER)]

**dĭmĭ′n|ĭsh** *v.t.* & *i.* Make or become smaller or less; lessen the reputation of (person); (in *p.p.,* Mus.) lessened by a semitone; **law of ~ishing returns,** (Econ.) fact that expenditure, taxation, etc., beyond a certain point does not produce proportionate yield; **~uĕ′ndō** *adv., a.,* & *n.* (*pl.* -os), (Mus.; passage performed) with gradual decrease of loudness; **~u′tion** *n.,* diminishing. [F f. L (MINUTE¹)]

**dĭmĭ′nŭtive. 1.** *a.* Remarkably small, tiny; (Gram., of word, suffix, etc.) implying smallness either actual or imputed in token of affection etc. **2.** *n.* (Gram.) Diminutive word. [F f. L (prec.)]

**dĭ′mĭtў** *n.* Cotton fabric woven with raised stripes or checks. [It. or L f. Gk (DI-², *mitos* thread)]

**dĭ′mpl|e. 1.** *n.* Small hollow or dent, esp. in cheek or chin; **~ў** *a.* **2.** *v.t.* & *i.* Produce dimples in; show dimples. [E]

**dĭn. 1.** *n.* Continued confused distracting noise. **2.** *v.t.* & *i.* (-nn-). Get (thing to be learnt) *into* person or person's *ears* by incessant repetition; make din. [E]

**dĭ′năr** (dē′-) *n.* Currency unit in Yugoslavia and in several countries of Middle East and N. Africa. [Arab. & Pers. f. Gk f. L DENARIUS]

**dine** *v.i.* & *t.* Eat dinner; entertain (persons) at dinner; **~ out** (away from home); **~ out on,** be invited to dinner mainly because of one's knowledge of (interesting event etc.); **dining-car** (for meals on train); **dining-room** (in which meals are eaten); **dining-table** (on which meals are served); **di′ner** *n.,* (esp.) railway dining-car, *restaurant, (small) dining-room. [F f. Rom. (DIS-, JEJUNE)]

**dǐng-dǒng** *adv.*, *n.*, & *a.* (With) alternating strokes as of two bells; with great energy (*hammer away at it ding-dong*); ~ **fight**, **race**, etc., in which advantage oscillates, hard fought); (colloq.) heated argument, riotous party. [imit.]

**dǐ'nghў** (-nggǐ, -ngī) *n.* Small boat of ship; small pleasure-boat; small inflatable rubber boat for emergency use. [Hindi]

**dǐ'ngle** (-nggel) *n.* Deep dell. [orig. unkn.]

**dǐ'ngō** (-nggō) *n.* (*pl.* ~**es**). Wild or half-domesticated Australian dog. [Aboriginal]

**dǐ'ngў** (-njī) *a.* (-**ily**, -**iness**). Dull-coloured, drab; dirty-looking. [orig. uncert.]

**dǐ'nkum.** (Austral. & N.Z. colloq.) **1.** *n.* Work, toil; the truth. **2.** *a.* Genuine, real; ~ **oil**, the honest truth. [orig. unkn.]

**dǐ'nkў** *a.* (colloq.) Neat, trim, small, dainty. [Sc. *dink*]

**dǐ'nner** *n.* Chief meal of day, whether at midday or evening (formal meal with several courses); banquet in honour of person or event; ~**dance**, dinner followed by dancing; ‖~**jacket**, man's short usu. black coat for evening wear; *dinner*-SERVICE[1] or SET[3]; ~**table** (at which dinner is eaten). [F (DINE)]

**dǐ'nosaur** *n.* Reptile (freq. huge) of Mesozoic era. [L f. Gk *deinos* terrible, SAURIAN]

**dǐnt. 1.** *n.* Mark made by blow or pressure, dent; (arch.) blow, stroke; **by ~ of**, by force or means of. **2.** *v.t.* Mark with dints, dent. [E]

**dǐ'ocèse** *n.* District under pastoral care of bishop; **dǐŏ'cèsan**, (*a.*) of a diocese, (*n.*) bishop in relation to diocese or its clergy, ‖member of diocese in relation to bishop. [F f. L f. Gk *dioikēsis* administration]

**Dǐonў'sǐăc, -ǐan**, *adjs.* Of (worship of) *Dionysus*, Gk god of wine. [L f. Gk]

**dǐora'ma** (-rah'-) *n.* Scenic painting in which changes in colour and direction of illumination simulate sunrise etc.; small representation of scene with three-dimensional figures, viewed through window etc.; small-scale model or film-set; **dǐora'mǐc** *a.* (-**ically**). [DI-[3], Gk *horaō* see]

**dǐŏ'xǐde** *n.* (Chem.) Oxide formed by combination of two atoms of oxygen with one of metal etc. (*carbon dioxide*). [DI-[2]]

**dǐp. 1.** *v.i.* & *t.* (-**pp**-). Put or let down into liquid, immerse, dye thus; go under water and emerge quickly; wash (sheep) in vermin-killing liquid; put hand, ladle, etc., *into* to take something out (~ **into** one's **pocket**, **purse**, etc., spend from it); lower (esp. flag, sail) for a moment, ‖lower (beam of vehicle's headlight) to reduce dazzle; have downward slope (esp. of strata, magnetic needle); go below any surface or level (*sun dips below horizon*; *bird dips and rises in flight*; *balance-scale dips*); look cursorily *into* (book etc.). **2.** *n.* Dipping (LUCKY *dip*); quantity dipped up; (colloq.) bathe in sea etc.; (sl.) pickpocket; downward slope of stratum, road, etc.; depression in skyline etc.; tallow candle; washing-preparation for sheep etc.; sauce or dressing into which food is dipped before eating; ~ **net**, small fishing net with long handle; ~ **pen** (that has to be dipped in ink, not fountain-pen); ~**stick**, rod for measuring depth of liquid; ‖~**switch** (for dipping vehicle's headlight beams). **3.** ~'**per** *n.*, (esp.) Anabaptist, Baptist, diving-bird, ladle. [E]

**Dǐp.** *abbr.* Diploma.

**dǐphthē̆r'ǐa** *n.* Infectious disease with membranous growth in throat etc.; ~**l**, **dǐphther̆i'tǐc**, *adjs.* [L f. F f. Gk *diphthera* skin, hide]

**dǐ'phth|ŏng** *n.* Union of two vowels (letters or sounds) pronounced in one syllable (as in *coin*, *loud*, *side*); compound vowel character, ligature, (as *æ*); ~**ŏ'ngal** (-ngg-) *a.* (-**lly**). [F f. L f. Gk (*phthoggos* voice)]

**dǐplŏ'ma** *n.* Document conferring honour or privilege; (certificate of) University or College degree or qualification; charter, official document; ~**cў** *n.*, management of, skill in managing, international relations, tact, adroitness in personal relations; **dǐ'plomăt** *n.*, one engaged in diplomacy, esp. accredited to court or seat of government, adroit negotiator; **diplomă'tǐc** (*a.*; -**ically**) of diplomacy (~**tic bag**, containing official mail from embassy etc.; ~**tic corps**, body of diplomats accredited to a government; ~**tic immunity**, exemption of diplomatic staff etc. abroad from arrest, taxation, etc.; ∼**tic service**, branch of public service concerned with representation of country abroad); tactful, skilled in diplomacy, proceeding by negotiation, (*n.*, also in *pl.*) palaeographic study of documents; ∼**tist** *n.*, diplomat. [L f. Gk. = folded paper (*diplous* double)]

**dĭ′pper.** See DIP.

**dĭpsomā′nĭ|a** *n.* Morbid craving for alcoholic liquor; ∼**ăc** *n.* (colloq. abbr. **dĭ′psō**). [Gk *dipsa* thirst]

**dĭ′pterous** *a.* (Of insect, e.g. fly, gnat) two-winged. [L f. Gk (*pteron* wing)]

**dĭ′ptўch** (-k) *n.* Painting, esp. altar-piece, on two boards etc. hinged so as to close like book. [L f. Gk. = pair of writing-tablets (*ptukhē* fold)]

**dīre** *a.* Dreadful; ominous; urgent (*in dire need*). [L]

**dĭrĕ′ct** *a., adv.,* & *v.* **1.** *a.* & *adv.* Straight, not crooked(ly) or oblique(ly) or round about, (*direct route*; *went direct to London*); straightforward, going straight to the point, frank(ly), not ambiguous(ly), (*direct answer, manner, threat*); without intermediaries, personal(ly), not by proxy, (*direct result, negotiations*; *deal with him direct*); (of descent) linear, not collateral; complete, greatest possible, (*direct contradiction, contrast, opposite*); ∼ **action**, exertion of pressure on the community by action (e.g. strike or sabotage) seeking immediate effect, rather than by Parliamentary means; ∼ **current** (Electr., flowing in one direction only); ‖∼ **grant** (of money given to certain schools by Government not local authority); ∼ **hit** (without ricochet, or exactly on target); ∼ **labour** (by employees without intervention of contractor); *direct* OBJECT; ∼ **proportion**, relation between quantities whose ratio is constant; ∼ **speech**, words quoted as actually spoken, not as modified in reporting; *direct* TAX. **2.** *v.t.* Tell (person) the way (*to*); give indications for delivery of (letter etc. *to* person or place); utter or write *to* or to be conveyed *to* (*I direct my remarks to you*); point, turn, (blow, thing, gunfire, eyes, attention, person, course, efforts, etc.) *to, at, towards*, person or thing; control, govern movements of; guide as adviser, principle (*duty directs my actions*), etc.; order (person) *to* do, thing *to be* done; super-

vise acting etc. of (film, play, etc.); give orders (*that*, or abs.). **3.** ∼**ion** *n.*, directing, (usu. in *pl.*) order or instruction what to do, point to or from, line along, which person or thing moves or looks (in the ∼ion of, towards; **sense of** ∼ion, ability to know without guidance the places towards which one is walking, etc.), scope, sphere, subject (*improvements in many directions*); **dĭrĕ′ctional** *a.*, (esp., Radio) transmitting in one direction only, giving direction from which signal comes; ∼**ĭve**, (*a.*) serving to direct, (*n.*) general instruction for procedure or action; ∼**lў**, (*adv.*) in a direct line or manner, at once, without delay, (*conj.*, ‖colloq.) as soon as (*get up directly the bell rings*); ∼**or** *n.*, (esp.) member of board managing affairs of company etc. (∼**or-general**, chief administrator), person who directs film, play, etc., (Eccl.) spiritual adviser; ∼**orate** *n.*, office of director, board of directors; ∼**ōr′ĭal** *a.* (-lly); ∼**orship**, ∼**rĕss**, *ns.*; ∼**orў** *n.*, (esp.) book with list of telephone subscribers, inhabitants of district, etc., with various details. [L *dirigo* (*rego rect*- guide)]

**dĭr′eful** (-īr′f-) *a.* (literary; ∼**ly**). Terrible, dreadful. [DIRE]

**dĭrge** *n.* Song of mourning; slow mournful song. [L *dirige* imper. (DIRECT), used in Office of the Dead]

**dĭ′rĭgible** (or -rī′-). **1.** *a.* (Esp. of balloon) capable of being guided. **2.** *n.* Dirigible balloon or airship. [DIRECT]

**dĭrk** *n.* Kind of long dagger (esp. of Sc. Highlander). [orig. unkn.]

**dĭr′ndl** *n.* Woman's dress imitating Alpine peasant costume with bodice and full skirt; ∼ (**skirt**), full skirt with tight waistband. [G]

**dĭrt** *n.* Unclean matter that soils; excrement; foul or scurrilous talk; anything worthless (**treat person like** ∼, entirely without respect; ∼ **cheap**, very cheap); earth, soil, (\*∼ **road,** road without made surface); **do** person ∼, (sl.) harm or injure him maliciously; **eat** ∼, put up with insult etc., \*make humiliating confession; ∼**-track**, course made of rolled cinders etc. for motor-cycle racing, or of earth for flat races; ∼′**ў**, (*a.*; ∼**ily,** ∼**iness**) like or connected with dirt, soiled, obscene, sordid, despicable, (of weather) rough, squally, (of colour) not pure or clear, (dirty road, house, face, linen, story, night, yellow); ~y dog, sl., despicable person; ~y look, colloq., look of disapproval or disgust; ~y money, paid to those who must handle dirty materials; ~y trick, despicable act; ~y word, obscene word, word denoting concept regarded as discreditable (compromise is a dirty word); ~y work, dishonourable behaviour, unpleasant task; do the ~y, play mean trick on), (adv., sl.) very (big etc.), (v.t. & i.) make or become dirty. [N]

dis- pref. forming ns., adjs., and vbs., w. stress & inflexion usu. unaltered, meaning (1) reverse of action or state (disaffiliate v.t. & i., disaffiliation n.; ||disafforest [L], v.t., disafforestation n.; disarrange v.t., disarrangement n.; disarray v.t., & n.; disassemble v.t.; disembark v.i. & t., disembarkation n.; disembarrass v.t.; disembody v.t., disembodiment n.; disencumber v.t.; disendow v.t., disendowment n.; disentail v.t. (land etc.); disentangle v.t., disentanglement n.; disenthral, *-ll, v.t., disenthral(l)ment n.; disentomb v.t., disentombment n.; disinfest v.t., disinfestation n.; disinter v.t.; disorganize v.t., disorganization n.; disorient(ate) vbs. t., disorientation n.; disrobe v.t. & i.; disunite v.t.), (2) direct contrary of the simple word (disaccord n., & v.i.; disadvantage n., disadvantageous a.; disamenity n.; disapprobation n.; disapprove v.t. & i., disapproval n.; disbelief n., disbelieve v.t. & i.; discomfort n., & v.t.; discountenance v.t.; discourteous a., discourtesy n.; disfavour, *disfavor, n., & v.t.; disharmony n., disharmonious a.; dishearten v.t., disheartenment n.; dishonest a., dishonesty n.; disingenuous a.; disloyal a., disloyalty n.; disobedience n., disobedient a., disobey v.i. & t.; dispraise n., & v.t.; dissimilar a., dissimilarity n.; distrust n., & v.t., distrustful a.; disunion, disunity, ns.), (3) removal of thing or quality (disbud v.t.; dishorn v.t.; dismast v.t., usu. in p.p.; dispeople v.t.). [F des- or L]

disa'ble v.t. Incapacitate from doing or for work etc.; (esp. in p.p.) cripple, deprive of or reduce power

of acting, walking, etc.; disabi'lity n., thing or lack that prevents one's doing something, physical incapacity caused by injury or disease; ~ment (-belm-) n. [DIS-]

disabu'se (-z) v.t. Undeceive; relieve of illusion etc.

disaccord, disadvantage(ous). See DIS- (2). [F]

disadva'ntaged (-ah′ntijd) a. In unfavourable conditions, esp. lacking normal social opportunities. [p.p. of disadvantage v.]

disaffe'ct|ed a. Unfriendly; ill-disposed, disloyal, esp. to one's superiors; ~ion n., political discontent. [DIS-]

disaffiliate, disaffiliation, disafforest [L], -ation. See DIS- (1).

disagree' v.i. ~ (with), differ in nature (from), be unlike, differ in opinion (from), dissent (from), quarrel (with); ~ with (of food, climate, etc.) prove unsuitable for, have bad effects on, (person, his health, etc.); ~able (or -gri′a-) a. (-bly), not to one's taste, unpleasant, ill-tempered; ~ment n. [F (DIS-)]

disallow' v.t. Refuse to sanction or accept as reasonable, prohibit.

disamenity. See DIS- (2).

disappear' v.i. Pass from sight or existence, vanish; ~ance n., fact of disappearing. [DIS-]

disappoi'nt v.t. Fail to fulfil desire or expectation of, break appointment with, (person, or abs.); disappointed at failure, in thing, of one's expected gain, in or with person; agreeably etc. ~ed, glad to find one's fears groundless; frustrate (hope, purpose, etc., person in love); ~ment n., event etc. that disappoints, resulting distress. [F (DIS-)]

disapprobation, disapproval, disapprove. See DIS- (2).

disar'm v.t. & i. Deprive of or of weapon(s); deprive (city, ship, etc.) of means of defence; reduce (army) to peace footing; deprive of power to injure; remove fuse of (bomb etc.); pacify hostility or suspicions of; ~ing, a., (esp.) removing suspicion or doubt; ~ament n., (esp.) reduction of military etc. forces and weapons of war. [F (ARM²)]

disarrange(ment), disarray, disassemble. See DIS- (1).

disa'st|er (-zah′-) n. Sudden or great misfortune; complete failure; ~er area (in which major disaster

has recently occurred); ~**rous** *a.*
[F or It. f. *L astrum* star]

**disavow'** *v.t.* Say one does not
know or have responsibility for or
approve of; ~**al** *n.* [F (DIS-)]

**disbǎnd** *v.t. & i.* (Of troops etc.)
break up, disperse; ~**ment** *n.*

**disbǎr'** *v.t.* (**-rr-**). Expel from
membership of the bar, deprive of
status of barrister; ~**ment** *n.* [DIS-]

**disbelief, disbelieve.** See DIS- (2).
**disbud,** DIS- (3).

**disbǔr'den** *v.t.* Relieve of or *of* a
burden; discharge (load, anxieties,
etc.). [DIS-]

**disbǔr'se** *v.t. & i.* Pay out
(money); ~**al** *n.*; ~**ement** (-sm-)
*n.*, (esp.) outlay. [F (DIS-, BOURSE)]

**disc, disk,** *n.* Thin circular plate
of any material (e.g. medal, coin,
counter); round flat or apparently
flat surface (*sun's disc*) or mark; layer
of cartilage between vertebræ
(**slipped** ~, one that has become
displaced and causes lumbar pain);
gramophone record; ~ **brake**
(using disc-shaped friction surfaces);
~ **jockey,** (colloq.) compère of
broadcast programme of gramophone records; ~ **parking,** system
in which parked vehicles must display disc showing time of arrival or
latest permitted time of departure.
[F, or L DISCUS]

**discǎrd. 1.** (-ǎr'-) *v.t. & i.* Cast
aside, give up, (garment, unwanted
material, habit, belief, friend, etc.);
throw out or reject from hand at
cards (specified card or abs.). **2.** (-ǐ'-)
*n.* Discarded thing(s). [CARD²]

**discěrn'** *v.t.* (~**ible**). Perceive
clearly with mind or senses; make
out by thought or by gazing, listening, etc.; ~**ing** *a.,* (esp.) having
quick or true insight (*a discerning
critic*); ~**ment** *n.,* (esp.) insight, keen
perception. [F f. L (*cerno cret-*
separate)]

**dischǎr'ge. 1.** *v.t. & i.* Relieve
(ship etc.) of cargo; fire (gun);
release electric charge of; dismiss;
release (prisoner); let go (patient,
jury); relieve (bankrupt) of residual
liability; put forth, send out, emit,
(missile, liquid, purulent matter,
abuse); unload from ship; (Law)
cancel (order of court); acquit oneself of, pay, perform, (duty, debt,
vow); undergo discharge of con-
tents; (of river) flow *into* sea etc. **2.**
(*or* -ǐ'-) *n.* Discharging or being dis-

charged; liquid or purulent matter
emitted; written certificate of discharge; liberation. [F (DIS-)]

**discī'ple** *n.* One of Christ's personal
followers, any early believer in
Christ; follower or adherent of any
leader of thought, art, conduct, etc.
[E f. L (*disco* learn)]

**dǐ'sciplin|e. 1.** *n.* Branch of in-
struction or learning; mental or
moral training, adversity as effecting
this; system of rules for conduct;
behaviour according to established
rules; order maintained among
schoolchildren, soldiers, etc.; control
exercised over members of organization; chastisement. **2.** *v.t.* Train to
obedience and order; punish. **3.**
~**ǎr'ian** *n.,* maintainer of discipline;
~**arў** (*or* -lǐ'n-) *a.,* of or promoting
discipline. [F f. L *disciplina* (prec.)]

**disclai'm** *v.t.* Renounce legal
claim to (thing or abs.); disavow
(*responsibility* etc.); ~**er** *n.,* (esp.)
renunciation, disavowal. [AF (DIS-)]

**disclō's|e** (-z) *v.t.* Expose to view,
make known, reveal; ~**ure** (-zher) *n.,*
disclosing, thing disclosed. [F (DIS-)]

**dǐ'scō** *n.* (colloq.; *pl.* ~**s**). Dis-
cothèque; party at which records are
played for dancing. [abbr.]

**disco'lour, *-lor,** (-ǔ'ler) *v.t. & i.*
Change or spoil colour of, stain,
tarnish; become stained etc.; **dis-
colorā'tion** (-ŭler-) *n.* [F or L (DIS-)]

**disco'mfǐt** (-ŭ'm-) *v.t.* Baffle, disconcert; (arch.) defeat; ~**ure** *n.* [F
(DIS-, CONFECTION)]

**discomfort.** See DIS- (2). [F]

**discompō'se** (-z) *v.t.* Disturb composure of; **discompō'sure** (-zher)
*n.,* discomposed state. [DIS-]

**disconcěr't** *v.t.* Spoil, upset, (plan
etc.); disturb self-possession of,
fluster; ~**ment** *n.* [F (DIS-)]

**disconně'ct** *v.t.* Break connection
of (thing *from* another); put (electric
apparatus) out of action by disconnecting parts; ~**ed** *a.,* (esp., of
speech or writing) incoherent, having
abrupt transitions; **disconně'ction,**
‖**-ě'xion,** (-kshon) *n.* [DIS-]

**discŏ'nsolate** *a.* Forlorn, down-
cast, disappointed. [L (DIS-, SOLACE)]

**discontě'nt. 1.** *n.* Dissatisfaction;
lack of contentment, grievance. **2.**
*v.t.* (esp. in *p.p.*) Make dissatisfied;
~**ment** *n.* [DIS-]

**discontǐ'nū|e** *v.t. & i.* (Cause to)
cease; cease from, give up (*doing,*
habit); ~**ance** *n.,* discontinuing (*of*)

**~ous** *a.*, lacking continuity in space or time, intermittent; **disconti‐nū'ity** *n.*, quality of being discontinuous. [F f. L (DIS-)]

**di'scŏrd** *n.* Opposition of views, strife; harsh noise, clashing sounds; lack of harmony between notes sounded together; **~ant** (-ôr'-) *a.*, not in harmony, disagreeing; **~ance** (-ôr'-) *n.* [F f. L (DIS-, *cor cord-* heart)]

**di'scothèque** (-tĕk) *n.* Club, café, etc., where records are played for dancing. [F, = record-library]

**discount. 1.** (-ĭ'-) *n.* Deduction from amount due or price of goods, e.g. when payment is prompt or in advance, or for special class of buyers; deduction from amount of bill of exchange etc. by one who gives value for it before it is due; **at a ~,** below nominal or usual price (cf. PREMIUM), (fig.) depreciated; **~ shop** etc., one that regularly sells goods at less than normal retail price. **2.** (-ow'-) *v.t.* Give or get present worth of (bill not yet due); disregard partly or wholly; reduce effect of (event etc.) by previous action. [F or It. (DIS-, COUNT¹)]

**discountenance.** See DIS- (2).

**discou'rage** (-kŭ'-) *v.t.* Deprive of courage, confidence, or energy; dissuade *from*; show disapproval of; **~ment** (-rĭjm-) *n.* [F (DIS-)]

**discourse. 1.** (dĭ'skôrs) *n.* (literary). Talk, conversation; lecture, sermon, dissertation. **2.** (-ôr's) *v.i.* Converse; speak or write at length on a subject (*of*, *on*, *upon*, or abs.); utter a discourse. [L (DISCURSIVE)]

**discourteous, discourtesy.** See DIS- (2).

**disco'ver** (-kŭ'-) *v.t.* Find out (fact etc., *that* etc., unknown country), become aware *that*; (arch.) exhibit, disclose, betray; **~y** *n.*, discovering, thing discovered. [F f. L (DIS-)]

**discre'dit. 1.** *v.t.* Refuse to believe; bring disrepute to; cause to be disbelieved. **2.** *n.* Loss of repute (*bring discredit on*; *bring into discredit*); person or thing causing loss of repute; lack of credibility; loss of commercial credit. **3. ~able** *a.* (**-bly**), bringing discredit, shameful. [DIS-]

**discree't** *a.* Judicious, prudent; circumspect in speech or action; unobtrusive. [F f. L (DISCERN)]

**discre'pan|cy** *n.* Difference, inconsistency, (*between* different ver‐

sions, amounts, etc.); **~t** *a.* [L *discrepo* be discordant]

**discre'te** *a.* Separate, individually distinct, discontinuous. [L (DISCERN)]

**discre'tion** *n.* Liberty of deciding as one thinks fit, absolutely or within limits (use one's **~,** make such decision); (Law) court's degree of freedom to decide sentence etc.; prudence, good sense, (**age, years, of ~,** age at which one is fit to manage one's own affairs); **~ary** *a.*, left to discretion. [F f. L (prec.)]

**discri'min|āte** *v.t. & i.* Be, set up, or act on the basis of, a difference between or *between*, distinguish *from* another; make a distinction esp. on grounds of race or colour (**~ate against,** select for unfavourable treatment by taxation etc.); observe distinctions carefully; have good judgement; **~ātĭng** *a.*, (esp.) discerning, acute; **~ā'tion,** **~ātor,** *ns.*; **~atĭve,** **~atorў,** *adjs.*, (esp. of treatment etc.) that varies with the object. [L *discrimino* (DISCERN)]

**discu'rsĭve** *a.* Expatiating, digressive, rambling. [L (*curro curs-* run)]

**di'scus** *n.* Heavy thick-centred disc thrown in ancient and modern athletic sports. [L f. Gk]

**discu'ss** *v.t.* Examine by argument, debate; hold conversation about; **~ion** (-shŏn) *n.* [L *discutio -cuss-* disperse]

**disdai'n. 1.** *n.* Scorn, contempt. **2.** *v.t.* Regard with disdain; think beneath oneself or one's notice (thing, *to* do, do*ing*). **3. ~ful** *a.* (**-lly**), scornful, showing disdain. [F f. L (DE-, DEIGN)]

**disea'se** (-zē'z) *n.* Unhealthy condition of body, plant, etc.; illness, sickness; particular kind of this with special symptoms or location; **~d** (-zd) *a.*, affected with disease, abnormal, disordered. [F (DIS-)]

**disembark(ation)** [F], **disembarrass, disembody, disembodiment.** See DIS- (1).

**disēmbow'el** *v.t.* (‖-ll-). Remove entrails of; **~ment** *n.* [DIS-]

**disencha'nt** (-ah'-) *v.t.* Free from enchantment or illusion; **~'ment** *n.* [F (DIS-)]

**disencumber, disendow(ment).** See DIS- (1).

**disēngā'ge** (-n-g-) *v.t. & i.* Detach, liberate, loosen; remove (troops) from (area of) fighting; become detached; **~d** (-jd) *a.*, (esp.)

at leisure to attend to any visitor or business that comes, vacant, uncommitted; ~**ment** (-jm-) *n.*, disengaging or being disengaged. [DIS-]

**disentail,   disentangle(ment), disenthral(l)(ment),   disentomb-(ment).** See DIS- (1).

**dĭsèstă′blĭsh** *v.t.* Terminate establishment of; deprive (Church) of State connection; ~**ment** *n.* [DIS-]

**disfavour, *favor.** See DIS- (2).

**dĭsfĭ′gure** (-ger) *v.t.* Spoil appearance of; ~**ment** *n.*, (esp.) blemish. [F (DIS-)]

**dĭsfrā′nchise** (-z) *v.t.* Deprive of rights as citizen or of franchise held; ~**ment** (-zm-) *n.* [DIS-]

**dĭsgōr′ge** *v.t. & i.* Eject (as) from throat (what has been swallowed, lit. or fig., esp. wrongfully taken, or abs.). [F (DIS-)]

**dĭsgrā′ce. 1.** *n.* Loss of favour, downfall from position of honour, ignominy (*is in disgrace*); thing or person involving dishonour, cause of reproach. **2.** *v.t.* Dismiss from favour, degrade from position of honour; be a disgrace to. **3.** ~**ful** (-sf-) *a.* (-lly), shameful, dishonourable, degrading. [F f. It. (DIS-)]

**dĭsgrŭ′ntled** (-teld) *a.* Discontented, sulky. [DIS-, GRUNT]

**dĭsguī′se** (-gī′z). **1.** *v.t.* Conceal identity of (*disguise oneself*, person or thing, *as* someone or something else, *with* false beard etc.); conceal, cover up, (*disguise one's intentions*). **2.** *n.* (Use of) changed dress or appearance for concealment or deception; disguised condition (BLESSING *in disguise*). [F (DIS-)]

**dĭsgŭ′st. 1.** *n.* Repugnance, strong aversion, indignation, (*at, for*); **in ~**, as a result of such feeling (*I left in disgust*). **2.** *v.t.* Cause disgust in (*disgusted with, at, by*). [F or It. (DIS-, GUSTO)]

**dĭsh. 1.** *n.* Shallow usu. flat-bottomed vessel of earthenware, glass, metal, etc., for holding food at meals or for cooking; food so held, particular kind of food (MADE *dish*; SIDE-*dish*); (colloq.) attractive person, esp. woman; dish-shaped receptacle, object, or cavity; (in *pl.*) all utensils used at meal (*wash the dishes*); ~**′cloth,** (for washing dishes); ~**′rag,** (for washing dishes); ~**′washer,** machine for washing dishes, water wagtail; ~-**water** (in which dishes have been

washed). **2.** *v.t.* Put (food) into dish ready for serving; make dish-shaped; (colloq.) circumvent, outmanœuvre; ~ **out,** (sl.) distribute, esp. carelessly or indiscriminately; ~ **up,** dish (food), prepare to serve (meal, or abs.), (fig.) present (facts, argument) attractively. [E f. L DISCUS]

**disharmony,   disharmonious, dishearten(ment).** See DIS- (2).

||**dĭshĕ′vel|led, *~|ed,** (-ld) *a.* (Of hair) loose, disordered; (of person) untidy, ruffled; ~**ment** *n.* [F (DIS-, *chevel* hair f. L *capillus*)]

**dishonest(y).** See DIS- (2). [F]

**dĭshŏ′nour, *dĭshŏ′nor,** (-sŏ′ner). **1.** *v.t.* Treat without honour or respect; refuse to accept or pay (cheque, bill of exchange); (arch.) violate chastity of. **2.** *n.* State of shame or disgrace, discredit; thing that causes such state. **3.** ~**able** *a.* (-bly), ignominious, causing disgrace (*to*), against dictates of honour, unprincipled, base. [F (DIS-)]

**dishorn.** See DIS- (3).

**dĭ′shў** *a.* (sl.) Very attractive. [DISH]

**dĭsĭllū′sion** (-zhon; *or* -ōō′-) *n.*, & *v.t.* Disenchant(ment), free(dom) from illusions; ~**ment** *n.* [DIS-]

**dĭsĭncĕ′ntĭve** *a. & n.* (Thing) that tends to discourage a particular (esp. economic) action etc.

**dĭsĭncl|ī′ne** (-n-k-) *v.t.* Make unwilling (*to* do, *for* course of action); ~**ĭnā′tion** *n.*, absence of liking or willingness.

**dĭsĭnfĕ′ct** *v.t.* Cleanse (room, clothes, etc.) of infection; ~**ant** *a. & n.*, (substance) having disinfecting qualities; ~**ion** *n.* [F (DIS-)]

**disinfest(ation).** See DIS- (1).

**dĭsĭnflā′tion** *n.* (Econ.) Policy designed to counteract inflation without producing disadvantages of deflation; ~**arў** *a.* [DIS-]

**disingenuous.** See DIS- (2).

**dĭsĭnhĕ′rĭt** *v.t.* Reject as one's heir, deprive of right of inheritance; ~**ance** *n.*, rejection from position of heir. [DIS-]

**dĭsĭ′ntĕgr|āte** *v.t. & i.* (~**able**). Separate into component parts; deprive of or lose cohesion; (Phys.) (cause to) undergo disintegration; ~**ā′tion** *n.*, (esp., Phys.) process in which nucleus emits particle(s) or divides into smaller nuclei; ~**ātor** *n.*

**disinter.** See DIS- (1). [F]

**dĭsĭ'nterĕst** (*or* -tr-) *n.* Absence of interest, unconcern; **~ĕd** *a.*, not influenced by one's own advantage, impartial, (*colloq.*) uninterested; **dĭsjoi'n** *v.t.*, separate, disunite, part; **dĭsjoi'nt** *v.t.*, take to pieces at the joints, dislocate, disturb working or connection of, (in *p.p.*, esp. of talk) incoherent, desultory; **dĭsjŭ'nction** *n.*, disjoining, separation; **dĭsjŭ'nctive** *a.*, disjoining, involving separation or alternative. [DIS-]

**dĭsk.** See DISC.

**dĭsli'ke. 1.** *v.t.* Not like, have aversion or objection to, (do*ing*, person, thing). **2.** *n.* Feeling that thing etc. is unattractive, unpleasant, etc.; object of this. [LIKE²]

**dĭ'slocǀāte** *v.t.* Disturb normal connection of (esp. joint in the body); put (machinery, affairs) out of order; **~ā'tion** *n.* [F or L (DIS-)]

**dĭslŏ'dge** *v.t.* Remove from established position; **~ment** (-jm-) *n.* [F (DIS-)]

**dĭsloyal(ty).** See DIS- (2). [F]

**dĭ'smal** (-z-) *a.* (**~ly**). Causing or showing gloom; miserable, sombre, dreary; (*colloq.*) feeble, inept. [AF f. L *dies mali* unlucky days]

**dĭsmă'ntle** *v.t.* Pull down, take to pieces; deprive of defences, equipment, etc. [F (DIS-)]

**dĭsmast.** See DIS- (3).

**dĭsmay'** *n.*, & *v.t.* (Fill with) consternation; discourage(ment); (reduce to) despair. [F f. Gmc (DIS-, MAY¹)]

**dĭsmĕ'mber** *v.t.* Tear or cut limbs from; partition (country etc.); divide up; **~ment** *n.* [F (DIS-)]

**dĭsmi'ss** *v.t.* (**~ible**). Send away, disperse, disband, (assembly, army); (Mil., in *imper.*) word of command at end of drilling; allow to go; send away (esp. dishonourably) from service or office (*was dismissed the*, or *from the*, *army*); put out of one's thoughts, cease to feel or discuss, treat (subject) summarily; (Law) send out of court, refuse further hearing to; (Crick.) put (batsman, side) out (*for* score); **~al** *n.*; **~ive** *a.* [F f. L (*mitto miss-* send)]

**dĭsmou'nt** *v.i.* & *t.* (Cause to) alight or fall from cycle, horseback, etc.; remove (thing) from its mount (esp. gun from carriage). [DIS-]

**disobedience, disobedient, disobey.** See DIS- (2). [F]

**dĭsobli'ge** *v.t.* Refuse to consider

convenience or wishes of. [F f. Rom. (DIS-)]

**dĭsŏr'der. 1.** *n.* Confusion; tumult, riot; disturbance of normal state of body, organ, etc.; ailment, disease. **2.** *v.t.* Disarrange, throw into confusion; put out of good health, upset. **3.** **~ly** *a.* (**-iness**), untidy, confused, riotous, contrary to public order or morality (*disorderly* HOUSE). [F (DIS-, ORDAIN)]

**disorganize, disorganization,** [F], **disorient(ate), disorientation.** See DIS- (1).

**dĭsow'n** (-ō'n) *v.t.* Refuse to recognize, repudiate, disclaim; renounce connection with or allegiance to. [DIS-]

**dĭspä'rage** *v.t.* (**~able** *pr.* -ĭja-). Speak slightingly of; bring into disrepute; **~ment** (-ĭjm-) *n.* [F (DIS-, PAR¹)]

**dĭ'sparate** *a.* Essentially different, unrelated, not comparable. [L *disparo* to separate]

**dĭspä'rĭtў** *n.* Inequality, difference, incongruity. [F f. L (DIS-)]

**dĭspä'ssionate** (-sho-) *a.* Free from emotion, impartial.

**dĭspä'tch,** ǁ**dĕs-. 1.** *v.t.* Send off to a destination or for a purpose; give the death-blow to, kill; get (task, business) promptly done, finish off; eat (food, meal) quickly. **2.** *n.* Dispatching; rapidity, efficiency; written message, esp. official communication on State or military affairs (mention in **~es**, distinction given by having one's actions etc. commended in these); **~-box**, **-case**, (for carrying these or other documents); **~-rider**, (esp.) motor--cyclist carrying military dispatches. [It. *dispacciare* or Sp. *despachar*]

**dĭspĕ'l** *v.t.* (**-ll-**). Disperse, scatter, (suspicions, fears, darkness). [L (*pello* drive)]

**dĭspĕ'nsǀe** *v.t.* & *i.* Distribute, deal out, administer (justice, sacrament); make up and give out (medicine etc.) according to prescription (**~ing** chemist, one qualified to do this); **~e with**, relax, give exemption from, (rule), render needless, do without; **~able** *a.* (**-bly**), that can be done without; **~arў** *n.*, place where medicines etc. are dispensed; **~ā'tion** *n.*, distributing, dealing out, ordering or management (esp. of the world) by Providence, arrangement made by Nature or Providence, exemption (*from* penalty or duty); ~**er** *n.*, (esp.) person who dispenses something, device that dispenses a selected quantity at a time. [F f. L (*pendo pens-* weigh)]

**dispeople.** See DIS- (3).

**disper'se** *v.t. & i.* Scatter; drive, go, or send in different directions; send to or station at different points; put in circulation, disseminate; separate (white light) into coloured constituents; ~**al** *n.* act of dispersing; ~**ion** *n.*, dispersing, being dispersed, **the D~ion**, the Jews dispersed among the Gentiles; ~**ive** *a.* [L *dispergo* (DI-[1], SPARSE)]

**dispi'rit** *v.t.* (esp. in *p.p.*) Make despondent. [DI-[1]]

**displa'ce** *v.t.* Shift from its place (~**d person**, one who has had to leave his home country as a result of war, persecution, etc.); remove from office; oust, take the place of, put something in the place of; ~**ment** (-sm-) *n.*, displacing or being displaced, amount by which thing is shifted from its place, amount of fluid displaced by thing floating or immersed in it (*a ship with a displacement of 11,000 tons*). [DIS-]

**display'. 1.** *v.t.* Exhibit, show; reveal, betray, allow to appear. **2.** *n.* Displaying, exhibition, show, (*is on display*); ostentation. [F f. L (*plico* fold)]

**displea'se** (-z) *v.t.* Offend, annoy, make indignant or angry, be unpleasing to; **be** ~**ed** (*at, with,* or abs.), disapprove, be indignant or dissatisfied; ~**ure** (-lĕ'zher) *n.*, displeased feeling, disapproval, dissatisfaction, anger. [F (DIS-)]

**dispor't.** (literary). **1.** *v.i. & refl.* Frolic, gambol, enjoy one*self*. **2.** *n.* Pastime. [AF (*porter* carry f. L)]

**dispo'se** (-z) *v.t. & i.* Place suitably, at intervals, or in order; bring (person, mind) into certain state (esp. in *pass.*, have a specified tendency of mind: *be well* or *ill disposed*; *not disposed to be lenient*); incline, make willing or desirous, *to* something or *to to* do; determine course of events (*man proposes, God disposes*); ~ **of**, do what one will with, get rid of, sell, settle, finish, kill, prove (claim, argument, opponent) to be incorrect, consume (food); ~**able**, (*a.*; -**bly**) that can be disposed of, made over, or used, at one's disposal, that is designed to be thrown away

after one use, (*n.*) disposable article; ~**al** *n.*, disposing *of*, disposing, (at one's ~**al**, available for one's use, subject to one's orders or decisions). [F (POSE)]

**disposi'tion** (-zǐ'-) *n.* Setting in order, arrangement, relative position of parts; (usu. in *pl.*) plan, preparations, (*make* one's *dispositions*), stationing of troops ready for attack, defence, etc.; temperament (*has a cheerful disposition*), natural tendency; inclination *to*. [F f. L (DIS-)]

**disposse'ss** (-oz-) *v.t.* Oust, dislodge, (person); deprive (*of*); **disposse'ssion** (-zĕ'shon), ~'**or**, *ns.* [F (DIS-)]

**dispraise.** See DIS- (2). [F]

**disproo'f** *n.* Refutation; **dispro've** (-ōō'v) *v.t.*, prove to be false. [DIS-]

**dispropor'tion** *n.* Lack of proportion; being out of proportion; ~**ate** *a.*, relatively too large or small. [DIS-]

**dispu'te. 1.** *v.i. & t.* Argue, hold disputation, (*with, against,* person, *on, about,* subject); discuss esp. heatedly (*whether, how,* etc.; point, question); controvert, call in question, (statement, view); resist (advance, landing); contend for, strive to win, (pre-eminence, possession, victory, etc.). **2.** (*or* dǐ'-) *n.* Controversy, debate, (**in** ~, being argued about; **beyond, past, without,** ~, certainly, indisputably); heated contention, quarrel, difference of opinion. **3. dispu'table** (*or* dǐ'-) *a.* (-**bly**), open to question; **dispu'tant** *n.*, party to discussion; **disputa'tion** *n.*, argumentative debate, formal attack on and defence of set question or thesis; **disputa'tious** (-shus) *a.*, fond of argument. [F f. L (*puto* reckon)]

**disqua'lif|y** (-ŏ'l-) *v.t.* Make or pronounce unfit, disable, (*for* some purpose or office); debar from competition because of infringement of rules; ~**ica'tion** *n.*, (esp.) thing that disqualifies. [DIS-]

**disqui'et. 1.** *n.* Uneasiness, anxiety, perturbation. **2.** *v.t.* Cause disquiet to. **3. disqui'etude** *n.*, state of disquiet.

**disquisi'tion** (-zǐ'-) *n.* Long or elaborate treatise or discourse on subject. [F f. L (*quaero quisit-* seek)]

**disregar'd. 1.** *v.t.* Pay no attention to, treat as of no importance. **2.** *n.* Indifference, neglect, (*of, for*). [DIS-]

**dĭsrĕpair'** *n.* Bad condition due to lack of repairs (*is in disrepair, in a state of disrepair*); **dĭsrĕ'pŭtable** *a.* (**-bly**), discreditable, of bad repute, not respectable in character or appearance; **dĭsrĕpū'te** *n.*, lack of good repute, discredit; **dĭsrĕspĕ'ct** *n.*, lack of respect, discourtesy; **dĭsrĕspĕ'ctful** *a.* (**-lly**), showing disrespect. [DIS-]

**dĭsrōbe.** See DIS- (1).

**dĭsrū'pt** *v.t.* Separate forcibly, shatter; interrupt flow or continuity of; **~ion** *n.*; **~ĭve** *a.* [L (RUPTURE)]

**dĭssă'tĭsǀfy** *v.t.* Fail to satisfy, make discontented; **~fǎ'ction** *n.*, fact or condition or cause of being dissatisfied. [DIS-]

**dĭssĕ'ct** *v.t.* Cut into pieces; cut up (animal, plant) to show its parts, structure, etc.; examine part by part, analyse, criticize in detail; **~ion, ~or,** *ns.* [L (SECTION)]

**dĭssĕ'mble** *v.t. & i.* Conceal or disguise (intention, character, feeling, etc.), practise such concealment; talk or act hypocritically. [F f. L (DIS-, SIMILAR)]

**dĭssĕ'mĭnǀāte** *v.t.* Scatter about, sow in various places (esp. fig. of doctrines, sedition, disease, etc.); *disseminated* SCLEROSIS; **~ā'tion, ~ātor,** *ns.* [L (DIS-, SEMEN)]

**dĭssĕ'nǀt. 1.** *v.i.* Refuse to assent, think differently or express such difference (*from*), esp. in religious doctrine from an established, national, or orthodox church. **2.** *n.* (Expression of) difference of opinion, refusal to accept doctrines of established, national, or orthodox church. **3. ~sion** (-shon) *n.*, discord arising from difference of opinion; **~ter** *n.*, (esp., *D-*) member of sect that has separated itself from the Church of England; **dĭssĕ'ntient** (-shĭ-, -shĕnt) *a. & n.*, (person) disagreeing with majority or official view. [L (DIS-, *sentio* feel)]

**dĭssertā'tion** *n.* Detailed discourse, esp. as submitted for higher degree in university. [L (*disserto* discuss)]

**dĭssĕr'vĭce** *n.* Ill turn done (*to*), esp. by misguided attempt to help. [DIS-]

**dĭ'ssĭdenǀt** *a. & n.* (Person) disagreeing, at variance, esp. with established government etc.; dissentient; **~ce** *n.* [F f. L (DIS-, *sedeo* sit)]

**dĭssimilar(ity).** See DIS- (2).

**dĭssĭmĭlā'tion** *n.* (Philol.) Tendency to avoid repetition of a sound (as in change of *cinnamom* to *cinnamon*); **dĭssĭ'mŭlate** *v.t. & i.* (**-lable**), dissemble; **dĭssĭmŭlā'tion** *n.* [L (DIS-, SIMILAR)]

**dĭ'ssĭpātǀe** *v.t. & i.* Dispel, disperse, (clouds, darkness, fears, etc.); squander (money), fritter away (energies, attention); break up entirely; **~ĕd** *a.*, given to dissipation; **dĭssipā'tion** *n.*, (esp.) frivolous or dissolute way of life; **~or** *n.* [L (DIS-, *sipo* shake)]

**dĭssō'cĭǀāte** (*or* -shī-) *v.t. & i.* (**~able**). Disconnect, separate, in thought or fact (*from*; **~ate** oneself **from**, declare oneself unconnected with); become dissociated; **~ā'tion** *n.*; **~ātive** (*or* -sha-) *a.* [L (DIS-, ASSOCIATE)]

**dĭssō'lve** (-z-) *v.t. & i.* Make or become liquid, esp. by immersion or dispersion in liquid (**~ into tears,** begin to weep copiously); (cause to) vanish (*ghost dissolves into thin air*); (Cinemat.) change gradually (*into* a different picture); dismiss or disperse (assembly, esp. parliament); put an end to (partnership etc.); annul; **dĭssŏ'lŭble** *a.* (**-bly**), that can be disintegrated, loosened, or disconnected; **dĭssŏlūbĭ'lĭtў** *n.*; **dĭ'ssolūte** (*or* -ōot) *a.*, lax in morals, licentious; **dĭssolū'tion** (*or* -lōō'-) *n.*, disintegration, undoing or relaxing *of* bond, partnership, marriage, etc., dismissal or dispersal of assembly esp. parliament for new election, death, coming or being brought to an end, disappearance. [L (DIS-, *solvo solut-* loosen)]

**dĭ'ssonanǀt** *a.* Not in harmony, harsh-toned, incongruous; **~ce** *n.* [F or L (DIS-, *sono* to SOUND[1])]

**dĭssuā'ǀde** (-swā'd) *v.t.* Give advice or exercise influence to discourage or divert (person *from*); **~sion** (-zhon) *n.*; **~sĭve** *a.* [L (DIS-, *suadeo* advise)]

**dĭssy'llable** etc. See DISYLLABLE etc.

**dĭ'staff** (-ahf) *n.* Cleft stick holding wool or flax wound for spinning by hand; corresp. part of spinning-wheel; **~ side,** female branch of family. [E]

**dĭ'stance. 1.** *n.* Being far off, remoteness; avoidance of familiarity, aloofness (*esp. keep* one's, or *at a, distance*); extent of space between (**within hailing, walking,** etc., **~,**

near enough to reach easily by that means); distant point (*to, from, a distance*; **at a ~,** far off, not very near); remoter field of vision (*in the distance*); **middle ~,** in painted or actual landscape, part between foreground and far part); space of time (*at this distance of time*). 2. *v.t.* Place or make seem far off; leave far behind in race or competition. 3. **di'stant** *a.*, far, or at a specified distance, away or *from* (*10 miles distant*), remote in position, time, resemblance, relation, (*distant prospect, ages, likeness, cousin*), not intimate, reserved, cool, (of railway signal) in advance of home signal to give warning of its setting; **distant early warning,** N. Amer. radar system for detection of missile attack. [F f. L (DI-[1], *sto* stand)]

**distă'ste** *n.* Dislike, repugnance, (slight) aversion, (*for*); **~'ful** (-tf-) *a.* (-**lly**), causing distaste, disagreeable *to*. [DIS-]

**distĕ'mper**[1]. 1. *v.t.* (arch.; usu. in *p.p.*) Derange (mind etc.; *a distempered fancy*). 2. *n.* Dog-disease with catarrh and weakness. [L (DIS-)]

**distĕ'mper**[2]. 1. *n.* Method of painting on plaster etc. without oil; paint so used. 2. *v.t.* Paint (wall etc.) in distemper. [F or L (prec.)]

**distĕ'n|d** *v.t.* & *i.* Swell out (balloon, vein, nostril, etc.) by pressure from within; **~sible** *a.* (-**bly**); **~sion** (-shŏn) *n.* [L (TEND[1])]

**di'stich** (-k) *n.* (Pros.) Couplet. [L f. Gk (*stikhos* line)]

**disti'l, *-l|l,** *v.i.* & *t.* (-**ll-**). Trickle down, come or give forth in drops; turn to vapour by heat, condense by cold, and re-collect (liquid, esp. to remove dissolved impurities or to separate mixed liquids); extract essence of (plant etc. or fig. doctrine etc.); drive (volatile constituent) *off* or *out* by heat; make (whisky, essence, etc.) by distilling raw materials; undergo distillation; **~lā'tion** *n.*; **~ler** *n.*, (esp.) maker of alcoholic liquor; **~lery** *n.*, factory etc. for distilling liquor. [L (DE-, *stillo* drip)]

**disti'nct** *a.* Not identical, separate, different in quality or kind, (*from*, or abs.); clearly perceptible, definite, unmistakable, positive, (*distinct change, advantage*; *I distinctly saw, heard*). [L (DISTINGUISH)]

**disti'nction** *n.* Making of a difference, discrimination; the differ-

erence made; being different; thing that differentiates (**draw a ~,** point out or lay down difference), name, mark, title; showing of special consideration (*treat with distinction*); mark of honour; distinguished character, excellence, (*a man of distinction*); **disti'nctive** *a.*, distinguishing, characteristic; **distingué** (dĭstă'ngā) *a.*, having distinguished air, features, manners, etc. [F f. L (prec.)]

**disti'nguish** (-nggw-) *v.t.* & *i.* Be, see, point out, the difference of (thing, thing *from* another); make out by listening, looking, etc.; differentiate, draw distinctions (between or *between*); be a mark or property of; make one*self* prominent or noteworthy (*by* gallantry etc.); **~ed** (-ĭsht) *a.*, (esp.) eminent, having distinction, *distingué*. [F or L (DI-[1], *stinguo stinct-* extinguish)]

**distŏ'rt** *v.t.* Pull out of shape, make crooked or unshapely, (actually or, as by curved mirror etc., apparently); misrepresent (motives, facts, statements); **~ion** *n.*, (also, Electr.) change in form of signal during transmission etc., usu. with impairment of quality. [L (*torqueo tort-* twist)]

**distră'ct** *v.t.* Draw (attention, the mind, etc.) away *from* or in different directions; divide or confuse the attention of, bewilder, (usu. in *p.p.*); madden; **~ion** *n.*, diversion of, thing that diverts, the mind, interruption, lack of concentration, amusement, relaxation from work, confusion, perplexity, frenzy, (**to ~ion,** almost to a state of madness). [L (DIS-, *traho tract-* draw)]

**distrai'nt** *n.* (Law). Seizure of goods as method of enforcing payment; **distrai'n** *v.i.*, levy distraint (*upon* person, his goods, or abs.). [F f. L (DI-[1], *stringo strict-* draw tight)]

**distrait** (dĭstrā') *a.* (*fem. ~e e̅pr̄ -ā't*). Absent-minded, not paying attention; distraught; **distrau'ght** (-aw't) *a.*, much agitated in mind, nearly crazy with worry etc. [F (DISTRACT)]

**distrĕ'ss. 1.** *n.* Severe pressure of pain, sorrow, etc.; anguish; lack of money or necessaries; damage or danger to ship etc. (*in distress*); exhaustion, breathlessness; misfortune; (Law) distraint; **~signal** (from ship in danger). 2. *v.t.* Subject to distress; cause anxiety to; vex;

make unhappy. **3.** ~ed (-č'st) *a.*, (esp.) impoverished; ‖~ed **area**, region of high unemployment; ~ful *a.* (literary) giving or suffering distress. [F f. Rom. (DISTRAINT)]

**distri'but|e** *v.t.* Deal out, give share of to each of a number; spread about, scatter, put at different points; divide into parts, arrange, classify; (Print.) separate (type that has been set up) and return each letter to its proper box in the case; ~ary̆ *n.*, river or glacier branch that does not return to main stream after leaving it (as in a delta); **distri-bū'tion** *n.*; ~**ive**, (*a.*) of, concerned with, produced by, distribution, (Logic, Gram.) referring to each individual of a class (*distributive* PRONOUN), (*n.*) distributive word (*each, neither, every*); ~**or** *n.*, (esp.) agent who markets goods, electric cable from which lines run to individual premises, device in internal combustion engine for passing current to each sparking-plug in turn. [L (*tribuo -but-* assign)]

**di'strict** *n.* Territory marked off for administrative purpose; ‖division of county; tract of country with common characteristics, region; \*~ **attorney**, prosecuting officer of a district; ‖~ **nurse**, nurse serving rural or urban district. [F f. L (DISTRAINT)]

**distrust(ful).** See DIS- (2).

**distür'b** *v.t.* Break the rest or quiet or calm of; agitate, worry; move from settled position (*nothing has been disturbed, don't let me disturb you, don't disturb yourself*); (Psych., in *p.p.*) emotionally or mentally unstable or abnormal; ~ance *n.*, interruption of tranquillity, agitation, tumult, uproar. [F f. L (DIS-, *turba* tumult]

**disunion, disunite, disunity.** See DIS- (2, 1).

**disü'se. 1.** (-z) *v.t.* Cease to use. **2.** (-s) *n.* Disused state. [F (DIS-)]

**disy'll|able, diss-,** *n.* Word or metrical foot of two syllables; ~ă'bĭc *a.* [F f. L f. Gk (DI-²)]

**ditch. 1.** *n.* Long narrow excavation, esp. to hold or conduct water or serve as boundary (**last ~**, place of final desperate defence; DIE² *in the last ditch*); ~**water** (stagnant in ditch; esp. *dull as ditch-water*). **2.** *v.i. & t.* Make or repair ditches (esp. *hedging and ditching*); provide with ditches, drain; (sl.) abandon, dis-

card, defeat, frustrate; (sl.) make forced landing on sea, bring (aircraft) down thus; drive (vehicle) into ditch. [E]

**di'ther** (-dh-). **1.** *v.i.* Tremble, quiver; vacillate. **2.** *n.* State of dithering; (colloq.) state of tremulous excitement or apprehension; ~y̆ *a.* [var. of didder DODDER²]

**di'thy̆r|ămb** (-m) *n.* Greek choric hymn, wild in character; passionate or inflated poem, speech, or writing; ~ă'mbĭc *a.* (-ically). [L f. Gk]

**di'ttany̆** *n.* Herb formerly supposed to have healing power. [F f. L f. Gk]

**di'ttō** *n.* (*pl.* ~s). (In accounts, inventories, etc., or colloq.) the aforesaid, the same or a similar thing. [It. f. L (DICTUM)]

**di'tty̆** *n.* Short simple song. [F f. L (DICTATE)]

**diūrě'tĭc** *a.* (~ally) & *n.* (Drug) causing increased excretion of urine. [F or L f. Gk (DI-³, *oureō* urinate)]

**diŭr'nal** *a.* (~ly). Of the day, not nocturnal; (Astron.) occupying a day; of each day; (Zool.) active in daytime. [L *diurnalis* (*dies* day)]

**di'va** (dē'-) *n.* Great woman singer, prima donna. [It. f. L, = goddess]

**di'vag|āte** *v.i.* (literary). Digress; ~ā'tion *n.* [L (DI-¹, *vagor* wander)]

**di'valent** (or divā'-) *a.* (Chem.) Having a valence of two. [DI-², VALENCE]

**divā'n** (or di'văn) *n.* Long low seat against room-wall; ~ (**bed**), couch or bed without head- or foot-board. [F or It. f. Turk. f. Arab. f. Pers.]

**dive. 1.** *v.i.* (~d, \*dove *pr.* dōv). Plunge, esp. head foremost, into water etc.; (of aircraft) plunge steeply downwards; (of submarine) submerge; put one's hand *into* water, vessel, pocket, handbag, etc.; penetrate or search mentally *into*; **diving-bell**, open-bottomed box or bell with air supplied by tube, in which person can be let down into deep water; **diving-board**, elevated board for diving from; **diving-suit**, watertight suit, usu. with helmet and air-supply for work under water. **2.** *n.* Act of diving; (colloq.) disreputable place of resort; ~**-bom-ber**, aircraft specially designed to aim and release bombs while diving towards target; ~**-bomb** *v.t.* **3.** **di'ver** *n.*; (esp.) user of diving-suit, diving bird (esp. loon). [E]

**divér'|ge** *v.i. & t.* (Cause to) go

in different directions from point; take different courses from each other; go aside *from* track (lit. or fig.); deflect; ~**gent** *a.*, diverging; ~**gence** *n.* [L (DI-[1], *vergo* incline)]

**di´vers** (-z) *a.* (arch.) Various, sundry, several. [F f. L (foll.)]

**diver´|se** *a.* Unlike in nature or qualities; varied, changeful; ~**sify** *v.t.* make diverse, vary, spread (investment) over several enterprises or products; ~**sion** (-shon) *n.*, deflecting, deviation, diverting *of* attention, manœuvre to secure this, recreation, pastime, ||alternative route when road is temporarily closed to traffic; ~**sity** *n.*, being diverse; ~**t** *v.t.*, turn aside (stream etc. *from, to,* or abs.) turn elsewhere, ward off, draw attention of (away *from* one thing *to* another), distract, amuse, (in *part.* as *a.*) amusing. [F f. L (DI-[1], *verto* vers-turn)]

**dive´st** *v.t.* Unclothe, strip *of* garment etc.; deprive, rid, *of* (~ oneself *of,* abandon). [F f. L (VEST)]

**divi´de.** 1. *v.t.* & *i.* Separate into or *in*(*to*) parts (**\*~d highway,** dual carriageway; ~**d skirt,** culotte); separate, part, cut off or *off,* (things, thing *from*); mark out into parts, specify different kinds of; cause to disagree, set at variance (*opinion is divided*; ~**d against itself,** formed into factions); distribute, deal *out* (*among, between*), share *with* others; find how many times number contains another (*divide 20 by 5*), do division, (of number) be contained in (number) without remainder; part (legislative assembly etc.) into two sets in voting, be thus parted. 2. *n.* Watershed; (fig.) dividing line. 3. **di´vidend** *n.*, number to be divided by divisor, sum payable as profit of joint-stock company or to creditors of insolvent estate, individual's share of this, (fig.) benefit from any action; ~**r** *n.*, (esp.) screen, piece of furniture, etc., to divide room into two parts, (in *pl.*) measuring compasses. [L *divido -vis-*]

**divi´ne** *a., n.,* & *v.* 1. *a.* (~**r, ~st**). Of, from, like God or a god (*divine beauty, purity,* etc.; ~ **right of kings,** doctrine that kings have authority independently of their subjects' will); sacred (~ **service,** meeting for worship); superhumanly excellent, gifted, or beautiful; (colloq.) excellent, delightful. 2. *n.* Theologian.

3. *v.t.* & *i.* Discover by inspiration, magic, intuition, etc.; foresee, conjecture; practise divination; **divining-rod** (see DOWSE[2]). 4. **divina´tion** *n.*, divining the future etc., skilful forecast, good guess; **divi´natory** *a.*; ~**r** *n.*, (esp.) expert in divination; **divi´nity** *n.*, being divine, a god, theology. [F f. L *divinus*]

**divi´sion** (-zhon) *n.* Dividing or being divided (~ **of labour,** improvement of efficiency by giving different parts of manufacturing process etc. to different persons); disagreement, discord, (*division of opinion*); process of dividing number by another (~ **sign, ÷**; **long ~,** with details of calculation written down; **short ~,** with quotient written down directly); dividing line; section; administrative etc. district; definite part (under single command) of army or navy, police, government or industrial organization, High Court, etc.; (Bot.) major taxonomic grouping; ||part of county or borough returning a Member of Parliament; ~**al** *a.* (**-lly**); **divi´sible** (-z-) *a.* (**-bly**), capable of being divided; **divisibi´lity** (-z-) *n.*; **divi´sive** *a.*, tending to divide, esp. in opinion etc.; **divi´sor** (-z-) *n.*, number by which dividend is to be divided, number that divides another without remainder. [F f. L (DIVIDE)]

**divor´ce.** 1. *n.* Legal dissolution of marriage; judicial separation of married pair; decree of nullity of marriage; (fig.) severance, separation. 2. *v.t.* Legally dissolve marriage between; separate (spouse) by divorce *from*; obtain divorce *from* (spouse); detach, separate (things, thing *from,* esp. fig.). 3. **divorcee´** *n.*, divorced person. [F f. L (DIVERSE)]

**di´vot** *n.* (Golf.) Piece of turf dislodged by club-head in making a stroke. [orig. unkn.]

**divu´lge** *v.t.* Disclose, reveal, (secret etc.); **divulga´tion** *n.* [L *divulgo* publish]

**di´vvy** (colloq.) 1. *n.* Dividend. 2. *v.t.* ~ (**up**), share out. [abbr.]

**Di´xie[1]** *n.* Southern States of U.S.; ~**land,** Dixie, kind of jazz. [orig. uncert.]

||**di´xie[2]** *n.* Large iron pot in which stew, tea, etc., are made or carried

by campers or soldiers. [Hind. f. Pers.]

**D.I.Y.** *abbr.* do-it-yourself.

**di′zzy. 1.** *a.* (**-ily, -iness**). Dazed, unsteady; making giddy (*dizzy height, speed*). **2.** *v.t.* Make dizzy, bewilder. [E]

**D.J.** *abbr.* ‖dinner-jacket; disc jockey.

‖**D.L.** *abbr.* Deputy Lieutenant.

**D.Litt.** *abbr.* Doctor of Letters. [L *Doctor Litterarum*]

**DM, D-mark,** *abbr.* Deutschmark.

**D.Mus.** *abbr.* Doctor of Music.

**DNA** *abbr.* deoxyribonucleic acid.

‖**D-notice** (dē′nōtĭs) *n.* Formal request to news editors not to publish items on specified subjects, for reasons of security. [*defence*, NOTICE]

**dō¹.** See DOH.

**do²** (dōō) *n.* (*pl.* **dos, do's;** colloq.) Hoax, swindle; ‖entertainment, elaborate operation etc.; (in *pl.*) share (**fair dos!,** share fairly); **dos and don'ts,** rules of behaviour. [foll.]

**do³** (dōō, do) *v.t., i.,* & *aux.* (**did;** DONE; DOING; **doable** *pr.* dōō′a-; 2 *sing. pres.* arch. **dost** *pr.* dŭ-, **doest** *pr.* dōō′ĭst; 3 *sing. pres.* **does** *pr.* dŭz, doz, arch. **doth** *pr.* dŭ- or **doeth** *pr.* dōō′ĭth; 2 *sing. past* arch. **didst, diddest;** *neg.* **do not,** colloq. **don't** *pr.* dōnt, **does not,** colloq. **doesn't** *pr.* dŭz′ent, **did not,** colloq. **didn't** *pr.* dĭd′ent). **1.** *v.t.* Perform, carry out, effect, complete, bring about, produce, make, provide, (*do work, duty, bidding, penance, good, right, wrong; do 30 miles to the gallon, 100 m.p.h.; do copies, painting, omelette; we do bed and breakfast; do one's* BEST; *easier said than done; do* BATTLE; *do one's* BIT¹; **do a degree,** study for and obtain it; DO-GOODER; *do the* HONOURS; **do it,** be successful; **do a play,** give performance(s) of it; **do something for** or **to,** colloq., enhance appearance or quality of; *do the* TRICK; **that's done it,** excl. of achievement or dismay; **do-it--yourself,** (to be) done or made by amateur handyman); operate on, deal with, (*do to* DEATH; **do the dishes,** wash up; **do the flowers,** arrange them; **do one's hair,** comb or arrange it; **do one's nut,** sl., be very worried or angry; **do a room,** clean it or paint it etc.); cook, esp. to the right degree (*do it in the oven; do* BROWN; *done to a* TURN; *overdone*);

solve (*do sum, problem*); translate or transform (*into* English, book *into* film etc.); work at (lesson, subject); play the part of, act like, (*did Lear; do the host*); **do a,** colloq., act like *Garbo* etc.); (colloq.) visit, see sights of, (place, entertainment; *do London, a show*); (sl.) rob, prosecute, convict, have sexual intercourse with; bestow, grant, impart, give, (*does him credit; do me a favour, a service; does me good, harm; do* JUSTICE *to*); (colloq.) provide food etc. for (*they do one very well here*); **do oneself well,** make liberal provision for one's own comfort); ‖satisfy (*that will do me nicely; do* PROUD); traverse (distance); (sl.) undergo (term of punishment); exhaust, tire out; (sl.) defeat, ruin, kill; **do (in the eye),** cheat, swindle. **2.** *v.i.* Act, proceed, perform deeds, (*do as the Romans do; would do well to refuse;* **do or die,** be undeterred by danger); make an end (*have* DONE *with*); be in progress (**nothing doing,** nothing happening, no prospect of success; **what is to do,** what is happening; TO-*do*); (of person or thing) fare, get on (well, badly, etc.; *mother and child doing well;* **do well for oneself,** prosper; **do well out of,** profit by; **how do you do?** conventional greeting on being introduced); be suitable or acceptable, suffice, serve the purpose, (*it doesn't do to worry;* MAKE *do;* **that will do,** no more is needed, as *int.* = stop it). **3.** *v. aux.* w. inf. as pres. or past or imper. (*a*) for special emphasis (*I do wish I could; do tell me*) esp. in contrast with what precedes or follows (*but I did see him; I did go but she wasn't in*), (*b*) for inversion (*rarely does it happen that, little did I imagine that, did he but know it*), (*c*) in questions and negations exc. w. some aux. vbs. (*do you dine; did he not come?; I did not go; he doesn't smoke; don't be silly*); **don't-care** *n.,* person who is careless or indifferent; **don't-know** *n.,* person who does not answer definitely to questionnaire item etc. **4.** *v. substitute.* (*a*) replacing v. and taking its construction (*I treat him as he does me*), (*b*) replacing v. and obj. etc. (*if you knew him as well as I do*), (*c*) as ellipt. aux. (*did you see him? —yes, I did; why don't you answer?—but I did!*), (*d*) with *so, it, which,* etc., (*I wanted to see him and I did so; when visiting London, as I seldom do; if you want to tell him, do it now*), (*e*) in emphatic repetition (*tell me, do!*; *you don't know me, do you?*). **5. do away with,** abolish, kill; **do by,** treat, deal with, in specified way; **do down,** (colloq.) overcome, cheat, swindle; **do for,** be satisfactory or sufficient for, (colloq.) destroy, ruin, kill, ‖(colloq.) act as housekeeper etc. for; **do in,** (sl.) ruin, kill, (colloq.) exhaust, tire out; **do out,** clean or redecorate (room); **do over,** (sl.) attack, beat, *(colloq.) do again; **do to,** = *do by*; **do up,** fasten, make into a parcel or bundle (*done up in brown paper*), refurbish, adorn (*oneself*), (sl.) ruin or beat; **do with,** accept, find useful or sufficient, use, treat, (*what shall we do with this food, these people?*; *not know what to do with oneself,* be embarrassed or bored); *could do with,* (colloq.) would be glad to have; *to do with,* concerned with, related to; *have to do with,* be concerned with, have dealings with; *what did you do with it?* where did you put it?; **do without,** forgo, complete one's task in the absence of (thing expressed or implied). **6. ~'er** *n.*, (esp.) one who acts rather than merely talking or thinking. [E]

**do.** *abbr.* ditto.

**dŏc** *n.* (colloq.) Doctor. [abbr.]

**dŏ'cĭle** *a.* Teachable, submissive, easily managed; **docĭ'lĭtў** *n.* [L (*doceo* teach)]

**dŏck**[1] *n.* Kind of coarse weed. [E]

**dŏck**[2] *v.t.* Cut short (animal's tail), cut short tail of (animal); lessen, deduct, deprive *of*, put limits on (person, wages, supplies, etc.). [E]

**dŏck**[3]. **1.** *n.* Artificial enclosed body of water in which ships may be loaded, unloaded, or repaired (**dry ~,** dry enclosure for repairing or building; **floating ~,** floating structure usable as dry dock; **in ~,** colloq., in hospital or repair-shop); (usu. in *pl.*) range of docks with wharves and offices, *ship's berth, wharf; **~'land,** district near docks; **~'yard,** area with docks and all shipbuilding and repairing appliances, esp. for naval use. **2.** *v.t.* Bring (ship), (of ship) come, into dock; furnish with dock(s); join (spacecraft) together in space, be thus joined. **3. ~'er** *n.*, labourer in docks. [Du. *docke*]

**dŏck**[4] *n.* Enclosure in criminal

court for prisoner; **in the ~,** on trial (lit. or fig.). [Flem. *dok* cage]

**dŏ'ckėt. 1.** *n.* ‖Document recording payment of customs duties, nature of goods delivered, jobs done, etc.; voucher, order form. **2.** *v.t.* Label with docket. [orig. unkn.]

**dŏ'ctor. 1.** *n.* Holder of highest university degree in any faculty (often honorary; used as prefix to surname); physician (**what the ~ ordered,** colloq., something beneficial or desirable); (colloq.) one who carries out repairs (lit. or fig.); (arch.) learned man. **2.** *v.t.* (colloq.) Treat (patient, *oneself*) medically; castrate, spay; patch up; adulterate; falsify. **3. ~al** *a.* (-lly), (esp.) of the degree of doctor, of learned authority; **~ate** *n.*, doctor's degree. [F f. L (*doceo* teach)]

**dŏ'ctrĭn|e** *n.* What is taught, body of instruction; religious, political, scientific, etc., belief, dogma, or tenet; **~air'e,** (*n.*) person who applies principles pedantically with no allowance for circumstances, (*a.*) theoretical and unpractical; **~air'ĭsm** *n.*; **dŏctrī'nal** (or dŏ'ktrī-) *a.* (-lly). [F f. L *doctrina* (prec.)]

**dŏ'cŭment. 1.** *n.* Thing, esp. title-deed, writing or inscription, that furnishes evidence (esp. in law or commerce). **2.** (-ĕnt) *v.t.* Prove by or provide with documents or evidence. **3. dŏcŭmĕ'ntalĭst** *n.*, person engaged in documentation; **dŏcŭmĕ'ntarў,** (*a.*; -ĭly) pertaining to or consisting of documents, factual, based on real events, (*n.*) documentary film etc.; **dŏcŭmĕntā'tion** *n.*, (esp.) accumulation, classification, and dissemination of information, material thus collected. [F f. L (prec.)]

**dŏ'dder**[1] *n.* Threadlike twining parasitic plant. [orig. uncert.]

**dŏ'dder**[2] *v.i.* Tremble owing to frailty, palsy, etc.; totter, be feeble; **~er** *n.*, feeble or inept person; **~ў** *a.* (-iness). [obs. dial. *dadder*]

**dōdĕ'ca-** in *comb.* Twelve; **~gon** *n.*, plane figure with 12 sides and angles; **~hĕ'dron** *n.*, solid with 12 faces; **~sўllable** *n.*, metrical line of 12 syllables. [Gk]

**dŏdge. 1.** *n.* Quick side-movement; trick, artifice, clever expedient. **2.** *v.i.* & *t.* Move to and fro, change position, move quickly *round, about,* or *behind*, obstacle so as to elude pursuer, blow, etc.; quibble, prevaricate; baffle by artfulness, trifle with; elude (pursuer, blow, etc.) by sideward deviation etc.; evade by trickery (*dodge paying* one's *fare*; *dodge the* COLUMN). **3.** dŏ'dgem *n.*, small electrically-powered car at fun-fair, in which driver bumps into similar cars in enclosure; dŏ'dger *n.*, (esp.) artful person; dŏ'dgy *a.* (-ily, -iness), cunning, (colloq.) awkward, tricky. [orig. unkn.]

dō'dō *n.* (*pl.* ~s). Extinct bird of Mauritius; as dead as the ~, entirely obsolete. [Port. *doudo* simpleton]

dōe *n.* Female of fallow deer, reindeer, hare or rabbit; ~'skin (dōs'-), skin of fallow deer. [E]

‖D.O.E. *abbr.* Department of the Environment.

doer, does, doesn't, doest, doeth. See DO³.

dŏff *v.t.* Take off (hat, clothing). [*do off*]

dŏg. **1.** *n.* Carnivorous quadruped of many breeds with and domesticated, one used for hunting, male of dog, wolf (also ~-wolf), or fox (also ~-fox), (BOTTOM *dog*; not a ~'s chance, not even the least chance; every ~ has his day, no one is always unlucky; die like a ~, miserably or shamefully; like a ~'s dinner, colloq., smartly or flashily (dressed, arranged, etc.); give a ~ a bad name and hang him, nicknaming or slander is effective; go to the ~s, be ruined; HAIR *of the dog that bit* one; HELP *lame dog over stile*; HOT *dog*; keep a ~ and bark oneself, do work for which one employs others; ~ in the manger, one who prevents others from enjoying what is useless to him; put on ~, colloq., behave pretentiously; RAIN *cats and dogs*; *let* SLEEP*ing dogs lie*; ‖the ~s, colloq., greyhound racing; TOP¹ *dog*; like a ~ with two tails, delighted); despicable person (esp. *dirty dog*), (colloq.) fellow (*sly, lucky, gay, dog*; SEA-*dog*); mechanical device for gripping etc.; FIRE*dogs*. **2.** *v.t.* (-gg-). Follow closely, pursue, track, (person, his *steps*). **3.** ~-biscuit (for feeding dogs); ~'cart, two-wheeled driving-cart with cross seats back to back; ~-clutch (with teeth of one part engaging in slots in the other); ~-collar, lit., and fig. of person's high straight collar divided at back, (colloq.) clerical collar; ~ days, hottest period of year; ~-eared, (of corner of book-page) turned down through use; ~-end (sl.) cigarette-end; ~'fight, fight (as) between dogs, general uproar, (colloq.) fight between aircraft; ~'fish, small shark; ~'house, *kennel; in the ~house*, (sl.) in disgrace; dog LATIN; ~-leg(ged), bent like a dog's hind leg; ~'rose, wild hedge-rose; ~'s-body, (colloq.) drudge; ~'s breakfast, (sl.) mess; ~'skin, leather of or imitating dog's skin, esp. as glove-material; ~'s life, life of misery (cf. LEAD¹); ~-star, Sirius, ~-tired, tired out; ~-tooth, small pointed ornament in Norman and Early English architecture; ~-violet (scentless wild kind); ~-watch, (Naut.) short half-watch of 2 hrs. (4–6, 6–8, p.m.); ~'wood, wild cornel. **4.** ~'gĕd (-g-) *a.*, tenacious, grimly persistent (it's ~ged as does it, colloq., persistence succeeds); ~'gie (-gǐ) *n.*, (pet name for) dog; ~'gō *adv.* (sl.; lie ~go, wait motionless or hidden); ~'gy (-gǐ), (*a.*, esp. devoted to dogs, (*n.*) = *doggie*; ~'like *a.* (esp. in devotion). [E]

dōge *n.* (Hist.) Chief magistrate of Venice or Genoa; dŏ'gāte *n.*, office of doge. [F f. It. f. L *dux* leader]

dogged. See DOG.

dŏ'ggerel (-ger-) *a.* & *n.* Trivial, worthless or irregular (verse). [app. f. DOG]

doggie, doggo, doggy, doglike. See DOG.

dŏ'gm|a *n.* Principle, tenet, doctrinal system, esp. as laid down by authority of Church; arrogant declaration of opinion; ~ă'tĭc *a.* (-ically), of dogma(s), doctrinal, (*dogmatic theology*), asserting dogmas or opinions (*about*), authoritative, arrogant; ~atism *n.*; ~atize *v.i.* & *t.*, make positive unsupported statements, speak authoritatively, express (principle etc.) as a dogma. [L f. Gk, = opinion]

do-gŏo'der (dōō-) *n.* Well-meaning but unrealistic philanthropist or reformer. [*do good*]

doh (dō), dō¹, *n.* (Mus.) First note of scale; note C. [It. *do*]

doi'ly, doy'ley, *n.* Small ornamental mat of paper, linen, etc., on plate for cakes etc. [person]

do'ing (dōō'-) *n.* (esp.) Activity,

effort; (colloq.) scolding, beating; (in *pl.*, sl.) things needed. [DO³]

**do′ldrums** (-z) *n.pl.* Low spirits; (fig.) state of stagnation; equatorial ocean region of calms, sudden storms, and light unpredictable winds. [orig. uncert.]

**dōle¹. 1.** *n.* Charitable distribution, charitable (esp. niggardly) gift of food, clothes, or money; ‖the ~, (colloq.) · benefit claimable by the unemployed from the State (on the ~, receiving this). **2.** *v.t.* Deal *out* sparingly, esp. as alms. [E]

**dōle²** *n.* Woe, lamentation, (arch.); ~′ful (-lf-) *a.* (-lly) dreary, dismal, melancholy. [F f. L (*doleo* grieve)]

**dŏll. 1.** *n.* Small model of human figure, esp. as child's toy (~′s **house,** *~′house,** miniature toy house for dolls, diminutive dwelling--house); ventriloquist's dummy; pretty but silly woman; (sl.) attractive person, young woman. **2.** *v.t. & i.* (colloq.) Dress *up* smartly. [pet form of *Dorothy*]

**dŏ′llar** *n.* Currency unit in U.S. and other countries (~ **mark, sign,** $); ~ **area** (in which currency is convertible with U.S. dollar); ~ **gap,** excess of country's import trade with dollar area over corresp. export trade. [LG *daler* f. G *taler*]

**dŏ′llop** *n.* (colloq.) Clumsy or shapeless lump of food etc. [perh. Scand.]

**dŏ′lly** *n.* (Pet-name for) doll; (colloq.) easily hit or caught ball at cricket; ~(-bird), (colloq.) attractive young woman; ~ **mixture** (of tiny variously shaped and coloured sweets); CORN¹ *dolly.* [DOLL]

**dŏ′lman** *n.* Kind of robe or cape; ~ **sleeve,** loose sleeve cut in one piece with body of coat etc. [Turk.]

**dŏ′lmĕn** *n.* Megalithic tomb with large flat stone laid on upright ones. [F]

**dŏ′lomite** *n.* Magnesian limestone. [*Dolomieu,* person]

**dŏ′lorous** *a.* (literary, joc.) Painful, sad, dismal; **dŏ′lour, *-lor,** (-ler), *n.* (literary) sorrow, distress. [F f. L (*dolor* pain)]

**dŏ′lphĭn** *n.* Marine mammal resembling porpoise but larger and with beaklike snout; (pop.) dorado; curved fish in heraldry, sculpture, etc. [L f. Gk *delphis* -in-]

**dōlt** *n.* Stupid person. [prob. rel. to obs. *dol* = DULL]

**Dŏm** *n.* Title prefixed to names of some R.C. dignitaries and Benedictine and Carthusian monks. [L *dominus* master]

**-dom** *suf.* forming *ns.* denoting (1) rank, condition, domain, f. *ns.* or *adjs.* (*earldom, freedom, kingdom*), (2) collective pl. or the ways of —s, f. *ns.* (*officialdom*). [E]

**domai′n** *n.* Lands held or ruled over, estate, realm; sphere of influence, province of thought or action, scope; ~**e** *n.*, vineyard. [F alt. f. *demesne*; see DEMESNE]

**dōme** *n.* Rounded vault as roof resting on circular, elliptical, or polygonal base; natural vault, canopy, (of sky, trees, etc.); rounded summit of hill etc.; (sl.) head; (poet.) stately building; ~**d** (-md) *a.*, having dome(s), shaped like dome, rounded. [F f. It. f. L *domus* house]

**domĕ′stĭc. 1.** *a.* (~ally) Of the home, household, or family affairs; of one's own country, not foreign or international (*domestic trade, policy*); native, home-made; (of animal) kept by or living with man; fond of home life; ~ **science,** study of household management. **2.** *n.* Household servant. **3.** ~**āte** *v.t.*, naturalize (plant etc.), bring (animal) under human control, tame, make fond of home life; ~**ā′tion,** ~**ātor,** *ns.*; **domĕstĭ′cĭty** *n.*, being domestic, home life or privacy. [F f. L (*domus* home)]

**dŏ′mĭcĭl|e, -ĭl,** *n.* Dwelling-place; (esp. Law) place of permanent residence, fact of residing; ~**ed** (-ld) *a.*, having domicile *at* or *in*; **dŏmĭcĭ′liarў** (-lyerĭ) *a.* (esp. of visit of doctor, officials, etc., to person's home). [F f. L (as prec.)]

**dŏ′mĭn|āte** *v.t. & i.* (~able). Have commanding influence over or *over*; (of person, power, sound, feature of scene) be the most influential or conspicuous; (of high place) overlook, hold commanding position *over*; ~**ant,** (*a.*) dominating, ruling, prevailing, (*n.*, Mus.) fifth note of diatonic scale of any key; ~**ance,** ~**ā′tion,** *ns.*, being dominant; ~**eer** *v.i.*, act imperiously, tyrannize. [L *dominor* (*dominus* lord)]

**domĭ′nical** *a.* Of Sunday (~ **letter,** the one of the seven A–G indicating dates of Sundays in Church calendar for the year); of Christ. [F, or L *dominicalis* (as prec.)]

**Domi'nican. 1.** *a.* Of St. Dominic or his order. **2.** *n.* Dominican friar or nun. [L (*Dominic*)]

**domi'nion** (-yon) *n.* Lordship, sovereignty, control; domains of feudal lord, territory of sovereign or government; (Hist.) title of self--governing territories of British Commonwealth. [F f. L (as prec.)]

**do'minō** *n.* (*pl.* ~es). Cloak with mask for upper part of face, worn to conceal identity esp. at masquerade etc.; one of usu. 28 small oblong pieces, marked with usu. 0–6 pips in each half, used in game of ~es (usu. treated as *sing.*); ~ **theory** (that political event etc. in one place will cause similar events in others). [F f. L (as prec.)]

**dŏn**[1] *v.t.* (**-nn-**). Put on (clothing). [*do on*]

**dŏn**[2] *n.* Head, fellow, or tutor, of college, esp. at Oxford or Cambridge; (**Don**) Spanish title prefixed to Christian name, Spanish gentleman, (*Don Quixote*); **Don Juan**, rake, libertine; ~**'nish** *a.*, like a college don, pedantic. [Sp. f. L *dominus* lord]

**donā'tion** *n.* Bestowal, presenting; thing presented, gift (esp. of money given to institution); **donā'te** *v.t.*, make donation of. [F f. L (*dono* give)]

**done** (dŭn) *a.* (esp.) Socially acceptable (colloq.; *the done thing*; *it isn't done*); ~ (**in, up**), (colloq.) tired out; (as *int.* in reply to offer etc.) accepted; **be ~ with**, have (been) finished with; **have ~**, cease; **have ~ with**, finish dealing with. [p.p. of DO[3]]

**dŏ'njon** (or dŭ'-) *n.* Great tower of castle. [arch. sp. of DUNGEON]

**dŏ'nkey** *n.* = ASS[1] (**talk the hind leg off a ~**, talk incessantly); stupid person; ~ **jacket**, workman's thick weatherproof jacket; ~**'s years**, (colloq.) a very long time; ~**-work**, drudgery. [perh. *Duncan* (cf. NEDDY)]

**dŏ'nna** *n.* (**D**~, title of) Italian or Spanish or Portuguese lady. [It. f. L *domina* mistress]

**dŏ'nnish.** See DON[2].

**dŏ'nor** *n.* Giver of gift; person or animal providing blood for transfusion, semen for insemination, organ for transplantation, etc. [AF f. L (DONATION)]

**dŏn't** *n.* Prohibition (DO[2]*s and don'ts*). [abbr. of DO[3] *not*]

**dŏo'dle. 1.** *v.i.* Scrawl or draw absent-mindedly. **2.** *n.* Scrawl or drawing so made; ~**-bug**, (colloq.) flying bomb. [orig. = foolish person]

**dŏom. 1.** *n.* Fate, destiny, (usu. evil); ruin, death; the Last Judgement (*crack, day, of doom*; *doomsday*); **till ~sday**, for ever. **2.** *v.t.* Condemn *to* some fate or *to* do; (esp. in *p.p.*) consign to misfortune or destruction. [E, = statute]

**door** (dŏr) *n.* Hinged or sliding barrier usu. of wood or metal for closing entrance to building, room, safe, etc., (*lives etc. next* ~, in next house or room, **three ~s away**, etc.; **next ~ to**, fig., nearly, near to; *at* DEATH's *door*); entrance, access, exit, (**close the ~ to**, make impossible; **foot in the ~**, chance of ultimate success; **leave the ~ open**, preserve possibility; **open the ~ to**, create opportunity for; **packed to the ~s**, entirely full; **show person the ~**, dismiss him); doorway; DARKEN person's *door*; **lay, lie, at the ~ of**, impute, be imputable, to; **out of ~s**, in(to) the open air; ~**'bell**, bell in house rung by handle or button outside door; ~**-keeper**, person who guards door; ~**'knob** (for turning to release latch of door); ~**'man** = *door--keeper*; ~**'mat**, mat for wiping mud from shoes, (fig.) despised passive person; ~**'nail** (with which doors used to be studded; DEAD *as a door-nail*); ~**'step**, step leading up to usu. outer door (*on one's or the ~step*, very near), (sl.) thick slice of bread; ~**'stop**, device for keeping door open or to prevent it from striking wall etc.; ~**-to-**~ *a.*, (of selling etc.) done at each house in turn, (of journey) from start to finish; ~**'way**, opening filled by door. [E]

**dŏp**|**e. 1.** *n.* Thick liquid; varnish; (sl.) drug esp. narcotic; drug etc. given to horse or greyhound to affect its performance; (sl.) misleading or not generally known information; (colloq.) stupid person; ~**e-fiend**, drug addict. **2.** *v.t.* & *i.* Treat with dope, drug; take narcotics; ~**e out**, (sl.) discover. **3.** ~**'ey** *a.* (sl.; ~**'iness**), stupefied (as with a drug), stupid. [Du., = sauce]

**doppelgänger** (dŏ'pelgĕngər) *n.* Wraith of living person. [G, = double-goer]

**Dŏ′ppler** n. ~ **effect**, apparent increase (decrease) in frequency of sound or other waves when source and observer become closer (more distant). [person]

**dor** n. Loud-humming flying insect. [E]

**dora′dō** (-ah′-) n. (pl. ~s). Blue and silver sea-fish showing brilliant colours when dying out of water. [Sp. = gilt]

**Dŏ′ric. 1.** a. (Of dialect) broad, rustic; ~ **order**, (Archit.) oldest and simplest Gk order. **2.** n. Dialect of Dorians in ancient Greece; rustic English or esp. Scots; Doric order. [L f. Gk (*Doris*, place)]

**dor′m|ant** a. Lying inactive as in sleep (of some animals through winter, undeveloped buds, volcano, potential faculties); not acting or in use; ~**ancy** n.; ~**er** n., projecting upright window in sloping roof; ~**itory** n., sleeping-room with a number of beds (colloq. abbr. **dorm**), suburban or country district of city workers' residences. [F f. L *dormio* sleep]

**dŏr′mouse** n. (pl. -mice pr. -mīs). Small hibernating rodent, resembling mouse and squirrel. [orig. unkn.]

**dŏr′my̆** a. (Golf). (Of player or side) as many holes ahead of opponent as there are holes left to play (*dormy one*, *five*, etc.).

||**Dŏ′rothy̆** n. ~ **bag**, woman's open-topped handbag closed by draw-string and slung by loops from the wrist. [fem. name]

**dŏr′sal** a. (Anat., Zool., & Bot.; ~**ly**). Of or on the back; ridge-shaped. [F or L (*dorsum* back)]

**dŏr′y̆**[1] n. (Also **John D**~) kind of edible sea-fish. [F *dorée* = gilded]

**dŏr′y̆**[2] n. Flat-bottomed skiff. [orig. unkn.]

**dōse. 1.** n. Amount of medicine to be taken at one time (lit., or fig. of flattery, punishment, etc.; **like a** ~ **of salts**, sl., very fast); amount of radiation received by person or thing exposed to it; (sl.) venereal infection. **2.** v.t. Give medicine to; treat (person or animal) *with*. **3. dō′sage** n., giving of dose, size of dose. [F f. L f. Gk *dosis* gift]

**dŏss** v.i. (sl.) Sleep, esp. in doss-house; ~ **down**, sleep on makeshift bed; ~**house**, cheap lodging-house. [prob. orig. seat-back cover, F f. L *dorsum* back]

**dŏ′ssïer** (or dŏ′syā) n. Set of documents, esp. record of information about person or event. [F]

**dost**. See DO[3].

**dŏt**[1]. **1.** n. Small spot, roundish pen-mark; such mark written or printed as part of *i* or *j*; (Mus.) such mark used to denote lengthening of note or rest, or staccato; decimal point; shorter signal of two in Morse code; **on the** ~, exactly on time; ||**the year** ~, (colloq.) very long ago. **2.** v.t. (-**tt**-). Mark with dot(s), place dot over (letter); ~ **the i's and cross the t's**, fig., be minutely accurate, emphasize details); partly cover as with dots (*sea dotted with ships*; *dot with butter*); scatter (*about, all over*) like dots; (sl.) hit (*dotted him one in the eye*); ~ **and carry (one)**, child's formula for remembering to carry in addition sum, (joc.) limp, limping(ly); ~**ted line**, (esp.) line of dots to show place left for signature etc. (*sign on the dotted line*, give formal agreement). [E]

**dŏt**[2] (dŏt) n. Dowry. [F f. L]

**dōt|e** v.i. Be silly, deranged, infatuated, or feeble-minded, esp. from age; ~**e on**, be excessively fond of; ~**age** n., feeble-minded senility (*is in his dotage*); ~**ard** n., one in his dotage, old fool. [orig. uncert.]

**doth**. See DO[3].

**dŏ′tterel** n. Kind of small plover. [DOTE]

**dŏ′ttle** n. Remnant of unburnt tobacco in pipe. [DOT[1]]

**dŏ′tt|y̆** a. (colloq.; ~**ily**, ~**iness**). Feeble-minded; silly.

**dou′ble** (dŭ′-) a., adv., n., & v. **1.** a. (-**bly**). Multiplied by two, having twofold relation; twice as much, many, large, good, etc., (*double the amount, the number*; *double thickness*); consisting of or combining two things; folded, stooping (*bent double*); having some part double, (of flower) with petals multiplied by conversion of stamens etc., (of domino) with same number of pips on each side; of extra size, strength, value, etc., (*a double whisky*); (Mus.) lower in pitch by an octave (*double bassoon* etc.); deceitful, hypocritical (*playing a double game*). **2. adv.** To twice the amount etc. (**see** ~, seem to see two things where there is only one; esp. of drunken person); two together (*sleep double*). **3.** n. Double quantity or thing, double measure of spirits etc., twice as much or many; counterpart of person or thing, understudy, wraith; pair of victories over same team or of championships at same game etc.; (Racing) bet on two horses etc. in different races, winnings and stake from one race being bet on the second; (Darts) hit on narrow ring between the two outer circles on the board, scoring double; (Bridge) doubling of a bid; (in *pl.*) game between two pairs of players; **at the ~**, running. **4.** *v.t.* & *i.* Make or become double, increase twofold, multiply by two, amount to twice as much as; fold, bend, or turn (paper, cloth, leaf, etc.) over upon itself, become folded; clench (fist); (of actor) play (two parts) in the same piece, play twofold role (*as*), be understudy etc. (*for*); move at double pace, run; turn sharply in flight or pursuit, take tortuous course, (**~ back**, take direction opposite to previous one); (Naut.) get round (headland); (Bridge) make call increasing value of points to be won or lost on (opponent's bid); **~ up**, put (passenger etc.) in same quarters as another, bet twofold (stake), bend one's body into stooping or curled-up position (fig., be convulsed with laughter or pain), cause (another) to do this by blow. **5.** *double* ACROSTIC; **~ agent**, one who spies for two rival countries etc.; **~-barrelled**, (of gun) having two barrels, (fig.) twofold, (of surname) hyphened; **~-bass**, lowest-pitched instrument of violin family; **~ bed** (for two persons); **~ bill**, programme with two principal items; **~ bind**, dilemma; **~ boiler**, saucepan with detachable upper compartment heated by boiling water in lower; **~-breasted**, (of coat etc.) having two fronts overlapping across body; **~-check**, verify twice or in two ways; **~ chin** (with fold of flesh under it); **~ cream**, thick cream with high fat-content; **~-cross** *n.*, & *v.t.*, (subject to) act of treachery or cheating; **~-dealing**, deceit(ful); *double*-DECKER, -DECLUTCH, DUMMY, DUTCH[1]; **~-dyed**, (fig.) deeply stained with guilt; *double* EAGLE; **~-edged**, (fig.) damaging to user as well as his opponent; *double entendre* (doōblahntah'ndr), phrase capable of two meanings (one usu. indecent), use of such phrases; *double* ENTRY,

EVENT; **~ exposure**, (Photog.) accidentally or deliberately repeated exposure of film etc.; **~-faced**, insincere; *double* FAULT; **~ feature**, cinema programme with two full--length films; *double* FIGURES; ‖**~ first**, (person winning) first-class honours in two subjects at university; **~ glazing**, (provision of) two sheets of glass in window to reduce heat loss etc.; **~ harness**, (fig.) matrimony or close partnership; *double* HELIX; **~-jointed**, having joints that allow unusual bending of fingers etc.; **~ life**, sustaining of two different characters in one's life, esp. one virtuous and the other not; **~-lock** *v.t.*, lock by double turn of key; *double* OBELUS; **~-parking**, parking of vehicle alongside one that is already parked at roadside; **~ pneumonia** (of both lungs); **~-quick**, at running pace (lit. or fig.); **~ or quits**, game, throw, toss, deciding whether person shall pay either twice his loss or debt, or nothing; **~ room**, bedroom for two persons; **~ saucepan**, = *double boiler*; *double* SHUFFLE; **~ standard**, rule etc. applied more strictly to some persons than to others; **~ star**, two stars actually or apparently very close together; **~-stopping**, (Mus.) sounding of two notes at once on stringed instrument; **~ take**, delayed reaction to situation etc. immediately after one's first reaction; **~-talk**, verbal expression that is (usu. deliberately) ambiguous; **~ time**, payment of employee at twice normal rate for work, (Mil.) regulation running pace. **6. dou'blet** (dŭ'-) *n.*, man's close body-garment in 14th–18th c. (**doublet and hose**, male costume), one of two words of same derivation but different sense (*fashion* and *faction*); **~ton** (-belt-) *n.*, two cards only of a suit [cf. SINGLETON]; **doubloo'n** (dŭ-, du-) *n.*, (Hist.) Spanish gold coin. [F f. L *duplus*]

**doubt** (dowt). **1.** *n.* Feeling of uncertainty (about), inclination to disbelieve (*of*, *about*), hesitation, (have one's *doubts about*; *have*, *make*, *no doubt that*); uncertain state of things, lack of full proof or clear signs of the future, (BENEFIT *of the doubt*; **beyond**, **without** a, ~, certainly; **in** ~, not certain; **no** ~, certainly, probably, admittedly). **2.** *v.t.* & *i.* Feel undecided or uncertain (about); be undecided about or *about*, hesitate to believe or trust; call in question (person, thing, *whether, if*; neg. or interrog. *that, but, but that*); have doubts *of* (esp. w. neg., *never doubted of success*); ~**ing Thomas**, incredulous or sceptical person (after John 20: 24–29). **3.** ~**ful** *a.* (**-lly**), feeling or causing doubt, uncertain in meaning, character, truth, or result, undecided (*doubtful ally*); ~**less** *adv.*, certainly, probably, admittedly. [F f. L *dubito* hesitate]

**douche** (dōōsh). **1.** *n.* Jet of liquid applied to body as form of bathing or for medicinal purpose; device for producing such jet. **2.** *v.t. & i.* Administer douche to; take douche. [F f. It. f. L (DUCT)]

**dough** (dō) *n.* Kneaded moistened flour, bread-paste; (sl.) money; ~**'boy**, boiled dumpling, (colloq.) U.S. infantryman; ~**'nut**, sweetened and fried dough-cake; ~**'y̆** (dō'ĭ) *a.* (~**ily**, ~**iness**), like dough (esp. of half-baked bread or pastry). [E]

**dou'ght|y̆** (dow'tĭ) *a.* (arch., joc.; ~**ily**, ~**iness**). Valiant. [E]

**doughy.** See DOUGH.

**dour** (door) *a.* (Sc.) Severe, stern, stubborn. [prob. Gael. *dúr* stupid]

**douse, dowse[1]**, *v.t.* Extinguish (light); throw water over, drench. [orig. uncert.]

**dove[1]** (dŭv) *n.* Pigeon (esp. RING[1]- -dove, TURTLE[1]-dove); Holy Spirit; gentle or innocent person, beloved person; person advocating negotiation rather than violence; ~**-colour**, warm grey; ~**'cot(e)**, pigeon-house (*flutter the ~cots*, alarm quiet people); ~**'tail**, (*n.*) joint made with tenon shaped like dove's spread tail, (*v.t. & i.*) put together with dovetails, (fig.) fit together compactly or neatly (*into, with*). [N]

**dōve[2].** See DIVE.

**dow'ager** *n.* Woman with title or property derived from her late husband (often in comb., *Queen dowager, dowager duchess*); (colloq.) dignified elderly lady. [F (DOWER)]

**dow'd|y̆. 1.** *a.* (~**ily**, ~**iness**). (Of dress etc.) unattractively dull, unfashionable; (of woman) shabbily, badly, or unfashionably dressed. **2.** *n.* Dowdy woman. [orig. unkn.]

**dow'el** *n.* Headless pin used in carpentry etc. [LG]

**dow'er. 1.** *n.* Widow's share for life of husband's estate; (arch., poet.)

dowry; (fig.) natural gift or talent; ||~ **house** (forming part of widow's dower). **2.** *v.t.* Give dowry to; endow *with* talent etc. [F f. L (*dos* dowry)]

**down[1]** *n.* ~(**'land**), open high land, esp. (in *pl.*) chalk uplands of S. England and elsewhere. [E]

**down[2]** *n.* First covering of young birds, bird's under-plumage; fine short hair, similar substance on plant, fruit, etc.; fluffy substance (THISTLE*down*); ~**'y̆** *a.* (~**ily**, ~**iness**), of or like down, (sl.) aware, knowing. [N]

**down[3]** *adv., prep., a., v., & n.* **1.** *adv.* (*superl.* ~**'most**). Towards, at, or in lower place, the ground, place regarded as lower, or the south, (*fall down*; UP *and down*; *blinds are down*; *down to the sea, the country*; *down in Devon*); in(to) helpless position, position of lagging or loss, fallen posture, low level, depression, humiliation, etc., (*hit a man when he's down*; *team was three goals down*; £5 *down on the transaction*; *many down with colds*; *river, sun, temperature, tide, is down*; *down to one's last penny* etc.); ||*away from, not in, capital or university*, (*down to Scotland from London*; *go, be, down*; SEND *down*); from bedroom etc. (*come down early in the mornings*); with current or wind; from earlier to later time (*custom handed down*); to finer consistency or smaller amount or size (*boil, grind, thin, wear, down*); into quiescence (*calm down*); cheaper, of lower value, (*eggs, shares, are down*); (as *int.*) lie, get, put, bring, etc., down (*down, Bonzo!*, and w. *with, down with the aristocrats!*); **be** ~ **on**, disapprove of; **cash, pay,** ~, (at once, as though on counter); DO[3] *down*; **howl, shout,** ~ (into silence); **run, ride, hunt,** ~, overtake and trap; WRITE, **copy,** ~ (on paper; *meeting is* ~ *for next week*; *he is* ~ *to speak at the meeting*, on programme). **2.** *prep.* Downwards along, through, or into; from top to bottom of; at or in a lower part of (*situated down the river*); along (*walk down the road*); UP *and down*. **3.** *a.* (*superl.* ~**'most**). Directed downwards. **4.** *v.t.* (colloq.) Knock, bring, swallow, (person, aeroplane, drink) down. **5.** *n.* Act of putting down; reverse of fortune (usu. UPs *and downs*); **have a** ~ **on**, (colloq.) dislike, have grudge against. **6.** ~ **and out**, unable to resume fight in boxing, (fig.) completely without resources or means of livelihood (so ~-and-out n.); *down at* (*the*) HEEL; ~ **beat**, (Mus.) accented beat; ~**'beat**, gloomy, relaxed, unemphatic; ~**'cast**, (of eyes) looking down, (of person) dejected; ~**'fall**, (cause of) fall from prosperity or power, downpour; ~**grade**, descending slope of road or railway, (fig.) deterioration; ~**'-grade** *v.t.*, lower in rank etc.; ~**-hearted**, dejected; ~**'hill**, (n.) downward slope, decline, (a.) sloping down, declining, (-ĭ'z, *adv.*) in descending direction; ~ **in the mouth,** down-hearted; *down on* one's LUCK; ~ **payment** (made in cash, esp. initially and to be followed by instalments); ~**'pipe** (from roof to drain); ~ **platform** (for arrival or departure of down train); ~**'pour,** heavy fall of rain etc.; ~**'right,** (a.) plain, straightforward, out-and-out, (*downright atheist, nonsense*), (*adv.*) thoroughly, quite, (*downright scared, insolent*); ~ **stage,** at or to front of theatre stage; ~**stair's** *adv., a., & n.,* down the stairs, (to, on, of) lower floor of house etc.; *~'state a. & n.,* (of) part of state remote from large cities, esp. southern part; ~**'stream** *a. & adv.,* in direction in which stream etc. flows; ~**-stroke** (made or written downwards); ~**-to-earth,** practical, realistic; ~ **tools,** cease work for the day etc., go on strike; ~ **to the ground,** (colloq.) completely; ~ **town,** into town from higher or outlying part, *to or in business part of city, *~**'town** *a. & n.,* (of) lower or more central part of town or city; ~ **train** (going or coming from capital or place regarded as higher); ~**'trodden,** oppressed; ~**'turn,** decline, esp. in economic or business activity; ~ **under,** in Australia etc.; ~ **(the) wind,** ~**'wind,** *a. & adv.,* in direction in which wind is blowing (*let go ~ the wind,* abandon); ~**'ward** *a. & adv.*; ~**'wards** (-z) *adv.* [*adown* (*off,* DOWN)]

**Dow'ning Street** *n.* British Government, Prime Minister, or Foreign (etc.) Office. [place]

**dow'ny.** See DOWN².

**dow'ry** (dow'erĭ) *n.* Property or money brought by bride to her husband. [AF, = F *douaire* DOWER]

**dowse¹.** See DOUSE.

**dows|e²** (-z) *v.i.* Search for hidden water or minerals with forked twig (~**ing-rod,** *divining-rod*) which dips suddenly when over right spot; ~**'er** *n.,* user of dowsing-rod. [orig. unkn.]

**dŏxŏ'logy** *n.* Formula of praise to God. [L f. Gk (*doxa* glory)]

**doy'en** (or dwah'yaṅ) *n.* (*fem.* **doyenne** *pr.* dwahyĕ'n). Senior member *of* a body of colleagues. [F (DEAN¹)]

**doy'ley.** See DOILY.

**doz.** *abbr.* dozen.

**dōze. 1.** *v.i.* Be half asleep, sleep lightly; ~ **off,** fall lightly asleep. **2.** *n.* Short light sleep. [orig. unkn.]

**do'zen** (dŭ'-) *n.* (*pl.* ~, ~s; for pl. usage see HUNDRED). Twelve, set of twelve, (*pack them in dozens*); ~**s of,** (colloq.) very many; **by the ~,** in large quantities; BAKER'*s,* long, ~, 13; *half a ~,* (about) 6; ||**talk nineteen to the ~** (incessantly). [F f. L *duodecim* twelve]

**dō'z|ỹ** *a.* (colloq.; ~**ily,** ~**iness**). Stupid; lazy. [DOZE]

**D.P.** *abbr.* displaced person.

**D.Phil.** *abbr.* Doctor of Philosophy.

**Dr.** *abbr.* debtor; Doctor.

**dr.** *abbr.* drachm(s); dram(s).

**drăb¹. 1.** *a.* (**-bb-**). Of dull light--brown colour; dull, monotonous. **2.** *n.* Drab colour; monotony. [obs. *drap* cloth f. F f. L]

**drăb²** *n.* Slut; prostitute. [LDu.]

**drăchm** (-ăm) *n.* Apothecaries' weight of 60 grains, ⅛ oz.; avoirdupois weight of 1/16 oz.; (**fluid**) ⅛, apothecaries' measure of 60 minims, ⅛ fluid oz.; **dră'chma** (-k-) *n.* (*pl.* ~ae, ~as), ancient or modern Gk coin. [F, or L f. Gk]

**Drācō'nĭan, -ŏ'nĭc,** (or dra-) *adjs.* (Of laws) rigorous, harsh, cruel. [*Draco,* person]

**draft** (-ah-). **1.** *n.* (Selection of) detachment from larger body for special duty or purpose; *(Mil.) conscription; drawing of money by written order; bill or cheque drawn, esp. by one branch of bank on another; sketch of work to be executed; preliminary copy of written matter; * = DRAUGHT; ~**'sman,** drafter of documents. **2.** *v.t.* Draw off (part of larger body) for special duty or purpose; *conscript; prepare draft of (writing, work). [phon. sp. of DRAUGHT]

**drăg. 1.** *v.t. & i.* (**-gg-**). Pull along with force, difficulty, or friction;

allow (feet, tail, etc.) to trail; trail or go heavily or tediously; use grapnel, search (river-bed etc.) with grapnels, nets, etc.; (colloq.) take (person *to* place etc., esp. against his will); (colloq.) suck *on* or *at* (cigarette); ~ one's **feet**, (fig.) be deliberately slow or reluctant to act; ~ **in**, introduce (subject) irrelevantly; ~ **on**, continue tediously; ~ **out**, protract; ~ **up**, (colloq.) rear (child) roughly, deliberately mention an event (usu. unpleasant) which is generally forgotten. **2.** *n.* Obstruction to progress, retarding force, retarded motion; boring or dreary performance, person, etc.; lure drawn before hounds as substitute for fox, hunt using this; = **drag-net**; apparatus for dredging etc.; (sl.) pull at cigarette, women's clothes worn by men, clothes in general, motor car, acceleration race between cars (~**ster**, car modified to take part in this); ~**-line**, excavator with bucket pulled in by wire rope; ~**-net**, net drawn through river or across ground to trap fish or game, (fig.) means of systematically discovering criminals etc. **3.** ~**gle** *v.t.* & *i.*, make dirty and wet or limp by trailing, hang trailing; ~**gle-tail(ed)**, (woman) with draggled skirts. [E or N]

**dragée** (drah'zhā) *n.* Chocolate-coated sweet; sugar-coated almond etc. [F]

**dra'ggle.** See DRAG.

**dra'gon** *n.* Mythical monster like reptile, usu. with wings and claws and often breathing fire; fierce person; ~**-fly**, long-bodied gauze-winged insect. [F f. L f. Gk, = serpent]

**dragoon'. 1.** *n.* Cavalryman (orig. mounted infantryman); fierce fellow. **2.** *v.t.* Subject to military oppression, persecute; force *into* submission etc. or do*ing*. [F *dragon* (prec.)]

**drain. 1.** *v.t.* & *i.* Draw (liquid) *off* or *away* by pipe, ditch, etc., make (land etc.) dry thus; (of river) carry off superfluous water of (district); drink (liquid), empty (vessel), to the dregs; deprive (person, thing) *of* property, strength, etc.; trickle *through*, flow *off* or *away*; (of wet cloth, vessel, etc.) get rid of moisture by its flowing away (*set it there to drain*); ‖~'**ing-board**, \*~'**board**, ~'**er** *n.*, sloping usu. grooved board on which washed dishes etc. are left to drain. **2.** *n.* Channel, conduit, or pipe carrying off water, liquid, sewage, etc., (**down the** ~, colloq., lost, wasted); ~**-pipe**, pipe for carrying off surplus water or liquid sewage from a building); constant outlet or expenditure (*is a great drain on my resources*). **3.** ~'**age** *n.*, draining, system of drains, what is drained off. [E (DRY)]

**drāke¹** *n.* Mayfly, esp. as used in fishing. [E, = DRAGON]

**drāke²** *n.* Male duck (*play* DUCK²*s and drakes*). [orig. uncert.]

**drăm** *n.* = DRACHM; small drink of spirit etc. [F, or L *drama* (DRACHM)]

**dra'ma** (-ah'-) *n.* Play for acting on stage, radio, etc. (**the** ~, art of writing and presenting plays); dramatic series of events; **dramă'tic** *a.* (**-ically**), (of the study of) drama, (of gesture etc.) theatrical, (of event etc.) sudden, striking, impressive; **dramă'tics** *n.*, performance of plays; **drămatis persō'nae** *n.pl.* (often treated as *sing.*), (list of) characters in a play; **dra'matist** *n.*, writer of dramas; **dra'matize** *v.t.* & *i.*, turn or make (novel etc.) into drama, behave dramatically; **dramatizā'tion** *n.* [L f. Gk (*draō* do)]

**drănk.** See DRINK.

**drāp|e.** **1.** *v.t.* Cover, hang, adorn, with cloth etc.; arrange (clothes, hangings) in graceful folds. **2.** *n.* Piece of drapery; \*curtain. **3.** ‖~'**er** *n.*, retailer of cloth, linen, etc.; ~'**ery** *n.*, ‖cloth or textile fabrics, ‖draper's trade, clothing or hangings disposed in folds. [F f. L *drappus* cloth]

**drā'stic** (*or* -ah'-) *a.* (~**ally**). Acting strongly or severely, vigorous, violent, (*drastic measures*, *remedy*, *aperient*). [Gk *drastikos* (DRAMA)]

**drăt** *v.t.* -**tt**-; esp. in 3 *sing. subj.*) (As mild imprecation) curse, bother; ~'**ted** *a.*, cursed. [(*Go*)*d rot*]

**draught** (-ahft) *n.* Traction; drawing of net, fish taken at one drawing; single act of drinking; amount so drunk; dose of liquid medicine; depth of water ship draws; current of air in room, chimney, etc. (**feel the** ~, sl., suffer from adverse (usu. financial) conditions; **forced** ~, provided by blower etc.); ‖(in *pl.*) game on ~**-board** (same as chess-board) with 12 uniform pieces on each side; = DRAFT; ~ **beer** (from cask, not bottled); ~**horse** (for drawing cart, plough, etc.); ~'**sman**, person who makes drawings, piece in draughts, = DRAFT*sman*; ~'**smanship** *n*.; ~'**y** *a*. (~ily, ~iness), (of room etc.) liable to draughts of air. [foll.]

**draw. 1.** *v.t.* & *i.* (**drew** *pr.* drōō; ~**n**). Pull (boat up from water, hat over face, belt tighter, pen across paper, friend aside); pull after one (plough, cart, etc.); pull at; bend (bow); pull (curtain, VEIL) open or shut; protract, stretch, elongate (*long drawn agony*); make (wire) by stretching; (of ship) need (specified depth of water); pull (ball at cricket or golf); take out (cork, tooth, gun-charge, nail, cricket stumps from ground at close of play, card from pack, pistol, sword from sheath); (abs.) draw one's sword or pistol; (abs.) draw LOTS; obtain by lot (*draw the winner*); drag (badger or fox) from hole; (abs.) chimney, *pipe*, ~**s well**, promotes or allows draught; haul up (water) from well; take or get from a source (*draw inspiration*, one's *salary*, *money from bank*); bring out (liquid from vessel, blood from body); extract liquid essence from; (of tea) infuse; (Cards) cause to be played (*draw all the trumps*); leave (game, battle, or abs.) undecided; elicit, evoke, bring about, entail, (*draw criticism*, *ruin*, *upon* one*self*); infer (conclusion); bring (person) out, make (him) reveal information, talent, irritation, etc.; induce (*to* do); attract, bring to oneself or to something, take in (*draw a deep breath*; *I felt drawn to him*; *drew my attention to the matter*; *display draws customers*); search (cover) for game; disembowel (fowl before cooking; criminal is **hanged, ~n and quartered**); trace (furrow, figure, line); make (picture), delineate, represent (object), by drawing lines, (abs.) practise this; frame (document) in due form, compose; formulate, institute, (comparisons, distinctions); write out (bill, cheque, draft *on* banker etc.); (abs.) make call *on* person or his faith, memory, one's imagination, etc., for money or service; make one's way, move, *towards, round, into, near, off, back*, etc. (*draw to an end* or *close*); (Racing) get farther *away* to the front, come *level*, gain *on*. **2.** draw a BEAD *on*; ~ **back**, withdraw from undertaking, ~'-

**back,** thing that impairs satisfaction, disadvantage, amount of excise or import duty paid back or remitted on goods exported, deduction *from*; ~ **bit, bridle, rein,** check horse or (fig.) oneself; *draw* (*a*) BLANK; ~'**bridge** (hinged at one end for drawing up to prevent passage or to open channel); ~ person's **fire,** deflect it from more important targets; ~**hoe** (used with pulling action); ~ **in,** persuade to join, (of day) close in, (of successive days) become shorter, (of train etc.) enter station etc.; *draw in* one's HORNS; ~ **it mild,** (colloq.) avoid exaggeration, be moderate; *draw* LOTS; ~ **off,** withdraw (troops); ~ **on,** lead to, bring about, allure, come nearer, put (gloves etc.) on; ~ **out,** lead out, detach or array (troops), prolong, elicit, induce to talk, write out in proper form, (of days) become longer, (of train etc.) leave station etc.; ~**string** (that can be pulled to tighten mouth of bag, waist of garment, etc.); ~ **one's sword against,** attack; ~ **the line at,** refuse to go as far as or beyond; ~ **up,** come up *with* or *to*= overtake, come to a halt, bring or come into regular order, compose (document etc.), make one*self* stiffly erect; ~**-well,** deep well with rope and bucket. **3.** *n*. Act of drawing; pull, strain; person or thing that draws custom, attention, etc.; drawing of lots, raffle; drawn game; act of whipping out revolver in order to shoot (*quick on the draw*, lit. or fig.); *suck on cigarette etc. **4.** ~**ee'** *n*., person on whom bill or draft is drawn; ~'**er** *n*., (esp., *pr.* also draw) receptacle sliding in and out of frame (**chest of** ~ers) or of table etc., (BOTTOM *drawer*, TOP *drawer*), (in *pl.*) knickers or other garment worn next to body below waist; ~**n** *a*., (esp.: of face etc.) distorted with pain or fear. [E]

**draw'ing** *n*. Act or fact of DRAW*ing*; art of representing by line, delineation without colour or with single colour, product of this; ~**-board,** board for stretching drawing-paper on (*back to the* ~*-board*, colloq., the enterprise has failed, we must begin afresh); ~**-paper** (stout, for drawing pictures etc. on); ||~**-pin** (for fastening paper to drawing-board etc.); ~**-room,** room for formal reception of company, to which ladies retire after dinner.

**drawl. 1.** *n.* Indolent or affected slowness of speech. **2.** *v.i.* & *t.* Speak or utter with drawl. [LDu.]

**dray** *n.* Low esp. brewer's cart without sides, for heavy loads. [DRAW]

**dread** (-ĕd) *v.*, *n.*, & *a.* **1.** *v.t.* Be in great fear of, look forward to with terror; ∼'**nought**, fearless person, (Hist., *D*-) type of heavily-armed battleship. **2.** *n.* Great fear, awe. **3.** *a.* Dreaded; (arch.) awful, revered. **4.** ∼'**ful** *a.* (-lly), terrible (∥**penny** ∼**ful**, cheap story-book full of horrors), troublesome, horrid. [E]

**dream. 1.** *n.* Series of pictures or events in mind of sleeping person (**like a** ∼, colloq., easily, effortlessly; WET *dream*); (**waking**) ∼, similar experience of one awake, = DAY- -*dream*; ideal, (esp. national) aspiration or ambition; person, dress, dish, etc., of dreamlike goodness, beauty, or refinement; ∼**land**, ideal or imaginary land. **2.** *v.i.* & *t.* (∼*t pr.* -ĕmt, ∼ed). Have visions etc. (as) in sleep; see, hear, etc., in sleep; imagine as in a dream; (w. neg. etc.) think of even in a dream, so much as contemplate possibility *of* (*would not dream of upsetting them*), believe possible (*never dreamt that he would behave so badly*), have any conception of; fall into reverie; spend (time) *away* unpractically; be inactive or unpractical; ∼ **up**, imagine, invent. **3.** ∼'**y** *a.* (∼ily, ∼iness), given to reverie, impractical, vague. [E]

**drear'y** (-ily, -iness), (poet.) **drear,** *adjs.* Dismal, gloomy, dull. [E]

**drĕdg**|**e¹. 1.** *n.* Apparatus for clearing out mud etc., or collecting oysters etc., from sea or river bottom. **2.** *v.t.* & *i.* Bring *up*, clear *away* or *out*, clean out, (as) with dredge; use dredge. **3.** ∼'**er¹** *n.*, esp. (boat with) machine used in dredging. [orig. uncert.]

**drĕdg**|**e²** *v.t.* Sprinkle with flour etc.; sprinkle (flour etc.) *over*; ∼'**er²** *n.*, container with perforated lid for sprinkling flour etc. [F (DRAGÉE)]

**drĕg** *n.* (usu. in *pl.*) Sediment, grounds (*drink*, *drain*, **to the** ∼**s**, leaving nothing); refuse. [N]

**drĕnch. 1.** *v.t.* Wet thoroughly (by immersion or by falling liquid); force (animal) to take dose. **2.** *n.* Dose for animal; a soaking. [E (DRINK)]

**drĕss. 1.** *v.t.* & *i.* Clothe; provide oneself with and wear clothes (*dress well* etc.); put on one's clothes; put on evening dress (esp. *dress for dinner*); deck, adorn (shop window with attractive goods, ship with flags); treat (wound) with remedies, apply dressing to; subject to cleansing, trimming, smoothing, etc.; prepare (bird, crab) for cooking or eating; brush, comb, do up, (hair); curry (horse, leather); manure; finish surface of (textile fabrics, building stone); (Mil.) correct the alignment of (companies etc. in relation to each other, or men in line), come into correct place in line etc. **2.** *n.* Clothing, esp. the visible part of it; woman's or girl's garment of bodice and skirt; external covering, outward form, (*birds in their winter dress*). **3.** ∥∼-**circle**, first gallery in theatre; ∼ **coat** (swallow-tailed for evening dress); ∼ **down**, (fig.) thrash, scold; ∼ **length**, piece of material sufficient to make a dress; ∼'**maker**, ∼'**making**, (woman) making women's dresses; ∼ **out**, attire conspicuously; ∼ **rehearsal**, (esp. final) one in costume; ∼ **up** (elaborately or in masquerade). **4.** ∼'**er** *n.*, (esp.) kitchen sideboard with shelves, one who helps to dress actors or actresses; ∼'**y** *a.* (∼ily, ∼iness), fond of or smart in dress, (of clothes) stylish. [F f. L (DIRECT)]

**drĕ'ssage** (-ahzh) *n.* Training of horse in obedience and deportment. [F]

**drĕ'ssĭng** *n.* Act or process of, thing used for, DRESSING; seasoning, sauce, stuffing, etc., for food; ∼-**case** (of toilet necessaries); ∼-**gown**, loose robe worn while one is resting, not fully dressed, etc.; ∼-**room**, place for dressing or changing clothes esp. in theatre, sports-ground, etc., or attached to bedroom; ∼-**table** (with mirror etc. for use while dressing). [DRESS]

**drew.** See DRAW.

**drĭ'bble. 1.** *v.t.* & *i.* (Let) flow in drops or trickling stream; run at the mouth; (Footb., Hockey, etc.) move (ball) forward with slight touches of feet or of stick. **2.** *n.* Act or process of dribbling; small trickling stream. **3. drĭb** *n.* (**dribs and drabs**, small scattered amounts); **drĭ'blĕt** *n.*, small quantity, petty sum. [obs. *drib* = DRIP]

**dried, dri′er, dri′èst.** See DRY.

**drift. 1.** *n.* Being driven by current; slow movement or variation; deviation due to currents or to projectile's rotation; controlled slide of racing-car etc.; merely awaiting events, inaction; intention, tenor, or scope, of person's words; driving mass, snow etc. heaped by wind; ∼(**-wood** etc.), material driven by water; (S. Afr.) ford; ∼(**-net**) (used in sea-fishing, allowed to drift with tide). **2.** *v.i.* & *t.* Be carried (as) by current of air or water, (of current) carry; heap or be heaped into drifts; move passively, casually, or aimlessly. **3.** ∼′**er** *n.*, (esp.) aimless person, boat with drift-net used in herring-fishing. [N & LDu. (DRIVE)]

**drill¹. 1.** *n.* Tool or machine for boring holes or sinking wells; instruction or training in military exercises, (fig.) rigorous discipline, (exact) routine, (colloq.) recognized procedure. **2.** *v.t.* & *i.* (Of person or tool) make hole with drill through (metal etc.); make (hole) with drill; subject to or undergo discipline by drill; impart (knowledge etc.) by strict method. [Du.]

**drill². 1.** *n.* Small furrow for sowing seed in; ridge with such furrow on top; row of plants so sown; machine for furrowing, sowing, and covering seed. **2.** *v.t.* Sow (seed) or plant (ground) in drills. [orig. unkn.]

**drill³** *n.* Coarse twilled fabric. [abbr. *drilling* f. G *drillich* f. L *trilix* having 3 threads]

**drill⁴** *n.* W. Afr. baboon. [native]

**dri′lў.** See DRY.

**drink. 1.** *v.i.* & *t.* (**drank; drunk**). Swallow liquid, swallow (liquid); swallow contents of (vessel); (of plant, sponge, etc.) absorb (moisture); take alcoholic liquor esp. to excess; bring (one*self to death* etc.) by drinking; spend (wages etc. *away*) on drink. **2.** *n.* Liquid for drinking; glass etc. or portion of this, esp. alcoholic; (**strong**) ∼, intoxicating liquor, excessive use of it (**in** ∼, drunk); **the** ∼, (colloq.) the sea. **3.** ∼ **deep**, take large draught(s); ∼ **down**, drink straight off; ∼ person's **health**, wish good health etc. to him by drinking; ∼ **in**, (fig.) contemplate or listen to with delight or

eagerness; ∼**ing-water** (reserved, or pure enough, for drinking); *drink like a* FISH¹; ∼ **off**, drink the whole (contents) at once; ∼ **to**, pledge, toast, wish success etc. to, by drinking; ∼ **under the table**, outlast (person) in ability to continue drinking liquor etc.; ∼ **up**, drink all or remainder of. **4.** ∼′**able** *a.*, suitable for drinking. [E]

**drip. 1.** *v.i.* & *t.* (**-pp-**). Fall or let fall in drops; let drops fall; be so wet (*with* blood etc.) as to shed drops (∼**ping wet**, very wet); ∼**-dry**, (*v.i.*) dry when hung up to drip, without wringing or ironing, (*a.*) that will drip-dry. **2.** *n.* Act of dripping, dripping liquid; (sl.) stupid or dull person, grumble, flattery, drivel; ∼**-feed**, feeding (esp. intravenously) by liquid a drop at a time; ∼ **mat**, small mat under glass etc.; ∼**-moulding**, ∼′**stone**, (Archit.) projection keeping rain from parts below. **3.** ∼′**ping** *n.*, (esp.) fat melted from roasted meat. [Da. (cf. DROP)]

**driv|e. 1.** *v.t.* & *i.* (**drove** *pr.* drōv; **driven** *pr.* drĭ′ven). Urge in some direction by blows, threats, violence, etc., (*away, back, in, out, from, to, through*, etc.); direct and control (vehicle, animal drawing it, locomotive, etc.); convey in vehicle; be competent to direct course of motor vehicle etc.; travel in private car or carriage; chase (wild beasts, enemy) from large area into small; impel, (of wind, water) carry along; throw, propel, send, cause to go, in some direction, (inanimate thing); (Crick.) return (ball) from freely swung bat to or past bowler; (Golf) strike (ball, or abs.) with driver from tee; (Tennis) hit (ball) with freely swung racket, impel forcibly, constrain, compel (*to, into, to* do); force into a state of being (*mad* etc.); overwork (*was very hard driven; tends to drive himself*); force (stake, nail) into ground etc.; bore (tunnel, horizontal cavity); (let) ∼**e**, aim blow or missile (*at*); (of steam or other power) set or keep (machinery) going; carry on, conclude, (*drove a roaring trade, a good bargain*); dash, rush, work hard *at*; be moved by wind, esp. rapidly (*driving rain*). **2.** *n.* Excursion or journey in vehicle; stroke made by driving in cricket, golf, tennis, etc.; transmission of power to machinery, wheels of motor vehicle, etc.; position of steering--wheel of motor vehicle (*left-hand drive*); energy, capacity or desire or organized effort, to achieve things; game of WHIST, bingo, etc., with many players; street or road, esp. scenic one; ~e('way), road for vehicles, esp. private one leading to house. **3.** ~e at, seek, intend, mean, (*what is he driving at?*); ~e home, make fully known, realized, or understood (message, meaning, etc.); ~e-in *a.* & *n.* (bank, cinema, etc.) that can be used without getting out of one's car; ~e out, oust, take place of; ~ing-licence, ~ing test, (concerned with competence to drive motor vehicle etc.); ~ing-wheel (communicating motive power in machinery). **4.** ~er *n.*, (esp.) person who drives vehicle, golf-club for driving from tee. [E]

**dri'vel. 1.** *v.i.* (‖-ll-). Run at mouth or nose; talk silly nonsense. **2.** *n.* Silly talk, twaddle. [E]

**dri'ven, dri'ver.** See DRIVE.

**dri'zzl|e. 1.** *n.* Spraylike rain; ~ў *a.* **2.** *v.i.* (Of rain) fall in drizzle. [E]

**drŏll** *a.* Amusing; odd, queer; drŏ'llў (-l-lĭ) *adv.*; ~'erў *n.*, quaint humour. [F]

**drŏ'mĕdarў** (*or* -ŭ'm-) *n.* Camel bred for riding, esp. one-humped or Arabian camel. [F or L f. Gk *dromas -ados* runner]

**drōne. 1.** *n.* Male or non-worker bee; idler; deep humming sound; bass-pipe of bagpipe or its continuous note; monotonous speech or speaker. **2.** *v.i.* & *t.* Buzz; talk or utter monotonously; be idle, idle (*away*) life etc. [E]

**drōōl** *v.i.* Drivel, slobber. [DRIVEL]

**drōōp. 1.** *v.i.* & *t.* Hang down, incline, as in weariness; (of eyes) look downwards; languish, flag; let (head, eyes) fall. **2.** *n.* Drooping attitude, loss of spirit. [N (foll.)]

**drŏp. 1.** *n.* Portion of liquid (water, tears, sweat, dew, rain, blood) such as hangs or falls separately or adheres to surface; (in *pl.*, Med.) liquid medicine to be measured by drops; minute quantity; glass etc. of intoxicating liquor (*take a drop; has had a ~ too much*, is drunk); pendant, hanging ornament; sweet (‖ACID, *pear*, etc., *drops*); act of dropping, fall of prices, temperature,

etc., (*at the drop of a* HAT; **get the ~ on**, colloq., have the advantage over); thing that drops or is dropped; distance dropped; abrupt fall or steep slope of surface, amount of this; (sl.) hiding-place for stolen or illicit goods etc., bribe; *box for letters etc. **2.** *v.t.* & *i.* (-pp-). (Let) fall in drops, shed (tears, blood); fall by force of gravity from not being held etc.; allow to fall, cease to hold; allow (supplies etc.) to fall by parachute; set down (passenger, parcel); utter or be uttered casually, as if unconsciously; send casually (*postcard, line, note*); lose (money, esp. in gambling); perform (curtsy); give birth to (esp. lamb); (Footb.) send (ball), make (goal), by drop-kick; omit (one's *h's, syllable*) in speech; cease to associate with, abandon, no longer deal with or discuss (*drop an acquaintance, the subject*); cease, lapse; sink to ground, esp. because exhausted, wounded, etc., (*fit, ready, to ~*, colloq., tired out); die; fall naturally *asleep*, (*back*) *into habit*, etc.; fall in direction, condition, amount, degree, pitch, (*price, voice, wind, drops*); go *down* stream, hillside, etc.; fall *behind, to the rear*, etc.; let (eyes) droop, lower (voice); place in lower position than usual (*dropped handlebars* of bicycle; *dropped waist* of garment); come or go casually *by* or in as visitor, *into* place, *across* person. **3.** *drop a* BRICK, *a* STITCH; ~ **anchor**, anchor ship; ~ **away**, decrease or depart gradually; ~(-**curtain, -scene**), (Theatr.) painted curtain or scenery let down on to stage; ~ **dead!**, sl. excl. of intense scorn; ‖~-**head**, adjustable canvas roof of car; ~ **in a bucket** or **the ocean**, infinitesimal factor; ~ **it!**, stop that; ~(-**kick**), kick at football made by dropping ball and kicking it as it touches ground; ~ **off**, drop away, fall asleep, drop (passenger); ~ **on**, reprimand or punish; ~ **out**, cease to appear or participate, esp. in course of study or in conventional society; ~-**out**, (colloq.) one who drops out; ~ **scone** (made by dropping spoonful of mixture on cooking surface); ~-**shot**, (Tennis) shot dropping abruptly after clearing net; ~ **to**, (sl.) become aware of. **4.** ~'**lĕt** *n.*; ~'**per** *n.*, (esp.) device for administering liquid in drops; ~'**pings** (-z) *n.pl.*, what falls or has fallen in drops (e.g. wax from candles), dung. [E]

**dro′ps|y** n. Disease with watery fluid collecting in body; ~**ical** a. [*hydropsy* f. F f. L f. Gk (HYDRO-)]

**dröss** n. Scum separated from metals in melting; impurities; refuse; ~**′y** a. (~**iness**). [E]

**drought** (-owt), (poet., Sc., Ir., & U.S.), **drouth**, n. Continuous dry weather; (fig.) prolonged lack of something; ~**′y** a. [E (DRY)]

**dröve¹** n. Herd or flock being driven or moving together; crowd esp. in motion; **dröve²**, see DRIVE; ~**′er** n., driver of or dealer in cattle; ~**′ing** n., drover's trade. [E (DRIVE)]

**drown** v.i. & t. Be suffocated or suffocate by submersion; drench, flood; (of sound etc.) overpower (weaker one); assuage (grief) with drink. [E]

**drow′s|y** (-zĭ) a. (~**ily**, ~**iness**). Half asleep; lulling, soporific; ~**e** (-z) v.i., be drowsy. [E]

**drŭb** v.t. (-bb-). Thump, belabour; beat in fight; beat (notion) *into, out of*, person; ~**′bing** n. [ult. f. Arab.]

**drŭdg|e**. **1.** v.i. Work slavishly *at* laborious or distasteful task. **2.** n. Servile worker, slave, hack. **3.** ~**′erў** n., condition or work of a drudge. [orig. uncert.]

**drŭg**. **1.** n. Medicinal substance used alone or as ingredient; (esp.) narcotic, hallucinogen, or stimulant, (*drug addict, habit, traffic*); **dangerous** ~, esp. one that can cause addiction); thing unsaleable from lack of demand (usu. ~ **on the market**); *~′store, chemist's shop also selling miscellaneous articles, light refreshments, etc. **2.** v.t. & i. (-gg-). Add drug (esp. narcotic or poison) to (drink, food); administer drugs, esp. narcotics, to; indulge in narcotics etc. **3.** ~**′gĭst** (-g-) n., dealer in drugs, pharmaceutical chemist. [F]

**drŭ′ggĕt** (-g-) n. (Carpet etc. of) coarse woven fabric. [F]

**druggist**. See DRUG.

**Dru′ĭd** (-ōō′-) n. Ancient Celtic priest and magician; officer of Welsh etc. Gorsedd; ~**ĕss**, ~**ĭsm**, ns.; **Drui′dĭc(al)** (-ōō-) adjs. [F or L f. Celt.]

**drŭm**. **1.** n. Musical instrument sounded by striking skin stretched over ends of cylindrical frame or metal hemisphere, its player; sound (as) of drum; (in *pl.*) percussion

section of jazz band etc.; = EAR¹--drum; cylindrical structure or object, cylinder or barrel in machinery on which something is wound or for other purposes; segment of pillar; cylindrical receptacle for packing dried fruit, holding oil, etc. **2.** v.i. & t. (-mm-). Play drum; beat, tap, or thump continuously on something (on piano, *at* door; *feet drum on floor*; *drumming in the ears*); strike (hands etc.) repeatedly (up)on something, play (as) on drum; (of bird, insect) make loud noise with wings; summon (*up*) by drumming, drive lesson *into* person by persistence. **3.** ~ **brake** (in which shoes on vehicle press against drum on wheel); ~**′fire**, heavy continuous rapid artillery fire usu. heralding infantry attack, (fig.) barrage of criticism etc.; ~**′head**, skin of drum (~*head court martial, service*, improvised or summary); ~ **major**, leader of marching band [orig. in charge of drummers]; ~ **out**, cashier by beat of drum, dismiss with ignominy; ~**′stick**, stick for beating drum, lower joint of cooked fowl's leg; ~**′mer** n., player of drum, commercial traveller. [LG]

**drŭnk**. **1.** a. Deprived of proper control of oneself by alcoholic liquor, (*blind, dead, half, drunk; drunk as a lord, fiddler*); (fig.) overcome *with* joy, success, etc. **2.** n. (sl.) Drinking-bout, period of drunkenness; drunken person. **3.** ~**′ard** n., person often drunk, drunken person; ~**′en** a. (usu. *attrib.*; **-nness** pr. -n-n-), drunk, often drunk, caused by or exhibiting drunkenness (*drunken brawl, frolic*). [p.p. of DRINK]

**drupe** (-ōōp) n. (Bot.) Stone-fruit (e.g. plum, olive). [L f. Gk]

**drў**. **1.** a. (**-ier, -iest; -ily** or ~**ly**, ~**ness**). Without moisture; not rainy, with deficient rainfall (*dry spell, season*; HIGH *and* dry); (of eyes) free from tears; not using, unconnected with, liquid (*dry distillation, shampoo*); parched, dried up, (colloq.) thirsty; not yielding water, milk, etc., (*well, cow, is dry*); (of country, state, legislation, etc.) teetotal, prohibiting sale of alcoholic liquor at some or all times; without butter etc. (*dry bread*); solid, not liquid, (*dry provisions*); (of liquid) having disappeared by evaporation, draining, wiping, etc.; (of wine) free from sweetness; impassive, stiff, cold, (of jest, sarcasm, etc.) expressed in matter-of-fact tone with pretended unawareness; plain, bare, not enlarged upon, (*dry facts*, *thanks*); uninteresting, unprofitable, (*dry as dust*). **2.** *v.t.* & *i.* Make or become dry; preserve food by removal of moisture (*dried egg*, *fruit*). **3.** ~ **battery, cell,** (Electr.) battery or cell in which electrolyte is absorbed in a solid; *dry*-BOB²; ~**-clean,** clean (clothes etc.) with organic solvents without using water; *dry* DOCK³; ~**-fly** *a.*, & *v.i.*, (fish) with artificial fly floating on water; *dry* ICE; ~ **land,** land as opp. sea etc.; ~ **measure** (for dry goods); *dry*-NURSE; ~ **out,** become fully dry, (of drug addict etc.) undergo treatment to cure addiction; ~**-point,** needle for engraving without acid, engraving so produced; ~ **rot,** decayed state of wood when not well ventilated, caused by certain fungi; ~ **run,** (colloq.) rehearsal; ~**-salter,** dealer in drugs, dyes, gums, oils, pickles, tinned meats, etc.; ~ **shave** (using electric razor etc.); ~**-shod** *a.* & *adv.*, without wetting the shoes; ~'**stone,** ~**-walling,** (without mortar); ~ **up,** make utterly dry, dry washed dishes, (of moisture) disappear utterly, (of well etc.) cease to yield water, (colloq., esp. in *imper.*) cease talking or doing something; ~ (**up**), (Theatr.) forget one's lines. **4.** **drī′er,** ~'**er,** *n.*, (esp.) machine for drying hair, laundry, etc. [E]

**drȳ′ăd** *n.* (Myth.) Nymph inhabiting tree. [F f. L f. Gk (*drus* tree)]

**drȳ′er.** See DRY.

**D.S.** *abbr.* dal segno; disseminated SCLEROSIS.

**D.Sc.** *abbr.* Doctor of Science.

**D.S.C., D.S.M., ‖D.S.O.,** *abbrs.* Distinguished Service Cross, Medal, Order.

**D.T.(s)** *abbr.* delirium tremens.

**dū′al. 1.** *a.* (~ly). Of two, twofold, divided in two, double, (*dual ownership*); ‖~ **carriageway,** road with dividing strip between traffic in opposite directions; ~ **control,** esp. of vehicle etc. controlled by instructor as well as by learner); (Gram.) denoting two (cf. *singular*, *plural*). **2.** *n.* (Gram.) Dual number or form. **3.** **dŭă′lĭtў** *n.*; ~**ĭsm** *n.*, duality, theory recognizing two independent principles (e.g. mind and matter, good and evil); ~**ĭst** *n.*;

~**ĭ′stĭc** *a.* (-ically); ~**ĭze** *v.t.* [L (*duo* two)]

**dŭb¹** *v.t.* (-bb-). Make (person) a knight by touching his shoulders with sword; give (person) specified name (*dubs me a crank*); apply dubbing to; ~'**bin(g)** *n.*, grease for softening and waterproofing leather. [F]

**dŭb²** *v.t.* (-bb-). Make another sound-track of (film) esp. in a different language; add (sound effects, music) to film or broadcast. [abbr. of DOUBLE]

**dū′bĭous** *a.* Hesitating, doubting, unreliable, of questionable value or truth (*dubious friend*, *claim*); of doubtful result (*dubious undertaking*); of suspected character (*dubious gains*); **dūbī′etў** *n.*, feeling of doubt; **dŭbĭtā′tion** *n.*, hesitation; **dū′bĭtatĭve** *a.*, expressing doubt. [L (*dubium* doubt)]

**dū′cal** *a.* (~ly). Of, like, bearing title of, duke. [F (DUKE)]

**dŭc′at** *n.* (Hist.) Gold coin once current in most European countries. [It., or L *ducatus* DUCHY]

**dŭ′chĕss** *n.* Duke's wife or widow, woman with own rank of duke; ‖(sl., *abbr.* dutch) costermonger's wife; **dŭ′chў** *n.*, duke's territory, royal dukedom of Cornwall or Lancaster. [F f. L *ducissa* (DUKE)]

**dŭck¹** *n.* Strong linen or cotton material for small sails and clothing; (in *pl.*) trousers of it. [Du.]

**dŭck². 1.** *n.* (*pl.* ~s, coll. ~). Swimming-bird esp. domesticated form of the mallard or wild duck, female of this, its flesh as food, (LAME *duck*; **like a (dying)** ~ **in a thunderstorm,** flabbergasted, distressed; **like water off a** ~'**s back,** producing no effect; *take to thing like* **a** ~ **to water,** very readily); ‖~(**s**), = DUCKY; (Crick.) ~('**s egg**), batsman's score of 0 (**break** one's ~, score one's first run). **2.** *v.i.* & *t.* Dip head under water and emerge; plunge (person) momentarily in or under water; bob down to avoid being seen or hit, or by way of bow or curtsy; (colloq.) withdraw, abscond, dodge. **3.** ~(**s**) **and drake(s),** game of making flat stone ricochet along water (*make* ~s *and drakes of*, *play* ~s *and drakes with*, squander); ~'**bill,** *duck*-billed PLATYPUS; ~**-boards,** narrow path of wooden slats in trench or over mud; ~'**weed,** a water-plant. **4.** ~'**lĭng** *n.*, young duck; ‖**~'ў,** (n.) darling, attractive thing, (a., colloq.) pretty, splendid. [E]

**dŭct. 1.** n. Channel, tube; (Anat.) tube in body conveying secretions etc. (**~'less gland,** one secreting directly into bloodstream). **2.** v.t. Convey through duct. [L *ductus* (*duco duct-* lead)]

**dŭ'ctile** a. Capable of being drawn into wire, tough; pliable, docile; **dŭcti'lĭtў** n. [F or L (prec.)]

**dŭd.** (sl.) **1.** n. Counterfeit article; shell etc. that fails to explode; futile plan or person; (in *pl.*) clothes, rags. **2.** a. Counterfeit; useless, futile. [orig. unkn.]

***dūde** n. (sl.) Foppish person; **~ ranch,** cattle ranch converted to holiday centre. [G dial. *dude* fool]

**dŭ'dgeon** (dŭ'jen) n. **In** (**high**) **~,** (a.), (very) angry, offended, resentful, (adv.) very angrily. [orig. unkn.]

**dūe** a., adv., & n. **1.** a. That ought to be given *to* person (*first place is due to Milton*; *it is due to him to admire his skill*); merited, appropriate, (*has his due reward*; *after due consideration*); to be looked for or foreseen, (*in due time*; *in due* COURSE); owing, payable, as a debt or obligation (**fall, become, ~,** e.g. of bill reaching maturity); to be ascribed *to* cause, agent, etc., (*the difficulty is due to our ignorance*; *the discovery is due to Newton*); under engagement *to do* something or arrive at certain time (*is due to speak tonight*; *train due at 7.30*). **2.** adv. (Of point of compass) exactly, directly, (*went due east*; *a due north wind*); **~ to,** because of (*was late due to an accident*). **3.** n. Person's right, what is owed him, (**give** person, esp. **the Devil** lit. or fig., **his ~,** not be unjust to him, however undeserving); what one owes (*pay one's dues*); (usu. in *pl.*) toll, fee, legally demandable (*harbour, university, dues*). **4. dū'lў** adv., rightly, properly, fitly, sufficiently, punctually. [F f. L (*debeo* owe)]

**dū'el. 1.** n. Fight with deadly weapons between two persons, in presence of two seconds, to settle quarrel; two-sided contest. **2.** v.i. (‖**-ll-**). Fight duel(s). **3. ~list** n., duel-fighter. [It. *duello* or L *duellum* war]

**dūe'nna** n. Older woman acting as governess and companion in charge of girls (orig. and esp. in Spanish

family); chaperon. [Sp. f. L *domina* (DON²)]

**dŭe't** n. (Mus.) (composition for) two voices or performers; (fig.) dialogue; **~tĭst** n. [G or It. f. L *duo* two]

**dŭff¹. 1.** n. Boiled pudding (PLUM *duff*); (sl.) worthless thing. **2.** a. (sl.) Counterfeit, useless. [var. of DOUGH]

**dŭff²** v.t. (sl.) Bungle; **~'er** n., (esp.) inefficient or stupid person. [orig. uncert.]

**dŭ'ffle, dŭ'ffel,** n. Coarse woollen cloth (**~ bag,** cylindrical canvas bag closed by draw-string; **~-coat,** hooded overcoat of duffle with toggle fastenings). [place]

**dŭg¹** n. Udder or breast, teat, nipple, (of female mammal or derog. of woman). [orig. unkn.]

**dŭg².** See DIG.

**dū'gŏng** (or doō'-) n. (*pl.* **~s, ~**). Herbivorous sea-mammal. [Malay]

**dŭ'g-out** n. Roofed shelter esp. for troops in trenches; hollowed tree as canoe; (sl.) retired officer etc. recalled to service. [DUG², OUT]

**dūke** n. (*fem.* DUCHESS). Person holding highest hereditary title of nobility (**royal ~,** one who is also royal prince); sovereign ruling duchy or small State; **~'dom** (-kd-) n., duchy, rank of duke. [F f. L *dux* leader]

**dŭ'lcĕt** a. (Of sound) sweet, soothing; **dŭ'lcĭmer** n., stringed instrument, prototype of piano. [F dim. f. L *dulcis* sweet]

**dŭll. 1.** a. (**~'y** pr. -l-lĭ, **~ness**). Slow of understanding, stupid; (of ears, eyes, etc.) without keen perception; (of pain etc.) indistinctly felt, not acute; (of colour, light, sound, taste) not bright, vivid, or keen; (esp. of edge) blunt; (of person, animal, trade, etc.) sluggish, stagnant; (of goods, stocks) not easily saleable; tedious, monotonous; (of weather) overcast, gloomy; listless, depressed. **2.** v.t. & i. Make or become dull (**~ the edge of,** blunt, make less sensitive or effective). **3. ~'ard** n., slow-witted person. [LDu.]

**dū'lў.** See DUE.

**dŭmb** (-m) a. Unable to speak, either abnormally (of human beings; *the dumb, the deaf and dumb,* as ns.) or normally (of animals); inarticulate, having no voice in government etc. (*the dumb millions*); silenced by surprise, shyness, etc.; taciturn, reticent;

stupid, ignorant; not expressed in words (*dumb agony*); giving no sound; ~~**bell**, short bar with weight at each end used in pairs for exercising muscles, (sl.) stupid person; ~ **blonde**, pretty but stupid blonde woman; ~ **cluck**, *\*~*'**head**, (sl.) stupid person; ~**fou'nd**, strike dumb, nonplus, [CONFOUND]; ~ **show**, gestures instead of speech; ~ **waiter**, movable table esp. with revolving shelves making waiter unnecessary in dining-room, lift for food etc. [E]

**du'mmy** *n.*, *a.*, & *v.* **1.** *n.* (Whist) imaginary player, his cards exposed and played by partner; (Bridge) partner of declarer, whose cards are exposed after first lead, this player's hand (**double** ~, play with two hands exposed, allowing every card to be located); person taking no real part, figure-head; stupid person; counterfeit object, object serving to replace real or normal one; tailor's model of body to hang clothes on; ventriloquist's model of person or animal as feigned talker etc.; baby's indiarubber teat; **sell the** or **a** ~, (Rugby Footb., colloq.) deceive opponent by feigning to pass ball. **2.** *a.* Sham; ~ **run**, practice attack etc., trial run, rehearsal. **3.** *v.i.* (Footb., colloq.) use feigned pass or swerve etc. [DUMB]

**dump. 1.** *v.t.* & *i.* Shoot, deposit, (rubbish); let fall with bump, fall with thud; send (superfluous goods) for sale at low price abroad with view to maintaining home price and capturing foreign market; (colloq.) abandon. **2.** *n.* Rubbish-heap; accumulated pile of ore, earth, etc.; temporary deposit of ammunition etc.; (colloq.) unpleasant or dreary place; ~ **truck** etc. (with body that tilts for unloading). [orig. uncert.]

**du'mp|ling** *n.* Mass of dough boiled or baked either plain or enclosing apple etc.; small fat person; ~**y** *a.* (~**ily**, ~**iness**), short and stout. [*dump* small round object]

**dumps** *n.pl.* (colloq.) Depression, melancholy (*in the dumps*). [LDu. (DAMP)]

**dun**[1]. **1.** *a.* Of dull greyish brown. **2.** *n.* Dun colour; dun horse etc. [E]

**dun**[2]. **1.** *n.* Importunate creditor; debt-collector. **2.** *v.t.* (**-nn-**). Importune for payment. [obs. *dunkirk* privateer]

**dunce** *n.* Bad learner, dullard. [*Duns* Scotus, person]

**du'nderhead** (-ĕd) *n.* Stupid person; ~**ĕd** *a.*, grossly stupid. [orig. unkn.]

**dūne** *n.* Mound or ridge of loose sand etc. formed by wind. [F f. Du. (DOWN[1])]

**dŭng. 1.** *n.* Faeces of animals; manure; ~~**beetle** (whose larvae develop in dung); ~'**hill**, heap of dung or refuse in farmyard. **2.** *v.t.* & *i.* Apply dung to (land); excrete dung. [E]

**dŭngaree'** (-ngg-) *n.* Coarse Indian calico; (in *pl.*) overalls etc. of dungaree or similar material. [Hindi]

**du'ngeon** (-njon) *n.* Subterranean cell for prisoners. [F f. L (DON[2])]

**dŭnk** *v.t.* & *i.* Dip (bread, cake, etc.) into soup or beverage while eating; immerse (lit. or fig.). [G *tunken* dip]

**Dŭnkĭr'k** (-n-k-) *n.* Scene of crisis or withdrawal; ~ **spirit**, refusal to surrender in time of crisis. [place]

**du'nlin** *n.* Red-backed sandpiper. [DUN[1]]

**du'nnage** *n.* Mats, brushwood, etc., stowed under or among cargo to prevent wetting and chafing; (colloq.) miscellaneous baggage. [AL *dennagium*]

‖**du'nnock** *n.* Hedge-sparrow. [DUN[1]]

**dū'ō** *n.* (*pl.* ~**s**). Pair of artistes (*comedy duo*); (Mus.) duet. [L, = two]

**dŭode'cĭm|al** *a.* (**-lly**). Of twelfths or twelve, proceeding by twelves; ~**ō** *n.* (*pl.* ~**os**), book-size in which each leaf is 1/12 of printing-sheet, book of this size; **dŭode'num** *n.*, (Anat.) part of small intestine next to stomach, 12 fingers' breadth long; **dŭode'nal** *a.* [L (*duodecim* twelve)]

**du'ologue** (-g) *n.* Dialogue of two speakers. [DUO, MONOLOGUE]

**dupe. 1.** *v.t.* Cheat, make a fool of. **2.** *n.* Victim of deception. [F]

**du'ple** *a.* ~ **time** (Mus.), with two beats to bar). [L *duplus*]

**du'plex** *a.* Having two elements, twofold. [L, = double]

**du'plic|ate**, *a.*, *n.*, & *v.* **1.** *a.* Having two corresponding parts, existing in two examples; doubled, twice as large or many; exactly like a thing (with any number of specimens etc.); ~ **bridge**, **whist**, (where same hands are played by different persons). **2.** *n.* One of two things

exactly alike, esp. that made after
the other; second copy of letter or
document. **3.** (-āt) *v.t.* Double, multiply by two; make in duplicate, make
or be exact copy of; repeat (action
etc.), esp. unnecessarily; ~**ā'tion** *n.*;
~**ā'tor** *n.*, (esp.) machine for making
copies from stencils etc.; **dūplī'cĭtў**
*n.*, deceitfulness. [L (DUPLEX)]

**dūr'|able** *a.* (-bly). Capable of
lasting; (of goods) remaining useful
for a period; resisting wear; ~**abi'-
lĭtў** *n.*; **dūra mā'ter** *n.*, outer
membrane of brain; ~**ance** *n.*,
(arch.) imprisonment (esp. *in durance
vile*); ~**ā'tion** *n.*, time thing, esp.
war, lasts (**for the ~ation**, until end
of war, fig. for a very long time).
[F f. L (*durus* hard)]

**dūrĕ'ss** (*or* dūr'ĕs) *n.* Forcible
restraint or imprisonment; threats
or other esp. illegal compulsion to
do something (*under duress*). [F f. L
(*durus* hard)]

**dur'ian** (door'-) *n.* S.E. Asian tree
bearing sweet-tasting but strong-
-smelling fruit. [Malay]

**dūr'ing** *prep.* Throughout the continuance of; at a point in the duration
of. [F f. L (DURABLE)]

**dūr'mast** (-ah-) *n.* Species of oak
with sessile flowers. [orig. unkn.]

**dŭrst.** See DARE.

**dŭsk** *n.* Partial darkness; shade;
~**ў** *a.* (~ily, ~iness), shadowy,
dim, dark-coloured. [E]

**dŭst. 1.** *n.* Powdered earth or other
matter lying on ground or other surface or carried along by wind (BITE
*the dust*; ~ **and ashes**, something
very disappointing; **in the ~**,
humiliated, dead; **shake the ~ off
one's feet**, depart indignantly;
**throw ~ in** person's **eyes**, mislead
him); cloud of dust (RAISE *a dust*),
(fig.) confusion, turmoil; pollen,
fine powder of any material (*gold
dust*); dead person's remains (*honoured
dust*); ||~**bin**, container for house-
hold refuse; ~ **bowl**, area denuded
of vegetation by drought and erosion
and so reduced to desert; ||~**cart**,
vehicle for collecting household
refuse; ~**cover**, removable cloth to
keep dust off furniture etc., = dust-
-JACKET; ||~**man**, man who re-
moves refuse from dustbins; ~**pan**
(into which dust is brushed from
floor); ~**sheet**, dust-cover for furniture; ~**trap**, something on which
dust readily collects; ~**up**, (colloq.)

fight, disturbance; ~**wrapper**, =
dust-JACKET. **2.** *v.t.* Sprinkle (powder
usu. *over* object, object *with* powder);
clear (furniture, room, etc.) of dust
(~ person's **jacket**, colloq., thrash
him). **3.** ~**er** *n.*, (esp.) cloth for
dusting furniture, woman's light
loose casual full-length coat; ~**ing**
*n.* (**crop-~ing**, sprinkling of powdered insecticide etc. on crops, esp.
from the air; ~**ing-powder**, esp.
talcum powder); ~**ў** *a.* (~**ily**,
~**iness**), full of or strewn with or
finely powdered like dust, uninteresting, (of colour) dull, vague, unsatis-
factory (*dusty answer*; ||**not so ~y**,
sl., fairly good); ~**y miller**, auricula
plant. [E]

**Dŭtch**[1]. **1.** *a.* Of the Netherlands,
its language, or its people; having
Dutch characteristics. **2.** *n.* The
Dutch language (CAPE[2] *Dutch*;
**double ~**, gibberish); **in ~**, (sl.) in
disgrace; **the ~**, (*pl.*) people of the
Netherlands. **3.** ~ **auction** (in which
auctioneer reduces price until purchaser is found); ~ **barn,** roof on
poles over hay etc.; ~ **cap**, (esp.)
contraceptive diaphragm; ~ **courage** (induced by drink); ~ **doll,**
jointed wooden doll; ~ **elm
disease,** fungous disease of elms;
*Dutch* HOE, OVEN; ~ **treat,** party
where each person pays for his own
share (**go ~**, share expenses thus);
**talk to** person **like a ~ uncle,**
lecture him with kindly severity. **4.**
~**man** *n.*, native of the Netherlands
(or **I'm a ~man, I'm a ~man if,**
forms of asseveration), Dutch ship;
~**woman** *n.* [Du.]

||**dŭtch**[2]. See DUCHESS.

**dū'tў** *n.* Moral or legal obligation,
what one is bound or ought to do,
binding force of what is right;
business, office, function, or engagement in these (HEAVY-duty; **on, off,
~**, actually so engaged or not; **do ~
for**, serve as or pass for (something
else)); payment to public revenue
levied on import, export, manufacture, or sale, of goods (CUSTOMS,
EXCISE[1], *duty*), transfer of property
(||DEATH or ESTATE *duty*), licences,
legal recognition of documents, etc.;
deference, expression of respect to
superior; ~**bound,** obliged by duty;
~ **officer** etc., the one currently on
duty; ~ **paid, -free,** (of goods) on
which customs or excise duty has
been paid, is not leviable; ~**free**

**shop**, one at which duty-free goods can be bought; **dū′teous** *a.*, (literary) dutiful; **dū′tiable** *a.*, liable to customs etc. duties; **dū′tiful** *a.* (-lly), regular or willing in obedience and service. [AF (DUE)]

**du′vet** (dōō′vā) *n.* Thick soft quilt used instead of bedclothes. [F]

**D.V.** *abbr. Deo volente.*

**dwarf** (-ôrf) *n.*, *a.*, & *v.* **1.** *n.* (*pl.* **-fs, -ves** *pr.* -vz). Much undersized person, animal, or plant; (Gmc Myth.) small supernatural being skilled in metal-working. **2.** *a.* Undersized, stunted. **3.** *v.t.* Stunt in growth or in intellect etc.; make look small by contrast or distance. [E]

**dwell** *v.i.* (**dwelt**). Keep one's attention fixed, write or speak at length, (*up*)*on* (~ **upon**, syllable), prolong it); (literary) make one's abode or live in specified place or state (*dwell in, at, near, apart, secure,* etc.); ~**ing** *n.*, (esp.) house, residence; ~**ing-house** (opp. shop, office, etc.). [E, = lead astray]

**dwi′ndle** *v.i.* Waste away, diminish gradually; lose importance. [E]

**dwt.** *abbr.* pennyweight.

**d.w.t.** *abbr.* dead-weight tonnage.

**dy′ad** *n.* The number two; set of two; **dy′ădic** *a.* (duo two) [L f. Gk]

**dye. 1.** *v.t.* (~**ing** *pr.* dī′i-; **dye′able**). Impregnate with colouring-matter (~**d in the wool, in grain**, fig., unchangeable); make (thing) specified colour thus (*dyes her hair brown*); colour, tinge. **2.** *n.* Colour produced (as) by dyeing, hue (lit. or fig., *scoundrel of the deepest dye*); ~**(′stuff)**, substance used for dyeing. [E]

**dy′ing.** See DIE[2]; **dyke**, see DIKE.

**dynă′mics** *n.pl.* (usu. treated as *sing.*) Branch of mechanics that treats of motion in itself, and of the motion of bodies or matter under the influence of forces; branch (of any science) in which forces or changes are considered (often with a specific prefix: *aerodynamics, population dynamics*); motive forces, physical or moral, in any sphere; (Mus.) variation or amount of volume of sound; **dynă′mic,** (*a.*; **-ically**) of dynamics, of motive force (opp. *static*), of force in actual operation (opp. *potential*), active, energetic, (*n.*) energizing or motive force; **dynă′mical** *a.* (**-lly**), of dynamics or dynamism, of force or mechanical power actually operative; **dy′namism** *n.*, energizing or dynamic action or power, (Philos.) theory that phenomena of matter and mind are due merely to the action of forces; **dy′namite,** (*n.*) high explosive of nitroglycerine combined with inert absorbent, (fig.) potentially dangerous person or thing, (*v.t.*) charge or shatter with dynamite; **dy′namo** *n.* (*pl.* **-os**), machine converting mechanical into electrical energy by electric induction (e.g. by rotating conductor in magnetic field), (fig.) energetic person; **dynamo′meter** *n.*, instrument measuring energy expended. [Gk (*dunamis* power)]

**dy′nasty** *n.* Line of hereditary rulers; succession of leaders in any field; **dy′nast** *n.*, member of dynasty; **dynă′stic** *a.* (**-ically**). [F or L f. Gk]

**dyne** *n.* (Phys.) Unit of force, force that, acting for 1 sec. on mass of 1 g, gives it velocity 1 cm per sec. [F f. Gk *dunamis* force]

**dys-** *pref.* (esp. Med. etc.) Bad, difficult, (opp. EU-); ~**menorrhoe′a**, painful menstruation. [Gk]

**dy′sentery** *n.* Inflammation of the bowels; **dysentĕ′ric** *a.* [F or L f. Gk (*entera* bowels)]

**dyslĕ′x|ia** *n.* Word-blindness; ~**ic, dyslĕ′ctic,** *adjs.* (**-ically**) & *ns.* [G f. Gk *lexis* speech]

**dyspĕ′p|sia** *n.* Indigestion; ~**tic** *a.* (**-ically**) & *n.*, (person) subject to dyspepsia or the resulting depression. [L f. Gk (*peptō* digest)]

**dy′strophy** *n.* Defective nutrition; **muscular ~**, hereditary progressive weakening and wasting of muscles. [L f. Gk -*trophia* nourishment]

# E

**E, e,** (ē) *n.* (*pl.* **Es, E's**). Fifth letter; (Mus.) third note in diatonic scale of C major.

**E.** *abbr.* east(ern).

**e-** *pref.,* form of EX-[1] bef. consonants exc. *c, f, h, p, q, s.*

**ea.** *abbr.* each.

**each. 1.** *a.* Every (person, thing, group) taken separately (*each man; on each occasion; five in each class*). **2.** *pron.* Each person or thing (*each has his or its claims, each of us has his claims; we have, they cost, £1 each*). **3.** **~ and every,** every single; **~ other** (used as compound reciprocal pron.; *they hate ~ other,* each hates the other); ||**~ way,** (of bet) backing horse etc. to win and to be placed. [E]

**ea'ger** (-g-) *a.* Full of keen desire, keen, enthusiastically impatient, (*eager to start, for fame; an eager glance; in eager pursuit*); *eager* BEAVER[1]. [F f. L *acer* keen]

**ea'gle** *n.* Large bird of prey with keen vision and powerful flight; figure of eagle, esp. as symbol of U.S., (Hist.) as Roman or French ensign; (Golf) hole played in two under par or bogey; **double ~,** figure of two-headed eagle; **~ eye,** keen sight or watchfulness; **~-owl,** large horned owl; **ea'glĕt** *n.,* young eagle. [F f. L *aquila*]

**ea'gre** (ā'ger, ē'ger) *n.* = BORE[3]. [orig. unkn.]

**E. & O. E.** *abbr.* errors and omissions excepted.

**ear**[1] *n.* Organ of hearing in man and animals, esp. external part of this (*bring storm, hornets' nest,* etc. **about** one's **~s,** down upon oneself, lit. or fig.; **all ~s,** listening attentively; *ears* BURN[2]; **give ~,** listen *to*; **give** one's **~s,** make any sacrifice *for* thing, *to* do, *if*; **~ to the ground,** alertness regarding rumours or trend of opinion; **have** person's **~,** have his favourable attention; **over head and ~s,** deeply immersed, lit. or fig.; **in (at) one ~ and out (at) the other,** heard but leaving no impression; **out on** one's **~,** dismissed

ignominiously; PRICK *up* one's **ears;** **set by the ~s,** cause to quarrel; **up to the ~s,** colloq., deeply involved *in;* **a word in your ~,** in private); faculty of discriminating sound (*an ear for music*); ear-shaped thing; **~'ache,** pain in ear-drum; **~-drops,** (1) medicinal drops for ear, (2) hanging ear-rings; **~-drum,** internal membrane of ear; **~'mark,** (*n.*) owner's mark on ear of sheep etc., (fig.) mark of ownership, (*v.t.*) mark (animal) thus, assign (money etc.) to a purpose; **~-muff,** device to protect ear against cold or noise; **~'phone,** device worn on ear to aid hearing or to listen to radio or telephone communication; **~-piece,** part of telephone &c. to be held to ear; **~-piercing,** shrill; **~-plug,** piece of wax etc. placed in ear to protect against water, noise, etc.; **~-ring,** ornament worn in or hanging from lobe of ear; **~'shot,** hearing-distance (*within earshot*); **~-splitting,** excessively loud; **~-trumpet,** tube used by partly deaf person; **~'wig,** insect with large terminal forceps (once thought to enter head through ear); **~'ful** (-ŏŏl) *n.,* (colloq.) large amount of talk etc., reprimand. [E]

**ear**[2] *n.* Spike, head, of corn containing flowers or seeds. [E]

**earl** (ẽrl) *n.* (*fem.* **countess**). British nobleman ranking between marquis and viscount; ||**E~ Marshal,** officer presiding over Heralds' College, with ceremonial duties; **~'dom** *n.* [E]

**ear'lў** (ẽr'-) *a.* & *adv.* (**-ier, -iest; -iness**). **1.** Before the due, usual, or expected time (*was early for my appointment*); forward in flowering, ripening, etc., (*early peaches*); not far on in day or night or time, (*early evening; seek an early opportunity for discussion;* **on Friday at earliest,** not before then); not far on in a period, development, or process of evolution. (*the early spring; the early part of the century; the early Christians; early man*). **2. ~ bird,** (joc.) person who arrives, rises, etc., early; **~ closing,** shutting of shops etc. on a particular afternoon of each week; **~ days,** early in time for something (to happen, etc.); **E~ English style,** (Archit.) first stage of English Gothic (13th c.); **keep ~ hours,** go to bed and rise early; **~ on,** at an early stage; **~ riser,** one who gets up unusually early from bed. [E (ERE)]

**earn** (ẽrn) *v.t.* (Of person, conduct, etc.) obtain or be entitled to as reward of work or merit; bring in as income or interest; **~'ings** (-z) *n.pl.,* money earned. [E]

**ear'nest**[1] (ẽr'-). **1.** *a.* Serious, not trifling, ardent, zealous. **2.** *n.* Seriousness; **in ~,** serious(ly), not joking(ly). [E]

**ear'nest**[2] (ẽr'-) *n.* Money paid as instalment esp. to confirm contract; foretaste, token, *(an earnest of future favours).* [L (*arrha* pledge)]

**earth** (ẽr-). **1.** *n.* Dry land; soil, mould; ground *(it fell to earth;* **come back to ~,** return to realities; DOWN[3]*-to-earth);* land and sea, opp. sky; (or *E~)* planet on which we live; present abode of man, opp. heaven or hell *(on ~,* existing anywhere; *happiest man on earth; what on earth do you mean?);* hole of badger, fox, etc., **(gone to ~,** fig., in hiding; **run to ~,** fig., find after extensive search); ‖(Electr.) connection to earth as completion of circuit; (colloq.) huge sum, vast amount, *(cost the earth; wants the earth).* **2.** *v.t.* & *i.* Cover (roots) with earth; ‖(Electr.) connect to earth. **3.** ‖**~-closet,** substitute for water-closet in which earth is used to cover excreta; **~- -moving,** excavation of large quantities of soil; **~-nut,** (edible tuber of) one of various plants, esp. PEA*nut;* **~'quake,** convulsion of earth's surface due to faults in strata or volcanic action, (fig.) social etc. disturbance; **~ sciences** (dealing with the earth or part of it); **~- -shaking** *a.,* (fig.) having violent effect; **~'work,** bank of earth in fortification etc.; **~'worm,** worm living in earth. **4.** **~'en** *a.,* made of earth or of baked clay; **~'enware,** *(a.)* made of baked clay, *(n.)* baked clay, vessels of this; **~'lỹ** *a.* (-iness), of the earth, terrestrial, *(earthly* PARADISE; **no ~ly use,** colloq., no use at all; **not an ~ly,** sl., no chance whatever); **~'ỹ** *a.* (**~iness),** of or

like earth or soil, grossly material, coarse *(earthy jokes).* [E]

**ease** (ēz). **1.** *n.* Freedom from pain or trouble; freedom from constraint *(at one's ease;* **put** person **at his ~,** avoid undue formality; **at ~,** Mil., in relaxed attitude, with feet apart; ILL *at ease);* facility *(did it with ease).* **2.** *v.t.* & *i.* Relieve from pain etc.; give mental ease to *(ease* one's *mind);* relax, slacken, (grip, rope, etc.); cause to move by gentle force *(ease into place);* **~ (off, up),** become less burdensome or severe. **3.** **~'ful** (-zf-) *a.* (-lly), (arch.) comfortable, soothing, at rest. [F f. L (ADJACENT)]

**ea'sel** (-z-) *n.* Frame to support picture etc. [Du. *ezel* ass]

**ea'sement** (-zm-) *n.* Right (esp. of way) over another's property. [F (EASE)]

**east** *n., a.,* & *adv.* **1.** *n.* Point of horizon where sun rises at equinoxes, compass point 90° to right of North **(to the ~ of,** in an eastward direction from); *(E~)* regions or countries lying to the east of Europe **(Far E~,** China, Japan, etc.; **Middle, Near, E~,** esp. countries from Egypt to Iran inclusive; **Near E~,** arch., Turkey and Balkan countries), part of country or town lying to the east, Communist States of eastern Europe; altar-end of church; **~-north-~, ~-south-~,** (compass point) midway between east and north-east, south-east. **2.** *a.* Towards, at, near, facing, east (‖**E~ End,** eastern part of London including docks; *East* INDIES; *\**E~ Side,** eastern part of Manhattan); coming from east *(east wind).* **3.** *adv.* Towards, at, near, the east (DUE *east; lies* etc. **~ and west,** lengthwise on line running from E. to W.; *east* BY *north, south;* **~ of,** in an eastward direction from). **4.** **~'erlỹ** *a.* & *adv.,* in eastern position or direction, (of wind) blowing (nearly) from east; **~'ern** *a.* (superl. **~ern- most),** of or dwelling in the east; **E~ern Church,** Orthodox Church; **~'erner** *n.,* inhabitant of the east; **~'ward** *a., adv.,* & *n.;* **~'wards** (-z) *adv.* [E]

**Ea'ster** *n.* Christian festival commemorating Christ's resurrection, held on a variable Sunday *(Easter Day, Sunday);* **~ egg,** artificial (esp. chocolate) egg or coloured hard- -boiled egg as gift at Easter. [E]

**ea'sỹ** (ē'zĭ) (-ily, -iness). **1.** *a.*

Free from bodily or mental pain, worry, etc., (*make your mind easy*; ~ **circumstances**, colloq. E~ Street, affluence); free from embarrassment, strictness, etc., (*easy manners*; FREE *and easy*); not difficult (*to do, of* access; ~ **on the eye**, pleasant to look at); compliant (I'm ~, colloq., I have no preference). **2.** *adv.* In effortless or relaxed manner, with ease; ~!, move gently; **go ~**, be sparing or cautious (*with*); **take it ~**, proceed gently, relax. **3.** ~ **chair** (designed for comfort); ~**going**, (of person) not strict, taking things as they are; ~ **mark**, **meat**, (colloq.) person or thing easily overcome, persuaded, etc.; ~ **money** (got without effort). [F (EASE)]

**eat** *v.t.* & *i.* (**ate** *pr.* ĕt, āt; **ea'ten**). Take into mouth, chew and swallow, swallow, (solid food, soup, etc.; ~ **out of** person's **hand**, be submissive to him; *eat* one's HAT; ~ **its head off**, (of animal) cost more to feed than it is worth; **what's** ~**ing you?**, (colloq.) why are you vexed?; ~ one's **words**, retract them abjectly); consume food, take a meal, (~ **out**, take a meal elsewhere than at home); destroy, consume, (*eat* one's HEART *out*); ~ **away**, **into**, destroy gradually, erode, (lit. or fig.; *eaten away with rust*); ~ **up**, consume completely (lit. or fig.; *eaten up with pride*), traverse (distance) rapidly; ~**able** *a.* & *n.* (usu. in *pl.*); ~**er** *n.*, one who or that which eats (*he is a big eater*), fruit that may be eaten raw; ~**ing** *n.* (~ing apple etc., that may be eaten raw; ~**ing-house**, restaurant); ~**s** *n.pl.*, (colloq.) food. [E]

**eau** (ō) *n.* ~-**de-Cologne** (ōdekolō'n), perfume made orig. at Cologne; ~-*de-vie* (ōdevē'), brandy. [F, = water]

**eaves** (ēvz) *n.pl.* Projecting lower edge of roof; ~'**drop**, (orig.) stand under eaves to overhear secrets, (fig.) listen secretly to private conversation; ~'**dropper**, one who does this (usu. fig.). [E]

**ebb. 1.** *n.* Outward movement of tide (*ebb and flow*; *ebb-tide*); decline, decay, (*at a low ebb*). **2.** *v.i.* Flow back; recede, decline. [E]

**e'bony. 1.** *n.* Hard heavy black wood from tropical tree. **2.** *a.* Made

of, black as, ebony; **e'bonīte** *n.*, = VULCANITE. [F f. L f. Gk]

**ebu'llien**|**t** (or -ōō'-) *a.* Boiling; exuberant; ~**ce**, ~**cy**, *ns.*; **ebulli'-tion** *n.*, boiling, (fig.) outburst (*of* anger etc.). [L *ebullio* (BOIL[2])]

**E.C.** *abbr.* East Central.

**ecce'ntric** (ĭks-). **1.** *a.* (~**ally**). Not concentric (*to another circle*); not placed, not having its axis placed; centrally; (of orbit) not circular; irregular, odd, whimsical, capricious; **ecce'ntric'ity** *n.* **2.** *n.* Eccentric person; (Mech.) disc fixed eccentrically on revolving shaft. [L f. Gk (CENTRE)]

‖**E'ccles** (ĕ'kelz) *n.* ~ **cake**, round cake of pastry filled with currants etc. [place]

**Eccles.** *abbr.* Ecclesiastes (O.T.).

**Ecclēsiā'stēs** (ĭklēzĭă'stēz) *n.* O.T. book ascribed to Solomon; **ecclēsiā'stic** (-zĭ-) *n.*, clergyman; **ecclēsiā'stical** (-zĭ-) *a.* (-**lly**), of the Church or clergy; **Ecclēsiā'sticus** (ĭklēz-) *n.*, book of maxims in Apocrypha; **ecclēsiō'logy** (-z-) *n.*, science of church building and decoration. [Gk (*ekklēsia* church)]

**Ecclus.** *abbr.* Ecclesiasticus (Apocrypha).

**E.C.G.** *abbr.* electrocardiogram.

**e'chelon** (-sh-; *or* ā'-) *n.* Arrangement of troops in parallel groups each with its end clear of those ahead or behind; similar arrangement of things (e.g. ships); group of persons at a particular level in an organization. [F (SCALE[3])]

**echi'dna** (-k-) *n.* Australian toothless burrowing egg-laying hedgehog--like animal. [L f. Gk, = viper]

**echī'n|us** (-k-) *n.* (Esp. common European) kind of sea-urchin; (Archit.) rounded moulding below abacus; ~**odĕrm** *n.*, animal of star-fish and sea-urchin group. [L f. Gk]

**e'chō** (ĕ'kō). **1.** *n.* (*pl.* ~**es**). Repetition of sound by reflection of sound-waves, secondary sound so produced, (*cheer* person etc. **to the** ~, loudly); reflected radio or radar beam; close imitation; ~**loca'tion**, location of objects by reflected sound; ~-**sounder**, sounding apparatus for determining depth of sea beneath ship by echo from bed. **2.** *v.i.* & *t.* (Of place) resound with echo, repeat (sound) thus; (of sound) be repeated, resound; repeat (person's words), imitate opinions of. **3.** ~**ic**

(-ō′-) *a.* (~ically), onomatopoeic. [F or L f. Gk]

**echt** (ĕxt) *a.* Authentic, genuine, typical. [G]

**éclair** (ā′klār, -ār′) *n.* Finger--shaped cake of choux pastry filled with cream and iced, usu. with chocolate icing. [F, = lightning]

**éclat** (ĕklah′, ā′klah) *n.* Brilliant success; prestige. [F]

**éclĕc′tic. 1.** *a.* (~ally). (Of philosopher) selecting doctrines from various schools of thought; borrowing freely from diverse sources; not exclusive in taste, opinions, etc. **2.** *n.* Eclectic person; ~ism *n.* [Gk (*eklegō* pick out)]

**éclī′pse. 1.** *n.* Interception of light of sun, moon, etc., by another body between it and the eye or between the luminous body and what illuminates it; loss of light, brilliance, or importance. **2.** *v.t.* (Of heavenly body) cause eclipse of (another); intercept (light); (fig.) outshine, surpass. **3.** **éclī′ptic** *n.,* sun's apparent path among stars during year. [F f. L f. Gk]

**é′clŏgue** (-g) *n.* Short poem, esp. pastoral dialogue. [L f. Gk (ECLECTIC)]

**ēcŏ′log|ў** *n.* Branch of biology dealing with relations of organisms to one another and to their surroundings; **ēcolŏ′gĭcal** *a.* (-lly); ~ĭst *n.*; **ēcŏ-** *comb. form.* [G f. Gk *oikos* house]

**ēconŏ′mĭc. 1.** *a.* (~ally). Of economics; maintained for profit, on business lines; paying or recouping (at least) expenditure; (of rent) high enough to compensate builder, owner, etc.; practical, considered with regard to human needs (*economic botany, geography*). **2.** *n.* (in *pl.,* treated as *sing.*) Science of production and distribution of wealth; application of this to particular subject (*the economics of publishing*). **3.** ~al *a.* (~ally), saving, avoiding waste, (*of*). [F or L f. Gk (foll.)]

**ēcŏ′nom|ў** *n.* (Administration or condition of) concerns and resources of a community (**political** ~**y,** study of economic problems of government, arch. economics); careful management of (esp. financial) resources, frugality, frugal use, (*make little economies; travel* ~**y class, buy an** ~**y** ticket, the cheapest available (esp. in air travel); ~**y**

size, of goods etc., so large as to be economically advantageous to the customer); ~**ĭst** *n.,* manager (of money etc.), thrifty person, expert on or student of economics; ~**ĭze** *v.i.* & *t.,* practise economy, reduce expenditure; ~**ize** (**on**), use sparingly; ~**izā′tion** *n.* [F or L f. Gk, = household management]

**ecru** (ā′krōō) *n.* Colour of unbleached linen, light fawn. [F]

**ĕ′cstas|ў** *n.* Exalted state of feeling, rapture, (**in** ~**ies,** of joy or delight); trance; **ĕcstă′tic** *a.* (-ically), of or in ecstasies. [F f. L f. Gk *ekstasis* standing outside oneself]

**E.C.T.** *abbr.* electroconvulsive therapy.

**ĕ′ctō-** *in comb.* Outside; ~**mŏrph** *n.,* lean-bodied person (with predominance of structures formed from outer layer of embryo) [Gk *morphē* form]; ~**plăsm** *n.,* viscous substance supposed to emanate from body of spiritualistic medium during trance [PLASMA]. [Gk *ektos* outside]

**-ĕ′ctomў** *suf.* forming *ns.,* denoting surgical operation in which some part is removed (*appendice′ctomy,* removal of the appendix; HYSTERECTOMY). [Gk *ektomē* excision]

**ēcūmĕ′nĭcal** *a.* (~ly). Of, representing, the whole Christian world; seeking world-wide Christian unity; world-wide; ~**ĭsm, ēcūmĕni′citў,** **ē′cūmenĭsm,** *ns.* [L f. Gk *oikoumenikos* of the inhabited earth]

**ĕ′czĕma** (or ĕ′ks-) *n.* Inflammation of skin with itching and discharge from vesicles. [L f. Gk]

**-ed** (ĭd after *d* or *t,* t after other voiceless consonant, d elsewhere) *suf.* forming *adjs.* f. *ns.,* meaning 'having, wearing, etc.' (*diseased, booted*), or f. *phrs.* of *adj.* & *n.* (*good-humoured, stout-hearted, three-cornered*); see also Inflexion, p. xii. [E]

**ed.** *abbr.* edited (by); edition; editor; educated.

**E′dăm** (ē′-) *n.* Spherical Dutch cheese, usu. yellow with red rind. [place]

**E′dda** (ĕ′-) *n.* Elder, Poetic, ~, collection of ancient Icelandic poems; Younger, Prose, ~, miscellaneous handbook (*c.* 1230) to Icelandic poetry. [N]

**ĕ′ddў. 1.** *n.* Small whirlpool; smoke, fog, etc., moving like this. **2.** *v.i.* & *t.* Move in eddies. [E *ed-* again, back]

**e′delweiss** (ā′delvīs) *n.* Alpine

white-flowered plant. [G, = noble--white]

**E'den** (ē'-) n. **(Garden of)** ~, abode of Adam and Eve at creation, (earthly) paradise; delightful place; state of supreme happiness. [L f. Gk f. Heb. (orig. = delight)]

**ĕdĕ'ntāte** a. & n. (Animal, esp. mammal, e.g. sloth, armadillo) having few or no teeth. [L (dens dent- tooth)]

**ĕdge. 1.** n. Cutting side of blade, (fig.) effectiveness, (knife has no ~, is blunt; **on** ~, excited or irritable; **set** person's **teeth on** ~, revolt him (as) by sour taste or grating noise; **take the** ~ **off**, blunt, dull, weaken; **rough** ~ of one's **tongue**, reviling; edge-shaped thing, esp. crest of ridge; meeting-line of surfaces; boundary-line of region or surface, brink of precipice (**on the** ~ **of**, almost involved in or affected by; **have the** ~ **on**, colloq., have an advantage over); ~~, ~**d**, **tool**, cutting-tool. **2.** v.t. & i. Sharpen (tool etc.); give or form border to; insinuate (thing, oneself, in etc.); advance, esp. gradually and obliquely. **3.** ~**ways** (-jwāz), ~**wise** (-jwīz), advs., with edge foremost or uppermost; **get a word in** ~**ways** or ~**wise** (in talkative person's pause); **ĕ'dging** n., (esp.) border, fringe; **ĕ'dgў** a. (-ily, -iness), sharp-edged, (fig.) having one's nerves on edge, testy. [E]

**ĕ'dĭb|le** a. & n. (Thing) fit to be eaten; ~**i'lĭtў** n. [L (edo eat)]

**ĕ'dĭct** n. Order proclaimed by authority. [L (edico proclaim)]

**ĕ'dĭfĭce** n. Building, esp. large imposing one. [F f. L (aedis dwelling)]

**ĕ'dĭf|ў** v.t. Improve morally; ~**ĭcā'tĭon** n. [F f. L (aedifico build)]

**ĕ'dĭt** v.t. Arrange, annotate, or otherwise prepare (another's work) for publication; take extracts from and collate (films etc.) to form unified sequence; reword for a purpose; act as editor of (newspaper etc.); **ĕdĭ'tĭon** n., edited or published form of a book etc., the copies of a book, newspaper, etc., issued at one time, (fig.) product of the same kind, person etc. resembling another (a smaller edition of his brother); ~**or** n., one who edits (another's work, a film, etc.), one who conducts a newspaper or a particular section of one (sports editor; city editor), head of

department of publishing house; ~**ōr'ĭal**, (a.; -lly) of an editor, (n.) newspaper article written or sanctioned by editor. [F, ult. f. L edo edit- give or put out]

**ĕ'dŭc|āte** v.t. (~**able**). Bring up (child) so as to form habits, manners, etc.; train intellectually and morally; provide schooling for; train (person etc., faculty, to do); ~**ated guess** (based on experience); ~**abĭ'lĭtў**, ~**ātor**, ns.; ~**ātive** a. [L educo -are rear]

**ĕdŭcā'tĭon** n. (Course of) systematic instruction (classical, commercial, FURTHER, HIGHer, education); development of character or mental powers; ~**al** a. (~**ally**); ~**(al)ĭst** ns., person concerned with education.

**ĕdū'ce** v.t. (~**ible**). Bring out, develop from latent or potential existence; **ĕdŭ'ctĭon** n. [L educo -ere draw out]

**Edwăr'dĭan** (ĕ-; or -ōr'-). **1.** a. Characteristic of Edward VII's reign (1901-10). **2.** n. Person belonging to this period. [Edward]

**-ee** suf. forming ns. expr. (1) person affected by vbl action (addressee, employee, payee), (2) person concerned with or described as (absentee, bargee, refugee), (3) object of smaller size (bootee, coatee). [F -é in p.p.]

**E.E.C.** abbr. European Economic Community.

**E.E.G.** abbr. electroencephalogram.

**eel** n. Snakelike fish; (fig.) slippery or evasive person or thing; ~**ў** a. [E]

**-eer** suf. forming (1) ns. denoting 'person concerned with' (auctioneer, mountaineer, profiteer), (2) vbs. denoting the actions of such ns. (electioneer). [F -ier f. L -arius]

**eer'|ĭe** a. (~**ily**, ~**iness**). Gloomy; strange, weird. [E]

**ef-.** See EX-[1].

**ĕff** v.i. & t. (sl.) Say fuck etc.; = FUCK (eff off); ~ **and blind**, use strong expletives. [name of letter F, as euphem. abbr.]

**ĕffā'ce** v.t. Rub or wipe out (mark, recollection, impression); surpass, eclipse; ~ **oneself**, treat oneself as unimportant; ~**'ment** (-sm-) n. [F (FACE)]

**ĕffĕ'ct. 1.** n. Result, consequence, (**in** ~, for practical purposes; **to that** ~, having that result or implication); efficacy (of no effect); being operative (**bring, carry, into** ~, accomplish; **give** ~ **to**, **take** ~, make, become, operative; **with ~ from**, coming into operation at (stated time)); combination of colour, form, etc., (*a pretty effect*); impression produced on observer (*done, said, only for effect*); (in *pl.*) property (*personal effects*; '**no ~s**', written by banker on dishonoured cheque), lighting, sounds, etc., as accompaniment to play, film, etc., (*sound effects*; *special effects*). **2.** *v.t.* Bring about, accomplish, cause to occur, (*effect a change, cure, sale*). **3. ~ive** *a.*, having effect, impressive, actual, existing, actually usable, equivalent in its effect; **~ual** *a.* (-lly), answering its purpose, valid; **~uāte** *v.t.*, cause to happen; **~uā'tion** *n.* [F or L (FACT)]

**effē'mina|te** *a.* Womanish, unmanly; **~cỹ** *n.* [L (*femina* woman)]

**efferve'sc|e** *v.i.* Give off bubbles of gas, bubble, (fig. of persons); **~ent** *a.*; **~ence, ~encỹ**, *ns.* [L (FERVENT)]

**effē'te** *a.* Worn out; feeble. [L]

**effica'cious** (-shus) *a.* Producing, sure to produce, desired effect (*efficacious remedy*); **e'fficacỹ** *n.* [L *efficax* (FACT)]

**effi'cien|t** (-shent) *a.* Producing effect (**~t cause**, that which makes a thing what it is); (of person) competent, capable; **~cỹ** *n.*, (also, Mech. & Phys.) ratio of useful work done to energy expended.

**e'ffigỹ** *n.* Portrait, image, (**burn person in ~**, burn a figure representing him). [L *effigies* (*fingo* to fashion)]

**efflore'sc|e** *v.i.* Burst into flower; **~ent** *a.*; **~ence** *n.* [L (*flos flor*-FLOWER)]

**e'ffluen|t** (-lōō-). **1.** *a.* Flowing out. **2.** *n.* Stream flowing from larger stream, sewage tank, industrial process, etc. **3. ~ce** *n.*, flowing out (of light, electricity, etc., or fig.), that which flows out; **efflu'vium** (-lōō'-) *n.* (*pl.* -ia), exhaled (esp. unpleasant) substance affecting lungs or sense of smell; **e'fflux, efflu'xion** (-kshon), *ns.*, effluence. [L (*fluo flux*- flow)]

**e'ffort** *n.* Strenuous exertion; vigorous attempt (*at, to* do); force exerted; (colloq.) something accomplished (*a reasonably good effort*). [F f. Rom. (L *fortis* strong)]

**effro'nterỹ** (-ŭnt-) *n.* Shameless insolence, impudence. [F f. L (*frons front*- forehead)]

**efful'gen|t** *a.* Radiant; **~ce** *n.* [L '*fulgeo* shine)]

**efffū's|e** (-z) *v.t.* Pour forth (liquid, light, influence, etc.); **effū'sion** (-zhon) *n.*, outpouring (often derog. of literary work); **effū'sive** *a.*, demonstrative, gushing. [L (*fundo fus*- pour)]

**eft** *n.* Newt. [E]

**E'fta** (ě'-), **E.F.T.A.**, *n.* European Free Trade Association. [abbr.]

**e.g.** *abbr.* for example. [L *exempli gratia* for the sake of example]

**egalitār'ian. 1.** *a.* Of, relating to, holding, principle of equality of mankind; **~ism** *n.* **2.** *n.* Egalitarian person. [F (*égal* equal)]

**egg**[1] *n.* Spheroidal body produced by female of birds etc. containing germ of new individual, esp. that of domestic fowl for eating (**have all one's ~s in one basket**, risk all on a single venture; **teach one's grandmother to suck ~s**, presume to advise person(s) of greater experience; **as sure as ~s is** or **are ~s**, undoubtedly); (Zool.) ovum; (pop.) pupa of ant etc.; (sl.) person or thing (*good, BAD, tough, egg*), bomb; **~-and-spoon race** (in which runners carry egg in spoon); **~-cup** (for egg boiled in shell); **egg** CUSTARD; **~-flip, -nog**, drink of hot or cold beer etc. with eggs and usu. milk stirred in; **~'head**, (colloq.) intellectual person; **~-plant**, = AUBERGINE; **~'shell**, shell of egg, fragile thing (*~shell china*, very thin kind), (of paint etc.) slightly glossy; **~-spoon**, small spoon for eating boiled egg; **~-timer**, device for timing the cooking of an egg; **~'ỹ** *a.* [N]

**egg**[2] *v.t.* **~ person on**, urge him (*to* an act, *to* do). [N (EDGE)]

**e'glantine** *n.* SWEET-brier. [F, f. L *acus* needle]

**e'gō** *n.* (*pl.* **~s**). (Metaphys.) conscious thinking subject; (Psych.) part of mind that reacts to reality and has sense of individuality; self-esteem; **~-trip**, (colloq.) activity etc. devoted to one's own interests or feelings. [L, =I]

**egocě'ntr|ic** *a.* (**~ically**). Self-centred, egoistic. [CENTRE]

**e'gō|ism** *n.* Ethical theory basing morality on self-interest; systematic selfishness; opinionatedness; egotism; **~ist** *n.*; **~i'stic(al)** *adjs.* (-ically). [EGO]

**e'got|ism** *n.* Practice of talking about oneself; too frequent use of 'I' and 'me'; self-conceit; selfishness; ~ist n.; ~i′stic(al) adjs. (-ically). [EGO + -ISM w. intrusive -t-]

**ègrē′gious** (-jǔs) a. Shocking (egregious fool, folly, blunder); (arch.) remarkable. [L (grex greg- flock)]

**ē′grĕss** n. (Right of) going out; way out. [L (egredior -gress- walk out)]

**ē′grĕt** n. Lesser white heron. [F aigrette]

**Egў′ptian** (ĭjĭ′pshǎn). **1.** a. Of Egypt. **2.** n. Native of Egypt; Hamitic language used in Egypt until 3rd c. **3.** Egўptŏ′logŷ (ē-) n., study of Egyptian antiquities; Egўptŏ′logĭst (ē-) n. [Egypt]

**eh** (ā) int. (colloq.) expr. inquiry or surprise, or inviting assent, or asking for repetition or explanation. [instinctive excl.]

**ei′der** (ī′-) n. ~ (duck), large northern duck; ~(-down), breast feathers of eider; ~down, quilt stuffed with eider-down etc. [Icel.]

**eidĕ′tic** (ī-) a. (Of mental image) unusually vivid and detailed. [G f. Gk (eidos form)]

**eight** (āt) a. & n. NUMERAL (figure of) ~, 8-shaped figure; 8-oared boat or its crew (~s, races between such boats); **have one over the ~**, (sl.) get slightly drunk; ~ee′n(th) (or ā′-) adjs. & ns., NUMERALS; ~′fŏld a. & adv.; ~h (ātth) a. & n., NUMERAL, ~′hlŷ (ā′tthlĭ) adv.; ~some a. & ; ~some (reel), lively Scottish dance for 8 persons; ~′ĭĕth, ~′ŷ, adjs. & ns., NUMERALS; 8vo, see OCTAVO. [E]

**eisteddfod** (īstĕ′dhvŏd) n. (pl. ~s, ~au pr. -ī). Congress of Welsh bards; national or local gathering for musical and literary competitions. [W (eistedd sit)]

**ei′ther** (ī′dh-, ē′dh-) a., pron., & adv. or conj. **1.** a. & pron. Each (one) of two (at either end was a lamp; either will do; either view is tenable); one or other of two (put the lamp at either end; either of you can go). **2.** adv. or conj. On one or other supposition, which way you will, (is either black or white; either come in or go out); (w. neg. or interrog.) any more than the other (if you do not go, I shall not either; there is no time to lose, either). [E]

**èjā′cŭlāt|e** v.t. & i. Utter suddenly, exclaim; eject (fluid etc., esp. semen) from body; èjăcŭlā′tion n.; ~orŷ a. [L (ejaculor dart out)]

**èjĕ′ct** v.t. Expel (person or thing from place etc.); emit; dispossess

(tenant) by legal process; ~ion, ~ment, ~or, ns. (~ion or ~or seat, device for ejection of pilot of aircraft etc. in emergency); ~ĭve a. [L ejicio eject- throw out]

**ēke** v.t. ~ out, supply deficiencies of (eke out one's salary with odd jobs), make (livelihood) or support (existence) with difficulty. [E]

**èlă′bor|ate. 1.** a. Minutely worked out; highly developed or complicated. **2.** (-āt) v.t. & i. Work out (system, theory, machine, etc.) in detail; produce by labour; explain thing in detail (I need not elaborate); ~ā′tion, ~ātor, ns.; ~ātĭve a. [L (LABOUR)]

**élan** (ā′lahṅ) n. Vivacity, dash. [F]

**ē′land** n. Large Afr. antelope. [Du.]

**èlă′pse** v.i. (Of time) pass away. [L elabor elaps- slip away]

**èlă′stĭc** (or -ah′-). **1.** a. (~ally) Spontaneously resuming its normal bulk or shape after contraction, dilation, or distortion, (elastic stocking; elastic band); springy; (of feelings or person) buoyant; flexible, adaptable (elastic conscience). **2.** n. Elastic cord or fabric, usu. woven with strips of rubber. **3.** ~ātĕd a., (of fabric) made elastic by weaving with rubber thread (elasticated waistband); èlăstĭ′cĭtŷ n.; ~ize v.t.; èlă′stomĕr n., natural or synthetic rubber or rubber-like plastic. [L f. Gk elastikos propulsive]

**èlā′t|e** v.t. Inspirit, stimulate; (esp. in p.p.) make proud; ~ion n. [L effero elat- raise]

**ē′lbow** (-ō). **1.** n. Joint between forearm and upper arm (at one's ~, close by; **bend, lift, the ~**, drink liquor immoderately); ~-grease, joc., vigorous polishing, hard work; **more power to** person's ~, approbatory wish for success; ~-room, plenty of room to move or work in; **up to the ~s**, busily engaged); part of sleeve of garment covering elbow (**out at ~s**, (of coat) worn out, (of person) ragged, poor); elbow-shaped bend etc. **2.** v.t. Thrust, jostle, (elbow oneself or one's way in, out, etc.). [E (ELL, BOW[1])]

**ĕ′lder**[1] n. White-flowered dark-fruited tree; ~-flower, ~(-berry), wine (made from elder flowers or berries). [E]

**ĕ′lder**[2]. **1.** a. (Of persons, esp. related ones) senior, of greater age, (*my elder brother*; *the elder children*; *which is the elder?*; ~ **statesman**, person of ripe years and experience whose advice is sought and valued). **2.** *n.* (in *pl.*) Persons of greater age (*respect your elders*) or venerable because of age (*your elders and betters*); official in early-Christian, Presbyterian, or Mormon Church. **3.** ~**lÿ** *a.*, somewhat old, (of person) past middle age; **ě'lděst** *a.*, first-born or oldest surviving (*eldest son, daughter*). [E (OLD)]

**ěldora'dō** (-ah'-) *n.* (*pl.* ~s). Fictitious land etc. rich in gold; place of great abundance. [Sp. *el dorado* the gilded]

**e'ldrĭtch** *a.* (Sc.) Weird, blood-curdling. [orig. uncert.]

**ělěcampā'ne** *n.* Plant with bitter leaves and root. [L *enula* this plant, *campana* of the fields]

**ělě'ct. 1.** *v.t.* Choose (thing, *to do*); choose by vote (*elect a chairman, elect him chairman* or *to the chair*); (of God) choose (person) for salvation. **2.** *a.* Chosen; select, choice; chosen by God; (after *n.*) chosen for office etc. (*president elect*). **3.** ~**ion** *n.*, electing, being elected; **general** ~**ion** (of representatives, esp. M.P.s, throughout the country etc.); **by-**~**ion** (of M.P. etc. to fill vacancy); ~**ioneer'** *v.i.*, busy oneself in political elections; ~**ive** *a.*, appointed, filled up, or conferred, by election, entitled to elect, (of course of study, surgical operation, etc.) optional; ~**or** *n.*, one who has right of electing, (Hist.; *E-*) one of German princes entitled to elect Emperor, *member of electoral college; ~**oral** *a.* (-lly); *~**oral college**, body of persons representing U.S. states who cast votes for election of President; ~**orate** *n.*, body of electors, dignity or dominions of German Elector. [L *eligo elect-* pick out]

**ělě'ctrĭc. 1.** *a.* (~**ally**). Of, charged with, worked by, capable of generating, electricity; suddenly exciting (*had an electric effect*). **2.** *n.* = electric light, motor car, etc.; (in *pl.*) electrical equipment. **3.** ~ **blanket** (heated by internal wires); ~ **blue**, steely or brilliant light blue; ~ **chair** (used in electrocution of criminals); *~ **cord**, = FLEX; ~ **eel**, eel-like fish able to give electric shock; ~ **eye**, photoelectric cell operating relay when beam of light is broken;

~ **fire**, electrically operated incandescent heater; ~ **hare**, dummy hare propelled by electricity, used in greyhound racing; ~ **ray**, RAY[2] able to give electric shock; ~ **shock**, effect of sudden discharge of electricity on person etc. **4.** ~**al** *a.* (-lly), relating to, connected with, of the nature of, electricity, suddenly exciting (*the effect was electrical*); **ělěctrĭ'cian** (-shan; *or* ělĭ-) *n.*; **ělěctrĭ'cĭty** (*or* ě-) *n.*, form of energy occurring in elementary particles (cf. ELECTRON, PROTON) and hence in macroscopic bodies, science of this, supply of electricity; **ělě'ctrĭfy** *v.t.*, charge (body) with electricity, convert (railway, factory, etc.) to electric working, (fig.) startle, excite; **ělěctrĭfĭcā'tion** *n.* [L f. Gk *ēlektron* amber]

**ělě'ctrō-** *in comb.* Of, by, caused by, electricity; ~**car'diogram**, record of electric currents generated by heartbeats; ~**car'diograph**, instrument for taking such records; ~**convulsive therapy** (using convulsive response to electric shocks); ~**cute** (-okūt), execute (criminal), kill in any way, by electricity; ~**cu'tion** (-okū'-) *n.*; **ele'ctrode** (-ōd), conductor through which electricity enters or leaves electrolyte, gas, vacuum, etc.; ~**dyna'mics**, study of electricity in motion; ~**ence'phalogram**, record of electrical activity of brain; ~**ence'phalograph**, instrument for taking such records; ~**lyse** (-olīz), *~**lyze**, *v.t.*, subject to or treat by electrolysis; ~**lysis** (-ŏ'lĭsĭs; *or* ě-), chemical decomposition, (Surg.) breaking up of tumours, hair-roots, etc., by electric action; ~**ly'tic** (-olĭ'-) *a.* (-ically); ~**lyte** (-olĭt), (substance that can dissolve to give a) solution able to conduct electric current; ~**ma'gnet**, piece of material made into magnet by electric current through coil surrounding it; ~**magne'tic**, having both electrical and magnetic character; *~magnetic radiation* etc., kind of radiation including visible light, radio waves, etc., in which electric and magnetic fields vary simultaneously; ~**ma'gnetism**, (study of) magnetic forces produced by electricity; ~**mo'tive** (-om-) *a.*, producing, tending to produce, electric current; *~motive force*, force set up by difference of potential in electric circuit; **~plate,** (*v.t.*) coat with chromium, silver, etc. by electrolysis, (*n.*) objects so produced; **~scope** (-ŏskŏp), instrument for detecting and measuring electricity; **~-sho'ck,** electric shock; **~-*shock treatment*,** medical treatment by means of electric shocks; **~sta'tics,** study of electricity at rest; **~techno'logy,** science of technological application of electricity. [ELECTRIC]

**elĕ'ctrŏn** *n.* Stable elementary particle with indivisible charge of negative electricity, found in all atoms and acting as carrier of electricity in solids; **~ microscope,** microscope with high magnification and resolution using focused electrons; **~-volt,** energy of electron passing through one volt difference of potential; **eléctrŏ'nĭc** (*or* ĕ-) *a.* (**~ically**), of electrons or electronics (**~ic brain,** colloq. = *electronic* COMPUTER; **~ic flash,** Photog., flash from electric discharge in rechargeable unit), (of music) produced electronically or electrically without pipes, strings, etc., (of musical instrument) operating thus; **eléctrŏ'nĭcs** (*or* ĕ-) *n.pl.* (treated as *sing.*), branch of physics and technology dealing with behaviour of electrons in vacuum, gas, semiconductor, etc. [ELECTRIC, -ON]

**elĕĕmŏ'sўnarў** (*or* -z-) *a.* Of, dependent on, alms; charitable. [L (ALMS)]

**e'lĕgan|t** *a.* Graceful, tasteful, (*elegant movements, writer, dress*); of refined luxury (*a life of elegant ease*); **~ce** *n.* [F or L (ELECT)]

**e'lĕgў** *n.* Song of lamentation, esp. for the dead (occas. used of other poems); poem in elegiac metre; **~ī'ăc,** (*a.*) used for elegies (**~iac couplet,** dactylic hexameter and pentameter), mournful, (*n.,* in *pl.*) elegiac verses. [F, or L f. Gk]

**e'lĕment** *n.* Component part (**reduced to its ~s,** analysed; *the elements of national wealth*); (Chem.) any of the (about 100) substances that cannot be resolved by chemical means into simpler substances; any of the **four ~s** (earth, water, air, and fire) in ancient and medieval philosophy, one of these as a being's natural abode or sphere (**in one's ~,** in one's accustomed or preferred surroundings); (Electr.) resistance wire in electric heater, cooker, etc.;

(in *pl.*) atmospheric agencies, esp. wind and storm; (in *pl.*) rudiments of learning (i.e. the ABC) or of an art etc.; (in *pl.*) bread and wine of Eucharist; **elĕmĕ'ntal** *a.* (**-lly**), of the four elements, of or like the powers of nature, tremendous, uncompounded, essential; **elĕmĕ'ntarў** *a.* (**-ily, -iness**), rudimentary, simple, unanalysable; **~ary particle,** (Phys.) one of several subatomic particles not known to consist of simpler ones; **~ary school** (teaching rudiments of subjects). [F f. L]

**e'lĕphant** *n.* Largest living land animal, with trunk and long curved ivory tusks; size of paper, 711 × 584 mm; **pink ~s,** hallucinations due to excessive indulgence in alcohol etc.; **white ~,** burdensome or useless possession; **~ seal,** large seal with prolonged snout in male; **~ī'asĭs** *n.,* skin disease causing gross enlargement of limb etc., (fig.) undue expansion or enlargement; **elĕphǎ'ntine** *a.,* of elephants, huge, clumsy, unwieldy, (*elephantine movements, humour*). [F f. L f. Gk]

**e'lĕvāt|e** *v.t.* Lift up, raise, (*elevate one's eyes, voice, hopes*; *elevate person to the peerage*; **~e the Host,** for adoration); **~ed railway** etc. (raised above ground level); (in *p.p.*, of rank, aims, style) exalted, colloq. slightly drunk; **elĕvā'tion** *n.,* (esp.) angle (esp. of gun or direction of heavenly body) with the horizontal, height above given (esp. sea) level, drawing etc. in projection on vertical plane, flat drawing of one side of house etc., grandeur; **~or** *n.,* (esp.) \*lift, hoisting-machine, movable part of aircraft's tailplane; **~orў** *a.* [L (*levo* lift)]

**elĕ'ven** *n.* & *a.* NUMERAL; team of 11 players at cricket, football, etc.; ||**~s(es)** *n.,* light refreshment about 11 a.m.; ||**~-plus,** examination taken at age 11–12 before entering secondary school; **~fŏld** *a.* & *adv.*; **~th** *a.* & *n.,* NUMERAL (**~th hour,** latest possible time). [E]

**elf** *n.* (*pl.* **elves** *pr.* -vz). Small or mischievous creature; mythical dwarfish being; **~-lock(s),** tangled mass of hair; **~'in** *a.,* of elves, elflike; **~'ish, ĕ'lvish,** *adjs.* [E]

**eli'cĭt** *v.t.* Draw out (latent thing; *elicit the truth, a reply from*). [L *elicio*]

**elī'de** *v.t.* Omit (vowel, syllable)

in pronunciation; **ĕlĭ′sion** (-zhon) *n*. [L *elido elis-* crush out]

**ĕ′lĭgĭb|le** *a*. (~ly). Fit or entitled to be chosen (*for* office, award, etc.); desirable, suitable, esp. as marriage--partner (*eligible bachelor*); ~i′lĭtȳ *n*. [F f. L (ELECT)]

**ĕlĭ′mĭn|āte** *v.t*. (~able). Remove, get rid of, expel, (waste matter *from* body, substance *from* a compound); exclude from competition etc. by defeat, or from consideration as irrelevant; ~ā′tion, ~ātor, *ns*. [L (*limen -min-* threshold)]

**elision.** See ELIDE.

**élĭt|e** (ālē′t) *n*. The pick, the best, (of a group); size of letters in type-writing (12 per inch); select group or class; ~ĭsm *n*., advocacy of, reliance on, leadership or dominance by a select group. [F (ELECT)]

**elĭ′xĭr** *n*. Alchemist's preparation designed to change metal into gold or (~ **of life**) to prolong life in-definitely; sovereign remedy; aro-matic solution used as medicine or flavouring. [L f. Arab.]

**Elĭzabē′than** (ĭ-) *a*. & *n*. (Person, writer) of the time of Queen *Elizabeth* I. [person]

**ĕlk** *n*. Large species of deer found in N. Amer. (where called MOOSE), N. Europe, and Asia. [E]

**ĕll** *n*. (Hist.) Measure = 45 in. (**give him an inch and he'll take an ~**, he takes undue advantage of slight concession). [E, = forearm]

**ĕllĭ′p|se** *n*. Regular oval, figure produced when cone is cut by plane making smaller angle with base than side of cone makes; (also ~sĭs, *pl*. ~ses *pr*. -sēz) omission of words needed to complete construction or sense, set of three dots etc. indicating such omission; ~soid *n*., solid of which all plane sections through one axis are ellipses and all other plane sections are ellipses or circles; **ĕllĭpsoi′dal** *a*.; ~tĭc(al) *adjs*. (-ically). [F f. L f. Gk *elleipsis* deficit]

**ĕlm** *n*. Tree with rough doubly--serrated leaves; its wood. [E]

**ĕlocū′tion** *n*. Art of expressive oral delivery; style of speaking; ~ȧry *a*.; ~ĭst *n*. [L (*loquor* speak)]

**ē′lŏng|āte** (-ngg-) *v.t*. Lengthen, extend, draw out; ~ā′tion *n*., lengthening, part (of line etc.) so formed. [L (*longus* long)]

**ēlŏ′pe** *v.i*. (Of woman) run away from husband, or from home for secret marriage, (*with* lover); (of couple) run away to get married; abscond; ~ment (-pm-) *n*. [AF]

**ĕ′loquen|ce** *n*. Fluent and power-ful use of language; ~t *a*., having eloquence, (fig.) clearly indicative (*of*). [F f. L (ELOCUTION)]

**else** *adv*. (With indef. or interrog. pron.) besides (*nobody else knew*; *what else?*; *who else's?*, *whose else?*); instead (*what else could I say?*); otherwise, if not, (*run*, (*or*) *else you will be late*); **or ~,** (colloq.) expr. warning or threat (*hand over the money or else*); ~′where, in, to, some other place. [E]

**ĕlū′cĭd|āte** (or -ōō′-) *v.t*. Throw light on, explain; ~ā′tion, ~ātor, *ns*.; ~ātĭve, ~ātorȳ, *adjs*. [L (LUCID)]

**ĕlū′|de** (or -ōō′-) *v.t*. (~dible). Escape adroitly from (blow, danger, grasp, person, observation); avoid compliance with or fulfilment of (law, request, obligation); baffle (person's memory, understanding); ~sion (-zhon) *n*.; ~sĭve, ~sorȳ, *adjs*. [L (*ludo* play)]

**ĕ′lver** *n*. Young eel. [EEL, FARE]

**elves, ĕ′lvĭsh.** See ELF.

**Elȳ′sĭ|um** (ĭlĭ′z-) *n*. (Gk Myth.) abode of the blessed after death; (place of) ideal happiness; ~an *a*. [L f. Gk]

**ĕm** *n*. (Print.) Unit of measurement equal to space occupied by m. [name of letter *M*]

**'em** *pron*. (colloq.) Them (*let 'em all come*). [obs. *hem* dat. pl. (E)]

**em-.** See EN-.

**ėmā′cĭ|āte** (or -shĭ-) *v.t*. Make thin or feeble (*emaciated face* etc.); ~ā′tion *n*. [L *macies* leanness]

**ĕ′man|āte** *v.i*. & *t*. (Cause to) issue, originate, proceed, (*from* source, person, etc.); ~ā′tion *n*., (thing) proceeding from a source (esp. fig., of virtues, qualities, etc.); ~ātĭve *a*. [L (*mano* flow)]

**ėmă′ncĭp|āte** *v.t*. Free from legal, social, political, intellectual, or moral restraint; ~ā′tion *n*., liberation, esp. from slavery, or from legal or political disabilities; ~ā′tionĭst *n*., advocate of this; ~ātor *n*.; ~ā′torȳ *a*. [L, = free from possession (*manus* hand, *capio* take)]

**ėmă′scŭl|āte. 1.** *v.t*. Castrate; en-feeble; weaken (writing) by excisions; ~ā′tion *n*.; ~ātorȳ *a*. **2.** (-at) *a*. Castrated; effeminate. [L (MALE)]

**ėmba′lm** (-ah′m) *v.t*. Preserve

(corpse) from decay, orig. with spices etc.; preserve from oblivion; make fragrant; ~'ment (-m-m-) n.;

**ĕmbă'nk** v.t., shut in, confine, (river etc.) by banks, stone structure, etc.; **ĕmbă'nkment** n., bank confining river or carrying road or railway. [EN-]

**ĕmbăr'gō** (or ĭ-). **1.** n. (pl. ~es). Order forbidding foreign ships to enter, or any ships to leave, the country's ports; suspension of commerce etc. (be under an embargo). **2.** v.t. Place (ships, trade, etc.) under embargo; seize (ship, goods) for State use. [Sp. (BAR¹)]

**ĕmbăr'k** v.t. & i. Put, go, on board ship (for destination); engage (in, on, enterprise etc.); **ĕmbărkā'tion** n., embarking on ship. [F (BARK²)]

**ĕmbă'rrass** v.t. Encumber; make (person) feel awkward or ashamed; perplex; complicate (question etc.); ~ment n. [F f. Sp. f. It. (BAR¹)]

**ĕ'mbassў** n. Ambassador's function, office, or residence; deputation. [F (AMBASSADOR)]

**ĕmbă'ttle** v.t. Set in battle array; furnish with battlements. [EN-]

**ĕmbĕ'd, ĭm-,** v.t. (-dd-). Fix in surrounding mass. [EN-, IN-¹]

**ĕmbĕ'llish** v.t. Beautify, adorn; heighten (narrative) with fictitious additions; ~ment n. [F (bel, BEAU)]

**ĕ'mber¹** n. (usu. in pl.) Small piece of live fuel in dying fire. [E]

**ĕ'mber²** a. ~ days, days of fasting and prayer, the Wed., Fri., and Sat., after 1st Sun. in Lent, Whit Sunday, Holy Cross Day (14 Sept.), and St. Lucy's Day (13 Dec.). [E]

**ĕ'mber³** n. ~ (-goose), a sea-bird, species of LOON². [Norw.]

**ĕmbĕ'zzle** v.t. Divert (money etc.) fraudulently to one's own use; ~ment (-zlm-) n. [AF]

**ĕmbĭ'tter** v.t. Make (life etc.) bitter; aggravate (evil); exasperate; ~ment n. [EN-]

**ĕmblā'zon** v.t. = BLAZON; ~ment, ~rў, ns.

**ĕ'mblem** n. Symbol, type, (of a quality, state, etc.); heraldic device or symbolic object as distinctive badge; ~ĕmă'tĭc(al) adjs. (-ically). [L f. Gk, = insertion]

**ĕmbŏ'dў** v.t. Clothe (spirit) with body; make concrete (idea etc. in action, words, etc.); (of thing) be an expression of; include, comprise;

~ĭment n.; **ĕmbō'lden** v.t., make bold, encourage (to do). [EN-]

**ĕ'mbolǁism** n. Obstruction of artery etc. by clot of blood, air-bubble, etc.; ~us n. (pl. ~i pr. -ī), object causing embolism. [L f. Gk]

**embonpoint** (ahṅbawṅpwă'n) n. Plumpness (of person). [F]

**ĕmbō'ss** v.t. Carve, mould, (figures etc.) in relief; adorn (surface) thus; ~ment n. [BOSS²]

**ĕmbow'er** v.t. Enclose as in bower. [EN-]

**ĕmbrā'ce. 1.** v.t. Hold (person etc.; in pl. abs. = embrace one another) closely in the arms, usu. as sign of affection; clasp, enclose; accept, adopt, (offer, course, doctrine, party); include, comprise; take in with eye or mind. **2.** n. Holding in the arms, clasp. [F f. L (BRACE)]

**ĕmbrā'sure** (-zher) n. Bevelling of wall at sides of window etc.; opening in parapet for gun. [F (embraser splay)]

**ĕmbrocā'tion** n. Liquid for rubbing on body to relieve muscular pain. [F or L f. Gk embrokhē lotion]

**ĕmbroi'der** v.t. Ornament (cloth etc.) with needlework; embellish (narrative); ~ў n., (esp.) embroidered work, inessential ornament. [AF f. Gmc]

**ĕmbroi'l** v.t. Bring (affairs etc.) into confusion; involve (person) in hostility (with another); ~ment n. [F (BROIL¹)]

**ĕ'mbrўǁō. 1.** n. (pl. ~os). Unborn or unhatched offspring; human offspring in first eight weeks from conception; rudimentary plant in seed; thing in rudimentary stage (in ~o, undeveloped); ~o'logў n.; ~o'nĭc a. (-ically). **2.** a. Undeveloped, immature. [L f. Gk (bruō grow)]

**ĕmĕ'nd** v.t. (Seek to) remove errors from, correct, (text of book etc.); **ĕmĕndā'tion, ĕ'mĕndātor,** ns.; ~atorў a. [L (menda fault)]

**ĕ'merald** n. Bright-green precious stone; ~ (green), colour of this; E~ Isle, Ireland. [F f. L f. Gk smaragdos]

**ĕmẽr'ǁge** v.i. Come up or out into view (from water, enclosed space, obscurity); come out (from a state); (of facts) become known as result of inquiry or trial; (of difficulty etc.) crop up; ~gence n.; ~gencў, (n.) sudden state of danger, conflict, etc., requiring immediate action, (patient with) condition needing immediate treatment, (*a.*) used in an emergency (*emergency door, exit*); ~**gent** *a.*, (esp., of nation) newly independent. [L (MERGE)]

**ĕmĕ′rĭtus** *a.* Retired and holding honorary title (*emeritus professor*). [L, = having earned discharge]

**ĕ′merў** *n.* Coarse corundum for polishing metal etc. [F f. It. f. Gk]

**ĕmĕ′tĭc** *a. & n.* (Medicine) that causes vomiting. [Gk (*emeō* vomit)]

**E.M.F.** *abbr.* electromotive force.

**ĕ′mĭgr|āte** *v.i.* Go to settle in another country; ~**ant,** (*a.*) emigrating, (*n.*) one who emigrates; ~**ā′tion** *n.*; ~**ātorў** *a.*; **émigré** (ĕ′mĭgrā) *n.*, emigrant, esp. political exile. [L (MIGRATE)]

**ĕ′mĭnen|t** *a.* Distinguished, notable, (*eminent lawyer, services, wisdom*); ~**ce** *n.*, distinction, recognized superiority, (**His, Your, E~ce,** cardinal's title), piece of rising ground; **éminence grise** (āmēnahñs grē′z) F, = grey cardinal), one who exercises power unofficially; ~**tlў** *adv.*, notably, decidedly. [L *emineo* jut out]

**ĕmir′** (-ēr′) *n.* Title of various Muslim rulers; ~**āte** *n.*, position, reign, or domain of emir. [AMIR]

**ĕ′mĭssarў** *n.* Person sent on special (occas. odious or underhand) mission. [foll.]

**ĕmī′|t** *v.t.* (-tt-). Give out, send forth, (stream, light, heat, cry, etc.); ~**ssion** (-shon) *n.*; ~**ssĭve** *a.* [L *emitto emiss-*]

**ĕ′mmĕt** *n.* (arch., dial.) Ant. [E]

**ĕmŏ′llĭent** (-lye-) *a. & n.* (Substance) that softens skin etc.; soothing (agent). [L (*mollis* soft)]

**ĕmŏ′lŭment** *n.* Profit from employment, salary. [F or L]

**ĕmŏ′tĭon** *n.* Disturbance of mind, mental sensation or state; instinctive feeling; **ĕmŏ′te** *v.i.*, act emotionally; ~**al** *a.* (-llў), of the emotions, expressing emotion, liable to excessive emotion; ~**alĭsm,** ~**ă′lĭtў,** *ns.*; **ĕmŏ′tĭve** *a.*, of or tending to excite emotion, arousing feeling. [F (MOVE)]

**ĕmpă′nel, ĭm-,** *v.t.* (||-ll-). Enter (jury) on panel. [EN-]

**ĕ′mpath|ў** *n.* (Psych.) Power of projecting one's personality into (and so fully comprehending) object of contemplation; ~**ĕ′tĭc, ĕmpă′-**

**thĭc,** *adjs.* (-ically); ~**īze** *v.t. & i.* [PATHOS]

**ĕ′mperor** *n.* Sovereign of an empire; ~ **penguin,** largest known species of penguin; **ĕ′mprĕss** *n.*, wife or widow of emperor, woman emperor. [F f. L *imperator* (*impero* command)]

**ĕ′mphas|ĭs** *n.* (*pl.* ~**es** *pr.* -ēz) Stress laid on word(s) to indicate special meaning or importance; importance assigned (*lay great emphasis on*); vigour, intensity, of expression, feeling, etc.; ~**īze** *v.t.*, lay stress on (word, fact, etc.); **ĕmphă′tĭc** *a.* (-ically), full of emphasis, forcibly expressive, (*emphatic tone, speaker, denial*), (of words) bearing stress, used to give emphasis. [L f. Gk]

**ĕmphўsē′ma** *n.* Swelling due to air in body tissues. [L f. Gk (*emphusaō* puff up)]

**ĕ′mpīre** *n.* Supreme and extensive (political) dominion; (period of) rule, territory, of an emperor; (Hist.) **the E~,** (usu.) British Empire or Holy Roman Empire; large commercial organization etc. owned or directed by one person; ~**building,** deliberately acquiring much additional territory, authority, etc.; \*E~ **City,** New York; \*E~ **State,** New York State. [F f. L *imperium* dominion]

**ĕmpī′rĭc** *a.* Relying on observation or experiment, not on theory; ~**al** *a.* (-llў), empiric; ~**ĭsm,** ~**ĭst,** *ns.* [L f. Gk (*en* in, *peiraō* try)]

**ĕmplā′cement** (-sm-) *n.* Putting in position; platform for gun(s). [F (PLACE)]

**ĕmplā′ne** *v.i. & t.* Go or put on board aeroplane. [PLANE²]

**ĕmploy′. 1.** *v.t.* Use (instrument, time, energies, etc., *in, on, for,* etc.); use services of, keep in one's service; keep occupied. **2.** *n.* In the ~ **of,** employed by. **3. ĕmployee′, \*ĕmployé′,** (*or* -oi′ē) *n.*, person employed for wages; ~**er** *n.*, (esp.) one who employs others; ~**ment** *n.*, (esp.) one's regular trade or profession; ~**ment agency,** business that finds employers or employees for those seeking them; ~**ment exchange,** State office with similar function. [F f. L *implicor* be involved]

**ĕmpŏr′ĭ|um** *n.* (*pl.* ~**ums,** ~**a**). Centre of commerce, market; large shop, store. [L f. Gk (*emporos* merchant)]

**empow′er** v.t. Authorize, enable, (person to do). [EN-]

**e′mpress.** See EMPEROR.

**e′mpty** a., n., & v. **1.** a. (-ily, -iness). Containing nothing (on an empty STOMACH; ~-handed, bringing no gift, carrying nothing away); (of house etc.) unoccupied, unfurnished; (colloq.) hungry; foolish, meaningless, vacuous; ~-headed, lacking common sense. **2.** n. Empty bottle, box, etc. **3.** v.t. & i. Remove contents of; transfer (contents of thing into etc.); become empty; (of river) discharge itself. [E]

**empŭr′ple** v.t. Make purple. [EN-]

**empўre′an** a. & n. (Of) the highest heaven, as sphere of fire or abode of God. [L f. Gk (pur fire)]

**e′mū** n. Large flightless Australian bird related to cassowary. [Port.]

**e′mŭl|āte** v.t. Try to equal or excel; imitate; ~ā′tion, ~ātor, ns.; ~ative, ~ous, adjs., zealously or jealously imitative (of), actuated by rivalry. [L (aemulus rival)]

**emū′l|sion** (-shon) n. Fine dispersion of one liquid in another, esp. as paint, medicine, etc.; (Photog.) mixture of silver compound in gelatin on plate or film; ~sify v.t., make an emulsion of; ~sĭve a. [F or L (mulgeo to milk)]

**ĕn** n. (Print.) Unit of width, half an EM. [name of letter N]

**en-** pref. (em- bef. b, m, p). **1.** = IN-[1], forming vbs. (1) f. ns., meaning 'put into or on' (engulf, entrust, embed), (2) f. ns. or adjs., meaning 'bring into condition of' (enslave), often w. suf. -EN (enlighten), (3) f. vbs., meaning 'in, into, on' (enfold) or intensively (entangle). **2.** In, inside, (energy, enthusiasm). [F f. L in-; Gk]

**-en** suf. forming vbs. f. adjs. (usu. w. sense 'make or become so or more so': deepen, moisten) or f. ns. (happen, heighten). [E]

**enā′ble** v.t. Give (person etc.) authority or means (to do); make possible. [EN-]

**enā′ct** v.t. Ordain, decree; play (part on stage or in life); ~ment n., (esp.) law enacted; ~ĭve a.

**enā′mel.** **1.** n. Glasslike (usu. opaque) ornamental or preservative coating on metal; hard smooth coating, cosmetic simulating this; hard coating of teeth; painting done in enamel. **2.** v.t. (||-ll-). Coat, inlay, portray, with enamel. [AF f. Gmc]

**enā′mour,** *enā′mor, (-mer) v.t. (esp. in p.p.) Inspire with love or liking (of). [F (amour love)]

**en bloc** (ahn blŏ′k) adv. In a block, all at the same time. [F]

**encă′mp** v.t. & i., settle in (military) camp, lodge in tents; ~ment n., (esp.) place where troops encamp. [EN-]

**encă′psŭl|āte** (ĭn-k-) v.t. Enclose (as) in a capsule; (fig.) summarize, isolate; ~ā′tion n. [CAPSULE]

**encā′se** (ĭn-k-) v.t. Confine (as) in a case; ~ment (-sm-) n. [EN-]

**||encă′sh** (ĭn-k-) v.t. Convert (bills etc.) into cash; receive in form of cash; ~ment n.

**encau′stic** (ĭn-k-) a. & n. (Painting, art of painting) by burning-in wax paint etc.; ~ brick, tile, (inlaid with differently coloured clays burnt in). [L f. Gk (CAUSTIC)]

**-ence.** See -NCE.

**enceinte** (ahnsă′nt). **1.** a. (Of woman) pregnant. **2.** n. (Fortif.) Enclosure. [F (CINCTURE)]

**ĕnc|ĕphă′lic** (or ĕn-k-) a. Of the brain; ~ĕphali′tĭs n., inflammation of the brain; ~ĕ′phălogrăm n., X-ray photograph of the brain; ~ĕ′phălograph (-ahf) n., instrument for recording electrical activity of brain. [Gk (kephalē head)]

**enchai′n** v.t. Chain up; hold fast (attention, emotions); ~ment n. [F (EN-)]

**enchă′nt** (-ah′-) v.t. Bewitch; charm, delight; ~ment, ~rĕss, ns.

**encī′pher** v.t. Write (message etc.) in cipher. [EN-]

**encir′cle** v.t. Surround; form a circle round; ~ment (-kelm-) n. (esp. by supposedly hostile nations).

**enclă′sp** (ĭn-klah′-) v.t. Clasp, embrace. [EN-]

**ĕ′nclāve** (-n-k-) n. Foreign territory surrounded by one's own territory. [F f. L clavis key]

**enclĭ′tĭc** (-n-k-). **1.** a. (~ally). (Of word) so unemphatic as to be pronounced as if part of preceding word. **2.** n. Such word, e.g. not in cannot. [L f. Gk (klinō lean)]

**enclō′s|e, ĭn-,** (ĭn-klō′z) v.t. Shut in, surround, (land etc. in or with walls, fence, etc.); shut up in receptacle (esp. in envelope besides letter); hem in on all sides; seclude (religious community) from outside world (*an enclosed order*); **~ure** (-zher) *n.*, act of enclosing, enclosed place esp. for specified persons at race-course etc. (*judges', members', enclosure*), paper etc. included with letter in envelope. [F f. L (INCLUDE)]

**encō'de** (ĭn-k-) *v.t.* Write (message etc.) in code or cipher. [EN-]

**encō'mǐ|um** (ĕn-k-) *n.* (*pl.* **-ums**, **~a**). Formal or high-flown praise. [L f. Gk (*kōmos* revelry)]

**enco'mpass** (ĭn-kŭm-) *v.t.* Surround, esp. to protect or attack; contain. [EN-]

**encore** (ŏngkōr', ŏ'-) *int.*, *n.*, & *v.* **1.** *int.* & *n.* (Audience's demand for song etc. to be performed) again, once more; further item given in response to such demand. **2.** *v.t.* Call for repetition of (song etc.); summon (performer) for this. [F, = *once again*]

**encou'nter** (ĭn-k-). **1.** *v.t.* Meet as adversary; meet, esp. by chance or unexpectedly. **2.** *n.* Meeting in combat or by chance. [F (CONTRA)]

**encou'rage** (ĭn-kŭ'-) *v.t.* Give courage to; urge (person *to* do); stimulate by help, reward, etc.; further, promote; **~ment** (-kŭ'rĭjm-) *n.* [F (EN-)]

**encroa'ch** (ĭn-k-) *v.i.* Intrude (*on* others' territory, rights, etc.); (fig.) make gradual inroads (*on*); **~ment** *n.* [F (*croc* CROOK)]

**encrŭ'st** (ĭn-k-) *v.t.* & *i.* Cover with, form, a crust; overlay with crust of silver etc. [F (EN-)]

**encŭ'mb|er** (ĭn-k-) *v.t.* Hamper, impede; fill (place *with* lumber); burden (person, estate, *with* debt); **~rance** *n.*, burden, impediment, (**without ~rance**, having no children), mortgage etc. on property. [F f. Rom.]

**-ency̆.** See -NCE.

**ency̆'clĭc(al)** *adjs.* & *ns.* (Letter issued by Pope) for extensive circulation. [L f. Gk (CYCLE)]

**ency̆clopae'd|ĭa, -pē'd|ĭa,** (*or* ĭ-) *n.* Book, set of books, giving information on every (branch of a) subject, usu. arranged alphabetically; **~ĭc** *a.*; **~ĭst** *n.*, person compiling encyclopaedia. [L f. spurious Gk, = all-round education]

**ĕnd. 1.** *n.* Limit (*no end to it*; *at one's* WIT'*s end*, *the end of* one's TETHER; **no ~**, colloq., many or much (*of*); **the ~**,

colloq., the limit of one's endurance or tolerance); farthest point (*the ends of the earth*); extreme point or part (*end of the line, road*; **all ~s up**, completely; *at a* LOOSE *end*; **deep ~**, end of swimming-pool where water is deepest, so **go in (off) the deep ~**, colloq., give way to emotion or anger; ||EAST, WEST, *End*; *end* ON; **~-paper**, blank leaf of paper at beginning or end of book; **~ to ~**, lengthwise continuously; **from ~ to ~**, throughout; **make (both) ~s meet**, live within one's income; **on ~**, upright, continuously (*for three weeks on end*)); remnant (*candle, cigarette, -ends*; ODDS *and ends*); portion, part, side, (*no problem at my end*; **keep** one's **~ up**, sustain one's part in an undertaking etc.); conclusion, latter part, (*the end of the world*; **~-product**, final product of manufacture, transformation, etc.; **come to an ~**, be finished or used up; **make an ~ of**, **put an ~ to**, stop, abolish; **there's an ~ to it**, there is no more to be said or done on a matter); destruction, death, (*a bad, an untimely, end*; **near** one's **~**, dying); result (*the end of it was*); purpose, object, (*to what end?*; **gain** one's **ends**; **ends** *and means*). **2.** *v.t.* & *i.* Bring or come to an end, finish, result, (*end the discussion*; one's *life*; *how will it end?*; thing **ends** in disaster etc.); **~ by doing**, eventually do (*will end by marrying a millionaire*); **~ it (all)**, colloq., commit suicide; **~ up**, conclude. **3.** **~'ing** *n.*, (esp.) end of word, verse, or story; **~'mŏst** *a.*, nearest the end; **~'ways**, **~'wise**, (-z) *adv.*, with end uppermost or foremost, end to end. [E]

**endā'nger** (-nj-) *v.t.* Bring into danger. [EN-]

**endear'** *v.t.* Make (person, thing, one*self*) dear (*to*); **~ment** *n.*, (esp.) act or utterance expressing affection.

**endea'vour, *-vor,** (-dĕ'ver). **1.** *v.t.* Try (*to* do); (arch.) strive (*after*). **2.** *n.* Attempt. [DEVOIR]

**ĕndē'mĭc. 1.** *a.* (**~ally**). Regularly or only found among (specified) people or in (specified) country. **2.** *n.* Endemic disease or plant. [F or L f. Gk (as DEMOTIC)]

**ĕ'ndĭve** *n.* Curly-leaved chicory, used as salad; *chicory crown. [F f. L *endivia* f. Gk]

**ĕ'ndlĕss** *a.* Infinite; continual; incessant; (colloq.) innumerable; **~**

belt, **chain**, etc., (with ends joined for continuous action over wheels etc.). [E (END)]

ĕ'ndŏ- *in comb.* Internal; ∼**crīne** *a.*, (of gland) secreting directly into blood, ductless [Gk *krinō* sift]; ∼**gĕnous** (-ŏ'j-) *a.*, growing or originating from within; ∼**mŏrph** *n.*, person of soft round body-build (with predominance of structures formed from inner layer of embryo) [Gk *morphē* form]. [Gk *endon* within]

**endŏr'se**, **ĭn-**, *v.t.* Write, esp. sign one's name, on back of (bill, cheque, etc.); write (comment etc. *on back* of document); confirm (statement, opinion); declare one's approval of; ‖make entry regarding offence on (motorist's, publican's, licence); ∼**ment** (-sm-) *n.* [L (*dorsum* back)]

**endow'** *v.t.* Bequeath or give permanent income to (person, institution, etc.); (esp. in *p.p.*) invest, furnish, (person *with* powers, qualities, etc.); ∼**ment** *n.*; ∼**ment assurance**, **insurance**, form of life insurance with payment of fixed sum to insured person on specified date, or to his estate on earlier death. [AF (DOWER)]

**endŭ'e**, **ĭn-**, *v.t.* Put on (clothes etc., lit. or fig.); clothe (person) *with*; furnish (person *with* powers, qualities, etc.). [F f. L (INDUCE)]

**endŭr'|e** *v.t. & i.* Undergo (pain etc.); tolerate, bear, (*cannot endure that fellow*); last; ∼**ance** *n.*, power of enduring (*beyond endurance*), ability to withstand prolonged strain (*endurance test*). [F f. L (*durus* hard)]

**E.N.E.** *abbr.* east-north-east.

ĕ'nĕma (*or* ĭnē'-) *n.* (Instrument for) injection of liquid etc. into rectum esp. to expel its contents; liquid etc. so used. [L f. Gk]

ĕ'nemў. **1.** *n.* Person hating another and striving to defeat or injure him; adversary, opponent (*of*, *to*), (be one's **own worst** ∼, be **nobody's** ∼ but one's own, be responsible for one's own misfortunes; **the E**∼, the Devil); member of hostile army or nation; hostile force or ship. **2.** *a.* Of or belonging to the enemy (*enemy aircraft*; *destroyed by enemy action*; ∼ **alien**, person living in a country with which his own is at war). [F f. L (IN-[2], *amicus* friend)]

ĕ'nerg|ў *n.* Force, vigour, activity; (*act*, *speak*, *with energy*; *what energy you have!*; *devote your energies to this*); ability of matter or radiation to do work; ∼**ĕ'tĭc** *a.* (-**ically**), full of energy, powerfully operative; ∼**īze** *v.t.*, infuse energy into, provide energy for operation of (device). [F or L f. Gk (*ergon* work)]

**e'nerv|āte** *v.t.* Deprive of vigour; ∼**ā'tion** *n.* [L (NERVE)]

*enfant terrible* (ahñfahñ tĕrē'bl) *n.* Child who asks awkward questions, repeats talk, etc.; person or thing causing embarrassment by unruliness. [F, = terrible child]

**enfee'ble** *v.t.* Make feeble; ∼**ment** (-belm-) *n.* [EN-]

**enfilā'de. 1.** *n.* Fire from guns etc. sweeping line from end to end. **2.** *v.t.* Subject (troops, road, etc.) to enfilade. [F (FILE[2])]

**enfō'ld** *v.t.* Wrap (person etc. *in*, *with*); clasp, embrace. [EN-]

**enfor'ce** *v.t.* Persist in, press home, (argument, demand); impose (action etc. (*up*)*on* person; compel observance of (law etc.); ∼**ment** (-sm-) *n.* [F f. L (FORCE[1])]

**enfrăn'ch|ise** (-z) *v.t.* Give (town) municipal rights, esp. representation in parliament; give (person) electoral franchise; release (slave etc.) from bondage; ∼**īsement** (-zm-) *n.* [F (FRANK[2])]

**engā'ge** (-n-g-) *v.t. & i.* Bind by contract or by promise (esp. of marriage); hire (employee, servant); arrange beforehand to occupy (cab, seat, etc.); employ busily, occupy, (*are you engaged tomorrow?*; *his telephone*, *the bathroom*, *is engaged*; *engage one's attention*); bring (troops), come, into conflict; come into conflict with; interlock (thing *with* another), (of thing) interlock; pledge oneself (*to* do, *that*); take part (*engage in politics*); ∼ **for**, (arch.) guarantee; *engagé* (ahñgah'zhā) *a.*, (of writer etc.) morally committed; ∼**ment** (īn-gā'jm-) *n.* (∼**ment ring**, given by man and worn by woman to whom he is engaged to be married); **engā'gĭng** (-n-g-) *a.*, (esp.) attractive, charming. [F (GAGE[1])]

**engĕ'nder** (-nj-) *v.t.* Give rise to (feeling etc.). [GENUS]

ĕ'ngine (-nj-) *n.* Complex mechanical contrivance, esp. as source of power; = FIRE, STEAM, -*engine*; locomotive (*is an engine-driver*); (arch.) machine or instrument of war, instrument, means. [F f. L (INGENIOUS)]

**ĕngĭneer'** (-nj-). **1.** *n.* One who designs and constructs military works, esp. a soldier so trained (ROYAL *Engineers*); (**civil**) ~, one who designs or maintains works of public utility (roads, bridges, canals, etc.); one who works in a branch of engineering, esp. as qualified professional (*chemical, electrical, mechanical, engineer*); maker of engines; person in charge of engine; *engine-driver.* **2.** *v.i.* & *t.* Act as engineer, construct, manage (bridge, work, etc.) as engineer; (colloq.) contrive, bring about. **3.** ~**ĭng** *n.*, application of science for control and use of power, esp. by means of machines (~**ing science,** engineering as field of study). [F f. L (prec.)]

**E'nglish** (ĭ'ngg-) *a., n.,* & *v.* **1.** *a.* Of England (*English* HORN; ~**man,** ~**woman,** one who is English by birth, descent, or naturalization; EARLY *English style*); of, written or spoken in, the English language. **2.** *n.* The language of England, now used in U.K., U.S., and most Commonwealth countries; **in plain** ~, in plain words; **the King's, Queen's,** ~, English language correctly spoken or written; **Middle** ~ (between about 1150 and 1500); **Old** ~ (before about 1150); **the** ~, (*pl.*) people of England. **3.** *v.t.* (*e*~; arch. or pedant.) Render into English. [E]

**ĕngra'ft, ĭn-,** (-n-grah'-) *v.t.* Insert (scion of one tree *into, upon* another); implant (idea *in* mind); incorporate thing *into* another). [EN-, IN-¹]

**ĕngrai'n** (-n-g-) *v.t.* (usu. fig.) Cause (dye etc.) to sink deeply in; (in *p.p.*; cf. INGRAINed) inveterate. [F, = dye in GRAIN]

**ĕngra've** (-n-g-) *v.t.* Inscribe, ornament, (hard surface *with* incised marks); carve (figures etc.) *on*; cut (design etc.) as lines on metal plate for printing; (fig.) impress deeply (*on* memory etc.); ~**ĭng** *n.*, (esp.) copy of picture from engraved plate. [GRAVE²]

**ĕngro'ss** (-n-g-) *v.t.* Write out in large letters or in legal form; fully occupy (person, attention, time); ~**ment** *n.* [AF (EN-)]

**ĕngu'lf** (-n-g-) *v.t.* Swallow up (as) in gulf; ~**ment** *n.* [EN-]

**ĕnha'nce** (-hah'-) *v.t.* Heighten, intensify, (quality, power, etc.); (arch.) exaggerate; ~**ment** (-sm-) *n.* [AF f. Rom. f. L *altus* high]

**ĕnĭ'gma** *n.* Riddle; puzzling person or thing; **ĕnĭgmă'tĭc(al)** *adjs.* (**-ically**). [L f. Gk]

**ĕnjă'mbment, -bem-,** (-m-m-) *n.* Continuation of sentence without pause beyond end of one line of verse into next. [F, = encroachment]

**ĕnjoi'n** *v.t.* Prescribe, impose, (action etc. *on* person); command (person *to* do, *that* thing be done); (Law) prohibit by injunction (*from* doing). [F f. L *injungo* attach]

**ĕnjoy'** *v.t.* Take delight in (thing, doing); ~**onesself,** experience pleasure; have use of (advantages etc.); experience (*enjoy poor health*); ~**able** *a.* (**-bly**), (esp.) pleasant; ~**ment** *n.* [F]

**ĕnkĭ'ndle** (-n-k- *v.t.* Cause (flame, war, passions, etc. to blaze up. [EN-]

**ĕnlá'ce** *v.t.* Encircle tightly; enfold; entwine. [F f. Rom. (LACE)]

**ĕnlár'ge** *v.t.* & *i.* Make or become larger or wider (lit. or fig.); (Photog.) reproduce on larger scale; expatiate (*upon*); ~**ment** (-jm-) *n.* [F (LARGE)]

**ĕnli'ghten** (-ĭ't-) *v.t.* Instruct, inform, (person *on* subject); free from superstition etc.; (poet.) shed light on; ~**ment** *n.* (**the E~ment,** 18th-c. philosophy of reason and individualism). [EN-]

**ĕnli'st** *v.t.* & *i.* Engage for military service; secure as means of help or support; ~**ment** *n.*

**ĕnli'ven** *v.t.* Animate, inspirit, brighten, (person, scene, etc.); ~**ment** *n.*

*en masse* (ahn mă's) *adv.* All together. [F]

**ĕnmě'sh** *v.t.* Entangle (as) in net. [EN-]

**ĕ'nmĭtў** *n.* Hatred; state of being an enemy. [F f. Rom. (ENEMY)]

**ĕnnŏ'ble** *v.t.* Make (person) a noble; make noble; ~**ment** (-belm-) *n.* [F (EN-)]

**ennui** (ŏ'nwē) *n.* Feeling of boredom, mental weariness caused by idleness or lack of interest; *ennuyé fem.* **-ée,** (ŏnwē'yā) *a.*, bored. [F (ANNOY)]

**ĕnŏr'm|ous** *a.* Extraordinarily large, vast, huge, (*enormous wasp, hall, profits*); ~**ĭtў** *n.*, monstrous wickedness, dreadful crime, serious error, magnitude, great size, (lit. or fig.). [L *enormis* (NORM)]

**ĕnou'gh** (ĭnŭ'f) *a., n.,* & *adv.* Not less than the required number, quantity, degree, as: (a.) *we have* *apples enough, enough apples, beer enough, enough beer, he made enough noise to wake the dead*; (n.) *we have enough of everything except beer, enough of* (stop) *this folly, enough!* (say no more), *enough* (no more need be) *said, enough is as good as a feast, cry 'enough'* (acknowledge defeat), *I have had enough* (am tired) *of him, you have done more than enough or enough and to spare*; (pred. a. or n.) *five men are enough, £5 is not enough*; (adv.) *it is boiled (just) enough, are you warm enough?, he is willing enough* (but incapable), *she sings well enough* (tolerably well), *you know well enough* (very well) *what I mean*; **oddly** etc. ~ (to justify the term *oddly* etc.); **sure** ~, undeniably, as was (or might have been) expected. [E]

**ènou'nce** *v.t.* Enunciate; pronounce (words). [F (ENUNCIATE)]

**en passant** (ahn pă'sahn) *adv.* By the way. [F, = in passing]

**en pension.** See PENSION².

‖**enquire, enquiry.** See INQUIRE, INQUIRY.

**ènra'ge** *v.t.* Make furious. [F (EN-)]

**ènra'pture** *v.t.* Delight intensely. [EN-]

**ènri'ch** *v.t.* Make rich(er); add to contents of (museum, collection, book); ~**ment** *n.* [F (EN-)]

**ènro'l, \*-ll,** *v.t. & i.* (-ll-). Write name of (person) on list, esp. of army; incorporate (person *in* a society etc.) as member; enter one's name on list etc.; ~**ment** *n.*

**en route** (ahn rōō't) *adv.* On the way (*to, for,* place etc., or abs.). [F]

**ènscô'nce** *v.t.* Establish (one*self* etc. *in* place) safely or snugly. [SCONCE²]

**ensemble** (ahnsah'nbl) *n.* (*Tout*) ~, thing viewed as a whole; general :ffect (Mus.) concerted passage in which all performers unite, group of musicians performing thus; group of dancers in ballet etc.; woman's outfit of harmonizing items. [F f. L *simul* at same time)]

**ènshri'ne** *v.t.* Enclose (as) in shrine; serve as shrine for. [EN-]

**ènshrou'd** *v.t.* Cover completely (as) with shroud; hide from view.

**è'nsign** (-ĭn, -ĭn) *n.* Banner, flag, esp. ‖with union in corner (**blue** ~ of government departments and formerly of naval reserve, **red** ~ of merchant service, **white** ~ of Royal Navy and Royal Yacht Squadron); standard-bearer; \*lowest commis-

sioned officer in navy; (Hist.) lowest commissioned infantry officer. [F (INSIGNIA)]

**è'nsĭlage** *n.* Storage in silo; green fodder so stored; **ènsī'le** *v.t.*, put, preserve, (fodder) in silo. [F (SILO)]

**ènslā've** *v.t.* Make (person) a slave (lit., or fig. *to* habit etc.); ~**ment** (-vm-) *n.*; **ènsnār'e** *v.t.*, entrap (lit. or fig.). [EN-]

**ènsū'e** *v.i. & t.* Happen later; result (*from, on*). [F f. Rom. (L *sequor* follow)]

**en suite** (ahn swē't) *adv.* Forming single unit (*bedroom with bathroom en suite*). [F, = in sequence]

**ènsur'e** (-shoor') *v.t.* Make safe (*against* risks); make certain, secure, (*ensure delivery*; *ensure that* thing shall happen; *ensure an income to, for,* person). [AF (ASSURE)]

**-ent.** See -NT.

**E.N.T.** *abbr.* ear, nose, and throat.

**ènta'blature** *n.* (Archit.) Part of order above column, including architrave, frieze, and cornice. [It. (TABLE)]

**èntai'l. 1.** *v.t.* Impose (labour etc. *on*); necessitate; settle (land etc.) on persons successively so that it cannot be bequeathed at pleasure. **2.** *n.* Such settlement; estate so secured. [TAIL²]

**ènta'ngle** (-nggel) *v.t.* Catch in snare etc.; involve in difficulties or illicit activities; tangle, complicate; ~**ment** *n.*, (also, Mil.) barrier, esp. of stakes and interlaced barbed wire, erected to impede enemy's progress. [EN-]

**ente'nte** (ahntah'nt) *n.* Friendly understanding, esp. between States; ~ **cordiale,** = *entente,* esp. of Britain and France 1904–. [F]

**è'nter** *v.t. & i.* Go or come in or into (*enter the room*; *thorn enters flesh*; 3rd pers. subjunctive as stage direction, = come on stage: *Enter Macbeth*); become member of (a society, army, etc.; *enter the* CHURCH); admit, procure admission for (child *at* school etc.); write (name, details, etc.) in list, book, etc.; record formally (before court of law or in minutes of debate etc.); make known (a protest etc.); announce oneself as, record name of person etc. as, competitor in race, contest, etc., (*have you entered for the long jump?*; *they entered the horse for the Derby*); ~ **into,** engage in (conversation, agreement, etc.), sympathize with (feelings), form part of (calculation, plan, etc.), bind oneself by (contract etc.); ~ (up)on, assume possession of (property) or functions of (office), begin, begin to deal with. [F f. L (*intra* within)]

**entĕ′rĭc 1.** *a.* Of the intestines; ~ fever, typhoid. **2.** *n.* Enteric fever. **3. ĕnterī′tĭs** *n.*, inflammation of the intestines, esp. the small intestine. [Gk (*enteron* intestine)]

**e′nterprĭs|e** (-z) *n.* Undertaking, esp. bold or difficult one; readiness to engage in such undertakings; ~ĭng *a.*, showing courage or imaginativeness. [F f. L *prehendo* grasp]

**ĕntertaɪ′n** *v.t.* Amuse, occupy agreeably; receive as guest (*at or* ||*to* meal; *they entertain a great deal*); harbour, cherish, consider favourably, (idea, feeling, proposal); ~er *n.*, (esp.) professional provider of amusement; ~ĭng *a.*, amusing; ~ment *n.*, (esp.) amusement, hospitality, public performance. [F f. Rom. (*teneo* hold)]

**ĕnthra′l, *-ll,** (-aw′l) *v.t.* (-ll-). Enslave (usu. fig.); charm, please greatly; ~ment *n.* [EN-]

**ĕnthrō′ne** *v.t.* Place (king, bishop, etc.) on throne, esp. with ceremony; exalt; ~ment (-nm-), **ĕnthrōnĭzā′tion, ĭn-,** *ns.*

**ĕnthū′sĭ|ăsm** (-zĭ-; *or* -ōō′-) *n.* Rapturous intensity of feeling, great eagerness, zeal, (*for, about,* person, cause, etc.); ~ăst *n.*, person full of enthusiasm, visionary; ~ă′stĭc *a.* (-ically); **ĕnthū′se** (-z; *or* -ōō′z) *v.i. & t.*, (colloq.) show, fill with, enthusiasm. [F or L f. Gk (*entheos* inspired by god)]

**ĕntī′ce** *v.t.* Persuade by offer of pleasure etc. (person *from* place, action, etc., *into* another; *to* do); ~ment (-sm-) *n.* [F f. L *titio* firebrand]

**ĕntī′re** *a.* Whole, complete; not broken; not castrated; unqualified, pure, (*an entire delusion, success*); in one piece, continuous; ~lў (-ĭr′lĭ) *adv.*, wholly, solely; ~tў (*or* -ĭr′tĭ) *n.*, completeness (**in its** ~**tў**, in its complete form), sum total (*of*). [F f. L (INTEGER)]

**ĕntī′tle** *v.t.* Give (book, person) the title of; (of circumstances, ticket, etc.) give (person) a claim (*to* thing, *to* do); ~ment (-tɘlm-) *n.* [AF f. L (TITLE)]

**e′ntĭtў** *n.* Thing's existence as opp.

to its qualities or relations; thing that has real existence. [F or L (*ens ent-* being)]

**ĕnto′mb** (-ōō′m) *v.t.* Place in tomb; serve as tomb for; ~ment (-m-m-) *n.* [F (TOMB)]

**ĕnto̅mŏ′lŏg|ў** *n.* Study of insects; **ĕntomolŏ′gical** *a.* (-lly); ~ĭst *n.* [F or L f. Gk *entomon* = INSECT]

**entourage** (ŏntoorah′zh) *n.* Surroundings; attendant persons. [F]

**entr′acte** (ŏ′ntrăkt) *n.* (Performance in) interval between acts of play. [F]

**e′ntrails** (-z) *n.pl.* Bowels, intestines; inner parts (*of the earth* etc.). [F f. L *intralia* (*intra* within)]

**ĕntraɪ′n** *v.t. & i.* Put (troops etc.), get, into a train. [EN-]

**ĕntra′nc|e¹** (-ah-) *v.t.* Throw into trance; overwhelm (*with* joy etc.); ~ĭng *a.*, (esp.) delightful; ~ement (-sm-) *n.*

**e′ntrance²** *n.* Going or coming in; coming of actor on stage; entering *into* or *upon* (office etc.); right of admission; ~ (**fee**), fee paid for admission to society, exhibition, etc.; passage, door, etc., by which one enters; **e′ntrant** *n.*, one who enters room, profession, etc., or *for* race. [F (ENTER)]

**ĕntra′p** *v.t.* (-pp-). Catch (as) in trap; beguile. [EN-]

**ĕntrea′t** *v.t.* Ask earnestly, beg; ~ў *n.*, earnest request.

**e′ntrecôte** (ŏ′ntrekōt) *n.* Boned steak off sirloin. [F, = between-rib]

**entrée** (ŏ′ntrā, ah′ntrā) *n.* Right, privilege, of admission; ||dish served between fish and meat courses; *main dish of meal. [F]

**ĕntre′nch** *v.t. & i.* Surround (post, army) with trench as fortification; apply extra safeguards to (rights etc. guaranteed by legislation); ~ (oneself), occupy well-defended position (lit. or fig.); ~ment *n.* [EN-]

**entre nous** (ŏntre nōō′) *adv.* Between you and me; in private. [F]

**entrepôt** (ŏ′ntrepō) *n.* Commercial centre for import and export, esp. free of duty; storehouse. [F]

**entrepreneur** (ŏntreprenĕr′) *n.* Person in effective control of commercial undertaking; one who undertakes an enterprise, with chance of profit or loss; contractor acting as intermediary; ~ĭal *a.* [F (ENTERPRISE)]

**e′ntropў** *n.* (Phys.) Measure of the

unavailability of a system's thermal energy for conversion into mechanical work; measure of the degradation or disorganization of the universe. [G f. Gk (EN-, *tropē* transformation)]

**entrŭ′st, in-,** *v.t.* Give with trust (person *with* duty, object of care; task, thing, etc. *to* person). [EN-, IN-[1]]

**e′ntrȳ** *n.* Going or coming in; liberty to do this (~ **permit**, authorization to enter a particular country; **no** ~, notice prohibiting vehicles or persons from going in); place of entrance, door, gate, etc.; passage between buildings; entering, item entered, in account-book, catalogue, diary, etc. (**double, single,** ~, in which each item is entered twice, once, in ledger); list of competitors for race etc.; person or thing competing in race, contest, etc. [F f. Rom. (ENTER)]

**entwi′ne** *v.t.* Interweave; wreathe (thing *with, about,* another). [EN-]

**enŭ′mer|āte** *v.t.* Count; specify (items); ~**ā′tion** *n.*; ~**ative** *a.*; ~**ātor** *n.* (esp. person employed in census-taking). [L (NUMBER)]

**enŭ′nci|āte** *v.t.* (~**able**). State (proposition, theory) in definite terms; proclaim; pronounce (words); ~**ā′tion,** ~**ātor,** *ns.*; ~**ative** (or (-sha-) *a.* [L (*nuntius* messenger)]

**enŭr′e.** See INURE.

**envĕ′lop** *v.t.* Wrap up (person, thing, *in* garment, flames, mystery); (of garment etc.) cover closely on all sides; (Mil.) effect the surrounding of (enemy); ~**ment** *n.* [F]

**e′nvelōpe** (or ŏ′n-) *n.* Folded and gummed cover of letter; wrapper, covering; gas container of balloon or airship.

**envĕ′nom** *v.t.* Put poison or venom on or into (weapon, air, feelings, words, etc.). [F (VENOM)]

**e′nviable, e′nvious.** See ENVY.

**envir′on** *v.t.* Form a ring round, surround, (person, place, thing) hostilely or protectively; ~**ment** *n.*, (esp.) surrounding objects or conditions, circumstances of life of person or society; ~**mĕ′ntal** *a.*; ~**mĕ′ntalist** *n.*, one who is concerned with protection of the environment; ~**s** (-z; or č′nvi-) *n.pl.*, district round town etc. [F, = round about (VEER)]

**envi′sage** (-z-) *v.t.* View (question etc.); imagine (thing not yet existing). [F (VISAGE)]

**envi′sion** (-zhon) *v.t.* Envisage, imagine. [EN-]

**e′nvoy** *n.* Messenger; ~ (**extraordinary**), minister plenipotentiary (below ambassador, above chargé d'affaires); (arch.; also **-oi**) short final stanza of ballade etc. [F (*envoyer* send f. L *via* way)]

**e′nv|ȳ. 1.** *n.* Bitter or longing contemplation (of more fortunate person; *of, at,* his advantages etc.); object of this. **2.** *v.t.* Feel envy of (*I envy him, his success, him his success*); ~**iable** *a.* (-bly), such as to cause envy; ~**ious** *a.*, feeling, full of, envy (*of*). [F f. L *invidia* (*video* see)]

**enwea′ve.** See INWEAVE.

**enwră′p** (-nr-) *v.t.* (-**pp**-). Wrap, enfold, (*in*). [EN-]

**e′nzȳme** *n.* (Chem.) Protein catalyst of a specific biochemical reaction. [G f. Gk (ZYMOTIC)]

**E′ocēne** (ē-) *a.* & *n.* (Geol.) (Of) second lowest division of Tertiary. [Gk *ēōs* dawn, *kainos* new]

*****ēō′lian.** See AEOLIAN.

**ĕoli′thic** *a.* Of the period preceding the palaeolithic age. [Gk *ēōs* dawn, *lithos* stone]

**ē′on.** See AEON.

**E.P.** *abbr.* electroplate; extended-play (record).

**e′paulĕtte, \*-ĕt,** (or -ōl-, ĕpelĕ′t) *n.* Ornamental shoulder-piece of uniform. [F (*épaule* shoulder)]

**épée** (āpā′) *n.* Sharp-pointed duelling-sword, used (blunted) in fencing. [F (SPATHE)]

**Eph.** *abbr.* Ephesians (N.T.).

**e′phedrīne** *n.* Alkaloid drug used against asthma etc. [*Ephedra,* genus of plants yielding it]

**ephĕ′mer|al** *a.* Lasting or living only a day or a few days; transitory; ~**a** *n.* (*pl.* ~**as,** ~**ae**), ~**on** *n.* (*pl.* ~**ons,** ~**a**), ephemeral insect or thing, insect of genus including mayfly; ~**ā′litȳ** *n.* [Gk (EPI-, *hēmera* day)]

**ĕpi-** *pref.* Upon, above, in addition. [Gk]

**e′pic** *a.* & *n.* (Poem) narrating continuously achievements of some hero(es) or embodying nation's conception of its history; (book, film, topic) of heroic type or scale; ~**al** *a.* (-lly). [L f. Gk *epos* song]

**e′picēne** *a.* & *n.* For or used by both sexes; (person) with characteristics of both sexes or without sexual characteristics; (Gram.) denoting either sex without change of gender. [L f. Gk (*koinos* common)]

**e'picĕntre** (-ter), ***-ter***, *n*. Point at which earthquake reaches earth's surface (also fig.). [Gk (CENTRE)]

**e'picūr|e** *n*. Person of refined tastes in food, literature, etc.; **~ĭsm** *n*., epicure's behaviour; **~ē'an** *a*. & *n*., (E-) (follower) of *Epicurus* (who taught that pleasure in its most refined form, calmness of mind, was the highest good), (person) devoted to pleasure, esp. refined sensuous enjoyment; **~ē'anĭsm** *n*. [person]

**epĭdĕ'mĭc** *a*. (**~ally**) & *n*. (Disease etc.) prevalent among community at special time (cf. ENDEMIC); **epĭdēmĭŏ'logў** *n*., science of epidemics. [F f. L f. Gk (as DEMOTIC)]

**epĭdẽr'm|ĭs** *n*. Outer layer of animal's skin, cuticle; **~al**, **~ĭc**, *adjs*. [L f. Gk (*derma* skin)]

**epĭdĭa'scōpe** *n*. Optical projector giving images of both opaque and transparent objects. [EPI-, DIA-, -SCOPE]

**epĭglŏ'tt|ĭs** *n*. Cartilage at root of tongue, depressed in swallowing; **~al**, **~ĭc**, *adjs*. [Gk *glōtta* tongue]

**e'pĭgŏne** *n*. (*pl*. **~s**, epigoni *pr*. -ĭ'goni). One of a later (and less distinguished) generation. [F f. L f. Gk, = born after]

**e'pĭgrăm** *n*. Short poem with witty ending; pointed saying; **epĭgrammă'tĭc** *a*. (-ically); **~matĭst** (-ră'-) *n*.; **~matīze** (-ră'-) *v.i*. & *t*., make epigrams (about). [F or L f. Gk (-GRAM)]

**e'pĭgraph** (-ahf) *n*. Inscription; **epĭ'graphў** *n*., study of epigraphs. [Gk (-GRAPH)]

**e'pĭl|āte** *v.t*. Remove hair from; **~ā'tion** *n*. [F (as DEPILATE)]

**e'pĭlĕpsў** *n*. Nervous disorder in which person suffers convulsions with or without loss of consciousness; **epĭlĕ'ptĭc**, (*a*.) of, subject to, epilepsy, (*n*.) such person. [F or L f. Gk (*lambanō* seize)]

**e'pĭlŏgue** (-g) *n*. Concluding part of book etc.; speech or short poem addressed to audience by actor at end of play. [F f. L f. Gk (LOGOS)]

**epĭ'phanў** *n*. (E~) manifestation of Christ to the Magi, festival of this (6 Jan.); manifestation of a superhuman being. [F f. L f. Gk (*phainō* show)]

**e'pĭphӯte** *n*. Plant growing on (usu. not fed by) another; vegetable parasite on animal. [Gk *phuton* plant]

**epĭ'scop|al** *a*. (**~ally**). Of, governed by, bishop(s), (E~al Church, Church of England in Scotland & U.S.); **~acў** *n*., episcopal government, *the* bishops; **~ā'lĭan** *a*. & *n*., (adherent) of episcopacy, (E-) (member) of Episcopal Church; **~ā'lĭanĭsm** *n*.; **~ate** *n*., office, position, tenure, of bishop, *the* bishops. [F or L (BISHOP)]

**e'pĭsōde** *n*. Incidental narrative or series of events; incident in narrative, part of serial story; event as part of sequence; **epĭsŏ'dĭc(al)** *adjs*. (-ically), (also) sporadic, irregularly occurring. [Gk (*eisodos* entrance)]

**epĭstĕm|ŏ'logў** *n*. Theory of method or grounds of knowledge; **~olŏ'gĭcal** *a*. (-lly). [Gk *epistēmē* knowledge]

**epĭ'stle** (-sel) *n*. Letter in N.T., written by apostle; (E~) extract from this read in church service; (usu. joc.) letter; poem etc. in form of letter; **epĭ'stolarў** *a*., of, for, carried on by, letters (*epistolary style*). [F f. L f. Gk *epistolē* (*stellō* send)]

**e'pĭtaph** (-ahf) *n*. Words (composed as if to be) inscribed on tomb. [F f. L f. Gk (*taphos* tomb)]

**epĭthē'lĭ|um** *n*. (*pl*. **~ums**, **~a**). Tissue forming outer layer of body or lining open cavity; epidermis of young cells; **~al** *a*. [L f. Gk *thēlē* teat]

**e'pĭthĕt** *n*. Adjective expressing quality or attribute; significant appellation; **epĭthĕ'tĭc** *a*. (-ically). [F or L f. Gk (*tithēmi* to place)]

**epĭ'tom|e** *n*. Summary, abstract; (fig.) thing that represents another in miniature, person who embodies a quality etc.; **~ize** *v.t*., make an epitome of. [L f. Gk (*temnō* cut)]

**E.P.N.S.** *abbr*. electroplated nickel silver.

**e'pŏch** (-k) *n*. Beginning of era in history, life, etc.; date; period marked by notable events; **~-making**, notable, significant; **~al** *a*. [Gk, = pause]

**e'pōde** *n*. Form of lyric poem with long line followed by shorter one; third section of ancient-Greek choral ode. [F or L f. Gk (ODE)]

**e'ponӯm** *n*. One who gives his name to place etc.; **epŏ'nӯmous** *a*., commemorated by adoption of name (*church and its eponymous saint*). [Gk (*onoma* name)]

**ĕpsī′lon** *n.* Fifth Gk letter (E, ε) = ĕ (cf. ETA). [Gk]

**E′psom** (ĕ′-) *n.* ~ **salt(s)**, magnesium sulphate used as purgative etc. [place]

**ĕ′quab|le** *a.* (~ly). Uniform, even; not easily disturbed; uniform and moderate (*equable climate*); ~i′lĭtў *n.* [foll.]

**ĕ′qual** *a., n.,* & *v.* **1.** *a.* (~ly). The same in number, size, degree, merit, etc., (*twice 3 is equal to 6*; *the totals are equal*; *speaks French and Dutch with equal ease*; *they are equal in ability*); having strength etc. adequate (*to the occasion, to doing*); uniform in operation etc. (*equal laws*); evenly balanced as regards power, entitlement, etc., (*equal fight*; ~ **pay** for same work done, esp. by either sex). **2.** *n.* Person equal to another in rank, power, etc., (*mix with one's equals*; *he has no equal*), (in *pl.*) equal things (*if equals be added to equals*). **3.** *v.t.* (||-ll-). Be equal to; do something that is equal to. **4.** **ĕqualitār′ian** (-ŏl-) etc.,= EGALITARIAN etc.; **ĕqua′lĭtў** (-ŏ′l-) *n.,* being equal; **~ize** *v.t.* & *i.,* make equal (*to, with*), become equal, (Footb. etc.) reach opponent's score; **~izā′tion** *n.;* **~izer** *n.,* (esp.) goal that equalizes. [L *aequalis*]

**ĕquani′mĭtў** *n.* Composure; acceptance of fate. [L *aequus* even, *animus* mind]

**ĕquā′t|e** *v.t.* State, assume, equality of (thing *to, with*); **~ion** (-zhon) *n.,* making equal, balancing, correction for inaccuracy (**personal ~ion**, allowance for person's time of reaction in making observations, fig. bias), (Math.) statement of equality between two expressions (conveyed by the sign =), (Chem.) formula indicating reaction by use of symbols; **~ional** (-zhon-) *a.* (-lly); **~or** *n.,* great circle of the earth, sun, etc., equidistant from poles, great circle of sky in plane perpendicular to earth's axis; **ĕquātor′ial** *a.* (-lly), of, near, the equator. [L *aequo aequat-* make EQUAL]

**ĕ′querry** (or ĭkwĕ′rĭ) *n.* Officer of British royal household, attending sovereign etc. [F *escurie* stable]

**ĕquĕ′stri|an. 1.** *a.* Of horse-riding (~ **statue**, of horseman). **2.** *n.* (*fem.* **-ie′nne**). Rider, performer, on horse; **~ĭsm** *n.* [L *equestris* (*equus* horse)]

**ĕqui-** *in comb.* Equal; **~a′ngular,** having equal angles; **~di′stant,** at equal distances; **~la′teral,** having all sides equal. [L (EQUAL)]

**ĕqui′lĭbr|āte** (or ēkwĭlī′-) *v.t.* & *i.* Cause (two things) to balance; balance; **~ā′tion** *n.;* **ĕquĭ′librĭst** *n.,* tightrope-walker, acrobat; **ĕquilĭ′brium** *n.* (*pl.* **-ia, -iums**), state of balance (lit. or fig.). [LIBRA]

**ĕ′quĭne** *a.* Of, like, a horse. [L (*equus* horse)]

**ĕ′quĭnŏx** *n.* Time or date at which sun crosses equator and day and night are equal (**spring** or **vernal** ~, about 20 Mar.; **autumn(al)** ~, about 22 Sept.); (in *pl.*) equinoctial points; **ĕquĭnŏ′ctial** (-shal), (*a.* -lly) of, happening at or near, equinox (*equinoctial gales*; **equinoctial line,** celestial EQUATOR; (*n.*) equinoctial line. [F f. L (*nox* night)]

**ĕquī′p** *v.t.* (-pp-). Supply (person, ship, etc., *with* requisites); furnish (one*self* etc.) with what is needed for journey etc.; **ĕ′quĭpage** *n.,* requisites, outfit, carriage and horses with attendants; **~ment** *n.,* (esp.) outfit, tools, apparatus, for expedition, job, etc. [F f. N (SHIP)]

**ĕ′quĭpoise** (-z). **1.** *n.* Equilibrium; counterbalancing thing. **2.** *v.t.* Counterbalance. [EQUI-]

**ĕquĭtā′tion** *n.* Riding on horse; horsemanship. [F or L (*equito* ride horse)]

**ĕ′quĭt|ў** *n.* Fairness; use of principles of justice to supplement law, system of law so developed; value of shares issued by a company; ||(*E*-) actors' trade union; (in *pl.*) stocks and shares not bearing fixed interest; **~able** *a.* (-bly), fair, just, valid in equity as opp. to law. [F f. L *aequitas* (EQUAL)]

**ĕquĭ′val|ent. 1.** *a.* Equal in value, amount, etc., (*to*); meaning the same; having same result; corresponding; **~ence, ~encў,** *ns.* **2.** *n.* Equivalent thing, amount, etc. [F f. L (VALUE)]

**ĕquĭ′voc|al** *a.* (-lly). Of double or doubtful meaning; of uncertain nature; questionable, dubious; **~ă′lĭtў** *n.;* **~āte** *v.i.,* use ambiguous words to conceal truth; **~ā′tion, ~ātor,** *ns.* [L (*voco* call)]

**ĕr** *int.* expr. hesitation. [imit.]

**-er**[1] *suf.* forming *ns.* f. *ns.*, *adjs.*, & *vbs.* (with spelling-rules as -ER[2]), meaning person, animal, that does (*maker*, *pointer*, *executioner*), person or thing that has or is (*three-decker*, *foreigner*), instrument, machine, action, etc., (*poker*, *computer*, *header*), person concerned with (*hatter*, *geographer*), person from place (*Londoner*, *villager*), sl. distortion of word (*rugger*, *soccer*). [E]

**-er**[2], **-est**, *sufs.* forming compar. & superl. of *adjs.* & *advs.* esp. of one or sometimes two syllables (*wider*, *widest*; *narrower*, *narrowest*; *sooner*, *soonest*); these words drop silent final *e* (*braver*, *nicest*), and change final *y* after a consonant into *i* (*happier*, *luckiest*; but *gayest*); see note on Suffixes, p. viii. [E]

**E.R.** *abbr.* King Edward [L *Edwardus Rex*]; Queen Elizabeth [L *Elizabetha Regina*]

**ēr′a** *n.* System of chronology starting from particular event etc. (*Christian era*); (date beginning) historical or other period; (Geol.) major division of time. [L, = number (pl. of *aes* money)]

**ėrä′dĭc|āte** *v.t.* (~able). Root out, extirpate, get rid of, (weeds, evils, etc.); ~**ā′tion**, ~**ātor**, *ns.* [L (RADIX)]

**ėrā′s|e** (-z) *v.t.* Rub out; obliterate, remove all traces of; remove recording from (magnetic tape); ~**er** *n.*, (esp.) piece of rubber etc. for rubbing out writing etc.; **ėrā′sure** (-zher) *n.* [L (*rado* scrape)]

**ere** (ār) *prep.* & *conj.* (poet., arch.) Before (*ere noon*; *ere he went*); ~**whi′le**, (poet., arch.) formerly. [E]

**ėrĕ′ct. 1.** *a.* Upright, vertical; (of hair) bristling; (of part of body) enlarged and rigid, esp. from sexual excitement. **2.** *v.t.* Raise, set upright; build, establish, (*erect a hospital*, *theory*); ~**īle** *a.*, that can be erected or become erect; ~**ion**, ~**or**, *ns.* [L (*erigo erect-* set up)]

**ė′rĕm|īte** *n.* Hermit (esp. Christian recluse); ~**ĭt′ĭc(al)** *adjs.* [F (HERMIT)]

**ĕrg** *n.* (Phys.) Unit of work or energy. [Gk *ergon* work]

**ĕr′gō** *adv.* Therefore. [L]

**ĕrgonŏ′m|ĭcs** *n.* Study of efficiency of persons in their working environment; ~**ĭc** *a.* (~ically); **ĕrgŏ′nomĭst** *n.* [Gk *ergon* work]

**ĕr′got** *n.* Disease of rye etc. caused by fungus; drug prepared from the fungus; ~**ĭsm** *n.*, disease produced by bread made from flour affected by ergot. [F]

**ė′rĭca** (or ĭri′ka) *n.* Kind of heath (plant). [L f. Gk]

**Erin** (ĕ′rĭn, ēr′ĭn) *n.* (Ancient or poet. name of) Ireland. [Ir.]

**ĕr′mĭne** *n.* Carnivorous animal of weasel family with fur brown in summer and white (exc. black tail--tip) in winter; its winter fur, used in robes of judges, peers, etc. [F]

**ĕrne**, ***ĕrn**, *n.* Sea eagle. [E]

‖**Er′nĭe** (ĕr′-) *n.* Device for drawing prize-winning numbers of Premium Bonds. [*electronic random number indicator equipment*]

**ėrō′d|e** *v.t.* (~ible). Eat away, wear out, destroy gradually; **ėrō′sion** (-zhon) *n.*; **ėrō′sĭve** *a.* [F or L (*rodo* gnaw)]

**ėrō′gėnous** *a.* Giving rise to sexual excitement. [EROTIC, Gk *gen-* become]

**Er′ŏs** (ēr′-) *n.* Earthly or sensual love; god of love, Cupid. [L f. Gk, as foll.]

**ėrŏ′tĭc** *a.* (~ally). Of sexual love, amatory, esp. tending to arouse sexual desire or excitement; ~**a** *n.pl.*, erotic literature or art; ~**ĭsm** *n.*, erotic spirit or character. [F f. Gk (*erōs* love)]

**ĕrr** *v.i.* Make mistake(s); (of statement etc.) be incorrect; sin; **ĕrrā′tum** (or -ah′-) *n.* (*pl.* -ta), error in printing etc.; **ĕrrō′nėous** *a.*, incorrect (*erroneous idea*, *statement*); **ĕ′rror** *n.*, mistake (*make*, *commit*, *an error*; **in error**, mistaken(ly), by mistake), condition of erring in opinion or conduct (*realize the error of one's ways*), wrong opinion, amount of inaccuracy in calculation or measurement. [F f. L (*erro* stray, wander)]

**ĕ′rrand** *n.* Short journey on which person goes or is sent to take message, deliver goods, etc., (*run*, *go*, (*on*) *errands*; *errand-boy*; ~ **of mercy**, journey to relieve distress etc.); object of journey. [E]

**ĕ′rrant** *a.* Roaming in quest of adventure (esp. KNIGHT errant); erring (*errant husband*); **ĕr′rancy** *n.*, erring state or conduct; ~**ry** *n.*, condition, conduct, notions, of a knight errant; **ĕrrā′tĭc** *a.* (-ically), uncertain, irregular, in movement, conduct, opinion, etc. [ERR; errant partly ult. f. L (*iter* journey)]

**erratum, ěrrō′nĕous, ě′rror.** See ERR.

**ĕr′sătz** (-zăts; or ār-) a. & n. Substitute; (inferior) imitation. [G]

**Erse** (ẽrs) a. & n. Irish Gaelic or (arch.) Scottish Gaelic (language). [early Sc. form of *Irish*]

**ẽrst** adv. (arch.) Formerly, of old; ~′**while**, (a.) former, previous, (adv., arch.) formerly. [E superl. (ERE)]

**ĕrŭctā′tion** n. Belching (of person or volcano). [L]

**ĕ′rŭd|ĭte** (or -rŏŏ-) a. Learned; showing learning; ~**i′tion** n. [L *eruditus* instructed (RUDE)]

**ĕrŭ′pt** v.i. Break out or through (lit. of teeth through gums, etc., or fig. of anger etc.); (of volcano) emit lava, rocks, etc.; (of rash) appear on skin; ~**ion**, n., outbreak (of volcano, anger, disease, war, etc.), breaking out or through (of rash, teeth, etc.); ~**ive**, a., (esp.) of, due to, tending to, volcanic eruption. [L *erumpo erupt-* break out]

**-erў, -rў,** suf. forming ns. meaning class of goods or other things (*drapery, greenery, machinery*) or of persons (*citizenry*), employment or condition (*archery, dentistry, slavery*), place of work or cultivation or breeding (*brewery, orangery, rookery*), behaviour (*mimicry*), (often derog.) all or something that is characteristic of or has to do with (*knavery, popery, tomfoolery*). [F f. L]

**ĕrўsĭ′pĕlas** n. Acute inflammation of skin, with deep red coloration. [L f. Gk]

**erўthē′ma** n. Superficial inflammation of skin in patches; **ĕrў′throcўte** n., red blood-corpuscle. [L f. Gk (*eruthros* red)]

**ĕ′scal|āte** v.t. & i. Increase, develop, by successive stages; ~**ā′tion** n.; ~**ātor** n., moving staircase; ~**ator clause** etc. (providing for change in price etc. under stated conditions). [F f. Sp. (SCALE[3])]

**ĕscă′llop** n. = SCALLOP; = foll. [foll.]

**ĕ′scalōpe** n. Slice of boneless meat, esp. from leg of veal. [F, orig. = shell]

**ĕscapā′de** n. Piece of irresponsible or unorthodox conduct. [foll.]

**ĕscā′pe.** 1. v.i. & t. Get free of (*from*) restriction or control; (of gas etc.) get out of container etc.; get off unpunished etc.; elude, avoid, (person, his grasp, task, do*ing*); elude notice or memory of (*nothing* escapes *you!*; the name escapes *me*); (of words, sigh, etc.) issue unawares from (person, lips). 2. n. (Means or act or fact of) escaping (~ **clause**, one specifying conditions under which contracting party is free from obligations; ~ **velocity**, minimum velocity needed to escape from gravitational field of a body); leakage (of gas etc.); garden plant growing wild; **ĕscā′pee′** (or ěskā′pē) n., one who has escaped; ~**ment** (-pm-) n., mechanism connecting motive power and regulator of watch etc.; **ĕscā′p-ĭsm** n., tendency to seek distraction or relief from reality; **ĕscā′pĭst** n. [AF f. Rom. (L *cappa* CAPE[1])]

**ĕscār′p(ment)** n. Long steep face of plateau etc. [F f. It. (SCARP)]

**ĕschat|ŏ′logў** (-k-) n. Doctrine of death, judgement, heaven, and hell, as the four last things; ~**olŏ′gĭcal** a. (-lly). [Gk *eskhatos* last]

**ĕschea′t.** (Hist.) 1. n. Lapse of property to government etc. on owner's dying intestate without heirs; property so lapsing. 2. v.t. & i. Hand over, revert, as an escheat; confiscate. [F f. L (*cado* fall)]

**ĕschew′** (-ōō′) v.t. Avoid, abstain from. [F f. Gmc (SHY[1])]

**eschschŏ′ltzia** (ĭskŏ′lsha, ĕshŏ′lt-sia) n. The yellow-flowered Californian poppy or allied plant. [*Eschscholtz*, person]

**escort.** 1. (ĕ′skŏrt) n. Body of armed men as guard to persons, baggage, etc.; person(s), ship(s), etc., accompanying another on journey for protection etc. or as courtesy; man accompanying woman socially. 2. (ĭskŏr′t) v.t. Act as escort to. [F f. It.]

**ĕ′scritoire** (-twär′) n. Writing-desk with drawers etc. [F f. L SCRIP-TORIUM]

**ĕscū′dō** n. (pl. ~s). Monetary unit of Portugal. [Sp. & Port., f. L *scutum* shield]

**ĕ′sculent** a. & n. (Thing) fit for food. [L (*esca* food)]

**ĕscū′tcheon** (-chŏn) n. Shield with armorial bearings (**blot on** one's ~, stain on one's reputation). [AF f. L *scutum* shield]

**Esd.** abbr. Esdras (Apocrypha).

**E.S.E.** abbr. east-south-east.

**E′skĭmō** (ĕ′-) n. (pl. ~**s**, ~) & a. (Member or language) of people inhabiting arctic coast of N. America and of E. Siberia; ~ **dog**, breed of powerful dog used by Eskimos to pull sledges etc. [Da. f. F f. Algonquian]

**E.S.N.** *abbr.* educationally subnormal.

*__eso'phagus.__ See OESOPHAGUS.

**ĕsotĕ'rĭc** *a.* (~ally). Meant for the initiated, not generally intelligible. [Gk (*esō* within)]

**E.S.P.** *abbr.* extra-sensory perception.

**ĕspadrĭ'lle** *n.* Canvas sandal with plaited fibre sole. [F f. Prov. (ESPARTO)]

**ĕspā'lier** *n.* Lattice-work for tree etc.; tree etc. trained on espalier. [F f. It.]

**ĕspā̆r'tō** *n.* ~ (**grass**), species of grass used in making paper. [Sp. f. L f. Gk *sparton* rope]

**ĕspē'cial** (-shal) *a.* Pre-eminent, exceptional, (*my especial friend; of especial importance*); ~lȳ *adv.*, particularly, more than in other cases, (*hate sugar, especially in tea*). [F f. L (SPECIAL)]

**Esperă̆'ntō** (ĕ-) *n.* Artificial universal language. [L *spero* hope]

**ĕspi'al** *n.* Espying. [F (ESPY)]

**ĕ'spĭonage** (*or* -ahzh) *n.* Spying; use of spies. [F (SPY)]

**ĕsplanā'de** (*or* -ah'd) *n.* Level space, esp. one used as promenade or separating fortress from town. [F f. Sp. f. L (*planus* level)]

**ĕspou's|e** (-z) *v.t.* Marry (arch.); (fig.) adopt, support, (cause); ~al *n.*, (fig.) espousing (*of* cause), (arch., usu. in *pl.*) marriage, betrothal. [F f. L (*spondeo* betroth)]

**ĕsprĕ'ssō** *n.* (*pl.* ~s). (Apparatus for) coffee made under steam pressure. [It., = pressed out]

**esprit** (ĕ'sprē, ĕsprē') *n.* Sprightliness, wit; ~ *de corps* (-dekŏr'), regard for honour, interests, etc., of a body by those belonging to it. [F (SPIRIT)]

**ĕspȳ'** *v.t.* Catch sight of. [F (SPY)]

**Esq.** *abbr.* Esquire.

**-ĕ'sque** (-ĕ'sk) *suf.* forming *adjs.* meaning 'after the style of' (*arabesque, Turneresque*). [F f. It. f. L *-iscus*]

**ĕsquir'e** *n.* ‖Title added to gentleman's name, or to name of any man without other title in formal use or in address of letter; (arch.) = SQUIRE. [F f. L (*scutum* shield)]

**-ĕss** *suf.* forming *ns.* denoting females (*actress, countess, enchantress, lioness, mayoress*). [F f. L f. Gk *-issa*]

**ĕssay. 1.** (ĕ'sā) *n.* Literary composition (usu. in prose and short) on any subject; attempt. **2.** (ĕsā') *v.t.* Attempt (task, *to do*); (arch.) try, test, (person, thing). **3. ĕ'ssayĭst** *n.*, essay-writer. [F f. L *exigo* weigh; cf. ASSAY]

**ĕ'ssence** *n.* All that makes a thing what it is; indispensable quality or element; extract got by distillation etc.; perfume, scent; **in** ~, fundamentally; **of the** ~, indispensable. [F f. L (*esse* to be)]

**Essē'ne** (ĕ-; *or* ĕ'-) *n.* Member of ancient-Jewish sect. [L f. Gk]

**ĕssĕ'ntial** (-shal). **1.** *a.* (~lȳ). Of, constituting, a thing's essence (*essential features, qualities*); ~ **oil**, volatile oil with characteristic odour etc.); indispensable (*to*); most important; **ĕssĕntiă'lĭtȳ** (-shi-) *n.* **2.** *n.* Indispensable or fundamental element or thing (*bare essentials*). [L (ESSENCE)]

**-ĕst.** See -ER².

**ĕstă'blĭsh** *v.t.* Set up (system, business, etc.) on permanent basis; settle (person etc. *in* office etc.); get generally accepted, place beyond dispute, (*establish a custom, belief, fact, that* thing is so); make (CHURCH) officially national; ~**ment** *n.*, establishing, church system established by law, organized body permanently maintained (e.g. army, navy, civil service), household, staff of servants etc., public institution, house of business, ‖(esp. **the E**~**ment**) social group exercising authority or influence and resisting change. [F f. L (STABLE)]

**ĕstā'te** *n.* Class forming part of body politic and sharing in government (**the Three E**~**s**, Lords Spiritual, Lords Temporal, Commons; **third** ~, usu., French bourgeoisie before Revolution; **fourth** ~, joc., the press); (person's holdings in) landed property (*real estate*) or movables (*personal estate*); one's assets and liabilities; property where rubber, tea, grapes, etc., are cultivated; residential, industrial, etc., district planned by one owner or local council; (arch.) state, condition, (*come to man's estate; holy estate of matrimony*); ‖~ **agent**, steward of estate, one who conducts business in sale or lease of houses and land; ‖~ (**car**), saloon motor car for carrying both passengers and goods; ‖~ **duty**, = DEATH duty. [F f. L (STATION)]

**estee'm. 1.** *v.t.* Think favourably of, regard as valuable; consider (*shall esteem it a favour*). **2.** *n.* Favourable opinion, regard. [F f. L (ESTIMATE)]

**e'ster** *n.* Compound formed when hydrogen in an acid is replaced by an organic radical such as ethyl. [G]

**Esth.** *abbr.* Esther (O.T. & Apocr.).

**e'stim|ate. 1.** *n.* Approximate judgement of number, amount, quality, character, etc.; price quoted by contractor for specified work. **2.** (-āt) *v.t.* Form an estimate or opinion of, *that*; fix (quantity etc. *at* so much) by estimate; **~able** *a.*, worthy of esteem; **~a'tion** *n.*, judgement of worth; **~ātor** *n.* [L *aestimo* fix price of]

**estŏ'p** *v.t.* (Law; -pp-). Bar, preclude, (*from*); **~page** *n.*; **~pel** *n.*, being precluded from a course of action by one's own previous behaviour. [F (STOP)]

**estrā'nge** (-nj) *v.t.* Cause (person) to turn away in feeling or affection (*from* another); **~ment** (-jm-) *n.* [F f. L (STRANGE)]

**e'stuary** *n.* Tidal mouth of river. [L (*aestus* tide)]

**e'ta** *n.* Seventh Gk letter (H, η) = ē (cf. EPSILON). [Gk]

**ĕt ăl.** *abbr.* and others. [L *et alii*]

**etc.** *abbr.* = foll.

**ĕt cē'tera, ĕtcē'tera. 1.** *phr.* And the rest, and so on. **2.** *n.* (in *pl.*) (The usual) sundries. [L]

**ĕtch** *v.t. & i.* Reproduce (picture etc.) by engraving metal plate with acid, esp. in order to print copies; engrave (plate) thus; practise this craft; (fig.) impress deeply (on); **~'ing** *n.*, (esp.) copy from etched plate. [Du. *etsen* f. G]

**etĕ'r'n|al** (or ē-) *a.* (**~ally**). That always (has existed and) will exist (*eternal life*; *Eternal* CITY; *eternal* TRIANGLE; **the E~al**, God); constant, too frequent (*eternal arguments*, *grumbling*); **~(al)ize** *vbs. t.*; **~ĭtỹ** *n.*, being eternal, infinite (esp. future) time, the future life, (colloq.) very long time. [F f. L *aeternus*]

**-eth.** See -TH.

**ĕ'thāne** *n.* A hydrocarbon gas of the paraffin series. [foll.]

**e'ther** *n.* Clear sky, upper air; medium formerly assumed to permeate space and transmit electromagnetic radiation; volatile liquid produced by action of acids on alcohol, used as solvent or anaesthetic; **ĕthĕr'ĕal** *a.* (-lly), light, airy, of unearthly delicacy of substance etc., heavenly; **~eal oil**, essential oil; **ĕthĕrĕ'lĭtỹ** *n.*; **ĕthĕr'ealize** *v.t.*; **~ize** *v.t.*, anaesthetize (patient) with ether. [F or L f. Gk]

**ĕ'thĭc. 1.** *a.* (**~ally**). Relating to morals or moral questions. **2.** *n.* Set of moral principles (*the Quaker ethic*); (in *pl.*, also treated as *sing.*) science of morals, moral principles or code. **3.** **~al** *a.* (-lly), ethic, morally correct, (of medicine or drug) not advertised to general public and usu. available only on doctor's prescription. [F or L (ETHOS)]

**ĕ'thnĭc. 1.** *a.* (**~ally**). Pertaining to race; (arch.) heathen; *originating from specified racial, linguistic, etc., group. **2.** *n.* *Member of ethnic group; (in *pl.*, usu. treated as *sing.*) ethnology. **3.** **~al** *a.* (-lly), ethnological; **ĕthnŏ'graphỹ** *n.*, scientific description of races of men; **ĕthnŏgrā'phĭc(al)** *adjs.* (-ically); **ĕthnŏ'logỹ** *n.*, science of human races; **ĕthnŏlŏ'gĭc(al)** *adjs.* (-ically); **ĕthnŏ'logĭst** *n.* [L f. Gk (*ethnos* nation)]

**ĕ'thŏs** *n.* Characteristic spirit or tone of a community etc.; **ēthŏ'logỹ** *n.*, science of animal behaviour. [L f. Gk *ēthos* (settled) character]

**ĕ'thỹl** *n.* (Chem.) Radical derived from ethane; **~ēne** *n.*, a hydrocarbon of the olefin series. [G (ETHER)]

**ē'tiol|āte** *v.t.* Make (plant) pale by excluding light; give sickly hue to (person); **~ā'tion** *n.* [F f. L (*stipula* straw)]

***ētiŏ'logỹ.** See AETIOLOGY.

**ĕ'tiquĕtte** (-kĕt) *n.* Conventional rules of manners; court ceremonial; unwritten code forbidding unprofessional conduct (*medical*, *legal*, *etiquette*). [F (TICKET)]

**E'ton** (ē'-) *n.* **~ collar** (broad and stiff, worn outside coat-collar); **~ crop**, woman's short hair-style; **~ĭan** (ētō'-) *a. & n.*, (member) of Eton College. [place]

**Etrŭ'scan** (ĭ-) *a. & n.* (Native, language) of ancient Etruria. [L]

**et seq(q).** *abbr.* and the following (pages, matter, etc.). [L *et sequentia*]

**-ĕ'tte** *suf.* forming *ns.*, meaning small (*cigarette*, *kitchenette*), imitation or substitute (*flannelette*, *leatherette*), female (*suffragette*, *usherette*). [F]

**étude** (ā′tūd, -ū′d) *n.* Short musical composition or exercise. [F, = study]

**ĕtў̆mŏ′log|ў̆** *n.* (Account of) a word's origin and sense-development; branch of linguistic science concerned with this; **ĕtў̆molŏ′gĭcal** *a.* (-lly); ~**ĭst** *n.*; ~**ĭze** *v.t.* & *i.*, give or trace etymology of, study etymology; **ĕ′tў̆mon** *n.* (*pl.* -**ma**), primary word from which another is derived. [F f. L f. Gk (*etumos* true)]

**eu-** *pref.* Well, easily (opp. DYS-). [Gk]

**eucalў̆′pt|(us)** *n.* Austral. etc. evergreen tree; ~**us** (**oil**), essential oil from this used as antiseptic etc. [L (EU-, Gk *kaluptos* covered)]

**Eu′char|ĭst** (-k-) *n.* Christian sacrament in which bread and wine are consecrated and consumed; consecrated elements, esp. bread; ~**ĭ′stĭc** *a.* [F f. L f. Gk, = thanksgiving]

**eu′chre** (-ker) **1.** *n.* Amer. card game. **2.** *v.t.* Gain advantage over (opponent) by his failure to take 3 tricks at euchre; (fig.) deceive, outwit. [orig. unkn.]

**eugĕ′nĭc** *a.* (~**ally**). Of the production of fine (usu. human) offspring by improvement of inherited qualities; ~**s** *n.pl.*, science of this; **eu′genĭst** *n.* [Gk *gen-* produce]

**eu′log|ў̆** *n.* Speech, writing, in praise of person; (expression of) praise; ~**ĭst** *n.*; ~**ĭ′stĭc** *a.* (-ically); ~**ĭze** *v.t.*, extol, praise. [L f. Gk]

**eu′nuch** (-k) *n.* Castrated man, esp. one employed in harem, or (esp. in the Orient or under Roman Empire) as court official; (fig.) person lacking effectiveness (*political eunuch*). [L f. Gk, = bed-keeper]

**euŏ′nў̆mus** *n.* Spindle-tree or kindred plant. [L f. Gk, = of lucky name]

**eupĕ′ptĭc** *a.* (~**ally**). Having good digestion. [Gk (*peptō* digest)]

**eu′phem|ĭsm** *n.* Substitution of mild for blunt expression; such substitute ('*touched*' *is a euphemism for* '*mad*'); ~**ĭ′stĭc** *a.* (-ically); ~**ĭze** *v.t.* & *i.*, express by euphemisms, use euphemisms. [Gk (*phēmē* speaking)]

**eu′phon|ў̆** *n.* Pleasing sound; pleasantness or smoothness of sound, esp. of words; **euphŏ′nĭc** *a.* (-ically); **euphŏ′nĭous** *a.*; ~**ĭze** *v.t.*; **euphŏ′nium**, *n.*, tenor tuba, bass saxhorn. [F f. L f. Gk (*phōnē* sound)]

**euphŏr′bĭa** *n.* Spurge plant. [*Euphorbus*, person]

**euphŏr′ĭa** *n.* Feeling of well-being, esp. one based on over-confidence; **euphŏ′rĭc** *a.* (-ically). [Gk (*pherō* bear)]

**eu′phrasў̆** *n.* The plant eyebright. [L f. Gk, = cheerfulness]

**eu′phu|ĭsm** *n.* Affected or high-flown style of writing; ~**ĭst** *n.*; ~**ĭ′stĭc** *a.* (-ically). [orig. of writing in imit. of Lyly's *Euphues*]

**Eurā′sian** (ūrā′zhan). **1.** *a.* Of mixed European and Asian parentage; of Europe and Asia. **2.** *n.* Eurasian person. [*Europe, Asia*]

**eurē′ka** (ūr-) *int.* 'I have (found) it!' (announcing discovery etc.). [Gk *heurēka* I have found]

**Eur′ō-** (ūr′ō-) *in comb.* Europe, European; ~**crat**, bureaucrat of European Communities; ~**dollar**, dollar held in bank in Europe etc.; ~**vision**, television of European range. [abbr.]

**Europē′an** (ūr-). **1.** *a.* Of, in, extending over, Europe (*European nations; has a European reputation*); ~**ĭze** *v.t.* **2.** *n.* Native or inhabitant of Europe; descendant of such; person interested in Europe as a whole rather than its individual countries. [F f. L (*Europe*)]

**Eustā′chian** (-shan) *a.* ~ **tube**, canal from pharynx to cavity of middle ear. [*Eustachi*, person]

**euthanā′sĭa** (-z-) *n.* Gentle and easy death; bringing about of this, esp. in case of incurable and painful disease. [Gk (*thanatos* death)]

**eV** *abbr.* electron-volt(s).

**evă′cŭ|āte** *v.t.* (~**able**). Empty (bowels etc., vessel); discharge (faeces etc.); (esp. of troops) withdraw from (place); remove (person) esp. from place considered to be dangerous; ~**ā′tion** *n.*; ~**ee′** *n.*, person removed from place of danger. [L (VACUUM)]

**evā′d|e** *v.t.* Escape from, avoid (person, attack, blow, designs); avoid doing, answering, etc., (*evade duty, question, tax*); frustrate (law etc., esp. while complying with its terms); elude, baffle; **evā′sion** (-zhon) *n.*; **evā′sĭve** *a.* (**evasive action**, action to avoid trouble etc.). [F f. L *evado* escape]

**evă′lŭ|āte** *v.t.* Find, state, the number or amount of; appraise, assess; ~**ā′tion** *n.*; ~**atĭve** *a.* [F (VALUE)]

**ĕvănĕ′s|ce** *v.i.* Fade from sight;

disappear; **~cent** a., quickly fading; **~cence** n. [L (VAIN)]

**èvă′ngel** (-nj-) n. (arch.) The gospel; any of the 4 Gospels; political or other creed. [F f. L f. Gk, = good news (ANGEL)]

**èvăngě′lical** (-nj-). **1.** a. (**~ly**). Of, according to, the teaching of the gospel or the Christian religion; of the Protestant school maintaining that doctrine of salvation by faith is essence of gospel. **2.** n. Member of evangelical school. **3.** **~ism** n., doctrine of evangelical school.

**èvă′ngelľ|ist** (-nj-) n. Writer of one of the 4 Gospels; preacher of the gospel; layman doing missionary work; **~ism** n., preaching, promulgation, of the gospel, evangelicalism; **~i′stic** a., of (esp. the 4) evangelists, evangelical; **~ize** v.t., preach the gospel to, convert to Christianity; **~izā′tion** n.

**èvă′por|āte** v.t. & i. (**~able**). Turn into vapour; (cause to) lose moisture as vapour (**~ated milk**, unsweetened milk concentrated by partial evaporation); (fig.) (cause) to be lost or disappear; **~atīve** a.; **~ā′tion**, **~ātor**, ns. [L (VAPOUR)]

**evasion, -sive.** See EVADE.

**Eve**[1] (ēv) n. First woman, in Hebrew tradition; **daughter of ~**, woman (often w. ref. to feminine curiosity etc.). [E f. L f. Heb., = life]

**ēve**[2] n. Evening or day before festival etc. (Christmas Eve, the eve of the funeral); time just before an event (on the eve of an election); (arch.) evening. [= foll.]

**ē′ven**[1] n. Evening (poet.); **~song**, evening prayer in Ch. of England; **~tide**, (arch.) evening; **~tide home** (for old people). [E]

**ē′ven**[2] a., v., & adv. **1.** a. (**~er**, **~est**, **~ness** pr. -n-n-). Level, smooth, (**on an ~ keel**, of ship, not rolling; also fig.); in same plane or line (with); uniform in quality (even work); equal in amount, value, etc., equally balanced, (even contest; **be or get ~ with**, have one's revenge on; BREAK even; **~ chance**, as much of success or failure; **~-handed**, impartial; **~ money**, ‖**~s**, betting odds offering gambler chance of winning the amount he staked); equable, calm (even temper); (of number such as 4, 6) integrally divisible by 2, bearing such number (no parking on even dates); not involving fractions (in even dozens). **2.** v.t. & i. **~ (up)**, make or become even or equal. **3.** adv. (Inviting comparison of the negation, assertion, etc., with a less strong one implied:) disputes even the facts (not merely the inferences); never even opened (let alone read) the letter; does he even suspect (not to say realize) the danger?; ran even faster (not just as fast as before); (introducing extreme case) even Jones must realize; might even run to £5; **~ now** (as well as previously); **~ so**, in that case as well as others. [E]

**ē′vening** (-vn-) n. Close of day, esp. from 6 p.m. to bedtime (phrs. as AFTERnoon); (colloq.) = GOOD evening; (fig.) decline (of life etc.); **~ dress** (prescribed by fashion for formal evening wear); **~ paper**, newspaper published after (usu.) midday; **~ primrose** (with flowers that open in evening); **~ star**, planet, esp. Venus, seen in west after sunset. [E (EVEN[1])]

**ĕvě′nt** n. Occurrence of a thing (**in the ~ of his death**, *that he dies*, if he dies; **double ~**, combined occurrence of two things; thing whose occurrence is noteworthy (quite an event); item of programme esp. in sports; result (**in any or either ~**, **at all ~s**, in any case; **in the ~**, as it turned out); **~ful** a. (**-lly**), marked by noteworthy events; **~ūal** a. (**-lly**), finally resulting; **~ūǎ′lĭty** n., possible event; **~ūāte** v.i., turn out (well etc.) as the result (in). [L (venio vent- come)]

**ē′ver** adv. At all times, always, (arch., exc.: **for ~**, ***for~(more)***, for all future time, incessantly; Wales etc. **for ever!**, expression of support; **yours ~**, in ending letter to friend); in comb. w. participles etc. (ever-present, ever-recurring); (w. negative, question, etc.) at any time (as good as ever; be as quick as ever you can; best thing I ever did; did you ever hear such nonsense?; nothing ever happens; **did you ~?**, i.e. see or hear the like, colloq.); (emphatic in question, assertion, etc.: how ever, what ever, who ever, why ever, etc., cf. WHATever; **~ so**, to any possible extent, colloq. very (much): ever so easy, thanks ever so; **~ such a**, vulg., a very: ever such a nice man); **~ after**, continuously from that time; **~ and anon**, (arch.) occasionally; **~green**, (a.) always green or fresh, always having green leaves, (n.) such tree or shrub; **~lasting**, (a.) lasting for ever or (too) long, (of plant) keeping shape and colour when dried, (n.) eternity (from everlasting), everlasting flower; **~more**, always; **~ since**, throughout period since (then). [E]

**e'very** (ĕ'vrĭ) a. Each single (heard every word of it; watched her every movement; comes every day, every other or second day = on alternate, or fig. on most, days, every third etc. day or three etc. days); **~ bit as**, (colloq.) quite as; **~body**, every person; **~day** a., occurring etc. every day, ordinary, commonplace; **~ now and then**, from time to time; **~ one**, each one (emphat.: every one of them); **~one**, **~ one**, everybody; **~ so often**, at intervals, occasionally; **~thing**, all things (everything depends on that), thing of first importance (speed is everything); **~ time**, (colloq.) without exception or hesitation; **~where**, in every place, (colloq.) in many places; **\*~ which way**, in every direction. [E (EVER, EACH)]

**E'verymǎn** (ĕ'vr-) n. Ordinary or typical human being. [character in 15th-c. morality play]

**evĭ'ct** v.t. Expel (tenant from land etc.) by legal process; **~ion**, **~or**, ns. [L evinco evict- conquer]

**e'vidence. 1.** n. Indication, sign, facts available as proof, (is there any evidence of or for this?; no evidence of corruption); (Law) information given personally c r drawn from document etc. and tending to prove fact, testimony admissible in court, (was called in evidence; not accepted as in evidence; ‖turn King's, Queen's, \*State's, ~, of accomplice in crime, testify for prosecution); obviousness (in ~, conspicuous). **2.** v.t. Be evidence of, indicate. **3. e'vĭdent** a., obvious, manifest; **evĭdĕ'ntial** (-shal) a. (-lly), **evĭdĕ'ntiarỹ** (-sherĭ) a., of evidence. [F f. L (video see)]

**e'vĭl** (or -il). **1.** a. (~ly). Bad, harmful; **an ~** (slanderous) **tongue**; **~ eye**, malicious look superstitiously believed to do material harm; **the E~ One**, the Devil; **fall on ~ days**, suffer misfortune. **2.** n. Evil thing, sin, harm; **~-doer, -doing**, sin(ner); **speak ~ of**, slander. [E]

**evĭ'nce** v.t. Show, indicate, (quality etc., that). [L (EVICT)]

**evĭ'scer|āte** v.t. Disembowel; **~ā'tion** n. [L (VISCERA)]

**evŏ'ke** v.t. Call up (spirit from the dead, memories, energies); **ēvocā'tion** n.; **evŏ'cative, evŏ'catorỹ**, adjs. [L (voco call)]

**evolū'tion** (-lōō'-) n. Evolving; origination of species by development from earlier forms; development (of organism, human society, universe, etc.); change in disposition of troops or ships; movement in dancing etc.; **~al (-lly), ~arỹ**, adjs.; **~ism** n., theory of evolution of species; **~ist** n. [L (volvo volut- roll)]

**evŏ'lve** v.t. & i. Unfold, open out; give off (gas, heat, etc.); develop by natural process; develop, deduce, (theory, facts, etc.).

**ewe** (ū) n. Female sheep; **~ lamb**, (fig.) most cherished possession [2 Sam. 12]. [E]

**ew'er** n. Water-jug with wide mouth. [AF f. Rom. (L aqua water)]

**ĕx¹.** (colloq.). **1.** a. Former; outdated. **2.** n. Former occupant of position etc., esp. former husband or wife. [EX-¹]

**ĕx²** prep. (Commerc.; of goods) sold from (ex ship, store); outside, without, exclusive of (**~-directory**, deliberately not listed in telephone directory; **~ dividend**, of stocks and shares, not including next dividend). [L, = out of]

**ex-¹** pref. (**ef-** bef. f; **ē-** bef. many consonants) forming (1) vbs. w. sense 'out', 'forth', (exclude, exit), 'upward' (extol), 'thoroughly' (excruciate), 'bring into a state' (exasperate), 'remove, free from' (expatriate, exonerate), (2) ns. f. titles of office, status, etc., w. sense 'formerly' (ex--convict, ex-president, ex-wife); ‖**~--ser'vice** a., having belonged to one of the fighting services, of former servicemen).

**ex-²** pref. = 'out' (exodus). [Gk]

**ĕxă'cerb|āte** v.t. Aggravate (pain etc.); irritate (person); **~ā'tion** n. [L (ACERBITY)]

**ĕxă'ct** (igz-). **1.** a. Precise, rigorous, (exact order of arrival); accurate, strictly correct, (exact description; **~ science**, one admitting of absolute precision). **2.** v.t. Demand and enforce payment etc. of (exact fees, retribution, from or of); demand, require urgently, insist upon. **3. ~ing** a., making great demands; **~ion** n., (esp.) illegal or exorbitant demand, extortion; **~itūde, ~or**, ns.; **~lỹ** adv., (esp., in reply) quite so, just as you say; **not ~ly**, (colloq.) by no means. [L *exigo exact-* require]

**exǎ'gger|āte** (ĭgzǎ'j-) *v.t.* Overstate, carry (story etc., or abs.) beyond truth, elaborate rhetorically; enlarge or otherwise alter beyond normal limits or proportions (*exaggerated features, politeness*); **~ā'tion, ~ātor,** *ns.*; **~ative** *a.* [L (*agger* heap)]

**exa'lt** (ĭgzaw'lt) *v.t.* Raise in rank, power, etc.; praise, extol, (*exalt to the skies*); make lofty or noble (*exalted aims, style*); **exǎltā'tion** (-awl-; *or* ĕgz-) *n.*, (esp.) elation, rapture. [L (*altus* high)]

**exā'mĭn|e** (ĭgz-) *v.t.* Inquire into nature, condition, etc., of; look closely at; ask questions of (person *on* matter); test proficiency of (pupil etc. *in* subject) by oral or written questions; **~ā'tion** *n.*, (esp. of pupil etc.; colloq. abbr. **exa'm**) **~ee', ~er,** *ns.* [F f. L (*examen* tongue of balance)]

**exa'mple** (ĭgzah'-) *n.* Thing illustrating general rule (**for ~**, by way of illustration); problem etc. set for this; specimen of a group or of art etc.; model, pattern, for (worthy) conduct (*give, set, a good* or *an example*); precedent (*without example*; **make an ~ of**, punish as warning to others). [F f. L *exemplum* (EXEMPT)]

**e'xarch** (-k) *n.* Orthodox Church bishop between patriarch and metropolitan; (Hist.) governor of Byzantine province; **~ate** *n.*, office, province, of exarch. [L f. Gk (*arkhō* rule)]

**exǎ'sper|āte** (ĭgz-; *or* -ah'-) *v.t.* Irritate (person to anger; *exasperated at, by*); **~ā'tion** *n.* [L (ASPERITY)]

**ex cathedra** (ĕkskathē'dra, -kǎ'-thĭ-) *adv.* & *a.* Authoritative(ly); (of papal pronouncement) given as infallible judgement. [L, = from the chair]

**e'xcav|āte** *v.t.* Hollow out; make (hole), remove (soil), reveal, extract, by digging; **~ā'tion** *n.*; **~ātor** *n.*, person engaged in, machine used for, excavating. [L *excavo* (CAVE[1])]

**excee'd** *v.t.* Go beyond, do more than is warranted by, (one's instructions, rights, etc.), be more than, (*exceed (all) expectation(s)*; *exceed the speed limit*); surpass (person etc. *in*); **~ing** *a.* & *adv.*, (arch.) surpassing(ly) in amount or degree, pre-eminent(ly); **~ingly** *adv.*, very. [F f. L *excedo -cess-* go beyond]

**excě'l** *v.t.* & *i.* (-**ll**-). Be superior to (others *in* quality, *in* doing); be pre-eminent (*in, at,* thing or doing). [L *excello* be eminent]

**ě'xcellen|t** *a.* Very good; **~ce** *n.*, great merit; **~cy** *n.*, title of ambassadors, governors, etc., and their spouses.

**excě'ntric** *a.* = ECCENTRIC. [EX-[1]]

**excě'pt** *v.*, *prep.*, & *conj.* **1.** *v.t.* Exclude from general statement etc. (*present company excepted*; *except him from the general amnesty*). **2.** *prep.* Not including, other than, (*all failed except him*; *always there except when he is wanted*; *is all right except (that) it is too long* or *except for the length*). **3.** *conj.* (arch.) Unless (*except he be born again*). **4.** **~ing** *prep.*, except. [L *excipio -cept-* take out]

**excě'ption** *n.* Excepting; thing or case excepted; **~ proves the rule,** the excepting of some cases, by their being noted as such, demonstrates the existence of the rule; **with the ~ of,** except; **take ~,** object (*to*); **~able** *a.* (-**bly**), open to objection; **~al** *a.* (-**lly**), forming an exception. unusual. [F f. L (prec.)]

**excě'rpt. 1.** (ĭksĕr'pt) *v.t.* (**~ible**). Extract, quote, (passage *from* book etc.); **excě'rption** *n.* **2.** (ĕ'ksĕrpt) *n.* Such passage. [L (*carpo* pluck)]

**excě'ss. 1.** *n.* Fact of exceeding (**in ~ of,** more than); amount by which one number or quantity exceeds another; agreed amount subtracted from claim under insurance; overstepping of limits of moderation, esp. intemperance in eating or drinking; extreme or improper degree (*in, to, excess*); (usu. in *pl.*) outrageous or immoderate behaviour. **2.** (ĕ'ksĕs) *a.* That is an excess (**~ baggage, luggage,** exceeding weight-allowance included in fare and so liable to extra charge; **~ fare,** payment due for travelling further or in higher class than ticket allows; **~ postage,** payment due when stamps on letter etc. received are insufficient). **3.** **~īve** *a.*, too much, too great. [F f. L (EXCEED)]

**exchā'nge** (-nj). **1.** *n.* Act or process of giving one thing and receiving another in its place (**~,** or **fair ~, is no robbery,** prov., freq. joc. as excuse for unfair exchange; **in ~,** as thing exchanged *for*); giving of money for its equivalent in money of same or another country (**rate of ~,**

price at which foreign currency may be bought, or difference between this and par); money-changer's trade; system of settling debts between persons (esp. in different countries) without use of money, by BILL³s of exchange; building used as place of assembly for transaction of business by merchants, brokers, etc., (*corn, stock, exchange*); place where potential employers and employees are made known (EMPLOYMENT *exchange*); district's central telephone office where connections are effected. **2.** *v.t.* & *i.* Give or receive (thing) in place of another; give and receive (blows, glances, prisoners, words, etc.); take part in exchange of positions etc. (*with* another). **3.** **~abi′lity** *n.* [F (CHANGE)]

**exche′quer** (-ker) *n.* ||Department for receipt and custody of public revenue (CHANCELLOR *of the Exchequer*); royal or national treasury; money of private person (*my exchequer is low*). [F f. L *scaccarium* chess-board, w. ref. to keeping of accounts on chequered table-cloth]

**e′xcise¹** (-z). **1.** *n.* Duty or tax levied on goods produced or sold within the country, and on various licences etc. **2.** *v.t.* Make (person) pay excise; charge excise on; **exci′sable** (-z-) *a.*, liable to excise. [Du. *excijs* f. Rom. (L CENSUS tax)]

**exci′se²** (-z) *v.t.* Cut out or away (passage of book, limb, etc.; **exci′sion** (-zhon) *n.* [L *excido* cut out]

**exci′te** *v.t.* Bring into play, rouse up, (feelings etc.); provoke, bring about (action, etc.); stimulate (bodily organ etc.) to activity; move (person) to strong emotion; **~able** *a.* (-bly), (esp., of person) easily excited; **~abi′lity** *n.*; **e′xcitant** *a.* & *n.*, stimulant; **excita′tion** *n.*, (esp.) stimulation; **~ative**, **~atory**, *adjs.*; **~ement** (-tm-) *n.*, (esp.) excited state of mind, cause of this; **~ing** *a.*, (esp.) arousing great interest or enthusiasm. [L (*cieo* stir up)]

**exclai′m** *v.i.* & *t.* Cry out, speak in anger, pain, surprise, etc.; utter, say, (quoted words, *that*) in this manner; **exclama′tion** *n.*; **exclamation mark, *point**, punctuation mark (!) indicating exclamation; **excla′matory** *a.* [F or L (CLAIM)]

**exclu′|de** (-lōō′d) *v.t.* Shut out (person, thing, *from* place, privilege, etc.); make impossible, preclude;

**~sion** (-zhon) *n.*; **~sive** *a.*, excluding, not inclusive (**~sive of**, not counting), (of society etc.) tending to exclude outsiders, (of pursuits, rights, etc.) followed, held, in such a way as to exclude all others, (of article in shop or newspaper, etc.) not to be had or not published elsewhere, high-class, expensive. [L *excludo -clus-* shut out]

**exco′git|ate** *v.t.* Think out, devise; **~a′tion**, **~ator**, *ns.* [L (*cogito* think)]

**excommu′nic|ate. 1.** *v.t.* (**~able**). Cut off (person) from sacraments or communication with the Church. **2.** (-at) *n.* Excommunicated person. **3.** **~a′tion**, **~ator**, *ns.*; **~ative**, **~atory**, *adjs.* [L (COMMON)]

**exco′r|iate** *v.t.* Remove part of skin of (person), strip off (skin), by abrasion etc.; (fig.) censure severely; **~a′tion** *n.* [L (*corium* hide)]

**e′xcrem|ent** *n.* Faeces; **~e′ntal**, **~enti′tious** (-shus), *adjs.*; **excre′te** *v.t.*, (of animal or plant) expel from system as waste; **excre′ta** *n.pl.*, faeces and urine; **excre′tion** *n.*; **excre′tive**, **excre′tory**, *adjs.* [F or L (*cerno cret-* sift)]

**excre′scen|t** *a.* Growing abnormally; redundant; (of sound etc. in word) due merely to euphony; **~ce** *n.*, abnormal or morbid outgrowth. [L (*cresco* grow)]

**excre′te** etc. See EXCREMENT.

**excru′ci|ate** (-krōō′shi-) *v.t.* Cause acute pain to, in body or mind; **~ating** *a.* (esp. colloq. of joke, pun, etc., shocking); **~a′tion** *n.* [L *excrucio* (*crux* cross)]

**e′xculp|ate** *v.t.* Free from blame; clear (person *from* charge); **~a′tion** *n.*; **excu′lpatory** *a.* [L (*culpa* blame)]

**excu′rsion** (-shon) *n.* Short journey, ramble, trip, taken for pleasure and with intention of returning to starting-point (**~ train**, for people on excursion, usu. at reduced rates); (arch.) sortie, raid; **alarums and ~s**, (joc.) confused noise and bustle [f. old stage-direction]; **~ist** *n.*, member of excursion party; **excu′rsive** *a.*, (esp.) digressive. [L (*excurro* run out)]

**excu′se. 1.** (-z) *v.t.* (Try to) lessen blame attaching to (person, act, fault); overlook, forgive, (fault or offence, person *for* this); **~ me**, as apology for lack of ceremony or for contradiction; **~-me dance**, in which one may take another's partner); gain exemption for (person, one*self*, *from* duty etc.; ~ oneself, ask permission or apologize for leaving); release, dispense, (person (*from* duty, attendance, etc.; **be ~d**, (colloq.) be allowed to leave room etc., e.g. to go to lavatory). **2.** (-s) *n.* Apology (*make my excuses*); (ground of) exculpation (*that is no excuse*). **3. excŭ'satŏrў** (-z-) *a.*, intended to excuse. [F f. L (*causa* accusation)]

**ĕx-dĭrĕ'ctorў.** See EX².

**ĕ'xĕāt** *n.* ‖Leave of absence from college etc. [L, = let him go out]

**ĕ'xĕcr|āte** *v.t.* & *i.* Express, feel, abhorrence for; utter curses; **~able** *a.* (-bly), abominable; **~ā'tion** *n.* [L *ex(s)ecror* curse (SACRED)]

**ĕ'xĕcūte** *v.t.* Carry (plan, design, orders, law, a will, etc.) into effect; perform (duty, function, operation, music); make (legal document) valid by signing, sealing, etc.; inflict capital punishment on; **ĕxĕ'cūtant** (ĭgz-) *n.*, performer esp. of music. [F f. L (*sequor* follow)]

**ĕxĕcū'tion** *n.* Carrying out, performance; skill in performing music; effective action (**do ~**, have destructive effect, of weapon, or fig.); infliction of capital punishment; **~er** *n.*, person carrying out sentence of death.

**ĕxĕ'cŭt|ĭve** (ĭgz-). **1.** *a.* Concerned with executing laws, agreements, etc., or with other administration or management. **2.** *n.* Person or body having executive authority or in executive position in business organization etc.; the executive branch of government etc. **3.** **~or** *n.*, person appointed by testator to execute his will; **~ŏr'ĭal** *a.*; **~rĭx** *n.* (*pl.* -trĭces *pr.* -ĭsēz), female executor.

**ĕxĕgē's|ĭs** *n.* (*pl.* **~es** *pr.* -ēz). Exposition esp. of Scripture; **ĕxĕgĕ'tĭc(al)** *adjs.* (-ically). [Gk (*hēgeomai* lead)]

**ĕxĕ'mpl|ar** (ĭgz-) *n.* Model, type; instance; **~arў** *a.* (-ily, -iness), fit to be imitated, illustrative; **~ifȳ** *v.t.*, give or be an example of; **~ĭfĭcā'tion** *n.* [F f. L (EXAMPLE)]

**ĕxĕ'mpt** (ĭgz-). **1.** *a.* Freed (*from* allegiance or liability); **~ from**, not liable, exposed, or subject to, (taxation, risk, charge, duty, etc.). **2.** *v.t.* Make exempt (*from*); **~ion** *n.* [L (*eximo -empt-* take out)]

**ĕ'xĕquĭes** (-kwĭz) *n.pl.* Funeral rites. [F f. L *exsequiae* (*exsequor* follow after)]

**ĕ'xĕrcĭse** (-z). **1.** *n.* Employment, application, (*of* organ, faculty, power); practice (of virtue, profession, function); use of muscles, limbs, etc., esp. for health; (task etc. set for) bodily or other training (**object of the ~**, essential purpose of action etc.); act of worship. **2.** *v.t.* & *i.* Use, apply, (faculty, power); perform (function etc.); give exercise to (limbs, horse, etc.); perplex, worry, (*exercised* in mind); take exercise. [F f. L (*exerceo* keep busy)]

**ĕxĕr't** (ĭgz-) *v.t.* Use, bring to bear, (influence, pressure, etc.); **~** oneself, use efforts or endeavours, strive, (*to* do); **~ion** *n.* [L *exsero exsert-* put forth]

*exeunt.* See EXIT².

**ĕxfō'lĭ|āte** *v.i.* Come off in scales or layers; (of tree) throw off bark thus; **~ā'tion** *n.* [L (*folium* leaf)]

*ex gratia* (ĕks grā'sha) *adv.* & *a.* (Done etc.) as act of grace and not under (esp. legal) compulsion. [L, = from favour]

**ĕxhā'le** *v.t.* & *i.* Give off, be given off, (as) in vapour; breathe out (air, life, words); **ĕxhalā'tion** (ĕksa-) *n.*, expiration of air, breath, vapour, emanation. [F f. L (*halo* breathe)]

**ĕxhau'st** (ĭgzaw'-). **1.** *v.t.* (**~ible**). Draw off (air); empty (vessel etc. of contents); consume, use up, the whole of; say, learn, all that is worth knowing of (subject; (esp. in *p.p.*) use up strength, resources, of; tire out. **2.** *n.* (Expulsion or exit of) motive fluid, steam, or gaseous products from engine cylinder; **~(-pipe)** (for this); **~ĭbĭ'lĭtў** *n.*; **ĕxhau'stĭon** (ĭgzaw'schǒn) *n.*; **~ĭve** *a.*, tending to exhaust, esp. a subject, comprehensive. [L (*haurio haust-* drain)]

**ĕxhĭ'bĭt** (ĭgzĭ'-). **1.** *v.t.* Show, display; manifest (quality etc.); show publicly in competition etc. or to entertain. **2.** *n.* Thing exhibited esp. as item in evidence in lawcourt, or at exhibition. **3.** **~or** *n.*, (esp.) one who exhibits thing in show etc. [L *exhibeo -hibit-*]

**ĕxhĭbĭ'tion** (ĕksĭ-) *n.* Display (**make an ~ of** oneself, behave so as to appear ridiculous or contemptible); public display of works of art, industrial products, etc.; ‖scholarship, esp. from funds of school, college, etc. (~**er** n., student holding exhibition); ~**ism** n., tendency towards display or extravagant behaviour, (Path.) perverted mental condition characterized by indecent exposure of genitals; ~**ist** n., one who displays exhibitionism. [F f. L (prec.)]

**exhī′lar|āte** (ĭgzĭ′-) v.t. Enliven, gladden, (person, spirits); ~**ā′tion** n. [L (HILARIOUS)]

**exhŏr′t** (ĭgzŏr′t) v.t. Admonish earnestly; urge (person to do, to conduct); **exhŏrtā′tion** (ĕksŏr-, ĕgz-) n.; ~**ative**, ~**atorý**, adjs. [F or L exhortor encourage]

**exhū′m|e** (ĭgzŭ′m) v.t. Dig out, unearth, (esp. buried corpse; lit. or fig.); ~**ā′tion** (ĕksū-) n. [F f. L (humus ground)]

**ex hypothesi** (ĕks hĭpŏ′thĭsī) adv. According to the hypothesis. [L]

**e′xĭg|ence**, ~|**encý**, (or ĕgz-) ns. Urgent need or demand; emergency; ~**ent** a., urgent, exacting; ~**ĭble** a., that may be exacted. [F f. L (exigo EXACT)]

**exi′gŭous** (ĕgz-, ĭgz-) a. (formal). Scanty, small; **exĭgū′itý** n. [L]

**e′xīle** (or ĕ′gz-). **1.** n. (State of) being expelled or long absence from one's native land etc.; person in exile. **2.** v.t. Condemn to exile (from). **3.** **exi′līc** (or ĕgz-) a., (esp.) of the Jews' exile in Babylon. [F f. L]

**exi′st** (ĭgz-) v.i. Have place in (objective) reality; (of circumstances etc.) occur, be found; live, sustain life; continue in being, ~**ence** n., fact, mode, of existing or living (**in** ~**ence**, existing), all that exists; ~**ent** a. [L existo]

**exĭstĕ′ntial** (ĕgz-; -shal) a. (~**ly**). Of or relating to existence; ~**ism** n., philosophical theory emphasizing existence of the individual as free and responsible agent determining his own development; ~**ist** n. & a., (adherent) of existentialism.

**e′xĭt**[1] (or ĕ′gz-). **1.** n. (Right of) going out; passage or door as way out; actor's departure from stage; death. **2.** v.i. Make one's exit; die. **exit**[2] (ĕ′ksĭt, -gz-) v.i. (pl. **exeunt** pr. ĕ′ksĭunt), (as stage direction) leaves stage (exit Macbeth; **exeunt omnes** pr. ŏ′mnēz, all go off). [L (exeo exit-go out)]

**e′xō-** in comb. External; ~**crĭne** a., (of gland) secreting through duct [Gk krinō sift]. [Gk exō outside]

**Exod.** abbr. Exodus (O.T.).

**e′xodus** n. Departure of many people; (O.T. book, E~, relating) departure of Israelites from Egypt. [L f. Gk (hodos way)]

**ex officio** (ĕks ŏfĭ′shĭŏ) adv. & a. By virtue of one's office. [L]

**exŏ′ner|āte** (ĭgz-) v.t. (~**able**). Free (person from blame, duty, etc.); exculpate; ~**ā′tion** n.; ~**ātĭve** a. [L (onus oner- load)]

**exor.** abbr. executor (of will).

**exŏr′bĭtan|t** (ĭgz-) a. (Of price, demand, etc.) grossly excessive; ~**ce** n. [L (ORBIT)]

**e′xŏrc|īse** (-z) v.t. Expel (evil spirit from person or place) by invocation etc.; free (person or place of evil spirits) thus; ~**ism**, ~**ist**, ns. [F f. L f. Gk (horkos oath)]

**exŏr′dĭ|um** n. (pl. ~**ums**, ~**a**). Introductory part of discourse or treatise; ~**al** a. [L (exordior begin)]

**exotĕ′ric** a. (~**ally**). Intelligible to outsiders (cf. ESOTERIC); ordinary, popular. [L f. Gk (exō outside)]

**exŏ′tic** (ĭgz-). **1.** a. (~**ally**). Introduced from abroad; remarkably strange or unusual. **2.** n. Exotic plant etc. **3.** ~**a** n.pl., exotic objects.

**expa′n|d** v.t. & i. Spread out; develop (into); dilate, increase in bulk or importance; express at length (condensed notes, algebraical expression, etc.); be genial or effusive; ~**se** n., wide area or extent of land, space, etc.; ~**sĭble** a.; ~**sĭbĭ′lĭtý** n.; ~**sion** (-shon) n.; ~**sionĭsm**, ~**sionĭst**, (-shon-) ns., advocacy, advocate, of increased amount of territory etc.; ~**sĭve** a., able or tending to expand, extensive, (of person etc.) effusive, genial. [L (pando pans- spread)]

**ex parte** (ĕks pär′tĭ) adv. & a. (Made or said) on, in the interests of, one side only. [L]

**expā′ti|āte** (-shĭ-) v.i. Speak, write, copiously (on); ~**ā′tion** n.; ~**atorý** (-sha-) a. [L (spatium SPACE)]

**expā′tri|ate. 1.** (-āt) v.t. Expel, remove oneself, from homeland. **2.** (-at) a. & n. Expatriated (person). **3.** ~**ā′tion** n. [L (patria native land)]

**expĕ′ct** v.t. Regard as likely, assume as future event, (I expect a storm; I expect to see him, him to come, (that) he will come; just what I expected of or from him; **be** ~**ing** (a baby, a child, etc.), be pregnant); look for as due (I expect obedience, you to obey, that *you will obey*); (colloq.) think, suppose, (*I expect it was the cat*); ~**ant** *a.*, expecting (*of*; ~**ant mother**, pregnant woman), having the prospect of possession etc.; ~**ancy** *n.*; **expectā'tion** *n.*, anticipation, what one expects, probability (*of* event), probable duration (*of life*), (in *pl.*) prospects of inheritance. [L (*specto* look)]

**expě'ctor|āte** *v.t. & i.* Cough or spit out (phlegm etc.) from chest or lungs; spit; ~**ant** *a. & n.*, (medicine) promoting expectoration; ~**ā'tion**, ~**ātor**, *ns.* [L (*pectus pector-* breast)]

**expē'dien|t. 1.** *a.* Advantageous, advisable, (*do whatever is expedient; it is expedient that he should go*); more politic than just; ~**ce**, ~**cy**, *ns.* **2.** *n.* Resource, means of attaining one's end. [foll.]

**e'xped|īte** *v.t.* Assist progress of, hasten, (action, measure, etc.); accomplish (business) quickly; ~**i'tion** *n.*, promptness, speed, (men, fleet, sent on) journey or voyage for definite purpose; ~**i'tionary** *a.*, (to be) employed on an expedition; ~**i'tious** (-shŭs) *a.*, acting or done with, marked by, speed. [L *expedio* (*pes ped-* foot)]

**expě'l** *v.t.* (-**ll**-). Cause to depart or emerge (person *from* place, bullet *from* gun, etc.) by use of force; compel departure of (person; *from* country, school, etc.); **expŭ'lsion** (-shŏn) *n.*; **expŭ'lsive** *a.* [L (*pello puls-* drive)]

**expě'nd** *v.t.* Spend (money, care, time, *on* or *in* object or doing); use up; ~**able** *a.*, (esp.) not regarded as worth preserving or saving, not normally re-used, that may be sacrificed to gain one's ends; ~**iture** *n.*, expending (*of* money etc.), amount expended. [L (*pendo pens-* weigh)]

**expě'nse** *n.* Spending of money (**at** person's *n*, causing him to spend money or fig. suffer ridicule etc.; **at the ~ of**, fig., so as to cause damage or discredit to); cost incurred, (usu. in *pl.*) outlay in executing commission etc., reimbursement of this, (*offered me £10 and expenses*; ~ **account**, list of employee's expenses payable by employer); **expě'nsive** *a.*, of high price, dear. [F f. L *expensa* (prec.)]

**expě'r|ience. 1.** *n.* (Knowledge, skill, based on) personal observation

or action or contact; event that affects one (*trying, pleasant, curious, experience*). **2.** *v.t.* Meet with, undergo, feel, (difficulty, treatment, pleasure, etc.). **3.** ~**d** (-st) *a.*, having had much experience, knowing life or a pursuit etc.; **experiě'ntial** (-shal) *a.* (-**lly**), based on experience. [F f. L (*experior -pert-* try)]

**expě'riment. 1.** *n.* Procedure tried on the chance of success, to test hypothesis etc., or to demonstrate known fact. **2.** (-ěnt) *v.i.* Make experiment (*on, with*). **3.** ~**al** (-ě'n-) *a.* (-**lly**), of, based on, making use of, experiment (*experimental philosophy, physics, psychology*); tentative; ~**alism**, ~**alist**, (-ě'n-), *ns.*; ~**alize** (-ě'n-) *v.i.*, use experiments; ~**ā'tion** *n.* [F or L (prec.)]

**e'xpert. 1.** *a.* Practised, skilful, well-informed, (*at, in*). **2.** *n.* Person expert in subject; (attrib.) of, being, an expert (*expert evidence, witness*). **3.** **expě'rtise** (-ē'z) *n.*, expert opinion or skill or knowledge. [F f. L (EXPERIENCE)]

**e'xpi|āte** *v.t.* (~**able**). Pay the penalty of, make amends for, (sin); ~**ā'tion**, ~**ātor**, *ns.*; ~**atory** *a.* [L *expio* (PIOUS)]

**expīr'|e** *v.i. & t.* Breathe out (air *from* lungs, or abs.); die; (of period) come to an end; (of law, patent, truce, etc.) become void, reach end of its term; **expirā'tion** *n.*; ~**atory** *a.*, of breathing out; ~**y** *n.*, expiring (*of* period, contract, etc.). [F f. L (*spiro* breathe)]

**explai'n** *v.t.* Make known in detail (facts, situation, *that, why*); make intelligible (one's meaning, one*self*, etc.); account for (conduct etc.); ~ **away**, minimize significance of; ~ oneself, justify one's conduct etc.; **explanā'tion** *n.*; **expla'natory** *a.* (-**ily**). [L *explano* (*planus* flat)]

**explē'tive** (or ě'-). **1.** *a.* Serving to fill out (esp. a sentence etc.). **2.** *n.* Expletive word, esp. oath. [L (*expleo* fill out)]

**e'xplic|able** (or -lī'k-) *a.* Explainable; ~**āte** (ě'ks-) *v.t.*, develop, explain, (idea etc.); ~**ative**, ~**atory**, *adjs.*, explanatory. [L *explico -plicit-* unfold]

**expli'cit** *a.* Stated in detail (~ **faith**, embracing nothing one has not examined, cf. IMPLICIT); expressly stated, not merely implied; definite; outspoken. [F or L (prec.)]

**explṓ|de** *v.i.* & *t.* (Of gas, gun-powder, bomb, etc.) expand suddenly with loud noise owing to release of internal energy; cause (gas etc.) to do this; give vent suddenly to emotion or violence; (of population etc.) increase suddenly or rapidly; expose, discredit, (theory etc.); **∼sion** (-zhon) *n.*; **∼sive** (or -z-), (*a.*) tending to explode (lit. or fig.), (*n.*) explosive substance (HIGH *explosive*). [L *explodo* -*plos*- hiss off the stage (PLAUDIT)]

**exploit. 1.** (ĕ́ksploit) *n.* Brilliant or daring feat. **2.** (ĭksploi't) *v.t.* Work (mine etc.); utilize (person, situation, etc.) for one's own ends; **exploitā́-tion** *n.* [F f. L (EXPLICABLE)]

**explōr'|e** *v.t.* Examine (country etc.) by going through it; examine by touch; inquire into; **explorā́tion** *n.*; **∼ative**, **∼atory**, (or -ō'r-) *adjs.* [F f. L *exploro* search out]

**explosion, -sive.** See EXPLODE.

**expṓ'nent** *n.* Person etc. that explains or interprets; executant; person who favours the use *of*; type, representative; (Math.) symbol showing what power of a factor is to be taken, index; **exponĕ́ntial** (-shal) *a.* (Math., or of more and more rapid increase; -lly) [L *expono* EXPOUND]

**ĕ'xpōrt. 1.** (or ĭkspō̄'rt) *v.t.* Send out (goods) to another country; **∼ā'tion** *n.* **2.** *n.* Exported article; exporting; (usu. in *pl.*) amount exported. [L (*porto* carry)]

**expṓ'|se** (-z) *v.t.* Leave unprotected esp. from weather; (Hist.) leave (child) out of doors to perish; subject *to* (risk, weather, light, criticism, etc.); (in *p.p.*) open (to the east etc.); exhibit (**∼se** oneself, expose one's body indecently); put up for sale; disclose, reveal, (secret, villain); **∼sure** (-zher) *n.*, (esp., Photog.) action of exposing plate or film to light, duration of this action, area of film etc. affected by it; **∼sé** (ĕ-; -zā) *n.*, orderly statement of facts, revealing (of discreditable thing). [F f. L (*pono* put)]

**exposition** etc. See EXPOUND.

*ex post facto* (ĕks pŏst fă̆'ktō) *a.* & *adv.* (Acting) retrospectively. [L, = from what is done afterwards]

**expṓ'stūlāt|e** *v.i.* Make protest, remonstrate, (*with* person *on*, *about*); **expŏstūlā'tion**, **∼or**, *ns.*; **∼ory** *a.* [L (POSTULATE)]

**exposure.** See EXPOSE.

**expou'nd** *v.t.* Set forth in detail; explain, interpret, (esp. Scripture); **exposi'tion** (-z-) *n.*, expounding, explanation, (Mus.) presentation of principal theme(s), exhibition of goods etc.; **expo'sĭtive**, **expo'sĭtory**, (-z-) *adjs.*; **expo'sĭtor** (-z-) *n.* [F f. L (*pono posit*- place)]

**expre'ss** *v.*, *a.*, *n.*, & *adv.* **1.** *v.t.* (**∼ible**). Represent, make known, in words or by gestures, conduct, etc., (∼ oneself, say what one means); squeeze out (juice etc.); send by express (messenger or delivery). **2.** *a.* Definitely stated, explicit, (*express orders*); (of messages or goods) delivered by special messenger or service; operating at high speed (∼ lift, not stopping at every floor; ∼ train, fast, stopping at few intermediate stations; **∼way**, urban motorway). **3.** *n.* Express train, messenger, etc.; *company undertaking transport of parcels etc. **4.** *adv.* At high speed, by express. **5.** **expre'ssion** (-shon) *n.*, (esp.) wording, word, phrase, (Math.) symbols expressing a quantity, aspect of face, tone (of voice), (Mus.) execution designed to express feeling etc., (Art) mode of expressing action etc.; **expre'ssional** (-shon-) *a.* (-lly); **expre'ssionism** (-shon-) *n.*, style of painting etc. in which artist etc. seeks to express emotional experience rather than impressions of physical world; so **expre'ssionist** (-shon-) *a.* & *n.*, (artist etc.) exhibiting this style or technique; **∼ive** *a.*, serving to express (*expressive of contempt*), significant; **∼lў** *adv.*, explicitly. [F f. L *exprimo* -*press*- squeeze out]

**exprō'prĭāt|e** *v.t.* Dispossess (person *from*); take away (property); **∼ā'tion**, **∼ātor**, *ns.* [L (*proprium* property)]

**expulsion, -sive.** See EXPEL.

**expu'nge** (-nj) *v.t.* Erase, omit, (passage *from* book etc.). [L *expungo* prick out (for deletion)]

**ĕ'xpurgāt|e** *v.t.* Purify (book etc.) by removing matter thought objectionable; remove (such matter); **expurgā'tion**, **∼or**, *ns.*; **expūrgatŏr'ĭal**, **∼orў**, *adjs.* [L (PURGE)]

**exqui'site** (-z-; or ĕ'kskwĭz-). **1.** *a.* Of extreme beauty or delicacy; acute, keen, (*exquisite pain, pleasure, sensibility*). **2.** *n.* Coxcomb, dandy. [L *exquiro* -*quisit*- seek out]

‖**ĕx-sēr′vĭce.** See EX-¹.

**ext.** *abbr.* exterior; external.

**ĕxtă′nt** (*or* ĕ′kstant) *a.* (Of document etc.) still existing. [L *ex(s)to* exist]

**ĕxtĕ′mpor|ĕ** *adv. & a.* Without preparation, offhand, (*speak extempore*; *an extempore speech*); **~ā′nĕous, ~ărў,** *adjs.*; **~ize** *v.t. & i.,* produce (speech, device, etc.) extempore, speak extempore; **~izā′tion** *n.* [L]

**ĕxtĕ′n|d** *v.t. & i.* Lay out (body, limbs, etc.) at full length; stretch out (hand, arm, etc.); accord (kindness etc. *to*); offer (invitation etc. *to*); (cause to) stretch or be continuous *over* space, *to* point; prolong (period, structure); **~ded-play** *a.,* of gramophone record containing a longer recording than is or was usual); enlarge (scope); (usu. in *pass.* or *refl.*) tax powers of (horse, athlete, etc.) to utmost; **~dible, ~sible,** *adjs.* (**-bly**); **~sǐbi′lǐtу** *n.*; **~sǐle** *a.,* that can be protruded or extended; **~sion** (-shon) *n.,* (esp.) enlargement, additional part, (number of) subsidiary telephone, extramural instruction by university etc.; **~sǐve** *a.,* large, far-reaching, (*extensive business, lands, plans*); **~t** *n.,* space covered, large space or tract, width of application, scope, degree, (**to a great ~t,** largely). [L *extendo -tens-* (TEND¹)]

**ĕxtĕ′nŭāt|e** *v.t.* (**-uable**). Lessen seeming seriousness of (guilt, offence) by partial excuse (*nothing can extenuate his behaviour*); **ĕxtĕnŭā′tion, ~or,** *ns.*; **~orў** *a.* [L *tenuis* thin]

**ĕxtĕ′r’|or.** 1. *a.* Outer, outward; coming from outside; (Cinemat.) outdoor. 2. *n.* Exterior aspect or part or (Cinemat.) scene. 3. **~ŏ′rǐtу** *n.*; **~orize** *v.t.,* externalize. [L]

**ĕxtĕr′mǐnāt|e** *v.t.* (**-nable**). Destroy utterly (disease, nation, etc.); **ĕxtĕrmǐnā′tion, ~or,** *ns.*; **~orў** *a.* [L *terminal*]

**ĕxtĕr′nal.** 1. *a.* (**~ly**). Of, situated on, the outside or visible part (**~ evidence,** that derived from source independent of thing discussed); (of remedy etc.) applied to outside of body; (of a country's foreign affairs; of students taking examinations of, but not attending, a university; outside the conscious subject (*the external world*). 2. *n.* (in *pl.*) External features or circumstances; non-essentials. 3. **ĕxtĕrnă′lǐtу** *n.*; **~ize** *v.t.,* give,

attribute, external existence to; **~izā′tion** *n.* [L (*externus* outer)]

**ĕxtī′nct** *a.* No longer burning, quenched, (*fire, life, hope, is extinct*); (of volcano) that has ceased erupting (**~ volcano,** fig., person no longer having remarkable energy etc.); that has died out, obsolete, (*extinct family, species, office, title*); **~ion** *n.,* making or becoming extinct, dying out; **ĕxtī′nguish** (-nggw-) *v.t.,* make extinct, terminate, douse, (light, fire, life, zeal), destroy, wipe out (debt); **ĕxtī′nguisher** (-nggw-) *n.,* (esp.) (**fire**) **extinguisher,** apparatus with jet for discharging liquid chemicals or foam to extinguish fire. [L *ex(s)tinguo -stinct-* quench]

**ĕ′xtīrpāt|e** *v.t.* Destroy, root out; **ĕxtīrpā′tion, ~or,** *ns.* [L *ex(s)tirpo* (*stirps* stem of tree)]

**ĕxtŏ′l** *v.t.* (**-ll-**). Praise enthusiastically. [L *tollo* raise]

**ĕxtŏr′t** *v.t.* Get (money, secret, etc., *from* person) by force, threats, persistent demands, etc.; force (meaning *from* words). [L *torqueo tort-* twist]

**ĕxtŏr′tion** *n.* Extorting, esp. of money; illegal exaction; **~ate** *a.,* given to extortion, exorbitant; **~er** *n.,* one who practises extortion.

**ĕ′xtra** *a., adv., & n.* **1.** *a.* Additional (**~ cover,** Crick., fieldsman on line between cover-point and mid-off but beyond these); more than is usual or necessary (**~ time,** further period of play at end of football etc. match when scores are equal). **2.** *adv.* More than usually (*extra long*); additionally (*is charged extra*); **~ special,** (fig.) exceptionally fine. **3.** *n.* Extra thing; thing charged extra (*dancing is an extra*); (Crick.) run not scored from hit with bat; special issue of newspaper etc.; (Cinemat.) person engaged temporarily for minor part. [prob. EXTRAORDINARY]

**ĕxtra-** *pref.* forming *adjs.* usu. f. *adjs.,* w. senses 'outside', 'beyond the scope of'; **~curri′cular,** outside the normal curriculum; **~judi′cial,** not made in court, not belonging to the case before the court, not legally authorized; **~ma′rital,** of sexual relationships outside marriage; **~mu′ndane,** outside our world or the universe; **~mur′al,** outside walls or boundaries (of town etc.), additional to ordinary university teaching or studies; **~-se′nsory,** derived by means other than known

senses (e.g. telepathically); ~·
**terre′strial**, outside the earth or its
atmosphere. [L (*extra* outside)]

**extráct. 1.** (ĭkstrǎ′kt) *v.t.* Take out
esp. by force (tooth, anything firmly
fixed); draw forth (money, admission, etc.) against person's will;
obtain (juice etc.) by pressure,
distillation, etc.; derive (pleasure
etc. *from*); (Math.) find (root of a
number); copy out, quote, (passage).
**2.** (ĕ′kstrăkt) *n.* Substance got by
distillation etc.; concentrated preparation (*malt extract*); passage from
book etc. **3. èxtra′ction** *n.*, extracting, lineage (*of Indian extraction*);
**extra′ctive** *a.* & *n.*, (thing) of the
nature of an extract; **~ive industry**
(obtaining coal, ore, etc.); **èx-
trá′ctor** *n.* (~**or fan**, ventilating
fan in window etc. to remove stale
air). [L (*traho tract-* draw)]

**extradi′tion** *n.* Delivery of fugitive
criminal or accused person to proper
foreign authorities; **ě′xtradite** *v.t.*,
give up (such criminal etc.), obtain
extradition of; **èxtradi′table** *a.*,
liable to, (of crime) warranting,
extradition. [F (TRADITION)]

**extrá′neous** *a.* Of external origin,
not naturally belonging, foreign (*to*
object to which it is attached). [L
(STRANGE)]

**extraôr′dinar|ỹ** (or ĭkstrôr′-) *a.*
(~**ily**, ~**iness**). Out of usual
course, additional, specially employed, (*extraordinary supplies*; ENVOY
*extraordinary*); exceptional, surprising,
(*an extraordinary man*; *what an extraordinary idea!*); unusually great (*an
extraordinary scarcity*). [L]

**extrá′pol|āte** *v.t.* & *i.* (Math. etc.)
Estimate from known values, data,
etc., (others which lie outside the
range of those known); **~ā′tion** *n.*
[EXTRA-, INTERPOLATE]

**extrá′vagan|t** (or -vĭg-) *a.* Passing
the bounds of reason, wild, absurd;
exorbitant (*extravagant price*); profuse, wasteful; **~ce** *n.*, extravagant
expenditure, extravagant idea, statement, or action; **èxtrăvagă′nza** *n.*,
fanciful composition (literary, musical, or dramatic), extravagant language or behaviour. [L (*vago·*
wander)]

**extrá′vas|āte** *v.t.* & *i.* Force out
(blood etc.) from its vessel; (of
blood, lava, etc.) flow out; **~ā′tion**
*n.* [L *vas* vessel]

**extrè′me. 1.** *a.* Outermost, farthest

from centre; reaching a high or the
highest degree (*extreme danger, old age*);
**an ~ case**, having some characteristic in the highest degree; severe,
going to great lengths, (*extreme
measures, opinions*); utmost; last (~
**unction**, R.C. & Orthodox Ch.,
anointing of dying person by priest).
**2.** *n.* Thing at either end, esp. (in *pl.*)
things as remote or as different as
possible (*extremes meet*); first or last of
a series; extreme degree (**go to ~s**,
take extreme course of action; **go to
the other ~**, take a diametrically
opposite course of action; **in the ~**,
to an extreme degree). **3. ~lỹ** (-mlĭ)
*adv.*, in an extreme degree, very;
**~nèss** (-mn-) *n.* (of opinions etc.).
**extrè′mĭsm, extrè′mĭst**, *ns.*, advocacy, advocate, of extreme measures; **extrè′mĭtỹ** *n.*, extreme point,
end, (in *pl.*) hands and feet, extreme
distress or embarrassment. [F f. L]

**ě′xtrĭc|āte** *v.t.* (~**able**). Disen-
tangle, free, (person, thing, *from*
entanglement, dilemma, etc.);
**~ā′tion** *n.* [L (*tricae* perplexities)]

**extrī′nsĭc** *a.* (~**ally**). Not inherent
or intrinsic; extraneous, not belonging, (*to*). [L *extrinsecus* outwardly]

**ě′xtrovert. 1.** *a.* (or **~ed**). Directing thoughts and interests to things
outside oneself; sociable, unreserved.
**2.** *n.* ditto person. [L *verto* turn]

**extrover′sion** (-shon) *n.* **2.** *n.*
Extrovert person. [L *verto* turn]

**extru′|de** (-rōō′-) *v.t.* Thrust out;
shape (metal, plastics, etc.) by
forcing through die; **~sion** (-zhon)
*n.*; **~sĭve** *a.* [L *extrudo -trus-* thrust
out]

**exū′ber|ant** (ĭgz-) *a.* Luxuriant,
prolific; (of health, emotion, etc.)
overflowing, abundant; (of person,
action, etc.) effusive, high-spirited;
(of language) high-flown, copious;
**~ance** *n.* [F f. L (*uber* fertile)]

**exū′de** (ĭgz-) *v.i.* & *t.* Ooze out;
give off (moisture); emit (smell);
show (pleasure etc.) abundantly;
**exūdā′tion** *n.* [L (*sudo* sweat)]

**exū′lt** (ĭgz-) *v.i.* Rejoice, triumph,
(*at, in*, thing; *over* person); **~ant** *a.*;
**~ancỹ, exūltā′tion** (or ĕgz-), *ns.* [L
*ex(s)ulto* (*salio salt-* leap)]

**-ey.** See -Y².

**eye** (ī). **1.** *n.* Organ or faculty of
sight in man and animals (**all ~s**,
watching intently; **all my ~**, sl.,
nonsense; **catch** person's ~, succeed
in attracting his attention; CLAP¹
*eyes on*; CRY one's *eyes out*; **do** (person)

in the ~, defraud or thwart; ~ **for an** ~, retaliation in kind (Exod. 21: 24); ~**s front, left, right,** Mil., turn eyes in direction stated; **get** one's ~ **in,** in sports, become accustomed to prevailing conditions; **half an** ~, the slightest degree of perceptiveness; **have an** ~ **for,** be capable of perceiving or appreciating; **have** ~**s for,** be interested in; **hit person in the** ~, fig., be very obvious; **in** or **through the** ~**s of,** from the point of view of, in the judgement of; **in the mind's** ~, in imagination; **in the public** ~, receiving much publicity; **keep an** ~ **on,** direct one's attention to; **keep an** ~ **open** or **out, keep one's** ~**s open,** (sl.) **peeled** or **skinned,** watch carefully (*for*); **look** person **in the** ~, directly or unashamedly at him; **make (sheep's)** ~**s,** look amorously (*at*); **my** ~, sl., nonsense! **one in the** ~, disappointment or discomfiture (*for* person); OPEN one's, person's, *eyes*; SEE[1] *eye to eye;* SET[1] *eyes on;* SIGHT *for sore eyes;* turn a BLIND *eye to;* **up to the** ~**s,** deeply engaged or involved in; **with an** ~ **to,** with a view to; **with one's** ~**s closed, shut,** (fig.) with great ease, innocently, unsuspectingly; iris of eye (*blue* etc. *eyes*); region round eye (BLACK *eye*); eyelike thing, e.g. spot on peacock's tail or butterfly's wing, hole of needle, calm region in centre of hurricane etc., loop of cord, leaf-bud of potato; GLASS *eye;* HOOK *and eye.* **2.** *v.t.* (~**ing,** eying, *pr.* i'ing). Observe, watch, esp. with curiosity, suspicion, disgust, etc. **3.** ~'**ball,** pupil of eye, eye within lids and socket (~*ball to* ~*ball,* colloq. confronting closely); ~-**bath,** vessel for applying lotion to eye; ~'-**bright,** euphrasy, plant formerly used as remedy for weak eyes; ~'**brow,** hair growing on ridge over eye (raise an ~*brow* or one's ~*brows,* show surprise; *up to the* ~*brows,* deeply involved); ~'**glass,** lens for defective eye, (in *pl.*) pair of these held by hand or frame or by spring on nose; ~'**hole,** hole containing eye, hole to look through; ~'**lash,** hair(s) on edge of eyelid, (fig.) very small distance, hairbreadth, (*be within an eyelash of winning*); ~'**lid,** either fold of skin that can cover eye; ~-**liner,** cosmetic applied as line round eye; ~-**opener,** surprising fact etc.; ~'**piece,** lens(es) at eye-end of microscope etc.; ~-**rhyme,** correspondence of words in spelling but not in pronunciation, as *dear, pear;* ~-**shade,** device to protect eyes from strong light; ~-**shadow,** cosmetic applied to skin round eyes; ~'**sight,** faculty, strength, of sight; ~'**sore,** ugly object, thing that offends the sight; ~-**strain,** weariness of eyes; ~-**tooth,** canine tooth under eye in either jaw; ~'**wash,** (sl.) bunkum; ~'**witness,** one who can testify from his own observation; ~'**ful** (ï'fŏŏl) *n.,* (esp., colloq.) thorough look, remarkable or attractive person or thing. [E]

**eye'let** (ï'l-) *n.* Small hole in leather, cloth, sail, etc., for lace, ring, rope, etc.; loophole. [F dim. (*oil eye* f. L *oculus*)]

‖**eyot.** See AIT.

**eyr'ie, aer'ie,** (ār'ĭ, ēr'ĭ, ïr'ĭ) *n.* Nest of bird of prey, esp. eagle, or of bird that builds high up; dwelling perched high up. [F *aire* lair f. L *agrum* piece of ground]

**Ezek.** *abbr.* Ezekiel (O.T.).

# F

**F, f,** (ĕf) *n.* (*pl.* **Fs, F's**). Sixth letter; (Mus.) fourth note in diatonic scale of C major.

**F.** *abbr.* Fahrenheit; farad(s); Fellow of; fine (pencil-lead).

**f.** *abbr.* female; feminine; focal length; folio; following page etc.; FORTE[2].

**fa.** See FAH.

**F.A.** *abbr.* ‖Football Association.

**fâb** *a.* (colloq.; **-bb-**). Marvellous. [abbr. FABULOUS]

**Fā'bïan** *a.* Cautiously persistent (*Fabian policy* etc.); ~ **Society** (of socialists aiming at gradual social change). [L (*Fabius,* person)]

**fā′ble. 1.** *n*. Story, esp. supernatural one, not based on fact; legendary tales (*in fable*; *fact and fable*); lie; thing only supposed to exist; short moral tale esp. about animals. **2.** *v.t.* (in *p.p.*) Celebrated in fable, legendary. **3.** **fā′bŭlist** *n*., composer of fables, liar. [F f. L *fabula* discouse]

**fă′brĭc** *n*. Thing put together; woven esp. material; structure (lit. or fig.); walls, floor, and roof of building; ~**āte** *v.t.*, construct (esp. product in final shape), invent (story), forge (document); ~**ā′tion**, ~**ātor**, *ns*. [F f. L (*faber* metal-worker)]

**fă′bŭlist.** See FABLE.

**fă′bŭlous** *a*. Famed in fable; legendary; incredible, absurd; (colloq.) marvellous. [F or L (FABLE)]

**faça′de** (-sah′d) *n*. (Principal) face of building towards street etc.; outward (esp. deceptive) appearance. [F (foll.)]

**fāce. 1.** *n*. Front of head from forehead to chin (~ **to** ~, confronted; **fly in the** ~ **of**, openly disobey; **in** (**the**) ~ **of**, despite; **look person in the** ~, confront him steadily; **set** one's ~ **against**, oppose; **show** one's ~, let oneself be seen; **to** person's ~, openly in his presence); expression of countenance (LONG *face*); grimace (*make, pull, a face or faces*); composure, effrontery, (**have the** ~, be shameless enough; **lose** ~, be humiliated; **save** one's, person's, ~, spare oneself, him, from humiliation); outward appearance, aspect, (**on the** ~ **of it**, judging by appearances; **put a good, bold,** ~ **on**, make the best of); surface; front; dial-plate of clock etc.; = TYPE-*face*. **2.** *v.t.* & *i.* Meet firmly, not shrink from (*face the facts*; ~ **the music**, not quail at moment of trial; ~ **up to**, confront, accept; present itself to (*the problem that faces us*); look or front towards, be opposite to; supply (garment, wall, etc.) with facing(s). **3.** ~ **about**, turn round; ~ **card**, = COURT-*card*; ~**-cloth**, **-flannel**, cloth for washing face; ~**-lift**, face-lifting, (fig.) improvement in appearance; ~**-lifting**, operation for removing wrinkles by tightening skin of face; ~ **value**, value stated on coin, note, etc. **4.** ~′**lĕss** (-sl-) *a*., (esp.) without identity, purposely not identifiable; **fā′cing** *n*., (esp.) material over part

of garment etc. for contrast or strength, coating of different material, (in *pl.*) cuffs, collar, etc., of (esp.) soldier's jacket. [F f. L *facies*]

**fā′cĕt** *n*. One side of many-sided body esp. cut gem; particular aspect of thing. [F (prec.)]

**facē′tious** (-shus) *a*. Given to or marked by (ill-timed) pleasantry or joking. [F f. L *facetia* jest]

**fā′cia** (-sha) *n*. Plate over shop-front with name etc.; instrument panel of motor vehicle. [FASCIA]

**fā′cial** (-shal). **1.** *a*. (~**ly**) Of the face. **2.** *n*. Beauty treatment for face. [L (FACE)]

**fā′cĭle** *a*. Easy; working easily, fluent; **facī′lĭtāte** *v.t.*, make easy, promote, (action, result); **facĭlĭtā′-tion** *n*.; **facī′lĭty̆** *n*., ease, absence of difficulty, fluency, dexterity, (esp. in *pl.*) opportunity or means *for* doing something. [F or L (*facio* do)]

**fā′cing.** See FACE 4.

**făcsǐ′mǐle** *n*. Exact copy of writing, picture, etc. [L, = make like]

**făct** *n*. Thing that is (known to be) true (*the fact that fire burns, of my being there*; ~**s and figures**, precise information; ~**s of life**, colloq., realities of a situation, esp. euphem. of human sexual functions); truth, reality, (**in** ~, in reality, in short; MATTER, POINT, *of fact*); thing assumed (*his facts are disputable*); wrongful act (*before the fact*); ~′**ŭal** *a*. (-**lly**), concerned with or involving facts. [L *factum* (*facio* do)]

**fă′ct|ion** *n*. Self-interested or unscrupulous party or group, esp. in politics; prevalence of party zeal; ~**ional** *a*.; ~**ious** (-shus) *a*., showing faction. [F f. L (FACT)]

**-fă′ction** *suf.* forming *ns*. of action f. *vbs.* in -FY (*petrifaction, satisfaction*). [L (FACT)]

**factī′tious** (-shus) *a*. Made for special purpose; artificial. [L (prec.)]

**fă′ctitive** *a*. ~ **verb**, one taking obj. & compl., w. sense of making, calling, or thinking (*appointed him captain*; *called it a swindle*; *thought her mad*). [L (FACT)]

**fă′ctor** *n*. Commission agent; (Sc.) land-agent, steward; agent, deputy; one of the numbers etc. whose product is a given number; thing contributing to a result; SAFETY *factor*; **făctor′ĭal** *a*.; ~**ĭze** *v.t.*, resolve into factors; ~**y̆** *n*., building(s) and equipment for manufacturing, (Hist.)

merchant company's foreign trading station. [F or L (FACT)]

**făctō'tum** n. Employee doing all kinds of work. [L (FACT, TOTAL)]

**fă'ctŭal.** See FACT.

**fă'cultǀy** n. Aptitude or competence for particular action; power inherent in the body or an organ; a mental power, e.g. will, reason; branch of art or science, those qualified to teach it, department of university teaching, \*staff of university or college; (esp. Eccl.) authorization; ∼**ative** a., of a faculty, optional. [F f. L (FACILE)]

**făd** n. Peculiar notion, craze; ∼**'dǐsh** a.; ∼**'dǧ** a. (-ily, -iness); ∼**'dǐst** n. [prob. FIDDLE-*faddle*]

**fāde.** 1. v.i. & t. ∼ (**away, out**), droop, wither; (cause to) lose freshness, colour, or strength; disappear gradually; (Cinemat.) cause (picture) to come gradually *in, out* (of, view); bring (sound) *in* or *out* (of audibility). 2. n. Action of fading; ∼**'lĕss** (-dl-) a. [F *fade* dull]

**fae'cēs,** \*fē'cēs, (-z) n.pl. Waste matter discharged from bowels; **fae'cal,** \*fē'cal, a. [L]

**fā'erǀie,** fā'erǀy, n. (arch.) Fairyland, the fairies. [FAIRY]

**făg[1].** 1. v.i. & t. (-gg-). Toil; tire, make weary; ‖(at schools, of junior) do service for senior, (of senior) use service of (junior). 2. n. ‖Drudgery, exhaustion; ‖(at schools) junior who fags; (sl.) cigarette; ∼**-end,** inferior remnant, (sl.) cigarette-end. [orig. unkn.]

**făg[2]** n. (sl.) Homosexual. [abbr. foll.]

**fă'ggot,** \*fă'got, n. Bundle of sticks or twigs for fuel; bundle of herbs, metal rods, etc.; ‖(usu. in *pl.*) seasoned chopped liver etc. baked or fried as ball or roll; unpleasant woman; (sl.) homosexual. [F f. It.]

**fah, fa,** (fah) n. (Mus.) Fourth note of scale; note F. [L *famuli*, wd arbitrarily taken]

**Fah'renheit** (fă'rĕnhīt) a. Pertaining to ∼ **scale** of temperature, on which water freezes at 32° and boils at 212°. [person]

**faience** (fah'yahns, f iah'ns) n. Decorated earthenware and porcelain. [F (*Faenza*, place)]

**fail.** 1. v.i. & t. Be absent or deficient, not suffice for, (supplies *fail*; **words** ∼ **me,** I cannot describe etc.); die away, break down (*engine*

*fails*; ∼ **safe,** revert to safe condition in event of breakdown etc.); disappoint hopes of, not succeed, (*failed me in my need*; *fail in persuading* or *to persuade*); neglect, not be able, (*failed to appear*; *fail to see the reason*); become bankrupt; adjudge or be unsuccessful as candidate (in). 2. n. Failure in an examination; **without** ∼, for certain, unconditionally. 3. ∼**ed** (-ld) a., unsuccessful; **fai'ling**[1] n., (esp.) foible, fault; **fai'ling**[2] prep., in default of (*failing this, failing whom*); **fai'lure** (-lyer) n., (act of) failing, non-occurrence, non-performance, running short, cessation or impairment of vital function (HEART *failure*), unsuccessful person or thing. [F f. L *fallo* deceive]

**fain.** (arch.) 1. pred. a. Willing or forced (*to* do something). 2. adv. Gladly (*would fain*). [E]

**faint** a., v., & n. 1. a. Feeble (*faint praise*); weak from hunger etc.; timid (∼ **heart,** timid spirit; ∼**-heart,** coward); dim, pale, (a *faint idea, glimmer*); ∼ or **feint lines** (of paper ruled for writing). 2. v.i. Lose consciousness (esp. through syncope). 3. n. Act, state, of fainting. [F (FEIGN)]

**fair**[1] n. Periodical gathering for sale of goods, often with entertainments; exhibition, esp. to display specified product(s); = FUN-*fair*. [F f. L *feriae* holiday]

**fair**[2] a., adv., & n. 1. a. Just, equitable, in accordance with rules, (*by fair means*; *fair* DO[2]*s*; ∼ **enough,** colloq., that's reasonable; *fair* GAME[1]; ∼ **play,** equitable conduct or conditions); clean, clear, unblemished, (*fair* COPY); ∼**'way,** navigable channel, mown grass between golf tee and green); of (only) moderate quality or amount (∼**-to-middling,** slightly above average); satisfactory, promising (**be in a** ∼ **way to,** have a good chance of); (of weather) dry and fine, (of wind) favourable, (∼**-weather friend,** not good in a crisis); blond, light or pale in colour (*fair complexion, hair*); beautiful (the ∼ **sex,** women). 2. adv. In a fair manner (BID *fair to*; ∼ **and square,** equitably, exactly; *fight fair*; *play fair*); exactly, completely. 3. ∼'s ∼, (colloq.) (reciprocal) fairness is desirable; ∼**'lǧ** adv., (esp.) completely, tolerably (*fairly good*), to a noticeable degree (*fairly narrow*). [E]

**Fair' Isle** (-īl) *a.* (Of jersey etc.) knitted in a characteristic coloured design. [place]

**fair'ў** *n.* Small mythical being with magical powers; (sl.) male homosexual; ~-**cycle**, low small-wheeled bicycle for children; ~ **godmother**, (fig.) benefactress; **F~land**, home of fairies; ~ **light**, small coloured light esp. for outdoor decorations; ~ **ring** (of darker grass caused by fungi); ~ **story, -tale**, tale about fairies, incredible story, falsehood. [F (FAY, -ERY)]

**fait accompli** (fātahkaw'n̂plē, -kŏ'mplĭ) *n.* Thing done and past arguing against. [F]

**faith** *n.* Trust (*in*); unquestioning confidence; strong belief, esp. in religious doctrines; religion (*the Christian, Jewish,* etc., *faith*); **the F~**, the true religion; things believed; promise; loyalty, trustworthiness (**bad ~**, dishonest intention; **good ~**, honest intention); ~-**cure, -healing**, etc., (by faith or prayer, not by drugs etc.). [F f. L *fides*]

**fai'thful** *a.* Showing faith; loyal, constant, (*to*); trustworthy; true (*a faithful account, copy*); **the ~**, believers, esp. Muslims; ~**lў** *adv.* (**yours ~ly**, formula in closing business etc. letter; **promise ~ly**, colloq., promise emphatically).

**fai'thless** *a.* Perfidious, false; unbelieving.

**fāke** *v., n.,* & *a.* **1.** *v.t.* Feign; make from poor or sham material; make plausible. **2.** *n.* Faking, faked thing; trick; spurious person or thing. **3.** *a.* Spurious, counterfeit. [G *fegen* sweep]

**fă'kir** (-ēr; *or* fakēr') *n.* Muslim or Hindu religious mendicant or ascetic. [Arab., = poor man]

**fa'lchion** (faw'lchon) *n.* Broad curved sword. [F f. L *falx* sickle]

**fa'lcon** (faw'-, fô'-) *n.* Diurnal bird of prey, esp. as trained to hunt game-birds for sport; ~**er** *n.,* one who keeps, trains, or hunts with hawks; ~**rў** *n.,* hunting with, breeding of, hawks. [F f. L *falco*]

**fa'ldstool** (faw'l-) *n.* Bishop's backless folding chair; ‖movable stool or desk for kneeling at; desk from which litany is said. [E f. L f. Gmc (FOLD², STOOL)]

**fall** (fawl). **1.** *v.i.* (**fell**; ~'**en**, with *be* or *have*). Go or come down freely, descend, (*rain falls*; ~**ing star**, meteor; *fall* SHORT); become detached, slope or hang down, drop off; (of river) discharge *into*; become lower, subside, (*price, wind, fell*); (of face) show dismay; lose high position (*fall from grace*); cease to stand, be overthrown or vanquished, perish (*fall* FLAT); yield to temptation; succumb (*to*); pass *in* or *into* a specified condition (*fall in love, into error, a rage*); become (*fall a prey, victim, to*; *fall asleep, due, ill*); take or have a particular direction or place (*accent falls on first syllable*; *companions fell behind*); come by chance or duty (*it fell to me to do the work*); occur (*Easter falls early this year*). **2.** ~ **about**, be helpless, esp. with mirth; ~ **away**, desert, become few or thin, vanish; ~ **back**, retreat (*fall* ~ *back on*, have recourse to); ~ **down (on)**, (colloq.) fail (in); ~ **for**, (colloq.) be captivated or deceived by; ~ **foul of**, collide or quarrel with; ~ **in**, (Mil.) (cause to) take place in parade, (of building etc.) collapse; ~ **into**, take one's place in, begin (conversation *with*), be caught in (trap etc.); ~ **in with**, meet (by chance), agree or coincide with; ~ **off**, decrease, deteriorate; ~ **on** (or **upon**), assault, meet; ~ **on one's face**, fail ridiculously; ~ **on one's feet**, be fortunate; ~ **out**, quarrel, result, occur, (Mil.) (cause to) leave place in parade; ~**-out** *n.,* radioactive debris from nuclear explosion; ~ **over**, (*prep.*) stumble at, (*adv.*) not stay upright (*fall over* BACK-WARDS); ~ **over** oneself, (colloq.) be very awkward or eager; ~ **through**, break down, fail; ~ **to**, (*prep.*) be killed etc. by, begin, (*adv.*) start working etc.; ~ **to the ground**, (of plan etc.) be abandoned, fail; ~ **under**, be classed among, be subjected to (scrutiny etc.). **3.** *n.* Act or manner of falling; amount of fall or that falls; overthrow; succumbing to temptation (**the F~** (**of Man**), Adam's sin and its results); waterfall (esp. in *pl.*; *Niagara Falls*); *autumn; wrestling-bout, throw in this (~**-guy**, sl., easy victim, scapegoat). [E]

**fă'llacў** *n.* Misleading argument; mistaken belief; delusiveness; (Logic) flaw in syllogism; **falla'cious** (-shŭs) *a.* [L (*fallo* deceive)]

**fă'llib|le** *a.* Liable to error; ~**ĭ'lĭtў** *n.* [L (as FALLACY)]

**Fallō'pian** *a.* ~ **tube**, oviduct in female mammals. [*Fallopius*, person]

**fă'llow¹** (-ō) *a.* & *n.* (Land) ploughed but left uncropped for a year; uncultivated (land). [E]

**fă'llow²** (-ō) *a.* Of pale brownish or reddish yellow; ~ **deer**, species smaller than red deer. [E]

**fals|e** (fawls, fŏls). **1.** *a.* Wrong, incorrect, (*false idea, note*); deceitful, treacherous, unfaithful *to*, (bear, give, ~e witness, tell lies, deceive); deceptive (*false* COLOURS); spurious, sham, artificial, (*false* COIN, *eyelashes, god,* KEEL¹, *teeth*); improperly so called (*false acacia,* RIB); ~e **alarm** (given without valid cause); ~e **bottom,** (disguised) horizontal partition in vessel, drawer, suitcase, etc.; ~e **card** (played unusually, to mislead); ~e **position** (that makes person seem to act against his principles); ~e **pretences,** misrepresentation(s) made with intent to deceive; ~e **quantity,** error as to length of vowel; ~e **step,** stumble, unwise or improper action. **2.** *adv.* Play person ~e, cheat or betray him. **3.** ~e'**hŏŏd** (-s-h-) *n.,* untrue thing, lie(s), lying; ~ě'**ttō** *n.* (*pl.* -os), high-pitched artificial voice esp. of male singer; ~'**ĭes** (-ĭz), (colloq.) devices to make breasts seem larger; ~**ĭfĭcā'tion** *n.,* action of falsifying; ~'**ĭfў** *v.t.,* fraudulently alter, misrepresent; ~'**ĭtў** *n.,* being false. [E and F f. L *falsus* (FAIL)]

**fa'lter** (fawl-, fŏl-) *v.i.* & *t.* Stagger; waver, flinch; speak or say hesitatingly. [orig. uncert.]

**fāme** *n.* Renown, glory; (arch.) reputation (HOUSE *of ill fame*); ~**d** (-md) *a.,* famous, much spoken of (*for* valour etc.). [F f. L *fama*]

**fami'lial** (-lyal) *a.* Of or relating to (members of) family. [F f. L (FAMILY)]

**fami'liar** (-lyer). **1.** *a.* Well acquainted (*with*; ~ **spirit,** demon attending witch etc.); (of subject etc.) well known (*to*); common, usual; (excessively) informal. **2.** *n.* Familiar friend or spirit. **3.** **familiă'rĭtў** *n.;* ~**ize** *v.t.,* make (fact etc.) familiar, make (person, one*self*) familiar (*with* fact etc.); ~**izā'tion** *n.* [F f. L (foll.)]

**fă'mĭlў** *n.* Set of parents and children or of relations (HOLY, ROYAL, *Family*); parents, children, servants, etc., forming household; person's children; all descendants of one ancestor, house, lineage; group of kindred peoples or of objects having common features; (Biol.) group of allied genera of animals or plants; ~ **allowance** (paid by State or employer to parent of family); ~ **Bible** (large, with pages for recording births etc.); ‖~ **butcher** etc. (supplying goods to families); ~ **doctor,** general practitioner consulted by members of a family; ~ **likeness,** general resemblance (like that) between relations; ~ **man,** husband and father, domestic man; ~ **name,** surname (esp. used as Christian name); ~ **planning,** birth-control; ~ **tree,** genealogical chart; **in the** ~ **way,** (colloq.) pregnant. [L *familia*]

**fă'mine** *n.* Extreme scarcity of food or specified thing in a district etc.; **fă'mĭsh** *v.t.* & *i.,* reduce, be reduced, to extreme hunger; **famished, famishing,** (colloq.) very hungry. [F (*faim* f. L *fames* hunger)]

**fā'mous** *a.* Well known, celebrated, (*for* quality etc.); (colloq.) excellent. [F f. L (FAME)]

**făn¹. 1.** *n.* Device (usu. sector-shaped when spread out) for agitating air to cool one's face etc.; thing so spread out, e.g. bird's tail; rotating apparatus for ventilation etc. **2.** *v.t.* & *i.* (-nn-). Move (air) with fan; drive air (as) with fan upon (face, flame) to cool or kindle (~ **the flame,** fig., increase passion etc.); spread (*out*) in fan shape. **3.** ~ **belt** (transmitting torque from motor-vehicle engine to fan that cools radiator); ~ **heater** (in which fan drives air over electric heater into room etc.); ~**jet,** jet engine with additional thrust from cold air drawn in by fan; ~'**light,** (fan-shaped) window over door; ~'**tail,** broad-tailed pigeon; ~ **tracery, vaulting,** kind of ornamental vaulting. [E f. L *vannus* winnowing-basket]

**făn²** *n.* Devotee of specified amusement, performer, etc., (*film, football, fan*); ~ **club,** organized group of person's devotees; ~ **mail,** letters from one's fans. [abbr. foll.]

**fanǎ'tic** *a.* & *n.* (Person) filled with excessive (mistaken) enthusiasm, esp. in religion; ~**al** *a.* (-lly); ~**ĭsm** *n.* [F or L (*fanum* temple)]

**fă'ncў** *n., a.,* & *v.* **1.** *n.* Faculty of imagination; mental image; unfounded belief, arbitrary supposition; caprice, whim; capricious or individual liking or preference (*for something*; *passing fancy*; *take a fancy to*; *took my fancy*); ~-**free**, not in love); **the** ~, followers of a certain pastime, esp. patrons of boxing; breeding of fancy animals; fancy cake. **2.** *attrib. a.* Ornamental, not plain, unusual, (*fancy bread, cake, goods*; ~ **dress**, fanciful costume, often historical or exotic); (of flower etc.) particoloured; whimsical, arbitrary; (of prices etc.) excessive; (of animal) bred for particular qualities; ~ **man**, (sl.) man living on earnings of prostitute; ~ **woman**, (sl.) mistress. **3.** *v.t.* Imagine, conceive, picture to oneself; freq. imper. as excl. of surprise (~ **that!**, **just** ~!, how strange or surprising!); be inclined to think (*that*); take a liking to, find attractive; (colloq.) have unduly high opinion of (one*self*, one's ability, etc.). **4.** **fă'ncĭer** *n.*, connoisseur (*dog-, pigeon-, fancier*); **fă'ncĭful** *a.* (-**lly**), indulging in fancies, quaint, imaginary, unreal. [contr. FANTASY]

**fặndă'ngō** (-nggō) *n.* (*pl.* ~**es**, ~**s**). (Music for) lively Spanish dance. [Sp.]

**fāne** *n.* (poet.) Temple. [L *fanum*]

**fǎ'nfāre** *n.* Short showy or ceremonious sounding of trumpets, bugles, etc. [F]

**făng** *n.* Canine tooth, esp. of dog or wolf; serpent's venom-tooth; (prong of) root of tooth. [E]

**fặntặ'stĭc** *a.* (~**ally**). Extravagantly fanciful, eccentric; grotesque, quaint; (colloq.) excellent, extraordinary. [F f. L f. Gk (foll.)]

**fă'ntasў, phặ'-. 1.** *n.* Faculty of imagination, esp. when extravagant; mental image, day-dream; fanciful invention, composition, speculation, etc.; fantasia. **2.** *v.t.* Imagine in visionary manner. **3.** **fặntă'sĭa** (-z-, -tazē'a) *n.*, musical or other composition in which form is of minor importance, or which is based on several familiar tunes; **fă'ntasĭze** *v.t.* & *i.*, have fanciful vision (of). [F f. L f. Gk *phantasia* appearance]

‖**F.A.N.Y.** *abbr.* First Aid Nursing Yeomanry.

**F.A.O.** *abbr.* Food and Agriculture Organization.

**fär.** (FARTHER, FURTHER; FARTHEST, FURTHEST). **1.** *adv.* At, to, by, a great distance, a long way (off), in space or time, or fig., *far away, off, out*; *far*

better, *otherwise, the best*; *talked far into the night*; **be** ~ **from** wishing, by no means wish). **2.** *a.* Distant, remote, (*a far* CRY; *Far* EAST; *in the far distance*); more distant (*the far end of the hall*). **3.** **as** ~ **as**, right to (a place), to the extent that; **by** ~, by a large amount; ~ **and away**, very much (*better* etc.); ~ **and near**, everywhere; ~ **and wide**, over a large area; ~-**away**, remote, (of look) dreamy, (of voice) sounding as if from distance; ~ **be it from me to**, I would on no account; ~ **between**, infrequent; ~-**fetched**, studiously sought out, unnatural; ~-**flung**, (rhet.) extending far; ~ **from**, very different from being, tending to the opposite of (*problem is far from easy*); ~ **gone**, advanced in time, very ill, mad, drunk, etc.; ~-**off**, remote; ~-**out**, distant, (fig.) avant-garde, excellent; ~-**reaching**, of wide application or influence; ~-**seeing**, prescient, prudent; ~-**sighted**, far-seeing, seeing distant things best; **from** ~, from a distance; **go** ~, (fig.) achieve or obtain much, contribute greatly *to(wards)*; **go too** ~, (fig.) go beyond limits of reason, politeness, etc.; **how** ~, to what extent; **in so** ~ **as**, to the extent that; **so** ~, to such an extent, to this point, until now; **so** ~ **as**, as far as, in so far as; **so** ~, **so good**, progress has been satisfactory. [E]

**fặ'rad** *n.* (Electr.) Fundamental unit of capacitance. [*Faraday*, person]

**fặrandō'le** *n.* (Music for) lively Provençal dance. [F f. Prov.]

**fäřc|e** *n.* Dramatic work meant merely to cause laughter, often by presenting ludicrously improbable events; this branch of drama; absurdly futile proceeding(s); ~'**ĭcal** *a.* (-**lly**); ~**ĭcǎ'lĭtў** *n.* [F f. L *farcio* to stuff, w. ref. to interludes etc.]

**fāre. 1.** *n.* Price of passenger's conveyance; passenger who pays to travel in public vehicle; food provided (*good, hard, fare*; **bill of** ~, menu). **2.** *v.i.* Get on (*well, ill*); (poet.) go, travel. **3.** ~**we'll** (-ārw-), (*int.*) goodbye!, (*n.*) departure, leave-taking. [E]

**farī'na** (*or* -ē'-) *n.* Flour or meal of corn, nuts, or starchy roots; **fărĭnă'ceous** (-sh‍us) *a.*, of, like, farina. [L]

**färm. 1.** *n.* Tract of land used under

one management for growing crops, raising animals, etc.; ~('house), dwelling-place on farm; place for breeding of animals (fish-, mink-, -farm); ~'stead, farm with buildings; ~'yard, yard of farmhouse. 2. v.t. & i. Use (land) for growing crops, raising animals, etc.; breed (fish etc.) commercially; take proceeds of (tax, office, etc.) on payment of fixed sum; ~ (out), dispose of (tax etc.) thus, delegate (work etc.) to others; maintain and care for, or arrange maintenance of, (person, esp. child) for payment; ~'er n., owner or manager of farm. [F *ferme* f. L *firma* fixed payment]

**far'ō** n. Gambling card-game. [F *pharaon* PHARAOH]

**farou'che** (-ōō'sh) a. Sullen, shy. [F f. L]

**farra'gō** (-rah'-) n. (pl. ~s, *~es). Medley, hotchpotch. [L, = mixed fodder (far corn)]

‖**fa'rrier** n. Smith who shoes horses; horse-doctor; ~y̆ n., farrier's work. [F f. L (*ferrum* iron, horseshoe)]

**fa'rrow** (-ō). 1. n. Giving birth to, litter of, pigs. 2. v.t. & i. (Of sow) produce (pigs). [E, = pig]

**fart.** (vulg.) 1. v.i. Emit wind from anus; fool (about, around). 2. n. Emission of wind from anus; contemptible person. [E]

**far'ther** (-dh-). 1. adv. More far (in space or time). 2. a. More distant or advanced; additional, more; ~most a., farthest. **far'thest** (-dh-), (a.) most distant, (adv.) to, at, the greatest distance. [FURTHER]

**far'thing** (-dh-) n. (Hist.) quarter of penny, coin worth this; least possible amount (*doesn't matter a farthing*; BRASS *farthing*). [E (FOURTH)]

**far'thingāle** (-dhĭngg-) n. (Hist.) Hooped petticoat to extend woman's skirt. [F f. Sp. (*verdugo* rod)]

**fă'scēs** (-z) n.pl. (Rom. Hist.) bundle of rods and an axe carried by lictor before magistrate; emblems of authority. [L, pl. of *fascis* bundle]

**fa'scia** (fă'shĭa, fā'sha) n. (Archit.) long flat surface of wood or stone; stripe, band; = FACIA. [L, = band, door-frame]

**fă'scicle, fă'scicule, fasci'cū-lus,** n. (Bot. etc.) bunch, bundle; instalment of book. [L dim. (FASCES)]

**fă'scin|āte** v.t. (Esp. of serpent) make (victim) powerless by one's look or presence; charm irresistibly;

~ā'tion, ~ātor, ns. [L (*fascinum* spell)]

**Fă'sc|ism** (fă'sh-) n. Principles and organization of Italian nationalist and anti-communist dictatorship (1922–43); similar action or movement in other countries; extreme right-wing or authoritarian views; ~ist n. & a.; ~ĭ'stic a. [It. (*fascio* bundle, organized group)]

**fă'shion** (-shon). 1. n. Make, shape, style, pattern, manner (*after, in, this fashion*; **after, in, a ~**, hardly satisfactorily; (as *suf.*) = -WISE (*learn parrot-fashion*); prevailing (usu. transient) custom or usages of society, esp. in dress (**in, out of (the) ~**, conforming, or not, with current usage; *lady, man of ~*, of high social standing as shown by dress etc.; **set the ~**, give lead in changing usages). 2. v.t. Form, shape, (*into*); shape (stocking) to fit leg. **~able** a. (-bly), following or suited to the fashion, characteristic of or patronized by those who are in fashion. [F f. L *factio* (FACT)]

**fast**[1] (-ah-). 1. v.i. Abstain from (some kinds of) food, esp. as religious observance; go without food. 2. n. Fasting; season or day for this; going without food (**break one's ~**, to breakfast). [E]

**fast**[2] (-ah-). 1. a. (no adv. in **-ly**). Rapid, quick-moving, causing quick motion (*fast and* FURIOUS); (of clock etc.) showing later than correct time; (of person) immoral, dissipated; (of photographic film) needing only short exposure; firm, fixed, firmly attached (HARD *and fast*; **play ~ and loose**, be unreliable); (of colour) not fading when washed etc.; (of friend) close. 2. adv. Quickly, in quick succession; firmly, tightly, (*stand, stick, fast*; **~ asleep**, in a deep sleep). 3. **~'back**, (motor car with) rear sloping to bumper; *~ **buck**, (sl.) quickly-earned money; **~ lane** (on road, for overtaking by fast-moving vehicles); **~ neutron** (with high kinetic energy); **~ one**, (sl.) unfair or deceitful action; **~ reactor** (nuclear, using fast neutrons); *~**talk**, (colloq.) persuade by rapid or deceitful talk; **~ worker**, one who makes rapid progress, esp. in amatory activities. **4. ~'nĕss** n., (esp.) stronghold. [E]

**fa'sten** (fah'sen) v.t. & i. Attach, fix, secure, (thing *to* another, *on, up,* etc., *fasten garment, parcel, door*; *fasten one's look, attention*, etc., *on*; *fasten nickname* etc. *on*); become fast (*door will not fasten*); ~ (**up**)**on**, seize upon (pretext etc.); ~**er** (fah'sn-), ~**ing**, *ns.*, (esp.) clasp etc. to fasten thing with. [E]

**făsti'dĭous** *a.* Easily disgusted, hard to please, carefully selective. [L (*fastidium* loathing)]

**făt** *a.*, *n.*, & *v.* **1.** *a.* (-tt-). Well-fed, plump, corpulent; (of animal) made plump for slaughter, so ~'**stock**; thick, solid (~-**head**, stupid person); greasy, oily; fertile, profitable (**a ~ lot**, sl., a large amount, usu. iron. = very little). **2.** *n.* Fat part of thing (**live off, on, the ~ of the land**, live luxuriously); oily or greasy substance, esp. that found in animal bodies (CHEW *the fat*; **the ~ is in the fire**, there will be a commotion). **3.** *v.t.* (-tt-). Fatten (**kill the ~ted calf**, celebrate, esp. at prodigal's return). [E]

**fā'tal** *a.* (~**ly**). Deadly, ending in death, (*fatal wound*); destructive, ruinous, (*to*); disastrous, ill-advised, (*fatal mistake*); of fate, inevitable, fated; ~**ism** *n.*, belief that all is predetermined, submission to all that happens as inevitable; ~**ist** *n.*; ~**i'stic** *a.* (-ically); **fatā'lĭtỹ** *n.*, supremacy of fate, predestined liability to disaster, fatal influence, calamity, death by accident etc. [F or L (FATE)]

**fāte. 1.** *n.* Power predetermining events from eternity; (usu. F~) goddess, esp. one of 3 Greek or Scandinavian goddesses, of destiny; what is destined (**as sure as ~**, absolutely certain); person's appointed lot or ultimate condition (*fate worse than* DEATH); death, destruction; ~'**ful** (-tf-) *a.* (-**lly**), controlled by or fraught with fate, decisive. **2.** *v.t.* (usu. in *pass.*) Preordain; (in *p.p.*) doomed to destruction. [It., & L *fatum*]

**fa'ther** (fah'dh-). **1.** *n.* Male parent (lit. or fig.; (**adoptive**) ~, adopter of child; **like ~, like son**, sons resemble, or behave like, their fathers; **the ~ and mother of a**, colloq., an extremely large, severe, etc.); forefather; originator, early leader (PILGRIM *Fathers*; F~**s** (**of the Church**), early Christian writers, esp. of 1st–6th cc.); (F~) God, esp. as 1st person of Trinity; confessor,

priest of religious order; (as prefixed title) priest; venerable person (*Father Christmas, Thames, Time*, as personifications); oldest member (*Father of the House of Commons*); (in *pl.*) elders, leading members (*City Fathers*); ~-**figure**, trusted leader, respected older man; ~-**in-law**, wife's or husband's father; ~**land**, native land (esp. Germany); F~'**s Day**, day, usu. 3rd Sunday in June, for tribute to fathers; *Father* SUPERIOR. **2.** *v.t.* Beget; originate (scheme etc.); appear as, confess oneself, father or author of; fix paternity of, or responsibility for, (child, book, etc.) on or upon. **3.** ~**hood** *n.*; ~**lỹ** *a.* (-iness), of or like a father. [E]

**fă'thom** (-dh-). **1.** *n.* Measure of 6 feet, esp. in soundings (*30 fathom* or *fathoms*). **2.** *v.t.* Measure depth of (water); (fig.) comprehend; ~**less** *a.*, too deep to fathom. [E]

**fati'gue** (-ē'g). **1.** *n.* Weariness from exertion; weakness in metals etc. from variations of stress; wearying task; soldier's non-combatant duty (~-**dress**, ~**s**, garments worn for this duty). **2.** *v.t.* Tire, cause fatigue in. [F f. L *fatigo* exhaust]

**fă'tt|en** *v.t.* & *i.* Make or become fat; ~**ỹ**, (*a.*) of or like fat (~**y degeneration**, with morbid deposition of fat), (*n.*) fat person (esp. as nickname). [FAT]

**fă'tŭous** *a.* Silly, purposeless; **fatū'ĭtỹ** *n.* [L *fatuus*]

**fau'cĕt** *n.* Tap for barrel etc.; \*any kind of tap. [F *fausset* vent-peg f. Prov. (*falsar* to bore)]

**fault** (or f ŏlt). **1.** *n.* Defect, blemish, in character, structure, etc., (*generous etc.* **to a ~**, excessively); offence, misdeed, responsibility or blame attaching, (*whose fault is it?*; **at ~**, wrong, blameworthy; **find ~ with**, complain of); (Tennis etc.) ball wrongly served (**double ~**, two consecutive faults losing point); (Hunting) loss of scent, check; (Geol.) break in continuity of strata etc.; ~-**finding** *a.* & *n.*, querulous(ness), censorious(ness). **2.** *v.t.* & *i.* Find fault with, blame; commit fault; (Geol.) cause fault in, have fault. **3.** ~'**ỹ** *a.* (~**ily**, ~**iness**). [F f. L *fallo* deceive]

**faun** *n.* Latin rural deity with horns and tail. [F, or L *Faunus*]

**fau'na** *n.* (*pl.* ~**e**, ~**s**). Animals of

a region or epoch; treatise on or list of fauna. [L *Fauna*, fem. (prec.)]

*faute de mieux* (fōtdmyởͤ') *adv.* & *a.* (Used) for want of any better alternative. [F]

*faux pas* (fōpah') *n.* (*pl.* same *pr.* -ah'z). Tactless mistake; compromising act. [F = false step]

**fā'vour, *fā'vor,** (-er). **1.** *n.* Liking, goodwill, approval, (CURRY[2], FIND, *favour*; *look with favour on*); kindness beyond what is due (*do me a favour*); partiality (*without* FEAR *or favour*; **in ~ of**, on behalf or in support of, to the advantage or account of); thing given or worn as mark of favour, badge etc. **2.** *v.t.* Regard, treat, with favour; oblige *with*; treat with partiality; support, promote, facilitate; (in *p.p.*) having unusual advantages; (colloq.) resemble in appearance; **ill** etc. **-~ed,** having such looks. [F f. L (*faveo* be kind to)]

**fā'vourable, *fā'vorable,** (-ver-) *a.* (-bly). Well disposed; commendatory, approving, promising, auspicious, satisfactory, helpful, suitable, (*favourable prospect*; *soil favourable to roses*).

**fā'vourit|e, *fā'vorit|e,** (-ver-). **1.** *a.* Habitually or specially preferred (*favourite author, colour, excuse*). **2.** *n.* Favourite person or thing, esp. person unduly favoured by king or superior; (Sport) competitor, horse, etc., generally expected to win; **~ism** *n.*, unfair favouring of one person or group at expense of another. [F f. It. (FAVOUR)]

**fawn[1]** *n., a., & v.* **1.** *n.* Fallow etc. deer in first year; light yellowish brown colour. **2.** *a.* Fawn-coloured. **3.** *v.t. & i.* Bring forth (fawn). [F f. L (FOETUS)]

**fawn[2]** *v.i.* (Of dog etc.) show affection by tail-wagging, grovelling, etc., lavish caresses (*on, upon*); (of person) behave servilely (usu. *fawn on, upon,* person). [E]

**fay** *n.* (literary). Fairy. [F f. L *fata* pl. the FATES]

***F.B.I.** *abbr.* Federal Bureau of Investigation.

**F.C.** *abbr.* Football Club.

‖**F.C.O.** *abbr.* Foreign and Commonwealth Office.

**Fe** *symb.* iron. [L *ferrum*]

**fē'altў** *n.* Feudal tenant's or vassal's (acknowledgement of obligation of) fidelity to his lord; allegiance. [F f. L (FIDELITY)]

**fear. 1.** *n.* Alarm, painful emotion caused by impending danger or evil, (*the fear of death*; *for fear of slipping, lest* or *that he should slip*; **without ~ or favour,** impartially; **in ~ of his life,** anxious lest he lose it); danger, likelihood, (*there is some fear of it*; **no ~,** colloq., not likely, certainly not); dread and reverence (*fear of God*; **put the ~ of God into,** terrify). **2.** *v.i. & t.* Be afraid (*I fear that we are too late*; **never ~,** there is no danger of that); be afraid or apprehensive of; hesitate (*to* do), shrink from (*doing*); revere (God); **~'ful** *a.* (-lly), terrible, afraid (*of, lest, to* do), (colloq.) annoying, extreme, (*a fearful mess*); **~'less** *a.,* feeling no fear, brave; **~'some** *a.,* formidable. [E]

**fea'sib|le** (-z-) *a.* (~ly). Practicable, possible; (colloq.) convenient, manageable, plausible; **~i'litў** *n.* [F (L *facio* do)]

**feast. 1.** *n.* Joyful religious anniversary (**movable ~,** festival of varying date); annual village festival; sumptuous (esp. public) meal; (fig.) something giving great pleasure. **2.** *v.i. & t.* Partake of feast, eat and drink sumptuously (*on*); regale (guests, one's *eyes on* beauty etc.). [F f. L (*festus* joyous)]

**feat** *n.* Notable or surprising act, esp. of dexterity or strength. [F f. L (FACT)]

**fea'ther** (fĕ'dh-). **1.** *n.* One of the appendages growing from bird's skin, consisting of horny stem fringed with barbs on both sides, piece of this as ornament etc., (**~ in one's cap,** achievement to be proud of; **white ~,** sign of cowardice); (collect.) plumage (BIRDS *of a feather*; **in fine, high, ~,** in good spirits); game-birds (*fur and feather*); (Rowing) feathering. **2.** *v.t. & i.* Furnish, line, coat, (as) with feathers (**~ one's nest,** enrich oneself; TAR *and feather*); turn (oar) so as to pass through air edgeways. **3. ~-bed,** (*n.*) mattress stuffed with feathers, (*v.t.*; **-dd-**) make things easy for, pamper; **~-brain(ed), -head(ed),** silly (person); **~weight,** very light thing or person, esp. boxer (see BOX); **~ing** *n.,* (esp.) plumage, feathers of arrow, feather-like structure or marking; **~ў** *a.* (~iness). [E]

**fea′ture. 1.** *n.* Part of face, esp. with regard to appearance, (usu. in *pl.*); notable or characteristic part of thing; prominent article in newspaper etc.; ~ (film), main item in cinema programme; ~**lèss** (-cherl-) *a.*, lacking distinct features. **2.** *v.t. & i.* Make special display of, give prominence to, (esp. in film etc.); be feature of; be participant (*in*). [F, f. L *factura* formation (FACT)]

**Feb.** *abbr.* February.

**fè′brĭfŭge** *n.* Medicine to reduce fever; cooling drink. [F f. L *febris* fever, *fugo* drive away]

**fè′brĭle** *a.* Of fever. [F or L (prec.)]

**Fĕ′bruarў** (-rŏŏ-) *n.* Second month. [F f. L (*februa* purification feast)]

*fē′cal, *feces. See FAECES.

**fè′cklèss** *a.* Feeble, futile, inefficient, aimless. [Sc. *feck* (*effeck* var. of EFFECT)]

**fè′cund** *a.* Prolific, fertile; fertilizing; ~**ate** *v.t.*, make fecund, = FERTILIZE; ~**ā′tion**, fĕcŭ′ndĭtў, *ns.* [F or L]

**fĕd.** See FEED[1].

**fĕ′deral** *a.* (~**ly**). Of system of government in which several States unite but remain independent in internal affairs; of such States or form of government; relating to or favouring central (as distinct from separate provincial or state) government; *of Northern States in Civil War; ~ **district, territory,** etc., region used as seat of federal government; ~**ĭsm, ~ĭst,** *ns.;* ~**ĭze** *v.t.;* ~**ĭzā′tion** *n.;* **fĕ′derāte,** (*v.t. & i.*) unite on federal basis or for common object, (-*at; a.*) so united; **fĕderā′tion** *n.,* act of federating, federal society; **fĕ′derātive** *a.* [L (*foedus* covenant)]

**fee. 1.** *n.* Sum due to public officer for performing function; professional man's pay for consultation etc.; money paid for transfer to another employer of footballer etc.; entrance money for examination etc.; (in *pl.*) regular payment for instruction at school etc.; = FEUD[2]; inherited estate (~**-tail**, ~ **simple,** limited, not limited, to one class of heirs). **2.** *v.t.* (~**′d,** ~**d**). Pay fee to; engage for fee. [AF, = F *feu* etc. f. L *feudum* perh. f. Gmc]

**fee′ble** *a.* (~**r,** ~**st;** -**bly**). Weak, deficient in character or intelligence (~**-minded,** mentally deficient, esp.

with mental age of 8 or 9); lacking energy, force, or clearness. [F f. L *flebilis* lamentable]

**feed[1]. 1.** *v.t. & i.* (**fed**). Supply with food; put food into mouth of; take food, eat, (esp. of animals, or colloq.); comfort (person *with* hope etc.); serve as food for; keep (fire, reservoir, etc.) supplied; put (material (*in*)to machine etc.); (Theatr. sl.) supply (actor) with cues; (Footb.) give passes to. **2.** *n.* Feeding (off one's ~, with no appetite; **out at** ~, grazing); (colloq.) meal, feast; (allowance of) fodder for cattle etc.; material supplied to machine etc.; (Theatr. sl.) actor etc. who supplies another with cues. **3.** ~ **a cold,** eat much when one has a cold; ~ **back,** return by or as FEEDBACK; ~**′ing--bottle** (for infant to suck); ~**′ing-time,** meal-time, esp. time when captive animals are fed; ~ **on,** consume, be nourished by; ~ **up,** give nourishing food to; **fed up, fed to death, fed to the (back) teeth,** (sl.) satiated, bored, (*with*); ~**′er** *n.,* one who feeds in a specified way, ‖child's bib, feeding-bottle, feeding apparatus in machine, tributary, branch road, railway line, etc., that links with main system. [E]

**feed[2].** See FEE.

**fee′dbăck** *n.* (Electr.) return of fraction of output signal to input of same or a preceding stage, signal so returned, (**negative, positive,** ~, decreasing, increasing, amplification etc.); (Biol., Psych., etc.) modification or control of process or system by its results or effects; information about result of experiment etc.; response. [FEED[1], BACK]

**fee′der.** See FEED[1].

**feel. 1.** *v.t. & i.* (**felt**). Examine or search by touch; perceive by touch, have sensation of, (*feel a pain; felt him move, moving, that he was cold;* **make** one's **presence felt,** have effect on others); be conscious of (emotion etc.); be consciously, consider oneself, (*feel* CHEAP, *fit, like an outcast; feel free to call on us*); experience, be affected by; sympathize (*with*), have pity (*for*); have vague or emotional impression (*I feel (that) I am right; feel in* one's BONES); consider, think, (*feel it necessary*); seem, produce impression of being, (*air feels cold; it feels like velvet*). **2.** *n.* Sense of touch (*firm to the feel*); act of feeling; sensation characterizing a material, situation, etc. **3.** ~ **bad** (ill or ashamed); ~ **good** (in good spirits or health); ~ **like**, (colloq.) desire (thing), be inclined towards do*ing*; ~ **out**, investigate (cautiously); ~ (**quite**) one**self**, be fit, self-possessed, etc.; ~ **up**, (sl.) caress sexually; ~ **up to**, be ready for or capable of; ~ one's **way**, proceed cautiously (lit. or fig.). **4.** ~**er** n., (esp.) organ in certain animals for testing things by touch, tentative suggestion etc.; ~**er gauge** (with blades for measuring gaps etc.). [E]

**fee′ling. 1.** n. Sense of touch; physical sensation; emotion (*a feeling of irritation*); (in *pl.*) susceptibilities, sympathies, (*strong feelings on the matter*; **hurts my** ~**s**, offends me); tenderness for others, considerateness; consciousness, belief, or opinion, not based solely on reason (*had a feeling of safety*; *the general feeling was against it*); general emotional effect of work of art. **2.** a. Sensitive; sympathetic; heartfelt (*a feeling protest*).

**feet.** See FOOT.

**feign** (fān) v.t. Pretend, simulate, (*that one is mad*, one*self mad*, *madness*); (arch.) invent (story etc.). [F f. L *fingo fict-* mould, contrive]

**feint** (fā-) n., v., & a. **1.** n. Sham attack, blow, etc., to deceive opponent; pretence (*of doing*). **2.** v.i. Make a feint. **3.** a. See FAINT. [F (prec.)]

**fě′ldspār.** See FELSPAR.

**felī′cit|āte** v.t. Congratulate (usu. on); ~**ā′tion** n. (usu. in *pl.*); ~**ous** a., well-chosen (*felicitous phrase*), (of person) pleasingly ingenious in choice of words etc.; ~**ў** n., (thing causing) great happiness, felicitous nature or thing. [L (*felix* happy)]

**fē′line. 1.** a. Of cats; catlike esp. in beauty or slyness; **felī′nitў** n. **2.** n. Animal of cat family. [L (*feles* cat)]

**fěll**[1] n. Animal's hide or skin with hair; human skin; thick matted hair or wool. [E]

‖**fěll**[2] n. Hill (in names, as *Scafell*); stretch of high moorland. [N]

**fěll**[3] a. Fierce, terrible, destructive, (poet.); **at one** ~ **swoop**, in a single (deadly) action. [F (FELON)]

**fěll**[4] v.t. Strike down by blow or cut; cut down (tree); stitch down (edge of seam). [E (FALL)]

**fěll**[5]. See FALL.

**fě′llah** (-ə) n. (*pl.* ~**in** *pr.* -*a*-hēn). Egyptian peasant. [Arab.]

**fě′llōe, fě′llў,** n. (Section of) outer circle of wheel, attached by spokes. [E]

**fě′llow** (-ō). **1.** n. Comrade, associate, (usu. in *pl.*); ~**feeling**, sympathy; counterpart, equal, one of same class; incorporated senior member of college; graduate receiving stipend for period of research; member of learned society; (colloq.) man (*my dear fellow*; *old fellow*; *stout fellow*). **2.** attrib. or a. Of same class, associated in joint action etc., (*fellow-citizen, -creature*; ~**countryman**, person from same country; ~**-traveller**, esp., non-Communist who sympathizes with aims of Communist Party). **3.** ~**shıp** n., sharing (*in*, *of*), community of interest, companionship, body of associates, position or income of fellow of college or learned society. [E f. N, = one who lays down money in partnership (FEE, LAY[4])]

**fě′llў.** See FELLOE.

**fě′lon** n. One who has committed felony; ~**ў** n., crime regarded by the law as grave; **felō′nious** a. [F f. L *fello*]

**fě′l(d)spār** n. Common white or flesh-red mineral containing aluminium and other silicates; ~**ă′thic** a. [G (*feld* field, *spat(h)* SPAR[2])]

**fělt**[1]. **1.** n. Cloth made by rolling and pressing, or by weaving and shrinking, wool etc.; ~(**-tipped**) **pen** (with point made of felt). **2.** v.t. & i. Make into felt; cover with felt; become matted. [E]

**fělt**[2]. See FEEL.

**felū′cca** n. Mediterranean coasting-vessel with oars or lateen sails. [It. *feluc(c)a* f. Sp. f. Arab.]

**fē′māle. 1.** a. Of the sex that can bear offspring or produce eggs; (of plants or their parts) fruit-bearing, having pistil and no stamens, or thought of as female because of colour etc., (~ **fern**, tall slender kind); of women (*female sex*, *suffrage*; ~ **impersonator**, male performer dressed and acting as woman) or female animals; (of SCREW, socket, etc.) made hollow to receive corresponding inserted part; *female* RHYME. **2.** n. Female person or animal; (derog. or joc.) woman, girl. [F f. L dim. of *femina* woman, assim. to *male*]

**fĕ'min|ĭne. 1.** *a.* Of women; womanly (*feminine intuition*); (Gram.) of gender proper to women's names; (Pros.) ~**ine ending,** ending of line with unaccented syllable after final stress; *feminine* RHYME. **2.** *n.* Feminine gender or word. **3.** ~**i'nĭtỹ** *n.*; ~**ĭsm** *n.*, advocacy of women's rights on ground of equality of sexes; ~**ĭst** *n.*; ~**ĭze** *v.t.* & *i.*, make or become feminine or female. [F or L (prec.)]

*femme fatale* (făm fătah'l) *n.* Dangerously attractive woman. [F]

**fē'mur** *n.* (*pl.* ~**s,** femora *pr.* fĕ'-). Thigh-bone; **fĕ'moral** *a.* [L]

**fĕn** *n.* Low marshy tract of land (the F~**s,** low-lying areas in Cambs. etc.); ~**nỹ** *a.* [E]

**fence. 1.** *n.* Barrier or railing enclosing field, garden, etc., (**mend one's ~s,** make peace with person; **sit on the ~,** remain neutral or undecided; **sunk ~,** see SINK); guard, guide, or gauge in machine; receiver, receiving-house, of stolen goods. **2.** *v.t.* & *i.* Surround (as) with fence, enclose, (*about, in, round, up*); separate (*off, out*) with fence; screen, protect; practise sword-fighting, esp. with foils; ~ **with,** avoid giving direct answer to (question, questioner); **fĕ'ncĭng** *n.,* (esp.) fences, material for fences. [DEFENCE]

**fĕnd** *v.t.* & *i.* Repel *from,* ward *off;* provide *for* (usu. one*self*); ~**'er** *n.,* thing used to ward something off, bumper, \*mudguard, of motor car etc., low frame around fireplace to prevent falling coal etc. from rolling into room. [DEFEND]

**fĕ'nnel** *n.* Yellow-flowered herb used in sauces etc.; related or similar plant. [E & F f. L (*fenum* hay)]

**fĕ'nnỹ.** See FEN.

**fĕ'nŭgreek** *n.* Leguminous plant with aromatic seeds. [F f. L, = Greek hay]

**feoff** (fĕf) *n.* = FEUD[2]. [AF var. FIEF]

**fēr'al** *a.* Wild, untamed, uncultivated; in wild state after escape from captivity; brutal. [L *ferus* wild]

*fer de lance* (fārdelah'ns) *n.* Large very venomous S. Amer. snake. [F, = lance-iron]

**fēr'ĭal** *a.* (Of day) not a festival or fast. [F, or L (*feria* FAIR[1])]

**fermĕnt. 1.** (fĕr'mĕnt) *n.* Leaven, fermenting-agent; fermentation; excitement, tumult. **2.** (fermĕ'nt) *v.i.* & *t.* Undergo, subject to, fermentation;

excite, foment. [F, or L *fermentum* (FERVENT)]

**fĕrmĕntā'tion** *n.* Process like that induced by leaven in dough, with effervescence, evolution of heat, and change of properties; excitement; **fermĕ'ntative** *a.* [L (prec.)]

**fērn** *n.* Vascular cryptogam, usu. with feathery fronds; (collect.) quantity of ferns; **fēr'erỹ** *n.,* place for growing ferns; ~**'ỹ** *a.* [E]

**ferō'cious** (-shŭs) *a.* Fierce, cruel; **ferŏ'cĭtỹ** *n.* [L *ferox*]

**-ferous** *suf.* forming *adjs.* (usu. w. *-i-*) w. sense 'bearing, having' (*auriferous, odoriferous*). [L *fero* bear]

**fĕ'rret. 1.** *n.* Variety or species of polecat used in catching rabbits, rats, etc.; ~**ỹ** *a.* **2.** *v.i.* & *t.* Hunt with ferrets; rummage, search, (*about, around, for*); search *out* (secret, criminal). [F f. L (*fur* thief)]

**fĕ'rrĭc** *a.* Of iron; (Chem.) containing iron in trivalent form (cf. FERROUS). [L *ferrum* iron]

**Fĕ'rrĭs** *n.* ~ **wheel,** giant revolving vertical wheel with passenger cars, in amusement parks etc. [person]

**fĕrrō-** *in comb.* Containing iron; of iron; ~**cŏ'ncrēte** (*or* -n-k-) *n.,* REINFORCED concrete. [FERRIC]

**fĕ'rrous** *a.* Containing iron (*ferrous and non-ferrous metals*); (Chem.) containing iron in divalent form (cf. FERRIC).

**ferru'gĭnous** (-rōō'-) *a.* Of iron-rust; rust-coloured, reddish-brown. [L *ferrugo* rust (FERRIC)]

**fĕ'rrule** (*or* -ōōl) *n.* Metal ring or cap strengthening end of stick etc. [F f. L (*viriae* bracelet)]

**fĕ'rrỹ. 1.** *v.t.* & *i.* Take or go in boat, work (boat), (of boat) pass to and fro, over river, lake, etc.; transport (persons or things) from one place to another, esp. as regular service. **2.** *n.* Place for, means of, service of, ferrying. [N]

**fēr't|ĭle** *a.* Bearing abundantly, fruitful, (lit. or fig.); (of seed, egg, etc.) capable of becoming new individual; able to become a parent; (of nuclear material) able to become fissile by capture of neutrons; ~**i'lĭtỹ** *n.;* ~**ĭlĭze** *v.t.,* make fertile, cause (egg etc. or female) to develop new individual; ~**ĭlĭzā'tion,** ~**ĭlĭzer,** *ns.* [F f. L]

**fĕ'rule** (-ōōl) *n.* Flat ruler with widened end for punishing boys. [L]

**fēr'v|ent** *a.* Hot, glowing; ardent,

intense; **∼ency, ∼our** (-*er*), **\*∼or**, *ns.*; **∼id** *a.*, ardent. [F f. L *ferveo* boil]

**fě'scue** *n.* Kind of grass valuable for pasture etc. [F f. L *festuca* stalk]

**fěss(e)** *n.* (Her.) Horizontal stripe across middle of shield. [F f. L *fascia* band]

**fě'stal** *a.* (∼ly). Of a feast; engaging in holiday activities; gay. [F f. L (FEAST)]

**fě'ster** *v.i. & t.* (Of wound etc.) become purulent; (of poison, disease) cause suppuration (of); (of grief, resentment, etc.) rankle; putrefy, rot. [F f. L FISTULA]

**fě'stival** *n.* Feast day, celebration, merry-making; periodic musical etc. performance(s). [F (foll.)]

**fě'stive** *a.* Of a feast; joyous; jovial; **fěsti'vity** *n.*, gaiety, festive celebration, (in *pl.*) festive proceedings. [L (FEAST)]

**fěstoo'n. 1.** *n.* Chain of flowers, ribbons, etc., hung in curve between two points; ornament representing this. **2.** *v.t.* Adorn (as) with, form into, festoons. [F f. It. (prec.)]

**Fě'stschrift** (-shr-) *n.* (*pl.* ∼en, ∼s). Collection of writings presented to scholar to mark an occasion in his life. [G, = festival-writing]

**\*fě'tal.** See FOETUS.

**fětch**[1]. **1.** *v.t. & i.* (Go for and) bring back (person or thing; *go and fetch a doctor*); cause to come, draw forth, (blood, tears, etc.); be sold for (price); heave (sigh), draw (breath); strike (a blow; *fetch him a box on the ears*); move the feelings of, delight, irritate; *fetch a* COMPASS; **∼ and carry**, be a mere servant; **∼ up**, vomit, come to rest, arrive. **2.** *n.* Act of fetching; trick. **3.** **∼'ing** *a.*, attractive. [E]

**fětch**[2] *n.* Wraith, double. [orig. unkn.]

**fête** (fāt). **1.** *n.* Bazaar-like function to raise money for charity; festival. **2.** *v.t.* Entertain, make much of, (person). [F (FEAST)]

**fě'tĭd, foe'tĭd** (fē'-), *a.* Stinking. [L (*feteo* stink)]

**fě'tĭsh** *n.* Inanimate object worshipped by primitive peoples; principle etc. irrationally reverenced; (Psych.) abnormal stimulus, or object, of sexual desire; **∼ĭsm, ∼ĭst**, *ns.*; **∼i'stĭc** *a.* [F f. Port. f. L (FACTITIOUS)]

**fě'tlŏck** *n.* Part of horse's leg where

tuft of hair grows behind pastern-joint. [FOOT]

**fě'tter. 1.** *n.* Shackle for the feet; bond, (in *pl.*) captivity; restraint. **2.** *v.t.* Bind (as) with fetters. [E]

**fě'ttle** *n.* Condition, trim, (*in fine fettle*). [E]

**\*fě'tus.** See FOETUS.

**feud**[1]. **1.** *n.* Lasting mutual hostility, esp. between tribes or families with murderous assaults in revenge for injury. **2.** *v.i.* Conduct feud. [F f. Gmc (FOE)]

**feud**[2] *n.* Land held under feudal system or in fee, fief. [L *feudum* FEE]

**feu'dal** *a.* (∼ly). Of a FEUD[2] (∼ **system**, medieval European form of government based on relation of vassal and superior arising from holding of land on condition of homage and service); of or resembling this system; **∼ĭsm, ∼ĭst**, *ns.*; **feuda'lĭty** *n.*, feudal system or principles, feud; **∼ĭze** *v.t.*; **∼ĭza'tion** *n.*; **feu'datŏry**, (*a.*) feudally subject (*to*), (*n.*) feudal vassal or land.

**fě'ver. 1.** *n.* Abnormally high temperature with excessive change and destruction of tissues; disease so characterized; nervous agitation (∼ **heat, pitch**, state of abnormal excitement). **2.** *v.t.* Throw into, affect with, fever or excitement (*fevered brow, imagination*). **3.** **∼ĭsh, ∼ous**, *adjs.*, having symptoms of fever, excited, restless. [E & F f. L *febris*]

**fě'verfew** *n.* Feathery-leaved aromatic herb formerly used as febrifuge. [FEBRIFUGE]

**few** *a. & n.* **1.** Not many, a small number (of), (*a man of few words*; *few and* FAR *between*; *every* ∼ *days* etc., once in every small group of days etc.; **no ∼er than**, as many as; **not a ∼**, a considerable number; **the ∼**, the minority). **2. A ∼**, some, several; **a good ∼, quite a ∼**, (colloq.) a fair number (of); **have a ∼**, (colloq.) take several alcoholic drinks; **some ∼**, some but not many. [E]

**fey** (fā) *a.* Unearthly, magical, whimsical; (Sc.) fated to die soon, mentally disordered. [E, = doomed to die]

**fěz** *n.* (*pl.* ∼'zes). Muslim man's flat-topped conical red cap with tassel. [Turk.]

**ff.** *abbr.* following pages etc.

**ff** *abbr.* fortissimo.

**fiancé** (fĭah'nsă) *n.* (*fem.* ∼**e** *pr.*

same). Person who is engaged to marry another. [F]

**fiă′scō** n. (pl. ~s). Failure; ignominious result. [It.; see FLASK]

**fī′ăt** (or -at) n. Authorization; decree, order. [L, = let it be done]

**fíb** n., & v.i. (-bb-). (Tell) trivial lie; ~′ber, ~′ster, ns. [perh. f. redupl. of FABLE]

**fī′bre** (-ber), *****fī′ber**, n. Threadlike cell or filament in animal and vegetable tissue or textile substance; threadlike piece of glass etc. (~**glass**, (plastic containing) fibrous glass woven as fabric or used as insulator etc.); substance, structure, formed of fibres; character (*lacks moral fibre*); ~**-board**, material of compressed wood etc. fibres; **fī′bril** n., small fibre; **fī′broid**, (a.) fibre-like, (n.) fibroid uterine tumour; **fībrō′sis** n., development of excessive fibrous tissue; **fibrosi′tis** n., rheumatic inflammation or disorder of fibrous tissue; **fī′brous** a. [F f. L *fibra*]

**fī′būl**a n. (pl. ~ae, ~as). Bone on outer side of lower leg; ~**ar** a. [L, = brooch]

**-fic** suf. forming adjs. (usu. w. -i-) w. sense 'producing, making' (*beatific, pacific*). [F or L *facio* make)]

**-ficā′tion** suf. forming ns. of action (usu. w. -i-) f. vbs. in -FY (*purification, simplification*).

**fiche** (fēsh) n. (pl. same). = MICRO-*fiche*. [abbr.]

**fī′ckle** a. (-kly). Inconstant, changeable. [E]

**fī′ction** n. Invention; invented statement or narrative; prose literature concerning imaginary events and characters; conventionally accepted falsehood (LEGAL, *polite, fiction*); ~**al** a. (-lly); ~**alize** v.t. [F f. L (FEIGN)]

**ficti′tious** (-shus) a. Not genuine; (of name etc.) assumed; imaginary.

**fī′ddle. 1.** n. Violin (colloq. or derog.; **as fit as a** ~, in good health or spirits; **play first, second,** ~, take leading, subordinate, position); (sl.) piece of cheating. **2.** v.i. & t. Play fiddle, play (tune) on fiddle; trifle (*at*), fidget (*with*), move aimlessly (*about*); (sl.) cheat, swindle, falsify, get by cheating. **3.** ~**-de-dee′** int. & n., nonsense; ~**-faddle**, (n.) trivial matters, (v.i.) fuss, trifle; ~**stick**, bow for fiddle, (usu. in pl., as int.) nonsense. **4.** **fī′ddler** n., player on fiddle, small crab, (sl.)

swindler; **fī′ddling, fī′ddlÿ**, adjs., (colloq.) trifling, awkward to do or use. [E]

**fidě′litÿ** n. Faithfulness, loyalty, (*to*); accuracy; (Radio etc.) precision of reproduction (HIGH *fidelity*). [F or L (*fides* faith)]

**fī′dget. 1.** n. Restless state with spasmodic movements, restless mood, (also in pl.); one who fidgets; ~**ÿ** a. (~iness). **2.** v.i. & t. Move restlessly; be or make uneasy. [obs. or dial. *fidge* to twitch]

**fidū′ciary** (-sherĭ). **1. a.** Of, held or given in, trust; (of paper currency) depending for its value on public confidence or securities. **2. n.** Trustee. [L (*fiducia* trust)]

**fie** int. expr. disgust or pretence of outraged propriety. [F f. L]

**fief** (fēf) n. = FEUD[2]; one's sphere of operation or control; ~′**dom** n. [F (FEE)]

**field. 1.** n. (Piece of) land, esp. for pasture or crops, usu. bounded by hedges etc.; area rich in some natural product (*coal, gold, oil, -field*); place of battle or campaign (**hold the** ~, not be superseded; **in the** ~, campaigning, fig. working outside headquarters etc.; **take the** ~, begin campaign); piece of land for specified purpose, esp. for games, (AIR*field;* PLAYING-*field*); participants in contest or sport; all competitors or all but specified one(s); expanse of ice, sea, snow, etc.; (Her.) surface of escutcheon; ground of picture, coin, flag, etc.; area of operation, influence, etc., (*field of view; gravitational, magnetic, field*); force exerted by magnetic etc. field on standard object. **2.** attrib. (Of animal etc.) found in open country, wild, (*field-mouse*); (of artillery etc.) light and mobile for use on campaign; carried out or working in the natural environment, not in laboratory etc., (*field test*). **3.** v.i. & t. Act as fieldsman in cricket etc., stop (and return) (ball); (fig.) deal with (succession of questions etc.); select (team or individual) to play in a game. **4.** ~**-day,** (Mil.) manœuvring-exercise or review, (fig.) important or successful day or occasion; ~ **events,** athletic contests other than races; ~′**fare,** species of thrush; ~**-glasses,** binoculars for outdoor use; ~ **hospital,** temporary hospital near battlefield; ||**F~ Marshal,** Army officer of highest rank; ~ **officer,** Army officer above captain and below general; ~'**sman,** (Crick., Baseball) person on side which is not batting; ~ **sports,** outdoor sports, esp. hunting, shooting, and fishing; ~**work,** temporary fortification, outdoor work of surveyor etc.; so ~**-worker.** [E]

**fiend** n. The Devil; demon; superhumanly wicked or cruel person; person causing mischief or annoyance; addict, devotee, (dope, fresh-air, fiend); ~'**ish** a., very wicked or cruel. [E]

**fierce** a. Violent in hostility; ardent, eager; raging, vehement; (of heat etc.) intense. [F & L ferus savage]

**fier'y** (fīr'ĭ) a. (-ily, -iness). Consisting of fire, flaming; blazing-red; (of eyes) flashing; hot as fire; producing burning sensation, inflaming; irritable, pugnacious, spirited; ~ **cross,** wooden cross burnt or set on fire as rallying signal in Scotland or *intimidating symbol. [FIRE]

**fiĕ'sta** (fĕ-) n. Festivity, holiday. [Sp.]

**fife** n. Shrill flute used with drum in military music; its player. [G pfeife PIPE or F fifre]

**fiftee'n** (or fĭf'-) a. & n. NUMERAL; (Rugby Footb.) team of 15 players; ~**th** a. & n. [E (FIVE, -TEEN)]

**fifth** a. & n. NUMERAL; *(colloq.) (bottle containing) fifth of a gallon of liquor; ~ **column,** organized body sympathizing with and working for the enemy within a country at war etc. [f. remark in Sp. Civil War 1936]; ~**co'lumnist,** member of fifth column, traitor, spy; ~ **wheel,** superfluous person or thing; ~'**ly** adv. [E (FIVE)]

**fi'fty** a. & n. NUMERAL; large indefinite number; ~-~, half and half, (shared) equally, (go fifty-fifty; on a fifty-fifty basis); ~'**ftieth** a. & n.

**fĭg**[1] n. ~(-tree), broad-leaved tree with soft pear-shaped many-seeded fruit eaten fresh or dried; fruit of this tree; valueless thing (don't care a fig for); ~**-leaf,** device for concealing something, esp. genitals; ~'**wort,** brown-flowered herb. [F & L ficus]

**fĭg**[2]. 1. v.t. (-gg-). ~ **out, up,** dress up (person). 2. n. Dress (in full fig). [obs. feague (FAKE)]

**fig.** abbr. figure.

**fight** (fīt). 1. v.i. & t. (**fought** pr. fawt). Contend or struggle physically in war, battle, single combat, etc.,

(against, with; for, on behalf of person or to secure thing); contend thus with (person); contend about (case, election, etc.); make one's way by fighting; strive to overcome (disease, fire, etc.); ~ **back,** resist; ~ **down,** suppress; ~ **off,** repel with effort; ~ **out,** settle (dispute etc.) by fighting; ~ **shy of,** avoid. 2. n. Fighting, battle, combat, (**make a ~ of it, put up a ~, show ~,** resist); boxing-match; (fig.) strife, conflict, struggle; power or inclination to fight (has fight in him). 3. ~**ing chance,** opportunity of succeeding by great effort; ~**ing fit,** very fit; ~**ing mad,** furiously angry. 4. ~'**er** n., (esp.) fast aircraft designed for attacking other aircraft. [E]

**fĭg'ment** n. Merely imaginary thing; invented statement. [L (FEIGN)]

**figūrā'tion** n. Act or mode of formation; ornamentation. [F or L (FIGURE)]

**fĭ'gŭrătĭve** (or -ger-) a. Metaphorical; abounding in figures of speech; emblematic; of pictorial or sculptural representation. [L (foll.)]

**fĭ'gure** (-ger). 1. n. External form; bodily shape (keep one's ~, not grow stout); (Geom.) space enclosed by line(s) or surface(s); person as seen (a figure emerged); ~ **of fun,** grotesque person) or as viewed mentally (FATHER-figure; **public ~,** well-known person); conspicuous appearance (cut a poor etc. ~, make poor etc. impression); representation of human form; type, typical person; image; ~ **(of speech),** expression using words differently from literal meaning, esp. metaphor or hyperbole; diagram, illustration; decorative pattern; series of movements forming a single unit in dancing, skating, etc.; symbol of number, numeral, esp. 0–9, (**double, three,** etc., ~**s,** 10–99, 100–999, etc.; figure of EIGHT); (in pl.) arithmetical calculations; value, amount of money; ~**head,** carved bust etc. over ship's prow, merely nominal leader etc. 2. v.t. & i. Represent in diagram or picture; imagine, picture mentally; be symbol of; appear, make appearance; embellish with pattern (figured satin); mark with numbers (figured BASS[3]) or prices; calculate, do arithmetic; *understand, consider; *(colloq.) be likely or understandable (*that figures*); *~ **on**, count on, expect; *~ **out**, work out by arithmetic or logic, *estimate, understand. [F f. L *figura* (FEIGN)]

**fi´gŭrine** (-ēn) *n.* Statuette. [F f. It. (prec.)]

**fi´lament** *n.* Threadlike body, fibre; conducting wire or thread in electric bulb or thermionic valve; part of stamen that supports anther; ~ar̆y̆, ~ous, (-ĕ´n-) *adjs.* [F or L (*filum* thread)]

**fi´lbert** *n.* (Nut of) cultivated hazel. [AF (because ripe about St. *Philibert*'s day)]

**filch** *v.t.* Steal, pilfer. [orig. unkn.]

**file**[1]. **1.** *n.* Instrument usu. of steel roughened for shaping or smoothing objects. **2.** *v.t.* Smooth or shape with file; elaborate, polish, (writing etc.); ~ **away**, **off**, remove (roughness etc.) with file; **fi´ling** *n.*, (esp., usu. in *pl.*) particle(s) rubbed off by file. [E]

**file**[2]. **1.** *n.* Stiff pointed wire on which papers are kept; folder etc. for holding papers arranged for reference; papers so kept, esp. in office or in lawcourt; collection of records for use by computer; line of persons etc. one behind another (**Indian**, **single**, ~, arrangement of marchers etc. in file, with no two abreast; RANK[1] *and file*). **2.** *v.t.* Place (papers) in or on file or among public records; submit (application for patent, petition for divorce, etc.); (of reporter) send (story etc.) to newspaper; march in file. [F f. L *filum* thread]

**fi´lial** *a.* (~ly). Of, due from, son or daughter. [F or L (*filius*, -*a*, son, daughter)]

**fi´libŭster**. **1.** *n.* One who engages in unauthorized warfare against foreign State; obstruction(ist) in legislative assembly. **2.** *v.i.* Act as filibuster. [Du. (FREEBOOTER)]

**fi´ligree** *n.* Fine tracery of gold etc. wire, fine metal open-work; similar delicate thing. [F -*grane* f. It. f. L *filum* thread, *granum* seed]

**fi´ling.** See FILE[1].

**Filipi´no** (-pē´-) *n.* (*pl.* ~s) & *a.* (Native) of the Philippine Islands. [Sp., = Philippine]

**fill. 1.** *v.t.* & *i.* Make or become full (*with*); (of sail) be distended by wind; stock abundantly, occupy completely, spread over, pervade,

(~ **the bill**, do all that is required, suffice); block up (cavity, hollow tooth); satisfy, satiate; hold or discharge duties of (office etc.); carry out or supply (order, commission, etc.); occupy (vacant time); appoint person to hold (vacant post); ~ **in**, add what is wanted to complete (document etc.), fill (hole etc.) completely, spend (time) in a temporary activity, act as substitute, *(colloq.) inform (person) more fully; ~ **out**, enlarge, become enlarged or plumper, to the proper size, * = *fill in* (document etc.); ~ **up**, fill completely, supply vacant parts etc. in, fill petrol tank of (motor vehicle), become full, = *fill in* (document etc.). **2.** *n.* As much as one wants or can bear of food etc. (*eat your fill*; *wept her fill*); enough to fill thing. **3.** ~´**er** *n.*, (esp.) material used to fill cavity or increase bulk; ~**er cap** (closing pipe to petrol tank of motor vehicle); ~´**ing** *n.* (esp. of hollow tooth or of sandwich); ~**ing station**, establishment selling petrol etc. to motorists. [E]

**fi´llĕt. 1.** *n.* Boneless piece of fish or meat; ~ (**steak**), undercut of sirloin; band worn round head, ribbon for binding hair etc.; narrow strip or ridge; (Archit.) narrow flat band between mouldings or flutes. **2.** *v.t.* Remove bones from (fish etc.); divide (fish etc.) into fillets; bind or provide with fillet(s). [F f. L (*filum* thread)]

**fi´llip. 1.** *n.* Sudden release of bent finger or thumb held back by thumb or finger; smart stroke so given; stimulus, incentive. **2.** *v.t.* & *i.* Propel, stimulate, (coin, memory) with fillip; give fillip (to). [imit.]

**fi´lly** *n.* Young female horse; (sl.) young, esp. lively, woman. [N]

**film. 1.** *n.* Thin coating or layer; (roll or sheet of) plastic or other flexible base coated with light--sensitive emulsion for exposure in a camera; story etc. recorded on cinematographic film; (in *pl.*) the cinema industry; dimness or morbid growth affecting eyes; slight veil of haze etc.; ~´**setting**, (Print.) photographic composing; ~ **star**, well--known actor or actress in films; ~-**strip**, series of transparencies in a strip for projection. **2.** *v.t.* & *i.* Cover, become covered, with a film; photograph (scene, story, etc.) on cinematographic film; be (*well*) suited for reproduction on film. **3.** ~'ў *a.* (~ily, ~iness), like a thin film. [E]

**fi′lter. 1.** *n.* Device for purifying liquid, air, etc., by passing it through a porous substance; ~ (**tip**), (cigarette containing) pad of absorbent material to purify smoke; screen for absorbing or modifying light, X-rays, etc.; (Electr.) circuit to weaken signals not of particular frequencies; arrangement for filtering of traffic; **~-paper**, porous paper for filtering. **2.** *v.t. & i.* Pass (liquid, light, etc.) or flow through filter; make way through, *through*, *into*, etc.; (fig. of news etc.) leak *out* or come *through*; (of road traffic) merge with other vehicles by passing on one side of a stream of stationary traffic; ~ **out**, separate or hold back (as) by filtering. **3.** **fi′ltrāte**, (*n.*) filtered liquid, (*v.t. & i.*) filter; **filtrā′tion** *n.* [F f. L f. Gmc (FELT[1])]

**filth** *n.* Loathsome dirt; corruption; vileness; obscenity; ~'ў, (*a.*; ~ily, ~iness) of or like filth (**~y lucre**, dishonourable gain, joc. money), colloq., of weather) very unpleasant, (*adv.*) filthily, extremely, (*filthy dirty, rich*). [E (FOUL)]

**fi′ltrāte, filtrā′tion.** See FILTER.

**fin** *n.* Fish's propelling and steering organ (**~-back**, ~ **whale**, rorqual); underwater swimmer's flipper; small projecting surface on aircraft or rocket to ensure stability; projection on other devices to improve heat transfer etc. or on motor car (esp. *tail-fin*). [E]

**fina′gle** *v.i. & t.* (colloq.) Act, obtain, dishonestly or by trickery. [dial. *fainaigue* cheat]

**fi′nal. 1.** *a.* (~ly). Situated at the end, coming last; conclusive, definite, unalterable; concerned with purpose (~ **cause**, ultimate purpose; ~ **clause**, Gram., clause expressing purpose). **2.** *n.* Final thing; last or deciding heat or game in sports etc.; (in *sing.* or *pl.*) final examination; last edition of day's newspaper. **3.** **fina′le** (-nah′-) *n.*, last movement, scene, etc., of musical piece, drama, etc., conclusion; **~ist** *n.*, competitor in final; **fina′lity** *n.*, quality or fact of being final; **~ize** *v.t.*, complete, bring to an end, put in final form, approve final form of; **~izā′tion** *n.* [F or L (*finis* end)]

**fina′nce** (*or* fi′-). **1.** *n.* Management of (esp. public) money; money support for an undertaking (~ **company, house**, company mainly concerned with providing money for hire-purchase transactions); (in *pl.*) money resources of State, company, or person. **2.** *v.t.* Provide with money, esp. capital. **3.** **fina′ncial** (-shal) *a.* (-lly; *financial* YEAR); **fina′ncier** *n.*, one skilled in finance, capitalist. [F (FINE[1])]

**finch** *n.* Small passerine bird. [E]

**find. 1.** *v.t.* (**found**). Discover, become aware of, or get possession of, by chance or by search, (*found dead*); receive, obtain, succeed in getting, (*can't find time to read*); ~ **favour**, be acceptable; ~ one's **feet** or **legs**, be able to stand, develop one's powers); recognize, acknowledge, experience, (*find no sense in it, difficulty in breathing*; *find* FAULT *with*); discover, learn, prove by trial, (*finds England too cold*; *I find it pay(s), that it pays*); ascertain by inquiry, calculation, etc., (*find the time of the next train, the cube root of 64*); reach by natural process (*water finds its level*); (Law) judge and declare (*the jury found him guilty, it murder, that*, or *abs.*); ~ **against, for**, decide against, in favour of, (person), judge to be guilty, innocent); provide, supply free of charge (**all found**, with board, lodging, etc., provided free); ~ **out**, discover, solve, detect; ~ one**self**, discover that one is, discover one's vocation; ~ one's or **its way**, arrive at place or position. **2.** *n.* Discovery of treasure etc.; thing found; person who comes to notice. **3.** ~'**er** *n.*, (esp.) small telescope attached to large one to locate object, viewfinder; **~ers keepers**, (colloq.) whoever finds a thing is entitled to keep it; ~'**ing** *n.*, (esp.) conclusion reached by judicial etc. inquiry. [E]

**fin de siècle** (făṅdesyä′kl) *a.* Characteristic of end of 19th c.; decadent. [F, = end of century]

**fine[1]. 1.** *n.* Sum of money (to be) paid as penalty for offence; **in ~**, to sum up, in fine. **2.** *v.t.* Punish by fine (*fined him £5*). [F *fin* settlement of dispute (L *finis* end)]

**fine[2]** *a., n., adv., & v.* **1.** *a.* Of high quality; pure, refined; (of gold or silver) containing specified proportion of pure metal; delicate, subtle, (*a fine distinction*); (of feelings) refined; very small, slender, sharp, (*not to* *put too fine a* POINT *on it*; **cut, run, it ~**, allow very little margin of time etc.); excellent (*fine performance*; iron., *a fine friend you are!*); of handsome appearance or size, beautiful, imposing; in good health; (of weather) bright, free from rain, (*one of these fine* DAYS); (of speech) complimentary; smart, showy, ornate, (~ **feathers,** gaudy dress); fastidious, affectedly refined; ~ **art,** (usu. in *pl.*) art appealing to mind or to sense of beauty, esp. painting, sculpture, architecture; ~**-tooth comb,** comb with narrow close-set teeth, (fig.) detailed search. **2.** *n.* Fine weather; (in *pl.*) small particles in mining, milling, etc. **3.** *adv.* Finely (~**-spun,** delicate, too subtle); (colloq.) very well (*that will suit me fine*). **4.** *v.t. & i.* ~ (**away, down, off**), make or become pure, clear, thinner, etc. **5. fi′nery** *n.*, showy dress or decoration. [F *fin* f. L *finio* to FINISH]

**fines herbes** (fēnzár′b) *n.pl.* Mixed herbs used in cooking, esp. as omelette-flavouring. [F, = fine herbs]

**finĕ′sse. 1.** *n.* Subtle manipulation; artfulness; (Cards) attempt to take trick with card that is not the highest and might lose to an opponent's card. **2.** *v.i. & t.* Use finesse; achieve by finesse; (Cards) make a finesse (with). [F (FINE[2])]

**fi′nger** (-ngg-). **1.** *n.* One of terminal members of hand (esp. other than thumb; BURN[2], CROSS, one's *fingers; finger in the* PIE[2]; one's ~**s are all thumbs,** one is clumsy; one's ~**s itch,** one is eager; **get, pull, take,** one's ~ **out,** sl., hurry up, begin work in earnest; **lay a ~ on,** touch, however slightly; **let slip through** one's ~**s,** lose hold of, miss opportunity of; **lift, move, raise, a ~,** make the slightest effort; **little ~,** finger farthest from thumb; **point ~ at,** esp. in scorn; **put** one's ~ **on,** locate or identify exactly; **twist round** one's **little ~,** persuade or manage (person) easily; part of glove for finger; finger-like object (FISH[1] *finger*); long narrow structure; breadth of finger, esp. (sl.) that depth of liquor in a glass. **2.** *v.t.* Feel, turn about, with the fingers; play (music or instrument) with the fingers, esp. in particular way; mark (music) with signs showing which fingers to use. **3.** ~ **alphabet,** deaf-and-dumb alphabet; ~**-board,** part

of neck of violin etc. on which fingers press strings; ~**-bowl** (for rinsing fingers during meal); *finger* LANGUAGE; ~**-mark,** mark left on surface by (dirty) finger; ~**-paint** *n.*, & *v.i.*, (use) paint that can be applied by the fingers; ~**-plate** (on door to prevent finger-marks); ~**-post,** signpost at road-junction; ~**print,** (*n.*) impression made on surface by fingers, esp. used for identifying criminals, (fig.) distinctive characteristic, (*v.t.*) record fingerprint(s) of (person); ~**-stall,** cover to protect finger; ~**tip,** tip of finger (**have at** one's ~**tips,** be fully conversant with; **to** one's ~**tips,** completely). **4.** ~**ing**[1] *n.*, (esp.) (indication of) use of fingers to play musical instrument. [E]

**fi′ngering**[2] (-ngg-) *n.* Fine wool for knitting. [perh. F *fin grain* fine grain]

**fi′nial** *n.* Ornamental top to gable, canopy, etc. [AF (FINE[1])]

**fi′nical** (~ly), **fi′nicking, fi′nicky,** *adjs.* Over-particular, fastidious; excessively detailed. [perh. FINE[2] + *-ical*]

**fi′nis** *n.* End, esp. of a book. [L]

**fi′nish. 1.** *v.t. & i.* ~ (**off, up**), bring or come to an end, come to the end of (thing, action, or do*ing*); make perfect, put final touches to; complete education of (girl at *finishing-school*); ~ **off,** (esp.) kill; ~ **with,** complete one's use of or association with. **2.** *n.* End, last stage, esp. of fox-hunt (*be in at the finish*, lit. or fig.); point at which race etc. ends; completed state, what serves to complete; mode of surface treatment (esp. of furniture); **fight to a** or **the ~** (till one party is defeated or exhausted). [F f. L (*finis* end)]

**fi′nite** *a.* Bounded, limited, not infinite; (Gram., of verb parts) having specific number and person. [L *finitus* (prec.)]

**Finn** *n.* Native of Finland; ~′**ic** *a.*; ~′**ish** *a. & n.*, (language) of the Finns. [E]

**fi′nnan** *n.* ~ (**haddock**), haddock cured with smoke of green wood, turf, or peat. [*Findhorn, Findon,* places]

**fiord, fjord,** (fy-) *n.* Narrow arm of sea between cliffs, as in Norway. [Norw.]

**fi′pple** *n.* Plug at end of whistle

etc.; ~ **flute**, flute played by blowing endwise. [orig. unkn.]

**fir** n. ~(-**tree**), evergreen coniferous tree with needles placed singly on the shoots (cf. PINE²); its wood; ~-**cone**, its fruit; ~'**rў** a. [N]

**fire. 1.** n. State of combustion, condition of burning, active principle operative in this, flame, incandescence, (CATCH or TAKE *fire*; **there is no smoke without ~**, rumour is never entirely baseless; **on ~**, burning, fig. excited; **play with ~**, take foolish risks; SET¹ *fire to, on fire*; **set the Thames or world on ~**, do something remarkable); burning fuel in grate etc. (*the* FAT *is in the fire*; *many* IRONS *in the fire*; PULL *out of the fire*); = ELECTRIC, GAS, etc., *fire*; destructive blaze (*the Fire of London*; *forest fire*; **go through ~ and water**, face all perils); burning heat, fever; fervour, spirit, vivacity, poetic inspiration, (~ **in** one's **belly**, ambition, enthusiasm); firing of guns (CEASE, HANG, LINE¹ *of fire*; **under ~**, being shot at, adversely criticized, etc.). **2.** v.t. & i. Set fire to with intention of destroying; catch fire; (of cylinder of internal combustion engine) undergo ignition of its fuel; become heated or excited; redden; bake or dry (pottery, bricks, etc.); supply (furnace etc.) with fuel; cause (gun, explosive) to explode or ignite (~ **a salute**, fire guns as salute); shoot (*at, on*, etc.); propel (missile) from gun etc.; stimulate (imagination); fill (person) with enthusiasm; ~ **away**, shoot continuously, (fig.) start talking etc.; ~ (\***out**), expel, dismiss (person). **3.** ~-**alarm**, device giving warning of fire; ~ **and brimstone**, torment in hell; ~'**arm**, (usu. in *pl.*) gun, pistol, etc.; ~-**ball**, large meteor, ball of flame from nuclear explosion, energetic person; ~-**bomb**, incendiary bomb; ~-**box**, fuel-chamber of steam-engine or boiler; ~'**brand**, piece of burning wood, (fig.) kindler of strife; ~-**break**, obstacle to spread of fire in forest etc.; ~-**brick**, fireproof brick for grate etc.; ~-**brigade**, organized body of firemen; ~-**bug**, (colloq.) pyromaniac; ~-**clay**, (kind used for fire-bricks); \*~-**cracker**, explosive firework; ~'**damp**, (miners' name for) methane; ~'**dog**, andiron; ~-**drill**, rehearsal of procedure to be used if

fire breaks out; ~-**eater**, conjurer who (allegedly) swallows fire, quarrelsome person; ~-**engine**, vehicle carrying equipment used to extinguish large fires; ~-**escape**, apparatus or emergency staircase for escape from building on fire; *fire* EXTINGUISHER; ~-**fighter**, one whose task is to extinguish fires; ~'**fly**, beetle emitting phosphorescent light; ~-**guard**, protective frame or grating in front of fireplace; ~ **insurance** (against losses by fire); ~-**irons**, tongs, poker, and shovel, for tending domestic fire; ~'**light**, light from fire in fireplace; ‖~-**lighter**, piece of inflammable material etc. to help start fire in grate; ~'**man**, one who tends furnace or steam-engine fire, man employed to extinguish fires; ~'**place**, grate or hearth for domestic fire; ~-**plug**, connection in water-main for hose; ~-**power**, destructive capacity of guns etc.; ~-**practice**, fire-drill; ~-**proof** a., & v.t., (render) incombustible; ‖~-**raising**, arson; ~'**side**, area round fireplace, home, home-life; ~ **station**, headquarters of fire brigade; ~-**storm**, high wind or storm following fire caused by bombs; ~-**trap**, building without proper exits in case of fire; ~-**walking** (barefoot over hot stones etc.); ~-**watcher**, person watching for fires (esp. those caused by bombs); ~-**water**, (colloq.) strong alcoholic liquor; ~'**wood**, wood for fuel; ~'**work**, device giving spectacular effects by use of combustibles, explosives, etc., (fig., in *pl.*) display of wit, anger, etc. **4.** fir'**ing** n., (esp.) fuel, discharge of guns; **firing-line**, front line of battle, lit. or fig.; **firing-party, -squad**, group which fires salute at military funeral or performs military execution. [E]

**firm**¹ n. (Partners carrying on) a business (LONG¹ *firm*); group of persons, esp. hospital doctors and assistants, working together. [Sp. & It. f. L *firma*; cf. foll.]

**firm**² a., adv., & v. **1.** a. Of solid structure; fixed, stable, steady; steadfast, resolute; (of prices; goods) maintaining their level or value; (of offer etc.) not liable to cancellation after acceptance. **2.** adv. Firmly (*stand, hold, firm*). **3.** v.t. & i. ~ (**up**), make or become firm or secure. [F f. L *firmus*]

**fir′mam|ent** n. (literary). Vault or arch of heaven; sky; ~**e′ntal** a. [F f. L (*firmus*, prec.)]

**fir′ry.** See FIR.

**first** a., n., & adv. (see also NUMERAL). **1.** a. Earliest in time or order, next encountered, (*the first cuckoo*; *first turning to the left*; *at first* BLUSH or SIGHT; *shall do it* etc. ~ **thing**, colloq., before anything else; ~ **things** ~, do the most important things before any others; **not know the** ~ **thing about**, know nothing about); basic, evident, (*first principles*); foremost in position, rank, etc., (HEAD *first*); most willing or likely (*be the first to admit it*); (Mus.) performing highest or chief part (*first violins*). **2.** n. First person or thing (**at** ~, at the beginning; **from** ~ **to last**, throughout; **from the** ~, from the beginning). **3.** adv. Before anyone or anything else (*first and foremost*; *first of all*; ~**-born** a. & n., eldest (child); ~ **come,** ~ **served,** those who arrive first will be served first); before someone or something else (*must get this done first*); in preference (*I'll see you damned first*); for the first time (*when did you first see her?*). **4.** ~ **aid,** help given to injured until medical treatment is available; *first* BASE[2], BLOOD; *First* CAUSE; ~ **class,** best group or category, best accommodation in train, ship, etc., (place in) highest category of achievement in examination; ~**-class** a. & adv., of or by the first class, excellent; *first* COUSIN; ~**-day cover,** envelope with stamps postmarked on first day of issue; *first* FLOOR; ~**-foot** n., & v.i., (Sc.) (be) first person to cross threshold in New Year; ~**-fruit,** (usu. in pl.) first produce of agriculture for the season esp. as offered to God, (fig.) first results of work etc.; *first* GEAR; ~**hand,** direct, original, (*at first hand*, directly); *F~ **Lady,** wife of U.S. President; ~ **light,** dawn; *First* LORD; ~ **name,** personal or Christian name; ~ **night,** first public performance of play etc.; ~ **offender** (against whom no previous conviction is recorded); ~ **officer,** mate on merchant ship; *first* PERSON, QUARTER; ~**-rate,** excellent(ly), (colloq.) very well (*feeling first-rate*); *first* REFUSAL; ~ **strike,** initial attack with nuclear weapons; *first* STRING, WATER; ~**ly** adv., NUMERAL. [E]

**firth, frith,** n. Arm of sea; estuary. [N (FIORD)]

**fi′scal** a. & n. **1.** a. (~ly). Of public revenue. **2.** n. Legal official in some countries; (Sc.) = PROCURATOR *fiscal*. [F, or L *fiscalis* (*fiscus* treasury)]

**fish[1]. 1.** n. (pl. usu. **fish**). Vertebrate cold-blooded animal with gills and fins (**drink like a** ~, excessively; **feed the** ~**es,** be drowned, be seasick; ~ **out of water,** person not in his element; *pretty* KETTLE *of fish*); any animal living in water (CUTTLE*fish,* JELLY*fish,* SHELL*fish*); (colloq.) person (*cold, queer, fish*); flesh of fish as food (*fish, flesh, and fowl*; **neither** ~, **flesh, nor good red herring,** of vague character; **other** ~ **to fry,** more important business to attend to); (in *sing.* or *pl.*) sign of ZODIAC. **2.** v.i. & t. Try to catch fish (~ **in troubled waters,** make profit out of disturbances; do this in (stream etc.); search (*for* thing) in water or concealed place; seek by indirect means *for* (compliments, secrets, etc.); ~ **out, up,** (colloq.) pull from pocket etc. **3.** ~ **and chips,** fried fish and fried chipped potatoes; ~**-bowl,** glass bowl for keeping fish in; ~ **cake,** small cake of shredded fish and mashed potato; ~**-eye,** (of lens) wide-angled; ~ **finger,** small oblong piece of fish in batter or bread-crumbs; ~**-fork** (for eating or serving fish); *fish-*HOOK; ~**-kettle,** oval pan for boiling fish; ~**-knife** (for eating or serving fish); ~**-meal,** ground dried fish as fertilizer etc.; ||~**′monger,** dealer in fish; ~**-net,** (of fabric) open-meshed; ~**-pond,** pond in which fish are kept, (joc.) the sea; ~**-slice,** carving-knife for fish, cook's implement for turning fish; ~**-tail,** (thing) shaped like fish's tail; ~**′wife,** woman selling fish. **4.** ~**′er** n., fishing animal, (arch.) fisherman; ~**erman,** man who lives by fishing, angler; ~**′ery** n., business of fishing, fishing-ground; ~**′ing** n.; ~**ing-line, -rod,** (used with baited hook in fishing). [E]

**fish[2]** n. Piece of wood or iron etc. to strengthen mast, beam, etc. (~**-plate,** one of two holding rails together). [F *ficher* f. L *figere* FIX]

**fi′sh|y** a. (~ily, ~iness). Of or like fish (*fishy smell, taste*); (of eye) dull; rich in fish; (sl.) dubious, open to suspicion. [FISH[1]]

**fi′ssile** a. Tending to split;

capable of undergoing nuclear fission. [L (FISSURE)]

**fi′ssion** (-shŏn). **1.** *n.* Division of cell etc. into new ones as mode of reproduction; (**nuclear**) ~, splitting of heavy atomic nucleus spontaneously or on impact of another particle, with release of energy (~ **bomb**, atomic bomb). **2.** *v.i. & t.* (Cause to) undergo fission. [L (foll.)]

**fi′ssure** (-sher). **1.** *n.* Opening, usu. long and narrow, made esp. by cracking or splitting; (Bot., Anat.) narrow opening in organ etc.; cleavage. **2.** *v.t. & i.* Split, crack. [F, or L (*findo fiss-* cleave)]

**fist. 1.** *n.* Clenched hand esp. as used in boxing; (joc.) hand (*give us your fist*), handwriting. **2.** *v.t.* Strike with fist. **3.** ~′**ic(al)** *adjs.*, (joc.) pugilistic; ~′**icuffs** *n.pl.*, fighting with fists. [E]

**fi′stul|a** *n.* Pipe-like ulcer; surgically made body-passage; ~**ar**, ~**ous**, *adjs.* [L, = pipe]

**fit¹** *n.* Sudden passing or recurring attack of an illness; sudden seizure of hysteria, apoplexy, fainting, paralysis, or epilepsy; (fig.) attack of strong feeling (*give person a* ~, surprise or outrage him; *have a* ~, be greatly surprised or outraged); sudden transitory state (*of energy*, idleness, etc., **by, in,** ~**s and starts,** spasmodically); mood (*when the fit was on him*). [E]

**fit²** *a., v., & n.* **1.** *a.* (-tt-). Well suited or qualified, competent, worthy, (*food fit for a king*); proper, befitting, (*it is fit that; see,* **think,** ~ **to,** decide esp. unwisely to); in suitable condition, ready, (*laughing fit to bust*); ~ **to be tied,** sl., extremely angry); in good health or condition (*fit as a* FIDDLE; SURVIVAL *of the fittest*). **2.** *v.t. & i.* (-tt-). Be in harmony with, befit; be of right size and shape (for) (*coat does not fit him, does not fit; the* CAP *fits*); cause to do this (~**ted carpet,** carpet cut to fit floor exactly; ~**ted coat,** coat shaped to fit person's figure); adapt (*for, to,* person or thing; *to do*); make competent (*for, to do*); supply (ship etc.) *with*; ~ **in,** (cause to) be in suitable or harmonious place or relation (*with* other things, *to* space), find space or time for (object, engagement, etc.); ~ **on,** put or go into position on, try on (garment); ~ **out, up,** equip (*with*). **3.** *n.* Way in

which garment, machine-part, etc., fits (*a bad, tight, fit*). **4.** ~′**ment** (-), piece of furniture; ~′**ter** *n.,* (esp.) person engaged in fitting, cutting, etc., of garments, mechanic who fits together and adjusts machine; ~′**ting,** (*n.,* esp.) action of fitting on a garment, (usu. in *pl.*) fixture(s), apparatus, furniture, (*a.,* esp.) proper, befitting. [orig. unkn.]

**fi′tchew** (-ōō) *n.* Polecat. [F f. Du.]

**fi′tful** *a.* (~**ly**) Active or occurring spasmodically or intermittently. [FIT¹]

**fi′tment, fi′tting.** See FIT².

**five** *a. & n.* NUMERAL; ~ **o′clock shadow,** beard-growth visible on man's face after about 5 p.m.; ‖~′**stones,** = JACKS; ~-**year plan** (of economic development, orig. in U.S.S.R.); ~′**fōld** (-vf-) *a. & adv.*; **fi′ver** *n.,* £5 or $5 note; ~**s** (-vz) *n.,* ball-game played with gloved hands or bat in court with 3 (**Eton** ~**s**) or 4 (**Rugby** ~**s**) walls. [E]

**fix. 1.** *v.t. & i.* Make firm or stable, fasten, secure; direct steadily (eyes, attention, *on*); attract and hold (attention, person); make or become rigid; (of plant) assimilate (nitrogen, carbon dioxide) by forming non-gaseous compound; congeal, stiffen; make (colour, photographic image, etc.) fast or permanent; single out (person *with* one's *eyes*); place definitely or permanently; determine exact nature, position, etc., of; identify, locate; decide, settle, specify, (price, liability, date, etc.); mend, repair; (colloq.) prepare, deal with, kill (person); (colloq.) obtain support of (person) esp. by bribery; (colloq.) arrange (result of match etc.) fraudulently; (sl.) inject (oneself) with narcotic; ~ **up,** arrange, organize, accommodate; ~ (**up**)**on,** choose, decide on. **2.** *n.* Dilemma, difficult position; act of finding position, position found, by bearings etc.; (sl.) dose of narcotic drug. **3.** ~**ā′te** *v.t.,* direct one's gaze on, (Psych.) cause to acquire abnormal attachment to persons or things; ~**ā′tion** *n.,* fixing, coagulation, process of combining gas to form solid, (Psych.) act, process, of being fixated, (pop.) obsession, concentration on one idea; ~′**ative,** (*a.*) tending to fix, (*n.*) substance used to fix colours etc.; ~**ed** (-kst) *a.,* (esp., *pred.,* colloq.) . situated as regards money etc.; ~ed idea, *idée fixe*; ~ed income (from pension, investment at fixed interest, etc.); ~ed odds (predetermined, in betting); *fixed* STAR; ~'èdlỹ *adv.*, intently; ~'èd-nèss *n.*; ~'er *n.*, (esp.) substance for fixing photographic image etc., one who makes (esp. illicit) arrangements; *\*~'ĭngs* (-z) *n.pl.*, equipment, trimmings of dress or dish; ~'ĭtỹ *n.*, fixed state, stability; ~'ture *n.*, thing fixed in position, (in *pl.*) articles annexed to house or land, person or thing established in one place, (date fixed for) race, match, etc. [L *figo fix*-]

**fizz. 1.** *v.i.* Hiss, splutter. **2.** *n.* Hissing sound; effervescence; (colloq.) effervescent drink; ~'ỹ *a.* (~iness). [imit.]

**fĭ'zzle** *v.i.*, & *n.* (Make) feeble fizz; ~ out, fail feebly. [imit.]

**fjord.** See FIORD.

**fl.** *abbr.* floruit; fluid.

**Fla.** *abbr.* Florida.

**flä'bbergast** (-gah-) *v.t.* (colloq.) Overwhelm with astonishment. [orig. uncert.]

**flă'bb|ỹ** *a.* (~ily, ~iness). (Of flesh etc.) limp, hanging loose; (fig.) feeble. [alt. *flappy* (FLAP)]

**flă'cc|ĭd** (-ks-) *a.* (Of flesh etc., or fig.) flabby; drooping; ~ĭ'dĭtỹ *n.* [F or L (*flaccus* limp)]

**flăg¹** *n.* Plant with bladed leaf, usu. growing on moist ground. [orig. unkn.]

**flăg².** **1.** *n.* ~('stone), flat slab of stone for paving; (in *pl.*) pavement of flags. **2.** *v.t.* (-gg-). Pave with flags. [prob. Scand.; cf. FLAKE]

**flăg³.** **1.** *n.* Piece of cloth or other material, usu. oblong or square, attached by one edge to pole, rope, etc., and used as standard, ensign, signal, etc. (black ~, of pirate or to announce execution; red ~, symbol of danger or of revolution; white ~, of truce or surrender; yellow ~, displayed by ship in quarantine; keep the ~ flying, usu. fig., continue to fight; show the ~, make official visit to foreign port etc., fig. ensure that notice is taken of oneself, one's country, etc.); metal plate showing that taxi is for hire. **2.** *v.t.* (-gg-). Communicate, inform, by flag-signals; mark with flag or tag; ~ (down), signal (vehicle or driver) to stop. **3.** ‖~-day (on which money is raised for a cause by sale of small

paper etc. flags to be worn as sign of having contributed); ~ of convenience, foreign flag under which ship is registered to avoid taxes etc.; ~-officer, admiral, vice-admiral, rear-admiral, or commodore of yacht club; ~ of truce (white, indicating desire to parley); ~'pole, flagstaff; ~'ship (with admiral on board); ~'staff, pole on which flag is hoisted. [orig. unkn.]

**flăg⁴** *v.i.* (-gg-). Become limp, feeble, or uninteresting.

**flä'gellant** (or *flajĕ'-*) *n.* & *a.* (One) who flagellates himself or others. [L *flagello* to whip (*flagellum* whip)]

**flä'gellāte** *v.t.* Scourge, whip, esp. as religious discipline or sexual stimulus; **flägellā'tion, flä'gellātor,** *ns.*

**flägeolĕ't** (-jol-; *or* flä'j-) *n.* Fipple flute with 2 thumb-holes. [F f. Prov.]

**flä'gon** *n.* Large nearly globular bottle for wine etc.; vessel, usu. with handle, lip, and lid, to hold wine for Eucharist or liquor at table. [F f. L *flasco* FLASK]

**flä'grant** *a.* (Of offence or offender) openly wicked, gross, scandalous; ~cỹ *n.* [F or L (*flagro* to blaze)]

**flail.** **1.** *n.* Hand threshing-implement, wooden staff with short heavy stick swinging at end. **2.** *v.t.* & *i.* Beat (as) with flail; wave, swing, wildly or erratically. [E f. L *flagellum* whip]

**flair** *n.* Instinct or ability for selecting or performing what is excellent, useful, etc. [F, = scent, f. L (FRAGRANT)]

**flăk** *n.* Anti-aircraft fire; (fig.) barrage of criticism; ~ jacket, protective jacket of heavy fabric reinforced with metal. [G, *Flieger*ab*wehrk*anone 'aviator-defence-gun']

**flāke.** **1.** *n.* Light fleecy piece, esp. of snow; thin broad piece peeled or chipped off (CORN*flakes*; *soap flakes*); dogfish as food. **2.** *v.i.* & *t.* Fall in, sprinkle with, flakes; take or come *away* or *off* in flakes; ~ out, (colloq.) faint, fall asleep from exhaustion etc.; **flä'kỹ** *a.* (-iness). [orig. unkn.]

**flambé** (flah'nbā) *a.* (Of food) covered with spirit and served alight. [F (foll.)]

**flä'mbeau** (-bō) *n.* (*pl.* ~s, ~x, *pr* -z). Torch, esp. of thick waxed wicks. [F (FLAME)]

**flămboy'an|t** *a.* Florid, showy; ~ce *n.* [F (prec.)]

**flâme.** **1.** *n.* (Portion of) ignited gas (**the ~s**, fire); visible combustion (*burst into flame*; *in flames*); bright light, brilliant (red) colour; passion, esp. love, (FAN[1] *the flame*); (joc.) sweetheart (*my old flame*); **~gun** (throwing flames to destroy weeds etc.); **~-thrower**, weapon for throwing spray of flame. **2.** *v.i.* Emit flames, blaze; (of passion) burst out; (of person) break out into anger (*flame out, up*); shine or glow like flame; **flā′ming** *a.*, (esp.) very hot or bright, (colloq.) passionate (*a flaming row*), = DAMNED. [F f. L *flamma*]

**flamē′ncō** *n.* (*pl.* **~s**). Spanish gipsy style of song or dance. [Sp., = foll.]

**flamī′ngō** (-nggō) *n.* (*pl.* **~s, ~es**). Tall long-necked bird with pink, scarlet, and black plumage. [Port. f. Prov. (FLAME)]

**flă′mmab|le** *a.* Inflammable; **~ı′lĭty** *n.* [L (FLAME)]

**flăn** *n.* Pastry or sponge cake spread or filled with jam, fruit, cheese, etc. [F f. L f. Gmc]

**flănge** (-nj) *n.* Projecting flat rim, collar, or rib, for strengthening or attachment. [orig. uncert.]

**flănk.** **1.** *n.* Fleshy part of side of body between ribs and hip; side of mountain etc. or of body of troops. **2.** *v.t.* Guard, strengthen, attack, on the flank; be at, move along, flank of. [F f Gmc]

**flă′nnel.** **1.** *n.* Woven woollen usu. napless cloth; (in *pl.*) flannel garments, esp. trousers; ‖piece of flannel etc. used in washing; (sl.) nonsense, blarney, flattery. **2.** *v.t.* & *i.* (‖-ll-). Wash with flannel; (sl.) flatter, use blarney. **3.** **~ĕ′tte** *n.*, napped cotton fabric resembling flannel. [W *gwlanen* (*gwlân* wool)]

**flăp.** **1.** *v.t.* & *i.* (-pp-). (Cause to) swing or sway about; move (wings) up and down; drive (flies etc. *away, off*) with flapper; (colloq., of ears) listen intently; (colloq.) be agitated or panicky. **2.** *n.* Broad piece hinged or held by one side and usu. hanging down, e.g. pocket-cover, envelope-seal, table-leaf; (Aeronaut.) aileron; up-and-down or side-to-side motion (of wing etc.); light blow, usu. with something broad; (colloq.) state of agitation or fuss; **~doo′dle**, (colloq.) nonsense; **~′jack**, small pancake, sweet oatcake. **3.** **flă′pper** *n.*, broad

flat device, flap; **flă′ppy** *a.*, that flaps. [prob. imit.]

**flāre.** **1.** *v.t.* & *i.* (Cause to) widen gradually; blaze with bright unsteady flame; **~ up**, burst into blaze, anger, etc. **2.** *n.* Dazzling unsteady light; outburst of flame; bright light used as signal (**~ path**, area illuminated to enable aircraft to land or take off at night); container of combustible material dropped from aircraft to illuminate target etc.; gradual widening, esp of skirt. [orig. unkn.]

**flăsh** *n.*, *v.*, & *a.* **1.** *n.* Sudden short blaze of flame or light (*flash of lightning*; **~ in the pan**, failure after showy start, impressive but unrepeated achievement etc.); brief outburst or transient display (*flash of hope, wit*); instant (*in a flash*); brief news dispatch on radio, telegraph, etc.; (Photog.) = *flashlight*; ‖(Mil.) cloth patch on uniform as emblem of unit etc. **2.** *v.i.* & *t.* Produce a flash; gleam; send or reflect like a flash or in flashes (*eyes flash fire, flash back defiance*); be suddenly perceived; move swiftly; cause to shine briefly (*flash headlights, sword, torch*); send (news etc.) by radio, telegraph, etc.; (colloq.) show suddenly or ostentatiously; (sl.) briefly display oneself indecently. **3.** *a.* (colloq.) Gaudy, showy, smart; connected with thieves etc. **4.** **~′back**, return, esp. in a film, to a past event; **~′bulb** (giving light for flashlight photograph); **~′light**, illuminating device for photographing in poor light, electric torch; **~-point**, temperature at which vapour from oil etc. ignites, (fig.) point at which anger etc. begins. **5.** **~′er** *n.*, (esp.) automatic device for switching lights rapidly on and off; **~′y** *a.* (**~ily**, **~iness**), gaudy, showy, cheaply attractive. [imit.]

**flă′shĭng** *n.* Strip of metal to prevent flooding or leakage at joint of roofing etc. [dial.]

**flask** (-ah-) *n.* Narrow-necked bottle for wine or oil, or for use in chemistry; traveller's pocket-bottle for spirits etc.; = VACUUM *flask*. [F & It. f. L *flasca, flasco*; cf. FLAGON]

**flăt** *a.*, *adv.*, & *n.* **1.** *a.* (-tt-). Horizontal, level; spread out, lying at full length, (*fall flat*; *flat against the wall*); smooth, without projection or indentation; absolute, downright, (*flat denial, refusal*; *that's ~*, colloq., that is definite); dull, uninteresting, monotonous, (**fall ~**, be a failure, not win applause); (of drink) that has lost its effervescence; (of battery etc.) unable to generate electric current; (Mus.) below correct or normal pitch (B, E, etc., ~, a semitone lower than B, E, etc.). **2.** *adv.* (**-tt-**). In a flat manner (*lies flat*; *sings flat*); (colloq.) absolutely, completely, (*turned it down flat*), exactly (*ten seconds flat*); **~ out**, at top speed, using all one's strength or resources. **3.** *n.* What is flat; flat part (*the flat of the hand*); ‖group of rooms, usu. on one floor, forming a residence; level ground (**the ~**, season of flat races for horses); low land; (Theatr.) section of scenery mounted on frame; (Mus.) (sign indicating) flat note; (colloq.) flat tyre. **4.** **~(-bottomed) boat** (with flat bottom for transport in shallow water); **~-fish**, sole, plaice, turbot, etc.; **~ foot**, foot with less than normal arch; **~-footed**, with flat feet, (colloq.) resolute, uninspired, unprepared); **~-iron** (for ironing linen etc.); **~ race** (over level ground, without jumps); **~ rate**, unvarying rate or charge; **~ spin**, (Aeron.) nearly horizontal spin, (colloq.) agitation or panic; **~ tyre** (deflated or punctured); **~'-ware**, plates etc.; **~'worm**, tapeworm, fluke, etc. **5.** ‖**~'let** *n.*, small flat, usu. of one or two rooms; **~'ten** *v.t. & i.*, make or become flat, humiliate, defeat decisively; **~ten out**, make or become flat, bring aircraft parallel to ground. [N]

**flă'tter** *v.t.* Pay obsequious attention to; overpraise; gratify vanity or self-esteem of; cause to feel honoured; please, delude, one*self* with the belief (*that*); (of portrait, painter) represent (person) too favourably; **~y** *n.*, overpraise. [F]

**flă'ttie, flă'tty,** *n.* (colloq.) Flat--heeled shoe. [FLAT]

**flă'tūlen|t** *a.* Causing formation of gas in alimentary canal; caused or accompanied by, troubled with, such gas; inflated, pretentious; **~ce, ~cy,** *ns.* [F, or L (*flatus* blowing)]

**flaunt** *v.t. & i.* Wave proudly; display oneself; show off (one*self*, finery, etc.). [orig. unkn.]

**flau'tist** *n.* Flute-player. [It. (FLUTE)]

**flă'vour, *-vor,** (*-er*) **1.** *n.* Mingled sensation of smell and taste; distinc-

tive taste; undefinable characteristic quality; slight admixture *of* a quality. **2.** *v.t.* Give flavour to, season. **3.** **flă'vorous, ~ful, ~some,** *adjs.*; **~ing** *n.*, thing used to flavour food or drink. [F]

**flaw¹. 1.** *n.* Imperfection, blemish, crack, breach; (Law) invalidating defect in document etc. **2.** *v.t. & i.* Make flaw in; spoil. [N]

**flaw²** *n.* Squall of wind. [LDu.]

**flăx** *n.* Plant grown for its textile fibre and its seeds; similar plant; fibres of flax; **~-seed**, linseed; **~'en** *a.*, of flax, (of hair) pale yellow. [E]

**flay** *v.t.* Strip off skin or hide of; peel off (skin, peel, etc.); (fig.) criticize severely. [E]

**flea** *n.* Small wingless jumping insect feeding on human and other blood (**with a ~ in** one's **ear**, discomfited by reproof etc.); **~'bane,** plant supposed to drive away fleas; **~-bite,** (fig.) slight injury, inconvenience, etc., reddish etc. spot on horse or dog; **~-bitten,** bitten by or infested with fleas, shabby, having reddish etc. spots. [E]

**flĕck. 1.** *n.* Skin-spot, freckle; small spot or streak of colour etc. **2.** *v.t.* Mark with flecks. [N or LDu.]

**\*flĕ'ction.** See FLEXION.

**flĕd.** See FLEE.

**flĕdge** *v.t.* Provide (bird, arrow, etc.) with feathers or down; bring up (young bird) till it can fly; (in *p.p.*) able to fly, (fig.) mature, independent; **flĕ'dg(e)ling** (-jl-) *n.*, young bird, inexperienced person. [obs. adj. *fledge* fit to FLY²]

**flee** *v.i. & t.* (**fled**). Run away (from), seek safety in flight; shun; vanish, pass away. [E]

**fleece. 1.** *n.* Woolly covering, esp. of sheep (**Golden F~**, Gk Myth., fleece of gold sought and won by Jason); wool shorn from a sheep in one operation; fleecelike thing (cloud, snow, etc.); **flee'cy** *a.* (-iness). **2.** *v.t.* Remove fleece from (sheep); strip or rob (person) of money, property, etc. [E]

**fleer.** **1.** *v.i.* Laugh mockingly, jeer, sneer. **2.** *n.* Mocking look or speech. [prob. Scand.]

**fleet** *v., n., & a.* **1.** *v.i. & t.* (usu. in *part.*) Glide, pass rapidly, last only a short time. **2.** *n.* Naval force, navy; ships sailing together; number of vehicles owned by one proprietor (*fleet of lorries, taxis*). **3.** *a.* (poet.)

Swift, nimble. [E, orig. = float, swim]

**Flĕ′mǐng** n. Native of Flanders. **Flĕ′mǐsh** a. & n., (language) of Flanders. [E]

**flĕsh. 1.** n. Soft substance between skin and bones, body as opp. to mind or soul, (**all ~**, whatever has bodily life; **~ and blood**, the human body, human nature, mankind; one's **own ~ and blood**, near relations; **in the ~**, in bodily form, alive; **one ~**, united as one personality; POUND³ *of flesh*; **the ~**, physical or sensual appetites; visible surface of human body; plumpness, fat; tissue of animal bodies (excluding fish and sometimes fowl) as food; pulpy substance of fruit or plant; **~-colour**(ed), yellowish pink; **~-pots**, luxurious living; **~-wound** (not reaching bone or vital organ). **2.** v.t. **~ out**, (fig.) fill out, make substantial. **3.** **~′lў** a. (-iness), mortal, material, worldly, (of desire etc.) sensual; **~′ў** a. (**~ily, ~iness**), of or like flesh, plump, pulpy. [E]

**fleur-de-lis, -lys,** (flĕrdelē′) n. (pl. **fleurs-** pr. same). Heraldic lily; (in sing. or pl.) former royal arms of France. [F, = flower of lily]

**flew.** See FLY².

**flews** (-z) n.pl. Hanging lips of bloodhound etc. [orig. unkn.]

**flĕx. 1.** v.t. Bend (joint, limb); move (muscle) to bend joint. **2.** ‖Flexible insulated wire for carrying current to electric lamp, iron, etc. **3.** **~′ible** a. (-bly), that will bend without breaking, pliable, manageable, adaptable, versatile; **~ibi′lity** n.; **~′ion** (-kshŏn), *flĕ′ction,* ns., bending, bent state or part, (Gram.) inflexion; **~′itĭme,** (system of) working-hours with set total but with times partly as chosen by employee; **flĕ′xure** (-kshѐr) n., bending, bent state or thing. [L (*flecto flex-* bend)]

**flŭbbertigĭ′bbĕt** n. Gossiping, frivolous, or restless person. [imit.]

**flĭck. 1.** n. Quick light blow with whiplash, finger, finger-nail, etc.; sudden movement, jerk; quick turn of wrist; (colloq.) cinema film, (in pl.) cinema; **~-knife** (with blade springing out when button etc. is pressed). **2.** v.t. & i. Strike or knock (*away, off*) with a flick; move with a flick; **~ through,** turn over (pages

etc.) by rapid movement of fingers. [imit.]

**flĭ′cker. 1.** v.i. (Of light, flame, etc.) shine or burn unsteadily or intermittently; move waveringly, flutter; (fig., of hope etc.) rise and subside alternately; **~ out,** die away after a final flicker. **2.** n. Flickering movement or light; brief feeling of hope etc. [E]

**flĭ′er.** See FLY².

**flight¹** (-īt). **1.** n. Act or manner of flying (**take, wing, one's ~,** fly); (fig.) act surpassing usual bounds (*flight of fancy*); group of birds etc. flying together (**in the first** or **top ~,** taking a leading place); volley (*of arrows etc.*); tail of dart; swift movement of projectile etc.; trajectory and speed of cricket-ball etc.; series (*of stairs in straight line, of hurdles etc. for racing*); (regular) journey by airline; (members of) R.A.F. unit of about six aircraft; **~-deck,** deck of aircraft-carrier for taking-off and landing, part of aircraft accommodating pilot, navigator, etc.; **~ lieutenant,** R.A.F. officer next below squadron leader; **~-recorder,** device in aircraft to record technical details for use in case of accident; **~ sergeant,** R.A.F. rank next above sergeant. **2.** v.t. Vary trajectory and speed of (cricket-ball etc.); provide (arrow) with feathers. **3.** **~′less** a., (of bird) unable to fly; **~′ў** a. (**~ily, ~iness**), fickle, changeable. [E (FLY²)]

**flight²** (-īt) n. Act or manner of fleeing, hasty retreat, (**put to ~,** rout; **take ~** or **to ~,** run away). [E (FLEE)]

**flĭ′ms‖ў** (-zĭ) a. (**~ily, ~iness**). Easily destroyed, frail; paltry, superficial, (*flimsy pretence*). [orig. uncert.]

**flĭnch** v.i. Draw back, shrink, (*from action, facts,* etc.); wince. [F f. Gmc]

**flĭng. 1.** v.t. & i. (**flung**). Throw, esp. forcefully or violently, hurl, (*flung out his arms; fling prudence* etc. *to the* WIND¹s); utter (words) forcefully; put *on* or take *off* (clothes) carelessly; rush, go angrily or hastily, (*had flung out of the room*). **2.** n. Action of flinging (**have a ~ at,** attempt, jeer at); vigorous dance (*Highland fling*); spell of indulgence in pleasure (*have one's fling*). [N]

**flĭnt** n. Hard silica found in lumps; piece of this esp. as prehistoric tool or weapon; anything hard and un-yielding; piece of flint etc. used with steel to produce fire; ~'lock, (Hist.) (lock of) gun discharged by spark from flint; ~'ў $a$. [E]

**flip** $n., v.,$ & $a.$ **1.** $n.$ Flick, fillip; turning over (~ **side**, reverse, or less important, side of gramophone record); drink of heated beer and spirit (EGG[1]-flip). **2.** $v.t.$ & $i.$ (**-pp-**). Propel or strike with a flip; move with a flick; turn over; ~ (one's **lid** or **wig**), (sl.) become wildly excited, go mad; ~ **through**, flick through. **3.** $a.$ (colloq.; **-pp-**). Glib, flippant. **4.** ~'**ping** $a.$ & $adv.,$ (sl.) = DAMNED. [prob. FILLIP]

**fli'ppan|t** $a.$ Treating serious things lightly; disrespectful; ~**cў** $n.$ [FLIP]

**fli'pper** $n.$ Limb used by turtle, seal, etc., in swimming; rubber etc. attachment to foot for underwater swimming; (sl.) hand.

**flirt. 1.** $v.t.$ & $i.$ Behave (with person) in enticing or loving manner without serious intentions; super-ficially interest or concern oneself (with idea etc.). **2.** $n.$ Person, usu. woman, who flirts. **3.** ~**ā'tion** $n.;$ ~**ā'tious** (-shʉs) $a.$ [imit.]

**flit. 1.** $v.i.$ (**-tt-**). Move lightly or rapidly (about etc.); make short flights; depart, change one's abode; ~'**ter** $v.i.,$ flit about (~**ter-mouse,** BAT[1]). **2.** $n.$ Change of abode, esp. to evade creditor etc. (MOONlight flit). [N (FLEET)]

**flitch** $n.$ Side of pork salted and cured. [E]

**float. 1.** $v.i.$ & $t.$ (Cause to) rest or move on surface of liquid; move or be suspended in liquid or gas; hover before eye or mind; (sl.) move in leisurely way; (of currency) (cause or allow to) have fluctuating exchange-rate; start (company, scheme, etc.). **2.** $n.$ Raft; cork, quill, used on fishing-line as indicator; cork supporting edge of fishing-net; structure enabling aircraft to float on water; floating device to control flow of water, petrol, etc.; (Theatr., in sing. or pl.) footlights; low-bodied cart, lorry, etc., esp. used in pro-cession; tool for smoothing plaster; sum of money for minor expendi-tures or change-giving; ~ **glass** (made by solidifying on surface of molten metal). **3.** ~**ā'tion,** = FLOTA-TION; ~'**ing** $a.,$ that floats (floating DEBT, DOCK[3], KIDNEY, RIB), fluctuat-

ing, not settled in definite place (floating population; ~**ing voter,** not attached to any political party). [E]

**flŏ'cculen|t** $a.$ Like tufts of wool; in or showing tufts; ~**ce** $n.$ [foll.]

**flŏck**[1] $n.$ Lock, tuft, of wool etc.; powdered wool or cloth; (in pl.) wool-refuse etc. for filling mattresses etc. [F f. L floccus]

**flŏck**[2]. **1.** $n.$ Number of animals, esp. birds, sheep, or goats, feeding, travelling, or kept together; large crowd of people; number of people in person's charge (a priest and his flock). **2.** $v.i.$ Move, assemble together, in great numbers. [E]

**flŏe** $n.$ Sheet of floating ice. [Norw.]

**flŏg** $v.t.$ & $i.$ (**-gg-**). Beat with whip, stick, etc., (~ **a dead horse,** waste one's efforts; ~ **to death,** colloq., talk about, promote, etc., ad nauseam); (sl.) defeat, steal, sell, proceed by violent or painful effort. [orig. unkn.]

**flood** (-ŭd). **1.** $n.$ (Coming of) great quantity of water, esp. over land (**the F**~, that described in Genesis); outburst, outpouring (of tears, words, etc.); inflow of tide; (colloq.) = floodlight; ~(-**tide**), rising tide; ~'**gate,** gate for admitting or excluding water, (fig.) barrier against rain, tears, etc.; ~'**light** $n.,$ & $v.t.,$ (illuminate with, lamp used for) copious artificial light from several directions. **2.** $v.t.$ & $i.$ Overflow, cover, or be covered, with flood (lit., or fig.: I was flooded with letters); come (in) in great quantities; drive out (of home etc.) by flood; have uterine haemorrhage. [E]

**floor** (-ôr). **1.** $n.$ Lower surface of room; part of legislative assembly etc. where members sit and speak; right to speak next in debate etc. (have, be given, the floor); rooms etc. on same level in building, storey, (||GROUND[1], *first, ~, floor on ground level; ||first, *second, ~, floor above this); level area; bottom of sea, cave, cavity, etc.; minimum of prices, wages, etc.; ~**board** (used for flooring); ~-**cloth** (for washing floors); ~ **show,** cabaret. **2.** $v.t.$ Provide with floor; knock down; nonplus, baffle; overcome; ~'**ing** $n.,$ (esp.) boards etc. used as floor. [E]

**floo'zie, -sie,** (-zǐ), $n.$ (colloq. Girl or woman, esp. disreputable one. [orig. unkn.]

**flŏp** $v., n.,$ & $adv.$ **1.** $v.i.$ (**-pp-**

Sway about heavily and loosely; move clumsily; sit, fall, etc. (*down*) awkwardly or suddenly; make dull flapping sound; (sl.) fail; (sl.) sleep; ~'**py** *a*. (-iness). **2.** *n.* Flopping motion or sound; (sl.) failure; ~**-house**, (sl.) doss-house. **3.** *adv.* With a flop. [var. of FLAP]

**flōr'|a** *n*. (*pl.* ~**ae**, ~**as**). Plants of a region, epoch, or environment; treatise on, list of, these; ~'**al** (*or* -ŏr-) *a*. (-**lly**), of flowers or flora(e), decorated with or depicting flowers. [L, name of goddess of flowers]

**Flō'rentine** *a*. & *n*. (Native) of Florence in Italy. [F or L]

**flŏr'ĕt** *n*. One of the small flowers of a composite flower; small flower. [L *flos* FLOWER]

**flŏ'rĭd** *a*. (Of style) ornate, flowery; showy; ruddy, flushed; **flori'dĭtў** *n*. [F or L (FLOWER)]

**flŏ'rĭn** *n*. (Hist.) Gold or silver coin, esp. English silver coin (2s.) of 19th–20th c. [F It. *fiorino* (foll.)]

**flŏ'rĭst** *n*. One who deals in or raises flowers. [L *flos* FLOWER]

**flŏr'uĭt** (-ŏŏ-; *or* flŏ'r-) *n*., & *v.i.* (Period at which person) lived or worked. [L, = he or she flourished]

**flŏss** *n*. Rough silk enveloping cocoon; untwisted silk thread for embroidery; CANDY-*floss*; DENTAL *floss*; ~ **silk**, rough silk used in cheap goods; ~'**y** *a*. (-**ily**, ~**iness**), of or like floss, (colloq.) showy. [F *floche*]

**flota'tion** *n*. Act of floating, esp. starting a company etc. [FLOAT]

**floti'lla** *n*. Small fleet; fleet of small ships. [Sp.]

**flŏ'tsam** *n*. Floating wreckage; ~ **and jetsam**, (fig.) odds and ends, vagrants, etc. [AF (FLOAT)]

**flounce**[1] **1.** *v.i.* Go, move, abruptly or impatiently (*about*, *away*, *out*, etc.). **2.** *n.* Fling, jerk, of body or limb(s). [orig. unkn.]

**flounce**[2] **1.** *n.* Ornamental strip round woman's skirt, with lower edge hanging loose. **2.** *v.t.* Trim with flounces. [alt. of *frounce* pleat f. F]

**floun'der**[1] *n.* Flat-fish, esp. of small edible species. [AF, prob. Scand.]

**floun'der**[2] **1.** *v.i.* Move or struggle clumsily or helplessly (*in* mud etc.); (fig.) act bunglingly or ineffectually. **2.** *n.* Act of floundering. [imit.]

**flour** (-owr) **1.** *n.* Powdery substance made by milling and usu.

sifting cereals, esp. wheat (CORN*flour*); fine soft powder; ~'**ў** *a*. (~**iness**). **2.** *v.t.* Sprinkle with flour. [diff. sp. FLOWER 'best part']

**flou'rish** (flŭ'-). **1.** *v.i.* & *t.* Grow vigorously; thrive, prosper; be active or in one's prime; be in good health; show ostentatiously; wave, move, (sword, limbs, etc.) about. **2.** *n.* Ornamental curve in writing; waving of sword, hand, etc. (*removed his hat with a flourish*); (Mus.) florid passage, extemporized addition or prelude, fanfare of brass instruments. [F f. L *floreo* (*flos* FLOWER)]

**flout. 1.** *v.t.* & *i.* Express contempt for (person, command) by word or act; scoff (*at*). **2.** *n.* Flouting speech or act. [Du. *fluiten* whistle (FLUTE)]

**flow** (-ō). **1.** *v.i.* Glide along as a stream; (of blood, money, electric current) circulate; move smoothly or in large numbers; hang easily, undulate, (*flowing hair, robe*); gush out, spring, (*from* source); result (*from*); (of tide) rise; (arch.) be plentifully supplied *with* (*land flowing with milk and honey*). **2.** *n.* Flowing movement; (amount of) flowing liquid; rise of tide (*ebb and flow*); outpouring, copious supply; ~ **chart, diagram, sheet**, diagram of movement, actions, etc., of things or persons in complex activity. [E]

**flow'er** (*or* flowr). **1.** *n.* Coloured (i.e. usu. not green) part of plant, from which fruit or seed is developed; (Bot.) reproductive organ in plant; blossom detached from plant, esp. as used in groups for decoration, wreaths, etc.; plant esteemed for its flowers; state of blooming (*in flower*); the best part or example of (*the flower of our manhood*); (in *pl.*) powder obtained by sublimation (*flowers of sulphur*); ~**-bed** (for growing flowers in garden); ~**pot** (in which plants are grown); ~**-show**, competitive or other exhibition of flowers. **2.** *v.i.* & *t.* (Cause to) bloom or blossom; decorate with flowers or floral designs. **3.** ~**ĕt** *n.*, small flower; ~'**ў** *a.* (~**iness**), abounding in flowers, (of language etc.) ornate, full of figures of speech. [F f. L *flos flor*-]

**flown.** See FLY[2].

**Flt. Lt., Flt. Sgt.,** *abbrs.* Flight Lieutenant, Sergeant.

**flu** (-ŏŏ) *n.* (colloq.) Influenza. [abbr.]

**flŭc′tŭ|āte** v.i. Vary irregularly, rise and fall; vacillate, waver; ~**ā′tion** n. [L (fluctus a wave)]

**flue** (-oo) n. Smoke-duct in chimney; tube etc. for conveying heat. [orig. unkn.]

**flu′en|t** (-oo′-) a. Expressing oneself quickly and easily; (of speech, style, etc.) copious, coming readily; flowing easily; ~**cy̆** n. [L (fluo flow)]

**flŭff. 1.** n. Light feathery stuff given off by blankets etc.; soft downy mass; (sl.) mistake made in speaking, music, etc.; ~**′y̆** a. (~**ily**, ~**iness**). **2.** v.t. & i. Shake (feathers etc. out, up) into soft mass; (sl.) make mistake in speaking, music, etc. [prob. dial. alt. flue fluff]

**flu′id** (-oo′-). **1.** a. Consisting of particles that move freely among themselves and yield to slightest pressure; not solid or rigid or stable (situation is fluid); fluid OUNCE[1]. **2.** n. Fluid substance, gas or liquid; liquid part or secretion. **3. flui′dify̆** (-oo-) v.t., make fluid; **flui′dĭty̆** (-oo-) n., fluid quality; ~**ize** v.t., make like fluid. [F, or L fluidus (FLUENT)]

**fluke[1]** (-ook) n. Flat-fish, flounder; trematode worm found in sheep's liver; triangular flat end of arm of anchor; lobe of whale's tail. [E]

**fluk|e[2]** (-ook). **1.** n. Lucky accidental stroke or success; chance breeze; **flu′k(e)y̆** (-oo′kĭ) a. (~**ily**, ~**iness**). **2.** v.t. Get, hit, etc., by a fluke. [orig. uncert.]

**flŭ′mmery̆** n. Sweet dish made with milk, flour, eggs, etc.; empty compliments, nonsense. [W llymru]

**flŭ′mmox** v.t. (colloq.) Bewilder, disconcert. [orig. unkn.]

**flŭng.** See FLING.

**\*flŭnk** v.i. & t. (colloq.) Fail, esp. in examination. [orig. unkn.]

**flŭ′nkey** n. (usu. derog.) Footman; toady, snob; \*cook, waiter, etc.

**fluor|ĕs′cence** (-oo-) n. Radiation produced from certain substances by incident radiation of shorter wavelength, electrons, etc.; ~**ĕ′sce** v.i., exhibit fluorescence; ~**ĕ′scent** a. (~**escent lamp**, radiating largely by fluorescence and usu. tubular). [FLUORSPAR]

**flu′or|ide** (-oo′-) n. Binary compound of fluorine; ~**idāte** v.t., add traces of fluoride to (drinking-water etc.), esp. to prevent tooth-decay; ~**ĭd(āt)ā′tion** n.; ~**ine** (-ēn) n., pale yellow highly reactive halogen gas; ~**ināte** v.t., = fluoridate; ~**spār** n., calcium fluoride as mineral, once used as flux. [fluor mineral used as flux (L, f. fluo flow)]

**flŭ′rry̆. 1.** n. Gust, squall; nervous hurry, agitation; sudden burst of activity. **2.** v.t. Confuse, agitate, (person). [imit.]

**flŭsh[1]** v.i. & t. (Cause to) take wing and fly up or away; reveal, drive out. [imit.]

**flŭsh[2]** v., n., & a. **1.** v.i. & t. Spurt, rush out; cleanse (drain, lavatory, etc.) by flow of water (~ **out**, cleanse or remove by flushing); dispose of thing thus (away, down); (cause to) glow or blush; inflame with pride or passion (flushed with success); make level. **2.** n. Rush of water; cleansing by flushing; rush of emotion, elation, etc., (in the first flush of youth); freshness, vigour; glow, blush; (hot) ~, feverish feeling. **3.** a. Full, in flood; having plenty of money etc.; level (with).

**flŭsh[3]** n. Hand of cards all of one suit; **straight** ~, flush that is also a sequence; **royal** ~, (Poker) straight flush headed by ace. [F f. L (FLUX)]

**flŭ′ster. 1.** v.t. & i. Agitate, confuse; make nervous; bustle. **2.** n. Agitation, flurry. [orig. unkn.]

**flute** (floot). **1.** n. Musical wind-instrument consisting of pipe with holes along it stopped by fingers or keys, and blow-hole in side; its player; vertical groove in pillar; similar groove elsewhere. **2.** v.t. & i. Play (on) flute; whistle, sing, or speak, in flutelike tones; make grooves in. **3. flu′t(e)y̆** (floo′tĭ) a., like flute in tone; **flu′ting** (-oo′-) n., (esp.) series of grooves; **flu′tist** (-oo′-) n., flute-player. [F]

**flŭ′tter. 1.** v.i. & t. Flap (wings) without flying or in short flights; fly or move with small flapping movements; go about restlessly; (cause to) be agitated (flutter the DOVEcots); quiver; (of pulse) beat feebly and irregularly. **2.** n. Fluttering; tremulous excitement (be, put, in a flutter); vibration; rapid variation of pitch or loudness of sound; ||(sl.) small bet or speculation. [E]

**flu′vĭa|l,** ~**tīle,** (floo′-) adjs. Of or found in river(s). [L (fluvius river)]

**flŭx** n. Flowing; inflow of tide; continuous succession of changes (state of flux); substance mixed with metal etc. to aid fusion. [F, or L *fluxus* (*fluo flux-* flow)]

**flȳ¹** *n.* Two-winged insect (**~ in the ointment,** trifling circumstance that spoils thing, situation, etc.; **~ on the wall,** unnoticed observer; *die* etc. **like flies,** in large numbers; **there are no flies on him,** sl., he is very astute; winged insect (BUTTER*fly*, FIRE*fly*, MAY²*fly*); disease of plants or animals caused by flies; natural or artificial fly as bait (DRY-*fly*); **~-blow,** fly's eggs in meat etc.; **~-blown,** tainted (lit. or fig.); **~'catcher,** trap for flies, bird that catches flies in air; **~-fish** *v.i.,* fish with fly; **~-paper** (for catching or poisoning flies); **~-spray,** liquid sprayed from canister to kill flies; **~-trap,** trap for flies, plant able to catch flies, esp. VENUS's *fly-trap*; **~'weight** (see BOX); **~-whisk** (for driving away flies). [E]

**flȳ².** **1.** *v.i.* & *t.* (**flew** *pr.* floo; **flown** *pr.* flōn). Move through air with wings (**~ high,** aim at, or reach, high standard); (cause to) move through air or space in or as aircraft or spacecraft (**~ in, out,** arrive, depart, by aircraft; **~ past,** fly aircraft in ceremonial formation); control flight of (aircraft); pass quickly through air; make (KITE) rise and stay aloft; (of flag, hair, etc.) wave; hoist (flag); travel or pass swiftly (*time flies*); flee (from); (colloq.) depart hastily (*I must fly*); hasten or spring violently (*at, on, to, upon; fly in the* FACE *of*); pass suddenly *into* (a rage etc.); come or be forced off suddenly (*door flew open*; *make feathers, fur, sparks, fly*; *fly off the* HANDLE; *sent me flying*, falling headlong; LET² *fly*). **2.** *n.* Flying; flap on garment, esp. trousers, to contain or cover fastening; (freq. in *pl.*) this fastening; part of flag farthest from staff; (Theatr., in *pl.*) space over proscenium. **3.** **~-ash** (from burning of powdered coal); **~-away** (of garment) streaming, loose; **~-by,** = *fly-past,* close approach of spacecraft to planet etc.; **~-by-night,** (*n.*) one who wanders about or departs suddenly at night, (*a.*) unreliable, dishonest; **~-half,** (Rugby Footb.) stand-off half; **~'leaf,** blank leaf, esp. at beginning or end of book; **~'over,** = *fly-past,* bridge carrying road etc. over another; **~-past,** ceremonial flight of aircraft past

some person or place; **~-post,** display (handbills etc.) rapidly in unauthorized places; **~-sheet,** handbill or small pamphlet; **~'wheel,** heavy wheel on revolving shaft to regulate machinery or accumulate power. **4. flȳ'er, fliʹer,** *n.,* (esp.) airman, (colloq.) ambitious or outstanding person, fast animal, vehicle, etc., flying jump. [E]

**flȳ³** *a.* (sl.; **~'ness**). Knowing, clever. [orig. unkn.]

**flȳ'ing. 1.** *n.* Flight; **~ machine,** (esp. heavier-than-air) machine able to fly; **~ officer,** R.A.F. officer next below flight lieutenant; **~ school,** place for learning to fly aircraft. **2.** *a.* That flies; fluttering (*with flying* COLOURs); hasty (*flying visit*); (of animal) able to make long leaps by use of membranes etc. (*flying lizard*); designed for rapid movement; **~ boat,** seaplane with boatlike fuselage; **~ bomb,** pilotless aircraft with explosive warhead; **~ buttress** (slanting from column etc. up to wall, usu. on arch); **~ fish** (rising into air by winglike fins); **~ fox,** fruit-eating bat; **~ jump, leap,** (with running start); **~ saucer,** unidentified saucer-shaped object reported as seen in the sky; **~ squad,** police detachment or other body organized for rapid movement; **~ start,** start in which starting-point is passed at full speed, (fig.) initial advantage; **~ tackle,** (Footb. etc.) tackle made while running or jumping; **~ trapeze,** trapeze on or from which acrobats swing to and fro. [FLY²]

**F.M.** *abbr.* Field Marshal; frequency modulation.

**f-nŭmber** (ĕ'f-) *n.* (Photog.) Ratio of focal length and effective diameter of lens. [*focal,* NUMBER]

**F.O.** *abbr.* Flying Officer; ‖(Hist.) Foreign Office.

**foal. 1.** *n.* Young horse, ass, etc.; **in** or **with ~,** (of mare etc.) pregnant. **2.** *v.t.* (Of mare etc.) bring forth (young, or abs.). [E]

**foam. 1.** *n.* Collection of small bubbles formed in liquid by agitation, fermentation, etc.; froth of saliva or perspiration; rubber or plastic in cellular mass; frothing substance used to extinguish fires; **~'ў** *a.* **2.** *v.i.* Gather or run in a foam; emit foam; **~ (at the mouth),** (fig.) be very angry. [E]

**fŏb**[1] *n.* Small pocket for watch etc. in waistband of trousers; ∼(-**chain**), chain attached to watch carried in fob. [G]

**fŏb**[2] *v.t.* (-**bb**-). ∼ **off**, trick or deceive (person) into accepting or being contented (*with* thing); palm or pass off (thing) *on*(*to*) or *upon* person. [cf. obs. *fop* to dupe]

**f.o.b.** *abbr.* free on board.

**fō'cal** *a.* (∼**ly**). Of or at a focus; ∼ **distance, length**, distance between centre of mirror or lens and its focus. [L (FOCUS)]

**fo'c's(')le.** See FORECASTLE.

**fō'cus. 1.** *n.* (*pl.* foci *pr.* -sī, ∼**es**). Point at which rays or waves meet after reflection or refraction; point from which rays etc. appear to proceed; place where object must be for lens or mirror to give well-defined image; adjustment of eye or lens to give clear image; (fig.) state of clear definition (*in, into, focus*); principal seat (of disease, activity, etc.); (Geom.) point whose distance from any point of a given curve satisfies a certain fixed equation; place of origin of earthquake. **2.** *v.t. & i.* (-**s**-, -**ss**-). Converge, make converge, to a focus; adjust focus of (lens, eye); bring into focus; concentrate or be concentrated *on*. [L, = hearth]

**fŏ'dder. 1.** *n.* Dried food, hay, etc., for stall-feeding cattle; CANNON-*fodder*. **2.** *v.t.* Give fodder to. [E]

**fōe** *n.* (poet., rhet.) Enemy; ∼'-**man**, (arch.) enemy in war. [E]

**foetid.** See FETID.

**foe't|us** (fē'-), *∗**fē't|us**, *n.* Unborn or unhatched offspring, esp. human embryo more than 8 weeks after conception; ∼**al** *a.* [L *fetus* offspring]

**fŏg**[1]. **1.** *n.* Thick cloud of water droplets or smoke suspended at or near earth's surface (**in a** ∼, puzzled); (Photog.) cloud obscuring image on negative etc. **2.** *v.t. & i.* (-**gg**-). Envelop or obscure (as) in fog; perplex; become covered with fog or condensed vapour. **3.** ∼**-bank**, mass of fog at sea; ∼**-bound**, unable to move because of fog; ∼**-horn**, instrument for warning ships in fog, (fig.) loud penetrating voice; ∼**-lamp** (used to improve visibility in fog). **4.** ∼**'gў** (-gĭ) *a.* (-iness), of or resembling fog, indistinct (**not have the foggiest**, colloq., have no idea

at all). [perh. back-form. f. *foggy* covered with coarse grass (foll.)]

**fŏg**[2] *n.* Aftermath; rank grass; a fodder-grass. [orig. unkn.]

**fō'gў, fō'gey**, (-gĭ) *n.* (**Old**) ∼, old-fashioned person. [orig. unkn.]

**foi'ble** *n.* Weak point in person's character, esp. one of which he is mistakenly proud. [F (FEEBLE)]

**foil**[1] *n.* Metal hammered or rolled into thin sheet (*gold, silver, tin, foil*); sheet of this, or of tin amalgam, as reflector behind mirror; leaf of foil placed under gem to enhance it; thing that sets something off by contrast; (Archit.) small arc or space between cusps of window. [F f. L *folium* leaf]

**foil**[2] *v.t.* Frustrate, baffle; defeat. [orig. = cross track to baffle hounds; perh. f. F *fouler* trample f. L *fullo* (FULL[2])]

**foil**[3] *n.* Light blunt-edged sword used in fencing. [orig. unkn.]

**foist** *v.t.* ∼ (**off**) **on** or **upon**, fob (thing) off on (person). [Du. *vuist* fist; orig. of palming false die]

**fōld**[1]. **1.** *n.* = SHEEP-*fold*; (fig.) body of believers, members of Church. **2.** *v.t.* Enclose (sheep) in fold. [E]

**fōld**[2]. **1.** *v.t. & i.* Double (flexible thing) over upon itself (∼ **away, up**), make compact by folding; bend part of (thing) *back, down*; become or be able to be folded (*folding boat, stool, table*); ∼**ing door**, usu. in *pl.*, door that folds back, esp. (one of) pair of doors with jambs on each side of opening; ∼**ing money**, colloq., paper money); clasp (arms etc.) *about, round*; embrace (*in* arms or *to* breast); lay (one's arms) together, usu. intertwined, across chest; clasp (one's hands); wrap, envelop, (*fold it in paper*); (Cookery) mix (ingredient) *in* without stirring or beating; ∼ (**up**), collapse (lit. or fig.), cease to function. **2.** *n.* Folding; folded part (*folds of dress*); line made by folding; hollow among hills; (Geol.) curvature of strata. **3.** ∼'**er** *n.*, (esp.) folding cover or holder for loose papers, a folded circular etc. [E]

**-fōld** *suf.* forming *adjs. & advs.* f. cardinal numbers, denoting: multiplied by, in amount multiplied by, (*twofold charm; repaid tenfold*). [orig. = folded in so many layers etc.]

**fōliā'ceous** (-shŭs) *a.* Of or like leaves; laminated; **fō'liage** *n.*, leaves, leafage, (**foliage plant,** cultivated for leaves not flowers); **fō′liate,** (*a.*) leaflike, having leaves, (-āt; *v.i.* & *t.*) split into laminae; **fōliā′tion** *n.* [L (FOIL¹)]

**fō′liŏ. 1.** *n.* (*pl.* ~**s**): Leaf of paper etc., esp. one numbered only on front; (Bookbinding) sheet of paper folded once (**in** ~, made of folios); book or volume in folio. **2.** *a.* (Of book etc.) made of folios, of largest size. [L, abl. of *folium* leaf]

**folk** (fōk) *n.* (*pl.* ~, ~**s**). Nation, race; (chiefly in *pl.* exc. arch. or dial.) people in general or of specified class (TOWN*sfolk*); one's parents or relatives; = **folk-music**; (*attrib.*) of the people, of popular origin, traditional, (*folk-art*, *-dance*, *-hero*, *-tale*); ~ **etymology,** popular modifying of word's form to make it seem derived from familiar words (e.g. *sparrowgrass* for *asparagus*); ~**′lore,** (study of) traditional beliefs etc.; ~ **memory,** recollection of past persisting among a people; ~**music, -song,** music or song (resembling that) of popular origin; ~**′weave,** coarsely woven fabric; ~**sў,** ~**′ў,** *adjs.,* having characteristics of ordinary people, resembling folk-art. [E]

**fŏ′llicle** *n.* Small sac or vesicle; small gland or cavity containing hair-root; **fŏlli′cular** *a.* [L dim. of *follis* bellows]

**fŏ′llow** (-ō) *v.t.* & *i.* Go or come after or *after* (moving thing or person; ~**-my-leader,** game in which each player does what leader does); accompany, serve; provide *with* sequel or successor; result *from*; take as guide or leader, conform to, (*follow* SUIT); go along (road etc.); practise (profession etc.); ~ **the plough, the sea,** be ploughman, sailor); understand meaning of (argument, speaker); be aware of present state or progress of (events etc.); come next in order or time (*my reasons are as follows*); be necessarily true (*it follows from this that*; *that does not follow*); ~ **on,** continue, (of cricket team) bat again immediately; ~ **out,** carry out, adhere strictly to (instructions etc.); ~ **through,** continue (action etc.) to conclusion; ~ **up,** pursue, develop, supplement (action, blow, etc., another or *by doing*); ~*-up* n., continuation or development of action, esp. second advertisement, letter, etc., referring to earlier one; ~**er** *n.*, (esp.) adherent; ~**ĭng,** (*n.,* esp.) group of adherents, (*a.,* esp.) now to be named (thing, or abs.: *the following is* or *are noteworthy*), (of wind) blowing in one's direction of travel, (*prep.*) as sequel to, coming after in time. [E]

**fŏ′llў** *n.* Foolishness; foolish act, conduct, idea, etc.; costly structure that is (considered) useless. [F *folie* (*fol* mad, FOOL)]

**fomě′nt** *v.t.* Bathe with lotion; apply warmth to; foster or instigate (sedition etc.); **fōmĕntā′tion** *n.* [F f. L (*foveo* heat, cherish)]

**fŏnd** *a.* Tender, loving, (~ **of,** having much love or liking for); doting; foolishly credulous or optimistic. [obs. *fon* fool, be foolish]

**fŏ′ndant** *n.* Soft sweetmeat of flavoured sugar. [F, = melting (FUSE¹)]

**fŏ′ndle** *v.t.* Caress. [FOND]

**fŏ′ndūe** (*or* -ōō) *n.* Dish of flavoured melted cheese. [F, = melted (FUSE¹)]

**fŏnt¹** *n.* Receptacle for baptismal water; ~**′al** *a.*, primary, baptismal. [E f. Ir. f. L *fons font-* fountain]

***fŏnt².*** See FOUNT¹.

**fŏntaně′lle, *fŏntaně′l,** *n.* Membranous space in infant's skull at angles of parietal bones. [F f. L *fontanella* little FOUNTAIN]

**fōōd** *n.* Substance taken into body to maintain life and growth; solid food (*food and drink*); nutriment for plants, skin, etc.; material for mental work (*food for thought*); ~ **poisoning,** illness due to bacteria etc. in food; ~**′stuff,** substance used as food. [E]

**fōōl** *n., a.,* & *v.* **1.** *n.* Person who acts or thinks unwisely or imprudently, stupid person, (*I was fool enough to agree*; **no** or **nobody's** ~, prudent person); (Hist.) jester, clown, (**act, play, the** ~, indulge in buffoonery, behave stupidly); dupe (ALL Fools′ *Day*; APRIL *fool*; MAKE *a fool of*); fruit stewed, crushed, and mixed with cream, custard, etc., (*gooseberry fool*). **2.** *a.* (*colloq.*) Foolish, silly. **3.** *v.i.* & *t.* Play the fool, trifle, (*about, around*); cheat (person) *out of* money etc. or *into* doing; dupe, play tricks on; ~ **away,** waste (time, money, etc.). **4.** ~**′-hardy** (-*iness*), foolishly bold, reckless; ~**′proof,** (of procedure, machine, etc.) so plain or simple as to be incapable of misuse or mistake;

~'**scap** (*or* -z-), size of paper, about $330 \times 200$ (or 400) mm; ~'**s errand** (fruitless); ~'**s paradise**, illusory happiness. 5. ~'**erȳ** *n.*, fooling, foolish act or thing; ~'**ish** *a.*, lacking good sense, ridiculous. [F f. L *follis* bellows, empty-headed person]

**foot. 1.** *n.* (*pl.* **feet**). End part of leg beyond ankle (**at** person's **feet**, as disciple, subject, or suppliant; *foot in the* DOOR; **feet of clay**, fundamental weakness (cf. Dan. 2: 33); **have** one's **feet on the ground**, be practical; **have one ~ in the grave**, be near death; **keep** one's **feet**, not fall; **my ~!**, colloq. excl. of contemptuous contradiction; **not put a ~ wrong**, make no mistakes; OFF one's **feet**; **on ~**, walking, not riding etc., (of project etc.) started, in operation; **on** one's **feet**, standing esp. to make speech, well enough to walk about; **on the right, wrong, ~**, in advantageous, disadvantageous, position; **put** one's **feet up**, have a rest; **put** one's **~ down**, be firm or insistent, accelerate motor vehicle; **put** one's **~ in it**, blunder; SET[1] *foot in, on*; **stand on** one's **own (two) feet**, be self-reliant or independent; **under** one's **feet**, obstructing one's progress; **under ~**, on the ground); step, pace, tread, (*he is fleet of foot*); (Hist.) infantry (*foot and horse*); lowest part or lower end of bed, grave, hill, page, table, etc.; part of sock etc. covering foot; (Pros.) division of verse including one stressed syllable; (*pl.* also **foot**) linear measure of 12 in., 30·48 cm (*six feet* or *foot long*; CUBIC, SQUARE, *foot*). **2.** *v.t.* Pay (bill); ~ **it**, walk, dance. **3.** ~-**and-mouth (disease)**, contagious virus disease of cattle etc.; ~'**ball**, (outdoor game played with) large inflated (usu. leather) ball (*football* POOL), (fig.) person or thing kicked or tossed about; ~'**baller**, football-player; ~'**bath**, (small bath for) washing feet; ~'**board** (in or on vehicle, for resting or placing feet); ~'**brake**, foot-operated brake on vehicle; ~'**bridge** (for pedestrians); ~'**fall**, sound of footstep; ||F~ **Guards**, Grenadier, Coldstream, Scots, Irish, and Welsh Guards; ~'**hill** (lying at base of mountain or range); ~'**hold**, support for feet (lit. or fig.); ~'**lights**, lights at front of stage at level of actors' feet; ~'**loose**, free to act as

one pleases; ~'**man**, liveried servant for carriage and waiting at table; ~'**mark**, footprint; ~-**muff** (for keeping feet warm); ~'**note** (at foot of page); ~'**pad**, (Hist.) unmounted highwayman; ~'**path** (for walkers, esp. ||pavement at side of road); ~'**plate**, driver's and fireman's platform in locomotive; ~'**print**, impression left by foot or shoe; ~-**race**, between persons on foot; ~-**rule**, wood or metal measuring device 1 foot long; ~-**slog** *n.*, & *v.i.*, (colloq.; -gg-) tramp, march; ~-**soldier**, infantryman; ~'**sore**, with sore feet, esp. from walking; ~'**stalk**, stalk of leaf, peduncle of flower, attachment of barnacle etc.; ~'**step**, tread, footprint, (*follow in* person's ~*steps*, do as he did); ~'**stool** (for resting feet on when sitting); ~'**way**, path for walkers; ~'**wear**, shoes, socks, etc.; ~'**work**, use or agility of feet in sports, dancing, etc. **4.** ~'**age** *n.*, length in feet, esp. of cinematographic film; ||~'**er** *n.*, (colloq.) football (game). [E]

**foo'ting** *n.* Foothold; secure position (lit. or fig.); relation, position, status, of person etc. towards others.

**foo'tl**|**e** *v.i.* (sl.) Play the fool; ~**ing** *a.*, trivial, silly. [orig. uncert.]

**fŏp** *n.* Dandy; ~'**perȳ** *n.*, behaviour of fop; ~'**pish** *a.*, like or befitting fop. [perh. obs. *fop* fool]

**for** (*or emphat.* fŏr). **1.** *prep.* In defence, support, or favour of (*are you for or against the proposal?; take my* WORD *for it*); for the sake or benefit of (*won a name for himself*; **that's** or **there's** *courage, gratitude,* etc., **for you!**, expr. enthusiasm or (ironical) satisfaction); suitable or appropriate to (*a book for children; it is for you to make a move*); representing (*member for Liverpool*); at price of, in exchange with, corresponding to, (60 *for 2 wickets; sold for* £1; WORD *for word*); with the object of (*go for a walk; for* SALE); in hope or quest of, in order to get, (*go* or *send for a doctor*; **O** or **oh for** thing, I wish I had!; RUN *for it*); in direction of, towards, to reach, (*left, sailed, for India; meeting is at 7.30 for 8*, so as to start promptly at 8); through or over (distance or period), during, (*walk for two hours, two miles; for* EVER); in respect or reference to, regarding, so far as concerns, (*fit for nothing; for all I know; time for a rest; too beautiful for words*;

AS[1] *for*; **be ~ it**, sl., be about to get punishment or other trouble; **there is nothing ~ it but to** *submit* etc., submission etc. is the only possible course); used with *n.* or *pron.* and *inf.* as noun-phrase: **it is wicked ~ him to smoke** (his smoking is wicked), **it is usual ~ hats to be worn** (hats are usually worn); in the character of, as being, (*for the last time*; *for* FREE; *for one* THING; *take for* GRANTED); because of, on account of, (*could not speak for laughing*; *the worse for* WEAR[1]); in spite of, notwithstanding, (*for all his boasting*; *for all (that) you say*); considering or making allowance required by the usual nature of (*quite active for a man of 80*). **2.** *conj.* Seeing that, since, because. [E, reduced form of FORE]

**for-** *pref.* forming *vbs.* etc. denoting: away, off, (*forget, forgive*), prohibition (*forbid*), abstention, neglect, (*forsake*), excess (*forlorn*). [E]

**f.o.r.** *abbr.* free on rail.

**fŏ′rage. 1.** *n.* Food for horses and cattle; foraging; **~cap,** infantry undress cap. **2.** *v.t. & i.* Collect forage from; supply with forage; rummage, search (*for* thing). [F f. Gmc (FODDER)]

**fŏrasmŭ′ch** (-z-) *adv.* (arch.) **~ as** *conj.*, since, because. [*for as much*]

**fŏ′ray** *n., & v.i.* (Make) incursion, raid. [F (FODDER)]

**forbad(e).** See FORBID.

**fŏr′bear[1], fŏr′ebear,** (fŏr′bār) *n.* (usu. in *pl.*). Ancestor. [FORE-, obs. *beer* (BE)]

**forbear′[2]** (-bā′) *v.t. & i.* (**for-bor′e; forbor′ne**). Abstain or refrain from or *from*; not use or mention; be patient; **~ance** *n.* [E (BEAR[2])]

**forbi′d** *v.t.* (**-dd-; forba′d** *pr.* -ă′d, **forba′de** *pr.* -ă′d; **forbi′dden**). Command (person etc.) not *to* do; not allow (person) to have etc. (thing; *forbid him wine*); not allow to exist or happen; *forbidden* DEGREES; **~den fruit,** thing desired because not allowed; *forbidden* GROUND[1]; God **~!**, may it not happen!; **~ding** *a.*, repellent, uninviting, stern. [E (BID)]

**forbŏr′(n)e.** See FORBEAR[2].

**fŏrce[1]. 1.** *n.* Strength, power, impetus, intense effort; military strength, body of armed men (**in ~,** in great numbers; **join ~s,** combine efforts); (in *pl.*) troops; body of police (**the ~,** the police); body of workers etc. (*labour force*); coercion, compulsion, (*by force*); influence, efficacy, (*force of circumstances*; *force of habit*); binding power, validity, effect, (*law comes into force, remains in force*; *saw the force of his remarks*); precise meaning; (Phys.) measurable influence tending to cause motion of a body, intensity of this, (fig.) person or thing likened to this (*he was a force for good*). **2.** *v.t. & i.* Compel (person) to do, *into* doing, or *into* course of action (**~ person's hand,** make him act prematurely or unwillingly); strain or increase to the utmost, overstrain, (**~ the bidding, ~** price at auction rapidly; **~ the pace,** adopt high speed in race to tire opponent); overpower, capture, make way through, or break open by force; drive or propel violently or against resistance; impose, press, (thing) *on* or *upon* person; cause or produce by effort (*force a smile*; *force the* ISSUE; **~** one's **way,** make a passage); artificially hasten growth or maturity of (plant, pupil, etc.); **~ down,** compel (aircraft) to land; **~ up,** cause (prices etc.) to rise. **3. ~d labour,** compulsory (usu. rigorous) labour; **~d landing,** unavoidable landing of aircraft in emergency; **~d march** (by troops etc., requiring special effort); **~-feed,** feed (prisoner etc.) by force. **4. ~′ful** (-sf-) *a.* (**-lly**), powerful, (of speech etc.) impressive. [F f. L *fortis* strong]

**fŏrce[2]** *n.* (N. Engl.) Waterfall. [N]

**force majeure** (fŏrsmahzhĕr′) *n.* Irresistible force, unforeseeable course of events excusing from fulfilment of contract. [F]

**fŏr′cemeat** (-sm-) *n.* Meat etc. chopped and seasoned for stuffing or garnish. [FARCE]

**fŏr′ceps** *n.* (*pl.* same). Surgical pincers; forceps-like organ. [L]

**fŏr′cib|le** *a.* (**-ly**). Done by or involving force; forceful. [F (FORCE[1])]

**fŏrd. 1.** *n.* Shallow place where river etc. may be crossed by wading or in vehicle. **2.** *v.t.* Cross (water) at ford. [E]

**fōre** *a., n., adv., & int.* **1.** *a.* Situated in front. **2.** *n.* Front part, bow of ship; **to the ~,** conspicuous (*come to the ~,* become prominent). **3.** *adv.* **~ and aft** *adv.,* at bow and stern, all over ship; **~-and-aft** *a.,* (of sail or rigging) lengthwise, not on yards. **4.** *int.* (Golf) (To person in probable line of flight of ball) look out! [E]

**fore-** *pref.* forming *vbs.* denoting: in front (*foreshorten*), beforehand (*foreordain*); forming *ns.* denoting: situated in front (*forecourt*, *fore-paw*), front part of (*forearm*), of or near bow of ship (*forecastle*, *forehold*), preceding (*forefather*).

**forearm. 1.** *n.* (fôr'ärm). Arm between elbow and wrist or fingertips. **2.** *v.t.* (fôrär'm). Arm beforehand, prepare. [ARM¹,²]

**forebear.** See FOREBEAR¹.

**forebo'd|e** (fôrb-) *v.t.* Betoken, portend; have presentiment of (usu. evil) or *that*; **~ing** *n.*, presentiment, omen. [FORE-]

**for'ecast** (fôr'kahst). **1.** *v.t.* (~, ~ed). Estimate or conjecture beforehand. **2.** *n.* Prediction or estimate of future thing, esp. weather. [FORE-]

**forecastle, fo'c's(')le** (fō'ksel) *n.* (Naut.) Forward part of ship where sailors live.

**foreclo's|e** (fôrklō'z) *v.t.* Exclude, prevent; gain possession of mortgaged property of (person) on non-payment of money due; stop (mortgage) from being redeemable; **~ure** (-zher) *n.*, act of foreclosing. [F (L *foris* out, CLOSE¹)]

**for'ecourt** (fôr'kôrt) *n.* Enclosed space in front of building; part of filling station where petrol is supplied; **foredoo'm** (fôrd-) *v.t.*, doom or condemn beforehand (*to*); **for'e-edge** (fôr'ej) *n.*, front or outer edge esp. of book pages; **for'efather** (fôr'fahdher) *n.* (usu. in *pl.*), ancestor, member of past generation of a family or race; **for'efinger** (fôr'-fingger) *n.*, finger next to thumb; **for'efoot** (fôr'-) *n.* (*pl.* **for'efeet**), front foot of animal; **for'efront** (fôr'-frunt) *n.*, foremost part. [FORE-]

**forego'** (fôrgō') *v.t. & i.* (**forewe'nt**; *foregone* pr. -gŏ'n, -gaw'n, *attrib.* fôr'-). **1.** (arch.) Precede. **2.** **~ne conclusion**, decision reached in advance of evidence etc., easily foreseen result; **~ing** (or fôr'g-) *a.*, (esp.) previously mentioned (thing, or abs.).

**for'eground** (fôr'g-) *n.* Part of view, esp. in picture, nearest observer; (fig.) most conspicuous position. [Du. (FORE-, GROUND¹)]

**for'ehand** (fôr'h-). **1.** *a.* (Tennis etc.) (Of stroke) made with palm of hand forward. **2.** *n.* Forehand stroke. **3.** **~ed** *a.*, forehand, *thrifty. [FORE-]

**forehead** (fŏ'rĭd, fôr'hĕd) *n.* Part of face above eyebrows.

**fŏ'reign** (-rĭn) *a.* Of, in, with, or characteristic of some country or language other than one's own (**~ aid**, money etc. given or lent by one country to another; **~ exchange**, (dealings in) foreign currency; *foreign* LEGION); dealing with matters concerning other countries (*Foreign and Commonwealth Office*; F**~ Minister**, ‖**Secretary**, minister dealing with such matters); of another district, society, etc.; of or proceeding from other persons or things; dissimilar or irrelevant *to*; introduced from outside (*foreign body*, *substance*); **~er** *n.*, person born or dwelling in foreign country etc. or speaking foreign language. [F f. L (*foris* outside)]

**foreknow'** (fôrnō') *v.t.* (**-knew'** pr. -nū'; **-known'** pr. -nō'n). Know beforehand; **~ledge** (fôrnŏ'lij) *n.*; **for'eland** (fôr'l-) *n.*, promontory, land lying in front; **for'eleg** (fôr'l-) *n.*, front leg of animal; **for'elimb** (fôr'lĭm) *n.*, front limb of animal; **for'elock** (fôr'l-) *n.*, lock of hair just above forehead (**take time** etc. **by the forelock**, seize opportunity). [FORE-]

**for'e|man** (fôr'm-) *n.* (*pl.* **~men**). Workman superintending others; principal juror.

**for'emast** (fôr'mahst) *n.* Forward (lower) mast of ship.

**for'emost** (fôr'm-; *or* -ost). **1.** *a.* Most advanced in position, front, (*dive head foremost*); most notable, best. **2.** *adv.* In the first place, most importantly, (*first and foremost*). [E]

**for'ename** (fôr'n-) *n.* First or Christian name; **for'enoon** (fôr'n-) *n.*, (Naut., Law, or arch.) day till noon, morning. [FORE-]

**fore'nsic** *a.* (**~ally**). Of or used in courts of law; **~ medicine**, application of medical knowledge to legal problems. [L *forensic* (FORUM)]

**foreord|ai'n** (fôrôr-) *v.t.* Predestinate; **~ina'tion** *n.*; **for'e-paw** (fôr'p-) *n.*, front paw of animal; **for'erunner** (fôr'-r- *n.*, predecessor, harbinger; **for'esail** (fôr's-; *or* -sel) *n.*, principal sail on foremast. [FORE-]

**foresee'** (fôrsē') *v.t.* (**foresaw'**; *foresee'n*). See or be aware of beforehand (thing, *that*); **~able**

**future,** period for which one can predict general course of events;

**fŏreshă'dow** (fōrshă'dō) v.t., be warning or indication of (future event); **fŏr'eshore** (fōr'sh-) n., part of shore between high- and low--water marks; **fŏreshŏr'ten** (fōrsh-) v.t., show or portray (object) with the apparent shortening due to visual perspective.

**fŏreshow'** (fōrshō') v.t. (p.p. ~n). Foretell, foreshadow.

**fŏr'esight** (fōr'sīt) n. Foreseeing; care for future; front sight of gun.

**fŏr'eskin** (fōr's-) n. Loose skin covering end of penis.

**fŏ'rĕst. 1.** n. Large area of land covered chiefly with trees and undergrowth; trees in this (lit. or fig.; forest of masts); ||(Hist.) unenclosed woodland district kept for hunting, usu. owned by sovereign. **2.** v.t. Plant with trees; make into forest. **3.** ~**er** n., officer in charge of forest, dweller in forest; ~**rў** n., (management of) forests. [F f. L forestis (FOREIGN)]

**fŏresta'll** (fōrstaw'l) v.t. Anticipate the action of, esp. so as to baffle; deal with beforehand. [FORE-, STALL]

**fŏretăste. 1.** (fōr't-) n. Partial enjoyment or suffering (of thing) in advance. **2.** (fōrtă'st) v.t. Have foretaste of. [FORE-]

**fŏretĕ'll** (fōrt-) v.t. (foreto'ld). Predict, prophesy; be precursor of; **fŏr'ethought** (fōr'thawt) n., care for the future; deliberate intention.

*****fŏrĕ'ver.** See for EVER.

**fŏrewar'n** (fōrwor'n) v.t. Warn beforehand. [FORE-]

**fŏr'ewom|an** (fōr'woóman) n. (pl. ~en). Woman worker supervising others; woman foreman of jury.

**fŏr'eword** (fōr'wĕrd) n. Preface; introductory remarks, esp. by person other than author.

**fŏr'feit** (-fĭt) n., a., & v. **1.** n. Thing surrendered as penalty for crime, negligence, etc.; penalty, (esp. trivial) fine. **2.** a. Lost or surrendered as a forfeit. **3.** v.t. Lose or surrender as penalty or as necessary consequence. **4.** ~**ure** n., act of forfeiting. [F forfaire transgress f. L foris outside, facio do]

**fŏrfĕ'nd** v.t. (arch.) Avert, prevent, (disaster); freq. abs. as excl. (God, Heaven, forfend!). [FOR-]

**fŏrgă'ther** (-dh-) v.i. Assemble, meet before, associate. [Du.]

**fŏrgă've.** See FORGIVE.

**fŏrge[1]. 1.** n. (Workshop with) furnace or hearth for melting or refining metal; blacksmith's workshop. **2.** v.t. Shape by heating and hammering (lit. or fig.); make (money etc.) or write (document, signature, etc.) in fraudulent imitation. **3.** **fŏr'gery** n., (making of) forged document etc. [F f. L fabrica (FABRIC)]

**fŏrge[2]** v.i. Move or advance gradually or steadily; ~ **ahead,** progress rapidly, (don't forget to ask; you forget that we saw it). [perh. alt. FORCE[1]]

**fŏrgĕ't** (-g-) v.t. & i. (-tt-; forgo't; forgo'tten, *forgo't). Lose remembrance of or about, not remember, (I forget the name, forget why); neglect, overlook, (don't forget to ask; you forget that we saw it); ~ oneself, act unworthily, neglect one's own interests); cease to think of (forgive and forget); ~ (about) it!, colloq., take no more notice of it); ~**-me--not,** plant with small blue flowers; ~**'ful** a. (-lly), liable to forget (forgetful of), that forgets. [E (FOR-)]

**fŏrgi've** (-g-) v.t. (forgă've; forgi'ven). Cease to resent, pardon, (forgive me, my sin, me my sin); remit (debt); ~**nĕss** (-vn-) n., act of forgiving, state of being forgiven.

**fŏrgŏ'** v.t. (forwĕ'nt; forgo'ne pr. -gō'n, -gaw'n). Go without, relinquish; omit or decline to take or use (pleasure, advantages, etc.).

**fŏrgŏ't(ten).** See FORGET.

**fŏrk. 1.** n. Pronged agricultural implement used for digging, lifting, etc.; pronged instrument used in eating and cooking; pronged device pushed under load to be lifted; forked support for bicycle wheel; (place of) divergence into branches or members, e.g. human legs; road, stick, etc., so diverging; ~**-lift** (truck etc.), vehicle with fork for lifting and carrying loads. **2.** v.i. & t. Form fork or branch; take one road at fork; dig, lift, throw, with fork; ~ **out,** (sl.) pay, usu. unwillingly. [E f. L furca pitchfork]

**fŏrlŏr'n** a. Forsaken; in pitiful condition; desperate; ~ **hope,** desperate enterprise, faint hope. [LORN; hope = Du. hoop troop (HEAP)]

**fŏrm. 1.** n. Shape, arrangement of parts, visible aspect; person or animal as visible or tangible (a form darkened the window); mode in which thing exists or manifests itself (*in, under, take, the form of*); species, kind; one of the ways in which a word may be spelt, pronounced, or inflected; class in school (usu. numbered from SIXTH down to *first*); arrangement and style in literary or musical composition; customary method (*in due form*); **common ~**, what is usual and of no special significance; **matter of ~**, mere routine); set order of words; (printed) document esp. with blanks to be filled up (**~ letter**, standardized letter for reply on recurring matters); formality; behaviour according to rule or custom (*good, bad, form*); correct procedure (*he knows the form*); (of horse, athlete, etc.) condition of health and training (**in, out of, ~**, fit, not fit, for racing etc.; **in good** or **top , on ~**, playing, performing, etc., well; **off ~**, playing etc. badly); (Racing etc.) details of previous performances; (sl.) criminal record; bench; (Print.) = FORME; hare's lair; structure to hold concrete while it sets; **~less** *a.*, without definite or regular form. **2.** *v.t.* & *i.* Fashion, mould, (thing *into* shape, *on* or *upon* pattern); mould by discipline, train; organize (*into* a company etc.); frame, make, develop, (structure, idea, habit, alliance, etc.); construct (word) by inflexion etc.; be material of, make up, be *one of* or *part of*; take shape, come into existence; (Mil.) draw up or *up* in order, move into formation. [F f. L *forma*]

**-form** *suf.* forming *adjs.* (usu. w. *-i-*) denoting: having the form of (*cruciform*), having such a number of forms (*multiform*).

**for′mal** *a.* (**~ly**). Of or concerned with (outward) form, esp. as distinct from content or matter; done etc. in accordance with rules or convention (*formal call, dress*); perfunctory; precise, symmetrical, (*formal garden* ; excessively stiff or methodical; valid or correctly so called because of its form, explicit, (*formal agreement, receipt, denial*); **~ism** *n.*, strict or excessive adherence to or concern with form or forms; **~ist** *n.*; **forma′lity** *n.*, formal act, regulation, or custom (often lacking real significance), primness, precision; **~ize** *v.t.*, make formal, give definite (esp. legal) form to; **~iza′-tion** *n.* [L (FORM)]

**forma′ldehyde** *n.* Aldehyde of formic acid, used as disinfectant and preservative and in manufacture of synthetic resins; **for′malin** *n.*, aqueous solution of formaldehyde. [FORMIC, ALDEHYDE]

**for′mat. 1.** *n.* Shape and size (of book etc.); style or manner of arrangement or procedure; arrangement of data etc. for computer. **2.** *v.t.* Arrange in format, esp. for computer. [F f. G f. L *formatus* shaped (FORM)]

**forma′tion** *n.* Forming; thing formed; arrangement of parts or of troops; a number of aircraft flying in company; (Geol.) set of rocks or strata with common characteristic. [F or L (FORM)]

**for′mative** *a.* Serving to form, of formation.

‖**forme** *n.* (Print.) Body of type secured in chase for printing at one impression. [var. FORM]

**for′mer** *a.* Of the past, earlier, (*former times*; *more like her former self*); **the ~** (with noun, or abs.), the first or first-mentioned of two (opp. *the latter*); **~ly** *adv.*, in former times. [FOREMOST]

**for′mic** *a.* **~ acid**, colourless irritant volatile acid contained in fluid emitted by ants. [L *formica* ant]

**for′midab|le** *a.* (**~ly**). That causes fear or dread; likely to be hard to overcome or deal with (*formidable opponent, obstacle, task*). [F or L (*formido* to fear)]

**for′mul|a** *n.* (*pl.* **~ae, ~as**). Fixed form of words for use on ceremonial or social occasion etc. or in enunciating principle; conventional or hackneyed usage or belief; principle that reconciles differences; recipe; *infant's food; (Math., Chem., etc.) rule or fact expressed by symbols or figures; classification of racing car esp. by engine capacity; **~a′ic** *a.*, that is a (mere) formula; **~ary**, (*a.*) of or using formulae, (*n.*) collection of formulae; **~ate** *v.t.*, express in a formula, set down definitely or systematically; **~a′tion** *n.* [L, dim. of *forma* FORM]

**for′nic|ate** *v.i.* Commit fornication; **~a′tion** *n.*, voluntary sexual intercourse between unmarried persons; **~ator** *n.* [L (*fornix* brothel)]

**fŏ′rrader.** See FORWARD 3.

**forsa′ke** *v.t.* (forsoo′k *pr.* -ŏŏ′k;

~n). Give up, renounce; withdraw help or companionship from. [E (FOR-)]

**forsōo'th** adv. (arch., iron., or derog.) Truly, no doubt. [E (FOR, SOOTH)]

**forswear'** ('-wār') v.t. (**forswor'e**; **forswor'n**). Abjure, renounce; perjure (oneself); (in p.p.) perjured. [E (FOR-)]

**forsy'thia** n. Ornamental shrub with bright-yellow flowers. [Forsyth, person]

**fort** n. Fortified building or position; (Hist.) trading-station, orig. fortified; **hold the ~**, act as temporary stronghold, cope with emergency. [F or It. (L fortis strong)]

**forte¹** (or -tĭ) n. Person's strong point, thing in which one excels. [fem. of F FORT]

**for'tě²** a., adv., & n. (Mus.) (Passage to be) performed loudly. [It. (FORT)]

**forth** adv. (arch. exc. ın set phrs.) Forward, into view, (bring, come, HOLD¹, set, forth); out from home etc. (set etc. forth); forwards (back and forth); onwards in time (from this time forth; henceforth); and so¹ forth; ~'coming (-kŭ-; or -kū'-) a., about to come forth, approaching, produced when wanted, (of person) informative or responsive; ~'right a., straightforward, outspoken, decisive, unhesitating; ~wi'th adv., at once, without delay. [E]

**for'tĭeth.** See FORTY.

**for'tĭfȳ** v.t. & i. Strengthen physically, mentally, morally, etc.; strengthen (wine) with alcohol; add extra nutrients, esp. vitamins, to (food); provide (town etc.) with defensive works, erect these; ~ĭcā'tion n., fortifying, (usu. in pl.) defensive work(s), wall(s), etc. [F f. L (fortis strong)]

**forti'ssĭm|ō** a., adv., & n. (pl. ~os, ~ĭ pr. -ē). (Mus.) (Passage to be) performed very loudly. [It., superl. of FORTE²]

**for'tĭtūde** n. Courage in pain or adversity. [F f. L (fortis strong)]

**for'tnĭght** (-īt) n. Two weeks (**to-day, Monday, ~**, a fortnight from today etc.); ~lý, (a. & adv.) (produced, occurring, done) once a fortnight, (n.) fortnightly magazine etc. [E (fourteen nights)]

**for'trèss** n. Military stronghold, esp. town fit for large garrison. [F f. L fortis strong]

**fortū'ĭtous** a. Happening by chance, accidental. [L (forte by chance)]

**for'tune** (-chǔn, -chōōn). **1.** n. Chance or luck as a power in human affairs (**F~**, goddess of fortune); (in sing. or pl.) luck that befalls person or enterprise; person's destiny (**tell** person **his fortune**, foretell his destiny; hence fortune-teller, -telling); good luck; prosperity, wealth, huge sum of money, (**~-hunter**, person seeking rich person to marry; **make** one's **~**, prosper; **make a ~**, become rich; **a small ~**, large sum of money). **2.** v.i. (arch. or poet.) Occur; come by chance (upon thing). **3.** for'tŭnate (or -chu-, -chōō-) a., lucky, prosperous, auspicious. [F f. L fortuna]

**for'tỹ** a. & n. NUMERAL; ‖the **Forties**, sea area between N.E. Scotland and S.W. Norway [named from its depth of 40 fathoms or more]; ROARıng forties; **~ winks**, short sleep; for'tĭeth a. & n.; ~fōld a. & adv. [E (FOUR)]

**for'um** n. (Rom. Ant.) assembly-place for judicial and other business, esp. at Rome; place of or meeting for public discussion; court, tribunal, (lit. or fig.). [L]

**for'ward** a., n., adv., & v. **1.** a. Of fore part of ship; lying in one's line of motion, onward or towards the front, (forward horizon, path); (Rugby Footb. etc., of pass) towards opponents' goal-line; (Commerc.) relating to future produce, delivery, etc., (forward contract); approaching maturity or completion; (of plant etc.) well advanced or early; precocious; pert. **2.** n. (Position of) an attacking player in football etc. **3.** adv. Towards the future (from this time forward; CARRIAGE forward; **look ~ to**, expect esp. with pleasure); in advance, ahead, (send him forward; ~-looking, progressive); to the front, into prominence, (BRING, COME, forward); (Naut., Aeron.) in, near, to, towards, bow or nose; onward so as to make progress (**get any ~er** or colloq. **forrader**, make any progress; **go ~**, be going on, progress); ~(s), towards front in direction one is facing, in normal direction of motion or traversal, with continuous forward motion, (*backwards and forwards*; *rushing forward*). **4.** *v.t.* Help to advance, promote; send (letter etc.) on to further destination; dispatch (goods etc.). [E (FORTH, -WARD)]

**fŏsse** *n.* Long narrow excavation, ditch, trench, esp. in fortification. [F f. L,=ditch (as foll.)]

**fŏ′ssil. 1.** *a.* Preserved in strata of earth and recognizable as remains or impressions of (usu. prehistoric) plant or animal; found buried, dug up, (~ **fuel**, coal, oil, etc., formed in geological past); antiquated, incapable of further development. **2.** *n.* Fossil object; antiquated or unchanging person or thing. **3.** ~**ize** *v.t. & i.*, turn into fossil; ~**izā′tion** *n.* [F f. L (*fodio foss-* dig)]

**fŏ′ster. 1.** *a.* Related not by blood but because of rearing or bringing up (*foster-brother*, *-child*, *-mother*); concerning care of orphans etc. (*foster care*, *home*); ~**ling** *n.*, foster-child. **2.** *v.t.* Promote growth of; nurse or bring up as foster-child; encourage or harbour (feeling); (of circumstances) be favourable to; (arch.) tend, cherish. [E (FOOD)]

**fought.** See FIGHT.

**foul** *a., n., adv., & v.* **1.** *a.* (~′ly *pr.* -l-lĭ). Offensive, loathsome, stinking; filthy, soiled; (colloq.) disgusting, awful; containing noxious matter (*foul air*, *water*); clogged, choked; (of ship's bottom) overgrown with weed etc.; (of language etc.) obscene, disgustingly abusive, (~-**mouthed**, using obscene language); (arch.) ugly (*fair or foul*); unfair, against rules, (*by fair means or foul*; *foul blow*); (of weather) rough, stormy; in collision (FALL *foul of*); (of rope etc.) entangled; ~ **line** (marking boundary of playing area etc.); ~ **play**, unfair play in games, (fig.) treachery, murder, or violence. **2.** *n.* Collision, entanglement; foul stroke or piece of play. **3.** *adv.* Unfairly, contrary to rules. **4.** *v.t. & i.* Make or become foul (*foul one's own* NEST); commit foul against (player); (cause to) become entangled; collide with; ~ **up**, entangle, block or jam (traffic etc.), make dirty or unpleasant, (fig.) spoil; ~-*up* n., muddle, confusion. [E]

**foulǎr′d** (fōōl-) *n.* (Handkerchief of) thin soft material of silk or silk and cotton. [F]

**found**[1] *v.t.* Establish esp. with endowment, originate, initiate, (institution etc.); lay base of (building); be original builder of (town etc.); construct or base (tale, theory, rule, one's fortunes) (*up*)*on*; **ill-, well-,** ~**ed**, (un)justified, (un)reasonable; **fou′nder**[1], **fou′ndrĕss**, *ns.*, (esp.) one who founds an institution. [F f. L (*fundus* bottom)]

**found**[2] *v.t.* Melt and mould (metal), fuse (materials for glass), make (thing) thus; **fou′nder**[2] *n.*; **fou′ndrў** *n.*, founder's work(shop). [F f. L *fundo fus-* pour]

**found**[3]. See FIND.

**foundā′tion** *n.* Establishing esp. of endowed institution; such institution (e.g. college, hospital, school) or its revenues (**on the** ~, entitled to benefit by its funds); solid ground or base on which building rests; (in *sing.* or *pl.*) lowest part of building usu. below ground-level; basis, underlying principle, (*report has no foundation*); material or part on which other parts are overlaid; ~ (**cream**), base for application of cosmetics; ~ (**garment**), woman's supporting undergarment, e.g. corset; ~-**stone**, (esp.) stone laid ceremonially to celebrate founding of edifice, (fig.) basis. [F f. L (FOUND[1])]

**fou′nder**[1,2]. See FOUND[1,2].

**fou′nder**[3] *v.i.* (Of ship) fill with water and sink; (of plan etc.) fail; (of horse or rider) fall to ground, fall from lameness, stick in mud etc. [FOUND[1]]

**fou′ndling** *n.* Deserted infant of unknown parents. [FIND]

**fou′ndrĕss** See FOUND[1]; **fou′ndrў**, see FOUND[2].

‖**fount**[1] (*or* fŏnt), *∗fŏnt[2], n.* (Print.) Set of type of same face and size. [F (FOUND[2])]

**fount**[2] *n.* Source; (poet.) spring, fountain. [back-form. f. foll.]

**fou′ntain** (-tĭn) *n.* Jet(s) of water made to spout for ornamental purposes, structure provided for this; spring; source (*of river, wisdom,* etc.); (**drinking-**)~, structure for public supply of drinking-water; reservoir for oil in lamp, ink in pen, etc., (~-**pen**, pen having this); = SODA-*fountain*; ~-**head**, source. [F f. L *fontana* (*fons font-* a spring)]

**four** (fŏr). **1.** *n.* NUMERAL; 4 players in game; 4-oared boat or its crew (~**s**, races between such boats); ~-**in-hand**, vehicle with 4 horses driven by one person, \*necktie knotted so that the two hanging ends are superposed; **on all ~s**, on hands and knees, (fig.) completely analogous or corresponding (*the case was on all fours with others*). 2. *a.* NUMERAL; **~-ball**, golf match between two pairs with each person using separate ball; **the ~ corners** (*of the world*, etc.), the remotest parts; **~-letter word**, vulgar monosyllable referring to sexual or excretory functions; ||**~'pence**, sum of 4p. or 4d.; ||**~'penny**, costing 4p. or 4d. (*~penny one*, colloq., hit, punch); **~-poster**, bed with 4 posts supporting canopy; **~'score**, (arch.) 80; **~-square**, square-shaped, solidly based or steady, resolute(ly); **~-stroke**, (of internal combustion engine) having a cycle of 4 strokes (intake, compression, combustion, exhaust); **~-wheel**, acting on all 4 wheels of vehicle (*four-wheel drive*). 3. **~'fōld** *a.* & *adv.*; **4to**, see QUARTO. [E]

**four'some** (fôr'-) *n.* Group or party of 4 persons; golf match between two pairs with partners playing same ball.

**fourtee'n** (fôrt-; *or* fôr'tēn) *a.* & *n.* NUMERAL; **~th** *a.* & *n.* [E (FOUR, -TEEN)]

**fourth** (fôr-) *a.* & *n.* NUMERAL; person who completes group of 4; *fourth* ESTATE; \*F**~ of July**, anniversary of independence in U.S.; **~'ly** *adv.* [E (FOUR)]

**fowl. 1.** *n.* (*pl.* **~s**, **~**). Domestic cock or hen kept for eggs and flesh; bird (arch. exc. in *comb.*: GUINEA-*fowl*, WILD*fowl*); flesh of birds as food (*fish, flesh, and fowl*). **2.** *v.i.* Hunt, shoot, or snare, wildfowl; **~'ing piece**, light gun. [E]

**fŏx. 1.** *n.* Red-furred bushy-tailed carnivorous quadruped preserved in England etc. as beast of chase, proverbial for cunning; its fur; animal of related species; (fig.) crafty person. **2.** *v.t.* Deceive, puzzle; (esp. in *p.p.*) discolour (pages of book etc.) with fox-marks. **3.** **~'glove**, tall plant with purple or white flowers like glove-fingers; **~'hole**, (Mil.) hole in ground used as shelter against missiles or as firing-point, (fig.) place of refuge or concealment; **~'hound** (bred to hunt foxes); **~-hunting** *a.* & *n.*, (given to) sport of chasing fox with hounds; **~-mark**, brown spot

or stain caused by damp in book etc.; **~'tail**, fox's tail, grass with brush-like spikes; **~-terrier** (short-haired, sometimes used for unearthing foxes but chiefly kept as pet); **~'trot** *n.*, & *v.i.*, (perform) ballroom dance with slow and quick steps, music for this. **4.** **~'ў** *a.* (**~ily**, **~iness**), foxlike, crafty(-looking), reddish-brown, damaged by mildew etc. [E]

**foyer** (foi'ā, fwah'yā) *n.* Large space in theatre etc. for audience's use during interval; entrance hall of hotel, cinema, etc. [F, = hearth, home, f. L FOCUS]

**Fr.** *abbr.* Father; French.

**fr.** *abbr.* franc(s).

**frā'cas** (-kah) *n.* (*pl.* same *pr.* -kahz, \*-es). Noisy quarrel. [F f. It.]

**frā'ction** *n.* Numerical quantity that is not a whole number (DECIMAL, IMPROPER, VULGAR, *fraction*); small part, piece, or amount, (*a mere fraction of the cost*); portion of mixture obtainable by distillation etc.; **~al** *a.* (**-lly**), of or by fraction(s), very slight; **~āte** *v.t.*, separate into fractions. [F f. L (*frango fract-* break)]

**frā'ctious** (-shus) *a.* Unruly, peevish. [prec. in obs. sense 'brawling']

**frā'cture. 1.** *n.* Breakage esp. of bone or cartilage. **2.** *v.t.* & *i.* Cause fracture in; undergo fracture. [F or L (FRACTION)]

**frā'gile** *a.* (**~ly**). Easily broken, weak; of delicate constitution or frame; **fragi'lĭtў** *n.* [F or L (prec.)]

**frā'gment. 1.** *n.* Part broken off; remainder of otherwise lost or destroyed whole; extant remains or unfinished portion of book etc. **2.** *v.t.* & *i.* (*or* -ĕ'nt). Break or separate into fragments. **3.** **~arў** *a.*; **fragmentā'tion** *n.*

**frā'gran|ce** *n.* Sweetness of smell; sweet scent; **~t** *a.*, sweet-smelling. [F or L (*fragro* smell sweet)]

**frail** *a.* (**~ly** *pr.* -l-lĭ). Fragile, delicate; transient; morally weak; **~'tў** *n.*, -frail quality, weakness, foible. [F f. L (FRAGILE)]

**frāme. 1.** *v.t.* Shape, direct, dispose, (thoughts or acts *for* or *to* purpose, *to* do); adapt, fit, *to* or *into*; construct, put together, devise, (complex thing, plot, statement, theory, etc.); articulate (words); set in frame; serve as frame for; (sl.) concoct false charge or evidence against, devise plot against; **~-up**

*n.*, (colloq.) conspiracy, esp. to make innocent person appear guilty. **2.** *n.* Construction, build, structure; established order or system (*frame of society*); ~ **of reference**, system of geometrical axes for defining position, set of standards etc. governing behaviour, thought, etc.); temporary condition (*frame of mind*); human or animal body (*man of gigantic frame*); skeleton, essential substructure of building, motor vehicle, aircraft, etc.; rigid part of bicycle, spectacles, etc.; case or border enclosing picture etc.; glazed portable structure protecting plants; single complete image or picture on cinema film or transmitted in series of lines by television; triangular frame for positioning snooker etc. balls or skittles, balls so set up; round of play at snooker etc.; *(sl.)* = *frame-up*; ~**-house** (of wooden skeleton covered with boards etc.); ~**-saw** (stretched in frame to make it rigid); ~**'work**, substructure (lit. or fig.). [E, = be helpful]

**franc** *n.* French, Belgian, Swiss, etc., currency unit. [F (FRANK¹)]

**fra'nchise** (-z). **1.** *n.* Right to vote in election esp. for Parliament etc.; full membership of corporation or State, citizenship; right or privilege granted to person or corporation; authorization to sell company's goods etc. in particular area. **2.** *v.t.* Grant franchise to. [F (*franc* FRANK²)]

**Franci'scan** *a. & n.* (Friar or nun) of order founded by St. Francis of Assisi. [F f. L (*Franciscus* Francis)]

**Fra'nco-** *in comb.* French (and) (*Franco-Ger'man*). [L (FRANK¹)]

**franglais** (frah'ñglā) *n.* Corrupt version of French using many words and phrases borrowed from English. [F (*français* French, *anglais* English)]

**Frank¹** *n.* Member of Gmc nation that conquered Gaul in 6th c. [E]

**frank²** *a., v., & n.* **1.** *a.* Candid, open, outspoken, undisguised, unmistakable. **2.** *v.t.* Mark (letter etc.) to record payment of postage; ~**'ing-machine** (for stamping letters etc. and recording cost of postage). **3.** *n.* Franking signature or mark. [F f. L *francus* free (FRANK¹)]

**Fra'nkenstein** (-tīn) *n.* ~('s **monster**), thing that becomes terrifying to its creator. [character in Mrs. Shelley's novel *Frankenstein*]

**fra'nkfurter** *n.* Seasoned smoked sausage. [G (*Frankfurt*, place)]

**fra'nkincense** *n.* Aromatic gum resin burnt as incense; turpentine from conifers. [F (FRANK² in obs. sense 'high-quality', INCENSE²)]

**fra'ntic** *a.* (~ally, ~ly). Wildly excited, frenzied; characterized by great hurry or anxiety, desperate, violent, (*frantic effort, haste*); (colloq.) extreme. [F f. L (PHRENETIC)]

**frappé** (frã'pā) *a.* (Esp. of wine) iced, cooled. [F]

**frater'n|al** *a.* (-lly). Of brothers, brotherly; ~**al twins** (developed from separate ova and not necessarily similar); ~**ity** *n.*, brotherliness, religious brotherhood, guild or group of same class or with same interests, *students' society in college or university; **fra'ternize** *v.i.*, associate, make friends, (*with, together*, or abs.), (of troops) enter into friendly relations *with* enemy troops or inhabitants of occupied country; **fraterniza'tion** *n.* [L (*frater* brother)]

**fra'tricid|e** *n.* One who kills his, killing of one's, brother or sister; ~**al** *a.* (-lly). [F or L (*frater* brother, *caedo* kill)]

**Frau** (frow) *n.* (*pl.* ~'en). Title of German wife or widow = Mrs.; German woman. [G]

**fraud** *n.* Criminal deception; dishonest artifice or trick (**pious** ~, deception meant to benefit victim, esp. to strengthen religious belief); impostor; disappointing person or thing; ~**'ulent** *a.*, of, involving, guilty of, fraud; ~**'ulence** *n.* [F f. L *fraus fraud-*]

**fraught** (frawt) *a.* Filled or attended *with* (danger, meaning, etc.); (colloq.) causing or suffering anxiety or distress. [LDu. *vracht* (FREIGHT)]

**Fräulein** (froi'līn) *n.* Title of German spinster = Miss; unmarried German woman. [G]

**fray¹** *n.* Fight, conflict, (lit. or fig., *ready for the fray*); brawl. [AFFRAY]

**fray²** *v.t. & i.* Wear through by rubbing; ravel out at end; become ragged at edge (lit., or fig. of nerves, temper, etc.). [F f. L *frico* rub]

**fra'zzle** *n.* Worn or exhausted state (*beaten to a frazzle*). [orig. uncert.]

**freak. 1.** *n.* Capricious or unusual idea, act, etc.; ~ (**of nature**), monstrosity, abnormal person or thing; one who freaks out; drug addict; unconventional person. **2.**

*v.i.* & *t.* (sl.) ~ (**out**), (cause to) undergo drug etc. hallucinations or strong emotional experience, adopt unconventional life-style; ~**ed** (-kt) *a.*, oddly flecked or streaked.

**frĕ′ckle. 1.** *n.* Light brown spot on skin. **2.** *v.t.* & *i.* Spot or be spotted with freckles. [N]

**free** *a., adv.,* & *v.* **1.** *a.* (**freer** *pr.* frē′er; **freest** *pr.* frē′ist). Not a slave; having personal rights and social and political liberty; (of State, citizens, institutions) subject neither to foreign domination nor to despotic government (*free press, society*; **it's a ~ country**, colloq., the action proposed is not illegal); unrestricted, unimpeded, not confined or fixed; independent; permitted (*he is free to go*); (of literary style) not observing strict laws of form; (of translation) not literal; open to all comers; clear of or *of* or *from* obstructions, engagements, obligations, etc.; not occupied or in use (*the bathroom is free now*); spontaneous, unforced; costing nothing; (**\*for**) ~, provided without payment; lavish, unstinted, (*free flow of water; free with his money*); frank, unreserved; familiar, impudent, (**be, make, ~,** take liberties *with*); (of talk, stories, etc.) slightly indecent; (Chem.) not combined; (of power or energy) disengaged, available; released or exempt *from* (*free from disease; free from the ordinary rules*); not subject to tax etc. **2.** *adv.* Freely; without cost or payment. **3.** *v.t.* Make free, set at liberty; relieve *from*; rid or ease *of*; clear, disentangle; ~**′dman,** emancipated slave. **4.** ~ **and easy,** informal, unceremonious; ~**′board,** part of ship's side between water-line and deck; ~-**born,** born as a free citizen; **F~ Church** (nonconformist, or free from State control); ~ **enterprise,** freedom of private business from State control; ~ **fall,** movement under force of gravity only; ~ **fight** (in which all present may join, without rules); ~-**for-all** *n.* & *a.,* free (fight), unrestricted (discussion etc.); ~ **gift** (not in return for anything, esp. object given away to promote sales); ~ **hand,** liberty to act at one's own discretion (*give* or *have a free hand*); ~-**hand,** (of drawing) done without artificial aid to the hand; ~-**handed,** generous; ~′**hold,** (*n.*) (tenure of) land, property, etc.,

possessed absolutely as one's own, (*a.*) owned thus; ~′**holder,** possessor of freehold; ‖~ **house,** inn or public house not controlled by brewery and therefore able to sell any brand of beer etc.; ~ **kick,** (Footb.) kick taken without interference from opponents as minor penalty; ~-**lance,** person working for no fixed employer (so ~-*lance* v.i.); ~ **list** (of persons or things to be admitted free of payment, duty, etc.); ~**li′ver,** one who indulges in pleasure, esp. eating and drinking; ~**loader,** (sl.) one who eats etc. at other's expense; ~ **love,** (doctrine favouring) sexual relations irrespective of marriage; ~′**man,** person not slave or serf, one who has freedom of city etc.; ~ **market** (in which prices are determined by unrestricted competition); **F~′mason,** member of a society for mutual help etc. having elaborate secret rituals; **F~′masonry,** system and institutions of Freemasons, (*f-,* fig.) instinctive sympathy; ~ **on board, rail,** etc., without charge for delivery to ship, railway wagon, etc.; ~ **pass,** authority to travel on railway etc. or enter place of entertainment etc. without payment; ~ **port** (open to all traders, or free from duty on goods in transit); ~-**range,** (of hens etc.) given freedom of movement in seeking food; ~ **speech,** liberty to express opinions of any kind; ~-**spoken,** not concealing one's opinions; ~-**standing,** not supported by another structure; ~′**stone,** fine-grained easily sawn sandstone or limestone, peach with stone loose when fruit is ripe; ~-**style,** (of swimming-race) in which any stroke may be used, (of wrestling) allowing more holds than Graeco-Roman wrestling; ~ **thinker,** rejector of authority in religious belief (so ~-*thinking* n. & *a.,* ~ **thought**); ~ **trade** (left to its natural course without import restrictions etc.); ~ **verse,** = VERS LIBRE; ~ **vote,** Parliamentary vote not subject to party discipline; ~′**way,** express highway esp. with limited access; ~ **wheel,** driving-wheel of bicycle able to revolve with pedals at rest; ~-*wheel* v.i., ride bicycle without pedalling, (fig.) move or act without constraint; ~ **will,** power of acting without constraint of necessity or fate, ability to act at one's own discretion, (*I did it of my own free will*); ~**will** *a.*, voluntary; ~ **world**, non-Communist countries' collective name for themselves. [E]

**-free** *in comb.* Free of or from (*disease*, DUTY, POST², *-free*).

**free′booter** *n.* Pirate (lit. or fig.). [Du. *vrijbuiter* (FREE, BOOTY)]

**free′dom** *n.* Personal or civil liberty (*freedom of* CONSCIENCE, *of the* PRESS¹); liberty of action (*to do*; **the four ~s**, of speech and religion, from fear and want); frankness, undue familiarity; exemption (*from*); privilege possessed by city or corporation; membership, honorary citizenship, (*of* company, city); unrestricted use (*of* house etc.). [E]

**free′sia** (-z-) *n.* Bulbous Afr. plant with fragrant coloured flowers. [*Freese*, person]

**freeze. 1.** *v.i.* & *t.* (**froze; fro′zen**; *pr.* frō-). Turn into ice or other solid by cold (**it is freezing**, there is frost; **freezing-mixture**, salt and snow used to freeze liquids; **freezing-point**, temperature at which liquid, esp. water, freezes); be or feel very cold; cover or become covered with ice; preserve (food) by refrigeration below freezing-point; make or become rigid from cold (~ person's **blood**, terrify him; ~ **to death**, die through extreme cold); adhere *to* or *together* by frost (~ **on to**, sl., take or keep tight hold of); (cause to) become motionless, fixed, unavailable, or inactive; ~**-dry**, freeze and dry by evaporation of ice in high vacuum; *\*~ **out**, (sl.) exclude from business, society, etc., by competition, boycotting, etc.; ~ **up**, freeze completely, obstruct by formation of ice etc. (so ~*-up n.*, period or conditions of extreme cold). **2.** *n.* State, coming, or period, of frost; fixing or stabilization of prices, wages, etc. **3. free′zer** *n.*, (esp.) refrigerated room or compartment, deep-freeze. [E]

**freight** (frāt). **1.** *n.* Hire of ship or aircraft for transporting goods; (charge for) transport of goods in containers or by water (or *\*by land); cargo, load; *\*~ (**train**), goods train. **2.** *v.t.* Load (ship); transport (goods) by freight; ~′**er** *n.*, (esp.) cargo ship, freight-carrying aircraft, \*freight-wagon. [LDu. *vrecht* var. of *vracht* FRAUGHT]

**Frěnch. 1.** *a.* Of France or its language or people; having French characteristics. **2.** *n.* The French language; (euphem.) bad language (*excuse my French*); dry vermouth (*gin and French*); **the ~**, the French people. **3.** ||~ **bean** (kind used as unripe sliced pods or as ripe seeds); ~ **bread** (in long crisp loaf); ~ **Canadian** *a.* & *n.*, (native) of French-speaking area of Canada; ~ **chalk**, kind of steatite used as marker, dry lubricant, etc.; ~ **cricket**, informal type of cricket without stumps, in which bowler aims to hit batsman's legs; ~ **dressing**, salad dressing of vinegar and oil, usu. flavoured; *\*~ **fried potatoes**, *\*~ **fries**, potato chips; *French* HORN; **take ~ leave**, depart or act without permission or notice; ~ **letter**, (colloq.) condom; ~′**man**, man of French birth or nationality; ~ **polish**, shellac polish for wood; ~ **vermouth** (dry); ~ **window**, glazed door in outside wall; ~′**woman**, woman of French birth or nationality. **4.** ~′**ify** (or *f-*) *v.t.*, (usu. in *p.p.*) make French in form, manners, etc. [E (FRANK¹)]

**frěně′tic** *a.* (~**ally**). Frantic; fanatic. [F f. L f. Gk (*phrēn* mind)]

**frě′nzy. 1.** *n.* Delirious fury; wild excitement. **2.** *v.t.* (usu. in *p.p.*) Drive to frenzy.

**frē′quency** *n.* Frequent occurrence (*the frequency of his references to himself*); commonness of occurrence; (Phys.) rate of recurrence (of vibration etc.), number of cycles of carrier wave per second, band or group of such values, (~ **modulation**, varying carrier-wave frequency). [foll.]

**frē′quent¹** *a.* Occurring often, common, happening in close succession, (*frequent pauses*; *a frequent practice*); habitual, constant, (*a frequent caller*). [F, or L *frequens -ent-* crowded]

**frěquě′nt²** *v.t.* Go often or habitually to (place, meetings, house); **frěquentā′tion** *n.*; ~**ative** *a.* & *n.*, (verb etc.) expressing frequent repetition or intensity of action. [F or L (prec.)]

**frě′sco** *n.* (*pl.* ~**s**, ~**es**). Method of painting, picture, in water-colour laid on wall etc. before plaster is dry. [It., =fresh]

**frěsh** *a.*, *adv.*, & *n.* **1.** *a.* New, novel, not previously known etc.;

other, different, (*a fresh chapter*); lately made or arrived, just come *from*, not stale or musty or faded, (*fresh eggs, fish, flowers, memories*; *fresh from the maker*); (of food) not preserved by salting, tinning, freezing, etc.; not salt (*fresh water*); ~**'water** *a.*, not of the sea); inexperienced (~**'man**, first-year student at university etc.); pure, untainted, refreshing, (*fresh air, complexion*); brisk, vigorous, cheeky, amorously impudent. **2.** *adv.* Newly, recently, (esp. in comb.: *fresh-baked, -caught, -cut*, etc.). **3.** *n.* Fresh part (*the fresh of the morning*); freshet. **4.** ~**en** *v.t. & i.*, make or become fresh; ||~**'er** *n.*, (sl.) freshman; ~**'et** *n.*, stream of fresh water flowing into sea, flood of river. [F f. Rom. f. Gmc]

**frĕt**[1] *v.t.* (**-tt-**). Variegate, chequer; adorn (ceiling etc.) with carved or embossed work; ~**'saw**, narrow saw stretched on frame for cutting thin wood in patterns; ~**'work**, wood cut with fretsaw, carved work in decorative patterns esp. of straight lines. [f *freter*]

**frĕt**[2]. **1.** *v.i. & t.* **-tt-**). Worry, annoy; distress oneself or one*self* with regret or discontent (*at*; ~ **and fume**, show angry impatience); wear or consume by gnawing or rubbing (lit. or fig.). **2.** *n.* Irritation, vexation, querulousness. **3.** ~**'ful** *a.* (**-lly**), querulous. [E (FOR, EAT)]

**frĕt**[3] *n.* Bar or ridge on finger-board of guitar etc. to guide fingering. [orig. unkn.

**Freu'dian** (froi'd-   *a. & n.* (Disciple) of the Austrian psychologist *Freud* or his methods of psycho-analysis (~ **slip**, unintentional error that seems to reveal subconscious feelings). [person]

**Fri.** *abbr.* Friday.

**fri'ab**|**le** *a.* (~**ly**). Easily crumbled; ~**ĭ'lĭty** *n.* [F or L (*frio* crumble)]

**fri'ar** *n.* Member of certain religious orders of men (**Austin, Black, Grey, White, F~s**, Augustinians, Dominicans, Franciscans, Carmelites); ~**'s** or ~**s' balsam**, tincture of benzoin etc. used esp. for inhaling; ~**y** *n.*, convent of friars. [F f. L *frater* brother]

**fri'cassee** (*or* -ē'). **1.** *n.* Meat cut up, fried or stewed, and served with sauce. **2.** *v.t.* Make fricassee of. [F]

**fri'cative** *a. & n.* (Consonant)

made by friction of breath in narrow opening (e.g. *f*, *th*). [L (*frico* rub)]

**fri'ction** *n.* Rubbing of two bodies; (Phys. etc.) resistance body encounters in moving over another; (fig.) clash of wills, temperaments, opinions, etc.; ~**al** *a.* (**-lly**). [F f. L (prec.)]

**Fri'day** (*or* -dĭ). **1.** *n.* Day of week, following Thursday; **Good ~**, Friday before Easter Sunday, commemorating Crucifixion; **girl ~**, **man ~** [f. Man ~ in Defoe's *Robinson Crusoe*], assistant doing general duties. **2.** *adv.* (colloq.) On Friday (*see you Friday*); ~**s**, on Fridays, each Friday. [E]

||**frĭdge** *n.* (colloq.) Refrigerator. [abbr.]

**friend** (frĕnd) *n.* Person, not usu. a relation or lover, who feels mutual affection and regard for another (**be, keep, make, ~s**, be or become friendly *with*); person (esp. stranger) already mentioned (*my friend in the brown hat now left me*; used in voc. as polite form or in irony; **my honourable ~**, **my noble ~**, used of another member of same party in House of Commons, House of Lords; **my learned ~**, of another lawyer in court); (**F~**) member of the Society of Friends, Quaker; sympathizer, helper, (**a ~ at court**, one whose influence may be useful); helpful thing or quality (*my shyness was my best friend*); one who is not an enemy (*friend or foe?*); (usu. in *pl.*) regular contributor of money, help, etc., to institution. [E]

**frie'ndl**|**y** (frĕ'-) *a., n., & adv.* **1.** *a.* (~**iness**). Acting or disposed to act as friend; characteristic of friends, showing or prompted by kindness; not hostile, on amicable terms (*with*), (~ **match**, match played for pleasure merely; not in competition for cup etc.; ||**F~ Society**, society for insurance against sickness etc.); ready to approve or help; opportune. **2.** *n.* Friendly match. **3.** *adv.* In friendly manner.

**frie'ndshĭp** (frĕ'-) *n.* Friendly relationship or feeling.

**fri'er.** See FRY[2].

**Frie'sian** (frē'zhan; *or* -zĭan) *a. & n.* (One) of a breed of usu. black and white Friesland dairy cattle. [var. FRISIAN]

**frieze**[1] *n.* Coarse woollen cloth with

nap usu. on one side only. [F f. L (*lana*) *frisia* FRISIAN (wool)]

**frieze²** *n.* Part of entablature between architrave and cornice; horizontal band of sculpture filling this; band of decoration, esp. along wall near ceiling. [F f. L *Phrygium* (*opus*) Phrygian (work)]

**fri'gate** *n.* Escort-vessel like large corvette; (Hist.) warship next in size to ships of the line; ~(-**bird**), tropical marine bird of prey. [F f. It.]

**fright** (frīt) *n.* Sudden or violent fear; instance of this (*you gave me a fright*); person or thing looking grotesque or ridiculous; ~**en** *v.t.*, fill with fright, drive by fright (*away*, *into* or *out of* doing, *into* submission etc., *off*); (in *p.p.*) alarmed (*at, by*), having fear (*of, that, to* do); ~**ful** *a.* (-lly), dreadful, shocking, ugly, (colloq.) very great (*a frightful bore*). [E]

**fri'gid** *a.* Cold (esp. of climate or air); lacking ardour or friendliness, formal, forced, dull; (of woman) sexually unresponsive; **frigi'dity** *n.* [L (*frigus* n. cold)]

**frill. 1.** *n.* Ornamental strip of material gathered at one edge; similar paper ornament on ham-knuckle etc.; natural fringe on bird etc.; (in *pl.*) unnecessary embellishments or accomplishments. **2.** *v.t.* Decorate with frill. **3.** ~**y** *a.*, having or like frill(s). [orig. unkn.]

**fring|e** (-nj). **1.** *n.* Border, edging, esp. of tassels or loose threads; front hair hanging over forehead; margin or outer limit of area, population, etc.; thing, area, etc., of secondary or minor importance (**lunatic** ~**e**, fanatical or eccentric or visionary minority of party etc.; ~**e benefit**, perquisite or benefit supplementing money wage or salary; *\*=fringe benefit*; ~**y** *a.* **2.** *v.t.* Adorn with fringe, serve as fringe to. [F f. L *fimbria*]

**fri'ppery** *n.* Finery; showy ornament esp. in dress; empty display esp. in literary style; knick-knack(s). [F *friperie*]

**Fri'sian** (-z-) *a.* & *n.* (Native, language) of Friesland. [L *Frisii* n.pl. f. OFris. *Frisa*]

**frisk. 1.** *v.i.* & *t.* Leap or skip playfully; (sl.) feel over or search (person) for weapon etc. **2.** *n.* Playful leap or skip; (sl.) search of person; ~**y** *a.*

(~**ily**, ~**iness**), lively, playful. [F *frisque* lively]

**frisson** (frē'sawn) *n.* Emotional thrill. [F]

**frith.** See FIRTH.

**friti'llary** (*or* frī't-) *n.* Liliaceous plant, esp. wild snakeshead; spotted butterfly. [L (*fritillus* dice-box)]

**fri'tter¹** *n.* Piece of fried batter, often containing slice of fruit, meat, etc. [F *friture* f. L (*frigo* FRY²)]

**fri'tter²** *v.t.* ~ **away**, waste (money, time, energy, etc.) triflingly or indiscriminately. [obs. *fritters* fragments]

**fri'volous** *a.* Paltry, trifling, futile; lacking seriousness, silly; **fri'vol** *v.i.* & *t.* (‖-ll-), be frivolous, throw (time etc.) *away* foolishly; **frivo'lity** *n.* [L]

**frizz. 1.** *v.t.* Crimp, form into mass of small curls, (hair); frizz hair of (person). **2.** *n.* Frizzed hair or state. **3.** **fri'zzle¹**, (*v.t.* & *i.*) curl (*up*, or of hair etc.) in small curls, (*n.*) frizzled hair; ~**ly**, ~**y**, *adjs.* (-iness). [*friser*]

**fri'zzle²** *v.i.* & *t.* Fry or cook with sputtering noise; burn or shrivel (*up*). [obs. *frizz* (FRY², w. imit. ending)]

**Frl.** *abbr.* Fräulein.

**frō** *adv.* See to. [N (FROM)]

**frock. 1.** *n.* Woman's or girl's dress; monk's or priest's gown; = SMOCK-*frock*; ~(-**coat**), man's long-skirted coat not cut away in front; military coat of like shape. **2.** *v.t.* Invest with priestly office. [F f. Gmc]

**frog¹** *n.* Tailless smooth-skinned leaping amphibian developing from tadpole; (derog.) Frenchman; ~ **in** one's **throat**, (colloq.) hoarseness; ~'**man**, person equipped with rubber suit and flippers etc. for underwater swimming; ~-**march**, (*n.*) carrying of person face downwards by 4 others holding a limb each, (*v.t.*) carry thus, or hustle forward after seizing from behind and pinning arms; **F~gy** (-gǐ) *n.*, (derog.) Frenchman. [E]

**frog²** *n.* Elastic horny substance in middle of horse's sole. [orig. uncert.]

**frog³** *n.* Ornamental coat-fastening of spindle-shaped button and loop. [orig. unkn.]

**fro'lic. 1.** *v.i.* (-ck-).Play pranks or games, gambol. **2.** *n.* Prank, merry-making; merry party; ~**some** *a.*, merry, sportive. [Du. *vrolijk* a. (*vro* glad)]

**from** (*or emphat.* -ŏm) *prep.* expr. separation or origin, followed by: person, place, time, etc., that is starting-point of motion or action (*called out from the window; comes from the clouds; from the beginning*); lower limit (*saw from 10 to 20 boats*); place, object, etc., whose distance or remoteness is stated (*10 miles from Rome; I am far from saying*); thing or person avoided, deprived, etc., (*took his gun from him; released her from prison; prevented from coming; refrain from laughing*); state changed for another (*from being the victim he became the attacker*); thing distinguished or unlike (*know black from white*); source, giver, sender, (*dig gravel from pit; quoted from Shaw; have had no news from him*); reason, cause, motive, (*died from fatigue; does it from malice*); advs. or adv. phrs. of place or time (*from abroad; from long ago*), or preps. (*from among the nettles*); ~ **a child**, since childhood; ~ **day to day**, daily; ~ **home**, out, away; ~ **life**, ~ **nature**, with the living form or natural object etc. in front of the artist; ~ **now on**, henceforward; ~ **time to time**, occasionally. [E]

**frŏnd** *n.* (Bot.) Leaflike organ usu. bearing fructification, esp. in ferns. [L *frons frond-* leaf]

**front** (-ŭnt) *n.*, *a.*, & *v.* **1.** *n.* Side or part normally nearer to or towards spectator or direction of motion; any face of building, esp. that of main entrance; (Mil.) foremost part of army, line of battle, ground towards enemy, scene of actual fighting; (fig.) sector of activity resembling military front (*the home front*), organized political group; forward or conspicuous position (**in** ~, in an advanced or facing position; **in** ~ **of**, before, in advance of, in presence of, confronting); appearance, face, demeanour, (*show a bold front*); bluff, pretext; person etc. serving to cover subversive or illegal activities; = *sea front*; auditorium of theatre. **2.** *a.* Of the front; situated in front; ‖~ **bench**, seats for leading members of Government and Opposition parties in Parliament (~-**be'ncher**, occupant of such seat); ~ **line**, foremost position of army in battle (lit. or fig.); ~ **office**, head office; ~ **page**, first page of newspaper, usu. with most important news; ~ PASSAGE; ~ **runner**, leading con-

testant. **3.** *v.i.* & *t.* Have one's or its front facing or directed (*on, to, towards, upon*); (sl.) act as cover or front *for*; furnish with front (*fronted with stone*); lead (band). [F f. L *frons front-* face]

**fro'ntag|e** (-ŭn-) *n.* Land abutting on street or water, or between front of building and road; extent of front; front of building; way a thing faces; outlook; ~**er** (-ij-) *n.*, owner of land abutting on street or water.

**fro'ntal** (-ŭn-). **1.** *a.* (~**ly**). Of or on front (*frontal attack*); of person facing spectator (*frontal nudity*); of forehead (*frontal bone*). **2.** *n.* Covering for altar-front; façade.

**fro'ntier** (-ŭn-) *n.* Part of country that borders on another country; \*border of civilization; limits of attainment in science etc.

**fro'ntispiece** (-ŭn-) *n.* Illustration facing title-page of book. [F *frontispice* or L (FRONT, *specio* look)]

**frŏst** (*or* -aw-). **1.** *n.* Freezing, prevalence of temperature below freezing-point of water (BLACK, WHITE, *frost*; JACK *Frost*; ‖**two, three**, etc., **degrees of** ~, 30°, 29°, etc., Fahrenheit); frozen dew or vapour; (sl.) a failure; ~**-bite**, inflammation or gangrene of skin from severe cold (~**-bitten**, affected with this). **2.** *v.t.* & *i.* Injure (plant etc.) with frost; cover (as) with frost; cover (cake etc.) with frostlike sugar etc.; give rough or finely granulated surface to; ~ **over**, become covered with frost. **3.** ~**ing** *n.*, (esp.) frostlike icing for cakes; ~**y** *a.* (~**ily**, ~**iness**), cold with frost, frigid, lacking warmth of feeling, covered (as) with frost. [E (FREEZE)]

**frŏth** (*or* -aw-). **1.** *n.* Collection of small bubbles in or on liquid, foam; scum; (fig.) idle talk, light substance; ~**y** *a.* (~**ily**, ~**iness**). **2.** *v.i.* & *t.* Emit or gather froth; make (beer etc.) froth. [N]

**fro'ward** (frō'erd) *a.* (arch.) Perverse, refractory. [FRO, -WARD]

**frown. 1.** *v.i.* & *t.* Knit brows, esp. in displeasure or deep thought; (of thing) have gloomy aspect; ~ **at, on, upon**, disapprove of. **2.** *n.* Action of frowning; look of displeasure or deep thought. [F]

**frowst.** (colloq.) **1.** *n.* Fusty warmth in room; ~**y** *a.* (~**ily**, ~**iness**). **2.** *v.i.* Stay in or enjoy frowst. [*frowsty* var. foll.]

**frow′z|ȳ** *a.* (∼ily, ∼iness). Fusty; slatternly, dingy. [orig. unkn.]

**frō′ze(n).** See FREEZE.

**F.R.S.** *abbr.* Fellow of the Royal Society.

**frŭ′ctif|ȳ** *v.i. & t.* Bear fruit (lit. or fig.); make fruitful; ∼icā′tion *n.*, fructifying, reproductive parts of ferns etc. [F f. L (FRUIT)]

**frŭ′ctōse** *n.* (Chem.) Sugar found in fruit juice, honey, etc. [L (FRUIT)]

**frū′gal** (frōō′-) *a.* (∼ly). Sparing, economical, esp. as regards food (*frugal meal*); **frugă′litỹ** (frōō-) *n.* [L]

**fruit** (frōōt). **1.** *n.* Product of plant or tree that contains seed and freq. is used as food; these collectively (*feeds on fruit*); (usu. in *pl.*) vegetable products fit for food (*fruits of the earth*); produce of action, result, (BEAR[2] *fruit*); (in *pl.*) profits (*fruits of industry*); ∼-**cake** (with currants etc.); ∼ **cocktail,** finely-chopped fruit salad; ∼-**knife** (with silver etc. blade unaffected by acid); ‖∼ **machine,** gaming machine in which aim is to get certain combinations of symbols often representing fruit; ∼ **salad,** various fruits cut up and mixed; ∼ **sugar,** fructose. **2.** *v.i. & t.* (Cause to) bear fruit. **3.** ∼′**erer** *n.*, dealer in fruit; ∼′**ful** *a.* (-lly), fertile, causing fertility, prolific (lit. or fig.), remunerative, productive; ∼′**less** *a.*, not bearing fruit, useless, vain. [F f. L *fructus* (*fruor* enjoy)]

**frui′tion** (frōō-) *n.* Enjoyment, realization of aims or hopes; bearing of fruit (lit. or fig.). [F f. L (prec.)]

**frui′t|ȳ** (frōō′-) *a.* (∼ily, ∼iness). Of or resembling fruit; (of wine) tasting of the grape; (colloq.) full of rich quality, rough humour, or (usu. scandalous) interest. [FRUIT]

**frŭmp** *n.* Dowdy old-fashioned woman. [perh. dial. *frumple* wrinkle]

**frŭstr|ā′te** (*or* -ŭ′-) *v.t.* Baffle, counteract, disappoint; (in *p.p.*) discontented through inability to achieve one's desires; ∼ā′tion *n.* [L (*frustra* in vain)]

**frŭ′st|um** *n.* (*pl.* ∼a, ∼ums). Remainder of cone or pyramid whose top is cut off by plane parallel to base. [L, = piece cut off]

**frȳ[1]** *n.* Young fishes fresh from spawn; young of salmon in second year; **small** ∼, young or insignificant beings, children etc. [N, = seed]

**frȳ[2]. 1.** *v.t. & i.* Cook in hot fat;

*∼, ∼ing, -pan,* shallow pan used in frying (**out of the ∼ing-pan into the fire,** from bad situation to worse); ∼ **up,** heat (cold food) in frying-pan (so ∼-*up n.*). **2.** *n.* Fried food; internal parts of animals usu. eaten fried (*lamb's fry*). **3.** ∼′**er,** *n.,* (esp.) vessel for frying fish, one who fries fish. [F f. L *frigo*]

**ft.** *abbr.* feet; foot.

**fūchsia** (fū′sha) *n.* Drooping-flowered shrub. [*Fuchs*, person]

**fŭck.** (vulg.) **1.** *v.t. & i.* Copulate (with); = DAMN; mess *about, around, up*; make *off.* **2.** *n.* Act of, person as partner in, copulation; slightest amount (*not care or give a fuck*). **3.** ∼′**er** *n.* (often as general term of abuse); ∼′**ing** *a. & adv.* (often as mere intensive). [orig. unkn.]

**fŭ′ddle. 1.** *v.t.* Confuse; intoxicate. **2.** *n.* Confusion; intoxication. [orig. unkn.]

**fŭ′dd|y-dŭddy** *n. & a.* (sl.) Old-fashioned or ineffectual (person).

**fŭdge. 1.** *n.* Soft toffee-like sweetmeat; deceit; nonsense. **2.** *v.t. & i.* Fit together or make up (thing) in makeshift or dishonest way; fake; deal with incompetently. [orig. uncert.]

**fū′el. 1.** *n.* Material for burning as fire or source of heat or power; material used as source of nuclear energy; food as source of energy; thing that sustains or inflames passion etc.; ∼ **cell** (producing electricity direct from chemical reaction). **2.** *v.t. & i.* (‖-ll-). Supply with fuel (lit. or fig.); ∼ (up), take in or get fuel. [F f. L (*focus* hearth)]

**fŭg** *n.* (colloq.) Stuffiness of air in room; ∼′**gỹ** (-gi) *a.* [orig. unkn.]

**fū′gal** *a.* (∼ly). Of or resembling fugue. [FUGUE]

**fuggy,** See FUG.

**fū′gitive. 1.** *a.* Fleeing, that runs or has run away; fleeting, transient; (of literature) of passing interest, ephemeral. **2.** *n.* One who flees e.g. *from* justice or enemy; refugee. [F f. L (*fugio* flee)]

**fūgue** (fūg) *n.* Piece of music in which short melodic theme is introduced by one part and successively taken up or developed by others. [F, or It. (L *fuga* flight)]

**-ful** *suf.* forming: (1) *adjs.* f. *ns.*, w. sense 'full of' (*beautiful*), 'having qualities of' (*masterful*), or f. *adjs.* (*direful*), or f. *vbs.* w. sense 'apt to' (*forgetful*); (2, *pr.* foŏl) *ns.* (*pl.* occas. -**sful**), w. sense 'amount that fills' (*handful, spoonful*). [FULL¹]

**fŭ'lcr|um** *n.* (*pl.* ~**a**). Point against or on which lever is placed to get support. [L (*fulcio* to prop)]

**fulfi'l, \*fulfi'll,** (foŏl-) *v.t.* (-**ll**-). Carry out (task, prophecy, promise, command, law); satisfy (conditions, desire, prayer); answer (purpose); ~ **oneself**, develop fully one's gifts and character; ~'**ment** *n.* [E (FULL¹, FILL)]

**full¹** (foŏl). **1.** *a.* Holding all its limits will allow, replete, (*full of water; full to the brim;* colloq. *full up*); replete with food; (of heart etc.) charged with emotion; having abundance of (*full of interest, mistakes, vitality*); engrossed in thinking of (*full of himself, of his subject*); ~ **of the news** etc., unable to stop talking about it); abundant, copious, satisfying, (*a full meal; full details; is very full on this point*); complete, perfect, reaching specified or usual or utmost limit, (*full daylight, membership, orchestra; in full bloom; waited a full hour; at full* LENGTH; *gained full marks; at full* SPEED; *in full* SWING); swelling, plump; (of clothes) containing much material in folds etc.; **in** ~, without abridgement, to or for the full amount; **to the** ~, to the utmost extent. **2.** *adv.* Very (*know full well*); quite, fully, (*full six miles*); exactly (*hit him full on the nose*); ~ **out**, (done) at full power or top speed. **3.** ~ **back**, (position of) player behind half-backs in football etc.; ~-**blooded**, vigorous, sensual, not hybrid; ~-**blown,** (of flower) completely open, (fig.) fully developed; ~ **board**, provision of bed and all meals at hotel etc.; ~-**bodied**, rich in quality, tone, etc.; ~-**bottomed wig** (long at back); ~ **brother, sister,** (with both parents same); *full* CIRCLE; ~ **dress**, dress worn on great occasions; ~-**dress** *a.,* (of debate etc.) of major importance; ~ **face** (entirely visible to spectator); ~ **house**, large or full attendance at theatre, in Parliament, etc., (Poker) hand with three of a kind and a pair; ~-**length**, not shortened or abbreviated, (of mirror, portrait) showing whole of human figure; ~ **moon**, moon with whole disc illuminated, time when this occurs; ~ **pitch**, = *full toss*; ~-**scale**, not reduced in size, complete; *full*

SCORE; ~ **sister** (see *full brother*); ~ **speed** or **steam ahead!** (order to advance at full speed or pursue course of action energetically); *on a full* STOMACH; ~ **stop**, punctuation-mark (.) used at end of sentence, complete cessation; *full* TILT¹; ~ **time**, total normal duration of work etc. (~-*time a.,* occupying or using all one's working time); ~ **toss**, (Cricket) ball pitched right up to batsman; **in** ~ **view**, entirely visible. [E]

**full²** (foŏl) *v.t.* Clean and thicken (cloth); ~'**er** *n.* (~**er's earth**, clay used in fulling). [*fuller* E f. L *fullo*]

**fu'l(l)nèss** (foŏl-) *n.* Being full; **the** ~ **of time** (or **years**), destined time. [FULL¹]

**fu'lly** (foŏ'-) *adv.* Completely, quite, (*fully aware; fully 60*); ~-**fashioned,** (of women's stockings etc.) seamed and shaped to body. [E (FULL¹)]

**fu'lmar** (foŏ'-) *n.* Arctic gull-sized sea-bird related to petrel. [N (FOUL, *mar* gull)]

**fŭ'lmin|āte** *v.i.* & *t.* Flash like lightning, explode; thunder forth (censure); issue censures or condemnations (*against*); (of disease) develop suddenly; ~**ant** *a.,* fulminating; ~**ā'tion, ~ātor,** *ns.;* ~**atory** *a.* [L (*fulmen -min-* lightning)]

**fulness.** See FULLNESS.

**fu'lsome** (foŏ'-) *a.* (Of flattery etc.) cloying, disgustingly excessive. [FULL¹]

**fŭ'mble. 1.** *v.i.* & *t.* Use the hands awkwardly, grope about, (*fumble at lock, for keyhole, with key*); handle awkwardly or nervously; (Games) not stop (ball) cleanly. **2.** *n.* Bungling attempt or catch. [LG *fummeln*]

**fūme. 1.** *n.* (Esp. malodorous or harmful) smoke, vapour, or exhalation; fit of anger (*in a fume*). **2.** *v.i.* & *t.* Emit fumes; issue in fumes; be angry or irritated (*at person*); subject to fumes, esp. of ammonia to darken oak etc. **3. fū'migāte** *v.t.,* apply fumes to, disinfect or purify with fumes; **fūmigā'tion, fū'migātor,** *ns.* [F f. L (*fumus* smoke)]

**fū'mitory** *n.* Herb formerly used against scurvy. [F f. L *fumus terrae* smoke of earth]

**fŭn. 1.** *n.* Sport, amusement, jest. (**for** ~, **for the** ~ **of it, in** ~, not seriously; **like** ~, vigorously, quickly, iron. not at all; **make** ~ **of**, poke

~ **at**, tease, ridicule); source of amusement; ~ (**and games**), (colloq.) exciting or amusing happenings; ~**-fair**, (part of) fair devoted to amusements and side--shows. 2. *a*. Amusing, entertaining, enjoyable. [obs. *fun, fon* (FOND)]

**fŭ'nction. 1.** *n*. Activity proper to person or institution or by which thing fulfils its purpose; official duty; profession, calling; public ceremony or occasion; (important) social gathering; (Math.) quantity whose value depends on varying values (*of* others). 2. *v.i.* Fulfil function, operate. 3. ~**al** *a*. (-lly), of function(s), affecting only functions of a bodily organ etc., (of building etc.) constructed with regard mainly to its function, practical, utilitarian; ~**al-ism**, ~**alist**, *ns.*; ~**arȳ** *n.*, person who has to perform functions or duties. [F f. L (*fungor funct-* perform)]

**fŭnd. 1.** *n*. Permanently available stock (*fund of knowledge, labour*); stock of money, esp. one set apart for a purpose (SINKing-*fund*); (in *pl.*) pecuniary resources (in ~**s**, having money to spend). 2. *v.t.* Make (debt) permanent at fixed interest; provide with money. [L *fundus* bottom]

**fŭ'ndament** *n*. Buttocks; anus. [F f. L (FOUND¹)]

**fŭndamĕ'ntal. 1.** *a*. (~**ly**). Of, affecting, serving as, base or foundation, essential, primary, (*fundamental change, rules, truths*; ~ **note**, lowest note of chord; ~ **particle**, elementary particle). 2. *n*. Fundamental note; (usu. in *pl.*) fundamental rule etc. 3. ~**ism** *n.*, strict maintenance of traditional orthodox Protestant beliefs; ~**ist** *n.*; **fŭndamĕntă'litȳ** *n.*

**fŭ'neral. 1.** *n*. Burial or cremation of dead person(s) with ceremonies; (sl.) one's (usu. unpleasant) concern (*that's your funeral*). 2. *attrib. a.* Of or used at funeral(s). 3. **fŭ'nerarȳ** *a.*, of funeral(s); **fŭnĕ'real** *a.* (-lly), of or appropriate to funeral, dismal, dark. [F f. L (*funus funer-*)]

**fŭ'ng|us** (-ngg-) *n.* (*pl.* ~**i** *pr.* -nggī *or* -njĭ, ~**uses**). Mushroom, toadstool, or allied plant; spongy morbid growth; **fŭ'ngicide** (-nj-) *n.*, fungus-destroying substance; ~**oid**, (*a.*) fungus-like, (*n.*) fungoid plant; ~**ous** *a.* [L]

**fŭni'cular** *a. & n.* Of rope or its

tension; ~ (**railway**), cable railway with ascending and descending cars counterbalanced. [L *funiculus* dim. of *funis* rope]

**fŭnk¹.** (sl.) **1.** *n*. Fear, panic, (BLUE *funk*; ‖~**-hole**, place of safety, esp. dug-out, where one can hide); coward; ~**'y¹** *a*. 2. *v.t. & i.* Be afraid (of); try to evade. [orig. uncert.]

**fŭnk²** *n.* (sl.) *Strong smell, stink; funky music; ~**'y²** *a*. (~**iness**), *smelly, (of music, behaviour, etc.) down-to-earth, emotional, fashionable.

**fŭ'nnel. 1.** *n*. Narrowing tube, or truncated cone and tube, for guiding liquid etc. into small opening; chimney of steam-engine or ship. 2. *v.t. & i.* (‖-ll-). (Cause to) move (as) through funnel. [Prov. *fonill* f. L (*in*)*fundibulum*]

**fŭ'nnȳ. 1.** *a.* (-ily, -iness). Amusing, comical; strange, hard to account for; (colloq.) slightly unwell, insane, etc. 2. *n*. (in *pl.*, colloq.) (Section of newspaper for) comic strips. 3. ~**-bone**, part of elbow over which ulnar nerve passes; ~ **business**, ~ **stuff**, comic behaviour, (sl.) misbehaviour or deception. [FUN]

**fŭr. 1.** *n*. Short fine hair of certain animals (**make the ~ fly**, cause disturbance or dissension); (dressed) animal skin with this hair on it, used esp. for trimming or lining; garment of or trimmed or lined with this; (collect.) furred animals (*fur and feather*); crust or coating formed on tongue in sickness, in kettle by hard water, etc. 2. *v.t. & i.* (-rr-). Provide, clothe, coat, with fur (esp. in *p.p.*); ~ (**up**), (of kettle etc.) become coated with fur. 3. **fŭ'rrier** *n.*, dealer in or dresser of furs; ~**'rȳ** *a.* (-iness). [F f. Gmc]

**fŭr'below** (-ō) *n.* Gathered strip or pleated border of skirt or petticoat; (in *pl.*, derog.) showy ornaments. [F *falbala*]

**fŭr'bish** *v.t.* ~ (**up**), polish, renovate (old thing). [F f. Gmc]

**fŭr'cāte. 1.** (*or* -at) *a.* Forked, branched. 2. *v.i.* Fork, divide; ~**ā'tion** *n.* [L]

**fŭr'ious** *a*. Raging, intense, frantic, very angry; **fast and ~**, with great speed, uproarious(ly). [F f. L (FURY)]

**fŭrl** *v.t. & i.* Roll up and bind (sail,

flag, etc., on yard, pole, etc.; umbrella); become furled. [F *ferler*]

**fŭr′lŏng** *n.* Eighth of mile. [E (FURROW, LONG)]

**fŭr′lough** (-lō). **1.** *n.* Leave of absence, esp. granted to soldier. **2.** \**v.t.* & *i.* Grant furlough to; spend furlough. [Du. (FOR-, LEAVE[1])]

**fŭr′nace** (-ĭs) *n.* Apparatus with combustion chamber for subjecting metals etc. to intense heat (BLAST--*furnace*); very hot place; (fig.) severe test (*tried in the furnace*); closed fire-place for central heating. [F f. L *fornax* (*fornus* oven)]

**fŭr′nish** *v.t.* Provide (thing, person *with* thing); fit up (house etc.) with furniture; **~ing** *n.*, (esp. in *pl.*) article of furniture. [F f. Gmc]

**fŭr′niture** *n.* Movable contents of building or room, i.e. tables, chairs, etc., (~ **van**, large van to move furniture from one building to another; **part of the ~**, colloq., person or thing taken for granted); ship's equipment; spec. tackle etc.; accessories, e.g. handles and lock on door, traffic signs etc. in street; (Print.) pieces of wood or metal to make blank space or fasten type in chase.

**fŭrŏr′e**, \**fŭr′ŏr**, *n.* Enthusiastic admiration; craze; uproar. [It. f. L (FURY)]

**fŭr′rier.** See FUR.

**fŭr′row** (-ō). **1.** *n.* Narrow trench made by plough; ship's track; rut, groove, wrinkle. **2.** *v.t.* Plough; make furrows in. [E]

**fŭr′ry.** See FUR.

**fŭr′ther** (-dh-) *adv.*, *a.*, & *v.* **1.** *adv.* = FARTHER (*nothing was further from his thoughts*; **I′ll see you ~ first**, in hell, as strong form of refusal); to greater extent (*inquire further*); ~**(more)**, in addition (*I may further mention*; *and further, we must remember*). **2.** *a.* = FARTHER (*further details*; ||~ **education**, for persons above school age; **till ~ notice**, to continue until explicitly changed). **3.** *v.t.* Promote, favour (scheme etc.). **4.** **~ance** *n.*, furthering (*of* plan etc.); **~mŏst** *a.*, most distant; **fŭr′thest** (-dh-) *a.* & *adv.*, = FARTHEST; at (the) **fur-thest**, at greatest distance, at the latest, at most. [E (FORTH)]

**fŭr′tive** *a.* Done by stealth; sly, stealthy. [F or L (*fur* thief)]

**fūr′y** *n.* Fierce passion, wild anger, rage; violence of storm, disease, etc.; (usu. in *pl.*; F~) avenging goddess of Gk myth; (fig.) avenging spirit; angry or malignant woman; **like ~**, (colloq.) with great force or effort. [F f. L *furia*]

||**fŭrz|e** *n.* Spiny yellow-flowered evergreen shrub, gorse; **~′y** *a.* [E]

**fūse**[1] (-z). **1.** *v.t.* & *i.* Melt with intense heat; blend into a whole by melting (of metals etc., or fig.); (Electr.) provide (circuit etc.) with fuse(s), (of appliance etc.) fail owing to melting of fuse, cause (appliance etc.) to do this. **2.** *n.* (Electr.) (Device with) strip or wire of easily-melted metal placed in circuit so as to interrupt excessive current by melting; **~-box**, small box or cupboard containing fuses for a building's circuits. [L (FOUND[2])]

**fūse**[2] (-z), \**fūze*. **1.** *n.* Tube etc. filled or saturated with combustible matter for igniting bomb etc.; component in shell, mine, etc., designed to detonate explosive charge after an interval (*time-fuse*) or on impact etc. **2.** *v.t.* Fit fuse to. [It. f. L *fusus* spindle]

**fū′selage** (-z; -z -ahzh). *n.* Body of aeroplane. [F (FUSE[2])]

**fū′sib|le** (-z-) *a.* That may be melted; **~i′litў** *n.* [L (FUSE[1])]

**fū′sĭl** (-z-) *n.* (Hist.) Light musket; **~ier′** *n.*, member of one of several British regiments formerly armed with fusils; **~lā′de** *n.*, continuous discharge of firearms, sustained outburst of criticism etc. [F (L *focus* fire)]

**fū′sion** (-zhon) *n.* Fusing, melting; blending; coalition; (**nuclear**) **~**, union of atomic nuclei to form heavier nuclei, with release of energy; this process as source of energy; **~ bomb** (using this process, esp. hydrogen bomb). [F or L (FUSE[1])]

**fŭss. 1.** *n.* Bustle, excessive commotion, (**make a ~**, complain vigorously; **make a ~ of, over**, treat (person) with excessive attention etc.); treatment of trifles as important; abundance of petty detail; **~-budget, -pot**, (colloq.) person who is always making a fuss; **~′ў** *a.* (**~ily, ~iness**), inclined to fuss, over-elaborate, fastidious. **2.** *v.i.* & *t.* Make fuss, bustle (*about, around*, etc.); agitate, worry. [orig. unkn.]

**fū′stian. 1.** *n.* Thick twilled cotton cloth usu. dyed dark; (fig.) bombast. **2.** *a.* Made of fustian; bombastic, worthless. [F]

**fŭ′st|ў** *a.* (~ily, ~iness). Stale-smelling, musty, stuffy; antiquated. [F (*fust* barrel f. L *fustis* cudgel)]

**fū′tile** *a.* Useless, ineffectual, frivolous; **fūtĭ′lĭtў** *n.* [L *futilis* leaky, futile]

**fū′ture. 1.** *a.* About to happen or be or become (~ **life**, existence after death); of time to come; (Gram., of tense) describing event yet to happen. **2.** *n.* Time to come (**for the ~, in ~**, from this time onwards); what will happen in the future; person's, country's, etc., future condition; prospect of success etc. (*there's no future in it*); (Gram.) future tense; (in *pl.*) goods etc. sold for future delivery. **3.** **fū′turism** (-cher-) *n.*, artistic or literary movement abandoning traditional forms; **fū′turĭst**

(-cher-) *n.*; **fūturĭ′stĭc** (-cher-) *a.*, of futurism, ultra-modern, pertaining to future; **fūtŭr′ĭtў** *n.*, future time, (in *sing.* or *pl.*) future events, future life; **fūturŏ′logў** (-cher-) *n.*, forecasting of future esp. from present trends in society. [F f. L *futurus*, fut. part of *sum* be]

***fūze.** See FUSE[2].

**fŭzz** *n.* Fluff; fluffy or frizzed hair; (sl.) police(man); ~′ў *a.* (~ily, ~iness), fluffy, frizzy, blurred, indistinct. [prob. LDu.]

**-fў** *suf.* forming (1) *vbs.* f. *ns.* w. sense 'make, produce' (*pacify*, *satisfy*), 'make into' (*deify*, *petrify*), (2) *vbs.* f. *adjs.* w. sense 'bring or come into state' (*Frenchify*, *solidify*), (3) *vbs.* w. causative sense (*horrify*, *stupefy*). [L *facio* make]

# G

**G, g,** (jē) *n.* (*pl.* **Gs, G's**). Seventh letter; (Mus.) fifth note in diatonic scale of C major.

**g** *abbr.* gram(s); (acceleration due to) gravity.

**Ga.** *abbr.* Georgia.

**găb** *n.* (colloq.) Talk, chatter; **gift of the ~**, eloquence, loquacity; ~′bў *a.*, talkative. [var. GOB[2]]

**gă′bardine** (-ēn) *n.* Twill-woven cloth esp. of worsted. [var. GABERDINE]

**gă′bble. 1.** *v.i.* & *t.* Talk, utter, inarticulately or too fast. **2.** *n.* Fast unintelligible talk. [Du., imit.]

**gă′berdine** (-ēn) *n.* (Hist.) loose long upper garment worn by Jews etc.; = GABARDINE. [F]

**gă′ble** *n.* (Triangular upper part of) wall at end of ridged roof; gable-shaped canopy. [N & F]

**găd**[1] *int.* (or by ~) expr. surprise or asseveration. [*God*]

**găd**[2] *v.i.* (-dd-). Go *about* idly or in search of pleasure; ~**about**, gadding (person). [obs. *gadling* companion]

**gă′dflў** *n.* Cattle-biting fly; irritating person. [obs. *gad* spike]

**gă′dgĕt** *n.* Small fitting or contrivance in machinery etc.; (useful) instrument; ~**rў** *n.*, gadgets. [orig. unkn.]

**gă′doid** *a.* & *n.* (Fish) of the cod family. [L f. Gk *gados* cod]

**gă′dwall** (-awl) *n.* Brownish-grey freshwater duck. [orig. unkn.]

**Gael** (gāl) *n.* Scottish Celt; Irish or Manx Celt; **Gae′lic** (gă′l-), (*a.*) of Gaels, (*n.*) their language. [Sc. Gael. *Gaidheal*]

**găff**[1]. **1.** *n.* Barbed fishing-spear; stick with iron hook for landing large fish; spar to which head of fore-and-aft sail is bent. **2.** *v.t.* Seize (fish) with gaff. [Prov. *gaf* hook]

**găff**[2] *n.* (sl.) **Blow the ~**, divulge plot or secret. [orig. unkn.]

**gă′ffe** *n.* Blunder, *faux pas.* [F]

**gă′ffer** *n.* Elderly rustic, old fellow, (also as title or *voc.*); ‖foreman of gang of workmen. [prob. GODFATHER]

**găg. 1.** *n.* Thing thrust into mouth to prevent speech or hold mouth open for operation; (Parl.) closure, guillotine; (esp. Theatr.) jest, comic business in play etc. **2.** *v.t.* & *i.* (-gg-). Apply gag to; silence, deprive of free speech; (esp. Theatr.) insert gags; choke, retch. [orig. uncert.]

**gă′ga** (*or* gah′gah) *a.* (sl.) Fatuous, senile, slightly crazy. [F]

**gāge**[1]. **1.** *n.* Pledge, thing deposited as security; (glove thrown down as, any symbol of) challenge to fight.

**2.** *v.t.* (arch.) Stake, offer as guarantee. [F f. Gmc (WAGE, WED)]

**gāge²**. See GAUGE.

**gāge³** *n.* Greengage. [abbr.]

**gǎ'ggle** *n.* Flock (of geese); (derog.) company (of women); (disorderly) group. [imit.]

**gai'etў, \*gay'etў**, *n.* Being gay, mirth; merry-making, amusement; bright appearance; **gai'lў**, see GAY. [F (GAY)]

**gain. 1.** *v.t. & i.* Obtain, secure, (*gain advantage*, one's *object*); win (sum) as profits etc., earn; make a profit, be benefited, improve or advance *in* some respect, *by* comparison or contrast; obtain as increment or addition (*gain momentum, weight*); win (land from sea, battle); persuade (*gain over*); reach (desired place); (of clock etc.) become fast, or fast by (specified time); *gain* GROUND¹; ~ **time**, obtain advantageous delay by pretexts or slow methods; ~ **(up)on**, come closer to (what is pursued). **2.** *n.* Increase of wealth etc., profit, improvement; acquisition of wealth; (in *pl.*) sums got by trade etc.; increase in amount; ~**'ful** *a.* (**-lly**), lucrative, paid (employment). [F f. Gmc]

**gain|say'** *v.t.* (arch., literary; ~**said** *pr.* -ā'd, -ĕ'd). Deny, contradict. [N (AGAINST, SAY)]

**gait** *n.* Manner of or carriage in walking; manner of forward motion of horse etc. [N]

**gai'ter** *n.* Covering of cloth, leather, etc., for leg below knee, for ankle, or for part of machine etc. [F *guêtre*]

**gǎl** *n.* (vulg.) Girl. [repr. var. pr.]

**Gal.** *abbr.* Galatians (N.T.).

**gal.** *abbr.* gallon(s).

**gā'la** (*or* gah'-) *n.* Festive occasion; ||festive gathering for sports. [F, *or* It. f. Sp., f. Arab.]

**galǎ'ctic** *a.* Of a galaxy or galaxies. [Gk (GALAXY)]

**gǎ'lantine** (-ēn) *n.* White meat boned, spiced, etc., and served cold. [F f. L]

**gǎ'laxў** *n.* (*G*~) irregular luminous band of stars indistinguishable to naked eye, Milky Way; independent system of stars, gas, dust, etc., existing in space; brilliant company (*of* beauties etc.). [F f. L f. Gk (*gala* milk)]

**gāle¹** *n.* (Sweet-)~, bog myrtle. [E]

**gāle²** *n.* Very strong wind; outburst esp. of laughter; (Naut.) storm; (poet.) breeze. [orig. unkn.]

**gall¹** (gawl) *n.* Bile of animals; (fig.) bitterness (*gall and wormwood*); asperity, rancour, (**dip** one's **pen in** ~, write virulently); (sl.) impudence; ~**-bladder**, vessel containing bile; ~**'stone**, calculus in gall-bladder. [N]

**gall²** (gawl). **1.** *n.* Sore made by chafing; (cause of) mental soreness; place rubbed bare. **2.** *v.t.* Rub sore; vex, humiliate. [LDu. *galle*]

**gall³** (gawl) *n.* ~**('nut)**, excrescence produced by insects (*gall-fly, gall-wasp*) etc., on trees, esp. on oak. [F f. L *galla*]

**gǎ'llant** (*or as below*) *a., n., & v.* **1.** *a.* Fine, stately, (*gallant ship, steed*); brave; (*or* galǎ'nt) very attentive to women, concerned with love, amatory. **2.** *n.* (arch.) Man of fashion; (*or* galǎ'nt) ladies' man, lover; ~**rў** *n.*, bravery, devotion to women, polite act or speech, sexual intrigue. [F (*galer* make merry)]

**gǎ'lleon** *n.* (Hist.) Ship of war (usu. Spanish). [Du. f. F or Sp. (GALLEY)]

**gǎ'llerў** *n.* Covered walk partly open at side, colonnade; narrow passage in thickness of wall or on corbels, open towards interior of building; balcony, esp. in hall or over part of area of church etc. (*minstrels' gallery*); (Theatr.) (occupants of) highest balcony (**play to the** ~, appeal to unrefined taste); group of spectators at golf match etc.; long narrow room (SHOOTING-*-gallery*), corridor; room or building for showing works of art; (Mining etc.) horizontal underground passage. [F f. It. f. L]

**gǎ'lley** *n.* (Hist.) low flat one-decked vessel usu. rowed by slaves or criminals; ancient Greek or Roman warship; ship's or aircraft's kitchen; (Print.) long tray for set-up type, ~ (**proof**), proof in long narrow form; ~**-slave,** (fig.) drudge. [F f. L *galea*]

**Gǎ'llic** *a.* Of Gaul(s); (often joc.) French; ~**an** *a. & n.*, (adherent) of the school of (French) Roman Catholics claiming partial autonomy; ~**ism** *n.*, French idiom; ~**ize** *v.i. & t.* [L *gallicus*]

**gǎllinā'ceous** (-shʊs) *a.* Of the order including domestic poultry, pheasants, etc. [L (*gallina* hen)]

**gállivă'nt** v.i. (colloq.) Gad about. [perh. corrupt. GALLANT 'to flirt']

**Gă'llō-** in comb. French. [L]

**gă'llon** n. Measure of capacity (4546 c.c.; for wine, or U.S., 3785 c.c.); (colloq., usu. in *pl.*) large amount. [F]

**gallōō'n** n. Narrow close-woven braid. [F]

**gă'llop. 1.** n. Quadruped's, esp. horse's, fastest pace, with all feet off ground together in each stride; ride at this pace. **2.** v.i. & t. (Of horse etc. or its rider) go at a gallop; make (horse) gallop; read, talk, etc., fast; progress rapidly (*galloping consumption, inflation*). [F (WALLOP)]

**gă'llows** (-ōz) n.pl. (usu. treated as *sing.*) Structure, usu. of two uprights and cross-piece, for the hanging of criminals. [N]

**Gă'llup** n. ~ poll, assessment of public opinion by questioning representative sample, esp. as basis of forecasts of voting etc. [person]

**gă'lop** n. (Music for) lively dance in duple time. [F (GALLOP)]

**galŏ're** adv. In plenty (*whisky galore*). [Ir.]

**galŏ'sh**, ||golŏ'sh, n. Overshoe usu. of rubber. [F]

**galŭ'mph** v.i. (colloq.) Go prancing in triumph; move noisily or clumsily. [see PORTMANTEAU]

**gălvă'nic** a. (~ally). Of electricity from a primary battery, (fig.) stimulating, full of energy; **gă'lvanize** v.t., stimulate (as) by electricity, (fig.) rouse by shock etc. (*into* action etc.), coat (iron) with zinc to protect from rust; **gălvanŏ'mĕter** n., instrument for measuring small electric currents. [*Galvani*, person]

**gă'mbĭt** n. Chess opening in which player sacrifices pawn or piece; (fig.) opening move in some action; trick, device. [It. *gambetto* tripping up]

**gă'mble. 1.** v.t. & i. Play games of chance for (esp. high) money stakes; risk much in hope of great gain; ~ away, lose by gambling; ~ on, act in hope of (event); ~r n., one who gambles habitually. **2.** n. Risky undertaking. [GAME[1]]

**gămbo'ge** (-ōō'zh, -ō'zh) n. Gum resin used as yellow pigment and as purgative. [*Cambodia*, place]

**gă'mbol** n., & v.i. (||-ll-). Caper, frisk. [*gambade* leap f. It. (*gamba* leg)]

**gāme**[1] n., a., & v. **1.** n. Contest bound by rules and decided by skill, strength, or luck, (**play a good, poor,** ~, be skilful or not; **be on, off,** one's ~, be playing well, badly; **play the** ~, observe rules, fig. behave honourably); (in *pl.*), (Gk & Rom. Ant.) athletic, dramatic, and other contests, gladiatorial etc. shows, (mod.) athletic contests (OLYMPIC *Games*); diversion, pastime, (*a game of ball*); scheme, undertaking, &c., (**play** person's ~, advance his schemes unintentionally; ~ **not worth the candle**, result not worth trouble etc. involved; **the** ~ **is up**, scheme is foiled; **give the** ~ **away**, reveal intentions; portion of play forming scoring unit e.g. in bridge or tennis; winning score in game, state of score (*the game is four all*); jest (**make** ~ **of**, ridicule); hunted animal (lit. or fig.; **fair** ~, legitimate object of pursuit etc.); (flesh of) animals, birds, &c., hunted for sport or food. **2.** a. Spirited (DIE[2] *game*); having the spirit or energy (*am game to go, game for a walk*). **3.** v.i. Gamble for money stakes. **4.** ~'**cock** (of kind bred for cock-fighting); ~'**keeper**, person employed to breed game, prevent poaching, etc.; ~'**smanship**, art of winning games by psychological means. [E]

**gāme**[2] a. (Of leg, arm, etc.) crippled. [orig. unkn.]

**gā'me|some** (-ms-) a. Sportive; ~**ster** (-ms-) n., gambler. [GAME[1]]

**gamē'te** (or -ă'-) n. (Biol.) Mature germ-cell uniting with another in sexual reproduction. [L f. Gk, = wife]

**gă'mĭn** (or gă'măn) n. (Street) urchin; impudent child; **gami'ne** (-ē'n) n., girl gamin, small attractively informal etc. young woman. [F]

**gă'mma** n. Third Gk letter (Γ, γ) = g; third-class mark in examination; ~ **radiation, rays**, X-rays of very short wavelength. [Gk]

**gă'mmon** n. Bottom piece of flitch of bacon with hind leg; pig's ham cured like bacon. [F (JAMB)]

**gă'mmy** a. (sl.) = GAME[2]. [dial. form of GAME[2]]

**gă'mut** n. Whole series of recognized musical notes; compass of voice etc.; (fig.) entire range. [L. *gamma ut*, wds arbitrarily taken as names of notes]

**gā′m**|**ў** *a.* (~ily, ~iness). Smelling or tasting like high game. [GAME¹]

**gă′nder** *n.* Male goose; fool; (sl.) look, glance, (*take a gander*). [E]

**găng¹. 1.** *n.* Set of workmen, slaves, or prisoners; band of persons associating esp. for criminal or (colloq.) other disapproved purpose; set *of* tools working in co-ordination; ~′**way,** opening in ship's bulwarks, bridge from this to shore, passage esp. between rows of seats. **2.** *v.i. & t.* Join *up*, act in concert *with*; arrange (tools etc.) to work in co-ordination. **3.** ‖~′**er** *n.,* foreman of gang of workmen; ~′**ster** *n.,* member of gang of violent criminals. [N]

**găng²** *v.i.* (Sc.) Go; ~ **agley,** (of plan etc.) go wrong. [E]

**gă′ngling** (-ngg-) *a.* (Of person) loosely built, lanky. [frequent. of prec.]

**gă′ngli**|**on** (-ngg-) *n.* (*pl.* ~a, ~ons). Enlargement or knot on nerve forming centre for reception and transmission of impulses; (fig.) centre of activity etc.; ~ŏ′**nic** *a.* [Gk]

**gă′ngr**|**ēne** (-ngg-). **1.** *n.* Necrosis of part of body, usu. caused by obstructed blood-circulation; (fig.) moral corruption; ~**ēnous** *a.* **2.** *v.t. & i.* Become affected, affect, with gangrene. [F f. L f. Gk]

**gă′ngue** (-ng) *n.* Valueless earth etc. in which ore is found. [F f. G (GANG¹)]

**gă′nnet** *n.* Sea-bird, esp. solan goose. [E]

**\*gă′ntlet.** See GAUNTLET².

**gă′ntrў** *n.* Structure supporting travelling crane, railway signals, equipment for rocket-launch, etc. [prob. *gawn* GALLON, TREE]

‖**gaol, jail,** (jāl). **1.** *n.* Public prison for persons committed by process of law; confinement in this; ~′**bird,** habitual criminal; ~′**break,** escape from gaol. **2.** *v.t.* Put in gaol; ‖**gao′ler, jai′lor, -er,** (jā′l-) *n.,* person in charge of (prisoners in) gaol. [F f. Rom. (CAGE)]

**găp** *n.* Breach in hedge or fence or wall; gorge, pass; empty space, interval, deficiency; wide divergence in views etc.; ~′**pў** *a.* [N]

**gāpe. 1.** *v.i.* Open mouth wide, (of mouth or comparable thing) open or be open wide; stare *at*; yawn. **2.** *n.* Yawn, open-mouthed stare; open mouth. [N]

**gă′rage** (*or* -ahzh, -ahj). **1.** *n.* Building for storing motor vehicle(s); establishment selling petrol etc., or repairing and selling motor vehicles. **2.** *v.t.* Put or keep (vehicle) in garage. [F]

**gărb. 1.** *n.* Dress, esp. characteristic dress, (*of* nation, class). **2.** *v.t.* (usu. in *pass.* or *refl.*) Dress, esp. in this. [F f. It. f. Gmc (GEAR)]

**gă′rbage** *n.* Refuse; domestic waste (\*~ **can,** dustbin); foul or rubbishy literature etc. [AF]

**gă′rble** *v.t.* Make (usu. unfair) selection from (facts, statement); unintentionally distort or confuse (facts, messages, etc.). [It. f. Arab.]

**gā′rden. 1.** *n.* Piece of ground for growing flowers, fruit, or vegetables, (LEAD¹ *up the garden* (*path*)); (*attrib.*) cultivated (*garden plants*; **common or** ~, colloq., ordinary); (esp. in *pl.*) grounds laid out for public resort (*botanical, zoological, gardens; beer garden*); ~ **city,** industrial or other town laid out with garden-like surroundings; ~ **party** (held on lawn or in garden). **2.** *v.i.* Cultivate garden; ~**er** *n.,* (esp.) person employed to tend garden. [F f. Rom. f. Gmc (YARD²)]

**gārdē′nia** *n.* Tree or shrub with large fragrant white or yellow flowers; its flower. [*Garden*, person]

**gă′rfish** *n.* (*pl.* same). Fish with long spearlike snout. [E, = spear-fish]

**gārgă′ntuan** *a.* Gigantic. [*Gargantua,* giant in Rabelais]

**gā′rgle. 1.** *v.t. & i.* Wash (throat) with liquid kept in motion by breath. **2.** *n.* Liquid so used. [F (foll.)]

**gā′rgoyle** *n.* Grotesque spout of gutter of building. [F, = throat]

‖**gă′riba′ldi** (-baw′l-) *n.* Biscuit containing layer of currants. [person]

**gā′rish** *a.* Obtrusively bright, showy, gaudy. [obs. *gaure* stare]

**gā′rland. 1.** *n.* Wreath of flowers etc. worn on head or hung on thing as decoration. **2.** *v.t.* Crown with garland; deck with garlands. [F]

**gā′rlic** *n.* Plant with pungent strong-smelling bulb used in cookery; ~**kў** *a.* [E, = spear-leek]

**gā′rment** *n.* Article of dress; (in *pl.*) clothes; outward covering. [F (GARNISH)]

**gā′rner. 1.** *v.t.* Store up; collect.

**2.** n. (literary). Storehouse, granary, (lit. or fig.). [F f. L (GRANARY)]

**gar′net** n. Vitreous silicate mineral, esp. red kind used as gem. [F f. L; cf. (POME)GRANATE]

**gar′nish. 1.** v.t. Decorate (esp. dish for table). **2.** n. Material(s) for this. [F garnir f. Gmc]

**garotte.** See GARROTTE.

**gă′rret** n. (Esp. wretched) attic or room in roof. [F, = watch-tower (foll.)]

**gă′rrison. 1.** n. Troops stationed in town etc. to defend it. **2.** v.t. Furnish with, occupy as, garrison. [F (garir defend, f. Gmc)]

**gar(r)ŏ′tte, *garrŏ′te. 1.** n. (Apparatus for) Spanish capital punishment by strangulation; highway robbery done by throttling victim. **2.** v.t. Execute, throttle, thus. [F or Sp.]

**gă′rrulous** (-rōō-) a. Talkative; **garru′lĭtў** (-rōō′-) n. [L]

**gar′ter** n. Band worn near knee to keep up a stocking; ‖**the G~**, (badge, membership, of) highest order of English knighthood; **~ stitch** (of all-plain knitting). [F]

**găs. 1.** n. (pl. **~es** pr. gă′sĭz). Any airlike or completely elastic fluid, esp. one not liquid or solid at ordinary temperatures (cf. VAPOUR); such fluid, esp. COAL gas, or natural **~** (found in earth's crust), used for lighting, heating, or cooking; *(colloq.) petrol, gasoline, (**step on the ~**, accelerate motor vehicle by pressing accelerator pedal with foot, fig. hurry); (**laughing-**)**~**, nitrous oxide gas as anaesthetic; (**poison**) **~**, substance to disable enemy in war; (colloq.) empty talk, boasting; **~′éous** (gă′-) a., of (the nature of) gas. **2.** v.t. & i. (**-ss-**). Expose to gas; talk emptily or boastfully; (in p.p.) disabled by gas. **3.** **~′bag**, gas-container in airship etc., (derog.) empty talker; **~ chamber** (used to kill animals or prisoners by gas poisoning); **~ cooker** (heated by gas); **~ fire**, domestic heater (usu. fixed) burning gas; **~-fired**, using gas as fuel; **~ helmet, mask**, appliances worn as defence against poison gas; **~′holder**, large receptacle for storing gas, gasometer; **~′light**, light given by esp. coal gas; **~ main**, main pipe supplying gas; **~ meter** (registering amount of gas consumed); **~ oven, =** gas

cooker or gas chamber; **~ poker**, hollow tube conveying gas to light a fire; **~ ring** (pierced with small holes and fed with gas for cooking etc.); *~ station**, petrol filling station; **~′works**, place where (coal-)gas is manufactured. [Du., after Gk (CHAOS)]

**găsh. 1.** n. Long deep cut, wound, or cleft. **2.** v.t. Make gash in, cut. [F]

**gă′sĭf|ў** v.t. Convert into gas; **~ĭcā′tion** n. [GAS]

**gă′skĕt** n. Small cord securing furled sail to yard; sheet or ring of rubber, asbestos, etc., to seal junction of metal surfaces. [F garcette]

*găsoline** (-ēn) n. Petrol. [GAS]

**găsŏ′mĕter** n. Reservoir from which gas is distributed by pipes. [F gazomètre (GAS, -METER)]

**gasp** (-ah-). **1.** v.i. & t. Catch breath with open mouth as in exhaustion or surprise; utter with gasp(s). **2.** n. Convulsive catching of breath; **at one's last ~**, at point of death, (fig.) exhausted. [N]

**gă′ssў** a. Of or like or full of gas; verbose. [GAS]

**gă′steropŏd.** See GASTROPOD.

**gă′strĭc** a. Of the stomach; **~ flu**, (colloq.) intestinal disorder of unknown cause; **~ juice**, digestive fluid secreted by stomach glands. [F (foll.)]

**găstr|ō-** in comb. Stomach; **~ŏ′-nomў** n., science of good eating and drinking; **~onŏ′mĭc** a. [Gk gastēr stomach]

**gă′st(e)ropŏd** n. Mollusc, e.g. snail, with locomotive organ placed ventrally. [F (GASTRO-, Gk pous foot)]

**gāte. 1.** n. (Also **~′way**) opening in wall etc. made for entrance and exit and closable with barrier; such barrier, of wooden or iron framework, solid or of bars etc., hinged, pivoted, or sliding; means of entrance or exit; numbered place of access to aircraft at airport; contrivance regulating passage of water in lock etc.; number entering by payment at gates to see football match etc.; **~(-money)**, amount of money thus taken; **~′crasher**, uninvited intruder at party etc. (so **~′crash** v.t. & i.); **~′leg(ged)**, (of table) with legs in gatelike frame swinging back to allow top to fold down. **2.** v.t. ‖Confine to college or school esp. after fixed hour. [E]

**gă′teau** (-tō) *n.* (*pl.* ~**s**, ~**x**, *pr.* -z). Large rich cream-cake. [F]

**gă′ther** (-dh-) *v.t.* & *i.* Bring or come together, assemble, accumulate, (**be** ~**ed** to one's **fathers**, die; **rolling stone** ~**s no moss**, constant change of employment etc. does not pay; **ship** ~**s way**, begins to move); summon up (energy etc.); pluck (flowers etc.); collect (grain etc.) as harvest; draw (garment, brow) together in folds or wrinkles, develop purulent swelling; pick *up* from ground; draw *up* (limbs, one*self*) into small compass; sum *up* (scattered facts); infer, deduce, (*that*); ~**ing** *n.*, assembly, purulent swelling, (Bookbinding) group of leaves taken together; ~**s** (-z) *n.pl.*, gathered-in part of dress. [E]

**G.A.T.T.** (găt) *abbr.* General Agreement on Tariffs and Trade.

**gauche** (gōsh) *a.* Tactless, socially awkward; ~**rie** (gō′sherē) *n.*, gauche manners or act. [F]

**gau′cho** (*or* gow′-) *n.* (*pl.* ~**s**). One of a mixed European and Amer. Ind. people of mounted herdsmen in S. America. [Sp. f. Quechua]

**gaud** *n.* Showy ornament; ~**y̆**, (*n.*) ‖annual entertainment, esp. college dinner for old members etc., (*a.*; ~**ily**, ~**iness**) tastelessly showy. [F f. L *gaudeo* rejoice]

**gauge** (gāj), *\****gāge²** (also ‖in Naut. sense). **1.** *n.* Standard measure esp. of capacity or contents of barrel, fineness of textile, diameter of bullet, or thickness of sheet metal; capacity; extent; distance between rails or opposite wheels; (Naut.) position relative to wind (**have the weather** ~ **of**, be to windward of, fig. have advantage of); instrument measuring rainfall, pressure, etc., testing dimensions of wire etc., or marking parallel lines; criterion, test. **2.** *v.t.* Measure exactly, test dimensions etc. of; measure content or capacity of (cask etc.); estimate (person, character). [F]

**Gaul** *n.* Inhabitant of ancient Gaul; ~**ish**, (*a.*) of the Gauls, (*n.*) their language. [F f. Gmc]

**gaunt** *a.* Lean, haggard; grim, desolate. [orig. unkn.]

**gau′ntlet¹** *n.* Stout glove with long loose wrist for driving, wicket-keeping, etc.; (Hist.) armoured glove (**throw down, pick up, the** ~, fig. issue, accept, a challenge). [F dim. of *gant* glove]

**gau′ntlet²**, *\****gă′ntlet**, *n.* Run the ~, pass between rows of men who strike one with sticks etc. as punishment, (fig.) undergo criticism etc. [Sw. *gatlopp* (*gata* lane, *lopp* course)]

**gauz|e** *n.* Thin transparent fabric of silk, cotton, wire, etc.; ~′**y̆** *a.* (~**iness**). [F (*Gaza*, place)]

**gāve.** See GIVE.

**gă′vel** *n.* Auctioneer's, chairman's, or judge's hammer. [orig. unkn.]

**gavŏ′tte** *n.* (Music for) medium-paced dance in common time. [F f. Prov.]

**gawk. 1.** *n.* Awkward or bashful or ungainly person; ~′**y̆** *a.* (~**iness**). **2.** *v.i.* (colloq.) Stare stupidly. [obs. *gaw* GAZE]

**gawp** *v.i.* (colloq.) Gawk. [YELP]

**gay** *a.* (gai′ly, ~′ness). Light-hearted, sportive, mirthful; showy, brilliant; (euphem.) dissolute; (sl.) homosexual. [F]

*\****gay′etў.** See GAIETY.

**gāze. 1.** *v.i.* Look fixedly (*at, on*). **2.** *n.* Intent look. [orig. unkn.]

**gazē′bō** *n.* (*pl.* ~**s**, ~**es**). Structure whence a view may be had. [perh. joc. f. *gaze* v.]

**gazĕ′lle** *n.* Small graceful soft-eyed antelope. [F f. Sp. f. Arab.]

**gazĕ′tte. 1.** *n.* ‖London G~, official journal with lists of government appointments, bankruptcies, etc.; newspaper (used in title). **2.** *v.t.* ‖Publish in official gazette. [F f. It.]

**găzetteer′** *n.* Geographical index.

**gazpa′cho** (gahspah′-) *n.* (*pl.* ~**s**). Spanish cold vegetable soup. [Sp.]

**gazŭ′mp** *v.t.* (sl.) Swindle; raise price after accepting offer from (buyer). [orig. unkn.]

**G.B.** *abbr.* Great Britain.

‖**G.B.E.** *abbr.* Knight (or Dame) Grand Cross (of the Order) of the British Empire.

‖**G.C.** *abbr.* George Cross.

‖**G.C.B.** *abbr.* Knight Grand Cross (of the Order) of the Bath.

‖**G.C.E.** *abbr.* General Certificate of Education.

‖**G.C.M.G.** *abbr.* Knight (or Dame) Grand Cross (of the Order) of St. Michael & St. George.

‖**G.C.V.O.** *abbr.* Knight (or Dame) Grand Cross of the Royal Victorian Order.

**G.D.R.** *abbr.* German Democratic Republic.

**gear** (g-). 1. *n.* Equipment; clothes, esp. (colloq.) for young people; apparatus; tackle, tools; set of (esp. toothed) wheels, levers, etc., that work together (**in** ~, connected or working; **out of** ~, disconnected or not working, lit. or fig.; **high, low,** ~, with faster, slower, revolutions of driven part of vehicle relatively to driving part; ‖**top,** ‖**bottom** or ‖**first** ~, available extremes); rigging; ~**'box,** ~**'case,** (enclosing gears of machine or vehicle); ~**-lever,** \*~**-shift,** (to engage or change gear); ~**'wheel,** cogwheel. 2. *v.t.* Harness (often *up*); put in gear, provide with gear; adjust or adapt *to*; ~**'ing** *n.,* set or arrangement of gears. [N]

**gĕ'ckō** (g-) *n.* (*pl.* ~s, ~es). Tropical house-lizard. [Malay]

**gee**[1]. 1. (Also ~**-ho',** ~**-up'**) *int.* of command to horse etc.: go on, faster, (occas.) to right. 2. *n.* ~(-~), ‖(colloq.) horse. [orig. unkn.]

**gee**[2], **gee whĭz,** *ints.* expr. asseveration, discovery, etc. [perh. abbr. *Jesus*]

**geese.** See GOOSE.

**gee'zer** (g-) *n.* (sl.) Old man; person. [dial. *guiser* mummer]

**Gei'ger** (gī'g-) *n.* ~ **counter,** device for detecting and measuring radioactivity etc. [person]

**gei'sha** (gā'-) *n.* Japanese woman trained to entertain men. [Jap.]

**gĕl** *n.* Semi-solid colloidal solution or jelly. [foll.]

**gĕ'latĭn,** ‖**gĕ'latine** (-ēn), *n.* Transparent tasteless substance got from skin, tendons, etc., and used in cookery, photography, etc.; **gĕlā'tĭnĭze** *v.t.* & *i.,* **gĕlā'tĭnous** *a.,* (esp.) of jelly-like consistency. [F f. It. (JELLY)]

**gĕld** (g-) *v.t.* Deprive (usu. male animal) of reproductive ability, castrate; ~**'ing** *n.,* gelded horse etc. [N]

**gĕ'lignĭte** *n.* Nitro-glycerine explosive. [GELATIN, IGNEOUS]

**gĕm.** 1. *n.* Precious stone, esp. cut and polished; thing of great beauty or worth; engraved (semi-)precious stone. 2. *v.t.* (**-mm-**). Adorn (as) with gems. [F f. L *gemma* bud, jewel]

**gĕ'mĭn|āte. 1.** *v.t.* Double, repeat; arrange in pairs; ~**ā'tion** *n.* 2. (-at) *a.* Combined in pairs. [L (foll.)]

**Gĕ'mĭnī** *n.* Sign of ZODIAC. [L, = twins]

**gĕ'mm|a** *n.* (*pl.* ~ae). (In cryptogams) small cellular body that separates from mother-plant and starts a new one; ~**ā'tion** *n.,* reproduction by gemmae. [L, see GEM]

‖**gĕn.** (sl.) 1. *n.* Information. 2. *v.t.* & *i.* (**-nn-**). ~ **up,** gain, give, information. [general information]

**Gen.** *abbr.* General; Genesis (O.T.).

**ge'ndârme** (zhŏ'n-) *n.* French soldier employed in police duties. [F *gens d'armes* men of arms)]

**gĕ'nder** *n.* (Gram.) classification (or one of the classes) corresponding roughly to the two sexes and sexlessness (see MASCULINE, FEMININE, NEUTER); (joc.) one's sex. [F f. L GENUS]

**gēne** *n.* (Biol.) Unit of heredity in chromosome, controlling a particular inherited characteristic of an individual. [G]

**gĕneă'log|y̆** *n.* Descent traced continuously from ancestor, pedigree; study of pedigrees; plant's, animal's, line of development from earlier forms; **gĕneălŏ'gical** *a.* (-lly); ~**ĭst** *n.* [F f. L f. Gk (*genea* race)]

**gĕ'nera.** See GENUS.

**gĕ'neral. 1.** *a.* Including or affecting or applicable to all or most parts or cases or things; not partial or particular; not specialized; prevalent, usual, (**in a** ~ **way, in** ~, usually; roughly correct or adequate (*as a general rule*); not detailed, indefinite (*general resemblance; in general terms*); (appended to titles, as *Attorney General*) chief, head, with unrestricted authority. 2. *n.* Officer next below Field Marshal or \*~ **of the army** or **air force** (highest-rank officer); = *lieutenant-general* or *major-general;* commander of army; strategist (*good* etc. *general*); chief of religious order, e.g. of Jesuits etc.; ~**ship** *n.* 3. ~ **anaesthetic** (affecting whole body); ‖**G~ Certificate of Education,** secondary-school examination, certificate from passing it; ~ **knowledge** (of miscellaneous facts); ~ **meeting** (open to all members); ~**officer** (above colonel); ~ **post,** general and rapid exchange of positions; ‖**G~ Post Office,** chief post office in city or town; ~ **practitioner,** doctor in ~ **practice,** i.e. treating cases of all kinds; ~ **staff** (assisting military commander in planning etc.); ~ **strike** (of workers in all or most trades). 4. ~**ĭty**

(-ă'l-) *n.*, general applicability, indefiniteness, general rule or statement, majority or bulk *of*; ~**ize** *v.t.* & *i.*, reduce to general statement, infer (law etc.) by induction, form general notions, make indefinite, speak indefinitely, bring into general use; ~**izā'tion** *n.*; ~**lў** *adv.*, in a general sense, without regard to particulars or exceptions (*generally speaking*), in most respects or cases (*made himself generally offensive*), usually. [F f. L *generali*]

**gĕnerali'ssimō** *n.* (*pl.* ~**s**). Commander of combined military and naval and air force, or of several armies. [It. superl.]

**gĕ'nerāt|e** *v.t.* Bring into existence, produce (heat, light, etc., feelings etc.); ~**ive** (*or* -at-) *a.*, of procreation, productive; ~**or** *n.*, apparatus for producing gas, steam, etc., dynamo. [L (GENUS)]

**gĕnera'tion** *n.* Procreation; production esp. of electricity; step in pedigree; all persons born about same time (~ **gap,** differences of opinion or attitude between different generations); average time in which children are ready to take place of parents (about 30 years). [F f. L (prec.)]

**gĕnĕ'rĭc** *a.* (~**ally**). Characteristic of a genus or class; applied to (any individual of) a large class; general, not specific or special.

**gĕ'ner|ous** *a.* Noble-minded, not mean; free in giving; abundant, copious; ~**o'sĭtў** *n.* [F f. L (GENUS)]

**gĕ'nĕsĭs** *n.* Origin, mode of formation or generation; (G~) first O.T. book, with account of Creation. [L f. Gk (*gen-* be produced)]

**gĕ'nĕt** *n.* (Fur of) kind of civet-cat. [F f. Arab.]

**gĕnĕ'tĭc** *a.* (~**ally**). Of or in origin; of genetics; ~ **code,** system of storage of genetic information in chromosomes; ~**s** *n.*, study of heredity and variation in animals and plants (so ~**ĭst** *n.*). [GENESIS]

**gĕ'nĭal** *a.* (~**lў**). (Of climate etc.) conducive to growth, mild, warm; cheering; jovial, kindly, sociable; **gēnĭă'lĭtў** *n.* [F f. L (GENIUS)]

**gĕ'nĭe** *n.* (*pl.* usu. genii *pr.* jē'nĭī). Jinnee, sprite or goblin of Arab. tales. [F *génie* GENIUS; see JINNEE]

**gĕ'nĭī.** See prec. and GENIUS.

**gĕnĭ'sta** *n.* Kind of flowering shrub, e.g. broom. [L]

**gĕ'nĭtal. 1.** *a.* (~**lў**). Of animal reproduction. **2.** *n.* (in *pl.*, also **gĕnĭtā'lĭa**). External genital organs. [F or L (*gigno genit-* beget)]

**gĕ'nĭt|ive** *a.* & *n.* (Gram. (Case) corresponding to *of*, *from*, etc., with noun representing source, possessor, etc.; ~**i'val** *a.* (-llў). [F or L (prec.)]

**gĕ'nĭus** *n.* (*pl.* ~**es,** **gĕ'nii** *pr.* -ĭī). Tutelary spirit of person, place, etc. (**good, evil,** ~, two opposed spirits attending each person, person influencing one powerfully for good or ill); prevalent feeling, taste, etc. (*of* nation etc.); character, spirit, (*of* a language etc.); associations etc. (*of* place); natural tendency; exalted intellectual, creative, imaginative, etc., power; (*pl.* ~**es**) person having this; ~ *loci* (lō'sĭ), presiding deity, associations, etc., of a place. [L]

**gĕ'nocĭd|e** *n.* Deliberate extermination of a people or nation; ~**al** (*or* -sī'-) *a.* [Gk *genos* race, L *caedo* kill]

**genre** (zhahnr) *n.* Kind or style of art etc.; painting of scenes from ordinary life. [F (GENDER)]

**gĕnt** *n.* Gentleman (vulg. or joc.); ~**s,** (in shops) men; ||**the G~s,** (colloq.) men's public lavatory. [abbr.]

**gĕntee'l** *a.* (~**lў** *pr.* -l-lĭ). Upper-class, stylish, elegant, (arch., iron., or vulg.); ~**ĭsm** *n.*, word used because thought to be less vulgar than usual word (e.g. *perspire* for *sweat*). [F *gentil* (GENTLE)]

**gĕ'ntian** (-shan, -shĭan) *n.* Plant with usu. blue flowers. [E f. L *gentiana* (*Gentius,* person)]

**gĕ'ntĭle** *a.* & *n.* (Person) not Jewish; heathen. [L *gentilis* (*gens* family)]

**gĕntĭ'lĭtў** *n.* Social superiority, good manners, upper-class habits. [F (foll.)]

**gĕ'ntle** *a.* (~**r,** ~**st**). Moderate (*gentle breeze, heat, slope*); not rough or severe, kind, mild, (*gentle rule,* a *gentle nature*); (of birth, pursuits, etc.) honourable, of or fit for gentlemen; quiet (**the** ~ **art, craft,** angling); ~**folk(s),** people of good family; **the** ~ **sex,** women. [F *gentil* f. L (GENTLE)]

**gĕ'ntleman** (-telm-) *n.* (*pl.* -**men**). Chivalrous well-bred man; man of good social position or of wealth and leisure (*country gentleman*); (polite or formal for) man; gentleman attached to royal household (*gentleman in* *waiting, usher*); (in *pl.*, voc.) male (part of) audience, also in letters = Dear Sirs; **old ~**, the Devil; ‖**the Gentlemen('s)**, (as *sing.*) men's public lavatory; **~-at-arms**, one of sovereign's bodyguard; **~'s** or **-men's agreement** (binding in honour, but not enforceable); **~lў** *a.*, behaving or looking like a gentleman, befitting a gentleman.

**gĕ'ntlewoman** (-telwŏŏman) *n.* (*pl.* **-women** *pr.* -wĭmĭn). (arch.) Woman of good birth or breeding.

**gĕ'ntlў** *adv.* Mildly, tenderly; quietly, moderately; (*int.* expr. remonstration) not so fast.

**gĕ'ntrў** *n.* People next below nobility; (derog., esp. *these gentry*) people. [F (GENTLE)]

**gĕ'nŭ**|**flĕct** *v.i.* Bend the knee esp. in worship; **~flĕ'xion** (-kshon) *n.* [L (*genu* knee, *flecto* bend)]

**gĕ'nŭine** *a.* Really coming from its reputed source etc.; not sham; pure-bred; properly so called. [L]

**gĕ'nŭs** *n.* (*pl.* **ge'nera** *pr.* jĕ'-). (Biol.) group of animals or plants with common structural characteristics and usu. containing several species; (Logic) kind of things including subordinate kinds or species; (pop.) kind, class. [L *genus -eris*]

**geo-** *in comb.* Earth. [Gk *gē*]

**gĕocĕ'ntric** *a.* (**~ally**). Considered as viewed from the earth's centre; having the earth as centre.

**gĕ'ōde** *n.* (Rock with) cavity lined with crystals. [L f. Gk *geōdēs* earthy]

**gĕŏ'd**|**ĕsў** *n.* Study of figure and area of (portions of) the earth; **gĕodĕ'sĭc, -ĕ'tĭc**, *adjs.* (**~esic line**, shortest possible line on surface between two points). [L f. Gk *geōdaisia*]

**gĕŏ'graph**|**ў** *n.* Science of earth's form, physical features, climate, population, etc.; features or arrangement of place; **~er** *n.*; **gĕogră'phĭc(al)** *adjs.* (**-ically**), of geography; *geographical* MILE. [F or L f. Gk]

**gĕŏ'log**|**ў** *n.* Science of earth's, moon's, etc., crust and strata, and their relations; geological features of district; **gĕolŏ'gĭcal** *a.* (**-lly**); **~ist** *n.* [L]

**gĕŏ'mĕt**|**rў** *n.* Science of properties and relations of magnitudes (e.g. line, surface, solid) in space; **gĕomĕ'trĭc(al)** *adjs.* (**-ically**), of geometry; **~rical progression** (with constant ratio between successive

quantities, e.g. 1, 3, 9, 27); **~er**, **gĕomĕtrĭ'cian** (-shan), *ns.*, person skilled in geometry. [F f. L f. Gk (-METRY)]

**gĕopŏ'lĭtics** *n.* Politics of a country as determined by its geographical features; **gĕopolĭ'tĭcal** *a.* [GEO-]

‖**Geor'die** (jôr'-) *n.* Native of Tyneside. [foll.]

**George** (jôrj) *n.* SAINT *George*; ‖**~ Cross**, **Medal**, decorations for gallantry; **by ~**, oath or exclamation. [L f. Gk *Geōrgios*, person]

**georgĕ'tte** (jôr-) *n.* A thin silk etc. dress-material. [person]

**Geor'gĭan¹** (jôr'-) *a.* Of the time of Kings George I–IV or of George V and VI. [*George*]

**Geor'gĭan²** (jôr'-) *a. & n.* (Native, language) of *Georgia* in U.S.S.R. or U.S.

**Ger.** *abbr.* German.

**gerā'nium** *n.* Herb or shrub bearing fruit shaped like bill of crane; (pop.) cultivated pelargonium. [L f. Gk (*geranos* crane)]

**gĕr'bĭl, jĕr'bĭl,** *n.* Mouselike desert rodent with long hind legs. [F f. L (JERBOA)]

**gĕrĭă'tr**|**ĭc** *a.* Relating to **~ics** *n.*, branch of medical science dealing with old age and its diseases; **gĕrĭatrĭ'cian** (-shan) *n.*, one skilled in geriatrics. [Gk *gēras* old age, *iatros* physician]

**gĕrm** *n.* Portion of organism capable of becoming a new one, rudiment of animal or of plant in seed (*wheat germ*); micro-organism or microbe, esp. one causing disease; (fig.) thing that may develop, elementary principle (**in ~**, undeveloped). [F f. L *germen* sprout]

**gĕr'man¹** *a.* **Brother, sister, cousin, ~** (in the fullest sense); (arch.) = GERMANE. [F f. L *germanus*]

**Gĕr'man². 1.** *a.* Of Germany or its people or language; **~ measles**, disease like mild measles; **~ sausage** (large, with spiced partly cooked meat); *\*~* **shepherd (dog)**, Alsatian; **~ silver**, white alloy of nickel etc. **2.** *n.* Native, language, of Germany (**High ~**, form orig. spoken in South, now in literary and cultured use throughout Germany; **Low ~**, dialects of Germany that are not High German); **~ism** *n.*, (imitation of) German idiom; **~ize** *v.t. & i.*; **Gĕr'mănō-** *comb. form.* [L *Germanus*]

**germă'nder** n. Kind of plant; ~ **speedwell**, speedwell with leaves like germander. [L f. Gk, = ground-oak]

**germă'ne** a. Relevant or pertinent *to* a subject. [var. GERMAN¹]

**Germă'nic. 1.** a. Having German characteristics; (Hist.) of the Germans. **2.** a. & n. (Primitive language) of Scandinavians, Anglo-Saxons, or Germans. [GERMAN²]

**gĕr'mĭcĭd|e** n. Substance destroying germs; ~**al** a. [L *caedo* kill]

**gĕr'mĭnal** a. (~**ly**). Of germs; in earliest stage of development; productive of new ideas etc. [GERM]

**gĕr'mĭnāte** v.i. & t. Sprout, bud, (lit. or fig.); cause to shoot, produce; ~**ā'tion** n.; ~**atĭve** a. [L (GERM)]

**gĕrŏntŏ'logў** (*or* g-) n. Scientific study of old age and process of ageing. [Gk *gerōn geront-* old man]

**gĕrrўmă'nder. 1.** v.t. Manipulate (constituency etc. boundaries) so as to give undue influence to some class etc. **2.** n. This practice. [*Gerry*, person]

**gĕ'rund** n. Cases of Latin infinitive constructed as noun but governing like verb; English verbal noun in -*ing* (*what is the use of my scolding him?*); **gĕrŭ'ndĭve**, (a.) of or like the gerund, (n.) Latin vbl adjective from gerund stem with sense 'that should be done' etc.; ~**ī'val** a. [L]

**gĕ'ssō** n. (*pl.* ~**es**). Gypsum as used in painting or sculpture. [It. (GYPSUM)]

**Gesta'pō** (gestah'-) n. Nazi secret State police; any comparable organization. [G *Geheime Staatspolizei*]

**gĕst|ā'tion** n. Carrying in womb between conception and birth; this period; (fig.) private development of plan etc.; ~**ā'te** v.t., carry (as) in gestation. [L (*gesto* carry)]

**gĕstĭ'cŭlāt|e** v.i. & t. Use expressive motion of limbs etc. with or instead of speech; express thus; **gĕstĭcŭlā'tion**, ~**or**, ns.; ~**ĭve**, ~**orў**, adjs. [L (foll.)]

**gĕ'sture. 1.** n. Significant movement of limb or body; use of gestures as rhetorical device etc.; (fig.) action to evoke response or to convey (esp. friendly) intention. **2.** v.i. & t. = prec. [L *gestura* (*gero* wield)]

**gĕt** (g-) v.t. & i. (-**tt**-; *past* **got**; *p.p.* **got**, in comb. or arch. or U.S. **go'tten**). Come into possession of, earn, gain, win, (*get one's living,*

£40 *a week, little by it, the prize*); procure, ascertain, fetch, catch, arrive at, (*get the facts for you, my book, a fish, a train,* 77 *as the average*); establish communication by telephone etc. with; prepare or (colloq.) eat (meal); be given, receive, (*got the job, the credit, a gift*); experience or suffer, have inflicted on one, contract (idea etc.), (*get a shock, six months in gaol, the notion, measles*); (in *perf.*) possess, have, be bound *to* do or be, (*have not got a penny*; *has got nothing to say*; *you have got to do it*); (cause to) become, (cause to) reach some state, (with *p.p., adj., or part.*; *get him elected, it done with,* one's *elbow dislocated, tired, married,* (*yourself*) *ready,* one's *feet wet, talking*); (cause to) come or go or arrive, (*get* (*him, it*) *to London, here, home, out* (*of bed*), *away*; *get a message to her*); (sl.) be off, clear out; (colloq.) catch in argument, understand, annoy, attract or obsess; (sl.) (deliberately) kill or injure; induce *to* do; (with *inf.*) acquire habit; (usu. of animals) beget; ~ **about**, go from place to place, begin walking after illness etc., (of news) be spread; ~ **across** *adv.,* (colloq.) be or make effective or acceptable; ~ **across** *prep.,* (sl.) annoy; ~ **along**, advance, fare *ill, well,* etc., live harmoniously *together or with*; ~ **along with you!,** (colloq.) be off!, nonsense!; ~ **at**, reach, get hold of, (colloq.) imply, (sl.) tamper with, bribe, etc., (colloq.) taunt; ~-**a't-able** a., accessible; ~ **away**, escape, start, (*imper.*) be off!; ~-*away* n., (esp. of criminals) escape; ~ *away with it*, succeed in one's endeavour, escape retribution; ~ **back**, come home etc., recover (lost thing); ~ *back at*, (colloq.) retaliate on; ~ one's *own back*, (colloq.) have revenge (*on*); ~ **by**, (colloq.) be acceptable, manage *without* etc.; ~ **by heart** (learn); ~ **down**, alight, swallow, record in writing, (colloq.) depress or weary; ~ *down to*, begin work on; *get person's* GOAT; ~ **his** etc., (sl.) be killed; *get* HOLD¹ *of*; ~ **in**, win election, obtain place at college etc., enter vehicle, arrive at destination, collect (debts etc.), fit (work etc.) into given time, become friendly *with*, place (blow) effectively; ~ **into**, (colloq.) put on (clothes), become interested in, take possession of (*what's got into you* *tonight?*); ~ **it**, be punished etc.; ~ *it bad*(*ly*), (sl.) be infatuated; ~ *it into* one's *head*, be convinced *that*; ~ **off** *prep.*, dismount from, obtain release from (duty etc.); ~ **off** *adv.*, escape, start, alight from public vehicle, (cause to) go to sleep, be acquitted or pardoned, be let off *with* or *for* slight penalty, procure acquittal or slight penalty for (person), send (letter etc.), (colloq.) become on amorous terms *with* member of opposite sex; ~ **on**, = *get along*; *get* a MOVE *on*; ~*ting on*, elderly; ~*ting on for*, approaching (an age, time, etc.); ~ **on** *to*, (colloq.) understand, become aware of, (fact), communicate with (person); ~ **out**, transpire, elicit, utter, publish, finish (puzzle etc.), alight from vehicle, (*imper.*) be off!, nonsense!; ~ **out of**, issue or escape from ( *got out of bed on the wrong side*, is in a bad temper), abandon (habit), evade (do*ing*), obtain (money, information) from (person); ~-*out* n., means of evasion; ~ **over** *prep.*, surmount, show (evidence etc.) to be unconvincing, recover from (illness etc.) or from surprise at; ~ **over** *adv.*, = *get across*; ~ **over** (*with*), finish (troublesome task); *get* RELIGION; *get* RID *of*; ~ **round** *prep.*, cajole, evade; ~ **round** *adv.*, (of news) be spread; ~ *round to*, find time etc. to deal with; ~ **there**, (sl.) succeed, understand what is meant; ~ **through** *prep.* & *adv.*, pass (examination etc., or abs.), (of Bill etc.) pass (Commons etc., or abs.), spend (money), (cause to) reach destination; ~ *through to*, (colloq.) reach attention or understanding of; ~ **together**, collect, unite in discussion, promotion of plan, etc., (sl.) put in order; ~-*together* n., (social) assembly; ~ **under** *adv.*, subdue (fire); ~ **under way**, make a start; ~ **up**, rise esp. from bed, (of fire, wind, sea) grow violent, organize, produce, arrange the appearance of (hair, one*self*, play, binding etc. of book), work up (anger etc., subject for examination); ~-*up* n., style of equipment, costume, etc.; ~ **with child**, make pregnant. [N]

**gē′um** n. Kind of rosaceous plant. [L *gaeum*]

**gew′gaw** (g-) n. Gaudy plaything or ornament; showy trifle. [orig. unkn.]

**gey′ser** n. **1.** (gī′z-, gā′z-). Inter-

mittent hot spring. **2.** ‖(gē′z-). Apparatus for heating water. [Icel. *Geysir*, = gusher]

**Ghanai′an** (gah-) a. & n. (Native) of Ghana. [place]

**gha′st**‖**y** (gah′-). **1.** a. (~**ily**, ~**iness**). Horrible, frightful; (colloq.) objectionable; deathlike; pallid; (of smile etc.) forced, grim. **2.** adv. Ghastlily (pale etc.) [obs. *gast* terrify]

**ghat, ghaut,** (gawt) n. (Ind.) Steps leading to river, landing-place (**burning-~**, level spot at top of river ghat where Hindus burn their dead). [Hindi]

**gher′kin** (gēr′-) n. Young or small cucumber for pickling. [Du.]

**ghě′ttō** (gě′-) n. (*pl.* ~**s**). Jews' quarter in city (Hist.); part of city occupied by minority group(s); segregated group or area. [It.]

**ghost** (gō-). **1.** n. Apparition of dead person or animal, disembodied spirit, (**raise, lay, ~**, cause it to appear or cease appearing); emaciated or pale person; shadow, semblance, (*not the ghost of a chance*); secondary or duplicated image in defective telescope or television--picture; ~ (**writer**), literary etc. hack doing work for which employer takes credit; **Holy G~**, Holy Spirit; ~ **town**, (almost) uninhabited town; **give up the ~**, die; ~′**ly** a. (~**liness**), as of a ghost, spectral. **2.** v.t. & i. Act as ghost writer etc. (of. *for*). [E]

**ghoul** (gōōl, gowl) n. Spirit preying on corpses in Muslim superstition; (fig.) person morbidly interested in death etc. [Arab.]

**G.H.Q.** *abbr.* General Headquarters.

‖**ghyll** (gĭl). See GILL[2].

**G.I.** (jēī′, jē′ī). **1.** a. Of or for U.S. armed forces or servicemen; ~ **bride**, foreign woman married to U.S. serviceman on duty abroad. **2.** n. (or ~ **Joe**). American private soldier. [*government* (or *general*) *issue*]

**gī′ant. 1.** n. A being of human form but superhuman size; (Gk Myth., *pl.*) sons of Gaea (Earth) and Uranus (Heaven) or Tartarus (Hell) who warred against the gods; very tall or large person, animal, plant, etc.; person of immense ability, strength, etc.; ~**ėss** n. **2.** a. Gigantic, (of animal, plant, etc.) unusually large. **3.** **~-killer,** one who defeats more powerful opponent. [F f. L f. Gk *gigas gigant-*]

**gǐ′bber** (or g-). **1.** *v.i.* Jabber inarticulately, chatter like ape. **2.** *n.* Such chatter. [imit.]

**gǐ′bberish** (or g-) *n.* Unintelligible speech, meaningless sounds.

**gǐ′bbét. 1.** *n.* Death by hanging; (Hist.) gallows, post with arm on which executed criminal was hung. **2.** *v.t.* Put to death by hanging; expose, hang up, on gibbet; hold up to contempt. [F *gibet*]

**gǐ′bbon** (g-) *n.* Long-armed S.E. Asian anthropoid ape. [F]

**gǐ′bb|ous** (g-) *a.* Convex (of moon etc.) having bright part greater than semicircle; humpbacked; **~ŏ′sǐtў** (g-) *n.* [L (*gibbus* hump)]

**gibe, jibe,** *v.i.* & *t.,* & *n.* Flout, jeer (at or *at*), mock, taunt. [perh. f. F *giber* handle roughly]

**gǐ′blét|s** *n.pl.* Liver, gizzard, etc., removed before bird is cooked (**~ soup,** made with these).

**gǐ′dd|ў** (g-) *a.* (**~ily, ~iness**). Dizzy, tending to fall or stagger; making dizzy (*giddy height, success*); mentally intoxicated, frivolous (**~y goat,** fool); flighty. [E]

**gift** (g-). **1.** *n.* Thing given, present, (*would not have it as a* ~, even gratis); natural endowment (*gift of the* GAB); giving (*the living is in his* ~, his to bestow); easy task; *gift--HORSE*; **~ shop** (selling articles suitable for gifts); **~ token, voucher,** (exchangeable for goods, used as gift); **~-wrap** *v.t.* (*-pp-*), wrap attractively (as gift). **2.** *v.t.* Endow with gifts (esp. in *p.p.*, talented), present *with* as gift; bestow as gift (*to* person; *away*). [E (GIVE)]

**gǐg**[1] (g-) *n.* Light two-wheeled one--horse carriage; light ship's-boat for rowing or sailing; rowing-boat esp. for racing. [prob. imit.]

**gǐg**[2] (g-) *n.* (colloq.) Engagement of musician(s) to play jazz etc., esp. for one night. [orig. unkn.]

**gǐgǎ′ntǐc** *a.* (**~ally**). Giant-like, huge. [L (GIANT)]

**gǐ′ggl|e** (g-). **1.** *v.i.* Have small bursts of half-suppressed laughter; laugh in silly manner. **2.** *n.* Such laugh; (colloq.) amusing person or thing, joke (*did it for a giggle*); **~ў** *a.* [imit.]

**gǐ′golō** (or zhǐ′-) *n.* (*pl.* **~s**). Pro-

fessional male dancing-partner or escort; young man paid by older woman for his attentions. [F]

**Gǐlbér′tian** (g-; *or* -shạn) *a.* Ludicrous or paradoxical, as in *Gilbert* & Sullivan's operas. [person]

**gǐld**[1] (g-) *v.t.* (*p.p.* sometimes **gilt** as adj. in lit. sense, otherwise **~′ed**). Cover thinly with gold (*gild the* LILY; **~ the pill,** soften down unpleasant necessity; tinge with golden colour. [E (GOLD)]

**gǐld**[2]. See GUILD.

**gǐll**[1] (g-) *n.* (usu. in *pl.*) Respiratory organ in fish etc.; flesh below person's jaws and ears (**rosy, green, about the ~s,** healthy-, sickly-looking); vertical radial plate on under side of mushroom etc.; **~-net** (for catching fish by gills). [N]

||**gǐll**[2], ||**ghўll,** (g-) *n.* Deep usu. wooded ravine; narrow mountain torrent. [N]

**gǐll**[3] *n.* Quarter-pint liquid measure; ||(dial.) half-pint. [F]

**gǐ′llie** (g-) *n.* Man or boy attending sportsman in Scotland. [Gael.]

**gǐ′llўflower** (g-) *n.* (Clove) ~, clove--scented pink; other similarly scented flower, e.g. wallflower. [F *gilofre*]

**gǐlt**[1]. See GILD[1].

**gǐlt**[2] (g-) *n.* Gilding (**take the ~ off the gingerbread,** strip thing of adventitious attractions); gilt-edged security; **~-edged,** (of securities, stocks, etc.) having high degree of reliability. [E (GILD[1])]

**gǐlt**[3] (g-) *n.* Young sow. [N]

**gǐ′mbal|s** (-z; *or* g-) *n.pl.* Contrivance of rings etc. for keeping instruments horizontal at sea; **~--ring,** (ring in) gimbals. [var. *gimmal* f. F *gemel* double finger-ring]

**gǐ′mcrǎck. 1.** *n.* Showy ornament etc., knick-knack. **2.** *a.* Flimsy, trumpery. [orig. unkn.]

**gǐ′mlét** (g-) *n.* Boring-tool usu. with wooden cross-handle, and screw at pointed end; **~ eye** (with piercing glance). [F]

**gǐ′mmǐck** (g-) *n.* (colloq.) Tricky device, esp. to attract attention or publicity; **~rў** *n.*; **~ў** *a.* [orig. unkn.]

**gǐmp, gўmp,** (g-) *n.* Twist of silk etc. with cord or wire running through it; fishing-line of silk etc. bound with wire. [Du.]

**gǐn**[1]. **1.** *n.* Snare, trap; kind of crane and windlass; machine separating cotton from seeds. **2.** *v.t.*

(**-nn-**). Trap; treat (cotton) in gin. [F (ENGINE)]

**gin**[2] n. Spirit made from grain or malt and flavoured with juniper berries (**pink ~**, gin flavoured with angostura bitters); *gin and* IT[2]; **~ rummy**, form of RUMMY[2]; *\*~ **sling**, cold drink of gin flavoured and sweetened. [abbr. *geneva* f. Du. f. F (JUNIPER)]

**gĭn̄ger** (-nj-). **1.** n. (Plant with) hot spicy root used in cooking and medicine and preserved in syrup etc.; mettle, spirit; stimulation; light reddish yellow; **~-ale, -beer, -pop,** ginger-flavoured aerated drinks; **~-bread,** (n.) ginger-flavoured treacle cake (cf. GILT[2]), (a.) gaudy, tawdry; ‖**~ group** (urging Parl. party etc. to more decided action); **~-nut, ~-snap,** kinds of ginger-flavoured biscuit; **~ wine** (made with bruised ginger); **~y̆** a. **2.** v.t. Flavour with ginger; (fig., transf. from horses) rouse *up* (person). [E & F f. L f. Gk f. Skr.]

**gĭn̄gerly̆** (-nj-). **1.** a. Such as to avoid making a noise or injuring oneself or what is touched. **2.** adv. In gingerly manner. [perh. F *gensor* delicate]

**gingham** (gĭng̍am) n. Plain-woven cotton cloth often striped or checked. [Du. f. Malay]

**ging|i′val** (-nj-) a. (**-lly**). Of the gums; **~ivī′tis** n., inflammation of the gums. [L *gingiva* GUM[1]]

**gĭn̄kgō** (g-; *or* -ngkō) n. (*pl.* **~s, ~es**). Tree with fan-shaped leaves and yellow flowers. [Jap. f. Chin., = silver apricot]

**gĭn̄sěng** n. (Root of) medicinal plant found in E. Asia and N. America. [Chin.]

**gĭ′ppy̆** a. (sl.) **~ tummy,** diarrhoea of visitors to hot countries. [EGYPTIAN]

**gĭ′psy̆, gy̆′psy̆, G-,** n. Member of a wandering race of Hindu origin; **~ rose,** scabious; **~'s warning,** cryptic or sinister warning.

**giră′ffe** (*or* -ah′f) n. African ruminant quadruped with spotted skin and long neck and forelegs. [F, ult. f. Arab.]

**gĭrd**[1] (g-) v.t. (literary; **~′ed,** girt). Encircle with waist-belt etc. esp. to confine clothes (**~ one**self, **(up) one's loins,** prepare for action); equip *with* sword in belt, fasten (sword etc. *on, to*) with belt; secure (clothes) with belt etc.; put (cord etc.) *round*; encircle. [E]

**gĭrd**[2] (g-) v.i., & n. Gibe (*at*). [orig. unkn.]

**gĭr′der** (g-) n. Beam supporting joists; iron or steel beam or compound structure for bridge-span etc. [GIRD[1]]

**gĭr′dle**[1] (g-). **1.** n. Belt, cord, used to gird waist; corset; thing that surrounds; bony support of limb (*shoulder or pectoral, pelvic or hip, girdle*). **2.** v.t. Surround with girdle. [E]

**gĭr′dle**[2] (g-) n. (Sc. etc.) Round iron plate set over fire or otherwise heated for baking etc. [var. GRIDDLE]

**gĭrl** (g-) n. Female child; young woman; woman working in office, factory, etc.; female servant; man's sweetheart; *girl* FRIDAY; **~-friend,** female friend, esp. boy's, man's, usual or preferred female companion; **~ guide,** = GUIDE; **the ~s,** group of women esp. with similar interests, (grown-up) daughters in family; **~'hood** n.; **~'ie,** (n.) little girl (as term of endearment), (a.; of publication etc.) erotically depicting young women usu. (almost) nude. [E]

**gĭr′ō** n. (*pl.* **~s**). System of credit transfer between banks, post offices, etc. [G f. It.]

**girt.** See GIRD[1].

**gĭrth** (g-) n. Band round body of horse etc. securing saddle etc.; measurement round a thing. [N (GIRD[1])]

**gist** n. Substance, point, essence. *of* a matter. [F f. L *jaceo* LIE[2]]

**gĭt** (g-) n. (sl.) Worthless person. [GET n., = fool]

**give** (g-). **1.** v.t. & i. (**gave; gĭ′ven;** gĭ′veable** *pr.* -va-). Transfer possession of gratuitously, make present of, confer ownership of; render (benefit etc.), grant, accord, bequeath; (of God etc.) grant (faculty etc., *to do*; in *imper.*, I prefer: *give me the good old times*); sanction marriage of (daughter etc.); deliver (without ref. to ownership), administer, (medicine, food, etc.; message, LOVE, SACK[1], etc.); consign, put, (*give in* CHARGE, *into custody*, etc.); pledge (one's *word, honour*); make over in exchange or payment; devote, addict, (one's *life* etc., one*self*, and in *pass.*, *to* habits etc.); exert (action, effort; *give a jump, a cry; give him a kick; give orders*); deliver (judgement etc.) authoritatively (give batsman out, not out); pro-vide (party, meal) as host; present, offer, hold out, (one's *hand, arm*, etc.; *good* etc. *example*; *the facts, reason*, etc.); perform, read, (play, lecture, etc.); impart, be source of, (*gave me his cold*; *give trouble*; *gave its name to the battle*); assume, grant, specify, (*given health, he will succeed*; *on a given straight line*); yield as result (*gives an average of 7*); cause or allow to have (*gave me much pain*; *this gives him a right to complain*); collapse, yield, shrink; (of window, road, etc.) look, lead, (*upon, into*). **2.** ~ **and take** v.i., & n., exchange of blows, or concessions; ~ **as good as one gets**, retort or retaliate adequately; ~ **away**, transfer as gift, hand over (bride) to bridegroom, betray or expose to ridicule or detection (*give the* GAME¹, SHOW, *away*); ~-**away** n., (colloq.) free gift, low price, in-advertent betrayal; ~ **back**, restore; ~ **forth**, emit, publish; ~ **in**, yield, succumb, hand in (document etc.) to proper official; ~ **it** person (**hot**), reprimand, punish, (severely); *~**n name**, first or Christian name; ~ **off**, emit (vapour etc.); ~ **oneself**, (of woman) yield sexually; ~ **or take**, (colloq.) add or subtract in estimating; ~ **out**, announce, emit, distribute, be exhausted, run short; ~ **over**, cease from doing, abandon (habit), desist, hand over, devote (*to*); ~ **person to understand, know**, etc., inform or assure him; ~ **up**, resign, surrender, part with (*give up the* GHOST), deliver (fugitive etc.) to pursuers etc., abandon (*oneself to despair* etc.), cease from effort or do*ing*, addict (*oneself to*), pronounce incurable etc., renounce hope (of); *give* WAY; ~ person **what for**, (sl.) punish, scold, him severely. **3.** n. (Capacity of) yielding to pressure. [E]

**gi'zzard** (g-) n. Bird's stomach for grinding food; muscular stomach of some fish etc.; **stick in** one's ~, be distasteful. [F]

**glacé** (-ǎ'sā, -ah'-) a. (Of cloth etc.) smooth, polished; (of fruit) iced, sugared; ~ **icing** (made from icing sugar and water). [F]

**glā'cial** (or -shal) a. (~**ly**). Of ice, icy, (lit. or fig.); (Geol.) character-ized, produced, by ice; ~ **period** (when large area was covered with ice-sheet); **glā'ciāted** a., marked

by ice-action, covered with glaciers or ice-sheet; **glācia'tion** n. [F or I. (*glacies* ice)]

**glā'cier** n. Slowly moving river or mass of ice formed by accumulation of snow on higher ground. [F (prec.)]

**glad** a. (-dd-). Pleased (*pred.*: *am glad of it, to hear it, (that) it is so*); expressing or giving joy, joyful, (*glad cry, news*); (of nature etc.) bright; ~ **eye**, (sl.) amorous glance; ~ **hand**, the hand of welcome; **be ~ of**, find useful to have; ~ **rags**, (colloq.) best clothes; ~'**den** v.t.; ~'**some** a., (poet.) cheerful, joyous. [E]

**glāde** n. Clear open space in forest. [orig. unkn.]

**glā'diātor** n. Trained fighter in ancient Roman shows; controver-sialist; ~**ator'ial** a. (-lly). [I. (*gladius* sword)]

**glādiō'lus** n. (*pl.* ~**i** *pr.* -ī, ~**uses**). Iridaceous plant with sword-shaped leaves and brightly coloured flower-spikes. [L, dim. of *gladius* (prec.)]

**Glā'dstone** a. & n. ~ (**bag**), kind of light portmanteau. [person]

**glair** n. (Viscous substance, esp. one prepared from) white of egg; ~'**eous**, ~'**y**, *adjs.* [F]

**Glam.** *abbr.* Glamorgan(shire).

**glā'm|our**, *-m|or*, (-*er*) n. De-lusive or alluring or exciting beauty or charm; (esp. feminine) physical attractiveness; ~**our girl**, young woman possessing this; ~**orize** v.t., make glamorous or attractive; ~**oriza'tion** n.; ~**orous** a. [var. of GRAMMAR in obs. sense 'magic']

**glance** (-ah-). **1.** v.i. & t. (Of weapon etc.) strike and glide off object (usu. *aside, off*); (of talk or talker) pass quickly (*over, off, from, subject*); ~ **at**, make only brief allu-sion to); (of light etc.) flash, dart; cast momentary look (*at, down*, etc.); ~ **over**, read cursorily); direct (one's *eye at, over*, etc.); (Crick.) deflect (ball) with glance-stroke. **2.** n. Swift oblique movement or im-pact; (sudden movement causing) flash, glance; brief look (*at* etc.; **at a ~**, as soon as one looks); (Crick.) stroke with bat's face turned slant-wise to ball. [orig. uncert.]

**gland** n. Organ secreting sub-stances for use in body or for ejec-tion; similar organ in plant; ~'**ular** a., of gland(s); ~**ular fever**, infectious disease with swelling of lymph-glands. [F f. L *glandulae* pl.]

**gla'nder|s** (-z) *n.pl.* Contagious horse-disease (communicable to man etc.); **~ed** (-erd), **~ous**, *adjs.* [F *glandre* (prec.)]

**gla'ndular.** See GLAND.

**glare. 1.** *v.i.* Shine oppressively; look fiercely or fixedly; **glaring error** (conspicuous, gross). **2.** *n.* Oppressive light; tawdry brilliance; fierce or fixed look. [LDu.]

**glass** (-ah-). **1.** *n.* Substance, usu. transparent, lustrous, hard, and brittle, made by fusing sand with soda, potash, etc.; substance of similar properties (FIBRE*glass*; WATER-*glass*); glass utensils, windows, greenhouses, etc.; glass drinking-vessel; ~('ful), amount this holds, drink (*a friendly glass*); glass covering of watch-face or picture; glazed frame for plants; lens; telescope; microscope; barometer; = HOUR*glass*, LOOK*ing-glass*; (esp. in *pl.*) = EYE-*glasses*, FIELD-*glasses*, OPERA[1]-*glass*(es). **2.** *v.t.* (usu. in *p.p.*) Fit with glass. **3.** ~**-blower**, one who blows and shapes glass; ~ **case** (glazed to protect exhibits etc.); ~ **cloth**, woven fabric of fine-spun glass; ~**-cloth**, cloth for drying glasses, cloth covered with ~**-dust** for polishing; ~ **eye**, false eye of glass; ~ **fibre**, filaments of glass made into fabric, or as reinforcement in plastic; ~'**house**, greenhouse, (sl.) military prison; ~**-paper** (covered with glass-dust, for smoothing etc.); ~'**ware**, articles made of glass; ~ **wool**, fine glass fibres for packing and insulation. **4.** ~'**y** *a.* (~**ily**, ~**iness**), like glass, (of eye, stare) fixed, dull, (of water) clear or smooth as glass. [E]

**Glaswe'gian** (or -z-, -jan) *a. & n.* (Native) of Glasgow. [after *Norwegian*]

**Glau'ber** (or -ow'-) *n.* ~'**s salt(s)**, crystalline (hydrated) sodium sulphate, esp. as laxative. [person]

**glauco'ma** *n.* Eye condition with increased pressure in eyeball and gradual loss of sight; ~**tous** *a.* [L f. Gk *glaukos* greyish blue]

**glaze. 1.** *v.i. & t.* Fit (window etc.) with glass or (building) with windows; cover (pottery etc.) with glaze; fix (colour *on* pottery) thus; put glaze on (cloth, pastry, etc.); cover (eye) with film; give glassy surface to; (of eye etc.) become glassy.

**2.** *n.* Vitreous substance for glazing pottery; smooth shiny coating on materials or food; coat of transparent paint to modify underlying tone; surface formed by glazing. **3.** **gla'zier** (*or* -zher) *n.*, one whose trade is to glaze windows etc. [GLASS]

‖**G.L.C.** *abbr.* Greater London Council.

**gleam. 1.** *n.* Subdued or transient light; faint or momentary show (of humour, hope, etc.). **2.** *v.i.* Emit gleams. [E]

**glean** *v.i. & t.* Gather corn left by reapers, gather (such corn), strip (field) thus; pick up (facts etc.) in small amounts; ~'**ings** (-z) *n.pl.*, what (esp. facts) one has been able to glean. [F]

**glebe** *n.* Land yielding revenue to benefice. [L *gl(a)eba* clod, soil]

**glee** *n.* Composition for three or more (prop. adult male) voices, one to each part; mirth, manifest joy; ~ **club**, society for singing glees etc.; ~'**ful** *a.* (-**lly**), joyful. [E]

**glen** *n.* Narrow valley. [Gael.]

**glenga'rry** (-n-g-) *n.* Kind of Highland cap with pointed front. [place]

**glib** *a.* (-bb-). Fluent, voluble rather than sincere or sound, (*glib speaker, tongue, words*). [obs. *glibbery* slippery, imit.]

**glide. 1.** *v.i. & t.* (Of ship, bird, train, snake, skater, etc.) pass, proceed, by smooth continuous movement; (of aircraft) fly without engine; go stealthily; pass gradually or imperceptibly; cause to glide (*glide the feet* in dancing). **2.** *n.* Gliding motion; (Crick.) = GLANCE; ~ **path**, aircraft's line of descent to land. **3.** **gli'der** *n.*, (pilot of) engineless aeroplane. [E]

**gli'mmer. 1.** *v.i.* Shine faintly or intermittently. **2.** *n.* Faint or intermittent light; gleam (of hope etc.; also ~**ing** *n.*). [prob. Scand.]

**glimpse** *n., & v.t.* Faint transient appearance; (have) brief view (of). [E]

**glint** *v.i., & n.* Flash, glitter. [prob. Scand.]

**glissa'de** (*or* -ah'd) *n., & v.i.* Slide down slope of snow etc. usu. on feet with help of ice-axe etc.; (make) gliding step in dance. [F]

**gli'sten** (-i'sen) *v.i., & n.* Glitter, sparkle; shine like (that of) wet or polished surface. [E]

**gli'tter** *v.i., & n.* (Shine with)

bright tremulous light, sparkle; be(ing) showy or splendid (*with*). [N]

**gloa′ming** n. Evening twilight. [E]

**gloat.** 1. *v.i.* Feast eyes or mind greedily, malignantly, etc., (*up*)*on*, *over*. 2. *n.* Look of triumphant satisfaction; act of gloating. [orig. unkn.]

**glōbe** n. Sphere; *the* earth; planet, star, sun; spherical map of earth or constellations; approximately spherical glass vessel, esp. lampshade, fish-bowl, electric-light bulb; globe ARTICHOKE; **~-fish** (inflating itself into globe form); **~-flower**, ranunculaceous plant with spherical yellow flowers; **~ lightning** (of rare globular form); **~-trotter, -trotting**, hurried travel(ler) for sightseeing; **glō′bal** *a.* (**-lly**), world-wide, embracing the totality of a group of items etc.; **glōbŏ′sĭtў** n.; **glō′būlar** a., globe-shaped, composed of globules; **glōbūlā′rĭtў** n.; **glō′būle** n., small globe or round particle, drop, pill; **glō′būlin** n., protein found usu. associated with albumin in animal and plant tissues. [F, or L *globus*]

**glŏ′ckenspiel** (*or* -nshp-) n. Musical instrument consisting of set of bells or metal tubes or bars struck by hammers. [G, = bell-play]

**glōom.** 1. *n.* Darkness; melancholy, depression. 2. *v.i. & t.* Look or be or make dark or dismal. 3. **~′ў** a. (**~ily, ~iness**), dark, depressed, depressing. [orig. unkn.]

**glŏr′ĭ|ў.** 1. *n.* Renown, honourable fame; adoring praise (**~y be!**, devout, or vulg. surprised, excl.); resplendent majesty, beauty, etc.; heavenly bliss and splendour (**go to ~y**, sl. die, be destroyed); exalted or prosperous state; source of renown, special distinction; halo of saint etc.; **~y-hole**, (sl.) untidy room, drawer, etc. 2. *v.i.* Take pride (*in*), be proud (*to do*). 3. **~ifў** *v.t.*, make glorious, invest with radiance, (try to) make (common or inferior thing) seem more splendid than it is; extol; **~ĭfĭcā′tion** n.; **~ĭous** a., possessing or conferring glory, splendid, excellent, (often iron., *a glorious muddle*), illustrious. [AF *glorie* f. L *gloria*]

**Glos.** abbr. Gloucestershire.

**glŏss¹.** 1. *n.* Word inserted in margin etc. to explain word in text; comment, paraphrase; misrepresentation of person's words; glossary. 2. *v.t. & i.* Insert glosses in (text) or concerning (word etc.); make (esp.

unfavourable) comments; explain away. 3. **~′arў** n., collection of glosses, dictionary or list of technical or special words. [alt. GLOZE after L]

**glŏss².** 1. *n.* Lustre of surface; specious appearance; **~ paint** etc. (containing varnish to give glossy finish). 2. *v.t.* Make glossy; **~ (over)**, make specious. 3. **~′ў** a. (**~ily, ~iness**), having a gloss, shiny. [orig. unkn.]

**glŏ′tt|ĭs** n. Opening at upper end of windpipe and between vocal cords; **~al** a. (glottal STOP); **~ic** a. [L f. Gk]

**Glou′cester** (glŏ′ster) n. Cheese made in Gloucestershire (now usu. **double ~**, orig. richer kind). [place]

**glove** (-ŭv) 1. *n.* Hand-covering, usu. with separated fingers, for protection, warmth, etc., (**fit like a ~**, fit exactly; HAND *in* or *and* glove; *throw down* etc. *the* glove or GAUNTLET¹) = BOXING-glove (**with the ~s off**, arguing or contending in earnest); **~ box, ~ compartment**, recess for small articles in motor-car dashboard; **~ puppet** (made to fit on hand like glove). 2. *v.t.* Cover or provide with glove(s). 3. **glō′ver** (-ŭ′v-) n., glove-maker. [E]

**glow** (-ō). 1. *v.i.* Emit flameless light and heat; shine like thing intensely heated; show warm colour; burn *with*, indicate, bodily heat or fervour; **~-worm**, beetle whose wingless female emits light from end of abdomen. 2. *n.* Glowing state; warmth of colour; ardour. [E]

**glow′er** *v.i.* Look angrily (*at*). [orig. uncert.]

**glŏxĭ′nĭa** n. Amer. tropical plant with bell-shaped flowers. [*Gloxin*, person]

**glōze** *v.i. & t.* Talk speciously (arch.); **~ (over)**, explain away. [F f. L *glossa* f. Gk, = tongue]

**glu′cōse** (-ōō′-; *or* -z) n. Sugar found in fruit-juice, blood, etc. [F f. Gk *gleukos* sweet wine]

**glue** (-ōō). 1. *n.* Hard gelatin got from hides and bones and used warm as adhesive; similar adhesive substance; **~′ў** a. (**-u′ier, -u′iest**). 2. *v.t.* Attach (as) with glue (*ear glued to keyhole*). [F f. L *glus* (GLUTEN)]

**glŭm** a. (**-mm-**). Dejected, sullen. [var. GLOOM]

**glume** (-ōō-) n. (Bot.) Husk; bract of some grasses etc. [L]

**glŭt. 1.** *v.t.* (-tt-). Feed to the full, sate (person, stomach, desire); fill to excess; overstock (market). **2.** *n.* Full indulgence, surfeit; excessive supply (*a glut in the market*). [F *gloutir* swallow (GLUTTON)]

**glu'tamāte** (-ōō'-) *n.* (Chem.) Salt or ester (esp. for flavouring food) of **gluta'mic acid,** amino-acid normally found in proteins. [foll.]

**glu'ten** (-ōō'-) *n.* Viscous animal--secretion; viscous part of flour left when starch is removed; **glu'tinous** (-ōō'-) *a.,* sticky, gluelike, viscous. [F, f. L *gluten -tin-* glue]

**glŭ'tton** *n.* Excessive eater; avid reader (*of books*), person insatiably eager (*for* work etc.); voracious animal of weasel family; **~ous** *a.;* **~y** *n.,* character, conduct, of a glutton. [F f. L (*gluttio* SWALLOW[1])]

**glў'cerǀine** (-ēn), *\*~ǀīn,* (Chem.) **~ǀŏl,** *ns.* Colourless sweet viscous liquid got from fats, used as ointment etc. and in explosives; **~ĭde** *n.* [F, f. Gk *glukeros* sweet]

**glў'cŏl** *n.* Compound intermediate between glycerine and alcohol.

**‖G.M.** *abbr.* George Medal.

**gm.** *abbr.* gram(s).

**\*G-man** (jē'măn) *n.* (sl.; *pl.* **G--men**) Federal criminal-investigation officer. [*Government*]

**G.M.T.** *abbr.* Greenwich Mean Time.

**gnârled** (nârld), **gnâr'lў** (n-), *adjs.* (Of tree, hands, etc.) knobbly, rugged, twisted; knurled. [rel. to KNURL]

**gnăsh** (n-) *v.i. & t.* (Of teeth) strike together; grind one's teeth, grind (one's *teeth* etc.). [N]

**gnăt** (n-) *n.* Small two-winged biting fly, \*esp. mosquito; insignificant annoyance. [E]

**gnaw** (n-) *v.t.& i.* (*p.p.* **~ed, ~n**). Bite persistently (*away, off, in two,* etc.; *at, into*), wear *away* thus; (of acid, pain, envy, etc.) corrode, torture. [E]

**gneiss** (gnīs, nīs) *n.* (Geol.) Coarse--grained metamorphic rock of quartz, felspar, and mica. [G]

**gnōme**[1] (nōm) *n.* Subterranean spirit, goblin; figure of gnome; (colloq., esp. in *pl.*) person with sinister influence, esp. in finance. [F]

**gnō'mǀē**[2] (n-; *or* nōm) *n.* Maxim, aphorism; **~ĭc** *a.,* of maxims, sententious. [Gk *gnōmē* opinion]

**gnō'mon** (n-) *n.* Rod, pin, etc., of sundial, showing time by its shadow. [F *or* L f. Gk, = indicator]

**gnō'sǀĭs** (n-) *n.* Knowledge of spiritual mysteries. [Gk, = knowledge]

**gnō'stǀic** (n-). **1.** *a.* (**~ally**). Of knowledge; having esoteric spiritual knowledge; (*G~*) of the Gnostics, mystic. **2.** *n.* (*G~;* usu. in *pl.*) Early Christian heretic claiming gnosis; **~ĭsm** *n.* [L f. Gk (prec.)]

**G.N.P.** *abbr.* gross national product.

**‖gns.** *abbr.* guineas.

**gnū** (nū) *n.* Oxlike antelope. [ult. Bantu *nqu*]

**gō** *v., n.,* & *a.* **1.** *v.i.* (**went; gone** *pr.* gŏn, gawn; *part.* GOING). Begin or be moving from some place, position, time, etc., travel, proceed, make one's way, (*go a walk, for a walk; go by car; go the same way; time goes by; went to find him; go and fetch it;* **who goes there?**, sentry's challenge; **be gone**, depart); lie in certain direction (*road goes to York, past the house*); be habitually or for a time (*go armed, hungry; 6 months* **gone with child**, in 7th month of gestation; **it is gone 9**, is past 9 o'clock); be current, pass, (*the* STORY[1] *goes*); be kept or put (*where do the forks go?*); be able to be put, (of number) be capable of being contained in another without remainder or at all, (*boots will go in the bag; 6 into 12 goes twice*); be on the average (*as cooks go nowadays*); have specified wording etc. (*forget how the chorus goes*); turn out, take a course or view, (*things went well; election went against him;* **how goes it?**, what progress?); be functioning, moving, etc., (*clock will not go*); get away, pass, (*go free, unnoticed*); (of money etc.) be spent *in, on*; be given up or abolished; die (*dead and gone*); collapse, give way, fail, (*the bulb has gone*); explode or collapse with sound (*go bang, crack, smash*), give forth sound (*the bell has gone*); be allotted (*the prize went to his rival*); contribute, tend, extend, reach, (*how many days go to the year?; that goes to show; is true as far as it goes*); pass into specified condition (*go blind, mad, mouldy, to sleep*); be successful (*make the party go*); (colloq.) be acceptable or permitted (*anything goes*), be accepted without question (*goes without* SAYING); *what he says goes*); (colloq. or U.S.) proceed to (do) (*go jump in the lake*); be sold (*go* cheap, for £1); carry action to certain point (*will go so far as to say, as high as £10*); **go!**, race-starter's word; **from the word go**, (colloq.) from the very beginning; **to go**, yet to elapse or be traversed (*ten days to go before Easter*; *two miles to go before I get home*); **go about**, endeavour to do, set to work at, (Naut.) change to opposite tack, be in the habit of doing; **go ahead**, proceed confidently; **go-ahead**, (*a.*) enterprising, (*n.*) permission to proceed; **go a long way**, have much effect *towards*, (of food, money, etc.) last long, buy much; **go along with**, = *go with*; **go and do** etc., (colloq.) be so foolish etc. as to; **go around**, be in the habit of doing, be regularly in company *with*; **go at**, attack, grapple with (task); **go away**, depart esp. for holiday etc.; **go back on**, fail to keep (promise etc.); *go* BAIL[1] (*for*); *go* BEGging; **go-between**, intermediary; **go by**, pass, be proportioned to or depend on (*promotion goes by merit*); judge or act (up)on (*I go by the barometer*; *go by the* BOOK); **give** person **the go-by**, pass him without notice, ignore him; *go by* DEFAULT; **go by the name of**, be called; **go doing**, make an expedition to do (*went shopping*), (colloq.) = *go and do*; **go down**, sink, succumb (*before conqueror*), be written down, be swallowed, find acceptance (*with*), leave university; *go down with*, begin to suffer from (disease); *go* FAR; **go for**, go to fetch, pass or be accounted as (*little* etc.), be applicable to, try to attain, prefer, choose, (sl.) attack; *go* FORWARD; **go-getter**, (colloq.) pushful enterprising person; **go-go**, unrestrained, energetic, (of investment) speculative; **go halves** (**with** person, **in** thing), take half each; **go in**, compete (*go in and win*), take or begin innings, (of sun) be obscured; *go in for*, take as one's object, pursuit, principle, etc.; **go into**, enter (profession etc.), frequent (society), fall into (a fit etc.), investigate; **go it**, (sl.) act vigorously etc., indulge in dissipation; **go-kart**, miniature racing car with skeleton body [CART]; **go like this**, make this motion; **go off**, explode, deteriorate, fall asleep, (of pain, excitement, etc.) abate, (of social function etc.) succeed *well* etc., begin to dislike; **go on**, continue (doing), persevere (*with*), talk at

undue length, proceed next *to* do, happen, conduct oneself (*shamefully* etc.), (of garment) be large enough for wearer, (colloq.) rail *at*, take a turn at bowling etc., (colloq.) = *go upon*, (colloq., *imper.*) nonsense!; **be gone on**, (sl.) be infatuated with; **go one better**, outbid or outdo rival; **go out**, leave room or house, be broadcast, be extinguished, cease to be fashionable, (colloq.) lose consciousness, mix in society, feel sympathy (*my heart went out to him*); **go over**, change sides, (of play etc.) be successful, examine, rehearse, retouch; **go round**, pay informal visit *to*, be long enough to encompass, suffice for all; **go shares** (**with** others, **in** thing), take a share each; **go short**, not have enough (*of*); *go* SICK[1]; **go slow**, (esp.) work at deliberately slow pace as industrial protest; **go through**, examine or revise, perform (ceremony etc.), undergo (trials etc.), make holes in, use up, spend (money); *go through with*, complete (task etc.); **go to**, spend as much as (*would go to £10*), have recourse or appeal to (*war, a higher court*), attend (*school, market, church*, etc.); **go together**, be concomitant or compatible; **go to it**, (colloq., esp. in *imper.*) begin work; **go-to-meeting**, Sunday-best (hat, clothes, etc.); **go under**, succumb; **go under the name of**, be called; **go up**, rise in price, explode, burn, enter university; **go upon**, judge by, base conclusions on; **go with**, match, suit, agree to, share views of; **go without**, not have, abstain from. **2.** *n.* (*pl.* **goes** *pr.* gōz). Act of going; animation, dash; (colloq.) vigorous activity (*it's all go*), state of affairs (*a rum go*), success (*make a go of it*), turn or try (*at*; *have a go*; *scored 7 at one go*); **all the go**, (colloq.) in fashion; **it's a go**, (colloq.) the bargain is agreed; **near go**, (colloq.) narrow escape; **no go**, (colloq.) hopeless; **on the go**, (colloq.) in constant motion. **3.** *a.* (colloq.) Functioning properly; fashionable, progressive. **4.** **gō'er** *n.*, person or thing that goes (*slow* etc. *goer*), person who goes to (*church-goer*), lively or persevering person. [E; *went* orig. past of WEND]

**gō²** *n.* Japanese board-game. [Jap.]

**goad. 1.** *n.* Spiked stick for urging cattle; thing that torments or incites. **2.** *v.t.* Urge with goad; irritate; drive (person *to* fury, *to* do, *into* do*ing*) thus. [E]

**goal** *n.* (~**less** *pr.* -l-l-). Point where race ends; object of effort; destination; pair of posts between which football etc. is to be driven, cage or basket used thus in other games, point(s) so won; ~**keeper**, (colloq.) ~**ie**, player protecting goal; ~**-line** (extended from goal-posts, forming end-boundary of field of play); ~**mouth**, space around goal-posts. [orig. unkn.]

**goat** *n.* Lively frisky usu. horned and (in the male) bearded ruminant; (*G~*) sign of ZODIAC; licentious or (colloq.) foolish person; **get** person's ~, (sl.) annoy him; ~**herd**, one who tends goats; ~**sucker**, = NIGHT*jar*; ~**ee** *n.*, beard like goat's; ~**y̆** *a.* [E]

**gŏb¹.** (vulg.) Clot of slimy substance. [F *go(u)be* mouthful]

**gŏb²** *n.* (sl.) Mouth; ~**stopper**, large hard sweet for sucking. [orig. uncert.]

**gŏ'bbĕt** *n.* Extract from text, set for translation or comment; (arch.) lump of meat etc. [F dim. of *gobe* GOB¹]

**gŏ'bble¹** *v.t.* & *i.* Eat hurriedly and noisily. [GOB¹]

**gŏ'bble²** *v.i.* (Of turkey-cock) make gurgling sound in throat; speak thus. [imit.]

**gŏ'bbledĕgōŏk, -dy̆g-,** (-bĕldĭ-; *or* -ōōk) *n.* (sl.) Pompous official etc. jargon. [imit. of turkey-cock]

**gŏ'blĕt** *n.* Glass with foot and stem; (arch.) bowl-shaped handleless drinking-cup of metal or glass. [F dim. of *gobel* cup]

**gŏ'blĭn** *n.* Mischievous ugly demon. [AF]

**gō'by̆** *n.* Small fish with ventral fins joined into disc or sucker. [L *gobius* f. Gk *kōbios* gudgeon]

**G.O.C.(-in-C.)** *abbr.* General Officer Commanding(-in-Chief).

**gŏd** *n.* Superhuman being worshipped as having power over nature and human fortunes; image or animal worshipped as symbolizing or embodying or possessing divine power, idol; adored or admired person; (Theatr., in *pl.*) (occupants of) gallery; (**God**) Supreme Being, Creator and Ruler of universe; ACT *of God*; **by God**, so HELP *me God*, (excl. of asseveration); **God, God Almighty, good God, my God,**

oh **God, 'ye gods,** (excl. of pain, grief, surprise, or anger; *ye* ~*s and little fishes,* joc. excl. of astonishment); **God-awful,** (sl.) extremely unpleasant; *God* BLESS *me, my soul, you, him,* etc.; ~**child,** child sponsored at baptism; **God damn** (*you* etc.; excl. of imprecation); ~**dam(n),** **-damned,** accursed, damnable; ~**-daughter,** female godchild; ~**-father,** male godparent, *person directing illegal organization; **God-fearing,** earnestly religious; **God forbid,** may it not be so; **God-forsaken,** devoid of all merit, dismal; ~ **from the machine,** *deus ex machina;* **God grant,** may it befall or prove (*that*); **God knows,** (1) it is beyond mortal or my knowledge, (2) assuredly; ~**mother,** female godparent; ~**parent,** sponsor at baptism; **God's Acre,** churchyard; *God* SAVE; **God's** (*own*) **country,** earthly paradise, esp. U.S. regarded as such; ~**send,** piece of luck, lucky acquisition; ~**son,** male godchild; **Godspee'd,** wish of 'God speed you!' to departing person; **God's truth,** the absolute truth; **God the Father, Son, Holy Ghost,** persons of Trinity; **God willing,** if conditions allow; **on the knees, in the lap, of the ~s,** beyond human control; **play God,** seek to be all-powerful; **under God** (qualifying attribution of full agency to man); **with God,** dead and in heaven; ~**dĕss** *n.,* female deity, adored woman; ~**head** (-hĕd) *n.,* divine nature, deity (**the Godhead,** God); ~**lĕss** *a.,* without god, not recognizing God, impious, wicked; ~**like** *a.,* like God or a god, like that of a god; ~**ly̆** *a.* (-iness), pious, devout. [E]

**godĕ'tia** (-shǎ) *n.* Showy-flowered hardy annual. [*Godet,* person]

**godow'n** *n.* Warehouse in E. Asia. esp. in India. [Port. f. Malay]

**gŏ'dwĭt** *n.* Wading bird like curlew but with straight or slightly upcurved bill. [orig. unkn.]

**gō'er, goes.** See GO¹.

**gŏ'ggle** *v.,* *a.,* & *n.* **1.** *v.i.* & *t.* Roll (eyes); look with wide-open eyes; (of eyes) be rolled, project. **2.** *a.* (Of eyes) protuberant, rolling. **3.** *n.* (in *pl.*) Spectacles for protecting eyes from glare, dust, etc.; ~**box,** (sl.) television set. [prob. imit.]

**gō'ĭng. 1.** *n.* State of ground for walking, riding, etc. (esp. for horse-

-racing); progress as helped, hindered, by this, lit. or fig. (**heavy ~**, slow or difficult progress; **while the ~ is good**, while conditions are favourable); **~-over**, (colloq.) inspection or overhaul, (sl.) thrashing; **~s-o'n**, strange conduct. 2. *a.* In action (*set the clock going*); existing, available, (*the best brand going*; *there is cold beef going*); currently valid (*the going rate*); **get ~** *v.t.* & *i.*, start talking, working, etc.; **to be ~ on with**, to start with, for the time being; **~ concern**, business in working order; **~ for** one, (colloq.) acting in one's favour; **~! gone!** (auctioneer's announcement that bidding is closing, closed); *going great* GUNS; **~ on** (**for**), approaching (a time, age, etc.); *going* STRONG; **~ to**, about to, intending or likely to. [part. of GO[1]]

**goi'tre** (-*ter*), **\*-ter**, *n.* Morbid enlargement of thyroid gland; **goi'-tred** (-*terd*) *a.*, having goitre; **goi'trous** *a.* [F (L *guttur* throat)]

**gŏld.** 1. *n.* Yellow non-rusting heavy precious metal; coins of this, wealth; beautiful or precious things, material, etc. (*a heart of gold*); colour of gold; = *gold medal*. 2. *a.* Of, coloured like, gold. 3. **~-beater**, one who beats gold into gold-leaf; **~brick**, (sl.) thing with only surface appearance of value, fraud; **~'crest**, very small bird with golden crest; **~-digger**, (fig., sl.) coquette who wheedles money out of men; **~-dust**, gold in fine particles as often found naturally; **~-field**, district yielding gold; **~'finch**, song-bird with yellow on wings; **~'fish**, small red Chinese carp (**~***fish bowl*, fig. situation lacking privacy); **~ foil, -leaf**, gold beaten into thin, thinner, sheet; **~ medal**, medal of gold usu. as 1st prize; **~-mine**, source of wealth (lit. or fig.); **~ plate**, vessels of gold, material plated with gold; **~-***plate* v.t., plate with gold; **~ of pleasure**, yellow-flowered annual; **~'rush** (to new gold-field); **~'smith**, worker in gold; *gold* STANDARD. [E]

**gŏ'lden** *a.* Of gold; yielding gold; coloured or shining like gold (*golden hair*); precious, excellent; *golden* AGE; **~ disc**, award to artiste after sale of a million copies of gramophone record made by him; **~ eagle** (with yellow-tipped head-feathers); *Golden* FLEECE; **~ handshake**, gratuity as compensation for dismissal or compulsory retirement; *golden* JUBILEE; **~ mean**, neither too much nor too little; **~ number** (of year in Metonic lunar cycle, used in fixing Easter); **~ opinions**, high regard; **~ opportunity** (exceptionally good); **~ rod**, plant with yellow flower-spikes; **~ rule**, 'do as you would be done by', basic principle of action; ‖**~ syrup**, pale treacle; *golden* WEDDING.

**gŏlf.** 1. *n.* Game in which small hard ball is struck with clubs towards and into hole on each of successive smooth greens separated by fairways and rough ground. 2. *v.i.* Play golf. 3. **~ ball** (used in golf, or colloq. spherical unit carrying the type in some electric typewriters); **~-club**, club used, (premises of) association, for playing golf; **~-course, -links**, area of land on which golf is played. [orig. unkn.]

**gŏ'lliwŏg** *n.* Black-faced soft doll with bright clothes and fuzzy hair. [orig. uncert.]

**gŏ'lly**[1] *int.* = (By) God. [GOD]

**gŏ'lly**[2] *n.* = GOLLIWOG. [abbr.]

‖**gŏlŏ'sh.** See GALOSH.

**-gon** *suf.* forming *n*s. denoting plane figures with given number of angles (*hexagon*). [Gk *-gōnos* -angled]

**gŏ'năd** *n.* Animal organ producing gametes, e.g. testis or ovary. [L f. Gk *gonê* seed]

**gŏ'ndol|a** *n.* Light flat-bottomed Venetian canal-boat; car suspended from airship or balloon; **~ier'** *n.*, rower of gondola. [It.]

**gone.** See GO[1].

**gŏ'ner** (*or* gaw'-) *n.* (sl.) Doomed or irrevocably lost person or thing. [prec.]

**gŏ'nfalon** *n.* Banner, often with streamers, hung from crossbar. [It.]

**gŏng** *n.* Metal disc with turned rim giving resonant note when struck; saucer-shaped bell; (sl.) medal. [Malay]

**gŏnorrhoe'a**, **\*-rrhē'a**, (-*orē'a*) *n.* Venereal disease with inflammatory discharge from urethra or vagina. [L f. Gk, = semen-flux]

**gŏŏ** *n.* (sl.) Viscous or sticky substance; (fig.) sickly sentiment; **~'ey** *a.* (**~ier, ~iest**). [orig. unkn.]

**gŏŏd** *a., adv.,* & *n.* **1.** *a.* (BETTER[1], BEST; *adv.* WELL[2]). Having the right qualities, adequate, (*a good fire*, bright, large; *meat keeps good*, untainted; *good soil*, fertile; *good theatre* etc., entertainment suited to specified medium; *is good eating*, pleasant to eat); commendable, worthy, (*good men and true*; *my good sir, man*, etc., usu. ironical or indignant; *the good man*, *your good lady* = your wife, etc., esp. patronizingly); proper, expedient; morally excellent, virtuous, (*do one's good deed for the day*); (of child) well-behaved (*as good as gold*); kind, benevolent, (*how good of you!*); agreeable (*good news*; in forms of greeting or parting, as *good afternoon, day* (formal), *evening, morning, night*); suitable, efficient, competent, reliable, safe, valid, (*a good driver*; *good English*; *the rule holds good*); financially sound (*his credit is good*); thorough, considerable, (*a good beating*; *a good number*); not less than (*waited a good hour*; *a good three miles from here*); **as ~ as**, practically (*as good as dead*); **make ~** *v.t. & i.*, compensate for, repair (damage or damaged part), pay (expense), effect (purpose), fulfil (promise), prove (statement, charge), gain and hold (position), succeed in an undertaking. **2.** *adv.* \*(colloq.) Well (*doing pretty good*); **~ and** (colloq., as intensive: *I was good and angry*). **3.** *n.* Profit, benefit, well-being, (*deceive him for his own good*; *what good will it do?*; *it is no good talking*; **do ~ to**, benefit; **for ~ (and all)**, finally, permanently; **to the ~**, having as net profit etc.; **up to no ~**, bent on mischief); (as *pl.*) virtuous persons (*the good go to heaven*); (in *pl.*) movable property, merchandise, ‖things to go by rail etc.; (in *pl.*, colloq.) objects one has undertaken to supply (DELIVER *the goods*), advantageous information (*have the goods on a person*), the real thing. **4. ~ at**, skilful in; *good* BOOK(s), BREEDING; *a good* DEAL²; **be ~ enough to** (please) do; **not ~ enough**, (colloq.) not worth doing, accepting, etc.; *good* FAITH; **~ fellow**, sociable person; **~-fe′llowship**, conviviality; **~ for**, beneficial to, having good effect on, able to undertake or pay (*good for a 20-mile walk*, *£100*); **~-for-nothing** *a. & n.*, worthless (person); **~ for you′**, (colloq.) well done!; *Good* FRIDAY; **~ God!, ~ gracious!, ~ heavens!**, (excl. of surprise etc.); **~-hearted**, kindly, well-meaning; **~ humour**, genial mood (esp. *in a good humour*); **~-hu′moured**, in genial mood, of genial disposition; *good* JOB¹; **~-**

**-loo′ker, -loo′king**, handsome (person); **~ looks**, personal beauty; **~ luck**, being fortunate, happy chance, (*good luck to you!*); **~ money**, genuine money, money that might have been better spent (THROW *good money after bad*), (colloq.) high wages; ‖**~ morrow**, (arch.) good morning; **~ nature**, kindly disposition; **~ old — (colloq. form of approval)**; *good* OLD *days*; **~ o′n you**, (Austral. sl.) well done!; **a ~ one**, (sl.) excellent joke, incredible lie or exaggeration; **~ people**, the fairies; **~ question** (not answerable immediately or easily); **~ sense**, practical wisdom; **~ show!**, (colloq.) well done!; **~ thing**, fortunate occurrence, source of satisfaction, profitable bargain etc., witty saying, (in *pl.*) luxuries: *a good* TIME; **in ~ time**, with no risk of being late; **all in ~ time**, in due course but without haste; **~-time** *a.*, recklessly pursuing pleasure; **~ times**, period of prosperity; **~ to drink, eat**, wholesome as food; **~ will**, intention that good shall result; **~wi′ll**, kindly feeling (*to, towards*), heartiness, zeal, right granted by seller of a business to trade as successor; **~ word**, brief commendation (*say a good word for*). [E]

**goodby′|e, \*-by̆′**, *int. & n.* (*pl.* **~es**, **\*~s**). Farewell (expr. good wishes on parting, ending telephone conversation, etc.); **kiss, wave, ~e to**, (fig.) accept loss of. [*God be with you*]

**goo′dly** *a.* (**-iness**). Handsome or imposing size etc. [E]

**goo′dness** *n.* Virtue; excellence; kindness (*have the goodness to wait*); (in excl.) God (*goodness knows*; *for goodness' sake*; *goodness gracious!*). [E]

**goo′dy** *n., a., & int.* **1.** *n.* Something good or attractive, esp. to eat; (colloq.) hero etc. (opp. *baddy*); goody-goody person. **2.** *a.* (**-iness**). **~(-goody)**, obtrusively or weakly or sentimentally virtuous. **3.** *int.* expr. childish delight or surprise. [GOOD]

**goo′ey.** See GOO.

**goof.** (sl.) **1.** *n.* Foolish or stupid person; mistake; **~y̆** *a.* **2.** *v.i. & t.* Blunder, bungle. [ult. f. L *gufus* coarse]

**goo′gly** *n.* (Crick.) Off-break ball bowled with apparent leg-break action. [orig. unkn.]

**goon** *n.* (sl.) Stupid person; person

hired by racketeer etc. to terrorize workers. [orig. uncert.]

**gōōsǎ′nder** *n.* Duck with sharp serrated bill. [foll.]

**gōōse** *n.* (*pl.* **geese** *pr.* gēs). Web-footed bird between duck & swan in size, female of this (opp. **gander**), flesh of goose as food, (**all his geese are swans,** he overestimates merits; cook person's *goose;* **kill the ~ that lays the golden eggs,** sacrifice future profit to present greed); simpleton; (*pl.* **~s**) tailor's smoothing iron (with handle like goose's neck); **~-flesh, -pimples,** bristling state of skin due to cold or fright; **~-grass,** cleavers; **~ step,** army recruit's balancing-drill, parading-step of marching soldiers with knees kept stiff. [E]

**gōō′seberrў** (-zb-) *n.* A thorny shrub, its edible berry; **play ~,** be chaperon or unwelcome companion to pair of lovers; **~ bush** (w. ref. to nursery explanation of source of babies). [orig. uncert.]

**\*G.O.P.** *abbr.* Grand Old Party (the Republican Party).

**gō′pher** *n.* American burrowing rodent, ground squirrel, or burrowing tortoise. [orig. uncert.]

‖**gorbli′mey** *int.* (vulg.) expr. surprise etc. [*God blind me*]

**Gŏr′dian** *a.* Cut the **~ knot,** solve problem by force or evasion. [*Gordius,* who tied a knot later cut by Alexander the Great]

**gōre¹** *n.* Blood shed and clotted; **gŏr′ў** *a.* (-ily, -iness). [E, = dirt]

**gōre²**. **1.** *n.* Wedge-shaped piece in a garment; triangular or lune-shaped piece in umbrella etc. **2.** *v.t.* Shape with gore. [E, = triangle of land]

**gōre³** *v.t.* Pierce with horn, tusk, etc. [orig. unkn.]

**gōrge**. **1.** *n.* Contents of stomach (one's **~ rises at,** one is sickened by); (rhet.) internal throat; gorging, surfeit; narrow opening between hills. **2.** *v.i.* & *t.* Feed greedily; satiate, devour greedily, choke up. [F, = throat]

**gŏr′geous** (-jŭs) *a.* Richly coloured, sumptuous; (colloq.) very pleasant, splendid, (*had a gorgeous time*). [F]

**gŏr′gon** *n.* (Gk Myth.) one of three snake-haired sisters whose look petrified beholder; terrible or repulsive woman. [L f. Gk (*gorgos* terrible)]

**Gŏrgonzō′la** *n.* Type of rich blue-veined cheese. [place]

**gori′lla** *n.* Large reputedly fierce arboreal anthropoid ape. [Gk, perh. f. Afr. = wild man]

**gŏr′mandize** *v.i.* Eat like a glutton. [GOURMAND]

**gŏr′mless** *a.* (colloq.) Foolish, lacking sense. [obs. *gaumless* f. dial. *gaum* understanding]

**gōrse** *n.* = FURZE; **gŏr′sў** *a.* [E]

**Gŏr′sĕdd** (-ĕdh) *n.* Meeting of Welsh etc. bards and druids (esp. as preliminary to eisteddfod). [W, lit. 'throne']

**gŏr′ў.** See GORE¹.

**gŏsh** *n.* (In excl. etc., for) God. [euphem.]

**gŏ′shawk** (-s-h-) *n.* Large short-winged hawk. [E (GOOSE, HAWK¹)]

**gŏ′sling** (-z-) *n.* Young goose. [N (GOOSE)]

**gŏ′spel** *n.* Glad tidings preached by Christ; Christian revelation; (*G~*) (one of) records of Christ's life in first four books of N.T.; portion from a Gospel read at Communion service; thing one may safely believe; principle one acts on, preaches, etc., (*gospel of soap and water*); **~ oath** (sworn on the Gospels); **~ truth,** truths contained in gospel, thing as true as gospel; **~ler** *n.,* reader of Gospel in Communion service; **hot ~ler,** rabid propagandist (for religion). [E (GOOD, SPELL¹ news) transl. I. *evangelica* EVANGEL]

**gŏ′ssamer**. **1.** *n.* (Thread of) filmy substance of small spiders' webs floating in calm air or spread over grass; flimsy thing; delicate gauze; **~ў** *a.* **2.** *a.* Light, flimsy, as gossamer. [orig. uncert.]

**gŏ′ssip**. **1.** *n.* Idle talk(er), tattler, esp. woman; informal talk or writing esp. about persons or social incidents (**~ column,** section of newspaper etc. containing this); **~ў** *a.* **2.** *v.i.* Talk or write gossip. [E, orig. 'familiar acquaintance', 'godparent'. = related in God, fellow godparent]

**gŏt.** See GET.

**Gŏth** *n.* Uncivilized or ignorant person, comparable to Goths who invaded Roman Empire in 3rd–5th c. [tribe-name]

**Gŏ′thĭc**. **1.** *a.* (**~ally**). Of the Goths; (Archit.) in the pointed-arch style prevalent in W. Europe in 12th–16th c. (**~ Revival,** reversion to this in 19th c.); barbarous, uncouth; (of novel etc.) in a popular horrific 18th–19th-c. style. **2.** *n.* Gothic language or architecture. [F or L (*Gothi* Goths)]

**gŏt′ten.** See GET.

**gouache** (gōōäsh′) *n.* (Painting in) opaque colours ground in water and thickened with gum and honey. [F f. It.]

**Gou′da** *n.* Flat round cheese, orig. Dutch. [place]

**gouge** (*or* gōōj) **1.** *n.* Concave-bladed chisel. **2.** *v.t.* Cut (as) with gouge; force (*out*, esp. eye with thumb) (as) with gouge, force out eye of (person) thus; ~ **out**, make or shape (cork, groove) with gouge. [F f. L *gubia*]

**gou′lȧsh** (gōō′-; *or* -ahsh) *n.* Highly seasoned stew of meat and vegetables. [Magyar *gulyás-hús*, = herdsman's meat]

**gourd** (goord) *n.* (Fleshy usu. large fruit of) trailing or climbing plant; dried rind of this fruit used as bottle. [F, ult. f. L *cucurbita*]

**gour′mand** (goor′-) *n.* Glutton; gourmet; ~**ise** (-mahndēz′), ~**ism**, *ns.*, gluttony. [F]

**gour′met** (goor′mā) *n.* Connoisseur of delicate food. [F]

**gout** *n.* Disease with inflammation of joints, esp. of big toe, and chalk-stones; drop, esp. of blood; splash; ~′**y̆** *a.* [F f. L *gutta* drop, w. ref. to old theory of humours]

**Gov.** *abbr.* Government; Governor.

**go′vern** (gŭ′-) *v.t. & i.* Rule with authority, conduct the policy and affairs of (State), regulate proceedings of (corporation etc.; ~**ing body**, managers of hospital etc.); be in military command of (fort etc.); curb, control, (one's passions, oneself); sway, influence, determine, (person, his acts, course of events); be a standard or principle for, serve to determine; (Gram., esp. of *v.* or *prep.*) have (noun, case) depending on it; ~**ance** *n.*, act, manner, function, of governing. [F f. L f. Gk *kubernaō* steer]

**go′vernȧ́ss** (gŭ′-) *n.* Female teacher, usu. of children in private household; ‖~**-car′t**, light two-wheeled vehicle with side seats face to face; ~′**y̆** *a.*, (esp.) prim.

**go′vernmȧnt** (gŭ′-) *n.* System of governing; act, manner, fact, of governing; form of organization of State; persons governing State; State as an agent; (usu. *G*~) ministry; \*~ **issue**, (equipment) provided by government; **G**~ **securities**, bonds etc. issued by government; ~ **surplus**, unused equipment sold by government; ~**al** (-č′n-) *a.* (-**lly**). [F (GOVERN)]

**go′vernor** (gŭ′-) *n.* Ruler; official governing province, town, etc.; representative of Crown in Commonwealth country (*Governor-General*) or colony; executive head of each State of U.S.; officer commanding fortress etc.; head, one of governing body, of institution; official in charge of prison; (sl.) one's employer or father, (as *voc.*) sir; automatic regulator of supply of steam etc. to machine. [F, f. L (GOVERN)]

**gown** *n.* Loose flowing garment, esp. woman's (elegant long) dress; ancient Roman toga; surgeon's overall; official robe of alderman, judge, clergyman, member of university (**town and** ~, non-members and members esp. at Oxf. and Camb.), etc.; ~**ed** (-nd) *a.*, attired in gown. [F f. L *gunna* fur]

**goy** *n.* (*pl.* ~**s**, ~**′im**). (Jewish name for) GENTILE. [Heb., = people]

**G.P.** *abbr.* general practitioner.

**Gp. Capt.** *abbr.* Group Captain.

**G.P.O.** *abbr.* ‖General Post Office; \*Government Printing Office.

**G.R.** *abbr.* King George. [L *Georgius Rex*]

**gr.** *abbr.* grain(s); gram(s); gross.

**grăb. 1.** *v.t. & i.* (-**bb**-). Seize suddenly; take greedily; capture; (sl.) attract attention of, impress; snatch (*at*). **2.** *n.* Sudden clutch or attempt to seize; rapacious proceedings in commerce etc.; (Mech.) device for clutching; \***up for** ~**s**, (sl.) easily available; \*~**-bag**, lucky dip; ~ **handle**, **rail**, etc., (to steady passengers in moving vehicle). [LDu.]

**grāce. 1.** *n.* Attractiveness, charm, esp. that of elegant proportions or of easy and refined motion, expression, manner, etc.; becomingness (*cannot with any grace ask it*; *had the grace to be ashamed*); air, bearing, (**with a good, bad,** ~, as if willingly, reluctantly); attractive feature, accomplishment, (*social graces*); (Mus.) note(s) added as embellishment of melody; (Gk Myth.; *G*~) one of three sister goddesses, bestowers of beauty and charm; goodwill, favour, (**act of** ~, concession not claimable as right; ~ **and favour** *house* etc., occupied by permission of sovereign; **by the** ~ **of God,** esp. in royal titles, through God's favour; **be in** person's **good** ~**s,** enjoy his favour); (Theol.) favour of God, divine regenerating and inspiring influence, state of being so influenced, (YEAR *of grace*); delay granted (*had a year's grace*); **days of** ~, time allowed by law for payment of due bill); thanksgiving before or after meal; **His, Her, Your, G**~ (said of or to duke, duchess, or archbishop). **2.** *v.t.* Add grace to, adorn, (often *with*). **3.** ~'**ful** (-sf-) *a.* (-**lly**), full of grace (first sense); ~'**less** (-sl-) *a.*, shameless, inelegant, ungracious, (arch. or joc.) depraved. [F f. L *gratia*]

**gra′cious** (-shŭs) *a.* Kind, indulgent and beneficent to inferiors, (esp. as polite epithet of royal persons or their acts; *the gracious speech from the throne*); (of God) merciful, benign, (in *int.* w. *God* omitted, *gracious!*, *good gracious!*, *gracious me!*); ~ **living,** elegant way of life. [F f. L (prec.)]

**grada′tion** *n.* (usu. in *pl.*) Stage of transition or advance; degree in rank, intensity, etc.; arrangement in gradations; **grada′te** *v.t.* & *i.*, (cause to) pass by gradations from one shade to another, arrange in gradations; ~**al** *a.* (-**lly**). [L (foll.)]

**grade. 1.** *n.* Degree in rank, merit, proficiency, etc.; class of persons or things of same grade; mark indicating quality of student's work; slope (**on the up, down,** ~, rising, falling; **make the** ~, succeed); *class, form, in school (*~ **school,** elementary school). **2.** *v.t.* & *i.* Arrange in grades; give grade to (student); reduce (road etc.) to easy gradients; pass gradually (*up, down,* etc.) between grades. [F, or L *gradus* step]

**gra′dient** *n.* (Amount of) slope in road etc.

**gra′dual** *a.* (~**ly**). Occurring by degrees, not rapid or steep or abrupt; ~**ism,** *n.,* policy of gradual but sudden change. [L (GRADE)]

**gra′du|āte. 1.** *v.i.* & *t.* Take academic degree; *admit to academic degree etc.; move up *to* (higher grade of activity etc.); mark out in degrees or parts; arrange in gradations, apportion (tax) according to scale; ~**a′tion,** ~**ātor,** *ns.*

**2.** (-*at*) *n.* Holder of academic degree (~**ate school,** university department for advanced work by graduates). [L *graduor* take a degree (GRADE)]

**Grae′co-** *in comb.* Greek (and); ~**o-Roman,** of the Greeks and Romans, (of wrestling) attacking only upper body; ~**ism** *n.,* (imitation of) Greek idiom, style, etc.; ~**ize** *v.t.,* give Greek character or form to. [L]

**graffi′t|o** (-fē′-) *n.* (*pl.* ~**i** *pr.* -ē). Drawing etc. scratched or scribbled on wall etc. [It. (*graffio* scratching)]

**graft¹** (-àh-). **1.** *n.* Shoot, scion, planted in slit of another stock; such slit; this process; (Surg.) piece of transplanted living tissue; (sl.) hard work. **2.** *v.t.* & *i.* Insert (scion *in, upon,* stock); insert grafts; (fig.) insert or fix *in* or *on* so as to unite; transplant (living tissue); (sl.) work hard. [F f. L f. Gk *graphion* stylus]

**graft²** (-àh-; colloq.) *n.*, & *v.i.* (Practices for securing, seek or make) illicit political or business gains. [orig. unkn.]

**Grail** *n.* (Holy) ~, cup or platter used by Christ at Last Supper and in which Joseph of Arimathea received Christ's blood at the Cross; this as object of lengthy quest (by medieval knights, or fig.). [F f. L *gradalis* dish]

**grain. 1.** *n.* Fruit or seed of cereal; (collect.) wheat or allied food-grass, its fruit, corn; particle of sand, SALT, etc.; unit of weight, 1/480 oz. troy, 1/7000 lb. avoirdupois; least possible amount (*without a grain of sense*); (Hist.) kermes, cochineal, dye from these (**dye in** ~, dye in kermes, in the fibre or thoroughly); roughness of surface; texture in skin, wood, stone, etc.; pattern of lines of fibre in wood or paper, lamination in stone etc., (fig.) nature, tendency, (**against the** ~, contrary to inclination); ~'**y** *a.* (~**iness**). **2.** *v.t.* & *i.* Form into grains; dye in grain; give granular surface to; paint in imitation of grain of wood etc. [F f. L *granum*]

**grăllātor′ial** *a.* Of the long-legged wading birds. [L *grallator* walker on stilts (*grallae*)]

**grăm¹** *n.* Chick-pea; any pulse used as horse-fodder. [Port. f. L *granum* grain]

**grăm², grămme,** *n.* Unit of mass in metric system, 1/1000 of

KILO*gram*; **~-atom, -equivalent,** mass in grams numerically equal to atomic weight, equivalent weight. [F (*-me*) f. Gk *gramma* small weight]

**-grăm** *suf.* forming *ns.* denoting thing (so) written or recorded (*diagram, monogram, telegram*); cf. -GRAPH. [Gk *gramma* thing written (*graphō* write)]

**grămĭn|ā′ceous** (-shus) *a.* Of or like grass; **~ĭ′vorous** *a.*, feeding on grass, cereals, etc. [L (*gramen* grass)]

**grā′mmar** *n.* Study or rules of a language's inflexions or other means of showing relation between words (as used in speech or writing) and its phonetic system; book on grammar; observance or correct use of rules of grammar (*good, bad, grammar*); **~ school** (‖orig. founded for teaching Latin, now a secondary school with academic curriculum; *intermediate between primary and high schools); **grammā′rĭan** *n.*, one versed in grammar or linguistics; **grammă′tical** *a.* (-lly), of or according to grammar. [AF *gramere* f. L f. Gk *grammatikē* (*gramma* letter of alphabet)]

**grămme.** See GRAM².

**grā′mophōne** *n.* Instrument reproducing recorded sound by stylus resting on rotating grooved disc. [inversion of PHONOGRAM]

**grā′mpus** *n.* Blowing spouting dolphin-like cetacean. [F f. L (*crassus piscis* fat fish)]

**grăn** *n.* (colloq. or childish). Grandmother. [abbr.]

**grănadĭ′lla, grĕ-,** *n.* Passion-fruit. [Sp. dim. of *granada* pomegranate]

**grā′narў** *n.* Storehouse for threshed grain; region producing (esp. exporting) much corn. [L (GRAIN)]

**grănd¹. 1.** *a.* (In titles) chief, of highest rank; of chief importance, final, ultimate, main, (*the grand question, result, staircase*); splendid, imposing, magnificent, lofty, noble; belonging to high society (*grand people*); (colloq.) excellent (*in grand condition*); (in names of relationships) in second degree of ascent or descent (**~′parent,** one's parent's parent; so **~′father, ~′mother;** (colloq. or childish) **~-dad(dy), ~′ma(ma), ~′pa(pa),** **~′child,** one's child's child; so **~′daughter, ~′son;** **~ air,** distinguished appearance; *Grand* CROSS; **~father clock** (in tall wooden case); **~ finale,** im-

pressive closing scene of opera etc. (or transf.); *Grand* INQUISITOR; *~* **jury** (to examine validity of accusation before trial); *grand* LODGE; **~ manner,** style suited to noble subjects; **~ master,** head of order of knighthood, Freemasons, etc., chess-player of highest ability; ‖G**~ National,** annual steeplechase at Liverpool; **~ old man,** venerated person, esp. Gladstone, Churchill; *grand* OPERA¹, PIANO², SEIGNEUR; **~′sire,** animal's sire's sire, (arch.) grandfather or ancestor or old man; *grand* SLAM²; **~′stand,** main stand for spectators at races etc. (*~stand finish,* close and exciting); **~ style,** = *grand manner;* **~ total,** sum of minor totals; **~ tour,** (arch.) tour of Europe completing education, (fig.) extensive tour. **2.** *n.* Grand piano; (sl.) thousand pounds, *dollars, etc. [AF, F f. L *grandis* full-grown]

**grand²** (grahṅ) *a.* **~ mal** (mah′l), epilepsy with loss of consciousness; G**~ Prix** (prē′), international motor-racing championship. [F (prec.)]

**grā′ndăd** *n.* = GRAND¹-dad.

**grā′ndăm, -āme,** *n.* Animal's dam's dam; (arch.) grandmother, old woman. [F (GRAND¹, DAME)]

**grande** (grahṅd) *a.* **~ dame** (dah′m), dignified lady; **~ passion** (pă′syawṅ), overwhelming love affair. [F (GRAND¹)]

**grāndee′** *n.* Spanish or Portuguese noble of high rank; great personage. [Sp., Port. *grande* (GRAND¹)]

**grā′ndeur** (-njer, -ndyer) *n.* High rank, eminence; nobility of character; majesty, splendour, dignity, of appearance or bearing. [F (GRAND¹)]

**grăndĭ′loquen|t** *a.* Pompous or inflated in language; **~ce** *n.* [L (GRAND¹, *-loquus* f. *loquor* speak)]

**grā′ndĭ|ōse** *a.* Producing or meant to produce imposing effect; planned on large scale; **~ŏ′sĭtў** *n.* [F f. It. (GRAND¹)]

**grānge** (-nj) *n.* Country house with farm-buildings. [F f. L *granica* (GRAIN)]

**gran|ĭ′ferous** *a.* Producing grain or grainlike seed; **~ĭ′vorous** *a.*, feeding on grain. [L (GRAIN)]

**grā′nĭte** *n.* Granular crystalline rock of quartz, mica, etc., used for building; **the ~ city,** Aberdeen; **granĭ′tic** *a.* [It. *granito* (GRAIN)]

**grā′nnў, grā′nnĭe,** *n.* (colloq. or childish). Grandmother; **~ (knot),**

insecure reef-knot crossed the wrong way. [abbr. *grannam* f. GRANDAM]

**grant** (-ah-). **1.** *v.t.* Consent to fulfil (request etc.); concede, allow, (thing to person); *God grant that we arrive safely*); give formally, transfer (property) legally; admit (proposition, *that*; **take for ~ed**, regard as necessarily true or certain to continue or occur). **2.** *n.* Granting; thing, esp. money, granted; conveyance by written instrument; ||**~-aided school** (receiving some financial aid from public funds). **3.** **~ee'**, **~or'**, *ns.*, person to, by, whom property etc. is legally transferred. [F *granter* var. of *creanter* f. L *credo* entrust]

**grǎ'nūl|ar** *a.* Of or like grains or granules; **~ǎ'rǐtȳ** *n.*; **~āte** *v.t. & i.*, form into grains, roughen surface of, (of wound) form small prominences as beginning of healing; **~ā'tion**, **~ātor**, *ns.*; **grǎ'nůle** *n.*, small grain. [L dim. of *granum* (GRAIN)]

**grāpe** *n.* Berry (usu. green, purple, or black) growing in clusters on vine, used as fruit and in making wine; **~'fruit**, large round yellow citrus fruit growing in clusters with acid juicy pulp; **~ hyacinth**, small plant with usu. blue flowers; **~-shot**, (Hist.) small balls as scattering charge for cannon; **~-vine**, vine, means of transmission of rumour; **sour ~s** (said when person disparages what he desires but cannot attain). [F]

**grǎph** (*or* -ahf). **1.** *n.* Diagram showing relation of two variable quantities each measured along one of a pair of axes; **~ paper** (with network of lines as help in drawing graphs); **grǎ'phǐcal** *a.* (-lly). **2.** *v.t.* Plot or trace on graph. [abbr. *graphic* formula]

**-graph** (-ahf) *suf.* forming *ns.* & *vbs.* denoting: thing written etc. in specified way (*holograph*), instrument that records (*telegraph*), write etc. in specified way (*photograph*); **-grapher** *suf.* forming *ns.* denoting person skilled in *-graphy* (*geographer, radiographer*); **-grǎ'phǐc(al)** *sufs.* forming *adjs.* from *ns.* in *-graph* or *-graphy*; **-graphy** *suf.* forming *ns.* denoting: style, method, of writing etc. (*stenography*), descriptive science (*geography*). [F f. L f. Gk (*graphō* write)]

**grǎ'phǐc. 1.** *a.* (**~ally**). Of writing, drawing, painting, etching, etc., (**~ arts,** arts of writing, printing, decorating, etc., on flat media); vividly descriptive. **2.** *n.* (esp. in *pl.*, usu. treated as *sing.*) Production or use of diagrams in calculation and design. [L f. Gk (*graphē* writing)]

**-grǎ'phǐc(al).** See -GRAPH.

**grǎ'phǐte** *n.* Crystalline allotropic form of carbon used in pencils, as lubricant, etc.; **graphǐ'tǐc** *a.* [G *graphit* f. Gk *graphō* write]

**graphǒ'log|ȳ** *n.* Study of handwriting esp. as guide to character; **~ǐst** *n.* [Gk (GRAPHIC)]

**-graphy.** See -GRAPH.

**grǎ'pnel** *n.* Iron-clawed instrument for seizing esp. enemy's ship; small many-fluked anchor. [AF f. F f. Gmc]

**grǎ'pple. 1.** *n.* Clutching-instrument, grapnel; hold (as) of wrestlers; close contest. **2.** *v.t. & i.* Seize (as) with grapple; grip with hands, come to close quarters with; **~ with,** contend with, try to deal with or accomplish; **grappling-iron,** grapnel. [F *grapil* f. Prov. f. Gmc]

**grasp** (-ah-). **1.** *v.t. & i.* Clutch, seize greedily, (**~ing,** avaricious); hold firmly (**~ the nettle,** tackle difficulty boldly); understand, realize, (fact, meaning); **~ at,** try to seize, accept eagerly. **2.** *n.* Firm hold, grip; mastery (*of* subject); mental hold; **within, beyond,** one's **~,** close, not close, enough to be grasped (lit. or fig.) [*grapse*, rel. to GROPE]

**grass** (-ahs). **1.** *n.* Herbage of which blades, leaves, etc., are eaten by cattle etc. (**not let the ~ grow under** one's **feet,** be quick to act); any species of this (Bot. incl. cereals, reeds, and bamboos); (sl.) marijuana; grazing (*be at, turn out to, grass*); pasture land; grass-covered ground, lawn, (*keep off the grass*); **~'ȳ** *a.* **2.** *v.t. & i.* Cover with turf; *provide with pasture; (sl.) betray, inform police. **3. ~-cloth,** linen-like cloth woven from ramie etc.; **~ court,** grass-covered lawn-tennis court; **~'-hopper,** jumping and chirping insect; **~'land** (covered with grass, esp. if used for grazing); **~ parakeet** (frequenting grassland); **~ roots,** fundamental level or source, esp. (Polit.) the voters; **~ skirt** (made of long grass and leaves fastened to waistband); **~ snake,** ||common ringed snake, *common green snake; **~ widow(er),** person whose husband, wife, is temporarily absent. [E]

**grāte**[1] n. (Metal frame confining fuel in) recess of fireplace or furnace. [F f. L *cratis* hurdle]

**grāte**[2] v.t. & i. Reduce to small particles by rubbing on rough surface; rub with harsh noise (*against, on*); grind (teeth); utter in harsh tone; sound harshly (*grating laugh*); have irritating effect (*on* person, nerves); creak. [F f. Gmc]

**grāte'ful** (-tf-) a. (~ly). Thankful, feeling or showing gratitude; pleasant, acceptable. [obs. *grate* f. L *gratus*]

**grā'tif̄|y** v.t. Please, delight; please by compliance; yield to (desire); ~icā'tion n. [F or L (GRATEFUL)]

*gratin* (grā'tan) n. Way of cooking, dish cooked, with crisp brown crust usu. of bread crumbs or grated cheese; *au* ~ (-ō-), so prepared. [F (GRATE[2])]

**grā'ting** n. Framework of parallel or crossed bars, wires, lines ruled on glass, etc. [GRATE[1]]

**grā'tis** (or -ah'-) adv. & a. Free of charge, for nothing. [L]

**grā'titūde** n. Being thankful for and ready to return kindness. [F or L (GRATEFUL)]

**gratū'it|ous** a. Got or done gratis; uncalled for, motiveless, (a *gratuitous lie, liar, insult*); ~y̆ n., money given in recognition of services, bounty on retirement etc. [L, = spontaneous]

**gravā'men** n. (pl. ~s, grava'-mina). Essence, worst part, (*of* accusation); grievance. [L (*gravis* heavy)]

**grāve**[1] n. (Mound, monument, over) hole dug for corpse (**dig** ~ **of**, cause downfall of; *one* FOOT *in the* grave; **would make** person **turn in his** ~, would have shocked him if alive); death (*carry the scar to* one's *grave*); receptacle of what is dead; ~**clothes**, wrappings of corpse; ~'**stone**, (inscribed) stone over or at head or foot of grave; ~'**yard**, burial-ground. [E]

**grāve**[2] v.t. (*p.p.* ~**n**, ~**d**). Fix indelibly (*in, on,* one's memory etc.); (arch.) engrave, carve; ~**n image**, idol. [E]

**grāve**[3] a. Serious, weighty, important, (*grave matter, question, fault*); dignified, solemn; sombre; (of sound) low-pitched, not acute. [F, or L *gravis* heavy]

**grāve**[4] v.t. Clean (ship's bottom)

by burning and tarring; **graving dock**, = *dry* DOCK[3]. [perh. F *grave, grève* shore]

**grāve**[5] (or grahv) a. & n. ~ (accent), mark (`) placed over vowels in some languages to show quality etc. [GRAVE[3]]

**grăv'el. 1.** n. Coarse sand and small stones, used for paths etc.; stratum of gravel esp. one containing gold; (disease with) formation of calculi in bladder; ~**ly** a.; ~(**ly**) **voice** (deep and rough-sounding). **2.** v.t. (**‖-ll-**). Lay with gravel; puzzle, nonplus. [F dim. (GRAVE[4])]

**grā'ven.** See GRAVE[2].

**Graves** (grahv) n. Light French wine made in *Graves*. [place]

**grăv'id** a. (literary, Zool.) Pregnant. [L *gravidus* (GRAVE[3])]

**gravi'mĕt|er** n. Instrument measuring difference in force of gravity between two places; ~**rȳ** n., measurement of weight; **grăvimĕ'tric** (-ically). [F f. L (GRAVE[3])]

*gravitas* (grā'vitahs) n. Gravity, seriousness. [L (GRAVE[3])]

**grā'vit|ȳ** n. Solemnity; importance, seriousness; weight (**centre of** ~**y**, centre of MASS[2] of rigid body, fig. point of chief importance; **specific** ~**y**, weight of substance compared with same volume of water or air); (intensity of) body's attraction to centre of earth etc.; gravitational force; ~**y feed**, supply of material by its fall under gravity; ~**āte** v.t. & i., move, tend, by force of gravity (*towards*), sink (as) by gravity, (fig.) move because, be, attracted (*towards*); ~**ā'tion** n., falling of bodies to earth, (movement or tendency towards centre of) attraction of each particle of matter on every other; **law of** ~**ation** (specifying force of this); ~**ā'tional** a. [F or L (GRAVE[3])]

**grā'vȳ** n. Juices exuding from meat in and after cooking; dressing for food, made of these; (sl.) unearned or unexpected money; ~**boat**, boat-shaped vessel for gravy. [perh. erron. f. F *grané* (*grain* spice, GRAIN)]

***gray.** See GREY.

**gray'ling** n. Silver-grey freshwater fish. [GREY, -LING]

**grāze**[1]. **1.** v.t. & i. Touch lightly in passing, move (*against, along,* etc.) with such contact; suffer slight abrasion of (part of body). **2.** n. Abrasion. [perh. f. foll. 'take off grass close to ground']

**grāz|e**² *v.i.* & *t.* (Of cattle etc.) feed, feed (cattle etc.), on growing grass; feed on (grass); pasture cattle; **~′ier** (*or* -zher) *n.*, one who feeds cattle for market, (Austral.) sheep-farmer; **~′ing** *n.*, grassland suitable for pasturage. [E (GRASS)]

**grease.** 1. *n.* Oily or fatty matter esp. as lubricant; melted fat of dead animal; **~-paint** (as actor's make-up). 2. (*or* -ēz) *v.t.* Lubricate with grease (**~ palm of**, bribe; *like greased* LIGHTNING). 3. **grea′sy̆** (*or* -zī) *a.* (**-ily, -iness**), of, like, smeared with, having too much, grease, slippery, (of person, manner) too unctuous. [F f. L (*crassus* adj. fat)]

**great** (-āt). 1. *a.* Occupying much space, large, big, (usu. with implied surprise, contempt, etc.; *made a great blot, look at that great wasp*; colloq. *great big cake, great thick stick*); **~(′er)**, the larger of the name (*greater celandine*; *great titmouse*; *Great Malvern*); more than ordinary (*great care, age, friends*); important, distinguished, pre-eminent, (*to a great extent*; *the great attraction*; *Peter the Great*); of remarkable ability, of lofty character, (*great painter*; *a truly great man*; *great thoughts*); (colloq.) very satisfactory (*had a great time*; *that's great!*); fully deserving the name of, doing a thing much or on a large scale, (*a great scoundrel, fiasco*; *a great one for travelling*; *great dancer, land-owner*); (prefixed once or more to *uncle, aunt, nephew, niece*, and to *grand-* in kinship wds) one degree more remote. 2. *n.* Great person or thing; **the ~**, (*pl.*) great persons; **the ~est**, (sl.) very remarkable person; **G~s**, Oxford univ. course, final examination, esp. in classics and philosophy. 3. **~ at**, skilful in (game etc.); *Great* BEAR¹; *great* CIRCLE; **~′coat**, heavy overcoat; *Great* DANE; *a great* DEAL²; **~er** London etc. (including adjacent urban areas); *greatest common* MEASURE; *Great* LAKE¹s; **~ on**, fond of talking, or well-informed, on (subject); **G~ Russian**, of principal U.S.S.R. ethnic group; **G~ Scott!** (joc. excl.); *Great* SEAL¹; **~ toe**, big toe; **G~ War** (of 1914–18); **~ with child**, (arch.) pregnant. 4. **~lȳ** *adv.*, much (usu. with vbs., and a few compar. adjs.; *adds greatly to the cost*; *greatly esteemed, superior*; *should greatly prefer*), nobly, loftily. [E]

**greave** *n.* (usu. in *pl.*) Armour for shin. [F, = shin]

**grēbe** *n.* A diving bird. [F]

**Grē′cian** (-shan). 1. *a.* (Of architecture or facial outline) Greek; **~ nose** (straight and continuing forehead line without dip). 2. *n.* Person skilled in Greek. [F or L (*Graecia* Greece)]

**greed** *n.* Insatiate desire esp. for food or wealth; **~′y̆** *a.* (**~ily, ~iness**), gluttonous, voracious, (*of*), avaricious, rapacious, (*of, for*), eager (*to* do). [E]

**Greek.** 1. *n.* Native of Greece (**~ meets ~**, said of encounter between equals); Greek language (**~ to me**, incomprehensible to me). 2. *a.* Of Greece or its people, Hellenic, of or in Greek (*Greek alphabet, philosophy*); *Greek* CALENDS; **~ Church**, ORTHODOX Church; **~ cross** (with four equal arms); **~ gift** (given with intent to harm); **~ god**, paragon of male beauty. [E f. Gmc f. L f. Gk *Graikos*]

**green** *a., n.,* & *v.* 1. *a.* (**~′ness** pr. -n-n-). Of colour between blue and yellow, coloured like grass, emerald, etc.; covered with herbage, in leaf, (**a ~ Christmas**, mild, snowless); pale, sickly-hued; (fig.) jealous, envious; vegetable (*green food*); (of fruit etc.) unripe; young, flourishing; not withered or worn out (*a green old age*); inexperienced, gullible; not dried, seasoned, smoked, or tanned; **~′er̆y̆** *n.*, vegetation. 2. *n.* Green colour, pigment, clothes or material (*dressed in green*), ball in snooker etc.; colour symbolizing Ireland; vigour, youth, (*in the green*); (in *pl.*) green vegetables; piece of grassy public land (*village green*); grass-plot (*bowling, putting, -green*); (Golf) putting-green, (occas.) fairway (**through the ~**, between tee and putting-green). 3. *v.i.* & *t.* Become or make green. 4. **\*~′back**, U.S. legal-tender note; **~ belt**, area of open land for preservation round city; **~ card**, motorist's international insurance document; **~ cheese**, whey cheese, cheese coloured with sage; ||**G~ Cloth**, Lord Steward's department of Royal Household; **~ eye, -eyed monster**, jealousy; **~′finch**, finch with yellow and green plumage; **~ fingers**, (colloq.) skill in gardening; ||**~′fly**, green aphid; **~′gage**, round green plum [Sir W. *Gage*]; ||~'-**grocer(y)**, (business of, things sold by) retailer of fruit and vegetables; ~'**horn**, simpleton, raw recruit; ~'**house** (of glass for rearing plants); ~'**keeper**, keeper of golf-course; ~ **light**, signal to proceed on road etc., (colloq.) permission to go ahead with a project; green MEAT; ||G~ **Paper**, tentative report of Governmental proposals, without commitment; green PEAS, PEPPER; ~ **revolution**, much increased crop production in developing countries; ~**room** (for actors off stage); ~'**sand**, green kind of sandstone; ~**stick**, bone-fracture, esp. in children, in which one side of bone is broken and one only bent; ~'**stone**, green eruptive rock containing felspar and hornblende, N.Z. kind of jade; ~'**stuff**, vegetation, green vegetables; ~'**sward**, grassy turf; ~ **tea** (made from steam-dried leaves); ~ **thumb**, (colloq.) = *green fingers*; ~'**wood**, woodlands in summer. [E]

**Gree'nwich** (grĭ'nĭj, grě'nĭch) *n.* ~ (**mean**) **time**, (mean) time on the meridian of Greenwich, used as international basis of time-reckoning. [place]

**greet**[1] *v.t.* Accost with salutation; salute, receive, (person, event, news, etc., *with* words, gestures, applause, hisses, etc.; or w. these as subject); (of a sight, sound, etc.) meet (eye, ear, etc.); ~'**ing** *n.* (act or words). [E]

**greet**[2] *v.i.* (Sc.) Weep. [E]

**grēgā̆r'ious** *a.* Living in flocks or communities; fond of company. [L (*grex gregis* flock)]

**Grēgŏr'ian** *a.* Of the plainsong ritual music named after Pope Gregory I; ~ **calendar**, correction of Julian calendar under Pope Gregory XIII in 1582. [persons]

**grĕ'mlin** *n.* (sl.) Mischievous sprite alleged to derange machinery etc. [orig. unkn.]

**grĕnā̆'de** *n.* Explosive shell thrown by hand (**hand-**~) or shot from rifle (**rifle-**~); glass vessel thrown to disperse chemicals for extinguishing fires etc.; **grĕnadier'** *n.*, (Hist.) soldier who threw grenades; ||**Grenadiers, Grenadier Guards**, first regiment of royal household infantry. [F (POMEGRANATE)]

**grĕnadi'lla.** See GRANADILLA.

**grĕ'nadīne** *n.* Pomegranate syrup;

dress-fabric of loosely-woven silk or silk and wool. [F]

**Grĕ'sham** *n.* ~'**s law**, (Econ.) tendency for money of lower intrinsic value to circulate more freely than money of higher intrinsic and equal nominal value. [person]

**grew.** See GROW.

**grey** (grā), *gray, a., n.*, & *v.* **1.** *a.* Between black and white, coloured like ashes or lead; clouded, dull, dismal; (of hair) turning white, (of person) with grey hair; aged, experienced, mature; ancient; (of person) anonymous, unidentifiable. **2.** *n.* Grey colour, pigment, clothes or material (*dressed in grey*); grey horse (||the (Scots) **Greys**, 2nd Dragoons). **3.** *v.i.* & *t.* Become or make grey. **4.** ~'**beard**, old man; ~ **cells**, = *grey matter*; ~ **eminence**, = *éminence grise* (see EMINENT); ~ **eye** (with grey iris); *Grey FRIARS*; ~ **goose**, European wild goose; ~**headed**, old, ancient; ~**hen**, female black grouse; ~'**lag**, = *grey goose*; ~ **mare**, (fig.) wife who dominates husband; ~ **matter** (of active part of brain); ~ **monk**, Cistercian; ~ **squirrel**, Amer. squirrel brought to Europe in 19th c. [E]

**grey'hound** (grā'-) *n.* Slender swift dog used in coursing; ~**racing**, sport in which mechanical hare is coursed by greyhounds on track as opportunity for betting. [E, = bitch-hound]

**grĭd** *n.* Grating; wire network between filament and anode of thermionic valve; system of numbered squares printed on map and forming basis of map references; network of lines, electric-power connections, gas-supply lines, etc.; pattern of lines marking starting-places on car-racing track; arrangement of town streets in rectangular pattern; gridiron (for broiling or *football); NATIONAL *grid*. [GRIDIRON]

**grĭ'ddle** *n.* = GIRDLE[2]. [F f. L (*cratis* hurdle)]

**grĭ'diron** (-īern) *n.* Barred metal broiling- or grilling-frame; *football field (with parallel marking-lines); ~ (**pendulum**), type of compensated pendulum. [GRIDDLE]

**grief** *n.* Deep or violent sorrow (**come to** ~, meet with disaster); (euphem.) God (*good grief!*); **grie'v-ance** *n.*, real or fancied ground of complaint; **grieve** *v.t.* & *i.*, (cause to) feel grief (*at*, *about*, *for*, *over*); **grie'vous** *a.*, injurious, (of pain etc.) severe, flagrant, heinous; **grievous bodily harm**, (Law) serious injury. [F f. L (GRAVE³)]

**gri'ffin, gry'phon,** *n.* Fabulous creature with eagle's head and wings and lion's body. [F f. L f. Gk]

**gri'ffon** *n.* = prec.; large vulture; coarse-haired terrier-like dog.

**grig** *n.* Small eel; cricket; **merry, lively, as a ~**, full of fun or life. [orig. unkn.]

**grill. 1.** *v.t.* & *i.* Cook on gridiron or under grill; subject to, undergo, torture or great heat; subject to severe questioning (esp. by police). **2.** *n.* Grilled food; device on cooker for radiating heat downwards; gridiron (first sense); **~(-room)**, informal restaurant; (also **grille**) grating or latticed screen in door, metal grid protecting motor-vehicle radiator. [F (GRIDDLE)]

**grilse** *n.* Young salmon that has been only once to the sea. [orig. unkn.]

**grim** *a.* (**-mm-**). Stern, merciless; of stern or harsh aspect (*hold on like ~ death*, tightly); ghastly, joyless, (*grim smile*); unpleasant, unattractive. [E]

**grima'ce. 1.** *n.* Distortion of face made in disgust etc. or in jest. **2.** *v.i.* Make grimace. [F f. Sp.]

**grime. 1.** *n.* Soot, dirt, ingrained esp. in skin; **gri'my** *a.* (**-ily, -iness**). **2.** *v.t.* Blacken, befoul. [LDu.]

**grin. 1.** *v.i.* & *t.* (**-nn-**). Show teeth in amusement or pain or in forced, unrestrained, or stupid smile (*at*); express by grinning; **~ and bear it**, take pain etc. stoically. **2.** *n.* Act or action of grinning. [E]

**grind. 1.** *v.t.* & *i.* (**ground**). Crush to small particles between millstones, teeth, etc., (*down, small, to dust*, etc.); produce (flour) thus; oppress, harass with exactions, (*grinding poverty*); sharpen or smooth by friction (*an* AXE *to grind*; **ground glass**, made opaque by grinding); work (hand-mill); turn handle of (barrel-organ etc.); produce or bring *out* with effort; study hard, toil; rub gratingly; rub (teeth) hard together. **2.** *n.* Grinding; hard dull work (**the daily ~**, colloq. one's usual day's work); size of ground particles. **3.** **~'stone**, thick revolving disc for grinding and polishing (**keep** person's

**nose to the ~stone**, make him work incessantly), stone used for this; **~'er** *n.*, (esp.) molar tooth, grinding machine. [E]

**grip. 1.** *n.* Firm hold, grasp, (**at ~s, come** or **get to ~s with**, of close combat, or purposeful approach to a subject); grasping power; way of clasping hands or of grasping or holding; mastery (of subject), intellectual hold, (*get a grip* on oneself; *lose* one's *grip*); gripping part of machine etc.; part of weapon etc. that is held; hair-grip; *~(-'sack*), suitcase, travelling-bag. **2.** *v.t.* & *i.* (**-pp-**). Grasp tightly; take firm hold esp. by friction; compel attention of. [E (foll.)]

**gripe. 1.** *v.t.* & *i.* Clutch, grip; oppress; affect with colic; (sl.) complain. **2.** *n.* Grip; (in *pl.*) colic; (sl.) complaint; **~-water**, carminative esp. for babies. [E]

‖**gri'skin** *n.* Lean part of loin of bacon pig. [obs. *gris* pig f. N]

**gri'sl̵y** (-z-) *a.* (**~iness**). Causing (esp. superstitious) terror. [E]

**grist** *n.* Corn to grind (**brings ~ to the mill**, is profitable; **all is ~ that comes to his mill**, he utilizes everything). [E (GRIND)]

**gri'stle** (-sel) *n.* Tough flexible tissue, cartilage; **~y** (-slĭ) *a.* [E]

**grit. 1.** *n.* Particles of sand etc. as causing discomfort, clogging machinery, etc.; **~('stone**, coarse sandstone; (colloq.) pluck, endurance; **~'ty** *a.* (**~tily, ~tiness**). **2.** *v.i.* & *t.* (**-tt-**). Make grating sound; grind, clench, (teeth); spread grit on (icy roads etc.). [E]

**grits** *n.pl.* Husked but unground oats; coarse oatmeal. [E]

‖**gri'zzle** *v.i.* (colloq.) (Esp. of child) cry fretfully. [orig. unkn.]

**gri'zzl̵y. 1.** *a.* Grey, grey-haired; **~y bear**, large fierce N. Amer. bear; **~ed** (-zeld) *a.*, grey(-haired). **2.** *n.* Grizzly bear. [*grizzle* a. f. F *grisel* grey]

**groan. 1.** *v.i.* & *t.* Make deep sound expressing pain, grief, etc., (**~ inwardly**, be distressed); utter with groans; be oppressed (*groan under injustice*; **~ing board**, well-loaded dining-table). **2.** *n.* The sound made by groaning. [E]

**groat** *n.* (Hist.) Silver coin with value of 4d. [LDu. (GREAT)]

**groats** *n.pl.* Hulled (and crushed) grain, esp. oats. [E]

**grō'cer** *n.* Dealer in tea, butter, flour, tinned foods, etc., and household stores; ~**y̆** *n.*, grocer's trade, shop, or (usu. in *pl.*) goods. [AF *grosser* f. L (*grossus* GROSS)]

**grŏg** *n.* Drink of spirit (orig. rum) and water; ~**'gy̆** (-gĭ) *a.* (~**gily**, ~**giness**), unsteady, tottering. [orig. uncert.]

**grŏ'gram** *n.* Coarse fabric of silk, mohair, etc. [F *gros grain* coarse grain]

**groin**[1]. **1.** *n.* Depression between belly and thigh; (Archit.) edge formed by intersecting vaults, arch supporting vault. **2.** *v.t.* Build with groins. [orig. uncert.]

**\*groin**[2]. See GROYNE.

**grŏ'mmĕt.** See GRUMMET.

**grōōm. 1.** *n.* ‖One of certain officers of Royal Household; person employed to take care of horses; bridegroom (~**'sman**, unmarried male friend attending bridegroom at wedding). **2.** *v.t.* Curry, tend, (horse); give neat appearance to (person); prepare (person) *as* political candidate, *for* career, etc. [orig. unkn.]

**grōōve. 1.** *n.* Channel, hollow, esp. one made to guide motion or receive ridge; spiral cut in gramophone record for needle (**in the** ~, sl., performing excellently, excellent); piece of routine, habit; (sl.) well-played jazz, something excellent; **grōō'vy̆** *a.*, of, like, a groove, (sl.) in the groove. **2.** *v.t. & i.* Make groove(s) in; settle *into* (routine etc.); (sl.) give pleasure to (person), enjoy well-played jazz, make progress, get on well *with* (person). [Du.]

**grōpe** *v.i. & t.* Feel about as in dark (*for*, *after*, etc.); search blindly (lit. or fig.); ~ one's **way**, proceed tentatively. [E]

**grō'sbeak** *n.* = HAW*finch*. [F *grosbec*, = large (GROSS) beak]

**grō'sgrain** (-ō'gr-) *n.* Corded silk etc. fabric. [F (GROGRAM)]

**gros point** (grō'pwǎn) *n.* Cross-stitch embroidery on canvas. [F (GROSS, POINT)]

**grŏss** *a., n., & v.* **1.** *a.* Luxuriant, rank; overfed, bloated; flagrant (*gross negligence*); total, not NET[2], (*gross tonnage*; ~ **national product**, annual total value of goods produced and services provided in a country); thick, solid; (of food) coarse (~ **feeder**, one liking gross food); (of senses etc.) dull; (of manners, morals,

person) coarse, unrefined, indecent. **2.** *n.* (*pl.* same). Twelve dozen; **by the** ~, in large quantities, wholesale. **3.** *v.t.* Produce as gross profit; ~ **up**, increase (net amount) to its value before deduction of tax etc. [F f. L *grossus*; n. f. F *grosse* (*douzaine* dozen)]

**grōtĕ'sque** (-sk). **1.** *n.* Decoration interweaving human etc. forms with foliage; comically distorted figure etc. **2.** *a.* In style of grotesque; distorted; incongruous, absurd. [F f. It. (foll.)]

**grŏ'ttō** *n.* (*pl.* ~**es**, ~**s**). Picturesque cave; artificial or simulated cave. [It. *grotta* f. L (CRYPT)]

‖**grŏ'tty̆** *a.* (sl.) Unpleasant, dirty, ugly, useless. [abbr. GROTESQUE]

**grouch.** (colloq.) **1.** *v.i.* Grumble. **2.** *n.* Discontented person; fit of grumbling or the sulks; ~**'y̆** *a.* [GRUDGE]

**ground**[1]. **1.** *n.* Bottom of sea (**touch** ~, fig. reach solid conclusion etc.); (in *pl.*) dregs, esp. of coffee; foundation, motive, (**on the** ~ **of**, by reason of); surface worked upon, undecorated part, prevailing colour; surface of earth (opp. Aeron., opp. *air*; **above, below,** ~, fig., alive, dead and buried; **cut** ~ **from under** person's **feet**, anticipate and defeat his arguments etc.; **down to the** ~, **from the** ~ **up**, colloq., completely; **fall to the** ~, (of plan, hope) fail; *feet on the ground*, see FOOT; **get off the** ~, start successfully; **go to** ~, (of dog, fox, etc.) enter burrow, (of person) withdraw from public notice; **into the** ~, to exhaustion etc.; **on the** ~, on the spot, in practical conditions; **on firm, solid,** etc., ~, fig., using soundly-based reasoning; **thin on the** ~, sparse); (in *pl.*) enclosed land attached to house; position, area, on earth's surface or fig. (**break new** ~, begin work on previously untouched ground, lit. or fig.; **cover much** ~, be far-reaching; **cover the** ~, deal adequately with subject; **gain** ~, advance, catch up *on* (person pursued); **give, lose,** ~, retreat, decline; **hold** one's ~, not retreat; *meet* person **on his own** ~, in his territory or on his terms; SHIFT, STAND, one's *ground*); (Electr.) earth; area of special kind or use (*camping-, cricket-, fishing-, ground*; **forbidden** ~, taboo subject; **in, out of, his** ~, of batsman in, out of, his lawful position); ‖floor of room etc.; (attrib., in names of birds) terrestrial, (of animals) burrowing, lying on ground, (of plants) dwarfish, trailing. **2.** v.t. & i. Run ashore, strand; base (principle etc. on fact etc., in pass. also in); instruct thoroughly (in subject); place, lay, (esp. Mil. arms) on ground; (Electr.) connect with earth as conductor; prevent (aircraft, airman) from flying; alight on ground. **3.** ~-**bait** (thrown to bottom to attract fish; lit. or fig.); ~ **bass**, (Mus.) theme in bass constantly repeated with upper part of music varied; ~-**fish** (living at bottom); ground FLOOR (get in on the ~ **floor**, be admitted to project, company, etc., as one of the initiators); ~ **frost** (on surface of ground or in top layer of soil); ~′**hog**, kind of N. Amer. marmot; *~′-**keeper**, = groundsman; ~-**nut**, (edible tuber of) N. Amer. wild bean, ‖pea-nut; ~-**plan**, plane drawing of divisions of building at ground level, general outline of anything; ~-**rent** (of ground leased for building); ~ **rule**, basic principle; ~′**sheet**, waterproof sheet for spreading on ground; ~′**sman** (in charge of cricket-ground etc.); ~ **speed**, aircraft's speed relative to ground; ~ **squirrel**, chipmunk, gopher, etc.; ~ **staff**, non-flying members of aerodrome staff, ‖cricket-club's paid players; ~ **swell**, heavy sea due to distant or past storm or earthquake; ~ **water** (in surface soil); ~′**work**, foundation (usu. fig.); ~ **zero**, point on ground under exploding bomb; ~′**ing** n., (esp.) drill in elements of subject; ~′**less** a., (of feeling, action, statement) without motive or foundation. [E]

**ground²**. See GRIND.

**grou′ndling** n. = GROUND¹-fish; spectator, reader, of inferior taste. [GROUND¹]

**grou′ndsel** n. Plant of which commonest species is used as food for cage-birds. [E]

**group** (-ōōp). **1.** n. Number of persons or things near together, or belonging or classed together; (Polit.) smaller unit than a party; number of commercial companies under one owner; division of air force; = POP² group; ~ **captain**, R.A.F. officer next below air commodore; ~ **practice** (medical, in which several

doctors are associated); ~ **sex**, sexual activity involving more than two persons simultaneously; ~ **therapy** (in which similarly affected patients are brought together to assist one another). **2.** v.t. Form into a group; place in a group (with, together) or groups. [F f. It. gruppo]

**grou′per** (-ōō′-) n. Marine food-fish. [Port.]

**grouse¹** n. (pl. same). Wild gallinaceous bird with feathered feet, esp. ‖(red) ~, reddish European game-bird; its flesh as food. [orig. uncert.]

**grouse²** v.i., & n. (sl.) Grumble. [orig. unkn.]

**grout¹. 1.** n. Thin fluid mortar. **2.** v.t. Apply grout to.

**grout²** v.i. & t. (Of pigs, or fig.) turn up earth, turn up, with snout. [obs. groot mud]

**grōve** n. Small wood, group of trees. [E]

**grŏv′el** v.i. (‖-ll-). Lie prone in abject humility, abase oneself; ~′**velling** a., abject, base, prone. [N phr., = on one's face]

**grow** (-ō) v.i. & t. (grew pr. grōō; ~n with be or have, or as a.). Develop or exist as living plant or natural product (~ **into one, together**, coalesce); increase in size, height, amount, intensity, etc., (~ **on**, have increasing charm etc. for; ~ **out of**, become too large to wear (garment), become too mature to retain (habit etc.); ~′**ing pains**, neuralgic pain in children's legs due to fatigue etc., (fig.) early difficulties in development of a project etc.; ~**n man** etc., adult); become gradually (grow rich); produce by cultivation; let (beard etc.) develop; (in pass.) be covered (over etc.) with growth; ~ **up**, advance to maturity (~**n-up** a. & n., adult), (of custom) arise; ~′**er** n., person growing produce, esp. fruit, plant that grows in specified way (free grower). [E]

**growl. 1.** n. Guttural sound of anger; rumble; angry murmur, complaint. **2.** v.i. & t. Make a growl; ~ **out**, utter with growl; ~′**er** n., (esp.) small iceberg, ‖(Hist.) four-wheeled cab. [imit.]

**grown**. See GROW.

**growth** (-ōth) n. Growing (of foreign ~, grown abroad); increase in size or value; what has grown or is growing; (Path.) morbid formation;

~ **industry** (developing faster than other industries). [GROW]

**groyne**, *\*groin²*, *n.* Structure of timber etc. run out to check shifting of sea beach. [dial. *groin* snout f. F f. L]

**grŭb. 1.** *v.i.* & *t.* (-bb-). Dig superficially; clear (ground) of roots etc., clear away (roots etc.); get, find, (*up*, *out*, lit., or fig. in books etc.) by digging; rummage (*for* etc.). **2.** *n.* Larva of insect, maggot; (sl.) food; ~**-screw** (headless); *\*~-stake* *v.t.*, & *n.*, (sl.) supply with outfit, provisions, etc., in return for share in profits; ~'**bў** *a.* (-ily, -iness), full of grubs, dirty. [F]

**Grŭ'b Street** *n.* & *a.* (Typical of) needy and hack authors. [place]

**grŭdge. 1.** *v.t.* Be unwilling to give or allow (*do you grudge me it?*). **2.** *n.* Resentment, ill will, (*have*, *\*hold*, *a grudge against*; *bear*, OWE, *person a grudge*). [F]

**gru'el** (-ōō'-). **1.** *n.* Liquid food of oatmeal etc. boiled in milk or water. **2.** *v.t.* (||-ll-). Exhaust, punish, esp. ~(l)**ing** *n.* & *a.* [F f. Gmc]

**grue'some** (-ōō's-) *a.* Horrible, grisly, disgusting. [Scand.]

**grŭff** *a.* Surly, rough-mannered, rough-voiced. [LDu. *grof* coarse]

**grŭ'mble. 1.** *n.* Faint growl, murmur; complaint. **2.** *v.i.* & *t* Utter grumble; complain (*at*, *about*); be discontented; ~**r** *n.*, (esp.) one who constantly grumbles. [obs. *grumme*]

**grŭ'mmĕt, grŏ'mmĕt,** *n.* Insulating washer round electric conductor passing through hole in metal; (Naut.) ring usu. of twisted rope as fastening etc.; stiffening ring in service cap. [F]

**grŭ'mp/ў** *a.* (~ily, ~iness). Ill-tempered, surly. [imit.]

**Grŭ'ndў** *n.* (**Mrs.**) ~, prudish person of conventional propriety. [character in play]

**grŭnt. 1.** *n.* Low guttural sound characteristic of pig. **2.** *v.i.* & *t.* Utter grunt; express discontent etc. thus; utter with grunt (*out*); ~'**er** *n.*, (esp.) pig, or Amer. fish grunting when caught. [E (imit.)]

**gruyère** (grōō'yār) *n.* Swiss cheese with many holes. [place]

**grў'phon.** See GRIFFIN.

**G-string** (jē'-) *n.* Narrow strip of cloth etc. covering genitals, attached to string round waist; (Mus.) string

on violin etc. sounding note G. [G, STRING]

**Gt.** *abbr.* Great.

**gua'nō** (gwah'-) *n.* (*pl.* ~s). Excrement of sea-fowl, used as manure and found esp. in islands off Peru; **fish** etc. -~, artificial manure. [Sp. f. Quechua]

**guărantee'** (gă-). **1.** *n.* Giver of guaranty or security; guaranty; thing esp. document serving as security for fulfilment of conditions etc. **2.** *v.t.* Be guarantee for, answer for fulfilment or genuineness or permanence of; give one's word (*that* thing is or will be so); secure (person *in* possession etc., *against* risk etc.); secure (thing *to* person); **guă'rantor** (gă'-; or -ŏr') *n.*; **guă'rantў** (gă'-) *n.*, written or other undertaking to answer for payment of debt or performance of obligation by the person primarily liable, ground of security. [WARRANT]

**guǎrd** (gärd). **1.** *n.* Defensive posture or motion in fencing, boxing, etc., defensive position of cricket-bat; watch, vigilant state, (*keep*, *be on*, *guard*; *on*, *off*, one's ~, ready, not ready, against attack, lit. or fig.); protector (*stand* ~ *over*, protect), sentry; ||official in charge of train; *\*prison warder; soldiers protecting place or person, escort, separate portion of army, (*advance*, *rear*, *-guard*; *guard of honour*; *mount*, *relieve*, ~, take up, take others' place on, sentry duty); ||(in *pl.*) household troops (*Foot*, *Horse*, *Life*, *Dragoon*, *Guards*); device to prevent injury or accident (*fire-*, *mud-*, *shin-*, *-guard*). **2.** *v.t.* & *i.* Protect, defend, (*from*, *against*); protect (door etc.) so as to control passage; secure by stipulations etc. from misunderstanding or abuse; keep (thoughts, speech) in check (~**ed language**, cautious, measured); take precautions (*against*). **3.** ~'**house**, ~'**room**, (accommodating military guard or securing prisoners); ~-**ring** (to keep other ring on finger); ~'**sman**, soldier belonging to guard or Guards. [F f. Gmc (WARD)]

**guǎr'dian** (gär'-) *n.* Keeper, protector; ||(Hist.) member of board administering poor-laws in parish etc.; (Law) one having custody of person or property of WARD (minor, lunatic, etc.); ~ **angel** (watching over person or place); ~**ship** *n.* [F (prec., WARDEN)]

**gua′va** (gwah′-) *n.* (Tropical Amer. tree with) edible orange acid fruit. [Sp.]

**gŭ′bbĭns** (-z) *n.* Trash; valueless thing; gadget; (colloq.) foolish person. [obs. *gobbons* fragments]

*****gŭbernatŏr′ĭal** *a.* Of governor. [L]

**gŭ′dgeon**[1] (-jon) *n.* Small freshwater fish used as bait; credulous person. [F f. L (*gobio* GOBY)]

**gŭ′dgeon**[2] (-jon) *n.* Kind of pivot or metal pin; socket for rudder. [F dim. (GOUGE)]

**guĕ′lder** (gĕ′-) *n.* ~ **rose,** shrub with round bunches of white flowers. [Du. (*Gelderland,* place)]

**guĕr′don** (gĕr′-) *n.,* & *v.t.* (poet.) Reward. [F f. Gmc]

**Guĕr′nsey** (gĕr′nzĭ) *n.* (One of) breed of cattle from Guernsey; (*g*~) thick knitted woollen jersey; ~ **lily,** kind of amaryllis. [place]

**guer(r)ĭ′lla** (ger-) *n.* Person taking part in irregular fighting (~ **war, warfare**) by small independently acting groups; URBAN *guerrilla.* [Sp. dim. (WAR)]

**guĕss** (gĕs). **1** *v.t.* & *i.* Estimate without calculation or measurement; form hypothesis about, conjecture, think likely, (thing, *that, how,* etc.); conjecture (answer to riddle etc.) rightly; ~ **at,** make guess concerning; *****I** ~, I think it likely, I suppose; **keep** person ~**ing,** (colloq.) leave him uncertain. **2.** *n.* Rough estimate, conjecture; ~**′work,** (procedure based on) guessing. [orig. uncert.]

**guĕ′s(s)timate** (gĕ′-) *n.* (colloq.) Estimate based on guesswork and reasoning. [prec., ESTIMATE]

**guĕst** (gĕst) *n.* Person invited to visit one's house or have meal etc. at one's expense (**paying** ~, boarder); person lodging at hotel etc.; occasional performer from outside company etc.; ~**house,** superior boarding-house. [N]

**gŭff** *n.* (sl.) Empty talk. [imit.]

**gŭ′ffaw** (*or* -aw′). **1.** *n.* Boisterous laugh. **2.** *v.i.* Make guffaw. [imit.]

**guide** (gīd). **1.** *n.* One who shows the way; tourist's, traveller's, hired conductor; person or thing by which others regulate movements; ||(G~) member of girls' organization similar to Scouts; adviser; directing principle; book of rudiments; ~**′book,** book of information for tourists (*to* cathedral, city, etc.); (Mech.) rod

etc. directing motion; thing marking position or guiding the eye; ~**dog** (trained to guide blind person); ~**line,** (fig.) directing principle. **2.** *v.t.* Act as guide to, lead; arrange course of (events); be the principle or motive of; ~**d missile** (under remote control or directed by equipment within itself); ~**d tour** (accompanied by guide); **gui′dance** (gī′-) *n.;* **Gui′der** (gī′-) *n.,* adult leader of Guides. [F f. Gmc]

**gui′don** (gī-) *n.* Pennant narrowing to point or fork at free end. [F f. It.]

**guild, gĭld**[2], (gĭ-) *n.* Society for mutual aid or with common object; G~**hall,** hall in which medieval guild met, town hall; ~ **socialism,** system by which each industry should be controlled by a council of its members. [LDu. *gilde*]

**gui′lder** (gĭ′-) *n.* Monetary unit of Netherlands; (Hist.) Dutch and German gold coin. [alt. Du. GULDEN]

**guile** (gīl) *n.* Treachery, deceit, cunning; ~**′ful** (-lf-) *a.* (-lly); ~**′lèss** (-l-l-) *a.* [F f. Scand.]

**gui′llemot** (gĭ′-) *n.* Kind of auk. [F]

**gui′llotine** (gĭ′lotēn; *or* -tē′n). **1.** *n.* Beheading-machine with knife-blade sliding in grooves; machine for cutting paper, metal, etc.; ||(Parl.) method of preventing delay by fixing times for voting on parts of Bill. **2.** *v.t.* Use guillotine on. [F (*Guillotin,* person)]

**guilt** (gĭ-) *n.* Fact of having committed specified or implied offence; (feeling of) culpability; ~ **complex,** (Psych.) mental obsession with idea of having done wrong. [E]

**guilt′lèss** (gĭ′-) *a.* Innocent (*of* offence); not having knowledge, possession, *of* (*guiltless* of Greek).

**guilt**|**y** (gĭ′-) *a.* (~ily, ~iness). Criminal, culpable; conscious of, due to, guilt (*guilty conscience, look*); having committed offence (*of*); ~**y, not** ~**y,** (verdicts in criminal trials).

**gui′nea** (gĭ′nĭ) *n.* ||Sum of £1·05; (Hist.) gold coin first coined for Afr. trade; ~**fowl,** gallinaceous bird with white-spotted slate-grey plumage; ~**pig,** S. Amer. rodent kept as pet or for research in biology, person used as subject for medical experiment etc. [place]

**gui′pure** (gē′poor) *n.* Heavy lace

of linen pieces joined by embroidery. [F]

**guise** (gīz) *n.* External esp. assumed appearance, pretence, (*under, in, the guise of*). [F f. Gmc (WISE²)]

**guitar′** (gĭ-) *n.* Six-stringed musical instrument played with fingers or plectrum; **electric** ~ (with built-in microphone); **~ist** *n.* [F or Sp. f. Gk *kithara* harp]

***gulch** *n.* Ravine esp. with torrent. [orig. uncert.]

**gu′lden** (gŏŏ-, gōō′-) *n.* = GUILDER. [Du., G, = golden]

**gules** (-lz) *n.* & *a.* (Her.) Red. [F *go(u)les* red-dyed fur neck-ornament]

**gulf** *n.* Piece of sea like bay but narrower at mouth (**G~ Stream**, warm current from Gulf of Mexico to Europe); deep hollow, chasm; impassable gap (Luke 16: 26); wide difference of feelings, opinion, etc. [F f. It. f. Gk *kolpos*]

**gull¹** *n.* Long-winged web-footed aquatic bird. [prob. W *gwylan*]

**gull²** *n.*, & *v.t.* Dupe, fool, (arch., dial.); **~ible** *a.*, easily cheated or duped; **~ibi′lity** *n.* [perh. obs. *gull* yellow (N)]

**gu′llet** *n.* Food-passage from mouth to stomach; throat. [F dim. (L *gula* throat)]

**gu′lly** *n.* Water-worn ravine; gutter, drain; (Crick.) fielding-position between point and slips. [F *goulet* (prec.)]

**gulp. 1.** *v.t.* & *i.* Swallow (*down*) hastily, greedily, or with effort (~ **back** or **down sobs, tears,** suppress weeping); swallow (*intr.*) with effort, gasp, choke. **2.** *n.* Act of gulping (*drained it at one gulp*); effort to swallow; large mouthful of a drink. [Du. *gulpen* (imit.)]

**gum¹** *n.* (usu. in *pl.*) Firm flesh around roots of teeth; **~′boil,** small abscess on gum; **~-shield,** pad protecting boxer's teeth and gums; **~′my¹** *a.,* toothless. [E]

**gum². 1.** *n.* Viscous secretion of some trees and shrubs, used esp. to stick paper etc. together; = *gum-tree*; sweet made of gelatin etc.; * = CHEWING-*gum*; *gum* ARABIC; **~′boot** (of rubber); ~ **resin,** secretion of resin mixed with gum, as gamboge; ***~′shoe,** galosh, (colloq.) stealthy action, (colloq.) detective or policeman; **~-tree,** tree exuding gum, esp. eucalyptus (*up a* **~-tree,** in great difficulties); **~′my²** *a.* (**-iness**),

sticky, exuding gum. **2.** *v.t.* (**-mm-**). Apply gum to, fasten thus; ~ **up,** interfere with, spoil, (*gum up the works*). [F f. L f. Gk *kommi* f. Egypt. *kemai*]

**gum³** *n.* (vulg.) God (in oaths, as *by gum!*). [corrupt. of *God*]

***gu′mbō** *n.* = OKRA; soup thickened with okra pods. [Negro wd.]

**gu′mmy¹,²** See GUM¹,².

**gu′mption** *n.* (colloq.) Resourcefulness, enterprise, go, (colloq. abbr. **gump**). [orig. unkn.]

**gun. 1.** *n.* Metal tube for throwing missiles with explosive propellant; cannon, rifle, carbine, pistol, (BIG *gun*); **blow great ~s,** blow a gale; **going great ~s,** moving vigorously towards success; **son of a ~,** contemptible person; **stick to one's ~s,** maintain one's position); starting-pistol (**beat, jump, the ~,** start before signal is given, lit. or fig.); device for discharging grease, electrons, etc., in desired direction; member of shooting-party; ***gun-man. 2.** *v.t.* & *i.* (**-nn-**). Shoot at or *down*; (colloq.) accelerate (engine etc.); go shooting; ~ **for,** seek with gun, (fig.) seek to harm or destroy. **3.** *~′***boat,** small warship with heavy guns (~*boat diplomacy,* supported by military force); *gun-*CARRIAGE; **~-cotton,** cotton steeped in nitric and sulphuric acids, used for blasting; ***~-fight,** (colloq.) fight with firearms; **~-fire,** firing of gun(s); **~-layer,** person who aims large gun; **~′man,** man with gun, assassin using gun; **~-metal,** bluish-grey alloy of copper and tin or zinc, formerly used for guns, colour of this; ~ **moll,** (sl.) gangster's mistress; **at ~′point,** threatened by gun; **~′powder,** fine green tea of granular appearance, explosive of saltpetre, sulphur, and charcoal; **Gunpowder Plot** (to blow up Parliament 5 Nov. 1605); ‖**~′room,** room in warship for junior officers or as lieutenants' mess, room for sporting-guns etc. in house; **~-runner, -running,** (person) illegally bringing guns into country; **~′shot,** shot from gun, range of gun (*within gunshot*). [perh. abbr. of Scand. *Gunnhildr* woman's name applied to cannon etc.]

**gung-hō′** *a.* Enthusiastic, eager. [Chin. *kung ho* work together]

**gunk** *n.* (sl.) Viscous or liquid material. [orig. P]

**gŭ′nnel.** See GUNWALE.

**gŭ′nner** *n*. Artillery soldier esp. as official term for private; (Naut.) warrant officer in charge of battery, magazine, etc.; airman who operates gun; game-shooter; **gŭ′nnerў** *n*., construction and management of large guns, firing of guns. [GUN]

**gŭ′nnў** *n*. Coarse sack(ing) usu. of jute fibre. [Hindi, Marathi]

**gŭ′nwale** (-nǎl), **gŭ′nnel,** *n*. Upper edge of ship's or boat's side. [GUN, WALE (formerly used to support guns)]

**gŭr′gle. 1.** *n*. Bubbling sound as of water from bottle. **2.** *v.i.* & *t*. Make, utter with, gurgles. [imit.]

**Gŭr′kha** (-ka; *or* goor′-) *n*. Member of dominant Hindu race in Nepal, forming regiments in British army. [Skr.]

**gŭr′nard, gŭr′nèt,** *n*. Sea-fish with large head, mailed cheeks, and finger-like pectoral rays. [F]

**gu′ru** (gōo′rōo) *n*. Hindu spiritual teacher or head of religious sect; influential or revered teacher. [Hindi]

**gŭsh. 1.** *n*. Sudden or copious stream; effusiveness. **2.** *v.i.* & *t*. Flow (*out* etc.) with gush; emit gush of (water etc.); speak, behave, with gush; ~**er** *n*., (esp.) oil-well emitting unpumped oil. [prob. imit.]

**gŭ′ssèt** *n*. Piece let into garment etc. to strengthen or enlarge; strengthening iron bracket. [F]

**gŭst. 1.** *n*. Sudden violent rush of wind; burst of rain, smoke, anger, etc.; ~′ў *a*. (~ily, ~iness). **2.** *v.i.* Blow in gusts. [N]

**gŭstā′tion** *n*. Tasting; **gŭ′statorў** *a*. [F or L (*gustus* taste)]

**gŭ′stŏ** *n*. (*pl.* ~es). Zest, enjoyment in doing thing. [It. f. L (prec.)]

**gŭt** *n., a.,* & *v*. **1.** *n*. Intestine; (in *pl*.) bowels or entrails, contents, (**has no** ~**s** in it, is of no real value or force; **hate** person's ~**s**, dislike him intensely; **sweat** one's ~**s out**, work very hard); material for violin etc. strings or surgical use made from intestines of animals or for fishing-line from those of silkworm; narrow passage on land or water; (in *pl.,* colloq.) pluck, force of character, staying power; ~′**less** *a*., (colloq.) lacking energy or determination. **2.** *a*. Fundamental, instinctive, (*a gut issue; a gut reaction*). **3.** *v.t.* (**-tt-**). Remove guts of (fish); remove, destroy, internal fittings of (building);

extract essence of (book etc.). **4.** ~′**sў** *a*., (colloq.) greedy, courageous. [E]

**gŭtta-pĕr′cha** (*or* -ka) *n*. Tough plastic substance from latex of various Malayan trees. [Malay]

**gŭ′tter. 1.** *n*. Shallow trough below eaves, channel at side of street, for carrying off rain-water; channel, groove; **the** ~, place of low breeding or vulgar behaviour; ~ **press,** sensational journalism; ~**snipe,** street urchin; ~**ĭng** *n*., material for gutter. **2.** *v.t.* & *i*. Furrow; flow in streams; (of candle) melt away by becoming channelled. [F f. L *gutta* drop]

**gŭ′ttural. 1.** *a*. (~ly). Of the throat; (Phon.) produced in throat or by back of tongue and palate. **2.** *n*. Guttural consonant (as *g, k*). [F or L (*guttur* throat)]

‖**gŭv,** ‖**gŭ′v'nor,** *ns*. (vulg. or colloq.) = GOVERNOR. [abbr.]

**guy**[1] (gī). **1.** *n*. Rope, chain, to steady crane-load etc. or secure tent. **2.** *v.t.* Secure with guys. [prob. LG]

**guy**[2] (gī). **1.** *n*. ‖Effigy of *Guy* Fawkes burnt on 5 Nov.; ‖grotesquely dressed person; (sl.) man. **2.** *v.t.* Exhibit in effigy; ridicule. [person]

**gŭ′zzle** *v.i.* & *t*. Drink, eat, greedily; consume (money etc.; *away*) thus. [F *gosiller* (*gosier* throat)]

**gȳbe, \*jībe,** *v.i.* & *t*. (Of fore-and-aft sail or boom) swing to other side; make (sail) gybe; (of boat etc.) change course thus. [Du.]

**gỹm** *n*. (colloq.) Gymnasium, gymnastics; ~**slip, -tunic,** schoolgirl's sleeveless usu. belted garment from shoulder to knee. [abbr.]

**gȳmkha′na** (-kah′-) *n*. Public place arranged for, display of, athletics; meeting for competition between horse-riders, vehicle-drivers, etc. [Hindi *gendkhāna* ball-house, assim. to foll.]

**gỹmnā′sĭ|um** (-z-) *n*. (*pl.* ~**ums,** ~**a**). Room etc. fitted up for gymnastics. [L f. Gk (*gumnos* naked)]

**gỹmnā′stĭc. 1.** *a*. (~ally). Of bodily or mental exercise or discipline; of gymnastics. **2.** *n*. Course, mode, of bodily or mental discipline; (in *pl.,* occas. treated as *sing*.) muscular exercises, esp. as done in gymnasium (also fig., *mental gymnastics*). **3.** **gỹ′mnăst** *n*., expert in gymnastics.

**gymp.** See GIMP.

**gỹnaec|o-** (g-) *in comb.* Woman;

~ŏ′cracў (gīnĭ-) *n.*, female rule. [Gk *gunē gunaikos* woman]

gȳnaecŏ′|logў (gīnĭ-) *n.* Science of physiological functions and diseases of women; \*~lŏ′gĭc, ~lŏ′gĭcal, (-ol-) *adjs.*; ~logĭst *n.*

‖gȳp¹ *n.* College servant at Cambridge and Durham. [orig. unkn.]

gȳp² *n.* (colloq.) Give person ~, scold, punish, defeat, pain, him severely.

gȳp³ *v.t.* (-pp-). Cheat, swindle. [orig. uncert.]

gȳ′ps|um *n.* Mineral used to make plaster of Paris or as dressing for crop-land; ~ĕous *a.*; ~ŏ′phĭla *n.*, garden plant with many small white flowers. [L f. Gk *gupsos*]

gȳ′psў. See GIPSY.

gȳrā′t|e *v.i.* Move in circle or spiral; ~ion *n.*; gȳrā′atorў *a.* [L f. Gk (GYRO-)]

gȳr′falcon (jĕr′faw-; *or* -fŏ-) *n.* Large northern falcon. [F f. N]

gȳr′o- *in comb.* Rotation; gyroscopic. [Gk *guros* ring]

gȳr′osc|ōpe *n.* (colloq. abbr. gȳr′ō). Rotating wheel whose axis is free to turn but maintains fixed direction unless perturbed, esp. for stabilization or to replace compass in ship etc.; ~ŏ′pĭc *a.* [F (prec.)]

# H

**H, h,** (āch) *n.* (*pl.* **Hs, H′s,** *pr.* ā′chĭz). Eighth letter; DROP one's *h*'s.

**H** *abbr.* hard (pencil-lead).

**h.** *abbr.* hecto-; hot; hour(s).

**H** *symb.* hydrogen.

**ha** (hah). **1.** *int.* expr. surprise, suspicion, triumph, etc. **2.** *v.i.* See HUM. [imit.]

**ha.** *abbr.* hectare(s).

**Hab.** *abbr.* Habakkuk (O.T.).

**hābĕas cŏr′pus** *n.* Writ requiring person to be brought before judge etc., esp. to investigate lawfulness of his restraint. [L, = you must produce the body]

**hă′berdāsher** *n.* ‖Dealer in small articles of dress and accessories etc.; \*dealer in men's wear; ~ў *n.*, such wares. [prob. AF]

**habĭ′liments** *n.pl.* Dress suited to any office or occasion, (joc.) clothes. [F f. L *habiller* fit out (ABLE)]

**hă′bĭt. 1.** *n.* Settled tendency or practice (*fall into bad habits*; *has, is in, the habit of* doing; **creature of** ~, one whose behaviour is guided by his habits; **make a** ~ **of**, do regularly); constitution (*habit of mind*; *man of corpulent habit*); dress esp. of religious order; (**riding-**)~, woman's riding--dress; (arch.) dress; (colloq.) practice of taking drugs as addict (*habit-forming*). **2.** *v.t.* (usu. in *p.p.*) Clothe. [F f. L (*habeo habit-* have)]

**hă′bĭt|able** *a.* (~ably). That can be inhabited; ~abĭ′lĭtў *n.*; ~ăt *n.*, natural home of plant or animal [L, = it inhabits]; ~ā′tion *n.*, inhabiting (*fit for human habitation*), house or home. [F f. L (*habito* INHABIT)]

**habĭ′tū|al** *a.* (~ally). Customary, continual, given to some habit (*habitual drunkard*); ~āte *v.t.*, accustom (*to thing, to doing*); ~ā′tion *n.*; **habitué** (habĭ′tūā) *n.*, habitual visitor or resident (*of*). [L (HABIT)]

**hă′bĭtūde** *n.* Mental or bodily disposition; custom, tendency. [F f. L *habitudo* (HABIT)]

**hăchūr′es** (-shūr′) *n.pl.* Lines on maps to indicate steepness of slope by their closeness. [F (HATCH³)]

**hăciĕ′nda** *n.* Plantation etc. with dwelling-house or factory in Spanish--speaking country. [Sp. f. L *facienda* things to be done]

**hăck¹. 1.** *n.* (Wound esp. from) kick with boot-toe; mattock, pick. **2.** *v.t. & i.* Cut, mangle; kick shin of (opponent at game); deal cutting blows (*at*); ~ing (short dry frequent) **cough;** ~-**saw** (for metal--cutting). [E]

**hăck². 1.** *n.*, *a.*, & *v.* **1.** *n.* Hired horse; horse for ordinary riding; common drudge; uninspired writer etc.; \*taxi. **2.** *a.* Typical of or used as a hack; commonplace. **3.** *v.t. & i.* Make common, hackney; ride (horse), ride horse, on road at ordinary pace. [abbr. of HACKNEY]

**hă′ckle. 1.** *n.* Steel flax-comb; long feathers on neck of domestic cock etc. (**with his** ~**s up, rising,** fig.

of dog or man, angry, ready to fight; fishing-fly dressed with hackle. **2.** *v.t.* Dress (flax, fly) with hackle. [E, var. HECKLE]

**hă′ckney. 1.** *n.* Horse for ordinary riding; ~ **cab, carriage**, etc., (kept for hire). **2.** *v.t.* Make common or trite by indiscriminate use (*a hackneyed phrase*). [perh. place]

**had.** See HAVE.

**hă′ddock** *n.* N. Atlantic fish allied to cod. [F]

**Hā′dēs** (-z) *n.* (Gk Myth.) lower world, abode of departed spirits; (euphem.) hell. [Gk, also used as name of god]

**hădj, hăjj,** *n.* Pilgrimage made by Muslim to Mecca; **hă′dji, hă′jji,** *n.,* Muslim who has been to Mecca as pilgrim. [Arab.]

**hadn't.** See HAVE.

**hae′m|al, *hě′-,*** *a.* Of the blood; **~ă′tĭc** *a.*, of or containing blood; ~ **atite** *n.*, reddish ferric oxide ore; **~ătŏ′logў** *n.*, study of physiology of blood; **~oglŏ′bĭn** *n.*, oxygen-carrying substance in red blood-cells of vertebrates. [Gk *haima* blood]

**haemophĭ′l|ĭa, *hě-,*** *n.* (Hereditary) tendency to prolonged bleeding from even a slight injury through failure of blood to clot normally; **~ĭăc** *n.*, sufferer from haemophilia; **~ĭc** *a.* [L f. Gk *haima* blood, *philia* loving]

**hae′morrhage, *hě′-,*** (hĕ′mĕrĭj) *n.* Escape (esp. profuse) of blood from blood-vessels. [F f. L f. Gk (*haima* blood, *rhēgnumi* burst)]

**hae′morrhoid, *hě′-,*** (hĕ′mĕroid) *n.* (usu. in *pl.*) Swollen veins in tissue near anus, piles. [F f. L f. Gk (*haima* blood, -*rhoos* -flowing)]

**haft** (-ah-). **1.** *n.* Handle of knife etc. **2.** *v.t.* Furnish with haft. [E]

**hăg** *n.* Ugly old woman, witch; **~ridden**, afflicted by nightmare, mentally harassed. [E]

**Hag.** *abbr.* Haggai (O.T.).

**hă′ggard. 1.** *a.* Wild-looking esp. from fatigue, worry, etc. **2.** *n.* Hawk caught when adult. [F *hagard*]

‖**hă′ggis** (-g-) *n.* Minced offal of sheep boiled in maw or artificial bag with oatmeal etc. [orig. unkn.]

**hă′ggle** *v.i.,* & *n.* Dispute esp. *about* or *over* price or terms. [N]

**hăgĭ|o-** (-g-) *in comb.* Of saints; **~ŏ′graphў** *n.*, writing of saints' lives; **~ŏ′logў** *n.*, literature of lives and legends of saints. [Gk *hagios* holy]

**ha ha** (hah hah′) *int.* expr. laughter. [E]

**ha-ha** (hah′hah) *n.* Sunk fence bounding park or garden. [F]

**hai′ku** (hī′kŏŏ) *n.* (*pl.* same). (English imit. of) Japanese three-line 17-syllable poem. [Jap.]

**hail**[1]**. 1.** *n.* Pellets of frozen rain falling in shower or **~′storm;** shower *of* missiles, questions, etc.; **~′stone,** pellet of hail. **2.** *v.i.* & *t.* It **~s,** is **~ing,** hail falls; (fig.) pour down (blows, words, etc.), come down violently (like hail). [E]

**hail**[2] *int., v.,* & *n.* **1.** *int.* of greeting (*to*); **~-fellow, ~-fellow-well-met,** (too) intimate *with;* **H~ Mary,** = AVE *Maria.* **2.** *v.t.* & *i.* Salute, greet (person etc. *as*) leader etc.; *hail him king*); call to (ship, person) to attract notice (**within ~ing distance,** able to do this, lit. or fig.); (of ship, person) have come *from* place. **3.** *n.* Hailing (**within ~,** close enough to be hailed). [N *heill* (WASSAIL)]

**hair** *n.* **1.** Any or (in *pl.* sense with *sing. vb.*) all of the fine filaments growing from skin of animals, esp. from human head; elongated cell growing from surface of plant; hairlike thing; very small quantity (**to a ~,** exactly); **a ~ of the dog that bit** one, further drink to cure effects of drink; **in** person's **~,** (colloq.) obstructing or annoying him; **keep** one's **~ on,** (sl.) remain calm; **let** one's **~ down,** (of woman) release it from chignon etc., (fig., colloq.) cease to be formal, behave in relaxed way or unrestrainedly; **not turn a ~,** show no sign of discomposure. **2.** **~′breadth,** **~′s breadth,** minute distance (*~breadth escape*, very narrow); **~′brush** (for smoothing hair); **~′cloth** (made of hair); **~′cut,** (style of) cutting hair; **~-do,** (colloq.; *pl.* **-os**) style or process of woman's hairdressing; **~′dresser,** one whose business is to dress and cut hair; ‖**~-grip,** flat hair-pin with ends close together; **~-line,** thin up-stroke in written or printed letter, edge of person's hair on forehead etc., very narrow crack or line; **~-piece,** quantity of false hair augmenting person's natural hair; **~′pin** (U-shaped for fastening the hair; **~pin bend,** very sharp doubling-back of road); **~-raising,** enough to make hair stand on end through fear or excitement; **~ shirt** (of haircloth for penitents or ascetics); ~**-slide**, hinged clip for keeping hair in position; ~**-splitting** a. & n., over-subtle(ty); ~**spring**, fine spring regulating balance-wheel in watch; ~**-style**, particular way of dressing hair; ~ **trigger**, secondary trigger releasing main one by slight pressure. **3.** ~**ȳ** a. (~ily, ~iness), having much hair, made of hair, (sl.) difficult, unpleasant, angry, or clumsy. [E]

**hăjj(ĭ).** See HADJ(I).

**hāke** n. Edible fish like cod. [orig. uncert.]

**hă'lberd** n. (Hist.) Combined spear and battleaxe; ~**ier'** n., man armed with halberd. [F f. G]

**hă'lcȳon** a. Calm, peaceful (halcyon days; (of period) happy, prosperous. [L f. Gk, = kingfisher, reputed to calm the sea at midwinter]

**hāle**[1] a. (Esp. of old person) robust, vigorous. [var. WHOLE]

**hāle**[2] v.t. (arch.) Drag or draw forcibly. [F f. N]

**half** (hahf) n. (pl. **halves** pr. hahvz), a., & adv. **1.** n. One of two (esp. equal) parts into which a thing is divided (half of 10 is 5; cut it in half, into halves; my half is bigger than yours; two hours and a half, two and a half hours; half of it is, half of them are, bad); (colloq.) = half-back, half-pint; ‖school term; one of two equal periods of football (or hockey etc.) match; half--price ticket; **better** ~, (joc.) wife; **by halves**, imperfectly (never does things by halves); **too** clever etc. **by** ~ (far more than is needed); GO[1] halves. **2.** a. Forming a half (a half length, share; amounting to half (half the men, stays at home half the TIME, half a pint (or a half-pint), half a dozen (or a half dozen), half a MIND. **3.** adv. To the extent of half, (loosely) to some extent, (only half cooked; a half-cooked potato; half dead, usu. joc., with cold etc.; I am half inclined to agree); **not** ~, by no means (not half long enough), (colloq.) not at all (not half a bad fellow), (sl.) extremely, violently, (he didn't half swear); ~ **past two**, thirty minutes after two o'clock. **4.** ~**-and--**~, (what is) half one thing and half another; ~ **as much** or **many again**, more by half; ~**-back**, (position of) player immediately behind forwards in football etc.; ~**-baked**, (fig.) not thorough, not

earnest; ~**-binding** (of book, with leather back and corners, cloth or paper sides); ~**-breed**, ~**-caste**, person of mixed race; ~**-brother, -sister**, (with one parent in common); half-COCK[1]; ‖~**-crow'n**, ‖~ **a crown**, (Hist.) coin or amount of 2s. 6d.; ~**-hardy**, (of plant) hardy except in severe frost; ~**-hearted**, lacking courage or zeal; ~ **holiday**, day of which (usu. latter) half is holiday; ~**-landing** (half-way up flight of stairs); ~**-life**, (Phys.) time after which radioactivity etc. is half its original value; ~**-light**, dim imperfect light; **at** ~**-ma'st** (of flag) lowered to half height of mast as mark of respect for the dead; ~ **measures** (not thorough); ~ **moon**, moon when disc is only half--illuminated, time when this occurs, semicircular object; ~(**-**)**nelson**, hold in wrestling with arm under opponent's and behind his back; ~ **pay**, reduced allowance to army etc. officer when retired or not in actual service; ~**-price**, reduced price (of admission etc.); ~**-seas-over**, (sl.) half-drunk; ~**-sister** (see half--brother); ~**-ter'm**, period about half-way through school term usu. with short holiday; ~**-timbered**, having walls with timber frame and brick or plaster filling; ~**-ti'me**, time at which half of game or contest is completed, interval then occurring; ~**-title**, title or short title of a book, usu. printed on recto of leaf preceding title-leaf; ~**-tone**, illustration printed from a block (produced photographically) in which lights and shades of original are represented by small and large dots; ~**-truth**, statement that (esp. deliberately) conveys only part of the truth; half-VOLLEY; ~**-way** a. & adv., at point equidistant between two others (MEET half-way); ~**-way house**, inn midway between two towns etc., (fig.) compromise; ~**-wit(ted)**, stupid or foolish (person). [E]

**hā'lfpennȳ** (hā'pni) n. (pl. as PENNY). British bronze coin worth half a penny; ~**-worth** (usu. pr. hā'perth), **ha'p'orth**, as much as can be bought for a halfpenny, a very small amount.

**hā'libut** n. Large flat-fish used for food. [HOLY (perh. as used on holy days), butt flat-fish]

**hălĭtō′sĭs** n. (Med.) Foul breath. [L (*halitus* breath)]

**hall** (hawl) n. Large public room in palace etc.; mansion, residence esp. of landed proprietor; university building used for residence or instruction of students, (in Engl. colleges etc.) common dining-room, dinner in this; building of guild (*Fishmongers' Hall*); large room or building for public gathering or business (*concert, town, hall*); entrance room or passage of house; ~'mark, (n.) mark used to show standard of gold, silver, and platinum, (fig.) token of excellence or quality, (v.t.) stamp with this; ~-stand (in hall of house, with mirror, pegs for coats, etc.). [E]

**hallelujah.** See ALLELUIA; **hă′llĭard**, see HALYARD.

**hallŏ′** int., n., & v. 1. int. calling attention or expr. ||surprise or ||informal greeting or ||beginning telephone conversation. 2. n. (pl. ~s), & v.i. (The) cry 'hallo'. [HOLLO]

**hallŏŏ′** int., n., & v. 1. int. inciting dogs to chase, calling attention, or expr. surprise. 2. n. The cry 'halloo'. 3. v.i. & t. Cry 'halloo!', esp. to dogs, urge (dogs etc.) with shouts; shout to attract attention (**don't ~ till you are out of the** ||**wood** or \***woods**, don't rejoice prematurely). [perh. *hallow* pursue with shouts]

**hă′llow** (-ō). 1. n. Saint; All H~s, H~mas, = All Saints' Day, 1 Nov.; H~e′en, (Sc. & U.S.) eve of this. 2. v.t. Make, honour as, holy. [E (HOLY)]

**hallu′cĭn|āte** (-lōō′-) v.t. Produce illusions in the mind of (person); ~ā′tion n., illusion, apparent presence of object not actually present; ~ātorў a.; ~ogĕn n., drug causing hallucinations. [L f. Gk]

**halm.** See HAULM.

**hā′lō.** 1. n. (pl. ~es). Circle of light around luminous body, esp. sun or moon; circle, ring; disc of light (shown) surrounding head of saint; (fig.) glory around idealized person etc. 2. v.t. Surround with halo. [L f. Gk *halōs* threshing-floor, disc of sun or moon]

**hă′logĕn** n. (Chem.) Any of the group of non-metallic elements (chlorine, iodine, etc.) which form a salt by simple union with a metal. [Gk *hals halos* salt, *gignomai* become]

**halt¹** (hawlt, hŏlt). 1. n. Temporary stoppage on march or journey; interruption of progress (*call a halt to*; *come to a halt*); ||railway stopping--place (without regular station--buildings etc.). 2. v.i. & t. Make a halt; cause (troops etc.) to halt. [G (HOLD)]

**halt²** (hawlt, hŏlt). 1. a. (arch.) Lame, crippled. 2. v.i. Walk hesitatingly; (of argument, verse, etc., esp. in *part.*) be defective; (arch.) be lame, limp. [E]

**ha′lter** (haw′l-, hŏ′l-). 1. n. Rope, strap, with noose or headstall for horses or cattle; rope with noose for hanging a person; strap round nape for low-cut dress. 2. v.t. Fasten (*up*) with halter. [E].

**halve** (hahv) v.t. Divide into halves, share equally; reduce to half; (Golf) play (hole) in same number of strokes as other player, win same number of holes in (match); **halves**, see HALF. [HALF]

**hă′lyard, hă′llĭard,** n. (Naut.) Rope or tackle for raising or lowering sail etc. [HALE²]

**hăm.** 1. n. Back of thigh, thigh and buttock; (meat from) thigh of pig salted and dried for food; (sl.) amateur (**radio** ~, operator of amateur radio station), inexperienced performer esp. actor, one who overacts; ~-fisted, -handed, (sl.) heavy--handed, clumsy; ~'mў a., (esp., sl.) of or like ham actors. 2. v.i. & t. (sl.; -mm-). Overact. [E]

**hă′mbŭrger** (-g-) n. Cake of minced beef usu. fried and eaten with onions, often in soft round bread roll. [*Hamburg,* place]

**Hamĭ′tĭc** a. Of group of African peoples incl. Berber, Tuareg, etc.; of group of African languages incl. ancient Egyptian, Berber, and Cushitic. [*Ham* (Gen. 10: 6ff.)]

**hă′mlet** n. Small village, esp. without church. [F *hamelet* dim.]

**hă′mmer.** 1. n. Instrument for beating, breaking, driving-in nails, etc., with hard solid head at right angles to handle; machine with metal block for same purpose; similar device for exploding charge in gun, striking piano-string, etc.; auctioneer's mallet indicating by rap that article is sold (**come under the** ~, be sold by auction); metal ball attached to wire in athletic contest of **throwing the** ~; ~ **and sickle,** symbols of industrial worker and peasant (as emblem on flag of U.S.S.R.) used to repr. international Communism; ~ **and tongs**, with great energy (and noise); ~**-head**, head of hammer, type of shark; ~**-toe** (bent permanently downwards). **2.** *v.t. & i.* Strike, drive, (as) with hammer (*hammer home the nail*, one's *advantage*; *hammer idea into* person's *head*); (colloq.) defeat heavily in game or fight; (St. Exch.) declare (person or firm) a defaulter; beat (as) with hammer, (fig.) work hard, (*at*); ~ **out**, devise laboriously. [E]

**hă′mmock** *n.* Bed of canvas etc. hung by cords at ends esp. used on ship. [Sp. f. Carib]

**hă′mmy.** See HAM.

**hă′mper¹** *n.* Basketwork packing-case; food etc. packed esp. as present (*Christmas hamper*). [F (*hanap* goblet f. Gmc)]

**hă′mper²** *v.t.* Obstruct movement of (person etc.) with material obstacles; (fig.) impede, hinder. [orig. unkn.]

**hă′mster** *n.* Ratlike hibernating rodent with short tail, and cheek-pouches; **golden** ~, kind much kept as pet etc. [G]

**hă′mstring. 1.** *n.* (In man) one of five tendons at back of knee; (in quadruped) great tendon at back of hock. **2.** *v.t.* (**ha′mstrung**, ~**ed**). Cripple (person, animal) by cutting hamstrings; (fig.) destroy or impair activity or efficiency of. [HAM]

**hănd. 1.** *n.* End part of human arm beyond wrist; similar member of all four limbs of monkey; forefoot of quadruped; control, disposal, (*in the hands of*; *child is in good hands*); agency (*at*, *by*, *the hands of*; *pass through many hands*; *the hand of God*); share in action (*bear, give, have, lend, take, a hand in*); pledge of marriage (*seek woman's hand*; *give* one's *hand to*); manual worker in factory, farm, etc.; person who does or makes something (*a picture by the same hand*; **all** ~**s**, the whole crew; **a good** ~, person skilful *at*; OLD *hand*); person etc. as source (FIRST, SECOND, etc., *hand*); skill (*a hand for pastry*; TRY one's *hand*); style of writing (*a legible hand*); signature (*witness my hand* and SEAL¹); handlike thing, esp. pointer of clock or watch; RIGHT or LEFT² side or direction relative to thing or person; measure of horse's height, = 4 in.;

playing-cards dealt to a player, such player, (*first*, *third*, *hand*; FORCE¹ person's *hand*; SHOW one's *hand*); (colloq.) applause (*got a big hand*). **2. at** ~, close by, soon to happen; **by** ~, by manual labour, in writing (not typed), by messenger (not by post); *live* **from** ~ **to** ~ **mouth**, precariously; **in** ~, at one's disposal, under one's control, receiving attention; OFF *hand*; **off** one's ~**s**, no longer one's responsibility; **on** ~, in one's possession, in attendance; **on** one's ~**s**, resting on one as a responsibility; **on the one** ~, **on the other** ~, (of contrasted points of view etc.); **out of** ~, without any delay, out of control; **to** ~, within reach; **to** one's ~, ready for one's purpose. **3. change** ~**s**, pass to different owner, use opposite hands for task; **come to** ~, turn up; ~ **and foot**, (bind) completely, (serve) assiduously; ~ **and** or **in glove**, on intimate terms (*with*); ~ **in** ~, with hands mutually clasped (in affection), (fig.) in close association; ~ **over** ~, **fist**, with each hand passing over the other as in climbing rope, (fig.) with steady or rapid progress; ~ **to** ~, (of fighting etc.) at close quarters; **get, have, keep,** one's ~ **in**, become or be in PRACTICE; ~**s down**, (win etc.) easily; ~**s off !**, do not touch (lit. or fig.); one's ~**s are tied**, (fig.) one is powerless to act; ~**s up!** (ordering persons to raise hand(s) to signify assent or surrender); **have** one's ~**s full**, be fully occupied; **hold** one's ~, refrain from stern action; **hold** person's ~, (fig.) give him close guidance or support; **hold** ~**s**, be hand in hand; **put, set, turn,** one's ~ **to**, start work on, engage in. **4.** (*attrib.*) Operated by hand (*hand-brake*); held or carried by hand (*hand-mirror*); done by hand not by machine (*hand-knitted*); ~**bag**, small bag esp. used by woman to hold purse etc.; *hand-*-BARROW²; ~**bell**, bell rung by hand; ~**bill**, printed notice circulated by hand; ~**book**, (usu. short) manual, guidebook; ~**cart** (pushed or drawn by hand); ~**clap**, clapping of hands; ~ **cream**, emollient for the hands; ~**cuff**, secure (prisoner) with ~**cuffs** (pair of lockable metal rings joined by short chain); *hand-*-GRENADE; ~**made**, (of paper, shoes, etc.) made by hand not machine; ~'**maid(en)**, (arch. or fig.) female servant; ~**-picked,** (of supporters etc.) carefully chosen; ~'**rail,** railing along edge of stairs etc.; ~'**saw,** saw held with one hand; ~'**shake,** shake of person's hand with one's own (GOLDEN *hand-shake*); ~'**spring,** somersault in which one lands first on hands and then on feet; ~'**stand,** feat of supporting body on hands only; *hand's* TURN; ~**-towel,** small towel for wiping hands after washing; ~'**writing,** way a person writes. **5.** *v.t.* Deliver, transfer by hand or otherwise (*over to* person, *down* or *on* to succeeding generations, *in* at office, *on, up,* etc.); serve (food *round*); ~ **down,** transmit (decision) from superior court etc.; ~**-me-down,** ready-made or second-hand (clothing, or fig.); ~**-out,** information given to the press etc., food etc. given to needy person; ~ **it to,** (colloq.) give credit to (person) for achievement. [E]

**h. & c.** *abbr.* hot and cold (water).

**hă'ndful** (-ŏŏl) *n.* Quantity that fills the hand; small number (*of* men etc.); (colloq.) troublesome person or task. [HAND]

**hă'ndĭcăp. 1.** *n.* Race, contest, in which competitors' chances are made more equal by difference in start, weight carried, etc.; extra weight or condition so imposed, (fig.) hindrance; number of strokes by which golfer normally exceeds par for course. **2.** *v.t.* (**-pp-**). Impose handicap on (competitor); (fig.) of circumstances) place (person) at disadvantage; (in *p.p.*) suffering from physical or mental disability. [phr. *hand i'* (=in) *cap* (deposit of stakes)]

**hă'ndĭcraft** (-ahft) *n.* Manual art, trade, or (esp. artistic) skill. [E (HAND, CRAFT)]

**hă'ndĭwork** (-wĕrk) *n.* Work done, thing made, by the hands or by personal agency. [E (HAND, WORK)]

**hă'ndkerchief** (hă'ngkĕrchĭf, -ēf) *n.* (*pl.* ~**s,** -**ieves** *pr.* -ēvz). Square of linen, cotton, silk, etc., usu. carried in pocket for wiping nose etc. [HAND, KERCHIEF]

**hă'ndle. 1.** *n.* Part of thing made to hold it by; fact that may be taken advantage of (*gave a* ~ *to his critics*); ~**bar** (with which bicycle is steered); **fly off the** ~, (colloq.) lose self-control; ~ **to** one's **name,**

(colloq.) title of nobility etc. **2.** *v.t.* Touch, feel, move, with the hands; manage, treat (person *roughly, kindly,* etc.), deal with (subject, problem, etc.); deal in (goods); **hă'ndler** *n.,* (esp.) person in charge of trained dog. [E (HAND)]

**hă'ndsel** (-ns-) *n.* (arch.) Thing given in advance or at New Year etc.

**hă'ndsome** (-ns-) *a.* (~**r,** ~**st**). Of fine form or figure; generous (*handsome present, treatment*); (of price, fortune, etc.) considerable. [HAND]

**hă'ndỹ** *a.* (-ily, -iness). Ready to hand; convenient to handle or use; clever with the hands; ~**man,** man able to do various odd jobs esp. in house maintenance.

**hăng. 1.** *v.t.* & *i.* (**hung,** exc. as below). Cause thing to be supported from above esp. by hooks etc. (on wall or line, from ceiling, etc.); place (meat) thus to improve quality; place (picture) on wall or in exhibition, attach (wallpaper) to wall; fit up (bells in belfry); set up (door) on hinges; (~**ed**) suspend or be suspended by neck as capital punishment (~**ing matter,** resulting in this), kill one*self* thus, (as imprecation) = DAMN, *be damned* (*I'll be hanged if I can see it*; *do it and hang the expense*); let droop (*hang one's head in shame*); remain, or be, hung (lit. or fig.; *dress hangs badly*; *punishment hangs over his head*); ~ **in the balance,** remain uncertain (*hang by a* THREAD); decorate *with* (things hung on). **2.** ~ **about, around,** loiter, not move away; ~ **back,** show reluctance; ~'**dog,** shamefaced; ~ **fire,** (of firearm) be slow in going off, (fig.) delay acting; ~**glider** (controlled by movements of person standing or lying in it); ~ **heav(il)y,** (of time) pass slowly; ~'**man,** executioner; ~'**nail,** agnail; ~ **on,** depend on, attend closely to, remain in office etc., stick or hold closely (*to*), (sl.) wait for a short time, (colloq.) not ring off when telephoning; ~ **out,** hang from window, clothes-line, etc., (sl.) reside; ~'**over,** remainder, unpleasant after-effects of (esp. alcoholic) dissipation; ~ **together,** be coherent, remain associated; ~ **up,** hang from hook etc., put aside, end telephone conversation, cause delay to (~**-up** *n.,* sl., difficulty, obsession). **3.** ~'**ing** *n.,* (esp., in *pl.*) drapery for walls etc. **4.** *n.* Way a thing hangs; **get the ~ of**, (colloq.) get the knack of, understand; **not** *care* **a ~**, (colloq.) not at all. [E]

**hă′ngar** (*or* -ngg-) *n.* Shed for housing aircraft etc. [F]

**hă′nger**[1] *n.* Person, thing, that hangs; loop, chain, etc., by which thing is hung; (**clothes-, coat-**)**~**, shaped piece of wood etc. from which clothes may be hung to keep their shape; **~o′n**, follower, dependant. [HANG]

**hă′nger**[2] *n.* Wood on side of steep hill. [E]

**hănk** *n.* Coil of yarn etc. [N]

**hă′nker** *v.i.* **~ after**, crave or long for. [obs. *hank*]

**hă′nky** *n.* (colloq.) Handkerchief. [abbr.]

**hă′nky-pănky** *n.* (sl.) Trickery; misbehaviour. [orig. unkn.]

**Hă′nŏver** *n.* **House of ~**, British sovereigns from George I to Victoria; **Hănověr′ian** *a.* & *n.* [place]

**Hă′nsărd** *n.* Official report of proceedings in Parliament. [person]

**Hăns|e** *n.* (Hist.) Political and commercial league of Germanic towns; **~ĕă′tĭc** *a.* [G]

**hă′nsom** *n.* **~** (**cab**), two-wheeled horse-drawn cab for two inside, with driver mounted behind. [person]

**Hănts.** *abbr.* Hampshire. [E]

**hăp.** (arch.) **1.** *n.* Chance, luck; chance occurrence. **2.** *v.i.* (**-pp-**) Come about by chance. [N]

**hăphă′zard** (-p-h-) *n., a.,* & *adv.* **1.** *n.* Mere chance (*at, by, haphazard*). **2.** *a.* & *adv.* Casual(ly), (at) random.

**hă′pl|ĕss** *a.* Unlucky; **~ў** *adv.,* (arch.) by chance, perhaps.

‖**ha′p′orth.** See HALFPENNY.

**hă′ppen** *v.i.* Occur, come to pass (**~ to**, be experienced by; **~ing** *n.,* event, performance esp. improvised); chance (*to* do); come by chance (*up*)*on* (person, thing). [HAP]

**hă′ppў** *a.* (-ily, -iness). (Of person or event) lucky, fortunate; contented, pleased; (of language etc.) apt; **~ event**, birth of a child; **~-go-′lucky**, taking things cheerfully as they happen; *happy* HUNTING-*grounds*; **~ medium**, means of satisfactory avoidance of extremes; **~ release**, (esp.) death; (as *suf.*) dazed etc. from (*bomb-happy*), irresponsible about (TRIGGER-*happy*).

**hăra-kī′rĭ** *n.* Suicide by disembowelling orig. as practised by Samurai in Japan when in disgrace etc. [Jap. *hara* belly, *kiri* cutting]

**harǎ′ngue** (-ng). **1.** *n.* Speech to an assembly; loud or vehement address. **2.** *v.i.* & *t.* Make harangue (to). [F f. L, perh. f. Gmc]

**hă′rass** *v.t.* Worry, trouble; vex by repeated attacks; **~ment** *n.* [F]

**hăr′binger** (-nj-) *n.* One who announces another's approach, forerunner. [F f. Gmc (foll.)]

**hăr′bour**, *\****hăr′bor**, (-er). **1.** *n.* Place of shelter for ships; shelter; **~age** *n.,* (place of) shelter. **2.** *v.t.* & *i.* Give shelter to (criminal), entertain (evil thoughts); come to anchor in harbour. [E, = army-shelter]

**hărd. 1.** *a.* Firm, unyielding to pressure, solid, not easily cut; not disputable (*hard facts*); difficult (*to* do or to understand; *hard task, question*); not easily allowing one *to* do (*she is hard to please*); (of person etc.) unfeeling, harsh, (*hard as* NAILS); difficult to bear, (of season or weather) severe; unpleasant to ear or eye (*hard voice, colours*); (of liquor) alcoholic, (of drug) potent and addictive, (of water) difficult to use soap with; (of prices, pornography, etc.) high, extreme; strenuous (*a hard worker*); (Phon.) guttural (as *c, g,* in *cat, go*). **2.** *adv.* Strenuously, severely, (*try hard*; DIE[2] *hard*; *raining hard*); **~ at it**, working hard; **~ by**, close by; **~ on, upon**, severe in criticism etc. of (*don't be too hard on him*), close to (*was hard on my heels*); **~ put to it**, in difficulties; **~ up**, short of money, at a loss *for*; **go ~ with** person, turn out very badly for him. **3. ~ and fast**, (of distinction made or rule) strict; **~′back** *n.* & *a.*, (book) bound in stiff covers; **~ bargain** (without concession); **~′-bitten**, tough in fight etc.; **~′board**, stiff board of compressed etc. wood-pulp; **~-boiled**, (of boiled egg) with solid white and yolk, (fig.) tough, shrewd; **~ case**, case of hardship, intractable person; **~ cash**, money in coin or as opp. to mere promises of payment; **~ core**, irreducible nucleus, ‖heavy material as road-foundation; **~ court**, lawn-tennis court made of asphalt etc.; **~ currency** (not likely to depreciate suddenly or fluctuate much in value); **~-earned** (with effort); **~ hat**, bowler hat, safety helmet; **~-headed**, practical, not sentimental;

~-hearted, unfeeling; ~ hit, severely troubled; ~-hitting, vigorous, not sparing feelings; ~ labour (esp. that imposed on criminals); ~ line, firm adherence to policy; ~ lines, luck, (on person), worse fortune than one deserves; ~ nut (to crack), difficult problem or person; ~ of hearing, somewhat deaf; ~ pad, form of distemper of dogs etc.; ~ palate, front part of palate; ~-pressed, closely pursued, burdened with urgent business; *hard* ROE²; ~ row to hoe, difficult task; ~ sell, aggressive salesmanship; ~ shoulder, strip on side of motorway for use only in emergency; ~sta'nding, firm area for vehicle to stand on when not in use; *hard* TACK³; ~ times (of economic difficulty etc.); ~'ware, ironmonger's goods, weapons, machinery, physical components of computer etc.; ~-wearing, able to stand much wear; ~'wood (of deciduous tree); ~ words, difficult words, angry talk; ~-working, diligent. 4. ~'en v.t. & i., make or become hard(er) or robust. [E]

**har'dihood** n. Boldness. [HARDY]

**har'di|ly** adv. With difficulty; scarcely; harshly; in hard manner; ~ship n., hardness of fate or circumstance, severe privation. [HARD]

**har'dy** a. (-ily, -iness). Bold, robust, capable of endurance; (of plant) able to grow in the open all the year; ~ annual, annual plant that sows itself or may be sown in the open, (fig., joc.) subject that comes up regularly. [F *hardi* f. Gmc (HARD)]

**hare**. 1. n. Mammal like large rabbit, with long ears, short tail, and hindlegs longer than forelegs; **start a ~**, raise topic of discussion; ~ and hounds, paper-chase; ~'bell, round-leaved bell-flower; ~-brained, rash, wild; ~'lip, congenital fissure of upper lip. 2. v.i. Run with great speed. [E]

**har'em** (or hahrē'm) n. Women's quarters of Muslim house; its occupants. [Arab., = sanctuary]

**hă'ricŏt** (-kō) n. Ragout (usu. of mutton or lamb); ~ (bean), (white dried seed of) kind of bean. [F]

**hark** v.i. Listen (to, at, or abs. in *imper.*); ~ back, retrace course to find scent, (fig.) revert (to subject). [E]

**har'lequin. 1.** n. (H~) Pantomime character in mask and particoloured tights. **2.** a. Gaily coloured. **3.** ~a'de n., piece of buffoonery, part of pantomime. [F, legendary person]

**har'lot** n., & v.i. (arch.) Prostitute (oneself); ~ry n. [F, = knave]

**harm** n., & v.t. Damage, hurt, (out of ~'s way, in safety); ~'ful a. (-lly), that does harm; ~'less a., that does or suffers no harm. [E]

**har'mon|y** n. Agreement, concord; (Mus.) combination of notes to form chords; sweet or melodious sound; collation of parallel narratives esp. of the Gospels; ~ic (-ŏ'n-), (a., ~ically) concordant, harmonious, (Mus.) relating to harmony (~ic tones, produced by vibration of aliquot parts of strings etc.), (n.) harmonic tone, component frequency of wave motion; ~ica (-ŏ'n-) n., mouth-organ; ~ious (-ō'n-) a., in concord, forming a consistent or agreeable whole, free from dissent, tuneful; ~ist n., person skilled in harmony; ~ium (-ŏ'n-) n., keyboard instrument with air blown through reeds; ~ize v.t. & i., bring into, be in, harmony (*with*), add notes to (melody) to form chords; ~izā'tion n. [f f. L f. Gk *harmonia* joining]

**har'ness. 1.** n. Gear of draught-horse or other animal, by which it is controlled etc. (**in ~**, in the routine of daily work); arrangement for fastening thing to person, resembling horse's harness. **2.** v.t. Put harness on (horse etc.); (fig.) utilize (natural forces) for motive power. [F f. N, = army-provisions]

**harp. 1.** n. Stringed musical instrument played by plucking with fingers, usu. as large triangular (orchestral) instrument. **2.** v.i. Play on harp (~er, ~ist, ns.); dwell tediously (*on* subject). [E]

**harpoo'n. 1.** n. Spearlike missile with rope attached, for catching whales etc.; ~-gun (for firing this). **2.** v.t. Strike or spear with harpoon. [F, f. L f. Gk *harpē* sickle]

**har'psichŏrd** (-k-) n. Musical instrument with mechanically plucked strings. [F *harpechorde* f. L *harpa* harp, *chorda* string]

**har'py** n. Mythical rapacious monster with woman's face and body and bird's wings and claws; rapacious person. [F or L f. Gk *harpuiai* snatchers]

**(h)ăr′quèbus** n. (Hist.) Portable gun supported on tripod by hook or on forked rest. [F f. G, = hook- -gun]

**hă′rrĭdan** n. Ill-tempered old woman. [orig. uncert.]

**hă′rrĭer** n. Hound used for hunting hares; one who harries; (in pl.) pack of hounds with huntsmen, group of cross-country runners; kind of falcon. [HARE, HARRY]

**Harrō′vian** a. & n. (Member) of Harrow School. [Harrow, place]

**hă′rrow** (-ō). **1.** n. Frame with iron teeth for breaking clods etc. on ploughed land (**under the ~**, in distress). **2.** v.t. Draw harrow over (land); distress, wound, (fig., feelings etc.; *harrowing details* of story). [N]

**hă′rrў** v.t. Ravage, despoil, (land, person); harass. [E]

**harsh** a. Rough to the touch etc.; unpleasing; severe. [LG]

**hart** n. Male of (esp. red) deer, esp. after 5th year; **~'s-tongue**, fern with narrow undivided fronds. [E]

**hăr′tèbeest** n. Large Afr. antelope with ringed horns. [Afrik.]

**harum-scar′um** a. & n. (colloq.) Reckless, wild, (person, conduct). [rhyming form. on HARE, SCARE]

**hăr′vèst. 1.** n. (Season for) reaping and storing of grain etc.; a season's yield; (fig.) product of any action. **2.** v.t. Reap and collect as harvest; take for food etc. **3.** ~ **festival**, thanksgiving festival in church for harvest; ~ **home**, close of harvest- ing; ~ **moon** (full within fortnight of 22 or 23 Sept.); ~ **mouse**, small species nesting in stalks of growing grain; **~er** n., reaper, reaping- -machine. [E]

**has.** See HAVE.

**hă′s-been** (-z-) n. (colloq.) Out- -of-date person or thing. [BEEN]

**hăsh. 1.** v.t. Cut (meat, often up) into small pieces; mutilate, mangle. **2.** n. Dish of hashed meat; old matter served up as if new; medley; **make a ~ of**, spoil in dealing with; **settle** a person's ~, (colloq.) make an end of or subdue him. [F hacher (hache HATCHET)]

**hă′shĭsh** n. Top leaves etc. of hemp, dried for smoking or chewing as narcotic (colloq. abbr. **hash**). [Arab.]

**hasn't.** See HAVE.

**hasp** (hah-) n., & v.t. (Fasten with) hinged clasp passing over staple and secured by pin etc. [E]

**hă′ssle** n., & v.i. (colloq.) Quarrel, struggle, wrangle. [dial.]

**hă′ssock** n. Thick cushion for kneeling on esp. in church; tuft of matted grass etc. [E]

**hāste. 1.** n. Urgency of movement (**in ~**, quickly, hurriedly; **make ~**, act quickly); hurry. **2.** v.i. Hasten. **3.** ~**'n** (-sen) v.i. & t., act, go, come, quickly, cause (person) to hasten, accelerate (work etc.); **hā′stў** a. (-ily, -iness), hurried, rash, quick- -tempered. [F f. Gmc]

**hăt** n. (Esp. outdoor) head- -covering, usu. with brim; ‖BAD hat; **at the drop of a ~**, promptly; **eat** one's ~, (promise expr. disbelief about event); **my ~!**, excl. of sur- prise; **old ~**, (colloq.) thing tediously familiar; **out of a ~**, by random selection or as if by magic; **pass the ~ round**, solicit contributions; **take off** one's ~ **to**, applaud merit of; **talk through** one's ~, (sl.) wildly, absurdly; **under** one's ~, in secrecy; **wear two ~s**, be present or act in two different capacities; **~'band**, ribbon etc. round hat; **~-pin** (to fasten hat); ~ **trick**, success 3 times in close succession esp. (Crick.) same bowler taking 3 wickets with suc- cessive balls, (Footb. etc.) scoring of 3 goals by same player in same match; **~'ful** (-ŏŏl) n.; **~'ter** n., maker, seller, of hats. [E]

**hătch¹** n. Lower half of divided door; opening in wall, floor, etc.; opening or door in aircraft etc.; cover for hatchway; **~'back**, vehicle with rear door hinged at top; **~'way**, opening in ship's deck for lowering cargo etc.; **down the ~**, (sl.) down the throat (in drinking); **under ~es**, below deck, (fig.) down out of sight. [E]

**hătch². 1.** v.t. & i. Bring (young bird etc.), come forth, from egg; incubate (egg); form (plot etc.). **2.** n. Hatching; brood hatched. [E]

**hătch³** v.t. Mark (usu. parallel) lines on. [F hacher (HASH)]

**hă′tchèt** n. Light short-handled axe; ~ **face** (narrow and sharp); ~ **man**, professional killer, malicious critic (so ~ **job**); BURY the hatchet. [F hachette dim. of hache (HASH)]

**hāte. 1.** v.t. Bear malice towards (thing, person); dislike greatly (to do, doing); **~'ful** (-tf-) a. (-lly), exciting hatred; **hā'trėd** n., intense dislike, ill will. **2.** n. Hatred; (colloq.) hated person or thing. [E]

**hau'ght|y̆** (haw'tĭ) a. (~ily, ~iness). Lofty and disdainful. [*haught*, *haut* f. F, = high]

**haul. 1.** v.t. & i. Pull, drag (thing, at thing, on rope) forcibly; transport by cart etc.; bring for reprimand or trial; *haul over the* COALS. **2.** n. Act of hauling; (fig.) amount gained or acquired (*made a good haul*); distance to be traversed; ~'age n., conveyance of goods, charge for it; ~'ier n., one who hauls, esp. firm or person engaged in road transport of goods. [var. HALE²]

‖**ha(u)lm** (hawm, hahm) n. Stalk, stem; (collect.) stalks, stems, of peas, beans, etc. [E]

**haunch** n. Part of side of body between last ribs and thigh; fleshy part of buttock and thigh; leg and loin of deer etc. as food. [F f. Gmc]

**haunt. 1.** v.t. Frequent (place), frequent company of (person); (of memories etc.) occur to person frequently; (in *p.p.*) visited or frequented by ghosts. **2.** n. Place of frequent resort (*his old haunts*; *the haunts of criminals*); range, feeding-place of animals. [F f. Gmc]

**Hau'sa** (how'-) n. & a. (Member) of Negroid people in Sudan etc.; their language, widely used in W. Africa. [native name]

**hautboy.** See OBOE.

**haute** (ōt) a. ~ *couture* (kōōtūr'), high-class dressmaking; ~ *cuisine* (kwēzē'n), high-class (French) cooking; ~ *école* (ākō'l), the harder feats of dressage. [F (HAUGHTY)]

**hauteur** (ōtêr') n. Haughtiness of manner. [F (HAUGHTY)]

**Havă'na** n. Cigar made at *Havana* or elsewhere in Cuba. [place]

**hăve** (or hav) v. (3 *sing. pres.* has *pr.* hăz, haz; *past* & *p.p.* **had** *pr.* hăd, had; colloq. abbr. **I've, we've,** etc., **I'd, he'd,** etc.; **'s** = **has**; colloq. neg. **haven't, hasn't, hadn't,** vulg. **ain't** = *haven't* or *hasn't*) & n. **1.** v.t. Hold in possession or at one's disposal; know (a language); possess (relation etc.; *I have no uncle, no equals*); contain as part or quality (*has blue eyes*; *trees have leaves*; *it has its advantages*); give birth to (baby); enjoy (*never had it so good*; *have a good time!*); suffer (*had a toothache, an acci-*

dent); be burdened with (*have my work to do*); permit (to), accept, (*I will not have you say such things, won't have it*); be provided with (*have nothing to do, wear*); let (feeling etc.) be present (*have no doubt*; *have nothing against her*); be influenced by quality etc. (*have mercy on us*); engage in (activity; *have breakfast, conversation, a look, a game, a try*); receive, take (food etc.), (*we had bad news*; *have a cup of tea*); cause (person or thing) to be, do, etc., (*have him dismissed*; *have one's hair cut*); ~ **it,** express view or win decision (*he will have it that*; *the ayes have it*), (colloq.) possess advantage, have found answer, (sl.) copulate; ~ **had it,** (colloq.) have missed one's chance, passed one's prime, been killed; ~ **it all** one's **own way,** without opposition; *have it* IN *for*; ~ **it out,** settle dispute (*with*); ‖**be had,** (sl.) be cheated; **let him** ~ **it,** (sl.) punish or reprimand him; ~ **on,** wear (clothes), have (engagement), (colloq.) play trick on, tease; ~ **out,** get (tooth) extracted, complete (*one's sleep etc.*); ~ **to,** (colloq.) ~ **got to,** be obliged to, must; ‖~ **up,** bring person to lawcourt, police, interviewer, etc. **2.** v. aux. w. *p.p.* of *vbs.*, forming past tenses (*I have, had, shall have, seen, added*); *had* BETTER¹, RATHER. **3.** n. One who has (esp. wealth etc.; ~s **and** ~**-nots,** rich and poor); (sl.) swindle. [E]

**hā'ven** n. Harbour; (fig.) refuge. [E]

**have-not, haven't.** See HAVE.

‖**hā'ver** v.i. Talk foolishly; hesitate. [orig. unkn.]

**hă'versăck** n. Canvas etc. bag carried on back or over shoulder by soldier, hiker, etc. [F f. G, = oats--sack]

**hă'voc** n. Devastation; confusion (*make havoc of, play havoc among, with,* often fig.). [AF f. F *havo(t)*]

**haw¹** n. (Fruit of) hawthorn; ~'finch, thick-beaked species of finch; ~'thorn, thorny shrub with small dark red berries. [E]

**haw².** See HUM.

**hawk¹. 1.** n. Bird of prey once much used in falconry; rapacious person; person advocating warlike action; ~-eyed, keen-sighted. **2.** v.i. & t. Hunt with hawk. [E]

**hawk²** v.i. & t. Clear throat

noisily; bring (phlegm etc. *up*) thus. [imit.]

**hawk**[3] *v.t.* Carry (goods) about for sale (lit. or fig.); ~**er** *n.*, one who does this for a living. [*hawker* f. LDu.]

**haw′ser** (-z-) *n.* (Naut.) Large rope or small cable. [F, = hoist (L *altus* high)]

**hay** *n.* Grass mown and dried for fodder; **hit the** ~, (sl.) go to bed; **make** ~, mow grass and turn it over for exposure to sun; **make** ~ **of,** throw into confusion; **make** ~ **(while the sun shines),** seize opportunity for profit; ~ **fever,** allergic irritation of nose, throat, etc., caused esp. by pollen; ~′**maker,** (fig., sl.) swinging blow; ~′**stack,** regular pile of hay with pointed or ridged top; ~′**wire,** poorly contrived, (colloq.) in disorder, distracted. [E]

**hă′zard. 1.** *n.* Chance, (source of) danger, risk; (Bill.) **winning** ~, pocketing object-ball, **losing** ~, pocketing own ball off another; (Golf) obstruction to play, e.g. bunker or water. **2.** *v.t.* Expose to hazard; run the risk of; venture on (a guess etc.). **3.** ~**ous** *a.*, risky. [F f. Sp. f. Arab.]

**hāze** *n.* Obscuration of atmosphere near earth by fine particles of water, dust, etc.; (fig.) mental obscurity, confusion. [HAZY]

**hā′zel** *n.* A bush whose fruit is the ~**-nut;** (stick of) its wood; (light) brown colour (esp. of eyes). [E]

**hā′z**|**y̆** *a.* (~**ily,** ~**iness**). Misty; vague, indistinct. [orig. unkn.]

**HB** *abbr.* hard black (pencil-lead).

**H-bomb** (ā′chbŏm) *n.* Hydrogen bomb. [*H* for HYDROGEN]

**H.C.** *abbr.* Holy Communion; House of Commons.

**h.c.** *abbr. honoris causa.*

**H.C.F.** *abbr.* highest common factor.

**hē**[1] (or hĭ) *pron., n.,* & *a.* **1.** *pron.* (*obj.* HIM, *refl.* HIMSELF, *poss.* HIS; *pl.* THEY etc.) The male previously mentioned or implied; person etc. of unspecified sex. **2.** *n.* Male, man. **3.** *a.* (usu. w. hyphen). Male (*he-goat*); ~**-man,** masterful or virile man. [E]

**hē**[2](-hē′) *int.* expr. amusement or derision. [E]

**H.E.** *abbr.* high explosive; His Eminence; His or Her Excellency.

**head** (hĕd). **1.** *n.* Foremost part of body of animal, upper part of human body, containing mouth, sense-organs, and brain; height or length of head as measure (*am taller, horse won, by a head*); seat of intellect, imagination (*made it up out of his own head*); mental aptitude (*a good head for business*); (**good** etc.) ~ **for heights,** lack of giddiness when standing close to edge of high cliff etc.); (colloq.) headache; life (*it cost him his head*); image of head on one side of coin; (usu. in *pl.*) this side turning up in toss of coin; person, individual, (*ten pence a* or *per head*); (in *pl.*) number present (*count heads*); individual animal, (collect.) animals (*twenty head*); (sl.) drug-addict (often *pot-head* etc.); thing like head in form or position, e.g. striking part of hammer, knobbed end of nail etc., mass of leaves or flowers at top of stem, closed end of cylinder in pump or engine, flat end of drum etc., signal-converting device on tape-recorder etc., foam on top of liquor, cream on milk; top (of stairs, list, page, etc.); upper end (of table, occupied by host; of lake, at which river enters; of bed etc., for one's head); front (of procession etc.); bows of ship; promontory; ruler, chief, leader, master etc. of college, headmaster (~′**ship** *n.*); (pressure of) confined body of water or steam; position of command (*at the head of*); division in discourse, category; culmination, climax or crisis, fully developed top of boil etc., (COME *to a head*). **2. above** one's ~, above one, esp. beyond one's comprehension; **come into,** or **enter,** one's ~, (of idea) be thought of; **from** ~ **to foot,** all over a person; GET *it into* one's *head*; **give** (horse, or fig. person) **his** ~, let him go freely; **go to** person's ~, (of liquor, success, etc.) impair his self-control, judgement, etc.; ~ **and shoulders,** (as measure of difference esp. fig.) considerably; ~ **first,** (of plunge etc.) with head foremost, (fig.) precipitately; *head in the* CLOUDS; *head in the* SAND; ~ **of hair,** hair on person's head esp. as noticeable feature; person's ~ **off,** (fig.) into a state of exhaustion (*beat, talk,* person's *head off*); ~ **over heels,** topsy-turvy, so as to turn completely over; **in** one's ~, by thought, not in writing; **keep** one's ~, remain calm; **keep** one's ~ **above water,** (fig.) keep out of debt; **lay, put,** ~s **together,** consult one another; LOSE one's *head*; *cannot* MAKE *head or tail of*; *off* one's ~, crazy; **off the top of** one's ~, (sl.) impromptu; **old ~ on young shoulders**, wisdom in young person's views; **on** one's ~, supported by head and arms not feet, (sl.) very easily; **on** one's **(own)** ~, (of responsibility etc.) falling on one; **over** one's ~, above one (esp. fig. of impending danger etc.), beyond one's comprehension, (of another's promotion) when one has prior or stronger claim; **put** into person's ~, suggest (idea etc.) to him; **take it into** one's ~, conceive notion; TURN person's *head*; **two ~s are better than one**, combination of two persons' ideas is superior to those of either alone. **3.** ~'**ache**, continuous pain in head (esp. forehead), (colloq.) troublesome problem; ~'**achy**, suffering from or causing headache; ~'**board** (forming head of bed etc.); ~-**dress**, covering (esp. ornamental attire) for the head; ~'**gear**, hat etc.; ~-**hunter**, savage who collects heads of enemies as trophies; ~'**land**, promontory; ~'**lamp**, ~'**light**, (beam from) lamp on front of car etc.; ~'**line**, line at top of page or newspaper article containing title etc., (in *pl.*) summary of broadcast news; ~'**long**, with head foremost, precipitately; ~'**man**, chief man (of tribe etc.); ~**ma'ster**, ~**mi'stress**, principal master, mistress, of school; ~**-on** *a.* & *(-ŏ'n) adv.*, (of collision etc.) with meeting head to head (lit. or fig.); ~'**phone**, telephone receiver held by band fitting over head; ~'**piece**, helmet, intellect; ~-**quar'ters**, (as *pl.* or *sing.*) chief place of business etc., quarters of officer commanding army etc.; ~-**rest**, support for head of seated person; ~'**room**, overhead space; ~-**shrinker**, head-hunter who shrinks enemies' heads, (sl.) psychiatrist; ~'**stall**, part of bridle or halter fitting round horse's head; ~ **start**, advantage granted or gained at the beginning of race (lit. or fig.); ~'**stone**, gravestone, chief stone in foundation (lit. or fig.); ~'**strong**, strongly self-willed, obstinate; ~-**up**, (of instrument) readable without lowering the eyes; ~'**waters**, streams from sources of river; ~'**way**, progress, (of ship) rate of progress, headroom; ~ **wind** (blowing from directly in front); ~'**word**, word forming heading. **4.** *v.t.* & *i.* Provide with head or heading; be, form, put oneself or be put at, put thing at, head of (troops, chapter, queue, etc.); (Footb.) strike (ball) with head; face (in specified direction); direct course (of); ~ **back, off**, get ahead so as to force to turn back, aside; ~ **for**, be moving towards (place, point, or fig. disaster etc.). **5.** ~'**er** *n.*, (esp.) (Footb.) act of heading the ball, brick etc. laid at right angles to face of wall (cf. STRETCHER), (colloq.) dive or plunge head first; ~'**ing** *n.*, (esp.) title etc. at head of page etc.; ~'**ў** *a.* (~**ily**, ~**iness**), impetuous, violent, (of liquor, success, etc.) apt to intoxicate (lit. or fig.). [E]

**heal** *v.t.* & *i.* Restore (person, injured part of body, etc.) to health; cure (person; *of* disease); (fig.) mend (any bad condition in person or situation); ~ **(over, up)**, (of wound or injured part) become sound or whole. [E (WHOLE)]

**health** (hĕl-) *n.* Soundness of body or mind; condition of body (*good, poor, health*); toast drunk in person's honour; ~ **food** (chosen for its unmodified natural qualities etc.); ~ **resort**, place visited for benefit of one's health; ~ **service**, public medical service; ~'**ful** *a.* (-lly), health-giving; ~'**ў** *a.* (~**ily**, ~**iness**), having, showing, conducive to, good health. [E (WHOLE)]

**heap. 1.** *n.* Group of things lying one on another; (in *sing.* or *pl.*, colloq.) large number or amount (*a heap of trouble; there is heaps of time; is heaps better*); **strike all of a** ~, (colloq.) dumbfound. **2.** *v.t.* Pile (things *up, together*, etc.) in a heap; load (vehicle, person, etc. excessively) *with* goods, benefits, etc.; pile large quantities of (insults etc. *on, upon*). [E]

**hear** *v.t.* & *i.* (~**d** *pr.* hĕrd). **1.** Perceive with ear (*I heard a groan, him groan, him groaning; he was heard groaning* or *to groan*); listen to (*hear him, a sermon*); listen judicially to (case, party); grant (prayer); obey (order); be informed (*that*); be told (*about*); ~ **from**, receive letter etc. from; ~ person **out** (to the end); ~ **say**, ~ **tell** (of), (arch.) be told (about); ~'**say**, gossip; ~ **of**, be told about, (w. neg.) consider (*will not hear of my paying for it*); ~!, ~! (as form of applause). **2.** ~**er** *n.*, (esp.) member of audience; ~'**ing** *n.* (HARD *of hearing*; **in** one's **or within, out of,** ~**ing,** near, not near, enough to be heard; **give a fair** ~**ing,** listen impartially *to*; ~**ing aid,** small sound-amplifier worn by deaf person). [E]

**hear'ken** (hār'-) *v.i.* (arch.) Listen (*to*). [E (HARK)]

**hearse** (hĕrs) *n.* Car for conveying coffin. [F *herse* harrow f. L *hirpex* large rake]

**heart** (hārt) *n.* **1.** Hollow muscular organ keeping up circulation of blood by contracting and dilating; breast, bosom; mind, seat of inmost thoughts; soul (**in** one's ~ **of** ~**s,** in one's inmost feelings; ~ **to** ~, with candour); seat of emotions, esp. love (**give, lose,** one's ~ **to,** fall in love with); ability to feel emotions (*has a tender heart*); courage (*pluck up or take, lose, heart*; **take** ~ **of grace,** summon up fresh courage); central or innermost part; compact head of cabbage etc.; essence (*the heart of the matter*); heart-shaped thing, figure of heart, playing-card of suit (~**s**) marked with red shape of heart. **2.** AFTER one's *own heart*; **at** ~, in one's inmost feelings or interests; **bless his** etc. ~ (excl. of fond pleasure); **bless my** ~ (excl. of surprise); **from the bottom of** one's ~, genuinely, deeply; **break** person's ~, crush him with grief; **by** ~, in, from, memory (*learn, say, by heart*); **change of** ~, conversion to different frame of mind; **does my** ~ **good,** rejoices me; **eat** one's ~ **out,** pine away; **find it in** one's ~, be (un)feeling enough (*to* do); **from the** ~, sincerely; **go to** person's ~, grieve him deeply; **have a** ~, (sl.) be merciful; **have no** ~, be unfeeling; **have the** ~, (esp. w. neg.) be hard-hearted or unfeeling enough (*to* do); ~ **and soul,** with all one's energy; *heart* BLEEDS; *to* one's *heart's* CONTENT²; one's ~ **goes out to,** one feels strong sympathy for; one's ~ **is in** one's **boots,** one is dejected or fearful; one's ~ **is in** one's **mouth,** one is much alarmed or startled; one's ~ **is in the right place,** one has good intentions; one's ~ **is not in it,** one is not really interested in succeeding; ~ **of oak,** courageous man; one's ~ **stands still,** one is paralysed with fright; **in** one's ~, secretly; **in** (**good**) ~, cheerful; **lay to** ~, think over seriously; **near** one's ~, dear to one; **set** one's ~ **on,** long for; **take to** ~, be much affected by; **wear** one's ~ **on** one's **sleeve,** let one's feelings be quite obvious; **win the** ~ **of,** gain person's affection; **with all** one's ~, sincerely, with all goodwill. **3.** ~'**ache,** mental anguish; ~ **attack,** deranged action of heart; ~'**beat,** pulsation of heart; ~-**break,** overwhelming distress; ~-**breaking, -broken,** causing, crushed by, great distress; ~'**burn,** burning sensation in chest, pyrosis; ~-**burn**(**ing**), jealousy, grudge; ~ **failure,** heart attack, esp. if fatal; ~'**felt,** sincere (emotion etc.); ~'-**land,** central part of an area; ~-**-lung machine,** machine which can temporarily take over functions of heart and lungs; ~-**rending,** distressing; ~-**searching,** examination of one's own feelings; ~'**sick,** despondent; ~'**sore,** grieved; ~-**strings,** (fig.) deepest affections; ~-**throb,** beating of heart, (sl.) object of one's infatuation; ~-**-warming,** emotionally moving and encouraging; ~'**wood,** dense hard inner part of tree-trunk. **4.** ~'**en** *v.t.* & *i.,* inspirit, cheer (*up* or *on*); ~'**less** *a.,* unfeeling, pitiless. [E]

**hearth** (hār-) *n.* Floor of fireplace; ~ **and home,** home and its comforts; ~'**rug** (laid before hearth); ~'**stone,** slab forming hearth, stone for whitening hearth. [E]

**hear't|ỹ** (hār'-) **1.** *a.* (~**iness**). Vigorous; genial; (of feelings) sincere, strong, (*a hearty dislike*); (of meal) copious. **2.** *n.* Hearty person. **3.** ~**ilỹ** *adv.,* in hearty manner, very (*heartily sick of it*). [HEART]

**heat. 1.** *n.* Being hot (RED, WHITE, *heat*); sensation of this; (Phys.) energy arising from motion of molecules of bodies (**latent** ~, heat required to convert solid into liquid or vapour, or liquid into vapour, not causing change of temperature); hot weather; inflamed state of body (PRICKLY *heat*); pungency of flavour; warmth of feeling, anger, (**in the** ~ **of the moment,** without pause for thought); receptive period of sexual cycle esp. in female mammals (*on, in, heat*); (**trial**) ~, race or contest the winner of which competes in **final** (~). **2.** *v.t.* & *i.* Make or become hot, inflame; (esp. in *p.p.*) inflame with rage or passion, excite; ~'**edly** *adv.* **3.** ~-**resistant**, = heat--PROOF; ~-**stroke**, prostration from excessive heat; ~ **wave**, (long) spell of hot weather. **4.** ~'**er** *n.*, stove, warming device. [E (HOT)]

**heath** *n.* Open flat waste tract of land, often covered with low shrubs; kind of shrub growing on such land; ~-**cock**, blackcock; ~'**y** *a.* [E]

**hea'then** (-dh-). **1.** *a.* Not member of a widely-held religion, esp. not Christian, Jewish, or Muslim. **2.** *n.* Heathen person (collect. *pl.*, **the** ~); unenlightened person; ~**dom**, ~**ism**, *ns.* [E (prec.)]

**hea'ther** (hĕ'dh-) *n.* Heath or similar shrub, esp. one with small purple flowers; **mixture**, a fabric of mixed hues like heather; ~**y** *a.* [orig. unkn.]

**Heath Rŏ'binson** *a.* Absurdly ingenious. [person]

**heave. 1.** *v.t.* & *i.* (~d, Naut. also **hove** *pr.* hōv). Lift (heavy thing); utter (groan, sigh) with effort; (Naut. or colloq.) throw; (Naut.) haul up, haul, by rope (~ **ho**, sailors' cry in heaving anchor; as *n.*, sl., dismissal; ~ **to**, bring (ship, or abs.) to stand-still with head to wind; ~ **in sight**, become visible); pull (*at* rope etc.); swell, rise, esp. with alternate falls, as waves; retch. **2.** *n.* Heaving. [E]

**hea'ven** (hĕ'-) *n.* The sky, apparent vault over earth, (usu. *pl.* exc. poet.); (or *H*~) abode of his angels, and beatified spirits, usu. placed beyond sky (**in the seventh** ~, in state of extreme delight; **move** ~ **and earth**, make every possible effort to do); (*H*~) God, Providence, (*it is Heaven's will*; in exclamations etc.: **by H**~!, **good H**~**s!**, **H**~**s above!**, **H**~ **forbid!**); place or state of bliss; ~-**sent**, providential; ~**ly** *a.* (~**liness**), of heaven, divine, (**the H**~**ly City**, Paradise), of the sky (~**ly bodies**, stars etc.), of divine or (colloq.) great excellence (*what a heavenly day!*). [E]

**hea'vy** (hĕ'-) *a.*, *n.*, & *adv.* **1.** *a.* (-ily, -iness). Of great weight; of great density; weighty from abundance (*a heavy crop*); (of guns etc.) of large calibre, firing heavy projectiles; (Mil.) carrying heavy arms (*the heavy brigade*); severe, extensive, (*heavy -ʰting, frost, losses*; behaving in

intense manner (*heavy drinker*); striking, falling, with force (*heavy blows, sea, storm*); (of ground) difficult to traverse; (of bread etc.) dense from not rising; (of food or fig. of writings) hard to digest; ungraceful (*heavy features*), unwieldy; (of person, style, etc.) dull, tedious, slow; (of newspaper etc.) serious in tone; (Theatr.) serious, sombre; dignified, stern, (*heavy father*); oppressive (*heavy fate*); drowsy; despondent; **lie** ~, make its weight felt (lit. or fig.); *time* HANGS heavy. **2.** ~-**duty**, intended to be resistant to much stress in use; ~-**handed**, ungraceful, oppressive; ~-**hearted**, doleful; ~ **hydrogen**, isotope of hydrogen, with atoms of about twice usual mass (~ **water**, oxide of this); ~ **industry** (concerned with production of metal, machines, etc.); ~ **metal**, heavy guns, metal of high density; ~ **traffic**, lorries etc., large number of vehicles; ~ **type** (thicker than normal type); *heavy* WEATHER; ~-**weight**, person of above average weight (see BOX), (fig.) very able or important person; **heavier--than-air**, (of aircraft) weighing more than the air it displaces. **3.** *n.* (Theatr.) villain etc.; (usu. in *pl.*) heavy vehicle, serious newspaper. **4.** *adv.* Heavily (esp. in *comb.*: heavy--laden . [E]

**Heb.** *abbr.* Hebrews (N.T.).

**Hē'brew** (-ōō). **1.** *n.* Member of a Semitic people, Israelite, Jew; language of ancient Jews, modern form of this used esp. in Israel. **2.** *a.* Of or in Hebrew; of the Jews etc. **3. Hēbrā'ic** (-ically); **Hē'braïsm** *n.*, Hebrew characteristic, idiom, religion, etc.; **Hē'braïst** *n.*, expert in Hebrew. [F f. L f. Gk f. Heb.]

**hĕ'catomb** (-ōōm) *n.* Sacrifice of many victims. [L f. Gk (*hekaton* hundred, *bous* ox)]

**hĕck** *n.* (sl.) Euphem. for HELL esp. in exclamations etc. [HELL]

**hĕ'ckle** *v.t.* Harass (speaker) with interruptions, questions, etc.; = HACKLE. [var. HACKLE]

**hĕ'ctare** *n.* Metric unit of square measure, about 2½ acres. [F (HECTO-, *are* = 100 sq. metres)]

**hĕ'ctic** *a.* (~**ally**). Feverish; (colloq.) exciting, restlessly active. [F f. L f. Gk (*hexis* habit of body)]

**hĕ'cto-** *in comb.* Hundred; ~**gram**, ~**litre**, ~**metre**, units in METRIC system. [F f. Gk *hekaton*]

**hĕ´ctor** *n.*, & *v.t.* & *t.* Bluster(er), bully. [person in *Iliad*]

**hĕdge. 1.** *n.* Fence of bushes or low trees, esp. as boundary of field, garden, etc.; barrier of turf, stone, etc., or of things or persons; (fig.) barrier; act or means of hedging bet; ~**´hog** (-jh-), small spiny insectivorous mammal rolling itself up for defence; ~**hop** *v.i.*, fly at low altitude; ~**´row**, row of bushes forming hedge; ~**sparrow**, common British etc. thrushlike bird. **2.** *v.t.* & *i.* Surround with hedge (lit. or fig.); shut (*off*, *in*) thus; make or trim hedges (so **hĕ´dger** *n.*); secure oneself against loss on (bet, speculation, or abs.) by compensating bets etc.; avoid committing oneself. [E]

**hē´don│ism** *n.* Doctrine that pleasure is the only proper aim; **hēdō´nĭc** *a.*, of pleasure; ~**ĭst** *n.*; ~**ĭ´stĭc** *a.* [Gk *hēdonē* pleasure]

**heed. 1.** *v.t.* Attend to, take notice of. **2.** *n.* Careful attention (*take*, *pay*, *give*, *heed*); ~**´ful** (-lly), ~**´less**, *adjs.*, giving, not giving, care or attention. [E]

**hee´-haw** *n.*, & *v.i.* Bray; (utter) loud laugh. [imit.]

**heel[1]. 1.** *n.* Back part of human foot below ankle (ACHILLES' *heel*); corresponding part of quadruped's hind limb, often above ground; part of sock etc. that covers, of boot etc. that supports, heel; heel-like thing, e.g. handle-end of violin bow, crook in head of golf-club; (sl.) despicable person; ~**´less** (-l-l-) *a.* **2. at, on, the ~s of**, close behind (person, event, etc.); **down at** (*\*the*) ~, (of shoe) with heel worn down, (of person) wearing such shoes, shabby; HEAD *over heels*; **kick** or **cool** one's ~**s**, be kept waiting; **lay by the ~s**, arrest, overthrow; **show a clean pair of ~s**, take to one's ~**s**, run away; **to, at,** ~, (of dog or fig.) close behind, under control; **turn on** one's ~, turn sharply round. **3.** ~**´ball**, shoemaker's polishing mixture of wax etc., this or similar substance used to make rubbings of church brasses etc.; ~**´tap**, a thickness of leather in heel, liquor left at bottom of glass after drinking. **4.** *v.i.* & *t.* Touch ground with heel, e.g. in dancing; furnish (boot etc.) with heel; (Rugby Footb.) pass ball *out* at back of scrum with heel; (in *p.p.*, colloq.), armed with a revolver,

supplied with money (*well-heeled*). [E]

**heel[2]. 1.** *v.i.* & *t.* (Of ship) lean over temporarily (cf. LIST[3]); make (ship) heel. **2.** *n.* (Amount of) heeling. [E]

**heel[3].** See HELE.

**hĕ´ft│y** *a.* (~ily, ~iness). Sturdy, stalwart, (*a mob of hefty fellows*); bulky, heavy. [*heft* weight (HEAVE)]

**hĕge´mony** (or -g-, hĕ´jĭ-) *n.* Leadership esp. by one State of confederacy; **hĕgĕmo´nĭc** (or -g-) *a.*, supreme. [Gk *hēgemōn* leader)]

**Hĕ´gĭra, -jĭra**, *n.* Muhammad's flight from Mecca to Medina, A.D. 622; Muslim era. [L f. Arab.]

**hē-hē´.** See HE[2].

**hei´fer** (hĕf-) *n.* Young cow esp. that has not had more than one calf; female calf. [E]

**heigh** (hā) *int.* expr. encouragement or inquiry; ~**-ho**, expr. boredom etc. [*heh*, imit.]

**height** (hīt) *n.* Measure from base to top; (great) elevation above ground or other (esp. sea) level; high point; top; highest degree (*at its height*; *the height of folly*); ~**´en** *v.t.*, make high(er), intensify, exaggerate. [E (HIGH)]

**hei´nous** (hā´n-) *a.* Utterly odious (*heinous crime, criminal*). [F (*haïr* hate)]

**heir** (ār) *n.* Person entitled to property or rank as legal successor of its former owner; (fig.) one fitted or fated to inherit; ~ **apparent, presumptive**, whose claim cannot, may, be superseded by birth of another heir; ~**´loom**, chattel that goes with real estate, piece of personal property that has been in family for generations; ~**´dom**, ~**´ess**, *ns.* [F f L (*heres* hered-)]

**Hĕ´jĭra.** See HEGIRA; **hĕld**, see HOLD.

**hēle, heel[3]**, *v.t.* Set (plant) in ground and cover its roots *in*. [E]

**hĕ´lĭcal.** See HELIX.

**hĕ´lĭcŏpter** *n.* Aircraft lifted and propelled by engine-driven blades revolving horizontally; **hĕ´lĭpŏrt** *n.*, helicopter station. [F f. Gk (HELIX, *pteron* wing)]

**hē´lĭo-** *in comb.* Sun; ~**graph** (-ahf-), (*n.*) signalling apparatus reflecting sunlight, message thus sent, (*v.t.*) send (message) thus; ~**trōpe** *n.*, plant with small clustered purple flowers, colour or scent of these. [Gk *hēlios* sun]

**hē′lĭum** *n.* Inert, light, non-inflammable gaseous element, used in balloons etc.

**hē′l\|ĭx** *n.* (*pl.* ~ices *pr.* -ĭsēz) Spiral (in one plane or inclined, e.g. curve of screw-thread); **double ~ĭx**, pair of parallel helices with common axis esp. in DNA molecule; **hē′lĭcal** *a.* [L f. Gk *helix*]

**hĕll** *n.* **1.** Abode of the dead or of devils and damned spirits, usu. regarded as below surface of earth; place or state of wickedness or misery; (in colloq. abuse etc.) = *the* DEUCE², *the* DEVIL, (*a* or *the hell of a*; *go to hell!*; *hell to pay*; PLAY hell *with*; RAISE hell; *what, who, in* or *the hell?*); **all ~ let loose**, utter chaos; (*tired* etc.) **as ~**, extremely; **beat** or **knock ~ out of**, pound heavily; **come ~ or high water**, whatever the obstacles; **for the ~ of it**, just for fun; **get ~**, be severely told off; **give person ~**, pain or punish him severely; **like ~**, recklessly, (iron.) not at all; **not a hope in ~**, no chance at all. **2.** ~**bent**, recklessly determined (*for* thing, *on* do*ing*); ~**fire**, fire(s) of hell; ~ **for leather**, at full speed (usu. of rider); ~**'s angel**, lawless young motor-cyclist. **3.** ~**'ish** *a.*, like or fit for hell. [E]

**hē′llĕbŏre** *n.* Plant of kinds once held to cure madness; plant of kind including Christmas rose. [F f. L f. Gk]

**Hĕ′ll\|ēne** *n.* Ancient Greek; subject of modern Greece; ~**ē′nĭc** *a.*; ~**ĕnĭsm** *n.*, Greek idiom, character, culture; ~**ĕnĭst** *n.*, non-Greek user of Greek language, expert in Greek; ~**ĕnĭ′stĭc** *a.*, (esp.) of Greek history etc. after Alexander. [Gk]

**hĕllō′** (or hĕ-). **1.** *int.* expr. surprise or informal greeting esp. on telephone. **2.** *n.* The call 'hello'. [var. HALLO]

**hĕlm¹** *n.* Tiller, wheel, by which rudder is controlled (**down, up, ~**, place helm so as to bring rudder to windward, to leeward); (fig.) government, guidance, (*take the helm*); ~**'sman**, steersman. [E]

**hĕlm²** *n.* (arch.) Helmet. [E]

**hĕ′lmĕt** *n.* Protective head-cover of soldier, policeman, fireman, motor-cyclist, etc.; hat of pith etc. for hot climate. [F f. Gmc (prec.)]

**hĕ′lmĭnth** *n.* Worm, esp. intestinal; ~**ĭc** (-mĭ′-) *a.* [Gk]

**hē′lot** *n.* Serf esp. in ancient Sparta. [L f. Gk]

**hĕlp. 1.** *v.t.* Provide with means to what is needed or sought, be useful to, (*help me*; *help me* (*to*) *lift it*; *help me in lifting it*; *help me on, off, with my coat*; *help me out of the car*; *help me with my work*; *help the work on*; ~ **lame dog over stile**, give aid at need; ~ **person out** (of a difficulty); ~ **person to**, serve him with (food)); distribute (food at meal); prevent (*it can't be helped*); **more than one can ~**, more than is avoidable; refrain from (*cannot help laughing*); (in oath etc.) **so ~ me God** (as I speak the truth etc.); **cannot ~ oneself**, cannot avoid undesired action; ~ **oneself** (*to*), take without seeking help or permission; ~**-yourself**, (of restaurant etc.) self-service; **a ~ing hand**, (fig.) assistance; ~**'ing** *n.*, (esp.) portion of food served. **2.** *n.* Act of helping (*we need your help*; *come to our help*); person or thing that helps; domestic servant(s), employee(s), (\|**home ~**, one who helps in household work; \|**mother's ~**, one who gives help with children); remedy etc. (*there is no help for it*); ~**'mate**, helpful companion etc., esp. husband or wife; ~**'ful** *a.* (-lly), useful, serviceable; ~**'less** *a.*, lacking help, unable to help oneself. [E]

**hĕ′lter-skĕlter** *adv.*, *a.*, & *n.* **1.** (In) disordered haste. **2.** *n.* Spiral slide at fun-fair. [imit.]

**hĕlve** *n.* Handle of weapon or tool. [E]

**hĕm¹. 1.** *n.* Border of cloth etc., esp. one made by sewing down turned-in edge; ~**line**, lower edge of skirt etc. **2.** *v.t.* (-mm-). Turn down and sew in edge of (cloth etc., or abs.); ~ **in, up**, etc., enclose, confine; ~**stitch** *n.*, & *v.t.*, (to hem with) an ornamental stitch. [E]

**hĕm²** (or hem) *int.*, & *v.* **1.** *int.* expr. hesitation or calling attention by clearing of throat. **2.** *n.* The sound *hem*. **3.** *v.i.* (-mm-). Say *hem*; hesitate in speech. [imit.]

**\*hē′mal** etc. See **haem-**.

**hē′mĭ-***pref.* Half; ~**pterous** (-ĭ′p-), of insect order including aphids, bugs, and cicadas, with base of front wings thickened. [Gk = L SEMI-]

**hē′mĭsphēre** *n.* Half sphere; half the celestial sphere; half the earth, containing (**Eastern ~**) Europe,

Asia, and Africa, or (Western ~) America, or as divided by equator (**Northern, Southern,** ~); each half of brain; **hĕmǐsphē'rǐc(al)** *adjs*. [L f. Gk (HEMI-, SPHERE)]

**hĕ'mlŏck** *n*. A poisonous plant; sedative, poison, got from it. [E]

**\*hemorrhage** etc. See **haem-**.

**hĕmp** *n*. Asian herbaceous plant; its fibre used for rope etc.; any of several narcotic drugs got from hemp; ~'**en** *a*., made of hemp. [E]

**hĕn** *n*. Female bird, esp. of domestic fowl; (in *pl*.) domestic fowls; female crab, lobster, or salmon; ~'**bane**, (drug got from) narcotic and poisonous plant; ~-**harrier**, a European falcon; ~-**party** (colloq., of women only); ~'**pecked**, domineered over by one's wife. [E]

**hĕnce** *adv*. From this time (**five years** ~, in five years' time from now; ~**forth**, ~**forward**, from this time onwards); as a result from this, as inference (*hence it appears that*), therefore; (arch.) (**from**) ~, from here, ~!, go away, **go** ~, die, ~ **with**, away with. [E]

**hĕ'nch|man** *n*. (*pl*. ~**men**). Trusty follower; political supporter; (Hist.) squire, page. [E (*hengest* horse, MAN)]

**hĕndĕ'ca-** *in comb*. Eleven. [Gk]

**hĕnge** (-nj) *n*. Monument of wood or stone as at *Stonehenge*. [place]

**hĕ'nna** *n*. Tropical shrub; reddish dye made from it and used esp. for hair. [Arab.]

**hĕp, hĭp**[1], *a*. (sl.; -**pp**-). Well-informed; stylish; ~-**cat**, hep person, jazz devotee. [orig. unkn.]

**hĕpă'tǐc** *a*. Of, good for, the liver; **hĕpatī'tǐs** *n*., inflammation of liver. [L f. Gk (*hēpar -atos* liver)]

**hĕ'pta-** *in comb*. Seven; ~**gon** *n*., plane figure with 7 sides and angles; ~**gonal** (-ǎ'g-) *a*. [Gk]

**hĕr** (or her). **1**. *pron*. Obj. case of SHE (colloq. also = SHE; *that's her, he is worse than her*); (arch.) = HER-SELF refl. (*laid her down to die*). **2**. *poss. pron. attrib.* Of her (*her hat; shook her head*); (in titles) that she is (*Her Majesty*); cf. HERS. [E dat. & gen. of SHE]

**hĕ'rald**. **1**. *n*. (Hist.) Officer who made State proclamations, regulated use of armorial bearings, etc.; ‖official of Heralds' COLLEGE concerned with pedigrees and bearings; messenger (often as newspaper-title); forerunner. **2**. *v.t.* (usu. fig.) Proclaim

approach of; usher in. **3. hĕră'ldǐc** *a*., of heraldry; ~**rў** *n*., knowledge or art of a herald, armorial bearings, heraldic pomp. [F f. Gmc, = army-rule]

**hĕrb** *n*. Plant whose stem is soft and dies down to the ground after flowering; plant whose leaves etc. are used for flavouring, food, medicine, scent, etc.; ~ **Robert**, common wild crane's-bill; ~ **tobacco**, herb-mixture smoked as substitute for tobacco or as medicine; ~**ā'ceous** (-shŭs) *a*., of, like, full of, herbs (~**aceous border,** border in garden etc. containing esp. perennial flowering plants); ~'**age** *n*., herbs collectively esp. as pasture for cattle etc.: ~**al** *a*. & *n*., (book with descriptions) of herbs; ~'**alǐst** *n*., writer on herbs, dealer in medicinal herbs; ~**ār'ǐum** *n*., a collection of dried herbs; ~'**ǐcǐde** *n*., toxic substance used to destroy unwanted vegetation; ~'**ǐvŏre** *n*., animal feeding on plants; ~**ǐ'vorous** *a*., feeding on plants; ~'**ў** *a*. [F f. L *herba*; -*cide*, -*vorous*, f. L *caedo* kill, *voro* devour]

**Hĕr'cūlēs** (-z) *n*. (Gk & Rom. Myth.) hero of great strength who performed 12 difficult tasks (**Pillars of** ~, rocks on each side of Strait of Gibraltar); very strong man; **Hĕr-cūlē'an** *a*., of, like, fit for, Hercules (*Herculean task*). [L alt. of Gk *Hēraklēs*]

**hĕrd**. **1**. *n*. Number of cattle etc. feeding or travelling together (also derog. of people, **the common** or **vulgar** ~); herdsman; ~-**book**, pedigree-book of cattle etc.; **the** ~ **instinct**, gregariousness; ~'**sman**, keeper of herds. **2**. *v.i.* & *t*. Go in a herd (*with others, together*); tend (cattle etc.), drive or crowd (people) like cattle. [E]

**hĕre** *adv., n., & int.* **1**. *adv*. In this place or position (*sit here; leave it down, over, up*, etc., *here; has lived here for years; here is your coat*); at this point (in speech, performance, writing, etc.); to this place or position (*come here; bring the book here;* LOOK *here!*); ~ (**below**), in this life (before death); ~ **goes!**, now I make the attempt etc.; ~'**s to**, I drink to the health of; ~ **and there**, in various places; **neither** ~ **nor there**, of no importance. **2**. *n*. This place (*lives near here; fill it up to here; leave here today*). **3**. *int*. calling attention or as command (*here, watch where you're going!*); = I am present (in answer to roll-call). **4.** ~**about'(s)**, near this place; ~**a'fter** *adv.* & *n.*, (in) the future, (in) the world to come; ~**by'**, by this means, as a result of this; ~**i'n**, (*formal*) in this place, book, etc.; ~**ina'fter**, ~**inbefor'e**, (*formal*) in later, earlier, part (of formal document); ~**o'f**, ~**to'**, (arch.) of, to, this; ~**tofore'**, (*formal*) formerly; ~**upo'n**, after or in consequence of this; ~**with'**, with this (esp. of enclosure in letter etc.). [E]

**herĕ'dit|able** *a.* That can be inherited; ~**ament** (or hĕrĭdĭ'-) *n.*, hereditable (esp. real) property, inheritance. [F or L (HEIR)]

**herĕ'dit|ary̆** *a.* (**-ily**, **-iness**). Descending by inheritance; holding hereditary office etc.; transmitted from one generation to another (*hereditary disease, instinct, feud*); ~**y̆** *n.*, tendency of like to beget like, sum of characteristics inherited from parents, genetic constitution. [L (HEIR)]

**Hĕ'rĕford** *n.* (One of a) breed of red and white beef cattle. [place]

**hĕ'rĕsy̆** *n.* Opinion contrary to doctrine of Christian Church or to accepted doctrine on any subject; **hĕ'rĕtic** *n.*, believer in a heresy; **herĕ'tĭcal** *a.* (**-lly**). [F f. L f. Gk (*hairesis* choice)]

**hĕ'rĭt|able** *a.* (**-bly**). That can be inherited or inherit; transmissible from parent to offspring; ~**age** *n.*, what is or may be inherited, one's portion or lot, inherited cultural influence, tradition, etc., (*the heritage of free speech*). [F (HEIR)]

**hĕrmă'phrod|ite** *n.* & *a.* (Person, animal) with characteristics of both sexes; (plant) in which same flower has stamens and pistils; ~**i'tĭc** *a.*; ~**ĭtĭsm** *n.* [L f. Gk, orig. the name of son of *Hermes* and *Aphrodite*]

**hĕrmĕ'tĭc** *a.* (~**ally**). Of alchemy; esoteric; ~ **seal**, airtight closure by fusion etc. [L (*Hermes*, Gk god regarded as founder of alchemy)]

**hĕr'mĭt** *n.* Person, esp. early Christian, living in solitude; ~**-crab** (living in mollusc's cast-off shell); ~**age** *n.*, hermit's abode, monastery, secluded residence. [F *ermite* or L f. Gk (*erēmos* solitary)]

**hĕr'nĭa** *n.* (Path.) Protrusion of

part of organ through aperture in enclosing membrane etc. [L]

**hē'rō** *n.* (*pl.* ~**es**). Man admired for great deeds and noble qualities; chief man in poem, play, or story; illustrious fighter (~**'s welcome**, such as is given to returning victor); ~**-worship(per)**, worship(per) of the ancient heroes or of heroic or admired person(s); **hē'rōĭne** *n.*, female hero. [L f. Gk *hērōs*]

**hērō'ĭc. 1.** *a.* (~**ally**). Of, fit for, having qualities of, a hero; attempting great things; ~ **poetry** (concerned with heroes); ~ **verse**, that used in heroic poetry, as E iambic pentameter. **2.** *n.* (in *pl.*) Heroic verse, high-flown language or sentiments. **3. hē'rōĭsm** *n.*, heroic conduct or qualities. [F or L f. Gk]

**hĕ'rōĭn** *n.* Sedative addictive drug prepared from morphine. [G]

**hē'rōĭne.** See HERO.

**hĕ'ron** *n.* A long-legged wading bird; ~**ry̆** *n.*, place where herons breed. [F f. Gmc]

**hĕr'pēs** (-z) *n.* Skin-disease of various kinds with blisters. [L f. Gk (*herpō* creep)]

**Herr** (hār) *n.* (*pl.* ~**en**). (Of a German) Mr.; German man; ~**'envolk** (hĕ'renfŏlk) *n.*, German nation, or other group, regarding itself as innately superior. [G]

**hĕ'rring** *n.* N. Atlantic fish used for food (RED *herring*); ~**-bone**, weave or stitch in cloth etc. suggesting bones of herring, zigzag pattern of bricks etc.; ~ **gull**, large N. Atlantic gull; ~**-pond**, (joc.) N. Atlantic. [E]

**hers** (-z) *poss. pron. pred.* (& *abs.*) Of her (*it is hers; hers is best; take one of hers; some friends of hers*). [HER]

**hersĕ'lf** *pron.*, emphat. & refl. form of SHE, HER; (*she went herself; she herself said it; she has hurt herself*; BY *herself*; *ask the girl herself*; **she is not** ~, not in normal state of body or mind); **be** ~, act in her normal manner. [E (HER, SELF)]

**Herts.** *abbr.* Hertfordshire.

**hĕrtz** (-ts) *n.* (*pl.* same). Unit of frequency, one cycle per second. [person]

**hĕ'sĭt|āte** (-z-) *v.i.* Feel or show indecision (*about, over*); scruple, be reluctant, (*to do*); ~**ant** *a.*, irresolute, hesitating; ~**ancy̆**, ~**ā'tion**, ~**ātor**, *ns.* [L (*haereo haes-* stick fast)]

**hĕ'ssĭan** *n.* A strong coarse cloth

used for furnishings, packing, etc. [*Hesse*, place]

**hĕst** *n.* (arch.) = BEHEST. [E]

**hĕt** *a.* ~ **up**, (sl.) excited. [= *heated*]

**hètaer'a** (-cī'*a*) *n.* (*pl.* ~**s**, ~**e**). Courtesan, mistress, esp. in ancient Greece. [Gk]

**hĕ'tero-** in comb. Other, different; ~**mŏr'phic** *a.*, of dissimilar forms; ~**mŏr'phism** *n.*, existence in various forms; ~**sĕ'xūal** (*or* -kshoo-) *a.* & *n.*, (person) characterized by attraction to opposite sex. [Gk *heteros* other]

**hĕ'terodŏx** *a.* Not orthodox; ~**ў** *n.* [L (HETERO-, Gk *doxa* opinion)]

**hĕ'terodȳne** *a.*, & *v.i.* (Radio). Relating to production of, produce, a lower (audible) frequency from the combination of two high frequencies. [HETERO-, Gk *dunamis* force]

**hĕterogĕ'nĕous** *a.* Diverse; composed of diverse elements; **hĕterogĕnē' itў** *n.* [L f. Gk (*genos* kind)]

**heurī'stic** (hūr-) *a.* (~**ally**). Serving to discover; using trial and error; teaching by enabling pupil to find things out. [Gk *heuriskō* find]

**hew** *v.t.* & *i.* (*p.p.* ~**n**, ~**ed**). Chop, cut (thing *down*, *off*, *to pieces*; *at* thing; one's *way*) with axe, sword, etc.; cut into shape. [E]

**\*hĕx. 1.** *v.i.* & *t.* Practise witchcraft (on). **2.** *n.* Witch; magic spell. [G]

**hĕ'xa-** in comb. Six; ~**chŏrd** (-k-), 6-note scale, 6-stringed instrument; ~**gon** *n.*, plane figure with 6 sides and angles; ~**gonal** (-ă'g-) *a.*; ~**grăm** *a.*, 6-pointed star formed by 2 intersecting equilateral triangles; ~**mēter** (-ă'-) *n.*, line of 6 metrical feet. [Gk]

**hey** (hā) *int.* calling attention or expr. joy, surprise, or inquiry; ~ **for** —, expr. applause or appreciation; ~ **presto !**, conjuror's formula of command. [cf. HEIGH]

**hey'day** (hā'-) *n.* Bloom, prime, (*the heyday of youth* etc.). [LG]

**H.F.** *abbr.* high frequency.

**Hg** *symb.* mercury. [L *hydrargyrum*]

‖**H.G.V.** *abbr.* heavy goods vehicle.

**H.H.** *abbr.* Her or His Highness; His Holiness.

**HH** *abbr.* double-hard (pencil-lead).

**hi** *int.* calling attention. [var. HEY]

**hiā'tus** *n.* Gap in series, argument, etc.; break between two vowels

coming together but not in same syllable. [L (*hio* gape)]

**hi'bern|āte** *v.i.* (Of animal) spend winter in torpid state; ~**ā'tion** *n.* [L (*hibernus* of winter)]

**Hibēr'nian** *a.* & *n.* (Native) of Ireland; **Hibēr'nicism** *n.*, Irish idiom or BULL[2]. [L *Hibernia* f. Gk f. Celt.]

**hibī'scus** *n.* Cultivated malvaceous plant or shrub. [Gk *hibiskos* marsh mallow]

**hi'ccup, hi'ccough** (-kŭp). **1.** *n.* Involuntary spasm of respiratory organs with abrupt coughlike sound. **2.** *v.i.* & *t.* Make, utter (words) with, hiccup. [imit.]

**\*hĭck** *n.* (colloq.) Yokel. [fam. form of *Richard*]

**hi'ckorў** *n.* N. Amer. tree allied to walnut, (stick of) its tough heavy wood. [Virginian]

**hid, hi'dden.** See HIDE[2].

**hidă'lgŏ** *n.* (*pl.* ~**s**). Spanish gentleman. [Sp., = son of something]

**hide**[1]. **1.** *n.* Animal's skin, raw or dressed; (joc.) person's skin; ~'-**bound**, (of ill-bred cattle) with skin clinging close, (fig.) rigidly conventional. **2.** *v.t.* (colloq.) Thrash (esp. **hi'ding** *n.*). [E]

**hide**[2]. **1.** *v.t.* & *i.* (**hid**; **hidden**, arch. **hid**). Put or keep (thing) out of sight intentionally or not (~ *one's* **head**, keep out of sight from shame etc.; *hide* one's *light under a* BUSHEL; *hidden by trees*); conceal oneself (**in hiding**, in fugitive state); conceal (fact *from* person); ~**-and-seek**, children's game in which player hides and is sought by others; ~**-out**, (colloq.) hiding-place. **2.** *n.* ‖Place of concealment used in observing or hunting wild animals. [E]

**hi'dĕous** *a.* Repulsive, revolting, (*hideous monster, crime, noise*); (colloq.) unpleasant. [AF *hidous*]

**hie** *v.i.* & *refl.* (poet.) Go quickly (*hie thee*, or *hie, to*). [E, = strive]

**hier'arch** (hīr'ärk) *n.* Chief priest; ~**ў** *n.*, graded priesthood or other organization; **hierâr'chic(al)** (hīr-, är'k-) *adjs.* (-ically). [L f. Gk (*hieros* sacred, *arkhō* rule)]

**hierā'tic** (hīr-) *a.* Of the priests (esp. of type of ancient Egyptian writing). [L f. Gk (*hieros* priest)]

**hier'o|glўph** (hīr'-) *n.* Figure of an object standing for word etc. as used in ancient Egyptian and other writing; (in *pl.*) such writing, (joc.) illegible writing; **~glẏ'phic** *a.* (-ically), & *n.* (in *pl.*). [F or L f. Gk *hieros* sacred, *gluphō* carve)]

**hi'-fī** *a.* & *n.* (colloq.)=HIGH *fidelity*; equipment for such sound--reproduction. [abbr.]

**higgledẏ-pi'ggledẏ** (-geldĭ) *adv.*, *a.*, & *n.* (colloq.) (In) utter confusion. [orig. uncert.]

**high** (hi) *a.*, *n.*, & *adv.* **1.** *a.* Of great or specified upward extent (*a high hill*; *one inch high*); situated far above ground, sea level, etc., (*high altitude*); coming above normal level (*jersey with high neck*); (of physical action) reaching, done at, a height (*high kick*, *flight*); of exalted rank or authority (**the Most H~**, God; *High Admiral*; *high card*); of superior quality (*high art*, *living*, *opinion of*, *principles*); extreme, intense, above the normal, (*high favour*, *fever*, *polish*, *prices*, *temperature*, *vacuum*, *wind*); extreme in opinion (*high Tory*); (of time) far advanced, fully reached, (*high summer*; *it is high time we left*); (of sound) shrill; (of meat etc.) beginning to go bad; (colloq.) intoxicated by or *on* alcohol or drugs. **2.** *n.* High or highest level or number; area of *high* PRESSURE; (sl.) euphoric state caused by drug; **from on ~**, from heaven or a high place. **3.** *adv.* Far up, aloft; in or to high degree; at a high price; (of sound) at or to high pitch; **play ~** (for high stakes); **run ~**, (of sea) have strong current with high tide, (fig. of feelings) be strong; **hunt ~ and low**, everywhere. **4.** **~ altar**, chief altar of church; **~ and dry**, (of ship) out of the water, (fig.) stranded; **~ and mighty**, (colloq.) arrogant; *\***~'ball**, drink of spirits and soda etc.; **~-born**, of noble birth; **~'brow** *a.* & *n.*, (colloq.) (person) of superior intellectual or cultural interests; **~ chair**, child's chair for use at meals with long legs and usu. tray; **H~ Church**, party revering authority of priests, ceremony, and role of sacraments; **~-class**, of high quality; **~ colour**, flushed complexion; **H~ Commission(er)**, (head of) embassy from one Commonwealth country to another; ‖**H~ Court (of Justice)**, supreme court of justice for civil cases; **~ day**, festal day; *higher* CRITICISM: **~er education** (at uni-

versity etc.); **~er mammal, plant**, etc., (more evolved); **~er mathematics** (beyond what is usu. taught in schools); **~ explosive** (with violent local effect); **~-falu'tin(g)** (-ōō'-) *a.* & *n.*, bombast(ic), pretentious(ness); **~ fidelity**, quality of sound-reproduction with little distortion; **~ finance** (dealing with large sums of money); **~-flown**, extravagant, bombastic; **~-flẏ'er**, **-fli'er**, ambitious person, person or thing with potential for great achievements; **~-flẏ'ing**, ambitious; **~ frequency** (esp. in Radio, 3–30 megahertz); *high* GEAR; **High German**[2], of high quality; **~-grade**, of high quality; **~-handed**, overbearing; **~-hat** *a.*, supercilious; *high* HORSE, JINKS; **~ jump**, athletic contest of clearing greatest height, (fig.) drastic punishment; *high* LATITUDES; **~-level**, (of negotiations etc.) conducted by persons of high rank; **~ life**, luxurious existence; **~'light**, (*n.*) bright part of picture, moment or detail of vivid interest, outstanding feature, (*v.t.*) bring into prominence; *high* MASS[1]; **~-minded**, virtuous, of firm moral principles; *high* OLD *time*; **~-pitched**, (of sound) high, (of roof) steep; **~ point**, maximum or best state reached; **~-powered**, having great power etc.; *high* PRESSURE; **~ priest**, chief priest (of Jews), head of cult; *high* RELIEF; **~-rise**, (of building) having many storeys; **~ road**, main road (*to*); **~ school** (for secondary education); *high* SEAs, SEASON; **~-speed**, (of tool etc.) operating at great speed; *high* SPIRITs; **~ spot**, (sl.) important place or feature (esp. in entertainment); **~ street**, principal shopping street of town etc.; **~-strung**, very sensitive; **~ table**, elevated table at public dinner or for fellows of college; *high* ‖TEA, TIDE, TREASON; **~-up**, (colloq.) person of high rank; **~ voltage**, electrical potential involving danger of injury etc.; **~ water**, high tide (**~-wa'ter mark**, level reached at high water, fig., recorded maximum in any fluctuation); **~ wire**, high tightrope in circus etc.; **~ words**, angry talk. **5.** **~'lẏ** *adv.*, in a high degree (*highly amusing*, *paid*, *probable*); **~-ly-strung**, = HIGH-*strung*), favourably (*think*, *speak*, *highly of*); **~'nèss** *n.*, title of British and other princes etc. (*His*,

*Her, Royal* etc. *Highness*), state of being high (esp. fig.). [E]

**hi′ghland** (hī′l-). **1.** *n.* (usu. in *pl.*) Mountainous country esp. (H∼s) of N. Scotland. **2.** *a.* Of highland or Scottish Highlands (*Highland dress*, FLING, etc.); H∼ **cattle** (with shaggy hair and long curved horns); (H)∼**er,** (H)∼**man,** *ns.* [E, = promontory (prec.)]

**hi′ghway** (hī′w-) *n.* Public road (**King′s, Queen′s,** ∼, seen as protected by royal power); main route; ‖H∼ **Code,** official handbook for road-users; ∼**man,** (Hist.) (usu. mounted) robber of stage-coaches etc. [HIGH, WAY]

**hi′jäck. 1.** *v.t.* Seize control of (lorry, aircraft in flight, etc.) by (threat of) violence; steal (goods etc. in transit). **2.** *n.* Hijacking. [orig. unkn.]

**hike.** (colloq.) **1.** *n.* Long walk for pleasure or exercise; *rise. **2.** *v.i.* Walk vigorously or laboriously; go for a long tramp. [orig. unkn.]

**hilār′ious** *a.* Cheerful, merry; **hilā′rĭtў** *n.* [L f. Gk *hilaros*]

‖**Hi′larў** *n.* ∼ **term,** legal or university term beginning in Jan. [person (Anglican festival 13 Jan.)]

**hĭll** *n.* Natural elevation of ground, small mountain; heap, mound, (*ant-, dung-, mole-, hill*); *∼**billy,** rustic person from hills etc.; ∼′**side,** lateral slope of hill; ∼′**ock** *n.,* small hill, mound; ∼′**ў** *a.* (∼**iness**). [E]

**hĭlt** *n.* Handle of sword or dagger (**prove** etc. **up to the** ∼, completely). [E]

**hĭm** *pron.*, obj. (& colloq. subj.) case of HE[1] (for use cf. HER). [E, dat. of HE[1]]

**hĭmsĕ′lf** *pron.*, emphat. & refl. form of HE[1], HIM, (for use cf. HER-SELF). [E (HIM, SELF)]

**hind**[1] *n.* Female of (esp. red) deer, esp. in and after 3rd year. [E]

‖**hind**[2] *n.* (arch.) Rustic. [E]

**hind**[3], **hi′nder**[1], *adjs.* At the back, posterior, (usu. *hind*, esp. of things in pair or pairs front and back, as *hind leg, -*QUARTERS, *wheel*); **hi′ndsight,** back sight of gun, wisdom after the event (opp. *foresight*); **hi′ndmŏst** (*or -o-*) *a.* [E]

**hi′nder**[2] *v.t.* Impede, obstruct, prevent, (*you will hinder him, his work, him from working*). [E (prec.)]

**Hi′ndi** (-ē) *a.* & *n.* (Of) a major group of dialects in N. India; (of)

literary form of Hindustani as used in India. [Urdu (*Hind* India)]

**hi′ndrance** *n.* Obstruction; obstacle. [HINDER[2]]

**Hĭndu′** (-dōō′; *or* hĭ′-). **1.** *n.* Adherent of Hinduism. **2.** *a.* Of the Hindus. **3.** **Hi′nduïsm** (-ōō-) *n.,* religious and social system esp. in India with worship of several gods etc. [Urdu, f. Pers. (*Hind* India)]

**Hĭndusta′ni** (-ah′nē). **1.** *a.* Of Hindustan(i). **2.** *n.* A colloquial language of N. India and Pakistan. [Urdu f. Pers. (prec., *stan* country)]

**hĭnge** (-nj). **1.** *n.* Movable joint such as that by which door is hung on post; (fig.) principle on which all turns. **2.** *v.t.* & *i.* Attach with hinge; (of door etc. or fig.) turn (*on* post, principle, etc.). [HANG]

**hi′nnў** *n.* Offspring of she-ass and stallion (cf. MULE[2]). [L *hinnus* f. Gk]

**hĭnt. 1.** *n.* Indirect suggestion, slight indication, (**broad** ∼, clear and unmistakable hint; **drop a** ∼, make hint; **take a** ∼, understand hint); small piece of practical information. **2.** *v.t.* & *i.* Suggest indirectly (thing, *that*); ∼ **at,** give a hint of. [obs. *hent* grasp]

**hi′nterländ** *n.* District behind coast or river′s banks; area served by port or other centre. [G]

**hĭp**[1] *n.* Projection of pelvis and upper part of thigh-bone (**smite** ∼ **and thigh,** Bibl., unsparingly); ∼**bath** (in which one sits immersed to the hips); ∼**bone,** bone forming hip; ∼**flask** (for spirits etc., carried in hip-pocket); ∼**joint,** joint of thigh-bone with pelvis; ∼**length** *a.,* reaching to hips; ∼**pocket** (just behind hip). [E]

**hĭp**[2] *n.* Fruit of (esp. wild) rose. [E]

**hip**[3] *int.* used in cheering (*hip, hip, hurrah*). [orig. unkn.]

**hĭp**[4]. See HEP.

**hi′ppĭe, hi′ppў,** *n.* (sl.) Person who rejects social conventions and adopts unusual style of dress, living habits, etc. [prec.]

**hi′ppō** *n.* (colloq.; *pl.* ∼s). Hippopotamus. [abbr.]

**Hĭppocrā′tic** *a.* ∼ **oath** (stating obligations and duties of physicians). [L f. Gk *Hippokratēs,* person]

**hi′ppodrōme** *n.* (Gk & Rom. Ant.) course for chariot races etc.; circus; name for theatre etc. [F or L f. Gk (*hippos* horse, *dromos* race)]

**hĭppopŏ′tam‖us** *n.* (*pl.* ∼**uses,**

~i *pr.* -i). Large African short-legged thick-skinned quadruped inhabiting rivers etc. [L f. Gk (*hippos* horse, *potamos* river)]

**hi′ppy.** See HIPPIE.

**hire. 1.** *n.* Payment by contract for use of thing, labour, etc.; engagement on these terms (**for, on** ~, open to hire); ‖~**-pur′chase** (**system**), by which hirer owns thing after a number of payments. **2.** *v.t.* Employ, procure (*from* person), on hire; ~ (**out**), grant use of (thing) on hire. **3.** ~′**ling** (hīr′l-) *n.*, (usu. derog.) one who works for hire. [E]

**hir′sūte** *a.* Having much hair. [L]

**his** (-z) *poss. pron.* Of him; for phrs. see HER, HERS. [E, gen. of HE[1]]

**Hispa′nic** *a.* Of Spain (and Portugal; and other Spanish-speaking countries). [L (*Hispania* Spain)]

**hiss. 1.** *v.i.* & *t.* (Of person, animal, water etc. poured on fire, etc.) make sharp sibilant sound of *s*, esp. as sign of disapproval; express disapproval of (person etc.) thus. **2.** *n.* Hissing sound. [imit.]

**hist** *int.* used to call attention, enjoin silence, incite dog, etc. [natural excl.]

**hi′stamine** (*or* -ēn) *n.* Substance present throughout the body and causing some allergic reactions. [HISTOLOGY, AMINE]

**hi′stogram** *n.* Statistical diagram in which frequency of values of a quantity is shown by columns. [Gk *histos* mast]

**histŏ′logў** *n.* Science of organic tissues. [Gk *histos* tissue]

**histŏr′ian** *n.* Writer of history (esp. as critical analyst etc., not mere compiler); student of history. [F (HISTORY)]

**histŏ′ric** *a.* Famous in history; (Gram., of tense) normally used for past events. [L f. Gk (HISTORY)]

**histŏ′ric|al** *a.* (~**ally**). Of history (*historical evidence*); belonging to the past, not to legend or rumour, not of the present; (of novel etc.) dealing with past period; (of study of subject) showing development over period of time; ~**ism** *n.*, belief that historical events are governed by laws, tendency to stress historical development and influence of the past etc.; **histori′cĭtў** *n.*, historical truth or authenticity. [L f. Gk (prec.)]

**histŏriŏ′graph|ў** *n.* Writing of history, study of historical writing; ~**er** *n.* [F *or* L f. Gk (as foll.: -GRAPH)]

**hi′storў** *n.* Continuous record of (esp. public) events; study of the past involving human affairs or of any related thing, person, place, time, or activity, (*the history of this jewel, Peter the Great, France, music,* etc.); systematic or critical analysis of, research into, past events etc.; similar record or account of natural phenomena; historical play etc.; (significant) sequence of past events; **make** ~, do something memorable. [L f. Gk *historia* inquiry]

**histriŏ′nic. 1.** *a.* (~**ally**). Of acting; stagy, theatrical. **2.** *n.* (in *pl.*) Theatricals; stagy behaviour (designed to impress others). [L (*histrio* actor)]

**hit. 1.** *v.t.* & *i.* (-tt-; hit). Strike with blow or missile; aim blow (lit. or fig.) *at*; of (moving body) strike (*against*); deliver (blow, person etc. a blow); have effect on person, cause to suffer, (*hard hit by the cold*); light (*up*)*on*, find, (*hit on a plan*), (colloq.) encounter (*hit a snag*); (Crick.) score (runs), hit (ball) *for* so many runs (‖~ **for six,** fig., defeat in argument etc.); ~ **and run,** do damage etc. and escape quickly; ~ **back,** retaliate; ~ **below the belt,** give unfair blow (Boxing or fig.); ~ **it off,** be congenial *with*; ~ **off,** represent exactly; ~**-or-miss,** (colloq.) casual, careless; ~ **out,** deal vigorous blows (lit. or fig.); *hit the* HAY; ~ **the** (**right**) **nail on the head,** give right explanation. **2.** *n.* Blow, stroke; stroke of satire etc. (*at*); stroke of good luck, success esp. in becoming popular or well-known; **make a** ~, be successful (as entertainer etc.). [E f. N]

**hitch. 1.** *v.t.* & *i.* Move (thing *up* etc.) with jerk; fasten with loop, hook, etc., (~ one's **wagon to a star,** utilize powers higher than one's own); become so fastened (*on to* etc.); **get** ~**ed,** (sl.) marry; ~(**-hike**), travel by means of lifts in vehicles. **2.** *n.* Jerk; (Naut.) kinds of noose or knot; impediment, stoppage. [orig. uncert.]

**hi′ther** (-dh-; literary). **1.** *adv.* To(wards) this place; ~ **and thither,** to and fro, in various directions; ~**to** (-tŏŏ′), up to now. **2.** *a.*

Situated on this side; the nearer (of two). [E]

**Hi′ttite** *n.* & *a.* (Member, language) of a powerful ancient people of Asia Minor and Syria. [Heb.]

**hive. 1.** *n.* Artificial home for bees (**bee′hive**); (fig.) busy swarming place; hive-shaped thing. **2.** *v.t.* & *i.* Place (bees) in hive; store (as) in hive; enter hive; ~ **off**, separate from larger group. [E]

**hives** (-vz) *n.pl.* Skin eruption, esp. nettle-rash. [orig. unkn.]

**H.K.** *abbr.* Hong Kong.

**H.L.** *abbr.* House of Lords.

**h′m** = HEM².

**H.M.** *abbr.* Her or His Majesty('s).

**H.M.I., H.M.S., H.M.S.O.,** *abbrs.* Her or His Majesty's Inspector (of Schools), Ship, Stationery Office.

‖**H.N.C., H.N.D.,** *abbrs.* Higher National Certificate, Diploma.

**hō** *int.* expr. surprise, triumph, derision, etc., calling attention, or added to other *ints.* (HEIGH-ho, WHAT ho) or (Naut.) to name of destination (*westward ho*); cf. HO-HO. [natural excl.]

**ho.** *abbr.* house.

**hoar. 1.** *a.* Grey-(haired) with age; greyish-white; ~**-frost**, frozen water vapour on lawns etc. **2.** *n.* Hoar-frost; ~′**y̆** *a.* (~**iness**), grey with age (esp. of hair), venerable, old and trite. [E]

**hoard. 1.** *n.* Stock, store, (of savings, treasure, facts, etc.). **2.** *v.i.* & *t.* Amass or keep in hoard; keep things in hoard (esp. food etc. in time of scarcity), or stored in the mind. [E]

**hoar′ding** *n.* Temporary board fence round building, often used for posting bills etc.; ‖permanent structure to carry advertisements. [*hoard* f. F (HURDLE)]

**hoarse** *a.* (Of voice) rough and deep, husky, (esp. from talking); having hoarse voice. [N]

**hoar′y̆.** See HOAR.

**hoax** *v.t.,* & *n.* Deceive (person), deception, by way of joke. [prob. contr. HOCUS(-POCUS)]

**hob** *n.* Side casing of fireplace, with surface level with top of grate; ~′**nail**, heavy-headed nail for boot-sole. [cf. HUB]

**hŏ′bbit** *n.* One of an imaginary race of small people. [invented by J. R. R. Tolkien]

**hŏ′bble. 1.** *v.i.* & *t.* Walk lamely, limp; act, speak, haltingly; cause to

hobble; tie legs of (horse), tie (horse's legs) together, to keep it from straying etc. **2.** *n.* Limping gait; rope, clog, for hobbling a horse. [prob. LG]

**hŏ′bbledĕhoy** (-beld-) *n.* Awkward half-grown youth; ~**hŏŏd** *n.* [orig. unkn.]

**hŏ′bby¹** *n.* Favourite occupation not one's main work or business; ~**-horse**, wicker figure of horse for morris dancer etc., child's stick with horse's head, rocking-horse, merry-go-round horse, topic to which one often recurs. [*Robin*, name]

**hŏ′bby²** *n.* A small falcon. [F]

**hŏ′bgŏblin** *n.* Mischievous imp, bogy. [HOBBY¹, goblin]

**hŏ′b-nŏb** *v.i.* (**-bb-**). Drink together; talk informally (*with*). [*hab nab* have or not have, give and take]

*****hō′bō** *n.* (*pl.* ~**s**). Wandering workman or tramp. [orig. unkn.]

**Hŏ′bson** *n.* ~'s choice, option of taking what is offered or nothing. [person]

**hŏck¹** *n.* Joint of quadruped's hind leg between knee and fetlock. [E]

‖**hŏck²** *n.* (Kind of) German white wine. [*Hochheim*, place]

*****hŏck³** *v.t.,* & *n.* (sl.) Pawn, pledge; **in** ~, in pawn, in prison, or in debt. [Du.]

**hŏ′ckey** *n.* Game played with ball and curved sticks on field, ice, etc., between goals. [orig. unkn.]

**hōcus-pō′cus. 1.** *n.* Conjuring deception or formula. **2.** *v.i.* & *t.* (**-ss-**). Play tricks on; hoax. [sham L]

**hŏd** *n.* Light trough on staff for carrying bricks etc.; receptacle for coal; ~′**man**, labourer carrying hod, (fig.) literary hack. [F *hotte* pannier]

‖**Hŏdge** *n.* Typical English farm-labourer. [fam. form of *Roger*]

**hodgepodge.** See HOTCHPOTCH.

**hōe. 1.** *n.* Long-handled tool for scraping up weeds etc.; **Dutch** ~, kind pushed forward by user. **2.** *v.t.* & *i.* (~′**ing**). Weed (crops), loosen (ground), remove (weeds), with hoe; use hoe. [F f. Gmc]

**hŏg. 1.** *n.* Domesticated pig, esp. castrated male for slaughter; swine; (fig.) coarse, gluttonous, or filthy person; **go the whole** ~, (sl.) do thing thoroughly; ~**('s)-back**, sharp hill-ridge; ~′**shead** (-z-h-), large cask, measure of beer etc. (usu. about

50 gal.); ~'**wash,** (fig.) worthless stuff; ~'**weed,** coarse weed of various kinds (eaten by animals); ~'**gish** (-g-) *a.* **2.** *v.t.* & *i.* (-gg-). Appropriate greedily or selfishly. [E]

‖**hŏ'ggĕt** (-g-) *n.* Yearling sheep.

**hŏ'gmanay** *n.* (Sc.) (Celebration of) New Year's Eve. [prob. F]

**hŏ-hŏ'** *int.* expr. surprise, triumph, or derision. [redupl. HO]

**hoick** *v.t.* (sl.) Lift or bring (*out* etc.) esp. with jerk. [perh. var. HIKE]

*hoi polloi* (hoi pŏ'loi; *or* -oi') *n.* Ordinary people, the majority, the masses. [Gk, = the many]

**hoist. 1.** *v.t.* Raise (esp. flag) aloft; raise with tackle etc.; ~ (as *p.p.* of obs. *hoise*) **with** one's **own petard,** caught by one's own devices. **2.** *n.* Hoisting; elevator, lift. [*hoise* f. I.Du.]

**hoity-toi'ty. 1.** *a.* Haughty. **2.** *int.* expr. surprise at person's presumption. [obs. *hoit* romp]

**hŏkey-pŏ'key** *n.* (colloq.) Cheap ice cream. [HOCUS-POCUS]

**hŏ'kum** *n.* (sl.) Theatrical plot or business, film scenario, meant for the uncritical; claptrap. [orig. unkn.]

**hŏld**[1]. **1.** *v.t.* & *i.* (**held;** arch. *p.p.* ~'**en** esp. w. ref. to formal meeting). Keep fast, grasp, (*hold* HANDS); sustain, keep thing in some position, (*hold the baby; hold it in the light*); grasp so as to control (*hold the reins*); keep (one*self,* one's head, etc.) in some attitude etc.; have capacity for, contain, (*jug holds two pints*); possess or own (land, property, shares, etc.); have gained (a degree, sports record, etc.); (Mil.) occupy, keep possession of (against attack); engross (person, his attention); dominate (*holds the stage*); keep (person) in place or condition (*hold him at bay, in suspense*); detain in custody; keep (person) *to* (promise, etc.); conduct, celebrate, (conversation, meeting, festival); restrain (*hold your fire*); (colloq.) cease (~ **everything!, it!,** cease action etc.; **there's no** ~**ing** him, he is restive or determined); think, believe, (thing, *that,* person etc. *to* be; ~ **it against** person, regard it as to his discredit *that*); (of judge or court) decide (*that*); regard (*hold* thing *cheap, dear; hold him in contempt, esteem*); remain unbroken (under pressure etc.); (of weather) continue fine; ~ (**good, true**), (of law etc.) be valid. **2.** ~'**all,** portable bag as luggage etc.; ~ **aloof,** keep oneself separate (*from*); ~ **back,** (fig.) restrain, hesitate, refrain *from*; hold one's BREATH; ~ **down,** repress, (colloq.) be competent enough to keep (one's job); ~'**fast,** clamp securing object to wall etc.; ~ **forth,** (usu. derog.) speak at length or publicly; hold one's GROUND, one's or person's HAND; ~ one's **head high,** behave proudly or confidently; ~ **in,** keep in check; ~ **off,** delay, keep one's distance, not begin; ~ **on,** maintain grasp, not ring off, (colloq., in *imper.*) stop; ~ **out,** offer (inducement etc.), maintain resistance, continue to make demand *for*; ~ **over,** postpone; hold one's OWN, one's PEACE; hold the FORT; ~ **the line,** not yield, maintain telephone connection; ~ **to,** adhere to (purpose etc.); ~ **together,** (cause to) cohere; hold one's TONGUE; ~ **up,** sustain (lit. or fig.), maintain (head etc.) erect, obstruct or stop (traffic etc.), (stop and) rob by (threat of) violence; ~-*up* **n.,** robbery of this kind, stoppage or delay; ~ **water,** (fig.) be sound, bear examination; ~ **with,** (sl., usu. neg.) approve of; *hold your* HORSES. **3.** *n.* Grasp (lit. or fig.; *catch, get, take,* etc., *hold of*; **get** ~ **of,** fig., acquire, make contact with); manner or means of holding, thing to hold by; **a** ~ **on, over,** influence over; **with no** ~**s barred,** all methods being permitted; **take** ~, (of plant, habit, custom, etc.) become established. **4.** ~'**er** *n.,* (esp.) occupant of office etc., device for holding something (*cigarette-holder* etc.); ~'**ing** *n.,* (esp.) tenure of land, land or stocks held; ~**ing company** (formed to hold shares of other companies); ~**ing operation** (to prevent change for the time being). [E]

**hŏld**[2] *n.* Cavity below deck of ship for cargo. [E (HOLLOW)]

**hŏle. 1.** *n.* Hollow place, cavity in solid body, aperture through surface, (*cheese, ground, stocking, is full of holes*); animal's burrow; wretched place; (sl.) dilemma, fix, (*in a hole*); cavity into which ball etc. must be got in various games, (Golf) point scored by doing this in fewest strokes, terrain from tee to hole; ~-**and--corner,** (of affair etc.) secret, underhand; **in** ~**s,** worn so much that holes have formed; ~ **in the**

**heart,** congenital defect in heart membrane; **make a ~ in,** use large amount of (one's supply); **pick ~s in,** find fault with; **square peg in round ~,** person not fitted for his place; **hŏ'ley** *a.* 2. *v.t.* Make holes in; (Naut.) pierce side of ship; send (golf-ball etc.) into hole. [E]

**hŏ'liday** (*or* -dǐ). **1.** *n.* Day, ‖(usu. in *pl.*) period, of cessation from work or of recreation (**make ~, take a ~,** stop work; **on ~,** in course of holiday; **the summer** etc. **~s,** esp. of school); **~-maker,** person on holiday. **2.** *v.i.* Spend a holiday. [E (HOLY, DAY)]

**hŏ'liness.** See HOLY.

**hŏ'lla.** See HOLLO. [F *holà* (ho HO, *là* there)]

**hŏ'lland** *n.* Hard-wearing linen fabric (**brown ~,** unbleached); **H~er** *n.,* native of Holland; **H~s** (-z) *n.,* Dutch gin; **~aise** (-z) *n.,* creamy sauce served with fish etc. [Du.]

**\*hŏ'ller** *v.i. & t., & n.* (Make, express with) loud cry or noise. [foll.]

**hŏ'llō, hŏ'lla.** 1. *int. & t.* Shout, call out. 2. *n.* Shout, cry. [HOLLA]

**hŏ'llow** (-ō) *a., n., adv., & v.* **1.** *a.* (**~er, ~est**). Having a hole or cavity, not solid; sunken (*hollow cheeks*); empty, hungry; (of sound) echoing, as if made in or on hollow container; (fig.) empty, insincere, false, (*hollow triumph, laugh, promises*). **2.** *n.* Hollow place, hole, valley; **in the ~ of one's hand,** entirely subservient to one. **3.** *adv.* Completely (*beaten hollow*). **4.** *v.t.* **~ (out),** excavate, make into hollow shape. **5. ~-eyed,** with eyes deep sunk; **~ square,** troops drawn up so as to enclose rectangular space; **~-ware,** hollow articles of metal, china, etc., e.g. pots, kettles, jugs. [E]

**hŏ'lly** *n.* Evergreen shrub with prickly dark-green leaves and red berries used to decorate houses and churches at Christmas. [E]

**hŏ'llyhŏck** *n.* Tall plant with large flowers of many colours. [E. = holly mallow]

**Hŏ'llywŏŏd** *n.* American cinema industry or its products. [place]

**hōlm** (hōm) *n.* **~(-oak),** evergreen oak with holly-like leaves, ilex. [dial. *holm* holly]

**hŏ'locaust** *n.* Wholesale sacrifice or destruction. [F f. L f. Gk (*holos* whole, *kaustos* burnt)]

**hŏ'logrăm** *n.* (Photograph of) pattern formed by interference of coherent light coming direct from source and diffracted etc. by object, capable of reproducing image of object when suitably illuminated. [Gk *holos* whole, -GRAM]

**hŏ'lograph** (-ahf) *a. & n.* (Document) wholly in handwriting of person in whose name it appears. [F or L f. Gk (*holos* whole, -GRAPH)]

‖**hŏls** (-z) *n.* (colloq.) Holidays. [abbr.]

**hŏ'lster** *n.* Leather case for carrying pistol. [Du.]

**hō'lỹ** *a.* Consecrated, sacred; belonging to, devoted to, God; of high moral or spiritual excellence (**holier-than-thou,** colloq., having attitude of superior sanctity); **H~ City,** city held sacred by adherents of one or more religions, esp. Jerusalem, Heaven; *Holy* COMMUNION; **~ day,** religious festival; **H~ Family,** the young Jesus depicted with his mother and St. Joseph (etc.); **H~ Father,** the Pope; **H~ Ghost** = *Holy Spirit*; *Holy* GRAIL²; **H~ Land,** Palestine as revered esp. in Christianity (and Judaism), region similarly revered in other religions; *Holy* OFFICE; **~ of holies,** inner chamber of sanctuary in Jewish temple, (fig.) innermost shrine, thing held most sacred; *holy* ORDERS; **~ place,** outer chamber of sanctuary in Jewish temple, (in *pl.*) objectives of religious pilgrimage etc.; *Holy* ROMAN *Empire,* SEPULCHRE; **H~ Spirit,** Third Person of the Trinity, God as spiritually acting; *holy* TERROR; **H~ Thursday,** Ascension Day or Thursday in Holy Week; *Holy* TRINITY; **~ water,** water (blessed by priest) dedicated to holy uses; *holy* WAR; **H~ Week** (before Easter Sunday); **H~ Writ,** holy writings esp. the Bible; **hō'liness** *n.* (His Holiness, title of Pope). [E (WHOLE)]

**hō'lỹstōne** *n., & v.t.* (Scour with) soft sandstone used for cleaning deck. [perh. f. being used while kneeling]

**hŏ'mage** *n.* (In feudal law) formal acknowledgement of allegiance; (fig.) reverence, tribute, paid (*to* person, merit). [F f. L (*homo* man)]

**Hŏ'mbŭrg** *n.* Soft felt hat with curled brim and dented crown. [place]

**hōme** *n., a., adv., & v.* **1.** *n.* Dwelling-place; fixed residence (**long**, **last**, **~**, grave); native land; place where thing is native or most common; institution for persons needing care, rest, etc., (*children's*, NURSING, *home*); (in games) finishing point in race, match or win; **at ~**, in one's own house etc., at ease (*make yourself at home*), familiar, well--informed, (*in*, *on*, *with*, subject), available to callers (*at-ho'me* n., reception of visitors within certain hours); **~ from ~**, place where one feels at home; **near ~**, (fig.) affecting one closely. **2.** *a.* Of, connected with, home; carried on, done, or made, at home; in one's own country, not foreign; played on one's own ground etc. (*home match*, *win*); that affects one closely (*home question*, *truth*). **3.** *adv.* To or at one's home (*come*, *go*, *home*; *is he home yet?*; *\*stay home*) to the point aimed at or as far as possible (*the thrust went home*; DRIVE *a nail home*); **come ~ to**, become fully realized by; **come home to** ROOST; **~ and dry**, having achieved one's aim; **nothing to write ~ about**, (colloq.) unexciting, trivial. **4. ~-** **-coming**, arrival at home; ||H~ Counties, those nearest to London; **~ economics**, domestic science; ||**~ farm** (worked by owner of estate); **~-grown**, grown or produced at home; **H~ Guard**, (member of) British volunteer army organized for defence in 1940; ||*home* HELP; **~land**, native land; **~--made**, made at home; **~ movie**, film made at home or of one's own activities; ||**H~ Office**, department of **H~ Secretary** or Secretary of State for Home Affairs, concerned with immigration, law and order, etc.; **H~ Rule**, government of a country or region by its own citizens; **~ run**, baseball hit allowing batter to go round all bases; **~'sick**, depressed by absence from home; **~'sickness** n.; **~'spun** *a.* & *n.*, (cloth of yarn) spun at home, (anything) plain, homely, etc.; **~'stead**, house with outbuildings, farm; **~ town** (of one's original or present residence); **~'work**, work (to be) done at home, esp. by school pupil, (fig.) any necessary preparation (*do one's homework*) for discussion etc. **5.** *v.i.* & *t.* (Of pigeon etc.) make way home; **~ (in)**, (of vessel, missile, etc.) be guided to destination e.g. by auto-

matic **homing device**); **hŏ'mer** n., homing pigeon, *home run; **hŏ'mǐng** *a.*, (of pigeon) trained to fly home from a distance. **6. ~'lў** (-mlĭ) *a.* (-iness), plain, unpretentious, *ugly; **~'ward(s)** (-mwerdz) *a.* (-d) & *adv.*, going towards home (**homeward bound**, esp. of ship). [E]

**\*hŏ'mĕopăth.** See HOMOEOPATH.

**Homĕ'ric** (or hō-) *a.* Of, in the style of, Homer; on a very large scale; **~ laughter** (loud and long, as of Homer's gods at the sight of lame Hephaestus hobbling). [L f. Gk]

**hŏ'mĭcīde** n. Killing, killer, of human being; **hŏmǐcī'dal** *a.* [F f. L (*homo* man, *caedo* kill)]

**hŏ'mĭlў** n. Sermon esp. for spiritual edification; tedious discourse; **hŏmǐlĕ'tǐc** *a.*, of homilies; **hŏmǐlĕ'tǐcs** *n.pl.*, art of preaching. [F f. L f. Gk]

**hŏ'mĭnĭd** n. & *a.* (Member) of the mammal family of existing and fossil man; **hŏ'mĭnoid** n. & *a.*, manlike (animal). [L (*homo -minis* man)]

**hŏ'mĭnў** n. Ground maize boiled in water or milk. [Algonquian]

**Hŏ'mō**[1] n. (Zool.) (Genus including) man; **~ sapiens** (să'pǐĕnz [L, = wise]), modern man regarded as a species. [L]

**hŏ'mō**[2] n. (*pl.* **~s**) & *a.* (colloq.) Homosexual. [abbr.]

**hŏ'mō-** in comb. Same; **~graph**, word spelt like another, but of different meaning or origin; **~phone**, word having same sound as another, but of different meaning or origin (e.g. *pair*, *pear*). [Gk *homos* same]

**hŏmoeŏ'path|ў** (-mĭ-), *-mĕŏ'-**, n. Treatment of disease by drugs (usu. in minute doses) that in healthy persons would produce its symptoms; **hŏ'm(o)eopăth**, **~ĭst** (-mĭ-) *ns.*, one who practises homoeopathy; **hŏm(o)eopă'thĭc** (-mĭ-) *a.* (-ically). [Gk *homoios* like, PATHOS]

**hŏmogĕ'nĕous** *a.* Of the same kind; formed of parts all of the same kind, uniform; **hŏmogĕnē'ĭtў** n. [L (HOMO-, Gk *genos* kind)]

**homŏ'gĕnize** *v.t.* Make homogeneous; treat (milk) so that cream does not separate.

**homŏ'log|ous** *a.* Having same relation, relative position, etc.; corresponding; (Biol.) similar in structure but not necessarily in function; **~ĭze** *v.i.* & *t.*, be or make homologous; **hŏ'mŏlŏgue** (-g), *-lŏg, n., homologous thing; ~y̆ n., homologous state or relation. [L (HOMO-, Gk *logos* ratio)]

**hŏ'mon|y̆m** n. Word of same form as another but different sense (e.g. POLE¹, POLE²; cf. HOMOgraph, -*phone*); namesake; ~y̆'mĭc, homŏ'ny̆-mous, *adjs.* [L f. Gk (HOMO-, *onoma* name)]

**hŏmosĕ'xŭal** (*or* -kshoŏ-) *a.* & *n.* (Person) having sexual attraction to persons of same sex. [HOMO-]

**Hon.** *abbr.* Honorary; Hono(u)rable.

**hōne** n., & *v.t.* (Sharpen on) whetstone, esp. for razors. [E]

**hŏ'nĕst** (ŏ'-) *a.* Fair, righteous, in speech and act; not lying, cheating, or stealing; sincere; blameless but undistinguished; fairly earned (*turn, earn, an honest penny*), unadulterated, unsophisticated; (of woman) chaste, virtuous, (**make an ~ woman of**, marry after seducing); ~(**-to-God**), ~**-to-goodness**, ~ **Injun**, (colloq.) genuine(ly), real(ly); ~y̆ *n.*, uprightness, truthfulness, plant with purple flowers and translucent pods. [F f. L *honestus* (HONOUR)]

**ho'ney** (hŭ'-) *n.* Sweet sticky yellow fluid made by bees from nectar collected from flowers; colour of this; (fig.) sweetness, sweet thing, excellent thing or person; (esp. as *voc.*) sweetheart, darling; ~**-bee**, common hive-bee; ~**-buzzard**, bird of prey feeding on larvae of bees etc.; ~**comb**, (*n.*) bees' wax structure of hexagonal cells for honey and eggs, pattern hexagonally arranged, (*v.t.*) fill with cavities, mark with honeycomb pattern; ~**dew**, sweet substance excreted by aphids found on leaves etc., tobacco sweetened with molasses, ideally sweet substance, sweet green-fleshed type of musk-melon; ~**moon**, (*n.*) holiday of newly married couple, (fig.) initial period of enthusiasm, (*v.i.*) spend honeymoon (*in, at*, place); ~**suckle**, climbing shrub with fragrant yellow and pink flowers; ~**ed, honied**, (hŭ'nĭd) *a.* (lit. or fig.). [E]

**hŏnk. 1.** *n.* Wild-goose's cry; sound of (motor) horn. **2.** *v.i.* & *t.* (Cause to) emit or give honk. [imit.]

**hŏ'nky̆-tŏnk** *n.* (colloq.) Cheap night-club, dance-hall, etc.; ragtime music as played in these. [perh. imit. of music]

**\*honor(able).** See HONOUR(ABLE).

**hŏnorār'ĭ|um** (ŏ-) *n.* (*pl.* ~**ums**, ~**a**). (Voluntary) fee esp. for professional services. [L (HONORARY)]

**hŏ'norary** (ŏ'-) *a.* Conferred, appointed, by way of honour without usual requirements (*honorary degree, member*); unpaid (*honorary secretary, treasurer*, etc.); **hŏnorĭ'fic** (ŏ-) *a.* (-**ically**) & *n.*, (form of words) implying respect.

**honoris causa** (ŏnōrĭs kow'za) *adv.* As mark of esteem (esp. of honorary degree). [L, = for the sake of honour]

**hŏ'nour, \*hŏ'nor,** (ŏ'ner). **1.** *n.* High respect, reputation; nobleness of mind; allegiance to what is right or accepted standard of conduct (*code of honour; upon my honour*); (of woman) chastity, reputation for this; exalted position (**your, his, H~**, said to, of, judge etc.); privilege (**have the honour to do, of doing**); thing conferred as distinction (esp. official award for bravery or achievement); (in *pl.*) hospitality to guests etc. (**do the honours**), specialized degree-course or special distinction in examination, mark of respect esp. at funeral; person, thing, that does credit to another (*is an honour to his profession*); (Golf) right of driving off first; (Whist) ace, king, queen, and jack of trumps (in Bridge the ten also; ~**s even**, equality in contest); **in ~** (celebration) **of; in ~ bound, on** one's ~, under moral obligation (*to* do); AFFAIR, POINT, *of honour*; ~**s list** (of persons awarded honours). **2.** *v.t.* Respect highly; confer honour on; accept or pay (bill, cheque) when due. [F f. L *honor* repute]

**hŏ'nourable, \*hŏ'nor-,** (ŏ'ner-) *a.* (-**bly**). Deserving, bringing, or showing honour (*honourable* MENTION); title given to younger sons of Earls, children of Viscounts and Barons, Maids of Honour, Justices of High Court, Lords of Session, Members of Parliament by one another, \*members of Congress, \*cabinet ministers, \*judges, etc.; ‖**Most H~** (title of Marquises etc.); ‖**Right H~** (title of Earls, Viscounts, Barons, Privy Councillors, Lords (Justices) of Appeal, some Lord Mayors and Lord Provosts). [F f. L (prec.)]

**\*hōōch** *n.* (colloq.) Crude alcoholic liquor. [Alaskan]

**hŏōd¹. 1.** *n.* Covering for head and

neck, often part of cloak etc.; garment worn over university gown to show degree; hood-shaped thing; *bonnet of motor car; ||collapsible top of motor car, pram, etc. 2. *v.t.* Cover, furnish, with hood; ~'wink *v.t.*, deceive, delude. [E]

**hood²** (or hŏŏd) *n.* (sl.) Gangster, gunman. [abbr. HOODLUM]

**-hood** *suf.* forming *ns.* of condition, quality, or grouping f. *ns.* & *adjs.* (*childhood, falsehood, sisterhood*). [E]

**hoo'dlum** *n.* Street hooligan, young thug. [orig. unkn.]

*hŏŏ'dŏŏ. 1. *n.* (Bringer of) bad luck, malignant spell. 2. *v.t.* Make unlucky. [var. VOODOO]

**hoo'ey** *n.* & *int.* (sl.) Nonsense. [orig. unkn.]

**hoo|f.** 1. *n.* (*pl.* ~fs, ~ves *pr.* -vz). Horny casing of foot of horse etc.; (joc.) human foot. 2. *v.t.* & *i.* Strike with hoof; (sl.) kick (person *out* etc.); (sl.) walk, dance. [E]

**hoo'-ha** (-ah) *n.* (colloq.) Uproar, trouble. [orig. unkn.]

**hŏŏk. 1.** *n.* Bent piece of wire etc. for catching hold or for hanging things on (fish-~, usu. barbed, for catching fish; ~ **and eye**, small metal hook and loop as dress--fastener); hooking stroke, short swinging blow in boxing; curved cutting instrument (*reaping-hook*); sharp bend in river etc.; (Mus.) cross-stroke in tail of quaver etc.; **by ~ or by crook**, by one device or another; ~, **line, and sinker**, (fig.) entire(ly); ~-**nose**(d), (with) aquiline nose; ~'worm, (disease caused by) kind of worm infesting men and animals; **off the ~**, no longer in difficulty, (of telephone receiver) not on its rest; ~ed (-kt) *a.*, (esp.) hook-shaped (*hooked nose*). 2. *v.t.* & *i.* Grasp, secure, with hook(s) (~ **on, in, up**, etc., attach or be attached (as) by hook; **be ~ed on**, sl., be addicted to or captivated by); catch (fish or fig. husband etc.) with hook; (sl.) steal; (Golf) pull (ball) slightly; (Cricket) drive to on side with upward stroke; (Rugby Footb.) secure and pass (ball) backward with foot in scrum (~'er¹ *n.*, player in front row who tries to do this); ~ **it**, (sl.) make off; ~-**up**, connection, esp. interconnection in broadcast transmission. [E]

**hoo'kah** (-ka) *n.* Tobacco-pipe with long tube, drawing smoke through vase of water. [Urdu f. Arab., = casket]

**hoo'ker¹** *n.* See HOOK 2.

**hoo'ker²** *n.* Kind of small Dutch or Irish sailing-ship (**the old ~**, said scornfully or fondly of any ship). [Du. *hoeker* (HOOK)]

*hoo'key *n.* **Play ~**, (sl.) play truant. [orig. unkn.]

**hoo'ligan** *n.* Young thug; member of a street gang. [orig. uncert.]

**hoop. 1.** *n.* Band of metal for binding cask etc.; wooden etc. circle trundled by child; iron arch used in croquet; circle of flexible material expanding woman's skirt etc.; large ring (with paper stretched over it) through which circus performer jumps (**go through the ~**(s), undergo ordeal); ~-**la**, game in which rings are thrown to capture prizes, (sl.) commotion, nonsense. 2. *v.t.* Bind, surround, with hoop. [E]

**hoo'poe** (-ōō) *n.* Bird with variegated plumage and large erectile crest. [F f. L *upupa* (imit.)]

**hooray'.** See HURRAH.

**hoot. 1.** *v.i.* & *t.* Make loud sounds, esp. of derision or (colloq.) merriment (often *at*); greet (person) thus; (of owl) utter cry; (of steam whistle, car horn, etc.) sound, cause (car horn etc.) to sound. 2. *n.* Inarticulate shout esp. of derision; (colloq.) (cause of) laughter; owl's cry; sound of horn, hooter, etc.; *do not care, does not matter*, etc., **a ~** or two **~s**, (sl.) at all; ~'er *n.*, (esp.) ||siren, steam-whistle, esp. as signal for start or end of work, ||car horn, (sl.) nose. [imit.]

**Hŏŏ'ver. 1.** *n.* Vacuum cleaner (prop. as made by Hoover company). 2. *v.t.* (colloq.) Clean (carpet etc.) with Hoover. [P]

**hooves.** See HOOF.

**hŏp¹. 1.** *n.* Climbing plant cultivated for its bitter cones used to flavour beer etc.; (in *pl.*) these cones. 2. *v.t.* & *i.* (-pp-). Flavour with hops; produce or pick hops. 3. ~-**bind, -bine**, climbing stem of hop; ~--**picker**, labourer or machine used to pick hops; ~-**pillow** (stuffed with hops, to induce sleep); ~'**sack**(**ing**), coarse sack, fabric, etc. [LDu.]

**hŏp². 1.** *v.i.* & *t.* (-pp-). Spring, (of person) on one foot, (of bird, frog, etc.) with all feet at once; (colloq.) quickly change position etc. (~ **in,**

**out,** get into, out of, car); **hop over** (ditch etc.); ~ **it,** (sl.) go away; ~**ping mad,** (colloq.) very angry; ~'**scotch,** child's game of pushing stone, with one foot while hopping, over marked lines [SCOTCH²]. **2.** *n.* (Action of) hopping (**on the** ~, colloq., bustling about, or unprepared); (colloq.) dance; distance travelled by air without landing; stage of flight or journey; ~, **skip** or **step, and jump,** athletic exercise or contest requiring these three movements in sequence. [E]

**hōpe. 1.** *n.* (in *sing.* or *pl.*) Expectation and desire (*of* thing, *of* do*ing, that*); trust (SET¹ one's *hopes on*); ground of hope, probability; person or thing that encourages hope; what is hoped for; **not a** ~, (iron.) **some** ~(**s**)!, (colloq.) no chance at all; ~'**ful** (-pf-) *a.*, ~'**lly,** often = *it is hoped that*), feeling hope, promising; ~'**lèss** (-pl-) *a.*, feeling, admitting, no hope (~**less case,** person in bad situation), inadequate, incompetent. **2.** *v.t.* & *i.* Expect and desire (thing, *that, to* do); feel hope (*for* thing); ~ **against** ~, cling to slight chance. [E]

**hŏ'pper¹** *n.* One who hops; hopping insect esp. flea or young locust; device for feeding grain into mill or other similar contrivance. [HOP²]

**hŏ'pper²** *n.* Hop-picker. [HOP¹]

**hŏrde** *n.* Troop of Tartar or other nomads; gang, troop. [Pol. f. Turk.]

**hŏr'ehound** (hŏr'h–) *n.* Herb with bitter aromatic juice used against coughs etc. [E, = hoary herb]

**hori'zon** *n.* Line at which earth and sky appear to meet (**artificial** ~, gyroscopic device showing position of aircraft relative to horizon plane); (fig.) boundary of mental outlook (**on the** ~, becoming apparent). [F f. L f. Gk (*horizō* bound)]

**hŏrĭzŏ'ntal. 1.** *a.* (~**ly**). Parallel to plane of horizon, at right angles to the vertical; involving firms, social groups, etc., concerned with similar work, of similar status, etc.; ~**ĭtŷ** (-ă'l-) *n.* **2.** *n.* Horizontal line, bar, etc.

**hŏr'm|ōne** *n.* Substance internally secreted that passes into the blood or sap and stimulates organs, growth, etc.; similar synthetic substance; ~**ō'nal** *a.* [Gk (*hormaō* impel)]

**hŏrn. 1.** *n.* Non-deciduous outgrowth, often curved and pointed, from head of animal; each of two deciduous branched appendages on head of (esp. male) deer; substance of horns; hornlike projection on other animals, as snail's tentacle, insect's antenna, (**draw in** one's ~**s,** check one's ardour, draw back); receptacle, instrument, made of horn (SHOE*horn*; ~ **of plenty,** cornucopia); wind instrument, orig. made of horn, now usu. brass, (**English** ~, cor anglais; **French** ~, instrument with coiled tube, valves, and wide bell); instrument giving warning (*car horn*; FOG¹-*horn*); horn-shaped projection; extremity of moon or other crescent, arm of river etc.; either alternative of a dilemma; **the H**~, Cape Horn; ~'**beam,** a tree with hard wood; ~'**bill,** bird with hornlike excrescence on bill; ~'**blende,** dark-brown etc. mineral, constituent of granite etc.; ~'**pipe,** lively dance esp. associated with sailors; ~-**rimmed,** (esp. of spectacles) having rims made of horn or similar material; ~**ed** (-nd) *a.* (~**ed owl,** with hornlike feathers on head); ~'**ÿ** *a.* (~**iness**), of or like horn, hard as horn, (sl.) lecherous. **2.** *v.t.* & *i.* Furnish with horns; ~ **in,** (sl.) intrude. [E]

**hŏr'nèt** *n.* Large kind of wasp (**bring a** ~**s'** nest about one's ears, stir up many enemies). [LDu.]

**hŏrŏ'logÿ** *n.* Clock-making; (study of) measurement of time; **hŏrŏlŏ'gĭcal** *a.* [F f. L f. Gk (*hōra* time)]

**hŏ'roscōpe** *n.* (Astrol.) Observation of, diagram showing, disposition of planets etc. at certain moment esp. at person's birth (**cast a** ~, make such a diagram etc.); prediction of person's future based on this. [F f. L f. Gk (*hōra* time, *skopos* observer)]

**horrè'ndous** *a.* (colloq.) Horrifying. [L (foll.)]

**hŏ'rrĭble** *a.* (-**bly**). Exciting horror; hideous, shocking; (colloq.) excessive, unpleasant, (*horrible noise, weather*); **hŏ'rrĭd** *a.*, terrible, frightful, (colloq.) disagreeable (*how perfectly horrid of you!*; *horrid weather*); **horrĭ'fĭc** *a.* (-**ically**), horrifying; **hŏ'rrĭfÿ** *v.t.*, shock, excite horror. [F f. L (*horreo* bristle, shudder at)]

**hŏ'rror. 1.** *n.* Painful feeling of loathing and fear; terrified shuddering; intense dislike (*of*); horrifying thing or person (**Chamber of H~s**, place full of horrors, orig. room of criminals etc. in Tussaud's waxworks); **~s!** (excl. of dismay); **the ~s**, fit of depression etc. esp. as in delirium tremens; **~stricken, -struck,** shocked. **2. *a.*** (Of literature, film, etc.) arousing feelings of horror; **~ comic,** paper like comic but describing much violence etc.

**hors** (ōr) *adv. & prep.* **~ *concours*** (-kawṅkoor'), not competing for prize, unrivalled; **~ *de combat*** (-dekaw'ṅbah), out of the fight, disabled; **~d'œuvre** (ōrdĕr'vr, -v), extra dish served usu. before meal as appetizer. [F, = outside]

**horse. 1.** *n.* Solid-hoofed quadruped with long mane and tail, ridden and used as beast of burden and draught; (esp.) adult male horse, stallion; wooden etc. likeness of horse (ROCK²*ing-horse*); (collect. *sing.*) cavalry (LIGHT² *horse*); similar animal (SEA-*horse*); gymnastic vaulting-block; supporting frame (*clothes-horse*); *put the* CART *before the horse*; **look a gift-~ in the mouth,** criticize gift; **on one's high ~,** haughty; **hold your ~s!,** (colloq.) wait, don't be hasty; *eat, work,* **like a ~,** with great vigour; **(straight) from the ~'s mouth,** (of news etc.) directly from person involved or authoritative source; **wooden ~** (by use of which Troy was taken); **on ~'back,** mounted on horse; **~box,** closed vehicle for transporting horse(s); **~chestnut,** (coarse bitter fruit of) tree with conical clusters of white or pink flowers; *horse*-COLLAR; **~coper,** dealer in horses [*cope* buy f. LDu.]; **~doctor,** veterinary surgeon attending horses; **~'flesh,** flesh of horse as food, horses collectively; **~fly,** insect (of various kinds) molesting horses; **‖H~ Guards,** cavalry brigade of household troops; **~'hair** (from mane or tail of horse); **~laugh,** loud coarse laugh; **~'man,** (skilled) rider on horseback; **~'manship,** skill in riding; *tell that to the* **horse** MARINES; **~'play,** boisterous play; **~'power,** unit of rate of doing work, about 750 watts; **~race,** (between horses with riders); **~racing,** holding of horse-races as sport; **~radish,** plant with pungent root often made into sauce; **~ sense,** (colloq.) plain common sense;

**~'shoe** (-s-sh-), iron shoe for horse, C-shaped thing; **~tail,** tail of horse, plant resembling it; **\*~trading,** dealing in horses, (fig.) shrewd bargaining; **~'whip,** (*n.*) whip for horse, (*v.t.*; -pp-) chastise person with this; **~'woman,** woman who rides horse; **hŏr'sў** *a.,* of or like horse, concerned with (race)horses, dressed or speaking like such person. **2.** *v.i.* (colloq.) Fool *around*. [E]

**hŏr'tat|ĭve, ~|orў,** *adjs.* Serving to exhort. [L (*hortor* exhort)]

**hŏr'tĭcŭlture** *n.* (Art of) cultivation of plants esp. in gardens; **hŏrtĭcŭ'ltural** (-cher-) *a.* (-lly); **hŏrtĭcŭ'lturĭst** (-cher-) *n.* [L *hortus* garden, CULTURE]

**Hos.** *abbr.* Hosea (O.T.).

**hōsă'nna** (-z-) *n.* Shout of adoration. [L f. Gk f. Heb.]

**hōse** (-z). **1.** *n.* Stockings collectively (**half-~,** socks); (Hist.) breeches (DOUBLET *and hose*); **~(-pipe),** flexible tube conveying water for watering plants, putting out fires, etc. **2.** *v.t.* Drench or water with hose. **3. hō'sier** (-zher) *n.,* dealer in hose etc.; **hō'sierў** (-zherĭ) *n.,* such goods. [E]

**hŏ'spice** *n.* Travellers' house of rest kept by religious order etc.; home for the destitute or sick. [F f. L (HOST²)]

**hŏ'spĭtab|le** *a.* (**~ly**). Giving, disposed to give, hospitality. [F, f. L *hospito* entertain (HOST²)]

**hŏ'spĭtal** *n.* Institution providing medical and surgical treatment for persons ill or injured; (Hist.) establishment of Knights Hospitallers; hospice; charitable institution; **~ ship, train,** (used to convey wounded soldiers); **~ize** *v.t.,* send to, treat in, hospital; **~izā'tion** *n.* [F f. L *hospitalis* (HOST²)]

**hŏspĭtă'lĭtў** *n.* Friendly and generous reception of guests or strangers or (fig.) of new ideas etc.

**hŏ'spĭtaller, \*-aler,** *n.* Member of charitable religious order (**Knight H~,** member of order of military monks founded *c.* 1048).

**hōst¹** *n.* Large number (*of*; *person is a ~ in himself*, equal to a large number of ordinary persons in ability, effect, etc.); (arch.) army (*Lord God of hosts*); **~(s) of heaven,** sun, moon, and stars, the angels. [F f. L *hostis* enemy, army]

**hŏst²**. **1.** *n.* One who receives or entertains another as guest; landlord of inn (**reckon without one's ~**, overlook opposition etc.); animal or plant having parasite, animal with transplanted organ etc.; **~′èss** *n.*, woman host (esp. employed in night-club etc.); AIR *hostess.* **2.** *v.t.* Act as host to (person) or at (event). [F f. L *hospes -pitis* host, guest]

**hŏst³** *n.* Bread consecrated in the Eucharist. [F f. L *hostia* victim]

**hŏ′stage** *n.* Person, thing, given or seized as pledge (**~ to fortune**, person, thing, one may suffer by losing). [F f. L *obses obsidis* hostage]

‖**hŏ′stel** *n.* House of residence for students or other special class (YOUTH *hostel*); (arch.; *or* **~rў**) inn. [F f. L (HOSPITAL)]

**hŏ′stile** *a.* Of an enemy, unfriendly; **hŏstī′lĭtў** *n.*, enmity, state or (in *pl.*) acts of warfare, opposition (in thought etc.). [F or L (HOST¹)]

**hostler.** See OSTLER.

**hŏt** *a.* & *v.*, (**-tt-**). **1.** *a.* Of or at high temperature, very warm (RED, WHITE, *-hot*); (of food etc.) heated and served without cooling; (of person) feeling heat; causing sensation of heat (*hot fever*); (of pepper, spices, etc.) pungent; having intense feeling, angry or upset; ardent, eager (*in hot pursuit*), excited, passionate; (of scent in hunting) strong; (of news etc.) fresh, recent; (of competitor, performer, feat) skilful, formidable (*a hot favourite*; **not so ~**, mediocre); (of music) rhythmical and emotional; (sl.) (of goods) stolen, esp. if difficult to dispose of, (dangerously) radioactive; **blow ~ and cold**, vacillate; **give it him ~**, (colloq.) chastise him severely; **~ and bothered**, agitated; **~ and cold** (of water supply); **go ~ and cold**, feel flushes of hot and cold due to fear etc.; **~ and strong**, vehement(ly); **make it** etc. (**too**) **~ for him**, persecute him; **~ under the collar**, angry, resentful, embarrassed. **2. ~ air**, (sl.) boastful or excited talk; **~′bed**, bed of earth heated by fermenting manure, (fig.) place favourable to growth (*of vice* etc.); **~-blooded**, ardent, passionate; *sell* etc. **like ~ cakes**, very rapidly; **~ cross bun** (marked with cross and eaten on Good Friday); **~ dog**, (colloq.) hot sausage sandwiched in roll of bread; *hot* FLUSH²;

**~′foot**, in eager haste; *hot* GOS-PELLER; **~′head(ed)**, impetuous (person); **~′house**, heated building usu. largely of glass for growing plants out of season etc.; **~ line**, direct communications link between distant places (for urgent messages); **~ money**, capital frequently transferred; **~′plate**, heated metal plate for cooking food or keeping it hot; **~′pot**, lamb etc. with vegetables cooked in oven in tight-lidded pot; *hot* POTATO; **~ rod**, motor vehicle modified to have extra power and speed; **~ seat**, (sl.) electric chair, awkward or responsible position; **~ spot**, place or area that is hot, (fig.) place with political etc. unrest; **~ stuff**, (sl.) person of high vigour, skill, or passions; **~ war** (with active hostilities); **~ water**, (colloq., fig.) disgrace, trouble, (*get into hot water*); **~-wa′ter bottle**, *****bag**, container filled with hot water used to warm bed etc. **3.** *v.t.* & *i.* ‖(colloq.) Warm *up*, make hot; become hot or (fig.) dangerous etc. [E]

**hŏ′tchpŏtch, hŏ′dgepŏdge** (-jp-), *n.* (Confused) mixture, medley; broth or stew of mixed vegetables etc. [F *hochepot* shake pot]

**hōtĕ′l** (*or* ō-) *n.* (Large) house or inn where food and accommodation are available to paying travellers; (Austral. & N.Z.) public house; **~ier** *n.*, hotel-keeper. [F (HOSTEL)]

**Hŏ′ttentŏt** *a.* & *n.* (Member or language) of pastoral Negroid people once occupying area of S. Africa near Cape. [Du.]

‖**hough** (hŏk). **1.** *n.* = HOCK¹. **2.** *v.t.* Hamstring. [E]

**hound. 1.** *n.* Dog for hunting, esp. one tracking by scent ‖in pack of foxhounds (*follow the hounds*); despicable man; runner following scent in paper-chase; dogfish; **~′s-tongue**, tall flower of borage family. **2.** *v.t.* Chase (as) with hound; set (hound, or fig. person) *at* (quarry etc.); urge (person) *on.* [E]

**hour** (owr) *n.* Period of 60 minutes, twenty-fourth part of day and night (*1700 ~s* etc., time of 17 etc. hours after midnight); **the ~**, the time o'clock, time of whole number of hours, (*what is the hour?*; *at half past the hour*; *the* ELEVENTH *hour*); (in *pl.*) fixed time for use of building, factory, etc., (*office hours, opening hours of* *museum, are* from 9 to 5; **after** ∼**s,** after closing time esp. of public house); short, indefinite period of time (*an idle hour*); *the* present time (*question of the hour*); time for action etc. (*the hour has come*); (prayers said at) one of (7 fixed) times of day in R.C. Church (*book of hours*); distance traversed in an hour (*we are an hour from Bath*); astron. measurement (15°) of longitude; **till all** ∼**s,** till very late; **small** ∼**s,** 1, 2, etc., a.m.; *regular* etc. ∼**s** (time for getting up or going to bed); ∼′**glass,** sandglass running for an hour; ∼**-hand** (showing hour on watch or clock); ∼**-long** *a. & adv.,* (lasting) for one hour; ∼′**lỹ** *a. & adv.,* (done etc.) every hour, frequent(ly). [F f. L f. Gk *hōra*]

**houri** (hoor′ĭ) *n.* Beautiful young girl or woman (in Muslim Paradise). [F f. Pers. f. Arab.]

**house. 1.** *n.* (*pl. pr.* -zĭz). Building for human habitation or occupation (∼ **of God,** church); inn, place of public refreshment etc., (*a drink on the* ∼, at innkeeper's expense; **disorderly** ∼, gaming-house, brothel); building for keeping animals or goods (*hen-house,* STORE*house,* WARE*house*); (place of residence incl. members of) religious order, university college, section of boarding--school incl.; division of day-school for games etc.; (building used by) legislative etc. assembly (Low²*er,* UPPER, *House;* House *of* COMMONS, LORDS, REPRESENTATIVE*s*); (place of business of) firm or institution (CLEAR*ing--house*); audience or performance in theatre etc. (FULL¹ *house; second house starts at* 9); household, family, dynasty (**the** H∼ **of** Windsor, British Royal Family); ‖(Army sl. etc.) gambling form of lotto (also *housey-housey*); ∼′**ful** (-sŏŏl) *n.* **2.** ∼ **of cards** (of playing cards as built by child; fig., insecure scheme etc.); ∼ **of ill fame,** (arch.) brothel; H∼ **of Keys,** elective branch of Manx legislature; ∼ **and home,** (emphat.) home; ∼**-to-**∼, at each house in turn; **keep** ∼, provide for a household; **keep open** ∼, provide general hospitality; **keep** (**to**) **the** ∼, = KEEP *indoors*; **like a** ∼ **on fire,** vigorously; **put, set,** one's ∼ **in order,** (fig.) introduce needed reforms; **as safe as** ∼**s,** perfectly safe; **set up** ∼, (esp. of married couple) begin to live in

separate dwelling. **3.** ‖∼**-agent** (for sale and letting of houses); ∼ **arrest,** detention in one's own house; ∼′**boat,** boat fitted up for living in; ∼**-bound,** unable to leave one's house through illness etc.; ∼′**-breaker,** ‖demolisher of old houses, burglar (esp. in daytime); so ∼′**-breaking** *n.;* ∼′**broken,** house--trained; ∼′**coat,** woman's usu. long garment for housework etc.; ∼**-dog** (kept to guard house); ∼**-flag** (flown by a firm's ship); ∼**-fly** (frequenting houses); ∼ **guest,** guest staying for some days in person's house; ∼**-hunting,** seeking house to live in; ∼′**keeper,** woman managing affairs of household, person in charge of house, etc., (∼′*keep* v., colloq.); ∼′**keeping,** management of household affairs, money allowed for this; ∼′**leek,** pink-flowered plant on walls and roofs; ∼ **magazine** (concerned with firm's activities); ∼′**maid,** female servant in house (∼*maid's knee,* inflammation of knee--cap); ∼′**man,** = ‖house officer; *house-*MARTIN; ∼′**master,** ∼′**mistress,** (of school boarding--house); *house* MOUSE; ∼ **officer, physician, surgeon,** resident doctor at hospital etc.; ∼**-parents** (also ∼**-father,** ∼**-mother**), persons in charge of house, esp. home for children; ∼ **party,** (of guests staying at country house etc.); ∼**-plant** (grown indoors); ∼**-proud,** (unduly) preoccupied with care and beauty of the home; ∼**-room,** space in house (*would not give it* ∼*-room,* would not take it even as a gift); ∼**-top,** roof of house (*proclaim from the* ∼*-tops,* announce publicly); ‖∼**-trained,** (of domestic animals) trained to be clean in the house, (colloq.) well-mannered; ∼**-warming,** celebration of move to new home; ∼′**work,** cleaning, cooking, etc. **4.** (-z) *v.t.* Receive (person etc.), store (goods), in house or as house does; provide houses for (families etc. in need); fix in socket, mortise, etc. [E]

**hou′sehold** (-s-h-) *n.* Occupants of house; domestic establishment; ∼ **gods,** (fig.) essentials of home life; ∼ **management,** art of managing domestic affairs; ‖∼ **troops** (employed to guard Sovereign); ∼ **word,** familiar saying or name; ∼**er** *n.,* one who occupies house as his own dwelling, head of household. [HOUSE, HOLD[1]]

**housewife** n. **1.** (how′swĭf). (Usu. married) woman supervising household; (good, bad) domestic manager; ∼lў (-swĭflĭ) a.; ∼rў (-swĭfrĭ) n. **2.** (hŭ′zĭf). Case for needles, thread, etc. [HOUSE, WIFE]

**hou′sĭng**[1] (-z-) n. Horse's cloth covering. [F f. Gmc]

**hou′sĭng**[2] (-z-) n. (Provision of) houses collectively; shelter; casing for part of machine etc.; ∼ **estate**, residential district planned as a unit. [HOUSE]

**hōve.** See HEAVE.

**hŏ′vel** n. Shed, outhouse; miserable dwelling. [orig. unkn.]

**hŏ′ver. 1.** v.i. (Of bird, helicopter, etc.) hang in the air (over, about, a spot); linger (about, around, person or place); remain undecided between alternatives. **2.** n. Hovering, state of suspense. **3.** ∼**craft**, ∼**train**, (moving on air-cushion over surface of sea or land).

**how. 1.** adv. In what way, by what means, (how does he do it?; show me how to do it; how does it differ?; how do plants grow?; how could you tell?); in what condition esp. of health (how are you?; how do you do?, also as formal greeting; how do things stand now?; how GO[1]es it?); to what extent (how far is it?; how far it is!; how would you like to go?; how he snores!); in whatever way, as, (do it how you can); (colloq.) = that (told us how the man ran away). **2.** n. The way a thing is done (the how of it). **3.** and ∼!, (sl.) very much so; ∼ **about**, = WHAT about; ∼**beit** (-bē′ĭt), (arch.) nevertheless; ∼**-do-you-do**, embarrassing situation; ∼e′**ver**, in whatever way, to whatever extent, nevertheless, = how EVER; ∼ **much?**, what amount, what price, (how much will the box hold, do I owe you?; how much is it?), (joc.) what? (asking for repetition); how so[1]?; ∼'**s that?**, how do you regard or explain that?, (Crick. to umpire) is batsman out or not?; ∼**soe′ver**, in whatsoever way, to whatsoever extent. [E]

**how′dah** (-a-) n. Seat usu. with canopy on elephant's back. [Urdu f. Arab.]

***how′dў** int. = HOW do you do? [corrupt.]

**how′itzer** (-ts-) n. Short gun for

high-angle firing of shells. [Du. f. G f. Czech]

**howl. 1.** v.i. & t. (Of animal) utter long loud doleful cry; (of person, esp. child) utter long cry of pain, derision, glee, etc. (a ∼**ing shame** etc., sl., great); (of wind etc.) make prolonged wailing noise; utter (words) thus; ∼ **down**, reduce to silence by howls of derision. **2.** n. Such cry; howling noise in loudspeaker; ∼'**er** n., a S. Amer. monkey, (sl.) glaring blunder. [imit.]

**hoy**[1] n. (Hist.) Small vessel usu. rigged as sloop and going short distance. [Du. hoei]

**hoy**[2] int. used to call attention, drive animals, or (Naut.) to hail or call aloft. [cf. AHOY]

**hoy′den** n. Boisterous girl. [Du. heiden (HEATHEN)]

**h.p.** abbr. high pressure; hire-purchase; horsepower.

**H.Q.** abbr. headquarters.

**H.R.H.** abbr. Her or His Royal Highness.

**hr(s).** abbr. hour(s).

**H.T.** abbr. high tension.

**hŭb** n. Central part of wheel, from which spokes radiate; (fig.) central point of interest etc. (hub of the universe). [orig. uncert.]

**hŭ′bble-bŭbble** n. Simple form of hookah; bubbling sound; confused talk. [imit.]

**hŭ′bbŭb** n. Confused din; disturbance, riot. [perh. of Ir. orig.]

**hŭ′bbў** n. (colloq.) Husband. [abbr.]

**hŭ′br∣ĭs** n. Insolent pride or presumption; ∼**i′stĭc** a. [Gk]

**hŭ′ckabăck** n. Rough linen or cotton fabric for towels etc. [orig. unkn.]

**hŭ′ckleberrў** (-kĕlb-) n. (Blue or black fruit of) shrub common in N. Amer. [prob. f. hurtleberry, WHORTLE-BERRY]

**hŭ′ckster. 1.** n. Hawker; mercenary person. **2.** v.i. & t. Haggle; be hawker; adulterate. [prob. LG]

**hŭ′ddle. 1.** v.t. & i. Heap, crowd (things etc.) promiscuously, nestle closely, (together etc.); ∼ oneself up, into small compass); put (clothes) on hurriedly. **2.** n. Confused heap etc.; confusion; (sl.) (secret) conference, esp. go into a ∼ (with). [perh. LG]

**hūe**[1] n. Colour, tint; variety of colour caused by admixture of another. [E]

**hŭe**[2] *n.* ~ **and cry**, clamour for pursuit of wrongdoer, outcry (*against*). [F (*huer* shout)]

**hŭff. 1.** *v.t.* & *i.* Bully; offend; take offence; (Draughts) remove (opponent's man) as forfeit; puff out air, (fig.) bluster (*huffing and puffing*). **2.** *n.* Fit of petulance (*in a huff*); (Draughts) huffing; **~·y** *a.* (**-ily, -iness**), offended, apt to take offence. [imit. of blowing]

**hŭg. 1.** *v.t.* (**-gg-**). Squeeze in one's arms, esp. with affection; (of bear) squeeze between forelegs; keep close to (kerb, shore, etc.); congratulate (one*self on, for*). **2.** *n.* Strong clasp with arms; wrestling grip. [prob. Scand.]

**hūge** *a.* (Of object etc.) very large of its kind (*huge fish, tree, mountain*); (of abstract thing) very great (*huge difference*); **~·ly** (-jlĭ) *adv.*, very much (*hugely amused*). [F *ahuge*]

**hŭ'gger-mŭgger** (-g-) *n., a.,* & *adv.* **1.** *n.* Secrecy; confusion. **2.** *a.* & *adv.* Secret(ly); confused(ly). [orig. uncert.]

**Hŭ'guenŏt** (-ge-; *or* -nō) *n.* (Hist.) French Protestant. [F]

**hŭh** (hŭ) *int.* expr. inquiry, contempt, etc. [imit.]

**hu'la** (hōō'-) *n.,* & *v.i.* ~(-~), (perform) orig. Hawaiian woman's dance; ~ **hoop**, large hoop for spinning round the body. [Hawaiian]

**hŭlk** *n.* Body of dismantled ship, esp. (in *pl.*, Hist.) as prison; unwieldy vessel; (fig.) big person or mass; **~'ing** *a.*, (colloq.) bulky, clumsy. [E]

**hŭll**[1]**. 1.** *n.* Outer covering, pod, of grain, beans, etc. **2.** *v.t.* Remove hull of. [E]

**hŭll**[2] *n.* Body of ship etc.; ~ **down**, (of ship) at such distance that masts are, but hull is not, visible. [perh. rel. to HOLD[2]]

**hŭllabalōō'** *n.* Uproar, clamour. [redupl. *hallo, hullo,* etc.]

**hŭllō'** = HALLO, HELLO.

**hŭm** *v., n.,* & *int.* **1.** *v.i.* & *t.* (**-mm-**). Murmur continuously like bee or top; make low inarticulate sound, esp., usu. ~ **and ha(w)**, of hesitation; sing (tune etc.) with closed lips; (colloq.) proceed briskly (*make things hum*); ‖(sl.) smell unpleasantly. **2.** *n.* Humming sound; sound of surprise etc.; ‖(sl.) bad smell. **3.** *int.* expr. dissent, doubt, etc. **4.** **~'ming-bird** (of kind whose

wings hum); **~'ming-top** (spinning with a hum). [imit.]

**hū'man. 1.** *a.* (**~ness** *pr.* -n-n-). Of or belonging to man (*human* NATURE; *human affairs*); of man as opp. to animals (*human being, race*) or in relation to God (*human creature*; *to err is human, to forgive divine*); showing (esp. the better) qualities of man (*a very human person*); of man as opp. to machines etc. (*the human element*); ~ **interest**, (story) involving personal emotions; ~ **relations** (between people as individuals); ~ **rights** (held to belong to all persons); **~·lў** *adv.*, (esp.) within human capabilities (*I will do it if it is humanly possible*), from the human point of view (*humanly speaking*). **2.** *n.* Human being. [F f. L *humanus*]

**hūmā'ne** *a.* Benevolent, compassionate; inflicting least possible pain (~ **killer**, instrument for painless slaughter of animals); (of studies esp. history, literature) tending to civilize, elegant.

**hū'man|ism** *n.* Devotion to human interests; system of thought concerned with human (not religious etc.) matters; literary culture, esp. in Renaissance; doctrine emphasizing common human needs and seeking solely rational ways of solving human problems; **~ist** *n.*

**hūmănĭtār'ian. 1.** *n.* One who promotes or practises humane actions, philanthropist; one who promotes human welfare. **2.** *a.* Of, holding, the views of humanitarians; **~ism** *n.*

**hūmā'nĭtў** *n.* Human nature or (in *pl.*) qualities; the human race; humaneness; (in *pl.*) learning or literature concerned with human culture, esp. Gk and L classics. [F f. L (HUMAN)]

**hū'maniz|e** *v.t.* Make human or humane; **~ā'tion** *n.* [F (HUMAN)]

**hŭ'mble. 1.** *a.* (**~r, ~st, -bly**). Having or showing low estimate of one's own importance (*humble apologies, opinion; your humble* SERVANT); lowly, modest, (thing) of small dimensions; **eat ~ pie**, submit to humiliation. **2.** *v.t.* Make humble, abase (one*self* etc.). [F f. L *humilis* (HUMUS)]

**hŭ'mble-bee** *n.* Bumble-bee. [LDu. *hummel*]

**hŭ'mbŭg. 1.** *n.* Sham, deception; nonsense; impostor; ‖kind of hard boiled peppermint sweet. **2.** *v.t. & i.* (-gg-.) Delude (person; *into, out of*); act like a humbug. [orig. unkn.]

**hŭ'mdĭnger** *n.* (sl.) Exceptionally good person or thing.

**hŭ'mdrŭm** *a.* Dull, commonplace, monotonous. [HUM]

**hŭ'mer|ŭs** *n.* Bone of upper arm; **~al** *a.* [L, = shoulder]

**hū'mĭd** *a.* Damp, moist; **hūmĭ'dĭfy̆** *v.t.*; **hūmĭ'dĭty̆** *n.*, humid state, degree of moisture esp. in atmosphere. [F, or L *humidus*]

**hūmĭ'lĭ|āte** *v.t.* Humble, abase; mortify; **~ā'tion** *n.* [L (HUMBLE)]

**hūmĭ'lĭty̆** *n.* Humbleness, meekness. [F (prec.)]

**hŭ'mmock** *n.* Hillock. [orig. unkn.]

‖**hū'mour, *hū'mor,** (-er) **1.** *n.* State of mind, mood, inclination, (**good, ill, ~,** temper; **out of ~,** displeased; **in the ~ for,** inclined to); comicality, facetiousness, (**sense of ~,** faculty of perceiving this and enjoying the ridiculous); (**cardinal**) **~,** (Hist.) one of 4 fluids of the body (blood, phlegm, choler, melancholy), held to determine physical and mental qualities of person (so **hū'moral** *a.*); transparent fluid part of eye (**aqueous, vitreous, ~,** before, behind, lens). **2.** *v.t.* Gratify, indulge, (person, mood, taste, etc.). **3.** **hū'morist** *n.*, facetious talker, writer, etc.; **hū'morous** *a.*, full of humour, comic; **hū'moursome** *a.*, capricious, peevish. [F f. L *humor* moisture]

**hŭmp. 1.** *n.* Normal or other protuberance, esp. on the back; rounded raised mass of earth etc. (**over the ~,** over the worst part); ‖(sl.) depression (*it gives me the hump*); **~'back,** (person having) back with hump; **~'backed,** having such a back; **~(back) bridge** (with steep approach to top); **~' y̆** *a.* **2.** *v.t.* Make hump-shaped; annoy, depress; (sl.) hoist, carry on one's back. [perh. LDu.]

**humph** (hmf) *int., n., & v.i.* (Utter) vague sound expr. doubt or dissatisfaction. [imit.]

**hū'm|ŭs** *n.* Organic constituent of soil, vegetable mould; **~ĭc** *a.* [L, = ground]

**Hŭn** *n.* One of nomadic warlike people who invaded Europe in 4th–5th c.; (derog.) German (esp. Prussian); **~'nĭsh** *a.* [E f. L f. Gk f. Turki]

**hŭnch. 1.** *n.* Hump; thick piece; presentiment, notion; **~'back(ed),** humpback(ed). **2.** *v.t.* Bend convexly; thrust (*out, up*) to form hump. [orig. unkn.]

**hŭ'ndred** *a. & n.* (*pl.* **~, ~s**). **1.** NUMERAL (*a, one, six, several, hundred, men, of them; hundreds of; some, several, many, hundreds of*); (**a**) **~ (and one),** large number of; *1700* etc. HOURS; *not a hundred* MILES *from;* **a ~ to one,** a high probability; LONG[1] *hundred;* **a or one ~ per cent,** entire(ly), complete(ly); **~s and thousands,** tiny coloured sweets used for decorating cake etc.; **the seventeen-~s,** years 1700–99. **2.** ‖(esp. Hist.) Subdivision of county or shire with own court; ‖CHILTERN HUNDREDS. **3.** **~fŏld** *a., adv., & n.;* (-)**~th** *a. & n.* (Old H~th, a hymn based on Ps. 100, its tune); **~weight** *n.* (*pl.* **-t, -ts**), measure of ‖112 lb. or *100 lb. (**metric ~weight,** 50 kg). [E]

**hŭng.** See HANG.

**Hŭngār'ian** (-ngg-) *a. & n.* (Native) of Hungary; Magyar (person or language). [L]

**hŭ'nger** (-ngg-). **1.** *n.* Painful sensation, exhaustion, due to lack of food; strong desire (*for, after*); **~-march** (protest by unemployed etc.); **~-strike,** refusal of food by prisoner in order to gain some benefit or as protest. **2.** *v.i.* Feel hunger; crave (*for, after*). [E]

**hŭ'ngry̆** (-ngg-) *a.* (**-ily, -iness**). Feeling hunger, showing hunger (*a hungry look*); inducing hunger (*hungry work*); eager, greedy; (of soil) poor.

**hŭnk** *n.* Large piece cut off (*a hunk of bread*). [prob. LDu.]

**hŭ'nkers** (-z) *n.pl.* The haunches (**on one's ~,** squatting). [Sc.]

**Hŭ'nnĭsh.** See HUN.

**hŭnt. 1.** *v.i. & t.* Pursue wild animals esp. foxes; chase (these) for food or sport; (of animal) chase its prey; drive (*away* etc.); scour (area) in search of game; use (horse, hounds) in hunting; seek (*after, for*); (in *p.p.,* of look etc.) showing terror as of one being hunted; **~ down,** bring to bay; **~ out, up,** find by search. **2.** *n.* Hunting; hunting district or society (**~ ball,** one given by members of a hunt). **3.** **~'er** *n.,* one who hunts or (fig.) seeks something (FORTUNE-*hunter*), horse for hunting, watch with hinged cover over glass;

**~er's moon,** next full moon after harvest moon; **~'ĭng** *n.*; *hunting*-CROP; **~ing-dog** (used for hunting); **~ing-ground,** place where one hunts (lit. or fig.) *happy ~ing-ground(s),* life after death esp. for Amer. Indians); *hunting*-PINK²; **~'rĕss** *n.,* woman who hunts or follows hounds; **~'sman** *n.,* hunter, man in charge of hounds. [E]

**hŭr'dle. 1.** *n.* Portable frame with bars etc. for temporary fence etc.; upright frame to be jumped over in **~-race** or **~s;** (fig.) obstacle; **~r** *n.,* hurdle-maker, hurdle-racer. **2.** *v.t.* Fence off etc. with hurdles; leap over (lit. or fig.). [E]

**hŭr'dỹ-gŭrdỹ** *n.* Musical instrument with droning sound played by turning handle; (colloq.) barrel-organ. [imit.]

**hŭrl. 1.** *v.t. & i.* Throw violently (*hurl stones, reproaches; hurled him from his throne*); play **~'ĭng** or **~'ey** *n.,* fast played with wooden sticks (**~eys**) and ball in Ireland. **2.** *n.* Violent throw; **~'ỹ-bŭrlỹ** *n.,* commotion, tumult. [imit.]

**hurrah', -ray',** (or hŏō-), **hŏōray',** *int., n., & v.i.* **1.** *int.* expr. joy or approval. **2.** *n., & v.i.* Cry 'hurrah' etc. [alt. HUZZA]

**hŭ'rrĭcane** *n.* Violent storm-wind, esp. W. Ind. cyclone (often fig.); **~-lamp** (with flame protected from wind). [Sp. & Port. f. Carib]

**hŭ'rrỹ. 1.** *n.* Great haste; eagerness (*in a hurry to go, for dinner*); (w. neg. or interrog.) need for haste (*there is no hurry*); (colloq.) *you will not beat that* **in a ~** (easily), *shall not ask again* **in a ~** (willingly); **~-scurry** *adv., a., & n.,* (in) disorderly haste. **2.** *v.t. & i.* Drive (person etc. *away, along, into,* etc.) with haste; move or act with great haste; (in *p.p.*) hasty, done rapidly; **~ along, up,** (colloq.) make haste. [imit.]

**hŭrst** *n.* Wooded eminence; wood. [E]

**hŭrt. 1.** *v.t. & i.* (**hurt**). Injure, damage, pain; distress, wound, (person, feelings); (colloq.) suffer harm or pain (*his hand hurts*). **2.** *n.* Wound, injury; harm; **~'ful** *a.* (-**lly**); **hŭr'tle** *v.t. & t.,* strike *against,* move with clattering sound or rapidly, hurl swiftly. [F *hurter* knock]

**hŭ'sband** (-z-). **1.** *n.* Married man esp. in relation to wife (*her* etc. *husband*). **2.** *v.t.* Economize, manage carefully; **~man,** farmer; **~rỹ** *n.,* farming, economy (*good, bad, husbandry*). [E, = house-dweller]

**hŭsh. 1.** *v.t. & i.* Silence; be silent (esp. **~!,** imper.); **~ up,** suppress (fact); **~'aby(e)** *int.* used to lull child; **~-hush** *a.,* (colloq.) highly secret. **2.** *n.* Silence; **~-money** (paid to prevent exposure). [*husht* imit. int. taken as *p.p.*]

**hŭsk. 1.** *n.* Dry outer covering of fruit or seed; (fig.) worthless outside part of anything. **2.** *v.t.* Remove husk(s) from; **~'ỹ¹** *a.* (**~ily, ~iness**), of, full of, dry as, husks, hoarse, (colloq. of person) strong, tough. [prob. LG]

**hŭ'skỹ²** *n.* Eskimo dog. [perh. corrupt. *Eskimo*]

**hussâr'** (hŏōz-) *n.* Light-cavalry soldier. [Magyar f. It. (CORSAIR)]

**hŭ'ssỹ** (or -zǐ), **-zzỹ,** *n.* Pert girl; worthless woman. [contr. HOUSE-WIFE]

**hŭ'stĭngs** (-z) *n.* (Parliamentary) election proceedings. [E, = house of assembly, f. N]

**hŭ'stle** (-sel). **1.** *v.t. & i.* Push roughly, jostle; hurry (person *into* place, act, *doing,* etc.); push one's way, bustle; (sl.) swindle, obtain by force. **2.** *n.* Hustling, bustle. [Du.]

**hŭt. 1.** *n.* Small simple or crude house or shelter (*bathing, gardening, workmen's, hut*); (Mil.) temporary housing for troops; **~'ment** *n.,* hutted encampment. **2.** *v.t.* (-**tt**-). Place (troops etc.) in huts; furnish with huts. [F *hutte* f. Gmc]

**hŭtch** *n.* Boxlike pen for rabbits etc.; (derog.) hut, cabin. [F *huche*]

**huzza'** (-ah') *int., n., & v.* (arch.) **1.** *int.* expr. joy or applause. **2.** *n., & v.i. & t.* (Make, greet with) the cry 'huzza'. [orig. uncert.]

**hỹ'acĭnth** *n.* Kind of bulbous plant with bell-shaped flower esp. of purple-blue; this colour; orange variety of zircon; **wild** or **wood ~,** kind of squill; **hỹacĭ'nthine** *a.* [F f. L f. Gk]

**hỹae'na.** See HYENA.

**hỹ'brĭd. 1.** *n.* Offspring of two animals or plants of different species etc.; person of mixed origins; thing, esp. word, composed of incongruous elements. **2.** *a.* Bred as hybrid, mongrel; heterogeneous, **~ism,** **hỹbrĭ'dĭtỹ,** *ns.;* **~ize** *v.t. & i.* [L]

**hỹ'dra** *n.* Thing hard to extirpate; water-snake; freshwater polyp. [Gk]

(Myth.) snake whose many heads grew again when cut off]

**hy̆dră′ngea** (-nja) n. Kind of shrub with white, blue, or pink flower-clusters. [L, f. Gk *hudōr* water, *aggos* vessel]

**hy̆′dr|ant** n. Water-pipe (esp. in street) with nozzle for hose; **~āte** (Chem.), (n.) compound of water with another compound, (v.t.) (cause to) combine with water; **~ā′tion** n. [HYDRO-]

**hy̆drau′lic.** 1. a. (**~ally**). Of water or other liquid conveyed through pipes etc.; involving water-power (*hydraulic brakes, lift, ram*; **~ press**, hydrostatic); hardening under water (*hydraulic cement*). 2. n.pl. Science of conveyance of liquids through pipes etc. esp. as motive power. [L f. Gk (*hudōr* water, *aulos* pipe)]

**hy̆′dride** n. Compound of hydrogen with metal. [HYDRO-]

**hy̆′drō** n. (colloq.; pl. **~s**). Hotel etc. providing hydropathic treatment; hydroelectric power plant. [abbr.]

**hy̆′dro-** in comb. Water, liquid; combined with hydrogen; **~car′bon**, compound of hydrogen and carbon; **~chlor′ic**, containing hydrogen and chlorine (*hydrochloric acid*); **~chlor′ide**, compound of organic base with hydrochloric acid; **~cya′nic**, containing hydrogen and cyanogen (*cyanic acid*, prussic acid); **~dynamics** n.pl., science of forces acting on or exerted by liquids; **~dynamic(al)** adjs.; **~ele′ctric**, producing electricity, of electricity produced, by water-power; **~foil**, (vessel equipped with) device under hull making it rise out of water at speed; **~graphy** (-ŏ′g-), study of seas, lakes, rivers, etc.; **~logy** (-ŏ′l-), science of the properties of water esp. of its movement in relation to land; **~meter** (-ŏ′m-), instrument for determining density of liquids; **~phone**, instrument for detection of sound-waves in water; **~plane**, finlike device enabling submarine to rise or fall, light fast motor boat designed to skim over surface; **~sphere**, waters of earth's surface. [Gk *hudro-* (*hudōr* water)]

**hy̆droce′phal|us** n. Disease of brain, esp. in young children, with accumulation of fluid within cra-

nium; **hy̆drocě̆phă′lǐc, ~ous,** adjs. [Gk *kephalē* head]

**hy̆′drogen** n. Colourless tasteless odourless gas, the lightest element, combining with oxygen to form water; **~ bomb**, immensely powerful bomb utilizing explosive fusion of hydrogen nuclei; *hydrogen* PEROXIDE; **~ sulphide**, unpleasant-smelling poisonous gas formed by rotting animal matter; **~ate** (or -ŏ′j-) v.t., charge, cause to combine, with hydrogen; **~ous** (-ŏ′j-) a. [F]

**hy̆drŏ′ly̆sis** n. Decomposition by chemical reaction with water; **hy̆′drolȳse** (-z), **\*-lȳze**, v.t., decompose thus; **hy̆droly̆′tĭc** a. [Gk (*lusis* dissolving)]

**hy̆drŏ′path|y** n. Medical treatment by external and internal application of water; **hy̆dropă′thic** a., of hydropathy; **~ĭst** n. [PATHOS]

**hy̆drophi̱′lĭc** a. Having affinity for water; wettable by water. [Gk (*philos* loving)]

**hy̆drophō′b|ĭa** n. Aversion to water, esp. as symptom of rabies in man; rabies; **~ĭc** a. (also, not wettable by water). [-PHOBIA]

**hy̆dropŏ′nics** n.pl. Soilless culture, art of growing plants without soil, in (sand etc. with) water impregnated with chemicals. [Gk *ponos* labour]

**hy̆drostă′tĭc.** 1. a. (**~ally**). Of the equilibrium of liquids and the pressure exerted by liquids at rest; **~ press**, machine in which pressure of water is multiplied by transmission to larger cylinder. 2. n.pl. Hydrostatic science. [STATIC]

**hy̆′drous** a. (Chem. & Min.) Containing water. [HYDRO-]

**hy̆drŏ′x|ide** n. (Chem.) Compound of element or radical with hydroxyl; **~y̆l** n., (Chem.) radical containing hydrogen and oxygen. [HYDRO-, OXYGEN]

**hy̆ē′na, hy̆ae′na,** n. Carnivorous strong-jawed quadruped allied to dog (**laughing ~**, kind with howl said to be like fiendish laughter). [I. f. Gk]

**hy̆′gien|e** (-jēn) n. Principles of maintaining health esp. by cleanliness; sanitary science; **~ĭc** (-jē′n-) a. (**~ically**); **~ĭst** n. [F f. Gk (*hugiēs* healthy)]

**hy̆′gro-** in comb. Moisture; **~meter** (-ŏ′m-) n., instrument measuring humidity of air etc.;

~**scōpe** *n.*, instrument showing humidity of air; ~**scŏ′pĭc** *a.*, (of substance) tending to absorb moisture from the air. [Gk *hugros* wet]

**hy̆′mĕn** *n.* (Anat.) Fold of membrane partly closing external orifice of virgin's vagina; ~**al** *a.* [Gk *humēn* membrane]

**hy̆měnŏ′pterous** *a.* (Zool.) With four membranous wings. [Gk, = membrane-winged]

**hy̆mn** (-m). **1.** *n.* Song of praise, esp. to God as sung in religious service; ~**-book** (of hymns). **2.** *v.t.* Praise, celebrate, in hymns. **3. hy̆′mnal**, (*a.*) of hymns, (*n.*) hymn-book; **hy̆′mnĭst** *n.*, writer of hymns; **hy̆′mnŏdy̆** *n.*, singing, making, of hymns; **hy̆′mnodĭst** *n.*; **hy̆mnŏ′logy̆** *n.*, study of hymns; **hy̆mnŏ′logist** *n.* [F f. L f. Gk]

**hy̆′oscine, hy̆oscy̆′amine**, (-ēn) *ns.* Poisonous alkaloids used as sedatives. [Gk *huoskuamos* henbane (*hus huos* pig, *kuamos* bean)]

**hy̆per-** *pref.* w. senses 'over', 'above', 'too'. [Gk *huper* over]

**hy̆pĕr′bola** *n.* (*pl.* ~s, ~e). Plane curve produced when double cone is cut by plane making larger angle with base than side of cone makes; **hy̆perbŏ′lĭc** *a.* [foll.]

**hy̆pĕr′bolē** *n.* Rhetorical exaggeration; **hy̆perbŏ′lĭcal** *a.* (-lly). [Gk (HYPER-, *ballō* throw)]

**hy̆percrĭ′tĭc|al** *a.* (-lly). Too critical; ~**ĭsm** *n.* [HYPER-]

**hy̆′permărkĕt** *n.* Very large self-service store, usu. outside town. [F (HYPER-, MARKET)]

**hy̆persĕ′nsĭtĭv|e** *a.* Abnormally or excessively sensitive; ~**ĭty̆** (-ĭ′v-) *n.* [HYPER-]

**hy̆persŏ′nĭc** *a.* Of speeds more than about 5 times that of sound; of sound frequencies above about 1,000 megahertz.

**hy̆pertĕ′ns|ion** (-shon) *n.* Abnormally high blood pressure; state of great mental tension; ~**ĭve** *a.*

**hy̆pĕr′troph|y̆** *n.* Enlargement (of organ etc.) due to excessive nutrition; **hy̆pertrŏ′phĭc**, ~**ĭed** (-ĭd), *adjs.* [HYPER-, Gk *trephō* feed]

**hy̆′phen. 1.** *n.* Sign (-) used to join words together (*pick-me-up*), join parts of word broken in line of printing (as here), divide word into parts for clarity (*re-echo*), etc. **2.** *v.t.* Join, divide, (words) with hyphen. **3.**

~**āte** *v.t.*, = hyphen; ~**ā′tion** *n.* [L f. Gk (HYPO-, *hen* one)]

**hy̆pnō′s|ĭs** *n.* (*pl.* ~es *pr.* -ēz). State like sleep in which the subject acts only on external suggestion; artificially produced sleep; **hy̆pnŏ′tĭc**, (*a.*: -ically) of or causing hypnosis or sleep, (*n.*) thing producing hypnosis; **hy̆′pnotĭsm** *n.*, (production of) hypnosis; **hy̆′pnotĭst** *n.*; **hy̆′pnotize** *v.t.* [L f. Gk *hupnos* sleep]

**hy̆′pō¹** *n.* (Photog.) Sodium thiosulphate (incorrectly called hyposulphite), used in fixing. [abbr.]

**hy̆′pō²** *n.* (*pl.* ~s). = HYPODERMIC.

**hy̆po-** *pref.* w. senses 'under', 'below', 'slightly'. [Gk *hupo* under]

**hy̆′pocaust** *n.* (Rom. Ant.) Hot-air channel under floor for heating house or bath from furnace. [L f. Gk (HYPO-, *kaustos* burnt)]

**hy̆pochŏ′ndr|ĭa** (-k-) *n.* Morbid anxiety esp. about one's health; ~**ĭăc**, (*a.*) of hypochondria, (*n.*) sufferer from hypochondria. [L f. Gk, = soft parts of body below ribs (whence melancholy was thought to arise)]

**hy̆pŏ′crĭsy̆** *n.* Simulation of virtue; dissimulation, pretence; **hy̆′pocrĭte** *n.*, person guilty of hypocrisy, dissembler, pretender; **hy̆pocrĭ′tĭcal** *a.* (-lly). [F f. L f. Gk, = acting, feigning]

**hy̆podĕr′mĭc. 1.** *a.* (~ally) (Med., of drug etc.) introduced beneath skin (*hypodermic injection*); ~**needle, syringe**, for hypodermic injection); lying under the skin. **2.** *n.* Hypodermic injection or syringe. [L f. Gk (HYPO-, *derma* skin)]

**hy̆′poid** *n.* Gear with off-centre pinion between non-intersecting shafts. [orig. uncert.]

**hy̆pŏ′phy̆s|ĭs** *n.* (*pl.* ~es *pr.* -ēz). Pituitary gland. [L f. Gk, = offshoot]

**hy̆pŏ′stas|ĭs** *n.* (*pl.* ~es *pr.* -ēz). (Metaphys.) underlying substance (as distinct from attributes); (Theol.) any one of the three Persons of the Trinity; **hy̆postă′tĭc** *a.* [L f. Gk (*stasis* standing)]

**hy̆potĕ′ns|ion** (-shon) *n.* Abnormally low blood pressure; ~**ĭve** *a.* [HYPO-]

**hy̆pŏ′tĕnūse** (-z) *n.* Side opposite right angle of right-angled triangle. [L f. Gk, = subtending line]

**hȳpŏ′thēc|āte** *v.t.* Pledge, mortgage; **~ā′tion** *n.* [L f. Gk (HYPO-, *tithēmi* place)]

**hȳpŏther′mĭa** *n.* (Med.) Condition of having body-temperature below normal. [HYPO-, Gk *thermē* heat]

**hȳpŏ′thĕs|ĭs** *n.* (*pl.* **~es** *pr.* -ēz). Supposition made as basis for reasoning, investigation, etc.; groundless assumption; **~ĭze** *v.i.* & *t.*, frame hypothesis, assume as hypothesis; **hȳpŏthĕ′tĭc(al)** *adjs.* (-lly), of, resting on, hypothesis. [L f. Gk, = foundation]

**hȳ′ssop** *n.* Small bushy aromatic herb formerly used medicinally; (Bibl.) plant used for sprinkling in Jewish rites. [E & F f. L f. Gk f. Semitic]

**hȳsterĕ′ctom|ȳ** *n.* Removal of womb; **~ĭze** *v.t.* [Gk (as foll., -ECTOMY)]

**hȳstēr′ĭa** *n.* Functional disturbance of nervous system, of psychoneurotic origin; morbid excitement; **hȳstĕ′rĭcal** *a.* (-lly), of or affected with hysteria; **hȳstĕ′rĭc** *n.*, hysterical person, (in *pl.*) fit(s) of hysteria. [Gk *hustera* womb (since hysteria formerly thought more frequent in women)]

**Hz** *abbr.* hertz.

# I

**I[1], i,** (ī) *n.* (*pl.* **Is, I′s**). Ninth letter; (as Roman numeral) 1.

**I[2]** (ī) *pron.* of 1st pers. sing. (*obj.* ME[1], *refl.* MYSELF, *poss.* MY, MINE[1]; *pl.* WE etc.; *I see; it is I*). [E]

**I.** *abbr.* Island(s); Isle(s).

**Ia.** *abbr.* Iowa.

**-ĭal.** See -AL.

**ĭă′mb|us** *n.* (*pl.* **~uses, ~i** *pr.* -ī). A metrical foot (⏑ –); **~ĭc,** (*a.*) of iambuses, (*n.*, usu. in *pl.*) iambic verse. [L f. Gk]

**-ĭan.** See -AN.

**I.A.T.A.** *abbr.* International Air Transport Association.

**ib.** *abbr.* ibidem.

**Ibēr′ĭan** (ī-) *a.* & *n.* (Inhabitant, language) of ancient Iberia; of Spain and Portugal. [L *Iberia* f. Gk]

**i′bĕx** *n.* Wild goat of Alps etc. with large recurved horns. [L]

**ibid.** *abbr.* = foll.

**ibidem** (ĭ′bĭděm, ĭbĭ′děm) *adv.* In the same book, passage, etc. [L, = in same place]

**i′bĭs** *n.* Storklike bird with curved bill (sacred **~**, white kind venerated in ancient Egypt). [L f. Gk]

**-ĭble** *suf.* forming *adjs.* (-ibly) w. senses as -ABLE (*terrible, forcible, possible*). [F or L]

**-ĭc** *suf.* forming *adjs.* & *ns.* (*Arabic, classic, public; critic, mechanic, music*); (Chem.) combined in higher valence etc. (*ferric, sulphuric*). [F or L or Gk]

**i/c** *abbr.* in charge; in command.

**-ĭcal** *suf.* forming *adjs.* esp. f. *ns.* in *-ic* or *-y* (*comical, historical*). [-IC, -AL].

**I.C.B.M.** *abbr.* inter-continental ballistic missile.

**ice.** **1.** *n.* Frozen water; sheet of this on surface of water (**break the ~**, fig., make a start, break through reserve; CUT *no ice*; **on ~**, colloq., held in reserve, quite certain; **on thin ~**, in risky situation); other similar solid or frozen substance (**dry ~**, solid carbon dioxide); frozen confection esp. ‖ice cream or water-ice; **~-age**, glacial period; **~-axe** (used by mountaineer); **~-blue**, very pale blue; *~′box*, refrigerator; **~-breaker**, boat used for breaking ice; **~-cap, -field**, permanent covering, expanse, of ice esp. in polar regions; **~ cream**, frozen flavoured cream; **~-cube**, small cube of ice (for drinks); **~ hockey** (played on skates); **~ lolly**, kind of water-ice on stick; **~-water** (ice-cold or cooled by ice); *ice*-YACHT. **2.** *v.t.* & *i.* Freeze; cover, mix, with ice; cool in ice; cover (cake, fruit) with icing; become covered (*over, up*) with ice. [E]

‖**I.C.E.** *abbr.* Institution of Civil Engineers.

**i′cebrg** (ī′sb-) *n.* Huge floating mass of ice; (fig.) unemotional person; **tip of the ~**, part of iceberg (about 1/9) that projects above surface of sea, (fig.) small evident part of something much larger. [Du.]

**I′celand** (ī′sl-) *n.* **~ spar**, transparent variety of calcite; **~er** *n.*, native of Iceland; **Icelǎ′ndǐc** (isl-) *a.* & *n.*, (language) of Iceland. [place]

**ichneu′mon** (ĭk-) *n.* Mongoose of N. Africa etc., noted for destroying crocodiles' eggs; **~-fly**, an insect that deposits its eggs on larva of another insect. [L f. Gk]

**i′chor** (ī′k-) *n.* (Gk Myth.) Fluid flowing like blood in veins of gods. [Gk]

**i′chthȳ|o-** (ĭk-) *in comb.* Fish; **~ǒ′graphy** *n.*, description of fishes; **~oid** *a.*, fishlike; **~ǒ′logȳ** *n.*, study of fishes; **~ǒ′phagous** *a.*, fish-eating; **~osaur′us** *n.*, extinct marine animal with long head, four paddles, and large tail. [Gk *ikhthus* fish]

**-i′cian** (ī′shan) *suf.* forming *ns.* chiefly with sense 'person skilled in', usu. corresp. to subject in *-ic(s)*. [F]

**i′cicle** *n.* Tapering hanging spike of ice formed from dripping water. [ICE, obs. *ickle* icicle]

**i′cǐng** *n.* Sugar etc. coating of cake etc. (‖**~ sugar**, finely powdered sugar); formation of ice on aircraft. [ICE]

**i′con, i′kon,** *n.* Image, statue; (Orthodox Ch.) sacred painting, mosaic, etc.; **iconǒ′logȳ** *n.*, study of icons. [f. Gk]

**icǒ′nocl|ǎst** *n.* Breaker of images; one who assails cherished beliefs; **~ǎsm** *n.*, breaking of images; **~ǎ′stǐc** *a.* [ICON, Gk *klaō* break]

**iconǒ′graphy** *n.* Illustration of subject by drawings etc.; study of portraits esp. of one person. [Gk (ICON)]

**icǒsi-** *in comb.* Twenty; **icosahě′dron** (-a-h-), solid figure with 20 faces. [Gk]

**-ics** *suf.* forming *ns.* denoting branches of study or action (*athletics, politics*). [F or L or Gk]

**i′ctus** *n.* Rhythmical or metrical stress. [L, = stroke]

**i′cȳ** *a.* (-ily, -iness). Abounding in or covered with ice; very cold (lit. or fig.: *icy wind, tone*). [ICE]

**id** *n.* (Psych.) Inherited instinctive impulses of the individual. [L, = that; transl. G]

**i.d.** *abbr.* inner diameter.

**-ide** *suf.* (Chem.) forming names of binary compounds of an element with another element or radical (*sodium chloride; calcium carbide*). [orig. in OXIDE]

**ide′a** *n.* Thing conceived by the mind (**man of ~s**, resourceful person; **have ~s**, be ambitious etc.; **put ~s into** person's **head**, suggest ambitions etc. he would not otherwise have had); way of thinking; vague belief, fancy, (*I had no, had an, idea you were there*); **the very ~!**, colloq., that is outrageous etc.; **that's an ~**, colloq., that proposal etc. is worth considering); conception, aim, plan, (**not my ~ of**, colloq., the opposite of; **has no ~**, colloq., is incompetent; **the big ~**, (supposedly) important scheme); archetype, pattern, esp. (Platonic) eternally existing pattern of which individual things are imperfect copies. [L f. Gk, = form, kind]

**ide′al. 1.** *a.* (**~ly**). Answering to one's highest conception; perfect; existing only in idea, visionary; of Platonic ideas. **2.** *n.* Perfect type; actual thing as standard for imitation. **3. ~ǐsm** *n.*, representation of things in ideal form, imaginative treatment, following after or forming ideals, philosophy in which object of external perception is held to consist of ideas; **~ǐst** *n.*; **~i′stǐc** *a.*; **~ǐze** *v.t.*, make or treat as ideal; **~izā′tion** *n.* [f. L (prec.)]

*idée fixe* (ēdāfē′ks) *n.* Idea that dominates the mind [F, = fixed idea]; *idée reçue* (ēdāresü′) *n.*, generally accepted notion. [F]

**idě′nti|cal** *a.* (-lly). (Of one thing at different times) the same; (of different things) agreeing in all details (*with*); (of twins) developed from a single fertilized ovum and thus of same sex and of very similar features; **~fȳ** *v.t. & i.*, treat (thing) as identical (*with*), associate (person, *oneself*), associate oneself, closely (*with* party, policy, etc.), recognize, select; **~fǐcā′tion** *n.* (**~fication, ~ty, card, disc,** etc., object carried, worn, etc., for identification; **~fication, ~ty, parade,** assembly of persons from whom suspect is to be identified); **~kit,** picture of person wanted by police, assembled from witnesses' descriptions of features; **~tȳ** *n.*, absolute sameness, individuality, personality, (Alg.) equality of two expressions for all values of quantities, expression of this; **~ty card** etc. (see above). [L (prec.)]

**ǐ′děo|grǎm, ~|graph** (-ahf-), *ns.* Numeral or Chinese etc. character indicating the idea of a thing without expressing the sounds in its name; **~grä'phĭc(al)** *adjs.*; **ĭdĕŏ'graphy** *n*. [IDEA, -GRAM, -GRAPH]

**ĭdĕŏ'lŏg|y̆** *n*. Ideas characteristic of some class etc. or at basis of some economic or political theory or system; **ĭdĕŏlŏ'gĭcal** *a.*; **~ĭst** *n.*; **ĭ'dĕŏlŏgŭe** (-g) *n.*, adherent of an ideology. [F (IDEA, -LOGY)]

**ides** (ĭdz) *n.pl.* Eighth day after nones in ancient Roman calendar. [F f. L *Idus*]

**ĭ'dĭŏcy̆** *n*. Extreme mental imbecility; utter foolishness. [IDIOT]

**ĭ'dĭŏm** *n*. Language of a people; form of expression or usage peculiar to a language, esp. one whose meaning is not given by those of its separate words; characteristic mode of expression in art etc.; **~ă'tĭc** *a.* (-ically), characteristic of a language, relating or conforming to idiom. [F, or L f. Gk (*idios* own)]

**ĭdĭŏsy̆'n|crasy̆** *n*. Mental (also physical) constitution, view, feeling, peculiar to a person; **~crä'tĭc** *a.* [Gk *idios* private, *sun* with, *krasis* mixture]

**ĭ'dĭŏt** *n*. Person too deficient in mind to be capable of rational conduct; (colloq.) stupid person; **ĭdĭŏ'tĭc** *a.* (-ically). [F f. L f. Gk, = private citizen, ignorant person]

**ĭ'dle.** 1. *a.* (~r, ~st; ĭ'dly). Lazy, indolent; not working; (of time etc.) unoccupied; useless, vain, (*idle protest*); purposeless (*idle talk*); groundless (*idle rumour*). 2. *v.i.* & *t.* Be idle, (of engine) revolve slowly without doing work; pass (time etc.) *away* in idleness; **~r** *n.*, indolent person. [E]

**ĭ'dol** *n*. Image of deity as object of worship; false god; object of excessive devotion; false conception. [F f. L f. Gk]

**ĭdŏ'lat|er** *n*. Worshipper of idol(s); devout admirer (*of*); **~rèss, ~ry̆**, *ns.*; **~rous** *a.* [F f. L f. Gk (IDOL, *latreuō* worship)]

**ĭ'dolĭz|e** *v.t.* Make an idol of; venerate, love, to excess; **~ā'tion** *n*. [IDOL]

**ĭ'dy̆ll** *n*. Short description usu. in verse of picturesque scene or incident esp. in rustic life, such incident etc.; **ĭdy̆'llĭc** *a.* (-ically); **~ĭst** *n*. [L f. Gk (*eidos* form)]

**-ĭe.** See -Y².

**i.e.** *abbr.* that is to say. [L *id est*]

**‖I.E.E.** *abbr.* Institution of Electrical Engineers.

**if. 1.** *conj.* On the condition or supposition that (*if you are* now or later *tired we will sit down*; *if he has found it he will send it*; *if he had fair warning, he has nothing to complain of*; w. past tense, implying that condition is not fulfilled: *if I were you, if I knew I would say, if I had known I would have said*); whenever (*if I feel doubt I ask*; *if I wanted him I rang*); whether (*ask, see, try, if you can turn the key*); expr. wish or surprise (*if I only knew!*; *if you wouldn't mind opening the door*; *if I haven't lost my watch!*); **as ~**, as the case would be if (*he talks as if he were drunk*; *as if you didn't know!*, you know very well; *it looks as if he meant*, colloq. *means, business*); **if** (there are) **any**; **if** (it is) **so.** 2. *n*. Condition, supposition, (*too many ifs about it*). [E]

**ĭ'glōo** *n*. Eskimo dome-shaped hut, esp. one built of snow. [Eskimo, = house]

**ĭ'gnĕous** *a*. Of fire; produced by volcanic action. [L (*ignis* fire)]

**ignĭs fä'tūus** *n*. Phosphorescent light seen on marshy ground; delusive hope or aim. [L, = foolish fire]

**ignĭ'te** *v.t.* & *i.* Set fire to; take fire; cause to burn, make intensely hot; **ignĭ'tion** *n.*, igniting, mechanism for or act of starting combustion in cylinder of motor engine (*ignition key*). [L *ignio ignit-* set on fire]

**ignō'ble** *a.* (-bly). Of low birth or position; mean, base. [F or L (IN-², NOBLE)]

**ĭgnomĭny̆** *n*. Dishonour, infamy; **ignomĭ'nĭous** *a.*, humiliating. [F or L (IN-², L (*g*)*nomen* name)]

**ignorā'mus** *n*. Ignorant person. [L, = we do not know (IGNORE)]

**ĭ'gnoran|t** *a*. (Uncouth because) lacking knowledge; uninformed (*of*, *that*); **~ce** *n.* [F f. L (foll.)]

**ignō'r'e** *v.t.* Refuse to take notice of; intentionally disregard. [F or L (*ignoro* not know)]

**igua'n|a** (ĭgwah'-) *n*. Large W. Ind. and S. Amer. tree lizard; **~odŏn** *n.*, large herbivorous dinosaur. [Sp. f. Carib]

**IHS** *abbr.* Jesus. [repr. Gk *Iēs(ous)*]

**ĭ'kon.** See ICON.

**il-¹,², ².** See IN-¹,².

**‖I.L.E.A.** *abbr.* Inner London Education Authority.

**ĭ'lĕ|um** *n*. (*pl.* ~a). Third and last portion of small intestine. [L *ilium*]

**ĭ'lĕx** *n*. Holm-oak; (Bot.) plant of genus including holly. [L]

**i′liăc** *a.* Of the flank (*iliac artery*). [L (*ilia* flanks)]

**ilk** *a.* (Sc.) same (*Guthrie of that ~, Guthrie of Guthrie*); (colloq.) that ~, that family, class, etc. [E]

**ill** *a. & adv.* (WORSE, WORST) *& n.* **1.** *a.* (no adv. in **-ly**). Out of health, sick, (usu. *pred.*: be, fall, be taken, ill with a fever, with anxiety, etc.); (of health) unsound; hostile (*ill feeling, will*); irritable (*ill humour, temper*); harmful (*ill effects; do an ill turn to* person); unfavourable (*ill luck, fortune*; *it's an ~ wind that blows nobody good*, most events benefit someone); improper, deficient, (*with an ~ grace*, sullenly; *~ success*, partial or complete failure). **2.** *adv.* Badly, unfavourably, (*take thing ~*, resent it; *it would go ~ with him*, he would come to grief); scarcely (*can ill afford to go there*); *~ at ease*, embarrassed, uneasy. **3.** *n.* Injury, harm, evil (*speak ~ of*, say something unfavourable of); (in *pl.*) misfortunes. **4.** *~*-adviˊsed(ly *pr.* -ĭdlĭ), imprudent(ly); *~*-behaved, having bad manners etc.; *~*-bred, badly brought up, rude; *~*-defined, not clearly defined; *~*-disposed, disposed to evil, unfavourably disposed (*towards*); *~*-faˊted, destined to, or bringing, bad fortune; *~*-favoured, unattractive, objectionable; *~*-gotten, gained by evil or unlawful means; *~*-juˊdged, unwise; *~*-maˊnnered, having bad manners; *~*-naˊtured(ly), churlish(ly); *~*-o′mened, attended by bad omens; *~*-starred, born under an evil star, unlucky; *~*-teˊmpered, morose, irritable; *~*-tiˊmed, unseasonable; *~*-treaˊt, *-u′se*, treat badly (*~*-*treatment, ~-use*, ns.). [N]

**Ill.** *abbr.* Illinois.

**illeˊgal** *a.* (*~ly*). Not legal, contrary to law; **illēgăˊlitў** *n.* [IN-²]

**illeˊgĭb|le** *a.* (*~ly*). Not legible; *~*iˊlitў *n.*

**illēgĭˊtĭm|ate** *a. & n.* Not authorized by law; improper; wrongly inferred; bastard; *~*acў *n.*

**illiˊberal** *a.* (*~ly*). Without liberal culture; sordid, narrow-minded, stingy; **illĭbĕrăˊlitў** *n.*; **illiˊcĭt** *a.*, unlawful, forbidden; **illiˊmĭtable** *a.* (*-bly*), limitless.

**illiˊter|ate** *a. & n.* Uneducated (person), esp. (one) unable to read; *~*acў *n.*

**iˊllnėss** *n.* Ill health, state of being ill, disease. [ILL]

**illŏˊgĭc|al** *a.* (*~lly*). Devoid of, contrary to, logic; *~*aˊlitў *n.* [IN-²]

**illu′mĭn|āte** (-ōō′-) *v.t.* Light up; enlighten spiritually or intellectually; help to explain (subject); shed lustre on; decorate (buildings etc.) profusely with lights as sign of festivity; decorate (initial letter in manuscript etc.) with gold or other bright colours; *~*ant, (*a.*) serving to illuminate, (*n.*) means of illumination, gas or lamp etc.; *~*āˊtion, *~*ātor, ns.; *~*ātĭve *a.*; *~*e *v.t.*, (literary) light up, enlighten spiritually. [L (*lumen* light)]

**illu′sion** (-zhon; *or* -ōō′-) *n.* Deceptive appearance, statement, or belief; *~*ĭst *n.*, producer of illusions, conjuror; **illu′sĭve, illu′sorў,** (*or* -ōō′-) *adjs.*, deceptive. [F f. L (*illudo* mock)]

**iˊllustr|āte** *v.t.* Make clear esp. by examples or drawings; provide (book, newspaper) with pictures; serve as example of; *~*āˊtion *n.*, (esp.) drawing etc. in book; *~*ātĭve *a.*, explanatory (*of*); *~*ātor *n.* [L (*lustro* light up)]

**illu′strĭous** *a.* Distinguished, renowned. [L *illustris* (prec.)]

**I.L.O.** *abbr.* International Labour Organisation.

**ĭm-¹,².** See IN-¹,².

**iˊmage. 1.** *n.* Imitation of object's external form, e.g. statue esp. as object of worship; counterpart in appearance (*he is the image of his father*); simile, metaphor; idea, conception, general impression of person or thing; optical counterpart produced by rays of light reflected from mirror etc. **2.** *v.t.* Make an image of, portray; reflect, mirror; describe vividly. **3.** *~*rў (-ĭj-) *n.*, images, statuary, carving, figurative illustration. [F f. L *imago imagin-*]

**ĭmăˊgĭn|e** *v.t.* Form mental image of, picture to oneself (something non-existent or not present); conceive (thing or person *to* be or do, *that* it is, how, etc.); guess (*I cannot imagine where he has gone*); suppose, be of opinion, (*that*); *~*arў *a.*, existing only in, due to, imagination; *~*āˊtion *n.*, mental faculty forming images or concepts of objects not existent or present, creative faculty of the mind; *~*ātĭve *a.*, of, given to, having a high degree of, imagination. [F f. L (prec.)]

**i'magist** *n.* One of group of 20th-c. poets aiming at clarity of thought etc. through use of precise images. [IMAGE]

**ĭmā'g̣|ō** *n.* (*pl.* ~ines *pr.* -jĭnēz, ~os). Final and perfect stage of insect e.g. butterfly. [L (IMAGE)]

**ima'm** (-ah'm) *n.* Leader of prayers in mosque; title of some Muslim leaders. [Arab.]

**ĭmbǎ'lance** *n.* Lack of balance; disproportion. [IN-²]

**i'mbēcĭle** (*or* -ēl). **1.** *a.* Mentally weak, idiotic; stupid; **ĭmbēcĭ'lĭc** *a.*; **ĭmbēcĭ'lĭtȳ** *n.* **2.** Person of weak intellect esp. adult like normal child of 5; stupid person. [F f. L]

**ĭmbě'd.** See EMBED.

**ĭmbi'be** *v.t.* Absorb (ideas, moisture, etc.); drink (liquid esp. alcoholic liquor); inhale (air etc.); **ĭmbĭbi'tion** *n.* [L (bibo drink)]

**i'mbrĭc|āte** *v.t. & i.* Arrange (leaves etc.), be arranged, so as to overlap; ~ā'tion *n.* [L (imbrex imbrictile)]

**ĭmbrō'gliō** (-ō'lyō) *n.* (*pl.* ~s). Confused heap; complicated situation. [It. (IN-¹, BROIL¹)]

**ĭmbrue'** (-ōō') *v.t.* Stain (hand, sword, *in* or *with* blood, slaughter, etc.). [F f. Gmc]

**ĭmbue'** *v.t.* Saturate, dye, (with); permeate, inspire (with feelings); = prec. [F, or L imbuo]

**‖I.Mech.E.** *abbr.* Institution of Mechanical Engineers.

**I.M.F.** *abbr.* International Monetary Fund.

**i'mĭt|āte** *v.t.* (~able). Follow example of; make copy of; mimic; be like; ~ā'tion *n.*, imitating, copy, counterfeit (often *attrib.*: imitation *leather*); ~ative *a.* (~ative word, whose sound reproduces a natural sound, e.g. fizz, or is otherwise suggestive, e.g. blob); ~ātor *n.* [L imitor -tat-]

**ĭmmǎ'cŭl|āte** *a.* Pure, spotless (I~ate Conception, of Virgin Mary as conceived and remaining free from taint of original sin); (usu. iron.) faultless; ~acȳ *n.* [L (IN-², macula spot)]

**i'mmanen|t** *a.* Inherent; (of God) permanently pervading the universe (opp. TRANSCENDENT); ~ce, ~cȳ, *ns.* [L (IN-¹, maneo remain)]

**ĭmmatēr'ial** *a.* (~ly). Not mater-

ial, not corporeal; unimportant; ~ĭtȳ (-ǎ'l-) *n.* [IN-²]

**ĭmmatūr'|e** (*or* ĭ'-) *a.* Not mature, unripe; ~ĭtȳ *n.*

**ĭmmea'surable** (-mě'zher-) *a.* (-bly). Not measurable, immense.

**ĭmmē'dĭa|te** *a.* (Of person or thing) without intervening medium, direct, nearest, not separated by others, (has no immediate connection with the decision; the immediate future; my immediate neighbour); occurring at once (immediate reply); ~cȳ *n.* [F or L (IN-²)]

**ĭmmēmōr'ial** *a.* (~ly). Ancient beyond memory or record (from time immemorial); very old. [IN-²]

**ĭmmě'nse** *a.* Unmeasured, vast, huge; (colloq.) great (an immense difference), (sl.) very good; ~lȳ (-slĭ) *adv.*, vastly, very much; **ĭmmě'nsĭtȳ** *n.* [F f. L (metior mens- measure)]

**ĭmmēr'se** *v.t.* Dip, plunge, (in liquid); lay (person) completely under water, baptize thus; embed; involve deeply (in debt, thought); ~ion (-shon) *n.* (~ion heater, electric heater designed to heat liquid by immersion esp. to produce hot water). [L (mergo mers- dip)]

**i'mmĭgr|āte** *v.i. & t.* Come, bring, (into a country) as settler; ~ant, (a.) immigrating, (n.) one who immigrates (‖esp. if a coloured person; also a descendant of such a person); ~ā'tion *n.* [IN-¹]

**i'mmĭnen|t** *a.* (Of danger etc.) about to happen; ~ce *n.* [L immineo be impending]

**ĭmmĭ'scĭb|le** *a.* That cannot be mixed, esp. (of one liquid) with another; ~ĭ'lĭtȳ *n.* [IN-²]

**ĭmmō'b|ĭle** *a.* Immovable, motionless; **ĭmmobĭ'lĭtȳ** *n.*; ~ĭlize *v.t.*, fix immovably, keep (limb, patient) still for healing purposes, prevent (troops, vehicle) from being moved; ~ĭlizā'tion *n.* [IN-²]

**ĭmmō'derate** *a.* Excessive, lacking moderation.

**ĭmmō'děst** *a.* Having no modesty, impudent, indecent; ~ȳ *n.*

**i'mmol|āte** *v.t.* Sacrifice (victim, fig. thing *to* another); ~ā'tion, ~ātor, *ns.* [L, = sprinkle with meal]

**ĭmmō'ral** *a.* (~ly). Not conforming to, opposed to, (esp. sexual) morality; depraved, dissolute; **ĭmmōrǎ'lĭtȳ** *n.* [IN-²]

**ĭmmōr'tal.** **1.** *a.* (~ly). Not mortal, living for ever, (immortal soul); divine; unfading; famous for all time. **2.** *n.* Immortal being, esp. (in *pl.*) gods of antiquity; person (esp. author) of enduring fame. **3.** **immŏrtǎ'lǐtў** *n.*; **~ǐze** *v.t.* [L (IN-²)]

**immo'vab|le** (ĭmōō'-) *a.* (**~lў**). That cannot be moved; motionless; unyielding; emotionless; (Law) consisting of land, houses, etc.; **~ǐ'lǐtў** *n.* [IN-²]

**immū'n|e** *a.* Having immunity (*from* taxation; *against* infection, poison; *to* criticism), exempt, secure; **~ǐtў** *n.*, (legal) exemption, freedom, (*from*), means by which organisms resist and overcome infection; **i'mmŭnize** *v.t.*, make immune; **~ǐzā'tion** *n.*; **ǐmmŭnǒ'logў** *n.*, study of resistance to infection. [L *immunis* exempt]

**immūr'e** *v.t.* Imprison, shut (one-*self* etc.) up. [F or L (*murus* wall)]

**immū'tab|le** *a.* (**~lў**). Unchange-able; **~ǐ'lǐtў** *n.* [L (IN-²)]

**imp** *n.* Child of the Devil; little devil; mischievous child. [E, = young shoot]

**impǎct. 1.** (ĭ'-) *n.* Striking (*on*, *against*), collision, (lit. or fig.); effect, influence. **2.** (-ǎ'-) *v.t.* Press, fix, firmly (*into*, *in*); (in *p.p.*, of tooth) wedged between another tooth and jaw; **~ion** (-ǎ'-) *n.* [L (IMPINGE)]

**impair'** *v.t.* Damage, weaken; **~ment** *n.* [F f. L, = make worse (*pejor*)]

**impǎ'la** (or -ah'-) *n.* Small S. Afr. antelope. [Zulu]

**impā'le** *v.t.* Transfix (body etc. upon, *with*, stake etc., esp. as capital punishment); place (two coats of arms) on one shield with vertical line between; **~ment** (-lm-) *n.* [F or L (*palus* PALE¹)]

**impǎ'lpab|le** *a.* (**~lў**). Not palp-able; not easily grasped by the mind, intangible; (of powder) very fine; **~ǐ'lǐtў** *n.* [F or L (IN-²)]

**impǎ'nel.** See EMPANEL.

**impar't** *v.t.* Give share of (thing *to*); communicate (news etc. *to*). [F f. L (PART)]

**impar'tial** (-shal) *a.* (**~lў**). Not partial, fair; **impártiǎ'lǐtў** (-shǐ-) *n.* [IN-²]

**impa'ss|able** (-pah'-) *a.* (**-blў**). That cannot be traversed; **~abǐ'lǐtў** *n.*; **~e** (or ǎ'mpahs) *n.*, blind alley, deadlock, dilemma.

**impǎ'ssǐb|le** *a.* (**~lў**). Not liable

to pain or injury; impassive; **~ǐ'lǐtў** *n.* [F f. L (PASSION)]

**impǎ'ssioned** (-shŏnd) *a.* Deeply moved, ardent. [It. *impassionato* (PASSION)]

**impǎ'ss|ǐve** *a.* Void of feeling or emotion; serene; **~ǐ'vǐtў** *n.* [IN-²]

**impǎ'stō** *n.* (*pl.* **~s**). Laying on of paint thickly. [It.]

**impā'tien|t** (-shent) *a.* Not patient; showing lack of patience; intolerant (*of*); eager (*for* thing, *to* do); **~ce** *n.* [F f. L (IN-²)]

**impea'ch** *v.t.* Call in question, dis-parage, (character etc.); accuse of treason or high crime before compe-tent tribunal; **~ment** *n.* [F *empecher* f. L (*pedica* fetter)]

**impě'ccab|le** *a.* (**~lў**). Not liable to sin; (of thing) faultless; **~ǐ'lǐtў** *n.*; **impĕcū'nious** *a.* [PECUNIARY], having little or no money; **impĕcūniŏ'sǐtў** *n.* [IN-²]

**impě'd|e** *v.t.* Retard by obstruct-ing, hinder; **~ance** *n.*, total effective resistance of electric circuit etc. to alternating current. [L *impedio* (*pes ped-* foot)]

**impě'dǐment** *n.* Hindrance (**~** in one's **speech**, lisp or stammer); (in *pl.*, and esp. in L form **-e'nta**) baggage esp. of army; **~al** (-ě'n-) *a.* [L (prec.)]

**impě'l** *v.t.* (**-ll-**). Drive, force, urge, (*to* action, *to* do); propel; **~lent** *a.*, impelling. [L (*pello* drive)]

**impě'nd** *v.i.* Hang (*over*); (of event, danger) be imminent (*impending disaster*). [L (*pendeo* hang)]

**impě'nétrab|le** *a.* (**~lў**). Not penetrable; impervious (*to, by*, ideas etc.); inscrutable; **~ǐ'lǐtў** *n.* [IN-²]

**impě'nǐten|t** *a.* Not penitent; **~ce** *n.*

**impě'rat|ǐve. 1.** *a.* (Gram.) ex-pressing command; peremptory; necessary, urgent. **2.** *n.* Imperative mood; **~ǐ'val** *a.* [L (*impero* com-mand)]

**impercě'ptǐb|le** *a.* (**~lў**). Not perceptible, very slight or gradual; **imperci'pient** *a.*, lacking in per-ception; **imperci'pience** *n.* [F or L (IN-²)]

**imper'fěct. 1.** *a.* Not perfect, in-complete, faulty; (Gram., of tense) denoting action going on but not completed (esp. in past, e.g. *was doing*). **2.** *n.* Imperfect tense. **3.** **imperfě'ction** *n.* imperfectness, fault, blemish. [F f. L]

**impēr′ial. 1.** *a.* (~ly). Of an empire or similar sovereign state; (Hist.) of the British Empire; of an emperor; supreme; majestic; (of weights and measures) used by statute in U.K.' (*imperial gallon* etc.). **2.** *n.* Small part of beard left growing beneath lower lip [partly after Emperor Napoleon III]. **3.** ~ism *n.*, an imperial system of government etc., (Hist.) extension of British Empire to protect trade etc. or unite policy for defence, commerce, etc., (military) extension of a country's power by the acquisition of dependencies, (usu. derog.) extension of a country's influence through trade, diplomacy, etc.; ~ist *n.*; ~i′stic *a.* [ f. L (*imperium* dominion)]

**impĕr′il** *v.t.* (‖-ll-). Endanger. [IN-¹]

**impēr′ious** *a.* Domineering; urgent. [L (as IMPERIAL)]

**impĕ′rishab|le** *a.* (~ly). Not perishable; ~i′litў *n.* [IN-²]

**impĕr′manen|t** *a.* Not permanent; ~ce, ~cў, *ns.* [IN-²]

**impĕr′mӗab|le** *a.* Not permeable; ~i′litў *n.*; **impermi′ssible** *a.*, not allowable; **impĕr′sonal** *a.* (-lly), having no personality or personal feeling or reference, (of verb) used only in 3rd sing. (e.g. *it snows*); **impersonā′litў** *n.*

**impĕr′son|āte** *v.t.* (~able). Personify; pretend to be (another person); play the part of; act (character); ~ā′tion, ~ātor, *ns.* [IN-¹, L PERSONA]

**impĕr′tinen|t** *a.* Insolent, saucy; irrelevant; ~ce *n.*; **impertûr′bable** *a.* (-bly), not excitable, calm; **imperturbabi′litў** *n.*; **impĕr′vious** *a.*, not affording passage (*to* water etc.), (fig.) inaccessible *to* argument etc. [IN-²]

**impĕti′gō** *n.* (*pl.* ~s). Contagious pustular skin disease. [L (*impeto* assail)]

**i′mpĕtus** *n.* Force with which body moves; moving force, impulse; **impĕ′tūous** *a.*, moving violently or fast, acting with rash or sudden energy; **impĕtūŏ′sitў** *n.*

**impi′etў** *n.* Lack of piety or reverence. [F or L (IMPIOUS)]

**impi′nge** (-nj) *v.i.* & *t.* (Cause to) make impact (*on*); encroach (*upon*); ~ment (-njm-) *n.* [L (*pango* pact-fix)]

**i′mpious** *a.* Not pious, wicked. [L (PIOUS)]

**i′mpish** *a.* Of, like, an imp; mischievous. [IMP]

**implă′cab|le** *a.* (~ly). Not appeasable; ~i′litў *n.* [F or L (IN-²)]

**implant** (-ah-). **1.** (-ah′-) *v.t.* Insert, fix, (*in*); instil (idea etc.) in person's mind; insert (tissue etc.) in a living object; plant; ~ā′tion *n.* **2.** (ĭ′-) *n.* Thing implanted, esp. piece of tissue etc. [F or L (PLANT)]

**implau′sib|le** (-z-) *a.* (~ly). Not plausible; ~i′litў *n.* [IN-²]

**i′mplӗment¹** *n.* Tool, instrument, utensil; (in *pl.*) equipment etc.; **i′mplӗment²** (*or* -mĕ′nt) *v.t.*, carry (contract, promise, etc.) into effect; **implӗmĕntā′tion** *n.* [L (*impleo* fulfil)]

**i′mplic|āte** *v.t.* Involve, include, (person *in* charge or crime); imply; ~ā′tion *n.*, (esp.) thing implied. [L (*plico* fold)]

**impli′cit** *a.* Implied though not expressed (*implicit* denial, *promise*); involved in some general principle (~ faith, esp. in doctrines of Church as such, cf. EXPLICIT; ~ obedience, absolute). [F or L (prec.)]

**implō′|de** *v.i.* & *t.* (Cause to) burst inwards; ~sion (-zhon) *n.*; ~sive (*or* -z-) *a.* [IN-¹; cf. EXPLODE]

**implōr′e** *v.t.* Beg earnestly (*implore his aid, him to go*). [F or L (*ploro* weep)]

**implȳ′** *v.t.* Involve truth of (thing not expressly stated, *that*); mean; insinuate; **impli′ӗdlў** *adv.* [F f. L (IMPLICATE)]

**impoli′te** *a.* Uncivil, rude; **impŏ′litĭc** *a.*, inexpedient; **impŏ′nderable**, (*a.*, -bly), weightless, very light, (fig.) that cannot be estimated, (*n.*) imponderable thing. [IN-²]

**import. 1.** (-ôr′t) *v.t.* Bring, introduce, (thing, esp. foreign goods *into* country; ~ā′tion, ~er, *ns.*); imply, mean; express, make known, (*that*). **2.** (ĭ′-) *n.* What is implied, meaning; importance; importing; (usu. in *pl.*) amount or article imported. [L (*porto* carry)]

**impôr′tan|t** *a.* Of great consequence (*to* person, plan, etc.), momentous; (of person) having high position of authority or rank; pompous; ~ce *n.*, being important, significance, weight.

**impôr′t|unate** *a.* Persistent, pressing, in solicitation; **~ū′nǐtў** n. [L *importunus* inconvenient]

**impŏrtū′ne** (or -ōī′-) v.t. Solicit pressingly (person); solicit for immoral purpose. [F or L (prec.)]

**impŏ′se** (-z) v.t. & i. Lay (pages of type) in proper order; lay (tax, duty, etc., *upon*); palm off (thing *upon* person); enforce compliance with; **~ upon**, overawe, impress, take advantage of (person, his good nature etc.), deceive; **impŏ′sǐng** (-z-) a., impressive, formidable, esp. in appearance. [F f. L (*pono* put)]

**imposǐ′tion** (-z-) n. Laying on (of *hands* in blessing etc.); impost, tax; piece of advantage-taking or deception; ||work set as punishment at school. [F or L (prec.)]

**impŏ′ssǐb|le** a. (**~ly**). Not possible; (loosely) not easy or convenient or credible; (colloq.) outrageous, intolerable, (*impossible hat, person*); **~ǐ′lǐtў** n. [F or L (IN-²)]

**i′mpŏst** n. Upper course of pillar, carrying arch; tax; duty, tribute. [F f. L (IMPOSE)]

**impŏ′st|or** n. One who assumes a false character or personality; swindler; **~ure** n., deception, sham. [F f. L (prec.)]

**i′mpoten|t** a. Powerless; decrepit; (of male) without sexual power; **~ce** n. [F f. L (IN-²)]

**impou′nd** v.t. Shut up (cattle etc.) in pound; take legal possession of; confiscate. [IN-¹]

**impŏ′verish** v.t. Make poor; **~ment** n. [F (POVERTY)]

**imprā′ctǐc|able** a. (**~ably**). Not practicable; (of person, thing) unmanageable; **~abǐ′lǐtў** n.; **\*~al** a., not practical, not practicable; **\*~ǎ′lǐtў** n. [IN-²]

**i′mprĕc|āte** v.t. Invoke (evil *upon*); **~ā′tion** n.; **~atorў** a. [L (*precor* pray)]

**imprĕc|ǐ′se** a. Not precise; **~ǐ′sion** (-zhon) n. [IN-²]

**imprĕ′gnab|le** a. (**~ly**). (Of fortress etc., or fig.) proof against attack; **~ǐ′lǐtў** n. [F (IN-², L *prehendo* take)]

**i′mprĕgn|āte** v.t. (**~atable**). Make (female) pregnant; fertilize (ovum); fill, saturate, (*with*; lit. or fig.); **~ā′tion** n. [L (PREGNANT)]

**imprĕsār′iŏ** n. (pl. **~s**). Organizer of public entertainment esp. opera or concert. [It.]

**imprĕscrī′ptǐble** a. That cannot

be legally taken away (*imprescriptible right*). [L (PRESCRIBE)]

**imprĕ′ss**¹ v.t. (Hist.) Force to serve in army or navy; **~ment** n. [IN-¹, PRESS²]

**imprĕss²**. **1.** (-ĕ′s) v.t. (**~ible**). Imprint, stamp, (mark etc. *on* thing, thing *with* mark); enforce, fix, (*impress idea on* person, his mind; *impress on* person *that, how*, etc.); affect, influence, deeply (*impress* person *with idea, one's importance*). **2.** (ǐ′-) n. Mark impressed; (fig.) characteristic mark. [F (PRESS¹)]

**imprĕ′ssion** (-shon) n. Impressing, mark impressed; print from type or engraving; copies forming one issue of book, newspaper, etc.; unaltered reprint from standing type or plates (as opp. to *edition*); effect produced (esp. on mind or feelings); representation of such effect by artist, mimic, musician, etc.; notion, belief, (*a vague, strong, mistaken, impression*; *I was under, had the, impression that*); **~able** a. (**-bly**), easily influenced; **~abǐ′lǐtў** n.; **~ǐsm** n., style of painting, music, or writing so as to give general effect without detail; **~ǐst** n.; **~ǐ′stǐc** a. [F f. L (prec.)]

**imprĕ′ssǐve** a. Able to excite deep feeling esp. of approval or admiration. [IMPRESS²]

**imprǐmā′tur** (or -ah′-) n. Licence to print (now usu. of R.C. Ch.); sanction. [L, = let it be printed]

**imprǐ′mǐs** adv. (arch.) In the first place. [L *in primis* among the first]

**imprint**. **1.** (-rǐ′-) v.t. Impress (mark *on*, idea etc. *on* or *in* mind); stamp (*thing with* figure). **2.** (ǐ′m-) n. Impression, stamp, (lit. & fig.). [F f. L (PRESS¹)]

**imprǐ′son** (-z-) v.t. Put into prison; (fig.) confine; **~ment** n. [F]

**imprŏ′bab|le** a. (**~ly**). Not likely; **~ǐ′lǐtў** n.; **imprŏ′bǐtў** n., wickedness, dishonesty. [IN-²]

**imprŏ′mptū** adv., a., & n. **1.** adv. & a. Extempore. **2.** n. Impromptu musical or other composition. [F, f. L *in promptu* in readiness (PROMPT)]

**imprŏ′per** a. Inaccurate, wrong, (**~ fraction**, with numerator greater than denominator); unseemly, indecent. [F or L (IN-²)]

||**imprŏ′prǐ|āte** v.t. Place (tithes, benefice) in hands of layman; **~ā′tion** n.; **~ātor** n., such layman. [L (PROPER)]

**impropri′etў** n. Incorrectness, unfitness, indecency; instance of this. [F or L (IN-²)]

**improve′** (-ōō′v) v.t. & i. Make or become better; make good use of (occasion, opportunities); (in part.) giving moral benefit (improving book); ~ **upon**, produce something better than; **improvabi′litў** (-ōōv-), ~**ment** (-vm-), ns. [AF f. F prou profit]

**imprŏ′viden|t** a. Unforeseeing; thriftless; ~**ce** n. [F (IN-²)]

**i′mprovis|e** (-z) v.t. Compose, utter, (verse, music, etc.) extempore; provide, construct, extempore; ~**ā′tion** n.; **improvi′satorў** (-z-) a. [F or It. f. L (PROVIDE)]

**impru′den|t** (-ōō′-) a. Rash, indiscreet; ~**ce** n. [L (IN-²)]

**i′mpūden|t** a. Shameless; insolent; ~**ce** n. [L (pudeo be ashamed)]

**impŭ′gn** (-ū′n) v.t. Call in question, challenge, (statement, act); ~**ment** n. [L (pugno fight)]

**i′mpŭlse** n. Impelling, push; impetus; sharp force producing change of momentum (e.g. blow of hammer); wave of excitation in nerve; mental incitement; sudden tendency to act without reflection (impulse buying); **impŭ′lsion** (-shŏn) n., impulse (usu. in first sense); **impŭ′lsĭve** a., tending to impel, apt to be moved or prompted by impulse. [L (PULSE¹)]

**impŭ′nitў** n. Exemption from punishment or injurious consequences (rob, drink, with impunity). [L (poena penalty)]

**impūr′e** (or ĭ′-) a. Dirty; unchaste; mixed with foreign matter, adulterated; **impūr′itў** n. [L (IN-²)]

**impūt′e** v.t. Attribute (esp. fault to); ~**ā′tion** n. [F f. L (puto reckon)]

**in** prep., adv., a., & n. **1.** prep. expr. inclusion or position within limits of space, time, circumstance, etc., (in Europe, Britain, Kent, Leeds, or any familiar or important place with emphasis on extent; in bed, prison, school; in a box, a crowd; in the car, the house, the rain, the street); wearing as dress (in blue, cotton; in a suit); with respect to (blind in one eye; weak in Latin; lacking in courage; a change in the weather; the finest thing in comfort; seven in number; a mile in length) as proportion of (one in three failed; gradient of one in six; she is one in a million); as member of (in the army, the orchestra, the union); concerned with (in politics, my opinion); as content of (there is something in what you say); (of condition: in CLOVER, bad health, LIQUOR); having as purpose (in search of; in reply to); (of arrangement: packed in tens; falling in folds); (of word) having as beginning or ending (words in 'pro-'); (of material or means: drawn in pencil; worker in gold; modelled in bronze; curtains in green velvet); (of musical key or language: symphony in G; written in French); (of person or person's writings etc.: found a friend in Mary; find the answer in Shaw); during the time of (in the night; in summer; in 1978; read it in two hours); after the time of (will be back in two hours); (of capacity: as far as in me lies; have it in one to do the job); (of animal) pregnant with (in calf); (with vb. of motion or change: put it in your pocket; cut it in two; throw him in the river); (with ind. obj.: believe in, trust in, his words; engage in, share in, the enterprise); (adv. phrs.: in any case, in fact, in short; inasmuch as, because; in so FAR as); **nothing, not much, in it**, no, not much, advantage to any competitor; **in that**, because, in so far as. **2.** adv. expr. position within limits or motion to such position; into room, house, etc., (come in, walk in); at home, in one's office, etc., (is he in?); in a publication (is the advert in?); on or to the inward side (coat with woolly side in; rub the ointment in); so as to be enclosed (hemmed, locked, in); in fashion, season, office, favour, etc., (long skirts, mushrooms, Labour, are in; my luck was in); functioning as batsman, elected candidate, etc.; (of fire etc.) with continued burning; (of transport, season, harvest, order, etc.) having arrived or been received; (of effective action: join in; the TIDE is in); **in and out**, sometimes in, sometimes out; **in at**, present at (the finish etc.); **in between**, in the space or time between; **in for**, about to undergo, competing in or for; **have it in for**, seek revenge on (person); **in off**, losing HAZARD; **in on**, sharing in (secret etc.); **in with**, on good terms with (person); **day, week, etc. in, day etc. out**, throughout a long succession of days, weeks, etc.; **in-swinger**, (Crick.) ball that swings towards batsman; **in-tray** (for incoming documents); as suf. denoting prolonged action esp. by

large numbers (SIT-*in*, TEACH-*in*). **3.**
*a.* Internal, living etc. inside (**in--patient**, one residing in hospital
during treatment); fashionable, eso-
teric, (**in-group**, persons with interest in common). **4.** *n.* ins and
outs, details (*of* procedure etc.). [E]
**in-**[1] *pref.* (**il-** bef. *l*; **im-** bef. *b, m, p*;
**ir-** bef. *r*). In, on, into, towards,
within, (*induce, influx, insight, intrude*).
[prec. or L]
**in-**[2] *pref.* (**il-** etc. as prec.) = UN- 4
(*inedible, insane, insignificant*). [L]
**in.** *abbr.* inch(es).
**inabi′lity** *n.* Being unable; lack of
power or means. [IN-[2]]
*in absentia* (ĭn ăbsĕ′ntĭa, -shĭa)
*adv.* In (his, her, their) absence. [L]
**inacce′ssib′le** (-ks-) *a.* (**~ly**) Not
accessible (*of person*) unapproachable; **ină′ccurate** *a.*, not accurate;
**ină′ccuracy** *n.* [IN-[2]]
**ină′ct|ion** *n.* Absence of action;
sluggishness; **~ive** *a.*, not active, indolent; **~ivate** *v.t.*, make inactive or
inoperative; **~i′vity** *n.*
**ină′dequa|te** *a.* Not adequate; in-
sufficient; incompetent; **~cy** *n.*
**inadmi′ssib′le** *a.* That cannot be
admitted or allowed; **~i′lity** *n.*
**inadver′ten|t** *a.* (Of action) un-
intentional; negligent, inattentive
[ADVERT[2]]; **~ce, ~cy,** *ns.*; **inad-
vi′sable** (-z-) *a.*, not advisable;
**ină′lienable** *a.* (**-bly**), not alien-
able; **inălienabi′lity** *n.*
**inămora′t|o** (-rah′-) *n.* (*fem.* **~a**
*pr. -a*). Lover. [It. *innamorato* (IN-[1],
*amor* love)]
**ină′ne** *a.* Empty, void; silly, senseless; **ină′nity** *n.* [L *inanis*]
**ină′nim|ate** *a.* Not endowed with,
or deprived of, animal life; spiritless,
dull; **~ā′tion** *n.* [L (IN-[2])]
**inani′tion** *n.* Emptiness esp. from
want of nourishment. [L (INANE)]
**ină′pplicab|le** *a.* (**~ly**). Not
applicable, unsuitable; **~i′lity** *n.*;
**ină′pposite** (-z-) *a.*, not apposite,
out of place; **inappre′ciable** (-sha-)
*a.* (**-bly**), not appreciable, not worth
reckoning; **inappre′ciative** (-shĭ-)
*a.*, not appreciative. [IN-[2]]
**ină′pprehe′nsible** *a.* (**-bly**). That
cannot be grasped (by senses or
intellect); **inappro′priate** *a.*, not
appropriate; **ină′pt** *a.*, not suitable,
unskilful; **ină′ptitude** *n.*
**inărti′culate** *a.* Not jointed; not
articulate, indistinct, dumb; unable
to express oneself clearly; **inărti′stic**

*a.* (**-ically**), contrary to, unskilled
in, art; **inatte′ntion** *n.*, lack of
attention, neglect of courteous attentions; **inatte′ntive** *a.*; **inau′dible**
*a.* (**-bly**), that cannot be heard;
**inaudibi′lity** *n.*
**inau′gur|ate** *v.t.* Admit (person)
to office, begin (undertaking), initiate public use of (building etc.),
with ceremony; begin, introduce;
**~al,** (*a.*; **-lly**) of inauguration,
(*n.*) inaugural speech or address;
**~ā′tion, ~ātor,** *ns.* [L (AUGUR)]
**inauspi′cious** (-shŭs) *a.* Not of
good omen, unlucky. [IN-[2]]
**i′nboard** *adv.* & *a.* (Situated)
within sides, towards centre, of ship,
aircraft, or vehicle. [IN]
**i′nborn, inbre′d,** *adjs.* Implanted
by nature, innate; **i′nbreeding** *n.*,
BREEDING in and in; **i′n-built** (-bĭ-)
*a.*, built-in.
*****Inc.** *abbr.* Incorporated.
**I′nca** (ĭ′-) *n.* King, royal or other
member of people, of Peru before
Spanish conquest. [Quechua, = lord]
**incă′lculab|le** (ĭn-k-) *a.* (**~ly**).
Beyond calculation; not calculable
beforehand, uncertain; **~i′lity** *n.*
[IN-[2]]
*in camera.* See CAMERA.
**incande′sce** (ĭn-k-) *v.i.* & *t.*
(Cause to) glow with heat; **~nt** *a.*,
glowing with heat, shining, (of
artificial light) produced by glowing
filament etc.; **~nce** *n.* [L (*candeo*
become white)]
**incantā′tion** (ĭn-k-) *n.* Magical
formula, spell, charm. [F f. L
(*canto* sing)]
**incă′pable** (ĭn-k-) *a.* (**-bly**). Not
capable (**~ of** doing, too honest
etc.; **drunk and ~,** so drunk as to
be incapable of rational conduct);
**incapabi′lity** (ĭn-k-) *n.* [IN-[2]]
**incapă′cit|y** (ĭn-k-) *n.* Inability
(*for* work, *for* doing); legal disquali-
cation; **~ate** *v.t.*, make incapable or
unfit (*for, from*).
**incăr′cer|ate** (ĭn-k-) *v.t.* Imprison;
**~ā′tion** *n.* [L (*carcer* prison)]
**incăr′nadine** (ĭn-k-) *v.t.* (poet.)
Dye crimson. [F f. It. (foll.)]
**incarnate. 1.** (ĭn-kăr′năt) *v.t.*
Embody in flesh; put (idea etc.)
into concrete form; be living
embodiment of (quality etc.). **2.**
(ĭn-kăr′nat) *a.* Embodied in flesh,
esp. in human form (*an incarnate
fiend*; *a devil incarnate*); in recognizable
or perfect form. **3. incarnā′tion**

(ĭn-k-) *n.*, embodiment in flesh (**the Incarnation**, of Christ), living type (*of* quality). [L *incarnor* be made flesh (as CARNAGE)]

**incau′tious** (ĭn-kaw′sh*u*s) *a.* Rash. [IN-²]

**ince′ndiar|y. 1.** *a.* Of, guilty of, malicious setting on fire of property; (fig.) inflammatory; ~**y bomb** (filled with material for causing fires, instead of explosive). **2.** *n.* Incendiary person (lit. or fig.); incendiary bomb; ~**ism** *n.*, incendiary practices. [L (*incendo -cens-* kindle)]

**ince′nse¹** *v.t.* Make angry. [F f. L (prec.)]

**i′ncense². 1.** *n.* Gum, spice, giving sweet smell when burned; smoke of this esp. in religious ceremonial; flattery. **2.** *v.t.* Burn incense to; fumigate, perfume, as with incense. [F f. L *incensum* (prec.)]

**ince′ntive. 1.** *a.* Inciting. **2.** *n.* Motive, incitement, (*to*); payment etc. encouraging effort in work. [L, = setting the tune (*cano* sing)]

**ince′pt|ion** *n.* Beginning; ~**ive** *a.*, beginning, initial; ~**ive verb** (denoting beginning of action). [F, or L (*incipio -cept-* begin)]

**ince′rtitude** *n.* Uncertainty, doubt. [F or L (IN-²)]

**ince′ssant** *a.* Continual, repeated. [F or L (*cesso* cease)]

**i′ncest** *n.* Sexual intercourse of near relations; **ince′stuous** *a.*, (guilty of) incest. [L (*castus* chaste)]

**inch. 1.** *n.* Twelfth of (linear) foot, 2·54 cm; used as unit of map-scale (= 1 inch to 1 mile) or as unit of rainfall (= 1 inch depth of water); **by ~es**, gradually; *is every ~* (thoroughly) *a king*; *flog* etc. person **within an ~ of his life**, almost to death; **a man of your ~es** (height). **2.** *v.t.* & *i.* Move gradually *in* etc. [E f. L *uncia* OUNCE¹]

**i′ncho|ate** (ĭ′n-k-). **1.** *v.t.* Begin, originate; ~**a′tion** *n.*; ~**ative** (or -kŏ′a-) *a.* **2.** (-at) *a.* Just begun; undeveloped. [L *inchoo, incoho* begin]

**i′ncidence** *n.* Falling on, contact with, a thing (**what is the ~ of the tax?**, on whom does it fall?); falling of line, ray, particles, etc., on surface (**angle of ~**, between such line and perpendicular to surface at point of incidence); range of influence. [F or L (foll.)]

**i′ncident. 1.** *a.* Apt to occur, naturally attaching, (*to*); (of rays etc.) falling (*upon*). **2.** *n.* Event, occurrence, esp. clash of armed forces (*frontier incident*); public event causing trouble; distinct piece of action in film, play, etc.; ~**al** (-ĕ′n-) *a.* (~**ally**), casual, not essential, liable to happen *to*; ~**al music** (played to accompany action of film, play, etc.). [F or L (*cado* fall)]

**inci′ner|ate** *v.t.* Consume (corpse, refuse) by fire; ~**a′tion** *n.*; ~**ator** *n.*, (esp.) furnace for incineration. [L (*cinis ciner-* ashes)]

**inci′pient** *a.* Beginning, in early stage. [L *incipio* begin]

**inci′s|e** (-z) *v.t.* Make a cut in; engrave; **inci′sion** (-zhon) *n.*; **inci′sive** *a.*, sharp, (fig.) acute, clear and effective, pointed; ~**or** *n.*, any tooth between canine teeth. [F f. L (*caedo* cut)]

**inci′te** *v.t.* Urge, stir up, (*to* action, *to* do); ~**ment** (-tm-) *n.* [F f. L (*cito* rouse)]

**inci′vi′lity** *n.* (Act of) rudeness. [F or L (IN-²)]

**incle′men|t** (ĭn-k-) *a.* (Of weather) severe, cold or stormy; ~**cy** *n.*

**inclin|a′tion** (ĭn-k-) *n.* Slope, slant, (~**ation** *of* line from the vertical or *to* another line, angle between them); propensity (*to* or *for* thing, *to* do); liking, affection; dip of magnetic needle. [F or L (foll.)]

**incline** (ĭn-k-). **1.** (-i′n) *v.t.* & *i.* (Cause to) lean from the vertical etc. (~**d plane**, sloping plane used e.g. to raise load with less force); bend (head, one*self*) forward or downward (**~ one's ear**, listen favourably to person etc.); dispose (*I am inclined to think so; this door is inclined to bang*); tend (*to* or *towards* fatness etc.). **2.** (ĭ′n-, -i′n) *n.* Inclined plane, slope. [F f. L (*clino* bend)]

**inclu′|de** (ĭn-kloo′d) *v.t.* Comprise, reckon in, as part of a whole (*7 were killed including the driver*); ~**sion** (-zhon) *n.*; ~**sive** *a.*, including (*of*; *pages 3 to 5 inclusive*, 3, 4, and 5; ~**sive terms** at hotel etc. including all or much). [L *includo -clus-* enclose (*claudo* shut)]

**inco′gnìto** (ĭn-k-; *or* -ē′to) *a.*, *adv.*, & *n.* **1.** *a.* & *adv.* Under false name, with identity concealed. **2.** *n.* (pl. ~**s**). (Pretended identity, anonymity, of) person who is incognito. [It., = unknown (IN-², COGNITION)]

**incoher′en|t** (ĭn-k-) *a.* Not coherent; **~ce** *n.* [IN-²]

**incombŭ′stĭb|le** (ĭn-k-) *a.* That cannot be burnt up; **~i′lĭtў** *n.* [L (IN-²)]

**i′ncome** (ĭn-k-) *n.* Periodical, esp. annual, receipts from one's work, lands, investments, etc.; **~ tax** (levied on income). [IN, COME]

**i′ncoming** (ĭ′n-kŭ-) *a.* Coming in, esp. succeeding (*incoming tenant*).

**incommĕ′nsur|able** (ĭn-k-; -sher-, -syer-) *a.* (**~ably**). Not commensurable; having no common measure integral or fractional (*with*); (Math.) irrational; **~abĭ′lĭtў** *n.*; **~ate** *a.*, disproportionate, inadequate (*to*), incommensurable. [L (IN-²)]

**incommō′d|e** (ĭn-k-) *v.t.* Trouble, annoy, impede; **~ious** *a.*, not affording comfort. [F or L (IN-²)]

**incommŭ′nicab|le** (ĭn-k-) *a.* (**~ly**). That cannot be shared or told; **~i′lĭtў** *n.* [L (IN-²)]

**incommŭ′nicadō** (ĭn-k-; -ah′-) *a.* Without means of communication, (of prisoner) in solitary confinement. [Sp. (-omu-)]

**incommŭ′nicatĭve** (ĭn-k-) *a.* Not communicative, taciturn; **incō′mparable** (ĭn-k-) *a.* (-bly), without an equal, matchless. [IN-²]

**incompă′tĭb|le** (ĭn-k-) *a.* (**~ly**). Opposed, discordant, inconsistent (*with*); **~i′lĭtў** *n.* [L (IN-²)]

**incŏ′mpéten|t** (ĭn-k-). **1.** *a.* Not qualified or able (*to* do); not able to function; not legally qualified; **~ce** *n.* **2.** *n.* Incompetent person. [F or L (IN-²)]

**incomplē′te** (ĭn-k-) *a.* Not complete. [L (IN-²)]

**incŏmprĕhĕ′ns|ĭble** (ĭn-k-) *a.* (**~ibly**). That cannot be understood; **~ibĭ′lĭtў** *n.*; **~ion** (-shŏn) *n.*, failure to understand.

**incomprĕ′ssĭb|le** (ĭn-k-) *a.* That cannot be compressed; **~i′lĭtў** *n.* [IN-²]

**inconcei′vab|le** (ĭn-kŏnsē′v-) *a.* (**~ly**). That cannot be imagined; (colloq.) strange, unlikely; **~i′lĭtў** *n.*; **inconclu′sĭve** (ĭn-kŏn-klōō′-) *a.*, (of argument, action, etc.) not decisive or convincing.

**incŏ′ngru|ous** (ĭn-kŏ′nggrōō-) *a.* Out of keeping (*with*); out of place, absurd; **~u′ĭtў** (-ōō′-) *n.* [L (IN-²)]

**incŏ′nsēqu|ent** (ĭn-k-) *a.* Dis-

connected, irrelevant; **~ĕ′ntial** (-shal) *a.*, unimportant, disconnected; **~ence** *n.* [IN-²]

**inconsī′der|able** (ĭn-k-) *a.* (**~ably**). Not worth considering; of small size, value, etc.; **~ate** *a.*, (of person or action) thoughtless, rash, lacking in regard for others' feelings. [L (IN-²)]

**inconsī′sten|t** (ĭn-k-) *a.* Discordant, incompatible, (*with*); acting at variance with one's own principles; **~cў** *n.* [IN-²]

**inconsō′lab|le** (ĭn-k-) *a.* (**~ly**). (Of person, grief) that cannot be consoled. [F or L (IN-²)]

**incŏ′nsonan|t** (ĭn-k-) *a.* Not harmonious (*with*, *to*); **~ce** *n.* [IN-²]

**inconspī′cŭous** (ĭn-k-) *a.* Not conspicuous. [L (IN-²)]

**incŏ′nstan|t** (ĭn-k-) *a.* Fickle, variable; **~cў** *n.* [F f. L (IN-²)]

**incontĕ′stab|le** (ĭn-k-) *a.* (**~ly**). That cannot be disputed. [F or L (IN-²)]

**incŏ′ntinen|t** (ĭn-k-) *a.* Lacking self-restraint (esp. in sexual desire); unable to control excretions voluntarily; **~ce** *n.* [F or L (IN-²)]

**incŏntrovĕ′tĭble** (ĭn-k-) *a.* (-bly). Indisputable. [IN-²]

**inconvĕ′nien|t** (ĭn-k-) *a.* Unfavourable to ease or comfort; awkward, troublesome; **~ce** *n.*, & *v.t.*, (cause to undergo, instance of) lack of ease or comfort. [F f. L (IN-²)]

**inconvĕ′rtĭble** (ĭn-k-) *a.* Not convertible; (esp. of currency) not convertible into another form; **~i′lĭtў** *n.* [F or L (IN-²)]

**incŏr′por|āte** (ĭn-k-). **1.** *v.t.* & *t.* Form into a corporation; admit as member of company etc.; unite (*in* one body, *with* others); **~ā′tion**, **~ātor**, *ns.* **2.** (-at) *a.* Incorporated. [L (*corpus* body)]

**incorp|ŏr′eal** (ĭn-k-) *a.* (-lly). Not composed of matter; (Law) having no material existence; **~orĕ′ĭtў** *n.*

**incorrĕ′ct** (ĭn-k-) *a.* Untrue, inaccurate; faulty. [F or L (IN-²)]

**incŏ′rrĭgĭb|le** (ĭn-k-) *a.* (**~ly**). (Of person or habit) incurably bad; **~i′lĭtў** *n.* [F or L (IN-²)]

**incorrŭ′ptĭb|le** (ĭn-k-) *a.* (**~ly**). That cannot decay or be corrupted (esp. by bribery); **~i′lĭtў** *n.*

**increase. 1.** (ĭn-krē′s) *v.i.* & *t.* Become, make, greater or more numerous e.g. by propagation;

advance (*in* power etc.). 2. (ĭ'n-krĕs) *n.* Growth, enlargement, (*is on the* ~, increasing); (of people, animals, plants) multiplication; (arch.) crops. [F f. L (*cresco* grow)]

**incre'd|ible** (ĭn-k-) *a.* (~ibly). That cannot be believed; (colloq.) surprising; ~ibi'lĭtў *n.*; ~ūlous *a.*, unwilling to believe; **incredū'lĭtў** *n.* [L (IN-²)]

**i'ncrement** (ĭn-k-) *n.* (Amount of) increase; profit. [L (*cresco* grow)]

**incri'min|āte** (ĭn-k-) *v.t.* Charge with crime; involve in accusation; ~ātor *n.*; ~ātorў *a.* [L (CRIME)]

**incrustā'tion** (ĭn-k-) *n.* Encrusting; crust, hard coating; deposit on a surface; (fig.) accretion of habit. [F or L (CRUST)]

**i'ncub|āte** (ĭn-k-) *v.t. & i.* Hatch (eggs) by sitting on them or by artificial heat; sit on eggs; cause (bacteria etc.) to develop; ~ā'tion *n.*, (esp.) development of disease germs before first symptoms appear; ~ātive, ~ātorў, *adjs.*; ~ātor *n.*, apparatus for hatching birds, rearing children born prematurely, or developing bacteria. [L (*cubo* lie)]

**i'ncub|us** *n.* (*pl.* ~uses, ~i *pr.* -ī). Evil spirit visiting sleeper; nightmare; oppressive person or thing. [L (prec.)]

**i'nculc|āte** (ĭ'n-k-) *v.t.* Impress (fact, habit, *in* or *upon* person) persistently; ~ā'tion, ~ātor, *ns.* [L (*calco* tread)]

**i'nculp|āte** (ĭ'n-k-) *v.t.* Accuse, blame; involve in charge; ~ā'tion *n.*; ~ātorў (-ŭ'-) *a.* [L (*culpa* fault)]

**incu'mben|t** (ĭn-k-). 1. *a.* Lying, resting, (*on*); **it is** ~**t on** you (is your duty) *to* do. 2. *n.* Holder of benefice or other office or place; ~cў *n.*, office, tenure of incumbent. [L *incumbo* lie upon]

**incūnā'būla** (ĭn-k-) *n.pl.* Early stages of thing; early printed books esp. from before 1501. [L, = swaddling-clothes]

**incur'** (ĭn-k-) *v.t.* (-rr-). Bring on oneself (danger, blame, loss). [L (*curro* run)]

**incūr'able** (ĭn-k-) *a.* (-bly) & *n.* (Person) that cannot be cured; ~abi'lĭtў *n.*; ~ious *a.*, devoid of curiosity, heedless; ~ĭŏ'sĭtў *n.* [L (IN-²)]

**incur'sion** (ĭn-kĕr'shŏn) *n.* Invasion; sudden attack; ~ive *a.* [L (INCUR)]

**incur'v|e** (ĭn-k-) *v.t.* Bend into curve; (esp. in *p.p.*) curve inwards; ~ā'tion *n.* [IN-¹]

**Ind.** *abbr.* Independent; Indiana.

**indê'btêd** (-dĕ't-) *a.* Owing money (*to*); obliged (*to* person etc. *for* thing). [F *endetté* (DEBT)]

**indê'cen|t** *a.* Unbecoming, unsuitable, (*indecent haste*); offending against decency (~**t assault**, sexual attack not involving rape); ~cў *n.* [F or L (IN-²)]

**indêci'pherab|le** *a.* (~ly). That cannot be deciphered. [IN-²]

**indêci'sion** (-zhon) *n.* Lack of decision, hesitation; ~ive (-ī's-) *a.* [F (IN-²)]

**indêcli'nable** *a.* (Gram.) That cannot be declined. [IN-²]

**indê'corous** *a.* Improper, in bad taste; **indêcŏr'um** *n.*, lack of decorum.

**indee'd** *adv.* In truth, really, admittedly, (*it is indeed lost*; emphat.: *I shall be very glad indeed*; *if indeed such a thing is possible*; *indeed it is*); ~**?**, really?; ~**!** (expr. incredulity, surprise, irony, etc.). [IN, DEED]

**indêfă'tĭgab|le** *a.* (~ly). Unwearying, unremitting, (*indefatigable worker, zeal*); ~i'lĭtў *n.* [F or L (FATIGUE)]

**indêfea'sĭb|le** (-z-) *a.* (~ly). (Of right, possession, etc.) that cannot be forfeited or annulled; ~i'lĭtў *n.* [IN-²]

**indêfê'nsĭb|le** *a.* (~ly). That cannot be defended (by force of arms or argument); ~i'lĭtў *n.* [IN-²]

**indêfi'nab|le** *a.* (~ly). That cannot be defined or exactly described. [IN-²]

**indê'finite** *a.* Vague, undefined; unlimited; (Gram.) not determining the person etc. referred to (~ **adjectives, pronouns, adverbs,** e.g. *some, someone, anyhow*; *indefinite* ARTICLE). [L (IN-²)]

**indê'lib|le** *a.* (~ly). That cannot be blotted out (*indelible ink, stain, disgrace*); that makes indelible marks (*indelible pencil*); ~i'lĭtў *n.* [F or L (*deleo* efface)]

**indê'lic|ate** *a.* Coarse, immodest; tactless; ~acў *n.* [IN-²]

**indê'mni|fу** *v.t.* Secure (person *from* or *against* loss); exempt from penalty (*for* actions); compensate; ~fĭcā'tion *n.*; ~tў *n.*, security against damage or loss, exemption from penalty, compensation, esp. sum exacted by victorious belligerent. [L *indemnis* free from loss]

**indent 1.** (-ĕ'-) *v.t.* & *i.* Make notches, dents, or recesses in; draw up (document) in duplicate (orig. on sheet divided by zigzag line); set back (beginning of paragraph etc.) inwards from margin; ‖make requisition (*on* person *for* thing), order (goods) by indent. **2.** (-ĕ'-, ĭ'-) *n.* Indentation; indenture; ‖official requisition for stores; ‖order (esp. from abroad) for goods. **3.** (ĭ'-) *n.* Dent, depression. **4.** ~ā'tion, **indĕ'ntion**, *ns.*, indenting, notch, deep recess. [AF f. L (*dens dentis* tooth)]

**indĕ'nture. 1.** *n.* Indented document; sealed agreement esp. (usu. in *pl.*) binding apprentice to master; formal list etc. **2.** *v.t.* Bind by indentures.

**indepe'ndent. 1.** *a.* Not depending on authority or control (*of*); not depending on another thing for validity etc., or on another person for one's opinion or livelihood (~t **income** etc., making it unnecessary to earn one's livelihood); (of broadcasting, school, etc.) not supported from public funds; acting independently of any political party; unwilling to be under obligation to others. **2.** *n.* Person who is politically independent. **3.** ~ce *n.*, being independent (**\*I~ce** Day, 4 July); ~cy *n.*, independent State. [IN-²]

**indescri'bable** *a.* (~ly). Vague; too great etc. to be described; ~i'lity *n.*; **indestru'ctible** *a.* (-bly), that cannot be destroyed; **indestrŭctibi'lity** *n.*

**indetĕr'minable** *a.* (-bly). That cannot be ascertained or settled; ~ate, *a.*, not fixed in extent, character, etc., left doubtful; *indeterminate* VOWEL; ~acў *n.*; ~ā'tion *n.*, lack of determination; ~ĭsm *n.*, doctrine that human action is not wholly determined by motives. [L (DETERMINE)]

**i'ndĕx. 1.** *n.* (*pl.* ~exes, ~ices *pr.* -ĭsēz). Forefinger; alphabetical list of subjects etc. with references, usu. at end of book; (R.C. Ch. Hist.) **the I~ex**, list of forbidden books; number expressing prices etc. in terms of a standard value; (Math.) exponent. **2.** *v.t.* Furnish (book) with index, enter in index; relate

(wages etc.) to value of price index, whence ~exā'tion *n.* [L]

**I'ndia** (ĭ'-) *n.* \*~ **ink**, Indian ink; ~**man**, (Hist.) ship in India trade; ~ **paper**, thin tough opaque printing-paper; **i~rubber**, RUBBER¹ (esp. for rubbing out pencil marks etc.). [place; E f. L f. Gk]

**I'ndian** (ĭ'-). **1.** *a.* Of India; of the subcontinent comprising India, Pakistan, and Bangladesh; of the original inhabitants of America and W. Indies; ~ **club**, bottle-shaped (for gymnast's use); ~ **corn**, maize; *Indian* FILE²; ‖~ **ink**, a black pigment; ~ **summer**, calm dry period in late autumn in Northern U.S. and elsewhere, (fig.) tranquil late period. **2.** *n.* Indian native; ‖**Red ~**, of aboriginal race of N. America, with reddish skin; **West ~**, native of W. Indies.

**i'ndic|āte** *v.t.* Point out, make known, show, state briefly, be sign of, suggest, call for, (indicate the house, the reason, that one consents; stronger measures are indicated); ~ā'tion *n.*; **indi'cative**, *a.* (Gram.) expressing fact, not command, wish, etc., (indicative mood), (or ĭ'ndĭkā-) suggestive *of*, (n.) indicative mood; ~ātor *n.*, person or thing that indicates, recording instrument on machine etc., board giving current information, device to show intended turn by vehicle; ~atorў *a.* [L (*dico* make known)]

**indices.** See INDEX.

**indi'ct** (-ī't) *v.t.* Accuse (person *for* offence, *as* offender, *on* charge). esp. by legal process; ~**able** *a.* (of person or offence); ~**ment** *n.* [F (INDITE)]

**I'ndies** (ĭ'ndĭz) *n.pl.* **East ~**. islands etc. east of India; **West ~**. islands of central America. [pl. of obs. *Indy* INDIA]

**indi'fferen|t** *a.* Impartial; having no interest in or inclination for or against (indifferent to); neither good nor bad; bad, poor, (in indifferent taste; **very ~t**, definitely bad); unimportant; ~ce *n.*, absence of interest or attention (to, towards); neutrality, unimportance; ~tĭsm *n.*, indifferent attitude esp. in religion; ~tĭst *n.* [F or L (IN-²)]

**indi'genous** *a.* Native, belonging naturally, (to the soil etc.). [L]

**i'ndigen|t** *a.* Needy, poor; ~ce *n* [F f. L (*egeo* need)]

**ĭndĭgĕ'st|ion** (-schon) n. (Case of, pain from) difficulty in digesting food (lit. or fig.); undigested condition; **~ĭble** a. (-bly), difficult to digest; **~ĭbi'lĭty** n. [F f. L (IN-²)]

**ĭndĭ'gn|ant** a. Moved by mingled anger and scorn or sense of injury (*at* thing, *with* person); **~ā'tion** n., such feeling; **~ĭty** n., unworthy treatment, insult. [L (*dignus* worthy)]

**ĭ'ndĭgō** n. (pl. **~s**). (Blue dye from) kind of leguminous plant; **~** (**blue**), blue-violet; **ĭndĭgō'tĭc** a. [Sp. & Port. f. L f. Gk *indikon* Indian (dye)]

**ĭndĭrĕ'ct** a. Not straight, not going straight to the point, not directly aimed at, (*indirect road*, *reply, result*); **~ lighting** (reflected, from concealed source); *indirect* OBJECT, QUESTION; **~ speech**, reported speech; *indirect* TAX. [F or L (IN-²)]

**ĭndĭscer'nĭb|le** a. (~ly). That cannot be distinguished; **ĭndĭ'scĭpline** n., lack of discipline; **ĭndĭscree't** a., injudicious, unwary; **ĭndĭscrē'tion** n., indiscreet conduct, imprudent immoral action; **ĭndĭscrĭ'mĭnate** a., confused, promiscuous, not discriminating; **ĭndĭscrĭmĭnā'tion** n. [IN-²]

**ĭndĭspĕ'nsab|le** a. (~ly). That cannot be dispensed with, necessary *to* or *for*; that cannot be evaded; **~ĭ'lĭty** n. [L (IN-²)]

**ĭndĭspō'se** (-z) v.t. Render unfit or unable (*for* thing; *to* do); make averse (*towards, from; to* do); (esp. in p.p.) make slightly unwell; **~osĭ'tion** (-zĭ'-) n., (esp.) slight illness; **ĭndĭspū'table** (*or* -dĭ'-) a. (-bly), that cannot be disputed or questioned; **ĭndĭssŏ'lūble** a. (-bly), lasting, stable. [IN-²]

**ĭndĭstĭ'nct** a. Not distinct; confused, obscure; **~ĭve** a., without distinctive features; **ĭndĭstĭ'nguĭshable** (-nggw-) a. (-bly), not distinguishable (*from*). [IN-²]

**ĭndĭ'te** v.t. Put (speech etc.) into words; (usu. joc.) write (letter etc.). [F f. L (*dicto* DICTATE)]

**ĭndĭvĭ'dŭal. 1.** a. Single; particular, not general; having distinct character; characteristic of particular person etc.; designed for use by one person. **2.** n. Single member of a class; single human being; (colloq.) person (*a tiresome individual*). **3.** **~ĭsm** n., egoism, social theory favouring free action by individuals;

**~ĭst** n.; **~ĭ'stĭc** a.; **~ĭty** (-ă'-) n., separate existence, (strong) individual character; **~ĭze** v.t., **ĭndĭvĭ'dŭate** v.t., give individual character to; **~lý** adv. personally, distinctively, one by one. [L (DIVIDE)]

**ĭndĭvĭ'sĭb|le** (-z-) a. (~ly). Not divisible or distributable; **~ĭ'lĭty** n. [L (IN-²)]

**I'ndō-** (ĭ-) in comb. Indian (and); **~-European, -Germanic**, of the family of languages spoken over greater part of Europe and Asia as far as N. India. [L f. Gk (INDIA)]

**ĭndō'ctrĭn|āte** v.t. Teach, instruct; imbue with or *with* a doctrine or opinion; **~ā'tion** n. [IN-¹]

**ĭ'ndolen|t** a. Slothful, lazy; **~ce** n. [L (*doleo* suffer pain)]

**ĭndŏ'mĭtab|le** a. (~ly). Unyielding, untiringly persistent. [L (DAUNT)]

**ĭ'ndoor** (-dŏr) a. Done, existing, used, within house or under cover (*indoor games*); **~s** (-ŏr'z) adv., within house, under roof. [IN]

**ĭndŏr'se.** See ENDORSE.

**ĭ'ndrawn** a. Drawn in, aloof. [IN]

**ĭndū'bĭtab|le** a. (~ly). That cannot be doubted. [F or L (*dubito* to doubt)]

**ĭndū'ce** v.t. (-cible). Prevail on, persuade, (*nothing shall induce me to go*); bring about; produce by induction; infer as induction; **~ment** (-sm-) n., what induces, attraction, motive. [L (*duco duct-* lead)]

**ĭndū'ct** v.t. Install (person *to* benefice, *into* seat etc.); **~ance** n., amount of induction of current.

**ĭndū'ct|ion** n. Inducting; inducing; bringing on by artificial means; inferring of general law from particular instances (cf. DEDUCTION); production of electric or magnetic state by proximity (without contact) of electrified or magnetized body, quantity giving measure of such influence; production of electric current by change of magnetic field; drawing of fuel mixture into cylinder(s) of internal combustion engine; **~ĭve** a., based on or using induction (cf. INDUCE)]

**ĭndū'e.** See ENDUE.

**ĭndū'lge** v.t. & i. Please (person, oneself) by compliance with wishes (*in* matter etc.); favour (person *with* thing given); yield freely to (desire etc.); take pleasure freely *in* (activity etc.); (colloq.) partake (too) freely of intoxicants; **~nce** *n.*, indulging (oneself), privilege granted, (R.C. Ch.) remission of punishment still due after sacramental absolution; **~nt** *a.*, (esp.) (too) willing to overlook faults etc. [L *indulgeo* give free rein to]

**i'ndūr| āte** *v.t. & i.* Make, become, hard; make callous; become inveterate; **~ā'tion** *n.*; **~ātive** *a.* [L (*durus* hard)]

**indū'strial** *a.* (**~ly**). Of industries; designed, or only fit for, industrial use (*industrial* ESTATE, *alcohol*); **~ nation** (having highly developed industries); **~ revolution**, rapid development of British industry through use of machines in late 18th and early 19th c.; **~ism** *n.*, system involving prevalence of industries; **~ist** *n.*, person engaged in management of industry; **~ize** *v.t.* [foll.]

**i'ndustry** *n.* Diligence; habitual employment in useful work; branch of trade or manufacture; trade or manufacture collectively; **indū'strious** *a.*, diligent. [F or L]

**i'ndwélling** *a. & n.* Dwelling within, inhabiting, (usu. fig.). [IN-¹]

**-ine** *suf.* forming *adjs.* w. senses 'belonging to', 'of the nature of', (*Alpine, asinine*), & *fem. ns.* (*heroine*). [F, L, & Gk]

**inē'brïate** *a.,n., & v.* **1.** *a.* Drunken. **2.** *n.* Drunkard. **3.** (-āt) *v.t.* Make drunk; **inēbrïā'tion** *n.*; **inēbri'etý** *n.*, drunkenness. [L (*ebrius* drunk)]

**inē'díb|le** *a.* Not edible, esp. by nature; **~i'lïtý** *n.*; **inē'dūcable** *a.*, incapable of being educated, esp. through mental retardation. [IN-²]

**inē'ffab|le** *a.* (**~ly**). Too great etc. for description in words; that must not be uttered. [F or L (*effor* speak out)]

**inēffa'ceab|le** (-sa-) *a.* (**~ly**), that cannot be effaced; **inēffē'ctive** *a.*, **inēffē'ctüal** *a.* (-lly), **inēffīcā'cious** (-shŭs) *a.*, not producing (desired) effect; **inēffī'cient** (-shĕnt) *a.*, not efficient or fully capable; **inēffī'ciencý** (-shen-) *n.*; **inēlă'stic** *a.* (-ically), not elastic, unadaptable; **inēlăsti'cïtý** *n.*; **inē'légant** *a.*, ungraceful, unrefined, (of style) unpolished; **inē'légance** *n.*; **inē'lĭgible** *a.* (-bly), not eligible, undesirable; **inēlĭgĭbi'lĭtý** *n.* [IN-²]

**inēlŭ'ctable** *a.* Against which it is useless to struggle. [L (*luctor* strive)]

**inē'pt** *a.* Absurd, silly; out of place; unskilful; **~itūde** *n.* [L (APT)]

**inē'quable** *a.* Unfair, not uniform; **inēqua'lĭtý** (-ŏ'l-) *n.*, lack of equality in any respect, variableness, unevenness of surface; **inē'quĭtable** *a.* (-bly), unfair, unjust; **inē'quĭtý** *n.*; **inēra'dĭcable** *a.* (-bly), that cannot be rooted out. [IN-²]

**inē'rt** *a.* Without inherent power of action, reaction, motion, or resistance; sluggish, slow; **inē'rtia** (-sha, -shya) *n.*, property by which matter continues in its existing state of rest or uniform motion in straight line unless that state is changed by external force; inertness; **~ia reel** (allowing automatic adjustment of safety-belt rolled round it); **~ia selling**, sending of goods not ordered in hope that they will not be refused. [L *iners -ert-* (ART²)]

**inēscā'pab|le** *a.* (**~ly**). That cannot be escaped. [IN-²]

**inēssē'ntial** (-shal) *a.* (**~ly**) & *n.*, unnecessary (thing); **inē'stĭmable** *a.* (-bly), too good, great, etc., to be estimated. [IN-²]

**inē'vĭtab|le** *a.* (**~ly**). Unavoidable, bound to happen or (re)appear (*ruin is inevitable, and* with *his inevitable camera*); **~i'lĭtý** *n.* [L (*evito* avoid)]

**inēxă'ct** (-gz-) *a.*, not exact; **~itūde** *n.*; **inēxcū'sable** (-za-) *a.* (-bly), that cannot be excused or justified; **inēxhau'stible** (-ĭgzaw'-) *a.* (-bly), that cannot be exhausted. [IN-²]

**inē'xorab|le** *a.* (**~ly**). Relentless; **~i'lĭtý** *n.* [F or L (*exoro* entreat)]

**inēxpē'dĭen|t** *a.*, not expedient; **~cý** *n.*; **inēxpē'nsive** *a.*, offering good value for the price; **inēxpē'rïence** *n.*, lack of (knowledge or skill from) experience; **inēxpē'rïenced** (-st) *a.*; **inē'xpert** *a.*, unskilled. [IN-²]

**inē'xpĭab|le** *a.* (**~ly**). That cannot be expiated or appeased; **inē'xplĭcable** (*or* -lĭ'k-) *a.* (-bly), that cannot be explained; **inēxplĭcabi'lĭtý** *n.*; **inēxprē'ssible** *a.* (-bly). that cannot be expressed in words.

**in extenso** (ĭn ĕkstĕ'nsō) *adv.* At full length; **in extremis** (ĭn ĕkstrē'mĭs) *a.*, at point of death, (fig.) in great difficulties. [L]

**inē'xtrĭcab|le** *a.* (**~ly**). That cannot be loosened, solved, resolved, or escaped from, (*inextricable knot*, *problem, confusion, dilemma*). [L (EX-TRICATE)]

**infǎ′llib|le** *a.* (~ly). Incapable of erring; (of method or remedy or test) unfailing; **~i′lǐtў** *n.* (esp. of Pope speaking *ex cathedra*). [F or L (IN-²)]

**i′nfam|ous** *a.* Notoriously vile or evil, abominable; **~ў** *n.*, evil reputation, infamous conduct. [L (IN-²)]

**i′nfan|t** *n.* Child during earliest period of life; (Law) person under 18; thing in early state of development; **~cў** *n.*; **infǎ′nta** *n.*, (Hist.) daughter of Spanish or Portuguese king; **infǎ′nticide** *n.*, murder(er) of infant (esp. with mother's consent) soon after birth; **~tile** *n.*, (as) of infants (**~tile paralysis**, poliomyelitis). [F f. L *infans* unable to speak]

**i′nfantrў** *n.* Soldiers marching and fighting on foot; **~man**, soldier of infantry regiment. [F f. It. (*infante* youth, foot-soldier, f. as prec.)]

**infǎ′tu|āte** *v.t.* Affect with extreme folly; inspire with extravagant love; **~ā′tion** *n.* [L (FATUOUS)]

**infě′ct** *v.t.* Contaminate (air etc.) with germs or other noxious matter; affect (person, body, mind, *with* disease etc.); imbue (person *with* opinion etc.); **~ion** *n.*; **~ious** (-shŭs) *a.*, infecting, able to be transmitted by infection; **~ive** *a.* [L *inficio -fect-* taint]

**infěli′cit|ous** *a.* Not felicitous; **~ў** *n.*, unhappiness, infelicitous expression or detail. [IN-²]

**infě′r** *v.t.* (-rr-). Deduce, conclude, (thing, *that*, *when*, etc.); (of fact or statement, colloq. of person) imply; **i′nferable** (*or* -ēr′-) *a.*; **i′nference** *n.*; **infere′ntial** (-shal) *a.* (-lly). [L (*fero* bring)]

**infēr′ior** *a.* 1. *a.* Situated below; lower in rank, quality, etc., (*to*); of poor quality; written or printed below the line. 2. *n.* Person inferior to another esp. in rank (*your inferiors*). 3. **inferiô′rǐtў** *n.*; **~ity complex**, unconscious feeling of inferiority to others, sometimes manifested in aggressive behaviour, (colloq.) sense of inferiority. [L compar. of *inferus* low]

**infer′nal** *a.* (~ly). Of hell; hellish; (colloq.) detestable, annoying; **~ machine**, (arch.) explosive apparatus for criminal destruction of life etc.; **infer′nō** *n.* (*pl.* -os), hell, scene

of horror or distress, esp. in fire. [F f. L (*infernus* low; *inferno* esp. w. ref. to Dante's *Divine Comedy*)]

**infer′t|ile** *a.* Not fertile; **~i′lǐtў** *n.* [F or L (IN-²)]

**infě′st** *v.t.* (Of vermin, pirates, etc.) haunt, swarm in, (disease etc.); **~ā′tion** *n.* [F or L (*infestus* hostile)]

**i′nfidel.** 1. *n.* Disbeliever in religion or in a specified religion. 2. *a.* Unbelieving; of infidels. 3. **infidě′lǐtў** *n.*, disbelief in Christianity, disloyalty esp. to one's husband or wife. [F or L (*fides* faith)]

**i′nfield** *n.* (Crick.) part of ground near wicket; (Baseball) area between bases; **~er** *n.*; **i′nfīghting** (-fīt-) *n.*, boxing within arms' length, (fig.) hidden conflict in an organization: **i′nfilling** *n.*, placing buildings in gaps between others. [IN]

**i′nfiltr|āte** (*or* -fī′-) *v.t. & i.* Pass (fluid *into*), (of fluid etc.) permeate, by (in)filtration; **~ā′tion** *n.*, (esp. Mil. & Polit.) gradual unobserved occupation of territory etc. by small groups and parties; **~ātor** *n.* [IN-¹]

**i′nfinite** *a.* Boundless, endless, (**the I~**, God; **the ~**, infinite space); very great or many; (of verb parts) having no specific person or number (e.g. infinitive, gerund; cf. FINITE); **infinitě′simal** *a.* (-lly), infinitely or very small, (of calculus) dealing with such quantities. [L (IN-²)]

**infi′nitǐve.** 1. *a.* (Of verb form) expressing verbal notion without predicating it of a subject (e.g. *see*, *to see*). 2. *n.* Infinitive form; **infīniti′val** *a.* (-lly).

**infi′nitūde, infi′nǐtў,** *ns.* Boundlessness; infinite number or extent.

**infir′m** *a.* Physically weak esp. from age; weak, irresolute, (*infirm of purpose*); **~ǐtў** *n.*; **~arў** *n.*, hospital, sick-quarters in school etc. [L (IN-²)]

**infi′x** *v.t.* Fix (thing *in*). [IN-¹]

*in flagrante delicto* (in flǎgrǎntǐ dělǐ′ktō) *a.* In the very act of committing an offence. [L, = in blazing crime]

**inflǎ′me** *v.t. & i.* Set ablaze; catch fire; light up (as) with flame; make hot or passionate; cause inflammation in; **inflǎ′mmable** *a.* (-bly), easily set on fire or excited; **inflǎmmabi′lǐtў** *n.*; **inflammǎ′tion** *n.*, inflaming, esp. condition of body-part with heat, swelling, redness, and usu. pain; **inflǎ′mma-**

**tory** *a.*, tending to inflame, of inflammation. [F f. L (IN-[1])]

**infla´te** *v.t.* Distend with air or gas; puff up (*with* pride etc.); raise (price) artificially; resort to inflation of (currency); (in *p.p.*) bombastic; **~ion** *n.*, inflating, (Econ.) inordinate rise in prices, increase in supply of money regarded as cause of such a rise; **~ionary** *a.* [L *inflo -flat-*]

**infle´ct** *v.t.* Bend, curve; change pitch of (voice); modify (word) to express grammatical relation; **~ion** *n.*, see INFLEXION; **~ive** *a.* (Gram.) [L (*flecto flex-* bend)]

**infle´xib|le** *a.* (**~ly**). Unbendable; unbending (*inflexible will*); **~i´lity** *n.* [L (IN-[2])]

**infle´xion** (-kshon), **infle´ction,** *n.* Inflecting; inflected word, suffix etc. used in inflexion; modulation of voice; **~al** *a.* (**-lly**). [F or L (INFLECT)]

**infli´ct** *v.t.* Deal, deliver forcibly, impose, (blow, wound, pain, penalty, one*self* or one's company, *on* or *upon*); **~ion** *n.*, (esp.) troublesome or boring experience; **~or** *n.* (L (*fligo flict-* strike)]

**inflore´scence** *n.* (Bot.) Arrangement of flowers in relation to axis and to each other; collective flower of plant; flowering (lit. or fig.). [L (IN-[1], FLOURISH)]

**i´nflow** (-ō) *n.*, **i´nflowing** (-ōing) *n. & a.* Flowing in; that which flows in. [IN]

**i´nfluence** (-lŏŏ-). **1.** *n.* Action invisibly exercised (*on*); ascendancy, moral power, (*over, with*); thing, person, exercising this; **under the ~,** (colloq.) drunk. **2.** *v.t.* Exert influence upon, affect. **3. influe´ntial** (-lŏŏe´nshal) *a.* (**-lly**), having great influence. [F or L (*influo* flow in)]

**influe´nza** (-lŏŏ-) *n.* Acute contagious and infectious febrile disorder caused by virus, usu. with fever and severe aching and catarrh, occurring in epidemics. [It. (prec.)]

**i´nflux** *n.* Flowing in (of stream *into* river, of persons etc. *into* place). [For L (FLUX)]

**i´nfo** *n.* (colloq.) Information. [abbr.]

**infor´m** *v.t. & i.* Tell (*inform him of* or *about it, that it is so*); inspire (person, mind, etc., *with* feeling etc.); bring charge or complaint (*against*); (in *p.p.*) knowing the facts, en-

lightened, (*an informed public, mind; well, ill, -informed*). [F f. L (FORM)]

**infor´mal** *a.* (**~ly**). Not in due form; without formality; **infor´ma´lity** *n.* [IN-[2]]

**infor´m|ant** *n.* Giver of information (*my informant says*); **informa´tion** *n.*, telling, what is told, knowledge, items of knowledge, news, charge or complaint lodged with court etc.; **~ation theory,** study of transmission of information by signals; **~ative** *a.*, giving information, instructive; **~er** *n.*, one who informs against others, esp. one who makes this his business. [INFORM]

**infra** (i´nfra) *adv.* Below or further on in book etc.; **~ dig.** [L *dignitatem*], (colloq.) beneath one's dignity. [L]

**i´nfra-** *pref.* Below; **~-re´d,** of or using invisible rays (just) beyond red end of spectrum; **~structure,** subordinate parts of an undertaking, esp. permanent installations forming a basis of defence. [L]

**infra´ction** *n.* Infringement. [L (INFRINGE)]

**infre´quen|t** *a.* Not frequent; **~cy** *n.* [L (IN-[2])]

**infri´nge** (-nj) *v.t. & i.* Act contrary to (law, another's rights, etc.), encroach, trespass, (*on*); **~ment** (-jm-) *n.* [L (*frango fract-* break)]

**infu´riate** *v.t.* Make furious. [L (FURY)]

**infu´s|e** (-z) *v.t. & i.* (**~able**). Pour (thing *into*); instil (life, quality, etc., *into*); steep (tea etc.), be steeped, in liquid to extract constituents; imbue *with* quality; **~ion** (-zhon) *n.*, infusing, liquid extract so obtained, infused element. [L *infundo -fus-* (FOUND[2])]

**infu´sib|le** (-z-) *a.* (**~ly**). That cannot be melted; **~i´lity** *n.* [IN-[2]]

**-ing**[1] *suf.* forming *ns.* f. *vbs.*, with sense of vbl action or its result (*asking, fighting, learning*). [E]

**-ing**[2] *suf.* forming *pres. part.* of *vbs.* (*asking, fighting*), often as *a.* (*charming, strapping*). [E]

**i´ngathering** (i´n-gădh-) *n.* Gathering in, esp. harvest. [IN]

**inge´nious** (-nj-) *a.* Clever at inventing, organizing, etc.; cleverly contrived. [F or L (*ingenium* cleverness)]

**ingénue** (ă´nzhānŏŏ, -ŭ) *n.* Artless young woman, esp. as stage role. [F (INGENUOUS)]

**ingenu´ity** (-nj-) *n.* Ingeniousness.

**ingĕ′nŭous** (ĭnj-) *a.* Frank; artless. [L *ingenuus* free-born, frank]

**ingĕ′st** (ĭnj-) *v.t.* Take in by swallowing or absorbing; ∼ion (-schon) *n.* [L (*gero* carry)]

**i′ngle** (ĭ′nggel) *n.* Fire on hearth; ∼-nook, chimney-corner. [perh. Gael. *aingeal*]

**inglōr′ious** (ĭn-g-) *a.* Shameful; obscure. [L IN-²]

**i′ngōing** (ĭn-g-) *a.* & *n.* Going in. [IN]

**i′ngot** (-ngg-) *n.* Mass, usu. oblong, of cast metal, esp. gold, silver, or steel. [orig. uncert.]

**ingraft.** See ENGRAFT.

**i′ngrain** (ĭ′n-g-) *a.* Dyed in grain; (fig.) deeply embedded, inveterate, also ∼ed (before *n.* ĭ′n-grānd, else -ā′nd) *a.* [GRAIN]

**i′ngrāte** (ĭn-g-) *a.* & *n.* (arch.) Ungrateful (person). [L (as GRATEFUL)]

**ingrā′tiāte** (ĭn-grā′shĭ-) *v.t.* Bring one*self* into favour (*with*). [L *in gratiam* into favour]

**ingră′titūde** (ĭn-g-) *n.* Lack of due gratitude. [F or L (INGRATE)]

**ingrē′dient** (ĭn-g-) *n.* Component part in mixture; **i′ngress** (ĭn-g-) *n.*, (right of) entrance. [L *ingredior* enter into]

**i′ngrowing** (ĭ′n-grō̅ī-) *a.* (Of nail) growing into the flesh. [IN]

**i′nguinal** (ĭ′nggw-) *a.* Of the groin. [L (*inguen* groin)]

**ingŭr′gĭtāte** (ĭn-g-) *v.t.* Swallow greedily; engulf; ∼ā′tion *n.* [L (*gurges -git-* whirlpool)]

**inhă′bĭt** *v.t.* Dwell in, occupy; ∼ant *n.*, person etc. who inhabits place; ∼ation *n.* [F or L (HABIT)]

**inhā′l|e** *v.t.* & *i.* Breathe in (air, gas, etc.); take (esp. tobacco-smoke) into lungs; **inhalā′tion** *n.*; ∼ant *n.*, medicinal substance to be inhaled; ∼er *n.*, (esp.) inhaling-apparatus for ether, vapour, etc. [L (*halo* breathe)]

**inharmō′nious** *a.* Not harmonious. [IN-²]

**inhēr′|e** *v.i.* (Of qualities etc.) exist, abide, essentially *in*; (of rights) be vested *in* person; ∼ent *a.*; ∼ence *n.* [L (*haereo haes-* to stick)]

**inhĕ′rĭt** *v.t.* Receive (property, rank) as heir; derive (qualities etc.) from parents, predecessor, etc.; ∼ance *n.*, inheriting, what is inherited; ∼or *n.* [F f. L (*heres* heir)]

**inhĕ′sion** (-zhon) *n.* Inhering. [I. (INHERE)]

**inhĭ′bĭt** *v.t.* Prohibit (*from* do*ing*); hinder, restrain, prevent, (action); **inhĭbĭ′tion** *n.*, (esp.) restraint of direct expression of instinct, (colloq.) emotional resistance to thought or action, so ∼ĕd *a.*; ∼orў *a.* [L *inhibeo -hibit-* hinder]

**inhŏmog|ĕ′nĕous** *a.* Not homogeneous; ∼enē′ĭtў *n.*; **inhŏ′s-pĭtable** *a.* (-bly), not hospitable, not affording shelter etc.; **inhŏs-pĭtă′lĭtў** *n.*, being inhospitable. [IN-²]

**inhū′man** *a.* Brutal, unfeeling, barbarous; **inhūmă′nĭtў** *n.*; **inhūmā′ne** *a.*, not humane. [L (IN-²)]

**inĭ′mĭcal** *a.* (∼ly). Hostile, harmful, (*to*). [L (*inimicus* enemy)]

**inĭ′mĭtab|le** *a.* (∼ly). Defying imitation. [F or L (IN-²)]

**inĭ′quĭt|ў** *n.* Wickedness; gross injustice; ∼ous *a.* [F f. L (*aequus* just)]

**inĭ′tial** (-shal) *a.*, *n.*, & *v.* **1.** *a.* (∼ly). Of, occurring at, the beginning (*initial expenses*); ∼ letter (of word). **2.** *n.* Initial letter, esp. (in *pl.*) of (esp. person's) name(s). **3.** *v.t.* (-ll-, -l-) Mark, sign, with initials. [I. (foll.)]

**inĭ′ti|āte** (-shĭ-). **1.** *v.t.* Originate, begin, set going; admit (person *into* office, secret, *in* or *into* mysteries) esp. with rites or forms; ∼ā′tion, ∼ātor, *ns.*; ∼atorў (-shya-, -sha-) *a.* **2.** (-at) *n.* Initiated person. [L (*initium* beginning)]

**inĭ′tiative** (-shya-, -sha-) *n.* First step (**take the** ∼, be first to take action; **on** one's **own** ∼, without others' prompting); power or right to begin (**have the initiative**); ability to initiate things, enterprise, (**has no initiative**). [F (prec.)]

**injĕ′ct** *v.t.* Force (fluid, medicine, etc., *into* cavity etc.) (as) by syringe; fill (*with* fluid etc.) thus; administer medicine etc. to (person) thus; place (quality etc.) where needed in something; ∼ion *n.*, (esp.) fluid etc. injected; ∼or *n.* [L *injicio -ject-* (*jacio* throw)]

**injudĭ′cious** (-jo͞odĭ′shus) *a.* Unwise, ill-judged. [IN-²]

**I′njun** (ĭ′-) *n.* (colloq., \*dial.) American Indian. [corrupt.]

**injŭ′nction** *n.* Authoritative order; judicial process restraining person from wrongful act, compelling restitution, etc. [L (ENJOIN)]

**i′njur|e** *v.t.* Do wrong to (**an** ∼ed

*voice*, showing one is offended); harm, impair; **injur'ious** (-joor'-) *a.*, wrongful, harmful, calumnious; **~y** *n.*, wrongful action or treatment, harm, damage; ‖**~y time**, extra playing-time allowed by referee because of that lost when players were hurt. [IN-², L *jus jur-* right]

**injŭ'stĭce** *n.* Unfairness; unjust act (you do me an **~**, judge me unfairly). [F f. L (IN-²)]

**ĭnk. 1.** *n.* Fluid (black, red, etc.) for writing with pen or marking; paste similarly used in printing or duplicating; black liquid ejected by cuttlefish etc.; **~'stand** (for one or more ink-bottles); **~-well** (pot fitted into hole in desk); **~'y** *a.*, of, black as, ink. **2.** *v.t.* Mark (in, over, etc.) with ink; cover with ink; **~ out**, obliterate with ink. [F f. L f. Gk *egkauston* Roman emperors' purple ink (EN-, CAUSTIC)]

**ĭ'nkling** *n.* Hint, slight knowledge or suspicion, (of). [orig. unkn.]

**ĭ'nland** (or -ă-) *n.*, *a.*, & *adv.* **1.** *n.* Interior of country. **2.** *a.* In the inland, remote from sea or border; within a country (*inland trade*); **~ duty** (on inland trade); ‖**~ revenue** (from taxes and inland duties). **3.** *adv.* In, towards, the inland. [IN]

**ĭ'n-law** *n.* (colloq.; usu. in *pl.*) Relative by marriage.

**ĭnlay'. 1.** (-ā') *v.t.* (**inlaid**). Embed (thing *in* another) so that their surfaces are even; ornament (thing *with* another) thus. **2.** (ĭ'-) *n.* Inlaid material or work; filling shaped to fit tooth-cavity. [IN, LAY⁴]

**ĭ'nlĕt** (or -ĕt) *n.* Small arm of sea, creek; way of admission, entrance; piece inserted. [IN, LET²]

*in loco parentis* (ĭn lŏkō perĕ'ntĭs) *adv.* In place of a parent. [L]

**ĭ'nlў** *adv.* (poet.) Inwardly, in the heart. [E]

**ĭ'nmāte** *n.* Occupant (*of* house, hospital, prison, etc.). [prob. INN, MATE²]

*in memoriam* (ĭn mĭmōr'ĭăm). **1.** *prep.* In memory of. **2.** *n.* Notice etc. in memory of deceased person. [L]

**ĭ'nmōst** (or -o-) *a.* Most inward. [E (IN)]

**ĭnn** *n.* House providing lodging etc. for payment, esp. for travellers; house providing alcoholic liquor; **~'keeper**, keeper of inn; ‖**Inns of Court**, four legal societies ad-

mitting persons to practise at English bar. [E (IN)]

**ĭ'nnards** (-z) *n.pl.* (colloq.) Entrails. [dial. etc. for INWARDS *n.*]

**ĭnnā'te** (or ĭ'-) *a.* Inborn, natural. [L (*natus* born)]

**ĭ'nner. 1.** *a.* Interior, internal; **~ man, woman**, soul, mind, (joc.) stomach; **~ tube**, separate inflatable tube in pneumatic tyre; **~mōst** *a.* **2.** *n.* (Shot striking) division of target next outside bull's-eye. [E, compar. of IN]

*\*ĭ'nning* *n.* Innings at baseball etc. [*in* v. = go in]

**ĭ'nnings** (-z) *n.* (*pl.* same). (Crick. etc.) batsman's turn of play, that part of game during which one side is batting; time of power etc. of political party etc.; period of person's chance to achieve something. [pl. of prec.]

**ĭ'nnocent. 1.** *a.* Sinless; not guilty (*innocent of crime*); (pretended as) guileless; harmless; **ĭ'nnocence** *n.* **2.** *n.* Innocent person, esp. child (**I~s' Day**, commemorating slaughter of children by Herod, Dec. 28). **3.** **ĭnnŏ'cŭous** *a.*, harmless (*innocuous snakes*). [F or L (*noceo* hurt)]

**ĭ'nnovāte** *v.i.* Bring in novelties, make changes *in*; **ĭnnovā'tion**, **~or**, *ns.*; **~orў** *a.* [L (*novus* new)]

**ĭnnuĕ'ndō** *n.* (*pl.* **~es**, **~s**). Allusive (usu. disparaging) remark or hint. [L, = by nodding at (IN-¹, *nuo* nod)]

**ĭnnu'mera|ble** *a.* (**~ly**). Too many to count; **~te** *a.*, not knowing basic mathematics and science; **~cў** *n.* [L (*numerus* number)]

**ĭnŏ'cŭl|āte** *v.t.* (**~able**). Impregnate (person etc. *with* agent of disease) esp. as protective measure; implant (disease *on*, *into*) thus; **~ā'tion**, **~ātor**, *ns.*; **~ātĭve** *a.* [L (*oculus* eye, bud)]

**ĭnoffĕ'nsĭve** *a.* Unoffending, not objectionable. **ĭnŏ'perable** *a.*, (of tumour etc.) that cannot suitably be operated on; **ĭnŏ'peratĭve** *a.*, not working or taking effect; **ĭnŏ'pportūne** *a.*, not appropriate, esp. as regards time. [IN-²]

**ĭnŏ'rdĭnate** *a.* Excessive. [L (OR-DAIN)]

**ĭnŏrgă'nĭc** *a.* Without organized physical structure; (Chem., of compound etc.) mineral not organic (**~ chemistry**, that of inorganic substances); extraneous. [IN-²]

*in partibus* (ĭn pär'tĭbŭs) *adv.* (Of R.C. bishop) in heretics' territory. [L, = in the regions (of the unbelievers)]

**i'nput** (-ŏot). **1.** *n.* What is put in; place of entry of energy, information, etc. **2.** *v.t.* (-tt-; ~, ~ted). Put in or *into*. [IN]

**i'nquěst** (*or* ĭ'n-kw-) *n.* Legal or judicial inquiry into matter of fact; (**coroner's**) ~ (held by coroner into cause of death). [F f. L (INQUIRE)]

**inqui'ětŭde** (*or* ĭn-kw-) *n.* Uneasiness. [F or L (QUIET)]

**inquīr'|e**, |**ěn-**, (*or* ĭn-kw-) *v.i.* & *t.* Search (*into* matter); seek information (*of* = from person *about* matter); ~**e after** *or* **for him**, esp. how he is); ask (*for* goods in shop etc.); ask to be told (*inquire his name, why, the reason*); ~**ÿ** *n.*, question, (official) investigation, (*make inquiries; hold an inquiry into*); ~**y office** (answering questions from callers etc.). [F f. L (*quaero* -*quisit*- seek)]

**inquīsi'tion** (-z-; *or* ĭn-kw-) *n.* Investigation, official inquiry; (R.C. Ch. Hist.; *I*~) tribunal for suppression of heresy esp. in Spain; ~**al** *a.*

**inqui'sitive** (-z-; *or* ĭn-kw-) *a.* Seeking knowledge; unduly curious, prying.

**inqui'sit|or** (-z-; *or* ĭn-kw-) *n.* Official investigator; officer of the Inquisition (**Grand I**~**or**, director of this in some countries; **I**~**or-General**, head of it in Spain); ~**ōr'ial** *a.* (-lly), inquisitor-like, prying.

*in re* (ĭn rē') *prep.* = RE². [L]

**I.N.R.I.** *abbr.* Jesus of Nazareth, King of the Jews. [L *Iesus Nazarenus Rex Iudaeorum*]

**i'nroad** *n.* Hostile incursion; encroachment; **i'nrŭsh** *n.*, violent influx. [IN]

**insalū'bri|ous** (*or* -loō'-) *a.* (Of climate etc.) unhealthy; ~**tÿ** *n.*; **insā'ne** *a.*, not of sound mind, extremely foolish; **insā'nitÿ** *n.*; **insă'nitary** *a.*, not sanitary, harmful to health.

**insā'ti|able** (-sha-) *a.* (-bly). That cannot be satisfied, very greedy; ~**abi'litÿ** *n.*; ~**ate** (-shyat) *a.*, never satisfied. [F or L (IN-²)]

**inscrī'be** *v.t.* Write (words etc. *in* or *on* stone, metal, paper, book); mark (sheet, tablet, etc., *with* characters); (Geom.) draw (figure)

within another so that points of it lie on the other's boundary; enter name of (person) on list or in book; place informal dedication in or on (book etc.); **inscri'ption** *n.*, inscribing, words inscribed; **inscri'ptional**, **inscri'ptive**, *adjs.* [L (*scribo* write)]

**inscru'tab|le** (-rŏō'-) *a.* (~**ly**). Mysterious, impenetrable; ~**i'litÿ** *n.* [L (*scrutor* to search)]

**i'nsěct** *n.* Small invertebrate animal with body in (usu.) three segments (head, thorax, abdomen), 2 antennae, and 3 pairs of legs, and usu. 1 or 2 pairs of wings, on thorax; ~**-powder** (for killing or driving away insects); **insě'cticide** *n.*, powder etc. for killing insects; ~**i'vorous** *a.*, insect-eating or (of plant) -trapping. [L (SECTION); -*cide*. -*vorous*, f. L *caedo* kill, *voro* devour]

**insēcūr'|e** *a.* Unsafe; liable to give way; ~**itÿ** *n.* [L (IN-²)]

**insě'min|āte** *v.t.* Sow (seed etc., lit. & fig., *in*); introduce semen into; ~**ā'tion** *n.* [L (SEMEN)]

**insě'nsāte** *a.* Without sensibility; stupid. [L (SENSE)]

**insě'nsi|ble** *a.* Too small or gradual to be perceived; unconscious; unaware (*of, to how*); callous; ~**bi'litÿ** *n.*; ~**blÿ** *adv.*, imperceptibly; ~**tive** *a.*, not sensitive (*to* touch, light, treatment, moral feeling); ~**ti'vitÿ** *n.*; **insě'ntient** (-shi-, -shent) *a.*, inanimate. [F or L (IN-²)]

**insě'parab|le. 1.** *a.* (~**ly**). That cannot be separated; ~**i'litÿ** *n.* **2.** *n.* (usu. in *pl.*) Inseparable person or thing, esp. friend. [L (IN-²)]

**insěrt. 1.** (-ěr't) *v.t.* Place, put, (thing *in, into, between*); introduce (letter, word, article, advertisement, *in* or *into* written matter, newspaper, etc.). **2.** (ĭ'-) *n.* Thing inserted. **3. insěr'tion** *n.*, inserting, thing inserted, ornamental work inserted in plain material. [L (*sero sert-* join)]

**insět. 1.** (ĭ'-) *n.* Extra piece inserted in book, garment, etc.; small map etc. within border of larger one. **2.** (-ět') *v.t.* (-tt-; ~, ~ted). Put in as inset. [IN]

**inshŏr'e** *adv.* & *a.* Near shore. [IN]

**insīde** *n.*, *a.*, *adv.*, & *prep.* **1.** (-ī'd) *n.* Inner side or part (*know* ~ **out**, thoroughly; *turned* ~ **out**, so that inner becomes outside, fig. utterly confused); (of path) side away from road; (colloq.) stomach and bowels; position on inner side (*open the door* *from the inside).* **2.** (ĭ′n-) *a.* Of or on or in the inside; nearer to centre of games field; **~ information** (not accessible to outsiders); **~ job,** (colloq.) burglary etc. by one living or working on the premises. **3.** (-ĭ′d) *adv.* On or in the inside; (sl.) in prison. **4.** (-ĭ′d) *prep.* Within, on the inside of; in less than (*inside an hour*). **5.** **insi′der** *n.* Person within a society etc. (opp. OUTSIDER), one who is in the secret. [IN]

**insi′dious** *a.* Treacherous, crafty; proceeding secretly or subtly (*insidious disease*). [L (*insidiae* ambush)]

**i′nsight** (-īt) *n.* Mental penetration (*into* character etc.); instance of this; **~ful** *a.* [IN¹]

**insi′gnia** *n.pl.* Badges, marks, (of office etc.). [L (*signum* sign)]

**insigni′fican|t** *a.* Unimportant; meaningless; **~ce** *n.;* **insincē′r′e** *a.,* not sincere or candid; **insince′rity** *n.* [IN-²]

**insi′nuat|e** *v.t.* Bring, get, (thing *into* place, oneself into place, favour, etc.) gradually or subtly; hint obliquely (idea, *that*); **insĭnŭā′tion, ~or,** *ns.;* **~ive** *a.* [L (*sinuo* to curve)]

**insi′pid** *a.* Flavourless; dull, lifeless; **insipi′dity** *n.* [F, or L (SAPID)]

**insi′st** *v.i.* & *t.* **~** (on), emphasize (*insist on this point*), maintain (*insist on his innocence, that he is innocent*); demand persistently (*insist on going, on his going, that he shall go*); **~ence, ~ency,** *ns.;* **~ent** *a.,* insisting, obtruding itself. [L (*sisto* stand)]

***in situ*** (ĭn sī′tū) *adv.* In its (original) place. [L]

**insobri′ety** *n.* Intemperance, esp. in drinking. [IN-²]

**insofar′** *adv.* = *in so* FAR.

**i′nsole** *n.* Removable inside sole for use in shoe; fixed inner sole of boot or shoe. [IN]

**i′nsolen|t** *a.* Offensively contemptuous, insulting; **~ce** *n.* [L (*soleo* be accustomed)]

**insŏ′lŭb|le** *a.* (**~ly**). That cannot be (dis)solved; **~i′lity** *n.;* **insŏ′lvent** *a.* & *n.,* (debtor) unable to pay debts; **insŏ′lvency** *n.* [F or L (IN-²)]

**insŏ′mni|a** *n.* Habitual sleeplessness; **~ăc** *a.* & *n.,* (person) suffering from insomnia. [L (*somnus* sleep)]

**insomŭ′ch** *adv.* To such an extent that; INASMUCH as. [orig. *in so much*]

**insou′cian|t** (-ōō′-, ăňsōō′syaňn) *a.* Carefree, indifferent; **~ce** (or -ňs) *n.* [F (*souci* care)]

**inspa′n** *v.t.* & *i.* (S. Afr.; **-nn-**). Yoke (oxen etc.) in team to vehicle, do this; harness (wagon, or abs.). [Du. (SPAN¹)]

**inspe′ct** *v.t.* Look closely into; examine officially; **~ion, ~or,** *ns.* (‖**police ~or,** officer next above sergeant); ‖**~or of taxes,** official assessing income tax payable; **~ŏr′ial** *a.* (**-lly**). [L (*specio* spect- look)]

**inspīr′|e** *v.t.* Breathe (air etc.) in; infuse thought or feeling into (person); animate (person etc. *with* feeling); **inspirā′tion** *n.,* (esp.) divine influence in poetry and Scripture, prompted thought, sudden brilliant idea; **~atory** *a.,* of breathing in. [F f. L (*spiro* breathe)]

**inspi′rit** *v.t.* Put life into, animate; encourage (*to* action, *to* do). [IN-¹]

**inst.** *abbr.* instant (*the 6th inst.*); institute; institution.

**instabi′lity** *n.* Lack of stability. [F f. L (IN-²)]

**insta′ll** (-aw′l) *v.t.* Place (person *in* office etc.) with ceremony; establish (person *in* place etc.; equipment ready for use in house etc.); **installā′tion** *n.* [L (STALL¹)]

**insta′lment,** *\*-ll-,* (-aw′l-) *n.* Any of successive parts in which a sum is (to be) paid; any of the parts of a whole successively delivered, published, etc. [AF (*estaler* fix)]

**i′nstance. 1.** *n.* Example, illustration of general truth (*many substances, for instance soda; soda is an instance*); particular case (*in your, this, instance*); request (*at the instance of*); **in the first ~,** originally, first. **2.** *v.t.* Cite (case) as instance. [F f. L *instantia* contrary example]

**i′nstant. 1.** *a.* Urgent, pressing; immediate; of the current month (*the 6th instant*); (of food) that can be prepared easily for immediate use. **2.** *n.* Precise moment (*went that instant*; **on the ~,** at once); short time, moment, (*in an instant*). **3.** **i′nstancy** *n.,* urgency; **~ā′neous** *a.,* occurring or done in an instant; **~ly,** (arch. or joc.) immediately; **instä′nter,** *advs.,* immediately, at once. [F f. L (*insto* be urgent)]

**instea′d** (-ĕ′d) *adv.* As a substitute (*this will do instead*); **~ of,** in place of (*instead of this, of going, of him*). [IN]

**i′nstep** *n.* Top of foot between toes and ankle; part of shoe etc. over or under instep. [ult. f. IN, STEP]

**i′nstigāte** *v.t.* Incite (person *to* action, *to* do esp. evil); bring about (revolt, murder, etc.) thus; ~**ā′tion,** ~**ātor,** ns. [L (*stigo* prick)]

**instī′l, \*-ll,** v.t. (-**ll**-). Put in (liquid *into* thing) by drops; put (ideas etc. *into* mind etc.) gradually; **instillā′tion,** ~**ment,** ns. [L (*stillo* to drop)]

**instinct. 1.** (ĭ′n-) n. Innate propensity, esp. in lower animals, to seemingly rational acts; innate impulse or behaviour; intuition; **instī′nctive, instī′nctual,** adjs. **2.** (-tĭ′-) a. Filled, charged, (*with* life, energy, etc.). [L (*stinguo* prick)]

**ĭ′nstitute. 1.** v.t. Establish, found; initiate (inquiry etc.); appoint (person *to*, *into*, benefice). **2.** n. Organized body for promotion of public object; its building. [L (*statuo* set up)]

**institū′tion** n. Instituting; established law, custom, or practice, (colloq.) well-known person; (esp. charitable) institute; ~**al** a. (~**ally**), of or like institution(s), (of religion) expressed or organized through churches etc., typical of charitable institutions; ~**alize** v.t. [F f. L (prec.)]

**instrŭ′ct** v.t. Teach (person *in* subject); inform (person *that* etc.); give information to (solicitor, counsel); direct (person *to* do); ~**ion** n., (esp., in pl.) direction, orders; ~**ional** a.; ~**ive** a., tending to instruct, enlightening; ~**or** n. [L *instruo -struct-* teach, furnish]

**ĭ′nstrument** (-rōō-). **1.** n. Thing used in an action; person so made use of; tool, implement, esp. for delicate or scientific work; measuring-device, esp. in aircraft to find position in fog etc.; (**musical**) ~, contrivance giving musical sounds by vibration of strings, membranes, or air in pipe etc.; formal (esp. legal) document. **2.** v.t. Arrange (music) for instruments; equip with instruments. **3.** ~**ā′tion** n., arrangement of music for, provision of or operation with, instruments. [F or L (prec.)]

**instrumě′ntal** (-rōō-) a. (~**ly**). Serving as instrument or means (*to* purpose, *in* work or do*ing*); of or due to instrument; performed with musical instruments; (Gram., of case) denoting means; ~**ist** n., performer on musical instrument; ~**ĭtў** (-ā′l-) n., agency or means.

**ĭnsubŏr′din|ate** a. Disobedient, unruly; ~**ā′tion** n.; **insubstǎ′ntial**

(-shal) a. (-**lly**), lacking reality or solidity; **ĭnsŭ′fferable** a. (-**bly**), unbearably conceited, intolerable; **ĭnsuffī′cient** (-shĕnt) a., not enough, inadequate; **insuffī′ciencў** (-shĕn-) n. [IN-²]

**ĭ′nsūlar** a. Of (the nature of) an island; of or like islanders; narrow-minded; ~**ism, ĭnsūlǎ′ritў,** ns. [L (foll.)]

**ĭ′nsūl|ate** v.t. Isolate, esp. by non-conductor of electricity, heat, or sound; ~**ā′tion,** ~**ātor** (substance or device), ns. [L *insula* island]

**ĭ′nsūlin** n. Hormone from the islets of Langerhans in the pancreas of animals, controlling sugar in body and used against diabetes.

**ĭnsŭlt. 1.** (ĭ′n-) n. Scornful abuse; offence to modesty or self-respect. **2.** (-ŭ′lt) v.t. Treat with insult. [F or L (*insulto* leap upon, assail)]

**ĭnsŭ′perab|le** (or -ōō′-) a. (~**ly**). That cannot be surmounted or overcome (*insuperable barrier*, *objection*); ~**ĭ′litў** n. [F or L (*supero* overcome)]

**ĭnsuppŏr′tab|le** a. (~**′y**). Unbearable; unjustifiable. [F [IN-²]

**ĭnsur′ance** (-shoor′-) n. Insuring; sum paid for or because of t. is; safeguard; ~ **agent** etc. (und.rtaking insurance dealings. [OF (EN URE)]

**ĭnsur′e** (-shoor′) v.t. Secure payment of money in event of (cgainst) loss, damage, or injury to (property, life, person) on payment of prenium; secure payment of (money) thus; **the** ~**d,** person in respect of whom such payment is ensured; ~**r** n., one who insures property in consideration of premium. [var. ENSURE]

**ĭnsŭr′gen|t. 1.** a. In revolt, rebellious; ~**cў** n. **2.** n. Rebel. [F f. L (*surgo surrect-* rise)]

**ĭnsurmou′ntab|le** a. (~**ly**). That cannot be surmounted or overcome. [IN-²]

**ĭnsurrě′ction** n. Incipient rebellion, rising in open resistance to authority; ~**al,** ~**arў,** adjs.; ~**ĭst** n., insurgent. [F f. L (INSURGENT)]

**ĭnsuscě′ptib|le** a. (~**ly**). Not susceptible (*of* treatment, *to* quality); ~**ĭ′litў** n. [IN-²]

**int.** abbr. interior; internal; international.

**ĭntă′ct** a. Untouched, unimpaired; entire. [L (*tango tact-* touch)]

**ĭntă′gli|ō** (-tă′l-, -tah′l-) n. (pl. ~**os**). Engraved design; gem with incised design. [It. (IN-¹, TAIL²)]

**i'ntāke** n. Action of taking in; (place of) taking water into pipe, fuel or air into engine, etc.; person(s) or thing(s) or quantity taken in or received. [IN]

**intă'ngĭb|le** (-nj-) a. (~ly). That cannot be touched, or mentally grasped; ~i'lĭtў n. [F or L (INTACT)]

**i'ntĕg|er** n. Whole number; ~ral a. (-lly), of or necessary to a whole, complete, forming a whole, of or denoted by an integer; ~ră'lĭtў n.; ~rāte v.t. & i. (~rable), complete by addition of parts, combine (parts) into a whole, bring or come into equal membership of society esp. disregarding race or religion, end (racial) segregation (of or at); ~rated circuit, small piece of material replacing electric circuit of many components; ~ră'tion, ~rātor, ns.; ~rātive a.; intĕ'grĭtў n., wholeness, soundness, honesty. [L, = untouched, whole]

**intĕ'gument** n. Skin, husk, rind, or other covering; ~al, ~arў, (-č'n-) adjs. [L (tego cover)]

**i'ntĕll|ĕct** n. Faculty of knowing and reasoning; understanding; person, persons collectively, with good understanding; ~ĕ'ctŭal, (a.; -lly) of or for or needing or using intellect, having good understanding or intelligence, enlightened, (n.) intellectual person; ~ĕ'ctŭalism n., doctrine that knowledge derives from reason, (excessive) use of intellect only; ~ĕctŭă'lĭtў n.; ~ĕ'ctŭalize v.t. [F or L (foll.)]

**intĕ'llig|ence** n. Intellect, understanding; quickness of understanding (~ence quotient, ratio of given person's intelligence to the normal or average); information, news, (~ence department, engaged in collecting information, esp. for military purposes); ~ent a., having or showing good intelligence, clever; ~ĕ'ntsĭa n., class of intellectuals, esp. regarded as cultured and politically enterprising; ~ĭble a. (-bly), that can be understood; ~ĭbĭ'lĭtў n. [F f. L (intelligo -lect-understand)]

**intĕ'mperate** a. Immoderate, unbridled; excessive in indulgence of appetite; addicted to drinking; ~ance n. [L (IN-²)]

**intĕ'nd** v.t. Have as one's purpose, destine, mean, (we intend to go, intend no harm, intend him to go, intend that

he shall go; ~ed, done on purpose; one's ~ed, colloq., fiancé(e); is this portrait ~ed for me?, meant to represent me, meant to be given to me; what do you intend by the word?). [F f. L (tendo tens-, tent- stretch)]

**intĕ'ns|e** a. (~er, ~est). Existing in high degree, violent, vehement, (intense disgust, desire); having a quality in high degree; eager, ardent, strenuous; feeling or apt to feel strong emotion; ~ifў v., make or become (more) intense; ~ifĭcā'tion n.; ~itў n., intenseness, (measurable) amount of force, brightness, etc.; ~ive a., of or in intensity, giving force, vigorous, thorough, concentrated on one point or area (intensive bombardment, study), serving to increase production from given area (intensive agriculture), (as suf.) making much use of (capital-, labour-intensive); ~ive care, medical treatment with constant supervision of patient.

**intĕ'nt. 1.** n. Intention, purpose, (with intent to defraud; to all ~s and purposes, practically, virtually). **2.** a. Resolved, bent, (on doing, on object); attentively occupied (intent on his task); earnest, eager, (intent gaze).

**intĕ'ntion** n. Intending (done without intention); purpose of doing or to do; thing intended, (ultimate) aim; ~al a. (-lly), done on purpose.

**intĕr'** v.t. (-rr-). Place (corpse etc.) in earth or tomb, bury. [F f. Rom. (L terra earth)]

**i'nter-** pref. Between, among, mutually, reciprocally; ~a'ct, act on each other; ~a'ction; ~a'ctive; ~bree'd, (cause to) produce hybrid individual; ~-ci'tў, existing or travelling between cities; ~commu'nicate, communicate mutually, have free passage into each other; ~communica'tion; ~commu'nion, mutual communion, mutual action or relation esp. of religious bodies; ~conne'ct, connect with each other; ~conne'ction; ~contine'ntal, connecting, situated or travelling between, different continents; ~conver'tible, interchangeable; ~denomina'tional, of more than one (religious) denomination; ~departme'ntal, of more than one department; ~depe'nd, depend on each other; ~depe'ndence, -encў; ~depe'ndent; ~discipli'nary (or -dĭ'-), of or involving different branches of learning; ~**governme'ntal**, of more than one government; ~**li'near**, written or printed between lines of text; ~**li'nk**, link together (things, one *with* another); ~**ma'rry**, (of tribes etc.) become connected (*with* others) by marriage; ~**ma'rriage**; ~**me'ddle**, concern oneself (*with*, *in*, esp. what is not one's business); ~**mi'ngle**, ~**mi'x**, mix together; ~**pe'netrate**, pervade, penetrate reciprocally; ~**penetra'tion**; ~**per'sonal**, (of relations) between persons; ~**pla'netary**, (of travel) between planets; ~**rela'ted**, mutually related; ~**rela'tion**(**ship**); ~**speci'fic**, formed from different species; *~**state**, existing or carried on between states esp. of U.S.; ~**ste'llar**, between stars; ~**war**, existing in period between two wars; ~**wea've**, weave together, blend intimately. [F or L (*inter* between, among)]

*inter alia* (ĭnter ā'lĭa) *adv*. Amongst other things. [L]

**inter'cal|ary** *a*. Inserted to harmonize calendar with solar year (*intercalary day, month*); ~**ary year**, having intercalary additions); interpolated; ~**āte** *v.t.*, insert (intercalary day etc.), interpose; ~**ā'tion** *n*. [L (*calo* proclaim)]

**interce'de** *v.i.* Interpose on another's behalf, mediate; plead (*with* person *for* another). [F or L (CEDE)]

**interce'pt** *v.t.* Seize, catch, stop, in transit or progress; cut off (light etc. *from*); ~**ion**, ~**or**, *ns*.; ~**ive** *a*. [L *intercipio* *-cept-* (*capio* take)]

**inter|ce'ssion** (-shon) *n*. Interceding; ~**ce'ssor** *n*.; ~**cĕssŏr'ial**, ~**cĕ'ssory**, *adjs*. [F or L (INTER-CEDE)]

**interchānge** (-nj). 1. (-ā'-) *v.t.* Put (things) in each other's place; make an exchange of (things) with each other; alternate. 2. (ĭ'-) *n*. Exchange of (things) between persons etc.; alternation; road junction where traffic streams do not intersect. [F (CHANGE)]

**i'ntercŏm** *n*. (colloq.) System of intercommunication esp. in aircraft. [abbr.]

**i'ntercourse** (-ôrs) *n*. Social communication between individuals; communication in trade etc. between countries etc.; = SEXUAL *intercourse*. [F f. L (COURSE)]

**interdi'ct**. 1. (-ĭ'kt) *v.t.* Forbid (action, thing *to* person); forbid use of; restrain (person *from* doing); **interdi'ction** *n*.; **interdi'ctory** *a*. 2. (ĭ'n-) *n*. Authoritative prohibition; (R.C. Ch.) sentence debarring person or place from ecclesiastical functions etc. [F f. L (*dico* say)]

**i'nterest** (*or* -tr-). 1. *n*. Legal concern, title, right, (*in* property); money stake (*in* a business); advantage (*it is in your interest to go*; *in the interests of truth*); thing in which one is concerned; principle which a party has in common, such party (*the brewing interest*); selfish pursuit of one's own welfare, self-interest; concern, curiosity, (*take an interest, no interest, in*); quality causing these (*is of no interest to me*); money paid for use of loan of money (**simple ~**, reckoned on principal only; **compound ~**, on principal and accumulated interest). 2. *v.t.* Cause interest of (person *in* thing); (in *p.p.*) having private interest, not impartial; ~ oneself, take active part *in*; ~**ing** *a*., causing curiosity, holding the attention. [F f. L, = it matters]

**i'nterfāc|e** *n*. Surface forming common boundary of two regions; place where interaction occurs between two systems etc. [INTER-]

**interfēr'|e** *v.i.* Meddle, intervene, (*with* person or thing, *in* matter, *between* persons); clash (*with*), be an obstacle; (of light-waves etc.) combine in different phases with partial or complete neutralization; ~**e with**, (euphem.) molest or assault sexually; ~**ence** *n*., (esp.) fading of received radio signals; ~**ing** *a*., (esp.) meddling. [F f. L *ferio* strike]

**interfū's|e** (-z) *v.t. & i.* (~**ible**). Blend (things, thing *with* another); ~**ion** (-zhon) *n*. [L (FUSE¹)]

**i'nterim**. 1. *n*. Intervening time. 2. *a*. Intervening; temporary, provisional. [L, = in the interim]

**intēr'ior**. 1. *a*. Situated or coming from within; inland; internal, domestic; existing in the mind. 2. *n*. Interior part, inside; inland region; (picture of) inside of room etc. (*interior decoration*); (department for) home affairs in some countries (*Minister of the Interior*). [L]

**interjĕ'ct** *v.t.* Utter (words) abruptly or parenthetically; ~**ion** *n*., exclamation esp. as part of speech (ah, whew, *are interjections*); **~ional** *a.* (**-lly**). [L (*jacio* jectthrow)]

**interlā′ce** *v.t.* & *i.* Bind intricately together, interweave (two things, thing *with* another); cross each other intricately; **~ment** (-sm-) *n.* [F (LACE)]

**interlār′d** *v.t.* Mix (writing, speech, *with* foreign etc. words). [F]

**interlea′ve** *v.t.* Insert (usu. blank) leaves between leaves of (book). [LEAF]

**interlŏck.** **1.** *v.i.* & *t.* Engage with each other by overlapping; lock or clasp in each other. **2.** *a.* (Of fabric) knitted with closely interlocking stitches. [LOCK²]

**interlŏ′cŭtor** *n.* One who takes part in conversation (**my ~**, person conversing with me); **interlocu′tion** *n.*, dialogue; **~ÿ** *a.*, of dialogue, (of decree etc.) given in course of a legal action. [L (*loquor* speak)]

**i′nterlōper** *n.* Intruder, one who thrusts himself into others' affairs, esp. for profit. [after *landloper* vagabond (Du. *loopen* run)]

**i′nterlūde** (*or* -ōod) *n.* (What fills) pause between acts of play; (Mus.) piece played between verses of hymn etc.; event etc. interposed, interval of different character. [L (*ludus* play)]

**intermē′dĭ|ate** *a.*, *n.*, & *v.* **1.** *a.* Coming between two things in time, place, character, etc. **2.** *n.* Intermediate thing, esp. in chemical reactions. **3.** (-āt) *v.i.* Mediate (*between*). **4.** **~ary̆,** (*a.*) acting between parties, intermediate, (*n.*) mediator, intermediate thing. [l. (MEDIUM)]

**intėr′ment** *n.* Burial. [INTER]

**intermĕ′zz|ō** (-tsō) *n.* (*pl.* **~i** *pr.* -ē, **~os**). Short light dramatic or other performance between acts of play etc.; short connecting movement in musical work, or similar but independent piece. [It. (INTERMEDIATE)]

**intėr′minab|le** *a.* (**~ly**). Endless; tediously long. [F or L (IN-²)]

**intermi′|t** *v.t.* & *i.* (**-tt-**). Suspend, discontinue, (of pulse, pain, etc.) stop for a time; **~ssion** (-shon) *n.*, pause, cessation, *interval in theatre etc.; **~ttent** *a.* [L (*mitto miss-* let go)]

**intėrn.** **1.** (-ėr′n) *v.t.* Oblige (prisoner, alien, etc.) to live within prescribed limits; **~ee′, intėr′n-ment,** *ns.* **2.** (ĭ′-) *n.* *Graduate etc. living in hospital and acting as assistant physician or surgeon. [F *interner* (foll.)]

**intėr′nal** *a.* (**~ly**). Of, in, the inside or invisible part; of the inner nature, intrinsic; relating or applied to interior of the body (*internal injury, organ, remedy*); of a country's domestic affairs; of students attending a university as well as taking its examinations; of mind or soul; **~ combustion engine** (in which motive power comes from explosion of gas or vapour with air in cylinder); **~ evidence** (derived from contents of the thing discussed); *~ (= inland) **revenue**; **~ĭtÿ** (-ă′l-) *n.*; **~īze** *v.t.* [L (*internus* inward)]

**internā′tional.** **1.** *a.* (**~ly**). Existing, carried on, between nations; agreed on by all or many nations (*international driving licence*); **~ law,** body of rules accepted as governing nations' mutual behaviour in peace and war; **~ system** (of physical units based on metre, kilogram, second, etc.); **~ unit,** standard quantity of vitamin etc. **2.** *n.* Contest (usu. in sports) between representatives of different nations; such representative; (*I~*) one of four successive associations for socialist or communist action. **3. I~e** (-ăh′l) *n.*, = *International* (**the I~e**, socialists' revolutionary song) [F]; **~ĭsm** *n.*, advocacy of community of interests among nations, support of International(s); **~ĭst** *n.*; **~ĭtÿ** (-ă′l-) *n.*; **~īze** *v.t.* [NATION]

**internē′cine** *a.* Mutually destructive. [L (*neco* kill)]

**internee′, intėr′nment.** See INTERN.

**intėr′nĭst** *n.* Specialist in internal diseases. [INTERNAL]

**i′nterplay** *n.* Reciprocal action. [INTER-]

**I′nterpŏl** (ĭ′-) *n.* International Criminal Police Commission. [abbr.]

**intėr′pol|āte** *v.t.* Make (esp. misleading) insertions in (book etc.); insert (words) thus; interject (remark) in talk; (Math.) insert (terms) in series, estimate (values) from known ones in same range; **~ā′tion, ~ātor,** *ns.* [L *interpolo* furbish]

**interpō′s|e** (-z) *v.t.* & *i.* Insert, make intervene, (thing *between* others); say (words) as interruption, speak thus; exercise, advance, (veto, objection) so as to interfere; intervene (*between* parties); **ĭnterposĭ′tion** (-z-) *n.* [F f. L (*pono* put)]

**inter′pret** *v.t.* & *i.* Explain (abstruse or foreign words, dream, etc.); make out or bring out meaning of; explain or understand in specified way; act as interpreter; ~**ā′tion** *n.*; ~**(ăt)ĭve** *adjs.*; ~**er** *n.*, (esp.) one who orally translates words of persons speaking different languages. [F or L (*interpres -pretis* explainer)]

**ĭnterrĕg′n|um** *n.* (*pl.* ~**ums**, ~**a**). Interval when State has no normal ruler, esp. between successive reigns; interval, pause. [L (*regnum* reign)]

**ĭntĕ′rrogāt|e** *v.t.* (-gable). Question (person) esp. closely or formally; obtain information-signal from (automatic device); **ĭntĕrrogā′tion** *n.*, questioning, question; **interro′gative**, (*a.*) of, like, used in, question(s), (*n.*) such word, e.g. *why?*; ~**or** *n.*; **interro′gatory**, (*a.*) of inquiry, (*n.*) question, set of questions, esp. formally put to accused person etc. [L (*rogo* ask)]

**ĭnterru′pt** *v.t.* Act so as to break the continuous progress of (action, speech, person speaking etc., series); obstruct (view etc.); ~**er**, ~**ion**, ~**or**, *ns.* [L (RUPTURE)]

**inter se** (ĭnter sē′) *adv.* Between or among themselves. [L]

**ĭntersĕ′ct** *v.t.* & *i.* Divide (thing) by crossing it (*lines* ~, cross each other); ~**ion** *n.*, (esp.) point, line, common to lines, planes, that intersect, place where two roads intersect. [L (SECTION)]

**ĭntersĕx** *n.* (Individual in) condition of being abnormally intermediate between male and female; ~**ūal** (-sĕ′-) *a.* (-lly), existing between the sexes, of intersex. [INTER-]

**ĭnterspăce**. **1.** *n.* Intervening space. **2.** *v.t.* Put space(s) between.

**ĭnterspēr′s|e** *v.t.* Scatter (things *between*, *among*); diversify (thing *with* others interspersed); ~**ion** (-shon) *n.* [L (SPARSE)]

**ĭntĕr′stice** *n.* Chink, crevice, gap; **interstĭ′tial** (-shal) *a.* (-lly), of or in interstices. [L *interstitium* (*sisto* stand)]

**ĭntertwĭ′ne**, **-twĭ′st**, *vbs. t.* & *i.* Twine, twist, closely together. [INTER-]

**ĭn′terval** *n.* Intervening time or

space, pause, break, (**at** ~**s**, here and there, now and then); difference of pitch between two sounds. [L = space between ramparts (*vallum*)]

**inter|vē′ne** *v.i.* Come in as extraneous thing; occur in mean time; be situated *between* others; interfere, modify course or result of events; ~**vĕ′ntion** *n.*, (esp.) interference, mediation. [L (*venio vent-* come)]

**ĭ′nterview** (-vū). **1.** *n.* Meeting of persons esp. for purpose of discussion; oral examination of applicant; conversation between reporter and person whose views he wishes to publish. **2.** *v.t.* Have interview with; ~**ee′** *n.* [F *entrevue* (INTER-, *vue* sight)]

**inter vivos** (ĭnter vĭ′vōs) *adv.* Between living persons (esp. as gift not legacy). [L]

**ĭntĕ′sta|te** *a.* & *n.* (Person) who has not made a will; ~**cў** *n.* [L (TESTAMENT)]

**ĭntĕ′stĭn|e**. **1.** *a.* (Of war etc.) internal, civil. **2.** *n.* (in *sing.* or *pl.*) Lower part of alimentary canal (**small, large,** ~**e**, parts of this); ~**al** *a.* (-lly), of the intestines. [L (*intus* within)]

**inthrōnizā′tion**. See ENTHRONE.

**ĭ′ntima|te[1]**. **1.** *a.* Closely acquainted, familiar, (*intimate friend, friendship, knowledge* of subject); (of relation between things) close; (of mixing) thorough; intrinsic; closely personal; promoting close personal relationships; (euphem.) having sexual intercourse *with*. **2.** *n.* Intimate friend. **3.** ~**cў** *n.*, being intimate, (euphem.) sexual intercourse. [L (*intimus* inmost)]

**ĭ′ntim|āte[2]** *v.t.* Make known, state, (fact, wish, *that*); imply, hint; ~**ā′tion** *n.* [L (prec.)]

**inti′mid|āte** *v.t.* Frighten, esp. in order to influence conduct; ~**ā′tion**, ~**ātor**, *ns.* [L (TIMID)]

**inti′nction** *n.* Dipping of Eucharistic bread in wine. [L (TINGE)]

**ĭ′nto** (or -tŏo) *prep.* expr. motion or direction to a point within, lit. or fig., (*go into the park; look into the box; inquire into it; get into trouble*) or change to a state (*turned into gold; divided into classes; flogged into submission*); (colloq.) interested in. [E (IN, TO)]

**ĭntŏ′ler|able** *a.* (-bly). That cannot be endured; ~**ant** *a.*, not tolerant, esp. of religious views differing from one's own; **~ance** n. [F or L (IN-²)]

**into'ne, i'ntonāte,** vbs. t. (**-nable**). Recite (prayers etc.) with prolonged sounds, esp. in monotone; utter with particular tone; **intonā'tion** n., intoning, modulation of voice, accent. [L (IN-¹)]

**in toto** (ĭn tō'tō) adv. Completely. [L]

**into'xĭc|āte** v.t. (**~able**). Make drunk; excite, elate, beyond self-control; **~ant** a. & n., intoxicating (liquor); **~ā'tion** n. [L (TOXIC)]

**intra-** pref. On the inside, within. [L intra inside]

**intră'ctab|le** a. (**~ly**). Not docile, refractory, not easily dealt with; **~i'lĭty** n. [L (IN-²)]

**intramūr'al** a. (**~ly**). Situated, done, within walls of city, house, etc.; forming part of ordinary university work. [L murus wall]

**intră'nsĭgen|t** (or -z-) a. & n. Uncompromising (person), esp. in politics; **~ce** n. [F, f. Sp. los intransigentes extremists (IN-², TRANSACT)]

**intră'nsĭtive** (or -z-, -ah'-) a. Not taking direct object (intransitive verb). [L (IN-²)]

**intra|-ū'terĭne** a. Within the womb; **~vē'nous** a., in(to) veins. [INTRA-]

**intrĕ'pĭd** a. Fearless, brave; **intrĕpĭ'dĭty** n. [F or L (trepidus alarmed)]

**i'ntrĭca|te** a. Perplexingly entangled or complicated (intricate mass, business); **~cy** n. [L IN-¹, tricae tricks)]

**intrī'gue** (-ē'g). 1. n. Underhand plot(ting); (arch.) secret amour. 2. v.i. & t. Carry on intrigue (with); employ secret influence (with); rouse the interest or curiosity of. [F f. It. (prec.)]

**intrī'nsĭc** a. (**~ally**). Inherent, essential, (intrinsic value, merit, cf. EXTRINSIC). [F f. L intrinsecus inwardly]

**intro-** in comb. Into, inwards. [L]

**introdū'c|e** v.t. (**~ible**). Bring in; insert; bring (custom etc.) into use; usher in, bring forward; come just before start of; make known esp. formally (person, oneself) to another; present to audience; extend understanding of (person to subject etc.) for first time; bring (bill) before Parliament etc.; **introdū'ction** n., introducing, thing introduced, pre-liminary explanation in book etc., introductory treatise, formal presentation of person to another; **introdū'ctory** a., that introduces, preliminary. [L (duco lead)]

**intrō'ĭt** (or ĭ'-) n. Psalm etc. sung while priest approaches altar for Mass or Communion. [F f. L introitus entrance]

**introspĕ'ction** n. Examining one's own thoughts; **~ĭve** a. [L (specio spect- look)]

**intro|vĕrt. 1.** (-ĕr't) v.t. (esp. in p.p.) Turn thoughts of (person), turn (mind, thought), inwards; **~vĕr'sion** (-shon) n. 2. (ĭ'n-) n. Person given to introversion. [L (verto turn)]

**intru'|de** (-rōō'-) v.t. & i. Thrust, force, (thing into place, thing or oneself on, upon, person); thrust oneself uninvited (into company, on or upon person); **~der** n., (esp.) burglar, raiding aircraft; **~sion** (-zhon) n., intruding, (Geol.) influx of molten rock between strata etc.; **~sive** a. (trudo trus- thrust)]

**intrŭ'st.** See ENTRUST.

**intū'ĭt** v.t. & i. Know by intuition or direct perception; **intū'tion** n., immediate apprehension by the mind without reasoning, immediate apprehension by a sense, immediate insight; **~ional** (-ūĭ'-) a. (**-lly**); **~ĭve** a., of, having, perceived by, intuition. [L (tueor tuit- look)]

**intūmĕ'scen|t** a. Swelling up; **~ce** n. [L (tumeo swell)]

**i'nŭnd|āte** v.t. Flood (land with water, person with letters etc.); **~ā'tion** n. [L (unda wave)]

**inūr'e, ĕn-,** v.t. & i. Accustom (inure oneself, be or become inured, to drudgery, drudging); (Law) be operative, take effect; **~ment** (-ūr'm-) n. [AF (IN, eure work f. L opera)]

**inūtĭ'lĭty** n. Uselessness. [F f. L (IN-²)]

**in vacuo** (ĭn vă'kūō) adv. In a vacuum. [L]

**invā'|de** v.t. Make hostile inroad into (country); (of disease etc.) assail; swarm into; encroach on (rights); **~sion** (-zhon) n.; **~sive** a. [L (vado vas- go)]

**i'nvalid¹** (-ēd) a., n., & v. **1.** (or -ĭd) a. & n. (Person) enfeebled or disabled by illness or injury; **~chair** etc. (for use by invalids). **2.** (or -ē'd) v.t. & i. Remove from active service, send away (home etc.), as an invalid; disable by illness; become an invalid. **3.** ~**ism** *n.*, state of being a confirmed invalid. [L (IN-²)]

**ĭnvă'lĭd²** *a.* Not valid; ~**āte** *v.t.* (~**able**), make invalid; ~**ā'tion**, **invalĭdĭty̆**, *ns.*

**ĭnvă'lūab|le** *a.* (~**ly**). Above price, inestimable. [IN-²]

**ĭnvā'rĭab|le** *a.* (~**ly**). Unchangeable; always the same; (Math.) constant; ~**ĭ'lĭty̆** *n.*; **ĭnvā'rĭant** *n.*; **ĭnvā'rĭance** *n.* [IN-²]

**invasion, -sive.** See INVADE.

**ĭnvě'ctĭve** *n.* Abusive speech or oratory. [L *invehor -vect-* assail]

**ĭnvei'gh** (-vā') *v.i.* Speak violently, rail loudly, (*against*).

**ĭnvei'gle** (-vē'-, -vā'-) *v.t.* Entice, tempt, (*into* place, conduct, do*ing*); ~**ment** (-gelm-) *n.* [AF f. F *aveugler* to blind]

**ĭnvě'nt** *v.t.* Create by thought, originate, (method, instrument); concoct (false story); ~**ion** *n.*, inventing, thing invented, esp. one patented, fictitious story, inventiveness; I~**ion** of the Cross, (3 May, festival of) finding of the Cross by Helena A.D. 326; ~**ĭve** *a.*; ~**or** *n.* [L *invenio -vent-* come upon, find]

**ĭ'nventory̆ 1.** *n.* Detailed list (of goods etc.); goods in this. **2.** *v.t.* Enter (goods) in inventory; make inventory of. [L (prec.)]

**invert. 1.** (-ẽr't) *v.t.* Turn upside down; reverse position, order, or relation, of; ||~**ed commas,** quotation-marks. **2.** (ĭ'-) *n.* Homosexual. **3. ĭnvẽr'se** (or ĭ'-), (*a.*) inverted in position etc. (**inverse proportion, ratio,** between two quantities one of which increases in proportion as the other decreases; **inverse square law,** by which intensity of light or force decreases in inverse ratio to square of distance), (*n.*) inverted state, thing that is direct opposite (*of* another); **ĭnvẽr'sion** *n.*, turning upside down, reversal of normal position etc. (e.g. of words), homosexuality; **ĭnvẽr'sĭve** *a.* [L (*verto versturn*)]

**ĭnvẽr'tebrate** (or -āt). **1.** *a.* Without backbone or spinal column, (fig.) weak-willed. **2.** *n.* Invertebrate animal or (fig.) person. [L (IN-²)]

**ĭnvě'st** *v.t.* & *i.* Clothe (person etc. *in, with*); cover as garment; clothe, endue, (person etc. *with* qualities, insignia); lay siege to; employ (money *in* stocks, property, etc.) esp. for profit; ~ **in,** put money into

(stocks etc.), (colloq.) buy; ~**ĭture** *n.*, formal investing of person(s) with honours etc.; ~**ment** *n.*, investing. money invested, property etc. in which money is invested; ~**or** *n.* (esp. of money). [F or L (*vestis* clothing)]

**ĭnvě'stĭgāt|e** *v.t.* (-**gable**). Examine, inquire into; **ĭnvě'stĭgā'tion,** ~**or,** *ns.*; ~**ĭve,** ~**ory̆,** *adjs.* [L (*vestigo* to track)]

**ĭnvě'tera|te** *a.* Deep-rooted, confirmed, (inveterate *habit, prejudice, smoker*); ~**cy̆** *n.* [L (*vetus* old)]

**ĭnvĭ'dĭous** *a.* Likely to excite ill-will against the performer, possessor, etc., (an invidious *task, position, honour*). [L *invidiosus* (ENVY)]

||**ĭnvĭ'gĭlāte** *v.i.* Maintain surveillance over examinees; ~**ā'tion,** ~**ātor,** *ns.* [L (VIGIL)]

**ĭnvĭ'gor|āte** *v.t.* Make vigorous; ~**ātĭve** *a.*; ~**ā'tion,** ~**ātor,** *ns.* [L (VIGOUR)]

**ĭnvĭ'ncĭb|le** *a.* (~**ly**). Unconquerable; ~**ĭ'lĭty̆** *n.* [F f. L (*vinco* conquer)]

**ĭnvĭ'ol|able** *a.* (-**bly**). Not to be violated or profaned (inviolable *law, shrine*); ~**abĭ'lĭty̆** *n.*; ~**ate** *a.*, not violated; ~**acy̆** *n.* [F or L (VIOLATE)]

**ĭnvĭ'sĭble** (-z-) *a.* (-**bly**). That cannot be seen (~ **exports, imports,** items for which payment is made by or to another country but which are not goods; ~ **ink,** for writing words invisible till heated etc.; ~ **mending,** of clothing etc., so carefully done as to be undetectable); **ĭnvĭsĭbĭ'lĭty̆** (-z-) *n.* [F or L]

**ĭnvĭ't|e. 1.** *v.t.* Request courteously to come (*to* dinner, *to* one's house, *in,* etc.); request courteously (*to* do); solicit (suggestions etc.) courteously; tend to call forth (criticism etc.); attract, be attractive; ~**ĭng** *a.*, attractive. **2.** (ĭ'n-) *n.* (colloq.) Invitation. **3. ĭnvĭtā'tion** *n.* [F or L]

**ĭnvocā'tion, -tory.** See INVOKE.

**ĭ'nvoice. 1.** *n.* List of goods shipped or sent, or services rendered, with prices. **2.** *v.t.* Make invoice of (goods); send invoice to (person). [orig. pl. of obs. *invoy* (ENVOY)]

**ĭnvō'ke** *v.t.* Call on (deity etc.) in prayer or as witness; appeal to (law, person's authority etc.); summon (spirit) by charms; ask earnestly for (vengeance etc.); **ĭnvocā'tion** *n.*, (esp.) appeal to Muse for inspiration.

preacher's prefatory words 'In the name of ...' (cf. ASCRIPTION); **invŏ'catorў** a. [F f. L (*voco* to call)]

**i'nvolūcr|e** (-ker; or -lōō-) n. (Bot.) whorl of bracts round inflorescence; (Anat.) covering, envelope; **~al** a. [F or L (INVOLVE)]

**invŏ'luntarў** a. (~ily, ~iness). Done without exercise of will; not controlled by will. [L (IN-²)]

**invŏ'lve** v.t. Wrap (thing in another); entangle (person, thing, in difficulties, mystery, etc.); implicate (person in charge, crime, etc.); include (in); imply, entail; (in p.p.) concerned (in), complicated in thought or form (*involved argument, sentence*); **~ment** (-vm-) n.; **i'nvolūte** (or -ōōt) a., involved, intricate, spirally curled; **involu'tion** (-lōō'-) n., involving, intricacy, curling inwards, part so curled. [L (*volvo* to roll)]

**invŭ'lnerab|le** a. (~ly). That cannot be wounded or hurt (esp. fig.); **~i'litў** n. [L (IN-²)]

**i'nward** a., n., & adv. 1. a. Situated within; mental, spiritual; directed towards the inside; going in. 2. n. (in pl.) Entrails. 3. ~, **~s** (-dz), advs., towards the inside, within mind or soul; **~lў** adv., on the inside, not aloud, in mind or soul; **~nĕss** n., inner nature, spirituality. [E (IN, -WARD)]

**inwĕa've, ĕnw-,** v.t. (-wo've; -wo'ven). Weave in (thing with another). [IN-¹, EN-]

**inwrou'ght** (inraw't, before n. i'n-) a. (Of fabric) decorated (with pattern); (of pattern) wrought (in, on, fabric). [IN¹, WORK]

**i'odĭne** (or -ēn) n. Black solid halogen element used in medicine and photography; tincture of this; **i'odĭde** n., binary compound of iodine; **iŏ'dĭnāte** (or i'o-), **i'odĭze** vbs. t., impregnate with iodine; **iŏ'dofŏrm** n., an antiseptic compound of iodine. [F *iode* f. Gk *iōdēs* violet-coloured (as its vapour is)]

**I.O.M.** abbr. Isle of Man.

**i'on** n. One of the electrically charged particles into which the atoms or molecules of certain substances are dissociated by solution in water, making it a conductor of electricity; a similarly charged molecule of gas e.g. in air exposed to X-rays. [Gk, = going]

**-ion** suf. (appearing as **-sion, -tion, -xion,** and esp. **-ation**) in nouns denoting verbal action (*excision*), an instance of this (a *suggestion*), or the resulting state (*vexation*) or product (*concoction*). [F or L]

**Iŏ'nĭc¹** (ī-) a. Of Ionia; **~ order** (with two lateral volutes of capital); **Iŏ'nĭan** (ī-) a. & n. [L f. Gk *lōnikos*]

**iŏ'nĭc²** a. Of or using ions; **i'onize** v.t., convert into ion(s); **ioniză'tion** n.; **iŏ'nosphēre** n., ionized region of upper atmosphere reflecting radio waves; **iŏnosphĕ'rĭc** a. [ION]

**iŏ'ta** n. Ninth Gk letter (I, ι) = i; smallest amount. [Gk *iōta*]

**IOU** (iōū') n. Signed document acknowledging debt in the form IOU (£5 etc.). [*I owe you*]

**I.O.W.** abbr. Isle of Wight.

**ipĕcăcuă'nha** (-na) n. Root of S. Amer. plant used as emetic etc. [Port., f. Tupi-Guarani, = emetic creeper]

**i.p.s.** abbr. inches per second.

**ipso facto** (ĭpsō fă'ktō) adv. By that very fact. [L]

**I.Q.** abbr. intelligence quotient.

**ir-¹,².** See IN-¹,².

**I.R.** abbr. infra-red.

**I.R.A.** abbr. Irish Republican Army.

**Irā'nian** (ĭr-). 1. a. Persian, (of language) of the Persian family. 2. n. Native of Iran (Persia). [Pers. *Irān* Persia]

**Ira'qi** (ĭrah'kī) a. & n. (Native or Arabic dialect) of Iraq. [Arab.]

**ĭră'scĭb|le** (or ĭr-) a. (~ly). Irritable, hot-tempered; **~i'litў** n.; **ĭră'te** (or ĭr-) a., enraged, angry; **īre** n., (rhet., poet.) anger; **īreful** (īr'f-) a. (-lly). [F f. L *irascor* grow angry (*ira* anger)]

**īrĕ'nĭc(al)** (or ĭr-) adjs. Aiming or aimed at peace. [Gk *eirēnikos*]

**īr'ĭs** n. Circular coloured membrane behind cornea of eye, with circular opening (pupil) in centre; perennial herbaceous plant usu. with tuberous roots, sword-shaped leaves, and showy flowers; diaphragm with hole of variable size; **īrĭdā'ceous** (-shus; or ĭr-) a., (Bot.) of iris family; **ĭrĭdĕ'scent** a., showing rainbow-like colours, changing colour with position; **ĭrĭdĕ'scence** n.; **īrĭ'dĭum** (or ĭr-) n., hard white metal of platinum group; **īrī'tĭs** n., inflammation of iris. [L f. Gk *iris iridos* rainbow (goddess)]

**Ir'ish** (īr'-). 1. a. Of Ireland (*Irish* BULL²; **~ stew,** of mutton, potato, and onion); like the Irish, esp. in supposed illogicality. **2.** *n.* Irish language; (as *pl.*) Irish people. **3.** ~**man**, ~**woman**, Irish native; ~**ism** *n.*, (esp.) an Irish idiom. [E] **ȋrk** *v.t.* Tire, bore, (*it irks me*); ~'**some** *a.*, tedious. [orig. unkn.]

**iron** (ī'ern) *n.*, *a.*, & *v.* **1.** *n.* Silver--white common strong metal much used for tools etc. (~ **entered into his soul**, he became permanently affected by ill-treatment etc.; *man* **of** ~, stern, unyielding; **rod of** ~, severe discipline; **strike while the** ~ **is hot**, act promptly at good opportunity); tool of iron, golf--club with iron or steel head and sloping face, implement with smooth flat base heated to smooth clothes etc., (**many** ~**s in the fire**, many undertakings or resources); (in *pl.*) fetters, stirrups, leg-supports to rectify malformations etc. **2.** *a.* Of iron; very robust; unyielding, merci-less. **3.** *v.t.* Smooth (clothes etc.) with iron; ~ **out**, (fig.) remove (difficulties etc.); ~**ing-board**, flat surface to support clothes etc. being ironed. **4.** I~ **Age**, era of iron imple-ments and weapons; ~**clad**, (*a.*) protected with iron, (*n.*, Hist.) ship cased in iron plates; I~ **Cross**, German military decoration; I~ **Curtain**, (fig.) barrier to passage of persons and information at limit of Soviet sphere of influence; ~**-grey**, colour of freshly broken iron; ~ **lung**, rigid case over patient's body for prolonged artificial respiration; ~**master**, manufacturer of iron; ~**monger**, dealer in hardware etc. (~**mongery**); ~**-mould**, spot caused by iron-rust or ink-stain; ~ **ration**, (soldier's) modicum of tinned etc. food for use in emergency only; ~**stone**, hard iron-ore, kind of hard white pottery; ~**ware**, ~**work**, things made of iron; ~**works**, (as *sing.* or *pl.*), place where iron is smelted or iron goods are made; ~**y**[1] *a.*, of or like iron. [E]

**īr'on**|**y**[2] *n.* Expression of meaning by language of opposite or different tendency, esp. mock adoption of another's views or laudatory tone to ridicule; ill-timed or perverse event or circumstance that would in itself be desirable; use of language with one meaning for privileged few and another for those addressed or concerned; **īrŏ'nĭc(al)** *adjs.* (**-lly**).

~**ĭst** *n.*, user of irony. [L, f. Gk *eirōneia* pretended ignorance]

**ĭrrā'dĭ|āte** *v.t.* (~**able**). Shine upon; throw light on (subject); light up (face *with* joy etc.); subject to sunlight or ultraviolet or other rays; ~**ance**, ~**ā'tion**, ~**ātor**, *ns.* [L *irradio* shine on (*radius* ray)]

**ĭrrā'tional** *a.* (~**ly**). Unreasonable, illogical; not endowed with reason; (Math.) not commensurable with the natural numbers; ~**ĭtý** (-ǎ'l-) *n.* [L (IN-[2])]

**ĭrrė'concilab|le** *a.* (~**ly**). Impla-cably hostile; incompatible; ~**ĭ'lĭtý** *n.*; **ĭrrėco'verable** (-kŭ'-) *a.* (**-bly**), that cannot be recovered or remedied; **ĭrrėdee'mable** *a.* (**-bly**), that can-not be redeemed, hopeless. [IN-[2]]

**ĭrrėdě'nt|ĭst** *n.* Advocate of return to Italy of all Italian-speaking districts; Greek, Pole, etc., of similar views; ~**ĭsm** *n.* [It. (*irredenta* un-redeemed)]

**ĭrrėdū'cĭb|le** *a.* (~**ly**). That can-not be reduced, simplified, or brought (*to* condition); **ĭrrė'fūtable** (*or* -rĭfū'-) *a.* (**-bly**), that cannot be refuted. [IN-[2]]

**ĭrrė'gŭl|ar. 1.** *a.* Contrary to rule or principle; abnormal; unsym-metrical, uneven, varying, (*irregular shape, surface, intervals*); (Gram.) not inflected normally; disorderly; (of troops) not in regular army; ~**ǎ'r-ĭtý** *n.* **2.** *n.* (in *pl.*) Irregular troops. [F f. L (IN-[2])]

**ĭrrė'lėvan|t** *a.* Not relevant, not applying, (*to*); ~**ce**, ~**cý**, *ns.*; **ĭrrėli'gion** (-jon) *n.*, hostility or indifference to religion; **ĭrrėli'gious** (-jus) *a.*; **ĭrrėmė'dĭable** *a.* (**-bly**), that cannot be remedied; **ĭrrėmo'vable** (-mōō'-) *a.* (**-bly**), that cannot be removed, esp. from office; **ĭrrė'parable** *a.* (**-bly**), that cannot be rectified or made good (*irreparable loss*); **ĭrrėplā'ceable** (-sa-) *a.* (**-bly**), that cannot be replaced; **ĭrrėprė's-ĭble** *a.* (**-bly**), that cannot be re-pressed or restrained; **ĭrrėproa'ch-able** *a.* (**-bly**), faultless, blameless; **ĭrrėsi'stible** (-zĭ'-) *a.* (**-bly**), too strong, delightful, etc., to be re-sisted; **ĭrrė'solūte** (-z-; *or* -ōōt) *a.*, hesitating, lacking in resoluteness; **ĭrrėsolū'tion** (-z-; *or* -ōō'-) *n.* [IN-[2]]

**ĭrrėspė'ctĭve** *a.* ~ **of**, not taking account of, without reference to (*chosen irrespective of age*).

**ĭrrėspŏ'ns|ĭble** *a.* (~**ĭbly**). Not

responsible for (one's) conduct; acting, done, without due sense of responsibility; **~ibĭ'lĭtў** n.; **~ĭve** a., not responsive (to).

**irrėtrie'vab|le** a. (**~ly**). That cannot be retrieved (irretrievable disaster, loss; took an irretrievable step); **irrė'verence** n.; lacking reverence; **irrė'verence** n.; **irrėvē'sĭble** a. (-bly), not reversible or alterable; **irrė'vocable** a. (-bly), unalterable, gone beyond recall.

**ĭ'rrĭg|āte** v.t. (**~able**). (Of stream etc.) supply (land) with water; water (land) with channels; (Med.) moisten continually; **~ā'tion**, **~ātor,** ns. [L rigo moisten]

**ĭ'rrĭt|āte** v.t. Excite to anger, annoy, (irritated at, by, with, against); excite, cause uneasy sensation in, (organ etc.); stimulate (organ) to action; **~able** a. (-bly), (esp.) easily annoyed; **~abĭ'lĭtў** n.; **~ant** a. & n., (substance or agent) causing irritation; **~ā'tion** n.; **~ātĭve** a. [L irrito]

**ĭrrŭ'ption** n. Invasion, violent entry. [L (RUPTURE)]

**is.** See BE.

**Is.** abbr Isaiah (O.T.); Island(s); Isle(s).

**I.S.B.N.** abbr. international standard book number.

**-ise.** See -IZE.

**-ĭsh** suf. forming adjs. (1) from ns., w. sense 'having the qualities of' (knavish), 'of the nationality of' (Danish); (2) from adjs., w. sense 'somewhat' (thickish), (3, colloq.) of approximate age or time (fortyish); these words drop silent final e; see note on Suffixes, p. viii. [E]

**I'shmael(ite)** (ĭ'-) ns. Outcast, one at war with society. [Gen. 16: 12]

**ĭ'sĭnglass** (ĭ'zĭngglahs) n. Kind of gelatin got from sturgeon etc. and used for jellies, glue, etc.; mica. [Du. huisenblas sturgeon's bladder]

**I'slăm** (ĭz-; or -ahm, -ah'm) n. Religion of Muslims, revealed through Muhammad; the Muslim world; **Islă'mĭc** (-z-) a. [Arab.,= submission to God)]

**I'sland** (ĭ'l-) n. Piece of land surrounded by water; = TRAFFIC island; (fig.) detached or isolated thing; **~er** n., inhabitant of island. [E, orig. iland; -s- f. foll.]

**isle** (īl) n. Island (poet. or with

proper name, as Isle of Man, and usu. of small islands); **ĭ'slėt** (ĭ'l-) n., small isle, detached portion of tissue (e.g. **~ts of Langerhans** in pancreas secreting insulin). [F ile f. L insula]

**ĭsm** n. (often derog.) Any distinctive doctrine or practice; **-ĭsm** suf. forming ns. expressing esp. a state or quality (barbarism, heroism), or a system or principle (Conservatism, jingoism), or peculiarity in language (Americanism). [F f. L f. Gk (-IZE)]

**isn't.** See BE.

**ĭ'so-** in comb. Equal; **~bār** n., line on map connecting places with same atmospheric pressure [Gk baros weight]; **~bă'rĭc** a.; **isŏ'chronous** (-k-) a., occupying equal time, occurring at same time; **~mēr** n., one of two or more substances whose molecules have same atoms in different arrangement [Gk meros share]; **~mĕ'rĭc** a.; **isŏ'merism** n.; **~mĕ'trĭc** a., of equal measure, (of drawing etc.) with plane of projection at equal angles to 3 principal axes of object shown; **~mŏr'phic, ~mŏr'phous,** adjs., having same form (and relations); **~thĕrm** n., line on map connecting places with same temperature; **~thĕr'mal** a.; **~trŏ'pĭc** a., having same physical properties in all directions; **isŏ'tropў** n. [Gk isos equal]

**ĭ'sol|āte** v.t. Place apart or alone; (Chem.) free (substance) from combination with others; (Electr.) insulate; **~ā'tion** n. (**~ation hospital,** for patients with contagious or infectious diseases); **~ā'tionism** n., policy of holding aloof from affairs of other countries or groups; **~ā'tionist, ~ātor,** ns. [F f. It. f. L (INSULATE)]

**isŏ'scelēs** (-z) a. (Of triangle) having two sides equal. [L (ISO-, Gk skelos leg)]

**ĭ'sotōpe** n. One of two or more forms of an element differing from each other in atomic weight, and in nuclear but not chemical properties; **isotŏ'pĭc** a. [ISO-, Gk topos place]

**I'srael** (ĭ'z-) n. The Jewish people; **~ī** (izrā'lī) a. & n., (inhabitant) of State of Israel in S.W. Asia; **~īte** n., Jew. [Heb. yisrā'ēl striver with God (Gen. 32: 28)]

**ĭ'ssūe** (or ĭ'shoo). **1.** n. Outgoing, outflow; way out; place of emergence of stream etc.; (Law) progeny, children, (*without male issue*); result, outcome, (**force the ~**, compel decision); point in question, important topic of discussion, esp. between parties in lawsuit (**at ~**, in dispute; **join, take, ~**, proceed to argue *with* person *on* point); giving out, issuing, (*of* shares, notes, stamps, etc.); quantity of coins, copies of newspaper, etc., issued at one time; one of regular series of magazine etc. (*in the May issue*). **2.** *v.i.* & *t.* Go or come out; emerge from a condition; be derived, result, (*from*); end, result, (*in*); send forth, publish, put into circulation; give out (book, orders *to* subordinate); supply (thing *to* person, person *with* thing) esp. for official use. [F f. L *exitus* (EXIT)]

**-ist** *suf.* forming personal *ns.* expressing esp. adherent of creed etc. in -ism (*Marxist*, *fatalist*), person concerned with something (*pathologist*, *tobacconist*), person who uses a thing esp. musical instrument (*organist*, *violinist*, *balloonist*, *motorist*), or person who does thing expressed by *v.* in -ize (*plagiarist*). [F & L f. Gk -*istēs* (-IZE)]

**i'sthm|us** (or **i'smus**) *n.* Narrow piece of land connecting two larger bodies; narrow connecting part; ~**ian** *a.* [L f. Gk]

**it**[1] *pron.* (*obj.* **it**, *refl.* ITSELF, *poss.* ITS; *pl.* THEY etc.). The thing previously named or in question (*took a stone and threw it*; *dog wags its tail*; *child lost its way*; **who is it?** that is knocking etc.; **it is I** who am knocking etc.); as subj. of impers. v. (*it rains*; *it is raining*; *it is cold*; *it is winter*; *it is Monday today*; *it is 6 o'clock*; *it is 6 miles to Oxford*); as substitute for deferred subj. (*it is absurd talking like that, to talk like that, that he should talk like that*; *it is seldom that he fails*; *it is to him that you must apply*); as substitute for deferred or vague obj. (*I take it that you agree*; *run for it*; *brazen it out*; **have done it**, have blundered); as antecedent to relative (*it was a purse that he dropped*); exactly what is needed; extreme limit of achievement etc.; (colloq.) sexual intercourse, sex appeal; **that's it**, (colloq.) that is the problem, what is wanted, or the end. [E]

||**it**[2] *n.* (colloq.) Italian vermouth (*gin and it*). [abbr.]

**ital.** *abbr.* italic (type).

**Ita'lian** (ĭtă'lyan). **1.** *a.* Of Italy; ~ **vermouth** (sweet). **2.** *n.* Native, language, of Italy. **3.** ~**ate** (or -ăt) *a.*, having Italian style or appearance. [It. *italiano* (*Italia* Italy)]

**itā'lic. 1.** *a.* (*I~*) of ancient Italy; ~ **hand**, (simulation of) original form of Italian handwriting; ~ **letters, type**, sloping kind now used esp. for emphasis or in foreign words (cf. ROMAN). **2.** *n.* Italic type, letter in this; ~**ize** *v.t.*, print in italics. [L *italicus* f. Gk (prec.)]

**itch. 1.** *n.* Irritation in skin; contagious disease with itch caused by ~**-mite**; impatient desire (*for* thing, *to* do); ~**y** *a.* (~**iness**), having or causing itch. **2.** *v.i.* Feel itch (*itching to tell you the news*; *my* FINGERS *itch to box his ears*); ~**ing palm**, avariciousness.

**-ite** *suf.* forming *ns.* w. sense 'person or thing belonging to or connected with' (*Israelite*, *graphite*, *dynamite*). [F f. L f. Gk -*itēs*]

**i'tem. 1.** *n.* Any one of enumerated things; detached piece of news etc.; ~**ize** *v.t.*, state by items. **2.** *adv.* Also (formally introducing an item). [L, = likewise]

**i'ter|ate** *v.t.* (~**able**). Repeat, state repeatedly, (quoted words, objection, etc.); ~**ā'tion**, ~**ātor**, *ns.*; ~**ative** *a.* [L (*iterum* again)]

**-i'tic** *suf.* forming *adjs.* corresp. to *ns.* in -ITE, -ITIS, (*Semitic*, *arthritic*). [F f. L f. Gk -*itikos*]

**iti'ner|ant** *a.* Travelling from place to place; (of justices) travelling on circuit; (of Methodists) preaching in various circuits; ~**a(n)cy** *ns.*; ~**āte** *v.i.*, be itinerant, esp. preach in circuits; ~**ā'tion** *n.*; ~**arȳ**, (*n.*) record of travel, guidebook, route, (*a.*) of roads or travelling. [L (*itiner-* journey)]

**-i'tis** *suf.* forming *ns.*, esp. names of inflammatory diseases (*appendicitis*) or (colloq.) of mental states fancifully regarded as diseases (*electionitis*). [Gk]

**its** *poss. pron.* Of it(self). [IT[1]]

**it's** = *it has, it is.*

**itse'lf** *pron.*, emphat. & refl. form of IT[1]; **by ~**, automatically, apart from its surroundings; **in ~**, viewed in its essential qualities (*not in itself a bad thing*). [E (IT[1], SELF)]

||**I.T.V.** *abbr.* independent television.

**-itȳ** *suf.* forming *ns.* of quality or

condition (*humility, purity*) or instance of this (*a monstrosity*). [F f. L *-itas*]

**-ive** *suf.* forming *adjs.* (and *ns.*) meaning esp. (*thing*) *tending to do* (*suggestive, corrosive, palliative, coercive, talkative*). [F f. L *-ivus*]

**i'vory** *n.* Hard white substance of tusks of elephant etc.; colour of this; (in *pl.*) articles made of ivory; (sl., in *pl.*) dice, billiard-balls, piano--keys, teeth; ~ **tower**, seclusion or withdrawal from (harsh realities of) the world. [F f. L *ebur*]

**i'vy** *n.* Climbing evergreen with shining usu. five-angled leaves; ~ **geranium**, pelargonium with ivy--like leaves; \***Ivy League**, group of famous colleges in eastern U.S. [E]

**i'xia** *n.* S. Afr. iridaceous plant with large showy flowers. [L f. Gk]

**-ize, -ise** (-z), *suf.* forming *vbs.* meaning esp. make or become such (*Americanize, volatilize*), treat by such method (*monopolize, pasteurize*); **-izā'tion, -isā'tion** (-z-), *n. suf.* [F f. L f. Gk *-izō*]

# J

**J, j,** (jā) *n.* (*pl.* **Js, J's**). Tenth letter.

**J.** *abbr.* jack; Judge; Justice.

**jăb. 1.** *v.t.* (**-bb-**). Poke roughly; thrust abruptly (thing *into*). **2.** *n.* Abrupt blow with pointed thing or fist; (colloq.) hypodermic injection. [var. of *job* = prod]

**jǎ'bber. 1.** *v.i.* & *t.* Chatter volubly; utter (words) fast and indistinctly. **2.** *n.* Chatter, gabble. [imit.]

**jǎ'bŏt** (zhǎ'bō) *n.* Ornamental frill or ruffle of lace etc. worn on front of man's shirt (usu. Hist.); similar frill on woman's blouse etc. [F]

**jăcară'nda** *n.* Tropical Amer. tree with hard scented wood, or one with blue flowers. [Tupi]

**jă'cĭnth** *n.* Reddish-orange gem, variety of zircon. [F or L (HYACINTH)]

**jăck. 1.** *n.* (*J~*) type of common man (**before you could say J~ Robinson**, in a moment, suddenly; **every man ~**, each individual man); = *Jack tar*; court-card = KNAVE; machine for turning spit or for lifting weights or for lifting wheel off ground; (usu. young) pike; ship's flag esp. one flown from bow and showing nationality (UNION *Jack*); (Bowls) small white ball for players to aim at; (in *pl.*, treated as *sing.*) game played with jackstones. **2.** *v.t.* ~ (**up**), raise (as) with jack; ~ **in, up**, (sl.) abandon (attempt etc.). **3.** ~**anapes** (-āps), pert child or fellow; ~**ass**, male ass, stupid person, (*laughing jackass*, Austral.

giant kingfisher with loud discordant cry); ~**boot**, large boot (Hist., with top reaching above knee), (fig.) oppressive behaviour; ~**daw**, thievish bird of crow family; J~ **Frost**, frost personified; ~**in--office**, pompous official; ~**in--the-box**, toy figure that springs out when box is opened; ||~**in-the--pulpit**, wild arum; ~**knife**, (*n.*) large pocket clasp-knife, dive in which body is first doubled up and then straightened, accidental folding of articulated vehicle (also as *v.i.* & *t.*); ~ **of all trades**, person who can turn his hand to anything; ~**plane** (for coarse joinery); ~**pot**, large esp. accumulating prize in lottery etc. (*hit the ~pot*, be remarkably lucky); \*~**rabbit**, large prairie hare with very long ears; ~**snipe**, small species of snipe; ~**stone**, small metal etc. object used with others in tossing-games; J~ **tar**, sailor; ~**towel**, roller towel. [pet form of JOHN]

**jǎ'ckal** (-awl) *n.* Wild animal related to dog, formerly supposed to find prey for lion; one who does preliminary drudgery etc. for another. [Pers.]

**jǎ'ckĕt** *n.* Sleeved short outer garment; thing similarly worn (LIFE--*jacket*, STRAIT *jacket*); outer covering round boiler etc. to prevent heat--loss etc.; (**dust-**)~, paper wrapper in which bound book is issued; animal's coat; skin of potato (*baked in their jackets*). [F]

**Jăcŏbē'an** *a.* Of James I's reign:

(of furniture) of colour of dark oak. [L (*Jacobus* James)]

**Jă'cobite** *n. & a.* (Person) adhering to cause of James II after his abdication or of the Stuarts.

**jă'conèt** *n.* Cambric-like plain cotton fabric, esp. waterproofed and used for poultices etc. [*Jagannath*, place]

**Jă'cquard** (-kärd) *n.* Apparatus with perforated cards to facilitate weaving of figured fabrics (~ **loom**, one fitted with this); fabric thus made. [person]

**jāde**¹ *n.* Poor or worn-out horse; (joc.) hussy; **jā'dėd** *a.*, tired out, surfeited. [orig. unkn.]

**jāde**² *n.* A hard green, blue, or white stone, silicate of calcium and magnesium; green colour of jade; ~**ite** (-dīt) *n.*, jadelike silicate of sodium and aluminium. [F f. Sp. *ijada* f. L *ilia* flanks (named as cure for colic)]

**jăg**¹. **1.** *n.* Sharp projection of rock etc. **2.** *v.t.* Cut or tear unevenly; make indentations in. **3.** ~**'gėd** (-g-) *a.*, with unevenly cut or torn edge. [imit.]

**jăg**² *n.* (colloq.) Drinking bout; period of indulgence in activity, emotion, etc. [orig. dial. = load]

**jă'gŭar** (or -gwer) *n.* Large Amer. carnivorous spotted animal of cat family. [Tupi]

**jail** etc. See GAOL etc.

**Jain** (jīn) *a. & n.* (Adherent) of Indian religion having doctrines like those of Buddhism; ~**ïsm**, ~**ïst**, *ns.* [Hindi]

**jāke** *a.* (sl.) Excellent, all right. [prob. abbr. *Jacob*]

**jă'lap** *n.* Purgative drug from tubers of a Mexican plant. [F f. Sp. f. Aztec *Xalapan* (place)]

**jalŏ'pў** *n.* (colloq.) Dilapidated old motor vehicle. [orig. unkn.]

**jă'lousie** (zhă'lōozē) *n.* Blind, shutter, with slats sloped upwards from outside. [F (JEALOUSY)]

**jăm**¹. **1.** *v.t. & i.* (-mm-). Squeeze (thing) between two surfaces; cause (machinery) to become wedged etc. so that it cannot work, become thus fixed; force or thrust violently (*jam on the brakes*; *into* confined space); push or cram together in compact mass; block (passage, road, etc.) by crowding; (Radio) make (transmission) unintelligible by causing interference; (Jazz colloq.) extem-

porize. **2.** *n.* Squeeze, crush; stoppage (of machine etc.) due to jamming; crowded mass (*log-jam, traffic jam*; ~**-packed**, colloq., very full); (colloq.) awkward position, fix; (Jazz colloq.) improvised playing by group (*jam session*). [imit.]

**jăm**² *n.* Conserve of fruit and sugar boiled until thick (~ **tomorrow,** pleasant thing continually promised but usu. never produced); ||(colloq.) something easy or pleasant (MONEY *for jam*); ~**'mў** *a.* (-**ily,** -**iness**), covered with jam, (colloq.) profitable. [perh. f. prec.]

**Jam.** *abbr.* Jamaica; James (N.T.).

**Jamai'ca** *n.* ~ **pepper,** = ALL-SPICE. [place]

**jămb** (-m) *n.* Side post, side, of doorway, window, or fireplace. [F *jambe* leg f. L]

**jămboree'** *n.* Celebration, merry-making; large rally of Scouts. [orig. unkn.]

**jă'mmў.** See JAM².

**Jan.** *abbr.* January.

**jāne** *n.* (sl.) Woman; **Jā'neíte** (-ni-) *n.*, admirer of Jane Austen's novels. [name]

**jă'ngle** (-nggel). **1.** *v.t. & i.* Make, cause (bell etc.) to make, harsh noise; irritate (nerves etc.) by discord etc. **2.** *n.* Harsh noise. [F]

**jă'nĭtor** *n.* Doorkeeper, caretaker of building. [L (*janua* door)]

**jă'nĭzarў** *n.* (Hist.) One of body of Turkish infantry forming Sultan's guard etc. [Turk., = new troops]

**Jă'nŭarў** *n.* First month. [AF f. L (*Janus*, guardian god of doors)]

**Jăp** *a. & n.* (colloq., often derog.) Japanese; ~ **silk,** kind of thin silk. [abbr.]

**japă'n**. **1.** *n.* Hard usu. black varnish, esp. kind brought orig. from Japan. **2.** *v.t.* (-**nn-**). Varnish with japan; make black and glossy. **3. Jăpăne'se** (-z) *a. & n.* (*pl.* same), (native, language) of Japan; **japŏ'n-ica** *n.*, ornamental red-flowered variety of quince. [place]

**jāpe** *v.i. & n.* (Practical) joke. [orig. unkn.]

**jär**¹. **1.** *v.i. & t.* (-**rr-**). (Of sound or vibration; fig. of words, manner, person, idea) strike discordantly, grate, (*on, upon,* person, ears, nerves); strike, make (thing) strike, vibratingly (*against* etc.); (of body affected) vibrate gratingly; (of fact etc.) be at variance (*with*); quarrel. **2.** *n.* Jar-ring sound, shock, or thrill. [imit.]

**jar**[2] *n.* Glass or pottery or plastic vessel, usu. cylindrical, with or without handle(s); contents of this; ||(colloq.) glass (of beer etc.). [F f. Arab.]

**jar**[3] *n.* (arch. or colloq.) **On the ~**, ajar. [obs. CHAR[1] turn]

**jardinière** (zhărdēnyār´) *n.* Ornamental pot or stand for display of growing flowers; dish of mixed vegetables. [F]

**jar´gon**[1] *n.* Barbarous or debased language; gibberish; speech full of technical terms etc. (*lawyers´, scientific, jargon*). [F]

**jar´gon**[2], **jărgōō´n**, *n.* Translucent, colourless, or smoky variety of zircon; **jārgonĕ´lle** *n.*, early-ripening variety of pear. [F, prob. ult. as ZIRCON]

**jă´smĭn(e)** (*or* -z-), **jĕ´ssamĭn(e)**, *n.* Shrub with white or yellow flowers (**white ~**, climbing fragrant kind); **red ~**, a red-flowered fragrant shrub. [F f. Arab. f. Pers.]

**jă´sper** *n.* Red, yellow, or brown opaque quartz. [F f. L f. Gk *iaspis*]

**jau´ndice. 1.** *n.* Morbid state due to obstruction of bile and marked by yellowness of skin etc.; disordered (esp. mental) vision; envy. **2.** *v.t.* Affect with jaundice; (fig.) affect (person etc.) with envy, resentment, etc. [F (*jaune* yellow)]

**jaunt. 1.** *n.* Pleasure excursion. **2.** *v.i.* Take a jaunt; **jaunting-car**, two-wheeled horse-drawn vehicle used in Ireland. [orig. unkn.]

**jau´ntÿ** *a.* (**-ily, -iness**). Airily self-satisfied; sprightly. [F (GENTLE)]

**Ja´van** (jah´-) *a.* & *n.* (Native) of *Java*; **~ĕ´se** (-z) *a.* & *n.*, (native, language) of Java. [place]

**jă´velin** (*or* -vl-) *n.* Light spear thrown as weapon or in sports. [F]

**jaw. 1.** *n.* Bone(s) containing the teeth and used in seizing and masticating food (*lower, upper, jaw*; **~-bone**, lower jaw of mammals; **~-breaker**, colloq., word hard to pronounce); (*pl.*) mouth, its bones and teeth, mouth of valley etc., gripping parts of machine etc., (fig.) grip (*of death* etc.); (colloq.) loquacity (**hold your ~**, stop talking), long or sermonizing talk. **2.** *v.t.* & *i.* (sl.) Speak esp. at length; admonish, lecture, (person). [F]

**jay** *n.* Noisy European bird with vivid plumage; silly chatterer; **~-walker**, pedestrian who crosses, or walks in, road without regard for traffic. [F f. L]

**jazz. 1.** *n.* Music of U.S. Negro origin usu. characterized by improvisation, syncopation, and regular or forceful rhythm; (sl.) pretentious talk or behaviour (*all that jazz*); **~´ÿ** *a.* (**~ily, ~iness**), of or like jazz, unrestrained, vivid. **2.** *v.t.* & *i.* Brighten or liven *up*; play or dance to jazz. [orig. uncert.]

||**J.C.R.** *abbr.* Junior Combination Room; Junior Common Room.

**jea´lous** (jĕ´l-) *a.* Watchfully tenacious (*of* rights etc.); afraid, suspicious, resentful, of rivalry in love or affection; envious (*of* person, his advantages); (Bibl., of God) intolerant of disloyalty; (of inquiry etc.) vigilant; **~ÿ** *n.*, being jealous. [F f. L (ZEALOUS)]

**jean** (*or* jān) *n.* Twilled cotton cloth; (*pl., pr.* jēnz) trousers of jean or denim. [F (L *Janua* Genoa)]

**Jeep** *n.* Small sturdy motor vehicle with four-wheel drive. [P; orig. U.S., f. initials of *general purposes*]

**jeer. 1.** *v.i.* & *t.* Scoff (*at*); deride. **2.** *n.* Scoff, taunt. [orig. unkn.]

**Jĕhō´vah** (-a), **Yah´veh** (-ā), **Yah´weh** (-ā), *ns.* Name of God in O.T.; **Jehovah´s Witness**, member of a fundamentalist millenary sect. [Heb. *yahveh*]

**jĕju´ne** (-ōō´n) *a.* Meagre, poor, barren; unsatisfying to the mind. [orig. = fasting (L *jejunus*)]

**jĕju´num** (-jōō´-) *n.* Part of small intestine between duodenum and ileum. [L (prec.)]

**Jĕ´kyll** *n.* **~ and Hyde**, person in whom two (opposing) personalities alternate. [characters in story by R. L. Stevenson]

**jĕll** *v.i.* (colloq.) Set as jelly; (fig.) take definite form. [back-form. f. JELLY]

**jĕ´llaba** *n.* Loose hooded woollen cloak worn by Arab men. [Arab.]

**jĕ´llÿ. 1.** *n.* Soft stiffish semitransparent food made of or with gelatin; similar preparation of fruit-juice, sugar, etc.; substance of similar consistency (**~ baby**, gelatinous sweet in shape of baby); **~fish**, marine animal with stinging tentacles and gelatinous body); (sl.) gelignite. **2.** *v.t.* & *i.* (Cause to) set as jelly, congeal; set (food) in jelly (*jellied eels*). [F *gelée* f. L (*gelo* freeze)]

‖**jě′mmy** n. Burglar's crowbar, usu. in sections. [name *James*]

**je ne sais quoi** (zhεnεsăkwah′) n. Indefinable something. [F, = I do not know what]

**jě′nny** n. = SPINning-jenny; she-ass; ~ **wren**, (pop.) wren. [name *Janet*]

**jeo′pard**y̆ (jě′p-) n. Danger esp. of severe harm; ~**ize** v.t., endanger. [obs. F *iu parti* divided play (JOKE, PART)]

**Jer.** abbr. Jeremiah (O.T.).

**jěr′bil.** See GERBIL.

**jěrbō′a** n. Small Afr. jumping rodent with long hind legs. [L f. Arab.]

**Jěrěmi′ah** (-a) n. Dismal prophet, denouncer of the times; **jěrěmi′ad** n., doleful complaint. [*Lamentations of Jeremiah*, in O.T.]

**Jě′richō** (-kō) n. **Go to ~**, (colloq.) go away. [place]

**jěrk**[1]. **1.** n. Sharp sudden pull, twist, twitch, start, etc.; spasmodic twitch of muscle; (sl.) fool, stupid person. **2.** v.t. & i. Move with a jerk; throw with suddenly arrested motion. **3.** ~′y̆ a. (-ily, -iness) often fig. of abrupt style etc.). [imit.]

**jěrk**[2] v.t. Cure (beef) by cutting in long slices and drying in the sun. [Sp. f. Quechua]

**jěr′kin** n. Sleeveless jacket; (Hist.) man's close-fitting jacket, often of leather. [orig. unkn.]

**jěrobō′am** n. Wine-bottle of 8–12 times ordinary size. [1 Kgs. 11: 28, 14: 16]

**jě′rry**[1] n. ~**-builder, -building**, builder, building, of unsubstantial houses with bad materials; ~**-built**, so built. [orig. uncert.]

**Jě′rry**[2] n. (sl.) German (soldier), the Germans; **j~can, je′rrican,** kind of (orig. German) petrol- or water-can. [prob. alt. *German*]

‖**jě′rry**[3] n. (sl.) Chamber-pot. [orig. unkn.]

**jěr′sey** (-zĭ) n. Knitted usu. woollen pullover or similar garment; plain-knitted (orig. woollen) fabric; (*J~*, a. & n.) (animal) of breed of dairy cattle from Jersey. [place]

**jě′ssamin(e).** See JASMINE.

**jěst. 1.** n. Joke (~**-book**, book of jests); fun (**spoken in** ~, not meant seriously); raillery, banter; object of derision. **2.** v.i. Joke, make jests. **3.**

~′**er** n., (esp. Hist.) professional joker of a court etc. [F f. L *gesta* exploits]

**Jě′suit** (-z-) n. Member of Society of Jesus (R.C. order initiated by Ignatius Loyola 1534); (derog., arch.) dissembling person; **Jěsuī′tical** (-z-) a. (-lly), (derog., arch.) crafty; ~**ry** n., principles, practice, of Jesuits. [F or L (foll.)]

**Jē′sus** (-z-) n. **Society of ~** (see prec.); ~ (**Christ**)!, (vulg.) excl. of surprise etc.; **Jě′sū** (-z-) n., (arch. voc.) Jesus. [person]

**jět**[1] n. & a. Hard black lignite taking brilliant polish; ~(**-black**), deep glossy black. [F f. L f. Gk]

**jět**[2]. **1.** n. Stream of water, steam, gas, flame, etc. shot esp. from small opening; spout, nozzle, for emitting water etc. thus; (colloq.) jet engine or plane. **2.** v.t. & i. (-tt-). Spurt out in jets; (colloq.) send or travel by jet plane. **3.** ~ **engine** (using jet propulsion for forward thrust, esp. of aircraft); ~ **lag**, delayed bodily effects felt after long flight, esp. owing to difference of local time; ~ **plane** (with jet engine); ~**-propelled**, having jet propulsion, (fig.) very fast; ~ **propulsion** (by backward ejection of high-speed jet of gas etc.); ~ **set**, wealthy élite frequently travelling by jet. [F *jet(er)* f. L *jacto* throw]

**jě′tsam** n. Goods thrown out of ship to lighten it and washed ashore; ~ (**Christ**)!, (vulg.) jet engine **jě′ttison**, (n.) such throwing out, (v.t.) throw out thus, drop from aircraft, (fig.) abandon. [*jetsam* contr. of *jettison* f. AF *getteson* (JET[2])]

**jě′tty** n. Pier, breakwater, constructed to defend harbour etc.; landing-pier. [F *jetee* (JET[2])]

**jeu** (zhêr) n. (*pl.* ~**x** *pr.* same). ~ **de mots** (demō′), play on words, pun; ~ **d'esprit** (děsprē′), witty or humorous (usu. literary) trifle. [F, = play, game, f. L *jocus* jest]

**Jew** (jōō). **1.** n. Person of Hebrew descent, person whose religion is Judaism, (WANDERing *Jew*); ~**-baiting**, persecution of Jews; ~**'s harp**, small musical instrument held between the teeth; (derog., colloq.) person who drives a hard bargain in trading, usurer. **2.** v.t. & i. (*j~*; derog., colloq.) Drive a hard bargain, cheat, haggle. **3.** ~′**ess** n.; ~′**ish** a., of or like Jews; ~**ry** (joor′ĭ) n., Jews collectively, (Hist.) Jews' quarter in town etc. [F f. L *judaeus* f. Gk *ioudaios* f. Aram.]

**jew'el** (jōō'-). **1.** *n.* Precious stone; personal ornament containing jewel(s); precious person or thing. **2.** *v.t.* (||-ll-). Adorn with jewels, fit (watch) with jewels for the pivot-holes. **3.** ~**ler**, *~er, *n.*, dealer in jewels or jewellery; ~(le)rў *n.* [F]

**Jew'ess, -ish, -ry.** See JEW.

**Je'zebel** *n.* Shameless woman. [~, wife of Ahab (1 Kgs. 16, 19, 21)]

**jib.** **1.** *n.* Triangular staysail from outer end of jib-boom to top of foremast or from bowsprit to mast-head (**cut of one's** ~, one's personal appearance); ~**-boom**, spar run out from end of bowsprit); projecting arm of crane. **2.** *v.t.* & *i.* (-bb-). Pull (sail) round to other side of ship, (of sail) gybe; (of horse, fig. of person) stop and refuse to go on, move backwards or sideways instead of going on, (~ **at**, object strongly to). [orig. unkn.]

**ji'be.** See GIBE, GYBE.

**jiff('ў)** *n.* (colloq.) Short time, moment, (*in a jiffy*). [orig. unkn.]

**jig.** **1.** *n.* Lively jumping dance, music for this; appliance that holds a piece of work and guides the tools operating on it; ~'**saw**, machine fretsaw; ~**saw** (**puzzle**), (puzzle of reassembling) picture pasted on board etc. and cut into irregular pieces. **2.** *v.i.* & *t.* (-gg-). Dance jig; work on or equip with jig; move quickly up and down.

**ji'gger**¹ (-g-) *n.* = CHIGGER. [corrupt.]

**ji'gger**² (-g-) *n.* (Small glass holding) measure of spirits etc.; (sl.) contrivance, gadget; (Bill. sl.) cue-rest. [partly f. JIG]

**ji'ggered** (-gerd) *a.* (colloq., as mild oath). Confounded (*I'll be jiggered*). [euphem.]

||**jiggerў-pō'kerў** (-g-) *n.* (colloq.) Deceitful or dishonest dealing, trickery. [orig. uncert.]

**ji'ggle** *v.t.* Rock or jerk lightly. [JIG]

**jilt** *v.t.* (Esp. of woman) capriciously discard encouraged lover. [orig. unkn.]

*****Jim Crow'** (-ō') *n.* (derog.) A Black; racial segregation esp. of Blacks. [nickname]

**ji'm-jams** (-z) *n.pl.* (sl.) Delirium tremens; fit of depression or nervousness. [fanciful redupl.]

**ji'ngle** (-nggel). **1.** *n.* Mixed noise as of shaken keys or links; repetition of same sounds in words, short verse of this kind used in advertising etc. **2.** *v.i.* & *t.* Make, cause (keys etc.) to make, a jingle; (of writing) be full of alliterations, rhymes, etc. [imit.]

**ji'ngō** (-nggō) *n.* (*pl.* ~**es**). Blustering patriot, supporter of bellicose policy (orig. f. use of **by** ~!, form of asseveration, in popular song); ~**ism**, ~**ist**, *ns.*; ~**i'stic** *a.* [conjuror's wd]

**jink.** **1.** *v.i.* & *t.* Move elusively, dodge, elude by dodging. **2.** *n.* Act of jinking; **high** ~**s**, boisterous fun. [orig. Sc.; imit.]

**ji'nnee'** (*pl.* **jinn**), **ji'nn,** *ns.* (Muslim Myth.) Spirit of supernatural power able to appear in human and animal forms. [Arab.]

**jinx** *n.* (colloq.) Person or thing that brings bad luck. [perh. var. *jynx* wryneck, charm]

**ji'tter.** (colloq.) **1.** *v.i.* Be nervous, act nervously; ~**bug**, (*n.*) nervous person, popular dance like jive, person fond of this or of jazz, (*v.t.*) dance jitterbug. **2.** *n.* (in *pl.*) Extreme nervousness; **have the** ~**s**, be frightened or nervous; ~**ў** *a.* (~**iness**), nervy, jumpy.

**jive.** (sl.) **1.** *n.* (Dance to) fast lively jazz music. **2.** *v.i.* Play or dance to jive.

**Jnr.** *abbr.* Junior.

**job**¹. **1.** *n.* Piece of work (to be) done; paid employment; (colloq.) difficult task; unscrupulous transaction; (sl.) a crime, esp. a robbery. **2.** *v.i.* & *t.* (-bb-). Do jobs; ||hire, let out for time or job; buy and sell (stock, goods) as middleman; deal corruptly with (matter). **3. bad, good,** ~, unsatisfactory, satisfactory, state of affairs etc.; ~ **lot**, lot of goods bought as speculation, miscellaneous group of articles; *jobs for the* BOYS; **just the** ~, (sl.) precisely what is wanted; **make a** (**good**) ~ **of**, do thoroughly or successfully. **4.** ~**ber** *n.* (esp. = STOCKjobber); ~**berў** *n.*, corrupt dealing; ~**less** *a.*, unemployed.

**Job**². The patriarch Job esp. as type of patience or destitution; ~**'s comforter,** one whose intended consolations increase distress. [person in O.T.]

**Jock** *n.* (sl.) Scottish soldier. [Sc. form of JACK]

**jo'ckey.** **1.** *n.* Rider, esp. professional, in horse-races (~ **cap,**

with long peak; ‖J~ **Club**, for regulation of racing). 2. *v.t.* & *i.* Cheat (person *into, out of, doing*); ~ **for position**, try to gain advantageous position esp. by skilful manœuvring or unfair action. [dim. of *prec.*]

**jŏ´ck-străp** *n.* Support or protection for male genitals, worn esp. by sportsmen. [vulg. *jock* genitals]

**jŏcō´se, jŏ´cūlar**, *adjs.* Given to joking, waggish, humorous; **jŏcō´s-ĭtỹ, jŏcŭlă´rĭtỹ**, *ns.* [L (*jocus* jest)]

**jŏ´cund** *a.* Merry, sprightly; **jŏcŭ´ndĭtỹ** *n.* [F f. L *jucundus* pleasant]

**jŏ´dhpurs** (-dperz) *n.pl.* Long breeches for riding etc., tight from knee to ankle. [place]

**jŏg. 1.** *v.t.* & *i.* (-gg-). Push, jerk; nudge (person); stimulate (person's memory); walk, run, ride, with jolting pace; proceed, trudge, go one's way, (*on, along*); *run slowly for exercise. 2. *n.* Push, jerk, nudge; slow walk or trot (~**trot**, slow regular trot). 3. ~**´gle**, (*v.t.* & *i.*) move to and fro in jerks, (*n.*) slight jog. [imit.]

**Jŏhă´nnine** *a.* Of the apostle John. [L (JOHN)]

**Jŏhn** (jŏn) *n.* ~ **Bull**, English nation, typical Englishman; ~ **Chinaman**, (derog.) typical Chinese; ~ **Doe**, fictitious character in law, *average man; *John* DORY[1]; ‖**jŏ´hnnỹ** (jŏ´nĭ) *n.*, (colloq.) fellow, man; ~**ny-come-lately**, newcomer; ~**ny Raw**, novice. [man's name; L *Jo(h)annes* f. Gk f. Heb.]

**joie de vivre** (zhwahdēvē´vr) *n.* Feeling of exuberant enjoyment of life; high spirits. [F, = joy of living]

**join. 1.** *v.t.* & *i.* Put together, fasten, unite, (things, one *to* another, *together*); ~ **battle**, begin fighting; ~ **hands**, clasp one's hands together, clasp each other's hands, fig. combine; connect (points etc.) by line etc.; unite (persons, one *with* or *to* another), be united in marriage, alliance, etc. (*join* FORCE[1]*s*); take part with others (*in* action etc.; ~ **in**, take part); take one's place with or in (company, procession, etc.; ~ **up**, enlist in army etc.); (of river, road, etc.) become continuous or connected with (another). 2. *n.* Point, line, or surface of junction. 3. ~**´er** *n.*, (esp.) maker of furniture and

light woodwork; ~**´erỹ** *n.*, such work. [F f. L *jungo junct-*]

**joint** *a., n.,* & *v.* **1.** *a.* Held or done by, belonging to, two or more persons etc. in common (*joint account, action*; **during their** ~ **lives**, till one of them dies; ~ **stock**, capital held jointly, so *joint-stock company*); sharing (*with* others in possession etc.; *joint author, ownership*). 2. *n.* Place at which two things join; structure by which two bones fit together (**out of** ~, dislocated, fig. out of order); point at which, contrivance by which, two parts of artificial structure are joined; section of animal's carcass used for food; (sl.) place of meeting or resort (CLIP[2]--*joint*), marijuana cigarette. 3. *v.t.* Connect by joint(s); divide (carcass) into joints or at a joint. [F (*prec.*)]

**joi´nt|ure. 1.** *n.* Estate settled on wife for period during which she survives husband. 2. *v.t.* Provide with jointure. 3. ~**rèss** *n.*, widow holding jointure. [F f. L (JOIN)]

**joist** *n.* One of parallel timbers stretched from wall to wall to carry ceiling laths or floor boards. [F *giste* f. L (*jaceo* lie)]

**jŏke. 1.** *n.* Thing said or done to excite laughter, jest, (**practical** ~, trick played on person); ridiculous circumstance, person, etc., (**no** ~, serious matter; **standing** ~, object of permanent ridicule). 2. *v.i.* & *t.* Make jokes; banter. 3. **jŏ´ker** *n.*, one who jokes, (highest) trump card in some games, (sl.) person; **jŏ´key, jŏ´kỹ**, *a.* (-ily, -iness). [L *jocus* jest]

**jŏ´llỹ[1]. 1.** *a.* (-ily, -iness). Joyful, festive, jovial, (~ **Roger**, pirates' flag, black usu. with skull and cross--bones); slightly drunk; (colloq., of person or thing) pleasant, delightful, (also iron., *a jolly shame*). 2. *adv.* (colloq.) Very (*jolly miserable*; *for he's a jolly good fellow*). 3. *n.* ‖(sl.) Royal Marine. 4. *v.t.* (colloq.) Flatter, cajole, (usu. *jolly along*); chaff, banter. 5. **jŏ´llĭfy** *v.i.* & *t.*, make merry, esp. in drinking; **jŏllĭfĭcā´tion** *n.*; **jŏ´llĭtỹ** *n.*, merry--making. [F *jolif* gay, pretty]

**jŏ´llỹ[2]** *n.* ~(-**boat**), clinker-built ship's-boat, smaller than cutter. [orig. unkn.]

**jŏlt. 1.** *v.t.* & *i.* Jerk (person etc.) from seat etc. esp. in locomotion; (of vehicle) move along with jerks; give mental shock to. **2.** *n.* Such jerk or shock; ~**'y** *a.* (~**ily,** ~**iness**).

**Jon.** *abbr.* Jonah (O.T.).

**Jō'nah** (-a) *n.* Person who brings, or is believed to bring, bad luck. [person in O.T.]

**Jō'nathan** *n.* (**Brother**) ~, personified people of, typical citizen of, U.S.; red-skinned Amer. dessert apple. [personal name]

**Jōnes** (-nz) *n.* DAVY JONES; KEEP up with the *Joneses*. [surname]

**jŏ'nquil** *n.* Species of narcissus with white or yellow fragrant flowers. [F or L (*juncus* rush plant)]

**Jŏr'dan** *n.* = almond, fine almond esp. from Malaga. [prob. F or Sp. *jardin* GARDEN, assim. to name of river]

\*jŏsh. (sl.) **1.** *n.* Good-natured joke. **2.** *v.t.* & *i.* Hoax, banter; indulge in ridicule. [orig. unkn.]

**Josh.** *abbr.* Joshua (O.T.).

**jŏss** *n.* Chinese idol (~**-house,** temple; ~**-stick,** of fragrant tinder and clay for incense); ‖~**'er** *n.*, (sl.) fool, fellow, (Austral.) clergyman. [perh. ult. Port. *deos* f. L *deus* god]

**jŏ'stle** (-sel). **1.** *v.i.* & *t.* Push, shove, knock, (*against*); struggle (*with* person *for* thing). **2.** *n.* Jostling, encounter. [JOUST]

**jŏt. 1.** *n.* Small amount, whit, (*not a jot*). **2.** *v.t.* (-**tt**-). Write (usu. *down*) briefly. **3.** ~**ter** *n.*, (esp.) small notebook etc. for memoranda; ~**'tings** (-z) *n.pl.*, jotted notes. [L f. Gk IOTA]

**joule** (jōōl) *n.* Unit of work or energy. [person]

**jounce** *v.t.* & *i.* Bump, bounce, jolt. [orig. unkn.]

**jour'nal** (jĕr'-) *n.* Daily record of events or of business transactions and accounts; log-book; daily or other newspaper, periodical; part of shaft or axle that rests on bearings; ~**ĕ'se** (-z) *n.*, style of language characteristic of (inferior) newspaper writing; ~**ism** *n.*, work of journalist; ~**ist** *n.*, editor of or writer for, public journal esp. newspaper; ~**i'stic** *a.* [F f. L (DIURNAL)]

**jour'ney** (jĕr'-). **1.** *n.* Distance travelled in specified time (*a day's, 4 days', journey*); expedition, round of travel (usu. by land; cf. VOYAGE); travelling of vehicle along route at stated time; ~**man**, qualified mechanic or artisan working for another, (fig.) mere hireling. **2.** *v.i.* Make a

journey. [F *jornee* day, day's work or travel f. L (*diurnus* daily f. *dies* day)]

**joust** (or jōō-). **1.** *n.* Combat with lances between two mounted knights etc. **2.** *v.i.* Engage in joust. [F f. L (*juxta* near)]

**Jōve** *n.* Jupiter (by ~!, excl. of surprise); **jō'vial** *a.* (-**lly**), merry, convivial, hearty; **jōviă'lity** *n.*; **Jō'vian** *a.*, of or like Jupiter, of the planet Jupiter. [L *Jupiter Jov-*]

**jowl** *n.* Jaw(bone); cheek (CHEEK by *jowl*); external throat or neck when prominent. [E]

**joy** *n.* Gladness, pleasure, (~**-ride,** colloq., pleasure-ride, usu. unauthorized, in motor car etc.; ~**stick,** sl., control-lever of aeroplane; **no** ~, colloq., no satisfaction or success; cause of this (cf. PRIDE); ~**'ful** *a.* (-**lly**); ~**'ous** *a.* [F f. L *gaudia* (*gaudeo* rejoice)]

**J.P.** *abbr.* Justice of the Peace.

**Jr.** *abbr.* Junior.

**jt.** *abbr.* joint.

**ju'bĭllāte** (jōō'-) *v.i.* Exult, manifest joy; ~**ance,** ~**ā'tion,** *ns.*; ~**ant** *a.*, exultant. [L *jubilo* to shout]

**ju'bilee** (jōō'-) *n.* (Jewish HIST.) year of emancipation etc. kept every 50 years; (R.C. Ch.) year, time, of remission from penal consequences of sin; anniversary (esp. 50th, **golden** ~; DIAMOND, SILVER, *jubilee*); (time of) rejoicing. [F f. L f. Gk f. Heb.]

**Jud.** *abbr.* Judith (Apocr.).

**Judā'ic** (jōō-) *a.* Of or characteristic of Jews; **Ju'dăism** (jōō'-) *n.*, monotheistic religion of the Jews, Jews collectively; **Ju'dăize** (jōō'-) *v.t.* & *i.*, make Jewish, follow Jewish customs. [L f. Gk (JEW)]

**Ju'das** (jōō'-) *n.* Infamous traitor; (*j*~) peep-hole in door; ~ **kiss,** act of betrayal (Matt. 26: 48). [person]

**jŭ'dder. 1.** *v.i.* Shake noisily, wobble. **2.** *n.* Shaking, wobbling. [imit.; cf. *shudder*]

**Judg.** *abbr.* Judges (O.T.).

**jŭdge. 1.** *n.* Officer appointed to try causes in court of justice (**grave, sober, as a** ~, entirely so); (of God) supreme arbiter (*as God is my judge*); person appointed to decide dispute or contest; person who decides a question; person fit to decide on merits of thing or question (*am no judge of that; good judge of claret*). **2.** *v.t.* & *i.* Pronounce sentence on (person) in court of justice; try (cause); decide (contest, question); form opinion about, estimate; conclude, consider, (thing *to be*, *that*, etc.; *from* or *by* evidence); act as judge. [F f. L *judex judic-*]

**ju'dgement, -dgm-,** (-jm-) *n.* Sentence of court of justice etc. (Last J~, by God at end of world); misfortune as sign of divine displeasure (often joc.: *it is a judgement on you for being late*); opinion (**against** one's **better** ~, contrary to what one really feels to be advisable); critical faculty, discernment; good sense; J~ **Day**, of Last Judgement; ~-**seat**, judge's seat, tribunal. [F (prec.)]

**ju'dicature** (jōō'-) *n.* Administration of justice (**Supreme Court of** J~, in England, consisting of Court of Appeal and High Court of Justice); judge's (term of) office; body of judges. [L (*judico* to judge)]

**judi'ci|al** (jōōdi'shal) *a.* (-**lly**). Of, by, a court of law (~**al murder**, legal but unjust death sentence; *judicial* SEPARATION); having the function of judgement (*judicial assembly*); of, proper to, a judge; critical (*judicial opinion*); impartial; ~**ary** *n.*, the judges of a State collectively; ~**ous** *a.*, sensible, prudent. [L (*judicium* judgement)]

**ju'do** (jōō'-) *n.* Modern development of JU-JITSU; ~**ka** (*pl.* same), ~**ist**, *ns.*, student of or expert in judo. [Jap., = gentle way]

**Ju'dy** (jōō'-) *n.* See PUNCH[3]; (colloq.) woman. [pet-form of *Judith*]

**jug. 1.** *n.* Deep vessel for liquids with handle and often with spout; (sl.) prison. **2.** *v.t.* (-**gg**-). Stew (hare) in jug etc. [orig. uncert.]

**Ju'ggernaut** (-g-) *n.* Idol of Krishna dragged yearly in procession on car under whose wheels devotees are said to have formerly thrown themselves; superstition etc. to which people sacrifice themselves or others; (j~) overpowering force or object, large heavy motor vehicle. [Hindi *Jagannath*, = lord of the world]

**ju'ggins** (-ginz) *n.* (sl.) Simpleton. [perh. f. surname]

**ju'ggle. 1.** *v.i.* & *t.* Perform feats of dexterity (*with* objects tossed up and caught); perform conjuring tricks; cheat (person etc. *out of* thing); get (thing *away*, *into*, etc.) by trickery; ~ **with**, deceive (person), misrepresent

(facts), rearrange adroitly. **2.** *n.* Trick, fraud. **3.** ~**r** *n.*, (esp.) entertainer performing such feats of dexterity; ~**rý** *n.* [L *joculor* to jest (JOKE)]

**Jugoslav.** See YUGOSLAV.

**ju'gular. 1.** *a.* Of neck or throat (~ **veins**, great veins of neck, conveying blood from head). **2.** *n.* Jugular vein. [L (*jugulum* collar-bone)]

**juice** (jōōs) *n.* Liquid part of vegetable or fruit; fluid part of animal body or substance; (sl.) petrol, electricity; **jui'cý** (jōō'-) *a.* (-**ily**, -**iness**), full of juice, (colloq.) interesting, (esp.) scandalous. [F f. L]

**ju-ji'tsu** (jōōji'tsōō) *n.* Japanese system of unarmed combat using opponent's strength and weight to his disadvantage. [Jap. *jūjutsu* gentle science]

**ju-ju** (jōō'jōō) *n.* (W. Afr.) Charm, fetish; magic attributed to this. [perh. F *joujou* toy]

**ju'jube** (jōō'jōōb) *n.* Sweet fruit-flavoured lozenge of gelatin etc. [F, or L ult. f. Gk *zizuphon*]

**juke-box** (jōō'k-) *n.* Machine that automatically plays selected gramophone record when coin is inserted. [U.S. Black wd *juke* disorderly]

**Jul.** *abbr.* July.

**ju'lep** (jōō'-) *n.* Sweet drink esp. as vehicle for medicine; medicated drink; *iced and flavoured spirit and water, esp. *mint julep*. [F f. Pers. *gulāb* rose-water]

**Ju'lian** (jōō'-) *a.* Of Julius Caesar (~ **calendar**, introduced by him, with year of 365 days and 366 every fourth year). [L (*Julius*)]

**julie'nne** (zhōō-, jōō-) *a.* & *n.* (Foodstuff esp. vegetables) cut into thin strips; clear soup to which are added such vegetables already cooked. [F (name *Jules* or *Julien*)]

**Ju'liet** (jōō'-) *n.* ~ **cap**, small network ornamental cap worn by brides etc. [Shakespeare's *Romeo & ~*]

**July'** (jōō-) *n.* Seventh month. [L (*Julius* Caesar)]

**ju'mble. 1.** *v.i.* & *t.* Move about in disorder, mix *up*. **2.** *n.* Confused heap etc., muddle; ||articles for jumble sale; ||~ **sale** (of miscellaneous usu. second-hand articles to raise funds for charity etc.). [imit.]

**ju'mbō. 1.** *n.* (*pl.* ~**s**). Big person, animal (esp. elephant), or thing; (**jet**), large jet plane able to carry several hundred passengers. **2.** *a.* Very large of its kind. [MUMBO- -JUMBO]

**jump. 1.** *v.i.* & *t.* Move up off ground etc. by sudden muscular tension, move suddenly with bound or start (*up*, *from*, *out*, etc.), (fig., of prices etc.) rise suddenly, cause to do this; clear (gate, brook, etc.) by jumping; cause (thing, animal esp. horse) to jump; come *to*, arrive *at*, (conclusion) hastily; (of train etc.) leave (rails); abscond from (*jump bail*, *ship*); pounce upon, attack, (person etc.); pass over to point beyond; take summary possession of (claim allegedly forfeit etc.); skip over (passage in book etc.); ~ **at**, (fig.) accept (offer etc.) eagerly; ~ **down** person's throat, reprimand or contradict him severely; ~ **for joy**, be overjoyed; ~ **in**, get quickly into vehicle etc.; ~-**off**, deciding round in show-jumping; ~**ing-o'ff** *a.*, starting (*place*, *point*; lit. or fig.); ~ **on**, attack crushingly (lit. or fig.); *jump out of* one's SKIN; *jump the* GUN; ‖~ **the queue**, take unfair precedence (lit. or fig.); ~ **to it**, act promptly and energetically; ~**ed up** (-pt-) *a.*, upstart. **2.** *n.* Act of jumping (be one ~ **ahead**, have progressed one stage farther than rival; \**broad* or ‖LONG¹ *jump*; HIGH *jump*); sudden movement caused by shock, excitement, etc. (**the** ~**s**, sl., nervousness etc., delirium tremens); abrupt rise in price etc.; sudden transition; obstacle to be jumped esp. by horse; SKI-*jump*; ~-**jet**, V.T.O.L. jet plane; ~ **suit**, one-piece garment for whole body. **3.** ~'**er¹** *n.*, (esp.) jumping insect e.g. flea; ~'**ў** *a.* (-ily, -iness), making sudden movements esp. from nervous excitement. [imit.]

**jŭ'mper²** *n.* Loose outer jacket of canvas etc. worn by sailors etc.; ‖woman's knitted pullover; \*pinafore dress. [prob. dial. *jump* short coat]

**Jun.** *abbr.* June; Junior.

**jŭ'nct|ion** *n.* Joining; joint, joining-point (~**ion box**, containing junction of electric cables etc.); place where railway lines or roads meet; ~**ure** *n.*, joining(-point); state of affairs, crisis, (*at this juncture*). [L (JOIN)]

**June** (jōōn) *n.* Sixth month, associated with roses and midsummer. [F f. L *Junius* month of JUNO]

**jŭ'ngle** (-nggel) *n.* (Area of) land overgrown with tangled vegetation, esp. in tropics (**law of the** ~, state of ruthless competition); tangled mass; (fig.) place of bewildering complexity or confusion or ruthless struggle. [Hindi f. Skr.]

**ju'nior** (jōō'-). **1.** *a.* The younger (esp. appended to name for distinction between two persons of same name, as son from father); inferior in age, standing, or position *to*, of low or lowest position, (opp. SENIOR; *junior partner*; ‖~ **combination** or **common room**, for use by junior members of college); (of school) for the younger pupils. **2.** *n.* Junior person (*office junior*; *my junior by 3 years*; cf. SENIOR); \*(colloq.) son of family. [L, compar. of *juvenis* young]

**ju'niper** (jōō'-) *n.* A coniferous evergreen shrub, esp. one with purple berry-like cones yielding **oil of** ~ (used for gin and medicine). [L *juniperus*]

**jŭnk¹. 1.** *n.* Old cables or ropes cut up for oakum etc.; discarded articles (*junk-shop*), rubbish; ‖lump, chunk; (Naut.) hard salt meat; (sl.) narcotic drug esp. heroin; ~'**ie** *n.*, (sl.) drug addict. **2.** *v.t.* \*Discard as junk. [orig. unkn.]

**jŭnk²** *n.* Flat-bottomed sailing vessel in China seas. [F f. Jav.]

**jŭ'nkèt. 1.** *n.* Dish of milk curdled by rennet and sweetened and flavoured; feast; pleasure outing; \*official's tour at public expense. **2.** *v.i.* Feast, picnic, go on a spree. [F *jonquette* rush-basket (used for junket) f. L *juncus* rush]

**Ju'nō** (jōō'-) (*pl.* ~**s**). Queenly woman; ~**ĕ'sque** (-sk) *a.*, of woman, (esp.) large and regal. [L name of Jupiter's wife]

**jŭ'nta, jŭ'ntō** (*pl.* ~**s**), *ns.* Political clique or faction after revolution etc. [Sp. (JOIN)]

**Ju'piter** (jōō'-) *n.* (Rom. Myth.) king of gods (*by Jupiter!*; cf. JOVE); largest of the planets. [L]

**jur'al** (joor'-) *a.* Of law, of (moral) rights and obligations. [L *jus jur-law*, right]

**Jurăssic** (joor-) *a.* & *n.* (Of) middle Mesozoic period or system, with prevalence of oolitic limestone. [F (*Jura* mountains)]

**juri'dical** (joor-) *a.* (~**ly**). Of

judicial proceedings; relating to law. [L (*jus jur-* law, *dico* say)]

**jurĭsdĭ′ction** (joor-) *n.* Administration of justice (*over, of*); (extent of) authority, territory it extends over; **~al** *a.* [F & L (prec., DICTION)]

**jurĭsprū′d|ence** (joorĭsprŏŏ′-) *n.* Science of, skill in, law; **~ĕ′ntial** (-ŏŏdĕ′nshal) *a.*, of jurisprudence. [L (prec., PRUDENT)]

**jur′|ĭst** (joor′-) *n.* One versed in law; **~ĭ′stĭc(al)** *adjs.* (-lly) [F or L (*jus jur-* law)]

**jur′y̆** (joor′ĭ) *n.* Body of persons sworn to render verdict in court of justice or coroner's court (**common, petty, trial, ~,** of 12 persons who try final issue of fact in civil or criminal cases and pronounce verdict; *\*GRAND[1] jury;* **~-box,** enclosure for jury in court; **~man, ~woman,** member of jury; **special ~,** of persons of particular standing in society); body of persons selected to award prizes in competition; **jur′or** (joor′-) *n.*, member of jury, one who takes oath (cf. NONjuror). [F *juree* f. L (*juro* swear)]

**jur′y̆-mast** (joor′ĭmahst) *n.* Temporary mast replacing one broken or lost; **jur′y̆-rigged** (joor′ĭrĭgd) *a.*, makeshift. [orig. unkn.]

**jŭst. 1.** *a.* Equitable, fair, (*just man, sentence,* etc.); deserved, due, (*a just reward*); well-grounded (*just fear, resentment*); right in amount etc., proper, (*just proportions*). **2.** *adv.* Exactly (*just three o'clock; just what I wanted; just how did you do it?;* **~ about,** colloq., almost (exactly), almost completely; **just so,** exactly arranged, exactly as you say; barely (*I just managed it*); exactly or nearly at this or that moment (**~ now,** at this moment, a little time ago); (colloq.) simply, merely, (*we are just good friends;* **~ in case,** as a precaution, positively (*just splendid*), quite (*not just yet*); (sl.) really, indeed, (*won't I just give him a dressing-down!*). [F f. L *justus* (*jus* right)]

**jŭ′stĭce** *n.* Justness, fairness, (**do ~ to,** treat fairly, appreciate duly; **do oneself ~,** perform in manner worthy of one's abilities); exercise of authority in maintenance of right (poetic(al) **~,** due allocation of reward of virtue and punishment of vice); judicial proceedings (*Court of Justice; was brought to justice*); judge, ‖esp. of Supreme Court of Judicature, ‖**Mr. J~ ——,** title of High Court Judge); magistrate (**J~ of the Peace,** unpaid lay magistrate appointed to hear minor cases in county, town, etc.). [F f. L *justitia* (*justus,* prec.)]

**jŭstĭ′ciary̆** (-shyerĭ) *n.* Administrator of justice; **Court of J~,** supreme criminal court in Scotland.

**jŭ′stĭf|y̆** *v.t.* Show justice or truth of (person, act, statement, claim); (of circumstances) be adequate ground for, warrant, (act, person *in doing*); (Print.) adjust (line of type) to fill a space evenly; **~ĭcā′tion** *n.;* **~ĭcātĭve, ~ĭcātŏry̆,** *adjs.* [F f. L (*JUST,* -FY)]

**jŭt. 1.** *v.i.* (-tt-). Project (*jut out*). **2.** *n.* Projection. [var. JET[2]]

**jute**[1] (jŏŏt) *n.* Fibre from bark of E. Ind. plants, used for sacking, mats, etc. [Bengali]

**Jute**[2] (jŏŏt) *n.* Member of Low German tribe invading Britain in 5th-6th c. [E]

**ju′venīle** (jŏŏ′-). **1.** *a.* Youthful; of, for, young persons; **~ court,** for trial of young offenders; **~ delinquency,** offences committed by persons below age of legal responsibility; **~ delinquent,** such offender. **2.** *n.* Young person; actor playing such part. **3. juvenī′lĭa** (jŏŏ-) *n.pl.,* works produced by author or artist in youth; **juvenī′lĭty̆** (jŏŏ-) *n.,* youthfulness, youthful manner etc. [L (*juvenis* young)]

**jŭxta|pō′se** (-z) *v.t.* Put side by side; **~posĭ′tion** (-z-) *n.* [F f. L (*juxta* next, *pono* put)]

# K

**K, k,** (kā) *n.* (*pl.* **Ks, K's**). Eleventh letter.

**K.** *abbr.* kelvin(s); King('s); Köchel (list of Mozart's works).

**k** *abbr.* kilo-.

**K** *symb.* potassium. [L *kalium*]

**Kaffir** *n.* Member or language of S. Afr. people of Bantu family; (derog.) Bantu inhabitant of S. Afr. [Arab., = infidel]

**Kafkaë'sque** (-sk) *a.* Nightmarish. [*Kafka*, person]

**kä'ftän.** See CAFTAN.

**kail('yard).** See KALE.

**kai'ser** (kī'z-) *n.* (Hist.) Emperor, esp. of Germany, Austria, or Holy Roman Empire. [L CAESAR]

**käle, kail,** *n.* Variety of cabbage, esp. one (**curly ~**) with wrinkled leaves (**~'yard**, Sc., kitchen garden; **Scotch ~**, kind with purplish leaves). [north. var. COLE]

**kalei'do|scope** (-lī'd-) *n.* Tube through which are seen symmetrical patterns, produced by reflections of pieces of coloured glass, and varied by rotation of the tube (often fig. of shifting colours, changing groups of objects, etc.); **~sco'pic** *a.* (-ically). [Gk *kalos* beautiful, *eidos* form, -SCOPE]

**kämikä'ze** *n.* In war of 1939–45, Japanese aircraft laden with explosives and deliberately crashed on target by pilot; pilot of this. [Jap., = divine wind]

**kängaroo'** (-ngg-) *n.* Australian marsupial with hind quarters strongly developed for jumping; **~ closure** (when chairman in committee selects some amendments for discussion and excludes others); **~ court**, illegal court held by strikers etc.; **~ rat**, small ratlike Austral. marsupial, Amer. pouched nocturnal rodent. [Aboriginal]

**Kans.** *abbr.* Kansas.

**kä'olin** *n.* Fine white clay used for porcelain. [F f. Chin. *kao-ling* high hill]

**kä'pŏk** *n.* Fine cotton-like material from tropical tree used to stuff cushions, soft toys, etc. [Malay]

**kä'ppa** *n.* Tenth Gk letter (K, κ) = k. [Gk]

**käpu't** (-ŏŏt) *a.* (sl.) Done for, ruined, out of order. [G]

**kä'rakul, cä'racul,** (-ŏŏl) *n.* Asian sheep whose lambs have dark curled fleece; fur made from or resembling this. [Russ.]

**kara'tè** (-ah'-) *n.* Japanese system of unarmed combat using hands and feet as weapons. [Jap., = empty hand]

**kär'ma** *n.* Buddhist's or Hindu's destiny as determined by his actions. [Skr., = action, fate]

**kar(r)oo'** *n.* S. Afr. high plateau waterless in dry season. [Hottentot]

**kärt** *n.* = GO¹-*kart*. [abbr.]

**kä'tÿdĭd** *n.* Large green grasshopper common in U.S. [imit.]

**kaur'i** (kowr'ĭ) *n.* Coniferous N.Z. timber-tree. [Maori]

**kay'äk** (kī'-) *n.* Eskimo one-man canoe of light wooden framework covered with sealskins; canoe developed from this. [Eskimo]

‖**K.B.E.** *abbr.* Knight Commander (of the Order) of the British Empire.

**K.C.** *abbr.* King's Counsel.

**kc(/s)** *abbr.* kilocycles (per second).

‖**K.C.B.** *abbr.* Knight Commander (of the Order) of the Bath.

‖**K.C.M.G.** *abbr.* Knight Commander (of the Order) of St. Michael & St. George.

‖**K.C.V.O.** *abbr.* Knight Commander of the Royal Victorian Order.

**kè'a** *n.* Green N.Z. parrot said to attack sheep. [Maori, imit.]

**kèbä'b** *n.* (usu. in *pl.*) Small piece(s) of meat, vegetables, etc., cooked on skewer. [Urdu f. Arab.]

**kèdge. 1.** *v.t.* & *i.* Move (ship) by hawser attached to small anchor. **2.** *n.* Small anchor for this purpose. [orig. uncert.]

**kě'dgeree** (*or* -ē') *n.* European dish of fish, rice, hard-boiled eggs, etc.; Indian dish of rice, pulse, onions, eggs, etc. [Hindi]

**keel. 1.** *n.* (**~'less** *pr.* -l-l-). Lowest longitudinal timber on which ship's framework is built up, iron substitute for this, (**false ~**, protecting true keel from underneath; **~-haul**, haul (person) under keel as punishment; *on an* EVEN[2] *keel*). 2. *v.t. & i.* Turn (ship) keel upwards; **~ over**, upset, capsize, (of person) fall over. [N]

**kee'lson.** See KELSON.

**keen[1]. 1.** *n.* Irish funeral song accompanied with wailing. 2. *v.i. & t.* Utter the keen; bewail (person) thus. [Ir. *caoinim* to wail]

**keen[2]** *a.* (**~'ness** *pr.* -n-n-). (Of edge, knife) sharp; (of sound, light, etc.) penetrating, vivid, strong; (of wind etc.) piercingly cold; (of pain etc.) acute, intense; (colloq.) excellent; ||(of price) competitively low; (of person, desire, interest) eager, ardent, (**~ as mustard**, very enthusiastic); (of eyes, sight, scent, etc.) highly sensitive; intellectually acute; **~ on**, colloq., much attracted by (person, thing, do*ing*). [E]

**keep. 1.** *v.t. & i.* (**kept**). Pay due regard to, observe, (law, *the* PEACE, TIME, promise, appointment, feast); guard, protect, (person, fortress, goal at football, etc.; *keep* WICKET); have charge of, retain possession of, (**~'sake**, thing treasured for giver's sake; **you can ~ it**, colloq. as derog. refusal); maintain (place etc.) in proper order (*keep* HOUSE, *open* HOUSE); carry on, manage, (shop etc.); maintain (diary, accounts, etc.) by making requisite entries; provide for sustenance of (family, one*self*, etc.); own and manage (cows, bees, etc.; *keep* DOG *and bark* one*self*); maintain in return for sexual favours (*kept man, woman*); have (commodity) habitually on sale; preserve in being; continue to have or do (*keep* COMPANY, GUARD, WATCH); maintain, remain, in specified condition, course, etc., (*keep cool; keep indoors; keep* (*to the*) *left*; **how are you ~ing?**, colloq. inquiry after person's health; *keep* one's HAIR *on*; *keep* one's HAND *in*, MIND *on*; *keep in* TOUCH); continue to follow (way, course; *keep* TRACK *of*); (of food etc., also fig. of news etc.) remain in good condition; detain (person *in prison* etc.; *what kept you so long?*); restrain (person, thing, one*self*, *from* do*ing, from* thing); **reserve** (thing *for* future time etc.; *keep in* MIND); conceal (secret etc.);

remain in (one's *bed, room, the* HOUSE, etc.); retain one's place in (saddle, one's seat, one's ground, etc.) against opposition. **2.** *n.* Maintenance, food, (*you don't earn your keep*); (Hist.) tower, stronghold; **for ~s**, (colloq.) permanently. **3. ~** (work, cause to work, persistently) **at**; **~ away**, avoid coming, prevent from coming; **~ back**, (cause to) stay at a distance, hinder, restrain, conceal (fact), reserve or deduct, (*from*); **~ down**, hold in subjection, keep low in amount, not vomit; **~ in**, restrain (feelings etc.), confine (esp. schoolchild after hours), keep (fire) burning, stay indoors, remain on good terms *with*; **~ off**, avoid (subject etc.), not go on (*the grass* etc.), ward off, not (allow to) touch; **~ on**, continue (do*ing*), ||nag (*at*); **~ out**, not let enter, stay outside; **~ to**, adhere to (course, promise), confine oneself to, (**~** thing, fact *to* one*self*, keep private; **~** one*self to* one*self*, remain aloof); **~ under**, hold in subjection; **~ up**, prevent (one's spirits, prices, etc.) from sinking, maintain (*keep* one's END *up*); **~ it up**, not relax or slacken), keep in efficient or proper state (*keep up* APPEARANCES, *your Greek*), cause (person) to remain out of bed at night, proceed at equal pace (*with*; **~ up with the Joneses**, strive to remain on terms of social equality with one's neighbours. **4. ~'er** *n.*, (esp.) gamekeeper, wicket-keeper, custodian of museum or art gallery or forest, ring to keep another on finger; **~'ing** *n.*, (esp.) custody (*in safe·keeping*), agreement, harmony, (*out of keeping with the décor*). [E]

**kee'shŏnd** (kā'z-h-) *n.* (Breed of) chowlike Dutch dog once kept esp. on barges. [Du.]

**kĕg** *n.* Small cask usu. under ||10 or *30 gal. [N]

**kĕlp** *n.* Large seaweed; calcined ashes of this yielding iodine etc. [orig. unkn.]

**kĕ'lpĭe** *n.* (Sc.) malevolent water-spirit usu. in form of horse; Austral. sheep-dog of Sc. origin.

**kĕ'lson, kee'lson,** *n.* Line of timber fixing ship's floor-timbers to keel. [LG (KEEL, SWINE as name of timber)]

**Kĕlt[1].** See CELT[1].

**kĕlt[2]** *n.* Salmon or sea trout after spawning. [orig. unkn.]

**kĕ'lvĭn** n. Degree (equal to Celsius degree) of **K~ scale** of temperature (with zero at absolute zero). [person]

**kĕn.** 1. v.t. (Sc.; -nn-; ~t). Know. 2. n. Range of knowledge or sight (*beyond my ken*). [E, = make known (CAN²)]

**kĕ'nnel.** 1. n. Small structure for shelter of house-dog or hounds; (in *pl.*) establishment where dogs are bred, or are cared for in owners' absence; pack of dogs; mean dwelling. 2. n. & i. (||-ll-|). Put or be put into, keep or live in, kennel. [AF f. L (*canis* dog)]

**kĕ'pi** n. French soldier's cap with horizontal peak. [F f. G]

**kĕpt.** See KEEP.

||**kĕrb** n. Stone edging to pavement or raised path; ~ **drill,** simple procedure to promote safety of pedestrians when about to cross roads; ~**stone,** one of stones forming kerb. [var. CURB]

**kĕr'chief** (or -ĭf) n. Cloth used to cover head; (poet.) handkerchief. [AF *courchef* (COVER, CHIEF)]

**kerfŭ'ffle** n. (colloq.) Fuss, commotion. [orig. Sc.]

**kĕr'mĕs** (-z) n. Female of an insect, formerly taken to be a berry; red dyestuff made of dried bodies of these. [F f. Arab.]

**kĕr'nel** n. Part within hard shell of nut or stone-fruit; seed within husk etc., e.g. grain of wheat; (fig.) central or essential part. [E (CORN¹)]

**kĕ'rosēne, -ine** (-ēn), n. (U.S. etc.) Fuel-oil got by distillation of petroleum or from coal or bituminous shale, paraffin oil. [Gk *kēros* wax]

**kĕr'sey** (-zĭ) n. Coarse usu. ribbed cloth woven from long wool. [prob. place]

**kĕr'seymēre** (-zĭ-) n. Twilled fine woollen cloth. [*cassimere* var. CASHMERE, assim. to prec.]

**kĕ'strel** n. Kind of small falcon. [orig. uncert.]

**kĕtch** n. Small two-masted usu. cutter-rigged coasting-vessel. [CATCH]

**kĕ'tchup** n. Sauce made from tomatoes, mushrooms, etc., with vinegar, spices, etc., and used as condiment. [Chin.]

**kĕ'tōne** n. (Chem.) One of a class of organic compounds including acetone. [G *keton* alt. *aketon* ACETONE]

**kĕ'ttle** n. Vessel, usu. of metal with spout and handle, for boiling water; FISH¹-*kettle*; **a** (pretty etc.) ~ **of fish,** (awkward) state of affairs; ~**drum,** tuned drum of hollow metal hemisphere with parchment etc. stretched across; ~**holder,** pad etc. for handling hot kettle. [N]

**key¹** (kē). 1. n. Instrument, usu. of metal, for moving bolt of lock forwards or backwards to lock or unlock (HOUSE *of Keys*); power of the ~**s,** papal authority; **St. Peter's ~s,** two keys crosswise as in papal coat of arms); what governs opportunity for or access to something; place that by its position gives control of sea, territory, etc.; solution to problem(s), explanation, word or system for solving cipher or code; (Mus.) system of notes definitely related and based on particular note (*key of C major*; key SIGNATURE), (fig.) tone, style, of thought or expression, (*high, low, key*; **in a minor ~,** sad, sadly); piece of wood or metal inserted between others to secure them; lever pressed by finger in piano, flute, typewriter, etc.; mechanical device for making or breaking electric circuit (IGNITION key); instrument for grasping screws, pegs, nuts, etc., esp. one for winding clock etc.; winged fruit of sycamore, ash, etc.; (*attrib.*) essential, of vital importance. 2. v.t. Fasten (*in, on,* etc.) with pin, wedge, bolt, etc.; ~ **up,** stimulate (person *to do, to condition* etc.), raise tone or standard of, raise (offer, demand, etc.). 3. ~'**board,** set of keys on typewriter, piano, etc.; ~'**hole** (by which key is put into lock); ||~ **money,** payment demanded from incoming tenant for provision of keys to premises; ~'**note,** (Mus.) note on which key is based, (fig.) dominant idea etc.; ~-**ring** (for keeping keys on); ~'**stone,** central stone of arch, (fig.) central principle; ~'**word,** key to cipher etc., significant word used in indexing. [E]

**key²** (kē) n. Reef, low island. [Sp. *cayo*]

**Key'nesĭan** (kā'nz-) a. & n. (Adherent) of economic theories of J. M. *Keynes,* esp. regarding State control of the economy through money and taxes. [person]

||**K.G.** abbr. Knight (of the Order) of the Garter.

**kg** abbr. kilogram(s).

**K.G.B.** (kājēbē´) *n.* U.S.S.R. Secret police since 1954. [Russ. abbr., = State security committee]

**Kgs.** *abbr.* Kings (O.T.).

**kha´kī** (kah´-). **1.** *a.* Dull brownish--yellow. **2.** *n.* Khaki cloth esp. as used in military uniforms. [Urdu, = dusty]

**khan** (kăn, kahn) *n.* Title of rulers and officials in Central Asia; **~´āte** *n.*, khan's rule or district. [Turki, = lord]

**kHz** *abbr.* kilohertz.

**kǐbbu´tz** (-ōō´ts) *n.* (*pl.* **~im** *pr.* -ē´m). Communal esp. farming settlement in Israel; **~nǐk** *n.*, member of kibbutz. [Heb., = gathering]

**kǐ´bōsh** *n.* (sl.) Put the ~ on, put an end to. [orig. unkn.]

**kǐck. 1.** *v.t.* & *i.* Strike (out) forcibly with foot or hoof esp. to inflict injury or show annoyance (**alive and ~ing**, colloq., fully active; *kick against the* PRICKs, *over the* TRACEs); (fig.) protest, show dislike, etc., (*against, at,* treatment etc.); strike (anything) with foot, esp. to propel (*kick one's* HEEL¹s, *the* BUCKET); score (goal) by a kick; drive or move by kicking or (fig.) forcibly and contemptuously (**~ out**, expel by force or with contumely; **~ person upstairs**, remove him from scene of action to ostensibly higher position esp. peerage); (sl.) abandon (habit). **2.** *n.* Kicking action or blow (**~ in the pants** or **teeth**, colloq., humiliating set-back; **more ~s than halfpence**, more rough treatment than kindness); recoil of gun when discharged; (colloq.) resilience (*has no kick left*), sharp stimulant effect, thrill, (*does it for kicks*), temporary interest or enthusiasm of specified kind (*on a health-food kick*). **3.** **~ about, around**, treat (person) roughly or scornfully, move idly from place to place, be unused or unwanted; **~´back**, recoil, refund, payment (esp. for illegal help); **~-down**, device for gear-changing in motor vehicle by full depression of accelerator; **~ off**, (*v.t.* & *i.*) remove (shoes) by kicking, (Footb.) begin game, (colloq.) start, (*n.*) start esp. of game of football; **~-start(er)**, device to start engine of motor cycle etc. by downward thrust of pedal; **~ up a**

fuss etc., (colloq.) cause disturbance by vigorous protest etc.

**kǐd. 1.** *n.* Young goat; kid-skin leather (**~-glove** *a.*, fig., avoiding exertion or unnecessary violence); (sl.) child (**~s' stuff**, something very simple or easy); (sl.) hoax, humbug. **2.** *v.t.* & *i.* (**-dd-**). (Of goat) give birth to kid; (sl.) hoax, deceive. **3.** **~´dǐe, ~´dy**, *n.*, (sl.) child. [N]

**kǐ´dnǎp** *v.t.* (**-pp-, *-p-**). Steal (child); carry off (person etc.) illegally esp. to obtain ransom. [KID, *nap* = NAB]

**kǐ´dney** *n.* Either of pair of glandular organs in abdominal cavity of mammals, birds, and reptiles, serving to excrete urine (**artificial ~, ~ machine**, apparatus performing functions of human kidneys instead of damaged organ; **floating ~**, abnormally mobile one; **~ bean**, kidney-shaped dwarf French bean, scarlet runner bean; **~ potato**, oval kind); kidney of sheep, pig, etc., as food; nature, kind, (*a man of that kidney*). [orig. unkn.]

**Kǐlkě´nnӯ** *n.* See CAT. [place]

**kǐll. 1.** *v.t.* Deprive of life, put to death, (**~ off**, get rid of by killing; **~ time**, spend it unprofitably while waiting; *kill two* BIRDs *with one stone*; **~ with kindness**, ruin with mistaken or excessive kindness); (colloq.) cause severe pain to (*my feet are killing me*); put an end to (feelings, etc.; **~´joy**, depressing person); overwhelm (person) with admiration or amusement (*dressed* etc. **to ~**, showily or fascinatingly); (Lawn Tennis etc.) strike (ball) so that it cannot be returned; totally defeat (Parliamentary bill). **2.** *n.* Act of killing; animal(s) killed, esp. by sportsman; destruction or disablement of submarine, aircraft, etc.; **in at the ~**, (fig.) present at the time of victory. **3.** **~´er** *n.*, (esp.) murderous person; HUMANE *killer*; **~´ing**, (*n.*, fig.) great (esp. financial) success, (*a.*, colloq.) very attractive or amusing. [E]

**kǐln** *n.* Furnace or oven for burning, baking, or drying, esp. for calcining lime, or baking bricks. [E f. L *culina* kitchen]

**kǐ´lō** (or kē´-) *n.* (*pl.* **~s**). Kilogram; kilometre. [F, abbr.]

**kǐ´lo-** *in comb.* Thousand; **~cycle (per second), ~hertz**, unit of frequency = 1,000 cycles per second; **~gram(me)**, unit of mass in METRIC system, approx. 2·205 lb.; **~litre**, measure of 1,000 litres, approx. 35·31 cu. ft.; **~metre** (or -ŏ′mĭ-), distance of 1,000 metres, approx. 0·62 mile; **~ton(ne)**, esp. unit of explosive power equivalent to 1,000 tons of T.N.T.; **~watt**, power of 1,000 watts, approx. 1·34 h.p.; **~watt-hour**, energy equal to 1 kilowatt working for 1 hour. [F f. Gk *khilioi*]

**kilt. 1.** *n.* Skirt, usu. tartan, heavily pleated at sides and back, reaching from waist to knee, traditionally worn by Highland man; similar garment worn by women and children. **2.** *v.t.* Tuck up (skirts) round body; gather in vertical pleats. [Scand.]

**kimō′nō** *n.* (*pl.* ~s). Long loose Japanese robe; European dressing-gown modelled on this. [Jap.]

**kin. 1.** *n.* Ancestral stock, family, (*of noble kin*); one's relatives (KITH and kin; of ~, akin; NEXT of kin). **2.** *pred. a.* Related (*we are kin; he is kin to me*); **~sfolk, ~s(wo)man,** blood relations; **~′ship** *n.* [E]

**-kin** *suf.* forming dim. *ns.* (*catkin, lambkin, napkin*). [Du.]

**kind. 1.** *n.* Race, natural group, of animals, plants, etc., (*human kind*); class, SORT, variety, (**something of the ~,** something like the thing in question; **nothing of the ~,** not at all like it; **of a ~,** derog., scarcely deserving the name (*it was coffee of a kind*); **two of a ~,** two that are similar in some important respect; (in transposed constr.) **what ~ of tree is this?,** of what kind is this tree?; **the ~ of thing I meant,** a thing of the kind I meant; **this** or (colloq.) **these ~ of men,** men of this kind; (implying loose or vague description) *a kind of stockbroker, a kind of sympathy;* **~ of,** colloq., to some extent, *felt kind of sorry for him*); (Eccl.) each of the two elements in the Eucharist; natural way, fashion, (*act after their kind*); character (*differ in degree but not in kind*; **in ~,** of payment, in goods or natural produce instead of money, fig. of repayment, in same form, as, *repay his insolence in kind* = with insolence). **2.** *a.* Of gentle or benevolent nature, friendly in one's conduct *to* (person etc.), considerate, (*kind-hearted*). **3.** **~′lў¹**

*adv.* (esp. in polite request or command: *kindly bring this letter with you, kindly leave the stage;* **take ~ to,** be pleased by); **~′lў² a.** (**-ily, -iness**), kind, good-natured, (of climate) pleasant, genial. [E]

**kĭ′ndergärten** *n.* School for young children, teaching esp. by object-lessons, games, etc. [G, = children's garden]

**kĭ′ndl|e** *v.t. & i.* Set on fire, light, (flame, fire, substance); inspire, animate, (passion *in* person, person *with* or *to* passion); become kindled, flame, glow; **~ing** *n.*, (esp.) small wood etc. for lighting fires. [N]

**kĭ′ndlў¹,².** See KIND.

**kĭ′ndred. 1.** *n.* Blood relationship; one's relations; resemblance in character. **2.** *a.* Related, allied, similar, (*kindred peoples, subjects*); **~ spirit,** person felt to be congenial. [E, = kinship]

**kine.** See COW¹.

**kĭnĕmă′tĭc** *a.* (**~ally**). Of motion considered abstractly without reference to force or mass; **~s** *n.*, science of pure motion. [Gk *kinēma -matos* motion (*kineō* move)]

**kinematograph.** See CINEMATO-GRAPH.

**kĭnĕ′tĭc** *a.* Of or due to motion; **~ art** (depending upon movement for its effect); **~ energy,** body's ability to do work by virtue of its motion; **~s** *n.*, science of relations between motions of bodies and forces acting upon them. [Gk *kinētikos* (*kineō* move)]

**king. 1.** *n.* Male sovereign (esp. hereditary) ruler of independent state; magnate, man pre-eminent in specified field, (*oil, tennis, king*); something regarded as supreme in its class (**~ of beasts,** lion; **~ of birds,** eagle); (*attrib.*) large or largest kind of (*king cobra, -crab, penguin*); chess piece to be protected from checkmate; crowned piece in draughts; court-card bearing representation of king and usu. ranking next below ace. **2.** *v.t.* Make (person) king; **~ it,** act the king, govern. **3.** **K~ Charles spaniel** (small black-and-tan kind); **~′cup,** buttercup, ‖marsh marigold; **~′fisher,** small bird with brilliant plumage, which dives for fish; **~′maker,** one who sets up kings by his power, esp. Earl of Warwick in reign of Henry VI; ‖**K~ of Arms,** chief herald; **K~ of**

~s, God, title assumed by many eastern kings; ~ **of terrors**, Death; ~'**pin**, main or large bolt, (fig.) essential or leading person or thing; ~**post**, upright post from tie-beam to rafter-top; ‖*King's* BENCH, COUNSEL, ENGLISH, EVIDENCE, HIGHWAY, PROCTOR, SHILLING; ~'**s evil**, scrofula, formerly held to be curable by royal touch; ~**size(d)** *a.*, larger than normal, very large. **4.** ~'**dom** *n.*, state, territory, ruled by king or queen (UNITED *Kingdom*); ~'**dom of heaven**, spiritual reign of God, sphere of this; ~'**dom-come**, sl., the next world), domain, province of nature (*animal, vegetable, mineral, kingdom*); ~'**lў** *a.* (-iness); ~'**shĭp** *n.* [E]

**kink. 1.** *n.* Short backward twist in wire or chain or rope such as may cause obstruction or a break; (fig.) mental twist. **2.** *v.i.* & *t.* (Cause to) form a kink. **3.** ~'**ў** *a.* (~ily, ~iness), having (many) kinks, bizarre, perverted (esp. sexually). [LDu.]

**kĭ'nkajou** (-ōō) *n.* Carnivorous nocturnal arboreal animal of central & S. America, allied to racoon. [F f. N. Amer. Ind.]

**kinsfolk** etc., **kĭ'nshĭp**. See KIN.

**ki'ŏsk** (kē'-) *n.* Light out-of-door or ‖indoor structure for sale of newspapers, food, etc.; bandstand etc.; structure in street etc. for public telephone. [F f. Turk. f. Pers.]

**kĭp.** (sl.) **1.** *n.* A sleep; common lodging-house; bed. **2.** *v.i.* (-pp-). Sleep. [cf. Da. *kippe* mean hut]

**ki'pper. 1.** *v.t.* Cure (herring, salmon, etc.) by splitting open, rubbing with salt etc., and drying in open air or smoke. **2.** *n.* Kippered fish esp. herring; male salmon in spawning season. [orig. uncert.]

‖**kĭrk** *n.* (Sc. & N. Engl.) Church; The K~ (**of Scotland**), Ch. of Scotland as opp. to Ch. of England or to Episcopal Ch. in Scotland; ~**session**, lowest court in Ch. of Scotland and (Hist.) other Presbyterian Churches, composed of ministers and elders. [N *kirkja* = E CHURCH]

**kir'sch(wasser)** (kēr'shvahs*er*) *n.* Spirit distilled from fermented liquor of wild cherries. [G, = cherry (water)]

**kĭ'smĕt** (*or* -z-) *n.* Destiny. [Turk. f. Arab.]

**kĭss. 1.** *n.* Touch given with lips;

(Bill.) impact between moving balls; ~**curl**, small curl of hair arranged on face or at nape; ~ **of death**, apparently friendly action with ruinous results; ~ **of life**, mouth-to-mouth method of artificial respiration; ~ **of peace**, ceremonial kiss in Eucharist as sign of unity. **2.** *v.t.* Touch with the lips, esp. as sign of love, affection, greeting, or reverence; express thus (*kiss me good night*); (abs., of two persons) touch each other's lips thus; (Bill., of ball) touch (another) lightly (also abs. of two balls); ~ **away**, remove (tears etc.) with kisses; *kiss* GOODBYE *to*; ~ **hands, the hand,** (of sovereign etc. as ceremonial salutation or appointment to office); ~ **one's hand to,** BLOW[1] kiss to; ~ **the book** (Bible, in taking oath); ~ **the dust,** yield abject submission, be overthrown; ~ **the rod,** accept chastisement submissively. **3.** ~'**er** *n.*, mouth, face. [E]

**kĭt[1]. 1.** *n.* (Articles carried in) soldier's or traveller's pack etc.; personal equipment esp. as packed for travelling (~'**bag**, for carrying soldier's or traveller's kit); workman's outfit of tools etc.; clothing etc. for particular activity etc. (*riding-kit; tropical kit*); set of parts sold together from which whole thing may be made; ‖wooden tub. **2.** *v.t.* & *i.* (-tt-). Fit out, be fitted out, with kit (often *out, up*). [Du.]

**kĭt[2]** *n.* Kitten; young fox etc. [abbr.]

**kĭ'tchĕn** *n.* Place where food is cooked; ~ **garden** (for growing one's own fruit and vegetables); *kitchen* MIDDEN; ~ **sink**, (fig.) extreme realism in painting, drama, etc., (*everything but the ~ sink*, everything imaginable); ~ĕ'tte *n.*, small room, alcove, etc., used as kitchen. [E f. L *coquina*]

**kite** *n.* Bird of prey of hawk family; light framework covered with paper etc. and flown in wind at end of long string as toy (BOX-*kite*; **fly a ~**, fig., make experiment to gauge public opinion etc.); ‖(sl.) aeroplane; ‖K~'**mark**, official mark (representing stylized kite) on goods approved by British Standards Institution. [E]

**kĭth** *n.* ~ **and kin**, friends and relations. [E, orig. 'knowledge' (CAN[2])]

**kitsch** (kĭch) *n*. Worthless pretentiousness in art; art of this type; **~y** *a*. [G]

**kitten. 1.** *n*. Young of cat; young ferret etc.; skittish young girl; **have ~s,** (colloq.) be very nervous or upset. **2.** *v.t.* & *i*. Give birth to (kittens). [AF dim. of *chat* CAT]

**kittiwāke** *n*. Kind of small sea-gull. [imit. of its cry]

**kittle** *a*. Hard to deal with, ticklish, (esp. **~ cattle,** usu. of persons or things). [orig. = tickle; N]

**kitty¹** *n*. (Pet-name for) kitten. [KIT²]

**kitty²** *n*. Pool in some card games; joint fund. [orig. unkn.]

**ki'wi** (kē'wē) *n*. Apteryx, flightless N.Z. bird; (**K~**; colloq.) New Zealander. [Maori]

**klaxon** *n*. Powerful electric (motor-)horn. [P]

**kleptomā'ni|a** *n*. Irresistible tendency to steal what one could afford to buy or does not need; **~ăc** *n*. & *a*. [Gk *kleptēs* thief]

**klōof** *n*. (S. Afr.) Ravine. [Du.]

**km** *abbr*. kilometre(s).

**kn.** *abbr*. (Naut.) knot(s).

**knăck** *n*. Acquired or intuitive faculty of doing a thing adroitly; trick, habit, of action, speech, etc. [orig. unkn.]

‖**knä'cker¹** *n*. Buyer of useless horses for slaughter or of old houses etc. for the materials.

‖**knä'cker²** *v.t.* (sl.) Kill; (fig., esp. in *p.p.*) exhaust, wear out. [orig. dial.]

**knä'psack** *n*. Soldier's or traveller's usu. canvas bag for necessaries, strapped to back. [G (*knappen* bite, SACK¹)]

**knä'pweed** *n*. Weed with purple flowers on globular head. [KNOP]

**knäv|e** *n*. Unprincipled or dishonest man, rogue; lowest-ranking court-card; **~ery** *n*., conduct of knave. [E, orig. = boy, servant]

**knead** *v.t.* & *i*. Work up (flour, clay) into dough or paste; make (bread, pottery) thus; treat with, make, such motions (in massaging etc.); (fig.) blend. [E]

**knee** *n*. Joint between thigh and lower leg in man (**bend, bow, the ~,** kneel esp. in submission); **bring person to his knees,** reduce him to submission; **on one's ~s, on bended ~(s),** kneeling in worship, supplication, or submission); cor-responding joint in animal; upper surface of thigh of sitting person (*hold child* etc. *on* one's *knee*); part of garment covering knee; **~-breeches** (reaching down to or just below the knee); **~'cap,** convex bone in front of knee, protective covering for knee; **~-deep,** immersed up to knees, (fig.) deeply involved *in*; **~-deep, ~-high,** so deep, high, as to reach the knees; **~-hole,** space for knees, esp. between columns of drawers in desk; **~-jerk,** sudden involuntary kick caused by blow on tendon below knee; **~-length,** so long as to reach the knees. [E]

**kneel** *v.i.* (**knelt,** *\*~ed*). Fall, rest, on the knee(s) esp. in prayer or reverence (*to* person); **~er** *n*., (esp.) hassock etc. to kneel on. [E (prec.)]

**knell** *n*. Sound of bell esp. after a death or at funeral; (fig.) announcement, event, etc., regarded as omen of death or extinction. [E]

**knelt.** See KNEEL.

**knew.** See KNOW.

**kni'ckerböcker|s** (-z) *n.pl.* Loose-fitting breeches gathered in at knee. [K~'s (W. Irving's) *History of New York* (1809)]

**kni'ckers** (-z) *n.pl.* ‖Female undergarment covering lower part of body and having separate legs or leg-holes; \*knickerbockers; \*boy's short trousers. [abbr. prec.]

**kni'ck-knäck, ni'ck-näck,** *n*. Light dainty article of furniture, dress, or food; trinket. [KNACK in obs. sense *trinket*]

**knife. 1.** *n*. (*pl.* knives *pr.* nīvz). Metal blade with long sharpened edge fixed in handle and used as cutting instrument or weapon (*before you can say* **~,** colloq., very quickly, suddenly; **get** one's **~ into,** show malicious or vindictive spirit towards; **that one could cut with a ~,** colloq., fig. of accent, atmosphere, etc., very obvious or oppressive; **the ~,** surgical operation(s); WAR *to the knife*); cutting-blade in machine; **~-edge,** edge of knife, (fig.) position of extreme uncertainty; **~-pleat** (narrow, flat, one of a series that overlap); **at ~-point,** threatened by knife. **2.** *v.t.* Cut, stab, with knife. [E]

**knight** (nīt). **1.** *n*. Man raised to rank below baronetcy as reward for personal merit or services to Crown or country; (Hist., or fig.) military follower, esp. devoted to service of lady as her attendant or champion in war or tournament; (Hist.) man raised to honourable military rank by king etc.; chess piece usu. with shape of horse's head; (with following n. in apposition etc.; pl. usu. ~s —): knight BACHELOR, HOSPITALLER, TEMPLAR, ~ **errant**, medieval knight wandering in search of chivalrous adventures, (fig.) man of such spirit; ~-e′rrantry, practice or conduct of knight errant. **2.** v.t. Confer knighthood on. **3.** ~′**hood** (-t-h-) n.; ~′**lў** a. (-iness). [E, orig. = boy]

**knit** v.t. & i. (-tt-; ~′ted or, esp. fig., knit). Form (texture, garment, or abs.) by interlocking loops of yarn or thread (~′**ting machine**, for mechanical knitting of garments etc.; ~′**ting-needle**, one of pair of slender pointed rods used in knitting; ~′**wear**, knitted garments); treat (yarn etc.) thus; make (plain stitch) in knitting; wrinkle (brow); make, become, close or compact (a well-knit frame); (fig.) unite (together) by common interests etc.; (of parts of broken bone) become joined (together) again as one; ~′**ting** n., (esp.) work being knitted. [E]

**knob. 1.** n. Rounded protuberance esp. at end or on surface of thing, e.g. handle of door, drawer, etc.; small lump (of butter, coal, etc.); ~**kerrie** [after Afrik. knopkierie], short stick with knobbed head as weapon of S. Afr. tribes; **with ~s on**, (sl., esp. as retort) that and more. **2.** v.t. (-bb-). Furnish with knob(s). **3.** ~′**bў** a. (-iness); ~′**ble** n., small knob, so ~′**blў** a. (-iness). [MLG knobbe knot, knob]

**knock. 1.** v.t. & i. Strike with audible sharp blow; strike door, at door etc. for admittance; drive (thing, person) in, out, off, by striking; make by knocking (knock a hole in); (of motor etc. engine) make thumping or rattling noise as result of mechanical defect, PINK³; (sl.) criticize, ||impress favourably. **2.** n. Act of knocking; sharp or audible blow; rap esp. at door; sound of knocking in engine; (colloq.) innings at cricket. **3.** ~ **about**, strike repeatedly, treat roughly, lead irregular life; ~′**about** a., (esp.) boisterous (freq. of theatrical per-

formance); ||~ **back**, (sl.) eat or drink esp. quickly, disconcert; ~ **down**, strike (person) to ground, demolish, (at auction) dispose of (article to bidder) by knock of hammer, (Commerc.) take (machinery, furniture, etc.) to pieces for ease of transport; ~-down a., (lit. or fig.) overwhelming, (of price) very low; ~ **for** ~ **agreement** (between insurers, whereby each pays his own policy-holders regardless of liability); ||~′**ing-shop**, (sl.) brothel; knock into ǎ COCK¹ed hat; ~ person **into the middle of next week**, (colloq.) send him flying; ~ **knees**, abnormal condition with leg(s) curved inward at the knee, so ~-**kneed** a.; ~ **off**, strike off with blow, leave off (work), (colloq.) dispatch (business) or rapidly compose (verses, picture, etc.), deduct (sum from bill etc.), (sl.) steal or kill; ~ **on**, (Rugby Footb.) knock ball forward with hand; ~ **on the head**, stun or kill (person etc.) by blow on head, (fig.) put an end to (scheme etc.); *~ **on wood**, = TOUCH wood; ~ **out**, empty (tobacco-pipe) by tapping, render unconscious by blow to head, disable (boxer) so that he cannot rise within usu. ten seconds, astonish, make useless, defeat esp. in knock-out competition; ~-**out** n. & a., (blow) that knocks boxer etc. out, (competition) in which loser of each match is eliminated, (sl.) outstanding person or thing; ~ **sideways**, (colloq.) shock, astound; knock SPOTS off; knock the BOTTOM out of; ~ **together**, construct hurriedly; ~ **up**, drive upwards with blow, make or arrange hastily, score (runs) rapidly at cricket, ||arouse (person) by knocking at door, make or become tired or ill, *(sl.) make pregnant; ~-**up** n., practice, casual game, at tennis etc.; **take a, the, ~**, sustain severe financial or emotional blow. **4.** ~′**er** n., (esp.) metal appendage hinged to door and struck against metal plate to call attention. [E]

**knoll** n. Small hill, mound. [E]

**knop** n. (Ornamental) knob; loop, tuft in yarn. [LDu.]

**knot¹. 1.** n. Intertwining of parts of one or more ropes, strings, etc., as fastening (tie person **in ~s**, colloq., confuse or baffle him); ribbon etc. so tied for ornament etc.; tangle (of hair, yarn, etc.);

group, cluster, (*of persons or things*); difficulty, problem; that which forms or maintains a union esp. wedlock; (hard mass formed in tree-trunk where branch grew out, causing) round cross-grained piece in board; (Naut.) division marked by knots in log-line, unit of ship's or aircraft's speed equal to one nautical mile per hour, (pop.) one nautical mile, (**at a rate of ~s**, colloq., very fast); **~-grass**, weed with intricate creeping stems and pink flowers; **~-hole** (in wooden board, where knot has fallen out). **2.** *v.t. & i.* (**-tt-**). Tie (string etc.) in knot; make knots (esp. for fringe); make (fringe) thus; unite closely or intricately; entangle. **3.** **~'ty** *a.* (**-ily, -iness**), full of knots, (fig.) puzzling, difficult. [E]

**knot²** *n.* Small wading bird of sandpiper family. [orig. unkn.]

**know** (nō). **1.** *v.t. & i.* (**knew** *pr.* nū; **~n** *pr.* nōn). Be aware of (fact), be aware, have in the mind, have learnt, (*that, how, why*, etc.), (in *p.p.*) of which there is knowledge as fact (*a known thief*); have understanding of (language, subject); recognize, identify, be able to distinguish (one *from* another); be acquainted with (thing, place, person) *by* SIGHT, *to speak to*, etc. (**~ by name**, have heard name of, be able to give name of); have personal experience of (fear etc.), be subject to (*her joy knew no bounds*); **all one ~s**, the utmost of one's powers; **before one ~s where one is**, with baffling rapidity; **don't I ~ it** (colloq., expr. rueful assent); **don't you ~** (colloq. parenthetic expletive: *it's such a bore, don't you know*); **for all I ~**, so far as my knowledge is concerned; **has been ~n to do**, is known to have done; **~ about**, have information about; **~-all**, person who appears to know everything (usu. derog.); *know* BETTER¹; **~-how**, practical knowledge, technical expertness; **~ of**, be aware of, have heard of, (*not that I ~ of*, not so far as I know); **~ one's own mind**, not vacillate; **~ a thing or two**, be experienced or shrewd; **~ person or thing to be** (that he etc. is); **~ what's what**, have proper knowledge of the world and of things in general; **not if I ~ it**, only against my will; **not want to ~**, refuse to take notice (of); **what do you know (about that)?**

(colloq. excl. of surprise); **you ~** (esp. colloq. as conversational filler); **you ~ something?, what?**, I am going to tell you something; **you never ~**, nothing future is certain. **2.** *n.* (colloq.). **In the ~**, knowing a secret or other thing in question. **3.** **~'ing**, (*a.*; esp.) cunning, shrewd, (*n.*) esp. *there is no ~ing*, one cannot tell; **~'ingly** *adv.*, in a knowing manner, consciously, intentionally. [E]

**know'ledge** (nŏ'l-) *n.* Knowing, familiarity gained by experience, (*of* person, thing, fact); person's range of information (*it came to my ~*, became known to me; **to my ~**, so far as I know, as I know for certain); theoretical or practical understanding (*of* language, subject); sum of what is known (*every branch of knowledge*); **~able** (nŏ'lĭjə-) *a.*, (colloq.) well-informed, intelligent.

**known.** See KNOW.

**knu'ckle. 1.** *n.* Bone at finger-joint, esp. at root of finger; projection of carpal or tarsal joint of quadruped, this with adjacent parts as joint of veal, ham, etc.; **near the ~**, (colloq.) verging on the indecent; **~-bone**, (esp., in *pl.*) sheep's bones used in game of JACKS; **~-duster**, metal guard worn over knuckles in fist-fighting esp. to increase violence of blow. **2.** *v.t. & i.* Strike, press, rub, with knuckles; **~ down**, apply oneself earnestly (*to* work etc.); **~ down, under**, give in, submit (*to*). [LDu. dim. (*knoke* bone)]

**knurl** *n.* Small projecting ridge etc. [LDu.]

**K.O.** *abbr.* knock-out.

**kōa'la** (-ah'-) *n.* **~ (bear)**, Australian tailless arboreal marsupial with thick grey fur and large ears. [Aboriginal]

**kohl** (kōl) *n.* Powder used in East to darken eyelids and outline eyes. [Arab.; see ALCOHOL]

**kohlra'bi** (kōlrah'-) *n.* Cabbage with turnip-like edible stem. [G f. It. f. L (COLE, RAPE²)]

**kō'la.** See COLA.

**koli'nský** *n.* (Fur of) Siberian mink. [Russ. (*Kola*, place)]

**kŏ'lkhŏz** (-kŏz) *n.* Collective farm in U.S.S.R. [Russ.]

**kōō'dōō, kudu** (kōō'dōō), *n.* Large white-striped spiral-horned Afr. antelope. [Xhosa]

**\*kŏŏk** n. & a. (sl.) Crazy or eccentric (person); ~′ў a. (~ily, ~iness). [prob. CUCKOO]

**kŏŏ′kaburra** n. (Austral.) Laughing JACKASS. [Aboriginal]

**kŏ′ppie, kŏ′pje** (-pĭ), n. (S. Afr.) Small hill. [Afrik. *koppie*, Du. *kopje*, dim. of *kop* head]

**Kŏra′n** (-ah′n) n. Sacred book of Muslims; ~ic (or -ă′-) a. [Arab., = recitation]

**kŏr′fball** (-awl) n. Game like basketball played by teams of 6 men and 6 women. [Du. *korfbal* (*korf* basket, *bal* ball)]

**kŏ′sher. 1.** a. (Of food or foodshop) fulfilling requirements of Jewish law; (colloq.) correct, genuine, legitimate. **2.** n. Kosher food or shop. [Heb., = proper]

**kowtow′, kōtow′. 1.** n. Chinese custom of touching ground with forehead as sign of worship or submission. **2.** v.i. Perform the kowtow; act obsequiously (*to* person etc.). [Chin., = knock the head]

**∥K.P.** abbr. Knight (of the Order) of St. Patrick.

**k.p.h.** abbr. kilometres per hour.

**kraal** (-ahl) n. S. Afr. village of huts enclosed by fence; enclosure for cattle or sheep. [Afrik. f. Port. *curral*, of Hottentot orig.]

**kraft** (-ah-) n. ~ (**paper**), smooth strong brown (wrapping-)paper. [G, = strength]

**Kraut** (-owt) n. (sl., derog.) German. [SAUERKRAUT]

**krě′mlin** n. Citadel within Russian town, esp. that of Moscow; **the K~**, the U.S.S.R. Government. [F f. Russ.]

**krĭll** n. Tiny plankton crustaceans eaten by whales etc. [Norw. *kril* tiny fish]

**kris** (or -ē-), **creese,** n. Malay dagger with wavy blade. [Malay]

**kromě′skỳ** n. Minced meat or fish rolled in bacon and fried. [Russ.]

**krō′n|a** n. Monetary unit of Sweden (*pl.* ~or) and of Iceland (*pl.* ~ur). [Sw. & Icel., = CROWN]

**krō′ne** (-e) n. (*pl.* ~r). Monetary unit of Denmark and of Norway. [Da. & Norw., = CROWN]

**Kru′ger** (-ōō′-) n. ~rand, S. Afr. gold coin bearing portrait of President Kruger. [person]

**K.T.** abbr. ∥Knight (of the Order) of the Thistle; Knight Templar.

**Kt.** abbr. Knight.

**kū′dŏs** n. (colloq.) Renown. [Gk]

**kudu.** See KOODOO.

**Kū′fic.** See CUFIC.

**\*Kū′-Klŭx(-Klă′n)** n. Secret society hostile to Blacks. [orig. uncert.]

**ku′krĭ** (kŏŏ′-). Heavy curved knife used by Gurkhas as weapon. [Hindi]

**kümmel** (kŏŏ′mel) n. Liqueur flavoured with caraway and cumin seeds. [G (CUMIN)]

**kumquat.** See CUMQUAT.

**kung fu** (kŭngfōō′, kŏŏ-) n. Chinese form of karate. [Chin.]

**Kŭr′dĭsh** (or koor′-) a. & n. (Language) of the Kurds, tall pastoral people in S.W. Asia. [native]

**kV** abbr. kilovolt(s).

**kW** abbr. kilowatt(s); **kWh,** kilowatt-hour(s).

**Ky.** abbr. Kentucky.

# L

**L, l,** (ĕl) n. (*pl.* **Ls, L's**). Twelfth letter; L-shaped thing; (as Roman numeral) 50.

**L.** abbr. Lake; ∥learner-driver; Liberal; Licentiate of.

**£,** abbr. POUND[3] (money). [L *libra*]

**l.** abbr. left; line; litre(s).

**la.** See LAH.

**La.** abbr. Louisiana.

**lăb** n. (colloq.) Laboratory. [abbr.]

**Lab.** abbr. Labour.

**lā′bel. 1.** n. Slip of paper, metal, etc., attached to an object to give some information about it, (fig.) classifying phrase applied to persons etc. **2.** v.t. (~ll-). Attach label to; assign to category; replace (atom) by usu. radioactive isotope for identification. [F]

**lā′bĭal. 1.** a. (~ly). Of the lips;

of the nature of a lip; (Phon.) pronounced with closed lips. **2.** *n.* (Phon.) Labial sound (e.g. *p, m, v*). [L (*labia* lips)]

***lā′bor*** etc. See LABOUR etc.

**labo′ratory** *n.* Place used for scientific experiments esp. in chemistry, or for research. [L (foll.)]

**lā′bour, \*lā′bor,** (-er). **1.** *n.* Bodily or mental work, exertion; toil tending to provide what is wanted by the community; body of those who do such work, such body as a political force; (*L~*) the Labour Party; task; pains of childbirth, process of giving birth; **L~ Exchange,** (colloq. or Hist.) employment exchange; **~ force,** body of workers employed; *labour- -intensive*; **~ of Hercules,** one needing enormous strength; **~ of love,** task one delights in; **L~ Party,** (Polit.) party representing esp. workers' interests; **~-saving,** designed to reduce or eliminate work. **2.** *v.i.* & *t.* Use labour, exert oneself, work hard, work as labourer; strive *to* do; have difficulty in maintaining normal motion; suffer *under* (delusion etc.); elaborate, work out in (excessive) detail, (*I will not labour the point*); (in *p.p.*) showing signs of effort, not spontaneous. **3. labor′ious** *a.,* hard-working, toilsome, showing signs of effort; **~er** *n.,* one who labours, (esp.) person doing for wages work needing strength or patience rather than skill; **~ite** *n.,* member of Labour Party. [F f. L]

**Lā′brador** *n.* (Dog of) retriever breed with black or golden coat. [place]

**labur′num** *n.* Tree with yellow hanging flowers. [L]

**lā′byr|inth** *n.* Network of passages difficult to find one's way in without guidance, maze, tangled affairs; complex cavity of inner ear; **~i′nthine** *a.* [F or L f. Gk]

**lăc**[1] *n.* Resinous substance secreted by the S.E. Asian ~ **insect** as protective covering. [Hind.]

**lăc**[2]. See LAKH.

‖**L.A.C.** *abbr.* Leading Aircraftman.

**lāce. 1.** *n.* Cord or strip put through eyelets or hooks for fastening or tightening shoes etc.; trimming- -braid (esp. *gold, silver, lace*); fine open fabric of threads usu. with pattern. **2.** *v.t.* & *i.* Fasten or tighten (shoe etc., often *up*) with lace(s); trim with lace; pass (cord etc.) *through*; flavour (coffee etc.) with spirits; ~ (**into**), lash, beat, defeat. [F f. L *laqueus* noose]

**lă′cer|āte** *v.t.* (~able). Tear (flesh, tissues, etc., or fig. heart, feelings, etc.); **~ā′tion** *n.* [L (*lacer* torn)]

**lă′chrym|al** (-k-) *a.* Of tears (esp. Anat., as *lachrymal duct, gland*); **~ā′tion** *n.,* flow of tears; **~atory** *a.,* of, causing, tears; **~ōse** *a.,* tearful, given to weeping. [L (*lacrima* tear)]

**lăck. 1.** *n.* Deficiency or want *of* (no ~, plenty; for ~ *of,* owing to absence of). **2.** *v.t.* & *i.* Not have when needed, be without, (*lacks courage, money,* etc.); ~ **for,** have none or insufficient of; be **~ing,** be undesirably absent or deficient (*money is lacking; is not lacking in courage*); **~′lustre,** (of eye etc.) lustreless, dull. [LDu.]

**lăckadai′sical** (-z-) *a.* (~ly). Languidly affected; unenthusiastic. [ALACK]

**lă′ckey. 1.** *n.* Footman; obsequious person. **2.** *v.t.* Play lackey to. [F f. Catalan f. Sp.]

**laco′nic** *a.* (~ally). Using, expressed in, few words; **~ism** *n.* [L f. Gk (*Lakōn* Spartan)]

**lă′cquer** (-ker). **1.** *n.* Kind of varnish, esp. that made of shellac and alcohol as coating for brass; substance sprayed on hair to keep it in place. **2.** *v.t.* Coat with lacquer. [F *lacre* = LAC[1]]

**lacrŏ′sse** (or -aw′s) *n.* Game like hockey with ball carried in crosse. [F (*la* the)]

**lă′ct|ic** *a.* Of milk (~**ic acid,** formed in sour milk); **~ā′tion** *n.,* suckling, secretion of milk; **~eal,** (*a.*) of milk, conveying chyle, (*n.pl.*) chyle-conveying vessels; **~e′scent** *a.,* looking like milk or yielding milky juice; **~e′scence** *n.;* **~i′ferous** *a.,* yielding milk or milky fluid; **~ōse** *n.,* a sugar present in milk. [L (*lac lact-* milk)]

**lacū′na** *n.* (*pl.* ~**e,** ~**s**). Gap in MS. where some part has been lost or obliterated, missing link in a chain or argument or any series, vacant interval, interstice. [L (LAKE[1])]

**lacŭ′strine** *a.* Of lakes.

‖**L.A.C.W.** *abbr.* Leading Aircraftwoman.

**lā′c|y̆** *a.* (~ily, ~iness). Lacelike in fineness or intricacy. [LACE]

**lăd** *n.* Boy, young fellow; man, fellow, (my ~, **the** ~s, cf. BOY; **my** ~s, = *my men* in addressing sailors, workmen, etc.); stable-man or -woman of any age; ~′**dĭe** *n.*, lad (in affectionate etc. use). [orig. unkn.]

**lă′dder. 1.** *n.* Pair of long pieces of wood or metal or cords joined at intervals by cross-pieces to serve as usu. portable means of ascending a building etc.; (fig.) means of rising in the world; ‖vertical flaw in stocking etc. caused by stitch(es) becoming undone; ~**back**, chair with back made of horizontal bars between uprights; ~ **tournament** (with contestants listed and each entitled to higher place if he can defeat the one just above him). **2.** *v.t. & i.* ‖Cause ladder in (stocking etc.), develop ladder. [E]

**lāde** *v.t.* (*p.p.* ~**n**). Load (ship), ship (goods); (in *p.p.*) loaded or burdened (*with*); **bill of lading**, ship's captain's detailed receipt for consignor. [E]

**la-dĭ-da′** (lahdĭdah′) *a. & n.* (Person or action) that is pretentious in manner and speech. [imit.]

**lā′dle. 1.** *n.* Long-handled large-bowled spoon for transferring liquids; vessel for transporting molten metal. **2.** *v.t.* Transfer with ladle; ~ **out**, (fig.) distribute lavishly. [E]

**lā′dy̆** *n.* Ruling woman (*lady of the house*; **Our L**~, Virgin Mary); mistress, (usu. arch. or vulg.) wife; (as fem. of *gentleman*) woman of or fitted for upper class, (polite or formal for) woman; ‖(*L*~) title used as less formal prefix to name of peeress below duchess, or to Christian name of daughter of duke, marquis, or earl, or to surname of baronet's or knight's wife or widow, (**my ~**, form of address to holder of title *Lady*); (*attrib.*, usu. polite or formal) female (*lady doctor, friend*); ‖**the Ladies(′)**, (as *sing.*) women's public lavatory; **ladies and gentlemen** (addressing company of both sexes); ~**bird**, *\**~**bug**, coleopterous insect usu. reddish-brown with black spots; **L**~ **Bountiful**, beneficent lady in village etc.; **L**~ **chapel** (in large church, usu. E. of high altar, dedicated to Virgin Mary); **L**~ **Day**, 25 Mar. (feast of Annuncia-

tion); ~**fern** (slender kind); ~**in-waiting**, lady attending royal lady; ~**killer**, man who flirts; ~**love**, man's sweetheart; **L**~ **Mayoress**, Lord Mayor's wife; **(Our) L**~'s **bedstraw**, yellow-flowered kind of bedstraw; ~'s-**maid**, personal maidservant of lady; **ladies′ man**, ~'s **man**, (fond of female society); ~**smock**, cuckoo flower; ~**like** *a.*, behaving as or befitting a lady; (of man) effeminate; ~**ship** *n.* (esp. with *her*, *your*, etc., as respectful substitute for titled lady's name, or iron.). [E, = loaf-kneader; cf. LORD]

**lăg**[1]. **1.** *v.i. & t.* (-gg-). Go too slow, not keep pace, fall behind others (often *behind* adv. or prep.). **2.** *n.* Lagging, delay; TIME-*lag*; (sl.) a convict (*old lag*). **3.** ~′**gard** *n.*, person who lags behind, procrastinator. [orig. uncert.]

**lăg**[2]. **1.** *n.* (Piece of) non-conducting cover of boiler etc. **2.** *v.t.* (-gg-). Enclose with lags; ~′**gĭng** (-g-) *n.*, (esp.) material for this. [N]

**la′ger** (lah′g-) *n.* Light beer (orig. of German kind). [G, = store]

**lagōō′n** *n.* Salt-water lake separated from sea by sandbank or enclosed by atoll. [F, It., Sp., f. L LACUNA pool]

**lah, la,** (lah) *n.* (Mus.) Sixth note of scale; note A. [L *labii*, wd arbitrarily taken]

**lā′ĭc(allў)**, **lā′ĭcīze**. See LAY[3]; **laid**, see LAY[4]; **lain**, see LIE[2].

**lair** *n.* Animal's lying-place; (fig.) person's hiding-place. [E]

**laird** *n.* Landed proprietor in Scotland. [LORD]

**laissez-aller** (lāsā ă′lā) *n.* Unconstrained freedom of manners or conduct; **laissez-faire** (lāsāfāī′) *n.*, government abstention from interference with individual action esp. in commerce. [F, = let go, act]

**lā′ĭty̆** *n.* Body of laymen in respect of religion or a profession. [LAY[3]]

**lāke**[1] *n.* Large body of water surrounded by land (**the L**~s, region in N. England; **the Great L**~s, on boundary of Canada and U.S.); ~**dwelling**, prehistoric habitation on piles over or near lake; ~**country**, **L**~ **District**, **L**~′**land**, the Lakes; ~′**lĕt** (-kl-) *n.* [F *lac* f. L *lacus*]

**lāke**[2] *n.* Pigment made from dye and mordant. [var. LAC[1]]

**lăkh** (-k), **lăc²**, *n.* (Ind.) 100,000 esp. *of rupees*. [Hind. *lākh* f. Skr.]

**lăm** *v.t. & i.* (sl.; -mm-). Hit with stick etc.; thrash. [perh. Scand.]

**Lam.** *abbr.* Lamentations (O.T.).

**la'ma** (lah'-) *n.* Tibetan or Mongolian Buddhist priest; Dalai (*pr.* dă'li) L~, head lama of Tibet; **lama'serў** (-mah'-) *n.*, lama monastery. [Tibetan]

**lămb** (-m). **1.** *n.* Young sheep; its flesh as food; young, innocent, weak, or dear person; **The L~** (of God), Christ; **like a ~,** unresistingly; **~'s-wool,** fine soft wool for knitted garments; **~'kin** (-mk-) *n.* **2.** *v.i. & t.* Give birth to lamb; (in *pass.*, of lamb) be born. [E]

**lămbă'ste, -bă'st,** *v.t.* (colloq.) Thrash, beat. [LAM, BASTE² thrash]

**lă'mbda** (-md-) *n.* Eleventh Gk letter (Λ, λ) = l. [Gk]

**lă'mben|t** *a.* (Of flame or light) playing about a surface, (of eyes, sky, wit, etc.) gently brilliant; **~cў** *n.* [L *lambo* lick]

**Lă'mbeth** *n.* **~ Conference,** regular assembly of Anglican bishops; **~ degree,** honorary degree conferred by Archbishop of Canterbury. [place]

**lāme. 1.** *a.* Disabled by injury or defect esp. in foot or leg, limping or unable to walk normally, (of person, limb, gait, etc.); (of excuse etc.) unconvincing; (of metre) halting; HELP *lame dog*; **~ duck,** disabled person, insolvent person or firm. **2.** *v.t.* Make lame, disable. [E]

**lamé** (lah'mā) *a. & n.* (Material) with gold or silver thread inwoven. [F]

**lamě'nt. 1.** *n.* Passionate expression of grief; elegy. **2.** *v.i. & t.* Utter lament (*for, over*); express or feel grief for or about, be distressed at, (in *p.p.*) mourned for (esp. *the late lamented*); **lă'mentable** *a.* (-bly), deplorable, regrettable; **lămentā'tion** *n.*, lament, lamenting; L~ations (of Jeremiah), O.T. book. [F or L (*lamentum* n., *-tor* v.)]

**lă'min|a** *n.* (Geol., Physiol., etc.; *pl.* ~ae). Thin plate or scale or flake or layer; **~āte¹** *v.t. & i.*, beat or roll (metal) into laminae, split into layers, overlay with metal plates; **~ā'tion** *n.*; **~ar, ~āte²,** **~ōse,** *adjs.*; **~āte³** *n.*, laminated structure, esp. of layers fixed together. [L]

**Lă'mmas** *n.* 1st day of August, formerly kept as harvest festival. [E (LOAF¹, MASS¹)]

**lămp** *n.* Vessel with oil and wick for giving light; transparent vessel enclosing source of light (esp. wire made incandescent by electricity when light is wanted); **smell of the ~,** betray nocturnal study, be laborious in style etc.; **~black,** pigment made from soot; **~'light** (given by lamp); **~'lighter,** (usu. Hist.) man who lights street lamps; **~'post** (supporting street lamp); **~'shade** (placed over lamp to soften or intercept its light). [F f. L f. Gk *lampas* torch]

**lămpoo'n. 1.** *n.* Piece of virulent or scurrilous satire on a person; **~ïst** *n.* **2.** *v.t.* Write lampoon(s) against. [F *lampon*]

**lă'mprey** *n.* Eel-like aquatic animal with sucker mouth. [F *lampreie* f. L *lampreda*]

**Lă'ncaster** *n.* **House of ~,** English sovereigns from Henry IV to Henry VI; **Lăncă'striăn,** (*a.*) of Lancaster, of Lancashire, of the family of John of Gaunt Duke of Lancaster or its party in Wars of the Roses (opp. *Yorkist*), (*n.*) Lancastrian person. [place]

**lance** (-ah-). **1.** *n.* Horseman's long wooden spear; similar implement for spearing fish etc.; **break a ~,** argue *for* or *with*; **~-corporal,** N.C.O. below corporal. **2.** *v.t.* Pierce with lance; (Surg.) prick or open with lancet. **3.** **~'lĕt** (-sl-) *n.*, small marine animal burrowing in sand; **lă'ncĕolate** *a.*, shaped like spearhead, tapering to each end; **la'ncer** (-ah'-) *n.*, soldier of cavalry regiment orig. armed with lances, (in *pl.*) (music for) kind of quadrille; **la'ncĕt** (-ah'-) *n.*, surgical instrument with point and two edges for small incisions, narrow arch or window with pointed head. [F f. L]

**Lancs.** *abbr.* Lancashire.

**lănd. 1.** *n.* Solid part of earth's surface (*travel by land*; *reach land after a sea voyage*; LIE² *of the land*; **how the ~ lies,** fig., what is the state of affairs); ground, soil, expanse of country; this as basis for agriculture, building, etc.; landed property, (in *pl.*) estates; country, nation, State. **2.** *v.t. & i.* Set or go ashore; bring (aircraft), come down, to ground or surface of water; bring to, (also **~**

up) reach or find oneself in, a certain place; deal (person blow etc.); present (with problem etc.); bring (fish) to land, (fig.) win (prize, appointment, etc.). **3.** ~-**agent**, ‖steward of estate, dealer in estates; ~-**breeze** (blowing seaward from land); ~-**crab** (living on land but breeding in sea); ~**fall**, approach to land esp. for first time on sea or air voyage; ~ **force(s)** (military, not naval or air); ‖~-**girl**, woman doing farmwork, esp. in wartime; ~'**lady**, woman keeping inn, boarding-house, or lodgings, or having tenants; ~-**line**, means of telegraphic communication over land; ~'**locked**, (almost) enclosed by land; ~'**lord**, keeper of inn, boarding-house, or lodgings, person who has tenants; ~'**lubber**, (Naut.) person unfamiliar with sea and ships; ~'**mark**, boundary-mark of estate etc., conspicuous object in district, event etc. marking stage in history; ~ **mass**, large area of land; ~-**mine**, explosive mine laid in or on ground; ~ **on** one's **feet**, get well out of difficulty; ~'**owner**, owner of land; ~'**rail**, corncrake; L~'s **End**, western point of Cornwall; ~'**slide**, landslip, (fig.) overwhelming majority for one side in election etc.; ~'**slip**, sliding down of mass of land on cliff or mountain; ~'**sman**, non-sailor; ~-**tax** (assessed on landed property); ~-**wind** (blowing seaward from land). **4.** ~'**ĕd** a., possessing land, consisting of land; ~'**ĭng** n., (esp.) place for disembarking (also ~**ing-place**), platform between flights of stairs, passage leading to rooms from top of flight of stairs; ~**ing-craft**, naval craft for putting ashore troops and equipment; ~**ing-gear**, undercarriage; ~**ing-net** (for landing large fish after hooking it); ~**ing-stage**, platform for disembarking passengers and goods; ~**ing-strip**, airstrip; ~'**lĕss** a., holding no land; ~'**ward** a., adv., & n.; ~'**wards** (-z) adv. [E]

**lă'ndau** n. Four-wheeled horse-drawn carriage with top whose front and back can be separately raised and lowered. [place]

**lă'ndĕd, lă'ndĭng, lă'ndlĕss.** See LAND.

**lă'ndscăpe** (or -ns-). **1.** n. Piece of inland scenery, picture of it, art of painting such pictures; ~ **garden-**ing, laying-out of grounds to imitate natural scenery. **2.** v.t. & i. Improve by, engage in, landscape gardening etc. [Du. (LAND, -SHIP)]

**lāne** n. Narrow road usu. between hedges; narrow usu. winding street; passage between rows of people; strip of road for one line of traffic; strip of track or water for competitor in race; regular course followed by ship or aircraft. [E]

**lă'nguage** (-nggw-) n. Words and the way of using them, faculty of speech; form of this prevalent in one or more countries, or in a profession etc.; method or style of expression; system of symbols and rules for computer programs; (**bad**) ~, oaths and abusive talk; **finger** ~, talk by conventional signs with fingers; **speak the same** ~, have similar outlook and style; STRONG language; ~ **laboratory**, room with tape-recorders etc. for learning foreign languages. [F f. L lingua tongue]

**lă'nguĭ|d** (-nggw-) a. Inert, lacking vigour or disposition to exert oneself; apathetic; (of trade, etc.) slow-moving; ~**sh** v.i., grow or be feeble, lose intensity, live under enfeebling or depressing conditions, droop, pine (for), adopt languid look; **lă'nguor** (-ngger) n., languid state, soft or tender mood or effect, oppressive stillness of air; **lă'nguorous** (-ngger-) a. [F or L (langueo languish)]

**langur'** (-nggoor') n. Asian long-tailed monkey. [Hindi]

**lănk** a. Lean and tall; (of grass, hair, etc.) long and limp; ~'**ў** a. (~ily, ~iness), ungracefully lean and tall or long (of a person, limb, etc.). [E]

**lă'nolĭn** n. Fat from sheep-wool used in ointments. [G, f. L lana wool, OIL]

**lă'ntern** n. (Lamp with) transparent case protecting flame of candle etc.; = MAGIC lantern; light-chamber of lighthouse; erection on top of dome or room, with glazed sides; ~ **jaws**, long thin jaws; ~-**slide** (for projection by magic lantern etc.). [F f. L f. Gk lamptēr torch]

**lă'nyard** n. (Naut.) Short cord attached to something to enable it to be handled or secured; cord hanging round neck or looped round shoulder, to which knife, whistle, etc., may be attached. [F *laniere*, assim. to YARD¹]

**Lāodĭcē'an** *n.* & *a.* (Person) lacking zeal esp. in religion or politics. [*Laodicea*, place (Rev. 3: 16)]

**Lao'tian** (low'sh-, lahō'sh-) *a.* & *n.* (Native, language) of Laos. [place]

**lăp¹. 1.** *v.i.* & *t.* (-**pp**-). Drink by scooping with the tongue (esp. of dogs and cats); drink (liquid, or fig.) greedily (usu. *up*, *down*); (of waves etc.) make lapping sound. **2.** *n.* Liquid food; (sl.) weak beverage; single act or amount of lapping; sound of wavelets. [E]

**lăp². 1.** *n.* Hanging part of garment etc.; front of skirt held up as receptacle; front of sitting person's body from waist to knees, with dress, as place for holding child or object (lit. or fig.; *in the lap of luxury*; *in the lap of the* GODS; **in** or **on** person's ~, as his responsibility); amount of overlap; single turn of thread etc. round reel etc.; one circuit of race-track etc. (~ **of honour**, ceremonial circuit by winner(s)); (fig.) section of journey etc. (*last lap*). **2.** *v.t.* & *i.* (-**pp**-). Coil, fold, wrap, (garment etc. *about*, *round*, advs. or preps.); enfold (*in* wraps); enfold caressingly; cause to overlap; lead (competitor in race) by one or more laps; project *over* (thing). **3.** ~-**dog**, small pet dog; *~**robe**, travelling-rug; **lapě'l** *n.*, part of coat-front folded back. [E]

**lă'pĭdarў. 1.** *a.* Concerned with stones; engraved on stone (*lapidary inscriptions*; ~ **style**, suitable for such inscriptions). **2.** *n.* Cutter, polisher, or engraver, of gems. **3. lăpĭs lă'zūlĭ** *n.*, a bright blue gem mineral, colour, and pigment. (*lapis lapid-* stone); *lazuli* as AZURE]

**Lăpp** *n.* Member of a N. Scandinavian Mongol race; its language; (attrib.) Lappish; **Lă'plănder** *n.*, inhabitant of Lapland; ~'**ĭsh**, (*a.*) of the Lapps or their language, (*n.*) the Lapp language. [Sw.]

**lă'ppĕt** *n.* Flap or fold of garment etc. or flesh; kind of large moth with side-lobed caterpillars. [LAP²]

**lăpse. 1.** *n.* Slip of memory etc., slight mistake; weak or careless deviation from what is right; passage *of* time. **2.** *v.i.* Fail to maintain position or state for want of effort or vigour; fall *back* (*into* inferior or previous or ordinary state); (of

right etc.) become void, revert *to* other person, by non-fulfilment, absence of heirs, etc., (in *p.p.*) that has lapsed. **3. lapsus calami, linguae,** (lăpsus kǎ'lamĭ, lĭnggwē) *ns.*, slip of the pen, of the tongue. [L *lapsus* (*labor laps-* slip); *calamus* reed, *lingua* tongue]

**lă'pwĭng** *n.* Pewit. [E (LEAP, WINK; f. mode of flight)]

**lăr'board** (-bèrd) *n.* & *a.* (Naut.; arch. or U.S.) = PORT⁴. [orig. *ladboard*, perh. 'side on which cargo was taken in' (LADE)]

**lăr'cen/ў** *n.* (Law). Theft of personal property; ~**ous** *a.* [AF f. L *latrocinium* (*latro* robber f. Gk)]

**lärch** *n.* Bright-foliaged deciduous coniferous tree; its wood. [G *larche* f. L *larix*]

**lärd. 1.** *n.* Pig fat prepared for use in cooking etc. **2.** *v.t.* Insert strips of bacon in (meat etc.) before cooking; garnish (talk etc.) *with* strange terms etc.; ~'**er** *n.*, room or cupboard for meat etc.; ~'**ў** *a.*; ~**y-cake** (made with lard, currants, etc.). [F = bacon, f. L *lardum*]

**lärge. 1.** *a.* Of considerable or relatively great magnitude (~ **of limb**, with large limbs); doing thing on a large scale (*large farmers*); of the larger kind (*large intestine*); of wide range, comprehensive; ~-**handed**, generous; ~-**hearted**, kindly; ~-**scale**, made or occurring on large scale or in large amounts. **2.** *n.* At ~, at liberty, with all details, as a body or whole, without specific aim; **in** ~, on a large scale. **3.** ~'**lў** (-jlĭ) *adv.*, (esp.) to a great or preponderating extent (*is largely due to*); **lärgě'ss(e)** *n.*, money or gifts freely given esp. on occasion of rejoicing. [F f. L *largus* copious]

**lär'gō** *adv.*, *a.*, & *n.* (*pl.* ~**s**). (Mus.) (Movement) in slow time with broad dignified treatment; **lärghě'ttō** (-g-) *adv.*, *a.*, & *n.* (*pl.* ~**s**), (movement) in fairly slow time. [It., = broad]

**lă'rĭat** *n.* Tethering-rope; lasso. [Sp. *la reata*]

**lärk¹** *n.* Kind of small bird, esp. the skylark (**rise with the** ~, get up early); ~'**spur**, plant with spur-shaped calyx. [E]

**lärk². (colloq.) 1.** *n.* Frolic, spree, amusing incident (**what a** ~!, how amusing!); ‖type of activity etc.;

~'ỹ *a.* (~**iness**), given to larks. **2.**
*v.i.* Indulge in a lark. [orig. uncert.]

**larn** *v.t. & i.* Joc. or vulg. var. of
LEARN; (colloq.) teach (*that'll larn
you*). [dial.]

**lă′rrĭkĭn** *n.* (Austral.) Young
street rowdy, hooligan. [perh. *Larry*
= *Lawrence*]

**lar′v|a** *n.* (*pl.* ~**ae**). Insect in the
stage between egg and pupa (e.g.
caterpillar); ~**al** *a.* [L, = ghost]

**lă′rўn|x** *n.* Cavity in throat holding
vocal cords; **larў′ngėal** (-nj-) *a.*;
~**gī′tĭs** (-nj-) *n.*; **larў′ngoscōpe**
(-ngg-) *n.*, mirror instrument for
inspecting larynx; ~**gŏ′tomў** (-ngg-)
*n.*, making of incision into larynx.
[L f. Gk]

**Lă′scar** *n.* E. Indian seaman. [ult.
Urdu *laškar* army, camp]

**lasci′vĭous** *a.* Lustful; inciting to
lust. [L]

**lā′ser** (-z-) *n.* Device giving strong
beam of radiation in one direction.
[*l*ight *a*mplification by *s*timulated
*e*mission of *r*adiation]

**lăsh. 1.** *v.i. & t.* Make sudden
violent movement of limb or tail;
pour or rush with great force; strike
violently *at* or *against*; hit or kick out,
break *out* into excess or angry words;
beat with thong etc.; move suddenly
and violently; (of rain etc.) beat
upon; castigate in words; urge as
with lash (~ *oneself* **into a fury**,
work up a rage); fasten (*down, together*, etc.) with cord or twine; ~**-up**
*a. & n.*, makeshift, improvised
(structure), (sl.) muddle or failure.
**2.** *n.* Stroke with thong etc., lit. or
fig.; flexible part of whip; eyelash.
**3.** ~**′ing** *n.*, (esp., in *pl.*, sl.) plenty
(*of*). [imit.]

**lăss** *n.* Girl (esp. Sc., N. Engl., or
poet.); ~**′ie** *n.*, lass (in affectionate
etc. use). [N]

**lă′ssĭtūde** *n.* Languor, disinclina-
tion to exert or interest oneself. [F or
L (*lassus* weary)]

**lă′ssō** (*or* lasōō′). **1.** *n.* (*pl.* ~**s**,
~**es**). Noosed rope used for catching
cattle. **2.** *v.t.* Catch with lasso. [Sp.
*lazo* (LACE)]

**last¹** (-ah-) *n.* Shoemaker's model
for shaping shoe etc. on (**stick to
one's** ~, not meddle with what one
does not understand). [E]

**last²** (-ah-) *n.* Commercial measure
of weight, capacity, or quantity,
varying with place and goods. [E]

**last³** (-ah-) *a., adv., & n.* **1.** *a.* After

all others, coming at or belonging to
the end, of lowest rank or estimation,
(**the** ~ **two**, last and last but one;
~ **but one, second** ~, next to last;
~ **but not least**, last to occur or be
mentioned but not least in importance); most recent, next before
specified time, (*last Christmas, Tuesday*; ~ **week** etc., (during) the week
etc. most recently past); only remaining (*last chance*); least likely,
willing, etc., to (*that is the last thing
to try*); L~ **Day**, Judgement Day;
*last* DITCH, HOME; **on** one's, **its**, ~
**legs**, near death or end of usefulness
etc.; ~ **minute, moment**, time
just before decisive event; ~ **name**,
surname; *last* OFFICES, QUARTER,
SLEEP, STRAW; L~ **Supper** (of
Christ and disciples on eve of
Crucifixion); ~ **thing**, (colloq. *adv.*)
as final act; ~ **word**, conclusive or
definitive or final statement, latest
fashion; ~ **words**, person's dying
words. **2.** *adv.* After all others (esp. in
comb.: *last-mentioned*); on the last
occasion before the present (*when did
you last see him?*); lastly. **3.** *n.* (*pl.*
same). Last-mentioned person or
thing; most recent letter etc.; last
day or moments, death (*the* or *his* etc.
*last*); last mention or sight (*shall never
hear the last of it, see the last of him*);
last performance of certain acts
(*breathe, look,* one's *last*); **at (long)**
~, in the end, after much delay.
[E, = *latest*]

**last⁴** (-ah-) *v.i. & t.* Remain
unexhausted or adequate or alive
for specified or long time (*this will
last me a month*); ~ **out**, not come to
an end before; ~**′ing** *a.*, permanent
(*no lasting benefit*), durable. [E]

**la′stlў** (-ah′-) *adv.* (In enumera-
tions) finally, in the last place.
[LAST³]

**lat.** *abbr.* latitude.

**lătch. 1.** *n.* Bar with catch and
lever as fastening of gate etc. (**on
the** ~, fastened by latch only);
small spring-lock preventing door
from being opened from outside
without key after being shut. **2.** *v.t.
& i.* Fasten with latch; ~ **on to**,
(colloq.) attach oneself to, understand. **3.** ~**′key**, key of outer door. [E]

**lāte** *a., adv., & n.* **1.** *a.* (~**r**,
LATTER; ~**st**, LAST³). (Doing or
done) after the due or usual time,
backward in flowering, ripening,
etc., far on in day or night or time

or period or development, (*was late for dinner*; *it is too late to go*; *late riser, rising*; *a few late roses*; *it is getting late*; *late* LATIN; *on Monday at* ~st, then if not before); no longer alive or having specified status (*my late husband*); of recent date (**of** ~ **years**, during the last few years). **2.** *adv.* (~r; ~st, LAST³). After the due or usual time, far on in time, at or till late hour, at late stage of development, (*better late than never*; *happened later on*; *sat up late*; *traces remained as late as 1900*); formerly but not now (*late of Oxford*); ~ **in the day**, (colloq.) at (unreasonably) late stage. **3.** ~ **Of** ~, recently. [E]

**latee'n** *a.* ~ **sail**, triangular sail on long yard at angle of 45° to mast; ~ **ship** (so rigged). [F (*voile*) *latine*, = Latin (sail)]

**lā'tely** (-tlĭ) *adv.* Not long ago, in recent times. [LATE]

**lā'ten|t** *a.* Concealed, dormant, existing but not developed or manifest, (*latent* HEAT); ~**cў** *n.* [L (*lateo* be hidden)]

**lă'teral. 1.** *a.* (~ly). Of, at, towards, from, the side(s), side-; sprung from brother or sister of person in direct line of descent; ~ **thinking**, seeking to solve problems by apparently illogical methods. **2.** *n.* Lateral shoot or branch. [L (*latus later-* side)]

**lā'tĕx** *n.* (*pl.* ~**es**, **la'tices** *pr.* -ĭsēz). Milky fluid of (esp. rubber) plant; synthetic substance like this. [L, = liquid]

**lath** (-ah-) *n.* (*pl. pr.* -dhz). Thin narrow strip of wood (~ **and plaster**, materials for facing inside of room-wall; **as thin as a** ~, of persons). [E]

**lāthe** (-dh) *n.* Rotating machine used in turnery and pottery for keeping object in circular motion while operated on. [orig. uncert.]

**lă'ther** (-dh-; *or* -ah'-). **1.** *n.* Froth of soap etc. and water; frothy sweat of horse; (fig.) state of agitation. **2.** *v.i. & t.* (Of soap) form lather; cover (chin etc. for shaving) with lather; thrash. [E]

**Lă'tĭn. 1.** *n.* Language of ancient Rome; **classical** ~ (75 B.C.–A.D. 200); **late** ~ (200–600); **medieval** ~ (600–1500); **modern** ~ (since 1500); **dog** ~ (incorrect or mongrel); **low** ~ (medieval, or late and medieval); **thieves'** ~, secret cant of

thieves. **2.** *a.* Of or in Latin; (of peoples) inheriting Roman customs etc., speaking a language based on Latin; of the Roman Catholic Church; ~ **America**, parts of Central & S. America where Sp. or Port. is main language; ~ **Church**, Western Church; ~ **cross** (with lowest arm longer than others); ~ **Quarter**, educational centre of Paris, with unconventional mode of life. **3.** ~**āte** *a.*, having character of Latin; ~**ĭst** *n.*, person familiar with Latin; ~**īze** *v.t. & i.*, put into Latin form; ~**izā'tion** *n.* [F or L (*Latium* district about Rome)]

**lă'tĭtūde** *n.* Freedom from restriction in action or opinion; (Geog.) angular distance on meridian, place's angular distance N. or S. of equator, (usu. in *pl.*) regions with reference to temperature (**high** ~s, near poles; **low** ~s, near equator); (Astron.) body's or point's angular distance esp. from ecliptic; **lătĭtūdĭnā'r'ĭan** *a. & n.*, (person) allowing latitude esp. in religion. [L (*latus* broad)]

**latri'ne** (-ēn) *n.* Place for urination and defecation, esp. in camp etc. [F f. L *latrina* (*lavo* wash)]

**lă'tter** *a.* Recent (esp. **in these** ~ **days**, opp. *in former times*); following another (*the latter part of the year*); mentioned later of the two or last of three or more; **the** ~, abs., the latter thing or person, opp. *the former*; ~ **day**, Judgement Day; ~**-day**, modern, newfangled; *L*~**-day Saints**, Mormons; ~ **end**, (esp.) death; ~**lў** *adv.*, in the later part of life or a period, of late. [E, = *later*]

**lă'ttĭce** *n.* Structure of laths or bars crossing each other with interstices as screen etc.; regular arrangement of atoms or molecules; ~ **window** (with small panes set in lead). [F *lattis* (*latte* LATH)]

**laud. 1.** *n.* Praise, song of praise (poet.); (Eccl., in *pl.*) first daily service. **2.** *v.t.* Praise, extol; ~**'able** *a.* (-bly), commendable; ~**abi'lĭtў** *n.*; ~**ā'tion** *n.*, praising, a panegyric; ~**'atorў** *a.* (-ily, -iness). [F f. L (*laus laud-*)]

**lau'danum** (-dn-; *or* lŏ'-) *n.* Tincture of opium. [L]

**laugh** (lahf). **1.** *v.i. & t.* Make the sounds and movements usual in expressing lively amusement, sense of the ludicrous, exultation, or scorn, (**don't make me** ~, colloq., that is ridiculous; **he ~s best who ~s last**, warning against premature exultation); utter with a laugh; get (person) *out of* habit etc. by ridicule. **2.** *n.* Sound, act, manner, of laughing; (colloq.) comical thing (*that's a laugh*). **3.** ~ **at**, ridicule; ~ **in** or **up** one's **sleeve** (covertly); ~ **off**, get rid of (embarrassment etc.) with a jest; ~ **out of court**, deprive of a hearing by ridicule; ~ **over**, discuss with laughter; ~**'able** *a.* (-bly), causing laughter, ludicrous; *laughing* JACK*ass*; ~**'ing** *n.* (no ~ing matter, serious thing; ~**ing-gas**, nitrous oxide as anaesthetic, with exhilarating effect when inhaled; ~**ing-stock**, person or thing generally ridiculed); ~**'ter** *n.*, laughing. [E]

**launch**¹ (or -ah-). **1.** *v.t. & i.* Hurl, discharge, send forth, (missile, blow, censure, threat, decree); burst (usu. *out*) *into* expense, strong language, etc.; start (person, enterprise, rocket) on a course, go *forth* or *out* on an enterprise; set (vessel) afloat; ~**'er** *n.*, (esp.) structure for rocket during launching. **2.** *n.* Launching of a ship, rocket, etc. [AN *launcher* (LANCE)]

**launch**² (or -ah-). *n.* Man-of-war's largest boat; motor-driven (pleasure-)boat on rivers etc. [Sp. *lancha*]

**lau'nd|er** *v.t. & i.* Wash, starch, iron, etc., (linen or other clothes); ~**(e)rĕ'tte** *n.*, establishment with automatic washing-machines for public use; ~**rĕss** *n.*, woman who launders; ~**rў** *n.*, clothes-washing place, batch of clothes sent to or from this. [F (LAVE)]

**laur'eate** (or lŏ'r-). **1.** *a.* Wreathed with laurel (Poet L~, poet receiving stipend as writer of poems for State occasions). **2.** *n.* Poet Laureate; ~**ship** (-tsh-) *n.* [L (foll.)]

**lau'rel** (lŏ'-). *n.* Kind of plant with dark green glossy leaves; (in *sing.* or *pl.*) wreath of bay-leaves as emblem of victory or poetic merit (*reap, win, laurels* or *the laurel*; *rest on* one's ~*s*, not seek further victories; **look to** one's ~**s**, take care not to lose preeminence); ~**led** (lŏ'reld) *a.*, wreathed with laurel; **laurusti'nus** (lŏ-) *n.*, an evergreen winter-flowering shrub. [F f. Prov. f. L *laurus* bay]

**lăv** *n.* (colloq.) Lavatory. [abbr.]

**la'va** (lah'-) *n.* Matter flowing from volcano and solidifying as it cools. [It. f. L *lavo* wash]

**lă'vatorў** *n.* (Room or building or compartment with) receptacle for urine and (usu.) faeces, usu. with means of disposal; ~ **paper**, = TOILET-*paper*. [L (prec.)]

**lāve** *v.t.* (literary). Wash, bathe; (of sea, stream) wash against, flow along. [F f. L *lavo* wash]

**lă'vĕnder** *n.* A fragrant-flowered shrub, its flowers and stalks used to perfume linen, colour of its flower (a pale blue tinged with red); ~**-water**, a scent. [AF f. L *lavandula*]

**lā'ver**¹ *n.* (Bibl.) large brazen vessel for priests' ablutions; (arch.) the font, baptism. [F f. L (LAVE)]

**lā'ver**² *n.* Edible seaweed. [L]

**lă'vĭsh. 1.** *a.* Giving or producing without stint, profuse or prodigal (*of* money etc., *in* giving etc.); very or over abundant. **2.** *v.t.* Bestow or spend (money, effort, blood, praise) lavishly. [F *lavasse* deluge (LAVE)]

**law** *n.* Rule or body of rules enacted or customary in a community and recognized as enjoining or prohibiting certain action(s), controlling influence of this, such rules as a social system or subject of study, branch of this subject, (*forbidden by law*, *under British law*; *the laws of cricket*, *of libel*; **at**, **in**, ~, according to the laws; whence SON-*in-law* etc., orig. w. ref. to lawful wedlock; **be a ~ unto** oneself, do what one feels is right, disregard custom; **lay down the ~**, be dogmatic; *necessity knows no ~*, justifies anything); (in *pl.*) jurisprudence (*doctor of laws*); **the** legal profession; judicial remedy, lawcourts providing it, (*go to law*; **have** or **take the ~ of**, sue; **take the ~ into** one's **own hands**, redress grievance by force); God's commandments as expressed in Bible or implanted in man's mind, precepts of the Pentateuch; ~ (**of nature**), statement of invariable sequence between specified conditions and phenomena (*Newton's laws of motion*); regularity in nature; ~**-abiding**, obedient to the laws; ~**'court**, COURT of law; ~**'giver**, one who makes (esp. code of) laws; ‖**Law Lord**, member of House of Lords qualified to perform its legal work; ~**'maker**, legislator; \*~**'man**, police officer, sheriff, etc.; ~ **officer**, legal functionary esp. ‖Attorney-General etc.; ~ (**of Moses**), the Pentateuch; ~ **of nations**,

INTERNATIONAL law; ~ **of nature** (see above); ~'**suit**, prosecution of claim in lawcourt; ~'**ful** a. (-lly), permitted or appointed or qualified or recognized by law, not illegal or (of child) illegitimate; ~'**less** a., having no (effective) laws, regardless of or disobedient to laws, unbridled. [E f. N, = thing laid down]

**lawn**[1] n. Fine linen or cotton used esp. for bishops' sleeves. [*Laon*, place]

**lawn**[2] n. Piece of turf kept mown and smooth in garden etc.; ~-**mower**, lawn-mowing machine; ||~ **sand**, mixture of sand with weed-killer and fertilizer; *lawn* TENNIS. [*laund* glade f. F f. Celt.]

**law'yer** (*or* loi'er) n. Person pursuing law as a profession, esp. ||solicitor; expert at law (*good, no*, etc., *lawyer*). [LAW]

**lax** a. Negligent, not strict, vague; ~'**ative** a. & n., (medicine) tending to cause evacuation of the bowels; ~'**ity** n. [L *laxus* loose]

**lay**[1]. See LIE[2].

**lay**[2] n. Minstrel's song, ballad. [F]

**lay**[3] a. Non-clerical, (of or done by persons) not in holy orders; non-professional, (of or done by persons) not in the class of those skilled in law or medicine or the like; ~ **brother, sister**, member of religious order excused duties other than manual labour; ~'**man**, person not in holy orders or without professional or special knowledge; ~ **reader**, layman licensed to conduct some religious services (see *lay brother*); **lā'ic** a. (-ically), non-clerical, secular; **lā'icīze** v.t. [F f. L f. Gk (*laos* people)]

**lay**[4]. **1.** v.t. & i. (**laid**). Deposit on a surface esp. horizontally or in proper or specified place, put or bring into specified position or state, make by laying, (*lay him here, on the floor, on his back*; *lay foundation, floor*; *scene is laid in London*); cause to subside or lie flat (*lay the dust*; *storm has laid the corn*); (of hen) produce (egg, or abs.); put down as wager, stake; (sl.) copulate with (woman); make ready (trap, plan); aim (large gun) for direction; prepare table for (meal); put fuel ready to light (fire); impute (fault) *to* person's CHARGE or *door*; impose (penalty, obligation, burden, blame) (*up*)*on*; coat, strew, (surface) *with* material; (Naut. or vulg.) = LIE[2] (||~'**about**, habitual loafer or tramp); ~ **about** one, hit out on all sides; ~ **a charge**, make accusation; ~ **aside**, put away, cease to use or practise or think of, abandon, save for future needs; *lay at the* DOOR *of*; ~ **back**, cause to slope back from vertical; ~ **bare**, denude, reveal; ~ (facts etc.) **before** person, exhibit or submit for consideration; ~ **by**, lay aside; ~**by** n. (pl. -*bys*), ||extra strip beside road where vehicles can stop without obstructing other traffic; ~ **claim to**, claim as one's own; ~ **down**, put on ground, relinquish (office), pay or wager (money), sacrifice (one's life), (begin to) build (ship), formulate (rule), store (wine) in cellar; ~ **down** one's **arms**, surrender; ~ one's **hand(s) on**, be able to find; ~ **hands on**, seize, attack, (of bishop) confirm; *lay* HEADS *together*; ~ **hold of**, seize, grasp; ~ **in**, provide oneself with stock of; ~ **into**, (sl.) belabour; ~ **low**, overthrow, humble; ~ **off**, discharge (temporarily) owing to shortage of work, (colloq.) desist; ~ **on**, impose (tax etc.), inflict (blows), apply coat of (paint; ~ *it on thick* or *with a trowel*, sl., exaggerate, be lavish in flattery), provide supply of (gas, water, refreshments, transport, etc.); ~ **open**, reveal, break skin of; ~ **out**, spread, expose to view, prepare (body) for burial, (colloq.) put (person) temporarily out of action, expend (money), dispose (grounds etc.) according to a plan, (*refl.*) take pains *to* do; ~'**out** n., disposing or arrangement of ground, house, printed matter, etc., drawing showing this; ~ **the table**, prepare it for meal; ~ **to rest** or **sleep**, (fig.) bury; ~ **under contribution**, compel to contribute; ~ **under obligation**, oblige; ~ **up**, store, save (money); **laid** a. (**laid paper**, with ribbed surface owing to wires used in making; **laid up**, confined to bed or house). **2.** n. Way, position, or direction in which something lies; (sl.) line of business, (woman partner in) copulation; **in ~**, (of hen) in condition to lay eggs; ~'**shaft**, secondary or intermediate transmission-shaft in machine. [E]

**lay'er. 1.** n. Person etc. that lays; a thickness of matter, esp. one of several, spread over a surface; a shoot fastened down to take root

while attached to the parent plant.
2. *v.t.* Propagate (plant) as layer.

**layĕ′tte** *n.* Clothes etc. needed for
new-born child. [F f. Du.]

**lay′ figure** (-ger) *n.* Jointed figure
used by artists for arranging draperies
on etc.; unreal character in novel
etc., person lacking individuality.
[Du. (*led* joint)]

**lā′zў** *a.* (**-ily, -iness**). Averse to
work, indolent; of or inducing
indolence; **~-bones,** lazy person; **~
Susan,** revolving food-stand for
table; **~-tongs,** arrangement of
zigzag levers for picking up distant
objects; **lāze,** (*v.i.,* colloq.) indulge
in laziness, (*n.,* colloq.) spell of
lazing. [perh. f. LG]

**lb.** *abbr.* pound(s) weight. [L *libra*]
**l.b.** *abbr.* leg-bye.
**l.b.w.** *abbr.* leg before wicket.
**l.c.** *abbr.* *loco citato*; lower case.
**‖L.C.J.** *abbr.* Lord Chief Justice.
**L.C.M.** *abbr.* least common multiple.
**L/Cpl.** *abbr.* Lance-Corporal.
**Ld.** *abbr.* Lord.

**lea** *n.* (poet.) Piece of meadow or
pasture or arable land. [E]

**L.E.A.** *abbr.* Local Education
Authority.

**leach** *v.t.* Make (liquid) percolate
through some material, subject
(bark, ore, ash, soil) to this action,
purge *away* or *out* thus. [E]

**lead¹. 1.** *v.t.* & *i.* (led). Cause to
go with one, help to go esp. by
going in front or alongside or by
contact or by taking person's hand
or animal's halter etc.; guide by
persuasion or example or argument
(*to do, to* conclusions), direct the
actions or opinions of; (of road etc.)
bring (person, or usu. abs.) (*in*)*to*
place (*all roads lead to Rome*); make
(rope, water) go *through* pulley,
channel; pass, go through, (life etc.
of specified kind); have first place in
(*lead the dance, the world*), go first, be
first in race or game; play (card, or
abs.) as first player in trick, play one
of (suit) thus; **~** person **a** (*dog's*)
**life,** harass him constantly; **~ by
the hand,** guide like a child; **~ by
the nose,** cajole into obedience;
**~-in,** introductory matter; **~ off,**
begin (action, or abs.); **~ on,** (esp.)
entice into going farther than was
intended; **~ to,** (fig.) have as result;
**~** person **to suppose** etc., deceive
him into thinking *that*; **~ up the**

**garden** (**path**), (colloq.) entice,
mislead; **~ up to,** form preparation
for, serve to introduce, direct conversation towards. **2.** *n.* Guidance
given by going in front, example,
(*give a lead to*); leader's place (*is in the
lead*; *has taken the lead*); amount by
which competitor is ahead of others;
(Electr.) conductor conveying current
to place of use; thong etc. for leading
or controlling a dog; (Cards) act
or right of playing first, card so
played; (Theatr.) (player of) chief
part; **~ story,** news item made most
prominent. **3.** **~′er** *n.,* (esp.) person
followed by others, front horse,
‖leading article, leading performer
in orchestra, quartet, etc., shoot at
apex of stem or main branch; **L~er
of the House,** member of Government with official initiative in
business; **~′ership** *n.;* **~′ing¹** *a.,*
(esp.) chief, most important; **~ing
aircraftman** etc. (ranking just
below N.C.O.); **‖~ing article,**
editorial expression of opinion shown
prominently in newspaper; **~ing
case** (serving as precedent for
deciding others); **~ing edge,** foremost edge of aircraft's wing; **~ing
lady, man,** (taking chief part in
play); **~ing light,** prominent influential person; **~ing note,** seventh
note of diatonic scale; **~ing question** (prompting desired answer);
**~′ing²** *n.,* (esp.) guidance (**in ~ing-
-strings,** in state of pupillage). [E]

**lead²** (lĕd). **1.** *n.* A heavy soft
grey easily melted metal (**red,
white, ~,** compounds of lead used
as pigments); = BLACKlead; stick of
graphite in or for pencil; bullet(s);
lump of lead used in sounding water
(‖swing the **~,** sl., malinger); (in
*pl.*) strips of lead covering roof,
piece of lead-covered roof, lead
frames holding glass of lattice etc.;
(Print.) metal strip to give space
between lines; (*attrib.*) made of lead;
**~ pencil** (of graphite enclosed in
wood); **~-poisoning** (by entry of
lead into the body); *lead* SHOT¹. **2.** *v.t.*
Cover, weight, frame, space, with
lead(s); **~′ing³** *n.* **3.** **~′en** *a.,* (as) of
lead, heavy, inert, lead-coloured. [E]

**leaf. 1.** *n.* (*pl.* -ves *pr.* -vz). Broad
flat usu. green part of plant often on
a stem; (collect.) leaves; state of
having leaves out (*is in leaf*); single
thickness of folded paper, esp. in
book with each side a page (*take a*

*leaf out of* person's BOOK; TURN *over a new leaf*); very thin sheet of metal etc.; hinged flap of door or shutter or table; extra section that can be added to table; ~**insect** (with wings like plant-leaf); ~**mould,** soil chiefly of decaying leaves; ~'**age** n., leaves of plants; ~'**lĕt** n., division of compound leaf, young leaf, paper single or folded but not stitched and containing facts etc. esp. for free distribution; ~'**ÿ** a. (~**ily,** ~**iness**). 2. *v.i.* Put forth leaves; ~ **through,** turn over pages of (book etc.). [E]

**league**[1] (-g) n. (arch.) Varying measure of travelling-distance, usu. about 3 miles. [L f. Celt.]

**league**[2] (-g). 1. n. Agreement for mutual help, parties to it, (**in ~ with,** allied with); group of sports clubs who contend for championship; class of contestants. 2. *v.t. & i.* Join in league. [F or It. f. L *ligo* bind]

**leak.** 1. n. Hole through which liquid etc. makes its way wrongly in or out; liquid etc.; (escape of) electric charge from imperfectly insulated conductor; disclosure of secret information. 2. *v.i. & t.* Pass, let liquid etc. pass, out or in through leak; disclose (secret); ~ (**out**), become known. 3. ~'**age** n., action or result of leaking; ~'**ÿ** a. (~**ily,** ~**iness**), having leak(s). [LDu.]

**lean**[1]. 1. a. (~**ness** *pr.* -n-n-). (Of person or animal) having no superfluous fat; (of meat) consisting chiefly of muscular tissue, not fat; meagre; ~ **years,** period of scarcity. 2. n. Lean part of meat. [E]

**lean**[2]. 1. *v.i. & t.* (~**ed** *pr.* lēnd, lĕnt, ‖~**t** *pr.* lĕnt). Take or be in or put in sloping position, incline from the perpendicular, (lean back, forward, out, over, etc.; *leaning tower*; ~ **against, on, upon,** for support; ~ **on** person, sl., put pressure on him in order to force him to be co-operative; *lean over BACKWARDS*; ~ (**up**)**on,** fig., rely, depend, on); be inclined or partial, have tendency, *to, towards.* 2. n. Deviation from perpendicular, inclination, (*has a decided lean to the right*). 3. ~'**ing** n., (esp.) tendency (*to* conduct etc.); ~**-to,** building with roof resting against larger building or wall. [E]

**leap** *v.i. & t.* (~**ed** *pr.* lēpt, lĕpt,

~**t** *pr.* lĕpt), & *n.* = JUMP; **by ~s and bounds,** with startlingly rapid progress; ~**-frog,** (n.) game in which player vaults with parted legs over another bending down, (*v.t. & i.*: -gg-) perform such vault (over), (fig.) overtake alternately; ~ **in the dark,** rash step or enterprise; ~ **year,** with 29 Feb. as intercalary day; ~**-year proposal,** (joc.) proposal of marriage by woman to man, traditionally allowable only in leap year. [E]

**learn** (lẽrn) *v.t. & i.* (~**ed** *pr.* -nd, -nt, ~**t**). Get knowledge of (subject) or skill in (art etc.) by study, experience, or being taught, (*from* study etc., *from* or *of* teacher); commit to memory (esp. ~ **by heart**); receive instruction, be informed (*of*), ascertain, find out, (*that, how,* etc.); (arch., joc., vulg.) teach; ~'**ĕd** a., deeply read, showing or requiring learning (*a learned treatise; the learned professions; my* ~**ed** *friend* etc., another lawyer), concerned with interests of learned persons (*a learned society*); ~**er** n., one who learns, beginner, (~**er-driver,** one who has begun to drive motor vehicle but has not yet passed driving test); ~'**ing** n., (esp.) knowledge got by study. [E]

**lease.** 1. n. Contract by which land or tenement is conveyed for specified time by its owner (the *lessor*) to a tenant (the *lessee*) usu. for rent; **on ~,** subject to such contract; **a new ~ of, \*on, life,** improved prospect of living or of use after repair; ~'**hold**(**er**), (person having) tenure, property held, by lease. 2. *v.t.* Grant or take on lease. [AF *les* (*lesser* let f. L *laxo* loosen)]

**leash.** 1. n. Thong for holding dog(s) (**hold in ~,** fig., control; **straining at the ~,** eager to begin). 2. *v.t.* Put leash on; hold in leash. [F *lesse* (*lesser,* prec.)]

**least** a., n., & adv. 1. a. Smallest, slightest, (**the ~,** esp. after neg., any however small; *least common* DE-NOMINATOR, MULTIPLE); very small (species or variety, e.g. *least tern*). 2. n. Least amount; **at ~,** at all events, even if a wider statement is disputable, at the lowest computation; (**in**) **the ~,** in the smallest degree, at all; ~ **said soonest mended,** discussion will only make things worse; **to say the ~ (of it),**

to put the case moderately. **3.** *adv.* In the least degree. [E, superl. of LESS]

**lea'ther** (lĕ'dh-). **1.** *n.* Skin of animal prepared for use by tanning etc.; article wholly or partly made from this (cloth for polishing, thong esp. for stirrup, sl. cricket-ball or football, in *pl.* leggings, breeches). **2.** *v.t.* Cover with leather; wipe or polish with leather; beat, thrash, (orig. with leather thong). **3.** ~-**back**, largest existing turtle, with flexible shell; ~-**cloth**, strong fabric coated to resemble leather; ~-**jacket**, ‖crane-fly grub with tough skin; **patent** ~ (with fine black varnished surface). **4.** ~**ĕt'te** *n.*, imitation leather; ~**n** *a.*, (arch.) made of leather; ~**ў** *a.* (-ily, -iness), (esp., of meat etc.) tough. [E]

**leave**[1] *n.* Permission (*to do*; **by your** ~, apology, often iron., for taking liberty; *without a 'with your* ~' *or a 'by your* ~', colloq., without even asking permission; **take** ~ **to**, venture or presume to); permission to be absent from duty, period for which this lasts, (*leave of absence*; **on** ~, absent thus); permission to withdraw; **take** (one's) ~ (**of**), bid farewell (to); **take** ~ **of** one's **senses**, go mad; ~-**taking**, a farewell. [E]

**leave**[2] *v.t. & i.* (**left**). Cause to or let remain, depart without taking, have at time of one's death, (*has left a permanent scar, a bad impression on us, his gloves; six from seven leaves one; leaves a wife and three sons*; ~ **much** etc. **to be desired**, be unsatisfactory); bequeath; abstain from consuming or dealing with, (in *pass.*) remain over or **over**, (**left**-**overs**, esp., food not eaten at earlier meal); let remain in specified state (*this* ~s me cool, cold, does not excite me; ~ **it at that**, colloq., abstain from comment or further action); commit or refer *to* another agent (*nothing was left to chance*; ~ **it to me**, let me deal with it); allow (person or thing) *to do* something without interference or assistance (~ **be**, colloq., not interfere with); deposit, entrust, (thing, message), station (person), to be seen to, delivered, etc., or to discharge function in one's absence, (‖**left luggage**, that deposited at railway etc. office for later retrieval); quit,

go away from, depart (*for* destination); cease to reside at or belong to or serve; abandon, forsake, desert, (**left at the post**, beaten from start of race); ~ **alone**, not interfere with; ~ **behind**, go away without, leave as consequence or sign of passage, pass; ~ **go**, (vulg.) let go; ~ **hold of**, cease holding; *leave in the* LURCH[1]; ~ **off**, cease to wear, discontinue (habit, do*ing*, work), (abs.) come to or make an end; ~ **out**, omit; ~ **over**, reserve for later attention; **lea'ving** *n.* (esp., usu. in *pl.*), what someone has left as worthless etc. [E]

**leaved** (-vd) *a.* Having leaves (esp. in *comb.*: *one-leaved table, large-leaved tree*). [LEAF]

**lea'ven** (lĕ'-). **1.** *n.* Substance (esp. yeast) used to make dough ferment and rise, (fig.) pervasive transforming influence, admixture of some quality. **2.** *v.t.* Ferment (dough) with leaven; permeate and transform, modify *with* tempering element. [F f. L (*levo* raise)]

**leaves.** See LEAF.

**Lĕbanĕ'se** (-z) *a. & n.* (Native) of *Lebanon.* [place]

**lebensraum** (lā'benzrowm) *n.* (Hist. or fig.) Territory which the Germans believed was needed for their natural development as a nation. [G, = living-space]

**lĕ'cher** *n.* Fornicator, debauchee; ~**ous** *a.*, lustful; ~**ў** *n.*, lecherous conduct. [F *lecheor* f. Gmc (LICK)]

**lĕ'ctern** *n.* Reading- or singing-desk in church; *similar desk for lecturer etc.; **lĕ'ctionary** *n.*, list of portions of Scripture appointed to be read in churches. [F f. L (*lectrum* f. *lego* read)]

**lĕ'cture. 1.** *n.* Discourse delivered for instruction of class or other audience; admonition, reproof, (**read** person a ~, reprove him). **2.** *v.t. & i.* Deliver lecture(s); admonish, reprimand. **3.** **lĕ'cturer** (-kcher-) *n.* (esp. as university post); ~**ship** (-kchersh-) *n.*, appointment as lecturer. [F or L (prec.)]

**lĕd.** See LEAD[1].

**lĕdge** *n.* Narrow horizontal surface projecting from wall or cliff or other vertical surface. [orig. uncert.]

**lĕ'dger. 1.** *n.* Book in which a firm's debit and credit accounts are kept. **2.** *a.* (Mus.) = LEGER. [Du.]

**lee** *n.* Shelter given by neighbouring

object (*under the lee of*); ~ **(side),** sheltered side, side away from wind, (opp. *windward, weather side*); ~ **shore,** shore to leeward of ship; ~**way,** lateral drift of ship to leeward of desired course, (fig.) allowable deviation (*make up ~way*, fig., struggle out of bad position, recover lost time etc.); ~**ward** (or, esp. Naut., lōō′erd), (a. & adv.) on, towards, the sheltered side, (n.) this direction. [E]

**leech**[1] *n.* (arch.) Physician. [E]

**leech**[2] *n.* Blood-sucking worm formerly used medicinally for bleeding (**sticks like a ~,** cannot be shaken off); (fig.) person who extorts profit from others. [E]

**leech**[3] *n.* Sail edge. [orig. uncert.]

**leek** *n.* Vegetable of onion family with long white bulb; this as Welsh national emblem. [E]

**leer** *n.,* & *v.i.* Glance with lascivious, malign, or sly expression; ~**y** *a.* (sl.; -ily, -iness), knowing, sly, wary *of.* [perh. obs. *leer* cheek]

**lees** (-z) *n.pl.* Sediment of wine etc. (**drink, drain,** etc., **to the ~,** lit. or fig.); dregs, worst part after the better is gone. [F]

**leeward.** See LEE; **left**[1], LEAVE[2].

**left**[2] *a., adv.,* & *n.* **1.** *a.* (opp. RIGHT). On or towards side of human body which in the majority of persons has the less-used hand, on or towards that part of an object which is analogous to person's left side or (with opp. sense) which is nearer to spectator's left hand (*left side, eye,* etc.); *left flank* of army etc.; *left* BANK[1]); (Polit., often *L~*) of the left (see sense 3); **have two ~ feet,** be clumsy; ~**-ha′nded,** using left hand by preference as more serviceable, made by or for the left hand, turning to the left, (fig.) awkward or clumsy, (of compliment, remark, etc.) ambiguous, of doubtful sincerity; ~**-hander,** left-handed person (esp. in games) or blow; ~**wing** (of army, football etc. team, or political party), whence ~**-wi′nger,** member of this; ~**′mōst** *a.,* furthest to the left; ~**′ward** *a. & adv.;* ~**′wards** (-z) *adv.* **2.** On or to the left side. **3.** *n.* Left-hand part, region, or direction; (blow with) left hand; (Polit., often *L~*) radicals collectively, more innovative etc. section of any group, so ~**′ish** *a.,* ~**′ism** *n.,* principles or policy of political left,

~**′ist** *n.;* ~**′y** *n.,* (colloq.) left--handed person, left-winger in politics. [E, = weak, worthless]

**lĕg. 1.** *n.* One of the limbs on which person or animal walks, runs, and stands, part of this from hip to ankle, (FIND one's *legs*; **give** person **a ~ up,** help him to mount or to get over obstacle, lit. or fig.; **keep** one's ~**s,** not fall; ~ **before wicket,** (of batsman) out because of illegal obstruction of ball that would otherwise have hit his wicket; *on* one's, *its,* LAST[3] *legs*; **pull** person's ~, deceive him jokingly, so ~**-pull,** a hoax; **shake a ~,** sl., dance, make a start; **show a ~,** sl., get out of bed; **has not a ~ to stand on,** cannot support argument by facts or sound reasons; **stretch** one's ~**s,** go for a walk); leg of animal as food (~**-of-mutton sail, sleeve,** so shaped); artificial leg (*wooden etc. leg*); part of garment covering leg; more or less leg-shaped support of chair, table, bed, machine, etc.; (Crick.) part of field on side where striker places his feet, opp. OFF, (*leg stump*; ~ **break,** ball which turns from leg side to off; *leg-*BYE[2]) (Naut.) run made on one tack; (colloq.) one of a progression of stages in journey, competition, etc.; ~**-room,** space for legs when sitting. **2.** *v.t.* (-gg-). ~ **it,** walk or run hard. **3.** (-)~**ged** (-gd) *a.;* ~**′ging** (-g-) *n.* (usu. in *pl.*), outer covering of leather etc. for leg from knee to ankle; ~**′gў** (-gĭ) *a.* (-iness), long-legged. [N]

**lĕ′gacў** *n.* Gift left by will; material or immaterial thing handed down by predecessor. [F f. L (*lego* bequeath, commit)]

**lē′gal** *a.* (~ly). Of, based on, concerned with, appointed or required or permitted by, law; ~ **aid,** payment from public funds for legal advice or proceedings; ~ **fiction,** assertion accepted as true (though probably fictitious) to achieve useful purpose esp. in legal matters; *legal* PROCEEDINGS, SEPARATION, TENDER[1]; ~**ĭsm** *n.,* exaltation of law or formula, red tape; ~**ĭst** *n.,* stickler for legality; ~**ĭ′stĭc** *a.;* **lēgă′lĭtỳ** *n.,* lawfulness; ~**ĭze** *v.t.,* (esp.) make lawful, bring into harmony with law; ~**ĭzā′tion** *n.* [F or L (*lex leg-* law)]

**lĕ′gate** *n.* Papal ambassador;

(arch.) ambassador; **lĕgā'tion** *n.*, body of deputies, diplomatic minister (esp. below ambassadorial rank) and his suite, his residence, legateship. [F f. L (*lego* depute)]

**lĕgatee'** *n.* Recipient of legacy. [L *lego* bequeath]

**lĕga'tō** (-ah'-) *a., adv.,* & *n.* (*pl.* ~s). (Mus.) (Passage to be performed) in smooth connected manner. [It., = bound (L *ligo* bind)]

**lĕ'gend** *n.* Traditional story, myth, such literature or tradition; inscription on coin or medal; caption; wording on map etc. explaining symbols used; ~**ary** *a.*, famous, or existent only, in legend, (colloq.) remarkable enough to be a subject of legend. [F f. L *legenda* things to be read]

**lĕ'ger** *a.* (Mus.) ~ **line**, short line added above or below staff for outside note(s). [var. LEDGER]

**lĕ'gerdemain** *n.* Sleight of hand, juggling; trickery, sophistry. [F, = light of hand]

**legging, leggy.** See LEG.

**lĕ'ghŏrn** (or līgŏr'n) *n.* (Hat of) fine plaited straw; (L~) breed of domestic fowl. [place]

**lĕ'gĭb**|**le** *a.* (~ly). Easily read (of handwriting or print); ~**i'lĭtÿ** *n.* [L (*lego* read)]

**lĕ'gion** (-jon) *n.* Division of 3,000–6,000 men in ancient Roman army; other large organized body (**foreign** ~, body of foreign volunteers in modern esp. French, army; L~ **of Honour,** French order of distinction; ||**Royal British L~,** national association of ex-service men, and now women, formed 1921); vast host, multitude, (**their name is L~, they are** ~, they are innumerable, cf. Mark 5: 9); ~**ary,** (*a.*) of legion's, (*n.*; also ~**nair'e**) member of legion. [F f. L *legio -onis*]

**lĕ'gĭslāt**|**e** *v.i.* Make laws; **lĕgĭslā'-tion** *n.*, law-making, laws made; ~**ive** *a.*; ~**or** *n.*; ~**ure** *n.*, legislative body of a State. [L *lex legis* law, *latus* p.p. of *fero* carry]

**lĕgĭ'tĭm**|**ate** [1] *a.* (Of child) born of parents married to one another; lawful, proper, regular, conforming to standard type, (~**ate theatre,** plays of established merit, plays containing spoken lines only, as opp. musical comedy etc.); logically admissible (*a legitimate inference*); ~**acÿ** *n.*, being legitimate; ~**āte** [2],

~**atīze,** ~**īze,** *vbs. t.*, make legitimate by decree or enactment, prove to be legitimate, serve as justification for; ~**ā'tion,** ~**izā'tion,** *ns.* [L *legitimo* legitimize (*lex legis* law)]

**lĕ'gūme** *n.* Fruit, edible part, pod, of leguminous plant; vegetable used for food; **lĕgū'mĭnous** *a.*, of the family including peas, beans, and other pod-bearing plants. [F f. L *legumen -minis* pulse, bean (*lego* pick, gather, as being picked by hand)]

**lei** (lā, lā'ē) *n.* Polynesian garland of flowers. [Hawaiian]

**Leics.** *abbr.* Leicestershire.

**lei'sure** (lĕ'zher) *n.* (Opportunity *to do, for,* afforded by) free time, time at one's own disposal; **at** ~, not occupied, in unhurried manner; **at** one's ~, when one has time; ~**d** *a.*, having (ample) leisure; ~**lÿ,** (*a.*; -**iness**) deliberate, not hurried, (*adv.*) without hurry. [AF *leisour* f. L *licet* it is allowed]

**leitmotiv, -if,** (lī'tmōtēf) *n.* (Mus. etc.) Theme associated throughout piece or work with some person or idea. [G (LEAD[1], MOTIVE)]

**lĕ'mming** *n.* Small arctic rodent reputed in migration to rush headlong into sea and drown. [Norw.]

**lĕ'mon**[1] *n.* ~ (**sole**), kind of plaice. [F *limande*]

**lĕ'mon**[2] *n.* Pale-yellow acid fruit used esp. for flavouring, its colour, tree bearing it, (~ **cheese** or **curd,** lemon conserve with consistency of cream cheese; ||*lemon* SQUASH[1]; ~--**squeezer,** for extracting juice from lemon); (sl.) simpleton, something bad, undesirable, disappointing, etc.; ~**ā'de** *n.*, drink made from lemons, sweetening, and water, and freq. aerated; ~**ÿ** *a.* [F *limon* f. Arab. (as LIME[2])]

**lĕ'mur** *n.* Nocturnal mammal of Madagascar allied to monkeys. [L *lemures* ghosts]

**lĕnd** *v.t.* (**lent**). Grant (*to* person) use of (thing) on understanding that it or its equivalent shall be returned; allow use of (money) at interest; bestow, contribute, (something of temporary service or effect, as *enchantment, aid, dignity*); ~ **an ear,** one's **ears,** listen; ~ **a hand,** help); accommodate one*self to* some policy or purpose; ~ **itself to,** (of thing) be serviceable for. [E (LOAN[1])]

**lĕngth** *n.* Measurement from end to end; greatest of a body's three dimensions; extent in, of, or with regard to, time (*a stay of some length*; *the length of a speech*); distance thing extends (*at* ARM¹'*s length*), length of horse, boat, etc., as measure of lead in race; long stretch or extent; piece of certain length (*length of cloth, piping*); full extent of one's body (*lay at full length*); degree of thoroughness in action (*went to great lengths*); (Pros.) vowel's or syllable's quantity; (Crick.) (proper) distance for pitching of ball in bowling; **at ~**, at last, after a long time; **at (full, great, some) ~**, in detail; **~'en** *v.t.* & *i.*, make or become longer; **~'ways** (-z) *adv.*; **~'wise** (-z) *adv.* & *a.*; **~'ў** *a.* (**~ily**, **~iness**), of unusual length, prolix, tedious. [E (LONG)]

**lē'nien|t** *a.* Tolerant, gentle, not disposed to severity, mild; **~ce, ~cў**, *ns.*; **lē'nitў** *n.*, gentleness, mercifulness. [L (*lenis* mild)]

**Lē'nin|ism** *n.* Political theories and practices of Russ. statesman *Lenin* (d. 1924); **~ist** *n.* [person]

**lē'nō** *n.* (*pl.* **~s**). Open-work fabric with warp yarns twisted in pairs before weaving. [F *linon* (*lin* flax f. L *linum*)]

**lĕns** (-z) *n.* Piece of transparent substance with one or both sides curved for concentrating or dispersing light-rays in spectacles, telescopes, etc.; combination of lenses in photography; transparent substance behind iris of eye. [L *lens lent-* lentil (from similarity of shape)]

**lĕnt¹.** See LEND.

**Lĕnt²** *n.* Period of fasting and penitence from Ash Wednesday to Easter Eve; ‖**~ lily**, (esp. wild) daffodil; ‖**~ term**, spring term at universities etc.; **Lĕ'nten** *a.*, of or in or suited to Lent (**Lenten fare**, without meat). [E, = spring]

**lĕ'ntil** *n.* Biconvex edible seed of a leguminous plant; **lĕnti'cŭlar** *a.*, lentil-shaped. [F *lentille* f. L (LENS)]

**lĕ'ntō** *a.* & *adv.* (Mus.) Slow(ly). [It.]

**Lē'ō** *n.* Sign of ZODIAC; **lē'onine** *a.*, lionlike, of lions. [F f. L (LION)]

**leo'pard** (lĕ'p-) *n.* Large African and S. Asian carnivorous animal with dark-spotted yellowish-fawn or (**black ~**) black coat, panther. [F f. L f. Gk (LION, PARD¹)]

**lē'otard** *n.* Close-fitting one-piece

garment worn by ballet-dancers, acrobats, etc. [person]

**lĕ'per** *n.* Person with leprosy; (fig.) person shunned on moral grounds. [F *lepre* leprosy f. L f. Gk (*lepros* scaly)]

**lĕpidŏ'pter|ous** *a.* Of the Lepidoptera or insects with four scale-covered wings including moths and butterflies; **~ist** *n.*, student of these. [Gk *lepis -idos* scale, *pteron* wing]

**lĕ'prechaun** (-k-) *n.* Small mischievous sprite in Irish folklore. [Ir. (*lu* small, *corp* body)]

**lĕ'pr|osў** *n.* Chronic infectious disease of skin and nerves causing mutilations and deformities (also fig.); **~ous** *a.* [LEPER]

**Lĕ'sbian** (-z-). **1.** *a.* Of women's homosexuality. **2.** *n.* (or *l~*). Female homosexual; **~ism** *n.* [*Lesbos*, place]

**lèse-mǎ'jĕstў** (-zm-), **lèse-majesté** (lāzmă'zhĕstā), *n.* Treason; affront to sovereign or ruler; (joc.) presumptuous conduct. [F f. L, = injured sovereignty]

**lē'sion** (-zhon) *n.* Damage, injury; (Path.) morbid change in action or texture of an organ. [F f. L (*laedo laes-* injure)]

**lĕss**, *a.*, *prep.*, *n.*, & *adv.* **1.** *a.* (Of size, degree, duration, number, etc.) smaller (opp. *greater*; *in a less degree*, *of less magnitude or importance*; *of two evils choose the less*; *5 is less than 6*); of smaller quantity, not so much (of), (opp. *more*; *find less difficulty*, *eat less meat*); NO¹ *less*. **2.** *prep.* Minus, deducting, (*a year less three days*; *dividend paid less tax*). **3.** *n.* Smaller amount, quantity, number, (*cannot take much less*; *for less than £10*; *is little less than disgraceful*; *in ~ than no time*, joc., very quickly or soon). **4.** *adv.* To smaller extent, in lower degree, (NONE the less). **5.** **~'en** *v.i.* & *t.*, diminish; **~'er** *a.* (usu. *attrib.*), not so great as the other or the rest, minor, (*the Lesser Celandine*; *the lesser evils of life*; opp. *greater*). [E]

**-lèss** *suf.* forming *adjs.* & *advs.* f. *ns.*, w. sense 'not having, without, free from', and f. *vbs.*, w. sense 'unable to be —ed', 'not —ing', (*doubtless, guileless, powerless, shell-less*; *fathomless, relentless, tireless*); see note on Suffixes, p. viii. [E]

**lĕssee'.** See LEASE; **lĕ'ssen**, **lĕ'sser**, see LESS.

**lĕ'sson** *n.* Thing learnt by pupil, spell of teaching, (in *pl.*) systematic instruction *in* subject (*give, take, lessons in*); experience that serves to warn or encourage (*let that be a lesson to you*); passage from Bible read aloud during church service. [F *leçon* f. L (*lego lect-* read)]

**lĕssŏr′.** See LEASE.

**lĕst** conj. In order that not, for fear that, (*lest we forget*); *fear* etc. ~, that. [E (LESS)]

**lĕt¹. 1.** *v.t.* (arch.; -tt-; ~′ted, let). Hinder, obstruct. **2.** *n.* (Rackets, Lawn Tennis, etc.) obstruction of ball or player, on account of which ball must be served again; **without** ~ **or hindrance**, unimpeded. [E]

**lĕt²** *v.t. & i. & aux.* (-tt-; let), & *n.* **1.** *v.t. & i.* Allow or enable or cause to, not prevent or forbid, (*we will let him try, see us, know*; LIVE *and let live*); ‖grant use of (rooms, land, etc.) for rent or hire (*to* person *for* period; **to** ~, offered for rent); allow, cause, (liquid, air) to escape (*let blood*); award (contract for work); ~ **alone,** ~ **be,** not interfere with, attend to, or do, (~ *alone, in imper.*, not to mention, far less or more; *hasn't got a radio, let alone television*); ~ **down,** lower (window etc.), fail to support (another, or user) at need, disappoint (~ *him down gently*, avoid humiliating him abruptly), lengthen (garment); ~*-down* n., disappointment; ~ **drop, fall,** drop (lit. or fig.) intentionally or by accident; ~ **fly,** release, discharge, (lit. or fig., usu. *at* person *with* weapon, abuse, etc.); ~ **go,** release, lose hold of, lose or relinquish hold *of*, dismiss from thought, cease to restrain (~ one*self go*, abandon restraint etc. for extreme behaviour); ~ **in,** admit, open door to (lit. or fig.), involve in loss etc., insert into surface of something; ~ *in for,* involve in (loss or difficulty); ~ **into,** allow to enter, insert into surface of, make acquainted with (secret etc.); ~ **loose,** release, unchain; ~ **off,** discharge (lit. or fig., gun, joke, etc.), not punish or compel, punish *with* light penalty, excuse (person penalty), allow or cause (liquid, STEAM, etc.) to escape, ‖let (part of house etc.); ~ **on,** (sl.) reveal secret, pretend (*let on that he had succeeded*); ~ **out,** open door for exit of, allow (person etc., secret, *that*) to depart or escape (*let the* CAT *out of the bag*), release from

restraint, make (garment) looser, put out to rent or to contract; ~*-out* n., opportunity to escape; ~ **up,** (colloq.) become less severe, diminish; ~*-up* n., cessation, diminution. **2.** *v. aux.* supplying 1st and 3rd persons of imper. in exhortations (*let us pray*; *let us,* colloq. *let's, go*), commands (*let it be done*), assumptions (*let AB be equal to CD*), and permission or challenge (*let him do his worst*). **3.** *n.* ‖Act of letting (house, room, etc.; *short, long, let*). [E]

**-lĕt** (or let) *suf.* forming *ns.* usu. dim. (*leaflet, ringlet, tartlet*) or denoting articles of ornament or attire (*armlet, necklet*). [F]

**lē′thal** *a.* (~ly). Causing, sufficient or designed to cause, death (*lethal dose*; ~ **chamber,** for killing animals painlessly); **lēthă′litÿ** n. [L (*lethum* death)]

**lĕ′thargÿ** n. Morbid drowsiness; torpid or apathetic state; lack of interest and energy; **lĕthăr′gĭc** *a.* (-ically). [F f. L f. Gk *lēthargia* drowsiness f. root 'forget']

**Lĕtt** n. Member of people living near Baltic, mainly in Latvia; ~′**ĭc** *a.,* = *Lettish*; ~′**ĭsh,** (*a.*) of the Letts, (*n.*) their language. [G *Lette* f. Lettish *Latvi*]

**lĕ′tter. 1.** *n.* Any of the symbols, representing sounds, of which written words are composed (~**s** after one's **name,** colloq., abbreviations of degrees, honours, etc.); written or printed communication usu. sent by post or messenger, (in *pl.*) addressed legal or formal document; precise terms of statement (**to the** ~, with adherence to every detail), strict verbal interpretation (**in** ~ **and in spirit,** in form and substance); (in *pl.*) literature, acquaintance with books, erudition, (**man of** ~**s,** scholar, author); ~*-bomb,* terrorist explosive device sent by post; ~*-box* (for delivery or posting of letters); ~*-card,* folded card with gummed edge for posting as letter; ~*-head*(*ing*), printed (heading on) stationery; *letter of* CREDENCE, *of* CREDIT; ~**press,** printed words in illustrated book, printing from raised type; ~**s of administration,** authority to administer intestate's estate; *letters of* MARQUE¹; *letters* PATENT; ~**ed** (-erd) *a.,* well-read. **2.** *v.t.* Inscribe letters on; classify with letters. [F f. L *littera*]

**lĕt′tuce** (-tĭs) *n.* Garden plant with crisp leaves used as salad, and milky juice. [F f. L *lactuca* (*lac lact-* milk)]

**leu′co-** *in comb.* White; ∼**cȳte** *n.*, white or colourless blood-corpuscle; ∼**tomȳ** (-ŏ′t-) *n.*, incision into white tissue of frontal lobe of brain to relieve some cases of mental disorder. [Gk *leukos* white]

**leukae′m|ia, *-kē′m-,** *n.* Progressive disease with abnormal accumulation of white corpuscles in tissues and usu. in blood; ∼**ĭc** *a.* [G (Gk *leukos* white, *haima* blood]

**Lev.** *abbr.* Leviticus (O.T.).

||**lĕvă′nt**[1] *v.i.* Abscond, esp. without paying one's debts. [ult. L *levo* lift]

**Lĕvă′nt**[2] *n.* The East-Mediterranean region; ∼**ine** (*or* lĕ′van-) *a.* & *n.*, of, trading to, inhabitant of, the Levant. [F, = point of sunrise, east, (*lever* rise f. L, as prec.)]

**lĕ′vee′** (-vĭ) *n.* Assembly of visitors esp. at formal reception; ||sovereign's assembly for men only. [F *levé* var. of *lever* rising (LEVY)]

***levee**[2] (lĭvē′, lĕ′vĭ) *n.* Embankment against river floods; river's natural embankment; landing-place. [F *levée* p.p. of *lever* raise (LEVY)]

**lĕ′vel** *n., a.,* & *v.* **1.** *n.* Instrument for giving or testing a horizontal line or plane; horizontal line or plane (**find** one's ∼, reach a position socially, intellectually, etc., suitable for one; **on a ∼ with**, in same horizontal plane as, fig. equal with; **on the ∼**, colloq., truthful(ly), honest(ly)); social, moral, or intellectual standard, plane of rank or authority (*discussions at Cabinet level*); height etc. reached (*eye level*); position on real or imaginary scale (*danger, energy, noise, level*); level surface, flat country. **2.** *a.* (∼**ly**). Horizontal; on a level or equality (*with*; ||∼**crossing**, of railway and road, or two railways, at same level; *level* PEG*ging*); even, equable, uniform, well-balanced, in quality, style, temper, judgement, etc., (**do** one's ∼ **best**, colloq., do one's utmost; ∼**headed**, well-balanced mentally, cool). **3.** *v.t.* & *i.* (||**-ll-**). Make or become level, even, or uniform; place on same level, bring *up* or *down* to a standard; raze (*to* or *with the ground*), abolish (distinctions); aim (missile, gun); direct (satire, accusation, etc., or abs.; *at, against*). **4.** ∼**ler, *∼er,** *n.,* (esp.) advocate

of abolition of social relations. [F f. L dim. (*libra* balance)]

**lĕ′ver. 1.** *n.* Bar or other tool used in prizing; bar or other rigid structure used as lifting device of which one point (*fulcrum*) is fixed, another is connected with the force (*weight*) to be resisted or acted upon, and a third is connected with the force (*power*) applied; (fig.) means of moral pressure. **2.** *v.i.* & *t.* Use lever; lift, move, etc., with lever (*along, out, up*, etc.). **3.** ∼**age** *n.,* action of lever, advantage gained by use of lever, (fig.) means of accomplishing a purpose. [AF f. L *levo* raise]

**lĕ′verĕt** *n.* Young (esp. first-year) hare. [AF dim. of *levre* f. L *lepus lepor-* hare]

**lēvi′athan** *n.* Sea monster (Bibl.); huge ship; anything very large of its kind, person of great power etc. [L f. Heb.]

**lē′vis** (-z) *n.pl.* Type of (orig. blue) denim jeans or overalls reinforced with rivets. [*Levi* Strauss, person; P]

**lĕ′vit|āte** *v.i.* & *t.* (Cause to) rise and float in air (esp. w. ref. to spiritualism); ∼**ā′tion** *n.* [L *levis* light, after *gravitate*]

**Lē′vite** *n.* Member of tribe of Levi, priests' assistant in Jewish temple-worship; **Lĕvi′tical** *a.* (-lly), of the Levites or their duties, of Leviticus; **Lĕvi′ticus** *n.,* O.T. book with ritual and law. [L f. Gk f. Heb. (*Levi*)]

**lĕ′vitȳ** *n.* Disposition to make light of weighty matters, frivolity, lack of serious thought. [L (*levis* light)]

**lĕ′vȳ. 1.** *n.* Collecting of tax or compulsory payment, enrolling of soldiers etc., amount or number thus enrolled, (in *pl.*) troops levied. **2.** *v.t.* Raise or impose compulsorily (troops, taxes, ransom, blackmail, etc.; ∼ **war**, proceed to make it by collecting men and munitions). [F *levée*, p.p. of *lever* raise f. L *levo*]

**lewd** *a.* Lascivious; indecent, obscene. [E, orig. = lay, vulgar, ill-mannered, base]

**lĕ′xĭcal** *a.* (∼**ly**). Of the words of a language (opp. *grammatical*); (as) of a lexicon. [foll.]

**lĕ′xĭc|on** *n.* Dictionary, esp. of Greek, Hebrew, Syriac, or Arabic; (fig.) vocabulary of person, of language, of branch of knowledge, etc.; **~ŏ′graphў, ~ŏ′grapher,** *ns.,* making, maker, of dictionaries; **~ográ′phĭcal** *a.* (-**ically**). [L f. Gk *lexis* word *f. legō* speak)]

**ley** (lā) *n.* Land temporarily under grass. [LEA]

**Ley′den** (lī′-) *n.* **~ jar,** kind of electrical condenser with glass jar as dielectric between sheets of tin foil. [*Leiden,* place]

**L.F.** *abbr.* low frequency.

**l.h.** *abbr.* left hand.

**li′able** *pred. a.* Legally bound, answerable *for,* subject *to* tax or penalty, under obligation *to* do; exposed or open *to,* apt *to* do or suffer, something undesirable; **~r′lĭtў** *n.,* being liable (‖**limited ~ility,** being legally responsible only to limited amount for debts of one's trading company), troublesome person or thing under one's responsibility, (in *pl.*) debts etc. for which one is liable. [AF f. F f. L (*ligo* bind)]

**liai′son** (-z-) *n.* Connection, co-operation, esp. (Mil.) between allied forces or units of same force; illicit sexual relationship; egg-yolk thickening for sauces; **liai′se** (-z-) *v.i.,* (colloq.) establish co-operation, act as link, *with, between.* [F (*lier* bind f. L, as prec.)]

**lia′na** (-ah′-) *n.* Climbing and twining plant in tropical forests. [F]

**li′ar.** See LIE[1].

**li′as** *n.* A blue limestone rich in fossils; **liă′ssic** *a.* [F *liois*]

**Lib.** *abbr.* Liberal; (colloq.) Liberation.

**libā′tion** *n.* (Pouring of) drink-offering to god; (joc.) toast-drinking etc. [L]

**li′bel. 1.** *n.* Published false statement damaging to person's reputation, publication of it; false defamatory statement or representation (**is a ~ on,** does injustice to); **~lous** *a.* **2.** *v.t.* (‖-**ll-**). Defame falsely, misrepresent maliciously, portray with less than justice; publish libel against. [F f. L *libellus* dim. of *liber* book]

**li′beral. 1.** *a.* (**~ly**). Given or giving freely, generous, not sparing *of,* abundant; open-minded, unprejudiced; not rigorous; directed to general broadening of mind, not professional or technical, (*liberal education, studies*); (Polit.) favouring (moderate) democratic reforms (*the Liberal Party*). **2.** *n.* Person of liberal

views; (*L~*) member of (esp. British) Liberal Party. **3. ~ism** *n.,* principles of Liberal Party; **libera′l-itў** *n.,* free giving, breadth of mind; **~ize** *v.t.,* (esp.) free from narrow-mindedness; **~izā′tion** *n.* [F f. L (*liber* free)]

**li′ber|āte** *v.t.* Set at liberty, release *from;* free (country) from enemy occupation; free (person) from oppressive social conventions (*liberated woman*); **~′ātion, ~ātor,** *ns.*

**li′bert|īne** (*or* -ēn) *n.* & *a.* Dissolute, licentious, (man). [L, = freedman (*liber* free)]

**li′bertў** *n.* Being free, freedom, freedom personified, right or power to do as one pleases or *to* do, (**at ~,** free, disengaged, having the right or permission *to* do); **civil ~,** freedom of action subject to the law; *liberty of* CONSCIENCE, *of the* PRESS[1]; **~ of the subject,** rights of subject under constitutional rule); setting aside of rules, licence, (**take liberties,** behave in unduly familiar manner (*with* person, or abs.), deal (unduly) freely *with* rules or facts; **take the ~ to do, of doing,** presume or venture *to* do); (in *pl.*) privileges enjoyed by prescription or grant; ‖**~ boat** (Naut., carrying liberty men); **~ bodice,** young girl's close-fitting under-bodice; **L~ Hall,** place where one may do as one likes; **~ horse** (performing in circus without rider); ‖**~ man,** sailor with leave to go ashore. [F f. L (LIBERAL)]

**libi′dō** (*or* -ē′-) *n.* (*pl.* **~s**). Psychic drive or energy, esp. that associated with sex instinct; **libi′dĭnal** *a.* (-**ally**); **libi′dĭnous** *a.,* lustful. [L, = lust]

**Li′bra** (*or* -ē′-) *n.* Sign of ZODIAC. [L, = pound weight, balance]

**li′brarў** *n.* (Room or building in which is kept) a collection of books, public or private, (‖**free, public, ~,** used by public without payment and usu. supported by local rates; **lending ~,** from which books may be temporarily taken away; **reference ~,** in which books may be consulted but not taken away); (place in which is kept) a collection of films, records, computer routines, etc.; series of books issued in similar bindings as connected in some way; **librā′rian** *n.,* custodian or assistant in library. [F f. L (*liber* book)]

**librĕ′tt|ō** *n.* (*pl.* **~i** *pr.* -ē, **~os**).

Text of opera or other long musical vocal work; **~ist** n., writer of this. [It., dim. of *libro* book f. L *liber*]

**lice.** See LOUSE.

**li′cence¹, \*li′cense¹,** n. Permit from government etc. to carry out some action etc. which without this permission would be illegal, (~ to drive, ‖own a dog, carry on some trade (esp. in alcoholic liquor), etc.; leave, permission; excessive liberty of action, disregard of law or property, licentiousness; writer's or artist's transgression of established rules for effect (*poetic licence*); **li′cense², -nce²,** v.t., grant licence to (person), authorize use of (premises) for certain purpose esp. sale etc. of alcoholic liquor, authorize publication of (book etc.) or performance of (play); **licensee′** n., (esp.) holder of licence to sell alcoholic liquor; **licě′ntiate** (-shĭat) n., holder of certificate of competence from collegiate or examining body; **licě′ntious** (-shŭs) a., immoral in sexual relations. [F f. L (*licet* it is allowed)]

**lichee, lichi.** See LITCHI.

**li′chen** (or lĭ′k-) n. Plant organism composed of fungus and alga in association, forming grey, green, or yellow crust on rocks etc. [L f. Gk]

**li′chgāte, lȳ′ch-,** n. Roofed gateway of churchyard where coffin awaits clergyman's arrival. [*lich* = corpse, GATE]

**li′cit** a. Not forbidden. [L (LICENCE¹)]

**lick. 1.** v.t. & i. Pass tongue over (~ person's **boots, shoes,** be servile to him; ~ one's **chops, lips,** in relish or anticipation of food, or fig.; ~ **into shape,** give proper form to, make presentable or efficient; ~ one's **wounds,** fig., remain in retirement after defeat); take *up* or *off,* make clean, by licking; (of waves, flame, etc.) play lightly over; (sl.) thrash, beat in fight etc., defeat (lit. or fig.; *this problem has me licked*), excel. **2.** n. Act of licking with tongue (**a ~ and a promise,** colloq., hasty performance of task, esp. of washing oneself); smart blow with stick etc.; (sl.) pace (*at a great lick*; **\*~ety--spli′t,** colloq., at full speed, headlong). [E]

**li′ckerish, li′quorish,** (-ker-) a. Fond of fine food, greedy; lecherous. [AF *lik-,* F LECHEROUS]

**li′corice.** See LIQUORICE.

**li′ctor** n. (Rom. Hist.) Officer attending consul or other magistrate, bearing fasces, and executing sentence on offenders. [L]

**lid** n. Hinged or detached cover for an opening, esp. at top of container (‖**put the ~ on,** sl., be the culmination of, put a stop to; **with the ~ off,** fig., with all horrors etc. exposed to view); = EYELid; (sl.) hat; (-)**li′dd-děd** a. [E]

**li′dō** (lē′-) n. (pl. ~s). Public open-air swimming-pool or bathing--beach. [place]

**lie¹. 1.** n. Intentional false statement (*tell a lie*; **act a ~,** deceive without verbal lying; **give person the ~,** accuse him of lying; **give the ~ to** *supposition* etc., serve to show its falsity; **~-detector,** instrument for measuring physiological changes so as to indicate tension accompanying the telling of lies; **white ~,** lie excused or justified by its motive); imposture, false belief. **2.** v.i. & t. (**ly′ing**). Tell lie(s) (*to* person); (of thing) be deceptive; get (one*self,* person) *into* or *out of* by lying. **3.** n. **li′ar** n., teller (esp. habitual) of lie(s). [E]

**lie². 1.** v.i. (**ly′ing; lay; lain**). (Of person or animal) be in or assume horizontal position on supporting surface, be at rest on something, (*lie asleep, sick, in* STATE); (of troops) be encamped *at, in, near,* a place; (of thing) be resting (flat) on surface (*lie at the* DOOR *of; lie* HEAVY; **~ in ruins, in the dust,** be overthrown, fallen); be kept or remain or be in specified state or place (*lie at the mercy of; lie fallow, in* WAIT; *money lying idle at the bank;* **~ low,** crouch, keep quiet or unseen, bide one's time); be spread out to view (*lie on the surface, before us, open*); be situated (*see how the* LAND *lies; ships lying* at anchor); (of abstract thing) exist, be in certain position or manner, (*knows where her interest lies; the remedy lies in education;* **as far as in me ~s,** to the best of my ability; **~s with you,** is your business or right *to* do); (Law) be admissible or sustainable (*action, appeal, will not lie*); **~-abed,** late riser; **~ about,** be left carelessly out of place; **~ down,** assume lying position (*take defeat, it,* etc., *lying down,* in abject manner), have brief rest in or on bed etc. (so ~-*down* n.); ~ *down under*, accept without protest; ~ **in**, be brought to bed in childbirth, ||(colloq.) remain in bed late in morning, so ~-*in* n.; ~ **over**, be deferred; ~ **to**, (Naut.) come as near to a standstill as possible without anchoring; ~ **up**, go into hiding, take to one's bed or room, (of ship) go into dock or be out of commission. **2.** *n.* Way, direction, position, in which thing lies (||~ **of the land**, fig., state of affairs); position of golf--ball to be struck. [E]

**lied** (lēt) *n.* (*pl.* ~'*er* pr. lē'dĕr). German song esp. of Romantic period. [G]

**lief** *adv.* (arch.) Gladly, willingly, (usu. I *had* or *would as lief* do one thing *as* another). [E, = dear]

**liege.** (usu. Hist.) **1.** *a.* Entitled to receive or bound to give feudal service or allegiance; ~ **lord**, feudal superior, sovereign; ~'**man**, sworn vassal. **2.** *n.* Liege lord; (usu. in *pl.*) vassal, subject. [F f. L prob. f. Gmc]

**li'en** (lē'ĕn) *n.* Right to hold another's property till debt on it is paid. [F f. L (*ligo* bind)]

**lieu** (lū) *n.* In ~, in the place, instead, (*of*). [F f. L *locus* place]

**Lieut.** *abbr.* Lieutenant.

**lieutě'n|ant** (lěft-, left-, in Navy lět-, let-) *n.* Deputy, substitute, who acts for a superior (||**Deputy** **L~ant**, deputy of LORD Lieutenant of county; ~**ant-governor**, acting or deputy governor of state, province, etc., under governor(-general)); army officer next below captain, naval officer next below lieutenant--commander; ||FLIGHT¹ *lieutenant*; ~**ant-colonel, -commander, -gen-** **eral**, officers ranking next below colonel etc.; ~**ancy̆** *n.* [F (LIEU place, TENANT holder)]

**life** *n.* (*pl.* **lives** pr. -vz). State of functional activity and continual change peculiar to animals and plants before death, animate existence, (**a matter of ~ and death**, issue upon which person's living or dying depends, fig., matter of great importance; **bring, come, to ~**, (cause to) emerge from unconsciousness or inactivity); state of existence as a living individual (**for one's ~**, **for dear ~**, (as if) to escape death; **cannot for the ~ of me**, could not even if my life depended on it; **lay** **down** one's ~, be willing to be

killed; *life and* LIMB²; **lose** one's ~, be killed; **not on your ~**, colloq., most certainly not; **save** one's ~, avoid death; **take ~**, kill persons or animals; **take** one's (**own**) ~, kill oneself; **take** one's ~ **in** one's **hands,** risk it); period during which life lasts, period from birth to present time, or from present time to death, (*have done so all my life; shall remember you all my life*; **get the fright, have** **the time,** etc., of one's ~, colloq., be frightened, enjoy oneself, etc., as never before; ~ (**sentence**), **an-** **nuity, membership**, etc., to continue for rest of person's life); living things and their activity (*a drawing done from life; is there life on Mars?*; **as large as ~**, life-size, joc., in person; **larger than ~**, exaggerated; **to the ~**, with fidelity to original; **true to ~**, accurately represented); energy, liveliness, animation, (*the life and soul of the party*; **put some ~ into it**, colloq., act more energetically); fresh start after narrowly escaped death; one of successive chances before being put out of game; individual's actions and fortunes, manner of existence or particular aspect etc. of this, (*one's* *private life; village life*; **in ~**, to be experienced anywhere; **make ~** **easy**, not create problems; **the** **other, the future, eternal, ever-** **lasting, ~**, state of existence after death; **this is the ~**, expr. contentment; **this ~**, on earth) written account of person's life, biography; active part of existence, business and pleasures of the world, (HIGH, LOW², *life*; SEE¹ *life*); (Theol.) salvation, regenerate condition; time for which manufactured or perishable product continues to function or be valid or saleable; *life* ASSURANCE; ~'**belt** (of buoyant material to support body in water); ~-**blood**, blood necessary to life, (fig.) vitalizing influence; ~'- **boat**, boat of special construction for rescue in storms, ship's boat for emergency use; ~'**buoy**, annular lifebelt; ~ **cycle**, (Biol.) cyclic series of changes undergone by an organism; ~-**guard**, bodyguard of soldiers; ||L~ **Guards**, regiment of royal household cavalry; ~ **insurance** (for payment on death of insured person); ~-**jacket** (as *lifebelt*); ~'**line**, rope used for life-saving, e.g., that attached to lifebuoy, (fig.) sole means of communication; ~'**long**, continued for a lifetime; ~-**office** (dealing in life insurance); ~ **peer(age)** (with title lapsing at death); ~-**preserver**, life-jacket etc., short stick with heavily loaded end; ~-**saver**, source of redemption from death or serious difficulty; ~ **sciences**, biology and kindred subjects; ~-**size(d)**, of same size as living person etc.; ~-**style**, (individual's) way of life; ~'**time**, duration of person's life (*chance* etc. *of a ~time*, such as occurs only once in a person's life), life of manufactured product etc.; ~-**work**, task pursued throughout life; ~'**less** (-fl-) *a.*, dead, lacking in animation; ~'**like** (-fl-) *a.*, (of representation) realistic or vivid; **li'fer** *n.*, (sl.) person sentenced to, sentence of, imprisonment for life. [E]

**lift. 1.** *v.t.* & *i.* Raise to higher position, take up, hoist, (*up*, *off*, *out*), elevate to higher plane of thought or feeling, give upward direction to, (eyes, face; **have one's face** ~**ed**, undergo face-lifting; ~ **a hand**, make the slightest effort, usu. *to do*; ~ **down**, pick up and bring to lower position; ~-**off**, (*a.*) removable simply by lifting, (*n.*) vertical take-off of spacecraft or rocket; ~ (**up**) one's **hands**, **heart**, in prayer etc.; ~ **up** one's **voice**, sing, speak, cry out); hold, or have, high (*church lifts its spire*); steal; plagiarize (passage); remove (barrier, restriction); dig up (bulbs, tubers); (of cloud, fog, darkness) rise, disperse; (of floor) swell upwards, bulge. **2.** *n.* Lifting; carrying of person as passenger in vehicle; transport by air, quantity thus transported; ‖apparatus for raising and lowering persons or things from floor to floor in building; apparatus for carrying persons up or down mountain etc.; supporting or elevating influence; upward force which air exerts on aircraft. [N, rel. to LOFT]

**li'gament** *n.* (Anat.) Band of tough fibrous tissue binding bones together. [L (*ligo* bind)]

**li'gature. 1.** *n.* Tie or bandage (esp. in Surg.); thing that unites, bond; (Mus.) slur, tie; (Print.) two or more letters joined (*fi, æ*, etc.). **2.** *v.t.* Bind or connect with ligature.

**light**[1] (lit) *n.*, *a.*, & *v.* **1.** *n.* The natural agent that stimulates sight

and makes things visible (opp. *darkness*; **come**, **bring**, **to** ~, be revealed, reveal); amount of illumination in place or person's share of this (**in a good**, **bad**, ~, easily, barely, visible; **stand in** person's ~, deprive him of this, fig. prejudice his chances); appearance of brightness (**northern**, **southern**, ~**s**, = AURORA *borealis*, *australis*); object from which light emanates such as sun, lamp, candle, lighthouse, (~ **of one's eyes** or **life**, fig., beloved person; ~**s out**, esp. Mil., signal for lights to be extinguished at end of day; **out like a** ~, deeply asleep or otherwise unconscious); eminent person (LEAD[1]*ing light*); (device for producing) flame or spark serving to ignite (**strike a** ~, produce this with match etc., ‖as sl. *int.* of surprise etc.); vivacity, inspiration, or inspiration in person's face, esp. in eyes; mental illumination, elucidation, (**by the** ~ **of nature**, without aid of revelation or teaching; **throw**, **shed**, ~ **on**, **upon**, help to explain); (in *pl.*) one's mental powers (*do one's best* etc. *according to* one's *lights*); aspect in which thing is viewed (**in the** ~ **of** *these facts*, with the help given by them; **place in a good** ~, represent favourably); (Theol.) brightness of heaven, illumination of soul by divine truth; window or opening in wall to let light in (ANCIENT *lights*), brighter part of picture etc.; (in crossword etc.) word to be deduced from clues; ~'**house**, tower or other structure containing beacon light to warn or guide ships at sea; ~ **meter**, instrument to measure intensity of light, esp. to show correct photographic exposure; ~'**ship**, moored or anchored ship with beacon light; ~-**year**, distance which light travels in one year, about 6 million million miles. **2.** *a.* Well provided with light, not dark; pale (often prefixed to *adjs.* & *ns.* of colour: *light-blue ribbon*; *light* BLUE). **3.** *v.t.* & *i.* (lit, ~'**ed**; as *attrib.* *a.* usu. ~*ed*). Set (lamp, fire, combustible) burning; give light to (room, street, etc.; often *up*); show (person his) way or surroundings with a light; (of eyes, face, etc.) (cause to) brighten with animation (usu. *up*); ~ **up**, (abs.) begin to smoke cigarette, pipe, etc., turn on electric etc. lights; ~**ing-u'p time** (after which vehicles on road must show pre-scribed lights); **lit up**, (sl.) drunk. [E]

**light²** (līt) *a., adv., & v.* **1.** *a.* Of little weight, not heavy; deficient in weight (*light coin* etc.); not abundant (*light traffic*); of low density (*light metal*); carrying, of suitable construction to carry, small load(s) (*light railway*); (of ship) unladen; easy to lift or wield (*light arms, weapons*); (Mil.) carrying only light arms, armaments, etc., (*light brigade, infantry*); (of building) elegant, graceful; acting gently, applied delicately, (*light blow, rain, touch*); not dense, friable, (*light soil, pastry*); easy to digest (*light meal*); (of wine, beer) not strong; slight, not im-portant, (**make ∼ of**, treat as of no consequence); trivial, jesting, fri-volous; unchaste, wanton, (esp. of woman or her conduct); nimble, quick-moving, (*light of foot; light rhythm*); easily borne or done (*light punishment, taxation, work*); aimed, aiming, merely at entertainment (*light comedy, literature,* OPERA¹); (of sleep) easily disturbed; free from sorrow, cheerful, (*light heart*); giddy (*light in the head*). **2.** *adv.* In light manner (*tread, sleep, light*); with minimum load (*travel light*). **3.** *v.i.* (lit, ∼ed). Come by chance (*up*)on; (sl.) ∼ **into**, attack, ∼ **out**, depart. **4.** ∼**er-than-air′**, (of aircraft) weigh-ing less than the air it displaces; ∼**-fingered**, apt to steal; ∼**-foot(ed)**, nimble; ∼ **hand**, (fig.) tactful management; ∼**-hea′ded**, giddy, delirious, frivolous; ∼**-hear′ted**, cheerful, (unduly) optimistic or casual; ∼ **horse(man)**, (member of) light-armed cavalry; ∼ **industry** (producing small or light articles); ∼**-mi′nded**, flighty, frivolous; ∼**′-weight** *a. & n.*, (person, animal, garment) below average weight (see BOX), (fig.) (person) of little ability or importance. **5.** ∼**′en¹** *v.t. & i.*, make or grow lighter, reduce weight or load of, bring relief to (heart, mind, etc.), mitigate (penalty); ∼**′some** *a.*, gracefully light, merry, agile. [E]

**li′ghten²** (līt-) *v.t. & i.* Shed light upon, make bright (lit. or fig.); (of face, eyes, sky, etc.) grow bright, shine, flash; (of sky, clouds, or *it*) emit lightning. [LIGHT¹]

**li′ghter¹** (līt-) *n.* (Esp.) automatic

device for lighting cigarettes etc. [LIGHT¹]

**li′ghter²** (līt-) *n.* Boat, usu. flat-bottomed, for transporting goods between ship and wharf etc. [Du. (LIGHT² 'unload')]

**li′ghtning** (līt-). **1.** *n.* Visible elec-tric discharge between clouds or cloud and ground (BALL¹ *lightning*; **forked ∼**, lightning-flash in form of zigzag or branching line; **sheet ∼**, lightning-flash of diffused bright-ness; **summer ∼**, sheet lightning without audible thunder, result of distant storm); **like (greased** colloq.) ∼, with greatest conceivable speed; *∼**-bug**, firefly; ∼**-conduc-tor**, *∼**-rod**, metal rod or wire fixed to exposed part of building or to mast to divert lightning into earth or sea. **2.** *a.* Very quick (*with lightning speed*); ∼ **strike**, (esp.) labour strike at short notice by way of surprise. [LIGHTEN²]

**lights** (līts) *n.pl.* Lungs of sheep, pigs, etc., used as food esp. for pets. [LIGHT²; cf. LUNG]

**lightsome.** See LIGHT².

**li′gn|eous** *a.* Of the nature of wood; (of plants) woody (opp. *herbaceous*); ∼**ite** *n.*, brown coal of woody tex-ture; ∼**um vi′tae** (or -vē′tī) *n.*, a hard-wooded tree. [L *lignum* wood; *vitae* L = of life]

**like¹** *a., prep., adv., conj., & n.* **1.** *a.* (**more, most, ∼**). Having the qualities of another or each other or the original, (*in like manner; as like as two peas; the two letters are very like; like* FATHER *like son*; ∼**-minded**, having same tastes, opinions, etc.); resembling, such as, as good as, (**what is he, it, ∼?**, what sort of person is he, thing is it?); LOOK *like*; **more ∼ it**, nearer that re-quired; *a critic ∼* **you**, of the class that you exemplify; **nothing ∼** (*as or so good, many,* etc., *or* abs.) not nearly; SOMETHING *like*); character-istic of (*it was like him to do that*); in suitable state or mood for do*ing* etc. (LOOK *like*; *feel like working*) or having (*feel like a rest, a cup of tea*); (arch. or colloq.) likely (*as like as not*; *like enough*; **be, have, ∼ to do**, be on the point of doing). **2.** *prep.* In the manner of, to the same degree as, (*cannot do it like him; don't talk like that*; *like* HELL); ∼ **anything, blazes,** FUN, **MAD,** etc., vigorously, intensely; freq. in proverbial etc.

phrs.: *drink like a fish, swear like a trooper*). **3.** *adv.* In the same manner as (arch.); (appended, vulg.) so to speak (*by way of argument, like*). **4.** *conj.* (colloq.) As (*can't cook like her mother does*); *as if (ate like he had not seen food for a week*). **5.** *n.* Counterpart, equal, like thing or person, (*we shall not see his like again*; *did you ever see the like of it?*; *compare like with like*; **the ~s of me, of you,** colloq., persons so humble as I, so distinguished as you); thing(s) of same kind (**and the ~,** and similar things, et cetera; **or the ~,** or other thing(s) of same kind); (Golf) *the* stroke that equalizes number of strokes played by each side. **6. li'ken** *v.t.*, find or point out resemblance in (thing or person) *to*; **~'ness** (-kn-) *n.*, resemblance (*between, to*), semblance (*in the likeness of*), representation, portrait; **~'wise** (-kwiz) *adv.*, also, moreover, too; **do ~wise,** act similarly. [E]

**like².** **1.** *v.t.* Find agreeable, congenial, or satisfactory, feel attracted by, wish, prefer, (*I like you, the offer,* (iron.) *his impudence, her to be within reach, to see or seeing them now and then, things settled*; *I should like to come, like you to come*; *I don't like to disturb her*; *I like my coffee black*; *would you like another cup?*; **if you ~,** expr. consent to request or suggestion: *I shall come if you like*). **2.** *n.* (usu. in *pl.*) Liking(s), predilection(s) (esp. *likes and dislikes*). **3. ~able** (-ka-) *a.* (**-bly**), pleasant, easy to like; **li'king** *n.*, one's taste (*is it to your liking?*), regard, fondness, taste, fancy, *for* (*have a liking for him*; *no liking for flattery*).

**-like** *suf.* forming *adjs.* f. *ns.*, w. sense 'similar to', 'characteristic of' (*godlike, ladylike, shell-like*); see note on Suffixes, p. ix.

**li'kel|ў** (-kli-). **1.** *a.* (**~iness**). Probable, such as might well happen or be or prove true or turn out to be the thing specified (*a likely story,* often iron.; *it is not likely that he will come*; *his most likely destination is Rome*; **not ~y,** colloq., certainly not, I refuse); to be reasonably expected *to* (*he is not likely to come*); promising, apparently suitable *for* purpose or *to do or be*, capable-looking, (*called at every likely house*; *a likely lad*; *the likeliest place to find him*). **2.** *adv.* Probably. **3. ~ihŏŏd** (-kl-) *n.*, probability (**in all ~ihood,** very probably). [N (**LIKE¹**)]

**li'lac.** **1.** *n.* Shrub with fragrant pale pinkish-violet, or white, blossoms. **2.** *a.* & *n.* (Of) pale pinkish-violet colour. [F f. Sp. f. Arab. f. Pers.]

**liliaceous.** See LILY.

**lilliput'ian** (-shan) *a.* & *n.* Diminutive (person or thing). [*Lilliput,* place in Swift's 'Gulliver's Travels']

**lilt.** (Sc. or literary.) **1.** *v.t.* & *i.* Sing, speak, with very rhythmical effect. **2.** *n.* Such effect, song marked by it; light springing gait. [orig. unkn.]

**li'lУ** *n.* (Flower of) bulbous plant bearing large showy white or reddish or purplish often spotted flowers on tall slender stem, esp. the white or madonna lily (**gild the ~,** try to improve what is already quite satisfactory); heraldic figure of it; (*attrib.*) delicately white (*lily hand*); **~-livered,** cowardly; **~ of the valley,** spring plant with fragrant white bell-shaped flowers; **~-pad,** floating leaf of WATER-*lily*; **lilia'ceous** (-shus) *a.*, of lily family. [F f. L *lilium*]

**limb¹** (-m) *n.* (Astron.) Specified edge (*eastern, lower,* etc., *limb*) of sun etc. [F, or L *limbus* hem, border]

**limb²** (-m) *n.* Leg, arm, or wing, (*escape* **with life and ~,** without grave injury; **tear ~ from ~,** dismember violently); large branch of tree (**out on a ~,** fig., isolated, stranded, at a disadvantage); arm of cross; **~** (**of Satan, of the devil**), mischievous child; **~ of the law,** lawyer, policeman. [E]

**li'mber¹.** **1.** *n.* Detachable front part of gun-carriage. **2.** *v.t.* Attach limber to (gun), connect parts of (gun-carriage), (often *up*). [perh. L *limo -onis* shaft]

**li'mber².** **1.** *a.* Flexible; (of persons etc.) lithe, agile. **2.** *v.i.* & *t.* **~ up,** make (oneself) limber in preparation for athletic etc. activity. [perh. prec.]

**li'mbō¹** *n.* (*pl.* **~s**). Supposed region on border of hell, abode of souls of unbaptized infants and pre-Christian righteous persons; prison, confinement; condition of neglect or oblivion; place for forgotten or unwanted things. [L (*in*) *limbo* (**LIMB¹**)]

**li'mbō²** *n.* (*pl.* **~s**). W. Ind. dance in which dancer bends backwards and passes under horizontal bar, the height of which is progressively lowered. [W. Ind. wd, perh. = LIMBER²]

**lime¹. 1.** *n*. White caustic alkaline substance got by heating limestone etc. and used for making mortar, as fertilizer, etc., (quick~, slaked ~, this before, after, combination with water); (arch.) = BIRD*lime*. **2.** *v.t.* Treat with lime. **3.** ~-kiln (for heating limestone); ~'light, intense white light got by heating cylinder of lime in oxyhydrogen flame, used formerly in theatres; *the ~light*, fig., full glare of publicity; ~'stone, rock composed mainly of calcium carbonate. [E]

**lime². 1.** *n*. Round fruit like lemon but smaller and more acid; ~(-green), (of) pale green colour of this; ~(-juice), antiscorbutic drink; *Li'mey *n. (sl.; or *~-juicer), British person (orig. sailor) or ship [because of enforced use of lime-juice in British Navy]. [F f. Arab.]

**lime³** *n*. ~(-tree), ornamental tree with heart-shaped leaves and fragrant yellow blossom. [alt. of *line* = lind = LINDEN]

**li'merick** *n*. Humorous five-line stanza. [orig. uncert.]

*Li'mey.** See LIME².

**li'mit. 1.** Bounding line, terminal point, (upper, lower, ~, largest, smallest, possible or permissible amount); line or point that may not or cannot be passed (within ~s, to some extent but not unrestrictedly; without ~, unlimited(ly); is the ~, sl., is the last straw, intolerable, etc.; *off ~s, out of bounds). **2.** *v.t.* Set limits to, serve as limit to, restrict *to*; (in *p.p.*) scanty. **3.** ||*limited* (LIABILITY) *company*; ~ed *edition* (with limited number of copies); ~ed *monarchy* etc. (subject to constitutional restrictions). **4.** ~ā'tion *n*., limiting, limited condition or disability (*has his ~ations*, is untalented in some directions), limiting rule or circumstance; ~ative *a*. [L *limes* limit- boundary, frontier]

**limn** (-m) *v.t.* (literary). Paint (picture); portray; **li'mner** *n*. [*lumine* f. F f. L *lumino* ILLUMINATE]

**limnŏ'logў** *n*. Study of fresh waters and their inhabitants; **limnŏ'gical** *a*. (-lly); ~ist *n*. [Gk *limnē* lake]

**li'mousine** (-ōōzēn) *n*. Motor car with closed body and partition behind driver; luxurious motor car. [F]

**limp¹. 1.** *v.i.* Walk lamely; (of damaged ship, aircraft, etc.) proceed slowly or with difficulty; (of verse) be defective. **2.** *n*. Lame walk. [perh. obs. *limp-halt* (HALT²)]

**limp²** *a*. Easily bent and not springing back to shape; (fig.) without will or energy. [perh. prec.]

**li'mpėt** *n*. Marine gastropod mollusc with shallow conical shell sticking tightly to rocks; ~ *mine* (attached to ship's hull and exploding after set time). [E]

**li'mp|id** *a*. Transparently clear (*limpid water, air, eyes, style*); ~i'dǐtў *n*. [F or L]

**li'nage** *n*. Number of lines in page etc., payment by the line. [LINE¹]

**li'nchpin** *n*. Pin passed through axle-end to keep wheel on; (fig.) element or person vital to an organization etc. [E *lynis* = axle-tree]

**Lincs.** *abbr.* Lincolnshire.

**li'nctus** *n*. Medicine, esp. soothing syrupy cough-mixture. [L (*lingo* lick)]

**li'nden** *n*. = LIME³. [E *lind(e)*]

**line¹. 1.** *n*. Piece of cord, rope, etc., serving usu. specified purpose (CLOTHES-*line*; FISH¹ing-*line*; HARD *lines*; PLUMB-*line*); (connection by) wire or cable for telephone or telegraph (*storms have damaged lines to Devon*; get one's, the, ~s crossed, fig., become confused; HOLD¹ *the line*); (in *pl.*, orig. Bibl.) one's lot in life; long narrow mark traced on surface, its use in art, (*boldness, purity, of line*; ~-drawing, done with pen or pencil; ~-engraving, with incised lines); thing resembling such traced mark, band of colour, furrow, wrinkle, (~ *of life*, in palmistry, crease on hand supposedly indicating length of life); (Games etc.) mark limiting court or ground or special parts of them, starting-point in race, (~'sman, umpire's assistant who decides whether ball falls within playing area or not); one of the very narrow horizontal sections in which scenes are televised; (Math.) straight or curved continuous extent of length without breadth, track of moving point; curve connecting all points having specified common property (the L~, the equator, so *crossing the Line*); straight line (**in ~**, so as to form a straight line (*with*); **~ of fire,** path of bullet etc. about to be shot; **~ of sight, vision,** along which observer looks); (Print.) level of base of most letters (*below the line*); contour, outline, lineament, (*the savage lines of his mouth*), shape to which garment is designed (*A line*); (in *pl.*) plan, draft, manner of procedure, (*along these lines*); limit, boundary, (*dividing line*; DRAW *the line*; **on the ~,** not clearly one thing or the other, offered without reserve; *lay on the line*); row of persons or things, *queue, direction as indicated by them, trend, (**come, bring, into ~**, conform or co-operate, induce to do so; **get a ~ on,** colloq., learn something about; **in ~ for,** likely to get; **in ~ with,** in accordance with; **~ abreast, ahead,** Naut., fleet-formations with ships parallel to, following, each other); **~ (of battle),** ships drawn up in battle array; **out of ~,** discordant; (Mil.) connected lines of field-works (FRONT *line*), arrangement of soldiers side by side (**all along the ~,** at every point, lit. or fig.), ‖*the* regular infantry regiments excluding Guards and Rifles (*regiments of the line*); row of printed or written words (**drop person a ~,** colloq., write him a short letter; ‖MARRIAGE *lines*; READ *between the lines*), a verse, (in *pl.*) piece of poetry, (in *pl.*) words of actor's part, (in *pl.*) ‖specified amount (*100* etc. *lines*) of verse, repeated admonition, etc., to be written out as school punishment; series, regular succession of steamers, buses, aircraft, etc., plying between certain places, company conducting this (*airline*; *shipping line*); connected series of persons following one another in time (*a long line of heroes*), esp. several generations of family, lineage, stock, (*comes of a good line*); direction, course, track, (*line of communication*); single track of railwa▼ (**up, down, ~** for UP, DOWN[3], trains), one branch of railway system (*main, branch, line*), whole system under one management; course of procedure, conduct, thought, etc., (HARD *line; line of least* RESISTANCE; **shoot a ~,** sl., boast, talk or act pretentiously); department of activity, province, branch of business, (**in the ~ of** *duty* etc., as a proper part of; **in, out**

of, one's **~,** interesting, concerning, one, or not); class of commercial goods (*sells a nice line in hats*); (as measure) $\frac{1}{12}$ inch. **2.** *v.t.* & *i.* Mark with lines (*a face lined with pain*; **~d paper,** ruled); post men or take post or stand at intervals along (*line the border with troops*; *people, trees, lined the road*); **~-out,** (Rugby Footb.) parallel lines of opposing forwards at right angles to touch-line when ball is thrown in; **~ up,** arrange, be arranged, in line(s); **~-up,** line of persons for inspection, arrangement of persons in team etc. **3.** **lī'nĕage** *n.,* lineal descent, ancestry; **lī'nĕal** *a.* (**-lly**), in the direct line of descent or ancestry, linear; **lī'nĕament** *n.* (usu. in *pl.*), distinctive feature or characteristic esp. of face; **lī'nĕar** *a.,* of or in lines, long and narrow and of uniform breadth; **Linear A, B,** forms of ancient writing in Crete and Greece; **lĭnĕă'rĭtў** *n.*; **lī'nĕr[1]** *n.,* ship, aircraft, belonging to regular line and used for passenger transport, train belonging to regular line, (**~r train,** fast freight train with detachable containers on permanently coupled wagons). [E & F f. L *linea* (*linum* flax)]

**line[2]** *v.t.* Apply layer of (usu. different) material to inside of (garment, box, etc.); fill (purse, pocket, stomach, etc.); serve as lining for; **lī'ner[2]** *n.*; **lī'nĭng** *n.,* such layer of material, contents of purse etc. [obs. *line* linen, used for linings]

**lī'nĕn. 1.** *n.* Cloth woven from flax; (collect.) articles made, or orig. made, of linen, as sheets, table--cloths, shirts, undergarments, (**wash one's dirty ~ at home, in public,** keep quiet, not keep quiet, about domestic quarrels etc.); ‖**~-draper,** dealer in linen, cotton, etc. **2.** *a.* Made of linen. [E, rel. to L *linum* flax]

**lĭng[1]** *n.* A sea-fish. [prob. Du.]

**lĭng[2]** *n.* Kind of heather. [N]

**-lĭng** *suf.* forming *ns.* denoting person or thing connected with (*hireling, sapling*) or having the property of being (*grayling, underling*) or undergoing (*starveling*), or denoting diminutive (*codling, duckling*), often derog. (*lordling*). [E; dim. f. N]

**lĭ'nger** (-ngg-) *v.i.* Be slow to depart, fail to arrive punctually, stay about, dally, (*round* place or person; *over, on, upon,* subject etc.); (of disease etc.) be protracted; (of moribund person or custom) be slow in dying. [N (LONG)]

**li'ngerie** (lă'nzherē) n. Women's underwear and night-clothes. [F (*linge* linen)]

**li'ngō** (-nggō) n. (*pl.* **~es**). (derog. or joc.) Foreign language; vocabulary of special subject or class of people. [prob. Port. *lingoa* f. L *lingua* tongue]

**lingua frä'nca** (-nggwa) n. Mixture of Italian with French, Greek, Arabic, and Spanish, used in the Levant; any language used by speakers whose native languages are different; system for mutual understanding. [It., = Frankish tongue]

**li'ngua|l** (-nggw-) a. (**-lly**). Of or formed by the tongue; of speech or languages; **~ist** n., person skilled in languages or in linguistics; **~i'stic** a. (-ically), of the study of languages, of language; **~i'stics** n. [L *lingua* tongue, language]

**li'niment** n. Embrocation, usu. made with oil. [L *linio* smear)]

**li'ning.** See LINE².

**link. 1.** n. One loop or ring of chain or of knitted work etc.; connecting part, thing or person that unites or provides continuity; state or means of connection; member of series (MISSING *link*); = CUFF-*link*; **~('man**, person providing continuity in broadcast programme. **2.** v.t. & i. Connect, join, (*together, to, with*); clasp or intertwine (hands, arms); be joined *on* or *in to* system, company, etc.; **~ up**, connect, combine; **~-up** n., act or result of linking up; **~'age** n., system of links, state of being linked. [N]

**links** n. (as *sing.* or *pl.*) Golf-course. [E, = rising ground]

**Linnae'an** a. & n. (Follower of) *Linnaeus* or his classification of plants. [person]

**li'nnet** n. Song-bird, the common brown or grey finch. [F f. *lin* flax (flax-seeds being its food)]

**li'nō** n. (*pl.* **~s**). Linoleum; **~cut**, (print made from) design cut in relief on block of linoleum. [abbr.]

**linō'leum** n. Floor-covering of canvas thickly coated with a preparation of linseed oil etc. [L *linum* flax, *oleum* oil]

**Li'notype** n. Composing-machine producing lines of words as single slugs of metal, used esp. for newspapers. [= *line of type*; P]

**li'nseed** n. Seed of flax. [E (LINE¹)]

**li'nsey-woo'lsey** (-z-; -zī) n. Fabric of coarse wool woven on cotton warp. [prob. *Lindsey* place + WOOL]

**li'nt** n. Linen with one side made fluffy by scraping, used for dressing wounds; fluff; **~-white**, flaxen in colour. [perh. F *linette* (*lin* flax)]

**li'ntel** n. Horizontal timber or stone across top of door or window. [F (LIMIT)]

**li'on** n. Large powerful tawny African and S. Asian carnivorous feline with tufted tail and (in the male) flowing shaggy mane (**~ (-heart)**, courageous person; **~-hearted**, brave; **~'s mouth**, perilous position; **~'s share**, largest or best part); celebrated person much sought after socially (*is a literary lion*); national emblem of Great Britain (**the British L~**, the nation personified); **~ and unicorn**, supporters of British royal coat of arms); representation of lion (esp. Her.); (*L~*) sign of ZODIAC; **~ess** n.; **~ize** v.t., treat (person) as celebrity. [AF f. L *leo leon-* f. Gk]

**lip. 1.** n. Either of the fleshy parts forming edges of opening of mouth (*upper, lower* or *under*, **lip**; **bite** one's **~** in vexation or to repress emotion, laughter, etc.; **curl** one's **~** in scorn; **lick, smack**, one's **~s**, in relish or anticipation of food, or fig.; not OPEN one's *lips*; **pass** person's **~s**, be eaten, spoken, etc.; **stiff upper ~**, firmness, fortitude); (sl.) impudence (*none of your lip!*); edge of cup, vessel, cavity, wound, etc., esp. part shaped for pouring from; **~-reading**, method used esp. by deaf persons to understand speech from lip movements, so **~-read** v.t. & i.; **~-salve** (to prevent or cure dry or sore lips; fig., flattery); **~-service**, insincere expression of support; **~-stick**, (n.) (stick of) cosmetic for colouring lips, (*v.t.*) apply lipstick to; (-)**~ped** (-pt) a. **2.** v.t. (**-pp-**). Touch with lips, apply lips to; touch lightly. [E]

**li'quid. 1.** a. Having a consistency like that of water or oil, incompressible but not resistant to change of shape, neither solid nor gaseous, (*liquid* PARAFFIN; **~ air, oxygen**, etc., reduced to liquid state by intense cold); watery, having the transparency, translucence, or brightness, of pure water (*liquid lustre, eyes, sky, blue*); (of sounds) clear, pure, not guttural or discordant, (*blackbird's liquid notes*); (of assets) easily converted into cash. **2.** *n.* Liquid substance (e.g. water, oil, wine, blood, molten metal); sound of *l* or *r*; **li′quefy** *v.t. & i.*, make or become liquid; **liquefa′ction** *n.*; **liqueur′** (-kūr′) *n.*, strong spirituous liquor sweetened and flavoured with aromatic substances and usu. drunk in small quantities after meals (**liqueur-glass**, very small glass for liqueurs); **~āte** *v.t. & i.*, pay off (debt), wind up affairs of (company, firm) by ascertaining liabilities and apportioning assets, put an end to or get rid of (often by violent means); **~ā′tion** *n.* (**go into ~ation**, of company, have its affairs wound up, become bankrupt); **~ātor** *n.*; **liqui′dity** *n.*, state of being liquid or having liquid assets; **~ize** *v.t.*, reduce to liquid state; **~izer** *n.*, machine used to make purées, emulsify, etc.; **li′quor** (-ker), (*n.*) liquid (usu. fermented or distilled) for drinking (**in liquor, the worse for liquor**, more or less drunk), liquid used in or resulting from some process, esp. cooking, (*v.t. & i.*, sl.) **liquor** (**up**), (cause to) drink much alcoholic liquor. [L (*liqueo* be liquid)]

**li′quorice** (-ker-), **li′co-**, *n.* Black substance used in medicine and as sweetmeat; plant from whose root it is obtained. [AF *lycorys* f. L f. Gk *glukus* sweet, *rhiza* root]

**liquorish.** See LICKERISH.

**lir′a** (lēr′a) *n.* (*pl.* lire *pr.* -ā, ~s). Italian and Turkish monetary unit. [It. f. Prov. f. L *libra* pound]

**lisle** (līl) *n.* ~ (**thread**), fine smooth cotton thread used for stockings etc. [*Lille*, place]

**lisp. 1.** *v.i. & t.* Substitute sound like (th) or (dh) for sibilants in speaking; (of child) speak with imperfect pronunciation; say lispingly. **2.** *n.* Such pronunciation. [E]

**li′ssom** *a.* Lithe, agile. [LITHE]

**list**[1]. **1.** *n.* Roll or catalogue or inventory of names, things to be done, etc., (**~ price**, as shown in published list); selvage, this torn off and used e.g. as material for slippers; (in *pl.*) palisades enclosing tilting-

-ground (**enter the ~s**, fig., issue or accept challenge to controversy etc.). **2.** *v.t.* Enter in list. [E]

**list**[2] *v.t. & i.* (arch.; 3 *sing. pres.* ~, ~′eth; *past* ~, ~′ed). Desire, choose, (to do, or abs.; *ye who list to hear*; *wind bloweth where it listeth*). [E (LUST)]

**list**[3] *n., & v.i.* Lean(ing) over to one side of (ship, owing to leak, shifting cargo, subsidence, etc.; also of building, fence, etc.). [orig. unkn.] [E]

**list**[4] *v.i. & t.* (arch.) Listen (to). [E]

**li′sten** (-sen) *v.i.* Make effort to hear something, hear with attention person speaking; give attention with ear *to* (person, sound, story); yield *to* temptation or request or advice or its author; ~ (**out**) **for**, seek to hear (sound etc.) by waiting alertly for it; ~ **in**, tap communication made by telephone, use radio receiver; **~ing-post**, point near enemy's lines for detecting his movements by sound, (fig.) place for gathering information from reports etc.; **~er** (-sn-) *n.*, one who listens (**good ~er**, one who habitually listens with interest or sympathy), person receiving broadcast radio programmes.

**li′stless** *a.* Without inclinations or energy, suffering from lassitude, languid. [E (obs. *list* inclination f. LIST[2])]

**lit.** See LIGHT[1] 3 and LIGHT[2] 3.

**li′tany** *n.* Series of petitions to be recited by priest etc. and responded to by congregation (**the L~**, that in Book of Common Prayer). [F f. L *litania* f. Gk = prayer]

**li(t)chi′, lichee′, lychee′**, (lēchē′) *n.* (Sweetish pulpy shelled fruit of) a Chinese tree. [Chin.]

**\*liter.** See LITRE.

**li′ter|al. 1.** *a.* (-lly). Of, in, expressed by, letter(s) of alphabet (**~al error**, misprint of a letter); exactly corresponding to the original words (*literal translation*); taking words in their usual sense without mysticism or allegory or metaphor (*literal interpretation*); **~al(-minded)**, (of person) prosaic, matter-of-fact; so called without exaggeration (*literal extermination*), (colloq.) so called with some exaggeration (*a literal avalanche of mail*). **2.** *n.* Literal error. **3. ~acy** *n.*, ability to read and write; ‖**literae hūmănĭŏr′ĕs** (-z) *n.*, POLITE letters (esp. name of school of classics and philosophy at Oxford University) [L, = the more humane studies]; ~**alīsm** n., insistence on literal interpretation, adherence to the letter; ~**alist** n.; ~**arў** a. (-**ily**, -**iness**), of, constituting, occupied with, literature or books or written composition (~**ary man**, author, scholar), (of word, idiom) not colloquial, used chiefly by writers; ~**ate**, (a.) able to read and write, (n.) literate person, ‖man admitted to Anglican orders without university degree; ~**a'ti** (-ah'tē, -ĭ) n.pl., men of letters, the learned class; ~**ature** n., books and written works esp. of kind valued for form and style, the production of these or their authors as a class, the realm of letters, the writings of a country or period, *the* books etc. *treating of a* subject, (colloq.) printed matter. [F or L (*littera* letter)]

**lithe** (-dh) a. Flexible, supple. [E]

**lĭ'thō** n. (pl. ~s), a., & v.t. (colloq.) (Produce by) lithographic process). [abbr.]

**lĭthŏ'graph|ў** n. Process of obtaining prints from stone or metal surface so treated that what is to be printed can be inked but the remaining area rejects ink; **lĭ'thograph** (-ahf), (n.) print thus produced, (v.t.) produce such print of; ~**er** n.; **lĭthŏgrǎ'phĭc** a. (-**ically**). [Gk *lithos* stone]

**lĭ'tĭg|āte** v.i. & t. (~**able**). Go to law, contest (point) at law; ~**ant**, (a.) engaged in lawsuit, (n.) party to lawsuit; ~**ā'tion** n.; **lĭtĭ'gious** (-jus) a., fond of litigation, contentious. [L (*lis lit-* lawsuit)]

**lĭ'tmus** n. Blue colouring-matter got from lichens that is turned red by acid and restored to blue by alkali; ~**-paper** (unsized and stained with litmus as test for acids or alkalis). [N, = dye-moss]

**lĭ'totēs** (-z) n. Ironic understatement esp. using negative to express contrary (*I shan't be sorry when it's over* = *I shall be very glad* etc.). [L f. Gk (*litos* plain, meagre)]

**lĭ'tre**, *lĭ'ter, (lē'ter) n. Unit of capacity in metric system, 1 cubic decimetre or about 1¾ pints. [F f. L f. Gk *litra*]

**Litt.D.** abbr. Doctor of Letters. [L *Litterarum Doctor*]

**lĭ'tter. 1.** n. Vehicle containing couch shut in by curtains and carried on men's shoulders or by beasts of burden; kind of stretcher for sick and wounded; straw etc. as bedding for animals; straw and dung of farmyard; odds and ends lying about, disorderly accumulation of papers etc. (\*~**bug**, ~**lout**, person who leaves rubbish in public places); the young animals brought forth at a birth. **2.** v.t. Provide (horse etc.) with litter as bedding, spread straw etc. on (stable-floor etc.); make (place) untidy; give birth to (whelps etc., or abs.). [AF f. L (*lectus* bed)]

**lĭttérateur** (lētĕrahter') n. Literary man. [F]

**lĭ'ttle** a., n., & adv. **1.** a. (LESS, LESSER, **lĭ'ttler**; LEAST, **lĭ'ttlest**; *also* **smaller**, **smallest**). Small (often with emotional implications not given by *small*; cf. GREAT), not great or big; working etc. on only a small scale (*the little shopkeeper against the supermarkets*); (as distinctive epithet) of smaller or smallest size etc. (*little* AUK, BEAR[1], FINGER, *toe*; L~ Venice etc., small area reminiscent of); young (*a little child*; ~ **man, woman,** boy, girl, esp. as joc. or affectionate *voc.*; ~ **ones**, children, cubs, etc.), younger (*little brother, sister*); as of child, evoking tenderness, condescension, amusement, etc., (*him and his little ways*; *so that is* **your ~ game,** what you hope to do undetected; **the ~ woman,** colloq., one's wife); short in stature, distance, or time, (*a little man; go a little way; wait a little while*); trivial, paltry, mean, (*exaggerates every little difficulty; little things please little minds; you little sneak*); not much (*very little butter left; did little or no damage*); **a** certain though small amount of (*give me a little butter*); **in ~,** on a small scale; **no ~,** considerable (*took no little trouble over it*). **2.** n. Not much, only a small amount, (*got little out of it; ~ or nothing,* hardly anything; *did not a ~ for us,* a great deal; THINK *little of*); *a* certain but no great amount (*knows a little of everything*; **a ~,** rather, somewhat; **not a ~** vexed etc., extremely); short time or distance (~ **by ~,** by degrees). **3.** adv. (LESS, LEAST). To a small extent only (*little-known authors; is little more than speculation*); not at all (*little does he know*). **4. little** BIRD; ~ **end,** smaller end of connecting-rod, attached to piston; **L~ Englander,** (Hist.) one opposed to British imperial policy; ~ **magazine** (literary, usu. with experimental writing and in small format); **the ~ people**, fairies; **L~ Russian**, Ukrainian; *little* SLAM². [E]

**li′ttoral. 1.** *a.* Of or on the shore. **2.** *n.* Region lying along the shore. [L (*littus litor-* shore)]

**li′turgy** *n.* Fixed form of public worship used in a church; *the Book of Common Prayer*; **litur′gical** *a.* (**-lly**). [F or L f. Gk, = public worship]

**live¹** *attrib. a.* That is alive, living; (joc.) actual, not pretended or toy, (*a real live burglar*); (of broadcast; also *pred.*) heard or seen during the occurrence of an event, not recorded or edited; full of power, energy, or importance, not obsolete or exhausted, (*a live issue*); glowing (*live coals*); (of shell, match, wire, etc.) unexploded, unkindled, charged with or carrying electricity; (of rock) not detached, seeming part of earth's frame; (of wheel etc. in machinery) moving or imparting motion; ~ **bait**, living fish, worms, etc., as bait; ~ **birth** (of living child); ~′**stock**, animals kept or dealt in for use or profit; ~ **weight** (of animal before being killed); ~ **wire**, (fig.) highly energetic forceful person; ~′**lihood** (-vl-) *n.*, means of living, sustenance; ~′**ly** (-vl-) *a.* (**-iness**), lifelike or realistic, full of life, energy, interest, or vividness, (*look ~*, move quickly or energetically), (joc.) exciting or dangerous (*police had a lively time*), bright, vivacious; **li′ven** *v.t. & i.*, (colloq.) brighten, cheer, (esp. *up*). [ALIVE]

**live²** *v.i. & t.* Be alive, have animal or vegetable life; subsist (*up*)*on*, depend for subsistence or (fig.) social position etc. (*lives on fruit, on his wife's earnings, on his reputation*); ~ **and let ~**, condone other's failings so as to secure same treatment for oneself; ~ **by one's wits**, esp. by deceit or fraud; *live from* HAND *to mouth*; ~ **on air**, (appear to) take no food); conduct oneself (honestly, viciously, like a saint, etc.; ~ **down**, cause (scandal, discreditable incident, etc.) to be forgotten by blameless conduct thereafter; ~ **up to one's principles**, **faith**, etc., put them into practice; ~ **up to one's promise**, **reputation**, etc., not fall short of it); arrange one's

habits, expenditure, feeding, etc., (~ **well**, on luxurious food); (w. cogn. obj.) spend, pass, (*live a virtuous*, DOUBLE, *life*; ~ **it up**, live gaily and extravagantly; ~ **one's own life**, follow one's own principles etc., live independently); express in one's life (*live a lie*); enjoy life to the full (*you haven't lived till you've seen Naples*); continue alive (*patient may live*; *lived to regret his decision*; ~ **and learn**, continually discover new facts; ~ **through**, survive; ~ **to**, survive and reach (*lived to a great age*); **long** ~ **the Queen!**, excl. of loyalty); (of thing) survive (*his memory lives*), (of ship) escape destruction; make one's permanent abode (‖~ **in**, **out**, of domestic etc. staff residing on premises or not; ~ **together**, esp. of man and woman not his wife, share dwelling-place; ~ **with**, share dwelling-place with, fig. tolerate, find congenial; **li′vable**, **li′veable**, (-va-) *a.*, (of life) worth living, (of house, person, etc.) fit to live in or with; **li′ver¹** *n.*, person who lives in specified way (*clean, loose, liver*; *good ~r*, esp. gourmand); **li′ving²** *n.*, (esp.) livelihood, ‖position as vicar or rector with income and/or property, (**cost of living**, of basic necessities of life; **good living**, luxurious feeding; **living-room**, for general day use; **living wage**, on which earner and family can live without privation); **li′ving²** *a.*, contemporary, now alive, (*the greatest living poet*; **in the land of the living**, still alive; **living death**, state of hopeless misery; **within living memory**, that of some persons still living), (of likeness) lifelike, exact, (of language) still in vernacular use, (of rock)= LIVE¹. [E]

**li′velŏng** (-vl-) *a.* (poet., rhet.) Whole length of (**the ~ day**, **night**, **summer**, delightfully or tediously long as it is). [LIEF, LONG, assim. to LIVE²]

**lively**, **li′ven**. See LIVE¹.

**li′ver¹**. See LIVE².

**li′ver²** *n.* Large glandular organ in abdomen of vertebrates, secreting bile; flesh of some animals' liver as food; ~**(-colour)**, dark reddish brown; LILY-*livered*; ‖~ **salts** (to cure dyspepsia or biliousness); ~ **sausage** (filled with cooked liver etc.); ~**wort**, lichen-like plant with liver-shaped leaves; ~**ish**, (colloq.)

~ў¹, *adjs.*, suffering from disorder of liver, peevish, glum. [E]

**Liverpǔ'dlian** *a.* & *n.* (joc.) (Native) of *Liverpool*. [place]

**li'very²** *n.* Allowance of provender for horses (**at ~,** of horse, kept for owner and fed and groomed for fixed charge; **~man,** keeper of, attendant in, **~ stable,** where horses are kept at livery or let out for hire); distinctive clothes worn by member of City Company or person's man-servant (**in, out of ~,** of servant, so attired or in plain clothes; ‖**~ company,** one of London City companies that formerly had distinctive cos-tume; ‖**~man,** member of such company); (fig.) distinctive guise or marking (*the stoat in his winter livery*; *the livery of grief*); **li'veried** (-id) *a.,* wearing livery. [AF *liveré,* p.p. of *livrer* DELIVER]

**li'vid** *a.* Of bluish leaden colour; ‖(colloq.) very angry. [F or L]

**li'ving¹,²** See LIVE².

**li'zard** *n.* Reptile having usu. long body and tail, four legs, movable eyelids, and scaly or granulated hide. [F *lesard* f. L *lacertus*]

‖**L.J.** *abbr.* (*pl.* L.JJ.) Lord Justice.

**'ll** *v.* (usu. after *prons.*) = SHALL, WILL, (*I'll, he'll, that'll*). [abbr.]

**lla'ma** (lah'-, lyah'-) *n.* S. Amer. woolly-haired ruminant used as beast of burden. [Sp. f. Quechua]

**LL.B., LL.D., LL.M.,** *abbrs.* Bache-lor, Doctor, Master, of Laws. [L *legum baccalaureus, doctor, magister*]

**Lloyd's** (loidz) *n.* Incorporated society of underwriters in London; **~ Register,** annual classified list of shipping. [*Lloyd,* person]

**ln** *abbr.* natural logarithm.

**lō** *int.* (arch.) drawing attention (**lo and behold,** joc. introduction to mention of surprising fact). [E]

**loach** *n.* Small freshwater fish. [F]

**load. 1.** *n.* What is (to be) carried, (fig.) weight of care, responsibility, etc., (**take a ~ off** person's **mind,** relieve him of anxiety); amount usu. or actually carried, this as weight or measure of some substances, (*cart--load of bricks*; *plane-load of refugees*; **get a ~ of,** sl., look at, listen to, attentively); (in *pl.,* colloq.) plenty *of*; material object or force acting as a weight etc.; (Electr.) amount of power supplied by a generating station or carried by an electric circuit; **~ line,** = PLIMSOLL line; **~'-**

stone, lo'destone, magnetic oxide of iron, piece of it used as magnet; (fig.) thing that attracts. **2.** *v.t.* & *i.* Put load on or aboard (person, animal, vehicle, ship, etc.); place (load, cargo) aboard ship, on vehicle, etc.; (of ship, vehicle, person) take load aboard or *up*; burden, strain; weight, add extra weight to, (**~ed dice,** so weighted as to fall with a certain face up; **~ed question,** fig., carrying hidden implication); supply, assail, overwhelmingly *with* (*loaded her with gifts, praise, work, abuse*; *air loaded with soot*), (in *p.p.,* sl.) rich, drunk, *drugged; charge (firearm); insert film in (camera). **3. ~'er** *n.,* **~'ing** *a.,* (gun, machine, etc.) loaded in specified way (*breech, muzzle, front, top, -loader, -loading*). [E, = way]

**loaf¹** *n.* (*pl.* **-ves** *pr.* -vz). Quantity of bread baked alone or as separate or separable part of batch, usu. of standard weight, (**half a ~ is better than no bread,** motto of compromise, opp. *all or nothing*); (sl.) head (**use one's ~,** use one's common sense); (**meat** etc.) **~,** minced or chopped meat moulded into loaflike shape and cooked, usu. to be eaten cold; (**sugar-**)**~,** conical moulded mass of sugar (**~ sugar,** this as whole or cut into lumps). [E]

**loaf²** *v.i.* Spend time idly, hang about. [orig. uncert.]

**loam.** *n.* Rich soil of clay, sand, and decayed vegetable matter; **~'ў** *a.* (-iness). [E]

**loan. 1.** *n.* Thing lent, sum to be returned with or without interest, money lent by individuals etc. to State usu. at stipulated interest, lending or being lent (*on loan*; **ask for the ~ of,** ask leave to borrow). **2.** *v.t.* Grant loan of. **3. ~ collection** (of pictures etc. lent for exhibition); **~-translation,** expression adopted by one language from another in more or less literally translated form (e.g. F *gratte-ciel* f. *skyscraper*); **~--word,** word adopted by one language from another in more or less modified form (e.g. *morale, naïve*). [E]

**loath, lōth,** *pred. a.* Disinclined, reluctant, (usu. *to do,* or abs.; *for* person *to do, that*; **nothing ~,** glad or gladly enough); **loathe** (-dh) *v.t.,* regard with disgust; **loa'thing**

(-dh-) *n.*; **loa'thly** (-dh-; **-iness**; arch. or literary), **loa'thsome** (-dh-), *adjs.*, causing nausea or disgust, repulsive, odious. [E]

**loaves.** See LOAF¹.

**lŏb. 1.** *v.t.* & *i.* (**-bb-**). Send (ball), send ball, with slow or high-pitched motion esp. in cricket and· lawn tennis. **2.** *n.* Such ball. [prob. LDu.]

**lŏ'bar, lŏ'bāte.** See LOBE.

**lŏ'bby̆. 1.** *n.* Porch, ante-room, entrance-hall, corridor; (in House of Commons etc.) large hall open to public used esp. for interviews between M.P.s and others, (also **division** ~) one of two corridors to which members retire to vote; body of those who lobby. **2.** *v.t.* & *i.* Seek to influence (members of legislature), get (bill etc.) *through*, by interviews etc. in lobby; solicit members' votes or influence (of person); frequent parliamentary lobby for this purpose; ~**ist** *n.* [L *lobia* LODGE]

**lŏbe** *n.* The lower soft pendulous part of the outer ear, similar flap of other natural objects often being one of several, (*lobes of the liver, of a leaf, of the brain*); **lŏ'bar, lŏ'bāte, lōbed** (-bd), *adjs.*; **lŏbŏ'tomy̆** *n.*, (Med.) = LEUCOtomy. [L f. Gk *lobos* lobe, pod]

**lobē'lĭa** *n.* Herbaceous plant with brightly coloured flowers and cleft corolla. [*Lobel*, person]

**lŏ'bscouse** *n.* Sailor's dish of meat stewed with vegetables and ship's biscuit. [orig. unkn.]

**lŏ'bster** *n.* Large edible marine crustacean with stalked eyes and heavy pincer-like claws, that turns from bluish black to scarlet when boiled; its flesh as food; ~**-pot,** basket in which lobsters are trapped. [E f. L *locusta* lobster, LOCUST]

**lŏ'būle** *n.* Small lobe; ~**ar** *a.* [LOBE]

**lŏ'bworm** (-wĕrm) *n.* Large earthworm used as fishing-bait. [LOB in obs. sense 'pendulous object']

**lō'cal. 1.** *a.* (~**ly**). In regard to place; belonging to, existing in, peculiar to, certain place(s) (*local customs, history*); of one's own neighbourhood (*the local doctor*); of or affecting a part and not the whole (*local anaesthetic, pain*); ||(on envelope) for delivery in this town or district; ||~ **authority,** body charged with administration of local government; ~ **call,** telephone call to nearby place, charged at low rate; ~

colour, touches of detail in story etc. designed to provide convincing background; ~ **Derby,** contest between two teams from same district; ||~ **government,** system of administration of county, district, parish, etc., by elected representatives of those who live there; ~ **preacher,** Methodist layman authorized to preach in his own circuit; ~ **time** (measured from position of sun at place concerned). **2.** *n.* Inhabitant of particular district; train stopping at all stations; ||(colloq.) *the* local public house. **3.** **loca'le** (-ah'l) *n.*, scene or locality of operations or events; ~**ism** *n.*, attachment to a place, limitation of ideas resulting from this; **locă'lĭty̆** *n.*, thing's position, site or scene of something, faculty of remembering and recognizing district or places, finding one's way, etc.; ~**ize** *v.t.*, invest with particular place's characteristics, assign to particular place, decentralize; ~**izā'tion** *n.*; **locā'te** *v.t.*, state locality of, discover exact place of, establish in a place, (in *pass.*) be situated; **locā'tion** *n.*, (esp.) particular place, place other than studio where (part of) film is made (*on location*); **lŏ'cative** *a.* & *n.*, (Gram.) (case) denoting place where; **locā'tor** *n.* [F f. L (*locus* place)]

**loc. cit.** *abbr. loco citato.*

**lŏch** (-χ, -k) *n.* Scottish lake or land-locked arm of the sea. [Gael.]

**lō'cī.** See LOCUS.

**lŏck¹** *n.* One of the portions into which the hair groups itself (in *pl.*) the hair (*her golden locks*). [E]

**lŏck². 1.** *n.* Mechanism for fastening door, lid, etc., with bolt that requires key of particular shape to work it (**under** ~ **and key,** locked up); mechanism for exploding charge of gun· (~, **stock, and barrel,** whole of thing, completely); section of canal or river confined within sluiced gates for shifting boats from one level to another; interlocked or jammed state; wrestling-hold that keeps opponent's arm etc. fixed; kinds of check in machinery; turning of front wheels of vehicle (**full** ~, maximum extent of this); ~ (**forward**), (Rugby Footb.) player in second row of scrum; ||~ **hospital** (for treatment of venereal disease); ~**-keeper,** ~**'sman,** keeper of canal etc. lock; ~**-knit,** (fabric) knitted with interlocking stitch; ~-**nut**, nut screwed down on another to keep it tight; ~'**smith**, maker and mender of locks; ~-**stitch**, secure sewing-machine stitch. **2.** *v.t. & i.* Fasten (door, box, etc.) with lock, shut *up* (house etc.) thus, (*lock the* STABLE-*door after the horse has bolted*); (of door etc.) be lockable; shut (person, thing) *up*, *in*, *into*; enclose, hold fast *in*; (fig.) store (*up*, *away*) inaccessible (*history locked up in hieroglyphics*; *capital locked up in land*); keep (person) *out* by locking door (esp. of employer refusing employees access to place of work until they accept his conditions); ~-**out** *n.*, this procedure); bring, come, into rigidly fixed position, (cause to) jam or catch, (*locked in an embrace*; *the wheels locked with the force of the collision*); ~'**jaw**, variety of tetanus in which the jaws are rigidly closed; ~ **on to**, (of radar, missile using it) locate and then track automatically, cause (radar etc.) to do this; ~-**up**, (time of) locking up school etc. for night, unrealizable state of invested etc. capital, house or room for temporary detention of prisoners, ||(premises etc.) that can be locked up. **3.** ~'**er** *n.*, (esp.) small cupboard e.g. one reserved for individual's use in public room, (Naut.) chest or compartment for clothes, stores, ammunition, etc., (DAVY JONES's *locker*; **not a shot in** one's, **the,** ~**er**, no money in one's pocket, no chance left). [E]

**lŏ´ckĕt** *n.* Small ornamental case containing portrait etc. as memento, and usu. hung from neck. [F dim. of *loc* latch, LOCK²]

**lŏ´cō¹** *n.* (*pl.* ~s). (colloq.) Locomotive engine. [abbr.]

\***lŏ´cō²** *a.* (sl.) Crazy. [Sp.]

*loco citato* (lŏkō sĭtä´tō, -ah´-) *adv.* In the passage already quoted. [L, = in the place cited]

**lŏcomō´tion** *n.* (Power of) motion from place to place; travel, way (esp. artificial) of travelling; **lŏ´comōtive** (*or* -mō´-), (*a.*) of or having or effecting locomotion, not stationary, (**locomotive engine**, esp., engine for drawing trains; **locomotive organs**, legs etc.), (*n.*) locomotive engine; **lŏ´comōtor**(ў̆) *adjs.*, of locomotion (*locomotor* ATAXY). [L LOCUS, MOTION]

**lŏ´cum** *n.* (colloq.) = foll. [abbr.]

**lōcum tĕ´nĕn|s** (-z) *n.* (*pl.* ~tes *pr.* -ĕ´ntēz). Deputy acting esp. for clergyman or doctor. [L, = (one) holding place]

**lō´cus** *n.* (*pl.* **lo´ci** *pr.* -sī). (Math.) curve etc. made by all points satisfying certain conditions, or by defined motion of point or line or surface; ~ *classicus*, best known or most authoritative passage on a subject. [L, = place]

**lō´cust** *n.* African or Asian grasshopper migrating in swarms and consuming all vegetation of districts; (fig.) person of devouring or destructive propensities; kinds of tree and their fruit. [F f. L (*locusta* locust, LOBSTER)]

**locū´tion** *n.* Style of speech; a phrase or idiom. [F or L (*loquor locut-* speak)]

**lōde** *n.* Vein of metal ore; ~'**star**, star that is steered by, esp. pole-star, (fig.) guiding principle, object of pursuit; ~'**stone**, = LOADstone. [var. LOAD]

**lŏdg|e. 1.** *n.* Small house, esp. one at entrance to park or grounds of large house, occupied by keeper of gate etc.; house in forest, on moor, etc., used in the hunting or shooting season; porter's room(s) at entrance or gateway of college, factory, etc.; residence of head of Cambridge college; (place of meeting for) members of branch of society such as Freemasons (**grand** ~**e**, governing body of Freemasons or similar society); beaver's or otter's lair. **2.** *v.t. & i.* Provide with sleeping--quarters, receive or establish as guest or inmate, reside or have one's quarters esp. as lodger (*in*, *at*, *with*); deposit for security or attention (*lodge money etc. with* person; *lodge a complaint about the food*); place (power etc.) *in*, *with*, *in the hands of*, (person); (make, let) stick without going further (*lodged a bullet, bullet lodged, in his brain*). **3.** ~'**er** *n.*, (esp.) person paying for accommodation in another's house; ~'**ing** *n.*, accommodation in hired rooms, dwelling-place, (in *pl.*) residence of head of Oxford college, (~**ing-house**, in which lodgings are let; ||**common** ~**ing-house**, usu. one with dormitory in which bed can be had for the night); ~'(**e**)**ment** (-jm-) *n.*, (esp.) stable position gained, foothold, accumulation of matter intercepted in fall or transit. [F *loge* f. L *lobia* f. Gmc (LEAF)]

**lō′ĕss** *n.* Deposit of fine wind-blown soil esp. in basins of large rivers. [Swiss G, = loose]

**lŏft** (or lawft). **1.** *n.* Attic; room over stable esp. for hay and straw; pigeon-house; gallery in church or hall (*organ-loft*, *rood-loft*); (Golf) backward slope on face of club, a lofting stroke. **2.** *v.t.* Hit, throw, kick, etc., (ball) high up. **3.** ~′ў *a.* (~ily, ~iness), of imposing height (*lofty mountain, flight*; not used of person), haughty or keeping aloof (*lofty disdain*), exalted, distinguished, high-flown, sublime, (*lofty ideals, strains*). [N, = air, upper room]

**lŏg¹. 1.** *n.* Unhewn piece of felled tree, any large rough piece of wood esp. cut for firewood, (*fall, lie, like a* ~, unconscious, immovable; **sleep like a** ~, sleep soundly); floating device attached to line (~-**line**) and trailed from ship to ascertain its speed; ~(-**book**), book in which are recorded details and events of ship's or aircraft's voyage(s), traveller's diary etc., regularly maintained record of progress or performance; ~-**book**, ‖book showing registration details of motor vehicle; ~ **cabin**, hut built of logs; ~-**rolling**, mutual help, esp. in politics [f. phr. *you roll my log and I'll roll yours*]; ~′**wood**, (wood, used in dyeing, of) a W. Ind. tree. **2.** *v.t.* (-**gg**-). Cut into logs; enter in ship's log-book; enter (data etc.) in regular record; attain (cumulative total thus recorded; *how many miles have we logged?*). [orig. unkn.]

**lŏg².** *n.* Logarithm. [abbr.]

**lō′ganbĕrrЎ** *n.* Fruit got by cross between raspberry and Amer. blackberry. [*Logan*, person]

**lō′gan(-stōne)** *n.* Poised heavy stone rocking at a touch. [*logan* = (dial.) *logging*, = rocking]

**lŏ′garithm** (-dhĕm, -thĕm) *n.* One of a series of reckoning-numbers tabulated to simplify computation by enabling addition and subtraction to be used instead of multiplication and division; **lŏgarī′thmic** (or -dh-) *a.* (-**ically**). [L f. Gk *logos* reckoning, *arithmos* number]

**lŏ′ggerhead** (-gerhĕd) *n.* At ~s, disagreeing or disputing (*with*). [prob. dial. (*logger* wooden block)]

**lŏ′ggia** (-jyа) *n.* Open-sided gallery

or arcade; open-sided extension to house. [It., = LODGE]

**lŏ′gĭc** *n.* Science of reasoning; particular scheme of or treatise on this; chain of reasoning, use of or ability in argument, arguments, (*argues with great learning and logic*; *is not governed by logic*; CHOP³ *logic*); force, power of convincing, (*the logic of events, necessity, war*, etc.); ~**al** *a.* (~**ally**), of logic, in conformity with the laws of logic, rightly deducible, defensible on ground of consistency, capable of correct reasoning; *logical* POSITIVISM; **lŏgĭcă′lĭtЎ** *n.*; **lŏgĭ′cian** (-shǝn) *n.* [F f. L f. Gk, = pertaining to reason (LOGOS)]

**-lŏ′gĭc(al)** *sufs.* forming *adjs.* corresp. esp. to *ns.* in -LOGY: *pathological*, *physiologic(al)*, *theological*, *zoological*. [Gk *-logikos* (-LOGY)]

**-logist** *suf.* forming *ns.* meaning 'person skilled in *-logy*' (*etymologist, geologist, zoologist*). [-LOGY, -IST]

**logi′stĭc|s** *n.pl.* Art of moving, lodging, and supplying troops and equipment; **logi′stĭc** *a.* (~**ally**). [F (*loger* to lodge)]

**lō′gō** *n.* (colloq.; *pl.* ~s). Logotype. [abbr.]

**Lŏ′gos** *n.* The Word of God, or Second Person of the Trinity. [Gk, = reason, discourse, (rarely) word]

**lō′gotЎpe** *n.* (Piece of type with) non-heraldic device as badge of an organization. [Gk *logos* word, TYPE]

**-logЎ** *suf.* forming *ns.* denoting character of speech or language (*eulogy, tautology*), subject of study (*mineralogy, sociology*), or discourse (*trilogy*). [F or L or Gk *-logia* (LOGOS)]

**loin** *n.* (In *pl.*) part of body on both sides of spine between false ribs and hip-bones (**fruit of** one's ~**s**, one's begotten offspring; GIRD¹ (*up*) one's *loins*; ~′**cloth**, cloth worn round loins esp. as sole garment; joint of meat that includes the loin vertebrae. [F f. L *lumbus*]

**loi′ter** *v.i.* Linger on the way, hang about, travel indolently and with pauses. [Du.]

**lŏll** *v.i. & t.* Recline or sit or stand in lazy attitude, rest (one's head or limbs) lazily on something; hang (one's tongue) *out*, (of tongue) hang *out*. [imit.]

**Lŏ′llard** *n.* One of the 14th-c. heretics holding views like those of Wyclif; ~**ĭsm** *n.* [Du., = mumbler]

**lŏ′llĭpŏp** *n.* Large usu. flat rounded

boiled sweet on small stick; ||~ **man** etc., (colloq.) official using circular sign on stick to stop traffic for children to cross road. [orig. uncert.]

**lŏ'llop** v.i. (colloq.) Flop about; move or proceed in lounging or ungainly way. [prob. LOLL, TROLLOP]

**lŏ'lly** n. (colloq.) Lollipop (**ice**(d) ~, frozen confection (esp. water-ice) on small stick); (sl.) money. [abbr. LOLLIPOP]

**Lŏ'mbard. 1.** n. One of the Germanic 6th-c. conquerors of Italy; native of Lombardy; **Lŏmbā'rdic** a. **2.** a. Of the Lombards or Lombardy; ~ **Street**, a London street noted for banks, the financial world or money market (~ **Street to a China orange**, long odds). [LDu. or F f. It. L f. Gmc]

**Lo'ndon** (lŭ'-) n. ~ **clay**, geological formation in lower division of Eocene in S.E. England; ~ **pride**, a pink-flowered saxifrage; ~**er** n., native or inhabitant of London. [place]

**lōne** attrib. a. Companionless, unfrequented, uninhabited, lonely, (poet. or rhet.); ~ **hand**, hand played or player playing against the rest at cards, (fig.) person or action without allies; lone WOLF; ~**'ly** (-nlĭ) a. (-ily, -iness), solitary, isolated, unfrequented, (sad because) companionless; **lŏ'ner** n., person or animal preferring not to associate with others; ~**'some** (-ns-) a., feeling or making feel lonely. [ALONE]

**lŏng¹** a., n., & adv. **1.** a. (~**'er**, ~**'est**, pr. -ngg-). Measuring much from end to end in space or time (a long line, journey, life; long in the TOOTH); (seemingly) more than the stated amount (ten long miles); (colloq., of person) tall; far-reaching, acting at a distance, involving great interval or difference; (usu. appended to measurement) having specified length or duration (tail 6 in. long; vacation is two months long; as BROAD as it is long); of elongated shape, remarkable for or distinguished by or concerned with length or duration; expressed by many digits or consisting of many individuals (~ **family**, with many children; ~ **figure**, **price**, heavy cost); of more than the usual numerical amount (long DOZEN; ~ **hundred**, 120); lasting, going far back or forward in time, (long fare-

well, friendship, memory); (of vowel or syllable) having the greater of two recognized durations, (of vowel) sounded like its name; (St. Exch., of stocks, stockbroker, etc.) bought, buying, etc., in large quantities in advance, with expectation of rise in price. **2.** n. A long interval or period (shall see you before long; shall not be away for long; will not take long); recital at length (**the ~ and the short of it**, all that can or need be said, the total upshot); long syllable or vowel; ||=long vacation. **3.** adv. (-er, -est, pr. -ngg-). For a long time (have long thought so; be ~ (in) doing, be ~, take much time, be slow, to do; **not be ~ for this world**, have only short time to live; so or **as ~ as**, whilst, provided that); by a long time (long before, after, since or ago; ~**-ago** a. & n., (belonging to the distant past); (appended to ns. of duration) throughout specified time (all day long); (in compar.) after implied point of time (shall not wait any longer; **no ~er**, not now or henceforth as formerly). **4.** ~ **arm**, far-reaching power; ~**'boat**, sailing ship's largest boat; ~**'bow** (drawn by hand and shooting long feathered arrow; draw the ~bow, tell exaggerated or invented stories); ~**-distance**, between distant places; long DIVISION; ~**-drawn**(-out), (unduly) prolonged; ~ **drink** (served in tall glass); ~ **face**, dismal expression; ||~ **firm**, swindlers who obtain goods but do not pay; ~**-hair**(ed), (person) with hair longer than usual, esp. intellectual or hippie; ~**'hand**, ordinary writing (opp. shorthand, typing, printing); ~**-hea'ded**, shrewd, far-seeing, sagacious; long HOME; ~ **hop**, (Crick.) short-pitched ball, easily hit; ~ **johns**, (colloq.) underpants with full-length legs; ||~ **jump**, athletic contest of jumping as far as possible along the ground in one leap; at long LAST³; ~**-lived** (-ĭvd), having a long life, durable; **make a ~ nose**, cock a SNOOK; ~ **odds** (very uneven); ~ **on**, (colloq.) well supplied with; ~**-playing**, (of gramophone record) playing about 10 to 30 minutes on each side; ~**-range**, having long range, relating to long period of future time; ~ **robe**, legal profession; **in the ~ run**, as ultimate outcome, in the end; ~ **ship**, (Hist.) Viking galley;

~'**shore**, found or employed on or frequenting the shore (~*shoreman*, landsman employed in loading and unloading ships) [ALONG]; ~ **shot**, wild guess or venture, bet at long odds, (Cinemat.) shot including objects at a distance, (*not by a ~ shot*, by no means); ~ **sight**, ability to see clearly only what is comparatively distant; ~-**sighted**, having long sight, (fig.) having imagination or foresight; *long* STANDING; ~-**stop**, (position of) cricket fieldsman behind wicket-keeper, (fig.) last resort; ~-**suffering**, bearing provocation patiently; ~ **suit**, many cards of one suit in a hand, (fig.) one's strong point; ~-**term**, occurring in or relating to a long period of time; *long* TON; ||~ **vacation**, summer vacation of lawcourts and universities; ~ **view(s)**, consideration of remote effects; *long* WAVE; ~ **wind**, ability to run long distance without rest or (fig.) to talk or write at tedious length; ~-**winded**, showing such ability. **5.** ~'**ways**, ~'**wise**, (-z) *advs.*, in a direction parallel with a thing's length. [E]

**lŏng**[2] *v.i.* Wish earnestly or vehemently *for* thing or *to* do; ~'**ing** *n.*, vehement desire. [E, =seem LONG[1] to]

**long.** *abbr.* longitude.

**lŏ'ngeron** (-nj-) *n.* (usu. in *pl.*) Longitudinal member(s) of aeroplane's fuselage. [F]

**lŏngē'vĭtÿ** (-nj-) *n.* Long life. [L (*longus* long, *aevum* age)]

**lŏ'ngĭt|ūde** (-nj-, -ngg-) *n.* (Geog.) Angular distance east or west from the meridian of Greenwich or other standard meridian to that of any place; (Astron.) body's or point's angular distance esp. along ecliptic; ~ū'dĭnal *a.* (-lly), of or in length, lying longways, of longitude. [L *longitudo* length (*longus* long)]

||**lŏŏ** *n.* (colloq.) Lavatory. [orig. uncert.]

**lŏŏ'fah** (-a) *n.* Pod of a plant used as flesh-brush. [Arab.]

**lŏŏk. 1.** *v.i.* & *t.* Use one's sight, turn eyes in some direction, (~ (**here**)!, ~ **you**!, demanding attention or expostulating; ~ **before you leap**, avoid rash action); make visual or (fig.) mental search; take care, make sure, *that*, expect *to* do; contemplate, examine, (*look a gift-* -HORSE *in the mouth*; *look person, death,* etc., *in the* EYE, FACE; ~ **person through and through**, observe him searchingly); indicate (emotion etc.) by one's looks (*look compassion*, DAGGERS); ascertain or observe by sight *what, how, whether*, etc.; (of thing) face, be turned, in some direction (*the house looks south*); have specified appearance, seem (to be), (*look a fool, foolish*); ~ **one's age**, seem as old as one really is; *look* ALIVE!; ~ **as if**, suggest by appearance the belief that; *look* BLACK, BLUE; ~ **like**, have appearance of, ||seem to be, threaten or promise, indicate presence of, (*looks like rain*; *he looks like an angel, a policeman, biting, winning*); *look* LIVE[1]*ly*; ~ **one**-**self again**, seem recovered; *look* SICK[1]; ~ **small**, be exposed as mean etc.; ~ **well** or **ill**, (of person) seem in good or bad health, (of thing; also ~ **good** or **bad**) seem to be going well or badly. **2.** *n.* Act of looking, gaze or glance; (in *sing.* or *pl.*) appearance of face, expression, personal aspect, (*good* ~s, beauty); (of thing) appearance (**for the ~ of the thing**, for the sake of appearances; **don't like the ~ of this**, find this alarming). **3.** ~ **about** (one), examine the surroundings, take time to form plans; ~ **after**, (esp.) attend to, take charge of; ~ **ahead**, (esp.) consider the future; ~ **at**, direct one's eyes or attention at, examine or consider; *to* ~ *at*, in outward appearance; *will not* ~ *at*, rejects, scorns; ~ **back**, (esp.) be half- -hearted in an enterprise, relapse or cease. *to* progress; ~ **down one's nose at**, (colloq.) regard with contempt or displeasure; ~ **down (up)on**, consider oneself superior to; ~ **for**, expect, try to find, (*look for* TROUBLE); ~ **forward to**, anticipate (usu. with pleasure); ~ **in**, (esp.) make short visit or call; ~-*in n.*, informal call or visit, chance of participation or success; ~'**ing-glass**, glass mirror; ~ **into**, examine inside of, investigate; ~ **on**, regard (*as*), be mere spectator; ~ **out**, direct one's sight or put one's head out of window etc., have or afford outlook *on, over*, etc., be vigilant or prepared (*for* person, event), ||search for and produce; ~-*out n.*, watch (*on the look-out for*), observation-post, person(s) or boat stationed to look out, view over landscape, prospect of luck (*it's a poor look-out for him*), person's own concern (*that's your look-out*); ~ **over**, inspect; ~ **round**, look in every or another direction, examine objects of interest; ~**see**, (sl.) inspection; ~ **sharp**, make haste; ~ **through**, (esp.) inspect exhaustively or successively; ~ **to**, consider, be careful about, rely on; ~ **up**, improve in price or prosperity, search for (information in book), (colloq.) go to visit (person), raise eyes; ~ *up to*, respect, venerate; ~ *person up and down*, scrutinize him keenly or contemptuously. 4. ~**er** *n.*, person of specified appearance (*good-looker*), (colloq.) attractive woman; ~**er-o′n**, mere spectator. [E]

**loom**[1] *n.* Weaving-machine. [E]

**loom**[2] *v.i.* Appear dimly, be seen in vague and often magnified shape, (lit. or fig.; often *loom large* etc.). [prob. LDu.]

**loon** *n.* Kind of diving bird; crazy person (cf. foll.). [N]

**loo′ny** *n. & a.* (sl.) Lunatic; ~**-bin**, mental home or hospital. [abbr.]

**loop. 1.** *n.* Figure produced by curve, or doubled string etc., that crosses itself; similarly shaped attachment or ornament used as fastening; metal ring etc. as handle etc.; ~(**-line**), contraceptive coil; railway or telegraph line that diverges from main line and joins it again; skating figure or aerobatic manœuvre describing shape of loop; (Electr.) complete circuit for current; endless strip of tape or film allowing continuous repetition. **2.** *v.t. & i.* Form (string etc.) into loop(s), enclose (as) with loop, fasten (*up, back, together*) with loop(s), (~ **the** ~, Aeron., perform loop), form loop. **3.** ~**er** *n.*, kind of caterpillar that moves by arching itself into loops; ~**y** *a.*, (sl.) crazy. [orig. unkn.]

**loop′hole** (-p-h-) *n.* Narrow slit in wall, (fig.) means of evading rule etc. without infringing letter of it.

**loose** *a., v., & n.* **1.** *a.* Released from bonds or restraint (LET[2] *loose*); detached or detachable from its place, not held together or contained or fixed, (*at a ~ end*, \**at ~ ends*, without definite occupation; *cut ~*, begin to act freely); slack, relaxed, (*with a ~ rein*, lit. of riding, fig. indulgently); not compact or dense (*loose scrum, soil*); inexact, indefinite, vague, incorrect, (*loose grammar, style,*

thinker, translation); morally lax. **2.** *v.t.* Release, free, untie, undo, detach from moorings; ~ (**off**), discharge (arrow), (abs.) discharge gun (*at*); relax (*loose hold*). **3.** *n.* State of unrestrainedness (**on the** ~, having a spree); open play in football (*in the loose*). **4.** ~ **ball** (Crick., inaccurately pitched; Footb., not in any player's possession); ~ **bowels**, tendency to diarrhoea; ~ **box**, stall in which horse can move about; ~ **build, make**, ungainly figure; ~ **change**, money as coins in pocket etc. for casual use; ~ **cover** (removable, for chair etc.); ~**-leaf**, (of book) with each leaf separately removable; ~**′strife** (-s-s-), kind of marsh plant. **5.** **loo′sen** *v.t. & i.*, make or become less tight or compact or firm (~**n** person's **tongue**, make him speak freely). [N]

**loot. 1.** *n.* Booty, spoil; (sl.) money. **2.** *v.t. & i.* Take loot (from), carry off (as) loot. [Hindi]

**lop**[1] *v.t.* (-pp-). Cut away some or all of the branches or twigs of, cut away (twigs or branches or head of tree, person's hair or head or limb; often *off, away*). [E]

**lop**[2] *v.i.* (-pp-). Hang limply; ~**-ear**, drooping ear, rabbit with such ears; ~**-eared**; ~**si′ded**, with one side lower etc., unevenly balanced. [rel. to LOB]

**lope** *v.i., & n.* (Run with) long bounding stride (esp. of animals). [N, rel. to LEAP]

**loqua′cious** (-shus) *a.* Talkative; **loqua′city** *n.* [L (*loquor* speak)]

**lo′quat** (-ŏt) *n.* (Small reddish fruit of) orig. Chinese and Japanese tree. [Chin., = rush orange]

‖**lor** *int.* (vulg.) = Lord. [abbr.]

**lord** *n., int., & v.* **1.** *n.* Master, ruler, chief, sovereign, (*our sovereign lord the King*; ~ **and master**, poet. or joc., husband); (rhet.) owner (*lord of a few acres*); magnate in some trade; (Hist.) feudal superior (*lord of the* MANOR); God (usu. **the L~**; **L~** (only) **knows**, colloq., I have no idea) or Christ (usu. **Our L~**; YEAR *of Our Lord*); peer of realm or person entitled by courtesy to title *Lord* as part of his ordinary style (*drunk* **as**, *swear* **like, a** ~, excessively; **live, treat, like a** ~, fare, entertain, sumptuously; **House of L~s, the L~s**, Upper House of Parliament, committee of specially qualified members of this (L~s of Appeal) appointed as ultimate judicial appeal court, building where these bodies meet; **my ~,** form of address to nobleman (below duke), bishop, lord mayor, lord provost, or judge of supreme court; the **L~s,** TEMPORAL and SPIRITUAL peers of Parliament); ||(L~; prefixed as designation of) marquis, earl, viscount, or baron, (whether peer or peer's eldest son holding his father's second title by courtesy; *the Earl of Derby* or *Lord Derby*), (prefixed to Christian name, with or without surname, of) younger son of duke or marquis; ||**L~s (Commissioners),** members of board performing duties of high State office (**First** L~, president of such board; **Sea L~,** naval member of Admiralty Board). 2. *int.* (colloq.) **L~!, oh L~(y)!, good L~!,** (expr. surprise or consternation); **L~ bless me** etc. (expr. surprise). 3. *v.t.* Rule over like a lord (esp. *lord it over* person). 4. **L~ Advocate,** principal law-officer of Crown in Scotland; **L~ Bishop** (ceremonious title of any bishop; ||**L~ Chamberlain,** head of management in Royal Household; *Lord (High)* CHANCELLOR; ||**L~ Chief Justice,** president of Queen's Bench Division; ||**~-in-waiting, ~ of the bedchamber,** nobleman attending queen, king; **L~ Justice (of Appeal),** judge in Court of Appeal; ||**L~ Lieutenant,** chief executive authority and head of magistrates in each county; *Lord* MAYOR; ||**L~ President,** chief judge of Court of Session; **L~ President of the Council,** Cabinet Minister presiding at Privy Council; ||*Lord* PRIVY Seal, RECTOR; **~s and ladies,** wild arum; **L~'s day,** Sunday; **L~'s Prayer,** the Our Father (Matt. 6: 9–13); **L~'s Supper,** Eucharist; **L~'s table,** Christian altar, Eucharist; ||*Lord (High)* STEWARD. 5. **~'ling** *n.;* **~'ly** *a.* (-iness), (as) of, fit for, a lord, haughty, imperious; **~'ship** *n.,* rule *over,* ownership of, domain, manor, being a lord (**his, your, ~ship,** as respectful substitute for a lord's name, or iron.). [E, = loaf-keeper (LOAF¹, WARD); cf. LADY.]

**lore** *n.* Erudition (arch.); body of traditions and facts on a subject (*ghost, bird,* etc., *lore*). [E (LEARN)]

**lorgnĕ'tte** (-nyĕ't) *n.* Pair of eye-

glasses or opera-glasses held up by long handle. [F (*lorgner* to squint)]

**lor'ĭs** *n.* Tailless nocturnal arboreal lemur of S.E. Asia. [F, perh. f. obs. Du. *loeris* clown]

**lorn** *a.* (arch. or joc.) Desolate, forlorn. [E, p.p. of LOSE]

||**lŏ'rry** *n.* Motor truck for transporting goods etc. [orig. uncert.]

**lŏr'y** *n.* Bright-plumaged parrot-like Asian bird. [Malay]

**lose** (lōoz) *v.t.* & *i.* (lost *pr.* lŏst, lawst). Be deprived of, cease by negligence, misadventure, death, etc., to have (person, part of body, possession); let or have pass from one's control or reach or power of finding; get rid of; spend (TIME, efforts, etc.) to no purpose; fail to obtain or catch or perceive (*lose a train, word*), be defeated in (game, race, lawsuit, battle), forfeit (stake, right to thing); suffer detriment, be the worse off, (*you will not lose by it*); cause person the loss of (*will lose you your place*); (of clock) become slow, become slow by (specified time); (in *pass.*) disappear, perish, die or be dead, (*the lost art of letter-writing; ship and all hands were lost*); **get lost,** (sl., usu. in *imper.*) leave me, us, alone; *lose* FACE, GROUND¹; **~ one's head,** be beheaded, become flustered; **lose** (one's) HEART; **~ in,** suffer loss as regards; **~ interest,** become uninterested or uninterested; **~ itself in,** be obscured or merged in; *lose* one's MIND; **~ out,** (colloq.) be unsuccessful, fail; *lose* (one's) PATIENCE; **~ oneself in, be lost in,** be engrossed in (book, thought, etc.); *lose* one's TEMPER, one's or *the* WAY; **losing battle, game,** (in which defeat seems inevitable); *losing* HAZARD; *lost* CAUSE; **lost souls,** the damned; **lost to,** no longer in the possession of, insensible or inaccessible to (*lost to pity, the world, all sense of decency*); **lost (up)on,** wasted on, not observed or appreciated by (*hints are lost upon him*); **lo'ser** (lōo'z-) *n.,* (esp.) person worsted in game, venture, etc., (**good, bad, loser,** accepting defeat with good, bad, grace), incompetent or unsuccessful person; **lŏss** (*or* laws) *n.,* losing, what is lost, detriment resulting from losing; **sold at a loss,** for less than was paid to buy it; **at a loss** (*for, to discover,* etc.), puzzled, uncertain; DEAD loss; person etc. **is a great, no great, loss,** the loss of him is a serious blow, a matter of indifference); **loss-leader,** article sold at a loss to attract customers. [E]

**lŏt** n. One of a set of objects used in securing a chance selection or apportionment (**cast, draw, ~s,** use these; CAST, THROW, *in* one's *lot with*); this method of deciding (*chosen by lot*), choice or share or office resulting from or given by it; person's destiny, fortune, condition, (*it falls to my lot; the lot fell upon me*); plot, allotment, of land, *esp. for specific purpose (*parking lot*); article or set of articles for sale at auction etc. (**bad ~,** disreputable or vicious person); number or quantity of associated persons or things (**the ~, the whole ~,** the total number or quantity); (colloq.) considerable or (in *pl.*) great quantity, amounts, or number (*a lot of accidents; plays rugby a lot; lots of beer left; take a ~ of doing,* be hard to do). [E]

**lŏth.** See LOATH.

**Lothăr′iō** (*or* -ār′-) n. (*pl.* ~s). Libertine. [character in play]

**lō′tion** n. Liquid preparation for skin as healing or cosmetic agent. [F or L (*lavo lot-* wash)]

**lŏ′ttery** n. Arrangement for distributing prizes by chance among purchasers of numbered tickets; (fig.) thing that defies calculation (*life, marriage, is a lottery*). [Du. (LOT)]

**lŏ′ttō** n. Game of chance similar to BINGO. [It.]

**lō′tus** n. Legendary plant inducing luxurious languor in the eater (~-**eater, ~-land,** person given to, place of, indolent enjoyment); kind of water-lily etc., esp. as used symbolically in Hinduism and Buddhism. [L f. Gk]

**loud. 1.** *a.* Strongly audible (~-**spea′ker,** Naut. ~ **hailer,** apparatus that converts (sound through) electrical signals into sounds loud enough to be heard at some distance); noisy; (of colour, dress, manners) obtrusive; ~ **pedal** (on piano, giving more sustained tone). **2.** *adv.* With loud voice (*don't talk so loud; who laughed loudest?*); loud-SPOKEN; **out ~,** aloud (*laughed out loud when I read it*). [E]

**lough** (lŏχ) n. (Ir.) Lake, arm of sea. [Ir. (LOCH)]

**lounge** (-nj). **1.** *v.i.* Loll, recline, stand about or move lazily, idle. **2.** n. Spell of, place for, public room for, lounging; place in airport etc. with seats for waiting passengers; sitting--room in house; ‖~ **suit,** man's suit for fairly formal dress, with tailless jacket. [orig. uncert.]

**lour, lower²,** (lowr) *v.i.* Frown, look sullen or (of sky etc.) dark and threatening. [orig. unkn.]

**louse. 1.** n. (*pl.* lice). Kind of parasitic insect; (sl., *pl.* ~s) contemptible person. **2.** *v.t.* Remove lice from; ~ **up,** (sl.) spoil, mess up. **3. lou′sy** (-zĭ) *a.* (**-ily, -iness**), infested with lice, (sl.) disgusting or bad, (sl.) abundantly supplied *with* (money etc.), (sl.) swarming *with*. [E]

**lout** n. Hulking or rough-mannered fellow. [orig. uncert.]

**lou′ver, -vre,** (loo′ver) n. Domed erection on roof with side openings for ventilation etc.; one of set of overlapping boards or glass strips like slats of Venetian blinds to admit air and exclude light or rain. [F *lover* skylight]

**love** (lŭv). **1.** n. Fondness, warm affection, paternal benevolence (esp. of God), (*of, for, to, towards*; *play for ~,* for the pleasure of it, not for stakes; **for ~ or money,** by any means; **for the ~ of,** for the sake of, in the name of (*God, Heaven,* sl. *Mike,* etc.), esp. in adjurations; **give, send,** one's, person's, **~,** convey affectionate message (*to*); LABOUR *of love*; **there's no ~ lost between them,** they dislike each other); sexual passion, Cupid or other personification of it, (**fall in ~,** become enamoured; **in ~ (with),** enamoured (*of* person or, fig., of a pursuit etc.); **make ~,** pay amorous attentions *to,* have or seek sexual intercourse; beloved one, sweetheart, (colloq., as form of address, also *my love*); (colloq.) delightful person or thing (*he is an old love*); (in games) no score, nothing, nil, (~ **all,** neither side has yet scored; ~ **game, set,** in which loser has not scored). **2.** *v.t. & i.* Be in love, be in love with, feel affection for; delight in, admire, be glad of the existence of; be (habitually) inclined, (colloq.) like, be delighted, (*children love to ape their elders; he loves to find or finding mistakes*). **3.** ~ **affair,** (usu. temporary) relationship between two people in love; ~**-bird**, parakeet esp. of kind said to pine away at death of its mate; ~**-child** (illegitimate); ~**-hate relationship** (involving ambivalent feelings of love and hate towards same object); ~**-in-a-mist**, blue-flowered garden plant; ~**-in-idle-ness**, wild pansy; ~**-knot**, ribbon interlaced in special way to symbolize true love; ~**-letter** (between sweet-hearts); ~**-lies-bleeding**, garden plant with drooping spikes of purple--red bloom; ~**'lorn**, pining with un-requited love; ~**-match**, marriage for love; ~**-seat**, armchair or sofa for two persons; ~**-sick**, languishing with love. **4.** **lo'vable** (lŭ'-) *a.* (-**bly**), inspiring affection; ~**less** (-vl-) *a.*, unloving or unloved or both; ~**'ly**, (*a.*; **-lily, -liness**) exquisitely beauti-ful, (colloq.) pleasing, delightful, (*n.*, esp.) glamorous showgirl; **lo'ver** (lŭ'-) *n.*, person (esp. man) in love with another (**lover's knot**, = *love--knot*), (in *pl.*) pair of lovers, admirer or devotee (*of*; *lover of music, dog--lover*); **lo'vey** (lŭ'-) *n.* (colloq., as term of affection); ~**y-dovey**, (*n.*) = *lovey*, (*a.*) fondly affectionate and sentimental; **lŏ'vĭng** (lŭ'-) *a.* & *n.*, (esp.) affection(ate); **loving-cup**, two-handled drinking cup passed round at banquets; **loving-kind-ness**, tenderness and consideration. [E]

**low**[1] (lō). **1.** *n.* The sound made by cows. **2.** *v.i.* Make this sound. [E]

**low**[2] (lō) *a., n.,* & *adv.* **1.** *a.* (no *adv.* -**ly**). Not high or tall or reaching far up, not elevated in position, (*low hills, house, forehead, stature, moon*); of or in humble rank or position (*of low birth*); not exalted or sublime, commonplace; abject, mean, vulgar, (*low cunning; low slang*); lacking vigour, dejected, (*low* SPIRITS); not intense (*low fever*), of small or less than normal amount (*low attendances, prices, temperature*), (of supply of anything) nearly exhausted; (of sound) not shrill or loud. **2.** *n.* Low or lowest level or number (*pound reached new low against the dollar*); area of low PRESSURE. **3.** *adv.* In or to low position (lit. or fig.; *aim low; bowed low; never stooped so low as to*); in low tone (*talk low*); (of sound) at or to low pitch; **bring** ~, depress or reduce in health, wealth, or position; LAY[4] *low*; LIE[2] *low*. **4.** ~**-born**, of humble birth; *~**'boy**, table with

drawers and fairly short legs; ~**'brow** *a.* & *n.*, (colloq.) (person) not highly intellectual or cultured; **Low Church**, less sacerdotal and ritualistic party in Church of Eng-land; ~**-class**, of low quality or social class; ~ **comedian**, actor in ~ **comedy** (in which subject and treatment border on farce); **Low Countries**, Netherlands (Holland), Belgium, and Luxembourg; ~**-down**, (*a.*) abject, mean, dis-honourable, (*n.*, sl.) true facts, inside information (*on*); ~ **dress** (with low neck); *lower* CASE[2], CRITICISM; ||**lower deck**, petty officers and men of Navy or of ship; **Lower House**, (esp.) House of Commons; **lower mammal, plant,** etc., (evolved to only slight degree, e.g. platypus, fungus); **lower regions**, hell, realm of the dead; **lower world**, the earth, hell; *lowest common* DE-NOMINATOR, MULTIPLE; ~ **frequency** (esp. in Radio, 30–300 kilohertz); *low* GEAR; *Low* GERMAN[2]; ~**-grade**, of low quality; ~**-key**, restrained; ~**'land** (-ănd) *a.* & *n.*, (of or in) low-lying country; **Lowlands** (-ăndz), less mountainous part of Scotland (*Lowlander*, inhabitant of Lowlands); *low* LATIN, LATITUDE; ~ **life** (of the lower classes); ~**-lying**, at low altitude (above sea level etc.); *low* MASS[1]; ~ **neck(line)** (of woman's dress etc., cut so as to expose neck and part of shoulders and breast); ~ **opinion** (of very un-favourable); ~**-pitched**, (of sound) low, (of roof) having only slight slope; *low* PRESSURE, PROFILE, RELIEF, SEASON; **Low Sunday** (next after Easter); ~ **tackle** (Rugby Footb., at or below waist); *low* TIDE; ~ **water**, low tide, time of extreme ebb, (in ~ *water*, short of money or other assets; ~*-wa'ter mark*, level reached at low water, fig. minimum recorded value, point of least excellence, etc.). **5.** ~**'er**[1] *v.t.* & *i.*, let or haul down, make or become lower, diminish height or elevation of (*lower one's eyes, one's gun*), de-grade; ~**'ermŏst** *a.*, lowest; ~**'ly** *a.* (**-iness**), humble, unpretending. [N]

**lower**[2]. See LOUR.

**loy'al** *a.* (~**ly**). Faithful (*to*), true to allegiance, devoted to the legiti-mate sovereign (~ **toast**, toast to sovereign); ~**ĭsm** *n.*, adherence to legitimate sovereign esp. in face of rebellion or usurpation; ~**ĭst** *n.*; ~**tў** *n.* [F f. L (LEGAL)]

**lŏ′zĕnge** (-nj) *n.* Rhombus, diamond figure, esp. as heraldic bearing; lozenge-shaped object, e.g. shield (for spinster's or widow's coat of arms), small pane of glass; small sweet or medicinal etc. tablet to be dissolved in mouth. [F]

**L.P.** *abbr.* long-playing (record).

‖**L-plāte** (ĕ′lp-) *n.* Sign bearing letter L, affixed to front and rear of motor vehicle to indicate that it is being driven by learner. [PLATE]

**L.S.D.** *abbr.* lysergic acid diethylamide, a powerful hallucinogenic drug.

**£.s.d.** (ĕlĕsdē′) *n.* Pounds, shillings, and pence (in former British currency); money, riches. [L *librae, solidi, denarii* pounds, shillings, pence]

**L.S.E.** *abbr.* London School of Economics.

**L.T.** *abbr.* low tension.

**Lt.** *abbr.* Lieutenant(-); light.

**Ltd.** *abbr.* Limited.

**lŭ′bber** *n.* Clumsy fellow, lout, (esp. LAND*lubber*); ~**lў** *a.* (-**iness**), awkward, unskilled. [orig. uncert.]

**lŭ′brĭc|āte** (*or* lōō′-) *v.t.* Apply oil or grease to reduce friction in (machinery), make slippery; ~**ant** *n.*, substance used to lubricate; ~**ā′tion**, ~**ātor**, *ns.*; **lubrĭ′cĭtў** (lōō-) *n.*, slipperiness, skill in evasion, lewdness. [L]

‖**lūcĕr′n(e)** *n.* A clover-like fodder-plant. [F f. Prov.,= glow-worm, w. ref. to shiny seeds]

**lū′cĭd** (*or* lōō′-) *a.* Free from obscurity, clearly expressed or arranged, (*lucid style, account,* etc.; ~ **interval,** period of sanity between fits of madness); ~**ĭtў** (-ĭ′d-) *n.*; **Lu′cĭfer** (lōō′-) *n.*, Satan. [F or It. f. L (*lux luc-* light); L *fero* bring]

**lŭck** *n.* (Chance as bestower of) good or ill fortune (*good, ill* or *bad, luck;* **as ~** would have it, (un)fortunately; **down** on one's ~, dispirited by misfortune, temporarily unfortunate; HARD *luck*; **just my ~,** I am unlucky as usual; PUSH one's *luck*; **try** one's ~, make a venture; **worse ~!,** excl. of disappointment; **you never know your ~,** you may be lucky); good fortune, success due to chance, (*in, out of, luck;* **for ~,** to bring good fortune; **no such ~,** unfortunately not); ~**′lèss** *a.,* invariably having

ill luck, ending in failure; ~**′ў** *a.* (~**ily,** ~**iness**), constantly attended by good luck, in luck, getting more luck than one deserves, due to luck rather than skill or design or merit, right by a fluke, (*lucky guess, shot; luckily it is still available*), presaging or bringing or worn etc. for luck (*lucky charm, day, penny*); ~**y-bag** of sweets etc., bought without full knowledge of its contents, or = ‖~**y dip,** ~**y-tub,** at bazaars etc. containing articles for which one may dip upon paying small sum). [LDu.]

**lucre** (lōō′ker) *n.* (derog.) Pecuniary gain as a motive (FILTHY *lucre*); **lu′crative** (lōō-) *a.,* yielding considerable profits. [F or L (*lucrum* gain)]

**Lŭ′ddīte** *n.* & *a.* (Member) of bands of English artisans (1811-16) who raised riots for destruction of machinery; (person) similarly engaged in seeking to obstruct progress. [Ned *Lud,* person]

**lū′dĭcrous** (*or* lōō′-) *a.* Absurd, ridiculous, laughable. [L (*ludicrum* stage-play)]

**lŭff** *v.i.* & *t.* Bring ship's head, bring head of (ship), nearer the wind; raise or lower (crane's jib). [F, prob. f. LG]

**lŭg. 1.** *v.t.* & *i.* (-**gg**-). Drag with effort or violence (*along* etc.); pull hard *at.* **2.** *n.* Hard or rough pull; (colloq. or joc., esp. Sc. & N. Engl.) ear; projection on object by which it may be carried, fixed in place, etc. **3.** ~**gage** *n.,* bags etc. (for) containing traveller's belongings; ~**ger** (-g-) *n.,* small ship with four-cornered sails (~**sails**) set fore and aft. [prob. Scand.]

**luge** (lōōzh). **1.** *n.* (Orig. Swiss) short raised toboggan. **2.** *v.i.* Ride on luge. [Swiss F]

**lugū′brious** (lōō-, lōō-; *or* -gōō′-) *a.* Doleful. [L (*lugeo* mourn)]

**lukewarm** (lōō′kwŏrm, -ŏr′m) *a.* Moderately warm, tepid; not zealous, indifferent. [E (now dial. *luke* warm)]

**lŭll. 1.** *v.t.* & *i.* Send to sleep, soothe, quiet (suspicion etc.) usu. by deception; (in *pass.*) be deluded *into* (undue confidence); (of storm or noise) lessen, fall quiet. **2.** *n.* Intermission in storm (lit. or fig.) or in any activity. **3.** ~**′abў** *n.,* soothing song to send child to sleep. [imit.]

**lu′lu** (lōō′lōō) *n.* (sl.) Remarkable

or excellent person or thing. [orig. uncert.]

**lŭmbā′gō** *n.* (*pl.* ~s). Rheumatic affection in muscles of loins; **lŭ′m-bar** *a.*, of the loins. [L (*lumbus* loin)]

**lŭ′mber. 1.** *n.* Disused and cumbersome articles (~-room, where such things are kept); useless stuff; *partly prepared timber (~jack, ~man, feller, dresser, or conveyer of lumber; ~jacket, warm jacket as worn by lumbermen). **2.** *v.t.* & *i.* Fill *up* inconveniently, obstruct (place); encumber *with* (esp. of person, *with* unwanted task or situation); move in blundering noisy way; cut and prepare forest timber. [orig. uncert.]

**lū′min|arў** (or lōō′-) *n.* Natural light-giving body, esp. sun or moon; person as source of intellectual, spiritual, etc., light; ~ĕ′scent *a.*, emitting light without heat; ~ous *a.*, shedding light (~ous paint, phosphorescent and so visible in darkness); ~ŏ′sitў *n.* [F or L (*lumen lumin-* light)]

**lŭmp**[1]. **1.** *n.* Compact shapeless or unshapely mass; (sl.) great quantity, lot; protuberance or swelling on a surface; heavy, dull, or ungainly person. **2.** *v.t.* & *i.* Put together in a lump, collect into lumps; treat as all alike (*lump together, with, in with, under* title etc.). **3. In the ~,** generally, taking things as a whole; ~(′fish), ugly spiny-finned fish clinging to objects by sucking-disc on belly; ~ **in the,** one's, **throat,** choking sensation caused by emotion; ~ **sugar** (broken or cut or shaped into lumps or cubes); ~ **sum,** sum covering number of items, money paid down at once (opp. *instalments*); |the ~, casual workers esp. in building trade who are paid in lump sums. **4.** ~′ish *a.*, heavy and clumsy, stupid, lethargic; ~′ў *a.* (-ily, -iness), full of or covered with lumps, (of water) choppy. [Scand.]

**lŭmp**[2] *v.t.* (colloq.) Be displeased at, put up with ungraciously, (used in contrast with *like: you can like it or lump it*). [imit.]

**lu′na|cў** (lōō′-) *n.* Insanity [orig. that attributed to changes of moon]; (Law) mental unsoundness interfering with civil rights or transactions; great folly; ~tĭc *a.* & *n.*, insane (person), eccentric, outrageously foolish, (person); ~tĭc

**asylum,** (Hist.) mental home or hospital; *lunatic* FRINGE. [F f. L (*luna* moon)]

**lu′nar** (lōō′-) *a.* Of, in, as of, concerned with, determined by, the moon; ~ **(excursion) module,** module for journey from spacecraft in orbit round moon to moon's surface and back; ~ **month,** period of moon's revolution, esp. = LUNATION, (pop.) period of four weeks; **lu′năte** (lōō′-) *a.*, crescent-shaped; **lunā′tion** (lōō-) *n.*, interval between new moons, about 29½ days. [L (as prec.)]

**lŭnch. 1.** *n.* Midday meal; light refreshment taken between breakfast and dinner (where latter is taken at midday). **2.** *v.t.* & *i.* Provide lunch for; take lunch. **3.** ~′eon (-nchŏn) *n.*, (formal) a midday meal; ||~eon **voucher** (given to employee as part of pay and exchangeable for meal at restaurants). [orig. uncert.]

**lun|e** (lōōn) *n.* Crescent-shaped figure; ~ĕ′tte *n.*, arched aperture in concave ceiling to admit light, crescent-shaped or semicircular space in ceiling etc. decorated with painting etc. [F f. L *luna* moon]

**lŭng** *n.* Either of the pair of air-breathing organs in man and most vertebrates; **good** ~s, (esp.) strong voice; ~-**fish** (having lungs as well as gills). [E, rel. to LIGHT[2]]

**lŭnge** (-nj). **1.** *n.* Thrust with sword etc.; sudden delivery of a blow or kick or throwing forward of the body in thrusting or hitting. **2.** *v.i.* & *t.* Deliver or make a lunge (*out, at,* etc.); drive (weapon, sting, etc.) violently in some direction. [F *allonger* (*long* LONG)]

**lu′pin(e**[1]) (lōō′-) *n.* Garden or fodder plant with long tapering spikes of flowers. [foll.]

**lu′p|ine**[2] (lōō′-) *a.* Of or as of wolves; ~us *n.*, ulcerous skin disease, esp. tuberculosis of skin. [L *lupinus* (*lupus* wolf)]

**lŭrch**[1] *n.* **Leave in the** ~, desert (friend, ally) in difficulties. [obs. F *lourche* kind of backgammon]

**lŭrch**[2]. **1.** *n.* Sudden shifting of the weight to one side as with drunken man or rolling ship. **2.** *v.i.* Make lurch(es), stagger. [orig. Naut., of uncert. orig.]

||**lŭr′cher** *n.* Cross-bred dog between collie or sheep-dog and greyhound used esp. by poachers. [LURK]

**lūre** (or loor). **1.** *n.* Falconer's apparatus for recalling hawk; thing used to entice; enticing quality *of* a pursuit etc. **2.** *v.t.* Recall with lure; entice (*away*, *into*). [F f. Gmc]

**lūr'id** (or loor'-) *a.* Ghastly, wan, glaring, stormy, or terrible, in colour etc. (**cast a ~ light on**, show or explain in a horrible way); sensational, horrifying, (*lurid details*); showy, gaudy, (*paperbacks with lurid covers*). [L]

**lŭrk** *v.i.* Keep out of sight, be hidden, *in*, *under*, *about*, etc.; exist unobserved, be latent, (*have a lurking sympathy for*). [perh. f. LOUR]

**lŭ'scious** (-shŭs) *a.* Richly sweet in taste or smell; (of style) over-rich in sound, imagery, or voluptuous suggestion; voluptuously attractive. [perh. rel. to DELICIOUS]

**lŭsh** *a.* Luxuriant and succulent (of grass etc.); (fig.) luxurious. [orig. uncert.]

**lŭst. 1.** *n.* Animal desire for sexual indulgence, lascivious passion; passionate enjoyment *of* or desire *of*, *for*, (*lust of battle*, *for power*); (Bibl. & Theol.) sensuous appetite regarded as sinful (*lusts of the flesh*); **~ful** *a.* (**-lly**). **2.** *v.i.* Have strong or excessive (esp. sexual) desire (*after*, *for*). [E]

**lŭ'stre** (-ter), *lŭ'ster, *n.* Gloss, shining surface, brilliance, splendour, (**add ~ to**, **throw, shed, ~ on**, enhance the glory etc. of); chandelier with prismatic glass pendants; iridescent glaze on pottery and porcelain; such pottery and porcelain; **lŭ'strous** *a.* [F f. It. (L *lustro* illumine)]

**lŭ'stȳ** *a.* (**~ily**, **~iness**). Healthy and strong; vigorous, lively. [LUST]

**lūt|e**[1] (or lōōt) *n.* Musical instrument with plucked strings, much used in 14th-17th c.; **~'anist**, **~'enist**, *n.*, lute-player. [F f. Arab.]

**lūte**[2] (or lōōt). **1.** *n.* Composition for making joints airtight etc. **2.** *v.t.* Treat with lute. [F, or L *lutum* mud]

**Lū'theran** (or lōō'-) *a. & n.* (Follower) of Martin *Luther*; (member) of Church accepting the Augsburg confession of 1530, with justification by faith alone as principal tenet; **~ism** *n.* [person]

**lŭxe** (or lŏŏks) *n.* Luxury; cf. DE LUXE. [F, f. L *luxus*]

**lŭxūr'|iant** (or -gz-, -gzhoor'-) *a.* Profuse of growth, exuberant, (of style) florid; **~iance** *n.*; **~iāte** *v.i.*

revel, feel keen delight, *in*, abandon oneself to enjoyment or ease; **~ious** *a.*, fond of or contributing to luxury, self-indulgent, voluptuous, very comfortable. [L (foll.)]

**lŭ'xurȳ** (-ksheri) *n.* (Habitual use of) choice or costly food, dress, furniture, etc.; thing desirable for comfort or enjoyment but not indispensable; thing one enjoys; (*attrib.*) comfortable and expensive (*luxury flat*). [F f. L (LUXE)]

**‖L.V.** *abbr.* luncheon voucher.

**LXX** *abbr.* Septuagint.

**-lȳ**[1] *suf.* forming *adjs.* esp. f. *ns.*, w. sense 'having the qualities of' (*kingly*, *lovely*, *rascally*), or 'recurring at intervals of' (*daily*, *hourly*). [E (LIKE[1])]

**-lȳ**[2] *suf.* forming *advs.* f. *adjs.* (*boldly*, *ethically*, *feebly*, *nastily*, *pathetically*, *soothingly*, *undoubtedly*, *volubly*); see note on Suffixes, p. ix

**Lȳcē'um** *n.* Garden at Athens where Aristotle taught, his followers, his philosophy. [L f. Gk]

**lychee.** See LITCHI.

**lȳ'chgāte.** See LICHGATE.

**lȳe** *n.* Water made alkaline with wood ashes or other alkaline solution for washing. [E]

**lȳ'ing.** See LIE[1], LIE[2].

**lymph** *n.* Colourless fluid from tissues or organs of body, like blood but without red corpuscles; exudation from sore etc.; (**calf, vaccine**) **~**, vaccine; (poet.) pure water; **~ă'tic**, (*a.*; **-ically**) of, secreting, conveying, lymph, (*lymphatic system*), (of person) flabby, pale, sluggish, [qualities formerly attributed to excess of lymph], (*n.*) veinlike vessel conveying lymph. [F, or L *lympha*]

**lynch. 1.** *n.* **~ law**, procedure of self-constituted illegal court that summarily executes or otherwise punishes person charged with offence. **2.** *v.t.* Execute (person) thus. [orig. U.S., earlier *Lynch's law*, after *Lynch* person]

**lynx** *n.* Animal of cat family with short tail, spotted fur, and proverbially keen sight; **~-eyed**, keen-sighted. [L f. Gk]

**lȳre** *n.* Ancient U-shaped stringed instrument used esp. for accompanying song; **~-bird**, Austral. bird, male with lyre-shaped tail display; **lȳ'ric**, (*a.*; **-ically**) of or for the lyre, meant to be sung, fit to be expressed in song, of the nature of song, (*lyric* *drama*), (of poem) expressing writer's emotions usu. briefly and in stanzas or groups, (of poet) writing in this manner, (*n.*) lyric poem, (Theatr.) words of song, (in *pl.*) lyric verses;

**lyr′ĭcal** *a.* (-lly), resembling, using language appropriate to, lyric poetry, (colloq.) highly enthusiastic; **lyr′ist** *n.*, (lĭr′-) player on lyre, (lī′r-) lyric poet. [F f. L *lyra* f. Gk]

# M

**M, m,** (ĕm) *n.* (*pl.* Ms, M's). Thirteenth letter; (as Roman numeral) 1,000; (Print.) em.

**M.** *abbr.* Master; mega-; Member of; *Monsieur*; ‖motorway.

**m.** *abbr.* maiden (over); male; married; masculine; metre(s); mile(s); milli-; million(s); minute(s).

**′m** *v.* (colloq.) = am in *I'm*. [abbr.]

**ma** (mah) *n.* (vulg.). Mother. [abbr. MAMMA]

**M.A.** *abbr.* Master of Arts.

**ma′am** (mahm, măm, mum) *n.* Madam (esp. used by servants or in addressing royal lady). [abbr.]

**măc.** See MACK.

**maca′bre** (-ah′br) *a.* Grim, gruesome. [F]

**maca′dam** *n.* Material for road--making with successive layers of broken stone compacted; TAR *macadam*; ~**ize** *v.t.* (McAdam, person)

**măcar|o̅′nĭ** *n.* Pasta formed into long tubes used as food; (*pl.* -ies) 18th-c. dandy; ~**oni cheese,** savoury dish of macaroni and cheese (sauce); ~**o̅′nĭc** *a.,* (of verse) of burlesque form and containing Latin or other foreign words, native words with Latin endings, etc.; ~**o̅o̅′n** *n.,* biscuit of ground almonds etc. [It. f. Gk]

**Maca′ssar** *a.* & *n.* ~ (**oil**), (Hist.) kind of oil for the hair. [place]

**macaw′** *n.* Long-tailed brightly coloured Amer. parrot. [Port. *macao*]

**Macc.** *abbr.* Maccabees (Apocrypha).

**McCoy′** (makoi′) *n.* (colloq.) **The real ~,** the real thing, the genuine article. [orig. uncert.]

**măce¹** *n.* (Hist.) heavy usu. metal--headed and spiked club; heavy club used by policeman etc.; staff of office; ‖symbol of Speaker's authority in House of Commons. [F f. Rom.]

**măce²** *n.* Dried outer covering of nutmeg as spice. [F f. L *macir*]

**mă′cédoine** (-ĭdwahn) *n.* Mixed fruit or vegetables esp. cut up small or in jelly. [F]

**mă′cer|āte** *v.t.* & *i.* Make or become soft by soaking; waste away by fasting; ~**ā′tion** *n.* [L]

**Mach** (mahχ, măk, mahk) *n.* ~ (**number**), ratio of speed of body to speed of sound in surrounding medium. [person]

**machĕ′tĕ** (or -ā′-) *n.* Broad heavy knife used in Central America and W. Indies. [Sp. f. L]

**măchiavĕ′llian** (-k-) *a.* Deceitful, perfidious, cunning. [*Machiavelli*, person]

**mă′chĭn|āte** (-k-) *v.i.* Lay plots, intrigue; ~**ā′tion,** ~**ā′tor,** *ns.* [L (foll.)]

**machi′n|e** (-shē′n). **1.** *n.* Apparatus for applying mechanical power, having several parts each with definite function; bicycle, motor cycle, etc.; aircraft; computer; person who acts mechanically; controlling system of an organization (*party, war, machine*). **2.** *v.t.* Make or operate on with machine (esp. of sewing or printing). **3.** ~**e age,** era of many mechanical devices; ~**e-gun,** (*n.*) mounted gun, automatically reloaded and fired, giving continuous fire, (*v.t.*; -**nn-**) shoot at with machine-gun; ~**e-made,** made by machine, monotonously regular; ~**e-readable,** in form that computer can respond to; ~**e tool,** mechanically operated tool for working on metal, wood, or plastics. **4.** ~**ery** *n.,* machines, mechanism, organized system, means arranged *for doing,* group of contrivances (esp. supernatural persons and incidents) used in literary work; ~**ist** *n.,* one who makes or controls machinery, one who works (esp. sewing-)-machine. [F f. L f. Gk]

**măc(k)** n. (colloq.) Mackintosh. [abbr.]

**mă′ckerel** n. (pl. ~, ~s). Sea-fish used as food; ~ **shark**, porbeagle; ~ **sky** (dappled with rows of small white fleecy clouds, like pattern on mackerel's back). [AF]

**mă′ckĭntŏsh** n. Cloth water-proofed with rubber; ‖coat etc. of this or of any waterproof material. [*Macintosh*, person]

**macra′mé** (-ah′mĭ) n. Art of knotting cord or string in patterns to make decorative articles; work so made. [Turk. f. Arab., = bedspread]

**mă′crŏ-** in comb. Long, large, large-scale; ~**bio′tic**, relating to or following diet intended to prolong life; ~**cosm**, the great world, the universe, any great whole; ~**sco′pic**, visible to the naked eye, regarded in terms of large units. [Gk (*makros* long)]

**mă′crŏn** n. Written or printed mark (⁻) of long or stressed vowel.

**mă′cŭl|a** n. (pl. ~ae). Dark spot; spot, esp. permanent one, in skin; ~**ā′tion** n. [L, = spot, mesh]

**măd. 1.** a. (-dd-). With disordered mind, insane, (**like** ~, furiously, violently); frenzied; extravagantly gay; (of person, conduct, idea) wildly foolish; wildly excited, infatuated, (*after, about, for, on*); (colloq.) annoyed (*I was mad at missing my train*); (of animal) rabid (*mad bull, dog*); ~**′cap** n. & a., wildly impulsive (person); ~**′house**, mental home or hospital, (fig.) confused uproar; ~**′man**, ~**′woman**, mad person. **2.** v.i. (-dd-). (arch.) Be mad, act madly. **3.** ~**′lў** adv., (also, colloq.) passionately, extremely. [E]

**mă′dam** n. Polite or respectful formal address or mode of reference to woman; (euphem.) woman brothel-keeper; (derog.) conceited, pert, etc., young woman. [foll.]

**Madame** (madah′m, mă′dam) n. (pl. **Mesdames** pr. mădă′m, mā-dah′m). Title used of or to French-speaking woman, corresponding to Mrs. or madam; (m~) = prec. [F *ma dame* my lady]

**mă′dden** v.t. & i. Make or become mad, irritate (*maddening delays, suspense*). [MAD]

**mă′dder** n. Herbaceous plant with yellowish flowers; red dye got from its root; synthetic substitute for this dye. [E]

**māde** a. (esp.) (Of person) built, formed, (*well-made*; *loosely-made*); ~ **dish**, food prepared from several separate foods; ~ **for**, ideally suited to; ~ **man** (who has attained success in life); ~ **of**, consisting of (*pipes are made of clay*); ~ **of money**, (colloq.) very rich; *made to* MEASURE; *made to* ORDER; **have it** ~, (sl.) be sure of success. [p.p. of MAKE]

**Madeir′a** (-dēr′a) n. Fortified white wine from *Madeira*; ~ **cake**, kind of rich sweet sponge-cake. [place]

**Mademoiselle** (mădam(w)azĕ′l) n. (pl. **Mesdemoiselles** pr. mădm-wazĕ′l). Title used of or to un-married French-speaking woman, corresponding to Miss or madam; (m~) young Frenchwoman, French governess. [F (*ma* my, *demoiselle* DAMSEL)]

**mădŏ′nna** n. (Picture or statue of) Virgin Mary; ~ **lily** (white kind freq. shown in pictures of Virgin Mary). [It., = my lady]

**mădră′s** n. Cotton fabric with coloured or white stripes etc. [place]

**mă′drĭgal** n. (Mus.) Part-song for several voices, usu. without instrumental accompaniment. [It.]

**mae′lstrom** (mā′l-) n. Whirlpool on W. coast of Norway; great whirlpool (lit. or fig.). [Du.]

**mae′năd** n. Bacchante (lit. or fig.). [L f. Gk (*mainomai* rave)]

**maĕ′str|ō** (mah-; or mī′s-) n. (pl. ~**os**, ~**i** pr. -ē). Great musical composer, teacher, or conductor; masterly performer in any sphere. [It.]

**Mae Wĕ′st** (mā-) n. (sl.) Inflatable life-jacket. [person]

**Mă′fĭ|a** (or mah′-) n. Organized international body of criminals esp. in U.S. and orig. among Italian immigrants; ~**ō′sō** n. (pl. ~**osi** pr. -ē), member of the Mafia. [It. dial. = bragging]

**măgazi′ne** (-ē′n) n. Store for arms, ammunition, and provisions, for use in war; store for explosives; chamber containing supply of cartridges fed automatically to breech of gun, similar device in camera, slide projector, etc.; (colloq. abbr. **mag**) periodical publication (now usu. illustrated) containing contributions by various writers. [F f. It. f. Arab.]

**magĕ′nta. 1.** n. Crimson aniline dye; colour of this. **2.** a. Coloured with or like magenta. [place]

**maggot** 523 **Magyar**

**ma'ggot** *n.* Larva esp. of blue-bottle or cheese-fly; whimsical fancy; ~**y** *a.*, (esp., of meat etc.) containing maggots. [perh. alt. *maddock* f. N]

**Mā'g|ī** *n.pl.* Priests of ancient Persia; **the (three)** ~**i**, the 'wise men' from the East (Matt. 2: 1). [L f. Gk f. Pers.]

**ma'gĭc. 1.** *n. & a.* (Of) the supposed art of influencing course of events by occult control of nature or of spirits (**black, white, natural,** ~, involving invocation of devils, angels, no personal spirit; SYMPA-THETIC *magic*); witchcraft; (inexplicable or remarkable influence) producing surprising results (**like** ~, very rapidly); ~ **carpet,** mythical carpet able to transport person on it to any place; ~ **eye,** small cathode-ray tube used to indicate correct tuning of radio receiver, photoelectric device used for automatic control; ~ **lantern,** simple form of image-projector using slides. **2.** *v.t.* (**-ck-**) Change or make (as if) by magic; ~ **away,** cause to disappear thus. **3.** ~**al** *a.* (**-lly**), of magic, resembling or produced as if by magic; **magi'cian** (-shan) *n.*, one skilled in magic, conjurer. [F f. L f. Gk *magikos* (MAGI)]

**ma'gĭs|trāte** *n.* Civil officer administering law; person conducting court of summary jurisdiction; ~**trates' court** (for minor cases and preliminary hearings); ~**tēr'ial** *a.* (**-lly**), of a magistrate, invested with authority, dictatorial; ~**tracy** *n.*, the magistrates, magisterial office. [L (MASTER)]

**Măgna C(h)ār'ta** (k-) *n.* Charter of liberty obtained from King John in 1215; any similar document of rights. [L, = great charter]

**măgn|ă'nǐmous** *a.* Noble, generous, not petty, in feelings or conduct; ~**anǐ'mǐtў** *n.* [L (*magnus* great, *animus* mind)]

**ma'gnāte** *n.* Wealthy or eminent man (*cotton, financial, magnate*). [L (*magnus* great)]

**măgnē'|sium** (or -z-, -shyum) *n.* Silver-white metallic element; ~**sia** (-sha) *n.*, magnesium oxide, (pop.) hydrated magnesium carbonate used in medicine (MILK *of magnesia*); ~**sian** (-shan) *a.*, of magnesia. [*Magnesia*, place]

**ma'gnĕt** *n.* Piece of iron, steel,

alloy, ore, etc., having properties of attracting iron and of pointing approx. north and south when suspended (**bar** ~**et,** in form of straight bar; **horseshoe** ~**et,** in shape of bar bent till ends nearly meet); = loadstone; (fig.) thing that attracts; ~**ĕ'tǐc** *a.* (**-ically**), having properties of magnet, produced or acting by magnetism, capable of acquiring properties of, or being attracted by, magnet, (fig.) very attractive, (*magnetic* FIELD; ~**etic mine,** submarine mine detonated by approach of large mass of metal, e.g. ship; *magnetic* NEEDLE, NORTH, POLE[2]; ~**etic storm,** disturbance of earth's magnetic field by charged particles from the sun etc.; *magnetic* TAPE); ~**ĕtǐsm** *n.*, (science of) magnetic phenomena, natural agency producing these, (fig.) attraction, personal charm; ~**ĕtīze** *v.t.,* give magnetic properties to, make into a magnet, attract (lit. or fig.) as magnet does; ~**ĕtīzā'tion** *n.*; ~**ĕ'tō** *n.* (pl. **-os**), electric generator using permanent magnets (esp. for ignition in internal combustion engine). [L f. Gk *magnēs -ētos* of Magnesia (prec.)]

**măgnǐ'fǐcen|t** *a.* Splendid, stately; sumptuously constructed or adorned; splendidly lavish; (colloq.) fine, excellent; ~**ce** *n.*; **măgnǐfý** *v.t.,* increase apparent size of (thing) as with lens (**magnifying glass**) etc., exaggerate, intensify, (arch.) extol; **măgnǐfǐcā'tion, măgnǐfier,** *ns.* [L *magnificus* (*magnus* great)]

**ma'gnǐtūde** *n.* Largeness; size; importance; (Astron.) (class of fixed stars arranged according to) degree of brightness (*first, seventh,* etc., *magnitude*); (fig.) **of the first** ~ (importance). [L (*magnus* great)]

**măgnō'lia** *n.* Tree with dark-green foliage and waxlike flowers. [*Magnol*, person]

**ma'gnum** *n.* (Bottle containing) two quarts of wine or spirits. [L (*magnus* great)]

**magnum opus.** See OPUS.

**ma'gpie** *n.* Kind of crow with long pointed tail and black-and-white plumage; random collector; (shot striking) outer division but one of target. [*Mag* abbr. of woman's name *Margaret,* PIE[1]]

**Mă'gyār** *a. & n.* (Member or language) of the people now predominant in Hungary (or mŏ'dyer);

~ (blouse), blouse with ~ sleeves (cut in one piece with main part of garment). [native name]

**maha|ra′ja(h)** (mah-*harah*′ja) n. (Hist.) Title of some Indian princes; **~ra′nee**, **~ra′ni**, (-rah′nĭ) n., maharajah's wife or widow. [Hindi, = great rajah]

**mahari′shi** (mah-ha-) n. Great Hindu sage. [Hindi]

**mahā′tma** (ma-h-) n. (Buddhism) one of class of persons with preternatural powers; person regarded with reverence. [Skr., = great soul]

**mah-jŏ′ng(g)** (-ng) n. Game played with 136 or 144 pieces. [Chin., = sparrows]

**mah′lstick.** See MAULSTICK.

**mahŏ′ganў** (ma-h-) n. Reddish-brown wood used for furniture; its colour. [orig. unkn.]

**Mahometan.** See MUHAMMADAN.

**mahou′t** (ma-how′t) n. Elephant-driver. [Hindi f. Skr.]

**Mahratta.** See MARATHA.

**maid** n. Girl, young (unmarried) woman, virgin, spinster, (arch., poet.); ~(′servant), female servant esp. for indoor work (HOUSEmaid, NURSEmaid); ~ of all work, female servant doing general housework, (fig.) person doing many jobs; ~ of honour, unmarried lady attending queen or princess, kind of custard tart, *principal bridesmaid; OLD *maid*. [abbr. foll.]

**mai′den. 1.** n. Girl, virgin, young unmarried woman, (arch., poet.); = maiden over, maiden horse. **2.** a. Unmarried (*maiden aunt, lady*); (of female animal) unmated; (of horse) that has never won prize; (of race) open only to such horses; (of speech by M.P.), voyage, etc.) first; **~hair**, fern with fine hairlike stalks and delicate fronds; **~head**, virginity, hymen; ~ **name**, woman's surname before marriage; ~ **over**, (Crick.) one in which no runs are scored. **3.** **~hŏŏd** n.; **~lў** a. (-iness). [E]

**mail**[1] n. Armour composed of metal rings or plates; defensive armour for the body (coat of ~), jacket covered with this); **~ed** (-ld) a., clad in mail (**~ed fist**, physical force). [F *maille* f. L MACULA]

**mail**[2]. **1.** n. Bag of letters for conveyance by post; the POST[2]; matter so conveyed; letters, parcels, etc., sent, collected, or delivered at one place on one occasion; ~ (**coach**, train, etc.), vehicle carrying post. **2.** v.t. Send (letters etc.) by post. **3.** **~-bag**, large bag for carrying mail; **~-boat** (carrying mail); *~′**box**, letter-box; **~′ing list** (of persons to whom advertising matter etc. is to be posted); *~′**man**, postman; ~ **order**, order for goods to be sent by post. [F *male* wallet]

**maim** v.t. Cripple, mutilate, (lit. or fig.). [F *mahaignier*]

**main**[1]. **1.** n. Principal channel, duct, etc. for water, sewage, etc., or (usu. in *pl.*) for supply of electricity; (arch. or poet.) mainland, high seas, (SPANISH *Main*); **in the** ~, for the most part; **with might and** ~, with all one's force. **2.** *attrib. a.* Exerted to the full (*by main force*); chief in size or extent (*the main body of an army*); principal, most important, as *the main point* (in argument), *the main road* (in district). **3.** ~ **brace**, (Naut.) brace attached to main yard (*splice the* ~ *brace*, Hist., serve extra rum ration); *have an eye to the* ~ **chance**, one's own interests; **~′land**, large continuous extent of land, excluding neighbouring islands etc., largest island in Orkney and in Shetland; **~′mast**, principal mast; **~′sail** (or -sal), (in square-rigged vessel) lowest sail on mainmast, (in fore-and-aft rigged vessel) sail set on after part of mainmast; **~′spring**, principal spring of watch, clock, etc., (fig.) chief motive power or incentive; **~′stay**, stay from maintop to foot of foremast, (fig.) chief support; **~′stream**, principal current of river etc., (fig.) prevailing trend of opinion, fashion, etc.; **~′top**, platform above, **~′topmast**, mast above, head of lower mainmast; ~ **yard**, yard on which mainsail is extended. **4.** **~lў** *adv.*, for the most part, chiefly. [E]

**main**[2] n. Match between fighting-cocks. [orig. uncert.]

**maintai′n** v.t. Cause to continue, continue one's action in, retain in being, (war, condition, position, attitude, relations, correspondence); cause (person etc.) to continue *in* (condition, possession of thing, etc.); support (life, one's state in life) by nourishment, expenditure, etc.; furnish (one*self*, one's family, etc.) with means of subsistence; provide means for (building or road to be repaired, garrison to be equipped, etc.; ‖**~ed**

**school**, one supported from public funds); take action to preserve (machine etc.) in good order; give aid to (cause, party); assert as true (opinion, statement, *that*); **mai'ténance** n., maintaining or being maintained, (provision of) enough to support life, alimony; **maintenance man** (employed to keep equipment etc. in repair). [F f. L *manus* hand, *teneo* hold]

**maison(n)é'tte** (-z-) n. Small house; part of a house let or sold separately (usu. not all on one floor). [F dim. of *maison* house]

**maître d'hôtel** (mātr dōtĕ'l) n. Major-domo; head waiter; ~ **butter, sauce,** (containing lemon-juice and chopped parsley). [F, = master of house]

**maize** n. Grain of) orig. N. Amer. cereal, Indian corn; yellow colour of its cobs. [F or Sp.]

**Maj.** abbr. Major(-).

**ma'jesty** n. Stateliness of aspect, bearing, language, etc.; sovereign power; **Your, His, Her, M~** (forms used in speaking to or of sovereign or sovereign's wife or widow: *Her Majesty the Queen; Her Majesty the Queen Mother; Her Majesty's Stationery Office*); **maje'stic** a. (-ically), possessing stateliness or grandeur, imposing. [F f. L *majestas* (MAJOR)]

**majo'lica** (or mayŏ'-) n. Renaissance Italian earthenware with coloured ornamentation on white enamel; modern imitation of it. [It., former name of *Majorca*]

**ma'jor** n., a., & v. **1.** n. Army officer next below lieutenant-colonel; officer in charge of section of band instruments (TRUMPET *major*); SERGEANT-major; DRUM *major*; person of full age; *student's special subject or course; *student specializing in a subject (*is a philosophy major*). **2.** a. Greater of two things, classes, etc.; of full age; ||(in schools) *Smith* etc. ~, the elder of the two Smiths or the first to enter the school; unusually important or serious or significant (*major road, war*); (of operation) presenting possible danger to patient's life; (Logic) (of term) occurring in predicate of conclusion of syllogism, (of premiss) containing major term; (Mus.) (of interval) normal or perfect (cf. MINOR), as in major scale (*major third*, (of key) in which scale has

major third, (of scale) with semitones above third and seventh notes. **3.** v.i. *(Of student) undertake study or qualify in as special subject. **4.** **~-domo** (*pl.* **-os**), chief official of Italian or Spanish princely household, house-steward, butler; **~-general**, Army officer next below lieutenant-general; ~ **part**, majority (*of*); *major* PLANET, PROPHET; ~ **suit**, (Bridge) spades or hearts. [L, compar of *magnus* great]

**majo'rity** n. Greater number or part (*of*); **the (great) ~**, (much) the larger part, the dead (*join the ~*, die); number by which votes cast on one side exceed those cast on other; party etc. receiving greater number of votes (**in the ~**, belonging to or constituting this); full age (*attained his majority*); rank of major; ~ **verdict** (given by more than half the jury but not unanimous); ABSOLUTE or *overall majority*. [F f. L (MAJOR)]

**make. 1.** v.t. & i. (MADE). Construct, frame, create, from parts or other substance (*God made the world*; *bees make cells of wax*); prepare (coffee etc.) for consumption; compose, write, prepare, (book, will, etc.); frame in the mind, feel, (*make a judgement*); bring about, give rise to, favour development of, (*make difficulties, a disturbance, a noise*; *it makes a* DIFFERENCE; *good fences make good neighbours*); establish, enact, (distinctions, rules, laws); cause (obj. of prep. *of*) to become (*make an* EXAMPLE, *an* EXHIBITION, *a fool, of* person or one*self*); cause to be (*make it hot, known*; *make oneself a* MARTYR, *him a* duke); cause, compel, (to), (*make him repeat it*; *he was made to repeat it*); represent as, cause to appear to do or to be, (*he makes Richard the king's son*); consider to be, consider, (*I make it 5 miles*); execute (bodily movement; *a* BOW$^2$, *a* FACE); perform (journey etc., and with many *ns*. expr. vbl action, as *an acquisition, effort, mistake, offer, promise, purchase, speech, start*); wage (war on, against, with); arrange and light materials for (a fire); (be sufficient to) constitute, amount to, (*hydrogen and nitrogen make ammonia*; *one* SWALLOW$^2$ *does not make a summer*; *2 and 2 make 4*); bring to (chosen value etc.; *add one and make it a round dozen*); form, be counted as, (*this makes the 10th time*; *will you make* one of the party?); serve for, become by development or training, (this makes pleasant reading; she will make a good wife; he would make a good preacher); gain, acquire, procure, obtain as result, (make money, a living, one's fortune; made a profit, a loss, on the transaction); (Cards) win (trick), play (card) to advantage, win number of tricks that fulfils (contract); (Crick.) score (runs); (sl.) catch (train etc.); achieve place in (prize-list, team, etc.); accomplish (distance, speed); arrive at; (Naut.) discern, come in sight of; secure advancement or success of; proceed (towards etc.), act as if with intention to do (he made to go). 2. ~ **a bag,** kill number of game; ~ **a book,** arrange series of bets on an event; ~ **a clean breast of,** confess fully; ~ **a clean sweep of,** completely abolish or expel, win all prizes etc. in; ~ **a day, night, week,** etc., **of it,** carry activity etc. on through the day etc.; ~ (eat) **a good breakfast** etc.; ~ **as if** or **though,** act as if one were about to do or as one would if one had etc.; ~ **a song and dance,** a fuss (about, over); ~ **away with,** get rid of, kill, squander; ~**-belief,** pretence; ~ **believe,** pretend (to do, that); ~**-believe** a. & n., pretended, pretence; make BOLD; ~ **bricks without straw,** perform the impossible; ~ one's **day,** etc., be essential factor in its success; ~ **do,** use (with) temporary expedients, manage with (something) as inferior or temporary substitute; make EYES at; ~ **for,** conduce to (happiness etc.), confirm (view), proceed towards (place), assail; make FREE, GOOD; cannot ~ **head or tail of,** understand at all; make heavy WEATHER of; ~ **it,** succeed in traversing a certain distance, (fig.) be successful; ~ **much, little, the best,** etc., **of,** derive much etc. advantage from, give much etc. attention to, attach much etc. importance to; ~ **no bones,** not hesitate or scruple; make NOTHING of; ~ **of,** construct from, (fig.) conclude to be the meaning or character of (can you make anything of it?); ~ **off,** depart hastily; ~ **off with,** carry away, steal; ~ **or break,** ~ **or mar,** cause success or ruin of; ~ **out,** draw up, write out, (list, document, cheque to or in favour of person), (try to) prove (how do you make that out?; you make me out (to be) a

hypocrite), understand (I can't make him out; I can't make out what he wants), decipher (handwriting etc.), distinguish by sight or hearing (I made out a figure in the distance), pretend, claim, (he made out that he liked it), (colloq.) fare, make progress, (how did you make out?); ~ **over,** transfer possession of (thing to person), refashion (garment etc.); ~ **sail,** spread (additional) sail(s); ~ one**self scarce,** (colloq.) make off, esp. surreptitiously, keep out of the way; make SHIFT; ~'**shift** a. & n., (serving as) temporary substitute or device; ~ **time,** find an occasion when time is available (for doing or to do); ~ **up,** serve or act to overcome (deficiency), complete (amount, party), compensate (make up lost ground; make up for lost time; we must ~ it up to (compensate) him somehow), compound, put together, prepare, (medicine, beds for use, etc.) sew together (parts of garment etc.), get together (company, sum of money), arrange (type) in pages, compile (list, account, document), concoct (story), (of parts) compose (whole), prepare (actor) for his part by dressing, false hair, etc., apply cosmetics (to), arrange (marriage etc.), settle (dispute; ~ it up) be reconciled); ~-**up** n., disguise of actor, cosmetics etc. used for this, (cosmetics for) woman's facial adornment, composition or constitution, person's character and temperament; make up one's MIND; ~ **up to,** court, curry favour with; ~'**weight,** small quantity added to make full weight (lit. or fig.). 3. n. (Of natural or manufactured thing) kind of structure or composition; build of body; mental or moral disposition; origin of manufacture, brand, (are these your own make?; different makes of car); on the ~, (sl.) intent on gain. 4. **mā′ker** n., esp. **the, our, Maker,** God. [E]

**mā′king** n. 1. (Esp.) Be the ~ of, ensure success or favourable development of; **in the ~,** in course of being made or formed. 2. (in pl.) Earnings, profits; essential qualities for becoming (he has the makings of a General). [E (MAKE)]

**măl-** pref. Bad(ly) (malpractice, maltreat), faulty (malfunction), not (maladroit). [F mal badly f. L male]

**Mal.** abbr. Malachi (O.T.).

**mă′lachite** (-k-) *n.* Green mineral used for ornament. [F f. L f. Gk]

**măladjŭ′st|ĕd** *a.* Not correctly adjusted; (of person) not satisfactorily adjusted to one's environment and conditions of life; ~ment *n.* [MAL-]

**mălad|mĭ′nĭster** *v.t.* Manage inefficiently or badly or improperly; ~mĭnĭstrā′tion *n.*

**mă′ladroit** (*or* -oi′t) *a.* Clumsy, bungling. [F (MAL-)]

**mă′lady** *n.* Ailment, disease, (lit. or fig.). [F *malade* sick)]

**Mălagǎ′sў** *a.* & *n.* (Language, native) of Madagascar. [native]

**malai′se** (-z) *n.* Bodily discomfort, esp. without development of specific disease; uneasy feeling. [F (EASE)]

**mălăpropŏ′s** (-pō′) *adv.*, *a.*, & *n.* (Thing) inopportunely (said, done, or happening); **mă′lapropˌ(ĭsm** *ns.*, ludicrous misuse of word esp. in mistake for one resembling it (e.g. a *nice derangement of epitaphs* for *arrangement of epithets*, f. Mrs. *Malaprop* in Sheridan's *Rivals*). [F (MAL-)]

**malār′|ĭa** *n.* Fever transmitted by bite of certain mosquitoes; ~ĭal, ~ĭan, ~ĭous, *adjs.* [It., = bad air]

**malār′key** *n.* (sl.) Humbug, nonsense. [orig. unkn.]

**Malay′** *a.* & *n.* (Language, member) of a people predominating in Malaysia and Indonesia; ~an *a.* & *n.*; ~ō- *comb. form.* [Malay *malāyu*]

**Mălaya′lam** (-yah′-) *n.* Language of Malabar district of India. [native]

**mă′lcontĕnt** *n.* & *a.* Discontented (person). [F (MAL-)]

**mal de mer** (măldemār′) *n.* Seasickness. [F]

**māle. 1.** *a.* Of the sex that can beget offspring by performing the fertilizing function; (of plants) whose flowers have stamens but no pistil, or thought of as male because of colour etc., (~ fern, commonest lowland fern in U.K.); of men or male animals or plants; (of parts of machinery etc.) designed to enter or fill the corresponding hollow part (*male* SCREW); *male* RHYME. **2.** *n.* Male person or animal. [F f. L *masculus* (*mas* male)]

**mălĕdĭc′t|ion** *n.* (Utterance of) curse; ~ory *a.* [L *maledictio* (MAL-)]

**mă′lĕ|făctor** *n.* Criminal; evil-doer; ~făc′tion *n.*; malĕ′fĭc *a.*, (of magical arts etc.) harmful; **malĕ′ficent** *a.*, criminal, hurtful (*to*);

**malĕ′ficence** *n.* [L (*male* ill, *facio fact-* do)]

**malĕ′volen|t** *a.* Wishing ill to others; ~ce *n.* [F or L (*volo* wish)]

**mălförmā′tion** *n.* Faulty formation; **mălför′med** (-md) *a.* [MAL-]

**mălfŭ′nction** *n.*, & *v.i.* Fail(ure) to function in normal manner.

**mă′lice** *n.* Active ill will, desire to tease, (bear ~ *to*, *towards*, *against*, cherish vindictive feelings against); (Law) wrongful intention esp. as increasing guilt of certain offences, esp. murder (*malice* AFORE-*thought* or PREPENSE); **mali′cious** (-shŭs) *a.*, given to or arising from malice. [F f. L (*malus* bad)]

**mali′gn** (-i′n). **1.** *a.* Malevolent; (of thing) injurious; (of disease) malignant. **2.** *v.t.* Speak ill of, slander. **3.** **mali′gnant** *a.*, harmful, feeling or showing intense ill will, (of disease) very virulent (*malignant cholera*), (of tumour) tending to spread and to recur after removal, cancerous; **mali′gnancў**, **mali′gnitў**, *ns.* [F or L (*malus* bad)]

**mali′nger** (-ngg-) *v.i.* Pretend, produce, or protract illness to escape duty. [F *malingre* sickly]

**mǎll** (*or* mawl) *n.* Sheltered walk as promenade; *shopping precinct. [*The M~*, street in London where game of *pall-mall* was played]

**mǎ′llard** *n.* Wild drake or duck; its flesh as food. [F]

**mǎ′lleab|le** *a.* (Of metal etc.) that can be shaped by hammering; (fig.) adaptable, pliable; ~ĭ′lĭtў *n.* [F f. L (foll.)]

**mǎ′llĕt** *n.* Hammer, usu. of wood; implement for striking croquet or polo ball. [F *mail* f. L *malleus* hammer]

**mǎ′llow** (-ō) *n.* Kind of flowering plant with hairy stems and leaves; **mǎlvā′ceous** (-shŭs) *a.* [E f. L *malva*]

**ma′lmsey** (mah′mzǐ) *n.* A strong sweet wine. [LDu. f. Gk *Monemvasia*, place]

**mălnūtrĭ′tion** *n.* Insufficient nutrition; condition where diet omits some foods necessary for health; **mălō′dorous** *a.*, evil-smelling. [MAL-]

**mălprǎ′ctice** *n.* Wrongdoing; (Law) physician's improper or negligent treatment of patient, illegal action for one's own benefit while in (esp. official) position of trust.

**malt** (mawlt, mŏlt). **1.** *n.* Barley or

other grain prepared by steeping, germination, and drying for brewing or distilling or vinegar-making; (colloq.) malt liquor; malt whisky. **2.** *v.t.* Convert (grain) into malt; **~ed milk** (made from dried milk and preparation of malt). **3.** **~-house** (for preparing and storing malt); **~ liquor** (made from malt by fermentation, not distillation, e.g. beer, stout); **~ whisky** (made from malted barley); **~'ing** *n.*, malt-house. [E]

**Maltē'se** (mawltē'z, mŏ-) *a.* & *n.* (*pl.* same). (Language, native) of *Malta*; **~ cross** (with arms broadened outwards, often indented at ends). [place]

**Mălthū'sǐan** (-z-) *a.* & *n.* (Adherent) of *Malthus*'s doctrine that population should be restricted to prevent increase beyond means of subsistence; **~ìsm** *n.* [person]

**măltrea't** *v.t.* Ill-treat; **~ment** *n.* [F (MAL-)]

**ma'ltster** (maw'l(t)ster, mŏ'-) *n.* One who makes malt. [MALT]

**malvaceous.** See MALLOW.

**mălversā'tion** *n.* Corrupt behaviour in position of trust; corrupt administration (*of* public money etc.). [F f. L (*male* ill, *versor* behave)]

**mama.** See MAMMA.

**mă'mba** *n.* Kind of venomous African snake. [Zulu *m'namba*]

**Mă'mèluke** (-ōōk) *n.* (Hist.) Member of military body that ruled Egypt 1254–1811. [F f. Arab.]

**mam(m)a'** (-ah') *n.* (Child's name for) mother. [imit. of child's *ma*, *ma*]

**mă'mm|al** *n.* Animal of class Mammalia characterized by secretion of milk to feed young; **~ā'lian** *a.*; **~arў** *a.*, of the breasts. [L (*mamma* a breast)]

**Mă'mmon** *n.* Wealth regarded as idol or evil influence; the worldly rich. [L f. Gk f. Aram.]

**mă'mmoth. 1.** *n.* Large extinct elephant, with hairy coat and curved tusks. **2.** *a.* Huge. [Russ.]

**mă'mmў** *n.* (Child's word for) mother, *Black woman in charge of white children. [MAMMA]

**măn. 1.** *n.* (*pl.* **men**). Human being, animal with power of articulate speech and upright posture, (member of) the human race, (*man is born unto trouble*; *man is a political animal*; **a ~ and a brother**, a fellow human being; **rights of ~**,

HUMAN rights); human being of particular historical period, esp. prehistoric type named from place where remains were found (*Renaissance man*; *Heidelberg, Java, Piltdown, Man*); (in indefinite or general application) person (*any, no, man*; *some, few, men*; **to a ~**, without exception); adult human male, opp. to woman, boy, or both, (**be a ~, play the ~,** be manly, not show fear; **separate, sort out, the men from the boys,** colloq., find who are truly virile or competent); individual (male) person, one's opponent, allocated assistant, etc., (**as one ~,** in unison; **as a ~,** viewed simply in regard to his personal character; **the (very) ~,** the most suitable man *for*; *if you want noise* **he is your ~,** can supply you; **be one's own ~,** be free to act, be independent, be in full possession of one's faculties etc.); **a ~,** one (*what is a man to do in such a case?*); husband (*man and wife*); manservant, valet, workman (*the employers held a meeting with the men*); (usu. in *pl.*) soldiers, sailors, etc., esp. those not officers; (as *voc.*) general mode of address among Blacks, hippies, etc., (*dig this, man*) or expressing impatience etc. (*nonsense, man!*; **my (good) ~,** patronizing); (as *suf.*, usu. *pr.* -man) man concerned or dealing or skilful with or describable as (*clergy*man, *country*man, *Dutch*man, *horse*man, *oars*man, *post*man); one of set of objects used in playing chess, draughts, etc. **2.** *v.t.* (-nn-). Furnish (fort, ship, industrial undertaking, etc.) with man or men for service or defence; act thus in respect of (*man the pumps*); fill (post). **3.** **~ about town,** fashionable idler; *man* ALIVE*!*; **~ and boy,** from boyhood upwards; **~-at-arms,** (arch.) soldier; **~-eater, ~-eating** *a.*, (cannibal, shark, or tiger) eating human flesh; **menfolk,** men in general, men in family; *man* FRIDAY; **~'handle,** move by human effort alone, (sl.) handle roughly; **~'hole,** opening in floor, sewer, etc., for man to pass through; **~-hour,** work done by one man in one hour; **~-hunt,** organized search for person (esp. criminal); **~ in the moon,** semblance of man seen in full moon; **~ in, *on, the street,** ordinary average man; *every man* JACK; **~-made,** (of textile etc.) artificially made, synthetic; *man of* FASHION; **~**

of God, saint, clergyman; *man of* LETTERS; ~ **of straw**, imaginary person set up as opponent, surety, etc., person undertaking financial commitment without adequate means; ~ **of the house**, householder; *man of the* MOMENT; *man of the* WORLD; ~**-of-war**, armed ship of country's navy (PORTUGUESE *man-of--war*); ~'**power**, number of persons available for military or other service; ~'**servant** (pl. *me'nservants*), male servant; ~**size(d)**, of size of or adequate to a man; ~'**slaughter**, (Law) unlawful killing of human being without malice aforethought; **menswear** (-z-), clothes for men; ~ **to** ~, (*adv.*) with candour; ~'**trap** (for catching men, esp. trespassers). **4.** ~'**ful** *a.* (**-lly**), brave, resolute; ~'**hŏŏd** *n.*, state of being a man, manliness, courage, the men of a country; ~'**ĭkĭn** *n.*, little man, dwarf, artist's lay figure, anatomical model of the body [Du.]; ~**kĭnd** *n.*, (-i'-) human species, (-ă'-) men in general; ~'**like** *a.*, having (good or bad) qualities of a man, (of woman) mannish, (of animal) resembling human being; ~'**lў** *a.* (**-iness**), having a man's virtues, courage, frankness, etc., (of woman) having a man's qualities, (of things, qualities, etc.) befitting a man; **mănned** (-nd) *a.*, (of aircraft, spacecraft, etc.) containing human crew; ~'**nĭsh** *a.*, (of woman, usu. derog.) masculine, characteristic of man as opp. to woman. [E]

**Man.** *abbr.* Manitoba.

**mă'nacle. 1.** *n.* (usu. in *pl.*) Fetter for the hand, handcuff, (fig.) restraint. **2.** *v.t.* Fetter with manacles. [F f. L *manus* hand)]

**mă'nag|e** *v.t.* & *i.* (~**eable** *pr.* -ĭja-). Handle, wield, control, (tool, undertaking, etc.); organize, regulate, be manager of, (household, institution, State, team, etc.); take control or charge of (person, animal, cattle, etc.); gain one's ends with (person etc.) by tact, flattery, dictation, etc.; succeed in achieving, contrive to do (*she managed a smile or to smile*; iron. *he managed to muddle it*); succeed in one's aim (often *with* inadequate material etc.); (with *can* or *be able to*) cope with, make proper use of, do what is suggested or appropriate regarding, (*can you manage this matter, another slice, lunch*

next *Friday?*; or abs., *can you manage by yourself?*); ~**ement** (-ĭjm-) *n.*, (esp.) trickery, deceit, administration of business concerns or public undertakings, persons managing a business (**the** ~**ement**, governing body, board of directors, etc.); ~**er** (-nĭj-) *n.*, person conducting a business, institution, etc., person controlling activities of person or team in sports, entertainment, etc.; **good, bad,** etc., ~**er** (of money, household affairs, etc.); ~**erĕss** (-ĭj-; *or* -č's) *n.*; ~**ēr'ial** *n.*; ~**ing** (-ĭj-) *a.*, (esp.) acting as manager, fond of being in control of affairs. [It. *maneggiare* f. L *manus* hand]

**mañana** (manyah'na) *adv.* & *n.* Tomorrow (as symbol of easy-going procrastination in Spanish-speaking countries); indefinite future. [Sp.]

**mănatee'** *n.* Large aquatic herbivorous sirenian mammal. [Sp. f. Carib]

**Mắncū'nĭan** *n.* & *a.* (Native) of Manchester; (past or present member) of Manchester Grammar School. [L *Mancunium*]

**mă'ndala** *n.* Circular figure as religious symbol of universe. [Skr.]

**mănda'mus** *n.* Judicial writ issued as command to inferior court, or ordering person to perform public or statutory duty. [L, = we command]

**mă'ndarĭn** *n.* Standard spoken Chinese language; party leader, bureaucrat, respected (esp. reactionary) person; (Hist.) Chinese official; ~ (**orange**), small flat loose-skinned deep-coloured orange. [Port. f. Malay f. Hindi *mantri*]

**mă'ndate. 1.** (mă'-) *n.* Judicial or legal command from superior; commission to act for another; politacal authority supposed to be given by electors to (party in) parliament. **2.** (-ā't) *v.t.* Commit (territory) *to* mandatary. **3.** ~'**atarў** *n.*, receiver or holder of a mandate; ~'**atorў** *a.* (**-ily**), of or conveying a command, compulsory. [L *mandatum*, p.p. of *mando* command]

**mă'ndĭble** *n.* Jaw, esp. lower jaw in mammals and fishes; upper or lower part of bird's beak; either half of crushing organ in mouth-parts of insect etc.; **măndĭ'būlar** *a.* [F or L (*mando* chew)]

**mă'ndolin(e)** *n.* Kind of lute with

paired metal strings, played with plectrum. [It.]

**măndră'gora, mă'ndrāke,** ns. Narcotic plant with large yellow fruit. [F f. L f. Gk]

**mă'ndrel** n. Lathe-shaft to which work is fixed while being turned; cylindrical rod round which metal or other material is forged or shaped. [orig. unkn.]

**mă'ndrill** n. Kind of large baboon. [app. MAN, DRILL⁴]

**māne** n. Long hair on neck of horse, lion, etc.; (fig.) long hair of person. [E]

**manège** (manā'zh) n. Riding-school; horsemanship; movements of trained horse. [F f. It.]

***maneuver.** See MANŒUVRE.

**mă'nful.** See MAN.

**mă'nganēse** (-ngganēz, -ē'z) n. Black mineral used in glass-making etc.; (Chem.) metallic element of which this is the oxide. [F f. It. (MAGNESIA)]

**măng|e** (-nj) n. Skin disease in hairy and woolly animals; ~'ў (-nj) a. (~ily, ~iness), having mange, squalid, shabby. [F (mangier eat f. L manduco chew)]

**mă'ngel(-wŭrzel), mă'ngold,** (-ngg-) n. Large kind of beet, used as cattle-food. [G, = beet(-root)]

**mă'nger** (-nj-) n. Long open box or trough in stable etc. for horses or cattle to eat from; DOG in the manger. [F f. Rom. f. L (MANGE)]

**mă'ngle¹** (-nggel). **1.** n. Machine of two or more cylinders for squeezing water from and pressing washed clothes etc. **2.** v.t. Press (clothes) in mangle. [Du. mangel]

**mă'ngle²** (-nggel) v.t. Hack, cut about, mutilate, by blows; cut roughly so as to disfigure; spoil (quotation, text, words, etc.) by gross blunders. [F ma(ha)ngler prob. rel. to MAIM]

**mă'ngō** (-nggō) n. (pl. ~es, ~s). (Indian tree bearing) fleshy fruit yellowish-red in colour, eaten ripe or used green for pickles etc. [Port. f. Malay f. Tamil mānkāy]

**mangold.** See MANGEL.

**mă'ngosteen** (-ngg-) n. (E. Ind. tree bearing) fruit with thick reddish-brown rind and white juicy pulp. [Malay]

**mă'ngrōve** (-ngg-) n. Tropical tree or shrub growing in shore-mud with

many tangled roots above ground. [orig. unkn.]

**mangy.** See MANGE; **mă'nhŏŏd,** see MAN.

**mā'ni|a** n. Mental derangement marked by excitement and violence; excessive enthusiasm (for thing, for doing); ~ăc a. & n., (person) affected by mania, raving madman; **-mā'nia** suf. forming ns. denoting special type of madness (kleptomania, megalomania) or (pop.) eager pursuit of admiration; **-mā'niăc** suf. forming ns. & adjs. w. sense '(person) affected with -mania'; **mani'acal** a. (-lly), of or affected by mania; **mā'nic** a., of or affected by mania; **manic-depressive,** (a.) relating to mental disorder with alternating periods of elation and depression, (n.) person having such disorder. [L f. Gk (mainomai be mad)]

**mă'nicūr|e. 1.** n. Cosmetic treatment of the finger-nails and hands. **2.** v.t. Apply manicure treatment to (hands, person); ~ĭst n. [F f. L manus hand, cura care]

**mă'nĭfĕst** a., n., & v. **1.** a. Clear, obvious, to eye or mind. **2.** n. Cargo-list for use of Customs officers; list of passengers in aircraft or trucks etc. in goods train. **3.** v.t. & i. Show plainly to eye or mind; be evidence of, prove; display, evince, (quality, feeling) by one's acts etc.; (of thing) reveal itself; record in a manifest; (of ghost) appear. **4.** ~ā'tion n.; ~ō (-ē's-) n. (pl. ~os), public declaration of policy by political party or other body. [F, or L manifestus]

**mă'nĭfōld. 1.** a. (literary). Having various forms, applications, component parts, etc.; performing several functions at once; many and various (manifold vexations). **2.** n. Manifold thing; (Mech.) pipe or chamber with several openings. [E (MANY, FOLD)]

**mă'nĭkin.** See MAN.

**Mani'l(l)a** n. Cigar or cheroot as made in Manila; ~ (hemp), strong fibre of a Philippine tree; **m~ (paper),** brown wrapping-paper made from Manila hemp, other paper of similar colour. [place]

**mă'nĭple** n. Subdivision of Roman legion; Eucharistic vestment, strip hanging from left arm. [F, or L manipulus handful (manus hand)]

**mani'pŭl|āte** v.t. (~able). Handle, treat, esp. with skill (material, thing, question); manage (person, property, etc.) by dextrous (esp. unfair) use of influence etc.; ~**ā′tion**, ~**ātive**, ~**ātor**, *ns*.; ~**ātive**, ~**atory**, *adjs*.

**mankind, mǎ′nīīke, mǎ′nlȳ.** See MAN.

**mǎ′nna** *n.* Substance miraculously supplied as food to Israelites in the wilderness (Exod. 16); unexpected benefit. [E f. L f. Gk f. Aram. f. Heb.]

**mǎ′nnequǐn** (-kǐn) *n.* Person, usu. woman, employed by dressmaker etc. to display clothes by wearing them; dummy for display of clothes in shop. [F = MANIKIN]

**mǎ′nner** *n.* Way thing is done or happens (*in this manner*; *after this manner*; **adverb of** ~, one that asks or tells how); outward bearing, style of utterance etc.; style in literature or art (*sketch in the manner of Rembrandt*); (in *pl.*) modes of life, conditions of society, (**comedy of** ~**s**, one with satirical portrayal of these in society), behaviour in social intercourse, polite social behaviour, (*good, bad,* etc., *manners*; *has no manners*); (arch.) kind, sort, (*what manner of man is he?*); mannerism; *manner of* MEAN[3]*s*; **all** ~ **of**, every kind of; **in a** ~ **(of speaking)**, in some sense, to some extent, so to speak; **no** ~ **of, no** . . . at all; ~**ed** (-ẽrd) *a.*, behaving in specified way (*ill, well, mannered*), showing mannerism; ~**ism** *n.*, excessive addiction to a distinctive manner in art or literature, trick of style, trick or gesture of speech (esp. of an actor); ~**ist** *n.*; ~**ĭ′stĭc** *a.* (-ically); ~**less** *a.*, unmannerly; ~**lȳ** *a.* (-iness) & *adv.*, well-behaved, polite(ly). [F f. L (*manus* hand)]

**mǎ′nnish.** See MAN.

**manœu′vr|e, *maneu′ver,** (-nōō′ver). **1.** *n.* Planned movement, (in *pl.*) large-scale exercise, of troops, warships, etc.; deceptive or elusive movement; skilful plan. **2.** *v.i.* & *t.* (~**able**). Perform, cause (troops, etc.) to perform, manœuvres; employ artifice; force, drive, manipulate, (person, thing, *into, out, away,* etc.) by scheming or adroitness. [F f. L *manu operor* work with the hand]

**mǎ′nor** *n.* English territorial unit, now consisting of lord's demesne and of lands from whose holders he may exact certain fees etc. (**lord of the** ~, person or corporation having rights of this; ~**house**, his mansion); (sl.) unit area of police administra-

tion; **manōr′ĭal** *a.* (-lly). [AF *maner* f. L *maneo* remain]

**manqué** (mah′nkā) *a.* (placed after *n.*). That might have been but is not, that has missed being, (*a comic actor manqué*). [F]

**mǎ′nsard** *n.* ~ (**roof**), curb roof. [person]

**mǎnse** *n.* Ecclesiastical residence, esp. Scottish Presbyterian minister's house. [L (MANOR)]

**mǎ′nsion** (-shon) *n.* Large residence (‖in *pl.* often of large buildings divided into flats); ‖~**house**, house of lord of manor or landed proprietor, official residence esp. (**the** M~ **House**) of Lord Mayor of London. [F f. L (MANOR)]

**mǎ′ntel** *n.* ~(**piece**), structure of wood, marble, etc., above and around fireplace, mantelshelf; ~(**shelf**), shelf projecting from wall above fireplace; **mǎntī′lla** *n.*, lace scarf worn by Spanish woman over hair and shoulders; **mǎ′ntle,** (*n.*) loose sleeveless cloak esp. of woman, (fig.) covering, fragile lacelike tube fixed round gas-jet to give incandescent light, (*v.t.*) clothe (as) in mantle, conceal, envelop, (*v.i.*) (of liquid) become covered with scum, (of blood) suffuse cheeks, (of face) blush. [F f. L *mantellum* cloak]

**mǎ′ntĭs** *n.* Praying ~, insect of species that holds forelegs in position suggesting hands folded in prayer. [Gk, = prophet]

**mǎ′ntra** *n.* Vedic hymn; Hindu or Buddhist devotional incantation. [Skr., = instrument of thought]

**mǎ′nūal. 1.** *a.* (-lly). Of, done with, the hands (*manual labour*); worked by hand, not by automatic equipment (*manual fire-engine, telephone exchange*); ~ **alphabet**, deaf-and-dumb alphabet. **2.** *n.* Small book for handy use; reference book; handbook; organ keyboard played with hands not feet. [F f. L (*manus* hand)]

**mǎnūfǎ′cture. 1.** *v.t.* Bring (material) into form fit for use; produce (articles) by labour, esp. by machinery on large scale, (derog. of literary work etc.); invent, fabricate, (evidence, story). **2.** *n.* Manufacturing of articles; branch of such industry (*woollen manufacture*); (derog.) merely mechanical production (*of* literature etc.). [F f. It., & L *manufactum* made by hand]

**manūr′e. 1.** *n.* Dung or other substance (to be) spread over or mixed with soil to fertilize it. **2.** *v.t.* Apply manure to (land etc., or abs.; lit. or fig.). [AF *mainoverer* = MAN-ŒUVRE]

**mă′nŭscript** *a.* & *n.* (Book, document) written by hand or typed, not printed; author's copy in this form, submitted for publication; manuscript state (*is in manuscript*). [L *manuscriptus* written by hand]

**Mănx. 1.** *a.* Of the Isle of Man. **2.** *n.* Language of Isle of Man; (as *pl.*) the Manx people. **3.** ~ **cat**, tailless variety; ~**man**, ~**woman**, native of Isle of Man. [N]

**ma′nў** (mĕ′-) *a.* (MORE, MOST) & *n.* Great in number, numerous, (*many* (*people*) *wish*; *many of us, there are many who, wish*; *many a man wishes*; *his reasons were many*; *did not find many*); ~**-sided**, having many sides, aspects, capabilities, interests, etc.; ~**'s the**, there are many —s that (*many's the tale he has told us*); **a good, a great,** ~, a fair, a large, number; **as** ~, that number of (*six mistakes in as many lines*); **as** ~ **again**, the same number additionally (*six now and as many again tomorrow*); **how** ~?, what number of?; **one too** ~, not wanted, in the way; **be (one) too** ~ **for**, baffle, outwit; **so**[1] *many*; **the** ~, the multitude of people. [E]

**Mao** (mow) *a.* Of style worn in Communist China (*Mao cap, jacket,* etc.); ~**′ism** *n.*, Communist doctrines of *Mao Tse-Tung*; ~**′ist** *n.* [person]

**Maor′ī** (mowr′ī) *n.* & *a.* (Member or language) of aboriginal New Zealand race. [native name]

**măp. 1.** *n.* Flat representation of (part of) earth's surface, showing physical and political features etc., or of the heavens, showing positions of stars etc.; (sl.) face. **2.** *v.t.* (-pp-). Represent on map. **3.** ~ **out**, arrange in some detail (course of conduct, one's time, etc.); (wipe) **off the** ~, (colloq.) (render) of no account, obsolete, in(to) oblivion, very distant; **on the** ~, (colloq.) to be reckoned with, important, (*put on the* ~, make prominent etc.). [L *mappa* napkin]

**mă′ple** *n.* Kind of tree or shrub grown for shade, ornament, wood, or sugar; its wood; ~**-leaf**, emblem of Canada; ~ **sugar** (got by evap-

orating sap of some kinds of maple); ~ **syrup** (made by evaporating maple sap or dissolving maple sugar). [E]

**maquĕ′tte** (-k-) *n.* Preliminary model or sketch. [F f. It. (*macchia* spot)]

**Ma′quis** (mah′kē) *n.* Secret army of patriots in France during German occupation (1940–5); member of this. [F, = brushwood]

**măr** *v.t.* (-rr-). Impair fatally, ruin, (esp. MAKE or mar); spoil, disfigure, impair perfection of. [E]

**Mar.** *abbr.* March.

**mă′rabou** (-bōō) *n.* Kind of stork; its down as trimming etc. [foll.]

**mă′rabout** (-bōōt) *n.* Muslim hermit. [F f. Port. f. Arab.]

**mară′ca** *n.* Hand-held clublike gourd containing beans, beads, etc., shaken (usu. in pairs) as percussion instrument. [Port.]

**măraschi′nō** (-kē′-) *n.* (*pl.* ~**s**). A sweet liqueur made from cherries; ~ **cherry** (preserved in this). [It.]

**Mara′th|a, Mahratt′|a,** (mară′-, -rah′-) *n.* Member of a warlike Indian race; ~**ĭ** *n.*, their language. [Hindi]

**mă′rathon** *n.* Long-distance foot--race, esp. as a principal event of modern Olympic Games; feat of endurance; undertaking of long duration. [*M*~ in Greece, scene of decisive battle in 490 B.C., whence messenger ran with news to Athens]

**marau′d** *v.i.* & *t.* Make plundering raid (on); go about pilfering. [F (*maraud* rogue)]

**măr′bl|e. 1.** *n.* Kind of limestone able to take high polish, used in sculpture and architecture; this as type of hardness or durability or smoothness (often *attrib.*); (in *pl.*) collection of sculptures (*Elgin Marbles*); small ball of glass etc. as toy; (in *pl.*) game using these; ~**ў** *a.* **2.** *v.t.* (esp. in *p.p.*). Stain, colour, (paper, edges of book, soap) to look like variegated marble; (in *p.p.*; of meat) with alternating layers of lean and fat. [F f. L *marmor* f. Gk]

**măr′casite** *n.* (Decorative piece of) crystalline iron sulphide. [L f. Arab. f. Pers.]

**Mărch**[1] *n.* Third month, associated with cold winds; ~ **hare**, hare in breeding season (*mad as a March hare*). [F f. L *Martius* (month) of MARS]

**mărch**[2]. **1.** *v.i.* & *t.* Walk in

military manner with regular and measured tread (*away, forth, past* (reviewing officer, sovereign), *out,* etc.); advance thus *on* (place to be attacked); walk or (fig. of events) proceed steadily; cause to march or go (*away, on, off,* etc.); ‖~'ing order, equipment or formation for marching; ~'ing orders, direction for troops to depart for war etc., (fig.) dismissal. 2. *n.* (Mil.) marching of troops; long toilsome walk, progress (*of* events, time, mind); distance covered by troops in a day (FORCE[1]*d march*; STEAL *a march* on); uniform step of troops etc. (*quick, slow, march*); (Mus.) composition meant to accompany march (DEAD *march*); ~ **past,** marching of troops in line past saluting-point at review. [F *marcher*]

**märch**[3]. 1. *n.* (Hist.) Boundary, frontier (often in *pl.*); tract of (often disputed) land between two countries. 2. *v.i.* (Of countries, estates, etc.) border *upon,* have common frontier *with.* [F f. L f. Gmc]

**marchioness.** See MARQUIS.

**mär'chpāne.** See MARZIPAN.

**Märdi Grā's** (märdēgrah') *n.* (Merry-making on) Shrove Tuesday; last day of carnival. [F = fat Tuesday]

**māre**[1] *n.* Female of horse or other equine animal; ~'s nest, illusory discovery; ~'s tail, tall slender marsh plant, (in *pl.*) long straight streaks of cirrus cloud. [E]

**mär'ē**[2] *n.* (*pl.* maria *pr.* mär'ïa). Large dark flat area on moon, once thought to be sea. [L, = sea]

**mär'garine** (-ēn; *or* -j-, -ē'n) *n.* Butter-substitute made from edible oils and animal fats with milk etc. [F f. Gk *margaron* pearl]

**märge**[1] *n.* (poet.) Margin. [F f. L (MARGIN)]

**märge**[2] *n.* (colloq.) Margarine. [abbr.]

**mär'gin. 1.** *n.* Edge or border of surface; plain space beside main body of print etc. on page; condition near the limit below or beyond which a thing ceases to be possible (*on the margin of bare subsistence*); extra amount (of time, money, etc.) over and above the necessary or minimum (*by a narrow margin*; *margin of profit, safety*); ~ **of error,** (slight) difference allowed for miscalculation or mischance. 2. *v.t.* Furnish with margin or marginal

notes. 3. ~al *a.* (-lly), of or written in the margin, of or at the edge, (of land) difficult to cultivate and yielding little profit, close to the limit (esp. of no further profit etc.), barely adequate or provided for (‖~al seat, one where M.P. has only small majority and is likely to be unseated at the next election); ~al cost (added by making one extra copy etc.); ~ā'lïa *n.pl.,* marginal notes. [L *margo -ginis*]

**mär'guerite** (-gerēt, -ē't) *n.* Ox-eye daisy or similar flower. [F f. L *margarita* pearl (f. Gk)]

**maria.** See MARE[2].

**Mär'ïan** *a.* & *n.* (Devotee) of the Virgin Mary, Mary I Queen of England, or Mary Queen of Scots; English Catholic of 1553–8. [L *Maria* Mary]

**mä'rïgöld** *n.* Plant with golden or bright yellow flowers; CORN[1], MARSH, marigold. [*Mary* (prob. the Virgin), *gold* (dial.) marigold]

**märïjua'na, -hua'na,** (märï-hwah'na) *n.* Dried leaves, flowering tops, and stems of common hemp, smoked as intoxicant. [Amer. Sp.]

**mari'mba** *n.* Xylophone of Afr. & Central-Amer. natives; modern orchestral instrument evolved from this. [Congo]

**mari'na** (-ē'na) *n.* Place with moorings for pleasure-yachts etc. [It. & Sp. f. L (MARINE)]

**märin|ā'de. 1.** *n.* Mixture of wine, vinegar, oil, herbs, etc., for steeping meat or fish; meat or fish so steeped. 2. *v.t.* Steep in marinade. 3. ~āte *v.t.,* marinade. [F f. Sp. (*marinar* pickle in brine; MARINE)]

**mari'ne** (-ē'n). 1. *a.* Of, found in, produced by, the sea; for use at sea; of shipping or naval matters (*marine insurance*). 2. *n.* Country's shipping, fleet or navy, (esp. *mercantile* or *merchant marine*); member of corps trained to serve on land or sea (‖*Royal Marines*; **tell that to the** (**horse**) ~s, colloq., you will not deceive me with that). 3. **mä'riner** *n.,* sailor, seaman. [F f. L (MARE[2])]

**märïonĕ'tte** *n.* Puppet worked by strings. [F (*Mary*)]

**mä'rïtal** (*or* meri'-) *a.* (~ly). Of a husband; of or between husband and wife; of marriage. [L (*maritus* husband)]

**mä'rïtime** *a.* Situated, living, or found, near the sea (*maritime town,* *plant*); connected with the sea or seafaring. [L (MARE²)]

**mår'joram** n. Aromatic herb used in cookery. [F f. L]

**mark¹** n. Currency unit in Germany, Finland, etc. [G]

**mark².** **1.** n. Target or other object to be aimed at, (sl.) intended victim of swindler etc., desired object, (*hit, miss,* OVERshoot, *the mark*; **beside, off, wide of, the ~,** not hitting it, fig. not to the point, irrelevant; EASY *mark*; one's ~, sl., what one prefers); visible sign left by person or thing, stain, scar, etc., (BIRTHmark; **make one's ~,** attain distinction; **of ~,** noteworthy; **(God) save the ~,** apology (often sarcastic or scornful) for mentioning unpleasant thing); sign, indication, (*of* quality, character, feeling, etc.); sign affixed or impressed for identification; cross etc. made in place of signature by illiterate person; written or printed symbol, this as sign of good or bad conduct or as characterizing quality of work, (PUNCTUATION *mark*; BLACK *mark*); unit of numerical award of merit in examination (*he gained 46 marks,* FULL¹ *marks*); line etc. serving to indicate position (**up to, below, the ~,** up, not up, to usual standard); runner's starting-point in race (*get on your marks*; **off the ~,** having made a start; **on the ~,** (smartly) ready to start); (Rugby & Austral. Footb.) heel-mark on ground made by player who has caught the ball; (followed by numeral) particular design of piece of equipment etc. **2.** v.t. & i. Make mark on (thing or person); put identifying mark or name to or on (clothes etc.); give distinctive character to, be a feature of, (*to mark the occasion*; *day was marked by storms*); attach figures indicating prices to (goods); (in *pass.*) have natural marks (*marked with silver spots*); name or indicate (place on map, length of syllable, etc.) by sign or mark; allot marks to (student's work etc.); see, notice, observe mentally (*mark my words*); ~ (**down**), note and remember spot to which (grouse etc.) has retired, choose as one's victim etc.; ‖(Footb. etc.) keep close to (opponent) so as to hamper him if he receives ball. **3.** ~ **down,** mark at lower price; ~ **off,** separate (thing *from* another, lit. or fig.) by boundary; ~ **out,** trace out boundaries for (ground), plan (course), destine (*marked out for slaughter*); ~ **time,** move feet as in marching, but without advancing, (fig.) act routinely or unprogressively, await opportunity to advance; ~ **up,** mark at higher price; ~-*up* n., amount added by shopkeeper to cost-price of goods to cover overhead charges and profit. **4.** ~**ed** (-kt) a., (esp.) (clearly) noticeable or evident (*a marked difference*); ~**ed man,** one whose conduct is watched with suspicion or hostility, one expected to reach eminence; ~**ˈedly** adv.; ~**ˈedness** n.; ~**ˈer** n., (esp.) one employed to mark game-birds, scorer esp. in billiards, thing that marks a position, bookmark; ~**ˈing** n., (esp.) colouring of feathers etc., identification symbol on aircraft etc.; ~**ing ink** (indelible for marking linen etc.); ~**ˈsman** n. (*pl.* -**men**), skilled shot esp. with rifle; ~**ˈsmanship** n. [E]

**mår'ket.** **1.** n. Gathering of people for purchase and sale of provisions, livestock, etc., open space or covered building used for market; demand (*for* commodity, service; *goods find a ready market*); place where there is such demand; conditions as regards, opportunity for, buying or selling; rate of purchase and sale. **2.** ~-**day** (on which market is held, usu. weekly); ~ **garden** (in which vegetables are grown for market); ~-**place,** open space in town, where market is held, (fig.) scene of actual dealings; ~ **research,** study of possible buyers for one's goods; ~ **town** (where market is held); ~ **value,** value as saleable thing; **in the ~ for,** wishing to buy; **on the ~,** offered for sale; (**European**) **Common M~,** ‖**the M~,** the European Economic Community, an economic and political association of certain (European) countries; **up-~,** in the direction of higher-priced goods. **3.** v.t. & i. Buy or sell in market; sell (goods) in market or elsewhere. [Gmc f. L (*mercor* buy)]

**mår'king, mår'ksman.** See MARK².

**mårl.** **1.** n. Soil consisting of clay and lime, used as fertilizer; ~**ˈy** a. (~**iness**). **2.** v.t. Apply marl to (ground). [F f. L *margila*]

**mår'lin|e** n. (Naut.) Line of two strands; ~(**e-)spike,** pointed tool used to separate strands of rope or wire. [Du. (*marren* bind, LINE[1])]

**mar'malade** *n.* Conserve of oranges or other citrus fruit, made like jam; ~ **cat** (with orange fur). [F f. Port. (*marmelo* quince, from which orig. made)]

**marmor'eal** *a.* (poet.; ~ly) Of or like marble. [L (as MARBLE)]

**mar'moset** (-z-) *n.* Small bushy--tailed monkey. [F]

**mar'mot** *n.* Burrowing rodent allied to squirrel. [F f. L *mus* mouse, *mons* mountain]

**mar'ocain** *n.* Dress-fabric of crêpe type, made in silk etc. [F, = Moroccan]

**maroo'n**[1] *a.* & *n.* (Of) brownish--crimson colour; explosive device giving loud report. [F f. It. f. Gk, = chestnut]

**maroo'n**[2] *v.t.* Put (person) ashore and leave him on desolate island or coast; (of floods etc.) make (person) unable to leave place safely. [orig. = marooned person, F f. Sp. *cimarrón* wild]

**marque**[1] (-k) *n.* (Hist.) **Letter**(s) **of** ~, licence to fit out armed vessel and employ it in capture of enemy's merchant shipping, (in *sing.*) ship carrying such licence. [F]

**marque**[2] (-k) *n.* Make of motor car, as opp. to specific type (*the Jaguar marque*). [F, = MARK[2]]

**marquee'** (-kē') *n.* Large tent. [F *marquise*]

**mar'quetry** (-kĭ-) *n.* Inlaid work in wood, ivory, etc. [F (MARQUE[2])]

**mar'quis, mar'quess,** *n.* Nobleman ranking between duke and (in U.K.) earl or (elsewhere) count; ~**ate** *n.*; **mar'quise** (-kē'z) *n.*, (in foreign nobility) marchioness. [F (MARCH[3])]

**mar'ram** *n.* A shore grass that binds sand. [N, = sea-haulm]

**mar'riage** (-rǐj) *n.* Condition of man and woman legally united for purpose of living together and usu. procreating lawful offspring, act or ceremony etc. establishing this condition (*give, take,* **in** ~, as husband or wife); particular matrimonial union (*children of a previous marriage*); ~ **bureau,** establishment arranging introductions between persons wishing to marry; ~ **certificate** (stating that marriage ceremony has taken

place); ~ **guidance,** assistance to married couples who have problems in living together harmoniously; ‖~ **lines,** marriage certificate; *marriage of* CONVENIENCE; ~ **settlement,** arrangement securing property to wife; CIVIL *marriage*; ~**able** (-ĭja-) *a.,* old enough to marry, (of age) fit for marriage. [F (*marier* MARRY[1])]

**marron glacé** (glah'sā) *n.* Chestnut preserved in and coated with sugar as sweetmeat. [F]

**ma'rrow** (-ō) *n.* Fatty substance in cavities of bones (chilled etc. **to the** ~, right through); (**vegetable**) ~, white-fleshed gourd cooked as vegetable; ~**bone,** bone containing edible marrow; ~(**fat**), kind of large pea; ~**y** *a.* (-iness). [E]

**ma'rry**[1] *v.t.* & *i.* (Of priest etc. or in *p.p.*) join (persons, one *to* another) in marriage; (of parent or guardian) give (daughter, son, etc.) in marriage; (of person) take (as) wife or husband in marriage; (fig.) unite intimately, correlate (things) as pair; ~ **into,** become member of (family) by marriage; ~ **off,** find wife or husband for (one's son or daughter); ~**ing** *a.,* (esp.) likely to marry (*not a marrying man*). [F f. L (*maritus* husband)]

**ma'rry**[2] *int.* (arch.) expr. surprise, asseveration, indignation, etc. [(the Virgin) *Mary*]

**Mars** (-z) *n.* Roman god of war; planet 4th from sun. [L *Mars Mart-*]

**Marsa'la** (-sah'-) *n.* Dark sweet fortified wine like sherry. [place]

**Marseillai'se** (-selǎ'z, -sāyǎ'z) *n.* National anthem of France. [F (*Marseille*, place)]

**marsh** *n.* Low land flooded in wet weather and usu. watery at all times; ~ **fever,** malaria; ~ **gas,** methane; ~ **mallow,** (confection made from root of) shrubby herb; ~'**mallow,** soft sweet made from sugar, albumen, gelatin, etc.; ~ **marigold,** golden-flowered plant growing in moist meadows; ~'**y** *a.* (~**iness**). [E]

**mar'shal.** 1. *n.* High-ranking officer of state or in armed forces (AIR, EARL, FIELD, *marshal*; ‖M~ **of the R.A.F.,** highest rank); officer arranging ceremonies, controlling procedure at races, etc.; PROVOST *marshal*. 2. *v.t.* (‖-**ll**-). Arrange in due order (soldiers, facts, one's thoughts, etc.); conduct (person) ceremoniously (*into* etc.); ~**ling yard,**

railway yard in which goods trains
etc. are assembled. [F f. L f. Gmc]

**mărsū'pĭal** *a.* & *n.* (Animal) of the
class of mammals having a pouch in
which to carry their young, which are
born incompletely developed. [L f.
Gk *marsupion* pouch]

**mărt** *n.* Market-place; auction-
room; trade centre. [Du. (MARKET)]

**mărtĕ'llŏ** *n.* (*pl.* ~s). ~ (tower),
circular fort usu. for coast-defence.
[Cape *Mortella*, place]

**mǎr'tĕn** *n.* Kind of weasel with
valuable fur. [Du. f. F]

**mǎr'tial** (-shal) *a.* (~ly). Of,
suitable for, appropriate to, warfare;
warlike, brave, fond of fighting; ~
**law,** military government, by which
ordinary law is suspended; **Mǎr'tian**
(-shan) *a.* & *n.*, (hypothetical inhabitant) of Mars. [F or L (MARS)]

**mǎr'tĭn** *n.* Bird of swallow family
(house-~, which builds nest on
house walls etc.); **M~mas** *n.*, St.
Martin's day, 11 Nov. [MASS[1]]. [*St.
Martin,* person]

**mărtĭnĕ't** *n.* Strict disciplinarian;
~**tĭsh** *a.* [person]

**Mărtī'nī** (-ē'nǐ) *n.* Cocktail made
of gin, vermouth, bitters, etc.

**mǎr'tyr. 1.** *n.* One who undergoes
death penalty for persistence in
Christian faith or obedience to law
of Church, or undergoes death or
suffering for any great cause; ~ **to,**
constant sufferer from (ailment);
**make a ~ of** oneself, (pretend to)
accept discomfort etc., in order to
be more highly thought of. **2.** *v.t.*
Put to death as martyr; torment. **3.**
~**dom** *n.*, sufferings and death of
martyr, torment; ~**ŏ'logў** *n.*, list or
register, history, of martyrs. [E f. L
f. Gk *martur* witness]

**mǎr'vel. 1.** *n.* Wonderful thing;
wonderful example *of* (quality). **2.**
*v.i.* (literary; ‖-ll-). Feel surprise (*at,
that*); wonder (*how, why,* etc.). **3.**
~**lous,** \*~**ous,** *a.*, astonishing,
extraordinary, excellent. [F f. L
(*miror* wonder at)]

**Mǎr'xĭan** *a.* & *n.* (Adherent) of
the doctrines of *Marx,* advocating
abolition of private property, and
State provision of work and sub-
sistence for all; ~**ĭsm** *n.*; ~**ĭst** *a.* & *n.*
[person]

**mǎr'zĭpǎn,** (arch.) **mǎr'chpāne,**
*n.* Paste of ground almonds, sugar,
etc., made up into small cakes or
used on top of large cakes. [G f. It.]

**mǎscǎr'a** *n.* Cosmetic for darkening eyelashes etc. [It., = mask]

**mǎ'scŏt** *n.* Person or animal or
thing supposed to bring luck. [F f.
Prov. (*masco* witch)]

**mǎ'scūlĭne** (or mah'-). **1.** *a.* Of
men; manly, vigorous; (of woman)
mannish; (Gram.) of gender proper
to men's names; (Pros.) ~ **ending,**
ending of line with stressed syllable;
*masculine* RHYME. **2.** *n.* Masculine
gender or word. **3.** **mǎscūlǐ'nǐtў** (or
mah'-) *n.* [F f. L (MALE)]

**mǎ'ser** (-z-) *n.* Device for amplify-
ing microwaves. [*microwave amplification by stimulated emission of
radiation*]

**mǎsh. 1.** *n.* Malt mixed with hot
water for use in brewing; mixture of
boiled grain, bran, etc., given warm
to horses etc.; soft pulp made by
crushing, mixing with water, etc.;
(colloq.) mashed potatoes (*sausage
and mash*); confused mixture. **2.** *v.t.*
Make (malt) into mash; crush to a
pulp; reduce (potatoes etc.) to
uniform mass by crushing. [E]

**mask** (-ah-). **1.** *n.* Covering for
all or part of face, worn as disguise
or for protection (e.g. by fencer), or
worn by surgeon etc. to prevent infection of patient; respirator used
to filter inhaled air or to supply gas
for inhalation; likeness of person's
face, esp. one made by taking mould
from face (DEATH-*mask*); (fig.) disguise (*throw off the mask*). **2.** *v.t.* Cover
(face etc.) with mask; (in *pass.*) be
disguised with mask; (Mil.) conceal
(battery etc.) from enemy's view;
disguise, conceal, (taste, one's feelings, etc.); protect from some
process; ~**ed ball** (at which masks
are worn). **3.** ~**'er** *n.*, masquer. [F f.
It. f. Arab.]

**mǎ'soch|ĭsm** (-k-; or -zo-) *n.* Form
of (esp. sexual) perversion in which
sufferer derives pleasure from his
own pain or humiliation (cf.
SADISM); (colloq.) enjoyment of
what appears to be painful or tire-
some; ~**ĭst** *n.*; ~**ĭ'stĭc** *a.* (-ically).
[von Sacher-*Masoch,* person]

**mǎ'son** *n.* One who builds with
stone; (M~) Freemason; **Masŏ'nĭc**
*a.* (-ically), of Freemasons; ~**rў** *n.*,
mason's work, stonework, (M-)
Freemasonry. [F]

**masqu|e** (mahsk) *n.* Amateur
dramatic and musical entertainment
esp. in 16th–17th c.; ~**'er** *n.*, one

who takes part in masque(rade);
**~erā´de** (*or* mă-), (*n*.) masked ball,
false show, pretence, (*v.i.*) appear in
disguise, assume false appearance
(*as*). [var. MASK]

**măss¹** (*or* -ah-) *n*. (A) celebration
(usu. R.C.) of the Eucharist; liturgy
used in this; musical setting of parts
of this; **high ~** (with incense, music,
etc.); **low ~** (with no music and
minimum of ceremony). [E f. L
*missa* dismissal]

**măss²**. **1.** *n*. Coherent body of
matter of indefinite shape; dense
aggregation of objects (*a mass of
fibres*); (in *sing.* or *pl.*) large number
or amount (*a ~ of*, full of or
covered with *mistakes, bruises*, etc.;
**the (great) ~,** the majority (*of*);
**the ~es,** the ordinary people; **in the
~,** in the aggregate); unbroken expanse (*of* colour etc.); (Phys.)
quantity of matter a body contains;
(*attrib.*) relating to large numbers of
persons or things, large-scale, (*mass
radiography*). **2.** *v.t.* & *i.* Gather into
mass; (Mil.) concentrate (troops).
**3. ~ grave** (in which many people
are buried at same time); **~
hysteria** (affecting many people at
same time); **~ media,** means of
communication (e.g. newspapers or
broadcasting) to large numbers of
people; **~ meeting,** large assembly
of people to express political etc.
views; **~ production** (of large
quantities of standardized article by
mechanical processes). [F f. L *massa*
f. Gk]

**Mass.** *abbr.* Massachusetts.

**mă´ssacre** (-ker). **1.** *n*. General
slaughter (of persons, occas. of animals); utter defeat or destruction.
**2.** *v.t.* Make a massacre of; murder
cruelly or violently (a number of
persons). [F]

**mă´ss|age** (-ahzh). **1.** *n*. Rubbing,
kneading, etc., of muscles and joints
of body with the hands, to stimulate
their action, cure strains, etc. **2.** *v.t.*
Treat (part, person) thus. **3. ~eur´**
(-ēr´) *n*. (*fem.* **~eu´se** *pr.* -ēr´z), one
who provides massage professionally.
[F]

**mă´ssif** (-ēf, -ē´f) *n*. Mountain
heights forming a compact group.
[F (foll.)]

**mă´ss|ive** *a*. Large and heavy or
solid; (of features, head, etc.) relatively large, of solid build; (fig.)
solid, substantial, impressive, im-

posing, unusually large; **~´ÿ** *a*.,
(arch. or rhet.; **~iness**), solid,
weighty. [F f. L (MASS²)]

**mast¹** (-ah-) *n*. Fruit of beech, oak,
etc., esp. as food for pigs. [E]

**mast²** (-ah-) *n*. Long pole of
timber, iron, etc., set up on ship's
keel to support sails (**before the ~,**
as ordinary sailor); flag-pole (HALF-
-*mast*); post, or lattice-work upright,
to support radio or television aerial;
**~-head,** highest part of mast, esp.
of lower mast as place of observation
or punishment, title etc. of newspaper etc. at head of front or
editorial page; **-~´er** *n*., ship with
so many masts. [E]

**măstě´ctomÿ** *n*. Excision or
amputation of a breast. [Gk *mastos*
breast]

**ma´ster** (-ah-´) *n*., *a*., & *v*. **1.** *n*.
Person having control (**be ~ of,**
have at one's disposal, know how to
control; **be one's own ~,** be independent or free to do as one wishes;
**make oneself ~ of,** acquire
thorough knowledge of or facility in
using); employer; owner of dog,
horse, etc., or slave; person in control
of pack (*of foxhounds* etc.); male head
of household; **~ (mariner),** captain
of merchant vessel; head of college,
school, etc.; presiding officer of
livery company, Masonic lodge, etc.;
one who has or gets the upper hand
(*we will see which of us is master*); male
teacher or tutor, esp. SCHOOL¹*master*;
revered teacher in philosophy etc.
(**the M~,** Christ); holder of university degree orig. giving authority
to teach in university (*Master of Arts*
etc.); skilled workman, or one in
business on his own account (*master
carpenter, mason*); (picture etc. by)
great artist (OLD *master*); (Chess etc.)
player of proved ability at international level; thing from which
series of copies (of film, gramophone
record, etc.) is made; (prefixed, esp.
by servants and in address of letter,
to name of boy or young man not
old enough for *Mr.*) *Master Tom,
Master (Tom or T.) Jones*; (arch.)
title of man of high rank, learning,
etc. **2.** *a*. Commanding, superior, (*a
master spirit*); main, principal, (*master
bedroom*); controlling others (*master
plan*). **3.** *v.t.* Overcome, defeat;
reduce to subjection; acquire complete knowledge of (subject) or
facility in using (instrument etc.);

rule as a master. **4.** ~ **aircrew,** R.A.F. rank equivalent to warrant officer; ~**-key** (opening many locks, each also opened by separate key); ~**-mind,** (n.) (possessor of) outstanding intellect, person directing an enterprise, (v.t.) plan and direct (an enterprise); **M~ of Ceremonies,** person in charge of ceremonies that are observed on state or public occasions, person introducing speakers at banquet or entertainers at variety show; *Master of* MISRULE; **M~ of the Horse,** third official in Royal Household; *Master of the* ROLLS; ~**piece,** consummate piece of artistry, one's best work; ~**-stroke,** surpassingly skilful act (of policy etc.); ~ **switch** (controlling electricity etc. supply to an entire system); ~ **touch,** masterly manner of dealing with something. **5.** ~**ful** *a.* (**-lly**), self-willed, imperious, masterly; ~**lў** *a.* (**-iness**), worthy of a master, very skilful; ~**shĭp** *n.*; ~**ў** *n.*, sway, dominion, *the* upper hand, masterly skill, masterly use or knowledge (*of* instrument, subject). [E & F f. L *magister*]

**mă′stĭc** *n.* Gum or resin exuded from certain trees; type of cement. [F f. L f. Gk]

**mă′stĭc|āte** *v.t.* (~**able**). Grind (food) with teeth, chew; ~**ā′tion,** ~**ātor,** *ns.*; ~**ātorў** *a.* [L f. Gk]

**ma′stĭff** (**-ah′-**) *n.* Large strong kind of dog. [F f. L (*mansuetus* tame)]

**mă′stŏdŏn** *n.* Extinct animal allied to elephant. [Gk *mastos* breast, *odous* tooth]

**mă′stoid.** (Anat.) **1.** *a.* Shaped like woman's breast. **2.** *n.* (Also ~ **process**) conical prominence on temporal bone; (colloq.) inflammation of mastoid process. [F or L f. Gk *mastos* (prec.)]

**mă′sturb|āte** *v.i.* & *t.* Produce sexual orgasm (of) by manual stimulation of genitals etc., not by sexual intercourse; ~**ā′tion** *n.*; ~**ātorў** *a.* [L]

**măt¹. 1.** *n.* Piece of coarse fabric of plaited rushes, straw, etc., for lying upon, packing furniture, etc.; piece of this or other material for wiping shoes upon, esp. doormat; piece of cork, rubber, plastic, etc., to protect surface from heat or moisture of object placed on it; small rug; piece of resilient material to protect falling wrestler etc.; **on the ~,** (sl.) in trouble. **2.** *v.t.* & *i.* (**-tt-**). Cover or furnish with mats; entangle (*together*) in thick mass (esp. in *p.p.*; *matted hair*); become matted. [E]

**măt².** See MATT.

**mă′tadŏr** *n.* Man appointed to kill bull in bull-fight. [Sp. f. *matar* kill (CHECKMATE)]

**mătch¹** *n.* Short thin piece of wood (~**′stick**), wax, etc., tipped with composition that bursts into flame when rubbed on rough or (**safety ~**) specially prepared surface; fuse for firing cannon etc.; ~**′box** (for holding matches); ~**′wood,** wood suitable for matches, minute splinters. [F *mesche*]

**mătch². 1.** *n.* Person able to contend with another as an equal (*find, meet,* one's *match; more than a match for*); person equal to another in some quality; person or thing exactly like or corresponding to another; contest of skill etc. in which persons or teams strive against each other; matrimonial alliance (**make a ~,** bring this about); person viewed in regard to eligibility for marriage. **2.** *v.t.* & *i.* Place (person etc.) in conflict or contest *against* another (**well ~ed,** fit to contend with each other, live together, etc., on equal terms); place (person or thing) in competition *with*; be equal, correspond in quantity, quality, colour, etc., *to* or *with* (thing etc., or abs.); find material etc. that matches with (another; *can you match this silk?*); find person or thing suitable for another (*matching unemployed workers with vacant posts*). **3.** ~**′board** (with tongue cut along one edge and groove along another, so as to fit with similar boards); ~**′maker,** person fond of scheming to bring about marriages; ~ **point,** state of a game when one side needs only one more point to win the match, this point; **to ~,** (fig.) corresponding in quality, number, etc., with what has been mentioned; ~**′less** *a.*, incomparable. [E]

**māte¹** *n.,* & *v.t.* (Chess) = CHECK-MATE. [F *mat* in *eschec mat* CHECKMATE]

**māte². 1.** *n.* Companion, fellow worker, (as general colloq. form of address among equals, esp. sailors or labourers); one of a pair, esp. of birds; fitting partner in marriage; (*in comb.*) fellow member or joint occupant of (*team-mate, room-mate*):

(Naut.) subordinate officer of merchant ship; assistant to a worker (*cook's, plumber's, mate*). 2. *v.t.* & *i.* Join (two persons, one *with* another) in marriage; marry (*with*, or abs.); come or bring together for breeding; keep company. 3. **ma′tey, ma′ty,** (*a*.; **-ier, -iest; -ily, -iness**) sociable, familiar and friendly (*with*), (*n.*, esp. as colloq. *voc.*) ‖mate, companion. [LG]

‖**mă′telŏt** (-tlō) *n.* (sl.) Sailor. [F]

‖**ma′ter** *n.* (sl.) Mother. [L]

**mater′ial.** 1. *a.* (~ly). Of matter, corporeal; (of conduct, point of view, etc.) not spiritual; concerned with bodily comfort etc. (*material well-being*; important, essential, (*to*, or abs.; *at the material time*). 2. *n.* Matter from which thing is made (RAW *material*); (in *sing*. or *pl*.) elements, constituent parts (*of substance, for historical composition* etc.); cloth, fabric; (in *pl*.) things needed for an activity (*building materials*); person(s) or thing(s) suitable for a purpose, got from a specified source, etc. (*academic, experimental, material*). 3. **~ism** *n.*, opinion that nothing exists but matter and its movements and modifications, tendency to prefer material possessions and physical comfort to spiritual values; **~ist** *n.*; **~i′stic** *a.* (-ically); **~ity** *n.*; **~ize** *v.t.* & *i.*, make or represent as material, make materialistic, cause (spirit) to appear, (of spirit) appear, in bodily form, make or become actual fact; **~izā′tion** *n.*; **matériel** (matērie̅ l) *n.*, available means, esp. materials and equipment in warfare (opp. *personnel*). [F f. L *materia* MATTER]

**mater′nal** *a.* (~ly). Of or like a mother, motherly; related through mother; of the mother in pregnancy and childbirth. [F or L (MATER)]

**mater′nity** *n.* Motherhood; motherliness; ~ **hospital, nurse,** etc., (for women during and just after childbirth); ~ **dress, wear,** etc., (suitable for pregnant woman).

**ma′tey.** See MATE[2].

**măthĕmă′tĭc|s** *n.pl.* (also treated as *sing*.) (**Pure**) **~s,** abstract science of space, number, and quantity; (**applied**) **~s,** this applied to branches of physics etc.; (as *pl*.) use of mathematics in calculation etc.; **~al** *a.* (-lly); **~ian** (-ati′shan) *n.* [F or L f. Gk (*manthanō* learn)]

‖**măths, *măth,*** *n.* (colloq.) Mathematics. [abbr.]

**mă′tĭn|s** (-z) *n.pl.* Morning prayer (or ‖-tt-); **~ée, *~ee,*** (-nā) *n.*, afternoon theatrical or musical performance; **~ée coat,** baby's short coat; **~ée idol,** handsome actor appealing to female playgoers etc. [F f. L (*matutinus* of the morning)]

**ma′triǎrch** (-k) *n.* Woman corresponding in status to patriarch (usu. joc.); **mātriǎr′chal** (-k-) *a.* (-lly); **~y** *n.*, social organization in which mother is head of family and descent is reckoned through female line. [L *mater* mother, on false analogy of *patriarch*]

**ma′tricid|e** *n.* One who kills his, killing of one's, mother; **~al** *a.* (-lly). [L (MATER, *caedo* kill)]

**matrĭ′cŭl|āte** *v.t.* & *i.* Admit (student) to membership of university; be thus admitted; **~ā′tion** (also as name of qualifying examination), **~ātor,** *ns.* [L (MATRIX)]

**mă′trĭ|mŏny** *n.* Rite of marriage; state of being married; a card-game; **~mō′nĭal** *a.* (-lly). [AF f. L *matrimonium* (MATER)]

**ma′tr|ĭx** *n.* (*pl.* **-ices** pr. -ĭsēz, **~ixes**). Womb; place in which thing is developed; mould in which printer's types, gramophone records, etc., are cast or shaped; mass of rock enclosing gems etc. [L]

**ma′tron** *n.* Married woman, esp. one of dignity and sobriety (~ **of honour,** married woman attending bride at wedding); woman in charge of nurses in hospital; woman managing domestic arrangements of school etc.; **~al, ~ly** (-iness; esp. w. ref. to stateliness or portliness), *adjs.* [F f. L *matrona* (MATER)]

**mătt, măt[2],** *a.* (Of colour etc.) dull, not lustrous. [F f. Arab. (MATE[1])]

**Matt.** abbr. Matthew (N.T.).

**mă′tter.** 1. *n.* Physical substance in general, as opp. to *spirit, mind*; (Physiol.) substance in or from the body (*faecal,* GREY, WHITE, *matter*); purulent discharge (so **~y** *a.*); material for thought or expression; substance of book, speech, etc., (often opp. to *manner* or *form*); what is or may be a good reason (*of* or *for* complaint, regret, etc.); thing(s) esp. of specified kind (*postal, printed, reading, matter*); affair, thing to be done or considered, esp. of specified kind (a HANGING *matter; no* LAUGHING matter; *money matters*); **a ~ of**, thing that pertains to or depends (solely) on (*a matter of common knowledge*; *only a matter of time before he goes*; *a matter of habit*), approximately (*a matter of £10, 10 years*); *a matter of* COURSE; **a ~ of fact**, what pertains to the sphere of fact (esp. opp. to *opinion* etc.), esp. *as a matter of fact* (often correcting another's misunderstanding); **~-of--fact** *a.*, unimaginative, prosaic; *a matter of* FORM; **for that ~, for the ~ of that**, so far as that is concerned, and indeed also (something further); **in the ~ of**, as regards; **no ~**, it is of no importance (*when, how*, etc., or abs.); **the ~**, thing that is amiss (*with; there is something the matter; what is the matter with him*); **what is the ~ with**, surely there is no objection to. **2.** *v.i.* Be of importance, signify, (*to person* etc.; *it matters how, when*, etc.; esp. w. neg.). [AF f. L *materia* timber, substance]

**mă'ttĭng** *n.* Fabric for mats (*coconut matting*). [MAT¹]

‖**mattins.** See MATINS.

**mă'ttŏck** *n.* Agricultural tool like pickaxe with an adze and a chisel edge as ends of head. [E]

**mă'ttrĕss** *n.* Fabric case stuffed with hair, straw, feathers, foam rubber, etc., as bed or support for bed (SPRING *mattress*). [F f. It. f. Arab.]

**matūr'e. 1.** *a.* (**~r, ~st**). Complete in natural development, ripe; with fully developed powers of body and mind, adult; (of thought, intentions, etc.) duly careful and adequate; (of bill etc.) due for payment. **2.** *v.t. & i.* Develop fully; ripen; perfect (plan etc.); come to maturity; (of bill etc.) become due for payment. **3. mă'tūr-āte** *v.i.*, (Med., of boil etc.) come to maturation; **mătūrā'tion** *n.*, maturing, development, (Med.) formation of purulent matter; **matūr'ĭtў** *n.* [L *maturus* timely]

**mătūtĭ'nal** (or mătū'tĭn-) *a.* Of, occurring in, the morning; early. [L (MATIN)]

**mā'tў.** See MATE².

**mau'dlĭn** *a.* Weakly or tearfully sentimental, esp. of tearful stage of drunkenness. [F *Madeleine* f. L (MAGDALEN)]

**maul. 1.** *n.* Special heavy hammer, commonly of wood; brawl; (Rugby Footb.) loose scrum. **2.** *v.t.* Beat and bruise; handle (thing, subject, quo-

tation) roughly or carelessly; damage by criticism. [F f. L *malleus* hammer]

**mau'lstĭck, mah'l-,** *n.* Stick used to steady the hand in painting. [Du. (*malen* paint)]

**mau'nder** *v.i.* Move or act listlessly or idly; talk in dreamy or rambling manner. [orig. unkn.]

**Mau'ndў** *n.* ‖Distribution of **~ money** (specially minted silver coins) by the Queen to the poor on **~ Thursday** (next before Easter). [F *mandé* f. L (MANDATE)]

**mausolē'um** *n.* Magnificent tomb. [L f. Gk (*Mausōlos*, person)]

**mauve** (mōv) *n. & a.* Pale purple. [F f. L (MALLOW)]

**mă'verĭck** *n.* Unorthodox or undisciplined person. [person, who owned unbranded cattle]

**maw** *n.* Stomach of animal or (joc.) person. [E]

**maw'kĭsh** *a.* Of faint sickly flavour; feebly or falsely sentimental. [obs. *mawk* MAGGOT]

**max.** *abbr.* maximum.

**mă'xĭ** *n.* (colloq.) Maxi-coat, -skirt, etc.; in comb., very large or long (*maxi-coat*). [abbr. MAXIMUM; cf. MINI-]

**măxĭ'llarў** (or mă'-) *a.* Of the jaw. [L (*maxilla* jaw)]

**mă'xĭm** *n.* A general truth or rule of conduct expressed in a sentence; **~al** *a.*, being or related to a maximum; **~alĭst** *n.*, person who holds out for the maximum of his demands and rejects compromises; **~ĭze** *v.t.*, increase or enhance to the utmost; **~ĭzā'tion** *n.*; **~um** *n.* (*pl.* **~a**) *& a.*, highest (amount) possible, attained or attainable, usual, etc. [F or L (*maximus* greatest)]

**may¹** *v. aux.* (*pres.* **may** exc. 2 *sing.* arch. **~st**, **~'est**; *neg.* **~ not**, colloq. **~n't**; *past night pr.* mĭt, exc. 2 *sing.* arch. **mi'ghtest**, *neg.* **might not**, colloq. **mightn't** *pr.* mĭ'tent; no other parts used). Expr. possibility (*it may be true*, opp. *it cannot be true*; *it may not be true*, opp. *it must be true*; *you may* (WELL²) *not see one*; *we ~ or* **might as well** *go* (as not); **that is as ~ be**, the truth of that is not yet determined; **be that as it ~**, irrespective of the situation regarding that); expr. permission (*you may go* opp. *you may not or must not or cannot go*; *I wish I might*); **you** etc. **might** (= I request you to) *call at* *the baker's*; **you** etc. **might (have)** *offer(ed) to help*, you ought to (have); (iron.) *who are you, may* or *might I ask?*); in purpose-clauses, and after *wish, fear*, etc., (*take, took, such a course as may, might, avert the danger; I hope he may, hoped he might, succeed*); expr. wish (*may the best man win!*); in questions emphasizing uncertainty (*who may* or *might you be?*); **might- -have-been**, a past possibility, a person who might have been more eminent. [E]

**May²** *n*. Fifth month (**Queen of the ~**, girl chosen to be queen of games on May Day); (*may*) hawthorn (blossom); **~ Day**, 1 May esp. as festival with dancing, or as international holiday in honour of workers; MAYDAY; **~'flower**, any flower that blooms in May; **may'fly**, insect which lives briefly in spring; **may'pole**, pole painted and decked with flowers and ribbons, for dancing round on May Day; **~ queen**, Queen of the May; **may'ing** *n*. & *a*., participating in May Day festivities. [F f. L *Maius* (month) of the goddess *Maia*]

**Ma'ya** (-ah'-) *n*. Member or language of early Central Amer. Ind. people; **~n** *a*. [native]

**may'bē** (*or* -bǐ), (arch.) **mayhǎ'p**, *advs*. Perhaps, possibly. [*it may be, it may hap*]

**may'day** *n*. International radio distress-signal used by ships and aircraft. [repr. pr. of F *m'aider* help me]

**may'hĕm** *n*. (Hist.) crime of maiming action; (fig.) violent or damaging action. [AF *mahem* (MAIM)]

**mayonnai'se** (-z) *n*. (Dish with) dressing of egg-yolks, oil, vinegar, etc. [F]

**mayor** (mār) *n*. Head of municipal corporation of city or borough (‖in some large cities **Lord M~**); ‖head of district council with status of borough; **may'oral** *a*.; **~'altў** *n*., mayor's (period of) office; **~èss** *n*., mayor's wife (**LADY** *Mayoress*), lady fulfilling ceremonial duties of mayor's wife. [F *maire* f. L MAJOR]

**măzari'ne** (-ē'n) *n*. & *a*. Deep blue. [*Mazarin*, person]

**māze. 1.** *n*. Labyrinth, network of paths and hedges designed as puzzle for those who try to penetrate it; (fig.) confusion, confused mass, etc. **2.** *v.t.* (esp. in *p.p.*) Bewilder, confuse. [AMAZE]

**mazū'rka** *n*. (Music for) lively Polish dance in triple time. [F or G f. Pol.]

**mā'zў** *a*. (-ily, -iness). Like a maze, full of turnings. [MAZE]

**M.B.** *abbr*. Bachelor of Medicine. [L *Medicinae Baccalaureus*]

‖**M.B.E.** *abbr*. Member (of the Order) of the British Empire.

**M.C.** *abbr*. Master of Ceremonies; ‖Military Cross.

**M.C.C.** *abbr*. Marylebone Cricket Club.

**McCoy.** See **MacCoy.**

**M.D.** *abbr*. Doctor of Medicine [L *Medicinae Doctor*]; Managing Director; mentally deficient.

**Md.** *abbr*. Maryland.

**mē¹** (*or* mǐ) *pron*. Obj. (& colloq. subj.) case of I (for use cf. HER), also used in excl. (*ah me! dear me!*). [E, acc. & dat. of I²]

**mē²**, **mi**, (mē) *n*. (Mus.) Third note of scale; note E. [L *mira*, wd arbitrarily taken]

**Me.** *abbr*. Maine.

**mead¹** *n*. Alcoholic liquor of fermented honey and water. [E]

**mead²** (poet.), **mea'dow** (mě'dō), *ns*. Piece of grassland esp. one used for hay; low well-watered ground, esp. near river; **meadow saffron**, lilac-flowered perennial plant; **meadowsweet**, a fragrant flowering plant; **mea'dowў** (mě'dōǐ) *a*. [E]

**mea'gre**, *mea'ger*, (-ger) *a*. (Of person etc.) lean; (esp. of meal) poor, scanty; (of literary composition, ideas, etc.) lacking fullness, unsatisfying. [AF *megre* f. L *macer*]

**meal¹** *n*. Grain or pulse ground to powder; (Sc.) oatmeal; *maize flour; powdery substance made by grinding. [E]

**meal²** *n*. Customary (or any) occasion of taking of food; food so taken; **make a ~ of**, consume as meal, make (task etc.) seem unduly laborious; **~-ticket**, (fig.) thing or person that provides for one; **~'time**, usual time of eating. [E]

**mea'lĭe** *n*. (S. Afr.; usu. in *pl.*) Maize. [Afrik. *milie* f. Port. *milho* MILLET]

**mea'lў** *a*. (-iness). Of, like, containing, meal; (of boiled potatoes) dry and powdery; **~(-mouthed)**, not outspoken, afraid to use plain expressions. [MEAL¹]

**mean¹** *a*. (**~ness** *pr*. -n-n-). (Of

capacity, understanding, etc.) inferior, poor, (**no** ~, a very good: *he is no mean scholar*); not imposing in appearance, shabby; ignoble, small-minded (*a mean trick*); malicious, ill-tempered; niggardly, not generous or liberal; \*vicious, nastily behaved; \*(colloq.) unwell, secretly ashamed (*feel mean*); \*(sl.) skilful; ~'**ie**, ~'**y̆**, *n.*, (colloq.) niggardly or small-minded person. [E]

**mean**² *v.t.* (~t *pr.* mĕnt). Have as one's purpose, have in mind, (*mischief*, BUSINESS; *to* do); design, destine, for a purpose etc. (*mean it to be used*; *mean it for a stopgap*; *it is* ~t *for you*, you are to receive it or take note of it; *I* ~ *you to* (am determined that you shall) *go*; ~ **well to, towards, by**, be kindly disposed towards); intend to convey or indicate or refer to (*I mean that it is impossible*; *I mean him, his own hat, Richmond in Surrey*); be of some (specified) importance *to* (person), esp. as source of benefit or object of affection etc.; (of words, event, person) signify, import, (thing, *that*); involve, portend, (*it means catching a bus*; *this means war*); **what do you** ~ **by it?**, can you justify such behaviour etc.?; ~'**ing**, (*n.*) what is meant, significance, (*a.*) expressive, significant; ~'**ingful** (-ly), ~'**ingless**, *adjs.* [E]

**mean**³. **1.** *a.* (Of quantity) equally far from two extremes; ~ **sea level** (half-way between levels of high and low water); **in the** ~ (intervening) **time** or **while. 2.** *n.* Condition, quality, virtue, course of action, equally removed from two opposite (usu. blameworthy) extremes (GOLDEN *mean*); term between first and last of arithmetical etc. progression esp. of three terms (**arithmetic** etc. ~); (in *pl.*, often treated as *sing.*) that by which a result is brought about (*it has been a means of extending our trade*; WAYS *and* means; ~**s of grace**, sacraments etc.); (in *pl.*) money resources (*he lives beyond his means*; ~**s test**, official inquiry as to proof of need before financial assistance is given); wealth (*a man of means*); **by all (manner of)** ~**s**, in every possible way, at any cost, certainly; **by no (manner of)** ~**s**, **not by any (manner of)** ~**s**, not at all, certainly not; **by** ~**s** (the agency, instrumentality) **of** (person, thing, do**ing**). **3.** ~'**time**, ~'**while**,

*advs.*, in the mean time. [AF f. L *medianus* MEDIAN]

**meă'nder. 1.** *n.* (in *pl.*) Sinuous windings of river; winding paths; circuitous journey. **2.** *v.i.* Wander at random; (of stream) wind about. [L f. Gk *Maiandros*, winding river in Phrygia]

**mea'nie, mea'ny̆.** See MEAN¹; **mea'ning, meant,** MEAN²; **means, mea'ntime, mea'nwhile,** MEAN³.

**mea'sles** (-zelz) *n.* (as *pl.* or *sing.*). Infectious virus disease marked by red rash (GERMAN² *measles*); a disease of pigs; **mea'sly** (-z-) *a.* (-iness), of or affected with measles, (sl.) inferior or contemptible or worthless. [LDu. *masel(e)*]

**mea'sure** (mĕ'zher). **1.** *n.* Size or quantity found by measuring (**for good** ~, as something beyond the minimum; **short, full,** ~, less, not less, than the professed amount; ǁ*clothes* made to ~, in accordance with measurements taken; **take** person's ~, measure him for clothes etc., fig. gauge his character, abilities, etc.); degree, extent, (esp. **in a** or **in some** ~, partly); rod, tape, vessel, etc., of standard size for measuring or for transferring fixed quantities of liquids etc.; system of measuring (*liquid, linear, measure*); that by which thing is computed (*a chain's weakest link is the measure of its strength*); quantity contained in another an exact number of times (**greatest common** ~, greatest number that is a factor of each of given numbers); prescribed extent or quantity (**set** ~**s to**, limit; **beyond** ~, excessively); poetical rhythm, metre; metrical group of dactyl or two disyllabic feet; time of piece, bar, of music; (arch.) dance (*tread a measure*); suitable action (*take measures to ensure that*); legislative enactment. **2.** *v.t.* & *i.* Find extent or quantity of (thing) by comparison with fixed unit or with object of known size; ascertain size and proportions of (person) for clothes etc.; mark off or *off* (line of given length); estimate (quality, person's character, etc.) by some standard; deal *out* (thing to person); bring (one*self*, one's strength, etc.) into competition *with*; be of specified size (*it measures 6 inches*); ~ **one's length**, accidentally fall flat on the ground; ~ **up (to)**, have necessary qualifications (for); **mea′suring- -jug, -tape**, etc., (marked at various points to assist measurement). **3.** ~**d** (mĕ′zherd) *a.*, rhythmical, regular in movement (*measured tread*), (of language) carefully weighed; ~**less** *a.*, not measurable, infinite; ~**ment** *n.*, act or result of measuring, (in *pl.*) detailed dimensions. [F f. L *mensura* (*metior* to measure)]

**meat** *n.* Animal flesh as food (BUTCHER'S *meat*); (arch.) food of any kind, a meal; chief part *of*; green ~, plants as food; **one man's ~ is another man's poison**, not everybody likes the same things; ~ **and drink**, source of great pleasure *to*; ~-**axe**, butcher's cleaver; *meat* LOAF¹; ~-**safe**, ventilated cupboard for storing meat; ‖~ **tea**, = *high* TEA; ~′**y** *a.* (~**iness**), full of meat, fleshy, (fig.) full of substance, of or like meat. [E]

**Mĕc′ca** *n.* Place one aspires to visit; birthplace of a faith, policy, etc. [Muhammad's birthplace]

**mĕchǎ′nic** (-k-) *n.* Skilled workman, esp. one who makes or uses machinery; (in *pl.*) branch of applied mathematics dealing with motion and tendencies to motion, science of machinery, method of construction or operation; ~**al** *a.* (-lly), of machines or mechanism, working or produced by machinery, of the nature of handicraft, (of person or action) like a machine, automatic, lacking originality, (of agency, principle, etc.) belonging to mechanics, of mechanics as a science; *mechanical* ENGINEER; *mechanical* POWERS; **mĕchani′cian** (-kani′shan) *n.*, person skilled in constructing machinery; **mĕ′chanism** (-k-) *n.*, structure, adaptation of parts, of machine (lit. or fig.), system of mutually adapted parts working (as) in machine, mode of operation of a process; **mĕ′chanize** (-k-) *v.t.*, give mechanical character to, introduce machines in, (Mil.) re-equip by substituting motor transport for horses; **mĕchaniză′tion** (-k-) *n.* [F & L f. Gk *mēkhanikos* (MACHINE)]

**Mĕd** *n.* (colloq.) Mediterranean Sea. [abbr.]

**med.** *abbr.* medium.

**mĕ′dal** *n.* Piece of metal, usu. in form of coin, struck or cast with inscription and device to commemorate event etc., or awarded as distinction to soldier, scholar, athlete, etc.; **mĕdǎ′llion** (-yon) *n.*, large medal, thing so shaped, e.g. decorative panel, portrait; ~**list**, *\**~**ist**, *n.*, (esp.) winner of (specified) medal (*gold medallist*). [F f. It. f. L (METAL)]

**mĕ′ddle** *v.i.* Busy oneself unduly (*with*), interfere (*in*); ~**some** (-dels-) *a.*, fond of meddling. [F f. L (MIX)]

**mĕ′dia.** See MEDIUM; **mĕdiae′val**, see MEDIEVAL.

**mĕ′di\al** *a.* (-lly). Situated in the middle; ~**an**, (*a.*) medial, (*n.*; Geom.) straight line drawn from any vertex of triangle to middle of opposite side; ~**ate**, (*a.*) connected not directly but through some other person or thing, (-āt; *v.i.* & *t.*) intervene (*between* two persons) for purpose of reconciling them, bring about (result) thus; ~**ā′tion**, ~**ātor**, *ns.*; ~**ator′ial**, ~**atory**, *adjs.* [L (*medius* middle)]

**mĕ′dic** *n.* (sl.) = MEDICO. [L *medicus* physician]

**mĕ′dic\al. 1.** *a.* (-lly). Of the art of medicine in general or as opp. to surgery etc.; ~**al certificate** (of fitness or unfitness to work etc.); ~**al examination** (to determine person's physical fitness); ~**al jurisprudence**, forensic medicine; ~**al man**, physician or surgeon; ~**al officer**, person in charge of health services of local authority or other organization; ~**al school** (in which physicians etc. are trained); ~**al student**, person studying for qualification in medicine. **2.** *n.* (colloq.) Medical examination. **3.** ~**ament** (or mĭdĭ′k-) *n.*, substance used in curative treatment; ~**āte** *v.t.*, treat medically, impregnate with medicinal substance; ~**ā′tion** *n.*; ~**ative** *a.* [F f. L (prec.)]

**mĕ′dicine** (mĕ′dsin, mĕ′dĭsin). **1.** *n.* Art of restoring and preserving health, esp. by means of remedial substances etc. as opp. to surgery etc.; substance, esp. one taken internally, used in this; (among primitive peoples) spell, charm, fetish, (~**man**, magician) ~ **chest**, box containing remedies; **a dose** etc. **of one's own ~**, treatment such as one is accustomed to giving others; **take one's ~**, submit to disagreeable thing. **2.** *v.t.* (arch.) Give medicine to. **3.** **mĕdǐ′cinal** *a.* (-lly), of medicine, having healing properties. [F f. L *medicina* (MEDIC)]

**mĕ'dĭcō** n. (pl. ~s). (colloq.) Medical practitioner or student. [It. f. L (MEDIC)]

**mēdĭē'val, -ae'val,** a. (~ly). Of or imitating the Middle Ages; (fig.) old-fashioned; ~ **history** (of 5th–15th c.); medieval LATIN; ~**ĭsm, ~ĭst,** n.; ~**ĭze** v.t. & i. [L medium aevum middle age(s)]

**mēdĭ|ō'cre** (-ker; or mē'-) a. Of middling quality; second-rate; ~**ŏ'crĭtÿ** n., mediocre quality or person. [F, or L mediocris]

**mĕ'dĭt|āte** v.t. & i. Plan mentally, design; exercise the mind in (esp. religious) contemplation (on, upon, subject); ~**ā'tion** n.; ~**ative** a., inclined to meditate, indicative of meditation; ~**ātor** n. [L meditor]

**Mĕdĭterrā'nēan** a. & n. = (Sea), that which separates Europe and Africa; (m~) of the region of the Mediterranean Sea. [L mediterraneus inland]

**mē'dĭum.** 1. n. (pl. mē'dia, ~s). Middle quality or degree (between extremes, or abs.; HAPPY medium); intervening substance through which impressions are conveyed to senses, e.g. air, (fig.) environment; agency, means, (by or through the medium of; ~ **of** circulation, coin etc.); (pl. ~s) person claiming to have communication with spirits of the dead etc. and reveal its results to others; means by which something is communicated, material or form used by artist, composer, etc.; (in pl.) = MASS² media. 2. a. Intermediate between two degrees or amounts; average, moderate; ~ **bowler, pace,** (Crick., neither fast nor slow); medium WAVE. 3. ~**ĭ'stĭc** a. (-ically), of a spiritualist medium. [L (medius middle)]

**mĕ'dlar** n. (Tree with) fruit like small apple, eaten when decayed. [F medler f. L f. Gk mespilē]

**mĕ'dley** n. Heterogeneous mixture, mixed company, miscellany. [F medlee f. L (MEDDLE)]

**mĕdŭ'lla** n. Marrow of bone; spinal marrow; ~ (**oblongata** pr. ŏblŏnggah'ta), hindmost section of brain; ~**rÿ** a. [L]

**mĕdū'sa** n. (pl. ~e, ~s). (Zool.) Jellyfish. [L f. Gk Medousa, name of Gorgon]

**meed** n. (literary or arch.) Reward; merited portion (of praise etc.). [E]

**meek** a. Tamely submissive. [N]

**meer'schaum** (-sham) n. Creamy clay used esp. for tobacco-pipe bowls; pipe with meerschaum bowl. [G, = sea-foam]

**meet¹** a. (arch.) Fitting, proper, (for thing, to do, that). [METE]

**meet².** 1. v.t. & i. (met). Come face to face (with); come together or into contact (with), (waistcoat won't ~, is too small in girth to be fastened; make ENDS meet); go to place to be present at arrival of (person, train, etc.); come by accident or design into the company of; make the acquaintance of; be assembled, (of qualities) be united in same person; pay (cost, bill at maturity); satisfy, conform with (person's wishes), give valid answer to (demand, objection, etc.); experience, receive, (one's death, fate, etc.); oppose, be in opposition, in contest etc.; ~ person's **eye,** see he is looking at one, look at him in one's turn; ~ (person) **half-way,** (fig.) respond to friendly advances of, make a compromise with; ~ **the case,** be adequate; ~ **the eye, ear,** be visible, audible (more in it than ~s the eye, hidden qualities or complications); ~ **up with,** (colloq.) happen to meet (person); ~ **with,** happen to meet (person, obstacle, etc.), encounter, experience. 2. n. Meeting of persons and hounds for hunt. 3. ~**'ing** n., (esp.) assembly of people for entertainment, discussion, or (esp. of Quakers) worship, (arch.) duel, race-meeting. [E]

**mĕ'ga-** in comb. Large (~**lĭth** n., large stone, esp. as monument, ~**lĭ'thĭc** a., [Gk lithos stone]); one million: ~**death,** death of one million people, (esp. as unit of results of war); megahertz; ~**ton,** one million tons, esp. = this quantity of T.N.T. as unit of equivalent explosive power; megavolt; megawatt. [Gk megas great]

**mĕgalomā'nĭa** n. Insanity of self-exaltation; passion for grandiose things.

**mĕ'gaphōne** n. Large speaking-trumpet for sending sound of voice to a distance. [Gk phōnē sound]

**meiō's|ĭs** (mī-) n. (pl. ~es pr. -ēz). = LITOTES; (Biol.) a process of division of cell nuclei before fertilization. [L f. Gk (meiōn less)]

**mĕ'lamine** (-ēn) n. ~ (**resin**), resilient kind of plastic. [arbitrary]

**mě'lanch|olў** (-n-k-). **1.** *n.* (Habitual or constitutional tendency to) sadness and depression; pensive sadness. **2.** *a.* Sad, gloomy; saddening, depressing; (of words etc.) expressing sadness. **3.** ~**ŏ'lĭa** *n.*, mental disease marked by depression and ill-founded fears; ~**ŏ'lĭc** *a.*, melancholy, liable to melancholy. [F f. L f. Gk (*melas* black, *kholē* bile)]

**mélange** (mālah'nzh) *n.* Medley. [F (*mêler* mix)]

**mě'lanin** *n.* Dark pigment in hair, skin, etc. [Gk *melas* black]

**Mě'lba** *n.* ~ **toast**, thin crisp toast; PEACH[2] *Melba*. [person]

*****měld** *v.t.* & *i.* Merge. [MELT, WELD]

**mêlée** (mě'lā) *n.* Confused fight or struggle; muddle. [F (MEDLEY)]

**mě'lior|āte** *v.t.* & *i.* Improve; ~**ā'tion** *n.* [L (*melior* better)]

**měllĭ'flu|ous**, ~|**ent**, (-lōō-) *adjs.* (Of words, voice, etc.) honey-sweet. [F or L (*mel* honey, *fluo* flow)]

**mě'llow** (-ō). **1.** *a.* (~**er**, ~**est**). (Of fruit) soft, sweet, and juicy; (of wine) well-matured; (of earth) rich, loamy; (of character) softened by age or experience; (of sound, colour, light) full and pure without harshness; genial, jovial; partly intoxicated. **2.** *v.t.* & *i.* Make or become mellow. [orig. unkn.]

**mě'lodў** *n.* Sweet music; musical arrangement of words; arrangement of single notes in musically expressive succession; principal part in harmonized music; **mělō'dĭc** *a.*, of melody; **mělō'dĭous** *a.*, of or producing melody, sweet-sounding; **mě'lodĭst** *n.*, singer, composer of melodies; **mě'lodrama** (-rah-) *n.*, sensational dramatic piece with crude appeals to emotions, behaviour or occurrence suggestive of this; **mělodramă'tĭc** *a.* (-ically). [F f. L f. Gk (*melos* song; ODE)]

**mě'lon** *n.* (Sweet fruit of) gourd, esp. MUSK-*melon*, WATER-*melon*. [F f. L f. Gk *mēlon* apple]

**mělt** *v.t.* & *i.* (*p.p.* ~**ed** or, as *a.* of substances not easily melted, **molten** *pr.* mō'-). Change from solid to liquid by heat; (of food) be easily dissolved *in the mouth*; (of person, feelings, etc.) be softened by or *with* pity or love; soften (person, feelings, etc.); pass by imperceptible degrees *into* (another form); ~ **away**, dis-

appear by liquefaction, dwindle away, (colloq. of person) depart unobtrusively; ~ **down**, (coin, plate, etc., to use metal as raw material); ~**'ing-point**, temperature at which solid melts; ~**'ing-pot**, (fig.) place of reconstruction or vigorous mixing. [E]

**mě'mber** *n.* Part or organ of body (**unruly** ~, arch., the tongue; ~ **of Christ**, fig., Christian); constituent portion of complex structure; person belonging to a society etc.; **M**~ (one formally elected to take part in proceedings) **of Parliament, of Congress**; ~**shĭp** *n.*, being a member, number of members, body of members; **mě'mbrāne** *n.*, pliable sheetlike connective tissue or lining in animal or vegetable body; **měmbrā'nēous**, **mě'mbranous**, *adjs.* [F f. L *membrum* limb]

**měmě'ntō** *n.* (*pl.* ~**es**, ~**s**). Object serving as reminder or warning, or kept as memorial of person or event. [L, imper. of *memini* remember]

**mě'mō** *n.* (colloq.; *pl.* ~**s**). Memorandum. [abbr.]

**mě'moir** (-wâr) *n.* Record of events; history written from personal knowledge or special sources of information; (esp. in *pl.*) (auto)biography; essay on learned subject specially studied by the writer. [foll.]

**mě'morў** *n.* Faculty by which things are recalled to or kept in the mind; this in an individual (**a good** ~**y**, ability to retain and recall much; **commit to** ~**y**, learn so as to recall); recovery of one's knowledge by mental effort (**from** ~**y**, without verification in books etc.; **in** ~**y of**, to keep alive the remembrance of); act of remembering; person or thing remembered, posthumous repute (*his memory has been censured*; *of happy memory*); length of time over which memory extends (*within living memory*, see LIVE[2]); store in computer; ~**able** *a.* (**-bly**), worth remembering, easily remembered; ~**ă'ndum** *n.* (*pl.* **-da**, **-dums**), note or record made for future use, informal business or diplomatic message; **měmō'rĭal**, (*a.*) of memory, (of statue, festival, religious service, etc.) serving to commemorate, (*n.*) memorial object, custom, etc., (usu. in *pl.*) record or chronicle, informal diplomatic paper, statement of facts as basis of petition etc.; **měmō'rĭalĭst** *n.*, signatory of memorial; **memŏr′ialīze** v.t., commemorate, address memorial to; **~īze** v.t., commit to memory. [F f. L *memoria* (*memor* remembering)]

**mĕm′sahīb.** See SAHIB.

**mĕn.** See MAN.

**mĕn′ace. 1.** n. Threat; dangerous or obnoxious thing or person. **2.** v.t. Threaten. [L *minax* (*minor* threaten)]

**ménage** (mănah′zh) n. Domestic establishment; **~ à trois** (ah trwah), household consisting of husband, wife, and lover of one of these; **ménâ′gerīe** n., collection of wild animals in captivity for exhibition etc. [F f. L (MANSION)]

**mĕnd. 1.** v.t. & i. Restore to sound condition, repair (broken article, torn clothes, damaged road, etc.); regain health; add fuel to (fire); **~ or end**, improve or abolish; mend one's FENCES; **~** one's **manners**, **ways**, improve them; **~ matters**, rectify or improve state of affairs; **~** one's **pace**, walk more quickly; LEAST *said soonest mended.* **2.** n. Repaired hole in material etc.; **on the ~**, improving in health or condition. [AF (AMEND)]

**mĕnd|ā′cious** (-shŭs) a. Lying, untruthful; **~ā′cĭtў** n. [L *mendax*]

**Mĕnde′lian** a. & n. (Adherent) of *Mendel*'s theory of heredity by genes; **~ĭsm, Mĕ′ndelĭsm,** ns. [person]

**mĕ′ndīcan|t. 1.** a. Begging; **~t friar** (living solely on alms); **~cў, mĕndi′cĭtў,** ns. **2.** n. Beggar; mendicant friar. [L (*mendicus* beggar)]

**menfolk.** See MAN.

**mĕ′nhir** (-ēr) n. Tall upright usu. prehistoric monumental stone. [Breton *men* stone, *hir* long]

**mĕ′nial. 1.** a. (**~lў**). (Of service) degrading, servile; (of servant, usu. derog.) domestic. **2.** n. Menial servant. [AF *meinie* retinue f. L (MANSION)]

**mĕnĭngī′tĭs** (-nj-) n. Inflammation of membrane (**meninx**) enclosing brain and spinal cord. [Gk *mēnigx* membrane]

**menī′sc|us** n. (pl. **~i** pr. -sī). Lens convex on one side, concave on the other; (Phys.) curved upper surface of liquid in tube. [L f. Gk dim. (*mēnē* moon)]

**mĕ′nopaus|e** (-z) n. Final cessation of menses; period of woman's life (usu. 40–50) when this occurs; **~al** a. [L f. Gk *mēn* month, PAUSE]

**mĕnŏr′ah** (-a) n. Seven-branched candelabrum used in Jewish worship. [Heb., = candlestick]

**mĕ′nsēs** (-z) n.pl. Monthly flow of blood etc. from lining of womb. [L pl. of *mensis* month]

**mĕ′nstru|al** (-ŏŏ-) a. (**-lly**). Of menses; **~āte** v.i., discharge menses; **~ā′tion** n.; **~ous** a., menstrual, menstruating; **~um** n. (pl. **~ua**), solvent (lit. or fig.). [F or L (*menstruus* monthly)]

**mĕnsūrā′tion** n. Measuring; (Math.) rules for finding lengths, areas, and volumes; **mĕ′nsūrable** a. (**-bly**), measurable, having fixed limits; **mĕ′nsūral** a. (**-lly**), of measure. [L (MEASURE)]

**-ment** suf. forming ns. expr. result or means of vbl action (*fragment, implement, ligament, ornament, abridgement, treatment*); also f. adjs. (*merriment, oddment*). [F f. L -*mentum*]

**mĕ′ntal** a. (**~lў**). Of the mind, done by the mind; ‖(colloq.) affected with mental disorder; **~ age**, degree of person's mental development expressed as age at which same degree is attained by average child; **~ arithmetic** (performed without use of written figures); **~ asylum, home,** hospital, establishment for care of mental patients; *mental* BLOCK; **~ cruelty,** infliction of suffering on another's mind; **~ defective, deficiency,** (condition of) mentally undeveloped person unable to deal with his ordinary affairs; **~ illness,** disorder of the mind; **~ patient,** sufferer from mental illness; *mental* RESERVATION; **mĕntă′lĭtў** n., (esp.) (degree of) intellectual power, mental character or outlook. [F or L (*mens ment-* mind)]

**mĕ′nthŏl** n. Camphor-like substance got from oil of peppermint etc., used as flavouring or to relieve local pain etc. [G f. L (MINT¹)]

**mĕ′ntion. 1.** v.t. Refer to, remark upon, specify by name; (in deprecation of apology or thanks) **don't ~ it;** (introducing fact or thing of secondary or, as rhet. artifice, of primary importance) **not to ~. 2.** n. Mentioning, formal reference to meritorious person (in mil. dispatches etc.; **honourable ~,** award of merit to candidate in examination, work of art, etc., not entitled to prize); **make (no) ~ of,** (not) refer to. [F f. L *mentio*]

**me̅'nto̅r** n. Experienced and trusted adviser. [person in *Odyssey*]

**me̅'nu̇** n. List of dishes to be served or available in restaurant. [F f. L (MINUTE²)]

**Mēphist|ŏ'phĕlēs** (-z) n. Fiendish person; **~ŏphĕlē'an, ~ophē'lian,** adjs. [G name of legendary evil spirit]

**me̅r'cantı̆l|e** a. Of trade, commercial; trading; **~e marine,** shipping employed in commerce. [F f. It. f. L (MERCHANT)]

**Me̅rca̅'tor** n. **~'s projection,** map projection of globe on cylinder, with straight lines of latitude and longitude at right angles. [person]

**me̅r'cĕnăry̆. 1.** a. (-ily, -iness). Working merely for money or other reward; hired. **2.** n. Hired soldier in foreign service. [L (MERCY)]

**‖me̅r'cer** n. Dealer in textile fabrics, esp. silks and other costly materials; **~y̆** n. [AF f. L (merx merc-goods)]

**me̅r'chandı̆se** (-z). **1.** n. Commodities of commerce; goods for sale. **2.** v.t. & i. Trade (in). [F (foll.)]

**me̅r'chant** n. Wholesale trader, esp. with foreign countries; (U.S. & Sc.) retail trader; (sl.) person fond of an activity etc. (SPEED-*merchant*); **~ bank** (dealing in commercial loans and financing); **~ fleet, \*marine, ‖navy, service,** mercantile marine; **~man, ~ ship,** ship conveying merchandise; **~ prince,** wealthy merchant; **~able** a., saleable. [F f. L (*mercor* to trade)]

**me̅r'cı̆ful, me̅r'cı̆less.** See MERCY.

**me̅r'cu̇ry̆** n. Silvery-white heavy normally liquid metal used in barometers, thermometers, etc., (**the ~ is rising,** weather is improving); (M~) planet nearest the sun; **mercu̇r'ial** a. (-lly), of or containing mercury, (of person) ready-witted, volatile; **mercu̇r'ic** a. (Chem.). [L *Mercurius,* Roman messenger-god]

**me̅r'cy̆. 1.** n. Compassion, forbearance, shown by one to another (esp. offender) who is in his power and has no claim to kindness, God's forbearance and forgiveness of sins, (**have ~ (up)on,** show mercy to; **~ (me)!, ~ (up)on us,** excl. of terror or surprise); compassionateness; act of mercy; **at the ~ of,** wholly in the power of, liable to danger or harm from; ERRAND *of mercy;* **left to the**

**tender mercies of,** at the mercy of, (usu., iron.) exposed to probable rough handling by; **that is a ~** (blessing, thing to be thankful for). **2.** a. Administered or performed out of mercy or pity for suffering person (*mercy killing*). **3.** me̅r'cı̆ful a. (-lly), having, showing, or feeling mercy; me̅r'cı̆less a., pitiless, showing no mercy. [F f. L *merces* reward, pity]

**me̅re¹** n. (arch., poet.) Lake. [E]

**me̅re²** attrib. a. That is solely or no more or better than (what the noun implies) (*a mere swindler; the merest buffoonery*); **no ~,** by no means only a; **~'ly̆** (me̅r'lı̆) adv., just, only. [AF f. L *merus* unmixed]

**me̅rĕtrı̆'cious** (-shŭs) a. (Of ornament etc.) showily but falsely attractive. [L (*meretrix* prostitute)]

**me̅rgă'nser** n. A diving duck. [L *mergus* diver, *anser* goose]

**me̅rg|e** v.t. & i. Lose, cause (thing) to lose, character or identity *in* (another); join or blend gradually; combine *with;* **~'er** n., combining of two commercial companies etc. into one. [L *mergo* dip]

**meri'dı̆|an** n. Circle of constant longitude, passing through given place and the terrestrial poles; corresponding line on map or sky; (arch.) point at which sun or star attains highest altitude; (fig.) prime, full splendour; (*attrib.*) of noon, of the period of greatest splendour, vigour, etc.; **~onal** a. (-lly), (of the inhabitants) of the south (esp. of Europe), of a meridian. [F or L (*meridies* midday)]

**meri'ngue** (-ă'ng) n. Confection made with white of egg, sugar, etc., baked crisp. [F]

**meri'no̅** (-rē'-) n. (*pl.* **~s**). **~** (sheep), variety of sheep with fine wool; soft woollen or wool-and-cotton material orig. of merino wool; fine woollen yarn. [Sp.]

**me̅'rı̆t. 1.** n. Quality of deserving well; excellence, worth; (usu. in *pl.*) thing that entitles to reward or gratitude; *judge* (proposal etc.) **on its ~s,** with regard only to its intrinsic excellences etc.; **‖Order of M~** (for distinguished achievement). **2.** v.t. Deserve (reward, punishment, consideration, etc.). **3.** **~ŏ'cracy̆** n., government by persons selected for merit; **~o̅r'ious** a., praiseworthy. [F f. L *meritum* value (*mereor* deserve)]

**mĕr′lĭn** *n*. Kind of falcon. [AF]

**mĕr′|maid** *n*. Imaginary half-human sea-creature with woman's head and trunk and fish's tail; ~′**man** *n*. [MERE¹ 'sea', MAID]

**Mĕrovĭ′ngian** (-nj-) *n*. & *a*. (Member) of Frankish dynasty founded by Clovis. [F f. L *Merovingi* (*Meroveus*, person)]

**mĕ′rry** *a*. (-ily, -iness). Joyous, full of laughter or gaiety; (colloq.) slightly tipsy; ~ **andrew**, mountebank's assistant, buffoon; ~ **Christmas!** (as salutation); ~ **or merrie** (pleasant) **England**; ~**-go-round**, revolving machine with wooden horses or cars for riding on at fair etc.; ~ **hell**, (sl.) great disturbance (*play merry hell with*); ~**-making**, festivity; **the M~ Monarch**, Charles II; **make ~**, be festive; **make ~ over**, make fun of; **mĕ′rriment** *n*., hilarious enjoyment, mirth, fun. [E]

*****mē′sa** (mā′-) *n*. High steep-sided tableland. [Sp., = table]

*mésalliance* (māză′lĭahṅs) *n*. Marriage with social inferior. [F]

**mĕ′scăl** *n*. Peyote cactus; ~ **buttons**, its disc-shaped dried tops; **mĕ′scaline** (-ēn), **-ĭn**, *n*., hallucinogenic alkaloid present in mescal buttons. [Sp.]

*Mesdames,   Mesdemoiselles*. See MADAME, MRS., MADEMOISELLE.

**mĕsĕmbryă′nthemum** (-z-) *n*. Kind of plant with flowers opening at about noon. [L f. Gk *mesembria* noon, *anthemon* flower]

**mĕsh. 1.** *n*. Open space in net, sieve, etc.; (in *pl*.) network, (fig.) snare; network fabric; **in ~**, (of teeth of wheels) engaged. **2.** *v.t.* & *i.* Catch in net (lit. or fig.); (of teeth of wheel) be engaged (*with* others); (fig.) be harmonious. [Du.]

**mĕ′smer|ĭsm** (mĕ′z-) *n*. (arch. or fig.) Hypnotic state produced in patient by operator's influence over will and nervous system; doctrine concerning, influence producing, this; **mĕsmĕ′ric** (-zm-) *a*. (-ically); ~**ĭst** *n*.; ~**ĭze** *v.t.* [*Mesmer*, person]

**mĕ′so-** (*or* -z-) *in comb.* Middle, intermediate; ~**lĭ′thic** *a*., of Stone Age between palaeolithic and neolithic [Gk *lithos* stone]; ~**mŏrph** *n*., person with compact muscular body-build [Gk *morphē* form]; **mĕ′sŏn** (-z-) *n*., (Phys.) elementary unstable particle intermediate in mass between proton and electron; **M~zō′ĭc** *a*. & *n*., (of) second geological era [Gk *zōion* animal]. [Gk *mesos* middle]

**mĕss. 1.** *n*. Portion of liquid or pulpy food (~ *of pottage*, material comfort etc. for which something higher is sacrificed); (derog.) disagreeable concoction or medley; dirty or untidy state of things; spilt liquid etc.; domestic animal's excreta; state of confusion, embarrassment, or trouble, (**make a ~ of**, bungle); company of persons who take meals together, esp. in the fighting services, meal so taken, room where such meals are taken; ~**-jacket**, short close-fitting coat worn at mess; ~**-kit**, soldier's cooking and eating utensils; ~′**mate**, one of the same (usu. ship's) mess. **2.** *v.t.* & *i.* ~ (**up**), make a mess of, dirty, interfere with, muddle (business); potter *about* or *around*; take one's meals (*with*, or abs.). [F f. L *missus* course of meal (foll.)]

**mĕ′ssage** *n*. Communication sent or transmitted by one person to another; prophet's, writer's, or preacher's inspired or significant communication; **get the ~**, (colloq.) understand what is meant; **mĕ′ssenger** (-nj-) *n*., person who carries message(s). [F f. L *mitto miss-* send]

**Mĕssī′ah** (-a) *n*. (Christ regarded as) promised deliverer of Jews; (would-be) liberator of oppressed people or country; **Mĕssiă′nic** *a*., of the, inspired by hope or belief in a, Messiah. [Heb., = anointed]

*Messieurs*. See MONSIEUR.

**Mĕ′ssrs.** (-serz) *n*. (used as *pl.* of MR., esp. as prefix to name of firm or to list of men's names). [abbr. prec.]

**mĕ′ssuage** (-swĭj) *n*. (Law). Dwelling-house with outbuildings and land. [AF, = dwelling]

**mĕ′ssy** *a*. (-ily, -iness). That is (accompanied by) a mess; untidy, difficult to deal with. [MESS]

**mĕt¹.** See MEET.

**mĕt²** *a*. (colloq.) Meteorological; metropolitan; **the Met**, ‖the Meteorological Office, *the Metropolitan Opera House (New York). [abbr.]

**mĕ′ta-** *pref.* denoting change of position or condition (*metabolism*), behind, after, (*metaphysics*), beyond (*metacarpus*). [Gk *meta* with, after)]

**mĕtă′bol|ĭsm** *n*. Changes undergone by nutritive material (**con-structive** ~**ism**) or protoplasm (**destructive** ~**ism**) in the body; **metabŏ′lic** a. (-ically); ~**ize** v.t. [META-, Gk *ballō* throw]

**mĕtacăr′p|us** n. (*pl.* ~**i** *pr.* -ī). (Set of bones in) hand between wrist and fingers; ~**al** a. [META-]

**me′tal. 1.** n. Any of a class of substances (such as gold, iron, tin) all crystalline when solid and many opaque, ductile, malleable, dense, good conductors of heat and electricity, and characterized by a peculiar lustre; alloy of these; (Mil.) tanks, armoured vehicles; ROAD-*metal*; ‖(in *pl.*) rails of railway line (**train leaves the** ~**s**, is derailed); (*attrib.*) made of metal. **2.** v.t. (‖-ll-). Furnish or fit with metal; ‖make or mend (road) with road-metal. **3.** **mĕta′llic** a. (-ically), (characteristic) of metal(s), sounding like struck metal; ~**li′ferous** a.; ~**lize**, *~**ize**, v.t., render metallic, coat with thin layer of metal; ~**lŏ′-graphy** n., descriptive science of metals. [F or L f. Gk *metallon* mine]

**mĕta′llurg|y̆** (*or* mĕ′talĕr-). n. Art of working metals, esp. of extracting metals from ores; **mĕtallŭr′gĭc(al)** *adjs.* (-ically); ~**ĭst** n. [Gk *metallon* (prec.), -*ourgia* working]

**mĕtamŏr′ph|osĭs** (*or* -fŏ′-) n. (*pl.* -**oses** *pr.* -ēz). Change of form (by magic, natural development, etc.); change of character, conditions, etc.; ~**ĭc** a. (-ically), (Geol.) of rock) that has undergone transformation by natural agencies; ~**ĭsm** n. (Geol.); ~**ōse** (-z) v.t., change in form, turn (*to, into*, new form), change nature of. [L f. Gk (*morphē* shape)]

**me′taph|or** n. Application of name or descriptive term or phrase to object or action where it is not literally applicable (*a glaring error*; *leave no stone unturned*; **mixed** ~**or**, combination of inconsistent metaphors (*this tower of strength will forge ahead*); ~**ŏ′ric(al)** *adjs.* (-ically). [F or L f. Gk]

**mĕtaphy̆s′|ics** (-z-) *n.pl.* (often treated as *sing.*) Theoretical philosophy of being and knowing; (pop.) abstract or subtle talk, mere theory; ~**ical** a. (-lly) ~**i′cian** (-shan) n. [F f. L f. Gk, as having followed physics in Aristotle's works]

**mĕta′stas|ĭs** n. (*pl.* ~**es** *pr.* -ēz). Transfer of disease etc. from one part

of the body to another. [L f. Gk, = removal]

**mĕtatăr′s|us** n. (*pl.* ~**i** *pr.* -ī). (Set of bones in) foot between ankle and toes; ~**al** a. [META-]

**mĕtă′thĕs|ĭs** n. (*pl.* ~**es** *pr.* -ēz). Transposition of sounds or letters in word (as in *bird*, earlier *brid*). [L f. Gk, = transposition]

**mēte** v.t. (literary). Measure (poet., Bibl.); ~ (**out**), allot (punishment, reward, etc.). [E]

**mĕtĕmpsy̆chō′s|ĭs** (-k-) n. (*pl.* ~**es** *pr.* -ēz). Supposed transmigration of human or animal soul at death into new body of same or different species. [L f. Gk (META-, *en* in, *psukhē* soul)]

**mē′tĕor** n. Small mass of matter from outer space rendered luminous by compression of air on entering earth's atmosphere; **mĕtĕŏ′rĭc** a. (-ically), of meteors, (fig.) like a meteor, dazzling, rapid, transient; ~**ite** n., fallen meteor, fragment of rock etc. reaching earth's surface from outer space; ~**ŏ′logy̆** n., study of phenomena of atmosphere esp. for weather forecasting; ~**olŏ′gĭcal** a. (-lly); ‖M~**ological Office**, government department providing weather forecasts etc.); ~**ŏ′logĭst** n. [Gk *meteōros* lofty]

**mē′ter¹. 1.** n. Instrument for recording quantity of substance supplied (GAS *meter*) or present; = PARK*ing-meter*, TAXIMETER. **2.** v.t. Measure by meter. [METE]

*\***mē′ter²**. See METRE.

-**mēter** (*or* -mē-) *suf.* forming names of automatic measuring instruments (*barometer, thermometer, voltmeter*) or (Pros.) of lines with specified number of measures (*dimeter, pentameter*). [Gk *metron* measure]

**mē′thāne** n. Inflammable hydrocarbon gas of the paraffin series. [METHYL]

**mĕth|ĭ′nks** v.i. impers. (arch.) *past* ~**ought** *pr.* -aw′t). It seems to me. [E (ME¹, THINK)]

**mĕ′thod** n. Special form of procedure esp. in mental activity; orderly arrangement of ideas; orderliness, regular habits; **there's** ~ **in his madness**, (joc.) his conduct or proposal is not so mad as it seems; **mĕthŏ′dical** a. (-lly), characterized by method or order; **M~ĭst** n., member of any of several Protestant religious bodies (now united) originating in an 18th-c. evangelistic movement; **M~ĭsm** *n.*; **~ŏ′logў** *n.*, science of method. [F or L f. Gk META-, *hodos* way)]

**methought.** See METHINKS.

**mĕ′thўl** *n.* (Chem.) Radical present in methane etc.; **~ alcohol**, a colourless volatile inflammable liquid; **~āte** *v.t.*, mix, impregnate (esp. alcohol to make it unfit for drinking), with methyl alcohol (*methylated spirit(s)*, colloq. **meths**). [G or F (Gk *methu* wine, *hulē* wood)]

**metī′cŭlous** *a.* (Over-)scrupulous about minute details; (colloq.) very careful, accurate. [L (*metus* fear)]

**métier** (mĕ′tyā) *n.* One's trade, profession, or department of activity; one's forte. [F f. L (MINISTER)]

**Mĕtŏ′nĭc** *a.* **~ cycle** (of 19 years covering all relative positions of moon, sun, and earth). [*Meton*, person]

**metŏ′nўmў** *n.* Substitution of name of attribute or adjunct for that of thing meant (e.g. *crown* for *king*, *wealth* for *rich people*). [L f. Gk (META-, *onuma* name)]

**mĕ′tre** (-ter), **\*mĕ′ter²**, *n.* Any form of poetic rhythm, determined by character and number of feet, metrical group, measure; unit of length in metric system (about 39.4 in.); **mĕ′trĭc** *a.* (-ically), of the metre; **metric system**, decimal measuring-system with metre, and litre and (kilo)gram determined by it, as units of length, capacity, and weight or mass, (**go metric**, colloq., adopt the metric system); *metric* HUNDREDWEIGHT, TON; **mĕ′trĭcal** *a.* (-lly), of, composed in, metre (*metrical psalms*), of or involving measurement (*metrical geometry*); **-mĕ′trĭc(al)** *sufs.* forming *adjs.* from *ns.* in *-meter* or *-metry*; **mĕtrĭcā′tion** *n.*, conversion to metric system. [F f. L f. Gk *metron* measure]

**mĕtrŏ′logў** *n.* Science or system of weights and measures; **mĕtrolŏ′gĭcal** *a.* (-lly). [Gk (METRE)]

**mĕ′tron|ōme** *n.* (Mus.) Instrument marking time at selected rate by means of pendulum etc.; **~ŏ′mĭc** *a.* (-ically). [Gk *metron* measure, *nomos* law]

**metrŏ′poli|s** *n.* Chief city of a country, capital, (‖**the ~s**, London); metropolitan bishop's see; **metropŏ′lĭtan**, (*a.*) of a or the metropolis, belonging to or forming (part of)

mother country as dist. from colonies etc., (**~tan bishop,** having authority over the bishops of a province), (*n.*) inhabitant of a metropolis, metropolitan bishop. [L f. Gk (*mētēr* mother, *polis* city)]

**-mĕtrў** *suf.* forming names of procedures and systems corresp. to instruments in **-METER** (*barometry*, *thermometry*). [Gk (METRE)]

**mĕ′ttle** *n.* Quality of person's disposition or temperament; natural ardour; spirit, courage; **on one's ~**, incited to do one's best; **~some** (-tels-) *a.*, spirited. [= METAL]

**mew¹** *n.* (Esp. common) gull. [E]

**mew².** 1. *v.i.* & *t.* Put (hawk) in mew; shut *up*, confine. 2. *n.* Cage for hawks; ‖(in *pl.*, treated as *sing.*) set of stabling round open yard or lane, now often converted into dwellings. [F f. L *muto* change]

**mew³.** 1. *v.i.* (Of cat or sea-bird) utter sound *mew*. 2. *n.* This sound, esp. of cat. 3. **~l** *v.i.*, cry feebly, whimper, mew like cat. [imit.]

‖**mews.** See MEW².

**Mĕ′xĭcan** *a.* & *n.* (Native, language esp. Nahuatl) of Mexico. [Sp.]

**mĕ′zzanine** (-ēn; *or* mĕ′tsa-) *n.* Low storey between two others (usu. between ground and first floors). [F f. It. f. L (MEDIAN)]

**mezzo** (mĕ′dzo, -tsō) *adv.* (esp. Mus.) Half, moderately; **~ forte**, **piano**, fairly loud, soft; **~soprano** (person with, part for) voice between soprano and contralto; **~tint**, method of engraving by scraping a uniformly roughened plate, print so produced. [It. f. L *medius* middle]

**mf** *abbr.* mezzo forte.

‖**M.F.H.** *abbr.* Master of Foxhounds.

**mg** *abbr.* milligram(s).

**Mgr.** *abbr.* Monseigneur; Monsignor.

**MHz** *abbr.* megahertz.

**mi.** See ME².

‖**M.I.** *abbr.* Military Intelligence.

**mĭaow** (mĭow′) *n.*, & *v.i.* (Make) cry of cat, mew. [imit.]

**mĭă′sm|a** (-z-) *n.* (*pl.* **~ata**, **~as**). Infectious or noxious emanation; **~al** (-lly), **~ă′tĭc** (-ically), *adjs.* [Gk, = defilement]

**Mic.** *abbr.* Micah (O.T.).

**mĭ′ca** *n.* Kind of mineral found as small glittering scales in granite etc. or in crystals separable into thin transparent plates. [L, = crumb]

**Micaw′ber** *n.* Person perpetually

idling and trusting that something good will turn up; **~ism** n. [character in Dickens]

**mice.** See MOUSE.

**Mich.** abbr. Michaelmas; Michigan.

**Mi′chaelmas** (-kel-) n. Feast of St. Michael, 29 Sept.; **~ daisy**, aster flowering at Michaelmas; **‖~ term** (in university etc., beginning at or near Michaelmas). [MASS¹]

**mi′ckey, mi′cky,** n. (sl.) Take the **~** (out of), act disrespectfully or teasingly (towards). [orig. uncert.]

**mi′ckle, mŭ′ckle,** n. (arch., Sc.) Large amount (in prov. many a little makes a mickle, erron. many a mickle makes a muckle). [N]

**mi′cro-** in comb. Small (**~bio′logy,** study of micro-organisms; **~circuit,** integrated circuit or other very small circuit; **~dot,** photograph of document etc. reduced to size of dot; **~electro′nics,** design, manufacture, and use of microcircuits; **~fiche** (-ēsh) pl. same), piece of film bearing microphotograph of document etc. [F fiche slip of paper]; **~film** n., & v.t., (photograph on) length of film bearing microphotograph of document etc.; **~organism,** organism not visible to naked eye, e.g. bacterium or virus; **~pho′tograph,** photograph reduced to very small size; **~wave,** electromagnetic wave of length between about 50 cm and 1 mm); one-millionth of (microgram, microsecond). [Gk (mikros small)]

**mi′crōbe** n. Minute living being (esp. of bacteria causing diseases and fermentation); **micro′bial** a. (-lly). [F f. Gk mikros small, bios life]

**mi′cro|cŏsm** n. Man viewed as epitome of universe, any community or complex unity so viewed; miniature representation (of); **~cŏ′smic** (-z-) a. [F or L f. Gk (COSMOS)]

**micrŏ′meter** n. Instrument for measuring small lengths or angles. [F (MICRO-)]

**mi′crŏn** n. One-millionth of a metre. [Gk mikros small]

**mi′crophŏne** n. Instrument for converting sound-waves into electrical energy which may be reconverted into sound elsewhere. [PHONO-]

**mi′crosc|ōpe** n. Instrument magnifying objects by means of lens(es) so as to reveal details invisible to naked eye; **~ŏ′pic** a. (-ically), of the microscope, too small to be visible (in detail) without micro-

scope; **~ŏ′pical** a. (-lly), of the microscope; **micrŏ′scopў** n., use of the microscope; **micrŏ′scopist** n. [-SCOPE]

**mictūri′tion** n. Urination. [L]

**mĭd** a. (superl. **~′most;** no adv. in -ly). That is in the middle of (usu. as comb.; in mid-air, -career, -stream; mid-week, from mid-June to mid--August); that is in the middle, medium, half; **~′field,** (Footb.) part of field away from goals; **~o′ff, ~o′n,** (Crick.) (position of) fieldsman near bowler on off, on side; **~′rib,** central rib of leaf; **~′way** (or -ā′) adv., in middle of distance between places; **~wi′cket,** (Crick.) (position of) fieldsman near leg boundary and opposite middle of pitch. [E]

**Mi′das** n. **~ touch,** ability to make money in all one's activities. [person in Gk myth]

**mi′dday** (-d-d-) n. (Time near) noon. [E (MID, DAY)]

**mi′dden** n. Dunghill, refuse-heap. [Scand., rel. to MUCK]

**mi′ddle** a., n., & v. **1.** attrib. a. (Of member of group) so placed as to have same number of members on each side; equidistant from extremities; intermediate in rank, quality, etc.; average (a man of middle height); middle AGE; **~aged,** of middle age (middle-age(d) SPREAD); **the M~ Ages** (about 1000–1400, in wider sense 600–1500); **~brow** a. & n., (colloq.) (person) claiming to be or regarded as only moderately intellectual; **~ C,** (Mus.) C near middle of piano keyboard, note between treble and bass staves; **~ class,** class of society between upper and lower, incl. professional and business workers; middle DISTANCE; **~ ear,** cavity behind ear-drum; Middle EAST, ENGLISH; **~ (longest) finger;** M~ Kingdom, China, or Egypt c. 2000–1800 B.C.; **~ life,** middle age; **~man,** any of traders who handle commodity between its producer and its consumer; **~ name,** name between first name and surname, (fig.) person's most characteristic quality (sobriety is his middle name); **~-of-the-road,** (of person or action) moderate, avoiding extremes; **~-sized,** of medium size; **~ term,** (Logic) term common to both premisses; **~ voice,** (Gram.) voice of (esp. Gk) verbs expr. reciprocal or reflexive action; ~**weight** (see BOX); *Middle WEST. **2.** *n.* Middle point or position or part (of); waist; middle voice or term; **in the ~ of,** while (doing), during (process); KNOCK *into the middle of next week.* **3.** *v.t.* Place in the middle; (Crick.) strike (ball) with middle of bat. **4. mĭ′ddling,** (*a.*; Commerc., of goods) of the second of three grades, (**fair to**) **middling,** moderately good or (colloq.) fairly well (in health), (*adv.*) fairly, moderately (*middling good*), (*n.*; in *pl.*) middling goods. [E]

**mĭ′ddỹ** *n.* (colloq.) Midshipman. [abbr.]

**mĭdg|e** *n.* Gnatlike insect; small person; ~′**ĕt** *n.* & *a.,* extremely small person, esp. when exhibited as curiosity, very small (thing). [E]

**mĭ′dland** *n.* Middle part of country; **the M~s,** the inland counties of central England. [MID]

**mĭ′dmŏst.** See MID.

**mĭ′dnĭght** (-nīt) *n.* The middle of the night; (time near) 12 o'clock at night; ~ **blue,** very dark blue; *midnight* OIL; ~ **sun,** sun visible at midnight during summer in polar regions.

**mĭ′drĭff** *n.* Diaphragm between thorax and abdomen; region of front of body over this. [E, = mid-belly]

**mĭ′dshĭpman** *n.* Naval officer ranking next above cadet. [MID]

**mĭdst. 1.** *n.* In the ~ **of,** among, in the MIDDLE of; **in our** etc. ~, among us etc. **2.** *prep.* (poet.) Amidst.

**mĭ′dsŭmmer** (*or* -ŭ′-) *n.* Period of or near summer solstice, about 21 June; **M~('s) Day,** 24 June; ~ **madness,** extreme folly.

**mĭ′dwĭ|fe** *n.* (*pl.* ~**ves** *pr.* -vz). Person (usu. woman) trained to assist others in giving birth; ~**ferỹ** (-ĭfrĭ) *n.* [orig. = with-woman]

**mĭdwĭ′nter** *n.* Period of or near winter solstice, about 22 Dec. [MID]

**mien** (mēn) *n.* (literary). Person's bearing or look. [prob. DEMEAN²]

**might¹.** See MAY¹.

**might²** (mīt) *n.* Great (bodily or mental) strength; power to enforce one's will (usu. in contrast with *right*); **with all one's ~,** to the utmost of one's power; *with might and* MAIN¹; ~′**ỹ,** (*a.*; ~**ily,** ~**iness**) powerful in body or mind, massive, bulky, (colloq.) great, considerable, (HIGH *and mighty*), (*adv.*) colloq. very (*that is mighty easy*). [E, rel. to MAY¹]

**mĭgnonĕ′tte** (mĭnyo-) *n.* Plant with fragrant grey-green flowers. [F dim. (*mignon* small)]

**mĭ′graine** (*or* mē′-) *n.* Recurrent paroxysmal headache, often with nausea and disturbance of vision. [F f. L f. Gk *hēmicrania* (HEMI-, CRANIUM)]

**mĭgr|ā′te** (*or* mī′-) *v.i.* Move from one place (country, town, college, house) to another; (of bird or fish) come and go with the seasons; **mĭ′grant,** (*a.*) that migrates, (*n.*) migrant bird etc.; ~**ā′tion,** ~**ā′tor,** *ns.*; **mĭ′gratorỹ** *a.* [L *migro*]

**mĭka′dō** (-ah′-) *n.* (*pl.* ~**s**). Emperor of Japan. [Jap., = august door]

‖**mike¹.** (sl.) **1.** *v.i.* Shirk work, idle. **2.** *n.* Idling (*on the mike*). [orig. unkn.]

**mike²** *n.* (colloq.) Microphone. [abbr.]

**mike³** *n.* (sl.) **For the love of M~,** for Heaven's sake. [*Michael*]

**mĭlā′dỹ** *n.* (Form used in speaking of or to) English noblewoman or great lady. [*my lady*]

**mĭlch** *a.* (Of domestic mammal) giving or kept for milk; ~ **cow,** (fig.) source of regular (and easy) profit. [E, rel. to MILK]

**mĭld** *a.* Gentle; (of rule, punishment, illness, etc.) not severe; (of weather, esp. in winter) moderately warm; (of medicine) operating gently; (of food, tobacco, etc.) not sharp or strong in taste; (of beer) not strongly flavoured with hops, opp. to bitter (DRAW *it mild*); ~ **steel** (tough but not easily tempered); ~′**lỹ** *adv.* (**to put it ~ly,** without any exaggeration). [E]

**mĭ′ldew. 1.** *n.* Growth of minute fungi on plants or on leather etc. exposed to damp; ~**ỹ** *a.* **2.** *v.t.* & *i.* Taint, be tainted, with mildew. [E]

**mile** *n.* Unit of linear measure (**statute ~,** 1,760 yds., about 1·6 km); **geographical, nautical, sea, ~,** approx. 2,025 yds. or 1·85 km); (colloq.) great distance or amount (STICK¹ *out a mile*; *miles apart, away, better, too big*; *beat him by miles*); race extending over a mile; ~′**stone,** stone set up on road to mark distance in miles, (fig.) stage, event, in life, progress, etc.; **not a hundred or a million ~s from,** (joc.) in or at or close to; ~′**age** (-lĭj) *n.,* number of miles travelled, used, etc., (fig.) benefit, profit; **mĭ′ler** *n.,* man or horse qualified or trained specially to run a mile. [E, ult. f. L *mille* thousand]

**mi'lfoil** *n.* Plant with small white flowers and finely divided leaves, yarrow. [F f. L (prec., FOIL¹)]

**milieu** (mē'lyêr) *n.* (*pl.* ~x, ~s, *pr.* -z). Environment, state of life, social surroundings. [F]

**mi'litan|t. 1.** *a.* Engaged in warfare (CHURCH *militant*); combative, aggressively active; ~cў *n.* **2.** *n.* Militant person. [foll.]

**mi'litar|ў. 1.** *a.* (~ily, ~iness). Of, done by, befitting, soldiers, the army, or all armed forces (*military service*); ~y academy (for training army officers); ~y band, wood-wind, brass, and percussion combination; ~y police (acting as police among soldiers). **2.** *n.* (as *sing.* or *pl.*) Soldiers, *the* army, (opp. police or civilians). **3.** ~ism *n.*, spirit or tendencies of the professional soldier, undue prevalence of military spirit or ideals; ~ist *n.*, student of military science, one dominated by military ideas; ~i'stĭc *a.*; ~ize *v.t.*, make military or warlike, equip with military resources, imbue with militarism; ~izā'tion *n.*; **mi'lĭtāte** *v.i.*, (of facts, evidence) have force, tell, (*against*, rarely *in favour of*, conclusion etc.); **milĭ'tia** (-sha) *n.*, military force, esp. one raised from civil population and supplementing regular army in emergency. [F or L (*miles milit-* soldier)]

**milk. 1.** *n.* Opaque white fluid secreted by female mammals for nourishment of their young; milk of cow etc. as food (CONDENSE*d milk*); **dried** or **powdered** ~, = milk-powder; *no use crying over spilt* ~, grieving over irremediable loss or error); milklike juice of plants, e.g. in coconut; milklike preparation of herbs, drugs, etc. **2.** *v.t.* Draw milk from; get money out of, exploit, (person); (sl.) tap (telegraph or telephone wires etc.). **3.** ~ **and honey**, abundant means of prosperity; ~ **and water**, feeble or insipid or mawkish discourse or sentiment; ~ **bar** (for sale of beverages made from milk, other non-alcoholic drinks, ice cream, etc.); ~ **chocolate** (for eating, made with milk); ~ **fever**, mild fever shortly after parturition; ‖~ **float**, light low vehicle used in delivering milk; ~

**for babes**, simple forms of literature, doctrine, etc. opp. to *strong meat*; ~'**ing-machine**, device for milking cows mechanically; ~'**maid**, woman who milks or works in dairy; ~'**man**, man who sells or delivers milk; ~ **of human kindness**, kindness natural to humanity; **M~ of Magnesia**, white suspension of magnesium hydroxide in water as antacid or laxative [P]; ~-**powder**, milk dehydrated by evaporation; ~ **pudding** (of rice, sago, tapioca, etc., baked with milk in dish); ~ **run**, (fig.) routine expedition or service journey; ~ **shake**, drink of milk, flavouring, etc., mixed by shaking or whisking; ~'**sop**, spiritless man or youth; ~-**tooth**, temporary tooth in young mammals; ~-**white**, white like milk. **4.** ~'ў *a.* (~ily, ~iness), of, like, mixed with, milk, (of liquid etc.) cloudy, not clear; **M~y Way**, the Galaxy. [E]

**mill¹. 1.** *n.* (Building fitted with) mechanical apparatus for grinding corn (WATER-*mill*; WIND*mill*; **put, go, through the** ~, subject to, undergo, training or experience or suffering); apparatus for grinding any solid substance to powder or pulp (COFFEE, PEPPER, -*mill*; (building fitted with) machinery for manufacturing-processes etc. (cotton, paper, -*mill*; SAW¹*mill*); ~'**board**, stout pasteboard; ~-**dam**, dam put across stream to make it usable by mill; ~-**pond** (formed by mill-dam; *like a* ~-*pond*, said of calm sea); ~-**race**, current of water that works mill-wheel; ~'**stone**, one of two circular stones for grinding corn, (fig.) heavy burden; ~-**wheel**, wheel used to drive water-mill; ~'**wright**, one who designs or erects mills. **2.** *v.t.* & *i.* Grind (corn), produce (flour), in mill; (esp. in *p.p.*) produce regular markings on edge of (coin); cut or shape (metal) with rotating tool; (of cattle or persons) move round and round in confused mass. [E, ult. f. L (*molo* grind)]

**\*mill² *n.* 1/1000 of dollar. [L (MILLESIMAL)]

**mi'llènarў** (or -ē'-) *a.* & *n.* (Period) of 1,000 years; (festival) of 1,000th anniversary; of, (person) believing in, millennium (also **mĭllènār'ĭan** *a.* & *n.*); **millè'nnium** *n.* (*pl.* -ums, -a), period of 1,000 years, esp. that of Christ's prophesied reign on earth (Rev. 20), (fig.) coming time of justice and happiness; **mǐllě′nnǐal** *a.* (-lly). [L (*milleni* 1,000 each); cf. BIENNIAL]

**mǐ′llĕpĕde, -ĭp-,** *n.* Small many--legged crawling animal; wood--louse. [L (*mille* 1,000, *pes ped-* foot)]

**mǐ′ller** *n.* One who works or owns (esp. corn-)mill; ~'s **thumb**, kind of small fish. [MILL¹]

**mǐllě′sǐmal** *a.* (~ly) & *n.* Thousandth (part); consisting of thousandths. [L (*mille* 1,000)]

**mǐ′llĕt** *n.* Cereal plant with small nutritious seeds. [F dim. f. L *milium*]

**mǐ′lli-** *in comb.* Thousand; one--thousandth (esp. of unit in METRIC system, as *milli*BAR², *milli*gram(me), *milli*litre); ~**mètre** (-ter), *-ter, n.,* about 0·04 inch. [L *mille* 1,000]

‖**mǐ′lliard** (-yerd) *n.* One thousand millions. [F (*mille* 1,000)]

**mǐ′llǐner** *n.* Person (usu. woman) who makes or sells women's hats; ~**ў** *n.* [*Milan*, place]

**mǐ′llion** (-yon) *a.* & *n.* (*pl.* ~, ~s; for pl. usage see HUNDRED). One thousand thousand (things, *of* things, or abs.); a million ‖pounds, *dollars; enormous number (*not a million* MILES *from*); **the** ~, the bulk of the population; ~**air′e** *n.*, person possess-ing a million pounds etc., very rich person; ~**fō′ld** *a.* & *adv.*; ~**th** *a.* & *n.*; see NUMERAL. [F, prob. f. It. (*mille* 1,000)]

**mǐ′llǐpĕde.** See MILLEPEDE.

**milŏ′mĕter** *n.* Instrument for measuring number of miles travelled by vehicle. [MILE, -METER]

**milt** *n.* Reproductive gland of male fish; spleen of mammals. [E]

**Miltŏ′nian, Miltŏ′nǐc** (-ically), *adjs.* Of, in the manner of, *Milton.* [person]

**mime.** See MIMIC.

**mǐ′meograph** (-ahf) *n.,* & *v.t.* (Reproduce by means of) apparatus for holding stencils of written pages, from which many copies may be taken. [Gk *mimeomai* imitate]

**mǐ′mǐc** *a., n.,* & *v.* **1.** *a.* Having aptitude for mimicry; imitating; imitative, esp. for amusement. **2.** *n.* Person skilled in ludicrous imitation. **3.** *v.t.* (-ck-). Ridicule by imitating (person, manner, etc.); copy minute-ly or servilely; (of thing) resemble closely. **4. mime,** (*n.*) (Gk & Rom. Ant.) simple farcical drama marked

by mimicry, (performer in) similar modern usu. wordless production with gestures, (*v.t.*) act with mimic gestures, usu. without words; **mǐ-mě′sǐs** *n.,* (Biol.) close external resemblance of an animal to another that is distasteful or harmful to predators of the first; **mǐmě′tǐc** *a.* (-ically), of, or addicted to, imita-tion, mimicry, or mimesis; ~**rў** *n.,* mimicking, thing that mimics an-other, mimesis; **mǐmŏ′sa** (*or* -z-) *n.,* kind of shrub with globular flower--heads, incl. sensitive plant. [L f. Gk *mimos* mime]

**min.** *abbr.* minim(um); minute(s).
**Min.** *abbr.* Minister; Ministry.

**mī′na, mȳ′na(h),** (-a), *n.* Mimic bird of starling family. [Hindi]

**mǐ′narět** (*or* -ě′t) *n.* Slender turret connected with mosque, from which muezzin calls at hours of prayer. [F or Sp. f. Turk. f. Arab.]

**mǐ′natorў** *a.* (-ily, -iness). Threatening, menacing. [L (*minor* threaten)]

**mǐnce. 1.** *v.t.* & *i.* Cut (meat etc.) very small (~ **matters,** usu. w. neg., use polite expressions in condemna-tion); restrain (one's words) within bounds of politeness; utter (words), walk, with affected delicacy. **2.** *n.* Minced meat; ~**′meat,** mixture of currants, sugar, spices, suet, etc., chopped small (make ~*meat of* per-son, argument, etc., utterly defeat); ~ **pie** (usu. small round) pie con-taining this. [F *mincier* f. L (MINUTE²)]

**mind. 1.** *n.* Seat of consciousness, thought, volition, and feeling; soul, opp. to body or material things (*mind may triumph over matter*); intellectual powers, opp. to will and emotions; normal condition of mental faculties (*in one's* RIGHT *mind*); **lose** one's ~, become insane; **out of** one's ~, insane); person as embodying mental qualities; candid opinion (SPEAK one's *mind*; *give* person *a* PIECE *of* one's *mind*); opinion (*in* or *to my mind he is a genius*; **be** in, **of,** a or **one** or **the same** ~, agree in opinion; **be in two** ~**s,** be undecided; **change** one's ~, adopt new plan or opinion; **have a** ~ **of** one's **own,** be capable of forming opinions independently; **have half a** ~, **a** (**good**) ~, feel (much) inclined or tempted *to* do; KNOW one's *own mind*; **make up** one's ~, decide, resolve, (*to* do, or abs.), reconcile oneself *to* inevitable fact; **read** person's ~, know what he is thinking without being told); direction of thought or desires (ABSENCE *of mind*); **cast** one's ~ **back**, recall an earlier time; **give, put, set, turn,** one's ~ **to**, direct one's attention to; **have it in** ~, intend; **have on** one's ~, be troubled by thought of; **keep** one's ~ **on**, continue to think about; PRESENCE *of mind*); way of thinking or feeling (FRAME, *state, of mind; the Victorian mind; to my mind it is wrong*); remembrance (*bear, have, keep, in mind*; **bring, call to,** ~, remember, cause to be remembered; **come to** ~, **come into** one's ~, be remembered; **put person in mind of,** make him remember; **put out of** one's ~, deliberately forget about; **time out of** ~, from before anyone can remember). **2.** *v.t. & i.* Bear in mind (chiefly in *imper.*), take heed of (*never mind the expense*); ~ (**you**) parenth., please take note); concern oneself about (**never** ~, imper., do not be troubled, I refuse to answer your question); apply oneself to (*mind* one's *own* BUSINESS); (usu. w. neg. or interrog.) object to (thing, person, *that, doing*; **I should not** ~, **don't** ~ **if I have,** (should like) *a drink*; **do you** ~?, iron., please stop that); remember and take care (*mind that* thing is done); ~ (**out for**), be on one's guard against, remember existence of (*mind the step*); have charge of (~ **the shop,** *store*, fig., have charge of affairs). **3.** ~ **away, out, your back,** (colloq.) let me pass; ~ **one's P's and Q's,** be careful as to speech or behaviour; ~**-reader,** = THOUGHT- *-reader*; *mind's* EYE. **4.** ~'**èd** *a.*, disposed (*to* do), inclined to think (in specified way: *mechanically minded*), (*in comb.*) having (specified kind of) mind (*high-minded*), inclined to concern oneself with (*car-minded*); ~'**er** *n.*, one whose business it is to attend to something, esp. child or machinery; ~'**ful** *a.* (-lly), taking thought or care (*of,* or abs.); ~'**lèss** *a.*, (esp.) stupidly ill-behaved. [E]

**mine**[1] *poss. pron. pred.* (& *abs.*) Of me (for phrs. see HERS); (arch. *attrib.* bef. vowel) my (*mine eyes*); **me and** ~ (my relations). [E]

**mine**[2] **1.** *n.* Excavation in earth for extracting metal, coal, salt, etc., (~'**worker,** one who works in

this); (fig.) abundant source (*of* information etc.); receptacle filled with explosive placed in or on ground or moored beneath or floating on or near surface of water for destroying enemy personnel, material, or ships; ~'**field,** area where mines have been laid, (fig.) area presenting many unseen hazards; ~'**layer,** ship or aircraft for laying mines; ~'**sweeper,** ship for clearing away floating or submarine mines. **2.** *v.t. & i.* Obtain (metal, coal, etc.) from mine; dig in (earth, etc., or abs.) for or *for* ore etc.; burrow or make subterranean passages in or under; (fig.) undermine; (Mil.) lay mines under or in. **3.** **mi′ner** *n.*, (esp.) mineworker. [F]

**mi′neral. 1.** *a.* Obtained by mining; not animal or vegetable; *mineral* KINGDOM; ~ **oil,** petroleum; ~ **water,** water found in nature impregnated with mineral substance, artificial imitation of this, other effervescent drink, e.g. ginger beer; *mineral* WOOL. **2.** *n.* Mineral substance or object; ‖(esp. in *pl.*) artificial mineral water. **3.** ~**ize** *v.t. & i.*, change (partly) into mineral; ~**izā′- tion** *n.*; ~**ogy** (-ă'l-) *n.*, science of minerals; ~**o′gical** *a.* (-lly); ~**ogist** (-ă'l-) *n.* [F or L (MINE[2])]

**minéstrō′nè** *n.* Thick soup containing vegetables and pasta or rice. [It.]

**Ming** *n.* Chinese porcelain of 14th–17th cc. [name of dynasty]

**mi′ngle** (-nggel) *v.i. & t.* Mix, blend; ~ **with,** go about among. [E]

‖**mi′ngy** (-nji) *a.* (colloq.; -ily). Mean, stingy. [M(EAN[1]), (ST)INGY]

**mi′nì** *n.* (colloq.) Minicar, miniskirt, etc. [abbr.]

**mi′nì-** *pref.* Miniature, very small of its kind (*minibus, minicar*); ~**skirt** (ending well above the knees). [abbr.]

**mi′nìatur|e** (*or* -nīcher) **1.** *n.* Small-scale minutely finished portrait; miniature thing; **in** ~**e,** on a small scale. **2.** *a.* Represented on small scale; smaller than normal. **3.** ~**ïst** *n.*, painter of miniatures; ~**ize** *v.t.*, make miniature, produce in smaller version. [It. f. L (*minium* red lead)]

**mi′nïm** *n.* ‖(Mus.) white-headed note with stem, = half semibreve; 1/60 of fluid drachm, about 1 drop; ~**al** *a.* (-lly), very minute or slight, being or related to a minimum;

~**alist** n., person ready to accept a minimum provisionally (opp. MAXI-MALIST); ~**ize** v.t., reduce to, estimate at, smallest possible amount or degree, estimate or represent at less than true value or importance; ~**um** n. (pl. ~a) & a., least (amount) possible, attained or attainable, usual, etc.; ~**um wage** (lowest allowed by law or agreement). [L *minimus* least]

**mi'nion** (-yon) n. (derog.) Favourite child, courtier, etc.; servile agent, slave; ~**s of the law**, gaolers, police, etc. [F *mignon*]

**mi'nist|er. 1.** n. Person employed in execution *of* (purpose, will, etc.); person at head of a government department; diplomatic agent accredited by one State to another; ~**er** (*of religion*), clergyman ‖esp. in Presbyterian and Nonconformist Churches; PRIME[1] *minister*; ‖M~**er of State**, departmental senior minister between department head and junior minister. **2.** v.i. & t. Render aid or service (*to* person, cause, etc.; ~**ering angel**, esp. of sick-nurse etc.). ~ **ēr'ial** a. (-lly) of minister or his office, siding with the Government against the Opposition; ~**rant** a. & n., (person) giving aid or service, esp. in religious matters; ~**rā'tion** n.; ~**rȳ** n., ministering, ministration, *the* body of ministers of the government or of religion, *the* clerical profession, government department headed by minister, building occupied by it, (period of tenure of) office as religious minister, priest, etc. [F f. L, = servant]

**mink** n. Small stoatlike animal; (coat made from) its fur. [Sw.]

**Minn.** abbr. Minnesota.

**mi'nnesinger** n. German lyric poet in 12th–14th cc. [G, = love-singer]

**mi'nnow** (-ō) n. Small freshwater fish. [E]

**Minō'an** a. & n. (Person) of Cretan Bronze-Age civilization (c. 3000–1000 B.C.). [Gk *Minōs*, legendary king of Crete]

**mi'nor** n., a., & v. **1.** n. Person under full age; *student's subsidiary subject or course. **2.** a. Lesser of two things, classes, etc.; not yet of full age; ‖(in schools) *Smith* etc. ~, the younger of the two Smiths or the second to enter the school; comparatively unimportant (*minor poet*); (of operation) presenting no danger

to patient's life; (Logic; of term) occurring as subject of conclusion of syllogism, (of premiss) containing minor term; (Mus.; of interval) less by a semitone than major interval, (of key) in which scale has minor third (*in a minor* KEY[1]). **3.** v.i. *(Of student) undertake study *in* as minor subject etc. **4.** ~ **canon**, clergyman not member of chapter, assisting in daily cathedral service; ~ **piece**, (Chess) bishop or knight; ~ **planet**, asteroid; *minor* PROPHET; ~ **suit**, (Bridge) diamonds or clubs. **5. minō'rĭtȳ** n., state of being under full age, period of this, smaller number or part (*of*), esp. smaller party voting together against majority, state of having less than half the votes, small group of persons differing from others in race, religion, language, opinion on a topic, etc., (*attrib.*) relating to or done by a minority. [L, = less]

**mi'nster** n. Church of monastery; large or important church (*York Minster*). [E (MONASTERY)]

**mi'nstrel** n. Medieval singer or musician; (Negro, nigger) ~, (usu. in *pl.*) one of a band of public entertainers, with blackened faces etc., performing songs and music ostensibly of Negro origin; ~**sȳ** n., minstrel's art or poetry. [F f. Prov. f. L (MINISTER)]

**mint**[1] n. Aromatic herb used in cooking; peppermint (sweetmeat); *mint* JULEP; ~ **sauce** (of finely chopped mint leaves with vinegar and sugar, eaten esp. with roast lamb). [E f. L *menta* f. Gk]

**mint**[2]. **1.** n. Place where money is coined, usu. under State authority; vast sum *of money*; **in** ~ **condition, state,** (of book, print, postage stamp, etc.) fresh, unsoiled, perfect. **2.** v.t. Make (coin) by stamping metal; invent, coin, (word, phrase). [E f. L *moneta*]

**minŭĕ't** n. Slow stately dance in triple measure; music for this, or in same rhythm or style. [F dim. (MENU)]

**mi'nus** prep., a., & n. **1.** prep. With subtraction of (symbol —); below zero (*temperature of minus 10°*); (colloq.) deprived of (*came back minus shoes and socks*). **2.** a. (Math.) negative; (Electr.) having negative charge; rather worse than (*beta minus*); *minus* SIGN. **3.** n. The symbol

(—); negative quantity; disadvantage. [L, neuter of MINOR]

**mi′nuscule** *a. & n.* Lower-case (letter); extremely small. [F f. L dim. (prec.)]

**mi′nute**[1] (-ĭt). **1.** *n.* Period of 60 seconds, sixtieth part of hour; distance traversed in a minute (*10 minutes from the shops*); short time, instant; exact point of time (**the ~,** colloq., the present time; **up to the ~,** having latest information, in the latest fashion; **the ~ that,** as soon as; LAST[3] **minute**); sixtieth part of angular degree; rough draft, memorandum; (in *pl.*) brief summary of proceedings of assembly, committee, etc.; official memorandum authorizing or recommending a course of action; **~hand** (showing minutes on watch or clock); **~ steak** (thin slice that can be cooked quickly). **2.** *v.t.* Record in minutes; send minute to (person); **~ (down),** make a note of. [F f. L (*minuo* lessen)]

**minū′te**[2] *a.* (**~r, ~st**). Very small; (of inquiry etc.) precise, going into details. [Same as MINUTE[1] (prec.)]

**minū′tia** (-shĭa) *n.* (usu. in *pl.* **~e**). Precise or trivial or minor detail. [L (MINUTE[1])]

**minx** *n.* Pert or sly girl. [orig. unkn.]

**Mi′ocène** *a. & n.* (Geol.) (Of) division of Tertiary below Pliocene. [Gk *meiōn* less, *kainos* new]

**mirabile dictu** (mĭrahbĭlă dĭ′ktoō) *adv.* Wonderful to relate. [L]

**mi′racle** *n.* Marvellous event due to supposed supernatural agency; remarkable occurrence; remarkable specimen (*of* ingenuity etc.); **~ (play),** dramatic representation in Middle Ages, based on Bible or lives of saints; **mirā′culous** *a.,* supernatural, surprising; **mira′ge** (-ah′zh; *or* mĭ′-) *n.,* optical illusion caused by atmospheric conditions, esp. appearance of sheet of water in desert or on hot road, illusory thing. [F f. L (*mirus* wonderful)]

**mire. 1.** *n.* Swampy ground, bog, (in the **~,** fig., in difficulties); mud. **2.** *v.t.* Plunge in mire; (fig.) involve in difficulties; defile, bespatter, (lit. or fig.). [N]

**mi′rror. 1.** *n.* Polished surface (usu. of amalgam-coated glass, or metal) reflecting image; (fig.) what gives faithful reflection or true description of thing (*hold the mirror up to*); **~ image** (with structure reversed). **2.** *v.t.* Reflect as in mirror (lit. or fig.). [F f. L *miro* look at (MIRACLE)]

**mirth** *n.* Merriment; laughter; **~′ful** *a.* (**-lly**). [E (MERRY)]

**mir′y** *a.* (**-ily, -iness**). Muddy, vile. [MIRE]

**mis-**[1] *pref.* to *vbs.* and vbl derivs., w. sense 'amiss', 'badly', 'wrongly', 'unfavourably', (*mislead, misshapen, mistrust*), or intensifying unfavourable meaning contained in *v.* (*misdoubt*). [E]

**mis-**[2] *pref.* to *vbs., adjs., & ns.,* w. sense 'amiss', 'badly', 'wrongly', or negative, (*misadventure, mischief*). [F f. L MINUS]

**misadve′nture** *n.* (Piece of) bad luck; (Law) death due to accident without crime or negligence. [MIS-[2]]

**misalli′ance** *n.* Alliance, esp. marriage, that is unsuitable. [MIS-[1]]

**mi′santhr|ōpe** (*or* -z-) *n.* Hater of mankind; one who avoids human society; **~ŏ′pic** *a.* (**-ically**); **misă′nthropy** *n.,* condition or habits of misanthrope. [F f. Gk (*misos* hatred, *anthrōpos* man)]

**misapplȳ′** *v.t.* Apply (esp. funds) wrongly; **misăpplica′tion** *n.*; **misăpprehĕ′nd** *v.t.,* misunderstand (words, person); **misăpprehĕ′n-sion** (-shon) *n.*; **misapprō′priate** *v.t.,* apply (usu. another's money) to wrong (esp. one's own) use; **misapprōpria′tion** *n.*; **misbĕgŏ′tten** *a.,* bastard, contemptible, disreputable; **misbĕhā′ve** *v.i.,* behave (oneself, or abs.) improperly; **misbĕhā′viour,** *\*-ior,* (-vyer) *n.* [MIS-[1]]

**misc.** *abbr.* miscellaneous.

**miscă′lcul|āte** *v.t.* Calculate (amount, results, etc., or abs.) wrongly; **~ā′tion** *n.*; **misca′ll** (-aw′l) *v.t.,* call by wrong name; **miscă′rry** *v.i.,* (of person, business, scheme) be unsuccessful, (of woman) have miscarriage, (of letter) fail to reach destination; **miscă′rriage** (-rĭj; *or* mĭ′-) *n.,* miscarrying (**miscarriage of justice,** failure of court to achieve justice), untimely delivery (of pregnant woman), abortion (esp. if spontaneous), (Med.) this in 12th–28th week of pregnancy; **misca′st** (-ah′-) *v.t.* (**misca′st**), add (accounts etc.) wrongly, allot unsuitable part to (actor). [MIS-[1]]

**miscĕgēnā′tion** *n.* Interbreeding

of races, esp. of whites with non-
-whites. [MIX, GENUS]

**miscellā′nĕ|ous** *a.* Of mixed com-
position or character; (w. *pl.* n.) of
various kinds; **miscĕ′llanў** *n.*,
mixture, medley, book containing
various literary compositions etc. [L
(*misceo* MIX)]

**mischa′nce** (-ah′-) *n.* (Piece of)
bad luck. [MIS-²]

**mi′schie|f** (-chĭf) *n.* Harm or
injury caused esp. by person (**do**
person **a** ~**f**, wound or kill him;
**make** ~**f**, create discord); cause(r)
of harm or annoyance; vexatious
but not malicious conduct esp. of
children, pranks, scrapes, (*get into
mischief*); playful malice, archness,
satire, (*eyes full of mischief*); ~**vous** *a.*,
(of thing) having harmful effects, (of
person, conduct, etc.) disposed to
acts of playful malice or mild
vexatiousness. [F (MIS-², *chever*
happen)]

**mi′scib|le** *a.* That can be mixed
(*with*); ~**i′litў** *n.* [L (MIX)]

**miscon|cei′ve** (-sē′v) *v.t. & i.*
Have wrong idea or conception of or
of or abs.; ~**cĕ′ption** *n.*, **misco′n-
duct¹** *n.*, improper conduct, esp.
adultery; ~**dŭ′ct²** *v.t. & refl.*;
~**strue′** (-ōō′) *v.t.*, put wrong construction on (word, action), mistake
meaning of (person); ~**strŭ′ction**
*n.*; **misco′py** *v.t.*, copy incorrectly;
**miscou′nt** *n., & v.t. & i.*, (make)
wrong count, esp. of votes, count
(things) wrongly. [MIS-¹]

**mi′scrĕant** *n.* Vile wretch, villain.
[F (MIS-², *creant* believer)]

**miscū′e** *n., & v.t.* (Bill. etc.)
Fail(ure) to strike ball properly with
cue; **misdā′te** *v.t.*, date (event,
letter, etc.) wrongly; **misdea′l** *n.*,
*& v.t. & i.* (-dea′lt), (make) mistake
in dealing (cards), misdealt hand;
**misdee′d** *n.*, evil deed. [MIS-¹]

**misdĕmea′n|our, *****or**, (-er) *n.*
Misdeed; (Law) indictable offence,
(in U.K. formerly) less heinous than
felony. [MIS-¹, DEMEAN²]

**misdĭrĕ′ct** *v.t.* Direct (person,
letter, blow, etc.) wrongly; ~**ion** *n.*;
**misdo′ing** (-ōō′-) *n.*, misdeed;
**misdou′bt** (-ow′t) *v.t.*, have doubts
as to truth or existence of, have mis-
givings or be suspicious about,
suspect (*that*). [MIS-¹]

**mise en scène** (mēzahñsă′n) *n.*
Scenery and properties of acted play;
(fig.) surroundings of an event. [F]

**mi′ser** (-z-) *n.* Person who hoards
wealth and lives miserably; **mi′ser-
able** (-z-) *a.* (-**bly**), wretchedly unhappy or uncomfortable, (of event
etc.) causing wretchedness, contemptible, mean, (*a miserable hovel*);
*misère* (mĭzār′) *n.*, undertaking at
cards to win no tricks; ~**lў** *a.*
(-**iness**); **mi′serў** (-z-) *n.*, wretched
state of mind or outward circumstances, thing causing this, wretched
or (colloq.) discontented or grumpy
person; **out of its misery,** (of
animal) released from suffering esp.
by being killed. [L, = wretched]

**misĕ′ricŏrd** (-z-) *n.* Projection
under seat in choir stall serving
(when seat was turned up) to support
person standing. [F f. L *misericordia*
pity]

**miserly, misery.** See MISER.

**misfī′re** *v.i., & n.* (Of gun, motor
engine, etc.) fail(ure) to go off or
start action or function regularly,
fail(ure) to have intended effect;
**mi′sfit** *n.*, garment etc. that does
not fit person it is meant for, person
unsuited to his environment or work;
**misfŏr′tune** (-chŭn, -chŏŏn) *n.*,
(instance of) bad luck; **misgi′ve**
(-g-) *v.t.* (-**ga′ve, -gi′ven**), (of person's mind, heart, etc.) fill (him)
with suspicion or foreboding (*about*
thing, *that*); **misgi′ving** (-g-) *n.*,
feeling of mistrust or apprehension;
**misgo′vern** (-gŭ′-) *v.t.*, govern
(State etc.) badly; **misgo′vern-
ment** (-gŭ′-) *n.*; **misguī′de** (-gī′d)
*v.t.*, (chiefly in *p.p.*) cause to err in
thought or action; **mishă′ndle**
(-s-h-) *v.t.*, handle (person or thing)
roughly or rudely, deal with incorrectly or ineffectively; **mi′shăp**
(-s-h-; *or* -ă′p) *n.*, unlucky accident;
**mishear′** (-s-h-) *v.t.* (-**hear′d**),
hear incorrectly or imperfectly;
**mi′shĭt** (-s-h-), (n.) faulty or bad
hit, (-ĭ′t; *v.t.*; -**tt-**; mishĭt) hit (ball)
faultily. [MIS-¹,]

**mi′shmăsh** *n.* Confused mixture.
[redupl. MASH]

**misin|fŏr′m** *v.t.* Give wrong in-
formation to; ~**formā′tion** *n.*;
~**tĕr′prĕt** *v.t.*, give wrong interpretation to, make wrong inference
from; ~**tĕrprĕtā′tion** *n.*; **mis-
jŭ′dge** *v.t. & i.*, judge wrongly, have
wrong opinion of or *of*; **mislay′** *v.t.*
(-**laid′**), put (thing) by accident
where it cannot readily be found;
**mislea′d** *v.t.* (-**le′d**), lead astray,

cause to go wrong in conduct or belief; **mĭsmă′nage** *v.t.*, manage badly or wrongly; **mĭsmă′nage- ment** (-ijm-) *n.*; **mĭsmă′tch,** (*v.t.*) match unsuitably or incorrectly, (-ĭ′-; *n.*) bad match; **mĭsnā′me** *v.t.*, miscall. [MIS-¹]

**mĭsnō′mer** *n.* Use of wrong name; wrong (use of) name or term. [AF (MIS-², *nommer* to name)]

**mĭsŏ′gўn|ĭst** (*or* -g-) *n.* One who hates all women; **~ў** *n.* [Gk *misos* hatred, *gunē* woman]

**mĭsplā′ce** *v.t.* Put in wrong place; bestow (affections, confidence) on wrong object; **~ment** (-sm-) *n.*; **mĭsplay′** *n.*, & *v.t.*, play(ing) in wrong or ineffective manner; **mĭs′- print,** (*n.*) mistake in printing, (-rĭ′-; *v.t.*) print wrongly. [MIS-¹]

**mĭsprī′sion** (-zhon) *n.* **~ of** treason or felony, (Law) conceal- ment of one's knowledge of treason- able or felonious intent. [AF (MIS-², *prendre* take)]

**mĭspron|ou′nce** *v.t.* Pronounce (word etc.) wrongly; **~ŭnciā′tion** *n.*; **mĭsquō′te** *v.t.*, quote wrongly; **mĭsquōtā′tion** *n.*; **mĭsrea′d** *v.t.* (misrea′d), read or interpret wrongly; **mĭsrĕmĕ′mber** *v.t.*, re- member incorrectly or imperfectly; **mĭsrĕpŏr′t** *v.t.*, & *n.*, (give) false or incorrect report (of); **mĭs- rĕprĕsĕ′nt** (-zĕ′-) *v.t.*, represent wrongly, give false account of; **mĭsrĕprĕsĕntā′tion** (-zĕ′-) *n.*; **mĭs- ru′le** (-ōō′l), (*n.*) bad government, disorder, (**Lord, Master, of Mis- rule,** Hist., person presiding over Christmas revels in nobleman's house), (*v.t.*) govern badly. [MIS-¹]

**mĭss¹. 1.** *v.t.* & *i.* (Of person or missile) fail to hit (mark etc. or abs.); fail to reach, find, get, meet, or catch (*miss a train*), or see (event), or hear or understand (remark, joke, etc.; **not ~ much,** be alert); let slip (opportunity); **~ (out),** leave out (words etc. in reading or writing); fail to keep (appointment) or per- form; feel the lack of (be **~ing,** not have); (of internal combustion engine) misfire; **~ fire,** (of gun, or fig.) = MISFIRE; **~ out (on),** fail to get (something), be unsuccessful; **~ the boat or bus,** (colloq.) lose an opportunity. **2.** *n.* Failure to hit or attain (**a ~ is as good as a mile,** failure or escape is what it is, how- ever narrow the margin; NEAR miss); give (thing) **a ~,** avoid, leave alone. **3. ~′ing** *a.*, (esp.) not found, not in its place, (of soldier) neither present after battle etc. nor known to have been killed, wounded, or captured; **~ing link,** thing lacking to complete a series, hypothetical intermediate type, esp. between apes and man. [E]

**mĭss²** *n.* (*M~*; as title of un- married woman or girl without higher title) *Miss Smith* (pl. *the Miss Smiths, the Misses Smith*), (as title of beauty queen from specified region) *Miss France, Miss World,* (as *voc.* without name, to teacher or shop assistant, or from servant etc.) young woman; (usu. derog. or playful) girl, esp. schoolgirl, often w. im- plication of silliness or sentimen- tality; **~′ish** *a.*, prim, affected, or sentimental. [MISTRESS]

**Miss.** *abbr.* Mississippi.

**mĭss′al** *n.* (R.C.) Book containing service of Mass for whole year; book of prayers. [L (*missa* MASS¹)]

**mĭss′el** *n.* **~(-thrush),** large thrush that feeds on mistletoe etc. berries. [E; = mistletoe]

**mĭsshā′pen** (-s-sh-) *a.* Ill-shaped, deformed; distorted. [MIS-¹, *shapen* arch. = *shaped*]

**mĭss′ile** *n.* Object or weapon suitable for throwing at target or for discharge from machine; weapon directed by remote control or auto- matically. [L (*mitto miss-* send)]

**mĭss′ing.** See MISS¹.

**mĭss′ion** *n.* Body of persons sent to conduct negotiations or propagate a religious faith; missionary post; task to be performed; journey for such purpose; operational sortie; dispatch of aircraft or spacecraft; person's vocation or divinely ap- pointed work in life; **~arў,** (*a.*) of religious or similar missions, (*n.*) person who goes on missionary work. [F or L (as MISSILE)]

**mĭss′ĭs, -us,** (*or* -sĭz) *n.* **The ~,** (vulg. or joc.) my or your wife; (vulg., as *voc.*) form of address to woman. [MISTRESS]

**mĭss′ĭve** *n.* Official or (joc.) long and serious letter. [L (as MISSILE)]

**mĭsspĕ′ll** (-s-s-) *v.t.* (-e′lt, -e′lled). Spell wrongly; **mĭsspĕ′nd** (-s-s-) *v.t.* (-e′nt), spend amiss or waste- fully; **mĭsstā′te** (-s-s-) *v.t.*, state wrongly; **mĭsstā′tement** (-s-s-; -tm-) *n.* [MIS-¹]

**mǐst. 1.** *n.* Water vapour near ground in droplets smaller than raindrops and causing obscuration of the atmosphere; dimness or blurring of sight caused by tears or bodily disorder; condensed vapour obscuring windscreens etc.; SCOTCH *mist.* **2.** *v.t. & i.* Cover, be covered, (as) with mist. [E]

**mǐstā́k|e. 1.** *v.t. & i.* (-tōo'k; -tā'ken). Misunderstand meaning or intention of (person, statement, purpose); wrongly take (one *for* another or abs., *mistake one's vocation*); **there's no ~ing,** one is sure to recognize); err in opinion; (in *p.p.*) wrong in opinion, (of action etc.) ill-judged, (*you are mistaken*; *mistaken kindness*); **~enlў** *adv.*; **~ennèss** (-n-n-) *n.* **2.** *n.* Misunderstanding of thing's meaning; thing incorrectly done or thought through ignorance or inadvertence; **and,** or **make, no ~e,** undoubtedly (emphasizing a statement). [N (MIS-¹, TAKE)]

**mǐ'ster** *n.* Person without title of nobility etc. (*a mere mister*); (vulg., as *voc.*) form of address to man. [MASTER; cf. MR.]

**mǐstī'me** *v.t.* Say, do, (thing) at wrong time. [MIS-¹]

**mǐ'stletōe** (-seltō) *n.* Parasitic plant growing on apple and other trees and bearing white berries. [E, = mistletoe-twig (MISSEL)]

**mǐstōō'k.** See MISTAKE.

**mǐ'stral** (*or* -ah'l) *n.* Cold N. or N.W. wind in S. France. [F & Prov. f. I. (MASTER)]

**mǐstrǎnsl|ā́te** (*or* -z-; *or* -trah-) *v.t.* Translate incorrectly; **~ā́tion** *n.*; **mǐstreā́t** *v.t.*, treat badly; **mǐstreā́'tment** *n.* [MIS-¹]

**mǐ'strèss** *n.* Woman in authority over servants; female head of household; woman who has power to control or dispose *of* or who has thorough knowledge *of* (**~ of the seas,** chief naval power); woman head of college, school, etc.; ||female teacher or tutor, esp. SCHOOL¹-*mistress*; woman loved and courted by a man; woman illicitly occupying place of wife or having permanent illicit relationship with man; (arch. or dial.) Mrs.; ||**M~ of the Robes,** lady charged with care of Queen's wardrobe; WARDROBE *mistress*; **~-shǐp** *n.* [F (*maistre* MASTER, -ESS)]

**mǐstrī'al** *n.* Trial vitiated by error; **mǐstrǔ'st,** (*v.t.*) feel no confidence in, be suspicious of, (*n.*) lack of confidence, suspicion; **mǐstrǔ'stful** *a.* (-lly), lacking confidence or trust. [MIS-¹]

**mǐ'stў** *a.* (-ily, -iness). Of, covered in, mist; of dim outline; (fig.) obscure, vague. [E (MIST)]

**mǐsŭnderstā́nd** *v.t.* (-stoo'd). Take (words etc., or abs.) in wrong sense; (esp. in *p.p.*) misinterpret words or actions of (person); **mǐsŭ'sage** (-zǐj) *n.*, wrong or improper usage, ill-treatment; **mǐsŭ'se,** (-z; *v.t.*) use wrongly, apply to wrong purpose, ill-treat, (-s; *n.*) wrong or improper use or application. [MIS-¹]

**mīte** *n.* Small arachnid, esp. cheese-**~** (found in cheese), ITCH--*mite*; modest contribution, best one can do, (*let me offer my mite of comfort*; **a ~,** *adv.*, colloq., somewhat); small object, esp. child; **a ~ of a** (a tiny) *child* etc. [E]

*__*mī'ter.** See MITRE.

**mǐ'tǐg|āte** *v.t.* (**~able**). Appease (anger), alleviate (pain), moderate (heat), reduce severity of; **~ā'tion,** **~ātor,** *ns.* [L (*mitis* mild)]

**mǐt|ō'sǐs** *n.* (*pl.* **~oses** *pr.* -ēz; Biol.) Division of cell or nucleus with lengthwise splitting of all chromosomes into pairs distributed equally between resulting two cells or nuclei; **~ǒ'tǐc** *a.* [L (Gk *mitos* thread)]

**mī'tre** (-ter), *__*mī'ter.** **1.** *n.* Bishop's and abbot's tall cap deeply cleft at top, esp. as symbol of episcopal office; joint of two pieces of wood etc. at angle of 90°, such that line of junction bisects this angle. **2.** *v.t.* Bestow mitre on; join with mitre. [F f. L f. Gk *mitra* turban]

**mǐtt** *n.* Glove with only one compartment for the four fingers (also **~'en**); knitted or lace glove leaving fingers and thumb-tip bare; *__*(sl.) hand; baseball-player's glove; **frozen ~,** (sl.) chilly reception; **give, get, the (frozen) ~en,** (sl.) dismiss (person), be dismissed. [F f. L (MOIETY)]

**Mī'ttў** *n.* Person with day-dreams of his imagined triumphs. [character in story]

**mǐx. 1.** *v.t. & i.* Put together, combine, (two or more substances, groups, qualities, etc., one *with* another) so that particles or members etc. of each are diffused among those of the others; prepare (compound, cocktail, etc.) by mixing ingredients; join, be mixed (*oil will not mix with water*); (of person) be harmonious or sociable (*with*), have dealings *with*, participate *in*; (of things) be compatible; ~ one's **drinks**, drink different alcoholic liquors in succession; ~ **in**, ~ **it**, (colloq.) start fighting; ~ **up**, mix thoroughly, confuse (esp. in thought, so ~*-up* n.); **be** ~ed **up**, be involved (*in* or *with* shady dealings etc.). 2. *n.* (colloq.) Mixture; proportion of materials in a mixture; ingredients prepared commercially for making cake etc. or for process such as concrete--making. 3. ~ed (-kst) *a.*, (esp.) of diverse qualities or elements, (of group of persons) containing persons from various classes, esp. of doubtful status, tangled, for persons of both sexes (*mixed school, bathing*); ~ed**-**(**-up**), (colloq.) mentally confused, muddled, ill-adjusted; ~ed **bag**, assortment of diverse things or persons; ~ed **blessing**, thing having advantages but also disadvantages; ~ed **doubles**, (Tennis etc.) doubles game with man and woman as partners on each side; ~ed **farming** (with crops and livestock); ~ed **feelings** (e.g. some pleasure and some dismay at same event); ~ed **grill**, dish of various grilled meats and vegetables; ~ed **marriage** (between persons of different race or religion); mixed METAPHOR; ~'**er** *n.*, (esp.) apparatus for mixing foods etc.; **good, bad,** ~**er**, (colloq.) one who gets on well, badly, with other people (esp. those of different social class); ~'**ture** *n.*, mixing, being mixed, thing or (fig.) person that is result of mixing, medical preparation of this kind (*cough mixture*; **the** ~**ture as before,** fig. the same treatment repeated); gas or vaporized petrol or oil mixed with air forming explosive charge in internal combustion engine; HEATHER *mixture*. [back-form. f. *mixed* f. F f. L (*misceo* mix)]

**mi'z(z)en** *n.* (Naut.) ~(**-sail**), lowest fore-and-aft sail of full--rigged ship's ~**-mast** (next aft of mainmast). [F *misaine* f. It. (MEZ-ZANINE)]

**Mk.** *abbr.* Mark (also N.T.).

**ml.** *abbr.* mile(s); millilitre(s).

**Mlle(s)** *abbr. Mademoiselle, Mesdemoiselles.*

**MM.** *abbr. Messieurs.*

‖**M.M.** *abbr.* Military Medal.

**mm** *abbr.* millimetre(s).

**Mme(s)** *abbr. Madame, Mesdames.*

**mnemo'nic** (n-). 1. *a.* (~**ally**). Of, designed to aid, the memory. 2. *n.* Mnemonic device; (in *pl.*) art of, system for, improving memory. [L f. Gk (*mnēmōn* mindful)]

**mō** *n.* (sl.; *pl.* **mos**). Moment (*wait a mo*). [abbr.]

**M.O.** *abbr.* Medical Officer; money order.

**Mo.** *abbr.* Missouri.

**mō'a** *n.* Extinct flightless N.Z. bird resembling ostrich. [Maori]

**moan.** 1. *n.* Long murmur expr. physical or mental suffering; low plaintive sound of wind etc.; complaint, grievance. 2. *v.i.* & *t.* Make moan(s); utter with moans. [E]

**moat** *n.* Defensive ditch round castle, town, etc., usu. filled with water; ~'**ed** *a.*, surrounded by moat. [F *mote* mound]

**mŏb.** 1. *n.* The populace; rabble; tumultuous crowd; (sl.) associated group of persons; ~ **law, rule,** (imposed and enforced by mob); ~'**ster** *n.*, (sl.) gangster. 2. *v.t.* (**-bb-**). (Of mob) attack; crowd round and molest or acclaim. [L *mobile vulgus* excitable crowd]

**mŏ'b-căp** *n.* (Hist.) Woman's large indoor cap covering all the hair. [obs. *mob*, orig. = slut]

**mō'bile.** 1. *a.* Movable, not fixed, able to move (easily); (of face etc.) readily changing its expression; (of troops) that may be easily moved from place to place; (of shop etc.) accommodated in vehicle so as to serve various places; (of person) able to change one's social status. 2. *n.* Structure of metal, plastic, cardboard, etc., that may be hung so as to turn freely. 3. **mobi'lity** *n.*; **mō'bilize** *v.t.*, (esp.) prepare (forces, or abs.) for active service; **mōbiliz̄ā'tion** *n.* [F f. L (*moveo* move)]

**mŏ'ccasin** *n.* Footwear of soft deerskin etc. as worn by N. Amer. Indians, with sole sewn to U-shaped flat vamp and no heel; similar shoe in ordinary wear. [Amer. Ind.]

**mŏck** *v., n.,* & *a.* 1. *v.t.* & *i.* Subject to ridicule; defy contemptuously; delude; mimic, counterfeit; scoff (*at*). 2. *n.* (arch.) Derision; thing deserving scorn (*make* (*a*) *mock of*); imitation. 3. *attrib. a.* Sham, imitation (esp.

without intent to deceive). **4.** ~**-heroic** *a.* & *n.*, burlesquing (of) heroic style; ~'**ing-bird** (that mimics notes of other birds); *mock* ORANGE[1]; ~ **turtle soup** (made from calf's head etc.); ~**-up**, experimental model showing appearance of (part of) proposed book, ship, etc. **5.** ~'**erў** *n.*, derision, subject or occasion of this, counterfeit or absurdly inadequate representation (*of*), ludicrously or insultingly futile action etc. [F *mocquer*]

**mŏd.** (colloq.) **1.** *n.* Modification. **2.** *a.* Modern; ~ **cons**, modern conveniences. [abbr.]

**mŏd**|e *n.* Way, manner, in which thing is done; method of procedure; prevailing fashion or custom; (Mus.) scale system; ~'**al** *a.* (**-lly**) of mode or form, not of substance, (Gram.) of mood of verb, (of verb, e.g. *would*) used to express mood of another verb; **modă′litў** *n.*, (esp.) (prescribed) method of procedure. [F, & L *modus* measure]

**mŏ′del** *n.*, *a.*, & *v.* **1.** *n.* Representation in three dimensions *of* existing person or thing or of proposed structure, esp. on smaller scale (WORK*ing model*); simplified description of system for calculations etc.; figure in clay, wax, etc., to be reproduced in other material; (copy of) garment etc. by well-known designer; design, style of structure, esp. of motor vehicle; person or thing proposed for imitation; person employed to pose for artist, or to display clothes etc. by wearing them. **2.** *a.* Exemplary, ideally perfect. **3.** *v.t.* & *i.* (‖**-ll-**). Fashion, shape, (figure) in clay, wax, etc.; form (thing) *after*, (*up*)*on*, model; act or pose as model; (of person acting as model) display (garment). [F f. It. *modello* f. L (prec.)]

**mŏ′der**|**ate** *a.*, *n.*, & *v.* **1.** *a.* Avoiding extremes, temperate in conduct or expression; fairly or tolerably large or good; (of wind) of medium strength; (of prices) low. **2.** *n.* One who holds moderate views in politics etc. **3.** (-āt) *v.t.* & *i.* Make less violent, intense, rigorous, etc.; (of fury, scorn, storm, etc.) become less vehement; act as moderator of or to). **4.** ~**ā′tion** *n.*, moderating, moderateness, (**in ~ation**, in moderate manner or degree); ~**ātor** *n.*, arbitrator, mediator, presiding offi-

cer, Presbyterian minister presiding over any ecclesiastical body. [L]

**mŏ′dern. 1.** *a.* Of present and recent times; in current fashion, not antiquated; ~ **English** (from 1500 onwards); ~ **history** (subsequent to Middle Ages); ~ **languages** (as subject of study, those spoken at present time, esp. in Europe). **2.** *n.* Person living in modern times. **3.** ~**ĭsm** *n.*, modern view(s) or method(s), esp. tendency in matters of religious belief to subordinate tradition to harmony with modern thought; ~**ĭst** *n.*; **moděr′nitў** *n.*; ~**īze** *v.t.* & *i.*, assimilate to modern needs or habits, adopt modern ways or views; ~**īzā′tion** *n.* [F f. L (*modo* just now)]

**mŏ′dĕst** *a.* Having humble or moderate estimate of one's own merits; diffident, bashful; (of woman) decorous in manner and conduct; (of demand, statement, etc.) not excessive or exaggerated (freq. iron.); (of thing) unpretentious in appearance, amount, etc.; ~**ў** *n.*, modestness. [F f. L]

**mŏ′dĭcum** *n.* Small quantity (*of* food, truth, etc.). [L (MODE)]

**mŏ′dĭf**|**ў** *v.t.* Make less severe or decided, tone down; make partial changes in; (Gram.) qualify sense of (word etc.); ~**ĭcā′tion** *n.*, modifying or being modified, change made; ~**ĭcătorў** *a.* [F f. L (MODE)]

**mŏ′dĭsh** *a.* Fashionable (derog.); **mŏdi′ste** (-ē′st) *n.*, dressmaker, milliner. [F (MODE)]

**mŏ′dŭl**|**āte** *v.t.* & *i.* Regulate, adjust; moderate; adjust or vary tone or pitch of (speaking voice); alter amplitude or frequency of (wave) by wave of lower frequency to convey signal; (Mus.) pass (*from one* key *to* another); ~**ā′tion**, ~**ātor**, *ns.* [L (foll.)]

**mŏ′dŭl**|e *n.* Standardized part or independent unit in construction esp. of furniture, building, spacecraft, or electronic system; ~**ar** *a.*; ~**us** *n.* (*pl.* ~**ĭ** *pr.* -ī), constant factor or ratio. [F, or L *modulus* (foll.)]

*modus* (mō′dŭs) *n.* ~ *operandi* (ŏperă′ndĭ), way a person goes about task, way a thing operates; ~ *vivendi* (vĭvĕ′ndĭ), arrangement between disputants pending settlement of debate, arrangement between people(s) who agree to differ. [L, = MODE of working, of living]

**mŏg, mŏ'ggie** (-gǐ), *ns.* (sl.) Cat. [dial.]

**Mogŭ'l** (*or* mō'-) *n.* Mongolian; **the (Great or Grand) ~**, emperor of Delhi in 16th–19th cc.; (**m~**; colloq.) important or influential person. [Pers. & Arab. (MONGOL)]

**M.O.H.** *abbr.* ‖Master of Otter--hounds; Medical Officer of Health.

**mŏ'hair** *n.* (Yarn or fabric from) hair of Angora goat. [ult. f. Arab., = choice]

**Mohă'mmĕdan.** See MUHAM-MADAN.

**moi'ety** *n.* (Law or literary) half; one of the two parts of a thing. [F f. L *medietas* (*medius* middle)]

**moil** *v.i.* Drudge, esp. **toil and moil**. [F f. L (*mollis* soft)]

**moire** (mwăr) *n.* ~ (**antique**), watered fabric, usu. silk; **moiré** (mwăr'ā) *a.*, (of silk) watered, (of metal) having clouded appearance like watered silk. [F (MOHAIR)]

**moist** *a.* Slightly wet, damp; (of season) rainy; **~'en** (-sen) *v.t.* & *i.*, make or become moist; **~'ure** *n.*, liquid diffused in small quantity as vapour, within solid, or condensed on a surface; **~'ūrīze** (*or* -scher-) *v.t.*, make less dry (esp. the skin by use of cosmetic). [F]

**mŏke** *n.* (sl.) Donkey. [orig. unkn.]

**mŏ'lar** *1. a.* (Usu. of mammal's back teeth) serving to grind. *2. n.* Molar tooth. [L (*mola* millstone)]

**molă'sses** (-z) *n.* Uncrystallized syrup drained from raw sugar; *treacle. [Port. f. L (*mel* honey)]

**\*mŏld** etc. See MOULD[1–3], MOULDER.

**mōle[1]** *n.* Abnormal pigmented prominence on human skin. [E]

**mōle[2]** *n.* Small burrowing insectivorous mammal with usu. blackish velvety fur and very small eyes, formerly thought to be blind; **~'hill**, small mound thrown up by mole in burrowing (*make a mountain out of a ~hill*, exaggerate obstacle etc.); **~'skin**, skin of mole as fur, kind of fustian like it. [LDu.]

**mōle[3]** *n.* Massive structure usu. of stone, as pier, breakwater, or causeway; artificial harbour. [F f. L *moles* mass]

**mŏ'lĕcule** *n.* Smallest particle (usu. group of atoms, or in some elements one of the single atoms) to which a substance can be reduced by subdivision without losing its chemical identity; **molĕ'cūlar** *a.* (**molecular**

**weight**, ratio between mass of one molecule of a substance and one--twelfth of mass of an atom of the isotope carbon-12); **molĕ'cūlă'rĭty** *n.* [F f. L dim. (prec.)]

**molĕ'st** *v.t.* Meddle hostilely or injuriously with (person); **molĕstā'tion** *n.* [F or L (*molestus* troublesome)]

**mŏll** *n.* (colloq.) Prostitute; gangster's female companion. [pet-form of *Mary*]

**mŏ'llĭf̄ȳ** *v.t.* Appease, soften; **~ĭcā'tion** *n.* [F or L (*mollis* soft)]

**mŏ'llusc, *-sk**, *n.* One of the group of soft-bodied usu. hard--shelled animals including snails, oysters, etc. [F f. L *molluscus* soft]

**mŏ'llycŏddle. 1.** *n.* Effeminate man or boy; valetudinarian. **2.** *v.t.* Coddle, pamper. [as MOLL; CODDLE]

**\*mŏlt.** See MOULT; **mŏ'lten,** see MELT.

**molto** (mŏ'ltō) *adv.* (Mus.) Very (preceding or following direction: *molto sostenuto; allegro molto*). [It. f. L *multus* much]

**molȳ'bdēnum** *n.* Silver-white metallic element used in steel for making high-speed tools etc. [L f. Gk (*molubdos* lead)]

**mō'ment** *n.* Very brief portion of time, instant; short period of time (*wait a moment*); **one, half a, just a, ~,** ellipt., wait a moment; **in a ~,** instantly, very soon; **not for a ~,** never; *timed to the ~*, with absolute accuracy; LAST[3] *moment*); exact point of time (*came the very ~ I heard of it*, as soon as; **the ~,** time that affords opportunity; *am, was, busy at the ~,* just now, then; *man of the ~,* important at time in question; PSYCHOLOGICAL *moment*; **~ of truth,** time of final sword-thrust in bull-fight, fig. time of crisis or test); importance (*of great, little, moment*); (Phys.) product of force and distance of its line of action from centre of rotation; **~ary** *a.* (-ily, -iness), lasting only a moment; **~lȳ** *adv.*, at every moment; **momĕ'ntous** *a.*, having great importance; **momĕ'ntum** *n.* (*pl.* -ta), quantity of motion of a moving body, product of its mass and its velocity, impetus gained by movement (lit. or fig.). [F f. L *momentum* (*moveo* to move)]

**\*mŏ'mma, -mmȳ,** (colloq. or childish). Mother. [MAMMA]

**Mon.** *abbr.* Monday.

**mŏ′nach|al** (-k-) *a.* (**-lly**). Monastic; **~ism** *n.* [F or L (MONK)]

**mŏ′năd** *n.* The number one, unit; ultimate unit of being (e.g. a soul, an atom, a person, God); **monă′dĭc** *a.* [F or L f. Gk *monas -ados* unit]

**mŏ′narch** (-k) *n.* Sovereign with title of king, queen, emperor, empress, or equivalent; supreme ruler (lit. or fig.); **monăr′chal**, **monăr′chĭc(al)**, (-k-) *adjs.* (**-ally**, **-ically**); **~ism** *n.*, principles of, attachment to, monarchy; **~ist** *n.*; **~y** *n.*, (State under) monarchical government (*constitutional* or LIMITED *monarchy*). [F or L f. Gk (MONO-, *arkhō* to rule)]

**mŏ′nastery** *n.* Residence of community of monks; **monă′stic** *a.* (**-ically**), of or like monks, nuns, friars, etc., of monasteries; *monastic* VOW; **monă′sticism** *n.*; **monă′sticize** *v.t.* [L *monasterium* f. Gk (*monos* alone)]

**Mo′nday** (mŭ′-; *or* -dĭ). **1.** *n.* Day of week, following Sunday. **2.** *adv.* (cf. FRIDAY 2). [E]

**mo′ney** (mŭ′-) *n.* Current medium of exchange in form of portable coins and of banknotes etc. (**paper ~**); (in *pl.*; also **monies**) sums of money; property viewed as convertible into money; rich person(s) (*marry money*); **~-bags**, wealth; **~-box**, closed box into which savings or contributions are dropped through slit; **~-changer**, one whose business it is to change money at stated rate; **|~ for jam** or **old rope**, (sl.) profit for little or no trouble; **~-grubber**, person sordidly intent on amassing money; **~-grubbing** *a.* & *n.*, (given to) this practice; **~-lender**, one whose business it is to lend money at interest; **~-making** *a.* & *n.*, (allowing) acquisition of wealth; **~-market**, sphere of operation of dealers in short-dated loans, stocks, etc.; *money of* ACCOUNT; *money* ORDER; **|~-spinner**, kind of small spider, thing that brings in much money (e.g. successful book); **~′s-worth**, anything recognized as equivalent to money, good value for one's money; **in the ~**, winning money prizes, having plenty of money; **make ~**, acquire wealth; **put ~ into**, make investment in; **the one for my ~** (that I prefer); **there is ~ in**, profit can be had from; **time is ~**, waste of time means loss of profit;

**mo′nètarў** (mŭ′-) *a.* (**-ily**), of the currency in use, (consisting) of money; **mo′nètarĭst** (mŭ′-) *n.*, one who advocates control of money as chief method of stabilizing the economy; **mo′nètize** (mŭ′-) *v.t.*, put (a metal) into circulation as money, give fixed value as currency; **~ed** (mŭ′nĭd) *a.*, rich, consisting of money. [F f. L *moneta*]

**mo′nger** (mŭ′ngg-) *n.* Dealer, trader, (chiefly in *comb.*; lit., as *fishmonger, ironmonger*; or fig., usu. derog., as *scandalmonger*). [E f. L *mango* dealer]

**Mŏ′ngol** (-ngg-) *n.* & *a.* (Member) of Asian people now inhabiting Mongolia; (person) with Mongoloid characteristics; (*m~*) (person) suffering from mongolism; **Mŏngō′lian** *a.* & *n.*, (native, language) of Mongolia, Mongol, Mongoloid; **m~ism** *n.*, congenital mental deficiency with Mongoloid appearance; **~oid** *a.* & *n.*, (person) resembling Mongolians in racial origin or in having broad flat (yellowish) face, mongol. [native name]

**mŏ′ngoōse** (-ngg-) *n.* (*pl.* **~s**). Small carnivorous tropical mammal, esp. a species common in India, able to kill venomous snakes unharmed. [Marathi]

**mo′ngrel** (mŭ′ngg-). **1.** *n.* Dog of no definable type or breed; other animal or plant resulting from crossing of different breeds or types; (derog.) person not of pure race. **2.** *a.* Of mixed origin, nature, or character. [rel. to MINGLE]

**mŏ′nĭ(c)ker** *n.* (sl.) Name. [orig. unkn.]

**mŏ′n|ĭsm** *n.* Any theory denying duality of matter and mind; **~ĭst** *n.*; **~ĭ′stic** *a.* [L, f. Gk *monos* single]

**mŏ′nĭt|or**. **1.** *n.* Senior pupil in school with duties of keeping order; pupil given specified duties in class etc.; shallow-draught warship of heavy gunpower; one who listens to and reports on foreign broadcasts etc.; tropical lizard supposed to warn of crocodiles; detector of radioactive contamination; television receiver used in selecting or verifying the broadcast picture. **2.** *v.t.* & *i.* Act as monitor (of); regulate strength of (recorded or transmitted signal); maintain regular surveillance (over). **3.** **~ŏr′ial** *a.* (**-lly**); **~rèss** *n.*; **mŏ′nĭtorў** *a.* (**-ily**), giving or serving as a warning. [L (*moneo* warn)]

**monk** (mŭ-) *n.* Member of community of men living apart under religious vows; ∼'**shood** (-s-h-), poisonous plant with hood-shaped flowers; ∼'**ish** *a.*, of monks, (usu. derog.) characteristic of monk. [E f. L f. Gk *monakhos* (*monos* alone)]

**mo'nkey** (mŭ'-). **1.** *n.* Mammal of a group closely allied to and resembling man, esp. small long-tailed member of order Primates; (as term of playful contempt, to or of person) *young monkey* etc.; (sl.) ‖£500, \*$500; ∼ **business**, (sl.) mischief; ∼-**jacket**, short close-fitting one worn by sailors etc.; ∼-**nut**, peanut; ∼-**puzzle**, prickly tree with interlaced branches; \*∼-**shines**, ‖∼--**tricks**, (sl.) mischief; ∼-**wrench** (with adjustable jaw); ‖**get one's** ∼ **up**, become angry; **make a** ∼ **of**, humiliate by making appear ridiculous. **2.** *v.t.* & *i.* Mimic, mock; play mischievous tricks (*with*); fool *about* or *around* (*with*). [orig. unkn.]

**mǒ'no** *a.* & *n.* (*pl.* ∼s). (colloq.) Monophonic (reproduction, record, etc.). [abbr.]

**mǒ'no-** *in comb.* (bef. vowel usu. **mon-**). One, alone, single. [Gk (*monos* alone)]

**mǒ'nochǒrd** (-k-) *n.* (Mus.) Instrument with single string, esp. for determination of intervals; ∼**romā'tic** *a.* (-ically), (of light or other radiation) containing only one colour or wavelength, executed in monochrome; ∼**rōme**, (*n.*) picture done in (different tints of) one colour, or in black and white only, (*a.*) having or using only one colour.

**mǒ'nocle** *n.* Single eye-glass. [F f. L (MONO-, *oculus* eye)]

**mǒnocǒtylē'don** *n.* Flowering plant with single cotyledon (abbr. **mǒ'nocǒt**); ∼**ous** *a.* [MONO-]

**monǒ'cŭlar** *a.* With or for one eye. [MONOCLE]

**mǒ'nodȳ** *n.* Ode sung by single actor in Greek play; poem in which mourner bewails someone's death; ∼**ist** *n.* [L f. Gk (MONO-, ODE)]

**monǒ'gamȳ** *n.* Practice or state of being married to one person at a time; (Zool.) habit of having only one mate at a time; ∼**ist** *n.*; ∼**ous** *a.* [F f. L f. Gk (*gamos* marriage)]

**mǒ'nogrăm** *n.* Two or more letters, esp. person's initials, inter-

woven as device; ∼**graph** (-ahf) *n.*, separate treatise on single object or class of objects; **monǒ'grapher, monǒ'graphist**, *ns.*, monograph-writer; ∼**grǎ'phic** *a.* [MONO-]

**mǒ'nolῑth** *n.* Single block of stone, esp. shaped into pillar etc.; person or thing like monolith in being massive, immovable, or solidly uniform; ∼**i'thic** *a.* [F f. Gk (*lithos* stone)]

**mǒ'nologue** (-g) *n.* Scene in drama where person speaks alone; dramatic composition for one performer; long speech by one person in a company. [F f. Gk *monologos* speaking alone]

**mǒnomā'nῑa** *n.* Obsession of mind by one idea or interest; ∼**ăc** *n.* [F (MONO-)]

**mǒnophǒ'nic** *a.* (Of reproduction of sound) using only one channel of transmission. [Gk *phōnē* sound]

**mǒ'noplāne** *n.* Aeroplane with one set of wings. [MONO-]

**monǒ'polȳ** *n.* Exclusive possession of the trade in some commodity; this conferred as a privilege by State; exclusive possession, control, or exercise (*of*, \*on); thing that is monopolized; ∼**ist** *n.*, one who has monopoly *of*; ∼**ize** *v.t.*, obtain exclusive possession or control of (trade, commodity, the conversation, person's attention, etc.); ∼**izā'tion** *n.* [L f. Gk (*pōleō* sell)]

**mǒ'norail** *n.* Railway in which track consists of single rail; ∼**sȳllable** *n.*, word of one syllable (**speak in** ∼**syllables**, answer little but *Yes* or *No*); ∼**sȳllǎ'bic** *a.* (-ically); ∼**thēism** *n.*, doctrine that there is only one god; ∼**thēist** *n.*; ∼**thēï'stic** *a.* (-ically); ∼**tōne** *n.* & *a.*, (utterance of successive syllables) without change of pitch, sameness of style in writing; **monǒ'tonous** *a.*, lacking in variety, wearisome through sameness; **monǒ'tonȳ** *n.*, monotonousness; **M∼tȳpe** *n.* [P], composing-machine that casts and sets up single types; **monǒ'xide** *n.*, oxide containing one oxygen atom. [MONO-]

**Monseigneur** (mawnsĕnyê̄r') *n.* Title given to eminent French person, esp. prince, cardinal, archbishop, or bishop. [F (*mon* my, SEIGNEUR)]

**Monsieur** (mŏsyê̄r') *n.* (*pl.* **Messieurs** *pr.* mĕsyê̄r'). Title used of or to French-speaking man, corresponding to Mr. or sir; Frenchman. [F (*mon* my, *sieur* lord)]

**Monsignor** (mŏnsēnyōr´) *n.* (*pl.* ~*i*). Title of various R.C. prelates. [It. (MONSEIGNEUR)]

**mŏnsōō´n** *n.* Wind in S. Asia, esp. in Indian Ocean, blowing from S.W. in summer and from N.E. in winter; rainy season accompanying S.W. monsoon. [Du. f. Port. f. Arab.]

**mŏ´nst|er.** 1. *n.* Misshapen creature or plant; imaginary animal compounded of incongruous elements, e.g. centaur, griffin; inhumanly cruel or wicked person, inhuman example *of* (cruelty etc.); animal or thing of huge size. 2. *a.* Huge. 3. ~**rance** *n.*, (R.C. Ch.) open or transparent vessel in which Host is exposed for veneration; ~**rŏ´sĭtў** *n.*, monstrousness, misshapen creature or plant, outrageous thing; ~**rous**, (*a.*) abnormally formed, of the nature of a monster, huge, outrageously wrong or absurd, atrocious, (*adv.*, arch.) extremely. [f. F L *monstrum* (*monstro* show)]

**mŏns Vĕ´nerĭs** (-nz-) *n.* Rounded mass of fat on woman's abdomen above vulva. [L., = mount of Venus]

**Mont.** *abbr.* Montana.

**mŏ´ntage** (-ahzh) *n.* Selection, cutting, and piecing together as consecutive whole, of separate sections of cinema or television film; (production of) composite whole from juxtaposed pieces of music, photographs, etc. [F (MOUNT)]

**mŏntbrē´tia** (-nbrē´sha) *n.* Iridaceous plant with orange-coloured flowers. [de *Montbret*, person]

**month** (mŭ-) *n.* (Calendar) ~, any of usu. 12 periods of time into which year is divided or any period between same dates in successive such portions; period of 28 days; LUNAR *month*; *month of* SUNDAYS; **this day** ~, in a month's time; ~**´lў**, (*a.* & *adv.*) (produced or occurring) once every month, (*n.*) monthly periodical. [E]

**mŏ´nŭment** *n.* Written record, anything enduring that serves to commemorate or make celebrated, esp. structure or building (‖**the M**~, column in London commemorating fire of 1666); stone or other structure placed over grave or in church etc. in memory of the dead; ~**al** (-ĕ´n-) *a.* (-lly), of, serving as, monument, (of literary work) massive and permanent, extremely great, stupendous (*monumental achievement, blunder*);

~**al mason**, maker of tombstones etc. [F f. L (*moneo* remind)]

**mōo** *v.i.*, & *n.* (Make) characteristic vocal sound of cattle, LOW[1]; ~**cow**, (childish name for) cow. [imit.]

**mōoch** *v.i.* & *t.* (sl.) Loiter *about*, walk slowly *along*; steal. [prob. F *muchier* skulk]

**mōod**[1] *n.* (Gram.) Form(s) of verb serving to indicate whether it is to express fact, command, wish, etc., (*indicative, imperative, subjunctive, mood*); (distinction of meaning expressed by) group of such forms. [alt. MODE]

**mōod**[2] *n.* State of mind or feeling; (in *pl.*) fits of melancholy or bad temper; **in the** ~, **in no** ~, inclined, disinclined, (*for* thing, *to* do); ~**´ў** *a.* (-ily, -iness), gloomy, sullen. [E]

**mōon.** 1. *n.* Satellite of the earth, revolving round it monthly, illuminated by sun and reflecting some light to earth; this in particular month, regarded as object distinct from that visible in other months (FULL, HARVEST, HUNTER'S, NEW, *moon*), or when visible (*no moon to-night*); (poet.) month; satellite of any planet; **the** ~, thing unlikely to be obtained (CRY *for the moon*), anything no matter how unattainable (*promised her the moon*); ~**beam**, ray of moonlight; ~**face** (round like full moon); ~**light**, (*n.*) light of moon, (*a.*) lighted by the moon (~*light flit*, removal of household goods by night to avoid paying rent), (*v.i.*, colloq.) have two paid occupations, esp. one by day and one by night; ~**lit**, lighted by the moon; ~**shine**, visionary talk or ideas, illicitly distilled or smuggled alcoholic liquor; ~**shot**, (launching of) spacecraft travelling to the moon; ~**stone**, felspar with pearly appearance; ~**struck**, deranged in mind; MAN *in the moon*; *once in a* BLUE *moon*; **over the** ~, in raptures, highly excited; ‖SHOOT *the moon*. 2. *v.i.* Move or look listlessly (*about, around,* etc.; ~ **over**, be inactive or inattentive because infatuated by). 3. ~**´ў** *a.* (-ily, -iness), of or like the moon, stupidly dreamy. [E]

**moor**[1] (or mŏr) *n.* Tract of open waste ground esp. if covered with heather; tract of ground preserved for shooting; ~**´fowl**, ~ **game**, red grouse; ~**´cock**, male of this; ~**´hen**, female of this, water-hen; ~**´land**, country abounding in heather. [E]

**moor²** (or mŏr) v.t. Attach (boat etc.) to fixed object; ~**age** n., place, charge made, for mooring; ~**ing** n. (usu. in pl.), permanent anchors and chains laid down for ships to be moored to, place where vessel is moored. [prob. LG]

**Moor³** (or mŏr) n. One of a Muslim people of N.W. Africa; ~**ish** a., of the Moors. [F f. L f. Gk *Mauros*]

**moose** n. (pl. same). N. Amer. animal closely allied to or same as European elk. [Narragansett]

**moot** n., a., & v. **1.** n. (Hist.) Assembly. **2.** a. Debatable (*it is a moot point*). **3.** v.t. Raise (question) for discussion. [E]

**mop.** **1.** Bundle of coarse yarn or cloth fastened at end of stick, for cleaning floors etc.; similarly-shaped instrument for various purposes; thick head of hair like mop; ~ ('head), person with this; ‖**Mrs. Mop**(p), (joc.) charwoman. **2.** v.t. (-pp-). Wipe or clean (as) with mop; wipe tears, sweat, etc., from (face, brow, etc.); wipe (tears etc.) thus; ~ **up**, wipe up (as) with mop, (sl.) absorb (profits etc.), (sl.) dispatch or make an end of, (Mil.) complete occupation of (district etc.) by capturing or killing troops left there, capture or kill (stragglers). [orig. uncert.]

**mope.** **1.** v.i. Abandon oneself to listless condition. **2.** n. One who mopes; **the ~s**, depression of spirits. [orig. unkn.]

**moped** n. Motorized bicycle. [Sw. *motor*, *ped*aler pedals]

**Mopp.** See MOP.

**moppet** n. (Endearing term for) baby, little girl, etc.; (colloq.) child. [obs. *moppe* baby, doll]

**moquette** (-kĕt´) n. Material of wool on cotton with pile or loops, used for upholstery etc. [F]

**moraine** n. Debris carried down and deposited by glacier. [F]

**moral.** **1.** a. (~ly). Concerned with goodness or badness of character or disposition or with the distinction between right and wrong; virtuous in general conduct; (of rights etc.) founded on moral law; capable of moral action (*man is a moral agent*); ~ **certainty**, probability so great as to allow no reasonable doubt; ~ **courage** (to meet contempt etc. rather than abandon right course of action); ~ **law**, conditions to be fulfilled by any right course of action; *moral* PHILOSOPHY; ~ **sense**, ability to distinguish right and wrong; ~ **support** (giving psychological rather than physical help); ~ **theology**, ethics as branch of theology; ~ **victory**, defeat that has some of the satisfactory elements of victory. **2.** n. Moral lesson (esp. at end) of fable, story, event, etc., (**draw the ~**, show what it is); moral maxim or principle (**point a ~**, illustrate or apply it); (in pl.) moral habits, e.g. sexual conduct. **3.** mora'le (-ah'l) n., moral condition esp. (of troops or workers) as regards discipline and confidence; ~**ist** n., one who practises or teaches morality, one who follows a natural system of ethics; ~**i'stic** a. (-ically); mora'lity n., science of morals, (in pl.) points of ethics, particular system of morals (*commercial morality*), degree of conformity to moral principles, (esp. good) moral conduct, moralizing; ~**ity** (**play**), (Hist.) kind of drama with abstract qualities as main characters and inculcating moral lesson; ~**ize** v.i. & t., indulge in moral reflection or talk (on subject), interpret morally, make (more) moral; ~**iza'tion** n. [L (*mos mor-* custom)]

**mora'ss** n. (literary). Marsh, bog; (fig.) entanglement (*morass of vice*). [Du. *moeras* f. F (MARSH)]

**morator'ium** n. (pl. ~**ums**, ~**a**). (Period of) legal authorization to debtors to postpone payment; temporary prohibition or suspension (*on activity*). [L (*moror* delay)]

**mor'bid** a. (Of mind, ideas, etc.) unwholesome, sickly; given to morbid feelings; (colloq.) melancholy; (Med.) of the nature of, indicative of, disease; ~ **anatomy** (of diseased organs). [L (*morbus* disease)]

**mor'dant.** **1.** a. (Of sarcasm etc.) caustic, biting, pungent, smarting; ~**cy** n. **2.** a. & n. Corrosive or cleansing (acid); (substance) serving to fix colouring-matter. [F f. L (*mordeo* bite)]

**more.** **1.** a. Existing in greater or additional quantity or degree (*there is more truth in it than you think*; *10 is 2 more than 8*; *bring some more water*); greater in degree (*more's the* PITY; *the more fool you*). **2.** n. Greater quantity or number (*more in it than* MEET²*the* *eye*; *hope to see more of you*, see you more often; *more than one person has found it so*). **3.** *adv.* In greater degree (*you must attend more to details*; *more in sorrow than in anger*; *more frightened than hurt*); moreover; again (*once, twice*, etc., *never, more*); (forming compar. of *adjs.* & *advs.*, esp. those of more than one syllable) *more absurd(ly), curious, easily, truly.* **4.** ~ **and** ~, in an increasing degree; *more LIKE it*; ~ **of**, to a greater extent (*more of a poet than a musician*); ~ **or less**, in greater or less degree, or thereabouts; ~ **so**, (the same) to a greater degree; ~ **than**, (colloq.) exceedingly (*happy* etc.), thing that . . . not (*you helped, which is more than I did*); **any** ~, (to) any greater or further quantity or extent; **neither** ~ **nor less than**, simply, literally, (*absurd, cheating*, etc.); NO[1] *more*; THE *more*; **what is** ~, as an additional point, moreover. **5.** ~**ō'ver** (-ōr̄ō'-) *adv.*, (literary) further, besides, (with new statement). [E]

**moree'n** *n.* Strong ribbed woollen or cotton material for curtains. [orig. unkn.]

**mor'eish** (-ōr̄'ĭ-) *a.* (colloq.) Pleasant to eat, causing desire for more. [MORE]

**morė'llō** *n.* (*pl.* ~s). Bitter kind of dark cherry. [It., = blackish]

**mor'ēs** (-z, -āz) *n.pl.* Customs or conventions regarded as essential to or characteristic of a community. [L pl. of *mos* custom]

**Morė'sque** (-k) *a.* Moorish in style. [F f. It. (MOOR[3])]

**mŏrgană'tĭc** *a.* (~**ally**). (Of marriage) between man of high rank and woman of lower rank, the wife and children having no claim to possessions or title of father; (of wife) so married. [F, or G f. L *morganaticus* f. Gmc, = morning gift (from husband to wife on morning after consummation of marriage)]

**mŏrgue** (-g) *n.* Mortuary; (Journ.) repository where miscellaneous material for reference is kept. [F, orig. name of Paris mortuary]

**mŏ'rĭbŭnd** *a.* At point of death (lit. or fig.). [L (*morior* die)]

**mŏ'rion** *n.* (Hist.) Helmet without beaver or visor. [F f. Sp. *morrion*]

**Mŏr'mon** *n.* (Nickname for) member of millenary religious body (Church of Jesus Christ of Latter-day Saints) founded on basis of revela-

tions in **Book of** ~ (named from its supposed author); ~**ĭsm** *n.* [name]

**mŏrn** *n.* (poet.) Morning. [E]

**mŏr'nay** *n.* Cheese-flavoured white sauce. [orig. uncert.]

**mŏr'nĭng** *n.* Early part of day, ending at noon or at hour of midday meal (phrs. as AFTER*noon*; **in the** ~, also, colloq., tomorrow); (colloq.) = GOOD *morning*; (fig.) early part (of life etc.); (*attrib.*) occurring or done in the morning; ~ **after,** (colloq.) hangover; ~ **coat** (with front cut away to form tails); ~ **dress,** daytime wear, man's morning coat and striped trousers; ~ **glory,** twining plant with trumpet-shaped flowers; ~ **paper,** newspaper published in the morning; ~**room,** sitting-room for the morning; ~ **sickness,** nausea in morning in early pregnancy; ~ **star,** planet esp. Venus, seen in east before sunrise. [MORN]

**Morŏ'cc|an** *a.* & *n.* (Native) of *Morocco*; **m**~**ō** *n.* (*pl.* ~**s**), fine flexible leather ' of goatskin tanned with sumac. [place]

**mŏr'ŏn** *n.* Adult with intelligence equal to that of average child of 8–12; (colloq.) very stupid or degenerate person; **morŏ'nĭc** *a.* [Gk *mŏros* foolish]

**morŏ's|e** *a.* Sullen, gloomy, and unsocial. [L (*mos mor-* manner)]

**Mŏr'pheus** *n.* Roman god of dreams (**in the arms of** ~, asleep); **mŏr'phĭne** (or -ēn), (pop.) **mŏr'phĭa,** *ns.*, narcotic principle of opium, used to alleviate pain. [L]

**morphŏ'log|ў** *n.* (Biol.) study of forms of animals and plants; (Philol.) study of forms of words, system of forms in a language; **mŏrpholŏ'gĭcal** *a.* (-lly); ~**ĭst** *n.* [Gk *morphē* form]

**mŏ'rrĭs** *a.* & *n.* ǁ~ (**dance**), traditional dance by persons in fancy costume, usu. as characters in legend, with ribbons and bells; ~ **dancer, man,** performer in this. [*morys* var. MOOR[3]*ish*]

**mŏ'rrow** (-ō) *n.* (literary). **The** ~, the following day; ǁGOOD *morrow*; **on the** ~ **of,** (fig.) in the time just following. [MORN]

**Mŏrse. 1.** *n.* & *a.* (Of) the alphabet or code in which letters are represented by various combinations of two signs, e.g. dot and dash, long and short flash, etc. **2.** *v.t.* & *i.* Signal by Morse code. [person]

**mŏr′sel** *n.* Mouthful; small piece (*of* food etc.); fragment. [F f. L *morsus* bite]

**mŏr′tal. 1.** *a.* (**~ly**). Subject to or causing death, fatal, (*to,* lit. or fig.; *mortal* SIN); (of battle) fought to the death; (of enemy) implacable; (of pain, fear, affront, etc.) intense, very serious; accompanying death (*mortal agony*); (sl.) long and tedious (*two mortal hours*), whatsoever (*every mortal thing*). **2.** *n.* Human being; (joc.) person (*a thirsty mortal*). **3. ~ĭtỹ** (-ă′l-) *n.,* mortal nature, loss of life on large scale, number of deaths in given period etc.; **~ity** (**rate**), death-rate. [F f. L (*mors* mort-death)]

**mŏr′tar. 1.** *n.* Vessel in which ingredients are pounded with pestle; short large-bore cannon for throwing shells at high angles; mixture of lime or cement, sand, and water, for joining stones or bricks, (**bricks and ~,** buildings); **~-board,** board for holding mortar, stiff square academic cap. **2.** *v.t.* Plaster or join with mortar; attack or bombard with mortars. [AF *morter* f. L *mortarium*]

**mŏr′tgage** (mŏr′gĭj). **1.** *n.* Conveyance of property by debtor to creditor as security for debt (esp. incurred by purchase of the property), with proviso that it shall be returned on payment of debt within certain period; deed effecting this; (loan resulting in) such debt. **2.** *v.t.* (**~eable** *pr.* -ĭja-). Convey (property) by mortgage. **3. ~ee′** (-jē′) *n.,* creditor in mortgage; **~er** (-jer), **~ŏr′** (-jor′), *ns.,* debtor in mortgage. [F, = dead pledge (GAGE¹)]

**mŏr′tĭce.** See MORTISE.

***mŏrtĭ′cian** (-shan) *n.* Undertaker of funerals. [L (as MORTAL)]

**mŏr′tĭf‖ỹ** *v.t.* **&** *i.* Bring (body, the flesh, passions, etc.) into subjection by self-denial or discipline; cause (person) to feel humiliated, wound (feelings); (of flesh) be affected by gangrene or necrosis; **~ĭcā′tion** *n.* [F f. L (as MORTAL)]

**mŏr′tĭse,** -**ĭce. 1.** *n.* Hole in framework to receive end of another part, esp. TENON; **~ lock** (recessed in frame of door etc.). **2.** *v.t.* Join (things *together,* one *to, into,* another) securely, esp. by mortise and tenon; cut mortise in. [F f. Arab.]

**mŏr′tŭarỹ. 1.** *a.* Of death or burial. **2.** *n.* Building in which dead bodies

may be kept for a time. [AF f. L (as MORTAL)]

**mŏsā′ĭc¹** (-z-) *n.* **&** *a.* (Form or work of art) in which pictures etc. are produced by joining together minute pieces of glass, stone, etc., of different colours; (fig.) diversified (thing). [F f. It. f. L f. Gk (MUSE²)]

**Mŏsā′ĭc²** (-z-) *a.* Of Moses. [F or L (*Moses,* person)]

**mŏsĕ′lle** (-z-) *n.* A dry German white wine. [*Moselle,* river]

**Moslem.** See MUSLIM.

**mŏsque** (-k) *n.* Muslim place of worship. [F *mosquée* f. It. f. Arab.]

**mŏsquī′tō** (-kē′-) *n.* (*pl.* **~es**). Gnat, esp. one of which the female punctures skin of man and animals and sucks their blood; **~-net** (to keep off mosquitoes). [Sp. & Port. dim. of *mosca* fly]

**mŏss** *n.* Small herbaceous cryptogam growing in crowded masses, in bogs or on surface of ground, trees, stones, etc., (*rolling stone* GATHERS *no moss*); (Sc. & N. Engl.) (peat-)bog; **~-grown,** overgrown with moss; **~-rose** (with mosslike growth on calyx and stalk); **~′ỹ** *a.* (-ĭly, -ĭness), (esp.) moss-grown. [E]

**mŏst. 1.** *a.* **&** *n.* (Existing in) greatest quantity or degree (*you have made most mistakes; see who can make the most noise; this is the most I can do*); **make the ~ of,** employ to the best advantage, represent at its best or worst); the majority (of) (*most people think so; most of it is, of them are, missing; his singing is better than most*); **for the ~ part,** in the main, usually). **2.** *adv.* In the highest degree (*this is most interesting; what most annoys me*); (forming superl. of *adjs.* & *advs.,* esp. those of more than one syllable) *most absurd*(*ly*), *curious, easily, most favoured* NATION, Most HONOURABLE, REVEREND. **3. at** (**the**) **~,** as the greatest amount; **ten at** (**the**) **~,** not more than; *this is at* **~** (no better than) *a makeshift*. **4. ~′lỹ** *adv.,* for the most part. [E]

**-most** (*or* -ō-) *suf.* forming *adjs.* w. superl. sense f. *preps.* & other *wds* indicating relative position (*foremost, inmost, topmost, uttermost*). [E]

**mot** (mō) *n.* (*pl. pr.* mōz). Witty saying; BON MOT; **~ juste** (zhōō′st), expression that conveys desired shade of meaning more precisely than any other. [F, = word]

‖**M.O.T.** *abbr.* Ministry of Transport; ~ **test**, (colloq.) compulsory annual test of motor vehicles of more than a specified age.

**mote** *n.* Particle of dust; ~, **beam, in** person's eye, fault that is trifling, great, compared to one's own (see Matt. 7: 3). [E]

**motě'l** *n.* Hotel or group of furnished cabins by roadside, where motorists and their vehicles may be accommodated. [*motor* ho*tel*]

**moth** *n.* Lepidopterous insect like butterfly but without knobbed antennae and mainly nocturnal, apt to scorch itself by fluttering about light; (**clothes**) ~, one breeding in cloth etc., on which its larvae feed; ~**-ball** (of naphthalene etc. for keeping moths away from clothes; in ~**-balls**, fig., stored out of use for considerable time); ~**-eaten**, destroyed by moths, (fig.) antiquated, time-worn; ~'**ў** *a.* (-iness), (esp.) infested with moths. [E]

**mo'ther** (mŭ'dh-). **1.** *n.* Female parent (EXPECTANT or *pregnant mother*; (**adoptive**) ~, woman adopter of child); quality, condition, etc., that gives rise to another (*necessity is the mother of invention*); head of female religious community (often *Mother* SUPERIOR); (title used to or of) elderly woman of lower class. **2.** *v.t.* Give birth to (also: fig.); protect as a mother. **3.** M~ Carey's chicken, stormy PETREL; ~ **country**, country in relation to its colonies; ~**craft**, skill in looking after one's children as a mother; ~ **earth**, earth as mother of its inhabitants, (joc.) the ground; ‖M~**ing** Sunday, 4th Sunday in Lent, with old custom of visiting parents with gifts; ~**-in--law**, wife's or husband's mother; ~**land**, native land; ~**-of-pearl**, smooth shining iridescent substance forming inner layer of oyster etc. shell; M~'s Day, ‖Mothering Sunday, *similar festival on 2nd Sunday in May; *mother's* HELP; ‖~ **ship** (in charge of torpedo-boats, submarines, etc.); ~**s' meeting** (in parish etc. for pastoral instruction or fig. for agitated discussion); ~ **tongue**, one's native language; ~ **wit**, common sense. **4.** ~**hŏŏd** *n.*; ~**lў** *a.* (-iness), having or showing the good qualities of a mother. [E]

**mōti'f** (-ē'f) *n.* Distinctive feature, dominant idea, in artistic or literary or musical composition; ornament of lace etc. sewn separately on garment; ornament on vehicle identifying maker etc. [F (MOTIVE)]

**mō'tion. 1.** *n.* Moving, manner of moving the body in walking etc., change of posture, gesture, (**go through the** ~**s**, simulate an action by gestures, fig. make pretence, do something only superficially; **in** ~, not at rest; **put** or **set in** ~, set going or working; ~ **picture**, cinema film); formal proposal in deliberative assembly; (Law) application by party etc. for rule or order of court); evacuation of bowels, (in *sing.* or *pl.*) faeces. **2.** *v.t.* & *i.* Direct (person *to, towards, away,* etc., *to do*) by sign or gesture; make gesture (*to* person) directing him (*to do*). **3.** ~**less** *a.*, still. [F f. L (MOVE)]

**mō'tiv**|e. **1.** *a.* Tending to initiate movement; concerned with movement; ~e **power**, moving or impelling power, esp. form of mechanical energy used to drive machinery. **2.** *n.* What induces a person to act, e.g. desire, fear, circumstance; motif. **3.** ~**āte** *v.t.*, supply motive to, be motive of, cause (person) to act in a particular way, stimulate interest of (person in studying etc.); ~**ā'tion** *n.* [F f. L *motivus* (MOVE)]

**mō'tley. 1.** *a.* Diversified in colour; of varied character (*a motley crew*). **2.** *n.* (Hist.) Jester's particoloured dress. [orig. unkn.]

**mō'tor** *n., a.,* & *v.* **1.** *n.* What imparts motion; machine supplying motive power for carriage or vessel, esp. internal combustion engine, or for other device with moving parts; ‖= *motor car.* **2.** *a.* Giving, imparting, or producing motion; driven by motor (*motor boat, coach*); of or for motor vehicles; ~ **bicycle**, motor cycle, moped; ~ **bike**, (colloq.) = *motor cycle*; ~**cade**, procession or parade of motor cars [CAVALCADE]; ‖~ **car**, car with motor engine for use on ordinary roads; ~ **cycle**, two-wheeled motor-driven road vehicle without pedal propulsion; ~**cyclist**; ~**man**, driver of underground train; ~ **nerve** (carrying impulses from brain or spinal cord to muscle); *motor* SCOOTER; ‖~ **spirit**, petrol or other fuel for internal combustion engine; ~ **vehicle** (with motor engine for use on ordinary roads); ‖~**way**, road specially constructed and controlled for fast motor traffic. **3.** *v.i.* & *t.* ‖Go or convey in motor car. **4.** ~**ist** *n.*, driver of motor car; ~**ize** *v.t.*, equip (troops etc.) with motor transport, furnish with motor for propulsion etc. [L (MOVE)]

**mŏ′ttle. 1.** *n.* Irregular arrangement of spots or confluent blotches of colour. **2.** *v.t.* (esp. in *p.p.*) Mark with mottle. [back-form. f. MOTLEY]

**mŏ′ttō** *n.* (*pl.* ~**es**) Sentence inscribed on some object (e.g. coat of arms) and expressing appropriate sentiment; maxim adopted as rule of conduct; verses etc. in paper cracker. [It., as MOT]

**mould**¹ (mōld), *mōld¹, n. Loose earth, upper soil of cultivated land, esp. when rich in organic matter. [E]

**mould**² (mōld), *mōld², n. Woolly fungous growth on things of animal or vegetable origin that lie for some time in moist warm air; ~**′y** *a.* (-**ily**, -**iness**), (esp.) covered with mould, (fig.) stale, out-of-date, (sl.) dull or miserable. [N]

**mould**³ (mōld), *mōld³. 1. n.* Hollow form into which metal, clay, etc., is poured or pressed in liquid or soft form to harden to required shape (**cast in** *heroic* etc. ~, fig., of such character); pattern or template used in making mouldings; metal or earthenware vessel used to give shape to puddings etc., pudding etc. so shaped; shape, esp. of animal body. **2.** *v.t.* Produce (object) in certain shape, *out of* (elements), (*up*)*on* (pattern), lit. or fig.; bring into certain shape. ~**′ing** *n.*, (esp.) ornamental variety of outline in cornices etc. of building, or similar shape of woodwork etc., strip of wood thus shaped for attachment; **picture-~ing** (for framing pictures, or along wall for hanging framed pictures from). [F *modle* f. L MODULUS]

**mou′lder** (mō′-), *mō′l-, v.i.* Decay to dust, rot *away*, (lit. or fig.). [perh. Scand.]

**moulding.** See MOULD³; **mouldy,** see MOULD².

**moult** (mōlt), *mōlt. 1. v.i.* & *t.* (Of bird) shed feathers, shed (feathers), in changing plumage (lit. or fig.); (of animal) shed hair, shell, etc. **2.** *n.* Moulting. [E f. L *muto* change]

**mound. 1.** *n.* Elevation of earth or stones, esp. of earth heaped over grave; hillock; heap, pile. **2.** *v.t.* Heap up in mounds. [orig. unkn.]

**mount. 1.** *n.* Mountain, hill, (arch. exc. bef. name, as *Mount Everest*; SERMON *on the Mount*); margin surrounding picture etc.; card on which drawing etc. is mounted; setting for gem etc.; horse for person to ride. **2.** *v.t.* & *i.* Ascend (hill, stairs, etc., or abs.); climb on to; get on (horse etc., or abs.) for purpose of riding; set on horseback; (in *p.p.*) serving on horseback etc. (*mounted police*); put or fix in position for use or exhibition; put (picture) in mount or (gem etc.) in gold etc.; fix (object) on microscope slide; prepare (specimens etc.) for display or preservation; put (play) on stage; take action to effect (programme etc., orig. Mil. of offensive; ~ **guard,** perform duty of guarding *over* thing etc.); move upwards; rise to higher rank or power; ~ (**up**), increase (considerably) in amount or intensity. [E & F f. L *mons mont-* mountain]

**mou′ntain** (-tǐn) *n.* Large or high and steep hill (*make a mountain out of a* MOLE²*hill*; **move ~s,** make every possible effort); large heap or pile, huge quantity *of*; ~ **ash,** tree bearing scarlet berries, rowan; ~ **dew,** (colloq.) Scotch whisky esp. illicitly distilled; ~ **goat,** white goatlike animal of Rocky Mountains etc.; ~ **lion,** puma; ~ **range,** line of mountains connected by high ground; ~ **sickness,** malady caused by rarefied air at great heights; ~**side,** slope of mountain below summit; ~**eer′,** (*n.*) dweller amongst mountains, one skilled in mountain--climbing, (*v.i.*) climb mountains as recreation; ~**ous** *a.*, abounding in mountains, huge. [F f. L (prec.)]

**mou′ntebănk** *n.* (Hist.) itinerant quack; clown, charlatan. [It., = mount on bench]

**Mou′ntie** *n.* (colloq.) Member of Royal Canadian MOUNTED Police. [abbr.]

**mourn** (môrn) *v.i.* & *t.* Feel sorrow or regret (*for* or *over* dead person, lost thing, loss, misfortune, etc.); sorrow for (dead person, regretted or past thing); show conventional signs of grief for period after person's death; ~**′er** *n.*, (esp.) one who attends funeral; ~**′ful** *a.* (-**lly**), expressing mourning, doleful, sad;

~**'ing** n., (esp.) (wearing of) black clothes as sign of sorrow. [E]

**mouse. 1.** n. (*pl.* **mice**). Small rodent, esp. (**house**) ~ (infesting houses etc.; **play cat and** ~ **with**, torment with suspense; ~**'trap**, for catching mice; ~**trap cheese**, of poor quality); small vole or shrew (FIELD, HARVEST, *mouse*); timid shy person; **mou'sy** a. (**-iness**). **2.** (*or* **-z**) *v.i.* (Of cat, owl, etc.) hunt mice. [E]

**moussaka** (mōōsah'-) n. Greek dish of minced meat, aubergines, eggs, etc. [Gk or Turk.]

**mousse** (mōōs) n. Dish of cold whipped cream, eggs, etc., flavoured with fruit, chocolate, or meat or fish purée. [F, = froth]

**mousta'che**, *\*mus-,* (mustah'sh) n. Hair on either side (usu. in *pl.*) or both sides of (usu. man's) upper lip. [F f. It. f. Gk *mustax*]

**mouth. 1.** n. (*pl. pr.* **-dhz**). External orifice in head, with cavity behind it containing apparatus of biting and mastication and vocal organs; this cavity; opening of bag, cave, cannon, trumpet, volcano, etc.; place where river enters sea. **2.** *v.t.* & *i.* (**-dh**). Utter or speak pompously, declaim; grimace, move lips silently. **3.** ~**-organ**, thin rectangular musical instrument played by blowing and sucking air through it; ~**'piece**, part of pipe, musical instrument, telephone, etc., placed between or near lips, person who speaks for another or others; ~ **to feed**, person, esp. child, who consumes food but does no useful work in return; ~**-to-**~**resuscitation** (in which person breathes into patient's lungs through mouth); ~**'wash**, liquid antiseptic etc. for use in mouth; *mouth* WATERS; DOWN³ *in the mouth*; **keep one's** ~ **shut**, (sl.) not reveal secret; *not* OPEN *one's* mouth; **out of** person's **own** ~, using his actual words; **put** one's **money where** one's ~ **is**, (sl.) be ready to support one's opinions by action; **put words into** person's ~, tell him what to say, represent him as having said them; **take words out of** person's ~, say what he was about to say; WORD *of mouth*. **4.** ~**'ful** (**-ŏŏl**) n., quantity of food that fills the mouth, small quantity (*of food* etc.), something difficult to say. [E]

**move** (mōōv). **1.** *v.t.* & *i.* Change

position (of); change position of (man), make a move, in chess etc.; put or keep in motion, rouse, stir; move house; change posture (of); (of inanimate thing) undergo change of position; cause (bowels) to be evacuated, (of bowels) be moved; go or pass (*about, away,* etc.) from place to place; be socially active *in* specified group etc. (*moves in the best circles*); (of merchandise) be sold; provoke (laughter, anger, etc., *in* person; person *to* these); affect (person *with* (emotion); prompt, incline, (person *to* action, *to* do; **the spirit** ~**s** person, he feels inclined *to* do); (fig.) initiate action (*moved to* halt *inflation*); make request or application *for*; propose (resolution, *that* thing be done) in deliberative assembly; ~ **along, on**, go to new place; *move* HEAVEN *and earth*; ~ **house**, change one's place of residence (~ **about**, do this often); ~ **in**, take possession of new abode, begin new job etc., so ~ **out**; ~ **over, up**, adjust one's position to make room for another. **2.** n. Moving of man at chess etc., player's turn to do this; (fig.) step taken to secure object; change of residence, business premises, etc.; **get a** ~ **on**, (sl.) hurry, bestir oneself; **make a** ~, initiate action; **on the** ~, progressing, moving about. **3. mov'able** (mōō'-) a., that can be moved (*movable* FEAST); ~**'ment** (**-vm-**) n., moving, moving part of mechanism, (Mus.) principal division of a musical work, (series of combined actions of) body of persons for special object (OXFORD *Movement*), motion of bowels; **mo'ver** (mōō'-) n., (esp.) one who moves proposition (**prime** ~**r**, initial source of motive power, fig. author of fruitful idea); *\***mo'vie** (mōō'-) n., (colloq.) cinema film; **mo'ving** (mōō'-) a., (esp.) affecting with emotion; **moving picture**, continuous picture got by projecting on screen etc. a sequence of photographs taken at very short intervals; **moving staircase**, escalator. [AF f. L *moveo*]

**mow¹** (mō) n. (U.S. or dial.) Stack of hay, corn, etc. [E]

**mow²** (mō) *v.t.* (*p.p.* ~**ed** *pr.* mōd, ~**n**). Cut (grass etc., or abs.) with scythe or machine; cut down produce of (field) or grass of (lawn) thus; ~ **down**, kill or destroy randomly or in great numbers; **~'er** *n.*, (esp.) mowing machine, lawn-mower. [E]

**M.P.** *abbr.* melting-point; Member of Parliament; military police(man).

**mp** *abbr. mezzo piano.*

**m.p.g.** *abbr.* miles per gallon.

**m.p.h.** *abbr.* miles per hour.

**Mr.** (mĭ'ster) *n.* (*pl.* MESSRS.) Title of man without higher title, or prefixed to designation of office etc., (*Mr. Jones*; *Mr. Speaker*); **Mr. Right**, (joc.) destined husband. [abbr. MISTER]

**Mrs.** (mĭ'sĭz) *n.* (*pl.* same, **Mesdames**). Title of married woman without higher title; *Mrs.* GRUNDY; ||*Mrs.* MOP(*p*). [abbr. MISTRESS]

**MS.** (ĕmĕ's) *abbr.* manuscript.

**Ms.** (mĭz) *n.* Title of woman without higher title, used like MR. without distinction between married and unmarried. [comb. of MRS., MISS²]

**M.S.** *abbr.* multiple sclerosis.

**M.Sc.** *abbr.* Master of Science.

**MSS.** (ĕmĕ'sĭz) *abbr.* manuscripts.

**Mt.** *abbr.* Mount.

**mū** *n.* Twelfth Gk letter (M, μ) = m. [Gk]

**much** *a., n.,* & *adv.,* (MORE, MOST). **1.** *a.* Existing in great quantity (*much trouble*; *too much, not much, noise*; **a bit ~**, colloq., somewhat excessive or immoderate; HOW, SO¹, THAT, THIS, *much*; **too ~ for**, more than a match for, beyond what is endurable by). **2.** *n.* Great quantity (*much of what you say is true*; MAKE, THINK, *much of*; *not much* IN *it*; **not ~ of a**, colloq., not a great, a somewhat poor; **not ~ to look at**, insignificant or unpleasing in appearance; **not come to ~**, have little success). **3.** *adv.* In great degree (*much to my surprise*; *I much regret, was much annoyed*); qualifying compar. or superl. adj.: *much better, much the most likely*); for a large part of one's time (*is much in society*); approximately (*much the* SAME; **~ of a size**, about the same size); **~ as**, though . . . much (*cannot come, much as I should like to*); *much* OBLIGED; **as ~**, that (quantity etc.; *I thought as ~*, I thought so; *as ~ again*, such as will double the amount). **4.** **~'lў** *adv.* (joc. only); **~'ness** *n.*, greatness in quantity or degree (**~ of a ~ness**, very nearly the same or alike). [MICKLE]

**mū'cilage** *n.* Viscous substance extracted from plants; adhesive gum. [F f. L (MUCUS)]

**muck. 1.** *n.* Farmyard manure; (colloq.) dirt, filth, mess (**make a ~ of**, bungle); **~-rake** (for collecting muck, usu. fig. of predilection for worthless or unsavoury matters); **~-raking** *a.* & *n.*; ||**~ sweat** (profuse). **2.** *v.t.* & *i.* Manure; make dirty; remove muck (*out*) from; ||**~ (up)**, (sl.) bungle; ||(sl.) **go aimlessly** *about*, fool *about with*; **~ in**, share tasks etc. equally (*with* another). **3.** **~'er** *n.*, ||(sl.) heavy fall (lit. or fig.); **~'ў a.** (**~ily, ~iness**). [Scand.]

**mŭ'ckle.** See MICKLE.

**mū'cus** *n.* Slimy substance secreted by mucous membrane; **mū'cous** *a.* (**mucous membrane**, skin lining nose and other cavities of the body); **mūcŏ'sitў** *n.* [L]

**mŭd** *n.* Wet soft earthy matter; hard ground from drying of area of this; (fig.) what is worthless or polluting (**fling, throw, ~**, make disgraceful imputations; **his name is ~**, his reputation is at present impaired); **~-flat**, stretch of muddy land uncovered at low tide; **~'-guard**, hood on wheel to protect rider, pedestrians, etc., from mud; **~'lark**, (esp.) street urchin; **~-pack**, cosmetic paste applied thickly to face; **~ pie**, mud made into pie shape by child; **as clear as ~**, (joc.) not at all clear; **here's ~ in your eye!** (sl. drinking toast); STICK¹-*in-the-mud*; **~'dle**, (*v.t.* & *i.*) bewilder, mix (things *up, together*) blunderingly, mismanage (*affair*), busy oneself (*with*) in confused and ineffective way (**~dle along** or **on**, progress in haphazard way; **~dle through**, attain one's end by tenacity not skill or efficiency), (*n.*) disorder, muddled condition; **~dle-headed**, stupid, confused; **~'dў**, (*a.*: **-ily, -iness**) like, abounding in, covered in, mud, (of liquid) turbid, mentally confused, obscure, (*v.t.*) make muddy. [G]

**mue'slĭ** (moō'z-) *n.* Food of crushed cereals, dried fruit, nuts, honey, etc. [Swiss G]

**mue'zzin** (moō-) *n.* Muslim crier who proclaims hours of prayer usu. from minaret. [Arab.]

**mŭff¹** *n.* Tubular covering esp. of fur in which hands are put to keep them warm; EAR¹, FOOT, -**muff**. [Du. *mof* f. L]

**mŭff².** **1.** *n.* Person who is awkward or stupid (orig. in athletic sport); failure. **2.** *v.t.* Bungle, miss

**mŭf′fin** n. (*English) ~, light flat round spongy cake eaten toasted and buttered. [orig. unkn.]

**mŭf′fle** v.t. Wrap, cover *up*, (oneself, one's throat, etc., or abs.) for warmth; wrap up (oars at rowlocks, bell, drum, etc.) to deaden sound; (usu. in *p.p.*) repress, deaden sound of, (curse etc.); ~**r** n., (esp.) wrap or scarf worn for warmth. [perh. F (*moufle* thick glove, MUFF[1])]

**mŭf′tī** n. Plain clothes worn by one who has right to wear uniform (esp. *in mufti*). [Arab.]

**mŭg**[1]. **1.** n. Drinking-vessel, usu. cylindrical, with or without handle; its contents; (sl.) mouth or face; *(sl.) hoodlum; ||(sl.) simpleton or gullible person (**a ~'s game**, senseless or unprofitable occupation). **2.** v.t. & i. (**-gg-**). Thrash, strangle, rob with violence, esp. in public place; (sl.) make faces. [Scand.]

**mŭg**[2]. (sl.) **1.** v.i. & t. (**-gg-**). Study hard (*at* subject, or abs.); ~ (**up**), learn (subject) by hard study. **2.** n. One who studies hard. [orig. unkn.]

**mŭg′gĭns** (-gĭnz) n. (colloq.; *pl.* ~**es**, same). Person who allows himself to be outwitted. [perh. surname]

**mŭg′gў** (-gǐ) a. (~**ily**, ~**iness**). (Of weather etc.) oppressively damp and warm. [N]

*mŭ′gwŭmp n. Great man, boss; one who holds aloof from party politics; one who refuses to commit himself. [Algonquin, = great chief]

**Mŭhă′mmadan**, **Mŏhă′mmedan**, **Măhŏ′metan** (-a-h-), n. & a. (Person believing in Allah as God according to revelations of Muhammad; Muslim; ~**ism** n. [person]

**mŭlā′ttō** n. (*pl.* ~**s**). Offspring of White and Black persons. [Sp. *mulato* young mule]

**mŭ′lberry** n. (Fruit of) tree bearing purple or white edible berries and leaves which are used to feed silkworms. [E f. L *morum* mulberry, + BERRY]

**mŭlch** (or -lsh). **1.** n. Mixture of wet straw, leaves, etc., spread to protect roots of newly planted trees etc. **2.** v.t. Treat with mulch. [E, = soft]

**mŭlct.** (literary). **1.** n. Fine imposed for offence. **2.** v.t. Fine (person (*in*) amount); deprive (person etc. *of*). [F f. L *mulcta* fine]

**mūle**[1] n. Backless slipper. [F]

**mūl|e**[2] n. Offspring (usu. sterile) of mare and he-ass, or (pop.) of she-ass and stallion (prop. HINNY), used as beast of draught and burden and undeservedly noted for obstinacy; hybrid plant or animal; kind of spinning-machine; ~**eteer′** n., mule-driver; ~**′ish** a., like a mule, obstinate. [F f. L *mulus*]

**mŭll**[1] v.t. & i. (colloq.) Ponder (*over*). [Du.]

**mŭll**[2] v.t. Make (wine, beer) into hot drink with sugar, spices, egg-yolk, etc. [orig. unkn.]

**mŭ′llein** (-lǐn) n. Herbaceous plant with woolly leaves and yellow flowers. [F *moleine*]

**mŭ′llet** n. Red, grey, ~, kinds of sea-fish valued for food. [F *mulet* f. L *mullus* f. Gk]

**mŭlligataw′nў** n. Highly seasoned soup orig. from India. [Tamil, = pepper-water]

**mŭ′llion** (-yon) n. Vertical bar dividing lights in window. [F *moinel* middle (MEAN[3])]

**mŭ′lti-** *pref.* Many; ~**colour**(ed), of many colours; ~**form**, having many forms, of many kinds; ~**la′teral**, having many sides, (of agreement, treaty, etc.) in which 3 or more parties participate; ~**li′ngual**, in or using many languages; ~**millionair′e**, person with fortune of several millions; ~**na′tional**, operating in several countries; ~~**purpose**, serving more than one purpose; ~**ra′cial**, (composed) of many races of men; ~~**storey**, having several (esp. similarly designed) storeys. [L (*multus* much, many)]

**mŭltifār′ious** a. Having great variety; (w. *pl. n.*) many and various. [L *multifarius*]

**mŭ′ltiple. 1.** a. Having several or many parts, elements, or individual components; (w. *pl. n.*) many and various; ~-**choice**, (of question in examination) accompanied by several possible answers from which what is incorrect is to be deleted; multiple SCLEROSIS; ~ ||**shop**, **store**, (with branches in various places). **2.** n. Quantity that contains another some number of times without remainder (*56 is a multiple of 7*; **least**, **lowest**, **common** ~, least quantity that is a multiple of two or more given quantities); **mŭ'ltĭplў**[1] *adv.* [F f. L *multiplus* (foll.)]

**mŭ'ltĭ|plĕx** *a.* Manifold, of many elements; **~plĭcă'nd** *n.*, quantity to be multiplied by multiplier; **~plĭcă'tion** *n.*, multiplying, esp. the arithmetical process (**~plication sign**, ×, as 2×3; **~plication table**, table of products of factors, esp. from 1 to 12, taken in pairs); **~plĭ'cătive** *a.*; **~plĭ'cĭtŷ** *n.*, manifold variety; **a ~plicity** (great number) **of**; **~plĭer** *n.*, (esp.) quantity by which multiplicand is multiplied; **~plŷ**[2] *v.t. & i.*, produce large number of (instances), breed (animals), propagate (plants), increase in number, esp. by procreation, (Math.) obtain from (number, or abs.) another that is a specified number of times its value (*multiply 6 by 4 or 4 by 6 and get 24*). [L (MULTI-, *-plex -plicis* -fold)]

**mŭ'ltĭtūde** *n.* Numerousness, great number (*of*), crowd of people (**the ~**, the common people); **multĭtū'dĭnous** *a.*, very numerous, consisting of many individuals. [F f. L]

**multum in parvo** (mŏŏltum ĭn pãr'vō, mŭ'-) *n.* Much in small compass. [L, = much in little]

**mŭm**[1] *int., a., & v.* **1.** *int.* (colloq.) Silence! (esp. *mum's the word*). **2.** *a.* (colloq.) Silent (*keep mum*). **3.** *v.i.* (**-mm-**). Act in dumb show. [imit.]

‖**mŭm**[2] *n.* (colloq.) = MUMMY[2].

**mŭ'mble. 1.** *v.i. & t.* Speak or utter indistinctly, bite, chew, (as) with toothless gums. **2.** *n.* Indistinct utterance. [MUM[1]]

**mŭmbō-jŭ'mbō** *n.* (*pl.* **~s**). Meaningless ritual; mystifying or obscure language etc., intended to confuse; object of senseless veneration. [name of supposed Afr. idol]

**mŭ'mchance** (-ah-) *a. & adv.* Silent(ly), saying nothing. [orig. = dumb show, f. G (MUM[1], CHANCE)]

**mŭ'mmer** *n.* Actor in traditional dumb show or (arch. sl.) in theatre; **~ў** *n.*, performance by mummers, ridiculous (esp. religious) ceremonial. [F *momeur* (MUM[1])]

**mŭ'mmĭf|ў** *v.t.* Preserve (body) as mummy; **~ĭcă'tion** *n.* [foll.]

**mŭ'mmŷ**[1] *n.* Body of human being or animal embalmed for burial, esp. in ancient Egypt. [F f. L f. Arab. f. Pers. *mūm* wax]

‖**mŭ'mmŷ**[2] *n.* (colloq.) Mother. [imit. of child's pronunc.]

**mŭmps** *n.* Infectious disease with swelling of neck and face. [imit. of mouth-shape]

**mŭnch** *v.t. & i.* Eat (food, or abs.) with marked action of jaws. [imit.]

**Mŭnchau'sen** (-z-) *n.* Extravagantly mendacious story(-teller). [character in book]

**mŭ'ndāne** *a.* Worldly; of this world; of the universe; dull, routine. [F f. L (*mundus* world)]

**mŭnĭ'cĭpal** *a.* (**~ly**). Of or under local self-government or corporate government of city or town; carried on by a municipality (*municipal trading, undertaking*); **mŭnĭcĭpă'lĭtŷ** *n.*, town, district, having local self-government, governing body of this; **~ĭze** *v.t.*, (esp.) bring under municipal control; **~ĭzā'tion** *n.* [L (*municipium* Roman city)]

**mŭnĭ'fĭcen|t** *a.* (Of giver or gift) splendidly generous; **~ce** *n.* [L (*munus* gift, -FIC)]

**mŭ'nĭment** *n.* (usu. in *pl.*) Document kept as evidence of rights or privileges. [F f. L (*munio* fortify)]

**mŭnĭ'tion. 1.** *n.* (in *pl.*) Military weapons, ammunition, equipment, and stores. **2.** *v.t.* Provide with munitions. [F f. L, = fortification (prec.)]

**mūr'al. 1.** *a.* (**~ly**). Of or like a wall; on a wall (*mural paintings*). **2.** *n.* Mural painting etc. [F f. L (*murus* wall)]

**mūr'der. 1.** *n.* Unlawful killing of human being with malice aforethought; (fig.) highly troublesome or dangerous state of affairs; exclamation of alarm (also as *int.*); **~ will out** (cannot be hidden); **cry blue ~**, (sl.) make extravagant outcry; **get away with ~**, (sl.) do whatever one wishes; JUDICIAL *murder*. **2.** *v.t.* Kill (human being) unlawfully with malice aforethought; kill wickedly or inhumanly; (colloq.) utterly defeat, spoil by bad performance, mispronunciation, etc. **3.** **~er**, **~ess**, *ns.*; **~ous** *a.*, (of person, weapon, action, etc.) capable of, bent on, involving, murder. [E]

**mūr'|ex** *n.* (*pl.* **~ices** *pr.* -ĭsēz, **~exes**). Mollusc yielding purple dye. [L]

**mūrk** *n.* Darkness; **~'ў** *a.* (**-ily, -iness**), dark, gloomy, (of darkness) thick, dirty. [Scand.]

**mūr'mur. 1.** *n.* Subdued continuous sound as of waves, brook, etc.; subdued expression of discontent; softly spoken or nearly inarticulate speech. **2.** *v.i.* & *t.* Make murmur; utter (words) softly; complain in low tones. **3.** ~**ous** *a.*, with murmuring sound. [F or L]

**mur̆′phy** *n.* (sl.) Potato. [Ir. surname]

**mŭr′rain** (-rĭn) *n.* Infectious disease in cattle; (arch.) **a** ~ (plague) **on you!** [AF *moryn*]

**mŭs′ca|dĭne** *n.* Musk-flavoured kind of grape; ~**t** *n.*, (wine made from) muscadine; ~**tĕl** *n.*, muscat, raisin from muscadine. [MUSK]

**mŭs′cle** (-sĕl). **1.** *n.* Any of the contractile fibrous bands or bundles that produce movement in animal body (**not move a** ~, be perfectly motionless); that part of the animal body which is composed of muscles, chief constituent of flesh; (muscular) power; ~**-bound**, with muscles stiff and inelastic through excessive exercise or training; ~**-man**, man with highly-developed muscles, esp. as intimidator). **2.** *v.i.* (sl.) ~ (**in**), intrude by violent means. [F f. L dim. of *mus* mouse]

**Mŭs′cov|ite** *n.* & *a.* (arch.) Russian; (citizen) of Moscow; ~**ў** *n.*, (arch.) Russia; ~**y duck**, MUSK-duck. [L (*Moscow*)]

**mŭs′cŭlar** *a.* Of or affecting muscle(s); having well-developed muscles; *muscular* DYSTROPHY; **mŭs̆culā′rĭtў** *n.* [MUSCLE]

**mūse**[1] (-z) *v.i.* & *t.* (literary). Ponder, meditate, (*on*, *upon*); say meditatively. [F]

**mūse**[2] (-z) *n.* The M~s, (Gk & Rom. Myth.) nine sister goddesses, inspirers of poetry, music, drama, etc.; **the** ~, poet's inspiring genius; **mūsē′um** (-z-) *n.*, building used for storing and exhibition of objects illustrating antiquities, natural history, arts, etc., (~**um piece**, specimen of art, manufacture, etc., fit for a museum, old-fashioned person or machine etc.). [F or L f. Gk *mousa*]

**mŭsh**[1] *n.* Soft pulp; \*maize porridge; feeble sentimentality; ~**ў** *a.* (-**ily**, -**iness**). [app. var. MASH]

**mŭsh**[2] *n.*, & *v.i.* (N. Amer.) (Go on) journey across snow with dog-sledge; (in *imper.* as command to sledge-dogs) get moving. [prob. corrupt. F *marchons* (MARCH[2])]

**mŭ′shröom** (*or* -ŏŏm). **1.** *n.* Edible fungus with stem and domed cap proverbial for rapid growth (~ **growth** etc., sudden development, thing suddenly developed); (fig.) upstart; ~ (**cloud**), cloud of mushroom shape, esp. from nuclear explosion. **2.** *v.i.* Gather mushrooms; spring up rapidly; expand and flatten like a mushroom cap. [F *mousseron* f. L]

**mū′sĭc** (-z-) *n.* Art of combining sounds of voice(s) or instrument(s) to achieve beauty of form and expression of emotion; sounds so produced; pleasant sound, e.g. song of bird, murmur of brook, etc. (~ **to one's ears**, something very pleasant to hear); (written or printed score of) musical composition(s); ‖~**-hall**, (place for) singing, dancing, variety entertainment, etc.; *music of the* SPHERES; ~**-paper** (with printed staves for writing music-score); ~**-stool** (with adjustable height of seat, for pianist); **face the** ~, face one's critics etc., not shirk consequences; **rough** ~, noisy uproar, esp. with vexatious intention; SET[1] (poem etc.) *to music*; ~**al**, (*a.*; -**lly**) of music, (of sound etc.) melodious or harmonious, fond of or skilled in music, set to or accompanied by music, (‖~**al box**, instrument that plays certain tunes mechanically; ~**al chairs**, a boisterous party game in which players are eliminated through failing to find seats when music stops; ~**al comedy**, light dramatic entertainment with songs; ~**al film**, in which music is important feature; *musical* INSTRUMENT; ~**al saw**, bent saw played with violin bow; ~**al sound**, produced by continuous regular vibrations), (*n.*) musical film or comedy; ~**ian** (-ĭ′shan) *n.*, person skilled in science or practice of music; ~**ŏ′logў** *n.*, study of music other than that directed to proficiency in performance or composition; ~**olŏ′gĭcal** *a.*; ~**ŏ′logĭst** *n.* [F f. L f. Gk (MUSE[2])]

**mŭsk** *n.* Substance secreted by male musk-deer used as basis of perfumes; plant (formerly) with musky smell; ~**-deer**, small hornless ruminant of Central Asia; ~**-duck** (with slight smell of musk); ~**-melon**, common yellow melon; ~**-ox**, shaggy ruminant with curved horns; ~**-rat**, (fur of) large N. Amer. aquatic rodent with musky smell; ~**-rose**, rambling rose with musky fragrance; ~'ў̆ a. (-ily, -iness), smelling like musk. [L *muscus* f. Pers.]

**mŭ′skĕt** n. (Hist.) Infantryman's (esp. smooth-bored) light gun; **~eer′** n., soldier armed with musket; **~rў̆** n., (art of using rifles or) muskets, troops armed with muskets. [F f. It. *moschetto* crossbow bolt]

**Mŭ′slĭm** (or mŏŏ′-), **Mŏ′slĕm**, (or -z-) a. & n. Believer in Islam; Muhammadan. [Arab. (ISLAM)]

**mŭ′slĭn** (-z-) n. Fine delicately woven cotton fabric. [F f. It. (*Mussolo* Mosul, place)]

**mŭ′squash** (-ŏsh) n. (Fur of) musk-rat. [Algonquian]

**\*mŭss.** (colloq.) **1.** v.t. ~ (**up**), throw into disorder, disarrange. **2.** n. Untidiness, mess; **~'ў̆** a. [MESS]

**mŭ′ssel** n. Edible bivalve mollusc. [E (MUSCLE)]

**mŭst**[1] n. Grape-juice before end of fermentation; new wine. [E f. L]

**mŭst**[2] (*unemphat.* mŭst). **1.** v.aux. (*pres.* & *past* **must**, neg. **must not**, colloq. **mustn't** pr. mŭ′sent; no other parts used). Be obliged to (do) (*you must find it*, opp. *you do not have to* or *need not find it*, past *you had to find it*; *you knew you must find it*; *it must be found*; *you must not do it*, opp. *you may do it*; *it must not be done*); (interrog., iron.) *must you slam the door?*; (ellipt.) *I must* (go) *away*, *if I will*; *ought to* (do) (w. necessity less emphasized: *we must see what can be done*; *I must ask you to retract that*; *you ~ know*, *I now tell you*; *I ~ say*, cannot refrain from saying); be certain to (do) (*you must lose whatever happens*, opp. *you cannot lose*; *you ~ be* (surely are) *aware of this*, *joking, the secretary*); (w. ref. to perverse destiny *just as I was busiest he must come worrying*; **~ have** done, surely did or has done (*you must have known what I meant*; *it must have stopped raining*); *must* NEEDS. **2.** n. (colloq.) Thing that cannot or should not be overlooked or missed. [E]

**\*mustache.** See MOUSTACHE.

**mŭ′stăng** n. Wild horse of Mexico etc. [Sp.]

**mŭ′stard** n. Plant with yellow flowers, seeds of which are ground and made into paste with water (‖**English ~**) or vinegar (‖**French ~**) and used as condiment esp. with meat; \*(sl.) thing that provides zest; **~ and cress** (used as seedlings for

salad); **~ gas**, colourless oily liquid whose vapour is a powerful irritant; **~ plaster** (containing mustard, applied to the skin as poultice); **~-pot** (for table mustard); KEEN *as mustard*. [F f. Rom. (MUST[1])]

**mŭ′ster. 1.** n. Assembling of persons for inspection etc. (**pass ~**, be accepted as adequate); **~-roll**, official list of officers and men. **2.** v.t. & i. Collect (orig. soldiers) for inspection, to check numbers, etc.; get together; ~ (**up**), summon (courage, strength, etc.). [F f. L (*monstro* show)]

**mŭ′stў̆** a. (-ily, -iness). Mouldy, stale, (fig.) antiquated. [perh. alt. *moisty* (MOIST)]

**mŭ′t|able** a. (**~ably**). Liable to change; fickle; **~abi′lĭtў̆** n.; **~ant** a. & n., (form) resulting from mutation; **~ā′te** v.t. & i., (cause to) undergo mutation; **~ā′tion** n., change, alteration, (Biol.) genetic change which when transmitted to offspring gives rise to heritable variation, (Gram.) umlaut; *mutatis mutandis* (mōōtahtĭs mōōtǎ′ndĭs) adv., with due alteration of details (in comparing cases). [L (*muto* change)]

**mūte** a., n., & v. **1.** a. Silent; not emitting articulate sound; (of person or animal) dumb; not expressed in speech (*mute appeal*, *adoration*); temporarily bereft of speech; (of letter) silent; ~ (common white) **swan. 2.** n. Mute consonant; dumb person (DEAF *mute*); actor whose part is in dumb show; hired mourner; clamp on bridge for deadening resonance of strings of violin etc., pad or cone for deadening sound of wind instrument. **3.** v.t. Deaden, muffle, sound of (esp. musical instrument); tone down, (in *p.p.*) subdued. [F f. L *mutus*]

**mŭ′tĭl|āte** v.t. Deprive (person etc.) of limb or organ; destroy use of (limb etc.); render (book etc.) imperfect by excision etc.; **~ā′tion**, **~ātor**, ns. [L (*mutilus* maimed)]

**mŭ′tĭn|ў̆. 1.** n. Open revolt against authority, esp. by soldiers etc. against officers. **2.** v.i. Revolt, engage in mutiny, (*against*, or abs.). **3. ~eer′** n., one who mutinies; **~ous** a., rebellious. [F f. Rom. (MOVE)]

**mŭtt** n. (sl.) Ignorant, stupid, or blundering person; (derog.) dog. [abbr. *mutton-head*]

**mŭ′tter. 1.** v.i. & t. Speak low in

barely audible manner; murmur, grumble, (against, at); utter (words etc.) in low tone; (fig.) say in secret. **2.** n. Muttering; muttered words. [rel. to MUTE]

**mŭ′tton** n. Flesh of sheep as food; (joc.) sheep (**return to** one's ∼**s**, [after F phr.] come back to one's main topic); ∼ **chop**, piece of rib or loin of mutton, usu. served fried or grilled (∼-chop whiskers, short bushy whiskers shaped like mutton chop); ∼**head,** (colloq.) dull, stupid person; **dead as** ∼, quite dead; LEG of mutton; ∼**y** a. [F f. L multo sheep]

**mū′tŭal** a. (∼ly). (Of feeling, action, etc.) felt, done, by each to-(wards) the other, standing in (specified) relation to each other, (mutual affection, suspicion, well-wishers); (colloq.) common to two or more persons (mutual friend, travels); ∼**ĭtў** (-ă′l-) n. [F f. L mutuus borrowed]

**mŭ′zzle. 1.** n. Projecting part of animal's head including nose and mouth; open end of firearm; contrivance of strap or wire etc. put over animal's head to prevent its biting, eating, etc.; ∼**loader,** gun that is loaded through the muzzle. **2.** v.t. Put muzzle on (animal, its mouth, or fig. person); impose silence on. [F musel f. L musum]

**mŭ′zz|ў** a. (∼ily, ∼iness). Dull, spiritless; mentally hazy; stupid from liquor-drinking. [orig. unkn.]

‖**M.V.O.** abbr. Member of the Royal Victorian Order.

**MW** abbr. megawatt(s).

**mў** poss. pron. attrib. Of me (in pred. & abs. use, & arch. bef. vowel, MINE[1]; for phrs. see HER); (in affectionate, sympathetic, jocular, or patronizing use, prefixed to some wds in voc.) my boy, child, dear (fellow), friend, man; (in excl. of surprise) my!, oh my!, my GOD!, my WORD!, etc.; my LADY, LORD. [MINE[1]]

**mў′all** n. Australian acacia. [Aboriginal]

**mўcŏ′log|ў** n. Study of fungi; ∼**ĭst** n. [Gk mukēs mushroom]

**myna(h).** See MINA.

**mў′ōpe** n. Short-sighted person.

**mў̄ō′pia** n., short-sightedness (lit. or fig.); **mў̄ŏ′pĭc** a. [F f. L f. Gk (muō shut, ōps eye)]

**mў′rĭad** a. & n. (poet., rhet.) Ten thousand; (of) indefinitely great number. [L f. Gk (murioi 10,000)]

**myr′mĭdon** (mẽr′-) n. Hired ruffian, base servant (∼ **of the law,** policeman, bailiff, etc.). [L f. Gk Murmidones followers of Achilles]

**myrrh** (mẽr) n. Gum resin used in perfumes, medicine, and incense. [E f. L myrrha f. Gk]

**myr′tle** (mẽr′-) n. Kind of plant, esp. **common** ∼, a shiny-leaved evergreen shrub with white scented flowers. [L f. Gk murtos]

**mўsĕ′lf** pron., emphat. & refl. form of I[2], ME[1], (for use cf. HERSELF). [E (ME[1], SELF)]

**mў′ster|ў**[1] n. Hidden or inexplicable matter (**make a** ∼ **of,** treat as impressive secret); secrecy, obscurity, (is wrapped in mystery); (practice of) making a secret of (unimportant) things; religious truth divinely revealed, esp. one beyond human reason; religious rite, esp. (in pl.) Eucharist; (in pl.) secret religious rites of Greeks, Romans, etc.; miracle play; ∼ (**novel, play,** etc.), fictional work with puzzling crime etc.; ∼ **tour, trip,** pleasure excursion to unspecified destination; **mўstē̆r′ious** a., full of, wrapped in, mystery, (of person) delighting in mystery. [F or L f. Gk mustērion (MYSTIC)]

**mў′ster|ў**[2] n. (arch.) Handicraft, trade, esp. (in indentures) art and mystery. [L ministerium MINISTRY]

**mў′st|ĭc. 1.** a. (∼ically). Spiritually allegorical or symbolic; occult, esoteric; of hidden meaning, mysterious; mysterious and awe-inspiring. **2.** n. One who seeks by contemplation and self-surrender to obtain union with or absorption into the Deity, or who believes in spiritual apprehension of truths beyond the understanding. **3.** ∼**ĭcal** a. (-lly), of mystics or mysticism, having direct spiritual significance; ∼**ĭcism** n.; ∼**ĭfў** v.t., hoax, bewilder, wrap up in mystery; ∼**ĭfĭcā′tion** n. [F or L f. Gk (mustēs initiated person)]

**mўsti′que** (-tē′k) n. Atmosphere of mystery and veneration investing some creeds, doctrines, arts, etc., or personages; any professional skill or technique which mystifies and impresses the layman. [F (MYSTIC)]

**myth** n. Traditional narrative usu. involving supernatural or fancied persons etc. and embodying popular ideas on natural or social phenomena etc.; allegory (*Platonic myth*); fictitious person or thing or idea; **~'ic** *a.* (**-ically**), (esp.) of or in primitive myths; **~ical** *a.* (**-lly**), (esp.) imaginary; **mȳthŏ'logȳ** *n.*, body of myths, study of myths; **mȳthŏlŏ'gĭcal** *a.* (**-lly**); **mȳthŏ'logĭst** *n.* [L f. Gk *muthos*]

**mȳxomatō'sĭs** (*or* -ōm-) *n.* Virus disease in rabbits. [Gk *muxa* mucus]

# N

**N, n,** (ĕn) *n.* (*pl.* **Ns, N's**). Fourteenth letter; (Print.) en; (Math.) indefinite number (**to the nth degree**, fig., to the utmost).

**N.** *abbr.* (chess) knight; New; newton(s); North(ern).

**n.** *abbr.* name; neuter; note.

**N** *symb.* nitrogen.

**Na** *symb.* sodium. [L *natrium*]

‖**N.A.A.F.I.** (nā'fĭ) *abbr.* Navy, Army, and Air Force Institutes (canteen for servicemen).

**năb** *v.t.* (sl.; **-bb-**). Apprehend, arrest; catch in wrongdoing. [orig. unkn.]

**nā'bŏb** *n.* (Hist.) Muslim official or governor under Mogul empire; (arch.) wealthy luxury-loving person esp. one who has returned from India with fortune. [Port. or Sp. f. Urdu (NAWAB)]

**năce'lle** *n.* Outer casing of aeroplane's engine; car of airship. [F f. L, = little ship]

**nā'cre** (-ker) *n.* (Shellfish yielding) mother-of-pearl; **nā'cr(e)ous** *adjs.* [F]

**nā'dir** (*or* -ēr) *n.* Point of heavens directly under observer (opp. ZENITH); (fig.) lowest point, state or time of greatest depression etc. [F f. Arab., = opposite]

**nae'v|us, *n̄e'v|us,** *n.* (*pl.* ~i *pr.* -ī). Red birthmark formed of blood-vessels of skin; = MOLE¹. [L]

**năg¹** *n.* (colloq.) (Esp. riding-) horse. [orig. unkn.]

**năg²** *v.i.* & *t.* (**-gg-**). Indulge in wearisome fault-finding (*at* person); worry (person) thus; (of pain etc.) be persistent. [dial.]

**Nah.** *abbr.* Nahum (O.T.).

**nai'ad** (nī'-) *n.* (*pl.* ~s, ~es *pr.* -ēz). Water-nymph. [L f. Gk]

*naïf* (nahē'f) *a.* = NAÏVE. [F masc. a.]

**nail. 1.** *n.* Horny covering of upper surface of tip of finger or toe (**bite** one's ~s, as habit, or in impatience, frustration, or anxiety); small metal spike hammered in to hold things together or serve as peg or ornament (**hard as ~s**, in good physical condition, callous; HIT the (*right*) **nail on** *the head*; ~ **in** person's **coffin**, thing hastening his death; **on the ~**, without delay, esp. of payment). **2.** *v.t.* Fasten with nail(s) (*nail* one's COLOURS *to the mast*); ~ (**to the counter, to the barn door**), expose as spurious or vile; fix or keep fixed (person, attention, etc.); secure, catch, get hold of, (person, thing); ~ **down**, bind (person *to* promise etc.), define precisely. [E]

**nai'nsŏŏk** *n.* Fine cotton fabric, orig. Indian. [Hindi]

**naïve** (nahē'v, nīē'v), **naive** (nāv), *a.* Artless, unaffected; amusingly simple; **naï'vetȳ** (nahē'vtĭ, nī-), **nai'vetȳ** (nā'vetĭ), **naïveté** (nahē'v-tā), *n.*, state or quality of being naïve, naïve action. [F fem. a. f. L *nativus* NATIVE]

**nā'kĕd** *a.* Unclothed, nude; defenceless, (of sword etc.) unsheathed, undisguised (*naked truth*), exposed, unprotected (*naked flame*); without trees, leaves, hair, etc.; without ornament or addition; **the ~ eye** (without telescope, microscope, etc.). [E]

‖**N.A.L.G.O.** (nă'lgō) *abbr.* National and Local Government Officers' Association.

**nămbȳ-pă'mbȳ** *a.* & *n.* Insipidly pretty, weakly sentimental (behaviour, style, or person). [derog. form. on name of *Ambrose* Philips]

**nāme. 1.** *n.* Word by which individual person, animal, place, or thing is spoken of or to (**by ~**, **by** or **of the ~ of**, called; **have to** one's ~, possess; **in ——'s ~**, **in the ~ of**, invoking: *in God's name*, as representing: *promised it in the King's name*;

KNOW *by name*; TAKE *person's name*; ~**-day**, day of saint after whom person is named; ~**-dropping**, familiar mention of names of the famous as form of boasting; ~**-plate**, affixed with name of occupant etc.; **the ~ of the game**, colloq., purpose or essence of action etc.; **what's in a ~?**, names are arbitrary labels); word denoting object of thought, esp. one applicable to many individuals (**call** person ~**s**, speak abusively to him); person as known, famed, etc., (*many great names were there*); family, clan; reputation (*a good name*; *has a name for honesty*; **make a ~ for** oneself, become famous); **in ~ only**, not in reality. **2.** *v.t.* (~**able** *pr.* -ma-). Give name to (AFTER, *for*), call by right name; nominate, appoint; mention, specify, cite, (~ ~**s**, mention specific persons' names, esp. in accusation; ~ **the day**, fix date, esp. of wedding; **you ~ it**, colloq., no matter what). **3.** ~'**less** (-ml-) *a.*, obscure, inglorious, left unnamed (*persons who shall be nameless*), anonymous, inexpressible, unmentionable, loathsome (*nameless vices*); ~'**ly** (-mlǐ) *adv.*, that is to say, in other words; ~**sake** (-ms-) *n.*, person or thing with same name as another (*his namesake*; *we are namesakes*) [prob. orig. *for the name's sake*]. [E]

**nă'ncy̌** *n.* & *a.* (sl.) Effeminate (man or boy); homosexual (male). [woman's name, pet-form of *Ann*]

**nănkee'n** *n.* Yellow cotton cloth; colour of this. [place]

**nă'nny̌** *n.* Child's nurse; ~(-**goat**), female goat. [NANCY]

**năp¹. 1.** *v.i.* (-**pp**-). Take short sleep esp. out of bed or by day (**catch** ~**ping**, take unawares, find remiss). **2.** *n.* Spell of such sleep. [E]

**năp²** *n.* Surface of cloth consisting of fibre-ends raised, cut even, and smoothed. [LDu.]

**năp³. 1.** *n.* A card game (**go** ~, take highest risk in this, also fig.); racing tip claimed to be almost a certainty. **2.** *v.t.* (-**pp**-). Name (horse) as almost certain winner. [*Napoleon*]

**nă'palm** (-ahm). **1.** *n.* Thickening agent made from naphthalene and coconut oil; jellied petrol made from this, used in bombs. **2.** *v.t.* Attack with napalm bombs. [NA(PHTHALENE), PALM]

**nāpe** *n.* Back *of the neck*. [orig. unkn.]

**nă'phth|a** *n.* Inflammable oil distilled from coal etc.; ~**alene** *n.*, white crystalline substance got in distilling coal-tar. [L f. Gk]

**nă'pkin** *n.* Piece of linen etc. for wiping lips etc. at table (*table-napkin*); ~**-ring**, to hold and distinguish person's napkin); ||**nappy**. [F *nappe* f. L *mappa* (MAP) + -KIN]

||**nă'pper** *n.* (sl.). The head. [orig. unkn.]

||**nă'ppy̌** *n.* Piece of absorbent material wrapped round waist and between legs of baby. [NAPKIN]

**nàrcī'ss|ĭsm** *n.* Morbid self-love or self-admiration; ~**ĭ'stĭc** *a.* [*Narkissos*, Gk youth who pined away from love of his own reflected image]

**nàrcī'ss|us** *n.* (*pl.* ~**i** *pr.* -ī, ~**uses**). Kind of flowering bulb including daffodil. [L f. Gk]

**nàrcŏ'tĭc. 1.** *a.* (~**ally**). Inducing drowsiness, sleep, stupor, or insensibility; of narcosis. **2.** *n.* Narcotic drug or influence. **3.** **nàrcŏ'sĭs** *n.*, narcotic action, insensible state; **nàr'cotize** *v.t.*, subject to narcotics. [F or L f. Gk *narkē* numbness)]

**nàrd** *n.* (Plant yielding) SPIKENARD. [L f. Gk]

||**nàrk.** (sl.) **1.** *n.* Police decoy or spy. **2.** *v.t.* Annoy, infuriate; ~ **it**, (imper.) stop that. [Romany *nāk* nose]

**nàrr|ā'te** *v.t.* Recount, tell facts of, relate as story, (abs.) employ narrative; ~**ā'tion**, ~**ā'tor**, *ns.*; **nă'rrative**, (*n.*) spoken or written recital of connected events in order, (*a.*) of, by, narration. [L *narro*]

**nă'rrow** (-ō) *a.*, *n.*, & *v.* **1.** *a.* (~**er**, ~**est**). Of small width in proportion to length (||~ **boat**, canal boat; ||~ **seas**, English Channel and Irish Sea); not broad, confined or confining, (lit. or fig., *in the narrowest sense*; *within narrow bounds*); careful, exact, (*examine it narrowly*); with little margin (*a narrow majority*, *escape*); ~(**-mi'nded**), illiberal, prejudiced, exclusive, self-centred. **2.** *n.* (usu. in *pl.*) Narrow part of a sound, strait, river, pass, or street. **3.** *v.i.* & *t.* Make or become narrower, lessen, contract. [E]

**nàr'whal** *n.* Arctic cetacean with tusk(s) developed into horn(s). [Du. f. Da.]

**nā'sal** (-z-). **1.** *a.* (~**ly**). Of the nose (~ **organ**, joc., nose); (of letter or sound) pronounced with nose passage open, as are *m, n, ng,* and F *en, un*; (of voice or speech) having many nasal sounds. 2. *n.* Nasal letter or sound. 3. **nasă′lĭtў** (-z-) *n.*; **~ize** (-z-) *v.i.* & *t.*, speak nasally, give nasal sound to. [F or L (*nasus* nose)]

**nă′scen|t** *a.* In process of birth, incipient, not mature; **~cў** *n.* [L (NATAL)]

**nastūr′tium** (-shŭm) *n.* Trailing garden plant with bright orange, yellow, or red flowers. [L]

**na′stў** (-ah′-) *a.* (-ily, -iness). Repulsively dirty; obscene, indecent; disagreeable to smell or taste, unpalatable (lit. or fig.); annoying, objectionable, (**~ piece of work**, colloq., unpleasant or contemptible person); (of weather etc.) foul, wet, stormy; hard to deal with or get rid of (*nasty sea, fence, blow, illness*; **a ~ one**, snub, disabling blow etc.); ill--natured, spiteful *to.* [orig. unkn.]

**Nat.** *abbr.* National(ist); Natural.

**nā′tal** *a.* (**~ly**). Of birth (one's *natal day*); **nată′lĭtў** *n.*, birth rate. [L *natalis* (*nascor nat-* be born)]

**natā′tion** *n.* (literary) Swimming; **nātatŏr′ial, nā′tatorў,** *adjs.* [L (*nato* swim)]

**nā′tion** *n.* A people or race distinguished by community of descent, language, history, or political institutions; **law of ~s**, international law; **most favoured ~** (to which State accords lowest scale of import duties); UNITED *Nations*; **~-wide**, extending over whole nation; **~-hŏŏd** *n.* [F f. L (NATAL)]

**nă′tional.** 1. *a.* (**~ly**). Of a or the, characteristic of a whole, nation (**~ anthem**, song adopted by nation to express patriotism or loyalty, e.g. 'God save the Queen'; ‖N**~ Assistance**, (former official name for) supplementary benefits under National Insurance; *National* DEBT; ‖**~ grid**, network of high-voltage electric power-lines between major power-stations, metric system of geographical co-ordinates used in maps of British Isles; \*N**~ Guard**, primary reserve force partly maintained by the states but available for federal use; ‖N**~ Health Service**, system of national medical service financed by taxation (1948–); ‖N**~ Insurance**, system of compulsory contribution from employee and employer to provide State assistance in sickness, unemployment, retirement, etc.; **~ park**, area of countryside under State supervision to preserve amenities; ‖**~ service**, service by conscription in armed forces; ‖N**~ Trust**, private body for preserving historic or beautiful places. 2. *n.* Citizen of specified country; one's fellow countryman (*consul's powers over his own nationals*); ‖(N**~**) = GRAND[1] *National*. 3. **~ism** *n.*, patriotic feeling, principles, or efforts, policy of national independence; **~ist** *n.*; **~ĭtў** (-ă′l-) *n.*, being national, distinctive national qualities, membership of a nation (*what is her nationality?*), race forming part of one or more political nations; **~ize** *v.t.*, make national, convert (land, railways, firm, industry, etc.) into national property; **~izā′tion** *n.* [F (prec.)]

**nā′tive.** 1. *a.* Inborn, innate, natural *to*, (*his native modesty, genius*); of one's birth, belonging to one by right of birth, (*native land; their native customs*); born in a place (esp. of non--Europeans), indigenous, of the natives of a place; (of metal etc.) found in pure or uncombined state; **go ~**, adopt (less civilized) mode of life of natives where one lives. 2. *n.* One born in a place (*a native of Scotland*); member of non-European or less civilized people; (S. Afr.) Black; indigenous animal or plant; British-reared oyster. 3. **natĭ′vĭtў** *n.*, (festival of) birth of Christ, the Virgin Mary, or St. John the Baptist, picture of the Nativity of Christ, (Astrol.) horoscope. [L (NATAL)]

**N.A.T.O., Nato,** (nā′tō) *abbr.* North Atlantic Treaty Organization.

**nā′tron** *n.* Native sodium carbonate. [F f. Sp. f. Arab. f. Gk (NITRE)]

‖**NATSOPA** (nătsō′pa) *abbr.* National Society of Operative Printers, Graphical & Media Personnel.

**nă′tter.** (colloq.) 1. *v.i.* Chatter idly, grumble. 2. *n.* Aimless chatter; grumbling talk. 3. **~jăck** *n.*, a small toad. [imit., orig. dial.]

**nă′tt|ў** *a.* (**~ily, ~iness**). Spruce, trim; deft. [cf. NEAT[2]]

**nă′tural** (-cher-). 1. *a.* Of, concerned with, according to, provided by, nature (*natural habitat, resources*;

*natural* GAS; ~ **history**, study esp. of animal or vegetable life, collection of facts about natural objects of a place or characteristics of a class of objects etc.; ~ **note**, Mus., not sharp or flat, so *B natural* etc.; ~ **philosophy**, arch., physics; ~ **religion**, based on reason not revelation; *natural* SCIENCE; ~ **selection**, process favouring survival of organisms best adapted to their environment; *natural* YEAR); physically existing (~ **law**, = LAW *of nature*; one's ~ **life**, duration of one's life on earth); normal, conforming to ordinary course of nature, not artificial, (~ **death**, by age or disease, not violence, accident, etc.; *natural* MAGIC); innate, instinctive, (*natural justice*); unaffected, easy-mannered; not surprising, to be expected, (*a natural mistake; the natural consequence*); spontaneous or easy to (*comes natural to him*); related by nature only, illegitimate, (*natural son*). 2. *n.* Half--witted person; person naturally endowed (*for* a role, activity, etc.), thing by nature suitable (*for* purpose etc.); pale fawn colour; (Mus.) natural note, sign denoting it. 3. ~**ĭsm** *n.*, action, morality, religion, philosophy, based on nature alone, adherence to nature in art and literature; ~**ĭst** *n.*, adherent of naturalism, student of animals or plants; ~**ĭs′tĭc** *a.* (-ically); ~**īze** *v.t.*, admit (alien) to citizenship, adopt or introduce (foreign word, custom, animal, plant), free from conventions; ~**īzā′tion** *n.*; ~**lў** *adv.*, (esp.) of course, as might be expected. [F f. L (foll.)]

**nā′ture** *n.* Thing's essential qualities (**by, from, in, the ~ of the case, of things**, inevitably); person's or animal's innate character (*it is not* (*in*) *her nature to act like that*; **by** ~, innately; so **-nā′tured** (-cherd) *a.*, as ILL-*natured*); (**human**) ~, general characteristics and feelings of mankind (TOUCH *of nature*); **against** ~, unnatural, immoral); kind, sort, class, (*things of this nature*; **in, of, the nature of a command**); vital force, functions, or needs, (*this diet will not support nature*; CALL *of nature*); physical power causing phenomena of material world, these phenomena as a whole (N~, these personified; *all nature looks gay*; *Nature is the best physician*); **against, contrary to,** ~,

miraculous(ly); **back to** ~, returning to supposedly natural conditions of living; DEBT *of nature*; FROM *nature*; LAW *of nature*; **one of N~'s,** a natural member of the class of *gentlemen* etc.; **state of** ~, unregenerate condition, condition of man before society is organized, uncultivated state of plants or animals, bodily nakedness; ~ **cure** (by seeking to aid natural recovery); ~ **trail**, path through woods etc. planned to show interesting natural objects. [F f. L *natura* (as NATAL)]

**naught** (nawt). 1. *n.* (arch.) Nothing, NOUGHT; **come to** ~, be ruined or baffled; **set at** ~, despise. 2. *pred. a.* (arch.) Worthless, useless. 3. ~**ў** *a.* (-ily, -iness), (of child etc.) ill-behaved, disobedient, wicked, indecent. [E (NO[1], WIGHT)]

**nau′sė|a** (*or* -z-, -sha) *n.* Inclination to vomit; loathing; ~**āte** *v.t.* & *i.*, disgust, loathe, feel nausea (*at*); ~**ous** *a.*, loathsome. [L f. Gk (*naus* ship)]

**nautch** *n.* Performance of Indian dancing-girls (~**-girl**, one of these). [Hindi]

**nau′tĭcal** *a.* (~**ly**). Of sailors or navigation; *nautical* MILE. [F *nautique* f. L f. Gk (*nautēs* sailor)]

**nau′tĭlus** *n.* (*pl.* ~**es**, -**li** *pr.* -**i**). Mollusc formerly thought to sail on sea. [L f. Gk (prec.)]

**nā′val** *a.* (~**ly**). Of the or a navy; of warships; of ships (*naval* ARCHITECT). [L (*navis* ship)]

**nāve**[1] *n.* Body of church (apart from choir or chancel, aisles, and transepts). [L (*navis* ship)]

**nāve**[2] *n.* Hub of wheel. [E]

**nā′vel** *n.* Depression on belly left by detachment of umbilical cord (**contemplate** one's ~, indulge in philosophical quietism; ~ **orange**, with navel-like formation on top); central point of anything. [E]

**nā′vĭg|āte** *v.i.* & *t.* Sail (in) ship; sail or steam over, up, down, etc., (sea, river); manage, direct course of, (ship, aircraft, etc.); (in car etc.) assist driver by indicating proper route; ~**able** *a.* (-bly), (of river, sea, etc.) affording passage for ships, seaworthy, (of balloon) steerable; ~**abĭ′lĭtў** *n.*; ~**ā′tion** *n.*, (esp.) methods of determining ship's or aircraft's position and course by geometry and astronomy (~**ation lights**, on ship or aircraft to indicate its position and direction at night); **~ător** n.; ‖**nă'vvy̆** n., & v.i., (work as) labourer excavating for roads, railways, canals, etc. [abbr. of *navigator*]; STEAM navvy. [L *navigo* (as NAVAL)]

**nā'vy̆** n. A State's warships with their crews and organization; officers and men of the navy; (poet.) a fleet; ‖MERCHANT navy; ~ (blue), dark blue as of naval uniforms; ‖N~ List (of officers' names etc.). [F f. L *navia* ship (as NAVAL)]

**nawa'b** (nawah'b, -aw'b) n. Title of nobleman in India (Hist.), or of distinguished Muslim in Pakistan. [Urdu f. Arab. = deputies]

**nay. 1.** adv. No (arch.); or rather, and even, and more than that, (weighty, nay, conclusive). **2.** n. The word 'nay'; **say ~**, refuse, contradict; YEA and nay. [N, = not ever]

**Năzăre'ne** n. & a. (Person) of Nazareth, esp. Christ; (in Jewish or Muslim use) Christian. [L f. Gk]

**Na'zi̇̆** (nah'tsĭ, -zĭ) n. & a. (Member) of German National Socialist Party led orig. by Hitler; **~idom, ~ism,** ns., its doctrines, institutions, etc. [repr. pronunc. of *Nati-* in G *Nationalsozialist*]

**N.B.** abbr. New Brunswick; no ball; *nota bene*.

‖**N.B.G.** abbr. (colloq.) no bloody good.

**N.C.** abbr. North Carolina.

**N.C.B.** abbr. National Coal Board.

**-nce, -ncy̆,** sufs. forming ns. of (instance of) quality (arrogance, fluency, impertinence, protuberance, constancy) or state (expectancy, infancy) or (-nce) action (assistance, penance, reference); cf. -NT. [L]

**N.C.O.** abbr. non-commissioned officer.

**N.D(ak).** abbr. North Dakota.

**n.d.** abbr. no date.

**N.E.** abbr. North-East(ern).

**Ně̆ă'nderthal** (-tahl) a. Of a type of man found in palaeolithic Europe, with retreating forehead and massive brow-ridges. [place]

**neap** a. & n. ~ (**tide**): see TIDE. [E]

**Nē̆apŏ'li̇tan** a. & n. (Native) of Naples; ~ **ice**, ice cream in layers of various colours and flavours. [L f. Gk *Neapolis* Naples]

**near** adv., prep., a., & v. **1.** adv. To, at, a short distance, in(to) closeness in space or time, or fig., (FAR and near); ~ **at hand**, ~ **by**,

not far off; **~'by**, close in position); closely (as near as one can guess; go ~ to do, **come** or **go** ~ (to) doing, nearly do). **2.** prep. Near to in space, time, condition, or semblance (comes near(er) the end; the time draws near Christmas; who comes nearest him in wit?); (in comb.) resembling, intended as substitute for, (near-beer), that is almost (near-hysterical; a near-Communist). **3.** a. (often governing n. in pred. use; so also in compar. & superl.). Closely related (near relation; near and dear), intimate (a near friend); close (to) in place or time (the nearest man; in the near future; the man near(est) you; is nearer (to) us; Near EAST; ~ **miss**, shot only just missing target and having some effect, also fig.; **~-sighted,** short-sighted); (of way) direct; close, narrow, (a near escape, GO[1], resemblance); ~ **thing**, narrow escape); niggardly; (of part of animal, vehicle, ‖road) left [orig. of side from which one mounted, opp. OFF] (near fore leg, ‖near side front wheel). **4.** v.t. & i. Draw near (to), approach. **5.** **~'ly̆** adv., closely (nearly related), almost (not **~ly,** nothing like). [N, orig. = NIGHer]

**neat[1]** n. (arch.) Ox, cow; (collect.) cattle. [E]

**neat[2]** a. (Of alcoholic drink) undiluted; elegantly simple, nicely made or arranged; cleverly phrased, pointed, epigrammatic; cleverly done, deft, dextrous; tidy. [F NET[2] f. L *nitidus* clean]

**neath** prep. (poet.) Beneath. [abbr.]

**Neb(r).** abbr. Nebraska.

**ně'bŭl|a** n. (pl. **~ae, ~as**). Luminous or dark patch in sky made by distant star-cluster or gas or dust; **~ar** a.; **~ous** a., cloudlike, vague, indistinct, turbid. [L, = mist]

**ně'cĕssar|y̆. 1.** a. Indispensable, requisite, that must be done; determined by predestination or natural laws and not by free will, inevitable. **2.** n. Thing without which life cannot be maintained or is unduly harsh; **the ~y,** (sl.) money, action, needed for a purpose (find, provide, do, the necessary). **3. nĕcĕssār'ian** n. & a., = NECESSITARIAN; **nĕcĕssār'ianism** n.; **~ily̆** (or -sĕ'r-) adv. [AF or L (necesse needful)]

**nĕcĕ'ssit|y̆** n. Constraint or compulsion regarded as a law prevailing through material universe and governing all human action (*physical necessity*; **logical** ~y, compulsion to believe that of which the opposite is inconceivable); constraining power of circumstances (**make a virtue of** ~y, take credit for doing what one must; ~y **knows no law,** absolves from any offence; **of** ~y, unavoidably); imperative need (*the necessity of protecting life and property*); indispensable thing; (in *sing.* or *pl.*) poverty, want, pressing need; ~ār′ian n. & a., (person) denying free will and maintaining that all action is determined by causes; ~ār′ianism n.; ~āte v.t., render necessary, involve as condition or accompaniment or result; ~ous a., poor, needy. [F f. L (prec.)]

**neck. 1.** n. Part of body connecting head with shoulders (**break** one's ~, dislocate it, esp. fatally; **get it in the** ~, colloq., suffer heavy blow, be severely reprimanded or punished; ~ **and crop,** headlong, bodily; ~ **and** ~, running level in race; ~ **or nothing,** desperately, staking all on success; **pain in the** ~, colloq., annoying or tiresome person or thing; *risk, save*, one's ~, one's life; STICK[1] one's **neck out; talk through the back of** one's ~, sl., talk foolishly or wildly; **up to** one's ~, colloq., very deeply involved *in*); length of horse's head and neck as measure of its lead in race (*win by a neck*); flesh of animal's neck as food (*neck of lamb*); part of garment around neck; (sl.) impudence; narrow part of anything (*neck of bottle, violin*), esp. connecting two larger parts (~ **of the woods,** colloq., locality). **2.** v.t. & i. (sl.) (Of couples) engage in amorous caresses. **3.** ~′band, part of garment around neck; ~′erchief (-chĭf), square of cloth worn round neck [KERCHIEF]; ~′lace (-lĭs), ornament of precious stones or metal, or beads etc., worn round neck; ~′line, outline of garment-opening at neck; ~′tie, band of material tied round shirt-collar; ~′wear, (Commerc.) collars and ties; ~′let n., ornament or fur garment for neck. [E]

**nĕcr**|**o-** *in comb.* Corpse; ~phi′lĭa, ~o′philĭsm, ~o′philў, ns., morbid (esp. erotic) attraction to corpses; ~o′polĭs n., (esp. ancient) cemetery [Gk *polis* city]; ~ō′sĭs n. (*pl.* ~o′ses *pr.* -ō′sēz),

(Path.) death of piece of bone or tissue; ~ŏ′tĭc a. [Gk (*nekros* corpse)]

**nĕ′cromănc**|**ў** n. Dealings with the dead as means of divination; magic; ~er n., diviner, wizard; **nĕcromă′ntic** a. (-ically). [F f. L f. Gk (*mantis* seer)]

**nĕ′ctar** n. (Gk & Rom. Myth.) drink of the gods; any delicious drink; sweet fluid produced by plants and made into honey by bees; ~ĭne (*or* -ēn) n., downless kind of peach; ~ous a.; ~ў n., plant's nectar-secreting organ. [L f. Gk]

||**N.E.D.C.** *abbr.* National Economic Development Council.

**nĕ′ddў** n. (colloq.) Donkey; ||(N~) = prec. [pet-form of name *Edward*]

**née** (nā) a. Born (used in adding married woman's maiden name after her surname: *Ann Smith, née Jones*). [F, fem. p.p. of *naître* be born]

**need. 1.** n. Circumstances requiring some course of action (*if need arise, be, were; feel the need, there is no need, to do, of doing, or abs.*); requirement, want, (*the need of further securities; my needs are few*; **have** ~ **of,** require); time of difficulty or crisis (*a friend in need; failed him in his need; **at** ~, in time of need*); destitution, poverty. **2.** v.i. & t. Stand in need of, require; be under necessity or obligation to or to do (*it needs to be done with care; need you ask?*); ellipt., *don't be away longer than you need*); (in 3 *sing. pres. neg. or interrog.* need *without to*: *he need not trouble himself; need she have come?*; colloq. *it needn't, doesn't need to, be finished*; ~ **not have done,** did not need to do). **3.** ~′ful a. (-lly), requisite (**the** ~**ful,** sl., money, action, required); ~′less a., unnecessary, uncalled for, (~less to say, parenth., I need not tell you); ~s (-z) adv., (arch.) of necessity; **must** ~s do, (esp.) foolishly insists or insisted on doing; ~′ў a. (-ily, -iness), poor, destitute. [E]

**nee′dle. 1.** n. Thin long round piece of smooth steel etc. pointed at one end and with eye for thread at other used in sewing (~ **in a hay-stack,** elusive concealed thing; ~'s **eye,** tiny aperture, esp. w. ref. to Matt. 19: 24; PINS *and needles*; **sharp as a** ~, lit., or fig. acute, observant); similar instrument without eye used in KNITting, crocheting, etc.; (**magnetic**) ~, indicator of magnetized steel on dial of compass, electric apparatus, etc.; pointed instrument or part of instrument used in etching, surgery, etc.; pointer on dial; pointed end of hypodermic syringe; thin pointed ~piece of metal etc. receiving and transmitting vibrations set up by revolving gramophone record; obelisk (*Cleopatra's Needle*); sharp rock, peak; needle-shaped crystal; leaf of fir or pine; ||(sl.) fit of nervousness, irritation, or bad temper. **2.** *v.t.* Sew, pierce, operate on, with needle; (colloq.) annoy, provoke. **3.** ~**cord**, finely ribbed fabric; ||~ **game, match**, (closely contested or arousing exceptional personal feeling); ~**point**, embroidery on canvas, lace made with needles not bobbins; ~**woman**, seamstress, *good* or *bad* user of sewing-needle; ~**work**, sewing or embroidery. [E]

**nee′dless, needs, nee′dy.** See NEED.

**ne′er** (nār) *adv.* (poet.) never (~ *a*, = NEVER *a*); ~**do-well, -weel**, good-for-nothing (person). [contr.]

**nefār′ious** *a.* Wicked. [L (*nefas* wrong)]

**neg.** *abbr.* negative.

**nega̅′t|e** *v.t.* Nullify, be the negation of; ~**ion** *n.*, denying, negative statement, absence or opposite of something actual or positive, negative or unreal thing. [L *nego* deny]

**ne′gative** *a., n.,* & *v.* **1.** *a.* Expressing or implying denial, prohibition, or refusal, (*negative answer, vote*); lacking, consisting in the lack of, positive attributes; marked by absence of qualities (*negative reaction; test gave a negative result; ~ evidence, instance*, of non-occurrence); (Alg., of quantity) less than zero, to be subtracted from others or from zero (*negative* FEEDBACK; ~ **quantity**, joc., nothing; *negative* SIGN); in direction opposite that regarded as POSITIVE; (Electr.) of, containing, producing, kind of charge carried by electrons (opp. POSITIVE); of opposite nature to thing regarded as positive (*debt is negative interest*); (Photog.) having lights and shades of actual object or scene reversed, or colours replaced by complementary ones. **2.** *n.* Negative statement or word (*it is hard to prove a negative*; *two negatives make an* AFFIRMATIVE; **in the ~**, negative(ly); *the answer is in the ~*, no); (Photog.) developed film etc.

bearing negative image, from which positive pictures are obtained. **3.** *v.t.* Veto, refuse consent to; serve to disprove; contradict (statement); neutralize (effect).

**neǧle̅′ct. 1.** *v.t.* Slight, not pay attention(s) to; leave uncared for; leave undone, be remiss about; omit *to* do or do*ing*. **2.** *n.* Neglecting or being neglected; disregard *of*; negligence. **3.** ~**ful** *a.* (**-lly**); **ne̅′g-ligence** *n.*, lack of proper care (**contributory negligence**, Law, on part of injured person who has failed to take proper precautions against accident), careless or easy indifference in appearance, style, etc.; **ne̅′gligent** *a.*; **ne̅′gligǐble** *a.* (**-bly**), that need not be considered. [L *neglego -ect-*]

**négligé, ne̅′gligee,** (ne̅′glǐzhā) *n.* Woman's informal garment, esp. (*-ee*) dressing-gown of thin fabric. [F, p.p. of *négliger* = prec.]

**nego̅′ti|a̅te** (-shǐ-) *v.i.* & *t.* Confer with a view to finding terms of agreement; arrange (affair), bring about (desired result), by negotiating; get, give, money value for (bill, cheque); deal successfully with (obstacle, difficulty); ~**able** (-sha-) *a.* (**-bly**); ~**a̅′tion, ~a̅tor,** *ns.* [L *negotium* business)]

**Negri′llo̅** *n.* (*pl.* ~**s**). One of dwarf Negro people in Central and S. Africa; **Negri′to̅** (-rē′-) *n.* (*pl.* ~**s**), one of small Negroid people in Malayo-Polynesian region. [Sp. dim. (foll.)]

**Ne̅′gro̅. 1.** *n.* (*pl.* ~**es**; *fem.* **Ne̅′gress**). Member of black-skinned (orig.) African race of mankind. **2.** *a.* Of this race, black-skinned, (*Negro* MINSTREL); occupied by, connected with, Negroes. **3. Ne̅′grǐtude** *n.*, quality of being a Negro, affirmation of the value of Negro culture [F]; **Ne̅′groid** *a.* & *n.* (member) of group having characteristics typical of Negro race (esp. black skin, woolly hair, and flat nose). [Sp. & Port., f. L *niger nigri* black]

**Ne̅′gus¹** *n.* (Hist.) Ruler of Ethiopia. [Amh., = king]

**ne̅′gus²** *n.* Hot sweetened wine and water. [person]

**Neh.** *abbr.* Nehemiah (O.T.).

**neigh** (nā) *v.i.* & *n.* (Utter) cry (as) of horse. [E]

**nei′ghbour, \*-bor,** (nā′ber). **1.** *n.*

Dweller next door, near, in same street or village or district or in adjacent country, (*my neighbour Jones; are next-door neighbours*; our *neighbours across the Channel*), esp. regarded as one who should be friendly (*good, bad, neighbours*) or as deserving help (*duty to one's ~*, to any fellow man); person or thing near or next to another (*my neighbour at dinner*; *falling tree brought down its neighbour*); (*attrib.*) neighbouring. **2.** *v.t. & i.* Adjoin, border on or (*up*)on. **3.** ~**hŏŏd** *n.*, district, people of a district, vicinity of (**in the ~hood of** £*100*, about); ~**lў** *a.* (-**iness**), like a good neighbour, friendly, helpful. [E (NIGH; rel. to BOOR)]

**nei′ther** (nī′dh-, nē′dh-) *adv., conj., a., & pron.* **1.** *adv.* (Introducing word, clause, etc., that is to be negatived equally with following one(s) attached to it by *nor*) not either, not on the one hand, (*neither knowing nor caring*; *would neither come in nor go out*; *neither fish nor flesh nor fowl*; *neither* HERE *nor there*); not either, also not, (*if you do not go, neither shall I*; *he did not go and neither did I*). **2.** *conj.* (arch.) Nor, nor yet, (*I do not know, neither can I guess*). **3.** *a. & pron.* Not either, not the one nor the other, (*neither accusation, neither of the accusations, is true*; *neither of them knows*). [E (NO, WHETHER)]

‖**nĕ′llў** *n.* **Not on your ~**, (sl.) certainly not. [perh. woman's name]

**nĕ′lson** *n.* Wrestling hold in which arm is passed under opponent's arm from behind and the hand applied to his neck. [app. person's name]

**nĕ′matŏde** *n.* Slender unsegmented worm. [Gk *nēma* thread]

*nem. con. abbr. nemine contradicente.*

**Nĕ′mĕsis** *n.* (Goddess of) retributive justice. [Gk]

*nemine* (nĕ′mĭnī, nā′-) *pron.* ~ *contradicente* or *dissentiente* (kŏntrădĭsĕ′ntī, -kĕ′-; dĭsĕntĭĕ′ntī), with no one dissenting. [abl. of L *nemo* nobody]

**nĕō-** *in comb.* New, modern, later, revived; ~**cla′ssic(al)**, of a revival of classical style or treatment in the arts; ~**li′thic**, of later Stone Age [Gk *lithos* stone]; ~**Pla′tonism**, 3rd-c. mixture of Platonic ideas with Oriental mysticism, similar doctrine in later times; **Neozō′ic**, of later period of geological history [Gk *zōion* animal]. [Gk (*neos* new)]

**nĕŏ′log|ĭsm, nĕŏ′log|ў,** *ns.* Word-coining; coined word; ~**ĭst** *n.*; ~**ize** *v.i.* [LOGOS]

**nē′ŏn** *n.* Inert gaseous element found in atmosphere and giving orange-red glow when electricity is passed through it in sealed low-pressure tube, whence its use in lights and illuminated advertisements (*neon light, sign*). [Gk, = new]

**nē′ophўte** *n.* New convert; religious novice; beginner. [L f. Gk (*phuton* plant)]

**nĕ′phew** (or -v-) *n.* Brother's or sister's son. [F *neveu* f. L *nepos*]

**nephr|ĭ′tĭc** *a.* Of or in the kidneys; of or for nephritis; ~**ī′tĭs** *n.*, inflammation of the kidneys. [Gk *nephros* kidney]

*ne plus ultra* (nē plŭs ŭ′ltra, nā plŏŏs ŏŏ′ltrah) *n.* Prohibition of advance; furthest point attained or attainable; acme, culmination. [L, = not further beyond]

**nĕ′pot|ĭsm** *n.* Favouritism to relatives in conferring offices; ~**ĭst** *n.* [F f. It. (*nepote* NEPHEW)]

**Nĕ′pt|ūne** *n.* (Roman god of) the sea; one of farthest planets of solar system; ~**ū′nian** *a. & n.*, of planet Neptune, (Geol.) produced by water action, (person) maintaining aqueous origin of certain rocks. [F or L]

**nēr′ĕĭd** *n.* Sea-nymph; (Zool.) long sea-worm or centipede. [L f. Gk]

**nērve. 1.** *n.* Fibrous connection conveying impulses of sensation and motion between brain or spinal cord or ganglionic organ and some part of body; material constituting these; (in *pl.*) bodily state as conditioned by relation between brain and other parts, disordered state in this respect, exaggerated sensitiveness, nervousness, (**bundle of ~s**, very nervous person; **fit of ~s**, nervous state; **get on** person's **~s**, be source of irritation etc. to him; WAR (of *nerves*); sinew, tendon, (poet.', arch.) (**strain every ~**, do one's utmost); presence of mind, coolness in danger, assurance, (**lose** one's **~**, become timid or irresolute); (colloq.) audacity, impudence, (*he had the nerve, you've got a nerve, to ask for more*); (Bot.) rib of leaf. **2.** *v.t.* Give strength, vigour, or courage, to; brace *oneself* to face danger or suffering. **3.** ~**cell** (transmitting impulses in nerve tissue); ~**centre**, group of closely connected ganglion-cells, (fig.) centre of control; ~ **gas**, poison gas that affects nervous system; ~**racking**, greatly straining the nerves. 4. **nĕr′vāte** *a.*, (Bot.; of leaf) ribbed; ~**′less** (-vl-) *a.*, (esp.) lacking vigour, (of style) diffuse; **nĕr′vous** *a.*, full of nerves, of the nerves, (**nervous system**, nerves and nerve-centres as a whole; CENTRAL *nervous system*), affecting or acting on the nerves (**nervous breakdown**, severe weakness or disorder of nerves), having disordered or delicate nerves, highly strung, timid, (‖nervous of doing, afraid to do), (of style) terse; **nĕr′vy** *a.* (-ily, -iness), nervous, (sl.) cool or confident or trying to the nerves. [L *nervus* sinew, tendon, bowstring]

**nĕ′scien|t** (or **nĕ′shyent**) *a.* & *n.* (Person) not having knowledge (*of*); ~**ce** *n.* [L (*ne*- not, *scio* know)]

**nĕss** *n.* Headland. [E]

**-ness** *suf.* forming *ns.* f. *adjs.*, expr. state or condition (*bitterness, clearness, conceitedness, happiness, redness, up-to-date-ness*), instance of this (*a kindness*), or material in a state (*foulness*); see note on Suffixes, p. ix. [E]

**nĕst. 1.** *n.* Structure, place, made or chosen by bird for laying eggs and sheltering young (FEATHER one's *nest*; **it's an ill bird that fouls its own ~**, one should not speak ill of home; ~**-egg**, real or imitation egg left in nest to induce hen to go on laying there, sum of money kept as reserve or nucleus); animal's or insect's breeding-place or lair; snug retreat, shelter, bed, haunt, fostering-place; brood, swarm; cluster or accumulation of similar objects (~ **of tables**, fitting one under another when not in use). **2.** *v.i.* & *t.* Make or have nest in specified place; set about nest-building; take wild birds' nests or eggs; (of boxes, tables) fit together or one inside another; (in *p.p.*) established (as) in nest. **3.** ~**le** (-sel) *v.i.* & *t.*, settle oneself, be settled, comfortably *down, into,* etc., lie half hidden or embedded, press oneself affectionately (*to, up to, close to,* etc.), push (head etc.) affectionately or snugly *in, into*; ~**ling** (-sl-) *n.*, bird too young to leave nest. [E]

**nĕt¹. 1.** *n.* Meshed fabric of cord, twine, thread, hair, etc.; piece of it used for catching fish, birds, etc., or for protecting fruit, confining hair, dividing or enclosing areas of ground esp. in sports (**the ~s**, wickets in net enclosures for cricket practice); snare. **2.** *v.t.* & *i.* (-tt-). Cover, confine, catch, with net(s); fish (water) with net, set nets in (water); put (ball) in net or goal; make cord etc. into net. **3.** ~**′ball**, game in which ball is to be thrown to fall through high horizontal ring from which net hangs; ~ **curtain** (of fine-meshed material); ~**′work**, (*n.*) arrangement with intersecting lines and interstices, complex system of railways etc., chain of interconnected persons or operations or electrical conductors, group of broadcasting stations connected for simultaneous broadcast of same programme, (*v.t.*) broadcast thus. **4.** ~**′ting** *n.*, netted string or thread or wire, piece of this serving some purpose. [E]

**nĕt². nĕtt. 1.** *a.* Free from deduction, remaining after necessary deductions (*of*), (~ **profit**, actual gain after working expenses have been paid, opp. *gross profit*); (of price) off which discount is not allowed; (of weight) excluding weight of container etc.; (of effect, result, etc.) ultimate, effective. **2.** *v.t.* (-tt-). Gain or yield (sum) as net profit. [F (NEAT²)]

**nĕ′ther** (-dh-) *a.* (arch. or joc.; *superl.* ~**most**). Lower (~ **garments** etc., trousers; ~ **regions, world,** hell, underworld); **N~lander** *n.*, **N~landish** *a.*, (native) of the **N~lands** (-z) *n.*, kingdom of Holland, (Hist.) Low Countries. [E]

**nĕ′tsuke** (-sōōkā) *n.* (*pl.* ~, ~**s**). Carved ornament formerly worn in Japanese dress to suspend articles from belt. [Jap.]

**nĕtt.** See NET²; **nĕ′tting**, see NET¹.

**nĕ′ttle. 1.** *n.* Plant covered with stinging hairs (GRASP *the nettle*; ~**-rash**, skin eruption like nettle-stings); other plant resembling this, esp. DEAD *nettle*. **2.** *v.t.* Sting with nettles; irritate, provoke, annoy. [E]

**neur′|al** (nūr′-) *a.* (-lly). Of the nerves; ~**ă′lgia** (-ă′lja) *n.*, intense intermittent pain in nerves esp. of face and head; ~**ă′lgic** *a.*; ~**ăsthĕ′nia** *n.*, debility of nerves causing fatigue etc.; ~**ăsthĕ′nic** *a.*; ~**i′tis** *n.*, inflammation of nerve(s); ~**ō-comb.** *form*, nerve(s); ~**ŏ′logў** *n.*, scientific study of nerve systems; ~**ŏn, ~ōne,** *n.*, nerve-cell and its appendages; ~**ō′sis** *n.* (*pl.* ~**oses**

*pr.* -ēz), functional derangement due to disorders of nervous system; ~ŏ'tic *a.* (-ically) & *n.*, (person) suffering from neurosis, (colloq.) showing undue adherence to unrealistic idea of things. [Gk *neuron* nerve]

**neu'ter** *a., n.,* & *v.* 1. *a.* (Gram.) (of noun etc.) neither masculine nor feminine; (Bot.) having neither pistils nor stamens; (Entom.) sexually undeveloped. 2. *n.* A neuter word; the neuter gender; sexually undeveloped female insect, esp. bee or ant; castrated animal. 3. *v.t.* Castrate. [F or L]

**neu'tral.** 1. *a.* (~ly). Not helping either of two belligerent States, belonging to a State that thus stands aloof; taking neither side, impartial; indistinct, vague, indeterminate, (~ **tint,** grey or slate colour; *neutral* VOWEL); (of gear) in which engine is disconnected from driven parts; (Chem.) neither acid nor alkaline; (Electr.) neither positive nor negative; (Entom. & Bot.) sexually undeveloped, asexual. 2. *n.* Neutral State or person; subject of neutral State; neutral gear. 3. **neutrǎ'lĭty** *n.;* ~**ize** *v.t.,* make neutral, render ineffective by opposite force or effect, exempt or exclude (place) from sphere of hostilities; ~**īzā'tion** *n.;* **neutrī'nō** (-ē'-) *n.* (*pl.* ~s), elementary particle with zero electric charge and prob. zero mass; **neu'trŏn** *n.,* elementary particle of about same mass as proton but without electric charge. [F, or L *neutralis* of neuter gender (as prec.)]

**Nev.** *abbr.* Nevada.

**nĕ'ver** *adv.* At no time, on no occasion, not ever, (*have never been there*; *never even looked*; *never-ending struggle*; *never before, since, yet*; *it is* ~ **too late to mend,** reformation is always possible; ~, ~ (emphat.); *never say* DIE[2]; NOW *or never*); not at all (*never fear*; *never* MIND); (colloq., expr. surprise or incredulity) surely not, it cannot be that, (*you never left the key in the lock!*; '*He ate the whole turkey.*'—'*Never!*'; I ~ did!, *Well, I* ~!, i.e. heard of such a thing); ~ **a,** not a, no . . . at all; ~ **a one,** none; ~**mor'e,** at no future time; ‖**never- -ne'ver,** (colloq.) hire-purchase; ~ **so,** (in concessive clause) to unlimited extent (*the task is beyond him, though he work never so hard*); ~ **the,**

(w. compar.) = NONE *the*; ~**thele'ss,** for all that, notwithstanding. [E, = not EVER]

*nē'vus. See NAEVUS.

**new.** 1. *a.* Now first made, invented, introduced, known, heard of, experienced, or discovered, (~ **star,** nova; *New* TESTAMENT; ~ **to** *me*, hitherto unknown to); renewed, fresh, further, additional, different, changed, (*a new morality*; *lead a new life*; *my new tailor*; *new* BROOM; ~ **deal,** new and improved arrangement; *New Deal,* U.S. reforms 1932–; **a ~ man,** converted or reformed; ~ **moon,** moon when first seen as crescent after conjunction with sun, time of such appearance; *new* STYLE[2]; TURN *over a new leaf*); (in place-names) discovered or founded later than and named after (**New England,** 6 N.E. states of U.S.; *New Zealand*); later, modern, (derog.) newfangled, advanced in method or doctrine, (freq. preceded by *the* as distinctive epithet: **the ~ mathematics,** using SET[2] theory etc. in elementary teaching; **the ~ poor, rich,** etc., classes recently impoverished, enriched, by social changes etc.; *the New* WORLD); of recent origin, growth, arrival, or manufacture, now first used, not worn or exhausted, (*new bread,* WINE, *clothes, countries*); *pleasures ever new*; *ten new members*; *new* CHUM; ~**'comer,** person lately arrived; ~ **look,** (colloq.) renovated appearance; ~ **potatoes** (earliest of the new crop); ‖~ **town,** established as completely new settlement with government sponsorship; ~ **year,** coming or lately begun year, first few days of year; **New Year's Day, Eve,** 1 Jan., 31 Dec.); ~**'lý** *adv.,* recently, afresh, new-; ~**ly-weds,** recently married couple. 2. *adv.* (usu. new-). Newly, recently, just, (*new-born, -come, -found, -made, -mown*; *new-laid eggs*); afresh, again. [E]

**new'el** *n.* Core of winding stairs; top or bottom post of stair-rail. [F f. L (*nodus* knot)]

**newfǎ'ngled** (-nggeld) *a.* (derog.) Different from the good old fashion, objectionably novel. [= new taken]

**Newfou'ndland** *n.* ~ (**= dog**), (dog of) large breed noted for sagacity and swimming powers. [place]

**news** (-z) *n.pl.* (usu. treated as *sing.*) New or interesting information, fresh events reported, (*have you heard the, this, news?; was in the news last year; that is news to me*; **bad, good, ~**, report of unwelcome, welcome, events etc.; *that is no ~*, already well known; **no ~ is good ~**, absence of information justifies optimism); broadcast report of news; **~′agent**, dealer in newspapers; **~-boy, ~-girl**, (who delivers or sells newspapers); **~ bulletin**, (esp. broadcast) collection of news items; **~′cast(er)**, radio or television broadcast(er) of news reports; **~-letter**, printed informal bulletin of club etc.; **~′monger**, a gossip; **~′paper** (-s-), printed publication usu. daily or weekly containing news, advertisements, correspondence, etc.; **~′print**, paper on which newspapers are printed; **~-reader**, = *newscaster*; **~-reel**, cinema film giving the news of the day; **~-room**, room for newspaper-reading, room where news is prepared for publication or broadcasting; **~-sheet**, simple newspaper; **~-stand**, stall for sale of newspapers; **~ theatre**, cinema showing cartoons and news-reels; **~′worthy**, important or interesting enough to be mentioned as news; **~′ў** *a*. (colloq.; -iness), abounding in news. [NEW]

**newt** *n*. Small tailed amphibian allied to salamander. [*a newt* f. *an ewt* (var. *ewet* EFT)]

**new′ton** *n*. (Phys.) Unit of force, force that, acting for 1 sec. on mass of 1 kg, gives it velocity of 1 metre per sec.; **Newtō′nian** *a*., of Sir Isaac *Newton* or his theories, devised etc. by Newton. [person]

**next** *a., adv., prep., & n*. **1**. *a*. Lying, living, being, nearest (*to; in the next house; the chair next to the fire; next* DOOR; **~ to**, fig., almost: *next to nothing, next to impossible*); soonest come to, first ensuing, immediately following or preceding, nearest in order etc. *to*, (*ask the next person you see; shall return next year, next Friday, on Friday next; she left (the) next day; the Sunday next before Easter; the next town to London in size*; **~-best**, second-best; *next* WORLD). **2**. *adv*. In next place or degree, on next occasion, as next step, (*in the week next ensuing; placed his chair next to hers; when I next see you*); **what(ever) ~?**, can anything beat this for impudence or strangeness? **3**. *prep*. (arch.) Next to. **4**. *n*. Next person or thing (*~ of kin,*

closest living relative; **~ please**, as call for next question, customer, etc.); next letter, issue, etc., (*to be continued in our next*); next year etc. (*the Friday, year,* etc., *after next*). [E, superl. of NIGH]

**ne′xus** *n*. Bond, connection, (**the cash ~**, consisting in money payments). [L *necto nex-* bind]

**NF., Nfld.,** *abbrs*. Newfoundland.

**n.g.** *abbr*. no good.

‖**N.G.A.** *abbr*. National Graphical Association.

**N.H.** *abbr*. New Hampshire.

‖**N.H.S.** *abbr*. National Health Service.

‖**N.I.** *abbr*. Northern Ireland.

**nib** *n*. Split pen-point; (in *pl*.) crushed coffee- or cocoa-beans. [LDu.]

**ni′bble**. **1**. *v.t. & i*. Take small bites at; bite gently or cautiously or playfully (**~ at**, lit., and fig. of dallying with temptation). **2**. *n*. Act of nibbling (esp. by fish); very small amount of food.

**nibs** (-z) *n*. (sl.) **His** etc. **~**, burlesque title based on *His Grace* etc. [orig. cant]

**nice** *a*. Fastidious, of critical taste, punctilious, particular, delicately sensitive, (*must not be too nice about the means; a nice judgement*); needing precision or care or tact, subtle, fine, minute, (*a nice distinction, negotiation, point, question, shade of meaning*); (colloq.) agreeable, attractive, well-flavoured, satisfactory, kind, friendly, considerate, generally commendable, (**~, ~ and,** satisfactor(il)y in respect of specified quality: *car is going nice and fast; it is nice and warm today; a nice stout stick*; **~-looking**, pretty, of engaging appearance; **~ work**, task well done), (iron.) disgraceful (*you've got me into a nice mess*). [orig. = foolish, f. F f. L *nescius* ignorant]

**Nicē′ne** (or nī′-) *a*. Of Nicaea in Bithynia (**~ Creed**, formal statement of Christian belief based on that adopted at Nicene Council of A.D. 325). [L]

**ni′cĕtў** *n*. Precision (**to a ~**, exactly); subtle quality (*a point of great nicety*); minute distinction, unimportant detail. [F (NICE)]

**niche** (or nēsh) *n*. Shallow recess in wall for statue or other ornament; (fig.) place destined or suitable for person's occupation (**~ in the**

**temple of fame**, place among memorable persons). [F f. L *nidus* nest]

**nick¹. 1.** *n.* Notch serving as catch, guide, mark, etc.; (sl.) prison, police station; **in good ~**, (colloq.) in good condition; **in the ~ of time**, at critical or opportune moment. **2.** *v.t.* Make nick(s) in, indent; ‖(sl.) catch, arrest, (criminal etc.), steal. [orig. unkn.]

**Nick²** *n.* Old ~, the Devil. [prob. fam. form of *Nicholas*]

**ni′ckel** *n.* Silver-white metallic element much used esp. in alloys (~ **silver,** alloy like German silver; ~ **steel,** alloy of nickel with steel); U.S. 5-cent piece. [G]

‖**ni′cker** *n.* (sl.; *pl.* same). £1 sterling. [orig. unkn.]

**ni′ck-näck.** See KNICK-KNACK.

**ni′ckname. 1.** *n.* Name added to or substituted for or altered from name of person, place, or thing (*William the Conqueror, the Iron Duke, Satchmo, Taffy, Bubbles, Ted, Auld Reekie, the Smoke, Big Ben*). **2.** *v.t.* Call (person, thing) by nickname; give nickname to. [EKE + NAME (*an eke = a nick-*); cf. NEWT]

**ni′cotin|e** (-ēn) *n.* Poisonous oily liquid got from tobacco; **nicoti′nic** *a.* (~**ic acid,** vitamin of B group). [F (*Nicot,* person)]

**ni′ctit|āte** *v.i.* Blink, wink; ~**ating membrane,** third or inner eyelid of many animals; ~**ā′tion** *n.* [L]

**niece** *n.* Brother's or sister's daughter. [F f. L *neptis* granddaughter]

‖**niff** *n.,* & *v.i.* (sl.) Smell, stink; ~**y** *a.* [orig. dial.]

**ni′ft|y** *a.* (sl.; ~**ily,** ~**iness**). Smart, stylish; clever, adroit. [orig. unkn.]

**ni′ggard** *n.* Stingy person, grudging giver; ~**ly** *a.* (-**iness**), parsimonious, scanty, given or giving grudgingly.

**ni′gger** (-g-) *n.* (derog.) Negro, dark-skinned person, (~ **in the woodpile,** sl., suspicious circumstance, something spoiling a good thing; *work* **like a ~,** very hard); ~(-**brown**), (arch. or colloq.) very dark brown; *nigger* MINSTREL. [F *nègre* f. Sp. NEGRO]

**ni′ggl|e** *v.i.* Spend time on petty details, find fault in petty manner; ~**ing** *a.,* petty, lacking in breadth, (of writing) cramped. [orig. unkn.]

**nigh** (nī) *adv., prep.,* & *a.* (arch., literary, dial.) = NEAR (w. same usage in compar. & superl.). [E]

**night** (nīt) *n.* Dark period between day and day, time from sunset to sunrise, (*all night; by night;* **at ~,** also, in the period 6 p.m. to midnight: *ten o'clock at night;* GOOD *night;* ~ **and day,** always); darkness (as) of night (*black as night*); nightfall (*shall not reach home before night*); weather, experiences, occupation, of (part of) a night (FIRST *night;* **have a good** or **bad ~,** sleep well or not, be comfortable or not during the night; **make a ~ of it,** spend night in festivity; ~ **out,** festive evening, servant's free evening); ‖~**-bell** (to summon person at night); ~**-bird,** (esp.) owl or nightingale, person who goes about at night; ~**′cap,** cap worn in bed, hot or alcoholic drink taken at bedtime; ~**-clothes** (worn in bed); ~**-club,** establishment open at night that provides refreshment and entertainment; *night*-COMMODE; ~**-dress, -gown,** woman's, girl's, or baby's loose garment worn in bed; ~**′fall,** end of daylight; ~**′ingale** (-ngg-), small bird of thrush family, the male singing much at night [E, = night-singer]; ~**′jar,** harsh-voiced nocturnal bird; ~**-life,** urban entertainment open at night; ~**-light** (providing dim light through night for child, invalid, etc.); ~**-long** *a.* & *adv.,* (lasting) all night; ~**′mare,** terrifying dream or (colloq.) experience (~**′marish** *a.*), (thing inspiring) haunting fear, [orig. female monster supposedly suffocating sleeper, incubus (*mare* goblin)]; ~**-owl,** (colloq.) person active at night; ~**-safe,** safe with opening in outer wall of bank for deposit of money etc. when bank is closed; *black, deadly, woody,* ~**′shade,** kinds of plant, some with poisonous berries; ~ **shift** (of workmen employed during night); ~**-shirt,** boy's or man's long shirt for sleeping in; ~**-time** (as state or opportunity); ~**-watch,** (person, party keeping) watch by night (*in the ~-watches,* during the wakeful, wearisome, etc., night); ~**-watchman,** person keeping watch by night, (Crick.) inferior batsman sent in near close of play to avoid dismissal of better one in adverse conditions; ~**-work** (that is, or must be, done by night); **~'ie**, **~'y̆**, *n.*, (colloq.) night-dress; **~'ly̆**, (*a.*) happening, existing, in the night, recurring every night, (*adv.*) every night. [E]

**ni'hil|ism** (or -i'ĭ-) *n.* Rejection of all religious and moral principles; (Philos.) doctrine that nothing has real existence; doctrines of extreme party completely opposed to the established order in 19th-20th c. Russia; **~ist** *n.*; **~ĭ'stĭc** *a.* [L *nihil* nothing]

**-nĭk** *suf.* forming *n*s. denoting person associated with specified thing or quality (*beatnik, kibbutznik*). [Russ. (as SPUTNIK) & Yiddish]

**nĭl** *n.* Nothing, no number or amount, esp. as score in games. [L]

**Nĭlŏ'tĭc** *a.* Of the Nile. [L f. Gk]

**nĭ'mble** *a.* (**~r**, **~st**; **-bly**). Agile, swift (of mind etc.) quick, clever. [E, = quick to take]

**nĭ'mb|us** *n.* (*pl.* **~i** *pr.* **-ī**, **~uses**). Cloud of glory, halo, aureole; (Meteor.) storm-cloud. [L, = cloud]

**nĭmĭny̆-pĭ'mĭny̆** *a.* Mincing; spiritless. [imit.]

**nĭ'ncompŏŏp** *n.* Fool, simpleton. [orig. unkn.]

**nīne** *a.* & *n.* NUMERAL; *dressed up* to the **~s**, very elaborately; **the N~**, the Muses; **~ days' wonder**, novelty attracting interest for short time; ‖**~'pins**, kind of skittles; **~ times out of ten**, nearly always; **~'fŏld** (-nf-) *a.* & *adv.*; **~tee'n(th)** (-nt-; *or* nī'-) *adjs.* & *ns.*, NUMERALS (1984, w. ref. to totalitarian state described in Orwell's novel *1984*; ‖*nineteen to the* DOZEN; **~teenth hole**, joc., golf club's bar); **~'ty̆**, **~'tĭĕth**, (-nt-) *adjs.* & *ns.*, NUMERALS. [E]

**nĭ'nny̆** *n.* Foolish person. [orig. uncert.]

**nĭ'non** (nē'nawn) *n.* Lightweight silk dress-fabric. [F]

**nĭnth('ly̆).** See NUMERAL.

**nĭp[1].** **1.** *v.t.* & *i.* (-pp-). Pinch, squeeze sharply, bite; pinch *off* (bud etc.); check growth of (esp. *nip in the* BUD; lit. or fig.); (of cold) affect injuriously; ‖(sl.) go nimbly (*in, out, past,* etc.). **2.** *n.* Pinch, sharp squeeze, bite; (check to vegetation caused by) coldness of air. **3.** **~'per** *n.*, ‖(sl.) young boy or girl, claw of crab etc., (in *pl.*) forceps, pincers, or other gripping or cutting tool; **~'py̆** *a.* (**-ily̆**, **-iness**), (colloq.) active,

nimble, (of weather etc.) chillingly cold. [LDu.]

**Nĭp[2]** *n.* & *a.* (sl., derog.) Japanese. [NIPPONESE]

**nĭp[3]** *n.* Small quantity of spirits. [*nipperkin* small measure]

**nĭ'pple** *n.* Point of mammal's (esp. of woman's) breast; teat of baby's bottle; nipple-like protuberance of glass, metal, etc.; **~-wort**, yellow-flowered weed. [*neble, nible* perh. f. *neb* tip]

**Nĭ'ppon** *n.* Japan; **~ĕ'se** (-z) *n.* (*pl.* same) & *a.*, Japanese. [Jap., = land of the rising sun]

**nĭ'ppy̆.** See NIP[1].

**nīrva'na** (-ah'-; *or* nēr-) *n.* (Buddhism & Hinduism). Beatitude attained by extinction of individuality. [Skr., = extinction]

**nĭ'si** *a.* (Law). Subject to conditions as regards taking effect (DECREE, *rule, nisi*). [L, = unless]

**Nĭ'ssen** *n.* **~ hut**, tunnel-shaped hut of corrugated iron with cement floor. [person]

**nĭt** *n.* Egg of louse or other parasite; (sl.) stupid person; **~-picking** *n.* & *a.*, (colloq.) fault-finding in petty manner. [E]

**nĭ'tr|āte[1]** *n.* Salt or ester of nitric acid; potassium or sodium nitrate as fertilizer; **~ā'te[2]** *v.t.*, treat, combine, impregnate, with nitric acid; **~ĭc** *a.*, of or containing nitrogen (**~ic acid**, pungent corrosive caustic liquid); **~ĭde** *n.*, binary compound of nitrogen; **~ĭfy̆** *v.t.*, turn into nitrite or nitrate; **~ĭficā'tion** *n.*; **~īte** *n.*, salt or ester of nitrous acid; **~ō-** *comb. form*, of, made with, nitric acid or nitre or nitrogen (**~o-glycerine**, yellowish oily violently explosive liquid made by adding glycerine to nitric and sulphuric acids); **~ogĕn** *n.*, gas forming four-fifths of the atmosphere; **~o'gĕnous** *a.*, containing nitrogen; **~ous** *a.*, of, like, impregnated with, nitre (**~ous acid**, containing less oxygen than nitric acid; **~ous oxide**, used as anaesthetic, laughing-gas). [foll.]

**nĭ'tre** (-ter), ***nī'ter**, *n.* Saltpetre. [F f. L f. Gk]

**nĭtty̆-grĭ'tty̆** *n.* (sl.) Realities or basic facts of a matter. [orig. uncert.]

**nĭ'twĭt** *n.* (colloq.) Stupid person; **~tĕd** *a.*, stupid. [perh. NIT, WIT]

**nĭx[1]** *n.* (*fem.* **~'ie**). Water-elf. [F *nix(e)*]

**nix²** *n.* (sl.) Nothing. [G colloq. *nix* = *nichts* nothing]

**N.J.** *abbr.* New Jersey.

**N.Mex.** *abbr.* New Mexico.

**N.N.E., N.N.W.,** *abbrs.* north--north-east, -west.

**nō¹** *a., adv., & n.* **1.** *a.* Not any (*no circumstances could justify it*; *king or no king*, regardless of the king, his kingship, etc.); not a, quite other than, (*is no genius*; *no* LITTLE; *no* SMALL); hardly any (*did it in no* TIME; **there is no —ing,** none is possible: *there's no accounting for tastes*, *no* SAYING); (ellipt. as notice, slogan, etc.) there is not any, no . . . is allowed (*no smoking*; *no surrender*); *no-* -BALL¹; **no'body,** (*pron.*) no person, (*n.*) person of no importance; *no* GO¹; **no man's land,** piece of waste, unowned, or debatable ground, (Mil.) space between opposed trenches, (fig.) area not clearly belonging to any one subject etc.; **no one,** (*pron.*) no person, (*a.*) no single (*no one man could lift it*); **no side,** (Rugby Footb.) (referee's announcement of) end of game; **no way,** (colloq.) it is impossible; NOWHERE. **2.** *adv.* (After *or*) not (*pleasant or no*, *it is true*; WHETHER *or no*); (w. *compar.*) by no amount, not at all, (**no better than she should be,** morally suspect; **no less (than),** as much (*n., a., adv.*) or many or important (as): *£50, no less*; *a no less fatal victory*; *no less a person than Gladstone*; **no more,** (*n.*) nothing further, (*a.*) not any more (*no more wine?*), (*adv.*) no longer (*is no more*, is dead), to no greater extent (*could no more do it than fly*), just as little, neither, (*you did not come and no more did he*); **no sooner . . . than,** hardly before: *no sooner said than done*); (equivalent to neg. sentence) the answer to the question is negative, the request or command will not be complied with, the statement etc. made is wrong, (**say no,** refuse request, deny statement; **take no for an answer,** accept refusal). **3.** *n.* (*pl.* noes *pr.* nōz). The word *no*, a denial or refusal, negative vote; **the noes have it,** are in the majority. [E]

**Nō².** See NOH.

**No.** *abbr.* number [L *numero*, abl. of *numerus* number].

**Nō'ah** (-a) *n.* ~'s ark, ship in which Noah, his family, and animals were saved, child's toy imitating this; **Nōā'chian, Nōā'chĭc,** (-k-)

*adjs.*, of the patriarch Noah or his time. [person: Gen. 6]

**nŏb¹** *n.* (sl.) Head. [KNOB]

||**nŏb²** *n.* (sl.) Person of wealth or high social standing; ~'**bў** *a.* (-ily). [orig. unkn.]

||**nŏ'bble** *v.t.* (sl.) Tamper with (racehorse) to prevent its winning; dishonestly get possession of; catch (criminal). [dial. *knobble* beat]

**Nō'bĕl** (or -ĕ'l) *n.* ~ **prize,** one of the annual prizes (for physics, chemistry, medicine, literature, economics, and promotion of peace) awarded mainly from bequest of A. Nobel, Sw. inventor of dynamite. [person]

**nō'ble. 1.** *a.* (~**r,** ~**st;** -**bly**). Illustrious by rank, title, or birth, belonging to the nobility; of lofty character, magnanimous, morally elevated; of imposing appearance; admirable; ~**man,** ~**woman,** peer(ess); ~ **metal,** gold etc. (resisting chemical attack). **2.** *n.* Nobleman, noblewoman. **3. nŏbi'lĭtў** *n.,* noble character, mind, birth, or rank, *the* or *a* class of nobles. [F f. L *nobilis*]

**noblesse** (nŏblĕ's) *n.* The nobility of a foreign country; ~ *oblige* (oblē'zh), privilege entails responsibility. [F]

**nŏck** *n.* Notch on bow or arrow for bowstring. [Du.]

**nŏctŭr'nal** *a.* (~ly). Of, in, done or active by, night; **nŏ'cturne** *n.,* dreamy musical piece, picture of night scene. [L (*nox* noct- night)]

**nŏd. 1.** *v.i. & t.* (-dd-). Incline head slightly and briefly in greeting (~**ding acquaintance,** very slight one *with* person or subject), assent, or command; let head droop, be drowsy, make sleepy mistake; (of plumes) dance up and down as result of motion; incline (head); signify (assent etc.) by nod. **2.** *n.* Nodding of head; **land of Nod,** sleep (w. pun on Gen. 4:16); **on the** ~, (colloq.) on credit, with merely formal assent. [orig. unkn.]

**nŏ'ddle** *n.* (colloq.) Head.

**nŏ'ddў** *n.* Simpleton; tropical seabird. [prob. obs. *noddy* foolish]

**nōde** *n.* Knob on root or branch; point at which leaves spring; hard swelling; intersecting-point of planet's orbit and ecliptic or of two great circles of celestial sphere; point or line of rest in vibrating body; point at which curve crosses itself;

**nŏ'd(ĭc)al** adjs. (-lly); **nodŏ'se** a., knotty, knotted; **nodŏ'sĭtў** n. [L *nodus* knot]

**nŏ'dŭl|e** n. Small rounded lump of anything; small node in plant; small knotty tumour, ganglion; **~ar,** **~ātĕd,** adjs.; **~ā'tion** n., arrangement of nodules. [L dim. (prec.)]

**Nŏë'l** n. Christmas (esp. as int. in carols). [F, f. L (NATAL)]

**nŏg**[1] n. Small block or peg of wood; **~'gĭng** (-g-) n., brickwork in wooden frame. [orig. unkn.]

**nŏg**[2] n. ||East Anglian strong beer; =EGG[1]-*nog*.

**nŏ'ggĭn** (-g-) n. Small mug; small (usu. ¼-pint) measure; (sl.) head.

**Noh** (nō), **Nŏ**[2], n. Traditional Japanese drama evolved from Shinto rites. [Jap.]

**noise** (-z). **1.** n. Clamour, din; any sound; (in *pl.*) utterances, esp. conventional remarks, (*made polite, sympathetic, noises*); irregular fluctuations with transmitted signal; BIG *noise*; **make a ~,** lit., or fig. talk or complain much *about*, be much talked of *in the world*; **~s off,** sounds made off stage but heard by audience. **2.** v.t. Make public, spread (person's fame, fact) *abroad*. **3.** **~'lĕss** (-zl-) a., without sound; **noi'sў** (-zĭ) a. (-ily, -iness), full of or making or attended with or given to making noise. [F f. L NAUSEA]

**noi'some** a. (literary). Noxious, disgusting esp. to smell. [ANNOY]

**nŏ'mad** n. & a. (Member of tribe) roaming from place to place for pasture; wanderer, wandering; **nomă'dĭc** a. (-ically), **~ĭsm** n. [F f. L f. Gk *nomas -ad-* (*nemō* to pasture)]

*nom de plume* (nŏmdĕplōō'm) n. (*pl. -ms pr.* same). Writer's assumed name. [sham F,= pen-name, after F *nom de guerre* (lit. war-name) in same sense]

**nŏ'měn** n. (Rom. Ant.) Second or family name (Marcus *Tullius* Cicero). [L,= name]

**nomě'nclature** (-n-k-; *or* nŏ'měn-klā-) n. System of names or naming, terminology. [L (prec., *calo* call)]

**nŏ'mĭnal** a. (~ly). Of, as, like, a noun (*nominal and verbal roots*); of, in, names (*nominal and essential distinctions*; *nominal list of officers*); existing in name only, not real or actual, (*nominal and real prices, rulers*); (of sum of money etc.) virtually nothing, much below actual value;

**~ value** *of coin, shares,* etc., face value; **~ĭsm** n., (Philos.) doctrine that abstract concepts are mere names (opp. *realism*), so **~ĭst** n., **~ĭ'stĭc** a. [F or L (NOMEN)]

**nŏ'mĭn|āte** v.t. (~able). Appoint, propose for election, to office; name or appoint (date etc.); **~ā'tion** n., (also) right of nominating (*have a nomination at your disposal*); **~ātor,** **~ee'**, ns. [L (NOMEN)]

**nŏ'mĭnative** a. & n. (Gram.) (case) used as or in agreement with subject of verb, word in this case, (**~** ABSOLUTE, independent construction in E with noun and participle or infinitive used as adverbial clause); (*pr. -ātĭv*) of, appointed by, nomination (*the nominative and the elective principles*); **nŏ'mĭnati'val** a. (Gram.; -lly). [F or L (prec.)]

**nŏ'mogrăm** n. Diagram giving value of a quantity from those of others when straight line is drawn between points. [Gk *nomos* law]

**nŏn-** pref. giving negation of sense of wds with which it is combined; **~-belli'gerent** a. & n., (country) taking no active or open part in war; **~-co'mbatant** a. & n., (person) not fighting (esp. in war as being civilian, army chaplain, etc.); **~-commi'ssioned** (esp. of officer) of grade below those with commissions; **~-commi'ttal** a. & n., avoiding committing oneself to definite opinion, course of action, etc.; **~-condu'cting, -condu'ctor,** (substance) that does not conduct heat or electricity; **~-contri'butory,** not involving contributions; **~-esse'ntial** a. & n., (thing) that is not essential; **~-event,** occurrence of no significance (usu. despite attempts to invest it with this); **~-fe'rrous,** (of metal) not iron or steel; **~-fi'ction,** literary matter based on fact (opp. novels etc.); **~-interfer'ence, ~-interve'ntion,** principle or practice of keeping aloof from others' disputes (esp. Polit.); **~-jur'ing, ~jur'or,** (Hist.) (beneficed clergyman) refusing oath of allegiance in 1689; **~-me'mber,** one who is not a member; **~-mo'ral,** unconcerned with morality (cf. *amoral, immoral*); **~-nu'clear,** not involving nuclei or nuclear energy; **~-par'ty,** independent of political parties; **~-playing,** (esp. of captain of sports team who does not himself take part); ~-**pro′fit**-(-**making**), (of enterprise) not conducted with a view to gain; ~-**prolifera′tion** (esp. of nuclear weapons); ~-**resi′stance**, policy of not resisting even wrongly exercised authority; ~-**ski′d**, (of tyre) designed to prevent skidding; ~-**smo′ker**, person who does not smoke, compartment in train etc. where smoking is forbidden; ~-**star′ter**, (fig., colloq.) idea, person, not worth consideration; ~-**stick**, (esp.) to which food will not adhere in cooking; ~-**stop**, (a.) (of train etc.) not stopping at intermediate stations, (of journey, performance, etc.) done without stop, (adv.) without stopping; ~-**U′**, (colloq.) not characteristic of upper class; ~-**u′nion**, not belonging to, not made by members of, trade union; ~-**vi′olence**, ~-**vi′olent**, abstaining from use of violence to gain one's ends; ~-**vo′ting**, (of shares) not entitling holder to vote; ~-**whi′te** a. & n., (person) belonging to other than white race. [F f. L *non* not]

**nŏ′nage** n. Being under age, minority; immaturity. [AF (NON-, AGE)]
**nŏnagēnār′ian** a. & n. (Person) from 90 to 99 years old. [L (*nonageni* 90 each)]

**nŏ′nagon** n. Plane figure with 9 sides and angles. [L *nonus* ninth, -GON]

**nŏnce** n. For the ~, for the occasion only; ~-**word** (coined for one occasion). [*for then anes* for the one; cf. NEWT]

**nŏ′nchalan|t** (-sh-) a. Unmoved, indifferent, cool; ~**ce** n. [F (*chaloir* be concerned)]

**non-com.** abbr. non-commissioned (officer).

**non compos (mentis)** (nŏn kŏ′mpŏs mĕ′ntĭs) a. Not in one's right mind. [L, = not having control of one's mind]

**nŏnconfor′m|ĭst** (-n-k-) n. One who does not conform to doctrine or discipline of an established Church, esp. (*N*-) member of (usu. Protestant) sect dissenting from Anglican Church; one who does not conform to a prevailing principle; ~**ĭtẏ** n., nonconformists or their principles etc., failure to conform (*to* rule etc.), lack of correspondence between things. [CONFORM]

**nŏ′ndĕscrĭpt** a. & n. Hard to classify, indeterminate, (person or thing). [DESCRIBE]

**none** (nŭn) pron., a., & adv. **1.** pron. Not any (one) *of* (none of them came; none of this concerns me; none can tell; none but fools have ever believed it); ~ **other**, no other person (than). **2.** a. (usu. = *no* with reference defined by earlier or later noun). No, not any, not to be counted in specified class, (*you have money and I have none; if a linguist is wanted, I am none; rather a bad reputation than none at all*). **3.** adv. By no amount, not at all, (w. *the* and compar.: *am none the wiser, none the better, for it; the pay is none too high*); ~ **the less**, nevertheless. [E, = not one]

**nŏnĕ′ntĭtẏ** n. Non-existence, non-existent thing; person or thing of no importance. [NON-]

**nōnes** (-nz) n.pl. In ancient Roman calendar by inclusive reckoning, ninth day before ides (7th day of Mar., May, July, Oct., 5th of other months); (Eccl.) office originally said at ninth hour. [L *nonus* ninth]

**nonesuch.** See NONSUCH.

**nŏ′npareil** (-ĕl) a. & n. Unrivalled or unique (person or thing). [F (*pareil* equal)]

**nŏnplŭ′s** v.t. (-ss-). Reduce to hopeless perplexity. [L *non plus* not more]

**nŏ′nsense. 1.** n. Absurd or meaningless words or ideas; foolish or extravagant conduct; arrangement etc. that one disapproves of. **2.** int. You are talking or proposing nonsense; it surely cannot be true. **3.** nŏnsĕ′nsĭcal a. (-lly). [NON-]

**non sequitur** (nŏn sĕ′kwĭter) n. Conclusion that does not logically follow from the premises. [L, = it does not follow]

**no′n(e)sŭch** (nŭ′ns-) n. Unrivalled person or thing, paragon; plant like lucerne. [*none such*]

**nŏ′nsuit** (-ūt, -ŏŏt; Law). **1.** n. Stoppage of suit by judge as unsustainable. **2.** v.t. Subject (plaintiff) to nonsuit. [AF *no(u)nsuit* (NON-)]

**nōō′dle**[1] n. Strip of dried dough made with eggs, used in soups. [G]

**nōō′dle**[2] n. Simpleton; (sl.) head. [orig. unkn.]

**nook** n. Secluded corner, recess.

**nōōn** n. Twelve o'clock in the day, midday; ~**′day**, ~**′tide**, midday. [E f. L *nona* (*hora*) ninth (hour); orig. 3 p.m. (cf. NONES)]

**nŏŏse. 1.** n. Loop with running knot, esp. in snare, lasso, or hangman's halter; snare, bond; **put one's head in a ~**, bring about one's own downfall. **2.** v.t. Catch with or enclose in noose. [F *no(u)s* f. L (NODE)]

**nor** (or emphat. nŏr). **1.** conj. And not, and no more, neither, and not either, (*had neither socks nor shoes*; *not a man nor a child in sight*; *I said I had not seen it, nor had I*; '*I can't find it*'—'*Nor can I*'; *all that is true, nor must we forget* . . .). **2.** adv. (poet., arch.). Neither (*nor gold nor silver*). [contr. obs. *nother* (NO¹, WHETHER)]

**nor'** = NORTH, esp. in compds. (*nor'ward*, *nor'wester*). [abbr.]

**Nŏr'dĭc** a. & n. (Person) of the tall blond long-headed Gmc people of N. Europe (esp. Scandinavia). [F (*nord* north)]

**Nŏr'folk** (-ok) n. ~ **jacket**, man's loose single-breasted belted jacket. [place]

**norm** n. Standard, pattern, type; standard amount (of work etc.); customary behaviour. [L *norma* carpenter's square]

**nŏr'mal. 1.** a. (~ly). Conforming to standard, regular, usual, typical; free from mental etc. disorder; (Geom.) at right angles, perpendicular. **2.** n. Normal value of temperature etc., esp. = BLOOD-*heat*; usual state, level, etc.; (Geom.) normal line. **3.** ~cў, **nŏrmă'lĭtў**, ns.; ~īze v.t.; ~īzā'tion n. [F, or L *normalis* (prec.)]

**Nŏr'man. 1.** n. Native of Normandy; descendant of mixed Scand. and Frankish people there established; Norman French or style. **2.** a. Of the Normans; *Norman* CONQUEST; ~ **French**, French as spoken by Normans or later in English law-courts; ~ **style** (Archit., with round arches and heavy pillars). [F f. N, = *Northman*]

**nŏr'mative** a. Of, establishing, norm(s). [F f. L (NORM)]

**Nŏrn** n. Any of the female Fates of Scand. mythology. [N]

**Nōrse. 1.** n. The Norwegian language; the Scandinavian language-group; **Old ~**, Gmc language of Norway and its colonies, or of Scandinavia, until 14th c. **2.** a. Of ancient Scandinavia, esp. of Norway; ~**man**. [Du. *noor(d)sch* northern]

**nŏrth** n., a., & adv. **1.** n. Point of horizon to left of person facing east (**to the ~ of**, in a northward direction from); compass point lying north (**magnetic ~**, point indicated by north end of compass-needle); (*N~*) part of country or town lying to the north. **2.** a. Towards, at, near, facing, north (*north window*); coming from north (*north wind*); ~ **light**, coming through north window. **3.** adv. Towards, at, near, north (DUE *north*; *lies* etc. ~ **and** *south*, lengthwise on line running from N. to S.; *north* BY *east*, *west*; ~ **of**, in a northward direction from). **4.** N~ **Britain**, (arch.) Scotland; ‖~ (**country**), northern part of England (north of Humber; so ~*cou'ntryman*) ; ~**-east**, -**west**, (compass point) midway between north and east, west; ~**ea'ster**, ~**we'ster**, N.E., N.W., wind; ~**-east**, ~**-west**, **passage**, ship-routes formerly supposed to exist round N. coast of Europe and Asia to the Orient, round N. coast of America from Atlantic to Pacific; ~**-~-east**, -**west**, (compass point) midway between north and north-east, north-west; N~'**man**, native of Scandinavia, esp. of Norway; *north* POLE²; N~ **Sea** (between Britain, Netherlands, Germany, and Scandinavia); N~ **star**, = POLE²-*star*. **5.** ~'**erlў** (-dh-) a. & adv., in northern position or direction, (of wind) blowing (nearly) from north; so ~**-ea'sterly**, ~**-we'sterly**; ~'**ern** (-dh-) a. (*superl.* ~**ernmost**), of or dwelling in the north (*northern* LIGHT¹*s*); so ~**-ea'stern**, ~**-we'stern**; ~'**erner** (-dh-) n., inhabitant of the north; **Nŏrthŭ'mbrĭan** a. & n., (native, dialect) of ancient Northumbria (England N. of Humber) or modern Northumberland; ~'**ward** a., adv., & n.; ~'**wards** (-z) adv. [E]

**Nŏrthă'nts.** abbr. Northamptonshire.

**Nŏrwē'gian** (-jan) a. & n. (Native, language) of Norway. [L *Norvegia* f. N, = north way]

**nŏr'-wĕ'ster** n. Northwester; = sou'wester. [NORTH*wester*]

**Nos.** abbr. numbers. [cf. No.]

**nōse** (-z). **1.** n. Organ of face or head of man or animal, above mouth, containing nostrils and serving for breathing and smelling (**as plain as the ~ on your face**, easily seen; *win race* etc. **by a ~**, by very narrow margin; **count ~s**, count supporters etc., decide by mere numbers; *cut off* one's *nose to* SPITE one's *face*; **follow one's ~**, go straight forward, be guided by instinct; **hold one's ~**, compress nostrils between fingers to avoid bad smell; **keep one's ~ clean**, sl., behave properly, avoid trouble; *keep one's nose to the* GRINDSTONE; LEAD¹ *by the nose*; LOOK *down* one's *nose at*; *make a* LONG¹ *nose*; **parson's, pope's, ~**, rump of (cooked) fowl; **pay through the ~**, have to pay exorbitant price; **poke, thrust**, one's **~**, pry or intrude *into* something or *in*; **put** person's **~** *out of joint*, displace, disconcert, him; **rub** person's **~ in it**, remind him humiliatingly of error, fault, etc.; **see no further than** one's **~**, be short-sighted (lit. or fig.); **speak through** one's **~**, pronounce words with nasal twang; THUMB one's *nose*; **turn up** one's **~**, show disdain; **under** person's **~**, straight before him; **with** one's **~ in the air**, haughtily); sense of smell (**has a good ~**, esp. of dog, fig. of detective etc.); odour, perfume, of hay, tea, wine, etc.; open end or nozzle of pipe etc.; prow, projecting part; front end of car, aircraft, etc.; (sl.) police informer. **2.** *v.t.* & *i.* Perceive smell of, discover by smell, smell *out*, (fig.) detect; thrust nose against or into; pry or search (*after*, *for*); (of ship etc.) make way along coast or channel. **3.** **~'bag** (containing fodder and hung on horse's head); **~'band**, lower band of bridle passing nose and attached to cheek-straps; **~'bleed**, a bleeding from the nose; **~-cone**, cone-shaped nose of aircraft, rocket, etc.; **~'dive**, (*n.*) aeroplane's downward plunge, (*v.i.*) make this; **~'gay**, bunch of flowers; **~'ring** (fixed in nose of bull etc. for leading, or of person for ornament); **~-wheel**, landing-wheel under nose of aircraft. **4.** **nō's(e)y** (-zǐ) *a.* (**-ier**, **-iest**; **-iness**), large-nosed, (sl.) inquisitive; **Nos(e)y Parker**, busybody. [E]

**nŏsh.** (sl.) **1.** *v.t.* & *i.* Eat or drink, esp. between meals; **~-up**, (large) meal. **2.** *n.* Food or drink, esp. snack. [Yiddish]

**nŏstǎ'lg|ia** (-ja) *n.* Homesickness; sentimental yearning for (some period of) the past; **~ĭc** *a.* (**-ically**).

[L f. Gk (*nostos* return home, *algos* pain)]

**nŏ'strĭl** *n.* Either opening in nose (**stink in the ~s of**, be loathed by); **(-)led** (-ld) *a.* [E, = nose-hole]

**nŏ'strum** *n.* Quack remedy, patent medicine; pet scheme esp. for political or social reform. [L, = of our own make]

**nŏt** *adv.* giving negation of vbs., participles, and infinitives, (often **n't** attached to auxiliary vbs. or BE) (*I do not, don't, know*, arch. *I know not*; *he will not, he won't*, arch. or dial. *he'll not, come*; *she is not, isn't*, vulg. *ain't, here*; *didn't you*, (formal) *did you not, tell me?*; *am I not, aren't I, clever?*; *do not, don't, worry*; *asked him not to do it*); used ellipt. for neg. sentence, verb, or phrase (*Are you ill? Not at all. Not so¹. Popular or not, it is right. I hope not. I would as soon do it as not*; **~ at all**, in polite reply to thanks, there is no need to thank me; **~ but**, **~ but that**, **~ but what**, I should however admit that; **~ that**, but it is not to be inferred that); variously in emphatic use (*He is not my son, but yours. They will not be outwitted, not they. Not a hair of your head will be hurt. Not a few* (= many) *people were there*); ‖*not* HALF; **~ least**, with considerable importance; **~ quite**, almost, noticeably not (*not quite proper*); **~ so** or **too well**, rather badly or ill; *not* VERY. [contr. NOUGHT]

**nota bene** (nōta bě'nā) *v. imper.* Observe, note this. [L, = note well]

**nō'tab|le.** **1.** *a.* (**~ly**). Worthy of note, striking, remarkable, eminent; **~ĭ'lĭtȳ** *n.*, (esp.) notable person. **2.** *n.* Eminent person. [F f. L (*noto* NOTE)]

**nō'tarȳ** *n.* **~ (public)**, person with authority to draw up deeds and perform other legal formalities; **notār'ial** *a.* (**-lly**). [L *notarius* secretary (NOTE)]

**notā'tion** *n.* Representing of numbers, quantities, sounds, etc., by symbols, any set of such symbols; *note*, annotation; SCALE³ *of notation*. [F or L (NOTE)]

**nŏtch.** **1.** *n.* V-shaped indentation on edge or convex surface. **2.** *v.t.* Make notches in; score (items etc.; often *up*, *down*) by notches (lit. or fig.); **~ȳ** *a.* [AF]

**nōte. 1.** *n.* Written sign representing pitch and duration of musical sound; key of piano etc.; single tone of definite pitch made by musical instrument, voice, etc.; bird's song or call; significant sound or way of expressing oneself (*a note of assurance in her voice; a note of optimism in his report*; **strike a false, the right, ~,** act inappropriately, suitably); sign, token, characteristic; brief record of facts, impressions, topics, for speech, article, etc., (usu. in *pl.*: make, take, *a note of* or *notes*); **~'book,** for memoranda); annotation in book etc.; short or informal letter (**~'paper,** for private correspondence); formal diplomatic communication; ~ (of **hand**), written promise to pay sum by certain time; ||= BANK²*note* (**~'case,** pocket wallet for banknotes); eminence (*critic, philosopher, person,* of ~, distinguished); notice, attention, (*worthy of* **note; take ~ of,** observe). **2.** *v.t.* Observe, notice, give attention to; set down or *down* as thing to be remembered or observed; (in *p.p.*) celebrated, well known *for*. **3. ~'let** (-tl-) *n.,* (esp.) folded card or paper with design etc. on label, used for informal letter; **~'worthy,** worthy of attention, remarkable. [F f. L *nota* a mark, *noto* to mark]

**no'thing** (nŭ'-). **1.** *n.* No thing (*nothing great is easy*); not anything (*nothing has been done; he did nothing but grumble*); **be ~ to,** be of no consequence to, be inferior in comparison with; **come to ~,** turn out useless, fail; **be, have, ~ to do with,** have no connection or dealings with; **for ~,** without payment, to no purpose (*count, go, for* ~, be unappreciated or profitless); **has ~ in him,** is insignificant, lacks individuality; **have ~ on,** colloq., be naked, possess no advantage over, know nothing discreditable about, be much inferior to; *feel, look,* etc., **like ~ on earth,** strange, ugly, wretched, etc., to an extreme degree; **make ~ of,** treat as trifling, be unable to understand or use or deal with; **mean ~ to,** not be understood, admired, desired, etc., by; **no ~** (as colloq. conclusion of list of negatives: *no bread, no butter, no cheese, no nothing*); *nothing* DO³*ing*; **~ if not,** primarily *thorough* etc.; **~ venture ~ win** (encouragement to bold action); *there is* **~ for it** *but to,* no alternative; **there is ~ in** or *to* **it,** it is untrue or unimportant or straightforward or (*in it*) evenly balanced; THINK *nothing of;* to SAY *nothing of*); (Arith.) no amount,

nought, (*multiply 6 by nothing, and the result is nothing*); non-existence, what does not exist; trifling thing, event, remark, or person, (*he is nothing without his money; whispering sweet nothings*), so (colloq.) as *a.,* unimportant, trivial. **2.** *adv.* Not at all, in no way, (*is nothing* LIKE¹ *so, as, good; nothing daunted; nothing* LOATH); *(as int., colloq.) not at all (Is it silver? Silver nothing, it's tin).* **3. ~ness** *n.,* non-existence, worthlessness, triviality, trifles. [E (NO¹, THING)]

**no'tice. 1.** *n.* Intimation, warning, (esp. formal) announcement, placard or paper conveying these, (**at short, a moment's, ten minutes', ~,** with such time for preparation; ||**~-board,** for posting notices on; **give a week's ~** etc. **~,** announce that contract etc. is then at an end; *notice to* QUIT; *till* FURTHER *notice*); heed, attention, cognizance, observation, (*brought it to his notice*); **come into, to, under, ~,** attract attention; **take (no) ~ of,** (not) observe, (not) act upon; **take ~,** show signs of intelligence or interest; **take ~ that,** I warn you); newspaper or magazine review, comment, or article. **2.** *v.t.* Perceive, take notice of; remark upon; treat with politeness or condescension; serve with notice; **~able** (-sa-) *a.,* noteworthy, perceptible. [F f. L (*notus* known)]

**no'tif|y** *v.t.* Report, give notice of; inform, give notice to, (person *of* fact, *that*); **~iable** *a.,* (of disease) that must be notified to health authorities; **~icā'tion** *n.*

**no'tion** *n.* Concept; idea, conception, (*I have not the faintest notion of what he means*); vague view or opinion (*has a notion that*); understanding or faculty or intention of (*has no notion of Greek, obeying, obedience, letting himself be put upon*); *(in pl.)* miscellaneous small articles esp. of haberdashery; **~al** *a.* (-lly), speculative, imaginary. [L *notio* (as NOTICE)]

**notōr'ious** *a.* (Of facts) known and talked of (*it is notorious that*); (of person or thing) known to deserve his or its bad repute (*notorious smuggler, offender, vice*); unfavourably known (*a ship notorious for ill luck*); **nōtori'ĕty̆** *n.* [L (*notus* known)]

**Notts.** *abbr.* Nottinghamshire.

**nŏtwithstǎ'nding** (or -dh-). **1.** *prep.* Without prevention by or regard to (*notwithstanding his resistance;*

*this notwithstanding*). **2.** adv. Nevertheless. [NOT, WITHSTAND]

**nou′gat** (nōō′gah) n. Sweetmeat made with sugar, honey, nuts, etc. [F f. Prov.]

**nought** (nawt) n. Figure 0, cipher, (‖~s and crosses, a paper-and-pencil game); (poet., arch.) nothing (cf. NAUGHT). [E (NOT, AUGHT)]

**noun** n. Word used as name of person, place, or thing. [AF f. L NOMEN]

**nou′rish** (nŭ′-) v.t. Sustain with food (lit. or fig.); cherish, nurse, (hope, resentment, etc.) in one's heart; ~**ing** a., containing much nourishment; ~**ment** n., sustenance, food. [F f. L *nutrio* feed]

**nous** (nows) n. (Philos.) mind, intellect; (colloq.) common sense, gumption. [Gk]

**nouveau riche** (nōōvō′ rē′sh) n. (pl. ~**ux** -es pr. same). One who has recently acquired (usu. ostentatious) wealth. [F, = new rich]

**Nov.** abbr. November.

**nō′va** n. (pl. ~**e**, ~**s**). Star showing sudden large increase of brightness and then subsiding. [L, = new]

**nŏ′vel. 1.** a. Of new kind, strange, hitherto unknown. **2.** n. Fictitious prose tale published as complete book; ~**ĕ′tte** n., short novel (‖freq. derog. of light romance; so ~**ĕ′ttish** a.); ~**ist** n., writer of novels; **novĕ′lla** n., short novel or narrative tale; ~**tȳ** n., new thing or occurrence, newness, small toy etc. of novel design. [F f. L (*novus* new)]

**Novĕ′mber** n. Eleventh month. [F f. L (*novem* nine; cf. DECEMBER)]

**novĕ′na** n. (R.C. Ch.) Devotion consisting of special prayers or services on nine successive days. [L (*novem* nine)]

**nŏ′vice** n. Probationary member of religious order; new convert; beginner; **novi′ciate, -tiate**, (-shǐ-) n., period of being novice, religious novice, novices' quarters. [F f. L *novicius* (NOVEL)]

**now** adv., conj., & n. **1.** adv. At the present or mentioned time; by this time; under present circumstances (*I cannot now believe*); immediately (*must go now*); in the immediate past (*just now*); on this further occasion (*what do you want now?*); (in narrative) then, next, by that time, (*Caesar now marched east*); (without temporal force, giving various tones to sentence) I beg, I insist, I warn you, you must know, surely, etc., (*Now what do you mean by that?. Oh, come now!. No nonsense, now!. Now Barabbas was a robber. Now then, now then, what's going on here?. You don't mean it, now*). **2.** conj. ~ (*that*), consequently upon or simultaneously with the fact that (*Now (that) I am grown up I understand it. You ought to write, now that you know the address*). **3.** n. This time, the present, (*before, by, till, now*; **as of** ~, at this time; **for** ~, until a later time: *goodbye for now*). **4.** (every) ~ **and then**, (every) ~ **and again**, from time to time, intermittently (~ . . . ~ . . ., ~ . . . **then** . . ., at one moment . . . at another . . .; ~ **for it!**, ~ **or never!**, this is the moment to act. **5.** ~**′adays** (-z) adv. & n., (at) the present day, (in) these (advanced) times. [E]

**nō′where** (nō′wār) adv. & pron. (In, to) no place; **be, come (in)** ~, not be placed in race or competition; **come from** ~, be suddenly evident or successful; **get** ~, make no progress, give (person) no success; **the middle of** ~, (colloq.) remote or inaccessible locality; ~ **near**, not nearly (*there's nowhere near enough milk left*). [E]

**nowt** n. (colloq. or dial.) Nothing. [NOUGHT]

**nŏ′xious** (-kshus) a. Harmful, unwholesome. [L (*noxa* harm)]

**noyau** (nwah′yō) n. (pl. ~**x** pr. -z). Liqueur of brandy flavoured with fruit-kernels. [F, = kernel, f. L *nux* nut]

**nŏ′zzle** n. Spout, end attached to bellows, hose, etc., for jet to issue from. [dim. NOSE]

**nr.** abbr. near.

**N.S.** abbr. new style; Nova Scotia.

‖**N.S.P.C.C.** abbr. National Society for the Prevention of Cruelty to Children.

**N.S.W.** abbr. New South Wales.

**n't.** See NOT.

**-nt** suf. forming adjs. denoting existence of action (*consequent, repentant*), and ns. denoting agent (*assistant, coefficient, deodorant, president*), usu. f. vbs. [F or L (-ant-, -ent-, part. stem of vbs.)]

**N.T.** abbr. New Testament; (Austral.) Northern Territory.

**nth.** See N.

**Nth.** abbr. North.

**nū** n. Thirteenth Gk letter (N, ν) = n. [Gk]

**nū'ance** (or -ah'ńs) n. Delicate difference in or shade of meaning, feeling, colour, etc. [F, ult. f. L *nubes* cloud]

**nŭb** n. Small lump, esp. of coal (also **nu'bble**); point or gist (of matter or story); **~'blў** a. [KNOB]

**nū'bile** a. (Of woman) marriageable or sexually attractive; **nūbi'litў** n. [L (*nubo* become wife)]

**nū'clear** a. Of, relating to, constituting, a nucleus; using nuclear energy; **~ bomb**, = ATOMIC *bomb*; **~ energy** (released or absorbed during reactions in atomic nuclei); **~ family**, father, mother, and child(ren); nuclear FISSION; **~ fuel**, source of nuclear energy; nuclear FUSION; **~ physics** (dealing with atomic nuclei); **~ power**, power derived from nuclear energy, country possessing nuclear weapons; nuclear REACTOR; **~ warfare**, = ATOMIC *warfare*. [foll.]

**nū'cle|us** (pl. **~i** pr. -ī). Central part or thing round which others collect, central part of atom, of seed, or of plant or animal cell; kernel, beginning meant to receive additions; **~āte** v.t. & i., form (into) nucleus; **nūclē'ic** a. (**~ic acid**, kind present in all living cells). [L, = kernel, dim. *nux nuc-* nut]

**nūde. 1.** a. Naked, bare, unclothed. **2.** n. Picture, sculpture, etc., of nude human figure; nude person; **the ~**, unclothed state, representation of undraped human figure. **3. nū'dist** n., person who advocates or practises going unclothed; **nū'dism** n.; **nū'ditў** n., nakedness. [L *nudus*]

**nūdge** v.t., & n. Push with elbow to draw attention privately; push in gradual manner. [orig. unkn.]

**nū'gator|ў** a. (**~ily**, **~iness**). Futile, trifling; inoperative, not valid. [L (*nugae* trifles)]

**nū'gget** (-g-) n. Lump of native gold etc. [app. dial. *nug* lump]

**nui'sance** (nū's-) n. Source of annoyance; obnoxious act, circumstances, thing, or person, (*make a nuisance of oneself*; *what a nuisance!*); **~ value** (due to capacity to harass or frustrate). [F, = hurt (*nuire nuis-* f. L *noceo* hurt)]

||**N.U.J.** abbr. National Union of Journalists.

**null** a. Void, not valid, (usu. *null and void*); characterless, expressionless; non-existent; **~'ifў** v.t., neutralize, invalidate; **~ifĭcā'tion** n.; **~'itў** n., being null, invalidity, (esp. of marriage). [F, or L *nullus* none]

||**N.U.M.** abbr. National Union of Mineworkers.

**Num.** abbr. Numbers (O.T.).

**nŭmb** (-m). **1.** a. Deprived of feeling or power of motion (*numb with cold, shock,* etc.). **2.** v.t. Make numb; (fig.) stupefy, paralyse. [obs. *nome* p.p. of *nim* take (NIMBLE)]

**nŭ'mber. 1.** n. Count, sum, aggregate, of or of persons or things or abstract units (**to the ~ of**, amounting to as many as); count of things etc. up to a certain one so as to show its position in series, symbol or figure representing such count, (**by ~s**, following simple instructions identified by numbers; GOLDEN *number*; **have** person's **~**, sl., understand his motives etc.; one's **~ is up**, colloq., one is doomed (to die); **~ one**, (n.) oneself, (a.) first in rank, quality, or importance; **~plate**, bearing number esp. of vehicle); person or thing (esp. single issue of magazine, song in programme) whose place in series is indicated by figure (BACK *number*); (in pl.; N~s) O.T. book containing census; company (*is of our ~*, included among us), collection, group, (*a large, small, number of birds*; *present in great, small, numbers*; **in ~s** = in great numbers); (in pl.) numerical preponderance (*won by force of numbers*); numerical reckoning (*laws of number and proportion*; **in ~**, numerically; **without ~**, **out of ~**, innumerable n.); (Gram.) class of word-forms including all singular, or all plural, words; (arch., in pl.) groups of musical notes, metrical feet, verses. **2.** v.t. Count; (in pass.) be restricted in number (**his days, years, are ~ed**, he does not have long to live); include *among, in, with,* some class; have or amount to specified number (*the population numbers 800*); **~ (off)**, assign number(s) to, distinguish with number(s). **3. ~less** a., innumerable; **nū'merable** a., countable; **numeral**, see foll.; **nū'merate** a., acquainted with basic principles of mathematics and science, so **nū'meracў** n.; **nūmerā'tion** n., numbering, calculation; **nū'merātor** n., number above line in vulgar fraction showing how many of the parts indicated by the denominator are taken (e.g. 2 in ⅔), person who numbers; **nŭmĕ′rĭcal** a. (-lly), of, in, denoting, number(s); **nŭmer-ŏ′lŏgў** n., study of occult significance of numbers; **nŭ′merous** a., comprising many units (a numerous class, family, library), (with pl. n.) many (numerous gifts). [AF numbre f. L numerus]

**nŭ′meral. 1.** a. Of, denoting, a number. **2.** n. Numeral word(s) or figure(s). **3.** The numerals comprise *cardinal numbers,* giving a measure of total quantity in a group, and *ordinal numbers,* giving a statement of position within a group. **Cardinal numbers** with notation in arabic and Roman figures (cf. ZERO): *one* 1 i; *two* 2 ii; *three* 3 iii; *four* 4 iv, occas. iiii; *five* 5 v; *six* 6 vi; *seven* 7 vii; *eight* 8 viii; *nine* 9 ix; *ten* 10 x; *eleven* 11 xi; *twelve* 12 xii; *thirteen* 13 xiii; *fourteen* 14 xiv; *fifteen* 15 xv; *sixteen* 16 xvi; *seventeen* 17 xvii; *eighteen* 18 xviii; *nineteen* 19 xix; *twenty* 20 xx; *twenty-one* (arch. one-and-twenty) 21 xxi; . . .; *twenty-nine* (arch. nine-and--twenty) 29 xxix; *thirty* 30 xxx; *thirty-one* (arch. one-and-thirty) 31 xxxi; . . .; *forty* 40 xl; . . .; *fifty* 50 l; . . .; *sixty* 60 lx; . . .; *seventy* 70 lxx; . . .; *eighty* 80 lxxx; . . .; *ninety* 90 xc; . . .; *a* or *one hundred* 100 c; *a* or *one hundred and one* 101 ci; . . .; *a* or *one hundred and ninety-nine* 199 cxcix; *two hundred* 200 cc; . . .; *three hundred* 300 ccc; . . .; *four hundred* 400 cd; . . .; *five hundred* 500 d; . . .; *nine hundred and ninety-nine* 999 cmxcix; *a* or *one thousand* 1,000 m; *a* or *one thousand and one* 1,001 mi; . . .; *one thousand one hundred* or *eleven hundred* 1,100 mc; . . .; *one thousand nine hundred* or *nineteen hundred* 1,900 mcm; . . .; *two thousand* 2,000 mm; . . .; *five hundred thousand* or *half a million* 500,000; . . .; *nine hundred and eighty-seven thousand six hundred and fifty-four* 987,654; . . .; *a* or *one million* 1,000,000; . . .; *one million two hundred and thirty-four thousand five hundred and sixty-seven* 1,234,567; see MILLIARD, BILLION, TRILLION, and see HUNDRED for the plural usage of this and higher numerals. Cardinal numbers are normally *adjs.;* they are used as *ns.* with the following general senses (where x and y stand for any cardinal numbers; see also the entries for particular numbers): *the number x* (13 is said to be unlucky),

*the symbol for x* (write a 7), *a set of x things* or *persons* (stack them in fifties), *a playing-card with x* (= 2 to 10) *pips, the hour x* (= 1 to 12) *o'clock, the year x* A.D. or B.C. or *of one's age, a hit for x runs,* (in pl.) *the decade from x* (= 20, 30, . . ., 90) *to x+9 of a century* or *the temperature* or *one's score* or *one's age* (in the thirties; in her twenties), *the size of gloves, shoes, etc., denoted by x, a sum of x pounds* or *pence* or *dollars, a banknote for such amount* (x = 1, 5, 10, etc.); **x figures** (see FIGURE; as measure of size of numbers; esp. x = 3 to 7); **xfold** (see -FOLD; esp. x = 2 to 9 and round numbers); **x to 1** (odds in betting etc.; esp. x = 2 to 6, 10, 50, 100, 1,000); **x.y,** time in hours and minutes (x = 0 to 23, y = 0 to 59) or minutes and seconds (x and y = 0 to 59), amount in pounds and pence or in dollars and cents (y = 0 to 99); **x/y/z,** date of ‖day *x*, month *y*, or *day *x*, month *x,* year (in full or of century) *z*. **Ordinal numbers** with notation in arabic figures: *first* 1st; *second* 2nd; *third* 3rd; *fourth* 4th; *fifth* 5th; *sixth* 6th; *seventh* 7th; *eighth* 8th; *ninth* 9th; *tenth* 10th; *eleventh* 11th; *twelfth* 12th; *thirteenth* 13th; *fourteenth* 14th; *fifteenth* 15th; *sixteenth* 16th; *seventeenth* 17th; *eighteenth* 18th; *nineteenth* 19th; *twentieth* 20th; *twenty-first* 21st; . . .; *twenty-ninth* 29th; *thirtieth* 30th; *thirty-first* 31st; . . .; *fortieth* 40th; . . .; *fiftieth* 50th; . . .; *sixtieth* 60th; . . .; *seventieth* 70th; . . .; *eightieth* 80th; . . .; *ninetieth* 90th; . . .; *hundredth* 100th; *hundred-and-first* 101st; . . .; *hundred--and-ninety-ninth* 199th; *two-hundredth* 200th; . . .; *three-hundredth* 300th; . . .; *nine-hundred-and-ninety-ninth* 999th; *thousandth* 1,000th; *thousand-and-first* 1,001st; . . .; *two-thousandth* 2,000th; . . .; *five-hundred-thousandth* or *half--millionth* 500,000th; . . .; *millionth* 1,000,000th; see BILLIONTH, TRIL-LIONTH. Ordinal numbers are normally *adjs.;* **xth part** (where *xth* stands for any ordinal number), one of *x* equal parts into which thing is or might be divided (x = 3 or more); they are used as *ns.* with the following general senses (see also the entries for particular numbers): *xth part, the one in xth position, xth* (= 1st to 31st) *day of month, musical interval spanning x alphabetical notes, note thus separated from given one, harmonic combination of notes thus separated, xth* (= 1st to 6th) *form in school,* (in *pl.*) *goods of xth quality,* (*person having*) *place in xth* (= 1st to 4th) *class in examination, xth* (= 1st to 5th) *gear;* they form *advs.* in **-ly** (FIRST or *firstly;* SECONDLY, *thirdly,* etc., = *in the xth* PLACE). [L (prec.)]

**nū′merate—nū′merous.** See NUMBER.

**nū′minous** *a.* Indicating presence of divinity; spiritual; awe-inspiring. [L (*numen* deity)]

**numism|ă′tic** (-z-) *a.* (-ically). Of coins or coinage or medals; **~ă′tics,** **nūmi′smatist** (-z-), **~atŏ′logy,** *ns.* [F f. L f. Gk *nomisma* coin]

**nū′mskull** *n.* (Head of) stupid person. [NUMB]

**nŭn** *n.* Member of community of women living apart under religious vows; **~'s veiling,** thin woollen fabric. [E & F f. L *nonna*]

**nū′nciō** (-shiō) *n.* (*pl.* **~s**). Pope's permanent diplomatic representative in another country; **nū′nciature** (-shat-) *n.,* (tenure of) this office. [It. f. L *nuntius* envoy]

**nū′ncup|āte** *v.t.* Declare (will, testament) by word of mouth only; **~ā′tion, ~ātor,** *ns.;* **~ātive** *a.* [L *nuncupo* to name]

**nū′nnery** *n.* Convent of nuns. [AF (NUN)]

**nū′ptial** (-shal). **1.** *a.* (**~ly**). Of marriage or wedding; **~ flight** (of ants, bees, etc., with mating). **2.** *n.* (usu. in *pl.*) Wedding. [F or L (*nubo nupt-* wed)]

**‖N.U.R.** *abbr.* National Union of Railwaymen.

**nūrse. 1.** *n.* Person trained for care of the sick or infirm; (**dry-**)**~,** woman employed to take charge of young children; = WET-*nurse;* country etc. that fosters some quality etc. (*the nurse of liberty*); nursing, being nursed, (lit., or fig. of estate etc.; *at,* *put out to, nurse*). **2.** *v.t. & i.* Be nurse (of), tend (sick person); suckle (child); (in *pass.*) be brought up (*in* luxury, certain place, etc.); foster, promote development of; manage with solicitude (‖**~ constituency,** keep electors' favour by continued attentions); cherish (grievance); hold or clasp (baby, one's knees) carefully or caressingly; treat carefully; sit close over (fire); (Bill.) keep (balls) together for series of cannons. **3. ~'maid,** girl in charge

of child(ren); **‖nursing home,** private hospital for surgical operations or medical treatment. **4.** **nū′rs(e)ling** (-sl-) *n.,* infant esp. in relation to its nurse (**~ling of,** person or thing bred in or fostered by). [F *nurice* f. L (NOURISH)]

**nū′rsery** *n.* Room, place, for children (and their nurses) (DAY *nursery;* **~ rhyme,** simple traditional song or story in rhyme; **~ school,** for young children esp. under 5; **~ slopes,** suitable for beginners at skiing); practice, institution, etc., that fosters certain abilities, qualities, etc., (*a nursery of politicians, of vice*); plot of ground where plants are reared (**~man,** owner of or worker in such establishment).

**nū′rture. 1.** *n.* Bringing up, fostering care; nourishment. **2.** *v.t.* Bring up, rear. [F f. *nourrir* (NOURISH)]

**‖N.U.S.** *abbr.* National Union of Seamen; National Union of Students.

**nŭt. 1.** *n.* Fruit consisting of hard or tough shell enclosing edible kernel, this kernel, (‖*can't shoot* etc. *for* **~s,** sl., even tolerably well; HARD or *tough nut;* **~s** (*to you*), sl. excl. of derision); pod containing hard seeds (EARTH-*nut,* PEAnut); (sl.) head (*off* one's **~,** crazy; *do* one's **~,** go crazy), crazy person, (in *pl.,* as *a.*) crazy, mad, (**~s about, on,** enthusiastic about, skilful at); (arch. sl.) showy young man; small lump of coal, butter, etc.; pierced piece, usu. hexagonal, screwed on end of bolt to secure it; **~s and bolts,** (fig.) practical details. **2.** *v.i.* (**-tt-**). Seek, gather, nuts (*go nutting*). **3.** **~-brown,** coloured like ripe hazelnut; **~-butter,** food like butter, made from nuts; **~-case,** (sl.) crazy person; **~′cracker,** (usu. in *pl.*) instrument for cracking nuts, prominent nose and chin that nearly touch, (*Nutcracker Man,* fossil hominid with large premolar teeth); **~′hatch** (-t-h-), small climbing bird feeding on nuts, insects, etc. [rel. to HATCH[2]]; **~-shell,** hard exterior covering of nut (*in a* **~***shell,* in few words, concisely); **~-tree,** esp. hazel. **4. ~′ty** *a.* (-iness), abounding in, tasting of, nuts, (sl.) crazy (**~ty about, on,** sl., = *nuts about*). [E]

**‖N.U.T.** *abbr.* National Union of Teachers.

**nūtā′tion** *n.* Nodding; oscillation of earth's axis. [L *nuto* nod]

**nŭt′mĕg** n. Hard aromatic seed of E. Ind. tree, used as spice etc. [F (*nois* nut, *mugue* MUSK)]

**nŭ′trĭa** n. Skin or fur of coypu. [Sp., = otter]

**nŭ′trĭ|ent** a. & n. (Substance) serving as or providing nourishment; **~ĭment** n., nourishing food (lit. or fig.); **~ĭ′tion** n., food, nourishment; **~ĭ′tious** (-shŭs) a., efficient as food; **~ĭtĭve** a., nutritious, of nutrition. [L *nutrio* nourish]

**nŭ′ttў.** See NUT.

**nŭx vŏ′mĭca** n. Seed of E. Ind. tree yielding strychnine. [L (*nux* nut, VOMIT)]

**nŭ′zzle** v.i. & t. Nose, burrow or press or rub or sniff with nose, press nose or press (nose) *into*, *against*; nestle, lie snug, (also *refl.*). [NOSE]

**N.W.** *abbr.* North-West(ern).

**N.Y.(C.)** *abbr.* New York (City).

**nў′lŏn** n. Very tough, light, elastic synthetic polymer, widely used in industry and in textile fabrics; fabric of this; (in *pl.*) stockings of nylon. [invented wd]

**nymph** n. (Myth.) semi-divine maiden of sea, mountains, woods, etc.; (poet.) maiden; (Zool.) immature form of some insects; **~′ĕt** (or -ĕ′t) n., (esp.) sexually attractive young girl; **~omā′nĭa** n., excessive sexual desire in women; **~omā′nĭăc** n. (colloq. abbr. **~′ō**, *pl.* **-os**). [F f. L f. Gk *numphē* nymph, bride]

**N.Z.** *abbr.* New Zealand.

# O

**O¹, o,** (ō) n. (*pl.* **Os, O's**). Fifteenth letter; (*O*) nought, zero.

**O²** (ō) *int.* (arch., poet., rhet.) prefixed to name in vocative (*O God our help*) or expr. wish, entreaty, etc., (*O* FOR; *O come, all ye faithful*). [natural excl.]

**o′** (*o*) *prep.* Of, on, (arch., poet., dial., exc. in some phrs.): *o'clock*, *will--o'-the-wisp*. [abbr.]

**-o** *suf.* forming usu. sl. or colloq. variants or derivatives (*beano*). [perh. OH as joc. suf.]

**-o-,** terminal vowel of comb. forms (*Franco-German, oscilloscope*). [orig. Gk]

**O.** *abbr.* Ohio; Old; ‖**O level,** = ORDINARY *level*.

**O** *symb.* oxygen.

**oaf** n. (*pl.* **~s, oaves** *pr.* -vz). Awkward lout. [N (ELF)]

**oak** n. Forest tree with hard wood, acorns, and lobed leaves; its wood (HEART *of oak*); allied or similar tree (HOLM-*oak*); (*attrib.*, =, but now more usu. than) oaken; **~-apple, -GALL³, -wart,** kinds of excrescence produced on oak by gall-flies; ‖**~-apple day,** 29 May (Charles II restored 1660), on which oak-apples or oak--leaves were worn to commemorate ROYAL-*oak* incident; **~-fern** (having three-branched fronds with subdivisions shaped like oak-leaves); ‖**the Oaks,** annual race at Epsom for fillies [f. name of estate]; **~′en** a., (arch.) made of oak. [E]

**oa′kum** n. Loose fibre got by picking old rope to pieces and used esp. in caulking (**pick ~**, make this). [E, = off-COMB]

**O. & M.** *abbr.* organization and methods.

‖**O.A.P.** *abbr.* old-age pension(er).

**oar** n. Pole with blade used to propel boat by leverage against water, esp. worked singly by one rower with both hands, (**have an ~ in**, be (meddlesomely) concerned with; **put one's ~ in**, interfere; **rest on one's ~s**, relax one's efforts); rower (*good, practised, oar*); **~′sman, ~′swoman,** rower; **~′smanship,** art of rowing. [E]

**ōā′s|ĭs** n. (*pl.* **-es** *pr.* -ēz). Fertile spot in desert (lit. or fig.). [L f. Gk]

**oast** n. Kiln for drying hops; **~-house,** building containing this. [E]

**oat** n. (in *pl.*) (Grain yielded by) hardy cereal grown as food for humans and horses (**feel one's ~s**, colloq., be lively; **off one's ~s**, colloq., lacking appetite for food); oat-plant, any variety of it (**wild ~**, tall grass resembling oats; **sow one's wild ~s**, indulge in youthful follies before becoming steady); (poet.) oat-stem used as shepherd's pipe, pastoral poetry; ~**cake**, thin un-leavened cake made of oatmeal, esp. in Scotland and N. England; ~**-grass**, wild oat; ~**meal**, meal from oats used esp. in oatcakes and porridge, greyish-fawn colour; ~**en** *a.*, made of oats or oat-stem. [E]

**oath** *n.* (*pl. pr.* ōdhz). Confirmation of statement by naming of God or other power or sacred thing (**make** ~, **take** *or* **swear an** ~, bind one-self thus; **on** ~, **under** ~, under the responsibility implied by an oath; **on** one's ~, with solemn assertion of truth); statement so confirmed (*oath of allegiance* etc.); name of God etc. used as expletive, piece of profanity. [E]

**O.A.U.** *abbr.* Organization of African Unity.

**ob-** *pref.* (usu. **oc-, of-, op-**, bef. *c, f, p* respectively) esp. in wds f. L, expr. exposure, meeting, facing, direction, compliance, opposition, resistance, hindrance, concealment, finality, completeness. [L (*ob* towards, against, in the way of)]

‖**O.B.** *abbr.* Old Boy; outside broad-cast.

**ob.** *abbr.* obiit.

**Obad.** *abbr.* Obadiah (O.T.).

**ŏbblĭgā′tŏ** (-ah′-). **1.** *a.* (Mus.) Forming an integral part of the composition, inseparable. **2.** *n.* (*pl.* ~**s**). Obbligato part or accompani-ment. [It., = obligatory]

**ŏ′bdūrate** (*or* -ūr′-) *a.* Hardened, stubborn; **ŏ′bdūracў** *n.* [L (*duro* harden)]

‖**O.B.E.** *abbr.* Officer (of the Order) of the British Empire.

**obē′dĭen\|t** *a.* Submissive to super-ior's will (‖*your obedient* SERVANT); ~**ce** *n.*, obeying, submission, com-pliance, (**in** ~**ce to**, at the dictates of), religious allegiance (*return to the obedience of Rome*). [F f. L (OBEY)]

**obei′s\|ance** (-ā′s-) *n.* Bow, curtsy, or other respectful gesture (*make an obeisance*); homage (*do, make, pay, obeisance*); ~**ant** *a.*, showing defer-ence, obsequious. [F (OBEY)]

**ŏ′belĭsk** (*or* -ĭl-) *n.* Tapering usu. monolithic stone shaft square or rectangular in section; = OBELUS. [L f. Gk (dim. of foll.)]

**ŏ′bel\|us** *n.* (*pl.* ~**i** *pr.* -ī). Mark placed against spurious word etc. in MS.; mark of reference (†; **double** ~**us**, ‡). [L f. Gk, = pointed pillar, spit]

**obē′s\|e** (*or* ō-) *a.* Very fat, corpu-lent; ~**ĭtў** *n.* [L (*edo* eat)]

**obey′** (obā′) *v.t. & i.* Perform bid-ding of, be obedient to; execute (command); be actuated by (force, impulse); do what one is told to do. [F *obéir* f. L *obedio* (*audio* hear)]

**ŏ′bfusc\|āte** *v.t.* Darken, obscure, confuse, (mind, judgement, topic, etc.); stupefy, bewilder; ~**ā′tion**, ~**ātor**, *ns.* [L (*fuscus* dark)]

**obiit** (ŏ′bĭit) *v.i.* 3 *sing. past.* Died (with date of death). [L *obeo* die]

**ŏ′bĭt** *n.* (Record of) date of death; (colloq.) obituary. [F f. L *obitus* death (prec.)]

**obiter dict\|um** (ŏbĭter dĭ′ktum) *n.* (*pl.* ~**a**). Judge's opinion expressed incidentally and without binding force; casual remark. [L, = thing said by the way]

**obĭ′tūar\|ў. 1.** *n.* Notice of death(s); account of deceased person. **2.** *a.* Of, in, serving as, obituary. **3.** ~**ĭst** *n.*, writer of obituaries. [L (OBIT)]

**object. 1.** (ŏ′bjĭkt) *n.* Thing pre-sented to senses, material thing, (~**-glass**, lens in telescope etc. nearest the object; ~**-lesson**, in-struction about an exhibited object, fig. striking practical example of some principle); person or thing of pitiable or ridiculous appearance; person or thing to which action or feeling is directed (*the Bible had been the object of his study*); ~**-ball**, that aimed at in billiards etc.); thing aimed at, end, purpose, (**no** ~, not an important matter: *distance, money, time,* etc., (*is*) *no object*); (Philos.) thing external to the thinking mind or subject; (Gram.) noun or noun-equivalent governed by active transitive verb or by preposition (**direct** ~, primary object of verbal action; **indirect** ~, person or thing affected by verbal action but not primarily acted on, e.g. *him* in *give him the book*). **2.** (objĕ′kt) *v.t. & i.* Adduce (quality, fact, *that*) as con-trary or damaging (*to, against*); announce opposition *to*, feel or ex-press dislike or reluctance to, (*I object to being treated like this*). **3.** **objĕ′ctifȳ** *v.t.*, make objective, em-body; **objĕ′ction** *n.*, objecting, ad-verse reason or statement, expression or feeling of disapproval or dislike; **objĕ′ctionable** *a.* (-bly), open to objection, undesirable, offensive; **objĕ′ctĭve,** (*a.*) external to the mind, actually existing, (of person, writing, discussion, etc.) dealing with outward things or exhibiting facts uncoloured by feelings or opinions (opp. *subjective*), (Gram.) constructed as or appropriate to the object (~**ive case,** in English that governed by transitive verb or preposition), (Mil., of point) towards which troops are directed to advance, (transf.) aimed at, (*n.*) objective case or point, object-glass; **obje̅'ctĭvĭsm** *n.*, tendency to lay stress on what is objective; **objĕctĭ'vĭtў** *n.*; **obje̅'ctor** *n.* [L (*jacio -ject-* throw)]

*objet d'art* (ŏbzhāda̅r') *n.* (*pl. -ets pr.* same). Small decorative object. [F, = object of art]

**o̅'bjur̄g|āte** *v.t.* (literary). Chide, scold; ~**ā'tion,** ~**ātor,** *ns.*; ~**ātorў** (*or* objĕr'ga-) *a.* (-ily). [L (*jurgo* quarrel)]

**ŏ'blāte**[1] *n.* Person dedicated to monastic or religious life or work. [F f. L (OFFER)]

**ŏ'blāte**[2] (*or* oblā't) *a.* (Geom., of spheroid) flattened at poles. [L (prec.; cf. PROLATE)]

**oblā'tion** *n.* Thing offered to God; (offering of the elements in) Eucharist; pious donation; ~**al, o̅'blatorў,** *adjs.* [F or L (OFFER)]

**oblī'ge** *v.t. & i.* Constrain, compel, *to do*; be binding on; gratify *by doing* or *with*, perform a service (for); (colloq.) make contribution to entertainment (*with* song etc., or *abs.*); (in *pass.*) be bound (*to* person) by gratitude (*for* service etc.; **much** ~**d,** thank you); (arch. or Law) bind (person) by oath, promise, contract, etc., *to* person, *to do*; **o̅'blĭ-gāte** *v.t.* (usu. in *p.p.*), bind (person, legally or morally) *to do*; **obligā'-tion** *n.*, binding agreement, written contract or bond, constraining power of law, contract, duty, etc., (**day of obligation,** one on which all are required to attend Mass or Communion), burdensome task, a duty, (indebtedness for) service or benefit (*be,* LAY[4], put, *under* (*an*) *obligation*; *repay an obligation*); **oblĭ'gatorў** (*or* o̅'blĭgă-) *a.* (-ily, -iness), binding, compulsory; **oblĭ'gĭng** *a.*, courteous, accommodating, ready to do service or kindness. [F f. L *obligo* bind]

**oblī'que** (-e̅'k) **1.** *a.* Declining from the vertical or horizontal, diverging from straight line or course; not going straight to the point, roundabout, indirect; (Gram., of case) other than nominative or vocative; **oblī'quĭtў** *n.* **2.** *n.* Oblique stroke (/). [F f. L]

**oblĭ'ter|āte** *v.t.* Blot out, efface, erase, destroy, leave no clear traces of; ~**ā'tion,** ~**ātor,** *ns.* [L *oblitero* erase (*litera* letter)]

**oblĭ'vĭ|on** *n.* State of having or being forgotten, disregard, (*buried in, fall* or *sink into, oblivion*); ~**ous** *a.* (~**ous to, of,** unaware, unconscious, of). [F f. L (*obliviscor* forget)]

**o̅'blŏng.** **1.** *a.* Rectangular with adjacent sides unequal. **2.** *n.* Oblong figure or object. [L *oblongus* somewhat long]

**o̅'blŏquў** *n.* Abuse; being generally ill spoken of. [L *obloquium* contradiction (*loquor* speak)]

**obnŏ'xious** (-kshus) *a.* Offensive, objectionable, disliked. [L (*noxa* injury)]

**o̅'bŏe,** (arch.) **hautboy** (ho̅'boi, *n.* Wood-wind double-reed treble instrument with piercing plaintive tone; its player; **o̅'bŏĭst** *n.* [It. f. F *hautbois* (*haut* high, *bois* wood)]

**obsce̅'ne** *a.* Indecent; lascivious; ||(Law, of publication) tending to deprave or corrupt; (colloq.) highly offensive; **obsce̅'nĭtў** *n.* [F, or L *obsc(a)enus* abominable]

**obscūr̄'|e. 1.** *a.* (~**er,** ~**est**). Dark, dim; dingy; indistinct; hidden, unnoticed, undistinguished; unexplained; not perspicuous; *obscure* VOWEL. **2.** *v.t.* Make obscure, dark, indistinct, or unintelligible; outshine; conceal. **3.** ~**ant** *n.*, opponent of inquiry, enlightenment, etc.; ~**antĭsm,** ~**antĭst,** (*or* ŏbskūrā'-) *ns.*; **ŏb-scūrā'tion,** ~**ĭtў,** *ns.* [F f. L]

**obse̅crā'tion** *n.* Earnest entreaty. [L (*obsecro* entreat)]

**o̅'bse̅quĭes** (-ĭz) *n.pl.* Funeral; **obse̅'quĭal** *a.* [AF f. L *obsequiae*; cf. EXEQUIES]

**obse̅'quĭous** *a.* Servile, fawning. [L (*obsequor* comply with)]

**obse̅r̄'v|e** (-z-) *v.t. & i.* Keep, follow, adhere to, perform duly, (law, command, appointed time, method, principle, silence, rite, anniversary, etc.); perceive, mark, watch, take notice of, become conscious of, (person, thing, *that*); examine and note (phenomena) without aid of experiment; say, esp. by way of comment; make remark(s) *on*; ~'**ance** *n.*, keeping or performance (*of* law, occasion, etc.), rite, ceremonial act; ~'**ant,** (*a.*) attentive in observance, acute in taking notice, (*n.*; *O-*) member of stricter branch of Franciscans; **ŏbservā'tion** (-z-) *n.*, noticing or being noticed (**under** ~**ation,** watched; ~**ation car,** in train esp. in U.S., so built as to afford good view; ~**ation post,** Mil., esp. for watching effect of artillery fire), faculty of taking notice, taking of sun's or star's altitude, comment, remark, statement; **ŏbservā'tional** (-z-) *a.* (**-lly**); ~'**atory** *n.*, building for astronomical or other observation; ~'**er** *n.*, (esp.) interested spectator (*Observer*, in newspaper titles), person trained to notice and identify aircraft, or carried in aeroplane to note enemy's position. [F f. L (*servo* watch, keep)]

**obsĕ'ss** *v.t.* Haunt, preoccupy, fill mind of; ~**ion** (-shon) *n.*; ~**ional** (-shon-), ~**ĭve,** *adjs.* [L (*obsideo -sess-* besiege)]

**obsĭ'dian** *n.* Dark vitreous lava. [L (*Obsius,* person)]

**ŏ'bsolēte** *a.* Disused, discarded, antiquated; ~**e'scent** *a.*, becoming obsolete; .~**e'scence** *n.* [L (*soleo* be accustomed)]

**ŏ'bstacle** *n.* Thing obstructing progress; ~**race** (with natural or artificial obstacles to be passed). [F f. L (*obsto* stand in the way)]

**obstĕ'trĭc(al)** *adjs.* (**-ically**). Of childbirth and processes immediately preceding and following it, as branch of medicine and surgery; **ŏbstĕtrĭ'cian,** ~**ĭcs,** *ns.* [L (*obstetrix* midwife f. *obsto* be present)]

**ŏ'bstĭnate** *a.* Stubborn, intractable; firmly continuing in one's action or opinion despite persuasion; ~**acў** *n.* [L (*obstino* persist)]

**obstrĕ'perous** *a.* Noisy, turbulent, unruly. [L (*obstrepo* shout at)]

**obstrŭ'ct** *v.t.* & *i.* Block up, make hard or impossible to pass; prevent or retard progress of, impede; ~**ion** *n.*, (esp.) hindering, esp. of Parliamentary business by deliberate delays, obstacle; ~**ionist** *n.*; ~**ĭve,** (*a.*) causing or meant to cause obstruction, (*n.*) obstructionist; ~**or** *n.* [L *obstruo -struct-* block up]

**obtai'n** *v.t.* & *i.* Acquire, secure, have granted to one, get; (of practice etc.) be in vogue, prevail. [F f. L (*teneo* hold)]

**obtru'|de** (-ōō'-) *v.t.* & *i.* Thrust (a matter, one*self*) importunately forward (*on, upon,* person or his notice); be, become, obtrusive; ~**sion** (-zhon) *n.*; ~**sĭve** *a.* [L *obtrudo* thrust against]

**obtū'se** *a.* Of blunt form, not sharp-pointed or sharp-edged; (of angle) greater than one and less than two right angles; (of the senses, a person, etc.) dull, slow of perception, stupid. [L (*obtundo -tus-* beat against, blunt)]

**ŏ'bverse** *n.* Side of coin or medal that bears the head or principal design (opp. *reverse*); front or proper or top side of a thing; counterpart. [L (*obverto -vers-* turn towards)]

**ŏ'bvĭāte** *v.t.* Clear away, get rid of, get round, (danger, hindrance, etc.). [L *obvio* prevent (*via* way)]

**ŏ'bvĭous** *a.* Seen or realized at the first glance, evident. [L (*ob viam* in the way)]

**oc–.** See OB-.

**O.C.** *abbr.* Officer Commanding.

**ŏcari'na** (-rē'-) *n.* Small egg-shaped musical wind-instrument. [It. (*oca* goose)]

**O'ccam** (ŏ'-) *n.* ~'**s razor,** principle that fewest possible assumptions are to be made in explaining a thing. [William of *Occam*]

**occā'sion** (-zhon). **1.** *n.* Suitable juncture, opportunity, (**take** ~, avail oneself of opportunity *to* do; **on** ~, when need arises, now and then); reason, ground, incentive, need, (*there is no occasion to be angry*); immediate but subordinate cause (*the cause of a revolution may be obscure while its occasion is obvious*); (particular time marked by) special occurrence (*on this festive occasion*; on the *occasion of her marriage*; *dressed, dismantled, for the occasion*; **rise to the** ~, show requisite ability, energy, etc.); (in *pl.*) affairs, business, (esp. *go about* one's *lawful occasions*). **2.** *v.t.* Cause, esp. incidentally. **3.** ~**al** *a.*, arising out of, intended for, acting on, special occasion(s), happening irregularly, not regular or frequent, (~**al table,** small table for use as required); ~**allў** *adv.*, as occasion suggests, sometimes, intermittently. [F or L (*occido -cas-* go down)]

**O'ccĭdent** (ŏ'ks-) *n.* (poet., rhet.) *The* west; western Europe; Europe, America, or both, as opp. countries east of them; European civilization.

[F f. L *occidens -entis* setting, sunset, west]

**ŏccĭdĕ'ntal** (ŏks-). **1.** *a.* (~ly). Of the Occident, western. **2.** *n.* (O~). Native, inhabitant, of the Occident. **3.** ~**ĭsm** *n.*, European ways; ~**ĭst** *n.*; ~**īze** *v.t.*

**ŏ'ccĭpŭt** (ŏ'ks-) *n.* Back of head (cf. *sinciput*); ~**ĭ'pĭtal** *a.* (-lly). [L (*caput* head)]

**occlu'|de** (-ōō'-) *v.t.* Obstruct, stop up; (Chem.) absorb (gases); ~**sion** (-zhon) *n.* [L *occludo -clus-* close up]

**ŏccŭ'lt** (*or* o-). **1.** *a.* Esoteric; recondite; involving the supernatural, mystical, magical; **the ~**, that which is occult. **2.** *v.t.* Conceal, (Astron.) hide by passing in front of. **3.** **ŏccultā'tion** *n.* (Astron.); ~**ĭsm** *n.*, mysticism; ~**ĭst** *n.* [L *occulo -cult-* hide]

**ŏ'ccŭp|ȳ** *v.t.* Take military possession of; reside in, be tenant of; hold (office); take up, fill, be in, (space, time, place); place oneself in (building etc.) esp. as political demonstration; (esp. in *pass.* or *refl.*) keep busy or engaged (*with* or *in* thing or do*ing*); ~**ant** *n.*, person holding piece of property or office, person or animal in a place; ~**ancȳ** *n.*; ~**ā'tion** *n.*, (esp.) employment, calling, pursuit; **army of** ~**ation** (left to hold occupied region till regular government is set up); ~**ā'tional** *a.*, pertaining to one's, or an, occupation; ~**ational disease, hazard,** (to which a particular occupation renders one especially liable); ~**ational therapy,** mental or physical activity to assist recovery from disease or injury; ||~**ĭer** *n.*, person in (esp. temporary or subordinate) possession of house etc. [F f. L *occupo* seize]

**occŭr'** *v.i.* (-rr-). Be met with or found in some place or conditions; come into one's mind (*it occurs to me that*); come into being as event or process, take place, happen; **ocçŭ'rrence** *n.*, happening (**is of frequent** ~**rence**, often happens), an incident. [L *occurro* befall]

**ō'cean** (ō'shan) *n.* Great body of water surrounding land of globe; large division of this (*Atlantic, Pacific, Indian, Arctic, Antarctic, Ocean*); *the sea*; immense expanse or quantity (*oceans of time*); ~**-going,** (of ship) able to cross the oceans; **Ŏcēă'nĭa** (ōshĭ-) *n.*, islands in and near Pacific;

the ocean, (O-) of Oceania; ~**ŏ'graphy** *n.*, study of the oceans. [F f. L f. Gk]

**ō'cēlot** *n.* Leopard-like feline of S. & Central America. [F f. Nahuatl]

**ŏch** (ŏχ) *int.* (Sc. & Ir.) = *oh, ah.* [Gael. & Ir.]

**ō'chre, *ō'cher,** (ō'ker) *n.* Earth used as yellow or brown or red pigment; pale brownish-yellow colour; **ō'chrous** (-k-) *a.* [F f. L f. Gk]

**o'clŏ'ck.** See o', CLOCK[1].

**Oct.** *abbr.* October.

**ŏct-, ŏcta-, ŏcto-,** in *comb.* Eight; **ŏ'ctachŏrd** (-k-) *n.*, 8-stringed instrument, series of 8 notes (e.g. diatonic scale); **ŏ'ctăd** *n.*, group of 8; **ŏ'ctagon** *n.*, plane figure with 8 sides and angles; **ŏctā'gonal** *a.*; **ŏctahē'dron** (-a-h-) *n.* (*pl.* -rons, -ra), solid figure contained by 8 plane faces and unu. by 8 triangles; **ŏctahē'dral** (-a-h-) *a.*; **ŏ'ctāne** *n.*, hydrocarbon of paraffin series (**high- -octane**, of fuel used in internal combustion engines, not detonating rapidly during power stroke); ~ **number**, representing certain properties of fuel); **ŏ'ctave** (-ĭv) *n.*, 8-line stanza, (Mus.) note 7 diatonic degrees from given note, these sounded together, interval between note and its octave, series of notes filling this; **ŏctā'vō** *n.* (*abbr.* 8vo; *pl.* -os), (size of) book or page given by thrice folding sheet(s) to form quire(s) of 8 leaves; **ŏctĕ't(te)** *n.*, group of 8, (Mus.) (composition for) group of 8 instruments or voices; **Octō'ber** (ŏ-) *n.*, tenth month [cf. DECEMBER]; **ŏctogēnār'ian** *a.* & *n.*, (person) from 80 to 89 years old; **ŏ'ctopus** *n.* (*pl.* -puses, octo'podes *pr.* -ŏ'podēz), cephalopod mollusc with 8 suckered arms round mouth, (fig.) formidable ramified power or influence [Gk *pous* foot]; **ŏcto- syllǎ'bĭc, ŏctosy'llable,** *adjs.* & *ns.*, 8-syllabled (verse). [L *octo*, Gk *oktō*, eight]

**ŏ'cŭl|ar** *a.* Of, for, by, with, etc., the eye(s) or sight, visual; ~**ĭst** *n.*, specialist in treatment of eye disorders or defects. [F f. L (*oculus* eye)]

**o.d.** *abbr.* outer diameter.

**ŏdd. 1.** *a.* Left over when rest have been distributed or divided into pairs; (of number such as 3, 5) not integrally divisible by two, bearing such number (*no parking on odd dates*);

(appended to number, sum, weight, etc.) with something over of lower denomination (**forty ~**, between 40 and 50; **twelve pounds ~**, between £12 and £13); by which round number, given sum, etc., is exceeded (*There are 1006; what shall we do with the odd six?*); additional, casual, beside the reckoning, unconnected, unoccupied, incalculable, (*picks up odd bargains; do it at odd moments; in some odd corner*); extraordinary, strange, queer, remarkable, eccentric. **2.** *n.* (Golf). *The* stroke which one player has played more than his opponent. **3.** **~'ball**, **~ fish**, (colloq.) eccentric person; **O'ddfellow**, member of fraternity similar to Freemasons; **~ job**, casual isolated piece of work; **~ man**, man who does odd jobs, person who has deciding vote in committee etc. with evenly divided members; **~ man out**, person or thing differing from all others of group in some respect; **~ numbers, volumes**, (belonging to incomplete sets of magazines, books). **4.** **~'ity** *n.*, strangeness, peculiar trait, queer person, fantastic object, strange event; **~'ment** *n.*, odd article, something left over, (in *pl.*) odds and ends. [N *oddi* point, angle, third or odd number]

**ŏdds** (-z) *n.pl.* (sometimes treated as *sing.*). Advantageous difference (*it makes no odds*; **what's the ~?**, what does it matter?); variance, strife, (*are at odds with fate, with their neighbours*); balance of advantage (*the odds are in our favour; won against all the odds*); handicap (*give, receive, odds*); ratio between amounts staked by parties to bet (**lay, give, ~ of three to one**, said of party offering higher amount; **~on**, a state when (betting odds indicate that) success is more likely than failure; **over the ~**, above generally agreed price etc.); chances in favour of or against some result (*it is long odds, the odds are, that he will do it*); **~ and ends**, (vulg.) **~ and sods**, remnants, stray articles.

**ŏde** *n.* Lyric poem of exalted style and tone, often of varied or irregular metre. [F f. L f. Gk *ōidē* song]

**ō'dĭum** *n.* Widespread dislike or disapproval attaching to person or action; **ō'dĭous** *a.*, hateful, repulsive. [L, = hatred]

**odŏ'mĕter** *n.* Instrument to meas-

ure distance travelled by wheeled vehicle. [F f. Gk *hodos* way]

**ō'dour**, **\*ō'dor**, (-er) *n.* Pleasant or unpleasant smell; fragrance; (fig.) savour, trace, (*no odour of intolerance attaches to it*), *good* or *bad* or ill repute or favour (*is in bad odour with the authorities*); **~ of sanctity**, reputation for holiness; **ŏdorī'ferous** *a.*, diffusing (usu. agreeable) odour; **ō'dorous** *a.* [F f. L *odor*]

**ŏ'dyssey** *n.* Adventurous journey. [title of Homeric epic on adventures of *Odysseus* (Ulysses)]

**O.E.C.D.** *abbr.* Organization for Economic Co-operation and Development.

**O.E.D.** *abbr.* Oxford English Dictionary.

**oedē'ma** (ēd-, ĭd-) *n.* Swollen state of tissue in body; **~tous** *a.* [L f. Gk (*oideō* swell)]

**Oe'dĭp|us** (ē'd-) *n.* **~us complex**, (Psych.) attachment of child to parent of opposite sex (esp. mother); **~al** *a.* [Gk *Oidipous*, who in ignorance married his mother]

**oenŏ'logȳ** (ē-) *n.* Knowledge or study of wines; **oe'nophile** (ē'-) *n.*, connoisseur of wines. [Gk *oinos* wine]

**o'er** (ōr) (poet.) = OVER *prep.*, *adv.*, & *pref.* [contr.]

**oesŏ'phag|us** (ēs-), **\*ēs-**, *n.* (*pl.* ~i *pr.* -jī, **~uses**). Canal from mouth to stomach, gullet. [Gk]

**of** (ŏv, ŏv) *prep.* indicating removal, separation, point of departure, deprivation, (*rid, independent, upwards, defraud, of*); origin, derivation, cause, agency, authorship, (*descended, born, buy, receive, die, works, of*; **of itself**, by or in itself), material, substance, closer definition, identity, (*house of cards; built of bricks; make an ass of; city of Rome; a fool of a man; your letter of 1 May*; **be of**, possess importance, interest, value, etc.), concern, reference, direction, respect, (*beware, think, suspect, guilty, of*), objective relation (*love of virtue; in search of food; redolent, lavish, destructive, of*), description, quality, condition, (*the hour of prayer; man of tact; girl of ten; on the point of leaving*), partition, classification, inclusion, selection, (*part, sort, member, best, of; six of the ten men*; **of all the impudence!**, which can be imagined; *plays chess* **of an evening**, colloq., at some time in the evenings; **of old, yore, late**, somewhere in the specified periods), belonging, connection, possession, (*articles of clothing*; *tip of the iceberg*; *topic of conversation*; *cause*, *result*, *counterpart*, *of*; *widow of*). [E]

**of-.** See OB-.

**öff** (or awf) *adv.*, *prep.*, *a.*, & *n.* **1.** *adv.* Away, at or to a distance, (*rode off*; *keep assailant off*; *is far*, *3 miles*, *2 years*, *off*; ~ **with his head!**, behead him; ~ **with you!**, go; **take oneself**, **be**, MAKE, ~, depart; **they're** ~!, horse-race has started); out of position, not on or touching or dependent or attached, loose, separate, gone, (*his hat is off*; *take his coat off*; *cut*, *break*, *throw*, etc., *off*; **be** ~ **with the old love**, have severed connection; ‖**a bit** ~, sl., rather annoying or unfair or unwell; LAUGH, SLEEP, **walk**, etc., ~, get rid of by such action; *the meat* etc. **is** ~, has begun to decay); off-stage (NOISES *off*); so as to break continuity or continuance, discontinued, stopped, not obtainable, (*turn off the gas*; *leave off work*; *the engagement*, *strike*, *is off*; *Mr. Jones is* ~ **sick**, not at work; *soup* etc. *is* ~, no longer available on menu etc.; BREAK *off*; ~ **and on**, intermittently, now and then); to the end, entirely, so as to be clear, (*clear*, *drink*, *pay*, POLISH[1], *work*, *off*; JUMP-~, PLAY-~, in sports, to decide a tie); situated as regards money, supplies, etc., (*well*, *better*, *badly*, etc., *off*). **2.** *prep.* From, away or down or up from, disengaged or distant from, no longer on or not yet on, (*chased off the grass*; *fell off a lorry*; *caught me off balance*; *eats off silver plate*; *took something off the price*; *is off duty or work*; *cut a slice off*, *dine off*, *the joint*; *was only a yard off me*; ~ **one's feet**, colloq., to a condition of no longer being able to stand; *carry*, *sweep*, *person* ~ *his feet*, make him enthusiastic or excited; ~ **one's food**, ~ **smoking**, not now attracted by it; *off the* MAP; ~ **the peg**, of clothes, ready-made; ~ **the point**, irrelevant; leading from, not far from, (*a street off the Strand*); at sea opposite (*sank off Cape Horn*); (Golf) with an official handicap of (*plays off 9*). **3.** *a.* Farther, far, (*on the off side of the wall*), (of part of animal, vehicle, ‖road) right (opp. NEAR; *the off front wheel*, *hind leg*); (Crick.) towards, in, coming from, that half of field (as divided by line through middle stumps) in which striker does not stand (opp. ON, LEG; *off break*, *drive*, *stump*; MID-*off*). **4.** *n.* (Crick.) the off side; start of horse-race. **5.** ~**-beat**, (*n.*, Mus.) unaccented part of bar, (*a.*) not coinciding with the beat, (fig.) eccentric, unconventional; ~ **chance**, bare possibility; ~ **colour**, not in good health, *somewhat indecent; ~**-cut**, remnant of paper, timber, etc., after cutting, usu. sold more cheaply; ~**-day** (when one is not at one's best); ~**ha'nd** *adv.* & *a.*, without preparation etc., unceremonious(ly), curt(ly); ~**ha'nded**, = *offhand* a.; *off* one's HANDS, HEAD; ~**-key**, out of tune (lit. or fig.); ‖~**-licence**, (place with) licence to sell beer etc. for consumption off the premises; ~**-li'ne** *a.* & *adv.*, not directly controlled by or connected to computer; ~**-load**, unload; ~**-peak**, (for use) away from peak of electricity consumption, traffic, etc.; ~**'print**, printed copy of article etc. that was orig. part of larger publication; ‖~**-putting**, (colloq.) repellent, disconcerting; ~**'scourings**, refuse, dregs, (*of*; lit. or fig.); ~**-season**, ~**-time**, (when business etc. is slack); ~**'shoot**, side-shoot or branch (lit. or fig.), derivative; ~**'shore**, situated at sea some distance from shore, (of purchases etc.) made or registered abroad, (of wind) blowing seawards; ~**si'de**, (Footb.) between ball and opponent's goal, esp. when player may not play the ball; ~**-sta'ge** *a.* & *adv.*, not on the stage and so not visible to audience; ~ **white** (with grey or yellow tinge). **6.** ~**'ing** *n.*, more distant part of visible sea (*was seen in the offing*; **in the** ~**ing**, fig., not far away, likely to appear); ~**'ish** *a.*, (colloq.) inclined to be aloof. [var. OF]

**Off.** *abbr.* Office; Officer.

**ö'ffal** *n.* Refuse, waste stuff, scraps, garbage; parts cut off as less valuable from carcass meant for food, esp. head, heart, liver, etc.; carrion, putrid flesh. [Du. *afval* (OFF, FALL)]

**offe'nd** *v.i.* & *t.* Stumble morally, do wrong, transgress, (*against*); hurt feelings of, anger, cause resentment or disgust in, outrage, (*am sorry you are offended*; *offended at*, *by*, thing, *with*, *by*, person; *offends the eye*, *his taste*, *her delicacy*, *my sense of justice*); ‖**offe'nce**, *-nse**, *n.*, attacking, aggressive action, wounding of the feelings, wounded feelings, umbrage, (*no offence was meant; too quick to take offence; give offence to*; **no offence**, colloq., I did not mean to offend you); transgression, misdemeanour, illegal act; ~**er** *n*., (esp.) guilty person (FIRST *offender*). [F f. L *offendo -fens-* strike against, displease]

**offe͞nsive. 1.** *a.* Aggressive, intended for or used in attack, (*offensive weapon, movement*); meant to give offence, insulting, (*offensive language*); disgusting, ill-smelling. **2.** *n.* Attitude of assailant, aggressive action, (*take, be on, the offensive*; also transf., as *peace offensive*); offensive campaign or stroke (*the long-expected German offensive*). [F or L (prec.)]

**o͞ffer. 1.** *v.t.* & *i.* Present by way of sacrifice or as token of devotion etc.; tender for acceptance or refusal or consideration, (*offered me a sweet, a job with prospects, an apology*; *offer one's services, opinions, comments*); give opportunity for, express readiness (*to do*); attempt (*violence, resistance, etc.*), show intention *to do* (*offered to strike me*); present to sight or notice (*each age offers its characteristic problems*), show for sale; present itself, occur, (*as opportunity offers*). **2.** *n.* Expression of readiness to do or give if desired, or to sell on terms (**on ~**, for sale at certain, e.g. reduced, price); proposal esp. of marriage; bid. **3.** ~**ing** *n.*, thing offered as sacrifice or as token of devotion; ~**torȳ** *n.*, (occasion of) collection of money at religious service. [E & F f. L *offero oblat-*]

**o͞ffice** *n.* Piece of kindness, service, (**ill ~**) disservice, (*by, through, the good, ill, offices of*); duty, task, function, (*it is my office, the office of the arteries, to*); position with duties attached to it, place of authority or trust or service esp. of public kind, (*was given an office under the Government*), tenure of official position (*take, enter upon, hold, leave, resign, office*); ceremonial duty (**the last ~s**, rites due to the dead); (Eccl.) authorized form of worship; place for transacting business, counting-house, room where administrative or clerical work is done; room etc. set apart for business of particular department of large concern (||*booking-office, lost-property office*) or local branch of dispersed organization (*our Manchester office*) or company for specified

purpose (*insurance-office*); (O~) quarters or staff or collective authority of a Government department etc. (*the ||*FOREIGN, ||HOME, POST²*, Office*); ||(in *pl.*) parts of house devoted to household work, storage, etc., (*with the usual offices*); **Holy O~**, the Inquisition; ~**bearer**, official, officer; ~**boy** (employed to do minor jobs in business office). [F f. L *officium* (*opus* work, *facio -fic-* do)]

**o͞fficer** *n.* Holder of office or position by election or appointment (*probation, returning, tax, officer*); president, secretary, treasurer, etc., of society; bailiff, constable; holder of authority in navy, army, air force, or mercantile marine, esp. with commission in armed forces; member of grade below commander in order of British Empire etc.

**offi͞cial** (-shal). **1.** *a.* (-lly). Of an office or its tenure; holding office; properly authorized. **2.** *n.* Person holding public office or engaged in official duties. **3.** ~**dom** *n.*; ~**ě'se** (-z) *n.*, officials' jargon; **offi͞ciate** (-shĭ-) *v.i.*, perform divine service, act in some official capacity esp. on particular occasion (*officiate as host, best man, etc.*); **offi͞cious** (-shŭs) *a.*, offering or doing unwanted service, intrusively kind, (Diplom.) opp. *official*) informal or not binding. [L (prec.)]

**o͞ffing, o͞ffish.** See OFF.

**o͞ffsĕt** (or aw'-). **1.** *n.* Side-shoot from plant serving for propagation; compensation, consideration or amount diminishing or neutralizing effect of contrary one; sloping ledge in wall etc.; bend in pipe etc. to carry it past obstacle; ~ (**process**), method of printing with transfer of ink from plate or stone to uniform rubber surface and thence to paper etc. **2.** *v.t.* (or -ĕ't; **-tt-;** offset). Counterbalance, compensate; print by offset process. [OFF, SET¹]

**o͞ffspring** (or aw'-) *n.* Person's child(ren) or descendant(s); animal's young or descendant(s); (fig.) result. [E (SPRING)]

**o͞ft** (or aw-) *adv.* (arch.) Often (*oft-told, oft-recurring*; *many a time and oft*); ~**times,** (arch.) often. [E]

**o͞ften** (or ŏ'fen, aw'-) *adv.* (~**er,** ~**est**). Frequently, many times, at short intervals, in many instances (*the victim often dies*); **every so ~**, from time to time; ~**times,** (arch.)

often; **once too ~** (w. ref. to discomfiture after several successes).

**o'gam.** See OGHAM.

**o'gee** (or -ē´) *n.* Sinuous line of double continuous curve as in S; moulding with such section. [OGIVE]

**o'g(h)am** (ŏ´gam) *n.* Ancient British and Irish alphabet; inscription in, letter of, this. [Ir.]

**o'give** (or oji´v) *n.* Diagonal rib of vault; pointed arch; **ogi'val** *a.*, with pointed arch(es). [F]

**o'gle. 1.** *v.i.* & *t.* Look amorously (at). **2.** *n.* Amorous glance. [prob. LDu.]

**o'gre** (-ger) *n.* Man-eating giant in folklore (also *fig.*); **o'gress** *n.*; **o'grish** *a.* [F]

**ōh**[1] (ō) *int.* expr. surprise, pain, entreaty, etc. [var. O[2]]

**ōh**[2] (ō) = O[1] (number).

**ohm** (ōm) *n.* Unit of electrical resistance. [person]

**O.H.M.S.** *abbr.* On Her (or His) Majesty's Service.

**ōhō´** *int.* expr. surprise or exultation. [O[2], HO]

**-oid** *suf.* forming *adjs.* & *ns.* w. sense '(something) having the form of or resembling' (*Negroid, rhomboid, thyroid*). [Gk *eidos* form]

**oil. 1.** *n.* One of various liquid, viscous, unctuous, usu. inflammable substances lighter than water and insoluble in it, \*petroleum, (**burn the midnight ~**, read or work far into the night; **~ and vinegar** or **water**, types of dissimilar or irreconcilable things or persons; **pour ~ on the flames**, *fig.*, aggravate fury, passion, etc.; **pour ~ on the waters, on troubled waters**, *fig.*, calm a disturbance with soothing words etc.; **strike ~**, find petroleum by sinking shaft, *fig.* attain prosperity or success); (often in *pl.*) = *oil-colour*, (colloq.) picture painted in oil-colours. **2.** *v.t.* & *i.* Apply oil to, lubricate, impregnate or treat with oil, (**~ the wheels**, *fig.*, make things go smoothly by courtesy, bribes, etc.; **~ed silk**, waterproofed with oil; **~ed**, *sl.*, drunk); supply oil to, (of ship etc.) take oil on board as fuel. **3. ~´cake**, compressed linseed from which oil has been expressed, used as cattle food or manure; **~´cloth**, fabric, esp. canvas, waterproofed with oil; **~-colour**, (usu. in *pl.*) paint made by grinding pigment in oil; **~´field**, district yielding mineral

oil; **~-fired**, using oil as fuel; **~´man**, maker or seller of oils, \*operator of oil-well; **~-paint**, = *oil-colour*; **~-painting**, art of painting, picture painted, in oil-colours (*she is no oil-painting*, colloq., she is ugly); *oil* RIG[2]; **~-shale** (yielding oil by distillation); **~´skin**, (garment or, in *pl.*, suit made of) cloth waterproofed with oil; *oil-*SLICK; **~-well** (from which mineral oil is drawn); **~´y** *a.* (**~ily**, **~iness**), of, like, covered or soaked with, oil, (of manner) fawning, insinuating, subserviently ingratiating. [AF f. L *oleum* olive oil]

**oi'ntment** *n.* Smooth greasy healing or beautifying preparation for the skin. [F f. L (*unguo* anoint)]

**O.K.** (ōkā´), **ōkay´**, *a.*, *adv.*, *n.*, & *v.* (colloq.) **1.** *a.* & *adv.* All right, satisfactor(il)y; (as *int.*) I agree. **2.** *n.* Approval, sanction. **3.** *v.t.* Mark 'O.K.'; approve, sanction. [orig. U.S., app. initials of *oll* or *orl korrect* joc. form of 'all correct']

**Okla.** *abbr.* Oklahoma.

**ō'kra** *n.* Tall orig. Afr. plant with seed-pods used for food. [W. Afr. native name]

**-ŏl** *suf.* (Chem.) in names of alcohols and other compounds. [(ALCOH)OL & L *oleum* oil]

**ōld. 1.** *a.* (cf. ELDER[2], ELDEST). Advanced in age, far on in natural period of existence, not young or near its beginning, (**the ~**, old people; **young and ~**, everyone); having characteristics, experience, feebleness, etc., of age (*child has an old face*; *old head on young* SHOULDERS); (appended to period of time) of age (*is ten years old*; *four* etc.**-year-~**, *pl.* **~s**, person or animal, esp. race-horse, of that age); practised, inveterate, (*old in crime, cunning, diplomacy*; *an old* STAGER, *trooper,* CAMPAIGNER, *offender*); made long ago, long in use, worn or dilapidated or shabby from passage of time; dating from far back, long established or known or familiar or dear, ancient, primeval, (*old as the hills*; *Old England*; *old friends*; *an old debt, grudge*; *an old name, family*; **any ~ thing**, *sl.*, anything no matter what, so **any ~ how** etc.; GOOD *old* —; **have a high** etc. **~ time**, *sl.*, be well amused or entertained; **of ~ standing**, long established; colloq. **~ chap, fellow, girl,** etc., *sl.* **~ bean, fruit, stick,**

thing, etc., esp. in *voc.*, intimate or person treated as such: **the ~ one** or **gentleman, Old Harry, Nick²**, *Scratch* [N *skratti* goblin], the Devil; **~ wine**, matured with keeping); belonging only or chiefly to the past, lingering on, former, **(the good ~ days, times,** customs etc. of earlier generations, regarded as better; **~ London** etc., London etc. as it once was, or the relics of its former state); (of language) as used in former or earliest times (*Old* ENGLISH). **2.** *n.* Of — *a.* & *adv.*, (living) in the old time (*the men of* ~; *of old there were giants*); *know him of* ~, since long ago. **3.** *old* AGE; *old-age* PENSION(ER); **~ bachelor,** man confirmed in bachelorhood; **~ bird,** wary person; *old* BONES; **~ boy,** former member of school, (colloq.) elderly man, (as *voc.*) = *old man*; **~ clothes** (worn or discarded); **~ clo'thes-man,** dealer in discarded clothes; **~ country,** the mother country of colonists etc.; **~-established,** long established; **~-fa'shioned,** (*a.*) in or according to old fashion(s), antiquated, (*n.*) *cocktail of whisky, bitters, etc.; **~ girl,** former member of school, (colloq.) elderly woman, (as *voc.*, term of endearment); *Old Glory,** U.S. flag; **~ gold,** dull brownish-golden colour; **~ guard,** original, past, or conservative members of party etc.; **~ hand,** practised workman, person with much experience (*at doing*); *old* HAT; **~ lady** (lit., or colloq. to or of mother or wife); **~ maid,** elderly spinster, precise tidy man, a card-game; **~-mai'dish,** fussy and prim; **~ man,** (sl.) headmaster, employer, ship's captain, (colloq.) husband or father, (as *voc.*) male person or animal regarded with affection or intimacy; **~ man's beard,** clematis, esp. traveller's joy; **~ master,** (painting by) great painter of former times, esp. of 13th–17th c. in Europe; ‖**Old Pals Act,** (joc.) doctrine that friends should always help each other; *old* SALT; **of the ~ school,** according to the older view of things; ‖**~ school tie,** necktie with characteristic pattern worn by members of a particular (usu. public) school; **~ soldier,** former or long-serving soldier, (fig.) experienced person; *old* STYLE²; *Old* TESTAMENT; **~-time dancing** (of long-established kinds of dance); *~-ti'mer,** person

with long experience or standing; *old wives' tale* (see WIFE); **~ woman,** (colloq.) wife or mother, (fig.) fussy or timid man; *the Old* WORLD; **~-world,** belonging to old times (also joc. *~e-worlde* pr. -dǐ-; -dǐ); **~ year,** year just ended or about to end. **4. ~'en** *a.,* (literary) of an earlier period (esp. *the olden time*); **~'ie** *n.,* (colloq.) old person or thing; **~'ster** *n.,* old person, one no longer a youngster. [E]

**ōlĕă'ginous** *a.* Having properties of or producing oil; oily (lit. or fig.). [F f. L (OIL)]

**ōlĕă'nder** *n.* Evergreen flowering Mediterranean shrub. [L]

**ōlĕă'ster** *n.* Wild olive. [L (OIL)]

**ō'lĕfīn(e)** *n.* (Chem.) Hydrocarbon of type containing less than maximum amount of hydrogen. [F *oléfiant* oil-forming]

**ōlfă'ctory** *a.* (-ily). Concerned with smelling (*olfactory nerves*). [L (*oleo* smell, *facio* make)]

**ō'ligărch** (-k) *n.* Member of oligarchy; **~y** *n.,* government, State governed, by small group of persons, members of such Government; **~ic(al)** (-ärk-) *adjs.* (-ically). [F or L f. Gk (*oligoi* few)]

**O'ligocēne** (ŏ'-) *a.* & *n.* (Geol.) (Of) division of Tertiary below Miocene. [Gk *oligos* little, *kainos* new]

**ō'liō** *n.* (*pl.* ~s). Mixed dish, hotchpotch, stew; medley. [Sp.]

**ŏ'live. 1.** *n.* Oval hard-stoned fruit, dusky yellowish green when unripe, and bluish black when ripe, yielding oil or eaten as relish; tree bearing it; leaves or branch or wreath of this as emblem of peace; its wood; (in *pl.*, **beef, veal, ~s**) slices of beef or veal rolled up with stuffing and stewed; colour of unripe olive. **2.** *a.* Coloured like unripe olive (*olive green*); (of complexion) yellowish-brown. **3. ~-branch,** (fig.) overture for peace or reconciliation; **~ crown,** garland of olive as sign of victory; **~ oil** (extracted from olives). **4. ōlivā'ceous** (-shŭs) *a.,* olive-green; **ŏ'livary** *a.,* olive-shaped; **ŏ'livīne** (or -ēn) *n.,* chrysolite. [F f. L *oliva* f. Gk]

**Olў'mpiăd** (o-) *n.* Period of 4 years between celebrations of Olympic games, used by ancient Greeks in dating events; celebration of modern Olympic games; regular international contest in chess etc. [F or L f. Gk *Olympias -ad-* (OLYM-PUS)]

**Oly͞m'pian** (o-). **1.** *a.* Of Olympus, celestial; (of manners etc.) magnificent, condescending, superior; = foll. **2.** *n.* Dweller in Olympus, Greek god; person of great attainments or superhuman calm. [OLYMPUS or foll.]

**Oly͞m'pic** (o-). **1.** *a.* Of or at Olympia in the Peloponnese; of the ~ **games**, ancient-Greek festival held every 4 years, modern international athletic and sports meetings at various places held every 4 years. **2.** *n.* (in *pl.*) Olympic games. [L f. Gk (foll.)]

**Oly͞m'pus** (o-) *n.* Divine abode of the Greek gods. [Gk *Olympos* (mountain)]

‖**O.M.** *abbr.* (Member of the) Order of Merit.

**o͞'mbuds|măn** (-bŏŏdz-) *n.* (*pl.* ~**men**). Official appointed to investigate individual's complaints against public authorities. [Sw., = legal representative]

**o͞'mĕga** *n.* Last letter (Ω, ω) of Gk alphabet, = ō (cf. OMICRON); last of series, final development. [Gk (*ō mega* = great O)]

**o͞'mĕlĕt(te)** (-ml-) *n.* Beaten eggs cooked in melted butter and folded (savoury ~, with herbs etc.; sweet ~, with jam etc.; **one cannot make an ~ without breaking eggs**, something must be sacrificed in order to achieve one's purpose). [F]

**o͞'mĕn** *n.* Occurrence or object portending good or evil; prophetic significance (*is of good* etc. *omen*); **o͞'mĭnous** *a.*, of evil omen, inauspicious. [L]

**omi'cron** *n.* Fifteenth Gk letter (O, o) = ŏ (cf. OMEGA). [Gk (*o micron* = small O)]

**omi't** *v.t.* (**-tt-**). Leave out, not insert or include; leave undone, neglect doing, fail *to* do; **omi'ssible** *a.*; **omi'ssion** (-shon) *n.* (**sins of omission**, neglect etc.). [L *omitto omiss-*]

**ŏmni-** *in comb.* All-; ~**fā̆r'ĭous** *a.*, of all sorts. [L (*omnis* all)]

**o͞'mnĭbus. 1.** *n.* Bus; omnibus book. **2.** *a.* Serving several objects at once, comprising several items, (*an omnibus bill, resolution,* etc.; ~ **book, volume**, low-priced volume containing several stories, plays, etc.,

freq. by one author). [F f. L, = for all]

**ŏmnĭ'potȩn|t** *a.* All-powerful; ~**ce** *n.*, infinite power. [F f. L (POTENT)]

**ŏmnĭprĕ'sȩn|t** (-z-) *a.* Ubiquitous; ~**ce** *n.* [L (PRESENT[1])]

**ŏmnĭ'sciȩn|t** (or -shye-) *a.* Knowing everything or much; ~**ce** (or -shens) *n.* [L (*scio* know)]

**ŏmnĭ'vorous** *a.* Feeding on many kinds of food, esp. on both plants and flesh; (fig.) reading, observing, etc., whatever comes one's way. [L (*voro* devour)]

**ŏn** *prep., adv., a., & n.* **1.** *prep.* (So as to be) supported by or attached to or covering or enclosing (*sat on the table; floats on the water; hangs on the wall; falls on his knees; lives on the Continent, on a grant; has a scar on his cheek; went on board; is on the committee; dog on a lead;* **on** one, carried with one, about one's person, *have you a pen on you?; on one's* HANDS, HEAD; **on-li'ne** *a. & adv.*, directly controlled by or connected to computer; **on-sta'ge** *a. & adv.*, on the stage, visible to audience); with axis, pivot, basis, motive, standard, confirmation, or guarantee consisting in, (*turn on one's heel; works on a ratchet; imprisoned on suspicion; on my conscience; had it on good authority; did it on purpose; a tax on petrol*); (so as to be) close to, in the direction of, touching, arrived at, against, just at, (*house is on the shore, road; Henley-on-Thames; marched on London; a punch on the nose; serve a writ on; lay hold on; bowling is on the wicket, is straight; drew a knife on me; turn one's back on it; a curse on him, it!; on* FORM; **o͞'nshore**, of wind, blowing landwards; **onsi'de**, Footb., not OFFSIDE); (of time) during, exactly at, contemporaneously with, immediately after or before, as a result of, (*on 29 May; shut on Sundays;* CASH *on delivery; on arriving, on examination, I found;* **on schedule, time, the minute**, punctual, -ly); in manner specified by *adj.* (*on the cheap, sly,* etc.); in state or action specified by *n.* (*on fire, lease, strike; on the look-out, run, move; on one's best behaviour*); concerning, about, (while) engaged with, so as to affect, (*keen, bent, set, on; die, rat, walk out, on; writes on finance; here on business, leave; is on antibiotics; the drinks are on me* colloq., at my expense; *went on an* errand; *draw cheque on bank*); added to (*ruin on ruin; a penny on the price of beer*). **2.** *adv.* On something (*has, put, his hat on; keep your* HAIR *on*); in some direction, towards something, farther forward, towards point of contact, in advanced position or state, with continued movement or action, in operation or activity, (*look on; getting on for two o'clock; happened later on; from that day on; left the light on*); **be on,** (of event) be due to take place, (colloq.) be willing to participate or approve, make bet, be practicable or acceptable; **be on at,** colloq., nag or grumble at; **be on to,** be aware of intentions etc. of, find fault with, nag (*he's always on to me*), notice, be able to make use of, realize importance of; **broadside, end,** etc., **on,** with that part forward; *bowler is* **on,** bowling; *play* etc. *is on,* being performed; HAVE *on;* **on and on,** continually on(wards); *on and off,* = OFF *and on;* **o'ncoming** *a.* & *n.,* approach(ing) from the front; **o'ngoing** (ŏ'n-g-) *a.,* continuing; **o'nlooker,** = LOOKer-*on;* **o'nrush,** onward rush; **o'nset,** attack, impetuous beginning; **on to, onto,** *compd. prep.* (corresp. to *on* as *into* to *in,* but usu. written as two words) to a position on (*jump on to the stage*); **speak, wait, work,** etc., **on,** continue to do so. **3.** *a.* (Crick.) Towards, in, part of field on striker's side and in front of his wicket (opp. OFF; *an on drive;* MID-*on*); ‖**on-licence,** (place with) licence to sell beer etc. for consumption on the premises. **4.** *n.* (Crick.) The on side (*a drive to the on*). **5. o'nwards** (-z) *adv.,* further on, towards the front, with advancing motion; **o'nward** *a.* & *adv.,* (directed) onwards. [E]

**o'nager** *n.* Wild ass. [L f. Gk (*onos* ass, *agrios* wild)]

**o'nanism** *n.* Masturbation. [F or L (*Onan,* Bibl. person)]

‖**O.N.C.,** ‖**O.N.D.,** *abbrs.* Ordinary National Certificate, Diploma.

**once** (wŭns) *adv., conj.,* & *n.* **1.** *adv.* For one time or on one occasion only, multiplied by one, by one degree, (*have read it more than once; once two is two; first* COUSIN *once removed*); **for** (**this, that**) **∼,** on this, that, occasion, even if on no other; **∼ again** *or* **more,** another time; **∼ bitten twice shy,** pain, loss, etc., teaches caution; **∼** (**and**) **for all,** in final manner, definitively; (**every**) **∼ in a while,** from time to time; (**for**) **∼ in a while** *or* ‖**way,** very rarely; **∼ or twice, ∼ and again,** a few times); even for one or the first time, ever, at all, (*if we once lose sight of him; when once he understands; once past the fence we are safe*); on a certain but unspecified past occasion (also **∼ upon a time**), at some period in the past, former(ly), (*once there was a giant; a once-famous doctrine*); **at ∼,** immediately, without delay, at the same time, (*do it at once, please; don't all shout at once; at once stern and tender; all at ∼,* all together, without warning); **∼-over,** (colloq.) rapid preliminary inspection. **2.** *conj.* As soon as, if once, when once, (*once he hesitates, we have him*). **3.** *n.* One time or occasion (*happened only the once*). [orig. gen. of ONE]

**one** (wŭn) *a., n.,* & *pron.* **1.** *a.* Single and integral in number, neither none nor fractional nor plural, a, (*one man's* MEAT; **for ∼ thing,** not to mention others; **∼ or two,** lit., or = a few); only, without others, forming a unity, united, identical, the same, unchanging, particular but undefined, to be contrasted with another, (*the one way to succeed; no one man can do it; is one and undivided; cried out with one voice; on the one* HAND; **be made ∼,** be married to each other; **become ∼,** coalesce; **neither ∼ thing nor the other,** of undesirably mixed nature; **∼ day,** on unspecified day, at some unspecified future date); single person or thing of kind expressed or implied (*one of the richest men in Wales; shall see you one of these days; that was a nasty one, one in the eye for the Liberals,* i.e. blow, lit. or fig.; **be ∼,** being one, even if alone, *I for one do not believe it*; **like ∼ o'clock,** colloq., vigorously; **∼ and all,** all singly and collectively; **∼ another,** formula of reciprocity with *one* orig. subjective and *another* objective or possessive: *struck one another; write to one another; scratch one another's backs*; **∼ by ∼, ∼ after another,** singly, successively; (**the**) **∼ . . . the other,** formula distinguishing two things: *one is good, the other bad*). **2.** *n.* (often used as substitute for repetition of previously expressed or implied noun). The NUMERAL one, thing numbered with it, a unit, unity, single thing or person or example, (*one is half of two*; *came in ones and twos*; *the big book and the little one*; *pick me out a good one, some good ones*; **at ~**, in agreement; **(all) in ~**, combined; **never a ~**, none), (colloq.) drink (QUICK *one*), story, joke, (*Have you heard the one about the parrot with a wooden leg?*). **3.** *pron.* A person of specified kind (*dear, little, loved, ones*; *behaved like one possessed*; *bought it from one Stephens*; *the* EVIL *One*); (arch.) a particular but unspecified person (*one came running*); any person, esp. the speaker or writer, as representing people in general (*if one cuts off one's nose, one hurts only oneself*; *then they give one a cup of tea*; *it offends one to be ignored*); (colloq.) I (*one let it pass, for one did not want to seem mean*). **4. ~-armed bandit**, (sl.) fruit-machine etc. operated by pulling down armlike handle; **~-eyed**, (esp., sl.) petty; **~-horse**, using a single horse, (sl.) petty, poorly equipped; **~-man**, requiring, consisting of, done or managed by, one man (*one-man band, bus, exhibition of paintings*); **~-night stand**, (colloq.) single performance of play, concert, etc., in a place; **~-off**, (colloq.) made as one (article etc.) only, not repeated; **~-sided**, lopsided, partial, unfair, prejudiced; **~-step**, vigorous kind of foxtrot in duple time; **~-track mind** (able to think of only one topic); **~-up**, scoring one point more than opponent, (fig.) maintaining a psychological advantage, whence **~-u'p-manship** (colloq.); **~-way street** (in which traffic may move in one direction only). **5. ~'ness** (wŭ'n-n-) *n.*, singleness, uniqueness, concord, sameness, changelessness; **~sě'lf** *pron.*, reflexive and emphatic appositional, form of the generalizing pronoun (*to starve oneself is suicide*; *to do right oneself is the great thing*). [E]

**ŏ'nerous** *a.* Burdensome. [F f. L (ONUS)]

**o'nion** (ŭ'nyŏn) *n.* (Plant with) edible bulb of pungent smell and flavour; **know one's ~s**, (sl.) be good at one's job; **~-skin**, outermost or any outer coat of onion, thin smooth translucent paper; **~ў** *a.* [AF f. L *unio -onis*]

**ŏ'nlў** *a.*, *adv.*, & *conj.* **1.** *attrib. a.* That is the one specimen, that are all the specimens, of the class (*an only child*; *the only instances known*; *my

one and only hope*); best or alone worth considering (*cricket is the only sport*). **2.** *adv.* Solely, merely, exclusively, and no one or nothing more or besides or else, and that is all, (*it is right only because it is customary*; *one and one only: I can only guess what happened*; *only just caught the train*; *I not only heard it, but saw it*; IF *only*; **~ too glad, true**, etc., glad etc. and not, as might be expected or desired, the opposite; no longer ago than (*came only yesterday*); with no better result than (*picked it up, only to drop it again*). **3.** *conj.* It must however be added that, but then, (*he makes good resolutions, only he never keeps them*); with the exception, were it not, that (*he does well, only (that) he is nervous at the start*; *I would describe it, only (that) you would be bored*). [E (ONE, -LY[1,2])]

‖**o.n.o.** *abbr.* or near offer.

**onŏmato|poe'ia** (-pē'a; *or* ŏnŏmă-) *n.* Formation of names or words from sounds that resemble those associated with the object or action to be named, or that seem suggestive of its qualities; such word (e.g. *cuckoo, sizzle*); **~poe'ic** (-pē'-), **~pŏe'tic**, *adjs.* (**-ically**). [L f. Gk (*onoma* name, *poieō* make)]

**ŏ'nslaught** (-awt) *n.* Fierce attack. [Du. (ON, *slag* blow)]

**Ont.** *abbr.* Ontario.

**onto.** See ON.

**ŏntŏ'log|ў** *n.* Branch of metaphysics dealing with the nature of being; **ŏntŏlŏ'gical** *a.* (**-lly**); **~ĭst** *n.* [Gk *ont*- being]

**ŏ'nus** *n.* Burden, duty, responsibility. [L *onus oner*- load]

**onward(s).** See ON.

**ŏ'nўx** *n.* Kind of chalcedony with coloured layers. [F f. L f. Gk]

**ōō'dles** (-dĕlz) *n.pl.* (colloq.) Superabundance (*oodles of money*). [orig. unkn.]

**ōōf** *n.* (sl.) Money, wealth. [abbr. Yiddish *ooftisch* for G *auf dem tische* on the table]

**ooh** (ōō) *int.* expr. surprised pleasure, excitement, pain, etc. [natural excl.]

**ŏ'ol|īte** *n.* Granular limestone; **~ĭ'tĭc** *a.* [F (Gk *ōion* egg)]

**ōōmph** *n.* (sl.) Attractiveness, esp. sex appeal; energy, enthusiasm. [orig. uncert.]

**ōōps** *int.* on making obvious mistake (cf. WHOOPS). [natural excl.]

**ōōze. 1.** *n.* Wet mud; sluggish flow

**2.** *v.i.* & *t.* Pass slowly through pores etc.; (of substance) exude moisture; (fig.) pass as if oozing *out* or *away* (*my courage is oozing away*); emit steadily (lit. or fig.; moisture, information, confidence); **ōō′zў** *a.* (**-ily, -iness**). [E]

**oop-.** See OB-.

**O.P.** *abbr.* Dominican [*Order of Preachers*; L *Ordo Praedicatorum*]; observation post; opposite prompt.

**o.p.** *abbr.* out of print; overproof.

**op.** *abbr.* & (colloq.) *n.* or *a.* = operation (Surg. or Mil.); operator; optical (*op art*); opus.

**opā′cǐtў** *n.* Opaqueness. [F f. L (OPAQUE)]

**ō′pal** *n.* Precious stone usu. milky or bluish with iridescent reflections; **~ĕ′scent, ~ine,** *adjs.*, iridescent; **~ glass** (white, translucent). [F or L]

**opā′que** (-k) *a.* (**~r, ~st**). Not transmitting light, impenetrable to sight; obscure. [L *opacus* shaded]

**op. cit.** *abbr.* in the work already quoted. [L *opere citato*]

**O.P.E.C.** *abbr.* Organization of Petroleum Exporting Countries.

**ō′pen** *a., n.,* & *v.* **1.** *a.* (**~er, ~est; ~ness** *pr.* -n-n-). Not closed or blocked up, allowing entrance or passage or access, having gate or door or lid or part of boundary withdrawn, unenclosed, unconfined, uncovered, bare, exposed, undisguised, public, manifest, not exclusive or limited, (*open gate, path, church, drawer, box, bottle, field, grave, drain, sore, sea, carriage, hostilities, scandal*; LAY⁴ *open; door flew open;* **~ to,** willing to receive *offers, persuasion,* etc., liable to *attack, misinterpretation,* etc., available to (*there are three courses open to us*); **throw ~,** cause to be suddenly or widely open, make accessible *to*); (of exhibition, shop, etc.) accessible to visitors or customers; (of race, competition, scholarship, etc.) unrestricted as to who may compete; (of bowels) not constipated; (of return ticket) without specified date of travel; expanded, unfolded, spread out, not close, with intervals, porous, communicative, frank, (*open book* lit., or fig.: *is an open book*, can be easily understood; **be ~ with,** speak frankly to; **with ~ eyes,** consciously or under no misapprehension, in eager attention or surprise); **(in the) ~ air,** outdoors; **~-and-shut case,** (colloq.) perfectly

straightforward matter; **~ boat** (undecked); **~cast,** (of mine or mining) with removal of surface layers and working from above, not from shafts; **~ champion,** winner of open competition; ||**~ cheque** (not crossed); **~ country** (affording wide views or free from houses, fences, etc.); **~ ears** (eagerly attentive); **~ended,** having no predetermined limit or boundary; **~ face** (ingenuous-looking); **~ hand,** generosity; **~ heart,** frankness, unsuspiciousness, kindliness, cordiality; **~heart surgery** (with heart exposed and no blood circulating through it); *keep open* HOUSE; **~ letter** (esp. of protest, printed in newspaper etc. but addressed to person by name); **~ market** (with free competition of buyers and sellers); **~ meeting** (admitting all persons, not only members etc.); **~ mind** (accessible to new ideas, unprejudiced or undecided); **~ mouth** (esp. as sign of gaping stupidity, surprise, or expectation); **~ order,** (Mil. etc.) formation with wide spaces between men, units, or ships; **~plan,** (of house, office, etc.) with few interior walls; **~ prison,** = PRISON *without bars;* **~ question,** matter on which differences of opinion are legitimate; **~ sandwich** (without bread on top); ||**~ season** (opp. CLOSE¹ *season*); *open* SECRET; ||**O~ University** (teaching mainly by broadcasting and correspondence, and open to those without scholastic qualifications); *open* VERDICT; **~work,** pattern with interstices in metal, lace, etc. **2.** *n.* The **~,** open space or country or air, public notice or view, (*bring it out into the open*); open championship etc. **3.** *v.t.* & *i.* Make or become open or more open (*shops open at 9 a.m.*; **~ bowels,** cause evacuation; **~s a prospect,** brings it to view; **~ the mind, heart,** etc., make it more sympathetic or enlightened); ceremonially declare (building etc.) open (*open* PARLIAMENT); start or establish or set going (business, account, innings, bidding, debate, campaign, etc.); make a start (*story opens with a murder*); begin speaking, writing, etc.; **not ~** one's **lips, mouth,** remain silent; **~** one's **eyes,** show surprise; **~** person's **eyes,** undeceive or enlighten him; **~ fire,** begin shooting; **~ into,** (of door etc.)

give or have communication with (room etc.); ~ **on**, (of door, window, eyes) give or get view of; ~ **out**, unfold, develop, expand, accelerate, become communicative; open SESAME; ~ **the case**, (of counsel in lawcourt) make preliminary statement before calling witnesses; ~ **up**, make accessible, bring to notice, reveal, accelerate, begin shooting or sounding. **4.** ~**er** (-pn-) *n.*, (esp.) device for opening bottles etc.; ~**ing** (-pn-), (*n.*, esp.) gap, aperture, opportunity, commencement, initial part, (*a.*, esp.) initial, first, (*his opening remarks*); ~**lỹ** *adv.*, publicly, frankly. [E]

ŏ'**pera**[1] *n.* Musical drama (**comic** ~, with spoken dialogue and humorous treatment; **grand** ~, sung throughout, with serious treatment; **light** ~, not on serious theme); ~-**glass(es)**, small binoculars for use at opera or theatre; ~-**hat**, man's collapsible top hat; ~-**house**, theatre for operas; SOAP opera; ŏ**peră'tic** *a.* (**-ically**), of or like opera. [It. f. L, labour, work]

ŏ'**pera**[2]. See OPUS.

ŏ'**perăt|e** *v.i.* & *t.* Be in action, produce effect, bring influence to bear, (*the medicine did not operate*; *the tax operates to our disadvantage*); perform surgical or strategic or financial operation(s); bring about; work (machine, system); ||~**ing-theatre**, room for surgical operation (orig. when done before students); ŏ'**perable** *a.*, that can be operated, suitable for treatment by surgical operation; ŏ'**perative**, (*a.*) in operation, having effect, practical, having principal relevance ('*may' is the operative word*), of or by surgery, (*n.*) worker, artisan; ~**or** *n.*, (esp.) person making connections of lines in telephone exchange, (colloq.) person engaging in business esp. shrewdly. [L *operor* work (OPUS)]

ŏperă'tion *n.* Working, action, way thing works, efficacy, validity, scope, (*is in, comes into, operation*; *its operation is easily explained*; *we must extend its operation*); ~**s research**, = *operational research*); active process, discharge of function, (*the operation of pruning, thinking*); financial transaction; piece of surgery; strategic manœuvre; ~**al** *a.*, engaged in or used for operations (||~**al research**, application of scientific principles to business etc. management for greater

efficiency), able to function. [F f. L (prec.)]

ŏpĕr'cŭl|um *n.* (*pl.* ~**a**). Fish's gill-cover; similar structure in plant; valve closing mouth of shell. [L (*operio* to cover)]

ŏpere'tta *n.* One-act or short opera; light opera. [It. dim of OPERA[1]]

ŏphī'dĭan *a.* & *n.* (Member of) suborder of reptiles including snakes; snake(like). [Gk *ophis* snake]

ŏphthă'lm|ĭa *n.* Inflammation of eye, esp. conjunctivitis; ~**ic** *a.* (**-ically**), of or for or affected with ophthalmia, of or for the eye; ||~**ic optician**, qualified to prescribe as well as dispense spectacles etc.; ~**ŏ'logỹ** *n.*, scientific study of the eye; ~**oscōpe** *n.*, instrument for examining the eye. [L f. Gk (*ophthalmos* eye)]

ō'**pĭate. 1.** *a.* Containing opium, narcotic, soporific. **2.** *n.* Drug containing opium and easing pain or inducing sleep; (fig.) soothing influence. [L (OPIUM)]

opī'ne *v.t.* Express or hold the opinion (*that*). [L *opinor* believe]

opī'nion (-yon) *n.* Belief based on grounds short of proof, view held as probable, what one thinks about something, (**be of (the)** ~ **that**, believe; **in my** ~, as it seems to me; **a matter of** ~, disputable point; ~ **poll**, = GALLUP *poll*); (**public**) ~, prevalent views on politics, morality, etc.; piece of professional advice (*you had better have another, a second, opinion*); estimate (*have a good, high, low, opinion of him*), favourable estimate (*has a great opinion of himself*); ~**ătĕd** *a.*, unduly confident in one's opinions. [F f. L (prec.)]

ō'**pĭum** *n.* Drug made from juice of the ~ **poppy** and smoked or eaten or used in medicines as sedative, narcotic, intoxicant, and stimulant; ~ **den**, haunt of opium-smokers. [L f. Gk *opion*]

opŏ'ssum *n.* American marsupial; Austral. phalanger like it. [Virginian Ind.]

**opp.** *abbr.* opposite.

oppŏ'nent *n.* One who opposes or belongs to opposing side. [L *oppono -posit-* set against]

ŏ'**pportūn|e** (*or* -ū'n) *a.* (Of time) well-chosen or especially favourable; (of action or event) well-timed; ~**ĭsm** *n.*, adaptation of policy to circumstances, preference of what can to what should be done; ~**ist** *n.*; **ŏppŏrtū′nĭtў** *n.*, favourable occasion, good chance, opening, (*of doing, to do, for action, or abs.; find, make, get, give, an opportunity*). [F f. L *opportunus* (of wind) driving towards PORT¹]

**oppŏ′se** (-z) *v.t.* Put into antagonism or contrast; place (thumb or big toe) against finger(s) or other toe(s) front to front; set oneself against, resist, propose the rejection of (resolution, motion, etc.); (in *p.p.*) contrary, opposite, adverse, (*to; good as opposed to bad; is firmly opposed to the merger*); ~**′able** *a.* (-bly), ~**abi′lĭtў** *n.*, (esp. of thumb). [F f. L (OPPONENT)]

**ŏ′ppŏsĭte** (-z-) *a., n., adv., & prep.* **1.** *a.* Contrary in position or kind, placed on other or farther side, facing or back to back, diametrically different, having any of these relations *to*, (*on opposite sides of the square; came from, went in, opposite directions; the tree opposite to the house; of a kind opposite to, from, what I expected*); ~ **number**, person or thing similarly placed in another set etc. to the given one; **the ~ sex**, men in relation to women or vice versa. **2.** *n.* Opposite thing or term (*wealth and poverty are opposites; you are bad-tempered, she is the opposite*). **3.** *adv.* In opposite position (*there was an explosion opposite*). **4.** *prep.* Opposite to (*the tree opposite the house*); ~ **prompt**, side of stage usu. to actor's right; **play ~**, (of actor, actress) have as leading lady or man.

**ŏppŏsĭ′tion** (-z-) *n.* Antagonism, resistance; party of opponents or competitors, esp. (‖**The O~**, **Her Majesty's O~**) chief Parliamentary party opposed to that in office (**in ~**, said of party out of office); contrast, antithesis; placing opposite; (Astrol. & Astron.) diametrically opposite position of two heavenly bodies (**planet is in ~**, opposite sun).

**oppre′ss** *v.t.* Govern tyrannically, exercise harsh dominion over; lie heavy on, weigh down, (mind, its owner, etc.); ~**ion** (-shon) *n.*; ~**ive** *a.*, (esp. of weather etc.) sultry, close; ~**or** *n.* [F f. L (PRESS)]

**opprŏ′brĭ|um** *n.* (Cause of) disgrace, evil reputation; ~**ous** *a.*, (of language) vituperative, abusive. [L, = infamy, reproach]

**oppŭ′gn** (-ū′n) *v.t.* Controvert, call in question. [L *oppugno* fight against]

**ŏpt** *v.i.* Make choice, decide, (*between* alternatives or *for* alternative); ~ **out** (**of**), choose not to participate (in). [F f. L *opto* choose, wish]

**ŏ′ptătive** (or -ā′-). **1.** *a.* (Gram.) Expressing wish (~ **mood**, verb-forms in Gk etc. used esp. in wishes). **2.** *n.* Optative mood or form. [F f. L (prec.)]

**ŏ′ptĭc. 1.** *a.* (~**ally**). Of eye or sight (*optic nerve*). **2.** *n.* Eye (arch. or joc.); ‖device fastened to neck of bottle for measuring out spirits [**P**]; (in *pl.*, treated as *sing.*) science of sight and related laws of light; ~**al** *a.* (~**ally**), visual (~**al art**, using contrasting colours to create illusion of movement; ~**al illusion**, involuntary mental misinterpretation of thing seen, due to its deceptive appearance), of the relations between sight and light, aiding sight, of or according to optics; ~**ian** (-ĭ′shan) *n.*, maker or prescriber of optical instruments, esp. spectacles. [F or L f. Gk (*optos* seen)]

**ŏ′ptĭm|ĭsm** *n.* Doctrine that the actual world is the best of all possible worlds; view that good must ultimately prevail over evil in the universe; (habitually) hopeful disposition, inclination to take bright views; ~**al** *a.*, = OPTIMUM; ~**ĭst** *n.*; ~**ĭ′stĭc** *a.* (-ically); ~**ĭze** *v.t.*, make optimum, make the most of; ~**um**, (*n., pl.* ~**a**) most favourable conditions (for growth etc.), best compromise, (*a.*) best or most favourable. [F f. L *optimus* best]

**ŏ′ptĭon** *n.* Choice, choosing, thing that is or may be chosen, (*take up an option; none of the options is satisfactory*); liberty of choosing (*imprisonment without the option of a fine*); **have no ~ but to**, must; **leave one's ~s open**, not commit oneself); (St. Exch. etc.) purchased right to call for or make delivery of specified stocks at specified rate within specified time; ~**al** *a.* (-lly), not obligatory. [F or L (OPT)]

**ŏptŏ′mĕt|er** *n.* Instrument for sight-testing; ~**rist**, ~**rў**, *ns.* [Gk *optos* seen]

**ŏ′pŭlen|t** *a.* Wealthy; abounding, abundant; luxurious; ~**ce** *n.* [L *opes* wealth]

**ŏ′pus** *n.* (*pl.* **o′pera**). Musician's

separate composition (esp. in citing by number; abbr. *op.*: *Beethoven op. 15*); *(magnum) opus*, great literary undertaking, artist's chief production; **opŭ'scŭle, -cŭlum** (*pl.* **-la**), *ns.*, minor composition. [L, = work]

**ŏr¹** *n.* (Her.) Gold. [F f. L *aurum* gold]

**ŏr²** *prep.* & *conj.* (arch.) Ere, before, esp. (poet.) *or ever* as conj. [E f. N]

**or³** (*emphat.* ŏr) *conj.* introducing alternatives: *white or black*; *red or blue or green*; *red, blue, or green*; *will you be there or not?*; *any Tom, Dick, or Harry*; *ripe tomatoes are red or yellow*; *common or garden heliotrope*; *one or two, five or six* (approximations); (explanation of preceding) *the common cormorant or shag*; *either take it or leave it*; *hurry up or (else) you will be late*; *ask him whether he was there or not*; *must do it whether I like it or dislike it*; *he doesn't know anything about it—or is he bluffing?*; **not A or B**, not A, and also not B. [E]

**-or** *suf.* forming *ns.* denoting esp. condition (*error, horror, tremor*) or agent (*actor, creator, emperor, escalator, tailor*), and compar. *adjs.* ult. f. L (*major, senior*). [F or L]

**ŏ'racle** *n.* Place at which ancient Greeks etc. consulted deities for advice or prophecy; response, often ambiguous or obscure, there given; divine inspiration or revelation; person or thing serving as infallible guide or test or indicator, wise or mysterious adviser or advice; WORK *the oracle*; **orā'cŭlar** *a.*, (esp.) authoritative or mysterious or ambiguous like ancient oracles. [F f. L *oraculum* (*oro* speak)]

**ŏr'al. 1.** *a.* (**~ly**). Spoken, verbal, by word of mouth; of the mouth; done or taken by the mouth (*oral sex, contraceptive*). **2.** *n.* (colloq.) Spoken (not written) examination. [L (*os oris* mouth)]

**ŏ'range¹** (-ĭnj). **1.** *n.* Roundish reddish-yellow juicy fruit, its colour, tree bearing it, (**mock ~**, tree with fragrant white flowers); orange pigment; **~-blossom,** fragrant white flowers of orange, often worn by bride at wedding; **~s and lemons,** children's singing game; ‖*orange* SQUASH¹; **~-stick,** small stick of orange-tree wood, with one pointed and one blunt end, used in manicuring nails. **2.** *a.* Orange-coloured. **3.** **~āde** *n.*, drink made from oranges, sweetening, and water, and freq.

aerated; **~rў** (-jerĭ) *n.*, building, hot-house, for orange-trees. [F f. Arab. *nāranj* f. Pers.]

**O'range²** (ŏ'rĭnj) *a.* Of the extreme Protestants in Ireland, esp. in Ulster; **~man,** member of political society formed 1795 to support Protestantism in Ireland (*~man's Day*, 12 July); **~ism** *n.* [place]

**ŏrăng-u'tăn, -ou'tăng,** (-ōō't-, -ută'-) *n.* Large arboreal anthropoid ape of E. Indies. [Malay, = wild man]

**orā'tion** *n.* A speech, esp. of ceremonial kind; **orā'te** *v.i.*, (joc.) hold forth, harangue; **ŏ'rator** *n.*, maker of a speech, skilful speaker (‖**Public Orator,** making ceremonial speeches in Latin at Oxford and Cambridge Universities); **ŏrătŏr'iō** *n.* (*pl.* **-os**), musical composition usu. on sacred theme for solo voices, chorus, and orchestra; **ŏ'ratory¹** *n.*, small chapel, place for private worship; **ŏ'ratory²** *n.*, rhetoric, speeches, eloquent language, highly coloured presentation of facts, so **ŏratŏ'rical** *a.* (**-lly**). [L *oratio* discourse, prayer (*oro* speak, pray)]

**ŏrb** *n.* Sphere, globe; globe surmounted by cross as part of regalia; heavenly body; (poet.) eyeball; **~ed** (ŏrbd, ŏr'bĭd) *a.*, rounded, bearing an orb; **~i'cŭlar** *a.*, spherical or circular. [L *orbis* ring]

**ŏr'bĭt. 1.** *n.* Eye-socket; curved course of planet, comet, satellite, etc.; state of motion in an orbit (*in, into, orbit*); **~al** *a.* **2.** *v.i.* & *t.* (Of satellite etc.) go round in orbit; put into orbit. [L (*orbitus* circular)]

**Orcā'dian** (ŏr-) *a.* & *n.* (Native) of Orkney. [L *Orcades* Orkney Islands]

**orch.** *abbr.* orchestra(ted by).

**ŏr'chard** *n.* Enclosure with fruit-trees. [E f. L *hortus* garden]

**ŏr'chėstr|a** (-k-) *n.* (Large) body of instrumental performers, part of modern theatre or concert-room assigned to them (**~a-pit** in theatre, in front of stage and on lower level; **~a stalls,** front rows of stalls); space in front of stage of ancient-Greek theatre where chorus danced and sang; **ŏrchė'stral** (-k-) *a.* (**-lly**), (Mus.) for, of, performed by, orchestra (*orchestral music, performance*); **~āte** *v.t.*, compose, arrange, or score, for orchestral performance, (fig.) combine (various elements harmoniously; ~**ā'tion** n. [L f. Gk (orkheomai dance)]

**ŏr'ch|id, ŏr'ch|is,** (-k-) ns. Kinds of flowering plant (~**is** is usual for wild British kinds, and ~**id** for hot-house exotics, many of which have fantastic and brilliant flowers); ~**idā'ceous** (-shus) a.; ~**idist** n., grower of orchids. [Gk]

**ŏrdai'n** v.t. Confer holy orders, esp. those of deacon or priest, upon; (of God, fate, law, authority, etc.) destine, appoint, enact. [AF f. L ordino (ORDER)]

**ŏrdea'l** (or -ē'al, ŏr'-) n. Experience that tests character or endurance, severe trial; primitive method of deciding suspected person's guilt or innocence by subjecting him to physical test such as holding red-hot iron, safe endurance of which was taken as divine acquittal. [E]

**ŏr'der. 1.** n. Social class or rank, its members; (the higher, lower, orders; the order of baronets); kind, sort, (talents of a high, another, order); grade of Christian ministry (holy ~**s**, those of bishop, priest, and deacon; **take** (holy) ~**s**, be ordained; **in** (holy) ~**s**, ordained); religious fraternity with common rule of life (the Franciscan order); company usu. instituted by sovereign to which distinguished persons are admitted as honour or reward (Distinguished Service Order; Order of the BATH, the GARTER, MERIT), insignia worn by members of this; (Archit.) mode of treatment with decoration and established proportions between parts (**the five classical** ~**s**, Doric, Ionic, Corinthian, Tuscan, and Composite, of column and entablature); ~ (**of magnitude**), class as regards size (**of, in, on, the** ~ **of**, having the order of magnitude specified by, errors of the order of one in a million, or approximately, of the order of 7%); (Biol.) classification-group below class and above family. **2.** Sequence, succession, (in alphabetical, chronological, order; in order of merit; follow the order of events; **in** ~, one after another on a principle; **out of** ~, not systematically arranged); regular array, condition in which every part or unit is in its right place, tidiness, normal or healthy or efficient state, (drew them up in order; **in bad, out of, not in,** ~, not working properly; **in** (**good**) ~, **in**

**working** etc. ~, ready or fit for use; OPEN order); (Mil.) style of dress and equipment; constitution of the world, way things normally happen, natural or moral or spiritual system with definite tendencies, (the order of nature, of things; the old order changeth); stated form of divine service (the order of confirmation); principles of decorum and rules of procedure accepted by assembly or meeting and enforced by its president (CALL to order; **point of** ~, inquiry whether procedure is **in** or **out of** ~, i.e. according or not according to rules etc.; ~ **of the day,** programme, business set down for treatment, fig. prevailing conditions, principal topic of action, procedure decided upon; ~**paper,** written or printed order of the day); prevalence of constituted authority, law-abiding state, absence of riot etc., (law and order; **keep** ~, enforce it); **in** ~ **to** do, with a view to, for the purpose of, doing; **in** ~ **that,** with the intention or to the end that. **3.** Command, injunction, authoritative direction or instruction, (give orders, an order, the order, for thing to be done, that it should be done, etc.; is obedient to orders; **by** ~, according to direction of the proper authority; ‖O~ **in Council,** sovereign's order on administrative matter given by advice of Privy Council); (Banking etc.) instruction to pay money or deliver property, signed by owner or responsible agent (**money** ~ for payment of specified sum, issued by bank or Post Office; ‖**postal** ~, ‖**post-office** ~, kinds of Post-Office money order; STANDING order); (Commerce etc.) direction to manufacturer, tradesman, waiter, etc., to supply or serve something (**made to** ~, made according to special directions, individual measurements, etc., opp. ready-made, fig. exactly what is wanted; **on** ~, ordered but not yet received; a TALL order); pass admitting bearer gratis, cheap, or as privilege to theatre, private house, etc., (~ **to view,** house-agent's request for client to be allowed to inspect premises). **4.** v.t. Put in order, array, regulate, (order one's affairs; ~ **arms,** Mil., stand rifle with butt on ground and hold it close to right side); (of God, fate, etc.) ordain; command, bid, prescribe, (order a retreat, thing to be done, person to do, *that* person or thing *should*); command or direct (person etc.) to go *to, away, home,* etc. (~ **about,** send hither and thither, domineer over); direct manufacturer, tradesman, etc., to supply, or waiter to serve. **5.** ~**lȳ,** (*a.*; ~**liness**) methodically arranged or inclined, tidy, not unruly, (Mil.) of or for orders (~**ly room** in barracks, for company's business), (*n.*) soldier in attendance on officer, attendant in (esp. military) hospital. [F f. L *ordo* ordin- row, array, degree, command, etc.]

**ŏr'dĭnal** *a.* & *n.* (Number) defining thing's position in a group ('*first*', '*twentieth*', etc., *are* ordinals *or* ordinal numbers; cf. NUMERAL). [L (prec.)]

**ŏr'dĭn|ance** *n.* Decree; religious rite; ~**ănd** *n.*, candidate for ordination. [F f. L (ORDAIN)]

**ŏr'dĭnarȳ. 1.** *a.* (-ily, -iness). Normal, customary, not exceptional, not above the usual, commonplace; ||*physician* etc. **in** ~, by permanent appointment, not temporary or extraordinary; **in the** ~ **way,** usually; **out of the** ~, unusual; ||~ **level,** G.C.E. examination of basic standard; ~ **seaman,** of lower rating than able seaman; *ordinary* SHARE*s.* **2.** *n.* Rule or book laying down order of divine service. [F & L (ORDER)]

**ŏr'dĭn|ate** *n.* (Math.) coordinate measured usu. vertically; ~**a'tion** *n.*, ordaining, conferring of holy orders. [L (ORDAIN)]

**ŏr'dnance** *n.* Mounted guns, cannon; government department for military stores (**O**~ **Survey,** government survey of U.K. orig. under Master of the Ordnance and producing accurate maps). [contr. *ordinance*]

**Ordovĭ'cian** (ŏr-; -shan) *a.* & *n.* (Of) Palaeozoic period or system below Silurian and above Cambrian. [L *Ordovices* ancient British tribe in N. Wales]

**ŏr'dūre** *n.* Dung. [F f. L *horridus* HORRID]

**ōre** *n.* Solid naturally-occurring mineral aggregate from which metal or other valuable constituent(s) may be usefully extracted; (poet.) metal, esp. gold. [E]

**ŏr'ĕăd** *n.* Mountain nymph. [L f. Gk (*oros* mountain)]

**Ore(g).** *abbr.* Oregon.

**ŏrĕga'nō** (-ah'-) *n.* Dried wild marjoram as seasoning. [Sp., = ORIGANUM]

**ŏr'gan** *n.* Musical instrument of pipes supplied with wind by bellows, sounded by keys, and distributed into sets or stops of special tone, which in turn form groups or partial organs each with separate keyboard (~-**loft,** gallery in church or concert-**room** for organ); harmonium; MOUTH-*organ;* = BARREL-*organ* (~-**grinder,** player of this); part of animal or vegetable body serving some special function (*organs of speech, digestion;* vocal, reproductive, *organs*); newspaper etc. representing a party or interest (*organ of the book trade*); **ŏrga'nĭc** *a.* (-ically), of bodily organs, (of disease, opp. *functional*) affecting structure of an organ, of animals or plants (opp. *inorganic*), having organs or organized physical structure, (of food) produced without artificial fertilizers or pesticides, (Chem., of compound etc.) containing carbon in its molecules (~**ĭc chemistry,** that of carbon compounds), constitutional, inherent, structural, (~**ĭc law,** stating formal constitution of country); systematic or co-ordinated or organized (*organic unity; an organic whole*); ~**ĭsm** *n.,* organized body, individual animal or plant; ~**ĭst** *n.,* player of organ, esp. as director of church choir; ~**ĭze** *v.t.,* furnish with organs or make organic or make into living tissue (esp. in *p.p.*), give orderly structure to, systematize, bring into working order, make arrangements for or initiate (undertaking requiring co-operation); ~**izā'tion** *n.,* (esp.) organized body or system or society. [F f. L f. Gk *organon* tool]

**ŏrga'ndĭe** (*or* ŏr'ga-) *n.* Fine translucent muslin, usu. stiffened. [F]

**ŏrga'nĭc** etc. See ORGAN.

**ŏrga'nza** *n.* Thin stiff transparent dress-fabric of silk or synthetic fibre. [P]

**ŏr'găsm** *n.* Climax of sexual excitement; **ŏrga'smĭc** (-z-), **ŏrga'stĭc,** *adjs.* [F or L f. Gk, = excitement]

**ŏr'gȳ** *n.* Drunken or licentious revel, (in *pl.*) revelry or debauchery; excessive indulgence in an activity (*an orgy of spending*); (Gk & Rom. Ant., in *pl.*) secret rites in worship of various gods esp. Bacchus, celebrated with wild drinking, dancing, singing;

**orgĭă′stĭc** *a.*, of the nature of an orgy. [F f. L f. Gk *orgia* pl.]

**or′iel** *n.* Part of upper room projecting from wall of house and containing window; ~ **(window)**, such window. [F]

**orient, 1.** (ŏr′ĭent) *n.* (O~) the East, the countries E. of Mediterranean, esp. E. Asia, (opp. *Occident*). **2.** (ŏr′ĭent, ŏr′-) *v.t.* & *i.* Place (building etc.) so as to face E., build (church) with chancel end due E.; turn eastward or in specified direction; ascertain compass-bearings of, (fig.) bring into clearly understood relations, direct *towards*; ~ oneself, determine how one stands in relation to surroundings. **3.** **ŏ′rientāte** (*or* ōr′-) *v.t.* & *i.*, orient; **ŏrĭentā′tion** (*or* ōr-) *n.*; **ŏrĭenteer′ing** *n.*, competitive sport of traversing rough country on foot with map and compass [Sw.]. [F f. L *oriens -entis* rising, rising sun, east]

**orĭe′ntal** (*or* ŏr-). **1.** *a.* (~ly). Of the Orient, of the eastern or (esp.) E. Asian world or its civilization. **2.** *n.* (O~). Native, inhabitant, of the Orient. **3.** ~**ism** *n.*, eastern ways; ~**ist** *n.*, (esp.) expert in oriental languages and history; ~**ize** *v.t.*

**o′rĭfice** *n.* Aperture, mouth of cavity, vent. [F f. L (*os or-* mouth, *facio* make)]

**ŏrĭga′mĭ** (-ah′-) *n.* Japanese art of folding paper intricately into decorative shapes. [Jap.]

**ori′ganum** *n.* Wild marjoram or similar plant. [L f. Gk]

**o′rĭgĭn** *n.* Source, starting-point, parentage; (Math.) point from which coordinates are measured. [F, or L *origo origin-* (*orior* rise)]

**ori′gĭn|al. 1.** *a.* (-lly). Existing from the first, primitive, innate, initial, earliest, (~**al** sin, innate depravity held to be common to all human beings in consequence of the Fall); that has served as pattern, of which copy or translation has been made, not derived or dependent or imitative, novel in character or style, inventive, creative, thinking or acting for oneself, (*where is the original picture?*; *what does the original Greek say?*; *made a very original remark*; *has an original mind*). **2.** *n.* Pattern, original model, thing from which another is copied or translated, (*several transcripts from the same original*; *the original is in the National Gallery*;

*reads Tolstoy in the original*); duplicate garment made by well-known designer. **3.** ~**ă′lĭtў** *n.*; ~**āte** *v.t.* & *i.*, initiate or give origin to or be origin of, have origin or begin (*from* or *in* thing or place, *with* or *from* person); ~**ā′tion**, ~**ātor**, *ns.*; ~**ative** *a.* [F or L (prec.)]

**ŏr′ĭōle** *n.* Bird, esp. **golden** ~ with black and yellow plumage in male. [F f. L (AUREOLE)]

**ŏ′rĭson** (-z-) *n.* (arch.) A prayer. [F f. L (ORATION)]

**ŏr′molu** (-lōō) *n.* Gilded bronze; a gold-coloured alloy; articles made of or decorated with these. [F *or moulu* powdered gold]

**ŏr′nament. 1.** *n.* Thing used or serving to adorn, quality or person whose existence or presence confers grace or honour; decorative work, embellishment, (*tower rich in ornament*; *more for ornament than use*); (in *pl.*) accessories of worship (e.g. altar, chalice, sacred vessels, service books). **2.** (-ĕ-) *v.t.* Adorn, beautify. **3.** **ŏrnamĕ′ntal** *a.* (-lly); **ŏrnamĕntā′tion** *n.* [F f. L (*orno* adorn)]

**ŏrnā′te** *a.* Elaborately adorned; (of literary style) embellished with flowery language.

***ŏr′ner|ў** *a.* (colloq.; ~**iness**). Of poor quality, coarse, unpleasant; cantankerous. [var. ORDINARY]

**ŏrnĭthŏ′log|ў** *n.* Study of birds; **ŏrnĭthŏlŏ′gĭcal** *a.* (-lly); ~**ĭst** *n.* [Gk *ornis ornith-* bird]

**ŏr|ŏ′graphў** (*or* ōr-) *n.* Physical geography of mountains; ~**ogră′phĭcal** *a.* (-lly). [Gk *oros* mountain]

**ŏ′rotŭnd** (*or* ōr′-) *a.* (Of utterance) dignified, imposing; pompous, boastful. [L *ore rotundo* with round mouth]

**ŏr′phan** *n.*, *a.*, & *v.* **1.** *n.* & *a.* (Child) bereaved of parent(s); ~**age** *n.*, institution for orphans; ~**hood** *n.* **2.** *v.t.* Bereave of parent(s). [L f. Gk, = bereaved]

**Or′phĭc, Orphē′an**, (ōr-) *adjs.* Of Orpheus or his mystic doctrines, oracular, (usu. *-ic*); like Orpheus's music, entrancing, (usu. *-ean*). [person in Gk legend]

**ŏr′pĭn(e)** *n.* Purple-flowered plant. [F]

**Or′pĭngton** (ōr′-) *n.* (Bird of) large-sized breed of buff white-legged poultry. [place]

**ŏ′rrerў** *n.* Clockwork model of planetary system. [person]

**ŏ′rrĭs** *n.* Kind of iris; ~**(-root)**,

violet-scented iris root used in perfumery etc. [alt. IRIS]

**ŏr'th|o-** *in comb.* Right, straight, correct; **~ochromă'tĭc** (-k-) *a.*, (Photog.) giving fairly correct relative intensity of visible colours by being sensitive to all except red; **~odŏ'ntĭcs** *n.*, correction of irregularities in teeth and jaws [Gk *odous odont-* tooth]; **~oĕpў** (*or* ŏrthŏ'ĭpĭ) *n.*, science of (correct) pronunciation [Gk *epos* word]; **~oĕpĭst** (*or* -ō'ĭp-) *n.*; **~ŏ'graphў** *n.*, spelling (esp. w. ref. to its correctness); **~ogră'phĭc(al)** *adjs.* -ically; **~opae'dĭcs, *-pē'-*,** *n.*, branch of surgery dealing with correction of deformities of bones or muscles, orig. in children [Gk *pais paidos* child]; **~opae'dĭc, *-pē'-*,** *a.* [Gk *orthos* straight]

**ŏr'thodŏx** *a.* Holding correct or accepted views esp. on religion, not heretical or original; generally accepted as right or true, approved, conventional; **O~ Church,** the Eastern or Greek Church, with Patriarch of Constantinople as head; **~ў** *n.*, adherence to the orthodox, orthodox views. [L f. Gk (*doxa* opinion)]

**ŏrthŏ'ptĭc** *a.* Relating to correct or normal use of eyes. [ORTHO-]

**ŏr'tolan** *n.* Eur. garden bird, eaten as delicacy. [F f. Prov. f. L (*hortus* garden)]

**-orў** *suf.* forming *ns.* denoting place (*dormitory, laboratory, refectory*), and *adjs.* (& *ns.*) w. sense of (person or thing) relating to or involving vbl action (*accessory, compulsory, predatory*). [AF f. L]

**O.S.** *abbr.* old style; ordinary seaman; ordnance survey; outsize.

**O'scar** (ŏ'-) *n.* Statuette awarded by Academy of Motion Picture Arts and Sciences for excellence in film acting, directing, etc. [man's name]

**ŏ'scĭll|āte** *v.i. & t.* (Cause to) swing to and fro; vacillate, vary between extremes of opinion, action, condition, etc.; (Electr., of current) undergo high-frequency alternations; **~ā'tion** *n.*; **~ātor** *n.*, (esp.) instrument for producing oscillations; **~ātorў** (*or* osĭ'la-) *a.* [L (*oscillo* swing)]

**oscĭ'llo-** *in comb.* Oscillation esp. of electric current; **~graph,** device for recording oscillations; **~scope,** device for viewing oscillations esp. on screen of cathode-ray tube.

**ŏ'scŭl|āte** *v.i. & t.* (joc.) Kiss; **~ar** *a.*, of or for kissing; **~ā'tion** *n.*; **~ātorў** *a.* [L (*osculor* kiss f. *os* mouth)]

**-ōse** *suf.* forming *adjs.* denoting possession of a quality (*bellicose, grandiose, morose, verbose*). [L]

**ō'sĭer** (-z-, ō'zher) *n.* (Shoot of) willow used in basketwork; **~-bed,** place where these are grown. [F]

**-ō'sĭs** *suf.* forming *ns.* denoting process or condition (*apotheosis, metamorphosis*), esp. pathological state (*neurosis, thrombosis*). [L or Gk]

**-ō'sĭtў** *suf.* forming *ns.* f. *adjs.* in -OSE or -OUS (*verbosity, curiosity*). [F or L]

**Osmă'nlĭ** (ŏs-, ŏz-) *a. & n.* = OTTOMAN. [Turk.]

**ŏsmō's|ĭs** (ŏz-) *n.* (*pl.* **~es** *pr.* -ēz) Tendency of solvent, when separated by suitable partition from more concentrated solution, to diffuse through into that solution; **ŏsmŏ'tĭc** (ŏz-) *a.* (-ically). [Gk *ōsmos* thrust, push]

**ŏ'smund** (*or* -z-) *n.* The flowering fern. [AF]

**ŏ'sprey** (*or* -ā) *n.* Large bird preying on inland fish; egret-plume used in millinery. [F, ult. f. L *ossifraga* (*os* bone, *frango* break)]

**ŏ'ss|ĕous** *a.* Bony, of bone, having bones; **~ĭcle** *n.*, small bone or piece of hard substance in animal structure. [L (*os oss-* bone)]

**O'ssĭe** (ŏ'zĭ) *n. & a.* (sl.) Australian. [abbr.]

**ŏ'ssĭf|ў** *v.t. & i.* Turn into bone, harden; make or become rigid or callous or unprogressive; **~ĭcā'tion** *n.* [F f. L (OSSEOUS)]

**ŏstĕ'ns|ĭble** *a.* (-bly) Professed, for show, used as a blind, (*his ostensible function was as interpreter*); **~ĭve** *a.*, directly showing; **~orў** *n.*, monstrance; **ŏstĕntā'tion** *n.*, pretentious display of wealth etc., showing off; **ŏstĕntā'tious** (-shus) *a.* [F f. L (*ostendo -tens-* show)]

**ŏ'stĕ|ŏ-** *in comb.* Bone; **~ŏ'logў** *n.*, science of bones; **~ŏ'pathў** *n.*, curative treatment (usu. manipulation) for disease supposedly caused by deformation of spine; **~opăth** *n.*, practitioner of this. [Gk *osteon* bone; PATHOS]

**‖ŏ'stler, hŏ'stler,** (-sl-) *n.* Stableman at inn. [HOSTEL]

**ŏ'strac|ize** *v.t.* Exclude from society, refuse to associate with; (in ancient Athens) banish for some years by popular vote without trial; **~ism** *n.*, ostracizing or being ostracized. [Gk *ostrakon* shell, potsherd (used in voting)]

**ŏ'strich** *n.* Large swift-running flightless African bird, swallowing hard substances to assist working of gizzard, and reputed to bury its head in sand when pursued, in the belief that it cannot be seen, (*has the digestion of an ostrich*, can digest any food; *following an ostrich policy*; **~-farm**, breeding ostriches for feathers; **~plume**, wing or tail feather of ostrich as ornament); (fig.) person who refuses to accept facts. [F (L *avis* bird, *struthio* (f. Gk) ostrich)]

**O.T.** *abbr.* Old Testament.

**o'ther** (ŭ'dh-) *a., n.* or *pron.*, & *adv.* **1.** *a.* Not the same as one or some already mentioned or implied, separate in identity, distinct in kind, alternative or further or additional, the only remaining, (*we have other evidence*; *other people think otherwise*; *have no other place to go*; *the other side of the fence*; *a few other examples would be useful*; *now open the, your, other eye*; ||*A. N. Other* (SEE ANOTHER); EVERY *other day* etc.; **the ~ day, night, week**, etc., (*adv.*) a few days etc. ago; **~ than**, different from (*a person other than yourself*; *would not wish her other than she is*); **~-wor'ldly**, concerned with the other WORLD or some imagined life to the neglect of the present or real one; **someone, something, some time**, etc., **or ~**, some unspecified or unknown person, thing, (at) some unspecified time, etc.; **how the ~ half lives**, other people's mode of life; **the ~ thing**, unexpressed alternative); (often ellipt. with numerals, as) ANOTHER (**the ~ two** etc., the other two etc. persons or things, of kind not needing specification). **2.** *n.* or *pron.* Other person or thing (*give me one other, another, some others, the two others*; *do good to others*; *one or other of us will be there*; *he acts while others talk*; *one or each neutralizes the other*; *they neutralize* EACH *other* or ONE *another*). **3.** *adv.* Otherwise (*other than cursorily, than by repeating it*). [E]

**o'therwise** (ŭ'dherwiz). **1.** *adv.* In a different way (*could not have acted otherwise*; *am otherwise engaged that day*; *Judas, otherwise* (called or known as) *Iscariot*; occas. preceded by *any* or *no*: *could do it no otherwise*); if

circumstances are or were or had been different, else, or else, (*seize the chance, otherwise you will regret it*); in other respects (*he is unruly, but not otherwise blameworthy*); **and ~, or ~**, = *and* or *or* followed by negation or opposite of what precedes (*the merits or otherwise of the Bill*, i.e. or demerits; *additions automatic and otherwise*, i.e. and not automatic). **2.** *a.* In a different state (*the matter is quite otherwise*). [E (WISE²)]

**ŏ'tic** *a.* Of or relating to the ear; **ŏto-** *comb. form.* [Gk (*ous ōt-* ear)]

**ŏ'tĭōse** (or -shĭ-) *a.* Not required, serving no practical purpose, functionless. [L (*otium* leisure)]

*ottava rima* (otahva rē'ma) *n.* Verse in stanzas of 8 lines, with rhymes *abababcc*. [It., = 8th rhyme]

**ŏ'tter** *n.* Furred aquatic fish-eating mammal; its fur; **~-dog, -hound**, (used in hunting otters). [E]

**ŏ'ttō.** See ATTAR.

**O'ttoman** (ŏ'-). **1.** *a.* Of *Osman* or Othman I or his descendants or their empire; Turkish. **2.** *n.* Turk; (o~) cushioned seat without back or arms, often box with cushioned top. [person]

**O.U.** *abbr.* ||Open University; Oxford University.

**oublĭĕ'tte** (ōō-) *n.* Secret dungeon with trapdoor entrance. [F (*oublier* forget)]

**ouch** *int.* expr. sharp or sudden pain. [natural excl.]

**ought¹** (awt) *n.* (colloq.) Figure 0, nought. [NOUGHT]

**ought²** (awt) *v.aux.* (the only form now in use is **ought** as pres. and past finite, *neg.* **~ not**, colloq. **~n't** *pr.* aw'tent) expr. duty, rightness, shortcoming, advisability, or strong probability; the past sense is usu. indicated by a following perf. inf.: *we ought to love our neighbours*; *it ought not to be allowed*; *you ought to know, to have known, better*; *he ought to be there by now*; *it ought to be done at once, to have been done long ago*; *ought I to say, to have said, that?*; *she ought to have been a lawyer, not a don.* [E, past tense of OWE]

**Ouija** (wē'jah, -yah, -*a*) *n.* **~** (-**board**), board marked with alphabet and other signs used with movable pointer to obtain messages in spiritualistic seances. [P; F *oui*, G *ja*, yes]

**ounce¹** *n.* Unit of weight, 1|16 lb. avoirdupois or 28 g, 1|12 lb. troy or apothecaries' weight; (fig.) small quantity (*hasn't got an ounce of common sense*); **fluid ~,** ‖1/20 pint, *1/16 pint. [F f. L *uncia* twelfth part of pound or foot]

**ounce**[2] *n.* Asian feline, the snow-leopard. [F (*l*)*once,* rel. to LYNX]

**our** *poss. pron. attrib.* Of or belonging to us (see WE), that we are concerned with or speaking or thinking of, (*in our midst; our friend will have to watch his step; for all our sakes*); **Our Father,** God, the LORD's Prayer; **Our LADY.** [E]

**ours** (-z) *poss. pron. pred.* (& abs.) Of us (for phrs. see HERS).

**oursě'l|f** *pron.* replacing MYSELF when used by sovereign, newspaper-writer, etc., who uses *we* instead of *I* (*we ourself are not able to attend*); **~ves** (-vz) *pron.,* emphat. & refl. form of WE, US (for use cf. HERSELF). [SELF]

**-ous** *suf.* forming *adjs.* meaning 'abounding in, characterized by, of the nature of' (*envious, fabulous, glorious, hazardous, ligneous, mountainous, poisonous*); (Chem.) combined in lower valence etc. (*ferrous, sulphurous*). [F f. L (-OSE)]

**ousel.** See OUZEL.

**oust** *v.t.* Put out of possession, eject, drive out, seize the place of; *~'er n.,* (Law & U.S.) ejection. [AF f. L *obsto* oppose]

**out** *adv., prep., n., a., int.,* & *v.* **1.** *adv.* Away from or not in a place, not in right or normal state, the fashion, etc., (*keep him out; get out (of here)!; on the voyage out; crinolines are out; workers are ~,* on strike; *arm, shoulder, is ~,* dislocated; *ball is ~,* beyond boundary of court in games; *batsman etc. is ~,* dismissed by being caught etc., opp. *not out; calculation, estimate, is ~,* in error; *fire etc. is ~,* no longer burning; *idea etc. is ~,* not worth considering; *person is ~,* not at home, not in his office, etc.; *jury is ~,* considering verdict in private; *a* NIGHT *out; ~* (*cold, for the* COUNT[1]), unconscious; *tooth is ~,* extracted; *Tories etc. are ~,* not in office; *~ with him!,* turn him out); in(to) the open, publicity, existence, notice, hearing, view, or clearness, (ALL *out; book is ~,* published; *chick is ~,* hatched; *flower is ~,* open; **~ and about,** engaging in outdoor activity; **~ for,** having one's interest or effort directed to, intent on; **~ to,** keenly striving to (do); *rash is ~,* visible; *secret is ~,* revealed; *shout ~,* loudly;

the best game etc. ~, known to exist; *murder, truth, etc., will ~,* is sure to be discovered; **~ with it,** say what you are thinking); to or at an end, completely, (*she had her cry out; tired out; hear me out; before the week is out;* **~ and away,** by far; **~ and ~,** thorough(ly), surpassing(ly): *an out and out liar*), in finished form (*have not typed it out yet*), (in radio conversation etc.) transmission ends; **~-tray** (for documents etc. dealt with and to be taken elsewhere). **2.** **~ of** *prep.,* from within, not within, from among, beyond range of, (so as to be) without, from, owing to, by use of (material), at specified distance from (town etc.), beyond, transgressing rules of, (*come out of the house; I was never out of England; nine people out of ten know that; is out of sight; was swindled out of his money; is out of breath, his mind, coffee; got money out of him; asked out of curiosity; chair made out of orange-boxes*); **~ of it,** not included, forlorn. **3.** *prep.* (arch. or U.S.) Out of (*from out the azure main;* *look out the window*). **4.** *n.* Way of escape; **at ~s,** at variance or enmity; INs *and* outs. **5.** *a.* (Of match) played away; (of island) away from mainland; **~-patient** (not residing in hospital during treatment). **6.** *int.* = *get* etc. *out!;* (arch.) expr. abhorrence, reproach, etc., (*Out upon you!*). **7.** *v.t.* Put out; (colloq.) eject forcibly; (Boxing) knock out. **8. ~'er,** (*a.*) farther from centre or inside, relatively far out, external, of the outside, objective, physical, not subjective or psychical, (**~er man, woman,** personal appearance, dress; **~er space,** universe beyond earth's atmosphere; **the ~er world,** people outside one's own circle), (*n.*) (shot striking) division of target farthest from bull's-eye; **~ermōst** *a.;* **~ing** *n.,* pleasure-trip, excursion. [E]

**out-** *pref.* meaning: (1) out of, away from, outward; (2) external, separate; (3) so as to surpass or exceed; **~'back,** (Austral.) remote inland districts; **~bi'd,** bid higher than; **~'board,** towards outside of ship, aircraft, or vehicle, (of motor) attached externally to stern of boat, (of boat) using such motor; **~'break,** breaking out of anger, war, disease, fire, etc.; **~'building,** outhouse; **~'burst,** bursting out esp. of

emotion in vehement words; ~**cast**
*a.* & *n.*, (person) cast out from home
and friends, homeless and friendless
(vagabond); ~**cla′ss**, surpass by a
wide difference; ~**come**, result,
issue; ~**crop**, emergence of stratum
etc. at surface, stratum thus emerging,
(fig.) noticeable manifestation; ~**′-
cry**, clamour, loud protest; ~**da′ted**,
out of date, obsolete; ~**di′stance**,
get far ahead of; ~**do′**, exceed, excel,
surpass; ~**door**, done, existing,
used, out of doors, not in buildings;
~**door′s** *n.* & *adv.*, (in, into) the
open air; ~**fa′ce**, abash by staring
or by confident manner; ~**fall**,
mouth of river, drain, etc.; ~**field**,
outlying land, outer part of cricket
or baseball pitch; ~**fit**, set of equipment or clothes, (colloq.) group of
persons, or organization; ~**fitter**,
supplier of equipment, esp. men's
clothing; ~**fla′nk**, extend beyond
flank of (enemy), outmanœuvre
(thus, or fig.); ~**flow**, outward flow,
what flows out; ~**fo′x**, (colloq.)
outwit; ~**ge′neral**, defeat by superior
generalship; ~**′going**, (*a.*) going
out, retiring from office, friendly,
(*n.*, in *pl.*) expenditure; ~**grow′**,
grow faster or taller than or too big
for, leave behind as one develops;
~**′growth**, offshoot, natural product; ~**′house**, shed etc. belonging
to main house and built against or
near it; ~**la′ndish**, looking or
sounding foreign, unfamiliar, bizarre
[*outland* foreign country]; ~**la′st**,
last longer than (person, thing, or
duration); ~**law**, (*n.*) person deprived of protection of law, (*v.t.*)
declare (person) outlaw, make illegal,
proscribe; ~**lawry**, condition of or
condemnation as outlaw; ~**lay**,
expenses; ~**let**, means of exit or
escape, market for goods; ~**line**,
(*n.*, in *sing.* or *pl.*) line(s) enclosing
visible object, contour, external
boundary, (in *sing.*) sketch containing only contour lines (*in* ~**line**, so
sketched), rough draft, summary,
(in *pl.*) main features or principles,
(*v.t.*) draw or describe in outline,
mark outline of; ~**li′ve**, live longer
than or beyond (period, date) or
through (an experience); ~**′look**,
view, prospect (esp. fig.), mental
attitude; ~**′lying**, far from a
centre, remote; ~**manœu′vre**, outdo in manœuvring; ~**ma′tch**, be
more than a match for; ~**mo′ded**,

out of fashion, obsolete; ~**nu′mber**,
exceed in number; ~**pa′ce**, go
faster than, outdo in contest; ~**play′**,
surpass in playing, play better than;
~**poi′nt**, score more points than;
~**′post**, detachment on guard at
some distance from army, distant
branch or settlement; ~**′pouring**,
what is poured out, (usu. in *pl.*)
expression of emotion; ~**put**, (*n.*)
amount produced by manufacture
etc., place where energy, information,
etc., leaves a system, (Electr.)
power etc. delivered by apparatus,
(*v.t.*: ~, ~**ted**) send out, (of computer) supply (results etc.); ~**ra′nk**,
be superior in rank to; ~**rider**,
mounted attendant riding ahead of
carriage, motor-cyclist similarly
guarding car(s); ~**′rigger**, spar or
framework projecting from or over
ship's side, iron bracket bearing rowlock outside boat, boat with these;
~**ru′n**, run faster or farther than,
escape, go beyond (specified point
or limit); ~**se′ll**, sell more than, be
sold in greater quantities than;
~**set**, start (*at*, *from*, *the outset*);
~**shi′ne**, shine brighter than, (fig.)
surpass in splendour or excellence;
~**size** *a.* & *n.*, (of) exceptionally
large size (in garments, measurements, etc., or fig.), outsize person or
thing; ~**skirts**, outer border of
town, district, subject, etc.; ~**-
smar′t**, (colloq.) outwit, be too
clever for; ~**spa′n**, (S. Afr.) unyoke,
unharness [cf. INSPAN]; ~**spo′ken**
(-*nness* *pr.* -n-n-), frank, unreserved,
(of speaker or words); ~**sprea′d**
*v.t.*, & *a.*, spread out, expand(ed);
~**sta′nding**, conspicuous, eminent,
not yet determined or settled;
~**′station**, remote (Austral., cattle
or sheep) station; ~**stay′**, stay
longer than (another) or beyond (*outstay* one's WELCOME); ~**stre′tched**,
stretched out; ~**stri′p**, pass in
running etc., surpass esp. com-
petitively; ~**-swinger**, (Crick.) ball
that swings away from batsman;
~**vo′te**, defeat by majority of votes;
~**wei′gh**, exceed in weight, value,
importance, or influence; ~**wi′t**, be
too clever for, overcome by greater
ingenuity; ~**′with** *prep.*, (Sc.) outside; ~**′work**, advanced or detached part of fortification; ~**wor′n**,
obsolete, worn out, exhausted.

**ou′ter, ou′ting.** See OUT.

**ou′trage. 1.** *n.* Forcible violation of

others' rights, sentiments, etc., gross or wanton offence or indignity (*an outrage upon common sense, decency,* etc.); strong resentment (*at*). 2. *v.t.* Subject to outrage, injure, insult, violate, ravish; infringe (law, morality, etc.) flagrantly; cause to feel strong resentment. 3. **~ous** (-ā′jŭs) *a.*, immoderate, violent, grossly cruel or immoral or offensive or abusive. [F (*outrer* exceed f. L *ultra* beyond)]

*outré* (ōō′trā) *a.* Eccentric, violating decorum. [F, p.p. of *outrer* (prec.)]

**outright** (-it). 1. (-i′-) *adv.* Altogether, entirely, once for all, not by degrees or instalments; without reservation, openly. 2. (ow′-) *a.* Downright, thorough. [OUT, RIGHT]

**outside** *n., a., adv., & prep.* 1. (-i′d, ow′-) *n.* External side or surface, outer part(s), (~ **in,** = INSIDE *out*); (of path) side next to road; external appearance, outward aspect; all that is without (*impressions from the outside*); position on outer side (*open the door from the outside*); (colloq.) highest computation (*there were 30 of them at the outside*). 2. (ow′-) *a.* Of or on or nearer the outside, outer, (‖~ **broadcast,** not made from studio; ~ **chance,** remote, unlikely; ~ **seat,** nearer the end; ~ **work,** done off the premises; nearer to outside of games field; not belonging to some circle or institution (*outside consultant*); greatest existent or possible or probable (*quote the outside prices*). 3. (-i′d) *adv.* On or to the outside, the open air, open sea, etc., not within or enclosed or included, (*is black outside and in;* **come ~,** i.e. from room or house, esp. as challenge to fight; ~ **of,** = sense 4; *get* ~ *of,* sl., eat or drink) (sl.) not in prison. 4. (-i′d) *prep.* External to, not included in, beyond the limits of, not in, to or at the outside or exterior of, (*forces outside our control; cannot go outside the evidence; meet me outside the library*). 5. ~**r** (-i′-) *n.*, non-member of some circle, party, profession, etc., uninitiated person, person without special knowledge, social background, etc., competitor thought to have no chance. [OUT-]

**ou′tward.** 1. *a.* Directed towards the outside; going out; bodily, external, material, visible, apparent, superficial, (**the ~ eye,** opp. *mind's eye;* ~ **form,** appearance; ~ **man,** body as opp. soul; ~ **things,** the

world around us; **to ~ seeming,** apparently). 2. *adv.* Outwards; ~ **bound,** (of ship or passenger) going away from home. 3. **~ly** *adv.*, in outward appearance, in externals, on the surface; **~ness** *n.,* external existence, objectivity, objective-mindedness; **~s** *adv.,* in an outward direction, towards the outside. [E (OUT, -WARD)]

**ou′zel, ou′sel,** (ōō′z-) *n.* Kind of small bird (RING[1] *ouzel, water ouzel*); (arch.) blackbird. [E]

**ou′zo** (ōō′-) *n.* Greek drink of aniseed-flavoured spirits. [Gk]

**ō′va.** See OVUM.

**ō′val.** 1. *a.* (**~ly**). Egg-shaped, ellipsoidal; having outline of egg, elliptical. 2. *n.* Egg-shaped or elliptical closed curve; thing with oval outline. [L (OVUM)]

**ō′varу** *n.* Either of two reproductive organs in which ova are produced in female animals; lower part of pistil in plant, from which fruit is formed; **ovā′rian** *a.*

**ovā′tion** *n.* Enthusiastic reception, general applause; (Rom. Ant.) lesser form of TRIUMPH. [L (*ovo* exult)]

**o′ven** (ŭ′-) *n.* Receptacle heated for baking food in (**Dutch ~,** metal box of which open side is turned towards ordinary fire, covered cooking-pot; **~ware,** dishes in which food can be cooked in oven). [E]

**ō′ver** *adv., n., a., & prep.* 1. *adv.* Outward and downward from brink or from erect position (*lean, fall, jump, knock, over*); so as to cover or touch whole surface (*brush, paint, it over;* **all ~,** in or on one's entire body, fig. in characteristic attitude or behaviour: *that is Jones all over;* ONCE-*over*); with motion above something, so as to pass across something, (*climb, look, boil, over*); so as to duce fold or reverse position, upside down, (*bend it over;* TURN *over; see over,* i.e. overleaf; *roll ~* **and ~,** so that same point comes uppermost repeatedly); (Crick., as umpire's call) change ends for bowling etc.; across a street or other space (*take this over to the pet-shop; is over in,* has come over from, *is going over to,* America; ~ **against,** in opposite situation to, adjacent to, in contrast with; **ask him ~,** to visit from place not far off); with transference or change from one hand, party, etc., to another (*went over to the enemy; hand it over; ~* (**to you**), in radio conversation etc. = I await your reply, action, etc.); too, in excess, in addition, besides, more, apart, till later time, (*shall have something over; £5 and over;* HOLD¹, STAND, *over;* **not ~ well** etc., rather badly etc.; ~ **and above**, in addition, moreover); from beginning to end, with repetition, with detailed consideration, (*read, count, over; did it six times over; talk, think, the matter over; start* etc. (**all**) ~ **again**, *\*~*, once again, again from the beginning; ~ **and ~**, many times); at an end, settled, (*the battle is over; get it over (and done) with;* **all ~**, completely finished). **2.** n. (Crick.) Number of balls (now 6 or 8) bowled between two calls of 'over', play resulting from this, (MAIDEN *over*). **3.** a. Upper, outer, superior, extra, (usu. as pref.; see OVER-). **4.** prep. Above, in or to position higher than, on, at all or various points upon, to and fro upon, all through, round about, concerning, engaged with, (*an umbrella over his head; projects over the street; bridge over the river; doubt hangs over the question; with his hat over his eyes; a change came over him; you may travel (all) over Europe, Europe over, and not find it; discuss it over a glass of wine; laugh over the absurdity of it; go to sleep over* one's *work;* **all ~** person, sl., effusively attentive to him; ~ **all**, from end to end; *over* one's HEAD); with or so as to get or give superiority or preference to, beyond, more than, in comparison with, (*reigns over her people; won a victory over; has no control over himself; give me preference over him; cost over £5; decrease of 25 over last year;* ~ **and above** fact, item, etc., besides, not to mention); out and down from, down from edge of, so as to clear, across, on or to the other side of, throughout, through duration of, till end of, (*fell over the cliff; stumble over a tree-root; jumped over the brook; look over the hedge; she spoke over her shoulder; riding over the moor; mislaid over the years; payments spread over two years; will not live over today;* ~ **the way**, on opposite side of street). **5.** ~**ly** adv., excessively, too. [E]

o´ver- *pref.* meaning: (1) over (as prec. entry); (2) upper, outer; (3) superior; (4) excessive(ly) (among the words given below, some are without

definitions; this implies that *over*-adds merely the sense *too* to an adjective or adverb, *excessive* to a noun, or *too much* to a verb); ~**a´ct**, act (role, emotion, etc.), act role, with exaggeration; ~**a´ctive** *a.*; ~**all**, (n.) ‖protective outer garment, (in *pl.*) protective outer trousers or suit, or ‖close-fitting cavalry trousers, (*a.*) from end to end (*overall length*), total, inclusive of all, (*or* -aw'l; *adv.*) in all parts, taken as a whole; ~**arm** *a. & adv.*, (esp. Crick. & Swimming) with arm raised above shoulder; ~**awe**, awe into submission; ~**ba´lance**, (cause to) lose balance and fall; ~**bear´**, bear down by weight or force, repress by power or authority; ~**bear´ing** *a.*, domineering, bullying; ~**bi´d**, (*v.t.*) make higher bid than, (Bridge) bid more on (one's hand, or abs.) than its strength warrants, overcall, (ō´-; *n.*) any such bid; ~**blouse**, loose upper garment worn over sweater etc.; ~**blow´n**, inflated or pretentious, (of flower, beauty) past its prime; ~**board**, from within ship into water (*go ~board*, colloq., be highly enthusiastic; *throw ~board*, lit., or fig. = abandon, discard); ~**bo´ld** *a.*; ~**boo´k**, make too many bookings for (aircraft flight etc., or abs.); ~**boot**, ~**shoe**, (worn over other boot or shoe for protection in wet weather etc.); ~**bur´den** *v.t.*; ~**ca´ll**, (Bridge) (*v.t.*) make higher bid than, ‖= *overbid*, (ō´-; *n.*) act or instance of this; ~**car´eful** *a.*; ~**ca´st**, (esp. in *p.p.*) cover (sky etc.) with clouds or darkness, stitch over (edge) to prevent unravelling; ~**char´ge**, (*v.t.*) charge too high a price for (thing) or to (person), charge (specified sum) beyond right price, put too much (explosive, electric, etc.) charge into, (ō´-; *n.*) excessive charge (of explosive etc. or of money); ~**check**, (cloth with) combination of two different-sized check patterns; ~**coat**, coat worn over indoor clothes, protective coat of paint etc.; ~**co´me**, prevail over, master, be victorious, (in *p.p.*) exhausted, made helpless, affected *with* or *by* emotion; ~*come with liquor* etc., drunk); ~**compensa´tion**, exaggerated correction of real or fancied defect of character; ~**co´nfidence** *n.*; ~**co´nfident** *a.*; ~**coo´ked**, cooked beyond its best;

~**crow'd**, cause too many people or things to be in (a place); ~**deve'lop**, (Photog.) treat with developer for too long or otherwise excessively; ~**do'**, carry to excess, go too far in, cook too much, exhaust, (~*do it, things*, work too hard, exaggerate, carry an action too far); ~**dose**, (*n.*) excessive dose (of drug etc.), (-ō's; *v.t.*) give such dose to; ~**draft**, overdrawing of bank account, amount by which sums drawn exceed credit balance; ~**draw'**, draw cheque in excess of (one's account), exaggerate in describing, (in *p.p.*) having overdrawn one's account; ~**dre'ss**, dress ostentatiously or with too much formality; ~**drive**, mechanism in car etc. providing gear ratio higher than that of usual gear; ~**du'e**, past the time when due or ready, not yet paid or arrived or born etc. though after expected time; ~~**ea'ger** *a.*; ~**ea't** *v.i.*; ~~**e'mphasis** *n.*; ~~**e'mphasize** *v.t.*; ~**e'stimate** *v.t.*, & *n.*, (form) too high an estimate (of); ~~**exci'te** *v.t.*; ~~**exer'tion** *n.*; ~-**expo'sure** *v.t.*; ~~**expo'sure** *n.*; ~**feed** *v.i.* & *t.*; ~**fi'll**, fill to overflowing; ~**fi'sh**, fish (stream, sea, etc.) to depletion; ~**flow'**, (*v.t.* & *i.*) flow over (brim etc.), flood (surface), (fig., of crowd etc.) extend beyond limits of (room etc.), (of receptacle etc.) be so full that contents overflow, (of kindness, harvest, etc.) be very abundant, (ō-; *n.*) what overflows or is superfluous, outlet for excess liquid, (~*flow meeting*, for those excluded from main meeting owing to lack of space); ~**fly'**, fly over or beyond (place or territory); ~**fo'nd** *a.*; ~**fulfi'lment**, completion of plan before appointed time; ~**fu'll** *a.*; ~**ground**, raised above the ground, not underground; ~**grow'**, (esp. in *p.p.*) (of plants) grow over, overspread; ~**growth** *n.*; ~**hand** *a.* & *adv.*, with hand above object held, = *overarm*; ~**ha'ng**, (*v.t.* & *i.*) jut out (over), impend (over), (ō-; *n.*) fact or amount of overhanging, overhanging part; ~**hau'l**, (*v.t.*) take to pieces for inspection and necessary repairs, examine state of, overtake, (ō-; *n.*) thorough examination with repairs if necessary; ~**hea'd**, (*adv.*) above one's head, in the sky or the storey above, (ō-; *a.*) placed overhead, (of expenses) arising from management,

office supplies, interest on borrowed capital, etc., as distinct from business transactions, (ō-; *n.*, in *pl.*) overhead expenses; ~**hear'**, hear as eavesdropper or as unperceived or unintentional listener; ~**hea't** *v.t.*; ~~**indu'lgence** *n.*; ~~**indu'lgent** *a.*; ~**joy'ed**, filled with extreme joy; ~**kill**, amount by which (capacity for) destruction (lit. or fig.) exceeds that necessary for victory over or annihilation of enemy; ~**la'den**, too heavily loaded; ~**la'nd**, (*adv.*) by land and not sea, (ō-; *a.*) entirely or partly by land (*overland route*); ~**la'p**, (*v.t.* & *i.*) partly cover, cover and extend beyond, partly coincide, (ō-; *n.*) fact or process or amount of overlapping, overlapping part; ~**lar'ge** *a.*; ~**lay'**, (*v.t.*) lay over, cover surface of *with* coating etc., overlie, (ō-; *n.*) thing laid over another; ~**lea'f**, on other side of leaf of book; ~**li'e**, lie on top of, smother (child) thus; ~**loa'd** *v.t.*; ~**load** *n.*; ~**lo'ng** *a.*; ~**loo'k**, have prospect of or over from above, be higher than, fail to observe, take no notice of, condone, superintend; ~**lord**, supreme lord; ~**ma'n**, provide with too many men as crew, staff, etc.; ~**mantel**, ornamental shelves etc. over mantelpiece; ~**ma'stering**, dominant; ~**mu'ch** *a.*, *n.*, & *adv.*; ~**ni'ce** *a.*; ~**ni'ght**, (*adv.*) on preceding evening with a view to, or as regarded from, next day, from one day to the next, (ō-; *a.*) done or for use etc. overnight; ~**pa'ss**, (*v.t.*) pass over, across, or beyond, surmount, (ō-; *n.*) road that crosses another by a bridge; ~**pa'ssed**, ~**pa'st**, gone by, past; ~**pay'** *v.t.*; ~**persua'de**, persuade (person) to some action or course in spite of his contrary judgement or inclination; ~**pi'tch**, (Crick.) bowl (ball) so that it pitches too near stumps, (fig.) exaggerate; ~**play'**, play (part) to excess, give undue importance to, (~*play* one's *hand*, Cards or fig., be unduly optimistic as to one's capabilities); ~**plus**, surplus, superabundance; ~**pow'er**, reduce to submission, subdue, make (thing) ineffective or imperceptible by greater intensity, (of heat, emotion, etc.) be too intense for, overwhelm; ~**prai'se** *v.t.*, & *n.*; ~**pri'nt**, print over (something already printed); ~~**produ'ce** *v.t.*;

~**produ′ction** n.; ~**proof,** containing more alcohol than proof spirit does; ~**ra′te,** have too high an opinion of; ~**rea′ch,** circumvent, outwit, (~*reach* one*self,* strain oneself by reaching too far, defeat one's object by going too far); ~**rea′ct,** respond more violently etc. than is justified; ~**refi′ne,** (esp.) make too subtle distinctions in; ~**ri′de,** (fig.) supersede arrogantly, have or claim superior authority or precedence over, make ineffective; ‖~**rider,** vertical attachment on motor-car bumper to prevent its becoming interlocked with bumper of another car; ~**ri′pe** a.; ~**ru′le,** set aside (decision, argument, proposal) by virtue of superior authority, annul decision or reject proposal of (person) thus; ~**ru′n,** flood, harry (enemy's country), (of vermin, weeds, etc.) swarm or spread over, exceed (limit); ~**sea(s)** a. & (~ē′) adv., across or beyond sea; ~**see′,** superintend (workmen, work); ~**seer,** superintendent; ~**se′ll,** sell more of (commodity etc., or abs.) than one can deliver, (fig.) exaggerate merits of; ~**se′nsitive** a.; ~**se′t,** overturn, upset; ~**sew,** sew (edges of material) with every stitch in same direction and thread passing across and outside edges near stitching; ~**se′xed,** having unusually great sexual desires; ~**sha′dow,** shelter from sun, cast into shade, make appear less important by one's own brilliance; ~**shoe** (see *overboot*); ~**shoo′t,** send missile, travel, beyond (*the mark* etc.; lit. or fig. of exaggeration, excess, etc.), (of aircraft) pass beyond limit of (runway etc.) when landing; ~**shot,** (of wheel) turned by water flowing above it; ~**si′de,** over side of ship (into smaller boat, or into sea); ~**sight,** omission to notice, inadvertent mistake, supervision; ~**si′mplify,** distort (problem, or abs.) by stating it in too simple terms; ~**slee′p,** miss intended time of rising by sleeping too long; ~**spe′nd,** spend too much (~*spend* one*self,* reduce one's means thus); ~**spill,** what is spilt over or overflows, (fig.) surplus population leaving one area for another; ~**sprea′d,** become diffused over, cover surface of, (in *pass.*) be covered with; ~**sta′ff,** provide too many people as staff for; ~**sta′te,** state too strongly, exaggerate, (so ~*sta′tement* n.); ~**stay,** stay longer than (time, one's welcome, etc.); ~**steer** v.i., & n., (of motor vehicle) (have) tendency to turn more sharply than was intended; ~**ste′p,** pass beyond (boundary, *the mark,* lit. or fig.); ~**sto′ck** v.t.; ~**strai′n** v.t., & n.; ~**stre′tch** v.t.; ~**stru′ng,** (of person, his nerves, etc.) (too) highly strung or intensely strained, (ō′-; of piano) with strings in sets crossing each other obliquely; ~**stu′ff,** stuff more than is necessary, (in *p.p.* of furniture) made soft and comfortable by thick upholstery; ~**-subscri′be,** (usu. in *p.p.*) subscribe more than amount of (shares offered for sale etc.); ~**ta′ke,** come abreast with (person or thing moving in same direction) by faster movement, catch up with and pass (such person or thing, or abs.) by faster movement (lit. & fig.), (of storm, misfortune, etc.) come suddenly or unexpectedly upon (person etc.); ~**ta′sk,** give or be too heavy a task to or for; ~**ta′x,** make excessive demands on (person for tax, or as regards his strength etc.); ~**throw′,** (v.t.) upset, knock down, cast out from power, vanquish, subvert, put an end to (institution etc.), (ō′-; n.) defeat, subversion, (Crick.) fielder's return throw of ball, not stopped near wicket, thus yielding further run(s); ~**time** n. & adv., (time during which person works) in addition to regular hours, payment for this; ~**tir′e** v.t.; ~**tone,** (Mus.) harmonic given by string, pipe, etc., (fig.) (subtle or elusive) secondary quality or implication; ~**to′p,** be or become higher than, surpass; ~**trick,** (Bridge) trick taken in excess of one's contract; ~**tru′mp,** play higher trump (than); ~**tur′n,** upset, (cause to) fall down or over, overthrow, subvert; ~*u′se* v.t., & n.; ~**va′lue** v.t.; ~**view,** general survey; ~**wee′ning,** arrogant, presumptuous; ~**weight,** (n.) preponderance, excessive weight, (~ā′t; a.) beyond allowed or suitable weight (*luggage, person, is overweight*), (~ā′t; v.t.) load unduly (*with*); ~**whe′lm,** bury or drown beneath superincumbent mass, submerge utterly, crush, bring to sudden ruin, overpower with emotion or *with* excess of business etc.,

(~whelming, irresistible by force of numbers, influence, amount, etc.); ~wi'nd, wind (watch etc.) beyond proper stopping-point; ~wor'k, (v.t. & i.) (cause to) work too hard, weary or exhaust with too much work, (n.) excessive work; ~wrou'ght, over-excited, suffering reaction from over-excitement; ~zea'lous a.

ō'vert (or -ẽr't) a. Openly done, unconcealed. [F, p.p. of ovrir open]

ō'verture n. Opening of negotiations, formal proposal or offer (esp. make overtures to); orchestral piece opening opera etc. or in this style.

ō'vi- in comb. Egg, ovum; ~duct, canal through which ova pass from ovary esp. in oviparous animals; ~form, egg-shaped; ~parous (-ĭ'-), producing young from eggs expelled from body before being hatched (cf. VIVIPAROUS). [OVUM]

ō'vine a. Of or like sheep. [L (ovis sheep)]

ō'void a. (Of solid) egg-shaped. [OVUM]

ŏ'vŭl|āte v.i. Discharge ovum or ova from ovary; produce ova; ~ā'tion n.; ~ātorȳ a.; ō'vŭle n., germ-cell in female plant, unfertilized ovum. [OVUM]

ō'vum n. (pl. ova). Germ-cell in female animal from which by fertilization with male sperm the young is developed; egg esp. of mammal, fish, or insect. [L, = egg]

ow int. expr. sudden pain. [natural excl.]

owe (ō) v.t. Be under obligation to (re)pay or render (money, person money, gratitude, etc.; money etc. to person; ~ person a grudge, cherish resentment against him; ~ it to oneself to do, need to do in order not to be unfair to oneself); (abs.) be in debt (for thing; I owe for my tea); be indebted for to person or thing (we owe to Newton the principle of gravitation; he owes his success to luck; I owe him much); ow'ing (ō'ĭ-) pred. a. yet to be paid, owed, due, (paid all that was owing); owing to, attributable to, caused by, (all this was owing to bad luck), (as prep.) on account of (owing to the weather, the match has been postponed). [E]

owl n. Nocturnal bird of prey with large head and eyes and hooked beak, supposed to look solemn and wise, (BARN, HORNED or long-eared, SCREECH-, SNOWY, tawny, owl); wise-looking

dullard; ~'ĕt n., small or young owl; ~'ish a., like an owl esp. dazzled by daylight, solemn and dull. [E]

own (ōn). 1. a. (After possessive) in full ownership, not another's, (saw it with my own eyes; has a charm all its own; may I have it for my (very) own?; be one's own MAN; call thing one's ~, possess it; my ~ (sweet etc.), expr. affection, esp. in voc.); (also used to emphasize not ownership, but subject's identity: cooks his own meals; every man his own lawyer); (abs.) private property etc. (come into one's ~, get possession of one's rightful property, be properly esteemed etc.; GET one's own back; hold one's ~, maintain position, not be beaten; of one's ~, belonging to one (exclusively): he has nothing of his own, I'll give you one of my own; on one's ~, independent(ly), on one's own account or responsibility or resources, alone, unrivalled; in a CLASS of or on its, one's, own); (without preceding possessive) ~ brother, sister, with both parents the same; ~ cousin, first cousin. 2. v.t. & i. Have as property, possess; (in p.p., in comb.) held as property by (State-owned); acknowledge paternity, authorship, or possession, of (child, pamphlet, hat, that nobody will own); admit as existent, valid, true, etc., (owns his deficiencies, himself indebted, that he does not know); confess to (owns to a sense of shame, to having done; ~ up, colloq., confess frankly); ~'er n., possessor (||~er-driver, -occupier, etc., one who both owns and drives vehicle, occupies house, etc.), (Naut. sl.) ship's captain; ~'ership n., possessing, identity of owner. [E]

ŏx n. (pl. o'xen). Any bovine animal, individual of kinds of large usu. horned cloven-footed ruminant used when domesticated for draught, milk, and meat; castrated male of domestic species of this; ox-eye, (esp.) plant with flower like eye of ox (ox-eye daisy, white ox-eye, having white petals with yellow centre; yellow ox-eye, corn marigold); o'x-herd, cowherd; o'xhide, (leather from) hide of ox; o'xlip, primula, (pop.) hybrid of primrose and cowslip; o'xtail, tail of ox, much used for soup-making; ox-tongue, tongue of ox, esp. for cooking. [E]

ŏxă'lic a. ~ acid, highly poisonous and sour acid orig. found in wood sorrel and other plants. [F f. L f. Gk *oxalis* wood sorrel]

‖**O'xbridge** (ŏ'-) *n.* (Characteristics of) *Oxford* and *Cambridge* universities, esp. in contrast to newer universities. [portmanteau wd]

**Oxf.** *abbr.* Oxford.

**O'xfam** (ŏ'-) *abbr.* Oxford Committee for Famine Relief.

**O'xford** (ŏ'-) *n.* ~ **accent,** pronunciation of English supposed affected and characteristic of members of Oxford University; ~ **blue** (dark, occas. with purple tinge); ~ **frame** (with sides which cross each other at corners and project); ~ **Movement,** Tractarianism; ~ **shoe,** *\*Oxford,** low shoe lacing over instep. [place]

**o'xide** *n.* Binary compound of oxygen; **o'xidize** *v.t. & i.,* cause to combine with oxygen, cover (metal) with oxide, make or become rusty, take up or combine with oxygen, (**oxidized silver,** incorrect name for silver with dark coating of silver sulphide); **oxid(iz)ā'tion** *n.* [F (OXYGEN)]

**O'xon.** (ŏ'-) *abbr.* Oxfordshire; of Oxford Univ. [L *Oxoniensis* (foll.)]

**Oxō'nian** (ŏ-) *a. & n.* (Member) of Oxford Univ.; (citizen) of Oxford. [*Oxonia* Latinized name of *Ox(en)-ford*]

**o'xy-** in *comb.* Oxygen; ~**-ace'tylene,** consisting of, involving use of, mixture of oxygen and acetylene (~**-acetylene blowpipe,** for producing intensely hot flame for welding etc.);

so ~**-hy'drogen** *blowpipe, flame, light,* etc. [OXY(GEN)]

**o'xygen** *n.* Colourless odourless tasteless gas essential to animal and vegetable life (~ **mask,** placed over nose and mouth to supply oxygen for breathing; ~ **tent,** enclosure to allow patient to breathe air with increased oxygen content); ~**āte,** ~**īze,** (*or* ŏksī'-) *vbs.t.,* supply or treat or mix with oxygen, oxidize. [F *oxygène* f. Gk *oxus* sharp, *gen-* root of *gignomai* become (because thought to be present in all acids)]

**oxymōr'on** *n.* Figure of speech with pointed conjunction of apparent contradictions (e.g. *cheerful pessimist*). [Gk, = pointedly foolish (*oxus* sharp, *mōros* dull)]

**ōyĕ'z, ōyĕ's,** *int.* uttered, usu. thrice, by public crier or court officer to call for attention. [AF imper. pl. of *oïr* hear f. L *audio*]

**oy'ster** *n.* Edible bivalve mollusc usu. eaten alive; something regarded as containing all that one desires (*the world is her oyster*); white colour with grey tinge; (sl.) taciturn person; ~**-bank, -bed, -farm, -park,** part of sea-bottom where oysters breed or are bred; ~**-catcher,** wading sea-bird. [F *oistre* f. L *ostrea* f. Gk]

**oz.** *abbr.* ounce(s). [It. (*onza* ounce)]

**ō'zōne** (*or* -ō'n) *n.* Form of oxygen with three atoms in molecule, having pungent refreshing odour; (pop.) invigorating air at seaside etc.; (fig.) exhilarating influence. [G f. Gk *ozō* to smell]

# P

**P, p,** (pē) *n.* (*pl.* **Ps, P's**). Sixteenth letter; MIND one's *P's and Q's.*

**P** *abbr.* (Chess) pawn.

**p.** *abbr.* page; (decimal) pence or penny; PIANO[1].

**pa** (pah) *n.* (vulg.) Father. [abbr. PAPA]

**P.A.** *abbr.* personal assistant; Press Association; public address.

**Pa.** *abbr.* Pennsylvania.

**p.a.** *abbr.* per annum.

**pă'bulum** *n.* Food (esp. fig.; *mental pabulum*). [L]

**pace**[1]. **1.** *n.* Single step in walking or running; space traversed in this as vague measure of distance (about 30 in.); mode of walking or running; any of various gaits of (esp. trained) horse etc.; speed in walking or running, rate of progression. **2.** *v.t. & i.* Walk with slow or regular pace; traverse by pacing; measure (distance *out*) thus; (of horse) amble; set pace for (rider, runner, etc.). **3.** ~'**maker,** rider, runner, etc., who sets pace for another in race etc., natural or electrical device for stimulating heart muscle; **go the ~**, go at great speed, (fig.) indulge in dissipation; **keep ~**, advance at equal rate (*with*); **put person through his ~s**, test his qualities in action etc.; SET[1] *the pace*. [F *pas* f. L *passus*]

**pace**[2] (pā′sĭ, pah′chā) *prep.* (In announcing contrary opinion) with all due deference to (person named). [L, abl. of *pax* peace]

**pacha.** See PASHA.

**pǎ′chў|derm** (-k-) *n.* Thick-skinned mammal, esp. elephant or rhinoceros; **~děr′matous** *a.* [F f. Gk (*pakhus* thick, *derma* skin)]

**pǎ′cif|ў** *v.t.* Appease (person, anger, etc.); bring (country etc.) to state of peace; **paci′fĭc**, (*a.*) tending to or characterized by peace, of peaceful disposition, tranquil, (*a.* & *n.*; P-) (of or adjoining) ocean between America eastward and Asia westward; **~ĭcā′tion** *n.*; **paci′fĭca-torў** *a.*; **~ism** *n.*, doctrine that abolition of war is desirable and possible; **~ĭst** *n.* [F or L (*pax pacis* peace)]

**pǎck**[1]. **1.** *n.* Bundle of things wrapped up or tied together for carrying, esp. on shoulder or back; (usu. derog.) lot or set (*a pack of fools, lies, nonsense*); number of hounds kept together for hunting, or of animals (esp. wolves) naturally associating; organized group of Cubs or Brownies; (Rugby Footb.) team's forwards; ||set of playing-cards; area of large crowded pieces of floating ice in sea; method of packing, or set of things packed, for selling (*pack of cigarettes*); application of medicinal or cosmetic substance to skin etc. (*face--pack*), substance so applied. **2.** *v.t. & i.* Put (things) together in bundle, box, bag, etc., for transport or storing (often **~ up**, esp. abs.); put closely together, crowd; cover (thing) with thing pressed tightly round; (sl.) carry (gun etc.), be capable of delivering (a punch) with skill or force; fill (bag, suitcase, etc.) with clothes etc. (**~ one's bags**, prepare to depart); depart with one's belongings (**send ~ing**, dismiss summarily); cram (space etc. *with*); fill (theatre etc.) with spectators; (of animals) form pack. **3.** **~-drill**, military punishment of walking up and down in full marching equipment (*no names no ~-drill*, discretion will prevent

punishment); **~ed meal** etc. (prepared beforehand and put in container for carrying to place of eating); **~ed out**, (colloq.) crowded; **~-horse** (for carrying packs); **~ in**, (sl.) end it, finish; **~ it up**, (sl.) desist; **~′man**, (arch.) pedlar; **~ off**, send or drive (person) away, esp. summarily; **~-saddle** (adapted for supporting packs); **~′thread**, stout thread for sewing or tying up packs; **~ up**, (sl.) retire from contest, activity, etc., (of machine etc.) cease to function, break down. **4.** **~′age**, (*n.*) bundle of things packed, parcel, box etc. in which things are packed; (**~age deal**, transaction agreed to as a whole, the less favourable items as well as the more favourable; **~age holiday, tour**, etc., with fixed route etc. at fixed inclusive price), (*v.t.*) make up into or enclose in a package; **~′aging** (-kĭj-), (making of) wrapper(s) or container(s) for goods; **~′ĕt** *n.*, small package, (colloq.) large sum of money won or lost; **~et(-boat)**, mail-boat; **~′ing** *n.*, (esp.) material closing joint or assisting in lubrication of axle, substance used to fill gaps in order to protect fragile objects; **~ing-case**, (usu. wooden) case for packing goods in. [LDu.]

**pǎck**[2] *v.t.* Select (jury etc.) so as to secure biased decision in one's favour. [PACT]

**pǎct** *n.* Agreement, treaty. [F f. L *pactum*]

**pǎd**[1]. **1.** *n.* Soft saddle; piece of soft stuff used to diminish jarring, raise surface, fill out hollows, absorb fluid, etc.; guard for leg and ankle in cricket etc. (SHIN-*pad*); number of sheets of blotting-, writing-, or drawing-paper fastened together at one edge; fleshy cushion forming sole of foot in some quadrupeds; flat surface for helicopter take-off or rocket launching; (sl.) bed, lodging, house; *water-lily leaf. **2.** *v.t.* (**-dd-**). Furnish with pad, stuff; fill out or *out* (book etc.) with superfluous matter; **~ded cell**, room with padded walls in mental hospital. [prob. LDu.]

**pǎd**[2] *v.t. & i.* (**-dd-**). Tramp along (road etc.) on foot; travel on foot; walk with soft dull steady sound of steps; ||**~ it**, ||**~ the hoof**, (sl.) go on foot. [LG *pad* PATH]

**pǎ′ddle**[1]. **1.** *n.* Small spadelike

implement with long handle; short broad-bladed oar used without rowlock (**double ~**, with blade at each end); one of the boards fitted round circumference of paddle-wheel or mill-wheel; paddle-shaped instrument; fin, flipper; action or spell of paddling; **~-wheel**, wheel for propelling ship (**~-boat** etc.), with boards round circumference so as to press backward against water. **2.** *v.i.* & *t.* Move on water, propel canoe, by means of paddles (**~ one's own canoe**, fig. be independent); row gently. [orig. unkn.]

**pă'ddle**[2]. **1.** *v.i.* Dabble with the feet or wade about in shallow water. **2.** *n.* Action or spell of paddling. [prob. LDu.]

**pă'ddock** *n.* Small field, esp. near stable or as part of stud farm; turf enclosure adjoining racecourse, where horses or cars are assembled before race. [*parrock*, var. PARK]

**Pă'ddy**[1] *n.* (Nickname for) Irishman; ||(*p~*); colloq.) rage, fit of temper. [Ir. *Padraig* Patrick]

**pă'ddy**[2] *n.* Rice before threshing or in the husk; **~(-field)**, field where rice is grown. [Malay]

**pă'dlŏck. 1.** *n.* Detachable lock hanging by pivoted hook on object fastened. **2.** *v.t.* Secure with padlock. [orig. unkn.]

**pa'dre** (pah'-; *or* -ā) *n.* (colloq.) Chaplain in army etc. [It., Sp., Port., = father, priest]

**pae'an** *n.* Song of praise or triumph. [L f. Gk]

**pae'derăst.** See PEDERAST.

**paediǎ'tr|ĭc, \*pēd-,** *a.* Relating to **~ĭcs** *n.pl.*, branch of medical science dealing with children and their diseases; **~ĭ'cian** (-shan), **~ĭst,** *ns.* [PAEDO-, Gk *iatros* physician]

**pae'dŏ-, \*pē'dŏ-,** *in comb.* Child; **~phi'lia,** sexual love directed towards children. [Gk *pais* paid- child]

**paĕ'lla** (pah-) *n.* Spanish dish of rice, chicken, seafood etc., cooked and served in large shallow pan. [Catalan, f. F f. L PATELLA]

**pā'gan** *n.* & *a.* Heathen; unenlightened or irreligious (person); **~ĭsm** *n.*; **~ĭze** *v.t.* [L *paganus* (*pagus* country district)]

**pāge**[1]. **1.** *n.* Boy or man, usu. in livery, employed to attend to door, go on errands, etc.; boy employed as personal attendant of person of rank, bride, etc.; **~-boy,** page, woman's hair-style with hair long and rolled under at ends. **2.** *v.t.* Summon (as) by page. [F]

**pāge**[2]. **1.** *n.* (One side of) leaf of book etc.; what is printed etc. on this; (fig.) episode that might fill page in written history etc. **2.** *v.t.* Put numbers on pages of (book etc.). [F, f. L *pagina*]

**pă'geant** (-jant) *n.* Brilliant spectacle, esp. procession, arranged for effect; spectacular procession, or play performed in the open, illustrating historical events; tableau etc. on fixed stage or moving vehicle; **~rỹ** *n.*, what serves to make a pageant, elements of display. [orig. unkn.]

**pă'gin|āte** *v.t.*, page; **~ā'tion** *n.* [L (PAGE[2])]

**pagō'da** *n.* Sacred building, esp. tower, usu. pyramidal, in the East; ornamental imitation of this. [Port.]

**pah** *int.* expr. disgust or contempt. [natural utterance]

**paid.** See PAY.

**pail** *n.* Vessel, usu. round, of wood, metal, or plastic for carrying liquids etc.; amount contained in this; **~ful** (-ŏŏl) *n.* [E]

**pain. 1.** *n.* Suffering or distress of body or mind (**in ~,** undergoing this); punishment (*pains and penalties*; **on, under, ~ of,** with *death* etc. as penalty) ; (in *pl.*) throes of childbirth, trouble taken (*take pains*; *be at pains to do*); *get a thrashing etc. for one's pains*); *pain in the* NECK; **~-killer,** medicine for alleviating pain; **~'s-taking** (-z-), careful, industrious. **2.** *v.t.* Inflict pain on; (in *p.p.*) expressing pain (*pained look*). **3.** **~'ful** *a.* (-lly), causing or (esp. of part of body) suffering pain, grievous, vexatious, causing trouble or difficulty, laborious; **~'lèss** *a.*, not suffering or causing pain. [F *peine* f. L *poena* penalty]

**paint. 1.** *n.* Colouring matter, esp. when suspended in liquid in order to impart colour to a surface; **~'box** (containing dry paints before use); **~'brush,** house-painter's or artist's brush. **2.** *v.t.* Portray (object, or abs.) in colours; make (picture) thus; cover surface of (object) with paint; apply paint of specified colour to (*paint the door green*); (fig.) represent (incident etc.) in words usually as by painting (**not so black as he is ~ed,** better than he is asserted to be); apply liquid or cosmetic to (face etc., or abs.); apply (liquid to skin etc.; *paint iodine on the cut*); ~'ed **lady**, orange-red butterfly with black and white spots; ~ **out**, efface with paint; *paint* (= *gild*) *the* LILY; ~ **the town red**, (sl.) cause commotion by riotous spree. **3.** ~'**er**¹ *n.*, one who paints pictures, workman who colours woodwork etc. with paint; ~'**ing** *n.*, (esp.) art of representing by colours on a surface, product of this. [F f. L *pingo pict-*]

**pai'nter**² *n.* Rope attached to bow of boat for making it fast; *cut the* ~, fig. effect a separation. [orig. unkn.]

**pair. 1.** *n.* Set of two persons or things; of things that usu. exist or are used in couples, as gloves, shoes, sculls, eyes); two playing--cards of the same denomination; article consisting of two corresponding parts not used separately (*pair of scissors, trousers*); engaged or married couple; mated couple of animals; ~ (**of horses**), two horses harnessed side by side; (Parl. etc.) two voters on opposite sides absenting themselves from division by mutual arrangement, person willing to act thus (*cannot find a pair*); the other member of a pair (*where is the pair to this sock?*); flight of stairs or steps. **2.** *v.t. & i.* Arrange (persons, things), be arranged, in couples; unite in love or marriage; (of animals) mate; unite (*with* one of opposite sex); ~ **off**, arrange or go off in pairs, (Parl. etc.) make a pair, (colloq.) marry (*with*). [F f. L *paria* (PAR¹)]

**Pai'sley** (-z-) *a.* (Of garment) made of soft wool with bright coloured design. [place]

**pajamas.** See PYJAMAS.

‖**Pǎk('ǐ)** *ns.* (sl.) Pakistani. [abbr.]

**Pakista'ni** (pah-; -ah'-) *a. & n.* (Native) of Pakistan. [Hind.]

**pǎl.** (sl.) **1.** *n.* Comrade, mate. **2.** *v.i.* (-ll-). ~ (**up**), associate (*with*) [Romany]

**pǎ'lace** *n.* Official residence of sovereign, president, archbishop, or bishop; stately mansion, spacious building; ~ **revolution**, overthrow of sovereign etc. without civil war. [F f. L *palatium*]

**pǎ'ladin** *n.* Any of Twelve Peers of Charlemagne's court; knight errant, champion. [F f. It. (PALATINE¹)]

**pǎ'laeo-, *-lēo-**, *in comb.* Ancient, of ancient times. [Gk *palaios*]

**palae|-, *pǎlē|ŏ'graphy,** *n.* Study of ancient writing and inscriptions; **~ogră'phic** *a.*; **~oli'thic** *a.*, of earlier Stone Age [Gk *lithos* stone]; **~ontŏ'logy** *n.*, study of life in geological past; **P~ozŏ'ic** *a. & n.*, (Geol.) (of) geological era containing oldest forms of highly organized life [Gk *zōion* animal].

**pǎ'lais** (-lā) *n.* ~ (**de danse**) (-dedah'ns), public hall for dancing. [F, = (dancing) hall]

**palanquin', -keen',** (-n-kēn) *n.* Eastern covered litter for one. [Port.]

**pǎ'lat|e** *n.* Structure closing upper part of mouth cavity in vertebrates; sense of taste; mental taste, liking; **~able** *a.* (-bly), pleasant to taste, (fig.) agreeable to the mind; **~al,** (*a.*; -lly) of the palate, (Phon., of sound) made by placing tongue against palate, (*n.*) palatal sound or letter. [L *palatum*]

**palā'tial** (-shal) *a.* (**~ly**). Like a palace; splendid. [L (as PALACE)]

**Pǎ'latine¹** *a.* (Count) ~, count having within his territory jurisdiction such as elsewhere belongs only to sovereign; **County** ~, his territory; **palā'tinate** *n.*, territory under Count Palatine. [F f. L (PALACE)]

**pǎ'latine²** *a.* Of the palate. [F (PALATE)]

**pala'ver** (-lah'-). **1.** *n.* Conference, (prolonged) discussion, esp. (Hist.) between African or other natives and traders etc.; profuse or idle talk, cajolery; (sl.) affair, business. **2.** *v.i. & t.* Talk profusely; flatter, wheedle. [Port. *palavra* f. L (PARABLE)]

**pāle¹** *n.* Pointed piece of wood for fence etc., stake; boundary (esp. fig., **beyond the** ~, outside bounds of civilized behaviour); (Her.) vertical stripe in middle of shield. [F *pal* f. L *palus*]

**pāle².** **1.** *a.* (Of person or complexion) of whitish or ashen appearance; (of colour) faint; faintly coloured; of faint lustre, dim; ~--**face**, supposed N. Amer. Ind. name for white man. **2.** *v.t. & i.* Grow or make pale; (fig.) become feeble in comparison (*before, beside*). [F f. L *pallidus*]

**pǎ'lēo-.** See PALAEO-.

**pǎ'lětte** *n.* Artist's thin wooden slab carried in hand and used for holding and mixing colours when painting; **~-knife**, thin steel blade with handle for mixing colours or applying them or for use in kitchen etc. [F dim. f. L *pala* spade]

**pǎ'lfrey** (or paw'-) *n.* (arch., poet.) Horse for ordinary riding, esp. for ladies. [F f. L (Gk *para* beside, L *veredus* horse)]

**pǎ'lǐ|mpsěst** *n.* Writing-material or manuscript on which original writing has been effaced to make room for other writing; monumental brass turned and re-engraved on reverse side; ~**ndrōme** *n. & a.*, (word, verse, etc.) that reads the same backwards as forwards (e.g. *rotator*); ~**ndrŏ'mǐc** *a.* (-ically). [Gk (*palin* again, *psēstos* rubbed, *drom-* run)]

**pā'lǐng** *n.* (in *sing.* or *pl.*) (Fence of) pale(s). [PALE¹]

**pǎlǐsǎ'de 1.** *n.* Fence of pales or of iron railings; strong pointed wooden stake. **2.** *v.t.* Enclose or furnish with palisade. [F (PALE¹)]

**pall¹** (pawl) *n.* Cloth spread over coffin, hearse, or tomb; kind of ecclesiastical vestment; (fig.) dark covering (*pall of smoke*); ~**'bearer**, person helping to carry coffin at funeral. [E f. L *pallium* cloak]

**pall²** (pawl) *v.i. & t.* Become uninteresting; satiate, cloy; ~ **on**, cease to interest or attract (person, mind, taste). [APPAL]

**Pallǎ'dǐan** *a.* (Archit.) In 16th-c. neoclassical style of *Palladio*. [person]

**pǎ'llĕt¹** *n.* Portable platform for transporting and storing loads. [F (PALETTE)]

**pǎ'll|ĕt²** *n.* Straw bed; mattress; ~**iǎsse** (-ly-) *n.*, straw mattress. [AF f. L *palea* straw]

**pǎ'llǐ|āte** *v.t.* Alleviate (disease) without curing; excuse, extenuate; ~**ā'tion**, ~**ātor**, *ns.*; ~**ative** *a. & n.*, (thing) that serves to palliate. [L *pallio* to cloak (PALL¹)]

**pǎ'll|ǐd** *a.* Pale, esp. from sickness; ~**or** *n.*, pallidness. [L (PALE²)]

**pǎ'll|ў** *a.* (colloq.; ~**iness**). Friendly. [PAL]

**palm** (pahm) **1.** *n.* Part of hand between wrist and fingers, esp. its inner surface, part of glove that covers this, (GREASE person's *palm*; **in the** ~ or HOLLOW² **of** one's **hand**); kind of chiefly tropical tree with upright unbranched stem and head of large fan-shaped leaves, leaf of this as symbol of victory; supreme excellence, prize for this (*bear, yield, the palm*); branch of various trees

substituted for palm in northern countries, esp. for Palm Sunday. **2.** *v.t.* Conceal (cards, dice, etc.) in the hand; ~ **off**, impose or thrust fraudulently (thing *on* person). **3.** ~**-oil**, oil from various palms, bribe-money; **P~ Sunday**, Sunday before Easter, on which Christ's entry into Jerusalem is celebrated by processions in which palm-branches are carried. **4.** **pǎ'lmar** *a.*, of or in palm of hand; **pǎ'lmāte** *a.*, shaped like palm of hand, having lobes etc. like spread fingers; ~**'er** *n.*, (Hist.) pilgrim returning from Holy Land with palm-leaf; **pǎlmě'ttō** *n.* (*pl.* ~s), (esp. small) palm-tree; ~**'ǐst** *n.*, practiser of ~**'ǐstrў** *n.*, divination from lines etc. in palm of hand; ~**'ў** *a.* (-ily), of, like, abounding in, palms, triumphant, flourishing (*palmy days*). [(of hand) F, (tree) E, f. L *palma*]

**pǎlomi'nō** (-mē'-) *n.* (*pl.* ~s). Golden or cream-coloured horse with light-coloured mane and tail. [Sp. (L *palumba* dove)]

**pǎ'lp|able** *a.* (-bly). That can be touched or felt; readily perceived by senses or mind; ~**abi'lǐtў** *n.*; ~**ā'te** *v.t.*, (Med.) examine by touch; ~**ā'tion** *n.* [L *palpo* feel]

**pǎ'lpǐt|āte** *v.i.* Pulsate, throb; tremble (*with* fear, pleasure, etc.); ~**ā'tion** *n.*, (esp.) increased activity of heart due to exertion, agitation, or disease. [L *palpito* frequent. (prec.)]

**pa'lsў** (paw'lzǐ, pǒ'-). **1.** *n.* Paralysis, esp. with involuntary tremors; (fig.) cause or condition of utter helplessness. **2.** *v.t.* Affect with palsy, paralyse (usu. fig.). [F (PARALYSIS)]

**pa'lter** (paw'-, pǒ'-) *v.i.* Shuffle, equivocate, (*with* person); haggle (*with* person *about* thing); trifle (*with* subject). [orig. unkn.]

**pa'ltrў** (paw'-, pǒ'-) *a.* (-ily, -iness). Worthless, contemptible, trifling. [*palt* rubbish]

**pǎ'mpas** (or -z) *n.pl.* Large treeless plains in S. America; ~**-grass**, large ornamental grass orig. from S. America. [Sp. f. Quechua]

**pǎ'mper** *v.t.* Over-indulge (person, taste, etc.); spoil (person) with luxury. [obs. *pamp* cram]

**pǎ'mphlet** *n.* Small usu. unbound treatise, esp. in prose on subject of current interest; ~**eer'**, (*n.*) writer of pamphlets, (*v.i.*) write pamphlets. [*Pamphilus*, name of medieval poem]

**păn¹. 1.** *n*. Metal or earthenware or plastic vessel, usu. shallow, for domestic purposes; panlike vessel in which substances are heated etc.; bowl of scales or of water-closet; part of lock that held priming in old guns (FLASH *in the pan*); hollow in ground (SALT-*pan*); ~'**ful** (-ŏŏl) *n.* **2.** *v.t.* & *i.* (**-nn-**). Criticize severely (colloq.); ~ **out**, (of gravel) yield gold, (fig., of action etc.) succeed (*well* etc.). [E]

**păn². 1.** *v.t.* & *i.* (**-nn-**). Swing (camera) horizontally to give panoramic effect or follow moving object; (of camera) be moved thus. **2.** *n*. Panning movement. [PANORAMA]

**pan-** *in comb.* All, relating to whole of continent, racial group, religion, etc., (*pan-American*). [Gk (*pan* neut. of *pas pantos* all)]

**pănacē'a** *n*. Universal remedy. [L f. Gk (PAN-, *-akēs* remedy)]

**pană'che** (-sh; *or* -ah'sh) *n*. Display, swagger, verve. [F, = plume]

**Pănam|a'** (-ah') *n*. ~**a** (hat), hat of strawlike material made from leaves of a pine-tree; ~**ā'nïan** *a.* & *n.*, (native) of Panama. [place]

**pă'ncāke** (-n-k-) *n*. Thin flat batter-cake fried in pan (**flat as a ~**, completely flat); flat cake (e.g. of make-up); P~ **Day**, Shrove Tuesday (on which pancakes are traditionally eaten); ~ **landing** (of aircraft descending vertically in level position). [PAN¹, CAKE]

**pănchromă'tĭc** (-n-kr-) *a*. (Photog., of film etc.) sensitive to all visible spectrum colours. [PAN-]

**pă'ncrē|as** *n*. Gland near stomach supplying digestive fluid and insulin; ~ă'tĭc *a*. [L f. Gk (*kreas* flesh)]

**pă'nda** *n*. Indian racoon-like animal; (**giant**) ~, large rare bear-like black-and-white mammal of China; ||~ **car**, police car (orig. with broad white stripe). [Nepali]

**pănde'mĭc** *a*. & *n*. (Disease) prevalent over whole country or world. [Gk (*dēmos* people)]

**păndēmō'nïum** *n*. Abode of all demons; (place of) uproar; utter confusion. [L (DEMON)]

**pă'nder. 1.** *n*. Go-between in illicit amours, procurer; one who ministers to evil designs. **2.** *v.i.* Minister (*to* base passion or evil designs). [character in Boccaccio and Chaucer]

**Păndŏ'ra** *n*. ~**'s box**, (Gk Myth.) box in which Hope alone remained when by its rash opening all ills were

let loose upon mankind. [person; Gk, = all-gifted]

||**p. & p.** *abbr.* postage and packing.

**pāne** *n*. Single piece of glass in (compartment of) window. [F *pan* f. L *pannus* a cloth]

**pănĕgў'r|ĭc** *n*. & *a*. Laudatory (discourse); ~**ĭcal** *a.*; ~**ĭst** *n.*, speaker or writer of panegyric; **pă'nĕgўrize** *v.t.*, speak or write in praise of. [F f. L f. Gk (*agora* assembly)]

**pă'nel. 1.** *n*. Distinct compartment of surface, esp. of wainscot, door, etc., often below or above general level; usu. vertical piece of material esp. of different kind or colour in woman's dress etc.; (list of) jury; team in broadcast or public quiz programme etc., body of experts assembled for discussion or consultation, (~ **game**, quiz etc. played by panel; ~**lĭst**, *~*ĭst, *n.*, member of panel). **2.** *v.t.* (||**-ll-**). Fit (wall, door, etc.), ornament (dress etc.), with panel(s); ~**lĭng**, *~*ĭng, *n.*, panelled work. [F f. L dim. of *pannus* (PANE)]

**păng** *n*. Shooting pain; sudden sharp mental pain. [obs. *pronge*]

**păngō'lĭn** (-ngg-) *n*. Scaly ant-eater. [Malay]

**pă'nĭc** *a., n.,* & *v.* **1.** *a.* (Of terror) unreasoning, excessive; excessively hasty through fear; for use in emergency (**panic stations**). **2.** *n.* Infectious fright, sudden alarm (e.g., in commerce) leading to hasty measures; ~**-stricken**, **-struck**, affected with panic; ~**kў** *a.* **3.** *v.t.* & *i.* (**-ck-**). Affect or be affected with panic. [F f. L f. Gk (*Pan*, rural god)]

**pă'nĭcle** *n*. (Bot.) Loose irregular compound inflorescence as in oats. [L *paniculum* dim. of *panus* thread]

**pănjă'ndrum** *n*. Mock title of exalted personage. [invented wd]

**pă'nne** *n*. ~ (**velvet**), velvet-like fabric of silk or rayon. [F]

**pă'nnier** (-nyer) *n*. Basket, esp. carried (usu. in pairs) by beast of burden or on bicycle, motor cycle, or shoulders; bag similarly carried. [F f. L (*panis* bread)]

**pă'nnĭkĭn** *n*. Small metal drinking-vessel. [PAN¹, -KIN]

**pă'noplў** *n*. Complete suit of armour; (fig.) complete or splendid array. [F or L f. Gk (*hopla* arms)]

**pănor|a'ma** (-rah'-) *n*. Picture or photograph containing wide view; continuous passing scene; unbroken view of surrounding region (lit. or fig.); **~ā'mĭc** *a.* (-ically). [Gk *horama* view]

**pă'n-pīpe(s)** *n.* Musical instrument made of series of reeds fixed together with mouthpieces in line. [*Pan*, Gk rural god]

**pănsў** (-zĭ) *n.* Garden plant with flowers of various rich colours; ~ (**boy**), (colloq.) effeminate man, male homosexual. [F *pensée* thought, pansy]

**pănt. 1.** *v.i.* & *t.* Gasp for breath; utter gaspingly (*out*); (fig.) yearn (*for, after*, thing; *to do*); (of heart etc.) throb violently. **2.** *n.* Gasp; throb. [F, ult. f. Gk (FANTASY)]

**pănte'chnicon** (-kn-) *n.* ~ (**van**), large van for removing furniture. [TECHNIC; orig. as name of bazaar]

**pă'nthe̊ism** *n.* Doctrine that God is everything and everything God; **~ist** *n.*, **~ĭ'stĭc(al)** *adjs.* (-ically). [Gk *theos* god]

**pă'nthĕon** (*or* -ē'on) *n.* Temple dedicated to all the gods; deities of a people collectively; building in which illustrious dead are buried or have memorials. [L f. Gk (*theion* divine)]

**pă'nther** *n.* Leopard. [F f. L f. Gk]

**pă'ntĭ|es** (-ĭz) *n.pl.* (colloq.) Short-legged or legless knickers worn by women and girls; **~hōse** (-z) *n.*, tights. [dim. PANTS]

**pă'ntile** *n.* Curved roof-tile. [PAN[1]]

**pă'ntograph** (-ahf) *n.* Instrument with jointed rods for copying plan etc. on any scale; jointed framework conveying current to electric vehicle from overhead wires. [PAN-, -GRAPH]

**pă'nto|mĭme** *n.* ||Dramatic entertainment usu. produced about Christmas and based on fairy-tale; dumb show; **~mĭ'mĭc** *a.* (-ically). [F or L f. Gk (PAN-, MIME)]

**pă'ntrў** *n.* Room in which bread and other provisions or (*butler's, housemaid's, pantry*) plate, table-linen, etc., are kept. [AF f. L (*panis* bread)]

**pănts** *n.pl.* (colloq.) Trousers or slacks (**pant(s) suit**, trouser suit; *bore, scare, talk*, **the ~ off**, sl., to a state of extremity; **with one's ~ down**, sl., in state of embarrassing unpreparedness etc.); ||underpants; panties. [abbr. *pantaloons*, F f. It. character in comedy]

**păp[1]** *n.* (arch., dial.) Nipple of breast. [Scand.]

**păp[2]** *n.* Soft or semi-liquid food for infants or invalids; undemanding reading-matter. [LDu.]

**papa'** (-ah') *n.* (arch., esp. childish). Father. [F f. L f. Gk]

**pā'pa|cў** *n.* Pope's (tenure of) office; papal system; **~l a.** (**~lly**), of the Pope or his office. [L *papatia* (POPE)]

**papāverā'ceous** (-shŭs) *a.* Of the poppy family; **papā'verous** *a.*, like or allied to the poppy. [L (POPPY)]

**papaw', pawpaw',** *n.* (Oblong orange edible fruit of) palmlike tropical Amer. tree. [Sp. & Port. *papaya*]

**pā'per** *n., a.,* & *v.* **1.** *n.* Substance used for writing etc. on, wrapping up parcels, etc., made of compactly interlaced fibres of rags, straw, wood, etc., in thin sheet, (**commit to ~**, write down; **on ~**, in theory, judging from statistics, etc., in writing; **put pen to ~**, begin writing); negotiable documents, e.g. bills of exchange; =*paper money*; (in *pl.*) documents proving person's or ship's identity etc., documents belonging to or relating to a person or matter; set of questions to be answered at one session in examination, written answers to these; =NEWS*paper*; piece of paper, esp. as wrapper etc.; document printed on paper (||GREEN, WHITE, *Paper*); essay, dissertation, esp. one read to learned society; **~ў** *a.*, like paper in texture. **2.** *a.* Made of, flimsy like, paper; conducted by means of writings (*paper warfare*); written on paper but not really existing (*paper profits*). **3.** *v.t.* Decorate (wall etc.) with paper (**~ over the cracks**, seek to disguise flaws or dissension). **4. ~back** *n.* & *a.*, (book) bound in paper; **~boy, -girl**, (who delivers or sells newspapers); **~-chase**, cross-country run with trail of torn-up paper laid by runner(s) to set course for the rest; **~-clip**, piece of bent wire by which a few sheets of paper may be held together; **~-hanger**, one whose business is to cover walls with wallpaper; **~-knife**, blunt knife of ivory, wood, etc., for opening envelopes etc.; **~-mill** (in which paper is made); *paper* MONEY, TIGER, TISSUE; **~weight**, small heavy object to prevent movement of loose papers; **~work**, office administration and record-keeping. [AF f. L PAPYRUS]

**papier mâché** (pă̆pyā mă̆'shā, mah'-) *n.* Moulded paper pulp used for boxes, trays, etc. [F, = chewed paper]

**papilionā'ceous** (-yonā'shŭs) *a.* (Bot.) With butterfly-like corolla. [L (*papilio* butterfly)]

**papi'lla** *n.* (*pl.* ~e). Small nipple-like protuberance in or on the body; **pă̆'pillary** *a.*, papilla-shaped; **pă̆'pillāte, pă̆'pillōse,** *adjs.*, having papillae. [L]

**pă̆'pist** *n.* Advocate of papal supremacy; (usu. derog.) Roman Catholic; **papi'stical** *a.* (-lly); ~**rȳ** *n.*, papistical views or policy. [F or L (POPE)]

**papōō'se** *n.* N. Amer. Indian young child. [Algonquin]

**pă̆'prika** (*or* pappré'-) *n.* Ripe (red) PEPPER; red condiment made from it. [Magyar]

**papy̆r'|us** *n.* (*pl.* ~**i** *pr.* -i). Aquatic plant of sedge family; (MS. written on) ancient writing-material from stem of this; **pă̆py̆rŏ'logist, pă̆py̆rŏ'logy,** *ns.*, student, study, of ancient papyri. [L f. Gk]

**par** *n.* Equality, equal footing, esp. *on a par* (*with*), (~ *of exchange*, recognized value of one country's currency in terms of another's; of stocks, shares, etc.: **at** ~, at face value, **above** ~, at a premium, **below** ~, at a discount); average or normal amount, degree, health, or condition, (*above, below, up to, par*); (Golf) number of strokes a first-class player should normally require for hole or course. [L, = equal]

**pă̆'ra.** *abbr.* paragraph.

**pă̆ra-**[1] *pref.* Beside (*parabola, paramilitary*); beyond (*paradox, paranormal*). [Gk]

**pă̆ra-**[2] *in comb.* Protect, ward off, (*parachute, parasol*). [F f. It. f. L (*paro* defend)]

**pă̆'rable** *n.* Narrative of imagined events used to typify moral or spiritual relations (*the parables of Christ in the Gospels*); allegory. [F f. L *parabola* f. Gk, = comparison]

**pară'bola** *n.* Open plane curve formed by intersection of cone with plane parallel to its side; **pă̆rabŏ'lic** *a.* (-ically), of or expressed in parable (also -ical), of or like parabola. [L f. Gk *parabolē* (prec.)]

**pă̆'rachut|e** (-shōōt). **1.** *n.* Umbrella-shaped apparatus of silk etc. allowing person or heavy object to descend safely from a height, esp. from aircraft; (*attrib.*) (to be) dropped by parachute (*parachute troops*). **2.** *v.t.* & *i.* Convey, descend, by parachute. **3.** ~**ïst** *n.*, user of parachute, (in *pl.*) parachute troops. [F (PARA-[2], CHUTE)]

**Pă̆'raclēte** *n.* The Holy Spirit as advocate or counsellor. [F f. L f. Gk (PARA-[1], *kaleō* call)]

**pară'de. 1.** *n.* Display, ostentation, esp. *make a parade of* (one's virtue etc.); public square or promenade; public procession; muster of troops for inspection; ~(**-ground**) (used for this); **on** ~, mustering thus, (fig.) displaying oneself formally or purposefully. **2.** *v.t.* & *i.* Assemble for parade; display ostentatiously; march through (streets etc.), march in procession, with display. [F f. It. & Sp. (L *paro* prepare)]

**pă̆'rad|igm** (-īm) *n.* Example or pattern, esp. of inflexions of noun, verb, etc.; ~**igmă̆'tic** *a.* [L f. Gk]

**pă̆'radis|e** *n.* (**Earthly**) ~**e**, garden of Eden; heaven; region or state of supreme bliss; ~**al** (-lly), **pă̆radi'siăc(al)** (-cally), *adjs.* [F f. L f. Gk]

**pă̆'radŏs** (*or* -dō) *n.* Elevation of earth behind fortified place to secure from rearward attack. [F (PARA-[2], *dos* back)]

**pă̆'rad|ŏx** *n.* Seemingly absurd though perhaps actually well-founded statement; self-contradictory or essentially absurd statement; person or thing conflicting with preconceived notions of what is reasonable or possible; paradoxical nature (*a lover of paradox*); ~**ŏ'xical** *a.* (-lly). [L f. Gk (PARA-[1], *doxa* opinion)]

**pă̆'raffin** *n.* Colourless tasteless odourless inflammable oily or waxy substance got by distillation from petroleum and shale and used for making candles etc. (~ **wax**, solid paraffin obtained by distillation from shale or petroleum; ||**liquid** ~, odourless tasteless mild laxative); ~ (**oil**), oil so obtained and used as illuminant or fuel or lubricant; (Chem.) hydrocarbon of type containing maximum amount of hydrogen. [G f. L, = having little affinity]

**pă̆'ragon** *n.* Model of excellence, supremely excellent person or thing; model (*of* virtue etc.). [F f. It. f. Sp.]

**pă̆'ra|graph** (-ahf). **1.** *n.* Distinct passage or section in book etc., usu.

marked by indentation of first line; symbol (usu. ¶) as reference mark; detached item of news etc. in newspaper. **2.** *v.t.* Arrange (article etc.) in paragraphs. **3.** ~**gră′phic** *a.* (**-ically**). [F or L f. Gk (PARA-¹, -GRAPH)]

**pă′rakeet, pă′roquĕt** (-kĕt), *n.* Small (esp. long-tailed) parrot. [F (PARROT)]

**pă′rallăx** *n.* (Angular amount of) apparent displacement of object, caused by actual change of point of observation; ~**ă′ctic** *a.* [F f. L f. Gk, = change]

**pă′rallĕl** *a.*, *n.*, & *v.* **1.** *a.* (no *adv.* in **-ly**). (Of lines) continuously equidistant, (of line) having this relation *to*; (fig.) precisely similar, analogous, or corresponding; ~ **bars,** pair of parallel rails on posts for gymnastics. **2.** *n.* ~ **(of latitude),** each of the parallel circles of constant latitude on earth's surface (*the 49th parallel*), or corresponding line on map; person or thing precisely analogous to another; comparison (*draw a parallel between two things*); two parallel lines (‖) as reference mark; **in** ~, (Electr., of circuits etc.) arranged so as to join at common points at each end. **3.** *v.t.* (**-l-**). Represent as similar, compare (things, one *with* another); find or mention something parallel or corresponding to; be parallel to, correspond to. **4.** ~**ĕ′pĭpĕd** (or -epĭ′pĭd) *n.*, (Geom.) solid bounded by parallelograms; ~**ĭsm** *n.*, being parallel (lit. or fig.), correspondence; ~**ogrăm** (-ĕ′-) *n.*, 4-sided plane rectilinear figure with opposite sides parallel. [F f. L f. Gk, = alongside one another]

**pă′ralȳse** (-z), **\*-ze,** *v.t.* Affect with paralysis; (fig.) render powerless, cripple; **pară′lȳsĭs** *n.*, nervous disease with impairment or loss of motor or sensory function of nerves, (fig.) state of utter powerlessness; ~**lȳ′tĭc** *a.* (**-ically**) & *n.*, (person) affected with paralysis (lit. or fig.), ‖(sl.) very drunk. [F f. Gk (PARA-¹, *luō* loosen)]

**păramă′tta.** See PARRAMATTA.

**pară′mĕter** *n.* (Math.) quantity constant in case considered, but varying in different cases; (esp. measurable or quantifiable) characteristic or feature. [L f. Gk PARA-¹, -METER]

**păramĭ′lĭtarȳ** *a.* Ancillary to and similarly organized to military forces. [PARA-¹]

**pă′ramount** *a.* Supreme; in supreme authority. [AF (*par* by, *amont* above; see AMOUNT)]

**pă′ramour** (-oor) *n.* (arch., rhet.) Illicit lover of married person. [F *par amour* by love]

**păranoi′|a** *n.* Mental derangement with delusions of grandeur, persecution, etc.; abnormal tendency to suspect and mistrust others; ~**ăc,** **pă′ranoid,** *adjs.* & *ns.*, (person) affected by paranoia. [L f. Gk (NOUS)]

**păranŏ′rmal** *a.* (~**ly**). Lying outside the range of normal scientific investigations etc. [PARA-¹]

**pă′rapĕt** (or -ĕt) *n.* Low wall at edge of roof, balcony, etc., or along sides of bridge etc.; (Mil.) defence of earth or stone to conceal and protect troops. [F or It. (PARA-², *petto* breast)]

**păraphernā′lĭa** *n.pl.* Personal belongings, miscellaneous accessories, etc. [L f. Gk (PARA-¹, *phernē* dower)]

**pă′raphrāse** (-z). **1.** *n.* Free rendering or amplification of a passage, expression of its sense in other words; one of various metrical paraphrases of passages of Scripture used in Church of Scotland etc. **2.** *v.t.* Express meaning of (passage) in other words. [F or L f. Gk (PARA-¹)]

**păraplĕ′g|ia** *n.* Paralysis of legs and part or whole of trunk; ~**ĭc** *a.* & *n.*, (victim) of this. [Gk (PARA-¹, *plēssō* strike)]

**părapsȳchŏ′logȳ** (-rasĭk-) *n.* Study of mental phenomena outside sphere of ordinary psychology (hypnosis, telepathy, etc.). [PARA-¹]

**pă′raquat** (-ŏt) *n.* Quick-acting herbicide, becoming inactive on contact with soil. [PARA-¹, QUATERNARY]

**pă′rasĭt|e** *n.* Self-seeking hanger-on, toady; unprofitable dependent; animal or plant living in or on another and drawing nutriment directly from it; **părasĭ′tĭc** *a.* (**-ically**); ~**ĭsm** *n.*; ~**ĭze** *v.t.*, infest as parasite. [L f. Gk (PARA-¹, *sitos* food)]

**pă′rasŏl** *n.* Light umbrella used to give protection from sunlight. [F f. It. (PARA-², *sole* sun)]

**pă′ratroop|s** *n.pl.* Parachute troops; ~**er** *n.*, one of these. [contr.]

**păratȳ′phoid** *n.* Fever resembling

typhoid, but caused by different bacterium. [PARA-¹]

**pår′boil** v.t. Partly cook by boiling; (fig.) overheat. [F f. L (*par-* = PER-, confused w. PART)]

**pår′cel** n., adv., & v. **1.** n. Goods etc. wrapped up in single package; bundle so wrapped; (Commerc.) quantity dealt with in one transaction; piece *of* land; PART and parcel; ~ **post**, branch of postal service concerned with parcels. **2.** adv. (arch.) Partly; ~ **gilt**, partly gilded, esp. of cup etc. with inner surface gilt. **3.** v.t. (‖-ll-). Divide (*out*) into portions; wrap (*up*) as parcel. [F f. L (PARTICLE)]

**pår′cĕn|ǎrỹ** n. Joint heirship; ~**er** n., joint heir. [AF f. L (PARTITION)]

**pårch** v.t. & i. (Of sun, thirst, etc.) make (earth, person, etc.) hot and dry; become hot and dry; roast (peas, corn, etc.) slightly. [orig. unkn.]

**pår′chment** n. (MS. written on) skin, esp. of sheep or goat, prepared for writing, painting, etc.; (**vegetable**) ~, high-grade paper made to resemble parchment. [F f. L (*Pergamum*, place)]

**pård¹** n. (arch.) Leopard. [F f. L f. Gk]

***pård²**, **pår′dner**, ns. (sl.) Partner, comrade. [corrupt.]

**pår′don. 1.** n. Forgiveness; (R.C. Ch.) = INDULGENCE; (Law) remission of legal consequences of crime or conviction; courteous forbearance; (**I beg your**) ~ (formula of apology for thing done, for dissent or contradiction, or for not hearing or understanding what was said). **2.** v.t. Forgive (person, offence, person his offence); make (esp. courteous) allowances for, excuse, (person, fault, person *for doing*); ~ **me**, = *I beg your pardon*; ~**able** a. (-**bly**), (esp.) easily excused. [F f. L *perdono* (PER-, *dono* give)]

**pår′e** v.t. Trim (thing) by cutting away irregular parts etc.; cut away skin, rind, etc., of (fruit etc.); (fig.) diminish little by little (*away*, *down*); shave, cut, *off*, *away*, (edges etc.); ~′**ing** n., (esp.) slip pared off. [F f. L *paro* prepare]

**pårĕgŏ′ric** n. Camphorated tincture of opium. [L f. Gk, = soothing]

**pår′ent** n. One who has begotten or borne offspring, father or mother; forefather; animal or plant from

which others are derived; (fig.) source, origin, (*of* evils etc.); ~ **teacher association**, organization promoting good relations between teachers and schoolchildren's parents; ~**age** n., lineage, descent from parents, (*his parentage is unknown*); **parĕ′ntal** a. (-**lly**); ~**hood** (-h-) n. [F f. L (*pario* bring forth)]

**parĕ′nthĕs|ĭs** n. (*pl.* ~**es** *pr.* -ēz). Word, clause, or sentence, inserted into a passage to which it is not grammatically essential, and usu. marked off by brackets, dashes, or commas; (pair of) round bracket(s) ( ) used for this; (fig.) interlude, interval; ~**ize** v.t., insert (words etc., or abs.) as parenthesis, put between marks of parenthesis; **părĕnthĕ′tic** a. (-**ically**), of, inserted as, parenthesis. [L f. Gk (PARA-¹, EN-, THESIS)]

***par excellence*** (pår ĕ′ksĕlahns) adv. Above all others that may be so called (*Mayfair was the fashionable quarter par excellence*). [F]

**pår′fait** (-fā) n. Rich iced pudding of whipped cream, eggs, etc.; layers of ice cream, fruit, etc., served in tall glass. [F (*parfait* PERFECT)]

**pår′gĕt. 1.** v.t. Plaster (wall etc.), esp. with ornamental pattern; roughcast. **2.** n. Plaster; roughcast. [F *pargeter* (*par* all over, *jeter* throw)]

**pă′riah** (-a; *or* parī′a) n. Member of low or no caste; (fig.) social outcast; ~ **dog**, = PYE-DOG. [Tamil]

**pari′etal** a. (-**lly**). Of the wall of the body or any of its cavities; ~ **bone**, one of pair forming part of skull. [F or L (*paries* wall)]

***pari passu*** (pårī pă′soo) adv. With equal pace; simultaneously and equally. [L]

**pă′rish** n. (**Ecclesiastical**) ~, area having its own church and clergyman; ‖(**civil**) ~, district constituted for purposes of civil government, orig. (Hist.) for poor-law administration; inhabitants of parish; ~ **clerk**, official performing various duties concerned with church; ‖~ **council**, administrative body in civil parish; ~ **pump** (fig., w. ref. to purely parochial or restricted outlook); ~ **register**, book recording christenings, marriages, and burials, at parish church; **pari′shioner** (-sho-) n., inhabitant of parish. [F f. L *parochia* f. Gk (*oikos* dwelling)]

**Parï′sian** (-z-) *a.* & *n.* (Native, inhabitant) of *Paris*. [place]

**pă′rĭtў** *n.* Equality, e.g. among members or ministers of church; parallelism, analogy, (*parity of reasoning*); (Commerc.) equivalence in another currency, being at PAR. [F, or L *paritas* (PAR)]

**park. 1.** *n.* Large enclosed piece of ground, usu. with woodland and pasture, attached to country house etc.; enclosure in town ornamentally laid out for public recreation; *sports ground; large tract of land kept in natural state for public benefit (*national park*); area for motor cars etc. to be left in; ~′land, open grassland with tree-clumps etc. **2.** *v.t.* Enclose (ground) in or as park; leave (vehicle, or abs.), usu. temporarily, in park or elsewhere; (colloq.) deposit and leave, usu. temporarily; ~ oneself, (sl.) sit down; *~′ing-lot, outdoor area for parking vehicles; ~′ing-meter, coin-operated meter which receives fees for vehicle parked in street and indicates time allowed; ~′ing-ticket, notice of fine etc. imposed for parking vehicle illegally. [F f. Gmc]

**păr′ka** *n.* Skin jacket with hood attached, worn by Eskimos; similar fabric garment of mountaineers etc. [Aleutian]

**Păr′kĭnson¹** *n.* ~'s disease, ~ĭsm *n.*, progressive disease of nervous system, with tremor, muscular rigidity, and emaciation. [person]

**Păr′kĭnson²** *n.* ~'s law, (joc.) fact that work will always last as long as the available time.

**păr′lance** *n.* (Particular) way of speaking (*in legal, medical, common, parlance*). [F f. *parler* speak ult. f. L *parabola* (PARABLE)]

**păr′ley. 1.** *n.* Conference to debate points in dispute, esp. (Mil.) discussion of terms for armistice etc. **2.** *v.i.* Discuss terms (of armistice *with* enemy etc.). [F *parler* (prec.)]

**păr′liament** (-lam-) *n.* (P~) council forming with the Sovereign the supreme legislature of United Kingdom, consisting of House of LORDS (Spiritual and Temporal) and House of COMMONS (representatives of counties, towns, etc.) (**Houses of P**~, these jointly, or the buildings where they meet; MEMBER *of Parliament*; open **P**~, (of Sovereign) declare its session open with cere-

monial); body of persons belonging to Parliament for period between successive dissolutions; corresponding legislative assembly in other countries; ~ār′ian *n.*, skilled debater in parliament, adherent of Parliament in Civil War; ~arỹ (-č′n-) *a.*, of parliament, (P-) enacted or established by Parliament, (of language) admissible in Parliament or (colloq.) civil. [F (prec.)]

**păr′lour,** *păr′lor, (-er) *n.* Ordinary sitting-room of family in private house; room in mansion, convent, inn, etc., for private conversation; *shop etc. providing specified goods or services (*beauty parlour, ice cream parlour*); ~ game, indoor game, esp. word-game; ~maid, maid who waits at table; ~ tricks, (usu. derog.) social accomplishments. [AF (PARLEY)]

**păr′lous.** (arch. or joc.) **1.** *a.* Perilous; hard to deal with. **2.** *adv.* Extremely. [PERILOUS]

**Părmèsă′n** (-z-; *or* -ār′-) *a.* & *n.* ~ (cheese), kind of hard cheese made orig. at *Parma*, used esp. in grated form. [F f. It. (place)]

**parō′chial** (-k-) *a.* (~ly). Of a parish; (fig., of affairs, views, etc.) confined to narrow area; ~ĭsm *n.*, concentration on or limitation to local interests. [F f. L (PARISH)]

**pă′rodỹ. 1.** *n.* Composition in which an author's characteristics are humorously imitated; feeble imitation, travesty; ~ĭst *n.* **2.** *v.t.* Compose parody of (literary work, manner, etc.). [L *or* Gk (PARA-¹, ODE)]

**parō′le. 1.** *n.* Word of honour; prisoner's promise not to attempt to escape if conditionally liberated, liberation on these terms (**on** ~, so liberated). **2.** *v.t.* Put (prisoner) on parole. [F,= word (PAROL)]

**părŏnomā′sia** (-z-) *n.* Play(ing) on words, pun. [L f. Gk (*onoma* name)]

**paroquet.** See PARAKEET.

**parō′tĭd. 1.** *a.* Situated near the ear (~ gland, salivary, in front of ear). **2.** *n.* Parotid gland. [F f. L f. Gk (PARA-¹, *ous ōt-* ear)]

**pă′roxỹsm** *n.* Fit of disease; fit (*of* rage, laughter, etc.); ~al (-ĭ′zm-) *a.* (-lly). [F f. L f. Gk (*oxus* sharp)]

**păr′quet** (-kĭ, -kā). **1.** *n.* Flooring of wooden blocks often of different kinds and arranged in pattern. **2.** *v.t.* Floor (room) thus. **3.** ~ĭng, ~rỹ,

(-kĭt-) *ns.*, parquet-work. [F, dim. of *parc* PARK]

**parr** *n.* Young salmon. [orig. unkn.]

**pǎr(r)amǎ'tta** *n.* Light dress--fabric of wool and silk or cotton. [place]

**pǎ'rri|cide, pǎ'tri|-,** *n.* One who kills his father or near relative; one who kills person regarded as sacred; person guilty of treason against his country; any of these crimes; ~**cī'dal** *a.* (-lly). [F or L]

**pǎ'rrot. 1.** *n.* Bird with short hooked bill, mainly tropical, of which many species have vivid plumage and some can be taught to repeat words; person who repeats another's words or imitates his actions unintelligently. **2.** *v.t.* Repeat (words, or abs.) mechanically. [F (dim. of *Pierre* Peter)]

**pǎ'rry. 1.** *v.t.* Turn aside, ward off, avert, (weapon, blow, awkward question), esp. with one's own weapon etc. **2.** *n.* Act of parrying. [prob. F f. It. *parare* ward off]

**parse** (-z) *v.t.* Describe (word in context) grammatically, stating inflexion, relation to sentence, etc.; resolve (sentence) into its component parts and describe them grammatically. [perh. F *pars* PARTS]

**par'sec** *n.* Unit of stellar distance, about 3¼ light-years. [PAR(ALLAX), SEC(OND)]

**Parsee** *n.* Adherent of Zoroastrianism; descendant of Persians who fled to India in 7th–8th cc.; ~**ism** *n.* [Pers., = Persian]

**par'sim|ony** *n.* Carefulness in employment of money etc. or (fig.) of immaterial things; excessive carefulness with money, meanness; ~**ō'nious** *a.* [L (*parco pars-* spare)]

**par'sley** *n.* Herb used for seasoning and garnishing dishes. [F f. L f. Gk (*petra* rock, *selinon* parsley)]

**par'snip** *n.* (Plant with) pale yellow tapering root used as culinary vegetable; *fine words* BUTTER *no parsnips*. [F f. L *pastinaca*]

**par'son** *n.* Rector; vicar or any beneficed clergyman; (colloq.) any (esp. Protestant) clergyman; *parson's* NOSE; ~**age** *n.*, parson's house; **parsō'nic(al)** *adjs.* (-ically), clerical. [F f. L (PERSON)]

**part** *n.*, *adv.*, & *v.* **1.** *n.* Some but not all of a thing or number of things (*part of it was spoilt*; *parts of it are excellent*; *a part of them have arrived*; the

most or greater part (the majority) *of them failed*; BETTER[1], BEST, *part*; *for the* MOST *part*; **in** ~(**s**), partly); division of book, broadcast serial, etc., esp. as much as is issued etc. at one time; portion of human or animal body (**the** ~**s**, genitals); component of machine etc.; each of several equal portions of a whole (cf. NUMERAL; **three** ~**s**, ¾; *gold content is 5 parts per million*; *take 3 parts of sugar, 5 of flour*, etc.); portion allotted, share; person's share in action, his duty, (*I have done my part*; *it was not my part to interfere*; *I will have no part in this affair*; **for my** ~, so far as I am concerned; **on the** ~ of, proceeding from, done etc. by, *there was no objection on my part*; **take** ~, assist *in* doing, *in* discussion etc.); character assigned to actor on stage, words spoken by actor on stage, copy of these, (**play** *a noble* etc. ~, fig. behave nobly etc.; **play a** ~, contribute by action etc., act deceitfully); (Mus.) melody or other constituent of harmony assigned to particular voice or instrument; (in *pl.*) abilities (*a man of parts*), region (*a stranger in these parts*; *from foreign parts*); side in agreement or dispute (**take the** ~ **of,** support, back up); ~ **and parcel,** essential part *of*; ~**-exchange,** transaction in which article is given as part of payment for more expensive one; ~ **of speech,** each of grammatical classes of words; ~**-owner,** one who owns in common with others; ~**-song,** song with three or more voice-parts, freq. without accompaniment; ~ **time,** less than FULL[1] time; ~**-time** *a.*, occupying or using only part of one's working time; ~**-timer** *n.*; ~**-work,** publication appearing in several parts at different times; **take** (words, actions) **in good** ~, not be offended at. **2.** *adv.* In part, partly, (*made part of iron and part of wood*; *is part iron part wood*). **3.** *v.t.* & *i.* Divide into parts (*the crowd parted and let him through*; *the cord parted*, broke); separate (hair of head on either side of parting) with comb; separate (combatants, fool and his money, etc.; *till death us do part*); quit one another's company (*let us part friends*); (colloq.) part with one's money, pay, (*he won't part*); *part* BRASS *rags with*, COMPANY; ~ **from,** with, say goodbye to; ~ **with,** give up, surrender, (property etc.). **4.** ~**'ing** *n.*, (esp.)

leave-taking (often attrib.: *parting words*; ~**ing** shot, = PARTHIAN *shot*), dividing line of combed hair; ~**ing of the ways**, point at which road divides into two or more, (fig.) point at which choice must be made between courses of action; ~**ly** *adv.*, with respect to a part, in some degree. [F f. L *pars part*-]

**partā́ke** *v.i.* (-tōo'k; -ta'ken). Take a share (*of* or in thing, *with* person); eat or drink some or (colloq.) all of (*partook of our fare, of a bun*); have some (*of* quality etc.; *his manner partakes of insolence*). [back-form. f. *partaker* = *part-taker*]

**parter're** (-tār´) *n.* Level space in garden occupied by flower-beds; part of ground-floor of auditorium of theatre, behind orchestra. [F, = on the ground]

**parthenoge'nesis** *n.* Reproduction from gametes without fertilization. [L f. Gk *parthenos* virgin]

**Par'thian** *a.* ~ **shot**, remark, glance, etc., reserved for moment of departure, like missile shot backwards by retreating Parthian horseman. [*Parthia*, place]

**par'tial** (-shăl) *a.* (~ly). Biased, unfair, (~ **to**, having a liking for); forming only a part, not complete (*a partial success*); ~ **eclipse** in which only part of the luminary is covered or darkened); ~**ity** (-shĭă'l-) *n.*, bias, favouritism, fondness (*for*). [F f. L (PART)]

**parti'cipate** *v.i.* Have share, take part, (*in* thing, *with* person); have something of (*his poems participate of the nature of satire*); ~**ant** *n.*, participator; ~**ā'tion**, ~**ātor**, *ns.* [L (*particeps -cip-* taking PART)]

**par'tici|ple** *n.* Verbal adjective qualifying noun but retaining some properties of verb, e.g. tense and government of object, as *qualifying* here; ~**i'pial** *a.* (-lly). [F f. L (prec.)]

**par'ticle** *n.* Minute portion of matter (ELEMENTARY *particle*); least possible amount (*has not a particle of sense*); minor part of speech, esp. short indeclinable one; common prefix or suffix such as *un-*, *-ship*. [L *particula* dim. of *pars* PART]

**par'ticoloured** (-ŭlerd) *a.* Partly of one colour, partly of another. [PART, COLOUR]

**parti'cular. 1.** *a.* Relating to one as distinguished from others; one considered apart from others, individual, (*this particular tax is no worse than others*); more than usual, special, (*took particular trouble; for no particular reason*); detailed (*full and particular account*); scrupulously exact, fastidious (*about, as to what* one eats etc.). **2.** *n.* Detail, item; (in *pl.*) detailed account or information; **in** ~, especially (*mentioned one case in particular*). **3.** ~**ity** (-ă'rĭ-) *n.*, (esp.) fullness or minuteness of detail in description; ~**ize** *v.t.* & *i.*, name specially or one by one, specify (items); ~**izā'tion** *n.*; ~**ly** *adv.*, (esp.) very, to an especial extent (*am particularly sorry; they are poisonous, particularly when green*). [F f. L (PARTICLE)]

**par'ting.** See PART.

**partisă'n** (-z-; *or* pär't-) *n.* (Esp. unreasoning) adherent of party, cause, etc.; guerrilla; ~**ship** *n.*, (esp.) party spirit, partisan action. [F f. It. (PART)]

**parti'tion. 1.** *n.* Division into parts; such part; structure separating two such parts, esp. slight wall. **2.** *v.t.* Divide into parts; ~ **off**, separate (part of room etc.) with partition. **3.** **par'titive** *a.* & *n.*, (Gram.) (word) denoting part of a collective whole (e.g. *some*, *any*). [F f. L *partior* divide]

**par'tly.** See PART.

**par'tner. 1.** *n.* Sharer (*with* person, *in* or *of* thing); person associated with others in business of which he shares risks and profits; wife or husband; companion in dance (esp. *dancing partner*); player associated with another in game and scoring jointly with him. **2.** *v.t.* Associate (persons, one *with* another) as partners; be partner of. **3.** ~**ship** *n.*, (esp.) pair of partners, joint business. [alt. PARCENER after PART]

**par'tridge** *n.* (*pl.* ~, ~**s**). Game-bird, esp. the brown and grey **common** or **grey** ~. [F *perdriz* f. L f. Gk *perdix*]

**partūr'ient** *a.* About to give birth (lit., or fig. of the mind etc.); ~**i'tion** *n.*, act of bringing forth young, childbirth, (lit. or fig.). [L *pario part*- bring forth)]

**par'ty** *n.* Body of persons united in a cause, opinion, etc., attachment to such body, taking of sides on public questions, (**the P**~, esp. the Communist party); body of persons travelling or working together

( *fishing, reading, -party* ); social gathering, esp. of invited guests at private house, (*dinner, tea, -party*); each of two or more persons making the two sides in legal action, contract, marriage, etc., (THIRD *party*); accessory (*to action*); (vulg. or joc.) person (*an old party with spectacles*); ~**-coloured,** = PARTICOLOURED; ~**line,** policy adopted by a political party, telephone line shared by two or more subscribers; ~ **spirit,** enthusiasm for social parties, (usu. derog.) zeal for a party of opinion; ~**-wall,** wall shared by occupiers of the two buildings etc. that it separates. [F f. Rom. (PART)]

**pár'venu** (-ōō) n. & a. (Person) of obscure origin but having gained wealth or position, upstart. [F]

**pas** (pah) n. (*pl.* same) ~ *de deux* (-dedēr') dance for two persons; ~ *seul* (-sēr'l), solo dance. [F, = step]

**pă'schal** (-k-) a. Of the Jewish Passover; of Easter; ~ **lamb,** lamb sacrificed at Passover, (fig.) Christ. [F f. L f. Heb.]

**pa'sha, pa'cha,** (pah'sha) n. (Hist.) Title (placed after name) of Turkish officer of high rank, e.g. military commander, governor of province, etc. [Turk.]

**pă'sque-flower** (-skf-) n. Kind of anemone. [F *passe-fleur*]

**pass¹** (-ah-) **1.** *v.t.* & *i.* (*p.p.* ~ed or as adj. PAST *both pr.* pahst). Move onward, proceed, (*along, down, on, over,* etc.); get through, effect a passage; go across (sea, frontier); leave (thing etc.) on one side or behind; overtake; surpass, be too great for (*it passes my comprehension*); (cause to) go by (*pass troops etc. in review; time passes rapidly; remark passed unnoticed*); move, (cause to) go, (*passed his hand across his forehead, flour through a sieve, a rope round it*); change (*into* something, *from* one state to another); die (usu. *pass hence, from among us,* etc.); come to an end (*kingdoms and nations pass; paroxysm has passed*); (of bill in Parliament, proposal, etc.) be sanctioned, (of bill) be examined and approved by (House of Commons etc.), cause or allow (bill in Parliament, candidate for examination, etc.) to proceed after scrutiny; reach standard required by (examiner, examination); (of candidate) satisfy examiner; go uncensured, be accepted as adequate

(*let the matter pass*); be accepted or currently known *as*; adjudicate (*upon*); utter (criticism, judicial sentence, *upon*); hand round, transfer, (*read this and pass it to Bob; please pass the salt*); (Footb. etc.) kick, hand, or hit, (ball, or abs.) to or to player of one's own side; (cause to) circulate, be current; happen, be done or said, (*I saw* or *heard what passed* or *what was passing*); (Cards) forgo one's opportunity, e.g. of making bid; spend (*time, the winter*); discharge from the body as or with excreta; ~ **away,** (fig.) die, cease to exist, come to an end; ~ **by,** walk etc. past, omit, disregard; ~**ed master,** = PAST *master*; ~ one's **eye over,** read (document) cursorily; ~ **for,** be accepted as; *pass* MUSTER; ~ **off,** (of feelings etc.) disappear gradually, (of proceedings) be carried through (*smoothly* etc.), palm off thing or person *on* person *for* or *as* what it etc. is not), evade or lightly dismiss (awkward remark etc.); ~ **on,** proceed on one's way, (fig.) die, transmit to next person in series; ~ **out,** depart, complete military training, (fig.) die, (colloq.) become unconscious; ~ **over,** omit, disregard, ignore claims of (person) to promotion etc., make no remark on (*pass over his subsequent conduct*), (fig.) die; *pass the* TIME *of day*; ~ **through,** experience; ~ **up,** (colloq.) refuse or neglect (opportunity etc.). **2.** *n.* Passing, esp. of examination or at cards; ‖attainment of standard that satisfies university examiners and entitles to ~ **degree** but not to honours degree; critical position (*things have come to a pass*); written permission to pass into or out of a place, or to be absent from quarters; = FREE *pass*; thrust in fencing, juggling trick, passing of hands over anything, as in conjuring or hypnotism, (**make a** ~ **at,** colloq., make amorous advances to); (Footb. etc.) transference of ball to player of one's own side; ~'**book,** book supplied by bank etc. to account-holder which shows all sums deposited and drawn, (S. Afr.) document to be carried by non-White persons; ~'**key,** private key to gate etc. for special purposes, master-key; ~'**word,** selected word or phrase known only to one's own side and used to distinguish friend from enemy; **bring to** ~, cause to happen; **come to ~**, happen. **3.** **~′able** *a.* (-bly), (esp.) that can pass muster, fairly good; **~′er** *n.*, (esp.) **~er-by**, one who goes past, esp. casually; **~′ing**, (*n.*, esp.) **in ~ing**, by the way, in course of speech, **~ing-bell** (rung to announce person's death), (*a.*, esp.) transient, fleeting, cursory, incidental, **~ing shot** (Tennis, intended to place ball beyond and out of reach of opponent), (*adv.*; arch.) very (*passing strange*). [F f. Rom. (L *passus* PACE[1])]

**pass**[2] (-ah-) *n.* Narrow passage through mountains (SELL *the pass*). [var. PACE[1]]

**pă′ssage** *n.* Passing, transit, (BIRD *of passage*); transition from one state to another; voyage or crossing from port to port; liberty or right to pass through; right of conveyance as passenger by sea or air (**work** one's **~**, earn this right by labour, lit. or fig.); passing of bill etc. into law; **~(way)**, way by which one passes (NORTH-*east, -west, passage*), corridor etc. giving communication between different rooms in house; duct etc. in the body (**back**, **front**, **~**, colloq., rectum, vagina); (in *pl.*) what passes between two persons mutually, interchange of confidences etc.; short part of book etc. (*famous, difficult, passage*); particular phrase or short section in piece of music; **~ of** or **at arms**, fight (lit. or fig.). [F (PASS[1])]

**passé** (pă′să) *a.* (*fem.* **~e** *pr.* same). Past the prime, esp. (of woman) past the period of greatest beauty; behind the times.

**pă′ssenger** (-nj-) *n.* Traveller in public conveyance by land or water or air; traveller in private conveyance (other than driver, pilot, etc.); (colloq.) member of team, crew, etc., who does, or can do, no effective work. [F *passager* (PASSAGE)]

**pă′sserine** *a.* & *n.* (Bird) of the sparrow order. [L (*passer* sparrow)]

**passim** (pă′sĭm) *adv.* (Of allusions, phrases, etc., to be found in specified author or book) in many places, here and there throughout (*this occurs in Milton passim*). [L]

**pă′ssion** (-shŏn) *n.* Strong emotion; outburst of anger (*flew into a passion*); sexual love; strong enthusiasm (*for thing*, *for doing*); (P~) the sufferings of Christ on the Cross, (musical setting of) narrative of this from Gospels; **~-flower**, plant with flower which was supposed to suggest instruments of Crucifixion; **~-fruit**, edible fruit of some species of passion-flower; **~-play**, miracle play representing Christ's Passion; **P~ Sunday**, fifth Sunday in Lent; **~ate** *a.*, dominated by or easily moved to strong feeling, due to passion, (of language etc.) showing passion; **~less** *a.*, cold, exempt from or lacking in passion. [F f. L (*patior pass-* suffer)]

**pă′ssive** *a.* Suffering action, acted upon; offering no opposition, submissive; not active, inert; (of verb etc.) in passive voice; **~ resistance**, non-violent refusal to co-operate; **~ voice**, (Gram.) that comprising those forms of transitive vbs. that indicate that subject undergoes action of verb (as *he was seen*; cf. ACTIVE); **pă′ssi′vĭtў** *n.* [F or L (prec.)]

**Pa′ssŏver** (-ah′-) *n.* Jewish spring festival commemorating liberation of Israelites from Egyptian bondage (Exod. 12); = PASCHAL *lamb*. [PASS[1], OVER]

**pa′sspŏrt** (-ah′-) *n.* Official document certifying identity and citizenship, permitting person(s) specified in it to travel to and from foreign country and entitling to protection; (fig.) thing that ensures admission (*flattery is the sole passport to his favour*). [F *passeport* (PASS[1], PORT[1])]

**past** (-ah-) *a.*, *n.*, *prep.*, & *adv.* **1.** *a.* Having passed; (just) gone by in time (*his prime is past; our past years; for the past month, for some time past*); (Gram.) expressing past action or state (*past participle*); relating to a former time (*past president*); **~ master,** one who has been master in guild, Freemasons' lodge, etc., (fig.) thorough master (*in, of*, a subject). **2.** *n.* Past time, esp. *the past*; what has happened in past time (*cannot undo the past*); person's past life or career, esp. if discreditable (*a woman with a past*); past tense. **3.** *prep.* Beyond in time or place (*stayed till past two o'clock; half past three; old man past seventy; two miles past the turning; ran past the house*); beyond range, duration, or compass of (*past belief, endurance, caring*, PRAYING *for*); **~ it,** (sl.) incompetent through senility etc.; **not put it ~** person (*to do*), (colloq.) regard him as morally capable (of doing). **4.** *adv.* So as to pass by (*hasten past*). [PASS[1]]

**pă'sta** (*or* -ah'-) *n.* (Dish made from cooked) flour paste used in Italian cooking in various shapes (spaghetti etc.). [It. (foll.)]

**păste. 1.** *n.* Flour moistened and kneaded, with fat etc., as cooking material; sweet doughy confection (*almond paste*); easily spread preparation of ground meat, fish, etc., (*anchovy paste*); cement of flour or starch and water; soft plastic mixture for any purpose (*toothpaste*); hard vitreous composition used in making imitation gems; mixture of clay, water, etc., used in making pottery; ~'**board,** stiff substance made by pasting together sheets of paper, (*attrib.*, *fig.*) unsubstantial, flimsy. **2.** *v.t.* Fasten with paste; (sl.) beat, thrash, bomb etc. heavily; ~**up,** document prepared for copying etc. by pasting various materials on a backing. [F f. L *pasta* lozenge f. Gk]

**pă'stel** (*or* -ĕ'l) *n.* Artists' crayon made of dried paste compounded of pigments with gum solution; drawing in pastel; ~ **colour** etc. (light and subdued). [F, or It. *pastello* dim. of PASTE]

**pă'stern** *n.* Part of horse's foot between fetlock and hoof. [F f. L]

**pă'steuriz|e** (-scher-, -ter-; *or* -ah'-) *v.t.* Subject (milk etc.) to Pasteur's method of partial sterilization by heating; ~**ā'tion** *n.* [person]

**păsti'che** (-ē'sh) *n.* Medley, esp. musical composition, or picture, made up from various sources; literary or other work of art composed in style of well-known author. [F f. It. *pasticcio* f. L *pasta* paste]

**pă'stille** (*or* -tēl) *n.* Small roll of aromatic paste burnt as fumigator etc.; medicinal lozenge. [F f. L]

**pa'stime** (-ah'-) *n.* Recreation, hobby; sport, game. [PASS[1], TIME]

**pa'stor** (-ah'-) *n.* Minister in charge of church or congregation; person exercising spiritual guidance; ~**al,** (*a.*; -**lly**) of shepherds, of flocks and herds, (of land) used for pasture, (of poem, picture, etc.) portraying country life, of a pastor, (*n.*) pastoral play, poem, picture, etc., letter from pastor (esp. bishop) to clergy or people; ~**ate** *n.*, pastor's (tenure of) office, body of pastors. [F f. L (*pasco past-* feed)]

**pă'stry** *n.* Baked flour-paste; article(s) of food made wholly or partly of this; ~**cook,** one who

makes pastry, esp. for public sale. [PASTE]

**pa'stur|e** (-ah'-). **1.** *n.* Herbage for cattle, sheep, etc.; (piece of) land covered with this (**common ~e,** use of herbage by cattle of several owners). **2.** *v.t. & i.* Lead or put (cattle etc.) to pasture; (of sheep etc.) eat down (grassland); put sheep etc. on (land) to graze; graze. **3.** ~**age** (-ah'scher-) *n.*, pasturing, pasture-(-land). [F f. L (PASTOR)]

**pă'sty**[1] (*or* -ah'-) *n.* Pie of meat, fruit, jam, etc., enclosed in paste and baked without dish. [F f. L (PASTE)]

**pă'sty**[2] *a.* (-**ily,** -**iness**). Of or like paste; ~(-**faced),** of pale complexion. [PASTE]

**păt**[1] *v., n., a., & adv.* **1.** *v.t.* (-**tt-**). Strike (thing) gently with flat surface; flatten thus; strike gently with inner surface of hand or fingers, esp. to mark sympathy, approbation, etc. **2.** *n.* Light stroke or tap, esp. with hand as caress etc.; small mass (esp. of butter) formed by patting; sound made by striking lightly with flat thing; ~ **on the back,** (*n.*; *fig.*, as token of approbation), (*v.t.*; *fig.*) express approbation of. **3.** *a. & adv.* Apposite(ly), opportune(ly) (*story came pat to his purpose*); (known thoroughly and) ready for any occasion (*has the story off pat*); **stand** ~, (Poker) retain hand dealt to one, (*fig.*) refuse to change, stick to one's decision etc. [prob. imit.]

**Păt**[2] *n.* (Nickname for) Irishman. [abbr. *Patrick*]

**Pat.** *abbr.* Patent.

**patch. 1.** *n.* Piece of cloth, metal, etc., put on to mend hole or rent (**not a ~ on,** colloq., very much inferior to); piece of plaster etc. put over wound; pad worn to protect injured eye; large or irregular distinguishable area on surface (∥**strike a bad ~,** go through period of bad luck or difficulty; **in ~es,** in isolated areas or periods of time); piece of ground; number of plants growing in one place; scrap, remnant; ~**pocket** (consisting of piece of cloth sewn on garment); ~'**work,** work made up of fragments of different kinds and colours (lit. or fig.). **2.** *v.t.* Put patch(es) on; (of material) serve as patch to; piece (things) together (lit. or fig.); ~ (**up),** repair with patches, (fig.) set to rights (matter, trouble, quarrel) esp. hastily or temporarily, put together hastily. **3.** ~'**y** *a.* (-ily, -iness), having patches, uneven in quality. [perh. F, var. PIECE]

**pă'tchoulĭ** (-ōō-) *n.* (Perfume from) an E. Ind. plant. [native name]

**pāte** *n.* (arch., colloq.) Head, often as seat of intellect. [orig. unkn.]

**pâté** (pă'tā, pah'-) *n.* Pie, patty; paste of meat etc.; ~ **de foie gras** (de fwah grah), paste or pie of fatted goose liver. [F, = PASTY[1]]

**patě'll|a** *n.* (*pl.* ~ae). Kneecap; ~**ar**, ~**ate**, *adjs.* [L, = pan, dim. *patina* (foll.)]

**pă'ten** *n.* Shallow dish used for bread at Eucharist. [F, or L *patina*]

**pă'tent** *n.*, *a.*, & *v.* **1.** *n.* Open letter from sovereign etc. conferring right, title, etc., esp. sole right for a period to make, use, or sell, some invention; government grant of exclusive privilege of making or selling new invention; invention or process so protected; ~ **agent**, *attorney, (specializing in procurement of patents); ~ **office** (from which patents are issued). **2.** *a.* Conferred or protected by patent; (of food, medicine, etc.) proprietary; (colloq.) such as might be patented, ingenious, well-contrived; (fig.) plain, obvious; ‖**letters** ~, = patent (1st sense); *patent* LEATHER. **3.** *v.t.* Obtain patent for (invention). **4.** pă'**tencў** *n.*, obviousness; ~**ee'** *n.*, taker-out or holder of a patent, person for time being entitled to benefit of patent. [F f. L (*pateo* lie open)]

‖**pă'ter** *n.* (sl.) Father. [L]

**pă'terfami'liǎs** *n.* (Rom. Law, or joc.) Head of family. [L]

**patě'rnal** *a.* (~ly). Of or like a father, fatherly; related through father; (of government, legislation, etc.) limiting freedom of the subject by well-meant regulations; ~**ism** *n.*, paternal government; ~**i'stĭc** *a.* [L (PATER)]

**patě'rnitў** *n.* Fatherhood; one's paternal origin; (fig.) authorship, source. [F or L (PATER)]

**păterno'ster** *n.* The Lord's Prayer, esp. in Latin; bead in rosary indicating that paternoster is to be said. [E, f. L *pater noster* our father]

**path** (pahth; *pl. pr.* pahdhz) *n.* Footway, esp. one merely made by walking, not specially constructed (also ~'**way**); track laid for foot or cycle races; line along which person

or thing moves; ~'**finder**, explorer. [E]

**Patha'n** (-tah'n) *n.* Member of a people inhabiting N.W. Pakistan and S.E. Afghanistan. [Hindi]

**pathě'tĭc** *a.* (~ally). Exciting pity or sadness or contempt; ~ **fallacy**, crediting inanimate things with human emotions. [F f. L f. Gk (*pathos* f. *paskhō* suffer)]

**pătho'lŏgĭcal** *a.* (~ly). Of pathology; (apparently) morbid (*a pathological dislike of dogs*); **patho'-logў** *n.*, science of bodily diseases, symptoms of a disease; **pathŏ'logĭst** *n.*; pă'**thŏs** *n.*, quality in speech, writing, events, etc., that excites pity or sadness.

**pā'tience** (-shens) *n.* Calm endurance of pain or of any provocation, perseverance, forbearance, quiet and self-possessed waiting for something, (**have no** ~ **with**, be irritated by, be unable to bear patiently; **lose** (one's) ~, become impatient *with*; **out of** ~ **with**, no longer able to endure); ‖game usu. for one player in which cards are to be brought into specified arrangement; **pā'tient** (-shent), (*a.*) having or showing patience, (*n.*) person under medical or dental or psychiatric treatment, person accepted by doctor etc. for treatment if this is needed in future. [F f. L (PASSION)]

**pă'tina** *n.* Incrustation, usu. green, on surface of old bronze; similar alteration on other surfaces; gloss produced by age on woodwork. [It. f. L (PATEN)]

**pă'tiŏ** *n.* (*pl.* ~s). Inner court open to sky in Sp.(-Amer.) house; paved usu. roofless area adjoining house. [Sp.]

**păti'sserie** *n.* Pastry-cook's shop or wares. [F f. L (PASTE)]

**pă'tois** (-twah) *n.* (*pl.* same *pr.* -z). Dialect of common people in a region, differing materially from the literary language; jargon. [F]

**pā'triarch** (-k) *n.* Father and ruler of family or tribe; (Bibl., in *pl.*) sons of Jacob, or Abraham, Isaac, Jacob, and their forefathers; (in Orthodox & R.C. Ch.) bishop of high rank; venerable old man; **pātriǎr'chal** (-k-) *a.* (-lly); ~**ate** *n.*, office, see, or residence of ecclesiastical patriarch, rank of tribal patriarch; ~**ў** *n.*, patriarchal system of society, government, etc. [F f. L f. Gk (*patria* family, *arkhēs* ruler)]

**patri′cian** (-shan). **1.** *n.* (Hist.) Ancient Roman noble. **2.** *a.* Noble, aristocratic; of the ancient Roman nobility. [F f. L *patricius* (PATER)]

**pă′tricīde.** See PARRICIDE.

**pă′tri|monў** *n.* Property inherited from father or ancestors; heritage (lit. or fig.); ∼mō′nial *a.* (-lly). [F f. L (PATER)]

**pă′triot** *n.* One who defends or is zealous for his country's freedom or rights; **pătriŏ′tic** *a.* (-ically); ∼ism *n.* [F f. L f. Gk (*patris* fatherland)]

**patrō′l. 1.** *n.* Going the rounds of garrison, camp, etc.; perambulation of town etc. by police (∼ **car**, used for this); detachment of guard, police constable(s), etc., assigned for patrol (∼**man**, *police constable); routine operational voyage of ship or aircraft; detachment of troops sent out to reconnoitre; unit of usu. 6 in Scout troop or Guide company. **2.** *v.t. & i.* (-ll-). Act as patrol; go round (camp, town, etc.) as patrol. [G *patrolle* f. F]

**pă′tron** *n.* One who countenances, protects, or gives influential support to (person, cause, art, etc.); (esp. regular) customer of shop etc.; ∼ **(saint)**, tutelary saint of person, place, etc.; ‖one who has right of presenting to benefice; **pă′tronage** *n.*, support or encouragement given by patron, ‖right of presenting to benefice or office, patronizing airs, customer's support; ∼**èss** *n.*; **pă′t-ronīze** *v.t.*, act as patron towards, support, encourage, treat (inferior) graciously. [F f. L *patronus* (PATER)]

**pătronŷ′mic** *a. & n.* (Name) derived from name of father or ancestor. [L f. Gk (*patēr* father, *onoma* name)]

**pă′tten** *n.* Shoe with sole set on iron ring etc. to raise wearer's foot out of mud etc. [F *patin*]

**pă′tter¹. 1.** *n.* Language of profession or class; deceptive speech of salesman etc.; rapid speech introduced into song. **2.** *v.t. & i.* Repeat (prayers etc.) in rapid mechanical way; talk glibly. [orig. *pater*, = PATERNOSTER]

**pă′tter². 1.** *v.i.* Make rapid succession of taps, as rain on window-pane; run with short quick steps. **2.** *n.* Rapid succession of taps or short light steps. [PAT¹]

**pă′ttern. 1.** *n.* Excellent or ideal example (*she is a pattern of virtue*); model or design or working instructions from which thing is to be made (*knitting pattern*); sample of tailor's cloth, wallpaper, etc.; (decorative) design as executed on carpet, wallpaper, cloth, etc.; regular form or order (*behaviour pattern*); pattern of one's *daily life*). **2.** *v.t.* Model (thing *after* or on design etc.); decorate with pattern. [PATRON]

**pă′ttў** *n.* Little pie or pasty; *small flat cake of minced meat etc. [F PÂTÉ, after PASTY¹]

**pau′citў** *n.* Smallness of number or quantity. [F or L (*paucus* few)]

**Pau′line. 1.** *a.* Of St. Paul. **2.** *a. & n.* (Member) of St. Paul's School. [L (*Paulus* Paul)]

**paunch** *n.* Belly, stomach; protruding abdomen; ∼′ў *a.* [AF *pa(u)nche* f. L *pantex -tic-* bowels]

**pau′per** *n.* Person without means of livelihood, beggar; (Hist.) recipient of poor-law relief; ∼ism *n.*, being a pauper; ∼ize *v.t.*, reduce to pauperism; ∼izā′tion *n.* [L, = poor]

**pause** (-z). **1.** *n.* Interval of inaction or silence, esp. due to hesitation; temporary stop (**give** ∼ **to**, cause to hesitate); break made in speech or reading; (Mus.) mark over note or rèst that is to be lengthened by some unspecified amount. **2.** *v.i.* Make pause, wait; linger *upon* (word etc.). [F, or L *pausa* f. Gk (*pauō* stop)]

**pă′van, pava′ne** (-ah′n), *n.* (Music of) stately dance in which dancers were elaborately dressed. [F f. Sp.]

**pāve** *v.t.* Cover (street, floor, etc.) with or (fig.) as with pavement; (fig.) prepare *the way* (*for* or *to* changes, reform, etc.); ∼′ment (-vm-) *n.*, covering of street, floor, etc., made of stones, tiles, wooden blocks, asphalt, etc., ‖esp. paved footway at side of road. [F *paver*, ult. f. L *pavio* to ram]

**pavi′lion** (-lyon) *n.* Tent, esp. large peaked one; light ornamental building; ‖building adjacent to cricket or other ground for players and spectators. [F f. L *papilio* butterfly]

**paw. 1.** *n.* Foot of animal having claws or nails; (colloq.) person's hand. **2.** *v.t. & i.* Strike with paw; (of horse) strike (ground), strike ground, with hoofs; (colloq.) handle awkwardly or rudely or indecently. [F *poue* f. Gmc]

‖**paw′ky** *a*. (-ily, -iness). (Sc. & dial.) Drily humorous; shrewd. [orig. unkn.]

**pawl** *n*. Lever with catch for teeth of wheel or bar; (Naut.) short bar to prevent capstan etc. from recoiling. [LDu. *pal*]

**pawn**¹ *n*. Chess-man of smallest size and value; (fig.) unimportant person subservient to others' plans. [AF *poun* f. L *pedo -onis* foot-soldier]

**pawn**². **1**. *n*. State of being pawned (*in pawn*); ~′**broker**, one who lends money at interest on security of personal property pawned; ~′**shop**, his place of business. **2**. *v.t*. Deposit (thing) as security for payment of money or performance of action; (fig.) pledge (one's life, honour, word). [F *pan* f. Gmc]

**pawpaw**′. See PAPAW.

**pay**. **1**. *v.t*. & *i*. (**paid**). Hand over money to discharge debt etc.; give (person) what is due in discharge of debt or for services done or goods received; hand over (money owed *to* person); hand over the amount of (debt, wages, ransom); suffer, undergo, (punishment, penalty, etc., or abs.); (fig.) reward, recompense, (*the* DEUCE² *or devil to pay*; **put paid to**, colloq., deal effectually with (person), terminate (hopes etc.)); recompense (work); render, bestow, (attention, respect, compliment, *to*; *a* CALL); (of business etc.) yield adequate return to (person), yield adequate return, be profitable or advantageous; (esp. Naut.) let rope *out* or *away* by slackening it. **2**. *n*. Payment, wages; **in the** ~ (employment) **of**. **3**. ‖~**-as-you-earn**, method of collecting income tax by deducting at source; ~ **back**, see *pay out*; ~**-bed**, hospital bed whose use is paid for by user; ~**-claim**, demand for increase of pay; ~**-day**, day on which payment is (to be) made, ‖(St. Exch.) day on which transfer of stock has to be paid for; ~ **for**, hand over price of, bear cost of, (fig.) be punished for (fault etc.); ~ **in**, pay to one's own or another's banking account; *paying* GUEST; *pay its* or one's WAY; ~′**load**, productive or useful part of load of aircraft, rocket, etc.; ~′**master**, official who pays troops, workmen, etc., (often fig.); ‖**Paymaster General**, minister at head of department of Treasury through which payments

are made; ~ **off**, pay in full and discharge or be quit of (ship's crew, creditor, debt, etc.), (colloq.) yield good results, succeed; ~*-off n.*, (sl.) act of payment, climax, final reckoning; ~ (person) **out** or **back**, punish him or be revenged on him; ‖~**-packet** (containing employee's wages); *~* **phone**, coin-box telephone; ~**-roll**, list of employees receiving regular pay; *pay the* PIPER, *through the* NOSE; ~ **up**, pay full amount of (arrears, or abs.; *paid-up member*, one who has made all necessary payments for membership). **4**. ~′**able** *a*. (-bly), that must or may be paid; ~**ee**′ *n*., person to whom money is (to be) paid; ~′**ment** *n*., paying, amount paid, (fig.) recompense. [F f. L *paco* appease (PEACE)]

‖**P.A.Y.E.** *abbr*. pay-as-you-earn.

**payo′la** *n*. Bribe(ry) offered in return for deliberate help in promoting commercial product by unsanctioned means. [PAY]

**P.C.** *abbr*. police constable; Privy Councillor.

**p.c.** *abbr*. per cent; postcard.

**pd.** *abbr*. paid.

**p.d.q.** *abbr*. (sl.) pretty damn quick.

**P.E.** *abbr*. physical education.

**pea** *n*. Hardy climbing leguminous plant whose seeds grow in pods and are used for food; its seed (**green ~s**, the seeds gathered unripe for food; **SPLIT** *peas*; **as like as two ~s (in a pod)**, indistinguishable); similar plant (CHICK-PEA, SWEET *pea*); ~**-green**, colour of green peas; ~**nut**, (plant whose fruit is a pod containing) seed used as food and yielding oil (~*nut butter*, paste of ground roasted peanuts; ~**nuts**, sl., paltry thing, esp. small amount of money); ~**-shooter**, toy tube from which dried peas are shot by blowing; ~ **soup** (made from esp. dried peas); ~**-sou′per**, (colloq.) thick yellow fog. [PEASE taken as *pl.*]

**peace** *n*. Freedom from or cessation of war (**make ~**, bring it about); *a* treaty of peace between powers at war; freedom from civil disorder (**the king's** or **queen's ~, the ~**, general peace of the realm as secured by law); quiet, tranquillity, (**hold** one's ~, keep silence); mental calm; *~***P~ Corps**, organization of young people to work in developing countries; ~′**maker**, one who brings about peace; **~-offering**, propitiatory or conciliatory gift; **~-pipe**, tobacco-pipe as token of peace among N. Amer. Indians; **~-time**, period when country is not at war; **at ~**, in state of friendliness or quietness, not at strife (*with*); **keep the ~**, prevent, or refrain from, strife; **make one's ~**, bring oneself back into friendly relations (*with*); **~'able** (-sa-) *a.* (**-bly**), disposed or tending to peace, free from disturbance, peaceful; **~'ful** (-sf-) *a.* (**-lly**), characterized by peace, belonging to state of peace, not violating or infringing peace. [F f. L *pax pac-*; ~*able* ult. f. L (PLEASE)]

**peach**[1] *v.i.* (sl.) Turn informer, inform (*against* or *on* accomplice). [obs. *appeach* (IMPEACH)]

**peach**[2] *n.* Large fruit, usu. round, with downy white or yellow skin flushed with red, highly flavoured sweet pulp, and rough stone; **~ (-tree)**, tree bearing this; (sl.) person or thing of superlative merit, attractive young woman; **~ Melba**, confection of ice cream and peaches [person]; **~'ÿ** *a.* (of flavour, colour of cheeks, etc.; sl., excellent). [F f. L *persica* Persian (apple)]

**pea'côck** *n.* Male peafowl, bird with splendid plumage and tail that can be expanded erect like fan (often as the type of ostentatious display; *proud as a peacock*); **~ (blue)**, lustrous blue of peacock's neck; **pea-chick**, young peafowl; **pea'fowl**, kind of pheasant, a peacock or peahen; **pea'hen**, female of peafowl; **~erÿ** *n.*, strutting vanity, piece of personal adornment. [*pea* (E f. L *pavo*), COCK[1]]

**pea-jäckĕt** *n.* Sailor's short double-breasted overcoat of coarse woollen cloth. [Du. *pijjakker*]

**peak**[1] *v.i.* Waste away (*peak and pine*); (in *p.p.*) sharp-featured, pinched; **~'ÿ**[1] *a.* (**-iness**), sickly, puny. [orig. unkn.]

**peak**[2]. **1.** *n.* Pointed top, esp. of mountain; point, e.g. of beard or hair (WIDOW'S *peak*); projecting part of brim of cap; highest point in curve or record of fluctuations (**~ hour**, time of most intense traffic etc.; **~-load**, maximum of electric power demand etc.); (Naut.) narrow part of ship's hold esp. at bow (*forepeak*) or stern (*after-peak*); upper outer corner of sail extended by

gaff. **2.** *v.i.* Reach highest value, quality, etc. **3. ~ed** (-kt), **~'ÿ**[2], *adjs.* [rel. to PICK]

**peal. 1.** *n.* Loud ringing of bell(s), esp. series of changes on set of bells; set of bells; loud outburst of sound, esp. of thunder or laughter. **2** *v.i.* & *t.* Sound forth in peal; utter sonorously; ring (bells) in peals. [APPEAL]

**pear** (pār) *n.* Fleshy fruit tapering towards stalk; **~-tree** (bearing this). [E, ult. f. L *pirum*]

**pearl**[1] (pêrl). **1.** *n.* Concretion, usu. white or bluish-grey, formed within shell of **~-oyster** or other bivalve mollusc, having beautiful lustre and highly prized as gem, imitation of this, (MOTHER-*of-pearl*; SEED-*pearl*); precious thing, finest example (*of* its kind; **cast ~s before swine**, offer good thing to one incapable of appreciating it); pearl-like thing, e.g. dewdrop, tear, tooth; **~ barley** (reduced by attrition to small rounded grains); **~ button**, of (imitation) mother-of-pearl; **~-diver** (who dives for pearl-oysters); **~ lamp**, frosted-glass electric-light bulb; **~ onion**, very small onion used in pickles. **2.** *v.t.* & *i.* Fish for pearls; form pearl-like drops; sprinkle with pearly drops. **3. ~'ÿ** (*a.*; **-iness**) resembling a pearl, containing pearls or mother-of-pearl, adorned with pearls, (P~y Gates, of Heaven; ‖~y king, queen, costermonger, his wife, wearing pearlies, (*n.*; in *pl.*) ‖costermongers' clothes decorated with mother-of-pearl buttons. [F f. Rom. *perla*]

**pea'sant** (pĕ'z-) *n.* Countryman, rustic, worker on the land, esp. labourer or small farmer; **~rÿ** *n.*, the peasants of a district etc. [AF *paisant* (*païs* country)]

**pease** (-z) *n.* (arch.) Peas (esp. **~-pudding**, pudding of boiled peas, eggs, etc.). [E *pise* f. L *pisa*]

**peat** *n.* (Cut piece of) vegetable matter decomposed in water and partly carbonized, used for fuel; **~'bog**, **~'moss**, bog composed of peat; **~'ÿ** *a.* (**-iness**). [perh. Celt., rel. to PIECE]

**pĕ'bble** *n.* Small stone worn and rounded by action of water (**not the only ~ on the beach**, not without competitors to be reckoned with); **~-dash**, mortar with pebbles in it as a coating for wall; **pĕ'bblÿ** *a.* (**-iness**). [E]

**pĕca'n** n. (Pinkish-brown smooth nut of) a hickory of the Mississippi region. [Algonquian]

**pĕ'cc|able** a. (-bly). Liable to sin; ~**abi'lity** n.; ~**adĭllŏ** n. (pl. -oes, -os), trifling offence, venial sin; ~**ant** a., sinning (lit. or fig.); ~**ancў** n. [F f. L pecco to sin]

**pĕ'ccary** n. American gregarious wild pig. [Carib]

**pĕck**[1] n. Measure of capacity for dry goods, = 2 gallons or 8 quarts; vessel used for this; **a** ~ (large number, amount) of trouble(s). [AF]

**pĕck**[2]. **1.** v.t. & i. Strike (thing) with beak (~**'ing order**, social hierarchy, orig. as observed among domestic fowls); ~ **out**, pluck out thus); make (hole) thus; strike at (thing) with beak; (fig.) carp at; kiss hastily or perfunctorily; (colloq.) eat (food, or abs.) esp. in nibbling or listless fashion. **2.** n. Stroke with beak, mark made with this; hasty or perfunctory kiss. **3.** ~**'er** n.; ‖**keep your ~'er up**, (sl.) maintain your courage; ~**'ish** a., (colloq.) hungry. [prob. LG]

**pĕ'ctĭn** n. (Chem.) Soluble gelatinous carbohydrate derivative acting as setting agent in jams and jellies. [Gk (pēgnumi make solid)]

**pĕ'ctoral. 1.** a. (~**ly**). Of or for the breast or chest; good for chest disease; worn on the breast; ~ **cross** (worn thus by bishop etc.); ~ **fin** (on side of fish). **2.** n. Ornamental breastplate esp. of Jewish high priest; pectoral fin, medicine, etc. [F f. L (pectus -tor- chest)]

**pĕ'cul|ate** v.t. & i. Embezzle (money); ~**ā'tion**, ~**ātor**, ns. [L (foll.)]

**pĕcu'liar** a. Belonging exclusively to; belonging to the individual, esp. one's own peculiar (character etc.); particular, especial, (a point of peculiar interest); strange, odd, (a peculiar flavour; he has always been a little peculiar); ~**ĭtў** (-ă'r-) n., being peculiar, characteristic, oddity. [L (peculium private property f. pecu cattle)]

**pĕcu'nĭar|ў** a. (~**ily**). (Consisting) of money (pecuniary aid, considerations); (of offence) having money penalty. [L (pecunia money f. pecu cattle)]

**pĕ'dagŏg|ue** (-g) n. (arch. or derog.) Schoolmaster, teacher; ~**ў**, ~**ĭcs**, (-ŏg-, -ŏj-) ns., science of

teaching; **pĕdagŏ'gĭc(al)** (or -ŏ'g-) adjs.; ~**(u)ĭsm** (-gĭ-) n. [L f. Gk (pais paid- boy, agō lead)]

**pĕ'dal** n., a., & v. **1.** n. (Mus., in organ) each of wooden keys played by feet; foot-lever in organ, piano, or harp, or in various machines, esp. for transmitting power to wheel of bicycle (~ **cycle**) or tricycle. **2.** (-ě'-) a. (Anat., Zool.). Of feet or foot **3.** v.t. & i. (‖-ll-). Play on organ pedals; work cycle pedals; ride bicycle; work (cycle) by pedals. [F f. L (pes ped- foot)]

**pĕ'dant** n. One who overrates or parades book-learning or technical knowledge or insists on strict adherence to formal rules; doctrinaire; **pĕdă'ntĭc** a. (-ically); ~**rў** n. [F f. It.]

**pĕ'ddle** v.i. & t. Follow occupation of pedlar; sell as pedlar; (fig.) deal out in small quantities, retail; busy oneself with trifles; *~**er** n.,= PEDLAR. [back-form. f. PEDLAR; in sense 'trifle' orig. var. PIDDLE]

**pĕ'derăst**, **pae'd-**, n. One who commits pederasty; ~**ў** n., sodomy with a boy. [L f. Gk (pais paid- boy, erastēs lover)]

**pĕ'destal** n. Base supporting column or pillar; base of statue etc. (put on a ~, fig., regard as highly admirable or important); each of two supports of knee-hole table; foundation (lit. or fig.); ~ **table** etc. (with single central support). [F piédestal f. It. = foot of stall]

**pĕdĕ'strian. 1.** a. Going or performed on foot; of walking; for walkers (~ **crossing**, part of road where pedestrians going across have priority over traffic; pedestrian PRECINCT); prosaic, dull. **2.** n. One who walks in street etc.; one who walks as athletic performance, whence ~**ĭsm** n. [F or L (PEDAL)]

*** pēdĭă'trĭc** etc. See PAEDIATRIC etc.

**pĕ'dĭcure. 1.** n. Care or treatment of feet, esp. of toe-nails; person who practises this. **2.** v.t. Treat (feet) by removing corns etc. [F f. L pes foot, curo to care]

**pĕ'dĭgree** n. Genealogical table; ancestral line (of man or animal); derivation (of word); ancient descent; (attrib.) having a recorded line of descent (pedigree cattle). [pedegru f. F pied de grue crane's foot, grees]

**pĕ'dĭment** n. Triangular part crowning front of building in Greek style, esp. over portico; similarly placed member in other styles. [*periment*, perh. corrupt. PYRAMID]

**pĕ'dlar** n. Travelling vendor of small wares usu. carried in pack; (fig.) retailer (*of* gossip etc.). [alt. obs. *pedder* f. dial. *ped* pannier]

**\*pĕdŏ-.** See PAEDO-.

**pĕdŏ'mĕter** n. Instrument' for estimating distance travelled on foot by recording number of steps taken. [F (L *pes ped-* foot; -METER)]

**pĕdŭ'ncle** (-ŭ'ngkl) n. (Bot.) stalk of flower, fruit, or cluster, esp. main stalk bearing solitary flower or subordinate stalks; ~**ŭlar**, ~**ŭlate**, adjs. [L *pedunculus* (prec.)]

**pee.** (colloq.) **1.** v.i. Urinate. **2.** n. Urination; urine. [PISS]

**peek** v.i., & n. Peep (*in, out*, etc.); (take) quick or sly look. [orig. unkn.]

**peel. 1.** n. Rind, outer coating, of fruit, potato, etc.; **candied** ~ (usu. of citrus fruits, used in cookery etc.). **2.** v.t. & i. Strip the peel, rind, bark, etc., from (orange, potato, tree, etc.); take *off* (skin, peel, etc.); (of tree, animal body, etc.) become bare of bark, skin, etc.; (of bark, surface, etc.) come off or *off* like peel; (sl., of person) strip for exercise etc.; keep one's EYES peeled; ~**'ĭng** n., (esp.) piece peeled off. [E f. L *pilo* strip of hair]

**peep¹. 1.** v.i. Look furtively or through narrow aperture (*at, into,* etc.); (of daylight, flower, distant object) come (*out*) slowly or partly into view, emerge; (fig., of quality etc.) show itself unconsciously; ~**ing Tom,** voyeur. **2.** n. Furtive or peering glance; first appearance, esp. *of* dawn or *day*; ~**-hole,** small hole to peep through; ~**-show,** small exhibition of pictures etc. viewed through lens in small orifice. [orig. unkn.]

**peep²** v.i., & n. (Make) feeble shrill sound (as) of young birds, mice, etc.; chirp, squeak. [imit.]

**peer¹** v.i. Look searchingly (*into, at,* etc.); appear, peep out. [orig. unkn.]

**peer²** n. Equal in civil standing or rank (*jury of his peers*); equal in any respect (*you will not easily find his peer*); ~ **group,** person's associates of same status as he); member of one of the

degrees (duke, marquis, earl, viscount, baron) of nobility in United Kingdom (LIFE *peer*; ~ **of the realm,** of class whose adult members may all sit in House of Lords); noble of any country; ~**'age** n., the peers, nobility, aristocracy, rank of peer or peeress (LIFE *peerage*), book containing list of peers; ~**'ĕss** n., peer's wife, female holder of peerage; ~**less** a., unequalled. [F f. L *par* equal]

**peev|e** n. (sl.) Cause of annoyance, mood of vexation; ~**ed** (-vd) a., (sl.) irritated, annoyed; ~**'ĭsh** a., querulous, irritable. [orig. unkn.]

**pee'wĭt.** See PEWIT.

**pĕg. 1.** n. Pin or bolt of wood, metal, etc., usu. round and slightly tapering, for holding together parts of framework etc., stopping up vent of cask, hanging hats etc. on, holding rope of tent, tightening or loosening string of violin etc., marking cribbage score, etc.; ||drink, esp. of spirits; ~**-board,** board with holes and pegs, esp. for game, as toy, or for commercial displays; ~**-leg,** (wearer of) artificial leg; ~**'top,** pear-shaped spinning-top with metal peg; **a** ~ **to hang** (discourse etc.) **on,** suitable occasion, pretext, or theme, for; ||CLOTHES-*peg;* **off the** ~, (of clothes) ready-made; *square peg in round* HOLE; **take** person **down a** ~ (or two), humble him. **2.** v.t. & i. (-gg-). Fix (thing *down, in, out,* etc.) with peg; (St. Exch.) prevent price of (stock etc.) from falling (or rising) by freely buying (or selling) at given price; stabilize (prices etc.); mark (score) with pegs on cribbage-board (**level** ~**ging,** even scores, lit. or fig.); mark *out* boundaries of (mining claim etc.); ~ (*away*), work persistently (*at*); ~ **down,** restrict (*to* rules etc.); ~ **out,** (Croquet) hit peg with ball as final stroke in game, (sl.) die. [prob. LDu.]

**P.E.I.** abbr. Prince Edward Island.

**pĕ'jorătĭve** (or pĭjŏ'r-) a. & n. Depreciatory (word). [F f. L (*pejor* worse)]

**Pĕkin(g)ē'se** (-z) n. & a. (Inhabitant) of *Pekin(g)* in China; small short-legged snub-nosed dog with long silky hair (colloq. abbr. **pĕke**). [place]

**pĕlărgō'nĭum** n. Plant with showy flowers and usu. fragrant leaves. [L f. Gk *pelargos* stork]

**pĕlf** n. (usu. derog. or joc.) Money, wealth. [F, rel. to PILFER]

**pĕ'lĭcan** n. Large gregarious water-fowl with pouch in bill for storing fish, fabled to feed its young with its own blood; ‖~ **crossing** (with traffic lights operated by pedestrians). [E & F f. L f. Gk]

**pĕlĭ'sse** (-ē's) n. Woman's mantle with armholes or sleeves, reaching to ankles; fur-lined mantle or cloak, esp. as part of hussar's uniform. [F f. L *pellicia* (cloak) of fur (*pellis* skin)]

**pĕllă'gra** n. Deficiency disease with cracking of skin. [It. *pelle* skin]

**pĕ'llĕt** n. Small ball of paper, bread, etc.; pill; small shot. [F *pelote* f. Rom. (L *pila* ball)]

**pĕ'llĭcle** n. Thin skin; membrane; film. [F f. L dim. (*pellis* skin)]

**pĕll-mĕ'll** adv. In disorder, confusedly; headlong, recklessly. [F *pêle-mêle*]

**pĕllū'cĭd** (or -ōō'-) a. Transparent, not distorting image or diffusing light; clear in style or expression or thought. [L (PER-)]

**pĕ'lmĕt** n. Valance or pendent border (esp. over window or door to conceal curtain rods). [prob. F]

**pĕlō'ta** n. Basque game with ball and wicker basket in walled court. [Sp., = ball]

**pĕlt**[1]. 1. v.t. & i. Assail with missiles (lit. or fig.); strike repeatedly with missiles; (of rain etc.) beat with violence; run fast. 2. n. Pelting; (at) full ~, as fast as possible. [orig. unkn.]

**pĕlt**[2] n. Skin of sheep or goat with short wool on; undressed skin of fur-bearing animal; raw skin of sheep etc. stripped of wool or fur; (joc.) human skin; ~'rў n., furs and skins. [F, ult. f. L *pellis* skin]

**pĕ'lv|ĭs** n. (pl. ~es pr. -ēz, ~ises). Basin-shaped cavity formed by bones of haunch with sacrum and other vertebrae; ~ĭc a. [L, = basin]

**pĕn**[1]. 1. n. Quill-feather with quill pointed and split in two, for writing with ink; similar instrument of steel, gold, etc., fitted into ~'holder of wood, plastic, etc., (BALL[1]-, FELT[1], FOUNTAIN-, pen; put pen to PAPER); (style of) writing (made a living with his pen; the pen is mightier than the sword); ~ and ink, (instruments of) writing; ~-and-ink a., drawn or written with these; ~friend, friend with whom one corresponds without

meeting; ~'knife, small knife usu. carried in pocket; ~'man, author, one who writes a (good, bad, etc.) hand; ~'manship, skill in writing, style of handwriting, action or style of literary composition; ~name, literary pseudonym; ~pal, (colloq.) = pen-friend; ~pusher, -pushing, clerical work(er). 2. v.t. (-nn-). (Compose and) write (letter etc.) [F f. L *penna* feather]

**pĕn**[2]. 1. n. Small enclosure for cows, sheep, poultry, etc. 2. v.t. (-nn-). Enclose, shut up or in; shut up (cattle etc.) in pen. [E]

**pĕn**[3] n. Female swan. [orig. unkn.]

**pē'nal** a. (~ly). Of punishment; concerned with inflicting this (penal laws); (of offence) punishable, esp. by law; inflicted as punishment (~ servitude, Hist., imprisonment with compulsory labour); inflicted as if by way of punishment (penal taxation); used as place of punishment (a penal colony); ~ĭze v.t., make or declare (action) penal, subject to penalty or comparative disadvantage. [F or L (*poena* penalty)]

**pĕ'nalt|ў** n. Punishment, esp. payment of sum of money, for breach of law, rule, or contract, money thus paid, (on or under penalty of dismissal etc.; the ~ of, disadvantage resulting from); disadvantage imposed on competitor in sports etc. for breaking rule or winning previous contest; ~ (bully, corner, kick, shot), action in various games allowed as redress to side against which foul has been committed; ~ area, (Assoc. Footb.) part of ground in front of goal in which foul by defenders involves award of penalty kick; **pĕ'nance** n., act of self-mortification as expression of penitence, esp. one imposed by priest, (do penance, perform such act).

**pĕnce.** See PENNY.

**penchant** (pah'nshahn) n. Inclination, liking, (for). [F]

**pĕ'ncil.** 1. n. Instrument for drawing or writing, esp. of graphite, chalk, etc., enclosed in cylinder of wood or metal etc. case with tapering end; similarly shaped device used as cosmetic etc.; ~sharpener, device with cutting edge for sharpening pencil by rotation. 2. v.t. (‖-ll-). Write with pencil; write tentatively. [F *pincel* f. L *penicillum* paint-brush]

**pĕ'ndant, -ent. 1.** a. (usu. -ent).

Hanging, overhanging; undecided, pending. 2. *n.* (usu. **-ant**). Hanging ornament, esp. one attached to necklace, bracelet, etc.; (Naut.) = PEN-NANT; (or *pr.* pah´ńdahń) match, parallel, companion, complement, (*to*). 3. **pĕ´ndency** *n.*, state of awaiting settlement. [F pres. part. of *pendre* hang]

**pĕ´nding.** 1. *a.* Undecided, awaiting decision or settlement, (*a suit was then pending*); about to come into existence (*patent pending*); ~**-tray** (to contain documents awaiting decision). 2. *prep.* During (*pending these negotiations*); until (*pending his return*). [after F (prec.)]

**pĕ´ndŭl|ous** *a.* Suspended, drooping, hanging down; oscillating; ~**um** *n.*, body suspended so as to be free to swing, esp. rod with weighted end regulating movement of clock's works (**the swing of the** ~**um**, tendency to alternation of power between political parties, or to oscillation of public opinion between extremes). [L *pendulus* (*pendeo* hang)]

**pĕ´nĕtr|āte** *v.t.* & *i.* (~**able**). Find access into or through, pass through; permeate; imbue (*with*); (fig.) see into, find out, discern, (person's mind, meaning, design, the truth); (of sight) pierce through (darkness, thicket, etc.); make a way (*into, through, to*); ~**abi´lĭty** *n.*; ~**āting** *a.*, (esp.) gifted with or suggestive of insight, (of voice etc.) easily heard through or above other sounds; ~**ā´tion** *n.*, (esp.) acute insight; ~**ātĭve** *a.*; ~**ātor** *n.* [L]

**pĕ´nguin** (-nggwĭn) *n.* Flightless sea-fowl of S. hemisphere with wings developed into flippers for swimming under water. [orig. unkn.]

**pĕnĭci´llĭn** *n.* Antibiotic of group produced naturally on moulds, able to prevent growth of certain disease bacteria. [L (PENCIL)]

**pĕnī´nsŭl|a** *n.* Piece of land almost surrounded by water or projecting far into the sea; ~**ar** *a.*, of (the nature of) a peninsula. [L (*paene* almost, *insula* island)]

**pĕ´nĭs** *n.* (*pl.* ~**es**, pe´nes *pr.* -ēz). Copulatory and (in mammals) urinary organ of male animal. [L]

**pĕ´nĭt|ent** *a.* & *n.* Repentant (sinner); person doing penance under direction of confessor; ~**ence** *n.*; ~**e´ntial** (-shal) *a.* (-lly); of penitence or penance; ~**e´ntiary**

(-sherĭ), (*n.*) *reformatory prison, (*a.*) of penance, of reformatory treatment. [F f. L (*paeniteo* repent)]

**Penn(a).** *abbr.* Pennsylvania.

**pĕ´nnant** *n.* (Naut.) tapering flag, esp. that flown at mast-head of vessel in commission; = PENNON. [blend of PENDANT and PENNON]

**pĕ´nnĭless** *a.* Having no money; poor, destitute. [PENNY]

**pĕ´nnon** *n.* Long narrow flag, triangular or swallow-tailed, esp. as military ensign of lancer regiments; long pointed streamer of ship. [F f. L *penna* feather]

**pĕ´nnў** *n.* (*pl.* usu. **pennies** for separate coins, **pence** for sum of money). British bronze coin worth 1/100 of pound; monetary unit represented by this, abbr. *p.*; (Hist.) British bronze coin worth 1/240 of pound, monetary unit represented by this, abbr. *d.*; **like a bad** ~, repeatedly present when not desired; **the** ~ **drops**, understanding dawns; **pennies from heaven**, unexpected benefits; *an* HONEST *penny*; **in for a** ~, **in for a pound**, thing once begun must be concluded at all costs; **in** ~ **numbers**, in small quantities at a time; **a pretty** ~, a large sum of money; SPEND *a penny*; **take care of the pence**, be economical in small outlays; **a** ~ **for your thoughts** (said to person deep in thought); **two a** ~, almost worthless though readily obtainable; ~ **black**, first adhesive postage stamp (U.K., 1840, value 1d., printed in black); *penny* DREAD*ful*; ‖~ **farthing**, (colloq.) old type of high bicycle; ~**-pinching**, (*n.*) niggardliness, (*a.*) niggardly; ~**weight**, unit of weight, 24 grains, 1/20 ounce troy; *penny* WHISTLE; ~ **wise**, (over-)careful in small expenditures, esp. *penny wise and pound foolish*, careful in small but wasteful in large matters; ~**wort**, plant with rounded leaves; ~**worth**, **penn´orth**, (pĕ´nĭ-wĕrth, pĕ´ner̄th), as much as can be bought for a penny (*not a pennyworth*, not the least bit). [E]

**pĕ´nnўroyal** *n.* Creeping species of mint cultivated for supposed medicinal virtues. [AF *puliol real* royal thyme]

**pēnŏ´log|ў** *n.* Study of punishment and of prison management; **pēnŏ-lŏ´gĭcal** *a.* (-lly); ~**ĭst** *n.* [L *poena* penalty]

**pĕ′nsile** *a.* Hanging down, pendulous; (of bird etc.) building pensile nest. [L (*pendeo pens-* hang)]

**pĕ′nsion**[1] (-shon). **1.** *n.* Periodic payment esp. by government, company, or employer, in consideration of past service or on retirement etc., or by government to person above specified age (*old-age pension*), widow, disabled person, etc. **2.** *v.t.* Grant pension to; ~ **off**, dismiss with pension, cease to employ (lit. or fig.). **3.** ~**able** *a.*, entitled or (of services etc.) entitling person to pension; ~**ary** *a.* & *n.*, (recipient) of pension; ~**er** *n.*, recipient of (esp. old-age) pension, ‖(Camb. Univ.) student without financial support from college. [F f. L (*pendo pens-* weigh)]

**pension**[2] (pah′ńsyawn). *n.* European boarding-house providing all or some meals at fixed rate; *live* **en** (prec.) ~, as boarder. [F (prec.)]

**pĕ′nsive** *a.* Plunged in thought. [F (*penser* think)]

**pĕnt** *a.* Closely confined, shut *in* or *up* (*pent-up fury*). [PEN[2]]

**pĕ′nta-** in *comb.* Five; ~**cle** *n.*, figure used as symbol, esp. in magic, e.g. pentagram; **pĕ′ntăd** *n.*, group of 5; ~**gon** *n.*, plane figure with 5 sides and angles (**\*the P~gon**, 5-sided Washington headquarters of leaders of U.S. defence forces); ~**gonal** (-ă′g-) *a.*; ~**grăm** *n.*, 5-pointed star formed by producing sides of pentagon both ways until they meet, formerly used as mystic symbol; ~**mĕter** (-ă′-) *n.*, line of 5 metrical feet; ~**prĭsm** *n.*, pentagonal prism used in viewfinder to get constant deviation of all rays of light through 90°; **P~teuch** (-k) *n.*, first 5 books of O.T. [Gk *teukhos* book]; ~**thlon** (-ă′-) *n.*, athletic contest comprising 5 different events for competitor; ~**tŏ′nĭc** *a.*, of 5-note musical scale. [Gk (*pente* 5)]

**Pĕ′ntĕcŏst** *n.* Jewish harvest festival on 50th day after 2nd day of Passover; Whit Sunday; **p~ŏ′stal** *a.* [E & F f. L f. Gk *pentēkostē* fiftieth (day)]

**pĕ′nthouse** (-t-h-) *n.* (*pl. pr.* -zĭz). Sloping roof, esp. as subsidiary structure attached to wall of main building; house or flat on roof of tall building. [F *apentis* f. L (APPEND)]

**pĕntstē′mon** (*or* pĕ′ntstĕ-) *n.* Bright-flowered garden plant. [PENTA-, Gk *stēmōn* stamen]

**pĕnŭ′lt** (*or* pē′-) *a.* & *n.* Last but one (page of syllable); **pĕnŭ′ltimate** *a.* & *n.*, last (syllable) but one. [L (*paene* almost, *ultimus* last)]

**pĕnŭ′mbr|a** *n.* (*pl.* ~**ae**, ~**as**). Partly shaded region round shadow of opaque body, esp. of moon or earth in eclipse; partial shadow; ~**al** *a.* [L (*paene* almost, UMBRA)]

**pĕ′nŭrў** *n.* Destitution, poverty; lack, scarcity, (*of*); **pĕnŭ′rious** *a.*, poor, scanty, grudging, stingy. [L]

**pĕ′on** (*or* pūn) *n.* (Ind. etc.) office-messenger, attendant; (Sp. Amer.) day-labourer. [PAWN[1]]

**pĕ′onў** *n.* Garden plant with large globular red, pink, or white flowers, in cultivation often double. [E f. L f. Gk]

**peo′ple** (pē′pel). **1.** *n.* Persons composing community, tribe, race, or nation, (*the English people*; *English-speaking peoples*; *a warlike people*); (as *pl.*) persons belonging to a place or forming a company or class etc., subjects of king etc., congregation of parish priest etc., armed followers, retinue, workers, parents or other relatives (*his people will be pleased*), *the* persons not having special rank or position in a country etc., persons in general (*people don't like to be kept waiting*); (as *sing.* or *pl.*) *the* body of enfranchised or qualified citizens. **2.** *v.t.* Fill with people, populate; fill (place *with* animals etc.); (of persons, animals, etc.) inhabit, occupy, fill, (esp. in *p.p.*; *a thickly peopled country*). [AF f. L *populus*]

**pĕp.** (sl.). **1.** *n.* Vigour, spirit; ~ **pill** (containing stimulant drug); ~ **talk**, exhortation to activity or courage. **2.** *v.t.* (-pp-). Fill with vigour, ginger *up.* **3.** ~′**pў** *a.*, (sl.) full of pep. [abbr. foll.]

**pĕ′pper. 1.** *n.* Pungent aromatic condiment got from dried berries of certain plants used whole or ground into powder when unripe (**black** ~) or when either ripe or husked (**white** ~); (fig.) anything pungent; capsicum plant; its fruit, used unripe (**green** ~) or ripe (**red** ~) as vegetable or source of condiment, (**sweet** ~, one with relatively mild taste); ~**-and-salt**, cloth of dark and light threads woven together, showing small dots of dark and light intermingled; ~**box**, small usu. round box with perforated lid for sprinkling pepper; ~**corn**, dried

pepper-berry esp. as nominal rent;
~-**mill** (for grinding peppercorns by
hand); ~-**pot**, pepperbox. 2. *v.t.*
Sprinkle or treat (as) with pepper;
pelt with missiles. 3. ~**mint** *n.*,
species of mint grown for its essential
oil, (lozenge or sweetmeat flavoured
with) this oil; ~**y** *a.* (-ily, -iness),
of, like, abounding in, pepper, (fig.)
pungent, hot-tempered. [E f. L *piper*
f. Gk f. Skr.]

**pĕ′p|sĭn** *n.* Enzyme contained in
gastric juice; ~**tĭc** *a.* (-ically), digestive; ~**tĭc ulcer** (in stomach or
duodenum). [G, f. Gk *pepsis* diges-
tion]

**pĕr** *prep.* Through, by, by means or
instrumentality of, (*per post, bearer*);
for each (*two pounds per man; five miles
per hour*); **as** ~, in accordance with
(*as per instructions*; **as** ~ **usual**, joc.,
as usual). [L]

**per-** *pref.* Through, all over, (*perforate, pervade*); completely, very,
(*perturb*); to destruction, to the bad,
(*pervert, perdition*). [L (prec.)]

**peradvĕ′nture** (or pĕr-; arch. or
joc.). 1. *adv.* Perhaps; **if, lest,** ~, if,
lest, it chance that. 2. *n.* Uncertainty,
chance, conjecture; doubt (*beyond or
without a peradventure*). [F (PER,
ADVENTURE)]

**perǎ′mbŭl|āte** *v.t. & i.* Walk
through, over, or about (streets,
country, etc.), or from place to
place; ~**ā′tion** *n.*; ‖~**ātor** *n.*, =
PRAM; ~**ātorў** *a.* [L *perambulo*
(AMBLE)]

**pĕr ǎ′nnum** *adv.* For each year. [L]

**percā′le** *n.* Closely woven cotton
fabric. [F]

**percei′ve** (-sē′v) *v.t.* Apprehend
with the mind, observe, understand,
(circumstance, *that, how*, etc.); apprehend through one of the senses, esp.
sight. [F f. L *percipio -cept-* seize,
understand]

**pĕr cĕ′nt(.),** *percĕ′nt. 1. *adv.* In
every hundred. 2. *n.* Percentage; one
part in every hundred (*half a per
cent*); **percĕ′ntage** *n.*, rate or proportion per cent, proportion (*only a
small percentage of books are worth
reading*). [PER, CENT]

**percĕ′pt|ĭble** *a.* (-bly). That can
be perceived by senses or intellect;
~**ĭbĭ′lĭtў** *n.*; ~**ĭon** *n.*, act or faculty
of perceiving, instinctive recognition
(*of truth, aesthetic quality*, etc.),
(Philos.) action by which the mind
refers its sensations to external object

as cause; ~**ĭve** *a.*, having or concerned in perception, discerning;
**pĕrcĕptī′vĭtў** *n.* [F or L (PERCEIVE)]

**pĕrch**[1]. 1. *n.* Horizontal bar for
bird to rest on; anything serving for
bird etc. to rest on; (fig.) elevated or
secure position; measure of length
esp. for land, 5½ yds.; (**square**) ~,
30¼ sq. yds. 2. *v.i. & t.* Alight or rest
like bird (*on* bough etc.); (esp. in *p.p.*)
place (as) on perch (*town perched on a
hill*). 3. ~**′er** *n.*, one of large class of
passerine birds with feet adapted for
perching. [F f. L *pertica* pole]

**pĕrch**[2] *n.* (*pl.* ~, ~**′es**). Spiny-
-finned freshwater food-fish. [F f. L
*perca* f. Gk]

**percha′nce** (-ah′-) *adv.* (arch.) By
chance; possibly, maybe. [AF (*par
by*)]

**percĭ′pĭen|t. 1.** *a.* Perceiving,
conscious; ~**ce** *n.* 2. *n.* One who per-
ceives esp. something outside range
of senses. [L (PERCEIVE)]

**pĕr′col|āte** *v.i. & t.* (Of liquid, or
fig.) filter, ooze, *through*, permeate;
(of person or strainer) strain (liquid,
powder) through pores etc.; prepare (coffee) by repeated downward
passage of boiling water through
ground beans; ~**ā′tion** *n.*; ~**ātor** *n.*,
(esp.) strainer of coffee-pot, coffee-
-pot with this. [L (*colum* sieve)]

**pĕr cŏ′ntra** *adv.* On the opposite
side (of account, assessment). [It.]

**percŭ′ssion** (-shon) *n.* Forcible
striking of one (usu. solid) body
against another; (Med.) gentle
tapping of body with finger or instrument for diagnosis etc.; (Mus.) playing by striking (*percussion band,
instrument*), group of such instruments
in orchestra; ~ **cap**, small metal or
paper device in (real or toy) firearm,
containing explosive powder and
exploded by fall of hammer; **per-
cŭ′ssĭve** *a.* [F or L (*percutio -cuss-*
strike)]

**perdĭ′tion** *n.* Damnation; eternal
death. [F or L (*perdo -dit-* destroy)]

**pĕ′rĕgrĭn|āte** *v.i. & t.* (arch. or
joc.) Travel, journey, (~**ā′tion**,
~**ātor**, *ns.* [L (foll.)]

**pĕ′rĕgrĭne** *n.* ~ (**falcon**), kind of
falcon much used for hawking. [L
*peregrinus* foreign]

**perĕ′mptor|ў** (or pĕ′rĭm-) *a.*
(~**ĭly**, ~**ĭness**). (Of statement or
command) admitting no denial or
refusal; (of person etc.) dogmatic,

imperious, dictatorial. [AF f. L *peremptorius* deadly, decisive]

**perĕ′nnial** (-nyal). **1.** *a.* (~ly). Lasting through the year; lasting long or for ever; (of plant) living several years (cf. ANNUAL). **2.** *n.* Perennial plant. [L *perennis* (*annus* year)]

**pĕr′fĕct** *a., n.,* & *v.* **1.** *a.* Complete, not deficient; faultless; thoroughly trained or skilled (*in* duties etc.); (colloq.) exceedingly satisfactory; exact, precise, (*a perfect* SQUARE, *circle*); entire, unqualified, (*a perfect stranger; perfect nonsense*); (Mus., of interval) that is fourth, fifth, or octave in major or minor scale of its lower note; (Gram., of tense) denoting completed event or action viewed in relation to the present. **2.** *n.* Perfect tense. **3.** (or perfĕ′kt) *v.t.* Complete, carry through; make perfect; improve. **4.** perfĕ′ctible *a.*; perfĕctibi′lity *n.*; perfĕ′ction *n.*, making perfect, full development, faultlessness (**to** ~ion, exactly, completely), comparative excellence, perfect person or thing, highest pitch or extreme or perfect specimen or manifestation (*of* quality etc.); perfĕ′ctionist *n.*, one who holds that perfection can or must be attained; ~lў *adv.*, (esp.) quite, completely. [F f. L *perficio* -*fect*- to complete]

**perfĕr′vid** *a.* Very fervid. [L (FERVID)]

**pĕr′fĭdў** *n.* Breach of faith, treachery; **perfĭ′dious** *a.* [L *perfidia* (*fides* faith)]

**pĕr′forāte** *v.t.* & *i.* (~able). Make hole(s) through, pierce, esp. make rows of holes in (sheet) to help to separate stamps, coupons, etc.; make opening into; pass or extend through; penetrate (*into, through,* etc.); ~ā′tion, ~ātor, *ns.* [L *perforo* pierce through]

**perfor′ce** *adv.* Unavoidably, necessarily. [F *per* (= by) *force*]

**perfor′m** *v.t.* & *i.* Carry into effect, be agent of, (command, promise, task); go through, execute, (public function, play, piece of music); act in play; play, sing, etc., ~ance *n.*, execution (*of* command etc.), carrying out, doing, notable or (colloq.) ridiculous action, performing of play etc., achievement under test; ~er *n.*, (esp.) one who performs before audience; ~ing *a.* (~ing arts, those

such as drama that require public performance). [AF (FURNISH)]

**pĕr′fūme. 1.** *n.* (Sweet) smell; fluid containing essence of flowers etc., scent. **2.** (or perfū′m) *v.t.* (esp. in p. p.) Impart sweet scent to. **3.** perfū′mer *n.*, maker or seller of perfumes; perfū′merў *n.* [F f. It. *parfumare* smoke through]

**perfŭ′nctor|ў** *a.* (~ily, ~iness). Done merely for sake of getting through a duty, acting thus, superficial, (*a perfunctory inspection, inquirer*). [L (FUNCTION)]

**pĕr′gola** *n.* Arbour or covered walk formed of growing plants trained over trellis-work. [It.]

**perhă′ps** (or prăps) *adv.* It may be, possibly, (*he has perhaps lost it; perhaps you would like to see it?*). [HAP]

**pĕ′ri-** *pref.* Round, about. [Gk]

**pĕ′riănth** *n.* Outer part of flower. [F (Gk *anthos* flower)]

**pĕ′ridŏt** *n.* Green variety of olivine, esp. as precious stone. [F]

**pĕ′rigee** *n.* Point (in orbit of moon etc.) that is nearest to earth. [F f. L f. Gk (*gē* earth)]

**pĕrĭhē′li|on** (or -lyon) *n.* (*pl.* ~a). Point of orbit nearest to sun. [L (Gk *hēlios* sun)]

**pĕ′ril** *n.* Danger; **in** ~ **of** (in danger of losing) one's *life* etc.; *you do it* **at your** ~, if you do it you take the risk; *keep off* **at your** ~ (take the risk if you do not); ~ous *a.* [F f. L *periculum*]

**perĭ′mēter** *n.* Circumference or outline of closed figure; length of this; outer boundary of camp, fortification, airfield, etc. [F f. L f. Gk (-METER)]

**pĕrĭnē′|um** *n.* (Anat.) Region between anus and scrotum or vulva; ~al *a.* [L f. Gk]

**pĕr′iod. 1.** *n.* Interval between recurrences of a phenomenon; distinct portion of history, life, etc.; (Geol.) time forming part of era; any portion of time (*showers and bright periods; spread the work over a period*); time allocated for lesson in school; time during which disease etc. runs its course; (time of) occurrence of menstruation; *the* part of history under discussion, or the present day, (*the girl, costume, catchwords, of the period*); complete sentence, esp. one consisting of several clauses; (in *pl.*) rhetorical language; full pause at end of sentence; = FULL[1] *stop*; (appended to statement, stressing its completeness; *we want the best, period*). **2.** *a.* (Esp. of furniture, dress, architecture) belonging to or characteristic of a particular (past) period. **3.** **pĕrĭŏ′dĭc** *a.* (-ically), (esp.) recurring at regular intervals; ~**ic table,** (Chem.) arrangement of elements by atomic number, with regular recurrence of properties; **pĕrĭŏ′dĭcal,** (*a.*; -**lly**) recurring at regular intervals, (*a.* & *n.*) (magazine) published at regular intervals; ~**ĭ′cĭt y** *n.*, recurrence at intervals. [F f. L f. Gk (*hodos* way)]

**pĕrĭpătĕ′tĭc. 1.** (*P*~) *a.* & *n.* Aristotelian [f. Aristotle's custom of walking while teaching]. **2.** *a.* (~**ally**). Going from place to place on one's business, itinerant. [F or L f. Gk (*pateō* walk)]

**pĕrī′phĕr y** *n.* Bounding line esp. of round surface; outer or surrounding surface or region; ~**al** *a.* (-**lly**), of periphery, of minor importance. [L f. Gk (*pherō* bear)]

**pĕrī′phrăs is** *n.* (*pl.* ~**es** *pr.* -ēz). Roundabout way of speaking or phrase, circumlocution; **pĕrĭphră′s tĭc** *a.* (-ically). [L f. Gk (PHRASE)]

**pĕ′rĭscōpe** *n.* Apparatus with tube and mirrors by which observer in trench, submerged submarine, rear of crowd, etc., can see things otherwise out of sight; ~**ŏ′pĭc** *a.*, of periscope(s), (of lens) allowing distinct vision over wide angle. [-SCOPE]

**pĕ′rĭsh** *v.i.* & *t.* Suffer destruction, lose life or normal qualities; come to untimely end; (of cold or exposure) reduce to distress or inefficiency (*we were perished with cold*; *in perishing cold*); ~ **the thought!,** I sincerely hope it will not be so; ~**able,** (*a.*) liable to perish, subject to speedy decay, (*n.*; in *pl.*) things (esp. foodstuffs in transit) subject to this; ||~**er** *n.*, (sl.) annoying person; ||~**ĭng** *a.* & *adv.*, (sl.) confounded(ly). [F f. L *pereo*]

**pĕrĭton e′um** *n.* (*pl.* ~**e′ums,** ~**e′a**). Membrane lining cavity of abdomen; ~**e′al** *a.*; ~**ī′tĭs** *n.*, inflammation of peritoneum. [L f. Gk (*peritonos* stretched round)]

**pĕ′rĭwĭg** *n.* (esp. Hist.) Wig. [alt. PERUKE]

**pĕ′rĭwĭnkle**[1] *n.* Evergreen trailing plant with blue or white flowers; their blue colour. [AF f. L *pervinca*]

**pĕ′rĭwĭnkle**[2] *n.* Winkle. [orig. unkn.]

**pĕr′jur e** (-jer) *v.refl.* ~**e** oneself, swear falsely; (in *p.p.*) guilty of or involving perjury; ~**ў** *n.*, swearing to statement one knows to be false, wilful utterance of false evidence while on oath. [F f. L (*juro* swear)]

||**pĕrk**[1] *n.* (colloq.; usu. in *pl.*). Perquisite. [abbr.]

**pĕrk**[2] *v.t.* & *i.* (colloq.) Raise (head etc.) briskly; smarten *up*; ~ (**up**), recover or restore confidence or courage (of); ~**ў** *a.* (~**ily,** ~**iness**), self-assertive, saucy, lively, cheerful. [orig. unkn.]

**pĕrm** *n.*, & *v.t.* (colloq.) (Give) permanent wave (to); (make) permutation (of). [abbr.]

**pĕr′mafrŏst** (*or* -awst) *n.* Subsoil remaining below freezing-point throughout year in polar regions. [foll.]

**pĕr′manen t** *a.* Lasting, intended to last or function, indefinitely (opp. *temporary*); ~**t magnet** (retaining its power without continued excitation); ~**t wave,** artificial wave in hair intended to last for some time; ||~**t way,** finished road-bed of railway; ~**ce** *n.*, duration or permanent quality; ~**cў** *n.*, (esp.) permanent thing or arrangement. [F, or L *permaneo* remain to the end]

**pĕr′me āte** *v.t.* & *i.* Penetrate throughout, pervade, saturate; diffuse itself *among, through,* etc.; ~**able** *a.* (-**bly**), admitting passage of fluid etc.; ~**abĭ′lĭtў** *n.*; ~**ā′tion** *n.* [L *permeo* pass through]

**Pĕr′mian** *a.* & *n.* (Of) latest Palaeozoic period or system, above Carboniferous. [*Perm,* place]

**permĭt. 1.** (-ĭ′-) *v.t.* & *i.* (-tt-). Give consent or opportunity (for) (*permit me to say*; *appeals are permitted*; *permit him access to it*); give opportunity (*weather permitting*); admit of (alteration, delay, etc.). **2.** (-ĕ′-) *n.* Written order giving permission to act, esp. for entry into a place, landing or removal of dutiable goods, etc.; permission. **3.** **permĭ′ssĭble** *a.* (-**bly**); **permĭssĭbĭ′lĭtў** *n.*; **permĭ′ssĭon** (-shon) *n.*, consent or liberty (*to* do); **permĭ′ssĭve** *a.*, giving permission, tolerant, liberal, esp. in sexual matters, (*the permissive society*). [L *permitto -miss-* allow]

**pĕrmŭtā′tion** *n.* Variation of order

of set of things; any one such arrangement; (pop.) combination or selection of specified number of items from larger group (esp. of matches in football pool); **permū́te** v.t., alter sequence or arrangement of. [F or L *permuto* change thoroughly]

**perni'cious** (-shŭs) a. Destructive, ruinous, fatal; ~ **anaemia** (severe progressive freq. fatal form). [L (*pernicies* ruin)]

**perni'ckĕtў** a. (colloq.) Fastidious, (over-)precise. [orig. unkn.]

**pĕ'ror|āte** v.i. Sum up and conclude speech; speak at length; ~ā́tion, ~ātor, ns. [L (*oro* speak)]

**perŏ'xide. 1.** n. Compound of oxygen with another element containing maximum proportion of oxygen; (**hydrogen**) ~, colourless liquid used in water solution (esp.) to bleach hair. **2.** v.t. Bleach (hair) with peroxide. [PER-]

**pĕrpĕndi'cŭlar. 1.** a. At right angles to plane of horizon; (of ascent, cliff) very steep; erect, upright; (joc.) in standing position; (Geom.) at right angles (*to* given line, plane, or surface); **P~ style,** (Archit.) third stage of English Gothic (15th–16th cc.), with vertical tracery in large windows; ~itў (-ǎ'r-) n. **2.** n. Perpendicular line; plumb-rule or other instrument for showing perpendicular line; **the ~,** perpendicular line or direction; *is out of* (*the*) ~, is not straight up and down. [L *perpendiculum* plumb-line]

**pĕ'rpĕtr|āte** v.t. (~able). Perform, commit, (crime, blunder, pun or other thing viewed as outrageous); ~ā́tion, ~ātor, ns. [L *perpetro* perform]

**perpĕ'tū|al** a. (-lly). Eternal; permanent during life; applicable or valid for ever or for indefinite time; continuous; (colloq.) frequent, repeated (*this perpetual nagging*); ~al **calendar** (that can be used for any year or over a long period); ~al **check,** (Chess) position where draw is obtained by repeated checking of king; *perpetual* CURATE; ~al **motion** (of hypothetical machine running for ever unless subject to external forces or wear); ~āte v.t. (~able), make perpetual, preserve from oblivion; ~ā́tion, ~ātor, ns.; **perpĕtū'itў** n., quality of being perpetual (**in, to, for,** ~ity, for

ever), perpetual possession or position or annuity. [F f. L *perpetuus* continuous]

**perplĕ'x** v.t. Bewilder, puzzle, (person, his mind); complicate, confuse (matter); ~ĕdly adv.; ~itў n., bewilderment, thing that bewilders. [F, or L *perplexus* involved]

**pĕr prō.** abbr. By proxy, through an agent. [L *per procurationem*]

**pĕr'quisite** (-z-) n. Casual profit additional to normal revenue or emolument; thing that has served its primary use and to which subordinate or servant has then a customary right; incidental benefit attaching to employment etc.; customary gratuity; (fig.) thing to which person has sole right. [L *perquiro* -*quisit*- search diligently for]

‖**pĕ'rrў** n. Drink made from fermented pear-juice. [F *peré* (PEAR)]

**per se** (pē'sē', -sā') adv. By or in itself, intrinsically. [L]

**pĕr'sĕcūte** v.t. Pursue with enmity and ill-treatment; subject to penalties on grounds of religious or political beliefs; harass, worry; importune (person with questions etc.); ~ū́tion n. (~ution mania, insane delusion that one is persecuted); ~ūtor n. [F f. L (*persequor* -*secut*-pursue)]

**pĕrsĕvēr'|e** v.i. Continue steadfastly, persist, (in course of action, *in* doing, *with* task, or abs.); ~ance n. [F f. L (SEVERE)]

**Pĕr'sian** (-shǎn) a. & n. (Native, language) of Persia (Iran); ~ (**cat**), breed of cat with long silky hair; ~ **lamb,** silky curled fur of young karakul. [F f. L (*Persia*)]

**pĕr'siflage** (-ahzh) n. Light raillery, banter. [F]

**persi'mmon** n. (Edible orange plumlike fruit of) an Amer. or E. Asian tree. [Algonquian]

**persi'st** v.i. Continue firmly or obstinately (*in* opinion, course of action, doing) esp. against obstacles, remonstrance, etc.; (of institution, custom, phenomenon, etc.) continue in existence, survive; ~ence, ~encў, ns.; ~ent a. [L (*sisto* stand)]

**pĕr'son** n. Individual human being (*a cheerful and forthright person*; *found a friend in the person of his landlord*); living body of human being (*he had a fine person*; *acting, appearing,* **in** (**his own**) ~, himself, personally); God as Father or Son or Holy Ghost;

character in play or story; (Gram.) one of three classes of personal pronouns, verb-forms, etc., denoting respectively person etc. speaking (**first ~**), spoken to (**second ~**), or spoken of (**third ~**). [F f. L (foll.)]

**perso͞o'na** n. (pl. ~**e**, ~**s**). Aspect of personality as perceived by others; ~ **grata** (grā'ta, -ah'-), person (esp. diplomat) acceptable to certain others; ~ **non grata** (nŏn), person not acceptable. [L, = actor's mask]

**pĕr'son**|**able** a. Handsome, comely, pleasing by one's appearance and demeanour; ~**age** n., person of rank or importance, person, character in play etc. [PERSON]

**pĕr'sonal** a. One's own, individual, private, (to suit his personal convenience; personal EQUATION, TOUCH; this is personal to myself); of the body (one's personal appearance, hygiene); done, made, etc., in person (personal service, acquaintance, interview); directed or referring to an individual (personal call, letter, abuse, remarks); (given to) making personal remarks (do not let us become personal); of, existing as, a person (a personal God); (Gram.) of or denoting one of the three persons, esp. personal PRONOUN; ~ **column**, part of newspaper devoted to short (semi-)personal advertisements; ~ **estate, property,** all property except land and those interests in land that pass to one's heirs; ~**ĭtў** (-ă'l-) n., being a person, personal existence or identity, distinctive personal character (SPLIT personality), person (esp. celebrity), (in pl.) personal remarks; ~**ĭze** v.t., personify, make personal esp. by marking with owner's name etc.; ~**lў** adv., in person, in one's own person, (he conducted them personally; writ was served on him personally), for one's own part (personally, I see no objection); ~**tў** n., personal estate; **pĕr'sonāte** v.t., play the part of (character in drama, or fig.), pretend to be (person) esp. for fraudulent purpose; **pĕrsonā'tion, pĕr'sonātor,** ns.; **perso͞o'nĭfў** v.t., attribute personal nature to (abstraction, thing), symbolize (quality) by figure in human form, (esp. in p.p.) embody in one's own person or typically exemplify (quality); **pĕrsonĭficā'tion** n., (esp.) person or thing viewed as striking example or embodiment of (quality etc.). [F f. L (PERSONA)]

**pĕr'sonnĕ'l** n. Body of persons employed in public undertaking, armed forces, factory, office, etc.; ~ **department** (for appointment, advising, training, etc., of employees). [F, = prec.]

**perspĕ'ctive. 1.** n. Art of delineating solid objects on plane surface so as to give same impression of relative positions, magnitudes, etc., as the actual objects do when viewed from particular point; picture so drawn; apparent relation between visible objects as to position, distance, etc.; (fig.) relation in which parts of subject are viewed by the mind; view, prospect, (lit. or fig.); **in ~**, drawn or viewed (lit. or fig.) according to rules of perspective. **2.** a. Of or in perspective. [L (perspicio -spect- look at)]

**Pĕr'spĕx, p-,** n. A tough light transparent plastic. [P; prec.]

**pĕrspĭc**|**ā'cious** (-shŭs) a. Having mental penetration or discernment; ~**ă'cĭtў** n. [L perspicax (PERSPECTIVE)]

**perspĭ'cūous** a. Easily understood, clearly expressed; (of person) expressing things clearly; **pĕrspĭcū'ĭtў** n. [L (as prec.)]

**perspīr'e** v.i. & t. Sweat; **pĕrspīrā'tion** n., sweat(ing). [F f. L (spiro breathe)]

**persuā'|de** (-sw-) v.t. Cause (person, oneself) to have belief (of fact, that thing is so); induce (person to do, into action); (in p.p.) convinced (of thing, that); ~**der** n., (esp., sl.) gun etc.; ~**sĭble** a.; ~**sion** (-zhon) n., (esp.) belief, conviction, religious belief, sect holding this (he is of the Roman Catholic persuasion); ~**sĭve** a., able to persuade. [L persuadeo -suas-induce]

**pĕrt** a. Saucy or impudent in speech or conduct; (of clothes etc.) neat and suggestive of jauntiness. [F apert f. L apertus open]

**pertai'n** v.i. Belong as part, appendage, or accessory, to; be appropriate to; have reference or relate to. [F f. L pertineo belong to]

**pĕrtĭn**|**ā'cious** (-shŭs) a. Stubborn, persistent, obstinate, (in a course of action etc.); ~**ă'cĭtў** n. [L pertinax (prec.)]

**pĕr'tĭnen**|**t** a. Pertaining, relevant, apposite, (to matter being considered etc.); to the point; ~**ce, ~cў,** ns. [F or L (PERTAIN)]

**pertur'b** *v.t.* Throw into confusion or disorder; disturb mentally; agitate; **perturbā'tion** *n.* [F f. L]

**peru'ke** (-ōō'k) *n.* (esp. Hist.) Wig. [F f. It.]

**peru'se** (-ōō'z) *v.t.* Read, esp. thoroughly or carefully; (fig.) examine (person's face etc.) carefully; **~al** *n.* [USE]

**Peru'vian** (-ōō'-). **1.** *a.* Of Peru; **~ bark** of (cinchona tree). **2.** *n.* Native of Peru. [L *Peruvia* Peru]

**pervā'|de** *v.t.* Spread through, permeate, saturate, (lit., or fig. of influences etc.); be rife among or through; **~sion** (-zhon) *n.*; **~sive** *a.* [L *pervado* penetrate]

**perver'|se** *a.* Persistent in error; different from what is reasonable or required; wayward; peevish; perverted, wicked; (of verdict) against weight of evidence or judge's direction; **~sity** *n.*; **~t,** (*v.t.*; **~tible**) turn aside (thing) from proper use or nature, misapply (words etc.), lead astray (person, mind) from right opinion or conduct or esp. religious belief, (in *p.p.*) showing perversion, (pĕr'-; *n.*) perverted person, apostate, person showing perversion of sexual instincts; **~sion** (-shon) *n.*, (esp.) preference of another form of sexual activity to normal intercourse. [F f. L (*verto vers-* turn)]

**per'vious** *a.* Affording passage (*to*); permeable; (fig.) accessible (*to* reason etc.). [L (*via* road)]

**pese'ta** (-sā'-) *n.* Spanish coin and currency unit. [Sp.]

***pe'sky** (-sk) *a.* (colloq.) Troublesome, annoying. [orig. unkn.]

**pe'so** (pā'-) *n.* (*pl.* **~s**). Silver coin and currency unit in several Latin-Amer. countries and in Philippines. [Sp.]

**pe'ssary** *n.* (Med.) Instrument worn in vagina to prevent uterine displacements or as contraceptive; vaginal suppository. [L f. Gk]

**pe'ssim|ism** *n.* Tendency to look at worst aspect of things (opp. OPTIMISM); doctrine that the actual world is the worst possible, or that all things tend to evil; **~ist** *n.*; **~i'stic** *a.* (**-ically**). [L *pessimus* worst]

**pĕst** *n.* Troublesome, annoying, or destructive person, animal, or thing; (arch.) pestilence, plague; **~'er** *v.t.*, trouble, annoy, importune, (*kept pestering me for an interview*), [prob. of diff. orig. but now assoc. w. *pest*]; **~'icide** *n.*, substance for destroying pests (esp. insects); **~i'ferous** *a.*, noxious, pestilential, (fig.) pernicious; **~'ilence** *n.*, fatal epidemic disease, esp. bubonic plague; **~'ilent** *a.*, destructive to life, deadly, (fig.) injurious to morals etc., (colloq.) troublesome, annoying, **~ilĕ'ntial** (-shal) *a.* (**-lly**), of pestilence, pestilent; **~'ology** *n.*, scientific study of pests (esp. harmful insects) and of methods of dealing with them. [F, or L *pestis* plague]

**pe'stle** (-sel) *n.* Club-shaped instrument for pounding substances in a mortar. [F f. L *pistillum* (*pinso* pound)]

**pĕt¹** *n., a., & v.* **1.** *n.* Animal tamed and kept as favourite or treated with fondness; darling, favourite. **2.** *a.* Kept as pet (*pet lamb*); of or for pet animals (*pet food, shop*); favourite (**~ aversion** etc., joc., thing or person particularly disliked); expressing fondness or familiarity (*pet-form* of name etc., *pet name*). **3.** *v.t.* (**-tt-**). Treat as pet; fondle (esp. person of opposite sex erotically; or abs.). [orig. unkn.]

**pĕt²** *n.* Offence at being slighted, ill-humour, (*be in a pet*); **~'tish** *a.*

**Pet.** *abbr.* Peter (N.T.).

**pe'tal** *n.* Each division of corolla of flower; **~led** (-ld) *a.* [L f. Gk *petalon* leaf]

**petär'd** *n.* (Hist.) Small bomb used to break down door etc. by explosion (HOIST *with* one's own *petard*). [F]

**Pēte** *n.* **For ~'s sake,** (sl.) for God's sake. [abbr. foll.]

**Pē'ter¹** *n.* BLUE Peter; **~ Pan,** person who retains youthful features etc. and seems not to age; **~ Pan collar** (flat, with rounded ends); **rob ~ to pay Paul,** take away from one to give to another, discharge one debt by incurring another. [man's Christian name]

**pē'ter²** *v.i.* **~ out,** (of stream, vein of ore, or fig.) give out, come to an end. [orig. unkn.]

**pē'tersham** *n.* Thick ribbed silk ribbon. [person]

**pē'tiole** *n.* (Bot.) Leaf-stalk. [F f. L]

***petit*** (petē') *a.* **~ four** (foor'), very small fancy cake etc.; **~ mal** (mah'l), mild form of epilepsy; **~ point** (pwăn), embroidery on canvas using small stitches, tent-stitch; **~e**

(-ĕ't; of woman) of small dainty build. [F, = little]

**pĕtĭ'tion. 1.** *n.* Asking, supplication, request; formal written request from one or more persons to sovereign etc., or (Law) to court for writ, order, etc. **2.** *v.t. & i.* Make petition to (sovereign etc. *for* thing, *to do*); ask humbly (*for* thing, *to* be allowed to do etc.). [F f. L (peto petit- ask)]

**pĕ'trel** *n.* Kind of sea-bird which flies far from land; **storm(y) ~**, small black and white long-winged petrel of N. Atlantic, (fig.) person causing unrest. [orig. unkn.]

**pĕ'trĭf̄ÿ** *v.t. & i.* Turn into stone (lit. or fig.); (fig.) paralyse or stupefy with astonishment, terror, etc.; **~ă'ction** *n.* [F f. L (petra f. Gk, = rock)]

**pĕtrŏchĕ'mĭcal** (-k-) *n.* Substance industrially obtained from petroleum or natural gas. [Gk petra rock]

**pĕ'trodŏllar** *n.* Dollar available in petroleum-exporting country. [PETROLEUM]

‖**pĕ'trol** *n.* Refined petroleum used as fuel in motor vehicles, aircraft, etc.; **~-pump**, machine for transferring this esp. from underground reservoir to tank in motor vehicle. [F pétrole f. L (foll.)]

**pĕtrō'lĕum** *n.* Hydrocarbon oil found in upper strata of earth, refined for use as fuel for heating and in internal combustion engines, as dry-cleaning agent, etc.; **~ jelly**, translucent solid mixture of hydrocarbons got from petroleum and used as lubricant etc. [L f. Gk petra rock + L oleum oil)]

**pĕ'ttĭcoat** *n.* Woman's or child's undergarment hanging from waist or shoulders (*she is a Cromwell in* **~s**, in all but her sex); woman or girl; (*attrib.*) feminine; **~ government**, predominance of women in the home or in politics. [petty coat]

**pĕ'ttĭfŏggĭng** (-g-) *a.* Practising legal chicanery; quibbling or wrangling about petty points. [orig. uncert.]

**pĕ'ttĭsh.** See PET[2].

**pĕ'ttÿ** *a.* (**-ily**, **-iness**). Unimportant, trivial; contemptible; minor, inferior, on a small scale, (*petty princes*); **~ cash**, (money for) small cash items of receipt or expenditure; *petty* JURY; **~ officer**, naval N.C.O.; *petty* SESSIONS. [F PETIT]

**pĕ'tŭlan|t** *a.* Peevishly impatient

or irritable; **~ce** *n.* [F f. L (peto seek)]

**pĕtŭ'nĭa** *n.* Plant with funnel-shaped flowers of vivid purple, white, red, etc.; dark violet or purple colour. [F petun tobacco]

**pew** *n.* (In church) enclosed compartment or fixed bench with back; (colloq.) seat (*take a pew*). [F f. L PODIUM]

**pĕ'wĭt, pee'-,** *n.* Kind of plover named from its cry. [imit.]

**pew'ter** *n.* Grey alloy of tin with lead or other metal; utensil(s) of this. [F peutre]

**peyō't|ĕ** (pā-) *n.* (Hallucinogenic drug prepared from) a Mexican cactus. [Amer. Sp., f. Nahuatl]

**pfĕ'nnĭg** *n.* Small German coin, worth 1/100 of a mark. [G]

**P.G.** *abbr.* paying guest.

**phă'gocȳte** *n.* Leucocyte etc. capable of absorbing foreign matter, esp. bacteria, in the body. [Gk phageat, kutos cell]

**phală'nger** (-nj-) *n.* Austral. & N.Z. arboreal marsupial with webbed hind feet. [F f. Gk phalaggion spider's web]

**phă'lăn|x** *n.* (*pl.* **~xes**, **~ges** *pr.* -njēz). (Gk Ant.) line of battle, esp. body of infantry drawn up in close order; set of persons etc. forming compact mass, or banded together for common purpose. [L f. Gk]

**phă'll|us** *n.* (*pl.* **~i** *pr.* -i, **~uses**). Image of (erect) penis, venerated in some religions as symbol of generative power; **~ĭc** *a.* [L f. Gk]

**phă'ner|ogăm** *n.* Plant having pistils and stamens, flowering plant; **~ogă'mĭc, ~ŏ'gamous,** *adjs.* [F f. Gk phaneros visible, gamos marriage]

**phă'n|tăsm** *n.* Illusion, phantom; supposed vision of absent (living or dead) person; **~tă'smal** (-z-) *a.* (**-lly**); **~tăsmagŏr'ĭa** (-z-) *n.,* shifting scene of real or imagined figures; **~tăsmagŏ'rĭc** (-z-) *a.*; **~tasȳ** *n.,* see FANTASY. [F f. L (foll.)]

**phă'ntom. 1.** *n.* (Mere) apparition, spectre; image (*of*); vain show, form without substance or reality; mental illusion. **2.** *a.* Merely apparent, illusive. [F f. L f. Gk phantasma]

**Phār'aoh** (fār'ō) *n.* Title of ruler of ancient Egypt. [L f. Gk f. Heb. f. Egypt.]

**Phă'rĭs|ee** *n.* One of ancient-Jewish sect distinguished by strict observance of traditional and written law; self-righteous person, hypocrite; ~ã'ĭc(al) *adjs.* (-ically); ~ãĭsm *n.* [E & F f. L f. Gk f. Aram. f. Heb.]

**phãrmac|eu'tĭcal** *a.* Of, engaged in, pharmacy; of use or sale of medicinal drugs; ~eu'tĭcs *n.*; ~ĭst *n.*, person engaged in pharmacy; ~ŏ'logў *n.*, science of action of drugs on the body; ~olŏ'gĭcal *a.* (-lly); ~ŏ'logĭst *n.*; ~opoe'ia (-pē'a) *n.*, book (esp. one officially published) containing list of drugs with directions for use, stock of drugs; **phãr'macў** *n.*, preparation and (esp. medicinal) dispensing of drugs, pharmacist's shop, dispensary. [F f. L f. Gk (*pharmakon* drug)]

**phã'rўn|x** *n.* Cavity behind mouth and nose; ~gē'al *a.*, ~gi'tĭs *n.*, (-nj-). [L f. Gk]

**phāse** (-z). 1. *n.* Stage of change or development; aspect of moon or planet, according to amount of illumination (esp. new moon, first quarter, full moon, or last quarter); (Phys.) stage in periodically recurring sequence of changes, e.g. of alternating current or light-vibrations. 2. *v.t.* Carry out (programme etc.) in phases or stages; ~ **in**, **out**, bring gradually into, out of, use. [F f. L f. Gk *phasis* appearance]

**Ph.D.** *abbr.* Doctor of Philosophy. [L *philosophiae doctor*]

**phea'sant** (fĕz-) *n.* Long-tailed game-bird. [F *faisan* f. L f. Gk (*Phasis*, river)]

**phē'nŏl** *n.* Hydroxyl derivative of benzene used as antiseptic. [F]

**phĕnŏ'mĕn|on** *n.* (*pl.* ~**a**). Thing that appears or is perceived, esp. thing the cause of which is in question; remarkable person, thing, occurrence, etc.; ~**al** *a.* (-lly), of the nature of a phenomenon, perceptible (only) by the senses, concerned with phenomena, remarkable; ~**alĭsm** *n.*, doctrine that phenomena are the only objects of knowledge; ~ŏ'logў *n.*, science of phenomena. [L f. Gk (*phainō* show)]

**phew** *int.* expr. impatience, disgust, or relief. [imit.]

**phi** *n.* Twenty-first Gk letter (Φ, φ) = ph. [Gk]

**phi'al** *n.* Small glass bottle, esp. for liquid medicine. [F *fiole* f. L f. Gk]

**phĭl-.** See PHILO-.

**-phil, -phile**, *suf.* forming *ns.* & *adjs.* w. sense '(one who is) fond of',

as *bibliophil(e)*. [Gk *philos* dear, loving]

**Phil.** *abbr.* Philippians (N.T.).

**phĭlaдĕ'lphus** *n.* Kind of shrub, esp. mock orange. [L f. Gk]

**phĭlä'nder** *v.i.* Flirt with or *with* woman; flirt habitually. [Gk (*anēr andr-* man)]

**phĭlä'nthrop|ў** *n.* Love of all mankind; practical benevolence; **phĭlanthrŏ'pĭc** *a.* (-ically); ~ĭst *n.* [L f. Gk *anthrōpos* human being)]

**phĭla'tel|ў** *n.* Collection and study of postage stamps; **phĭlatĕ'lĭc** *a.*; ~ĭst *n.* [F f. Gk *atelēs* tax-free]

**-phile.** See -PHIL.

**Philemon.** *abbr.* Philemon (N.T.).

**phĭlharmŏ'nĭc** (or -lär-) *a.* Fond of music (*philharmonic society*). [F f. It. (HARMONIC)]

**phĭli'ppĭc** *n.* Bitter invective. [L f. Gk (*Philip*, person)]

**Phi'listine.** 1. *n.* Member of a people in ancient Palestine hostile to Israel; (or *p*~) uncultured person, one whose interests are material and commonplace, so **phĭ'listinĭsm** *n.* 2. (or *p*~) *a.* Uncultured, commonplace, prosaic. [F or L f. Gk f. Heb.]

**phĭlo-** in comb. (**phil-** bef. vowel or h). Liking, fond of. [Gk *philos* friend)]

**phĭlŏ'log|ў** *n.* Science of language; **phĭlolŏ'gĭcal** *a.* (-lly); ~ĭst *n.*; ~ĭze *v.i.* [F f. L f. Gk (LOGOS)]

**phĭloprogĕ'nĭtĭve** *a.* Prolific; loving one's offspring. [PROGENITOR]

**phĭlŏ'soph|ў** *n.* Seeking after wisdom or knowledge, esp. that which deals with ultimate reality, or with the most general causes and principles of things, physical phenomena (*natural philosophy*), and ethics (*moral philosophy*); higher learning in general (*doctor of philosophy*); philosophical system; system for conduct of life; serenity, calmness; ~**er** *n.*, seeker after wisdom, person skilled in philosophy or in one of its branches, one who regulates his life by philosophy or shows philosophic calmness in adversity, (~**er's' stone**, supreme object of alchemy, supposed to change other metals into gold or silver); **phĭlŏsŏ'phĭc(al)** *adjs.* (-ically), of or consonant with philosophy, skilled in or devoted to philosophy (*philosophical society*), wise, calm under adverse but irremediable circumstances; ~**ĭze** *v.i.*, play the philtre 664 photo-

philosopher, speculate, moralize. [F f. L f. Gk (*sophia* wisdom)]

**phi′ltre** (-ter), *phi′lter**, *n*. Drink supposed to be able to excite sexual love. [F f. L f. Gk (*phileō* love)]

**phleb|ī′tĭs** *n*. Inflammation of walls of vein; ~i′tic *a*. [Gk *phleps phleb-* vein]

**phlĕgm** (flĕm) *n*. Thick viscous substance secreted by mucous membranes of respiratory passages, esp. when morbid or excessive and discharged by cough etc.; (Hist.) this substance regarded as a HUMOUR; calmness, sluggishness; **phlĕgmă′tĭc** *a*. (-ically), not easily agitated, sluggish; ~y̆ *a*. (-iness). [F f. L f. Gk *phlegma*]

**phlogi′ston** (*or* -g-) *n*. Substance formerly supposed to exist in all combustible bodies, and to be released in combustion. [L f. Gk (*phlox phlog-* flame)]

**phlŏx** *n*. Plant with clusters of flowers of various colours. [L f. Gk (prec.)]

**-phōbe** *suf*. forming *ns*. & *adjs*. w. sense '(person) disliking or fearing' (*Anglophobe*); **phō′bĭa** *n*., (morbid) fear or aversion; **phō′bĭc** *a*. & *n*.; **-phō′bĭa** *suf*. forming abstract *ns*. corresp. to *adjs*. in *-phobe* (*xenophobia*); **-phō′bĭc** *adj. suf*. [L f. Gk (*phobos* fear)]

**Phoe′bus** (fē′b-) *n*. (poet.) The sun. [L f. Gk *Phoibos* sun-god]

**Phoeni′cian** (fĭnī′shan; *or* -nē′-) *a*. & *n*. (Inhabitant) of *Phoenicia* (ancient name for part of coast of Syria) or its colonies. [F f. L (place)]

**phoe′nix** (fē′-) *n*. (Myth.) bird, the only one of its kind, that burnt itself on pyre and rose from the ashes with renewed youth to live again; unique person or thing. [E & F f. Gk]

**phōne** *n*., & *v.i.* & *t*. (colloq.) Telephone; ~-in, broadcast programme during which listeners telephone and participate. [abbr.]

**phonĕ′tĭc** *a*. (~ally). Of or representing vocal sounds, esp. (of system of spelling) using always same symbol for same sound; ~s *n.pl*. (usu. treated as *sing*.), (study of) phonetic phenomena; **phonĕti′cian** (-shan), **phō′nĕtĭst**, *ns*.; **phō′nĭc** *a*. (-ically), of (vocal) sound. [L f. Gk (*phōneō* speak)]

**phō′ney**, **-ny̆**. (sl.) **1**. *a*. (-ier, -iest; -ily, -iness). Sham, counter-

feit, fictitious. **2**. *n*. Phoney person or thing. [orig. unkn.]

**phō′no-** *in comb*. Sound; ~**grăm** *n*., sound-record made by early gramophone; ~**graph** (-ahf) *n*., ‖early form of gramophone, *gramophone; ~**logy̆** (fonŏ′l-) *n*., study of sounds in a language; ~**lŏ′gĭcal** *a*. (-lly). [Gk *phōnē* voice, sound]

**phō′ny̆**. See PHONEY.

**phŏ′sph|āte** *n*. Salt or ester of phosphoric acid, esp. used as fertilizer; ~**īde** *n*., binary compound of phosphorous; ~**īte** *n*., salt or ester of phosphorous acid; ~**or** *n*., synthetic fluorescent or phosphorescent substance; ~**oré′sce** *v.i.*, show ~**oré′scence** *n*., radiation similar to fluorescence but detectable after excitation ceases, emission of light without combustion or perceptible heat; ~**oré′scent** *a*.; ~**ŏ′rĭc**, ~**orous**, *adjs*. (esp. Chem., having phosphorus in higher, lower, proportion); ~**orus** *n*., non-metallic element existing in allotropic forms, incl. a yellowish waxlike substance luminous in dark. [L f. Gk (*phōs* light, *-phoros* bringing)]

**phō′tō** *n*. (*pl*. ~s), & *v.t.* Photograph; ~ **finish**, close finish of race (photographed to enable judge to decide winner etc.), or of any contest. [abbr.]

**phō′tō-** *in comb*. Light; photography; ~**cŏpĭer** *n*., machine for photocopying documents; ~**cŏpy̆** *n*., & *v.t.*, (make) photograph of document for use as a copy; ~**ělĕ′ctrĭc** *a*. (-ically), with or using emission of electrons from substances exposed to light (~*electric cell*, device using this effect to generate current); ~**ělĕctrĭ′cĭty** *n*.; ~**gĕ′nĭc** *a*. (-ically), producing or emitting light, apt to be a good subject for photographs; ~**graph** (-ahf), (*n*.) picture taken by chemical action of light or other radiation on sensitive film, (*v.t.*) take photograph of (person etc., or abs.); ~**grapher**, ~**graphy̆** (-ŏ′g-) *ns*.; ~**gră′phĭc** *a*. (-ically); ~**gravū′re** *n*., picture produced from photographic negative transferred to metal plate and etched in [F *gravure* engraving]; ~**lĭthŏ′graphy̆** *n*. (with plates made by photography); ~**mēter** (-ŏ′m-) *n*., instrument for measuring light; ~**mě′trĭc** *a*. (-ically); ~**mĕtry̆** (-ŏ′m-) *n*.;

**phŏ′tŏn** n., quantum of electromagnetic radiation energy, proportional to frequency; **~sĕ′nsĭtive** a., reacting chemically etc. to light; **P~stăt** (P; n., & v.t.), photocopy; **~sȳ′nthĕsis** n., process in which energy of sunlight is used by green plants to form complex substances from carbon dioxide and water. [Gk *phōs phōt-* light]

**phrās|e** (-z). 1. n. Mode of expression, diction; an idiomatic expression; small group of words usu. without predicate, esp. preposition with word(s) it governs, equivalent to adjective, adverb, or noun (e.g. the house *on the hill*, I refuse *to do it*); short pithy expression; (Mus.) short more or less distinct passage; **~e-book** (listing frequent expressions with equivalents in foreign language for use by tourists etc.). 2. v.t. Express in words; divide (music) into phrases, esp. in performance. 3. **~′al** a. (Gram.), (-lly), consisting of phrase; **~ĕŏ′logȳ** n., choice or arrangement of words, mode of expression; **~ĕolŏ′gĭcal** a. (-lly). [L f. Gk *phrasis* (*phrazō* tell)]

**phrĕn|ĕ′tic** (-ically). = FRENETIC; **~ŏ′logȳ** n., study of external conformation of cranium as supposed index to development and position of organs belonging to various mental faculties; **phrĕnolŏ′gĭcal** a. (-lly); **~ŏ′logĭst** n. [F f. L f. Gk (*phrēn* mind)]

**phthi′s|ĭs** (*or* thī′-, tī′-) n. Progressive wasting disease, now esp. pulmonary tuberculosis; **phthi′sĭcal** (-z-; *or* thī′-, tī′-) a. (-lly), of or having phthisis. [L f. Gk (*phthinō* to decay)]

**phŭt. 1.** n. Dull sound of impact, collapse of inflated object, etc. **2.** adv. Go **~,** (colloq.) collapse (lit. or fig.). [Hindi *phaṭna* to burst]

**phȳlă′cterȳ** n. Small box with Heb. texts worn by Jews at prayer. [F f. L f. Gk (*phulassō* guard)]

**phȳ′l|um** n. (pl. **~a**). Major division of animal or plant kingdom. [L f. Gk *phulon* race]

**phȳ′sĭc** (-z-). **1.** n. Art of healing; medical profession; (arch.) medicine (*a dose of physic*). **2.** v.t. (-ck-). Dose with physic (lit. or fig.). [F f. L f. Gk (*phusis* nature)]

**phȳ′sĭcal** (-z-) a. (-lly). Of matter, material, (*physical force*, opp. to *moral*); of, according to the laws of,

nature (*a physical impossibility*); belonging to physics; bodily (*physical examination, strength, love, education*); **~ chemistry** (applying physics to study chemical behaviour); **~ geography** (dealing with natural features); **~ jerks,** (colloq.) physical exercises; **~ science,** study of inanimate natural objects. [L (prec.)]

**phȳsĭ′cian** (-zĭ′shan) n. One who practises the healing art; one legally qualified in both medicine and surgery; (esp.) specialist in medical diagnosis and treatment; (fig.) healer. [F (PHYSIC)]

**phȳ′sĭc|s** (-z-) n. Science dealing with properties and interactions of matter and energy; **~ist** n. [L *physica* (pl.) f. Gk (PHYSIC)]

**phȳsĭŏ′gnom|ȳ** (-zĭŏ′n-) n. Art of judging character from features of face or form of body; cast of features, type of face; external features of country etc.; **phȳsĭognŏ′mĭc(al)** (-zĭŏn-) adjs. (-ically); **~ist** n., expert or believer in physiognomy. [F f. L f. Gk (PHYSIC, GNOMON)]

**phȳsĭŏ′graph|ȳ** (-z-) n. Description of nature or natural phenomena, or of a class of objects; physical geography; **phȳsĭŏgră′phĭc(al)** (-z-) a. (-lly); **~er** n., expert in physiography. [F (PHYSIC, -GRAPHY)]

**phȳsĭŏ′log|ȳ** (-z-) n. Science of functions and phenomena of living organisms and their parts; these functions; **phȳsĭolŏ′gĭc(al)** (-z-) a. (-lly); **~ist** n. [F or L (PHYSIC, -LOGY)]

**phȳsĭothĕ′rap|ȳ** (-z-; *or* -ō-) n. Treatment of disease or injury or deformity by massage, heat, exercises, etc., not by drugs; **~ist** n., expert in physiotherapy. [PHYSIC, THERAPY]

**phȳsĭ′que** (-zē′k) n. Bodily structure, organization, and development. [F (PHYSIC)]

**pī** n. Sixteenth Gk letter (Π, π) = p; (Math., π) symbol of ratio of circumference of circle to diameter (approx. 3·14). [Gk]

**pia mā′ter** n. Delicate inner membrane enveloping brain and spinal cord. [L = tender mother]

**pĭa′n|ō¹** (-ah′-) a., adv., & n. (pl. **~os,** ~i pr. -ē). (Mus.) (Passage to be) performed softly; so **piani′ssĭmō** (very softly). [It. (-*issimo* superl.) f. L *planus* flat, (of sound) soft]

**pĭă′nō²** n. (pl. **~s**). Musical instrument with metal strings struck by hammers worked by levers from keyboard, with pedals regulating tone; **grand ~**, large full-toned piano with horizontal strings; **upright ~**, with vertical strings; **~-accordion**, accordion with melody played from small piano-like keyboard; **~-player**, pianist, contrivance for playing piano automatically; **pi'anist** (pē′a-) n., player of piano; **~fŏr'tè** n., (arch. or formal name for) piano; **P~la** (pēanō′-) n., kind of automatic piano-player [P]. [It. *piano* (*e forte*) soft (& loud)]

**pi'brŏch** (pē′brŏk) n. Martial or funeral bagpipe music. [Gael.]

**pi'ca** n. Unit of type-size (⅙ inch); size of letters in typewriting (10 per inch). [L (PIE¹)]

**pi'cadŏr** n. Mounted man with lance in bullfight. [Sp.]

**picare'sque** (-k) a. (Of style of fiction) dealing with adventures of rogues. [F f. Sp. *pícaro* rogue]

**\*picayu'ne** (-yōō′n). **1.** n. Small coin; (colloq.) insignificant person or thing. **2.** a. (colloq.) Mean, contemptible, petty. [F *picaillon*]

**piccali'lli** n. Pickle of chopped vegetables, mustard, and spices. [orig. unkn.]

**‖piccani'nny**, **\*pick-**, n. Small Black or Austral. Aboriginal child. [W. Ind. Negro, f. Sp. *pequeño* little]

**pi'ccolo** n. (*pl.* **~s**). (Player of) small flute, sounding an octave higher than the ordinary. [It., = small]

**pick. 1.** n. Tool consisting of iron bar usu. curved with point at one end and point or chisel-edge at other, with wooden handle passing through middle perpendicularly, used for breaking up hard ground, masonry, etc., and in quarries etc.; instrument for picking; plectrum; picking, selection; right to select (*he had first pick from the collection*); *the best part of* (**the ~ of the bunch**, the best of the lot). **2.** *v.t.* & *i.* Break surface of (ground etc.) (as) with pick; make (HOLES etc.) thus; probe (teeth with toothpick, nostril with finger, etc.) to remove unwanted matter; clear (BONE, carcass) of adherent flesh; detach (flower, fruit, etc.) from place where it grew; (of person) eat (food, or meal, or abs.) in small bits; select carefully (*pick* one's *words*, *way*, *steps*; *picked men*); pull apart (*pick* OAKUM; **~ to**

**pieces**, fig., criticize hostilely). **3. ~ and choose**, select carefully or fastidiously; **~ and steal**, pilfer; *pick a* QUARREL²; **~ at**, nag at, eat without interest; *pick* person's BRAINS; **~ lock**, open it (esp. with intent to rob) with pointed instrument; **~-me-up**, tonic (lit. or fig.) to relieve depression; **~ off**, pluck off, shoot (persons etc.) deliberately one by one; **~ on**, nag at, find fault with, select; **~ out**, take from larger number, distinguish from surrounding objects, relieve (ground colour *in* or *with* another), make out (meaning of passage etc.), play (tune) by ear on piano etc.; **~ over**, select best from; **~** person's **pocket**, steal its contents from him; **~'pocket**, one who steals thus; **~ up**, lay hold of and take up from ground etc., accept responsibility for paying (bill etc.), raise (feet) clear of ground, raise one*self* after fall etc., gain or acquire (livelihood, germ, knowledge of language, profit, tricks, information), succeed in seeing with telescope or searchlight, hearing with radio, etc., take (person, or thing overtaken) along with one, make acquaintance of (person) casually, regain (lost path etc.), recover health, (of weather, share-prices, etc.) improve, (of motor engine) recover speed or accelerate quickly etc.; **~-up** n., picking up, person met casually, small open motor truck, part of record-player carrying stylus, detector of vibrations etc. **4. ~'ings** (-z) *n.pl.*, gleanings, remaining scraps, perquisites, pilferings. [PIKE]

**pi'ck-a-bàck**, **\*pi'ggÿbàck** (-g-). **1.** *adv.* (Carried) on back or top of larger person or object. **2.** n. Ride thus given. [orig. unkn.]

**\*pickani'nnÿ**. See PICCANINNY.

**pi'ckàxe**, **\*-àx. 1.** n. = PICK (first sense). **2.** *v.t.* & *i.* Break (ground etc.), work, with pickaxe. [F, rel. to PIKE]

**pi'ckèt. 1.** n. Pointed stake or peg driven into ground to form palisade, tether horse, etc.; (Mil.) small body of troops sent out to watch for enemy etc., party of sentries, outpost; (usu. in *pl.*) person stationed by trade union to dissuade workers from working during strike etc. **2.** *v.t.* & *i.* Secure (place) with stakes; tether (animal); post as pickets; beset (factory, workers) with pickets; act as picket. [F (*piquer* prick)]

**pi'ckle. 1.** *n.* Brine, vinegar, or similar liquor in which food is preserved; food, esp. (in *pl.*) vegetables, preserved in pickle; (colloq.) plight (*in a pickle*). **2.** *v.t.* Preserve in or treat with pickle; (in *p.p.*, sl.) drunk. [LDu. *pekel*]

**Pickwi'ckian** *a.* (joc.) (Of words or their sense) not in accordance with usual meaning, conveniently understood so as to avoid offence etc. [*Pickwick*, character in Dickens]

**pi'cnic. 1.** *n.* Pleasure party including outdoor meal; (colloq.) something agreeable or easily accomplished (**no ~**, not an easy job). **2.** *v.i.* (**-ck-**). Take part in picnic. [F *pique-nique*]

**pi'cot** (pē'kō) *n.* Small loop of twisted thread in edging to lace etc. [F, dim. of *pic* peak, point]

**Pict** *n.* One of an ancient people in N. Britain. [L]

**pi'ctogr|aph** (-ahf), **~|ăm**, *ns.* Pictorial symbol; primitive record consisting of these, (**-ically**). [L *pingo pict-* to paint]

**pictōr'ial. 1.** *a.* (**~ly**). Of, expressed in, picture(s); illustrated. **2.** *n.* Journal, postage stamp, etc., with picture(s) as main feature. [L *pictor* painter (foll.)]

**pi'cture. 1.** *n.* Painting or drawing of person(s) or object(s) esp. as work of art; portrait; beautiful object (*her hat is a picture*); scene, total visual or mental impression produced, (**in the ~**, fully informed or noticed; **the very ~**, a perfect example *of health, of misery*); (visible presentation of) cinema film; image on television screen; ||(in *pl.*) cinema (performance); **~-book** (consisting chiefly or wholly of pictures); **~-card**, court-card; **~-gallery**, (hall etc. containing) collection of pictures; **~-goer**, one who frequents the cinema; **~ hat**, lady's wide-brimmed and highly decorated hat as in pictures by Reynolds and Gainsborough; *picture-*MOULD³*ing*; **||~-palace, -theatre**, cinema; **~ postcard** (with picture on one side); **~ window**, large window facing attractive view; **~-writing**, mode of recording events etc. by pictures as in early hieroglyphs etc. **2.** *v.t.* Represent in picture; describe graphically; imagine (*to oneself*). **3. pi'cturĕ'sque** (-kcherĕ'sk) *a.*, like, or fit to be subject of, a striking picture, (of language etc.) strikingly graphic, vivid. [L (*pingo pict-* to paint)]

**pi'ddl|e** *v.i.* Work or act in trifling way; (colloq. or childish) urinate; **~ing** *a.*, (colloq.) trifling, trivial. [orig. uncert.]

**pi'dgĭn, pi'geon²** (-jĭn, -jŏn). **1.** *a.* **~ English**, jargon chiefly of English words used orig. between Chinese and Europeans. **2.** *n.* Simplified language used between persons of different nationality etc.; (colloq.) (a person's) business, job, or particular concern. [corrupt. *business*]

**pi'-dŏg.** See PYE-DOG.

**pie¹** *n.* Magpie. [F, f. L *pica*]

**pie²** *n.* Dish of meat, fish, fruit, etc., enclosed in or covered with paste etc. and baked (*easy* etc. **as ~**, very easy etc.; **have a finger in the ~**, be, esp. officiously, concerned in the matter; **~ in the sky**, prospect of future happiness after present suffering); similar object (MUD *pie*); confused mass of printers' type, (fig.) chaos; **~ chart** (representing relative quantities by areas of sectors of circle); **~'crust**, baked paste of pie; **~'man**, vendor of pies. [orig. uncert.]

**pi'ebald** (pī'bawld). **1.** *a.* (Usu. of animal, esp. horse) of two colours irregularly arranged, esp. black and white; (fig.) motley, mongrel. **2.** *n.* Piebald animal. [PIE¹, BALD]

**piece. 1.** *n.* One of the distinct portions of which thing is composed; fragment (**in one ~**, unbroken, fig. unharmed; **in ~s**, broken; **go to ~s**, fig. collapse; PICK, PULL, *to pieces*; **take to ~s**, separate the parts of, be divisible thus); one of the things of which a set is composed (*piece of furniture*); enclosed portion (of land; **~ of water**, small lake etc.); detached portion (*of* substance; **give person a ~ of** one's mind, scold or reprimand him); definite quantity in which thing is made up for sale etc. (**~ of work**, thing made by working, lit. or fig.; NASTY *piece of work*); example, specimen, (*a piece of impudence*; *fine piece of painting, cricket*); item (*piece of news*; (derog.) person, esp. woman (**~ of goods**, joc., person); firearm; artillery weapon; chess-man (esp. other than pawn), man at draughts etc.; coin (*penny piece*; **~ of eight**, i.e. REAL¹*s*, Spanish dollar); picture, (usu. short) literary or musical composition;

a drama; ~**goods**, textile fabrics woven in standard lengths; ~**rates, -work**, (paid by the piece); *paid by* the ~ (according to amount done); *of* a ~, uniform, consistent, (*with*); **say** one's ~, (fig.) give one's opinion, make prepared statement. **2.** *v.t.* Put together, form into a whole; eke *out*; make *out* by combination of parts; join *together*; patch *up*. [AF, prob. f. Celt.]

*pièce de résistance* (pēas de rāzē'stahns) *n.* (*pl.* *pièces pr.* same). Most substantial dish at meal; most important or remarkable item. [F]

**pie′cemeal** (-sm-) *adv.* & *a.* (Done etc.) piece by piece or part at a time. [PIECE, MEAL²]

**pied** (pīd) *a.* Particoloured; P~ **Piper**, delusive enticer. [PIE¹]

*pied-à-terre* (pyādahtār′) *n.* (*pl. -ds- pr.* same). Place kept available as temporary quarters when needed. [F, lit. 'foot to earth']

**pie-dog.** See PYE-DOG.

**pier** *n.* Breakwater, mole; structure of iron or wood open below running out into sea and used as promenade and landing-stage; support of arch or of span of bridge, pillar; solid masonry between windows etc. (~**glass**, large mirror, orig. used to fill this up). [L *pera*]

**pierce** *v.t.* & *i.* (Of sharp instrument etc., or fig. of cold, pain, grief, glance, discernment, discerning person, shriek, etc.) penetrate; prick (substance *with* pin etc.); make hole in (cask, ear-lobe for ear-ring, etc.); force one's way through or into; penetrate *through*, *into*, etc. [F *percer* f. L]

**pier′rot** (pēr′ō) *n.* (*fem.* **pierr-e′tte**). French pantomime character; itinerant minstrel with whitened face and loose white costume. [F]

**pietà** (pyātah′) *n.* Picture or sculpture of Virgin Mary holding dead body of Christ on her lap. [It.,—foll.]

**pi′et**|**ў** *n.* Quality of being pious; act etc. showing this; ~**ism** *n.*, pious sentiment, exaggeration or affectation of this. [F f. L (PIOUS)]

**pi′ffl**|**e** (sl.) **1.** *v.i.* Talk or act feebly, trifle; ~**ing** *a.*, trivial, worthless. **2.** *n.* Nonsense; empty discourse. [imit.]

**pig. 1.** *n.* Non-ruminant omnivorous ungulate bristly mammal (**sow in** ~, pregnant); flesh of (usu. young or sucking) domesticated pig as food; similar animal (GUINEA-*pig*);

(colloq.) greedy, dirty, sulky, obstinate, or annoying person (**make a ~ of** oneself, overeat etc.); (sl., derog.) policeman; oblong mass of metal (esp. iron or lead) from smelting-furnace; **bleed like a** (**stuck**) ~ (copiously); **buy a ~ in a poke** (thing unseen or of unknown value); ~**headed**, obstinate; ~**-iron**, crude iron from smelting-furnace; ~**s might fly**, (iron.) that is unlikely; ~**-nut**, = EARTH-*nut*; ~'**skin**, (leather made of) pig's skin; ~'**sticking**, hunting of wild boar with spear on horseback; ~'**sty**, = STY¹; ~'**swill**, ~'**wash**, swill of brewery or kitchen fed to pigs; ~**tail**, plait of hair hanging from back of head. **2.** *v.t.* & *i.* (-**gg**-). Herd together like pigs, behave like pig; ~ **it**, live in disorderly or untidy fashion. **3.** ~'**gerў** (-g-) *n.*, pig-breeding establishment, pigsty, piggishness; ~'**gish** (-g-) *a.*, greedy, dirty; ~'**gў** (-gĭ), (*n.*) little pig (*~**gyback**, see PICK-A-BACK; ~'**gy bank**, pig-shaped hollow pot for saving money in), (*a.*) like (that of) pig; ~'**let**, ~'**ling**, *ns.* [E]

**pi′geon¹** (-jĭn, -jon) *n.* Bird with many varieties, wild or domesticated, bred selectively, trained to carry missives etc., (**carrier** ~, trained to carry home messages tied to its neck or leg, = HOMING *pigeon*); simpleton, person easily swindled; **clay** ~, clay saucer thrown into air from trap as mark for shooting; ~**-breast**, deformed human chest with breastbone projecting; ~**-hole**, (*n.*) one of set of compartments for papers etc. in cabinet etc., (*v.t.*) deposit (document) in this, put aside (matter) for future consideration or neglect, assign (thing) to definite place in memory; ~**-toed**, having toes turned inwards. [F f. L *pipio -on-*]

**pigeon².** See PIDGIN.

**piggery—piggy.** See PIG.

**pi′gment. 1.** *n.* Colouring-matter used as paint or dye; natural colouring-matter of animal or plant tissue; ~**al** (-ĕ′n-), ~**arў**, *adjs.*; ~**ā′tion** *n.*, (esp.) excessive colouring of tissue by deposition of pigment. **2.** *v.t.* Colour (as) with pigment. [L (*pingo* paint)]

**pi′gmў.** See PYGMY.

**pike** *n.* (Hist.) long wooden shaft with pointed metal head; ‖peaked top of hill; (*pl.* same) large voracious freshwater fish with long narrow snout; **~staff**, wooden shaft of pike (*plain as a ~staff*, quite plain or obvious). [E]

**pilä'ff** *n*. Oriental dish of rice or wheat with meat, spices, etc. [Turk.]

**pilä'ster** *n*. Rectangular column, esp. one fastened into wall. [F f. It. f. L (PILE¹)]

**pilch** *n*. Infant's garment or wrapper worn over nappy. [E f. L (PELISSE)]

**pi'lchard** *n*. Small sea-fish allied to herring. [orig. unkn.]

**pile¹. 1.** *n*. Heap of things laid more or less regularly upon one another; (**funeral**) ~, heap of wood etc. on which corpse is burnt; (colloq.) large quantity esp. of money (*make a pile*; **make** one's ~, make as much money as one wants); lofty mass of building(s); series of plates of dissimilar metals laid alternately to produce electric current; (**atomic**) ~, nuclear REACTOR. **2.** *v.t. & i.* ~ (**up, on**), heap up; load (table etc. *with*); crowd *in, into,* or *on* vehicle, *out of* place etc.; ~ **on the agony**, (colloq.) intensify painful description etc.; ~ **it on**, (colloq.) exaggerate; ~ **up**, accumulate, cause (vehicle or aircraft) to crash; **~-up** *n.*, collision of several motor vehicles. [F f. L *pila*]

**pile²** *n*. Pointed stake or post; heavy beam driven vertically into ground as support for bridge etc.; **~-driver**, machine for driving piles. [E f. L *pilum* javelin]

**pile³** *n*. Soft surface on velvet, plush, etc., or on carpet. [AF f. L *pilus* hair]

**pile⁴** *n*. Haemorrhoid. [L *pila* ball]

**pi'lfer** *v.t.* Steal (thing, or abs.) esp. in small quantities; **~age** *n.*, act of pilfering. [F *pelfre*, rel. to PELF]

**pi'lgrim** *n*. One who journeys to sacred place as act of religious devotion; traveller; **P~ Fathers**, English Puritans who founded colony in Massachusetts 1620; **~age** *n.*, pilgrim's journey. [Prov. f. L (PEREGRINE)]

**pill** *n*. Small ball or flat piece of medicinal substance for swallowing whole (**the** ~, colloq., oral contraceptive; GILD¹ *the pill*); (fig.) something that has to be done willy-nilly, a humiliation etc., (*swallow the pill*; *a bitter pill*); (sl. or joc.) ball; **~'box**, shallow cylindrical box for holding pills, hat of similar shape, (Mil.)

small isolated chiefly underground concrete fort. [LDu. f. L (PILULE)]

**pi'llage. 1.** *n*. Plundering esp. in war. **2.** *v.t.* Sack, plunder, (place, person, or abs.). [F (*piller* plunder)]

**pi'llar** *n*. Vertical structure of stone etc. slender in proportion to height, used as support or ornament; post supporting a structure; (fig.) person who is a main supporter (*a pillar of the faith*); upright mass of air, water, rock, etc.; **from ~ to post**, (driven etc.) to and fro, from one resource to another; ||**~-box**, hollow pillar in which letters may be posted (**~-box red**, bright red colour of this); **Pillars of** HERCULES. [AF *piler* f. Rom. (L *pila* PILE¹)]

**pi'llion** (-lyon) *n*. Seat for passenger behind motor-cyclist etc. (**ride** ~, be such passenger). [Gael. *pillean* small cushion f. L *pellis* skin]

**pi'llory. 1.** *n*. (Hist.) Wooden framework with holes for head and hands of offender exposed to public ridicule etc. **2.** *v.t.* Put in pillory; (fig.) expose to ridicule. [F]

**pi'llow** (-ō) **1.** *n*. Cushion as (usu. oblong) support for head in reclining esp. in bed; pillow-shaped block or support; **~case**, **~slip**, washable case of linen etc. for pillow; **~-fight**, mock fight with pillows in bedroom. **2.** *v.t.* Rest, or prop up, on pillow(s). [E f. L *pulvinus* cushion]

**pi'llule**. See PILULE.

**pi'lot** *n., a., & v.* **1.** *n*. Person qualified to take charge of ships entering or leaving a harbour (**drop the** ~, fig., dismiss trusted adviser); person who operates controls of aircraft; (fig.) guide; **~-light**, small gas-burner kept alight to light another, electric indicator light or control light; ||**~ officer**, lowest commissioned rank in R.A.F. **2.** *a*. Experimental, small-scale, (*pilot plant, scheme*). **3.** *v.t.* Conduct as pilot (lit. or fig.). [F f. L f. Gk]

**pi'l(l)üle** *n*. (Small) pill. [F f. L (*pila* ball)]

**pimë'ntō** *n. (pl. ~s)*. Allspice (tree); (also **pimiĕ'ntō**) sweet pepper. [Sp. f. L (PIGMENT)]

**pimp** *n., & v.i.* (Act as) one who solicits clients for prostitute or brothel; ponce. [orig. unkn.]

**pi'mpernĕl** *n*. (**Scarlet**) ~, small annual plant with flowers closing in cloudy or rainy weather. [F f. Rom. (L *piper* PEPPER)]

**pi'mpl|e** *n.* Small hard inflamed spot on skin; similar slight swelling on surface; ~**y** *a.* [E]

**pin. 1.** *n.* Thin usu. cylindrical piece of wire with sharp point and round flattened head for fastening together parts of dress, papers, etc.; thing of small value (*for two pins I'd resign*); peg of wood or metal for various purposes (SPLIT *pin*); (in *pl.*, colloq.) legs (*quick on his pins*); 4½ gal. cask; ~**s and needles**, tingling sensation in limb recovering from numbness; ~**-ball**, game in which small metal balls are shot across sloping board and strike against pins; ~**'cushion**, small cushion for sticking pins in to keep them ready for use; ~**-head**, (fig.) minute thing, (colloq.) stupid person; ~**-hole** (made by pin or into which peg fits); ~**-hole camera** (with pin-hole aperture and no lens); ~**-money**, annual allowance to woman for dress expenses etc., allowance settled on wife, or money earned by her, for private expenditure; ~**-point**, (*n.*) point of pin, (fig.) something very small or sharp, (*a.*, of target) small and requiring very accurate aim, (*v.t.*) locate or designate with high precision; ~**'prick**, (fig.) trifling irritation; ~**-stripe**, very narrow stripe in cloth; ~**-table**, table used in pin-ball; ~**'tail**, duck or grouse with pointed tail; ~**-tuck**, very narrow ornamental tuck; ~**-wheel**, small Catherine wheel. **2.** *v.t.* (**-nn-**). Fasten (thing *to* another, *up*, etc., things *together*) with pin(s); (fig.) fix responsibility for deed *on* (person); transfix with pin, lance, etc.; seize and hold fast (*against* wall etc.); ~ **down**, bind (person etc.) *to* (promise, arrangement), restrict actions of (enemy etc.), specify (thing) precisely; ~ one's **faith** or **hopes** (rely implicitly) *on* (person etc.); ~**-up** *n.*, (colloq.) picture of attractive or famous person, pinned up on wall etc. [E f. L *pinna* wing, feather]

**pi'nafore** *n.* Child's or woman's washable covering worn over dress etc. to protect it from dirt; ~ **dress** (without collar and sleeves, worn over blouse or jumper). [PIN, AFORE]

**pince-nez** (păʹnsnā) *n.* (*pl.* same). Pair of eyeglasses with spring to clip nose. [F = pinch-nose]

**pi'ncer|s** (-z) *n.pl.* (**Pair of**) ~**s**, gripping-tool of two pivoted limbs forming pair of jaws with pair of handles to press them together with; similar organ of crustaceans etc.; ~ **movement**, (Mil.) converging movement against enemy position. [foll.]

**pinch. 1.** *v.t.* & *i.* Grip tightly between two surfaces, esp. between tips of finger and thumb, (lit., or fig. of cold, hunger, etc., esp. *pinched with cold*; **where the shoe ~es**, where one's difficulty or trouble is); stint (person etc. *in, of, for*, food etc.); be niggardly; (sl.) steal (thing), arrest. **2.** *n.* Pinching, squeezing; (fig.) stress (*of* poverty etc.; *feel the pinch*; **at** or **in a ~**, in an emergency, if necessary); as much as can be taken up with tips of finger and thumb (*a pinch of snuff, of salt*). [F *pincer*]

**pi'nchbĕck. 1.** *n.* Goldlike alloy of copper and zinc used in cheap jewellery etc. **2.** *a.* Counterfeit, sham. [person]

**pine**[1] *v.i.* Languish, waste *away* from grief, disease, etc.; long eagerly (*for, after, to* do). [E]

**pine**[2] *n.* ~(-**tree**), evergreen coniferous tree with needle-shaped leaves growing in sheathed clusters of two or more (cf. FIR), many species of which yield timber, tar, and turpentine; its wood; = *pineapple*; ~**'apple**, (large juicy edible fruit of) stiff-leaved tropical plant [from fruit's resemblance to pine-cone]; ~**-cone**, fruit of the pine; **pi'neal** *a.*, (Anat.) shaped like pine-cone (~**al gland**, eyelike conical gland of unknown function in brain). [E f. L *pinus*]

**ping** *n.*, & *v.i.* (Make) abrupt single ringing sound as of rifle bullet in flight, electric bell, etc.; ~**-pŏng** *n.*, [\*P] table tennis. [imit.]

**pi'nion**[1] (-nyon). **1.** *n.* Terminal segment of bird's wing; (poet.) wing; flight-feather. **2.** *v.t.* Cut off pinion of (bird, wing) to prevent flight; bind arms of (person), bind (arms); bind (person etc.) fast *to* (thing). [F f. L *pinna* PIN]

**pi'nion**[2] (-nyon) *n.* Small cogwheel engaging with larger one; cogged spindle engaging with wheel. [F f. L *pinea* PINE[2]-cone]

**pink**[1] *v.t.* Pierce slightly with sword; cut scalloped or zigzag edge on; ~**ing scissors, shears**, dressmaker's serrated shears for cutting zigzag edge. [perh. LDu.]

**pink². 1.** *n.* Garden plant with sweet-smelling white, pink, crimson, or variegated flowers; pale red colour slightly inclining to purple; **the ~** (embodied perfection) *of elegance* etc.; **the ~** (most perfect condition) *of health* (**in the ~**, sl., very well); (hunting-)**~**, fox-hunter's red coat, cloth for this, fox-hunter. **2.** *a.* Of pale red colour of various kinds; (Polit. sl.) mildly communist; pink ELEPHANTS, GIN². [orig. unkn.]

**pink³** *v.i.* (Of vehicle engine) emit high-pitched explosive sounds from detonation of mixture. [imit.]

**pi′nnace** *n.* (War)ship's small boat. [F]

**pi′nnacle** *n.* Small ornamental turret crowning buttress, roof, etc.; natural peak; (fig.) culmination, climax. [F f. L (*pinna* PIN)]

**pi′nnate(d)** (-at, -ātĭd) *adjs.* (Bot., of compound leaf) with series of leaflets on each side of petiole. [L *pinnatus* feathered (as prec.)]

**pi′nny** *n.* (childish or colloq.) Pinafore. [abbr.]

**pint** *n.* Measure of capacity for liquids etc., ⅛ gal.; ‖this quantity of liquid, esp. milk or beer; **~-sized**, (colloq.) diminutive. [F]

‖**pin′ta** *n.* (colloq.) Pint of milk etc. [corrupt. *pint of*]

**pi′ntle** *n.* Bolt or pin, esp. one on which some other part turns. [E]

**pioneer′. 1.** *n.* (Mil.) member of infantry group preparing road for main body of troops; initiator of enterprise; original explorer or settler. **2.** *v.i. & t.* Act as pioneer (to); open up (road etc.) as pioneer; originate (course of action etc. followed later by others). [F *pionnier* (PAWN¹)]

**pi′ous** *a.* Devout, religious (*pious* FRAUD); hypocritically virtuous; dutiful. [L]

**pip¹. 1.** *n.* Seed of apple, orange, grape, etc. **2.** *v.t.* (-pp-). Remove pips from (fruit). [abbr. PIPPIN]

**pip²** *n.* Each spot on playing-cards, dice, or dominoes; ‖star (1–3 acc. to rank) on shoulder of army officer's uniform. [orig. unkn.]

**pip³** *n.* Disease of poultry, hawks, etc.; (sl.) fit of disgust, depression, or bad temper, (*he gives me the pip*). [LDu.]

‖**pip⁴** *v.t.* (colloq.; -pp-). Black-

ball; defeat (**~ at the post**, defeat at the last moment). [orig. unkn.]

‖**pip⁵** *n.* Short high-pitched sound (*the 6 pips of the time-signal*). [imit.]

**pi′pal** (pē′-) *n.* Large Ind. fig-tree allied to banian. [Hindi]

**pipe. 1.** *n.* Tube of wood, metal, etc., esp. for conveying water, gas, etc.; (Mus.) wind-instrument of single tube, each tube by which sound is produced in organ; (in *pl.*) = BAG*pipes*; (sounding of) boatswain's whistle; tubular organ, vessel, etc., in animal body; (tobacco-)**~**, narrow tube with bowl at one end for drawing in smoke of burning tobacco, quantity of tobacco held by this (*light, smoke, a pipe*; PEACE-*pipe*; **put that in your ~ and smoke it**, colloq., consider that fact etc. and accept it if you can); cask for wine, esp. as measure usu. = 105 gal.; **~′clay**, fine white clay for tobacco-pipes or for whitening leather etc.; **~-cleaner**, flexible fabric-covered wire to clean inside a tobacco-pipe; **~-dream**, groundless hope or scheme, as indulged in when smoking (orig. opium) pipe; **~′line**, (esp.) pipe conveying petroleum to a distance, fig. channel of supply of goods, information, etc. (*in the ~line*, awaiting completion or processing); **~-stem**, shaft of tobacco-pipe. **2.** *v.i. & t.* Play (tune etc., or abs.) on pipe(s); lead or bring (person etc.) by sound of pipe; summon (crew *up, to* meal, work, etc.) by sounding whistle; utter in shrill voice; trim (dress etc.), ornament (cake etc.), with piping; furnish with pipes; convey (oil, water, gas, etc.) by pipes; transmit (music, broadcast programme, etc.) by wire or cable for hearing elsewhere; **~ down**, (Naut.) dismiss from duty, (colloq.) be quiet or less insistent; **~ up**, begin to play, sing, etc. **3.** **pi′per** *n.*, one who plays on pipe, esp. itinerant musician, bagpipe-player; **pay the ~r** (**and call the tune**), bear the cost (and have control) of a proceeding etc.; **pi′ping** (*n.*, esp.) ornamentation of dress, upholstery, etc., by means of cord enclosed in pipelike fold, ornamental cordlike lines of sugar on cake, (*a.*, esp.) **piping** (hissing) **hot**. [E f. Rom. (L *pipo* chirp)]

‖**pip ĕ′mma** *adv. & n.* (colloq.) =

P.M. [formerly signallers' names for letters *P.M.*]

**pipě'tte** *n.* Slender tube for transferring or measuring small quantities of liquids. [F dim. (PIPE)]

**pi'pit** *n.* Small bird resembling lark. [imit.]

**pi'ppin** *n.* Apple grown from seed; dessert apple; (sl.) excellent person or thing. [F]

**pi'p-squeak** *n.* (sl.) Insignificant or contemptible person or thing. [imit.]

**pi'quan|t** (pē'k-) *a.* Agreeably pungent, sharp, appetizing; (fig.) pleasantly stimulating, or disturbing, to the mind; ~**cÿ** *n.* [F (*piquer* prick)]

**pique** (pēk). 1. *v.t.* Irritate, wound the pride of; arouse (curiosity, interest); plume one*self* on. 2. *n.* Enmity, resentment, (*in a fit of pique*). [F (as prec.)]

**piquě't** (-k-) *n.* Card-game for two players with pack of 32 cards. [F]

**pī'racÿ.** See PIRATE.

**pira'nha** (-ah'nya), **pira'ya** (-ah'ya), *n.* Voracious S. Amer. freshwater fish. [Port.]

**pīr'|ate. 1.** *n.* (Ship used by) sea-robber; marauder; one who infringes another's business rights; one who broadcasts without official authorization (freq. *attrib.*: *pirate radio station*); ~**acÿ** *n.;* ~**ǎ'tic(al)** *adjs.* (-ically). 2. *v.t.* Plunder; reproduce (book etc.) without permission for one's own benefit. [L *pirata* f. Gk]

**pirouě'tte** (-rōō-) *n.,* & *v.i.* (Make) ballet-dancer's spin on one foot or point of toe. [F, = spinning-top]

*pis aller* (pēzǎlā') *n.* Course of action etc. followed for want of better. [F]

**pi'sc|atory,** ~**|atōr'ial,** *adjs.* Of fishermen or fishing; **Pi'scēs** (-z; or -skēz) *n.,* sign of ZODIAC; ~**icŭlture** *n.,* artificial rearing of fish; ~**i'na** (or -sē'-) *n.* (*pl.* -ae, -as), (Eccl.) perforated stone basin near altar in church for carrying away water used in rinsing chalice etc.; ~**i'vorous** *a.,* fish-eating. [L (*piscator* angler f. *piscis* fish)]

**piss.** (vulg.) **1.** *v.t.* Urinate; discharge (blood etc.), wet, with urine; (in *p.p.,* sl.) drunk; ~ **off,** (sl.) go away, (in *p.p.*) annoyed. 2. *n.* Urine; act of urinating; ~**pot,** chamber-pot. [F, imit.]

**pistǎ'chiŏ** (-sh-; *or* -ah'-) *n.* (*pl.* ~**s**). (Tree yielding) nut with greenish edible kernel. [Sp. & It. f. L f. Gk f. Pers.]

*piste* (pēst) *n.* Ski-track of compacted snow. [F, = racetrack]

**pi'stil** *n.* Female organ of flower, comprising ovary, style, and stigma; ~**late** *a.,* having pistils. [F or L (PESTLE)]

**pi'stol. 1.** *n.* Small firearm held and fired by one hand (hold ~ to person's **head,** coerce him by threats); implement of similar shape; ~**-grip,** handle of pistol-butt shape; ~**-shot,** range of, shot fired from, pistol; ~**-whip** *v.t.,* beat with pistol. 2. *v.t.* ||(-ll-). Shoot with pistol. [F f. G f. Czech]

**pi'ston** *n.* Disc or short cylinder of wood, metal, etc., fitting closely and moving up and down in tube, used in steam or petrol engine to impart motion by means of ~**rod,** or in pump to receive motion; sliding valve in cornet etc. [F, f. It. (PESTLE)]

**pit. 1.** *n.* Natural hole in ground; hole made in digging for mineral etc. or for industrial purposes (*chalk, gravel, tan,* -*pit*); covered hole as trap (dig a ~ for, fig., try to ensnare; the (bottomless) ~, hell); hollow on a surface (~ of the stomach, depression below bottom of breastbone); ||that part of auditorium of theatre which is on floor of house, esp. the part of this behind stalls; sunken area in workshop floor for access to underside of motor vehicles; place where racing cars are refuelled etc. during race; ~**fall,** covered pit as trap for animals etc., (fig.) unsuspected snare or danger; ~**head,** (area surrounding) top of coal-mine shaft; ~**prop,** balk of wood used as temporary support in a mine. 2. *v.t.* (-tt-). Put into pit; set (cock, dog, etc.) to fight (*against* another); (fig.) match (person, wits, *against*); (esp. in *p.p.*) make pits, esp. scars, in. [E f. L *puteus* well]

**pi't-a-păt** *adv.* & *n.* (With) sound as of light quick steps, (with) faltering sound, (*feet, heart, went pit-a-pat*). [imit.]

**pitch[1]. 1.** *n.* Dark tenacious resinous substance from distillation of tar or turpentine, used for caulking seams of ships etc.; ~**black,** ~**-darkness,** (with no light at all); ~**blende,** uranium oxide found in pitchlike masses and yielding radium; ~**pine,** pine-tree yielding much resin. **2.** *v.t.* Cover, coat, smear, with pitch. **3.** ~'ỹ *a.* (-iness), of, like, dark etc. as, pitch. [E f. L *pix pic-*]

**pitch²**. **1.** *v.t.* & *i.* Erect and fix (tent, camp); fix or plant (thing) in definite position (~ **wickets**, Crick., fix stumps in ground and place bails); (Mus. etc.) set at particular pitch, (fig.) express in particular style or at particular level; throw, fling; (Crick.) cause (bowled ball) to strike ground, (of ball) strike ground, (at specified point etc.); fall heavily (on one's head, *into*, etc.); (of ship, vehicle, etc.) plunge in longitudinal direction (cf. ROLL); (sl.) tell (tale, yarn); ~**and-toss**, game of skill and chance played with coins; ~**ed battle** (planned beforehand and fought on chosen ground, not casual skirmish, fig. vigorous argument etc.); ~'**fork**, (*n.*) long-handled fork with two prongs for pitching hay etc., (*v.t.*) cast (as with pitchfork, (fig.) thrust (person) forcibly (*into* position, office, etc.); ~ **in**, (colloq.) set to work vigorously; ~ **into**, (colloq.) assail forcibly with blows, words, etc., make vigorous attack on (person, food, etc.); ~ (**up**)**on**, happen to select. **2.** *n.* Pitching (e.g. of ship); mode of delivering cricket-ball in bowling; advertising or recommendation by salesman etc.; ‖place at which street performer, bookmaker, etc., is stationed (QUEER *the* pitch); (Crick.) area between or near wickets; area for playing football etc. on; height, degree, intensity, (*of* quality etc.); (Mus.) quality of sound governed by rate of vibration of string etc., degree of acuteness or graveness of tone (*high, low, pitch*); distance between successive ridges of screw, teeth of cog, etc.; degree of slope (~**ed roof**, not flat); ~**pipe**, small pipe blown by mouth to set pitch for singing or tuning. **3.** ~'**er¹** *n.*, (esp.) player who delivers ball in baseball. [orig. uncert.]

**pi'tcher²** *n.* Large vessel with handle or two ears and usu. a lip shaped for pouring, for holding liquids, jug, (**little** ~**s have long ears**, children are apt to overhear); ~**plant** (with pitcher-shaped leaves). [F, rel. to BEAKER]

**pi'tchỹ.** See PITCH¹.

**pi'téous** *a.* Deplorable, deserving or causing pity. [F f. Rom. (PITY)]

**pith** *n.* Spongy cellular tissue in plant stems and branches or lining rind of orange etc. (~ **helmet**, one made from dried pith of sola etc.); (fig.) essential part (*pith and marrow of*); physical strength, vigour; ~'ỹ *a.* (-ily, -iness), (fig.) condensed and forcible, terse. [E]

**pi'ti|able** *a.* (-bly). Deserving or causing pity or contempt; ~**ful** *a.* (-lly), (of thing) causing pity, contemptible; ~**less** *a.*, showing no pity (lit. or fig.). [F (PITY)]

**pi'ton** (pē'-) *n.* Peg driven in to support climber or rope. [F]

**pi'ttance** *n.* Allowance or remuneration, esp. scanty one (*a mere pittance*). [F f. Rom. (PITY)]

**pi'tter-pätter** = PIT-A-PAT. [imit.]

**pitū'itarỹ**. **1.** *a.* ~ **gland**, small ductless gland at base of brain. **2.** *n.* Pituitary gland. [L (*pituita* phlegm)]

**pi'tỹ**. **1.** *n.* Feeling of sorrow aroused by person's distress or suffering (*cannot help feeling pity for him*); **take** ~ **on**, feel or act compassionately towards; *for* ~'**s sake**, = *for God's* SAKE¹); regrettable fact, regrettableness, (*what a pity!*; *it is a thousand pities you did not mention it*; *more's the* ~, so much the worse). **2.** *v.t.* Feel (often contemptuous) pity for (*he is much to be pitied*; *I pity you if you think that*). [F f. L (PIETY)]

**pi'vot**. **1.** *n.* Short shaft or pin on which something turns or oscillates; (fig.) cardinal or crucial person or point. **2.** *v.t.* & *i.* Furnish with or attach by pivot; turn (as) on pivot; hinge (*up*)*on* (lit. or fig.); ~**al** *a.*, (esp.) of cardinal importance. [F]

**pi'xie, -xỹ,** *n.* Supernatural being akin to fairy; ~ **hat, hood,** (with pointed crown). [orig. unkn.]

**pi'zza** (pē'tsa) *n.* Open pie containing tomatoes, cheese, etc. [It., = pie]

*pizzicat|o* (pĭtsĭkah'tō) *adv., a.,* & *n.* (*pl.* ~**os,** ~**i**). (Note or passage performed by) plucking string of violin etc. with finger instead of using bow. [It.]

**pl.** *abbr.* place; plate; plural.

**plä'cab|le** *a.* (-lỹ). Easily appeased, mild, forgiving; ~**r'litỹ** *n.* [F or L (*placo* appease)]

**plä'cärd**. **1.** *n.* Document printed on one side of single sheet for posting up, poster. **2.** *v.t.* (*or* plakár'd). Set up placards on (wall etc.); advertise (wares etc.) by placards; display (poster etc.) as placard. [F f. Du. *placken* to glue]

**placa'te** *v.t.* Conciliate, pacify; ∼**ory** *a*. [L *placo* appease]

**place. 1.** *n.* Particular part of space, part of space occupied by person or thing, (**in** ∼**s**, at some places but not at others); city, town, village, etc. (**go** ∼**s**, fig., be successful); group of houses in town etc.; residence, dwelling, (*he has a place in the country*; *come round to my place*); country-house with surroundings; building or area devoted to specified purpose (*place of amusement*; *bathing-place*); particular spot on surface etc. (*a sore place on his arm*); passage in book etc.; rank, station, (*servants must know their* ∼, be respectful; **put him in his** ∼, restrain his presumption); (Racing) position among placed competitors, esp. other than winner; position of figure in series as indicating its value in decimal etc. notation (*calculated to 5 decimal places*); step in progression of argument, statement, etc., (*in the first place*); proper or natural or suitable position (*take your places*; *is in*, *out of*, (*its* or *his*) *place*; **in** ∼ **of**, in exchange for, instead of; **take the** ∼ **of**, be substituted for); space, seat, accommodation, for person etc. at table, in vehicle, etc.; office, employment, esp. government appointment; duties or entitlements of office etc. (*it is not my place to inquire into that*); ∼**kick**, (Footb.) kick made with ball placed on ground; ∼**mat**, small mat on table at person's place; ∼**name**, name of town, hill, field, etc.; ∼**setting**, set of dishes and implements for one person to eat with; **all over the** ∼, in disorder (lit. or fig.); **give** ∼ **to**, make room for, yield precedence to, be succeeded by; **take** ∼, (esp. of prearranged event) occur. **2.** *v.t.* Put (thing etc.) in particular place or state; arrange (set of things) in their proper places; find situation, living, etc., for; invest (money); dispose of (goods) to customer; give (order for goods etc.) to firm etc.; have (confidence etc. *in*, *on*); assign rank to; locate; (fully) identify, assign to a class, (*I know that man's face but I can't place him*); state position of (usu. any of first 3 horses or runners) in race (**be** ∼**d**, be among

first 3 or *be second); ∼**ment** (-sm-) *n.* [F f. L *platea* broad way f. Gk]

**place'bo** *n.* (*pl.* ∼s). Medicine given to humour, rather than cure, the patient; dummy pill etc. used as control; blank sample in test. [L, = I shall be acceptable]

**place'nt**|**a** *n.* (*pl.* ∼**ae**, ∼**as**). Organ in uterus of pregnant mammal (expelled after parturition) and helping to nourish foetus; (Bot.) part of carpel to which seeds are attached; ∼**al** *a*. [L f. Gk, = flat cake]

**pla'cer** *n.* Deposit of sand, gravel, etc., in bed of stream etc. containing valuable minerals in particles. [Amer. Sp.]

**pla'cid** *a*. Mild, peaceful; not easily disturbed; **placi'dity** *n.* [F or L (*placeo* please)]

**pla'cket** *n.* Opening or slit esp. in woman's skirt, for fastenings or access to pocket. [var. PLACARD]

**pla'giar**|**ize** *v.t.* Take and use another person's (thoughts, writings, inventions, or abs.) as one's own; ∼**ism**, ∼**ist**, *ns.* [L *plagiarius* kidnapper]

**plague** (-g). **1.** *n.* Affliction, esp. as divine punishment; (colloq.) unusual infestation *of* (rats etc.), nuisance, trouble; pestilence (the ∼ = BUBONIC *plague*); (arch., as imprecation) *plague on it!* etc.; ∼**spot**, (fig.) source or symptom of moral corruption. **2.** *v.t.* Afflict with plague; (colloq.) annoy, bother. [L *plaga* stroke, infection]

**plaice** *n.* (*pl.* same). Eur. flat-fish, much used as food. [F f. L *platessa*]

**plaid** (*or* plăd). **1.** *n.* Long piece of twilled woollen cloth, usu. with chequered or tartan pattern, outer article of Highland costume; cloth used for this. **2.** *a*. Made of plaid; having plaidlike pattern. [Gael.]

**plain** *a., adv., & n.* **1.** *a.* (∼'ness *pr.* -n-n-). Clear, evident, simple, readily understood, (*plain words*, *English*; *plain as a* PIKE*staff*); not in code; not intricate (*plain cooking*, *sewing*) or embellished or coloured; (of food) not rich or elaborate or highly seasoned; not luxurious (*plain living*); outspoken, straightforward, (**be** ∼ **with**, tell home truths to); unsophisticated (*I am a plain man*); of homely manners, dress, or appearance; ugly (*a pity the girl is so plain*). **2.** *adv.* Clearly (*see it plain*); simply (*that is plain silly*). **3.** *n.* Level tract of country; ordinary stitch in knitting (opp. PURL²). **4.** ~**chant**, = *plain-song*; ~ **chocolate** (without milk added in manufacture); ~ **clothes**, unofficial dress, esp. of policeman on duty but not in uniform; ~ **dealing**, candour, straightforwardness; ~ **sailing**, sailing in straightforward course, (fig.) simple situation or course of action; ~'**sman**, inhabitant of a plain; ~'**song**, traditional church music in free rhythm depending on accentuation of words, and sung in unison; ~**spoken**, outspoken. [F f. L *planus*]

**plaint** *n.* ||(Law) accusation, charge; (literary) lamentation, complaint; ~'**iff** *n.*, party who brings suit into lawcourt; ~'**ive** *a.*, mournful--sounding. [F *plaint(e)* f. L *plango* lament]

**plait** (plăt). **1.** *n.* Interlacing of 3 or more strands of hair, ribbon, straw, etc.; material thus interlaced. **2.** *v.t.* Form into plait. [F *pleit* f. L *plico* to fold]

**plan. 1.** *n.* Drawing etc. made by projection on horizontal surface (cf. ELEVATION), esp. one showing relative position of parts of (one floor of) building; large-scale detailed map of town or district; scheme of arrangement; formulated or organized method by which thing is to be done; project, design; way of proceeding (*the better plan is to peel them after boiling*; *plan of campaign*). **2.** *v.t.* & *i.* (-nn-). Make plan of (ground, existing building); design (building to be constructed etc.); arrange beforehand (procedure etc.); make plans; (in *p.p.*) conducted in accordance with plan; ~ **on**, (colloq.) aim at do*ing*. **3.** ~'**ner**, ~'**ning**, *ns.* (esp. w. ref. to controlled design of buildings and development of land). [F]

**plănchĕ'tte** (-sh-) *n.* Small board on two castors and pencil, said to trace letters etc. without conscious direction when person's fingers rest lightly on board. [F dim. (PLANK)]

**plāne¹** *n.* A tall spreading broad--leaved tree. [F f. L *platanus* f. Gk]

**plāne²** *n., a., & v.* **1.** *n.* Surface such that straight line joining any two points in it lies wholly in it; imaginary surface of this kind in which points or lines in material bodies lie; level surface; (main supporting surface of) aeroplane; (fig.) level (*of* thought, attainment, knowledge,

etc.); tool for smoothing surface of wood by paring shavings from it; ~ **sailing**, art of determining ship's position by assuming that she is moving on a plane, (fig.) = PLAIN *sailing*. **2.** *a.* Level as, lying in, a plane. **3.** *v.t.* & *i.* Smooth (wood) with plane; pare *away* or *down* (irregularities) with plane; travel, glide (*down* etc.) in aeroplane; soar. [F f. L (*planus* PLAIN)]

**plă'nĕt** *n.* Heavenly body revolving in approximately circular orbit round sun; the earth; **major** ~, Jupiter, Saturn, Uranus, or Neptune; **minor** ~, asteroid; ~**ār'ium** *n.* (*pl.* **-ums**, **-a**), orrery, device for projecting image of night sky as seen at various times and places; ~**arў** *a.* [F f. L f. Gk, = wanderer]

**plă'ngent** (-nj-) *a.* (Loudly) lamenting. [L (PLAINT)]

**plank. 1.** *n.* Long wide piece of timber, a few inches thick; item of political or other programme; **walk the** ~, (Hist., of pirates' captive etc.) be made to walk blindfold into sea along plank laid over side of ship. **2.** *v.t.* Furnish, cover, floor, with planks; (colloq.) put *down* roughly or violently, esp. pay (money, or abs.) *down* on the spot; ~'**ing** *n.*, (esp.) planks. [F f. L *planca*]

**plă'nktŏn** *n.* (Chiefly microscopic) drifting or floating organisms in seas, lakes, etc. [G f. Gk, = wandering]

**plă'nner, plă'nning.** See PLAN.

**plant** (-ah-). **1.** *n.* Organism capable of living wholly on inorganic substances and having neither power of locomotion nor special organs of sensation or digestion, member of the vegetable kingdom; small plant (other than trees and shrubs); fixtures, implements, machinery, etc., used in industrial processes; factory; (sl.) planned swindle or burglary, hoax, thing deliberately placed for discovery by others; ~**louse**, small insect that infests plants. **2.** *v.t.* Place (tree, shoot, bulb, seed, crop, etc.) in ground or soil so that it may take root and grow; fix (stake, feet, etc.) firmly (*in*, *on*, ground etc.); station (person), esp. as spy; establish (community etc.); settle (person) as colonist; cause (idea etc.) to take root *in* (mind); furnish (land *with* plants, district *with* settlers etc.); deliver (blow, thrust) with definite aim; (sl.) conceal (stolen goods etc.), esp. with view to misleading a later discoverer; ~ **out**, transfer (plant) from pot or frame to open ground, set out (seedlings) at intervals; ~ **oneself**, take up a position. **3.** ~**ā′tion** (or plă-) n., assemblage of planted growing plants (esp. trees), estate on which cotton, tobacco, etc., is cultivated (formerly by slave labour), (Hist.) colony; ~**′er** n., (esp.) occupier of plantation (*tea--planter*), container for decorative plants. [F f. L *planta*]

**Plăntă′gĕnĕt** n. Member of family ruling England in 12th–14th cc. [person]

**plă′ntain**[1] (-tĭn; or -ah′-) n. Low herb with broad flat leaves spread out close to ground and seeds much used for cage-birds. [F f. L *plantago*]

**plă′ntain**[2] (-tĭn; or -ah′-) n. (Fruit of) treelike tropical herbaceous plant bearing banana-like fruit. [Sp.]

**plantation, planter.** See PLANT.

**plăque** (-k, -ahk) n. Ornamental tablet of metal, porcelain, etc. [F f. Du. *plak* tablet (PLACARD)]

**plă′sma** (-z-) n. Colourless coagulable part of blood, lymph, or milk, in which corpuscles or fat--globules float; protoplasm; (Phys.) gas of positive ions and free electrons in about equal numbers. [L f. Gk (*plassō* to shape)]

**plă′ster** (-ah′-). **1.** n. Curative or protective substance spread on fabric and applied to the body; soft plastic mixture, esp. of lime and sand for spreading on walls etc. to form smooth surface and harden by drying; ~**board**, board with core of plaster for walls etc.; ~ **of Paris**, fine white plaster of gypsum for making moulds or casts, in bandages for immobilizing limbs etc., or as cement etc.; ~ **saint**, person regarded as being without moral faults and human frailty. **2.** v.t. Cover (wall etc.) with plaster or the like; coat, bedaub; apply medical plaster to; stick or fix (thing) like plaster on surface; make smooth with fixative etc. (*hair plastered down*); (sl.) bomb or shell heavily, (in *p.p.*) drunk. [E & F f. L (*em*)*plastrum* f. Gk]

**plă′stic** (or -ah′-). **1.** a. (~**ally**). Moulding, giving form to, clay, wax, or other yielding solid (~ **arts**, those concerned with modelling, e.g. sculpture, or with representation of solid objects; ~ **surgery**, repairing or replacing deficient structure esp. by transfer of tissue; ~ **surgeon**); produced by moulding; capable of being (easily) moulded; (fig.) pliant, supple; made of plastic (*plastic bag, flowers, wood*). **2.** n. Synthetic resinous etc. polymeric substance that can be given any permanent shape. **3.** P~**ine** (-ēn) n., plastic substance used for modelling [P]; **plăstĭ′cĭty** n., quality of being (easily) moulded; ~**ize** v.t.; ~**izer** n., substance that produces or promotes plasticity. [F or L f. Gk (PLASMA)]

**plāte. 1.** n. Flat thin usu. rigid sheet of metal etc. with even surface and fairly uniform thickness; (impression from) smooth piece of metal etc. for engraving; illustration on special paper in book; piece of metal with name or inscription for affixing to something (**put up** one's ~, begin practice as doctor etc.); thin sheet of metal, glass, etc., coated with sensitive film for photography; (collect. *sing.*) ‖table and domestic utensils of silver, gold, or other metal, (objects of) plated metal; silver or gold cup as prize for (orig. horse-)race, such race, (**selling** ~, = SELLING-*race*); shallow usu. circular vessel from which food is eaten or served (*cake, dinner, soup, -plate*; **on a** ~, colloq., to be taken without need of effort; **on one's plate**, colloq., for one to deal with or consider); contents of this (*a plate of strawberries*); similar vessel used for collection in churches etc. (*put a coin in the plate*); thin piece of plastic material, moulded to shape of gums, etc., to which artificial teeth are attached; (colloq.) denture; ~ **glass** (of fine quality orig. cast in plates, for shop windows etc.); ‖~**′layer**, man employed in fixing and repairing railway rails; ~**powder** (for cleaning silver); ‖~**-rack** (in which plates are kept or placed to drain). **2.** v.t. Cover (esp. ship) with plates of metal; cover (other metal) with thin coat esp. of silver, gold, or tin. **3.** ~**′ful** (-t‖ool) n. (lit. or fig.). [F f. L *platta* (*plattus* flat)‖

**plă′teau** (-tō) n. (*pl.* ~**x**, ~**s**, *pr.* -z). Tableland; state of little variation following an increase. [F (prec.)]

**plă′ten** n. Plate in printing-press by which paper is pressed against type; corresponding part in typewriter etc. [F *platine* (PLATE)]

**plǎ'tform** n. Raised level surface, natural or artificial terrace; thick sole of shoe; floor area at entrance to bus; ‖raised surface along side of line at railway station; (~ **ticket**, for access to this by non-traveller); raised flooring in hall or open air from which speaker addresses audience; (fig.) political basis of party etc., declared policy of political party. [F (PLATE, FORM)]

**plǎ'tinum** n. White heavy ductile malleable metallic element unaffected by simple acids and melting only at very high temperature; ~ **blonde**, (woman with) silvery-blonde (hair); ~ **group** (of platinum and similar metals). [L f. E *platina* f. Sp. dim. (*plata* silver)]

**plǎ'tĭt|ūde** n. Commonplace remark, esp. one solemnly delivered; ~**ū'dĭnous** a. [F (PLATE)]

**Platǒ'nǐc** a. (~**ally**). Of the Greek philosopher *Plato* or his doctrines; confined to words or theory, not leading to action, harmless; ~ **love**, purely spiritual love usu. for one of opposite sex; **Plā'tonism** n., doctrines of Plato; **Plā'tonĭst** n. [L f. Gk]

**platoō'n** n. (Mil.) subdivision of a company; group of persons acting together. [F *peloton*, dim. of *pelote* PELLET]

*\***plǎ'tter** n. Flat dish or plate, esp. for food (make a ~, = on a PLATE). [AF *plater* (PLATE)]

**plǎ'tӯpus** n. Austral. egg-laying aquatic and burrowing mammal with ducklike beak and flat tail. [Gk, = flat foot]

**plau'dĭt** n. (usu. in *pl.*) Round of applause; emphatic expression of approval. [L *plaudite*, imper. of *plaudo plaus-* clap]

**plau'sĭb|le** (-z-) a. (~**ly**). (Of argument, statement, etc.) specious, seeming reasonable or probable; (of person) persuasive but deceptive; ~**ĭ'lĭtӯ** n. [L (prec.)]

**play.** 1. *v.i.* & *t.* Move about in lively or unrestrained manner, pass gently (*around* etc.), strike lightly (*on*); emit light, water, etc., (*on*; *fountains* playing); amuse oneself, frolic, pass time pleasantly *with*; (sl.) act as required (*he wouldn't play*); employ oneself in a game or in game of (cricket etc.); gamble (*on*);

pretend for fun *that*; be in specified condition for playing on; contend against (person) in game; include (person), occupy (specified position), in team for game; strike (ball, or abs.) in specified manner; move (chess-man) etc.; take (playing-card) from hand and display it on table, (fig.) make use of (advantage available; *play* one's *ace*); allow (fish) to exhaust itself pulling against line; perform, execute, (trick, joke, *on* person; stroke etc. in game); perform on or *on* (musical instrument); perform (piece of music etc.); cause (gramophone, record, etc.) to produce music or other sound; perform role on stage (*in* drama); perform (drama, role, etc.) on stage, (fig.) act in real life the part of (*play truant, the fool*); give dramatic performance at (theatre etc.). 2. *n.* Brisk, light, or fitful movement; activity, operation, (**come into** ~, begin to operate; **in** ~, engaged, occupied; **make** ~ **with**, use effectively or ostentatiously); freedom of movement, space or scope for this; recreation, amusement, esp. as spontaneous activity of children; (manner of, action in) playing of game (**make a** ~ **for**, sl., seek to acquire; *ball is* **in** ~, being used in ordinary course of game, **out of** ~, temporarily out of use according to rules); dramatic piece (**as good as a** ~, very amusing or interesting); gambling. 3. ~ **about** or **around**, behave irresponsibly (*with*); ~ **at**, engage in (game, or trivial or half-hearted action); ~ **back**, use defensive stroke in cricket, make audible (what has been recorded); ~**'bill** (announcing theatre programme); ~**'boy**, irresponsible pleasure-loving usu. rich man; ~ **by ear**, perform without aid of written music, perform step by step according to results; ~ one's **cards well,** (fig.) make good use of one's opportunities; ~ **down**, minimize; ~**ed out**, exhausted of energy or usefulness; ~ **fair**, play or act fairly; ~**'fellow**, playmate; ~ **person for**, (colloq.) regard him as being or having; *play for* TIME; ~**'goer**, frequenter of theatre; ~**'-ground**, school or park recreation ground; ~**-group**, group of young children who play together under supervision; ~ **hell with,** (colloq.) affect adversely; ~**'house**, theatre;

~ **into** person's **hands**, act so as to give him advantage; ~'**mate**, companion in children's playing; ~ **off**, play extra match to decide draw or tie (so ~-**off** n.), oppose (person etc. *against* another) esp. for one's own advantage, complete (game etc.) that is to be played; ~ **on**, = *play upon*, (Crick.) be out by playing ball on to own wicket; ~**pen, -suit**, portable enclosure, garment, for young child to play in; ~ **safe**, act with caution; ~ one**self in**, become accustomed to prevailing conditions; *play the* GAME[1], *the* MAN; ~ **the market**, speculate in stocks etc.; ~'**thing**, toy; ~'**time**, time assigned for playing or recreation; ~ **up**, put all one's energy into game, make the most of, (colloq.) behave annoyingly; ~ **upon**, make use of (person's fears etc.); ~ *upon words*, (make) pun; ~ **up to**, act so as to support (other actor), (fig.) flatter; *play with* FIRE; ~'**wright**, dramatist. **4.** ~'**er** n., (esp.) person engaged in or skilful in game, performer on musical instrument, actor; ~'**ful** a. (**-lly**), frolicsome, humorous; ~'**ing** n. (~**ing-card**, oblong piece of pasteboard used in games, usu. in pack of 52; ~**ing-field**, used in outdoor game); ~'**let** n., short dramatic piece. [E]

**plea** n. Pleading, excuse; appeal, entreaty; (Law) formal statement by or on behalf of defendant. [AF f. L *placitum* decree (PLEASE)]

**pleach** v.t. Entwine, interlace, (esp. branches to form hedge). [F f. L (PLEXUS)]

**plead** v.i. & t. Address court as advocate; maintain (cause) in court; allege formally as plea, (fig.) allege as excuse etc. (*I plead ignorance*); make appeal or entreaty; ~ **guilty, not guilty**, confess, deny, liability or guilt; ~ **with**, make earnest appeal to; ~'**ing** n., (esp., usu. in *pl.*) formal statement of cause of action or defence. [AF *pleder* (PLEA)]

**plea'sant** (-ĕ'z-) a. (~**er**, ~**est**). Agreeable to mind, feelings, or senses; ~**rў** n., jocularity, humorous speech, joking remark. [F (foll.)]

**please** (-z) v.t. & i. Be agreeable to (*meant only to please the eye*; *this book will please you*; ~ oneself, do as one likes; be ~**d with**, derive pleasure from; be ~**d** = glad to do, esp. as polite form of consent or offer; be

~**d** = graciously willing to do, in formal or iron. deference, *your lordship was pleased to doubt my veracity*; with *it* as subj. expressed or omitted, representing prec. or foll. infinitive, clause, or sentence, esp. as in last use, *it has never pleased him to explain*; *may it please you*, *I have none*); think fit (*take as many as you please*; **if you** ~, (1) with your permission, as polite form of request esp. for trifling services, *I will take another cup, if you please*, (2) if I may say so and be believed, iron. with implication that nothing could be more unreasonable, *and now, if you please, he expects me to pay for it!*); give pleasure (*anxious to please*); in *imper.* with request, orig. = *may it please you*: *ring the bell, please*; *may I come in, please?*; *won't you please come in?*; *please return it soon.* [F *plaisir* f. L *placeo*]

**plea'sur|e** (plĕ'zher). **1.** n. Feeling of satisfaction or joy; sensuous enjoyment as object of life (*a life given up to pleasure*); **man of** ~**e**, profligate); source of pleasure (*it is a pleasure to talk to him*); gratification (*do me the pleasure of dining with me*; **take** (a) ~**e** in, like doing); will, desire, (*can be altered at pleasure*); gracious wish (of monarch etc.); ~**e-boat** etc. (for pleasure, not business); ~**e-ground** (laid out for pleasure). **2.** v.t. Give (esp. sexual) pleasure to. **3.** ~**able** a. (**-bly**), causing pleasure. [F (prec.)]

**pleat. 1.** n. Fold or crease, esp. flattened fold in cloth doubled upon itself. **2.** v.t. Fold (cloth etc.) thus. [PLAIT]

**plĕb** n. (sl.) Person of lower classes. [abbr. foll.]

**plĕbei'an** (-bē'-). **1.** n. Commoner esp. in ancient Rome. **2.** a. Of low birth, of the common people; uncultured; coarse, ignoble. **3.** plĕ'**bĭscĭte** n., direct vote of all electors of State on important public question, public expression of community's opinion; **plĕbĭ'scĭtarў** a. [L (*plebs plebis* common people, *scisco* vote for)]

**plĕ'ctrum** n. (*pl.* -**a**, -**ums**). Small pointed piece of ivory, quill, etc., for plucking strings of guitar etc. [L f. Gk (*plēssō* strike)]

**plĕdg|e. 1.** n. Thing given to person as security for fulfilment of contract, payment of debt, etc., and liable to forfeiture in case of failure; thing put in pawn; thing given as token of favour etc. or of something to come;

drinking of health, toast; promise (*under pledge of secrecy*); solemn engagement to abstain from intoxicants (*take the pledge*). **2.** *v.t.* (~**eable** *pr.* -ja-). Deposit as security, pawn; promise solemnly by pledge of (one's honour, word, etc.); bind (person, one*self*) by solemn promise; drink to the health of. [F f. Gmc]

**Plei'adēs** (plī'adĕz) *n.pl.* Cluster of stars in constellation Taurus, usu. taken as 7 in number. [L f. Gk]

**Plei'stocēne** (plī's-) *a.* & *n.* (Geol.) (Of) division above Pliocene, and forming lower part of Quaternary. [Gk *pleistos* most, *kainos* new]

**plē'nar|y̆** *a.* (~**ily**). Entire, unqualified (*plenary indulgence*); (of assembly) to be attended by all members. [L *plenus* full)]

**plĕnipotĕ'ntiary̆** (-sherĭ) *a.* & *n.* (Person, esp. diplomat) invested with full power of independent action. [L (prec., POTENT)]

**plē'nitude** *n.* Fullness, completeness; abundance. [F f. L (PLENARY)]

**plĕ'nt|y̆** *n.*, *a.*, & *adv.* **1.** *n.* Abundance, quite enough (*of* thing, or abs.; *plenty of cake*; *there are plenty of apples*; *apples in plenty*; *we are in plenty of time*). **2.** *a.* (colloq.) Plentiful (*apples are plenty*). **3.** *adv.* (colloq.) Fully (*it is plenty big enough*). **4.** ~**eous** (rhet.), ~**iful** (-lly), *adjs.*, existing in ample quantity. [F f. L *plenitas* (PLENARY)]

**plĕ'on|ăsm** *n.* Use of words not needed to give the sense (*hear with one's ears*); ~**ă'stic** *a.* (-ically). [L f. Gk (*pleon* more)]

**plĕ'thor|a** *n.* Morbid condition with excess of red corpuscles in the blood; (fig.) over-supply, glut; ~**ĭc** *a.* (-ically). [L f. Gk, = fullness]

**pleur'|isy̆** (ploor'-) *n.* Inflammation of the membrane (pleura) enveloping the lungs; ~**ĭ'tic** *a.* [F f. L f. Gk (*pleura* rib)]

**plĕ'xus** *n.* (Anat.) Network of nerves or vessels in animal body (SOLAR *plexus*). [L *plecto* plex- plait]

**pli'a|ble** (~**bly**), **pli'a|nt**, *adjs.* Bending easily, supple; (fig.) yielding, compliant; ~**bĭ'lity̆**, ~**ncy̆**, *ns.* [F (PLY[1])]

**pli'ers** (-z) *n.pl.* (Pair of) pincers having long jaws with parallel surfaces for holding small objects, bending wire, etc. [dial. *ply* bend (prec.)]

**plight[1]** (-īt) *v.t.* (arch.; esp. in *p.p.*). Pledge (one's TROTH, *faith*, *word*);

engage one*self* (*to* person; *plighted lovers*). [E]

**plight[2]** (-īt) *n.* Condition, state, esp. unfortunate one. [AF *plit* PLAIT]

**Pli'msoll** *a.* & *n.* ~ **line**, ~ **mark**, marking on ship's side showing limit of legal submersion under various conditions; ||(*p*~) rubber-soled canvas sports shoe. [person]

**plĭnth** *n.* Lower square member of base of column; projecting part of wall immediately above ground; base supporting vase, statue, etc. [F or L f. Gk. = tile]

**Pli'ocēne** *a.* & *n.* (Geol.) (Of) highest division of Tertiary. [Gk *pleiōn* more, *kainos* new]

**P.L.O.** *abbr.* Palestine Liberation Organization.

**plŏd** **1.** *v.i.* (-**dd**-). Walk doggedly or laboriously, trudge, (*on*, *along*, etc.); work steadily, drudge (*at* etc.). **2.** *n.* Piece of plodding. [prob. imit.]

**plŏnk** *n.* (sl.) Cheap or inferior wine. [orig. unkn.]

**plŏp** *n.*, *adv.*, & *v.* **1.** *n.* Sound as of smooth object dropping into water without splash. **2.** *adv.* With a plop. **3.** *v.i.* & *t.* (-**pp**-). (Cause to) fall thus. [imit.]

**plŏ'sive** (or -z-) *a.* & *n.* (Consonant) pronounced with sudden release of breath. [EXPLOSIVE]

**plŏt.** **1.** *n.* Piece (usu. small) of ground; plan of main events in play, poem, novel, etc.; conspiracy (*Gunpowder Plot*); secret plan. **2.** *v.t.* (-**tt**-). Make plan or map of (existing object, place, or thing to be laid out, constructed, etc.); mark (point etc.) on diagram; make (curve etc.) by marking out a number of points; plan, contrive, (crime etc., or abs.); plan secretly. [E, & F *complot*]

**plough** (plow), **\*plow.** **1.** *n.* Implement for cutting furrows in soil and turning it up, consisting of cutting blade (~**'share**) fixed in frame drawn by horses etc. and guided by ~**'man**, (put one's **hand to the** ~, undertake task); instrument resembling plough (SNOW-*plough*); ploughed land; the **P**~, the Great BEAR[1] or its seven bright stars; ~**boy** (who leads plough-horses etc.); ~**man's lunch**, meal of bread and cheese etc. **2.** *v.t.* Turn up (earth, or abs.), bring *out* or *up*, with plough; furrow, scratch, (surface) as with plough; produce (furrow, line) thus (~ **a lonely**

**furrow,** carry on without help); (of ship) make way through (surface of water etc.); ||(sl.) fail in examination; move like plough *through* or *into* obstacles; advance laboriously (*through* snow, book, etc.); ~ **back,** plough (grass etc.) into soil to enrich it, (fig.) reinvest (profits) in same business etc. [E]

**plo'ver** (-ŭ'-) *n.* Gregarious medium-sized wading bird, e.g. pewit. [AF f. Rom. (L *pluvia* rain)]

**\*plow.** See PLOUGH.

**ploy** *n.* (colloq.) Manœuvre to frustrate opponent etc. [orig. unkn.]

||**P.L.R.** *abbr.* Public Lending Right.

**plŭck. 1.** *v.t. & i.* Pull off, pick, (flower, feather, hair); (arch.) pull, snatch; (*away, off, out,* etc.); pull at; twitch; tug or snatch *at*; strip (bird) of feathers; plunder, swindle; ~ **up** one's (take) **courage. 2.** *n.* Plucking, twitch; animal's heart, liver, and lungs, as food; courage, spirit; ~'**y** *a.* (-**ily, -iness**), brave, spirited. [E]

**plŭg. 1.** *n.* Piece of solid material fitting tightly into hole, used to fill gap or cavity or act as wedge or stopper; device of metal pins in insulated casing, fitting into holes in socket for making electrical connection; (colloq.) electric socket; (colloq.) release-mechanism of water--closet flushing-apparatus (*pull the plug*); = FIRE, SPARK*ing,*-*plug*; tobacco pressed into cake or stick, piece of this for chewing; (colloq.) favourable reference to commercial product etc. **2.** *v.t. & i.* (-**gg-**). Stop (hole etc. *up*) with plug; (sl.) shoot (person etc.); (colloq.) plod (*away at* work etc.), seek to popularize (song, policy, etc.) by constant repetition and favourable mention; ~ **in,** connect electrically by inserting plug into socket; ~**in** *a.,* able to be connected thus. [LDu.]

**plŭm** *n.* (Tree bearing) roundish fleshy fruit with sweet pulp and flattish pointed stone; dried grape or raisin as used for plum-cake etc.; (fig.) good thing, best of a collection, prize in life etc., well-paid position; ~**-cake** (containing raisins, currants, etc.); ~ **duff,** plain flour pudding with raisins or currants; ~ **pudding,** rich boiled pudding of flour, suet, raisins, currants, etc., eaten esp. at Christmas; ~'**my** *a.* (-**iness**), of or abounding in plums, (colloq.) good,

desirable, (of voice) rich in tone. [E, ult. f. L (PRUNE¹)]

**plu'mage** (-ōō'-) *n.* Bird's feathers. [F (PLUME)]

**plŭmb** (-m) *n., a., adv., & v.* **1.** *n.* Ball of lead, esp. attached to mason's ~**-line** (string for testing perpendicularity of wall etc.; also fig.; *out of* ~, not vertical); sounding-lead, plummet. **2.** *a.* Vertical; (fig.) downright, sheer; (Crick., of wicket) level, true. **3.** *adv.* Vertically; (fig.) exactly (*points plumb in the same direction*); \*(sl.) quite, utterly, (*plumb crazy*). **4.** *v.t.* Sound (sea) or measure (depth, lit. or fig.) with plummet, make vertical; work as plumber. **5.** ~**ā'gō** (-mb-) *n.* (*pl.* **-os**), graphite, plant with greyish-blue flowers; ~'**er** *n.,* workman who fits and repairs water-pipes, cisterns, etc.; ~'**ic** (-mb-) *a.,* (Chem.) containing lead; ~'**ing** *n.,* plumber's work, system of water-pipes etc. [F f. Rom. (L *plumbum* lead)]

**plum|e** (-ōō-). **1.** *n.* Feather, esp. large one used for ornament (BORROW*ed plumes*); ornamental feather(s) or horsehair, esp. as attached to helmet or hat, or worn in hair; trail of smoke from chimney, blown snow from mountain, etc. **2.** *v.t.* Furnish with plume(s); pride one*self* (*on* esp. something trivial or to which one has no claim); (of bird) preen (it*self,* its feathers). [F f. L *pluma*]

**plŭ'mmet. 1.** *n.* (Weight attached to). plumb-line; sounding-lead; weight attached to fishing-line to keep float upright. **2.** *v.i.* Fall rapidly. [F (PLUMB)]

**plŭ'mmy.** See PLUM.

**plŭmp** *a., v., & adv.* **1.** *a.* (Esp. of person or animal or part of body) full, rounded, fleshy, filled out. **2.** *v.i. & t.* Make or become plump; fatten *up*; swell *out* or *up*; drop or plunge with abrupt descent (*down upon* etc.); ||vote *for* (one candidate alone, when one might vote for two), (fig.) go whole-heartedly *for* one of alternative choices. **3.** *adv.* (colloq.) With sudden or heavy fall. [LDu.]

**plu'my** (-ōō'-) *a.* Plumelike, feathery; adorned with plumes. [PLUME]

**plŭ'nder. 1.** *v.t.* Rob (place, person) forcibly of goods, esp. as in war; rob systematically; steal, embezzle, (goods, or abs.). **2.** *n.* Violent or dishonest acquisition of property; property so acquired; (sl.) profit, gain. [G *plündern*]

**plŭnge** (-nj). **1.** *v.t.* & *i.* Thrust violently into (liquid, cavity, etc.); (fig.) thrust (person etc. *into* condition, action, etc.; esp. in p.p., *plunged in gloom*); immerse completely; throw oneself, dive, *(into* water, difficulty, discussion, etc.); enter impetuously (*into* room, *down* stairs, etc.); descend violently or suddenly; (of horse) start violently forward; (of ship) pitch; (sl.) gamble deeply, run into debt; **plunging** (low) **neckline. 2.** *n.* Plunging, dive, (~-**bath**, one large enough to dive into); (fig.) decisive step (*take the plunge*). **3.** **plŭ'nger** (-nj-) *n.*, (esp.) part of mechanism that works with plunging or thrusting motion, rubber cup on handle for removal of blockages by suction, (sl.) reckless gambler. [F f. Rom. (PLUMB)]

**pluper'fĕct** (-ōō-; *or* -ōō'-) *a.* & *n.* (Gram.) (Tense) denoting action completed prior to some past point of time (e.g., *he had said*). [L (*plus quam perfectum* more than perfect)]

**plur'al** (-oor'-) *a.* & *n.* ~ (**number**), (form or class of forms of noun, verb, etc.) denoting more than one; more than one in number; ~ **vote** (of one person in more than one constituency); ~**ĭsm** *n.*, holding of more than one office (esp. benefice) at a time; ~**ĭst** *n.*; ~**ĭ'stĭc** *a.*; **plură'lĭty** (-oor-) *n.*, state of being plural, pluralism, benefice or office held with another, (\*non-absolute) majority (*of* votes etc.); ~**ĭze** *v.t.*, make plural, express in plural. [F f. L (full.)]

**plŭs** *prep.*, *a.*, & *n.* **1.** *prep.* With addition of (symbol +; *3 plus 4 equals 7*); (colloq.) with, having gained, possessing; above zero; ~**-fours,** long wide knickerbockers worn esp. by golfers. **2.** *a.* Additional, extra; (after number etc.) at least (*fifteen plus*), rather better than (*beta plus*); (Math.) positive; (Electr.) having positive charge; *plus* SIGN. **3.** *n.* The symbol (+); additional quantity, positive quantity; advantage. [L *plus plur-* more]

**plŭsh. 1.** *n.* Cloth of silk, cotton, etc., with long soft nap. **2.** *a.* Made of plush; plushy. **3.** ~'**ў̆ ă.** (-iness), stylish, luxurious. [F f. L (PILE[3])]

**Plu'tō** (-ōō'-) *n.* Farthest known planet of solar system. [L f. Gk name of god of underworld]

**pluto'cracў̆** (-ōō-) *n.* (State under) rule of the wealthy; (ruling class of) wealthy persons; **plu'tocrăt** (-ōō'-) *n.*, member of plutocracy, wealthy man; **plutocră'tĭc** (-ōō-) *a.* (-ically). [Gk *ploutos* wealth]

**Plut|ō'nĭan** (-ōō-) *a.* Infernal, of the infernal regions; ~**ō'nĭc** *a.*, Plutonian, (*p-*; of rock) formed as igneous rock by solidification at great depth (*p*~**onic theory**, attributing most geological phenomena to action of internal heat); **p**~**ō'nĭum** *n.*, radioactive metallic element used in nuclear weapons and fuel. [PLUTO]

**plu'vĭ|al** (-ōō'-) *a.* Of rain, rainy; (Geol.) caused by rain; ~**ŏ'mĕter** *n.*, rain-gauge. [L (*pluvia* rain)]

**plỹ[1]** *n.* Fold, thickness, layer, or cloth etc.; strand of rope, yarn, etc.; ~'**wood,** strong thin board made by gluing layers with the grain crosswise. [F *pli* (PLAIT)]

**plỹ[2]** *v.t.* & *i.* Use, wield vigorously, (tool, weapon); work at or at (one's business, task, trade); supply (person etc.) persistently *with* (food etc.); assail vigorously (person *with* questions etc.); (of vessel or its master, bus, etc.) go to and fro *between* (places); (of boatman, porter, cabman) attend regularly for custom (*at* place). [APPLY]

**Plỹ'mouth** (-mu-) *n.* ~ **Brethren,** a religious body with no formal creed and no official order of ministers; ~ **Rock,** breed of domestic fowl. [places]

**P.M.** *abbr.* Prime Minister.

**p.m.** *abbr.* after noon [L *post meridiem*]; post-mortem.

**pneumă'tĭc** (n-) *a.* (~**ally**). (Acting by means) of wind or (esp. compressed) air; ~ **drill,** machine for breaking up road surface etc. and driven by compressed air; ~ **tyre** (inflated with air). [F or L f. Gk (*pneuma* wind)]

**pneumō'nĭa** (n-) *n.* Inflammation of the substance of one (**single** ~) or both (**double** ~) lungs. [L f. Gk (*pneumōn* lung)]

**pō** *n.* (colloq.; *pl.* **pos**). Chamber-pot; **po-faced,** solemn-faced, humourless. [POT, after F pr.]

**P.O.** *abbr.* Petty Officer; Pilot Officer; postal order; Post Office.

**poach** *v.t. & i.* Cook (egg) without shell with boiling water; cook (fish etc.) by simmering in water, milk, etc.; capture (game, fish) by illicit or unsportsmanlike methods; encroach, trespass, (on person's preserves etc., lit. or fig.). [F (POKE²)]

**pō′chard** (or -k-) *n.* Diving duck with bright reddish-brown head and neck. [orig. unkn.]

**pŏck** *n.* Eruptive spot esp. in smallpox; ~**-marked**, bearing marks (like those) left by smallpox. [E]

**pŏ′ckĕt** *n., a., & v.* 1. *n.* Small bag inserted in or attached to coat, trousers, etc., for carrying small articles (**in person's ~**, close to or intimate with him, completely under his control; **put one's pride in** one's ~, submit to mortification); pouchlike compartment in suitcase, car door, etc.; (fig.) pecuniary resources (*it is beyond my pocket*; **put** one's **hand in** one's ~, spend or give money; **in, out of, ~**, having gained, lost, in a transaction; **out-of-~ expenses**, actual outlay incurred); bag, sack, (esp. of hops); pouch at corner or on side of billiard-table into which balls are driven; cavity in earth filled with gold or other ore; cavity in rock esp. (Geol.) filled with foreign matter; (Mil.) (troops occupying) isolated area in battle (*pockets of resistance*); isolated group (of unemployed persons etc.); = AIR *pocket*; ~**ful** (-ŏŏl) *n.* 2. *a.* Of suitable size or shape for carrying in pocket (*pocket calculator, dictionary, -watch*); ~**-book**, notebook, booklike case for papers or paper money carried in pocket, (fig.) pecuniary resources (*hurt one's pocket-book*), \*large handbag; ‖*pocket* BOROUGH; ~ **handkerchief** (carried in pocket; fig. of small garden etc.); ~**-knife** (with folding blade(s), to be carried in pocket); ~**-money** (for occasional expenses, esp. that allowed regularly to children). 3. *v.t.* Put into (one's) pocket; confine as in pocket; appropriate, usu. dishonestly; submit to (affront, injury); conceal, suppress, (feelings). [AF dim. (POKE²)]

**pŏd.** 1. *n.* Long seed-vessel esp. of pea, bean, etc. 2. *v.i. & t.* (**-dd-**). Bear or form pods; remove (peas etc.) from pods. [orig. unkn.]

**pŏ′dgў** *a.* (**-ily, -iness**). (Of person) short and fat; (of face etc.) soft and fat. [*podge* short fat person]

**pō′dǐ|um** *n.* (*pl.* ~**a**). Continuous projecting base or pedestal round room, house, etc.; conductor's or speaker's rostrum. [L, f. Gk *podion* dim. of *pous pod-* foot]

**pō′ĕm** *n.* A metrical composition, esp. of elevated character; elevated composition in prose or verse (*prose poem*); (fig.) something not in words but akin or compared to a poem (*their lives are a poem*); **pō′ĕsў** (or -zĭ) *n.*, (arch., poet.) art or composition of poetry, poems collectively; **pō′ĕt** *n.*, writer of poems, writer in verse, esp. one possessing high powers of imagination, expression, etc.; *Poet* LAUREATE; **Poets' Corner**, part of Westminster Abbey containing graves and monuments of several poets; **pōĕtă′ster** *n.*, paltry or inferior poet; **pō′ĕtĕss** *n.*; **pŏĕ′tĭc** *a.* (**-ically**), of, or proper to, poets or poetry (*poetic* JUSTICE, LICENCE), having the good qualities of poetry; **pŏĕ′tĭcal** *a.* (**-lly**), poetic, written in verse (*poetical works*); **pō′ĕtrў** *n.*, art or work of the poet, elevated expression of thought or feeling in metrical form, poems, quality that calls for poetical expression. [F or L f. Gk (*poieō* make)]

**pō′gō** *n.* (*pl.* ~**s**). Stiltlike toy with spring, used to jump about on. [orig. uncert.]

**pŏ′grom** *n.* Organized massacre (orig. of Jews in Russia). [Russ.]

**poi′gn|ant** (poi′n-, poi′ny-) *a.* Sharp or pungent in taste or smell; painfully sharp (*poignant hunger, regret*); pleasantly piquant; causing sympathy; ~**ancў** *n.* [F f. L (POINT)]

**poinsĕ′ttǐa** *n.* Plant with large scarlet bracts surrounding small yellowish flowers. [*Poinsett*, person]

**point.** 1. *n.* Very small mark on surface; punctuation-mark; = DECIMAL *point* (*four* ~ *six*, 4·6); single item, particular, (**at all** ~**s**, in every part or respect; **in ~ of**, as a matter of *fact* etc.; *point of* ORDER); unit of scoring in games etc. or fig. in debate (*win on* ~**s**, by scoring more points than boxing-opponent, not by knock-out), or in evaluation of exhibit, share-prices, etc.; (Geom.) that which has position but no magnitude; precise place or moment (~ **of no return**, in long journey when one must continue for lack of means to return to starting-place, or in action after which one cannot withdraw);

(Hunting) (place aimed at in) straight run (~-to-~ **race**, over course defined only by landmarks); ‖ = POWER *point*; stage or degree in progress or increase (*full to bursting--point; gave up at that point;* **up to a ~**, by no means wholly), level of temperature esp. at which change of state occurs (*freezing-point*); precise moment (*at the point of death*), esp. for action (*when it came to the point, he refused;* **at, on, the ~ of**, on the verge of); distinctive feature (*singing is not his strong point*); significant or essential thing, thing actually intended or under discussion, (*that is just the point; what was the point of your question?; come to the point;* **beside the ~**, irrelevant(ly); **carry one's ~**, secure one's object; **in ~**, apposite; **make a ~ of**, treat as essential; **make** or **prove a ~**, establish proposition, OFF *the point; I* TAKE *your point;* **to the ~**, relevant(ly); **you have a ~ there**, that is valid and relevant); sharp or operative end of tool, weapon, pin, pen, etc., (**come to a ~**, taper to sharp end; **not to put too fine a ~ on it**, to speak bluntly); tip, extreme end, promontory, (Ballet) tip of toe, (in *pl.*) extremities of horse, dog, etc.; sharp-pointed tool; tine of deer's horn (*buck of 8 points*); ‖(usu. in *pl.*) tapering movable rail to direct railway train from one line to another; one of 32 directions marked at equal distances on compass; corresponding direction towards horizon (CARDINAL *points*); salient feature of story, joke, remark, etc., (*don't see the point*); effectiveness, value, (*his remarks lack point; saw no point in going*); (Crick.) (position of) fieldsman near batsman on the off side and nearly in line with popping-crease; **~-bla'nk**, with aim or weapon level, at very close range, (fig.) direct(ly), flat(ly); ‖**~-duty** (of constable etc. stationed to regulate traffic); **~ lace** (made wholly with needle, or imitating such); **~ of honour**, thing that vitally affects one's honour; **~ of view**, position from which thing is viewed, (fig.) way of looking at or thinking about a matter. **2.** *v.t. & i.* Provide with point(s); give force to (words, actions); fill joints of (brickwork etc.) with smoothed mortar or cement; mark (Psalms etc.) with signs for chanting; (of dog) indicate

presence of game by acting as pointer; direct (finger, weapon, etc., *at* or *towards*, person etc. *to*); direct attention (*to, at*); aim or be directed *at, to, towards*; **~ out**, indicate, draw attention to; **~ to, towards**, be evidence of; **~ up**, emphasize. **3.** **~'ĕd** *a.*, (esp., of remark etc.) having point, cutting, emphasized; **~'er** *n.*, (esp.) index hand of clock, balance, etc., rod for pointing to words etc. on blackboard or map, (colloq.) hint, dog of breed that stands rigid looking towards where game is scented, (in *pl.*) two stars in Great Bear in line with pole-star; **~'illĭsm** (pwǎ'n-) *n.*, method of producing effects of light in painting by crowding a surface with small spots of various colours, blended by spectator's eye; **~'illĭst** (pwǎ'n-) *n.*; **~'lĕss** *a.*, (esp.) without point or force, meaningless, purposeless. [F f. L (*pungo punct-* prick)]

**poise** (-z). **1.** *v.t. & i.* Balance; hold or be suspended or supported; carry (one's head etc.). **2.** *n.* Equilibrium (lit. or fig.), composure; carriage (of head etc.). [F f. L (*pendo pens-* weigh)]

**poi'son** (-z-). **1.** *n.* Substance that when introduced into or absorbed by living organism causes death or injury, esp. one that kills by rapid action even in small quantity (**slow ~**, of which repeated doses are eventually injurious; **hate person like ~**, bitterly); (fig.) baneful principle, doctrine, etc.; *poison* GAS; **~ ivy**, N. Amer. climbing plant secreting irritant oil from leaves; **~ pen**, (practice of) anonymous writer of libellous or scurrilous letters; **~ous** *a.* **2.** *v.t.* Administer poison to (person, animal), kill or injure thus; infect (air, water, etc.) with poison, (esp. in *p.p.*) smear (weapon) with poison; corrupt, pervert, (person, mind); destroy, spoil, (person's pleasure etc.). [F f. L (POTION)]

**pōke¹. 1.** *v.t.* Thrust or push (thing *in, up, down,* etc.) with hand, arm, point of stick, etc.; thrust end of finger etc. against; stir (fire) with poker; produce (hole etc. *in* thing) by poking; thrust forward, esp. obtrusively, (lit. or fig.); make thrusts with stick etc. (*at* etc.); be thrust forward *through* opening, *up, down,* etc.; pry (*about, into*); potter *about* or *around*; *poke* FUN *at*, one's

NOSE *into*. **2.** *n.* Poking, thrust, nudge; projecting brim or front of woman's bonnet or hat; ~(**-bonnet**), bonnet with this. **3.** **pō′ker¹** *n.*, stiff metal rod with handle, for poking fire (**as stiff as a** ~**r**, esp. of person's bearing or manners; **red-hot** ~**r**, plant with spikes of scarlet or yellow flowers), implement used in ~**r--work**, (design made by) burning white wood etc. with heated metal rod; **pō′ký** *a.* (**-ily**, **-iness**), (of place, room, etc.) confined, mean, shabby. [LDu.]

**pōke²** *n.* Bag, sack, (usu. dial. exc. *buy a* PIG *in a poke*). [F dial.]

**pō′ker²** *n.* Card-game in which players bet on value of their hands and may win by holding strongest hand or by bluffing others into ceasing to compete; ~ **dice** (with card designs from ace to nine instead of spots); ~**face**, (person with) impassive countenance appropriate to poker-player. [orig. unkn.]

**pō′ký.** See POKE¹.

**pō′lar** *a.* Of or near either pole of earth or celestial sphere (~ **circles**, parallels at 23° 27′ from poles; ~ **star**, = POLE²-*star*); living in north polar regions (*polar bear*); having electric or magnetic polarity; (fig.) analogous to pole of earth or to pole-star; directly opposite in character; **polā′rity** *n.*, tendency of loadstone, magnetized bar, etc., to point with its ends to earth's magnetic poles, tendency of body to lie with axis in particular direction, possession of two poles having contrary qualities (lit. or fig.), electrical condition of body as positive or negative, (fig.) attraction towards an object; ~**ize** *v.t.* & *i.*, restrict vibrations of (transverse waves, esp. light) so that they have different amplitudes in different planes, give electric or magnetic polarity to, (fig.) divide into two opposing groups; ~**izā′tion** *n.* [F or L (POLE²)]

**pō′lder** *n.* Piece of low-lying land reclaimed from sea or river, esp. in Netherlands. [Du.]

**pōle¹** *n.* Long slender rounded piece of wood or metal esp. as support for tent, telegraph wires, bean-plant, etc., (**under bare** ~**s**, with no sails set; **up the** ~, sl., in a difficulty, crazy, drunk); (as measure) = PERCH¹; ~**-jump**(ing), ~**-vault-** (ing), (with help of pole held in hands). [E f. L *palus* stake]

**pōle²** *n.* (**north and south**) ~**s**, two points in celestial sphere about which stars appear to revolve, ends of earth's axis of rotation, (**magnetic**) ~**s**, points near these where magnetic needle dips vertically, (**from** ~ **to** ~, throughout the world); each of two points on surface of magnet at which magnetic forces are concentrated; each of two terminals (**positive** and **negative** ~) of electric cell, battery, etc.; (fig.) each of two opposed principles etc. (**be** ~**s apart**, differ greatly); ~**-star**, star in Little Bear, now about 1° distant from north pole of heavens, (fig.) thing serving as guide. [L f. Gk, = axis]

**Pōle³** *n.* Native of Poland. [G f. Pol.]

**pō′le-ăxe**, **\*-ăx**, (**-lă-**). **1.** *n.* Battle-axe; halberd; butcher's axe for slaughtering, with hammer at back. **2.** *v.t.* Slaughter or strike (animal) with pole-axe. [LDu. (POLL¹, AXE)]

**pō′lecăt** (**-lk-**) *n.* ‖Small dark-brown stinking carnivorous mammal of weasel family. [orig. unkn.]

**polĕ′mic** **1.** *a.* (also ~**al**; ~**ally**). Controversial, disputatious. **2.** *n.* Controversial discussion, (in *pl.*) practice of this; controversialist. [L f. Gk (*polemos* war)]

**polï′ce** (**-ē′s**) **1.** *n.* Civil force responsible for maintaining public order; (as *pl.*) members of this (*the police are on his track*); force with similar functions of enforcing regulations (*military police*); ‖*police* CONSTABLE; ~ **dog** (trained and used by police to track criminals); ~**man**, ~**-officer**, ~**woman**, member of police force; ~ **state**, totalitarian State controlled by esp. secret police supervising citizens' activities; ~ **station**, office of local police force. **2.** *v.t.* Control (country etc.) by means of police; furnish with police; (fig.) keep order in, control. [F f. L (foll.)]

**pŏ′licÿ¹** *n.* Prudent conduct, sagacity; course of action (to be) adopted by government, party, person, etc. (*honesty is the best policy*). [F f. L *politia* POLITY]

**pŏ′licÿ²** *n.* Document containing contract of insurance. [F *police* ult. f. Gk *apodeixis* proof]

**pŏliōmÿĕli′tĭs** *n.* (Path.; colloq.

*abbr.* **pŏ′liŏ**). Infectious viral inflammation of nerve cells in grey matter of spinal cord, with temporary or permanent paralysis. [Gk *polios* grey, *muelos* marrow]

**pŏ′lish**[1]. **1.** *v.t. & i.* Make or become smooth and glossy by friction; (fig., esp. in *p.p.*) make elegant or cultured, refine; smarten *up*; ~ **off**, finish off quickly. **2.** *n.* Smoothness or glossiness produced by friction; substance used to produce smooth surface; (fig.) refinement. [F f. L *polio*]

**Pŏ′lish**[2] *a. & n.* (Language) of Poland or the Poles. [POLE[3]]

**poli′te** *a.* (~**r**, ~**st**). Having refined manners, courteous; cultivated, cultured; well-bred; (of literature etc.) refined, elegant, (*polite letters*). [L *politus* (POLISH[1])]

**pŏ′litic. 1.** *a.* (Of person) sagacious, prudent; (of action etc.) judicious, expedient; **body** ~, State, or similarly organized system. **2.** *v.i.* (**-ck-**). Engage in politics. [F f. L f. Gk (as POLITY)]

**poli′tical** *a.* (~**ly**). Of or affecting the State or its government; of public affairs; of politics; belonging to, or taking, a side in politics; relating to person's or organization's status or influence (*a political decision*); *political* ASYLUM, ECONOMY; ~ **geography** (dealing with boundaries and possessions of States); ~ **prisoner**, person imprisoned for political offence; **pŏlĭti′cian** (-shan) *n.*, one skilled or interested or engaged in politics, esp. as profession; **poli′ticize** *v.i. & t.*, engage in or talk politics, give political character to; **poli′tico** *n.* (*pl.* **-os**), one interested or engaged in politics, esp. as profession; **pŏ′litics** *n.pl.* (also treated as *sing.*), science and art of government, political affairs or life (*politics is a dirty business*), political principles (*what are his politics?*); **not practical politics**, not likely or practicable enough to be worth discussing. [L (prec.)]

**pŏ′litỹ** *n.* Form or process of civil government; organized society, State. [L *politia* f. Gk (*politēs* citizen f. *polis* city)]

**pŏ′lka. 1.** *n.* (Music for) lively dance of Bohemian origin; ~ **dot**, round dot as one of many forming regular pattern on textile fabric etc.

**2.** *v.i.* Dance the polka. [F & G f. Czech]

**pŏll**[1]. **1.** *n.* Human head, part of this on which hair grows (*flaxen poll*), (~**-tax**, levied on every person); counting of voters esp. at parliamentary or other election; voting at election (*go to the poll*); result of voting; number of votes recorded; = GALLUP *poll*; hornless animal, esp. ox. **2.** *v.t. & i.* Cut off top of (tree, plant), esp. make pollard of; (esp. in *p.p.*) cut off horns of (cattle); take vote(s) of; (of candidate) receive (so many votes); give (vote); give one's vote. **3.** ~**′ster** *n.*, person who organizes Gallup poll. [perh. LDu.]

**pŏll**[2] *n.* ~ **parrot**, tame parrot, user of conventional phrases and arguments. [*Poll*, conventional name for parrot]

**pŏ′llack, -ock,** *n.* Marine food-fish allied to cod. [orig. unkn.]

**pŏ′llard. 1.** *n.* Animal that has cast or lost its horns; ox, sheep, or goat, of hornless breed; tree polled so as to produce close rounded head of young branches. **2.** *v.t.* Make (tree) pollard. [POLL[1]]

**pŏ′ll|en** *n.* Fine powdery substance discharged from anther, male element that fertilizes seeds; ~**en count**, index of amount of pollen in air published as warning to those allergic to it; ~**ĭnāte** *v.t.*, fertilize or sprinkle with pollen; ~**ĭnā′tion** *n.* [L]

**pŏ′llock.** See POLLACK.

**pollū′t|e** (*or* -ōō′t) *v.t.* Destroy purity or sanctity of; make foul or filthy; contaminate or defile (environment); ~**ion** *n.* [L *polluo* -lut-]

**pŏ′lō** *n.* Game like hockey played on horseback with long-handled mallet (~**-stick**); ~**-neck**, high round turned-over collar; WATER *polo*. [Balti, = ball]

**pŏlonai′se** (-z) *n.* (Music for or in style of) slow processional dance of Polish origin. [F (POLE[3])]

||**pŏlō′nỹ** *n.* Sausage of partly cooked pork etc. [prob. *Bologna*, place]

**pŏ′ltergeist** (-gī-) *n.* Noisy mischievous ghost, esp. one manifesting itself by physical damage. [G]

**pŏltrōō′n** *n.* Spiritless coward; ~**erỹ** *n.* [F f. It (*poltro* sluggard)]

**Pŏ′lỹ** *n.* (colloq.; *pl.* ~**s**). Polytechnic. [abbr.]

**pŏ′lў-** *pref.* Many (*polygamy*); poly-merized (*polyester*); **~ăndrў** *n.*, polygamy in which one woman has more than one husband, **~ă′ndrous** *a.*, [Gk *anēr andr-* man]; **~ă′nthus** *n.*, cultivated primrose from hybridized primulas [Gk *anthos* flower]; **~chrŏmă′tĭc** (-kr-) *a.* (-ically), many-coloured, (of radiation) consisting of more than one wavelength; **~chrŏme** (-kr-) *a.* & *n.*, (work of art) in many colours; **~ĕ′ster** *n.*, a synthetic resin or fibre; **~ĕ′thўlēne** *n.*, polythene; **polў′gamous** *a.*, having more than one wife or (less usu.) husband at once, (Zool.) having more than one mate, **polў′gamĭst, polў′gamў,** *ns.*, [Gk *gamos* marriage]; **~glŏt** *a.* & *n.*, of many languages, (person) speaking or writing several languages, (book, esp. Bible) with text and translation into several languages, [Gk *glōtta* tongue]; **~gon** *n.*, figure (usu. plane recti-linear) with many (usu. 5 or more) angles and sides; **polў′gonal** *a.* (-lly); **polў′gўnў** (or -g-) *a.*, polygamy in which one man has more than one wife, **polў′gўnous** (or -g-) *a.*, [Gk *gunē* wife]; **~hĕ′dron** *n.* (*pl.* -ra), solid figure with many (usu. 7 or more) faces, **~hĕ′dral** *a.* (-lly); [Gk *hedra* base]; **~măth** *n.*, person of varied learning, great scholar, [Gk *manthanō* math- learn]; **~mer** *n.*, (Chem.) compound whose molecule is formed from many repeated units of one or more compounds, **~mĕ′rĭc** *a.*, **~merize** *v.t.* & *i.*, combine into polymer, **~merĭzā′tion** *n.*, **polў′merous** *a.*, (Biol.) having many parts, [Gk (*meros* part)]; **~mŏr′phous** *a.*, varying in individuals, passing through successive variations, [Gk *morphē* form]; **~nŏ′mĭal** *a.* & *n.*, (algebraic expression) of 3 or more terms, esp. (sum) of various powers of variable(s), [BINOMIAL]; **~p** *n.*, (Zool.) individual member of colony of corals etc., (Path.) small tumour of mucous membrane, [F (POLYPUS)]; **polў′phonў** *n.*, (Mus.) simultaneous combination of several individual melodies, **~phŏ′nĭc** *a.*, [Gk (*phōnē* sound)]; **~stўr′ēne** *n.*, hard colour-less plastic [*styrene* f. Gk *sturax* a resin]; **~sўllable** *n.*, polysyllabic word; **~sўllă′bĭc** *a.* (-ically), marked by polysyllables, (of word) having many syllables; **~tĕ′chnĭc**

(-k-) *a.* & *n.*, (institution, esp. college) dealing with or devoted to various esp. technical subjects; **~thĕism** *n.*, belief in, worship of, many gods or more than one god; **~thĕĭst** *n.*, **~thĕĭ′stĭc** *a.* (-ically); **~thēne** *n.*, tough light plastic [POLYETHYLENE]; **~ūrĕ′thāne** (or -ūr′-) *n.*, synthetic resin or plastic used esp. as foam [UREA, ETHANE]; **~vī′nўl** *a.* (**~vinyl chloride**, vinyl plastic used for insulation or as fabric). [Gk (*polus* many)]

**pŏ′lўpus** *n.* (*pl.* **~i** *pr.* -ī, **~uses**; Path.) = POLYP. [Gk (*pous* foot)]

**pŏm** *n.* Pomeranian dog; = POMMY. [abbr.]

**po′mace** (pŭ′mĭs) *n.* Mass of crushed apples in cider-making. [L (*pomum* apple)]

**poma′de** (-ah′d) *n.* Scented ointment for hair and skin of head. [F f. It. (prec.)]

**pomă′nder** *n.* Ball of mixed aromatic substances; (spherical) container for this. [AF f. L]

**pŏ′mĕgranate** (or -mg-) *n.* (Tropical tree bearing) orange-sized fruit with tough rind and reddish pulp enclosing many seeds. [F *pome grenate* f. Rom. = many-seeded apple]

**po′melō** (pŭ′-) *n.* (*pl.* **~s**). Shaddock or grapefruit. [orig. unkn.]

**Pŏmerā′nian** *a.* & *n.* **~** (dog), small dog with long silky hair. [*Pomerania*, place]

||**pŏ′mfrĕt-cāke** (or pŭ′-) *n.* Small round flat liquorice sweetmeat. [*Pontefract*, place]

**po′mmel** (pŭ′-). **1.** *n.* Knob esp. at end of sword-hilt; upward projecting front of saddle. **2.** *v.t.* (||-ll-) = PUMMEL. [F dim. (L *pomum* apple)]

**pŏ′mmy, -ie,** *n.* (Austral. & N.Z. sl.) British person, esp. recent immigrant. [orig. uncert.]

**pŏmp** *n.* Splendid display, splendour; specious glory. [F f. L f. Gk]

**pŏ′m-pŏm¹** *n.* Automatic quick-firing gun. [imit.]

**pŏ′m-pŏm²**, **pŏ′mpŏn**, *n.* Ornamental tuft or bunch of ribbon, flowers, etc., on women's or children's hats, shoes, etc.; dahlia etc. with small tightly-clustered petals. [F]

**pŏ′mpous** *a.* Self-important, consequential; (of language) pretentious, unduly grand in style; **~ŏ′sĭtў** *n.* [F f. L (POMP)]

**pŏnce. 1.** *n.* Man who lives off prostitute's earnings. **2.** *v.i.* Act as ponce; move *about* effeminately etc. [orig. unkn.]

**pŏ'nchō** *n.* (*pl.* ~s). S. Amer. cloak of oblong piece of cloth with slit in middle for head; cycling-cape or other garment of similar design. [S. Amer. Sp.]

**pŏnd** *n.* Fairly small body of still water formed naturally or by hollowing or embanking; ~-**life**, animals (esp. invertebrates) living in ponds; ~'**weed**, aquatic herb growing in still water. [var. POUND²]

**pŏ'nder** *v.t.* & *i.* Weigh mentally, think over (matter, *how*, etc.); think *on*, muse *over*; ~**able** *a.* (-bly), having appreciable weight (lit. or fig.); ~**abi'lity** *n.*; ~**ous** *a.*, heavy, unwieldy, (of style) dull, tedious; ~**ŏ'sity** *n.* [F f. L *pondero* weigh]

**pŏng** *n.*, & *v.i.* (colloq.) Stink. [orig. unkn.]

**pŏ'niard** (-yerd) *n.*, & *v.t.* (Pierce, stab, with) dagger. [F *poignard* f. L (*pugnus* fist)]

**pŏns ăsĭnŏr'um** (-nz-) *n.* Name given to 5th proposition of 1st book of Euclid; anything found difficult by beginners. [L, = bridge of asses]

**pŏ'ntĭff** *n.* (Sovereign, supreme) ~**iff**, the Pope; bishop, chief priest; ~**i'fical**, (*a.*; -lly) of or befitting pontiff, pretending to infallibility, pompously dogmatic, (*n.*) (in *pl.*, also ~**ifĭcā'lia**) vestments and insignia of bishop; ~**i'ficate**, (*n.*) (period of) office of bishop or Pope, (-āt; *v.i.*) play the pontiff, pretend to infallibility. [F f. L *pontifex* -*fic*-priest]

**pŏntŏō'n** *n.* Flat-bottomed boat used as ferry-boat etc.; one of several boats etc. used to support temporary bridge; *vingt-et-un*. [F f. L *ponto*-*un* = punt]

**pŏ'ny** *n.* Horse of any small breed; ~-**tail**, woman's or girl's hair drawn back, tied, and hanging behind like pony's tail; ~-**trekking**, travelling across country on ponies for pleasure. [perh. F *poulenet* foal]

**pŏō'dle** *n.* Breed of dog with long curling hair often elaborately clipped and shaved. [G *pudel*]

**pŏōf** *n.* (colloq.) Effeminate man; male homosexual. [orig. unkn.]

**pŏŏh** (pōō) *int.* expr. impatience or contempt; ~~' *v.t.*, express contempt for, ridicule. [imit.]

**pŏōl¹** *n.* Small body of still water,

usu. of natural formation; small shallow body of any liquid; deep place in river; = SWIMMING-*pool*. [E]

**pōōl²**. **1.** *n.* (Cards) collective amount of players' stakes and fines, receptacle for these; ‖game on billiard-table in which winner takes all stakes; \*game on billiard-table with usu. 16 balls (~'**room**, place for playing this, betting, etc.); (collective stakes in) joint gambling venture (**football** ~, form of gambling in which entry money is awarded in prizes to those who (most) correctly forecast results of certain football matches; **the** ~**s**, various such competitions conducted week by week); arrangement between competing parties by which prices are fixed and business divided to avoid competition; common fund, e.g. of profits of separate firms; common supply of persons, commodities, etc.; group of persons sharing duties etc. **2.** *v.t.* Throw into common fund, share in common. [F *poule*]

**pōōp** *n.* Stern of ship; aftermost and highest deck. [F *pupe* f. L *puppis*]

**poor** *a.* Not having means to procure comforts or necessaries of life (*poor in* SPIRIT); ill supplied, deficient, (*in a possession or quality*); (of soil) unproductive; scanty, inadequate, less (good) than is expected, (*the crop, visibility, was poor; had a poor night; is a poor driver; in poor* SPIRITS); paltry, sorry, (*that is a poor consolation; came a poor second in the race; it is a poor look-out if that happens*); spiritless, despicable, (*he is a poor creature*); humble, insignificant, (often iron. or joc.; *in my poor opinion*); (expr. pity or sympathy) unfortunate, hapless, (*poor fellow!; the poor child is inconsolable*); **take a** ~ **view of,** regard with disfavour or pessimism; ~-**box**, money-box esp. in church for relief of the poor; ~-**house**, (Hist.) workhouse; ~-**law**, (Hist.) law relating to support of paupers; ~ **man's**, inferior or cheaper substitute for; ~ *man's weather-glass*, pimpernel; ~ **relation**, (fig.) inferior or subordinate member of group; ~-**spirited**, timid, cowardly; \*~ **white**, (derog.) member of socially inferior group of white people; ~'**ly**, (*adv.*) scantily, defectively, with little success, (*pred. a.*) unwell (*he is looking very poorly*); ~'**ness** *n.*, defectiveness, lack of some good quality or constituent. [F *povre* f. L *pauper*]

**pŏp**[1] *n., v.,* & *adv.* **1.** *n.* Abrupt explosive sound; (colloq.) effervescing drink; ||(sl.) pawning (**in ~**, in pawn). **2.** *v.t.* & *i.* (**-pp-**). (Cause to) make small quick explosive sound(s) as of cork when drawn; put (thing), move, go, come, (*in, out, up, down,* etc.) unexpectedly or quickly or suddenly; ||(sl.) pawn. **3.** *adv.* With sound of pop (*heard it go pop*); **~ goes the weasel**, a country dance). **4.** **~'corn**, maize parched till it bursts open; **~-eyed**, (colloq.) with eyes bulging or wide open; **~'gun**, child's toy gun shooting pellet etc. by compression of air with piston, (derog.) inefficient firearm; **~ off**, (colloq.) die; **~ the question**, (colloq.) propose marriage; **~-up** *a.*, (of toaster etc.) operating so as to move object quickly upwards. **5.** **~'ping** *n.*; **~ping-crease**, (Crick.) line in front of and parallel to wicket within which batsman must keep bat or foot grounded to avoid risk of being stumped. [imit.]

**pŏp**[2]. (colloq.) **1.** *n.* Popular concert, record, music, etc. **2.** *a.* Popular (*pop music*); performing popular music etc. (*pop group*); **~ art** (based on modern popular culture and mass media). [abbr.]

**pŏp**[3] *n.* (colloq., esp. as *voc.*) Father; any older man. [PAPA]

**pōpe** *n.* (P**~**) Bishop of Rome as head of Roman Catholic Church; *pope's* NOSE; **pō'pery** *n.*, (derog.) papal system, Roman Catholic religion; **pō'pish** *a.*, (derog.) of popery. [E f. L *papa* f. Gk *papas*]

**pŏ'pĭnjay** *n.* Fop, conceited person. [F *papingay* f. Sp. f. Arab.]

**pŏ'plar** *n.* Tree of rapid growth with straight trunk and freq. tremulous leaves. [AF f. L *populus*]

**pŏ'plĭn** *n.* Plain-woven fabric usu. of cotton, with corded surface. [F *papeline*]

**pŏ'ppét** *n.* (colloq. esp. as term of endearment). Small or dainty person. [ult. f. L *pu(p)pa* doll]

**pŏ'ppў** *n.* Herb with milky juice, narcotic properties, and showy esp. scarlet flowers; ||emblem of dead in World Wars, esp. artificial poppy worn on **P~ Day** (Remembrance Sunday); **opium ~** (from which opium is obtained). [E f. L *papaver*]

**pŏ'ppўcŏck** *n.* (sl.) Nonsense. [Du. *pappekak*]

**pŏ'psў, -sĭe,** *n.* (colloq., esp. as term of endearment). Young woman. [POPPET]

**pŏ'pŭlace** *n.* The common people. [F f. It. (foll.)]

**pŏ'pŭlar** *a.* Of, carried on by, the people; adapted to the understanding, taste, or means, of the people (*in popular language*; *popular science*; **~ music**, songs etc. not seeking to appeal to refined or classical taste); liked or admired by the people or by people generally or by specified class, (*popular teachers*; *is popular with his men*); prevalent among the people (*popular fallacies*); **~ĭtў** (-ǎ'r-) *n.*, being generally liked; **~ĭze** *v.t.*, make popular, present (technical subject) in popular form; **~ĭzā'tion** *n.* [AF or L (*populus* PEOPLE)]

**pŏ'pŭl|āte** *v.t.* Inhabit, form population of, (country, town); supply with inhabitants (*densely populated district*); **~ā'tion** *n.*, degree to which place is populated, total number of inhabitants of town, country, etc., *the* inhabitants of a place (*the population turned out to welcome him*), total number of things in a place (*the population of the world*); **~ation explosion**, large sudden increase of population of world or country; **~ist** *n.* & *a.*, (adherent) of political party claiming to represent all the people; **~ous** *a.*, thickly inhabited. [L (prec.)]

**pŏrbea'gle** *n.* Shark with pointed snout. [orig. unkn.]

**pŏr'celain** (-slĭn) *n.* Fine earthenware with translucent body and transparent glaze; thing(s) made of this. [F f. It. dim. (*porca* sow)]

**pŏrch** *n.* Covered approach to entrance of building; (P**~**) colonnade at Athens where Zeno taught, Stoic school or philosophy (cf. ACADEMY). [F f. L *porticus*]

**pŏr'cĭne** *a.* Of or like pig. [F or L (PORK)]

**pŏr'cŭpĭne** *n.* Rodent with body and tail covered with erectile spines. [F *porc espin* f. L (PORK, SPINE)]

**pōre**[1] *n.* Minute opening in surface, through which fluids may pass. [F f. L f. Gk *poros*]

**pōre**[2] *v.i.* **~ over,** be absorbed in studying (book etc.), (fig.) meditate, think intently upon, (subject). [orig. unkn.]

**pŏrk** *n.* Flesh (esp. unsalted) of

pig used as food; **~-butcher** (who slaughters pigs for sale, or sells pork rather than other meats); **~ pie** (of minced etc. pork, eaten cold); **~-pie hat** (with flat rimmed crown and brim turned up all round); **~'er** n., pig raised for pork; **~'y** a. (**~iness**), of or like pork, esp. (colloq.) fleshy. [F f. L *porcus* pig]

**porn('ō)** n. (colloq.) = foll. [abbr.]

**porno'graph|y** n. Explicit presentation of sexual activity in literature, films, etc., to stimulate erotic not aesthetic feelings; literature etc. containing this; **~er** n.; **pornogră'phĭc** a. (-ically). [Gk *pornē* prostitute]

**por'ous** a. Full of pores (lit. or fig.); **poro'sĭty** n. [F f. L (PORE[1])]

**por'phyry** n. Hard rock composed of crystals of red or white felspar in red matrix. [ult. f. Gk (PURPLE)]

**por'poise** (-pus) n. Small whale with blunt rounded snout. [F f. Rom. (PORK, L *piscis* fish)]

**po'rridge** n. Soft food of oatmeal or other meal or cereal boiled in water or milk (SAVE one's *breath to cool* one's *porridge*); **po'rringer** (-nj-) n., (arch.) small soup-basin esp. for child. [alt. POTTAGE]

**port**[1] n. Harbour (lit. or fig.; FREE *port*); town or place possessing harbour; **~ of call**, place where ship or (fig.) person stops during journey. [E f. L *portus*]

**port**[2] n. Opening in side of ship for entrance, loading, etc.; porthole; aperture in wall etc. for gun to be fired through; **~'hole**, (esp. glazed) aperture in ship's side for admission of light and air. [F f. L *porta* gate]

**port**[3] 1. v.t. (Mil.) Carry (rifle) diagonally across and close to the body (esp. command *port arms!*). 2. n. External deportment, carriage, bearing (arch.); (Mil.) position taken in porting arms. [F f. L *porto* carry]

**port**[4] 1. n. Left-hand side of ship or boat or aircraft looking forward (cf. STARBOARD); *port* TACK[1]. 2. v.t. Turn (helm) to port. [prob. orig. side turned towards PORT[1]]

**port**[5] n. **~ (wine)**, strong sweet dark-red (occas. brown or white) fortified wine. [*Oporto*, place]

**por't|able. 1.** a. (-bly). Easily movable, convenient for carrying, (*portable furnace, radio*). **2.** n. Portable object, esp. radio or typewriter. **3.** **~abĭ'lĭty** n.; **~age** (n.) carrying of

boats or goods between two navigable waters, place at which this is necessary, (v.t.) convey (boat, goods) over portage. [F or L (PORT[3])]

**por'tal. 1.** n. Door(way), gate(way), esp. elaborate one. **2.** a. (Anat.) **~ vein** (conveying blood to liver or other organ exc. heart). [F f. L (PORT[2])]

**portcŭ'llĭs** n. Strong heavy grating sliding up and down in vertical grooves, lowered to block gateway in fortress etc. [F, = sliding door]

**portĕ'n|d** v.t. Foreshadow, as an omen; give warning of (*this portends a renewal of the conflict*); **por'tĕnt** n., omen, significant sign of something to come, prodigy, marvellous thing; **~tous** a., (also = pompously solemn). [L *portendo* (PRO-[1], TEND[1])]

**||por'ter**[1] n. Gate-keeper, door-keeper, esp. of large building etc.; **~ress** n. [AF f. L (PORT[2])]

**por'ter**[2] n. Person employed to carry burdens, esp. railway or airport or hotel employee who handles luggage; dark beer brewed from charred or browned malt; **~house steak**, a choice cut of beef; **~age** n., hire of porters. [F f. L (PORT[3])]

**portfō'lĭo** n. (*pl.* **~s**). Case for loose drawings, sheets of paper, etc.; list of investments held by person, company, etc.; (fig.) office of minister of State (||**Minister without ~**, not in charge of any department of State). [It. *portafogli* sheet-carrier]

**por'tĭcō** n. (*pl.* **~es**, **~s**). Colonnade, roof supported by columns at regular intervals, usu. attached as porch to building. [It. f. L *porticus* porch]

**portière** (pŏrtyãr') n. Curtain hung over door(way). [F (PORT[2])]

**por'tion. 1.** n. Part, share; amount of food allotted to one person; dowry; one's destiny or lot. **2.** v.t. Divide (thing) into shares; distribute *out*; give dowry to. [F f. L *portio*]

**Pŏr'tland** n. **~ cement** (manufactured from chalk and clay); **~ stone**, valuable building limestone. [place]

**por'tl|y** a. (**~iness**). Bulky, corpulent. [PORT[3]]

**portmă'nteau** (-tō) n. (*pl.* **~s**, **~x**, *pr.* -z). Leather trunk for clothes etc., opening into two equal parts; **~ word**, factitious word blending sounds and combining meanings of two others (*chortle* =

chuckle and snort, *galumph* = gallop triumphant). [F (PORT³, MANTLE)]

**portray'** *v.t.* Make likeness of; describe graphically; **por'trait** (-rĭt) *n.*, likeness of person or animal made by drawing, painting, photography, etc., graphic description; **por'traitist** (-rĭt-) *n.*, one who paints or takes portraits; **por'traiture** (-rĭcher) *n.*, portraying, portrait, graphic description; **~al** *n.* [F *portraire* -trait depict]

**Portuguē'se** (-gē'z) *a.* & *n.* (*pl.* same). (Native, language) of Portugal; **~ man-of-war**, dangerous jellyfish with sail-shaped crest and poisonous sting. [Port. f. L]

**pōse** (-z). **1.** *v.t.* & *i.* Propound (question, problem); place (artist's model etc.) in certain attitude; assume attitude, esp. for artistic purposes, or to impress others; set up, give oneself out, *as* (connoisseur etc.); puzzle (person) with question or problem. **2.** *n.* Attitude of body or mind, esp. one assumed for effect (*his philanthropy is a mere pose*). **3.** **pō'ser** (-z-) *n.*, (esp.) puzzling question or problem; **pōseur'** (-zer') *n.* (*fem.* **poseuse** *pr.* -zer'z), person who poses for effect or behaves affectedly. [F f. L *pauso* PAUSE; confused w. L *pono* place]

**pŏsh** *a.* (sl.) Smart, stylish; first-rate. [perh. sl. *posh* money, a dandy]

**pŏ'sit** (-z-) *v.t.* Assume as fact, postulate. [L *pono* posit- place]

**posi'tion** (-z-). **1.** *n.* Way in which thing or its parts are placed or arranged; configuration of chess-men etc. during game; mental attitude, way of looking at question; place occupied by person or thing; proper place (*in, out of, position*); (Mil.) place where troops are posted for strategical purposes; being advantageously placed (*manœuvring for position*; **in a ~**, enabled by circumstances or resources or information *to do, state*, etc.); (fig.) situation in relation to others (*difficult for a person in my position*); rank, status, (high) social standing; paid (official or domestic) employment; **~al** *a.* **2.** *v.t.* Place in position. [F or L (prec.)]

**pŏ'sitive** (-z-). **1.** *a.* Formally or explicitly stated, definite, unquestionable, (*positive assertion*; *here is proof positive*); (of person) convinced, confident in opinion, cocksure; (Gram., of *adj.* or *adv.*) in primary form expressing simple quality without comparison (cf. COMPARATIVE, SUPERLATIVE); absolute, not relative; (colloq.) downright, out-and-out, (*it would be a positive miracle*); dealing only with matters of fact, practical, (*positive philosophy*); constructive (*a positive suggestion*); marked by presence, not absence, of qualities (cf. NEGATIVE; (Alg., of quantity) greater than zero (*positive SIGN*); in direction naturally or arbitrarily taken as that of increase or progress (*clockwise rotation is positive*; *positive FEEDBACK*); (Electr.) of, containing, producing, kind of charge produced by rubbing glass with silk; (Photog.) showing lights and shades or colours as in original image cast on film etc. (opp. NEGATIVE). **2.** *n.* Positive adjective, photograph, quantity, etc. **3.** **~ism** *n.*, philosophical system recognizing only positive facts and observable phenomena (**logical ~ism**, form of this in which symbolic logic is used and linguistic problems emphasized); **~ist** *n.*; **~i'stic** *a.* [F or L (POSIT)]

**pŏ'sitron** (-z-) *n.* Elementary particle with mass of electron and charge same as electron's but positive. [*positive electron*]

**pŏ'ssè** *n.* Body (*of* constables); strong force or company. [L, = be able]

**possė'ss** (-z-) *v.t.* Hold as property, own; have (faculty, quality, etc.; *they possess a special value for us*); maintain (*oneself*, one's mind, soul, *in* patience etc.); (of demon etc. or cause of infatuation) occupy, dominate, (person etc.) (*possessed by a devil, by* or *with an idea*; **like one ~ed**, with great energy; **what ~ed you?**, how could you be so foolish?); **~ oneself of**, take or get for one's own; **be ~ed of**, own, have. [F f. L *possideo* possess-]

**possė'ssion** (-zě'shon) *n.* Possessing or being possessed; occupancy, (**in ~**, (of thing) possessed, (of person) possessing; **in ~ of**, having in one's possession; **in the ~ of**, held or owned by; **take ~**, become owner or possessor *of*); thing possessed, (in *pl.*) property, wealth; subject territory; **possė'ssive** (poz-), (*a.*) showing desire to possess or retain what one possesses, of possession (**possessive case**, e.g. *Anne's, the baker's*;

*possessive* PRONOUN), (*n.*) possessive case or word; **posse´ssor** (poz-) *n.* [F or L (prec.)]

**po´sset** *n.* Drink of hot milk with wine, spice, etc., formerly much used as remedy for colds etc. [orig. unkn.]

**po´ssib|le. 1.** *a.* That can exist, be done, or happen (*it is quite possible to say, that he knows* or *may know; there are three possible excuses,* that may be made; *get the greatest possible assistance, all the assistance possible; come if possible,* if you can; *come as early as possible,* as you can); that is likely to happen etc. (*few thought her election possible*). **2.** *n.* Highest possible score esp. in shooting; possible candidate, member of team, etc. **3.** ~**i´lit̄y** *n.,* state or fact of being possible (*the possibility of miracles; there is no possibility of his coming; it is within the range of possibility*), capability of being realized, improved, etc., thing that may exist or happen (*what are the possibilities?*); ~**l̄y** *adv.,* in accordance with possibility (*cannot possibly do it; how can I possibly?*), perhaps, maybe, for all one knows to the contrary. [F or L (POSSE)]

**po´ssum** *n.* (colloq.) = OPOSSUM; **play** ~, pretend to be unconscious, feign ignorance. [abbr.]

**po̅st¹. 1.** *n.* Long stout vertical piece of timber or metal as support in building; stake or stout pole to mark boundary, carry notices, etc., (**deaf as a** ~, completely deaf; *from* PILLAR *to post*); pole etc. marking point in race, esp. STARTing-post (**left at the** ~, outdistanced immediately) or WINning-post (**beaten at the** ~, defeated at the last moment). **2.** *v.t.* ~ (**up**), attach (paper etc.) to post or in prominent place, advertise (fact, thing, person) by placard or in published list; ~**er** *n.,* (esp.) placard in public place. [E f. L *postis*]

**po̅st². 1.** *n.* Official conveying of letters, parcels, etc., single collection or delivery of these or place where it is done, (*send it by post; missed the last post; the post has come; take it to the post;* **by return of** ~, by next post in opposite direction); appointed place of soldier etc. on duty, situation of paid employment, (force of soldiers occupying) defensible position, fort, trading-station; **last** ~, (Mil.) bugle-call sounded at bedtime and at funerals. **2.** *v.t. & i.* Put

(letter etc.) into post office or letter-box for transmission by post; travel with haste; carry (entry) from auxiliary account-book to journal or ledger, (also ~ **up**) complete (ledger) thus, (fig., esp. in *p.p.*) supply (person) with full information (*keep me posted*); place (soldier etc.) at his post, appoint to post or command. **3.** ||~**-bag**, mail-bag; ~**-box**, postal letter-box; ~**´card** (for conveyance by post without envelope); ||~**-code**, group of letters and figures in postal address to assist sorting; ||~**-free**, carried free of charge by post; ~**-ha´ste**, with great speed; ~**´man** (who delivers or collects letters etc.); ~**´mark**, (*n.*) official mark on letter usu. giving place and date, and serving to cancel stamp, (*v.t.*) mark with this; ~**´master**, ~**´mistress**, official in charge of a post office; **P~ Office**, public department or corporation providing postal and kindred services; ~ **office**, room or building for postal business (~**-office box**, numbered place in post office where letters are kept until called for; *post-office* ORDER); ~**-paid**, on which postage has been paid; ~**-town** (with main post office). **4.** ~**´age** *n.,* amount charged for carriage of letter etc. by post; ~**age stamp**, small adhesive label affixed for prepayment of postage; ~**age due**, postage not prepaid and usu. demanded by special postage stamp; ~**´al** *a.* (**-lly**), of the post, by post; ~**al code**, post-code; *postal* ORDER. [F f. It. *posta* f. L (POSIT)]

**po̅st-** *pref.* After, behind; ~**-da´te**, affix or assign a date later than the actual one to (document, event, etc.); ~**-gra´duate**, (*a.*) (of course of study) carried on after taking first degree, (*n.*) student taking such course; **P~-Impre´s-sionism**, artistic aims and methods [so named as reaction from impressionism] directed to expressing individual artist's conception of objects represented; **P~-Impre´ssionist** *n.*; ~**-na´tal**, existing or occurring after (child)birth; ~**-war**, occurring or existing after a war (||~**-war credits,** resulting from reduced income-tax allowances in 1939–45 war). [L *post* adv. & prep.]

**po̅´stage, po̅´stal.** See POST²; **po̅´ster**, see POST¹.

*poste restante* (po̅st re̅stah´nt) *n.*

Department in post office where letters are kept till called for. [F]

**pŏstēr′i|or. 1.** *a.* Later, coming after in series, order, or time; hinder; **~ŏ′rĭty** *n.* **2.** *n.* (in *sing.* or *pl.*) Buttocks. [L compar. of *posterus* (POST-)]

**pŏstĕ′rĭty** *n.* Descendants of a person; all succeeding generations (*deserves the gratitude of posterity*); **pŏ′stern** *n.*, (arch.) back or side entrance. [F f. L (prec.)]

**pŏ′sthūmous** (-tū-) *a.* (Of child) born after death of its father; (of book etc.) published after author's death; occurring after death. [L *postumus* last]

**posti′l(l)ion** (-lyon) *n.* Rider on near horse drawing coach etc. without coachman. [F f. It. (POST²)]

**pŏst-mŏr′tem. 1.** (-ĕm) *adv.* After death. **2.** (-em) *a.* & *n.* (Examination) made after death, esp. to determine its cause; (colloq.) (discussion) after conclusion (of game, election, etc.). [L]

**pŏstpŏ′ne** (*or* po-; *or* -sp-) *v.t.* Cause to take place at later time; **~ment** (-nm-) *n.* [L (*pono* place)]

**pŏstprā′ndïal** *a.* (usu. joc.) After lunch or dinner. [POST-]

**pŏ′stscript** (*or* pŏ′sk-) *n.* Additional paragraph esp. at end of letter after signature. [L (SCRIPT)]

**pŏ′stŭl|āte. 1.** *v.t.* (**~able**). Demand, require as necessary condition, claim, take for granted (thing, *that, to* do); **~ant** *n.*, candidate esp. for admission to religious order; **~ā′tion** *n.* **2.** (-at) *n.* Thing postulated. [L *postulo*]

**pŏ′stur|e. 1.** *n.* Relative position of parts esp. of body, attitude of body or mind; condition, state, (of affairs etc.); **~al** (-cher-) *a.* **2.** *v.t.* & *i.* Dispose limbs of (person) in particular way; assume posture (lit. or fig.) esp. for effect. [F f. It. f. L (POSIT)]

**pŏ′sў** (-zĭ) *n.* Small bunch of flowers; (arch.) inscribed motto in ring etc. [contr. POESY]

**pŏt¹. 1.** *n.* Rounded vessel of earthenware, metal, or glass, for holding liquids or solids; = CHAMBER-, COFFEE-, FLOWER-, TEA-POT; contents of pot (*a pot of tea*); such vessel for cooking (**the ~ calls the kettle black,** person blames another for fault he too has; **keep the ~ boiling,** make a living, keep anything going briskly);

vessel, usu. of silver, as prize in athletic sports, (sl.) any prize in these; (colloq.) large sum (*made a pot or pots of money*); total amount bet; **~(-belly),** (person with) protuberant belly; **~-boiler,** work of literature or art done merely to make a living, writer or artist who does this; **~-herb** (grown in kitchen garden); **~-hole,** (*n.*) depression in road surface caused by traffic etc., (Geol.) deep cylindrical hole in rock, (*v.i.*) explore pot-holes; **~-hook,** hook over fireplace for hanging pot etc. on or for lifting hot pot, curved stroke in handwriting esp. as made in learning to write; **~-house,** (derog.) public house; **~-hunter,** sportsman who shoots anything he comes across, person who takes part in contest merely for sake of prize; **~ luck,** whatever is to be had (for a meal, or fig.; *come and take pot luck with us*); **~′man,** publican's assistant; **~ plant** (grown in flowerpot); **~-roast,** (*n.*) meat cooked slowly in covered dish, (*v.t.*) cook thus; **~′sherd,** (esp. Archaeol.) broken piece of earthenware; **~-shot,** shot taken at game-bird etc. merely to provide a meal, shot aimed at animal etc. within easy reach, random shot; BIG pot; **go to ~,** (colloq.) be ruined or destroyed. **2.** *v.t.* & *i.* (-tt-). Place (plant) in soil in pot; (esp. in *p.p.*) place (food, usu. salted or seasoned) in pot etc. to preserve it; abridge, epitomize; (Bill. etc.) pocket; kill (animal) by pot-shot; shoot (*at*, or *abs.*); seize, secure; (colloq.) make (esp. child) sit on chamber-pot; **~′ting-shed** (in which plants are grown in pots for later planting out). [E f. L]

**pŏt²** *n.* (sl.) Marijuana. [Mex. Sp. *potiguaya*]

**pŏ′table** *a.* Drinkable. [F or L (*poto* drink)]

**pŏta′ge** (-ah′zh) *n.* Thick soup. [F (POT¹)]

**pŏ′tăsh** *n.* Alkaline substance, crude potassium carbonate; **caustic ~,** potassium hydroxide; **potă′s′sium** *n.*, soft silver-white metallic element. [Du. (POT¹, ASH²)]

**pŏtā′tion** *n.* Drinking; (usu. in *pl.*) tippling; a drink. [F f. L (POTION)]

**pŏtā′tō** *n.* (*pl.* **~es**). Plant with farinaceous tubers used as food, its tuber; **hot ~,** (sl.) thing awkward to deal with; **small ~es,** insignificant person or thing; **sweet ~**, (root of) tropical climbing plant with sweet tuberous roots used for food. [Sp. *patata* f. Taino *batata*]

**pŏt(h)ee′n** n. (Ir.) Whisky from illicit still. [Ir. *poitín* dim. (POT¹)]

**pō′ten|t** a. (Of reason etc.) cogent; (of drug etc.) strong; (of a man) able to procreate; (literary) powerful, mighty; **~cy** n.; **~tāte** n., monarch, ruler. [L *potens* -ent- (POSSE)]

**potĕ′ntial** (-shal). **1.** a. (**~ly**). Capable of coming into being or action; **~ energy**, (Phys.) ability to do work by virtue of position, stress, etc. **2.** n. (Phys.) Quantity determining energy of mass in gravitational field, of charge in electric field, etc.; possibility (*reached its highest potential*); usable resources. **3. ~ity** (-shiă′l-) n., (esp.) possibility or promise of development. [F or L (prec.)]

**pŏthee′n**. See POTEEN.

**pŏ′ther** (-dh-) n. (literary). Noise, din, verbal commotion (*made a pother about it*). [orig. unkn.]

**pō′tion** n. Dose or draught of liquid medicine or of drug or poison. [F f. L (*poto* drink)]

**pot-pourri** (pōpoorē′, -oor′ĭ) n. Mixture of dried petals and spices in jar for its perfume; musical or literary medley. [F, = rotten pot]

**pŏ′ttage** n. (arch.) Soup, stew; MESS *of pottage*. [F (POT¹)]

**pŏ′tter¹** v.i. Work in desultory manner (*at, in*, subject or occupation); dawdle, loiter, (*about* etc.). [dial. *pote* push]

**pŏ′tter²** n. Maker of earthenware vessels; **~'s wheel**, horizontal revolving disc to carry clay during moulding; **~y** n., vessels etc. made of baked clay, potter's work(shop). [E (POT¹)]

**pŏ′tty¹** a. (sl.) Insignificant, trivial, foolish or crazy (*about* person or thing). [orig. unkn.]

**pŏ′tty²** n. (colloq.) Chamber-pot, esp. for child. [POT¹]

**pouch. 1.** n. Small bag or detachable outside pocket; baggy area of skin (under eyes etc.); pocket-like receptacle in which marsupials carry young during lactation. **2.** v.t. Put or make into pouch; take possession of, pocket. [F (POKE²)]

**pouffe** (pōof) n. Large cushion as low seat; soft stuffed couch. [F]

**poult** (pōlt) n. Young of domestic fowl, turkey, or game-bird. [contr. PULLET]

**poult-de-soie** (pōodeswah′) n. Fine corded silk. [F]

**poul′terer** (pō′-) n. Dealer in poultry and usu. game. [*poulter* (POULT)]

**poul′tice** (pō′-). **1.** n. Soft mass of bread, bran, kaolin, etc., usu. made with boiling water and spread on muslin etc. and applied to sore or inflamed part. **2.** v.t. Apply poultice to. [L *pultes* pl. of *puls* pottage]

**poul′try** (pō′-) n. Domestic fowls, ducks, geese, turkeys, etc., *esp.* as source of food. [F (POULT)]

**pounce. 1.** v.i. Make sudden attack (*up*)*on*; (fig.) seize eagerly (*up*)*on* (blunder etc.). **2.** n. Pouncing, sudden swoop. [orig. unkn.]

**pound¹** v.t. & i. Crush or bruise with repeated strokes; thump, pummel, with fists etc.; knock, beat, (thing *to* pieces, *into* a jelly, etc.); deliver heavy blows, fire heavy shot, (*at, on, away at*); walk, run, ride, make one's way, heavily (*along* etc.); (of heart) beat heavily; **~ out**, produce (as if) with heavy blows. [E]

**pound²** n. Enclosure for detention of stray cattle, officially removed vehicles, etc., till redeemed. [E]

**pound³** n. Unit of weight, 16 oz. avoirdupois (454 g), 12 oz. troy (373 g), (**~ of flesh**, fig. any legal but unconscionable demand); **~ (sterling)** (*pl.* **~s** or **~**), monetary unit of U.K., abbr. £ (*five pounds* or *pound* = £5); monetary unit of some other countries; **~ note**, banknote for £1; **~age** n., commission or fee of so much per pound sterling or weight; **~er** n., thing that, or gun carrying shell that, weighs a pound or (-**~er**) so many pounds (*a three-pounder*). [E f. L *pondo*]

**pour** (pôr) v.t. & i. Cause (liquid, granular substance, light, etc.) to flow esp. downwards, discharge copiously, (*pour hot water on it*; *pour out the tea*; *river pours itself into the sea*; *pour COLD water on, OIL on the flames* or *on troubled waters*); (of liquid etc.) flow (*forth, out, down*) in stream, (of rain) descend heavily (**it never rains but it ~s**, fig. events esp. misfortunes always come several together); discharge (missiles, crowd from building etc.; *forth, out*) copiously or in rapid succession; (fig.) come *in, out*, etc., abundantly;

send *forth* or *out* (words, music, etc.). [orig. unkn.]

**pourboire** (poorbwär′) *n.* Gratuity, tip. [F]

**pou′ssin** (pōō′săň) *n.* Young chicken bred for eating. [F]

**pout. 1.** *v.t.* & *i.* Protrude (lips), protrude lips, (of lips) protrude, esp. as sign of (mock) displeasure. **2.** *n.* Such protrusion; burbot or blenny. **3.** ~′er *n.*, (esp.) kind of pigeon with great power of inflating its crop. [orig. unkn.]

**pŏ′vertў** *n.* Being poor, indigence, want; scarcity, deficiency, (*in*, *of*); inferiority, poorness, meanness; ~ line, minimum income level needed to get necessities of life; ~-stricken, poor (lit. or fig., *a poverty-stricken language*). [F f. L (PAUPER)]

**P.O.W.** *abbr.* prisoner of war.

**pow′der. 1.** *n.* Mass of dry particles, dust; medicine in form of powder; cosmetic powder applied to face, skin, or hair; = GUN*powder* (**not worth ~ and shot**, not worth shooting, or fighting or striving for); ~ **blue**, pale blue; ~-**magazine**, place where gunpowder is stored; ~-**puff**, soft pad for applying powder to skin; ~-**room**, ladies' lavatory in public building. **2.** *v.t.* Sprinkle powder on, cover (*with* powder etc.); apply powder to (nose, hair, or abs.); (esp. in *p.p.*) reduce to (fine) powder (*powdered milk*). **3.** ~ў *a.* (-iness), consisting of or covered with powder. [F f. L *pulvis -ver-* dust]

**pow′er. 1.** *n.* Ability to do or act (*will do all in my power*; *has the power of changing its colour*); particular faculty of body or mind (*taxes his powers to the utmost*); vigour, energy, (*more power to you* or *to your* ELBOW); active property (*has a high heating power*); government, influence, authority, (*over*; **in** person's ~, under his control); personal ascendancy (*over*); political or social ascendancy (*the party now in power*); ~ **politics**, political action based on threats of force); authorization, delegated authority, (*power of* ATTORNEY); influential person, body, or thing, (**the** ~s **that be**, constituted authorities); State having international influence; deity (*merciful powers!*); (colloq.) large number or amount (*has done me a power of good*); (Math.) **third**, **tenth**, etc., ~ of a

number, product obtained from three, ten, etc., factors equal to that number (*the third power of 2 is 8*); instrument for applying energy to mechanical purposes (**the mechanical** ~s, simple machines, e.g. lever, inclined plane); mechanical or electrical energy as opp. to hand labour, (*attrib.*) operated by this, (~ **cut**, temporary withdrawal or failure of electric power supply; ~**house**, = *power-station*, (fig.) source of drive or influence; ‖~ **point**, socket for connection of electrical apparatus to mains; ~-**station**, building etc. where electric power is generated for distribution); capacity for exerting mechanical force, esp. HORSE*power*; magnifying capacity of lens. **2.** *v.t.* Supply with mechanical or electrical energy. **3.** ~**ful** *a.* (-**lly**), having great power or influence (*powerful grasp*, *horse*, *mind*, *odour*); ~**less** *a.*, without power, wholly unable (*to* help etc.). [AF f. L (POSSE)]

**pow′wow** *n.* Magic ceremonial, conference, of N. Amer. Indians; political or other meeting esp. for discussion. [Algonquian]

**pŏx** *n.* Virus disease with pocks (usu. in comb. as CHICKEN-*pox*, SMALL*pox*; **a ~ on him**, arch. excl. of impatience); (colloq.) syphilis. [alt. POCKS]

**pp.** *abbr.* pages.

**p.p.** *abbr. per pro.*

**pp** *abbr.* pianissimo.

**p.p.m.** *abbr.* parts per million.

‖**P.P.S.** *abbr.* Parliamentary Private Secretary; additional postscript [POST-*postscript*].

**P.R.** *abbr.* proportional representation; public relations.

**pr.** *abbr.* pair.

**P.R.A.** *abbr.* President of the Royal Academy.

**pră′ctĭce[1]** *n.* Habitual action or carrying on (*makes a practice of saving*); action as opp. to theory; habit, custom, (*has been the regular practice*); repeated exercise in an art, handicraft, etc., (*practice makes perfect*); spell of this (*target practice*); professional work, business, or connection, of lawyer, doctor, etc., (*has a large practice*); **good ~**, satisfactory procedure, means of improving one's skill; **in ~**, in the realm of action (*would never work in practice*); **put into ~**, make actual), skilled by having recently had practice; **out of** ~, no longer possessing former skill; **prä'cticable** a. (-bly), that can be done, feasible, (of road or passage) that can be used or traversed; **präcticabi'lity** n.; **prä'ctical,** (a.) of, concerned with, shown in, practice (opp. *theoretical*; *practical agriculture*, *examination,* JOKE; **for practical purposes**, in effect), useful in practice, engaged in practice, inclined or suited to action rather than speculation (*appeals to practical minds*; *a practical man good at improvising*), that is such in effect though not nominally, virtual, (*a practical atheist*, *has practical control*), feasible (*practical* POLITICS), (n.) practical examination; **präctica'lity** n.; **prä'ctically** adv., (esp.) virtually, almost (*practically nothing*); **prä'ctise, \*-ice²** v.t. & i., perform habitually, carry out in action, (*practise the same method, what you preach*), exercise, pursue, (profession or activity), exercise oneself in or on (art, instrument, or abs.; *practise music, the piano, running*), (esp. in *p.p.*) exercise (*person*, one*self*, *in action* or subject); **practise (up)on**, impose upon, take advantage of, (person, his credulity, etc.); **präcti'tioner** n., professional or practical worker, esp. in medicine (GENERAL *practitioner*). [F f. L f. Gk]

**praeno'men** n. (Rom. Ant.) First or personal name (*Marcus* Tullius Cicero). [PRE-, NOMEN]

**prae'tor, \*prē't-,** n. Ancient-Roman magistrate below consul; ~**ōr'ian** a. (~**orian guard**, bodyguard of Roman emperor etc.). [F *préteur* or L]

**prägmä'tic** a. (~**ally**). Treating facts of history with reference to their practical lessons; dealing with matters according to their practical significance; **prä'gmatism** n., matter-of-fact treatment of things, (Philos.) doctrine that evaluates assertions solely by practical consequences and bearing on human interests; **prä'gmatist** n. [L f. Gk *pragma -mat-* deed]

**prair'ie** n. Large treeless tract of grassland esp. in N. America; ~**-dog**, N. Amer. rodent with bark like dog's; ~ **oyster**, raw egg seasoned and swallowed whole. [F f. Rom. (L *pratum* meadow)]

**praise** (-z). **1.** v.t. Express warm approbation of, commend merits of;

glorify, extol attributes of, (God etc.). **2.** n. Praising, commendation, (*won high praise*); SING *the praises of*; ~'**worthy** a., worthy of praise, commendable. [F *preisier* f. L (*pretium* price)]

**pra'line** (prah'lēn) n. Sweet made by browning nuts in boiling sugar. [F]

||**prām** n. Carriage for one or two children, with usu. 4 wheels, pushed by person on foot. [abbr. PERAMBULATOR]

**prance** (-ah-). **1.** v.i. (Of horse) raise forelegs and spring from hind legs; (fig.) walk or behave in elated or arrogant manner. **2.** n. Prancing (movement). [orig. unkn.]

**prä'ndial** a. (joc.) Of dinner. [L *prandium* a meal]

||**präng.** (sl.) **1.** v.t. Bomb (target) successfully; crash (aircraft or vehicle); damage by impact. **2.** n. Act or instance of pranging. [imit.]

**pränk¹** v.t. & i. Dress, deck, (*out, up*); adorn, spangle, (field *with* flowers etc.); show oneself off. [LDu.]

**pränk²** n. Mad frolic, practical joke; ~'**ster** n., person fond of playing pranks. [orig. unkn.]

**prate. 1.** v.i. Chatter, talk too much; talk foolishly or irrelevantly. **2.** n. Prating, idle talk. [LDu.]

**prä'tfall** (-awl) n. (colloq.) Fall on buttocks; humiliating failure. [*prat* buttocks]

**prä'ttle. 1.** v.i. & t. Talk in childish or artless way; say thus. **2.** n. Childish chatter; inconsequential talk. [LG *pratelen* (PRATE)]

**prawn** n. Marine crustacean like large shrimp. [orig. unkn.]

**pray** v.t. & i. Make devout supplication to (God, object of worship); beseech earnestly (God, person, *for* thing, *to do, that*); ask earnestly for (permission etc.); engage in prayer, make entreaty, (*to* God or person, *for* thing, *for* or *on behalf of* person, *to do, that*; **past** ~**ing for**, hopeless); = *I pray* (*pray God she is safe*); ~ (I beg or urge you to) *consider* etc.; *what is the use of that,* ~ (tell me)?; ~'**er¹** n., one who prays; *praying* MANTIS. [F f. L *precor*]

**prayer²** (prār) n. Solemn request or thanksgiving to God or object of worship; formula used in praying, e.g. the LORD's *prayer*; form of divine service consisting largely of prayers (*morning prayer*; *family prayers*); action or practice of praying; entreaty to person; thing prayed for; ~**book**, book of forms of prayer, esp. Book of COMMON Prayer; ~**mat**, small carpet used by Muslims when praying; ~**meeting**, religious meeting at which several persons offer prayer; ~**wheel**, revolving cylindrical box inscribed with or containing prayers, used esp. by Buddhists of Tibet; ~**ful** a. (**-lly**), (of deliberation etc.) accompanied by prayer, (of person) fond of praying. [F f. L (PRECARIOUS)]

**prē-** *pref.* Before (in time, place, order, degree, or importance); ~**-arra'nge**(ment), arrange(ment) beforehand; ~**ca'st**, (esp. in *p.p.*) cast (concrete) in blocks before use; ~**-Chri'stian**, before Christ(ianity); ~**cogni'tion**, (esp. supernatural) foreknowledge; ~**-concei've**, form (idea, opinion, etc.) beforehand; ~**conce'ption**, (esp.) prejudice; ~**-concer't**, agree on beforehand; ~**condi'tion** (that must be fulfilled beforehand); ~**-da'te**, antedate; ~**decea'se**, (*v.t.*) die earlier than (another person), (*n.*) death preceding that of another; ~**deter'mine**, decree beforehand, predestine; ~**dige'st**, render (food, or fig.) easily digestible before ingestion; ~**dispo'se**, render liable, subject, or inclined (*to* feeling, disease, etc., *to* do); ~**disposi'tion**; ~**-e'minent**, excelling others, distinguished beyond others in some quality; ~**-e'minence**; ~**-exi'sting**, **-exi'stent**, **-exi'stence**, previous(ly) existing; ~'**fab**, (colloq.) prefabricated building; ~**fa'bricate**, manufacture sections of (building etc.) prior to their assembly on a site; ~**fi'gure**, represent beforehand by figure or type; ~**for'm**, form beforehand; ~**hea't**, make hot or warm beforehand; ~**histo'ric**, of the period antecedent to written history, (colloq.) utterly out of date; ~**hi'story**; ~**ju'dge**, pass judgement on (person) before trial or proper enquiry, form premature judgement on; ~**-ma'rital**, of the time before marriage; ~**me'ditate**, (esp. in *p.p.*) think out, design, (action etc.) beforehand; ~**medita'tion**; ~**-me'nstrual**, immediately before menstruation; ~**mo'lar**, (tooth) in front of true molars; ~**na'tal**, existing or occurring before (child)-

birth; ~**ordai'n**, appoint beforehand; ~**pa'ck(age)**, pack (goods) ready for sale before distributing them; ~**pay'**, pay (charge, postage), pay postage on (letter, parcel, etc.), beforehand; ~**pay'ment**; ~**posse'ss**, (usu. in *pass.*, of idea etc.) take possession of (person), prejudice (usu. favourably and at first sight; esp. ~*possessing*, attractive); ~**posse'ssion**; ~'**print**, printed document issued before its general publication; **Pre-Ra'phaelite** (-făel-, -fel-), artist emulating spirit that prevailed before the time of Raphael; ~**recor'd**, record beforehand; ~**re'quisite**, (thing) required as pre-condition (*for*, *of*, *to*); ~**school**, of time before child is old enough to attend school; ~**se't**, set beforehand; ~**shri'nk**, treat (fabric, garment) so as to shrink during manufacture, not after; ~**stre'ss**, (esp. in *p.p.*) strengthen (concrete) by means of stretched wires etc. in it; ~**suppo'se**, assume beforehand (thing, *that*), imply; ~**supposi'tion**, thing assumed beforehand as basis of argument etc.; ~**ta'x**, (of income) before deduction of taxes; ~'**view**, (*n.*) view or examination of film, play, book, etc., before it is seen by the general public, (*v.t.*) view in advance of public presentation; ~**war'**, (occurring or existing) before a war. [L *prae* before]

**preach** *v.i. & t.* Deliver sermon or religious address; deliver (sermon); give moral advice in obtrusive way; proclaim, expound, (the Gospel etc.) in public discourse; advocate, inculcate, (quality, conduct, principle, etc.) thus. [F f. L *praedico* declare]

**preă'mble** *n.* Preliminary statement in speech or writing; introductory part of statute, deed, etc. [F f. L (AMBLE)]

**pre'bend** *n.* Stipend of canon or member of chapter; portion of land or tithe from which this is drawn; ~**al** a., of a prebend; ~**ary** *n.*, holder of prebend, honorary canon. [F f. L (*praebeo* grant)]

**precā'rious** a. Dependent on chance, uncertain; insecure, perilous; **prě'catory** a. (**-ily**), expressing request. [L *precarius* (PRAY)]

**precau'tion** *n.* Action taken beforehand to avoid evil or ensure good result; ~**ary** a. (**-ily**). [F f. L (CAUTION)]

**precē'de** *v.t.* (Of person or thing) go before in rank or importance (*such duties precede all others*); come before (thing etc., or abs.) in order; walk etc. in front of (*preceded by our guide*); come before in time (*in the years preceding his accession*); cause (thing) to be preceded *by* (*must precede this measure by milder ones*); **prē'cēdence, -cȳ,** (*or* prisē'-) *ns.*, priority in time or succession, higher position, right of preceding others in ceremonies etc., (**take ~nce of,** have or claim right to precede); **prē'cēdent,** (*n.*) previous case taken as example for subsequent cases or as justification (*there is no precedent for this; that would create a precedent*), (*or* prisē'-; *a.*) preceding in time, order, rank, etc. [F f. L (CEDE)]

**precē'ntor** *n.* One who leads singing or (in synagogue) prayers of congregation. [F, or L *praecentor* (*cano* sing)]

**prē'cēpt** *n.* Command, maxim; moral instruction (*example is better than precept*); writ, warrant; ‖order for collection or payment of money under a rate; **precē'ptor** *n.*, teacher, instructor; **~ōr'ial** *a.* (-lly). [L *praeceptum* maxim, order]

**precē'ssion** (-shon) *n.* **~ of the equinoxes,** (Astron.; earlier occurrence of equinoxes in successive sidereal years, due to) slow retrograde motion of equinoctial points along ecliptic. [L (PRECEDE)]

**prē'cīnct** *n.* Space enclosed by walls or other boundaries of place or building, esp. around place of worship; (in *pl.*) environs; district in town where traffic is prohibited, esp. *pedestrian precinct.* [L (*praecingo -cinct-* encircle)]

**prē'cious** (-shŭs). **1.** *a.* Of great price, costly, (~ **metals,** gold, silver, platinum metals; ~ **stone,** piece of mineral having great value, esp. as used in jewellery); of great non-material worth (*precious words, privilege*); beloved (person, or abs.); affectedly refined in language, workmanship, etc.; (colloq.) very bad, considerable, (*made a precious mess of it*). **2.** *adv.* (colloq.) Extremely, very, (*took precious good care of that; precious little of it*). **3.** **prē'ciŏ'sĭtȳ** (-shŏ'-) *n.*, over-refinement in art, esp. in choice of words. [F f. L *pretium* price]

**prē'cĭpice** *n.* Vertical or steep face of rock, cliff, mountain, etc.; **prē-**

**cĭ'pĭtance, -ncȳ,** *ns.,* rash haste; **precĭ'pĭtāte,** (*v.t.:*) -**itable**) throw down headlong, (fig.) hurl or fling (person etc. *into* condition etc.), hurry, urge on, (course of events etc.), hasten occurrence of (*served to precipitate his ruin*), (Chem.) cause (substance) to be deposited in solid form from solution, (Phys.) condense (vapour) into drops and so deposit, (-*at; a.*) headlong, violently hurried, (of person or act) hasty, rash, inconsiderate, (-*at; n.*) (Chem.) substance precipitated from solution, (Phys.) moisture condensed from vapour by cooling and deposited, e.g. rain, dew; **precĭpĭtā'tion** *n.,* precipitating, being precipitated, precipitateness, (Meteor.) (quantity of) rain, snow, etc., falling to ground; **precĭ'pĭtous** *a.,* of or like precipice, dangerously steep, precipitate. [F or L (*praeceps -cipit-* headlong)]

**précis** (prā'sē). **1.** *n.* (*pl.* same *pr.* -ēz). Summary, abstract. **2.** *v.t.* Make précis of. [F]

**precī'se** *a.* Accurately expressed, definite, exact; punctilious, scrupulous in observance of rules etc.; **the ~** (exact, identical) *moment* etc.; **~lȳ** (-slī) *adv.,* in precise manner, in exact terms, (in emphatic or formal assent) quite so; **precī'sian** (-zhan) *n.,* one who is rigidly precise or punctilious; **precī'sion** (-zhon) *n.,* accuracy, degree of refinement in measurement etc., (*attrib.*) marked by or adapted for precision (*precision instruments*). [F f. L (*praecido* cut short)]

**preclū'de** (-ōō'd) *v.t.* Prevent (*from*), make impossible, (*so as to preclude all doubt*). [L *praecludo* (CLOSE¹)]

**precō'cious** (-shŭs) *a.* (Of person) prematurely developed in some faculty or characteristic; (of action etc.) indicating such development; **~ŏ'cĭtȳ** *n.* [L *praecox -cocis* early ripe]

**precū'rsor** *n.* Forerunner, harbinger; one who precedes in office etc. [L (*praecurro -curs-* run before)]

**predā'cious** (-shŭs) *a.* (Of animal) predatory. [L *praeda* booty]

**prē'dator** *n.* Predatory animal; **~ȳ** *a.,* of or addicted to plunder or robbery, (of animal) preying naturally upon others. [L (prec.)]

**prē'dēcessor** *n.* Former holder of office or position, with respect to later holder, (*Anne's predecessors; his* *immediate predecessor*); thing to which another has succeeded (*will share the fate of its predecessor*). [F f. L *decessor* (as DECEASE)]

**prèdě'stǐn|e** *v.t.* Determine beforehand, appoint as if by fate, (of God; also ~**ăte**) ordain in advance to salvation or *to* a fate or *to* do; ~**ā'tǐon** *n.* [F or L (PRE-)]

**prě'dǐc|ăte. 1.** *v.t.* Assert or affirm as true or existent. **2.** (-at) *n.* (Logic & Gram.) What is predicated, what is affirmed or is denied of a subject (e.g. *mortal* or *are mortal* in *all men are mortal*). **3.** ~**able** *a.* (-bly), that may be predicated or affirmed; **prě-dǐ'cament** *n.*, thing predicated, unpleasant or trying or dangerous situation; ~**ant** *a.*, (of religious order) engaged in preaching; ~**ā'-tǐon** *n.*, act of predicating; **prě-dǐ'cative** *a.*, (esp., Gram., of *a.* or *n.*; cf. ATTRIBUTIVE) forming part or all of the predicate (e.g. *old* in *the dog is old* but not in *the old dog*). [L *praedico* -*dicat*- declare]

**prèdǐ'ct** *v.t.* Foretell, prophesy; ~**abǐ'lǐty**, ~**ion**, ~**or**, *ns.*; ~**ǐve** *a.* [L *praedico* -*dict*- foretell]

**prèdǐlě'ctǐon** *n.* Mental preference, liking, (*for*). [F f. L (*praediligo* prefer)]

**prèdŏ'mǐn|ăte** *v.i.* Have control (over); be superior; be stronger or main element; ~**ance** *n.*; ~**ant** *a.* [PRE-]

**prě-ě'mpt** *v.t.* Obtain by pre--emption; ~**ion** *n.*, purchase or taking by one person etc. before opportunity is offered to others; ~**ǐve** *a.*, relating to pre-emption, (Mil.) intended to prevent attack by disabling threatening enemy, (Bridge, of bid) intended to be so high that further bidding esp. by opponents is impeded. [L (*emo empt*-buy)]

**preen** *v.t.* (Of bird) tidy (feathers) with beak; (of person) smarten (one-*self*); ~ **oneself**, congratulate oneself, show self-satisfaction. [F]

**prě'fa|ce. 1.** *n.* Introduction to book stating subject, scope, etc.; preliminary part of a speech. **2.** *v.t.* Furnish with preface; introduce (act, speech, *with*); (of event etc.) lead up to (another); ~**torў** *a.* (-ily). [F f. L *praefatio*]

**prě'fěct** *n.* Chief administrative officer of French, Japanese, etc., department; senior pupil in school,

authorized to maintain discipline; ~**ŏr'ǐal** *a.* (-lly); ~**ūre** *n.*, (period of) office, official residence, district under government, of prefect. [F f. L (*praeficio* -*fect*- set in authority over)]

**prèfer'** *v.t.* (-rr-). Choose rather, like better, (*gentlemen prefer blondes*; *prefer water to wine*; *prefer to leave it alone, that it should be left*; *preferred* SHARE etc.); submit (information, accusation, etc., *to* person in authority etc., *against* offender etc.); promote (person *to* office); **prě'fer-able** *a.* (-bly); **prě'ference** *n.*, liking *of* or *for* one thing better than (*to* or *over*) another (*do this in preference to that*), thing one prefers, prior right esp. to payment of debts (||*preference* SHARE etc.), favouring of one person or country before others in business relations, esp. favouring of a country by admitting its products at lower import duty; **prěferě'ntial** (-shal) *a.* (-lly), of, giving, or receiving preference, (of customs tariff etc.) favouring particular countries; ~**ment** *n.*, promotion to office, an ecclesiastical or other post. [F f. L *praefero* -*lat*-]

**prě'fǐx. 1.** (or -ǐ'ks) *v.t.* Add as introduction; join as prefix (*to* word). **2.** *n.* Verbal element placed at beginning of word to qualify meaning (e.g. *be-, ex-, pre-*); title placed before name (e.g. *Mr.*). [L (FIX)]

**prě'gnan|t** *a.* (Of woman or female animal) having developing child(ren) or young in womb; teeming with ideas etc.; fruitful in results, plentifully furnished *with* (consequences etc.); (of words or acts) having hidden meaning, significant, suggestive; ~**cў** *n.* [F, or L *praegnans*]

**prěhě'nsǐle** *a.* (Of tail or limb) capable of grasping. [F f. L *prehendo* -*hens*- seize]

**prě'jud|ice** (-jŏŏ-). **1.** *n.* Preconceived opinion, bias, (*against, in favour of*, person or thing); injury that results or may result from some action or judgement (*to the prejudice of*; *without* ~**ice**, without detriment to or to any existing right or claim). **2.** *v.t.* Impair validity of (right, claim, statement, etc.); (esp. in *p.p.*) cause (person) to have prejudice (*against* or *in favour of*). **3.** ~**ǐ'cial** (-shal) *a.* (-lly), causing prejudice, detrimental (*to* rights, interests, etc.). [F f. L (JUDGE)]

**prē′la|te** n. High ecclesiastical dignitary, e.g. (arch)bishop; **~cy̆** n., church government by prelates, *the* prelates, office, rank, see, of prelate; **prēlă′tical** a. (.-ily). [F f. L (PREFER)]

**prēli′m** n. (colloq.) Preliminary examination. [abbr.]

**prēli̇̌′minary̆. 1.** a. (-ily). Introductory, preparatory. **2.** adv. Preparatory. **3.** n. (usu. in pl.) Preliminary action or arrangement. [F or L (*limen* threshold)]

**prē′lūde. 1.** n. Performance, action, event, condition, serving as introduction (*to* another); introductory part of poem etc.; (Mus.) introductory movement or first piece of suite, short piece of music of similar type on one theme. **2.** v.t. & i. Serve as prelude to; introduce (with a prelude). [F or L (*ludo lus-* play)]

**prē′mature** a. Occurring or done before usual or proper time; too hasty; **~ baby** (born 3–12 weeks before expected time; cf. *miscarriage*); **prēmatŭr′ity̆** n. [L (MATURE)]

**prē′mier. 1.** a. First in position, importance, order, or time. **2.** n. Prime minister, esp. in Great Britain and in provinces etc. of Commonwealth countries. **3.** *première* (prē′myār) n., & v.t., (give) first performance of or in play, film, etc. [F, = first]

**prē′mise** n. (Logic) premiss; (in pl.) aforesaid or foregoing matters, esp. (Law) *the* aforesaid houses, lands, or tenements; (in pl.) house or building with grounds and appurtenances; **on the ~s**, in the house etc. concerned; **prē′miss** n., (Logic) previous statement from which another is inferred, esp. MAJOR and MINOR premisses in syllogism. [F f. L *praemissa* set in front]

**prē′mium** n. Reward, prize (**put a ~ on**, provide, or act as, incentive to); amount to be paid for contract of insurance; sum added to interest, wages, etc.; **at a ~**, above nominal or usual price (cf. DISCOUNT), (fig.) in high esteem; ||**P~** (**Savings**) **Bond**, government security with chances of cash prizes but zero interest. [L *praemium* reward]

**prēmoni′tion** n. Forewarning, presentiment; **prēmŏ′nitory̆** a. (-ily), serving to warn. [F or L (*moneo* warn)]

**prē′ntice** n. (arch.) Apprentice,

esp. **~** (inexperienced) **hand**. [APPRENTICE]

**prēŏ′ccup|y̆** v.t. Engage beforehand, engross; **~ā′tion** n., (esp.) occupation or business taking precedence of others, mental absorption. [PRE-]

**prĕp.** (colloq.) **1.** n. ||(Time for) preparation of school work. **2.** a. Preparatory (*prep school*). [abbr.]

**prēpār′e** v.t. & i. Make (person, one*self*, thing) ready (*for*); make ready (food, meal) for eating; make (person) mentally ready or fit (*for* news, *to* hear, etc.; **be ~d**, be ready or willing *to* do); get (lesson, speech, sermon) ready by study; get (person) ready by teaching (*for* examination etc.); prepare oneself or things (*for*, *to* do, etc.); make (chemical product etc.) by regular process; **prēparā′-tion** n., preparing, being prepared, (usu. in pl.) thing done to make ready (*for*; **make preparations**, prepare *for*), ||work done by pupils to prepare for lessons as part of school routine, substance (e.g. food or medicine) specially prepared; **prē-pǎ′rative** a. & n., preparatory (act); **prēpǎ′ratory̆**, (a.; -ily) serving to prepare, introductory (*to*; **preparatory school**, where pupils are prepared ||for higher school, *for college or university*), (adv.) in preparatory manner (*am packing it up preparatory to sending it by post*). [F or L (*paro* make ready)]

**prēpĕ′nse** a. (usu. after n.) Deliberate, intentional, (**malice ~**, intention to injure). [F *purpensé* premeditated]

**prēpŏ′nder|āte** v.i. Weigh more, be heavier, (**~ate over**, exceed in number, quantity, etc.); be of greater moral or intellectual weight; be the chief element, predominate; **~ance** n.; **~ant** a. [L (*pondus -der-* weight)]

**prēposi′tion** (-z-) n. Word governing (and normally preceding) noun or pronoun, expressing latter's relation to another word (e.g. the italic wds in: found him *at* home, the bed he slept *on*, won *by* waiting, came *through* the roof); **~al** a. (-lly). [L (*praepono -posit-* place before)]

**prēpŏ′sterous** a. Contrary to nature, reason, or common sense; perverse, foolish; utterly absurd. [L (= before behind)]

**pre′puce** n. Foreskin; similar structure of clitoris. [L *praeputium*]

**prerŏ′gative** n. Sovereign's right, theoretically subject to no restriction; exclusive right or privilege. [F or L (*praerogo* ask first)]

**Pres.** abbr. President.

**pre′sage. 1.** n. Omen, portent; presentiment, foreboding. **2.** (or -ĭsā′j) v.t. Portend, foreshadow; give warning of (event etc.) by natural means; (of person) predict or have presentiment of. [F f. L *praesagium*]

**pre′sbyt|er** (or -z-) n. (In Episcopal Ch.) minister of second order, priest, (in Presbyterian Ch.) elder; **P~ēr′ian,** (a., of church) governed by elders all of equal rank, esp. national Church of Scotland, (n.) adherent of Presbyterian system, member of Presbyterian church; **P~ēr′ianism** n.; **~erў** n., body of presbyters, esp. court next above kirk-session, eastern part of chancel, R.C. priest's house. [L f. Gk, = elder]

**pre′scien|t** (or -shĭ-) a. Having foreknowledge or foresight; **~ce** n. [L *praescio* know before]

**prescr|i′be** v.t. Lay down or impose authoritatively (*prescribe to him what he is to do or how to do it*); advise use of (medicine etc., or abs., to or for patient, for complaint; lit. or fig.); **pre′script** n., ordinance, command; **~i′ption** n., prescribing, physician's (usu. written) direction for composition and use of medicine, medicine thus prescribed, (Law) use or possession as giving title or right, or limitation of time within which action or claim can be raised; **~i′ptive** a., prescribing, based on prescription (*prescriptive right*), prescribed by custom. [L *praescribo*]

**pre′sent¹** (-z-). **1.** a. Being in the place in question (usu. *pred.*; *no one else was present*); **~ company excepted,** excluding those who are here now); being dealt with, discussed, etc., (*in the present case*); now existing, occurring, or being such (*the present king*; *during the present month*; **the ~** author, writer, etc., I who am writing); **~-day** a., of this time, modern); (Gram.) expressing action etc. now going on or habitually performed in past and future. **2.** n. The time now passing (**at ~**, now; **for the ~,** just now, as far as the present is concerned); (Gram.) present

tense; (Law or joc.) (*know all men* etc.) **by these ~s,** by this document. **3. pré′sence** (-z-) n., being present (*your presence is requested*; *in the presence of a large company*), place where person is (*admitted to his presence*), personal appearance, (esp. imposing) bearing (*a man of fine presence*), person or thing that is present; **presence of mind,** calmness and self-command in sudden emergency; **~lў** adv., soon, after a short time, (U.S., Sc., etc.) at the present time, now. [F f. L *praesens -ent-*]

**pre′sent²** (-z-) n. Gift; **make a ~ of,** give. [F (prec.)]

**prèse′nt³** (-z-) v.t. Introduce (person to another), introduce (person) to sovereign at court; (**~ oneself,** appear esp. as candidate for examination etc.); introduce or offer (actor, play, new product, theory, etc.) to the public; recommend (clergyman) to bishop for institution (to benefice); exhibit (thing to person etc.; *present a ragged appearance*; *presented its front to me*); show (quality etc.; *cases that present some difficulty*); (of idea etc.) offer or suggest *itself*; (Law) bring formally under notice (complaint, offence, to authority); aim (weapon at), hold out (weapon) in position for aiming, (**~ arms,** Mil., hold rifle etc. vertically as deferential position in saluting); offer or give (thing to person) as gift; offer (compliments, regards, to); deliver (cheque, bill, etc., to person etc.) for acceptance etc.; **~ person with** thing, present it to him, cause him to have it (*this presented me with a problem*); **~able** a. (-bly), of decent appearance, fit to be introduced or go into company, suitable for presentation (as gift etc.); **~abi′lĭtў** n.; **prèsentā′tion** (-z-) n., presenting or being presented, exhibition, theatrical representation, formal introduction esp. at court; **~ment** n., theatrical representation, delineation, description. [F f. L *praesento* (PRESENT¹)]

**prèsĕ′ntiment** (or -z-) n. Vague expectation, foreboding, (*of coming event, esp. evil*). [F (PRE-)]

**presently.** See PRESENT¹; **presentment,** see PRESENT³.

**prèsĕr′ve** (-z-). **1.** v.t. Keep safe (*from harm, decay, etc.*); keep alive (memory etc.); maintain (state of things); retain (quality, condition:

well ~d, of elderly person, showing little sign of ageing); prepare (food) by boiling with sugar, pickling, etc., to prevent decomposition or fermentation; keep from decomposition by refrigeration, chemical treatment, etc.; keep (game, river, or abs.) undisturbed for private use. 2. *n.* (in *sing.* or *pl.*) Preserved fruit, jam; ground set apart for protection of game; (fig.) sphere regarded by person as being for him alone. 3. **preservā′tion** (-z-) *n.*, preserving, being preserved; **preser′vative** (-z-) *a.* & *n.*, (quality, course of action, etc.) tending to preserve, substance for preserving perishable foodstuffs. [F f. L (*servo* keep)]

**presī′de** (-z-) *v.i.* Occupy chair of authority (*at* or *over* a meeting); sit at head of table; exercise control, sit or reign supreme, (lit. or fig.); **pre′sident** (-z-) *n.*, head of temporary or permanent body of persons who presides over their meetings and proceedings, elected head of republican State, presiding officer of legislative body, head of some colleges and U.S. universities, person presiding over meetings of literary or scientific society etc., *person directing general policy of bank or company, head of advisory council or board; **pre′sidency** (-z-) *n.*, (period of) office of president; **presidē′ntial** (-z-; -shal) *a.* (-lly); **presī′dium** (*or* -z-) *n.*, standing committee in Communist organization. [F f. L (*sedeo* sit)]

**press**[1]. 1. *v.t.* & *i.* Exert steady force against (thing in contact); ~ **the button**, set electric machinery in motion, fig. take decisive initial step); do this as sign of affection etc. (*he pressed my hand*); move (thing *up, down, against,* etc.) by pressing; squeeze (juice etc. *out of, from,* etc.); compress or squeeze (thing) to flatten or shape or smooth it or to extract juice etc.; (of enemy, attacking force, etc.) bear heavily on (esp. in p.p.; *hard pressed*; **be** ~**ed for**, have barely enough *space, time, money,* etc.); urge, entreat, (person *to* do; person, or abs., *for* answer etc.); urge (course of action, opinion, *upon* person); force (offer, gift, etc., *upon*); insist on (*did not press the point*); exert pressure (*on, against,* etc.); be urgent, demand immediate action; make insistent demand *for*; crowd

(*up, round,* etc.); hasten *on, forward,* etc. 2. *n.* Crowding; crowd (*of* people etc.); pressure of affairs; pressing (*give it a slight press*); instrument for compressing, flattening, shaping, extracting juice, etc.; = PRINTING-*press*; printing-house or establishment; publishing company (*Oxford University Press*); *the* art or practice of printing (**at** or **in** (the) ~, being printed; *send, go,* **to** (the) ~, to be printed; **freedom** or **liberty of the** ~, right to print and publish anything without censorship); *the* newspapers etc. generally (**get** or **have a good** etc. ~, receive good etc. notice); large usu. shelved cupboard for clothes, books, etc. 3. ~ **agent**, person employed to attend to advertising and press publicity; ~-**box**, reporters' enclosure esp. at sports event; ~-**button**, = PUSH-*button*; ~ **conference**, interview given to journalists to make announcement or answer questions; ||~ **cutting** (from newspaper etc.); ~-**gallery** (for reporters esp. in legislative assembly); ~′**man**, journalist; ~ **of sail**, (Naut.) as much as wind etc. will allow; *press* RELEASE; ||~-**stud**, small device fastened by pressing to engage two parts; ~-**up**, (usu. in *pl.*) exercise in which prone body is raised by pressing down on hands to straighten arms. 4. ~′**ing**, (*a.*, esp.) urgent (*pressing need*), importunate (*a pressing invitation*), (*n.*, esp.) thing made by pressing (e.g. part of vehicle, gramophone record, or series of these made at one time). [F f. L *premo* press-]

**press**[2] *v.t.* (Hist.) force (man, or abs.) to serve in army or navy; (fig.) bring into use as makeshift (*was pressed into service*); ~-**gang**, (*n.*) body of men employed to press men, (fig.) group using similar coercive methods, (*v.t.*) force into service (as if) by press-gang. [obs. *prest* f. F, = loan]

**pre′ssure** (-sher). 1. *n.* Exertion of continuous force, force so exerted, on or against body by another in contact with it; amount of this, expressed by force on unit area, esp. that of atmosphere (*atmospheric pressure*; **high, low,** ~, condition of atmosphere with pressure above, below, average, pressure in engines higher, lower, than atmospheric, fig. high, low, degree of activity,

# prestidigitator 702 prevent

speed, etc.); affliction, trouble, embarrassment (*under financial pressure*); urgency (*work under pressure*); constraining influence (*put pressure on him*); **~cooker**, apparatus for cooking under high pressure and in short time; **~ gauge** (for showing pressure of steam etc.); **~ group**, group of persons seeking to coerce legislature etc. e.g. by concerted action. **2.** Apply pressure to; coerce, persuade. **3. prĕ′ssurize** (-sherĭz) *v.t.*, pressure, raise to high pressure, (esp. in *p.p.*) maintain normal atmospheric pressure in (aircraft cabin etc.) at high altitude; **prĕssurizā′tion** (-sheriz-) *n.* [L (PRESS¹)]

**prĕstĭdĭ′gĭt|ātor** *n.* Conjurer; **~ā′tion** *n.* [F (PRESTO, DIGIT)]

**prĕsti′ge** (-ēzh). **1.** *n.* Influence or good reputation derived from past achievements, associations, etc. **2.** *a.* Having or conferring prestige. **3. prĕsti′gious** (-jŭs) *a.*, having or showing prestige. [F, = illusion]

**prĕ′stō** *adv., a.,* & *n.* (*pl.* **~s**). (Mus.) quick (movement); (*adv.*; in conjuror's formulae at moment of sudden change etc.) quickly (*hey presto!*). [It. f. L *praestus* quick]

**prĕsū′m|e** (-z-) *v.t.* & *i.* Suppose to be undoubtedly true, take for granted (*I presume that he has seen them*); take the liberty, be impudent enough, venture, (*to do*, or *abs.*); **~e** (**up**)**on**, take advantage of, make unscrupulous use of (person's good nature, one's acquaintance with him, etc.); **~ably** *adv.*, it is or may reasonably be presumed. [F f. L *praesumo*]

**prĕsū′mption** (-z-) *n.* Arrogance, assurance; taking for granted, thing that is or may reasonably be taken for granted, (*this was a mere presumption; the presumption is that he had gone*); ground for presuming (*there is a strong presumption against it*). [F f. L (prec.)]

**prĕsū′mpt|ive** (-z-) *a.* Giving grounds for presumption (*presumptive evidence*); HEIR *presumptive*; **~uous** *a.*, unduly confident. [F f. L (PRESUME)]

**prĕtĕ′n|d** *v.t.* & *i.* Feign, give oneself out, (*to be* or *do; does not pretend to be a scholar*); make oneself seem (*to do*), make it seem (*that*), in play; profess falsely to have (*pretend illness*); allege falsely (*that*); (in *p.p.*) falsely avowed as such (*a pretended friend*); lay claim to (right, title, etc.);

**~d to**, profess to have (quality etc.); **~ce, *****~se**, *n.*, claim (*to merit* etc.), ostentation (*devoid of all pretence*); false profession of purpose, pretext, (*under the pretence of helping*; FALSE *pretences*), pretending, make-believe; **~der** *n.*, one who makes (esp. baseless) claim (*to* title etc., or *abs.*; **Old, Young, P~der**, son, grandson, of James II); **~sion** (-shŏn) *n.*, assertion of claim (*to* thing, or *abs.*), justifiable claim (*to* thing, *to be* or *do*; *he has no pretensions to the name*), pretentiousness; **~tious** (-shŭs) *a.*, making claim to great merit or importance, ostentatious. [F, or L *praetendo* (TEND¹)]

**prēter-** *pref.* Beyond, outside range of, more than; **~na′tural**, outside the ordinary course of nature, supernatural. [L *praeter* beyond]

**prĕ′terite, *****-ĭt**, *a.* & *n.* (Gram.) (Tense) expressing past action or state. [F, or L *praeteritum* past]

**prĕ′tĕxt** *n.* Ostensible reason, excuse; (**up**)**on** or **under the ~ of** or **that**, professing as one's object etc. [L *praetextus* (TEXT)]

**prĕ′ttУ. 1.** *a.* (**-ily, -iness**). (Of woman or child) attractive in dainty or graceful way; attractive to eye, ear, or aesthetic sense, (*pretty cottage, song, story*); good of its kind (*has a pretty wit*); (iron.) considerable (*cost me a pretty* PENNY); (ellipt.) **my ~** (one, child); **~-pretty**, aiming too much at prettiness. **2.** *adv.* Fairly, moderately, (*am pretty well; find it pretty difficult*); **~ much** or **well**, very nearly (*the same thing* etc.); **sitting ~**, (colloq.) comfortably placed. [E]

**prĕvai′l** *v.i.* Gain the mastery, be victorious, (*against, over*); be the more usual or prominent; exist or occur in general use or experience; **~ (up)on**, persuade (*to do*); **prĕ′valent** *a.*, generally existing or occurring, predominant; **prĕ′valence** *n.* [L *praevaleo* (AVAIL)]

**prĕvă′ricāte** *v.i.* Speak or act evasively or misleadingly; quibble, equivocate; **~ā′tion, ~ātor,** *ns.* [L, = walk crookedly]

**prĕvĕ′nt** *v.t.* Hinder, stop, (*this may prevent him from writing, his* or colloq. *him writing*; *wish to prevent a dispute*); **~ion** *n.*; **~(at)ive,** (*a.*) serving to prevent, esp. (Med.) to keep off disease, (‖**~ive detention**, imprisonment of habitual criminal for corrective training etc.; **P~ive**

**Service,** department of Customs concerned with prevention of smuggling), (*n.*) preventive agent, measure, drug, etc. [L *praevenio -vent-hinder*]

**prĕ′vĭous. 1.** *a.* Coming before in time or order; prior *to*; done or acting hastily (*you have been a little too previous*). **2.** *adv.* ~ **to**, before (*had called previous to writing*). [L *praevius* (via *way*)]

**prey** (prā). **1.** *n.* Animal(s) hunted or killed by other animal for food (**beast, bird, of ~**, one that kills and devours other animals); person or thing that falls a victim (*to* enemy, disease, fear, etc.). **2.** *v.i.* ~ (**up**)**on**, seek or take (animal etc.) as prey, plunder (person), (of disease, emotion, etc.) exert harmful or destructive influence (up)on. [F f. L *praeda*]

**price. 1.** *n.* Money or other consideration for which thing is bought or sold (*price £5 each*; *offered at reduced prices*; **above, beyond, without, ~**, so valuable that no price can be stated; **at a** (relatively high) ~; **of** (**great**) ~, valuable; **set a ~ on**, announce amount for which thing will be sold; **set a ~ on** person's **head** or **life**, offer specified reward for his capture or death); odds in betting (*the* STARTING *price of a horse*); (fig.) what must be given, done, sacrificed, etc., to obtain a thing (*must be done at any price*; *every man has his price*, can be won over by some inducement; *would not do it* etc. **at any ~**, on any terms, for any sacrifice or consideration; ‖**what ~ . . . ?**, (sl.) what is the chance of . . . ?, the vaunted . . . has failed); ~**-fixing**, determination of prices by agreement between sellers; ~**-list**, list of current prices of commodities; ~**-tag**, cost (lit. or fig.). **2.** *v.t.* Fix or find price of (thing for sale); (fig.) estimate value of; ~ **oneself out of the market**, charge a prohibitive price. **3.** ~′**lĕss** (-sl-) *a.*, invaluable, (sl.) very amusing or incredibly absurd; **pri′cey** *a.* (-**cier, -ciest**), (colloq.) expensive. [F f. L *pretium*]

**prick. 1.** *v.t.* & *i.* Pierce slightly, make minute hole in, (*prick the* BUBBLE); (fig.) cause sharp pain to (*my conscience pricked me*); feel pricking sensation; make thrust (*at, into,* etc.) as if to prick; mark off (name etc. in list) by pricking, ‖select (sheriff) thus; mark (pattern *off, out*) with pricks or dots; ~ **in, off, out,** plant (seedlings etc.) in small holes pricked in earth; ~ **up** one's **ears,** (of dog) erect the ears when on the alert, (fig., of person) become suddenly attentive. **2.** *n.* Pricking, puncture, (~**s of conscience,** remorse); mark made by pricking; (arch.) goad for oxen, esp. (fig.) **kick against the ~s,** hurt oneself by useless resistance; (vulg.) penis, (vulg., derog.) man; ~**-ears,** erect pointed ears of some dogs etc. **3.** ~′**er** *n.,* (esp.) pricking instrument, e.g. awl; **pri′ckle,** (*n.*) small thorn, hard-pointed spine of hedgehog etc., (*v.t.* & *i.*) affect or be affected with sensation as of pricks; ~**lў** *a.* (**-iness**), armed with prickles, (fig., of person) ready to take offence, tingling; ~**ly heat,** inflammation of skin near sweat glands with eruption of vesicles and prickly sensation, common in hot countries; ~**ly pear,** (cactus with) usu. pear-shaped edible fruit. [E]

**pride. 1.** *n.* (Unduly) high opinion of one's own qualities, merits, etc., arrogant bearing or conduct, (~ **of place,** exalted position, consciousness of this); (**proper**) ~, sense of what befits one's position, preventing one from doing unworthy thing, (*put* one's *pride in* one's POCKET); feeling of elation and pleasure (**take a ~ in,** be proud of); object of this feeling (*he is his mother's pride and joy*; LONDON *pride*); best condition, prime. **2.** *v.refl.* ~ **oneself** (**up**)**on,** be proud of (thing, quality, do*ing*). [E (PROUD)]

**prie-dieu′** (prēdyẽr′) *n.* Kneeling-desk for prayer. [F, = pray God]

**priest** *n.* Ordained minister of R.C., Anglican, or Orthodox Church (in Anglican Church, above deacon and below bishop); official minister of non-Christian religion (HIGH *priest*); ~′**ĕss** *n.,* female priest of non-Christian religion; ~**hŏŏd** (-h-) *n.,* condition of being a priest, the priests in general; ~**lў** *a.* (**-iness**), of, like, befitting, a priest. [E f. L PRESBYTER]

**prig** *n.* Precisian in speech or manners or morals, conceited or didactic person; ~**gerў** (-g-) *n.,* priggish conduct; ~**gish** (-g-) *a.* [orig. unkn.]

**prim** *a.* (**-mm-**). (Of person, manner, speech, etc.) formal and precise, demure; (esp. of woman) prudish. [ult. f. F (PRIME¹)]

**pri'ma** (prē'-) *fem. a.* ~ **balleri'na**, chief female performer in ballet; ~ **do'nna**, chief female singer in opera, (transf.) temperamental person. [It. (PRIME¹)]

**pri'macў** *n.* Office of a primate; pre-eminence. [F f. L (PRIMATE)]

**prima fā'cĭe** (*or* -shĭē) *adv. & a.* (Arising) at first sight, (based) on the first impression, (*has prima facie a good case; see a prima facie reason for it*). [L]

**pri'mal** *a.* (~ly). Primitive, primeval; chief, fundamental. [L (PRIME¹)]

**pri'marў. 1.** *a.* (-ily). Earliest, original; of first rank in series, not derived, (*the primary meaning of a word*); of the first importance, chief; (Geol.) of lowest series of strata; (Biol.) of first stage of development; ~ **battery** (producing electricity by irreversible chemical action); *primary* COLOUR; ~ **education** (beginning with rudiments of knowledge, elementary); \*~ **election** (to appoint party conference delegates or to select candidates for principal election); ~ **feather,** large flight-feather of bird's wing; ~ **school** (where primary education is given). **2.** *n.* Primary period, feather, election, etc. [L (PRIME¹)]

**pri'mate** (*or* -āt) *n.* Archbishop; member of order Primates; **Primā'tēs** (-z; *or* pri'māts) *n.pl.,* (Zool.) highest order of mammals, including man, apes, and monkeys. [F f. L *primas* -*at*- chief (foll.)]

**prime¹. 1.** *a.* Chief, most important; first-rate (esp. of cattle and provisions), excellent; primary, fundamental; (Arith., of a number) divisible only by itself and unity (e.g. 2, 3, 5, 7, 11); ~ **cost,** = COST *price*; ~ **minister,** principal minister of sovereign or State; *prime* MOVER; ~ **time** (at which highest rates are charged, esp. to television advertisers). **2.** *n.* State of highest perfection (*in the prime of life*); *the best part* (*of* thing); beginning; (office of) second canonical hour of prayer; prime number. [F f. L *primus* first]

**prime²** *v.t.* Prepare (explosive) for detonation; pour liquid into (pump) to make it start working; equip, ply, (person *with* information, liquor,

etc.); cover (wood etc.) with first coat of paint, or with oil etc. to prevent paint from being absorbed; **pri'mer¹, pri'ming,** *ns.,* (esp.) substance used to prime wood etc. [orig. unkn.]

**pri'mer²** *n.* Elementary school-book for teaching children to read; small introductory book. [AF f. L (PRIME¹)]

**primē'val** *a.* (~ly). Of the first age of the world; ancient, primitive. [L (PRIME¹, *aevum* age)]

**pri'mitive. 1.** *a.* Early, ancient; old-fashioned, undeveloped, at an early stage of civilization; original, primary. **2.** *n.* Painter of period before Renaissance, modern imitator of such, untutored painter with direct naïve style; picture by such painter. [F or L (PRIME¹)]

**primogĕ'niture** *n.* Fact of being first-born child; right of succession belonging to the first-born, esp. feudal rule by which whole real estate of intestate passes to eldest son. [L (PRIME¹, *genitura* birth)]

**primôr'dial** *a.* (~ly). Existing at or from the beginning, primeval. [L (PRIME¹, *ordior* begin)]

**primp** *v.t.* Make (hair, clothes, etc.) tidy; smarten (one*self*). [var. PRIM]

**pri'mrose** (-z) *n.* (Plant bearing) pale yellow spring flower; colour of this flower; EVENING *primrose;* **the ~ path,** unjustified pursuit of ease or pleasure. [F & L, = first rose]

**pri'mŭla** *n.* Herbaceous perennial with flowers of various colours. [L dim. (PRIME¹)]

**Pri'mus** *n.* Brand of portable stove burning vaporized oil for cooking etc. [P]

**prince** *n.* Sovereign ruler (rhet.; P~ **of Peace,** Christ; ~ **of darkness, this world,** the Devil); ruler of small State, actually or nominally subject to king or emperor; male member of royal family; (rendering foreign title) noble usu. ranking next below duke; (fig.) the greatest (*of* novelists etc.); ~ **consort,** husband of reigning queen who is himself a prince; ~ **of the Church,** cardinal; P~ **of Wales,** (title usu. conferred on) heir apparent to British throne; P~ **Regent,** prince acting as regent, esp. the future George IV; ~'s **feather,** tall plant with red plumes; ~'**ling** (-sl-) *n.,* young or petty prince; ~'**ly** (-slĭ) *a.* (-iness), (worthy) of a prince, sumptuous, splendid; **prĭ'ncĕss** (*or* -ĕ's) *n.*, wife of prince, female member of royal family; ~**ss dress** etc. (made in panels with flared skirt and without seam at waist); ~**ss royal**, (title conferrable on) sovereign's eldest daughter. [F f. L *princeps -cĭp-*]

**prĭ'ncĭpal. 1.** *a.* (usu. *attrib.*) First in rank or importance, chief, (*the principal town of the district*); main, leading, (*a principal cause of his failure*; ~ **boy, girl,** actress who takes leading male, female, part in pantomime); (Gram.) ~ **sentence, clause,** one to which another is subordinate, ~ **parts** of verb, those from which all others can be deduced. **2.** *n.* Head, ruler, superior; head of some schools, colleges, and universities; leading performer in concert, play, etc.; ‖civil servant of grade below Secretaries; person directly responsible for crime, either as actual perpetrator or as aiding; person for whom another is agent or surety or second; capital sum as opp. to interest or income. **3.** ~'**ly** *adv.*, for the most part, chiefly. [F f. L (prec.)]

**prĭncĭpā'lĭty** *n.* Government of or State ruled by a prince; ‖**the P**~, Wales. [F f. L (prec.)]

**prĭ'ncĭple** *n.* Fundamental source, primary element; fundamental truth as basis of reasoning etc.; (Phys.) general law (*Archimedes' principle*); general law as guide to action (*moral, conservative, principles*; *a dangerous principle*; **in** ~, as regards fundamentals but not necessarily in detail); (in *pl.* or collect. *sing.*) personal code of right conduct (*a man of high principle*; *has ability but no principles*; **on** ~, from settled moral motive); law of nature forming basis for construction or working of machine; (Chem.) constituent of a substance, esp. one giving rise to some quality etc., (*bitter principle in quinine*); ~**d** (-peld) *a.*, based on or having (esp. praiseworthy) principles of behaviour. [AF f. L *principium* source (PRINCE)]

**prĭnk** *v.t.* Smarten (one*self* etc.); dress one*self up*; (of bird) preen. [orig. unkn.]

**print. 1.** *n.* Indentation in or mark on surface preserving the form left by pressure of some body (FINGER*print*; FOOT*print*); printed cotton fabric; language embodied in printed form; printed lettering, (SMALL *print*); state of being printed (*book is in* ~, in printed form, on sale; **out of print**, sold out; **appear in** ~, have one's work published; **rush into** ~, write to newspaper etc. on insufficient grounds); printed publication, esp. newspaper; picture or design printed from block or plate; (Photog.) picture produced from negative. **2.** *v.t.* Impress, stamp, (surface e.g. of wax, *with* seal etc.; mark or figure *on* or *in* surface); (fig.) impress (idea, scene, etc., *on* mind, memory); produce (book, picture, etc., or abs.) by applying inked types, blocks, or plates, to paper etc.; express or publish in print; write (words, letters, or abs.) without joining, in imitation of typography; mark (textile fabric) with decorative design in colours; ~**ed circuit** (Electr.; with thin conducting strips on sheet); ~ (**out**), produce (photograph) by transmission of light through negative; ~**-out** *n.*, computer output in printed form. **3.** ~'**er** *n.*, (esp.) one who prints books etc., owner of printing business; *printer's* DEVIL; ~'**ing** *n.*, (esp.) impression of a book; ~**ing-ink, -press,** (for printing on paper etc. from types etc.). [F f. L *premo* (PRESS[1])]

**prĭ'or** *n., a.,* & *adv.* **1.** *n.* Superior officer of religious house or order; (in abbey) deputy of abbot. **2.** *a.* Earlier; coming before in time, order, or importance, (*to*). **3.** *adv.* ~ **to,** before (*existing prior to his appointment*). **4.** ~**ĕss** *n.*; **prĭo'rĭty** *n.*, being earlier or antecedent, precedence in rank etc., an interest having prior claim to consideration; ~**y̆** *n.*, monastery or nunnery governed by prior(ess). [F f. L, = earlier]

‖**prise.** See PRIZE[3].

**prĭ'sm** *n.* Solid figure whose two ends are equal parallel rectilinear figures, and whose sides are parallelograms; transparent body of this form, usu. triangular, with refracting surfaces at acute angle with each other; ~ **binoculars** (in which triangular prisms are used to shorten the instrument); ~**ǎ'tĭc** (-zm-) *a.* (-ically), of or like prism (~**atic binoculars,** = PRISM *binoculars*), (of colours) formed, distributed, etc., (as if) by transparent prism. [L f. Gk]

**prĭ'son** (-z-) *n.* Place where person

is kept in captivity, esp. building to which persons are consigned while awaiting trial or for punishment; custody, confinement, (*in prison*); ~ **without bars**, area to which offenders are confined although without physical restraints. [F f. L (*prehendo* seize)]

**pri'soner** (-zn-) *n.* Person kept in prison; (fig.) person or thing confined by illness, another's grasp, etc.; ~ (**at the bar**), person in custody on criminal charge and on trial; *prisoner of* CONSCIENCE; ~ **of State** (confined for political reasons); ~ (**of war**), one who has been captured in war; **take** (person) ~, seize and hold as prisoner. [AF (prec.)]

**pri'ss|y** *a.* (~**ily**). Prim, prudish. [perh. PRIM, SISSY]

**pri'stine** (*or* -ēn) *a.* Ancient, primitive, old and unspoiled; fresh as if new. [L *pristinus* former]

**pri'vate. 1.** *a.* (Of person) not holding public office or official position; kept or removed from public knowledge or observation (*the matter was kept private*; *we are quite private here*); not open to the public (*private door*); one's own (*my private property*); individual, personal, not affecting the community, (*motives of private malice*); confidential (*asked for a private discussion*); (of place) secluded; **in** ~, privately; ~ **bill** etc. (of legislation affecting individual or corporation only); ||~ **company** (with restricted membership); *private* DETECTIVE; ~ **enterprise**, business-(es) not under State control, (fig.) individual initiative; ~ **eye**, colloq.) private detective; ~ **hotel** (not necessarily accepting all comers); ~ **house**, dwelling-house of private person; ~ **life** (as private person, not as official, public performer, etc.); ~ **means**, income from investments etc.; ~ **member**, M.P. not holding Government appointment; ~ **parts**, genitals; ||~ **patient**, patient treated by doctor etc. otherwise than under National Health Service; ~ **prac- tice** (of doctor etc. who is not only an employee); ~ **school**, ||school supported wholly by payment of fees, *school not supported mainly by State; *private* SECRETARY; ~ **soldier**, ordinary soldier, not officer; ~ **view** (of picture etc. exhibition before it is opened to the public).

**2.** *n.* Private soldier; (in *pl.*) genitals. **3. pri'vacy** *n.*, being withdrawn from society or public interest, being alone and undisturbed; **privateer'** *n.*, armed vessel holding letters of MARQUE[1], commander or (in *pl.*) crew of this. [L *privatus* (foll.)]

**priva'tion** *n.* Lack of comforts or necessaries of life (*died of privation*; *suffered many privations*); **pri'vative** *a.*, consisting in or showing loss or absence of a quality or attribute. [L (*privo* deprive)]

**pri'vet** *n.* Bushy evergreen shrub with smooth dark-green leaves, much used for hedges; ~**hawk**, large species of moth. [orig. unkn.]

**pri'vilege. 1.** *n.* Right, advantage, or immunity, belonging to person, class, or office, esp. freedoms of members of legislative assembly when speaking therein; special advantage or benefit (*to converse with him was a privilege*). **2.** *v.t.* Invest with privilege; (esp. in *p.p.*) allow (person *to do*) as privilege. [F f. L (foll., *lex leg-* law)]

**pri'vy. 1.** *a.* (-**ily**). (Of thing, place, etc.) hidden, secluded; (of action) secret; **P~ Council**, sover- eign's or governor-general's private counsellors (in U.K. now chiefly honorary); ~ **counsellor, council- lor,** (esp.) member of Privy Council; ||~ **purse**, allowance from public revenue for monarch's private expenses; ||~ **seal**, seal formerly affixed to documents that are after- wards to pass, or that do not require, the Great Seal; ||**Lord P~ Seal**, senior Cabinet Minister without official duties (formerly keeper of privy seal); ~ **to**, in the secret of (person's plans etc.). **2.** *n.* (arch. or U.S.) Lavatory. [F *privé* f. L (PRIVATE)]

**prize**[1] *n.*, *a.*, & *v.* **1.** *n.* Reward given as symbol of victory or superior- ity; (fig.) anything striven for or worth striving for (*missed all the great prizes of life*); money or thing offered for competition in lottery etc. **2.** *a.* To which prize is adjudged in show, competition, etc., (*prize bull*, *poem*, etc.); supremely excellent or out- standing of its kind. **3.** *v.t.* Value highly (*prized possessions*). **4.** ~**fight**, boxing-match for money; ~**fighter**, ~**fighting**, (one who engages in) professional boxing; ~**man**, win- ner of prize; ~**ring**, enclosed area (now usu. square) for, (fig.) practice of, prize-fighting. [F (PRAISE)]

**prize²** n. Ship or property captured at sea by rights of war, (fig.) valuable find (*see what a prize I have found!*). [F *prise* f. L *prehendo* seize]

**prize³, prise** (-z), v.t. Force (lid etc. *up, out,* box etc. *open*) by leverage against fulcrum. [F *prise* (prec.)]

**prō¹** n. (colloq.; *pl.* ~s). Professional. [abbr.]

**prō². 1.** *a. & prep.* ~ **and con**(tra), (of arguments or reasons) for and against. **2.** *n.* ~s **and con**(tra)**s**, reasons for and against. [L, = for, on behalf of]

**prō-¹** *pref.* meaning substitute(d) or deputy for, (person) favouring or siding with (opp. ANTI-); forwards (*produce*); forwards and downwards (*prostrate*); onwards (*proceed*); in front of (*protect*). [L *pro* in front (of), for]

**pro-²** *pref.* Before (in time, place, order, etc.) (*problem, prophet*). [Gk *pro* before]

**P.R.O.** *abbr.* public relations officer.

**prō´bab|le. 1.** *a.* (~ly). That may be expected to happen or prove true, likely, (*reckon the probable cost; it is probable that he forgot*). **2.** *n.* A probable candidate, member of team, etc., (cf. POSSIBLE). **3.** ~**i´lit|y** *n.*, quality of being probable (**in all** ~**ility,** most probably), likelihood, (most) probable event (*the probability is that he will come*), (Math.) extent to which event is likely to occur (measured by ratio of favourable cases to all possible cases). [F f. L (PROVE)]

**prō´bāte** (*or* -ăt) *n.* Official proving of will; verified copy of will with certificate as handed to executors. [L (*probo* PROVE)]

**probā´tion** *n.* Testing of conduct or character of person (esp. of candidate for employment or membership; **on** ~, undergoing this before full admission etc.); (Law) system of suspending sentence on selected offenders subject to good behaviour under supervision of ~ **officer** (*was put on probation*); ~**arў** *a.*; ~**er** *n.*, person on probation (e.g. hospital nurse at early stage of training), offender on probation; **prō´bative** *a.*, affording proof. [F f. L (prec.)]

**prōbe. 1.** *n.* Blunt-ended surgical instrument usu. of metal for exploring wound etc.; unmanned explora-

tory spacecraft transmitting information about its environment; (fig.) penetrating investigation. **2.** *v.t.* Explore with probe; penetrate (thing) with sharp instrument; (fig.) examine closely (person, motive, etc.). [L *proba* (PROVE)]

**prō´bitў** *n.* Uprightness, honesty. [F or L (*probus* good)]

**prō´blem** *n.* Doubtful or difficult question (often *attrib.*: ~ **child,** difficult to control, unruly); thing hard to understand (*his whole conduct is a problem to me*); (Geom.) proposition in which something has to be constructed (cf. THEOREM); (Phys. & Math.) inquiry starting from given conditions to investigate a fact, result, or law; (Chess, Bridge, etc.) arrangement of men, cards, etc., in which solver is challenged to accomplish specified result, often under prescribed conditions; ~**ă´tic(al)** *adjs.* (-ically), doubtful, questionable, (*the whole question is problematical*). [L f. Gk]

**probo´scis** *n.* Elephant's trunk; long flexible snout of tapir etc.; elongated part of mouth of some insects. [L f. Gk (*boskō* feed)]

**procē´dur|e** (-dyer) *n.* Mode of conducting business (esp. in parliament) or legal action; ~**al** *a.*, of or relating to procedure. [F (foll.)]

**procee´d** *v.i.* Go on, make one's way, (*to place*); go on (*with* or *in* action, investigation, remarks, etc.; *to* another subject, *to* do); adopt course of action (*how shall we proceed?*); (abs.) go on to say ('*in either case*', he *proceeded,* '*our course is clear*'); take legal proceedings *against* person; (of action) be carried on (further), take place, (*the case, the play, will now proceed*); come forth, issue, originate, (*sobs heard to proceed from her bed*); ~**ing** *n.,* (esp.) action, piece of conduct, (*a high-handed proceeding*); **legal** ~**ings,** (steps taken in) legal action), (in *pl.*) published report of discussions or conference; **prō´ceeds** (-z) *n.pl.,* money produced by sale, performance, etc. [F f. L (*cedo cess-*go)]

**prō´cĕss¹. 1.** *n.* Progress, course, (**in** ~ **of** construction etc., being constructed etc.); course of action, proceeding, esp. series of operations in manufacture, printing, etc.; natural or involuntary operation, series of changes; action at law, summons or writ (~-**server**, sheriff's officer); (Biol.) natural appendage, outgrowth, protuberance. 2. *v.t.* Treat (material, food esp. to prevent decay) by particular process. [F f. L (prec.)]

**procĕ'ss**[2] *v.i.* Walk in procession (colloq.); ~**ion** (-shon) *n.*, proceeding of body of persons, boats, etc., in orderly succession esp. as religious ceremony or political demonstration or on festive occasion, body of persons doing this, (fig.) race in which no competitor is able to overtake another; ~**ional** (-shon-), (*a.*; -**lly**) of processions, used, carried, or sung, in processions, (*n.*) processional hymn. [*procession* F f. L (PROCEED)]

**proclai'm** *v.t.* Announce officially (thing, *that*); declare (war, peace); officially announce accession of (sovereign); declare (person, thing) officially to be (traitor etc.); declare publicly or openly (thing, *that*); make known as being (*his accent proclaimed him a Scot*); **prŏclamā'-tion** *n.* [L (CLAIM)]

**proclĭ'vĭtў** *n.* Tendency (*to* or *towards* action or habit, esp. bad one; *to* do). [L (*clivus* slope)]

**procrā'stĭn|āte** *v.i.* Defer action, be dilatory; ~**ā'tion**, ~**ātor**, *ns.* [L (*cras* tomorrow)]

**prŏ'crĕ|āte** *v.t.* Bring into existence by natural process of reproduction, generate, (offspring, or abs.); ~**ā'tion** *n.*; ~**ātive** *a.* [L (CREATE)]

**Procrŭ'stĕan** *a.* Seeking to enforce uniformity by violent methods. [Gk *Prokroustēs* robber who fitted victims to bed by stretching or lopping]

‖**prŏ'ctor** *n.* Each of two university officers appointed annually at Oxf. & Camb. and having various functions esp. discipline; **Queen's** or **King's P~**, official who has right to intervene in probate, divorce, and nullity cases when collusion or suppression of facts is alleged; **prŏctō'rĭal** *a.* (-**lly**); ~**shĭp** *n.* [PROCURATOR]

**procŭr'|e** *v.t.* & *i.* Obtain by care or effort, acquire, (*must procure you a copy; cannot procure employment*); bring about (action by others; *procured his dismissal*); act as procurer or procuress (*of*); **prŏcūrā'tion** *n.*, (esp.) function or authorized action

of attorney; **prŏ'cūrātor** *n.*, agent, proxy, esp. with power of attorney (**procurator fiscal**, coroner and public prosecutor of district in Scotland; **procurator general**, head of Treasury law department); ~**atŏr'-ĭal** *a.*; ~**ement** (-ūr'm-) *n.*; ~**er** *n.*, (esp.) who obtains women to gratify another's lust; ~**ĕss** *n.*, female procurer. [F f. L (*curo* look after)]

**prŏd. 1.** *v.t.* & *i.* (-**dd-**). Poke with finger, pointed instrument, end of stick, etc.; (fig.) stimulate to action; make prodding motion *at.* 2. *n.* Poke, thrust; stimulus to action. [orig. unkn.]

**prŏ'dĭgal** *a.* (~**ly**) & *n.* Recklessly wasteful (person); lavish *of*; ~ (**son**), repentant wastrel, returned wanderer, (Luke 15); ~**ĭtў** (-ă'l-) *n.* [L (*prodigus* lavish)]

**prŏ'dĭgў** *n.* Marvellous thing, esp. one out of the ordinary course of nature; wonderful example *of* (some quality); person with surprising qualities or abilities, esp. precocious child; **prŏdĭ'gious** (-jus) *a.*, marvellous, enormous, abnormal. [L *prodigium* portent]

**produce. 1.** (-ū'-) *v.t.* (-**cible**). Bring forward for inspection or consideration (*will produce evidence, reasons*; *produce your tickets*); bring (play, performer, book, etc.) before the public; (Geom.) extend, continue, (line *to* a point); manufacture (goods) from raw materials etc.; cause, bring about, (a reaction, a sensation, etc.); bring into existence; (of land etc.) yield (agricultural etc. products); bear, yield, (offspring, fruit). 2. (-ŏ'-) *n.* (Amount of) what is produced, esp. agricultural and natural products generally (*dairy produce*). 3. **prŏdū'cer** *n.*, (esp.; Econ.) one who produces article for use (opp. *consumer*), person generally responsible for production of film or play, ‖director of play or broadcast programme; **prŏ'duct** *n.*, thing or substance produced by natural process or manufacture, result (*the product of his labours*), (Math.) quantity obtained by multiplying; **prŏdū'ction** *n.*, producing, being produced or manufactured esp. in large quantities (*go into production*), total yield, thing produced, esp. literary or artistic work; **prŏdū'ctive** *a.*, producing, tending to produce, (*productive of figs, of great annoyance*),

(Econ.) producing commodities of exchangeable value (*productive labour*), producing abundantly (*a productive soil, writer*); **prŏductī'vĭty** *n.*, capacity to produce, effectiveness of productive effort esp. in industry. [L (*duco -duct-* lead)]

**prō'ĕm** *n.* Introductory discourse. [F or L f. Gk]

**Prof.** *abbr.* Professor.

**profā'ne. 1.** *a.* Not belonging to what is sacred or biblical; not initiated into religious rites or esoteric knowledge; (of rite etc.) heathen; irreverent, blasphemous. **2.** *v.t.* Treat (sacred thing) with irreverence or disregard; violate, pollute, (what is entitled to respect). **3. prŏfanā'tion** *n.*; **profā'nĭty** *n.*, blasphemy. [F or L (*fanum* temple)]

**profĕ'ss** *v.t.* Lay claim to (quality, feeling), pretend (*to* be or do), (*does not profess to be a scholar*); declare (*they profess ignorance, themselves quite content*); affirm one's faith in or allegiance to (religion, Christ); teach (subject) as professor; ~**ed** (-st) *a.*, self-acknowledged (*a professed Christian*), having taken religious vows, alleged, ostensible; ~**ĕdly** *adv.* [F f. L *profiteor -fess-* declare]

**profĕ'ssion** (-shon) *n.* Declaration, avowal, (*accept my sincere professions of regard*); declaration of belief in a religion; vow made on entering, fact of being in, a religious order; vocation or calling (esp. in some branch of advanced learning or science; *the military profession*; *a carpenter by profession*; **the learned** ~**s**, divinity, law, medicine; **the oldest** ~, prostitution); body of persons engaged in a profession (**the** ~, Theatr. sl., actors). [F f. L (prec.)]

**profĕ'ssional** (-shon-). **1.** *a.* (~**ly**). Of, belonging to, connected with, a profession, (*professional men, etiquette*); ~ *politician* etc., making a trade of politics etc.; ~ *golf(er)* etc. (performing for monetary reward; opp. AMATEUR). **2.** *n.* Professional person, esp. golfer etc. **3.** ~**ism** *n.*, qualities or typical features of profession(als); **profĕ'ssor** *n.*, one who makes profession (esp. of a religion), teacher of high rank (esp. holder of chair or *senior teaching appointment in university); **profĕ'ssorate** *n.*, professoriate, professorship; **prŏ'fĕssōr'ĭal** *a.* (-lly); **prŏfĕssŏr'iate**

*n.*, the professors of a university etc.; **profĕ'ssorship** *n.*

**prŏ'ffer** *v.t.* (esp. in *p.p.*) Offer (gift, services, hand, etc., arch. *to* do). [F (PRO-[1], OFFER)]

**profĭ'cien|t** (-shent) *a.* & *n.* Expert, adept, (*in* or *at* an art etc.; *in* doing); ~**cȳ** *n.* [L *proficio -fect-* advance]

**prō'file** *n.* Drawing, silhouette, or other representation, of side view esp. of human face (*drawn* etc. **in** ~, as seen from one side); outline (esp. of human face) as seen from one side; short printed or broadcast biographical or character sketch; **keep a low** ~, remain inconspicuous. [It. *profilare* draw in outline]

**prŏ'fĭt. 1.** *n.* Advantage, benefit (*have studied it to my profit*); pecuniary gain, excess of returns over outlay, (*sold at a* ~, for more than one paid to get it; ~ **and loss account,** in which gains are credited and losses debited to show net profit or loss at any time; ~**-sharing,** sharing of profits esp. between employer and employed). **2.** *v.t.* & *i.* (Of thing) bring advantage to (person etc.; *it will not profit him to act thus*); be of advantage; (of person etc.) be benefited or assisted (*hope to profit from your advice*). **3.** ~**able** *a.* (-bly), beneficial, yielding profit, lucrative; ~**abi'lĭty** *n.*; ~**eer'**, (*v.i.*) (seek to) make excessive profits out of others' needs esp. in times of scarcity, (*n.*) person who profiteers. [F f. L *profectus* (PROFICIENT)]

**profĭ'terōle** *n.* Small hollow cake of choux pastry with sweet or savoury filling. [F dim. (PROFIT)]

**prŏ'flĭg|ate. 1.** *a.* Licentious, dissolute; recklessly extravagant; ~**acȳ** *n.* **2.** *n.* Profligate person. [L *profligo* ruin)]

**prō fŏr'ma** *adv.*, *a.*, & *n.* **1.** *adv.* & *a.* (Done) for form's sake. **2.** *a.* & *n.* ~ (*invoice*), invoice sent to purchaser in advance of goods for completion of business formalities. [L]

**profou'nd** *a.* (~**er**, ~**est**). Having or showing great knowledge or insight (*profound statesman, treatise*); demanding deep study or thought (*profound doctrines*); (of state or quality) deep, intense, (*fell into a profound sleep*; *simulated a profound indifference*); (rhet.) deep; **profu'ndĭty** *n.* [F f. L *profundus*]

**profū'se** *a.* (~**r**, ~**st**). Lavish,

extravagant, (*in* or *of* gifts, expenditure, etc.); (of thing) exuberantly plentiful (*profuse bleeding, variety*); **profū'sion** (-zhon) *n.* [L (*fundo fus- pour*)]

**progĕ'nĭtor** *n.* Ancestor of person, animal, or plant; (fig.) predecessor, original; **prŏ'gĕny̆** *n.*, offspring of person or animal or plant, (fig.) issue, outcome. [F f. L (*progigno beget*)]

**prŏgn|ŏ'sĭs** *n.* (*pl.* -es *pr.* -ēz). Prognostication, esp. (Med.) forecast of course of disease; **~ŏ'stĭc**, (*n.*) advance indication, omen, (*of*), prediction, (*a.*) foretelling, predictive, (*of*); **~ŏ'stĭcāte** *v.t.* (-cable), foretell or foresee (event, *that*), (of thing) betoken; **~ŏstĭcā'tion, ~ŏ'stĭcātor,** *ns.* [F f. L f. Gk (*gignōskō* know)]

‖**prŏ'grămme,** (U.S. & Computers) **prŏ'grăm.** **1.** *n.* Descriptive notice of series of events, e.g. of course of study, play, concert, etc.; such series of events (*a programme of lectures*); broadcast performance; definite plan of intended proceedings; series of instructions to control operation of computer; **prŏgrammă'tĭc** *a.* (-ically). **2.** *v.t.* (-mm-). Make programme of; express (problem) or instruct (computer) by means of program. [L f. Gk (*graphō* write)]

**progrĕss. 1.** (-ō'-) *n.* Forward or onward movement in space (*made slow progress*; **in ~,** in course of occurrence, going on); advance or development esp. to better state (*made no progress in his studies*; **~ report,** account of progress made); ‖(arch.) state journey, esp. by royal person. **2.** (-ogrĕ's) *v.i.* Move forward or onward, be carried on, advance or develop esp. to better state. **3.** **progrĕ'ssion** (-shon) *n.*, progressing (*mode of progression*), succession, series, (Math.) ARITHMETICAL, GEOMETRICAL, progression. [L (*progredior -gress-* go forward)]

**progrĕ'ssive. 1.** *a.* Moving forward (*progressive motion*); proceeding step by step, successive; (of card-game, dance, etc.) with periodic change of partners; (of taxation) at rates increasing with the sum taxed; advancing in social conditions, character, efficiency, etc., (*a progressive nation*); (of tense) expressing action in progress; (of disease, violence, etc.) continuously increasing

in severity or extent; favouring progress or reform (*progressive party*). **2.** *n.* Advocate of progressive policy. [F (prec.)]

**prohĭ'bĭt** *v.t.* Forbid, debar, (action, thing, person's doing, person *from* doing; prohibited DEGREES); **prŏhĭbĭ'tion** (*or* -ōĭb-) *n.*, forbidding, being forbidden, edict or order that forbids, forbidding by law of the manufacture and sale of intoxicants; **prŏhĭbĭ'tionĭst** (*or* -ōĭb-) *n.*, advocate of such legislation; **~ĭve** *a.*, prohibiting, such as to prevent use or abuse or purchase of thing (*prohibitive tax, price*); **~or** *n.*; **~ory̆** *a.* [L *prohibeo -hibit-*]

**projĕct. 1.** (-ē'-) *v.t.* & *i.* Plan, contrive, (scheme etc.); cast, throw, impel, (body *into* space etc.); extrapolate (results *to* future time etc.); go out of one*self into* another's feelings, the future, etc.; cause (light, shadow) to fall on surface etc.; cause (image) to be visible *on* screen etc.; (fig.) cause (idea etc.) to take shape or become known; make projection of (earth, sky, etc.); protrude, jut out. **2.** (-ŏ'-) *n.* Plan, scheme; planned undertaking, esp. by student(s) for presentation of results at specified time. **3.** **projĕ'ctile,** (*a.*) impelling (*projectile force*), capable of being projected by force esp. from gun, (*or* prŏ'jĭk-; *n.*) projectile missile; **projĕ'ction** *n.*, projecting, thing that projects or is projected, representation on plane surface of (any part of) surface of earth or of celestial sphere (e.g. MERCATOR's *projection*), mental image viewed as objective reality; **projĕ'ctionĭst** *n.*, person who operates cinema projector; **projĕ'ctive** *a.*; **projĕ'ctor** *n.*, apparatus for projecting rays of light or projecting image on screen. [L *projicio -ject- throw forth*]

**prŏ'lăpse[1], prolă'psus,** *ns.* Slipping forward or downward of part or organ, esp. of womb or rectum. [L (LAPSE)]

**prolă'pse[2]** *v.i.* Undergo prolapse.

**prŏ'lāte** *a.* (Geom., of spheroid) lengthened along polar diameter. [L, = brought forward, prolonged]

**prŏlĕgŏ'mĕna** *n.pl.* Preliminary discourse or matter prefixed to book etc. [L f. Gk (*legō* say)]

**prŏlĕtār'ĭ|at** *n.* (Rom. Hist., or derog. of modern society) lowest class of community; (Econ.) wage-earners, esp. on daily labour for subsistence; ~**an** *a.* & *n.*, (member) of proletariat; **proli′ferate** *v.i.* & *t.*, reproduce itself or grow by multiplication of elementary parts, produce (cells etc.) thus, increase rapidly in numbers etc.; **prolifera′tion** *n.*; **proli′fic** *a.* (-**ically**), producing (much) offspring, abundantly productive (*of*), abounding *in.* [F f. L (*proles* offspring)]

**pro′lix** *a.* Lengthy, tediously wordy; **proli′xity** *n.* [F or L]

**pro′logue** (-g) *n.* Preliminary discourse, poem, etc., esp. introducing play; (fig.) act or event serving as introduction (*to*). [F f. L f. Gk (LOGOS)]

**prolo′ng** *v.t.* Extend (action, condition, etc.) in duration; extend in spatial length; **prolonga′tion** (-ngg-) *n.* [L (*longus* long)]

**prom** *n.* (colloq.) Promenade (‖concert). [abbr.]

**prŏmena′de** (-ah′d). **1.** *n.* Walk etc. for exercise, amusement, or display, or as social ceremony; place, esp. paved public walk (‖at seaside), for this; ~ **concert** (at which part of audience is not seated and can move about); ~ **deck**, upper deck on passenger ship, where passengers may promenade. **2.** *v.i.* & *t.* Make a promenade (through); lead (person) about a place esp. for display; ~**r** *n.* (esp. at promenade concert). [F]

**pro′minen|t** *a.* Jutting out, projecting; conspicuous, distinguished; ~**ce** *n.*, being prominent (also ~**cy** *n.*), prominent thing. [L *promineo* project]

**promi′scuous** *a.* Of mixed and indiscriminate composition or kinds; indiscriminate (*promiscuous massacre, hospitality*); (of person) having sexual relations unrestricted by marriage or cohabitation; (of sexual relations) of this kind; (colloq.) casual, carelessly irregular; **promiscu′ity** *n.* [L (*misceo* mix)]

**pro′mis|e. 1.** *n.* Assurance given to a person that one will do or not do something or will give or get him something (*a promise of help, to help*; BREACH *of promise*; **land** *of* ~**e**, = *promised land*); (fig.) ground of expectation of future achievements or good results (*a book, writer, of great promise*). **2.** *v.t.* & *i.* Make (person) a promise to give or get

him (thing; *I promise you a fair hearing*); make (person, or abs.) a promise (*to do, that* thing shall be done etc.); (colloq.) assure (*I promise you, it will not be easy*); (fig.) afford expectation of, seem likely (*to* do); ~**ed land**, Canaan (Gen. 12), heaven, any place of expected felicity; ~**e** one**self**, look forward to (a pleasant time etc.); ~**e well** etc., offer good etc. prospect. **3.** ~**ing** *a.*, likely to turn out well, hopeful, full of promise; ~**sory** *a.*, conveying or implying a promise; ~**sory note**, signed document containing written promise to pay stated sum. [L *promissum* (as MISSILE)]

**pro′montory** *n.* Point of high land jutting out into sea etc., headland. [L]

**promo′t|e** *v.t.* Advance (person *to* position or higher office); help forward, encourage, (process, result); initiate (project), take necessary steps for passing of (private bill in parliament); publicize and sell (product); ~**er** *n.*, (esp.) one who promotes formation of joint-stock company, one who is financially responsible for sporting event, theatrical production, etc.; ~**ion** *n.*; ~**ional** *a.* [L *promoveo* -*mot*-]

**prŏmpt** *a., adv., v.,* & *n.* **1.** *a.* Ready in action, acting with alacrity; made, done, etc., readily or at once (*prompt reply, payment*). **2.** *adv.* Punctually (*at six o'clock prompt*). **3.** *v.t.* Incite, move, (person etc. *to* action, *to* do); inspire, give rise to, (feeling, action); help (actor, reciter, or abs.) by supplying words that come next; assist (hesitant person) with suggestion etc. **4.** *n.* Thing said to help memory esp. of actor; ~ **side** of stage (usu. to actor's left). **5.** ~′**er** *n.*, (esp., Theatr.) person unseen by audience who prompts actors; ~**itude** *n.*, promptness. [F or L]

**pro′mulg|ate** *v.t.* Make known to the public, disseminate (creed etc.), proclaim (decree, news); ~**a′tion, ~ātor,** *ns.* [L]

**prōne** *a.* Lying face downwards; lying flat, prostrate; disposed, liable, (*to* usu. bad quality, action, or condition; *to* do); (in *comb.*) more than usually likely to suffer (*accident-prone person*). [L]

**prŏng** *n.* Each of two or more projecting pointed parts at end of fork etc. [orig. unkn.]

**pronŏ′mǐnal** *a.* (~**ly**). Of (the nature of) pronoun. [L (foll.)]

**prŏ′noun** *n.* Word used instead of noun to designate (without naming) person or thing already mentioned or known from context or forming subject of inquiry; pronominal adjective; **demonstrative** ~ (*this, that*); **distributive** ~ (*each, either,* etc.); **impersonal** or **indefinite** ~ (*any, some, anyone, something,* etc.); **interrogative** ~ (*who?, what?, which?*); **personal** ~ (*I, we, thou, you, he, she, it, they*); **possessive** ~, adjective representing possessive case (*my, her, our,* etc., with absolute forms *mine, hers, ours,* etc.); **reciprocal** ~ (*one another,* etc.); **reflexive** ~ (*myself, oneself,* etc.); **relative** ~ (*who, what, which, that*). [PRO-¹]

**pronou′nce** *v.t. & i.* Utter, deliver, (judgement, curse, etc.) formally or solemnly, state to be in one's opinion (*apples were pronounced excellent*); pass judgement, give one's opinion (*on, for, against*); utter, speak (words, or abs.) *pronounce more distinctly*), esp. with reference to different ways (*how do you pronounce 'fulsome'?; cannot pronounce French*); ~**able** (-sa-) *a.* (esp. of word or language); ~**d** (-st) *a.*, (esp.) strongly marked, decided, (*pronounced tendency, flavour*); ~**ment** (-sm-) *n.*, formal statement, declaration; **pronŭnciamĕ′ntŏ** *n.* (*pl.* ~**s**), proclamation, manifesto, [Sp.]; **pronŭncĭã′tion** *n.*, way in which word is pronounced, person's way of pronouncing words. [F f. L (*nuntio* announce)]

**prŏ′ntŏ** *adv.* (sl.) Promptly, quickly. [Sp. f. L (PROMPT)]

**proof** *n., a., & v.* **1.** *n.* Fact or evidence or argument sufficing or helping to establish a fact (*as (a) proof of his esteem; proof* POSITIVE *of his intention* or *that he intended*); proving, demonstration, (*not capable of proof; in proof of my assertion*); test, trial, (*the proof of the pudding is in the eating*); standard of strength of distilled alcoholic liquors (~ **spirit**, alcohol–water mixture having this standard strength; **above** ~, stronger than this); photographic print made for selection; trial impression taken from printing-type or engraved plate for correction; ~-**reader**, ~-**reading**, (person employed in) reading and correcting proofs; ~-**read** *v.t.*; ~-**sheet**, sheet of proof. **2.** *a.*

Impervious to penetration or damage or undesired action (*proof against the severest weather*; esp. in comb.: *bullet, burglar, damp,* FOOL, *heat, moth, sound, -proof*). **3.** *v.t.* Make proof of (printed work); make (thing) proof, esp. make (fabric etc.) waterproof, (also in comb.: *sound-proof,* WATER-*proof*). [F f. L *proba* (PROVE)]

**prŏp¹. 1.** *n.* Rigid support, esp. not structural part of thing supported; (fig.) person etc. who upholds institution etc. **2.** *v.t.* (-**pp**-). Support (as) by prop (lit. or fig.); hold *up* thus. [LDu.]

**prŏp²** *n.* (colloq.) Aircraft propeller; (Theatr.) stage property. [abbr.]

**prŏpagǎ′nd|a** *n.* Organized scheme etc. for propagation of a doctrine or practice; (usu. derog.) doctrines, information, etc., thus propagated; ~**ist** *n.*, one who disseminates propaganda. [L (foll.)]

**prŏ′pag|āte** *v.t. & i.* Multiply specimens of (plant, animal, disease, etc.) by natural process from parent stock; (of plant, animal, etc.) reproduce (*itself*); disseminate, diffuse, (statement, belief, practice); transmit (vibration, earthquake, etc.); undergo propagation; ~**ā′tion**, ~**ātor,** *ns.* [L *propago*]

**prŏ′pāne** *n.* A hydrocarbon of the paraffin series. [*propionic acid* (PRO-², Gk *pīōn* fat)]

**prope′l** *v.t.* (-**ll**-). Drive or push forward, give onward motion to, (lit. or fig.); ~**lant** *n.*, propelling agent; ~**lent** *a.*; ~**ler** *n.*, (esp.) revolving shaft with blades (usu. SCREW-*propeller*) for propelling ship or aircraft; ~**ling** *a.* (~**ling pencil**, with lead moved forward by turning outer case). [L (*pello puls-* drive)]

**prope′nsǐtý** *n.* Inclination or tendency (*to* condition, quality, thing, *to* do, *for* doing). [L *propensus* inclined]

**prŏ′per** *a.* Belonging or relating exclusively or distinctively (*to*); accurate, correct, (*in the proper sense of the word*); (usu. placed after *n.*) strictly so called, real, genuine, (*within the sphere of architecture proper*; ~ **fraction**, one less than unity, with numerator less than denominator); (colloq.) thorough, complete, (*there will be a proper row about this*); fit, suitable, right, (*choose the proper time*; *do it the proper way*); in conformity with demands of society, respectable; ~ **name, noun,** (Gram.) name used to designate an individual person, animal, town, ship, etc. (*Ruth, Neddy, York, Victory*); ~**lў** *adv.*, fittingly, suitably, (*do it properly*), accurately, correctly, (*properly speaking*), rightly, duly, (*he very properly refused*), with decency or good manners (*behave properly*), (colloq.) thoroughly (*puzzled him properly*). [F f. L *proprius*]

**prŏ'pertў** *n.* Owning, being owned; thing owned, possession(s), esp. real estate, (*the book is his property*; **common** ~, = COMMON knowledge; **man of** ~, rich; PERSONAL *property*; ~ **tax,** one levied directly on property; (Theatr.) article of costume, furniture, etc., used on stage; attribute, quality, (*the properties of soda*; *has the property of dissolving grease*); **prŏ'pertied** (-ĭd) *a.*, having (a landed) property. [F f. L *proprietas* (prec.)]

**prŏ'phĕt** *n.* Inspired teacher, revealer or interpreter of God's will (**the P~,** Muhammad); prophetical writer of O.T. (**major** ~**s,** Isaiah, Jeremiah, Ezekiel, Daniel; **minor** ~**s,** Hosea to Malachi); spokesman, advocate, (*of principle* etc.); one who foretells events (*am no weather prophet*); **prŏ'phĕcў** *n.*, faculty of a prophet, prophetic utterance, foretelling of future events; **prŏ'phĕsў** *v.i. & t.*, speak as prophet, foretell future events, foretell (*event, that, who,* etc.); ~**ĕss** *n.*; **prophĕ'tĭc(al)** *adjs.* (**-ically**), of a prophet, predicting or containing a prediction of (event etc.). [F f. L f. Gk *prophētēs* spokesman]

**prŏphўlǎ'ctĭc** *a.* (**-ically**) & *n.* (Medicine or course of action) tending to prevent disease or other misfortune; ~**ǎ'xĭs** *n.* (*pl.* **-es** *pr.* -ēz), preventive treatment against disease etc. [F f. Gk, = keeping guard before]

**propī'nquitў** *n.* Nearness in place; close kinship. [F or L (*prope* near)]

**propī'tĭāte** (-shī-) *v.t.* (~**able**). Appease (offended person etc.); ~**ā'tion,** ~**ātor,** *ns.*; ~**atorў** (-sha-) *a.* (**-ily**), serving or intended to propitiate; ~**ous** (-shŭs) *a.*, well-disposed, favourable, (of omen etc.) auspicious, (of weather, occasion, etc.) suitable *for*, favourable *to*, (purpose). [L (*propitius* propitious)]

**propō'nent** *a. & n.* (Person) who puts forward a proposal. [L (PROPOSE)]

**propŏr'tion. 1.** *n.* Comparative part, share, (*a large proportion of the earth's surface, of the profits*); comparative relation, ratio, (*the proportion of births to the population*; *price will be raised in* ~ *to the cost* etc., or abs., by the same factor); correct relation of one thing to another or between parts of a thing (*his success bore no proportion to his abilities*; *exaggerated out of all proportion*); (in *pl.*) dimensions, size, (*building of magnificent proportions*); (Math.) equality of ratios between two pairs of quantities (*3, 5, 9, and 15 are in proportion*); DIRECT, INVERSE, *proportion.* **2.** *v.t.* Make (thing etc.) proportionate *to* (*must proportion the punishment to the crime*). **3.** ~**able** *a.* (**-bly**), proportionate; ~**al** *a.* (**-lly**), in due proportion, corresponding in degree or amount (~**al representation,** electoral system such that all parties are represented in proportion to their voting strength); ~**ate** *a.*, that is in due proportion (*to*); ~**ment** *n.* [F or L (PORTION)]

**propō's|e** (-z) *v.t. & i.* Put forward for consideration, propound; set up as an aim (*the object I propose to myself*); nominate (person) as member of society etc.; offer (person's health, person) as subject for drinking of toast; put forward as a plan (*we propose* (making) *a change, that a change should be made*); intend, purpose, (*to do, doing*); make proposal (*man proposes, God disposes*); make offer of marriage (*to*); ~**al** *n.*, act of proposing something, offer of marriage, course of action etc. proposed; **prŏposi'tion** (-z-) *n.*, statement, assertion, (Math.) formal statement of theorem or problem often including demonstration, proposal, scheme proposed, (colloq.) problem, undertaking, opponent, prospect, etc., that is to be dealt with (*a difficult, a paying, proposition*; **not a** ~**ition,** unlikely to succeed). [F *proposer* f. L *propono*; see POSE]

**propou'nd** *v.t.* Offer for consideration, propose, (question, problem, scheme, *to* person). [*propo(u)ne* f. L (prec.)]

**proprī'et|or** *n.* Holder of property, owner esp. of business; ~**arў** *a.*, of a proprietor (*proprietary rights*), holding property, held in private ownership; ~ary medicines (-shon) (protected by patent etc.); ~ōr'ĭal a. (-lly); ~rĕss n. [*proprietary* f. L *proprietarius* (PROPERTY)]

propri'etỹ n. Fitness, rightness, (*doubt the propriety of refusing*); correctness of behaviour or morals; (in *pl.*) details of correct conduct (*must observe the proprieties*). [F (PROPERTY)]

propŭ'ls|ion (-shon) n. Driving or pushing forward; ~ĭve a. [PROPEL]

pro rata (prō rā'ta, rah'-) adv. & a. Proportional(ly). [L]

prorō'gue (-g) v.t. & i. Discontinue meetings of (parliament etc.) without dissolving it; (of parliament etc.) be prorogued; prōrogā'tion n. [F f. L *prorogo* extend]

prosā'ĭc (-z-) a. (~ally). Like prose, lacking poetic beauty; unromantic, commonplace, dull, (a *prosaic life, person, view of things*). [F or L (PROSE)]

prōscē'nĭ|um n. (*pl.* ~ums, ~a). Part of theatre stage in front of drop or curtain, esp. with the enclosing arch. [L f. Gk (SCENE)]

proscr|ībe v.t. Put (person) outside protection of law; banish, exile, (esp. fig.); reject, denounce, (practice etc.) as dangerous etc.; ~ĭ'ption n.; ~ĭ'ptĭve a. [L, = publish in writing]

prōse (-z). 1. n. Ordinary non-metrical form of written or spoken language (*Milton's prose works*; *prose* POEM); matter-of-fact quality (*the prose of existence*); tedious discourse. 2. v.i. Talk tediously. [F f. L *prosa* (*oratio*) straightforward (discourse)]

prō'sĕc|ūte v.t. Follow up, pursue, (inquiry, studies); carry on (trade, pursuit); institute legal proceedings against (person) or with reference to (claim, crime, etc.), or abs.; ~ū'tion n., prosecuting (*of pursuit* etc.), (Law) institution and carrying on of criminal charge before court, carrying on of legal proceedings against person, prosecuting party (*the prosecution denied this*); ||director of public ~utions, public prosecutor; ~ūtor n., one who prosecutes esp. in criminal court; public ~utor, law officer conducting criminal proceedings in public interest. [L *prosequor -secut-* pursue]

prō'sel|ỹte n. Person converted from one opinion, creed, or party, to another; Gentile convert to Jewish faith; ~ỹtĭsm n., (condition of) being a proselyte, practice of proselytizing; ~ỹtize v.t., (seek to) make proselyte of (person, or abs.). [L *proselytus* f. Gk]

prō'sod|ỹ n. Science of versification; study of speech-rhythms; prosō'dĭc a. (-ically); ~ĭst n. [L f. Gk (*pros* to, ODE)]

prospĕct. 1. (-ŏ'-) n. Extensive view of landscape etc. (*a fine prospect*); mental scene; what one is to expect (*offers a gloomy prospect*; *no developments in prospect*); possible or probable customer, subscriber, etc. 2. (-ĕ'-) v.i. & t. Explore region (*for gold etc.*); explore (region) for gold etc.; (fig.) look out *for*. 3. prospĕ'ctĭve a., concerned with or applying to the future, expected, some day to be, (*prospective bridegroom, profit*); prospĕ'ctor n., person who prospects for gold etc.; prospĕ'ctus n., printed document describing chief features of school, commercial enterprise, forthcoming book, etc. [L *prospicio -spect-* look forward]

prō'sper v.i. & t. Be successful, thrive; ~ĭtỹ (-ĕ'r-) n., state of prospering; ~ous a., succeeding, thriving, auspicious (a *prosperous wind*). [F or L *prospero*]

prō'stāte n. ~ (gland), large gland round neck of bladder, accessory to male genital organs; prostă'tĭc a. [F f. Gk *prostatēs* one who stands before]

prō'sth|ĕsĭs n. (*pl.* ~ses *pr.* -sēz). (Part supplied for) making up of bodily deficiencies e.g. by artificial limb; ~ĕ'tĭc a. (-ically). [L f. Gk, = placing in addition]

prō'stĭt|ūte. 1. n. Woman who offers her body for promiscuous sexual intercourse esp. for payment; man who undertakes homosexual actions for payment. 2. v.t. Make prostitute of (esp. one*self*); (fig.) sell (one's honour etc.) unworthily, put (abilities etc.) to wrong use, debase; ~ū'tion n. [L (*prostituo -tut-* offer for sale)]

prŏstrāte. 1. (-ŏ'-) a. Lying with face to ground, esp. in submission or humility; lying in horizontal position; overcome, overthrown, (*prostrate with grief*); physically exhausted. 2. (-ā'-) v.t. Throw oneself down prostrate (*at shrine, before* person etc.); (fig.) overcome, make submissive; (of fatigue etc.) reduce to extreme physical weakness; **prŏstrā'tion** n. [L *prosterno -strat-* throw in front]

**prō'sў** (-zĭ) a. (**-ily, -iness**). Commonplace, tedious, wearisomely dull, (*prosy talk, talker*). [PROSE]

**prŏtă'gonĭst** n. Chief person in drama or plot of story; principal performer; champion or advocate *of* course, method, etc. [Gk (PROTO-, *agōnistēs* actor)]

**prō'tĕan** (*or* -ē'an) a. Variable, versatile; taking many forms. [*Proteus*, Gk sea-god who took various shapes]

**protĕ'ct** v.t. Keep safe, defend, guard, (person or thing *from* or *against* danger, injury, etc.); (Econ.) guard (home industry) against competition by import duties on foreign goods; **~ion** n., protecting, defence, protecting person or thing (*a dog is a protection against burglars*), (Econ.) system of protecting home industries, immunity from molestation obtained by payment under threat of violence, money so paid; **~ionĭsm, ~ionĭst,** *ns.*, principle or practice, advocate, of economic protection; **~ive** a., serving or seeking or intended to protect; **~ive colouring** (of animal or plant against predator); **~ive custody**, detention of person actually or allegedly for his own protection; **~or** n., person who protects, thing or device that protects, regent in charge of kingdom during minority, absence, etc., of sovereign (**Lord P~or of the Commonwealth**, title of O. & R. Cromwell 1653–9); **~orate** n., office of protector of kingdom or State, period of this, protectorship of weak or underdeveloped State by stronger one, such territory; **~orship, ~ress,** *ns.* [L (*tego tect-* cover)]

**protégé** (prŏ'tĕzhā) n. (*fem.* **~e** *pr.* same). Person to whom another is protector or patron. [F f. L (prec.)]

**prō'tein** (-ēn) n. (Chem.) One of a class of organic compounds important in all living organisms. [F & G f. Gk (*prōtos* first)]

*pro tempore* (prō tĕ'mperĭ) a. & adv. (colloq. abbr. **prŏ tĕ'm**). For the time being (esp. of appointment). [L]

**protĕst. 1.** (-ĕ'-) v.t. & i. Affirm solemnly (one's innocence etc., *that*, or abs.) esp. in reply to accusation etc.; write or obtain protest in regard to (bill); \*object to (decision etc.); make (often written) protest *against* (action, proposal). **2.** (-ō'-) n. Formal statement or action of dissent or disapproval, remonstrance, (*made a protest; paid it under protest*); written declaration that bill has been presented and payment or acceptance refused. **3. Prŏ'tĕstant** n. & a., (member or adherent) of any of the Christian bodies that separated from the Roman communion in the Reformation (16th c.) or their offshoots; **Prŏ'tĕstantĭsm** n.; **prŏtĕstā'tion** n., solemn affirmation (*of, that*), protest (*against*); **protĕ'stor** n. [F f. L *protestor* declare formally]

**prō'to-** in comb. First. [Gk *prōtos*]

**prō'tocŏl. 1.** n. Original draft of diplomatic document, esp. of agreed terms of treaty; (observance of) official formality and etiquette. **2.** v.t. & i. (**-ll-**) Draw up protocol(s); record in protocol. [F f. L f. Gk (*kolla* glue)]

**prō'tŏn** n. (Phys.) Elementary particle with unit positive electric charge, forming part or (in hydrogen) whole of atomic nucleus. [Gk (*prōtos* first)]

**prō'to|plăsm** n. Viscous translucent colourless substance forming main constituent of cells in organisms; **~plăsmă'tĭc, ~plă'smĭc,** (-z-) *adjs.* [Gk (PROTO-, PLASMA)]

**prō'totÿpe** n. An original thing or person in relation to a copy, imitation, representation, later specimen, improved form, etc.; trial model, preliminary version, esp. of aeroplane etc. [F or L f. Gk (PROTO-)]

**prōtozō'|on** n. (*pl.* **~a**). Unicellular microscopic animal; **~an** a. & n. [L (PROTO-, Gk *zōion* animal)]

**protră'ct** v.t. Prolong, lengthen, make last long(er); **~ion** n.; **~or** n., (esp.) instrument for measuring angles, usu. in form of graduated semicircle. [L (*traho tract-* draw)]

**protru'|de** (-ōō'-) v.t. & i. Thrust forth, (cause to) project, extend beyond or above the surrounding surface; **~sion** (-zhon) n.; **~sĭve** a. [L (*trudo -trus-* thrust)]

**protū'beran|t** a. Bulging out, prominent; **~ce** n. [L (TUBER)]

**proud. 1.** a. Valuing oneself (too) highly, esp. on ground *of* (qualities, rank, possessions, etc.); **~-hearted**, haughty, arrogant; feeling oneself greatly honoured (*am proud of his* *acquaintance, of knowing him, that I know him, to know him*); having a proper pride (*too proud to complain*; HOUSE-*proud*); (of action etc.) showing pride; of which one is or may be justly proud (*a proud day for us*); (of thing) imposing, splendid; slightly projecting; (of flesh) overgrown round healing wound. **2.** *adv.* (colloq.) **Do** (person, one*self*) ~, treat with great generosity or honour. [E f. F *prud* valiant]

**Prov.** *abbr.* Proverbs (O.T.).

**prov|e** (-ōōv) *v.t.* & *i.* (*p.p.* ~ed *or* esp. U.S., Sc., & literary, ~'en). Make certain, demonstrate by evidence or argument, (fact, *the truth of*, thing. *to be, that*; ~e oneself, show one's abilities etc.; (Sc. Law, as verdict in criminal trial) **not** ~en, evidence is insufficient to establish guilt or innocence); establish genuineness and validity of (will); be found (*to be, to do*); be found to be (*will prove the best*); cause (dough) to rise; (arch.) test qualities of; the EXCEPTION *proves the rule*. [F f. L *probo* test, approve]

**prŏ'vĕnance** *n.* (Place of) origin. [F (*provenir* f. L)]

**Prŏvença'l** (prŏvahṅsah'l) *a.* & *n.* (Inhabitant or language) of Provence. [F (PROVENCE)]

**prŏ'vĕnder** *n.* Fodder; (joc.) food for human beings. [F f. L (PREBEND)]

**prŏ'vĕrb** *n.* Short pithy saying in general use; person or thing that is widely known (*his ignorance is a proverb*; *he is a proverb for ignorance*); (**Book of**) P~s, O.T. book of maxims; **prover'bial** *a.* (-lly), of or expressed in proverbs (*proverbial wisdom; the proverbial ill wind*), notorious. [F, or L *proverbium* (*verbum* word)]

**provi'd|e** *v.i.* & *t.* Make due preparation (*for* possible event, *against* attack etc.); make due preparation of maintenance (*for* person); (of person, law, etc.) stipulate *that*; cause to have possession or use of (person *with* thing, thing *for* or *to* person); ~ed (that), ~ing (that), on the condition or understanding that; **prŏ'vidence** *n.*, timely care, thrift, beneficent care of God or nature, (P-) God in this aspect; **prŏ'vident** *a.*, having or showing foresight, thrifty (‖P~ent Society, = FRIENDLY *Society*); **prŏvidĕ'ntial** (-shal) *a.* (-lly), of or by divine foresight or

intervention, opportune, lucky; ~er *n.*, (esp.) breadwinner of family etc. [L *provideo* -*vis*- foresee]

**prŏ'vince** *n.* Principal administrative division of country etc.; (**the ~s**, whole of a country outside capital); (Eccl.) district under archbishop or metropolitan; (Rom. Hist.) territory outside Italy under Roman governor; sphere of action, business, (*is not within my province*); branch of learning etc. (*in the province of aesthetics*); **provi'ncial** (-shal), (*a.*; -lly) of province(s), having the manners, speech, narrow views, etc., attributed to inhabitants of the provinces, (*n.*) inhabitant of the province(s); **provi'ncialism** (-shal-) *n.*, provincial manner or expression; **provincia'lǐty** (-shǐă'l-) *n.*; **provi'ncialize** (-shal-) *v.t.* [F f. L *provincia*]

**provi'sion** (-zhon). **1.** *n.* Providing (*for, against*; esp. *make provision*); provided amount *of* something; (in *pl.*) supply of food and drink; (clause of) legal or formal statement providing for something. **2.** *v.t.* Supply with provisions. **3.** ~al *a.* (-lly), providing for immediate needs only, temporary; ~ă'lǐty *n.*; ~ment *n.*, provisioning. [F f. L (PROVIDE)]

**provi's|ō** (-z-) *n.* (*pl.* ~os). Stipulation, clause of stipulation or limitation in document; ~ory *a.* (-ily). [L, = it being provided]

**provo'ke** *v.t.* Rouse, incite, (person *to* anger, *to* do); annoy, irritate, (person *into* doing); instigate, tempt, allure; call forth, cause, (indignation, inquiry, etc.); **prŏvocā'tion** *n.*, incitement esp. to anger etc., irritation, (*did it under severe provocation*; *down tools at* or *on the slightest provocation*), cause of annoyance; **prŏvŏ'cative** *a.*, tending or intended to cause provocation (*of* curiosity, anger, lust, etc.). [F, or L *provoco* call forth]

**prŏ'vost** *n.* ‖Head of some colleges at Oxford, Cambridge, etc.; (Sc.) head of municipal corporation or burgh; ~ (provŏ') (**marshal**), head of military police in camp or on active service. [E & F f. L *propositus* (*pono* place)]

**prow** *n.* Part adjoining stem of boat or ship; pointed projecting front part. [F *proue* f. L *prora* f. Gk]

**prow'ĕss** *n.* Valour, gallantry, skill, expertness. [F (PROUD)]

**prowl. 1.** *v.i.* & *t.* Go about in search of prey or plunder (lit. or fig.); traverse (streets, place) thus. **2.** *n.* Prowling (*on the prowl*). [orig. unkn.]

**prox.** *abbr.* proximo.

**pro′xĭmate** *a.* Nearest, next before or after (in place, order, time, connection of thought, causation, etc.); approximate. [L (*proximus* nearest)]

**prŏxi′mĭtý** *n.* Nearness in space, time, etc., (*to*); ~ **fuse**, radio device causing projectile to explode when near target; **prŏ′xĭmō** *a.*, (Commerc.) of next month (*the 3rd proximo*). [F or L (prec.)]

**prŏ′xÿ** *n.* Agency of substitute or deputy (*voted, was married, by proxy*); person authorized to act for another (*stood proxy for the godmother*); document authorizing person to vote on behalf of another, vote so given. [obs. *procuracy* procuration]

**prud│e** (-ōō-) *n.* Person of extreme (esp. affected) propriety in conduct or speech, esp. as regards sexual matters. [F (PROUD)]

**pru′d│ent** (-ōō-) *a.* (Of person or conduct) careful to avoid undesired consequences; circumspect, discreet; ~**ence** *n.*; ~**ĕ′ntial** (-shal) *a.* (**-lly**), of or involving or marked by prudence. [F or L *prudens -ent-* (PROVIDENT)]

**pru′d│erý** (-ōō′-) *n.* Being a prude, conduct etc. of a prude; ~**ĭsh** *a.* [PRUDE]

**prune**[1] (-ōō-) *n.* Dried plum. [F f. L *prunum* f. Gk]

**prun│e**[2] (-ōō-) *v.t.* Trim (tree etc., often *down*) by cutting away dead or overgrown branches etc. with ~**′ing-hook** etc., esp. to promote growth; lop (branches etc.) *off*, *away*, (fig.) remove (superfluities), reduce (costs etc.), clear (book etc. *of* what is superfluous). [F *prooignier* f. Rom. (ROUND)]

**prur′ĭen│t** (-oor′-) *a.* Given to or arising from indulgence of lewd ideas; ~**ce** *n.* [L *prurio* to itch]

**Prŭ′ssian** (-shan) *a.* & *n.* (Native) of *Prussia*; ~ **blue**, deep blue pigment; **prŭ′ssic** *a.*, of, got from, Prussian blue; **prussic acid**, a highly poisonous liquid. [place]

**prÿ** *v.i.* Look or peer inquisitively (*into*); inquire impertinently *into* (person's affairs, conduct, etc.). [orig. unkn.]

**P.S.** *abbr.* postscript.

**Ps(s).** *abbr.* Psalm(s) (O.T.).

**psalm** (sahm) *n.* Sacred song, hymn; (**Book of**) **P~s**, book of these in O.T.; ~**book**, book containing the Psalms, esp. metrical version for public worship; ~**′ĭst** *n.*, author of psalm(s); ~**odý** (*or* sǎ′lm-) *n.*, practice or art of singing psalms etc. esp. in public worship; **psa′lter** (saw′l-, sŏ′l-) *n.*, the Book of Psalms, copy or version of this (*Scottish Metrical Psalter*); **psa′lterÿ** (saw′l-, sŏ′l-) *n.*, ancient and medieval instrument like dulcimer but played by plucking strings. [E & F f. L *psalmus* f. Gk]

**psĕphŏ′log│ÿ** (*or* s-) *n.* Study of trends in elections and voting; ~**ĭst** *n.* [Gk *psēphos* pebble, vote]

**pseud, pseu′dō,** (s-) *a.* & *n.* (*pl.* ~**s**). Sham, spurious, insincere (person). [foll.]

**pseu′dō-** (s-) *in comb.* False, apparent, supposed but not real. [Gk (*pseudēs* false)]

**pseu′d│onÿm** (s-) *n.* Fictitious name, esp. one assumed by author; ~**ŏ′nÿmous** *a.*, written under a fictitious name; ~**onÿ′mĭtÿ** *n.* [F f. Gk (prec., *onuma* name)]

**pshaw** (*or* sh-) *int.* expr. contempt or impatience. [imit.]

**psī** *n.* Twenty-third Gk letter (Ψ, ψ) = ps; parapsychology. [Gk]

**psŏrī′as│ĭs** (s-) *n.* (*pl.* ~**es** *pr.* -ēz). Skin disease with red scaly patches. [L f. Gk (*psōra* itch)]

**psst** *int.* to attract attention surreptitiously. [imit.]

‖**P.S.V.** *abbr.* public service vehicle.

**psÿchĕd│ĕ′lic** (sīk-) *a.* Expanding the mind's awareness; suggesting such experiences. [Gk *psukhē* mind, *dēlos* clear]

**psÿchi′atr│ÿ** (sīk-) *n.* Study and treatment of mental disease; **psÿchĭā′trĭc(al)** (sīk-) *adjs.* (**-ically**); ~**ĭst** *n.* [PSYCHO-, Gk *iatros* physician]

**psÿ′chĭc** (sī′k-). **1.** *a.* (~**ally**). Psychical, able to exercise psychical or occult powers. **2.** *n.* Person susceptible to psychical influence, medium; (in *pl.*) study of psychical phenomena. **3.** ~**al** *a.* (**-lly**), of the soul or mind, of phenomena and conditions apparently outside domain of physical law (*psychical research*). [Gk *psukhē* soul, mind]

**psÿ′ch│ō-** (sī′k-) *in comb.* Mind, soul; ~**ō-anǎ′lÿsĭs**, therapeutic method for treating mental disorders by investigating interaction of conscious and unconscious elements in the mind; ~ō-ă′nalȳse (-z) *v.t.*; ~ō--ă′nalȳst *n.*; ~ō-analȳ′tĭc(al) *adjs.* (-ically); ~olō′gĭcal *a.* (-lly), of the mind, of psychology; ~ological moment, the psychologically appropriate moment, (colloq.) the most appropriate time; ~ological warfare (achieving aims by acting on enemy's minds); ~ŏ′logĭst *n.*; ~ŏ′logȳ *n.*, science of human mind, treatise on or system of this, (colloq.) mental characteristics; ~ōneurō′sĭs (-nūr-) *n.*, neurosis esp. with indirect expression of emotional feelings; ~ōneurŏ′tĭc (-nūr-) *a.*; ~opăth *n.*, person suffering chronic mental disorder esp. with abnormal social behaviour, mentally or emotionally unstable person [PATHOS]; ~opă′thĭc *a.*; ~opăthŏ′-logȳ *n.*, science of mental disorders; ~ŏ′pathȳ *n.*, state or condition of a psychopath; ~ŏ′sĭs *n.* (*pl.* ~oses *pr.* -ō′sēz), severe mental derangement involving the whole personality; ~ōsomă′tĭc *a.* (-ically), of mind and body, (of disease etc.) caused or aggravated by mental stress; ~ōsŭr′gerȳ *n.*, brain surgery as means of treating mental disorder; ~ōthĕ′rapȳ *n.*, treatment of mental disorder by psychological means; ~ōthĕrapeu′tĭc *a.*; ~ōthĕ′rapĭst *n.*; ~ŏ′tĭc *a.* & *n.*, of, (person) suffering from, psychosis. [Gk (prec.)]

**P.T.** *abbr.* physical training.

**pt.** *abbr.* part; pint; point; port.

**P.T.A.** *abbr.* parent–teacher association.

**ptăr′mĭgan** (t-) *n.* Bird of grouse family, with plumage black or grey in summer and white in winter. [Gael.]

**Pte.** *abbr.* Private (soldier).

**ptĕrodă′ctȳl** (t-) *n.* Extinct winged reptile. [Gk *pteron* wing, DACTYL]

**P.T.O.** *abbr.* please turn over.

**Ptŏlĕmă′ĭc** (t-) *a.* Of or according to the theory of *Ptolemy* that the earth is the stationary centre round which sun and stars revolve. [person]

**ptomaine** (tō′mān, tomă′n) *n.* Any of various amines (some toxic) in putrefying animal and vegetable matter. [F f. It. f. Gk *ptōma* corpse]

‖**pŭb** *n.* (colloq.) Public house; ~ crawl, journey to several pubs with drinking at each. [abbr.]

**pŭ′b|ertȳ** *n.* Functional capability

of procreation reached through natural development; ~ertal *a.*; ~ēs (-z) *n.*, lower part of abdomen; ~ĕ′scence *n.*, arrival at puberty, soft down on plant or animal; ~ĕ′scent *a.*; ~ĭc *a.*, of pubes or pubis; ~ĭs *n.* (*pl.* ~es *pr.* -ēz), bone forming front of each half of pelvis. [F or L (*puber* adult)]

**pŭ′blĭc. 1.** *a.* (~lȳ). Of or concerning the people as a whole (*public holiday, interest*); representing, done by or for, the people (*public assembly, expenditure*); open to or shared by the people (*public* LIBRARY, *meeting, road*); open to general observation, done or existing in public, (*made his views public*; **go** ~, become public company); of or engaged in the people's affairs or service (*public life, money*); ~-address system, equipment of loudspeakers etc. to enable speaker, musician, etc., to be heard by audience; ~ bar, least expensive bar in public house; ~ bill (of legislation affecting the people as a whole); ‖~ company (with shares available to all buyers); *public* EYE, FIGURE; ~ health, protection of the public from disease by adequate sanitation etc.; ~ house, inn, esp. ‖providing alcoholic liquor for consumption on the premises; ~ law, law of relations between persons and State; ~ lending right, right of authors to payment when their books etc. are lent by public libraries; *public* OPINION, ORATOR; ~ ownership (by the State); *public* PROSECUTOR, PURSE; ~ relations, (esp. good) relations between organization etc. and the public (~ *relations officer*, employee concerned with these and issuing information to newspapers `etc.); ~ school, endowed grammar (usu. boarding-) school preparing pupils esp. for universities or public services, (Sc., U.S., etc.) school managed by public authorities; *public* SERVANT; ~ spirit, ~-spi′rited, (being) ready to do things for the benefit of people in general; ~ transport, buses, trains, etc., available to public and having fixed routes; ~ utility, organization supplying water, gas, electricity, etc., and regarded as a public service; *public* WORKS, WORSHIP. **2.** *n.* The (members of the) community in general; section of the community (*the reading public*); **in** ~, openly, publicly. **3.** ~**an** *n.*, ‖keeper of public house; ~**ā'tion** *n.*, making publicly known, issuing of book etc. to the public, book etc. so issued; ~**ist** *n.*, writer on or person skilled in current public topics, publicity agent; ~**ĭtў** (-ĭ'sĭ-) *n.*, being open to general observation, notoriety, the business of advertising (goods or persons); ~**ity agent,** person employed to keep the name of an actor etc., well known to the public; ~**ize** *v.t.*, make publicly known, esp. by advertisement; **pŭ'blĭsh** *v.t.*, make generally known, announce formally, promulgate (edict etc.), read (banns of marriage), (of author, editor, or publisher) issue copies of (book etc., or abs.) for sale to the public; **pŭ'blĭsher** *n.*, (esp.) one who produces copies of book etc. and distributes them to booksellers or to the public. [F or L]

**pūce** *a.* Flea-colour, purple-brown. [F f. L *pulex* flea]

**pŭck**[1] *n.* Mischievous sprite; ~**ĭsh** *a.*, impish. [E]

**pŭck**[2] *n.* Rubber disc used in ice hockey. [orig. unkn.]

**pŭ'cker. 1.** *v.t. & i.* ~ (**up**), contract, gather, (of brow, seam, material) into wrinkles, folds, or bulges, intentionally or as fault e.g. in sewing. **2.** *n.* Such bulge etc.

**pud** (pŏŏd) *n.* (colloq.) = foll. [abbr.]

**pu'dding** (pŏŏ'-) *n.* Soft or fairly firm food consisting of ingredients mixed with or enclosed in flour etc. and cooked by boiling, steaming, or baking (MILK, PLUM, YORKSHIRE, *pudding*; the PROOF *of the pudding*); sweet (course of meal); part of intestine of pig etc. stuffed with oatmeal, blood, etc., (BLACK *pudding*); person or thing of pudding-like appearance etc.; **in the ~ club,** (sl.) pregnant; ~ **face,** large fat face; ~**head,** stupid person; ~**stone,** conglomerate rock of rounded pebbles in siliceous matrix; ~**ў** *a.*, of consistency or shape of pudding. [F f. L *botellus* sausage]

**pŭ'ddle. 1.** *n.* Small dirty pool esp. of rain on road etc.; clay made into watertight coating. **2.** *v.t. & i.* Stir (molten iron) to produce wrought iron by expelling carbon. **3.** **pŭ'ddlў** *a.*, abounding in puddles. [E]

**pŭ'dencў** *n.* Modesty; **pŭdĕ'nda** *n.pl.*, genitals, esp. of woman. [L (*pudeo* be ashamed)]

**pū'er|īle** *a.* Boyish, childish; ~**ĭ'lĭtў** *n.*; **pūĕr'peral** *a.*, of or due to childbirth (~**peral fever,** following childbirth and caused by uterine infection). [F or L (*puer* boy, *pario* bear)]

**pŭff. 1.** *n.* Short quick blast of breath or wind; sound (as) of this; small quantity emitted at a puff; round soft protuberant mass of material (*puff sleeve*), hair, etc.; = POWDER-*puff*; piece of light (esp. puff) pastry; unduly laudatory review of book, advertisement of goods, etc.; ~**adder,** large venomous Afr. viper inflating upper part of body when excited; ~**ball,** fungus with ball-shaped spore-case; ~ **pastry** (light and flaky); ‖~**puff,** (childish for) steam-engine, train. **2.** *v.i. & t.* Emit puff of air or breath; (of air etc.) come *out* or *up* in puffs; ~ (**and blow**), breathe hard, pant; (of steam-engine, person smoking, etc.) emit puffs, move with puffs; become inflated, swell, (*up, out*); put out of breath; blow (dust, smoke, light object, *out, up, away,* etc.) with puff; smoke (pipe) in puffs; blow *out, up,* inflate; advertise (goods) with exaggerated or false praise; ~ **out,** utter pantingly; ~ **up,** elate, make proud, (esp. in *p.p.,* with pride etc.). **3.** ~'**erў** *n.*, advertisement, puffing; ~'**ў** *a.* (~**ily,** ~**iness**), gusty, short-winded, puffed out, corpulent. [imit.]

**pŭ'ffĭn** *n.* N. Atlantic auk with large bill. [orig. unkn.]

**pŭg** *n.* ~(-**dog**), dwarf breed of dog with broad flat nose and wrinkled face; ~**nose(d),** (with) short squat or snub nose. [orig. unkn.]

**pū'gĭl|ĭst** *n.* Boxer; ~**ĭsm** *n.*; ~**ĭ'stĭc** *a.* (-ically). [L *pugil* boxer]

**pŭgnā'cious** (-shŭs) *a.* Disposed to fight; ~**ā'cĭtў** *n.* [L *pugnax -acis* (*pugno* fight)]

**puī'snē** (pū'nĭ) *a. & n.* ~ (**judge**), judge of superior court inferior in rank to chief justice. [F (cf. PUNY)]

**pū'issan|t** (*or* pwī's-) *a.* (literary). Having great power or influence, mighty; ~**ce** *n.*, (in show-jumping) test of horse's ability to jump high obstacles, (arch.) great power or influence. [F f. Rom. (POTENT)]

**pūke** *v.i. & t., & n.* Vomit. [imit.]

**pŭ'kka** *a.* (Anglo-Ind.) Of full weight; genuine; permanent. [Hindi]

**pŭ'lchrĭt|ūde** (-kr-) *n.* (literary).

Beauty; **~ū′dĭnous** *a*. [L (*pulcher* beautiful)]

**pūle** *v.i.* Whimper, cry querulously or weakly. [imit.]

**pull** (-ŏŏ-). **1.** *v.t.* & *i.* Exert force on (thing etc.) to move it to oneself; cause to move towards oneself or in direction so regarded (*pull your cap over your ears*); draw (knife etc.) out of sheath etc. for use (*on person*); damage (muscle etc.) by abnormal strain; check (horse) esp. so as to lose race; exert pulling force; proceed with effort (*up* hill etc.); move (boat) by pulling, (of boat etc.) be caused to move, esp. in specified direction; attract (customers); remove (cork, tooth) by pulling; draw (liquor) from barrel etc.; pluck (plant *up*) out of ground; (colloq.) accomplish (*pull a* FAST² *one*); strike (ball) to leg in cricket, so as to deviate on side towards player in golf; make (grimace) by contorting muscles (*pull a face*); print (proof etc.); **~ about**, treat roughly; **~ at**, try to move by pulling, tear or pluck at, draw or suck at (tankard, pipe); **~ apart**, forcibly separate parts of, (fig.) criticize unfavourably; **~ back**, (cause to) retreat; **~ down**, demolish (building), lower in health or spirits or price; **~ in**, acquire (profit etc.), (colloq.) arrest, (of train etc.) enter station etc., (of vehicle) move to side of or off road (**~**-*in* n., place for doing this); *pull* person's LEG; **~ off**, remove garment etc. by pulling, succeed in winning or achieving; **~ out**, depart, withdraw from undertaking, (of train etc.) leave station etc., (of vehicle) move from side of road, or from normal position to overtake; **~** *out of the fire*, save (apparently hopeless game); **~′over**, (usu. knitted) outer garment for upper body, put on over head; **~** one's **punches**, fail to give full force in boxing (lit. or fig.); **~ round, ~ through** *adv.* & *prep.*, get safely through (danger, illness); **~ together**, work in harmony, recover control of one*self*; **~ to pieces**, = *pull apart*; **~ up**, cause to stop moving, reprimand, check oneself, improve one's relative position in race etc., pull out of ground; **~** one's **weight**, row with effect proportionate to one's weight, (fig.) do fair share of work. **2.** *n.* Act of pulling; force thus exerted; (fig.) advantage, means of exerting influence; printer's

rough proof; (Crick., Golf) pulling stroke; deep draught of liquor; handle etc. for applying pull. [E]

**pu′llĕt** (pŏŏ′-) *n.* Young domestic fowl, esp. hen that has begun to lay but not yet moulted. [F dim. of *poule* f. L *pullus*]

**pu′lley** (pŏŏ′-) *n.* Grooved wheel(s) for cord etc. to pass over, set in block and used for changing direction of force; wheel or drum fixed on shaft and turned by belt, used esp. to increase speed or power. [F *polie*, rel. to POLE²]

**Pu′llman** (-ŏŏ-) *n.* **~** (**car, coach**), railway carriage or motor coach with especially comfortable seats etc.; sleeping-car. [person]

**pŭ′llŭlāte** *v.i.* Grow, develop; abound *with*; **~ā′tion** *n.* [L *pullulo* sprout]

**pŭ′lmonarў** *a.* (-ily). Of, in, connected with, lungs (*pulmonary diseases*); affected with or subject to lung-disease. [L (*pulmo -onis* lung)]

**pulp. 1.** *n.* Fleshy part of fruit; any fleshy or soft part of animal body; soft shapeless mass, esp. that of rags, wood, etc., from which paper is made; **~ magazine** etc. (printed orig. on rough paper, often with sensational or poor-quality writing); **~′ў** *a.* (**~ily**, **~iness**), of, with, like, pulp. **2.** *v.t.* & *i.* Reduce to, become, pulp. [L]

**pu′lpĭt** (pŏŏ′-) *n.* Raised enclosed platform usu. with desk from which preacher in church or chapel delivers sermon; *the* profession of preaching; preachers. [L *pulpitum* platform]

**pŭ′lsȧr** *n.* Cosmic source of regularly and rapidly pulsating radio signals. [*pulsating star*, after *quasar*]

**pŭls|ā′te** (*or* -ŭ′-) *v.i.* Expand and contract rhythmically, throb (lit. or fig.); vibrate, quiver, thrill; **~ā′tion** *n.*; **pŭ′lsatorў** *a.* [F f. L (*pello puls-* drive, beat)]

**pŭlse¹. 1.** *n.* Rhythmical throbbing of arteries as blood is propelled along them, esp. as felt in wrists, temples, etc. (**feel the ~ of**, lit. to ascertain state of health, or fig. = cautiously ascertain intentions or sentiments of); each successive beat of arteries or heart; (fig.) throb or thrill of life or emotion, latent sentiment; single vibration of sound, light, electric current, etc., esp. as signal. **2.** *v.i.* Pulsate (lit. or fig.).

**pŭlse²** n. (as *sing.* or *pl.*) Edible seeds of leguminous plants, e.g. peas, beans, lentils; any kind of these. [F f. L *puls*]

**pŭ'lveriz|e** v.t. & i. Reduce to powder or dust; crumble to dust; (fig.) demolish, crush, smash; ~ā'tion n.; ~er n., (esp.) machine for pulverizing. [L (*pulvis -ver-* dust)]

**pŭ'ma** n. Large tawny Amer. feline. [Sp. f. Quechua]

**pŭ'mice** n. ~(-stone), (piece of) light porous lava for removing stains from skin etc., as powder for polishing, etc. [F *pomis* f. L *pumex -ic-*]

**pŭ'mmel** v.t. (‖-ll-). Strike repeatedly esp. with fist. [POMMEL]

**pŭmp¹.** 1. n. Machine, usu. cylinder in which piston etc. is moved up and down by rod, for raising water; machine of this kind or with rotary action etc. to move liquids or gases, (fig. of heart etc.); ~-room, building where pump is worked, esp. at spa where medicinal water is dispensed. 2. v.i. & t. Work a pump; remove or raise (water, air, etc., esp. *in, out, up*) with pump; make (ship, well, etc.) *dry* by pumping; cause to move, pour forth, be sent *out*, etc., as if by pumping; elicit information from (person) by persistent questioning; move vigorously up and down as if pumping; ~ up, inflate (pneumatic tyre). [orig. uncert.]

**pŭmp²** n. Light shoe usu. without fastening, worn for dancing, tennis, etc.; *court shoe. [orig. unkn.]

**pŭ'mpernickel** (or pŏŏ'-) n. German wholemeal rye bread. [G]

**pŭ'mpkin** n. (Plant bearing) large orange-coloured fruit with edible layer next to rind, used in cookery and as food for cattle. [F *pompon* f. L f. Gk *pepōn* melon]

**pŭn.** 1. n. Humorous use of word to suggest different meanings, or of words of same sound with different meaning (*no punishment if no pun is meant*). 2. v.i. (-nn-). Make pun(s) (*on* word or subject). [orig. unkn.]

**pŭnch¹.** 1. v.t. Strike esp. with closed fist; pierce (metal, leather, ticket to show it has been used, etc.) as or with punch; pierce (hole) thus; ‖~-ball, inflated ball held by elastic bands etc. and punched as form of exercise; ~(ed) **card, tape,** etc., (perforated according to specified code, for conveying instructions to computer etc.); ~-up, fist-fight,

brawl. 2. n. Blow with fist (*a punch on the head*; PULL one's *punches*); ~-drunk, stupefied through having been severely or repeatedly punched, lit. or fig.); ability to deliver this; (sl.) vigour, effective force; instrument or machine for cutting holes or impressing design in leather, metal, paper, etc.; ~-line, words giving point of joke etc.; ~'y a., having vigour. [var. *pounce* emboss]

**pŭnch²** n. Drink usu. of wine or spirits mixed with hot or cold water or milk, sugar, lemons, spice, etc., ~-bowl, bowl in which punch is mixed, round deep hollow in hill(s). [orig. unkn.]

**pŭnch³** n. ‖(Suffolk) ~, short-legged thickset draught horse; (*P~*) grotesque humpbacked figure in puppet-show called *Punch and Judy* (**as pleased** or **as proud as P~**, showing great pleasure or pride). [abbr. *Punchinello*, chief character in It. puppet-show]

**pŭncti'li|ō** (-lyō) n. (*pl.* ~os). Delicate point of ceremony or honour; etiquette of such points; petty formality; ~ous a., attentive to punctilio(s) or to details of conduct, duties, etc. [It. & Sp. (POINT)]

**pŭ'nctŭ|al** a. (-lly). Observant of appointed time; neither early nor late; ~ă'lity n. [L (POINT)]

**pŭ'nctŭ|āte** v.t. Insert stops in (writing), mark or divide with stops; (fig.) interrupt at intervals (speech *with* exclamations etc.); emphasize, accentuate; ~ā'tion n. (~ation mark, stop).

**pŭ'ncture.** 1. n. Prick(ing), esp. accidental piercing of pneumatic tyre; hole thus made. 2. v.t. & i. Prick, pierce, (lit. or fig.); undergo puncture.

**pŭ'ndĭt** n. Learned Hindu; learned expert or teacher; ~rў n. [Hind. f. Skr.]

**pŭ'ngen|t** (-nj-) a. (Of reproof, satire, etc.) biting, caustic; mentally stimulating, piquant; affecting organs of smell or taste, or skin etc., with pricking sensation (*pungent gas, sauce*); ~cў n. [L (POINT)]

**pŭ'nish** v.t. Cause (offender) to suffer for offence; chastise; inflict penalty on (offender); inflict penalty for (offence); (colloq.) inflict severe blows on (opponent), (of race, other competitor) tax severely the powers of (competitor), subject to severe treatment; **~ment** *n.*, punishing, penalty; **pū'nĭtive** *a.*, inflicting or intended to inflict punishment. [F f. L *punio*]

**Pŭnja'bĭ** (-ah'-) *a. & n.* (Native, language) of the *Punjab*. [place]

**pŭnk** *n.* (colloq.) Worthless stuff, nonsense; worthless person. [orig. unkn.]

**pŭ'nkah** (-ka) *n.* Large swinging fan worked by cord or electrically. [Hindi]

‖**pŭ'nnĕt** *n.* Small chip basket for fruit etc. [orig. unkn.]

**pŭ'nster** *n.* (Esp. inveterate) maker of puns. [PUN]

**pŭnt¹. 1.** *n.* Flat-bottomed shallow boat, broad and square at both ends, propelled by long pole thrust against bottom of river etc. **2.** *v.t. & i.* Propel with such pole; convey in punt; use punt-pole, travel in punt. [LDu]

**pŭnt². 1.** *v.t.* Kick (football) after it has dropped from the hands and before it reaches ground. **2.** *n.* Such kick; **~about**, kicking about of football for practice. [orig. unkn.]

**pŭnt³** *v.i.* (In some card-games) lay stake against bank; ‖(colloq.) bet on horse etc., speculate in shares etc. [F *ponter*]

**pŭ'n|ў** *a.* (~ily, ~iness). Undersized, weak, feeble. [F *puisné* born afterwards]

**pŭp. 1.** *n.* Young dog (*bitch in ~*, pregnant; **sell person a ~**, swindle him esp. by selling thing on prospective value); young wolf, rat, seal, etc. **2.** *v.t.* (-pp-). (Of bitch, etc.) bring forth (young, or abs.). [PUPPY]

**pū'pa** *n.* (*pl.* ~e). Insect in passive development between larva and imago. [L, = doll]

**pū'pil** *n.* One who is taught by another, schoolchild, disciple; circular opening in centre of iris of eye; **~lage** *n.*, nonage, being a pupil; **~lary** *a.*, under guardianship, of pupil(s), of the pupil of the eye. [F, or L *pupillus*]

**pŭ'ppĕt** *n.* Figure, usu. small, representing human being and moved by various means as entertainment in **~-show**; person whose acts are controlled by another; **~ state**, country professing to be independent but actually under the control of some greater power; **~rў** *n.* [var. POPPET]

**pŭ'ppў** *n.* Young dog; vain empty-

-headed young man; **~dog**, (childish) = *puppy*; **~-fat**, temporary fatness of child or adolescent; **~-love**, = CALF¹-*love*. [F (POPPET)]

**pŭr'blind** *a.* Partly blind, dim-sighted; (fig.) obtuse, dull. [*pur(e)* (= utterly) *blind*]

**pŭr'chase. 1.** *v.t.* Buy; acquire (victory, freedom, etc., *with* one's blood, toil, etc.). **2.** *n.* Buying; thing bought; annual rent or return from land (fig., **is not worth an hour's ~**, of person's life etc., cannot be expected to last an hour longer); mechanical advantage, leverage, (lit or fig.). [AF (PRO-¹, CHASE¹)]

**pŭr'dah** (-da) *n.* (Ind. etc.) Curtain, esp. one serving to screen Muslim or Hindu women from being seen by men or strangers. [Urdu]

**pūre** *a.* Unmixed, unadulterated, (*pure white, air, water*); (of sound) not discordant, esp. (Mus.) perfectly in tune; of unmixed origin (*pure* MATHEMATICS, SCIENCE); mere, simple, nothing but, sheer, (*knowledge pure and simple*; *pure nonsense*); not corrupt, morally undefiled; guiltless, sincere; sexually undefiled, chaste; **~lў** (-ūr'-lĭ) *adv.*, (esp.) merely, exclusively, solely, entirely. [F f. L *purus*]

**purée** (pūr'ā) *n.* Pulp of vegetables, fruit, etc., reduced to uniform mass. [F]

**pŭrge. 1.** *v.t.* Make physically or spiritually clean (*of* or *from* impurities, sin, etc.); remove by cleansing process (lit. or fig.), clear *away*, *off*, *out*; clear (bowels, person, or abs.) by evacuation; clear (person, one*self*, *of* charge, suspicion); (Law) atone for, wipe out, (offence esp. contempt of court, sentence) by expiation and submission; rid (political party etc.) of persons regarded as undesirable. **2.** *n.* Such clearance; purgative. **3.** **pŭrga'tion** *n.*; **pŭr'gative** *a. & n.*, strongly laxative (medicine), (thing) serving to purify; **pŭr'gatorў** *n.*, condition or place of spiritual purging, esp. (R.C. Ch.) of souls departing this life in grace of God but having to expiate venial sins etc., place or state of temporary suffering or expiation; **pŭrgatō'rĭal** *a.* (-lly). [F f. L *purgo* (PURE)]

**pŭr'if|ў** *v.t.* Make pure, cleanse, (*of*, *from*, impurities, sin, etc.); make ceremonially clean; clear of extraneous elements; **~ĭca'tion** *n.*, purifying or being purified, ritual

cleansing; ~**icătory** *a*. [F or L
(PURE)]

**pūr'ĭst** *n*. Stickler for or affecter of
scrupulous purity esp. in language
or art; ~**ism** *n*.; ~**i'stĭc** *a*. (-ically).
[F (PURE)]

**pūr'ĭtan. 1.** *n*. (Hist.; P~) one of
the English Protestants who regarded
Reformation as incomplete and
sought to abolish unscriptural and
corrupt ceremonies etc.; purist member of any party; person practising
or affecting extreme strictness in
religion or morals; **pūrĭtă'nic(al)**
*adjs*. (-ically); ~**ism** *n*.; ~**ĭze** *v.t.*
**2.** *a*. Of Puritans; scrupulous in
religion or morals. [foll.]

**pūr'ĭty** *n*. Pureness, cleanness,
freedom from physical or moral
pollution. [F f. L (PURE)]

**pûrl¹** *v.i.* (Of brook etc.) flow with
swirling motion and babbling sound.
[imit.]

**pûrl². 1.** *n*. ‖Chain of minute loops,
picot; stitch in knitting with needle
moved in opposite to normal (PLAIN)
direction. **2.** *v.t.* Make (stitch, or abs.)
purl. [orig. unkn.]

**‖pûr'ler** *n*. (colloq.) Throw or
blow that hurls one head foremost;
**come a ~**, fall headlong. [*purl* over-
turn]

**pûr'lieu** (-lū) *n*. ‖(Hist.) tract on
border of forest; one's bounds, limits,
usual haunts; (in *pl*.) outskirts,
outlying region (lit. or fig.). [AF
*puralé* (*aller* go)]

**pûr'lĭn** *n*. Horizontal beam along
roof. [L]

**purloi'n** *v.t.* Steal, pilfer. [AF
*purloigner* (*loign* far)]

**pûr'ple. 1.** *n*. & *a*. (Of) colour
between red and blue; (Tyrian) *n*.
(of) crimson colour got from some
molluscs; purple robe, esp. as dress
of emperor etc. (**born in the ~**,
born in reigning family, fig. belonging to most privileged class); scarlet
official dress of cardinal; ~ **heart**,
‖heart-shaped stimulant tablet; ~
**passage** or **patch**, ornate passage in
literary composition. **2.** *v.t.* & *i*. Make
or become purple. [E f. L *purpura* f.
Gk *porphura* shellfish yielding dye]

**purpôrt. 1.** (-ôr't) *v.t.* (Of document
or speech) have as its meaning,
convey, state, (fact, *that*); profess, be
intended to seem (*to do*; *a letter
purporting to be written by you*). **2.**
(pêr'-) *n*. Ostensible meaning; sense

or tenor of document or statement.
[AF f. L (PRO-¹, PORT³)]

**pûr'pose. 1.** *n*. Object to be
attained, thing intended, (*could not
effect my purpose*; *this will answer* or
*serve our* or *the purpose*; *for the purpose
of easier access*; ~**-built, -made**, etc.,
built etc. for a specific purpose; **on
~**, in order (*to do, that*); **on ~, of
set ~**, designedly, not by accident;
**serve no ~**, be useless; **to the ~**,
relevant, useful for one's purpose;
**to little, some, no, ~**, with little
etc. result or effect); intention to act;
resolution, determination. **2.** *v.t.*
Have as one's purpose, design,
intend. **3.** ~**ful** (-sf-) *a*. (-lly),
having or indicating (conscious)
purpose, intentional; ~**lў** (-slĭ) *adv.*,
on purpose; **pûr'posive** *a*., having,
serving, done with a, purpose,
purposeful. [F f. L *propono* PROPOSE]

**pûrr. 1.** *v.i.* & *t*. (Of cat or other
feline, fig. of person) make low
vibratory sound expressing pleasure;
(of machine etc.) make similar
sound; utter, express, (words, contentment) thus. **2.** *n*. Such sound.
[imit.]

**pûrse. 1.** *n*. Small pouch of leather
etc. for carrying money on the
person, orig. closed by drawing
strings together; *handbag; (fig.)
money, funds, (**heavy or long ~**,
wealth; ‖PRIVY *purse*; **the public ~**,
national treasury; sum collected,
subscribed, or given, as present or
as prize for contest; ~**-proud**,
arrogant through wealth; ~**-strings**,
strings for closing mouth of purse
(*hold the ~-strings*, have control of
expenditure). **2.** *v.t.* & *i*. ~ (**up**),
contract (lips, brow) in wrinkles;
become wrinkled. **3.** **pûr'ser** *n*.,
officer on ship who keeps accounts,
esp. head steward in passenger
vessel. [E f. L *bursa* f. Gk, = leather
bag]

**pûr'slane** (-ĭn) *n*. Herb formerly
much used in salads and pickled. [F
f. L *porcil*(*l*)*aca*]

**pursǔ'e** *v.t.* & *i*. Follow with
intent to overtake or attract or
capture or kill; (fig., of consequences,
penalty, disease, etc.) persistently
accompany; seek after, aim at,
(pleasure etc., one's object); proceed
in compliance with (plan etc.);
proceed along, continue, (road,
inquiry, conduct); continue to investigate or discuss (topic); follow

(studies, recreation, profession); go in pursuit (*after*, or abs.); **~ū'ance** *n.*, carrying out, pursuing, (of plan, object, idea, etc.; *in pursuance of the regulations*); **~ū'ant** *adv.*, conformably to (*the Act* etc.); **~ui't** (-ū't, -ōō't) *n.*, pursuing (esp. *in ~uit of* animal, person, one's object), profession or employment or recreation that one follows. [F f. L (PROSECUTE)]

‖**pūr'suivant** (-sĭ-, -swĭ-) *n.* Officer of College of Arms below herald. [F (prec.)]

**pūr's‖y̆¹** *a.* (**~ily**, **~iness**). Short-winded, puffy, corpulent. [AF *porsif* f. F *polsif* (L *pulso* PULSATE)]

**pūr's‖y̆²** *a.* (**~ily**, **~iness**). Puckered. [PURSE]

**pūr'ulen‖t** (-ōōl-) *a.* Of, full of, discharging, pus; **~ce** *n.* [L (PUS)]

**purvey'** (-vā') *v.t.* & *i.* Provide or supply (articles of food) as one's business; make provision, act as purveyor, (*for* person, army, etc.); **~or** *n.* [AF f. L (PROVIDE)]

**pūr'view** (-vū) *n.* Scope, intention, range, (extent, content, scheme, occupation, etc.); range of physical or mental vision. [AF p.p. (PURVEY)]

**pŭs** *n.* (Med.) Yellowish viscous matter produced from inflamed or infected tissue. [L *pus puris*]

**push** (-ōō-). **1.** *v.t.* & *i.* Exert force on (thing etc.) to move it away from oneself; cause to move thus; exert such force; thrust forward or upward; make one's way (*ahead, on*), make (one's way), by force or persistence; make persistent demands *for*; exert oneself esp. to surpass others; urge, impel, (*on*, *to do*, *to* effort, *into* action); pursue (claim etc.); press adoption, use, sale, etc., of; sell (drug) illegally; tax abilities or tolerance of (**~ed for**, colloq., scarcely able to find enough of); (cause to) project, thrust *out* or *forth*. **2.** *n.* Act of pushing; force thus exerted; use of influence to advance a person; vigorous effort (*to do* etc.); (Mil.) attack in force; pressure of affairs, crisis; enterprise, determination to succeed; push-button; ‖**give**, **get**, **the push**, (sl.) dismiss, be dismissed. **3.** **~ along**, (colloq.) depart; **~ around**, bully; ‖**~-bike**, (sl.) pedal cycle; **~-button**, (*n.*) button to be pushed esp. to operate electrical device, (*a.*) operated by pushing a button; **~-chair**, child's folding chair on wheels; **~** one's

**luck**, take undue risks; **~ off**, push with oar etc. to get boat out into stream etc., (sl.) go away; **~-over**, opponent or difficulty easily overcome; **~ the boat out**, (colloq.) celebrate; **~ through**, bring to a conclusion, compel acceptance of. **4.** **~'er** *n.*, (esp.) illegal seller of drugs; **~'ful** *a.* (**-lly**), (colloq.) **~'y̆** *a.* (**-ily**, **-iness**), showing determination to get on, self-assertive; **~'ing** *a.*, (esp.) pushful, (colloq.) having nearly reached (specified age). [F f. L (PULSATE)]

**Pŭ'shtu** (-ōō) *n.* & *a.* (Of) Iranian language of Pathans. [Pers.]

**pūsĭll‖a'nimous** *a.* Lacking courage, timid; **~ani'mĭty̆** *n.* [L (*pusillus* petty, ANIMUS)]

**puss** (pŏōs) *n.* Cat (esp. as *voc.*); (colloq.) playful or coquettish girl; **~'y̆** *n.*, (childish name for) cat (also **~y-cat**), (vulg.) vulva; **\*~'y̆foot** *v.i.*, move stealthily, act (over-) cautiously or non-committally; **~y willow** (with silky catkins). [LDu.]

**pŭ'stūl‖e** *n.* Pimple; **~ar**, **~ous**, *adjs.*; **~āte** *v.t.* & *i.*, form into pustules. [F, or L *pustula*]

**put** (-ōō-). **1.** *v.t.* & *i.* (**-tt-**; **put**). Transfer to specified place or position or state or application (*put it in your pocket, right way up, out of action*; *puts me on my guard, in a difficulty*; *put a tax on windows, the blame on her, a question to the candidate*; **not know where to ~ oneself**, be much embarrassed or uncomfortable); hurl (*the* SHOT¹ etc.) from hand as athletic exercise; substitute (thing *for* another); imagine oneself (*in* another's *place* etc.); express in specified way (*put the idea into words*). **2.** *n.* Throw of shot; (St. Exch.) option of selling stock at given date. **3.** **~ about**, distress, disseminate (rumour), put (ship) on opposite tack; **~ across**, make acceptable or effective or understood; **~ amount at**, estimate it as; **~ horse at**, bring it to jump (fence etc.); **~ away**, lay aside for future use, (colloq.) put into confinement, (colloq.) kill (old etc. animal), (colloq.) consume (food, drink); **~ back**, return to harbour or shore, restore to former place, move back the hands of (CLOCK¹); **~ by**, lay aside for future use; **~ down**, suppress by force, snub, record in writing, enter on list, reckon *as*, take *for*, (*put him down as* or *for a fool*), attribute to (*put it down to his nervousness*), preserve for future use, cease to read (book), put (baby) to bed, kill (old etc. animal), allow to alight; ~ **forth**, exert (effort), (of plant) send out (buds, leaves); ~ **forward**, thrust into prominence, advance (theory), advance the hands of (clock); ~ **in**, enter harbour or come to shore, install, formally present (document, defence, claim) for consideration, interpose (remark, blow), make claim or be candidate *for*, perform (spell of work), colloq.) spend (time); ~ **into**, translate into (other language); ~ **it across**, (sl.) get even with or deceive (person); ~ **it to** person, challenge him to deny *that*; ~ **money into**, invest in; ~ **money on**, bet on (horse etc.); ~ **off**, postpone, postpone engagement with (person), evade (person *with* excuse etc.), hinder or dissuade *from*, offend, disconcert, remove (clothes), start from shore or ship; ~ **on**, clothe (oneself) with, take on (character, appearance), feign (emotion), develop additional (weight of body), stage (play etc.), add (amount, runs *to* score), advance the hands of (clock), bring (pressure etc.) into action, cause (cricketer) to bowl or (electric light) to shine or (electrical device) to operate or (train) to run; ~ **out**, dislocate, cause (batsman, side) to be out, extinguish, disconcert, annoy, give (work) to be done elsewhere; *put (out) to* SEA; ~ **over**, = *put across*; ~ **through**, carry out (task), complete (transaction), connect by telephone *to* another person, make (telephone call); ~ **horse to**, harness it to vehicle; ~ **together**, make from parts, combine (parts) into whole; ~ **up**, build, raise (price etc.), offer (prayer), present (proposal), present oneself as candidate, provide (money as backer), cause (game) to rise from cover, publish (banns), offer for sale or competition, pack up in receptacle, sheathe sword, lodge or be lodged as guest (*at*), concoct; ~*-up* a., fraudulently concocted; ~ person *up to*, inform him about, instigate him in (doing etc.); ~ *up with*, submit to, tolerate (annoyance, insult); ~ **upon**, (colloq.) unfairly burdened or deceived. [E]

**pu'tative** a. Reputed, supposed,

(his *putative father*). [F or L (*puto* think)]

**pu'tr|efy** v.i. Become putrid, go bad; fester, suppurate; become morally corrupt; ~**efa'ction** n.; ~**efa'ctive** a.; ~**e'scent** a., in process of rotting, of or accompanying this process; ~**e'scence** n.; ~**id** a., decomposed, rotten, foul, noxious, (fig.) corrupt, (sl.) of poor quality, very unpleasant; ~**i'dity** n. [L *putrefy* rot]

**putsch** (pŏŏch) n. Attempt at revolution. [Swiss G]

**pŭtt. 1.** v.i. & t. Strike (golf-ball) gently with club to get it into or nearer to hole on smooth grass area (~*'ing-green*). **2.** n. Such stroke. **3.** ~*er* n., (esp.) golf-club used in putting. [PUT]

**pu'ttee** (-ĭ) n. Long strip of cloth wound spirally round leg from ankle to knee for protection and support. [Hindi]

**pu'tty. 1.** n. Powder of tin oxide for polishing glass or metal; fine mortar of lime and water without sand; cement of whiting, raw linseed oil, etc., for fixing panes of glass, filling up holes in woodwork, etc.; (fig.) compliant person; ||~ **medal**, (joc.) fit reward for small service. **2.** v.t. Cover, fix, join, fill up, with putty. [F *potée* (POT)]

**pu'zzle. 1.** n. Bewilderment; perplexing question; problem or toy designed to test knowledge, ingenuity, or patience. **2.** v.t. & i. Perplex; be perplexed (*about, over*, problem etc.); find *out* by patience and ingenuity. **3.** ~**ment** (-zelm-) n., state of being puzzled; ~**r** n., (esp.) difficult question or problem. [orig. unkn.]

**PVC** abbr. polyvinyl chloride.

||**P.W.** abbr. Policewoman.

**pȳae'mĭa**, *-ē'mĭa*, n. Blood-poisoning with formation of abscesses in viscera. [L f. Gk *puon* pus, *haima* blood]

**pȳ'e-dŏg**, **pī(e)-dŏg**, n. Ownerless mongrel of the East. [Hindi]

**pȳ'gmy**, **pi'gmy. 1.** n. One of a legendary diminutive race; one of a group of very short people in equatorial Africa; dwarf (fig. of intellectual inferiority etc.). **2.** a. Of pygmies; (of person or animal) dwarf. [L f. Gk]

||**pȳja'ma|s**, *\*paj-*, (-ah'măz) n.pl. Suit of loose trousers and jacket for

sleeping etc.; ~ **jacket, trousers,** (forming part of this). [Urdu, ≈ leg-clothing]

**pȳ'lon** n. Tall structure erected as support (esp. for electric-power cables) or boundary or decoration. [Gk (*pulē* gate)]

**pȳorrhoe'a, *-ē'a,** (-rē'a) n. Discharge of pus, esp. in disease of tooth-sockets. [Gk *puon* pus, *rheō* flow]

**pȳ'ramid** n. Monumental (esp. ancient Egyptian) structure of stone etc. with polygonal or (usu.) square base, and sloping sides meeting at apex; solid of this shape with base of 3 or more sides; pyramid-shaped thing or pile of things; **pyrā'midal** a. (-lly), shaped or arranged like pyramid. [L f. Gk *puramis* -mid-]

**pȳre** n. Heap of combustible material, esp. funeral pile for burning a corpse. [L f. Gk (PYRO-)]

**pȳrē'thrum** n. Chrysanthemum with finely divided leaves; insecticide from its dried flowers. [L f. Gk]

**pȳrě'|tĭc** a. Of, for, producing, fever; ~**xĭa** n., fever. [L f. Gk *puretos* fever]

**pȳrī'tēs** (-z) n. (**Iron**) ~, yellow lustrous iron sulphide mineral. [L f. Gk (PYRE)]

**pȳr'|ō-** in comb. Fire; ~**ōmā'nĭa,** ~**ōmā'nĭăc,** ns., (person suffering from) incendiary mania; ~**ō'mĕter** n., instrument for measuring high temperatures; ~**otě'chnĭc** (-tě'k-), (a.; also **-ical; -ically**) of (the nature of) fireworks, (fig.) brilliant, sensational, (n.; in pl.) art of making, or display of, fireworks (lit. or fig.); ~**otě'chnĭst,** ~**otěchnȳ,** (-těk-) ns., (expert in) pyrotechnics. [Gk (*pur* fire)]

**pȳrō'sĭs** n. Burning sensation in lower chest. [L f. Gk (prec.)]

**Pȳ'rrhĭc** (-rĭk) a. ~ **victory** (gained at too great cost, like that of *Pyrrhus* 279 B.C.); p~ (**dance**), war-dance of ancient Greeks. [persons]

**Pȳthăgorě'an** a. & n. (Follower) of *Pythagoras,* philosopher said to have believed in transmigration of souls; **Pytha'goras' theorem** (that square on hypotenuse of right-angled triangle is equal to sum of squares on other two sides). [L f. Gk (person)]

**pȳ'thon** n. Large snake that crushes its prey. [L f. Gk name of monster]

**pyx** n. (Eccl.) Vessel in which consecrated bread is kept. [L *pyxis* f. Gk (BOX)]

# Q

**Q, q,** (kū) n. (pl. **Qs, Q's**). Seventeenth letter; MIND one's *P's and Q's.*

**Q.** abbr. Queen('s); question.

**Q.C.** abbr. Queen's Counsel.

**Q.E.D.** abbr. which was the thing to be proved. [L *quod erat demonstrandum*]

**Qld.** abbr. Queensland.

**Q.M.(S.)** abbr. Quartermaster (Sergeant).

**qr.** abbr. quarter(s).

**qt.** abbr. quart(s).

**quā** (or **-ah**) conj. In the capacity of (*does it not qua father, but qua judge*). [L, = (in the way) in which]

**quăck**[1]. 1. n. Harsh sound made by ducks. 2. v.i. Utter quack; talk loudly and foolishly; **quack-quack,** (childish name for) duck. [imit.]

**quăck**[2] n. Pretender to medical or other skill, charlatan; ~ **remedy** etc. (such as quacks advertise); ~**'erȳ** n., quack methods. [abbr. *quacksalver* f. Du. (*quack* = prec., *salver* seller of salves, ointments)]

**quad** (-ŏd) n. (colloq.) = QUAD-RANGLE, QUADRAPHONIC, QUADRAT, QUADRUPLET. [abbr.]

**quadragēnār'ian** (-ŏd-) a. & n. (Person) from 40 to 49 years old. [L *-arius* (*quadrageni* 40 each)]

**Quadragě'sĭma** (-ŏd-) n. First Sunday in Lent. [L *quadragesimus* fortieth, w. ref. to 40 days of Lent]

**qua'dr|ăngle** (kwŏ'drănggel) n. Four-sided figure, esp. square or rectangle; four-sided court esp. in colleges; ~**ăngūlar** (-ngg-) a. [F f. L (QUADRI-, ANGLE[1])]

**qua'drant** (-ŏ'd-) n. Quarter of circle's circumference; quarter of circle as cut by two diameters at right angles; quarter of sphere as cut by two planes intersecting at right angles at centre; graduated quarter--circular strip of metal etc., instrument including this for taking angular measurements; **quadra′ntal** a. [L *quadrans -ant-*]

**quadraphŏ′nĭc** (-ŏd-) a. (~ally). (Of sound-reproduction) using 4 transmission channels. [QUADRI-, (STEREO)PHONIC]

**qua′drat** (-ŏ′d-) n. (Print.) Small metal block used in spacing; ~e a., square or rectangular; **quadră′tĭc**, (a.) involving the square and no higher power of unknown quantity or variable (esp. *quadratic equation*), (n.) quadratic equation; **qua′drature** (-ŏ′d-) n., (Math.) finding square with area equal to that of given figure, (Astron.) position of heavenly body in relation to another 90° away. [L (*quadro* make square)]

**quadrĕ′nnĭ|al** a. (-lly). Lasting, recurring every, 4 years; ~**um** n. (*pl.* ~**ums**, ~**a**), period of 4 years. [L *quadriennium* (foll.; cf. BIENNIAL)]

**qua′drĭ-** (-ŏ′d-) *in comb.* Four; ~**la′teral** a. & n., 4-sided (figure or area). [L (*quattuor* four)]

**quadri′lle** n. A square dance; music for it. [F]

**quadrĭplē′gĭ|a** (-ŏd-) n. Paralysis of all 4 limbs; ~**c** a. & n., (victim) of this. [L (Gk *plēgē* a blow)]

**quadri|sy̆llă′bĭc** (-ŏd-) a. 4-syllabled; ~**sy̆′llable** n., word of 4 syllables. [QUADRI-]

**quadroo′n** n. Offspring of white and mulatto, person of one-quarter Negro blood. [Sp. (*cuarto* fourth)]

**qua′drupĕd** (-ŏ′droŏ-) a. & n. Four-footed (animal, esp. mammal); **quadru′pĕdal** (-roŏ′-) a. [F or L (QUADRI-, *pes ped-* foot)]

**qua′druple** (-ŏ′droŏ-) a., n., & v. **1.** a. (-ply). Fourfold, having 4 parts or parties (*quadruple alliance*); ~ **time**, Mus., with 4 beats in bar); being 4 times as many or much as. **2.** n. Quadruple number or amount. **3.** v.t. & i. Multiply by 4. **4.** ~**t** (-ĭt; or -ŏdroŏ′-) n., one of 4 children born at a birth; **quadru′plĭcate** (-ŏŏ′-), (a.) fourfold, of which 4 copies are made (**in quadruplicate**, so copied), (-āt; v.t.) multiply by 4, make 4 copies of. [F f. L (QUADRI-)]

**quaff** (-ah-, -ŏ-) v.i. & t. (literary). Drink deeply; drain (cup etc.) in copious draughts. [perh. imit.]

**quăg** (or -ŏ-) n. Quagmire; ~**′gy̆**

(-gĭ) a.; ~**′mīre** n., quaking bog, marsh, slough. [imit.]

**quail**[1] n. Bird allied to partridge. [F *quaille* f. L, imit.]

**quail**[2] v.i. Flinch, show fear, (*before*, *at*). [orig. unkn.]

**quaint** a. Piquantly or attractively unfamiliar or old-fashioned, daintily odd. [F *cointe* f. L (*cognosco* ascertain)]

**quăk|e. 1.** v.i. (Of earth, trodden bog, person *with* or for fear or cold) tremble, rock to and fro; ~**′ing-grass**, kind trembling in wind; **Q~′er** n., member of the religious Society of Friends, devoted to peaceful principles, formerly noted for plain dress and simple living; **Q~er(s′) meeting**, silent company, w. ref. to their silence in the meeting-house till one is moved by the Spirit; **Q~′erĕss** n.: **Q~′erĭsh** a., (esp.) having Quaker simplicity of dress or speech; **Q~′erĭsm** n. **2.** n. (colloq.) Earthquake. [E]

**qua′lĭf|y̆** (-ŏ′l-) v.t. & i. Attribute a quality to, describe *as*; make competent or fit or legally entitled (*for being* or *doing, to be* or *do, for post*, or *abs.*); ~**ying examination** etc., to ensure that stated minimum level of ability or maximum number of competitors is complied with); fulfil condition, esp. by passing test of eligibility, (*for post*); modify, make less absolute, limit, (statement etc.); moderate, mitigate, make less extreme; ~**ĭcā′tion** n., qualifying, thing that qualifies (*statement with many qualifications*), accomplishment fitting person or thing (*for post*); ~**ĭcātory̆** a. [F f. L (*qualis* such as, of what kind)]

**qua′lĭt|y̆** (-ŏ′l-) n. Degree of excellence, relative nature, (*of poor etc.* quality; *made in three qualities*; *quality matters more than quantity*; **in the** ~**y of**, as); general excellence (**has** ~**y**, is excellent); attribute, trait, faculty, (*has many good qualities*; *the quality of courage*; *the qualities of a ruler*); (arch.) social standing (**people of** ~**y, the** ~**y**, the upper classes); (of voice or sound) timbre; ~**ătĭve** (or -tā-) a., concerned with or depending on quality (opp. *quantitative*).

**qualm** (-ahm, -awm) n. Momentary faint or sick feeling; misgiving, uneasy doubt, scruple of conscience. [orig. uncert.]

**qua′ndary̆** (-ŏ′n-) n. Perplexed state, practical dilemma.

**quand même** (kahṅ mā'm) *adv.* Despite consequences, all the same. [F]

**quanta.** See QUANTUM.

**qua'ntit̆y̆** (-ŏ'n-) *n.* Property of things that is measurable; size or extent or weight or amount or number; specified or considerable portion or number of amount (*a small quantity of blood; a quantity of bubbles; buys in quantity, in large quantities*); (in *pl.*) large amounts or numbers; length or shortness of vowel sounds; (Math.) thing having quantity (**negligible, unknown, ~y,** fig., person etc. that need not, cannot, be reckoned with); **~y surveyor,** person who measures and prices work of builders; **qua'ntif̆y̆** (-ŏ'n-) *v.t.,* determine quantity of, express as quantity; **quantif̆icā'- tion** (-ŏn-) *n.;* **~ative** (*or* -tā-) *a.,* measured or measurable by, concerned with, quantity (opp. *qualitative*), based on vowel quantity (*quantitative verse*). [F f. L (*quantus* how much)]

**qua'nt̆um** (-ŏ'n-) *n.* (*pl.* **~a**). (Required, desired, allowed) amount; (Phys.) unit quantity of energy proportional to frequency of radiation (**~um theory,** assuming that energy exists in such units). [L (*quantus* how much)]

**qua'rantine** (kwŏ'răntēn) **1.** *n.* (Period of) isolation imposed on ship or persons or animals to prevent infection or contagion. **2.** *v.t.* Put in quarantine. [It. (*quaranta* forty)]

**quärk** (*or* -ōr-) *n.* (Phys.) Hypothetical component of elementary particles. [wd used by Joyce in *Finnegans Wake*]

**qua'rrel**[1] (kwŏ'-) *n.* (Hist.) Cross-bow bolt. [F *quar(r)el* (L *quadrus* square)]

**qua'rrel**[2] (kwŏ'-). **1.** *n.* Occasion of complaint (*have no quarrel against, with;* **pick a ~,** invent or seize on opportunity for one); violent contention or altercation, rupture of friendly relations, (*between, with*). **2.** *v.i.* (**||-ll-**). Find fault with (**~ with** one's **bread and butter,** esp., abandon the employment one lives by); contend violently, fall out, (*with* person, *for, about, over,* thing). **3. ~some** *a.,* given to contention. [F f. L *querela* (*queror* complain)]

**qua'rry̆**[1] (kwŏ'-) *n.* Intended prey or victim, object of pursuit. [F f. L *cor* heart]

**qua'rry̆**[2] (kwŏ'-). **1.** *n.* Place from which stone is extracted for building etc.; store of available information; **~ (tile),** unglazed floor-tile; **~man,** worker in quarry. **2.** *v.t. & i.* Extract (stone, facts) from quarry; search in books etc. (*for*). [L f. F f. L *quadrum* square]

**quart** (kwôrt) *n.* Quarter of gallon, two pints, (**put ~ into pint pot,** make the less contain the greater); vessel containing quart; ⅛ gal. of wine or spirits; **~'an** *a. & n.,* (fever) recurring twice in 4 days. [F f. L *quartus* fourth]

**quar'ter** (-ōr'-). **1.** *n.* One of 4 equal parts (*can get it for a quarter, a quarter of, the price;* **~ mile,** quarter of a mile); amount or coin of 25 U.S. or Canadian cents; one of 4 parts into which carcass is divided; (in *pl.*) hind legs and adjoining parts of quadruped, hindquarters; either side of ship from middle to stern; ||grain-measure of 8 bushels; weight of ||28 or *25 lb.; side of boot or shoe from back to vamp; part of year ending on quarter-day; quarter of lunar month, moon's position between first two (**first ~**) or last two (**last ~**) of these; point of time 15 minutes before or after any hour o'clock (*a quarter to or past six*); (region at) point of compass, direction, district, source of supply (*offers of help from all quarters*); division of town esp. as occupied by particular class (*the residential quarter*); (in *pl.*) lodgings, abode, station of troops (CLOSE[1] *quarters*); exemption from death on condition of surrender (**cry ~,** ask for this; **give no ~ to,** fig., attack relentlessly). **2.** *v.t.* Divide into quarters; (Hist.) divide (traitor's body) thus; put (troops etc.) into quarters; provide with lodgings; (Her.) divide (shield) into quarters. **3. ~binding** (of book, with narrow leather at back only); **~day** (on which payments are due for preceding 3 months); **~deck,** upper deck between stern and after-mast, officers of ship or navy; **~-final,** match or round preceding semi-final; ||**~light,** window other than main door-window in side of carriage or motor vehicle; **~master** (Naut.) man in charge of steering, hold--stowing, etc., (Mil.) regimental officer in charge of quartering, rations, etc., (~*master sergeant*, his assistant); *quarter* SESSIONS; ~**staff**, stout pole 6–8 ft. long formerly used as peasant's weapon. **4.** ~**ing** *n.*, (esp., in *pl.*, Her.) coats of arms arranged on one shield to denote alliances of families; ~**lỹ**, (*a. & adv.*) (occurring, published, done) once in each quarter of year, (Her., of shield) quartered, (*n.*) quarterly review or magazine; ~**n** *n.*, (arch.) 4-pound loaf; **quartě't(te)** (-ō̆r-) *n.*, group of 4, (Mus.) (composition for) group of 4 instruments or voices; **quar'tŏ** (-ō̆r-) *n.* (*abbr.* **4to;** *pl.* **-os**), (size of) book or page given by twice folding sheet(s) to form 4 leaves. [AF f. L *quartarius* (prec.)]

**quartz** (-ôrts) *n.* Silica in various mineral forms; ~ **lamp**, quartz tube with mercury vapour as light-source. [G f. Slav.]

**quā'sȧr** (or -z-) *n.* (Astron.) Star-like object with large red-shift. [contr. *quasi-stellar*]

**quash** (kwŏsh) *v.t.* Annul, reject as not valid, esp. by legal procedure; suppress, crush. [F *quasser* f. L]

**quā'si-** (or -zī, kwah'zī) *pref.* Seeming(ly), not real(ly), almost. [L *quasi* as if]

**qua'ssia** (-ŏ̆sha) *n.* S. Amer. tree; its wood or bark or root; bitter tonic made from these. [*Quassi*, person]

**quǎtėrcěntě'narў** (or kwŏ̆-) *a. & n.* (Festival) of 400th anniversary. [L *quater* 4 times]

**quatėr'n|arў** *a. & n.* Having 4 parts; (Geol.; *Q*-) most recent (period or strata). [L (*quaterni* 4 each)]

**qua'train** (-ŏ̆t-) *n.* Four-line stanza; **quǎ'trefoil** (k-) *n.*, 4-cusped figure, 4-lobed leaf or flower. [F (*quatre* four)]

**quattrŏcě'nt|ō** (-ahtrŏch-) *n.* Italian art of 15th c.; ~**ĭst** *n.*, quattrocento artist. [It. = 400 used for 14—]

**quā'ver. 1.** *v.i. & t.* (Of voice or sound) vibrate, shake, tremble, trill (note etc., or abs.), say (*out*) in trembling tones. **2.** *n.* Trill, tremulousness in speech; ||(Mus.) note with hooked symbol, = half crotchet; ~**ў** *a.*, (of voice etc.) tremulous. [imit.]

**quay** (kē) *n.* Solid stationary artificial landing-place lying along or projecting into water for (un)loading ships; ~**'age** (kē'ĭj) *n.*, quay accommodation or dues; ~**'side**, land of or near quay. [F]

**Que.** *abbr.* Quebec.

**quean** *n.* (arch.) Bold girl or woman, hussy. [E]

**quea's|ỹ** (-zī) *a.* (~**ily**, ~**iness**). (Of digestion or conscience or its owner) easily upset, feeling or liable to qualms or scruples, over-fastidious; (of food etc.) causing queasiness. [orig. uncert.]

**queen. 1.** *n.* King's wife; female sovereign of kingdom; worshipped female; ancient goddess; sweetheart, wife, mistress; belle or mock sovereign on some occasion (*Queen of the* MAY[2]); personified best example (*the queen of roses*); woman, country, etc., regarded as supreme in the class; (sl.) male homosexual; perfect fertile female of bee etc.; most powerful piece in chess; court-card bearing representation of queen and usu. ranking next below king. **2.** *v.t. & i.* Make (person) queen; (Chess) convert (pawn) to queen when it reaches opponent's end of board, (of pawn) be thus converted; ~ **it**, act the queen. **3.** Q~**Anne**, style of English design in early 18th c.; **Q~ Anne is dead** (retort to stale news); ~**-cake**, small soft currant cake; ~ **consort**, king's wife; ~ **mother**, king's widow who is mother of sovereign; ~ **of hearts**, any beautiful woman; ~**-post**, one of two upright posts between tie-beam and main rafters; ||*Queen's* BENCH, COUNSEL, ENGLISH, EVIDENCE, HIGHWAY, PEACE, PROCTOR, SHILLING. **4.** ~**lỹ** *a.* (-**iness**), fit for or appropriate to or like a queen. [E]

**queer** *a., v., & n.* **1.** *a.* Strange, odd, eccentric; of questionable character, shady, suspect; out of sorts, giddy or faint, (*feeling queer*); (sl., esp. of man) homosexual; **in Q~ Street**, (sl.) in debt or trouble or disrepute. **2.** *v.t.* (sl.) Put out of order; ~ **the pitch for**, secretly spoil the chances of. **3.** *n.* (sl.) (Esp. male) homosexual. [orig. uncert.]

**quĕll** *v.t.* (literary). Suppress, put down, crush, (rebels, rebellion, fear, etc.). [E]

**quĕnch** *v.t.* Slake (thirst); extinguish (fire, light, fig. eyesight, life); cool esp. with water, cool (hot substance) rapidly in cold water etc.; stifle or suppress (desire etc.). [E]

**quenĕ′lle** (ke-) *n.* Ball of fish or meat pounded and seasoned. [F]

**quern** *n.* Hand-mill for grinding corn etc. [E]

**que′rulous** (-rōō-) *a.* Complaining, peevish. [L (*queror* complain)]

**quer′y. 1.** *n.* A question, esp. one disputing a fact etc.; question mark or the word *query* spoken or written as mark of interrogation. **2.** *v.t.* Ask, inquire, (*whether, if*); call in question, dispute accuracy of. [L *quaere* imper. of *quaero* inquire]

**quĕst. 1.** *n.* Seeking, thing sought, by inquiry or search (**in ~ of,** trying to find or get). **2.** *v.i.* Search (*about*) for something (esp. of dogs seeking game). [F (L *quaero quaesit-* seek)]

**quĕ′stion** (-schon). **1.** *n.* Sentence with order of or choice of words or punctuation or tone such as to elicit information (*put a question to; ask a question of*; ~ **and answer,** alternate questions and answers as in catechism; **indirect ~,** made into dependent clause, as: I know *who it was*; ~ **mark,** punctuation mark (?) indicating question; ~ **master,** chairman of broadcast quiz etc.; ‖~ **time,** period when M.P.s may question ministers); (raising of) doubt or dispute about thing's truth, credibility, advisability, etc., (**beyond all ~,** certainly; CALL *in question*; **make no ~ of,** admit; problem for solution, matter depending on conditions *of* (**is a ~ of time,** will certainly come sooner or later); subject of discussion or voting (**in ~,** being mentioned or discussed; **come into ~,** be discussed, be of practical importance; *is* **not the ~,** not what we are discussing or voting on; **out of the ~,** too impracticable to be worth discussing; **put the ~,** require vote to be taken). **2.** *v.t.* Ask questions of, subject to examination, (person); call in question, throw doubt on, (*question the honesty, accuracy, of*). **3.** **~able** *a.* (**-bly**), of doubtful truth or quality or honesty or wisdom; **~ary,** **~naire′** (or kĕstĭo-), *ns.*, (document containing) formulated series of questions. [F f. L (prec.)]

**queue** (kū). **1.** *n.* Hanging plaited tail of hair, pigtail; line of persons or vehicles awaiting their turn. **2.** *v.i.* ~ (*up*), join or stand in queue. [F f. L *cauda* tail]

**qui′bble. 1.** *n.* Play on words, pun; equivocation, evasion, argument depending on ambiguity of word or phrase, merely verbal or trivial point of criticism. **2.** *v.i.* Use quibbles. [orig. uncert.]

**quiche** (kēsh) *n.* Open pie with usu. savoury filling. [F]

**quick** *a., n.,* & *adv.* **1.** *a.* Lively, alert, ready, prompt, acute, intelligent, (*quick understanding, wits, eye, child; quick to take offence*); ~ **temper,** tendency to be easily irritated); (arch.) alive (*the quick and the dead*); taking only short time to move or do or obtain, with little interval (*in quick succession*); (of fire, oven) with strong heat; **be ~,** act in quick manner, make haste. **2.** *n.* Tender or sensitive flesh below nails or skin or sore; seat of feeling or emotion (*insult stung him to the quick*). **3.** *adv.* Quickly, at rapid rate, in fairly short time, (*come as quick as you can; quick-drying paint*). **4.** **~-change,** (of actor etc.) quickly changing costume or appearance to play another part; ~ **fire,** firing of shots in quick succession; **~-firing,** (of gun) having special mechanism for quick fire; **~-freeze,** freeze (food) rapidly to preserve natural qualities; **~′lime,** unslaked lime; **~march,** march in quick time (esp. as command to start); ~ **one,** (colloq.) a quickly taken drink; **~′sand,** (bed of) loose wet sand readily swallowing up heavy objects; **~′set,** (hedge) formed of live plants set to grow in ground; **~′silver,** mercury metal, mercurial temperament; **~′step,** fast foxtrot; ~ **time,** marching at about 120 paces per minute; **~-witted,** having quick wits. **5.** **~′en** *v.t.* & *i.,* give life or vigour to, rouse, accelerate, make or become quicker, (of woman or foetus) reach stage of pregnancy when movements of child have been felt; **~′ie** *n.,* (colloq.) thing made or done quickly. [E]

‖**quid**[1] *n.* (sl.; *pl.* same). One pound sterling; **~s in,** able to profit. [prob. L *quid* what]

**quid**[2] *n.* Lump of tobacco for chewing. [dial.= CUD]

**qui′ddity** *n.* Essence of a thing, what makes a thing what it is; quibble, captious subtlety. [L *quidditas* (*quid* what)]

**quid prō quō′** *n.* Thing given as compensation. [L,= something for something]

**quiĕ′scen|t** *a.* Inert, dormant; ~ce *n.* [foll.]

**qui′et** *n.*, *a.*, & *v.* **1.** *n.* Undisturbed state, tranquillity; repose; stillness, silence. **2.** *a.* (~er, ~est). With little or no sound or motion; of gentle or peaceful disposition; unobtrusive, not showy; not overt, disguised; undisturbed, uninterrupted, free or far from vigorous action; informal (*quiet wedding*); enjoyed in quiet (*a quiet pipe*); not anxious or remorseful; **be ~**, (colloq.) cease talk etc.; **keep ~**, say nothing (*about*); **on the ~**, secretly. **3.** *v.t.* & *i.* Make or become quiet, calm. **4.** ||~**en** *v.t.* & *i.*, quiet; ~**ism** *n.*, passive contemplative attitude to life, as form of religious mysticism; ~**ist** *n.* & *a.*; **qui′étude** *n.*, quietness; **quiē′tus** *n.*, release from life, final riddance, (*get his, its, quietus*). [F f. L (*quiesco* become calm)]

||**quiff** *n.* Lock of hair plastered down or brushed up on forehead. [orig. unkn.]

**quill** *n.* (Hollow stem of) large feather of wing or tail; pen etc. made of quill; (usu. in *pl.*) porcupine's spine(s). [prob. LG *quiele*]

**quilt. 1.** *n.* Coverlet esp. of quilted material. **2.** *v.t.* Make (coverlet, garment) of padding held between two layers of cloth etc. by cross lines of sewing. [F *cuilte* f. L *culcita* cushion]

**quin** *n.* (colloq.) Quintuplet. [abbr.]

**quince** *n.* (Tree bearing) acid pear-shaped fruit used in jams etc. [pl. of obs. *quoyn*, F f. L *Cydonia*, place]

**quincĕntē′nary** *a.* & *n.* (Festival) of 500th anniversary. [L *quinque* five]

**qui′nc|ŭnx** *n.* Centre and 4 corner points of square or rectangle, 5 trees etc. so placed; ~**ŭ′ncial** (-shal) *a.* (-lly). [L, = five-twelfths]

**quingentē′nary** (-nj-) *a.* & *n.* = QUINCENTENARY. [L *quingenti* 500]

**qui′nine** (-ēn) *n.* A bitter drug got from cinchona bark and used as febrifuge and tonic. [*quina* cinchona bark, Sp. *kina* bark f. Quechua]

**qui′nqu|e-** in comb. Five; ~**agēnā′rian** *a.* & *n.*, (person) from 50 to 59 years old; ~**agē′nary** *a.* & *n.*, (festival) of 50th anniversary; **Q~agē′sima** *n.*, Sunday before Lent; ~**ĕ′nnial** *a.* (-lly), lasting, recurring every, 5 years; ~**ĕ′nnium** *n.* (*pl.* -iums, -ia), period of 5 years; ~**ĕrēme** *n.*, ancient galley with 5

banks of oars. [L (*quinque* 5, *quinquaginta* 50, *remus* oar; cf. BIENNIAL)]

**qui′nsy̆** (-zī) *n.* Abscess forming round tonsils. [F f. L *quinancia* f. Gk]

**quint|ĕ′ssence** *n.* Purest and most perfect form or manifestation or embodiment *of* a quality etc.; highly refined extract; ~**ĕssĕ′ntial** (-shal) *a.* (-lly). [F f. L *quinta essentia* fifth substance (underlying the 4 elements)]

**quint|ĕ′t(te)** *n.* Group of 5, (Mus.) (composition for) group of 5 instruments or voices; ~**ŭ′ple**, (*a.*; -ply), fivefold, having 5 parts, being 5 times as many or much as, (*n.*) quintuple number or amount, (*v.t.* & *i.*) multiply by 5; ~**ŭ′plĕt** *n.*, one of 5 children born at a birth; ~**ŭ′plicate** *a.*, fivefold, of which 5 copies are made. [F f. It. (*quinto* fifth f. L *quintus*)]

**quĭp. 1.** *n.* Clever saying, epigram. **2.** *v.i.* (-pp-). Make quips. [perh. L *quippe* forsooth]

**quire¹** *n.* 24 sheets of writing-paper; one of the folded sheets that are sewn together in book-binding (**in ~s**, unbound). [F *qua(i)er* f. L (QUATERNARY)]

**quire².** See CHOIR.

**quirk** *n.* Quip; trick of action or behaviour, flourish in writing; ~**′y̆** *a.* (~ily, ~iness). [orig. unkn.]

**qui′sling** (-z-) *n.* Fifth-columnist, traitor. [person]

**quit. 1.** *v.t.* (-tt-). Give up, let go, abandon; cease, stop, (*quit grumbling*); depart from, leave, (place, person, or abs.: *notice to ~*, order to tenant to vacate premises); **~ oneself**, behave *well* etc. **2.** *pred. a.* Rid *of*. **3.** ~**′rent**, (usu. small) rent paid in lieu of service; ~**s** *pred. a.*, on even terms by retaliation or repayment (**cry ~s**, acknowledge that things are now even, agree not to continue quarrel etc.; DOUBLE *or* quits); ~**′tance** *n.*, (arch.) release *from* obligation, acknowledgement of payment; ~**′ter** *n.*, deserter, shirker. [F f. L (QUIET)]

**quitch** *n.* Weed with long creeping roots, COUCH²-grass. [E]

**quite** *adv.* Completely, wholly, entirely, altogether, to the utmost extent, nothing short of, in the fullest sense, positively, absolutely, (*quite covers it*; *was quite by myself*; *I quite agree*; **~ other**, very different; **~ another**, very different; *is* **~ something**, a remarkable thing; *is* **~ the thing**, fashionable or well;

NOT *quite*); rather, to some extent, (*it took quite a long time*; ~ **a few**, a fair number); ~ (**so**), I grant the truth of that. [var. QUIT]

**quits, qui′ttance, qui′tter.** See QUIT.

**qui′ver**[1] *n*. Case for holding arrows (~ **full of children,** ~ful (-ōol) *n*., large family; **an arrow left in** one's ~, a resource). [AF f. Gmc]

**qui′ver**[2]. **1.** *v.i.* Tremble or vibrate with slight rapid motion. **2.** *n*. Quivering motion or sound. [obs. *quiver* nimble]

*qui vive* (kēvē′v) *n*. **On the** ~, on the alert. [F, = (long) live who? (as sentry's challenge)]

**Qui′xote** *n*. Enthusiastic visionary, person who utterly neglects his interests in comparison with honour or devotion; **quixo′tic** *a*. (-ically); **qui′xotism, qui′xotry,** *ns*. [Don ~, hero of book]

**quiz. 1.** *v.t.* (-zz-). Examine by questioning; (arch.) make sport of, mock at, regard critically or curiously. **2.** *n*. (*pl*. ~′zes). Interrogation, examination; test of knowledge in radio or television or other entertainment programme; ~′zical *a*. (-lly), quizzing or quizzable, comical. [orig. unkn.]

**quŏd** *n*. (sl.) Prison (*in quod*). [orig. unkn.]

**quoin** (koin) *n*. Angle or corner of building; corner-stone; wedge used in printing and gunnery. [var. COIN]

**quoit** (koit) *n*. Heavy iron ring for throwing at mark or to encircle peg in game of ~s; rope or rubber ring for similar game. [orig. unkn.]

**quŏ′ndăm** *a*. That once was, sometime, former, (*a quondam friend of mine*). [L adv. = formerly]

**quŏr′um** *n*. Number of members that must be present to constitute valid meeting. [L, = of whom]

**quŏ′ta** *n*. Share to be contributed to or received from a total by one of the parties concerned; quantity of goods which under government controls must or may be manufactured, exported, imported, etc.; number of yearly immigrants allowed to enter a country, students allowed to enrol for course, etc. [L *quotus* (*quot* how many)]

**quŏt|e. 1.** *v.t.* & *i.* Cite or appeal to (author, book) in confirmation of some view; repeat or copy out passage(s) from; repeat or copy out (borrowed passage) usu. with indication that it is borrowed, make quotations, (*from* author, book, speech, etc.); adduce or cite *as*; enclose (words) in quotation-marks; (regularly) state price of (usu. *at* figure). **2.** *n*. (colloq.) Passage or price quoted; (usu. in *pl*.) quotation-mark. **3.** ~′able *a*., (esp.) worth quoting (from); ~abi′lity *n*.; quŏ-tā′tion *n*., quoting, passage or price quoted; ~ation-marks, inverted commas (' ' or " ") used at beginning and end of quoted passages or words. [L *quoto* mark with numbers]

**quŏth** *v.t.* (arch.) ~ **I, he, she,** said I etc. [E]

**quoti′dian** *a*. Daily; everyday, commonplace; (of fever) recurring every day. [F f. L (*quotidie* daily)]

**quŏ′tient** (-shent) *n*. Result of division sum (cf. DIVIDEND, DIVISOR) [L *quotiens -ent-* how many times]

**q.v.** *abbr*. which see (in references) [L *quod vide*]

**qy.** *abbr*. query

<br/>

# R

**R, r,** (är) *n*. (*pl*. **Rs, R′s**). Eighteenth letter; **the three Rs,** reading, (w)riting, (a)rithmetic.

**R.** *abbr*. Railway; rand; *Regina*; registered as trademark; *Rex*; River; (Chess) rook; Royal.

**r.** *abbr*. right; run(s).

**R.A.** *abbr*. Royal Academician; Royal Academy; Royal Artillery.

**ră′bbet. 1.** *n*. Step-shaped channel etc. cut along edge or face of wood etc. usu. to receive edge or tongue of another piece. **2.** *v.t.* Join or fix with rabbet; make rabbet in. [F *rab(b)at* (REBATE).]

**ră′bb|ĭ** *n*. Jewish scholar or teacher esp. of the law (so ~**ĭ′nĭcal** *a*.); Jewish religious leader; ~**ĭnate** *n*., (tenure of) office of rabbi. [Heb., = my master]

**ră′bbit. 1.** *n.* Burrowing gregarious herbivorous mammal of hare family; *hare; ||(colloq.) poor performer at game (esp. cricket, golf, lawn tennis); ~ **punch**, short chop with edge of hand to opponent's nape; WELSH[1] *rabbit*; ~**y** *a.* **2.** *v.i.* Hunt rabbits. [orig. uncert.]

**ră′bble** *n.* Disorderly crowd, mob; contemptible or inferior set of people; *the* lower or disorderly classes of the populace; ~-**rouser**, one who stirs up rabble in agitation for social or political change.

**Rabelai′sian** (-zyan) *a.* Of or like *Rabelais* or his writings; marked by exuberant imagination and language and coarse humour and satire. [person]

**ră′bid** *a.* Furious; violent; unreasoning, headstrong; (esp. of dog) affected with rabies, mad; of rabies; **rabi′dĭtў** *n.*; **ră′bies** (-z) *n.*, contagious virus disease of dogs etc., hydrophobia. [L (*rabio* rave)]

||**R.A.C.** *abbr.* Royal Armoured Corps; Royal Automobile Club.

**raccoo′n.** See RACOON.

**race[1]. 1.** *n.* Contest of speed between runners, ships, vehicles, horses, etc., or persons doing anything; (in *pl.*) series of these for horses, dogs, etc., at fixed time on regular course (~′**course**, ground for horse-racing; ~′**goer**, one who frequents horse-races; ~′**horse**, bred or kept for racing; ~-**meeting**, horse-racing event; ~-**track**, usu. oval track for horse or vehicle races); onward movement; strong current in sea or river; channel (MILL[1]-*race*). **2.** *v.i.* & *t.* Compete in speed *with*; have race with, try to surpass in speed; cause to race (*raced his car against a train*); go, (cause to) move or work, at full or excessive speed; indulge in horse-racing (*a racing man*). **3.** **ră′cer** *n.*, (esp.) horse etc. used for racing. [N]

**race[2]** *n.* Group of persons or animals or plants connected by common descent, posterity *of* (person); house, family, tribe, or nation regarded as of common stock; distinct ethnical stock (*the Caucasian race*); genus or species or breed or variety of animals or plants, any great division of living creatures (*the human race*); descent, kindred; class

of persons etc. with some common feature (*the race of poets, dandies*, etc.); ~ **relations** (between members of different races in same country); ~ **riot**, outbreak of violence due to racial antagonism. [F f. It. *razza*]

**race′me** *n.* Flower-cluster with flowers attached by short equal stalks at equal distances along stem. [L *racemus* grape-bunch]

**ră′cer.** See RACE[1].

**ră′cial** (-shal) *a.* (~**ly**). Of, in regard to, due to, characteristic of, race; ~**ism** *n.*, belief in superiority of a particular race, antagonism between races; ~**ist** *n.* & *a.*; **ră′cism** *n.*, racialism, theory that human abilities etc. are determined by race; **ră′cist** *n.* & *a.* [RACE[2]]

**răck[1]. 1.** *n.* Fixed or movable frame of wooden or metal bars to hold fodder; framework with rails, bars, pegs, or shelves, for keeping or placing articles on or in (*plate, luggage*, etc., -*rack*); instrument of torture stretching victim's joints by turning of rollers to which wrists and ankles were tied (**on the ~**, fig., in distress or under strain); cogged or indented bar or rail engaging with wheel or pinion or worm, or serving with pegs etc. to adjust position of something (~-**railway**, with cogged rail between bearing rails). **2.** *v.t.* Place in or on rack; stretch joints of (person) by pulling esp. with rack; (of disease or bodily or mental agony) inflict torture on (*racked with pain*); shake violently, injure by straining; ~ one's **brain**(s), make great mental effort *for* something to say, a plan, etc.; ~-**rent**, excessive rent. [LDu.]

**răck[2]** *n.* Destruction (*go to rack and ruin*). [WRACK]

**ră′ckĕt[1]**, **ră′cquĕt** (-kit), *n.* Bat having frame strung with catgut, nylon, etc., used in tennis, rackets, etc., (in *pl.*) ball-game with rackets in a court of 4 plain walls. [F *raquette* f. It. f. Arab.]

**ră′ckĕt[2]. 1.** *n.* Disturbance, uproar, din; busy activity; (sl.) dodge, game, line of business; scheme for obtaining money, or effecting some other object, by fraudulent (and often violent) means; ordeal, trying experience, (**stand the ~**, come successfully through test, face costs or other consequences of action). **2.** *v.i.* ~ (**about**), live gay life, move *about* noisily. **3.** ~**eer'** *n.*, one who operates a fraudulent racket; ~**eer'-ing** *n.*; ~**y** *a.*, (esp.) noisy, rowdy. [perh. imit.]

**răcŏnteur'** (-tēr') *n.* (*fem.* **-euse** *pr.* -êr'z). Teller of anecdotes. [F (RECOUNT)]

**rac(c)ōo'n** *n.* Greyish-brown furry bushy-tailed sharp-snouted N. Amer. nocturnal carnivore. [Amer. Ind.]

**racquet.** See RACKET[1].

**rā'c|y** *a.* (~**ily**, ~**iness**). Of distinctive quality or vigour, not smoothed into sameness or commonness, retaining traces of origin; *risqué.* [RACE[2]]

||**R.A.D.A.** (colloq. rah'da) *abbr.* Royal Academy of Dramatic Art.

**rā'dăr** *n.* System for ascertaining direction and range, or presence, of aircraft, ships, coasts, and other objects by sending out short radio waves which they reflect; apparatus used for this; ~ **trap**, arrangement using radar to detect vehicles etc. travelling faster than speed limit. [*radio detection and ranging*]

**ră'ddle. 1.** *n.* Red ochre. **2.** *v.t.* Colour with raddle, or with much rouge crudely used; (in *p.p.*) dilapidated. [var. RUDDLE]

**rā'di|al. 1.** *a.* (**-lly**). Of or in rays; arranged like rays or radii, having position or direction of a radius; (of tyre,'also ~**al-ply**) having fabric layers parallel and tread strengthened; having spokes or radiating lines; acting or moving along lines that diverge from a centre; relating to radius of forearm. **2.** *n.* Radial-ply tyre. **3.** ~**an** *n.*, angle at centre of circle formed by radii of arc with length equal to radius; ~**ant**, (*a.*) emitting rays of light, (of eyes or looks) beaming with joy or hope or love, (of light) issuing in rays, (of beauty) splendid or dazzling, operating radially, (~**ant heat**, transmitted by radiation), (*n.*) point or object from which light or heat radiates esp. in electric or gas heater; ~**ance**, ~**ancy**, *ns.*; ~**āte**[1] *v.t.* & *i.*, emit rays of light, heat, etc., (of light or heat) issue in rays, diverge or spread from central point, emit (light or heat) from central point, disseminate as from central centre, give manifest evidence of (life, love, joy, etc.); ~**āte**[2] *a.*, having parts radially arranged; ~**ā'tion** *n.*, radiating, emission of energy as electromagnetic waves, energy thus transmitted esp. invisibly (~**ation sickness**, caused by exposure to excessive radiation); ~**ātor** *n.*, (esp.) apparatus for heating room etc. by radiation of heat, engine-cooling apparatus in motor vehicle or aeroplane; ~**ator grille**, **mascot**, etc., (at front end of motor car, where radiator is usu. placed). [L (RADIUS)]

**rā'dĭcal. 1.** *a.* (~**ly**). Of root(s); inherent, essential, fundamental, (*a radical error*); forming the basis, primary; affecting the foundation, going to the root (*radical change*); (of politician) desiring radical reforms; (of measure etc.) advanced by or according to principles of radical politicians; (Math.) of the root of a number or quantity; (Philol.) of the roots of words. **2.** *n.* (Philol.) root; (Math.) quantity forming or expressed as root of another; (Chem.) element or atom, or group of these, normally forming part of compound and remaining unaltered during compound's ordinary chemical changes; (Polit.) person holding radical views or belonging to radical party. **3.** ~**ism** *n.*, radical politics; ~**ize** *v.t.* & *i.*; **ră'dĭcle** *n.*, part of plant embryo that develops into primary root, rootlet. [L (RADIX)]

**rā'dĭi.** See RADIUS.

**rā'dĭō** *n.*, *a.*, & *v.* **1.** *n.* (*pl.* ~**s**). Transmission and reception of messages etc. by electromagnetic waves without connecting wire; message so sent; (esp. sound) broadcasting; apparatus for receiving signals by radio; broadcasting station (*Radio Luxembourg*). **2.** *a.* Of or relating to, sent by, used in or using, radio, (~ **cab, car**, vehicle equipped with radio for communication); of or concerned with stars or other celestial bodies from which radio waves are received or reflected (*radio astronomy*, TELESCOPE); ~ **star**, small celestial object emitting strong radio waves. **3.** *v.t.* & *i.* Send (message), send message to (person), by radio; communicate or broadcast by radio. [abbr. *radio-telegraphy* etc.]

**rā'dĭ|ō-** *in comb.* Connected with rays, radiation, radioactivity, or radio; ~**ŏă'ctĭve** *a.*, of or exhibiting radioactivity; ~**ŏăctĭ'vĭty** *n.*, property of spontaneous disintegration of atomic nuclei usu. with emission of penetrating radiation or particles;

~ō-car'bon, radioisotope of carbon, esp. that of mass 14 used in dating ancient organic materials; ~ō--contro'lled (-ld) a., controlled from a distance by radio; ~ōgram n., radio-telegram; ~ograph (-ahf), (n.) instrument for recording intensity of radiation, picture obtained by X-rays etc., (v.t.) obtain such picture of; ~ō'grapher, ~ō'graphy, ns.; ~ōī'sotōpe n., radioactive isotope; ~ōlocā'tion n., = RADAR; ~ō'logy n., scientific study of X-rays and other high-energy radiation esp. as used in medicine; ~ō'scopy n., examination by X-rays etc. of objects opaque to light; ~ō-tě'lěgram n. (sent by radio); ~ō'-tělě'graphy, ~ō-tělě'phony, ns. (using radio); ~ō-thě'rapy n., treatment of disease by X-rays or other forms of radiation. [RADIUS]

**ra'dish** n. (Plant with) fleshy pungent root often eaten raw as relish in salads. [E & F f. L RADIX]

**ra'dium** n. Radioactive metallic element obtained from pitchblende etc., used esp. in luminous materials and in radio-therapy. [foll.]

**ra'di|us** n. (pl. ~i pr. -ī, ~uses). Thicker and shorter bone of forearm in man, corresponding bone in animal's foreleg or bird's wing; (Math.) straight line from centre to circumference of circle or sphere, radial line from focus to any point of curve; length of radius of circle etc., (fig.) distance from a centre (all within a radius of 20 miles); any of set of lines diverging from point like radii of circle; object of this kind, e.g. spoke. [L]

**ra'di|x** n. (pl. ~ces pr. -sēz). Number or symbol used as basis of numeration scale. [L radix -icis root]

||**R.A.F.** (colloq. răf) abbr. Royal Air Force.

**ra'ffia** n. Palm-tree orig. of Madagascar; fibre from its leaves used for tying up plants and making hats, baskets, mats, etc. [Malagasy]

**ra'ffish** a. Disreputable, dissipated, tawdry. [raff rubbish]

**ra'ffle.** 1. n. Sale of article, esp. for charity, by taking entry-fee from any number of persons and assigning the article by lot to one of them. 2. v.t. Sell by raffle. [F rafle a dice-game]

**raft** (-ah-). 1. n. Collection of logs, casks, etc., fastened together in the water for transportation; flat floating structure of timber etc. esp. as substitute for boat in emergency. 2. v.t. & i. Transport as or on raft; form into raft; cross (water) on raft(s); work raft (across water etc.); ~'er[1] n., man who rafts timber. [N]

**ra'fter[2]** (-ah'-) n. One of the sloping beams forming the framework of a roof. [E]

**răg[1]** n. Torn or frayed piece of woven material (CHEW the rag; in ~s, much torn; RED rag); (in pl.) old and torn clothes (GLAD rags; in ~s, in old clothes; ~s to riches, poverty to affluence); (usu. w. neg.) smallest scrap of cloth or sail (not a rag to cover him); (collect.) rags used as material for paper, stuffing, etc.; remnant, odd scrap, irregular piece, (flying rags of cloud; cooked to ~s, till it falls to pieces); (derog.) flag, handkerchief, curtain, newspaper, etc.; ||~-and--bone man, itinerant dealer in old clothes etc.; ~-bag, bag in which scraps of fabric etc. are kept for use, (fig.) miscellaneous collection; ~--bolt (with barbs to keep it tight when driven in); ~ book, child's book of untearable cloth; ~ doll, stuffed cloth doll; ~ paper (made from rags); ~'tag (and bobtail), riff-raff, ragged or disreputable people; ~'time, (n.) popular music of U.S. Black origin with much syncopation, (a.) farcical (a ragtime army); ~ trade, (colloq.) business of designing, making, and selling women's clothes; ~'weed, ~'wort, yellow-flowered ragged-leaved plant. [prob. back-form. f. RAGGED]

**răg[2]** n. ~('stone), hard coarse stone breaking up in thick slabs. [orig. unkn.]

**răg[3].** (sl.) 1. v.t. & i. (-gg-). Torment, play rough jokes on; ||engage in rough play; be noisy and riotous. 2. n. ||Noisy disorderly conduct or scene; rowdy celebration; annual comic parade etc. of students esp. to collect money for charity; prank.

**răg[4]** n. (Piece of) RAG[1]time. [abbr.]

**ra'gamuffin** n. Person in ragged dirty clothes. [prob. RAG[1]]

**rāge.** 1. n. (Fit of) violent anger; violent operation of natural force; vehement desire (for); object of widespread temporary enthusiasm (judo was (all) the rage); (poet.) poetic or prophetic or martial ardour. 2. v.i. Rave, storm, speak madly or furiously, (at, against, or abs.), be full of anger; (of wind, passion, battle, pain, etc.) be violent, be at its height. [F f. L RABIES]

**ră′gged** (-g-) *a.* Having broken jagged outline or surface; faulty, imperfect, lacking finish or smoothness or uniformity, (*ragged rhymes, time* in rowing, etc.); torn, frayed; (of person) in ragged clothes, almost exhausted (*was run ragged*); ∼ **robin,** crimson-flowered campion with tattered petals. [N]

**ră′glan** *n.* Overcoat without shoulder seams, the sleeve running up to the neck; ∼ **sleeve** (of this kind). [person]

**ră′gout** (-ōō) *n.* Meat in small pieces stewed with vegetables and highly seasoned. [F]

**raid. 1.** *n.* Sudden attack made by military party, ship(s), or aircraft; predatory incursion usu. relying on surprise and speed; surprise visit by police etc. to arrest suspected persons or seize illicit goods. **2.** *v.t.* & *i.* Make raid in, *into,* etc. [Sc. form of ROAD]

**rail¹. 1.** *n.* Level or sloping bar or series of bars used to hang things on, as top of banisters, as part of fence, as protection against contact or falling over, or for similar purpose; iron bar or continuous line of bars laid on ground usu. as one of two forming railway track (**off the** ∼**s,** disorganized, out of order, not working right); railway (*send it by rail*; FREE *on rail*; *rail travel*, *unions*); ∼′**car,** self-propelled railway carriage; ∼′**head,** farthest point reached by railway under construction, point on railway at which road transport of goods begins; ∼′**man,** railwayman; *∗∼′**road,** railway. **2.** *v.t.* Furnish or enclose (place) with rail(s) (*in, off*); ∼′**ing** *n.,* fence or barrier with rails. [F *reille* f. L *regula* rule]

**rail²** *n.* Small wading bird, esp. LANDrail, *water-rail.* [F]

**rail³** *v.i.* Use abusive language (*at, against*); ∼′**lery** *n.,* (piece of) good-humoured ridicule. [F *railler*]

**rai′ling.** See RAIL¹.

**rai′lway** *n.* Track or set of tracks of iron or steel rails for passage of trains of carriages or trucks drawn by locomotive engine and conveying passengers and goods; tracks of this kind worked by single company; organization and persons required for their working; ∼**man,** railway employee. [RAIL¹, WAY]

**rai′ment** *n.* (arch. or literary). Clothing. [*arrayment* (ARRAY)]

**rain. 1.** *n.* Condensed moisture of atmosphere falling visibly in separate drops, fall of such drops, (*as* RIGHT *as* rain; ∼ **or shine,** whether it rains or not); (in *pl.*) falls of rain (**the** ∼**s,** rainy season in tropical countries); (rainlike descent of) falling liquid or solid particles or objects (lit. or fig.); ∼′**coat,** waterproof or water-resistant coat; ∼′**drop,** single drop of rain; ∼′**fall,** shower, quantity of rain falling within given area in given time; ∼ **forest,** luxuriant tropical forest with heavy rainfall; ∼**-gauge,** instrument measuring rainfall; ∼**-water** (collected from rain, not got from wells etc.). **2.** *v.i.* & *t.* It ∼**s** or **is** ∼**ing,** rain comes down, it ∼**ed** *frogs, invitations,* etc., there was a rain of them, (∼ **cats and dogs,** very hard; *it never rains but it* POURS; **it** ∼**s in,** rain penetrates house etc.); of sky, clouds, etc.) send down rain (*it,* fig., send down, like rain (*blows rain, rain blows, upon him*); ∼ **off,** *∗***out,** (esp in *p.p.*) prevent or stop (event) etc. by rain. **3.** ∼′**y** *a.* (∼**ily,** ∼**iness,**) (of weather, day, region, etc.) in or on which rain is falling or much rain usually falls (∼**y day,** fig. time of need esp. of money), (of clouds, wind, etc.) laden with or bringing rain. [E]

**rai′nbow** (-ō). **1.** *n.* Arch showing sequence of colours formed in sky (or across cataract etc.) opposite sun by reflection, twofold refraction, and dispersion of sun's rays in falling raindrops etc.; similar effect from moon, fog, sea spray, etc.; **all the colours of the** ∼, many colours. **2.** *a.* Many-coloured; ∼ **trout,** large trout orig. of N. Amer. Pacific coast. [E (RAIN, BOW¹)]

**raise** (-z). **1.** *v.t.* Cause to stand up or *up,* bring back to or towards vertical position, rouse (∼ **a dust,** fig., cause turmoil, obscure the truth; ∼ **from the dead,** restore to life; ∼ **the wind,** fig., procure money for a purpose); build up or *up,* create, breed, educate, cause to be heard, start, set up, (*raise palace, blister, large family, shout, controversy, objection, hopes*); ∼ **a laugh,** cause others to laugh); put or take into higher position, extract from earth, increase amount of, cause (bread) to rise, bet more than (another player), multiply quantity *to a* power, (~ one's **eyebrows**, look supercilious or shocked; ~ one's **eyes**, look upwards; ~ one's **glass to**, drink health of; ~ one's **hand to**, make as if to strike; ~ one's **hat**, remove it in courtesy or respect; ~ one's **voice**, speak, esp. louder); levy, collect, get together, (*raise tax, money, army*); (cause enemy to) relinquish (blockade, siege, etc.); remove (barrier); cause (GHOST etc.) to appear; (colloq.) find (person etc. wanted); ~ **hell** or **the devil**, = raise CAIN; **~d pastry, pie,** etc., (standing without support). **2.** *n.* Increase in stake or bid or *salary. [N]

**rai′sin** (-z-) *n.* Partially dried grape. [F f. L (RACEME)]

**raison d'être** (rāzawǹdā′tr, -ĕ′-) *n.* Purpose etc. that accounts for or justifies or originally caused thing's existence. [F]

**raj** (-ah-) *n.* (Ind. Hist.) Sovereignty (*the British raj in India*); **~′a(h)** (-*a*) *n.,* Indian king or prince, petty dignitary or noble in India. [Hindi]

**rāke¹. 1.** *n.* Implement of pole with end cross-bar toothed like comb, or with several tines held together by cross-piece, for drawing together hay etc. or smoothing loose soil or gravel; implement like rake used for other purposes, e.g. to draw in money at gaming-table. **2.** *v.t.* & *i.* Collect, draw *together*, gather *in* or *up*, pull *out*, clear *off*, (as) with rake (*rake out the fire; rake up* or *together all possible charges*); clean or smooth with rake; search (as) with rake, ransack; scratch, scrape; enfilade, send shot along (ship) from stem to stern, sweep with the eyes; use rake, search as with rake (*have been raking among* or *in* or *into old records*); **~-off,** (colloq., usu. derog.) commission, share of profits; ~ **over, up,** revive memory of (past quarrels, grievances, etc.). [E]

**rāke²** *n.* Dissipated or immoral man of fashion; **rā′kish** *a.* [*rakehell* (RAKE¹, HELL)]

**rāke³. 1.** *v.i.* & *t.* (Of ship or its bow or stern) project at upper part of bow or stern beyond keel; (of mast, funnel) incline from perpendicular towards stern; give backward inclination to (back of seat etc.). **2.** *n.* Amount by which thing rakes, raking position or build. [orig. unkn.]

**rāllentā′nd|ō** *adv., a.,* & *n.* (*pl.*

~os, ~i). (Mus.) (Passage performed) with gradual decrease of speed. [It.]

**rǎ′llỹ¹. 1.** *v.t.* & *i.* Reassemble, get together again, after rout or dispersion; (cause to) renew conflict; bring or come together as support or for action; revive (faculty etc.) by effort of will, assume or rouse to fresh energy; throw off prostration or illness or fear; (of share-prices etc.) increase after fall. **2.** *n.* Act of reassembling forces or renewing conflict, reunion for fresh effort; recovery of energy after or in the middle of exhaustion or illness; (Tennis etc.) series of strokes before point is decided; competition for motor vehicles over public roads; mass meeting of supporters or persons having a common interest. [F *rallier* (RE-, ALLY)]

**rǎ′llỹ²** *v.t.* Subject to good-humoured ridicule, banter. [F *railler* (RAIL³)]

**rǎm. 1.** *n.* Uncastrated male sheep; (*Ram*) sign of ZODIAC; = BATTERing--ram; (battleship with) projecting beak at bow for charging side of other ships; falling weight of pile--driving machine; hydraulic water--raising or lifting machine. **2.** *v.t.* (**-mm-**). Beat down (soil etc., or abs.) into solidity with wooden block etc.; drive (pile etc.) *down, in, into,* by heavy blows; squeeze or force into place by pressure; cram *with* stuffing etc.; (of ship, vehicle, etc.) strike (as) with ram; dash or violently impel (thing) *against, at, on, into;* **~′mer** *n.,* (esp.) block of wood used for ramming soil. [E]

‖**R.A.M.** *abbr.* Royal Academy of Music.

**Rǎmada′n** (-ah′n) *n.* Ninth month of Muslim year, in which rigid fasting is observed during all daylight hours. [Arab.]

**rǎ′mbl|e. 1.** *v.i.,* & *n.* Walk for pleasure. **2.** *v.i.* Wander in discourse, talk or write disconnectedly. **3.** ~**er** *n.,* (esp.) straggling or climbing rose; ~**ing** *a.,* (esp., of house, street, etc.) irregularly arranged, (of plant) straggling, climbing. [Du. *rammelen*]

‖**R.A.M.C.** *abbr.* Royal Army Medical Corps.

**rǎ′mekin** *n.* Small ovenware dish for (baking and) serving individual portion of food; food thus (baked and) served. [F *ramequin*]

**ră′mie** n. Tall E. Asian etc. plant; strong fibre from its bast, woven into durable material. [Malay]

**ră′mǐf|y̆** v.i. & t. Form branches or subdivisions or offshoots, branch out; (usu. in pass.) cause to branch out, arrange in branching manner; **~ĭcā′tion** n. [F f. L (*ramus* branch)]

**ră′mmer.** See RAM.

**‖rămp¹.** (sl.) **1.** n. Swindle, racket, esp. by exorbitant prices. **2.** v.t. & i. Engage in ramp; subject (person etc.) to ramp. [orig. unkn.]

**rămp².** **1.** v.i. & t. (Of lion etc.) stand on hind legs with fore-paws in air; take threatening posture; furnish or build with ramp; rampage. **2.** n. Slope joining two levels of ground, floor, etc.; stairs for entering or leaving aircraft. **3. ~ā′ge,** (v.i.) rage, storm, rush *about*, (n.; or ră′-) violent behaviour (**on the ~age**, rampaging); **~ā′geous** (-jus) a.; **~′ant** a., ramping (Her., esp. of lion; after n.), violent or extravagant in action or opinion, aggressive, unchecked, (*rampant theorists, violence*), rank, luxuriant; **~′ancy̆** n. [F *ramper* crawl]

**ră′mpȧrt** n. Broad-topped usu. stone-parapeted walk on defensive wall; (fig.) defence, protection. [F (*remparer* fortify)]

**ră′mrŏd** n. Rod for ramming down charge of muzzle-loaded firearm; (fig.) thing that is very straight or rigid. [RAM, ROD]

**ră′mshăckle** a. (Usu. of house or vehicle) tumbledown, rickety. [earlier *ramshackled* p.p. of obs. *ransackle* RANSACK]

**răn.** See RUN.

**ranch** (-ah-). **1.** n. Cattle-breeding establishment esp. in U.S. & Canada; farm where other animals are bred (*mink ranch*); \*DUDE *ranch*. **2.** v.i. Conduct ranch. [Sp. *rancho* persons eating together]

**ră′ncǐd** a. Smelling or tasting like rank stale fat; **~ǐ′dǐty̆** n.; **~our,** \***~or,** (-ker) n., malignant hate, inveterate bitterness; **~orous** a. [L *rancidus* stinking]

**rănd** (or rahnt) n. Monetary unit of S. Afr. countries. [place]

**R. & D.** abbr. research and development.

**ră′ndom. 1.** n. At **~**, without aim or purpose or principle. **2.** a. Made, done, etc., at random (*random sample, selection*). [F *randon* f. Gmc]

**ră′nd|y̆** a. (**~ily, ~iness**). Lustful, eager for sexual gratification; (Sc.) loud-tongued, boisterous. [perh. rel. to RANT]

**ra′nee, ra′nǐ,** (rah′nǐ) n. Hindu queen; raja's wife or widow. [RAJ]

**răng.** See RING².

**range** n. **1.** v.t. & i. Place in row(s) or in specified arrangement; traverse in all directions; reach, lie spread out, be found over specified area, vary between limits; rove, wander, (*over, through,* etc.). **2.** n. Row, line, tier, series, esp. of buildings or mountains; large open area for grazing or hunting; open or enclosed area with targets for shooting; area over which thing is found or has effect or relevance; scope, (region between) limits of variation, distance attainable or to be covered by gun or projectile or by vehicle without refuelling, extent of time covered by forecast etc.; cooking fireplace; **~-finder,** instrument to estimate distance of object for shooting, photography, etc. **3. rā′nger** (-nj-) n., (esp.) keeper of royal park or forest, ‖senior Guide; **rā′ngy̆** (-nji) a., tall and slim. [F (RANK¹)]

**rani.** See RANEE.

**rănk¹. 1.** n. Row, line; place where taxis await customers; soldiers in single line abreast (**the ~s, the ~ and file,** common soldiers, fig. ordinary undistinguished people; **close ~s,** maintain solidarity; **other ~s,** soldiers other than officers; **rise from the ~s,** of common soldier given commission, or of self-made man, advance by one's own exertions); order, array, (**keep, break, ~,** remain, fail to remain, in line); place in a scale; position in hierarchy, grade of advancement; distinct social class, grade of dignity, (high) station, (*people of all ranks;* in the front or top rank of performers; **pull ~,** make unfair use of one's seniority etc.; **~ and fashion,** high society). **2.** v.t. & i. Arrange (esp. soldiers) in rank; classify, give certain grade to; have rank or place (*ranks among the Great Powers, next to the king,* etc.); \*have senior position among members of hierarchy etc.; **~′er** n., (commissioned officer who has been) soldier in the ranks. [F *ranc* f. Gmc]

**rănk²** a. Too luxuriant, coarse, choked with or apt to produce weeds or excessive foliage; foul-smelling, loathsome, indecent, corrupt; flagrant, virulent, gross, complete, (*rank treason, poison, nonsense, outsider*). [E]

**ră′nker.** See RANK[1].

**ră′nkle** *v.i.* (Of envy, disappointment, etc., or their cause) be bitter, give intermittent or constant pain. [F (*d*)*rancler* fester f. L *dra*(*cu*)*nculus* little serpent]

**ră′nsack** *v.t.* Thoroughly search (place, receptacle, person's pockets, one's conscience, etc.); pillage, plunder, (house, country, etc.). [N *rannsaka* (*rann* house, *saka* seek)]

**ră′nsom. 1.** *n.* (Liberation of prisoner in consideration of) sum of money or value paid for release; **hold person to ~,** be willing to release him for such consideration, (fig.) demand concessions from him by threat of damaging action; **worth a king's ~,** of immense value. **2.** *v.t.* Redeem, buy freedom or restoration of; hold to ransom, release for a ransom. [F f. L (REDEMPTION)]

**rănt. 1.** *v.i.* & *t.* Use bombastic language; declaim, recite theatrically; preach noisily. **2.** *n.* Piece of ranting. [Du.]

**ranŭn′cūl|us** *n.* (*pl.* ~uses, ~i *pr.* -ī). Plant of genus including buttercup; **~ā′ceous** (-shŭs) *a.* [L dim. of *rana* frog]

‖**R.A.O.C.** *abbr.* Royal Army Ordnance Corps.

**răp[1]. 1.** *n.* Smart slight blow (~ **on** or **over the knuckles,** fig., reproof); sound made by knocker on door or (Spiritualism) by some agency on table or floor; (sl.) blame, punishment, (**take the ~,** suffer the consequences); (sl.) a conversation. **2.** *v.t.* & *i.* (**-pp-**). Strike smartly; make sound called rap (*rapped at the door*); criticize adversely; (sl.) talk; ~ **out,** utter abruptly, (Spiritualism) express by raps. [prob. imit.]

**răp[2]** *n.* A small amount, the least bit, (*don't care a rap*). [abbr. Ir. *ropaire* counterfeit coin]

**rapā′cious** (-shŭs) *a.* Grasping, extortionate, predatory; **rapā′cĭtÿ** *n.* [L *rapax* (foll.)]

**rāpe[1]. 1.** *v.t.* Commit rape on (woman). **2.** *n.* Forcible or fraudulent sexual intercourse esp. imposed on woman; (poet.) carrying off by force; (fig.) forcible violation with institution, country, etc., violation *of*. [AF *raper* f. L *rapio* seize]

**rāpe[2]** *n.* Plant grown as food for sheep and for its seed from which oil is made. [L *rapum, rapa* turnip]

**ră′pĭd. 1.** *a.* (~**er,** ~**est**). Quick, swift; acting or completed in short time; (of slope) descending steeply; ~**-fire,** firing shots, asking questions, etc., in quick succession; **rapĭ′dĭtÿ** *n.* **2.** *n.* (usu. in *pl.*) Steep descent in river-bed with swift current. [L (RAPE[1])]

**rā′pier** *n.* Light slender sword for thrusting only; ~**-thrust,** (fig.) delicate or witty repartee. [prob. LDu. f. F *rapière*]

**ră′pĭne** *n.* (rhet.) Plundering. [F or L (RAPE[1])]

**ră′pist** *n.* One who commits rape. [RAPE[1]]

**rappor′t** (-ōr′) *n.* (Esp. useful) communication, (harmonious) relationship or connection; **răppor′teur′** (-ēr′) *n.,* person who reports from committee to higher body. [F (L *porto* carry)]

**rapprochement** (răprŏ′shmahn) *n.* Resumption of harmonious relations esp. between States. [F (APPROACH)]

**răpscă′llion** (-yon) *n.* (arch. or joc.) Rascal. [perh. f. RASCAL]

**răpt** *a.* Carried away bodily or in spirit from earth, life, consciousness, or ordinary thoughts and perceptions (*away, up,* etc.); absorbed, enraptured, intent, (*listen with rapt attention*); ~**or′ial** *a.* & *n.,* predatory (animal or bird); ~**′ure** *n.,* ecstatic delight, (in *pl.*) vehement pleasure or the expression of it (**be in, go into, ~ures,** be enthusiastic, talk enthusiastically); ~**′urous** (-cher-) *a.* [L *raptus* (RAPE[1])]

**rara avis** (rāī′a ā′vĭs, rāī′a ă′vĭs) *n.* Rarity, kind of person or thing rarely encountered. [L, = rare bird]

**rāre[1]** *a.* With only loosely packed substance, of less than usual density, (*the rare atmosphere of the mountain tops*); few and far between, uncommon, unusual, exceptional, seldom found or occurring (*it is rare for* person etc. *to do,* it is *rarely that* person etc. does); of uncommon excellence, remarkably good, very amusing; ~ **bird,** *rara avis*; WELSH[1] *rarebit*; ~ **earth,** (oxide of) any of a group of similar metallic elements; **rār′efÿ** *v.t.* & *i.,* lessen density or solidity of, refine, make (idea etc.) subtle, become less dense; **rārefǎ′ction** *n.;*

**~'lў** (rār'lĭ) *adv.*, (esp.) seldom, not often; **rār'ĭtў** *n.*, rareness, uncommon thing. [L *rarus*]

**rāre²** *a.* (Of meat) underdone. [E]

**rār'ĭng** *a.* (colloq.) Enthusiastic, eager, (*to go* etc.). [part. of *rare*, dial. var. ROAR or REAR¹]

**ra'scal** (-ah'-) *n.* Rogue, knave, (often joc., esp. to child: *you lucky rascal!*); **rască'lĭtў** *n.*; **~'lў** *a.* [F *rascaille* rabble]

**rase.** See RAZE.

**răsh¹** *n.* Eruption of skin in spots or patches; (fig.) sudden widespread onset of (*a rash of strikes*). [orig. unkn.]

**răsh²** *a.* Hasty, impetuous, reckless, acting or done without due consideration. [E]

**ră'sher** *n.* Thin slice of bacon or ham. [orig. unkn.]

**rasp** (-ah-). **1.** *n.* Coarse kind of file having separate teeth. **2.** *v.t. & i.* Scrape with rasp, scrape roughly, scrape *off* or *away*; grate upon (person or his feelings), make grating sound, say gratingly. [F *raspe(r)*]

**ra'spberry** (-ah'zb-) *n.* (Bramble bearing) usu. red berry like blackberry; (sl.) sound or gesture expressing derision or dislike; **~-cane**, raspberry plant. [orig. unkn.]

**răt. 1.** *n.* Rodent like large mouse (**like a drowned ~**, of person, wet through; **Rats!**, sl. nonsense!, drat it!; **smell a ~**, have suspicions of foul play etc.); similar rodent (MUSK, WATER, *-rat*); (Polit.) person who deserts his party in difficulties; blackleg; (colloq.) unpleasant person; **~-catcher** (who kills houses of rats); **~ race**, fiercely competitive struggle, struggle to maintain one's position in work or life; **~'sbane**, thing poisonous to rats. **2.** *v.i.* (-tt-). Hunt or kill rats; play the rat in politics; **~ on**, desert (person). [E & F f. Rom.]

**rătafi'a** (-fē'a) *n.* Liqueur flavoured with almonds or fruit-kernels; kind of biscuit similarly flavoured. [F]

**ratatouille** (rahtahtoo'ĭ) *n.* Provençal stew of vegetables. [F dial.]

**ră'tchĕt** *n.* Set of teeth on edge of bar or wheel with catch allowing motion in one direction only; **~(--wheel)**, wheel with rim so toothed. [F *rochet* lance-head]

**rāte¹. 1.** *n.* Stated numerical proportion between two sets of things (*moving at a rate of 10 m.p.h.*); amount etc. stated for application to all comparable cases; standard or way of reckoning; (measure of) value or cost (*rate of exchange, of interest*); **at any ~**, in every possible case, even if a stronger statement may be true; **at that** or **this ~**, colloq., if this is a fair specimen or true assumption); rapidity of movement or change (*travelling, increasing, at a great rate*); class (FIRST, SECOND, THIRD, TENTH, *-rate*); ‖assessment by local authorities levied on value of buildings and land owned, (in *pl.*) amount thus paid by householder etc.; ‖**~'payer**, person liable to pay rates. **2.** *v.t. & i.* Estimate or assign worth or value of; consider, regard as; ‖subject to payment of local rate, value for assessment of rates; *be worthy of, deserve; rank or be rated *as*; **~'able** (-ta-) *a.* (-bly), (‖esp.) liable to local rates (**~able value** of house etc., as assessed for these); **rā'tĭng¹** *n.*, (esp.) ‖ amount fixed as local rate, ‖non-commissioned sailor, tonnage-class of racing yacht, estimated size of audience to show popularity of a broadcast, estimated standing of person as regards credit etc. [F f. L *rata* (RATIO)]

**rāte²** *v.t. & i.* Scold angrily. [orig. unkn.]

**rateable.** See RATE¹.

**rā'tel** (or -ah'-) *n.* African and Indian nocturnal carnivorous burrowing mammal. [Afrik.]

**ra'ther** (rah'dh-) *adv.* More truly, to a greater extent, or to be more precise, (*is rather good than bad*; *late last night*, or rather, *early this morning*; **the ~ that**, so much the more because); in a modified way, to some extent, (*I rather think you know him*; *the performance was rather a failure*, *was rather good, fell rather flat*); by preference, as an alternative chosen sooner *than* another (of same grammatical form, or *inf.* after finite v.; *would much rather not go*; *the desire to seem clever rather than honest*; **had ~**, would rather); ‖(colloq., in answer) most emphatically, yes without doubt, (*Have you been here before?—Rather!*). [E compar. (*rathe* early)]

**ră'tifу** *v.t.* Confirm or accept (agreement made in one's name) by formal consent, signature, etc.; **~icā'tion** *n.* [F f. L (RATE¹)]

**rā'tĭng¹.** See RATE¹.

**rā'tĭng²** *n.* Angry reprimand. [RATE²]

**rā'tĭō** (-shĭ-) *n.* (*pl.* ~s). Quantitative relation between two similar magnitudes determined by the number of times one contains the other integrally or fractionally (*are in the ratio of three to two*; INVERSE *ratio*); **rătĭŏ'cĭnāte** *v.i.*, reason, use syllogisms; **ratĭŏcĭnā'tion** *n.*; **rātĭŏ'cĭnative** *a.*; **rā'tion**, (*n.*; usu. in *pl.*) fixed daily allowance of food served out esp. for members of Services, fixed allowance of food etc. for civilians in time of shortage (**~n book, card**, document entitling holder to ration), single portion *of* provisions, fuel, clothing, etc., (*v.t.*) limit (persons, food, clothing) to fixed ration, share (*out*) food etc. in fixed quantities; **rā'tional** *a.* (-**lly**), endowed with reason, sensible, moderate, of or based on reason(ing), rejecting what is unreasonable or cannot be tested by reason in religion or custom, (Math., of quantity or ratio) expressible as ratio of integers; **rătiona'le** (-ah'l, -ah'lĭ) *n.*, fundamental reason, logical basis, *of*; **rā'tionalism** *n.*, practice of treating reason as ultimate authority in religion as elsewhere, theory that reason is the foundation of certainty in knowledge; **rā'tionalist** *n. & a.*; **rătionali'stic** *a.* (-ically); **rătionă'lĭtỹ** *n.*; **rā'tionalize** *v.t. & i.*, explain (away) by rationalism, bring into conformity with reason, make (an industry) more efficient by scientifically reducing or eliminating waste, (colloq.) find 'reasons' for irrational or unworthy behaviour; **rătionalizā'tion** *n.* [L (*reor rat-reckon*)]

**rā'tlĭn(e), -lǐng**, *n.* (usu. in *pl.*) One of the small lines fastened across ship's shrouds like ladder-rungs. [orig. unkn.]

**rattă'n** *n.* Palm with long thin many-jointed pliable stems; piece of rattan stem used as cane etc. [Malay]

**răt-tă't** *n.* Rapping sound, esp. of knocker. [imit.]

**ră'ttle. 1.** *v.i. & t.* Give out rapid succession of short sharp hard sounds, cause such sounds by shaking something (*he rattled at the door*); talk in lively thoughtless way; move or fall with rattling noise, drive vehicle or ride or run briskly (*down, along, past*, etc.); make (chain, window, crockery, etc.) rattle; say or recite (stories, list) rapidly (*off, out*, etc.); (sl.)

agitate, frighten. **2.** *n.* Instrument or plaything made to rattle esp. to give alarm or to amuse babies; set of horny rings in rattlesnake's tail; plant with seeds that rattle in their cases when ripe; rattling sound (DEATH-*rattle*); uproar, bustle, noisy gaiety, racket; **~-brain, -head, -pate**, (person with) frivolous mind; **~snake**, venomous Amer. snake with rattling structure in tail; **~trap** *n. & a.*, rickety (vehicle etc.). **3. ră'ttler** *n.*, *(*esp.*)* rattlesnake; **ră'ttling**, (*a.*, esp.) brisk, vigorous, (*a rattling pace*), (*adv.*) remarkably (*good* etc.). [prob. LDu.]

**ră'ttỹ** *a.* Relating to or infested with rats; (sl.) irritable, touchy. [RAT]

**rau'cous** *a.* Harsh-sounding, hoarse. [L]

**ră'vage. 1.** *v.t. & i.* Devastate, plunder; make havoc (in). **2.** *n.* Devastation; (esp. in *pl.*) destructive effect *of*. [F alt. RAVINE rush of water]

**rāve. 1.** *v.i.* Talk wildly or furiously (as) in delirium (*about, against, at*; **raving mad**, uncontrollably mad so as to rave); (of sea, wind, etc.) howl, roar; speak with rapturous admiration *about, over*, go into raptures. **2.** *n.* (colloq.) Highly enthusiastic review of film, play, etc.; (sl.) infatuation. [prob. F dial. *raver*]

**ră'vel. 1.** *v.t. & i.* (∥-ll-). Entangle, become entangled; confuse, complicate (thread etc. or fig. question, problem); fray out; ~ (**out**), disentangle, unravel, distinguish separate threads or subdivisions of. **2.** *n.* Tangle, knot, complication. [perh. Du. *ravelen*]

**rā'ven**[1] *n.* Large glossy blue-black hoarse-voiced crow; (*attrib.*, of hair etc.) glossy black. [E]

**ră'ven**[2] *v.i. & t.* Plunder, seek *after* prey or booty; devour (food, or abs.) voraciously; **~ous** *a.*, rapacious, voracious, very hungry; **ravi'ne** (-ēn) *n.*, deep narrow gorge. [F *raviner* f. L (RAPINE)]

**răvĭŏ'lĭ** *n.* Small pasta cases containing meat etc. [It.]

**ră'vish** *v.t.* Commit rape on (woman); enrapture, fill with delight; (arch.) carry off by force; **~ment** *n.* [F f. L (RAPE[1])]

**raw. 1.** *a.* Uncooked; unripe; in unwrought or untreated state; not (completely) manufactured; (of silk) as reeled from cocoons; (of alcoholic spirit) undiluted; crude in artistic quality, lacking finish; inexperienced, untrained, (*is a raw lad*; *raw* RECRUIT); stripped of skin, having flesh exposed, sensitive to touch from being so exposed; (of edge of cloth) without hem or selvage; (of atmosphere, day, etc.) damp and chilly; **~-boned**, gaunt; *raw* DEAL²; **~'hide**, (rope or whip of) untanned leather; **~ material**, that from which process of manufacture makes articles. **2.** *n.* Raw place on person's or esp. horse's skin; **in the ~**, in its natural state without mitigation (*life in the raw*), naked; **touch** person **on the ~**, wound his feelings on point(s) where he is sensitive. [E]

**ray¹** *n.* Single line or narrow beam of light from small or distant source; straight line in which radiation is propagated to given point, (in *pl.*) radiation of specified type (X-RAYS; **~ gun**, imaginary weapon causing injury by emission of rays); (fig.) remnant or beginning of enlightening or cheering influence (*a ray of hope*); any of set of radiating lines or parts or things; marginal part of composite flower e.g. daisy. [F f. L RADIUS]

**ray²** *n.* Large marine food-fish allied to shark. [F *raie* f. L *raia*]

**ray³**, **re¹** (rā), *n.* (Mus.) Second note of scale; note D. [L *resonare*, wd arbitrarily taken]

**ray'ŏn** *n.* Textile fibre or fabric made from cellulose. [P]

**rāze, rāse** (-z), *v.t.* Completely destroy, level with the ground, (house, town, etc.); usu. *raze to the ground*); erase, scratch out, (esp. fig.). [F f. L *rado ras-* scrape]

**rā'zor** *n.* Instrument with sharp edge(s) used in cutting hair esp. from skin (SAFETY *razor*); **~-bill**, auk with sharp-edged bill; **~-blade**, flat piece of metal with usu. two sharp edges used in safety razor; **~-edge**, keen edge, sharp mountain ridge, critical situation, sharp line of division, (*on a ~-edge* or *~'s edge*, in great danger); **~-fish, -shell**, bivalve with shell like handle of cutthroat razor. [F *rasor* (prec.)]

**ră'zzle(-dă'zzle)** *n.* (sl.) Excitement, bustle, spree (*on the razzle*); noisy advertising. [redupl. DAZZLE]

**răzz(a)mătă'zz** *n.* (colloq.) = prec.; old-fashioned, sentimental, or

insincere actions; humbug. [prob. alt. prec.]

**R.C.** *abbr.* Roman Catholic.

‖**R.C.A., R.C.M., R.C.O., R.C.P.,** *abbrs.* Royal College of Art, Music, Organists, Physicians.

‖**R.C.S.** *abbr.* Royal College of Science; Royal College of Surgeons; Royal Corps of Signals.

**Rd.** *abbr.* road.

**rē²** *prep.* (Law etc.) In the matter of (as first word in headline stating matter to be dealt with); (colloq.) about, concerning. [L, abl. of *res* thing]

**'re** *v.* (colloq., usu. after *prons.*) = *are* (see BE). [abbr.]

**rē-¹** (or **rĕ**) *pref.* in vbs. and vbl derivs. (sometimes **red-** before vowels: *redeem, redolent*), denoting: in return, mutual(ly), (*react, resemble*), opposition (*repel, resist*), behind, after, (*relic, remain*), retirement, secrecy, (*recluse, reticence*), off, away, down, (*recede, relegate, repress*), frequentative or intensive force (*redouble, refine, resplendent*), negative force (*recant, reveal*). [L]

**rē-²** (or **rĕ**) *pref.* attachable to almost any vb. or vbl deriv., denoting *once more, again, anew, afresh*, (esp. to alter or improve or renew); *back, with return to previous state*. The following list contains the more established words of obvious meaning; unless otherwise stated, the pronunciation is that of the main word with (rē) prefixed.

**readdress**; **readjust(ment)**; **re-admit(tance)**, **-ission**; **reaffirm-(ation)**; **reafforest(ation)**; **re-align(ment)**; **reanimate, -tion**; **reappear(ance)**; **reapply**; **re-appoint(ment)**; **reappraise, -sal**; **rearm(ament)**; **rearrange(ment)**; **reascend**; **reassemble**; **reassert-(ion)**; **reassess(ment)**; **reassign-(ment)**; **rebind**; **rebirth**; **reborn** *v.* & *n.*; **re-cede** (cf. RECEDE); **re-capture** *v.* & *n.*; **re-cede** (cf. RECEDE); **re-charge** *v.* & (rē'-) *n.*; **reclothe**; **recoat** (cf. RECOIL); **re-collect** (cf. RECOLLECT); **recolour**; **recombine, -nation**; **recom-mence(ment)**; **reconquer, -quest**; **reconvert, -ersion**; **re-count** *v.* & (rē'-) *n.* (cf. RECOUNT); **re-cover** (cf. RECOVER); **re-create, -tion** (cf. RECREATE, -TION); **recross**; **re--deal**; **redecorate, -ation**; **re-**

descend; redesign; redirect(ion); rediscover(y); redissolve; re-distribute, -tion; redivide, -ision; re-do; re-dress (cf. REDRESS); redye; re-elect(ion); re-eligible; re-embark(ation); re-emerge, -ence, -ent; re-enact(ment); re-engage(ment); re-enter, -trance, -try; re-establish(ment); re-examine, -nation; re-export v. & n.; reface; refashion; refill v. & (rē'-) n.; refloat; re-form(ation) (cf. REFORM); refuel; refurbish; refurnish; re-fuse (cf. REFUSE); regrind; regroup; rehang; re-hear; reheat; rehouse; reignite; reimport v. & n.; reimpose, -sition; reincarnate v. & a., -tion; reincorporate v.; reinsert-(ion); reinter(ment); reinterpret-(ation); reintroduce, -uction; reinvest(ment); reinvigorate, -tion; reissue n. & v.; rejoin¹ (cf. REJOIN²); rekindle; relabel; re-lay (cf. RELAY); reline; relive; reload v.; remake n. & (rē'-) n.; remarry, -riage; remilitarize; remint; re-model; remonetize; re-mount; rename; renationalize; re-number; reoccupy, -pation; re-open; reorder; reorganize, -zation; reorient(ate); repack; repaint; repaper; repartition v.; repass(age); repatriate, -tion; repeople; replant(ation); re-point; repolish; repopulate; re-possess(ion); repot; reprint v. & (rē'-) n.; republish, -ication; re-purchase; repurify, -fication; re-read; re-route; rerun; resale; reseat; resell; reset; resettle-(ment); reshape; re-sign (cf. RESIGN); resole; re-sort (cf. RE-SORT); respell; restart; restate-(ment); restock; re-strain (cf. RESTRAIN); restructure; resurface; resurvey v. & n.; retake; retell; retranslate, -tion; retread¹; re-trim; returf; retype; reunite; re-urge; reuse v. & n.; revaccinate, -tion; revictual; revisit; revital-ize; rewind; rewire; reword; re-work; rewrite.

||**R.E.** *abbr.* Royal Engineers.

**reach. 1.** *v.t.* & *i.* Stretch out, extend, (*out* etc.; *reached out his hand, its branches*; *fog reaching from coast to coast*); stretch out the hand etc., make reaching motion or effort (lit. or fig.); (Naut.) sail with wind abeam or abaft the beam; get as far as, attain to, arrive at, (specified point or object of destination, or abs.), succeed in affecting with the hand or instrument or missile or influence, (*reached land*; *is on vacation and cannot be reached*; *your letter reached me today*; *has reached agreement with them, middle age, its sixth edition*; *number of applications reached 200*); hand, pass or take with outstretched hand, (*reached him the book*; *reached down his bat*); ||∼-me-**-down** *a.* & *n.*, (sl.) ready-made (garment). **2.** *n.* Act of reaching out; extent to which hand etc. can be reached out, influence be exerted, motion carried out, or mental powers be used (**within** one's ∼, **above, out of, beyond,** one's ∼, possible, impossible, of being grasped by stretching out the hand, or (fig.) of attainment or performance; *within easy reach of the airport*; *no help was within reach*); continuous extent, esp. part of river that can be looked along at once between two bends, or part of canal between locks; (Naut.) distance traversed in reaching. [E]

**rē̆ǎ'ct** *v.i.* Produce reciprocal or responsive effect; (Chem. of substance, Phys. of particle etc.) be cause of activity or interaction *with* another; respond *to* stimulus, under-go change or show behaviour due to some influence; be actuated by repulsion *against*, tend in reverse or backward direction; ∼**ion** *n.*, re-acting, responsive feeling (*what was his reaction to the news?*), occurrence of condition after its opposite (e.g. glow after cold bath), (esp. Polit.) ten-dency to oppose change or to return to former system; ∼**ionary** *a.* & *n.*, (Polit.) (person) showing reaction; ∼**ivate** *v.t.*, restore to state of activity; ∼**ive** *a.*, showing reaction; ∼**or** *n.*; (nuclear) ∼**or**, assembly of materials in which controlled nuclear chain reaction takes place. [RE-¹]

**read. 1.** *v.t.* & *i.* (read *pr.* rĕd). Interpret mentally, declare inter-pretation of, (read *dream, riddle, others' thoughts*, person's MIND, **cards** or person's **hand** as fortune-teller); (be able to) convert into intended words or meaning (written or other symbols or things so expressed, or abs.; *reads* or *can read* shorthand, music, *Dutch*; *cannot read or write*); (of com-puter) copy or transfer (data); reproduce mentally or (often *aloud, out,* or w. ind. obj.) vocally, while following symbols with eyes or fingers, the words of (author, book, letter, etc., or abs.; *read the story over or through*; *read it to me*; *have no time to read*; ~ person a **lecture** or **lesson**, reprove him; *the Bill was* ~ **for the first etc. time**, allowed its first etc. READING; ~**s well**, has good intonation or expressiveness; **take as** ~, dispense with actual reading of); study by reading (esp. subject at university; *is reading for the Bar*); (in *p.p.* w. act. sense as *a.*) versed in subject or literature by reading (*well read*); find thing stated in print etc. (*I have read somewhere that all is vanity*); interpret (statement, action) in certain sense (*my silence is not to be read as consent*); assume as intended or deducible from writer's words; bring into specified state by reading (*read myself to sleep*); (of recording instrument) show (figure etc.; *thermometer reads 20°*); convey meaning when read (*name reads from left to right*); sound or affect hearer or reader when read (*reads like a translation*); ~ **between the lines,** search for and discover hidden meaning; ~ **into,** assume to be implicit in (words); ~ **up,** make special study of (subject). **2.** *n.* Spell of reading. **3.** ~'**able** *a.* (-**bly**), able to be read with interest; ~'**er** *n.*, (esp.) publisher's employee who reports on submitted MSS., printer's proof-corrector, ‖university lecturer of high grade, person appointed to read aloud esp. in church, book of extracts for learning a language, device to produce image that can be read from microfilm etc.; ~'**ership** *n.*, (esp.) readers of newspaper etc.; ~'**ing** *n.*, (esp.) literary knowledge, entertainment at which something is read, (specified quality of) matter to be read (*is dull reading*), word(s) read or given by editor as text, figure etc. shown by recording instrument, interpretation or view taken *of* facts etc., one of three occasions on which a Bill must be presented to legislature for acceptance; ~**ing-lamp** (to give light for reading); ~**ing matter,** books etc. to read; ~**ing-room** (in club, library, etc., for those wishing to read). [E]

**rea′dy** (rĕ′-) *a.*, *adv.*, *n.*, & *v.* **1.** *a.* With preparations complete (*dinner is ready*); in fit state (*are ready to march*); with resolution nerved (*am ready to risk my life*); willing, inclined, (*is too ready to suspect*; *was ready to swear with rage*); about to (*a bud just ready to burst*); prompt, facile, (*is very ready with excuses*; *has a ready pen, wit*); provided beforehand; within reach, easily secured, (*a ready source of revenue*); fit for immediate use (*found an instrument ready to hand*); unreluctant (*found ready acceptance*); easy (*its ready solubility in water*); **make** ~, prepare (*they made ready for the attempt* or *to fight*); ~ **money,** actual coin or notes, payment on the spot; ~ **reckoner,** book or table of results of arithmetical computations of kind commonly wanted in business etc.; ~, **steady, go!** (formula for starting race). **2.** *adv.* Beforehand, so as not to require doing when the time comes, (*please pack everything ready*); ~**-made,** (of clothes) made in standard shapes and sizes, not to customer's individual measure, (fig.) commonplace, available without special effort; ~**-to-eat,** (of food) not needing to be cooked. **3.** *n.* (sl.) Ready money; **at the** ~, ready for action. **4.** *v.t.* Make ready, prepare. **5. rea′dily** (rĕ′-) *adv.*, without showing reluctance, willingly, without difficulty (*the facts may be readily ascertained*); **rea′diness** (rĕ′-) *n.*, willingness, facility, quickness in argument or action, ready or prepared state (*all is in readiness*). [E]

**rēā′gent** *n.* Substance used to cause chemical reaction, esp. to detect another reagent. [RE-¹]

**rē′al¹** (*or* rā′-, räah′l) *n.* (Hist.) Silver coin in Spanish-speaking countries. [Sp. (ROYAL)]

**rē′al²**. **1.** *a.* Actually existing as thing or occurring in fact, genuine, rightly so called, not artificial, (~ **life,** as lived by actual people, opp. fiction etc.; ~ **money,** coin, cash; **the** ~ **presence,** of Christ's body and blood in Eucharist; *real* TENNIS; **the** ~ **thing,** not makeshift or inferior; ~ **time,** actual time of process analysed by computer; **for** ~, sl., genuine); (Law) consisting of immovable property such as land or houses (*real estate*); appraised by purchasing power (*real wages*). **2.** *adv.* (Sc. & U.S. colloq.) Really, very. **3.** ~**ism** *n.*, practice of regarding things in their true nature and dealing with them as they are, fidelity to nature in representation, showing of life etc. as it is in fact, (Philos.) doctrine that abstract concepts have objective existence; ~**ĭst** *n*.; ~**ĭ'stĭc** *a*. (-ically); **rĕä'lĭtў** *n*., being real, resemblance to original, real existence, what is real or existent or underlies appearances, (in ~**ĭty**, in fact); ~**ĭze** *v.t.*, convert into fact (usu. in *pass.*), present or conceive as real, understand clearly, convert into money, acquire (profit), be sold for (specified price); ~**ĭzā'-tion** *n.*; **rĕ'ally** *adv.*, in reality (often *really and truly*), indeed, I assure you, I protest; **not** ~**ly**, in fact not; ~**ly?**, is that so?; \***tor** *n.*, real-estate agent; ~**tў** *n.*, real estate. [AF, & L *realis* (*res* thing)]

**realm** (rělm) *n*. Sphere, domain, (*the realm(s) of fancy, poetry*); (rhet. or Law) kingdom. [F f. L REGIMEN]

**ream** *n*. Twenty quires of paper; (usu. in *pl.*) large quantity of writing. [F ult. f. Arab., = bundle]

**reap** *v.t.* Cut (grain etc., or abs.) with sickle in harvest; gather in thus or with machine as harvest; (fig.) receive as consequence of one's own or others' actions (*reap the fruits of one's forethought*; ~ **where one has not sown,** profit by others' toil); harvest crop of (field etc.); ~**'ing-hook,** sickle; ~**'ing-machine** (for cutting grain and often binding sheaves without manual labour); ~**'er** *n.* (fig. of death personified). [E]

**rear**[1] *v.t.* & *i.* Bring up, foster, educate, cultivate, (cattle, children, crops, etc.); (of horse etc.) raise itself on hind legs; (rhet.) set upright, build, hold upwards, extend to great height. [E]

**rear**[2]. **1.** *n.* Hindmost part of army or fleet; space behind, (position at) back of, army or camp or person (**bring up the** ~, come last; **in the** ~, behind; **take in the** ~, attack from behind); back part of anything (**at the** ~ **of,** behind); (colloq.) buttocks, ‖lavatory. **2.** *a.* Hinder, back-; *rear-*ADMIRAL; ~**'guard,** [F *rereguarde*] body of troops detached to protect rear esp. in retreats (~*guard action,* engagement between rearguard and enemy, lit. or fig.); ~**-lamp, -light,** (usu. red, at rear of vehicle). **3.** ~**'mŏst** *a.*, furthest back; ~**'ward,** (*n.*) [AF *rerewarde* = *rear-guard*] rear, esp. in prep. phrs.: *to the rearward of*; *in the rearward*, (*a.* &

*adv.*) to the rear; ~**'wards** (-z) *adv.* [prob. abbr. *rearward* or *rearguard* (cf. VAN[2])]

**rea'son** (-z-). **1.** *n.* (Fact adduced or serving as) motive, cause, or justification (*give reasons for; I saw reason to be suspicious; there is no reason to suppose*); intellectual faculty characteristic esp. of human beings by which conclusions are drawn from premisses; sanity (*has lost his reason*); sense, sensible conduct, what is right or practical or practicable, moderation; **Age of R~,** 18th c. in England and France; **bring to** ~, induce to cease vain resistance; **by** ~ **of,** owing to; **in** ~, within the bounds of moderation; **listen to** ~, allow oneself to be persuaded by logic; *neither* RHYME *nor,* SEE[1], STAND *to, reason*; **with** ~, not unjustifiably; **within** ~, = *in reason*. **2.** *v.i.* & *t.* Use argument *with* person by way of persuasion; form or try to reach conclusions by connected thought silent or expressed (*from premisses, about subject*); conclude, assume as step in argument, say by way of argument, *that*; express in logical or argumentative form (*a reasoned exposition*), embody reason in (amendment etc.); persuade or bring by argument *out of* or *into* (*tried to reason him out of his fears*); think out (consequences etc.). **3.** ~**able** *a.* (-bly), having sound judgement, sensible, moderate, not expecting too much, ready to listen to reason, in accordance with reason, not greatly less or more than might be expected, inexpensive, not extortionate, tolerable, fair, (arch.) endowed with faculty of reason. [F f. L RATIO]

**rĕassŭr'|e** (-*a*shoor') *v.t.* Restore confidence to, dispel apprehensions of; confirm in opinion or impression; ~**ance** *n.* [RE-[2]]

‖**reave** *v.t.* (**reft**). (arch. or poet.; esp. in *p.p.*) Forcibly deprive *of*; take by force, carry off, (*away, from*). [E]

**rĕbar'batĭve** *a.* (literary). Repellent, unattractive. [F (*barbe* beard)]

**rĕbā'te. 1.** (or rĕ'-) *n.* Deduction from sum to be paid, discount. **2.** (or rā'bĭt) *n.*, & *v.t.* = RABBET. [F *rabattre* (RE-[1], ABATE)]

**rebel. 1.** (rĕ'bel) *n.* Person who fights against, resists, or refuses allegiance to, the established government; person or thing that resists authority or control; (*attrib.*) rebellious, of rebels, in rebellion. **2.** (rĭbĕ'l) *v.i.* (**-ll-**). Act as rebel (*against*); feel or manifest repugnance (*against* custom etc.). **3. rĕbĕ'llion** (-lyon) *n.*, organized armed resistance to established government (**the Great R~lion**, period of English history 1642–51), open resistance to any authority; **rĕbĕ'llious** (-lyus) *a.*, in rebellion, disposed to rebel, defying lawful authority, (of thing) unmanageable, refractory. [F f. L (RE-[1], *bellum* war)]

**rebound. 1.** (rĭbow'-) *v.i.* Spring back after impact; recoil *upon* agent (*their evil example will rebound upon themselves*). **2.** (rē'-) *n.* Act of rebounding, recoil; reaction after emotion (**take person on the ~**, utilize such reaction to persuade him to contrary of previously intended action etc.). [F *rebonder* (BOUND[2])]

**rĕbŭ'ff. 1.** *n.* Rejection of one who makes advances, proffers help or sympathy, shows interest or curiosity, makes request, etc.; repulse, snub. **2.** *v.t.* Give rebuff to. [F f. It.]

**rĕbū'ke. 1.** *v.t.* Subject to protest or censure (*for* fault etc.); reprove. **2.** *n.* Rebuking or being rebuked; reproof. [AF]

**rē'bus** *n.* Enigmatic representation of name, word, etc., by pictures etc. suggesting its syllables. [F f. L *rebus*, abl. pl. of *res* thing]

**rĕbŭ't** *v.t.* (**-tt-**). Force or turn back, check; refute, disprove, (evidence, charge); **~tal**, **~ment**, *ns.* [AF *rebuter* (BUTT[4])]

**rĕcă'lcĭtran|t** *a.* & *n.* (Person) objecting to restraint or obstinately disobedient; **~ce** *n.* [L *recalcitro* kick out (*calx* heel)]

**rĕca'll** (-aw'l). **1.** *v.t.* Summon to return from a place or from different occupation, inattention, digression, etc.; cancel or suspend appointment of (official sent to distance, esp. overseas); bring back to or *to* memory, serve as reminder of; recollect, remember; revive, resuscitate; revoke, annul, (action, decision); take back (gift). **2.** *n.* Summons to come back; cancelling or suspension of appointment abroad; possibility of recalling esp. in sense of annulling (*beyond* or *past recall*); act of remembering, ability to remember (**total ~**, ability to remem-

ber every detail of one's experience clearly). [RE-[2]]

**rĕcă'nt** *v.t.* & *i.* Withdraw and renounce (opinion, statement, etc.) as erroneous or heretical; disavow former opinion, esp. with public confession of error; **rēcăntā'tion** *n.* [L (CHANT)]

**rē'căp.** (colloq.) **1.** *v.t.* (**-pp-**). = foll. **2.** *n.* Recapitulation. [abbr.]

**rĕcapĭ'tŭlăte** *v.t.* & *i.* (**~able**). Go over main points or headings of, summarize, go briefly through again; **~ā'tion**, **~ātor**, *ns.*; **~ātĭve**, **~ātorў**, *adjs.* [L (CAPITAL)]

**rēca'st** (-ah'-). **1.** *v.t.* (**recast**). Put into new form, improve arrangement of. **2.** *n.* Recasting; recast form. [RE-[2]]

**rē'ccė** (rĕ'kĭ). (sl.) **1.** *n.* Reconnaissance. **2.** *v.t.* & *i.* Reconnoitre. [abbr.]

**rēcē'de** *v.i.* (for *re-cede* see RE-[2]). Go or shrink back or farther off; be left at increasing distance by observer's motion; slope backwards; withdraw (*from* engagement, opinion, etc.); decline in value etc. [L *recedo* -*cess-* (CEDE)]

**rēcei'pt** (-sē't). **1.** *n.* Amount of money etc. received (usu. in *pl.*); fact or action of receiving or being received (*goods will be sent on receipt of remittance*); written acknowledgement of this, esp. of payment of sum due; (*arch.*) recipe. **2.** *v.t.* Place written receipt on (bill). [AF *receite* (foll.)]

**rēcei'v|e** (-sē'v) *v.t.* Accept delivery of, take (proffered thing) into one's hands or possession; accept (stolen goods though knowing of the theft, or abs.); consent to hear (confession, oath) or consider (petition); bear up against, stand force or weight of, encounter with opposition; admit, consent or prove able to hold, provide accommodation for, submit to, serve as receptacle of, (*had to receive the visits, attentions*, etc. *of*); admit to membership of church etc.; be marked (lit. or fig.) more or less permanently with (impression etc.); convert (broadcast signals) into sound or picture; entertain (person as guest, company at formal reception, or abs.); greet, welcome, esp. in specified manner, (*you stay here and receive him; how did she receive his offer?*; *was received with cries of 'Traitor'; news* *was received with horror*); (esp. in *p.p.*) give credit to, accept as authoritative or true, (*an axiom universally received*; **~ed pronunciation,** form of English speech used, with local variations, by majority of educated English-speaking people); acquire, get, be given, be provided with, have sent to or conferred or inflicted on one, (*have not yet received my fee*; *receive a letter, news*; *receive the name of Thomas*; *pleasant to receive sympathy*; *deserves more attention than it receives*; *receive orders to march*); (abs.) partake of; **be at or on the ~ing end,** (colloq.) bear the brunt of something unpleasant; **~er** *n.,* (esp.) person appointed by court's **~ing-order** to administer property of bankrupt or insane person or property under litigation, person who receives stolen goods, receptacle etc. for receiving something in machine or instrument (esp. part of telephone that contains ear-piece), radio or television receiving apparatus. [F f. L *recipio -cept-* get back again]

**re̅ce̅n|t** *a.* Not long past, that happened or began to exist or existed lately; not long established, lately begun, modern; **~cy̆** *n.* [F or L *recens -ent-*]

**re̅ce̅p't|acle** *n.* Containing vessel, place, or space; (Bot.) common base of floral organs, axis of cluster; **~ion** *n.,* receiving or being received (esp. of person into place or company), ||place where guests register on arriving at hotel etc., formal or ceremonious welcome, occasion of receiving guests, assembly held for this esp. after wedding, (**~ion room,** one available or suitable for receiving company or visitors), welcome or greeting of specified kind, demonstration of feeling towards person or project, receiving of broadcast signals, efficiency with which these are received; **~ionist** *n.,* person employed by hotel, dentist, etc., to receive clients; **~ive** *a.,* able or quick to receive impressions or ideas; **re̅ce̅pti'vity** *n.* [F or L (RECEIVE)]

**re̅ce̅'ss. 1.** Temporary cessation from work, esp. of Parliament; niche or alcove of wall; remote or secret place. **2.** *v.t.* & *i.* Place in a recess; provide with recess(es); *take recess, adjourn. **3.** **~ion** (-shŏn) *n.,* receding or withdrawal from place or point, temporary decline in economic ac-

tivity or prosperity; **~ional** (-shŏn-) *a.* & *n.,* (hymn) sung while clergy and choir withdraw after service; **~ive** *a.,* tending to recede. [L *recessus* (RECEDE)]

**recherché** (resha̅r′sha̅) *a.* Devised or got with care or difficulty; (excessively) far-fetched or thought out. [F]

**re̅chri̅'sten** (-krī′sen) *v.t.* Christen again; (fig.) give new name to. [RE-2]

**re̅ci̅'divi̅s|t** *n.* One who relapses into crime; **~m** *n.* [F f. L *recidivus* falling back (RECEDE)]

**re̅'cipe** *n.* Statement of ingredients and procedure for preparing dish etc. in cookery; medical prescription; expedient. [L, 2nd sing. imper. of *recipio* RECEIVE]

**re̅ci̅'pient** *n.* Person who receives thing. [F f. It. or L (as prec.)]

**re̅ci̅'proc|al. 1.** *a.* (**-lly**). In return (*reciprocal help*); mutual (*reciprocal love*); (Gram.) expressing mutual relation ('*each other*' is a reciprocal PRONOUN). **2.** *n.* (Math.) Expression or function so related to another that their product is unity ($\frac{1}{5}$ *is the reciprocal of* 5). **3.** **~ate** *v.t.* & *i.* (**~able**), give and receive mutually, interchange, (influence etc.), requite (affection etc.), make a return (*with thing so given*), (Mech.) go with alternate backward and forward motion; **~a'tion,** **~ator,** *ns.;* **re̅ci̅pro̅'ci̅ty** *n.,* reciprocal condition, mutual action, give-and-take. [L *reciprocus* moving to and fro]

**re̅ci̅'t|e** *v.t.* & *i.* Repeat aloud or declaim (poem, passage) from memory; give recitation (**~ing-note,** that held for indefinite number of syllables in chanting); (Law) rehearse (facts) in document, enumerate; **~al** *n.,* detailed account *of* connected things or facts, narrative, act of reciting, performance of programme by one musician with or without accompanist (*vocal, piano, recital*); **re̅cita̅'tion** *n.;* **re̅citati̅'ve** (-e̅′v) *n.,* musical declamation of kind usual in narrative and dialogue parts of opera and oratorio. [F, or L *recito* read out]

**re̅ck** *v.i.* & *t.* (rhet. or poet., in neg. & interrog. sents. only.) Care, be troubled, concern oneself; **~ of,** pay heed to; **~'less** *a.,* regardless of consequences, danger, etc. [E]

**rĕ′ckon** *v.t. & i.* Ascertain (number, amount), ascertain number or amount of, by counting or usu. by calculation, compute; start *from*, go on *to*, in counting (things, or abs.); count *up*, sum *up* character of; arrive at as total (*I reckon 53 of them*); include in computation, count *in*, place in class *among* or *with* or *in*, take *for*, regard *as*, consider (*to be*); conclude after calculation, be of the confident opinion, (*that*); make calculations, cast up account or sum, (~ **with**, take into account); reckon *without* one's HOST²); settle accounts *with* person; rely or count or base plans (*up*)*on*; ~**ing** *n.*, (esp.) bill in public house etc.; **day of** ~**ing**, time when something must be atoned for or revenged; DEAD *reckoning*; **out** in one's ~**ing**, mistaken in a calculation or expectation. [E]

**rĕclai′m. 1.** *v.t.* Win back or away from vice or error or waste condition; bring under cultivation esp. from state of being flooded by sea or marsh; ask for return of (one's property); **rĕclamā′tion** *n.* **2.** *n.* Reclaiming or being reclaimed. [F f. L *reclamo* exclaim]

**rĕclī′ne** *v.t. & i.* Assume, be in, horizontal or leaning position; (in *p.p.*, of person) lying thus; sit with back or side supported at considerable inclination to vertical; lay (esp. one's head, body, or limbs) in such position. [F f. L *reclino*]

**rĕclu′se** (-lōō′s) *a. & n.* (Person) given to or living in seclusion or isolation, esp. as religious discipline. [F f. L *recludo -clus-* shut away]

**rĕ′cognīze** *v.t.* Acknowledge validity or genuineness or character or claims or existence of, discover or realize nature of, treat *as*, acknowledge *for*, realize or admit *that*; know again, identify as known before; ~**ī′tion** *n.*, recognizing or being recognized; ~**ĭzable** *a.* (-bly), (esp.) that can be identified or detected; ~**ĭzabĭ′lĭtў** *n.*; **rĕcŏ′gnĭzance** (*or* -kŏ′n-) *n.*, bond by which person engages before court or magistrate to observe some condition, e.g. to keep the peace, pay a debt, or appear when summoned, sum pledged as surety for such observance. [F f. L *recognosco*]

**rĕcoi′l. 1.** *v.i.* (for *re-coil* see RE-²). Suddenly move or spring back, shrink mentally, in horror or disgust or fear; rebound after impact; (of gun) be driven backwards by discharge; ~ **upon**, have adverse reactive effect on (its originator). **2.** *n.* Act or fact or sensation of recoiling. [F *reculer* f. L *culus* buttocks]

**rĕcollĕ′ct** *v.t.* (for *re-collect* see RE-²). Succeed in remembering, call to mind; ~**ion** *n.*, act or power of recollecting, thing recollected, person's memory, time over which it extends, (*happened within my recollection*). [L *recolligo* (COLLECT²)]

**rĕcommĕ′nd** *v.t.* Commend *to* God or a person or his care etc.; speak or write of or suggest as fit for employment or favour or trial (*to* person, *for* post, promotion, *as* remedy, etc.); (of qualities, conduct, etc.) make acceptable, serve as recommendation of; advise (course of action or treatment, person *to do*, *that* thing should be done); ~**ā′tion** *n.*; ~**atorў** *a.* [L (RE-¹)]

**rĕ′compĕnse. 1.** *v.t.* Requite, reward or punish, (person or action); make amends to (person) or for (loss etc.). **2.** *n.* Reward, requital, retribution. [F f. L (COMPENSATE)]

**rĕ′concīle** *v.t.* Make friendly after estrangement (persons to one another, person *to* or *with* another, person to oneself); (usu. in *refl.* or *pass.*) make acquiescent or contentedly submissive (*to* what is disagreeable, *to* doing, or abs.); settle (quarrel etc.); harmonize, make compatible, show compatibility of by argument or in practice; ~**ment** (-lm-), **rĕconcĭliā′tion**, *ns.* [F or L (CONCILIATE)]

**rĕ′condite** (*or* rĭkŏ′n-) *a.* (Of subject or knowledge) abstruse, out of the way, little known; (of author or style) dealing in recondite knowledge or allusion, obscure. [L (*recondo -dit-* put away)]

**rĕcondĭ′tion** *v.t.* Overhaul, renovate, make usable again. [RE-²]

**rĕcŏ′nnaissance** (-nĭs-) *n.* Military etc. examination of region to locate enemy or ascertain strategic features; preliminary survey; **rĕconnoi′tre** (-ter), *-ter, v.t. & i.*, make reconnaissance of (enemy, district), make reconnaissance. [F (RECOGNIZE)]

**rĕconsi′der** *v.t.* Consider again, esp. for possible change of decision; ~**ā′tion** *n.* [RE-²]

**rĕcŏ′nstĭtūte** *v.t.* Build up again from parts; restore previous constitution of (dried food etc.) by adding water; piece together (past events) into intelligible whole; re-organize; ~**u′tion** n.

**rĕconstrŭct′** v.t. Build again; restore mentally; reorganize; ~**ion** n.

**record. 1.** (rĭkor′d) v.t. Set down for remembrance or reference, put in writing or other permanent form; convert (sound, broadcast programme, etc.) to permanent form for later reproduction. **2.** (rĕ′-) n. State of being recorded or preserved in writing etc. (**on ~**, legally or otherwise recorded; **go on ~**, act so that one's words etc. are recorded; **court of ~**, whose proceedings are recorded and valid as evidence of fact; **matter of ~**, thing established as fact by being recorded); official report of proceedings and judgement in cause before court of record, copy of pleadings etc. constituting case to be decided by court (**keep to the ~**, abstain from introducing irrelevant matter); piece of recorded evidence or information, account of fact preserved in permanent form, document or monument preserving it, (**for the ~**, official(ly), for sake of recording facts; **off the ~**, unofficial(ly), secret(ly); **put the ~ straight**, correct a misapprehension; (**Public R~ Office**, institution keeping official archives for public inspection); object serving as memorial, portrait etc.; trace made by recording instrument on disc or cylinder for subsequent reproduction by gramophone; similar trace on magnetic tape etc.; disc etc. bearing copy of such trace (~**-player**, apparatus for reproducing sound from gramophone records); facts known about person's past (*has an honourable record of service*; **have a ~**, have been convicted on previous occasion); (often *attrib.*) best performance or most remarkable event of its kind on record (**break** or **beat the ~**, outdo all predecessors). **3.** rĕcor′der n., (esp.) judge in certain courts, recording instrument, recording-apparatus, = TAPE-*recorder*, (Mus.) vertical (English) flute; **rĕcor′ding** n., (esp.) process of recording sound etc. for later reproduction, sound etc. thus recorded, television programme recorded on film, material on which it has been recorded. [F *record(er)* f. L (*cor cord-* heart)]

**rĕcou′nt** v.t. (for *re-count* see RE-[2]). Narrate, tell in detail. [AF *reconter* (RE-[2], COUNT[1])]

**rĕcou′p** (-ōō′p) v.t. & i. Compensate (loss, person loss or *for* loss); ~ (oneself), recover what one has expended or lost; ~**ment** n. [F *recouper* cut back]

**rĕcour′se** (-ors′) n. Resorting to possible source of help (**have ~ to**, adopt as adviser, helper, or expedient); person or thing resorted to. [F f. L (COURSE)]

**rĕco′ver** (-kŭ′-) v.t. & i. (for *re-cover* see RE-[2]). Regain possession or use or control of, acquire or find (out) again, reclaim, (~ oneself, regain consciousness, calmness, control of limbs, senses; ~ one's feet or legs, stand up after fall); secure (restitution, compensation, damages, or abs.) by legal process; retrieve, make up for, cease to feel effects of, (*must try to recover lost time*); come back to consciousness, health, or normal state or position (*have or am quite recovered from my illness*; *sat down to recover from his agitation*); ~**ў** n., act or process of recovering or being recovered. [AF *recoverer* f. L (RE-CUPERATE)]

**rĕ′crean|t** a. & n. (rhet. or poet.) Craven, coward(ly), apostate; ~**cȳ** n. [F f. *recroire* surrender f. L (CREED)]

**rĕ′cre|āte** v.t. & i. (for *re-create* see RE-[2]). (Of pastime etc., or *refl.* of person) refresh, entertain, agreeably occupy; indulge in recreation; ~**ā′tion** n., (means of) recreating oneself, pleasurable exercise or employment, (~**ation ground**, public land for games etc.); ~**ātĭve** a. [L *recreo* (CREATE)]

**rĕcrī′mĭn|āte** v.i. Make mutual or counter accusations; ~**ā′tion** n.; ~**ātĭve**, ~**ātorȳ**, adjs. [L (CRIME)]

**rĕcrūdĕ′sce** (-ōō-) v.i. (Of sore, disease, etc., or fig. of discontent etc.) break out again; ~**nce** n.; ~**nt** a. [L (CRUDE)]

**rĕcrui′t** (-rōō′t). **1.** n. Newly enlisted and not yet fully trained soldier; person who joins a society etc.; (**raw**) ~, beginner. **2.** v.t. & i. Enlist recruits for (army, crew, society, etc.), enlist (person) as recruit; get or seek recruits; replenish, reinvigorate, (numbers, stock, strength, etc.); ~**ment** n. [F dial. *recrute* (CREW)]

**rĕ´ctal** *a.* Of or by means of rectum. [RECTUM]

**rĕ´ctăng**‖**le** (-nggel) *n.* Four-sided plane rectilinear figure with 4 right angles, esp. one with adjacent sides unequal; **~ular** (-ă´ngg-) *a.*, (having base or sides or section) shaped like rectangle, (having parts or lines) placed at right angles; **~ulă´rĭtў** *n.* [F or L]

**rĕ´ctĭ‖fў** *v.t.* Make right, adjust, (method, calculation, statement, position, instrument); exchange for what is right (anomaly, error, grievance); (Chem.) purify or refine by repeated distillation or other process; (Electr.) convert (alternating current) to direct current; **~ficā´tion** *n.*; **~fier** *n.* (esp. Electr.) [F or L (*rectus* straight)]

**rĕctĭlī´nĕar, -ĕal,** *a.* In or forming a straight line; bounded or characterized by straight lines. [L (as prec.)]

**rĕ´ctĭtūde** *n.* Moral uprightness, righteousness, correctness. [F or L (*rectus* right)]

**rĕ´ctŏ** *n.* (*pl.* **~s**). Right-hand page of open book, front of leaf (cf. VERSO). [L, = on the right (side)]

**rĕ´ctor** *n.* (In Ch. of England) incumbent of parish where all tithes formerly passed to incumbent (cf. VICAR); (in R.C. Ch.) head priest of church etc.; head of university, college, school, or religious institution; (**Lord**) **R~**, students' elected representative on governing body of Sc. univ.; **rĕctor´ĭal** *a.* (-lly); **~ship** *n.*; **~ў** *n.*, ‖rector's benefice, rector's house. [F or L (*rego rectrule*)]

**rĕ´ct‖um** *n.* (*pl.* **~ums, ~a**). Final section of large intestine, terminating at anus. [L, = straight]

**rĕcŭ´mben‖t** *a.* Lying down, reclining; **~cў** *n.* [L (*cumbo* lie)]

**rĕcŭ´per‖āte** (*or* -ōō´-) *v.t. & i.* (**~able**). Restore, be restored or recover, from exhaustion, illness, loss, etc.; **~ā´tion** *n.*; **~atĭve** *a.* [L *recupero*]

**rĕcŭr´** *v.i.* (-rr-; *part. pr.* -ĕr´-, -ŭ´r-). Go back in thought or speech *to*; (of idea etc.) come back *to* one's mind etc., return to mind; (of problem etc.) present itself again; occur again, be repeated, (**~ring decimal**, decimal fraction in which same figures are repeated indefinitely); **rĕcŭ´rrence** *n.*; **rĕcŭ´rrent** *a.*, recurring. [L (*curro* run)]

**rĕcŭr´v‖e** *v.i. & t.* Bend backwards; **~ate** *a.*, recurved. [L (RE-²)]

**rĕ´cūsan‖t** (-z-) *a. & n.* (Person) refusing submission to authority or compliance with regulation (*against*); (Hist.) (person) who refused to attend Anglican services; **~cў** *n.* [L *recuso* refuse]

**rēcy´cle** *v.t.* Return to previous stage of cyclic process, esp. convert (waste) to reusable material. [RE-²]

**rĕd. 1.** *a.* (-dd-). Of colour from crimson to orange, as seen in blood, sunset clouds, rubies, glowing coals, human lips, and fox's hair; flushed in face with shame, anger, etc.; (of hands) blood-stained; (of eyes) bloodshot, or sore with weeping; (of hair) reddish-brown, tawny; (as distinguishing epithet) *red deer, ant, cabbage,* etc.; having to do with bloodshed, burning, violence, or revolution (SEE¹ *red*; *a red republican*); anarchistic or communistic (*Red*) Russian, Soviet, (*the Red Army*); *red* ADMIRAL; **~-blooded,** virile, vigorous; **~´breast,** robin; ‖**~´-brick,** (of university) of modern foundation; **~´cap,** ‖military policeman, *railway porter; ~ **carpet,** privileged treatment of important visitor; **~ cell,** erythrocyte; *~ **cent,** smallest (orig. copper) coin; **~´coat,** (Hist.) British soldier; **~ corpuscle,** erythrocyte; **Red Cross,** (in Muslim countries) **Red Crescent,** (emblem of) international ambulance etc. service; *red* CURRANT, ENSIGN, FLAG³, ‖GROUSE¹; **~-ha´nded,** in the act of crime (*caught red-handed*); **~ hat,** cardinal's hat, (symbol of) cardinal's rank; **~´head,** person with red hair; **~ heat,** being red-hot (lit. or fig.), temperature of red-hot thing; **~ herring,** herring(s) reddened by being cured in smoke (*neither* FISH¹, *flesh, nor good red herring*), (fig.) irrelevant diversion; **~-hot,** heated to redness, highly exciting or excited, enthusiastic, furious; *red-hot* POKE¹r; ‖**Red INDIAN;** *red* LEAD²; **~-letter,** (of day) marked with red letter(s) in calendar as saint's day or festival, (fig.) memorable as date of joyful occurrence; **~ light,** red lamp as danger-signal on road, railway, etc. (*see the ~ light*, fig., realize approach of disaster); **~-light district** (containing many brothels); **~ man,** = Red Indian; **~ meat,** beef, mutton, etc., (opp. *white meat*); **~-**

**pepper,** CAYENNE pepper, ripe fruit of PEPPER; **~'poll,** red-crested bird similar to linnet; **~ rag,** thing that excites person's rage as red object enrages bull; red ROAN[1]; **~ rose,** emblem of Lancashire or Lancastrians; **~'shank,** large kind of sandpiper; **~-shift,** (Astron.) movement of spectrum to longer wavelengths in light from distant galaxies etc.; **~'skin,** = Red Indian; **~ squirrel,** native English species; **~'start,** red-tailed song-bird [obs. steort tail]; **~ tape,** excessive use of or adherence to formalities esp. in public business; **~ wine** (coloured red by grape-skins); **~'wing,** thrush with red wing-coverts; **~'wood,** tree yielding red wood. **2.** n. Red colour, pigment, clothes or material (dressed in red), ball in billiards etc.; debit side of account (**in the ~,** in debt); revolutionary radical or republican; anarchist, communist. **3. ~'den** v.i. & t.; **~'dish, ~'dy,** adjs. [E]

**red-.** See RE-[1].

**rèdee'm** v.t. Recover by expenditure of effort or by stipulated payment (redeem one's rights or honour, mortgaged land); make single payment to cancel (regular charge or obligation); convert (tokens etc.) into goods or cash; fulfil (promise); purchase freedom of (person), save (person's life) by ransom; save, rescue, reclaim, (of God or Christ) deliver from sin and damnation; make amends for, counterbalance, compensate, (fault, defect; has one redeeming feature); save from a defect or oneself from blame; **~er** n. (esp. Christ); **rèdè'mption** n., redeeming or being redeemed (**past** or **beyond redemption,** such that there is no hope of redemption), thing that redeems. [F redimer or L (emo buy)]

**rèdeploy** v.t. Send (troops, workers, etc.) to new place or task; **~ment** n.; **rèdiffū'sion** (-zhŏn) n., relaying of broadcast programmes esp. by wire from central receiver. [RE-[2]]

**rĕ'dolen|t** a. Fragrant; having strong smell, (fig.) strongly suggestive or reminiscent, of or with; **~ce** n. [F or L (oleo smell)]

**rèdou'ble** (-dŭ'-). **1.** v.t. & i. Make or grow greater or more intense or numerous, (redouble one's efforts; the clamour redoubled); (Bridge)

double again a bid already doubled by opponent. **2.** n. (Bridge). Redoubling of a bid. [F (RE-[1])]

**rèdou'bt** (-ow't) n. Outwork or field-work without flanking defences. [F redoute (REDUCE)]

**rèdou'btab|le** (-ow't-) a. (**~ly**). (Of opponent etc.) formidable. [F (DOUBT)]

**rèdou'nd** v.i. Result in contributing, make great contribution, to one's credit, advantage, etc. [F f. L (unda wave)]

**rèdrĕ'ss. 1.** v.t. (for re-dress see RE-[2]). Readjust, set straight again, remedy, rectify, (wrong, grievance, etc.); **~ the balance,** restore equality. **2.** n. Reparation for wrong; redressing of grievance etc. [F (DRESS)]

**rèdū'c|e** v.t. & i. (**~ible**). Convert to or other (esp. simpler or more general) form (reduce fraction to its lowest terms, oral traditions to writing, compound to components); make suitable or conformable or adapted to, bring by classification or analysis to (reduce observations to formula); bring by force or necessity to some state or action, subdue, bring back to obedience, (was reduced to despair, to borrowing); bring lower; weaken (is in a very reduced state); diminish (reduce liquid to half its bulk; reduce the prices of the goods, the temperature of the mixture); impoverish (**~ed circumstances,** poverty after prosperity); (Chem.) convert (oxide etc.) to metal; lessen one's weight or size. [L (duco duct-lead)]

**reductio ad absurdum** (rĭdŭktĭō ăd absĕr'dum) n. Proof of falsity by showing absurd logical consequence; carrying of principle to unpractical lengths. [L, = reduction to the absurd]

**rèdŭ'ct|ion** n. Reducing or being reduced; amount by which prices etc. are reduced; reduced copy of picture etc.; **~ive** a. [F or L (REDUCE)]

**rèdŭ'ndan|t** a. Superfluous; ||(of industrial worker) liable to dismissal as being no longer needed for any available job; that can be omitted without loss of significance; **~cy̆** n. [L (REDOUND)]

**rèdū'plic|ate** v.t. (**~able**). Make double, repeat; repeat (letter, syllable), form (tense) thus; **~ā'tion** n., (esp.) repetition of syllable (exactly or with change of vowel etc.: *hurly--burly*, *see-saw*); ~**ative** a. [L RE-²]

**rē-ĕ'chŏ** (-kō) v.t. & i. Echo; echo again and again, resound. [RE-¹]

**reed** n. (Tall and straight stalk of) firm-stemmed water or marsh plant (**broken** ~, unreliable person or thing; vibrating part of some musical wind-instruments; (usu. in *pl.*) such instrument(s); ‖~**mace**, tall waterside plant with brown flower-spikes; ~**pipe**, musical pipe of reed, reeded organ-pipe; ~**stop**, reeded organ-stop; ~**'ĕd** a., (esp.) with vibrating reed; ~**'ў** a. (-ily, -iness), full of reeds, like reed, like reed-instrument in tone. [E]

**reef.** 1. n. One of several strips along top or bottom of sail that can be taken in or rolled up to reduce sail's surface in high wind (**take in a** ~, lit., or fig. proceed cautiously; ~**knot**, double knot made symmetrically); ridge of rock, sand, etc., at or near surface of water; (fig.) hazardous obstacle; lode of ore, bedrock surrounding this. 2. v.t. Take in reef(s) of (sail); ~**'er** n., (esp.) marijuana cigarette. [LDu. f. N]

**reek.** 1. n. Foul or stale smell; (Sc. or literary) smoke, vapour, visible exhalation. 2. v.i. Smell unpleasantly (*of* garlic, tobacco, blood; fig. *of* corruption, affectation, etc.); emit smoke, vapour, etc. [E]

**reel.** 1. n. Cylindrical device on which thread, silk, yarn, paper, film, wire, etc., are wound; quantity of thread etc. thus wound; contrivance for winding and unwinding line as required esp. in fishing (**off the** ~, fig., without pausing); revolving part in various machines; reeling motion (lit. or fig.); (music for) lively esp. Scottish dance. 2. v.t. & i. Wind (thread, fishing-line, etc.) on reel; draw (fish etc.) *in* or *up* by use of reel; rattle (story, list, verses) *off* without pause or apparent effort; stand or walk or run unsteadily, be shaken physically or mentally, rock from side to side, or swing violently, (*his mind, the ship, reeled under the shock*; *reel to and fro like a drunken man*); dance reel. [E]

**rē-ĕ'ntrant** a. & n. (Angle) pointing inwards (opp. *salient*; esp. in Fortif.); reflex (angle). [RE-²]

**reeve¹** n. (Hist.) Chief magistrate of town or district. [E]

**reeve²** v.t. (**rove**, ~**d**). (Naut.) Thread (rope, rod, etc.) *through* ring or other aperture; fasten (rope, block, etc.) *in, on, round, to,* something by reeving. [prob. Du. *reven*]

**reeve³.** See RUFF¹. [orig. unkn.]

**rĕf** n. (colloq.) Referee. [abbr.]

**rĕfĕ'ct|ion** n. Slight meal; refreshment by food or drink; ~**ory** (or rĕ'fĭ-) n., room for meals in monastery, college, etc.; ~**ory table** (long and narrow). [F f. L *reficio* renew]

**rĕfĕr'** v.t. & i. (-rr-). Trace or ascribe *to* person or thing as cause or source, consider as belonging *to* certain date or place or class; send on or direct (person, question *for* decision), make appeal or have recourse, *to* some authority or source of information, (abs.) cite authority or passage, (*for proof I refer to Proverbs 10: 19*; *referred to his watch for the exact time*; *let us refer the dispute to Socrates*; ~ *to drawer*, banker's note suspending payment etc. of cheque); send (person) to medical specialist etc.; send proposal etc. *back to* lower body, court, etc.; interpret (statement etc.) as being directed *to*; (of statement etc.) have relation, directed, *to* (*these remarks refer only to deliberate offences*); (of person speaking etc.) make allusion, direct attention, *to*; fail (candidate); ~**able** (or rĕ'fer-) a.; ~**referee'**, (n.) person to whom dispute is (to be) referred for decision, umpire esp. in football or boxing, ‖person willing to testify to character of applicant for employment etc., (v.i. & t.) act as referee (*for*). [F f. L *refero relat*- carry back]

**rĕ'ference** (-fr-) n. Referring of matter for decision or settlement or consideration to some authority; scope given to such authority (TERMS *of reference*); relation, respect, correspondence, *to* (*success seems to have little reference to merit*; **in** or **with** ~ **to**, regarding, as regards, about; **without** ~ **to**, not taking account of); allusion *to* (*made reference, a* or *no reference, to our previous conversation*); direction *to* (page etc. of) book etc. where information may be found (*gives many, verify your, references*, CROSS-*reference*), book or passage so cited, (~ **mark**, used to refer reader of text to note or to part of diagram, esp. asterisk \*, obelisk or dagger †, double obelisk ‡, section §, parallel

‖, paragraph ¶); act of looking up passage etc., or of referring another or applying to person, for information (*reference to the dictionary would have enlightened him*; *please give me a reference to your last employer*); ~ (**book**), book to be used not for continuous reading but for consulting on occasion; person willing to testify to character of applicant for employment or of would-be credit-account customer etc.; testimonial; **refere̱'ntial** (-shal) *a*.

**refere̱'nd|um** *n*. (*pl*. ~**a**, ~**ums**). Referring of political question to electorate for direct decision by general vote; **refe̱r'ral** *n*., referring of person to medical specialist etc. [L (REFER)]

**refı̱'ne** *v.t. & i*. Free from impurities or defects; make elegant or cultured, make delicate in feeling or taste, polish manners or appearance of; improve (*up*)*on* by refinements; become pure or clear or improved in polish or delicacy; employ subtlety of thought or language, make fine distinctions; ~**ment** (-nm-) *n*., (esp.) fineness of feeling or taste, polished manners etc., subtle or ingenious manifestation *of* (*a refinement of reasoning, torture*), piece of elaborate arrangement, instance of improvement (*up*)*on*, piece of subtle reasoning, fine distinction; ~**r** *n*., (esp.) person whose business is to refine crude oil, sugar, etc.; ~**ry** *n*., place where oil etc. is refined. [RE-¹]

**refı̱t. 1.** (-ı̱'-) *v.t. & i*. (-tt-). Make or become fit again (esp. of ship undergoing renewal and repairs). **2.** (-e̱'-) *n*. Refitting. [RE-²]

**refla̱'tion** *n*. (Econ.) Inflation following deflation to restore previous condition; **refla̱'te** *v.t.*, cause reflation of (currency, economy, etc.). [RE-², after DEFLATION, INFLATION]

**refle̱'ct** *v.t. & i*. (Of surface or body) throw back (heat, light, sound, object, etc.); (of mirror etc., or transf.) show image of, reproduce to eye or mind, correspond in appearance or effect to, (~**ing telescope**, reflector); (of action, result, etc.) bring back or cause to redound (credit etc.), (abs.) bring discredit, (*up*)*on* person or method responsible; go back in thought, meditate, or consult with oneself (*on*, *upon*, or abs.), remind oneself or consider (*that*, *how*, etc.); make disparaging remarks (*up*)*on*; ~**ion**, ‖**refle̱'xion** (-kshon), *n*., (esp.) reflected light or heat or colour or image, (piece of) censure (*on* or *upon*), thing bringing discredit (*up*)*on*, reconsideration (*on reflection, I feel I was wrong*), idea arising in the mind, comment (*on*, *upon*); ~**ive** *a*., (of surface etc.) giving back reflection or image, (of mental faculties) concerned in reflection or thought, (of person, mood, etc.) thoughtful, given to meditation; ~**or** *n*., (esp.) piece of glass or metal for reflecting light in required direction, (telescope etc. using) mirror to produce images; **re̱'flex**, (*n*.) reflected light or image, secondary manifestation (*law is a reflex of public opinion*), a reflex action (*doctor tested patient's reflexes*; cf. CONDITION), (*a*.) bent backwards (**reflex angle**, exceeding 180°); **reflex action** (independent of the will, as automatic response to nerve-stimulation, e.g. sneeze); **reflex** (**camera**), camera in which image is reflected by mirror to allow focusing up to moment of exposure; **refle̱'xed** (-kst) *a*., bent back; **refle̱'xive** *a. & n*., (Gram.) (word or form) implying subject's action on himself or itself (*pride oneself*); reflexive PRONOUN. [F or L (*flecto flex-* bend)]

**refo̱'rm. 1.** *v.t. & i*. (for *re-form* see RE-²). Make (person, institution, procedure), (of persons) become, better by removal of faults or errors; abolish, cure, (abuse, malpractice). **2.** *n*. Removal of abuse(s) esp. in politics; improvement made or suggested. **3. refo̱rma̱'tion** *n*., (esp.) radical change for the better in political, religious, or social affairs; **the R~ation**, 16th-c. movement for reform of abuses in Roman Church ending in establishment of **Reformed** (= Protestant) **Churches**; **reforma̱'tional** *a*.; ~**ative**, ~**atory**, *adjs*., tending or intended to produce reform; ~**er** *n*., (esp.) leader in the Reformation, advocate of reform. [F or L (RE-²)]

**refra̱'ct** *v.t.* (Of water, air, glass, etc.) deflect (ray of light etc.) at certain angle when it enters obliquely from another medium of different density; ~**ion** *n*.; ~**ive** *a*.; ~**or** *n*., refracting medium or lens, telescope using lens to produce image. [L *refringo -fract-* break open]

**refra̱'ctory. 1.** *a*. (-ily, -iness).

Stubborn, unmanageable, rebellious; (of disease, wound, etc.) not yielding to treatment; (of substance) hard to fuse or work. **2.** *n.* Substance specially resistant to heat, corrosion, etc. [L (prec.)]

**refrai'n**[1] *n.* Recurring phrase or line(s) esp. at end of stanzas; music accompanying this. [F f. L (REFRACT)]

**refrai'n**[2] *v.i.* Abstain from doing something; abstain *from* act or do*ing.* [F f. L (*frenum* bridle)]

**refra'ngib|le** (-nj-) *a.* (~ly). That can be refracted. [L (REFRACT)]

**refre'sh** *v.t.* (Of food, drink, rest, etc., or person providing these, esp. in ~ oneself) give fresh spirit or vigour to; freshen up (memory, esp. by consulting source of information); ~er *n.*, (esp.) extra fee to counsel in prolonged case, (colloq.) a drink; ~er course (reviewing previous studies, or giving instruction in modern methods etc.); ~ment *n.*, refreshing or being refreshed in mind or body, thing (esp. usu. in *pl.*, drink or food) that refreshes. [F (FRESH)]

**refri'ger|ate** *v.t.* & *i.* (~able). Make or become cool or cold; subject (food etc.) to cold in order to freeze or preserve; ~ant *a.* & *n.*, (substance) that cools; ~a'tion *n.*; ~ator *n.*, (esp.) cabinet or room in which food etc. is refrigerated. [L *refrigero* (*frigus* cold)]

**reft.** See REAVE.

**re'fug|e** *n.* (Place of) shelter from pursuit or danger or trouble (*seek refuge*; *take refuge in a cave*, *in lying*); person, thing, course, that gives shelter or is resorted to in difficulties; traffic island; ~ee' *n.*, person taking refuge, esp. in foreign country from religious or political persecution, or from war, earthquake, etc. [F f. L *refugium* (*fugio* flee)]

**refu'lgen|t** *a.* Shining, gloriously bright; ~ce *n.* [L *refulgeo* shine brightly]

**refu'nd. 1.** (-ŭ'-) *v.t.* & *i.* Pay back (money, expenses, or abs.), reimburse. **2.** (-ē'-) *n.* Refunding, repayment. [F or L (*fundo* pour)]

**refu's|e. 1.** (rifū'z) *v.t.* & *i.* (for *re-fuse* see RE-[2]). Say or convey by action that one will not accept or submit to or give or grant or gratify or consent (*refuse offer, gift, chance, person* as husband etc., *orders, obedience*; *refuse* to do; *car refuses to*

*start*); not grant request made by (person); (of horse) be unwilling to jump (fence etc., or abs.); make refusal. **2.** (rĕ'fūs) *n.* & *a.* (What is) rejected as worthless or left over after use. **3. refu'sal** (-z-) *n.*, refusing or being refused; (**first**) ~al, right or privilege of deciding to take or leave a thing before it is offered to others. [F]

**refu'te** *v.t.* Prove falsity or error of (statement etc., person advancing it); rebut by argument; **refuta'tion** *n.* [L *refuto*]

**regai'n** *v.t.* Recover possession of (*regain consciousness*); reach (place) again; recover (one's *balance* or *feet* or *footing* or *legs*). [F (RE-[2])]

**re'gal** *a.* (~ly). Of or by king(s); fit for a king, magnificent, (*regal splendour*); **rega'lia** (-lya) *n.pl.*, insignia of royalty used at coronations, insignia of an order or of civic dignity; **rega'lity** *n.* [F or L (*rex reg-* king)]

**rega'le** *v.t.* Entertain choicely (often iron.) with food or *with* talk etc.; (of beauty, flowers, etc.) give delight to. [F *regaler* (GALLANT)]

**rega'rd. 1.** *v.t.* & *i.* Gaze upon (usu. w. adv.; *found him regarding me with curiosity, intently*); give heed to, take into account, (person, advice, etc., or abs.); look upon or contemplate mentally in specified manner (*regard it in that light*) or with specified feeling (*I still regard him kindly*), or *as* being (*regard it as madness* or *indispensable*, him *as among my friends*); (of thing) concern, have relation to, have some connection with; **as ~s, ~ing** (*part.* or *prep.*), about, concerning, in respect of, so far as it concerns, (*considerations regarding war*; *am innocent as regards* or *regarding the former*). **2.** *n.* Gaze, steady or significant look; respect, point attended to, (*in this* etc. *regard*; **in** ~ **to** or **of, with** ~ **to,** regarding, in respect of; **in** person's ~, concerning or about or towards him); attention, heed, care, (*to* or *for*; *regard must be had* or *paid to general principles*; *act without regard to* or *for decency*; *pays no regard to advice*); esteem, kindly feeling or respectful opinion, (*for*; *have little* or *a great regard for him*, *no* or *a high regard for his judgement* or *advice*); (in *pl.*) expression of friendliness in letter etc., compliments, (*kind regards to*

*you all; give him my regards).* **3.** ~**ful**
*a.* (-**lly**), not neglectful *of;* ~**less** *a.*
& *adv.,* without paying attention,
without regard or consideration (*of*
expense etc., or abs.). [F *regard*(*er*)
(GUARD)]

**regă′tta** *n.* Meeting for boat or
yacht races. [It.]

**rĕ′gency** *n.* Office of regent; commission acting as regent; regent's or
regency commission's period of
office (**the R~**, 1810–20; **R~
stripes**, broad coloured equal stripes
on fabric etc.). [L *regentia* (REGENT)]

**rĕgĕ′ner|āte. 1.** *v.t.* & *i.* (~**able**).
Invest with new and higher spiritual
nature; improve moral condition of,
breathe new and more vigorous and
spiritually higher life into, (person,
institution, etc.); generate again,
bring or come into renewed existence. **2.** (-*at*) *a.* Spiritually born
again, reformed. **3.** ~**rā′tion,** ~**ātor,**
*ns.;* ~**ative** *a.* [L (RE-[2])]

**rĕ′gent. 1.** *n.* Person appointed to
administer State esp. kingdom during
minority, absence, or incapacity of
monarch. **2.** *a.* (placed after *n.*)
Acting as regent (*Prince Regent*). [F
or L (*rego* rule)]

**rĕ′ggae** (-ā) *n.* W. Ind. style of
music with strongly accented subsidiary beat. [W. Ind.]

**rĕ′gicide** *n.* Killer or (participator
in) killing of a king; **rĕgici′dal** *a.*
(-**lly**). [L (*rex reg*- king, *caedo* kill)]

**regi′me, ré-,** (răzhē′m) *n.* Method
or system of government, prevailing
system of things; **rĕ′gimen** *n.,*
(Med.) prescribed course of exercise,
way of life, and esp. diet; **rĕ′giment**
(*or* -jm-), (*n.*) permanent unit of
army usu. commanded by (Lieu-
tenant-)Colonel and divided into
several companies or troops or batteries, operational unit of artillery
etc., large array or number (usu. *of*),
(arch.) government (*monstrous regiment
of women*), (*v.t.*) form into regiment(s),
organize (esp. oppressively) in groups
or according to a system; **rĕgi-
mĕ′ntal,** (*a.*; -**lly**) of a regiment,
(*n.*; in *pl.*) dress worn by regiment,
military uniform; **rĕgimĕntā′tion**
*n.* [F f. L *regimen* (*rego* rule)]

**Regina** (rijī′na) *n.* Reigning queen
(abbr. *R.,* in signatures to proclamations: *Elizabeth R.*; in titles of Crown
lawsuits: ~ **v. Jones,** the Crown
*versus Jones*). [L, = queen (REX)]

**rĕ′gion** (-jon) *n.* Tract of land,

space, place, having more or less
definitely marked boundaries or
characteristics (*region between Elbe and
Rhine; a fertile region*); separate part
of world etc. (LOW[2]*er,* UPPER,
*regions*); sphere or realm *of* (*you are
getting into the region of metaphysics*);
**in the ~ of,** approximately); part
of the body (*the lumbar region*); ~**al**
(-jo-) *a.* (-**lly**). [F f. L (*rego* rule)]

**rĕ′gist|er. 1.** *n.* Book in which
items are recorded for reference;
official list e.g. of births, marriages,
and deaths, of shipping, of professionally qualified persons, of qualified voters in constituency, (~**er
office,** a registry); (Mus.) (sliding
part in organ controlling) set of
pipes; compass of voice or instrument, part of voice-compass; adjustable plate for widening or narrowing
an opening and regulating draught
esp. in fire-grate; indicator recording
speed, force, etc.; CASH *register.* **2.** *v.t.*
& *i.* (~**rable**). Set down (name,
fact, etc.) formally, record in writing;
(fig.) make mental note of; enter or
cause to be entered in particular
register (~**er a letter,** entrust it to
post office for transmission as ~**ered
post** with special precautions for
safety and for compensation in case
of loss; ~**ered nurse,** with State
certificate of competence in nursing);
put one's name on electoral etc.
register, or as guest in register kept
by hotel etc.; (of instrument) record
automatically, indicate; express
(emotion) facially or by gesture;
make impression on person's mind
(*name did not register with me*). **3.** ~**rār**
(*or* -ā′r′) *n.,* person charged with
keeping register (esp. in university),
doctor undergoing hospital training
as specialist; ~**rā′tion** *n.,* registering,
being registered; ~**ration mark,
number,** combination of letters and
figures identifying motor vehicle;
~**rў** *n.,* place or office where
registers or records are kept; ~**ry
(office),** place where marriages are
conducted without religious ceremony. [F or L (*regero* -*gest*- transcribe, record)]

‖**Rĕ′gius** *a.* ~ **professor,** holder
of chair founded by sovereign (esp.
one at Oxf. or Camb. instituted by
Henry VIII) or filled by Crown
appointment. [L, = royal (REX)]

**regrĕss. 1.** (rē′-) *n.* Going back;
relapse, backward tendency. **2.**

(rĭgrĕ's) *v.i.* Move backwards (lit. or fig.); **rĕgrĕ'ssion** (-shon) *n.*, backward movement, relapse, reversion, return to earlier stage of development; **rĕgrĕ'ssive** *a.* [L *regredior -gress-* go back]

**rĕgrĕt'. 1.** *v.t.* (**-tt-**). Feel sorrow for loss of, wish one could have again; be distressed about or sorry for (event, fact), grieve at, repent, (action etc.); be sorry *to* say etc. or *that* (esp. in polite refusal of invitation etc.). **2.** *n.* Sorrow for loss of person or thing; repentance or annoyance concerning thing done or not done; vexation or disappointment caused by occurrence or situation (*express regret, hear with regret of* or *that*; *refuse with much regret* or *many regrets*). **3.** ∼**table** *a.* (**-bly**), (esp., of events or conduct) undesirable, unwelcome, deserving censure; ∼**ful** *a.* (**-lly**), (of person, mood, etc.) full of regret. [F *regretter*]

**rĕ'gŭlar. 1.** *a.* (Of shape, structure, arrangement, or of objects in these respects) following or exhibiting a principle, harmonious, systematic, symmetrical, (*regular nomenclature, formation, features*); acting, done, recurring, uniformly or calculably in time or manner, habitual, constant, orderly, (*regular working, footsteps, sequence, employment*; **keep** ∼ **hours,** do same thing at same time daily; **a** ∼ **life,** one lived in orderly manner, esp. without excesses); (of person) defecating or menstruating at predictable times; conforming to a standard of etiquette or procedure; (Gram., of verb, noun, etc.) following normal type of inflexion; properly constituted or qualified, devoted exclusively or primarily to its nominal function, (∼ **army, soldiers,** opp. volunteers or militia or temporary levies); (colloq.) thorough, indubitable, (*is a regular rascal, hero*; *had a regular smash*); (Eccl.) bound by religious rule, belonging to religious or monastic order, (opp. *secular*). **2.** *n.* One of the regular clergy; regular soldier; (colloq.) regular customer, visitor, etc. **3.** ∼**ĭtў** (-ă'r-) *n.*; ∼**īze** *v.t.*; ∼**izā'tion** *n.*; **rĕ'gŭlate** *v.t.* (**-lable**), control by rule, subject to restrictions, adapt to requirements, alter speed of (machine, clock) so that it may work accurately; **rĕgŭlā'tion,** (*n.*) regulating or being regulated, prescribed

rule, (*a.*) in accordance with regulations, of correct pattern etc., usual; **rĕ'gŭlative** *a.*; **rĕ'gŭlător** *n.* (esp. of machine, clock, etc.). [F f. L (*regula* rule)]

**rĕgŭr'gĭtate** *v.i.* & *t.* Gush back; (of person, animal, stomach, or receptacle) cast or pour out again; ∼**ā'tion** *n.* [L (as INGURGITATE)]

**rĕhabĭ'lĭtate** *v.t.* (∼**able**). Restore to privileges, reputation, or proper condition, or to effectiveness by training (esp. after imprisonment or illness); ∼**ā'tion** *n.* [L (RE-², ABILITY)]

**rĕhăsh. 1.** (-ă'-) *v.t.* Put (old material) into new form without essential change or improvement. **2.** (-ē'-) *n.* Rehashing; material rehashed. [RE-²]

**rĕhear'se** (-hĕr's) *v.t.* Recite, say over; give list of, enumerate; have rehearsal of (play etc., part in it, or abs.); practise or train for later public performance; ∼**al** *n.*, rehearsing, performance of play or other entertainment preparatory to public performance (DRESS *rehearsal*). [AF (HEARSE)]

*Reich* (rīk, rīχ) *n.* The German commonwealth as a whole (**Third** ∼, Nazi regime 1933–45). [G]

**reign** (rān) **1.** *n.* Sovereignty, rule, (*Reign of* TERROR); period during which sovereign reigns (*in the reign of Anne*). **2.** *v.i.* Be king or queen (lit. or fig.; *reigned over France*); hold sway, prevail, (**silence** ∼**s,** all is quiet). [F f. L *regnum* (REX)]

**rĕimbur'se** *v.t.* Repay (person who has expended money, person's expenses); ∼**ment** (-sm-) *n.* [RE-², *imburse* (PURSE)]

**rein** (rān). **1.** *n.* (in *sing.* or *pl.*) Long narrow strap with each end attached to bit used to guide or check horse etc. in riding or driving, similar device to restrain child etc., (fig.) means of control, (**draw** ∼, stop one's horse; **give horse the** ∼(**s**), let it go its own way; **give** (**free**) ∼ **to,** let it go (one's imagination etc.) have free scope; **keep a tight** ∼ **on,** allow little freedom to). **2.** *v.t.* Check or manage with reins, (fig.) govern, restrain, control; pull *up* or *back* with reins, hold *in* with reins (horse, or abs.; lit. or fig.). [F *rene* f. L (RETAIN)]

**rei'ndeer** (rā'n-) *n.* (*pl.* usu. same). Subarctic deer used for drawing sledges and kept in herds for its milk, flesh, and hide. [N]

**rĕinfŏr'ce** v.t. Strengthen or support by additional men or material or by increase of numbers, quantity, size, etc. (lit. or fig.); **~d concrete** (with metal bars etc. embedded to increase its strength); **~ment** (-sm-) n., (esp., in pl.) additional men, ships, aircraft, etc., for military or naval force. [F renforcer]

**rĕinstā'te** v.t. Restore to or replace in lost position, privileges, etc.; restore to health or proper order; **~ment** (-tm-) n. [RE-², IN-¹]

**rĕinsur'|e** (-shoor') v.i. & t. Insure again (esp. of insurer securing himself by transferring risk to another insurer); **~ance** n. [RE-²]

**rĕi'ter|āte** v.t. Say or do again or repeatedly; **~ā'tion** n.; **~ātive** a. [L (ITERATE)]

**rĕjĕc't.** 1. v.t. Put aside or send back as not to be accepted, practised, believed, chosen, used, complied with, etc.; refuse acceptance of; vomit; **~ion, ~or,** ns. 2. (rē'-). Person or thing rejected. [L reicio -ject- throw back]

**rĕjoi'c|e** v.t. & i. Cause joy to, make glad; feel great joy; be glad that or to do, take delight in or at, (**~e in,** be blessed in the possession of, joc. have); make merry, celebrate some event; **~ings** (-z) n.pl., merry-making. [F rejoir (JOY)]

**rĕjoi'n²** v.t. & i. (for rejoin¹ see RE-²). Say in answer, retort; (Law) reply to charge or pleading; **~der** n., what is rejoined or said in reply, retort. [F rejoindre (JOIN)]

**rĕju'ven|āte** (-ōō'-) v.t. & i. Make or become young again; **~ā'tion, ~ātor,** ns. [L juvenis young]

**rĕlă'pse.** 1. v.i. Fall back, sink again, (into worse state after improvement). 2. n. Act or fact of relapsing, esp. deterioration in patient's condition after partial recovery. [L (labor laps- slip)]

**rĕlā'te** v.t. & i. Narrate, recount; bring into relation (to, with, or abs.; cannot relate the phenomena with or to anything we know or to each other); (in p.p.) connected, allied, akin by blood or marriage (is related to the royal family); have reference to, stand in some relation to, (notices nothing but what relates to himself). [L (REFER)]

**rĕlā'tion** n. Narration, a narrative; what one person or thing has to do with another, way in which one stands or is related to another, kind of connection or correspondence or contrast or feeling that prevails between persons or things, (**in ~ to,** as regards); (in pl.) dealings with others (PUBLIC relations), sexual intercourse; = relationship; kinsman, kinswoman, relative, (the squire and his relations; is he any relation to you?; he is no relation); **~al** a. (-lly); **~ship** n., state of being related, condition or character due to being related, kinship (lit. or fig.). [F or L (REFER)]

**rĕ'lativ|e.** 1. a. (Gram.) (of adj., adv., or PRONOUN) referring, and attaching a subordinate clause, to expressed or implied antecedent, (of clause) attached to antecedent by relative word; having mutual relations, corresponding in some way, related to each other; comparative (what are the relative merits of the two?); in relation to something else (relative density, humidity, pitch); proportioned to something else (supply is relative to demand); implying comparison ('heat', 'speed', 'strength', are relative words); not having absolute existence but conditioned (beauty is relative to the beholder's eye); having reference, relating, to (detailed the facts relative to the matter). 2. n. (Gram.) relative word, esp. relative pronoun; kinsman, kinswoman; relation by blood or by marriage; species related to another by common origin. 3. **~ĭtў** (-ĭ'v-) n., relativeness, (Phys.) (special) **~ity,** theory based on the principle that all motion is relative and that light has constant velocity, **general ~ity,** theory extending this to gravitation and accelerated motion; **~i'stic** a. (-ically), (of phenomena etc.) accurately described only by relativity theories. [F f. L (REFER)]

**rĕlă'x** v.t. & i. Cause or allow to become loose or slack or limp, enfeeble, mitigate, abate, (relax muscles, discipline, one's grasp or attention or efforts; **~ing climate,** causing sluggish feeling, opp. bracing); grow less tense or rigid or stern or ceremonious or energetic or zealous (his hold, hands, severity, features, manner, endeavours, relaxed; must not relax in my efforts); cease work or effort (take one's coat off and relax); **rĕlăxā'tion** n., (esp.) recreation, amusements, diminution of tension or severity or precision. [L *relaxo* (LAX)]

**rē′lay** (for *re-lay* see RE-²). **1.** *n.* Set of fresh horses substituted for tired ones; gang of men, supply of material, etc., similarly used; (Electr.) device activating a circuit; ~ (**race**), race between teams of which each person does part of the distance, the 2nd etc. members of a team starting when the 1st etc. finish. **2.** (*or* relā′) *v.t.* Receive (esp. broadcast message) and transmit to others. [F *relai* f. L (prec.)]

**relea′se. 1.** *v.t.* Set free, liberate, unfasten, (*from*); allow to move from fixed position; make (information, gramophone record, etc.) public; (Cinemat.) issue (film etc.) for (esp. general) exhibition. **2.** *n.* Liberation from restriction, fixed position, trouble, life, duty, etc.; handle, catch, etc., that releases part of machine etc.; document etc. made available for publication (*news, press, release*); film, record, etc., that is released; releasing of document, film, etc., thus. [F *reles*(*ser*) f. L (RELAX)]

**rē′lēg|āte** *v.t.* (~**able**). Banish to place of exile, consign or dismiss to inferior position; (Sport) transfer (team) to lower division of league etc.; ~**ā′tion** *n.* [L *relego* send away]

**relē′nt** *v.i.* Relax severity, abandon harsh intention, yield to compassion; ~**less** *a.*, unrelenting. [L (*lentus* flexible)]

**rē′lĕvan|t** *a.* Bearing on or pertinent *to* the matter in hand; ~**ce**, ~**cy̆**, *ns.* [L *relevo* (RELIEVE)]

**relī′|able** *a.* (-**bly**). That may be relied on; ~**abī′lĭty̆** *n.*; ~**ance** *n.*, trust, confidence, (*have, place, reliance on, in*), thing depended on (*the well is our chief reliance*); ~**ant** *a.* [RELY]

**rē′lĭc** *n.* Part of holy person's body or belongings kept after his death as object of reverence; memento, souvenir; (in *pl.*) dead body or remains of person, what has survived destruction or wasting or use; surviving trace or memorial *of* a custom, belief, period, people, etc.; object interesting because of age or associations; **rē′lĭct** *n.*, object surviving in primitive form, (arch.) widow *of.* [F *relique* f. L *reliquiae* remains (RELINQUISH)]

**relie′f** *n.* Alleviation of or deliverance from pain, distress, anxiety, etc., (*the medicine brought relief; gave a*

*sigh of relief; it is a relief to come across an optimist*; ~ **bus** etc., supplementing ordinary service; ~ **road,** by which traffic can avoid congested area); feature etc. that diversifies monotony or relaxes tension (*a blank wall without relief; a comic scene by way of relief*); assistance given to persons in special danger or need or difficulty (*a relief fund for the earthquake victims*); reinforcement (esp. raising of siege) *of* besieged town; (replacing of person or persons on duty by) person(s) appointed to take turn of duty; (esp. Law) redress of hardship or grievance; method of moulding or carving or stamping in which design stands out from surface with depth more (**high** ~) or less (**low** ~) closely approximating to that of objects imitated; piece of sculpture etc. in relief; appearance of being done in relief given by arrangement of line or colour or shading, distinctness of outline (lit. or fig.), vividness, (*stands out in relief; bring out the facts in full relief*); ~ **map,** showing hills and valleys by shading or colouring etc. rather than by contour lines alone. [F & It. (as foll.)]

**relie′v|e** *v.t.* Bring, give, be a, relief to (*besieged town was relieved; am much relieved to hear it; relieve distress or the distressed*); release (person) from duty by taking his place or providing a substitute; ~**e one's feelings,** use strong language or vigorous behaviour when annoyed etc.; ~**e nature,** one**self,** urinate or defecate; ~**e person of,** take (load, duties, restriction, or joc. purse etc.) from him; ~**ō** *n.* (*pl.* -**os**), = RELIEF (in sculpture etc.). [F f. L *relevo* raise again, alleviate

**relĭ′gion** (-jon) *n.* Particular system of faith and worship (*the Christian, Muslim, Buddhist, religion*; **freedom of** ~, right to follow whatever religion one chooses); human recognition of superhuman controlling power and esp. of a personal God or gods entitled to obedience and worship; effect of such recognition on conduct etc. (**get** ~, vulg. or joc., be converted to such recognition); life under monastic conditions (*her name in religion is Sister Mary*); thing that one is devoted to (*make a religion of football*); **relĭ′gious** (-jus), (*a.*) imbued with religion, pious, devout, of or concerned with religion, of or belonging to a monastic order; scrupulous, conscientious, (n.; pl. same) person bound by monastic vows. [F f. L (religio bond)]

**rèli'nquish** v.t. Give up, cease from, (habit, plan, hope, belief); resign, surrender, (right, possession); relax hold of (object held); ~ment n. [F f. L relinquo -lict- leave behind]

**rě'liquary** n. Receptacle for relic(s). [F or L (RELIC)]

**rě'lish. 1.** n. Flavour, distinctive taste of, slight dash or tinge of some quality; appetizing flavour, attractive quality, (sweets, jokes, lose their relish); enjoyment of food or other things, liking for, zest, (eat, read, etc., with relish; has no relish for poetry); thing eaten with plainer food to add flavour. **2.** v.t. & i. Serve as relish to, make piquant etc.; get pleasure out of, be pleased with, (do not relish the prospect); taste, savour, suggest presence, of. [F reles remainder (RELEASE)]

**rèlu'ctan|t** a. Unwilling, disinclined, (to do, or abs.; gave me reluctant assistance); ~ce n. [L (luctor struggle)]

**rèly'** v.i. Depend with confidence or assurance (up)on person or thing (I rely on you to do it, its being done, today). [F f. L religo bind closely]

**rèmai'n** v.i. Be left over after removal of or use of or dealing with the other part(s) etc. (the few pleasures that remain to an old man; outcome remains to be seen); be in same place or condition during further time, continue to exist, be left behind, (remain in London till Easter; let it remain as it is); (w. compl.) continue to be (one thing remains certain; remain faithful etc.); ~der, (n.) residue, remaining persons or things, (Law) residual interest in estate, or right of succession to title etc. on holder's decease, (Arith.) number left after subtraction or division, copies of book left unsold when demand has almost ceased (often offered at reduced price), (v.t.) treat or dispose of copies of (book) as remainder; ~dership n., possession of legal remainder; ~s (-z) n.pl., what remains over, surviving members or parts or amount, (the remains of a nation, a meal, a building, one's strength, etc.), relics of antiquity, works (esp. those not before or yet published) left by author (literary remains), dead body. [F f. L remaneo]

**rèma'nd** (-ah'-). **1.** v.t. Send back (esp. prisoner into custody to allow further inquiry). **2.** n. Recommittal to custody; **on ~**, in state of being remanded; ‖~ **centre, home,** institution for detention of juvenile offenders. [L remando]

**rèmā'rk. 1.** v.t. & i. Take notice of, regard with attention, (person, thing, fact, that, etc.); say by way of comment (that); make comment (up)on. **2.** n. Noticing (**worthy of ~**, remarkable); written or spoken comment, anything said, (let it pass without remark; **make a ~**, utter a comment). **3.** ~**able** a. (-bly), worth notice, exceptional, striking. [F remarquer (MARK²)]

‖**R.E.M.E.** abbr. Royal Electrical and Mechanical Engineers.

**rě'mėdy. 1.** n. Cure for or against disease, healing medicine or treatment; means of removing or counteracting or relieving any evil; redress, legal or other reparation. **2.** v.t. Rectify, make good. **3. rėmė'diable** (-bly) a.; **rėmė'dial** a., affording a remedy, intended to remedy disease or deficiency. [AF f. L remedium (medeor heal)]

**rėmě'mb|er** v.t. Keep in the memory, not forget, bring back into one's thoughts, know by heart, (person, thing, fact, that, to do, how to do, when, why, etc., or abs.; ~**er** oneself, remember one's manners or intentions after a lapse); make present to, tip, (remembered me in his will; remember the waiter); mention in one's prayers; convey greetings from (person) to another (asked to be remembered to you); ~**rance** n., remembering or being remembered (‖R~rance Sunday, nearest 11 Nov., when those who were killed in the wars of 1914–18 and 1939–45 are commemorated), keepsake, souvenir, (in pl.) greetings conveyed through third person. [F f. L (MEMORY)]

**rèmi'nd** v.t. Make (person) have recollection (of, to do, that, how, etc., or abs.); ~**er** n., thing that reminds or is memento (of). [RE-²]

**rèmini'scen|ce** n. Remembering; remembered (and related) fact or incident, (in pl.) collection of these in literary form; feature of thing reminding or suggestive of other thing; **rėmini'sce** v.i., (colloq.)

indulge in reminiscence(s); ∼**t** a., recalling past things, given to or concerned with retrospection, reminding or suggestive *of*. [L (*reminiscor* remember)]

**rĕmí'ss** a. Careless of duty, lax, negligent; ∼**íble** a., that may be remitted; ∼**ion** (-shon) n., forgiveness (*of* or of sins etc.), remitting of debt, penalty, etc., shortening of convict's prison sentence on account of his good behaviour, diminution of force or effect or degree (esp. of disease or pain); ∼**íve** a. [foll.]

**rĕmí't. 1.** v.t. & i. (-**tt**-). (Usu. of God) pardon (sins etc.); refrain from exacting or inflicting or executing (debt, punishment, sentence); abate, slacken, mitigate, partly or entirely cease from or cease, (remit *one's efforts; pain begins to remit*); refer (matter for decision etc.) *to* some authority, send back (case) to lower court; postpone, defer, *to* or *till;* transmit (money etc.), send by post etc.; ∼**tance** n., money sent to person, sending of money; ∼**tent** a., that abates at intervals. **2.** n. (or rē'-). Item(s) remitted for consideration. [L *remitto -miss-*]

**rĕ'mnant** n. Small remaining quantity or piece or number of persons or things; piece of cloth etc. left when greater part has been used or sold. [F (REMAIN)]

*****remold.** See REMOULD.

**rĕ'monstrāte** (*or'* rĭmŏ'n-) v.i. & t. Make protest, expostulate, (*against* course of action, *with* person; *on* or *upon* matter, or abs.); urge in remonstrance (*that*); **rĕmŏ'nstrance** n. [L (*monstro* show)]

**rĕmŏr'se** n. Bitter regret for wrong committed; compunction, compassionate reluctance to inflict pain (esp. *without remorse*); ∼**ful** (-sf-) a. (-**lly**), filled with repentance; ∼**lèss** (-sl-) a., without compassion. [F f. L (*mordeo mors-* bite)]

**rĕmŏ'te** a. (∼**r**, ∼**st**). Far apart or away in place or time (*lies remote from the road; came from the remotest parts of the earth; memorials of remote ages*); not closely related (*a remote ancestor*); distant or widely different or by nature separate *from* (*remote effects*); ∼ **control**, control of apparatus etc. from a distance by means of electrically operated device, radio, etc.); out-of-the-way, secluded, (*a remote village*); aloof, not friendly;

(esp. in *superl.*, of idea etc.) slight(est), faint(est), least, (*have not the remotest, have only a very remote, conception of what he means*). [L *remotus* (REMOVE)]

**rēmou'ld** (-ō'-), *****rēmō'ld. 1.** v.t. Mould again, refashion; reconstruct tread of (tyre). **2.** (rē'-) n. Remoulded tyre. [RE-²]

**rĕmo'v|e** (-ōō'v). **1.** v.t. & i. Take off or away from place occupied, convey to another place, change situation of, get rid of, dismiss, (*remove one's hat, magistrate from office; this will remove all doubts;* ∼**e furniture**, as special trade for persons changing house; ∼**e mountains**, do miracles; change one's place of residence, go away *from*, go *to* another place, (*am removing from London to Oxford*); (in *p.p.*) distant or remote *from* (*is not many degrees removed from the brute*); *once, twice*, etc., ∼**ed**, (of COUSINS). **2.** n. Distance, degree of remoteness; stage in gradation, degree, (*is only a few removes from*); ||promotion to a higher form at school (*has got his remove*); ||a form or division in some schools. **3.** ∼**al** n., act of removing or being removed, transfer of furniture etc. to different house. [F f. L *removeo -mot-*]

**rĕmū'ner|āte** v.t. (∼**able**). Reward, pay for service rendered; serve as or provide recompense for (toil etc.) or to (person); ∼**ā'tion** n., (esp.) what is received as pay; ∼**ative** a., (esp., of work) profitable. [L (*munus -ner-* reward)]

**Renai'ssance** (*or* rĭ-, -sahns) n. Revival of art and letters in 14th– 16th cc., period of its progress, style of art and architecture developed by it; (r∼) any similar revival. [F (*naissance* birth)]

**rē'nal** a. Of the kidneys. [F f. L (*renes* kidneys)]

**rĕnǎ'sc|ence** n. Rebirth, renewal; (R-) = RENAISSANCE; ∼**ent** a., springing up anew, being reborn. [L (*renascor* be born again)]

**rĕnd** v.t. & i. (**rent**). (arch. or rhet.) Tear or wrench (∼ one's **garments** or **hair**, in grief etc.); split or divide in two or in pieces or into factions; ∼ **the air**, sound piercingly. [E]

**rĕ'nder** v.t. Give in return; (arch.) give back; pay (tribute etc.), show (obedience etc.), give (assistance etc.), do (service etc.), (*to*); produce for inspection, submit, (**account**

**~ed,** bill previously sent in and not yet paid); reproduce, portray, give representation or performance or effect of, execute, translate, (*her expression, the quartet, Iago, the Latin, was well rendered*); make, cause to be, convert into (*age had rendered him peevish; the tone rendered it an insult*); **~ (down),** melt (fat) down; **~ing** *n.*, (esp.) translation or performance or portrayal. [f. Rom. (L *reddo* give back)]

**re'ndezvous** (rŏ'ndǐvōō, -dā-). **1.** *n.* (*pl.* same *pr.* -ōōz). Place appointed for assembling; place where people often meet; meeting-place agreed on, meeting by agreement. **2.** *v.i.* (**~es,** **~ed,** **~ing,** *pr.* -ōōz, -ōōd, -ōōing). Meet at rendezvous. [F, = present yourselves]

**rendi'tion** *n.* Interpretation, rendering, *of* dramatic role, musical piece, etc. [F (RENDER)]

**re'negade** *n.* Deserter of party or principles; **reně'g(u)e** (-g) *v.t. & i.,* deny, renounce; **renege on,** fail to keep (promise etc.), disappoint (person). [Sp. f. L (*nego* deny)]

**renew'** *v.t. & i.* Make (as good as) new, revive, regenerate; patch, fill up, reinforce, replace; get, begin, make, say, or give, anew, continue after intermission, (*renew attack, acquaintance, efforts; renew one's vows* etc.); grant or be granted continuation of (lease, subscription, licence, etc., or abs.); recover (one's youth, strength, etc.); **~al** *n.* [RE-²]

**re'nnet** *n.* Curdled milk found in stomach of unweaned calf, or preparation of stomach-membrane or of plant, used in curdling milk for cheese, junket, etc. [E (RUN)]

**renou'nce** *v.t. & i.* Consent formally to abandon, surrender, (claim, right, peerage, possession); repudiate, refuse to recognize any longer, decline association or disclaim relationship with, withdraw from, discontinue, forsake, (*renounce treaty, principles, person's authority, all thought of, attempt, friend, friendship*). [F f. L (*nuntio* announce)]

**re'nov|āte** *v.t.* (**~able**). Restore to good condition or vigour, repair; **~ā'tion, ~ātor,** *ns.* [L (*novus* new)]

**renow'n** *n.* Fame, high distinction; **~ed** (-nd) *a.,* famous, celebrated. [F (*renomer* f. L NOMEN)]

**rĕnt¹.** See REND.

**rĕnt²** *n.* Large tear in garment etc.; opening in clouds etc. [REND]

**rĕnt³. 1.** *n.* Tenant's periodical payment to owner or landlord for use of land or premises; payment for use of storage space, machinery, etc. **2.** *v.t. & i.* Take, occupy, use, at a rent (*from*); let or hire (*out*) for rent (*to*); be let *at* specified rent. **3. ~'al** *n.,* income from rents, amount paid or received as rent, act of renting. [F f. Rom. (RENDER)]

**rentier** (rah'ntǐā) *n.* Person living on dividends. [F]

**renŭnciā'tion** *n.* Renouncing; self-denial, giving up of things; **renŭ'nciative, renŭ'nciatory,** (-sha-) *adjs.* [F or L (RENOUNCE)]

**rĕp¹, rĕpp,** *n.* Textile fabric with corded surface used in curtains and upholstery. [F *reps*]

**rĕp²** *n.* (sl.) Immoral person. [perh. *reprobate*]

**rĕp³** *n.* (colloq.) Representative, esp. commercial traveller. [abbr.]

**rĕp⁴** *n.* (colloq.) Repertory (theatre or company).

**\*Rep.** *abbr.* Representative (in Congress); Republican.

**repair'¹** *v.i.* Resort, have recourse, go often or in great numbers or for a specific purpose, *to.* [F f. L (RE-PATRIATE)]

**repair'². 1.** *v.t.* Restore (garment, building, machine, tissue, strength, etc.) to good condition, renovate or mend by replacing or refixing parts or compensating loss or exhaustion; remedy, set right again, make amends for, (loss, wrong, error). **2.** *n.* Restoring to sound condition (*health, bicycle, house, needs repair*); act of doing this (*repairs done while you wait*); good condition, relative condition, for working or using (*is in, out of, repair; must be kept in good, is in bad, repair*). **3. rĕ'parable** *a.* (-bly), (of loss etc.) that can be made good; **repară'tion** *n.,* making of amends, compensation. [F f. L (*paro* make ready)]

**repartee'** *n.* (Making of) witty retort(s). [F *repartie* f. *repartir* reply promptly (PART)]

**repa'st** (-ah'-) *n.* (Food supplied for or eaten at) meal (esp. of specified kind; *rich, slight,* etc., *repast*). [F f. L *repasco -past-* feed]

**repā'tri|āte. 1.** *v.t. & i.* Return to native land; **~ā'tion** *n.* (-at) *n.* Repatriated person. [L *repatrio* go back home (*patria* native land)]

**rēpay'** v.t. & ι. (**repai'd**). Pay back (money); return (blow, visit, service, etc.); give in recompense *for*; make repayment to (person); make return for, requite, (action); make repayment; ∼**ment** n. [F (RE-²)]

**rèpea'l. 1.** v.t. Annul, revoke, (law etc.). **2.** n. Repealing. [F (APPEAL)]

**rèpea't. 1.** v.t. & i. Say or do over again, recite, rehearse, report, reproduce, give imitation of, (*not*, ∼ *not*, emphatically not; *language* will not bear ∼ing, is too foul etc. to repeat; ∼ *itself*, recur in same form; ∼ *oneself*, say or do same thing over again); (of watch etc.) strike last quarter etc. again when required; (of firearm) fire several shots without reloading; recur, appear again or repeatedly; (of food) be tasted intermittently for some time after being swallowed. **2.** n. Repeating esp. of item in programme in response to encore; repeated broadcast programme; (Mus.) passage intended to be repeated, mark indicating this; pattern repeated in wallpaper etc. **3.** ∼**èdlý** adv., several times; ∼**er** n., (esp.) firearm or watch that repeats. [F f. L (*peto* ask)]

**repêchage** (rĕ'peshahzh) n. (Rowing etc.) Extra contest in which runners-up in eliminating contests compete for place in final. [F]

**rèpĕ'l** v.t. (-ll-). Drive back, ward off, refuse admission or approach or acceptance to; be repulsive or distasteful to; ∼**lent** a. & n., (substance) that repels (esp. insects etc.). [L *repello* -*puls*-]

**rèpĕ'nt** v.t. & i. Think with contrition of or *of*, be regretful about or *of*, wish one had not done, resolve not to continue wrongdoing in, (action etc., or abs.; *you shall repent, repent this, repent of it*); ∼**ance** n.; ∼**ant** a. [F f. L *paenitet*]

**rĕpercŭ'ssion** (-shŏn) n. Echo; recoil after impact; indirect effect or reaction *of* event or act. [F or L (RE-²)]

**rĕ'pert|oire** (-twär) n. Stock of pieces etc. that performer or company knows or is prepared to give; stock of regularly performed pieces, regularly used techniques, etc.; ∼**orÿ** n., place for finding something, store or collection, esp. of information, instances, facts, etc., repertoire, theatrical performance of various

plays for short periods by one ∼**tory company**. [F f. L (*reperio* find)]

**rĕpĕti'tio|n** n. Repeating or being repeated; copy, replica; piece set to be learnt by heart; ∼**us** (-shŭs), **rèpĕ'titive**, adjs. [F or L (REPEAT)]

**rèpī'ne** v.i. Fret, be discontented, (*at, against*, or abs.). [PINE¹, after *repine*]

**rèplā'ce** v.t. Put back in place; take place of, succeed, be substituted for, (in *pass.*) be succeeded or superseded or have one's or its place filled *by*; fill up place of (*with, by*), find or provide substitute for; ∼**ment** (-sm-) n., replacing or being replaced, person or thing that takes the place of another. [RE-²]

**rēplay. 1.** (-ā') v.t. Play (match, recording, etc.) over again. **2.** (-ē'-) n. Replaying (of match, recording of incident in game, etc.). [RE-²]

**rèplĕ'nish** v.t. Fill up again (*with*); (in *p.p.*) fully stored, full (*with*); ∼**ment** n. [F *replenir* (*plein* full)]

**rèplĕ't|e** a. Filled, well stocked, stuffed, *with*; gorged, sated, (*with*); ∼**ion** n. [F or L (*pleo* fill)]

**rĕ'plic|a** n. Duplicate made by original artist of his picture etc., exact copy; model, esp. on smaller scale; ∼**āte** a. (∼**able**), make replica of; ∼**ā'tion** n., copy, copying. [It. (*replicare* REPLY)]

**rèplý'. 1.** v.t. & i. Make answer, respond, in word or action (*to*); say in answer. **2.** n. Act of replying; what is replied, response; ∼**paid**, (of telegram) with cost of reply prepaid by sender, (of envelope etc.) for which addressee undertakes to pay postage. [F f. L *replico* fold back]

**rèpor't. 1.** v.t. & i. Bring back or give account of; state as fact or news, narrate or describe or repeat esp. as eye-witness or hearer etc. (*to*); relate as spoken by another; make official or formal statement about; specify (offence, offender) *to* authorities or abs.; present (one*self*), present oneself *to* (person), as returned or arrived; take down word for word or epitomize or write description of for publication (*report law case, proceedings, meeting*, or abs.); make, draw up, or send in report; be responsible *to* (superior, supervisor, etc.); ∥∼ **progress**, state what has been done so far; *report* SICK¹; ∼**ed speech**, speaker's words with changes of person, tense, etc., usual in reports.

**2.** *n.* Common talk, rumour; way person or thing is spoken of, (arch.) repute, (*things of good report*); account given or opinion formally expressed after investigation or consideration, description or epitome or reproduction of scene or speech or law case esp. for newspaper publication; periodical statement on school pupil's work, conduct, etc.; sound of explosion (*went off with a loud report*). **3. repŏrta′ge** (-ah'zh) *n.*, (style of) reporting events; ~**er** *n.*, (esp.) person employed to report news etc. for newspaper or broadcast. [F *report(er)* f. L (PORT³)]

**repŏ′s|e¹** (-z) *v.t.* Place (trust etc.) *in*; ~**al** *n.* [RE-¹, POSE]

**repŏ′se²** (-z) **1.** *v.t. & i.* Rest (oneself, or abs.); lay (one's head etc.) to rest (*on* pillow etc.); give rest to; lie, be lying or laid, esp. in sleep or death (*in, on,* or abs.); be supported or based *on* (*the whole system reposes on fear*). **2.** *n.* Cessation of activity or excitement or toil; sleep, peaceful or quiescent state, tranquillity. **3.** ~**ful** (-zf-) *a.* (-**lly**), inducing or exhibiting repose. [F *reposer* f. L (PAUSE)]

**repŏ′sitorў** (-z-) *n.* Receptacle; place where things are stored or may be found, warehouse, museum; recipient *of* secrets etc. [F or L (REPOSE¹)]

**repou′ssé** (repŏŏ′sā) *a. & n.* (Ornamental metalwork) hammered into relief from reverse side. [F (PUSH)]

**repp.** See REP¹.

**reprehĕ′n|d** *v.t.* Rebuke, blame; ~**sible** *a.* (-**bly**), blameworthy; ~**sion** (-shon) *n.*, censure, blame. [L (*prehendo* seize)]

**represĕ′nt** (-z-) *v.t.* Call up in the mind by description or portrayal or imagination, place likeness of before mind or senses, serve or be meant as likeness of; try to bring (facts influencing conduct) home (*to*), state by way of expostulation or incentive, (*represented to him the rashness of it, that it could not succeed, that it must succeed*); make out *to be* etc., allege *that*, describe or depict *as*, (*am not what you represent me to be* or *as*; *represents that he has, himself to have, seen service*); act (play etc.), play part of on stage; symbolize, act as embodiment of, stand for, correspond to, be specimen of, (*sovereign represents majesty of State*; *inch of rain represents 100 tons per acre*;

*by-election result does not represent country's views*; *symbol χ represents guttural sound*; *camels are represented in the New World by llamas*; *Welsh football is represented in the team by Morgan*); fill place of, be substitute or deputy for, be entitled to act or speak for, be sent as member to legislature or delegate to meeting etc. by, (*Queen was represented by the Duke*; *members representing urban constituencies*); ~**ā′tion** *n.*, representing or being represented, thing that represents, (esp. in *pl.*) statement made by way of allegation or to convey opinion; PROPORTIONAL *representation*; ~**ā′tional** *a.*, (esp., of art) seeking to portray reality. [F or L (PRESENT³)]

**represĕ′ntative** (-z-). **1.** *a.* Typical of class(es), containing typical specimens of all or many classes, (*a meeting of representative men*; *a very representative collection*); consisting of elected deputies or representatives; based on representation of nation etc. by such deputies (*representative government*); serving as portrayal or symbol of (*groups representative of the virtues*). **2.** *n.* Sample, specimen, typical embodiment, *of*; person's or firm's agent; delegate, substitute; deputy in representative assembly (**House of R~s**, lower house of U.S. Congress and other national Parliaments). [F or L (prec.)]

**reprĕ′ss** *v.t.* (~**ible**). Keep under, quell; suppress, prevent from sounding or bursting out or rioting; (Psych.) actively exclude (unwelcome thought) from conscious awareness, (usu. in *pass.*) subject (person) to repression of his thoughts; ~**ion** (-shon) *n.*; ~**īve** *a.*; ~**or** *n.* [L (PRESS¹)]

**reprie′ve. 1.** *v.t.* Postpone or remit execution of (condemned person); (fig.) give respite to. **2.** *n.* Reprieving or being reprieved; (warrant for) remission or commutation of capital sentence; respite. [*repry* f. F *reprendre -pris* take back]

**rĕ′primand** (-ah-) *n.*, & *v.t.* Official(ly) rebuke (*for* fault). [F f. Sp. f. L (REPRESS)]

**repri′sal** (-z-) *n.* Act of retaliation. [AF *reprisaille* f. L (REPREHEND)]

**repri′se** (-ē′z) *n.* Repeated passage in music; repeated song etc. in musical programme. [F (REPRIEVE)]

**reproa′ch. 1.** *v.t.* Scold, censure, express disapproval to (person; *with* his offence or *for* fault); rebuke (offence); (of look etc.) convey protest or censure to (*his eyes reproach me*). **2.** *n.* Thing that brings disgrace or discredit (*to*); disgraced or discredited state (*the things that had brought reproach upon him*; **above or beyond** ~, perfect); scolding, rebuke, censure, (*heap reproaches on*; *the mute reproach in his eyes*; **term of** ~, word implying censure). **3.** ~ful *a.* (-lly), (of words, look, etc.) conveying reproach, (of person) inclined to reproach. [F *reproche(r)* f. L *prope near*]

**rĕ'prŏb|āte. 1.** *v.t.* Express or feel disapproval of, censure; (of God) reject, exclude from salvation. **2.** *a.* & *n.* (Person who is) rejected by God, hardened in sin, of highly immoral character, or unprincipled. **3.** ~ā'tion *n.*, (esp.) rejection by God. [L (PROVE)]

**rĕprŏ|dū'ce** *v.t.* & *i.* (-cible). Produce copy or representation of; cause to be seen, heard, etc., again; produce offspring of (one*self*, it*self*); produce further members of same species by natural means; ~dŭ'ction *n.*, reproducing, copy of painting etc., (*attrib.* of furniture etc.) made in imitation of earlier style; ~dŭ'ctive *a.* [RE-²]

**rĕprōō'f** *n.* Blame (*a word, glance, of reproof*); rebuke, words expressing blame; **rĕprō've** (-ōō'v) *v.t.*, rebuke, scold, (person, conduct, etc.). [F *reprover* f. L (REPROBATE)]

**rĕ'ptile. 1.** *n.* Member of the class of animals including snakes, lizards, crocodiles, turtles, and tortoises; mean, grovelling, or repulsive person. **2.** *a.* (Of animal) creeping; mean and grovelling; **rĕptī'lian** (-lyan) *a.* & *n.* [F or L (*repo rept-* creep)]

**rĕpŭ'blic** *n.* A State in which supreme power is held by the people or its elected representatives or by elected or nominated president, not by monarch etc.; (fig.) society with equality between members; ~an, (*a.*) of, constituted as, characterizing, republic(s), (*a.* & *n.*) (person) advocating or supporting republican government, *(R-)* (member) of party opposed to Democratic Party; ~anism *n.*; ~anize *v.t.* [F f. L (*res* concern; PUBLIC)]

**rĕpŭ'di|āte** *v.t.* Disown, disavow, reject; refuse dealings with, deny; refuse to recognize or obey (authority,

treaty) or discharge (obligation, debt); divorce (one's wife; esp. of the ancients or non-Christians); ~ā'tion, ~ātor, *ns.* [L (*repudium* divorce)]

**rĕpŭ'gnan|ce** *n.* Aversion, antipathy (*to, against*); inconsistency, incompatibility, of ideas, statements, tempers, etc. (*of, between, to, with*); ~t *a.*, distasteful, contradictory, (*to*). [F or L (*pugno* fight)]

**rĕpŭ'ls|e. 1.** *v.t.* Drive back (attack, attacking enemy) by force of arms, (fig.) foil in controversy; rebuff (friendly advances or their maker), refuse (request, offer, or its maker); be repulsive to. **2.** *n.* Repulsing or being repulsed, rebuff. **3.** ~ion (-shon) *n.*, aversion, disgust, (Phys., or fig.) tendency of bodies to repel each other; ~ive *a.*, causing aversion or loathing, loathsome, disgusting. [L (REPEL)]

**rĕ'pŭt|able** *a.* (-bly). Of good repute, respectable; ~ā'tion *n.*, what is generally said or believed about person's or thing's character (*has not justified his reputation*; *place has a bad reputation*), state of being well thought of, respectability, (*persons of reputation*), *the* credit or discredit *of* doing (*has the reputation of swindling*); **rĕpū'te**, (*v.t.*; in *pass.*) be generally considered (w. compl. or *to* be or do; *is reputed the best doctor* or *to be the best*), be generally *well*, *ill*, etc., thought or spoken of, (in *p.p.* as *a.*) passing as being but probably or possibly not being (*his reputed father*), (*n.*) reputation. [L (*puto* reckon)]

**rĕquĕ'st. 1.** *n.* Asking for something, thing asked for, (*came at his request*; *made two requests*; *you shall have your request*; **by** or **on** ~, in response to expressed wish; ~ **programme** etc., of items requested by audience; ~ **stop**, where bus etc. stops only on passenger's request); state of being sought after, demand, (*is now in great request*). **2.** *v.t.* Ask to be given or allowed or favoured with (*request consideration*, person's *presence*, etc.); ask *that*; seek permission, ask (person), *to* do. [F f. L (REQUIRE)]

**rĕ'quiĕm** *n.* (Music of) special Mass for repose of souls of the dead. [L, = rest]

**rĕquīr'e** *v.t.* Order (person), demand (*of* or *from* person), *to* do; demand or ask in words (person's action, act *of* person, *that*, etc.) esp. as *of* right; lay down as imperative

(had done all that was required by the
Act; Gray's 'Anatomy' is required reading
for nurses); need, depend on for
success or fulfilment, (the emergency
requires it, that it should be done; irony
requires care in its use; place would
require an army to take it); ~ment
(-īr'm-) n., (esp.) thing required;
rĕ'quīsīte (-z-) a. & n., (thing)
needed (for some purpose). [F f. L
requiro -quisit- seek]

rĕquīsī'tion (-z-). 1. n. Demand
made, esp. formal and usu. written
demand that some duty should be
performed; order given by authorities
laying claim to use of property or
materials; being called or put into
service (under or in ~, being used
or applied). 2. v.t. Demand use or
supply of esp. by requisition order.
[F or L (prec.)]

rĕqui'te v.t. Make return for,
reward or avenge, (service, wrong,
injury, treatment; with what is given
etc. thus); make return to, repay with
good or evil, (person; for treatment
received, with treatment given); ~al
n. [RE-¹, quite = QUIT]

rĕr'edŏs (-ĕr'd-) n. Ornamental
screen covering wall above back of
altar. [AF (ARREAR, dos back)]

rĕscī'|nd v.t. Abrogate, revoke,
cancel; ~ssion (-zhon) n. [L
rescindo -sciss- cut off]

rĕ'script n. Roman emperor's or
Pope's written reply to appeal for
decision; ruler's or government's or
official edict or announcement. [L
rescribo -script- reply in writing]

rĕ'scūe. 1. v.t. Set free from or from
attack, custody, danger, or harm.
2. n. Rescuing or being rescued (come
to person's rescue). [F f. Rom. (L as
RE-¹, EX-¹, QUASH)]

rĕsear'ch (-sĕr'-; or rĕ'-). 1. n.
Endeavour to discover new or collate
old facts etc. by critical study (his
researches have been fruitful; engaged in
research); careful search after or for or
into. 2. v.i. & t. Make researches (into
or for). [F (SEARCH)]

rĕsĕ'mbl|e (-z-) v.t. Be like, have
similarity to or same appearance as;
~ance n. (to, between). [F (sembler
seem)]

rĕsĕ'nt (-z-) v.t. Show or feel indignation at or retain bitter feelings
about (doing, insult, or injury sustained); ~ful a. (-lly), feeling resentment; ~ment n. [F f. L (sentio feel)]

rĕsĕr've (-z-). 1. v.t. Postpone use

or enjoyment or treatment of, keep
back for later occasion (~ oneself
for, not expend one's energies till);
postpone delivery of (judgement);
retain possession or control or use of
by stipulation (for or to person); destine for some use or fate; (in pass.)
be left by fate for, fall first or only to;
(in p.p. as a.) reticent, slow to reveal
emotions or opinions, uncommunicative. 2. n. Thing reserved for future
use, extra amount; company's profit
added to capital; (in sing. or pl.) assets kept readily available, troops
withheld from action to reinforce or
protect others, forces outside regular
ones but available in emergency;
reservist; extra player chosen as
possible substitute in team; state of
being kept unused but available (has
it in reserve); place reserved for
special use, esp. for occupation by
animals; limitation or exception
attached to something (accepted
without ~, fully; sale without ~,
not subject to a lowest acceptable
price or ~ price); self-restraint,
reticence, coolness of manner. 3.

rĕservā'tion (-z-) n., (esp.) express
or tacit limitation or exception
(mental reservation, tacit qualification of statement, oath, etc.),
strip of land between carriageways
of road, *tract of land reserved for
occupation by Indian tribe, booking
of berth on ship, room in hotel, etc.,
place so booked, retention of part of
Eucharistic elements after celebration; rĕsĕr'vist (-z-) n., member of
reserve forces; rĕ'servoir (-zerv-
wär) n., receptacle for fluid, esp. one
built or dug for storing water, reserve
supply or collection of facts etc. [F f.
L (servo keep)]

rĕshŭ'ffle. 1. v.t. Shuffle (cards)
again; interchange posts of (Government ministers etc.). 2. n. Reshuf-
fling. [RE-²]

rĕsī'de (-z-) v.i. Have one's home,
dwell permanently, at, in, abroad,
etc.; (of power, right, etc.) be vested
in person etc.; (of quality) be present
or inherent in; rĕ'sĭdence (-z-) n.,
residing (have, take up, one's
~nce, dwell, begin to dwell; in
~nce, dwelling at specified place esp.
for performance of duties etc.), place
where one resides, abode of, house
esp. of considerable pretension;
rĕ'sĭdent (-z-), (a.) residing, dwelling in a place in fulfilment of duty,

having quarters on the spot (*resident housekeeper, surgeon*), located in (*a right resident in the nation*), (*n.*) permanent inhabitant *of* town or neighbourhood; **rĕsĭdĕ′ntial** (-z-; -shal) *a.* (**-lly**), suitable for or occupied by private house (*residential area, estate*), used as residence (*residential hotel*), connected with residence (*residential qualification for voters*); **rĕsĭdĕ′ntiarў** (-z-; -sherĭ) *a.*, subject to, requiring, of or for, official residence. [F f. L (*sedeo* sit)]

**rĕsĭ′dū|al** (-z-) *a.* (**-lly**) & *n.* (Quantity) left as residue or residuum; **~arў** *a.*, of the residue of an estate (*residuary legatee*), of or being a residuum, residual; **rĕ′sĭdūe** (-z-) *n.*, remainder, what is left or remains over, what remains of estate after payment of charges, debts, and bequests; **~um** *n.* (*pl.* **~ua**), what remains, esp. (Chem. etc.) substance left after combustion or evaporation. [*residue* f. F f. L *residuum* (prec.)]

**rĕsĭ′gn** (-zī′n) *v.t.* & *i.* (for *re-sign* see RE-²). Relinquish, surrender, (office, claim, property, charge, task, life, hope; *to* person); reconcile oneself (*to* one's *fate* etc., *to* doing); accept the inevitable without repining; give up office, retire, (*as* chairman etc., *from* chairmanship etc.); **rĕsĭgnā′tion** (-z-) *n.*, resigning esp. of an office, document conveying it (*send in* one's *resignation*), uncomplaining endurance of sorrow or other evil; **~ed** (-nd) *a.* (**~edly** *pr.* -ĭdlĭ), having resigned oneself, content to endure, full or indicative of resignation. [F f. L (*signo* sign)]

**rĕsĭ′lien|t** (-zĭ′lye-) *a.* Resuming original form after compression etc.; (of person) readily recovering from depression etc.; **~ce** *n.* [SALIENT]

**rĕ′sĭn** (-z-). **1.** *n.* Adhesive inflammable substance secreted by most plants and exuding naturally or upon incision esp. from fir and pine; (**synthetic**) **~**, organic compound made by polymerization etc. and used esp. as or in plastics; **~ous** *a.* **2.** *v.t.* Rub or treat with resin. [F]

**rĕsĭ′st** (-zĭ′-) *v.t.* & *i.* (**~ible**). Stop course of, withstand action or effect of, prevent from reaching or penetrating, repel, abstain from, (weapon, cutting edge, frost, heat, attack, temptation, influence, suggestion, etc., *doing*; **cannot ~** *a joke* etc., feels obliged to make it if it

suggests itself, is certain to be amused by it); strive against, try to impede, refuse to comply with, (*resist arrest*); offer resistance, make opposition; **~ance** *n.*, (power of) resisting (*showed resistance to* complying, *to wear and tear*; PASSIVE *resistance*· **~ance** (*movement*), secret organization resisting authority, esp. in conquered country), hindrance, impeding or stopping effect, exerted by material thing on another (*overcome the resistance of the air*; **take line of least ~ance**, fig. adopt easiest method or course), (Phys.) property of failing to conduct (electricity, heat, etc.), (Electr.) resistor; **~ant, ~ive**, *adjs.*; **~or** *n.*, (Electr.) device having resistance to passage of current. [F or L (*sisto* stop)]

**rĕsĭ′t** *v.t.* (**-tt-; -sa′t**). Take (examination) a second time after failing. [RE-²]

**rĕsŏ′lŭble** (-z-) *a.* That can be resolved; analysable *into*. [F or L (RESOLVE)]

**rĕ′sŏl|ūte** (-z-; *or* -ōōt) *a.* (Of person or his mind or action) determined, bold, not vacillating or shrinking; **~ū′tion** (*or* -ōō′-) *n.*, separation into components, conversion *into* other form, (Mus.) causing discord to pass into concord, (Phys.· etc.) smallest interval measurable by an instrument, solving of doubt or problem or question, formal expression of opinion by legislative body or public meeting, thing resolved on (**good ~utions**, intentions that one formulates mentally for virtuous conduct), resolute temper or character. [L (foll.)]

**rĕsŏ′lve** (-z-). **1.** *v.t.* & *i.* Dissolve (*into*), break up into parts, convert or be converted *into*, reduce by mental analysis *into*, (*resolve thing, thing is resolved*, or *resolves itself*, or *resolves, into its elements*; *telescope resolves nebula into stars*); (Mus.) convert (discord) or be converted into concord; solve, explain, settle, (*all doubts were resolved*; *the problem of its origin has not yet been resolved*); decide upon, make up one's mind (*up*)*on* action or doing or *to* do, form mentally or (of legislative body or public meeting) pass by vote the resolution *that*, (of circumstances etc.) bring (person) to resolution to do or (*up*)*on* action or doing (*resolved that nothing should induce him, that he would* do, on or *upon doing*; *this discovery resolved us on going or to go*); (in *p.p.* as *a.*) resolute. **2.** *n.* Mental decision (*kept her resolve*); (poet.) resoluteness (*deeds of high resolve*). [L (SOLVE)]

**rĕ'son|ant** (-z-) *a.* (Of sound) echoing, resounding, continuing to sound, reinforced or prolonged by vibration or reflection; (of body, room, etc.) tending to reinforce or prolong sounds esp. by vibration; (of place) resounding *with*; ~**ance** *n.*; ~**āte** *v.i.*, produce or show resonance, resound. [F (RESOUND)]

**rĕsôr't** (-z-; for *re-sort* see RE-²). **1.** *v.i.* Turn for aid *to* (*resort to force*); go in large numbers or often *to* (*visitors resorted to the shrine by the hundred; the inn to which he was known to resort*). **2.** *n.* Thing to which recourse is had, what is turned to for aid, expedient, recourse, (**in the last** ~, when all else has failed, as final attempt); frequenting or being frequented; place frequented usu. for specified purpose or quality (*health, seaside, resort*). [F (*sortir* go out)]

**rĕsou'nd** (-z-) *v.i.* & *t.* (Of place) ring or echo (*with*); (of voice, instrument, sound, etc.) produce echoes, go on sounding, fill place with sound; (of fame, event, etc.) be much talked of, produce sensation, (*through* Europe etc.); (of place) re-echo (sound); ~**ing** *a.*, (esp.) unmistakable, emphatic (*a resounding success*). [F or L (SOUND¹)]

**rĕsou'rce** (-sôr's, -z-), *n.* Means of supplying what is needed, stock that can be drawn on, (usu. in *pl.*); (in *pl.*) country's collective means for support and defence; expedient, device, (*flight was his only resource; am at the end of my resources*); skill in devising expedients (*is full of resource*); leisure occupation; **left to** one's **own** ~**s**, given no help in passing time or dealing with problems; ~**ful** (-sf-) *a.* (**-lly**), good at devising expedients. [F (SOURCE)]

**rĕspĕ'ct. 1.** *n.* Reference, relation, (*to; is true with respect to the French*); heed or regard *of*, attention *to*; particular, detail, aspect, (*of; is admirable in respect of style; in all, many, some, respects*); deferential esteem felt or shown towards person or quality (*has won the respect of all; have the greatest respect for him, for his ability; with respect, I suggest you are quite wrong*); (in *pl.*) one's polite messages or

attentions (*give him my respects*; **pay** one's ~**s**, make polite visit; **pay** one's **last** ~**s**, attend funeral). **2.** *v.t.* Regard with deference, esteem, or honour; avoid degrading or insulting or injuring or interfering with or interrupting, treat with consideration, refrain from offending or corrupting or tempting, (*respect person's feelings or innocence, the rule of the road; respect neutrality, privileges, property*); ~ oneself, have self-respect. **3.** ~**able** *a.* (**-bly**), deserving respect (*his motives were respectable*), of fair social standing, having the qualities necessary for such standing, honest and decent, befitting respectable persons, considerable in number or size or amount, of some merit or importance, fairly good, (*a respectable hill, painter, score, minority; respectable talents*); ~**abi'lity** *n.*; ~**ful** *a.* (**-lly**), showing deference; ~**ing**, (*a.*) having reference to (*legislation respecting property*), (*prep.*) in respect of (*am at a loss respecting his whereabouts*). [F or L (*respicio -spect-* look back at)]

**rĕspĕ'ctive** *a.* Pertaining or proper to each, individual, several, comparative, (*go to your, put them in their, respective places*; *were given places according to their respective rank or ranks*; *he and I contributed respective amounts of £10 and £1*); ~**ly** (-vlĭ) *adv.*, (esp.) for each separately or in turn, and in the order mentioned (*he and I contributed £10 and £1 respectively*). [F or L (prec.)]

**rĕspīr'e** *v.i.* & *t.* Breathe air, inhale and exhale air; breathe (air etc.); **rĕspirā'tion** *n.*, breathing, single inspiration and expiration, a breath; ARTIFICIAL *respiration*; **rĕ'spirător** *n.*, apparatus worn over mouth and nose to warm or filter inhaled air or to prevent inhalation of poison gas etc., apparatus for maintaining artificial respiration; **rĕ'spirătŏry** (or rĭspī'rat-, rĭspīr'at-) *a.* [F or L (*spiro* breathe)]

**rĕ'spīte. 1.** *n.* Delay permitted in the discharge of an obligation or suffering of a penalty; interval of rest or relief. **2.** *v.t.* Grant or bring respite to. [F f. L (RESPECT)]

**rĕsplĕ'nden|t** *a.* Brilliant, dazzlingly or gloriously bright; ~**ce**, ~**cỹ**, *ns.* [L (*splendeo* shine)]

**rĕspŏ'nd** *v.i.* Make answer; (of congregation) make set answers to priest etc.; act or behave in answering or corresponding manner (*responded with a kick*); show sensitiveness *to* by behaviour or change (*does not respond to kindness*; *nerve responds to stimulus*); ~**ent**, (*a.*) in position of defendant, (*n.*) defendant esp. in appeal or divorce case; **rèspŏ'nse** *n.*, answer given in word or act, reply, (*in response to*; *made no response*), feeling, movement, change, etc., caused by stimulus or influence, any part of the liturgy said or sung in answer to priest. [F f. L *respondeo -spons-*]

**rèspŏ'ns|ible** *a.* (-**bly**). Liable to be called to account (*to person, for thing, or abs.*); (of ruler, government) not autocratic; morally accountable for actions, capable of rational conduct; of good credit or position or repute, respectable, evidently trustworthy; being the primary cause *for* (result etc.); involving responsibility (*a responsible task*); ~**ĭbi'lĭtў** *n.*, being responsible (*refuses all responsibility for it*; *will take the responsibility of doing it*; **on** one's **own** ~**ibility**, without authorization), charge for which one is responsible (*a family is a great responsibility*); ~**ive** *a.*, answering, by way of answer, responding readily to or to some influence, sympathetic. [F f. L (prec.)]

**rèsprāy'** *v.t.* Spray again (esp. to change colour of paint on vehicle). [RE-²]

**rèst¹. 1.** *v.i. & t.* Be still, cease or abstain or be relieved from exertion or action or movement or employment, lie in sleep or death, lie buried (*in churchyard* etc.), be tranquil, be let alone, (*waves that never rest*; *rest from one's labours*; *could not rest till he got his wish*); (of matter under discussion) be left without further investigation; lie, be spread out or supported or based, depend, rely, (of look etc.) alight or be steadily directed, (*up*)*on* (*shadow, light, rests on his face*; *roof rests on four arches*; *hand resting on the table*; *science rests on observation*); be propped *against*; repose trust in (*be content to rest in God*); give relief or repose to, allow to rest, (*rest your men for an hour*; *says the goggles rest his eyes*; ~ one's **case**, conclude presentation of it); (in *p.p.*) refreshed or reinvigorated by resting; place for support or foundation (*up*)*on* (*rest one's elbow, load, on the table*; *rest one's case on equity*); ||**be** ~**ing**, (of actor) be out of work;

~**'ing-place**, place provided or used for resting (*last* ~**ing-place**, the grave); *rest on* one's OARS; *~ up*, rest oneself thoroughly. **2.** *n.* Repose or sleep esp. in bed at night (*go, retire, to rest*; *take* one's *rest*; *get a good night's rest*); (period of) resting (*a rest from work*; *give* person, horse, machine, fig. topic of discussion, *a rest*; *take a short rest*; *at* ~, not moving, not agitated or troubled, esp. of the dead; **set** person's **mind** or **heart at** ~, settle, relieve; **day of** ~, Sabbath; LAY¹ *to rest*); prop or support or steadying-piece for resting thing on, e.g. for gun in aiming, telephone-receiver, billiard-cue, foot; (Mus.) (sign denoting) interval of silence; ~**-cure**, rest usu. of some weeks in bed as medical treatment; ~**-day**, day spent in rest, day of rest; ~**-room**, public lavatory in factory, shop, etc. [E]

**rèst². 1.** *v.i.* Remain in specified state (*rest assured, satisfied*); ~ **with**, be left in the hands or charge of (*it rests with you to decide*). **2.** *n.* The remaining part(s) or individuals *of*, the remainder of some quantity or number, *the* others, (**for the** ~, as regards anything beyond what has been specially mentioned). [F *reste(r)* f. L (*sto* stand)]

**rè'staur|ant** (-torahn, -rŏnt) *n.* Public premises where meals or refreshments may be had; ||~**ant car**, dining-car; ~**ateur'** (-toratēr') *n.*, restaurant-keeper. [F (RESTORE)]

**rè'stful** *a.* (~**ly**). Favourable to repose, soothing. [REST¹]

**rè'st-hărrow** (-ō) *n.* Tough-rooted herb. [ARREST, HARROW]

**rèstĭtū'tion** *n.* Restoring of or of thing to proper owner, reparation for injury, (esp. *make restitution*). [F or L]

**rè'stĭve** *a.* (Of horse) jibbing, refractory; (of person) unmanageable, rejecting control; fidgety, restless. [F (REST²)]

**rè'stless** *a.* Finding or affording no rest; uneasy, agitated; constantly in motion or fidgeting. [E (REST¹)]

**rèstōr'|e** *v.t.* Give back; (attempt to) bring back to original state by rebuilding, repairing, etc., (*church, picture, text, has been restored*); make representation of supposed original state of (extinct animal, ruin, etc.); reinstate; bring back to or *to* health etc.; bring back to former place or condition or use; **rĕstōrā′tion** n., restoring or being restored, (period of) re-establishment of monarch etc. (**the R~ation**, return of Charles II in 1660), model or drawing representing supposed original form of extinct animal, ruined building, etc.; **rĕstō′rative** a. & n., (food etc.) that tends to restore health or strength. [F f. L *restauro*]

**rĕstrai′n** v.t. (for *re-strain* see RE-²). Check or hold in *from*, keep in check or under control or within bounds, repress, keep down; confine, imprison; ~**t** n., restraining or being restrained (**in ~t of**, in order to restrain; **without ~t**, freely, copiously), controlling agency or influence, confinement esp. because of insanity, self-control, avoidance of excess or exaggeration, austerity of literary expression, reserve of manner. [F f. L *restringo -strict-*]

**rĕstri′ct** v.t. Confine, bound, limit, (*to, within*; *has a very restricted application*; *am restricted to advising*; *is restricted within narrow limits*); ~**ion** n., (esp.) limitation placed upon action; ~**ive** a., imposing restrictions; ~**ive practice**, agreement to limit competition or output in industry. [L (prec.)]

**rĕsŭ′lt** (-z-). **1.** v.i. Arise as actual or follow as logical consequence (*from*); have outcome or end in specified manner esp. *in* failure etc. (*resulted badly, in a large profit*). **2.** n. Consequence, issue or outcome of something; satisfactory outcome (**without ~**, in vain, fruitless); (in *pl.*) list of scores, winners, etc., in sporting events; quantity or formula obtained by calculation. **3.** ~**ant**, (*a.*) resulting esp. as total outcome of more or less opposed forces, (*n.*) force etc. equivalent to two or more acting in different directions at same point. [L *resulto* spring back]

**rĕsū′me** (-z-) v.t. & i. Get or take again or back; begin again, go on (with) after interruption, begin to speak or work or use again, recommence (*resume work, the thread of one's discourse, one's maiden name*); **résumé** (rĕ′zōōmā) n., summary; **rĕsŭ′mption** (-z-) n.; **rĕsŭ′mptive** (-z-) a. [F or L (*sumo sumpt-* take)]

**rĕsŭ′rgen|t** a. Rising or arising again; ~**ce** n. [L (foll.)]

**rĕsurrĕ′ction** (-z-) n. (R~) rising of Christ from the grave, rising again of dead at the Last Judgement; exhumation (lit. or fig.); revival after disuse or inactivity or decay; **rĕsurrĕ′ct** (-z-) v.t., (colloq.) revive practice or memory of, take from grave, dig up. [F f. L *resurgo -surrect-* rise again]

**rĕsŭ′scit|āte** v.t. & i. (~**able**). Revive from unconsciousness or apparent death; return or restore to vogue, vigour, or vividness; ~**ā′tion**, ~**ātor**, ns.; ~**ātive** a. [L (CITE)]

**rē′tail** n., a., adv., & v. **1.** n. Selling of things in small quantities at a time and usu. not for resale. **2.** a. & adv. By retail (*buys wholesale and sells retail*). **3.** v.t. & i. Sell by retail; (of goods) be retailed (esp. *at* or *for* specified price); recount, relate details of. [F f. L *taillier* cut (TALLY)]

**rĕtai′n** v.t. Keep possession of, not lose, continue to have or practise or recognize, not abolish or discard or alter; succeed in remembering; keep in place, hold fixed; secure services of (esp. barrister) by engagement and preliminary payment (~**ing fee**, paid to secure services thus); ~**er** n., (esp.) retaining fee, (Hist.) dependant or follower of person of rank (**old ~er**, joc., old and faithful servant). [AF f. L *retineo -tent-*]

**rĕtā′li|āte** v.t. & i. Repay (injury, insult, etc.) in kind; cast (accusation) back *upon* person; do as one is done by, esp. return evil; ~**ā′tion**, ~**ātor**, ns.; ~**ative**, ~**atory**, (-lya-) adjs. [L (*talis* such)]

**rĕtā′rd** v.t. Make slow or late, delay progress or arrival or accomplishment or happening of; (in *p.p.*, esp.) backward in mental or physical development; **rētārdā′tion**, ~**ment**, ns. [F f. L (*tardus* slow)]

**rĕtch. 1.** v.i. Make motion of vomiting esp. ineffectually and involuntarily. **2.** n. Such motion or sound of it. [E]

**retd.** abbr. retired; returned.

**rĕtē′nt|ion** n. Retaining or being retained; ~**ive** a., tending to retain, (of memory) not forgetful; ~**ive of**, (of substance) apt to retain (moisture etc.). [F or L (RETAIN)]

**rē′think. 1.** v.t. (**re′thought**). Consider afresh, esp. with view to making changes. **2.** n. Rethinking, reassessment. [RE-²]

**rĕ′tĭcen|ce** *n.* Avoidance of expressing all one knows or feels or more than is necessary; disposition to silence, taciturnity; **~t** *a.* (*on*, *about*). [F f. L (*reticeo* keep silent)]

**rĕtī′cūl|āte¹** *v.t.* & *i.* Divide or be divided in fact or appearance into a network; **~ate²** *a.*, reticulated; **~ā′tion** *n.*, (usu. in *pl.*) netlike marking or arrangement; **rĕ′tĭcŭle** *n.*, (arch.) lady's netted or other bag to serve as pocket. [L (*reticulum* dim. of *rete* net)]

**rĕ′tĭna** *n.* (*pl.* **~s**, **~e**). Layer at back of eyeball sensitive to light; **~l** *a.* [L (*rete* net)]

**rĕ′tĭnūe** *n.* Suite or train of persons attending great personage. [F (RE-TAIN)]

**rĕtī′re** *v.i.* & *t.* Withdraw, go away, retreat, seek seclusion or shelter, recede, go (as) to bed, (**~ from the world**, become recluse; **~ into** oneself, become uncommunicative or unsociable); cease *from* or give up office or employment, (Crick.) voluntarily terminate or be compelled to suspend one's innings, (*retire from the army, on a pension*; *batsman retired hurt*; **retiring age**, at which persons usually retire); compel, order, (employee, troops, etc.) to retire; **~d** (-īr′d) *a.*, withdrawn from society or observation, secluded, (*lives a retired life*; *a retired valley*), who has retired (*a retired grocer*); **~d list** (of retired officers); **~ment** (-īr′m-) *n.*, (esp.) seclusion, secluded place, condition of having retired; **rĕtīr′-ing** *a.*, (esp.) shy, fond of seclusion. [F (*tirer* draw)]

**rĕtŏr′t.** **1.** *v.t.* & *i.* Repay (insult, attack) in kind; cast (mischief etc.), fling (charge, sarcasm), back (on or *upon* originator or aggressor); make (argument) tell against *or against* its user; say by way of witty reply or counter-charge or counter-argument; make retort. **2.** *n.* Incisive reply, repartee; turning of charge or argument against its originator; vessel with long downward-bent neck for distilling liquids; vessel for heating coal to generate gas. [L (*retorqueo* -*tort*- twist)]

**rĕtŏu′ch** (-ŭ′-) *v.t.* Improve (composition, picture, photograph, etc.) by fresh touches or alterations. [F (RE-²)]

**rĕtrā′ce** *v.t.* Trace back to source or beginning, recall the course of in

memory, go back over (one's *steps* or *way*; lit., or fig. of undoing actions).

**rĕtrā′ct** *v.t.* & *i.* Draw (esp. part of one's body) or be drawn back or in (snail retracts its horns); draw (undercarriage etc.) into body of aircraft; withdraw, refuse to abide by, acknowledge falsity or error of, (statement, promise, opinion, etc., or abs.); **rĕtrāctā′tion** *n.*, revoking, recanting; **~ile** *a.*, capable of being retracted; **~i′lĭty** *n.*, **~ion** *n.*; **~ive** *a.*, serving to draw back; **~or** *n.* [L *retraho* -*tract*- draw back]

**rĕtrea′d²** (-ĕd) (for *retread¹* see RE-²). **1.** *v.t.* Put fresh tread on (tyre). **2.** (rē′-) *n.* Retreaded tyre. [RE-²]

**rĕtrea′t.** **1.** *v.i.* Go back, retire, relinquish a position, (esp. of army etc.); recede. **2.** *n.* Act of, (Mil.) signal for, retreating (**beat a ~**, retreat, abandon undertaking; **make good** one's **~**, get safely away); (Mil.) bugle-call at sunset; withdrawing into privacy or security, (place of) shelter or seclusion; (Eccl.) temporary retirement for religious exercises. [F f. L (RETRACT)]

**rĕtrĕ′nch** *v.t.* & *i.* Cut down, reduce amount of, (expense or its cause, literary work); cut off, deduct; cut down expenses, introduce economies; **~ment** *n.* [F (TRENCH)]

**rĕtrī′al** *n.* Retrying of a case. [RE-²]

**rĕtrĭbū′tion** *n.* Recompense usu. for evil done; vengeance; **rĕtrĭ′būtĭve** *a.* [L (AS TRIBUTE)]

**rĕtrie′v|e.** **1.** *v.t.* & *i.* Regain possession of, recover by investigation or effort of memory; find again (stored information); rescue *from* bad state etc., restore to flourishing state; repair, set right, (loss, disaster, error); (of dog, esp. of special breed) find and bring in (killed or wounded game etc., or abs.). **2.** *n.* Possibility of recovery (*beyond, past, retrieve*). **3.** **~al** *n.*; **~er** *n.*, (esp.) dog of breed used for retrieving. [F (*trouver* find)]

**rĕ′tr|ō-** *pref.* Backwards, back again, in return, behind; **~ŏā′ctĭve** *a.*, having retrospective effect; **~ocē′de** *v.t.*, cede (territory) back again; **~ocē′ssion** (-shon) *n.*; **~ōchoir** (-kwīr) *n.*, part of cathedral or large church behind high altar. [L]

**rĕ′trŏ|grāde. 1.** *a.* Directed backwards, reversing esp. to inferior state, declining, reversed, (*retrograde motion, order*). **2.** *v.i.* Move backwards, recede; decline, revert. **3.** **~grĕ′ss**

*v.i.*, move backwards, deteriorate; ~**gre′ssion** (-shǒn) *n.*, reversal of development, deterioration, backward movement; ~**gre′ssive** *a.* [L (*retrogradior -gress-* move backwards)]

**re′tro-rocket** *n.* Auxiliary rocket for slowing down spacecraft etc. [ROCKET²]

**re′trospject** *n.* Regard or reference *to* precedent or authority or previous conditions; survey of past time or events (**in ~ect**, when looked back on); ~**e′ction** *n.*, action of looking back esp. into the past; ~**e′ctive** *a.*, of, in, proceeding by, retrospection, (of statute etc.) not restricted to the future, having application to what is past, (of view) lying to the rear. [RETRO-, PROSPECT]

**retroussé** (retrōō′sā) *a.* (Of nose) turned up at tip. [F]

**retrȳ′** *v.t.* Try (defendant, law case) again. [RE-²]

**retúrn′** *n.* **1.** *v.i.* & *t.* Come or go back (*gone never to return; return home, by the way one came; shall return to the subject; unto dust shalt thou return*); bring, convey, give, yield, put, send, or pay, back or in requital (*return fish to the water, borrowed book, undelivered letter to sender; investments return a profit; return the compliment* lit. or fig.; *a blow,* person's *greeting, love, gun-fire,* etc.); throw, strike, etc., (ball) back in cricket, tennis, etc.; (Cards) lead (suit) previously led or bid by partner; say in reply (~ **thanks**, express thanks esp. in grace at meals or in response to toast or condolence), retort; state, mention, or describe, officially esp. in answer to writ or formal demand (*liabilities were returned at £5,000; were all returned guilty*); (of constituency) elect as M.P. etc. (‖~**ing officer**, official conducting election in constituency and announcing name of person elected). **2.** *n.* Coming or going back; = *return of* POST²; ‖~ (**ticket**), ticket for journey to place and back to starting-point (so ~ **fare**); **many happy ~s (of the day)** (birthday or festival greeting); (in *sing.* or *pl.*) (coming in of) proceeds or profit of undertaking (*the returns were large; brings an adequate return*; **small profits and quick ~s**, motto of cheap shop relying on large trade); giving, sending, putting, or paying, back, thing so given etc., returning (of ball, suit at cards, etc.), (*must

ask for the return of the book; received a ticket in return for his fare;* SALE *or* return); formal report compiled or submitted by order (*income-tax return*); ~ (**match, game**), second match etc. between same opponents. [F f. Rom. (TURN)]

**reū′nion** (-nyon) *n.* Reuniting or being reunited; social gathering esp. of intimates or persons with a common interest. [F (RE-²)]

**rev.** (colloq.) **1.** *n.* Revolution (of engine). **2.** *v.i.* & *t.* (-vv-). (Of engine) revolve; ~ **up**, increase speed of revolution; ~ (**up**), cause (engine) to run quickly (esp. when starting). [abbr.]

**Rev.** *abbr.* Revelation (N.T.); Reverend.

**revā′lūe** *v.t.* Give new value to (esp. currency, opp. *devalue*); ~**ā′tion** *n.* [RE-²]

**revǎ′mp** *v.t.* Vamp or patch up again; renovate, revise, improve.

**Revd.** *abbr.* Reverend.

**reveal′** *v.t.* (Esp. of God) make known by inspiration or supernatural means (~**ed religion**, opp. *natural religion*); disclose, divulge, betray; display, show, let appear (~ **itself**, come to sight or knowledge). [F or L (*velum* veil)]

**reveille′** (-vă′lǐ, -vě′lǐ) *n.* Military waking-signal. [F *réveillez* wake up]

**re′vel. 1.** *v.i.* (‖-ll-). Make merry, be riotously festive; take keen delight *in*. **2.** *n.* Revelling; (in *sing.* or *pl.*) (occasion of indulgence in) merry-making. [F f. L (REBEL)]

**revelā′tion** *n.* Disclosing of knowledge, or knowledge disclosed, to man by divine or supernatural agency; (**the R~ (of St. John the Divine**), colloq. (**the**) **R~s**, last book of N.T.); striking disclosure (*it was a revelation to me*). [F or L (RE-VEAL)]

**re′velrȳ** *n.* Revelling. [REVEL]

**revě′nge** (-nj). **1.** *v.t.* & *i.* Satisfy oneself, (in *pass.*) be satisfied, with retaliation (*for* offence, *on* or *upon* offender); retaliate (offence; *on* or *upon* offender); avenge (person). **2.** *n.* (Act done in) revenging; desire to revenge, vindictive feeling; (in games) opportunity given for reversing former result by return game (*give* person *his revenge*). **3.** ~**ful** (-njf-) *a.* (**-lly**), eager for revenge. [F f. L (VINDICATE)]

**re′venue** *n.* Income, esp. of large

amount, from any source; (in *pl.*) items constituting this; State's annual income from which public expenses are met (‖INLAND or \*INTERNAL *revenue*); department of civil service collecting this. [F *revenu(e)* (*revenir* return)]

**rêvêr'berāte** *v.i.* & *t.* (Of sound, light, heat) be returned or reflected; return (sound etc.) thus; ~ā'tion *n.*, (esp.) echo; ~ant, ~ative, *adjs.* [L *verbero* beat]

**rêvêr'e** *v.t.* Hold in deep and usu. affectionate or religious respect. [F or L (*vereor* fear)]

**rê'verence. 1.** *n.* Revering or being revered, capacity for revering, (*hold in, regard with, reverence; feel reverence for, pay reverence to; lacks reverence*); (arch.) obeisance. **2.** *v.t.* Regard with reverence. [F f. L (prec.)]

**rê'verend** *a.* Deserving reverence, revered, (esp. as title of clergyman; **Very R~**, of dean; **Right R~**, of bishop; **Most R~**, of archbishop or Ir. R.C. bishop; **the ~ gentleman**, the clergyman in question); **R~ Mother**, Mother Superior of convent. [F, or L *reverendus* (REVERE)]

**rê'ver|ent** *a.* Feeling or showing reverence; ~ê'ntial (-shal) *a.* (-lly), of the nature of, due to, characterized by, reverence. [L (REVERE)]

**rê'verie** *n.* (Fit of) abstracted musing (*lost in* (*a*) *reverie*). [F]

**rêver's** (-vêr') *n.* (*pl.* same *pr.* -z). Turned-back edge of garment revealing under-surface; material on this surface. [F (foll.)]

**rêvêr's|e** *a., v.,* & *n.* **1.** *a.* Opposite or contrary (*to*) in character or order, inverted, back(ward), upside down; ~e gear (used to make vehicle etc. travel backwards). **2.** *v.t.* & *i.* Turn the other way round or up or inside out, convert to opposite character or effect, (*reverse motion, policy, order,* etc.); make (vehicle) travel backwards, (of vehicle) travel backwards, (~ing light, operated when vehicle is travelling backwards); make (engine etc.) work in contrary direction; revoke, annul, (decree, act, etc.); ~e arms, hold rifles butt upwards; ‖~e the charge(s), make recipient of telephone call responsible for payment. **3.** *n.* The contrary (*of*); contrary of usual manner (*name printed in reverse*; **the ~e of**, far from *complimentary* etc.); reverse gear or mo-

tion; (device on) subordinate side of coin etc. (lit. or fig.; opp. *obverse*); reverse side; verso of leaf; piece of misfortune, disaster, esp. defeat in battle, (*the reverses of fortune; suffered a reverse*). **4.** ~al *n.*, reversing or being reversed; ~ible *a.* (-bly); ~ĭbi'litȳ *n.*; ~ion *n.* (-shon), (return to grantor or passing to ultimate grantee of, right of ultimate succession to) estate granted till specified date or event (esp. death of original grantee), return to a previous state, habit, etc., esp. (Biol.) to ancestral type; ~ionarȳ (-shon-) *a.*; **rêvêr't** *v.i.* & *t.*, (of property, office, etc.) return by reversion, return *to* former state etc., recur *to* subject in talk or thought; **rêvêr'tĭble** *a.* (-bly), (of property) subject to reversion. [F f. L (*verto vers-* turn)]

**rêvê't** *v.t.* (-tt-) Face (rampart, wall, etc.) with masonry esp. in fortification; ~ment *n.* [F *revêtir* (VEST)]

**rêview'** (-vū'). **1.** *n.* Display and formal inspection of troops etc. (~ **order**, dress and arrangement usual at reviews; **pass in ~**, lit. or fig., examine or be examined); (esp. Law) revision; retrospect, survey of the past; general survey or reconsideration of subject or thing; published account or criticism of book etc.; periodical publication with articles on current events, new books, art, etc. **2.** *v.t.* View again; subject to esp. legal review; survey, glance over, look back on; hold review of (troops etc.); write review of (book etc., or abs.); ~er *n.*, (esp.) writer of reviews. [F f. *revoir* (VIEW)]

**rêvī'le** *v.t.* Call by ill names, speak unkindly to, rail at. [F (VILE)]

**rêvī's|e** (-z). **1.** *v.t.* (Re-)examine and improve or amend (literary matter, printers' proofs, law, constitution, etc.; **R~ed Version**, \***R~ed Standard Version**, revisions of Bible made 1870–84, 1946–57); read again (work learnt or done, or abs.) for improvement of one's knowledge or of work's quality. **2.** *n.* (Print.) Proof-sheet embodying corrections made in earlier proof. **3.** **rêvī'sion** (-zhon) *n.*, revising, revised edition or form; **rêvī'sionism** (-zhon-) *n.*, policy of revision or modification, esp. of Marxist-Leninist doctrine; **rêvī'sionist** (-zhon-) *n.*; ~orȳ *a.* of revision. [F, or L *reviso* (*video vis-* see)]

**rĕvī′v|e** *v.i.* & *t.* Come or bring back to consciousness, life, existence, vigour, notice, use, activity, validity, or vogue; **~al** *n.*, reviving or being revived (**~al of learning, letters**, etc., at Renaissance), new production of old play etc., (campaign to promote) reawakening of religious fervour; **~alism, ~alist**, *ns.*, organization, organizer, of religious revival; **rĕvī′vĭfȳ** *v.t.*, restore to animation, activity, vigour, or life; **rĕvīvĭfĭcā′tion** *n.* [F or L (*vivo* live)]

**rĕvō′ke. 1.** *v.t.* & *i.* Rescind, withdraw, cancel, (decree, promise, etc.); (Cards) make revoke; **rĕ′vocable** *a.* (**-bly**) **rĕvocā′tion** *n.* **2.** *n.* Card-player's failure to follow suit when able to do so. [F or L (*voco* call)]

**rĕvō′lt. 1.** *v.i.* & *t.* Fall away *from* or rise *against* ruler, go over *to* rival power; feel strong disgust *at*, rise in repugnance *against*, turn in loathing *from*; affect with strong disgust. **2.** *n.* Act of rebelling; insurrection (**in ~**, having revolted); sense of loathing, mood of protest or defiance. **3.** **~ing** *a.*, (esp.) disgusting, horrible. [F f. It. (REVOLVE)]

**rĕvolu′tion** (-lōō′-) *n.* Revolving, (time taken for) single completion of orbit or rotation, cyclic recurrence; reversal of conditions, fundamental reconstruction, esp. forcible action by nation etc. to substitute new ruler or system of government; **~arȳ** *a.* & *n.*, involving great and usu. violent change, (instigator or supporter) of political revolution; **~ize** *v.t.*, completely change or reconstruct. [F or L (foll.)]

**rĕvō′lv|e** *v.t.* & *i.* Turn round (and round), move in orbit, (*mechanism for revolving the turntable*; *Earth revolves round sun and on its own axis*; *as the seasons revolve*); ponder (problem etc.) in the mind; **~er** *n.*, (esp.) pistol with revolving chambers enabling user to fire several shots without reloading; **~ing** *a.*; **~ing door**, (with several partitions turning round central axis, to exclude draughts of air). [L *revolvo -volut-*]

**rĕvūe′** *n.* Theatrical entertainment reviewing (esp. satirically) current events etc. [F (REVIEW)]

**rĕvŭ′ls|ion** (-shon) *n.* Sudden violent change of feeling; abhorrence; **~ive** *a.* [F or L (*vello vuls-* pull)]

**rĕwar′d** (-wǒr′d). **1.** *n.* Return or recompense for service or merit, requital for good or evil; sum offered for detection of criminal, recovery of lost property, etc. **2.** *v.t.* Repay, requite, recompense (service or doer of it, offender, offence). **3.** **~ing** *a.*, (of task, book, etc.) well worth doing, reading, etc. [AF *reward(er)* REGARD]

**Rex** (rĕks) *n.* Reigning king (in use as REGINA). [L, = king]

**Rey′nard** (rĕ′n-, rā′n-) *n.* (Proper name for) fox. [F *Renart*]

‖**R.F.C.** *abbr.* Rugby Football Club.

**r.h.** *abbr.* right hand.

**rhä′psod|y̆** *n.* Enthusiastic high-flown utterance or composition; emotional irregular piece of music; (Gk Ant.) (part of) epic poem of length for one recitation; **rhăpsō′dical** *a.* (**-lly**); **~ist** *n.*, person who rhapsodizes; **~ize** *v.i.*, talk or write rhapsodies (*on, about*, etc.). [L f. Gk (*rhaptō* stitch, ODE)]

**Rhĕ′nish.** (arch.) **1.** *a.* Of the Rhine. **2.** *n.* Rhine wine. [AF *reneis* f. L (*Rhenus* Rhine)]

**rhē′sus** *n.* Small Ind. monkey; **R~ factor**, antigen occurring in red blood cells of most persons and some animals (e.g. rhesus monkey); **R~-po′sitive, R~-ne′gative**, having, not having, the Rhesus factor. [L f. Gk *Rhēsos*, mythical king]

**rhĕ′toric** *n.* Art of persuasive or impressive speaking or writing; language designed to persuade or impress (often with implication of insincerity, exaggeration, etc.); **rhĕtŏ′rical** *a.* (**-lly**), expressed with view to persuasive or impressive effect, of the nature of rhetoric; **~al question** (asked not for information but to produce effect, as *who cares?* for *nobody cares*); **rhĕtorĭ′cian** (-shan) *n.* [F f. L f. Gk (*rhētōr* orator)]

**rheum** (rōōm) *n.* Watery secretion or discharge such as tears, saliva, or mucus (arch.); catarrh; **~ă′tic**, (*a.*: **-ically**) of, suffering from, subject to, causing, or caused by rheumatism, (*n.*; in *pl.*, colloq.), rheumatism; **~atic fever** (with pain in joints); **~ă′ticky̆** *a.*, (colloq.) like, having, rheumatism; **~′atism** *n.*, disease marked by inflammation and pain in the joints, muscles, or fibrous tissue; **~′atoid** *a.*, having the character of rheumatism (**~atoid arthritis**, chronic progressive disease causing inflammation and stiffening of joints). [F f. L f. Gk (*rheô* flow)]

**Rhine** *n.* ~**'land,** region adjoining the Rhine; **r~'stone,** imitation diamond; **~ wine,** (usu. white) wine from Rhine vineyards. [river]

**rhī'nō**[1] *n.* (sl.) Money. [orig. unkn.]

**rhī'nō**[2] *n.* (sl.; *pl.* same, **~s**). = foll. [abbr.]

**rhīnŏ'ceros** *n.* Large thick-skinned quadruped with horn or two horns on nose. [L f. Gk (*rhis* nose, *keras* horn)]

**rhī'zōme** *n.* Prostrate or subterranean rootlike stem emitting both roots and shoots. [Gk *rhizoma*]

**rhō** *n.* Seventeenth Greek letter (P, ρ) = r. [Gk]

**Rhōdes** (-dz) *n.* ~ **Scholar,** holder of any of a number of ~ **Scholarships** awarded annually and tenable at Oxford Univ. by students from certain Commonwealth countries, S. Africa, W. Germany, and U.S. [person]

**rhŏdodĕ'ndron** *n.* Evergreen shrub with large trumpet-shaped flowers. [L f. Gk (*rhodon* rose, *dendron* tree)]

**rhŏmb** (-m) *n.* Rhombus. [F or L f. Gk *rhombos*]

**rhŏ'mb|ĭc** *a.* (~**ically**). Rhombus-shaped; ~**oid** *n.,* quadrilateral of which only opposite sides and angles are equal; ~**oi'dal** *a.* (-lly); ~**us** *n.* (*pl.* ~**uses,** ~**i** *pr.* -ī), oblique equilateral parallelogram, e.g. diamond on playing-cards.

**rhu'bárb** (rōo'-) *n.* (Fleshy leaf-stalks, used like fruit, of) a garden plant; (purgative made from) root of a Chinese plant. [F f. L f. Gk *rha rhubarb, barbaros* foreign]

**rhỹme, rīme**[1]. **1.** *n.* Identity of sound between words or verse-lines extending from end to last fully accented vowel and (in E Pros., strictly) not further (**male, masculine,** ~, between words ending in stressed syllables; **female, feminine,** ~, of two syllables, with the second unstressed; **neither ~ nor reason,** no reasonable character; ~**-scheme,** arrangement of rhymes within a piece of verse); poem with rhymes, (in *pl.* or *sing.*) verse having rhymes, use of rhyme (NURSERY *rhyme; prefer blank verse to rhyme*; *am sending you some rhymes*); word providing a rhyme (*to* another; *can't find a rhyme to* '*teacups*'). **2.** *v.i. & t.* Write rhymes; put or make (story

etc.) into rhyme; (of words or lines) exhibit rhyme; (of word) supply or act as rhyme *to* or *with*; treat (word) as rhyming *with*; **rhyming slang** (replacing words by rhyming words or phrases, e.g. *stairs* by *apples and pears*). **3. rhỹ'mer,** ~**'ster** (-ms-), *ns.,* writer of rhymes. [F *rime* f. L (foll.)]

**rhỹ'thm** (-dhm, -thm) *n.* Measured flow of words and phrases in verse or prose determined by various relations of long and short or accented and unaccented syllables; aspect of musical composition concerned with periodical accent and the duration of notes (~ **and blues,** popular music with blues themes and strong rhythm); movement with regular succession of strong and weak elements; regularly recurring sequence of events (~ **method,** contraception by avoiding sexual intercourse near times of ovulation); ~**ic(al)** (-dhm-) *adjs.* (-**ically**). [F or L f. Gk *rhuthmos*]

**R.I.** *abbr.* Rhode Island; Royal Institute; Royal Institution.

**rĭb. 1.** *n.* One of the curved bones articulated in pairs to spine and protecting thoracic cavity and its organs (**true, sternal,** ~, joined also to breastbone, opp. **false, floating, short,** ~); POKE[1] person *in the ribs*; ~(**s**) *of beef* etc. (as joint of meat; SPARE-*rib*); ridge or long raised piece often of stronger or thicker material across surface or through structure serving to support or strengthen or adorn, e.g. part of framework of leaf, spur of mountain, one of ship's curved timbers to which planks are nailed or corresponding ironwork, arch supporting vault, hinged rod of umbrella frame; combination of plain and purl stitches producing ribbed somewhat elastic fabric. **2.** *v.t.* (-**bb**-). Provide with ribs; (colloq.) make fun of, tease. **3.** ~**bed** (-bd) *a.,* having ribs or riblike markings; ~**bing** *n.,* ribs or riblike structure. [E]

**rĭ'bald. 1.** *a.* (Of language or its user) scurrilous, obscene, irreverent, coarsely humorous. **2.** *n.* Ribald person; ~**rỹ** *n.,* ribald talk. [F (*riber* be licentious)]

**rĭ'bbon, rĭ'band,** *n.* (Piece or length of) silk or other material woven into narrow band esp. for adorning hair or costume; ribbon of special colour etc. worn to indicate award of medal etc. or membership of knightly order, club, athletic team, etc. (BLUE *ribbon*); long narrow strip of anything, e.g. inked material struck by typewriter types to print on paper; (in *pl.*) ragged strips (*torn to ribbons*); ~ **development**, building of houses along main road outwards from town. [F *riban* f. Gmc]

**ri′bes** (-z) *n.* Plant of genus including currants and gooseberries. [L f. Arab.]

**ribonŭclē′ic** *a.* ~ **acid**, substance controlling protein-synthesis in cells. [*ribose* sugar, NUCLEIC]

**rice** *n.* (Seeds, used as staple food in many Eastern countries, and elsewhere in puddings, cakes, etc. and savoury dishes, of) chiefly oriental grass grown in marshes; ~~**paper** (made from pith of an oriental tree and used for painting and in cookery). [F *ris* f. It. f. L f. Gk *oruza*]

**rich** *a.* (Of person, society, State, etc.) having riches; (of country, period, soil, etc.) abounding in or *in* natural resources or some valuable possession or production, fertile, (**strike it** ~, find source of prosperity); valuable (*rich offerings, harvest*); (of dress, furniture, building, banquet, etc.) splendid, costly, elaborate; (of food or diet) containing or involving much fat, oil, spice, etc.; (of colour, voice, sound, smell) mellow, deep, full, not thin; abundant, ample (*a rich supply of ideas*); (of incident, assertion, etc.) highly amusing or ludicrous or entertaining; (of mixture in internal combustion engine) containing more than normal proportion of fuel; ~′ĕs (-z) *n.*, (usu. as *pl.*) abundant means, valuable possessions, ownership of these; ~′lў̆ *adv.*, (esp.) fully, thoroughly, (*richly deserves a thrashing, to succeed*). [E & F]

**rick**[1] *n.* Stack of hay etc. [E]

‖**rick**[2], **wrĭck**, *n.*, & *v.t.* Slight(ly) sprain or strain. [LG *wricken*]

**ri′ckĕt|s** *n.* (as *sing.* or *pl.*) Children's deficiency disease with softening of bones; ~ў̆ *a.* (**-ily, -iness**), suffering from rickets, shaky, weak-jointed, insecure. [orig. uncert.]

**ri′ckră̆ck.** See RICRAC.

**ri′cksha(w)** *n.* Light two-wheeled hooded vehicle drawn by one or more persons. [abbr. *jinricksha(w)* f. Jap.]

**ri′cochet** (-shā, -shĕt). **1.** *n.* Skipping or rebounding of projectile esp. shell or bullet on surface; hit made after this. **2.** *v.i.* & *t.* (**-t-, -tt-,** *pr.* -shăd *or* -shĕtĭd, -shāing *or* -shĕtĭng, etc.) (Of projectile) skip or rebound once or more on water etc. [F]

**ri′crăc, ri′ckrăck,** *n.* Zigzag braided trimming for garments. [RACK[1]]

**rĭd** *v.t.* (**-dd-; rid**). Make (person, place) free *of* (esp. in *p.p.*; *glad to be, must get, rid of it*); ~′**dance** *n.*; **good** ~**dance**, thing or person one is glad to be rid of. [N]

**ri′dden.** See RIDE.

**ri′ddle**[1]. **1.** *n.* Question, statement, or description, designed or serving to test ingenuity or give amusement in divining its answer or meaning or reference; puzzling fact, thing, or person. **2.** *v.t.* Speak in or propound riddles; solve (riddle); ~ **me**, (arch.) solve my riddle (if you can); **ri′ddling** *a.*, expressed in riddles. [E (READ)]

**ri′ddle**[2]. **1.** *n.* Coarse sieve. **2.** *v.t.* Pass through riddle, sift (lit. or fig.); fill (ship, person) with holes esp. of gunshot; refute (person, theory) with facts; (in *p.p.*) filled *with* (faults etc.). [E]

**ride. 1.** *v.t.* & *i.* (**rode** *pr.* rōd; **ri′dden** *pr.* rĭ′-). Sit on and be carried by horse etc., go on horseback etc. or on bicycle etc. or in train or other public conveyance (cf. DRIVE), sit or go or be *on* something as on horse esp. astride, sit on and manage horse, lie at anchor, float buoyantly, (of moon etc.) seem to float, rest *in* or *on* while moving, (**let** thing ~, leave it undisturbed); traverse on horseback etc., ride over or through; ride on, sit heavily on, oppress, dominate, tyrannize over, (*ride a bicycle*; *ship rides the waves*; *cliché*, HAG, -*ridden*); be carried by, travel on; yield to (blow) so as to reduce its impact; give ride to, cause to ride (*ride child on* one's *back*); (of rider) cause (horse etc.) to move forward (*at fence* etc.); ride-a-COCK-horse; ~ **down**, overtake or trample on horseback; ~ **for a fall**, ride or (fig.) act recklessly, risk defeat; ~ **high**, (fig.) be successful; ~ **to hounds**, be fox-hunter; ~ **out**, come safely through (storm; lit. or fig.); ~ **over,**

WALK over; (in horse-race); *ride* ROUGH*shod*; ~ **up**, (of garment) work upwards when worn. **2.** *n.* Journey in esp. public conveyance, spell of riding on horse, bicycle, person's back, etc., (**take for a ~**, sl., deceive, hoax); path (esp. through woods) for riding on; quality of sensations when riding (*gives a bumpy ride*). **3. ri′der** *n.*, (esp.) additional clause amending or supplementing document, corollary, ‖recommendation etc. added to verdict, (Math.) problem given as corollary of theorem etc.; **ri′ding**[1] *n.*; *riding*-HABIT; **riding-school** (where horse--riding is taught). [E]

**ridge** *n.* Line of junction of two surfaces sloping upwards towards each other; long narrow hill-top, mountain range, watershed; (Agric.) one of set of raised strips separated by furrows; (Meteor.) elongated region of high barometric pressure; any narrow elevation across surface; ~-**pole**, horizontal pole of long tent; ~′**way**, road along ridge; **ri′dgy** *a.* (-iness). [E]

**ri′dicule. 1.** *v.t.* Make fun of, subject to ridicule, laugh at. **2.** *n.* Making or being made object of derision or mockery; **ridi′culous** *a.*, deserving to be laughed at, unreasonable. [F or L (*rideo* laugh)]

**ri′ding**[1]. See RIDE.

‖**ri′ding**[2] *n.* (Hist.) division (**East**, **North**, **West**, **R**~) of Yorkshire. [E f. N, = third part]

**rife** *pred. a.* Of common occurrence, met with in large numbers or quantities, current. [E f. N]

**riff** *n.* Short repeated phrase in jazz and similar music. [orig. unkn.]

**ri′ff-räff** *n. The* rabble, disreputable or undesirable persons. [F *rif et raf*]

**ri′fle. 1.** *v.t.* Search and rob; make spiral grooves in (gun or its barrel or bore) to produce rotatory motion of projectile. **2.** *n.* Firearm with rifled barrel (esp. fired from shoulder--level); (in *pl.*) riflemen; *rifle*--GRENADE; ~**man**, soldier armed with rifle; ~**range**, distance coverable by shot from rifle, place for rifle-practice. **3. ri′fling** *n.*, (esp.) arrangement of grooves in rifle. [F]

**rift** *n.* Fissure, chasm, crack, split; disagreement, dispute. [Scand., rel. to RIVE]

**rig**[1]. **1.** *n.* ‖Trick, dodge, way of swindling. **2.** *v.t.* (-gg-). Manage or conduct fraudulently (*a rigged election*; ~ **the market**, cause artificial rise or fall in prices). [orig. unkn.]

**rig**[2]. **1.** *v.t.* (-gg-). Provide (ship) with spars, ropes, etc.; fit (*out*, *up*, or abs.) with or *with* or *in* clothes or other equipment (‖~-**out** *n.*, such clothes etc.); assemble and adjust parts of (aircraft); set *up* hastily or as makeshift or by utilizing odd materials. **2.** *n.* Way ship's masts, sails, etc., are arranged; (oil) ~, equipment for drilling an oil-well, person's look as determined by clothes etc. **3.** -**rigged** (-gd) *a.*, having specified rig (*square*, *schooner*, -*rigged*); ~′**ger** (-g-) *n.*, (esp.) one who attends to rigging of aircraft; ~′**ging** (-g-) *n.*, (esp.) ship's spars, ropes, etc. [perh. Scand.]

**right** *a.*, *v.*, *n.*, & *adv.* **1.** *a.* (Of conduct etc.) just, required by morality or equity or duty, (*it is only right to tell you, that you should know*; ~--**minded**, having natural inclination to favour what is right); correct, true, (*right use of words*; *a right account of the matter*); the preferable or most suitable, *the* less wrong or not wrong, (*which is the right way to proceed?*; *the right man in the right place*; *a fault on the right side*; MR. *Right*; ~ **side** of fabric etc., side meant for show or use; **on the ~ side of**, in favour with (person); **on the ~ side of** *forty*, not yet 40 years old); in good or normal condition, sound, sane, satisfactory, well--advised, not mistaken, (*all's right with the world*; *is not quite right in the head*; **as ~ as rain**, **as** a TRIVET, etc., entirely normal; **in** one's ~ **mind**, not mad etc.; **put** or **set** ~, restore to order, health, etc., correct mistaken ideas of (person); SEE[1] *person right*; ~ **whale**, kind yielding best whalebone; ~ (**you are**)!, ‖~ **oh!**, colloq. excl. of assent to order or proposal; (arch. or colloq.) real, properly so called, (*made a right mess of it*); on or towards side of human body which in the majority of persons has the more-used hand, on or towards that part of an object which is analogous to person's right side or (with opp. sense) which is nearer to spectator's right hand, (*right side, eye*, etc.; *right flank* of army etc.); ~ **about** (**face** or **turn**), right turn continued to face rear, reversal of policy, hasty retreat; ~ **angle**

(neither acute nor obtuse, made by lines meeting with equal angles on either side); at ~ angles, placed with right angle; ~ **arm**, (fig.) one's most reliable helper; right BANK¹; ~-**hand**, (fig.) indispensable or chief assistant; ~-**hand**, placed on the right hand; ~-**hand man**, indispensable or chief assistant; ~-**-handed**, using right hand by preference as more serviceable, made by or for the right hand, turning to right; ~-**hander**, right-handed person (esp. in games) or blow; ~ **wing** (of army, football etc. team, or political party, see sense 3), whence ~-**wi'nger**, member of this; ~'**most** a., furthest to the right; ~'**ward** a. & adv.; ~'**wards** (-z) adv. v.t. Restore to proper or straight or vertical position; make reparation for or to, avenge, (wrong, wronged person); vindicate, justify, rehabilitate; correct (mistakes etc.), correct mistakes in; (usu. refl.) set in order (a fault that will right itself). **3.** n. What is just, fair treatment, the juster cause, (by ~(s), if right were done; do person ~, do ~ by person, treat or think of him fairly; **in the** ~, having justice or truth on one's side); justification, fair claim, being entitled to privilege or immunity, thing one is entitled to, (has a, the, no, right to thing, to do, of doing; belongs to him of or as of or by right; rights and duties; **in** one's **own** ~, not through marriage, adherence, etc.; ~ **of way**, right established by usage to pass over another's ground, path subject to such right, precedence in passing granted to one vehicle etc. over another; **Bill of R~s**, ‖constitutional settlement of 1689, *constitutional amendments of 1791, statement of rights of a class of persons; ~**s issue**, offer of new shares at reduced price in proportion to holdings of old shares; **within** one's ~**s**, not exceeding one's authority or entitlement); (in pl.) right condition, true state, (**set** or **put to** ~**s**, arrange properly), true statement (do not know the rights of the case); right-hand part, region, or direction; (blow with) right hand; (Polit., often R~) conservatives collectively, so ~'**ism** n., principles or policy of political right, ~'**ist** n. **4.** adv. Straight (go right on; wind was right behind us); (colloq.) immediately (I'll be right back; ~ **away, off,**

immediately, without pausing); all the way to, round, through, etc., completely off, out, etc., (sank right to the bottom; turned right round); exactly, quite, (right here, now; right in the middle); (arch.) very, to the full, (know right well; ‖Right HONOURABLE, REVEREND); justly, properly, correctly, truly, satisfactorily, (whether they act right or wrong; does not hold his pen, do the sum, right; nothing goes right with me; if I remember right; guessed right); on or to the right side; ~ **and left**, to or on both sides, on all sides, (he was abused right and left); ~, **left, and centre**, on all sides. **5.** ~'**eous** (rī'chus) a., (of person, life, action) morally right, upright, virtuous, law-abiding; ~'**ful** a. (-lly), (of action etc.) equitable, fair, (of person) legitimately entitled to position etc. (the rightful king), (of property etc.) that one is entitled to; ~'**ly** adv., justly, properly, correctly, justifiably; ‖~'**ō** int. = RIGHT oh. [E]

**ri'gid** a. Not flexible, that cannot be bent; inflexible, harsh, strict, precise; **rigi'dity** n. [F or L]

**ri'gmarole** n. Rambling or meaningless talk or tale. [orig. ragman roll catalogue]

**ri'gour, \*ri'gor¹**, (-ger) n. Severity, strictness, harshness, (in pl.) harsh measures; strict enforcement of rules etc.; extremity or excess of weather, hardship, etc., great distress; austerity of life; logical exactitude; **ri'gorous** a.; **ri'gōr²** (or rī'ger) n., (Path.) sudden chill with shivering; **rigor mor'tis**, stiffening of body after death. [F & L]

**rile** v.t. (colloq.) Anger, irritate. [F f. L]

**rill** n. Small stream. [prob. LDu.]

**rim** n. Outer ring of wheel not including tyre; raised edge or border, margin, verge; (-)~**med** (-md) a. [E]

**rime¹.** See RHYME.

**rime².** 1. n. Frost; (poet.) hoar-frost. **2.** v.t. Cover with rime. [E]

**rind** n. Bark of tree or plant; peel of fruit or vegetable; hard outer layer of cheese etc.; skin of bacon etc. [E]

**ri'nderpĕst** n. Disease of ruminants (esp. cattle). [G]

**ring¹. 1.** n. Circlet usu. of precious metal and often set with gem(s) worn esp. on finger as ornament or token (esp. of betrothal or marriage); (usu. small) circular band of any material; raised or sunk or otherwise distinguishable line or band round, or rim of, cylindrical or circular object; fold, coil, bend, piece, structure, part, or mark, having form of circular band; persons or things arranged in a circle, such arrangement; combination of traders, politicians, spies, etc., acting together for control of operations; circular or other enclosure for circus, boxing, betting at races (**the ~**, bookmakers), showing of cattle, etc.; circular or spiral course (**make** or **run ~s round**, go or do things very much better or quicker than); **~-dove**, large species of pigeon; **~-fence** (completely enclosing estate etc.); **~-finger**, third finger esp. of left hand; **~'leader**, leading instigator in mutiny, riot, etc.; **~ main**, electrical supply through cable in closed ring providing alternative paths; **~-master**, director of circus performance; **~ ouzel**, thrush allied to blackbird; **~ road**, bypass encircling town; **~'side** *a.*, (of seat etc.) close to scene of action; **~'worm**, contagious fungous skin-disease forming circular patches esp. on child's scalp. **2.** *v.t.* Encompass (*round, about, in*); put ring on (bird etc.). [E]

**ring**[2]. **1.** *v.i.* & *t.* (**rang; rung**). Give clear resonant sound (as) of vibrating metal (*bell, coin, rings; shot rang out*); (of bell) be sounded for specified purpose; sound in specified way (**~ false, true**, of coin and fig. of sentiments): lack, have, tone of genuineness); (of place) resound (*with* sound, *to* sound or its cause, *with* fame etc. or its theme, *with* talk of; **~ in** one's **ears**, linger in one's hearing); (of ears) be filled with sensation of ringing; make (bell) ring (**~ a bell**, colloq., begin to revive a memory; **~ the bell**, colloq., be successful); ring bell esp. as summons; ‖make telephone call (to; also **~ up; ~ back**, ring person who has earlier rung oneself; **~ off**, end telephone call); sound (peal, the CHANGES) on bells; cause (theatre curtain) to go *up* or *down* by bell; usher *in* or *out* with bell-ringing. **2.** *n.* Ringing sound or tone; specified feeling conveyed by utterance (*has a melancholy ring*); (sound caused by) act of ringing bell; (colloq.) telephone call (*give me a ring*); set of (church) bells. [E]

**ri'nglet** *n.* Curly lock of hair; **~ěd, ~y̆,** *adjs.* [RING[1]]

**rink** *n.* Stretch of ice, team, in game of curling; sheet of natural or artificial ice, floor, for (roller-)skating; strip of green, team, at bowls. [app. F *renc* RANK[1]]

**rinse. 1.** *v.t.* Wash out or *out* (vessel, mouth) by filling with clean water etc., moving about or shaking, and emptying; pour liquid over or wash lightly; put (clothes) through clean water to remove soap etc.; clear (impurities) *out* or *away* by rinsing. **2.** *n.* Rinsing; solution for temporary tinting of hair. [F *rincer*]

**ri'ot. 1.** *n.* Tumult, disorder, disturbance of the peace by a crowd (‖R~ **Act**, by which persons not dispersing after official reading of part of it incur guilt of felony; *read the R~ Act*, joc., insist that disobedience etc. is to cease); loud revelry; unrestrained indulgence in or display or enjoyment *of* (*a riot of emotion, colour, sound*); (colloq.) very amusing thing or person; **run ~**, (of person or his tongue or fancy) throw off all restraint; **~ous** *a.* **2.** *v.i.* Make or engage in riot. [F]

**rip**[1]. **1.** *v.t.* & *i.* (**-pp-**). Cut or tear (thing) quickly or forcibly away or apart (*rip out the lining*), make (hole etc.) thus, make long cut or tear in, (**~ off**, sl., defraud, steal; so **~-off** n.); come violently asunder, split; rush along (of ship, or transf.; **let ~**, not check speed of or interfere). **2.** *n.* Act of ripping; long tear or cut; stretch of rough water. **3.** **~-cord**, cord for releasing parachute from its pack; **~-roaring**, wildly noisy; **~-saw** (for sawing wood along the grain). [orig. unkn.]

**rip**[2] *n.* Worthless horse; dissolute person. [perh. = REP[2]]

**R.I.P.** *abbr.* (May he, she, they) rest in peace. [L *requiesca(n)t in pace*]

**ripār'ian** *a.* Of or on river-bank. [L (*ripa* bank)]

**ripe** *a.* Ready to be reaped, gathered, eaten, drunk, used, or dealt with, mature, in fit state *for*, (*ripe corn, fruit, cheese, wine, judgement, experience, beauty*; *time is ripe for speaking the truth*); (of person's age) advanced; **ri'pen** *v.t.* & *i.* [E]

**ripŏ'ste. 1.** *n.* Quick return thrust in fencing; (fig.) retort. **2.** *v.i.* Deliver riposte. [F f. It. (RESPOND)]

**ri'ppl|e. 1.** *n.* Ruffling of water's

surface, small wave(s); wavy appearance in hair etc.; gentle lively sound that rises and falls (*ripple of applause, laughter*); ~ỹ *a*. 2. *v.i.* & *t.* Form, flow in, show, sound like, ripples. [orig. unkn.]

**Rĭp văn Wĭ'nkle** *n*. Person with utterly antiquated ideas or information. [hero of tale, who slept 20 years]

**rise** (-z). 1. *v.i.* (rose *pr.* rōz; ~n *pr.* ri'zen). Get up from lying or sitting or kneeling or from bed, (of meeting etc.) cease to sit for business, recover standing or vertical position, become erect, leave ground, come to life again or *again* or *from the dead*; cease to be quiet or submissive, rebel, (of wind) begin to blow; come or go up, grow or project or swell or incline upwards, become higher, reach higher position or level or intensity or amount, come to surface, become or be visible above surroundings or horizon; (of bread) swell by action of yeast etc.; (of river etc.) have origin, begin to flow *from, in, at*; (of person's spirits) become more cheerful; (of fish) come to surface to feed; ~ *above*, be superior to (petty feelings etc.); ~ *to*, develop powers equal to (occasion). 2. *n*. Act or manner or amount of rising; upward slope, hill; social advancement, upward progress, increase in power, rank, price, amount, height, ‖wages, etc.; movement of fish to surface (**get a ~ out of**, fig., cause to display temper or characteristic behaviour); origin (*has* or *takes its rise in* or *from*; **give ~ to**, cause, induce, suggest). 3. **ri'ser** (-z-) *n*., (esp.) vertical piece between treads of staircase; **ri'sing** (-z-), (*n*., esp.) insurrection, (*a*., esp.) advancing to maturity (*the rising generation*) or high standing (*a rising young lawyer*), approaching (specified age), (of ground) sloping upwards. [E]

**ri'sĭb|le** (-z-) *a*. (~ly). Inclined to laugh; laughable, ludicrous; ~**i'lĭtỹ** *n*. [L (*rideo ris-* laugh)]

**rising.** See RISE.

**risk.** 1. *n*. Chance of or of bad consequences, loss, etc., (*there is the risk of his catching cold; at the risk of his life*); person or thing causing risk; **at ~**, exposed to danger; **at** person's **~**, with him to bear any loss etc. resulting; **run ~s, a ~, the ~**, expose oneself or be exposed to loss etc. (*of*); **take ~s** etc., expose oneself so.

2. *v.t.* Expose to chance of injury or loss; venture on, accept the chance of, (*risk the jump, a sprained ankle*). 3. ~ỹ *a*. (-ily, -iness), full of risk, *risqué*. [F *risque*(*r*) f. It.]

**rĭsŏ'ttō** (-z-) *n*. (*pl.* ~s). Italian dish of rice with stock, meat, onions, etc. [It.]

**risqué** (ri'skā) *a*. (Of story etc.) slightly indecent. [F (RISK)]

**ri'ssōle** *n*. Fried ball or cake of meat mixed with bread crumbs etc. [F]

**ritărdă'nd|ō** (rē-) *adv., a.*, & *n*. (*pl.* ~os, ~i). (Mus.) = RALLENTANDO. [It.]

**rite** *n*. (Action required or usual in) religious or solemn observance (*the rite of confirmation*; **last ~s**, for dying person); body of usages characteristic of a Church. [F, or L *ritus*]

**ritĕnu't|ō** (rētĕnōō'-) *adv., a.*, & *n*. (*pl.* ~os, ~i). (Mus.) (Passage performed) with immediate slowing-down. [It.]

**ri'tūal.** 1. *a*. (~ly). Of, with, or involving rites. 2. *n*. Prescribed order of performing rites; performance of ritual acts. 3. ~**ism** *n*., (excessive) practice of ritual; ~**ĭst** *n*.; ~**i'stĭc** *a*. (-ically). [L (RITE)]

**ri'tzỹ** *a*. (colloq.) High-class, luxurious; ostentatiously smart. [*Ritz*, name of luxurious hotels]

**ri'val** *n., a.*, & *v.* 1. *n*. Person's competitor for prize (esp. another's love) or in some activity or quality; thing that equals another in quality. 2. *attrib. a*. Being rival(s). 3. *v.t.* (‖-ll-). Be rival of or comparable to; seem or claim to be as good as. 4. ~**rỹ** *n*., being rivals, emulation. [L (*rivus* stream)]

**rīve** *v.t.* & *i.* (~**d**; ~'**n** *pr.* ri'ven). (arch., poet.) Strike or rend asunder, wrench *away* or *off* or *from*; be split. [N]

**ri'ver** *n*. Copious natural stream of water flowing in channel to sea etc.; copious flow *of* (*a river of lava*; ~**s of blood**, much bloodshed); **sell down the ~**, (colloq.) defraud or betray; ~**side**, ground along river-bank; ~**ain**, ~**ine**, *adjs.*, of or on river. [AF *rivere* f. Rom. (L *ripa* bank)]

**ri'vĕt.** 1. *n*. Nail or bolt for holding together metal plates etc., its headless end being beaten out or pressed down after passing through two holes. 2. *v.t.* Clench (bolt etc.); join or fasten with rivets; fix, make immovable; concentrate, direct intently, (eyes, attention, etc., *on* or *upon*); engross (attention), engross attention of. [F (*river* clench)]

**rĭ′vŭlĕt** *n.* Small stream. [F, perh. f. It. (L *rivus* stream)]

‖**R.L.** *abbr.* Rugby League.

**rly.** *abbr.* railway.

**rm.** *abbr.* room.

‖**R.M.** *abbr.* Royal Marines.

‖**R.M.A.** *abbr.* Royal Military Academy.

‖**R.N.** *abbr.* Royal Navy.

**RNA** *abbr.* ribonucleic acid.

**roach** *n.* Small freshwater fish of carp family. [F]

**road** *n.* (Specially prepared) line of communication between places for pedestrians, riders, and vehicles (**by** ~, using transport along roads; **one for the** ~, colloq., final drink before departure; **on the** ~, travelling, esp. as commercial traveller, itinerant performer, or vagrant; **rule of the** ~, custom regulating side to be taken by vehicles, riders, or ships, meeting or passing each other; **take the** ~, set out); way of getting *to* (*the road to* York, ruin); (as name of thoroughfare) *Edgware Road*; one's way or route (**in the** ~, colloq., obstructing); (usu. in *pl.*) piece of water near shore in which ships can ride at anchor; ~**-block,** obstruction on road to detain traffic; ‖~ **fund** (Hist., for construction and maintenance of roads and bridges); ‖~ **fund licence,** (colloq.) vehicle excise tax certificate; ~**-hog,** reckless or inconsiderate motorist or cyclist; ~**-holding,** stability of moving vehicle; ~**-house,** inn or club on main road in country district; ~**man** (repairing roads); ~**-metal,** broken stone for road-making; ~ **sense,** capacity for safe behaviour on the road, esp. in traffic; ~ **show,** theatrical performance by company on tour; ~′**side,** border of road; ~ **sign** (giving information to drivers etc.); ~′**stead,** road for ships; ~ **test** (of vehicle by use on road); ~′**way,** (central part of) road, part of bridge or railway used for traffic; ~**-works,** construction or repair of roads; ~′**worthy,** fit to go on the road; ~′**ster** *n.,* open car without rear seats, horse or bicycle for use on road. [E (RIDE)]

**roam. 1.** *v.i.* & *t.* Ramble, wander; walk or travel unsystematically over or through or about. **2.** *n.* Act of roaming, ramble. [orig. unkn.]

**roam**[1]**. 1.** *a.* (Of animal) with coat of which prevailing colour is thickly interspersed with another, esp. bay or sorrel or chestnut mixed with white or grey (*red roan*); **strawberry** ~, red with white or grey. **2.** *n.* Roan horse or cow. [F]

**roan**[2] *n.* Soft sheepskin leather used instead of morocco in bookbinding. [perh. = *Rouen*, place]

**roar** *v.i.* & *t.,* & *n.* (Utter, send forth) loud deep hoarse sound (as) of lion, person(s) in pain or rage, the sea, thunder, cannon, engine, furnace, etc.; (utter) loud laughter; travel in vehicle at high speed with engine roaring; say, sing, utter, (words, chorus, oath, etc., *out*) in loud tone; ~′**ing,** (*a.*; esp.) riotous, noisy, brisk (*a roaring trade*); ~**ing forties,** stormy ocean tracts 40–50° S.), (*adv.*) very (*roaring drunk*). [E]

**roast** *v., a.,* & *n.* **1.** *v.t.* & *i.* Cook (esp. meat) by exposure to open fire or in oven; heat (coffee-beans) before grinding; expose (victim for torture, one*self* or some part for warmth) to fire or great heat; (in *part.*) very hot; *censure; undergo roasting. **2.** *attrib. a.* (Of meat, potato, chestnut, etc.) Roasted. **3.** *n.* (Dish of) roast meat (RULE *the roast*); meat for, operation of, roasting. **4.** ~′**er** *n.,* (esp.) fowl etc. suitable for roasting. [F *rost* (*ir*) f. Gmc]

**rŏb** *v.t.* (**-bb-**). Deprive (person etc., or abs.) of or *of* property by (threat of) violence, feloniously plunder (person or place, *of*), deprive *of* what is due or normal; ~**ber,** ~**berў,** *ns.* [F *rob*(*b*)*er* f. Gmc]

**rŏbe. 1.** *n.* Long loose outer garment; dressing-gown; (often in *pl.*) long outer garment worn as indication of wearer's rank, office, profession, etc. **2.** *v.t.* & *i.* Clothe (person) in robe; dress; put on robes. [F]

**rŏ′bĭn** *n.* ~ (redbreast), small brown red-breasted bird. [F pet name f. *Robert*]

**rŏ′bŏt** *n.* Apparently human automaton, intelligent and obedient but impersonal machine; machine-like person. [Czech]

**robŭ′st** *a.* (**-er, -est**). (Of person) having strong health and physique, (of animal, plant, body, health, etc.) not slender or delicate or weakly; (of exercise, discipline, etc.)

invigorating, vigorous; (of equipment etc.) strongly built; (of intellect etc.) not given to nor confused by subtleties; **~ious** (*or* -schus) *a.*, boisterous, self-assertive, noisy. [F or L (*robur* strength)]

**rŏc** *n.* Gigantic bird of Eastern legend. [Sp. f. Arab.]

‖**R.O.C.** *abbr.* Royal Observer Corps.

**rŏ′chĕt** *n.* Surplice-like vestment of bishop or abbot. [F f. Gmc]

**rŏck¹** *n.* Solid part of earth's crust underlying soil; sure foundation or protection; mass of rock projecting and forming hill, cliff, etc., or standing up into or out of water from bottom (**the R~**, Gibraltar); (fig.) source of danger or destruction (**on the ~s**, colloq., short of money, having broken down, (of drink) served with ice cubes); hard compact material of which rock consists; large detached stone; *stone of any size; hard usu. cylindrical sweetmeat of candied sugar with flavouring esp. of peppermint; **~-bottom**, (colloq., of prices etc.) very lowest (level); **~-bound**, (of coast) having many rocks; **~-cake**, bun with rugged surface; **~-crystal**, transparent colourless quartz usu. in hexagonal prisms; **~-dove,** = *rock-pigeon*; **~-garden**, artificial mound or bank of stones with rock-plants etc. in the interstices, garden in which rockeries are chief feature; **~-pigeon**, wild dove frequenting rocks; **~-plant** (growing on or among rocks); ‖**~ salmon**, (trade name for) dogfish; **~-salt**, common salt as solid mineral. [F *roque, roche*]

**rŏck².** **1.** *v.t.* & *i.* Move gently to and fro (as) in cradle, set or keep or be in such motion; sway from side to side, shake, oscillate, reel, (*earthquake rocks house*; *house rocks*; **~ the boat**, colloq., disturb equilibrium of situation); **~′ing-chair** (mounted on rockers, or with seat arranged to rock); **~′ing-horse**, wooden horse on rockers for child; **~′ing-stone**, poised boulder easily rocked. **2.** *n.* Rocking motion; rocking or swinging music; **~ (and roll)**, (popular dance to) music with heavy beat and simple melody. **3.** **~′er** *n.*, (esp.) one of the curved bars on which cradle etc. rocks (**off** one's **~er**, sl., crazy), rocking-chair. [E]

**rŏ′ckerў** *n.* Pile of rough stones

with soil between them for growing rock-plants on. [ROCK¹]

**rŏ′ckĕt¹** *n.* One of various kinds of flowering plant. [F *roquette* f. It. f. L *eruca*]

**rŏ′ckĕt².** **1.** *n.* Cylindrical paper or metal case that can be projected to height or distance by ignition of contents, used as firework or signal, to carry line to ship in distress, etc.; projectile moved by reaction of continuous jet of gases released in combustion of propellant within it, used to propel military warhead or spacecraft; rocket-propelled bomb etc.; ‖(sl.) reprimand. **2.** *v.t.* & *i.* Bombard with rockets; move rapidly upwards or away. **3.** **~rў** *n.*, science, practice, or rocket propulsion. [F *roquette* f. It.]

**rŏ′ckў** *a.* (**-ily, -iness**). Of or like rock; full of rocks (**the R~ Mountains, the Rockies,** range in western N. Amer.); (colloq.) unsteady, tottering. [ROCK¹,²]

**rocŏ′cŏ** *a.* & *n.* (*pl.* **~s**). (Of) a style of decoration prevalent in 18th-c. Europe; (of furniture, architecture, etc., or literary style) highly ornamented, florid. [F]

**rŏd** *n.* Slender straight round stick or metal bar; cane or birch for use in flogging (**the ~**, use of this; **make a ~ for** one's **own back**, prepare trouble for oneself; κιss *the rod*; **~ in pickle**, punishment prepared; *rod of* ιRON); (as measure) = PERCH¹; = FISH¹*ing-rod*. [E]

**rŏde.** See RIDE.

**rŏ′dent** *n.* Animal with strong incisors and no canine teeth (e.g. rat, squirrel, beaver); ‖**~ officer**, official rat-catcher. [L *rodo* gnaw]

**rŏ′dĕŏ** (*or* -dā′ŏ) *n.* (*pl.* **~s**). Round-up of cattle on ranch for branding etc.; exhibition of cowboys' skill in handling animals. [Sp.]

**rŏdomontā′de** *n.* Boastful talk. [F f. It.]

**rŏe¹** *n.* (*pl.* **~s, ~,** ♀). **~(-deer)**, a small kind of deer; **~′buck**, male roe. [E]

**rŏe²** *n.* (**Hard**) **~**, mass of eggs in female fish's ovary; (**soft**) **~**, male fish's milt; **~-stone**, oolite. [LDu.]

**rogā′tion** *n.* (Eccl.; usu. in *pl.*) Litany of the saints chanted on the 3 days (**R~ days**) in **R~ Week** before Ascension Day and following **R~ Sunday.** [L *rogo* ask]

**rŏ′ger.** **1.** *n.* JOLLY¹ Roger. **2.** *int.*

(In signalling etc.) your message has been received and understood; (sl.) I agree. [man's Christian name]

**rŏgue** (-g) n. Dishonest or unprincipled person, (joc.) mischievous child or waggish or arch person, (**~s' gallery**, collection of photographs of known criminals etc.); inferior or defective specimen among many acceptable ones; **~** (**elephant** etc.) wild animal driven or living apart from the herd and of savage temper; **~rӯ** (rō′gerī) n.; **rŏ′guish** (-gǐ-) a. [orig. unkn.]

**roi′ster** v.i. Revel noisily, be uproarious. [F *rustre* f. L (RUSTIC)]

**rôle, rôle,** (rōl) n. Actor's part; what a person or thing is appointed or expected to do. [F (foll.)]

**rŏll. 1.** n. Cylinder formed by turning flexible material over and over on itself without folding; similar structure of pastry etc. (SAUSAGE, SWISS, *roll*); document in this form (‖Master of the R~s, judge in charge of public records); catalogue, list, (**~ of honour,** esp. list of those who died for their country in war; ‖strike off the ~s, debar from practising as solicitor); more or less (semi-)cylindrical mass (*roll of butter, hair, tobacco*); small loaf esp. for one person at one meal; rolling motion or gait; spell of rolling; (Aeron.) complete revolution about longitudinal axis; continuous rhythmic sound of thunder or drum. **2.** v.t. & i. Move or send or go in some direction by turning on axis esp. to lower level; wallow, (of horse etc.) lie on back and kick about, sway or rock, walk with swaying gait, (of ship or vehicle) sway to and fro sideways; undulate, show undulating surface or motion (*rolling hills, smoke*), go or propel or carry with such motion; sound with vibration or trill (*roll one's* rs); (of vehicle) advance or convey on wheels; (of person) be so conveyed; flatten by passing under or between rollers; turn over and over into cylindrical or spherical shape, make thus (*roll a cigarette*). **3. ~-call,** calling over of list of persons to detect absentees; **~ed gold** (thin coating applied by roller to base metal); **~ed into one,** combined in one person etc.; **~ one's eyes,** show the whites in various directions; **~ in,** arrive in great numbers; **~′mop,** rolled pickled herring fillet;

**~ on,** put on by rolling, (of time) pass; **~-on,** (n.) light elastic corset, girdle; put on by rolling, (a., of ship) on to which motor vehicle can be driven; **~-top desk** (with flexible cover sliding in curved grooves); **~ up,** make into or form roll, (Mil.) drive flank of (enemy line) back so as to shorten or surround it, (colloq.) arrive in vehicle or on the scene; *roll up* one's SLEEVES. **4. ~′er** n., (esp.) hard cylinder used alone or in machine for smoothing, flattening, crushing, wringing, spreading ink or paint, etc., long swelling wave, small cylinder on which hair is rolled for setting; **~er-coaster,** switchback at fair etc.; roller-SKATE²; **~er towel** (with ends joined, hung on roller); **~′ing** n. & a.; **~ing in,** (colloq.) plentifully supplied with (money etc.); **~ing-mill** (for rolling metal into shape); **~ing-pin,** roller for pastry; **~ing-stock,** company's railway or *road vehicles; **~ing stone,** person of unsettled habits (cf. GATHER). [F f. L *rotulus* dim. (ROTA)]

**rŏ′llicking** a. Jovial and boisterous. [orig. unkn.]

**rŏlӯ-pō′lӯ. 1.** n. **~** (**pudding**), pudding made of sheet of paste covered with jam etc. formed into roll, and boiled or baked. **2.** a. (Usu. of child) podgy, plump. [ROLL]

**Rom.** *abbr.* Romans (N.T.).

**rom.** *abbr.* roman (type).

**Rō′man. 1.** a. Of ancient Rome or its territory or people; surviving from period of Roman rule (*Roman road*); of papal Rome, esp. = *Roman Catholic*; of medieval or modern Rome; **~ alphabet,** letters A–Z as in W. Eur. languages; **~ candle,** firework in form of tube discharging coloured balls; **~ Catholic** a. & n., (member) of part of Christian Church acknowledging the Pope as its head; **~ Catholicism; ~ Empire** (established 27 B.C., divided A.D. 395 into Western and Eastern Empires, of which the Eastern lasted until 1453, and the Western after lapsing 476 was revived 800 by Charlemagne and continued to exist as the **Holy ~ Empire** till 1806); **~ law,** code developed by ancient Romans and forming basis of many modern codes; **~ nose** (with high bridge, aquiline); **~numerals,** letters I = 1, V = 5, X = 10, L = 50, C = 100, D = 500, M = 1,000 used in writing numbers (opp. *arabic numerals*); **r~ type** or **letters**, plain upright type used in ordinary print; **Rōmā'nŏ**comb. form. **2.** *n.* Inhabitant of Rome, member of ancient-Roman State; = *Roman Catholic*; (in *pl.*) Christian of ancient Rome (*Epistle to the Romans*); (Print; *r~*) roman type. [L]

**romă'nce. 1.** *n.* R~ (**languages**), languages descended from Latin (French, Spanish, Italian, etc.); (*R~*) vernacular language of old France mainly developed from Latin, or corresponding language of Italy, Spain, Provence, etc.; medieval tale of chivalry usu. in verse [named as being written in Romance]; tale with scene and incidents remote from ordinary life, class of literature consisting of, episode (e.g. love affair) suggesting, atmosphere characterizing, such tales; tendency to be influenced by romances, sympathetic imaginativeness; (an) exaggeration, (a) picturesque falsehood. **2.** *v.i.* Exaggerate or distort the truth, esp. fantastically. [F *romanz* f. Rom. (ROMANIC)]

**Rōmā'nesque** (-k) *n.* Style of art and architecture prevalent in Romanized Europe between classical and Gothic periods. [F (-ESQUE)]

**Rōmā'nian, Rumā'nian** (rŏŏ-), *n.* & *a.* (Native, language) of *Romania*. [place]

**Romă'nic** *a.* & *n.* (Of) ROMANCE; descended from, inheriting civilization etc. of, the ancient Romans; Romance-speaking. [L *Romanicus* (ROMAN)]

**rŏ'man|ize** *v.t.* Make Roman (Catholic) in character; put into Roman alphabet or roman type; **~izā'tion** *n.*; **~ism**, **~ist**, *ns.*, **~i'stic** *a.* (-ically), (usu. w. ref. to religion). [-IZE]

**Romă'nsh, Rou-, Ru-,** (*ro-*, rŏŏ-; *or* -ah'-) *n.* & *a.* (Of) a Romance dialect of Switzerland. [ROMANCE]

**romă'ntic. 1.** *a.* (~ally). Characterized by or suggestive of or given to romance, imaginative, visionary, (*a romantic scene, story, adventure, girl*); (of project etc.) fantastic, unpractical; (of literary or artistic method etc.) preferring grandeur or picturesqueness or passion or irregular beauty to finish and proportion, subordinating whole to parts or form to matter, (opp. *classic, classical*). **2.** *n.* Romanticist. **3.** **~ism** *n.*, ad-

herence to romantic methods; **~ist** *n.*, writer or artist of the romantic school; **~ize** *v.t.* & *i.*, invest with romance, write in the romantic manner.

**Rŏ'manў** *a.* & *n.* Gipsy; (of) the gipsy language. [Romany *Romani* (*Rom* gipsy)]

**Rōme** *n.* Roman Empire; Roman Catholicism (so **Rō'mish** *a.*, derog.); **all roads lead to ~**, the place finally reached does not depend on the route chosen; **~ was not built in a day**, achievements take time; **when in ~ do as ~ does, as the Romans do**, one should conform to local practices. [F, & L *Roma* Rome]

**rŏmp. 1.** *v.i.* (Of children etc.) play about together, wrestle with and chase each other; (colloq.) get *past* etc. without effort, come *in* or *home* as easy winner. **2.** *n.* Child fond of romping, tomboy; spell of romping. **3.** **~er** *n.*, (in *sing* or *pl.*) young child's play-garment usu. covering trunk only. [perh. RAMP²]

**rŏ'ndeau** (-dō), **rŏ'ndel,** *ns.* Short poem with only two rhymes throughout and opening words used twice as refrain. [F (ROUND); cf. ROUNDEL]

**rŏ'ndō** *n.* (*pl.* **~s**). Piece of music with leading theme which returns from time to time. [It., f. F RONDEAU]

**Rŏ'neō** *n.* (*pl.* **~s**), & *v.t.* (Reproduce on) machine for duplicating documents etc. from stencils. [P]

**Rö'ntgen** (rŭ'ntyen) *n.* **~ rays,** X-rays. [person]

**rŏŏ** *n.* (Austral. colloq.) Kangaroo. [abbr.]

**rŏŏd** *n.* The cross of Christ (arch.); crucifix, esp. one raised on middle of rood-screen (**~-loft,** gallery on top of rood-screen; **~-screen,** wooden or stone carved screen separating nave and choir); quarter-acre. [E]

**rŏŏf. 1.** *n.* Upper covering of building (**under one ~**, in same building; **under person's ~**, in his house; **go through, hit, raise, the ~**, colloq. become very angry; **a ~ over** one's **head,** somewhere to live); overhead rock in cave, mine, etc.; top of covered vehicle; **~ of the mouth,** palate; **~-garden** (on flat roof of building); **~-rack,** framework to carry luggage etc. on motor-car roof; **~-top,** outer surface of roof; **~-tree,** ridge-piece of roof. **2.** *v.t.* Cover (*in, over*) with roof; be roof of. **3.** **~er** *n.*, (esp.) maker or mender of roofs; **~'ing** *n.*, material used·for roof. [E]

**rŏŏk¹** *n.* Chess piece with battle-ment-shaped top. [F f. Arab.]

**rŏŏk².** **1.** *n.* Black hoarse-voiced crow nesting in colonies. **2.** *v.t.* Win money from at cards etc. esp. by swindling; charge (customer) extortionately. **3.** **~'erȳ** *n.*, colony of rooks, penguins, or seals. [E]

**rŏŏ'kie** *n.* (sl.) Recruit. [corrupt.]

**rŏŏm** (or rŏŏm). **1.** *n.* Space that is or might be occupied by something, capaciousness or ability to accommodate contents, (*takes up too much room*; *there is plenty of room*); **make ~,** vacate standing-ground etc. or post etc. for or *for* another, clear a space *for* person or thing by removal of others); space in or on (*house-, shelf-, room*); opportunity, scope, *to* do or *for* (**there is ~ for improvement,** things might be better); part of house enclosed by walls or partitions, floor, and ceiling, (in *pl.*) set of these occupied by person or family, apartments or lodgings; **leave the ~,** colloq., go to lavatory; **~-mate,** person occupying same room as another; **~ service,** of food etc. to hotel guest in his room. **2.** *v.i.* *Have room(s), lodge, board; **~'ing-house,** lodging-house. **3.** **-~ed** (-md) *a.*, having (so many) rooms; **~'ful** (-ŏŏl) *n.* (esp. *of* people); **~'ȳ** *a.* (**-ily, -iness**), capacious of ample size to contain. [E]

**rŏŏst.** **1.** *n.* Bird's perching or resting place, esp. place where fowls sleep; **come home to ~,** recoil upon originator; RULE *the roost.* **2.** *v.i.* (Of bird or person) settle for sleep, be perched or lodged for the night; *~'er *n.*, domestic cock. [E]

**rŏŏt¹.** **1.** *n.* Part of plant that attaches it to earth and conveys nourishment from soil; (in *pl.*) fibres or branches of this, (fig.) what attaches one emotionally to a place; small plant with root for transplanting; (plant with) edible root; embedded part of hair, tongue, tooth, etc.; source or origin of (*the root of all evil*; **~ idea** etc., from which the rest originated); basis, means of continuance, (*has its root in selfishness*); (Math.) value of quantity such that given equation is satisfied, number that when multiplied by itself a given number of times yields a given number (CUBE *root*), esp. = SQUARE *root*;

(Philol.) ultimate element of language from which words have been made by addition or modification; **pull up by the ~s,** uproot (lit. or fig.); **~ and branch,** thoroughly, radically; **~-stock,** rhizome, source from which offshoots have arisen; **strike at the ~(s) of,** set about destroying; **strike** or **take ~,** begin to draw nourishment from root, (fig.) become established; **~·lĕt** *n.* **2.** *v.t.* & *i.* (Cause to) take root; (esp. in *p.p.*) fix or establish firmly (*has a rooted objection to*); drag or dig up by the roots; **~ out,** exterminate. [E]

**rŏŏt²,** **rout²,** *v.t.* & *i.* Turn up ground, turn *up* (ground etc.), with snout or beak in search of food; search *out,* hunt *up*; rummage (*among, in*); *~ **for,** (sl.) encourage by applause or support. [E & N]

**rōpe.** **1.** *n.* (Piece of) stout cord made by twisting together strands of hemp, flax, nylon, wire, etc.; **the ~,** esp. halter for hanging a person; **the ~s,** those enclosing boxing-ring etc. (*on the ~s,* near defeat), the conditions in some sphere of action (*know the ropes*); **give person ~,** **~ enough to hang himself,** leave him to bring about his own discomfiture; **~ of onions, pearls,** quantity of these strung together; **~-dancer, -dancing,** performer, performing, on tightrope; **~-ladder,** two long ropes connected by short cross-pieces as ladder; **~-trick,** supposed Indian feat of climbing unsupported rope; **~-walk,** long piece of ground where ropes are made; **~-walker, -walking,** = *rope-dancer, -dancing.* **2.** *v.t.* & *i.* Fasten or secure or catch with rope; (Mount.) connect (party) with rope, attach (person) to rope; enclose, close *in* or *off,* (space) with rope; **~ in,** persuade to take part. **3.** **rō'pȳ** *a.* (**-iness**), (colloq.) poor in quality. [E]

**Rŏ'quefŏrt** (-kfŏr) *n.* Blue cheese orig. made from ewes' milk. [place]

**rō'quet** (-kā, -kǐ). **1.** *v.t.* & *i.* Cause one's ball to strike, (of ball) strike, (another ball at croquet); strike another ball thus. **2.** *n.* Act or fact of roqueting. [arbitr. f. CRO-QUET]

**rŏr'qual** *n.* Whale with dorsal fin. [F f. Norw.]

**rosā'ceous** (-zā'shus) *a.* (Bot.) Of the large family Rosaceae, of which the rose is the type. [L (ROSE¹)]

**rō'sarȳ** (-z-) *n.* Rose-garden, rose-bed; (R.C. Ch.) form of devotion made up of repeated prayers, string of beads for keeping count in this. [L *rosarium* rose-garden]

**rōse¹** (-z). **1.** *n.* (Prickly bush or shrub bearing) a beautiful and usu. fragrant flower usu. of red or yellow or white colour (BED OF *roses*); **gather** ~s, seek pleasure; ~ **without a thorn**, impossible happiness, unalloyed delight); flowering plant resembling this (CHRISTMAS *rose*); rose-flower as emblem of innocence, beauty, etc., (**under the** ~, *sub rosa*; **Wars of the R~s**, 15th-c. civil wars between Yorkists with white and Lancastrians with red rose as emblem), representation of the flower (esp. as English national emblem); rose-shaped design e.g. on compass card, rosette; sprinkling-nozzle of watering-pot or hose; light crimson colour, pink; (usu. in *pl.*) rosy complexion (*roses in her cheeks*); ~**bay**, a willow-herb; ~**bud**, (thing resembling) bud of rose, pretty girl; ~**bush**, rose plant; ~**colour**, rosy red, pink; ~**coloured**, rosy, (fig.) optimistic, sanguine, cheerful, (*takes rose-coloured views*; *see things through rose-coloured spectacles*); *rose*-HIP²; ~**leaf**, leaf or usu. petal of rose; ~**pink** = *rose-coloured*; ~**water**, perfume made from roses; ~**window** (circular, usu. with roselike or spokelike tracery); ~**'wood**, valuable close-grained cabinet wood of one of various kinds, named from their fragrance. **2.** *a.* Coloured like a pale red rose, of warm pink. [E & F f. L *rosa*]

**rose².** See RISE.

**rosé** (rōzā') *n.* Light pink wine. [F]

**rō'sėate** (-z-) *a.* Rose-coloured (lit. or fig.). [L *roseus*]

**rō'semarȳ** (-zm-) *n.* Evergreen fragrant shrub. [*rosmarine* (L *ros* dew, MARINE)]

**rō'serȳ** (-z-) *n.* Rose-garden. [ROSE¹]

**rosė'tte** (-z-) *n.* Rose-shaped ornament of ribbons etc., esp. as supporter's badge or (symbol of) award in competition, or carved in stone etc. [F dim. (ROSE¹)]

**Rŏsĭcru'cian** (-zĭkrōō'shan) *n.* & *a.* (Member) of 17th–18th-c. society devoted to occult lore, or of similar later society. [*Rosenkreuz*, person]

**rŏ'sĭn** (-z-). **1.** *n.* Resin, esp. in solid form. **2.** *v.t.* Rub etc. (esp. bow of violin etc.) with rosin. [alt. RESIN]

‖**RoSPA** *abbr.* Royal Society for the Prevention of Accidents.

**rŏ'ster. 1.** *n.* List or plan showing turns of duty etc. **2.** *v.t.* Put on roster. [Du. *rooster*, lit. gridiron]

**rŏ'str|um** *n.* (*pl.* ~**a,** ~**ums**). Platform for public speaking; (Rom. Ant.) beak of war-galley; ~**al** *a.* [L]

**rō'sȳ** (-zĭ) *a.* (**-ily, -iness**). Coloured like pink or red rose (esp. of complexion as indicating health, of blush, sky, etc.), (fig.) = ROSE¹-coloured. [ROSE¹]

**rŏt** *v., n.,* & *int.* **1.** *v.t.* & *i.* (**-tt-**). Undergo natural decomposition, putrefy, (~ **off**, drop from stem etc. through rottenness); (fig.) gradually perish from want of vigour or use; cause to rot, make rotten; ‖(sl.) chaff, banter, tease; ~**gut** *a.* & *n.*, (liquor) injurious to stomach. **2.** *n.* Decay, rottenness, (DRY *rot*); (sl.) nonsense, absurd statement or argument etc., foolish course, undesirable state of things; sudden series of (freq. unaccountable) failures (*a rot set in*; *must try to stop the rot*). **3.** *int.* (expr. incredulity or ridicule). [E]

**rō'ta** *n.* List of persons acting, or duties to be done, in rotation; roster; **Rotār'ian** *a.* & *n.*, (member) of Rotary; ~**rȳ,** (*a.*) acting by rotation (*rotary drill, pump*), (*a.* & *n.*) (the) **R~ry, R~ry International,** world-wide society of business men with many branches (R~ry *Clubs*) for international service to humanity, orig. named from members entertaining in rotation; **rōtā'te** *v.i.* & *t.*, move round axis or centre, revolve, arrange (esp. crops) or take in rotation; **rōtā'tion** *n.*, rotating or being rotated, recurrence, recurrent series or period, regular succession of various members of a group, (*take office in or by rotation*); ~**tion of crops,** growing of different crops in regular order to avoid exhausting soil); **rōtā'tional** *a.* (**-lly**); ~**tive** *a.*; **rōtā'tor** *n.*, (esp.) revolving apparatus or part; ~**torȳ** *a.* (**-ily**). [L, = wheel]

**rōte** *n.* **By** ~, by mere habituation, from unintelligent memory. [orig. unkn.]

**rotĭ'sserie** *n.* Cooking device for roasting food on revolving spit. [F]

**rō'tor** *n.* Rotary part of machine;

horizontally-rotating vane of helicopter. [ROTA]

**rŏ′tten** a. (~er, ~est; ~ness pr. -n-n-). Perishing from decay, falling to pieces or friable or easily breakable or tearable from age or use; morally or politically corrupt, effete; inefficient, worthless; (sl.) disagreeable, ill-advised; rotten BOROUGH; **rŏ′tter** n., (sl.) (morally) objectionable person. [N (ROT)]

**rŏtŭ′nd** a. (~er, ~est). (Of person) plump, podgy; (of speech, literary style, etc.) sonorous, grandiloquent; ~a n., building with circular ground plan, esp. one with dome; ~ĭty n. [L rotundus (ROTA)]

**rou′ble** (rōō′-) n. Russian monetary unit. [Russ.]

**roué** (rōō′ā) n. (Esp. elderly) debauchee, rake. [F]

**rouge** (rōōzh) **1.** n. Red cosmetic used to colour cheeks and lips; ~-et-noir (-ānwãr), gambling game with red and black marks on table for placing of stakes. **2.** v.t. & i. Colour, adorn oneself, with rouge. [F f. L rubeus red]

**rough** (rŭf) a., adv., n., & v. **1.** a. Having uneven surface, not smooth or level, (rough skin, paper, road, country); not mild or quiet or gentle, violent, harsh, jerky, inconsiderate, unfeeling, unpleasant, severe, astringent, (rough manners, sea, wind, ride, usage, voice, cider); taxing (had a rough time); deficient in finish or elaboration or delicacy, (partly) unwrought, approximate, preliminary, (rough kindness, sketch, circle, estimate; roughly SPEAKING). **2.** adv. In rough manner (sleep ~, not in proper bed). **3.** n. Rough ground (esp. off fairway in golf); hardship (take the rough with the smooth); hooligan; the unfinished or natural state. **4.** v.t. Turn (feathers etc.) up by rubbing; sketch in, shape or plan out, roughly; ~ it, do without ordinary comforts; ~ up, (sl.) treat with violence. **5.** ~-and-ready, not elaborate or over-particular, just good or effective enough; ~-and-tumble, (a.) irregular, disorderly, (n.) haphazard fight; ~cast, (coat, coated, with) plaster of lime and gravel for walls; ~ copy, original draft, copy showing essentials only; rough DEAL², DIAMOND; ~-dry, dry but not iron (clothes); ~ house, (sl.) disturbance, horseplay; ~ justice,

treatment approximating to fairness; ~ luck (worse than one deserves); rough MUSIC; *~′neck, a rowdy; ~ passage, crossing over rough sea (lit. or fig.); ~-rider, one who rides unbroken horses; ~shod, with horseshoe nail-heads projecting (ride ~shod over, treat inconsiderately or arrogantly); ~ shooting (over unprepared land); ~ work, violence, task needing force, unfinished work. **6.** ~age n., indigestible material eaten to stimulate intestinal action; ~′en v.t. & i. [E]

**roulĕ′tte** (rōō-) n. Gambling game on table with revolving compartmented wheel with ball rolls randomly. [F dim. f. L ROTA]

**Roumansh.** See ROMANSH.

**round** a., n., adv., prep., & v. **1.** a. Spherical or circular or cylindrical or nearly so (square peg in round HOLE), convex in outline or surface; done with circular motion; entire, continuous, complete, candid, (a ~ dozen, that and no less). **2.** n. Round object; rung of ladder; slice across loaf; sandwich made from whole slices of bread; solid form of sculpture etc. (in the ~, fig., with all features shown or considered, with audience all round theatre-stage); circumference, extent, of; revolving motion, circular or recurring course, series, group of houses etc. to which goods are regularly delivered, (the daily ~, day's ordinary occupations; go one's ~s, take customary tour of inspection; go the ~s, passed from person to person); playing of all holes in golf-course once; (Mus.) canon for voices at same pitch or in octaves; allowance served out to each member of a group, one spell of play etc., one stage in competition; ammunition to fire one shot. **3.** adv. With (nearly) circular motion, with return to starting-point or change to opposite position (lit. or fig.; summer comes round; all the year round; wheels go round; he turned round when I shouted; soon won him round); measuring (specified distance) in girth; to or at or affecting all or many points of circumference or area or members of a company etc., in every direction from a centre or within a radius, (ALL round; get ~ to, eventually deal with; pass the HAT round; SHOW round); by circuitous way (go a long way *round*; **ask** person ~, from his house into one's own). **4.** *prep.* So as to encircle or enclose (*tour round the world*; *put a blanket round her*); with successive visits to, at or to points on the circumference of (*seated round the table*); in various directions from (*the fields round Oxford*); as axis or central point; so as to pass in curved course, having thus passed, in position thus reached (*go, be, find him, round the* BEND¹). **5.** *v.t. & i.* Give or take round shape; ~ (**off**), make (angle) less sharp; make (number etc.) round by omitting units etc.; ~ (**off, out**), bring to complete or symmetrical state; pass round (cape, corner, etc.). **6.** ~ **about**, in a ring (about), all around, on all sides (of), circuitously, approximately; ~'**about**, (*n.*) circuitous way, ||road junction where all traffic must travel in curve, ||merry-go-round, (*a.*) circuitous; ~ **and** ~, several times round; ~ **dance** (in which couples circulate round room or dancers form ring); ~ **figures**, round number; ~ **game** (in which each player plays for himself alone); R~'**head**, member of Parl. party in Civil War [from close-cut hair]; ~ **number** (without odd units etc.); ~ **of beef**, thick disc from haunch as joint; ~ **on**, make unexpected retort to; ~ **robin**, petition with signatures in circle to conceal order of writing; ~ **shot**, (Hist.) spherical cannon-ball; ~ **shoulders** (bent forward so that back is convex); ~'**sman**, ||tradesman's employee going round for orders and with goods; ~ **sum** (considerable); R~ **Table** (of King Arthur and knights, where none had precedence); ~-**table conference** (with all present on equal footing); ~ **trip**, circular tour, \*esp. by same route both ways; ~ **up**, gather up (cattle etc.) by riding round (lit. or fig.); ~-*up* n. (lit., or fig. summary of events); ~'**worm** (opp. *flatworm*). **7.** ||~'**ers** (-z) *n.*, game with bat and ball where players run through round of bases; ~'**lỹ** *adv.*, (esp.) bluntly, severely, (*told them roundly that he would not*; *was roundly abused*). [F f. L (ROTUND)]

**rou'ndel** *n.* Small disc, medallion; circular identifying mark; = RON-DEAU. [F *rondel(le)* (prec.)]

**rou'ndelay** *n.* Short simple song

with refrain; (arch.) bird's song. [alt. F *rondelet* dim. (prec.)]

**rouse** (-z) *v.t. & i.* Bring out of sleep, stir up or *up*, startle from or *from* or *out of* sleep or inactivity or confidence or carelessness (*to action* etc.; ~ **oneself**, overcome one's indolence); provoke anger of; evoke (feelings); ~ (**up**), cease to sleep, become active; **rou'sing** (-z-) *a.*, exciting, stirring, (*a rousing cheer, sermon*). [orig. unkn.]

**rout**¹. **1.** *n.* Disorderly retreat of defeated troops (**put to** ~, utterly defeat); company esp. of revellers or rioters; ||(arch.) large evening party. **2.** *v.t.* Put to rout. [F (ROUTE)]

**rout**². See ROOT².

**route** (rōōt, Mil. freq. rowt). **1.** *n.* Way taken (esp. regularly) in getting from starting-point to destination; ~ **march**, training-march of battalion etc. **2.** *v.t.* (~'*ing* pr. -tī-). Send by a certain route. [F *route* road f. L *rupta* (*via*)]

**routi'ne** (rōōtē'n). **1.** *n.* Regular course of procedure, unvarying performance of certain acts; (Theatr.) set sequence in dance or other performance; (Computers) sequence of instructions for performing a task. **2.** *a.* Performed by rule (*routine duties* etc.). [F (prec.)]

**roux** (rōō) *n.* (*pl.* same). Mixture of fat and flour for making sauce etc. [F]

**rōve**¹. See REEVE².

**rōv|e**² *v.i.* Wander without settled destination; (of eyes) look in changing directions (~*ing eye*, person's tendency to ogle). [prob. Scand.]

**rō'ver**¹ *n.* Wanderer; (Croquet) (player of) ball that has passed all hoops but not pegged out.

**rō'ver**² *n.* Pirate. [LDu. *rover* robber]

**row**¹ (rō) *n.* More or less straight line of persons or things (**in a** ~, colloq., in succession); ~ (**of houses**), street with houses along one or each side; line of seats in theatre etc. (*in the third row*). [E]

**row**² (rō). **1.** *v.i. & t.* Propel (boat), convey (passenger) in boat, with oars etc.; row race with; ~-**boat**, ||~'**ing-boat**, (propelled by oars). **2.** *n.* Spell of rowing. [E]

**row**³. (colloq.) **1.** *n.* Disturbance, commotion, noise, dispute, (**make, kick up, a** ~, raise noise, make protest); shindy, free fight; condition of being reprimanded (*shall get into a row*). **2.** *v.t.* & *i.* Reprimand; make, engage in, row. [orig. unkn.]

**row'an** (*or* rō'-) *n.* (Sc. & N. Engl.) ~(-**tree**), mountain ash; its scarlet berry. [Scand.]

**row'dy** *n.* & *a.* (-**ily**, -**iness**). Rough disorderly noisy (person); ~**ism** *n.* [orig. unkn.]

**row'el** *n.* Spiked revolving disc at end of spur. [F f. L *rotella* dim. (ROTA)]

**row'lock** (rŏ'-, rŭ'-) *n.* Pair of thole-pins or other contrivance serving as fulcrum for oar. [*oarlock* (E; OAR, LOCK²)]

**roy'al.** **1.** *a.* (~**ly**). Of, from, suited to, worthy of, in service or under patronage of, a king or queen (after *n.* in some phrs.: BLOOD *royal*, PRINCESS *royal*); belonging to king or queen, of family of king or queen; splendid, on great scale, of exceptional size etc., (*gave us royal entertainment*; BATTLE *royal*). **2.** *n.* Size of paper about 620 × 500 mm; (colloq.) member of royal family. **3.** *Royal* ACADEMY (*of Arts*); R~ **Air Force**, air force of Britain or Commonwealth country; ||~ **blue**, deep pure vivid blue; ||*Royal* COMMISSION; *royal* DUKE; ||R~ **Engineers**, engineering branch of Army; R~ **Family** (to which sovereign belongs); *royal* FLUSH³, HIGHNESS; R~ **Institution**, British society founded 1799 for diffusion of scientific knowledge; *Royal* MARINE; R~ **Navy**, navy of Britain or Commonwealth country; ~ **oak**, sprig of oak worn on 29 May to commemorate restoration of Charles II (1660), who hid in oak after battle of Worcester (1651); ~ **road to**, way of attaining without trouble; R~ **Society** (founded 1662 to promote scientific discussion); ~ **stag** (with head of 12 or more points); ~ **standard**, banner bearing royal heraldic arms; *Royal* VICTORIAN *Order*; ~ **warrant** (authorizing tradesman to supply goods to royal person). **4.** ~**ist** *n.*, supporter of monarchy or of the royal side in Civil War etc.; ~**ty** *n.*, being royal, royal persons, member of royal family, royal right (now esp. over minerals) granted by sovereign to individual or corporation, sum paid to patentee for use of patent or to author etc. for each copy of his book etc. sold or for each public performance of his work. [F f. L *rex* king]

**r.p.m.** *abbr.* resale price maintenance; revolutions per minute.

**Rs.** *abbr.* rupees.

**R.S.M.** *abbr.* Regimental Sergeant-Major.

||**R.S.P.C.A.** *abbr.* Royal Society for the Prevention of Cruelty to Animals.

**R.S.V.P.** *abbr.* (In invitation etc.) please answer. [F *répondez s'il vous plaît*]

**rt.** *abbr.* right.

||**Rt. Hon.** *abbr.* Right Honourable.

**Rt. Rev(d).** *abbr.* Right Reverend.

||**R.U.** *abbr.* Rugby Union.

**rub. 1.** *v.t.* & *i.* (-**bb**-). Press one's hand or an object on and slide it along over or up and down the surface of (~ *one's* **hands**, each with the other usu. in sign of keen satisfaction or for warmth; ~ **shoulders**, come into contact lit. or fig. *with* other people; ~ (**up**) **the wrong way**, irritate or repel as by stroking cat upwards); polish, clean, abrade, chafe, make dry or sore or bare, by rubbing; reproduce design of (sepulchral brass or stone) by rubbing paper laid on it with heelball or chalk; slide (hand, object) *against* or in or on or over something, (objects) together or *together*, with friction; use rubbing (lit. or fig.) to bring (stain etc.) *out* or (nap etc., or fig. novelty, shyness, etc.) *off* or *away*, or to force (liniment etc., or fig. humiliating fact etc.) *in* or *into*, or to reduce *to* powder etc., or to force *through* sieve, or to bring size or level or *down*, or to dry (horse, oneself) *down*, or to polish or brush (tarnished object, or fig. one's memory, Greek, etc.) *up*; come into or be in sliding contact, exercise friction, *against* or *on*; (fig., of person, process, etc.) go *on*, *along*, *through*, with more or less restraint or difficulty; (of cloth, skin, etc.) get frayed or worn or sore or bare with friction; ~ **it in**, (fig.) continue to refer to person's failure etc.; ~ **off**, be transferred by contact (lit. or fig.); ~ **out**, erase with rubber, (sl.) kill. **2.** *n.* Spell of rubbing; inequality of ground impeding or diverting BOWL²; impediment or difficulty (**there's the** ~, that is the point at which doubt or difficulty arises). **3.** ~'**bing**

*n.*, (esp.) reproduction made by rubbing. [LG]

**rŭ′b-a-dŭb** *n.* Sound of drum. [imit.]

**ruba′tō** (rōōbah′-) *a.* (Mus.) Performed with momentary variation of speed. [It., = robbed]

**rŭ′bber**[1] *n.* Elastic solid made from latex of tropical plants or synthetically and used in pneumatic tyres etc.; piece of this or other substance for erasing pencil-marks; (sl.) condom; *(in *pl.*) galoshes; ~ **band,** loop of rubber to hold papers etc.; *~-neck *n.*, & *v.i.*, (be) gaping sightseer or inquisitive person; ~ **plant,** plant yielding rubber, esp. a kind grown as ornamental dwarf; ~ **stamp,** device for inking and imprinting on surface, (fig.) one who mechanically copies or agrees to others' actions, indication of such agreement; ~**-stamp** *v.t.*, (fig.) approve automatically without proper consideration; ~**ў** *a.* [RUB]

**rŭ′bber**[2] *n.* Match of usu. 3 successive games between same sides or persons at bridge, cricket, lawn tennis, etc.; **the ~,** winning of two games in rubber, third game when each side has won one. [orig. unkn.]

**rŭ′bbish** *n.* Waste or worthless matter, litter, trash; absurd ideas or suggestions, nonsense (often as excl. of contempt); ~**ў** *a.* (**-iness**), of no value, not worth considering. [AF *rubbous*]

**rŭ′bbl|e** *n.* Waste fragments of brick, stone, etc.; ~**ў** *a.* [AF *robel* f. F *robe* spoils]

**rubě′lla** (rōō-) *n.* German measles. [L *rubellus* reddish]

**Ru′bicon** (rōō′-) *n. The* boundary by passing which one becomes committed to an enterprise (*cross the Rubicon*). [ancient name of stream on frontier of Italy]

**ru′bĭcŭnd** (rōō′-) *a.* (Of face, complexion, or person in these respects) ruddy, high-coloured. [F or L (*rubeo* be red)]

**ru′brĭc** (rōō′-) *n.* Heading or passage in red or special lettering; direction for conduct of divine service inserted in liturgical book; explanatory words. [F or L (*ruber* red)]

**ru′bў** (rōō′-). **1.** *n.* Rare precious stone with colour varying from deep crimson to pale rose (*above rubies*, of inestimable value). **2.** *a. & n.* (Of

glowing red colour; ~ **wedding,** 40th anniversary. [F *rubi* f. L]

**ruche** (rōōsh) *n.* Frill or gathering of lace etc.; ~**d** (rōōsht) *a.* [F f. L f. Celt.]

**rŭck**[1] *n.* Main body of competitors not likely to overtake leaders; (fig.) undistinguished crowd of persons or things. [app. Scand.]

**rŭck**[2], ‖**rŭ′ckle,** *vbs. i. & t.* ~ (**up**), crease, wrinkle. [N]

**rŭ′cksăck** (*or* rōō′-) *n.* Bag slung by straps from both shoulders and resting on back. [G]

**rŭ′ction** *n.* (colloq.) Disturbance, tumult, row. [orig. unkn.]

**rŭdd** *n.* (*pl.* same). Freshwater fish resembling roach. [app. rel. to *rud* red]

**rŭ′dder** *n.* Flat piece hinged to vessel's stern or rear of aeroplane for steering with; ~**lèss** *a.* (esp. fig.). [E]

**rŭ′ddle. 1.** *n.* Red ochre. **2.** *v.t.* Mark (esp. sheep) or colour (as) with ruddle. [rel. to *rud* red]

**rŭ′ddў** *a.* (**-ily, -iness**). (Of face or its owner) freshly or healthily red; (of light, sky, etc., or in animal name) reddish; ‖(sl.) bloody, damnable. [E]

**rude** (rōōd) *a.* Primitive, simple, in natural state, uncivilized, uneducated, roughly made or contrived or executed, coarse, lacking subtlety or accuracy, (*rude times, men, simplicity, ignorance, plough, beginnings, path, verses, fare, writer, version, classification*); violent, not gentle, startling, sudden, (*rude passions, shock, awakening, reminder*); vigorous, hearty, (*rude health*); insolent, impertinent, offensive, (*rude remarks*; *say rude things*; *be ~ to*, insult). [F f. L *rudis*]

**ru′dĭm|ent** (rōō′-) *n.* (In *pl.*) elements or first principles of or *of* knowledge or some subject, imperfect beginning of something undeveloped; part or organ imperfectly developed as being vestigial or having no function (e.g. the breast in males); ~**ě′ntarў** *a.* (**-ily**), not advanced or developed, of the nature of a rudiment. [F or L (prec.)]

**rue**[1] (rōō) *n.* A bitter-leaved evergreen shrub. [F f. L *ruta* f. Gk]

**rue**[2] (rōō). **1.** *v.t.* (~′**ing, ru′ing,** *pr.* rōō′-). Repent of, wish undone or non-existent, (*you shall rue it*; *rue the hour when* one did thing etc.). **2.** *n.*

(arch.) Repentance, dejection; compassion, pity. **3.** ~**ful** a. (-lly), expressing (mock) sorrow. [F]

**rŭff**[1] n. Projecting starched frill worn round neck esp. in 16th c.; projecting or conspicuously coloured ring of feathers or hair round bird's or animal's neck; kind of pigeon; (fem. **reeve**) bird of sandpiper family. [perh. = ROUGH]

**rŭff**[2]. n., & v.i. & t. Trump(ing) at cards. [F ro(u)ffle]

**rŭ'ffĭan** n. Violent lawless turbulent person; ~**ĭsm** n.; ~**lў** a. [F f. It. ruffiano]

**rŭ'ffle. 1.** v.t. & i. Disturb smoothness or tranquillity of (feathers, hair, water, temper, person); undergo ruffling. **2.** n. Frill of lace etc. worn esp. round wrist or neck; rippling effect on water; perturbation. [orig. unkn.]

**ru'fous** (roo'-) n. (Esp. of animals) reddish-brown. [L rufus]

**rŭg** n. Thick woollen wrap or coverlet; floor-mat of shaggy material or thick pile; **pull the ~ from under,** (fig.) remove support or concealment of (person). [prob. Scand.]

**Rŭ'gbў** n. ~ (**football**), game played with oval ~ **ball** that may be kicked or carried; ||~ **League,** professional Rugby football with teams of 13; ||~ **Union,** amateur Rugby football with teams of 15; **Rŭgbei'an** (-bē'an) a. & n., (member) of Rugby School. [place]

**rŭ'ggĕd** (-g-) a. (~**er,** ~**est**). Having rough uneven surface (rugged ground etc.); (of features) irregular and strongly marked; unpolished, lacking gentleness, harsh-sounding, austere, unbending, (rugged manners, kindness, verse, honesty); sturdy. [prob. Scand.]

||**rŭ'gger** (-g-) n. (colloq.) Rugby football. [RUG(BY)]

**ru'ĭn** (roo'-). **1.** n. Downfall, fallen or wrecked or impaired state, lit. (of building or structure) or fig. (the ruin of my hopes); complete loss of property or position (bring to ruin); (in sing. or pl.) what remains of building, town, structure, or fig. of person, that has suffered ruin (the ruins of Baalbek; is but the ruin of what he was; lies in ruins; lives in an old ruin); what causes ruin (will be the ruin of us). **2.** v.t. (esp. in p.p.) Reduce (place) to ruins; bring to ruin,

utterly impair or wreck. **3.** ~**ā'tion** n., bringing to ruin, ruining, being ruined; ~**ous** a., in ruins, dilapidated, bringing ruin, disastrous. [F ruine(r) f. L (ruo fall)]

**rule** (rool). **1.** n. Principle to which action conforms or should conform, dominant custom, standard, normal state of things, (the rules of decorum, cricket, the ROAD; **as a ~,** usually, more often than not; **by ~,** in regulation manner, mechanically; EXCEPTION proves rule; GOLDEN rule; **~ of thumb,** based on experience or practice, not on theory; WORK to rule); government, dominion, (under British rule; the rule of force, of law); (Eccl.) code of discipline of religious order; (Law) order made by judge or court w. ref. to particular case only; graduated straight measure used by carpenters etc. (**run the ~ over,** fig. examine cursorily for correctness; SLIDE-rule); ||(Print.) thin line in punctuation etc. **2.** v.t. & i. Exercise sway or decisive influence over, keep under control, curb, (person, conduct, one's passions; **ruling passion,** motive that habitually directs one's actions); (arch., in pass.) consent to follow advice, be guided by; have sovereign control of or over, (rules over many millions; kings should rule by love; **~ the roast** or **roost,** be in control); pronounce authoritatively (that; rule person or thing out of order; **~ out,** exclude, pronounce irrelevant or ineligible); make parallel lines across (paper), make (straight line), with ruler or mechanical help. **3. ru'ler** (roo'-) n., person or thing bearing (esp. sovereign) rule (of), straight strip or cylinder of wood, metal, etc., used in ruling paper or lines; **ru'lĭng** (roo'-) n., (esp.) authoritative pronouncement. [F f. L regula]

**rŭm**[1] n. Spirit distilled from sugar-cane or molasses. [orig. unkn.]

||**rŭm**[2] a. (colloq.; -mm-). Queer, strange. [orig. unkn.]

**Rumanian.** See ROMANIAN; **Rumansh,** see ROMANSH.

**rŭ'mba** n. Cuban Black dance; ballroom dance imitative of this. [Amer. Sp.]

**rŭ'mble**[1]. **1.** v.i. Make sound (as) of thunder or heavy machinery; go along, by, etc., making or in vehicle making such sound. **2.** n. Rumbling sound. [prob. Du. rommelen]

**rŭ′mble²** v.t. (sl.) See through, detect. [orig. unkn.]

**rŭmbŭ′stious** (or -schus) a. (colloq.) Boisterous, uproarious. [prob. var. ROBUSTIOUS]

**ru′min|āte** (rōō′-) v.i. Chew the cud; (fig.) meditate, ponder, (over, about, on, etc.); **~ant**, (n.) animal that chews the cud, (a.) belonging to the ruminants, ruminative; **~ā′tion** n.; **~ative** a., **~ātor** n., (fig.) [L (rumen throat)]

**rŭ′mmage. 1.** v.t. & i. Make thorough search in or in, make search; bring out or up from among other things. **2.** n. Search; things got by rummaging; miscellaneous accumulation; **~ sale**, = JUMBLE sale. [F arrumage (arrumer stow cargo)]

**rŭ′mmy¹** a. (-ily, -iness; colloq.) ≐ RUM². [RUM²]

**rŭ′mmy²** n. Card-game played usu. with two packs. [orig. unkn.]

**ru′mour, *-mor,** (rōō′mer). **1.** n. General talk, report, or hearsay, of doubtful accuracy. **2.** v.t. (usu. in pass.) Report by way of rumour (the rumoured disaster; it is rumoured that he will come). [F L rumor noise]

**rŭmp** n. **1.** Tail-end, buttocks, of animal or bird or person; **the R~**, (Hist.) remnant of Long Parliament after either 1648 or 1659; **~ steak** (cut from ox's rump). [prob. Scand.]

**rŭ′mple** v.t. Crease, tousle, disorder, (fabric, hair, leaves, etc.). [Du. rompelen]

**rŭ′mpus** n. (colloq.) Row, uproar, brawl. [orig. unkn.]

**rŭn. 1.** v.i. & t. (-nn-; ran; run). (Of person) go at pace faster than walk with both feet never on ground at once; (of animal) amble, canter, gallop, etc.; flee (**~ for it**, seek safety by fleeing); go with haste or for short time; be allowed to grow or stray wild; compete in race, finish race in specified position, seek election; (Crick.) traverse pitch to score run; (of ship) go straight and fast; advance (as) by rolling or on wheels or smoothly or easily, be in action or operation (left the engine running); (of public conveyance) ply, be in course of plying (train is running late); spread rapidly (shiver ran down my spine); (of colour or ink) spread beyond proper place; (of liquid, sand, etc., or its container, or fig.) flow, be wet, flow with, (BLOOD runs cold); extend, have course or order

or tendency or average (road runs along the ridge; story runs as follows; my inclination does not run that way; prices run high); traverse, make way through or over, perform, (course, race, distance, ERRANDS, a run at cricket); chase, hunt; cause to run or go (run ship aground, car into garage, pin into finger, hand along or over thing, water into bath, fingers through hair); smuggle (guns etc.); enter (competitor for contest); cause (machine, vehicle, business, etc.) to operate or be conducted; own and use (vehicle); take (person) for journey in vehicle; allow (account) to accumulate for a time before paying. **2.** n. Act or spell of running (**at a ~**, running; **have a ~ for** one's **money**, get some reward for expenditure or effort; **on the ~**, fleeing, bustling about); short excursion; distance travelled; (Crick.) traversing of pitch by both batsmen, (Baseball) return of batter after touching all bases, point thus or otherwise scored; rapid or rhythmical motion; ladder in stocking; general tendency; regular route; continuous or long stretch or spell or course (had a run of luck; in the LONG¹ run); general demand (**~ on the bank**, sudden demand for cash by many customers); quantity produced at one time; general or average type or class; animal's regular track, enclosure for fowls, range of pasture; permission for free use of (gave him the run of the house). **3. ~ about**, hurry from one to another, (of child) play or wander freely; **~′about** n., light motor car; **~ a chance of being**, may be; **~ across, against**, happen to meet; **~ after**, pursue with attentions; **~ along**, (colloq.) depart; **~ a temperature**, be feverish; **~ away**, flee, elope, (of horse) bolt; **~′away** n., fugitive; **~ away with**, carry off, win easily, lead to expense of (money), accept (notion) hastily; **~ close**, nearly overtake or equal; **~ its course**, proceed naturally to the end; **~ down**, (of unwound clock etc.) stop, (of person or health) become feeble from overwork or underfeeding, reduce numbers of (staff etc.), knock down or collide with, discover after search, disparage; **~-down**, (n.) reduction in numbers, detailed analysis, (a.) decayed from prosperity; **~ dry**, cease to flow; **~ one's eye over**, examine cursorily; ~ **high** (of tide, waves, passions, prices, stakes); ~ **in**, bring (new engine etc.) into good working order by careful running, (colloq.) arrest; ~ **in** one's **head**, (of tune, idea) constantly recur to the mind; ~ **in the family**, (of trait) be found in all or many members of it; ~ **into**, fall into (absurdity etc.), incur (debt), be continuous or coalesce or collide with, happen to meet, reach as many as (*runs into 6 volumes*); *run it* FINE[2]; ~ **low**, become or have too little; ~ **off**, flee, (cause to) flow away, write or recite fluently, produce (copies etc.) on machine, decide (race) after tie or heats; ~ **off** one's **feet**, very busy; ~ **of the mill**, ordinary or average product or specimen; ~ **on** *prep.*, be constantly reverting to (subject), use as fuel (*runs on diesel oil*); ~ **on** *adv.*, continue in operation, elapse, speak volubly, (Print.) continue in same line; ~ **out**, come to end, jut out, complete (race), put down wicket of (running batsman), exhaust one's stock *of*; ~ **over** *prep.*, review, (of vehicle) pass over (animal, prostrate person); ~ **over** *adv.*, (of vessel or contents) overflow; *run* RING[1]*s round*, RIOT, RISK; ~ **short**, = *run low*; *run the* GAUNTLET[2]; ~ **the show**, (colloq.) dominate in an undertaking; ~ **through** *prep.*, examine or rehearse briefly, peruse, deal successively with, consume by reckless or quick spending, pervade; ~ **through** *adv.*, pierce with sword etc.; ~ **to**, reach (amount, number), have money or ability for, (of money) be enough for, (of person) show tendency to (fat etc.); *run to* EARTH, *to* SEED; ~ **up**, (cause to) grow quickly, amount *to*, accumulate (debt etc.) quickly, erect or construct to great height or in unsubstantial or hurried way, raise (flag) on mast etc.; ~**-up** *n.*, approach to action or event; ~ **up against**, meet with (difficulty etc.); ~ **upon** (of thoughts) be engrossed by; ~'**way**, specially prepared airfield surface for taking off and landing. **4.** ~'**ner** *n.*, (esp.) messenger, twining plant esp. bean, sliding ring on rod etc., rod or groove or blade on which thing slides, long narrow ornamental cloth, creeping plant-stem that can take root; ~**ner- -u'p**, competitor taking second place; ~'**ning**, (*n.*, esp.) way race

proceeds (**make the** ~**ning**, set the pace, lit. or fig.; **in**, **out of**, **the** ~**ing**, with good, no, chance of winning), (*a.*, esp.) consecutive (*happened three days running*), continuous (*running battle*, usu. fig.); ~**ning-board**, footboard of motor vehicle; ~**ning commentary**, oral description of events in progress; ~**ning-dog**, (derog.) servile follower; ~**ning jump** (in which jumper runs to take-off); ~**ning knot** (that slips along rope etc. and changes size of loop); ~**ning repairs**, minor repairs and replacements; ~**ning sore** (suppurating); ~**ning water** (available from stream or taps); ~'**nÿ** *a.* (**-ily**, **-iness**), tending to run or flow. [E]

**run|e** (roon) *n.* Any letter of earliest Gmc alphabet; similar mark of mysterious or magic significance; ~'**ic** *a.* [N]

**rŭng**[1] *n.* Short stick fixed as crossbar in chair etc.; this or corresponding piece of rope etc. in ladder (lit. or fig.; *lowest rung of life's ladder*). [E]

**rŭng**[2]. See RING[1].

**rū'nic**, see RUNE.

**rŭ'nnel** *n.* Brook; gutter. [E]

**rŭ'nner**, **rŭ'nning**, **rŭ'nnÿ**. See RUN.

**rŭnt** *n.* Small animal of its kind; weakling or undersized person. [orig. unkn.]

**rupee'** (roo-) *n.* Monetary unit of India, Pakistan, etc. [Hind.]

**rŭ'pture. 1.** *n.* Breaking; breach; breach of harmonious relations, disagreement and parting; (Path.) abdominal hernia. **2.** *v.t. & i.* Burst (cell, membrane, etc.); sever (connection); affect with or suffer hernia. [F or L (*rumpo rupt-* break)]

**rur'al** (roor'-) *a.* (~**ly**). In, of, suggesting, the country (opp. *urban*; ||*rural* DEAN[1]; ~ **district**, ||Hist., group of country parishes governed by elected council); ~**itÿ** (-ă'l-) *n.*; ~**ize** *v.t.*; ~**izā'tion** *n.*; **rurĭdĕcā'nal** (roor-; *or* -dĕ'ka-) *a.*, of rural dean(ery). [F or L (*rus rur-* the country)]

**ruse** (rooz) *n.* Stratagem, trick. [F]

**rŭsh**[1] *n.* Marsh plant with slender pith-filled stems, used for making chair-bottoms or baskĕts etc., a stem of this; ~ **candle** (made by dipping pith of a rush in tallow); ~'**light**, rush candle, (fig.) faint glimmer of intelligence or knowledge. [E]

**rŭsh**[2]. **1.** *v.t. & i.* Impel or carry along forcefully and rapidly (*patient* *was rushed to hospital; emergency legislation was rushed through Parliament*); ~ person (**off his feet**), force him to act hastily; (Mil.) take by sudden vehement assault; swarm upon and take possession of (platform at meeting, etc.); pass (obstacle) with a rapid dash (~ **one's fences**, act with undue haste); (sl.) overcharge (customer); run precipitately, violently, or with great speed, go or resort without proper consideration (*in*)*to*, (*rush into* or *out of the room*; *rush to extremes*; ~ **at**, attack impetuously; ~ **into print**, write to newspaper etc. on insufficient grounds); flow, fall, spread, roll, impetuously or fast (*river rushes past*; *a rushing mighty wind*; *blood rushed to his face*; *his past life rushed into his memory*). **2.** *n.* Act of rushing, violent or tumultuous advance, charge, onslaught, period of great activity, (*the rush of the tide*; *a rush of blood to the head*; *a sudden rush of business*); (Cinemat., colloq.) first print or preliminary showing of film before cutting; sudden migration of large numbers; strong run *on* or *for* a commodity; ~**-hour** (at which traffic is busiest); ~ **job** etc. (done with minimum delay). [AF *russher*, F *ruser* (RUSE)]

**rŭ'shў** *a.* Abounding in rushes. [RUSH¹]

**rŭsk** *n.* Piece of bread pulled or cut from loaf and rebaked usu. as light biscuit. [Sp. *rosca* twist]

**rŭ'ssèt. 1.** *a.* Reddish-brown. **2.** *n.* Russet colour; rough-skinned russet apple. [F f. L *russus*]

**Rŭ'ssian** (-shɑn). **1.** *n.* Native or language of *Russia*. **2.** *a.* Of or from Russia; of or in Russian; ~ **roulette**, firing of revolver held to one's head with one chamber loaded; ~ **salad** (of mixed diced vegetables with mayonnaise). **3.** ~**ize**, **Rŭ'ssifў**, *vbs. t.*, make Russian in character; ~**ĭzā'tion, Rŭssĭfĭcā'tion,** *ns.*; **Rŭ'ssō-** *comb. form.* [place]

**rŭst. 1.** *n.* Reddish or yellowish--brown corrosive coating formed on iron or steel by oxidation; (fig.) im-

paired state due to disuse or inactivity; plant-disease with rust--coloured spots. **2.** *v.i.* & *t.* Become rusty; affect with rust; lose quality or efficiency by disuse or inactivity. [E]

**rŭ'stĭc. 1.** *a.* (~**ally**). Having appearance or manners of country people or peasants, unsophisticated, uncouth; of rude or country workmanship (~ **seat, bridge,** etc., structure of untrimmed branches or rough timber); **rŭstĭ'cĭtў** *n.* **2.** *n.* Countryman, peasant. **3.** ~**āte** *v.i.* & *t.* (~**able**), retire to or live in the country, send down temporarily from university as punishment, make rural; ~**ā'tion** *n.* [L (*rus* the country)]

**rŭ'stle** (-sel). **1.** *n.* Sound (as) of dry leaves blown or pattering rain. **2.** *v.i.* & *t.* (Cause to) make rustle; go with rustle (*along* etc.); *steal (cattle or horses); ~ **up,** (colloq.) produce when needed; **rŭ'stler** (-sl-) *n.* [imit.]

**rŭ'st|ў** *a.* (~**ily,** ~**iness**). Rusted, affected by rust; rust-coloured, (of black clothes) discoloured by age; stiff with age or disuse, impaired by neglect, (*his Greek is rusty*); (of voice) croaking. [E (RUST)]

**rŭt¹** *n.* Track sunk by passage of wheels; beaten track, groove; **in a** ~, following fixed pattern of behaviour difficult to change; ~**'tĕd,** ~**'tў,** *adjs.* [prob. F (ROUTE)]

**rŭt². 1.** *n.* Periodic sexual excitement of male deer etc.; ~**'tĭsh** *a.* **2.** *v.i.* (-tt-). Be affected with rut. [F f. L (*rugio* roar)]

**ruth** (rōōth) *n.* Pity, compassion, (arch. exc. in ~**'lèss** *a.*) [RUE²]

**R.V.** *abbr.* Revised Version (of Bible).

**-rў.** See -ERY.

**rўe** *n.* (Grain of) a N. Eur. cereal used for bread esp. in northern Continental countries and for fodder; ~ (**whisky**), whisky distilled from rye. [E]

**rў'e-grass** (rī'grahs) *n.* One of various kinds of fodder-grass. [alt. of *ray-grass*]

# S

**S, s,** (ĕs) *n.* (*pl.* **Ss, S's,** *pr.* ĕ'sĭz). Nineteenth letter; S-shaped thing.

**S.** *abbr.* Saint; Society; South(ern).

**s.** *abbr.* second(s); shilling(s) [orig. f. L *solidus*]; singular; son.

**'s** *abbr.* has, is, us (*he's done it; it's time; let's see*).

**S** *symb.* sulphur.

**S.A.** *abbr.* Salvation Army; sex appeal; South Africa; South Australia.

**Să'băŏth** (or -bā'-) *n.pl.* **Lord (God) of ~,** Lord God of HOST¹s. [L f. Gk f. Heb., = hosts]

**să'bbath** *n.* ~ **(day)**, religious rest-day appointed for Jews on the last, and for Christians on the first, day of the week; WITCHES' SABBATH; **săbbatā'rĭan** *a.* & *n.*, (person) observing sabbath strictly; **săbbatā'rĭanĭsm** *n.*; **sabbă'tical,** (*a.;* **-lly**) of the sabbath (**sabbatical year,** year's leave granted at intervals to university professor etc. for study, travel, etc.), (*n.*) sabbatical year. [E f. L & F f. Gk f. Heb., = rest]

*****să'ber.** See SABRE.

**Să'bine** *a.* & *n.* (Member) of people of ancient Italy inhabiting central Apennines. [L]

**să'ble. 1.** *n.* Small dark-furred arctic carnivorous quadruped; its fur or skin; (Her., poet., rhet.) the colour black. **2.** *a.* (Her., poet., rhet.) Black, dark, gloomy (**his ~ Majesty,** the Devil). [F f. L f. Slav.]

**să'bŏt** (-ō) *n.* Wooden(-soled) shoe; **să'botage** (-ahzh), (*n.*) malicious or wanton damage or destruction, esp. by dissatisfied workmen or by hostile agents, (*v.t.*) commit sabotage on, (fig.) destroy, spoil; **săboteur'** (-tér') *n.,* one who commits sabotage. [F]

**să'bre** (-ber), *****să'ber,** *n.* Cavalry sword with curved blade; light fencing-sword with tapering blade; **~-rattling,** display or threats of military force; **~-toothed lion, tiger,** extinct mammal with long curved upper canines. [F f. G *sabel*]

**săc** *n.* Membranous bag in animal or vegetable organism. [F or L (SACK¹)]

‖**S.A.C.** *abbr.* Senior Aircraftman.

**să'ccharĭn** (-k-) *n.* Very sweet substance used as substitute for sugar; **~e** (-kerēn) *a.,* sugary (lit. or fig.). [G f. L *saccharum* sugar]

**săcerdō'tal** *a.* (**~ly**). Of priest(s); ascribing or giving great power to priests; **~ĭsm, ~ĭst,** *ns.;* **~ĭze** *v.t.* [F or L (*sacerdos -dot-* priest)]

**să'chet** (-shā) *n.* Small bag or packet, esp. of perfumed substance. [F dim. (SAC)]

**săck¹. 1.** *n.* Large usu. oblong bag for storing or conveying goods, often made of coarse flax or hemp; quantity contained in sack; woman's sacklike dress; *****(sl.) bed (**hit the ~,** go to bed); **the ~,** (colloq.) dismissal (*get, give* person, *the sack*); plundering of town etc.; **~'cloth,** coarse fabric of flax or hemp, (fig.) mourning or penitential garb, esp. *sackcloth and ashes* (orig. Bibl.); **~ race** (between competitors enclosed in sacks up to waist or neck). **2.** *v.t.* Put into sack(s); (colloq.) dismiss from job etc.; plunder (captured town etc.). **3. ~'ful** (-ŏol) *n.;* **~'ĭng** *n.,* sackcloth. [E f. L *saccus* f. Gk]

**săck²** *n.* (Hist.) White wine formerly imported from Spain and Canary Is. [orig. (*wyne*) *seck* f. F *vin sec* dry wine]

**să'ckbut** *n.* Renaissance trombone; (Bibl., as wrong transl.) triangular harp. [F]

**să'cral** *a.* (Anat.) of sacrum; (Anthrop.) of or for sacred rites. [SACRUM]

**să'crament** *n.* Symbolic religious ceremony or act, esp. baptism and Eucharist, often also confirmation, penance, extreme unction, ordination, matrimony; (**Blessed** or **Holy**) **~,** *the* Eucharist; sacred thing, influence, etc.; **~al** (-ĕ'-) *a.* (**-lly**), [F f. L (foll.)]

**să'crĕd** *a.* Connected with religion; dedicated or appropriated to God or a god or *to* some person or purpose; safeguarded or required by religion;

reverence, or tradition, inviolable; **~ book** (embodying laws etc. of a religion); **~ cow**, (fig.) idea or institution unreasonably held to be immune from questioning or criticism. [p.p. of obs. *sacre* consecrate f. F *sacrer* f. L (*sacer* holy)]

**să'crif|ice. 1.** *n.* Slaughter of animal or person, surrender of a possession, as offering to a deity; what is thus slaughtered or surrendered; giving up something (usu. valuable) for sake of something else, thing so given up, loss so entailed; **~i'cial** (-shal) *a.* **(-lly). 2.** *v.t. & i.* Offer or kill (as) sacrifice; give up, devote to. [F f. L (prec.)]

**să'cril|ege** *n.* Violation of what is sacred; **~e'gious** (-jus) *a.* [F f. L (SACRED, *lego* take)]

**să'cring** *n.* (arch.) Consecration of Eucharistic bread and wine; ordination and consecration of bishop etc.; **~-bell** (rung at elevation of Eucharistic bread and wine); **să'cristan** *n.*, (arch.) sexton; **să'cristy** *n.*, repository for church's vestments, vessels, etc. [*sacre* (SACRED)]

**să'cro|sănct** *a.* Most sacred, inviolable; **~să'nctity** *n.* [L (SACRED, SAINT)]

**să'crum** *n.* Composite triangular bone forming back of pelvis. [L *os sacrum* sacred bone]

**săd** *a.* **(-dd-).** Sorrowful, unhappy; deplorably bad, incorrigible, (*sad deterioration, slut*); **~'den** *v.t. & i.* [E]

**să'ddle. 1.** *n.* Seat of leather etc., usu. raised at front and rear, fastened on horse etc. (**in the ~**, on horseback, fig. in office or control); seat for rider of bicycle etc.; joint *of* mutton or venison consisting of the two loins; ridge rising to a summit at each end; **~back**, saddlebacked hill or roof, black pig with white stripe across back; **~backed**, with upper outline concave; **~bag**, one of pair of bags laid across back of horse etc., bag attached behind saddle of bicycle etc.; **~bow** (-bō), arched front or rear of saddle. **2.** *v.t. & i.* Put saddle on (horse etc.); burden (person) *with* task etc.; put (burden etc.) (*up*)*on* person; **~r** *n.*, maker of or dealer in saddles etc.; **~ry** *n.*, saddler's trade or goods. [E]

**Să'ddŭcee** *n.* Member of Jewish sect at time of Christ that denied resurrection of the dead, existence of spirits, and obligation of traditional oral law; **Săddŭcē'an** *a.*; **~ism** *n.* [E f. L f. Gk f. Heb.]

**sa'dhu** (sah'dōō) *n.* (Ind.) Holy man, sage, ascetic. [Skr.]

**să'd|ĭsm** *n.* (Sexual perversion characterized by) love of cruelty to others; **~ĭst** *n.*; **sadĭ'stĭc** *a.* **(-ically).** [de *Sade*, person]

**s.a.e.** *abbr.* stamped addressed envelope.

**safa'rī** *n.* (Hunting or scientific) expedition or journey, esp. in Africa (*go on safari*); **~ park**, area where lions etc. are kept in the open for viewing. [Swahili f. Arab.]

**safe. 1.** *a.* Uninjured, out of danger; affording security or not involving risks (**it is ~ to say, it may ~ly be said**, one may say without exaggeration or falsehood; **be on the ~ side**, have margin of security against risks); cautious, unenterprising; reliable, certain; prevented from escaping or doing harm (*have got him safe*); **~ and sound**, unharmed; **~ conduct**, (document granting) immunity from arrest or harm; **~ deposit**, building containing strong-rooms and safes let separately; **~'guard**, (*n.*) proviso, circumstance, etc., that tends to prevent something undesirable, (*v.t.*) guard or protect (rights etc.); **~ period**, time during and near menstrual period when conception is unlikely. **2.** *n.* Strong lockable repository for valuables; = MEAT-*safe*; \*condom. [F *sauf* f. L *salvus*]

**să'fety** (-ftĭ) *n.* Being safe (**play for ~**, avoid risks; **~ first**, caution is of prime importance); **~-belt**, strap securing person safely, esp. holding occupant to seat in motor car, aircraft, etc.; **~-catch**, device for locking gun-trigger, preventing fall of lift, etc.; **~ curtain**, fireproof curtain in theatre to divide auditorium from stage in case of fire etc.; **~ factor, factor of ~**, ratio of material's strength to expected strain, (fig.) margin of security against risks; **~-glass**, glass that will not splinter when broken; **~ lamp**, miner's lamp so protected as not to ignite firedamp; **~ match** (igniting only on specially prepared surface); **~ net** (placed to catch acrobat etc. in case he falls); **~-pin** (with point that is bent back to head and can be held in guard so that user may not be pricked nor pin come out); ~ **razor** (with guard to prevent blade from cutting skin); ~ **valve**, valve releasing excessive pressure in boiler etc., (fig.) means of harmlessly releasing excitement, anger, etc. [F f. L (prec.)]

**să'ffron. 1.** n. Orange-coloured stigmas of crocus used for colouring and flavouring; colour of this. **2.** a. Saffron-coloured. [F f. Arab.]

**săg. 1.** v.i. (-gg-). Sink or subside, esp. unevenly; have downward bulge or curve in middle; fall in price. **2.** n. State or amount of sagging. [LDu.]

**sa'ga** (-ah'-) n. Story of heroic achievement, esp. medieval tale of Icelandic or Norwegian heroes; series of connected books telling story of a family etc. [N (SAW²)]

**sagā'cious** (-shus) a. Having or showing insight or good judgement; **sagā'cǐty** n. [L sagax -acis]

**sāge¹** n. Kitchen herb with dull greyish-green leaves; ~-**brush**, growth of plants in some alkaline regions of U.S.; ~ **green**, colour of sage-leaves. [F f. L SALVIA]

**sāge². 1.** a. Wise, judicious, experienced; (often iron.) wise--looking. **2.** n. Very wise man (often iron.). [F f. L sapio be wise]

**Săgĭttār'ius** n. Sign of ZODIAC. [L, = archer]

**sā'gō** n. (pl. ~s). (Palm with pith yielding) starch used in puddings etc. [Malay]

**sah'ĭb** n. (fem. mě'm~). (Ind.; arch.) European gentleman (often as honorific affix: Colonel Sahib, Jones Sahib). [Urdu f. Arab., = lord]

**said.** See SAY.

**sail. 1.** n. Piece of canvas or other material extended on rigging to catch the wind and propel vessel (fore~, main~, etc., on similarly named mast) (collect.) some or all of ship's sails (take in ~, furl sails, fig. moderate one's ambitions etc.; under ~, with sails set); ship, esp. as discerned from its sails; voyage or excursion in sailing-vessel (go for a sail); wind-catching apparatus on windmill; *~'boat, sailing-boat; ~'cloth, canvas for sails, canvas-like dress-material; ~-fish (with large dorsal fin); ~'plane, glider designed for soaring. **2.** v.i. & t. Travel on water by use of sails etc. (sail close to or near the WIND¹; ~ing-boat, -ship,

etc., ship moved by sails); navigate (sea, ship, etc.); start on voyage; set (toy boat) afloat; glide or move smoothly; (esp. of woman) move in stately manner; ~ **in**, enter energetically into argument etc.; ~ **into**, (colloq.) attack (person etc.) vigorously; ~ **through**, pass (examination etc.) easily. [E]

**sai'lor** n. Seaman or mariner, esp. one below rank of officer; **good, bad,** ~, person not liable, very liable, to sea-sickness; ~ **hat, suit,** etc., (resembling those now or formerly worn by sailors); ~**lÿ** a., of or befitting a sailor. [orig. sailer (-ER¹)]

**sai'nfoin** n. Pink-flowered fodder plant. [F f. L, = holy hay]

**saint** a. (unemphat. sent; usu. abbr. St., S., in pl. Sts., SS.), n., & v. **1.** a. Holy; canonized or officially recognized by the Church as exceptionally holy (usu. as prefix to name of person or archangel); **St. Andrew**, patron saint of Scotland; **St. Andrew's cross** (×-shaped); **St. Andrew's Day**, 30 Nov.; **St. Anthony('s) cross** (T-shaped); **St. Anthony's fire**, erysipelas, ergotism; **St. Bernard** (dog), very large dog of breed kept orig. in Alps to rescue travellers; **St. David**, patron saint of Wales; **St. David's Day**; 1 Mar.; **St. Elmo**, patron saint of seamen; **St. Elmo's fire**, corposant; **St. George**, patron saint of England; **St. George's cross** (+-shaped, red on white ground); **St. George's Day**, 23 Apr.; COURT of St. James's; **St. John's wort**, yellow-flowered plant; ‖**St. Leger**, horse-race at Doncaster for 3-year--olds; St. Martin's SUMMER; **St. Patrick**, patron saint of Ireland; **St. Patrick's Day**, 17 Mar.; **St. Swithin's Day**, 15 July, on which rain or its absence is said to presage the same for 40 days; St. VALENTINE's Day; **St. Vitus's dance**, disease producing involuntary convulsive movements of the body. **2.** n. Canonized person or member of the company of heaven (ALL Saints' Day); **communion of** ~s, fellowship of Christians past and present; PATRON saint; ~'s **day**, Church festival in memory of saint; very holy or virtuous person (would try the patience of a saint). **3.** v.t. Canonize; call or regard as saint; (in p.p.) worthy to be so regarded, sacred. **4.** ~'hood

(-h-) *n.*; ~'**lў** *a.* (-iness), very holy or virtuous. [F f. L *sanctus*]

**saith.** See SAY.

**sāke**[1] *n.* For the ~ of, for my etc. ~, out of consideration for, in the interest of, because of, owing to, in order to please, honour, get, or keep, (*for the sake of uniformity*; *for conscience*(') *sake*; *for my own sake as well as yours*; *for both our sakes*); for Christ's, God's, goodness', Heaven's, (sl.) Pete's, etc., ~ (excl. of exasperation or urgent supplication); for old ~'s or times' ~, in memory of former days. [E]

**sa'kē**[2] (-ah'-) *n.* Japanese fermented liquor made from rice. [Jap.]

**salaa'm** (-lah'm). 1. *n.* Oriental salutation, 'Peace'; Indian obeisance, a bow with right palm on forehead; (in *pl.*) respectful compliments. 2. *v.i.* Make salaam. [Arab.]

**salā'cious** (-shŭs) *a.* Erotic; lecherous; **salā'citў** *n.* [L *salax -acis* (SALIENT)]

**să'lad** *n.* Mixture of raw or cold vegetables, herbs, etc., usu. seasoned with oil, vinegar, etc., and often eaten with or including cold meat, cheese, etc.; vegetable or herb suitable for eating raw; FRUIT *salad*; ~ **days**, one's period of youthful inexperience; ~**-dressing**, mixture of oil, vinegar, etc., used with salad; ~ **oil**, olive or other vegetable oil for salad-dressing. [F f. Prov. (L *sal* salt)]

**să'lamănder** *n.* Lizard-like animal formerly supposed to be able to live in fire; kind of tailed amphibian. [F f. L f. Gk]

**sala'mĭ** (-lah'-) *n.* Italian sausage highly salted and often flavoured with garlic. [It.]

**săl ammō'nĭăc** *n.* Ammonium chloride, hard white crystalline salt. [L (*sal* salt, *ammoniacus* of Jupiter Ammon)]

**să'larў.** 1. *n.* Fixed regular payment, usu. monthly or quarterly, made by employer to employee. 2. *v.t.* (esp. in *p.p.*) Pay salary to. [AF f. L (*sal* salt)]

**sāle** *n.* Exchange of commodity for money etc., act or instance of selling, (for, on, ~, offered for purchase); ~ **or return**, arrangement by which retailer can return to wholesaler without payment any goods he fails to sell); amount sold (*the sales were enormous*); occasion when goods are sold (‖JUMBLE = RUMMAGE, WHITE, *sale*); ~ **of work**, selling of goods made by parishioners etc. for charity); offering of goods at reduced prices for a period; ~**-room** (in which auctions are held); *~s clerk**, shop assistant; ~'**sgirl**, ~'**slady**, saleswoman; ~'**sman**, man employed to sell goods in shop etc. or as middleman between producer and retailer; ~'**smanship**, skill in selling goods; ~**s talk**, persuasive talk to promote sale of goods or (fig.) acceptance of an idea; ~'**swoman**, female salesman. [E]

**sā'leab|le** (-la-) *a.* Fit to be sold, finding purchasers; ~**i'litў** *n.*

**Să'lic** *a.* ~ **law** (excluding females from dynastic succession). [F or L (*Salii* a Frankish tribe)]

**sălicў'lic** *a.* ~ **acid**, antiseptic and analgesic substance. [F (L *salix* willow)]

**sā'liěnt.** 1. *a.* Prominent, conspicuous; standing or pointing outwards. 2. *n.* Salient angle; (Mil.) bulge in line of attack or defence. [L *salio* leap]

**sā'line** (or sali'n). 1. *a.* Of salt(s); containing or tasting of salt(s); **sali'nĭtў** *n.* 2. *n.* Saline substance, esp. medicine; salt lake, spring, etc. [L (*sal* salt)]

**sali'va** *n.* The colourless liquid produced by glands in mouth; ~**rў** *a.*; **să'livāte** *v.i.*, secrete or discharge saliva esp. in excess; **sălivā'tion** *n.* [L]

**să'llow**[1] (-ō) *n.* Low-growing willow; a shoot or the wood of this. [E]

**să'llow**[2] (-ō). 1. *a.* (-er, -est). Of sickly yellow or pale brown (esp. of complexion). 2. *v.i.* & *t.* Grow or make sallow. [E]

**să'llў.** 1. *n.* Rush of besieged upon besiegers, sortie; excursion; lively or witty remark, esp. as good--humoured attack on person etc. 2. *v.i.* Make a sally, go *forth* or *out* on journey, walk, etc. [F *saillie* f. L (SALIENT)]

**Să'llў Lŭ'nn** *n.* Kind of teacake. [person]

**sălmagŭ'ndĭ** *n.* Highly seasoned dish of chopped meat, anchovies, eggs, etc.; medley; **să'lmi** (-ē) *n.*, ragout esp. of game-birds. [F]

**să'lmon** (să'm-). 1. *n.* (*pl.* usu. same). Silver-scaled fish with orange--pink flesh, valued for food; the colour of its flesh; ~-**trout**, sea trout. **2.** *a.* Orange-pink. [F f. L *salmo*]

**sălmonĕ'lla** *n.* Kind of bacterium causing food poisoning. [*Salmon*, person]

**să'lon** (-awṅ) *n.* (Meeting of notables in) reception-room at house of (esp. French) lady of fashion; room or establishment where hair-dresser, couturier, etc., receives clients. [F (foll.)]

**saloo'n** *n.* Large room suitable for assemblies, exhibitions, etc.; public room for ship's passengers; ||public room(s) for specified purpose (*billiard, hairdressing, saloon*), *public bar*; ||~ (**bar**), first-class bar in public house; ||~ (**car**), motor car with closed body and no partition behind driver. [F f. It. (*sala* hall)]

**sălpĭglŏ'ssĭs** *n.* Garden-plant with trumpet-shaped flowers. [Gk, = trumpet-tongue]

**să'lsĭfy̆** *n.* Plant with long fleshy root cooked as vegetable. [F f. It.]

**salt** (sawlt, sŏlt) *n., a.,* & *v.* **1.** *n.* (Common) ~, substance that gives sea-water its characteristic taste, got in crystalline forms by mining or by evaporation of sea-water etc., and used esp. for seasoning or preserving food (ROCK[1]-, SEA-, *salt*; **table salt**, powdered salt for use at table; **take with a grain** or **pinch of** ~, be sceptical about (statement etc.); **the ~ of the earth**, the finest people, those who keep society wholesome [Matt. 5: 13]; WORTH **one's** *salt*); = *salt-cellar* (above, be-**low, the** ~, Hist., in a superior, inferior, position at table); piquancy, pungency, wit; (often in *pl.*) sub-stance resembling salt in taste, form, etc. (BATH, EPSOM, SMELLing-, *salts*); (in *pl.*) such substance used as laxative (**like a dose of** ~**s**, sl., very quickly); (Chem.) compound of basic and acid radicals, acid with whole or part of its hydrogen replaced by metal or metal-like radical; ~(-**marsh**), marsh overflowed by sea; (**old**) ~, experienced sailor; ~-**cellar**, container for salt at table [orig. *saler*, f. as SALARY]; ~-**lick**, place where animals lick salt im-pregnated with salt; ~-**mine**, mine yielding rock-salt, (fig.) place of unremitting toil; ~-**pan**, depres-sion near sea, or vessel, used for getting salt by evaporation; ~-**spoon**, small spoon usu. with roundish deep bowl for taking table salt. **2.** *a.* Impregnated with, containing, tast-ing of, cured or preserved or seasoned with, salt; (of tears, grief) bitter; pungent; indecent. **3.** *v.t.* Cure, preserve, or season with salt or brine; sprinkle (road etc.) with salt; (sl.) make fraudulent entries in (accounts etc.); ~ **away, down**, (colloq.) save, deposit, or hide (money etc.) for the future. **4.** ~**'ing** *n.*, (esp.) marsh overflowed by sea; ~**'y̆** *a.* (-iness), = sense 2. [E]

**S.A.L.T.** (sawlt, sŏlt) *abbr.* Strategic Arms Limitation Talks.

**să'ltĭre** *n.* (Her.) St. Andrew's cross dividing shield etc. into four compartments. [F *sautoir* stile f. L (SALIENT)]

**saltpĕ'tre,** *saltpĕ'ter,* (sawl-, sŏl-; *-ter*) *n.* White crystalline salty substance used as constituent of gunpowder, in preserving meat, and medicinally. [F f. L, = salt of rock]

**salty.** See SALT.

**salu'brĭous** (*or* -loo'-) *a.* (Of climate, air, etc.) healthy; ~**ĭty̆** *n.* [L (*salus* health)]

**salu'kĭ** (-loo'-) *n.* Tall slender silky-coated dog. [Arab.]

**să'lūtăry̆** *a.* (-ily, -iness). Pro-ducing good effects; **sălūtā'tion** *n.*, (use of) words expressing pleasure at meeting or communicating with person, courteous recognition of his arrival, etc.; **salū'tatory̆** *a.* [foll.]

**salū'te** (*or* -oo't). **1.** *n.* Gesture of respect, homage, or courteous recog-nition; (Mil. etc.) prescribed move-ment of hand, firing of gun(s), use of flag(s), etc., as sign of respect (**take the** ~, acknowledge salutes from members of procession etc.). **2.** *v.t.* & *i.* Make salute to (person etc.); accost or receive *with* smile, oath, etc. [L (*salus -ut-* health)]

**să'lvage. 1.** *n.* (Payment made or due for) rescue of property from loss at sea, fire, etc.; property so saved; saving and utilization of waste materials; materials salvaged. **2.** *v.t.* (~**able** *pr.* -ĭja-). Save from wreck etc.; make salvage of. [F f. L (SAVE)]

**sălvā'tion** *n.* Act of saving or being saved, esp. from sin and its conse-quences (**work out** one's **own** ~, find unaided how to avoid disaster etc.); religious conversion; person or thing that saves from loss, calamity, etc.; **S**~ **Army**, religious and missionary organization on military model for revival of religion and helping the poor, whence **S~ism, S~ist,** ns. [F f. L (SAVE)]

**să'lve¹** (or sahv). **1.** Healing ointment (usu. poet.); = LIP*salve*; thing that soothes wounded feelings or uneasy conscience. **2.** v.t. Soothe (pride, conscience, etc.). [E = ointment, anoint]

**sălv|e²** v.t. Save from wreck, fire, etc.; ~'or n. [back-form. f. SALVAGE]

**să'lver** n. Tray, usu. metal, on which refreshments, letters, etc., are handed. [F *salve* or Sp. *salva* assaying of food (SAVE)]

**să'lvĭa** n. Garden plant of sage family, esp. species with red flowers. [L, = SAGE¹]

**să'lvŏ** n. (pl. ~es, ~s). Simultaneous firing of artillery or other guns, esp. as salute or in sea-fight; number of bombs released from aircraft at same moment; round of applause. [F f. It. *salva*]

**săl volă'tĭle** n. Solution of ammonium carbonate, used as restorative in fainting etc. [L, = volatile salt]

**Sam.** abbr. Samuel (O.T.).

**Samă'rĭtan** n. & a. (Native) of *Samaria* (good ~, genuinely charitable or helpful person, w. ref. to Luke 10: 33 etc.); member of an organization helping persons in despair. [L f. Gk (place)]

**să'mba. 1.** n. (Ballroom dance imitative of) a Brazilian dance. **2.** v.i. Dance samba. [Port.]

**Să'mbŏ** n. (derog.; pl. ~s, ~es). Nickname for Negro. [Sp. *zambo*]

**Săm Brow'ne** n. Army officer's belt, and strap supporting it. [person]

**sāme** a., pron., & adv. **1.** a. (~'ness pr. -mn-). The ~, (the) identical, not different, unchanged, unvarying, (all planets travel in the same direction; the same car was later used in another crime; gave the same answer as before; at the same TIME; by the same TOKEN; in the same BOAT; just the ~, one and the ~, the very ~, emphatically the same (thing); much the ~, not very different); that, these, this, those, ~, the aforesaid, the person(s) or thing(s) previously alluded to or thought of (this same man was later my tutor; derog., these same politicians would now deny it). **2.** pron. The ~, the same thing (it was just more of the same; we must all do the same; the ~ to you!, colloq., I hope you will have

the same thing; be all or just the ~, make no difference (to person); much the ~, not appreciably different); the ~, (arch., colloq., or Law) the aforesaid person or thing (grace to fulfil the same; was that person Smith?—the same); (colloq.) = the same (~ here, the same applies to me, I agree). **3.** adv. The ~, in the same way, similarly, (people work the same here or elsewhere; ALL the same; just the ~, nevertheless); (colloq.) = the same (we enjoy ourselves same as you do). [E]

**să'mite** n. (Hist.) Rich medieval dress-fabric of silk. [F f. L f. Gk, = 6-thread]

**să'mĭzdăt** n. Secret circulation of U.S.S.R. banned literature. [Russ.]

**să'movăr** n. Russian tea-urn. [Russ., = self-boiler]

**Să'moyĕd** (-mo-) n. Member of Mongol people of Siberia; white Arctic breed of dog. [Russ.]

**să'mpăn** n. Small boat used in Far East. [Chin.]

**să'mphīre** n. Cliff plant used in pickles. [F, = herb of St. Peter (St. Pierre)]

**sa'mple** (-ah'-). **1.** n. Small part taken from thing or quantity to show what whole is like; specimen; illustrative or typical example. **2.** v.t. Take, give, samples of; try qualities of; get representative experience of; ~r n., (esp.) piece of embroidery worked in various stitches as specimen of proficiency. [AF (EXAMPLE)]

**Să'mson** n. Person of great strength or otherwise resembling Samson (see Judg. 13–16). [L f. Gk f. Heb.]

**să'murai** (-oorī) n. (pl. same). Japanese army officer; (Hist.) member of military caste in Japan. [Jap.]

**sănatŏr'ĭ|um** n. (pl. ~ums, ~a). Establishment for treatment of invalids, esp. of convalescents and the chronically sick; room or building for sick persons in school etc. [L (sano heal)]

**să'nct|ĭfy** v.t. Consecrate, make or observe as holy; free from sin; (in p.p.) sanctimonious; justify, sanction; ~ĭfĭcā'tion n.; ~ĭmō'nious a., pretending to be holy; ~ion, (n.) penalty for disobeying a law or reward for obeying it, consideration helping to enforce obedience to any rule of conduct, (esp. in pl.) economic or military action to coerce a State to conform with (esp. international) agreement etc., confirmation or ratification of law etc., permission, approval or encouragement given to action etc. by custom or tradition, (v.t.) authorize, countenance, or agree to (action etc.), ratify, attach penalty or reward to (law); ~itẏ n., holiness, sacredness; ~uarẏ n., holy place, place where fugitives are safe from arrest, violence, etc., this immunity (take ~uary, resort to place of refuge), place where wild animals, birds, etc., are protected and preserved; ~um n., holy place, part of chancel containing altar, person's private room etc. (~um sanctor′um, holy of holies, person's sanctum). [F f. L (SAINT)]

**sänd. 1.** n. Substance resulting from wearing down of esp. siliceous rocks and found on sea-shore, river-beds, deserts, etc. (built on ~, unstable; **head in the ~**, refusal to acknowledge obvious danger; ~s **are running out**, time of grace etc. is nearly at end); (in pl.) grains of sand, expanse of sand, sandbank; ~′bag, (n.) bag filled with sand esp. for making temporary defences, (v.t.; -gg-) defend or hit with sandbag(s); ~′bank, deposit of sand forming shallow place in sea or river; ~-blast n., & v.t., (treat with) jet of sand driven by compressed air or steam for cleaning or roughening glass etc.; **as happy as a ~′boy**, very happy; ~-castle, structure of sand made by child on sea-shore; ~-glass, wasp-waisted reversible glass container with two bulbs containing enough sand to take a definite time in passing from upper to lower bulb; ~-hill, dune, ~′man, personification of sleep(iness); ∥~-martin, bird nesting in sandy banks; ~′paper n., & v.t., (treat with) paper with sand or other abrasive stuck to it for smoothing or polishing; ~′piper, bird inhabiting wet sandy places; ~-pit, (esp.) pit etc. containing sand for children to play in; ~-shoe (for wearing on sea-shore etc.); ~′stone, sedimentary rock of compressed sand; ~′storm, storm with clouds of sand raised by wind; sand-YACHT. **2.** v.t. Sprinkle, cover, treat, with sand; smooth or polish with sand(paper) etc. [E]

**sä′ndal**[1] n., & v.t. (∥-ll-). (Equip with) shoe having upper that consists mainly of straps. [L f. Gk]

**sä′ndal**[2]**(wŏŏd)** n. (Tree with) scented wood. [L, ult. f. Skr.]

**sä′ndwïch** (or -ïj). **1.** n. Two or more slices of (usu. buttered) bread with meat, jam, etc., between; cake of two or more layers with jam, cream, etc., between; ~-board, one of two advertisement boards carried by sandwich-man; ~ **course** of training with alternate periods of practical and theoretical work); ~-man (walking in street with sandwich-boards hanging before and behind). **2.** v.t. Put (thing, statement, etc.) between two others of different kind. [person]

**sä′ndẏ** a. (~ily, ~iness). Abounding in sand; (of hair) yellowish-red. [E (SAND)]

**säne** a. Of sound mind, not mad; (of views etc.) moderate, sensible. [L sanus healthy]

**säng.** See SING.

**sang-froi′d** (sahnfrwah′) n. Composure, coolness, in danger or under agitating circumstances. [F, = cold blood]

**sä′nguin**∣**arẏ** (-nggwï-) a. (-ily, -iness). Accompanied by or delighting in bloodshed, bloody, bloodthirsty; ~e a., optimistic, (of complexion) bright and florid, (literary, tech.) blood-red; ~éous (-ï′n-) a., of blood, blood-red. [L (sanguis -guin- blood)]

**Sä′nhêdrïn, -rïm,** (-nï-) n. Highest court of justice and supreme council in ancient Jerusalem. [Heb. f. Gk sunedrion council]

**sä′nït**∣**arẏ** a. (-ily, -iness). Of, aimed at, or assisting, the protection of health; ~ary *napkin, ∥towel, absorbent pad used during menstruation; *~ar′ium n., sanatorium; ~ā′tioɴ n., (maintenance or improvement of) sanitary conditions, disposal of sewage and refuse etc.; ~ẏ n., saneness. [F f. L sanitas (SANE)]

**sänk.** See SINK.

**säns** (-z) prep. (arch. or joc.) Without (sans teeth, sans eyes, sans taste, sans everything); ~cūlŏ′tte (or sahnk-) n., extreme republican or revolutionary; **sänsĕ′rïf, säns-sĕ′rïf,** (sänsĕ′-) n. & a., (type-face) without SERIFS. [F f. L sine]

**Sä′nskr**∣**ït** n. & a. (Of, in) the ancient and sacred language of Hindus in India, oldest Indo-European language; ~ï′tïc a. [Skr. = composed]

**Sǎ'nta Claus** (-z), (colloq.) **Sǎ'nta,** *n.* Person said to fill children's stockings with presents on night before Christmas. [Du., = St. Nicholas]

**sǎp**[1]. **1.** *n.* Vital juice circulating in plants; (fig.) vitality; (sl.) foolish person; ~(**'wood**), soft outer layers of tree. **2.** *v.t.* (-pp-). Drain or dry (wood) of sap; (fig.) exhaust vigour of, weaken. **3.** ~**'ling** *n.*, young tree; ~**'pȳ** *a.* (~**pily, ~piness**), full of sap, young and vigorous. [E]

**sǎp**[2]. **1.** *n.* (Making of) tunnel or trench to conceal assailants' approach to fortified place; (fig.) insidious undermining of belief etc. **2.** *v.t. & i.* (-pp-). Make sap(s); undermine (wall etc.); (fig.) destroy insidiously, weaken (cf. prec.); ~**'per** *n.*, one who saps, ‖soldier of Royal Engineers (esp. as official term for private). [F *sappe* or It. *zappa* spade]

**sapē'lè** *n.* (Mahogany-like wood of) a W. Afr. tree. [W. Afr. name]

**sā'pǐd** *a.* Savoury, palatable; (literary; of writings etc.) not insipid or vapid; **sapǐ'dǐtȳ** *n.*; **sā'pǐent** *a.*, (literary) (pretending to be) wise; **sā'pǐence** *n.*; **sǎpǐě'ntial** (-shal) *a.* (-lly), consisting of wise sayings. [L (*sapio* have savour, be wise)]

**sǎ'plǐng.** See SAP[1].

**sǎponā'ceous** (-shus) *a.* Of, like, containing, soap; soapy (lit. or fig.). [L (*sapo* soap)]

**sǎ'pper.** See SAP[2].

**Sǎ'pphǐc** (sǎ'fǐk) *a. & n.* Of Sappho or Sapphism; ~**s, ~ stanza, verse,** verse-form invented by Sappho, esp. 4-line stanza with third fourth line; **Sǎ'pphǐsm** (sǎ'f-) *n.*, Lesbianism. [F f. L f. Gk (person)]

**sǎ'pphǐre** (sǎ'fīr) *n.* **1.** *n.* Transparent blue precious stone; its bright blue colour. **2.** *a.* Of sapphire blue. [F f. L f. Gk]

**sǎ'ppȳ.** See SAP[1].

**sǎ'prophyte** *n.* Vegetable organism living on decayed organic matter. [Gk *sapros* rotten, *phuō* grow]

**sǎ'rabǎnd** *n.* (Music for) slow Spanish dance. [F f. Sp.]

**Sǎ'rac|en** *n.* Arab or Muslim of time of Crusades; ~**ě'nǐc** *a.* (esp. of Islamic architecture). [F f. L f. Gk]

**sǎr'c|ǎsm** *n.* (Use of) bitter or wounding remark(s), esp. ironically worded; ~**ǎ'stǐc** *a.* (-ically). [F or L f. Gk (*sarkazō* speak bitterly)]

**sǎrcŏ'phag|us** *n.* (*pl.* ~**i** *pr.* -gī,

-jī). Stone coffin. [L f. Gk, = flesh--consumer]

**sardǐ'ne** (-ē'n) *n.* Young pilchard, or similar small fish allied to herring, often tinned tightly packed in oil; **like ~s,** crowded close together. [F f. L]

**sǎrdŏ'nǐc** *a.* (~**ally**). Grimly jocular, full of bitter mockery, cynical. [F f. L f. Gk]

**sǎr'donyx** *n.* Onyx in which white layers alternate with yellow or orange ones. [L f. Gk]

**sǎrgǎ'ssō** *n.* (*pl.* ~**s, ~es**). Seaweed with berry-like air-vessels. [Port.]

**sǎrge** *n.* (sl.) Sergeant. [abbr.]

**sǎr'ǐ, sǎr'ee,** *n.* Length of cotton or silk draped round body, worn as main garment by Hindu women. [Hindi]

**sǎrk** *n.* (Sc., N. Engl.) Shirt, chemise. [N]

**saro'ng** *n.* (Esp. Malay or Javanese) garment of long strip of cloth tucked round waist or under armpits. [Malay]

**sǎrsaparǐ'lla** (or -sp-) *n.* Tropical Amer. smilax; (tonic made from) its dried roots. [Sp.]

**sǎr'sen** *n.* Sandstone etc. boulder, relict carried by ice in glacial period. [SARACEN]

**sǎr'senět** (-sn-) *n.* Soft silk fabric used esp. as lining. [AF f. *sarzin* SARACEN]

**sartōr'ial** *a.* (~**ly**). Of clothes or tailoring. [L *sartor* tailor]

**sǎsh**[1] *n.* Long strip or loop of cloth etc. worn usu. as part of uniform or insignia over one shoulder or round the waist. [Arab., = muslin]

**sǎsh**[2] *n.* Frame holding glass in ~**-window,** usu. made to slide up and down in grooves and kept at any height by ~**-weights** attached to sash by ~**-cord** or ~**-line**. [CHASSIS]

**Sask.** *abbr.* Saskatchewan.

**sǎ'ssafrǎs** *n.* (N. Amer. tree with) a medicinal bark. [Sp. or Port.]

**Sǎ'ssenǎch** (-χ, -k) *n. & a.* (Sc. & Ir., usu. derog.) English(man). [Gacl. f. L (SAXON)]

**sǎt.** See SIT.

**Sat.** *abbr.* Saturday.

**Sā'tan** *n.* The Devil; **satǎ'nǐc** *a.* (-ically), of Satan, devilish; ~**ǐsm** *n.*, deliberate wickedness, diabolical disposition, worship of Satan. [E f. L f. Gk f. Heb., = enemy]

**sǎ'tchel** *n.* Small bag of leather etc.

usu. hung from shoulder for carrying books etc., esp. to and from school. [F f. L (SACK¹)]

**sāte**¹ *v.t.* Satiate. [prob. dial. *sade* satisfy (SAD), after *satiate*]

**sāte²**. See SIT.

**satee'n** *n.* Glossy cotton fabric woven like satin. [alt. SATIN]

**să'tell|ite. 1.** *n.* Heavenly or artificial body revolving round earth or other planet; follower, hanger-on, underling; **~ĭ'tic** *a.* **2.** *a.* Minor, secondary; controlled by or dependent on another (State, town, etc.). [F, or L *satelles -lit-* attendant]

**sā'tiāte. 1.** (-shǐ-) *v.t.* Gratify fully; surfeit. **2.** (-shyat) *a.* (poet.) Sated. **3. sā'tiable** (-shạ-) *a.*; **sātiā'tiǒn** (-shǐ-) *n.*; **satī'etў** *n.*, glutted state, feeling of having had too much, (**to satiety**, in excessive measure). [L (*satis* enough)]

**să'tin** *n., a., & v.* **1.** *n.* Silk etc. fabric with glossy surface on one side; **~wood**, kind of choice glossy timber; **~ĕ't(te)** *n.*, satin-like fabric; **~ў** *a.* **2.** *a.* Smooth as satin. **3.** *v.t.* Give glossy surface to (paper). [F f. Arab.]

**să'tīre** *n.* Composition etc. ridiculing vice or folly or lampooning individual(s); use of ridicule, irony, or sarcasm to expose folly, vice, etc.; **satī'ric(al)** *adjs.* (-ically); **să'tīrĭst** *n.*, writer or performer of satires; **să'tīrīze** *v.t.*, assail with satire, describe satirically. [F, or L *satira* medley]

**sătisfă'ct|ion** *n.* Satisfying or being satisfied (*at, in, with*, thing) in regard to desire or want or doubt, thing that satisfies desire or gratifies feeling (**to one's ~ion**, so as to satisfy or convince one); payment of debt, fulfilment of obligation, atonement (*for*); apology or else duel (*demand satisfaction*); **~orў** *a.* (-ily, -iness), causing satisfaction, satisfying expectation or need, adequate. [F f. L (foll.)]

**să'tĭsfў** *v.t. & i.* Meet expectations or desires (of); be accepted as adequate by (person etc.); content, please; adequately meet, pay, fulfil, comply with, (conditions, debt, obligations, demand, expectation, etc.); put an end to (an appetite or want); rid (person) of an appetite or want; convince (*of* fact, *that*; **~ oneself**, become certain). [F f. L *satisfacio*]

**să'trăp** *n.* Provincial governor in

ancient Persian empire. [F or L f. Gk f. Pers.]

**să'tsuma** (*or* -sōō'-) *n.* Kind of mandarin orange. [place]

**să'tūr|āte** (*or* -cher-) *v.t.* Fill with moisture, soak; imbue *with*, steep *in*, (learning, tradition, prejudice, etc.); cause (substance) to absorb, hold, or combine with greatest possible amount of another substance; **~ā'tion** *n.*, act or result of being saturated (**~ation bombing**, aimed at destroying everything in an area; **~ation point**, stage beyond which no more can be absorbed or accepted). [L (*satur* full)]

**Să'turday** (*or* -dǐ). **1.** *n.* Day of week, following Friday. **2.** *adv.* (cf. FRIDAY 2). [E f. L (foll.)]

**Să'turn** *n.* Planet with 10 moons, and broad flat rings; **~ā'lĭa** *n.*, ancient-Roman festival of Saturn observed as time of unrestrained merry-making, (freq. *s-*) scene or time of wild revelry or tumult; **Satūr'nian** *a.*; **s~ine** *a.*, of sluggish gloomy temperament, (of looks etc.) suggestive of or produced by such temperament. [L, name of god of agriculture]

**să'tyr** *n.* (Gk & Rom. Myth.) half-human half-animal woodland deity; lustful or sensual man; **~ī'asĭs** *n.*, excessive sexual desire in men. [F or L f. Gk]

**sauce. 1.** *n.* Liquid or soft preparation used as relish with food (APPLE, BREAD, MINT¹, *sauce*; **~ for the goose is ~ for the gander**, what is permissible in one case etc. should be allowed in others that are comparable; **white ~**, sauce of flour, melted butter, etc.); (fig.) thing that adds piquancy; impudence, impertinent speech or action, (*none of your sauce!*); **~-boat**, boat-shaped vessel for sauce; **~-pan** (-an), metal cooking-vessel, usu. round and with long handle at side, for use on top of stove etc. **2.** *v.t.* (colloq.) Be impudent to (person). **3. sau'cer** *n.*, small concave dish esp. for standing cup on to catch spilt tea etc. (FLYING *saucer*); **~r eyes** (large and round); **sau'cerful** (-ŏŏl) *n.*; **sau'cў** *a.* (-ily, -iness), impudent, cheeky, (colloq.) smart-looking. [F f. Rom. (L *salsus* salted)]

*sauerkraut* (sowr'krowt) *n.* German dish of chopped pickled cabbage. [G]

**sau'na** (or sow'-) n. (Building for) Finnish-style steam-bath. [Finn.]

**sau'nter. 1.** v.i. Walk in leisurely way. **2.** n. Leisurely ramble or gait. [orig. unkn.]

**saur'ian** a. & n. (Of or like) a lizard. [L f. Gk]

**sau'sage** (sŏ'-) n. Minced meat seasoned and stuffed into cylindrical case of thin membrane; a length of this (**not a ~**, sl., nothing at all); sausage-shaped object; **||~-dog**, (colloq.) dachshund; **~-machine** (for making sausages); **~-meat**, meat minced and seasoned for use in sausages or as stuffing etc.; **~ roll**, sausage-meat baked in cylindrical pastry-case. [F *saussice* f. L (SAUCE)]

**sauté** (sō'tā) a., n., & v. **1.** a. & n. (Food) quickly fried in hot pan with little fat. **2.** v.t. (**~d**, **~ed**, pr. -ād). Cook thus. [F (*sauter* jump)]

**Sauter'ne(s)** (sōtār'n) n. Sweet white French wine. [*Sauternes*, place]

**sauve qui peut** (sōvkĕpĕ') n. Precipitate flight in various directions. [F, = 'save (himself) who can']

**sa'vag|e** a., n., & v. **1.** a. Uncivilized, primitive; fierce, cruel; (colloq.) very angry. **2.** n. Member of savage tribe; barbarous or brutally cruel person. **3.** v.t. (Of dog, horse, etc.) attack and bite or trample; (of critic etc.) attack fiercely. **4.** **~ery** (-Ijrĭ) n., savage behaviour or state. [F f. Rom. (L *silva* a wood)]

**savă'nna(h)** (-ə) n. Grassy plain in (sub)tropical region. [Sp.]

**să'vant** (-ahn) n. (fem. **~e** pr. -ahnt). Learned person, esp. distinguished scientist.

**save** v., n., prep., & conj. **1.** v.t & i. Rescue or preserve (*from* danger, harm, discredit, etc.; *save* the DAY, one's or person's FACE, one's LIFE, one's SKIN; **~ the situation**, avert imminent disaster); (God) **~**, may God preserve or protect (*God save the Queen*; (God) **~ us!**, excl. of surprise); effect spiritual salvation of, preserve from damnation; keep (money etc.) for future use or enjoyment (**~ one's breath** (**to cool** one's **porridge**), abstain from talking etc.; **~ oneself**, limit one's exertions); **~** (**up**), abstain from spending (money); relieve (person) from need of spending or using

(money etc.) or experiencing (trouble etc.); obviate need for, reduce requisite amount of, (*machines save labour*; *stitch in time saves nine*); avoid losing (*saved the game*); (Footb. etc.) prevent opponent from scoring; **||~-as-you-earn**, method of saving by regular deduction from earnings. **2.** n. (Footb. etc.) Act of preventing opponent from scoring. **3.** prep. (arch., poet., rhet.) Except, but. **4.** conj. (arch.) Unless, except. [AF f. L *salvo* (*salvus* safe)]

**să'veloy** n. Highly seasoned dried sausage. [alt. F *cervelat* f. It.]

**să'ving** n., a., & prep. **1.** n. Act of rescuing or preserving; (usu. in pl.) money saved (**~s bank**, bank receiving small deposits at interest; **||~s certificate**, interest-bearing document issued by Government for savers). **2.** a. That saves or redeems; that makes economical use of (labour etc.); (of clause etc.) stipulating exception or reservation. **3.** prep. Except, with the exception of; without offence to (**~ your reverence**, arch. apology for use of coarse term). [SAVE]

**să'viour**, **\*să'vior**, (-vyer) n. Deliverer, redeemer (our, the, S**~**, Christ); person who saves a State etc. from destruction etc. [F f. L (SAVE)]

**savoir-faire** (săvwārfār') n. Quickness to see and do the right thing, tact. [F]

**\*să'vor**(**ў**¹). See SAVOUR, SAVOURY.

**să'vory**² n. Aromatic herb used in cookery. [E f. L *satureia*]

**să'vour**, **\*să'vor**, (-er). **1.** n. Characteristic taste or flavour; power to affect the taste (lit. or fig.); suggestion or suspicion *of* a quality. **2.** v.t. & i. Appreciate or perceive taste of (lit. or fig.), esp. lingeringly or with deliberation; suggest the presence *of* (*the offer savours of impertinence*). [F f. L *sapor*]

**să'vour|ў**, **\*să'vor|ў**¹, (-verĭ). **1.** a. (**~ily**, **~iness**). With appetizing taste or smell; (of food) having salt or piquant and not sweet taste. **2.** n. ||Savoury dish, esp. served at beginning or usu. end of meal.

**savoy'** n. Cabbage with wrinkled leaves; S**~ard** n. & a., (native) of Savoy, enthusiast for, performer in, Gilbert & Sullivan operas. [places]

**să'vvy** v., n., & a. (sl.) **1.** v.i. & t. Know; **no ~**, I do, he etc. does, not know or understand. **2.** *n.* Knowingness, understanding. **3.** *a.* \*Knowing, wise. [Negro & Pidgin E, f. Sp.]

**saw**[1]. **1.** *n.* Tool with sharp usu. steel toothed blade or edge for cutting wood, metal, stone, etc., by to-and-fro or rotary motion, worked by hand or mechanically; (Zool. etc.) serrated organ or part; ~'**dust**, tiny wood-fragments produced in sawing; ~'**fish**, large sea-fish with toothed end of snout; ~-**horse**, rack supporting wood for sawing; ~'**mill** (for mechanical sawing of wood); ~-**tooth(ed)** *a.*, shaped like teeth of saw, serrated. **2.** *v.t.* & *i.* (*p.p.* ~**n**, ~**ed**). Cut (wood etc.) with saw; make (boards etc.) with saw; move to and fro, divide (the air etc.) with motion as of saw or person sawing; ~ **off**, remove by sawing (||~**n-**, ~**ed-off**, of gun etc. shortened by having part of barrel sawn off, colloq. of undersized person). [E]

**saw**[2] *n.* Old saying, maxim. [E (SAY)]

**saw**[3]. See SEE[1]; **sawn**, see SAW[1].

**saw'yer** *n.* Workman who saws timber. [SAW[1]]

**săx** *n.* (colloq.) Saxophone. [abbr.]

**săxe** *n.* ~ (**blue**), light blue with greyish tinge. [F, = Saxony]

**să'xhŏrn** *n.* Valved brass musical instrument. [*Sax*, persons]

**să'xifrage** (*or* -āj) *n.* Rock plant with tufted foliage. [F or L (*saxum* rock, *frango* break)]

**Să'xon** *n.* & *a.* (Member, language) of Germanic people that conquered parts of England in 5th–6th cc.; = ANGLO-SAXON; **s~ў** *n.*, (cloth made from) a fine wool. [F f. L *Saxo -onis*]

**să'xophŏn|e** *n.* Keyed brass wind instrument with reed like that of clarinet; ~**ĭst** (*or* -ksŏ'fo-) *n.*, saxophone-player. [SAXHORN]

**say.** **1.** *v.t.* & *i.* (**said** *pr.* sĕd; 3 *sing. pres.* **says** *pr.* sĕz, arch. **saith** *pr.* sĕth; 2 *sing. pres.* arch. ~**st**, ~**est**, *past* **saidst, saidest**). Utter (specified words); speak words of (prayers, grace, etc.); state, promise, prophesy, (*that*); put into words, express, (*cannot say what I feel; that was well said*); convey information (*spoke for an hour but didn't say much*); indicate, show (*clock said half past six*); adduce, plead, (*much to be said on both sides*); form or give opinion or decision (as to) (*it's hard to say who it was*); select as example etc., take (amount etc.) as near enough, assume as true, (*anyone, let us say yourself, might have done it; a few of them, say a dozen*); **and so ~ all of us**, that is our opinion too; **have nothing to ~ for** oneself, not be able to say anything in conversation, one's defence, etc.; **how ~ you?** (asking jury for verdict); **I cannot, could not, ~**, I do not know; *I* DARE *say*; **I'll ~**, (colloq.) yes indeed; **I'm not ~ing**, I refuse to answer the question; ||**I ~!** (excl. drawing attention, opening conversation, or expressing surprise); **it is said**, the rumour, belief, etc., is (*that*); NO[1] *sooner said than done*; **not to ~**, and indeed; **said he, said I**, (used in reporting conversation); \*~!, = *I say!*; ~ **a good word for**, commend or excuse; ~ **away**, say what you have to say; ~ **much, something**, etc., for, indicate high quality of; *say* NAY; *say* NO[1]; ~ **no more**, cease speaking, I understand you; ~ **nothing to**, (fig.) leave (person) unmoved; ~ **on**, = *say away*; ~ **out**, express fully or candidly; ~ **over**, recite, esp. to fix in memory; **says he, says I**, (colloq., used in reporting conversation); ~-**so** *n.*, power of decision, mere assertion; ~ **something**, make a short speech; ~s **or** sez **you**, (vulg. *int.*) I disagree; ~ **the word**, give the order etc.; ~ **when**, say when process is to start or stop, esp. when enough drink has been poured; *say* YES; **so you ~**, that is what you say (but you may be mistaken); **that is to ~**, in other words, more explicitly, or at least; **the said**, (Law or joc.) the previously mentioned; **they ~**, = *it is said*; **to ~ nothing of**, even disregarding, in addition to; **what do you ~ to**, (colloq.) would or do you like; **when all is said and done**, after all, in the long run; **you can ~ that again**, you said it, (colloq.) I agree emphatically; **you don't ~ (so)** (excl. of surprise or incredulity). **2.** *n.* (Opportunity of saying) what one wishes to say (*said his say; let him have his say*); share in discussion or decision (*had no say in the matter*); power of final decision. **3.** ~'**ing** *n.*, (esp.) frequent or proverbial remark (**as the** ~**ing goes or is**, in the words of the proverb); **go without** ~**ing**, be obvious; **there is no** ~**ing**, it is impossible to know. [E]

‖**S.A.Y.E.** *abbr.* save-as-you-earn.

**S.C.** *abbr.* small capitals; South Carolina; special constable.

**sc.** *abbr.* scilicet.

**scăb. 1.** *n.* Crust formed over sore in healing; kind of skin-disease or plant-disease; blackleg in strike; **~'bў** *a.* (-ily, -iness). **2.** *v.i.* (-bb-). Form scab, heal over; act as blackleg. [N; cf. SHABBY]

**scă'bbard** *n.* Sheath of sword etc. [AF]

**scă'bbў.** See SCAB.

**scă'b|ies** (-z) *n.* Contagious disease, the itch; **~ious** *n.*, a wild or garden flower; **~rous** *a.*, (of subject, situation, etc.) hard to handle with decency, indecent, (Bot., Zool., etc.) rough-surfaced. [L; *scabious* named as curing scabies]

**scă'ffold** *n.* Platform on which criminals are executed (**the ~,** death by execution); scaffolding; **~ing** *n.*, temporary structure of poles or tubes and planks providing platforms for workmen building or repairing houses etc., materials for this, temporary framework (lit. or fig.). [F f. Rom. (EX-¹, CATAFALQUE)]

**scă'lar** *a.* & *n.* (Math.) (Quantity) having magnitude but not direction. [L (SCALE³)]

**scalawag.** See SCALLYWAG.

**scald¹** (-aw-, -ŏ-). **1.** *v.t.* Injure or pain with hot liquid or vapour (**~ing tears,** tears of bitter grief); rinse (vessel *out*) with boiling water; heat (milk) to near boiling-point (**~ed cream,** made from scalded milk). **2.** *n.* Injury to skin by scalding. [AF f. L *excaldo* (*calidus* hot)]

**scald²**, **skald**, (-aw-, -ŏ-) *n.* Ancient-Scandinavian poet. [N]

**scăle¹. 1.** *n.* One of the small thin horny overlapping plates protecting the skin of many fishes and reptiles; thin plate or flake resembling this (**the ~s fall from** one's eyes, one is no longer deceived); incrustation inside boiler etc.; tartar on teeth. **2.** *v.t.* & *i.* Remove scale(s) from; form or drop off in scales. **3.** **scă'lў** *a.* (-iness). [F *escale* f. Gmc (foll.)]

**scăle². 1.** *n.* Pan of weighing-balance (**throw into the ~,** cause to be factor in contest or debate; **tip, turn, the ~(s),** outweigh opposite scale, fig. be decisive); (in *pl.*) weighing-instrument (**pair of ~s,** simple balance; **the S~s,** sign

of ZODIAC). **2.** *v.t.* Be found to weigh (specified weight). [N *skál* bowl]

**scăle³. 1.** *n.* Series of degrees, ladder-like arrangement, graded system (*high in the social scale*); (Mus.) set of sounds belonging to a key, arranged in order of pitch (**play, sing, ~s,** perform notes in such sequence esp. as exercise for fingers or voice); relative dimensions (**on a large ~,** extensively), ratio of reduction or enlargement in map, picture, etc. (**in ~,** in proportion *with* surroundings etc.; **to ~,** with uniform reduction or enlargement); set of marks at measured distances on line for use in measuring etc.; rule determining intervals between these; piece of metal etc. on which they are marked; **~ (of notation),** basis of numerical system (**binary ~** with places denoting units, twos, fours, etc.; **denary ~,** units, tens, hundreds, etc.). **2.** *v.t.* Climb (wall, precipice, etc.) with ladder or by clambering; represent in dimensions different from but proportional to the actual ones (**~ down, up,** make smaller or larger in proportion, reduce or increase in size). [L *scala* ladder]

**scă'lēne** *a.* (Of triangle etc.) unequal-sided. [L f. Gk *skalēnos* unequal]

**scă'llion** (-yon) *n.* Shallot; long-necked bulbless onion. [AF f. L (*Ascalon*, place)]

**scă'llop** (*or* skŏ'-), **scŏ'llop. 1.** *n.* Bivalve shellfish with nearly circular ridged shell edged with small rounded lobes; **~(-shell),** one shell of this esp. used for cooking or serving food on; shallow pan used like scallop-shell for food; (in *pl.*) ornamental edging in fabric etc. **2.** *v.t.* Cook in scallop; ornament (material etc.) with scallops; **~ing** *n.*, scallop-edging. [F ESCALOPE]

**scă'llўwăg, scă'lawăg** (-*a*-w-) *n.* Scamp, rascal. [orig. unkn.]

**scălp. 1.** *n.* Skin and hair of top of head; this cut off as trophy by Amer. Indian. **2.** *v.t.* Remove scalp of; criticize savagely; *\*(colloq.)* resell at high or quick profit. [prob. Scand.]

**scă'lpel** *n.* Small surgical knife. [F or L (*scalpo* scratch)]

**scă'lў.** See SCALE¹.

**scă'mmonў** *n.* (Plant yielding) a purgative resin. [F or L f. Gk]

**scămp. 1.** *n.* (derog. or joc.) Rascal, rogue. **2.** *v.t.* Do (work etc.) perfunctorily or inadequately. **3.** ~**er** *v.i.*, & *n.*, (take) quick, short, or impulsive run or journey (lit. or fig.). [prob. Du.]

**scă'mpĭ** *n.pl.* Large prawns. [It.]

**scăn. 1.** *v.t.* & *i.* (**-nn-**). Test metre of (line etc. of verse) by examining nature and number of feet and syllables; read with emphasis on rhythm; (of line etc.) be metrically correct; look at all parts successively of (horizon, face, etc.), esp. quickly; traverse (region) with controlled (radar etc.) beam; resolve (picture) into its elements of light and shade for television transmission. **2.** *n.* Act or process of scanning. **3.** ~**sion** (-shon) *n.*, metrical scanning. [L *scando* climb, scan]

**scă'ndal** *n.* (Thing that causes) general feeling of outrage or indignation; malicious gossip; ~**monger**, person who disseminates scandal; ~**ize** *v.t.*, offend moral feelings or sense of propriety of; ~**ous** *a.*, containing or arousing scandal, outrageous, shocking. [F f. L f. Gk, = snare]

**Scăndĭnā'vĭan** *a.* & *n.* (Native, family of languages) of Scandinavia (Denmark, Norway, Sweden, Iceland). [L]

**scansion.** See SCAN.

**scănt. 1.** *a.* (arch., literary). Barely sufficient, deficient, with scanty supply of, (*with scant regard for my feelings*; *scant of breath*). **2.** *v.t.* (arch.) Skimp, stint, provide grudgingly, (supply, material, person). **3.** ~**ies** (-ĭz) *n.pl.*, (colloq.) women's short panties; ~**y** *a.* (**-ily, -iness**), small, barely sufficient. [N]

**scă'ntling** *n.* Small beam; narrow board; size to which stone or timber is to be cut. [F *escantillon* pattern]

**scă'ntў.** See SCANT.

**scăpe**[1] *n.* Shaft of column; (Bot.) long flower-stalk springing from root. [L f. Gk]

**scăpe**[2] *n.*, & *v.t.* Escape (arch.); ~**'goat** (-pg-), person bearing blame due to others (with ref. to Lev. 16); ~**'grace** (-pg-), rascal (often playfully of child). [ESCAPE]

**scă'pŭla** *n.* (*pl.* ~ae). Shoulder-blade; ~**ar**, (*a.*) of the scapula, (*n.*) monastic short cloak. [L]

**scăr**[1]**. 1.** *n.* Mark left by damage, esp. on skin by healed wound or on

plant by loss of leaf etc.; (fig.) lasting effect of grief etc. **2.** *v.t.* & *i.* (**-rr-**). Mark with scar(s); (of wound etc.) form or heal into a scar. [F *escharre* f. L f. Gk]

**scăr**[2]**, scaur,** *n.* Precipitous craggy part of mountain-side or cliff. [N, = reef]

**scă'rab** *n.* Kind of beetle; sacred dung-beetle of ancient Egypt; gem cut in form of beetle. [L *scarabaeus* f. Gk]

**scārce. 1.** *a.* Not plentiful, insufficient for demand or need, (usu. *pred.*: *food, money, is scarce*); seldom found, rare, (*a scarce book*); **make oneself ~**, go away, esp. surreptitiously, keep out of the way. **2.** *adv.* (arch., literary). Scarcely. **3.** ~**lў** (-slĭ) *adv.*, hardly, not quite, only just, surely not (*he can scarcely have known*), (mild form of) not (*I scarcely think so*); ~**ness** (-sn-) *n.*, rarity; **scăr'cĭtў** *n.*, insufficiency. [AF *scars* f. Rom. (L *excerpo* EXCERPT)]

**scāre. 1.** *v.t.* & *i.* Strike or be struck with sudden terror, startle and frighten; drive *away, off,* etc., by fright; keep (birds) away from sown land; (in *p.p.*) frightened *of, to* do, (of facial expression etc.) betraying terror; ~**'crow**, figure of man dressed in old clothes and set up in field to keep birds away, badly-dressed or grotesque person. **2.** *n.* (Unreasoning) terror, esp. baseless general apprehension of war, invasion, epidemic, etc.; ~**monger**, person who starts or spreads scare(s); **scăr'ў** *a.*, (colloq.) frightening. [N]

**scărf**[1] *n.* (*pl.* **scarves** *pr.* -vz, ~**s**). Long narrow strip of material worn for ornament or warmth round neck etc.; square piece of material worn round neck or over woman's hair (‖~**pin, -ring**, ornamental device for fastening this). [F *escarpe*]

**scărf**[2]**. 1.** *n.* Joint made by thinning ends of two pieces of timber etc. so that they overlap without increase of thickness and fastening them with bolts etc. **2.** *v.t.* Join with scarf. [prob. F *escarf*]

**scăr'ĭfў** (*or* -ă'r-) *v.t.* Loosen surface of (soil etc.); (Surg.) make slight incisions in, cut off skin from; (fig.) criticize etc. mercilessly; ~**fĭcā'tion** *n.*; ~**fĭcātor, ~fĭer,** *ns.*, device for scarifying. [F f. L f. Gk (*skariphos* stylus)]

**scăr'lĕt** *n.* & *a.* (Of) brilliant red

colour inclining to orange; scarlet clothes or material (*dressed in scarlet*); ~ **fever**, infectious fever with scarlet rash; ~ **hat**, cardinal's hat, (symbol of) cardinal's rank; ~ **runner**, (scarlet-flowered climbing plant bearing) kind of bean; **scarlati'na** (-tē´-) n., scarlet fever. [F *escarlate*]

**scarp. 1.** n. Steep slope, esp. inner side (cf. *counterscarp*) of ditch in fortification. **2.** v.t. Make steep or perpendicular; provide with scarp and counterscarp; (in *p.p.*, of hillside etc.) precipitous or steep. [It. *scarpa*]

**scar'per** v.i. (sl.) Escape, run away. [prob. It. *scappare* escape, infl. by rhyming sl. *Scapa Flow* go]

**scar'ỹ.** See SCARE.

**scăt¹** v.i. (-tt-), & int. (colloq.) Depart quickly. [perh. abbr. SCATTER]

**scăt²** n., & v.i. (-tt-). (Sing) wordless jazz song using voice as instrument. [prob. imit.]

**scāthe** (-dh). **1.** v.t. Harm, injure, (poet.); (esp. in *part.*) wither with severe language (*scathing criticism*). **2.** n. (arch.) Harm, injury. [N]

**scătŏ'logỹ** n. Preoccupation with obscene literature or with excrement; **scătolŏ'gical** a. (-lly); **scatŏ'phagous** a., feeding on dung. [Gk *skŏr skat-* dung]

**scă'tter. 1.** v.t. & i. Throw, send, or go in many different directions (*the police scattered the crowd*; *the crowd scattered*); cover by scattering (*scatter road with gravel*); rout or be routed; dissipate (cloud, hopes, etc.); (Phys.) deflect or diffuse (light, particles, etc.); (in *p.p.*) not situated together, wide apart, (*scattered houses, instances*); ~**-brain**, heedless or flighty person; ~**-brained**, heedless, desultory. **2.** n. Act of scattering; small amount scattered (*a scatter of hail*); extent of distribution esp. of shot; ~ **cushions, rugs,** etc., (to be placed here and there in a room). [prob. var. SHATTER]

**scă'ttỹ** a. (sl.; -**ily,** -**iness**). Feeble-minded, hare-brained. [SCATTER-brained]

**scaur.** See SCAR².

**scă'věnge** (-nj) v.t. & i. Act as scavenger (of); remove dirt, waste, impurities, etc., from; ~**er** n., person who searches among or collects things unwanted by others, animal or bird that feeds on carrion. [AF *scawager*, rel. to SHOW]

**Sc.D.** abbr. Doctor of Science [L *Scientiae Doctor*]

**scène** n. Place of actual or fictitious action(s) or occurrence(s) (*the scene of action, of operations*; *the scene of the disaster was the North Sea*; **come on the** ~, appear, arrive; **quit the** ~, depart, die); portion of play, during which action is continuous, subdivision of an act, (*in the third scene of Act II*; *the famous duel scene*); similar portion of film, book, etc.; (description of) incident or part of person's life etc. (*scenes of clerical life*; *distressing scenes occurred*); agitated or bad-tempered conversation or behaviour, emotional outburst, (*please don't make a scene*); piece of painted canvas, woodwork, etc., used to represent scene of action on stage etc., whole of these together, or place represented by them, (**behind the** ~**s**, behind the stage, out of sight of the audience, fig. not known to the public, working secretly; **set the** ~, fig. describe location of events etc.); landscape or view spread out before spectator (**change of** ~ or ~**ry**, variety of surroundings esp. gained by travel); (sl.) area or subject of activity or interest, way of life, (*the drug, jazz, social, scene*; *poetry is not my scene*); ~**-shifter,** ~**-shifting,** (person engaged in) changing scenes in theatre; **scènar'io** (or -är´-) n. (pl. -os), script or synopsis of film, play, etc., imagined sequence of future events; **scē'nerỹ** n., furnishings used in theatre to represent supposed scene of action, features (esp. picturesque) of landscape; **scē'nic** a. (-**ically**), of or on the stage, of scenery, picturesque (**scenic railway**, miniature railway running through picturesque scenery at fair etc.). [L f. Gk *skēnē* tent, stage]

**scĕnt. 1.** n. Characteristic odour, esp. pleasant; smell or trail left by animal, enabling hounds to track it; (fig.) line of investigation or pursuit (**false** ~, laid to deceive as to course, lit. or fig.; **on the** ~, having a clue, following the right track; **off the** ~, misled by false information etc.); power of detecting or distinguishing smells or discovering presence of something (*greyhound has little scent*; *has a wonderful scent for talent*); ||liquid perfume. **2.** v.t. Discern by smell; sniff out; begin to suspect presence or existence of (*I scent* *treachery, trouble*); make fragrant, apply perfume to; ~ out, discover by smelling about or by search. [F *sentir* perceive f. L (SENSE)]

**scě′ptic** (sk-), *skě′ptic, *n*. Person who doubts truth of a (religious) doctrine, theory, etc.; person inclined to question truth of facts, inferences, etc.; philosopher who questions the possibility of knowledge; ~al *a*. (~ally); ~ism *n*. [F f. L f. Gk (*skeptomai* observe)]

**scě′ptre** (-ter), *scě′pter, *n*. Staff borne as symbol of sovereignty. [F f. L f. Gk]

*schadenfreude* (shah′denfroide) *n*. Malicious enjoyment of others′ misfortunes. [G, lit. damage-joy]

**schě′dule** (sh-). **1.** *n*. Table of details or items, esp. as appendix to document; *timetable; **according to** ~, as planned; **behind, on,** ~, not at, at, time expected. **2.** *v.t.* Make schedule of; include in schedule, esp. ‖include (building) in list of those to be preserved; ~d **flight, service,** etc., (according to regular timetable). [F f. L dim. (*scheda* leaf f. Gk)]

**schēme** (sk-). **1.** *n*. Systematic arrangement proposed or in operation (COLOUR *scheme*); tabulated statement, outline, syllabus; plan of construction, action, etc.; artful or underhand design. **2.** *v.i. & t.* Make plan(s) esp. in secret or underhand way; plan to bring about. **3. schě-mǎ′tic** (sk-; *or* -ē-) *a*. (-ically) & *n*., (diagram) of scheme, representing objects by symbols etc.; **schě′matize** (sk-) *v.t.*, put in schematic form. [L f. Gk *skhēma* -*mat*- shape]

**scher′zo** (skār′tsō) *n*. (*pl.* ~s). Vigorous, often playful, movement in symphony, sonata, etc.; lively musical composition. [It., = jest]

**schi′sm** (sĭ′-, sĭz′-) *n*. Separation of a Church into two or secession of part of a Church owing to difference of opinion on doctrine or discipline; offence of causing or promoting such separation; dividing of group into mutually opposing parties; ~ǎ′tic *n. & a.*, ~ǎ′tical *a.*, (-ically), (-z-) (person) inclined to or guilty of schism. [F f. L f. Gk *skhisma* -*mat*- cleft]

**schist** (sh-) *n*. Crystalline rock whose components are arranged in layers. [F f. L f. Gk (prec.)]

**schi′zo** (skĭ′tsō) *a. & n*. (colloq.; *pl.* ~s). Schizophrenic. [abbr.]

**schi′zoid** (skĭ′ts-). **1.** *a*. Of or resembling schizophrenia or a schizophrenic. **2.** *n*. Schizoid person. [foll.]

**schizo|phrē′nia** (skĭts-) *n*. Mental disease marked by disconnection between thought, feelings, and actions; ~phrē′nic *a*. (-ically) & *n*. [Gk *skhizō* split, *phrēn* mind]

**schmaltz** (shmawlts) *n*. Sugary sentimentalism. [Yiddish]

**schnäpps** (shn-) *n*. Strong Hollands gin. [G]

**schni′tzel** (shnĭ′ts-) *n*. Veal cutlet; **Wiener** ~, one breaded, fried, and garnished. [G]

**schnorkel.** See SNORKEL.

**schŏ′lar** (sk-) *n*. Person who learns (*proved an apt scholar*); (arch.) pupil at school; learned person, esp. expert in language or literature; (vulg. or dial.) person able to read and write; student awarded money to (help) pay for his education at school, college, etc.; ~ly *a*. (~liness), erudite, (as) of learned man; ~ship *n*., (right to) award to (help) pay for one′s education, erudition, methods or achievements of scholars; **scholǎ′stic** (sk-) *a*. (-ically), of schools or education, (as) of the schoolmen, dealing in logical subtleties; **scholǎ′sticism** (sk-) *n*.; **schō′liǎst** (sk-) *n*., writer of scholia; **schō′lium** (sk-) *n*. (*pl.* -ia), explanatory note, esp. by ancient grammarian on passage in classical author. [F f. L (foll.)]

**schōōl¹** (sk-). **1.** *n*. Institution for educating children or giving instruction ‖usu. of more elementary or more technical kinds than that given at universities (PRIVATE, PUBLIC, SUMMER, SUNDAY, *school*; ‖OLD *school tie*); buildings or pupils of such institution; time during which teaching is done (go to ~, attend lessons); process of being educated in a school (at ~, *in ~, in course of this; go to, leave, ~, begin, cease, this); circumstances or occupation serving to educate or discipline (*in the school of adversity*); medieval lecture-room (the ~s, medieval universities and their professors, teaching, etc.); ‖branch of study at university (*the history school*); (department of) *university; group of thinkers, artists, etc., sharing same principles, methods, characteristics, or inspiration (*the Dutch school of* *painting*; ~ **of thought**, group of thinkers, way of thinking); ||group of card-players or gamblers. **2.** *v.t.* Educate; send to school; discipline; deliberately train or accustom (*to* patience etc.). **3.** ~ **age**, age-range in which children normally attend school; ~**-board**, (U.S. or Hist.) local education authority; ~**-book** (for use in schools); ~'**boy**, ~'**child**, (who attends school); ~**-days**, time of being at school, esp. as looked back upon; ~ **fee(s)**, amount periodically paid to school by parent etc. for teaching of pupil(s); ~'**-fellow**, past or present member of same school; ~'**girl** (who attends school); ~'**house**, building of esp. village school; ~ **house**, (orig. headmaster's) house at boarding-school; ~**-kid**, (colloq.) schoolchild; ||~**-leaver**, child leaving school on reaching ~**leaving age**, specified (esp. minimum) age at which children leave school; *~**-ma'am**, (colloq.) schoolmistress; ~'**man**, teacher in medieval European university, theologian applying Aristotelian logic to religious doctrines; *~**-marm**, (colloq.) schoolmistress; *~**-marmish**, (colloq.) prim and fussy; ~'**master**, **-mistress**, male, female, teacher in school; ~'**room** (used for lessons in school or private house); ~'**teacher**, teacher in the (esp. infant or primary) school; *school* YEAR. [E & F f. L *schola* f. Gk]

**school²** (sk-). **1.** *n.* Shoal of fish etc. **2.** *v.i.* Form shoals. [LDu.]

**schoo'ner** (sk-) *n.* Fore-and-aft--rigged ship with more than one mast; measure for, or large glass of, sherry, beer, etc. [orig. uncert.]

**schŏtti'sche** (shŏtē'sh) *n.* Kind of slow polka. [G, = Scottish]

**schwa** (shwah, shvah) *n.* (Phon.) Indeterminate VOWEL; symbol (ə) representing this. [G f. Heb.]

**sciă'tĭc** *a.* (~**ally**). Of the hip (~ **nerve**, large nerve from pelvis to thigh); affecting hip or sciatic nerve; suffering from, liable to, sciatica; ~**a** *n.*, neuralgia of hip and thigh. [F f. L f. Gk (*ischion* hip)]

**sci'ence** *n.* (Pursuit or principles of) systematic and formulated knowledge; branch of knowledge; organized body of knowledge on a subject; expert's skill, esp. in sport; **applied** ~ (studied for practical purposes); EXACT *science*; (**natural**)

~ (dealing with natural or material phenomena, e.g. chemistry or biology); PHYSICAL *science*; **pure** ~ (studied without consideration of practical applications, or depending on deductions from self-evident truths); ~ **fiction**, fanciful fiction based on postulated scientific discoveries, environmental changes, etc., and freq. dealing with space travel or life on other planets; SOCIAL *science*; **scienti'fic** *a.* (-ically), of science, used or engaged in science, following the systematic methods of science, having, using, or requiring trained skill; **sci'entism** *n.*, (use of) methods or doctrines of science; **sci'entist** *n.*, student or expert in science; **sciento'logy** *n.*, religious system based on study of knowledge and seeking to develop highest potentialities of mankind; **sciento'logist** *n.* [F f. L (*scio* know)]

**sci'-fi** *n.* (colloq.) Science fiction. [abbr.]

**sci'lĭcĕt** *adv.* That is to say (introducing word to be supplied or explanation of ambiguous word). [L]

**sci'mĭtar** *n.* Curved Oriental sword. [F & It.]

**scĭnti'lla** *n.* Spark, glimmer, (usu. fig.; *not a scintilla of evidence*); **sci'ntĭllāte** *v.i.*, sparkle, twinkle, (fig.) talk or act cleverly or wittily; **scĭntillā'tion** *n.* [L]

**sci'olism** *n.* (Display of) superficial knowledge; ~**ist** *n.*; ~**i'stic** *a.* (-ically). [L *sciolus* dim. of *scius* knowing]

**sci'on** *n.* Shoot or plant, esp. one cut for grafting; descendant, young member *of* family. [F]

**sci'ssors** (-zerz) *n.pl.* (**Pair of**) ~, cutting-instrument made of two blades so pivoted that their cutting edges close on what is to be cut (*I want a pair of, some, scissors*; ~ **and paste**, compiling of book etc. from extracts etc., or without independent research). [F f. L (*caedo* cut, as CHISEL)]

**scler̄o'sĭs** (or -ēr-) *n.* Morbid hardening of tissue; **disseminated** or **multiple** ~**osis** (spreading to all or many parts of body); **scler̄o'sed** (-zd) *a.*, affected by sclerosis; ~**o'tĭc** *a.* & *n.*, of or having sclerosis, (of) membrane forming the white of the eye. [Gk (*sklēros* hard)]

**scŏff¹. 1.** *v.i.* Speak derisively, esp.

of religion or object of respect; jeer or mock *at*; ~**′er** *n.*, (esp.) person who gibes at religion. **2.** *n.* Mocking words, taunt; laughing-stock. [perh. Scand.]

**scŏff**[2]. (sl.) **1.** *n.* Food, meal. **2.** *v.t.* & *i.* Eat greedily. [Afrik. *schoff*, f. Du.]

**scŏld. 1.** *v.t.* & *i.* Severely or noisily rebuke (child, servant, etc.); find fault noisily; ~**′ing** *n.*, severe rebuke. **2.** *n.* One who scolds, esp. nagging or complaining woman. [prob. N (SCALD[2])]

**scŏ′llop.** See SCALLOP.

**scŏnce**[1] *n.* Wall-bracket holding candlestick or light-fitting. [F f. L (*ab*)*sconsa* covered (light)]

**scŏnce**[2] *n.* Small fort or earthwork. [Du. *schans* brushwood]

**scŏne** *n.* Small soft cake of flour etc. baked quickly. [orig. uncert.]

**scoop. 1.** *n.* Short-handled deep shovel; long-handled ladle-shaped dipping-vessel; excavating part of digging-machine etc.; device for serving portions of ice cream etc.; quantity taken with scoop; act or motion of scooping; large profit made quickly or by anticipating one's competitors; exclusive item in newspaper etc. **2.** *v.t.* Lift (*up*) or hollow (*out*) (as) with scoop; secure (large profit etc.) by sudden action or stroke of luck; forestall (rival newspaper etc.) with news scoop. [LDu.]

**scoot** *v.i.* (colloq.) Run, dart, make off esp. hastily; ~**′er** *n.*, child's toy propelled by foot, consisting of footboard with wheel at front and back, and long steering-handle; (**motor**) ~**er**, low-powered motor cycle shaped somewhat like child's scooter, with seat. [orig. unkn.]

**scope**[1] *n.* Reach or sphere of observation or action, extent to which it is permissible or possible to range, develop, etc., opportunity, outlet. [It. f. Gk, = mark for shooting]

**scope**[2] *n.* (colloq.) Microscope, oscilloscope, etc. [abbr.]

**-scope** *suf.* forming *ns.* denoting thing looked at or through (*kaleidoscope, telescope*), or instrument for observing or showing (*gyroscope, oscilloscope*). [L f. Gk *skopeō* look at]

**-scŏ′pic** *suf.* forming *adjs.* w. sense 'looking at' (*macroscopic*) or 'pertaining to instrument with name in -SCOPE' (*gyroscopic*).

**scŏrbū′tic** *a.* & *n.* Of or like, (person) affected with, scurvy. [L *scorbutus* scurvy]

**scorch. 1.** *v.t.* & *i.* Burn or discolour surface of with dry heat, become so discoloured etc., (~ed earth policy, policy of burning crops etc. and removing or destroying anything that might be useful to enemy); (sl.) go at very high speed. **2.** *n.* Mark made by scorching. **3.** ~**′er** *n.*, (esp. colloq.) very hot day. [orig. unkn.]

**score. 1.** *n.* Scratch, notch, or line made on surface; record of money owing (**pay** one's ~, settle reckoning; **pay off old** ~**s**, fig., get revenge); number of points, goals, etc., made by player or side in game etc., detailed table of these, (**keep the** ~, register score as it is made; **know the** ~, fig., be aware of essential facts); (Mus.) copy of composition with parts on series of staves (**full** ~, showing every part); point, subject, reason, (**on that** ~, so far as that matter is concerned; **on the** ~ **of**, for the reason or motive of); (colloq.) remark or act by which person scores off another; (*pl.* ~, ~**s**; for pl. usage see HUNDRED) (set of) 20, (in *pl.*) great numbers; ~**-board**, **-book**, **-card**, **-sheet**, (on which score in game is entered or displayed). **2.** *v.t.* & *i.* Mark with incisions or lines; make (line etc.) with something that marks; ~ (**up**), enter in score, record, esp. mentally (offence *against* or to offender); make (points etc.) in game; win or gain (success, victory, etc.); allot score to (competitor etc.); keep the score; secure an advantage, be successful, have good luck; (Mus.) orchestrate or arrange (*for* instruments); ~ **off**, (colloq.) humiliate, defeat in argument or repartee; ~ **out**, delete; **scŏr′er** *n.*, (esp.) one who keeps the score at cricket. [E f. N (SHEAR)]

**scŏr′i|a** *n.* (*pl.* ~**ae**) Slag; clinker-like mass of lava; ~**ā′ceous** (-shŭs) *a.* [L f. Gk]

**scorn. 1.** *n.* Disdain, contempt, derision; object of contempt. **2.** *v.t.* Hold in contempt, consider beneath notice; abstain from, refuse to do, as unworthy (*scorns lying*, *a lie*, *to lie*); ~**′ful** *a.* (-lly), contemptuous (*of*). [F *escarnir* f. Gmc]

**Scŏr′piŏ** *n.* Sign of ZODIAC. [L f. Gk (*skorpios* scorpion)]

**scor′pion** *n.* Lobster-like arachnid with jointed stinging tail; (S~) sign of ZODIAC.

**scot**¹ *n.* Tax or rate (Hist.); ~**-free**, unharmed or unpunished (*go scot-free*). [N & F f. Gmc]

**Scot**² *n.* Native of Scotland. [E f. L *Scottus*]

**Scotch**¹. **1.** *a.* Of Scotland, its inhabitants, or its language; ~ **broth**, soup made from beef or mutton with vegetables, pearl barley, etc.; ~ **egg**, hard-boiled egg enclosed in sausage-meat; ~ **fir**, type of pine-tree; *Scotch* KALE; ~′**man** = SCOTSman; ~ **mist**, thick mist and drizzle; \*~ **tape** [P], sellotape; ~ **terrier** (small rough-haired short-legged kind); ~ **whisky** (distilled in Scotland); ~′**woman**, = SCOTS-woman. **2.** *n.* Form of English used in (esp. Lowlands of) Scotland; Scotch whisky; **the** ~, (*pl.*) Scotch people. [SCOTTISH]

**scotch**² **1.** *v.t.* Decisively put an end to; frustrate (plan etc.); (arch.) wound without killing. **2.** *n.* Line on ground for hopscotch. [orig. unkn.]

**scotch**³ *n.* Wedge or block against wheel to stop downhill movement.

**Scotland Yar′d** *n.* Headquarters of London Metropolitan Police; its Criminal Investigation Department. [place]

**Scots** *a.* & *n.* (esp. Sc.) Scotch (language); ~′**man**, ~′**woman**, native of Scotland; ~ **pine**, = *Scotch fir.* [SCOTTISH]

**Sco′tt∣ie** *n.* (colloq.) Scotsman; Scotch terrier; ~**ish** *a.*, of Scotland or its inhabitants. [SCOT²]

**scou′ndrel** *n.* Unscrupulous person, villain; ~**ly** *a.* [orig. unkn.]

**scour**¹ **1.** *v.t.* Rub (metal, clothes, pots, etc.) bright or clean; rub (rust, stain, etc.) *away* or *off*; clear out (channel, harbour, etc.) by flow through or over; ~**er** *n.*, (esp.) abrasive pad or powder. **2.** *n.* Act or process of scouring. [LDu. f. F f. L (EX-¹, CURE)]

**scour**² *v.t.* & *i.* Search rapidly or thoroughly; hasten (over or along), esp. in search or pursuit. [orig. unkn.]

**scourge** (skêrj). **1.** *n.* Person or thing regarded as instrument or manifestation of divine or other vengeance or punishment; whip for chastising persons. **2.** *v.t.* Chastise,

afflict; whip. [F f. L (EX-¹, *corrigia* whip)]

‖**scouse** *n.* & *a.* (sl.) (Native) of Liverpool; Liverpool dialect. [LOB-SCOUSE]

**scout**¹. **1.** *n.* Person sent out to get information (esp. Mil., about enemy or surroundings; TALENT-*scout*); act of seeking such information;\* aircraft or ship designed for reconnoitring; college servant at Oxford; (colloq.) fellow, person, (*a good scout*); (S~) member of boys' organization (S~ **Association**) intended to develop character (**King's, Queen's, S~**, Scout of highest proficiency; S~**master**, officer in charge of Scouts). **2.** *v.i.* Act as scout; ~ **about, around**, search (*for*); ~′**er** *n.* (esp. S~**er**, adult member of Scout Association). [F *escoute(r)* f. L *ausculto* listen]

**scout**² *v.t.* Reject with scorn (proposal, idea, etc.). [Scand.]

**scow** *n.* Flat-bottomed boat. [Du.]

**scowl** *v.i.*, & *n.* (Have) sullen or bad-tempered look on one's face. [Scand.]

‖**S.C.R.** *abbr.* Senior Combination Room; Senior Common Room.

**scra′bble**. **1.** *v.i.* Scratch or grope (*about*) to find or collect something. **2.** *n.* Act of scrabbling; (S~; P) game in which players build up words from letter-blocks on a board. [Du.]

**scrag. 1.** *n.* Skinny person or animal; ~(**-end**), inferior end of neck of mutton. **2.** *v.t.* (**-gg-**). (sl.) Strangle, hang; seize roughly by the neck; handle roughly, beat up. **3.** ~′**gy** (-gi) *a.* (~**gily**, ~**giness**), thin and bony. [orig. uncert.]

**scram** *v.i.* (-**mm-**). (sl., esp. in *imper.*) Go away. [perh. foll.]

**scra′mble**. **1.** *v.i.* & *t.* Make way by clambering, crawling, etc.; struggle with competitors (*for* thing or share of it); mix together indiscriminately; cook (eggs) by heating them when broken with butter, milk, etc., in pan (~**d egg**, joc., gold braid on officer's cap); change speech frequency of (telephone conversation etc.) so as to make it unintelligible without special receiver; move hastily; (of aircraft or pilots) take off quickly in emergency. **2.** *n.* Climb, walk, or motor-cycle race over rough ground; eager struggle or competition (*for* something). **3.** ~**r**

*n.*, (esp.) device for scrambling telephone conversations. [imit.]

**scrap**[1]. **1.** *n.* Small detached piece, fragment; (w. neg.) smallest piece or amount (*not a scrap of evidence*); cutting taken from newspaper etc. for keeping in a collection (~-**book,** into which these are pasted); rubbish, waste material, (~-**heap,** collection of waste material, lit. or fig.; ~-**iron, -metal,** etc., collected for re-use; ~-**merchant,** dealer in scrap; ~-**yard,** place where scrap is collected) (in *pl.*) odds and ends, bits of uneaten food. **2.** *v.t.* (**-pp-**). Discard as useless. **3.** ~'**pỹ** *a.* (~**pily,** ~**piness**), consisting of scraps, incomplete, not properly arranged. [N (SCRAPE)]

**scrap**[2] *n.*, & *v.i.* (**-pp-**). (colloq.) (Have) fight or scrimmage, esp. of unpremeditated kind. [perh. foll.]

**scrap**|**e. 1.** *v.t.* & *i.* Level, clean, smooth, or abrade by causing hard edge to move across surface (*scrape the* BARREL); leave no food on (plate); dig (hollow) by scraping; take (projection, surface layer, etc.) *away*, *off*, *out*, etc., by scraping; draw or move with sound (as) of scraping, produce such sound (from); draw back foot in making clumsy bow (**bow and** ~**e,** be ceremoniously or obsequiously deferential); move while (almost) touching; get *along*, *by*, *through*, etc., with difficulty; gain with effort or by parsimony, contrive to bring (*together*, *up*); be economical; ~**e** (**an**) **acquaintance,** form acquaintance (*with* person) by persistent effort. **2.** *n.* Act or sound of scraping; scraped place; ‖thinly applied butter etc. on bread; awkward predicament esp. resulting from escapade. **3.** ~'**er** *n.*, device used for scraping (~**erboard,** card with blackened surface removable by scraping for making white-line drawings); ~'**ing** *n.*, (esp., in *pl.*) fragments produced by scraping. [N]

**scrā'ppỹ.** See SCRAP[1].

**scratch** *v.*, *n.*, & *a.* **1.** *v.t.* Score surface of, make long narrow superficial wound(s) in, with nail(s), claw(s), or other pointed thing(s) (~ **the surface,** fig., make only a superficial investigation etc. *of* a subject); get (oneself or some part of one's body) scratched; make or form (letters, hole, etc.) by scratch-

ing; scrape without marking, esp. with finger-nails to relieve itching (~ one's **head,** esp. as sign of perplexity; ~ **my back and I'll** ~ **yours,** I shall return your help, flattery, etc.); get (thing) *together*, *up*, etc., by scratching or with difficulty; strike *off*, *out*, *through*, with pencil etc.; erase (horse's name from list of entries for race, competitor's or *election candidate's name); withdraw from competition; ~ **about,** (lit. or fig.) dig here and there for; ~ **out,** delete, outline or draw with scratches. **2.** *n.* Mark, wound, or sound made by scratching; spell of scratching oneself; (colloq.) trifling wound; (sl.) money; line from which competitors, esp. those not receiving handicap, start (**start from** ~, start at the very beginning or without advantage or preparation; **up to** ~, at or to a state of readiness or of doing what is required); ~ **pad,** pad of paper for jotting or scribbling. **3.** *a.* Collected by chance, collected or made from whatever is available, heterogeneous, (*a scratch crew*, *meal*, *team*); with no handicap given (*scratch player*, *race*). **4.** ~'**ỹ** *a.* (~**ily,** ~**iness**), (of drawing etc.) done in scratches, careless or unskilful, (of pen etc.) tending to make scratches or scratching noise, tending to cause itchiness, inclined to be irritable or spiteful. [orig. uncert.]

**scrawl. 1.** *v.i.* & *t.* Write in hurried untidy way; cross *out* thus. **2.** *n.* Hurried writing; scrawled note. [orig. uncert.]

**scraw'nỹ** *a.* Lean, scraggy. [dial.]

**scream. 1.** *v.i.* & *t.* Emit piercing cry (as) of pain or terror; speak or sing (words etc.) in such tone; make, move with, shrill sound like scream; laugh uncontrollably; be blatantly obvious; ~ **out,** emit (as) a scream. **2.** *n.* Act or sound of screaming; (colloq.) irresistibly funny occurrence or person. [E]

**scree** *n.* (in *sing.* or *pl.*) (Mountain slope covered with) small loose stones. [N, = landslip]

**screech** *v.i.* & *t.*, & *n.* Scream with or of fright or pain or anger, or in harsh or uncanny tone; ~-**owl,** owl that screeches instead of hooting, esp. barn-owl. [E (imit.)]

**screed** *n.* Long tiresome harangue (esp. list of grievances) or letter. [prob. SHRED]

**screen. 1.** *n.* Movable piece of furniture designed as shelter from observation or draughts or excessive heat or light; partition of wood or stone separating one part of church, room, etc., from another (ROOD--*screen*); thing used as shelter esp. from observation (SMOKE-*screen*), measure adopted for concealment, protection afforded by this; = SIGHT--*screen*, WIND*screen*; blank surface on which film, televised picture, radar image, etc., is projected (**the ~,** moving pictures collectively); (frame with) fine wire netting to keep out flies, mosquitoes, etc.; large sieve; system for showing presence or absence of disease, quality, etc.; (Print.) transparent finely-ruled plate or film used in half-tone reproduction; **~′play,** script of film; **~-printing,** process like stencilling with ink forced through prepared sheet of fine material; **~ test** (of person's suitability for appearing in films). **2.** *v.t.* Shelter, hide partly or completely; protect from detection, censure, etc.; prevent from causing electrical interference; show (film etc.) on screen; sieve; test (person) for presence or absence of disease, quality, etc., esp. for reliability or loyalty; **~ off,** shut off or hide with screen. [F]

**screw** (-ōō). **1.** *n.* Cylinder or cone with spiral ridge round it outside (*male screw*) or inside (*female screw*); (**wood-**)**~,** metal male screw with slotted head and sharp point for fastening things (esp. of wood) together (**have a ~ loose,** colloq., be slightly mad); wooden or metal screw used to exert pressure; (*in sing.* or *pl.*) instrument of torture operating thus (**put the ~(s) on,** exert pressure, esp. to extort or intimidate); **~(-propeller),** propeller acting like screw; one turn of a screw; ||(Bill. etc.) oblique curling motion of ball; ||small twisted-up paper *of* tobacco etc.; (colloq.) miser; ||(sl.) amount of salary or wages, prison warder; (vulg.) (partner in) copulation; \***~′-ball** *a.* & *n.,* (sl.) mad or eccentric (person); **~-cap, -top,** (that screws on to bottle etc.); **~′driver,** tool like narrow chisel for turning screws by the slot. **2.** *v.t.* & *i.* Fasten or tighten with screw(s); turn (screw); twist or turn round like screw; (of ball etc.) swerve; put the screw on,

oppress; extort (consent, money, etc.) *out of*; contort or contract (one's face etc.); (vulg.) copulate (with); **~ up,** contract or contort (one's eyes, face, etc.), summon up (one's courage), (sl.) bungle or mismanage; **~ed** (-ōōd) *a.,* (esp., sl.) drunk; **~′y** *a.,* (sl.) mad, eccentric, absurd. [F *escroue*]

**scri′bble. 1.** *v.i.* & *t.* Write hurriedly or carelessly; be author or writer (esp. **~r** *n.* in self-depreciatory use); **~ out,** obliterate. **2.** *n.* Scrawl, hasty note etc. [L *scribillo* dim. (foll.)]

**scribe. 1.** *n.* Ancient or medieval copyist of manuscripts; (Bibl.) ancient-Jewish record-keeper or professional theologian and jurist; pointed instrument for making marks on wood etc.; **scri′bal** *a.* **2.** *v.t.* Mark with scribe. [L *scriba* (*scribo* write)]

**scrim** *n.* Open-weave fabric for lining, upholstery, etc. [orig. unkn.]

**scri′mmage** *n.,* & *v.i.* (Engage in) tussle, confused struggle, or brawl. [SKIRMISH]

**scrimp** *v.t.* & *i.* Skimp. [orig. unkn.]

||**scri′mshănk** *v.i.* (sl.) Shirk.

**scrip**[1] *n.* Provisional certificate of money subscribed entitling holder to dividends, (collect.) such certificates; extra share(s) instead of dividend. [abbr. *subscription receipt*]

**scrip**[2] *n.* (arch.) Traveller's satchel. [F *escrep(p)e*]

**script. 1.** *n.* Handwriting, written characters; type imitating handwriting; alphabet or system of writing; text of play, film, talk, etc., (**~-writer,** writer for broadcasting, films, etc.); ||examinee's written answer. **2.** *v.t.* Write script for (film etc.). **3.** **~ōr′ium** *n.* (*pl.* -ia, -iums), writing-room, esp. in monastery. [F l. L *scriptum* (*scribo* write)]

**scri′pture** *n.* Sacred book; (Holy) S**~,** the (Holy) S**~s,** the Bible; **scri′ptural** (-choor-, -cher-) *a.* (-lly), of or based on the Bible. [L prec.)]

**scri′vener** *n.* (Hist.) Drafter of documents, copyist, notary. [F *escrivein* f. L (SCRIBE) + -ER[1]]

**scro′fŭl|a** *n.* Disease with glandular swellings, prob. a form of tuberculosis; **~ous** *a.* [L *scrofa* sow)]

**scrŏll** *n.* Roll of parchment or paper esp. with writing; book of the ancient roll form; ornamental design imitating roll of parchment; ~**ed** (-ld) *a.*, having scroll ornament. [orig. (*sc*)*rowle* ROLL]

**Scrōoge** *n.* Miser. [character in Dickens]

**scrŏ't|um** *n.* (*pl.* ~**a**, ~**ums**). Pouch of skin containing the testicles; ~**al** *a.* [L]

**scrounge** (-nj) *v.t.* & *i.* (sl.) Obtain (things) illicitly or by cadging. [dial. *scrunge* steal]

**scrŭb**[1] **1.** *v.t.* & *i.* (-bb-). Rub hard so as to clean, esp. with scrubbing--brush and soap and water; use scrubbing-brush etc.; use water to remove impurities from; (sl.) cancel, scrap, (plan, order, etc.); ~ **up**, (of surgeon etc.) clean hands and arms by scrubbing before operation. **2.** *n.* Scrubbing or being scrubbed. **3.** ~**ber** *n.*, (esp.) apparatus for scrubbing gases. [LDu.]

**scrŭb**[2] *n.* (Land covered with) brushwood or stunted forest growth; stunted or insignificant person etc.; ~**bў** *a.* (~**bily**, ~**biness**). [SHRUB]

**scrŭff** *n.* Back of neck (*seize*, *take*, etc., *by the scruff of the neck*). [orig. unkn.]

**scrŭ'ff|ў** *a.* (colloq.; ~**ily**, ~**iness**). Shabby, slovenly, untidy; scurfy. [*scruff* = SCURF]

**scrŭm** *n.* = foll.; ~**-half**, half-back who puts ball into scrum. [abbr.]

**scrŭ'mmage** *n.* (Rugby Footb.) Grouping of all forwards on each side to push against those of the other and seek possession of ball thrown on ground between them. [SCRIMMAGE]

**scrŭ'mptious** (-psh*us*) *a.* (colloq.) Delicious, delightful. [orig. unkn.]

**scrŭnch** *n.*, & *v.t.* & *i.* Crunch. [alt. CRUNCH]

**scru'p|le** (-ōō'-). **1.** *n.* Weight of 20 grains; (reluctance caused by) doubt about morality or propriety of an action etc. **2.** *v.i.* Feel or be influenced by scruples; (esp. w. neg.) be reluctant because of scruples or to do. **3.** ~**ūlous** *a.*, careful to avoid doing wrong, conscientious or thorough even in small matters, punctilious, over-attentive to details; ~**ūlŏ'sitў** *n.* [F or L]

**scru'tĭn|ў** (-ōō'-) *n.* Critical gaze, close investigation, examination into details; official examination of ballot--papers to check their validity or accuracy of counting; ~**eer'** *n.*,

person who scrutinizes ballot-papers; ~**ize** *v.t.*, subject to scrutiny. [L *scrutinium* (*scrutor* examine)]

**scū'ba** (*or* -ōō'-) *n.* Self-contained underwater breathing apparatus. [acronym]

**scŭd. 1.** *v.i.* (-dd-). Run or fly straight and fast, skim along; (Naut.) run before the wind. **2.** *n.* Spell of scudding, scudding motion; vapoury driving clouds or shower. [perh. alt. SCUT]

**scŭff. 1.** *v.i.* & *t.* Walk with drag-ging feet, shuffle; graze or brush against; mark, wear out, (shoes etc.) thus. **2.** *n.* Mark of scuffing. [imit.]

**scŭ'ffle** *v.i.*, & *n.* (Engage in) confused struggle or disorderly fight at close quarters. [prob. Scand. (SHOVE)]

**scŭll. 1.** *n.* One of pair of small oars; oar used to propel boat from stern, usu. by twisting motion; (in *pl.*) sculling race. **2.** *v.t.* Propel (boat, or abs.) with sculls; ~**'er** *n.*, user of scull(s), boat for sculling. [orig. unkn.]

**scŭ'llerў** *n.* Back kitchen; room in which dishes are washed etc. [AF *squillerie* (*escuele* dish f. L *scutella* salver)]

**scŭ'llion** (-yon) *n.* (arch.) Cook's boy, dish-washer. [orig. unkn.]

**scŭ'lptur|e. 1.** *n.* Art of forming representations of objects in the round or in relief by chiselling stone, carving wood, modelling clay, casting metal, etc.; a work of sculpture. **2.** *v.t.* & *i.* Represent in, shape like, adorn with, sculpture; do sculpture. **3.** *sculpt v.t.* & *i.*, (colloq.) sculpture; **scŭ'lptor** *n.*, one who does sculpture; **scŭ'lptrĕss** *n.*; ~**al** (~**ally**) *a.* [L (*sculpo sculpt-* carve]

**scŭm. 1.** *n.* Layer of dirt, froth, impurities, etc., at top of liquid; (fig.) worthless part or person(s); ~**mў** *a.* **2.** *v.t.* & *i.* (-mm-). Remove scum from; form scum (on). [LDu.]

**scŭ'pper. 1.** *n.* Hole in ship's side to carry off water from deck. **2.** *v.t.* ||(sl.) Sink (ship, crew); defeat or ruin (plan etc.); kill. [perh. AF deriv. of F *escopir* spit]

**scŭrf** *n.* Flakes on surface of skin cast off as fresh skin develops below, esp. on the head; ~**'ў** *a.* (~**ily**, ~**iness**). [E]

**scŭ'rrĭlous** *a.* Grossly or obscenely abusive; **scŭrrĭ'lĭtў** *n.* [F or L (*scurra* buffoon)]

**scŭ′rrў. 1.** *v.i.* Run or move hurriedly esp. with short quick steps, scamper. **2.** *n.* Act or sound of scurrying; flurry of rain or snow. [abbr. *hurry-scurry* redupl. HURRY]

**scŭr′v|ў. 1.** *a.* (~ily, ~iness). Paltry, dishonourable, contemptible. **2.** *n.* Deficiency disease from lack of vitamin C, attacking those (esp. formerly sailors) who live without fresh vegetables. [SCURF; *n.* prob. infl. by F *scorbut* (SCORBUTIC)]

**scŭt** *n.* Short tail, esp. of rabbit, hare, or deer. [orig. unkn.]

**scŭ′tter** *v.i.,* & *n.* (colloq.) Scurry. [perh. alt. SCUTTLE³]

**scŭ′ttle¹** *n.* Coal-box; ‖part of motor-car body between windscreen and bonnet. [N, f. L *scutella* dish]

**scŭ′ttle². 1.** *n.* Hole with lid in ship's deck or side or in roof or wall; ~**butt,** (sl.) rumour. **2.** *v.t.* Make hole(s) in or open sea-cocks of (ship), esp. for purposes of sinking. [obs. F *escoutille* f. Sp. *escotilla* hatchway]

**scŭ′ttle³. 1.** *v.i.* Scurry; flee from danger or difficulty. **2.** *n.* Hurried gait; precipitate flight or departure. [cf. dial. *scuddle* frequent. of SCUD]

**Scy′lla** *n.* ~ **and Charybdis,** two dangers or extremes such that one can be avoided only by approaching the other. [monster and whirlpool in Gk Myth.]

**scythe** (-dh). **1.** *n.* Mowing and reaping implement with long blade swung over ground. **2.** *v.t.* Cut with scythe. [E]

**S.D**(ak). *abbr.* South Dakota.

**S.E.** *abbr.* South-East(ern).

**sea** *n.* **1.** Expanse of salt water that covers most of earth's surface, any part of this as opp. land or fresh water, (**at** ~, away from, esp. out of sight, of land, fig. perplexed, confused; **by** ~, in ship(s); **follow the** ~, be sailor; **go to** ~, become sailor; **high** ~**s,** beyond limit of territorial jurisdiction; **on the** ~, in ship etc., situated on coast; **put** (**out**) **to** ~, leave land or port; **the** (**seven**) ~**s,** all the sea areas of the world, esp. the Arctic, Antarctic, N. & S. Pacific, N. & S. Atlantic, and Indian, Oceans); tract of salt water partly or wholly enclosed by land and having special name (*Caspian, Dead, Mediterranean, Sea*); large lake (*Sea of Galilee*); local motion or state of the sea, swell, large wave, (HALF-*seas*-*over*); vast quantity or expanse of (*a sea of faces, flame, troubles*); (attrib.) living or used in, on, or near the sea (often prefixed to name of marine animal, plant, etc., having superficial resemblance to what it is named after). **2.** ~ **air,** air at seaside, esp. as recommended for invalids; ~ **anchor,** bag to retard drifting of ship; *sea* ANEMONE; ~**bed,** floor of the sea; ~**bird** (frequenting sea, or land near sea); ~**board,** seashore, coast region, line of coast; ~**borne,** conveyed by sea; ~ **breeze,** any breeze at sea; ~**breeze** (blowing landward from sea); ~ **captain,** captain of ship, great sailor or commander at sea; ~ **change,** (unexpected or notable) transformation; ~**cock,** valve to let sea water into ship's interior, grey plover; ~**cow,** sirenian, walrus, hippopotamus; ~**dog,** old sailor, (Elizabethan) sea captain, seal; ~ **eagle,** fish-eating eagle; ~**farer,** sailor; ~**faring** *a.* & *n.,* traversing the seas, esp. regularly; ~**food,** edible salt-water (shell)fish; ~ **front,** part of town facing sea, esp. promenade; ~**girt,** (poet., rhet.) surrounded by sea; ~**going,** (of ships) fit for crossing the sea, (of person) seafaring; ~**green** *a.* & *n.,* (of) bluish green (~-*green incorruptible,* orig. of Robespierre); ~**gull,** = GULL¹; ~**horse,** small fish with head suggestive of horse's, mythical creature with horse's head and fish's tail; ~**kale,** herb with young shoots used as vegetable; ~**legs,** ability to walk on deck of rolling ship; ~**level,** mean level of sea's surface, used in reckoning height of hills etc. and as barometric standard; ~**lion,** large eared seal; ‖*Sea* LORD; ~**man,** one whose occupation is on the sea, sailor, esp. below rank of officer; ~**manlike,** ~**manly,** *adjs.,* (characteristic) of a good sailor; ~**manship,** skill in managing ship or boat; ~**mark,** conspicuous object used to direct course at sea; ~**mew,** = MEW¹; *sea* MILE; ~ **monster,** huge, terrible, or strange sea-animal; ~**pink,** seashore or Alpine plant with pink flowers; ~**plane,** aircraft designed to take off from, and land on, water; ~**port,** town with harbour; ~ **power,** (State with) ability to control or make use of the sea, esp. in naval warfare; ~**room,** space for ship to turn etc. at sea; ~

rover, pirate (ship); ~-salt (got by evaporating sea-water); ~'scape, (picture of) scene at sea; **Sea Scout**, member of maritime branch of Scout Association; ~ serpent, sea snake, serpentine sea monster; sea-SHANTY²; ~ shell, shell of salt--water mollusc; ~-shore, land close to sea; ~'sick, vomiting, or inclined to vomit, from motion of ship etc.; ~'sickness, being seasick; ~'side, (place or places on) sea--coast esp. as holiday resort(s), edge of sea; ~ trout, trout resembling salmon; ~-urchin, small sea--animal with prickly shell; ~-wall, wall or embankment to prevent encroachment by the sea; ~-way, ship's progress, place where ship lies in open water, inland waterway open to seagoing ships; ~'weed, plant growing in sea; ~'worthy, fit to put to sea. 3. ~'ward a., adv., & n.; ~'wards (-z) adv. [E]

**seal¹. 1.** n. (Engraved piece of metal etc. used to stamp design on) piece of wax, lead, paper, etc., attached to document as guarantee of authenticity or to receptacle, envelope, etc., to prevent its being opened without owner's knowledge (**given under my hand and ~**, signed and sealed by me; ‖**Great S~**, used on important State papers; ‖**PRIVY** seal; **set the ~ on**, set one's ~ **to**, authorize, confirm); adhesive stamp used to aid a charity etc.; act, thing, etc., regarded as confirmation or guarantee; substance or device to close aperture etc., esp. water in drain-trap preventing ascent of foul air; ~**s of office**, those held during tenure esp. by Lord Chancellor or Secretary of State. **2.** v.t. Fix seal to; certify as correct with seal or stamp; stamp or fasten with seal, close securely or hermetically, (**my lips are ~ed**, I must not speak; ~ed **book**, thing utterly obscure to; ~ed **orders**, instructions that are not to be examined until specified time); settle or decide (his fate is sealed; seal a bargain); ~ **off**, prevent entry to or exit from (area); ~ (**up**), confine securely; ~'**ing-wax**, mixture of shellac and rosin softened by heating and used for seals; ~'ant n., material for sealing. [AF f. L sigillum]

**seal². 1.** n. Fish-eating amphibious marine mammal with flippers; ~('skin), its skin or prepared fur,

garment made from this. **2.** v.i. Hunt seals; ~'er n., ship or man engaged in hunting seals. [E]

**Sea'lyham** (-liəm) n. ~ (**terrier**), wire-haired short-legged terrier. [place]

**seam. 1.** n. Line where two edges join, esp. of pieces of cloth turned back and sewn together or of boards fitted alongside one another (**bursting** etc. **at the ~s**, full to bursting or overflowing); fissure between parallel edges; wrinkle; stratum of coal etc.; ~ **bowler** (Crick., who causes ball to spin, esp. by use of its seam). **2.** v.t. Join by seam; (esp. in p.p.) mark or score with seam, fissure, or scar. **3.** ~'er n., (esp.) seam bowler; ~'stress, sě'mpstress (sě'ms-) n., woman who sews; ~'y a. (~'ily, ~iness), marked with or showing seams; ~y side, (fig.) disreputable or unattractive side. [E]

**se'ance** (sā'-), séance (sā'ahṅs), n. Meeting for exhibition or investigation of spiritualistic phenomena. [F]

**sear. 1.** v.t. Scorch, cauterize; make (conscience, feelings, etc.) callous. **2.** a. (literary; also **sere**). Withered, dried up, (**the ~, the yellow leaf**, old age). [E]

**search** (sě'r-). **1.** v.t. & i. Look or feel or go over (person, his face or pockets, receptacle, place, book, etc.) for what may be found or to find something whose presence is suspected (~ **me!**, colloq., I do not know); probe or penetrate into (lit. or fig.); make search or investigation (for); (in part., of examination) thorough, leaving no loopholes; ~ **out**, look for, seek out. **2.** n. Act of searching, investigation, (for, of, after; **in ~ of**, trying to find; **right of ~**, belligerent's right to search neutral ship); ~'**light**, (light from) electric lamp with powerful concentrated beam that can be turned in any direction esp. for discovering hostile aircraft, enemy movements, etc.; ~-**party**, group of persons looking for lost or concealed person or thing; ~-**warrant**, official authority to enter and search a building. [AF f. L circo (CIRCLE)]

**sea'son** (-z-). **1.** n. One of the divisions of the year associated with a type of weather and a stage of vegetation (**the four ~s**, spring, summer, autumn, winter); proper or suitable time, time when something is plentiful, active, in vogue, etc., (*the strawberry, cricket, holiday, season*); **a word in** ~, opportune advice etc.; **high, low,** ~, period of greatest, smallest, activity at holiday resort etc.; **in** ~, (of food) available in good condition and plentifully, (of animal) on heat; **in and out of** ~, at all times indiscriminately; time of year when there is much activity in fashionable society (*London in the season*); indefinite period (*may endure for a season*); ~(**-ticket**), ticket entitling holder to any number of journeys, admittances, etc., in a given period. **2.** *v.t. & i.* Make or become suitable or in desired condition, esp. by exposure to air or weather; flavour or make palatable with or *with* salt, condiments, wit, etc.; temper, moderate, (*let mercy season justice*). **3.** ~**able** *a.* (~**ably**), suitable or usual to the season, opportune, meeting the needs of the occasion; ~**al** *a.* (~**ally**), of, depending on, or varying with the season(s); ~**ing** *n.*, (esp.) flavouring for food. [F f. L *satio* sowing]

**seat. 1.** *n.* Thing made or used for sitting on (**take a** ~, sit down); place for one person in theatre etc.; occupation of this or right to occupy it, esp. as member of House of Commons; manner of sitting on horse etc.; buttocks, part of trousers etc. covering them (**by the** ~ **of** one's **pants,** by instinct rather than logic); part of chair etc. on which sitter's weight directly rests; part of machine that supports or guides another part; site or location; country mansion, esp. with large grounds; ~**-belt,** safety-belt for seated person in vehicle or aircraft. **2.** *v.t.* Cause to sit; (in *p.p.*) sitting (**be** ~**ed,** sit down); provide (person(s), room, etc.) with seat(s); put or fit in position; ~**'er** *n.*, vehicle, aircraft, etc., with specified number of seats; ~**'ing** *n.*, (esp.) seats collectively. [N (SIT)]

**sĕbā'ceous** (-shŭs) *a.* Fatty, secreting or conveying oily matter. [L (*sebum* tallow)]

**sec** (sĕk) *a.* (Of wine) dry. [F]

**Sec.** *abbr.* Secretary.

**sec.** *abbr.* second(s).

||**sĕ'cateurs** (-ērz) *n.* Pruning-clippers used with one hand. [F]

**sĕcē'de** *v.i.* Withdraw formally from a Church, federation, or similar body; **sĕcē'ssion** (-shon) *n.*, **sĕcē'ssionĭst** (-shon-) *n.* [L *secedo -cess-*]

**sĕclu'|de** (-ōō'd) *v.t.* Keep (person, place, one*self*) retired or away from company, screen from view; ~**sion** (-zhon) *n.*, secluded state or place. [L *secludo -clus-*]

**sĕ'cond** *a., n., & v.* (see also NUMERAL). **1.** *a.* Next after first (*the world's second largest city*); other besides one or the first, additional, (*a second man now arrived*); of subordinate importance, position, etc., (*to*), inferior; (Mus.) performing lower or subordinate part (*second violins*); metaphorical, such as to be comparable to, (*a second Daniel*). **2.** *n.* Second person etc. in race or competition (**a good** ~, close to winner); another person or thing besides the previously mentioned or principal one; assistant to combatant in boxing-match, duel, etc.; sixtieth part of minute of time or angle, (colloq.) short time (*wait a second*); (in *pl.*) second helping of food or second course of meal. **3.** *v.t.* Support, back up; formally support (nomination, resolution, etc., or its proposer); ||(*pr.* sĭkǒ'nd) transfer (person) temporarily to another department etc. **4.** ~ **advent,** = *second coming*; ~**-best** *a. & n.*, (what is) next after the best (*come off* ~**-best,** be beaten); ~ **chamber,** upper house of parliament; ~ **childhood,** dotage; ~ **class,** second-best group or category or accommodation; ~**-class** *a. & adv.*, of or by the second or inferior class, position, quality, etc.; ~ **coming,** return of Christ esp. on Judgement Day; *second* COUSIN, FIDDLE, FLOOR; ~ **gear,** next-to-lowest gear in motor vehicle or bicycle; ~**-hand,** (*a.*) (of goods) bought after being used by previous owner(s), (of shops etc.) where such goods can be bought, (of information etc.) obtained from others and not by original observation or research, (*adv.*) from a secondary source; **at** ~ **hand,** indirectly; ~(**s**) **hand,** hand showing seconds on watch or clock; ~ **home,** subsidiary place of residence, place which one loves or feels comfortable in; ~ **in command,** next in rank to chief officer; ~ **lieutenant,** Army officer next below lieutenant; ~ **master, mistress,** deputy to head teacher; ~ **name,**

surname; ~ **nature,** acquired tendency that has become instinctive; ~ **officer,** assistant mate on merchant ship; *second* OPINION, PERSON; ~-**rate,** rated in second class, inferior; *second* SELF; ~ **sight,** power of perceiving future or distant events; *second* STRING; ~ **teeth,** those of adults; ~ **thoughts,** opinion or resolution formed by reconsideration; ~ **to none,** unsurpassed; *second* WIND[1]. **5.** ~**arỹ** *a.* (-ily, -iness), next below, coming after, derived from, depending on, or supplementing what is PRIMARY, (of education, school, etc.) for those who have had primary education; ~**lỹ** *adv.,* in the second place, furthermore; ~**ment** (sǐkǒ'nd-) *n.,* transfer of person to another department etc. [F f. L *secundus*]

**sě'crět. 1.** *a.* (To be) kept private, unknown, or hidden from all or all but a few (*secret agreement, passage, process*); fond of secrecy; having faculty of secrecy; ~ **agent,** spy; ~ **ballot** (in which voting is not made public); ~ **police** (operating in secret esp. for political ends); ~ **service,** government department concerned with espionage; ~ **society** (whose members are sworn to secrecy about it). **2.** *n.* A secret matter (**in** ~, secretly; **in the** ~, sharing the knowledge of it; **keep a** ~, not reveal it; **open** ~, thing unknown only to those who do not inquire); mystery, thing for which explanation is unknown or not widely known (*the secrets of nature*); true but not generally understood method for attainment of (*the secret of success*). **3. sē'crecỹ** *n.,* Keeping of secrets as a fact, habit, or faculty (**sworn to secrecy,** having promised to keep a secret). [F f. L (*secerno -cret-* separate)]

**sē'cretarỹ** *n.* Official appointed by society etc. to conduct its correspondence, keep its records, etc.; (**private**) ~, person employed by another to assist with correspondence, keep records, make appointments, etc.; principal assistant of government minister, ambassador, etc.; ~**bird,** long-legged crested African bird; S~-**General,** principal administrator of an organization; S~ **of State,** ‖head of a major government department, * = Foreign Secretary; **secretār'ial** *a.*; **secretār'iat**

*n.,* (members or premises of) administrative office or department; ~**ship** *n.* [L (prec.)]

**sěcrē'te** *v.t.* Conceal (object, person, one*self*); (Physiol.) separate (substance) in gland etc. from blood or sap for function in the organism or for excretion; **sěcrē'tion** *n.,* act of secreting, secreted substance; **sē'cretive** (*or* sǐkrē't-) *a.,* inclined to make or keep secrets, uncommunicative; **sěcrē'torỹ** *a.,* of physiological secretion. [SECRET]

**sěct** *n.* Body of persons agreed upon religious doctrines usu. different from those of an established or orthodox Church from which they have separated; (derog.) nonconformist or other Church; religious denomination; followers of a particular philosopher or philosophy or school of thought in politics etc.; ~**ār'ian** *a.* & *n.,* (member) of sect, esp. bigoted; ~**ār'ianism** *n.*; ~'**arỹ** *n.,* member of sect. [F or L (*sequor* follow)]

**sě'ction. 1.** *n.* Part cut off; one of the parts into which thing is divided or divisible or out of which a structure can be fitted together; subdivision of book, statute, group of people, etc.; *area of land; *district of town; (Mil.) subdivision of platoon; separation by cutting; cutting of solid by plane, (area of) resulting figure, (CROSS-*section*); ~ (-**mark**), sign (§) used to indicate start of section of book etc. **2.** *v.t.* Arrange in or divide into sections. **3.** ~**al** *a.* (~**ally**), of a section, made in sections, local rather than general, partisan; ~**alism** *n.*; **sě'ctor** *n.,* branch of an activity, (Mil.) portion of battle area, (Geom.) plane figure enclosed between two radii of circle, ellipse, etc., and the arc cut off by them. [F or L (*seco sect-* cut)]

**sě'cular** *a.* Concerned with the affairs of this world, not sacred, not ecclesiastical, not monastic; lasting for ages; (of change etc.) slow but persistent; occurring once in an age or century; ~**ism** *n.,* (esp.) doctrine that morality or education should not be based on religion; ~**ist** *n.*; **sěcŭlă'rĭtỹ** *n.*; ~**ize** *v.t.* [L (*saeculum* an age)]

**sěcūr'e. 1.** *a.* (~**r,** ~**st**). Untroubled by danger or fear; impregnable; reliable, certain not to fail or give way or get loose or be lost;

having sure prospect *of*, safe *against* or *from*. **2.** *v.t.* Fortify (town etc.); confine, enclose, fasten, or close, securely; guarantee, make safe; succeed in getting, obtain, (esp. something competed for or coveted). [L (*se-* without, *cura* care)]

**secūr'itў** *n.* Secure condition or feeling; thing that guards or guarantees (**in ~ for**, as guarantee for); (organization for ensuring) safety of State, company, etc., against espionage, theft, or other danger; thing deposited or pledged as guarantee of fulfilment of undertaking or payment of loan, to be forfeited in case of failure, (**on ~ of**, using as guarantee); document as evidence of loan, certificate of stock, bond, etc.; **~ risk**, person of doubtful loyalty. [F or L (prec.)]

**sedā'n** *n.* **~(-chair)**, (Hist.) vehicle for one person, carried on poles by two men; *enclosed motor car for four or more persons. [orig. uncert.]

**sedă't|e.** **1.** *a.* (Of person or his manner, look, writing, etc.) tranquil, equable, serious. **2.** *v.t.* Put under sedation. **3.** **~ion** *n.*, calming (esp. by sedative(s); **se'dative** *a.* & *n.* (medicine etc.) tending to calm or soothe; **se'dentarў** *a.* (**-ily, -iness**), sitting, (of work etc.) characterized by much sitting and little physical exercise, (of person) having or inclined to work etc. of this kind. [L (*sedo* settle, calm)]

**sedg|e** *n.* Waterside or marsh plant resembling coarse grass; **~'ў** *a.* [E]

**sedī'lia** *n.pl.* Stone seats for priests in S. wall of chancel usu. canopied and 3 in number; **se'diment** *n.*, matter that settles to bottom of liquid, dregs, (Geol.) water- or wind--borne matter that settles and may form rocks; **sedimě'ntarў** *a.*; **sedimĕntā'tion** *n.* [L pl. of *sedile* (*sedeo* sit)]

**sedī'tio|n** *n.* Conduct or speech inciting to rebellion; **~us** (-shus) *a.* [F, or L *seditio*]

**sedū'ce** *v.t.* (**-cible**). Lead astray; induce to commit sin, crime, or folly; persuade (person) to abandon principles, esp. chastity; persuade by being tempting or attractive, coax; **sedū'ction** *n.*, seducing or being seduced, tempting or attractive thing or quality; **sedū'ctive** *a.*; **sedū'ctress** *n.*, woman who seduces. [L (*se-* away, *duco* duct- lead)]

**se'dūlous** *a.* Persevering, unremitting, painstaking; **sedū'litў** *n.* [L *sedulus* zealous]

**se'dum** *n.* Fleshy-leaved plant with pink, white, or yellow flowers, e.g. stonecrop. [L, = houseleek]

**see**[1] *v.t.* & *i.* (**saw**; **seen**). **1.** Discern by use of eyes, descry, observe, look at or over, watch, (*children should be seen and not heard*; *saw him fall* or *falling*; *was seen falling* or *to fall*; *see page 15*; *see a film, game,* etc.); have or use power of discerning objects with eyes (*sees best at night*); give interview to, be visited by, pay visit to, meet, (*refused to see me*; *too ill to see anyone*; *should see a doctor*; *see you in church*); (in gambling, esp. poker) equal (a bet), equal bet of (player); discern mentally, apprehend, understand, ascertain, consider, foresee, (*can't see a* or *the joke*; *do you see what I mean?*; *must see what can be done*; *saw myself having to continue indefinitely*; **~?**, colloq., do you understand?); find attractive (*can't think what he sees in her*); learn from newspaper etc. (*I see that the record was broken yesterday*); reflect, wait until one knows more, (*we'll have to see*; WAIT *and see*); experience, have presented to one's attention, (*have seen five reigns*; *never saw such a mess*); have opinion of, take view of, (*I see life, things, differently now*); imagine (*cannot see him agreeing to it*); accept, consent to, prefer to have, (**I'll ~ person blowed, damned**, etc. **first**, I refuse categorically to do what he asks or to trouble about it); escort or conduct (*may I see you home?*); supervise, ensure, (*see that it is done*; *stay and see the doors locked*). **2. as far as I can ~**, to the best of my understanding or belief; **as I ~ it**, in my opinion; **has ~n better** or **its** etc. **best days**, has declined from former prosperity etc.; (**I'll**) **be ~ing you**, (colloq.) *au revoir*; **I ~**, I understand your explanation; **let me ~** (appeal for time to think); **~ about**, attend to (*shall ~ about that*, iron., do not intend that to happen); **~ after**, take care of; **see** DOUBLE; **~ eye to eye**, agree (*with* person); *see* FIT[2] *to*; **~ for** oneself, look so as to be convinced or satisfied; **~ here!**, (colloq.) look here!, how dare you!; **~ in**, celebrate arrival of (New Year etc.); **~ into**, investigate; **~ life**, gain experience of people and places, lea𝐜' dissipated life; ~ **off**, accompany to place of departure, ensure departure of (person); ~ **out**, accompany out of a building etc., last for (a period), last until death of (person), not abandon (project etc.) before its completion; see OVER (*adv.*); ~ **over** (*prep.*), tour and examine (house etc.); ~ **reason**, regard it as justifiable (*to* do, etc.), understand or accept the truth; ~ **red**, (fig.) become enraged; ~ **person right**, ensure that he is safe, rewarded, etc.; ~ **round**, = see over prep.; see SERVICE; ~ **stars**, see lights before one's eyes as result of blow on head; ~ **the back of**, be rid of (unwanted person or thing); ~ **the light**, realize one's errors etc., undergo religious conversion; ~ **the light (of day)**, be born or published; ~ **things**, have hallucinations; ~ **through**, (*prep.*, fig.) not be deceived by, detect nature of, (*adv.*) support (person) during difficult time, not abandon (project etc.) before its completion; ~-**through** *a.*, (esp. of clothing) transparent; ~ **to**, attend to, repair; ~ **to it**, ensure (*that*); ~ **one's way (clear)**, feel able or entitled (*to* do, *to* doing); ~ **you (later)!**, (colloq.) *au revoir*; **we shall** ~, we shall eventually know the outcome etc.; **will never** ~ **50** etc. **again**, is over that age; **you** ~, you understand, you will understand when I explain. [E]

**see**[2] *n.* (Jurisdiction of) area committed to (arch)bishop; **Holy See, See of Rome**, papacy or papal court. [AF *se(d)* f. L *sedes* seat]

**seed. 1.** *n.* Flowering plant's unit of reproduction (esp. a grain) capable of developing into another such plant; (collect.) seeds in any quantity esp. as collected for sowing (**go, run, to** ~, cease flowering as seed develops, fig. become degenerate, habitually unkempt, etc.); se-men; prime cause, beginning, (*seeds of doubt, strife*; **sow the** ~ **or** ~**s of**, first give rise to); (Bibl.) offspring; (colloq.) seedling player; ~-**bed**, bed of fine soil in which to sow seeds, (fig.) place of development; ~-**cake** (containing whole seeds esp. of caraway); ~-**coat**, outer coating of seed; ~-**pearl** (very small); ~-**potato** (kept for seed); ~'**sman**, dealer in seeds; ~-**time**, sowing season. **2.** *v.t.* & *i.* Place seed(s) in;

sprinkle (as) with seed; sow seeds; produce or drop seed; remove seeds from (fruit etc.); place crystal etc. in (cloud) to produce rain; (esp. Tennis) designate (competitor in knock-out tournament) so that stronger competitors do not meet each other till later rounds, arrange (order of play) thus. **3.** ~**ling** *n.*, young plant, esp. raised from seed and not from cutting etc.; ~'**y** *a.* (~ily, ~iness), full of seed, going to seed, shabby-looking, (colloq.) unwell. [E]

**see'ing. 1.** *n.* Use of the eyes (~ **is believing**, one's own observation is the best evidence). **2.** *conj.* ~ (**that**), considering that, inasmuch as, (*seeing* (*that*) *you don't know, I'll tell you*). [SEE[1]]

**seek** *v.t.* & *i.* (**sought** *pr.* sawt). Make search or inquiry (*for*); try or want to find, get, or reach; endeavour *to* do; (arch.) aim at, attempt; **not far to** ~, readily found; ~ **out**, look for and find, single out for companionship etc.; **sought-after**, much in demand. [E]

**seem** *v.i.* Have the air, appearance, or feeling of being, be apparently found *to* do or have done (*it seems ridiculous*; *I seem to see him still*); **can't** ~ **to**, (colloq.) seem(s) unable to; **it** ~s, it appears to be true or the fact (*that*); **it would** ~ (in guarded or iron. statement); ~ **good to**, be adopted as best course of action by (person); ~'**ing** *a.*, apparent but perhaps not real; ~'**ly** *a.* (~liness), decorous, becoming. [N]

**seen.** See SEE[1].

**seep** *v.i.* Ooze out, percolate slowly; ~**age** *n.*, act of seeping, quantity that seeps. [E]

**seer** *n.* One who sees; person who sees visions, prophet. [SEE[1]]

**seer'sücker** *n.* Striped material of linen, cotton, etc., with puckered surface. [Pers.]

**see-saw** *a.*, *adv.*, *n.*, & *v.* **1.** *a.* & *adv.* With up-and-down or backward-and-forward motion. **2.** *n.* Game played on long plank balanced on central support, with persons sitting one at each end and moving each other up and down alternately; plank thus balanced; up-and-down or to-and-fro motion; (fig.) contest in which the advantage repeatedly changes from one side to the other. **3.** *v.i.* Play on see-saw; move up and down as on see-saw; vacillate in policy etc. [redupl. SAW¹]

**seethe** (-dh) *v.i.* & *t.* Boil, bubble over; be agitated. [E]

**sĕ′gm|ent. 1.** *n.* Part cut off or separable or marked off as though separable from the other parts of something (e.g. one ring of worm, division of limb, wedge of orange); (Geom.) part of circle, sphere, etc., cut off by line or plane intersecting it; ~e′ntal *a.* (-lly). **2.** (*or* -mĕ′-) *v.t.* & *i.* Divide into segments; ~enta′tion *n.* [L (*seco* cut)]

**sĕ′grĕg|āte** *v.t.* & *i.* (~able). Put or come apart from the rest, isolate; separate (esp. racial group) from the rest of the community; ~a′tion, ~a′tionĭst, ~ātor, *ns.* [L (*grex greg-* flock)]

**seigneur′** (sānyē̆r′), **sei′gnior** (sā′nyer), *n.* Feudal lord, lord of manor; **grand seigneur,** (person resembling) great nobleman; **seigneur′ial** (sānyē̆r′-), **seigniŏr′-ial** (sānyŏr′-), *adjs.* [F f. L SENIOR]

**seine** (sān). **1.** *n.* ~(-net), fishing--net for encircling fish, with floats at top and weights at bottom edge. **2.** *v.i.* & *t.* Fish or catch with seine. [E & F f. L *sagena* f. Gk]

**seise.** See SEIZE.

**sei′sm|ĭc(al)** (sī′z-) *adjs.* (~ically). Of earthquake(s); ~ogrăm, record given by ~ograph (-grahf) or ~ŏ′mĕter *or* ~oscŏpe, instruments showing force, direction, etc., of earthquakes; ~ŏ′graphў, ~ŏ′logў, *ns.,* study or recording of seismic phenomena; ~ŏ′grapher, ~ŏ′log-ĭst, *ns.* [Gk *seismos* earthquake (*seiō* shake)]

**seize** (sēz) *v.t.* & *i.* Take hold or possession (of), esp. forcibly or suddenly or by legal power; comprehend quickly or clearly; (Law, *also* **seise** *pr.* sēz) put in possession of (~d, seised, of, possessing legally, fig. aware or informed of); (Naut.) fasten by binding with turns of yarn etc.; ~ (up), (of moving part in machine etc.) become stuck or jammed from undue heat, friction, etc.; ~ (up)on, seize eagerly; **sei′zure** (sē′zher) *n.,* seizing or being seized, sudden attack of apoplexy etc., stroke. [F *saisir* f. Gmc]

**sĕ′ldom** *adv.* Rarely, not often. [E]

**sĕlĕ′ct. 1.** *a.* Chosen for excellence or fitness; (of society, etc.) exclusive, cautious in admitting members;

~ **committee,** small parliamentary committee appointed to conduct special inquiry. **2.** *v.t.* Choose, esp. as best or most suitable. **3.** ~ion *n.,* selecting, what is selected, (Biol.) process by which some animals or plants thrive more than others, as factor in evolution (NATURAL *selection*); ~ĭve *a.,* using or characterized by selection; **sĕlĕctĭ′vĭtў** *n.,* (esp.) ability of radio receiver to respond to a chosen frequency without interference from other frequencies; ~or *n.* (esp. selecting representative team). [L *seligo -lect-*]

**sĕlē′nium** *n.* Non-metallic element of sulphur group; **sĕlēnŏ′graphў** *n.,* study, mapping, of the moon. [Gk *selēnē* moon]

**sĕlf** *n.* (*pl.* selves *pr.* -vz), *a.,* & *pron.* **1.** *n.* Person's or thing's own individuality or essence (*he showed his true self*); person or thing as object of introspection or reflexive action (*the study of the self; the consciousness of self*); (concentration on) one's own interests or pleasure (*cares for nothing but self*); (Commerc., vulg., or joc.) myself, yourself, himself, etc. (*cheque drawn to self; ticket admitting self and friend*); one's **former** etc. ~, oneself as one formerly etc. was; one's **second** ~, intimate friend, right--hand man; **my humble** ~, **your good selves,** etc., (forms of *myself, yourselves,* etc., when divided). **2.** *a.* Of same colour throughout. **3.** *pron.* See HERSELF, HIMSELF, ITSELF, MYSELF, ONESELF, OURSELVES, THEMSELVES, THYSELF, YOURSELF. **4.** ~′ish *a.,* deficient in consideration for others, concerned chiefly with one's own personal profit or pleasure, actuated by or appealing to self-interest; ~′lĕss *a.,* oblivious of self, incapable of or resisting selfishness. [E]

**sĕlf-** *pref.* repr. *itself, oneself,* or other refl. prons. in senses 'of, on, by, in, or relating to oneself or itself'; ~-abu′se, masturbation, reviling of oneself; ~-a′cting, automatic; ~--addre′ssed (of envelope, to oneself); ~-adhe′sive, able to be stuck or sealed without moistening; ~-ana′lysis (of oneself); ~--appointed (by oneself); ~-asser′-tion, -asser′tive(ness), (being) determined to assert oneself, one's claims, etc.; ~-assur′ance, self--confidence; ~-ce′ntred, preoccupied with oneself or one's own affairs; ~-co'loured, of same colour throughout, of colour not changed by dyeing, cultivation, etc.; ~-conde'mned (by oneself); ~-confe'ssed, openly confessing oneself to be; ~-co'nfidence, ~-co'nfident, (having) confidence in one's own abilities etc.; ~-co'nscious, aware of one's own existence, thoughts, actions, etc., shy, embarrassed; ~-consi'stent (with itself); ~-contai'ned, not dependent on others, uncommunicative, (‖esp. of living accommodation) complete in itself; ~-contro'l, control of oneself, one's behaviour, etc.; ~-cri'tical, ~-dece'ption, (of oneself); ~-defea'ting, that defeats its own purpose; ~-defe'nce, defence of one's own body etc., esp. by judo, boxing, etc., (in ~-defence, in the process of defending oneself); ~-deni'al, going without things one would like, e.g. in order to help others; ~-determina'tion, making of one's own decisions, esp. nation's right or act of deciding its own allegiance or form of government; ~-di'scipline (of oneself); ~-dri've, (of hired vehicle) driven by hirer; ~-e'ducated, educated with little or no help from schools or teachers; ~-effa'cement (of oneself); ~-effa'cing; ~-employ'ed, working as owner of business etc.; ~-estee'm, good opinion of oneself; ~-e'vident, evident without proof; ~-examina'tion (of oneself); ~-expla'natory, that needs no (further) explanation; ~-fer'tile, ~-fer'tilized, fertilized by its own pollen; ~-fulfi'lling, fulfilling one's own potentiality etc., (of prophecy etc.) that is inevitably fulfilled; ~-fulfi'lment (of oneself); ~-go'verning, governing oneself or itself; ~-go'vernment; ~-heal, plant believed to have healing properties; ~-he'lp, use of one's own abilities etc. to achieve success; ~-impor'tance, ~-impor'tant, having high opinion of oneself, pompous(ness); ~-impo'sed, (of task etc.) imposed on and by oneself; ~-impro'vement (of oneself); ~-indu'ced (by oneself or itself); ~-indu'ction, (Electr.) production of electromotive force in circuit when its current is varied; ~-indu'lgence, ~-indu'lgent, yielding to temptations of ease or pleasure; ~-infli'cted (by and on oneself); ~-i'nterest(ed), (activated by or absorbed in) what one thinks is for one's own advantage; ~-invi'ted, having had to ask for, having come without, an invitation; ~-know'ledge (of oneself); ~-loa'ding, that loads, locks, itself; ~-lo've, love of oneself, selfishness, tendency towards self-indulgence; ~-made, (of person) that has risen from poverty or obscurity by his own exertions; ~-opi'nionated, stubbornly adhering to one's own opinions; ~-pi'ty (for oneself); ~-por'trait, portrait (pictorial, literary, etc.) made of oneself; ~-posse'ssed, ~-posse'ssion, being calm esp. in agitating circumstances; ~-prai'se (of oneself); ~-preserva'tion, (instinct for) keeping oneself from death or harm; ~-prope'lled (by its own power); ‖~-rai'sing, (of flour) not needing addition of baking-powder etc.; ~-recor'ding, (of scientific instrument etc.) automatically recording its own operations; ~-regar'd (for oneself); ~-re'gulating, that regulates oneself or itself; ~-reli'ance, ~-reli'ant, being reliant on or confident in one's own abilities etc.; ~-reproa'ch (of oneself); ~-respe'ct, respect for oneself, feeling that one is behaving with honour, dignity, etc.; ~-respe'cting, having self-respect; ~-restrai'ned, ~-restrai'nt, being or showing oneself able to restrain one's own emotions; ~-ri'ghteous, convinced of one's own righteousness or rightness; ~-ri'ghting, (of boat) that rights itself; ~-sa'crifice, ~-sa'crificing, subordinating one's own interests or desires to those of others; ~'same, the very same, identical; ~-satisfa'ction, ~-sa'tisfied, showing (undue) satisfaction with oneself or one's achievements; ~-sea'ling, having means of automatically sealing small punctures; ~-see'king a. & n., seeking one's own welfare before that of others; ~-ser'vice, (esp. attrib.) system by which customers serve themselves with food or goods and pay cashier, or put money into and take food or goods from machine, (colloq.) shop etc. using this system; ~-sow'n, grown from seed that has dropped naturally from the plant;

~**star'ter**, electric device for starting internal combustion engine; ~**styled**, using a title, name, etc., that one has given oneself (without authorization or right); ~**suffi'ciency**, ~**suffi'cient**, **-sufficing**, being capable of supplying one's own needs; ~**suppor'ting**, that supports oneself or itself, self-sufficient; ~**sustai'ning**, that sustains oneself or itself; ~**tau'ght**, that has taught oneself; ~**wi'll(ed)**, being obstinately determined to follow one's own wishes, intentions, etc.; ~**wi'nding**, (of watch etc.) that winds itself automatically.

**sĕll. 1.** *v.t.* & *i.* (sold *pr.* sō-). Make over or dispose of in exchange for money (~ one's **life dearly**, do much injury before being killed; ~ **the pass**, betray a cause etc.); keep stock of for sale (*do you sell candles?*); cause to be sold (*the author's name will sell many copies*); (of goods) be purchased (*sell like hot* CAKES); have specified price (*it sells at* or *for* £5); betray or offer dishonourably for money or other reward (*sell one's body, country, honour*); advertise or disseminate merits of; inspire with desire to buy, acquire, accept, etc. (*sold on*, enthusiastic about); (sl.) disappoint, deceive; ~ **off**, sell remainder of (goods) at reduced prices; ~ **out**, sell (all one's stock, shares, etc., or abs.), betray, be treacherous or disloyal; ~*out*, selling of all tickets for a show etc., a commercial success, betrayal; *sell* SHORT; ||~ **up**, sell one's business, house, etc. **2.** *n.* (colloq.) Manner of selling (HARD, SOFT, *sell*); deception, disappointment. **3.** ~**'er** *n.*, one who sells (~**er's market**, where goods are scarce and expensive), article that sells well (BEST *seller*); ~**'ing** *n.* (~**ing-point**, an advantage; ~**ing-race**, in which winning horse must be auctioned). [E]

**sĕ'llŏtăpe, S-,** *n.,* & *v.t.* (Fix with) adhesive usu. transparent cellulose tape. [P]

**sĕ'lvage, -ĕdge,** *n.* Edge of cloth so woven that it cannot unravel, or made of other material or with inferior finish. [SELF, EDGE]

**selves.** See SELF.

**sĕmă'ntic. 1.** *a.* (~**ally**). Of meaning(s) in language. **2.** *n.* (in *pl.*, usu. treated as *sing.*) Branch of philology concerned with meanings. [F f. Gk *sēmainō* to mean)]

**sĕ'maphôre. 1.** *n.* Signalling apparatus of post with movable arm(s) etc. used on railways etc.; military signalling by operator's two arms or two flags. **2.** *v.i.* & *t.* Signal or send by semaphore. [F f. Gk *sēma* sign, *pherō* bear]

**sĕ'mblance** *n.* Outward or superficial appearance *of* something. [F (L *simulo* SIMULATE)]

**sĕ'mĕn** *n.* Generative fluid of males, containing spermatozoa. [L *semen semin-* seed]

**sĕme'ster** *n.* Half-year course or term in (esp. German and U.S.) universities. [G f. L *semestris* (*sex* six, *mensis* month)]

||**sĕ'mi** *n.* (colloq.) Semi-detached house. [abbr.]

**sĕ'mi- *pref.*** denoting half of (*semicircle*), on one of two sides (*semidetached*), in some direction or particular (*semi-infinite*), partly (*semicivilized, -liquid*), little more or rather less than, not total(ly) (*semi-barbarian, -conscious, -official*); occurring, published, etc., twice in specified period (*semi-annual*); ~**ba'sement**, storey partly below ground level; ||~**breve**, (Mus.) longest note in common use; ~**circle**, ~**cir'cular**, (in form of) half of circle or of its circumference; ~**co'lon**, punctuation-mark (;) of intermediate value between comma and full stop; ~**condu'ctor**, substance that when impure or at high temperature has electrical conductivity intermediate between insulators and metals; ~**deta'ched**, (of house) joined to another on one side only; ~**fi'nal**, match or round preceding final; ~**fi'nalist**, competitor in semifinal; ~**me'tal**, substance with some of the properties of metals; ~**pre'cious**, (of gem) less valuable than a precious stone; ||~**quaver**, (Mus.) note with two-hooked symbol, half a quaver; ~**ski'lled**, having or needing less training than skilled work(er); ~**tone**, half a tone in musical scale; ~**trai'ler**, trailer having wheels at back and supported at front by towing vehicle; ~**tro'pical**, subtropical; ~**vowel**, (letter representing) sound intermediate between vowel and consonant (e.g. *w, y*). [F or L]

**sĕ'minal** *a.* Of seed or semen or

reproduction, germinal; (of ideas etc.) providing basis for future development; **sĕ′mĭnȧr** *n.*, small class for discussion etc., short intensive course of study; **sĕ′mĭnȧry** *n.*, training-college for priests etc.; **sĕ′mĭnȧrist** *n.* [L (SEMEN)]

**Sĕ′mīte** *n.* & *a.* (Member) of any of the races supposedly descended from Shem (Gen. 10), including esp. Jews and Arabs; **Sĕmĭ′tĭc** *a.*, of Semites, esp. of Jews or of languages of family including Hebrew and Arabic; **Sĕ′mĭtĭsm, Sĕ′mĭtĭst,** *ns.* [L f. Gk *Sēm* Shem]

**sĕmolī′na** (-lē′-) *n.* Hard grains left after milling of flour, used in milk puddings etc.; ~ **(pudding),** pudding made of this. [It. *semolino*]

**sĕmpĭtĕr′nal** *a.* (~ly). (rhet.) Eternal. [F f. L *semper* always, ETERNAL)]

**sempre** (sĕ′mprā) *adv.* (Mus.) Always, throughout. [It.]

**sempstress.** See SEAMSTRESS.

‖**S.E.N.** *abbr.* State Enrolled Nurse.

**Sen.** *abbr.* Senator; Senior.

**sĕ′nāt|e** *n.* Upper and usu. smaller legislative assembly in U.S., France, etc.; (rhet.) any legislature, its proceedings, its members; governing (academic) body of university or *college; (Rom. Hist.) state council of republic and empire; ~or *n.*, member of senate; ~ōr′ĭal *a.* (-lly). [F f. L *senatus* (*senex* old man)]

**sĕnd** *v.t.* & *i.* (sent). Order or cause to go or be conveyed (*to* place, person; *sends goods all over the world*; *send person* FLY²*ing,* PACK*ing, to* COVENTRY); ~ **word,** get message conveyed); send message or letter (*he sent to warn me*); (of God, Providence, etc.) grant, bestow, inflict, bring about, cause to be, (*send rain, a judgement, her victorious*); (sl.) affect emotionally, put into ecstasy, (*that singer sends me*); ~ **away,** dispatch, cause to depart, send money etc. to dealer *for* thing; ~ **down,** rusticate or expel from university, put in prison, (Crick.) bowl (ball or over); ~ **for,** summon (person, help, etc.), order (thing) esp. by post; ~ **in,** cause to go in, submit (entry etc.) for competition etc.; ~ **off,** get (letter, parcel, etc.) dispatched, send away (*for* thing), attend departure of (person) as sign of respect etc., (Footb. etc., of referee) order (player) to take no further part in game;

~-*off* *n.*, demonstration of goodwill etc. at departure of person, start of project, etc.; ~ **on,** transmit to further destination or in advance of one's own arrival; ~ **up,** cause to go up, transmit to higher authority, (colloq.) satirize, or ridicule by mimicking; ~-*up* *n.*, (colloq.) satire or parody. [E]

**sĕnĕ′scen|t** *a.* Growing old; ~ce *n.* [L (*senex* old)]

**sĕ′nĕschal** (-shȧl) *n.* Steward of medieval great house. [F f. L f. Gmc, = old servant]

**sĕ′nīle** *a.* Incident to, showing feebleness etc. characteristic of, old age; **sĕnĭ′lĭty** *n.* [F or L (as prec.)]

**sĕ′nĭor. 1.** *a.* More advanced in age, older or oldest in standing, superior in age or standing *to,* of high or highest position, (opp. JUNIOR); (placed after person's name) senior to another of same name; ‖~ **citizen,** old person, esp. old-age pensioner; ‖~ **combination** or **common room** (for use by senior members of college); ~ **school** (for the older pupils); ‖~ **service,** Royal Navy; **sĕnĭŏ′rĭty** *n.*, state of being senior. **2.** *n.* Senior person; one's elder or superior. [L compar. of *senex* old]

**sĕ′nna** *n.* (Laxative prepared from) cassia. [Arab.]

**señor** (*pl.* **señores**), **señora**, **señorita,** (sĕnyōr′, -ōr′ĕz; -ōr′a; -erē′ta) *ns.* (used of or to Spaniards or Spanish-speakers as SIGNOR etc.). [Sp. f. L SENIOR]

**sĕnsā′tion** *n.* Consciousness of perceiving or seeming to perceive some condition of one's body, senses, mind, feelings, etc., (*a sensation of giddiness, pain, comfort, falling, pride*); (manifestation of) stirring of emotions or intense interest among a community, audience, etc., literary or other use of material calculated to cause such effect, event or person causing such effect, (*the news created a sensation; he was a great sensation*); ~al *a.* (~ally), causing or designed to cause a sensation; ~alism, ~alist, *ns.*, pursuit, pursuer, of the sensational. [L (as foll.)]

**sĕnse. 1.** *n.* Any of the bodily faculties through which sensation is caused (**the five ~s,** sight, hearing, smell, taste, and touch; **sixth ~,** supposed faculty giving intuitive or extra-sensory knowledge); sensitiveness of all or any of these (*a keen sense of smell*); ability to perceive or feel; consciousness of (*a sense of having done well*, one's *own importance, shame*); quick or accurate appreciation, understanding, or instinct (*sense of* DIRECTION, HUMOUR; *aesthetic, moral, sense*); (conformity to) practical wisdom, judgement, = COMMON *sense*, (*good, sound, sense; there's no sense in talking like that*; **have the ~ to**, be wise or sensible enough to); meaning of word etc., intelligibility or coherence, (**in a** or **one ~**, if the statement is taken in a particular way; **make ~**, be intelligible or practicable; **make ~ of**, show or find meaning of); prevailing opinion (**take the ~ of the meeting**, ascertain this by putting questions etc.); (in *pl.*) person's sanity or normal state of mind (**bring person, come, to his ~s**, out of unconsciousness or mad folly; **frighten** person **out of his ~s**, so that he behaves excitedly, uncontrollably, etc.; **in** one's **~s**, sane; **out of** one's **~s**, insane; **take leave of** one's **~s**, go mad); **~'less** (-sl-) *a.*, unconscious, wildly foolish, meaningless, purposeless. **2.** *v.t.* Perceive by sense(s); be vaguely aware of; realize; (of machine etc.) detect. [L *sensus* (*sentio sens-* feel)]

**sĕ'nsĭb|le** *a.* (~ly). Having or showing wisdom or common sense, reasonable, judicious; (of clothing) unpretentiously practical; perceptible by the senses, great enough to be perceived; (arch.) sensitive *to*, aware *of*; **~ĭ'lĭtÿ** *n.*, capacity to feel, (exceptional or excessive) sensitiveness or susceptibility, (in *pl.*) tendency to feel offended etc. [F or L (prec.)]

**sĕ'nsĭt|ĭve** *a.* Very open *to* or acutely affected by external stimuli or mental impressions, having sensibility *to*; (of person) quick to take offence or have the feelings hurt; (of instrument etc.) responsive *to* or recording slight changes; (of photographic paper etc.) prepared so as to respond to action of light; (of topic etc.) subject to restriction of discussion to prevent embarrassment, ensure security, etc.; **~ĭve plant**, mimosa or other plant that droops or closes when touched, (fig.) sensitive person; **~ĭ'vĭtÿ** *n.*, quality or degree of being sensitive; **~ĭze** *v.t.*, make sensitive; **~ĭzā'tion** *n.* [F or L (foll.)]

**sĕ'nsor** *n.* Device to detect, record, or measure a physical property; **~ÿ** *a.*, of sensation or the senses. [L (*sentio sens-* feel)]

**sĕ'nsūal** (or -shŏŏ-) *a.* (~ly). Of, given to, or depending on the senses or their gratification; self-indulgent, esp. in regard to sexual enjoyment or food and drink, voluptuous, licentious; indicative of sensuality (*sensual lips, mouth*); sensory; **~ĭsm**, **~ĭst**, **~ĭtÿ** (-ă'l-), *ns.*; **~ĭze** *v.t.*; **sĕ'nsŭous** *a.*, of, derived from, or affecting the senses, esp. aesthetically. [L (SENSE)]

**sĕnt.** See SEND.

**sĕ'ntence. 1.** *n.* Decision of lawcourt, esp. (declaration of) punishment allotted to person convicted in criminal trial (lit. or fig.; **under ~ of**, condemned to *death* etc.); set of words (occas. one word) containing or implying a subject and a predicate, and expressing a statement, question, exclamation, or command, (**complex ~**, with subordinate clause(s); **compound ~**, with more than one subject or predicate; **simple ~**, with one subject and one predicate). **2.** *v.t.* Announce sentence of (convicted criminal etc.); declare condemned *to*. **3. sĕntĕ'ntial** (-shal) *a.*, (Gram.) of sentence(s); **sĕntĕ'ntious** (-shus) *a.*, affectedly or pompously formal or moralizing, aphoristic, moralistic. [F f. L *sententia* (*sentio* consider)]

**sĕ'ntĭen|t** (-shĭ-, -shent) *a.* Having or able to have perception by the senses; **~ce**, **~cÿ**, *ns.* [L *sentio* feel]

**sĕ'ntĭ|ment** *n.* A mental feeling; the sum of what one feels on some subject, verbal expression of this; an opinion as distinguished from the words meant to convey it; a view based on or coloured with emotion, such views collectively, esp. as an influence; tendency to be swayed by feeling rather than by reason; (display of) mawkish tenderness; **those are,** (joc.) **them's, my ~ments**, that is what I think about it; **~mĕ'ntal** *a.* (-lly), of, characterized by, appealing to, or prone to sentiment (**~mental value**, value of thing to particular person because of its associations); **~mĕ'ntalĭsm**, **~mĕ'ntalĭst**, **~mĕntă'lĭtÿ**, *ns.*; **~mĕ'ntalize** *v.i.* & *t.* [F f. L (prec.)]

**sĕ'ntĭnel** *n.* Sentry; **~** (the) **~**, crab with long eye-stalks; **sĕ'ntrÿ** *n.*, soldier etc. stationed to keep guard;

**sentry-box**, wooden cabin large enough to shelter standing sentry; **sentry-go**, duty of pacing up and down as sentry. [F f. It.]

**se′pal** n. (Bot.) Division or leaf of calyx. [F f. L (foll., PETAL)]

**se′parate. 1.** a. Physically disconnected, forming unit that is or may be regarded as apart or by itself, distinct, individual, of individuals, (*the separate volumes may be had singly; one is quite separate from the other*). **2.** n. An offprint; (in pl.) separate articles of dress suitable for wearing together. **3.** (-āt) v.t. & i. (**se′parable**). Make separate, sever; prevent union or contact of; secede *from*; go different ways; cease to live together as married couple; divide or sort into parts or sizes; ~ (out), get (cream, refuse, etc.) by such process. **4. separā′tion** n., separating or being separated (**judicial** or **legal separation**, separation of husband and wife under **separation order** made by court); **se′paratist** n., one who favours separation, esp. for political or ecclesiastical independence; **se′paratism** n.; **se′parative** a.; **se′parātor** n. [L *separo* v.]

**Sèphär′d|i** n. (pl. ~im). Jew of Spanish or Portuguese descent (cf. ASHKENAZI); ~**ic** a. [Heb., = Spaniard]

**se′pïa** n. Dark reddish-brown colour or paint. [L f. Gk, = cuttle-fish]

**se′poy** n. (Hist.) Native Indian soldier under European, esp. British, discipline. [Pers. *sipāhī* soldier]

**se′ps|is** n. (pl. ~es pr. -ēz). Septic condition. [Gk (SEPTIC)]

**sept** n. Clan, esp. in Ireland. [alt. SECT]

**Sept.** abbr. September.

**Septe′mber** n. Ninth month of year; **septe′nnïal** a. (-lly), lasting, recurring every, 7 years. [L (*septem* seven; cf. DECEMBER)]

**septe′t(te)** n. Group of 7, (Mus.) (composition for) group of 7 instruments or voices. [G f. L *septem* seven]

**se′ptic** a. (~ally). Putrefying, contaminated by bacteria; ~ **tank** (in which sewage is disintegrated through bacterial activity). [L f. Gk (*sēpō* rot)]

**septicae′m|ïa** (-sē′m-), **\*-cē′m|ïa**, n. Blood-poisoning; ~**ic** a. [prec., Gk *haima* blood]

**septūag|ēnār′ïan** a. & n. (Person) from 70 to 79 years old; **S~ē′sïma** n., Sunday before Sexagesima; **S~ïnt** n., ancient-Greek version of O.T. including Apocrypha. [L -*arius* (*septuaginta* 70)]

**se′pt|um** n. (pl. ~a). (Anat., Bot., Zool.) Partition such as that between nostrils or the chambers of a poppy-fruit or shell. [L *s(a)eptum* (*saepio* enclose)]

**se′ptupl|e** a. & n. Sevenfold (number or amount); ~**ét** n., one of 7 children born at a birth. [L (*septem* seven, QUINTUPLE)]

**se′pulchre, \*-cher**, (-ker). **1.** n. Tomb esp. cut in rock or built of stone or brick; **the Holy S~**, in which Christ was placed; **whited ~**, hypocrite. **2.** v.t. Place in sepulchre; serve as sepulchre for. **3. sepŭ′l-chral** (-kral) a. (-lly), of sepulchre(s) or sepulture, (of voice, manner, etc.) gloomy, funereal; **se′pulture** n., burying, placing in grave. [F f. L (*sepelio* bury)]

**se′quel** n. What follows esp. as result; continuation or resumption of story etc. after pause or intended or provisional ending. [F or L (*sequor* follow)]

**se′quence** n. (Order of) succession, set of things belonging next to one another, unbroken series, (*follow the sequence of events*; **in ~**, one after another); part of cinema film dealing with one scene or topic; set of 3 or more playing-cards next to each other in value; **se′quent** a., following esp. as consequence; **sèquë′ntïal** (-shal) a. (-lly), forming sequence or consequence. [L (prec.)]

**sèquě′st|er** v.t. Seclude, isolate, (*a sequestered cottage, life*); sequestrate; ~**rāte** (or sē′kwïs-) v.t. (**-trable**), (esp. Law) confiscate, take temporary possession of (debtor's estate etc.); **sèquèstrā′tion**, **se′quèstrā′tor, ns.** [F or L (*sequester* trustee)]

**se′quïn** n. Circular spangle on dress; ~(**n)ed** (-nd) a., having sequins. [F f. It. *zecchino* a gold coin f. Arab.]

**sèquoi′a** n. Californian coniferous tree of great height. [L f. *Sequoiah*, person]

**sēr′a**. See SERUM.

**sera′glio** (-ah′lyō) n. (pl. ~s). Harem; (Hist.) Turkish palace. [It. f. Turk. f. Pers.]

**sě′raph** n. (pl. ~im, ~s). Member

of the highest of the 9 orders of angels, esp. associated with love; **seră′phĭc** *a.* (**-ically**), of or like seraph(s), exaltedly beautiful or devoted. [L f. Gk f. Heb.]

**Serb**(′ĭan) *adjs.* & *ns.* (Native, language) of Serbia. [Serbo-Croatian *Srb*]

**Sĕr′bō-** *in comb.* Serbian; **~-Cro′at,** **~-Croa′tian,** (of) Slavonic language of Serbs and Croats.

**sēre.** See SEAR 2.

**sĕrenā′de. 1.** *n.* Piece of music (suitable to be) sung or played at night, esp. by lover under his lady's window; orchestral suite for small ensemble. **2.** *v.t.* Sing or play serenade to. [F f. It. (SERENE)]

**sĕrendĭ′pĭt|ў** *n.* Faculty of making happy discoveries by accident; **~ous** *a.* [coined by Horace Walpole]

**sĕrē′ne** (*or ser-*) *a.* (**~r, ~st**). Clear and calm; tranquil, unperturbed; **sĕrē′nĭtў** *n.,* serene condition or quality. [L]

**sĕrf** *n.* (Hist.) labourer not allowed to leave the land on which he worked; oppressed person, drudge; **~′age,** **~′dom, ~′hŏŏd,** *ns.,* serf's condition. [F f. L *servus* slave]

**sĕrge** *n.* Durable twilled worsted etc. fabric. [F f. L (SILK)]

**ser′geant** (sär′jant) *n.* Non-commissioned Army or R.A.F. officer next below warrant officer, police officer below inspector; COMPANY *sergeant-major*; ‖(**regimental**) **~-major,** warrant officer assisting adjutant of regiment or battalion. [F f. L *serviens -ent-* servant (SERVE)]

**sēr′ĭal. 1.** *a.* (**~ly**). Of, in, forming, a series; (of story etc.) published etc. in instalments (**~ rights,** copyright of such publication); (Mus.) using transformations of a SERIES of notes. **2.** *n.* Serial story etc.; periodical. **3.** **~ize** *v.t.,* publish or produce in instalments. [foll.]

**sēr′ies** (*or* -ĭz) *n.* (*pl.* same). Number of things, events, etc., of which each is similar to or connected with the preceding one (**in ~,** in ordered succession); number of radio programmes, films, etc., with same actors, theme, etc., but each complete in itself; set of successive issues of periodical etc.; (Electr.) set of batteries etc. having positive electrode of each connected with negative electrode of next, set of circuits arranged **in ~,** so that same

current passes through each circuit; (Mus.) arrangement of 12 chromatic notes as basis for serial music. [L (*sero* join)]

**sĕ′rĭf** *n.* (Typ.) Cross-line finishing off a stroke of a letter as in T (compare SANSERIF T). [orig. uncert.]

**sĕrĭŏ-cŏ′mĭc** *a.* (**~ally**). Combining the serious and the comic. [foll.]

**sēr′ĭous** *a.* Thoughtful, earnest, sedate, not (merely) frivolous; important, demanding thought, not slight or negligible, (*serious matter, allegation, illness*); sincere, in earnest, not ironical or jesting. [F, or L *seriosus*]

**ser′jeant** (sär′jant) *n.* **~(-at-law),** (Hist.) barrister of highest rank; **~-at-arms,** official of court, city, or parliament with ceremonial duties; ‖**Common S~,** circuit judge at Central Criminal Court. [SERGEANT]

**sēr′mon** *n.* Spoken or written discourse on religion, scripture, morals, etc., esp. delivered from pulpit (**S~ on the Mount,** discourse of Christ in Matt. 5–7); piece of moral reflection, admonition, or reproof, lecture; **~ize** *v.t.* & *i.,* deliver moral lecture (to). [F f. L *sermo -mon-* speech]

**sēr′ous** *a.* Of or like serum, watery; (of gland etc.) having serous secretion; **sērŏ′sĭtў** *n.* [SERUM]

**sēr′pent** *n.* Snake esp. of large kind, or in rhet. use (**the S~,** the Devil); (fig.) sly or treacherous person; **~ine,** (*a.*) of or like serpent, coiling, tortuous, cunning, treacherous, (*n.*) soft usu. dark green rock, sometimes mottled. [F f. L *serpo* creep]

**sĕrrā′t|ĕd** *a.* With toothed edge like a saw; **~ion** *n.* [L (*serra* saw)]

**sĕ′rried** (-rĭd) *a.* (Of ranks of soldiers etc.) close together. [*serry* press close f. F *serrer* to close]

**sēr′|um** *n.* (*pl.* **~a, ~ums**). Amber-coloured liquid which separates from clot when blood coagulates, esp. used for inoculation; watery fluid in animal bodies. [L, = whey]

**sĕr′vant** *n.* Person who carries out orders of employer, esp. person employed in house on domestic duties and receiving wages, board, and lodging (CIVIL *servant*; **public ~,** State official; **~s' hall,** room in which servants of large household have meals etc.; **your humble** or **obedient ~,** formulae used at close of official letters); devoted follower, person willing to serve another; something useful esp. as means rather than end (*fire is a good servant but a bad master*). [F part. of *servir* (foll.)]

**serve. 1.** *v.t. & i.* Be servant (to), do service (for), (~ **on**, be member of *committee* etc.; ~ **two masters**, be divided in one's loyalty); be employed (*in* organization, esp. armed forces); be useful (to), meet needs (of), be adequate or suitable (for), perform function, (*serves only to prove my point*; *sofa serves as, for, a bed*; *if my memory serves me*; ~ **one's** or **the purpose** or **turn,** be adequate to one's requirements); go through due period of (office, apprenticeship, prison sentence, etc.); act as waiter (*at table*); set (dish) on table; dish *out* or *up*; distribute (food etc.); supply (person *with*); attend to (customer in shop etc.); (Mil.) keep (gun etc.) firing; copulate with (mare etc.); make legal delivery of (writ etc.; ~ **person with** writ etc., ~ writ etc. **on** him, deliver it to him in legally formal manner); (Tennis etc.) set (ball etc.) in play; treat, act towards, (person in specified way; ~(s) **him right!,** his misfortune, failure, etc., is deserved). **2.** *n.* (Tennis etc.) Act or manner of serving ball etc.; person's turn to serve. **3. ser'ver** *n.,* (esp., Eccl.) celebrant's assistant; **ser'very** *n.,* room from which meals etc. are served; **ser'ving** *n.,* (esp.) quantity of food for one person. [F *servir* f. L *servio*]

**ser'vice**[1]. **1.** *n.* Being servant, employment or position as servant, (*the girl is in service*; **take into** one's ~, employ as servant); (persons or employment in) department of royal or public employ (*the public services*); **on active** ~, employed in armed forces in wartime; **see** ~, have experience of serving esp. in armed forces, (of thing) be used or worn); **the** (**armed** or **fighting**) ~**s,** navy, army, and air force; (*attrib.*) of the kind issued to the armed services (*service rifle*); ||(in *pl.*) public supply of water, electricity, etc.; (transport provided by) system of vehicles etc. plying at stated times (*a fast service of buses, trains, to London*); person's benefit, help, or behalf, (*can I be of service to you?*; **at** person's ~, ready to obey orders or be used; ||**on Her, His, Majesty's** ~, frank stamped

on official envelopes etc.); work done, doing of work, for employer, superior, community, etc., benefit conferred on or exertion on behalf of someone, readiness to perform these, (*typist, typewriter, has given good service*; *offered my services*; YEOMAN *service*); serving of food etc., extra charge nominally made for this (*added 10 per cent service to the bill*); set of dishes, plates, etc., required for serving meal (*dinner, tea, -service*); serve in tennis etc., game in which one serves, (*his service is weak*; *she lost her service*); legal serving of writ etc.; liturgical form for use on some occasion, meeting of congregation for worship, musical setting of whole or part of liturgy, (*the burial, communion, marriage, service*; **attend morning, evening, service**; DIVINE *service*); provision of what is necessary for due maintenance of thing or process; assistance or advice given to customers after sale of goods; ~ **area,** area near road for supply of petrol, refreshments, etc., area served by broadcasting station; ~ **charge,** additional charge for service rendered; ||~ **flat** (in which domestic service and sometimes meals are provided by the management); ~ **industry** (providing services, not goods); ~**man,** man in armed services, man providing service or maintenance; ~ **pipe** (conveying water or gas from main to building); ~ **road** (to serve houses lying back from main road); ~ **station,** place where service (esp. of petrol etc.) is available; ~**woman,** woman in armed services. **2.** *v.t.* Provide service for, esp. maintain or repair (car, machine, etc.); ~**able** (-sa-) *a.* (~**ably**), useful or usable, able to render service, durable, suited for use rather than ornament; ~**abi'lity** (-sa-) *n.* [F, or L *servitium* (*servus* slave)]

**ser'vice**[2] *n.* ~ (**tree**), a European fruit-tree. [E, ult. f. L *sorbus*]

**ser'viette** *n.* Table-napkin. [F (SERVE)]

**ser'v|ile** *a.* Of or like slave(s); slavish, fawning, completely dependent; ~**i'lity** *n.*; ~**itor** *n.,* (arch. or poet.) servant, attendant; ~**itude** *n.,* slavery (lit. or fig.), subjection; PENAL *servitude*. [L (foll.)]

**ser'vo** (*pl.* ~**s**). Servo-motor or -mechanism; (*in comb.*) means of powered automatic control of larger system (*servo-assisted, -mechanism, -motor*). [F f. L *servus* slave]

**sĕ'samė** *n.* Annual E. Ind. plant with oil-yielding seeds; its seeds; (**open**) ~, [w. ref. to *Arabian Nights*] magic words used to cause door to open, magical or mysterious means of access to what is usu. inaccessible. [L f. Gk]

**sĕ'squi-** *pref.* denoting 1½; **~peda'lian** (-ā'l-), having many syllables, cumbrous and pedantic. [L]

**sĕ'ssile** *a.* (Bot., Zool.) (Of flower, leaf, eye, etc.) attached directly by base without stalk or peduncle; fixed in one position, immobile; ~ **oak**, durmast. [L (*sedeo sess-* sit)]

**sĕ'ssion** (-shon) *n.* Assembly for deliberative or judicial business, single meeting for such purpose, period during which such meetings are regularly held, period between meeting and prorogation or dissolution of legislative body, (**in ~**, assembled for business, not on vacation); period spent continuously in an activity (JAM[1] session); **Court of S~**, supreme civil court in Scotland; **petty ~s**, meeting of two or more magistrates for summary trial of certain offences; (‖Hist.) **quarter ~s**, court with limited criminal and civil jurisdiction usu. held quarterly; **~al** *a.* (**~ally**). [F or L (as prec.)]

**sĕ'stĕrce, sĕstĕr'tius** (-shus; *pl.* **-tii** *pr.* -shiī), *ns.* Ancient-Roman silver (and later bronze) coin = ¼ denarius or 2½ (later 4) asses. [L *sestertius*, = 2½]

**sĕstĕ't** *n.* Sextet. [It. (L *sextus* sixth)]

**sĕt**[1]. **1.** *v.t.* & *i.* (-**tt-**; **set**). Put, lay, stand, (*set load* or *passenger ashore*; *set one brick on another*; *set pen to paper*); station, place ready, place or turn in correct or specified position or direction; dispose suitably for use or action or display; put hands of (clock, watch) to right time; arrange for (alarm-clock) to sound at desired time; cause (hen) to sit on eggs; place (eggs) for hen to sit on; arrange (butterfly etc.) as specimen; make (trap) ready to act; give sharp edge to (razor etc.); *start (a fire); lay (table) for meal; join, attach, fasten; fix, determine, decide, (~ **great, little,** etc., **store by** or **on,** value greatly, little, etc.); appoint, settle, establish, (*set in* authority); put parts of (broken or dislocated bone, limb, etc.) into correct posi-

tion for healing, deal thus with (fracture, dislocation); fix (hair) while damp so that it dries in desired style; insert (jewel) in ring, framework, etc.; ornament or provide (surface) *with* (*sky set with stars*); set up (type, book, etc.); bring by placing, arranging, or other means, into specified state, cause to be, (*set things going, in motion, in order*; *set it on fire*); cause (person, one*self*) *to do* specified thing (~ one*self*, resolve or undertake *to do*); start (person etc.) *doing* (*set the* BALL[1] *rolling*); exhibit as type or model (*set, set him, an example*); present or impose as work to be done, material to be dealt with, problem to be solved, etc.; initiate (fashion etc.); *establish (a record etc.); set to music; solidify or harden (*cement, jelly, has* or *is set*); (of blossom) form into fruit, (of fruit) develop from blossom, (of tree) develop fruit; (of face) assume hard expression; (of eyes etc.) become motionless; (of sun, moon, etc.) move towards or below earth's horizon; (of tide, current, etc.) have motion; gather force, show or feel tendency, (lit. or fig.); (of dancer) take position facing partner; (of hunting dog) take rigid attitude indicating presence of game; (dial. or vulg.) sit. **2.** ~ **about,** begin or take steps towards (task, doing, etc.), attack; ~ thing **against,** reckon it as counterpoise or compensation for; ~ **apart,** separate, differentiate, reserve; ~ **aside,** PUT aside, reserve, disregard, reject, annul; ~ **back,** place farther back in space or time, impede or reverse progress of, (sl.) cost (person) specified amount; **~-back** *n.,* reversal or arrest of progress, relapse; *set one's* CAP *at;* ~ **down,** record in writing, allow to alight, attribute *to,* explain or describe to oneself *as;* ~ **eyes on,** catch sight of; *set one's* FACE *against;* ~ **foot in, on,** enter or go to (place etc.); ~ **forth,** begin journey or expedition, make known, expound; ~ **free,** release, liberate; *set one's* HAND *to,* HEART *on;* ~ one's **hopes on,** long for, be resolved to get; ~ **in,** begin (and seem likely to continue), become established, insert; *set one's* MIND *to;* ~ **off,** begin journey, serve as adornment or foil to, enhance, use as compensating item *against,* detonate, initiate, stimulate, cause (person) to start laughing, talking, etc.; ~ **on**, set upon, instigate; ~ **out**, begin journey, aim or intend *to* do, demonstrate, exhibit, arrange, mark out, declare; ~ person **over**, give him control or command of; ~ **sail**, hoist sail, begin voyage; ~ **the pace**, determine the speed, esp. by leading; *set the* SCENE, *the* SEAL *on*; ~ one's **teeth**, clench them, (fig.) make up one's mind inflexibly (*against*); ~ **to**, begin doing something vigorously, esp. fighting, arguing, or eating; ~*-to* n. (pl. ~*-tos*), fight or argument; ~ **to music,** provide (words, poem, etc.) with music for singing; *set to* RIGHTS, *to* WORK; ~ **up**, place (notice, statue, etc.) in position or in view, start (business, institution, etc.), establish (person, oneself) in some capacity, establish (a record), cause (condition or situation), prepare (task etc. for another), equip (person), compose (type for printing, book etc.), begin uttering (shriek, protest, etc.) loudly, restore or enhance health of (person); ~ (*oneself*) *up as*, pretend or claim to be; ~*-up* n., (manner, structure, or position of) arrangement or organization; ~ **up** *house*, establish one's home, begin to live together as husband and wife; ~ **up** (*shop*), start business or profession (*as grocer, solicitor,* etc.); ~ **upon**, cause or urge to attack person etc., attack. **3.** **sě′tter** n., (esp.) long-haired dog trained to stand rigid when it scents game; **sě′tting** n., (esp.) music to which words are set, frame for jewel, surroundings or accessories esp. as setting thing off, cutlery for one person at table, (Theatr.) scenery etc. of play. [E]

**sět**[2] a. Unmoving, unchanging, fixed, (*set smile, purpose*) (of phrase, speech, etc.) having invariable or predetermined wording, not extempore; (of book etc.) specified for reading in preparation for examination; (of batsman) fully accustomed to prevailing conditions; (of meal) served according to fixed menu; prepared for action (*get set*); **all** ~, (colloq.) ready to start; ~ **fair**, (of weather) fine without sign of breaking; ~ **on**, determined to get, achieve, etc.; ~ **piece**, formal or elaborate arrangement esp. in art or literature, fireworks arranged on

scaffolding etc.; *set* PURPOSE; ~ **scrum** (in Rugby Footb., ordered by referee); ~ **square**, right-angled triangular plate for drawing lines esp. at 90°, 60°, 45°, or 30°; ~ **upon**, = *set on*. [p.p. of SET[1]]

**sět**[3] n. **1.** Number of things or persons that belong together, resemble one another, or are usually found together, collection, group, (*set of golf-clubs, novels; a fine set of men*); section of society consorting together or having similar interests etc. (*the racing, smart, set*); collection of implements, vessels, etc., needed for a specified purpose (*cricket, dinner, tea-, toilet-, set*); (Math.) collection of things sharing a property (~ **theory,** study of such collections); radio or television receiver; ~ (**of teeth**), one's natural or artificial teeth collectively; (Tennis etc.) group of games counting as unit towards match for player or side that wins greater number of games (~ **point**, state of a set in lawn tennis when one side needs only one more point to win it, this point). **2.** Direction or position in which something sets or is set; setting of hair or (poet.) sun; (**dead**) ~, action of setter pointing at game (**make a dead** ~ **at,** attack esp. by argument or ridicule, try to win affections of); setting, stage furniture, etc., for play, film, etc.; (also **sett**) badger's burrow, granite paving-block, (square in) tartan pattern, (Hort.) young plant or bulb ready to be planted. [sense 1 f. F *sette* f. L (SECT); sense 2 f. SET[1]]

**sěttee′** n. Long seat, with back and usu. arms, for more than one person. [orig. uncert.]

**sě′tter, sě′tting.** See SET[1] 3.

**sě′ttle**[1] v.t. & i. Determine, agree upon, decide, resolve, (question, date, quarrel, etc.; ~ one's **affairs,** (esp.) make will etc. when death is imminent); terminate (lawsuit) by mutual agreement; deal effectively with, get rid of, (*settle* person's HASH); pay (money owed, account, etc., or abs.); subside, come down esp. on surface, or to(wards) bottom of a liquid; colonize, establish or become colonists or dwellers in (country etc.); ~ (**down**), establish or become established in abode or place or way of life, (cause to) sit or come down to stay for some time; bring to or attain fixity, certainty, clarity, composure, or quietness, give one's full attention *to* (work etc.); (in *p.p.*) not soon changing (*settled weather*); ~ **down**, begin to live the routine life said to be typical of married persons; ~ **for**, accept or agree to (esp. a less desirable alternative); ~ **in**, become established in a place; ~ **on,** = *settle for*, give (property etc.) to (person) esp. for rest of his life; ~ **the matter**, leave no more to be discussed; ~ **up**, pay (money owed, account, etc.), agree and settle account with, finally arrange (a matter); ~ **with**, pay (agreed part of) money owed to (creditor etc.), get revenge on; ~**ment** (-telm-) *n.* (esp.) (deed stating) terms on which property is given to person, colony, group of social workers living in poor district to assist inhabitants; ~**r** *n.*, (esp.) one who goes to live in new colony. [E (SIT)]

**se'ttle²** *n.* Bench with high back and often with box below seat.

**se'ven** *a.* & *n.* NUMERAL; *the seven deadly* SINS; ~**-league boots** (in fairy-tale, enabling wearer to travel 7 leagues at each stride); *the seven* SEAS, WONDERS; ~**fōld** *a.* & *adv.*; ~**tee'n(th)** (or sě'-) *adjs.* & *ns.*, NUMERALS (**sweet ~teen**, age of girlish beauty); ~**th** *a.* & *n.*, NUMERAL (S~**th-day Adventist**, member of millenary and sabbatarian sect; *seventh* HEAVEN); ~**thlў** *adv.*, ~**tǐeth**, ~**tў**, *adjs.* & *ns.*, NUMERALS. [E]

**se'ver** *v.t.* & *i.* Divide, break, make separate, esp. by cutting; end employment contract of (person); ~**ance** *n.*, severing, severed state; ~**ance pay**, amount paid to employee on termination of employment. [AF f. L (SEPARATE)]

**se'veral** *a.* & *pron.* A few, more than two but not many, (*have called several times*); *went fishing and caught several*); separate, diverse, individual, respective, (*went their several ways*); ~**lў** *adv.*, separately, respectively. [AF f. L (*separ* distinct)]

**sevēr'e** *a.* (~**r**, ~**st**). Rigorous, strict, harsh, unsparing, (*severe critic, discipline, sentence*); vehement or extreme (*a severe winter, attack of influenza*); (of weather) very cold or stormy; arduous, trying, exacting, (*severe competition, requirements*); unadorned, not florid or luxuriant, (*severe architecture, simplicity, style*);

serious (*severe shortage*); ~**lў** (-ēr'lǐ) *adv.*, in severe manner (**leave, let,** ~**ly alone**, abstain from dealing or meddling with); **sěvě'rǐtў** *n.* [F, or L *severus*]

**Sě'vǐlle** *n.* ~ **orange**, small bitter orange used for marmalade. [place]

**sew** (sō) *v.t.* & *i.* (*p.p.* ~**n** *pr.* sōn, ~**ed** *pr.* sōd). Fasten, join, enclose, or make with stitches; use needle and thread or sewing-machine; ~ **up**, join or enclose by sewing, (colloq., esp. in *p.p.*) arrange or finish dealing with (a project etc.); ~'**ing-machine**, machine for sewing or stitching. [E]

**sew'age** (or sōō'-) *n.* Matter conveyed in sewers (~ **farm, works**, place where sewage is treated, purified, etc.); **sew'er** *n.*, conduit, usu. under ground, for carrying off drainage water, excrementitious matter, etc. (**sewer-gas**, foul air of sewers; **sewer rat**, common brown rat); **sew'erage** *n.*, system of, drainage by, sewers. [AF *sever(e)* f. Rom. (EX-¹, *aqua* water)]

**sewn.** See SEW.

**sěx. 1.** *n.* Being male or female or hermaphrodite (*what is its sex?*); males or females collectively (**the fair, gentle, second, softer, weaker,** ~, women; **the sterner** ~, men); sexual instincts, desires, etc., or their manifestation (*Christian attitudes to sex*); ~ **life**, person's activities in this respect); (colloq.) sexual intercourse (*have sex with*). **2.** *a.* Of or pertaining to sex (*sex education*); arising from difference or consciousness of sex (*sex antagonism, instinct*); ~ **appeal**, attractiveness due to difference of sex; ~ **change**, (esp.) apparent change of sex by surgical means; ~ **maniac**, person needing excessive gratification of sexual desires; ~'**pot**, (colloq.) sexy woman; ~**-starved**, lacking adequate sexual gratification. **3.** *v.t.* Determine sex of; (in *p.p.*) equipped with sexual characteristics (esp. *highly* etc. *sexed*). **4.** ~'**ism** *n.*, prejudice or discrimination against people (esp. women) because of their sex; ~'**ist** *a.* & *n.*; ~'**lèss** *a.*, neither male nor female, lacking sexual desire or attractiveness; ~**o'logў** *n.*, study of sexual life or relationships. [F, or L *sexus*]

**sěxag|ènār'ian** *a.* & *n.* (Person) from 60 to 69 years old; S~**ě'sǐma**

*n.*, Sunday before Quinquagesima; **~ĕ'sĭmal** *a.* (**-lly**), of sixtieths or sixty, in sixtieths. [L *-arius (sexaginta* 60)]

**sĕ'xtant** *n.* Instrument with graduated arc of 60° used in navigation and surveying for measuring angular distance of objects by means of mirrors. [L *sextans -ntis* sixth part]

**sĕxtĕ't(te)** *n.* Group of 6, (Mus.) (composition for) group of 6 instruments or voices. [alt. SESTET after L *sex* six]

**sĕ'xton** *n.* Person who looks after church and churchyard, often acting as bell-ringer and grave-digger. [F *segerstein* f. L *sacristanus*]

**sĕ'xtŭpl|e** *a.* & *n.* Sixfold (number or amount); **~ĕt** *n.*, one of 6 children born at a birth. [L (*sex* 6, QUINTUPLE)]

**sĕ'xŭal** (*or* -kshŏŏal) *a.* (**~ly**). Of sex(es); pertaining to relations between the sexes, esp. w. ref. to mutual attraction and to gratification of resulting desires; **~ intercourse**, insertion of man's penis into woman's vagina, usu. followed by ejaculation of semen; **~ĭtў** (-ă'l-) *n.*, sexual characteristics or activity; **sĕ'xў** *a.* (**-ily, -iness**), sexually stimulating, attractive, or provocative, unduly engrossed in sex. [L (SEX)]

**sĕz.** See SAY.

**S.F.** *abbr.* science fiction.

**sf** *abbr.* = foll.

**sfòrză'ndō** (-ts-) *a.* & *adv.* (Mus.) With sudden emphasis. [It.]

**Sgt.** *abbr.* Sergeant.

**shă'bb|ў** *a.* (**~ily, ~iness**). Threadbare, dilapidated, very worn; poorly dressed (**~y-genteel**, shabby but attempting to appear genteel); in bad repair or condition; contemptible or dishonourable (*played a shabby trick on me*). [rel. to SCAB]

**shă'ck.** 1. *n.* Roughly built hut or cabin. 2. *v.i.* (sl.) **~ up**, cohabit *with* or *together*. [perh. Mex. *jacal* wooden hut]

**shă'ckle.** 1. *n.* Metal loop or link, closed by bolt, to connect chains etc.; fetter enclosing ankle or wrist, (fig.) restraint or impediment (*the shackles of convention*). 2. *v.t.* Fetter; impede (lit. or fig.). [E]

**shăd** *n.* (*pl.* **~s, ~**). Large edible fish. [E]

**shă'ddock** *n.* (Tree bearing) large citrus fruit. [person]

**shāde.** 1. *n.* Comparative darkness (and usu. coolness); place sheltered from sun; (in *pl.*) darkness *of* night or evening; ‖(in *pl.*) wine-vaults; (fig.) comparative obscurity (**in the ~**, outshone, surpassed, caused to appear insignificant or poor); darker part of picture etc.; a colour esp. with regard to its depth or as distinguished from one nearly like it, (fig.) slightly differing variety, (*all shades of green, opinion*); slight amount or difference (*am a shade better today*); insubstantial thing; ghost (**the ~s**, Hades); screen excluding or moderating light; translucent cover for lamp etc. 2. *v.t.* & *i.* Screen from light; cover or moderate or exclude light of; darken, esp. with parallel pencil lines to represent shadow etc.; change or pass by degrees (*away, off; into* other colour, state, etc.). [E]

**shā'dow** (-dō). 1. *n.* (Patch of) shade; region not reached by light, sound, etc., because of intervening object; dark figure projected by body intercepting rays of light, this regarded as person's or thing's appendage, (**cast a long ~**, fig., be significant); (fig.) one's inseparable attendant or companion; foreshadowing, premonition; slightest trace (*without a shadow of doubt*); insubstantial or counterfeit thing; ghost (**the ~ of** one's former self, much weakened or emaciated; **worn to a ~**, exhausted); **~-boxing** (against imaginary opponent, as form of training); ‖**S~ Cabinet, Chancellor**, etc., (of members of opposition party who would probably be Cabinet ministers if that party became the Government). 2. *v.t.* Cast shadow over; secretly follow and watch all movements of; set *forth* dimly, in outline, allegorically, or prophetically. 3. **~ў** *a.*, having or like shadow(s). [E (prec.)]

**shā'd|ў** *a.* (**~ily, ~iness**). Giving or situated in shade; disreputable, of doubtful honesty; **on the ~y side of**, more than (specified age). [SHADE]

**shaft** (-ah-) *n.* (Long slender stem of) arrow or spear; (fig.) remark aimed to hurt or stimulate (*shafts of ridicule, wit*); ray *of* light; stroke *of* lightning; stem or stalk; column, esp. between base and capital; long and narrow part supporting or connecting or driving part(s) of greater thickness etc.; part of golf-club between handle and head; handle of tool etc.; one of pair of poles between which horse of vehicle is harnessed; long narrow space, usu. vertical, for access to a mine, for a lift in a building, for ventilation, etc. [E]

**shǎg** n. Rough growth or mass of hair; coarse tobacco; (crested) cormorant; ~'gў (-gǐ) a. (~gily, ~giness), hairy, rough-haired, unkempt; ~y-dog story, long inconsequential narrative or joke. [E]

**shagree'n** n. Kind of untanned leather with granulated surface; shark-skin. [var. CHAGRIN]

**shah** n. Ruler of Iran. [Pers.]

**shāke. 1.** v.t. & i. (shook pr. -ŏŏk; sha'ken, arch. or colloq. shook). Move (thing or person) violently or quickly up and down or to and fro (shook the mat to get the dust out; shook him by the shoulders); (cause to) tremble, quiver, rock, vibrate, or wave, (explosion shook the house; the earth shook; shake a LEG, one's SIDEs); make threatening gesture with (one's fist, stick, etc.); agitate, shock, disturb, (colloq.) upset composure of, (was much shaken by, with, at, the news; that'll shake him); weaken, impair, make less convincing or firm or courageous (his credit, faith, was shaken); (of voice etc.) make tremulous or rapidly alternating sounds, trill; (colloq.) shake hands (we shook on the bargain); ~ person by the hand, shake hands with him; ~ down, settle or cause to fall by shaking, become comfortably settled or established, get into harmony, ~'down n., makeshift bed esp. on floor, (attrib., of cruise etc.) used to try out new ship etc.; ~ hands, clasp right hands (with person), esp. at meeting or parting, in reconciliation or congratulation, or as sign of bargain; ~ one's head, move one's head from side to side in refusal, denial, disapproval, or concern; ~ in one's shoes, tremble with apprehension; ~ off, get rid of (unwanted thing; shake the DUST off one's feet), evade (companion); ~ out, empty by shaking, spread or open (sail, flag, etc.) by shaking; ~-out n., radical upheaval or reorganization; ~ up, mix (ingredients) by shaking, restore (pillow etc.) to shape by shaking, disturb or make uncomfortable, rouse from lethargy,

apathy, conventionality, etc.; ~-up n., action or result of shaking up. **2.** n. Shaking or being shaken (no great ~s, colloq., not very good; the ~s, fit of trembling); = MILK shake; jerk, shock; (Mus.) trill; (colloq.) moment; in a brace of ~s, in two etc. ~s (of a lamb's tail etc.), very quickly. **3.** ~able (-ka-), shā'kable, adjs.; shā'ker n., (esp.) container for shaking together ingredients of cocktails etc. [E]

**Shākespear'ian** (-ks-) a. & n. (Student) of Shakespeare. [person]

**shă'kō** n. (pl. ~s). Cylindrical plumed peaked military hat. [F f. Magyar]

**shā'k|ў** a. (~ily, ~iness). Unsteady, apt to shake, trembling, unsound, infirm; unreliable, tottering, wavering. [SHAKE]

**shāl|e** n. Soft rock that splits easily, resembling slate; ~'ў a. [G (SCALE[2])]

**shall** (or emphat. -ăl) v. aux. (pres. **shall**, or 'll after I or we, exc. 2 sing. arch. **shalt**, neg. **shall not**, colloq. **shan't** pr. shahnt; past **should** pr. shŏŏd, shud, or 'd after I or we, exc. 2 sing. arch. **shouldst** pr. shŏŏdst, **shouldest** pr. shŏŏ'dĭst, neg. **should not**, colloq. **shouldn't** pr. shŏŏ'dĕnt; no other parts used) expressing (see also WILL) future event, situation, etc., (we shall hear about it tomorrow), (strong) intention (I shall return; you shall regret this), condition (if it should happen; I should have been killed if I had gone), command or duty (thou shalt not steal), obligation (I should tell you; he should have been more careful), likelihood (they should be there by now), or tentative suggestion (I should like to disagree); ~ I, do you want me to. [E]

**shă'llop** n. Light open boat. [F chaloupe f. Du. (SLOOP)]

**shallŏ't** n. Onion-like plant with cloves like those of garlic [F (SCALLION)]

**shā'llow** (-ō) a., n., & v. **1.** a. (~er, ~est). Of little depth; (fig.) superficial, trivial. **2.** n. Shallow place. **3.** v.i. & t. Become or make shallow. [E]

**shalŏ'm** n. & int. (Excl. of) salutation at meeting or parting, used among Jews. [Heb.]

**shălt.** See SHALL.

**shăm** v., n., & a. **1.** v.t. & i. (-mm-). Feign, pretend (to be). **2.** n. Imposture, pretence; person or thing pretending or pretended to be something that he or it is not. **3.** *a.* (**-mm-**). Pretended, counterfeit. [orig. unkn.]

**shă′man** *n.* Witch-doctor, priest claiming to communicate with gods etc.; **~ĭsm** *n.*; **~ĭ′stĭc** *a.* [Russ.]

**shă′mateur** (-tūr, -tēr) *n.* Sports player classed as amateur though often profiting like professional; **~ĭsm** *n.* [SHAM, AMATEUR]

**shă′mble** *v.i.*, & *n.* (Walk or run with) shuffling or awkward gait. [perh. rel. to foll.]

**shă′mbles** (-belz) *n.pl.* (usu. treated as *sing.*). Butcher's slaughter-house; scene of carnage; (colloq.) mess, muddle. [pl. of *shamble* stall, E f. L *scamellum* bench]

**shāme. 1.** *n.* Humiliated or distressed feeling caused by consciousness of one's guilt, shortcomings, offensiveness, or folly; restraint imposed by, desire to avoid, capacity for experiencing, this feeling (*has no sense of shame*; **for ~!**, reproof to person for not showing shame); state of disgrace, regret, ignoring, or discredit, (*brought shame on himself*); **put** person **to ~**, disgrace him esp. by exhibiting one's superior qualities etc.; **~ on you!**, you should be ashamed of yourself!); person or thing that brings disgrace etc., thing that is wrong or regrettable, (**what a ~!**, how disgraceful, how unfortunate!). **2.** *v.t.* Bring shame on, make ashamed; put to shame; force by shame *into* or *out of* doing, conduct, etc. **3.** **~′făced** (-mfāst) *a.*, showing shame, bashful, shy [FAST²]; **~′ful** (-mf-) *a.* (**-lly**), disgraceful, scandalous; **~′lĕss** (-ml-) *a.*, having or showing no shame, impudent. [E]

**shă′mmў** *n.* Chamois-leather. [CHAMOIS]

**shămpoo′. 1.** *v.t.* Wash (one's hair). **2.** *n.* (Substance used for) washing hair, carpet, car, etc. [Hind.]

**shă′mrŏck** *n.* Trefoil, used as national emblem of Ireland. [Ir.]

**shă′ndў(găff)** *n.* Beer mixed with ginger-beer or lemonade. [orig. unkn.]

**shănghai′** (-hī′) *v.t.* Force (person) to be sailor on ship, usu. by trickery; put into detention or awkward situation by trickery. [place]

**Shă′ngrĭ-La** (-nggrĭlah; *or* -ah′) *n.*

Imaginary paradise on earth. [place in book]

**shănk** *n.* Leg (**S~s′s mare, pony,** one's own legs as means of conveyance); lower part of leg; shin-bone; shaft or stem of anchor, tool, nail, key, spoon, etc. [E]

**shan′t.** See SHALL.

**shăntŭ′ng** *n.* Soft undressed Chinese silk, usu. undyed. [place]

**shă′ntў¹** *n.* Hut, cabin, hovel; **~ town** (consisting of shanties). [orig. unkn.]

**shă′ntў²** *n.* (Sea-)**~**, song sung by sailors while hauling ropes etc. [prob. F *chanter* (CHANT)]

**shāpe. 1.** *n.* External form, appearance, total effect produced by thing's outlines (*spherical in shape*; *has the shape of a boat*); specific form or embodiment (*showed me politeness in the shape of an invitation*); description, sort, way, (*not in any shape or form*); symmetrical, definite, orderly, or proper arrangement (*give shape to one's ideas*; *keep in shape*; LICK, *put, into shape*); condition (*in bad, good, shape*); person or thing as seen, esp. indistinctly seen or imagined (*a shape loomed through the mist*); mould or pattern; jelly etc. shaped in mould; piece of material, paper, etc., made or cut in a particular form. **2.** *v.t.* & *i.* Give (desired) shape or form to, fashion, create; direct (one's course); adapt or make conform *to*; frame mentally, imagine; assume or develop into shape; give signs of future shape, development, or success; **~ up**, take· (specified) form, show promise, progress *well*. **3.** **~′lĕss** (-pl-) *a.*, lacking proper shape or shapeliness; **~′lў** (-plĭ) *a.* (**-iness**), well formed or proportioned, of elegant or pleasing shape or appearance. [E]

**shărd** *n.* = POT¹*sherd*. [E]

**shāre. 1.** *n.* Portion that person receives or is entitled to from jointly owned amount, portion that one should or does contribute to fund or combined effort, (*get a, my, share of the profits*; *do your share of the work*; GO¹ *shares*; LION's *share*; **~ and ~ alike**, with equal division); part-proprietorship of property, business, etc., esp. one of the equal parts into which company's capital is divided entitling owner to proportion of profits (**deferred, ordinary, pre-ference** or **preferred, ~,** share with least, ordinary, or most, se-curity for payment of dividends); ~-**cropper**, tenant farmer who pays part of crop as rent; ~'**holder**, owner of shares; ~-**index**, number indicating how prices of shares have fluctuated. 2. *v.t. & i.* ~ (**out**), divide and distribute (*share the sweets between you*); give away part of (*would share his last crust*); get, have, or give share (of) (~ **and** ~ **alike**, make equal division); ~-**out** *n.*, division and distribution esp. of profits or booty. [rel. to SHEAR]

**shark** *n.* Large voracious sea-fish; rapacious person, swindler; ~-**skin**, skin of shark, smooth dull-surfaced fabric. [orig. unkn.]

**sharp** *a., n., & adv.* **1.** *a.* Having edge or point able to cut or pierce; tapering to point or edge; abrupt, angular, (*sharp corner, incline*); well--defined, clean-cut, (*sharp contrast, features*); keen, pungent, acid, tart, shrill, piercing, biting, harsh, acri-monious, severe, intense, painful, (*sharp flavour, sauce, voice, frost, words, temper, reproof*); acute, sensitive, quick to see, hear, notice, under-stand, etc., (*sharp ears, eyes, wits*; **as** ~ **as a needle**, very intelligent; ~'**shooter**, skilled marksman); quick to take advantage, artful, un-scrupulous, dishonest, (~ **practice**, dishonest or barely honest dealings); vigorous or brisk (*take a sharp walk*); ~'**s the word**, colloq., speed is required); (Mus.) above correct or normal pitch (**C, F,** etc., ~, a semitone higher than C, F, etc.). **2.** *n.* (Mus.) (sign indicating) sharp note; (colloq.) swindler, cheat. **3.** *adv.* Punctually (*at six o'clock sharp*); suddenly (*pulled up sharp*); at a sharp angle (*turn sharp right*); (Mus.) above true pitch (*sings sharp*); LOOK *sharp*. **4.** ~'**en** *v.t. & i.*, make or become sharp; ~'**er**, swindler esp. at cards; ~'**ish** *a. & adv.*, (colloq.) fairly sharp(ly), quite quickly. [E]

**shả'tter** *v.t. & i.* Break suddenly in pieces, utterly destroy, dissipate, (*shattered nerves, hopes*); (fig.) severely discompose. [rel. to SCATTER]

**shảve. 1.** *v.t. & i.* (*p.p.* ~**d** or, esp. as *a.*, **sha'ven**). Remove (hair), clear (chin etc.) of hair, remove hair from chin etc. of (person), with razor, do this to oneself; pare surface of (wood etc.); (fig.) reduce amount of; pass close to without touching,

miss narrowly. **2.** *n.* Shaving or being shaved; narrow miss or escape; tool for shaving wood etc. **3.** **shả'ver** *n.*, (esp.) electrically driven razor, (colloq.) lad, youngster; **shả'ving** *n.*, (esp., in *pl.*) thin parings of wood; **sha'ving-brush** (for lathering chin etc. before shaving); **sha'ving--cream, -soap,** etc., (applied to chin etc. to assist shaving). [E]

**Shả'vian** *a. & n.* (Admirer, in the manner) of the writer G. B. Shaw. [*Shavius*, L form of *Shaw*]

**shawl. 1.** *n.* Piece of fabric, usu. rectangular and often folded into triangle, worn over shoulders, round neck, etc., or wrapped round baby. **2.** *v.t.* (esp. in *p.p.*) Put shawl on (person). [Urdu f. Pers.]

**shẽ** (or shĭ) *pron., n., & a.* **1.** *pron.* (*obj.* HER, *refl.* HERSELF, *poss.* HER, HERS, *pl.* THEY etc.). The female previously mentioned or implied; thing personified as female (ship, nation, motor vehicle). **2.** *n.* Female, woman, (*is the puppy a he or a she?*). **3.** *a.* (usu. w. hyphen). Female (*she--ass*); ~-**cat, -devil**, spiteful, dan-gerous, or malignant woman. [E]

**sheaf. 1.** *n.* (*pl.* **sheaves** *pr.* -vz). Group of things laid lengthwise to-gether and usu. tied, esp. bundle of corn-stalks tied after reaping. **2.** *v.t.* (or **sheave**). Make into sheaves. [E]

**shear. 1.** *v.t. & i.* (*past* ~**ed**; *p.p.* **shorn,** ~**ed**). Cut (off) with scissors, shears, etc.; clip wool off (sheep etc.); (fig.) strip bare *of*, deprive *of*; dis-tort, be distorted, or break (*off*). **2.** *n.* Strain produced by pressure in structure of substance; (**pair of**) ~**s**, clipping or cutting instrument shaped like scissors. [E]

**sheath** *n.* (*pl. pr.* -dhz, -ths). Close--fitting cover esp. for blade of knife; woman's close-fitting dress; condom; ~-**knife**, dagger-like knife carried in sheath; ~**e** (-dh) *v.t.*, put into sheath, encase or protect with sheath. [E]

**sheave**[1] *n.* Grooved wheel in pulley-block etc. for rope to run on. [E]

**sheave**[2], **sheaves.** See SHEAF.

**shẽbee'n** *n.* (Ir.) Unlicensed house selling alcoholic liquor. [Ir.]

**shẽd**[1] *v.t.* (-**dd**-; **shed**). Let fall off, lose, (*tree sheds leaves*; *snake sheds skin*; *bather sheds clothes*); reduce (electrical power load) by disconnection etc.; cause to fall or flow (*shed blood, tears*);

disperse, diffuse, radiate, (*shed perfume, radiance,* etc., *around* one; *shed* LIGHT[1] *on*). [E]

**shĕd**[2] *n.* One-storeyed building, often open on one or more sides, for storage, shelter, or as workshop etc. [SHADE]

**sheen** *n.* Splendour, radiance, brightness; gloss on surface; ~'ў *a.* [E, = beautiful]

**sheep** *n.* (*pl.* same). Timid gregarious woolly animal, esp. kept in flocks for its wool or meat (BLACK *sheep*; like ~, acquiescently, subserviently; *make sheep's* EYES; **as well be hanged for a ~ as for a lamb**, one may as well commit a large crime as a small one [ref. to sheep-stealing]; ~ **and goats**, the good and the wicked [Matt. 25: 33]; WOLF *in sheep's clothing*); bashful or docile person; (usu. in *pl.*) member of minister's flock, parishioner; sheepskin leather; ~**-dip**, (place where sheep are dipped in) preparation for cleansing sheep of vermin etc.; ~**-dog**, dog trained to guard and herd sheep, type of dog suitable for this; ~**-fold**, enclosure for sheep; ~'**-shank**, knot used to shorten rope temporarily; ~'**skin**, garment or rug of sheep's skin with wool on, leather of sheep's skin used in bookbinding etc.; ~'**ish** *a.*, bashful, embarrassed through shame. [E]

**sheer**[1]. **1.** *a.* Mere, simple, unqualified, absolute, (*is sheer bad luck, stupidity, waste; a sheer impossibility*); (of cliff, ascent, etc.) perpendicular; (of textile) diaphanous. **2.** *adv.* Perpendicularly, directly, (*rises sheer from the water; cut sheer through an iron plate*). [E]

**sheer**[2] *v.i.* Swerve or change course; ~ **off**, go away, esp. from person etc. that one dislikes or fears. [orig. uncert.]

**sheer**[3] *n.* ~**s**, ~**-legs**, hoisting-apparatus used in dockyards or on dismasted ship (~**-hulk**). [SHEAR]

**sheet.** **1.** *n.* Large rectangular piece of cotton, linen, nylon, etc., used esp. in pairs as inner bedclothes (**between the ~s**, in bed); broad usu. flat piece of paper (CLEAN *sheet*), glass, iron, etc.; complete piece of paper as it was made; newspaper; wide expanse *of* water, snow, ice, flame, colour, etc.; rope etc. attached to lower corner of sail for regulating its position etc. (**three ~s in the**

wind, sl., very drunk); ~**-anchor**, second anchor for use in emergencies, (fig.) thing depended on for security or as one's last hope; ~ **metal** (formed into thin sheets by rolling, hammering, etc.); *sheet* LIGHTNING; ~ **music** (published in separate sheets). **2.** *v.t.* Provide or cover with sheets; form into sheets; (of rain etc.) move in sheets. [E]

**sheikh, sheik, shaik(h)**, (-āk, -ēk) *n.* Chief, head of Arab tribe, family, or village; Muslim leader; ~'**dom** *n.* [Arab.]

**shei'la** (-ē'-) *n.* (Austral. & N.Z. sl.) Young woman, girl. [orig. uncert.]

**shĕ'kel** *n.* Ancient Jewish etc. weight and silver coin; (in *pl.*, colloq.) money, riches. [Heb.]

**shĕ'l|drāke** *n.* (*fem.* & *pl.* ~**duck, sheld duck**). Bright-plumaged wild duck. [prob. dial. *sheld* pied, DRAKE[2]]

**shĕlf** *n.* (*pl.* **shelves** *pr.* -vz). Horizontal board, slab, etc., projecting from wall or forming one tier of bookcase or cupboard (**on the ~**, put aside, finished with, esp. of person past work or of unmarried woman thought unlikely to marry); ledge, horizontal steplike projection in cliff face etc.; reef or sandbank; CONTINENTAL *shelf*; ~**-life**, time for which stored thing remains usable; ~**-mark** (on book, showing its place in library). [LG]

**shĕll.** **1.** *n.* Hard outer case enclosing nut-kernel, egg, seed, fruit, animal (esp. marine mollusc) or part of it, (**come out of** one's ~, become communicative); walls or framework of unfinished or gutted building, ship, etc.; framework or case for something; light rowing-boat for racing; hollow case containing explosives for cartridge, firework, etc.; explosive projectile for firing from large gun etc.; outward show, mere semblance; ~'**fish**, mollusc(s) or crustacean(s); ~**-pink**, delicate pale pink; ~**-shock**, nervous breakdown resulting from exposure to bombardment and other battle conditions. **2.** *v.t.* & *i.* Take out of shell, remove shell or pod from; fire shells at; ~ **out**, (sl.) pay up (money). **3.** **shĕllā'c**, (*n.*) resinous substance used for making varnish etc., (*v.t.*; -ck-) varnish with shellac; **shĕlled** (-ld) *a.*, having a shell, deprived of its shell; ~**less** *a*.; ~'**ỹ** *a*., of or like shell(s), abounding in shells. [E]

**Shě'lta** *n*. Ancient hybrid cant language of Irish gipsies and pipers, Irish and Welsh travelling tinkers, etc. [orig. unkn.]

**shě'lter. 1.** *n*. (Thing or place providing) protection from wind, rain, danger, attack, etc., (**air-raid ~**, structure giving protection from air--raid). **2.** *v.t.* & *i*. Provide with shelter; defend *from* blame, trouble, etc.; protect (industry etc.) *from* competition; take shelter *under, in, from,* etc.

**shělv|e** *v.t.* & *i*. Put (books etc.) on shelf; (fig.) abandon or defer consideration of (plan etc.), remove (person) from active work etc.; fit (cupboard etc.) with shelves; (of ground etc.) slope gently; ~**es**, see SHELF; ~'**ing** *n*., (esp.) shelves collectively. [SHELF]

**shěmo'zzle** *n*. (sl.) Rumpus, brawl; muddle. [Yiddish]

**shěná'nigan** *n*. (colloq.) Nonsense; trickery; high-spirited behaviour. [orig. unkn.]

**shě'pherd** (-perd). **1.** *n*. Man who takes care of sheep; (fig.) minister, priest, etc. (**the Good S**~, Christ); ~'**s pie**, minced meat baked under mashed potatoes; ~**ess** *n*. **2.** *v.t.* Tend (sheep, lit. or fig.) as shepherd; marshal or conduct or drive (crowd etc.) like sheep. [E (SHEEP, HERD)]

**Shě'raton** *n*. Style of furniture introduced in England *c*. 1790. [person]

**shě'rbet** *n*. Sweet flavoured drink or powder, usu. effervescent. [Turk. & Pers. f. Arab.]

**shěrd** *n*. = POT[1]*sherd*. [E]

**shě'riff** *n*. ‖(High) ~, chief executive officer of Crown in county, with legal and ceremonial duties; ‖honorary officer elected annually in some towns; ~(-**depute**), (Sc.) chief judge of county or district; *chief law-enforcing officer of county. [E (SHIRE, REEVE[1])]

**Shě'rpa** *n*. (One of) a Himalayan people living on borders of Nepal and Tibet. [native name]

**shě'rry** *n*. White usu. fortified wine orig. from S. Spain. [*Xeres,* place]

**Shě'tland** *a*. ~ **pony,** small hardy rough-coated pony; ~ **wool,** fine wool from Shetland sheep. [place]

**shew.** See SHOW.

**shǐ'bbolěth** *n*. Old-fashioned doctrine or formula of party or sect; catchword; word, custom, principle, etc., regarded as revealing person's orthodoxy etc. [Heb. (Judg. 12: 6)]

**shield. 1.** *n*. Piece of defensive armour carried in hand or on arm to protect the body when fighting, usu. curving to a point at the bottom; (Her.) drawing etc. of this used for displaying person's coat of arms; trophy in form of shield; protective plate or screen in machinery etc.; person or thing that protects one; shieldlike part in animal or plant. **2.** *v.t.* Protect or screen, esp. from censure or punishment (often implying illegitimate concealment of facts). [E]

**shǐft. 1.** *v.t.* & *i*. Change or move from one position to another (~ one's **ground,** take new position in argument etc.); change form or character; *change gear in motor vehicle; use expedients, manage to do something, make a living, etc., (~ **for** oneself, depend on one's own efforts); (sl.) move quickly, consume (food or drink); ~ (**off**), get rid of (responsibility etc.) to another. **2.** *n*. Change of position or form or character; group of workmen working at same time, period for which they work, (*night shift*); expedient, stratagem, resource, (**make ~,** manage or contrive *to* do, get along somehow *with, without*); dodge, trick, piece of evasion or equivocation; woman's dress of oblong shape; (arch.) chemise; displacement of lines of spectrum; change of position of typewriter type--bars to type capitals etc.; *gear--change in motor vehicle. **3.** ~'**less** *a*., lacking resourcefulness, inefficient, lazy; ~'**ỹ** *a*. (~**ily,** ~**iness**), evasive, deceitful. [E]

**shǐlle'lagh** (-ā'lǐ, -ā'la) *n*. Irish cudgel. [place]

**shǐ'lling** *n*. Former British monetary unit and coin = twelve pence (CUT *off with a shilling;* **take the King's** or **Queen's ~,** enlist as soldier); monetary unit in E. Afr. countries. [E]

**shǐ'llỹ-shǎllỹ** *v., n.,* & *a*. **1.** *v.i.* Vacillate, be undecided, hesitate to act or choose one's course of action. **2.** *n*. Vacillation, indecision. **3.** *a*. Vacillating. [*shall I?*]

**shǐm. 1.** *n*. Thin wedge used in

machinery etc. to make parts fit. **2.** *v.t.* (-mm-). Fit or fill up thus. [orig. unkn.]

**shi′mmer** *v.i.*, & *n.* (Shine with) tremulous or faint light. [E]

**shin. 1.** *n.* Front of leg below knee; ~-**bone**, inner and usu. larger of two bones from knee to ankle; ~-**guard**, **-pad**, protective pad worn at football, hockey, etc.; ~ (lower foreleg) **of beef. 2.** *v.t.* & *i.* (-nn-). Climb (*up, down,* tree etc.) by using arms and legs, not on ladder etc. [E]

**shi′ndig, -dy,** *ns.* (colloq.) Festive gathering, esp. boisterous one; brawl, disturbance, noise. [perh. alt. SHINTY]

**shine. 1.** *v.i.* (shone *pr.* -ŏn). Emit or reflect light, be bright, glow; (of sun, star, etc.) be visible, not be obscured by clouds etc.; be brilliant, excel; (colloq.; ~**d**) cause (shoes, brass, etc.) to shine. **2.** *n.* Brightness, lustre, polish, (**take the ~ out of,** impair brilliance or newness of, surpass); light, sunshine, (RAIN *or* shine); *polishing of shoes etc.; (sl.) prank, disturbance; *****take a ~ to,** (sl.) take a fancy to. **3. shi′ner** *n.*, (esp., sl.) black eye; **shi′ny** *a.* (-ily, -iness), having shine, (of clothes) with nap worn off. [E]

**shi′ngle¹** (-nggel). **1.** *n.* Rectangular piece of wood used as roof-tile; (hair shaped by) shingling. **2.** *v.t.* Roof with shingles; cut (woman's hair) short so that it tapers from back of head to nape of neck, cut hair of (head, person) thus. [L *scindula*]

**shi′ngle²** (-nggel) *n.* Pebbles in a mass, as on sea-shore; ~**y** (-ngg-) *a.* [orig. uncert.]

**shi′ngles** (-nggelz) *n.pl.* (usu. treated as *sing.*) Acute painful viral inflammation of nerve ganglia, with skin eruption often forming girdle round middle of body. [L *cingulum* belt]

**Shi′ntō** *n.* Japanese religion revering ancestors and nature-spirits; ~**ism**, ~**ist**, *ns.* [Chin., = way of the Gods]

‖**shi′nty** *n.* Game like hockey but with taller goals; stick or ball used in it. [orig. uncert.]

**shi′ny.** See SHINE.

**ship. 1.** *n.* Large seagoing vessel (*when my* etc. ~ **comes home** or **in,** fortune is made; **take ~,** embark); (colloq.) spacecraft, *aircraft; ~**('s)

**biscuit,** hard coarse biscuit; ~**′board,** used or occurring on board ship; *on* ~**′board,** on board ship; ~-**breaker,** contractor who breaks up old ships; ~**′builder,** ~**′building,** (person engaged in) business of constructing ships; ~-**canal** (allowing ships to go inland); ~**′load,** quantity of cargo or passengers that ship can carry; ~**′mate,** person belonging to or sailing on same ship as another; ~**′owner,** person owning (shares in) shi (s); ~**'s boat** (carried on ship); ~**'s company,** entire crew; ~**′shape** *adv.* & *pred.a.*, in good order, neat and tidy; ~**'s papers,** documents est. blishing ownership, nationality, etc., of ship; ~-**way,** sloping structure on which ship is built and from which it is launched; ~**′wreck,** (*n.*) destruction of ship by storm, collision, etc., (fig.) ruin *of* one's *hopes* etc., (*v.t.* & *i.*) inflict shipwreck (lit. or fig.) on, suffer shipwreck; ~**′wright,** shipbuilder, ship's carpenter; ~**′yard,** place where ships are built. **2.** *v.t.* & *i.* (-pp-). Send, take, or put in ship; (Commerc.) deliver (goods) to agent for forwarding; fix (mast, rudder, etc.) in its place on ship; embark; (of sailor) engage for service on ship; take (oars) from rowlocks and lay them inside boat; ~ **water, a sea,** etc., have water come into boat etc. over gunwale; ~**′ment** *n.*, placing of goods on ship, amount shipped; ~**′per** *n.*, (esp.) importer or exporter; ~**′ping** *n.*, (esp.) ships collectively. [E]

**-ship** *suf.* forming *ns.* denoting condition or quality of being so-and- -so, status, office, honour, (*authorship, friendship, hardship, lordship*), tenure of office (*during his chairmanship*), skill in certain capacity (*horsemanship, marksmanship*), (number of) those who are (*membership*). [E]

‖**shire** *n.* County (**the ~s,** the midland counties of England, English fox-hunting district mainly in Leics. and Northants.); ~-**horse,** heavy powerful draught-horse; **-shire** (-sher) *suf.* forming names of counties or districts. [E]

**shirk** *v.t.* Avoid or get out of (duty, work, etc., or abs.) from laziness, cowardice, etc. [G *schurke* scoundrel]

**shirt** *n.* Loose sleeved garment of

cotton, linen, nylon, etc., for upper part of body (**in** one's **∼-sleeves,** not wearing jacket; **keep** one's **∼ on,** sl., keep one's temper; NIGHT--shirt; **the ∼ off** one's **back,** one's last remaining possessions); (sl.) all one's money (bet, put, one's shirt on a horse); **∼ dress,** woman's dress with bodice like shirt; **∼-front,** breast of shirt esp. if starched; *∼'waist,** woman's blouse resembling shirt; **∼'waister,** = shirt dress; **∼'ing** n., material for shirts; **∼'y** a. (**∼ily, ∼iness**), (sl.) angry, bad-tempered. [E]

**shi'sh kebăb** n. Pieces of marinated meat and vegetable cooked on skewers. [Turk. (KEBAB)]

**shit.** (vulg.) 1. v.i. & t. (-tt-; shit). Defecate; get rid of as excrement. 2. n. Faeces; act of defecating; nonsense; contemptible person; (as int.) expr. annoyance. [E]

**shi'ver¹.** 1. v.i. Tremble with cold, fear, etc. 2. n. Momentary shivering movement; **the ∼s,** attack of shivering, feeling of fear or horror; **∼y** a. (**∼iness**), characterized or affected by shivers. [orig. uncert.]

**shi'ver².** 1. n. (usu. in pl.). Small fragment, splinter. 2. v.t. & i. Break into shivers; **my timbers** (reputed naut. imprecation). [rel. to dial. shive slice]

**shoal¹.** 1. n. Multitude, great number, esp. of fish swimming together(s). 2. v.i. (Of fish) form shoal(s). [Du.; cf. SCHOOL²]

**shoal².** 1. n. Shallow place in sea, submerged sandbank esp. that shows at low water; (fig., usu. in pl.) hidden danger; **∼y** a. (**∼iness**), full of shoals. 2. v.i. Get shallow(er). [E]

**shŏck¹.** 1. n. Violent collision, concussion, or impact; violent tremor of earth's surface in earthquake; sudden and disturbing physical or mental impression (the news was a great shock); = ELECTRIC shock; (Path.) acute state of prostration following sudden violent emotion, severe injury, etc.; great disturbance of or injury to organization, stability, etc.; **∼ absorber,** device on vehicle etc. for absorbing shocks; **∼ tactics,** sudden violent action, esp. use of massed troops in attack; **∼ therapy, treatment,** treatment of psychiatric patients by means of electric shock or drug that induces convulsions

etc.; **∼ troops** (specially trained for assault); **∼ wave,** air-wave caused by explosion or by body moving faster than sound. 2. v.t. & i. Affect (person) with electrical or mental shock; appear horrifying or outrageous to; **∼'er** n., (colloq.) person or thing that shocks, very bad specimen of something, sordid or sensational novel, film, etc.; **∼'ing,** (a.) causing shock, scandalous, (colloq.) very bad, (adv., colloq.) shockingly. [F choc, choquer]

**shŏck².** 1. n. Group of corn-sheaves propped up together in field. 2. v.t. Arrange (corn) in shocks. [LDu.]

**shŏck³** n. Unkempt mass of hair; **∼-headed,** having such hair. [orig. unkn.]

**shŏd.** See SHOE.

**shŏ'dd|y** a. (**∼ily, ∼iness**). Of poor quality, counterfeit, shabby. [orig. unkn.]

**shoe** (-ōō). 1. n. Outer foot-covering of leather etc., esp. ‖one not reaching above ankle (**dead men's ∼s,** position or property which person expects to inherit or succeed to; **in** person's **∼s,** in his position, plight, etc.; SHAKE in one's shoes); metal rim nailed to horse's hoof; thing like shoe in shape or use; = BRAKE⁴-shoe; **∼'black,** person who cleans shoes for payment; **∼'horn,** curved piece of horn, metal, etc., for helping heel into shoe; **∼-lace,** cord for lacing shoe; **∼-leather** (save ∼-leather, avoid walking); **∼'maker, -making,** (of boots and shoes); *∼'shine,** polishing of shoes; **∼-string,** shoe-lace, (colloq.) small or inadequate amount of money, (attrib.) barely adequate; **∼-tree,** shaped block for keeping shoe in shape. 2. v.t. (shod; **∼'ing**). Fit (esp. horse) with shoe(s); protect (end of pole etc.) with ferrule; (in p.p.) having shoes etc. of a specified kind (DRY-, ROUGH-, SLIP²shod). [E]

**shŏne.** See SHINE.

**shoo** int., & v.i. & t. (Utter) sound used to frighten birds etc. away; drive away thus. [imit.]

**shook.** See SHAKE.

**shoot.** 1. v.t. & i. (SHOT²). Send out, discharge, propel, violently or swiftly; cause (gun, bow, or abs.) to discharge missile; kill or wound (person, animal) with missile from gun etc.; hunt game etc. with gun;

(Footb. etc.) score (goal), take shot at goal; pass swiftly down (rapids etc.) or under (bridge); (esp. Cinemat.) film or photograph; *(colloq.) play game of (craps etc.); *(as *int.*, sl.) say what you have to say; come or go swiftly, suddenly, or abruptly; (of plant) put forth buds, (of bud) appear; (of cricket-ball) dart along ground after pitching; (of pain) pass with stabbing sensation; **be** or **get shot** (= SHUT) **of**; *shoot a* LINE¹; ~ **down**, kill (person) cold-bloodedly by shooting, cause (aircraft or its pilot) to fall to ground by shooting, (fig.) argue effectively against (proposal etc.); ~'**ing star**, small meteor appearing like star, moving quickly and disappearing; ~ **it out**, (sl.) engage in decisive gun-battle; *~ one's **mouth off**, (sl.) talk freely, indiscreetly, or boastfully; ~-**out** *n.*, decisive gun-battle; ~ **over**, shoot game etc. on (an estate etc.); ‖~ **the moon**, (sl.) remove goods by night to avoid paying rent; ~ **up**, rise or grow rapidly, terrorize or destroy (district etc.) by (usu. indiscriminate) shooting. **2.** *n.* Young branch or sucker, new growth of plant; expedition, party, practice, land, etc., for shooting; chute; **the whole ~**, (sl.) everything. **3.** ~'**ing** *n.*, (esp.) right of shooting over particular land, estate rented to shoot over; ‖~**ing-box**, sportsman's lodge for use in shooting-season; ‖~**ing-brake**, estate car; ~**ing-gallery**, place for shooting at targets with rifles etc.; ~**ing-range**, ground with butts for rifle etc. practice; ~**ing-stick**, walking-stick which can be adapted to form seat. [E]

**shóp. 1.** *n.* Building, room, etc., for retail sale of goods, services, etc., (**all over the ~**, sl., in every direction, in disorder, wildly; BETting-*shop*; **shut up ~**, cease business or work for the day or permanently); place where manufacturing or repairing is done (CLOSED *shop*); (talk about) one's work or profession or things connected with it; (sl.) institution, establishment, place of business, etc.; ‖~-**assistant**, employee in retail shop; ~-**boy**, -**girl**, young shop-assistant; ~-**floor**, (work-place of) workers as dist. from management; ~'**keeper**, owner and manager of shop; ~-**lifter**, -**lifting**, (customer) stealing goods in shop; ~'**man**, shopkeeper('s assistant); ‖~-**soiled**, soiled or faded by display in shop (lit. or fig.); ~-**steward**, person elected by fellow-workers in factory etc. as their spokesman in dealings with employer; ‖~'**walker**, supervisor in large shop; ~-**window**, window in shop for display of goods (lit. or fig.). **2.** *v.i.* & *t.* (-**pp**-). Go to shop(s) to make purchases etc. (~ **around**, look for best bargain); (sl.) inform against, imprison; ~'-**ping** *n.*, going to shops (WINDOW-*shopping*), goods purchased in shops; ~**ping centre**, **street**, (containing many shops). [F *eschoppe* f. LG]

**shóre¹** *n.* Land that adjoins sea or large body of water (**on ~**, ashore); ~ **leave**, (Naut.) (permission for) period spent ashore. [LDu.]

**shóre².** **1.** *n.* Prop, beam set obliquely against wall, ship, etc., as support. **2.** *v.t.* Support, hold *up*, with shore(s).

**shórn.** See SHEAR.

**short** *a.*, *adv.*, *n.*, & *v.* **1.** *a.* Measuring little from end to end in space or time, or from head to foot (*a short life, line, person, time*; *make short* WORK *of*); not far-reaching; deficient, inadequate in quantity, scarce, (*we are one short*; *supplies are short*; GO¹ *short*); (seemingly) less than the stated amount etc. (*short weight*; *a few short years of happiness*); (St. Exch., of stocks, stockbroker, etc.) sold, selling, etc., when the amount is not in hand (**sell ~**, fig. disparage, underestimate); (Crick., of ball) pitching relatively near bowler, (of fielder or his position) relatively near batsman; (of person's memory) retaining only things from the immediate past; concise, brief, (**for ~**, as a short name; **in ~**, concisely); curt, sullenly or snappishly reticent, uncivil; (of vowel or syllable) having the less of two recognized durations, having sound that is not long; (of pastry etc.) easily crumbled; ~ **and sweet**, brief and pleasant (usu. iron.); ~'**bread**, crisp crumbly cake made with flour, butter, and sugar; ~'**cake**, shortbread, cake of short pastry usu. served with fruit; ~ **change**, insufficient money given as change; ~-**change** *v.t.*, rob thus, cheat; ~ **circuit**, electric circuit through small resistance, esp. instead of through normal circuit; ~-**circuit**

*v.t. & i.*, cause short circuit in, have short circuit, (fig.) shorten or avoid by taking short cut; ~'**coming**, failure to reach required standard, deficiency; *short* COMMONS; ~ **cut**, shorter way than that usually followed; ~**-dated**, due for early payment or redemption; *short* DIVISION; ~ **drink**, small drink of spirits etc.; ~'**fall**, deficit; ~ **for**, an abbreviation for; **have by the** ~ **hairs**, (colloq.) completely control (person); ~'**hand**, method of rapid writing for keeping pace with speaker etc., (fig.) abbreviated or symbolic mode of expression; ~**-ha'nded**, undermanned, understaffed; ~ **head**, (Racing) distance less than length of head of horse etc.; ~'**horn**, one of breed of cattle with short horns; ‖~ **list** (of selected candidates from which final choice will be made); ‖~**-list** *v.t.*, put on short list; ~**-lived** (-ĭvd), having a short life, ephemeral; ~ **odds**, nearly even chances in betting; ~ **of**, not having enough of (*short of money*), distant from, less than (*nothing short of a miracle*; **come, fall,** ~ **of**, fail to reach or amount to); ~ **on**, (colloq.) having little or none of; ~**-range**, having short range, relating to short period of future time; ~ **shrift**, curt attention or treatment; ~ **sight**, ability to see clearly only what is comparatively near; ~**-sighted**, having short sight, (fig.) lacking imagination or foresight; ~**-sleeved**, with sleeves not reaching below elbow; ~**-sta'ffed**, understaffed; ~ **story** (shorter than novel); ~ **temper**, self-control soon or easily lost; ~**-term**, occurring in or relating to short period of time; ~ **time**, condition of working for less than the normal time; *short* TON, WAVE; ~**-winded**, easily becoming breathless, (fig.) lacking persistence. **2.** *adv.* Abruptly, suddenly, before the natural or expected time or place, in short manner, (**taken** ~, put at disadvantage, colloq. suddenly wishing to defecate; ~ **of**, without going as far as, except). **3.** *n.* Short thing, esp. short syllable or vowel or film or (colloq.) circuit or drink; (in *pl.*) trousers reaching only to or above knees, *\*underpants; the* LONG[1] *and the short of it.* **4.** *v.t. & i.* Short-circuit. **5.** ~'**age** *n.*, (amount of) deficiency; ~'**en** *v.t. & i.*, make or

become short(er), (Naut.) reduce amount of (sail spread); ~'**ening** *n.*, (esp.) fat used for making short pastry; ~'**ly** *adv.*, soon, in a short time, in a short manner; ~'**ie**, ~'**y**, *n.*, (colloq.) person or garment shorter than the average. [E]

**shot**[1] *n.* Attempt to hit something by shooting, throwing, etc., (*first shot scored a bull's-eye*; *a lucky shot at goal*); attempt to do something (*had a shot at learning Greek*); stroke in golf, cricket, tennis, billiards, etc.; (sound of) discharge of gun, cannon, etc. (*several shots were fired, heard*; EAR[1]*shot*; **like a** ~, very quickly, without hesitation, willingly; ~ **in the dark**, a mere guess); launch of space-rocket; single missile for gun, cannon, etc., esp. non-explosive projectile; heavy metal ball thrown in athletic competition called the ~**-put** or **putting the** ~; (lead) ~ (*pl.* same), small lead pellet of which several are used for single charge; possessor of specified skill in shooting (*is a good shot*; BIG *shot*); photograph, film sequence taken by one camera; injection of drug etc. (~ **in the arm**, fig., stimulus or encouragement); (colloq.) dram of spirits; (one's share of) bill at inn etc.; ~**-blasting**, cleaning of metal etc. by impact of stream of shot; ~'**gun** (for firing small shot at short range; ~*gun wedding*, enforced esp. because of bride's pregnancy). [E]

**shot**[2]. **1.** See SHOOT. **2.** *a.* That has been shot; (of fabric) woven or dyed so as to show different colours at different angles; ~ **through**, permeated or suffused (*with*). [SHOOT]

**should(n't).** See SHALL.

**shou'lder** (shō'l-). **1.** *n.* Part of body to which arm or wing or foreleg is attached, either lateral projection below or behind neck, (in *pl.*, fig.) body regarded as bearing burden, blame, etc., (**broad** ~**s**, ability to bear heavy load or responsibility; **put** one's ~ **to the wheel**, make strong effort; RUB *shoulders with*; ~ **to** ~, side by side, with closed ranks or united effort; **straight from the** ~, (of blow) well delivered, (fig., of criticism etc.) frank, direct); part or projection resembling human shoulder; part of garment covering shoulder; strip of land adjoining metalled road-surface; animal's upper foreleg as joint of meat; ~**-bag,**

handbag that can be hung from shoulder; ~**-blade**, either large flat bone of upper back; ~**-high**, as high as one's shoulders; ~**-holster** (in armpit); ~**-pad** (used to raise shoulder of garment); ~**-strap**, strap (usu. one of two) suspending garment from wearer's shoulders, strap from shoulder to collar of garment, esp. with indication of military rank. **2.** *v.t.* & *i.* Push with one's shoulder, make way thus; take (burden, lit. or fig.) on one's shoulder(s); ~ **arms**, (Mil.) move rifle to position with barrel against shoulder and butt in hand. [E]

**shout. 1.** *n.* Loud utterance or vocal sound calling attention or expressing joy, (dis)approval, defiance, etc.; (Austral. & N.Z. colloq.) one's turn to buy drinks for the company. **2.** *v.i.* & *t.* Emit shout(s), speak or say or call loudly, (**it is all over bar the ~ing**, contest etc. is virtually decided; ~ **down**, reduce to silence by shouting); (Austral. & N.Z. colloq.) treat (person) to drinks etc. [perh. rel. to SHOOT]

**shove** (-ŭv). **1.** *v.t.* & *i.* Push vigorously; (colloq.) put somewhere (*shove it in the drawer*); ~**-halfpenny**, game in which coins etc. are pushed along marked board; ~ **off**, start from shore in boat, (colloq.) depart. **2.** *n.* Act of shoving. [E]

**sho'vel** (-ŭ'-). **1.** *n.* Spade-like concave implement for shifting coal etc.; (part of) machine with similar function; ~ **hat** (broad-brimmed). **2.** *v.t.* (‖-ll-). Move (as) with shovel; move vigorously in large quantities (*shovel food into mouth*). **3.** ~**board**, game played esp. on ship's deck by pushing discs over marked surface; ~**ful** (-ōol) *n.*, amount held by shovel; ~(**l)er** *n.*, (esp.) duck with shovel-like beak. [E]

**show** (-ō). **1.** *v.t.* & *i.* (*p.p.* ~**n**, ~**ed** *pr.* -ōd; also arch. **shew, shewn, shewed**, w. same pronunc.). Allow or cause to be seen, disclose, manifest, offer for inspection, exhibit, produce, (*window shows the interior*; *white clothes show the dirt*; *show me your ticket*; *showed a profit on his business*; *show* CAUSE, *a clean pair of* HEEL[1]*s*, one's COLOUR*s*, one's FACE, FIGHT, *the* FLAG[3]; ~ one's **hand**, reveal one's cards, fig. disclose one's plans; *show a* LEG; **nothing to ~ for** *effort* etc.,

no visible result; ~ **oneself**, be seen in public, let it be seen that one is *honest, a rogue*, etc.); give (specified treatment; *showed me kindness*; *show no mercy*); demonstrate, prove, point out, cause to understand, (*shows that it is false*; *show me how to write*; **it all** or **just** or **only goes to ~**, the fact is again demonstrated or proved; *show* person *the* DOOR); conduct (*showed us round the house*); be or become visible or noticeable, have specified appearance, (*stain will never show*; *it shows white at a distance*); ~ **in** or **out**, direct or accompany (person) to entrance or exit, open door for person's entrance or exit; ~ **off**, display to advantage, try to impress people by displaying one's skill, wealth, etc.; ~-**off** *n.*, person who shows off; ~ **round**, take (person) to all points of interest; ~ **through**, be visible (lit. or fig.) although behind something else; ~ **up**, make or be visible or conspicuous, expose, humiliate, (colloq.) appear or arrive or be present. **2.** *n.* Showing (DUMB *show*); spectacle, exhibition, pageant, display, (*a fine show of blossom*; *dog, flower, motor*, etc., -*show*); (colloq.) public entertainment or performance; (sl.) concern, undertaking, business, (**bad** or **poor** ~!, that was badly done or unfortunate; **good** ~!, that was well done or fortunate; **give the ~ away**, betray inadequacies or pretensions); outward appearance, impression produced, ostentation, mere display, (*made a great show of being reasonable*; *only done for show*); discharge of blood from vagina at approach of labour or onset of menstruation. **3.** ~ **business**, (sl.) ~'**biz**, the entertainment (esp. theatrical) profession; ~**-case**, glazed case for displaying goods, exhibits, etc.; ~**-down**, (Poker) laying down of cards with faces up, (fig.) final test, battle, etc., disclosure of achievements or possibilities; ~'**girl**, girl who appears, often merely decoratively, in revue etc.; ~**-jumping**, competitive jumping on horseback; ~'**man**, proprietor or organizer of public entertainment, person skilled in showmanship; ~'**manship**, (fig.) capacity for exhibiting one's wares or capabilities to best advantage; ~ **of force**, demonstration that one is ready to use force; ~ **of hands**, raising of hands to vote for or against proposal etc.; **~-piece,** excellent specimen suitable for display; **~-place** (that tourists etc. go to see); **~-room** (where goods are displayed or kept for inspection); **~-stopper,** (colloq.) performance receiving prolonged applause; **~ trial,** judicial trial allegedly designed to impress public opinion favourably. **4. ~'ing** *n.,* (esp.) quality or appearance of performance, achievement, etc., (*made a poor showing*), evidence, putting of case, (*on your own showing it must be true*); **~'y** *a.* (**~ily, ~iness**), making good or conspicuous display, gaudy. [E]

**show'er. 1.** *n.* Brief fall of rain, missiles, water, dust, (fig.) incoming gifts, honours, etc.; group of meteors moving thus; \*party for giving presents to prospective bride etc.; ‖(sl.) contemptible or unpleasant person(s); **~(-bath),** (device or place for) bath in which water is sprayed from above; **~'y** *a.* (**~iness**), of or characterized by rain-showers. **2.** *v.t. & i.* Discharge (water, missiles, etc.) in shower; lavishly bestow (gifts etc. *on, upon*); descend in a shower; use shower-bath. [E]

**showing, shown, showy.** See SHOW; **shrănk,** see SHRINK.

**shră'pnel** *n.* Fragments of metal scattered from exploding projectile. [person]

**shrĕd. 1.** *n.* Piece torn, scraped, or broken off, scrap, rag, fragment, least amount, (*clothes were in shreds; not a shred of evidence, truth*); **tear to ~s,** completely destroy or refute. **2.** *v.t.* (**-dd-**). Tear or cut into shreds. [E]

**shrew** (-ōō) *n.* Small long-snouted mouselike insectivorous animal; bad-tempered or scolding woman; **~d** *a.,* sagacious, astute, judicious, (arch. or literary, of blow, thrust, etc.) severe, effective, malicious; **~'ish** *a.,* scolding, bad-tempered. [E]

**shriek. 1.** *n.* Shrill scream or sound. **2.** *v.i. & t.* Make a shriek; **~ (out),** say in shrill tones; **~ (with laughter),** laugh uncontrollably. [N]

**shrĭft** *n.* Shriving (arch.); SHORT *shrift.* [E (SHRIVE)]

**shrīke** *n.* Bird with strong hooked and toothed bill. [E]

**shrĭll. 1.** *a.* (**~'y** *pr.* -l-lĭ). Piercing and high-pitched in sound; (fig.)

sharp, unrestrained. **2.** *v.t. & i.* Utter or sound shrilly. [orig. uncert.]

**shrĭmp. 1.** *n.* Small edible crustacean, pink when boiled, (*pl.* also **~**); diminutive person. **2.** *v.i.* Go catching shrimps.

**shrine** *n.* Tomb or casket containing sacred relics; place hallowed by some memory, association, etc. [E f. L *scrinium* bookcase]

**shrĭnk. 1.** *v.i. & t.* (**shrank; shrunk** *or,* esp. as *a.,* **shru'nken**). Become or make smaller, esp. by action of moisture or heat or cold; recoil, retire, flinch *from,* be averse *from* doing; **~-wrap,** enclose (article) in material that shrinks tightly round it. **2.** *n.* Act of shrinking; shrinkage; (sl.) psychiatrist, 'head-shrinker'. **3. ~age** *n.,* process or degree of shrinking. [E]

**shrive** *v.t.* (**shrove** *pr.* -ōv; **~'n** *pr.* -ĭ'vn). (arch.) Hear confession of, assign penance to, and absolve; submit one*self* for this. [E f. L *scribo* write]

**shrĭ'vel** *v.i. & t.* (‖-ll-). Contract into wrinkled or curled-up state. [perh. N]

**shroud. 1.** *n.* Winding-sheet; something which conceals; (in *pl.*) ropes supporting ship's mast. **2.** *v.t.* Clothe (corpse) for burial; cover or conceal. [E, = garment]

**Shrōve[1]** *n.* **~ Tuesday,** day before Ash Wednesday, on which and the two preceding days (**~-tide**) it was customary to be shriven. [SHRIVE]

**shrōve[2].** See SHRIVE.

**shrŭb** *n.* Woody plant smaller than tree and usu. with separate stems from or near root; **~'ber̄ẙ** *n.,* area planted with shrubs; **~'b̄ẙ** *a.,* of or like shrub(s). [E]

**shrŭg. 1.** *v.t. & i.* (**-gg-**). Slightly and momentarily raise (one's shoulders) to express indifference, helplessness, doubt, etc.; **~ off,** dismiss as unimportant. **2.** *n.* Shrugging movement. [orig. unkn.]

**shrŭnk('en).** See SHRINK.

**\*shŭck. 1.** *n.* Husk, pod, shell; (in *pl.,* as *int.*) expr. disgust or regret. **2.** *v.t.* Remove shucks from. [orig. unkn.]

**shŭ'dder** *v.i.,* & *n.* (Experience) sudden or convulsive shivering or quivering; feel strong repugnance, fear, etc. (*I shudder to think of it*); (have) vibrating motion. [LDu.]

**shŭ'ffle. 1.** *v.t. & i.* Move (esp.

one's feet) with dragging or sliding or difficult motion; keep shifting one's position (lit. or fig.); prevaricate, be evasive; intermingle or rearrange (esp. cards); ~-board, shovelboard; ~ off, remove or get rid of (clothes, responsibility, &c.), esp. clumsily or evasively. 2. *n.* Shuffling action or movement; shuffling dance (double ~, scraping twice with each foot in turn); general change of relative positions. [LG]

**shŭn** *v.t.* (-**nn**-). Keep clear of, avoid, eschew. [E]

**shŭnt. 1.** *v.t.* & *i.* Move (railway train etc.) to another track, esp. to clear line for more important traffic (so ~'er *n.*); ||(of train etc.) be shunted; (fig.) evade (subject), put aside (person). 2. *n.* Act of shunting; (Electr.) conductor joining two points of circuit for diversion of current; (Surg.) alternative path for circulation of blood; (sl.) collision of vehicles. [perh. SHUN]

**shŭsh. 1.** *int.* Hush! 2. *v.i.* & *t.* Call for silence (from), be silent. [imit.]

**shŭt** *v.t.* & *i.* (-**tt**-; **shut**). Move (door, window, lid, etc.) into position to block aperture; shut door etc. of (room, box, eye, etc.); bar access to (place); (of door etc.) become or admit of being closed; catch or pinch (finger, dress, etc.) by shutting something on it; bring (book, hand, telescope, etc.) into folded-up or contracted state; (in *p.p.*, sl.) *be* or *get rid of* (person, thing); ~ down, terminate operation of (factory etc.), (of factory etc.) cease working, whence ~-down *n.*; ~ one's ears, eyes, heart, mind, to, refuse to hear, see, consider, have sympathy for; ~-eye *n.*, (sl.) sleep; ~ in, encircle, enclose, confine; ~ off, stop flow of (water, gas, etc.), separate *from* access etc.; ~ out, exclude, prevent, block; ~ the door on, make impossible; ~ up, close securely, decisively, or permanently, imprison (person), put (thing) away in box etc., (colloq., esp. in *imper.*) stop talking; *shut up shop*; ~ your face, mouth, trap, (vulg.) stop talking; ~'ter, (*n.*, esp. movable cover for window (**put up the ~ters**, cease business for the day or permanently), (Photog.) device that opens and closes lens aperture of camera, (*v.t.*) provide with shutter(s), put up shutter(s) of. [E]

**shŭ'ttle. 1.** *n.* Weaving-implement by which weft-thread is carried between threads of warp; thread-carrier in sewing-machine; train, bus, etc., going to and fro over short route on ~ **service**; spacecraft travelling repeatedly e.g. between earth and space station; ~(**cock**), object struck to and fro in badminton, consisting usu. of rounded piece of cork with feathers on it, (fig.) thing passed back and forth. 2. *v.t.* & *i.* (Cause to) move to and fro like shuttle. [E (SHOOT)]

**shy**[1] *a.*, *v.*, & *n.* **1.** *a.* (~'er or shi'er, ~'est or shi'est, *pr.* -i'-; ~'ly; ~'ness). Self-conscious or uneasy in company, bashful; easily startled, avoiding observation; avoiding company of person, chary of doing, (FIGHT *shy of*); (as *suf.*) showing fear of or distaste for (GUN-, WORK-, *shy*). 2. *v.i.* Start aside in alarm (esp. of horse *at* noise or object, or of person *at*, *away from*, proposal etc.). 3. *n.* Act of shying. [E]

**shy**[2] *v.t.*, & *n.* (colloq.) Fling or throw; a ~ at, a try to hit, get, or achieve. [orig. unkn.]

**Shy'lŏck** *n.* Hard-hearted usurer. [character in Shakespeare]

**shy'ster** *n.* (colloq.) Person, esp. lawyer, who acts unscrupulously or unprofessionally. [orig. unkn.]

**si.** See TE.

**S.I.** *abbr.* international system of units of measurement. [F *Système International*]

**Siamē'se** (-z) *a.* & *n.* (*pl.* same). (Native, language) of *Siam* (Thailand); ~ (**cat**), cream-coloured brown-faced short-haired breed of cat; ~ **twins**, two persons joined together from birth, (fig.) any very closely associated pair. [place]

**sĭb** *n.* Sibling; ~'**ling** *n.*, one of two or more children having one or both parents in common. [E, = akin]

**sĭ'bĭl|ant** *a.* & *n.* (Letter) sounded with a hiss, hissing; ~**ance**, ~**ancy̆**, *ns.* [L]

**sĭ'bling.** See SIB.

**sĭ'bўl** *n.* Pagan prophetess; ~**line** *a.*, uttered by or characteristic of a sibyl, mysteriously prophetic. [F or L *f.* Gk]

**sic** (sĭk) *adv.* (usu. *parenth.*) Thus used, spelt, etc. (confirming, or calling attention to, form of quoted words). [L, = so]

**sice** *n.* 'Six' on dice. [F *sis* six]

**sick**[1] *a.*, *v.*, & *n.* **1.** *a.* Ill, feeling effects of disease, (**fall ~**, become ill; **go** or **report ~**, report oneself as ill); ||vomiting or tending to vomit (AIR*sick*; **look ~**, sl., be unimpressive or discomfited; SEA*sick*); disordered, perturbed, unhappy, disgusted, surfeited or tired *of*, pining *for*, (HOME*sick*; LOVE*sick*); (of humour) finding amusement in, or making fun of, misfortune or macabre things; **~ and tired**, (colloq.) fed up, tired *of*; **~ at heart**, despairing; **~-bay**, place for sick persons; **~-bed**, invalid's bed; ||**~-benefit**, money paid to person absent from work through illness; **~ headache**, headache as in migraine; **~-leave**, leave of absence granted because of illness; **~-list**, list of those who are ill (*on the* **~-*list***, ill); **~-nurse** (caring for the sick); **~-pay** (to employee etc. on sick-leave); **~-room** (ready for, or occupied by, sick person). **2.** *v.t.* **~ (up)**, (colloq.) vomit. **3.** *n.* (colloq.) Vomit. **4.** **~'en** *v.t.* & *i.*, (cause to) become sick, disgusted, despairing, etc.; **~en for**, be in first stages of (illness). [E]

**sick**[2] *v.t.* (usu. in *imper.*) Set upon; **~ him!** etc. (urging dog to attack rat etc.). [dial. var. SEEK]

**si'ckle** *n.* Semicircular-bladed implement used for reaping, lopping, etc.; **~ cell**, sickle-shaped red blood-corpuscle, esp. as found in severe hereditary anaemia. [E]

**si'ckl‖y̆** *a.* (**~iness**). Liable to be ill, of weak health; suggesting sickness, languid, faint, pale; causing ill health; inducing or connected with nausea; mawkish, weakly sentimental; **si'ckn̂ess** *n.*, being ill, disease, vomiting. [SICK[1]]

**side. 1.** *n.* One of the surfaces bounding an object, esp. vertical inner or outer surface or one of those distinguished from top and bottom or front and back or ends (*cube has six sides*; *four*, or *two*, *sides of box*, *drawer*, *house*); either surface of thing regarded as having only two (*both sides of sheet of paper*, *board*, *gramophone record*; BACK*side*); amount of writing filling one side of sheet of paper; one of the lines bounding a triangle, rectangle, etc.; part of person's or animal's body that is on right or left, esp. such part of person's trunk or animal's carcass (**by the ~ of**, close to or compared with; **shake** or

**split** one's **~s**, laugh heartily; **~ by ~**, standing close together, esp. for mutual encouragement); part of object, place, etc., that faces specified direction or that is on observer's right or left; marginal part or area of thing, region nearer or farther than, or to right or left of, a real or imaginary dividing line, (*side of road*, *table*, etc.; **on one ~**, not in the main or central position, aside; **on the** RIGHT, WRONG, *side of*; **on the ~**, as a sideline, *as a side-dish*; SEA*side*); direction (**from all ~s**, **from every ~**, from all directions; **on all ~s**, **on every ~**, in all directions, everywhere); partial aspect of thing, aspect differing from or opposed to other aspects, (*study all sides of the question*; *look on the bright, dark, side of life, things*; **on the high**, *low*, *fat*, etc., **~**, fairly, somewhat; *be on the SAFE side*); (cause represented by, position in company with) one of two sets of opponents in war, politics, games, etc., (**let the ~ down**, fig., frustrate one's colleagues' efforts; NO[1] *side*; OFF*side*); **on the ~ of**, favouring; **take ~s**, support one or other cause); line of descent through one parent (*cousin on my mother's side*); ||(Bill. etc.) spinning motion given to ball by striking it on one side; ||(sl.) assumption of superiority, swagger, (*puts on side*); **~-bet** (additional to the ordinary stakes); **~'board**, table or flat-topped chest for supporting and containing dishes, crockery, cutlery, etc., (in *pl.*, sl.) side-whiskers; **~'burns**, short side-whiskers; **~-car**, small car for passenger(s) attachable to side of motor cycle; **~-dish**, extra food subsidiary to main dish; **~-door**, door at side of building, (fig.) indirect means of access; **~-drum**, small double-headed drum of type orig. hung at drummer's side; **~-effect**, secondary (usu. undesirable) effect; **~-glance**, sideways or brief glance (lit. or fig.); **~-issue**, point that distracts attention from what is most important; *~'kick*, (colloq.) close associate; **~'light**, light from side, light at side of moving ship or at side of front of motor vehicle, (fig.) piece of incidental information; **~'line**, work etc. carried on in addition to one's main activity, (in *pl.*) (space just outside) lines bounding sides of football-pitch, tennis-court, etc., place for spectators as opp. participants; ~**-road**, minor or subsidiary road; ~**-saddle**, (n.) saddle, esp. for woman, made so that rider may have both feet on same side of horse, (adv.) sitting thus on horse; ~**-show**, small show at a fair or exhibition, minor or subsidiary activity or affair; ~**-slip** v.i., & n., skid, move(ment) sideways; ~'**sman**, church official who shows worshippers to seats, takes the collection, etc.; ~**-splitting**, causing violent laughter; ~**-step**, (n.) step sideways, (v.t.) avoid (thus, or fig.); ~**-street**, minor or subsidiary street; ~**-swipe**, (hit with) glancing blow along side, (fig.) indirect or incidental criticism etc.; ~**-track** v.t., shunt into siding, (fig.) divert (person) from his purpose, postpone or evade treatment or consideration of; ~ **view**, profile; \*~'**walk**, pavement at side of road; ~**-whiskers** (growing on cheek); ~ **wind** (from one side). **2.** v.i. Be on same side, take part, with disputant etc. **3.** -sī'dĕd a., having specified number or type of sides; ~'lŏng (-dl-) adv. & a., oblique(ly); ~'**ways** (-dwāz), ~'**wise** (-dwīz), advs. & adjs., to, towards, or from a side; sī'dĭng n., short railway track into which train etc. may be shunted. [E]

sidēr'ĕal a. (~ly). Of, determined or measured by means of, the stars; ~ **day**, time between successive passages of any given star over meridian. [L (sidus sider- star)]

sī'dle v.i. Walk obliquely, move timidly or furtively. [SIDELong]

siege n. (Period of) surrounding and blockading of fortified place (lay ~ to, conduct siege of; raise ~, end it). [F sege seat]

siĕ'nna n. Pigment or its colour of reddish-brown (burnt ~) or brownish-yellow (raw ~). [place]

siĕ'rra n. Long jagged mountain-chain in Spain or Spanish America. [Sp. f. L serra saw]

siĕ'sta n. Afternoon nap or rest, esp. in hot countries. [Sp. f. L sexta (hora) sixth (hour)]

sieve (sĭv). **1.** n. Utensil with network or perforated bottom through which liquids or fine particles can pass while solid or coarser matter is retained; head, memory, like a ~, poor memory. **2.** v.t. Sift. [E]

sĭft v.t. & i. Separate with or make pass through sieve; sprinkle (sugar etc.) from perforated spoon etc.; (of snow etc.) fall as if from sieve; subject (facts, evidence, etc.) to close scrutiny or analysis. [E]

sigh (sī). **1.** n. Long deep audible breath expressing sadness, weariness, longing, relief, etc.; act of making this; sound resembling it. **2.** v.i. & t. Make a sigh; express with sighs; yearn for (person or thing desired or lost). [E]

sight (-īt). **1.** n. Faculty of seeing by response of brain to action of light on eyes (know by ~, be familiar with appearance of); seeing or being seen (at first ~, on first glimpse or impression; at or on ~, as soon as person or thing is seen; catch ~ of, begin to see or be aware of; get, have, a ~ of, manage to see; lose ~ of, cease to see or be aware of); way of regarding, opinion, (found favour in his sight); range of or region open to vision (in ~, visible, imminent; in or within ~ of, so as to see or be seen from; out of ~, not visible, sl. marvellous; out of my ~!, rhet. order to depart; out of ~ out of mind, we forget those absent); thing seen, visible, or worth seeing (a ~ for sore eyes, person or thing one is glad to see; ~ unseen, without previous inspection); (in pl.) noteworthy or attractive features of town etc. (see the sights); a (perfect etc.) ~, (colloq.) person or thing of ridiculous, repulsive, dishevelled, etc., appearance; (colloq.) a great quantity (will cost a sight of money; he's a sight too clever); (device for assisting) precise aim with gun or observation with optical instrument (set one's ~s on, fig. aim at); ~**-reading** (of music at sight); ~**-screen**, (Crick.) large white screen placed near boundary in line with wicket to help batsman see ball; ~'**seer** (-sēer), ~'**seeing**, (person) visiting sights of town etc. **2.** v.t. Get sight of (land, game, etc.) esp. by coming near; observe presence of (aircraft, unidentified flying object, unusual species, etc.); aim (gun etc.) with sights. **3.** ~'lĕss a., blind; ~'lў a. (~liness), attractive to the sight, not unsightly. [E (SEE¹)]

sī'gma n. Eighteenth Gk letter (Σ, σ or, when final, ς) = s. [L f. Gk]

sign (sīn). **1.** n. Mark traced on

surface etc. (~ **of the cross,** cross traced with finger(s) in the air, or between forehead and breast and across breast); symbol, word, etc., representing phrase, idea, instruction, etc., (**positive, plus, ~, +**; **negative, minus, ~, −**; **road, traffic, ~,** displayed to give information or order to road-users); indication or suggestion or symptom *of* or *that* (*violence is a sign of weakness* or *that one is weak*; **hands up in sign of** *surrender*; ~ **of the times,** thing showing the current state of affairs); miracle evidencing supernatural power, portent; ~('**board**), device, often painted on a board, displayed by shopkeeper etc.; motion or gesture used instead of words to convey information, demand, etc., (*gave me a sign to withdraw*); one of the 12 divisions of the zodiac; ~-**language,** series of signs used esp. by deaf or dumb people for communication; ~**-painter,** ~-**writer,** (of signboards); ~'**post,** (*n.*) post etc. showing directions of roads, (*v.t.*) provide with signpost(s), lit. or fig. **2.** *v.t.* & *i.* Write one's name, initials, or recognized mark on (letter, petition, picture, etc.) to show that one is the author etc. or that one accepts or agrees with the contents; write (one's name) on document etc. for such purpose; ~ (**on, up**), engage or acknowledge being engaged for undertaking to which person binds himself by signature; communicate by gesture; ~ **away,** convey or relinquish (property, rights, etc.) by signing deed etc.; ~ **off,** end contract, work, etc. (of), indicate end of broadcast etc.; ~ **on,** indicate start of broadcast etc. [F f. L *signum*]

**si'gnal** *n., v.,* & *a.* **1.** *n.* Visual or audible (esp. prearranged) sign conveying information or direction esp. to person(s) at a distance, message made up of such signs, (*give, receive, the signal for retreat*); device on railway giving instructions or warnings to train-drivers etc. (*train stopped at the red signal*); event which causes immediate activity (*the earthquake was the signal for panic*); (Electr.) transmitted (sequence of) impulse(s) or radio wave(s); (Bridge) prearranged mode of bidding or play to convey information to one's partner; ∥~-**box,** building from which railway signals

are controlled; ~**man** (responsible for display of naval, railway, etc., signals). **2.** *v.i.* & *t.* Make signal(s) (to); transmit (order, information) by signal(s); announce (event, *that*) by signal(s); direct (person *to do*) by signal(s). **3.** *a.* (~**ly**). Remarkably good or bad, noteworthy. **4.** ~**ize** *v.t.,* make noteworthy or remarkable; ~**ler** *n.,* signalman. [F f. L (prec.)]

**si'gnatory** *n.* & *a.* (Party, esp. State) that has signed an agreement, esp. a treaty. [L (prec.)]

**si'gnature** *n.* Person's name, initials, or mark used in signing; act of signing; (**key, time**) ~, (Mus.) indication of key or tempo following clef; (Print.) letter or figure placed at foot of one or more pages of each sheet of book, such sheet after folding; ~ **tune,** tune used esp. in broadcasting to announce a particular programme, performer, etc.; **si'gnet** *n.,* small seal esp. one set in finger-ring (**si'gnet-ring**).

**si'gnif|y** *v.t.* & *i.* Mean, have as meaning, ('*D.D.*') signifies '*Doctor of Divinity*'); communicate, make known, (*he signified his agreement*); be a sign or indication or presage of (*lunar halo signifies rain*); be of importance (*it doesn't signify*); ~**icance** (-ĭ'f-) *n.,* (real) meaning, importance; ~**icant** (-ĭ'f-) *a.,* having a (esp. suggestive or noteworthy) meaning, important; ~**ica'tion** *n.,* meaning (esp. *of* word etc.); ~**icative** (-ĭ'f-) *a.,* significant, serving as evidence *of*. [F f. L (prec.)]

**signor** (*pl.* **signori**), **signora, signorina,** (sē'nyŏr, sēnyŏr'ē; sēnyŏr'a; sēnyerē'na) *ns.* (Titles used of or to Italians corresponding to) Mr. or sir, Mrs. or madam, Miss or madam (to unmarried woman). [It. f. L SENIOR]

**Sikh** (sēk, sĭk) *n.* Member of Indian monotheistic sect. [Hindi, = disciple]

**si'lage** *n.,* & *v.t.* Ensilage, ensile. [ENSILAGE]

**si'lence. 1.** *n.* Absence of sound, abstinence from speech or noise, taciturnity, avoidance of mentioning a thing, betraying a secret, etc.; **break** ~, speak; **in** ~, without speech or other sound; **keep** ~, not speak; **S~!** (order to cease from speech or noise); ~ **is golden,** it is often best to say nothing. **2.** *v.t.* Make silent, esp. by force or superior argument. **3.** ~**r** *n.,* device for reducing noise of gun, ||vehicle engine, door, etc.; **si'lent** *a.*, making or accompanied by little or no sound or speech, (**silent majority**, those of moderate opinions who rarely make themselves heard; \***silent partner**, = SLEEP*ing partner*), (of letter) written but not pronounced, e.g. *b* in *doubt*, (of film) without sound-track. [F f. L (*sileo* be silent)]

**silhouê'tte** (-lŏŏ-). **1.** *n.* Picture of person or thing showing outline only, all inside the outline being usu. black, on white ground or cut out in paper; appearance of person or thing as seen against light so that outline only is distinguishable (**in ~**, so seen or placed). **2.** *v.t.* Represent or (usu. in *pass.*) show in silhouette. [person]

**si'lic|a** *n.* Mineral occurring as quartz and as main constituent of sandstone and other rocks; **~āte** *n.*, compound of metal(s), silicon, and oxygen; **~eous, ~ious**, (-ǐ'shŭs) *adjs.*; **~on** *n.*, non-metallic element occurring in silica and silicates; **~ōne** *n.*, one of many organic compounds of silicon, used esp. in polishes, paints, lubricants, etc.; **~ō'sǐs** *n.* (*pl.* **~ō'ses** *pr.* -ēz), lung disease caused by inhaling dust containing silica. [L *silex* -*lic*- flint]

**silk** *n.* Fine strong soft lustrous fibre composing silkworms' cocoons, thread or cloth made from this, (**artificial ~**, rayon; ||**take ~**, become K.C. or Q.C. and so have right to wear silk gown); ||(colloq.) K.C. or Q.C.; (in *pl.*) kinds or garments of such cloth, esp. as worn by jockey in horse-owner's colours; (*attrib.*) made of silk; **~ hat**, tall cylindrical hat covered with silk plush; **~-screen printing**, = SCREEN-*printing*; **~'-worm**, caterpillar which spins cocoon of silk; **~'en** *a.*, of or resembling silk, soft or smooth or lustrous; **~'y̆** *a.* (**~ily, ~iness**), like silk in softness, smoothness, etc., suave. [E f. L *sericus* f. Gk *Seres* an oriental people]

**sill** *n.* Slab of wood, stone, etc., at foot of window, doorway, etc. [E]

**si'llabŭb.** See SYLLABUB.

**si'lly̆. 1.** *a.* (**-ily, -iness**). Foolish, imprudent, unwise; weak-minded; (Crick., of fielder or his position) very close to batsman; **~billy**, (colloq.) foolish person; ||**the ~ season**, summer holiday period

when newspapers lack important news. **2.** *n.* (colloq.) Foolish person. [E, = happy]

**si'lō** *n.* (*pl.* **~s**). Pit or airtight structure in which green crops are stored for fodder; tower or pit for storage of cement, ||grain, etc.; underground place where guided missile is kept ready for firing. [Sp. f. L]

**silt. 1.** *n.* Sediment deposited by water in channel, harbour, etc. **2.** *v.t. & i.* Block or be blocked (*up*) with silt; **~ā'tion** *n.* [perh. Scand.]

**Sĭlū'rian** *a. & n.* (Of) Palaeozoic period or system above Ordovician and below Devonian. [*Silures*, British tribe]

**si'lvan, sy̆'-,** *a.* Of the woods; having woods, rural. [F or L (*silva* a wood)]

**si'lver** *n., a., & v.* **1.** *n.* White lustrous precious metal; coins, cutlery, utensils, etc., made of or looking like this; colour of silver; = *silver medal*. **2.** *a.* Of, coloured like, silver (**born with a ~ spoon in** one's **mouth**, destined to be wealthy; **every cloud has a ~ lining**, every misfortune has its consolations). **3.** *v.t. & i.* Coat or plate with silver; provide (mirror-glass) with backing of tin amalgam etc.; give silvery appearance to; (of hair) turn grey or white. **4.** *silver* AGE; ||**~ band** (playing silver-plated brass instruments); **~ birch**, common birch with silver-coloured bark; **~-fish**, silver-coloured fish, silvery wingless insect; **~ fox**, (fox with) black white-tipped fur; **~ gilt**, gilded silver, imitation gilding of yellow lacquer over silver leaf; **~-grey**, lustrous grey; **~ jubilee**, 25th anniversary; **~ medal**, medal of silver usu. as 2nd prize; **~ paper**, tin foil; **~ plate**, cutlery, utensils, etc., of silver, material plated with silver; **~-plate** *v.t.*, plate with silver; **~ sand** (fine pure kind for gardening); ||**~side**, upper (best) side of round of beef; **~smith**, worker in silver; *silver* WEDDING. **5.** **~y̆** *a.* (**~iness**), resembling silver, esp. in whiteness or lustre. [E]

**si'lvĭcŭlture, sy̆'-,** *n.* Cultivation of forest trees. [F. f. L *silva* forest, CULTURE]

**si'mian** *a. & n.* (Resembling) ape or monkey. [L *simia* ape]

**si'mĭl|ar** *a.* Like, alike; having resemblance (*to*); of same kind, nature, shape, or amount; ~**ă'rĭtў** *n.*; ~**ē** *n.*, writer's or speaker's comparison of one thing with another as illustration or ornament, use of such comparisons; **simi'lĭtude** *n.*, guise, outward appearance, (expression of) comparison. [F or L (*similis* like)]

**sĭ'mmer. 1.** *v.i.* & *t.* Be or keep bubbling or boiling gently; (fig.) be in state of suppressed anger or laughter; ~ **down**, become less agitated. **2.** *n.* Simmering condition. [perh. imit.]

‖**sĭ'mnel** *n.* ~ (**cake**), rich ornamental cake baked esp. at Easter, Christmas, and Mid-Lent, often with marzipan layer and decoration. [F f. L or Gk]

**simon-pūr'e** *a.* Absolutely pure, genuine. [character in play]

**sĭ'monў** *n.* Buying or selling of ecclesiastical preferment. [F f. L (*Simon Magus*; see Acts 8:18)]

**simoō'm** *n.* Hot dry dust-laden desert wind. [Arab.]

**sĭ'mper. 1.** *v.i.* & *t.* Smile in silly or affected way; express by or with simpering. **2.** *n.* Such smile. [orig. unkn.]

**sĭ'mple** *a.* (~**r**, ~**st**). Not complicated or elaborate or involved or highly developed or sophisticated, plain, natural, (**the ~ life**, living without luxuries and artificial amusements); absolute, unqualified, straightforward, (*tell the simple truth*; *hold in* FEE *simple*); not compound, consisting of or involving only one element, operation, etc., (~ **fracture**, of bone only; *simple* INTEREST, SENTENCE); easily understood or done, presenting no difficulty, (*a simple task*; *written in simple English*); foolish, ignorant, gullible, feeble-minded, (*am not so simple as to suppose*); ~**-minded**, unsophisticated, ingenuous, feeble-minded; ~**ton** (-pelt-) *n.*, foolish, gullible, or half-witted person; **simpli'cĭtў** *n.*, fact or quality of being simple (**be simplicity itself**, be extremely easy to do etc.); **simpli'fў** *v.t.*, make simple(r); **simplĭfĭcā'tion** *n.*; **sĭ'mplĭsm** *n.*, unjustifiable simplification of problem etc., affected simplicity; **simpli'stic** *a.*; **sĭ'mplў** *adv.*, in simple manner, absolutely, without doubt, merely, (*he simply doesn't understand*). [F f. L *simplus*]

**sĭ'mŭl|āte** *v.t.* Pretend to be, have, or feel, imitate, counterfeit; imitate conditions of (situation etc.) e.g. for training; **simŭlā'crum** *n.* (*pl.* -**cra**), (shadowy or deceptive) likeness of something; ~**ā'tion**, ~**ātor**, *ns.* [L (SIMILAR)]

**simŭltā'nĕous** *a.* Occurring or operating at the same time (*with*); **simŭltănē'ĭtў** *n.* [L (*simul* at the same time)]

**sĭn. 1.** *n.* Transgression, esp. conscious, against divine law or principles of morality (*ugly etc.* **as ~**, colloq., exceedingly; **deadly** or **mortal ~**, such as causes death of the soul or is fatal to salvation; **for** one's ~**s**, joc., as judgement or punishment on one; **live in ~**, colloq., cohabit without being married; ORIGINAL *sin*; **the seven deadly ~s**, pride, covetousness, lust, anger, gluttony, envy, sloth); offence against good taste, propriety, etc. **2.** *v.i.* (-**nn-**). Commit sin, offend *against*. **3.** ~**'ful** *a.* (-**lly**), (of person) full of sin, wicked, (of act) involving or characterized by sin; ~**'ner** *n.* (also joc. = rascal etc.). [E]

**since** *prep., conj.,* & *adv.* **1.** *prep.* Through or in period between (specified time or event) and time present or being dealt with (*has happened, been going on, since 1960*; *have eaten nothing since yesterday*). **2.** *conj.* From the time when, during the time after that when (*what have you been doing since we met?*); for the reason that, because, (*since that is so, there is no more to be said*). **3.** *adv.* Since that time or event (*tree has since been cut down*; *have not seen her since*); ago (*happened many years since*). [E, = after that]

**sincēr'e** *a.* (~**r**, ~**st**). Free from pretence or deceit, the same in reality as in appearance or profession, genuine, honest, frank; ~**lў** (-**ēr'lĭ**) *adv.*, in sincere manner (*yours* ~**lў**, customary formula for closing letter to friend or acquaintance); **sincē'r-ĭtў** *n.* [L]

**sĭ'ncĭput** *n.* Head from forehead to crown (cf. *occiput*). [L (SEMI-, *caput* head)]

**sīne** *n.* (Math.) Ratio of side opposite angle (in right-angled triangle) to hypotenuse. [L SINUS]

**sĭ'necūre** *n.* Position that requires little or no work but usu. yields profit or honour. [L *sine cura* without care]

*sine die* (sīnī dī'ē, sĭnā dē'ā) *adv.*
(Of business adjourned indefinitely)
with no appointed date. [L]

*sine qua non* (sĭnā kwah nō'n) *n.*
Indispensable condition or qualification. [L, = without which not]

**si′new** *n.* (Piece of) tough fibrous
tissue joining muscle to bone; (in
*pl.*) muscles, bodily strength; (fig.)
that which strengthens or sustains
(**the ~s of war,** money); ~**ў** *a.*
(~iness), having strong sinews. [E]

**si′nful.** See SIN.

**sing** *v.i.* & *t.* (**sang; sung**). Utter
(words or sounds) in tuneful succession, esp. according to set tune
(~ **the praises of,** praise enthusiastically or continually); utter or produce (song, TUNE); (sl.) act as informer; (of wind, kettle, etc.) make
humming, buzzing, or ringing
sound; (of ears) be affected with
ringing or buzzing sound; put *to
sleep* etc. with singing; ~ (**of**),
celebrate (hero, event, etc.) in verse
or song; ~ **out,** shout; ~′**song** *a.* &
*n.,* (uttered with) monotonous
rhythm or cadence, ‖session of informal singing; ~ **small,** cease
boasting; ~ **up,** sing (more) loudly.
[E]

**singe** (-nj) **1.** *v.t.* & *i.* (~**ing** *pr.*
-njĭ-). Burn superficially or lightly,
burn off tips or ends of (hair etc.)
**2.** *n.* Superficial burn; act of singeing.
[E]

**Singhalese.** See SINHALESE.

**si′ngle** (-nggl) *a., n.,* & *v.* **1.** *a.*
(-gly). One only, not double or
multiple, united, undivided, designed for or used or done by one
person etc., solitary; not married;
taken separately (*every single thing*);
‖(of ticket) valid for one journey
only, not return; (w. neg. or interrog.) even one (*did not see a single
person*); (of flower) having only one
set of petals; ~**breasted** (of coat
etc.) with only one set of buttons,
not overlapping; *single* COMBAT,
ENTRY, FILE²; ~**handed** *a.* & *adv.,*
(done etc.) with one hand or without
help from another person; ~**minded,** having or intent on only one
purpose; ~**wicket,** cricket with only
one batsman at a time. **2.** *n.* Single
ticket, issue of journal, etc.; ‖£1 or
*\$1 note; hit for one run in cricket;
gramophone record with one piece
of music etc. on each side; (usu. in
*pl.*) game with one player on each

side. **3.** *v.t.* Choose *out* for special
attention etc. **4.** ‖~**t** (-glĭt) *n.,* vest,
sleeveless garment worn under or
instead of shirt; ~**ton** (-gelt-) *n.,*
single person or thing, esp. player's
only card of a suit [F f. L *singulus*]

**si′ngul|ar** (-ngg-). **1.** *a.* Unique,
much beyond the average, extraordinary; eccentric, strange; (Gram.)
denoting one person or thing;
~**ă′rĭtў** **2.** *n.* (Gram.) Singular
word or number. [F f. L (prec.)]

**Sĭnhalē′se** (-z; *or* -na-), **Singha-
lē′se** (-nggalē′z), *a.* & *n.* (*pl.* same).
(Member, language) of an Aryan
people from N. India now forming
majority of population of Sri Lanka.
[Skr.]

**si′nĭster** *a.* Suggestive of evil,
looking malignant or villainous;
wicked, criminal; of evil omen;
(Her.) on left-hand side (i.e. to
observer's right) of shield etc., opp.
*dexter.* [F or L, = left]

**sink. 1.** *v.i.* & *t.* (**sank, sunk;
sunk** or, as *a.,* **su′nken**). Fall or
come slowly downwards, decline,
disappear below horizon or surface
of liquid, settle down, droop, gradually expire or perish or cease, (*sun sank
in the west; sink into degradation, the
grave, sleep, a chair;* ~ **or swim,** *v.i.*
fail or succeed, *adv.* at the risk of
complete failure or destruction); (of
ship etc.) go to bottom of sea etc.;
cause or allow to sink (*sink the ship;
dog sank its teeth into my leg*); inlay;
conceal, ignore, forget, (*let us sink our
differences*); dig (well), bore (shaft);
engrave (die); invest (money) so that
it is not readily realizable or is lost;
cause (ball) to enter pocket at
billiards, hole at golf, etc., achieve
this by (stroke etc.); cause failure
of (plan etc.) or discomfiture of
(person); penetrate, make way, *in*
or *into*; be absorbed *in* or *into* mind
etc. (*paused to let his words sink in*).
**2.** *n.* Fixed basin with outflow pipe,
esp. with water supply for washing-
up etc. (KITCHEN *sink*); place where
foul liquid collects; (fig.) place of
rampant vice etc. **3.** ~**′er** *n.,* (esp.)
weight used to sink fishing- or
sounding-line (HOOK, *line, and sinker*);
~**′ing** *n.,* (esp.) internal bodily
sensation caused by apprehension or
hunger; ~**ing-fund,** money set
aside for gradual repayment of debt;
**su′nken** *a.,* (esp., of cheeks, eyes,
etc.) shrunken, hollow; **sunken**

**garden,** garden below ground level of surroundings; **sunk fence** (formed by, or along bottom of, ditch). [E]

**si′nner.** See SIN.

**Sinn Fein** (shĭn fā′n) *n.* Political movement and party advocating independent republican government for the whole of Ireland. [Ir., = we ourselves]

**Sī′nŏ-** *in comb.* Chinese (and) (*Sino-American*; *Sinophobia*); **sĭno′lo-gist, sĭ′nōlŏgue** (-g), *ns.,* person skilled in **sĭnŏ′logȳ** *n.,* study of China. [Gk *Sinai* the Chinese]

**sī′nter** *n.,* & *v.t. & i.* (Form into) solid coalesced by heating. [G (CINDER)]

**sī′nŭ|ous** *a.* With many curves, undulating, meandering; ~**ŏ′sĭtȳ** *n.,* (esp.) bend in stream etc. [F or L (foll.)]

**sī′nus** *n.* Cavity of bone or tissue, esp. in skull communicating with nostrils; ~**ī′tĭs** *n.* [L, = recess, curve] **-sion.** See -ION.

**Siou|x** (sōō) *n.* (*pl.* same) & *a.* (Member, language) of a group of N. Amer. Indian tribes; ~**an** (sōō′an) *a.* [F (native name)]

**sip. 1.** *v.t. & i.* (-pp-). Drink in repeated small mouthfuls or spoonfuls. **2.** *n.* Small mouthful of liquid; act of taking this. [perh. var. SUP[1]]

**sī′phon. 1.** *n.* Pipe or tube shaped like inverted V or U with unequal legs to convey liquid from container to lower level by atmospheric pressure; bottle from which aerated water is forced out by pressure of gas. **2.** *v.t. & i.* Conduct or flow (as) through siphon. [F or L f. Gk]

**sī′ppĕt** *n.* = *croûton.* [dim. SOP]

**sĭr** *n.* used as voc. to man superior in rank or age, or to whom one wishes to show respect (*please sir, may I go now?*; *here is your change, sir*; *dinner is served, sir*); used as voc. to inferior who is being rebuked (*you shall pay for this, sir!*); (*Sir*) used as titular prefix to name of knight or baronet (*Sir John* or *J. Moore*; *Sir John*); (**Dear**) **Sir(s)** (words used to begin formal letter); (colloq.) person addressed as 'sir' (esp. schoolmaster) or (*S-*) person with title of 'Sir'. [foll.]

**sīre. 1.** *n.* Male parent of animal, esp. stallion kept for breeding; (arch.) used as voc. to king, father, or other respected man. **2.** *v.t.* (Esp. of stallion) beget. [F, f. L SENIOR]

**sĭr′en** *n.* (Device for making) loud prolonged sound for warning, information, etc.; (Gk Myth.) any of several women or winged creatures whose singing lured unwary sailors on to rocks; dangerously fascinating woman, temptress; (*attrib.*) irresistibly tempting; **sīrē′nian** *a. & n.,* (member) of an order of large aquatic herbivorous mammals. [F f. L f. Gk]

**sĭr′loin** *n.* ‖Upper and choicer part of loin of beef; *rump steak. [F (SUR-[2], LOIN)]

**sĭrŏ′ccŏ** *n.* (*pl.* ~s). Hot moist wind in S. Europe. [F f. It. f. Arab.]

**sĭr′rah** (-a) *n.* (arch. derog., as voc.) Sir. [SIR]

***si′rup.** See SYRUP.

**sĭs** *n.* (colloq.) Sister. [abbr.]

**sī′sal** *n.* Fibre from leaves of agave. [place]

**sĭs′kin** *n.* Small song-bird. [Du.]

**sĭ′ssȳ** *n. & a.* (Typical of) effeminate or cowardly person. [SIS]

**sĭ′ster** *n.* Daughter of same parent(s) (HALF-*sister*); close woman friend; female fellow member of class or sect or human race; member of sisterhood (**S~ of Mercy,** member of religious order engaged in teaching, nursing, etc.); ‖female hospital nurse in authority over others; ‖(colloq.) any female nurse; (*attrib.*) of same type, design, origin, etc., (*sister nations, ship, university*); ~**-in--law,** one's husband's or wife's sister, one's brother's wife; ~**hŏŏd** *n.,* relationship (as) of sisters, society of women bound by monastic vows or devoting themselves to religious or charitable work; ~**lȳ** *a.* (~**liness**). [E]

**Sĭsȳphē′an** *a.* (Of toil) endless and fruitless as that of Sisyphus (whose task in Hades was to push uphill a stone that at once rolled down again). [L f. Gk]

**sit. 1.** *v.i. & t.* (-tt-; **sat,** arch. **sate**). Take or be in a position in which body is supported more or less upright by buttocks resting on ground, raised seat, etc.; cause to sit, place in sitting position; keep or have one's seat on (horse etc.); be engaged in occupation (e.g. eating) in which sitting position is usual; (of parliament, court, etc.) be in session; (of birds and some animals) rest with (hind) legs bent and body close to ground or perch; remain on nest to hatch eggs; be in more or less permanent position or condition; (of clothes etc.) fit, suit, hang; ~ **(in)**, act as baby-sitter; undergo or be candidate for (examination etc.), ~ **at** person's feet, be his pupil; ~ **back**, relax one's efforts; ~ **down**, sit after standing, cause to sit, suffer tamely (*under* humiliation etc.); ~- -*down* a., (of meal) eaten sitting; ~-*down strike* (in which workers refuse to leave their place of work); ~ **for**, pose for (portrait etc.), be candidate for (examination etc.), be member of Parliament etc. for (constituency); ~ **heavy on**, oppress, burden; ~ **in**, occupy place as protest; ~-*in* n., such protest; ~ **in judgement**, assume right of judging others, be censorious (*on*, *over*, *others*); ~ **in on**, be present as guest etc. at (meeting); ~ **on**, be member of (committee etc.), hold session or inquiry concerning, (colloq.) delay action about, (sl.) repress or rebuke or snub; *sit on the* FENCE; ~ **out**, take no part in (something, esp. particular dance), sit outdoors, stay till end of (performance, ordeal, etc.); ~ **tight**, (colloq.) remain firmly in one's place, not yield; ~ **up**, rise from lying to sitting position, sit erect without lolling, not go to bed (until later than usual time), (colloq.) become interested, surprised, aroused, etc.; ~ **upon**, = *sit on*; ~-*upon* n., (colloq.) buttocks; *sit* **well on**, suit, fit. 2. ~**ter** n., (esp.) person sitting for portrait, baby-sitter, (sl.) easy catch or shot; ~**ting**, (*n.*, esp.) time for which person, assembly, etc., sits continuously (~**ting-room**, a room for sitting in, space enough to accommodate seated persons), (*a.*, esp. of animal, bird, etc.) not running or flying; ~**ting duck**, **target**, person or thing easily attacked; *sitting* PRETTY; ~**ting tenant**, one already occupying house etc. [E]

**si'tar** (*or* -ar´) n. Long-necked Indian guitar-like instrument. [Hindi]

**si'tcom** n. (colloq.) Situation comedy. [abbr.]

**site. 1.** n. Ground on which town or building stood, stands, or is to stand; place of or for specified activity (*camping, caravan, launching, site*). **2.** v.t. Locate, place. [AF, or L *situs*]

**si'tter, si'tting.** See SIT 2.

**si'tu|āte** v.t. (usu. in *p.p.*), also arch. ~**ate** a.) Put in (specified) position or circumstances; ~**ā'tion** n., place and its surroundings, set of circumstances, state of affairs, condition, employee's position or job; ~**ation comedy**, broadcast comedy involving same characters in series of episodes; ~**ā'tional** a. [L *situo* (SITE)]

**six** n. & a. NUMERAL (**at ~es and sevens**, in confusion or disagreement; **it is ~ of one and half-a--dozen of the other**, difference is merely nominal; **hit** or **knock for ~**, colloq., utterly surprise or defeat); *~-**gun**, -**shooter**, 6-chambered revolver; ||~**pence**, sum of 6p., (silver coin worth) 6d.; ||~**penny**, costing or worth 6p. or 6d.; ~**'er** n., leader of group of 6 Brownies or Cubs; ~**fōld** a. & adv.; ~**tee'n(th)** (*or* si´-), ~**th**, adjs. & ns., NUMERALS (~**th form**, highest form in secondary school; *sixth* SENSE); ~**'thly** adv., ~**tieth**, ~**'ty**, adjs. & ns., NUMERALS; ~**ty-four (thousand) dollar question**, difficult and crucial question. [E]

**size. 1.** n. Relative bigness, dimensions, magnitude, (**be the ~ of**, be as big as; **cut down to ~**, fig., show true (un)importance of; **of a ~**, having the same size; OUT*size*; **the ~ of it**, colloq., the truth of a matter; **try thing for ~**, see if it fits, lit. or fig.); one of the (numbered) classes into which similar garments are divided according to size (*takes size 7 in shoes*; *is three sizes too big*); gelatinous solution used in glazing paper, stiffening textiles, etc. **2.** v.t. Sort in sizes or according to size; treat (paper, textiles, etc.) with size; ~ **up**, estimate size of, (colloq.) form judgement of (person etc.); ~**'able** (-za-) a., of (fairly) large size; ~**d** (-zd) a., (esp., in comb.) of specified size (*good-, under-, -sized*). [ASSIZE]

**si'zzle** v.i., & n. (Make) sound (as) of frying; (colloq.) (be in) state of great heat, excitement, etc. [imit.]

**S.J.** abbr. Society of Jesus.

**sjä'mbŏk** (sh-) n. (S. Afr.) Rhinoceros-hide whip. [Afrik. f. Malay f. Urdu]

**skald.** See SCALD².

**skāte¹** n. (*pl.* ~, ~**s**). Kind of RAY². [N]

**skāte². 1.** n. One of pair of (boots with attached) steel blades (or sets of rollers on **roller-~**), enabling wearer to glide over ice (or other surface); **get** one's **~s on**, (sl.) make haste; **~'board**, short narrow board on roller-skate wheels allowing quick movement along pavement etc. **2.** *v.i.* & *t.* Move, perform (specified figure), on skates (**~ on thin ice**, deal with subject needing tactful treatment); pass lightly *over* (esp. fig.); **ska'ting-rink**, (place with) specially-prepared surface for skating. [Du. *schaats* f. F]

**\*skāte³** *n.* (sl.) (**Cheap**) **~**, contemptible or dishonest person. [orig. uncert.]

**skĕdă'ddle.** (colloq.) **1.** *v.i.* Depart quickly. **2.** *n.* Hurried departure. [orig. unkn.]

**skeet** *n.* Shooting sport in which clay target is thrown from trap to simulate flight of bird. [N (SHOOT)]

**skein** (-ān) *n.* Loosely coiled bundle of yarn or thread; flock of wild geese etc. in flight; (fig.) tangle, confusion. [F *escaigne*]

**skĕ'lĕton** *n.* Hard framework (e.g. bones, cartilage, shell, or wood) of person or animal or plant; dried bones of person or animal fixed in same relative positions as in life (**~ at the feast**, something that spoils one's pleasure; **~in the ||cupboard** or **\*closet**, discreditable or humiliating fact kept secret); very thin person or animal; remaining part of something after life or usefulness is gone; outline sketch, epitome; framework or essential part of anything; (*attrib.*) having only the essential or minimum number of persons, parts, etc., (*skeleton crew, plan*); **~ key** (fitting many locks); **skĕ'lĕtal** *a.* [L f. Gk]

**skĕp.** See SKIP²; **\*skĕ'ptic**, see SCEPTIC.

**skĕ'rry** *n.* Reef, rocky island. [N]

**skĕtch. 1.** *n.* Preliminary, rough, slight, or unfinished drawing or painting; rough draft or general outline; short usu. humorous play; short descriptive piece of writing; **~-block, -book**, pad of drawing-paper; **~-map** (with outlines but few details). **2.** *v.t.* & *i.* Make or give sketch of; draw sketches; **~ (in, out)**, indicate briefly or in outline. **3. ~'y** *a.* (**~ily**, **~iness**), like a sketch, unsubstantial or imperfect esp. through haste. [Du. *schets* or G *skizze* ult. f. Gk *schedios* extempore]

**skew** *a.*, *n.*, & *v.* **1.** *a.* Set askew, oblique, distorted; **||~-whi'ff**, (colloq.) askew. **2.** *n.* Slant (**on the ~**, askew). **3.** *v.t.* & *i.* Make skew; distort; move obliquely. [F (ESCHEW)]

**skew'bald** (-awld) *a.* & *n.* (Animal, esp. horse) with irregular patches of white and another colour. [orig. uncert.]

**skew'er.** **1.** *n.* Long pin designed for holding meat compactly together while cooking. **2.** *v.t.* Fasten together or pierce (as) with skewer.

**ski** (skē). **1.** *n.* (*pl.* **~s**, **~**). One of pair of long narrow pieces of wood etc. usu. pointed and curved upwards at front, fastened under feet for travelling over snow; similar device under vehicle; WATER-*ski*; **~ boots**, **pants**, etc., (for wear when skiing); **~-jump**, (jump made from) steep slope levelling off before sharp drop to allow skier to leap through the air; **~-lift**, device for carrying skiers up slope, usu. on seats hung from overhead cable; **~-run**, slope suitable for skiing. **2.** *v.i.* (**~'d**, **~ed**, *pr.* skēd). Travel on skis; **~'er** *n.* [N]

**skĭd. 1.** *n.* Piece of wood etc. serving as support, fender, etc. (**on the ~s**, colloq. about to be discarded or defeated; **put the ~s under**, hasten to downfall); braking device, esp. wooden or metal shoe on wheel; runner beneath aircraft for use when landing; act of skidding; **~-lid**, (sl.) crash-helmet; **||~-pan**, slippery surface prepared for vehicle-drivers to practise control of skidding; **\*~ row**, district frequented by vagrants, alcoholics, etc. **2.** *v.i.* & *t.* (**-dd-**). (Of vehicle etc.) slide esp. sideways or obliquely on slippery road etc.; cause (vehicle) to skid; support, protect, check, with a skid. [orig. unkn.]

**skier.** See SKI.

**skĭff** *n.* Light rowing or sculling boat. [F *esquif* (SHIP)]

**skĭll** *n.* Expertness, practised ability, facility *in* an action or in do-*ing* or *to* do something; **ski'lful**, **\*~'ful,** *a.* (**-lly**), having or showing skill; **~ed** (-ld) *a.*, skilful, (of worker) highly trained or experienced, (of work) requiring skill or special training. [N, = difference]

**ski'llĕt** *n.* ||Small metal cooking-pot with long handle and usu. legs; **\*frying-pan. [F]

**skĭm** *v.t.* & *i.* (**-mm-**). Take cream or scum from surface of (liquid), take (cream etc.) from or *off* surface of liquid; keep touching lightly or nearly touching (surface) in passing over; go thus *along* or *over* surface, glide along; read or look at cursorily; ∼ **milk** (from which cream has been skimmed). [F (SCUM)]

**skimp** *v.t.* & *i.* Supply (person etc.) with or use meagre or insufficient amount of (food, money, material, etc.); ∼**'y** *a.* (∼**ily**, ∼**iness**), meagre, not ample. [cf. SCRIMP]

**skin. 1.** *n.* Flexible continuous covering of human or animal body (**be** ∼ **and bone**, be very thin); **by the** ∼ **of** one's **teeth**, by a narrow margin; **get under** person's ∼, colloq., interest or annoy him intensely; **jump out of** one's ∼, be extremely surprised; **no** ∼ **off** one's **nose**, colloq., of no concern to one; **risk, save,** etc., one's ∼, one's life; **thick, thin,** ∼, imperviousness, sensitiveness, to affront or reproach; *soaked, wet,* etc., **to the** ∼, right through one's clothing); colour or complexion of skin; (material made from) skin of flayed animal with or without the hair; container for liquid, made of animal's skin; outer covering of plant, fruit, sausage, etc.; ship's planking or plating; ∼**-deep,** superficial, not deep or lasting; ∼**-diver,** one who swims under water without diving-suit, usu. with aqualung and flippers; ∼**-flick,** (sl.) pornographic film; ∼**-food,** cosmetic intended to nourish the skin; ∼**-game,** (sl.) swindle; ∼**-graft** (transplanting of) skin transferred from one (part of) body to another; ‖∼**'head,** young hooligan with close--cropped hair; ∼**-tight,** very close--fitting. **2.** *v.t.* & *i.* (**-nn-**). Remove skin from (*keep* one's EYES *skinned*); cover or become covered *over* (as) with skin; (sl.) swindle, fleece; ∼**'-flint,** miser. **3.** ∼**'ful** (-ŏŏl) *n.,* as much liquor as one can drink; ∼**'ny** *a.,* niggardly, thin, emaciated. [N]

**skint** *a.* (sl.) Having no money. [= *skinned* (prec.)]

**skip**[1]. **1.** *v.i.* & *t.* (**-pp-**). Caper, frisk, dance along; jump lightly from ground e.g. so as to clear skipping--rope; move quickly *from* or *to* subject, occupation, place, etc.; omit, make omissions in, reading book, dealing with series or subject, etc.; (colloq.) not participate in; (colloq.) flee; ∼ **it!,** (sl.) abandon topic

etc.; ∼**'ping-rope,** \*∼**-rope,** length of rope (usu. with two handles) revolved over head and under feet during jumping as game or exercise. **2.** *n.* Skipping movement or action (HOP[2], *skip, and jump*). [prob. Scand.]

**skip**[2] *n.* Large container for refuse etc.; cage, bucket, etc., in which men or materials are raised or lowered in mines etc.; (also **skep**) straw or wicker beehive, (quantity contained in) wooden or wicker basket. [N]

**skip**[3] *n.* Skipper at bowls or curling. [abbr. foll.]

**ski'pper. 1.** *n.* Captain of ship, esp. of small trading or fishing vessel; captain of aircraft; captain of side in games. **2.** *v.t.* Act as captain of. [LDu. *schipper* (SHIP)]

**skirl** *v.i.,* & *n.* (Make) shrill sound characteristic of bagpipes. [prob. Scand.]

**skir'mish. 1.** *n.* (Unpremeditated or slight) fight esp. between small or outlying parts of armies or fleets; short argument, contest of wit, etc. **2.** *v.i.* Engage in skirmish. [F f. Gmc]

**skirt. 1.** *n.* Woman's outer garment hanging from the waist; (**bit of**) ∼, (vulg. sl.) woman; part of coat etc. that hangs below waist; hanging part round base of hovercraft; edge, border, extreme part; ∼ (**of beef**), diaphragm etc. as food, ‖meat from lower flank. **2.** *v.t.* & *i.* Go or be along or round the edge of; go *along* coast, wall, etc.; ‖∼**'ing(-board),** board etc. along bottom of room--wall. [N (SHIRT)]

**skit** *n.* Light, usu. short, piece of satire or burlesque; ∼**'tish** *a.,* (of horse etc.) nervous, inclined to shy, excitable, (of person, esp. woman) frivolous, coquettish, very lively. [perh. N (SHOOT)]

**ski'ttle. 1.** *n.* Pin used in skittles; (in *pl.*) game played with usu. 9 wooden pins set up to be bowled or knocked down (BEER *and skittles*). **2.** *v.t.* ∼ **out,** (Crick.) get (batsmen) out in rapid succession. [orig. unkn.]

**skive** *v.i.* & *t.* (sl.) Evade (a duty); ∼ **off,** depart evasively. [N]

‖**ski'vvy** *n.* (colloq., derog.) Female domestic servant. [orig. unkn.]

**sku'a** *n.* Large predatory sea-bird. [N]

**skul(l)du'ggery** (-g-) *n.* Trickery; unscrupulous behaviour. [orig. unkn.]

**skulk** *v.i.* Move stealthily, lurk, or

hide, esp. in cowardice, with evil intent, or to shirk duty. [Scand.]

**skull** *n.* Bony case of brain of vertebrate; (representation of) bony framework of head (~ **and cross-bones,** representation of skull with two thigh-bones crossed below it as emblem of piracy or death); head as site of intelligence (**thick ~,** stupidity); **~cap** (close-fitting peakless). [orig. unkn.]

**skunk** *n.* Black white-striped bushy-tailed Amer. carnivorous animal, emitting powerful stench when attacked; contemptible person. [Amer. Ind.]

**sky. 1.** *n.* Region of the atmosphere and outer space seen from the earth (in *sing.* or *pl.*; the ~'s the limit, there is almost no limit; **to the skies**, fig. very highly, *praised to the skies*; **under the open ~,** out of doors); **~-blue** *a.* & *n.,* colour(ed) like clear sky; **~-diving,** parachuting in which parachute is opened only at last safe moment; **~-high** *adv.* & *a.,* (as if) reaching the sky, very high(ly); **~'jack** *v.t.,* (sl.) hijack (aircraft); **~'lark,** (*n.*) lark that soars while singing, (*v.i.*) play tricks and practical jokes; **~'light,** window in roof; **~'line,** outline of hills, buildings, etc., defined against sky; **~-rocket,** (*n.*) rocket exploding high in air, (*v.i.*) rise steeply (lit. or fig.); **~'scraper,** very tall building; **~-writing,** (making of) legible smoke-trails from aeroplane esp. for advertising; **~'ward(s)** (-z) *adv.* & *a.* **2.** *v.t.* Hit (cricket-ball) high into air. [N, = cloud]

**Skye** *n.* ~ (**terrier**), short-legged long-haired Scotch terrier. [place]

**slab** *n.* Flat thick usu. square or rectangular piece of stone, cake, etc. [orig. unkn.]

**slack¹** *a., n.,* & *v.* **1.** *a.* Sluggish; lacking energy, activity, firmness, or tautness; negligent; (of tide etc.) neither ebbing nor flowing. **2.** *n.* Slack period, part of rope, etc.; (colloq.) spell of inactivity; (in *pl.*) informal trousers. **3.** *v.t.* & *i.* Slacken; (colloq.) take a rest, be lazy; ~ **off,** loosen, (cause to) lose vigour; ~ **up,** reduce speed. **4.** ~ **'en** *v.t.* & *i.,* make or become slack, slack *off;* **~'er** *n.,* (esp.) indolent person. [E]

**slack²** *n.* Coal-dust. [prob. LDu.]

**slag. 1.** *n.* Refuse left after ore has been smelted etc.; **~-heap,** hill of

refuse from mine etc.; **~'gy** ('-gĭ) *a.* **2.** *v.i.* & *t.* (-gg-). Form (as) slag. [LG]

**slain.** See SLAY.

**slake** *v.t.* Assuage or satisfy (thirst, revenge, etc.); disintegrate (lime) by combination with water. [E (SLACK)]

**slalom** (*or* -ah'-) *n.* Obstacle race on skis or in canoes. [Norw.]

**slam¹. 1.** *v.t.* & *i.* (-mm-). Shut (esp. door) with loud bang; put, knock, come, or move with similar sound or violently; (sl.) criticize severely, hit, beat, gain easy victory over. **2.** *n.* Sound or action of slamming. [prob. Scand.]

**slam²** *n.* Gaining of every trick at cards; **grand, little** *or* **small, ~,** winning of 13, 12, tricks in bridge; **grand ~,** (fig.) winning of all of group of championships in a sport. [orig. uncert.]

**slander** (-ah'-). **1.** *n.* (Uttering of) malicious false and injurious statement about person; **~ous** *a.* **2.** *v.t.* Utter slander about. [F *esclandre* (SCANDAL)]

**slang. 1.** *n.* Words and phrases, or particular meanings of these, in common informal use but generally not regarded as standard English; such expressions used by specified profession, class, etc. **2.** *v.t.* & *i.* Use abusive language (to); **~'ing-match,** prolonged exchange of insults etc. **3.** **~'y** *a.* (**~ily, ~iness**), resembling or using slang. [orig. unkn.]

**slant** (-ah-) *v., n.,* & *a.* **1.** *v.i.* & *t.* Slope, (cause to) lie or go obliquely to vertical or horizontal; present (news etc.) in biased or unfair way. **2.** *n.* Slope, oblique position, (**on a** *or* **the ~,** aslant); (esp. biased) point of view. **3.** *a.* Sloping, oblique; **~-eyed,** having slanting eyes, esp. Mongoloid; **~'wise** (-z) *adv.,* aslant. [Scand.]

**slap. 1.** *v.t.* & *i.* (-pp-). Strike (as) with palm of hand or so as to make similar noise; lay forcefully (*slapped the money on the table, a large fine on the offender*); put hastily or carelessly (*slap paint on the walls*); ~ **down,** (colloq.) reprimand; ~ (= CLAP¹) **on the back;** **~'stick,** boisterous knockabout comedy. **2.** *n.* Slapping stroke or sound; ‖**~ and tickle,** (colloq.) boisterous esp. amorous amusement; ~ **in the face,** (fig.)

rebuff, insult; ~ **on the back**, congratulations; ~**-happy**, (colloq.) punch-drunk, cheerfully casual. **3.** *adv.* Directly, suddenly, fully, (*ran slap into him*; *hit me slap in the eye*); ~**-bang**, violently, noisily, headlong; ~'**dash** *adv.* & *a.*, reckless(ly), careless(ly); ~**-up** *a.*, (sl.) done regardless of expense, first-class. [LG, imit.]

**slăsh. 1.** *v.i.* & *t.* Make sweeping cut(s) with sword, knife, whip, etc.; (in *part.*) vigorously incisive or effective; make long gash(es) in or sweeping cut(s) at; reduce (prices etc.) drastically; censure vigorously. **2.** *n.* Slashing cut or stroke. [orig. unkn.]

**slăt** *n.* Thin narrow piece of wood etc., esp. used in sets in Venetian blind, bedstead, etc. [F *esclat* splinter]

**slāte. 1.** *n.* Grey, green, or bluish--purple metamorphic rock easily split into flat smooth plates; piece of such plate used as roofing-material; piece of it usu. framed in wood for writing on (**clean ~**, no discreditable history; **clean the ~**, remove obligations, grievances, etc.; ‖**on the ~**, recorded as debt, on credit); colour of slate; ~**-pencil**, small rod of soft slate for writing on slate; **slā′tў** *a.* **2.** *v.t.* Cover with slates; *make arrangements for (event etc.); *nominate for office etc.; ‖(colloq.) criticize severely. [F *esclate* fem. of *esclat* (SLAT)]

**slă′ttern** *n.* Slovenly woman; ~**lў** *a.* (~**liness**). [orig. uncert.]

**slau′ghter** (-aw′t-). **1.** *n.* Killing of animal(s) for food; killing of many persons or animals at once or continuously; ~**house**, place for slaughter of animals for food. **2.** *v.t.* Kill thus; (colloq.) defeat utterly. [N (SLAY)]

**Slav** (-ah-) *n.* & *a.* (Member) of group of peoples in Central and Eastern Europe speaking Slavonic languages; ~′**ic** *a.* & *n.*, Slavonic (language-group). [L *Sclavus*, ethnic name]

**slāve. 1.** *n.* Person who is owned by another and has to serve him (WHITE *slave*); drudge, person working very hard; helpless victim *of* or *to* some dominating influence (*slave of fashion*); ~**-driver**, overseer of slaves at work, (fig.) hard taskmaster; ~**-trade**, procuring, transporting, and selling slaves, esp. African Ne-

groes. **2.** *v.i.* Work very hard (*at*, *over*). **3. slā′ver**[1] *n.*, ship or person engaged in slave-trade; **slā′verў** *n.*, condition or work of slave, drudgery, custom of having slaves; **slā′vish** *a.*, of or like slave(s), without originality. [F *esclave* f. L *Sclavus* SLAV (captive)]

**slā′ver**[2]. **1.** *n.* Saliva running from mouth; (fig.) flattery, drivel. **2.** *v.i.* Let saliva run from mouth, dribble. [LDu.; cf. SLOBBER]

**Slavŏ′nĭc. 1.** *a.* Of Slavs; ~ **languages**, group of Indo-Eur. languages such as Russian, Polish, Czech. **2.** *n.* Slavonic language-group. [SLAV]

**slay** *v.t.* (**slew** *pr.* -ōō; **slain**). (literary or joc.) Kill. [E]

**slea′z|ў** *a.* (~**ily**, ~**iness**). Slatternly, tawdry, squalid. [orig. unkn.]

**slĕdge**[1], *****slĕd. 1.** *n.* Vehicle on runners instead of wheels for conveying loads or passengers esp. over snow. **2.** *v.i.* & *t.* Travel or convey in sledge. [Du. *sleedse*, LDu. *sledde*]

**slĕdge**[2] *n.* ~(**-hammer**), large heavy hammer; ~**-hammer** *a.*, (as if) given by or using this (*sledge-hammer blows*, *arguments*). [E (SLAY)]

**sleek. 1.** *a.* (Of hair, skin, etc.) smooth and glossy; looking well-fed and comfortable; (fig.) ingratiating, wily. **2.** *v.t.* Make sleek. [var. SLICK]

**sleep. 1.** *n.* Condition that normally recurs for some hours each night in which eyes are closed, muscles and nerves relaxed, and consciousness suspended (**get to ~**, manage to fall asleep; **go to ~**, enter state of sleep, (of limb) become numbed; **in** one's ~, while asleep; **last ~**, death; **put to ~**, anaesthetize, kill (animal etc.) painlessly; **the ~ of the just**, sound sleep); *a* period of sleep; (fig.) rest, quiet, death; ~**-walker**, **-walking**, (person) walking or performing other actions during sleep. **2.** *v.i.* & *t.* (**slept**). Be in state of sleep, fall asleep, (**let ~ing dogs lie**, avoid stirring up trouble); ~ **like a log** or **top**, soundly); be inactive or dead; spend the night *at*, *in*, etc.; have sexual intercourse in bed *together* or *with*; provide sleeping accommodation for (*house sleeps six*); ~ **around**, (colloq.) be sexually promiscuous; ~ **away**, pass (time) by sleeping; ~ **in**, sleep by night at one's place of work, sleep late; ~′**ing-bag**, lined or padded bag to sleep in esp. when camping etc.; ~′**ing-car(riage**, railway coach with beds or berths; ~**'ing-draught, -pill,** (to induce sleep); ~**ing partner** (not sharing in actual work of a firm); ~**ing sickness,** tropical disease causing extreme lethargy; ~ **off,** get rid of (illness etc.) by sleeping; ~ **on,** continue sleeping, not decide (question) till next day; ~ **out,** sleep outdoors, sleep by night away from one's place of work; ~ **through,** fail to be woken by (sound etc.). **3.** ~**'er** n., (esp.) ‖wooden beam etc. supporting rails, (berth in) sleeping-car; ~**'less** a., lacking sleep, continually active; ~**'y** a. (~**ily,** ~**iness**), drowsy, indolent, inactive, (of fruit, esp. pear) over-ripe; ~**yhead,** sleepy or inattentive person (esp. in voc.); ~**y sickness,** inflammation of brain causing extreme lethargy. [E]

**sleet. 1.** n. Snow and rain together; hail or snow melting as it falls; ~**'y** a. **2.** v.i. **It** ~**s,** sleet falls. [E]

**sleeve** n. Part of garment that encloses arm (LAUGH in or up one's sleeve; **roll up** one's ~**s,** prepare to work or fight; **up** one's ~, concealed but ready for use; wear one's HEART on one's sleeve); tube enclosing rod or smaller tube; wind-sock; cover of gramophone record; ~**-board,** small ironing-board for pressing sleeves; ~**-note,** descriptive matter on record-sleeve; (-)~**d** (-vd) a., having sleeves. [E]

**sleigh** (slā). **1.** n. Sledge, esp. one for riding on; ~**-bell,** one of set of tinkling bells on sleigh-horses' harness. **2.** v.i. Travel on sleigh. [Du. slee (SLEDGE[1])]

**sleight** (slīt) n. ~**(-of-hand),** dexterity, conjuring. [N (SLY)]

**slě'nder** a. Of small girth or breadth, gracefully thin; relatively small, scanty, meagre, inadequate; ~**ize** v.t. & i., make or become slender. [orig. unkn.]

**slěpt.** See SLEEP.

**sleuth** (slōō-) n. Detective; ~**-hound,** bloodhound (lit. or fig.). [N]

**slew[1], slue,** (slōō). **1.** v.i. & t. Turn or swing forcibly or with effort (round) to new position. **2.** n. Such turn. [orig. unkn.]

**slew[2].** See SLAY.

**slice. 1.** n. Thin broad piece cut off or out esp. from bread, cake, meat, or large fruit; share, part; implement with broad flat blade for serving fish etc. or for scraping or chipping; (Golf) slicing stroke; ~ **of life,** realistic representation of everyday experience. **2.** v.t. & i. Cut (up) into slices; cut (piece) off; cut (into or through) (as if) to remove slice; (Golf) strike (ball) so that it deviates away from one. [F esclice f. Gmc]

**slick** a., n., & v. **1.** a. (colloq.) Sleek, smooth; (superficially or pretentiously) skilful or efficient; shrewd, wily. **2.** n. Smooth patch of oil esp. on sea. **3.** v.t. (colloq.) Make sleek or smart; flatten down (one's hair etc.); *~**'er** n., = CITY slicker. [E]

**slide. 1.** v.t. & i. (slid pr. -id). (Cause to) move along smooth surface touching it always with same part; move or go smoothly, gradually, or quietly (down, in, out, etc.); glide over ice on foot without skates; take its own course (let things ~, be negligent, allow deterioration); ~ **over,** barely touch upon (delicate subject etc.). **2.** n. Act of sliding; track for sliding esp. on ice; inclined plane down which children, goods, etc., slide to lower level; part of machine or instrument that slides; thing slid into place (esp. glass holding object for microscope, mounted picture usu. placed in projector for viewing on screen); ~**-rule,** ruler with sliding central piece, graduated logarithmically to allow ease in calculations. **3. sliding door** (pulled across opening, not turning on hinges); **sliding scale,** scale of fees, taxes, wages, etc., that varies as a whole according to changes in some standard. [E]

**slight** (-īt) a., v., & n. **1.** a. Small, inconsiderable, not serious or important, inadequate, (**not in the** ~**est,** not at all; **not the** ~**est,** not even a little); slender, frail-looking. **2.** v.t. Treat (person etc.) with disrespect or as not worth attention, markedly ignore. **3.** n. Act of slighting. [N]

**slim. 1.** a. (-mm-). Slender; not fat or overweight; clever, artful; ~**'line,** of slender design. **2.** v.i. (-mm-). Make oneself slimmer by dieting, exercise, etc. [LDu.]

**slim|e** n. Oozy or sticky substance; ~**'y** a. (~**ily,** ~**iness**), like slime, covered with or full of slime, disgustingly obsequious. [E]

**sling[1]. 1.** n. Strap etc. used to support or raise thing; bandage supporting injured arm; strap or string used to throw small missile; ~**-back,** shoe held in place by strap above and behind heel. **2.** *v.t.* (**slung**). Hurl, throw; suspend with sling, arrange so as to be held or moved from above; ~ one's **hook,** (sl.) make off; *~**-shot,** child's catapult. [N or LDu.]

*sling[2] *n.* Sweetened drink of spirits (esp. gin) and water. [orig. unkn.]

**slink** *v.i.* (**slunk**). Go in stealthy, guilty, or sneaking manner (*away, by, off,* etc.); ~'**y** *a.* (~**ily,** ~**iness**), stealthy, (of garment) close-fitting and sinuous. [E]

**slip**[1]. **1.** *v.i.* & *t.* (-**pp**-). Slide unintentionally or momentarily, lose footing or balance, (*slipped in the mud* or *over the edge; ring slips off finger*); go with sliding motion (*the catch slips into place; slipped* DISC); get away by being slippery or hard to hold or not grasped (**let** ~, release esp. from leash, miss (opportunity), utter inadvertently); go unobserved or quietly or quickly (*across, away, in, out,* etc.); make careless or casual mistake; deteriorate; release from restraint or connection; release (motor-vehicle clutch) momentarily; pull (garment etc.) hastily *on, off;* place stealthily, casually, or with sliding motion (*slipped a coin into his hand*); evade; escape from; (*dog slips his collar; the point had slipped my attention* or *mind*); ~ **up,** (colloq.) make mistake, fail; ~*-up n.,* (colloq.) mistake, blunder. **2.** *n.* Act of slipping (**give** person **the** ~, escape from or evade him); blunder, accidental or slight error (~ **of the pen, tongue,** thing written or said unintentionally); loose covering or garment, e.g. petticoat, (GYM-*slip*; PILLOW*slip*); (in *sing.* or *pl.*) slope on which boats are landed, ships repaired, etc.; (Crick.) fieldsman close behind wicket usu. on off side, (in *sing.* or *pl.*) this part of ground (*was caught in the slips* or *at slip*); finely ground clay mixed with water for coating or decorating earthenware; reduction in movement or speed of pulley, propeller, etc. **3.** ~**-case, -cover,** fitted cover for book, furniture, etc.; ~**-knot,** knot that can be undone by a pull, running knot; ~**-on,** ~**-over,** (shoe, garment, etc.) that can be easily slipped on or off; ||~**-road** (for entering or leaving motorway

etc.); ~'**shod,** having shoes down at heel, slovenly, careless, un-systematic; ~'**stream,** current of air or water driven backward by propeller; ~'**way,** shipbuilding or landing slip. **4.** ~'**per** *n.,* light loose shoe for indoor wear etc.; ||~**-per-bath,** bath for use by the public; ~'**perў,** (colloq.) ~'**pў,** *adjs.* (-**ily, -iness**), (of surface) on which one is liable to slip or slide, (of subject) requiring careful treatment, (of object or person) hard to hold firmly, (of person) unreliable, unscrupulous; ||**look** ~**py,** (colloq.) hurry. [prob. LDu. *slippen*]

**slip**[2] *n.* Long narrow strip of thin wood, paper, etc.; printer's proof on such paper; small piece of paper for making notes etc.; cutting from plant for grafting or planting (**a** ~ **of a,** a slim *girl* etc.). [LDu.]

**slit.** **1.** *v.t.* (-**tt**-; **slit**). Make slit in; cut into strips. **2.** *n.* Straight narrow incision or opening; ~ **trench,** (Mil.) narrow trench. [E]

**sli'ther** (-dh-). **1.** *v.i.* Slide or slip unsteadily; ~**ў** *a.* **2.** *n.* Act of slithering. [alt. *slidder* (SLIDE)]

**sli'ver. 1.** *n.* Thin strip of wood etc. **2.** *v.t.* & *i.* Break off as sliver; break or form into slivers. [E]

**slŏb** *n.* (colloq.) Stupid, careless, ill--mannered, or fat person. [Ir. *slab* mud]

**slŏ'bber** *v.i.* & *t.,* & *n.* Slaver; show excessive sentiment (*over* person etc.); ~**ў** *a.* [Du.]

**slŏe** *n.* (Small bluish-black fruit of) blackthorn; ~**-eyed,** having eyes of this colour. [E]

**slŏg. 1.** *v.i.* & *t.* (-**gg**-). Hit hard and usu. wildly; work or walk doggedly (*along, away, on,* etc.). **2.** *n.* Hard random hit; (spell of) hard steady work. [orig. unkn.]

**slŏ'gan** *n.* Short catchy phrase used in advertising etc.; party cry, watch-word. [Gael., = war-cry]

**sloop** *n.* Small one-masted fore-and--aft-rigged vessel. [Du. *sloep*]

**slŏp**[1]. **1.** *v.i.* & *t.* (-**pp**-). Spill, (allow to) flow over edge of vessel; make (floor etc.) wet or messy thus; carry slops *out* (in prison etc.); gush, be effusive (*over* person). **2.** *n.* Liquid spilled or splashed; sentimental utterance; (in *pl.*) dirty water or liquid, waste contents of kitchen or bedroom vessels; (in *sing.* or *pl.*) unappetizing liquid food; ||~**-basin**

(for dregs of cups at table); ~**-pail** (for removing bedroom slops). [E]

**slŏp²** n. (sl.) Policeman. [*ecilop*, back-slang for *police*]

**slōpe. 1.** n. Inclined position, direction, or state; difference in level between two ends or sides of thing; piece of rising or falling ground; place for skiing on side of mountain etc. **2.** v.i. & t. Have or take slope, slant; cause to slope (~ **arms,** place rifle in sloping position against shoulder); ~ **off,** (sl.) go away, esp. to evade work etc. [ASLOPE]

**slŏ'pp|y̆** a. (~ily, ~iness). Wet with slops, rain, etc.; (of food) watery and unappetizing; (of work etc.) unsystematic, careless; (of garment) untidy, ill-fitting (~y Joe, loose sweater); (of sentiment etc.) weakly emotional, maudlin. [SLOP¹]

**slŏsh. 1.** n. Slush; sound or act of splashing; ||(sl.) heavy blow; ~'y̆ a. **2.** v.t. & i. Splash or flounder (*about*); (colloq.) pour (liquid) clumsily, pour liquid on; ||(sl.) hit esp. heavily; ||(in *p.p.*, colloq.) drunk. [var. SLUSH]

**slŏt. 1.** n. Slit or other aperture in machine etc. for something (esp. coin) to be inserted or work in; allotted place in an arrangement; ~**-machine** (worked by insertion of coin, esp. delivering small purchased articles or providing amusement). **2.** v.t. & i. (**-tt-**). Put or be placed (as if) into slot; provide with slot(s). [F *esclot* hollow of breast]

**slŏth** n. Laziness, indolence; S. Amer. long-haired slow-moving arboreal mammal; ~'**ful** a. (-lly) lazy. [SLOW]

**slouch. 1.** n. Lounging ungainly attitude of body; downward bend of hat-brim; (sl.) incompetent or slovenly worker etc.; ~ **hat** (with wide flexible brim). **2.** v.i. & t. Stand or move or sit with slouch; give slouch to (hat). [orig. unkn.]

**slough¹** (-ow) n. Swamp, miry place; S~ **of Despond,** state of hopeless depression. [E]

**slough²** (slŭf). **1.** v.t. & i. Cast or drop off or *off* as slough. **2.** n. Dead skin or other part of animal (esp. snake) cast off. [orig. unkn.]

**Slō'văk** n. & a. (Member, language) of people of Slovakia. [native name]

**slo'ven** (-ŭ'-) n. Untidy, lazy, or careless person; ~**ly̆,** (a.; ~**liness**) of or like sloven, (adv.) in manner of sloven. [orig. uncert.]

**slow** (-ō) a., adv., & v. **1.** a. Not quick, lacking speed, taking a relatively long time to traverse a distance, do a thing, act, develop, or be done (*slow music, train, growth*; ~ **but sure,** successful despite slowness); (of clock etc.) showing earlier than correct time; dull-witted, stupid; (of fire, oven) not very hot; uninteresting, tedious; (of photographic film) needing long exposure; reluctant *to* do; not prone to anger etc. **2.** adv. Slowly (used when slowness is the point; GO¹ *slow*). **3.** v.i. & t. ~ (**down, up**), (cause to) move, act, or work less quickly or energetically; ~*-down* n., action of slowing down. **4.** ~'**coach,** slow or indolent person; ~ **march** (of troops in funeral procession etc.); ~ **motion,** speed of film in which actions appear much slower than usual, simulation of this in real action; *slow* POISON. [E]

**slow-worm** (slō'werm) n. Small Eur. legless lizard. [E; not f. prec.]

**slŭdg|e** n. Thick greasy mud; sewage; muddy or slushy sediment; ~'y̆ a. [cf. SLUSH]

**slue.** See SLEW¹.

**slŭg¹** n. Shell-less gastropod destructive in gardens etc.; bullet of irregular shape; missile for airgun; (Print.) metal bar used in spacing, line of type in linotype printing; \*tot of liquor; ~'**gard** n., lazy person; ~**gish** (-g-) a., inert, slow-moving. [Scand.]

\***slŭg²** v. (-**gg**-) & n. Hit hard. [cf. SLOG]

**sluice** (-ōōs). **1.** n. ~(**-gate, -valve**), sliding gate or other contrivance for regulating flow or level of water; water above or below or issuing through sluice-gate; ~(**-way**), artificial water-channel; (place for) rinsing. **2.** v.t. & i. Provide or wash with sluice(s); rinse; pour water freely upon; (of water) rush out (as) from sluice. [F *escluse* f. L (EXCLUDE)]

**slŭm. 1.** n. Overcrowded, squalid, and poor district or house in city; ~ **clearance,** demolition of slums and movement of their inhabitants to better housing; ~'**my̆** a. (-**iness**). **2.** v.i. (-**mm**-). Visit slum(s) esp. in search of amusement; behave like inhabitant of slum. [orig. unkn.]

**slŭ'mber** v.i. & t., & n. (often in *pl.*; literary or poet.) Sleep (lit. or fig.); ~ **away**, spend (time) in slumber; **slŭ′mb(e)rous** *a.* [E]

**slŭmp. 1.** *n.* Sudden or rapid or large fall in prices, values, demand, etc. **2.** *v.i.* Fall thus; subside limply. [imit.]

**slŭng.** See SLING; **slŭnk**, see SLINK.

**slŭr. 1.** *v.t.* & *i.* (**-rr-**). Sound or write (words, musical notes, etc.) so that they run into one another; put slur upon (person, character); pass lightly or deceptively *over*. **2.** *n.* Imputation of wrongdoing, reproach; action of slurring; (Mus.) curved line joining notes to be slurred; **slŭ′rry** *n.*, thin semi-liquid mixture of cement, mud, etc. [orig. unkn.]

**slŭrp** *n.*, & *v.t.* (colloq.) Eat(ing) or drink(ing) noisily. [Du.]

**slŭsh** *n.* Thawing snow; watery mud; (fig.) silly sentiment; ~ **fund** (used to bribe public servants); **~′y** *a.* (**~iness**). [orig. unkn.]

**slŭt** *n.* Slovenly woman; hussy; **~′tish** *a.*

**slý** *a.* (**~′er**, **~′est**; **~′ly**, **~′ness**). Crafty, wily, secretive, underhand, (**on the ~**, secretly; ~ **dog**, person secretive about his peccadilloes or pleasures); knowing, mischievous. [N, rel. to SLAY]

**smăck¹** *n.*, *v.*, & *adv.* **1.** *n.* Sharp sound as of surface struck with palm of hand, of lips parted suddenly, etc.; slap; hard hit at cricket; loud kiss; **have a ~ at**, (colloq.) attempt; **~ in the eye** or **face**, (fig.) rebuff. **2.** *v.t.* Slap; move with smack; *smack* one's LIPS. **3.** *adv.* (colloq.) With a smack; suddenly, directly, or violently. **4. ~′er** *n.*, (sl.) loud kiss, ||£1, *\$1. [imit.]

**smăck²** *v.i.*, & *n.* (Have) flavour, taste, or suggestion (*of* a quality or constituent, esp. undesirable). [E]

**smăck³** *n.* Single-masted sailing-boat. [LDu.]

**small** *a.* (-awl) *a.*, *n.*, & *adv.* **1.** *a.* Not large, little, (but often without emotional implications of *little*); of small importance, amount, power, etc., (**feel**, **look**, ~, be humiliated or ashamed); consisting of small particles (*small shot*); doing thing on small scale (*small farmer*); not much (*paid small attention to etiquette*; **no ~**, considerable, much; ~ **wonder**, that is not surprising); socially undistinguished, poor, humble; mean, ungenerous, paltry; *small*

ARM²*s*, BEER; ~ **capital**, letter shaped like capital but only about as high as lower-case letter; ~ **card** (of low rank in suit); ~ **change**, coins opp. notes, (fig.) trivial remarks; *small* FRY¹; ||**~′holder**, owner or user of **~′holding**, piece of agricultural land smaller than farm; *small* HOURS; ~ **letter** (not capital); **~-minded**, petty or rigid in one's views; **~′pox**, acute contagious disease with fever and pustules usu. leaving permanent scars; ~ **print**, matter printed small, esp. limitations in contract; **~-scale**, made or occurring on a small scale; ~ **talk**, trivial conversation(s); **~-time**, unimportant, petty; *in a small* WAY; **the ~est room**, (colloq.) lavatory in house. **2.** *n.* The slenderest part of something, esp. ~ **of the back**, hinder part of waist; ||(in *pl.*, colloq.) small articles of laundry, esp. underwear. **3.** *adv.* Into small pieces (*chop it small*). [E]

**smärm** *v.t.* (colloq.) Smooth, plaster *down* (hair etc.); flatter fulsomely; **~′y** *a.*, ingratiating. [dial.]

**smärt** *a.*, *v.*, & *n.* **1.** *a.* Clever, ingenious, quick-witted, (~ **a′lec(k)** (ă′lĭk), **~′y**(**-pants**), would-be clever person); bright and fresh in appearance, neat, fashionable; stylish, conspicuous in society; quick, brisk, (**look ~**, make haste); painfully severe, sharp, vigorous; **~′en** *v.t.* & *i.* (usu. *up*). **2.** *v.i.* Feel or give acute pain or distress; rankle; suffer *for* (one's behaviour etc.). **3.** *n.* Bodily or mental sharp pain, stinging sensation. [E]

**smăsh** *v.*, *n.*, & *adv.* **1.** *v.t.* & *i.* Break (*up*) into pieces; bring or come to sudden or complete destruction, defeat, or disaster; move with great force (*into*, *through*, etc.); break in with crushing blow; hit (ball etc.) with great force esp. downwards; **~-and-grab**, (colloq., of robbery etc.) in which thief smashes window and seizes goods; **~-up** *n.*, complete smash, violent collision. **2.** *n.* Act or sound of smashing; ~ **hit**, *\*~, (sl.) notably successful play, film, song, etc. **3.** *adv.* With a smash. **4. ~′er** *n.*, (esp., colloq.) very pleasing or beautiful person or thing; **~′ing** *a.*, (esp., colloq.) excellent, very beautiful. [imit.]

**smă′tter(|ing)** *n.* Slight knowledge of something; **~er** *n.*, person with a smattering esp. of many subjects. [orig. unkn.]

**smear. 1.** *v.t.* Daub or stain with or *with* greasy or sticky substance; smudge; (seek to) discredit or defame. **2.** *n.* Action or result of smearing; (specimen of) material smeared on microscope slide etc. for examination; (attempt at) discrediting or defaming; ~'**y** *a.* (~**ily**, ~**iness**). [E]

**smell. 1.** *n.* That one of the five senses special to the nose, by which odours or scents are perceived; quality in substances that affects this sense, odour, (*has no, a sweet, smell*); unpleasant odour; act of inhaling to ascertain smell (*take a smell at it*); ~'**y** *a.* (~**iness**), evil-smelling. **2.** *v.t.* & *i.* (**smelt, ~ed**). Perceive or detect by smell (*smell gas, a* RAT); examine by sense of smell (*of dog*) hunt *out* by smell, (fig., of person) find *out* (secret etc.) by investigation; have or use sense of smell; emit odour; seem by smell to be; be redolent *of* (*smell of the* LAMP); stink; ~'**ing-bottle**, small bottle of ~'**ing-salts**, sharp-smelling substances to be sniffed as cure for faintness etc. [E]

**smelt**[1] *v.t.* Extract metal from (ore) by melting; extract (metal) thus. [LDu. (MELT)]

**smelt**[2] *n.* (*pl.* ~**s**, ~). Small edible green and silver fish. [E]

**smelt**[3]. See SMELL.

**smew** *n.* Small kind of merganser. [orig. unkn.]

**smi'lax** *n.* A climbing plant. [L f. Gk]

**smile. 1.** *n.* (Change of) facial expression, usu. with parting of lips and upward turning of their ends, expressing amusement, pleasure, affection, scepticism, contempt, etc.; (fig.) pleasant or encouraging appearance. **2.** *v.i.* & *t.* Make or have a smile (**come up smiling**, colloq., recover from adversity and face future optimistically); look pleasantly, encouragingly, propitiously, or scornfully (*at, on*, etc.; lit. or fig.); express by smiling (*smiled a welcome, her appreciation*); give (smile) of specified kind. [perh. Scand.]

**smirch. 1.** *v.t.* Besmirch. **2.** *n.* Blot, stain, (lit. or fig.). [orig. unkn.]

**smirk** *v.i.*, & *n.* (Give) silly or conceited smile. [E]

**smite** *v.t.* & *i.* (**smote** *pr.* -ōt;

**smi'tten** *pr.* -ĭ'-). (arch., literary, or joc.) Strike, hit; chastise, defeat; have sudden effect on; seize *with* disease, emotion, fascination, etc. [E]

**smith** *n.* Worker in metal (GOLD-smith; TIN*smith*); blacksmith; (fig.) one who creates (*song-smith*). [E]

**smitheree'ns** (-dh-; -z) *n.pl.* Small fragments (*smashed to smithereens*). [dial. *smithers*]

**smi'thy** (-dhĭ) *n.* Blacksmith's workshop, forge. [SMITH]

**smi'tten.** See SMITE.

**smock. 1.** *n.* Loose overall; ~(-**frock**), loose shirtlike garment, often ornamented with smocking. **2.** *v.t.* Decorate with ~'**ing** *n.*, ornamentation on cloth made by gathering it tightly with stitches. [E]

**smog** *n.* Fog intensified by smoke; ~'**gy** (-gĭ) *a.* [portmanteau wd]

**smoke. 1.** *n.* Visible vapour from burning substance (**end in** ~, come to nothing; ||**the** (**big**) ~, sl., city, esp. London; *no smoke without* FIRE); (colloq.) period of tobacco-smoking; (sl.) cigar(ette); ~ **abatement**, reduction of amount of smoke from chimneys etc. in towns; ~-**bomb** (emitting dense smoke on bursting); ~-**dried**, cured in smoke; ~-**screen**, cloud of smoke (lit. or fig.) to hide military etc. operations; *smoke-*-**STACK. 2.** *v.i.* & *t.* Emit smoke or visible vapour; inhale and exhale smoke of (cigarette, pipe, tobacco, marijuana, etc., or *abs.*; *put that in your* PIPE *and smoke it*); colour, darken, preserve, by action of smoke; ~ **out**, remove (wasps from *nest*, etc.) by injecting smoke, (lit. or fig.). **3.** ~'**less** (-kl-) *a.*, (of area) free from smoke, or where smoke from chimneys is not allowed, (of fuel) producing little or no smoke; **smō'ker** *n.*, (esp.) person who habitually smokes tobacco (**smoker's cough** etc., ailment due to excessive smoking), smoking--**compartment**; **smō'king** *n.*, (esp.) act of smoking tobacco (**smoking--compartment**, train compartment in which smoking is permitted; **smoking-room**, room in hotel etc. where smoking is permitted); **smō'ky** *a.* (**-ily**, **-iness**), (often) producing smoke, veiled or filled with smoke, obscured (as) with smoke, suggestive of smoke. [E]

**\*smō'lder.** See SMOULDER.

**smooch** *v.i.*, & *n.* (colloq.) (Engage in) period of kissing and caressing or slow dancing close together. [imit.]

**smooth** (-dh) *a.*, *adv.*, *v.*, & *n.* **1.** *a.* Having even surface, free from roughness and projections and lumps and indentations; that can be traversed without hindrance; (of water etc.) free from waves; not harsh or jerky; unaffected by difficulties or adverse conditions; (of person, his behaviour, etc.) equable, polite, conciliatory, flattering; ~**tongued**, insincerely flattering. **2.** *adv.* Smoothly (*course of true love never did run smooth*). **3.** *v.t.* & *i.* Make or become smooth (often *down*, *out*); get rid of (impediments etc.; often *away*, *over*). **4.** *n.* Smoothing touch or stroke (*gave his hair a smooth*). [E]

**smŏr'gasbŏrd** *n.* Swedish hors-d'œuvres; buffet meal with variety of dishes. [Sw.]

**smōte.** See SMITE.

**smo'ther** (-ŭ'dh-). **1.** *v.t.* & *i.* Suffocate, stifle; have difficulty in breathing; overwhelm *with* kisses, gifts, kindness, etc.; cover entirely *in* or *with*; extinguish (fire) by heaping with ashes etc.; ~ (**up**), suppress or conceal. **2.** *n.* (Obscurity caused by) cloud of smoke, dust, etc. [E]

**smou'lder** (-ō'-), **\*smō'lder. 1.** *v.i.* Burn slowly without flame or in suppressed way (often fig. of discontent etc.). **2.** *n.* Such burning. [orig. unkn.]

**smŭdg|e. 1.** *n.* Blurred or smeared mark, blot, etc.; ~'**y** *a.* (**-ily**, ~**iness**). **2.** *v.t.* & *i.* Make smudge(s) on or of; become smeared or blurred.

**smŭg** *a.* (**-gg-**). Self-satisfied, consciously respectable, complacent. [LG *smuk* pretty]

**smŭ'ggle** *v.t.* Import or export (goods) illegally, esp. without paying customs duties; convey secretly *in*, *out*, etc. [LG]

**smŭt. 1.** *n.* (Spot or smudge made by) small piece of soot etc.; obscene talk or pictures or stories; (fungus causing) cereal-disease turning parts of ear to black powder; ~'**tÿ** *a.* (**-ily**, **-iness**). **2.** *v.t.* & *i.* (**-tt-**). Mark or infect with smut(s); contract smut disease. [orig. unkn.]

**snăck** *n.* Slight or casual or hurried meal; ~**bar**, place where snacks may be obtained. [Du.]

**snä'ffle. 1.** *n.* Simple bridle-bit without curb. **2.** *v.t.* Put snaffle on; (sl.) take, steal. [prob. LDu.]

**snăg. 1.** *n.* Jagged projecting point or stump, esp. as possible danger; tear in material caused by snag; (fig.) unexpected or hidden obstacle or drawback; ~**ged** (-gd), ~**gÿ** (-gĭ), *adjs.* **2.** *v.t.* (**-gg-**). Catch or tear on snag. [prob. Scand.]

**snail** *n.* Mollusc with spiral shell, esp. slow-moving kind destructive in gardens; ~'**s pace**, very slow movement. [E]

**snake. 1.** *n.* Long limbless reptile; ~ (**in** one's **bosom** or **the grass**), treacherous person, secret enemy; ~**charmer**, **-charming**, (person exhibiting) control of snakes by music etc.; ~**s and ladders**, game with counters moved along board with sudden advances up 'ladders' or returns down 'snakes' depicted on the board; ~'**s-head**, plant with part like snake's head; **snä'kÿ** *a.* (**-ily**, **-iness**), of or like a snake, venomous, sinuous, treacherous. **2.** *v.i.* Move, twist, etc., like snake. [E]

**snăp** *v.*, *n.*, *adv.*, & *a.* **1.** *v.i.* & *t.* (**-pp-**). Make sudden audible bite; say something irritably or spitefully; bite off (~ = BITE) person's **head off**); break with sharp crack; (cause to) emit sudden sharp sound (~ one's **fingers**, make audible fillip esp. lit. or fig. *at* person etc. in defiance or contempt); open or close with snapping sound; move quickly; take snapshot of; ~ **out**, say irritably; ~ **out of**, (sl.) get out of (mood, habit, etc.) by sudden effort; ~ **up**, pick up or buy hastily or eagerly. **2.** *n.* Act or sound of snapping; catch that fastens with a snap; crisp brittle cake or biscuit; snapshot; ‖card-game in which players call 'snap' when two cards of equal rank are exposed (also as *int.* at unexpected similarity of two things); vigour, liveliness; (**cold**) ~, sudden brief spell of cold weather. **3.** *adv.* With snapping sound. **4.** *a.* Done or taken quickly or unexpectedly (*snap decision*, *vote*). **5.** ~'**dragon**, plant with bag-shaped flower; ~ **shot**, shot taken with little or no time for aiming; ~'**shot**, casual photograph taken rapidly with hand-camera. **6.** ~'**per** *n.*, (esp.) a food-fish; ~'**pĭsh** *a.*, inclined to snap, irritable, petulant; ~'**pÿ** *a.* (**-ily**, **-iness**), (colloq.) brisk, zestful, neat and elegant; **make it ~py**, be quick. [prob. LDu.]

**snāre. 1.** *n.* Trap, esp. with noose, for catching birds or animals; thing that tempts one to risk capture, defeat, etc.; (freq. in *pl.*) arrangement of twisted gut, wire, etc., stretched across lower head of side--drum to produce buzzing etc. sound; ~ (**drum**), drum thus fitted. **2.** *v.t.* Catch in snare; ensnare. [N]

**snarl¹. 1.** *v.t. & i.* ~ (**up**), twist, tangle, confuse and hamper movement of (traffic etc.); ~*-up* n., confusion or jam of traffic etc. **2.** *n.* Tangle.

**snarl². 1.** *v.i. & t.* Make quarrelsome growl with bared teeth; ~ (**out**), speak discontentedly, irritably, or cynically. **2.** *n.* Act or sound of snarling. [*snar* f. LG]

**snatch. 1.** *v.t. & i.* Seize quickly, eagerly, or unexpectedly; obtain quickly or with difficulty; carry suddenly *away, from*, etc.; ~ **at**, try to seize; (fig.) take (offer etc.) eagerly. **2.** *n.* Act of snatching; fragment of song, talk, etc.; short spell of activity etc. [rel. to SNACK]

**snă′zz|y̆** *a.* (~**ily**, ~**iness**). (sl.) Smart, attractive, excellent. [orig. unkn.]

**sneak** *v., n., & a.* **1.** *v.i. & t.* Go or take furtively; ‖(school sl.) tell tales, turn informer; (sl.) carry off unobserved. **2.** *n.* Cowardly underhand person; ‖(school sl.) tell-tale. **3.** *a.* Acting or without warning; secret; ~**-thief**, petty thief, person who steals from open windows etc. **4.** ~′**ers** (-z) *n.pl.*, (sl.) soft-soled shoes; ~′**ing** *a.*, (esp., of feeling, suspicion, etc.) unavowed, persistent and puzzling; ~′**y̆** *a.*, like a sneak. [orig. uncert.]

**sneer. 1.** *n.* Derisive smile or remark. **2.** *v.i. & t.* Make a sneer (*at*); utter sneeringly. [perh. LDu.]

**sneeze** *v.i., & n.* (Make) sudden involuntary explosive expulsion of air from irritated nostrils; **not to be ~d at**, passable, not contemptible. [E]

**snĭb. 1.** *n.* Fastening or catch of door, window, etc. **2.** *v.t.* (**-bb-**) Fasten, bolt. [orig. uncert.]

**snick. 1.** *v.t.* Make small notch or incision in; (Crick.) deflect (ball) slightly with bat. **2.** *n.* Such notch or

deflection. [*snickersnee* long knife ult. f. Du.]

**snĭ′cker** *v.i.,* & *n.* Snigger; whinny, neigh. [imit.]

**snide** *a.* (colloq.) Sneering, slyly derogatory; counterfeit; *mean, underhand. [orig. unkn.]

**sniff. 1.** *v.i. & t.* Draw up air audibly through nose; smell (scent etc.), smell scent of, by sniffing; ~ **at**, try the smell of, show contempt for or disapproval of; ~ (**up**), take into the nose by sniffing. **2.** *n.* Act or sound of sniffing; ~′**y̆** *a.* (colloq.; ~**ily**, ~**iness**), disdainful. [imit.]

**snĭ′ffle. 1.** *v.i.* Sniff repeatedly or slightly. **2.** *n.* Act of sniffling; (in *pl.*) cold in the head causing sniffling. [imit.; cf. SNIVEL]

**snĭ′fter** *n.* (sl.) Small drink of alcoholic liquor. [dial. *snift* sniff]

**snĭ′gger** (-g-) *v.i.,* & *n.* (Utter) half-suppressed laugh. [SNICKER]

**snĭp. 1.** *v.t. & i.* (**-pp-**) Cut with scissors or shears esp. in small quick strokes. **2.** *n.* Act of snipping; piece snipped off; ‖(sl.) something cheaply acquired or easily done. [LDu. (imit.)]

**snipe. 1.** *n.* (*pl.* ~**s**, ~). Wading bird with long straight bill. **2.** *v.i.* Fire shots from hiding usu. at long range; (fig.) make sly critical attack *at*. [prob. Scand.]

**snĭ′ppĕt** *n.* Small piece cut off; (usu. in *pl.*) scrap or fragment of information, knowledge, etc., short extract from book etc.; ~′**y̆** *a.* [SNIP]

**snĭtch** *v.t.* (sl.) Steal. [orig. unkn.]

**snĭ′vel. 1.** *v.i.* (‖**-ll-**). Weep with sniffling; show maudlin emotion; run at the nose. **2.** *n.* Act of snivelling; running mucus. [E]

**snŏb** *n.* Person who has exaggerated respect for social position or wealth or who despises people with inferior rank, attainments, tastes, etc.; ~′**ber̆y̆** *n.*; ~′**bish** *a.* [orig. unkn.]

**snŏg** *v.i.* (**-gg-**), & *n.* (sl.) (Engage in) spell of kissing and caressing. [orig. unkn.]

**snŏod** *n.* Loose net worn by woman to keep hair in place. [E]

**snook** (*or* -ōō-) *n.* (colloq.) **Cock a ~**, make contemptuous gesture *at* with thumb to nose and fingers spread (also fig.). [orig. unkn.]

**snōō′ker. 1.** *n.* Game played with 15 red and 6 other coloured balls on billiard-table; position in this game where direct shot would lose points.

**2.** *v.t.* Subject (player) to snooker; (sl., esp. in *pass.*) thwart, defeat. [orig. unkn.]

**snoop.** (colloq.) **1.** *v.i.* Pry into other's private affairs; sneak *about* or *around* looking for infractions of the law or rules. **2.** *n.* Act of snooping; ∼'ў *a.* (∼ily, ∼iness), inquisitive, sneaky. [Du.]

**snoot** *n.* (sl.) Nose. [SNOUT]

**snoo't|ў** *a.* (∼ily, ∼iness). (colloq.) Supercilious, conceited, snobbish. [orig. unkn.]

**snooze** *v.i.*, & *n.* (Take) short sleep esp. in daytime. [orig. unkn.]

**snore** *v.i.*, & *n.* (Make) snorting or grunting noise in breathing during sleep. [imit.]

**snor'kel, schnor'kel** (shn-). **1.** *n.* Device for supplying air to underwater swimmer or submerged submarine. **2.** *v.i.* (‖-ll-). Swim with snorkel. [G *schnorkel*]

**snort. 1.** *n.* Explosive sound made by sudden forcing of breath through nose, esp. expr. indignation or incredulity; similar sound made by engine etc.; (colloq.) small drink of liquor. **2.** *v.i.* & *t.* Make, express or utter with, a snort; ∼'er *n.*, (esp., sl.) something notably vigorous, difficult, etc. [imit.]

**snot** *n.* (vulg.) Nasal mucus; contemptible person; ∼'tў *a.* (-ily, -iness), (vulg.) running or foul with nasal mucus, (colloq.) contemptible or bad-tempered or supercilious. [prob. LDu.]

**snout** *n.* Projecting nose (and mouth) of animal; (derog.) human nose; pointed front of thing. [LDu.]

**snow** (-ō). **1.** *n.* Frozen vapour falling to earth in light white flakes; fall of this, layer of it on ground; thing, esp. dessert, resembling snow in whiteness, texture, etc.; (sl.) cocaine; ∼-**ball,** (n.) snow pressed or rolled into ball esp. for use as missile, (*attrib.*) increasing or growing rapidly, (*v.t.* & *i.*) pelt (one another) with snowballs, (fig.) increase rapidly; ∼'**ball-tree,** guelder rose; ∼-**berry,** garden shrub with white berries; ∼-**blind(ness),** (being) blinded by glare from snow etc.; ∼-**bound,** prevented by snow from going out or travelling; ∼-**capped,** (of mountain) covered at top with snow; ∼-**drift,** bank of snow heaped by wind; ∼'**drop,** spring-flowering plant with white

drooping flowers; ∼'**fall,** amount of fallen snow; ∼'**flake,** one of the small collections of crystals in which snow falls; ∼-**goose,** arctic white goose; ∼-**leopard,** OUNCE[2]; ∼-**line,** level above which snow never melts entirely; ∼'**man,** figure made of snow usu. by children (ABOMINABLE *Snowman*); *∼'**mobile** (-ēl), motor vehicle for travel over snow; ∼-**plough,** device for clearing road or railway of snow; ∼-**shoe,** contrivance like racket attached to foot for walking on snow without sinking in; ∼'**storm,** heavy fall of snow esp. with wind; ∼-**white,** white as snow. **2.** *v.i.* & *t.* Fall as or like snow (it ∼s or is ∼ing, snow falls); (fig.) come in large numbers or quantities; *(sl.) deceive or impress; ∼ed **in** or **up,** snow-bound; ∼ **under,** (usu. in *pass.*) cover (as) with snow, overwhelm with large numbers etc. **3.** ∼'ў *a.* (∼ily, ∼iness), of or like snow (∼y **owl,** large white owl), covered with snow. [E]

**S.N.P.** *abbr.* Scottish National Party.

**Snr.** *abbr.* Senior.

**snub** *v.*, & *a.* **1.** *v.t.* (-bb-). Rebuff or humiliate with sharp words or marked lack of cordiality. **2.** *n.* Act of snubbing. **3.** *a.* (Of nose) short and stumpy or turned up. [N, = chide]

**snuff**[1]. **1.** *v.t.* & *i.* Remove snuff from (candle); ∼ **it,** (sl.) die; ∼ **out,** extinguish (candle) by snuffing, (fig.) kill or put an end to (hopes etc.), (sl.) die; ∼'**er** *n.*, device for snuffing or extinguishing candle. **2.** *n.* Charred part of candle-wick. [orig. unkn.]

**snuff**[2]. **1.** *n.* Powdered tobacco or medicine taken by sniffing it up nostrils; a sniff; ∼-**box,** small box for holding snuff; ∼-**colour(ed),** (of) dark yellowish-brown. **2.** *v.i.* & *t.* Take snuff; sniff. **3.** **snu'ffle,** (*v.i.* & *t.*) make sniffing sounds, speak or say nasally or whiningly, breathe noisily (as) through partly blocked nose, (*n.*) snuffling sound or tone. [Du.]

**snug. 1.** *a.* (-gg-). Sheltered, comfortable, cosy, well enclosed or placed or arranged; closely fitting; (of income etc.) adequate for comfort. **2.** *n.* ‖Bar-parlour of inn. **3.** ∼'**gerў** (-g-) *n.*, snug place, esp. person's private room; ∼'**gle** *v.i.* &

*t.*, settle or draw into warm, comfortable position. [prob. LDu.]

**sō**[1] *adv. & conj.* In this or that way, in the manner or position or state described or implied, to that extent, (*why are you panting so?*; *did not expect to live so long*); to a great or notable degree (*I am so glad!*; *cricket is so boring*); (with *vbs.* of saying, thinking, etc.) thus, this, that, (*I think so*; *so he said*); consequently, therefore, (*so you see you were wrong*; *the shops were closed, so I couldn't buy any*); indeed, in actual fact, (*you said it was good, and so it is*); also (*I was wrong, but so were you*); **and so forth** or **on**, et cetera, and the like; EVER *so*; EVERY *so often*; **how so?**, how is it so?, how can it be?; IF *so*; (*in*) *so* FAR *as*; JUST, MORE, NEVER, *so*; **not so**, it is not so, that is not correct; **not so (very) difficult** etc. (as had been expected or predicted); **not so much as**, not even, less . . . than (*is not so much unintelligent as uneducated*); **or so**, approximately; QUITE *so*; **so-and-so** (*pl.* **so-and-so's**), particular person or thing not needing to be specified (*tells me to do so-and-so*), (colloq.) unpleasant or contemptible person (*he's an old so-and-so*); **so as to**, in order to, in such a way as to; **so be it** (expr. acceptance of or resignation to event etc.); **so-called**, called or named thus (but perhaps wrongly or inaccurately); *so* FAR; *so* HELP *me God*; **so long**, (colloq.) goodbye; *so* LONG *as*; **so many**, **so much**, a definite number or amount, nothing but; **so much for**, that is all that need be said or done about; **so much so that**, to such an extent that; **so much the better**, *worse*, etc., it is that much; **so-so** *adv. & pred.a.*, indifferent(ly), not very well or good; *so* SOON *as*; **so that**, = *so as to*; **so to say** or **speak** (apology for exaggeration, metaphor, imprecision, etc.); *so* WHAT?; **I told you so**, I warned you in vain; **why** (is it) *so?*; *you don't* SAY *so*. [E]

**sō**[2]. See SOH.

**-sō** *suf.* = -SOEVER.

**soak. 1.** *v.t. & i.* Make or become thoroughly wet through saturation with or in liquid (lit. or fig.); (of rain etc.) drench; take (liquid) in or *up*; drink heavily; (sl.) extort money from; ‖**~-away**, arrangement for disposal of water by percolation through soil; **~** one**self** in, absorb

(lit. or fig.); **~ through**, (of moisture) penetrate, make thoroughly wet. **2.** *n.* Soaking; (colloq.) hard drinker. [E]

**soap. 1.** *n.* Cleansing substance yielding lather when rubbed in water (SOFT *soap*); **~-box**, (packing-) box for holding soap, crude vehicle, makeshift stand for street orator; **~-bubble** (of air in film of soapy water); **~-dish**, holder for soap in bathroom etc.; **~-flakes**, flakes of soap prepared for washing clothes etc.; **~ opera**, sentimental domestic broadcast serial; **~ powder** (esp. with additives, for washing clothes etc.); **~'stone**, steatite; *soap*SUDS; **~'y** *a.* (**~ily**, **~iness**), of, like, containing, smeared with, soap, (fig.) unctuous, flattering. **2.** *v.t.* Apply soap to; rub with soap. [E]

**soar** *v.i.* Fly or rise high (lit. or fig.); fly without flapping wings or using engine. [F *essorer* f. L (EX-[1], AURA)]

**sob. 1.** *v.i. & t.* (**-bb-**). Draw breath in convulsive gasps usu. with weeping; **~ (out)**, utter with sobs. **2.** *n.* Act or sound of sobbing; **~-story**, (colloq.) narrative meant to evoke sympathy; **~-stuff**, (colloq.) pathos, sentimental writing or behaviour. [imit.]

**sō'ber. 1.** *a.* (**~er**, **~est**). Not drunk (**as ~ as a judge**, completely sober); not given to drink; moderate, sane, tranquil, sedate; not exaggerated; (of colour etc.) quiet and inconspicuous; **sobrī'etў** *n.*, soberness. **2.** *v.t. & i.* **~ (down, up)**, make or become more sober. [F f. L]

**sō'brĭquet** (-kā), **sou'-** (sōō'-), *n.* Nickname. [F]

**Soc.** *abbr.* Socialist; Society.

**sŏ'ccer** (-k-) *n.* (colloq.) Association football. [Assoc.]

**sō'ciab|le** (-sha-) *a.* (**~ly**). Liking, fitted, for the society of other people; (of meeting, behaviour, etc.) friendly; **~ĭ'lĭtў** *n.* [F or L (*socius* comrade)]

**sō'cial** (-shǎl). **1.** *a.* (**~ly**). Living in communities, gregarious, unfitted for solitary life, interdependent, co-operative; concerned with mutual relations of (classes of) human beings (**~ contract**, agreement to co-operate for social benefits, esp. involving submission to restrictions on individual liberty; **~ science**, scientific study of human society and social relationships; **~ security**,

State assistance to those lacking adequate money or welfare; ~ **services,** education, health, housing, insurance, pensions, etc., as provided by the State; **~ worker,** person working to alleviate social problems); of, in, towards, society (~ **climber,** person seeking to gain higher rank in society). **2.** *n.* Social gathering, esp. one organized by club, congregation, etc. **3.** ~**ism** *n.*, political and economic theory of social organization advocating State ownership and control of commercial activities, policy or practice based on this theory; ~**ist** *n.*; ~**i′stic** *a.*; ~**ite** *n.*, person prominent in fashionable society; **sŏciă′lĭtў** (-shĭ-) *n.*; ~**ize** *v.t. & i.*, make social, organize in socialistic manner, behave sociably; ~**izā′tion** *n.* [F or L (prec.)]

**soci′etў** *n.* Social mode of life, the customs and organization of a civilized nation; a social community; the distinguished or fashionable members of a community, the upper classes; mixing with other people, companionship, company; association of persons sharing common aim, interest, etc., (S~ **of Friends,** Quakers; **S~ of Jesus,** Jesuits); **soci′etal** *a.*; **sŏciŏ-** (or -shĭ-) *comb. form,* of society or sociology (and); **sŏciŏ′logў** (or -shĭ-) *n.*, science of society and social problems; **sŏciŏ-lŏ′gĭcal** *a.* (-lly), **sŏciŏ′logĭst** *n.*, (or -shĭ-). [F f. L (prec.)]

**sŏck**[1] *n.* (*pl.* ~**s,** \***sox**). Short stocking usu. not reaching knee (‖**pull** one's ~**s up,** colloq., make an effort; ‖**put a** ~ **in it,** sl., be quiet); insole; WIND[1]-*sock.* [E f. L *soccus* slipper f. Gk]

**sŏck**[2]. (sl.) **1.** *v.t.* Hit (person) hard; ~ **it to,** attack or address (person) vigorously. **2.** *n.* Hard blow. [orig. unkn.]

**sŏ′ckĕt** *n.* Natural or artificial hollow for something to fit into or stand firm or revolve in, esp. device receiving plug, light-bulb, etc., to make electrical connection. [AF]

**Socră′tĭc** *a.* (~**ally**). Of, like, following, the ancient-Gk philosopher *Socrates*; ~ **irony,** pose of ignorance assumed to entice others into refutable statements; ~ **method,** dialectic, procedure by question and answer. [L f. Gk]

**sŏd**[1] *n.* (Piece of) turf; surface of ground (**under the** ~, in the grave), [LDu.]

**sŏd**[2]. (vulg.) **1.** *n.* Unpleasant or despised person; fellow. **2.** *v.t. & i.* (**-dd-**). Damn; (in *part.*) damned; ~ **off,** go away. [abbr. SODOMITE]

**sō′da** *n.* Compound of sodium in common use, esp. carbonate (**washing-**~), bicarbonate (**baking-**~), or hydroxide (**caustic** ~); ~(-**water**), water made effervescent with carbon dioxide and used as drink alone or with spirits etc.; ~-**bread** (leavened with baking-soda); ~-**fountain,** (shop equipped with) device supplying soda-water. [perh. L *sodanum* f. Arab.]

**sŏ′dden** *a.* (~**ness** *pr.* -n-n-). Saturated with liquid, soaked through; rendered stupid, dull, etc., with drunkenness. [obs. p.p. of SEETHE]

**sō′dium** *n.* Soft silver-white metallic element; ~ **lamp** (giving yellow light from electrical discharge in sodium vapour). [SODA]

**sŏ′domite** *n.* Person practising **sŏ′domў** *n.*, unnatural copulation-like act esp. between males or between person and animal. [L (*Sodom*; Gen. 18, 19)]

**sŏē′ver** *adv.* (literary, or as *suf.* to *rel. prons., advs.,* or *adjs.*) Of any possible kind or extent. [SO[1], EVER]

**sō′fa** *n.* Couch with raised ends and back. [F, ult. f. Arab.]

**sŏ′ffĭt** *n.* Under-surface of arch, lintel, etc. [F or It. (SUFFIX)]

**S. of S.** *abbr.* Song of Solomon (O.T.).

**sŏft** (or saw-). **1.** *a.* Not hard, yielding to pressure, malleable, plastic, easily cut; (of hair, skin, cloth, etc.) smooth or fine in texture, not rough; (of air etc.) mild, balmy; (of water) free from mineral salts and hence good for washing etc.; (of colour, light, etc.) not brilliant or glaring; (of sound) not loud or strident; (Phon.) sibilant; (of outline etc.) not sharply defined; (of action, manner, etc.) gentle, conciliatory, complimentary, amorous; (of heart, feelings, etc.) compassionate, sympathetic; (of character etc.) feeble, effeminate, silly, sentimental; (sl., of job etc.) easy; (of drug) not likely to cause addiction; ~ **answer,** conciliatory response to abuse or accusation; ~~**boiled,** (of egg) boiled but not hard-boiled; ~ **currency,** currency not (easily) convertible to gold or other currencies; ~ **drink** (non--alcoholic); ||~ **fruit,** small stoneless fruit; ||~**furnishings,** curtains, rugs, etc.; ~**headed,** idiotic, foolish; ~**hearted,** easily affected by others' pain, grief, etc.; ~ **on,** (colloq.) in love with, not sufficiently rigorous towards; ~ **option,** the easier alternative; ~ **palate,** back part of palate; ~ **pedal** n. (on piano, making tone softer); ~**pedal** v.t. & i., play (piano) with soft pedal down, (fig.) refrain from emphasizing; *soft* ROE[2]; ~ **sell,** restrained salesmanship; ~ **soap,** liquid soap, (fig.) flattery; *soft-*SPOKEN; ~ **spot,** sentimental affection *for*; *soft* TACK[3]; ~ **touch,** (sl.) person readily parting with money; ~'**ware,** programs etc. for computer, or other interchangeable material for performing functions; ~ **wicket** (with moist or sodden turf); ~**witted,** idiotic, stupid; ~'**wood** (of coniferous tree). **2.** *adv.* Softly. **3.** ~'**en** (-fen) v.t. & i., make or become soft(er); ~**en** (**up**) weaken (defences) by bombing or other preliminary attack; ~'**ie,** ~'**y,** n., (colloq.) weak or silly person. [E]

||**SOGAT** (sō'găt) *abbr.* Society of Graphical and Allied Trades.

**sŏ'gg**|**ў** (-gĭ) a. (~**ily,** ~**iness**). Sodden, saturated. [dial. *sog* marsh]

**soh** (sō), **sŏ²,** n. (Mus.) Fifth note of scale; note G. [L *solve,* wd arbitrarily taken]

**soi-disant** (swahdē'zahṅ) a. Self--styled, pretended. [F]

**soigné** (swah'nyā) a. (*fem.* ~**e** *pr.* same). Carefully finished or arranged, well-groomed. [F]

**soil¹. 1.** v.t. Make dirty, smear or stain with dirt; defile (lit. or fig.). **2.** n. Dirty mark; filth, refuse matter; ~**-pipe,** discharge-pipe of water--closet. [F *soill*(*i*)*er* ult. f. L *sus* pig]

**soil²** n. The ground, upper layer of earth; ground belonging to (esp. one's own) nation; ~**léss** (-l-l-) a., (esp.) using no soil. [AF f. L *solium* seat, *solum* ground]

**soirée** (swăr'ā) n. Evening party esp. for conversation or music. [F]

**sŏ'journ** (-ern, -ĕrn) v.i., & n. (Make) temporary stay *in* place or *with* person(s). [F f. Rom. (L SUB-, *diurnum* day)]

**sŏl** n. Liquid solution or suspension of colloid. [SOL(UTION)]

**sŏ'la** n. Pithy-stemmed E. Ind.

swamp plant (~ **topi,** sun-helmet made from its pith). [Urdu]

**sŏ'lace** n., & v.t. Comfort in distress or disappointment or tedium. [F f. L *solatium* (*solor* console)]

**sŏ'lan** n. ~ (**goose**), large goose--like gannet. [N]

**sō'lar** a. Of or reckoned by the sun; ~ **battery, cell,** device converting solar radiation into electricity; ~ **day,** interval between meridian transits of sun; ~ **plexus,** complex of radiating nerves at pit of stomach; ~ **system,** sun and the heavenly bodies whose motion is governed by it; *solar* YEAR; **solār'ium** n. (*pl.* **-ia**), place for enjoyment or medical use of sunshine. [L *sol* sun]

**solā'tĭ**|**um** (-shĭ-) n. (*pl.* ~**a**). Thing given as compensation or consolation. [L (SOLACE)]

**sŏld.** See SELL.

**sŏ'lder** n. **1.** Fusible alloy used to join less fusible metals, wires, etc. **2.** v.t. Join with solder; ~**ing-iron,** tool to melt and apply solder. [F f. L (SOLID)]

**sō'ldier** (-ljer) **1.** n. Member of army (OLD, PRIVATE, TIN, TOY, *soldier*); (**common**) ~, private or N.C.O. in army; military commander of specified ability (*a great, poor, soldier*); ~ **of fortune,** adventurous person ready to serve any State or person, mercenary; ~ (fighting) **ant;** ~**ly** a.; ~**y** n., soldiers esp. of a specified character. **2.** v.i. Serve as soldier; ~ **on,** (colloq.) persevere doggedly. [F f. *sou*(*l*)*er* (soldier's) pay f. L (SOLID)]

**sōle¹. 1.** n. Under-surface of foot; part of shoe, sock, etc., below foot, esp. part other than heel; lower surface or base of plough, golf-club head, etc.; flat-fish esteemed as food. **2.** v.t. Provide (shoe etc.) with sole. [E f. L *solea* sandal]

**sōle²** a. One and only, single, exclusive. [F f. L *solus*]

**sŏ'léc**|**ism** n. Offence against grammar, idiom, or etiquette; ~**i'stĭc** a. [F or L f. Gk]

**sŏ'lemn** (-m) a. (~**ness**). Accompanied with religious or other ceremony, formally regular; mysteriously impressive; weighty, serious, slow--moving or -acting; solemn rite; **sŏ'lemnĭty** n., solemnness, solemn rite; **sŏ'lemnize** v.t., duly perform (ceremony esp. of marriage), make solemn; **sŏlemnĭzā'tion** n. [F f. L *solemnis*]

**sō′lĕnoid** *n.* Cylindrical coil of wire acting as magnet when carrying electric current. [F f. Gk *sōlēn* tube]

**sŏl-fa′** (-ah′) *n.* System of syllables representing musical notes (TONIC *sol-fa*). [*sol* var. of SOH, FA]

**soli.** See SOLO.

**soli′cĭt** *v.t.* & *i.* Ask repeatedly or earnestly for or seek or invite (business etc.); (of prostitute) accost (person) for immoral purpose; ~ā′tion *n.*; ~or *n.*, (esp.) ‖member of legal profession competent to advise clients and instruct barristers; S~or- -General, law officer below Attorney- -General or Lord Advocate; ~ous *a.*, anxious, concerned, (*about*, *for*, etc.), eager *to* do, desirous *of*; ~ūde *n.*, being solicitous. [F f. L (*sollicitus* anxious)]

**sŏ′lĭd. 1.** *a.* (~er, ~est). Of stable shape (opp. *liquid*, *fluid*); of such material throughout (opp. *hollow*); of the same material throughout (opp. *plated* etc.); (of printing) without spaces between lines etc.; of three dimensions; concerned with solids (*solid geometry*); of strong material or construction or build (opp. *flimsy*, *slender*, etc.); reliable or real (opp. *specious* etc.); (of person or his work) sensible but not brilliant; financially sound; (colloq., of time) uninterrupted (*worked for two solid hours*); (colloq.) unanimous, undivided; ~ **angle** (formed by planes etc. meeting at point); ~ **solution** (of one solid uniformly distributed in another); ~ **state**, state of matter that retains its boundaries without support; ~-*state* *a.*, (esp.) using electronic properties of solids to replace those of valves. **2.** *n.* Solid substance or body; (in *pl.*) solid food. **3.** ~ă′rĭtÿ *n.*, unity, mutual dependence, community of interests, feelings, and action; **solĭ′dĭfÿ** *v.t.* & *i.*; **solĭdĭfĭcā′tion** *n.*; **solĭ′dĭtÿ** *n.*; ~**us** *n.* (*pl.* ~**i** *pr.* -ī), oblique stroke (/). [F, or L *solidus*]

**solĭ′loquÿ** *n.* (Period of) talking without, or regardless of, hearers, esp. in a play; ~**īze** *v.i.*, talk thus. [L (as foll., *loquor* speak)]

**solĭ′psĭsm** *n.* View that self is all that exists or can be known; ~**ĭst** *n.* [L *solus* alone, *ipse* self]

**sŏ′lĭtarÿ. 1.** *a.* (~ily, ~iness). Living alone, not gregarious, without companions, lonely; secluded, unfrequented; single, sole; ~**y con- finement**, isolation in separate cell. **2.** *n.* Recluse; (sl.) solitary confine-

ment. **3. sŏlĭtair′e** *n.*, (ear-ring etc. with) jewel set by itself, game played on special board by one person who removes objects one at a time by jumping others over them, *card- -game for one person; **sŏ′lĭtūde** *n.*, being solitary, solitary place. [L (prec.)]

**sō′lō. 1.** *n.* (*pl.* ~s, in 1st sense also **soli** *pr.* sō′lē). Piece of music performed by one person with or without subordinate accompaniment; performance by one person, esp. unaccompanied flight by pilot in aircraft; ~ (*whist*), card-game like whist in which one player may oppose the others; winning of 5 tricks thus; ~**ĭst** *n.*, performer of solo. **2.** *a.* & *adv.* Performed as solo, unaccompanied, alone, (*solo flight*, *flute*). [It. f. L (SOLE[2])]

**Sŏ′lomon** *n.* Very wise person; ~**'s seal**, flowering plant esp. with drooping green and white flowers. [person]

**sŏ′lstĭce** *n.* Either time (**summer**, **winter**, ~ about 21 June, 22 Dec.) when sun is farthest from equator; **sŏlstĭ′tial** (-shal) *a.* (-lly). [F f. L (*sol* sun, *stit-* stand)]

**sŏ′lūble** *a.* (~ly). That can be dissolved (esp. in water) or solved; ~**ĭ′lĭtÿ** *n.* [F f. L (SOLVE)]

**solū′tion** (or -lōō′-) *n.* Dissolving, being dissolved; conversion of solid or gas into liquid by mixture with liquid; state resulting from this; liquid so produced; (method for) solving *of*, *for*, *to*, a problem, doubt, etc. [F f. L (foll.)]

**sŏlv|e** *v.t.* Find answer to (problem, puzzle) or way out of (difficulty); ~**′ent** *a.* & *n.*, (liquid etc.) able to dissolve or form a solution with something, having enough money to meet one's liabilities (so ~**′encÿ** *n.*). [L *solvo solut-* release]

**Som.** *abbr.* Somerset.

**somă′tĭc** *a.* (~ally). Of the body, not of the mind. [Gk (*sōma* -*mat-* body)]

**sŏ′mbre** (-ber), *sŏ′mber, *a.* Dark, gloomy, dismal. [F f. Rom. (SUB-, UMBRA)]

**sŏmbrer′ō** (-ār′ō) *n.* (*pl.* ~s). Broad-brimmed hat worn esp. in Latin American countries. [Sp. (prec.)]

**some** (sŭm, sum) *a.*, *pron.*, & *adv.* **1.** *a.* An unspecified amount or number of (*buy some apples*, *bread*; *some of them* *were late*); an unknown or unnamed (person or thing; *some fool has locked the door*; *will tell you some day*); an appreciable or considerable amount or number of (*went to some trouble, some miles out of our way*; *some* FEW; ~ **little, small,** etc., a significant amount of); approximately so many or so much of (*waited some 20 minutes*); at least a small amount of (*do have some consideration*); such to a certain extent (*that is some guide*); (sl.) such in a notable or excellent sense, truly worthy of the name, (*this is some war*; *I call that some poem*). **2.** *pron.* Some people or things, some number or amount, (*some say he is right*; *have just drunk some*; **and then ~,** sl., more than that). **3.** *adv.* (colloq.) To some extent (*do it some more*). **4.** ~**'body,** some person, important person; ~**'how,** in some unspecified or unknown way, for some reason or other; ~**'one,** somebody; *~**'place,** somewhere; ~**'time,** at some time, former(ly); ~**'times,** at some times; ~**'what,** in some degree, rather; ~**'where,** in or to some place; *get ~-where,* colloq., achieve success; ~*where about,* approximately. [E]

**-some, -som,** *suf.* forming *adjs.* w. sense 'adapted to, productive of' (*cuddlesome, fearsome, quarrelsome*), 'characterized by being' (*fulsome, lissom*), or 'apt to' (*tiresome, wearisome*); forming *ns.* f. numerals in sense 'group of' (*foursome*). [E]

**so'mersault** (sŭ'-; *or* -ŏlt) *n.,* & *v.i.* (Perform) leap or roll in which one turns head over heels. [F (*sobre* above, *saut* jump)]

**so'mething** (sŭ'mth-). **1.** *n.* & *pron.* Some thing, esp. unspecified, unknown, unimportant, or forgotten; a quantity or quality expressed or understood (*there is something* (of truth etc.) *in what you say*; *is something* (some official) *in the Treasury*; *take a drop of something* (liquor); *has something* (impressive) *about him*; *it is something* (praiseworthy etc.) *to have got so far*); important or notable person or thing (*the party was quite something*); **see ~ of,** meet (person) occasionally or for short time; **or ~** (indicating absence of definite information); **~ like,** somewhat like, approximately; **~ li'ke,** (colloq.) impressive, a fine specimen of; **~ of,** to some extent; **~ or other** (as substitute for unknown or forgotten

description). **2.** *adv.* (arch.) Somewhat. [E (SOME, THING)]

**sŏmnă'mbul|ism** *n.* Sleep-walking; ~**ant** *a.*; ~**ist** *n.*; ~**i'stic** *a.* (-ically). [L *somnus* sleep, *ambulo* walk]

**so'mnol|ent** *a.* Sleepy, drowsy; inducing drowsiness; ~**ence** *n.* [F or L (prec.)]

**son** (sŭn) *n.* Male child in relation to his parents; male descendant, male member *of* family etc.; person viewed as inheriting an occupation, quality, etc., (*sons of toil*); (*my*) ~ (form of address by old man to young man, confessor to penitent, etc.); ~**-in-law,** daughter's husband; ~ **of a bitch,** (vulg.) disliked person or thing; *son of a* GUN; **the Son of God** or **of Man,** Christ; ~ **of the soil,** one who lives or works on the land, farmer, native of a district; **the ~s of men,** mankind. [E]

**sō'nant** *a.* & *n.* (Phon.) (Sound) uttered with vocal vibration (e.g. *b, d, g, v, z*). [L *sono* to sound]

**sō'năr** *n.* (Apparatus for) system of detecting objects under water by reflected or emitted sound. [*sound navigation* (and) *ranging*]

**sona'ta** (-ah'-) *n.* (Mus.) Composition for one or two instruments, normally with 3 or 4 movements; **sŏnati'na** (-ē'-) *n.,* simple or short sonata. [It., = sounded]

**son et lumière** (sŏn ā loo'myār) *n.* Entertainment by night at historic building etc. with recorded sound and lighting effects to give dramatic narrative of its history. [F, = sound and light]

**sŏng** *n.* Singing, (piece of) vocal music, short poem etc. set to music or meant to be sung; (arch.) poetry; (Mus.) composition suggestive of a song; **for a ~,** very cheaply; MAKE *a song and dance*; ~**-bird** (with melodious cry); ~**-book,** collection of songs; S~ **of S~s** or **of Solomon,** O.T. book; *song*-THRUSH[1]; *~**'ster** *n.,* singer, song-bird; ~**'stress** *n.,* female singer. [E (SING)]

**sŏ'nĭc** *a.* Of, relating to, or using sound(-waves); ~ **bang, boom,** noise made when aircraft passes speed of sound; ~**barrier,** = SOUND[1] barrier. [L *sonus* sound]

**sŏ'nnět** *n.* Poem of 14 lines, in English usu. having 10 syllables per line. [F, or It. *sonetto* (SOUND[1])]

**so'nnў** (sŭ'-) *n.* (colloq., as familiar

form of address to) boy or younger man. [SON]

**so'norous** (or sonŏr'-) a. Having a loud, full, or deep sound; (of speech etc.) imposing; **sonŏ'rĭtў** n. [L]

**sōon** adv. After no long interval of time (shall soon know the result); relatively early (why must you go so soon?); (after as or in compar.) readily or willingly (I would just as soon, I would sooner, stay at home); **as or so ~ as**, at the moment that, not later than, as early as, (I came as soon as I heard it; did not arrive as (or so) soon as expected); **no¹ sooner**; **~er or later**, at some future time, eventually. [E]

**sŏŏt. 1.** n. Black powdery substance rising in smoke and deposited by it on surfaces; **~ў** a. (**~ily**, **~iness**), covered with soot, (brownish-)black. **2.** v.t. Cover with soot. [E]

**sōoth** n. (arch.) Truth; **sōothe** (-dh) v.t., calm (person, nerves, passions), soften or mitigate (pain etc.); **~'say-er** n., one who foretells the future, diviner. [E]

**sŏp. 1.** n. Piece of bread etc. soaked in gravy etc.; thing given or done to pacify or bribe; MILKsop. **2.** v.t. & i. (**-pp-**). Soak (up); (in part.) drenched (clothes are sopping, sopping wet). [E]

**so'ph|ism** n. False argument, esp. one intended to deceive; **~ĭst** n., captious or fallacious reasoner, quibbler; **sophi'stĭc(al)** adjs. (**-ically**); **~ĭstry** n., use of sophisms, a sophism. [L f. Gk (sophos wise)]

**sophi'stĭc|āte. 1.** v.t. (esp. in p.p.) Make (person etc.) worldly-wise, cultured, or refined; make (equipment, techniques, etc.) highly developed or complex; **~ā'tion** n. **2.** (**-at**) a. & n. Sophisticated (person).

*****so'phomor|e** n. Second-year university or high-school student; **~ĭc** a. [sophom obs. var. SOPHISM]

**sopŏri'fic** a. (**~ally**) & n. (Drug) tending to produce sleep. [L sopor sleep]

**so'pp|ў** a. (**~ily**, **~iness**). Soaked with water; (colloq.) mawkishly sentimental, silly. [SOP]

**sopra'n|ō** (-ah'-) n. (pl. **~os**, **~i** pr. **-ē**). Highest singing voice of female or boy; singer with, part written for, this; high(est)-pitched member of group of similar instruments. [It. (sopra above)]

**sŏr'bĕt** n. Water-ice; sherbet. [F f. It. f. Turk. f. Arab.]

**sŏr'cer|er** n. Magician, wizard; **~ĕss**, **~ў**, ns. [F sorcier (SORT)]

**sŏr'dĭd** a. Ignoble, mean, mercenary; dirty, squalid. [F, or L sordidus]

**sōre** a., n., & adv. **1.** a. (Of part of body) painful from injury or disease (FOOTsore); (of person) suffering pain, aggrieved, touchy, vexed (at); (of subject etc.) arousing painful feelings, irritating; (arch. or poet.) distressing, grievous, severe; sore THROAT; **stick out like a ~ thumb**, (colloq.) be very obvious; **~'lў** (sŏr'lĭ) adv., (esp., fig.) very much (tempted, in need of). **2.** n. Sore place, subject, etc. **3.** adv. (arch.) Grievously, severely, (sore afflicted). [E]

**sŏr'ghum** (-gu-) n. Tropical cereal grass. [L f. It. sorgo]

**sorŏ'rĭtў** n. Devotional sisterhood; *women's society in university or college. [L (soror sister)]

**sŏ'rrel¹** n. Sour-leaved herb. [F f. Gmc (SOUR)]

**sŏ'rrel²** a. & n. (Of) light reddish-brown colour; sorrel animal, esp. horse. [F]

**sŏ'rrow** (-ō). **1.** n. (Cause of) mental distress or misfortune; **~ful** a. (**-lly**), feeling or causing sorrow. **2.** v.i. Feel sorrow; mourn. [E]

**sŏ'rrў** a. (**-ily**, **-iness**). (pred.) pained or regretful or repentant (about, for, that); feeling pity or sympathy or mild contempt (for person); (so) **~!**, (colloq.) I am sorry, I beg your pardon; **~ for oneself**, (colloq.) dejected; (attrib., literary) wretched, paltry, of poor quality (a sorry fellow, plight). [E (SORE)]

**sŏrt. 1.** n. Kind, variety, group of things etc. with similar attributes; (colloq.) person of specified sort (a good sort); nothing, something, etc., of the **~** (forms of denial or qualified assent); **of a ~**, **of ~s**, not fully deserving the name; **out of ~s**, slightly unwell, in low spirits; **~ of**, (colloq.) as it were, to some extent. **2.** v.t. & i. Sort out; (arch.) correspond or agree with; **~ out**, separate into sorts, select (things of one or more sorts) from miscellaneous group, disentangle (lit. or fig.), put into order, solve, (sl.) deal with or punish. [F f. L sors sort- lot]

**sŏr'tie** (or **-ē**) n. Sally, esp. from besieged garrison; operational flight by military aircraft. [F]

**SOS** (ĕsōē's) n. International code-

-signal of extreme distress; urgent appeal for help etc. [letters easily recognized in Morse]

**sŏstenu′tō** (-ōō′-) *adv., a.,* & *n.* (*pl.* ~**s**). (Mus.) (Passage performed) in sustained or prolonged manner. [It.]

**sŏt** *n.* Habitual drunkard; ~**tish** *a.* [E & F f. L]

*sotto voce* (sŏtō vō′chĭ) *adv.* In an undertone. [It.]

**sou** (sōō) *n.* Former French coin of low value; (colloq.) very small amount of money (**not a** ~, no money at all). [F f. L (SOLID)]

**soubrĕ′tte** (sōō-) *n.* (Actress taking part of) pert maidservant etc. in comedy. [F]

**soubriquet.** See SOBRIQUET.

**soufflé** (sōō′flā) *n.* Light spongy dish usu. made with stiffly beaten egg-whites. [F, = blown]

**sough** (sŭf, sow) *n.,* & *v.i.* (Make) moaning or whispering sound as of wind in trees. [E]

**sought.** See SEEK.

**souk** (sōōk) *n.* Market-place in Muslim countries. [Arab.]

**soul** (sōl) *n.* Spiritual or immaterial part of man, regarded as immortal; moral, emotional, or intellectual part of person or animal; person (*not a soul to speak of*), esp. as embodying moral or intellectual qualities; personification or pattern *of* (**the** ~ **of honour,** extremely honourable person); person regarded with familiarity, pity, contempt, etc., (*she's a good, simple, soul; the poor little soul had lost his way*); (person regarded as) animating or essential part (*he was the* (*life and*) *soul of the party*); emotional or intellectual energy or intensity, esp. as revealed in work of art (*the fellow, picture, has no soul*); Black American culture, music, etc. (~ **music,** also music played with strong emotional fervour); ALL **Souls′ Day**; **cannot call his** ~ **his own,** is dominated by another person; *keep* BODY *and soul together*; **sell** one's ~ **for,** make any sacrifice to get; ~**-destroying,** deadeningly monotonous etc.; ~ **mate,** person ideally suited to another; ~**-searching,** examining one's own conscience; **upon my** ~, = *upon my* WORD; ~**ful** *a.* (**-lly**), having, expressing, or evoking deep feeling; ~**less** (**-l-l-**) *a.,* having no soul, lacking noble qualities or deep emotion, undistinguished, uninteresting. [E]

**sound**[1]. **1.** *n.* Sensation due to vibration of air; what is or may be heard; idea of something conveyed by words (*don't like the sound of it*); mere words (*sound and fury*); ~ **barrier,** high resistance of air to objects moving at speeds near that of sound; ~ **effect,** sound other than speech or music used in broadcast, film, etc.; ~**-film** (having sound-track); ~**-proof** *a.,* & *v.t.,* (render) impervious to sound; ~**-track,** (sound recorded on) narrow strip on side of cinema film; ~**-wave** (of condensation and rarefaction, by which sound is transmitted in air etc.). **2.** *v.i.* & *t.* (Cause to) emit sound; convey an impression by sound (lit. or fig.; in *part.,* fig., having more sound than sense or truth; *sounding rhetoric, titles, promises*); utter, pronounce; give notice of (alarm, retreat, etc.) with bell, trumpet, etc.; test condition of (lungs, wheel, etc.) by noting sound produced; ~**ing-board,** canopy over pulpit etc. to project sound towards audience, (fig.) means of disseminating opinions etc.; ~ **off,** (colloq.) talk loudly, express one's opinions forcefully. [F f. L *sonus*]

**sound**[2]. **1.** *a.* Healthy, not diseased or injured or rotten; (of views, policy, etc.) correct, orthodox, well-founded; financially secure; thorough, complete, (*sound sleep, thrashing*). **2.** *adv.* Soundly; fast *asleep.* [E]

**sound**[3] *v.t.* Test depth or quality of bottom of (sea, channel, pond, etc.); ~ (**out**), inquire (esp. cautiously or discreetly) into opinions, feelings, etc., of (person); ~**ings** (-z) *n.pl.,* measurements obtained by sounding, region near enough to shore to allow sounding. [F f. L (SUB-, *unda* wave)]

**sound**[4] *n.* Strait (of water). [E, = swimming]

**soup** (sōōp). **1.** *n.* Liquid food made by stewing bones, vegetables, etc., (**in the** ~, sl., in difficulties or trouble); ~**-kitchen,** establishment supplying free soup etc. to the poor or in times of distress; ~**-plate,** large deep plate; ~**ў** *a.* **2.** *v.t.* ~ (**up**), (colloq.) increase power of (engine, car, etc.). [F]

**sou′pçon** (sōō′psawň) *n.* Very small quantity, trace or tinge, *of.* [F (SUSPICION)]

**sour. 1.** *a.* Having acid taste

or smell (as) from unripeness or fermentation; (of soil) dank; (of person or temper) peevish or morose; (of thing) unpleasant; **go, turn, ~,** (fig.) turn out badly, lose one's keenness (*on*); sour GRAPES; **~'puss,** (sl.) bad-tempered person. **2.** *v.t.* & *i.* Make or become sour (lit. or fig.). [E]

**source** (sôrs) *n.* Place from which river or stream issues; place from which thing comes or is got; document etc. providing evidence; **at ~,** at point of origin or issue; **~-book** (providing material for historical study etc.). [F (SURGE)]

**souse. 1.** *v.t.* & *i.* Immerse in pickle or other liquid; soak (thing *in* liquid); (in *p.p.*, sl.) drunk. **2.** *n.* Pickle made with salt; *food in pickle; plunge or soaking in water. [F f. Gmc (SALT)]

**souta'ne** (sōōtah'n) *n.* Cassock of R.C. priest. [F f. It. (*sotto* under)]

**south** *n., a.,* & *adv.* **1.** *n.* Point of horizon to right of person facing east (**to the ~ of,** in a southward direction from); compass point lying south; (S~) part of country or town lying to the south. **2.** *a.* Towards, at, near, facing, south; coming from south (*south wind*). **3.** *adv.* Towards, at, near, the south (DUE *south*; *south* BY *east, west*; **~ of,** in a southward direction from). **4.** **S~ African,** (native) of Republic of South Africa; **~-east, -west,** (compass point) midway between south and east, west; **~ea'ster, ~we'ster,** S.E., S.W., wind; **~-~-east, -west,** (compass point) midway between south and south-east, south-west; **~'paw,** (colloq.) left-handed (person esp. boxer); **south** POLE². **5.** **~'erly** (sŭ'dh-) *a.* & *adv.,* in southern position or direction, (of wind) blowing (nearly) from south; so **~'ea'sterly, ~'we'sterly; ~'ern** (sŭ'dh-) *a.* (*superl.* **~'ern-most**), of or dwelling in the south (S~ern Cross, constellation with stars forming cross); so **~'ea'stern, ~'we'stern; ~'erner** (sŭ'dh-) *n.,* inhabitant of the south; **~'ward** *a., adv.,* & *n.; ~'wards** (-z) *adv.* [E]

**souvenir'** (sōōvenēr') *n.* Thing given, bought, kept, etc., as reminder of person, place, event, etc. [F]

**sou'wĕ'ster** *n.* Wind from S.W.; waterproof hat with broad flap at back. [SOUTHwester]

**sŏ'vereign** (-vrĭn). **1.** *a.* Supreme; unmitigated; exempt from external control; royal; (of remedy etc.) very good or effective; **~tÿ** *n.* **2.** *n.* Supreme ruler, esp. monarch; ||British gold coin (now rarely used) worth nominally £1. [F *soverain* (SUPER-)]

**sŏ'viet. 1.** *n.* Council elected in district of U.S.S.R. (**Supreme S~,** governing council of U.S.S.R. or of one of its constituent republics); **S~ Union, Union of S~ Socialist Republics,** the Russian nation since 1917. **2.** *a.* (S~). Russian; of the Soviet Union. [Russ.]

**sow¹** (sō) *v.t.* (**~ed; ~n, ~ed**). Put (seed) on or in the earth for purpose of growth; plant (land *with* seed); (fig.) initiate, arouse; *sow the* SEED(s) *of.* [E]

**sow²** *n.* Adult female pig. [E]

**soy** *n.* ~ (**sauce**), sauce made from pickled soya beans; **~ or ~'a (bean),** (seed of) leguminous plant yielding edible oil and flour. [Jap.]

**sŏ'zzled** (-zeld) *a.* (sl.) Very drunk. [dial. *sozzle* slop together, imit.]

**S.P.** *abbr.* starting price.

**spa** (-ah) *n.* (Place with) curative mineral spring. [place]

**spāce. 1.** *n.* Continuous extension; interval between points or objects; interval of time; = OUTER *space*; large region; amount of paper used in writing etc.; blank between printed, typed, or written words etc.; (Print.) piece of metal providing this; (*attrib.*) of or used for travel etc. in outer space (*spacecraft, space flight, rocket, shuttle, travel(ler)*); **~ age,** era of space travel; **~-bar** (in typewriter, for making spaces between words etc.); **~-heater,** self-contained device for heating room; **~'man,** space traveller; **~-saving,** occupying little space; **~ station,** artificial satellite as base for operations in outer space; **~'suit,** garment allowing wearer to breathe etc. in outer space; **~-time,** fusion of concepts of space and time as 4-dimensional continuum. **2.** *v.t.* Set or arrange at intervals; put spaces between; **~ out,** put (more or wider) spaces or intervals between. **3.** **spā'cious** (-shŭs) *a.,* having ample space, roomy. [F *espace* f. L *spatium*]

**spāde¹** *n.* Digging-tool with sharp-edged broad usu. metal blade (**call a ~ a ~,** speak plainly or bluntly); similar tool for various purposes;

~'**work**, (fig.) hard preparatory work; ~'**ful** (-dŏŏl) n. [E]

**spāde**² n. Playing-card of suit (~s) denoted by black figures shaped like inverted heart with small handle; *in ~s, (fig., sl.) to a high degree, with great force. [It. *spade* pl. f. L f. Gk, = sword]

**spaghě'ttï** (-gě'-) n. Thin macaroni. [It.]

**Spăm** n. Tinned meat made from ham. [P (*spiced ham*)]

**spăn**¹. **1.** n. Full extent from end to end; maximum distance between tips of thumb and little finger, esp. as measure = 9 in.; maximum lateral extent of aeroplane or its wing; each part of bridge between supports. **2.** v.t. (-nn-). Extend from side to side or end to end of; bridge (river etc.). [E]

**spăn**². See SPICK.

**spă'ndrel** n. Space between curve of arch and the surrounding rectangular moulding or framework, or between curves of adjoining arches and moulding above. [orig. uncert.]

**spă'ngle** (-nggel). **1.** n. Small piece of glittering material esp. one of many as ornament of dress etc. **2.** v.t. Cover (as) with spangles (esp. in p.p., STAR-*spangled*). [obs. *spang* f. Du.]

**Spă'niard** (-yerd) n. Native of Spain; **spă'niel** (-yel) n., dog with long silky coat, drooping ears, and docile disposition. [F (*Espaigne* Spain)]

**Spă'nish. 1.** a. Of Spain or the Spaniards or their language; *Spanish* CHESTNUT; ~ **fly**, dried insect used in medicine etc.; ~ **Main**, (Hist.) N.E. coast of S. America and adjoining part of Caribbean Sea; ~ **onion** (large and mild-flavoured). **2.** n. Language of Spain. [place]

**spănk. 1.** n. Slap on buttocks. **2.** v.t. & i. Slap thus; (of horse etc.) move briskly; ~'**er** n., (esp., Naut.) fore-and-aft sail on after side of mizen-mast; ~'**ing** a. & adv., (esp., colloq.) striking(ly), excellent(ly), brisk. [imit.]

||**spă'nner** n. Tool for turning nut on bolt etc.; ~ **in the works**, up-setting element or influence. [G]

**spār**¹ n. Stout pole as used for ship's mast etc.; main longitudinal beam of aeroplane wing. [N *sperra* or F *esparre*]

**spār**² n. Easily cleavable crystalline mineral. [LG]

**spār**³. **1.** v.i. (-rr-). Make motions of attack and defence with closed fists, use the hands (as) in boxing; (fig.) engage in argument etc.; ~'**ring partner**, boxer employed to practise with another in training for a fight, (fig.) person with whom one enjoys arguing. **2.** n. Sparring motion; boxing-match. [E]

**spāre** v., a., & n. **1.** v.t. & i. Refrain from hurting or destroying or using or bringing into operation (**if I am ~d**, if I live so long); dispense with (**to ~**, left over, additional to what is needed); be parsimonious or grudging (with) (**not ~ oneself**, exert one's utmost efforts); let (person etc.) have (thing etc. esp. that one does not need); **spā'ring** a., frugal, grudging, restrained. **2.** a. Superfluous, not required for ordinary or present or (colloq.) others' use; reserved for emergency or occasional use; (of person etc.) lean, thin; frugal; ||**go ~**, (sl.) become very annoyed; ~ **part**, duplicate to replace lost or damaged part; ~-**rib**, closely-trimmed rib of meat, esp. pork; ~ **time**, leisure; ||~-**tyre**, (fig., colloq.) circle of fatness round or above waist. **3.** n. ||Spare part. [E]

**spārk. 1.** n. Fiery particle thrown from burning substance, or still visibly alight in ashes, or struck by impact of flint etc.; flash of light between electric conductors etc.; such discharge serving to fire explosive mixture in internal combustion engine; (fig.) flash of wit etc.; (usu. w. neg.) minute amount *of* a quality etc.; (arch.) lively or elegant young fellow; ~-**plug**, sparking-plug. **2.** v.t. & i. Emit spark(s) (||~'**ing-plug**, device for making spark in internal combustion engine); ~ (**off**), stir into activity, initiate. **3.** **spār'kle**, (v.i.) (seem to) emit sparks, glitter, glisten, scintillate, (of wine) effervesce, (n.) sparkling, glitter; ~'**ler** n., (esp.) sparkling firework, (sl.) diamond. [E]

**spă'rrow** (-ō) n. Small brownish-grey bird (HEDGE-*sparrow*); ~-**hawk**, a small hawk. [E]

**spārs|e** a. Thinly scattered, infrequent; ~'**itў** n. [L *spargo spars-* scatter]

**Spār'tan** a. & n. (Native) of Sparta

in ancient Greece; austere, rigorous, (person). [L]

**spă′sm** n. Sudden involuntary muscular contraction; sudden convulsive movement, emotion, etc.; **~ŏ′dĭc** (-zm-) a. (**-ically**), of or occurring in spasms, vigorous but intermittent; **spă′stĭc** n. & a. (**-ically**), (person) suffering from cerebral palsy with spasm of muscles. [F, or L f. Gk (spaō pull)]

**spăt¹** n. Spawn of shellfish esp. oyster. [AF]

**spăt²** n. (usu. in pl.) Short gaiter covering instep and reaching little above ankle. [abbr. spatterdash (SPATTER)]

**spăt³.** See SPIT².

**spă′tchcŏck** v.t. (colloq.) Insert or interpolate esp. incongruously. [orig. = fowl killed and quickly cooked]

**spāte** n. River-flood; (fig.) large or excessive amount. [orig. unkn.]

**spāthe** (-dh) n. Large bract(s) enveloping flower-cluster. [L f. Gk]

**spā′tial** (-shal) a. (**~ly**). Of space. [L (SPACE)]

**spă′tter. 1.** v.t. & i. Splash or scatter in drips. **2.** n. Spattering; pattering. [imit.]

**spă′tŭl|a** n. Broad-bladed instrument for mixing pigments, picking up powder, etc.; **~ate** a., with broad rounded end. [L dim. (SPATHE)]

**spă′vĭn** n. Disease of horse's hock with hard bony swelling; **~ed** (-nd) a. [F]

**spawn. 1.** v.t. & i. (Of fish, frog, mollusc, etc.) produce (eggs), be produced as eggs or young; (derog.) produce (offspring), (fig.) produce or generate in large numbers. **2.** n. Eggs of fish, frogs, etc.; (derog.) human or other offspring; white fibrous matter from which fungi grow. [AF espaundre (EXPAND)]

**spay** v.t. Remove ovaries of (female animal). [AF (ÉPÉE)]

**speak** v.i. & t. (**spoke**; **spo′ken**, pr. -ŏ′-, arch. or joc. **spoke**). Utter words in ordinary way, utter or pronounce (words), use (specified language) in speaking (cannot speak French); converse; make a speech; make known (one's opinion, the truth, etc.); make mention about or of; convey ideas (actions speak louder than words); (of gun, musical instrument, etc.) make a sound; **not** or **nothing to ~ of,** not or nothing worth mentioning, practically none or nothing; so¹ to speak; *~easy, (sl.) place where liquor is sold illicitly; ~ person fair, address him politely; ~ for, act as spokesman for, speak in defence of, bespeak; ~ for itself, be sufficient evidence; ~ for oneself, give (only) one's own opinions; ~ one's mind (frankly, bluntly, etc.); ~ out, speak loudly or freely, give one's opinion etc. without hesitation or fear; ~ to, address (person etc.), speak in confirmation of or in reference to; ~ up, = speak out; ~ volumes, be very significant; ~ volumes etc. for, well for, be abundant evidence of, place in favourable light; **~′er** n., (esp.) one who speaks in public, person of specified skill in speech-making, one who speaks specified language, loudspeaker, (S-) presiding officer of legislative assembly; **~′ing** n. & a., (esp.) **generally, roughly, strictly,** etc., **~ing,** in the general etc. sense of the word(s); **on ~ing terms,** sufficiently acquainted or friendly with person to speak to him; ‖**~ing clock,** telephone service giving correct time in words; **~ing likeness,** lifelike portrait; **~ing-tube** (for conveying voice from one room etc. to another); **-spŏken** a., (given to) speaking thus, having such a voice, (loud-, soft-, well-, spoken). [E]

**spear. 1.** n. Hunter's or footsoldier's thrusting or hurling weapon of stout staff with point usu. of steel; **~′head,** (n., esp. fig.) person or group leading a thrust or attack, (v.t.) act as spearhead of (attack etc.); **~′mint,** common garden mint, used in cookery and to flavour chewing-gum. **2.** v.t. Pierce or strike (as) with spear. [E]

**spĕc** n. (colloq.) Speculation; **on ~,** as a speculation. [abbr.]

**spĕ′cial** (-shal). **1.** a. (**~ly**). Of particular or peculiar kind, not general; for particular purpose; exceptional in amount, degree, etc. **2.** n. Special constable, edition of newspaper, dish on menu, etc. **3.** ‖**S~ Branch,** police department dealing with political security; ~ **constable** (assisting police in routine duties or in emergencies); ~ **correspondent** (appointed by newspaper to report on special event or facts); ~ **delivery** (of mail in advance of regular delivery); **~ edition** (of newspaper, including later news than ordinary edition); *special* JURY; **~ pleading**, (Law) allegation of special or new matter, (pop.) biased argument. **4. ~ist** n., one who devotes himself to particular branch of profession (esp. medicine), study, etc., or gives special attention to a thing; **~ity** (-shĭă'-) n., special feature, pursuit, product, operation, etc., thing in which a person, place, etc., specializes; **~ize** v.i. & i., become or make special, be(come) specialist *in* (subject etc.); **~iza'tion** n.; **~ty** n., speciality. [F (ESPECIAL) or L (foll.)]

**spě'cies** (-shēz, -shĭz) n. (*pl.* same). Class of things having some common characteristics; (Biol.) subdivision of genus; a kind, sort; **spě'cie** (-shē, -shĭ) n., coin as opp. to paper money. [L (*specio* look)]

**specĭ'fĭc. 1.** a. (**~ally**). Definite, distinctly formulated; particular, not general or vague; of or concerned with a species; (of medicine etc.) having distinct effect in curing a certain disease; *specific* GRAVITY. **2.** n. Specific medicine or aspect. **3. specĭficā'tion** n., (esp., usu. in *pl.*) detail of design, materials, etc., for work (to be) undertaken; **specĭfĭ'cĭty** n.; **spě'cĭfy** v.t., name expressly, mention definitely, include in specifications. [L (prec.)]

**spě'cĭmen** (*or* -ĭn) n. Individual or part taken as example of class or whole, esp. when used for investigation; (colloq., usu. derog.) person of specified sort; **spě'cĭous** (-shŭs) a., seeming good or correct but not being really so, plausible. [L (as prec.)]

**spěck. 1.** n. Small spot or stain; particle. **2.** v.t. (esp. in *p.p.*) Mark with specks. **3. ~le**, (n.) speck, esp. one of many markings on skin etc., (*v.t.*, esp. in *p.p.*) mark with speckles. [E]

**spěcs** n. pl. (colloq.) (Pair of) spectacles. [abbr.]

**spě'ctacle** n. A public show; object of sight, esp. of public attention; **make a ~** (= EXHIBITION) of oneself; (**pair of**) **~s**, pair of lenses to correct or assist defective sight, or to protect eyes, set in frame to rest on nose and ears (ROSE[1]-*coloured spectacles*); **~d** (-keld) a., wearing spectacles; **spěctā'cŭlar**, (a.) of or

like a public show, striking, lavish, (n.) spectacular performance; **spě-tā'tor** n., one who watches a show, game, incident, etc., (**spectator sport**, sport which attracts many spectators). [F f. L (*specio* spect-look)]

**spě'ctr|al** a. (**~ally**). Of spectres or spectra; ghostlike; **~oscope** n., instrument for producing and examining spectra; **~osco'pic** a. (-ically); **~o'scopў** n.; **~um** n. (*pl.* **~a**), band of colours as seen in rainbow etc., image formed by rays of light etc. in which parts are arranged according to wavelength, (fig.) entire or wide range of anything arranged by degree, quality, etc. [foll.]

**spě'ctre** (-ter), *spě'cter, n. Ghost; haunting presentiment (the spectre of ruin). [F, or L spectrum (*specio* look)]

**spě'cŭl|āte** v.i. Indulge in conjectural thought or talk or writing (on, upon, about); engage in risky financial transactions (esp. w. implication of recklessness); **~ā'tion**, **~ātor**, ns.; **~ātive** a. [L (*specula* watch-tower, as prec.)]

**spěd.** See SPEED.

**speech** n. Act, faculty, or manner of speaking (FIGURE *of speech*; **freedom of ~**, right to express one's views freely; PART *of speech*); talk or address given in public (‖King's or Queen's ~, ~ from the throne, prepared by Government and read by sovereign at opening of Parliament, outlining proposed legislation etc.); language of a nation, group, etc.; ‖**~-day**, annual celebration at school with speeches, distribution of prizes, etc.; **~ therapy**, treatment to improve defective speech; **~'ifў** v.i., (joc. or derog.) make speech(es); **~léss** a., (esp.) temporarily deprived of speech by anger, joy, etc. [E (SPEAK)]

**speed. 1.** n. Rapidity of movement, quick motion, (**at ~**, moving quickly; **at full ~**, as fast as one can go or work); rate of motion or action; gear appropriate to a range of speeds on bicycle etc.; (Photog.) relative sensitivity of film to light, light-gathering power of lens; (arch.) success, prosperity; (sl.) a stimulant drug; **~'boat**, motor boat designed for high speed; **~ limit**, maximum permitted speed of vehicle on road etc.; **∼-merchant,** (colloq.) motorist etc. who travels at high speed; **∼'way,** (arena for) motor-cycle racing, *road or track for fast traffic. **2.** *v.i.* & *t.* (**sped**). Go or send quickly; (of motorist etc.; **∼'ed**) travel at illegal or dangerous speed; (arch.) be or make prosperous or successful; **∼ up,** (cause to) move or work faster; **∼'well,** small plant with usu. bright-blue flowers. **3. ∼'ō** (colloq.; *pl.* **∼os**), **∼ö'mèter,** *ns.,* device indicating speed of vehicle; **∼'ster** *n.,* person who travels at high speed, esp. illegally; **∼'y̆** *a.* (**∼ily, ∼iness**), rapid, prompt, not long delayed. [E]

**spĕlĕŏ'logy̆** *n.* Scientific study of caves. [F f. L f. Gk *spélaion* cave]

**spĕll¹. 1.** *v.t.* & *i.* (**spelt, ∼ed** *pr.* -lt). Write or name correctly the letters of (word); (of letters) make up (word); (fig., of circumstances etc.) have as consequence, involve, (*floods spell ruin to the farmer*); **∼ out,** make out (words etc.) laboriously or slowly, (fig.) explain in detail; **∼'ing-bee,** competition in spelling. **2.** *n.* Words used as charm, incantation, etc., effect of these, fascination exercised by person or activity, (**break the ∼,** make it ineffectual, spoil a mood etc.; **under a ∼,** mastered (as) by a spell); **∼'bind,** (esp. in *p.p.*) bind (as) by spell, fascinate. [E]

**spĕll². 1.** *n.* (Short) period of time or work. **2.** *v.t.* Relieve or take turns with (person etc.). [E, = substitute]

**spĕlt¹** *n.* Kind of wheat giving very fine flour. [E]

**spĕlt².** See SPELL¹.

**spĕ'ncer** *n.* Thin jumper worn under dress. [person]

**spĕnd** *v.t.* & *i.* (**spent**). Pay out (money; **∼ a penny,** colloq., urinate or defecate); use up, consume, (material, energy, etc.); pass or occupy (time etc.); (in *p.p.*) having lost original force or strength; **∼'thrift,** extravagant person. [E f. L (EXPEND)]

**spĕrm** *n.* (*pl.* **∼s, ∼**). Semen; spermatozoon; **∼ (whale),** large whale yielding **∼acē'tī** *n.,* white waxy substance used for ointments etc.; **∼ă'tĭc** *a.* (-ically), of sperm; **∼atozō'on** *n.* (*pl.* -zoa), fertilizing element in semen; **∼ĭcīde** *n.,* substance killing spermatozoa. [L f. Gk *sperma -mat-*]

**spew,** (arch.) **spūe,** *v.t.* & *i.* Vomit (lit. or fig.). [E]

**sphā'gn|um** *n.* (*pl.* **∼a**). Moss growing in bogs and peat, used as packing etc. [L f. Gk *sphagnos*]

**sphēre** *n.* (Surface of) solid figure with every point on its surface equidistant from centre; globe, ball; each of the revolving shells in which heavenly bodies were formerly thought to be set (**harmony, music, of the ∼s,** sound supposedly produced by their movement); field of action, influence, or existence, (**∼ of influence,** area in which State etc. claims, or is recognized as having, certain interests); **sphē'rical** *a.* (-lly), shaped like sphere, of spheres); **sphēr'oid** *n.,* spherelike but not perfectly spherical body; **sphēroi'- dal** *a.* [F f. L f. Gk *sphaira* ball]

**sphī'ncter** *n.* Ring of muscle closing and opening orifice. [L f. Gk]

**sphinx** *n.* (Egypt. Ant.) figure with lion's body and man's or animal's head, esp. (**the S∼**) colossal one near the Pyramids at Giza; (Gk Myth.; **S∼**) winged monster with woman's head and lion's body, who posed riddle solved by Oedipus; (fig.) enigmatic or inscrutable person. [L f. Gk]

**spice. 1.** *n.* Aromatic or pungent vegetable substance used to flavour food; spices collectively; (fig.) touch, flavour, piquant quality. **2.** *v.t.* Flavour with spice or *with* wit etc. **3. spi'cer̆y̆** *n.,* spices; **spi'cy̆** *a.* (-ily, -iness), of or flavoured with spice, (fig.) piquant, improper. [F *espice* f. L SPECIES]

**spĭck and spă'n** *a.* Smart and new; clean and tidy. [emphat. extension of obs. *span new* (N, = new as a chip)]

**spī'der** *n.* Eight-legged arthropod, many species of which spin webs esp. to capture insects as food; thing resembling spider esp. in having radiating legs etc.; **∼-crab** (with long thin legs); **∼-man** (working at great height on building); **∼ monkey** (with long limbs and long prehensile tail); **∼'y̆** *a.,* (esp.) very thin or long. [E (SPIN)]

**spiel.** (sl.) **1.** *n.* (Esp. glib or long) speech or story. **2.** *v.i.* & *t.* Speak lengthily or glibly. [G, = game]

**spī'got** *n.* Small peg or plug;

device for controlling flow of liquor from cask etc. [foll.]

**spike**[1] n. (Sprig of) inflorescence with many sessile flowers on long axis. [L *spica* ear of corn]

**spike**[2]. **1.** n. Sharp point; pointed piece of metal, e.g. one of set forming top of iron fence or worn on bottom of running-shoe to prevent slipping; (in *pl.*) running-shoes fitted with spikes; large nail; pointed metal rod standing upright on base and used e.g. to hold unused matter in newspaper office; ~**nard**, (costly aromatic ointment formerly made from) tall sweet-smelling plant; **spi′ký** a. (**-ily, -iness**), like a spike, having spike(s), (colloq.) rigid or dogmatic or touchy or bad-tempered. **2.** v.t. Put spike(s) on or into; fix on spike(s); (Hist.) plug vent of (gun) with spike (~ person's **guns**, fig., spoil his plans); (colloq.) add alcohol to (drink). [LDu. (SPOKE)]

**spill**[1] n. Thin strip of wood, paper, etc., for lighting tobacco-pipe etc.; ~**ïkïn** n., splinter of wood etc., (in *pl.*) game in which heap of these is removed by taking one at a time without disturbing others. [LDu.]

**spill**[2]. **1.** v.t. & i. (**spilt**, ~**ed**). Allow (liquid, powder, etc.) to fall or run out from container esp. accidentally or wastefully (*no use crying over spilt* MILK; ~**way**, passage for surplus water from dam) (of liquid etc.) run out thus (~ **over**, be surplus or excessive); shed (others' blood); throw from saddle or vehicle; (sl.) disclose (information etc.; ~ **the beans**, divulge secret etc. indiscreetly or accidentally); ~**age** n., action of spilling, amount spilt. **2.** n. Spilling or being spilt; being thrown from saddle etc.; tumble, fall. [E]

**spin**. **1.** v.t. & i. (**-nn-**; **spun**). Draw out and twist (wool, cotton, etc.) into threads; make (yarn) thus; (of spider, silkworm, etc.) make (web, cocoon, etc.) by extruding viscous thread; (fig.) tell or compose (story etc.); (cause to) turn round quickly; (of person's head etc.) be in a whirl through dizziness or astonishment; toss (coin); ~**-drier**, machine for drying clothes by spinning them in rotating drum; ~**-dry**, dry (clothes) thus; ~**′ning-jenny**, (Hist.) machine for spinning fibres with more than one spindle at a time; ~**′ning-top**, = TOP[2]; ~**′ning-**

**-wheel**, household implement for spinning yarn or thread, with spindle driven by wheel with crank or treadle; ~ **off**, throw off by centrifugal force; ~-**off** n., incidental result(s), esp. benefit from industrial or technological development; ~ **out**, prolong (discussion etc.), (Crick.) dismiss (batsman, side) by spin bowling; **spun silk**, cheap material of short-fibred and waste silk, often mixed with cotton. **2.** n. Revolving motion, whirl; rotating dive of aircraft (FLAT *spin*); secondary revolving or twisting motion e.g. of cricket or tennis ball (~ **bowling**, causing cricket ball to do this); short or brisk run or spell of driving, rowing, cycling, etc. **3.** ~**ner** n., (esp.) manufacturer engaged in (esp. cotton-)spinning, real or artificial fly or revolving bait for fishing, spinneret, (Crick.) spin bowler or spun ball; ~**nerět** n., spinning-organ of spider etc., device for forming synthetic fibre. [E]

**spina bi′fida** n. Congenital defect of spine, with protruding membranes. [L, = cleft spine]

**spi′nach** (**-nïj**) n. Vegetable with succulent leaves cooked as food. [prob. Du. f. F, ult. f. Pers.]

**spi′nal** a. (~**ly**). Of spine (~ **column**, spine; ~ **cord**, cylindrical nervous structure within spine). [L (SPINE)]

**spi′ndle** n. Slender bar or rod, often with tapered ends, to twist and wind thread; pin or axis that revolves or on which thing revolves; ~**shanks**, person with long thin legs; ~**tree** (with hard wood used for spindles); **spi′ndlý** a., slender, tall and thin. [E (SPIN)]

**spi′ndrift** n. Spray blown along surface of sea. [Sc. var. of *spoondrift* f. obs. *spoon* scud]

**spine** n. Series of vertebrae extending from skull, backbone; central feature; sharp ridge or projection; sharp needle-like outgrowth of animal or plant; part of book's cover or jacket that encloses its page-fastening part and usu. faces outwards on shelf; ~**chiller, -chilling**, (book, film, etc.) causing thrill of terror; ~**less** (**-nl-**) a., lacking backbone or resoluteness, timid, weak; **spi′ný** a. (**-iness**), having (many) spines. [F *espine* L. *spina*]

**spině′t** (or **-ï′nït**) n. (Hist.) Small

harpsichord with one string to each note. [F f. It. *spinetta* dim. (prec.)]

**spi′nnaker** n. Large triangular sail carried opposite mainsail of racing-yacht running before wind. [*Sphinx*, yacht first using it]

**spi′nner(ĕt).** See SPIN.

‖**spi′nney** n. Small wood, thicket. [F f. L *spinetum* (SPINE)]

**spi′nster** n. Unmarried woman; (elderly) woman thought unlikely to marry. [orig. = woman who spins]

**spi′ny.** See SPINE.

**spīrae′a** n. Garden plant related to meadowsweet. [L f. Gk (foll.)]

**spir′al** a., n., & v. 1. a. (~ly). Coiled in a plane or as round a cylinder or cone, having this shape, (~ **staircase**, staircase rising round central axis); ~**ity** (-ă′l-) n. 2. n. Spiral curve; (**vicious**) ~, a progressive rise or fall usu. resulting from interaction of factors (*the spiral of rising wages and prices*). 3. v.i. (‖-ll-). Move in spiral course. [F or L (*spira* coil f. Gk)]

**spir′ant** a. & n. (Phon.) (Consonant) uttered with continuous expulsion of breath. [L *spiro* breathe]

**spīre** n. Tapering structure like tall cone or pyramid rising above tower; any tapering body. [E]

**spi′rit.** 1. n. Animating or vital principle of person or animal, intelligent or immaterial part of person, soul (**in** ~, inwardly); person from intellectual or moral viewpoint (KINDRED *spirit*); disembodied person or incorporeal being (HOLY *Spirit*; *the spirit* MOVES); person's mental or moral nature (**poor in** ~, arch., meek); courage, self-assertion, vivacity, (*infused spirit into his men*); attitude, mood, (*approached it in the wrong spirit*; *enter into the spirit of the thing*; PUBLIC *spirit*); (in *pl.*) state of mind (**in good** or **high**, **low** or **poor**, ~**s**, cheerful, depressed); tendency prevailing at particular time etc. (*the spirit of the age*); principle or purpose underlying the form of a law etc. (opp. *letter*); volatile liquid got by distillation; purified alcohol (METHYLAted *spirit*); (usu. in *pl.*) strong distilled liquor esp. alcohol, e.g. brandy, whisky, gin, rum; ~ **gum**, quick-drying gum for attaching false hair; ~**-lamp** (burning methylated or other volatile spirit instead of oil); ~**-level**, device with glass tube nearly filled with liquid used to test levelness by position of air-bubble; ~**-rapper**, person professing to converse with departed spirits by means of their raps on table etc. 2. v.t. Convey *away*, *off*, etc., rapidly or mysteriously (as) by agency of spirits. 3. ~**ed** a., full of spirit, lively, courageous, having specified spirit(s) (*mean*, *proud*, *-spirited*); ~**less** a., lacking courage, vigour, or vivacity; ~**ual**, (a.; -**lly**) of or concerned with the spirit, religious, divine, inspired, (‖**lords** ~**ual**, bishops in House of Lords), (n.) religious song (characteristic of Amer. Blacks); ~**ualism** n., belief that departed spirits communicate with the living (esp. through mediums), system of doctrines or practices founded on this; ~**ualist** n.; ~**uali′stic** a. (-ically); ~**uă′lity** n., spiritual quality; ~**ualize** v.t.; ~**ualizā′tion** n.; ~**uous** a., alcoholic, distilled and not only fermented. [AF f. L *spiritus* (SPIRANT)]

**spirt.** See SPURT.

**spit**[1]. 1. n. Rod on which meat is fixed for roasting over fire etc.; small point of land projecting into sea; long narrow underwater bank; spade-depth of earth. 2. v.t. (-tt-). Pierce (as) with spit. [E]

**spit**[2]. 1. v.i. & t. (-tt-; spat, spit). Eject (saliva) from mouth; do this as gesture of contempt; eject (blood, food, etc., *out*) from mouth; (fig.) utter (oaths, threats, etc.) vehemently (~ **it out**, colloq., speak quickly or candidly); make noise as of spitting; (of fire, gun, etc.) send out sparks, missiles, etc.; (of rain) fall lightly; ~**′fire**, fiery-tempered person; ~**ting image**, exact counterpart or likeness *of* (person). 2. n. Spittle (CUCKOO-*spit*); spitting (~ **and polish**, soldier's cleaning and polishing work); **the** (**dead** or **very**) ~, spitting image *of*. [E]

**spite.** 1. n. Ill will, malice; **in** ~ **of**, notwithstanding; **in** ~ **of oneself**, though one would rather have done otherwise; ~**′ful** a. (-lly), animated by spite, malicious. 2. v.t. Mortify, annoy; **cut off** one's **nose to** ~ one's **face**, injure oneself by spiteful conduct. [F (DESPITE)]

**spi′tt‖le** n. Saliva esp. as ejected from mouth; ~**oo′n** n., vessel to spit into. [SPIT[2]]

‖**spiv** n. (sl.) Man living by his wits without regular work, esp.

engaging in petty black-market dealings; flashily-dressed man; ~**vish**, ~**vỹ**, *adjs*. [orig. unkn.]

**splåsh. 1.** *v.t. & i.* Agitate (liquid) so that drops or scattered portions of it fly about; wet or stain by splashing (*with* water, mud, etc.); (of liquid) fly about thus; move *about, along*, etc., with splashing of liquid; step, fall, etc., *into* (water etc.) so as to splash it; decorate with scattered colour; display (news) prominently; spend (money) recklessly or ostentatiously. **2.** *n.* Act or noise of splashing (**make a ~**, attract much attention); quantity of liquid splashed; mark etc. made by splashing; patch of colour; prominent or ostentatious display; ‖(colloq.) small quantity of soda--water etc. (in drink); ~**ỹ** *a.* (~**ily**, ~**iness**). **3.** ~**back**, panel behind sink etc. to protect wall from splashes; ~**-board**, guard in front of vehicle or over wheel to keep mud etc. off occupants; ~**-down**, alighting of spacecraft on sea. [imit.]

**splå´tter** *v.i. & t., & n.* Splash up with continuous or noisy action; spatter. [imit.]

**splay** *v., n., & a.* **1.** *v.t. & i.* Construct (aperture) with divergent sides; make (window, doorway) wider at one side of wall; (of aperture or its sides) be so shaped or set; spread (elbows, feet, etc., *out*). **2.** *n.* Surface at oblique angle to another. **3.** *a.* Splayed. [DISPLAY]

**spleen** *n.* Abdominal organ maintaining proper condition of blood; moroseness, irritability; ~**´wort**, kind of fern. [F *esplen* f. L f. Gk *splēn*]

**splě´nd|id** *a.* Magnificent, gorgeous, sumptuous, glorious, brilliant; (colloq.) excellent, very fine; dignified, impressive; ~**i´ferous** *a.*, (colloq.) splendid; ~**our**, \*~**or**, (-*er*) *n.*, splendidness, great or dazzling brightness. [F or L (*splendeo* shine)]

**splěně´tic** *a.* (~**ally**). Bad--tempered, peevish; **splě´nĭc** *a.*, of or in the spleen. [L (SPLEEN)]

**splice. 1.** *v.t.* Join pieces of (ropes) by interweaving strands; join (pieces of wood, tape, etc.) in overlapping position; (colloq.; esp. in *pass.*) join in marriage; *splice the* MAIN[1] *brace*. **2.** *n.* Junction made by splicing. [prob. Du. *splissen*]

**splint. 1.** *n.* Strip of wood etc. bound to arm, leg, etc., esp. to keep broken bone in right position while it heals. **2.** *v.t.* Secure with splint. [LDu.]

**spli´nter. 1.** *n.* Pointed, sharp--edged, or narrow fragment broken off from wood, stone, etc.; ~ (**group, party**), group (esp. small) that has broken away from larger one; ~**-proof** (against splinters of bursting bombs etc.); ~**ỹ** *a.* **2.** *v.t. & i.* Break into splinters; break off as or like splinter. [Du., rel. to prec.]

**split. 1.** *v.t. & i.* (-**tt**-; **split**). Break, esp. lengthwise or with the grain or plane of cleavage; break forcibly; cause fission of (atom); divide into parts, thicknesses, etc.; remove or be removed by breaking or dividing (*off*); divide into disagreeing or hostile parties (*on* or *over* question etc.); = *split* one's SIDEs.; (of head) feel acute pain from headache (~**´ting headache**, acute); (sl.) betray secrets, inform *on* (accomplice etc.). **2.** *n.* Act or result of splitting; schism; half bottle of mineral water; half glass of liquor; dish made of fruit, esp. bananas, split open, with ice cream etc.; (‖in *pl.*) feat of sitting down or leaping with legs widely spread out at right angles to body. **3.** ~ **hairs**, make over-subtle distinctions; ~ **infinitive** (with adverb etc. inserted between *to* and verb); ~**-level**, (of house etc.) having some room(s) a fraction of a storey higher than adjacent part; ~ **mind**, schizophrenia; ~ **pea** (dried and split for cooking); ~ **personality**, change of personality as in schizophrenia; ~ **pin**, pin, bolt, etc., held in place by gaping of its split end; ~ **ring**, metal ring, with usu. two spiral turns, for holding keys etc.; ~ **second**, very short period of time; ~ **shift** (comprising two or more separate periods of duty); *split the* DIFFER*ence*; ~ **the vote**, (of candidate) attract votes from another so that both are perhaps defeated by a third; ~ **up**, split, esp. (of married couple etc.) cease living together. [Du.]

**splŏsh.** (colloq.) **1.** *v.t. & i.* Move with splashing. **2.** *n.* Act or noise of this; quantity of water suddenly dropped or thrown down. [imit.]

**splŏtch, splŏdge,** *n., & v.t.* Daub, blot, smear. [orig. uncert.]

**splurge** *n., & v.i.* (Make) noisy or

ostentatious display or effort. [prob. imit.]

**splŭt'ter** v. & n. Sputter (esp. of speech). [SPUTTER]

**spoil. 1.** v.t. & i. (~t, ~ed pr. -ld or -lt). Make or become useless or unsatisfactory; ruin the character of (person etc.) by indulgence (*spare the rod and spoil the child*); decay, go bad, (be ~ing for, eagerly or pugnaciously desire); (arch. or literary) plunder; ~-sport, one who spoils others' enjoyment. **2.** n. Earth etc. thrown up in digging etc.; (in pl. or collect. sing.) plunder, stolen goods, (fig.) profits, advantages accruing from success, public office, etc. [F espoille n., -llier v. f. L spolio]

**spōke¹. 1.** n. Any of the bars or rods running from hub to rim of wheel; rung of ladder; each radial handle of ship's steering-wheel; **put a ~ in** person's **wheel**, hinder or thwart his purpose; ~'shave, tool for planing spokes etc. **2.** v.t. Furnish with spokes; obstruct (wheel etc.) by thrusting spoke in. [E]

**spōke², spō'ken.** See SPEAK.

**spō'kes|man** (-ks-) n. (pl. ~men, fem. ~woman). One who speaks for others, esp. to express a group's views. [prec.]

**spōliā'tion** n. Plundering, pillage. [L (SPOIL)]

**spō'nd|ee** (or -dī) n. A metrical foot (‒ ‒); ~ā'ic a. [F, or L spondeus f. Gk]

**sponge** (-ŭnj). **1.** n. Aquatic animal with porous body-wall and tough elastic skeleton; this skeleton used as absorbent in bathing, cleansing surfaces, etc., piece of porous rubber etc. used similarly, (**throw up the ~,** abandon contest, admit defeat); thing of spongelike absorbency or consistency; sponge-cake; act of sponging; ‖~-bag, waterproof bag for holding sponge etc.; ~-cake, ~ pudding, (light, of spongelike consistency); ~ rubber (made porous like sponge). **2.** v.t. & i. Wipe or cleanse with sponge; wipe out or efface (as) with sponge; take up (water etc.) (as) with sponge; obtain (food etc.) by begging etc.; ~ (up-) on, live as a parasite on, be merely dependent on, (person etc.). **3.** spo'nger (-ŭ'nj-) n., (esp.) person who habitually sponges on others; spo'ngy̆ (-ŭ'njĭ) a. (-ily, -iness),

like sponge, porous, elastic, absorbent. [E & F f. L spongia f. Gk]

**spŏ'nsor. 1.** n. Person who makes himself responsible for another, presents candidate for baptism, introduces legislation, or contributes to charity in return for specified activity by another; advertiser who pays for broadcast which includes advertisements of his wares; **spŏn-sōr'ial** a. (-lly); ~ship n. **2.** v.t. Be sponsor for. [L (spondeo spons-pledge)]

**spŏntā'néous** a. Acting, done, or occurring without external cause or incitement; automatic, instinctive, natural; (of bodily movement, literary style, etc.) gracefully natural and unconstrained; ~ **combustion**, ignition of substance caused by chemical changes etc. within it; **spŏntanē'itў** n. [L (sponte of one's own accord)]

**spoof** n., & v.t. (colloq.) Hoax, swindle; parody. [invented wd]

**spook** n. (joc.) Ghost; ~'y̆ a. (~ily, ~iness). [LDu.]

**spool. 1.** n. Reel on which yarn, photographic film, etc., is wound; revolving cylinder of angler's reel. **2.** v.t. Wind on spool. [F espole or LDu. spole]

**spoon. 1.** n. Utensil with oval or round bowl and handle for conveying food (esp. liquid) to mouth, stirring, etc., (**dessert, table, tea, -~,** of medium, large, small, size, esp. as recognized measure for medicine or culinary ingredients); spoon-shaped thing; ~(-**bait**), revolving spoon-shaped metal fish-lure; ~'bill, wading-bird with broad flat tip of bill; ~-feed, feed (baby etc.) with spoon, (fig.) give help etc. to (person) without demanding any effort from the recipient; ~'ful (-ōōl) n. **2.** v.t. & i. Take liquid (up, out) with spoon; hit (ball) feebly upwards; (colloq.) behave in amorous way, esp. foolishly. [E]

**spōō'nerism** n. Transposition, usu. accidental, of initial letter etc. of two or more words. [Spooner, person]

**spoor** n. Animal's track or scent. [Du.]

**sporă'dic** a. (~ally). Occurring only here and there or occasionally; **spōre** n., minute reproductive cell of cryptogamous plants, resistant form of bacterium etc. [L f. Gk (sporas -ad- dispersed)]

**spŏ′rran** n. Pouch worn in front of kilt. [Gael. f. L (PURSE)]

**spŏrt. 1.** n. Pastime, game, esp. outdoor pastime, e.g. hunting, racing, cricket; these collectively; ‖(**athletic**) ~**s**, (meeting for competing in) running, jumping, throwing discus, etc.; amusement, diversion, fun, (**in** ~, jestingly; **make** ~ **of**, ridicule); (colloq.) good fellow, sporting person; animal or plant deviating suddenly or strikingly from normal type; ~**s car** (of low-built fast type); ~**s coat** (suitable for outdoor sports or informal wear); ~**′sman**, person fond of sport, person who behaves fairly and generously; ~**′smanlike** a.; ~**′smanship** n. **2.** v.i. & t. Engage in sport; wear or exhibit, esp. ostentatiously. **3.** ~**′ing** a., interested or concerned in sport, sportsmanlike (a ~**ing chance**, some possibility of success); ~**′ive** a., playful; ~**′y** a. (~**ily**, ~**iness**), (colloq.) fond of sport, rakish, showy. [DISPORT]

**spŏt. 1.** n. Particular place, definite locality; particular part of one's body or (fig.) character (SOFT, WEAK, spot); (colloq.) one's (regular) position in an organization, programme of events, etc.; small mark differing in colour, texture, etc., from the surface it is on; pimple; small circle or dot used to distinguish faces of dice etc.; (fig.) blemish on character; ‖(colloq.) small quantity of something (a spot of lunch, whisky, culture); drop (of rain etc.); spotlight; **in a** (**tight** etc.) ~, (colloq.) in difficulties; **knock** ~**s off**, (colloq.) easily defeat or surpass; **on the** ~, without delay or change of place, at scene of action or event, (of person) wide awake, (colloq.) compelled to take some action; **put on the** ~, *(sl.) decide to murder; **run on the** ~, raise feet alternately as in running but without moving forwards or backwards; ~ **cash**, money paid immediately after sale; ~ **check**, test made on the spot or on randomly selected subject; ~**′-light**, (n.) (projector giving) beam of light on particular part of theatre stage, particular part of road in front of vehicle, etc., (fig.) full attention or publicity, (v.t.) illuminate with spotlight (lit. or fig.); ~**o′n**, (colloq.) precise(ly); ~ **welding** (between points of metal surfaces in contact). **2.** v.t. & i. (-**tt**-). Mark or become

marked with spot(s); make spots, rain slightly; (colloq.) pick out, recognize, catch sight of; (Mil.) locate (enemy's position etc.); watch for and take note of (trains, talent, etc.); (in *p.p.*) marked or decorated with spots (~**ted Dick**, or **dog**, Dalmatian dog, ‖sl. plum duff). **3.** ~**less** a., (esp.) absolutely clean; ~**′ty** a. (-**ily**, -**iness**), marked with (many) spots, patchy, irregular. [perh. LDu.]

**spouse** (-z) n. Husband or wife. [F f. L *sponsus -sa* (as SPONSOR)]

**spout. 1.** n. Projecting tube or lip through which liquid etc. is poured from teapot, jug, kettle, roof-gutter, fountain, etc., (**up the** ~, sl., pawned, useless, broken, in trouble [f. sense 'pawnbroker's lift']); jet or column of liquid etc. **2.** v.t. & i. Discharge or issue forcibly in jet; utter in declamatory manner. [Du.]

**sprain. 1.** v.t. Wrench (ankle, wrist, etc.) and so cause pain or swelling. **2.** n. Such injury. [orig. unkn.]

**sprăng.** See SPRING.

**sprăt** n. Small sea-fish; **a** ~ **to catch a herring** or **mackerel** or **whale**, a little risked to gain much. [E]

**sprawl. 1.** v.i. & t. Sit, lie, or fall with limbs flung out or in ungainly way; spread (one's limbs) thus; (of plant, town, writing, etc.) be of irregular or straggling form. **2.** n. Sprawling position, movement, or mass. [E]

**spray**[1]. **1.** n. Water or other liquid flying in small drops; liquid preparation to be applied in this form with atomizer etc.; device for such application. **2.** v.t. Throw (liquid) in form of spray; sprinkle (object) thus, esp. (plants etc.) with insecticides; ~**-gun**, gunlike device for spraying paint etc. [orig. uncert.]

**spray**[2] n. Sprig of plant or small branch of tree, esp. graceful one with flowers and leaves used as ornament; artificial ornament in similar form. [E]

**spread** (-ĕd). **1.** v.t. & i. (**spread**). (Cause to) become widely known or felt (is *spreading rumours*; *rumours are spreading*); cover surface of (*bread spread with butter*); lay (table); ~ (**out**), extend surface of, cause to cover larger surface, display thus, have wide or specified or increasing extent; ~ one**self**, be lavish or discursive; ~ **eagle**, figure of eagle with legs and wings extended as emblem; ~-**ea'gle** v.t., place (person) in position with arms and legs spread out, defeat utterly. 2. n. Action, capability, or extent of spreading; breadth; increased bodily girth (*middle-age(d) spread*); diffusion (*of* education etc.); = BED*spread*; paste for spreading on bread etc.; printed matter spread across two facing pages or across more than one column; range of prices, rates, etc.; (colloq.) meal esp. feast. [E]

**spree** n. Lively frolic, bout of drinking etc., (**on the ~**, engaged in this); **buying, shopping, spending, ~**, occasion of lavish spending. [orig. unkn.]

**sprig. 1.** n. Small branch, shoot; ornament resembling this, esp. on fabric; (usu. derog.) young man. **2.** v.t. (**-gg-**). Ornament with sprigs (*sprigged muslin*). [LG *sprick*]

**spri'ghtl|y** (-ī't-) a. (~**iness**). Vivacious, lively, brisk. [SPRITE]

**spring. 1.** v.i. & t. (**sprang; sprung**). Rise rapidly or suddenly, leap; move rapidly (as) by action of a spring; originate or arise (*from* source, ancestors, etc.); (cause to) act or appear suddenly or unexpectedly; (of wood etc.) split; rouse (game) from covert etc.; contrive escape of (person *from* prison etc.); (usu. in *p.p.*) provide (chair, vehicle, etc.) with springs; develop (leak); ~ (thing, situation, etc.) **on**, present it suddenly or unexpectedly to (person); ~ **up**, come into being, appear. **2.** n. Jump, leap; first season of year, when vegetation begins to appear; (fig.) early stage of life etc.; place where water, oil, etc., wells up from earth, basin or flow so formed; recoil; elasticity; elastic contrivance usu. of bent or coiled metal used esp. to drive clockwork or for cushioning furniture or in vehicles; (fig.) motive for or origin of action, custom, etc.; ~ **balance** (measuring weight by tension of spring); ~**board**, elastic board giving impetus in leaping, diving, etc., (fig.) source of impetus; ~**bok**, S. Afr. gazelle; ~ **chicken**, young fowl for eating, (fig.) youthful person; ~-**clean** n., & v.t., clean(ing) (house, room) thoroughly, esp. in spring; ~ **gun** (contrived to go off

when trespasser or animal touches wire connected to trigger); ~ **mattress** (containing springs); ~ **onion** (taken from ground before bulb has formed, and eaten raw); *spring* TIDE; ~'**tide** (poet.), ~'**time**, season of spring (lit. or fig.). **3.** ~**e** (-nj) n., noose or snare for catching small game; ~'**er** n., (esp.) support from which arch springs, small spaniel, springbok; ~'**y** a. (~**ily**, ~**iness**), elastic. [E]

**spri'nkl|e.** v.t. Scatter in small drops or particles; subject (ground, object) to sprinkling (*with* liquid etc.); (of liquid etc.) fall thus on; (fig.) distribute in small amounts; ~**er** n., (esp.) device for sprinkling water on lawn or to extinguish fires; ~**ing** n., (esp.) *a* few or *a* little here and there *of*. **2.** n. Light shower (*of* rain etc.). [orig. uncert.]

**sprint. 1.** v.i. & t. Run short distance, run (specified distance), at full speed. **2.** n. Such run; similar short effort in cycling, swimming, etc. [N]

**sprit** n. Small diagonal spar from mast to upper outer corner of sail; ~'**sail** (*or* -sal), sail extended by sprit. [E]

**sprite** n. Elf, fairy. [*sprit*, contr. of SPIRIT]

**spro'cket** n. Each of several teeth on wheel engaging with links of chain. [orig. unkn.]

**sprout. 1.** v.t. & i. Put forth (shoots, hair, etc.); begin to grow. **2.** n. Shoot of plant; (in *pl.*, colloq.) = BRUSSELS *sprouts*. [E]

**spruce**[1] (-ōōs). **1.** a. Neat in dress and appearance, smart. **2.** v.t. & i. Smarten (one*self* etc., usu. *up*). [perh. foll.]

**spruce**[2] (-ōōs) n. Conifer with dense conical foliage; its wood. [obs. *Pruce* Prussia]

**sprung.** See SPRING.

**spry** a. (~'**er**, ~'**est**; ~'**ly**, ~'**ness**). Lively, nimble. [orig. unkn.]

**spud. 1.** n. Small narrow spade for weeding; (sl.) potato; ~-**bashing**, (orig. Services' sl.) task of peeling potatoes. **2.** v.t. (**-dd-**). Remove (weeds *up*, *out*) with spud.

**spue.** See SPEW.

**spum|e** n., & v.i. Froth, foam; ~'**y** a. (~**ily**, ~**iness**). [F, or L *spuma*]

**spun.** See SPIN.

**spunk** n. Touchwood; (colloq.)

courage, mettle, spirit; (sl.) semen; ~'**y** a., brave, spirited. [orig. unkn.]

**spŭr. 1.** n. Device with small spike(d wheel) attached to rider's heel for urging horse forward (**win** one's ~**s**, Hist. gain knighthood, fig. gain distinction or fame); (fig.) stimulus, incentive, (**on the ~ of the moment**, impromptu, on a momentary impulse); spur-shaped thing, esp. hard projection on cock's leg, projection from mountain (range), branch road or railway. **2.** v.t. & i. (**-rr-**) Prick (horse) with spur; incite (person *on to* effort, *to do*, etc.); stimulate (interest etc.); ride hard (*on, forward*, etc.); (esp. in *p.p.*) provide with spurs. [E]

**spŭrge** n. Plant with acrid milky juice. [F *espurge* f. L (EXPURGATE)]

**spŭr'ious** a. Not genuine, not what it purports to be. [L]

**spŭrn** v.t. Reject with disdain, treat with contempt; repel with one's foot. [E]

**spŭrt. 1.** v.i. & t. (Cause to) gush out in jet or stream (also **spĭrt**); make a spurt. **2.** n. Sudden gushing out, jet, (also **spĭrt**); short sudden effort or increase of pace in racing etc. [orig. unkn.]

**spŭt'nik** (*or* -ōō'-) n. Russian artificial earth satellite. [Russ.]

**spŭt'ter. 1.** v.i. & t. Speak or emit with spitting sound; emit spitting sounds; speak rapidly or incoherently. **2.** n. Sputtering speech or sound. [Du. (imit.)]

**spŭt'um** n. (*pl.* ~**a**). Saliva; expectorated matter esp. used to diagnose disease. [L]

**spy̆. 1.** n. Person secretly collecting and reporting information on activities or movements of enemy, competitor, etc.; person keeping (secret) watch on others. **2.** v.i. & t. Act as spy (*on* person or proceedings); pry (*into* secret etc.); discern, esp. by careful observation (**I ~**, children's game of guessing visible object from initial letter of its name); **~ out**, explore or discover, esp. secretly; **~ out the land**, (fig.) examine or assess the situation. **3.** ~'**glass**, small telescope; ~'**hole**, peep-hole. [F *espie*(r) f. Gmc]

**sq.** *abbr.* square.

**Sqn. Ldr.** *abbr.* Squadron Leader.

**squab** (-ŏ-). **1.** n. Short fat person; young esp. unfledged pigeon or other bird; stuffed cushion, esp. ‖as

part of seat in motor car; sofa, ottoman. **2.** a. Short and fat, squat. [perh. Scand.]

**squa'bble** (-ŏ'-) v.i., & n. (Engage in) petty or noisy quarrel. [prob. imit.]

**squad** (-ŏ-) n. Small group of people sharing task etc., esp. small number of soldiers (**awkward ~**, of awkward or incompetent recruits; FLYING *squad*); *\*~ car*, police car having radio link with headquarters; ~'**die**, ~'**dy**, n., ‖(sl.) recruit, private; ~'**ron** n., organized body of persons etc., esp. cavalry division of 2 troops, detachment of warships employed on particular service, unit of R.A.F. with 10 to 18 aircraft (~**ron leader**, officer commanding this, next below wing commander). [F *escouade* f. It. (SQUARE)]

**squa'lid** (-ŏ'-) a. Dirty, filthy; mean or poor in appearance; wretched, sordid; ~**or** n. [L]

**squall** (-awl). **1.** n. Sudden or violent gust(s) of wind, esp. with rain, snow, or sleet; discordant cry, scream (esp. of baby); ~'**y** a. (~**iness**). **2.** v.i. & t. Utter (with) squall(s); scream. [prob. alt. SQUEAL after BAWL]

**squa'nder** (-ŏ'-) v.t. Spend wastefully. [orig. unkn.]

**squāre** a., adv., n., & v. **1.** a. Having shape of a square (**~ foot** etc., square whose side is one foot etc., its area); rectangular; at right angles *to*; level or parallel (*with*); angular, not round; having breadth nearer length or height than is usual (*a man of square frame*); properly arranged, settled; not in debt; (**all**) ~, with no debit remaining, (Golf) having won same number of holes as opponent; fair, honest; thorough, direct, uncompromising, (*met with a square refusal*); (sl.) conventional, old-fashioned, unsophisticated; ~ **dance** (with usu. 4 couples facing inwards from 4 sides); ~ **deal**, bargain or treatment; ~ **leg**, (Cricket) (position of) fieldsman at or some distance from batsman's leg-side and nearly opposite stumps; ~ **meal** (substantial, satisfying); ~ **measure** (expressed in square feet etc.); *square peg in round* HOLE; ~-**rigged**, with principal sails at right angles to length of ship; ~ **root**, number that multiplied by itself gives a specified number; ~-

**-shouldered,** with broad, not sloping or rounded, shoulders; **~-toed,** (having boots or shoes) with square toes, (fig.) formal, prim. **2.** *adv.* Squarely (*hit him square on the jaw*); fairly; honestly; FAIR² *and square.* **3.** *n.* Equilateral rectangle; object of (approximately) this shape; square scarf; small square area on game-board (**back to ~ one,** colloq., back to starting-point with no progress made); open area (usu. quadrilateral) in town surrounded with buildings; area of cricket-field for use as wicket; area within barracks etc. for drill (**~-bashing,** Services sl., drill on barrack-square); L- or T-shaped instrument for obtaining or testing right angles (*T-square*; **out of ~,** not at right angles; SET² *square*); product of number multiplied by itself (*the square of 9 is 81*; **perfect ~,** square of an integer); square arrangement of persons, letters, figures, etc.; (sl.) person who is conventional, old-fashioned, or unsophisticated; **on the ~,** honest(ly), fair(ly). **4.** *v.t.* & *i.* Make square (**~ the circle,** construct square equal in area to given circle, fig. do what is impossible); mark out in squares; place (shoulders etc.) squarely facing forwards; multiply (number) by itself; adjust, make or be suitable *to* or consistent *with*, reconcile; settle, pay, (bill etc.); (colloq.) pay or bribe (person); (Golf) make score of (match) all square; **~ (*off**),** assume attitude of boxer; **~ up to,** move towards (person) in this attitude, (fig.) face and tackle (difficulty etc.) resolutely. [F *esquare* (L EX-¹, *quadra*)]

**squash¹** (-ŏ-). **1.** *v.t.* & *i.* Squeeze flat or into pulp; force or make one's way (*into*) by squeezing; crowd; (fig.) silence (person) with crushing retort etc. **2.** *n.* Crowd(ed state); sound (as) of something being squashed; ‖drink made of crushed fruit (*lemon, orange, squash*); **~** (**rackets**), game played with rackets and fairly soft ball in closed court. [F *esquasser* (EX-¹, QUASH)]

**squash²** (-ŏ-) *n.* (Gourd of) trailing annual plant. [Narraganset]

**squat** (-ŏ-) *v., a.,* & *n.* **1.** *v.i.* & *t.* (-tt-). Sit on one's heels, or on ground with knees drawn up, or in hunched posture; put (*oneself,* person) into squatting position;

(colloq.) sit down; act as squatter. **2.** *a.* Squatting; (of person etc.) short and thick, dumpy. **3.** *n.* Squatting posture; being squatter; place occupied by squatter(s). **4.** **~'ter** *n.,* (esp.) Austral. sheep-farmer, person who takes unauthorized possession of unoccupied premises etc. [F *esquatir* flatten]

**squaw** *n.* N. Amer. Ind. woman or wife. [Narraganset]

**squawk** *v.i.,* & *n.* (Utter) loud harsh cry esp. of bird; complain(t). [imit.]

**squeak. 1.** *n.* Short shrill cry (as) of mouse; slight high-pitched sound (as) of rusty hinge; (**narrow ~,** narrow escape, success barely attained; BUBBLE *and squeak*; **~'y̌** *a.* (**~ily, ~iness**). **2.** *v.i.* & *t.* Make a squeak; utter (words) shrilly; (colloq.) pass narrowly *by, through,* etc.; (sl.) turn informer. [imit. (foll. SHRIEK)]

**squeal. 1.** *n.* Shrill cry (as) of child etc. **2.** *v.i.* & *t.* Make a squeal; utter (words) with squeal; (sl.) protest vociferously, turn informer. [imit.]

**squea'mish** *a.* Easily nauseated (lit. or fig.); fastidious, over-scrupulous. [AF *escoymos*]

**squeegee'** *n.,* & *v.t.* (Treat with) instrument with rubber edge, roller, etc., and handle, used to remove liquid from surfaces. [*squeege,* alt. of foll.]

**squeeze. 1.** *v.t.* & *i.* Exert pressure on from opposite or all sides, esp. to extract moisture; press (person's hand) with one's own as sign of sympathy, affection, etc.; extract moisture (*out* of something), reduce size of, alter shape of, by squeezing; force (one*self,* person, thing), make one's way, into or through small or narrow space; bring pressure (lit. or fig.) to bear on, harass by exactions, extort money etc. from, get by entreaty or extortion (money etc. *out of*). **2.** *n.* Action or result of squeezing; small quantity produced by squeezing; crowd(ed state); extortion or exaction; (Econ.) (policy of) restriction on borrowing and investment; **~ bottle,** flexible container whose contents are extracted by squeezing it. [orig. unkn.]

**squĕlch. 1.** *n.* Make sucking sound (as) of treading in thick mud; move with squelching sound; disconcert, silence. **2.** *n.* Act or sound of squelching. [imit.]

**squib** *n.* Small firework burning with hissing sound and usu. with final explosion (**damp ~**, unsuccessful attempt to impress etc.); short satirical composition. [perh. imit.]

**squid** *n.* Ten-armed marine cephalopod. [orig. unkn.]

**squiffed** (-ft), **squi'ffy**, *adjs.* (sl.) Slightly drunk. [orig. unkn.]

**squi'ggl|e** *n.* Short curling line, esp. in handwriting; **~ỹ** *a.* [imit.]

**squill** *n.* Bulbous plant resembling lily. [L *squilla* f. Gk]

**squint. 1.** *v.i.* Have the eyes turned in different directions; look esp. obliquely or with half-shut eyes (*at* etc.). **2.** *n.* Squinting condition of eyes; stealthy or sidelong glance; (colloq.) glance, look; oblique opening in church wall affording view of altar. [obs. *asquint*, perh. f. LDu. (Du. *schuinte* slant)]

**squire. 1.** *n.* Country gentleman, esp. *the* chief landowner in country district; woman's escort or gallant; (Hist.) knight's attendant. **2.** *v.t.* (Of man) attend or escort (woman). **3.** **~'archỹ** (-ī'árkĭ) *n.*, landowners collectively. [ESQUIRE]

**squirm. 1.** *v.i.* Wriggle, writhe; (fig.) show or feel embarrassment or discomfort. **2.** *n.* Squirming movement. [imit.]

**squi'rrel. 1.** *n.* Bushy-tailed usu. arboreal rodent (GREY, RED, *squirrel*); its fur. **2.** *v.t.* (‖-ll-). Hoard (*away*). [AF f. L (*sciurus* f. Gk)]

**squirt. 1.** *v.t. & i.* Eject (liquid etc.) in a jet; be ejected thus. **2.** *n.* (Device for ejecting) jet of water etc.; (colloq.) insignificant self-assertive person. [imit.]

**squish** *v.i.*, & *n.* (Move with) slight squelching sound; **~'ỹ** *a.* [imit.]

**‖squit** *n.* (sl.) Small or insignificant person. [cf. SQUIRT]

**Sr.** *abbr.* Senior; Señor.

**S.R.N.** *abbr.* State Registered Nurse.

**SS.** *abbr.* Saints.

**S.S.** *abbr.* steamship; (Hist.) Nazi special police force [G *Schutz-Staffel*].

**S.S.E., S.S.W.,** *abbrs.* south-south-east, -west.

**St.** *abbr.* SAINT; Street.

**st.** *abbr.* stone; stumped by.

**stab. 1.** *v.t. & i.* (-bb-). Pierce or

wound with (usu. short) pointed tool or weapon; aim blow with such weapon (*at*); (fig.) cause sharp pain to (person, feelings, etc.). **2.** *n.* Act or result of stabbing (lit. or fig.); (colloq.) attempt (*have a stab at it*); **~ in the back,** (fig.) treacherous or slanderous attack. [orig. unkn.]

**stabi'lity** *n.* Being stable; **stā'bil-ize** *v.t. & i.*, make or become stable; **stābilizā'tion** *n.*; **stā'bilizer** *n.*, (esp.) device to keep ship or aircraft steady. [F f. L (foll.)]

**stā'ble** *a.*, *n.*, & *v.* **1.** *a.* (**-bly**) Firmly fixed or established, not easily moved, changed, or destroyed; resolute, constant. **2.** *n.* Building in which horses are kept; place where racehorses are kept and trained; racehorses of particular stable; (persons, products, etc., having) common origin or affiliation; **~-companion, -mate,** horse of same stable, (fig.) member of same organization; **lock** or **shut the ~-door after** or **when the horse is stolen,** take preventive action too late. **3.** *v.t.* Put or keep (horse) in stable; **stā'bling** *n.*, (esp.) accommodation for horses. [F *estable* f. L (*sto* stand)]

**staccā'tō** (-ah'-) *a.*, *adv.*, & *n.* (*pl.* **~s**). (Piece of music etc.) with each sound or spoken phrase sharply distinct from the others. [It.]

**stack. 1.** *n.* Pile or heap, esp. in orderly arrangement (HAY*stack*); part of library where books are compactly stored; ‖high detached rock esp. off coast of Scotland; stacked group of aircraft; (colloq.) large quantity (*a stack of work*; *has stacks of money*); (**chimney-**)**~**, number of chimneys standing together; tall factory chimney; (**smoke-**)**~**, funnel of locomotive or steamship. **2.** *v.t.* Pile in stack(s); arrange (cards, or fig. circumstances etc.) secretly for cheating; cause (aircraft) to fly round at different levels while waiting to land. [N]

**stā'dium** *n.* Enclosed athletic or sports ground with tiers of seats for spectators. [L f. Gk]

**staff** (-ahf). **1.** *n.* (*pl.* **~s**, arch. exc. Mus. **staves** *pr.* -āvz). Stick or pole esp. as weapon or support or as symbol of office; group of persons carrying on work under manager etc. (‖**~ nurse,** nurse ranking just below a sister); those in authority in a school etc.; (Mil. etc.) body of officers assisting officer in high command (GENERAL *staff*; ||~ **college,** where officers are trained for staff duties; ~ **officer,** serving on staff; ~ **sergeant,** senior sergeant in cavalry or engineers); (Mus.) set of usu. 5 parallel lines to indicate pitch of notes by position. 2. *v.t.* Provide (institution etc.) with staff. [E]

**Staffs.** *abbr.* Staffordshire.

**stǎg** *n.* Male deer; ||(St. Exch.) one who seeks to buy new shares and sell at once for profit; (*attrib.,* colloq.) (suitable) for men only (*stag film, -party*); ~**-beetle** (with branched mandibles like antlers); ~**'hound,** large hound used in hunting deer. [E]

**stǎge. 1.** *n.* Platform, esp. on which plays etc. are performed before audience; (fig.) the drama, acting profession, dramatic art or literature, (**go on the** ~, become actor or actress); scene of action (**hold the** ~, dominate conversation etc.); point or period of development or process (*reached a critical stage; is in the larval stage*); (regular) stopping place on route, distance between two of these; (**fare-**)~, (end of) section of bus etc. route for which fixed fare is charged; surface in microscope where object is put for inspection; section of space-rocket with separate engine; ~**-coach,** (Hist.) large closed coach running regularly by stages between two places; ~**'craft,** skill or experience in writing or staging plays; ~ **direction,** instruction in a play about actor's movement, sounds heard, etc.; ~ **door,** entrance from street to backstage part of theatre; ~ **fright,** nervousness on facing audience esp. for first time; ~**-hand,** person handling scenery etc.; ~**-manage,** be stage-manager of, (fig.) arrange and control for effect; ~**-manager,** person responsible for lighting, mechanical arrangements, etc., of play; ~ **play** (opp. broadcast etc.); ~**-struck,** strongly wishing to be actor or actress; ~ **whisper,** an aside, loud whisper meant to be heard by others than the person addressed. 2. *v.t.* Present (play etc.) on stage; organize, arrange occurrence of, esp. dramatically; **stǎ'ger** *n.* (esp. *old* ~**r,** experienced person); **stǎ'gy** *a.* (**-ily, -iness**), theatrical, artificial, exaggerated. [F *estage* f. Rom. (L *sto* stand)]

**stǎg'ger** (-g-). **1.** *v.i.* & *t.* (Cause to) walk or move unsteadily; (of news etc.) cause shock or confusion to (person); arrange (events, hours of work, etc.) so that they do not coincide; arrange (objects) so that they are not in line. 2. *n.* Staggering movement; (in *pl.*) disease, esp. of horses and cattle, causing staggering. 3. ~**'ĭng** *a.,* (esp.) bewildering, astonishing. [N]

**stǎ'gĭng** *n.* Presentation of play etc.; (temporary) platform; shelves for plants in greenhouse; ~ **post,** regular stopping-place, esp. on air route. [STAGE]

**stǎg'n|ant** *a.* (Of liquid) motionless, having no current; (of life, mind, etc.) inactive, dull, sluggish; ~**ā'te** *v.i.,* be or become stagnant; ~**ancy̆,** ~**ā'tion,** *ns.* [L (*stagnum* pond)]

**stǎ'gy̆.** See STAGE.

**staid** *a.* Of quiet and sober character or demeanour, sedate. [p.p. of STAY]

**stain. 1.** *v.t.* (Of liquid, vapour, etc.) sink into or mingle with and change colour of, make coloured patch(es) on thus, discolour; (fig.) sully or blemish (reputation, character, etc.); colour (wood, glass, microscopic specimen, etc.) with substance that penetrates the material. 2. *n.* Act or result of staining; substance used in staining; (fig.) blot, blemish (*without a stain on his character*); ~**'lèss** *a.,* without stain(s), not liable to stain (~*less steel,* chrome steel that resists rust and corrosion). [*distain* f. F f. Rom. (DIS-, TINGE)]

**stair** *n.* Each of a set of fixed indoor steps; (in *pl.*) set of these (BACK *stairs*; **below** ~**s,** in basement, esp. as the part occupied by servants); ~**'case,** (part of building containing) flight(s) of stairs; ~**-rod** (for securing carpet in angle between two steps); ~**'way,** (way up) a flight of stairs. [E]

**stāke. 1.** *n.* Stout stick pointed for driving into ground as support, boundary mark, etc.; (Hist.) post to which person was tied to be burnt alive, this death as punishment; money etc. wagered on event, esp. deposited with third party (~**'holder**) by each of those who make a wager (**at** ~, wagered, risked, to be won or lost); interest or concern, esp. financial (*in something; has a*

~ *in the country*, as landowner etc.); (in *pl.*) money to be contended for, esp. in horse-race, such race; **~-boat** (anchored to mark course for boat race etc.). **2.** *v.t.* Secure or support with stake(s); mark (area) *off*, *out*, with stakes (*stake* (*out*) *a* CLAIM, lit. or fig.); wager (money etc. *on* event); *(colloq.) give financial or other support to; **\*~ out**, (colloq.) place under surveillance. [E]

**Stakha′nov|ite** (-kah′-) *n.* (Esp. Russian) worker whose high output wins special awards; **~ism** *n.* [*Stakhanov*, person]

**stă′lactite** *n.* Icicle-like deposit of calcium carbonate hanging from roof of cave etc.; **stă′lagmite** *n.*, similar deposit rising like spike from floor. [L f. Gk *stalaktos* dripping]

**stale. 1.** *a.* Not fresh; musty, insipid, or otherwise the worse for age or use; lacking novelty, trite, (*stale joke*, *news*); (of athlete, musician, etc.) having ability impaired by excessive exertion, practice, etc. **2.** *v.i.* & *t.* Become or make stale. **3.** **~′mate** (-lm-), (*n.*) state of chess-game counting as draw, in which one player cannot move without going into check, (fig.) deadlock in proceedings, (*v.t.*) bring (player) to stalemate, (fig.) bring to standstill. [AF (*estaler* come to a stand)]

**Sta′lin|ism** (-ah′-) *n.* Policy followed by *Stalin* in governing U.S.S.R.; **~ist** *n.* [person]

**stalk**[1] (-awk) *n.* Stem, esp. main stem of herbaceous plant or slender stem supporting leaf, flower, fruit, etc.; similar support of organ etc. in animals. [dim. of obs. *stale* rung]

**stalk**[2] (-awk). **1.** *v.t.* & *i.* Pursue or approach (wild animal, enemy) stealthily; stride, walk in stately or haughty manner; **~′ing-horse**, horse behind which hunter hides, (fig.) pretext concealing one's real intentions or actions. **2.** *n.* Stalking of game; imposing gait. [E, rel. to STEAL]

**stall** (-awl). **1.** *n.* (Compartment for one animal in) stable or cowhouse (**~-feed**, fatten in stall); trader's booth in market etc. (‖BOOK-*stall*); fixed seat in choir or chancel, more or less enclosed at back and sides; ‖(usu. in *pl.*) each of seats on ground floor of theatre; compartment for one person in shower-bath, one horse at start of race, etc.;

= FINGER-*stall*; (condition resulting from) stalling of engine or aircraft. **2.** *v.t.* & *i.* Put or keep (cattle etc.) in stall(s); (of motor vehicle or its engine) stop because of inadequate fuel-supply, overloading of engine, etc.; (of aircraft) get out of control because speed is insufficient; cause (engine, vehicle, aircraft) to stall; play for time when being questioned etc.; delay or obstruct (person etc.). **3.** **stă′llion** (-yon) *n.*, uncastrated male horse. [E]

**sta′lwart** (-awl′-). **1.** *a.* Strongly built, sturdy; courageous, resolute. **2.** *n.* Stalwart person, esp. loyal uncompromising partisan. [E, = place-worthy]

**stă′měn** (*or* -en) *n.* Male fertilizing organ of flowering plant; **stă′mĭna** *n.*, vigour, ability to endure prolonged strain on body or mind. [L, = warp-thread]

**stă′mmer. 1.** *v.i.* & *t.* Speak with halting articulation, esp. with pauses or rapid repetitions of same syllable; ~ (**out**), utter (words) thus. **2.** *n.* Act or habit of stammering. [E]

**stămp. 1.** *v.t.* & *i.* Bring down (one's foot) heavily on ground etc., crush or flatten thus, (**~′ing-ground**, favourite place of resort or action); impress (pattern, mark, etc.) on; impress with pattern, mark, etc.; affix postage or other stamp to; (fig.) assign specific character to, mark out, (*this stamps him as a genius*); ~ **on**, impress on (the memory etc.), suppress; ~ **out**, produce by cutting out with die etc., put an end to, destroy. **2.** *n.* Instrument for stamping; mark or design made by this; act or sound of stamping of foot; = POSTAGE *stamp*; mark impressed on, label etc. fixed to, commodity as evidence of quality etc.; characteristic mark or quality (*her face bears the stamp of suffering*); **~-collector** (of postage stamps); **~-duty** (imposed on certain kinds of legal document); **~-hinge**, small piece of gummed paper to fix postage stamp in collector's album; **~-machine** (for selling postage stamps); **~-paper**, gummed marginal paper of sheet of postage stamps. **3.** **~ē′de**, (*n.*) sudden hurried movement of (usu. frightened) cattle, people, etc., uncontrolled or unreasoning action by large number of people, (*v.i.* & *t.*) (cause to) take part in stampede. [E]

**stănce** (*or* -ah-) *n*. Position adopted for stroke at golf, cricket, etc.; (fig.) attitude, standpoint. [F f. It. STANZA]

**stanch**[1], **staunch**[2], (-ah-, -aw-) *v.t.* Stop flow of (esp. blood); stop flow from (esp. wound). [F *estancher* (STAUNCH[1])]

**stanch**[2]. See STAUNCH[1].

**sta'nchion** (-ah'nshon) *n*. Upright post or support; device for confining cattle in stall etc. [AF]

**stănd. 1.** *v.i.* & *t*. (**stood** *pr*. -ŏŏd). Have, take, or maintain upright position, esp. on feet or base; be of specified height (*stands ten feet high*); be (situated) (*the house stands at the end of the road*); be in specified condition (*stands convicted of treason, in need of help; the matter stands thus*); act as (*stand proxy*); assume stationary position, cease to move; maintain position, avoid falling, moving, or being moved, (*don't stand arguing; whether we stand or fall; stand fast or firm*); remain valid or unaltered (*the former conditions may stand*); move to and remain in specified position (lit. or fig.; *stand aloof, aside, back, clear*); (Naut.) hold specified course (*stand in for the shore*); set in upright or specified position (*stand the jug on the table*); endure, tolerate, (*can't stand pain, that fellow*); undergo (trial); provide (person) with (thing, esp. drink) at one's own expense; **as it ∼s**, in its present condition; *not a* LEG *to stand on; stand a* CHANCE; **∼ alone**, be unsupported or unequalled; **∼ and deliver**, stop and hand over your valuables (as highwayman's order); **∼ between**, act as mediator or protector; **∼ by**, uphold or support (person), adhere to (terms, promise, beliefs, stand ready for action, stand near, look on without interfering; **∼-by** *n*. (pl. -bys), thing or person that is kept for emergency or that can be depended on; **∼ corrected**, accept that one was wrong; **∼ down**, withdraw from position or candidacy, leave witness-box or similar place; ||**∼ easy**, (Mil.) stand in more relaxed position than 'at ease'; **∼ for**, represent, signify, imply, support (a cause etc.), ||be candidate for (office, Parl. constituency), (colloq.) endure, tolerate; **∼ one's ground**, maintain one's position (lit. or fig.); **∼ in**, deputize *for*; **∼-in** *n*., deputy, substitute esp. for actor or actress; *stand*

person *in good* STEAD; **∼ off**, move or keep away, ||temporarily dispense with services of (employee); **∼-off** (**half**), (Rugby Footb.) half-back who forms link between scrum-half and three-quarters; **∼-o'ffish**, cold or distant in manner; **∼ on**, insist on, observe scrupulously; *stand on one's own* (*two*) *feet* (see FOOT); **∼ out**, be prominent or outstanding, persist in resistance (*against*) or support (*for*); **∼ over**, stand close to, esp. to supervise or control, be postponed; *stand* PAT[1]; **∼-pipe** (vertical, for fluid to rise in); **∼'point**, point of view; **∼'still**, stoppage, inability to proceed, (*work is at a standstill*); **∼ to**, abide by, be likely or certain to (*win* etc.); **∼ to reason**, be provable by reason, be clear to every reasonable person; **∼ treat**, pay for others' food, entertainment, etc.; **∼ up**, get on one's feet from sitting or other position, maintain upright position, be valid, (colloq.) fail to keep appointment with; **∼-up** *a*., (of collar) upright, (of meal) eaten standing, (of fight) violent and thorough; **∼ up for**, support, side with; **∼ upon**, = *stand on*; **∼ up to**, face (opponent) courageously, be resistant to harmful effects of (wear, use, etc.); **∼ well** *with*. **2.** *n*. Act or condition of standing; resistance to attack or compulsion (*made a stand against the enemy*); (Crick.) prolonged stay at wicket by two batsmen; position adopted (lit. or fig.; *take* one's **∼**, base argument or reliance *on*); rack, pedestal, etc., on or in which things may be placed (*hat, music, umbrella, -stand*); stall in market etc. (NEWS-*stand*); standing-place for vehicles (*cab-stand*); raised structure for persons to sit or stand on (BAND*stand*; GRAND[1]*stand*); *∗witness--box; group of growing trees etc.; halt made by touring-company etc. to give performance(s) (ONE-*night stand*). [E]

**stă'ndard. 1.** *n*. Measure, specification, object, etc., to which others (should) conform or against which others are judged, criterion, (*by present-day standards*; DOUBLE *standard*); document specifying agreed properties for manufactured goods etc. (*British Standard*); required degree of excellence etc. (*does not come up to standard*); thing recognized as model for imitation etc.; average quality (*his work was of a low standard*); ordinary procedure, design, etc.; prescribed proportion of fine metal in gold or silver coin (**gold ~**, system whereby value of money is based on gold); distinctive flag; (fig.) rallying principle (*raise the standard of revolt*); upright support or pipe; treelike shrub (grafted) on upright stem. **2.** *a.* Serving or used as standard; having recognized and permanent value (*a standard work of reference*); authoritative; of normal or prescribed quality, size, etc.; (of language) conforming to established educated usage (*Standard English*). **3. ~-bearer**, person who carries a distinctive flag, (fig.) prominent leader in cause; ‖**~ lamp** (with tall pillar standing on floor); **~ of living**, degree of material comfort enjoyed by person, class, or community; **~ time** (established in a country or region by law or custom). **4. ~ize** *v.t.*, make conform to a standard; **~iza'tion** *n.* [AF (EX-TEND, w. sense infl. by prec.)]

**stǎndee'** *n.* (colloq.) Person who stands, esp. when all seats are occupied. [STAND]

**stǎ'nding. 1.** *n.* Act of standing; estimation in which one is held, (high) repute, position, (*men of high standing*) duration (*a dispute of long standing*); **~ room**, space to stand in. **2.** *a.* That stands; established, permanent; (of race, jump, start, etc.) performed from rest without run-up; **leave** person **~**, make far more rapid progress than he; **long-~**, that has long existed; **~ army** (maintained even in peacetime); *standing* COMMITTEE; **~ corn** (unreaped); *standing* JOKE; **~ order**, instruction to banker to make regular payments, or to newsagent etc. for regular supply of a periodical etc.; **~ orders**, rules governing procedure in Parliament, council, etc.; **~ type** (Print., not yet distributed after use); **~ water** (stagnant).

**stǎnk**. See STINK.

**stǎ'nz|a** *n.* Group of (usu. 4 or more rhymed) lines as repeated metrical unit; **~ǎ'ic** *a.* [It.]

**stǎphy̆locǒ'cc|us** *n.* (*pl.* **~i** *pr.* -kī). Form of pus-producing bacterium; **~al** *a.* [L f. Gk *staphulē* bunch of grapes, *kokkos* berry]

**stǎ'ple². 1.** *n.* U-shaped metal bar or piece of wire with pointed ends,

driven into wood etc. to hold something or into sheets of paper to fasten them together. **2.** *v.t.* Fasten or furnish with staple. [E]

**stǎ'ple². 1.** *n.* Important (usu. principal) article of commerce in a district or country; (fig.) chief element or material (*formed the staple of conversation*); fibre of cotton, wool, etc., as determining its quality. **2.** *a.* Principal (*staple commodities, diet*); important as product or export. [F *estaple* market f. LDu. (prec.)]

**stǎr. 1.** *n.* Celestial body appearing as luminous point in night sky (SHOOTING *star*); (fixed) ~, such body so far from earth as to appear motionless (opp. *planet, comet,* etc.); celestial body regarded as influencing person's fortunes etc. (*born under an unlucky star; you may thank your (lucky) stars you were not there*); thing resembling star in shape or appearance (SEE¹ *stars*); figure or object with (often 5) radiating points e.g. as decoration or rank-mark or asterisk or showing category of excellence; famous or brilliant person, esp. actor, actress, or other performer; principal performer in play, film, etc.; **S~ Chamber**, ‖(Hist.) a court noted for its arbitrary procedure, (fig.) arbitrary oppressive tribunal; **~-dust**, multitude of stars looking like dust; **~'fish**, star-shaped sea creature; **~-gazer**, (joc.) astronomer or astrologer; **~'light**, (*n.*) light of stars, (*a.*) = *starlit*; **~'lit**, lighted by stars, with stars visible; **S~ of David**, figure of two interlaced equilateral triangles used as Jewish and Israeli symbol; **S~s and Stripes**, U.S. flag; **~-spangled**, spangled with stars (esp. of U.S. flag); **~-studded**, including many famous people; **~ turn**, main item in an entertainment etc. **2.** *v.t.* & *i.* (-rr-). Mark or adorn (as) with star(s); present as theatrical, film, etc., star; appear as star (*in* play, film, etc.). **3. ~'dom** *n.*, position or fame of star in plays, films, etc.; **~'lĕt** *n.*, little star, esp. young film actress likely to become a star; **~'rў** *a.* (-ily, -iness), starlike, full of or bright with stars; **~ry-eyed**, (colloq.) bright-eyed, (fig.) visionary but impractical. [E]

**stǎr'board** (-ẽrd). **1.** *n.* Right-hand side of ship or boat or aircraft looking forward (cf. PORT⁴); *starboard* TACK¹.

2. *v.t.* Turn (helm) to starboard. [E, = *steer board*]

**starch. 1.** *n.* White carbohydrate in cereals, potatoes, and all other plants except fungi; preparation of this for stiffening linen etc.; (fig.) stiffness of manner, formality; ~'y *a.* (~ily, ~iness). **2.** *v.t.* Stiffen with starch (lit. or fig., esp. in *p.p.*). [E, rel. to STARK]

**stare. 1.** *v.i.* & *t.* Look fixedly with eyes wide open, esp. with curiosity, surprise, or horror (**stark staring mad,** completely mad); reduce (person) to specified condition by staring; ~ person **in the face,** be evident to, be right in front of, be imminent for, him. **2.** *n.* Staring gaze. [E]

**stark. 1.** *a.* Desolate, bare; sharply evident (*in stark contrast*); downright, sheer, (*stark madness*); completely naked; (arch.) stiff, rigid. **2.** *adv.* Completely, wholly, (*stark mad, naked*). [E]

**star'ling** *n.* Small blackish-brown bird noted for its chatter and mimicry. [E]

**star'ry.** See STAR.

**start. 1.** *v.i.* & *t.* Begin journey, begin or cause beginning of (journey, work, undertaking, fire, race, etc.; doing, *to* do); (of engine etc.) begin running; cause (engine, clock, etc.) to begin operating; cause to begin doing (*smoke started me coughing*); conceive (baby), cause (baby) to be conceived; cause or enable (person) to commence business etc.; give signal to (persons) to start in race; (cause to) be loose or displaced (timbers etc.); make sudden movement from surprise, pain, etc., (*started with fright, at the sound of my voice*); spring out, up, etc., rouse (game, *a* HARE) from lair; ~ **at,** have as first item; ~ **in,** (colloq.) begin (*to* do), *make a beginning *on*; ~ **life,** be born or created, begin one's career etc.; ~ **off,** begin, start to move; ~ **on,** make a beginning with, cause (person) to start; ~ **out,** begin, begin journey, (colloq.) proceed as intending (*to* do); ~ **something,** (colloq.) cause trouble; ~ **up,** rise suddenly, come or bring into existence or action; ~ **with,** = *start at* (**to ~ with,** in the first place, at the beginning). **2.** *n.* Beginning (**for a ~,** colloq., to start with); beginning or starting-place of race;

advantage granted in beginning a race; advantageous initial position in life, business, etc., (**get the ~ of,** gain advantage over); sudden movement of surprise, joy, pain, etc.; FIT[1]s *and* starts. **3.** ~'er *n.,* (esp.) person giving signal for start of race, horse or competitor starting in race, (automatic) apparatus for starting engine of motor vehicle etc., first course of meal; **for ~ers,** (sl.) to start with; **under ~er's orders,** (of horses etc.) ready to start race; ~'ing *n.*; ~ing-block, shaped block against which runner braces feet at start of race; ~ing-gate, mechanically-operated barrier used to start horse-races; ||~ing-handle, crank for starting motor-engine; ~ing-pistol (giving signal for start of race); ~ing-post (from which race starts); ~ing price, final odds before start of horse-race etc.; star'tle *v.t.,* give shock or surprise to. [E]

**starve** *v.i.* & *t.* (Cause to) die of hunger or suffer from lack of food; compel (garrison etc. *into* surrender, *out,* etc.) thus; (cause to) be deprived or short of supplies, love, etc., (SEX-*starved*); (colloq.) feel very hungry (*am simply starving*); **starva'tion** *n.*; ~'ling (-vl-) *n.,* starving person or animal. [E, = *die*]

**stash.** (sl.) **1.** *v.t.* Conceal, put *away* in safe place. **2.** *n.* Hiding-place; thing hidden; *house. [orig. unkn.]

**sta's|is** *n.* (*pl.* ~es *pr.* -ēz). Stoppage of flow or circulation. [Gk]

**state** *n., a.,* & *v.* **1.** *n.* Existing or position of thing or person (*in a state of depression, a bad state of repair*); (colloq.) condition of being untidy, excited, anxious, etc.; pomp (*arrived in great state*); (often S~) organized political community under one government, such community forming part of federal republic, civil government (*Church and State*); of S~, = sense 2; **the S~s,** the UNITED States. **2.** *a.* Of, for, from, or concerned with the State; of, used for, or done on ceremonial occasions (*state apartments, carriage, opening of Parliament*). **3.** *v.t.* Express, esp. fully or clearly, in speech or writing; say *that*; fix or specify (date, time, etc.); (Law) specify facts of (case) in court; (Mus.) play (theme etc.) esp. for the first time. **4. lie in ~,** (of deceased great personage) be laid in public place of honour before burial; SECRETARY *of State*; ~**'craft**, art of conducting affairs of State; *\*S~ Department* (of foreign affairs); ~ **of affairs**, existing conditions; *state of* NATURE; ~ **of play**, cricket score, (fig.) state of affairs esp. between two parties in dispute etc.; ~ **of things**, existing conditions; ~**'room**, state apartment, private compartment in passenger ship or *\*train*; *State's* EVIDENCE; ~**'sman**, person skilled in affairs of State, sagacious far-sighted politician; ELDER *Statesman*; ~**'smanlike** *a.*; ~**'smanship** *n.* **5.** ~**'hood** (-t-h-) *n.*; ~**'less** (-tl-) *a.*, (esp.) having no nationality or citizenship; ~**'ly** (-tlı̆) *a.* (~**liness**), dignified, imposing (‖~**ly home**, large magnificent house, esp. one open to visits by public); ~**'ment** (-tm-) *n.*, stating or being stated, expression in words, thing stated, formal account of facts, esp. of transactions in bank account or of amount due to tradesman. [partly ESTATE, partly L *status*]

**stă'tic. 1.** *a.* (~**ally**). Stationary, not acting or changing; concerned with bodies at rest or forces in equilibrium; ~ **electricity** (not flowing as current). **2.** *n.* Static electricity; atmospherics; ~**s** *n. pl.* (usu. treated as *sing.*), = static, science of static bodies or forces. [L f. Gk]

**stă'tion. 1.** *n.* Place, building, etc., where person or thing stands or is placed or where particular activity, esp. public service, is based or organized (*took up a convenient station*; *trading-station*; ACTION *stations*; FILLING *station*); (buildings at) stopping-place for railway-trains, buses, etc.; position in life, rank, status, (*married above her station*); (inhabitants of) military or naval base; (Austral.) sheep- or other farm, usu. large; (Eccl.) ~ **(of the Cross)**, each of series of scenes from the Passion successively venerated in some churches etc., such venerations; *\*~***house**, police station; ~**master**, official in charge of railway-station; ~**wagon**, estate car. **2.** *v.t.* Assign station to; put in position. **3.** ~**ary** *a.* (**-ily, -iness**), not moving, not intended to be moved, not changing in amount or quantity; ~**er** *n.*, dealer in stationery; ~**ery** *n.*, writing materials, office supplies, etc.;

‖**S~ery Office**, Government publishing-house. [F f. L (*sto stat-* stand)]

**stati'stic** *n.* Statistical fact or item; ~**al** *a.* (**-lly**), of or pertaining to statistics; ~**s** *n. pl.*, numerical facts systematically collected (VITAL *statistics*), (usu. treated as *sing.*) science of collecting or using statistics; **stătis-ti'cian** (-shan) *n.* [G (STATE)]

**stă'tū|e** (*or* -chōō) *n.* Sculptural, cast, or moulded figure of person, animal, etc., usu. of or above life size; ~**arў**, (*a.*) of or for statues, (*n.*) (making, maker of) statues; ~**ě'sque** (-sk) *a.*, like, having dignity or beauty of, a statue; ~**ě'tte** *n.*, small-scale statue; **stă'ture** (-tyer) *n.*, height of (esp. human) body, (fig.) eminence, (great) mental or moral quality. [F f. L (*sto* stand)]

**stă'tus** *n.* Social position, rank, relation to others, relative importance; superior social etc. position (~ **symbol**, possession etc. indicating person's high status); ~ **quo**, (previously) existing or unchanged situation. [L (as prec.)]

**stă'tūte** *n.* Law passed by Parliament etc.; ordinance of corporation etc. intended as permanent; ~**book**, (book) containing) the statute law; ~ **law**, a statute, the statutes collectively; *statute* MILE; **stă'tūtable** *a.* (**-bly**), **stă'tūtorў** *a.* (**-ily**), enacted or (as) required by statute. [F f. L (*statuo* set up)]

**staunch¹, stanch²** (-aw-, -ah-) *a.* Trustworthy, loyal; (of ship, joint, etc.) watertight, airtight. [F *estanche*]

**staunch²**. See STANCH¹.

**stāve. 1.** *n.* Each of the curved pieces of wood forming sides of cask, pail, etc.; (Mus.) staff; stanza, verse. **2.** *v.t.* (stove *pr.* -ōv, ~**d**). ~ **(in)**, break a hole in, knock out of shape; ~ **off**, avert or defer (danger, misfortune, etc.). [STAFF]

**staves**. See STAFF.

**stay¹. 1.** *v.i.* & *t.* Continue to be in same place or condition, not depart or change, (*stay here till I return*; *never stays sober for long*); dwell temporarily (*at hotel etc.*, *in town etc.*, *with* person); (cause) to stop or pause; postpone (judgement etc.); assuage (hunger etc.) esp. for short time; show endurance; ~**er** *n.*, (esp.) person or animal with great endurance. **2.** *n.* Action or period of staying (*made a long stay in London*);

suspension or postponement of execution of a sentence etc. **3. has come to ~, is here to ~,** (colloq.) must be regarded as permanent; **~-at-home** a. & n., (person) remaining habitually at home; **~ in,** remain indoors, esp. in school after hours as punishment; **~'ing-power,** endurance; **~ put,** (colloq.) remain where it is placed or where one is; **~ the course,** continue to end of race, struggle, etc.; **~ the night,** remain until next day; **~ to,** stay long enough to partake of (meal etc.); **~ up,** not go to bed. [AF f. L (*sto* stand)]

**stay**[2] n. Prop, support, (lit. or fig.); rope etc. supporting mast, flagstaff, etc.; tie-piece in aircraft; (in *pl.*) corset, esp. stiffened with whalebone etc.; **~'sail** (or -sal), sail extended on stay. [F & E f. Gmc]

**S.T.D.** abbr. subscriber trunk dialling.

**stead** (-ĕd) n. **In** person's or thing's **~,** instead of him or it, as a substitute; **stand** person **in good ~,** be advantageous or serviceable to him; **~'fast** (or -fah-) a., constant, firm, unwavering. [E, = place]

**stea'dy** a., adv., n., & v. **1.** a. (-ily, -iness). Firmly in position, not tottering or rocking or wavering; done, moving, acting, happening, in uniform and regular manner (*ran at a steady pace; a steady increase in numbers*); constant, unchanging; of industrious and temperate habits; **~ (on)!** (exhortation to avoid or cease erratic or boisterous behaviour, hasty or premature action, etc.); **~ state,** unvarying condition, esp. in physical process. **2.** adv. Steadily; **go ~ with,** (colloq.) be regular sweetheart of. **3.** n. (colloq.) Regular sweetheart. **4.** v.t. & i. Make or become steady. [prec.]

**steak** (stāk) n. Thick slice of meat (esp. beef) or fish, usu. grilled or fried; **~-house,** restaurant specializing in beefsteaks. [N]

**steal. 1.** v.t. & i. (**stole; sto'len;** pr. stō-). Take (another's property) secretly, illegally, or without permission (**~ the show,** outshine other performers esp. unexpectedly; *steal* person's THUNDER); obtain surreptitiously or by surprise (*stole a kiss*; **~ a march on,** gain advantage over by acting surreptitiously or anticipating); move or come (*away,*

*over, up,* etc.) secretly, silently, or gradually; **~ (away),** gain insidiously, artfully, etc. **2.** n. (colloq.) Stealing, theft; (unexpectedly) easy task or good bargain. **3. stealth** (stĕ-) n., secret or surreptitious behaviour; **stea'lthy** (stĕ-) a. (-ily, -iness), practising, done etc. by, stealth. [E]

**steam. 1.** n. Gas into which water is changed by boiling; (esp. water) vapour; power obtained (colloq. as if) from this; FULL[1] *steam ahead*; **get up ~,** generate enough power to work steam-engine, (fig.) become energetic, excited etc.; **let off ~,** (fig.) relieve one's pent-up energy or feelings; **run out of ~,** lose impetus; **under one's own ~,** (fig.) without help from others. **2.** v.i. & t. Give out steam; move by power of steam; cook, soften, etc., with steam; get (envelope) *open* by steaming its gum; (colloq.) work or move vigorously or rapidly (*steam ahead, away*); **~ up,** cover or become covered with condensed steam, (sl., esp. in *p.p.*) make (person) excited or angry. **3. ~'boat** (propelled by steam); **~-coal** (used to heat boilers); **~-engine** (worked by steam); **~-hammer,** forging-hammer worked by steam; **~ iron,** electric iron emitting steam from its flat surface; ||**~ navvy, -shovel,** excavator worked by steam; **~ radio,** (colloq.) radio broadcasting regarded as antiquated by comparison with television; **~-roller,** (n.) heavy slow-moving locomotive with roller used in road-making, (fig.) a crushing power or force, (v.t.) crush or move along as with steam-roller; **~'ship** (propelled by steam); **~ train** (driven by steam, esp. opp. electric or diesel train); **~ turbine, -whistle,** (worked by steam). **4. ~'er** n., (esp.) steamship, utensil for steaming food etc.; **~'y** a. (~ily, ~iness), of, like, or full of steam, (colloq.) erotic. [E]

**stě'atite** n. Kind of usu. grey talc with greasy feel. [F f. Gk *stear steat-* tallow]

**steed** n. (poet., rhet., or joc.) Horse. [E]

**steel. 1.** n. Malleable alloy of iron and carbon, much used for tools, weapons, machines, etc., (**cold ~,** cutting or thrusting weapons; *a grip, muscles, a heart,* etc., **of ~,** very strong or hard); steel rod for sharpening knives; (poet. or rhet.; not in *pl.*) sword; ~ **band** (orig. W. Ind., with musical instruments made from oil--drums); ~ **wool**, mass of steel shavings used as abrasive; ~'**yard**, weighing-apparatus with graduated arm along which a weight slides. **2.** *v.t.* Harden, make resolute, (one-*self*, one's heart etc., *to do*, *against*, etc.). **3.** ~'**y** *a.* (~**iness**), of or like steel, inflexibly severe. [E]

**steep**[1]. **1.** *a.* Sloping sharply, hard to climb, (*steep hill*, *stairs*); (of rise or fall) rapid; (colloq.) exorbitant, unreasonable, exaggerated, incredible; ~'**en** *v.i.* & *t.* **2.** *n.* Steep slope, precipice. [E]

**steep**[2]. **1.** *v.t.* Soak or bathe in liquid; ~ **in**, (fig.) pervade or imbue with, make deeply acquainted with (subject etc.). **2.** *n.* Action of, liquid for, steeping. [E]

**stee'ple** *n.* Lofty structure, esp. tower surmounted by spire, above roof of church; ~**chase**, (*n.*) horse--race with obstacles such as fences to jump, cross-country foot-race, (*v.i.*) go on steeplechase; ~**jack**, person who repairs steeples, tall chimneys, etc. [E (STEEP[1])]

**steer**[1] *v.t.* & *i.* Guide (vessel, vehicle, aircraft, etc.) by rudder, helm, wheel, etc.; direct or guide (one's course, other people) in specified direction; ~ **clear of**, take care to avoid; ~'**ing-column** (on which steering-wheel is mounted); ~'**ing committee** (deciding order of business, general course of operations, etc.); ~'**ing-wheel**, wheel by which vessel, vehicle, etc., is steered; ~'**s-man**, one who steers ship; ~'**age** *n.*, steering, part of ship for passengers travelling at cheapest rate. [E]

**steer**[2] *n.* Young male ox, esp. bullock. [E]

**stein** (stīn) *n.* Large earthenware mug esp. for beer. [G]

**stē'l|a** (*pl.* ~**ae**), ~'**e** (*or* -ēl), *n.* (Archaeol.) Upright slab or pillar, usu. inscribed and sculptured, esp. as gravestone. [L *stela*, Gk *stēlē*]

**stē'llar** *a.* Of star(s). [L (*stella* star)]

**stĕm**[1]. **1.** *n.* Main body or stalk of plant; stalk supporting fruit, flower, or leaf; stem-shaped part, e.g. slender part of wineglass between body and foot, vertical stroke in letter or musical note; tube of

tobacco-pipe; main upright timber at bow of ship (**from ~ to stern**, from end to end of ship); (Gram.) root or main part of noun, verb, etc., to which case-endings etc. are added. **2.** *v.i.* (-**mm**-). Spring or originate *from*. [E]

**stĕm**[2] *v.t.* & *i.* (-**mm**-). Check, stop, make headway against, (stream etc., lit. or fig.). [N]

**Stĕn** *n.* ~ (**gun**), lightweight machine-gun. [*S T* (inventors' initials) + -*en* as in BREN]

**stĕnch** *n.* Offensive or foul smell. [E (STINK)]

**stĕ'ncil**. **1.** *n.* Thin sheet in which pattern is cut, used to produce corresponding pattern on surface beneath it by applying ink, paint, etc.; pattern so produced. **2.** *v.t.* (||-**ll**-). Produce (pattern) with stencil; mark (surface) thus. [F f. L (SCINTILLA)]

**stĕnǒ'graph|er** *n.* Writer of shorthand; ~'**y** *n.* [Gk *stenos* narrow]

**stĕntŏr'ian** *a.* (Of voice etc.) loud and powerful. [Gk *Stentōr*, person]

**stĕp**. **1.** *v.i.* & *t.* (-**pp**-). Lift and set down foot or alternate feet as in walking; go or come in specified direction (as) by stepping (lit. or fig.; *step back*, *forward*, *into the door* or *breach*); measure (distance *off* or *out*) by stepping; perform (dance); (Naut.) put (mast) into step; ~ **down**, (fig.) resign; ~ **in**, enter, intervene; ~ **on it**, (colloq.) = *step on the* GAS; ~ **out**, take long steps, (colloq.) go out for entertainment, sociability, etc.; ~'**ping-stone**, raised stone usu. as one of set in stream or muddy place to help in crossing, (fig.) means of progress; ~ **this way** (deferential for 'follow me'); ~ **up**, come up or forward, increase rate, volume, etc., of. **2.** *n.* Action of stepping, complete movement of one leg in walking, running, dancing, etc.; distance gained by stepping (lit. or fig.); act done esp. for purpose (*take steps to prevent it*; *a prudent*, FALSE, *step*); short distance (*only a step from my door*); mark or sound made by foot; manner of stepping; surface provided or utilized for placing foot on in ascending or descending, stair, tread; (in *pl.*) step--ladder; degree in scale of promotion, precedence, etc.; (Naut.) socket, block, etc. holding base of mast; **break ~**, get out of step; **change ~**, begin to keep step with opposite leg;

in ~, putting foot to ground at the same time as others, esp. in marching, (fig.) conforming to what others are doing etc.; **in** person's ~**s**, following his example; **keep** ~, remain in step; **mind** (= WATCH) one's ~; **out of** ~, not in step; **pair of** ~**s**, step-ladder; ~ **by** ~, gradually, cautiously; ~**-ladder**, short ladder with flat steps and prop; **turn** one's ~**s**, go in specified direction; WATCH one's *step*. [E]

**stĕp-** *pref.* denoting relationship like one specified but resulting from parent's remarriage: ~'**child**, ~'-**daughter**, ~'**son**, spouse's child by previous marriage; ~'**father**, ~'**mother**, ~'**parent**, mother's or father's later spouse; ~'**brother**, ~'**sister**, child of previous marriage of one's stepparent. [E, = orphaned]

**stĕphanō'tĭs** *n.* Fragrant tropical climbing plant. [L f. Gk]

**stĕppe** *n.* Level treeless plain. [Russ.]

**-ster** *suf.* denoting agent (*gangster, trickster, youngster*). [E, orig. fem.]

**stĕ'rĕō** (*or* -ēr'-) *n.* (*pl.* ~**s**) & *a.* Stereophonic (record-player etc.); stereophony, -scope, -scopic, -type. [abbr.]

**stĕ'rĕ|o-** (*or* -ēr'-) *in comb.* Solid, having three dimensions; ~**ophŏ'nic** *a.* (-ically), using two or more transmission channels so that sound reaches listener from more than one direction; ~**ŏ'phony** *n.*; ~**oscōpe** *n.*, device by which two slightly different photographs etc. are viewed together, giving impression of depth and solidity; ~**oscŏ'pic** *a.* (-ically); ~**otȳpe**, (*n.*) printing-plate cast from mould of composed type, (fig.) unchanging and unoriginal opinion, (*v.t.*) make stereotype(s) of, print from stereotype(s), (fig., esp. in *p.p.*) make unchangeable, formalize. [Gk *stereos* solid]

**stĕ'rĭle** *a.* Not producing seed, offspring, fruit, result, etc.; free from living germs; lacking originality, emotive power, etc.; **steri'lity** *n.*; **stĕ'rĭlize** *v.t.*, make sterile, deprive of power of reproduction; **stĕrĭlizā'tion** *n.* [F or L]

**stĕr'ling.** **1.** *a.* Of or in British money (*pound sterling*); (of coin or precious metal) genuine, of standard value or purity (~ **silver**, of 92½% purity); (of person, qualities, etc.) of solid worth, genuine, reliable. **2.** *n.*

British money (*paid in sterling*); ~ **area**, countries keeping reserves mainly in sterling and transferring money freely between themselves. [E, = penny]

**stĕrn**[1] *a.* (~**ness** *pr.* -n-n-). Severe, grim, enforcing discipline or submission; **the** ~**er sex**, men. [E]

**stĕrn**[2] *n.* Rear part of ship or boat; buttocks, rump; foxhound's tail; ~**-post**, central upright timber etc. of stern, usu. bearing rudder. [N (STEER[1])]

**stĕr'n|um** *n.* (*pl.* ~**ums**, ~**a**). Breastbone; ~**al** *a.* (*sternal* RIB). [L f. Gk]

**stĕr'|oid** (*or* -ēr'-) *n.* Any of various organic compounds incl. some hormones and vitamins; ~**ŏl** *n.*, complex solid alcohol important in vitamin synthesis. [CHOLESTEROL etc. f. Gk *stereos* stiff]

**stĕr'torous** *a.* (Of breathing etc.) laboured and noisy. [L *sterto* snore]

**stĕt** *v.i.* & *t.* (-tt-). (Usu. as *imper.*, written on proof-sheet etc.) ignore or cancel correction or alteration, let original form stand. [L, = let it stand]

**stĕ'thosc|ōpe** *n.* Instrument used in listening to heart, lungs, etc.; ~**ŏ'pic** *a.* (-ically). [F f. Gk *stēthos* breast]

**stĕ'tson** *n.* Slouch hat with very wide brim and high crown. [person]

**stĕ'vedōre** *n.* Man employed in loading and unloading ships. [Sp. *estivador*]

**stew.** **1.** *v.t.* & *i.* Cook by long simmering in closed vessel with liquid (~ **in** one's **own juice**, undergo consequences of one's own actions etc., usu. without help); sweat or swelter in hot atmosphere; (in *p.p.*, of tea) bitter or strong with too long infusing; (in *p.p.*, sl.) drunk. **2.** *n.* Dish of stewed meat etc.; (colloq.) agitated or angry condition; ~**-pan**, **-pot**, vessel used for stewing. [F *estuver* f. Rom.]

**stew'ard** *n.* Person who manages another's property; person who arranges supplies of food etc. for college, club, ship, etc.; passengers' attendant on ship, aircraft, or train; official who superintends race-meeting, show, public meeting, etc.; **Lord High S~**, **Lord S~**, (Hist.) **S~ of Scotland**, high officers of State; SHOP-*steward*; ~**ĕss** *n.*, female steward esp. on ship etc.; ~**shĭp** *n.*, rank, duties, period of office, of steward. [E, = house-warden]

**stick**[1] *v.t.* & *i.* (**stuck**). Insert or thrust point of (pin, bayonet, etc., *in, into, through*); stab; fix (*up*)on pointed thing, be fixed (as) by point *in*(*to*) or *on* (*to*); fix or become or remain fixed (as) by glue or other means of adhesion; (colloq.) put or remain in specified place, (of accusation etc.) be regarded as valid (*couldn't make the charges stick*); ||(sl.) endure, tolerate, (*can't stick that fellow*); lose or deprive of power of motion or action through friction, jamming, or other impediment (*is stuck on a sandbank*; *wrote ten lines and then got stuck*); **get stuck in, into** (*job* etc.), (sl.) start in earnest; ~ **around,** (sl.) linger, remain at same place; ~ **at,** (colloq.) work persistently at (task etc.); ~ **at nothing,** allow nothing, esp. no scruples, to deter one; ~**'ing-plaster,** adhesive plaster for wounds etc.; ~**-in-the-mud,** unprogressive or old-fashioned (person); ~ **in** one's **throat** etc., be unable to be swallowed or spoken (lit. or fig.); ~ **it out,** (colloq.) endure something unpleasant; ~ one's **neck out,** (fig., colloq.) behave boldly (esp. and so expose oneself to danger); ~ **out,** (cause to) protrude, hold out persistently *for* (something demanded); ~ **out a mile,** be very obvious; *\**~**'pin,** tie-pin; ~ **to,** remain fixed on or to, remain faithful to (friend, promise, etc.), keep to (subject etc.); ~ **together,** (colloq.) remain united or mutually loyal; ~ **up,** (cause to) protrude, be or make erect, fasten to upright surface, (sl.) rob or threaten (person etc.) with gun; ~ **up for,** support or defend (cause; esp. absent person, oneself); ~ **with,** stay close or faithful to; **stuck for,** at a loss for, needing; **stuck on,** (sl.) captivated by; **stuck-up,** conceited, snobbish; **stuck with,** (colloq.) unable to get rid of; ~**'er** *n.,* (esp.) adhesive label, persistent person. [E]

**stick**[2] *n.* Thin branch cut, broken, or fallen from tree or bush, esp. trimmed for use as support in walking or as bludgeon; thin rod of wood etc. for particular purpose (BROOM-, DRUM-, JOY*stick*); (colloq.) piece of wood as part of house or furniture (*house pulled down and not a stick left standing*; *has only a few sticks*

*of furniture*); implement used to propel ball in hockey, polo, etc.; gear-lever; conductor's baton; more or less cylindrical piece of celery, sealing-wax, dynamite, etc.; punishment (lit. or fig.); (colloq.) person, esp. one who is dull or unsociable; **the** ~**s** (sl.) remote rural area(s), hurdles, football goal; ~ **figure,** drawing of human figure with single straight lines for body and limbs; ~ **insect** (with twiglike body). [E]

**sti'cklebăck** (-kelb-) *n.* Small spiny-backed fish. [E, = thorn-back]

**sti'ckler** *n.* ~ **for,** person who insists on or pertinaciously supports or advocates (accuracy, authority, etc.). [obs. *stickle* be umpire]

**sti'ck|ў** *a.* (~**ily,** ~**iness**). Tending or intended to stick or adhere; glutinous, viscous, (of weather) humid; (colloq.) making or likely to make objections (*she was very sticky about giving me leave*); (sl.) very unpleasant or painful (*he'll come to a sticky end*); ~**y wicket,** (Crick., or fig.) wet wicket difficult for batsmen. [STICK[1]]

**stiff.** 1. *a.* Rigid, not flexible, hard to bend, move, stir, etc.; hard to cope with, needing strength or effort, severe, (*stiff examination, climb, breeze, penalty*); (of person, manners, etc.) formal, haughty, constrained; (of muscle, limb, etc., or person as regards these) aching when used, owing to previous exertion; (of an alcoholic drink) strong; (*pred.,* colloq.) thoroughly, (almost) to the point of death, exhaustion, etc., (*bored, scared, stiff*); ~**-necked,** obstinate or haughty; *stiff upper* LIP; ~ **with,** (sl.) abundantly provided with; ~**'en** *v.t.* & *i.* **2.** *n.* (sl.) Corpse; (**big**) ~, foolish, intractable, etc., person. [E]

**sti'fle** *v.t.* & *i.* Smother, cause or experience constraint of breathing or suppression of utterance etc. [orig. uncert.]

**sti'gma** *n.* (*pl.* ~**s,** Eccl. ~**ta**). Mark or sign of disgrace or discredit; (Bot.) part of style or ovary-surface which receives pollen; (Eccl., usu. in *pl.*) mark(s) corresponding to those left on Christ's body by the Crucifixion; ~**tize** *v.t.,* describe opprobriously. [L f. Gk *stigma -mat-* brand, dot]

**stile** *n.* Set of steps, rungs, etc., arranged to allow persons but not cattle etc. to get over or through fence, hedge, or wall. [E]

**stilĕ'ttō** n. (pl. ~s, ~es). Short dagger; pointed implement for making eyelets etc.; ~ **heel**, long tapering heel of shoe. [It. dim. (STYLE)]

**still¹** a., n., v., & adv. 1. a. (adv. ~y pr. -l-lĭ). (Almost) without motion or sound, tranquil; (of wine etc.) not effervescing; ~ **birth**, birth of dead child; ~'**born**, born dead, (fig.) abortive; ~ **life** (pl. -fes, -ves), painting of inanimate objects, e.g. fruits; ~ **small voice**, voice of conscience; *still waters run* DEEP. 2. n. Silence (*in the still of the night*); ordinary static photograph (as opp. motion picture), esp. single shot from cinema film. 3. v.t. & i. (literary) Make or become still, quieten. 4. adv. Without moving (*sit still*); even till or at a particular time (*why are you still here?*); nevertheless, all the same; even, yet, increasingly, (*urged to still greater efforts*). [E]

**still²** n. Apparatus for distilling spirituous liquors etc.; ||~-**room**, room for distilling, housekeeper's store-room in large house. [obs. *still* v. = DISTIL]

**stilt** n. One of pair of poles with supports for feet enabling user to walk at a distance above the ground; one of set of piles or posts supporting building etc.; ~'**ĕd** a., (as) on stilts, (of literary style etc.) stiff and unnatural, bombastic. [LDu.]

**Sti'lton** n. Rich blue-veined cheese. [place]

**sti'mŭl|ant** a. & n. (Substance) that stimulates, esp. that increases bodily or mental activity; ~**āte** v.t. (~**able**), animate, excite, rouse; ~**ā'tion**, ~**ātor**, ns.; ~**ātīve** a.; ~**us** n. (pl. ~**ī** pr. -ī), stimulating thing or effect. [L (*stimulus* goad)]

**sting.** 1. n. Sharp wounding organ of insect or snake or nettle; (infliction of) wound so made, pain caused by it; (fig.) wounding or painful quality or effect, keenness or vigour; (sl.) swindle, robbery; ~ **in the tail**, (fig.) unexpected final pungency; ~-**ray**, broad flat-fish with stinging tail. 2. v.t. & i. (**stung**). (Be able to) wound with sting; give or feel tingling physical pain or sharp mental pain; incite by such mental effect (*was stung into replying*); (sl.) involve (person) in expense, swindle;

~'**ing-nettle**, nettle that stings (opp. DEAD *nettle*). 3. ~'**er** n., (esp.) sharp painful blow; ~'**y** (-nji) a. (~**ily**, ~**iness**), niggardly, mean. [E]

**stink.** 1. v.i. & t. (**stank, stunk**; **stunk**). Have strong offensive smell (*stink in the* NOSTRILS *of*); (fig.) be or seem very unpleasant; ~ **out**, drive (person etc.) out by stink, fill (place) with stink. 2. n. Strong offensive smell; (colloq.) loud complaint, fuss, (*kick up a stink about it*); ||(in pl., sl.) chemistry or science as subject of study; **like** ~, (sl.) intensely. 3. ~-**bomb**, device emitting stink when exploded. 4. ~'**er** n., (esp., sl.) very objectionable person or thing, difficult task, letter etc. conveying strong disapproval; ~'**ing**, (a.) that stinks (CRY *stinking fish*), (adv.,) extremely and usu. objectionably (*stinking rich*). [E]

**stint.** 1. v.t. Supply (food, aid, etc.) in niggardly amount or grudgingly; keep (person etc.) thus supplied. 2. n. Limitation of supply or effort (usu. *without, no, stint*); fixed or allotted amount of work (*do a daily stint*); small sandpiper. [E]

**sti'pĕnd** n. Salary, esp. of clergyman; **stĭpĕ'ndiary** a. & n., (person) who receives stipend; ||~**iary** (**magistrate**), paid professional magistrate. [F f. L *stipendium*]

**sti'pple.** 1. v.t. & i. Draw, paint, etc., with dots instead of lines; roughen surface of (paint, cement, etc.). 2. n. (Effect of) stippling. [Du.]

**sti'pŭlāte** v.t. & i. Demand or specify as part of bargain or agreement; ~**ate for**, mention or insist upon as essential; ~**ā'tion** n. [L *stipulor*]

**stir¹.** 1. v.t. & i. (-**rr**-). Move esp. slightly, (begin to) be in motion; rise from bed (*is not stirring yet*); move spoon etc. round and round in (liquid) to mix ingredients; arouse, inspire, excite, (emotions etc., or person as regards these; *stirring events, music*); ~ **in**, mix (ingredient) with substance by stirring; ~ **one's stumps**, (colloq.) walk or move faster; ~ **the blood**, inspire enthusiasm; ~ **up**, mix thoroughly by stirring, make (sediment etc.) rise from bottom of liquid by stirring, (fig.) stimulate. 2. n. Act of stirring; commotion, excitement, sensation. [E]

**stir²** n. (sl.) Prison. [orig. unkn.]

**sti'rrup** n. Horse-rider's foot-rest;

~-**cup,** drink offered to person about to depart, orig. on horseback; ~-**leather, -strap,** strap attaching stirrup to saddle; ~-**pump,** hand--operated water-pump with foot-rest, used to extinguish small fires. [E, = climbing-rope]

**stitch. 1.** *n.* Single pass of needle, result of this, in sewing, knitting, crocheting, etc.; thread etc. between two needle-holes; particular method of sewing, knitting, etc.; least bit of clothing (*didn't have a stitch on*); acute pain in side induced by running etc.; **a ~ in time saves nine,** a timely remedy saves much trouble; **drop a ~,** let loop fall off end of knitting--needle; **in ~es,** (colloq.) laughing uncontrollably. **2.** *v.t. & i.* Sew, make stitches (in); ~ **up,** join or mend by sewing. [E (STICK¹)]

**stoat** *n.* Ermine, esp. in its brown summer coat. [orig. unkn.]

**stocha′stic** (-k-) *a.* (~ally). Governed by laws of probability. [Gk (*stokhos* aim)]

**stock** *n., a., & v.* **1.** *n.* Store of goods etc. ready for sale, distribution, or use, supply of anything, (lit. or fig.; **in, out of, ~,** available, not available, without being procured specially; **take ~,** examine one's stock so as to know what one has; **take ~ of,** review (situation etc.), observe so as to estimate quality); equipment or raw material for trade or pursuit (ROLLing-*stock*); liquor made by stewing bones, vegetables, etc., as basis for soup etc.; farm animals (LIVE¹*stock*) or implements; (shares in) capital of a business company; ‖money lent to government at fixed interest, right to receive such interest (**take ~ in,** concern oneself with); one's reputation or popularity (*his stock is rising*); ancestry, (source of) family or breed, (*he comes of Cornish stock*); base, support, or handle for implement, machine, etc.; butt of rifle etc. (LOCK², *stock, and barrel*); plant into which a graft is inserted; main trunk of tree etc.; fragrant-flowered cruciferous plant; (in *pl.*) supports for ship during building (**on the ~s,** fig., in construction or preparation); (in *pl.*, Hist.) timber frame with holes for feet where offenders were confined as public punishment; wide band of material worn round neck; piece of silk etc. worn below clerical

collar; ~-**breeder,** raiser of live-stock; ~′**broker,** ~′**broking,** (person) buying and selling stocks and shares for clients; ~-**car,** car used in racing where deliberate bumping is allowed, *railway cattle--truck; ~′**dove,** small wild pigeon; ~ **exchange,** place where stocks and shares are publicly bought and sold, dealers working there; ~′**holder,** owner of stocks or shares; ~-**in--trade,** all requisites of a trade or profession; ~′**jobber,** ~′**jobbing,** ‖(person) dealing in stocks to profit from price-fluctuations; ~-**market,** (transactions on) stock exchange; ~′**pile** *n. & v.,* accumulate(d) stocks of commodities, or materials to be held in reserve; ~-**pot** (for soup--stock); ~-**room** (for storage of goods); ~**s and stones,** inanimate objects, unfeeling people; ~-**still,** motionless; ~-**taking,** review of stock in shop etc., or fig.; ~′**yard,** enclosure for sorting or temporary keeping of cattle. **2.** *a.* Kept in stock and regularly available (*a stock item, size*); (fig.) perpetually repeated, hackneyed, conventional. **3.** *v.t. & i.* Have (goods) in stock; provide (shop, farm, etc.) with goods, requisites, livestock, etc.; fit (gun etc.) with stock; ~ **up,** provide with or get stocks or supplies; ~ **up with,** gather stock of (food, fuel, etc.); ‖~′**ist** *n.,* one who stocks (certain) goods for sale. [E]

**stocka′de** *n., & v.t.* (Fortify with) line or enclosure of upright stakes. [F f. Sp. (STAKE)]

**sto′cking** *n.* Covering for foot and (part of) leg, usu. woven or knitted of wool, nylon, silk, etc., (**in one's** ~(**ed**) **feet,** not wearing shoes); differently-coloured lower part of leg of horse etc.; ~ **cap,** knitted usu. conical cap; ~-**filler,** small present for putting in stocking hung up for Santa Claus; ~ **mask,** nylon stocking worn over head as criminal's disguise; ~-**stitch** (of alternate rows plain and purl); **sto′ckiné′t(te)** *n.,* elastic knitted material. [STOCK]

**sto′ck|y** *a.* (~ily, ~iness). Short and strongly built.

**stodg|e.** (colloq.) **1.** *n.* Food esp. of thick heavy kind; unimaginative person or work. **2.** *v.i. & t.* Stuff (oneself) with food etc.; trudge through mud etc. **3.** ~**y** *a.* (~ily, ~iness), heavy and thick, indigestible (lit. or fig.), uninteresting. [imit., after *stuff* and *podge*]

**stŏ′ic** *a.* & *n.* (Person) having great self-control, fortitude, or austerity; (*S~*) (typical of) philosopher of ancient Greek school noted for these qualities and emphasizing virtue and ethics; **~al** *a.* (**-lly**); **~ism** *n.* [L f. Gk (*stoa* portico, w. ref. to teaching--place)]

**stōke** *v.t.* & *i.* ~ (**up**), feed and tend (furnace, fire, etc.); ~ **up**, (colloq.) consume food esp. steadily and in large quantity; **~′hold**, **~′hole**, place where steamer's fires are tended; **stō′ker** *n.* (esp. on steamer or steam-engine). [Du.]

**stōle**[1] *n.* Strip of silk or other material worn over shoulders by women, priests, etc. [E f. L *stola* f. Gk]

**stōle**[2], **stō′len**. See STEAL.

**stŏ′lid** *a.* (Seemingly) lacking emotion or animation; not easily excited or moved; **stolĭ′dĭtў** *n.* [F or L]

**stŏ′mach** (-ŭ′mak). **1.** *n.* Internal organ in which chief part of digestion occurs (**on an empty ~**, not having recently eaten; **on a full ~**, after large meal); one of several digestive organs of animal; lower front of body; appetite (lit. or fig.); **~-ache**, pain in belly, esp. in bowels; **~--pump**, syringe for emptying stomach or forcing liquid into it; **~ upset**, temporary slight digestive disorder. **2.** *v.t.* Eat with relish or toleration; (fig.) endure, put up with. **3. ~er** *n.*, (Hist.) pointed front-piece of woman's dress, often jewelled or embroidered. [F f. L f. Gk]

**stŏmp. 1.** *n.* Lively jazz dance usu. with heavy stamping. **2.** *v.i.* & *t.* Tread heavily (on); dance stomp. [STAMP]

**stōne** *n.*, *a.*, & *v.* **1.** *n.* Rock, solid mineral matter that is not metallic, esp. for building (**have a heart of ~**, be hard-hearted); piece of this, usu. not larger than that used in building or road-making or as missile (**cast** or **throw ~s**, fig., make aspersions on character etc.; *kill two* BIRD*s with one stone*); **leave no ~ unturned**, try every possible means; **those who live in glass houses should not throw ~s**, aspersions made by the vulnerable can provoke damaging retort; ROLL*ing stone*; **a ~'s throw**, distance stone can be thrown, short

or moderate distance); = PRECIOUS *stone*; piece of stone of definite shape or for particular purpose (GRAVE[1]-, GRIND-, MILL[1]-, TOMB-, WHET*stone*); thing resembling stone in hardness or pebble in shape, e.g. hard morbid concretion in the body (or disease in which this occurs), hard case of fruit-kernel, pellet of hail; (*pl.* same) ‖weight of 14 lb. **2.** *a.* Made of stone. **3.** *v.t.* Pelt with stones; remove stones from (fruit); (sl.; esp. in *p.p.*) stupefy or stimulate with drink, drug, etc. **4.** S~ **Age**, stage of civilization when tools and weapons were of stone not metal; **~′chat**, small black and white bird; **~-cold**, completely cold; **~′crop**, creeping rock-plant; **~-dead**, **-deaf**, (completely so); **~-fruit** (with flesh or pulp enclosing stone); **~-ground** *a.*, ground with millstones; **~′mason**, dresser of or builder in stone; **~′wall**, obstruct by **~wa′lling**, excessively cautious batting, ‖obstruction of discussion etc.; **~′ware**, pottery made from very siliceous clay or from clay and flint; **~′work**, masonry. **5. stō′nў** *a.* (**-ily**, **-iness**), full of stones, hard, rigid, unfeeling, unresponsive; **sto′ny(-broke)**, (sl.) entirely without money. [E]

**stŏŏd**. See STAND.

**stŏŏge**. (colloq.) **1.** *n.* Butt, foil, esp. for comedian; assistant or subordinate, esp. for routine or unpleasant work. **2.** *v.i.* Move *about*, *around*, etc., esp. aimlessly; act as stooge *for*. [orig. unkn.]

**stŏŏl** *n.* Seat without back or arms, usu. for one person (**fall between two ~s**, fail from vacillation between two courses etc.); = FOOT*stool*; low bench for kneeling on; (place for) defecation (*go to stool*); faeces; root or stump of tree or plant from which shoots spring; **~-ball**, game resembling cricket; **~-pigeon**, pigeon as decoy, police informer. [E]

**stŏŏp**[1]. **1.** *v.i.* & *t.* Bend (one's head, body, etc.) forwards and downwards; carry one's head and shoulders bowed forward; (fig.) deign or condescend *to* do, descend or lower oneself *to* (some conduct). **2.** *n.* Stooping posture. [E]

\***stŏŏp**[2] *n.* Porch, small veranda, or set of steps in front of house. [Du. *stoep*]

**stŏp. 1.** *v.t.* & *i.* (**-pp-**). Put an end to progress, motion, operation, etc.

(of), effectively hinder or prevent (*from*), discontinue (do*ing*); defeat, (cause to) cease action, (sl.) receive (blow etc.); not permit or supply as usual (wages, food, etc.); ~ (**payment of**), direct one's banker not to honour (cheque); (colloq.) remain, stay, sojourn, (*shall stop in bed, at home, with friends in Cornwall*); = *stop up*, plug, (hole, leak, etc.); put filling in (tooth); (Mus.) obtain desired pitch from (string of violin etc.) by pressing at appropriate point with finger; ~ **at nothing**, be ruthless or unscrupulous; *~ **by***, call at (place, or abs.); ~ **dead** (abruptly); ~ **down**, (Photog.) reduce aperture of (lens, or abs.); ~ **one's ears**, prevent oneself from hearing (lit. or fig.); ~ **person's mouth**, (fig.) induce him by bribery etc. to keep silent about something; ~ **off**, ~ **over**, break one's journey; ~'**off**, ~'**over**, a break in one's journey; ‖~'**ping train** (stopping at many intermediate stations); ~ **short** (abruptly); ~ **thief!** (cry of pursuer); ~ **up**, (almost) close by plugging, obstructing, etc. **2.** *n.* Stopping or being stopped (*put a stop to*; *come to a stop*); place where bus, train, etc., regularly stops; sign to show pause in written matter, esp. comma, semicolon, colon, or FULL stop; device for stopping motion at particular point; (Mus.) change of pitch effected by stopping string, (in organ) row of pipes of one character, knob etc. operating these (**pull out all the ~s**, fig., use extreme effort, appeal to all the emotions); (Opt., Photog.) diaphragm, (device reducing) effective diameter of lens; (Phon.) = PLOSIVE (**glottal** ~, formed by sudden opening or closing of glottis). **3.** ~'**cock**, externally operated valve to regulate flow in pipe etc.; ~'**gap**, temporary substitute; ~**go**, alternate cessation and recommencement of progress; ~-**lamp**, -**light**, light on rear of motor vehicle showing when brakes are applied; ‖~-**press**, (late news) inserted in newspaper after printing has begun; ~-**watch** (with mechanism for instantly starting and stopping it, used in timing races etc.). **4.** ~'**page** *n.*, condition of being blocked or stopped; ~'**per**, (*n.*, esp.) plug for closing bottle etc. (**put a ~per on**, put an end to), (*v.t.*) close

or provide with stopper; ~'**ping** *n.*, (esp.) tooth-filling. [E (STUFF)]

**stor'age** *n.* (Method of, space for, cost of) storing of goods, data, etc.; COLD *storage*; ~ **battery, cell,** (for storing electricity); ~ **heater,** electric heater accumulating heat outside peak hours for later release. [foll.]

**store. 1.** *n.* Quantity of something ready to be drawn on; (arch.) abundance; place where things are sold, *shop, ‖large shop (DEPARTMENT *store*); warehouse for temporary keeping of furniture etc.; device in computer for storing retrievable data etc.; (in *pl.*) articles for particular purpose accumulated for use, supply of them or place where they are kept; **in ~**, kept in readiness, coming in the future, destined or intended *for*; **lay, put,** or **set ~ by** or **on**, consider to be important; ~ **cattle** etc. (kept for breeding or as ordinary stock, not being fattened); ~'**house**, place where things are stored (lit. or fig.); ~'**keeper,** storeman, *shopkeeper; ~'**man** (in charge of, or handling, stored goods); ~-**room** (in which household or other supplies are kept). **2.** *v.t.* Put in store, lay *up*, *away*, etc., for future use; equip (house, mind, etc.) plentifully with useful contents; contain, hold, keep. [F *estore(r)* f. L *instauro* renew]

**stor'ey, stor'y**[2], *n.* Any of the parts into which a building is divided horizontally, the whole of the rooms etc. having a continuous floor; thing forming horizontal division; **upper ~**, (joc.) the brain; (-)**stor'eyed,** (-)**stor'ied**[1], (-id) *a.* [AL (HISTORY, perh. w. ref. to tier of painted windows)]

**stor'ied**[2] (-rĭd) *a.* (literary). Celebrated in, associated with, stories or legends. [STORY[1]]

**stork** *n.* Tall usu. white wading bird, sometimes nesting on buildings, and in the nursery the pretended bringer of babies. [E]

**storm. 1.** *n.* Violent disturbance of atmosphere with thunder (THUNDER-*storm*) or strong wind or heavy rain etc. (SNOW-, HAIL*storm*; ~ **in a teacup**, great excitement over trivial matter); (fig.) violent disturbance or commotion in human affairs etc.; violent shower *of* missiles or outbreak *of* execration, applause, etc.; direct assault on (and capture of) defended place by troops etc. (**take by ~**, capture thus, fig. speedily captivate); **~-centre**, centre of (cyclonic) storm, (fig.) subject etc. upon which agitation is concentrated; **~-cloud**, heavy rain-cloud, (fig.) something threatening; ‖**~-cone**, cone-shaped device displayed as warning of impending storm; **~-door**, additional outer door; **~-troops**, shock-troops, Nazi political militia (**~-trooper**, member of this). **2.** *v.i.* & *t.* Rage, be violent, bluster; move violently or angrily (*stormed out of the room*); attack or capture by storm. **3.** **~'y** *a.* (**~ily**, **~iness**), violent, raging, of or marked by storms (lit. or fig.; *stormy* PETREL). [E]

**stor'y¹** *n.* Account of imaginary or past events, narrative, tale, anecdote, (**but that is another ~**, formula for breaking off narrative; **it is another ~ now**, things have changed; SHORT *story*; **the old ~**, fig., the very familiar course of events; **the ~ goes**, it is said; **to cut a long ~ short**, omitting details); past course of life of person, institution, etc.; **~(-line)**, narrative or plot of novel, play, etc.; facts or experiences that deserve narration; (colloq.) fib; **~-teller**, one who tells or writes stories, (colloq.) liar. [AF *estorie* f. L (HISTORY)]

**stor'y²**. See STOREY.

**stoup** (-ōōp) *n.* Flagon, beaker, (arch.); holy-water basin. [N]

**stout. 1.** *a.* Rather fat, corpulent, bulky; of considerable thickness or strength; brave, resolute, vigorous, staunch. **2.** *n.* Strong dark beer. [AF f. Gmc]

**stōve¹** *n.* Closed apparatus in which heat is produced by burning fuel or electrically, for warming of rooms, cooking, etc.; ‖(Hort.) artificially heated hothouse; **~-enamel** (heat-proof); **~-pipe** (conducting smoke and gases from stove to chimney). [LDu.]

**stōve²**. See STAVE.

**stow** (-ō) *v.t.* Pack (goods etc.) tidily in right or convenient place(s); (sl., esp. in *imper.*) abstain or cease from (**~ it**, cease talking etc.); **~ away**, place (thing) where it will not cause obstruction, hide oneself on board ship etc. to travel free or escape unseen; **~'away**, person who

does this; **~'age** *n.*, (space for) stowing. [BESTOW f. E, = place]

**strabǐ'sm|us** (-z-) *n.* Squint(ing). **~al**, **~ǐc**, *adjs.* [Gk (*strabos* squinting)]

**strǎ'ddle. 1.** *v.i.* & *t.* Sit or stand (across) with legs wide apart; part (one's legs) widely; drop shots or bombs short of and beyond (target etc.). **2.** *n.* Act of straddling. [STRIDE]

**strafe** (-ahf) *v.t.*, & *n.* (sl.) Bombard(ment); abuse, punish(ment). [G, = punish]

**strǎ'ggl|e. 1.** *v.i.* Lack or lose compactness or tidiness; be(come) dispersed or sporadic; trail behind others in march, race, etc. **2.** *n.* Straggling group; **~y** *a.* [orig. uncert.]

**straight** (-āt) *a.*, *n.*, & *adv.* **1.** *a.* Without curve or bend or flare, not crooked or curly; direct; undiluted, unmodified; successive (*ten straight wins*); level, tidy, in proper order or place or condition, (*put things straight*); honest, candid, (*gave him a straight answer*); (of thinking etc.) logical, unemotional; (of drama etc.) ordinary, without music, (opp. *variety* etc.); (colloq., of music) classical; (sl., of person etc.) conventional, respectable, heterosexual; **~ bat** (Crick., held vertically); **~ eye**, ability to detect deviation from straightness; **~ face** (intentionally expressionless, esp. avoiding smile though amused); ‖**~ fight**, contest between two candidates only; *straight* FLUSH³; **~ man**, performer who says things for comedian to make jokes about; *****~ ticket**, (voting for) party programme or candidate-list without modification; **~ tip**, hint from good authority about possible outcome. **2.** *n.* Straight condition (**on the ~**, direct, not on the bias; **out of the ~**, crooked); sequence of 5 cards in poker; straight part of something, esp. concluding stretch of racecourse; (sl.) straight person. **3.** *adv.* In a straight line, direct; in right direction, correctly; **go ~**, live honestly, esp. after being criminal; **~ away**, immediately; **~for'ward**, honest, frank, (of task etc.) uncomplicated; *straight from the* SHOULDER; **~ off**, (colloq.) immediately; **~ out**, immediately, bluntly. **4.** **~'en** *v.t.* & *i.*, make or become straight (**~en up**, stand erect after bending). [orig. p.p. of STRETCH]

**strain**¹ *n.* Breed or stock of animals, plants, etc. [E, = begetting]

**strain**². **1.** *v.t. & i.* Stretch tightly, make or become taut or tense; exercise (one*self*, senses, thing, etc.) intensely or excessively, press to extremes, make intense effort, wrest or distort from true intention or meaning; overtask or injure by over-use or excessive demands; clear (liquid) of solid matter by passing it through sieve etc., filter (solids) *out* from liquid; (in *p.p.*) constrained, forced, artificial, (of relationship) mutually distrustful or impatient; ~ **at a gnat**, be unduly scrupulous or fussy; ~'**er** *n.*, (esp.) device for straining liquids. **2.** *n.* Act of straining; (exertion required to meet) demand or force (*on*) that tries strength, cohesion, stability, etc., (lit. or fig.); strained condition, quantity measuring this; snatch or spell of music or poetry; moral tendency as part of character (*there is a strain of mysticism in him*); tone or tendency in speech or writing (*continued in another strain*). [F *estrei*(*g*)*n*- f. L *stringo*]

**strait.** **1.** *n.* (in *sing.* or *pl.*) Narrow passage of water connecting two large bodies of water; (usu. in *pl.*) difficulty, trouble, distress. **2.** *a.* (arch.) Narrow, limited, strict. **3.** ~-**jacket**, (*n.*) strong garment put on violent person to confine arms, (fig.) restrictive measures, (*v.t.*) restrict thus (lit. or fig.); ~-**laced**, (fig.) severely virtuous, puritanical; ~'**en** *v.t.*, restrict, (in *p.p.*) of or marked by poverty. [F *estreit* f. L (STRICT)]

**strāke** *n.* Line of planks or plates along ship. [orig. uncert.]

**stramo'nium** *n.* Drug used against asthma; plant yielding it. [orig. unkn.]

**strānd**¹. **1.** *v.t. & i.* Run aground; (in *p.p.*) in difficulties, without money or means of transport, left behind while others advance. **2.** *n.* (literary). Margin of sea, lake, or river, esp. foreshore. [E]

**strānd**² *n.* One of the strings or wires twisted round each other to make rope etc.; (fig.) element in character, theme in story, etc. [orig. unkn.]

**strānge** (-nj) *a.* Unusual, peculiar, surprising, eccentric, (~ **to say**, parenth., it is surprising that); unfamiliar, alien, foreign; unaccustomed *to* (*am strange to the work*); not at ease. [F *estrange* f. L *extraneus*]

**strā'nger** (-nj-) *n.* Person in place or company that he does not know or belong to or where he is unknown; person strange to one or *to* something; **be a, no,** ~ **to**, be unknown, known, to (person), have had no, much, experience of. [F *estrangier* f. L (prec.)]

**strā'ngle** (-nggel) *v.t.* Squeeze windpipe or neck of, esp. so as to kill; (fig.) hamper, suppress; ~**hold**, strangling or deadly grip (lit. or fig.); **strā'ngūlāte** (-ngg-) *v.t.*, prevent circulation through (vein, intestine, etc.) by compression; **străngūlā'tion** (-ngg-) *n.*, strangling, strangulating. [F *estrangler* f. L *strangulo* f. Gk]

**străp.** **1.** *n.* Strip of leather etc., often with buckle, for holding things in place, as means of chastisement, etc.; loop for grasping to steady oneself in moving vehicle; ~'**hanger**, train or bus passenger standing and holding strap for lack of seat. **2.** *v.t.* (-**pp**-). Secure or bind (*up* etc.) with strap; chastise with strap. **3.** ~'**less** *a.*, (esp., of garment) without shoulder-straps; ~'**ping** *a.*, big, tall, sturdy. [dial., = STROP]

**strata.** See STRATUM.

**strā'tagem** *n.* (An) artifice, trick(ery). [F f. L f. Gk]

**strā'těg|ў** *n.* The art of war (lit. or fig.), esp. planning of movements of troops, ships, etc., into favourable positions; (a plan using) skill in business, politics, etc.; **stratē'gĭc** *a.* (-**ically**), of, by, or serving the ends of strategy, (of materials) essential in war, (of bombing) designed to disorganize or demoralize the enemy; ~**ĭst** *n.* [F f. Gk]

**strāth** *n.* (Sc.) Broad valley; ~**spey'** (-ā'), (music for) a slow Scottish dance. [Gael.; *Spey* river]

**strā'tĭf|ў** *v.t.* (esp. in *p.p.*) Arrange in strata, grades, etc.; ~**ĭcā'tion** *n.* [F (STRATUM)]

**strā'tosph|ēre** *n.* Layer of atmosphere above troposphere; ~**ě'rĭc** *a.* [foll.]

**strā't|um** (or -ah'-) *n.* (*pl.* ~**a**). Layer of rock, atmosphere, etc.; social grade or class. [L (*sterno* strew)]

**straw** *n.* Dry cut stalks of grain as material for bedding, thatching, packing, hats, etc. (MAKE *bricks without*, MAN *of*, *straw*); single stalk or piece of straw, insignificant trifle, (catch at a ~, try hopeless expedient in desperation; ~ **in the wind**, slight hint of future developments; **the last** ~, addition to burden, task, etc., that makes it unbearable); hollow tube for sucking drink through; CHEESE[1] *straw*; ~**-board**, coarse cardboard from straw pulp; ~**-colour(ed)**, (of) pale yellow; ~ **poll, vote**, unofficial ballot as test of opinion; ~'ў̆ *a.*, of or like straw. [E]

**straw'berry** *n.* (Plant bearing) pulpy red fruit having surface studded with yellow seeds; **crushed** ~, dull crimson colour; ~ **blonde**, yellowish-red (hair), woman with such hair; ~**-mark**, reddish birth-mark; ~**-tree**, evergreen with strawberry-like fruit. [E (prec., for unkn. reason)]

**stray** *v., n.,* & *a.* **1.** *v.i.* Wander or get separated from or *from* flock or companions or right place, lose one's way, go astray (lit. or fig.). **2.** *n.* Strayed animal or thing or person (WAIFS *and strays*). **3.** *a.* Strayed; scattered, sporadic, occurring or met with infrequently, casually, or un-expectedly; unwanted, uninten-tional. [AF *strey* (ASTRAY)]

**streak. 1.** *n.* Long thin usu. irregular line or band, esp. dis-tinguished by colour; flash of lightning (**like a** ~ **of lightning**, swiftly); (fig.) strain or element in character; spell, series, (*had a long winning streak*); ~'ў̆ *a.* (~**ily**, ~**iness**), (esp., of bacon) with alternate streaks of fat and lean. **2.** *v.t.* & *i.* Mark with streak(s); move very rapidly; (colloq.) run naked through public place. [E, = pen-stroke]

**stream. 1.** *n.* Flowing body of water, brook, small river; (current or direction of) flow of liquid, onward-moving fluid mass or crowd, esp. (in *sing.* or *pl.*) large quantity, (**go with the** ~, do as others do); ‖group of schoolchildren selected as being of similar ability; ~**line**, (*n.*) natural course of water or air current, shape of aircraft or boat or vehicle presenting least resistance to motion, (*v.t.*) give streamline form to, (fig.) make simple, more efficient, or better organized; ~ **of con-sciousness**, (literary style depicting) continuous flow of person's thoughts, emotions, etc.; ~'lĕt *n.* **2.** *v.i.* & *t.* Move as stream; run with liquid;

(of banner, hair, etc.) float or wave in the wind; emit stream of (blood etc.); ‖arrange (school-pupils) in streams; ~'er *n.*, (esp.) long narrow flag, long narrow ribbon of paper, banner headline. [E]

**street** *n.* Road in city, town, or village, this with its contiguous houses or buildings, (MAN *in the street*; **on the** ~**s**, working as prostitute; ~**s ahead** (**of**), colloq., much superior (to); **up** one's ~, colloq., within one's range of knowledge, interest, etc., acceptable; WALK *the streets*); persons who live or work in a particular street; (as name of thoroughfare) *Oxford Street*; ~ **arab**, homeless child; *\*~'car*, tram; ~**-walker**, prostitute seeking cus-tomers in street. [E f. L *strata* (*via*)]

**strength** *n.* Being strong, degree or type of strongness, (*argue* etc. **from** ~, from a strong position; **from** ~ **to** ~, with ever-increasing success; **on the** ~ **of**, relying on, encouraged by, arguing from); what makes strong (*God is our strength*); number of persons present or available (*were present in great strength*); **in** ~, in large numbers); full complement (*below, up to, strength*; **on the** ~, on muster-roll); ~**en** *v.t.* & *i.*, make or become strong(er); ~**en** person's **hand**(s), encourage him to vigorous action. [E (STRONG)]

**stre'nuous** *a.* Making or requiring great exertions, energetic. [L]

**strĕpto|cŏ'ccus** *n.* (*pl.* **-cci** *pr.* **-kī**). Bacterium causing serious infections; ~**cŏ'ccal** *a.*; ~**mȳ'cin** *n.*, antibiotic effective against some disease-producing bacteria. [Gk *streptos* twisted, *kokkos* berry, *mukēs* fungus]

**strĕss. 1.** *n.* Pressure, tension, quantity measuring this; compul-sion; demand on physical or mental energy; emphasis (**lay** ~ **on**, indicate as important), esp. on syllable or word; ~**ful** *a.* (-**lly**), causing stress. **2.** *v.t.* Lay stress on, accent, emphasize; subject to stress. [DISTRESS, or F *estresse* (STRICT)]

**strĕtch** *v., n.,* & *a.* **1.** *v.t.* & *i.* Make or become taut; place or lie at full length or spread out; extend (one's limbs, or abs.; ~ one's **legs**, exercise oneself by walking; ~ one-**self**, tighten muscles thus after sleep etc.); draw, be drawn, or admit of being drawn out into greater length or size; have specified length or extension, extend; strain or exert extremely or excessively, exaggerate, (~ **a point**, agree to something not normally allowed); ~ **out**, extend (hand, foot, etc.), (cause to) last for long(er) period. **2.** *n.* Stretching or being stretched; continuous extent, expanse, or period (*a stretch of road*; *works ten hours at a stretch*); (sl.) period of imprisonment; *straight part of race-track. **3.** *a.* Able to stretch, elastic, (*stretch fabric*). **4.** ~**er** *n.*, (esp.) appliance (often of canvas, stretched on two poles) for carrying disabled or dead person on, board in boat against which rower presses feet, brick etc. laid along face of wall (cf. HEADER); ~**ў** *a.* (~**iness**), (colloq.) able or tending to stretch. [E]

**strew** (-ōō) *v.t.* (*p.p.* ~**n**, ~**ed**). Scatter (sand, flowers, small objects) over a surface, spread (surface) with or *with* sand etc. [E (STRAW)]

**stri´|a** *n.* (*pl.* ~**ae**). Slight furrow or ridge on surface; ~**a´tĕd** *a.*, marked with striae; ~**a´tion** *n.* [L]

**stri´cken.** See STRIKE.

**strict** *a.* Precisely limited or defined, accurate, without irregularity or exception or deviation; requiring complete obedience or exact performance; ~**ly speaking**, if one uses words in their strict sense; ~**ure** *n.*, (usu. in *pl.*) critical or censorious remark (*on, upon*). [L *stringo strict*- draw tight]

**stride. 1.** *v.i. & t.* (**strode** *pr.* -ōd; **stri´dden** *pr.* -ĭ'd-). Walk with long steps; cross with one step; bestride. **2.** *n.* Single step esp. in respect of length, distance of this, gait as determined by length of stride; (fig., usu. in *pl.*) progress (*has made great strides*); **get into** one's ~, (fig.) settle into job etc.; **take in** one's ~, clear (obstacle) without changing gait to jump, (fig.) find no serious impediment in. [E]

**stri´den|t** *a.* Of loud harsh sound; ~**cў** *n.* [L *strido* creak]

**strife** *n.* Conflict, struggle between opposed persons or things. [F *estrif* (STRIVE)]

**strike. 1.** *v.t. & i.* (**struck**, **struck**, arch. exc. in *comb.* **stri´cken**). Subject to impact, deliver (blow), come or bring sharply into contact with, (cause to) penetrate, propel or divert with blow; secure hook in mouth of (fish) by jerking tackle; produce (sparks, musical note, etc.) by striking; ignite (match) by rubbing against something; (of clock) indicate (time), (of time) be indicated, by sounding of bell etc.; make (coin) by stamping; agree on (bargain); afflict; make (person *blind, deaf*, etc.) suddenly; reach or achieve (*strike a balance, the* HAPPY *medium*); put oneself theatrically into (attitude); discover (track etc.); come to attention of, appear to, (person; *it strikes me as ridiculous*; *the idea suddenly struck me*); lower or take down (flag, tent, etc.); (of employees) engage in strike, cease work as protest; take specified direction. **2.** *n.* Act of striking; employees' concerted refusal to work till some grievance is remedied, similar refusal to participate in other expected activity, (**on** ~, acting thus; ~**-breaker**, employee brought in to replace striker; ~ **pay**, subsistence-allowance paid to strikers by trade union); sudden find or success, esp. from the air. **3.** ~ **a blow for**, act to support, protect, etc.; **strike a** LIGHT[1]; ~ **down**, knock down (lit., or fig. of illness etc.); ~ **home**, deal effective blow (lit. or fig.); ~ **it rich**, become rich; ~ **lucky**, have lucky success; ~ **me pink!** (vulg. *int.* expr. surprise); ~ **off**, remove with stroke, delete (name etc., esp. = *strike off the* ROLLS); *strike* OIL[1]; ~ **out**, hit from the shoulder or violently, swim or act vigorously, delete (item, name, etc.); *strike* ROOT[1]; ~ **through**, delete with pen-stroke; ~ **up**, start (an acquaintance, conversation etc.), esp. casually, begin playing (a tune etc.); ~ **upon**, devise (idea, plan, etc.) suddenly or unexpectedly; *strike while the* IRON *is hot*; **struck on**, (sl.) infatuated with. **4. stri´ker** *n.*, (esp.) employee on strike, player who is to strike ball in game, (Footb. etc.) player whose main function is to try to score goals; **stri´king**, (*a.*, esp.) impressive, attracting attention, (*n.*, esp.) **striking-distance**, distance short enough to strike a blow (lit. or fig.), **striking-force**, military body ready to attack at short notice. [E, = rub, go]

**string. 1.** *n.* Twine or narrow cord, piece of this or similar material for tying, lacing, drawing or holding together, working puppet, etc., (APRON-*strings*; **first, second, ~,** person or thing that one chiefly, alternatively, relies on; **on a ~,** under one's control or influence; **pull ~s,** exert esp. hidden influence; **pull the ~s,** control actions of another; **two ~s to one's bow,** more than one resource; **with no ~s attached,** not subject to conditions); piece of catgut, wire, etc., on musical instrument, producing note by vibration; (in *pl.*) stringed instruments in orchestra etc.; (*attrib.*) relating to or consisting of stringed instruments (*string orchestra, quartet*); set of things strung together, series or line of persons or things, (*a string of beads, cars, oaths*); group of race-horses trained at particular stable; **~ bag** (made of string, for parcels etc.); **~ bass,** double-bass; *****~ bean,** French or kidney bean with strings; **~-course,** raised horizontal band of bricks etc. on building; **~ vest** (made of large meshes). **2.** *v.t. & i.* (**strung**). Supply with string(s); tie with string; thread (beads etc.) on string; arrange in or as string; remove strings from (beans); place string ready for use on (bow); (fig., esp. in *p.p.*) tighten *up* or make ready or excited (nerves, resolution, etc.); **~ along,** (colloq.) deceive (person), keep company *with* (person); **~ up,** hang up on strings etc., kill by hanging. **3.** (-)**~ed** (-ngd) *a.,* (of musical instruments) having strings; **~'er** *n.,* (esp.) longitudinal structural member in framework esp. of ship or aircraft, newspaper correspondent not on regular staff; **~'y** *a.* (**~ily, ~iness**), like string, fibrous. [E]

**strĭ'ngen|t** (-nj-) *a.* (Of rules etc.) strict, severe, leaving no loophole or discretion; **~cy̆** *n.* [L (STRICT)]

**strĭp¹. 1.** *v.t. & i.* (-**pp**-). Remove clothes or covering from, undress, (**~ped to the waist,** wearing nothing above waist); take (covering, appurtenances, property, etc.) off or *off* from or *from* person or thing; tear thread from (screw); **~ (down),** remove accessory fittings of or take apart (machine etc.). **2.** *n.* Act of stripping esp. of undressing in strip-tease; ||(colloq.) clothes worn by footballer etc.; **~ club** (where strip-

-tease is performed); **~-tease** *n.,* & *v.i.,* (perform in) entertainment in which woman gradually undresses before audience. **3.** **~'per** *n.,* (esp.) device or solvent for removing paint etc., strip-tease performer. [E]

**strĭp²** *n.* Long narrow piece (**tear person off a ~,** sl., rebuke him); AIR*strip*; **~ (cartoon),** = COMIC *strip*; **~ light,** tubular fluorescent lamp; **~'ling** *n.,* youth not fully grown. [LG *strippe* strap]

**strīpe** *n.* Long narrow band or strip on surface from which it differs in colour or texture (STARS *and Stripes*); (Mil.) chevron etc. denoting rank; *****type of character, opinion, etc., (*a man of that stripe*); (arch., usu. in *pl.*) blow with scourge or lash; (-)**~d** (-pt), **strī'py̆,** *adjs.,* having stripes. [perh. LDu.]

**strīve** *v.i.* (**strove** *pr.* -ōv; **stri'ven** *pr.* -ĭ'v-). Struggle, contend, try hard, (*to do, for* or *after* desired end, *with* or *against* opponent etc.). [F *estriver*]

**strŏb|e** *n.* (colloq.) Stroboscope; **~'oscŏpe** *n.,* lamp flashing intermittently, device using this to determine speeds of rotation etc.; **~oscŏ'pĭc** *a.* [Gk *strobos* whirling]

**strŏde.** See STRIDE.

**strōke. 1.** *n.* Act of striking (*a stroke of lightning*; *20 strokes of the cane*; **at a ~,** by a single action; **finishing ~,** final and fatal blow); sudden disabling attack esp. of apoplexy (SUN*stroke*); action or movement esp. as one of series or in game etc. (**off** one's **~,** not performing so well as usual); slightest such action (*has not done a stroke of work*); (Rowing) mode or action of moving oar, **~ (oar),** oarsman nearest stern, who sets time of stroke; mode of moving limbs in swimming (BACK*stroke*, BREAST--*stroke*); effort or action *of* specified kind (*a stroke of diplomacy, genius, wit*; MASTER-*stroke*); **~ of luck,** unexpected opportune occurrence); (mark made by) movement in one direction of pen, paintbrush, etc., (**with a ~ of the pen,** merely by writing signature etc.); detail contributing to general effect; act or spell of stroking; sound made by a striking clock (**on the ~,** punctually; **on the ~ of** nine, just before or exactly at nine o'clock). **2.** *v.t.* Pass hand gently along surface of (hair, fur, etc.); act as stroke of (boat, crew). [E, rel. to STRIKE]

**stroll. 1.** *v.i.* Saunter, go for stroll; go from place to place giving performances etc. (*strolling players*). **2.** *n.* Short leisurely walk. [prob. G (*strolch* vagabond)]

**strŏng** (*in compar.* & *superl. pr.* -ngg-). **1.** *a.* Having power of resistance, not easily broken or torn or worn or injured or captured or disturbed, tough, firm, healthy; capable of exerting great force or of doing much, muscular, powerful; (of argument etc.) convincing, striking; powerfully affecting the senses or emotions (*strong light, perfume, acting*); (of group) having specified number (*we were 200 strong*); (of solution, tea, medicine, etc.) containing large proportion of the substance in water or other solvent; forcible, energetic, vigorous, decided, drastic, (*strong wind, protest, suspicion*); ~ **arm**, use of force; ~**box**, strongly made small chest for valuables; *strong* DRINK; ~**hold**, fortified place, secure refuge, centre of support for a cause etc.; ~ **language** (esp. profane or abusive); ~ **meat**, doctrine, action, etc., acceptable only to strong-minded or instructed people; ~**-mi′nded**, having a vigorous or determined mind; ~ **point**, fortified position, (fig.) thing at which one excels; ~**-room** (designed to protect valuables); ~ **suit**, suit at cards in which one can take tricks, (fig.) thing at which one excels; ~ **verb** (forming inflections by vowel-change within stem). **2.** *adv.* Strongly, vigorously; COME it strong; going ~, continuing vigorously. [E]

**strŏ′ntium** (*or* -shum) *n.* Soft silver-white metallic element; ~ **90**, radioactive isotope of strontium concentrating selectively in bones when ingested. [*Strontian*, place]

**strŏp. 1.** *n.* Device, esp. strip of leather, for sharpening razors. **2.** *v.t.* (-pp-). Sharpen on or with strop. [LDu.]

**strŏ′phē** *n.* Section of ancient-Greek choral ode. [Gk, = turning]

‖**strŏ′ppy** *a.* (sl.) Bad-tempered, awkward to deal with. [orig. uncert.]

**strŏve.** See STRIVE; **strŭck,** see STRIKE.

**strŭ′ctur|e. 1.** *n.* Manner in which thing is constructed; supporting framework or essential parts; thing constructed, complex whole. **2.** *v.t.* Give structure to, organize. **3.** ~**al** (-kcher-) *a.* (~**ally**), (esp.) of the (essential) framework; ~**alĭsm** (-kcher-) *n.*, doctrine that structure rather than function is important. [F or L (*struo struct-* build)]

**strū′del** (-ōō-) *n.* Confection of thin pastry filled esp. with apple. [G]

**strŭ′ggle. 1.** *v.i.* Throw one's limbs or body about in violent effort to get free; make violent or determined efforts under difficulties; strive hard to do, *for* thing; contend *with* or *against*; make one's way with difficulty *through, up, along,* etc.; (in *part.*) having difficulty in getting one's living or recognition. **2.** *n.* Act or period of struggling; hard or confused contest. [orig. uncert.]

**strŭm. 1.** *v.i.* & *t.* (-mm-). Touch strings or keys of (guitar, piano, etc.) esp. carelessly or unskilfully. **2.** *n.* Strumming sound. [imit.; cf. THRUM[2]]

**strŭ′mpĕt** *n.* (arch.) Prostitute. [orig. unkn.]

**strŭng.** See STRING.

**strŭt. 1.** *n.* Bar forming part of framework and designed to resist compression; strutting gait. **2.** *v.i.* & *t.* (-tt-). Walk in stiff pompous way; brace with strut(s). [E]

**'struth** (-ōō-) *int.* (colloq., used as mild oath). [*God's truth*]

**strȳ′chnine** (-knēn) *n.* Highly poisonous alkaloid used in small doses as stimulant. [F f. L f. Gk *struchnos* nightshade]

**Stū′art** *n.* & *a.* (Member) of family of British sovereigns from James I to Anne. [STEWARDS of Scotland]

**stŭb. 1.** *n.* Remnant of pencil, cigarette, etc., after use; counterfoil of cheque, receipt, etc.; stump, stunted tail etc.; ~**by** *a.* (-iness), short and thick. **2.** *v.t.* (-bb-). Strike (one's toe) against something; ~ (out), extinguish (cigarette etc.) by pressing lighted end against something. [E]

**stŭ′bbl|e** *n.* Cut stalks of cereals left sticking up after harvest; short hair on unshaven chin or cheek; ~**y** *a.* (~**iness**). [AF f. L *stupula*]

**stŭ′bborn** *a.* (~**ness** *pr.* -n-n-). Obstinate, inflexible, intractable. [orig. unkn.]

**stŭ′ccō. 1.** *n.* (*pl.* ~**es**). Plaster or cement for coating walls or moulding into architectural decorations. **2.** *v.t.* Coat with stucco. [It.]

**stŭck.** See STICK.

**stŭd¹. 1.** *n.* Large-headed nail, boss, or knob, projecting from a surface esp. for ornament; = COLLAR--stud. **2.** *v.t.* (-**dd**-). Set (as) with studs; (in *p.p.*) thickly set or strewn *with* (jewels, stars, etc.). [E, = post]

**stŭd²** *n.* Number of horses kept for breeding etc., place where these are kept (**at** ~, of stallion, available for breeding on payment of fee); stallion; (sl.) young man (esp. one noted for sexual prowess); ~**-book** (containing pedigrees of horses); ~**-farm**, place where horses are bred; ~ (**poker**), poker with betting after dealing of successive cards face up. [E]

**stŭ′dding-sail** (stŭ′nsal) *n.* Extra sail set in light winds. [LDu.]

**stŭ′dent** *n.* Person who is studying, esp. at university or other place of higher education; (*attrib.*) studying in order to become (*student nurse, teacher*). [L (STUDY)]

**stŭ′diŏ** *n.* (*pl.* ~**s**). Work-room of painter, photographer, etc.; place where motion-pictures are made; place where radio or television programmes are made and transmitted; **stŭ′dious** *a.*, assiduous in study or reading, painstaking, deliberate, taking care *to* do or *in* doing, anxiously desirous *of* doing. [It. f. L (foll.)]

**stŭ′dÿ. 1.** *n.* Acquiring of information or knowledge, esp. from books (often in *pl.*); thing that is or deserves to be investigated (*the proper study of mankind is man*); thing worth observing closely (*his face was a study*); piece of work, esp. drawing, done as practice or experiment; portrayal in literature or other art--form of an aspect of behaviour, character, etc.; (Mus.) composition designed to develop player's skill; room used for reading, writing, etc.; BROWN *study* (of persons meeting to study a particular subject). **2.** *v.t. & i.* Make a study of, investigate or examine (subject); apply oneself to study (*for* examination); scrutinize or earnestly contemplate (visible object); try to learn (words of one's role etc.); take pains to achieve (result) or pay regard to (subject, principle, etc.; *studies his own interests*; *going to study war no more*); (in *p.p.*) deliberate, intentional, affected, (*with studied politeness, unconcern*). [F *estudie*(*r*) f. L *studium*]

**stŭff. 1.** *n.* Material, substance or things of uncertain kind or not needing to be particularized or of inferior quality (*the stuff that dreams, heroes, are made of*; *do you call this stuff butter?*); woollen fabric; **do** one's ~, perform one's tricks etc., get on with one's job; GREEN-, HOT-, *stuff*; **know** one's ~, be master of one's subject, trade, etc.; ~ **and nonsense!** (excl. of incredulity or ridicule); **that's the** ~ (**to give 'em** or **to give the troops**), (colloq.) that is what is required; **the** ~, colloq.) supply of something, (sl.) money. **2.** *v.t. & i.* Pack tightly or cram (receptacle *with*, things or matter *into* receptacle or *in*); fill out skin of (animal, bird, etc.) with material to restore original shape (~**ed shirt**, colloq., pompous person); fill (fowl, rolled meat, etc.) with minced seasoning etc. before cooking; make (person or animal) eat to repletion (~ one**self**, eat greedily), eat thus; push, esp. hastily or clumsily; (usu. in *pass.*) block *up* (nose etc.); (vulg.) copulate with (woman); (sl.) dispose of as unwanted, damn, (*you can stuff the job*; **get** ~**ed**, go away, shut up). **3.** ~**'ing** *n.*, material used for stuffing chairs, fowls, etc. (**knock** or **take the** ~**ing out of**, colloq., render weak, defeat utterly); ~**'ÿ** *a.* (~**ily**, ~**iness**), (of room etc.) lacking ventilation or fresh air, (of nose etc.) stuffed up, (colloq.) sulky or ill--tempered or prim or narrow--minded. [F *estoffe*(*r*) f. Gk *stuphō* pull together]

**stŭ′ltif|ÿ** *v.t.* Make foolish, absurd, or useless; negate, neutralize; impair; ~**icā′tion** *n.* [L (*stultus* foolish)]

**stŭ′mbl|e. 1.** *v.i.* Lurch forward or have partial fall from catching or striking or misplacing foot, walk with repeated stumbling; make blunder(s); come accidentally (*up*)*on*, *across*; ~**ing-block**, obstacle, circumstance causing difficulty or hesitation. **2.** *n.* Act of stumbling. [cogn. w. STAMMER]

**stŭmp. 1.** *n.* Projecting remnant of cut or fallen tree, similar remnant of broken branch, amputated limb, worn-down pencil, etc.; (in *pl.*, joc.) legs (STIR[1] one's *stumps*); stump of tree, or other place, used by orator (~ **oratory**, **speech**, inflammatory or ranting speech); (Crick.) one of the 3 uprights of a wicket. 2. *v.i.* & *t.* Walk (as) on wooden leg(s); (Crick.) put (batsman) out by touching stumps with ball while he is outside his crease; (of question etc., colloq.) be too hard for (person); (in *p.p.*) at a loss, at one's wit's end; traverse (district) making stump speeches; ||~ **up**, (sl.) pay or produce (money required, or abs.). 3. ~**er** n., (esp., colloq.) wicket-keeper; ~**ÿ** a. (~**ily**, ~**iness**), short and thick. [LDu.]

**stŭn** v.t. (-nn-). Knock senseless, stupefy, overwhelm; ~**ner** n., (esp., colloq.) stunning person or thing; ~**ning** a., (esp., colloq.) extremely good or attractive. [F (ASTONISH)]

**stŭng.** See STING; **stŭnk.** See STINK.

**stŭnt**[1] v.t. Retard growth or development of, dwarf. [obs. *stunt* foolish, short]

**stŭnt**[2]. (colloq.) 1. *n.* Something unusual done to attract attention; trick or daring manoeuvre, esp. with aeroplane; ~ **man** (employed to take actor's place in performing dangerous stunts). 2. *v.i.* Perform stunts, esp. aerobatics. [orig. unkn.]

**stŭ′pĕf|ÿ** v.t. Make stupid or insensible; ~**ăction** n.; **stŭpĕ′ndous** a., amazing, prodigious, esp. by its size or degree. [F f. L (*stupeo* be amazed)]

**stŭ′pĭd** a. (~**er**, ~**est**). Unintelligent, slow-witted, foolish; typical of stupid persons; boring; in a state of stupor; ~**ĭtÿ** (-ĭ′d-) n.; **stŭ′por** n., dazed or torpid or helplessly amazed state.

**stŭr′d|ÿ** a. (~**ily**, ~**iness**). Robust, hardy, strongly built. [F *esturdi*]

**stŭr′geon** (-jon) n. Large edible fish yielding caviare. [AF f. Gmc]

**stŭ′tter.** 1. *v.i.* & *t.* Speak with checks and repetitions of certain sounds, esp. initial consonants; ~ (**out**), utter (words) thus. 2. *n.* Act or habit of stuttering. [dial. *stut*]

**stÿ**[1] n. Enclosure for pigs (usu. **pi′g~**); filthy room or abode. [E]

**stÿ**[2], **stÿe**, n. Inflamed swelling on edge of eyelid. [E]

**Stÿ′gĭan** a. (As) of Styx or Hades;

murky. [L f. Gk (*Styx*, river encompassing Hades)]

**style.** 1. *n.* Manner of writing, speaking, or doing; distinctive manner of person or school or period; (as *suf.*) = -WISE (*dressed cowboy-style*); correct way of designating person or thing (*is entitled to the style of 'Right Honourable'*; **new**, **old**, ~, of date reckoned by Gregorian, Julian, Calendar); superior quality or manner (*let us do it in style*); fashion in dress etc.; kind, sort, esp. in regard to appearance, shape, pattern, (*what style of house do you require?*); ancient writing-implement for scratching letters on wax-covered tablets, thing of similar shape esp. for engraving; (Bot.) narrow extension of ovary supporting stigma. 2. *v.t.* Design, make, etc., in particular (esp. fashionable) style; designate in specified way. 3. **stÿ′lĭsh** a., fashionable, elegant, superior; **stÿ′lĭst** n., person concerned with style, esp. writer having or aiming at good literary style, or designer of fashionable styles; **stÿlĭ′stĭc** a. (-**ically**), of literary style; **stÿ′lĭze** v.t., (usu. in *p.p.*) make (work of art etc.) conform to rules of a conventional style; **stÿ′lus** n. (*pl.* -**li** *pr.* -lī), needle-like point for producing or following groove in gramophone record, ancient pointed writing-implement (see STYLE). [F f. L *stilus*]

**stÿ′mĭe.** 1. *n.* Situation in golf when opponent's ball is between one's own ball and the hole; (fig.) difficult situation. 2. *v.t.* Subject (person etc.) to stymie; (fig.) obstruct, thwart. [orig. unkn.]

**stÿ′ptĭc** a. (~**ally**) & n. (Substance) that checks bleeding. [L f. Gk (*stuphō* contract)]

**suā′s|ion** (swā′zhon) n. Persuasion (as opposed to force); ~**ĭve** a. [F or L (*suadeo suas*- urge)]

**suav|e** (swahv) a. Urbane, gracious, refined; ~′**ĭtÿ** n. [F, or L *suavis*]

**sŭb.** (colloq.) 1. *n.* Sub-editor; submarine; subscription; substitute. 2. *v.i.* & *t.* (-**bb-**). Act as substitute *for* someone; sub-edit. [abbr.]

**sub-** *pref.* denoting: at, to, or from lower position, under, of lesser degree, (*subcutaneous*, *subnormal*, *subsoil*, *substandard*, *substructure*, *subzero*); subordinate(ly), secondary, deputy,

(*subclass, subcommittee, subculture, sub-
family, subheading, sub-lieutenant, sub-
-plot, subsection, subspecies, substation,
subtotal*); nearly, more or less, (*subarctic*). [L]

‖**sŭ′baltern** *n.* (Mil.) Officer below
rank of captain. [L (ALTERNATE)]

**sŭbă′qua** *a.* (Of sport etc.) taking
place under water; **sŭbaquă′tĭc,
sŭbă′quĕous,** *adjs.,* underwater;
**sŭbătŏ′mĭc** *a.,* occurring in or
smaller than an atom; **sŭbcŏ′n-
scious** (-shᵾs) *a. & n.,* (of) part of
mind that is not fully conscious but
is able to influence actions etc.; **sŭb-
cŏ′ntĭnent** *n.,* land-mass of great
extent not classed as continent.
[SUB-]

**sŭbcontrăct. 1.** (-ŏ′-) *n.* Arrangement by which one who has contracted to do work arranges for it
to be done by others. **2.** (-ă′-) *v.t. & i.*
Make subcontract (for); **sŭbcon-
tră′ctor** *n.* [SUB-]

**sŭ′bdĭvide** (*or* -ī′d) *v.t. & i.* Divide
again after first division; **sŭ′b-
dĭvision** (-zhᴏn) *n.,* subdividing,
subordinate division. [L (SUB-)]

**subdū′e** *v.t.* Conquer, suppress,
tame; (esp. in *p.p.*) make soft(er) or
gentle(r). [F f. L *subduco*]

**sŭb-ĕ′dĭt** *v.t.* Act as sub-editor of;
~**or** *n.,* assistant editor, ‖one who
prepares material for printing in
newspaper, book, etc.; ~**or′ĭal** *a.*
[SUB-]

**sŭ′bfŭsc** (*or* -fŭ′-) *a. & n.* Dull-
-coloured (formal clothing in some
universities). [L (*fuscus* dark brown)]

**sŭbhū′man** *a.* Less than human;
not fully human. [SUB-]

**sŭ′bject** (*or* -ĕ-) *a., adv., n., & v.*
**1.** *a.* Under control or government,
owing obedience *to*; liable or exposed *to* (*is subject to colds, damage,
delays*). **2.** *a. & adv.* ~ **to,** condition-
al(ly) upon, on the assumption of,
without precluding, (*the arrangement
is subject to your approval; subject to
correction, these are the facts*). **3.** *n.*
Person subject to political rule, any
member of a State except the sovereign; person owing obedience to
another; (Logic & Gram.) the term
about which something is predicated
in a proposition, noun or noun-
-equivalent with which verb of sentence is made to agree in number etc.;
(Philos.) the conscious self as opp.
to all that is external to the mind, the
substance as opp. to the attributes

of something; theme of discussion,
description, representation, or music,
matter (to be) treated or dealt
with, person (to be) studied or
thought about, (*never talks on serious
subjects; what is the subject of the poem,
story, picture?*); **change the** ~, talk of
something else, esp. to avoid embarrassment); circumstance, person,
or thing that gives occasion for
specified feeling or action (*is a subject for ridicule*); department of study
(*was examined in six subjects*); (esp.
Med.) person with specified usu.
undesirable bodily or mental tendency (*a hysterical subject*); ~ **catalogue** etc. (listing subjects treated);
~**-matter,** matter dealt with in
book, lawsuit, etc. **4.** (subjĕ′kt) *v.t.*
Expose or make liable *to* (*he was
subjected to criticism; subject the metal
to great heat*); subdue (nation etc. *to*
rule, control, etc.); **subjĕ′ction**
*n.* [F f. L *subicio* -ject- (*jacio* throw)]

**subjĕ′ctive** *a.* Of or due to the
consciousness or thinking or per-
cipient subject as opp. real or external things, not objective, imaginary; (of art, artists, history, etc.)
giving prominence to or depending
on personal opinions or idiosyncrasy;
(Gram.) of the subject; ~**ĭsm** *n.,*
doctrine that knowledge is merely
subjective and incapable of objective
proof; **subjĕctĭ′vĭty** *n.* [L (as
prec.)]

**subjoi′n** *v.t.* Add (anecdote, illustration, etc.) at the end. [F f. L
*subjungo* -junct-]

**sub judice** (sŭb jōō′dĭsĭ, sŏŏb
ū′dĭkă) *a.* Under judicial consideration, not yet decided (and therefore
not to be commented on). [L]

**sŭ′bjug|ăte** (-jŏō-) *v.t.* (~**able**).
Conquer, bring into subjection or
bondage; ~**ā′tion,** ~**ātor,** *ns.* [L
(*jugum* yoke)]

**subjŭ′nctive** *a. & n.* (Designating)
mood of verb used esp. for what is
imagined, wished, or possible (*if I
were you; suffice it to say*). [F or L
(SUBJOIN)]

**sŭ′blease¹** *n.,* **sŭblea′se²** *v.t.,*
**sŭblĕ′t** *v.t.* (-tt-; **suble′t**). Lease to
subtenant. [SUB-]

**sŭ′blĭm|āte. 1.** *v.t.* Convert (sub-
stance) from solid into vapour by
heat (and usu. allow to solidify
again); (fig.) refine, purify; (Psych.)
divert energy of (primitive impulse
etc.) into culturally higher activity;

~**ā'tion** *n.* 2. (-at) *a.* & *n.* Sublimated (substance). [L (foll.)]

**subli'me. 1.** *a.* (~**r**, ~**st**). Exalted, of greatest or highest sort, awe--inspiring; (of indifference, impudence, etc.) like that of one too exalted to fear consequences; **subli'mĭtў** *n.* 2. *v.t.* & *i.* Make sublime; sublimate; undergo sublimation. [L]

**sŭbli'mĭnal** *a.* (~**ly**). (Psych.) Below threshold of consciousness; too faint or rapid to be consciously perceived. [L *limen -min-* threshold]

**sŭb-machi'ne-gŭn** (-shē'-) *n.* Lightweight machine-gun held by hand. [SUB-]

**sŭbmari'ne** (-ē'n; *or* sŭ'-). **1.** *a.* Existing, occurring, done, or used, below surface of sea. **2.** *n.* Submarine vessel, esp. warship capable of operating on or under water-surface.

**submer'|ge** *v.t.* & *i.* Place or go beneath water, flood, inundate (lit. or fig.; **the ~ged tenth,** poorest section of the population); ~**gence,** ~**sion** (-shon), *ns.*; ~**sible** *a.* & *n.*, (vessel) capable of submerging. [L (*mergo mers-* dip)]

**sŭbmicrosco'pic** *a.* Too small to be seen by microscope. [SUB-]

**submi'|t** *v.t.* & *i.* (-tt-). Surrender (one*self*, oneself) *to* control, orders, treatment, etc., or *to* person for these; yield, cease to resist; present (document, theory, etc.) *for* consideration or decision; urge or represent deferentially (*I submit that there is no case to answer*); ~**t to,** cause to undergo; ~**ssion** (-shon) *n.*, submitting, thing submitted, submissiveness; ~**ssive** *a.*, willing to submit, unresisting, meek. [L (*mitto miss-* send)]

**subôr'dĭn|ate** *a.*, *n.*, & *v.* **1.** *a.* Of inferior importance or rank, secondary, subservient, (*to*); ~**ate clause** (serving as *n.*, *a.*, or *adv.* in sentence). **2.** *n.* Subordinate person. **3.** (-āt) *v.t.* (~**able**). Make or treat as subordinate (usu. *to*); ~**ā'tion** *n.*; ~**ative** *a.* [L (ORDAIN)]

**subôr'n** *v.t.* Induce esp. by bribery to commit perjury or other crime. [L (*orno* equip)]

**subpoe'na** (-ē'-; *or* sup-). **1.** *n.* Writ commanding person's attendance in lawcourt. **2.** *v.t.* (~**ed** *pr.* -ad, ~**'d**). Serve subpoena on. [L, = under penalty]

*sub rosa* (sŭb rō'za) *a.* & *adv.* (Done) in confidence or secretly. [L]

**subscri'be** *v.t.* & *i.* (Agree to) pay (specified sum) esp. regularly for membership of an organization, receipt of a publication, etc.; contribute *to* a fund or *for* a purpose; write (esp. one's name) at foot of document, etc. (~ **oneself,** sign one's name), sign (document) thus; ~ **to,** arrange to receive (periodical etc.) regularly, agree with (opinion or resolution); ~**r** *n.*, (esp.) person paying regular sum for hire of telephone (~**r trunk dialling,** making of trunk-calls by subscriber without assistance of operator); **sŭ'bscript** *a.* & *n.*, (symbol) written below another symbol; **subscri'ption** *n.*, amount subscribed, act of subscribing (**subscription concert** etc., paid for mainly by those who subscribe in advance). [L (*scribo script-* write)]

**sŭ'bsĕquent** *a.* Following a specified or implied event; ~ **to,** later than, after. [F or L (*sequor* follow)]

**subsĕr'v|e** *v.t.* Serve as means towards (purpose, action, etc.); ~**ĭent** *a.*, subserving, subordinate *to*, obsequious; ~**ĭence** *n.* [L *subservio*]

**subsi'de** *v.i.* (Of water, esp. flood) sink to low(er) level; (of ground) cave in, sink; (of building, ship, etc.) settle lower in ground or water; (of suspended matter) fall to bottom; (of swelling etc.) become less; (of storm, emotion, etc.) become tranquil; (of person, usu. joc.) sink (*into chair,* etc.); ~**nce** (*or* sŭ'bsī-) *n.* [L *subsido*]

**subsi'dĭar|ў. 1.** *a.* (~**ily,** ~**iness**). Serving to help or supplement, not of primary importance; (of company) controlled by another. **2.** *n.* Subsidiary company or thing or person. **3. sŭ'bsĭdize** *v.t.*, provide, or reduce cost of, with subsidy; **sŭ'bsĭdў** *n.*, money contributed by State, public body, etc., to keep prices at desired level or to assist in meeting expenses etc. [L (*subsidium* help)]

**subsi'st** *v.i.* (Continue to) exist, get sustenance or livelihood (*on* food etc., *by* occupation); ~**ence** *n.*, (means of) subsisting; ~**ence allowance** (granted for maintenance esp. while travelling on business); ~**ence farming** (in which almost all crops are consumed by farmer's household); ~**ence level, wage,** (merely enough to provide bare necessities of life). [L *subsisto*]

**sŭb̄soil** n. Soil immediately below surface soil; **sŭb̄so̅′nĭc** a. (~**ally**), relating to speeds less than that of sound. [SUB-]

**sŭb̄stance** n. (Particular kind of) material (a heavy, porous, yellow, substance); essence or most important part, real meaning, (can give you the substance of her remarks; **in ~**, in the main points, apart from details); theme, subject; reality, solidity, (there is no substance in the argument); wealth and possessions (a man **of ~** with much property); **sŭbstă′ntial** (-shăl) a. (-**lly**), having substance, actually existing, of real importance or value, of considerable amount, solid, well-to-do, essential, practical; **substăntiă′lĭty** (-shĭ-) n.; **sŭbstă′ntiāte** (-shĭ-) v.t. (-**tiable**), support or prove the truth of; **sŭbstăntiā′tion**, **substă′ntiātor**, (-shĭ-) ns. [F f. L substantia]

**sŭ′bstantīve** (or substă′-). **1.** a. Having independent existence, not subordinate; actual, real, permanent. **2.** n. Noun; **sŭbstanti′val** a. (-**lly**). [F or L (prec.)]

**sŭb̄stĭt̄ute** n., a., & v. **1.** n. & a. (Person or thing) acting or serving in place of another. **2.** v.t. & i. Put, use, or serve as a substitute (for); (vulg.) replace by; ~**ū′tion** n.; ~**ū′tional**, ~**ūtive**, adjs. [L substituo -tut-]

**sŭbstrā′t|um** (or sŭ′-, -ah-) n. (pl. ~**a**). Underlying layer, basis (lit. or fig.). [L (SUB-)]

**subsū′me** v.t. Include (instance etc.) under a rule or class. [L (sumo take)]

**sŭb̄tĕnan|t** n. Person renting room, house, etc., from one who is a tenant; ~**cȳ** n. [SUB-]

**subtĕ′nd** v.t. (Geom.) (Of line) be opposite (angle, arc). [L (TEND¹)]

**sŭb̄terfūge** n. (Piece of) evasion or trickery to escape censure, defeat, etc. [F or L]

**sŭbterrā′nean** a. Underground. [L (terra land)]

**sŭb̄tītle. 1.** n. Subordinate or additional title of book etc.; caption of cinema film, esp. translating dialogue in foreign film. **2.** v.t. Provide with subtitle(s). [SUB-]

**sŭb̄tle** (sŭ′tel) a. (-**er**, -**est**; -**tly**). Hard to detect or describe, fine, delicate, (a subtle charm, distinction, flavour); ingenious, clever, (a subtle explanation, observer); ~**tȳ** n. [F f. L subtilis]

||**sŭb̄to̅′pĭa** n. (derog.) (Region of) unsightly suburban buildings, esp. disfiguring a rural area. [SUB(URB), (U)TOPIA]

**subtră′ct** v.t. Deduct (number etc. from greater number); ~**ion** n.; ~**ĭve** a. [L (TRACT)]

**sŭb̄tro̅′pĭcal** a. (Characteristic of regions) bordering on the tropics. [SUB-]

**sŭ′būrb** n. Outlying district of city; **subŭ′rban** a., (characteristic) of suburb(s), (derog.) provincial in outlook; **subŭ′banite** n.; **Subŭr′-bĭa** n., (usu. derog.) the suburbs and their inhabitants. [F or L (urbs city)]

**subvĕ′ntion** n. Subsidy. [F f. L (subvenio assist)]

**subvĕr′|sion** (-shon) n. (Attempted) destruction or overthrow, esp. of government; ~**sĭve** a. & n., (person) attempting subversion; ~**t** v.t., effect subversion of. [F or L (verto vers- turn)]

**sŭ′bway** n. Underground passage, esp. for pedestrians; *underground railway. [SUB-]

**suc-** pref. assim. form of SUB- bef. c in wds f. Latin.

**succee′d** (-ks-) v.i. & t. Have success, not fail in doing, prosper; follow in order, be subsequent (to or to), come by inheritance or in due order (to title, office, etc.). [F, or L succedo -cess- come after]

**succĕ′ss** (-ks-) n. Favourable outcome, accomplishment of what was aimed at, attainment of wealth, fame, or position, (**nothing succeeds like ~**, one success leads to others); thing or person that turns out well; outcome (ill success); ~**ful** a. (-**lly**), having success, prosperous. [L (prec.)]

**succĕ′ssion** (-ksĕ′shon) n. A following in order (**in ~**, one after another; **in quick ~**, following one another at short intervals); series of things in succession (a succession of defeats); (right of) succeeding to the throne or any office or inheritance, series of persons having such right (**apostolic ~**, uninterrupted transmission of spiritual authority from Apostles through popes and bishops; **in ~ to**, as successor of); ~**al** a. (-**lly**); **succĕ′ssive** (-ks-) a., following in succession, consecutive; **succĕ′ssor** (-ks-) n., person or thing that succeeds (*to*) another. [F or L (SUCCEED)]

**succi'nct** (-ks-) *a.* Concise, brief. [L (*cingo cinct-* girdl)]

**su'ccour, \*su'ccor,** (-ker). (literary). **1.** *n.* Help given in time of need. **2.** *v.t.* Give succour to. [F f. L (*curro* run)]

**su'cculen|t. 1.** *a.* Juicy (of food, lit. or fig.); (Bot.) thick and fleshy; ~**ce** *n.* **2.** *n.* (Bot.) Succulent plant. [L (*succus* juice)]

**succu'mb** (-m) *v.i.* Be overcome, give way (*to*), die (owing *to* injuries, disease, etc.). [F or L (*cumbo* lie)]

**such. 1.** *a.* (no *compar.* or *superl.*; the order with **a(n)** is ~ **a(n)**, not **a** ~). Of the kind or degree indicated by context or circumstances (*such things make one despair; such is life; not such a fool as to believe that; no such* LUCK; *such* ANOTHER); (formal) the aforesaid, of the aforesaid kind, (*whoever shall make such return falsely*); so great(ly) or so extreme(ly), of a very notable kind, (*was in such a hurry; used such horrid language; we have had such fun!* EVER *such a*); ~**-and-~**, (person, thing) of particular kind but not needing to be specified (*will be in such-and-such a place at such-and-such a time*); ~ **as,** of the same kind or degree as (*such people, people such, as these; there is such a thing as loyalty*), of the or a kind that (*such a light as makes the eyes ache*), for example (*insects, such as bees*); ~ **as it is** (used to suggest that thing is of poor quality, of little value, etc.). **2.** *pron.* Such person(s) or thing(s), that, (*I haven't many specimens but I will send you such as I have; I may have offended but such was not my intention*); all ~, all persons of such character; as ~, as being what has been named (*in country places a stranger is welcome as such*); ~**like,** (colloq.) (things) of such kind. [E, = so-like]

**suck. 1.** *v.t.* & *i.* Draw (liquid) into mouth by making vacuum with lip-muscles etc.; (fig.) imbibe or gain (knowledge, advantage, etc.); roll tongue round, squeeze (sweet etc.) in mouth; draw liquid, sustenance, or advantage from (*suck the breast*); use sucking action or make sucking sound (*sat sucking at his pipe*); ~ **dry,** exhaust of contents by sucking (lit. or fig.); *suck* EGG[1]*s*; ~ **in,** absorb, engulf; ~ **up,** absorb, (sl.) toady (*to*). **2.** *n.* Act or period of sucking

(give ~, arch., allow baby to suck one's breast); ~**s (to you)!** (sl. excl., esp. of children, expr. derision or contempt). **3.** ~'**er** *n.*, (esp.) shoot springing from plant's root beside (not from) stem, organ in animals or part of apparatus for adhering by suction to surfaces, (sl.) gullible person, greenhorn; ~'**ing** *a.*, (esp.) not yet weaned; ~'**le** *v.t.*, feed (young) from breast or udder; ~'**ling** *n.*, unweaned child or animal. [E]

**su'crose** (or sōō'-) *n.* (Chem.) Sugar obtained from sugar-cane, sugar-beet, etc. [F *sucre* sugar]

**su'ction** *n.* Sucking; production of partial vacuum causing adhesion of surfaces or enabling external atmospheric pressure to force liquid etc. in. [L (*sugo suct-* suck)]

**Sudanē'se** (sōōdanē'z) *a.* & *n.* (*pl.* same). (Native) of (the) *Sudan*. [place]

**su'dden. 1.** *a.* (~**ness** *pr.* -n-n-). Occurring, come upon, made, or done abruptly, hurriedly, or unexpectedly; ~ **death,** (colloq.) decision by result of single event. **2.** *n.* (All) **of** (arch. **on**) **a** ~, suddenly. [AF f. L *subitaneus*]

**sudori'fic** (or sōō-) *a.* & *n.* (Drug) causing sweating. [L (*sudor* sweat)]

**suds** (-z) *n.pl.* (Soa'p)~, froth of soap and water; ~'**ÿ** *a.* [prob. LDu. *sudde, sudse* marsh, bog]

**sue** (or sōō) *v.t.* & *i.* Prosecute (person) in court; make application (*to* person or court, *for* redress or favour). [AF *suer* f. Rom. (L *sequor* follow)]

**suede** (swād) *n.* Kid or other skin with flesh side rubbed to a nap; cloth imitating it. [F, = Sweden]

**su'et** (or sōō'-) *n.* Hard fat of kidneys and loins of oxen, sheep, etc.; ~ **pudding** (made with suet and usu. steamed); ~'**ÿ** *a.* [AF f. L *sebum*]

**suf-** *pref.* assim. form of SUB- bef. *f* in wds f. Latin.

**su'ffer** *v.t.* & *i.* Undergo, be subjected to, (pain, defeat, change, etc.); undergo pain, grief, damage, disablement, or martyrdom; tolerate (*does not suffer fools gladly*); (arch.) permit, allow, (*to* come etc.); ~**ance** *n.*, tacit consent, abstention from objection, (**on** ~**ance,** in virtue of this). [F f. Rom. (L *suffero*)]

**suffi'ce** *v.i.* & *t.* Be enough or adequate (*to* do, *for* person or purpose; ~ **it to say,** I will content myself with saying *that*); meet the needs of (person etc.); **suffi′ciency** (-shen-) *n.*, a sufficient amount; **suffi′cient** (-shent), (*a.*) sufficing, adequate, (SELF-*sufficient*), (*n.*, esp.) a sufficient amount. [F f. L *sufficio*]

**su′ffix. 1.** *n.* Letter(s) added at end of word to form derivative. **2.** *v.t.* (or -ĭ′-). Append, esp. as suffix. [L (*figo fix-* fasten)]

**su′ffoc|ate** *v.t. & i.* Impede or stop breathing of (person etc.), choke or kill thus; be or feel suffocated; **~ā′tion** *n.* [L *suffoco* (*fauces* throat)]

**su′ffrag|e** *n.* Right of voting in political elections (**manhood ~e**, of all adult males; **universal ~e**, of all adults); vote, opinion or consent expressed in voting; (Eccl., esp. in *pl.*) intercessory petition in liturgy; **~an** *a. & n.*, (bishop) appointed to help diocesan bishop; **~ĕ′tte** *n.*, (Hist.) woman who agitated for women's suffrage. [F, or L *suffragium*]

**suffū′s|e** (-z) *v.t.* (Of colour, moisture, etc.) spread (as) from within over surface of; **~ion** (-zhon) *n.* [L (FOUND²)]

**Su′f|i** (-ōō′-) *n.* Muslim mystic; **~ic** *a.*; **~ism** *n.* [Arab.]

**sug-** *pref.* assim. form of SUB- bef. *g* in wds f. Latin.

**su′gar** (shŏŏ-). **1.** *n.* Sweet crystalline substance from sugar-cane, sugar-beet, and other plants, used in cookery, confectionery, etc., (BROWN, WHITE, *sugar*); (Chem.) soluble usu. sweet crystalline carbohydrate, e.g. glucose; (fig.) something to reconcile person to what is unpalatable; *(as colloq. term of address) darling, sweetheart; **~-basin, -bowl**, (holding sugar for use at table); **~-beet** (from whose roots sugar is made); *sugar*-CANDY; **~-cane**, perennial tropical grass with very tall stems from which sugar is made; **~-coated**, (of food, pill, etc.) enclosed in sugar, (fig.) made superficially attractive; **~-daddy**, (sl.) elderly man who lavishes gifts on a young woman; *sugar*-LOAF¹; **~ soap**, alkaline compound for cleaning or removing paint; **~-tongs**, small tongs for picking up lump sugar. **2.** *v.t.* Sweeten or coat with sugar. **3.** *v.t.* (**~iness**), containing or resembling sugar, (fig.) attractively or excessively sweet or pleasant. [F f. It. f. L f. Arab.]

**suggĕ′st** (suj-) *v.t.* Cause (idea) to present itself, bring (idea) into the mind, (**~ itself**, come into mind); propose (theory, plan, *that*), put forward for consideration or as a possibility; **~ible** *a.*, (esp.) open to (hypnotic) suggestion; **~ibi′lity** *n.*; **~ion** (-schon) *n.*, suggesting, thing suggested, insinuation of a belief or impulse into the mind (AUTO-SUGGESTION), a hint or slight trace *of*; **~ive** *a.*, conveying a suggestion (*of*), suggesting something indecent. [L *suggero* -*gest*-]

**su′icide** (or sōō′-) *n.* (Person who commits) intentional self-killing; (fig.) action destructive to one's own interests, reputation, etc.; **~ pact**, agreement between persons to commit suicide together; **~ pilot** etc. (undertaking mission likely to result in his own death); **su′icidal** (or sōō′-, -ī′d-) *a.* (-lly), of or tending to suicide, (fig.) destructive to one's own interests etc. [L (*sui* of oneself, *caedo* kill)]

**sui generis** (sūī jĕ′nerĭs, sōōē g-) *a.* Of its own kind, unique. [L]

**suit** (sūt, sŏŏt). **1.** *n.* Set of outer clothes, esp. of same cloth, consisting usu. of jacket (and for men sometimes waistcoat) and trousers or skirt; costume for particular purpose (SPACE*suit*; SWIM-*suit*); set of pyjamas, armour, etc.; any of the 4 sets (spades, hearts, diamonds, clubs) into which pack of cards is divided (**follow ~**, play card of same suit as was led, fig. conform to another's actions); lawsuit; (arch.) suing, seeking of woman's hand in marriage; **~′case** (for carrying clothes etc., usu. with handle and flat hinged lid). **2.** *v.t. & i.* Adapt, make appropriate, *to* (**~ the action to the word**, carry out one's promise or threat at once); satisfy, meet requirements or interests of, agree with, (*does not suit all tastes*); **~ person** or his **book**, be convenient for him; **~ oneself**, do as one chooses, find something that satisfies one); go well with, be in harmony with; be convenient or agreeable (*that date will suit*); (in *p.p.*) appropriate *to*, well adapted or having the right qualities *for*. **3.** **~′able** *a.* (**~ably**), suited *for* or *to*, right or appropriate for the purpose, occasion, etc.; **~abi′lity** *n.*; **suite** (swēt) *n.*, set of rooms or furniture, group of attendants, (Mus.) set of instrumental pieces usu. with related themes; ~**'ĭng** n., (esp.) cloth for suits; ~**'or** n., wooer, plaintiff or petitioner. [AF *siute* f. Rom.; see SUE]

**sŭ'lfa, *sŭ'lfur,** etc. See SULPHA, SULPHUR, etc.

**sŭ'lk|y̆. 1.** a. (~ily, ~iness). Silent, inactive, or unsociable from resentment or bad temper. **2.** n. Light two-wheeled one-horse vehicle. **3. sŭlk** (v.i.) be sulky (n., usu. in pl.) sulky condition. [perh. obs. *sulke* hard to dispose of]

**sŭ'llen** a. (~ness pr. -n-n-). Passively resentful, unforgiving, unresponsive, stubbornly ill-humoured. [AF (*sol* SOLE[1])]

**sŭ'lly̆** v.t. Diminish purity or splendour of (reputation etc.). [F *souiller* (SOIL[1])]

**sŭ'lpha, -fa,** a. Sulphonamide (*sulpha drug*). [abbr.]

**sŭ'lph|ur, *sŭ'lf|ur,** n. Pale-yellow non-metallic element burning with suffocating smell and blue flame; pale slightly greenish yellow colour; yellow butterfly; ~**āte** n., salt of sulphuric acid; ~**ĭde** n., binary compound of sulphur; ~**ĭte** n., salt of sulphurous acid; ~**ŏ'namĭde** a., a type of antibiotic drug; ~**ūr'éous** a., of or like sulphur; **sŭlphūrĕ'ttĕd, *sŭlfūrĕ'tĕd,** a., containing sulphur in combination; ~**ūr'ĭc** a., containing sulphur in a higher valency (~**uric acid,** dense oily colourless highly acid and corrosive fluid much used in industry); ~**ūrous** a., sulphureous, (or -ūr'-) containing sulphur in a lower valency (~**urous acid,** unstable weak acid used as reducing and bleaching agent); ~**ury̆** a., sulphureous. [AF f. L]

**sŭ'ltan** n. Muslim sovereign; (sweet) ~, a sweet-scented plant; **sŭlta'na** (-ah'-) n., sultan's wife, mother, concubine, or daughter, kind of seedless raisin; ~**āte** n., position of, territory ruled by, sultan. [F or L f. Arab.]

**sŭ'ltr|y̆** a. (~ily, ~iness). (Of weather etc.) hot and close; (of person etc.) passionate, sensual. [obs. *sulter* v., rel. to SWELTER]

**sŭm. 1.** n. Particular amount of money (LUMP[1] *sum*); (working out of) arithmetical problem; ~ (**total**), total resulting from addition of items, substance, summary, (**in** ~, briefly, to sum up). **2.** v.t. & i. (-mm-). ~ **up,** find or give total of,

express briefly or summarize (evidence, arguments, etc.), form or express judgement or opinion of (person, situation), (esp. of judge) recapitulate evidence or argument. [F f. L *summa*]

**sŭ'mmăc(h)** (-k; or sōō'-, shōō'-) n. (Shrub yielding) leaves dried and ground for use in tanning and dyeing. [F f. Arab.]

**sŭ'mmar|y̆. 1.** n. Brief account giving chief points. **2.** a. (~ily, ~iness). Brief, without details or formalities. **3.** ~**ize** v.t., make or be summary of; **summā'tion** n., finding of total, summarizing. [L (SUM)]

**sŭ'mmer** n., a., & v. **1.** n. Warmest season of the year (INDIAN *summer*; ||St. **Martin's** ~, fine weather about 11 Nov.); (fig.) mature stage of life etc.; ~**y̆** a. (~iness). **2.** a. Characteristic of or fit for summer; ~**-house,** light building in garden etc. providing shade in summer; *summer* LIGHTNING; ~ **school,** series of lectures etc. in summer, esp. at university; *summer* SOLSTICE; ~**-time,** season or weather of summer; ||~ **time** (shown by clocks advanced in summer for DAYlight saving). **3.** v.i. & t. Pass summer (*at, in,* place). [E]

**sŭ'mmĭt** n. Highest point, top, (lit. or fig.); ~ (**meeting** etc.), discussion between heads of governments. [F f. L *summus* highest]

**sŭ'mmon** v.t. Demand presence of, call together; call upon (*to* surrender etc.); muster *up* (courage etc., usu. *to* do or *for* task); ~**s** (-z), (n.) authoritative call to attend or do something, esp. to appear before judge or magistrate, (v.t.) serve with summons. [F f. L *summoneo*]

**sŭmp** n. Container, pit, or drain for (esp. superfluous) water, oil (esp. below crankcase in internal combustion engine), or other liquid. [LDu.]

**sŭ'mptū|ary̆** a. Limiting (esp. private) expenditure; ~**ous** a., (looking) rich and costly. [L (*sumptus* cost)]

**sŭn. 1.** n. The star that the earth travels round and receives light and warmth from, such light or warmth or both (*let in the sun*); any fixed star; *make* HAY *while the sun shines*; MIDNIGHT *sun*; *empire* etc. **on which the** ~ **never sets,** world-wide; **place in the** ~, favourable situation or condition; **rise with the ~**, get up at dawn; **take the ~**, expose oneself to sun's light and heat; **touch of the ~**, slight sunstroke; UNDER *the sun*. **2.** *v.t.* & *i.* (**-nn-**). Expose (oneself) to the sun. **3.** **~'bathe**, expose one's body to the sun; **~'beam**, ray of sun; ‖**~'blind**, window awning; **~'bonnet** (to shade face and neck from sun); **~'burn**, tanning or inflammation of skin by exposure to sun; **~'burnt**, affected by sunburn; **~'dew**, a hairy-leaved bog-plant; **~'dial**, instrument showing time by shadow of pointer in sunlight; **~'down**, sunset; **~'fish**, large globular fish; **~'-flower**, tall garden-plant with large golden-rayed flowers; **~glasses**, = DARK *glasses*; **~god**, the sun worshipped as a deity; **~hat**, **-helmet**, (designed to protect head from sun); **~lamp** (giving ultra-violet rays for therapy or artificial sun-tan); **~'light**, **~'lit**, (illuminated by) light from sun; **~ lounge**, room designed to receive much sunlight; **~rays**, sunbeams, ultra-violet rays used therapeutically; **~'rise**, (moment of) sun's rising; **~'roof**, = *sunshine roof*; **~'set**, (moment of) sun's setting, western sky with colours of sunset; **~'shade**, parasol, awning; **~'shine**, light of sun (**~shine roof**, sliding roof of motor car), area illuminated by it, fair weather, (fig.) cheerfulness or bright influence; **~'spot**, dark patch on sun's surface; **~'stroke**, acute prostration from excessive heat of sun; **~tan**, tanning of skin by exposure to sun; **~tanned** *a.*, coloured thus; **~trap**, sunny place, esp. sheltered from wind; *~**up**, sunrise. [E]

**Sun.** *abbr.* Sunday.

**su'ndae** (-dā, -dĭ) *n.* Confection of ice cream with fruit, syrup, etc. [perh. f. foll.]

**Su'nday** (*or* -dĭ). **1.** *n.* Day of week following Saturday, Christian day of rest and worship, (**month of ~s**, very long period); newspaper published on Sundays; **~** (BEST, GO[1]-*to-meeting*) **clothes** etc., one's best clothes (kept for Sunday use); **~ school** (for religious instruction etc. of children on Sundays). **2.** *adv.* (cf. FRIDAY 2). [E]

**su'nder** *v.t.* (literary). Sever. [E (cf. ASUNDER)]

**su'ndry. 1.** *a.* Various, several,

(**all and ~**, all collectively and individually). **2.** *n.* (in *pl.*) Oddments, accessories, items not needing to be specified. [E (prec.)]

**sŭng.** See SING; **sŭnk('en)**, see SINK.

**su'nn|ў** *a.* (**~ily**, **~iness**). Bright with or as sunlight; exposed to or warm with the sun; (fig.) cheerful. [SUN]

**sŭp. 1.** *v.t.* & *i.* (**-pp-**). Drink by sips or spoonfuls; take supper; (colloq.) drink (beer etc.). **2.** *n.* Mouthful of liquid (*neither bite nor sup*); (colloq.) drink of beer etc. [E]

**sup-** *pref.* assim. form of SUB- bef. *p* in wds f. Latin.

**su'per** (*or* soō'-). **1.** *n.* (colloq.) Supernumerary; superintendent. **2.** *a.* (sl.) (**-duper**), excellent, splendid. [abbr.]

**su'per-** (*or* soō'-) *pref.* denoting: at, to, or from higher position, above, beyond, of greater degree, (*superimpose, supernormal*); extreme(ly), excessive(ly), very much, very large, (*superabundance, superabundant, superheat, supersaturate, supertanker*). [L]

**supera'nnu|āte** (*or* soō'-) *v.t.* (**~able**). Dismiss or discard as too old; send into retirement with pension; (in *p.p.*) too old for work or use; **~ā'tion** *n.*, (esp.) (payment made to obtain) pension. [L (*annus* year)]

**supe'rb** (*or* soō-) *a.* Magnificent, splendid; (colloq.) excellent. [F or L, = proud]

**su'percārgō** (*or* soō'-) *n.* (*pl.* **~es**). Person in merchant ship managing sales etc. of cargo. [Sp. *sobrecargo*]

**su'perchārge** (*or* soō'-) *v.t.* Charge to extreme or excess (*with energy* etc.); use supercharger on; **~r** *n.*, device forcing extra air or fuel into internal combustion engine. [SUPER-]

**superci'lious** (*or* soō-) *a.* Contemptuous, haughty. [L *supercilium* eyebrow]

**super|erogā'tion** (*or* soō-) *n.* Doing of more than duty requires; **work of ~erogation** (beyond what is needed for one's own salvation); **~ĕrŏ'gatorў** *a.* (**-ily**, **-iness**). [L (*supererogo* pay in addition)]

**super|fi'cial** (-shəl; *or* soō-) *a.* (**-lly**). Of or on the surface only; without depth or knowledge, feeling, etc.; (of measure) square; **~fĭci-ă'litў** (-shĭă'-) *n.* [L (FACE)]

**sŭ′perfine** (*or* sōō-) *a.* Extremely fine or refined. [L (FINE²)]

**sŭper′fluous** (-floo-; *or* sōō-) *a.* More than is needed or wanted, useless; **sŭperflu′ĭty** (-floo-; *or* sōō-) *n.*, superfluous amount or thing, being superfluous. [L (*fluo* flow)]

**sŭper′hū′man** (*or* sōō-) *a.* Exceeding (normal) human capacity or power; **∼ĭmpō′se** (-z) *v.t.*, superpose; **∼ĭmposī′tion** (-z-) *n.*; **∼incŭ′mbent** (-n-k-) *a.*, lying on something else. [L (SUPER-)]

**sŭperĭntĕ′nd** (*or* sōō-) *v.t. & i.* Manage, watch and direct (work etc.); **∼ence** (-t-) *n.*; **∼ent** *n.*, ∥police officer above rank of inspector, *head of police department.

**sŭpēr′|ĭor** (*or* sōō-, su–). **1.** *a.* Situated above; higher in rank, quality, etc., (*to*); written or printed above the line; better or greater in some respect; high-quality (*made of superior leather*); priggish (*with a superior air*); unlikely to yield or not resorting *to* (bribery, temptation, etc.); **∼ĭŏ′rĭty** *n.* **2.** *n.* Person superior to another esp. in rank; head of monastery etc. (esp. *Father, Mother, Superior*). [F f. L compar. (SUPER-)]

**sŭpēr′lative** (*or* sōō-). **1.** *a.* Of the highest degree, excellent; **∼ adjective, adverb**, one in the **∼ degree**, expressing the highest or a very high degree of a quality (*bravest, most wickedly*). **2.** *n.* Superlative degree or (form of) word. [F f. L]

**sŭ′per|măn** (*or* sōō-) *n.* (*pl.* **∼men**). Man of superhuman powers or achievement; **∼mărkĕt** *n.*, large self-service store usu. selling food and some household goods; **∼nă′tural** (-chər-) *a.* (-lly), of or manifesting phenomena not explicable by natural or physical laws; **∼nŏr′mal** *a.*, supernatural, beyond what is normal. [SUPER-]

**sŭpernō′va** (*or* sōō-) *n.* (Astron.; *pl.* **∼e**, **∼s**). Star that suddenly increases very greatly in brightness. [SUPER-]

**sŭpernŭ′merary** (*or* sōō-) *a. & n.* (Person, thing) in excess of normal number; (person) engaged for extra work; (actor) appearing in unimportant part. [L (NUMBER)]

**sŭperphŏ′sphāte** (*or* sōō-) *n.* Fertilizer made from phosphate rock. [SUPER-]

**sŭper|pō′se** (-z; *or* sōō-) *v.t.* Place (thing) on or (*up*)on or above something else; **∼posī′tion** (-z-) *n.* [F (POSE)]

**sŭ′perpower** (*or* sōō-) *n.* Extremely powerful nation. [SUPER-]

**sŭ′per|scrĭbe** (*or* sōō-) *v.t.* Write (inscription) at top of or outside document etc.; **∼scrĭpt** *a. & n.*, (symbol) written above another symbol; **∼scrĭ′ption** *n.*, (esp.) words superscribed. [L (*scribo* write)]

**sŭper|sē′de** (*or* sōō-) *v.t.* Take the place of; put or use another in place of; **∼sē′ssion** (-shon) *n.* [F f. L *supersedeo*]

**sŭpersŏ′nĭc** (*or* sōō-) *a.* (**∼ally**). Of speed greater than that of sound. [SUPER-]

**sŭperstĭ′t|ion** (*or* sōō-) *n.* Credulity regarding the supernatural; irrational fear of the unknown or mysterious; misdirected reverence; a religion or practice or opinion based on such tendencies; widely held but wrong idea; **∼ious** (-shus) *a.* [F or L]

**sŭ′per|strŭcture** (*or* sōō-) *n.* Structure built on top of something else (lit. or fig.); **∼tăx** *n.*, & *v.t.*, = SURTAX. [SUPER-]

**sŭper|vē′ne** (*or* sōō-) *v.i.* Occur as interruption in or change from some state; **∼vĕ′ntion** *n.* [L *supervenio*]

**sŭ′per|vīse** (-z; *or* sōō-) *v.t.* Superintend, oversee; **∼vī′sion** (-zhon) *n.*; **∼vīsor** (-z-) *n.*; **∼vīsory** (-z-) *a.* [L *supervideo* -vis-]

**sŭ′pine** (*or* sōō-). **1.** *a.* Lying face upwards; inactive, indolent. **2.** *n.* Latin verbal noun used to denote purpose or make adj. specific. [L]

**sŭ′pper** *n.* Last meal of the day, esp. evening meal less formal and substantial than dinner, LAST³, LORD's, *Supper*; **sing for one's ∼**, do something in return for a benefit. [F *souper*]

**sŭpplă′nt** (-ah-) *v.t.* Take the place of, esp. by underhand means. [F, or L *supplanto* trip up]

**sŭ′pple** *a.* (**∼r**, **∼st**; **∼ly**, *pr.* -pel-lĭ, -plĭ). Flexible, pliant. [F f. L *supplex*]

**sŭ′pplĕment. 1.** *n.* Thing or part added to remedy deficiencies or amplify information; separate addition to newspaper etc.; **∼al**, **∼ary**, (-mĕ′n-) *adjs.* **2.** *v.t.* (-ĕnt, -ē′nt) Make supplement to; **∼ā′tion** *n.* [L (*suppleo* SUPPLY)]

**sŭ'pplǐ|ant** *n.* & *a.* (literary). Supplicating (person); **~cāte** *v.i.* & *t.*, make humble petition to or *to* person, for or *for* thing; **~cā'tion** *n.*; **~cātorў** *a.* [F f. L *supplico* (SUPPLE)]

**supplŷ'. 1.** *v.t.* Furnish or provide (thing needed, person *with* thing, etc.); make up for, meet, (deficiency, need, etc.). **2.** *n.* Providing of what is needed; stock, store, amount of something provided or obtainable, (in SHORT supply; **~ and demand**, quantities available and required, as factors regulating price of commodities); (in *pl.*) collected necessaries for army, expedition, etc., grant of money by Parliament for cost of government; person, esp. schoolteacher or clergyman, acting as temporary substitute for another (on **~**, acting thus). [F f. L *suppleo* fill up]

**suppŏ'rt. 1.** *v.t.* Carry (part of) weight of, keep from falling, sinking, or failing; provide for (*support oneself, a family*); strengthen, encourage, give help or corroboration to; speak in favour of (a resolution etc.); take secondary part to (actor etc.); endure, tolerate; **~ing film**, less important film in cinema programme. **2.** *n.* Supporting or being supported (in **~** of, so as to support); person or thing that supports. **3. ~er** *n.*, (esp.) person who is interested in a particular team or sport, (Her.) figure shown holding or standing by escutcheon; **~ǐve** *a.* [F f. L *porto* carry]

**suppŏ'se** (-z) *v.t.* Assume as a hypothesis, imagine; (in *imper.* or *part.*) if (*suppose your father saw you what would he say?*; *supposing black were white you might be right*); (in *imper.* as formula of proposal) *suppose we try another*; *suppose we went for a walk*; (of theory, result, etc.) require as condition (*that supposes a mechanism without flaws*; *design in creation supposes a creator*); assume, presume, be inclined to think, (*I suppose she'll be back soon*; *what do you suppose he meant?*; **I ~ so**, form of hesitating assent); (in *p.p.*) generally accepted as being so (*his supposed brother, generosity*); **be ~d to**, be expected or required to, (w. *neg.*, colloq.) ought not to, not be allowed to; **~dlў** (-zĭd-) *adv.*; **supposi'tion** (-zĭ'-) *n.*, thing supposed, supposing; **supposi'tious** (-zĭ'shŭs) *a.*, hypothetical; **sup-posǐti'tious** (-zĭtĭ'shŭs) *a.*, spurious; **suppŏ'sǐtorў** (-z-) *n.*, medical preparation inserted into rectum or vagina to melt. [F (POSE)]

**supprě'ss** *v.t.* (**~ible**). End the activity or existence of, esp. forcibly; prevent (groan, feelings, look, evidence, etc.) from being seen, heard, or known; (Electr.) partly or wholly eliminate (interference etc.), equip (device) to reduce interference due to it; **~ion** (-shŏn), **~or**, *ns.* [L (PRESS¹)]

**sŭ'ppŭrāte** *v.i.* Form pus, fester; **~ā'tion** *n.* [L (PUS)]

*supra* (sū'pra, soo'-) *adv.* Above or previously in book etc. [L]

**sŭ'pra-** (or soo'-) *pref.* Above; **~na'tional**, transcending national limits.

**sŭprē'me** (or soo-) *a.* Highest in authority or rank (**the S~ Being**, God; **S~ Court**, highest judicial court in State etc.); greatest, most important; (of penalty, sacrifice, etc.) involving one's death; **sŭprě'macў** (or soo-) *n.*, being supreme, highest authority; **sŭprē'mō** (or soo-) *n.* (*pl.* -os), supreme leader. [L]

**sur-¹** *pref.* assim. form of SUB- bef. *r* in wds f. Latin (*surrogate*).

**sur-²** *pref.* = SUPER- (*surcharge, surface, surrealism*). [F]

**surcea'se** (arch.) **1.** *n.* Cessation. **2.** *v.i.* Cease. [F *sursis* p.p. f. L (SUPERSEDE)]

**sŭr'charge. 1.** *n.* Additional charge, esp. as penalty e.g. for false tax-claim or unauthorized expenditure; excessive or additional load. **2.** (or -ār'-) *v.t.* Exact surcharge from; exact (sum) as surcharge; overload. [F (SUR-²)]

**sŭrd** *a.* & *n.* (Math.) irrational (number, esp. root of integer); (Phon.) (sound) uttered with breath and not voice (e.g. *f, k, p, s, t*). [L, = deaf]

**sure** (shoor). **1.** *a.* Having or seeming to have adequate reason for belief, convinced (*of, that*), having certain prospect or confident anticipation or satisfactory knowledge *of*, (*you may be sure of his honesty, that he is honest*; **I'm ~**, I assert or swear); reliable or unfailing (*as sure as* FATE); certain (*to do*; **be ~**, take care, not fail, *to do* etc.); undoubtedly true or truthful (**for ~**, colloq., without doubt; **make ~**, ascertain a supposition, take measures to be satisfied that something is or will be as desired or believed; **to be ~**, it is undeniable or admitted, or as excl. of surprise); **~-fire**, (colloq.) certain (to succeed); **~-footed**, never stumbling (lit. or fig.); **~ thing**, (*n.*) a certainty, (*int.*) certainly! **2.** adv. (colloq.) Certainly (cf. EGO¹); **~ enough**, in fact, with practical certainty. **3.** **~'ly** *adv.*, with certainty or safety, if strong belief, experience, probability, or right is to count for anything (*surely I have met you before*; *surely you wouldn't desert me*), (colloq., as answer) certainly ('*May I use your phone?*' '*Surely.*'); **~'ty** *n.*, person who makes himself responsible for another's performance of undertaking or payment of debt. [F f. L *securus*]

**surf. 1.** *n.* Foam of sea breaking on shore or reefs; **~-board**, long narrow board for **~-riding**, sport of being carried over surf to shore on board etc. **2.** *v.i.* Go surf-riding. [orig. unkn.]

**sur'face** (-ĭs) *n.*, *a.*, & *v.* **1.** *n.* The outside of a thing, (any of) the limits terminating a solid, the top of a liquid, soil, etc., outward aspect, what is apprehended of something on casual view or consideration, (*its smooth, wide, upper, surface*; **come to the ~**, fig., become perceptible after being hidden; **on the ~**, superficially); (Geom.) that which has length and breadth but no thickness. **2.** attrib. *a.* Of the surface (only), superficial, (*surface area, density, politeness*); **~ mail** (not carried by air); **~ tension** (of surface of liquid, tending to minimize its surface area); **~-water** (that collects on and runs off surface of ground). **3.** *v.t.* & *i.* Give (special) surface to (road, paper, etc.); bring (submarine) to the surface; come to the surface; (fig.) become visible or known or (colloq.) conscious. [F (SUR-²)]

**sur'feit** (-fĭt) **1.** *n.* Excess esp. in eating or drinking, resulting satiety. **2.** *v.t.* & *i.* Overfeed; (cause to) be wearied (*with*) through excess. [F (SUR-², FEAT)]

**surge. 1.** *v.i.* Move to and fro (as) in waves; move suddenly and powerfully (*forwards, upwards*, etc.). **2.** *n.* Wave(s), surging motion; (fig.) impetuous onset. [F f. L *surgo* rise]

**sur'g|eon** (-jon) *n.* Person skilled in surgery; naval or military medical officer; TREE *surgeon*; **~erў** *n.*, manual or instrumental treatment of injuries or disorders of the body (PLASTIC *surgery*), ‖place where or time when doctor, dentist, etc., gives advice and treatment, or (colloq.) M.P., lawyer, etc., is available for consultation; **~ical** *a.* (**-lly**), of or by surgeons or surgery, (of appliance) used in conditions suitable for surgery; ‖**~ical spirit**, methylated spirits used for cleansing etc. [AF f. L *chirurgia* surgery f. Gk]

**sur'l|ў** *a.* (**~ily**, **~iness**). Bad-tempered, unfriendly, churlish. [obs. *sirly* haughty (SIR)]

**surmi'se** (-z). **1.** *n.* Conjecture. **2.** *v.t.* & *i.* Make conjecture (about), infer doubtfully. [AF f. L *supermitto -miss-* accuse]

**surmou'nt** *v.t.* Overcome, get over, (difficulty, obstacle); (in *p.p.*) capped or crowned (*by, with*). [F (SUR-²)]

**sur'name. 1.** *n.* Name common to all members of a family, person's hereditary name. **2.** *v.t.* Give surname to. [obs. *surnoun* f. AF (SUR-²)]

**surpa'ss** (-ah's) *v.t.* Outdo, be greater or better than; (in *part.*) pre-eminent, matchless. [F (SUR-²)]

**sur'plice** *n.* Loose white linen vestment worn by clergy and choristers. [AF f. L (SUPER-, PELISSE)]

**sur'plus. 1.** *n.* Amount left over when requirements have been met; excess of revenue over expenditure. **2.** *a.* Exceeding what is needed or used. [AF f. L (PLUS)]

**surpri'se** (-z). **1.** *n.* Catching of person(s) unprepared, (emotion caused by) something unexpected or astonishing, (**by ~**, unexpectedly; **~, ~!**, excl. of ironical surprise; **to** person's **~**, much against his expectations); (*attrib.*, of attack, visit, etc.) unexpected, made, done, etc., without warning. **2.** *v.t.* Affect with surprise, turn out contrary to expectations of; shock, scandalize; capture or attack by surprise; come upon (person) off his guard (*surprised him in the act*); hurry (person) by surprise *into* conduct or act or do*ing*. [F]

**surrḗ'al|ism** *n.* 20th-c. movement in art and literature aiming to express the subconscious mind; **~ist** *a.* & *n.*; **~i'stĭc** *a.* (**-ically**). [SUR-², REAL²]

**surrĕ'nder. 1.** *v.t.* & *i.* Hand over, relinquish possession of, (fortress, one*self*, freedom, hopes, etc.); accept enemy's demand for submission; submit (*to*; cf. BAIL¹); give one*self* over *to* habit, emotion, etc.; give up rights under (insurance policy) in return for smaller sum received immediately. **2.** *n.* Surrendering; ~ **value**, amount payable to one who surrenders insurance policy. [AF (SUR-²)]

**surrepti'tious** (-shŭs) *a.* Done by stealth, underhand. [L (*surripio* seize secretly)]

**sŭ'rrogate** *n.* Deputy, esp. of bishop; substitute. [L (*rogo* ask)]

**surrou'nd. 1.** *v.t.* Come or be all round; ~**ed by, with**, having on all sides. **2.** *n.* ‖Border, edging, esp. (floor-covering for) area between walls and carpet. **3.** ~**ings** (-z) *n.pl.*, things in neighbourhood of, or conditions affecting, a person or thing. [AF f. L (SUR-², *unda* wave)]

**sŭr'tăx. 1.** *n.* Additional tax, esp. on incomes above a certain amount. **2.** *v.t.* Impose surtax on. [F (SUR-²)]

**survei'llance** (-vāl-) *n.* Close observation, esp. of suspected person. [F (SUR-², *veiller* watch)]

**survey. 1.** (-vā') *v.t.* Take or present a general view of; examine condition of (building etc.); determine boundaries, size, shape, ownership, etc., of (district, estate, etc.); ~**or** *n.* (esp. as profession). **2.** (sĕr'vā) *n.* Act or result of surveying (ORDNANCE *Survey*); inspection or investigation; map or plan made by surveying. [AF f. L (SUPER-, *video* see)]

**survi've|e** *v.t.* & *i.* Continue to live or exist (longer than); come alive through or continue to exist in spite of (danger, accident, etc.); ~**al** *n.*, surviving (~**al of the fittest**, result of natural selection); relic; ~**or** *n.* [AF *survivre* f. L (SUPER-, *vivo* live)]

**sŭs** *n.*, & *v.t.* (-ss-). (sl.) Suspect; suspicion; ~ (**out**), investigate, inspect, understand. [abbr.]

**sus-** *pref.* assim. form of SUB- before *c*, *p*, or *t*, in wds f. Latin.

**suscĕ'ptĭb|le** *a.* (~**ly**). Impressionable, sensitive, easily moved by emotion; (*pred.*) admitting *of* (proof etc.), open or liable or sensitive *to* (pain, kindness, beauty, etc.); ~**ĭ'lĭtў** *n.*, being susceptible, (in *pl.*)

person's sensitive feelings. [L (*suscipio* -*cept*- take up)]

**suspĕct. 1.** (-ĕ'-) *v.t.* Have an impression of the existence or presence of, half believe *to be*, be inclined to think (*that*); mentally accuse *of*, doubt the innocence or genuineness or truth of. **2.** (sŭ'-) *n.* Suspected person. **3.** (sŭ'-) *a.* Subject to suspicion or distrust (*enemy statements are suspect*). [L *suspicio* -*spect*-]

**suspĕ'n|d** *v.t.* Hang up; keep inoperative or undecided for a time; debar temporarily from function, office, etc.; (in *p.p.*, of solid in fluid) sustained or floating between top and bottom; ~**ded sentence** (remaining unenforced on condition of good behaviour); ~**der** *n.*, (esp., in *pl.*) ‖attachments to hold up stockings or socks by their tops (~**der belt**, woman's undergarment with suspenders) or *pair of braces; ~**se** *n.*, suspended condition, anxious uncertainty; ~**sion** (-shon) *n.*, suspending or being suspended (~**sion bridge**, with roadway suspended from cables supported by towers), substance consisting of particles suspended in fluid, means by which vehicle is supported on its axles; ~**sible**, ~**sive**, ~**sorў**, *adjs.* [F, or L *suspendo* -*pens*-]

**suspi'cion** (-shon) *n.* Feeling of one who suspects; suspecting or being suspected (**above** ~, too obviously good etc. to be suspected; **under** ~, suspected); soupçon (*of*); **suspi'cious** (-shŭs) *a.*, prone to, feeling, indicating, or justifying suspicion. [AF f. L (SUSPECT)]

**sustai'n** *v.t.* Bear weight of, support, esp. for long period; endure, stand, (*could not sustain the shock*); undergo or suffer (defeat, injury, loss, etc.); (of court etc.) decide in favour of, uphold, (objection etc.); substantiate or corroborate (statement, charge); keep up (role, effort, etc.); **sŭ'stenance** *n.*, nourishment, food, means of support. [AF *sustenir* f. L]

**sŭ'tler** *n.* (Hist.) Camp-follower selling food etc. [Du. *soeteler*]

**su'ture** (sōō'-; Surg.) **1.** *n.* Uniting of edges of wound by stitching; thread etc. used for this. **2.** *v.t.* Stitch (wound). [F, or L (*suo* sut-sew)]

**sŭ'zerain** (*or* sōō'-) *n.* Feudal overlord; sovereign or State having some control over another State that is internally autonomous; ~**ty** *n*. [F]

**svělte** *a*. Slender, lissom, graceful. [F f. It.]

**S.W.** *abbr.* South-West(ern).

**swab** (-ŏb). **1.** *n.* Mop or other absorbent device for cleaning or mopping up; absorbent pad used in surgery; specimen of morbid secretion taken for examination; (sl.) contemptible person. **2.** *v.t.* (**-bb-**). Clean with swab; take *up* (moisture) with swab. [Du.]

**swa'ddl|e** (-ŏ'-) *v.t.* Swathe (esp. infant) in garments, bandages, etc.; ~**ing-clothes,** (fig.) restrictive influences. [SWATHE]

**swăg** *n.* (Representation of) ornamental festoon of flowers etc.; (sl.) booty of burglars etc.; (Austral.) traveller's bundle; ~**ger** (-g-), (*v.i.*) walk or behave arrogantly or self--importantly, (*n.*) swaggering gait or behaviour, smartness, (~**ger--stick,** short cane carried by military officer), (*a.*, colloq.) smart or fashionable, (of coat) cut with loose flare from shoulders. [prob. Scand.]

**Swahi'li** (swahhē'-) *n.* (Member of) Bantu people of Zanzibar and adjacent coasts; their language, widely used in E. Africa. [Arab.]

**swain** *n.* (arch., poet.) Young rustic; (bucolic) lover or suitor. [N, = lad]

**swa'llow**[1] (-ŏ'lō). **1.** *v.t.* & *i.* Cause or allow (food etc.) to pass down one's throat; perform muscular movement (as) of swallowing something; accept meekly or credulously (affront, assertion, etc.), repress (tears, resentment, etc.); pronounce (sounds) indistinctly; ~ (up), engulf, absorb, exhaust, cause to disappear, (*expenses swallow up earnings*). **2.** *n.* Act of swallowing; amount swallowed. [E]

**swa'llow**[2] (-ŏ'lō) *n.* Migratory swift-flying fork-tailed insectivorous bird (**one** ~ **does not make a summer,** beware of hasty inferences); ||~**-dive** (with arms outspread till close to water); ~**-tail,** (butterfly etc. with) deeply forked tail, (in *sing.* or *pl.*, colloq.) tailcoat. [E]

**swăm.** See SWIM.

**swamp** (-ŏ-). **1.** *n.* Piece of wet spongy ground; ~**y** *a*. **2.** *v.t.* Overwhelm, flood, or soak with water;

overwhelm or make invisible etc. with excess or large amount of something. [orig. uncert.]

**swan** (-ŏn). **1.** *n.* Large web-footed usu. white water-bird with long flexible neck; (fig.) poet (esp. **S~ of Avon,** Shakespeare); ~**'sdown,** down of swan used in trimmings etc., thick cotton cloth with soft nap on one side; ~**-song,** legendary song of dying swan, (fig.) person's final composition, performance, etc.; ||~**-upping,** annual taking up and marking of Thames swans; ~**nery** *n.,* place where swans are kept. **2.** *v.i.* (**-nn-**). (sl.) Go aimlessly or casually (*around, off,* etc.). [E]

**swănk.** (colloq.) **1.** *n.* Ostentation, swagger; ||~**'pot,** person behaving with swank; ~**'y** *a.* (~**iness**) **2.** *v.i.* Behave with swank. [orig. unkn.]

**swap** (-ŏp), **swŏp.** (colloq.) **1.** *v.t.* & *i.* (**-pp-**), & *n.* Exchange by barter (lit. or fig.). **2.** *n.* Thing suitable for swapping. [orig. = 'hit', imit.]

**sward** (-ŏrd) *n.* (literary) Expanse of short grass. [E, = skin]

**swarf** (-ŏrf) *n.* Chips, filings, etc., of wood, metal, wax, etc. [E]

**swarm**[1] (-ŏrm). **1.** *n.* Large number of insects, birds, persons, etc., moving in a cluster; (in *pl.*) great numbers *of*; cluster of bees emigrating with queen to form new home. **2.** *v.i.* Move in or form swarm; (of place) be crowded or infested *with*. [E]

**swarm**[2] (-ŏrm) *v.i.* Climb *up* (rope, tree, etc.) by clasping or clinging with hands, knees, etc. [orig. unkn.]

**swar'th|y** (-ŏr'dhi) *a.* (~**ily,** ~**iness**). Dark(-complexioned). [obs. *swarty* (*swart* black f. E)]

**swa'shbückl|er** (-ŏ'-) *n.* Swaggering bully or ruffian; ~**ing** *a.* & *n.* [*swash* strike noisily, BUCKLER]

**swa'stika** (-ŏ'-) *n.* Symbol formed by cross with equal arms each continued as far again at right angles and all in same direction, esp. as symbol of Nazis. [Skr.]

**swat** (-ŏt). **1.** *v.t.* (**-tt-**). Hit hard; crush (fly etc.) with blow; ~**ter** *n.* (FLY[1]*-swatter*). **2.** *n.* Act of swatting. [dial. var. of SQUAT]

**swatch** (-ŏ-) *n.* Sample, esp. of cloth; collection of samples. [orig. unkn.]

**swath** (-aw-; *pl. pr.* -ths, -dhz), **swāthe**[1] (-dh), *n.* Ridge of grass, corn, etc., lying after being cut; space left clear after one passage of mower etc.; broad strip. [E]

**swāthe**[2] (-dh) v.t. Bind or enclose in bandages, garments, etc. [E]

**sway. 1.** v.i. & t. (Cause) to move in different directions alternately, oscillate irregularly, waver; control motion or direction of, have influence or rule over. **2.** n. Swaying motion; rule, government, (*under his sway*). [orig. uncert.]

**swear** (-ār) v.t. & i. (**swore**; **sworn**). Say solemnly or (colloq.) emphatically, promise or take oath (*that, to do*); cause to take oath (*sworn to* SECRECY); use profane or obscene language (*at* person); ~ **by**, appeal to (sacred being or thing) as witness or guarantee of oath (also ~ **to**), (colloq.) recommend or have great confidence in (remedy etc.); ~ **in**, induct into office etc. by administering oath; ~ **off**, (colloq.) promise to abstain from (drink etc.); ~ **to**, (colloq.) say that one is certain of; **sworn brothers** or **friends**, close intimates; **sworn enemies** (irreconcilable); ~**-word**, (colloq.) profane or obscene word. [E]

**sweat** (-ĕt). **1.** n. Moisture exuded from skin esp. when one is hot or nervous (**by the ~ of one's brow**, by dint of toil); state or period of sweating (**a cold ~**, induced by fear, illness, etc.); (colloq.) state of anxiety (*in a sweat*); (colloq.) drudgery, effort, laborious task or undertaking; (**no ~**, there is no need to worry; ||**old ~**, old soldier, person with much experience); condensed moisture on a surface; ~**-band**, band of absorbent material inside hat or round wrist etc. to soak up sweat; ~**-shirt**, sleeved cotton sweater; ~**-shop** (in which sweated workers are employed); ~**-suit** (of sweat-shirt and close-fitting trousers). **2.** v.i. & t. (~'ed, *~). Exude sweat; (fig.) be terrified, suffering, etc., (of wall etc.) exhibit surface moisture; emit like sweat (~ **blood**, work strenuously, be extremely anxious); make (horse, athlete, etc.) sweat by exercise; (cause to) toil or drudge (~**ed goods** etc., produced by sweated labour; ~**ed labour, workers**, etc., employed for long hours at low wages); ~ **it out**, (colloq.) endure to the end, persevere; *sweat* one's GUTS *out*. **3.** ~'**er** n., (esp.) jersey or pullover

(~**er girl**, colloq., woman wearing sweater to emphasize well-developed bust); ~'**y** a. [E]

**swēde** n. Native of Sweden (*S~*); large yellow-fleshed turnip orig. from Sweden; **Swē'dish** a. & n., (language) of Sweden. [LDu.]

**sweep. 1.** v.i. & t. (**swept**). Glide swiftly, speed along with unchecked motion, go majestically (*she swept from the room*); have continuous extent (*coast sweeps northward*); (*in part.*) of wide range, regardless of limitations or exceptions, (*sweeping changes, generalization, victory*); impart sweeping motion to (*swept his hand across*); carry along, down, etc., in impetuous course; clear off or away or out of existence etc. or from (~ **away**, abolish swiftly); traverse swiftly or lightly; swiftly cover or affect (*epidemic, fashion, sweeping America*); ~ (**up**), clear dust, litter, etc., from (room etc.), collect or move (as) with broom; push aside, away, etc., (as) with broom; ~'**stake**(s), (prize won in) race or contest where all competitors' stakes are paid to winner(s); ~ **the board**, win all the money in gambling-game, (fig.) win all possible prizes etc.; *sweep under the* CARPET; **swept-back**, (of hair) not over the face, (of aircraft wing) placed at acute angle to axis of aircraft; **swept-up**, upswept; **swept-wing**, (of aircraft) having swept-back wings; ~'**er** n., (esp.) one who cleans a place by sweeping; = CARPET-*sweeper*. **2.** n. Act or motion of sweeping (MAKE *a clean sweep*); curve in road etc.; sortie by aircraft; range of something that has sweeping action (lit. or fig.; *within or beyond the sweep of the net, telescope, eye, intelligence*); long oar; sail of windmill; = CHIMNEY-*sweep*; (colloq.) sweepstake. [E]

**sweet. 1.** a. Tasting like sugar or honey; (of wine) having sweet or fruity taste (opp. *dry*); smelling pleasant like rose or perfume; melodious or harmonious (*sweet singer, sounds, voice*); fresh, not salt or sour or bitter or stinking, (*is the meat, milk, butter, still sweet?*; *keep the room clean and sweet*); highly gratifying or attractive, beloved, amiable, pleasant, (colloq.) pretty or delightful, (*a sweet nature, air, sleep*; *isn't the baby sweet!*; **keep** person ~, placate him, ingratiate oneself with him); ~

**on,** colloq., fond of or in love with); selfish (**at one's own ~ will,** just as or when one pleases, arbitrarily). **2.** *n.* Sweetmeat; ||sweet dish forming course of meal; sweet part (*of something*); (in *pl.*) delights, gratifications, (*the sweets of success*); (esp. in *voc.*) darling. **3. ~-and-sour,** cooked in sauce with both sweet and sour ingredients; **~'bread,** pancreas or thymus gland of animal, esp. as food; **~-brier,** small wild rose; *sweet* CHESTNUT; **~ corn,** sweet-flavoured maize; **~'heart,** one of pair of lovers; **~'meat,** small shaped piece of confectionery, usu. chiefly of sugar or chocolate; **~ pea,** climbing garden annual with variously-coloured sweet-scented flowers; *sweet* PEPPER, POTATO, SULTAN; *\*~-talk,* blandish(ment); **~ tooth,** liking for sweet-tasting things; **~-wi'lliam,** garden plant with close-clustered sweet-smelling flowers often particoloured. **4. ~'en** *v.t. & i.*; **~'ener** *n.*, (esp.) bribe; **~'ening** *n.*, (esp.) thing that sweetens; **~'ie** *n.*, (colloq.) sweetmeat or (also **~ie-pie**) sweetheart. [E]

**swell** *v., n., & a.* **1.** *v.i. & t.* (*p.p.* **swo'llen** *pr.* swō'-, **~ed**). (Cause to) grow bigger, louder, or more intense, rise or raise up from surrounding surface, bulge *out*, (**~ed** or **swollen head,** colloq., conceit); (of heart) feel like bursting with emotion; **~ with,** be hardly able to restrain (pride etc.). **2.** *n.* Act or state or swelling; heaving of sea with waves that do not break; protuberant part; (Mus.) crescendo, mechanism in organ etc. for obtaining crescendo or diminuendo; (colloq.) person of distinction or of dashing or fashionable appearance. **3.** *a.* (colloq.) Smart, fashionable; fine, splendid, excellent. **4. ~'ing** *n.*, (esp.) abnormal protuberance on the body. [E]

**swe'lter. 1.** *v.i.* Be uncomfortably hot. **2.** *n.* Sweltering condition. [E]

**swept.** See SWEEP.

**swerve. 1.** *v.i. & t.* (Cause to) change direction, esp. suddenly. **2.** *n.* Swerving movement. [E, = scour]

**swift. 1.** *a.* Rapid, soon coming, (literary); prompt, quick, (*to do*). **2.** *n.* Long-winged swiftly-flying insect-ivorous bird. [E]

**swig.** (colloq.) **1.** *v.t. & i.* (**-gg-**). Take deep draughts (of). **2.** *n.* (Act

of taking) a (deep) draught of liquor. [orig. unkn.]

**swill. 1.** *v.t. & i.* Rinse or flush (*out*); drink greedily. **2.** *n.* Rinsing; mainly liquid refuse as pig-food; inferior liquor. [E]

**swim. 1.** *v.i. & t.* (**-mm-;** **swam;** **swum**). Progress at or below surface of water by working limbs, fins, etc., traverse (stream, distance, etc.) thus; float on or at surface of liquid (SINK *or* swim); appear to undulate or reel or whirl, have dizzy effect or sensation, (*everything swam before her eyes; my head is swimming*); be flooded (*in* or *with* liquid); **~'ming-bath, -pool,** pool constructed for swimming; **~'ming-costume, ~-suit,** bathing-suit. **2.** *n.* Spell or act of swimming; (fig.) main current of affairs (**in the ~,** engaged in or acquainted with what is going on). **3. ~'mingly** *adv.*, with easy and unobstructed progress. [E]

**swi'ndle. 1.** *v.t. & i.* Cheat (person, money *out of* person, person *out of* money). **2.** *n.* Act of swindling; person or thing represented as what it is not; **~-sheet,** (colloq.) expense account. [back-form. f. *swindler* f. G]

**swin|e** *n.* (*pl.* same). (U.S. or formal or Zool.) pig; (colloq.) disgusting or unpleasant person or thing; **~'ish** *a.*, bestial, filthy. [E]

**swing. 1.** *v.i. & t.* (**swung**). (Cause to) move with to-and-fro or curving motion, sway, hang so as to be free to sway, (*not room to swing a* CAT; *swing the* LEAD[2]); (cause to) oscillate or revolve; move *round* to opposite direction (lit. or fig.); go with swinging gait; move by gripping something and leaping etc. (*swing from bough to bough*); attempt to hit or punch (*at* person etc.); play (music) with swing rhythm; (sl.) be lively, up-to-date, or promiscuous, enjoy oneself; have decisive influence on (voting etc.); (sl.) be competent to) deal with or achieve; (sl.) be executed by hanging; **swung dash,** (Typ.) dash (**~**) with alternate curves. **2.** *n.* Act, motion, or extent of swinging (**in full ~,** fully active); swinging or smooth gait, rhythm, or action (*goes with a swing*; *get into the swing of things*); seat slung by ropes, chains, etc., for swinging on or in, spell of swinging thus, (**lose on the ~s what you make on the round-abouts,** end without profit or loss);

smooth rhythmic jazz or jazzy dance-music, rhythmic feeling or drive of jazz; amount by which votes, points scored, etc., change from one side to another; \*(circular) tour; ~-**boat**, boat-shaped carriage hung from frame for swinging in at fair etc.; ~ **bridge** (that can be swung aside to let ships pass); ~-**door** (able to open in either direction and close itself when released); ~-**wing**, aircraft wing that can be moved backwards and forwards. **3.** ~'**eïng** (-njĭ-) *a.*, forcible, daunting, huge, (*swingeing blow, damages, taxation*). [E, = beat]

**swipe. 1.** *v.t.* & *i.* Hit hard and recklessly (colloq.); (sl.) steal. **2.** *n.* (colloq.) Reckless hard (attempt to) hit. [perh. var. SWEEP]

**swirl. 1.** *v.i.* & *t.* Eddy; carry (object) or be carried with eddying motion. **2.** *n.* Eddying motion; twist, curl. [perh. LDu.]

**swish** *v., n.,* & *a.* **1.** *v.t.* & *i.* Swing (cane, scythe, etc.) audibly through air, grass, etc., cut (flower etc.) *off* thus; move with or make swishing sound. **2.** *n.* Swishing action or sound. **3.** *a.* (colloq.) Smart, fashionable. [imit.]

**Swiss** *a.* & *n.* (*pl.* same). (Native) of Switzerland; ~ **roll**, thin flat sponge-cake spread with jam etc. and rolled up. [F *Suisse*]

**switch. 1.** *n.* Mechanism for making and breaking connection in electric circuit; railway points; transfer, change-over, deviation; flexible shoot cut from tree, light tapering rod. **2.** *v.t.* & *i.* Turn (electric light, radio or television set, etc.) *on* or *off* (~**ed on**, sl., up-to-date, aware of what is going on, excited, under the influence of drugs); ~ (**over**), change or transfer (positions, roles, subject, etc.); swing or snatch (thing) suddenly; whip or flick with switch. **3.** ~'**back**, zigzag or up-and-down railway or road, ‖railway at fair etc. in which train's ascents are effected by momentum of previous descents; ~-**blade**, pocket-knife with blade released by spring; ~'**board**, apparatus for varying connections between electric circuits, esp. in telephony. [LG]

**swi'vel. 1.** *n.* Coupling between two parts enabling one to revolve without the other; ~ **chair** (with

seat turning horizontally). **2.** *v.i.* & *t.* (‖-**ll**-). Turn (as) on swivel. [E]

‖**swiz(z)** *n.* (sl.; *pl.* -**zzes**). Swindle, disappointment. [orig. unkn.]

**swi'zzle** *n.* (colloq.) Compounded intoxicating drink esp. of rum or gin and bitters made frothy; ‖(sl.) = prec.; ~-**stick** (used for frothing or flattening drinks). [orig. unkn.]

**swŏ'llen.** See SWELL.

**swŏŏn** *v.i.,* & *n.* (literary). Faint. [E]

**swŏŏp. 1.** *v.i.* Come down or *down* like bird of prey; make sudden attack (*on*). **2.** *n.* Swooping or snatching movement or action (*at one* FELL[3] *swoop*). [E]

**swŏp.** See SWAP.

**sword** (sŏrd) *n.* Weapon with long blade and hilt with hand-guard (**cross** or **measure** ~**s**, have fight, controversy, or rivalry *with*; **put to the** ~, kill; **the** ~, war, military power); ‖~-**bearer** (carrying sovereign's etc. sword on certain occasions); ~-**dance** (in which performer brandishes swords or steps about swords laid on ground); ~'**fish**, large sea-fish with swordlike upper jaw; ~-**play**, fencing, (fig.) repartee or lively arguing; ~'**sman**, person of (usu. specified) skill with sword; ~'**smanship**; ~-**stick**, hollow walking-stick containing blade that can be used as sword; ~-**swallower**, entertainer who (ostensibly) swallows sword-blade. [E]

**swŏre, swŏrn.** See SWEAR.

‖**swŏt** (sl.) **1.** *v.i.* & *t.* (-**tt**-). Study hard; ~ **up**, study (subject) hard or hurriedly. **2.** *n.* Person who swots; hard study. [dial. var. of SWEAT]

**swŭm.** See SWIM; **swŭng**, see SWING.

**sy̆'bar|īte** *n.* Self-indulgent or voluptuous person; ~**i'tĭc** *a.* (-ically). [*Sybaris*, place]

**sy̆'camōre** *n.* Large maple; \*plane-tree; wood of these. [F f. L f. Gk]

**sy̆'coph|ant** (or -ă-) *n.* Flatterer, toady; ~**ancy̆** *n.*; ~**ă'ntĭc** *a.* (-ically). [F f. L f. Gk]

**sy̆l-** *pref.* assim. form of SYN- bef. *l.*

**sy̆'llable** *n.* Unit of pronunciation forming (part of) word and usu. having one vowel-sound often with consonant(s) before or after ('*inform*' has two syllables, '*inferno*' has three; in **words of one** ~, simply, plainly); character(s) representing syllable;

**sȳ′llabarȳ** n., list of characters representing syllables; **sȳllăˈbĭc** a. (-ically), of or in syllables; **sȳllăbĭ(fĭ)cāˈtion** n., division into or utterance in syllables; **(-)~d** (-bĕld) a., having (specified number of) syllables. [AF f. L f. Gk (lambanō take)]

**sȳˈllabŭb, sĭ′-,** n. Dish of cream or milk curdled or whipped with wine etc. [orig. unkn.]

**sȳˈllabˈus** n. (pl. ~uses, ~i pr. -ī). Programme or conspectus of a course of study, teaching, etc. [L, erron. f. Gk sittuba label]

**sȳllĕˈpsˈis** n. (pl. ~es pr. -ēz). Figure of speech applying word to two others in different senses (took the oath and his seat). [L f. Gk (as SYLLABLE)]

**sȳˈllogˈism** n. Form of reasoning in which from two propositions a third is deduced; **~ĭˈstĭc** a. (-ically). [F or L f. Gk (logos reason)]

**sȳlph** n. Elemental spirit of the air; slender graceful woman or girl. [L]

**sȳˈlvan, sȳˈlvĭcŭlture.** See SILVAN etc.

**sȳm-** pref. assim. form of SYN- bef. b, m, p.

**sȳmbĭˈōˈsˈĭs** n. (pl. ~oˈses pr. -ōˈsēz). (Usu. mutually advantageous) association of two different organisms living attached to each other or one within the other (also fig. of co-operating persons); **~ōˈtĭc** a. (-ically). [L f. Gk (SYM-, bios life)]

**sȳˈmbol** n. Thing generally regarded as typifying, representing, or recalling something (white is a symbol of purity; the Cross is the symbol of Christianity); mark or character taken as conventional sign of some object, idea, process, etc.; **sȳmbŏˈlĭc(al)** a. (-ically); **~ĭsm** n., (use of) symbols, artistic movement or style using symbols to express ideas, emotions, etc.; **~ĭst** n.; **~ĭze** v.t., be symbol of, represent by means of symbols. [L f. Gk]

**sȳˈmmĕtrˈȳ** n. (Beauty resulting from) correct proportion of parts; (possession of) structure that allows an object to be divided into parts of equal shape and size, repetition of exactly similar parts facing each other or a centre; **sȳmmĕˈtrĭc(al)** a. (-ically); **~ĭze** v.t., make symmetrical. [F or L f. Gk]

**sȳˈmpathˈȳ** n. (Capacity for) being simultaneously affected with the same feeling as another; sharing (with person etc.) in emotion, sensation, or condition; compassion, approval, (for); (in sing. or pl.) agreement (with person etc.) in opinion or desire; **in ~y,** having, showing, or resulting from sympathy (with another); **~ĕˈtĭc** a. (-ically), of, exhibiting, expressing, or due to sympathy, likeable, not antagonistic; **~etic magic** (seeking to affect person through associated object); **~ĭze** v.i., feel or express sympathy (with). [L f. Gk, = fellow-feeling]

**sȳˈmphonˈȳ** n. Elaborate composition for full orchestra, usu. with several movements; instrumental passage in oratorio etc.; **~ orchestra,** \*~, large orchestra playing symphonies etc.; **sȳmphŏˈnĭc** a. (-ically). [F f. L f. Gk]

**sȳˈmphysˈĭs** n. (pl. ~es pr. -ēz). Growing together; (place or line of) union between two bones or other parts. [L f. Gk (SYM-, phuō grow)]

**sȳmpōˈsĭˈum** (-z-) n. (pl. ~a). Collection of essays etc., conference, on a particular subject; philosophical or other friendly discussion. [L f. Gk (sumpotēs fellow-drinker)]

**sȳˈmptom** n. Manifestation of disease or injury; sign of the existence of something; **~ăˈtĭc** a. (-ically). [L f. Gk (piptō fall)]

**sȳn-** pref. expr. combination, simultaneity, similarity, etc. [Gk (sun with)]

**sȳˈnagŏˈgue** (-g) n. (Place of meeting for) Jewish assembly for religious observance and instruction; **~al, ~ical** (-gŏˈg-, -gŏˈj-), adjs. (-lly). [F f. L f. Gk, = assembly]

**sȳnc(h)** (-ngk; colloq.). **1.** n. Synchronization. **2.** v.t. Synchronize. [abbr.]

**sȳˈnchromĕsh** (-ngkr-) n. & a. (System of gear-changing, esp. in motor vehicles) in which gear-wheels revolve at the same speed during engagement. [abbr. synchronized mesh]

**sȳnchrˈŏˈnĭc** (-ngkr-) a. (Ling. etc.; -ically). Describing a subject as it exists at a particular time (opp. diachronic); **~ˈonĭsm** n., synchrony, synchronizing; **~ˈonize** v.t. & i., make or be synchronous with; **~onizāˈtion** n.; **~ˈonous** a., existing or occurring at same time (with), having same or proportional speed; **~ˈonȳ** n., being or treating as synchronous or synchronic. [L f. Gk (*khronos* time)]

**sy̆'ncop|āte** *v.t.* Displace beats or accents in (music); shorten (word) by dropping interior letter(s); **~ā'-tion** *n.*; **~ĕ** *n.*, syncopation, (Med.) unconsciousness through fall of blood-pressure. [L (*syncope* f. Gk)]

**sy̆ncrĕ'tĭc** *a.* Attempting, esp. inconsistently, to unify or reconcile differing schools of thought; **sy̆'ncrētĭsm, sy̆'ncrĕtĭst,** *ns.*; **sy̆ncrĕtĭ'stĭc** *a.*; **sy̆'ncrĕtīze** *v.i.* & *t.* [L f. Gk]

**sy̆'ndic** *n.* One of various university or government officials; **~alĭsm** *n.*, movement for transferring means of production and distribution to workers' unions; **~alĭst** *n.*; **~ate,** (*n.*) combination of commercial firms, persons, etc., to promote some common interest, association supplying material simultaneously to a number of periodicals, committee of syndics, (-āt; *v.t.*) form into, publish (material) through, a syndicate; **~ā'tion** *n.* [F f. L (*syndicus* f. Gk, = advocate)]

**sy̆'ndrōm|e** (*or* -drŏmĭ) *n.* Group of concurrent symptoms of disease; characteristic combination of opinions, emotions, etc. [L f. Gk (SYN-, *dromos* course)]

**sy̆nĕ'cdochĕ** (-kĭ) *n.* Figure of speech in which part is named but whole is understood, or conversely, (*new faces in the team*; *England beat India at cricket*). [L f. Gk]

**sy̆'nod** *n.* Ecclesiastical council of bishop(s) and delegated clergy (and laity); **~al, sy̆nŏ'dĭc(al),** *adjs.* [L f. Gk, = meeting]

**sy̆'nony̆m** *n.* Word or phrase that means exactly or nearly the same as another in same language; **sy̆non-ŏny̆'mĭty̆** *n.*; **sy̆nŏ'ny̆mous** *a.* (*with*); **sy̆nŏ'ny̆my̆** *n.* [L f. Gk (*onoma* name)]

**sy̆nŏ'p|sĭs** *n.* (*pl.* **~ses** *pr.* -sēz). Summary, outline; **~tĭc** *a.* (**~tic-ally**), of or giving synopsis; **S~tĭc Gospels,** those of Matthew, Mark, and Luke. [L f. Gk (*opsis* view)]

**sy̆nŏ'vĭ|a** *n.* (Physiol.) Viscous fluid lubricating joints etc.; **~al** *a.* (**~al membrane,** connective tissue secreting synovia); **sy̆novī'tĭs** *n.*, inflammation of synovial membrane. [L]

**sy̆'ntăx** *n.* (Rules or analysis of)

grammatical arrangement of words; **sy̆ntă'ctĭc** *a.* (**-ically**). [F or L f. Gk, = arrangement]

**sy̆'nthĕs|ĭs** *n.* (*pl.* **~es** *pr.* -ēz). (Result of) combining of elements into a whole (opp. *analysis*); artificial production of (esp. organic) substances from simpler ones; **~īze** *v.t.*, make synthesis of; **~īzer** *n.*, electronic musical instrument producing a great variety of sounds; **sy̆nthĕ'tĭc,** (*a.*; **-ically**) of, made by, or showing synthesis, artificial, (colloq.) affected or insincere, (*n.*) synthetic substance. [L f. Gk (SYN-)]

**sy̆'phĭl|ĭs** *n.* A contagious venereal disease; **~ĭ'tĭc** *a.* (**-ally**). [character in poem]

**Sy̆'rĭ|ăc** *n.* & *a.* (In) language of ancient Syria; **~an** *a.* & *n.*, (native) of Syria. [L f. Gk]

**sy̆rĭ'nga** (-ngg-) *n.* Mock orange; (Bot.) lilac. [L (foll.)]

**sy̆'rĭnge** (-nj; *or* -rĭ'-). **1.** *n.* Device for drawing in liquid by suction and then ejecting it in fine stream. **2.** *v.t.* Sluice or spray with syringe. [L *syringa* f. Gk *surigx* -*rigg*- pipe]

**sy̆'rup, \*sĭ'rup,** *n.* Water (nearly) saturated with sugar, often flavoured or medicated; condensed sugar-cane juice, molasses, treacle, (‖GOLDEN, MAPLE, *syrup*); (fig.) excessive sweetness of manner; **~y̆** *a.* [F or L f. Arab. (SHERBET)]

**sy̆'stem** *n.* Complex whole, set of connected things or parts, organized body of things (SOLAR *system*); set of organs in body with common structure or function, *the* human or animal body as a whole (**get thing out of** one's **~,** fig., be rid of its effects); method, organization, considered principles of procedure, (principle or section of) classification; (Geol.) major group of strata; **~s analysis,** analysis of an operation to improve its efficiency by using computer; **~ă'tĭc** *a.* (**-ically**), methodical, according to a system, deliberate; **~atīze** *v.t.*, make systematic; **~atīzā'tion** *n.*; **sy̆stĕ'mĭc** *a.* (**-ically**), of the bodily system as a whole, (of insecticide etc.) entering plant tissues via roots and shoots. [F or L f. Gk *sustēma* -*mat*-]

**sy̆'stolē** *n.* Contraction of heart rhythmically alternating with diastole. [L f. Gk (*stellō* place)]

# T

**T, t,** (tē) n. (*pl.* **Ts, T's**). Twentieth letter (**cross the t's**, fig., be minutely accurate; *suits me*, etc., **to a T**, exactly, to a nicety); T-shaped thing (esp. *attrib.*: **T-bone**, T-shaped bone esp. in steak from thin end of loin; **T-joint**; **T-shirt**, short-sleeved buttonless casual shirt; **T-SQUARE**).

**t.** *abbr.* ton(s); tonne(s).

‖**ta** (tah) *int.* (childish or colloq.). Thank you. [infantile form]

‖**T.A.** *abbr.* Territorial Army.

**tăb. 1.** *n.* Small flap or strip attached for grasping, suspending, fastening, or identifying garment etc.; similar object as part of garment etc.; ‖(Mil.) mark on collar distinguishing staff officer; (colloq.) account, tally, *bill, *price, (**keep ~(s)** or **a ~ on**, keep account of, have under observation or in check). **2.** *v.t.* (**-bb-**). Provide with tab(s). [prob. dial.; cf. TAG]

**tă'bard** *n.* (Hist.) knight's short emblazoned garment worn over armour; herald's short official coat emblazoned with arms of sovereign; woman's or girl's garment of similar shape. [F]

**tă'bbў** *n.* Kind of watered silk; **~ (cat)**, female cat, grey or brownish cat with dark stripes. [F f. Arab. (place of silk manufacture)]

**tă'bernăcl|e** *n.* (Jewish Hist.) tent used as sanctuary before final settlement of Jews in Palestine; Nonconformist meeting-house; canopied niche or receptacle esp. for Eucharist. [F or L (TAVERN)]

**tă'bla** (*or* -ah'-) *n.* Pair of small Indian drums played with hands. [Urdu f. Arab., = drum]

**tă'ble. 1.** *n.* Piece of furniture with flat top and one or more usu. vertical supports, providing level surface on which things may be placed for use or display (**at ~**, while taking meal at table; **lay** measure, report, etc., in Parliament etc. **on the ~**, postpone it indefinitely, ‖submit it for discussion; CARDS *on the table*; **under the ~**, drunk); food provided at table (*keeps a good table*); slab of wood, stone, etc., matter inscribed on it, (**the ~s of the law** etc., the Ten COMMANDMENTS); set of facts or figures systematically arranged esp. in columns, matter contained in such set (*table of contents, of weights and measures*; MULTIPLICATION *tables*); flat surface; each half or quarter of folding backgammon-board (**turn the ~s on**, or abs., reverse relations with, esp. pass from inferior to superior position). **2.** *v.t.* Lay on the table; bring forward for discussion or consideration. **3. ~-cloth** (spread on table, esp. for meals); **~-knife** (for use at meals); **~land**, extensive elevated region with level surface; **~ licence** (to serve alcoholic drinks with meals only); **~-lifting, -rapping, -turning**, lifting etc. of table apparently without physical force, as spiritualistic phenomenon; **~-linen**, table-cloths, napkins, etc.; **~ manners**, ability to behave properly while eating at table; **~-mat** (to protect table from hot dishes); *table* SALT, -SPOON; **~-talk**, miscellaneous informal talk at table; **~ tennis**, indoor game based on lawn tennis, played with small bats and celluloid ball bouncing on table divided by net; **~-water**, mineral water bottled for use at table; **~ wine** (for drinking with meal). [F f. L *tabula* board]

**tă'bleau** (-lō) *n.* (*pl.* **~x** *pr.* -z). Picturesque presentation; group of silent motionless persons arranged to represent a scene; dramatic or effective situation suddenly brought about. [F, = picture, dim. of prec.]

**table d'hôte** (tahbl-dō't) *n.* Meal at fixed time and price in hotel etc., with less choice of dishes than à la carte. [F, = host's table]

**tă'blĕt** *n.* Small slab esp. for display of inscription; small flat piece of prepared substance (e.g. soap); fixed amount of drug compressed into convenient shape. [F f. L dim. (TABLE)]

**tă'bloid** *n.* Newspaper, usu. popular in style, printed on sheets of half size; anything in compressed or concentrated form. [orig. P (prec.)]

**taboo′, tabu′** (-ōō′), n., a., & v. **1.** n. (Among Polynesians etc.) system or act of setting apart person or thing as sacred or accursed; ban, prohibition. **2.** a. Prohibited; consecrated; avoided or prohibited by social custom (*taboo word*). **3.** v.t. Put under taboo; exclude or prohibit by authority or social influence (*the subject was tabooed*). [Tongan]

**ta′bor** n. Small drum, esp. used to accompany pipe. [F]

**tabu.** See TABOO.

**ta′bul|ar** a. Of, arranged in, tables (*tabular results, statements*); broad and flat like table; (formed) in thin plates (*tabular structure*); ~**āte** v.t., arrange (figures, facts) in tabular form; ~**ā′tion** n.; ~**ātor** n., (esp.) attachment to typewriter for advancing to sequence of set positions in tabular work. [L (TABLE)]

**ta′chograph** (-kograhf) n. Device in motor vehicle to record speed and travel-time; **tacho′meter** (-k-) n. (colloq. abbr. **ta′chō** pr. -kō, pl. ~s), instrument for measuring velocity or speed of rotation (esp. of vehicle engine). [Gk *takhos* speed]

**ta′cit** a. Understood, implied, or existing, without being stated, (*tacit consent, agreement, understanding*); ~**ūrn** a., reserved in speech, saying little, uncommunicative; ~**ūr′nity** n. [L (*taceo* be silent)]

**tack¹. 1.** n. Small sharp broad-headed nail; *=* THUMB*tack*; long stitch used in fastening materials lightly or temporarily together; (Naut.) rope for securing corner of some sails, sail-corner to which this is fastened, direction in which vessel moves as determined by position of sails (**port, starboard,** ~, with wind on that side), temporary change of direction in sailing to take advantage of side wind etc.; (fig.) course of action or policy (*is on the right tack; try another tack*); sticky condition of varnish etc. **2.** v.t. & i. Fasten (*down* etc.) with tacks; stitch (pieces of cloth etc.) lightly together; (fig.) annex, append, (thing *to, on to*, another); (Naut.) change ship's course (*about*) by turning head to wind, make series of such tacks; (fig.) change one's conduct, policy, etc. [prob. rel. to F *tache* clasp, nail]

**tack²** n. Riding-harness, saddles,

etc.; ~**-room** (where tack is kept). [TACKLE]

**tack³** n. Food (**hard** ~, ship biscuit; **soft** ~, bread); (derog.) stuff, rubbish. [orig. unkn.]

**ta′ckle** (Naut. tā′-). **1.** n. (**Block and**) ~, mechanism, esp. of ropes, pulley-blocks, hooks, etc., for lifting weights, managing sails, etc.; windlass with its ropes and hooks; requisites for a task or sport (*fishing-tackle*); act of tackling in football etc. **2.** v.t. Grapple with, grasp with endeavour to hold or manage or overcome, (opponent, problem); enter into discussion with (person esp. *about* or *on* awkward matter); (Footb. etc.) obstruct, intercept, or seize and stop (player running with ball). [LG]

**ta′cky** a. (-iness). (Of glue, varnish, etc.) in the sticky stage before complete dryness. [TACK¹]

**tact** n. Intuitive perception of right thing to do or say, adroitness in dealing with others or with difficulties due to personal feeling; ~**′ful** (-lly), ~**′less**, adjs., having or showing tact, no tact. [F f. L (*tango tact-* touch)]

**ta′ct|ics** n.pl. (also treated as sing.) Art of disposing armed forces esp. in contact with enemy; procedure calculated to gain some end, skilful device(s), (*cannot approve of these tactics*); ~**ic** n., (piece of) tactics; ~**ical** a. (-lly), of tactics, (of bombing) done in immediate support of military or naval operations, adroitly planning or planned; ~**i′cian** (-shan) n. [Gk *taktika* (*tasso* arrange)]

**ta′ct|ile** a. Of, perceived by, connected with, sense of touch, also ~**ual** a. (-lly); tangible; (Paint.) producing or having to do with effect of solidity (*tactile values*); ~**i′lity** n. [L (as TACT)]

**ta′dpole** n. Larva of frog, toad, etc., from time it leaves egg till loss of gills and tail. [TOAD, POLL¹]

**ta′ffeta** n. Fine plain-woven lustrous silk(like) fabric. [F or L f. Pers.]

**ta′ffrail** (or -ril) n. Rail round ship's stern. [Du. *taffereel* panel]

**Ta′ffy** n. (colloq.) (Nickname for) Welshman. [supposed W pronunc. of *Davy* = David]

**tag¹. 1.** n. Metal or plastic point of shoelace etc. used to assist insertion;

loop or flap or label for handling or hanging or marking a thing; loose or ragged end; trite quotation, stock phrase; ∼′**rag,** = RAG¹*tag.* **2.** *v.t. & i.* (**-gg-**). Furnish with tag(s); join (thing *to* or *on to* another, things *together*); find rhymes for (verses), string (rhymes) together; (colloq.) follow closely, trail behind, go *along with.* [orig. unkn.]

**tag². 1.** *n.* Children's game of chasing and touching. **2.** *v.t.* (**-gg-**). Touch in game of tag.

**tagliate′lle** (tahlyah-), **-lli** (-ē), *n.* Ribbon-shaped form of pasta. [It.]

**tail¹. 1.** *n.* (∼**less** *pr.* -l-l-). Hindmost part of animal esp. when prolonged beyond (rest of) body (**on** person's ∼, closely following him; **turn** ∼, turn one's back, run away; **with** ∼ **between legs,** discomfited; **with** ∼ **up,** fig. of person, in good spirits); thing like tail in form or position, hind or lower or subordinate or inferior part, slender part or prolongation, e.g. luminous train of comet, outer corner *of the eye,* rear part of aeroplane containing rudder etc., part of shirt below waist, hanging part of back of coat, end of procession etc., weaker members of side batting at cricket etc., foot of page, back of cart, string and paper appendage of kite, stem of musical note, part of letter *g* etc. below line; (sl.) person following or shadowing another; (in *pl.*, colloq.) (evening dress with) tailcoat; (usu. in *pl.*) reverse of coin turning up in toss (*heads or tails?*). **2.** *v.t. & i.* Furnish with tail; remove stalks of (fruit); dock tail of (lamb etc.); (sl.) shadow, follow closely; join (thing *on to* another); ∼ **after,** follow closely; ∼ **away, off,** fall behind or away in scattered line, become fewer or smaller or slighter, end inconclusively. **3.** ∼**-board,** hinged or removable back of lorry etc.; ∼′**coat,** man's coat with long skirt divided at back into tails and cut away in front; ∼**-end,** hindmost or lowest or last part; ∼**-gate,** (*n.*) lower end of canal lock, = *tail-board* or hinged rear door of estate car, *(*v.i.*) drive too close behind another vehicle; ∼**-lamp,** ∼**-light,** (carried at back of train, car, bicycle, etc.); ∼′**piece,** (esp.) decoration in blank space at end of chapter etc., final appendage; ∼′**pipe,** exhaust pipe of motor

vehicle; ∼′**plane,** horizontal stabilizing surface of aeroplane tail; ∼**-race,** part of mill-race below water-wheel; ∼**-spin,** spin of aircraft, (fig.) state of panic; ∼ **wind** (blowing in direction of one's travel). [E]

**tail². (Law). 1.** *n.* Limited ownership, esp. of estate limited to a person and his heirs; **in** ∼, under such limitation. **2.** *a.* So limited (FEE-*tail*). [F f. *tailler* cut (TALLY)]

**tai′lor. 1.** *n.* Maker of (esp. men's) outer garments esp. to order; ∼**-bird,** small Asian bird sewing leaves together to form nest; ∼**-made,** (*a.*) made by tailor usu. with special attention to cut and fit, (fig.) entirely appropriate to purpose, (*n.*; sl.) ready-made cigarette. **2.** *v.i. & t.* Be, work as, tailor; make (clothes esp. to order) as tailor; (esp. in *p.p.*) make clothes for; (in *p.p.*, of woman's suit etc.) simple and well fitted. [AF *taillour* (prec.)]

**taint. 1.** *n.* Spot or trace of decay or corruption or disease (lit. or fig.), corrupt condition, infection, (*a taint of insanity in the family; free from moral taint; without taint of commercialism*). **2.** *v.t. & i.* Introduce corruption or disease into, infect, affect slightly *with,* be infected, (*tainted meat; taints all it touches; meat will taint readily in hot weather*). [F f. L (TINGE)]

**take. 1.** *v.t. & i.* (**took** *pr.* -ŏŏk; **ta′ken**). Lay hold of, grasp, seize, capture, win, gain, (*took him by the throat; take it up with tongs; take a fortress, prisoners,* person *captive,* king *with ace,* £*100 a week in fees*); be successful or effective (*inoculation did not take*); get possession of, acquire, use, (*someone has taken my pen; take a wife, a dozen eggs, the opportunity* to do or *of doing*); occupy (position) esp. as right (*take a or the* CHAIR); copulate with (woman); obtain after fulfilling conditions (*take a degree*); regularly buy (periodical etc.); get use of by purchase etc. (*take tickets, lessons*); use as instance (*let us take Hitler*); consume, use up, (*take food, medicine, a cup of tea; do you take sugar?; it will only take me 10 minutes*); have as necessary accompaniment or part (*verb taking the dative; these things take time; have* **what it** ∼**s,** necessary qualities esp. for success); cause to come or go with one, remove, dispossess person of, (*take letters to the post; bus takes you past the* station; *took all the fun out of it*; *was taken from us by a stroke*); catch, be infected with, (fire, fever, etc.); conceive, experience, exert, (*take courage, fright, offence, pleasure* or *pride in, revenge*); ascertain and record (name and address, temperature); grasp mentally, understand, (*I take your meaning, his reply as a refusal*; **I ~ your point,** I grant the validity of what you have said); treat or regard in specified way (*take it easy, minutes as* READ); accept, submit to, choose, (*take the offer,* him *or his bet, a risk, us as you find us, my advice, my* WORD *for it, a different view of the matter*); derive (*takes its name from the inventor*); perform, deal with, (*take notes, a decision, an oath, a look at this, the corner too fast, the evening service*); teach, be taught or examined in, (subject); make (photograph), photograph (person etc.). **2. ~ after,** resemble (parent etc.); **~ against,** begin to dislike; **~** person **all his time,** (colloq.) tax his powers; **~ away,** subtract, remove, buy (food) to eat elsewhere; **~ back,** retract (statement), convey to original position, carry (person) in thought to past time; **~ down,** write down (spoken words), remove (structure) by separating into pieces; **~ for,** regard as being (*do you take me for a fool?*); **~ from,** subtract, weaken, detract from; **~-home,** (of pay etc.) given to employee after deduction of taxes etc.; **~ in,** receive as lodger etc., undertake (work) at home, include, make (garment, sail) smaller, understand, cheat; **~ in hand,** undertake, start doing or dealing with, undertake control or reform of; **~ it,** assume *that*, (colloq.) endure punishment etc. bravely; **~ it badly, ill, well,** be upset, resentful, neither of these; **~ it from me,** I am well informed and I assure you; **~ it or leave it,** I do not care whether you accept or not; **~ it out of,** have revenge on, exhaust strength of; **~ it out on,** relieve frustration by attacking; **~** person's **name in vain,** use it lightly or profanely, (joc.) mention it; **~n by, with,** attracted or charmed by; **~n ill,** suddenly affected by illness; **~ off,** remove (clothing) from body, deduct, mimic, jump from ground, become airborne, regard (day) as holiday; **~** one*self off,* depart; **~-off**

n., place from which one jumps, act of mimicking or becoming airborne; **~ on,** undertake (work), acquire (new meaning etc.), engage (employee), agree to oppose at game, (colloq.) show violent emotion, = *take upon*; **~ out,** cause to come out, procure (patent, summons, etc.); **~** person *out of himself,* make him forget his worries etc.; **~ over,** succeed to management or ownership of, assume control; **~-over** n., assumption of control (esp. of business); *take* ROOT[1], STOCK; **~ that!** (accompanying a blow etc.); **~ the biscuit, the cake,** (sl.) carry off the honours, surpass everything; *take the* PLACE *of*; **~** one's **time,** not hurry; **~ to,** begin, fall into habit of do*ing,* have recourse to, adapt oneself to, form liking for; **~ to** (remain ill in) one's *bed*; **~ up,** lift up, absorb (moisture, time), engage, allow (passenger) into vehicle, adopt as protégé or pursuit, begin (residence), interrupt or correct (speaker), begin to consort *with*; **~** person **up on,** accept (his offer etc.); **~ it upon** one(*self*), venture or presume *to* do. **3.** *n.* Amount taken or caught; (Cinemat.) scene or sequence photographed at one time without stopping camera. **4. tā′ker** n., (esp.) one who takes a bet etc.; **tā′king,** (n., in *pl.*) money taken in business, (*a.*) attractive, captivating. [E f. N]

**tălc(′um)** n. Translucent mineral often found in thin glasslike plates; **talcum (powder), talc,** powdered talc for toilet use, usu. perfumed. [F, or L *talcum* f. Arab. f. Pers.]

**tāle** n. True or usu. fictitious narrative, story, (*tell me a tale*; *old wives' tale,* see WIFE; TELL one's, *its, own tale*); report of alleged fact, freq. malicious, (TELL *tales*; **~′bearer,** person maliciously spreading such reports or secrets); (arch.) full number (*tale is complete*; *shepherd tells his tale,* i.e. counts his sheep). [E]

**tă′lent** n. Special aptitude, faculty, gift, (*for* music etc., *for* do*ing*; see Matt. 25), high mental ability; persons of talent (*looking out for local talent*; **~-scout, ~-spotter,** seeker-out of talent esp. for entertainment industries); ancient weight and money unit among Assyrians, Greeks, Romans, etc.; **~ĕd** *a.,* having high ability. [E & F f. L f. Gk]

**tă′lĭsman** (-z-) n. Object supposed

to be endowed with magic powers esp. of averting evil from or bringing good luck to its holder; ~ǐc (-ǎ'n-) a. [F & Sp. f. Gk]

**talk** (tawk). **1.** v.i. & t. Converse, communicate ideas, by spoken words (was talking with, to, a friend; do the ~'ing, be spokesman; know what one is ~'ing about, be expert; money ~s, has influence; now you're ~'ing, sl., I can welcome that offer; people will ~, there will be gossip or scandal; talk TALL; ~ing book, recorded reading of book, esp. for the blind; ~'ing of, while we are discussing (talking of food, what time is dinner?); ~'ing point, topic for discussion; you can, can't, ~, colloq., you are just as bad yourself); have the power of speech (child is learning to talk); betray secrets (we have ways of making you talk); express, utter, discuss, in words, (they are talking nonsense, cricket; *~ turkey, colloq., be straightforward and realistic; use (a language) in speech (was talking Welsh); bring into specified condition etc. by talking (talked himself hoarse, out of the difficulty; could talk the hind leg off a DONKEY). **2.** n. Conversation (SMALL, TABLE-, TALL, talk); discussion (talks were held); short address or lecture in conversational style (esp. when broadcast); (theme of) gossip (there is talk of a new appointment; they, their quarrels, are the talk of the town); mode of speech (sailors' talk). **3.** ~ about, discuss, make subject of gossip; ~ back, reply defiantly, respond on two-way radio system; ~ down, silence (person) by superior loudness or persistency, speak patronizingly or condescendingly to, bring (pilot or aircraft) to landing by radio instructions from ground; ~ of, discuss or mention, express some intention of (doing); ~ out, get rid of (bill in Parliament) by prolonging discussion till time of adjournment; ~ over, discuss at length; ~ person over, round, win him over by talking; ~ round, discuss (subject) at length without reaching conclusion; talk through one's HAT; ~ to, colloq., reprove (gave him a talking-to). **4.** ~'ative a., fond of talking. [TALE or TELL]

**tall** (tawl). **1.** a. (no adv. in -ly). (Of person) of more than average height, or of specified height (he is six feet tall); (of tree, steeple, mast, ship, etc.) higher than the average or than surrounding objects (~'boy, tall chest of drawers); (sl.) extravagant, boastful, excessive, (a tall story; tall talk; a ~ order, an exorbitant or unreasonable demand). **2.** adv. In a tall way (talk ~, boast; walk ~, be proud). [E, = swift]

**tǎl'low** (-ō) n. Harder kinds of (esp. animal) fat melted down for use in making candles, soap, etc.; ~ȳ a. [LG]

**tǎ'llȳ. 1.** n. (Hist.) piece of wood scored across with notches for items of an account and then split into halves of which each party kept one, account so kept; score, reckoning, mark registering fixed number of objects delivered or received, such number as unit; ticket, label, for identification; corresponding thing, counterpart, duplicate, (of). **2.** v.i. Agree, correspond, (with; goods do not tally with invoice). [AF tallie f. L talea rod]

**tǎllȳ-hō'** int., n. (pl. ~s), & v. **1.** int. & n. Huntsman's cry to hounds on seeing fox. **2.** v.i. & t. Utter, indicate (fox) or urge (hounds) with, this. [cf. F taïaut]

**Tǎ'lmud** (or -ŏŏd) n. Body of Jewish civil and ceremonial law and legend; **Tǎlmŭ'dǐc(al)** a.; ~ǐst n., compiler or adherent or student of Talmud. [Heb., = instruction]

**tǎ'lon** n. (usu. in pl.) Claw esp. of bird of prey. [F, = heel f. L talus ankle]

**TAM** abbr. television audience measurement.

**tǎ'marǐnd** n. (Tropical tree with) fruit whose acid pulp is used for cooling or medicinal drinks. [Arab., = Indian date]

**tǎ'marǐsk** n. Feathery-leaved evergreen shrub common at seaside. [L]

**tǎ'mbour** (-oor) n. Drum; circular frame for holding fabric taut while it is being embroidered; ~i'ne (-berē'n) n., musical instrument of hoop with parchment stretched over one end and loose jingling discs in slots. [F (TABOR)]

**tāme. 1.** a. (Of animal) domesticated, tractable, not wild or shy, (joc., of person) kept amenable and available; lacking or showing lack of spirit, uninteresting, insipid, (tame acquiescence, description, scenery, speaker).

**2.** *v.t.* (~'able *pr.* -ma-). Make tame, domesticate, break in; subdue, humble. [E]

**Tă'mĭl** *n.* & *a.* (Member, language) of a people inhabiting S. India and Sri Lanka. [native name]

**tăm-o'-shä'nter, tă'mmỹ,** *n.* Round woollen etc. Scottish cap. [character in Burns]

**tămp** *v.t.* Plug (blast-hole) with clay etc. to intensify force of explosion; ram down. [*tampion* stopper for gun-muzzle f. F *tampon*]

**tă'mper** *v.i.* ~ **with,** meddle with, make unauthorized changes in (will, MS., etc.), exert secret or corrupt influence upon, bribe. [var. TEMPER]

**tă'mpon. 1.** *n.* Plug of cotton-wool etc. used to absorb secretions or stop haemorrhage. **2.** *v.t.* Plug with tampon. [F (TAMP)]

**tăn** *v.,* *n.,* & *a.* **1.** *v.t.* & *i.* (-nn-). Convert (raw hide) into leather by soaking in liquid containing tannic acid or by use of mineral salts etc. (so ~'ner *n.*; ~'nerỹ *n.*, place where hides are tanned); make or become brown by exposure to sun; (sl.) beat, thrash. **2.** *n.* Bark of oak etc. bruised and used to tan hides; colour of this, yellowish-brown; bronze of sunburnt skin. **3.** *a.* Of tan colour. [E f. L *tanno*, perh. f. Celt.]

**║T.&A.V.R.** *abbr.* Territorial and Army Volunteer Reserve.

**tă'ndem. 1.** *adv.* With two or more horses harnessed one behind another (*drive tandem*). **2.** *n.* Vehicle driven tandem; bicycle etc. with two or more seats behind each other; group of two persons, machines, etc., with one behind or following the other; **in** ~, thus arranged. [L, = at length]

**tăng. 1.** *n.* Part of tool by which blade is held firm in handle; strong taste or flavour or smell, characteristic property. **2.** *v.t.* Furnish or affect with tang. **3.** ~'ỹ *a.*, having strong taste, smell, etc. [N *tange* point]

**tă'ngent** (-nj-) *n.* Straight line that meets a curve or curved surface at a point but if produced does not intersect it at that point (**fly, go, off at a** ~, diverge suddenly from previous course of motion or thought or talk or action); (Math.) ratio of sides opposite and adjacent to angle in right-angled triangle; **tăngĕ'ntial**

(-njĕ'nshal) *a.* (-**lly**). [L *tango tact-* touch]

**Tăngeri'ne** (-njĕrĕ'n) *n.* & *a.* (Native) of *Tangier*; t~ (**orange**), kind of small flat orange, its deep orange-yellow colour. [place]

**tă'ngĭb┃le** (-nj-) *a.* (~**ly**). Perceptible by touch; definite, clearly intelligible, not elusive or visionary, (*tangible advantages, distinction*); ~**i'l-ĭtỹ** *n.* [F or L (TANGENT)]

**tă'ngle**[1] (-nggel) **1.** *v.t.* & *i.* Intertwine (threads, hair, etc.), become involved in, confused mass; entrap; complicate (*a tangled affair*); become involved (esp. in conflict) *with.* **2.** *n.* Confused mass of intertwined threads etc., confused state, (*skein, business, is in a tangle*). **3.** **tă'nglỹ** (-ngg-) *a.*, tangled. [orig. uncert.]

**tă'ngle**[2] (-nggel) *n.* Coarse or leathery seaweed. [prob. Norw.]

**tă'ngō** (-nggō). **1.** *n.* (*pl.* ~**s**). (Music for) S. Amer. slow ballroom dance. **2.** *v.i.* Dance tango. [Amer. Sp.]

**tă'ngrăm** (-ngg-) *n.* Chinese puzzle square cut into 7 pieces to be combined into various figures. [orig. unkn.]

**tănk. 1.** *n.* Large receptacle for storing liquid, gas, etc.; (Mil.) armoured motor vehicle carrying guns and moving on caterpillar tracks; ~**-engine,** railway engine carrying fuel and water receptacles on its own frame, not in tender; ~**top,** short tight sleeveless upper garment. **2.** *v.i.* ~ (**up**), fill tank of vehicle etc., (sl.) drink heavily. **3.** ~**'er** *n.*, ship or aircraft or road vehicle with tank(s) for carrying liquids (esp. mineral oils) in bulk. [orig. Ind. = pond, f. Gujarati]

**tă'nkard** *n.* Tall mug of pewter etc. for beer. [Du. *tankaert*]

**tă'nker.** See TANK; **tă'nner,** see TAN.

**tă'nnĭ┃c** *a.* Of tan; ~**c acid,** ~**n** *n.*, any of several astringent substances got from oak-galls and various tree-barks, used in preparing leather and in making ink etc. [F *tanin* (TAN)]

**tă'nsỹ** (-zĭ) *n.* Aromatic herb with yellow flowers. [F f. L f. Gk *athanasia* immortality]

**tă'ntal┃ize** *v.t.* Torment with disappointment, raise and then dash the hopes of; ~**izā'tion** *n.*; ~**um** *n.*, rare hard white metallic element;

**~us** n., stand in which spirit-decanters are locked up but visible. [*tantalus* L f. Gk *Tantalos*, mythical king punished in Hades with sight of inaccessible water and fruit]

**tă'ntamount** *pred. a.* ~ **to**, coming to the same thing as, equivalent to. [AF f. It. *tanto montare* AMOUNT so so much]

**tă'ntra** n. Each of a class of Hindu or Buddhist mystical and magical writings. [Skr., = groundwork, doctrine]

**tă'ntrum** n. Outburst of petulance or bad temper. [orig. unkn.]

**Tao|ïsm** (tah'ō-, tow'-) n. A Chinese religious doctrine; **~ïst** n. [Chin. *tao* (right) way]

**tăp¹. 1.** n. Tubular plug with device by which flow of liquid or gas from cask, pipe, etc., can be controlled (on ~, ready to be drawn, fig. ready for immediate use; **~'room**, in which liquor on tap is sold and drunk; **~root**, tapering root growing vertically downwards); taproom; act of tapping telephone etc. **2.** *v.t.* Furnish (cask) with tap, let out (liquid) thus; draw sap from (tree) by cutting into it; get into communication with, establish trade etc. in, (district etc.); divert part of current from (telegraph or telephone wires etc.) to detect message; make screw-thread in. [E]

**tăp². 1.** *v.i.* & *t.* (**-pp-**). Strike gentle but audible blow, rap, (*at, on*, door etc.); strike lightly (*tap the door with your knuckles*; *tapping his teeth with a pencil*); cause (thing) to strike lightly *against* etc. (*tapped his stick against the window*). **2.** n. Light blow, rap; sound of this (*a tap at the door*); **~-dancing**, stage dancing with rhythmical tapping of feet. [imit.]

**tāpe. 1.** n. Narrow woven cotton etc. strip used as flat string (RED *tape*); such strip stretched across racing-track at finishing-line; (**adhesive**) ~, strip of paper, transparent film, etc., coated with adhesive for fastening packages etc.; continuous strip of paper on which messages are printed e.g. in tape-machine; (**magnetic**) ~, impregnated or coated plastic strip for electromagnetic recording and reproduction of signals; **~machine** (for receiving and recording telegraph messages); **~(-measure)**, strip of tape or thin flexible metal marked

for measuring length; **~recorder**, apparatus for recording sounds etc. on magnetic tape and afterwards reproducing them; ~(**-recording**), such record or reproduction; **~-worm**, tapelike worm parasitic in alimentary canal. **2.** *v.t.* Furnish, tie up, join, with tape; measure with tape (||**have** person, thing, **~d**, sl., have summed him up, fully understand it); record on magnetic tape. [E]

**tā'per** n., a., & v. **1.** n. Wick coated with wax etc. for conveying flame. **2.** a. (esp. poet., rhet.) Diminishing in thickness towards one end (*taper fingers*). **3.** *v.t.* & *i.* ~ (**off**), make or become taper, (cause to) grow gradually less, (*the upper part tapers, is tapered (off), to a point*). [E]

**tă'pèstr|ý** n. Thick textile fabric in which coloured weft threads are woven (orig. by hand) to form pictures or designs; ||(piece of) embroidery usu. in wools on canvas imitating this; (-)**~ïed** (-rĭd) a. [*tapissery* f. F (TAPIS)]

**tăpiŏ'ca** n. Starchy substance in hard white grains got from cassava and used for puddings etc. [Tupi-Guarani]

**tā'pir** (or -ēr) n. Piglike mammal of tropical America and Malaya, with short flexible proboscis, allied to rhinoceros. [Tupi]

**tapis** (tă'pē, -pǐs) n. **On the ~**, (of subject) under discussion or consideration. [F, = carpet, table-cloth]

**tă'ppèt** n. Arm, collar, cam, etc., used in machinery to give intermittent motion. [TAP²]

**tă'pster** n. Attendant drawing and serving liquor at bar etc. [E (TAP¹)]

**tär. 1.** n. Dark thick inflammable liquid distilled from wood, coal, etc., and used as preservative of wood and iron, antiseptic, etc., (**touch of the ~-brush**, admixture of Negro or Indian blood as shown by colour of skin; ~ **macadam**, road-materials of stone or slag bound with tar); similar substance formed in combustion of tobacco etc. (colloq.) sailor [TARPAULIN]. **2.** *v.t.* (**-rr-**). Cover with tar; ~ **and feather**, smear with tar and then cover with feathers as punishment; **~red with the same brush**, having same faults. **3.** ~**rý** a. (**-iness**), of, smeared with, tar. [E]

**tă'r(r)adĭddle** n. (colloq.) Fib; nonsense. [cf. DIDDLE]

**tărantĕ'lla** n. (Music for) rapid whirling S. Ital. dance once supposed to be cure for or effect of tarantism. [It. f. L f. Gk]

**tă'rantĭsm** n., (Hist.) dancing mania, esp. in S. Italy attributed to bite of tarantula; **tară'ntŭla** n., large black spider of S. Europe, large hairy tropical spider. [It. (*Taranto*, place)]

**tarbōo'sh** n. Cap like fez. [Arab. f. Pers.]

**tăr'd|ў** a. (~ily, ~iness). Slow to act or come or happen, delaying or delayed beyond right or expected time, (*tardy retribution, arrival, consent*). [f f. L *tardus* slow]

**tāre¹** n. Vetch, esp. as corn-weed or fodder; (Bibl., in *pl*.) injurious corn-weed. [orig. unkn.]

**tāre²** n. Allowance made for weight of box etc. in which goods are packed; weight of motor vehicle without fuel or load. [F f. L f. Arab.]

**tãrge** n. (arch.) Small round shield; **tăr'gĕt** (-g-) n., shooting-mark, esp. round or rectangular one divided by concentric circles, anything fired at (also *attrib.*; *target area*), (fig.) objective, result aimed at (*export, savings, target*), butt for scorn etc., (arch.) targe. [F f. Gmc]

**tă'riff** n. List of duties or customs to be paid on imports or exports; duty on particular class of goods; table of fixed charges (*railway, postal, hotel, tariff*). [f f. It. f. Turk. f. Arab., = notification]

**tăr'latan** n. Thin stiff open muslin. [F; prob. orig. Ind.]

**Tăr'măc. 1.** n. = TAR *macadam*; runway etc. made of this. **2.** *v.t.* (-ck-). Apply Tarmac to. [abbr.; P]

**tãrn** n. Small mountain lake. [N]

**tăr'nĭsh. 1.** *v.t.* & *i.* Lessen or destroy lustre of (*has been tarnished by damp*; fig., *a tarnished reputation*); lose lustre (*silver tarnishes easily*). **2.** n. Loss of lustre; blemish, stain. [F *ternir* (*terne* dark)]

**tăr'ō** n. (*pl.* ~s). Tropical plant of arum family with tuberous root used as food esp. in Pacific islands. [Polynesian]

**tă'rŏt** (-ō) n. Game played with, each card of, pack of 78 cards used also for fortune-telling. [F]

**tãrpau'lĭn** n. Waterproof cloth esp. of tarred canvas, sheet or covering of this. [TAR, PALL¹]

**tă'rradĭddle.** See TARADIDDLE.

**tă'rragon** n. Plant allied to worm-

wood; ~ **vinegar** (flavoured with this). [L f. Gk]

**tăr'rў¹.** See TAR.

**tă'rrў²** *v.i.* (literary). Defer going or coming, linger, be tardy, stay, wait. [orig. unkn.]

**tăr's|us** n. (*pl.* ~i *pr.* -i). The ankle-bones; shank of bird's leg; ~**al** a.; ~**ĭer** n., small large-eyed arboreal nocturnal E. Ind. animal. [Gk]

**tãrt¹** a. Of acid taste; cutting, biting, (*a tart reply*). [E]

**tãrt²** n. Pastry case, usu. open, containing usu. fruit or sweet filling, (*apple, jam, tart*); ~**lĕt** n. [F *tarte*]

**tãrt³. 1.** n. (sl.) Girl or woman, esp. of immoral character; ~**ў** a. **2.** *v.t.* & *i.* (colloq.) ~ **up**, dress up gaudily, (fig.) smarten up. [prob. abbr. *sweetheart*]

**tãr'tan** n. Cloth woven in coloured stripes crossing at right angles, worn orig. by Scottish Highlanders in distinctive patterns denoting their clans. [orig. uncert.]

**tãr'tar¹** n. Substance deposited in cask by fermentation of wine (CREAM *of* tartar); incrustation that forms on the teeth; **tărtă'rĭc** a. (~**ic acid,** organic acid present in many plants, esp. unripe grapes); **tãr'trāte** n., salt of tartaric acid. [F f. L f. Gk]

**Tãr'tar². 1.** a. & n. (Native) of Central Asia E. of Caspian Sea, (member) of group of peoples including Turks, Mongols, etc., (t~ **sauce,** of mayonnaise, chopped gherkins, etc.); violent-tempered, intractable, or savage person; **catch a** ~, meet with unexpectedly difficult adversary. [L or F]

**tãr'tãre** a. ~ **sauce,** = TARTAR² *sauce*. [F, = prec.]

**tărtă'rĭc, tãr'trāte.** See TARTAR¹.

**Tãr'zan** n. Man of great agility and powerful physique. [character in stories of Africa by E. R. Burroughs]

**Tas.** *abbr.* Tasmania.

**task** (-ah-). **1.** n. Piece of work to be done, esp. one imposed or under-taken; **take** person **to** ~, accuse him of fault, rebuke him *for* (doing); ~ **force, group,** specially organized unit for task; ~'**master,** one who imposes task or burden. **2.** *v.t.* Assign task to; exact labour from, put strain upon, tax, (person's powers, intellect, etc.). [F *tasque* f. L *tasca* = *taxa* TAX]

**Tăsmā'nian** (-z-) a. & n. (Native) of *Tasmania*; ~ **devil,** savage-

-looking nocturnal carnivorous marsupial. [place]

**tă′ssel** n. Tuft of hanging threads, cords, etc., attached as ornament to cushion, scarf, etc.; tassel-like catkin etc. [F tas(s)el clasp]

**tāste. 1.** n. Sensation caused in tongue etc. by contact of some soluble things, flavour, (*loathes the taste of garlic*; *white of egg has no taste*; **bad, nasty, ~ in the mouth**, fig., unpleasant after-feeling); faculty of perceiving this sensation (**~-bud**, group of cells on surface of tongue etc. through which this faculty operates); small portion (*of* food etc., or fig.) taken as sample, slight experience of, (*a taste of brandy, of the whip*); liking, predilection, (*has no taste for sweet things*; *a taste for beer, drawing, argument*; **is not to my ~**, does not please me; **~s differ,** different people like different things; *there is no accounting for tastes*; *add salt* etc. **to ~**, so as to produce desired result); aesthetic discernment in art or literature or conduct, conformity to its dictates, (*a man of taste*; *good, bad, taste*; *remark was in bad taste*). **2.** v.t. & i. (**~able** pr. -ta-). Learn, examine, flavour of (food etc., or abs.) by taking it into mouth; eat or drink (even a) small portion of (*has not tasted food for days*); perceive flavour of (*can taste nothing when you have a cold*); have experience of (*has never tasted* BLOOD, *success*); have specified flavour, smack of, (*tastes sour, of aniseed*). **3.** ~**′ful** (-tf-) a. (**-lly**), done in, having, good taste; ~**less** (-tl-) a., flavourless, having or done in bad taste; **tă′ster** n., (esp.) person employed to judge teas, wines, etc., by taste; **tă′sty** a. (colloq.; **-ily, -iness**), of pleasing flavour, appetizing. [F f. Rom.]

**tăt**[1]. See TATTING.

**tăt**[2] n. Tattiness; tatty thing(s) or person. [back-form. f. TATTY]

**ta-ta′** (tătah′) int. (childish or colloq.) Goodbye. [orig. unkn.]

**tă′tter** n. (usu. in pl.) Rag, irregularly torn piece of cloth, paper, etc.; (fig.) useless remains (*left his argument in tatters*); ~**dĕmă′lion** n., ragamuffin; ~**ed** (-erd) a., in tatters. [N]

**tă′tting** n. Kind of knotted lace made by hand with small shuttle and used for trimming etc.; **tăt**[1] v.i.

& t. (**-tt-**), do, make by, tatting. [orig. unkn.]

**tă′ttle. 1.** v.i. Prattle, chatter, gossip idly. **2.** n. Gossip, idle talk. [Flem. *tatelen*, imit.]

**tattoo′**[1]. **1.** n. Evening drum or bugle signal recalling soldiers to quarters; elaboration of this with music and marching as entertainment; drumming or rapping; **devil's ~**, idle drumming or tapping with fingers etc. **2.** v.i. Rap quickly and repeatedly; beat devil's tattoo (*on*). [earlier *tap-too* f. Du. *taptoe*, lit. 'close the tap' (of cask)]

**tattoo′**[2]. **1.** v.t. Mark (skin etc.) with indelible pattern by puncturing and inserting pigment, make (pattern) thus. **2.** n. Such pattern. [Polynesian]

**tă′tty** a. (colloq.) Tattered, shabby, inferior, tawdry. [orig. Sc., = shaggy, app. rel. to TATTER]

**tau** (*or* -ow) n. Nineteenth Gk letter (T, τ) = t; **~ cross** (T-shaped). [Gk]

**taught.** See TEACH.

**taunt. 1.** n. Thing said to anger or wound a person. **2.** v.t. Assail with taunts, reproach (person *with* conduct etc.) contemptuously. [F *tant pour tant* tit for tat, smart rejoinder]

**taupe** (tōp) n. Grey colour with brownish etc. tinge. [F, = MOLE[2]]

**Taur′us** n. Sign of ZODIAC. [L, = bull]

**taut** a. (Of rope etc.) tight, not slack; (of nerves) tense; (of ship etc.) in good condition; ~**en** v.t. & i. [perh. = TOUGH]

**tautŏ′log|ў** n. Saying of same thing twice over in different words, esp. as fault of style (e.g. *arrived one after the other in succession*); **tautolŏ′gical** a. (**-lly**); ~**ize** v.i.; ~**ous** a. [L f. Gk *tauto* the same)]

**tă′vern** n. (literary). Inn or public house. [F f. L *taberna*]

**taw′drў** a. (**-ily, -iness**). Showy but worthless, gaudy, of the nature of cheap finery. [*tawdry lace* f. *St. Audrey's lace*]

**taw′nў** a. (**-ily, -iness**). Of orange-brown colour. [AF *tauné* (TAN)]

**tăx. 1.** n. Contribution to State revenue legally levied on or *on* persons, property, or business (**direct ~**, levied on income etc.; **indirect ~**, paid as price increase for taxed goods); strain, heavy demand, (*up*)on (person, his energies, etc.); ~-collector, official who collects taxes; ~-deductible, (of expenses) that may be paid out of income before deduction of income tax; ~-free, exempt from taxes; ~ haven, country etc. where income tax is low; ~'payer, one who pays taxes; ~ return, declaration of income for taxation purposes; *tax* YEAR. **2.** *v.t.* Impose tax on (persons, goods, etc.), pay tax on (*income taxed at source*); make demands upon, demand exertion from, (person's resources, powers, etc.); (Law) examine and fix proper amount of (costs); charge (person *with* fault, *with* doing), call to account. **3.** ~ā'tion *n.*, imposition or payment of tax(es). [F f. L *taxo* to censure, compute]

**tă'xĭ. 1.** *n.* ~(-**cab**), motor car plying for hire and usu. fitted with taximeter (~-**driver, -man,** driver of this); boat etc. similarly used. **2.** *v.i.* & *t.* (~**ing, ta'xying**). Go, convey, in taxi; (Aeron., of aircraft or pilot) go along ground or surface of water under machine's own power before or after flying. [abbr. *taximeter cab*]

**tă'xĭderm|y̆** *n.* Art of preparing, stuffing, and mounting skins of animals with lifelike effect; ~**ist** *n.* [Gk *taxis* arrangement, *derma* skin]

**tă'xĭmeter** *n.* Automatic fare-indicator fitted to taxi. [F (TAX)]

**tăxŏ'nom|y̆** *n.* (Principles of) biological etc. classification; **tăxŏnŏ'mĭc(al)** *adjs.* (-**ically**); ~**ist** *n.* [F f. Gk *taxis* arrangement, *-nomia* distribution]

**T.B.** *abbr.* tubercle bacillus, hence (colloq.) tuberculosis.

**T.D.** *abbr.* Territorial (Officer's) Decoration.

**tē, tĭ,** (tē), **sĭ** (sē), *n.* (Mus.) Seventh note of scale; note B. [*si*, F f. It.]

**tea** *n.* ~(-**plant**), evergreen shrub or small tree grown in China, India, etc.; its dried leaves; infusion of tea-leaves as (usu. hot) drink (**early morning** ~, usu. drunk before getting up; ~ **and sympathy,** colloq., friendly treatment of the unhappy); infusion etc. of leaves of other plants or of other substance (*camomile, beef, tea*); meal at which tea is customarily the only drink

(**afternoon** ~, light afternoon meal with tea; ‖**high** or ‖**meat** ~, evening meal with tea and usu. meat etc.); ~-**bag,** small permeable bag of tea-leaves for infusion; ~-**break,** interval from work when tea is drunk; *tea*-CADDY[1]; ‖~'**cake,** light flat usu. sweet bun eaten at tea, often toasted; ~ **ceremony,** elaborate Japanese ritual of serving and drinking tea; ~-**chest,** light metal-lined wooden box in which tea is exported; ~-**cloth,** tea-table, tea-towel; *tea*-COSY; ~'**cup** (from which tea is drunk; STORM *in a teacup*); ~ **dance,** *thé dansant*; ~-**garden** (in which tea is grown, or is served to public); ~-**house** (in which tea etc. is served in China and Japan); ~-**leaf,** leaf of tea esp. (in *pl.*) after infusion or as dregs, (rhyming sl.) thief; ~-**party,** afternoon tea with guests; ~-**planter,** proprietor or cultivator of tea plantation; ~'**pot,** spouted vessel in which tea is made and from which it is poured; ~-**room, -shop,** (for serving tea etc. to public); ~-**rose** (with scent like tea); *tea*-SERVICE[1], -SET[3], -SPOON; ~-**things** (used for serving tea); ~-**towel** (for drying washed crockery etc.); ~-**urn** (for boiling or holding water for tea). [prob. Du. *tee* f. Chin.]

**teach** *v.t.* & *i.* (**taught** *pr.* tawt). Enable, cause, (person etc. *to do*) by instruction and training (*teach him to swim; experience taught him to trust no one*); give lessons at school or elsewhere in or on (subject, game, instrument, etc., *to* person; *taught him Greek; teaches the violin; I was never taught music*); be teacher, give lessons esp. at school; give instruction to, educate, (~-**in,** series of lectures and discussions on subject of public interest); explain, show, state by way of instruction, (fact etc., *how, that, to* person; *taught her how to dance; I was never taught this*); cause (person) by punishment etc. *to do* (*this will teach you to speak the truth*); (colloq.) make (person) disinclined (*to offend etc.; I will teach him to meddle in my affairs*); ~'**able** *a.* (-**bly**), (esp.) apt at learning; ~**abĭ'lĭty̆** *n.*; ~'**er** *n.*, (esp.) one who teaches in a school; ~'**ing** *n.*, (esp.) teachers' profession, doctrine, what is taught, (~**ing hospital,** where medical students are taught). [E]

**teak** n. (Orig. E. Ind. tree with) heavy durable timber. [Port. f. Malayalam]

**teal** n. (pl. same). Small freshwater duck. [orig. unkn.]

**team. 1.** n. Set of draught animals; set of players forming one side in game (*cricket team*); set of persons working together; **~-mate**, fellow member of team; **~ spirit**, willingness to act for group's rather than individual's benefit; **~-work**, combined effort, co-operation. **2.** v.t. & i. **~ up**, join in or as team, join in common action, (*with*). **3.** **~'ster** n., driver of team, *lorry-driver. [E]

**tear**[1] (tār) **1.** v.t. & i. (**tore**; **torn**). Pull apart with some force (*tore up the letter*; *has torn his coat*; *tear it in half*; *torn to pieces by a tiger*; fig., *country was torn by factions*, *was torn* (distracted at having to make a choice) *between love and duty*; **that's torn it**, sl., chances or plans have been spoiled); make (hole, rent) thus; pull violently or with some force (lit. or fig.) esp. *down*, *off*, *away*, etc., (*one's hair*, pull it in anger, perplexity, or despair); **~ oneself away**, go away despite strong allurement to stay); run, walk, travel, hurriedly or impetuously (*tore down the hill*); undergo tearing (*tore down the middle*); **~'away**, (a.) impetuous, (n.) hooligan, ruffian; **~'ing** a., (esp.) violent, overwhelming, (*tearing hurry*, *rage*). **2.** n. Hole made, damage caused, by tearing; torn part of cloth etc.; WEAR[1] and tear. [E]

**tear**[2] n. **~(-drop)**, drop of clear saline liquid ordinarily serving to moisten and wash the eye but falling from it in grief, laughter, etc., (**in ~s**, weeping; **without ~s**, fig., presented so as to be easily learned etc.); tearlike thing; e.g. drop of fluid, solid drop of resin etc.; **~-duct** (carrying tears to eye or from eye to nose); **~-gas**, lachrymatory gas used to disable opponents; **~-jerker**, (colloq.) story calculated to evoke sadness or sympathy; **~'ful** a. (**-lly**), in or given to or accompanied with tears. [E]

**tease** (-z). **1.** v.t. Irritate playfully or maliciously, vex with jests, questions, or petty annoyances; pick (wool etc.) into separate fibres, comb or card; dress (cloth) with teasels; **~ out**, separate by disentangling (lit. or fig.). **2.** n. (colloq.)

Person fond of teasing others. **3. tea'sel** (-z-), **-zle**, n., dried prickly flower-head used for raising nap on cloth, plant producing these; **tea'ser** (-z-) n., (esp., colloq.) hard question or task. [E]

**teat** n. Mammary nipple esp. of animal; device of rubber etc. for sucking milk from bottle. [F f. Gmc]

**tĕc** n. (sl.) Detective (novel). [abbr.]

**Tĕch** (-k) n. (colloq.) Technical college, institute, or school. [abbr.]

**tĕ'chnĭc** (-kn-) n. Technique; (in pl.) technology, technical terms or details; **~al** a. (**-lly**), of or in particular art, science, craft, etc., (*technical terms*; **~al hitch**, interruption or breakdown due to mechanical failure), of, for, in, applied science or vocational training (*technical college*), in strict legal interpretation (*technical assault*, *knock-out*); **~ă'lĭtў** n., technicalness, technical expression, (merely) technical distinction (*was acquitted on a technicality*); **~ian** (-ĭ'shan) n., person skilled in technique of an art or craft, person expert in practical application of science; **T~olor** (-ŭl-) n., a process of colour cinematography [*P]; **tĕchni'que** (-knē'k) n., mode of artistic expression in music, painting, etc., mechanical skill in art, means of achieving one's purpose (esp. skilfully); **tĕchnŏ'cracў** (-kn-) n., government or control of society or industry by technical experts; **tĕ'chnocrăt** (-kn-) n., advocate of this; **tĕchnŏ'logў** (-kn-) n., (science of) practical or industrial art(s), ethnological study of development of such arts, application of science; **tĕchnolŏ'gĭcal** (-kn-) a. (**-lly**); **tĕchnŏ'logĭst** (-kn-) n. [L f. Gk (*tekhnē* art)]

**tĕ'chў**. See TETCHY.

**Tĕ'ddў** n. **~ (bear)**, (or *t~*) child's toy bear [pet-name of *Theodore* Roosevelt]; **~ boy** (or *t~*; colloq.; abbr. **Tĕd**) youth with supposedly Edwardian style of dress [pet-form of *Edward*].

**Te Deum** (tē dē'um, tā dā'-) n. Expression of thanksgiving or exultation. [L, = Thee, God, (we praise), first wds of hymn]

**tĕ'dĭ|ous** a. Tiresomely long, wearisome, irksome; **~um** n., tediousness. [F or L (*taedet* it bores)]

**tee**[1] n. Letter T. [phon. sp.]

**tee². 1.** *n.* (Golf) cleared space from which ball is struck at beginning of play for each hole, small pile of sand or small appliance of wood, rubber, etc., on which ball is placed before being thus struck; mark aimed at in bowls, curling, quoits, etc. **2.** *v.t. & i.* Place (ball) on golf tee; ~ **off**, make first stroke in golf, (fig.) start, begin; ~ **up**, place ball on tee. [orig. unkn.]

**teem¹** *v.i.* Swarm *with*, be prolific, (*forest teems with snakes; fish teem in these waters*). [E, = give birth to]

**teem²** *v.i.* (Of water etc.) flow copiously, pour. [N]

**-teen** *suf.* forming NUMERALS 13–19. [E (TEN)]

**teen|s** (-z) *n.pl.* Years of one's age from 13 to 19; ~**age**, (characteristic) of ~**ager**, person in teens; ~**'y-bopper**, (colloq.) teenager (usu. girl) following latest fashions in clothes, pop music, etc. [-TEEN; cf. BOP]

**tee'nў(-weenў)** *a.* (childish or colloq.) Tiny. [var. TINY]

**tee'ter** *v.i.* Totter, move unsteadily. [dial.]

**teeth.** See TOOTH.

**teeth|e** (-dh) *v.i.* Grow or cut (esp. milk-)teeth; ~**'ing** *n.*; ~**ing-ring**, small ring for infant to bite on while teething; ~**ing troubles**, (fig.) initial troubles in an enterprise etc. [TEETH]

**teeto'tal** *a.* Of or advocating total abstinence from intoxicants; ~**ĭsm** *n.*; ~**ler** *n.*, person advocating or practising total abstinence from intoxicants. [redupl. TOTAL]

**teeto'tum** *n.* Children's four-sided top with sides lettered to decide spinner's luck; any top spun with the fingers (**like a** ~, spinning). [*T* (letter on one side), L *totum* whole (stakes), for which it stood]

**tēhee'** *n.,* & *v.i.* (Give) restrained or contemptuous laugh. [imit.]

**Tel.** *abbr.* Telegraph(ic); Telephone.

**tĕ'lĕ-** *in comb.* **1.** Far, at a distance; ~**communication**, communication over long distances by cable, telegraph, telephone, or radio, (usu. in *pl.*) this branch of technology; ~**pho'to, ~photogra'phic,** *adjs.*, ~**photo'graphy** *n.*, photographing distant object with combined lenses; ~**printer, T~type**, telegraph instrument for sending messages by typing. **2.** Television; ~**prompter**, device

that slowly unrolls (television) speaker's text in large print [*P]. [Gk (*tēle* far off)]

**tĕ'lĕgraph** (-ahf). **1.** *n.* (Apparatus for) transmitting messages or signals to a distance esp. by making and breaking electrical connection (~**-line, -pole** or **-post, -wire**, used in providing telegraphic connection); semaphore apparatus; ~(**-board**), board on which numbers are put up so as to be visible at a distance. **2.** *v.i. & t.* Send message, send (message), by telegraph (*telegraph the news to her; telegraph to him to come, that we cannot come*); make signals (*to person to do, that*). **3.** **tĕ'lĕgrăm** *n.*, message sent by telegraph and then usu. delivered in written etc. form to addressee; ~**er** (or **tĭlĕ'gra-**), **tĕlĕ'-graphĭst,** *ns.*, person skilled or employed in telegraphy; **tĕlĕ-grăphĭc** *a.* (-ically), of telegraphs or telegrams, (of style) economically worded; **tĕlĕ'graphў** *n.*, use or construction of telegraph. [F (-GRAPH)]

**tĕlĕ'mĕter** (or tĕ'lĭmē-). **1.** *n.* Apparatus to record readings of instrument at distance, usu. by radio. **2.** *v.i. & t.* Record readings thus; transmit (reading) to distant receiver; **tĕlĕ'mĕtrў** *n.* [METER]

**tĕlĕo'log|ў** *n.* Doctrine of final causes, view that developments are due to purpose or design that is served by them; **tĕlĕolŏ'gĭcal** *a.* (-lly); ~**ĭst** *n.* [Gk *telos* end]

**tĕlĕ'pathў** *n.* Communication between minds other than by known senses; **tĕ'lĕpăth** *n.*, person with ability to communicate thus; **tĕlĕ-pă'thĭc** *a.* (-ically). [PATHOS]

**tĕ'lĕphōne. 1.** *n.* Apparatus for transmitting sound (esp. speech) to a distance by wire or cord or radio, esp. by converting to electrical signals; (transmitting and) receiving instrument used in this; *the* system of communication by network of telephones; **on the** ~, having such instrument connected to network, by use of or (while) using the telephone; ~ **book, directory,** (listing names and numbers of telephone subscribers); ~ **booth,** ‖~**-box,** ~ **kiosk,** (containing telephone for public use); ~ **number** (assigned to particular subscriber and used in making connections to his telephone). **2.** *v.t. & i.* Send (message etc.), speak to (person), by telephone; make telephone call. **3. tĕlĕphŏ'nĭc** *a.* (-ically); **tĕlĕ'phonĭst** *n.*, (esp.) operator in telephone exchange; **tĕlĕ'phonў** *n.* (as *telegraphy*). [PHONO-]

**tĕ'lĕscōpe. 1.** *n.* Optical instrument using lenses or mirrors or both to make distant objects appear nearer and larger; **radio ~**, directional aerial system for collecting radio waves from celestial objects. **2.** *v.t. & i.* Press, drive, (sections of tube, colliding vehicles, etc.) together so that one slides into another like sections of telescope, compress (lit. or fig.) forcibly; close, be driven, be capable of closing, thus. **3. tĕlĕscŏ'pĭc** *a.* (-ically), of, made with, telescope (*telescopic observations*); **telescopic sight,** telescope used for sighting on rifle etc.), consisting of sections which telescope (*telescopic umbrella*). [It. or L (-SCOPE)]

**tĕ'lĕvision** (-zhon; *or* -vĭ'-) *n.* System for reproducing actual or recorded scene, with sound, at a distance on screen etc. by radio transmission; vision of distant objects obtained thus; televised programmes etc.; **~ (set)**, apparatus for displaying pictures transmitted thus; **tĕ'lĕvīse** (-z) *v.t.*, transmit by television; **tĕlĕvĭ'sŭal** (-z-, -zhŏŏ-) *a.*, of television. [VISION]

**tĕ'lĕx, T-. 1.** *n.* System of telegraphy using teleprinters and public telecommunication network. **2.** *v.t.* Send, communicate with, by telex. [TELE(PRINTER), EX(CHANGE)]

**tĕll** *v.t. & i.* (told *pr.* tō-). Relate or narrate (*tell me a story*; **~ a tale**, of fact etc., be significant; **~ its own tale**, need no comment; **~ one's own tale**, give one's own account of the matter; **~ tales (out of school)**, report esp. maliciously what is meant to be secret); make known, express in words, divulge, (*tell me your name, what to do, all about it*; **don't ~ me** *it's here already*, expr. incredulity; *I told you* so[1]; **~ it not in Gath**, usu. joc., let this not reach and gladden the enemy [2 Sam. 1: 20]; *tell that to the (horse)* MARINES; **~ the world**, announce openly; **you're ~ing me**, sl., I am fully aware of that); utter (*tell lies*); give information or description (*of, about*; HEAR *tell of*); reveal secret (**~ on**, colloq., inform against; **time will ~**, we shall know

eventually); decide, determine, distinguish, (*how do you tell when to begin?*; *cannot tell them apart*; **~ the time**, read it from face of clock etc.; **you never can ~**, appearances and probabilities are deceptive); assure (*it's not easy, I can tell you*); produce marked effect (*strain began to tell on him*); count (*we were 18 men all told*; **~ one's beads**, use rosary in praying; **~ off**, colloq., reprimand, scold); direct, order, (person) *to do* something (*tell him to wait for me*); **~-tale**, person who discloses another's private affairs, automatic registering device, (*attrib.*) serving to reveal or betray something (*a tell-tale blush, stain*); **~'er** *n.*, (esp.) person appointed to count votes in House of Commons, person appointed to receive or pay out money in bank etc.; **~'ing** *a.*, (esp.) having marked effect, striking. [E (TALE)]

‖**tĕ'llў** *n.* (colloq.) Television (set). [abbr.]

**tĕmĕ'rĭtў** *n.* Rashness; **tĕmĕrā'r-ĭous** *a.*, reckless. [L (*temere* rashly)]

**tĕmp** *n.* (colloq.) Temporary employee. [abbr.]

**tĕ'mper. 1.** *v.t.* Bring (clay, metal) to proper consistency or hardness; modify, mitigate, (justice etc.) by blending *with* (mercy etc.); moderate, restrain. **2.** *n.* Condition of metal as regards hardness and elasticity; habitual or temporary disposition of mind (**in a bad ~**, peevish, angry; **in a good ~**, in an amiable mood) esp. as regards composure (*keep, control*, one's temper; **lose** one's **~, out of ~**, angry); irritation, anger, (*in a fit of temper*; **have a ~**, be prone to outbursts of anger; **show ~**, be petulant). **3. ~a** *n.*, method of painting like DIS-TEMPER[2], esp. in fine art on canvas [It.]; **~ament** *n.*, individual character of person's physical constitution permanently affecting behaviour; **~amĕ'ntal** *a.* (-lly), (esp., of person) liable to erratic or peculiar moods; **~ance** *n.*, moderation or self-restraint esp. in eating and drinking, moderation in use of or (esp.) total abstinence from alcoholic drink; **~ate** *a.*, avoiding excess, moderate, of mild temperature; **~ature** *n.*, degree or intensity of heat of a body in relation to others esp. as shown by thermometer (**take** person's **~ature**, ascertain any variation from normal in illness etc.) or perceived by touch, (colloq.) body temperature above normal (*have a temperature*), (fig.) degree of excitement in discussion etc. [E f. L *tempero* mingle]

**tĕ′mpėst** *n.* Violent storm; **tĕmpĕ′stŭous** *a.*, stormy, turbulent. [F f. L (*tempus* time)]

**tĕ′mplāte, tĕ′mplėt,** *n.* Thin board or metal plate used as guide in cutting or drilling. [dim. of *temple* device in loom to keep cloth stretched, alt. after *plate*]

**tĕ′mple**[1] *n.* Building treated as the dwelling-place, or devoted to worship, of god(s) (**the T~**, that of Jehovah at Jerusalem; **Inner, Middle, T~**, two Inns of Court on site of establishment of Knights Templars in London; **Tĕ′mplar** *n.*, member of religious and military order (**Knights Templars,** suppressed 1312) for protection of pilgrims to Holy Land. [E & F (L *templum*)]

**tĕ′mple**[2] *n.* Flat part of either side of head between forehead and ear. [F f. L]

**tĕ′mplėt.** See TEMPLATE.

**tĕ′mp|ō** *n.* (*pl.* ~os, ~i *pr.* -ē). Speed at which music is (to be) played, esp. as characteristic (*waltz tempo*); (fig.) rate of motion or activity. [It., f. L *tempus -por-* time]

**tĕ′mpor|al** *a.* (-lly). Of this life, secular, esp. opp. to *spiritual* (*temporal affairs*; ||**lords** ~**al,** members of House of Lords not bishops; ~**al power,** of ecclesiastic esp. Pope in temporal matters); of, in, denoting, time; of TEMPLE[2]s (*temporal bone, artery*); ~**ā′lĭtȳ** *n.*, (esp., in *pl.*) religious body's or ecclesiastic's temporal possessions; ~**arȳ,** (*a.*; -ily, -iness) lasting or meant to last only for a time, (*n.*) person employed temporarily; ~**ize** *v.i.*, avoid committing oneself, act so as to gain time, comply temporarily with requirements of occasion. [F or L (prec.)]

**tĕmpt** *v.t.* Risk angering, defy, (*would be tempting Providence to try it*); entice, incite, (*to do, to* esp. evil action, *into* doing; *I am* ~**ed** (strongly disposed) *to question this*); allure, attract; (arch.) test resolution of; ~**ā′tion** *n.*, tempting, being tempted, incitement esp. to sin, attractive thing or course of action, (arch.) putting to the test (*lead us not into*

*temptation*); ~**er** *n.* (esp. **the T~er,** the Devil); ~**′rèss** *n.*; ~**′ing** *a.*, (esp.) attractive, inviting. [F f. L *tempto, tento* try, test]

**tĕn** *a.* & *n.* NUMERAL; *Ten* COMMANDMENTS; ~**-gallon hat,** cowboy's large broad-brimmed hat; ~**′pins,** kind of skittles; ~**′fōld** *a.* & *adv.*; ||~**′ner** *n.*, (colloq.) £10 note; ~**th** *a.* & *n.*, NUMERAL (~**th-rate,** of extremely poor quality). [E]

**tĕ′nab|le** *a.* That can be maintained against attack or objection; (of office etc.) that can be held *for* period or *by* class of person; ~**ĭ′lĭtȳ** *n.* [F (*tenir* hold)]

**tĕ′nace** *n.* Pair of playing-cards ranking above and below opponent's card. [F f. Sp., = pincers]

**tēnā′cious** (-shŭs) *a.* Holding tightly, not easily separable, tough; keeping firm hold (*of* property, principles, life, etc.); (of memory) retentive; **tēnă′cĭtȳ** *n.* [L *tenax -acis* (*teneo* hold)]

**tĕ′nant** *n.* Person who rents land or house from landlord; occupant of place; ~ **farmer** (farming hired land); **tĕ′nancȳ** *n.*, tenant's position; ~**rȳ** *n.*, tenants of estate etc. [F (as TENABLE)]

**tĕnch** *n.* (*pl.* same) European freshwater fish of carp family. [F f. L *tinca*]

**tĕnd**[1] *v.i.* Be moving, be directed, hold a course, (lit or fig.: *tends in our direction, to the same conclusion*); be apt or inclined, serve, conduce, (*to* action, quality, etc., *to do*); ~**′encȳ** *n.*, tending, leaning, inclination, (*towards, to,* thing; *to do*); ~**ĕ′ntious** (-shŭs) *a.*, (derog. of writing etc.) designed to advance a cause; ~**er**[1], (*v.t.* & *i.*) make offer of or present for acceptance (money in payment, one's services or resignation), send in a tender (*for* execution of work etc.), (*n.*) offer, esp. in writing to execute work or supply goods at fixed price; **legal** ~**er,** currency that cannot legally be refused in payment of debt; **put out to** ~**er,** seek offers in respect of (work etc.). [F f. L *tendo tens-* or *tent-* stretch]

**tĕnd**[2] *v.t.* Take care of, look after, (sheep, invalid, machine); ~**′er**[2] *n.*, (esp.) vessel attending larger one with stores etc., carriage attached to locomotive with coal etc. [ATTEND]

**tĕ′ndencȳ, tendentious, tĕ′nder**[1]. See TEND[1]; **tĕ′nder**[2], see TEND[2].

**tĕ'ndër**[3] *a.* (~**er**, ~**est**). Not tough (*tender steak*); easily hurt or wounded, susceptible to pain or grief, (*a tender heart*); ~ **spot**, fig., subject on which one is touchy); delicate, fragile, (lit. or fig.); **of ~ age, years**, immature, young); loving, affectionate, (*wrote tender verses*); requiring tact, ticklish, (*a tender subject*); ~**foot**, novice, newcomer; ~**loin**, ‖middle part of pork loin, *undercut of sirloin; ~**ize** *v.t.*, (esp.) render (meat) tender by beating etc. [F f. L *tener*]

**tĕ'nd|on** *n.* Cord of strong tissue attaching muscle to bone etc.; ACHILLES *tendon*; ~**ïnous** *a.* [F, or L *tendo* f. Gk]

**tĕ'ndrïl** *n.* One of the slender leafless shoots by which some climbing plants cling. [prob. F *tendrillon*, ult. rel. to L *tener* TENDER[3]]

**tĕ'nëment** *n.* Dwelling-place, esp. set of rooms let separately from rest of house; ~(-**house**), house divided into and let in tenements. [AF f. L (*teneo* hold)]

**tĕ'nët** *n.* Doctrine held by party, sect, etc. [L, = he holds]

**Tenn.** *abbr.* Tennessee.

**tĕ'nnër.** See TEN.

**tĕ'nnïs** *n.* Racket and ball game for 2 or 4 players played on court divided by net; (**lawn**) ~, development of real tennis played on outdoor orig. grass or hard court; **real** ~, original form of tennis played on indoor court; ~ **elbow**, sprain caused (as) by playing tennis; TABLE *tennis*. [prob. F *tenez* take! (as server's call)]

**tĕ'non** *n.* Projection that fits into MORTISE. [F (*tenir* hold f. L, as foll.)]

**tĕ'nor** *n.* Prevailing course of one's life or habits; general purport of document or speech; (Mus.) male voice between baritone and alto or counter-tenor, singer with or part written for this voice, instrument with range of this voice. [F f. L (*teneo* hold)]

**tĕnse**[1] *n.* Form taken by verb to indicate time (also continuance or completeness) of action etc.; set of such forms for various persons and numbers. [F f. L *tempus* time]

**tĕns|e**[2]. **1.** *a.* Stretched to tightness, strained or highly strung, (*tense muscle, nerves, emotion*); causing tenseness (*a tense moment*). **2.** *v.t* & *i.* Make or become tense. **3.** ~**ïle** *a.*, of tension (~**ile strength**, resistance to breaking under tension), capable of being stretched; ~**ï'lïtỹ** *n.*; ~'**ïon** (-shon) *n.*, stretching or being stretched, mental strain or excitement, strained (political, social, etc.) state or relation, effect produced by forces pulling against each other (SURFACE *tension*), electromotive force (*high, low, tension*). [L *tensus* (TEND[1])]

**tĕnt**[1] *n.* Portable shelter or dwelling of canvas, cloth, etc., supported by pole(s) and ropes attached to ~**pegs** driven into ground; OXYGEN *tent*; ~ **coat, dress**, (cut very full); ~-**stitch**, (one of) series of parallel diagonal stitches [perh. f. another wd]. [F *tente* f. L (TEND[1])]

**tĕnt**[2] *n.* Deep red wine used esp. as sacramental wine. [Sp. *tinto* (TINGE)]

**tĕ'nt|acle** *n.* Long slender flexible appendage of animal, used for feeling, grasping, or moving; (fig.) thing used like tentacle as feeler etc.; ~**acled** (-keld), ~**ă'cŭlar**, *adjs*. [L (TEMPT)]

**tĕ'ntative** *a.*, done by way of trial, experimental, hesitant, not definite, (*tentative suggestion*). [L (TEMPT)]

**tĕ'ntër** *n.* Cloth-stretching frame; ~**hooks** (to which cloth is fastened); **on ~hooks**, in state of suspense, distracted by uncertainty. [AF f. L *tentorium* (TEND[1])]

**tĕnth.** See TEN.

**tĕ'nūous** *a.* Thin, slender, small; rarefied; (of distinction etc.) subtle, over-refined; **tĕnū'ïtỹ** *n.* [L *tenuis*]

**tĕ'nure** (-nyer) *n.* Condition, form of right or title, under which (esp. real) property is held; (period of) holding (*during his tenure of office*); *permanent appointment of teacher etc. [F (*tenir* hold f. L *teneo*)]

**tenuto** (tenōō'tō) *a.* & *adv.* (Mus., of note etc.) sustained, given its full time-value. [It., = held]

**tĕ'pee** *n.* N. Amer. Indian's conical tent. [Dakota]

**tĕ'pïd** *a.* Slightly warm (lit. or fig.); **tĕpï'dïtỹ** *n.* [L]

**tĕquï'la** (-kĕ'-) *n.* Mexican liquor from agave. [place]

**tĕratŏ'log|ỹ** *n.* Study of animal and vegetable monstrosities; **tĕratolŏ'gïcal** *a.* (-lly); ~**ïst** *n.* [Gk *teras terat-* monster]

**tĕr'cel, tier'cel,** *n.* Male hawk. [F. f. Rom. dim. of L *tertius* third]

**tĕrcĕntĕ'narỹ** (or -sĕ'ntï-) *a.* & *n.* (Festival) of 300th anniversary. [L *ter* 3 times]

**tĕ'rĕb|ïnth** *n.* S. Eur. turpentine-yielding tree; ~**ï'nthine** *a.*, of the terebinth, of turpentine. [F or L f. Gk]

**tere′dō** n. (pl. ~s). Mollusc that bores into submerged timber. [L f. Gk]

**tĕrgĭvèrsā′tion** n. Turning one's back on thing; change of party or principles; making of conflicting statements. [L (*tergum* back, *verto* turn)]

**tĕrm. 1.** n. Appointed limit (arch.; *set a term to his existence*); limited period (esp. of office, tenure, pregnancy, imprisonment); period of action or of contemplated results (*in the short term*); period during which instruction is given in school or university, or ‖during which lawcourt holds sessions; word used to express definite concept esp. in branch of study etc. (*golfing, legal, term*); **in ~s of**, in the language peculiar to, using as basis of expression or thought); (in *pl.*) language used, mode of expression, (*in the most flattering, no uncertain, terms; state etc. in ~s*, explicitly); (in *pl.*) conditions, stipulations, (*I'll do it on my own terms; terms of surrender*); **bring** person **to ~ s**, cause him to accept conditions; **come to ~s**, yield, give way; **come to** or **make ~s**, conclude agreement *with*, reconcile oneself *with* difficulties etc.; **on ~s**, fig., of friendship or equality; ‖**~s of reference**, points referred to an individual or body of persons for decision or report, (definition of) scope of inquiry etc.; **~s of trade**, ratio of prices paid for imports and received for exports, charge, price, (*his terms are £5 a lesson; hire-purchase on easy terms*), relation, footing, (*am on good,* SPEAKING, *terms with her*); (Math.) each quantity in ratio or series, item of compound algebraic expression (*a* + *bc* − *2x* has three *terms*); (Logic) word(s) that may be subject or predicate of a proposition (MAJOR, MIDDLE, MINOR, *term*). **2.** v.t. Denominate, call, (*the music termed plainsong; this he termed sheer robbery*). [F f. L TERMINUS]

**tĕr′magant** n. Overbearing woman, virago. [F *Tervagan* f. It.]

**tĕr′min|al. 1.** a. (~ly). Of or forming the last part or terminus (*terminal section, joint, station*); of, done etc., each term (*terminal examinations*); (Med.) forming or undergoing last stage of fatal disease. **2.** n.

Terminating thing, extremity, esp. point of connection for closing electric circuit; terminus for trains or long-distance buses; = AIR *terminal*; apparatus for transmission of messages to and from computer, communications system, etc. **3.** ~**āte** v.t. & i. (~**able**), bring or come to an end, end *in*; ~**ā′tion** n., ending, way something ends, word's final syllable or letter(s); ~**ātor** n.; ~**ŏ′logȳ** n., science of proper use of terms, system of terms used in a science, art, etc.; ~**olŏ′gĭcal** a. (-lly; ~**ological inexactitude**, joc., a lie); ~**us** n. (pl. ~**i** pr. -ī, ~**uses**), point at end of railway or bus route or of pipeline etc. [L (*terminus* end, limit, boundary)]

**tĕr′mīte** n. Social insect destructive to timber. [L *termes* -*mitis*]

**tĕrn** n. Sea-bird like gull but usu. smaller and with forked tail. [Scand.]

**tĕr′narȳ** a. Composed of 3 parts. [L (*terni* 3 each)]

**Tĕrpsĭchorē′an** (-k-) a. Pertaining to dancing. [*Terpsichore*, Muse of dancing]

**tĕr′race** (or -ĭs) n. Raised level space, natural or artificial, esp. for walking or standing; row of houses on raised level or built in one block of uniform style (*terrace house*); ~**d** (-st) a., formed into or having terrace(s); ~**d roof**, flat roof esp. of Eastern house. [F f. L *terra* earth]

**tĕrracŏ′tta** n. Unglazed usu. brownish-red fine pottery used as ornamental building-material and in statuary; statuette of this; its colour. [It., = baked earth]

**terra firma** (tĕra fĕr′ma) n. Dry land, firm ground. [L]

**tĕrrai′n** n. Tract of land as regards its natural features. [F f. Rom. f. L (TERRENE)]

**tĕ′rrapin** n. N. Amer. edible freshwater tortoise; (*T*~; **P**) type of prefabricated one-storey building. [Algonquian]

**tĕrrār′ĭ|um** n. (pl. ~**a**, ~**ums**). Vivarium for terrestrial animals; sealed transparent globe etc. containing growing plants. [L (*terra* earth), after *aquarium*]

**tĕrra′zzō** (-tsō) n. (pl. ~**s**). Flooring-material of stone chips set in concrete and given a smooth surface. [It., = terrace]

**tĕrrē′ne** a. Of earth, earthly;

terrestrial; **terre'strial** a. (-lly), of or on the earth (*terrestrial globe, life*), of or on dry land (*terrestrial birds*). [AF f. L *terrenus* (*terra* earth)]

**te'rrib̄|le** a. Causing or fit to cause terror, dreadful; (colloq.) very great or bad (*he is a terrible bore*), incompetent (*I'm terrible at tennis*); **~ly̌** adv. (esp., sl.) very, extremely, (*he was terribly nice about it*). [F f. L (*terreo* frighten)]

**te'rrier** n. Small active dog bred orig. for turning out foxes etc. from their earths; ||*T~*; colloq.) member of Territorial Army etc. [F (*chien*) *terrier* f. L (*terra* earth)]

**terri'fic** a. (~ally). Causing terror; (colloq.) of great size, excellent (*did a terrific job*), excessive (*made a terrific noise*); **te'rrify** v.t., frighten severely. [L (as TERRIBLE)]

**terri'ne** (-ē'n) n. (Pâté or other food cooked in) earthenware vessel. [TUREEN]

**terrĭtor'ial. 1.** a. (~ly). Of territory or districts; ||T~ **Army**, volunteer reserve force organized by localities, now **T~ and Army Volunteer Reserve**; ~ **waters** (under a State's jurisdiction, esp. part of sea within stated distance of shore). **2.** n. ||Member of Territorial Army etc. [L (foll.)]

**te'rritory̌** n. Extent of land under jurisdiction of sovereign, State, city, etc.; (fig.) sphere, province; area over which commercial traveller etc. operates; (*T~*) organized division of a country esp. if not yet admitted to full rights of a State; area defended by animal(s) against others of same species, or by team etc. in game. [L (*terra* land)]

**te'rror** n. Extreme fear (~--stricken, -struck, affected with terror); person or thing causing terror; (holy) ~, (colloq.) formidable person, troublesome child, etc.; **Reign of T~, the T~**, period of French Revolution 1793–4, similar period of bloodshed by revolutionaries or reactionaries; **~ism** n., practice of using terror-inspiring methods of governing or of securing political or other ends; **~ist** n.; **~ize** v.t., fill with terror, coerce by terrorism; **~iza'tion** n. [F f. L]

**te'rry̌** n. & a. (Pile fabric) with loops uncut, used esp. for towels. [orig. unkn.]

**terse** a. Concise, brief and forcible in style; curt. [L (*tergo ters-* wipe)]

**ter'tian** (-shan) a. & n. (Fever) recurring twice in 3 days; **ter'tiary̌** (-sheri), (a.) of third order, rank, formation, etc., (n.) bird's flight-feather of third row, (Geol.; *T~*) period or system subsequent to Secondary. [L (*tertius* third)]

**te'ry̌lēne** n. Synthetic polyester used as textile fibre. [P; *terephthalic* acid +ETHYLENE]

**te'sse|llātĕd** a. Of or resembling mosaic, having finely chequered surface; **~llā'tion** n., tessellated chequering; **~ra** n. (pl. -ae), one of the small cubes or blocks of which mosaic consists. [L (*tessella*, dim. of *tessera*)]

**test¹. 1.** n. Critical examination or trial of person's or thing's qualities (ACID, BLOOD, MEAN³s, *test*; **put to the ~**, cause to undergo this; **stand the ~**, not fail or incur rejection); means, standard, circumstances, suitable for or serving such examination; (colloq.) test match. **2.** v.t. Put to the test, make trial of, (~ **out**, put to practical test); try severely, tax; (Chem.) examine by means of reagent. **3.** ~ **bed**, equipment for testing aircraft engines before general use; ~ **case**, (Law) case whose decision is taken as settling other cases involving same question of law; ~ **match** (in cricket tour etc., usu. between different countries and as one of series); ~ **paper**, minor examination-paper, (Chem.) paper impregnated with substance changing colour under known conditions; **~-tube**, thin glass tube closed at one end used for chem. tests etc.; **~-tube baby**, (colloq.) one conceived by artificial insemination, or developing elsewhere than in a mother's body. [F f. L *testu(m)* = *testa* (foll.)]

**test²** n. Hard continuous shell of some invertebrates; **~'a** n. (pl. -ae), (Bot.) seed-coat; **~ā'ceous** (-shus) a., having hard continuous shell. [L *testa* earthen pot, jug, shell, etc. (whence words for 'head' in F & It., giving E *tester* & *testy*)]

**te'stament** n. A will (usu. *last will and testament*); (Bibl.) covenant, dispensation, (**Old, New T~**, divisions of the Bible concerned with Mosaic, Christian, dispensation); (*T~*) copy of the N.T.; (colloq.)

(written) statement of one's beliefs etc.; **tĕstamĕ'ntarÿ** *a.*, of or by or in a will; **tĕ'stāte** (*or* -at) *a.* & *n.* (person) who has left a valid will at death; **tĕ'stacÿ** *n.*, being testate; **tĕstā'tor** *n.*, person who has made a will, esp. one who dies testate. [L *testamentum* f. *testor* be a witness (*testis*)]

**tĕ'ster** *n.* Canopy esp. over four-poster bed. [L *testerium* (TEST²)]

**tĕ'sticle** *n.* Male organ that secretes spermatozoa etc., esp. one of pair in scrotum behind penis of man and most mammals. [L, dim. of *testis* witness (of virility)]

**tĕ'stifÿ** *v.i.* & *t.* (Of person or thing) bear witness (*to* fact, state, assertion, *against* person etc.); (Law) give evidence; affirm, declare, (one's regret etc., *that, how,* etc.); (of thing) be evidence of. [L *testificor* (*testis* witness)]

**tĕ'stim|onÿ** *n.* Evidence, demonstration; (Law) oral or written statement under oath or affirmation; declarations, statements, (*the testimony of history, of historians*); ~**ō'nïal** *n.*, certificate of character or conduct or qualifications, gift presented to person (esp. in public) as mark of esteem. [L *testimonium* (*testis* witness)]

**tĕ'st|is** *n.* (*pl.* ~**es** *pr.* -ēz). (Anat. & Zool.) Testicle. [L, = witness (cf. TESTICLE)]

**tĕ'st|ÿ** *a.* (~**ily,** ~**iness**). Irascible, short-tempered. [AF (TEST²)]

**tĕ'tanus** *n.* Bacterial disease with continous painful contraction of some or all voluntary muscles. [L f. Gk (*teinō* stretch)]

**tĕ'(t)ch|ÿ** *a.* (~**ily,** ~**iness**). Peevish, irritable, touchy. [*teche* blemish, fault]

**tête-à-tête** (tātahtā't) *n.* & *adv.* (Conversation or interview) between two persons in private (often *attrib.; a tête-à-tête lunch*). [F, lit. head-to--head]

**tĕ'ther** (-dh-). **1.** *n.* Rope, chain, halter, by which grazing animal is confined; (fig.) scope of one's knowledge, resources, etc.; **at the end of** one's ~, having reached the limit of one's abilities, resources, patience, etc. **2.** *v.t.* Tie (animal) with tether. [N]

**tĕ'tra-** *in comb.* Four; ~**chŏrd** (-k-) *n.*, 4-note half-octave scale, 4--stringed instrument; **tĕ'trăd** *n.*, group of 4; ~**gon**, plane figure with

4 sides and angles; ~**gonal** (-ă'g-) *a.*; ~**hĕ'dron** (-a-h-) *n.* (*pl.* -**ra,** -**rons**), 4-sided solid, triangular pyramid [Gk *hedra* base]; ~**hĕ'dral** (-a-h-) *a.*; ~**logÿ** (tītră'l-) *n.*, group of 4 related literary or operatic works; ~**mĕter** (tītră'm-) *n.*, (Pros.) verse of 4 measures. [Gk (*tettares* 4)]

**Teu't|on** *n.* Member of a Teutonic nation, esp. a German; ~**ŏ'nïc,** (*a.*) of Teutons, (allegedly characteristic) of Germanic peoples or languages, German, (*n.*) Germanic language. [L *Teutones,* ethnic name]

**Tex.** *abbr.* Texas.

**tĕxt** *n.* Original words of author esp. opp. to paraphrase or commentary (*not mentioned in the text*); passage of Scripture quoted, or esp. chosen as subject of sermon etc.; subject, theme; main body of book opp. to notes, pictures, etc., (in *pl.*) books prescribed for study; \*textbook; ~**'book,** (*n.*) manual of instruction, standard book in branch of study, (*a.*) accurate, exemplary; ~**'ūal** *a.* (-lly), of or in the text; *textual* CRITICISM. [F f. L (*texo* text- weave)]

**tĕ'xt|īle.** **1.** *a.* Of weaving, woven, (*textile industry, fabrics*). **2.** *n.* Woven material. **3.** ~**ure** *n.*, arrangement of threads in textile fabric, quality of a surface or substance when felt or looked at (*fine, loose, rough, texture; texture of linen, wood, bread*); ~**ural** (-kscher-, -kstür-) *a.* (-lly). [L (as prec.)]

‖**T.G.W.U.** *abbr.* Transport & General Workers' Union.

**-th, -ĕth** (after -*ty*), *suf.* forming ordinal and fractional numbers with all simple numbers from *four* onwards (see NUMERAL). [E]

**Thai** (tī) *a.* & *n.* (Native, language) of Thailand. [Thai, = free]

**thalī'domīde** *n.* Sedative drug found in 1961 to cause malformation of limbs of embryo when taken by mother early in pregnancy. [*phthalimidoglutarimide*]

**Thames** (tĕmz) *n.* ‖*Set the Thames on* FIRE; FATHER *Thames.* [river]

**than** (dhăn, *emphat.* dhăn) *conj.* introducing second member of comparison (*you are taller than he, than he is,* colloq. *than him; I know you better than he* (*does*), *better than* (*I know*) *him; would do anything rather than let this happen; than whom no one is better able to judge*) or statement of difference (*any person other than himself; not known* *elsewhere than in Britain*). [E; orig. = THEN]

**thāne** *n.* (Hist.) Holder of land from Engl. king etc. by military service, or from Sc. king and ranking below earl, clan-chief. [E]

**thănk. 1.** *v.t.* Express gratitude to (person *for* thing); ~ **God, goodness, heaven**(s), etc., (expr. pious gratitude, or colloq. relief etc.); (**I**) ~ **you** (polite formula acknowledging gift, service, accepted offer, etc.; *no,* ~ *you,* polite refusal of offer); ~ **you for nothing** (as contemptuous denial that any thanks are due); **I will** ~ **you** (usu. iron. implying reproach: *I will thank you to leave the biscuit-tin alone*); **he can, may,** ~ **himself, has only himself to** ~, **for that,** it is his fault; ~**-you** *n.*, (colloq.) expressing of thanks (*took it without a thank-you*). **2.** *n.* (in *pl.*). (Expression of) gratitude (*give thanks to Heaven*; *many thanks for your help*; *small, iron. much, thanks I got for it*; *give* ~**s,** say grace at meal; **small, no,** ~**s to,** despite; ~**s to** *my foresight, your interference,* as good or bad result of it; ~**-offering,** gift made in gratitude; ~**'sgiving,** expression of gratitude esp. to God; \***T**~**sgiving** (*Day*), 4th Thurs. in Nov. in U.S.); (as formula) thank you (esp. colloq., *thanks awfully, very much,* etc.). **3.** ~**'ful** *a.* (**-lly**), grateful, pleased, expressive of thanks; ~**'less** *a.,* not feeling or expressing thanks, (of task etc.) unprofitable. [E]

**that** *a., pron., adv.,* & *conj.* **1.** dem. *a.* & *pron.* (*pr.* dhăt; *pl.* **those** pr. dhōz). The (person, thing), the person or thing, pointed to or drawn attention to or already named or understood (*do you see that dog over there?*; *who is that* (*man*) *in the garden?*; *I heard that* (*remark*); *that's not fair*; *those were the days*); (coupled or contrasted with THIS; *would you like this apple or that* (*one*)?); **and** (**all**) **that,** and all or various associated things, and so forth; **wouldn't give** ~ (a snap of the fingers) **for it; like** ~, of that kind, in that manner, etc., (*don't talk like that*), without effort (*did it just like that*), of that character (*he wouldn't accept any payment—he is like that*); ~**'s right!** (expr. approval or colloq. assent); ~**'s** *a dear* etc., (colloq.) thank you (by your obedience etc.); ~**'s** ~ (concluding narrative or task); ~ **will do,** no more is

needed or desirable. **2.** *pron.* (replacing *the* and noun, w. sense completed by *rel. pron.* expressed or omitted, or by *a.* or equivalent: *those who drink water think water*; *hold fast that which is good*; *all those* (*that*) *I saw*; *those unfit for use*; *a dress like that described above*; *those persons most affected by the tax*). **3.** *adv.* (*pr.* dhăt; colloq.) To such a degree, so, (*will go that far*; *have done that much*); (**all**) ~, very (*not all that, not that, expensive*). **4.** *rel. pron.* (*pr.* dhăt; *pl.* same; used to introduce defining clause and often omitted; cf. WHICH, WHO: *the book* (*that, which*) *I sent you*; *the man* (*that, whom*) *you saw*; *this is all* (*that*) *I have*). **5.** *conj.* (*pr.* dhăt, *emphat.* dhăt, introducing subord. clause indicating esp. statement or hypothesis, purpose, or result, and often omitted: *they say* (*that*) *he is better*; *he lives that he may eat*; *am so sleepy* (*that*) *I cannot keep my eyes open*). [E]

**thătch. 1.** *n.* Roofing of straw or rushes; (colloq.) hair of the head. **2.** *v.t.* Roof with thatch. [E]

**thaw. 1.** *v.t.* & *i.* Release or escape from frozen state, warm into liquid state or into life or animation or cordiality. **2.** *n.* Thawing; warmth of weather that thaws. [E]

**the** (*before vowel* dhĭ, *before consonant* dhe, *emphat.* dhē). **1.** *a.* serving to describe as unique (*the Thames*; *the Queen*; ~ *Mackintosh* etc., chief of clan), or assist in defining w. *adj.* (*Alfred the Great*), or distinguish as the best-known (stressed: *do you mean the Kipling?*), or particularize as needing no further identification (*book of the year*; *I dislike the book*), or indicate following defining clause or phrase (*the horse you mention*; *the rings on her fingers*), or confer generic or representative or distributive value on (*the cat loves comfort*; *the stage,* = acting; *only 5p in the pound*), or precede *adj.* used abs. (*from the sublime to the ridiculous*; *none but the brave*). **2.** *adv.* (preceding comparatives in expressions of proportional variation) in or by that (*or* such) degree, on that account, (*the more the merrier*; *am not the more inclined to help him because he is poor*; *that makes it all the worse*; *so*[1] *much the worse for you*). [E]

**thē'atre** (-ter), \***-ter,** *n.* Building or outdoor area for dramatic performances (~**-goer, -going,** frequenter, frequenting, of theatre);

cinema; plays and acting (*is interested in the theatre*); room or hall for lectures etc. with seats in tiers (‖**operating-theatre**, see OPERATE; **~ sister**, nurse assisting at surgical operations); scene or field of action (*the theatre of war*); **theă′trĭcal**, (*a.*, **-lly**) of or for theatre or acting, (of manner, language, persons, etc.) calculated for effect, showy, (*n.*, in *pl.*) dramatic performances, esp. *amateur theatricals*; **theătrĭcă′lĭtў** *n.* [F or L f. Gk *theatron*]

**thé dansant** (tā dahṅsah′ṅ) *n.* Afternoon tea with dancing. [F]

**thee.** See THOU[1].

**theft** *n.* (Act or instance of) stealing. [E (THIEF)]

**their** (dhār) *poss. pron. attrib.*, **theirs** (dhārz) *poss. pron. pred.* (& abs.), of or belonging to them(selves) (for phrs. see HERS). [N]

**the′|ism** *n.* Belief in divine creation and conduct of the universe without denial of revelation as in DEISM; **~ist** *n.*; **~i′stĭc** *a.* (-ically). [Gk *theos* god]

**them.** See THEY.

**theme** *n.* Subject or topic (*of talk* etc.); *school exercise on given subject; (Mus.) leading melody in a composition (**~ song**, recurrent melody in musical play or film); **themă′tĭc** *a.* (Mus.; -ically). [L f. Gk *thema -mat-*]

**themse′lves** (dhemse′lvz) *pron.* Emphat. & refl. form of THEY and *them* (for use cf. HERSELF, ITSELF). [THEY, SELF]

**then** (dh-) *adv., a.,* & *n.* **1.** *adv.* At that time (*was then too busy to help*; *Sir Winston, then Mr., Churchill*; NOW *and then*); happened etc. **~ and there**, immediately and on the spot); next, after that, and also, (*and then leave it to dry*; *it is a problem but then* (after all) *that is what he is here for*); in that case, accordingly, it follows that, (*then you should have said so*; (of grudging or impatient concession) *all right then, have it your own way*; (resumptively) *the new Governor, then, came prepared*). **2.** *a.* Existing etc. at that time (*the then Duke*). **3.** *n.* That time (*before, till, by, from, then*; *every* NOW *and then*). **4. thence** (dh-) *adv.* & *n.* (arch. or literary), from or *from* that place, for that reason (*a discrepancy thence results*; *it thence appears*); **~cefor′th, ~cefor′ward**, from that time on. [E]

**the′o-** *in comb.* God or god; **theŏ′cracў** *n.*, form of government by God or god directly or through a priestly order etc.; **~cră′tĭc** *a.* (-ically). [Gk (*theos* god)]

**theŏ′dolĭte** *n.* Surveying-instrument for measuring horizontal and vertical angles with rotating telescope. [orig. unkn.]

**theŏ′logў** *n.* Study or system of (esp. Christian) religion; **theŏlŏ′gĭan** *n.*, person learned in theology; **theŏlŏ′gĭcal** *a.* (-lly), of, in, for the study of, theology. [F f. L f. Gk (THEO-)]

**the′orem** *n.* General proposition not self-evident but demonstrable by argument (esp. Math.; cf. PROBLEM); algebraical etc. rule, esp. one expressed by symbols or formulae. [F or L f. Gk (*theōreō* look at)]

**the′or|ў** *n.* Supposition or system of ideas explaining something, esp. one based on general principles independent of particular things to be explained, (*atomic theory*; *theory of evolution*); speculative (esp. fanciful) view (*one of my pet theories*); sphere of abstract knowledge or speculative thought (*this is all very well in theory*); exposition of principles of a subject etc. (*the theory of music*); (Math.) collection of propositions to illustrate principles of a subject (*probability theory*); **~e′tĭc(al)** *a.* (-ically), concerned with knowledge but not with its practical application, speculative, unpractical; **~eti′cian** (-shan) *n.*, person concerned with theoretical part of a subject; **~ist** *n.*, holder or inventor of a theory; **~ize** *v.i.*, evolve or indulge in theories. [L f. Gk (prec.)]

**theŏ′sophў** *n.* Any of various philosophies professing to achieve knowledge of God by spiritual ecstasy, direct intuition, or special individual relations, esp. one following Hindu and Buddhist teachings and seeking universal brotherhood; **theosŏ′phical** *a.* (-lly). [L f. Gk (THEOsophos wise concerning God)]

**therapeu′tic** *a.* (**~ally**). Of, for, tending to, the cure of disease; **~s** *n.pl.* (usu. treated as *sing.*), branch of medicine concerned with treatment and remedying of ill health; **the′rapў** *n.*, curative medical treatment; **the′rapĭst** *n.* [F or L f. Gk (*therapeuō* wait on, cure)]

**there** (dhār) *adv., n.,* & *int.* **1.** *adv.*

In or at that place or position (*put it there*; *put it down, in, over, under, up, there*; *do you still live there?*; ALL *there*; *neither* HERE *nor there*; ~ **and then,** = THEN *and there*; ~ **it is,** that is the (unalterable) situation; ~ **you are,** this is what you wanted; (calling attention) *hallo there!*, *move along there!*, *there goes the bell*, *there's* (= THAT's) *a dear*); in that respect, at that point, (*I agree with you there*; *there you go misquoting me again*; **so** ~, that is my final decision whether you like it or not); to that place or position (*shall not go there again*; **get** ~, sl., succeed, understand what is meant); (*pr. dher*; merely expletive or introductory, used esp. w. *be*: *there are fairies at the bottom of our garden*; *what is there for supper?*; *there was nothing in it*; *there fell a deep silence*). **2.** *n.* That place (*lives somewhere near there*; *the tide comes up to there*). **3.** *int.* expr. confirmation, triumph, dismay, reassurance, etc., (*there* (*now*), *what did I tell you?*; *there, there, never mind*). **4.** ~**about'(s),** near that place (*ought to be somewhere thereabouts*), near that number, quantity, etc., (*two litres or thereabouts*); ~**a'fter,** (formal) after that; ~**by'** (*or* -ār'-), by that means, as result of that (~*by hangs a tale*, in which connection there is something to be told); ~**'fore,** for that reason, accordingly, consequently; ~**i'n,** (formal) in that place or respect; ~**o'f,** (formal) of that or it; ~**to',** (formal) to that or it, in addition; ~**upo'n,** in consequence of that, soon or immediately after that. [E]

**therm** *n.* Unit of heat, esp. ‖statutory unit of calorific value in gas-supply (100,000 British thermal units); ~**al,** (*a.*; **-lly**) of heat (~**al unit,** for measuring heat; *British* ~*al unit*, amount of heat needed to raise 1 lb. of water 1°F.), (*n.*) rising current of heated air (used by gliders to gain height); ~**iŏ'nic** *a.* (~**ionic** ‖**valve,** *\*tube,* device giving flow of electrons in one direction from heated substance, used esp. in rectification of current and in radio reception). [Gk *thermē* heat]

**ther'mō-** *in comb.* Heat; ~**dyna'mics,** science of relations between heat and other (mechanical, electrical, etc.) forms of energy; ~**nu'clear,** relating to nuclear reactions that occur only at very high temperatures, (of bomb etc.) using such reactions; ~**pla'stic,** (substance) becoming plastic on heating and hardening on cooling; ~**se'tting,** (of plastics) setting permanently when heated; ~**stat,** device for automatic regulation of temperature; ~**sta'tic** *a.*

**thermŏ'mĕt|er** *n.* Instrument for measuring temperature, esp. graduated narrow glass tube containing mercury or alcohol; **thèrmomĕ'trĭc** *a.*; ~**rў** *n.* [F or L (prec., -METER)]

**Thĕr'mos** *n.* ~ (**flask** etc.), (brand of) vacuum flask. [P]

**thèsaur'|us** *n.* (*pl.* ~**i** *pr.* -ī). Storehouse of information, esp. dictionary or encyclopaedia; list of concepts or words arranged according to sense or chosen for use in indexing etc. [L f. Gk (TREASURE)]

**these.** See THIS.

**thĕ's|is** *n.* (*pl.* ~**es** *pr.* -ēz). Proposition to be maintained or proved; dissertation, esp. by candidate for degree. [L f. Gk, = putting]

**Thĕ'spian. 1.** *a.* Of tragedy or the drama. **2.** *n.* Actor or actress. [*Thespis*, Gk tragedian]

**Thess.** *abbr.* Thessalonians (N.T.).

**thē'ta** *n.* Eighth Gk letter (Θ, θ) = th. [Gk]

**thews** (-z) *n.pl.* (literary). Person's muscular strength. [E, = habit]

**they** (dhā) *pron.* (*obj.* them *pr.* dhem *or emphat.* dhĕm; *refl.* THEMSELVES; *poss.* THEIR, THEIRS). Pl. of HE[1], SHE, IT[1]; people in general (*they say*); those in authority (*they have raised the fees*); **them,** (colloq.) they, (vulg.) those. [N]

**thick** *a., n.,* & *adv.* **1.** *a.* Of great or specified depth (between opposite surfaces) or diameter (*bread is cut too thick*; *a board, a rope, two inches thick*; ‖**a bit** ~, sl., unreasonable, excessive in some disagreeable quality; LAY[4] *it on thick*); (of line etc.) broad, not fine; (of script, type, etc.) consisting of thick lines; arranged closely, crowded together, dense, (*thick hair, forest, fog*); packed *with* (*air thick with snow*); firm in consistency, containing much solid matter, muddy, cloudy, impenetrable by sight, (*thick paste, soup, puddles, weather, darkness*); stupid, dull; (of voice) indistinct; (colloq.) intimate (*thick as thieves*; *those two are very thick with each other*). **2.** *n.* Thick part of anything; **in the** ~ **of it, of things,** in busiest part of fight, activity, etc.; **through ~ and thin**, under all conditions, in spite of all difficulties. **3.** *adv.* Thickly (*snow was falling thick*; *blows came thick and fast*). **4.** ‖**~ ear**, (sl.) external ear swollen by blow; **~ head**, stupidity, muzziness; **~'head**, blockhead; **~-headed**, stupid; **~'set**, set or growing closely together, heavily or solidly built; **~-skinned**, (fig.) not sensitive to reproach or rebuff, stolid; **~-skulled, -witted**, stupid. **5. ~'en** *v.t.* & *i.*, make or become thick(er) (**the plot ~ens**, becomes more complicated); **~'ening** *n.*, (esp.) substance used to thicken gravy; **~'ĕt** *n.*, tangle of shrubs or trees; **~'nĕss** *n.*, being thick, dimension other than length and breadth, layer of material of known thickness (*three thicknesses of cardboard*). [E]

**thief** *n.* (*pl.* **-ves** *pr.* **-vz**). One who steals esp. secretly and without violence; **thieve** *v.i.* & *t.*, be a thief, steal (*thing*); **thie'verỹ** *n.*, stealing; **thie'vish** *a.*, given to stealing. [E]

**thigh** (thi) *n.* Part of leg between hip and knee. [E]

**thi'mble** *n.* Metal or plastic cap with usu. closed end, worn to protect finger and push needle in sewing; **~rig** *n.*, & *v.i.*, (play) swindling sleight-of-hand trick with three thimble-shaped cups, one of which covers a pea; **~rigger**, sharper conducting this; **~ful** (-beĺfool) *n.*, (esp.) small quantity (*of spirits etc.*) to drink. [E (THUMB)]

**thin** *a.*, *adv.*, & *v.* **1.** *a.* (**-nn-**; **~'ness** *pr.* **-n-n-**). Having opposite surfaces close together, of small thickness or diameter, (*thin card, ice, string*); not dense or copious (*thin haze, hair*); of slight consistency (*thin paste, gruel*); lacking an important ingredient (*thin beer, blood, humour, voice*); (fig., of disguise, excuse, etc.) flimsy, transparent; lean, not plump; (of line) narrow, fine, (of script, type, etc.) consisting of fine lines; (sl.) wretched, uncomfortable, (*have a thin time*); **~ air**, (fig.) condition of invisibility or non-existence (*appear out of, disappear into, thin air*); **~ on the ground**, few in number; **~ on top**, balding; **~-skinned**, (fig.) sensitive to reproach or rebuff; **through** THICK **and thin**. **2.** *adv.* Thinly (*cut the bread very thin*). **3.** *v.t.* & *i.* (**-nn-**). Make or become thin(ner); **~ out**, remove some (plants) so as to give others more room for growth; **~'ner** *n.*, (esp.) volatile liquid used to make paint etc. thinner. [E]

**thine.** SEE THY.

**thing** *n.* Any possible object of thought including persons, material objects, events, qualities, circumstances, ideas, utterances, and acts (*take that thing away*; *platinum is a costly thing*); expr. contempt, pity, affection etc., esp. of person: *poor thing, you spiteful thing, a dear old thing*; *a foolish thing to do, a big thing to undertake, that's not the same thing at all, made a mess of things*; **and ~s**, colloq., and the like; **do the** *decent* etc. **~ by**, treat decently etc.; **do ~s to**, affect remarkably; **for one ~**, as one of several reasons; **have a ~ about**, colloq., be obsessed or prejudiced about; **know a ~ or two**, be experienced or shrewd; **make a ~ of**, regard as essential, cause a fuss about; **not a ~**, nothing (*did not mean a thing to me*); **one of those ~s**, something unavoidable; SEE[1] *things*; **the ~**, what is conventionally proper or fashionable, what is needed or required, what is in question (*for the fun, the look, of the thing*), what is most important (*the thing is, what shall we do about it?*); specimen, type of work, etc., (*the latest thing in hats*; *a little thing of mine that you might like to hear*); one's special interest or concern (esp. colloq. *do one's own thing*); (colloq.) something remarkable (*now there's a thing!*); (in *pl.*) personal belongings, (esp. outer) clothing, equipment, the world in general (*not in the nature of things*), (w. following *a.*, often joc.) all that is so describable (*things Japanese*); **~'umajïg, ~'ummỹ**, etc., *ns.*, (colloq.) person or thing whose name one forgets or does not know. [E]

**think. 1.** *v.t.* & *i.* (**thought** *pr.* **thawt**). Consider, be of opinion, (*we think* (*that*) *he will come*; *is thought to be a fraud*; *what do you think of, about, my idea?*; **I do'n't ~**, sl. addition to ironical statement: *she's a model of tact, I don't think*); intend, expect, (*thinks to deceive us*), (colloq.) remember (*did not think to lock the door*); form conception of (*cannot think the infinite*; colloq., *I can't think how you do it*); recognize presence or existence of (*child thought no harm*); reduce to specified condition by thinking (*cannot think away a toothache*); exercise the mind (*let me think for a moment*; ~ **for** oneself, have independent mind); have half-formed intention (*I think I'll try*); ~ **about**, consider, esp. consider practicability of (scheme, do*ing*); ~ **again**, revise one's plans or opinions; ~ **aloud**, utter one's thoughts as soon as they occur; *think* BIG, FIT²; ~ **of**, consider, be aware of, imagine, propose to oneself, entertain the idea of, hit upon, (~ *better of*, decide on second thoughts to abandon (intention); ~ *little* or *nothing of*, treat as insignificant or contemptible; ~ *much*, *a lot*, *well*, *highly*, *of*, esteem); ~ **out**, consider carefully, devise (plan etc.); ~ **over**, reflect upon in order to reach decision; ~ **through**, reflect fully upon (problem etc.); ~ **twice**, use careful consideration, avoid hasty action etc.; ~ **up**, (colloq.) devise, produce by thought. **2.** *n.* (colloq.) Act of thinking (*must have a think about that*); ~**-tank**, organization providing advice and ideas on national and commercial problems. **3.** ~'**er** *n.*, (esp.) one who thinks in specified way (*original thinker*), person with skilled or powerful mind; ~'**ing**, (*n.*, esp.) opinion, judgement (**put on** one's ~**ing-cap**, meditate on a problem; **to my** (**way of**) ~**ing**, in my opinion, (*a.*, esp.) thoughtful, intellectual. [E]

**thiosŭ'lphāte** *n.* Sulphate in which some oxygen is replaced by sulphur. [Gk *theion* sulphur]

**thĭrd** *a.* & *n.* NUMERAL; ~ **class** (next after second in accommodation, examination-list, etc.); *third* DEGREE, ESTATE; ~ **man**, (Crick.) fieldsman beyond slip(s) and point; ~ **party**, another party besides the two principals, bystander etc., (~-*party insurance*, against damage or injury suffered by person other than the insured); ~ **person**, = *third party*, (Gram.) see PERSON; ~**-rate**, inferior, very poor; *Third* REICH; T~ **World**, developing countries of Asia, Africa, and Latin America; ~**lў** *adv.* [E (THREE)]

**thĭrst. 1.** *n.* Suffering caused by lack of drink; desire for a drink; (fig.) ardent desire, craving, (*of*, *for*, *after*, glory, person's blood, etc.). **2.** *v.i.* Feel thirst, be thirsty, (fig. *for*, *after*, or arch. lit.). **3.** ~'**ȳ** *a.* (~**ily**, ~**iness**), feeling thirst, (of

country or season) dry, parched, (fig.) eager (*for*, *after*), (colloq.) causing thirst (*thirsty work*). [E]

**thĭrtee'n** (or thĕr'-) *a.* & *n.* NUMERAL; ~**th** *a.* & *n.*; **thĭr'tў** *a.* & *n.*, NUMERAL (**Thirty-nine Articles**, assented to by person taking orders in Church of England); **thĭr'tĭĕth** *a.* & *n.*; **thĭr'tўfōld** *a.* & *adv.* [E (THREE)]

**thĭs** (dh-). **1.** *dem. a.* & *pron.* (*pl.* **these** *pr.* dhēz). The (person, thing), the person or thing, close at hand or touched or indicated or already named or understood (*observe this dog lying here*; *whose are these* (gloves)?; *what flower is this?*; *fold it like this*; *this isn't fair*; *things are easier* (in) *these days*); (of time) the present (day, etc.; *I am busy all this week*; *should have been ready before this*; *this morning*, i.e. of today); (colloq., in narrative) a previously unspecified (*then up comes this policeman*); ~ **and that**, various ones, various things; ~, **that, and the other**, various things; ~ **much**, this amount, esp. = what I am about to state (*this much I do know, he's left home*). **2.** *adv.* (colloq.) To this degree, so, (*knew him when he was this high*); so as to correspond to the present time, place, etc., (*not likely to get this far*). [E]

**thĭ'stle** (-sel) *n.* Prickly composite herbaceous plant usu. with globular heads of purple flowers; (figure of this as) Scottish national emblem; **Order of the T~**, Scottish order of knighthood; ~**down**, DOWN² containing thistle-seeds, esp. w. ref. to its lightness; **thĭ'stlў** (-slĭ) *a.*, overgrown with thistles. [E]

**thĭ'ther** (dhĭ'dh-) *adv.* (arch.) To(wards) that place. [E]

**thōle** *n.* ~(**-pin**), pin in gunwale of boat as fulcrum for oar; each of two such pins forming rowlock. [E]

**thŏng** *n.* Narrow strip of hide or leather. [E]

**thŏr'ă**|**x** *n.* (*pl.* ~**ces** *pr.* -asēz, ~**xes**). (Anat. & Zool.) Part of trunk between neck and abdomen; **thŏră'cĭc** *a.* [L f. Gk]

**thŏrn** *n.* Stiff sharp-pointed process on plant (**a** ~ **in** one's **flesh** or **side**, a constant annoyance; **on** ~**s**, in anxiety and suspense); thorn-bearing shrub or tree; ~'**ȳ** *a.* (~**ily**, ~**iness**), abounding in thorns, (fig., of subject) hard to handle without offence. [E]

**tho'rough** (thŭ'ro) *a.* Complete,

unqualified, not superficial, (*his work is seldom thorough*; *caught a thorough chill*; *a thorough scoundrel*); thorough (= *figured*) BASS³; ~**bred** *a.* & *n.*, (animal, esp. horse, or fig. person) of pure breed, high-spirited; ~**fare**, road or path open at both ends esp. for traffic; *no* ~*fare*, (as notice) no public right of way; ~**going**, uncompromising, extreme; ~**paced**, (lit., of horse) trained to all paces, (fig.) complete, unqualified, (*a thoroughpaced rascal*). [THROUGH]

**those.** See THAT.

**thou¹** (dh-) *pron.* of 2nd pers. sing. (*obj.* thee *pr.* dhē; *poss.* THY, thine; *pl.* YE¹, YOU) now replaced by YOU (exc. in addressing God, in Quaker use, and in arch., poet., or dial. use). [E]

**thou²** *n.* (colloq.; *pl.* ~**s, ~**). Thousand(th). [abbr.]

**though** (dhō). **1.** *conj.* Notwithstanding the fact that (*though it was late, late though it was, we decided to start*); ellipt. *though annoyed, I agreed*); (even) on the supposition that (*it is better to ask him (even) though he refuse or refuses*; *as* ~, *as* IF; **what** ~, arch., what does it matter if *the way be long?*); and yet, nevertheless, (*I have no doubt he will understand—though you never know*; *she read on, though not to the very end*). **2.** *adv.* (colloq.) However, all the same, (*I wish you had told me, though*). [N]

**thought¹** (thawt) *n.* Process or power or manner of thinking, faculty of reason, sober reflection, consideration, (*give* ~ *to*, consider; *take* ~, consider matters; **have, take, no** ~ **for**, neglect, not heed; **in** ~, meditating; **quick as** ~, very quick); idea, conception, reasoning, intention, etc., produced by thinking (*an essay full of striking thoughts*; *had some thoughts of resigning*; *my one thought was how to escape*; **a happy** ~, a well-timed or apposite idea or suggestion; SECOND *thoughts*); (usu. in *pl.*) what one is thinking, one's opinion(s), (*tell me your thoughts on the matter*; *you are always in my thoughts*; *a* PENNY *for your thoughts*); **a** ~, a little, somewhat, (*cut it a thought shorter*); ~**-reader, -reading**, (person capable of) direct perception of what another is thinking, ~**-transference**, telepathy; ~'**ful** *a.* (-**lly**), engaged in or given to meditation, (of book, writer, etc.) giving signs of original

thought, (of person or conduct) considerate (*of*); ~'**less**, careless of consequences or of others' feelings, caused by lack of thought. [E (THINK)]

**thought².** See THINK.

**thou'sand** (-z-) *a.* & *n.* (*pl.* ~, ~**s**). NUMERAL (for pl. usage see HUNDRED); **one in a** ~, (fig.) a rare or excellent one; **(a)** ~ **(and one)**, (fig.) myriad, numberless, (*the thousand and one small worries of life*); **a** ~ *thanks, pardons*, etc., (polite forms of emphasis); ~**fold** *a.* & *adv.*; (-)~**th** *a.* & *n.* [E]

**thral|l** (-awl) *n.* (literary). Slave (*of, to*, person or thing, lit. or fig.); bondage (*in thrall*); ~'**dom** *n.*, bondage. [N]

**thrash** *v.t.* & *i.* = THRESH (corn etc.); beat, esp. with stick or whip, conquer, surpass; (of paddle-wheel, branch, etc.) act like flail, deliver repeated blows; move violently *about* or *around* (*in* water etc.); ~ **out**, arrive at, obtain, (truth etc.) by repeated trial, discuss (problem etc.) exhaustively. [E]

**thread** (-rĕd). **1.** *n.* (Length of) spun-out cotton, silk, glass, etc., yarn, thin cord of twisted yarns used esp. in sewing and weaving, (**has not a dry** ~ **on him**, is wet through; **hang by a** ~, fig. of person's life or momentous issue etc., be in precarious or still undecided state; ~'**bare**, (of cloth) so worn that nap is lost and threads are visible, (of person) wearing such clothes, (fig.) hackneyed); (fig.) anything regarded as threadlike w. ref. to its continuity or connectedness (*the thread of life, a narrative, an argument*); spiral ridge of screw; ~'**worm**, threadlike intestinal nematode. **2.** *v.t.* Pass thread through (needle's eye, beads); arrange (material in strip form, e.g. film) in proper position on equipment; pick one's way through (maze, crowded place, etc.), make one's *way* thus. [E (THROW)]

**threat** (-rĕt) *n.* Intimidatory declaration of intention to punish or hurt; indication of proximity of something undesirable (*there is a threat of rain*); ~'**en** *v.t.*, use threats towards (person etc., or abs., *with* harm etc.; *threatened me with death*; *am threatened with a visit*), give warning of infliction of (harm etc., or abs.), announce one's intention (*to* do) as punishment or in revenge etc., (*threatens terrible torments, to resign; fig., clouds threaten* (*rain, to interrupt us,* etc.); *the practice threatens to become general*). [E]

**three** *a.* & *n.* NUMERAL; RULE *of three*; ~**-card trick** (in which bets are made on which is the queen among 3 cards lying face downwards); *three* CHEERS; ~**-cornered**, triangular, (of contest etc.) between 3 parties each for himself; ~**-decker**, warship with 3 gun-decks, sandwich with 3 slices of bread, 3-volume novel; ~**-dimensional**, having or appearing to have length, breadth, and depth; ~**-handed** *a.* (esp. of card-game) for 3 players; T~ **in One**, the Trinity; ~**-legged race** (-gd-, -gĭd-), race between pairs with right leg of one tied to other's left leg; ‖*three-line* WHIP; ~ **parts**, ¾; ‖~**pence** (-ĕ'p-, -ĭ'p-, -ŭ'p-), sum of 3 pence; ‖~**penny** (same pr.), costing or worth 3 pence; ‖~**penny** (**bit**) (same pr.), former coin worth 3d.; ~**-ply** *n.* & *a.*, (wool etc.) having 3 strands, (plywood) having 3 layers; ‖~**-point turn**, method of turning vehicle round in narrow space; ~**-quarter(s)**, of ¾ of normal size or numbers, (of portrait) going down to hips or showing ¾ of face; ~**-quarter**, (Rugby Footb.) any of 3 or 4 players just behind half-backs; *three* Rs; ~**'score**, (arch.) 60 (~*score and ten*, age of 70 as normal limit of life); ~**-way**, involving three ways or participants (*resulted in a three-way tie*); ~**'fŏld** *a.* & *adv.*; ~**'some** *n.*, group or party of 3 persons. [E]

**thrĕ'nŏdy** *n.* (Song of) lamentation esp. on person's death. [Gk]

**thrĕsh** *v.t.* & *i.* Beat out or separate grain from (corn etc.) with flails etc. on hard level ~**'ing-floor**, or by power-driven machinery (~**'ing-machine**); = THRASH (3rd sense). [THRASH]

**thrĕ'shŏld** *n.* Plank or stone forming bottom of doorway and crossed in entering house etc.; (fig.) point of entry (*on the threshold of a revolution, of a new century*); limit below which stimulus causes no reaction. [E (THRASH in sense 'tread')]

**threw.** See THROW.

**thrice** *adv.* (arch., literary). Three times; (esp. in *comb.*) highly (*thrice-blessed*). [THREE]

**thrĭft** *n.* Frugality, economical management; the sea-pink; ~**lĕss** *a.*, wasteful; ~**y** *a.* (-ily, -iness), economical. [N (THRIVE)]

**thrĭll. 1.** *n.* Wave or nervous tremor of emotion or sensation (*a thrill of joy, of recognition*); throb, pulsation. **2.** *v.t.* & *i.* Penetrate (person etc.) with, be penetrated by, thrill of emotion or sensation, (of emotion) pass *through, over, along*; quiver, throb, (as) with emotion. **3.** ~**'er** *n.*, (esp.) sensational or exciting play, story, etc. [E, = pierce, rel. to THROUGH]

**thrĭps** *n.* Kind of small insect injurious to plants. [L f. Gk, = woodworm]

**thrive** *v.i.* (**throve** *pr.* -ōv, ~**d**; **thri'ven** *pr.* -ĭ'ven, ~**d**). Prosper, flourish; grow rich; (of animal or plant) grow vigorously. [N]

**throat** *n.* (Front part of neck containing) windpipe, gullet, (CLEAR one's *throat*; **cut** person's ~, slash this esp. with intent to kill by severing jugular vein; **cut one's own** ~, fig., bring about one's own downfall; **cut one another's** ~s, fig., compete ruinously; JUMP *down* person's *throat*; **give** person **the lie in his** ~, accuse him of lying grossly; **ram, thrust, down** person's ~, force (thing) on his attention; **sore** ~, inflammation of lining membrane of gullet etc.; STICK[1] in one's *throat*; **take by the** ~, try to throttle); narrow passage or entrance or exit; ~**'y** *a.* (~**ily**, ~**iness**), (of voice) deficient in clarity, hoarsely resonant. [E]

**thrŏb. 1.** *v.i.* (**-bb-**). (Of heart, temples, etc.) palpitate, pulsate esp. with more than usual force or rapidity; (fig.) quiver, vibrate, (as) with emotion or with persistent rhythm. **2.** *n.* Throbbing; palpitation, (esp. violent) pulsation. [imit.]

**throe** *n.* (usu. in *pl.*) Violent pang(s), esp. of childbirth or death, or fig. of authorship etc.; **in the** ~s, (colloq.) struggling with the task of (*spring-cleaning* etc.). [E, alt. of orig. *throwe* perh. by assoc. w. *woe*]

**thrŏmb|ō'sĭs** *n.* (*pl.* ~**oses** *pr.* -ō'sēz). Coagulation of blood in blood-vessel or organ during life; ~**ŏ'tĭc** *a.* [L f. Gk, = curdling]

**throne. 1.** *n.* Chair of state for sovereign, bishop, etc.; sovereign power (*came to the throne; lost his* throne). **2.** *v.t.* Enthrone (lit. or fig.). [F f. L f. Gk]

**throng. 1.** *n.* Crowd of people; multitude (*of* people, things) esp. in small space. **2.** *v.i.* & *t.* Come in great numbers; flock into or crowd round or fill (as) with crowd. [E]

**thrŏ'stle** (-sel) *n.* (esp. poet. or dial.) Song-thrush. [E]

**thrŏ'ttle. 1.** *n.* Throat, gullet, windpipe; ~(-**valve**), valve controlling flow of steam, fuel, etc., in engine; ~(-**lever**), lever etc. operating this valve. **2.** *v.t.* Choke, strangle; prevent utterance etc. of; control (steam etc., engine) with throttle--valve; ~ **back, down,** reduce speed of (engine, vehicle) thus. [THROAT]

**through, *thru,** (-rōō) *prep., adv.,* & *a.* **1.** *prep.* From end to end or side to side of, between the sides or walls or parts of, (*marched through the town; blade went through his hand; look through a telescope, the window; swam through the waves; read through the whole book;* fig. *went through many trials, got through her examinations; I saw through his hypocrisy; flashed through his mind*); by reason or agency or means or fault of (*came about through a misunderstanding; concealed it through shame; it's through you that we're late*); *up to and including (Monday through Friday).* **2.** *adv.* Through a thing, from side to side or end to end or beginning to end, (*would not let us through; ice gave and I fell through; read it through carefully*); ~ **and** ~, thoroughly, completely; **be** ~, have finished (*with*), cease to have dealings (*with*), have no further prospects, be connected to desired telephone etc.; ~'**put,** amount of material put through a manufacturing etc. process. **3.** *a.* (Concerned with) going through, esp. of travel where whole journey is made without change of line or vehicle etc. (*through carriage, train*) or with one ticket; (of traffic) going through a place to its destination; **no** ~ **road,** = *no* THOROUGHfare. **4.** ~**ou't,** (*adv.*) in every part or respect (*timber was rotten throughout*), (*prep.*) right through, from end to end of, (*throughout the 18th century*). [E]

**thrŏve.** See THRIVE.

**throw** (-ō). **1.** *v.t.* & *i.* (**threw** *pr.* -ōō; ~**n**). Release (thing) after imparting motion, propel through

space, send forth or dismiss esp. with some violence, (fig.) compel to be in specified condition, (*threw the ball at the stumps, threw him the ball; mortars throw shells; threw himself down, on his knees; ship was thrown on the rocks; was thrown into prison, upon his own resources;* ~ **good money after bad,** incur further loss in hopeless attempt to recoup previous loss; ~ oneself **at,** blatantly seek as spouse, friend, etc.; ~ oneself **into,** engage vigorously in; ~ oneself (**up**)**on,** attack, put one's reliance on; *throw* STONES); project (rays, LIGHT[1] lit. or fig.); (Crick.) bowl (ball) with illegal jerk by straightening elbow; cast (shadow, spell); (of wrestler) bring (antagonist) to the ground, (of horse) unseat (rider), colloq.) disconcert (*his question threw me for a moment*); put (clothes etc.) carelessly or hastily *on, off, over* one's *shoulders,* etc.; (of animal) give birth to (young); cause (dice) to fall on table etc., obtain (specified number) thus; twist (silk etc.) into yarn or thread; shape (round pottery) on wheel; turn, direct, move esp. quickly (esp. part of body), (*threw a glance backwards, her head up*), cause to pass or extend suddenly to another state or position (*throw army or bridge across river; throw switch to 'on'*); *lose (contest, race, etc.) intentionally; have (fit, tantrum, etc.), (sl.) give (a party). **2.** *n.* Act of throwing; distance a missile is or may be thrown (*record throw with the hammer; a STONE's throw*); being thrown in wrestling. **3.** ~ **about, around,** throw in various directions, spend (one's money) ostentatiously, make vigorous use of (one's WEIGHT; lit. or fig.); ~ **away,** (fig.) part with unwanted, lose by neglect, waste, discard (card), (Theatr.) speak (lines) with deliberate under--emphasis; ~-*away* a. & n., (thing) to be thrown away after (one) use, deliberately under-emphasized; ~ **back,** revert to ancestral character, (usu. in *pass.*) compel to rely *on*; ~-*back* n., (instance of) reversion to ancestral character; ~ **down,** cause to fall; *throw down the* GAUNTLET[1] or *glove;* ~ **in,** (esp.) add as makeweight, interpose (word, remark), throw (football) from edge of pitch where it has gone out of play; ~ one's

**hand in,** (lit.) abandon one's chances in card-game esp. poker, (fig.) give up, withdraw from contest; ~ in one's **lot with,** decide to share fortunes of; ~ **off,** discard (clothes, acquaintance, disguise), contrive to get rid of (illness, companion), produce or deliver (poem, epigram) in off hand manner; *throw* OPEN; ~ **out,** put out forcibly or suddenly, reject (proposal, bill in Parliament), (Crick., Baseball) put out (batsman etc.) by throwing ball to wicket or base; ~ **over,** desert, abandon; ~ **together,** assemble hastily, bring into casual contact; ~ **up,** lift (sash-window) quickly, erect (building), bring to notice, renounce (task), resign (office), vomit; ~ **up** one's **eyes** (as sign of pious horror etc.); *throw up the* SPONGE. [E, = twist]

**\*thru.** See THROUGH.

**thrum**[1] *n.* Unwoven end of warp-thread, or the whole of such ends, left when finished web is cut away; any short loose thread. [E]

**thrum**[2] **1.** *v.t. & i.* (**-mm-**). Play monotonously or unskilfully on or *on* (guitar, harp, etc.); drum, tap, idly on or *on* (table etc.). **2.** *n.* Such playing; resulting sound. [imit.]

**thrush**[1] *n.* Kind of small bird, e.g. blackbird, nightingale; *song-~*, common kind noted for singing. [E]

**thrush**[2] *n.* Fungoid infection of throat esp. in children, or of vagina. [orig. unkn.]

**thrust. 1.** *v.t. & i.* (thrust). Push with sudden impulse or with force (lit. or fig.); *thrust the letter into his pocket; I thrust out my hand; some have greatness thrust upon them; any objection was thrust aside;* ~ one**self,** one's **nose, in,** obtrude, interfere); pierce (person etc.) *through,* make sudden lunge *at* (person etc., *with* dagger etc.); make one's *way* by force, force oneself *through, past,* etc. **2.** *n.* Sudden or forcible push or lunge; forward force exerted by propeller, jet, etc.; strong attempt to penetrate enemy's line or territory; remark aimed at a person; stress between parts of arch etc. [N]

**thud** *v.i.* (**-dd-**), & *n.* (Make, fall with) low dull sound as of blow on non-resonant thing. [E]

**thug** *n.* Vicious or brutal ruffian; (*T~*; Hist.) member of religious organization of robbers and assassins in India; *~***gerў** (**-g-**) *n.,* brutal behaviour. [Hindi]

**thumb** (**-m**). **1.** *n.* Short thick finger set apart from and opposable to the other 4 (RULE *of* thumb; *like a* SORE *thumb*; *~***s down,** gesture of rejection; *~***s up!,** sl. excl. of satisfaction; **under** person's ~, completely dominated by him); part of glove for thumb. **2.** *v.t. & i.* Wear, soil, (pages etc.) with thumb, turn over pages (as if) with thumb, (*a well-thumbed novel; thumbed through the directory*); use thumb in gesture; ~ **a lift,** (try to) get lift in passing vehicle by indicating desired direction with thumb; ~ one's **nose,** cock a SNOOK (*at*). **3.** *~***-index** *n.,* & *v.t.,* (provide with) set of lettered grooves cut or tabs fixed in fore-edge of dictionary etc. to assist use; *~***-nail sketch,** small or hastily done portrait, brief word-picture; *~***-print,** impression of thumb esp. as used for identification; *~***'screw,** instrument of torture for squeezing thumbs; *~***-stall,** cover like finger-stall to protect thumb; *~***-sucking** (esp. as infant's habit); *\*~***'tack,** drawing-pin. [E]

**thump. 1.** *v.t. & i.* Beat or strike heavily esp. with fist; deliver blows *at, on,* etc. **2.** *n.* Heavy blow, bang. **3.** *~***'er** *n.,* (esp., colloq.) large or impressive person or thing; *~***'ing** *a.,* (colloq.) big (*a thumping majority, lie,* etc.). [imit.]

**thu'nder. 1.** *n.* Loud noise heard after lightning and due to disturbance of air by discharge of electricity; (fig.) resounding loud deep noise (*thunders of applause*); (in *sing.* or *pl.*) authoritative censure or threats; **steal** person's ~, (fig.) forestall him; *~***bolt,** flash of lightning with crash of thunder, imaginary bolt or shaft as destructive agent esp. as attribute of god; *~***box,** primitive lavatory; *~***clap** (esp. fig. or in simile, of sudden terrible event or news); *~***-cloud,** storm-cloud charged with electricity and producing thunder and lightning; *~***storm** (with thunder and lightning and usu. heavy rain or hail); *~***struck,** struck by lightning, (fig.) amazed. **2.** *v.i. & t.* Give forth thunder (esp. *it thunders, is thundering*); make noise like thunder (*voice thundered in my ears*); move with loud noise (*train thundered past*); make violent threats etc. *against* etc.; utter (threats etc.) loudly. **3.** ~**ing** *a*. & *adv*., (colloq.) very big or great, very, (*a thundering nuisance*; *a thundering great fish*); ~**ous** *a*., as loud as thunder; ~**y** *a*., (of weather etc.) oppressive. [E]

**thur′ible** *n*. Censer. [F or L (*thus thur-* incense)]

**Thur(s).** *abbr.* Thursday.

**Thur′sday** (-z-; *or* -dǐ). **1.** *n*. Day of week, following Wednesday; HOLY *Thursday*. **2.** *adv.* (cf. FRIDAY 2). [E]

**thŭs** (dh-) *adv.* (formal). In this way, in the way (to be) indicated; accordingly, as a result or inference; to this extent, so, (*thus far*; *thus much*); ~**′nĕss** *n*., (joc.) state of being thus. [E]

**thwăck** *v.t.*, & *n*. Hit esp. with stick. [imit.]

**thwart** (-ôrt). **1.** *v.t.* Frustrate, foil, (person, wish, purpose). **2.** *n*. Rower's seat. [N, = across]

**thy̆** (dhi) *poss. pron. attrib.* (now replaced by YOUR exc. as described at THOU[1]). Of thee (in *pred.* & *abs.* use, & usu. bef. vowel, **thine**): *thy lips*; *the fault is thine*; *thine eyes*; for phrs. see HER, HERS. [THOU[1]]

**thy̆m|e** (tim) *n*. Herb with fragrant aromatic leaves (*garden, lemon, wild, thyme*); **thy̆′mŏl** *n*., antiseptic made from oil of thyme; ~**′y̆** *a*. (esp. of scent). [F f. L f. Gk]

**thy̆′mus** *n*. (Anat.) Organ near base of neck. [L f. Gk]

**thy̆r′oid** *a*. & *n*. (Anat. & Zool.) ~ **cartilage**, large cartilage of larynx, projection of which in man forms Adam's apple; ~ (**gland**), large ductless gland near larynx, secreting a hormone which regulates growth and development, extract from this gland of animals used in treating goitre etc. [F or L f. Gk (*thureos* oblong shield)]

**thy̆sĕ′lf** (dh-) *pron.*, emphatic. & refl. form of THOU and THEE (for use cf. HERSELF). [E (THEE, SELF)]

**ti.** See TE.

**tiăr′a** *n*. Pope's three-crowned diadem; jewelled ornamental band worn on front of woman's hair; ~**′d** *a*. [L f. Gk]

**ti′bĭa** *n*. (*pl.* ~**e**). (Anat.) Shin-bone; ~**l** *a*. [L]

**tĭc** *n*. Habitual spasmodic contraction of muscles esp. of face; kind of neuralgia. [F f. It.]

**tĭck**[1]. **1.** *n*. Slight recurring click, esp. that of watch or clock (‖**on the** ~, with exact punctuality); ~**-tack**, kind of manual semaphore signalling by racecourse bookmakers; *~**-tack--toe**, noughts and crosses; ~**-tock**, ticking of large clock etc.); ‖(colloq.) moment, instant; small mark set against items in list etc. in checking. **2.** *v.i.* & *t.* (Of clock etc.) make ticks; mark (item, usu. *off*) with tick; ~ **off**, (sl.) reprimand; ~ **over**, (of engine or fig.) idle; **what makes** person ~, his motivation. [imit.]

**tĭck**[2] *n*. Parasitic arachnid or insect on animals. [E]

**tĭck**[3] *n*. Cover of mattress or pillow; ticking. [LDu., ult. f. Gk *thēkē* case]

**tĭck**[4] *n*. (colloq.) Credit (*buy goods on tick*). [app. abbr. TICKET in *on the ticket*]

**ti′cker** *n*. (colloq.) Watch, tape-machine; (joc.) heart; *~**-tape**, paper strip from tape-machine, esp. as thrown from windows to greet a celebrity. [TICK[1]]

**ti′ckĕt.** **1.** *n*. Written or printed piece of paper or card entitling holder to enter place, participate in event, travel by public transport, etc., (*theatre, library, lottery, railway, cloak-room, -ticket*); certificate of discharge from army or of qualification as ship's master, pilot, etc.; label attached to thing and giving price etc.; official notification of traffic offence etc. (*parking ticket*); *(Polit.) list of candidates put forward by party, (fig.) principles of a party; **the** ~, (sl.) the correct or desirable thing. **2.** *v.t.* Attach ticket to. [obs. F *étiquet*]

**ti′cking** *n*. Stout usu. striped linen or cotton material to cover mattresses etc. [TICK[3]]

**tĭckl|e.** **1.** *v.t.* & *i.* Apply light touches or stroking to (person, part of his body, or abs.) so as to excite nerves and usu. produce laughter and spasmodic movement, feel this sensation, (~**e** person's **ribs**, fig., cause him great amusement); excite agreeably, amuse, divert, (person, his sense of humour, fancy, vanity, etc.; ~**ed pink** or **to death**, colloq., extremely amused etc.); catch (trout) by stroking with the hand. **2.** *n*. Act or sensation of tickling, **3.** ~**ish** *a*., sensitive to tickling, (of matter, person, to be dealt with) difficult, requiring careful handling. [prob. dial. *tick* touch or tap lightly]

**ti′dal.** See TIDE.

**\*ti′dbit.** See TITBIT.

‖**ti′ddler** *n.* (childish or colloq.) Small fish, esp. stickleback or minnow; unusually small thing. [perh. rel. to *tiddly* 'little']

‖**ti′ddly** *a.* (sl.) Slightly drunk; **~-wink** *n.*, counter flicked by another into cup etc. on centre of table in game of **~-winks.** [orig. unkn.]

**tide. 1.** *n.* Periodical rise (**flood-~**) and fall (**ebb-~**) of sea due to attraction of moon and sun, water as moved by this, (**~ is in, out,** water is at high, low, level; **high, low, ~,** completion of flood, ebb, -tide; **spring, neap, ~,** tide of maximum, minimum, height; **~-mark,** mark made by tide at high water, colloq. line of dirt around bath, or on body of person showing extent of washing; **~′way,** tidal part of river); (fig.) trend of opinion or fortune or events (*go with, against, the tide*; **the ~ turns,** events take new direction; **turn the ~,** reverse trend of events); time, season, (arch. exc. in *comb.*: noontide, *Christmastide*). **2.** *v.i.* & *t.* Be carried by the tide; (enable or assist to) get *over* (difficulty etc., or abs.). **3.** **ti′dal** *a.* (**-lly**), of or due to or like or affected by the tide (**tidal wave,** exceptionally large ocean wave e.g. one attributed to earthquake, fig. widespread manifestation of feeling etc.). [E, = time]

**ti′dings** (-z) *n.* (literary; as *sing.* or *pl.*) (Piece of) news, information. [N]

**ti′dy** *a., n.,* & *v.* **1.** *a.* (**-ily, -iness**). Neat, orderly, methodically arranged; (colloq.) considerable (*cost a tidy sum*). **2.** *n.* Cover for chair-back etc.; receptacle for odds and ends. **3.** *v.t.* **~ (up),** make (room etc., one*self*, or abs.) neat, put in good order. [TIDE; orig. = timely]

**tie. 1.** *v.t.* & *i.* (**ty′ing** *pr.* ti′-i-). Attach or fasten with cord etc. (*together, back, down,* etc.), form (ribbon, string, necktie, shoe-lace, etc.) into knot or bow, restrict (person etc.) *to* or *down to* conditions or place (*FIT to be tied*); **~ and dye, ~-dye,** method of producing dyed patterns by tying string etc. to protect parts of fabric from dye; **~ in, up,** (cause to) agree or be closely associated *with*; **~ up,** fasten with cord etc.,

obstruct, make (money etc.) not immediately available esp. by annexing conditions to its use); bind (rafters etc.) by cross-piece etc.; (Mus.) unite notes by tie; make tie with or *with* (competitor; *for* place or prize); ‖(in *p.p.*) of (public house, etc.) bound to supply only a particular brewer's liquor, (of dwelling-house) occupied subject to tenant's working for house's owner. **2.** *n.* Cord, chain, etc., used for fastening; necktie (‖OLD *school tie*; **~-clip, -pin,** to hold tie in place); (fig.) thing that unites or restricts persons (*ties of blood, friendship*); **~-beam, -piece, -rod,** rod or beam holding parts of structure together; **\*rail sleeper;** (Mus.) curved line above or below two notes of same pitch that are to be joined as one; equality of score or draw or dead heat among competitors (**~-break,** deciding winner among such competitors); match between any pair of players or teams. [E]

**tier** *n.* Row or rank or unit of structure, as one of several placed one above another (*tiers of seats*); **~ed** (tērd) *a.* (*three-tiered wedding cake*). [F *tire* (*tirer* draw, elongate)]

**tier′cel.** See TERCEL.

**tiff** *n.* Slight or petty quarrel. [orig. unkn.]

**ti′ffin** *n.* (Ind.) Lunch. [obs. *tiff* take small drink]

**ti′ger** (-g-) *n.* Large Asian striped carnivorous maneless feline; fierce or energetic person, (colloq.) formidable opponent in game; **paper ~,** threatening but ineffectual person or thing; **~-cat,** any moderate-sized feline resembling tiger, e.g. ocelot; **~(′s)-eye,** yellow-brown gem of brilliant lustre; **~-lily,** tall garden lily with dark-spotted orange flowers; **~-moth** (with richly spotted and streaked wings); **ti′gress** *n.,* female tiger. [F f. L f. Gk]

**tight** (tīt) *a., n.,* & *adv.* **1.** Closely held or drawn or fastened or fitting or constructed (*tight knots*; *cork is too tight*; *tight joint, ship*); impermeable, impervious, esp. (in *comb.*) to specified thing (*airtight, watertight*); tense, stretched (**~′rope,** one on which acrobats etc. perform); (colloq.) drunk; (of money or materials) not easily obtainable; produced by, requiring, great exertion or pressure (*a tight squeeze*), (of precautions, programme, etc.) stringent, demanding, (~ **corner, place,** colloq. **spot,** fig., difficult situation); ~**(-fisted),** stingy; ~**-lipped,** with lips compressed to restrain emotion or speech. 2. *n.* (in *pl.*) Thin close-fitting elastic garment worn by dancer, acrobat, etc., to cover legs and lower half of body; similar garment worn by women in place of stockings. 3. *adv.* Tightly (*hold tight; tight-fitting*). 4. ~'**en** *v.t.* & *i.* (~en one's *belt,* go without food, lit. or fig.). [N]

**ti'gress.** See TIGER; **tike,** see TYKE.

**ti'lde** (-*e*, -ā) *n.* Mark (~) put over letter, e.g. Spanish *n* when pronounced *ny* (so *señor*); swung dash. [Sp. f. L (TITLE)]

**tile. 1.** *n.* Thin slab of baked clay for roof, pavement, drain, etc., or (glazed) for hearth, wall, etc.; **have a ~ loose,** (sl.) be slightly crazy; **on the ~s,** (sl.) on a debauch. 2. *v.t.* Cover etc. with tiles. [E f. L *tegula*]

**till¹. 1.** *prep.* Up to, as late as (specified time; *wait till evening, 5 o'clock, then*); up to the time of (expected event; *was true till death; waited till the end, till his arrival*). 2. *conj.* Up to the time when (*ring till you get an answer; walk on till you come to the gate*), so long that (*laughed till I cried*). [N, rel. to TILL³]

**till²** *n.* Money-drawer in counter of bank, shop, etc. [orig. unkn.]

**till³** *v.t.* Cultivate (land); ~'**age** *n.,* preparation of land for crop-bearing, tilled land. [E, = strive]

**ti'ller** *n.* Bar by which rudder is turned. [AF *telier* weaver's beam]

**tilt¹. 1.** *v.i.* & *t.* (Cause to) assume sloping position from vertical or horizontal, heel over, (*table is apt to tilt; tilt the cask so as to drain it*); strike, thrust, run, *at* weapon, engage in contest *with.* 2. *n.* Tilting; sloping position; (of medieval knights etc.) charging with lance against opponent or mark (*go etc.* **full ~,** at full speed, with full force); **have a ~ at,** assail with argument or satire. [E (*adj.*) = unsteady]

**tilt²** *n.* Awning of cart. [obs. *tild,* perh. alt. after TENT¹]

**tilth** *n.* Tillage, cultivation (lit. or fig.); soil tilled. [E (TILL³)]

**Tim.** *abbr.* Timothy (N.T.).

**ti'mber** *n.* Wood prepared for building, carpentry, etc.; piece of wood, beam, esp. (Naut.) as rib of vessel (SHIVER² *my timbers*); large

standing trees; (esp. as *int.*) tree about to fall; ~**line** (above which no trees grow); ~**wolf,** large N. Amer. grey wolf; ~**ed** (-*ĕrd*) *a.,* made (partly) of timber, (of country) wooded. [E, = building)]

**timbre** (tă̄br, tă̄'mbĕr) *n.* Distinctive character of musical sound or voice apart from its pitch and intensity; **ti'mbrel** *n.,* (arch.) tambourine. [F f. Rom. f. Gk (TYMPANUM)]

**time. 1.** *n.* The successive states of the universe regarded as a whole in which every state is either before or after every other, indefinitely continued existence, progress of this as affecting persons or things, (*will stand for all time; has stood the test of time*); more or less definite portion of time belonging to particular events or circumstances (*in the time of Victoria; prehistoric times; at a time like this*); allotted or available portion of time (*had no time to discuss it; waste no more time; will last for a time; gave him time to pay*); lifetime (*will last my time*); prison sentence (*is doing time*); apprenticeship (*served his time*); moment or definite portion of time destined or suitable for a purpose (*now is the time to act; it is time (that) I was going*); period of gestation, date of childbirth or death; (in *sing.* or *pl.*) conditions of life or of a period (*hard times; times have changed; went through a bad time;* **have a ~ of it,** undergo trouble or difficulty; **have a good ~,** enjoy oneself); occasion (*the first or only time (that) I saw it; wait till next time; have told you time* AFTER *time, many a time, many times;* expr. multiplication: *three times four is twelve; is three times as big as mine*); (amount of) time as reckoned by conventional standards (*time allowed is one hour; it is 7 a.m. New York time*); point of time esp. in hours and minutes (*what is the time?; the time is 4.15*); measured time spent in work (*workmen on* SHORT *time*); (Mus.) duration of note, style of movement depending on beats in bar, rate of performance. 2. **against ~,** with utmost speed so as to finish by specified time; **ahead of ~,** earlier than expected; **ahead of** one's ~, too enlightened for one's contemporaries; ALL *the* time; *six at a* ~, in groups of six; **at no ~,** never; **at one ~,** in a known but unspecified past period, simultaneously; **at the**

same ~, at a time which is the same for both or all, nevertheless; **at ~s**, intermittently; **before** (one's) ~, = *ahead of* (one's) *time*; BETWEEN *times*; FROM *time to time*; GAIN *time*; **in** GOOD *time*; **half the** ~, (colloq.) as often as not; **have no ~ for**, be unwilling or unable to spend time on, dislike; **have the** ~, be able to spend time needed, know what the time is; **in** ~, not late, early enough (*to do*, *for* thing), sooner or later, in accordance with time of music etc.; **in one's** ~, at some previous period of life; **in one's own** ~, outside working hours, at rate decided by oneself; **keep** ~, walk, sing, etc., in time, (of clock etc.) record time (accurately); **lose** ~, waste time *in doing* or *on* thing; MAKE *time*; **no** ~, (colloq.) very short interval; **on** ~, in accordance with timetable; **out of** ~, too late, not in time; **play for** ~, seek to gain time by delay; TAKE (one's) *time*; **the** ~(**s**), the age now or then present (BEHIND *the times*); **The T~s**, as name of newspaper); **what** ~, (poet., arch., joc.) while, when. **3.** **~ and** (**~**) **again**, on many occasions; **~ and a half** (of work paid for at 1½ times normal rate); **~-and-motion**, concerned with measuring efficiency of industrial etc. operations; **~ bomb** (designed to explode at set time after being dropped or placed); **~-consuming**, using or wasting much time; **~ enough**, soon enough (*for* purpose, *to* do), there is no hurry; **~ exposure** (of photographic film for longer than an instant); **~ factor**, passage of time as limiting what can be achieved; **~-honoured**, venerable by antiquity, traditional; *time* IMMEMORIAL; **~'keeper**, watch or clock in respect of accuracy, one who records time esp. of workmen or in game; **~-lag**, time interval between cause and effect; **~-limit** (within which thing must be done); **~ of day**, hour by clock (*know the* ~ *of day*, be well informed; *pass the* ~ *of day*, colloq., exchange greeting or casual remarks); **~ off** or *\*out*, time used for rest or different activity; **~ of one's life**, period of exceptional (pleasant or unpleasant) excitement; *time out of* MIND; **~'piece**, time-measuring instrument; **~-scale**, sequence of events as measure of historical etc. duration; **~-server**,

one who adapts himself to opinions of the times or of persons in power; **~-sharing**, use of computer by several persons at same time; **~-signal**, visible or audible announcement of exact time of day; *time* SIGNATURE; **~-switch** (acting automatically at set time); **~'table**, scheme of school work etc., table showing times of public transport services; **~ was**, there has been a time *when*; *time* ZONE. **4.** *v.t.* Choose time for, do at chosen or correct time; arrange time of arrival of; ascertain time taken by; **ti'mer** *n.*, person or device that measures time taken. **5.** **~less** (-ml-) *a.*, (rhet.) not affected by passage of time; **~'ly** (-mlĭ) *a.* (-iness), opportune, coming at right time. [E]

**ti'mĭd** *a.* (**~er**, **~est**). Easily frightened, apprehensive; **timi'dĭtў** *n.*; **ti'morous** *a.*, timid, frightened. [F or L (*timeo* fear)]

**ti'mpan|ŏ** *n.* (usu. in *pl.* **~i** *pr.* -ē). Kettledrum; **~ĭst** *n.* [It., = TYMPANUM]

**tin. 1.** *n.* White metal used esp. in alloys and for coating sheet iron and sheet steel to form **~ plate** as material for containers, kitchen utensils, toys, etc.; ‖vessel of tin or tin plate esp. for preserving food; ‖(sl.) money. **2.** *v.t.* (**-nn-**). Cover or coat with tin; ‖pack (food) in tin for preservation. **3.** **~ foil** (made of tin, aluminium, or tin alloy, and used to wrap food for cooking, keeping fresh, etc.); **~ god**, object of unjustified veneration; **~ hat**, (Army sl.) modern soldier's steel helmet; ‖**~-opener**, tool for opening tins; **~-pan alley**, world of composers and publishers of popular music; **~'pot** *a.*, (derog.) cheap, inferior; **~'smith**, worker in tin and tin-plate; **~ soldier** (toy made of tin etc.); **~-tack**, tinned iron tack; **~ whistle**, = *penny* WHISTLE. **4.** **~nў** *a.* (-ily, -iness), (esp.) sounding like struck tin. [E]

**ti'ncture. 1.** *n.* Medicinal solution *of* drug in alcohol (*tincture of quinine*); slight flavour, smack, (*of* thing, fig. *of* moral quality etc.), tinge (*of* colour). **2.** *v.t.* Colour slightly, tinge, flavour; (fig.) affect slightly (*with* quality). **3.** **tincto'r'ial** *a.* (-lly), of or for dyeing. [L (TINGE)]

**ti'nder** *n.* Dry substance readily

taking fire from spark; ~-box (containing tinder, flint, and steel, for kindling fires); ~ӯ a. (-iness). [E]

**tine** n. Prong or tooth or point of fork, comb, antler, etc. [E]

**tinge** (-nj). 1. v.t. Colour slightly (with; often fig., tinged with envy). 2. n. Tendency to or trace of some colour; slight admixture of a feeling or quality. [L tingo tinct- dye]

**ti'ngle** (-nggel). 1. v.i. Feel slight pricking or stinging or throbbing sensation esp. in ears or hands; cause this (the reply tingled in his ears). 2. n. Tingling sensation. [TINKLE]

**ti'nker.** 1. n. Itinerant mender of kettles, pans, etc. (don't care a ~'s cuss, damn, at all); (Sc. & Ir.) gipsy; (colloq.) mischievous person or animal. 2. v.i. Work as tinker or in amateurish or clumsy fashion at or with (thing) by way of repair or alteration. [orig. unkn.]

**ti'nkle.** 1. n. Sound (as of small bell; ||give person a ~, (colloq.), telephone him. 2. v.i. & t. Make, cause (bell) to make, tinkle. [imit.]

**ti'nny.** See TIN.

**ti'nsel** n. Glittering decorative metallic strips, threads, etc.; (fig.) superficial brilliance or splendour; (attrib.) showy, gaudy, flashy; ~led (-ld) a. [F estincele f. L SCINTILLA]

**tint.** 1. n. A variety of a colour, esp. made by adding white; tendency towards, admixture of, a different colour (red of, with, a blue, bluish, tint); faint colour spread over surface. 2. v.t. Apply tint to, colour (lit. or fig.). [tinct TINGE]

**tintinnābūlā'tion** n. Ringing or tinkling of bells. [L]

**ti'n|y̌** a. (~ily, ~iness). Very small or slight. [orig. unkn.]

**-tion.** See -ION.

**tip¹.** 1. n. Extremity, end, esp. of small or tapering thing (the tips of the fingers; tip of a cigarette, of a bird's wing; **on the ~ of** one's **tongue**, just about to be said, or remembered and spoken); leaf-bud of tea; small piece or part attached to end of thing, e.g. ferrule, leather cap on billiard--cue, cork filter on cigarette. 2. v.t. (-pp-). Furnish with tip. 3. ~'staff, (metal-tipped staff as badge of) sheriff's officer; ~-tilted, (of nose) turned up at tip; ~'toe, (n.) the tips of the toes, (adv.) on tiptoe, with heels off the ground, (v.i.) walk (as if) on tiptoe; ~'top (or -ŏ'p), (n.) highest

point of excellence, (a. & adv.) excellent(ly). [N]

**tip².** 1. v.t. & i. (-pp-). (Cause to) lean or slant (over, up, etc.; tip the SCALE²); overturn or cause to overbalance (into etc.), ||discharge (contents of truck, jug, etc., out, into, etc.) thus, (~'cat, short piece of wood struck with stick, game with this; ~-up, able to be tipped, e.g. of seat as used in theatres etc. to allow of free passing); strike or touch lightly (||~ and run, form of cricket in which batsman must run if bat touches ball); (sl.) throw lightly, give, communicate (esp. information), in informal manner (~ person off, give him warning, hint, or inside information; ~-off n., a hint; ~ person the wink, give him private information or warning); make usu. small present of money to (esp. for service given). 2. n. Slight push or tilt; light stroke; ||place where material (esp. refuse) is tipped; private or special information about horse-racing, stock-market, etc., (STRAIGHT tip), piece of advice, (~'ster n., one who gives tips); small money present esp. for service. [perh. Scand.; partly f. prec.]

**ti'ppet** n. Covering of fur etc. for the shoulders worn by women and as part of some official costumes. [orig. unkn.]

**ti'pple.** 1. v.i. & t. Drink intoxicating liquor habitually; drink (liquor) repeatedly in small amounts. 2. n. (colloq.) (Esp. strong) drink.

**ti'ps|y̌** a. (~ily, ~iness). Slightly intoxicated; caused by or showing intoxication (a tipsy lurch); ~y-cake, sponge-cake soaked in wine or spirits and served with custard. [TIP²]

||**TIR** abbr. Transport International Routier (F, = international road transport).

**tirā'de** (or tĭr-) n. Long vehement denunciation or declamation. [F f. It.]

**tire¹.** 1. n. Band of metal placed round rim of wheel to strengthen it; * = TYRE; (arch.) head-dress, attire. 2. v.t. Place tire on (wheel); (arch.) adorn (hair), dress. [ATTIRE]

**tire²** v.t. & i. Make or grow weary; exhaust patience or interest of, bore; (in p.p.) having had enough of (thing, doing), exhausted with, (fig.) hackneyed; ~'less (-īr'l-) a., of inexhaustible energy; **tīr'esome**

(-īr's-) a., wearisome, tedious, (colloq.) annoying. [E]

**tīr′ō, tȳr′ō,** (pl. ~s). Beginner, novice. [L, = recruit]

**'tis** (-z) (arch. or poet.) It is. [contr.]

**ti′ssue** (or -shōō) n. Fine woven esp. gauzy fabric; (fig.) interwoven series, set, (of lies etc.); (Biol.) any of the coherent substances of which animal or plant bodies are made (muscular, nervous, tissue); ~(-paper), thin soft unsized paper for wrapping etc.; (paper) ~, disposable piece of thin soft absorbent paper for wiping, drying, etc. [F tissu p.p. of tistre weave f. L (TEXT)]

**tit**[1] n. = TITMOUSE; blue ~ (with bright blue tail, wings, and top of head); COAL-tit; ~′lark, kind of pipit. [abbr.]

**tit**[2] n. ~ for tat, blow for blow, retaliation. [= TIP[2] for tap]

**tit**[3] n. (vulg.) Nipple; (in pl.) woman's breasts. [E]

**Tit.** abbr. Titus (N.T.).

**Ti′tan** n. (Gk Myth.) member of a gigantic race; person of superhuman size, intellect, strength, etc.; **titā′nic** a. (-ically), (esp.) gigantic, colossal; **titā′nium** n., grey metallic element. [L f. Gk]

**ti′tbit, *ti′db-,** n. Dainty morsel; piquant item of news etc. [dial. tid delicate]

‖**ti′tfer** n. (sl.) Hat. [abbr. TIT[2] for tat, rhyming sl.]

**tithe** (-dh). **1.** n. (Hist.) tax of one-tenth, esp. tenth part of annual produce of land or labour taken for support of clergy and church (~**barn**, built to hold tithes paid in kind); (rhet.) tenth part (not a tithe of). **2.** v.t. Subject to tithes. [E, = tenth]

**Ti′tian** (-shan) a. (Of hair) bright golden auburn, as often painted by Titian. [person]

**ti′tillāte** v.t. Tickle, excite pleasantly; ~ā′tion n. [L]

**ti′tiv|āte** v.t. (colloq.) Adorn, smarten, put finishing touches to, (oneself etc., or abs.); ~ā′tion n. [earlier tid-, perh. f. TIDY after cultivate]

**ti′tle** n. Name of book or work of art, heading of chapter, poem, document, etc.; (contents of title-page of) book; caption, CREDIT title, of film; form of nomenclature indicative of person's status (queen, judge,

professor, duchess, baron, lord, knight, M.A.) or used in addressing or referring to person (Lord, Lady, Mr., Mrs., Miss, Doctor, Her Majesty, Your Grace); championship in sport (a Wimbledon title; title-fight); (Law) right to ownership of property with or without possession, facts constituting this, just or recognized claim (to); ~**-deed**, legal instrument as evidence of right; ~**-page**, page at beginning of book giving particulars of subject, authorship, publication, etc.; ~**-role**, part in a play that gives name (e.g. Othello); **ti′tled** (-teld) a., having title of nobility or rank. [F f. L titulus]

**ti′t|mouse** n. (pl. ~**mice**). Kind of small active bird. [E tit little, mose titmouse, assim. to MOUSE]

**ti′tr|āte** (or -ā′t) v.t. Ascertain amount of constituent in (substance) by using standard reagent; ~**ā′tion** n. [F (titre title)]

**ti′tter. 1.** v.i. Laugh covertly, giggle. **2.** n. Such laugh. [imit.]

**ti′ttle** n. Small written or printed stroke or dot; particle, whit, (esp. not one jot or tittle). [L (TITLE)]

**ti′ttle-tāttle** n., & v.i. (Engage in) petty gossip. [redupl. TATTLE]

**ti′ttup. 1.** v.t. Go friskily or jerkily, bob up and down, canter. **2.** n. Such gait or movement. [imit.]

**ti′tular** a. Held by virtue of a title (titular possessions); relating to a title (titular hero of a book); ~ **saint**, after whom church is named); existing, that is such, only in name (titular sovereignty); ~ **bishop**, R.C. bishop of former Christian see esp. in now Muslim countries). [F (TITLE)]

**ti′zzy** n. (sl.) State of nervous agitation (in a tizzy). [orig. unkn.]

**T.N.T.** abbr. trinitrotoluene.

**to** (to bef. consonant, tŏŏ bef. vowel, emphat. tōō). **1.** prep. introducing noun (of place, time, person, thing, condition, quality, etc.) expr. what is reached or touched (fall to the ground; fight hand to hand; rotten to the core; to the value of £10) or approached (‖five minutes to six; face to face) or aimed at (throw it to me; on my way to the theatre) or followed (made to order; very much to the purpose) or regarded (with a view to securing; hold it to the light; accustomed to that) or affected (give to the poor; it is nothing to me; talking to himself; unkind to her) or caused or produced (do to death;

*found to his dismay; tear to pieces*) or compared (*equal to the occasion; nothing to what it might be; ten* etc. *to one*, cf. NUMERAL) or increased (*add one to another*) or included or involved (**to all eternity**, for ever; **that's all there is to it**, it's that and nothing more); introducing infinitive that is subject (*to err is human*) or object (*I like to think so*) or complement (*was seen to fall*) or in apposition (*have the honour to be*) or adjectival (*has nothing to do; the first to arrive*) or adverbial expr. purpose (*we eat to live*), consequence (*wise enough to know*), cause (*am sorry to hear*), limitation or relation (*good to eat*; *awoke to find her gone*; to *be honest, I can't face it*), etc.; as substitute for *to*+infinitive (*meant to call but forgot to; but you promised to*); BE *to*. **2.** *adv.* To or in normal or required position or condition, esp. to stand-still (HEAVE *to*); (of door) just not shut. **3. to and fro**, backwards and forwards, repeatedly, between same places; **to-do′** *n.*, bustle, fuss. [E]

**toad** *n.* Froglike amphibian breeding in water but living chiefly on land; repulsive person; ∼′**flax**, a yellow-flowered plant; ∼-**in-the--hole**, sausages or other meat baked in batter; ∼′**stool**, (esp. poisonous) fungus with round top and slender stalk; ∼′**y̆**, (*n.*) sycophant, obsequious hanger-on, (*v.t.* & *i.*) behave servilely (*to*), fawn upon; (contr. *toad-eater*) ∼′**y̆ism** *n.* [E]

**toast. 1.** *n.* Bread slice(s) browned on both sides by heat (*sardines* etc. **on** ∼, laid on it and served; **have person on** ∼, sl., at one's mercy; **as warm as** ∼, glowing with warmth; ∼-**rack**, for holding slices of toast at table); person (Hist. esp. woman) or thing in whose honour company is requested to drink, call to drink or instance of drinking thus, (∼-**master**, person announcing toasts at public dinner). **2.** *v.t.* & *i.* Brown, cook, (bread, teacake, cheese, etc.) by heat, warm (one's feet, one*self*) at fire etc.; drink to the health or in honour of; ∼′**ing-fork** (with long handle, for making toast); ∼′**er** *n.*, (esp.) electrical device for making toast. [F *toster* roast f. L (TORRID)]

**toba′cco** *n.* (*pl.* ∼s). ∼(-**plant**), plant of Amer. origin with narcotic leaves used for smoking, chewing, or snuff; its leaves esp. as prepared for smoking etc.; *tobacco*-PIPE;

∼-**pouch** (for carrying small quantity of tobacco); **toba′cconĭst** *n.*, dealer in tobacco, esp. by retail. [Sp. *tabaco*, of Amer. Ind. orig.]

**tobŏ′ggan. 1.** *n.* Long light narrow sledge for going downhill esp. over prepared snow or ice. **2.** *v.i.* Ride on toboggan. [Can. F f. Algonquian]

**tŏ′by̆** *n.* ∼ (**jug**), jug or mug in form of old man with three-cornered hat. [fam. form of name *Tobias*]

**tocca′ta** (-kah′-) *n.* (Mus.) Composition for keyboard instrument designed to exhibit performer's touch and technique. [It., = touched]

‖**Tŏc H** (-ā′ch) *n.* Society with many branches for Christian fellowship and service. [*toc* = signallers' former name for letter *T*, + *H*, for *T*albot *H*ouse, soldiers' club started 1915 in memory of G. *T*albot]

**tŏ′csĭn** *n.* (Bell rung as) alarm--signal. [F *touquesain*, *toquassen* f. Prov., ult. rel. to TOUCH, SIGN]

‖**tŏd**[1] *n.* (dial.) Fox. [orig. unkn.]

‖**tŏd**[2] *n.* (sl.) **On** one's ∼, alone, on one's own. [perh. *on* one's *Tod Sloan*, rhyming sl.]

**to(-)day′** *adv.* & *n.* (On) this present day; nowadays, (in) modern times. [E]

**tŏ′ddle. 1.** *v.i.* Walk with small child's short unsteady steps; (colloq.) take casual or leisurely walk, depart. **2.** *n.* Toddling walk; (colloq.) stroll. **3.** ∼**r** *n.*, (esp.) child just learning to walk. [orig. unkn.]

**tŏ′ddy̆** *n.* Drink of spirit with hot water and sugar; (fermented liquor from) palm-tree sap. [Hindi, = palm]

**tōe. 1.** *n.* One of terminal members of foot (*toe-nail*; **the light fantastic** ∼, joc., dancing; **on** one's ∼**s**, alert, eager; **turn up** one's ∼**s**, sl., die; ∼-**cap**, reinforced part of shoe covering toes; ∼-**hold**, slight foothold, lit. or fig.); corresponding part of animal or bird; part of footwear that covers toes; lower end or tip of implement etc. **2.** *v.t.* Touch with toe(s) (esp. *the line*, *mark*, before start of race; ∼ **the line**, fig., conform esp. under pressure to requirements of one's party). [E]

‖**tŏff** *n.* (sl.) Distinguished, or well--dressed fashionable, person. [perh. TUFT in arch. sl. sense 'titled undergraduate']

**tŏ′ffee** (-fǐ) *n.* Sweetmeat made by boiling sugar, butter, etc.;

‖small piece of this; *can't shoot* etc. *for* ~, (sl.) is incompetent at shooting etc.; ~**-apple**, toffee-coated apple on stick; ‖~**-nose(d)**, (sl.) snob(bish), pretentious (person). [orig. unkn.]

**tŏg** (sl.) **1.** *n.* (usu. in *pl.*) Garment. **2.** *v.t.* Dress (person, one*self*, *out* or *up*). [app. orig. cant & ult. rel. to L TOGA]

**tō'ga** *n.* Ancient Roman citizen's loose flowing outer garment; ~'**d**, ~**ed** (-ad), *adjs.* [L]

**togĕ'ther** (-gĕ'dh–) *adv.* In company or conjunction (*walking together*; *were at school together*); simultaneously (*both exclaimed together*); one with another (*fighting together*); into conjunction, so as to unite, (*sew them together*; *put* TWO *and two together*); into company or companionship; (colloq.) well organized or controlled; uninterruptedly (*he could talk for hours together*); ~ **with**, as well as, and also. [E (TO, GATHER)]

**tŏ'ggle** *n.* Device for fastening with cross-piece which can pass through hole or loop in one position but not in another; ~**-switch**, electric switch with projecting lever to be moved usu. up and down. [orig. unkn.]

**toil. 1.** *v.i.* Work laboriously or incessantly (*at*, *on*, *through*, task); make slow painful progress (*up* hill, *through* book, *along*, etc.). **2.** *n.* Severe labour, drudgery; ~**less** (-l-l-) *a.*; ~**some** *a.*, involving toil. [AF *toil(er)* dispute]

**toi'let** *n.* Process of washing oneself, dressing, etc., (*make* one's *toilet*; *attrib. toilet soap*; ~**-set**, of utensils for the toilet; ~**-table**, dressing-table usu. with looking-glass; ~ **water**, scented liquid used after washing); (arch.) (style of) dress, costume; (room containing) lavatory (~**-paper**, for use in lavatory; ~**-roll**, of toilet-paper; ~**-training**, of young child to use lavatory); ~**ries** (-ĭz) *n. pl.*, articles used in making one's toilet. [F *toilette* dim. of *toile* cloth]

**toils** (-z) *n. pl.* Net, snare, (lit. or fig.). [*toil* f. F (prec.)]

**Tokay'** *n.* A sweet Hungarian wine. [place]

**tō'ken** *n.* Indication, thing serving as symbol or reminder or keepsake or distinctive mark or guarantee (*as a token of*, *in token of*, *my affection* or *esteem*; **by this** or **the same** ~,

similarly, moreover, in corroboration of what I say); anything used to represent something else, esp. money; voucher exchangeable for goods; (*attrib.*) perfunctory (*token effort*); ~ **payment**, payment of small proportion of sum due as indication that debt is not repudiated, nominal payment; ~ **resistance**, ~ **strike**, (brief, to demonstrate strength of feeling only); ~ **vote**, Parliamentary vote of money in which the amount stated to allow discussion is not meant to be binding; ~**ism** *n.*, making of only a token effort, or granting only minimum concessions. [E]

**tōld.** See TELL.

**tŏ'ler|āte** *v.t.* Allow the existence or occurrence of without authoritative interference, leave unmolested, not be harmed by, find or treat as endurable, (*tolerate polygamy*, *infringement of copyright*, *penicillin*, *slang*, *crude colours*, *bores*); ~**able** *a.* (-bly), not beyond endurance, fairly good; ~**ance** *n.*, willingness or ability to tolerate, forbearance, permissible variation in dimension or weight; ~**ant** *a.*, disposed or accustomed to tolerate others or their acts or opinions, enduring or patient *of*; ~**ā'tion** *n.*, (esp.) allowing of differences in religious opinion without discrimination. [L *tolero*]

**tōll**[1] *n.* Charge payable for permission to pass barrier or use bridge, road, market, etc., (~**-bar**, **-gate**, preventing passage until toll is paid; ~**-road**, maintained by tolls collected on it); (fig.) cost or damage necessarily and regrettably caused by disaster or incurred in achievement (**take its** ~, be accompanied by loss, injury, etc.). [E f. L *toloneum* f. Gk (*telos* tax)]

**tōll**[2]. **1.** *v.t.* & *i.* Sound with slow uniform succession of bell-strokes (*for* death or dead person), ring (knell) or strike (hour) or announce or mark (death etc.) thus. **2.** *n.* Tolling or stroke of bell. [orig. (now dial.) = entice, pull]

**tolū'** (or tō'-) *n.* Fragrant brown balsam from S. Amer. tree; **tŏ'luĕne**, **tŏ'lŭŏl**, *ns.*, colourless aromatic liquid hydrocarbon derivative of benzene, orig. got from tolu, used in manufacture of explosives etc. [place]

**tŏm** *n.* ~**-(-cat)**, male cat; PEEP[1]*ing Tom*; ~'**boy**, wild romping girl;

**Tom, Dick, and Harry,** (usu. derog.) persons taken at random, ordinary people, *every* ordinary person; ~**foo′l,** (*n.*) fool, (*a.*) extremely foolish; ~**foo′lery,** foolish behaviour or ornamentation; **Tom Thumb,** legendary dwarf, any diminutive person; ~**′tit,** titmouse, esp. blue tit. [abbr. of name *Thomas*]

**tŏ′mahawk** (-a-h-) *n.* N. Amer. Indian war-axe (*BURY the tomahawk*). [Renape]

**toma′tŏ** (-ah′-) *n.* (*pl.* ~**es**). (Plant bearing) glossy red or yellow pulpy edible fruit. [F f. Mex. *tomatl*]

**tomb** (toōm) *n.* A grave; burial-vault; sepulchral monument; **the** ~, state of death; ~**′stone** (standing or laid over grave, usu. with epitaph). [AF *tumbe* f. L f. Gk]

**tŏ′mbola** (or -bō′-) *n.* Kind of lottery resembling bingo. [F or It.]

**tōme** *n.* Large book or volume. [F f. L f. Gk (*temnō* cut)]

**tŏ′mmy** *n.* (Usu. *T*~) British private soldier [*T*~ *Atkins,* orig. *Thomas Atkins,* name used in specimens of completed official forms]; ~**-bar** (for use with spanner that fits over nut); ~**-gun,** Thompson sub-machine-gun; ~**-rot,** (sl.) nonsense. [TOM]

**to(-)mŏ′rrow** (-ō) *adv.* & *n.* (On) the day after today; the (near) future; **like there's no** ~, (sl.) with complete disregard of future needs. [TO, MORROW]

**tŏ′m-tŏm** *n.* Primitive drum beaten with the hands. [Hindi *tamtam,* imit.]

**ton**[1] (tŭn) *n.* Measure of weight, **long** ~ (2240 lb.) **or short** ~ (2000 lb.) **or metric** ~ (1000 kg.); unit of measurement for ship's tonnage; (colloq.) large number or amount (*tons of people, love, money*); **weighs (half) a** ~, is very heavy); ‖(sl.) £100, speed of 100 m.p.h. (~**-up boys,** motor-cyclists who travel at such speeds); ~**′nage** *n.,* ship's internal cubic capacity or freight-carrying capacity, charge per ton on cargo or freight; ~**ne** (tŭn, tŭ′nĭ) *n.,* metric ton [F]. [diff. sp. of TUN]

**ton**[2] (tawn) *n.* Prevailing mode, fashion; fashionable style or society. [F]

**tōne. 1.** *n.* Sound, esp. w. ref. to pitch, quality, and strength; modu-lation of voice to express emotion, sentiment, etc., (*impatient, bantering, suspicious, tone*); corresponding style in writing; (Mus.) musical sound, esp. of definite pitch and character (~**-deaf,** unable to perceive these accurately), ‖interval of major second, e.g. C–D; prevailing character of morals, sentiments, etc., in a group (*lower the tone of the nation etc.; tone of the market is confident; set the tone with a dignified speech*); general effect of colour or of light and shade in picture, tint or shade of colour; (Med.) proper firmness of bodily organs, state of (good) health. **2.** *v.t.* & *i.* Give desired tone to, modify tone of, attune (*to*); be in harmony (esp. of colour) *with*; ~ **down,** lessen emphasis or vigour of, undergo such lessening; ~ **up,** provide with or receive higher tone or greater vigour. **3. tŏ′nal** *a.* (-lly); **tonă′litу** *n.,* (esp.) relationship between tones of a musical scale, colour-scheme of picture. [F f. L f. Gk *tonos* (*teinō* stretch)]

**tŏngs** (-z) *n. pl.* **(Pair of)** ~, two-limbed instrument for grasping and holding esp. substances that should not be touched (*fire-tongs,* for coal; HAMMER *and* tongs); **would not touch** (repulsive person or thing even) **with a pair of** ~. [E]

**tongue** (tŭng) *n.* Fleshy muscular organ in mouth used in tasting, licking, swallowing, and (in man) speech (**put out one's** ~, as grimace or for medical inspection; **with** one's ~ **hanging out,** thirsty or fig. eager; ~**-tied,** having speech impediment due to malformation of tongue, fig. too shy to speak; ~**-twister,** sequence of words difficult to pronounce quickly and correctly); faculty of, tendency in, speech (*has a ready, fluent, sharp, tongue*); **have, speak with,** one's ~ **in** one's **cheek,** speak insincerely or with sly irony; **keep a civil** ~ **in** one's **head,** avoid rudeness; **have lost, find,** one's ~, be too bashful or surprised to speak, recover power of speech after this; **give** ~, (of hounds) bark esp. on finding scent, (of person) speak loudly; *on the* TIP[1] *of* one's *tongue*; **hold** one's ~, be silent); language of nation etc. (*the German tongue*); one's **native,** MOTHER, *tongue*; **gift of** ~**s,** power of speaking unknown languages, esp. as miraculously conferred on early Christians, Acts 2); tongue of ox etc. as food; thing like tongue in shape, e.g. long low promontory, strip of leather protecting instep from laces etc. of shoe, clapper of bell, pin of buckle; (-)~d (tŭngd) a. [E]

**tŏ'nic. 1.** a. (~ally) (Of medicine, medical treatment, etc., or fig. of success, misfortune, punishment) serving to invigorate (~ **water**, carbonated drink with quinine); (Mus.) of tones, esp. of the keynote (~ **sol-fa**, musical notation used esp. in teaching singing). **2.** n. Tonic medicine etc. (lit. or fig.); tonic water; (Mus.) keynote. [F or L (TONE)]

**to(-)nï'ght** (-nï't) adv. & n. (On) the present evening or night, (on) the evening or night of today. [E]

**tonnage, tonne.** See TON[1].

**tŏ'nneau** (-nō) n. Part of motor car that contains the back seats. [F, lit. cask]

**tŏ'nsil** n. Either of two small organs on each side of root of tongue; ~**lar** a.; ~**lĕ'ctomў, ~lï'tĭs,** ns. [F or L]

**tŏ'nsure** (-sher). **1.** n. Shaving of crown of head or entire head as clerical or monastic symbol; bare patch so made. **2.** v.t. Give tonsure to. **3.** tŏnsŏ'rial a. (joc.; -lly), of a barber or his work. [F or L (tondeo tons- shave)]

**tōŏ** adv. In a higher degree than is admissible or desirable for a purpose, standard, etc., (too ripe for cooking; too good to be true; too sweet for my taste; the rumour is all too true; intervals are too long; ~ **much** (of a good thing), intolerable; too MUCH for; **none** ~ **good** etc., rather less than; ~**-too** a. & adv., extreme(ly), excessive(ly)); (colloq.) very (you are too kind; am not too well today); also, as well, (take the others too; I too have suffered); moreover (achieved, too, at small cost). [stressed form of TO]

**tōŏk.** See TAKE.

**tōŏl. 1.** n. Mechanical implement, usu. held in hand, for working upon something (carpenter's tools; DOWN[3] tools; also fig.: the computer as a research tool); simple machine, e.g. lathe; person used by another merely for his own purposes; (sl.) penis. **2.** v.i. & t. Dress (stone) with chisel; impress design on (leather book-cover); (sl.)

drive, ride, (along, around, etc.) esp. in casual or leisurely manner. [E]

**tōŏt. 1.** n. (Esp. short) sound (as) of horn or trumpet. **2.** v.i. & t. Sound (horn etc.) thus; give out such sound. [imit.]

**tōŏth** n. (pl. teeth). Each of a set of hard structures in jaws of most vertebrates, used for biting and chewing, (**false, artificial,** ~, made to replace missing one); toothlike projection or thing, e.g. cog of gear-wheel, point of saw, comb, etc.; sense of taste (SWEET tooth); **armed to the teeth** (completely, elaborately); **cast, fling,** thing in person's teeth, reproach him with it; CUT one's teeth; **escape by the skin of one's teeth** (narrowly); **fight** ~ **and nail** (fiercely, with utmost effort); **get** one's **teeth into,** begin serious work on; **in the teeth of,** in spite of (opposition etc.), in opposition to (instructions etc.), directly against (the wind etc.); KICK in the teeth; **long in the** ~, old; **put teeth into,** make (law etc.) effective; **set** person's teeth on EDGE; **show** one's **teeth,** adopt threatening manner; ~**'ache,** pain in teeth; ~**-brush** (for cleaning teeth); ~**-comb,** = FINE[2]-tooth comb; ~**'paste, -powder,** (for cleaning teeth); ~**'pick,** small sharp instrument for removing food etc. lodged between teeth; **(-)~ed** (-tht) a.; ~**'ful** (-ŏŏl) n., small draught of spirits; ~**'lĕss** a., (esp.) having lost teeth by age; ~**'some** a., (of food) delicious; ~**'ў** a., having large, numerous, or prominent teeth. [E]

**tōŏ'tle** v.i. Toot gently or repeatedly; (colloq.) move casually along, around, etc. [TOOT]

**tōŏ'tsў(-wōŏtsў)** n. (joc. or childish). Foot. [orig. uncert.]

**tŏp[1]** n., a., & v. **1.** n. Highest point or part (at the ~ (of the tree), fig., in highest rank in profession; **come to the** ~, win distinction; **from** ~ **to toe,** from head to foot, completely; **on** ~, above, in superior position; **on** ~ **of,** fig., fully in command of, in close proximity to, in addition to; **on** ~ **of the world,** exuberant; **over the** ~, over parapet of trench, fig., into final or decisive state or state of excess); surface (of ground, table, etc.), upper part, cover, garment for upper part of body, (usu. in pl.) leaves etc. of plant grown chiefly for its root (*turnip tops*); (person occupying) highest rank, foremost place, (*came out (at the) top of the form*); more honourable end (*top of the table*); utmost degree, height, (*called out at the top of his voice*); (in *pl.*, *pred.*) person or thing of very best quality; (Naut.) platform round head of lower mast; || = *top* GEAR in motor vehicle. 2. *a.* Highest in position or degree or importance (*the top landing*; *singer reached her top note*; *at top speed*; *top prices paid*; *is top secret*; *was given top priority*). 3. *v.t.* (-**pp**-.) Furnish with *top* or *cap* (*cake topped with icing, hills topped with snow*); remove top of (plant) to improve growth etc., remove withered calyx of (fruit; *top and tail the gooseberries*); reach top of (hill etc.); be higher than, be superior to, surpass, be at top of (*top the list*); (Golf) hit (ball) above centre; ~ (**off, up**), put an end or a finishing touch to; ~ **out**, put highest stone on (building); ~ **up**, fill up (partly empty container). 4. ~-**boot** (having high top usu. of different material or colour); ~**brass**, (colloq.) high-ranking officers; ~'**coat**, overcoat, outer coat of paint etc.; ~ **dog**, (sl.) victor, master; ~'**drawer**, (fig.) high social position or origin; ~**dress**, apply manure or fertilizer on the top of (earth), not plough it in; ~-**flight**, in highest rank of achievement; ~ **hat**, tall silk hat; ~-**heavy**, overweighted at top and so in danger of falling (lit. or fig.); ||~-**hole**, (sl.) first-rate; ~'**knot**, knot, bow of ribbon etc., tuft, crest, worn or growing on head; ~'**mast** (or -ast) (next above lower mast); ~-**notch**, (colloq.) first-rate; ~'**side**, outer side of round of beef, side of ship above water-line; ~'**soil**, top layer of soil, opp. *subsoil*. 5. ~'**less** *a.*, without a top, (of garment) having no upper part, (esp. of woman) wearing only such garment(s); ~'**most** *a.*, uppermost, highest; ~**per** *n.*, (esp., colloq.) top hat; ||~'**ping** *a.*, (sl.) excellent. [E]

**tŏp²** *n.* Toy, usu. conical or pear-shaped, rotating on sharp point at bottom when set in motion; SLEEP *like a top.* [E]

**tŏ'păz** *n.* A gem of various colours, esp. yellow. [F f. L f. Gk]

**tōpe¹** *n.* Kind of small shark. [perh. Corn.]

**tōpe²** *v.i.* (arch.) Drink intoxicating liquor to excess, esp. habitually; **tō'per** *n.* [orig. uncert.]

**tŏ'pĭ, -pee**, (-ĭ) *n.* (Anglo-Ind.) Hat, esp. SOLA *topi.* [Hindi]

**tŏ'piarў** *a.* & *n.* (Of) art of clipping shrubs etc. into ornamental shapes. [F f. L *topia* landscape gardening f. Gk (*topos* place)]

**tŏ'pĭc** *n.* Theme for discussion, subject of conversation or discourse; ~**al** *a.* (-**lly**), dealing with esp. current or local topics. [L f. Gk (*topos* place, commonplace)]

**topŏ'graph|ў** *n.* Local geography, natural and artificial features of a district, knowledge or description of these; ~**er** *n.*, expert in topography; **tŏpŏgră'phĭc(al)** *adjs.* (-**ically**)

**topŏ'logy** *n.*, study of geometrical properties unaffected by changes of shape and size. [L f. Gk (*topos* place)]

**tŏ'pper, tŏ'pping.** See TOP¹.

**tŏ'pple** *v.i.* & *t.* (Cause to) fall (*over, down*) from vertical to horizontal position (lit. or fig.); **tŏpsy̆-tŭr'vy̆** *adv.* & *a.* (-**ily**, -**iness**), upside down, in utter confusion, (often fig.; *topsy-turvy procedure*). [TOP¹, obs. *terve* topple]

**tōque** (-k) *n.* Woman's brimless hat. [F]

**tŏr** *n.* Rocky hill-top. [E]

**tŏrch** *n.* Piece of resinous wood or twisted flax etc. soaked in tallow etc. for carrying lighted in hand; ||(**electric**) ~, electric lamp with battery in portable case; (fig.) source of heat or illumination; **carry a ~ for**, have (esp. unreturned) admiration of; **hand on the ~**, keep tradition of knowledge etc. alive. [F *torche* f. L (as TORT)]

**tŏre.** See TEAR¹.

**tŏ'reădor** *n.* Bullfighter, esp. on horseback. [Sp. (*toro* bull f. L *taurus*)]

**tŏrmĕnt. 1.** (-ŏr'-) *n.* (Cause of) severe bodily or mental suffering (*is in torment*; *suffer torments*; *is a torment to him*). **2.** (-ĕ'-) *v.t.* Subject to torment; tease or worry excessively; **tŏrmĕ'ntor** *n.* [F f. L *tormentum* (as TORT)]

**tŏr'mentĭl** *n.* Trailing yellow-flowered herb. [F f. L]

**tŏrn.** See TEAR¹.

**tŏrnă'dō** *n.* (*pl.* ~**es**). Violent storm over small area, esp. rotatory one travelling in narrow path, (fig.) outburst or volley (of cheers, hisses, missiles). [Sp. *tronada* thunderstorm]

**tŏrpē'dō. 1.** *n.* (*pl.* ~**es**). Cigar-

-shaped self-propelled underwater or aerial missile that can be aimed at ship etc. and explodes on impact with it (**~-boat**, small fast lightly armed warship for carrying or discharging torpedoes); (Zool.) electric ray. **2.** *v.t.* Destroy or attack with torpedo(es); (fig.) paralyse, make (policy, institution, etc.) ineffective. [L, = electric ray (as foll.)]

**tor'pid** *a.* (Of hibernating animal) dormant; numb; sluggish, inactive, apathetic; **torpi'dity** *n.*; **tor'por** *n.*, suspended animation, apathy. [L (*torpeo* be numb)]

**torque** (-k) *n.* Twisting or rotary force esp. in machine; twisted metal necklace worn by ancient Britons, Gauls, etc. [F f. L (as TORT)]

**torr** *n.* Unit of pressure, 1/760 of atmosphere. [*Torricelli*, person]

**to'rrent** *n.* Rushing stream of water, lava, etc.; (in *pl.*) great downpour of rain; (fig.) violent flow (*of* abuse, questions); **torre'ntial** (-shal) *a.* (**-lly**). [F f. It.]

**to'rrid** *a.* (Of land etc.) parched by sun, very hot; (fig.) intense, zealous, (*torrid passion*). [F or L (*torreo* tost- parch)]

**tor'sion** (-shon) *n.* Twisting; **~al** *a.* (**-lly**). [F f. L (as TORT)]

**tor'so** *n.* (*pl.* **~s**). Statue lacking head and limbs; trunk of statue or of human body; (fig.) unfinished or mutilated work. [It. f. L *thyrsus* rod]

**tort** *n.* (Law). Breach of duty (other than under contract) with liability for damages; **~'ious** (-shus) *a.* [F f. L *tortum* wrong (*torqueo* tort- twist)]

**torti'lla** (-ē'lya) *n.* Latin Amer. thin flat maize cake eaten hot. [Sp., = little cake]

**tor'toise** (-tus) *n.* Land or freshwater slow-moving reptile with body in horny shell; **~-shell** (*or* -tesh-), yellowish-brown mottled and clouded turtle-shell; **~-shell butterfly, cat,** (with markings suggesting tortoise--shell). [F f. L *tortuca*]

**tor'tuous** *a.* Winding, indirect, involved, (*tortuous stream, tale*); **~ō'sity** *n.* [F f. L (as TORT)]

**tor'ture** *n.* **1.** Infliction of severe bodily pain e.g. as punishment or means of persuasion; severe physical or mental pain. **2.** *v.t.* Subject to torture; (fig.) force out of natural shape or meaning, distort. [F f. L *tortura* twisting (as TORT)]

**Tor'y** *n.* & *a.* (colloq. or derog.) (Member) of Conservative party; **~ism** *n.* [orig. = Irish outlaw]

**tosh** *n.* (sl.) Rubbish, nonsense. [orig. unkn.]

**toss** (*or* taws). **1.** *v.t.* & *i.* Move with fitful to-and-fro motion, fling or roll or wave about (*tossing sea, ship, branches, plumes*; *toss hay about*; *child tosses in its bed*); throw (thing *to* person, *away, aside, out*, etc.) lightly or carelessly; throw up (ball etc.) with the hand, (of bull etc.) throw (person etc.) up with the horns; throw (coin) into air to decide choice etc. by way it falls, settle question or dispute with (person *for* thing) thus; coat (food) with dressing etc. by gentle shaking; *toss the* CABER; **~ one's head**, throw it back esp. in contempt or impatience; **~ off**, drink (liquor) off at a draught, dispatch (work) rapidly or easily; **~ a pancake**, jerk it upwards from pan so that it falls back upside-down; **~ up**, toss coin; **~-up** *n.*, tossing of coin, doubtful matter (*it is a toss-up whether he comes or not*). **2.** *n.* Tossing of ball, coin, head, etc., (**win, lose, the ~**, have, not have, its decision in one's favour; **argue the ~**, dispute about a choice; FULL[1] *toss*; PITCH[2]*-and-toss*); ||throw from horseback etc. (**take a ~**, be thrown). [orig. unkn.]

**tot**[1] *n.* (colloq.) Small child, esp. *a tiny tot*; small drinking-glass etc.; dram of liquor. [orig. dial.]

**tot**[2]. (colloq.) **1.** *n.* Addition sum or its total. **2.** *v.t.* & *i.* (**-tt-**). Add (usu. *up*; **~ting-u'p**, adding of separate items, esp. of convictions towards disqualification from driving); (of items) mount up (**~ up to**, amount to). [abbr. TOTAL or L *totum* the whole]

**to'tal** *a., n.,* & *v.* **1.** *a.* (**~ly**). Complete, comprising the whole, (*the total number of persons, population*; SUM *total*); absolute, unqualified, (*was in total ignorance of it*; *total* ABSTINENCE, *abstainer*); **~ eclipse** (in which whole disc is obscured); *total* RECALL; **~ war** (in which all available weapons and resources are employed). **2.** *n.* Total number or quantity. **3.** *v.t.* & *i.* (**||-ll-**). Find total of; amount in number to; amount *to*. **4.** **totalitār'ian** *a.*, relating to form of government permitting no rival loyalties or parties;

**totă′lĭtў** *n.*; **~ĭzātor** *n.*, device showing number and amount of bets staked on race when total will be divided among those betting on winner, this betting system; **~īze** *v.t.*, combine into a total. [F f. L (*totus* entire)]

**tōte¹** *v.t.* (colloq.) Convey, carry as load, (gun, supplies, timber, etc.); **~ bag** (large and capacious for parcels etc.). [orig. U.S.; prob. dial.]

**tōte²** *n.* (sl.) Totalizator. [abbr.]

**tō′tem** *n.* (Image of) natural object (esp. animal) adopted among N. Amer. Indians as emblem of clan or individual; **~-pole** (on which totems are carved or hung, often in tall vertical array); **tōtē′-mĭc, ~ĭ′stĭc,** *adjs.* (-ically); **~ĭsm** *n.*, stage of development of which totems are characteristic. [Algonquian]

**t(′)o′ther** (tŭdh-) *a. & pron.* The other; **tell ~ from which,** (joc.) tell one from the other. [(*tha*)*t other*]

**tŏ′tter. 1.** *v.i.* Stand or walk unsteadily or feebly; (of tower etc., or fig. of State, system, etc.) be shaken, be on the point of falling; **~ў** *a.* **2.** *n.* Unsteady or shaky movement or gait. [Du.]

**tou′can** (tōō′-) *n.* Tropical Amer. bird with large bill. [Tupi]

**touch** (tŭch). **1.** *v.i. & t.* Be placed or move so as to meet at one or more points; put one's hand etc. so as to meet thus, cause (two things) to meet thus, establish this relation towards (thing *with* one's hand etc.), (w. neg.) move or harm or affect or attempt in any degree, have any dealings with; strike lightly, affect with such stroke; strike (keys or strings of musical instrument); (momentarily) reach as far as, (fig.) approach in excellence (*nobody can touch him for speed*); affect with tender or painful feelings; (in *p.p.*) slightly crazy; affect slightly, modify. **2.** *n.* Act or fact of touching (*felt a touch on my arm*; *got a touch to the ball*; **at a ~,** if touched however lightly; **to the ~,** when touched); faculty of perception through response of brain to contact esp. with fingers; light stroke of pencil etc. in drawing (**finishing ~es,** lit. or fig. of completing any matter); small amount, tinge or trace, (*needs a touch of salt*; *has a touch of flu*; *a touch of frost in the air*); manner of touching keys or strings, response

of keys etc. to this, distinctive manner of workmanship or procedure (**personal ~,** way of treating a matter typical of or designed for an individual); mental correspondence, communication, (**in ~,** in correspondence or personal relations; **keep in ~,** continue thus; **out of ~,** no longer in touch; **put in(to) ~,** cause to communicate *with*); (Footb.) part of field beyond side limits; (sl.) act of getting money from person, person from whom money may be got. **3. ~-and-go,** uncertain as regards result, risky; **~ at,** (Naut.) call at (port etc.); **~ bottom,** reach bottom of water with feet, (fig.) reach lowest or worst point or firm facts; **~ down,** touch ground behind goal with football, (of aircraft) alight; **~′down** *n.*, act of touching down; **~ person for,** (sl.) get (money) from him as loan or gift; **~ one's hat** (as salutation); **~-line,** side limit of football field; **~ off,** explode by touching with match etc., (fig.) initiate (process) suddenly; **~ of nature,** natural trait, exhibition of feeling that evokes sympathy; **~ on, upon,** refer to or mention briefly or casually, verge on; **~-paper** (impregnated with nitre to burn slowly and ignite firework etc.); **~′stone,** dark schist or jasper for testing alloys by marks they make on it, (fig.) criterion; **~-typing,** typewriting without looking at keys; **~ up,** correct, give finishing touches to; **~ upon,** = touch on; **~ wood,** hand on something wooden to avert ill luck; **~′wood,** readily inflammable rotten wood or similar substance. **4. touché** (tōō′shā) *int.* acknowledging hit by fencing-opponent or justified accusation by another in discussion [F]; **~′ing,** (*a.*) pathetic, moving, (*prep.* arch. or literary) concerning; **~ў** *a.* (**~ily,** **~iness,** apt to take offence, over-sensitive. [F *tochier*, prob. imit.]

**tough** (tŭf). **1.** *a.* Hard to break or cut or tear or chew; (of clay etc.) stiff, tenacious; able to endure hardship, hardy; stubborn, difficult, (*he's a tough customer,* NUT; *it's a tough job*); (colloq. of luck etc.) hard; (colloq.) acting sternly or vigorously (*get tough with*); *(sl.) vicious, ruffianly; **~′en** *v.t. & i.* **2.** *n.* Tough person, esp. ruffian. [E]

**tou′pee, toupet,** (tōō′pā) *n.* Wig

or artificial patch of hair worn to cover bald part of head. [F]

**tour** (toor). **1.** *n.* Pleasure journey including stops at various places and ending where it began, journey or expedition with any of these characteristics, (*walking tour*; *go on a tour of inspection*; GRAND[1] *tour*; **on ~**, going from place to place to give performances etc.); spell of military or diplomatic duty. **2.** *v.i.* & *t.* Go on a tour, travel through (country etc.) so. **3. ~ de force** (-defôr´s) *n.*, feat of strength or skill; **~'ism** *n.*, organized touring or service for tourists, esp. on commercial basis; **~'ist** *n.*, holiday traveller (**~ist class**, lowest class of passenger accommodation in ship, aeroplane, etc.); **~'istў** *a.*, (derog.) suitable for, visited by, tourists. [F f. L (TURN)]

**tour'maline** (toor´-; or -ēn) *n.* Mineral with unusual electric properties and used as gem. [F, f. Sinh.]

**tour'n|ament** (toor´-) *n.* (Hist.) medieval spectacle in which two sides contended with usu. blunted weapons; (modern) display of military exercises, contests, etc., (*Royal Tournament*); any contest of skill between a number of competitors (*chess tournament*); **~edōs** (-ō) *n.* (*pl.* same), small fillet of beef in strip of suet; **~'ey** (or têr´-) *n.*, & *v.i.*, (take part in) tournament; **~iquet** (-kā) *n.*, bandage etc. for stopping flow of blood through artery by compression. [F (TURN)]

**tou'sle** (-zel) *v.t.* Pull about roughly, make (hair, clothes) untidy. [dial. *touse*]

**tout. 1.** *v.i.* & *t.* Pester possible customers with requests (*for orders*), solicit custom of (person) or for (thing); ‖spy out movements and condition of racehorses in training. **2.** *n.* Person who touts. [E, = peep]

**tout court** (tōō koor´) *adv.* (Of name etc.) without addition of title or explanation. [F, lit. = quite short]

**tout ensemble** (tōōt ahñsah´ñbl) *n.* See ENSEMBLE. [F (*tout* whole, ENSEMBLE)]

**tow[1]** (tō) *n.* Fibres of flax or hemp prepared for spinning; **~-headed**, having head of very light-coloured or tousled hair. [LG *touw*]

**tow[2]** (tō). **1.** *v.t.* (Of vessel, horse on bank, etc.) pull (boat etc.) along in water by rope or chain; (of

vehicle) pull another along behind it; pull (person, thing) along behind one. **2.** *n.* Towing or being towed; **take** or **have** in or on **~**, (fig.) be accompanied by, assume direction of, take possession of, (person); **on ~**, being towed; **~('ing)-line, -rope**, (used in towing); **~('ing)-path** (along river or canal, orig. for towing). [E]

**toward(s)** (tôrd(z), twôrd(z), to-wô'r´d(z)) *prep.* In the direction of (*looks towards the sea*; *set out towards town*); as regards, in relation to, (*felt animosity toward him*; *his attitude towards death*); for, for the purpose of, (*saved something towards his education*); near (*towards noon*; *toward the end of our journey*). [E, = future (TO, -WARD)]

**tow'el. 1.** *n.* Absorbent cloth etc. for drying with after washing (*paper towel*; **throw in the ~**, Boxing or fig., admit defeat; **~-horse**, frame for hanging towels on); ‖ = SANITARY *towel*. **2.** *v.t.* & *i.* (‖-ll-). Wipe or dry (one*self* etc.) with towel, wipe or dry oneself thus; ‖(sl.) thrash. **3. ~ling**, *\*~ing**, *n.*, material for towels. [F *toaille* f. Gmc]

**tow'er. 1.** *n.* Tall structure often forming part of castle, church, or other large building; similar structure housing machinery etc. (*control, cooling, tower*); tall building containing offices or dwelling-places; fortress etc. having a tower (**~ of strength**, fig., champion, comforter, etc.); IVORY *tower*; **~ed** (-erd) *a.*, having tower(s). **2.** *v.i.* Reach high (*above, over*, surroundings, lit., or fig. of eminent person: *towers above his contemporaries*); (of eagle etc.) soar or be poised aloft; (in *part.*) high, lofty, (fig., of rage etc.) violent. [F f. L f. Gk *turris*]

**town** *n.* Considerable collection of dwellings, densely populated settlement esp. opp. country or suburbs; London or the chief city or town in one's neighbourhood (*went up to town*; *the best coffee in town*), central business area of one's neighbourhood (*went into town today*); **go to ~**, act or work with energy and enthusiasm; **man about ~**, fashionable idler; *woman* etc. **of the ~**, belonging to disreputable side of town life; **on the ~**, in carefree pursuit of urban pleasures; PAINT *the town red*; *town and* GOWN; **~ clerk**, officer of town corporation, in charge of records etc.; ‖∼ **council(lor)**, (member of) elective governing body in municipality; ∼ **crier** (making official announcements in public places); ∼ **gas**, manufactured inflammable gas for domestic use; ∼ **hall**, building for town's official business, often also used for public entertainment etc.; ∼ **house**, one's town (as opp. country) residence, house in planned (esp. terraced) group in town; ∼ **planning** (for regulated growth of towns); ∼'**scape**, visual appearance of town(s); ∼'**sfolk**, inhabitants of particular town(s); ∼'**ship**, one of the parishes into which a large original parish has been divided, (U.S. & Can.) administrative division of county, or district 6 miles square, (Austral. & N.Z.) small town or settlement; ∼'**sman**, ∼'**s-woman**, ∼'**speople**, inhabitant(s) of a town; ∼**ee'**, ∼'**ie**, n., (derog.) inhabitant of town, esp. opp. country person or (in university town) opp. member of university. [E]

**tŏxae′mĭa**, *-ē′mĭa*, n. Blood-poisoning; condition of increased blood-pressure in pregnancy. [as foll., Gk *haima* blood]

**tŏ′xĭc** a. (∼ally). Of or caused by or acting as poison; ∼**ŏ′logy̆**, ∼**ŏ′logist**, ns.; **tŏ′xĭn** n., poison esp. of animal or vegetable origin, poison secreted by micro-organism and causing particular disease. [L f. Gk *toxikon* poison for arrows]

**toy. 1.** n. Thing to play with, trinket or curiosity, trifling thing that one makes much of or regards as a child its playthings; (*attrib.*) mimic, not meant for real use, hardly deserving the name, (∼ **dog**, of diminutive breed; ∼ **soldier**, of lead etc., or of army that has no fighting to do). **2.** *v.i.* Play or fiddle or dally *with* (person's hair, etc., one's food, thing held in fingers, idea or proposal). [orig. unkn.]

**trăce. 1.** n. Mark left behind, as track of animal, footprint, line made by moving pen; perceptible sign of what has existed or happened (*of these buildings no trace remains; traces of sorrow in her face; has vanished, sunk, without trace*); small quantity (*contains a trace of iron, of irony*; ∼ **element**, occurring or required only in minute amounts); each of two side-straps, chains, or ropes by which horse draws vehicle (**kick over the ∼s**,

fig. of person, become insubordinate or reckless). **2.** *v.t.* ∼ (**out**), delineate, mark out, sketch, write esp. laboriously; ∼ (**over**), copy (drawing etc.) by marking its lines on superimposed sheet (esp. of transparent **tracing-paper**) or on sheet placed below with carbon paper etc.; follow or mark track, path, or position of; find vestiges or signs of (*cannot trace any such papers*); pursue one's way along (path etc.); ∼ **back**, go back along the course of (*can trace my family back to the time of Henry I; the report has been traced back to you*). **3.** ∼** abĭ′lĭty̆** (*-sa-*) n.; **trā′cer** n., (Mil.) projectile whose course is made visible by flame etc. emitted (*tracer bullet*), artificial radioisotope whose course in human body etc. can be followed by radiation it produces; **trā′cery̆** n., stone ornamental open-work esp. in head of Gothic window, decorative lacy pattern suggesting this; **trā′cĭng** n., (esp.) copy of lines of drawing, map, etc., done with tracing- or carbon paper. [F f. Rom. (L *traho* draw)]

**trachē′a** (-k-, trā′kĭa) n. (Anat.) The windpipe; **trāchĕŏ′tomy̆** (-k-) n., surgical incision of trachea. [L f. Gk]

**trăck. 1.** n. Mark, series of marks, left by person, animal, or vehicle etc., in passing along, (in *pl.*) such marks esp. footprints, (**in one's ∼s**, sl., where one stands, there and then; **off the ∼**, fig., away from subject; **on person's ∼**, in pursuit of him, lit. or fig.; **on the wrong ∼**, following wrong line of inquiry etc.; **cover one's ∼s**, conceal evidence of what one has done; **keep, lose, ∼**, follow, fail to follow, course or development (*of*); **make ∼s**, sl., go or run away; **make ∼s for**, sl., go in pursuit of or towards); course taken (*followed in his track; track of comet;* ONE-*track mind*); path esp. one beaten by use, (fig.) course of life or routine; prepared racing-path (∼ **events**, running-races; ∼ **record**, fig., person's past achievements; ∼ **suit**, worn by athletes etc. during training); racecourse for horses etc.; continuous railway-line; band round wheels of tank, tractor, etc.; = SOUND[1]-*track*; groove on gramophone record; particular recorded section on gramophone record or magnetic tape. **2.** *v.t. & i.* Follow track of (animal, person, *to* lair etc.; spacecraft etc.; ~ **down**, reach or capture by tracking); trace (course, development, etc.) from vestiges; (of cine-camera) move along set path while taking picture. [F *trac*]

**trăct** *n.* Region or area of indefinite (usu. large) extent; (Anat.) area of organ or system (*digestive tract*); short treatise or discourse esp. on religious subject; ~'**able** *a.* (-bly), (of person, material, etc.) easily handled, manageable, docile; ~**abĭ'lĭtў** *n.*; T~**ār'ĭan** *a.* & *n.*, (adherent or promoter) of T~**ār'ĭan**-**ĭsm** *n.*, 19th-c. High-Church movement towards primitive sacramental Catholicism voiced in 90 *Tracts for the Times*; ~'**ĭon** *n.*, hauling, pulling force, (Med.) therapeutic sustained pull on limb etc.; ~**ĭon-engine**, steam or diesel engine for drawing heavy load on road or across fields etc.; ~'**or** *n.*, traction-engine, self--propelled vehicle for hauling other vehicles, farm machinery, etc. [L (*traho tract-* draw)]

**trăd** *a.* & *n.* (colloq.) Traditional (jazz). [abbr.]

**trade.** 1. *n.* Business, esp. mechanical or mercantile employment opp. to *profession*, carried on as means of livelihood or profit, skilled handicraft, (*a carpenter, butcher, by trade*; *learn a trade*; **be in** ~, be a retailer, keep a shop; **trick of the** ~, device for attracting custom); exchange of commodities for money or other commodities (**is good, bad, for** ~, induces, discourages, buying), business done with specified class or at specified time (*tourist, Christmas, trade*); *the* persons engaged in one trade (*the book trade*; esp. ||(colloq.) *the* licensed victuallers; (usu. in *pl.*) trade wind. 2. *v.i.* & *t.* Buy and sell, engage in trade (*in* commodity or fig. *in* favours etc. *with* person), exchange (goods) in commerce; have a transaction (*with* person *for* thing), carry merchandise (*to* place); ~ (**in**), give (used car etc.) in (part) payment or exchange *for*; ~ **off**, exchange as compromise; ~ **on**, take (esp. unscrupulous) advantage of (person's credulity, one's reputation, etc.). 3. ||~ **cycle**, recurring succession of trade conditions between prosperity and depression; ~ **mark**, device or word(s) legally registered to distinguish goods of a

particular manufacturer etc., (fig.) distinctive feature of person's activities etc.; ~ **name** (by which a thing is known in the trade, or given by manufacturer to proprietary article, or under which business is carried on); ~ **plates**, number-plates used by dealer etc. on various unlicensed cars; ~ **price** (charged by manufacturer etc. to retailer); ~ **secret**, device or technique used in trade and giving advantage because not generally known; ~'**sman**, person engaged in trade, esp. shopkeeper; ~(**s**) **union**, organized association of workpeople of a trade or group of allied trades formed to further their common interests; T~**s Union Congress**, official representative body of British trade unions; ~**-u'nionism**, system of trade unions; ~**-u'nionist**, advocate of this, member of trade union; ~ **wind**, constant wind blowing towards equator from N.E. or S.E. 4. **trä'der** *n.*, person, ship, engaged in trading; **trä'ding** *n.*; **trading estate** (occupied by industrial and commercial firms); **trading stamp** (given by tradesman to customer and exchangeable in quantity for various articles). [LG,= track (TREAD)]

**trădĕscă'ntĭa** *n.* Perennial herb with large blue, white, or pink flowers. [L (*Tradescant*, person)]

**tradĭ'tion** *n.* Opinion or belief or custom handed down, handing down of these, from one generation to another esp. orally; artistic or literary principle(s) based on usage or experience; ~**al** *a.* (-lly), of, based on, obtained by, tradition, (of jazz) based on early style; ~**alĭsm** *n.*, (excessive) respect for tradition; ~**alĭst** *n.* [F f. L *trado -dit-* hand on, betray]

**tradŭ'ce** *v.t.* (-cible). Slander; ~**ment** (-sm-) *n.* [L,= disgrace]

**trä'ffĭc.** 1. *v.i.* & *t.* (-ck-). Trade (*in* commodity, lit. or fig., esp. what should not be bought and sold); deal in. 2. *n.* Trade, esp. trafficking (*in* commodity; *the traffic in drugs*); coming and going of persons and vehicles and goods by road, rail, air, sea, etc., (~ **island**, paved etc. area in road to direct traffic and provide refuge for pedestrians; *traffic* JAM[1]; ~**-light(s)**, **-signal**, signal controlling road traffic by coloured lights; ||~ **warden**, person employed to control movement of traffic, esp. parking of vehicles); number or amount of persons or goods conveyed; (amount of) use of a service (*telephone traffic*); dealings between persons etc. 3. ‖~**ātor** *n.*, device on side of vehicle used to show intended change of direction. [F f. It.]

**trăˊgacănth** *n.* Vegetable gum used in pharmacy etc. [F f. L f. Gk]

**trăˊgĕdy̆** *n.* Drama of elevated theme and diction and with unhappy ending; sad event, serious accident, calamity; **tragèˊdĭan** *n.*, author of or actor in tragedy; **tragĕdĭĕˊnne** *n.*, actress in tragedy; **trăˊgĭc** *a.* (-ically), of or like tragedy, sad or calamitous or distressing (*a tragic tale, event*; also **trăˊgĭcal**); **trăgĭcŏˊmĕdy̆** *n.*, drama of mixed tragic and comic events; **trăgĭcŏˊmĭc** *a.* (-ically). [F f. L f. Gk]

**trail.** 1. *v.t.* & *i.* Draw along, be drawn along, as appendage; drag (one*self*, one's limbs) along wearily etc., walk wearily (*along* etc.); follow the trail of, pursue, shadow; hang loosely, (of plant) hang or spread downwards; be losing in contest; tail *away* or *off*; ~ **arms**, (Mil.) let rifle etc. hang balanced in hand and ‖parallel to ground; trail one's COAT; ~**ˊing edge**, rear edge of aircraft's wing. 2. *n.* Part drawn behind or in wake of thing, long (real or apparent) appendage, (*vapour trails*; *the trail of a meteor*); track, scent, or other sign of passage left behind (*slimy trail of slug*; *vandals left a trail of wreckage*); beaten path esp. through wild region (BLAZE[2] *a trail*; so ~**blazer**, esp. fig.); (Mil.) position with rifle trailed. 3. ~**ˊer** *n.*, (esp.) trailing plant, set of short extracts from film shown in advance to advertise it, wheeled vehicle drawn by another and used to carry (additional) load, \*caravan. [F or LG]

**train.** 1. *v.t.* & *i.* Bring (person, animal, etc.) to desired state or standard by instruction and practice (*was trained for the ministry*; *a trained nurse*); teach and accustom (person, animal, *to* do, *to* action); bring (horse, athlete, one*self*) or come to physical efficiency by exercise and diet (*he is training them*, *they are training*, *for the boat race*, *the Derby*); guide growth of (plant; *up*, *along*, etc.); point, aim, (gun, camera, *on* object etc.). 2. *n.* Thing drawn along behind or forming hinder part, esp. elongated part of woman's skirt or of official robe (~**-bearer**, person holding up train of another's robe); body of followers, retinue, (**in the** ~ **of**, as sequel to); succession or series of persons or things (*train of camels*; *wagon train*; *train of thought*; **in** ~, properly arranged or directed); series of railway carriages or trucks drawn by same engine(s) (~**-ferry**, vessel conveying train across water; ~**ˊ-sick(ness)**, travel-sick(ness) through motion of train; ~**-spotter**, collector of locomotive-numbers seen); line of combustible material to lead fire to charge of explosive. 3. ~**ee** *n.*, person being trained (for occupation); ~**ˊer** *n.*, (esp.) person who trains horses, athletes, etc., aircraft or device simulating it used to train pilots; ~**ˊing** *n.*, (esp.) process of training for sport, contest, or occupation. [F f. Rom. (L *traho* draw)]

**traiˊn-oil** *n.* Whale-blubber oil. [LDu. *trān*; OIL]

**traipse** *v.i.* (colloq.) Tramp or trudge wearily; go *about* on errands. [orig. unkn.]

**trait** (trā) *n.* Distinguishing feature in character, appearance, habit, or portrayal. [F, f. L f. L *tractus* (TRACT)]

**traiˊtor** *n.* Person guilty of betrayal, one who acts disloyally (*to* country, leader, cause, etc.); ~**ous** *a.*; **traiˊtrĕss** *n.* [F f. L *traditor* (as TRADITION)]

**trajĕˊctory̆** (*or* trăˊjĭ-) *n.* Path of body (e.g. comet, bullet) moving under given forces. [L (*traicio* -*ject*- throw across)]

**trăm** *n.* ‖~**(ˊcar)**, passenger car running on rails in public road; 4- -wheeled car used in coal-mines; ‖~**-lines**, rails for tramcar (also ‖~**ˊway**), (colloq.) either pair of parallel lines at edge of tennis etc. court. [LDu. *trame* beam]

**trăˊmmel.** 1. *n.* Kind of fishing- net; (usu. in *pl.* and fig.) impedi- ment(s) to movement or action (*the trammels of routine*). 2. *v.t.* (‖-ll-). Hamper. [F *tramail* f. L *tremaculum*]

**trămp.** 1. *v.i.* & *t.* Walk with firm heavy tread; trudge, go on walking expedition; live as tramp; traverse or cover (streets, country, distance) on foot with effort. 2. *n.* Sound (as) of person(s) walking or marching; person who tramps the roads in search of work or as vagrant, this mode of life; (sl.) dissolute woman; (**ocean**) ~, freight-vessel, esp. steamer, on no regular line. **3.** ~**le** *v.t.* & *i.*, tread heavily on or *on* (*trampled to death by elephants*, fig. *tramples on everyone's susceptibilities*). [Gmc]

**trä'mpoline** (-ēn). **1.** *n.* Canvas sheet connected by springs to horizontal frame, used by acrobats etc. **2.** *v.i.* Use trampoline. [It. *trampolino*]

**trance** (-ah-) *n.* Sleeplike state without response to stimuli; hypnotic or cataleptic state; mental abstraction from external things, rapture, ecstasy. [F (*transir* f. L *transeo* pass over)]

**trä'nnȳ** *n.* (sl.) Transistor radio. [abbr.]

**trä'nquil** *a.* (~**ly**). Serene, calm, undisturbed, (*tranquil mind, surface of lake*); ~**litȳ** (-ĭ'l-) *n.*; ~**lize**, \*~**ize**, *v.t.*, make tranquil esp. by drug etc.; ~**(l)izer** *n.*, drug used to diminish anxiety. [F or L]

**trans-** (*or* -ah-, -z) *pref.* Across, through, beyond, to or on farther side of; ~**a'lpine**, on north side of Alps; ~**atla'ntic**, crossing or beyond the Atlantic, ‖American, \*European; ~**contine'ntal**, extending across a continent~**ocea'nic**, crossing or beyond the ocean; ~**po'ntine**, on south side of Thames. [L]

**trä'nsä'ct** (*or* -z-, trah-) *v.t.* Perform, carry through, (business); ~**ion** *n.*, transacting *of*, any piece of commercial or other dealing (*mixed up in shady transactions*), (in *pl.*) reports of discussions and lectures at meetings of learned society. [L (ACT)]

**trä'nscei'ver** (-nsē'v-; *or* -ah-) *n.* Combined radio transmitter and receiver. [portmanteau wd]

**trä'nscě'nd** (*or* -ah-) *v.t.* Be beyond range or domain or grasp of (human experience, reason, description, belief, etc.); excel, surpass; ~**ent** *a.*, of supreme merit or quality, (of God) existing apart from, or not subject to limitations of, material universe (opp. IMMANENT); ~**ence**, ~**encȳ**, *ns.*; **trä'nscendě'ntal** (*or* trah-) *a.* (-**lly**), a priori, not based on experience, intuitively accepted, innate in the mind, consisting of or dealing in or inspired by abstraction, (~**ental meditation**, seeking to induce detachment from problems and relief from anxiety; ~**ental philosophy**, that takes account of transcendental things); **trä'nscendě'ntalism**, **-ĭst**, (*or* trah-) *ns.*, belief, believer, in a transcendental philosophy. [F or L (*scando* climb)]

**trä'nscri'be** (*or* -ah-) *v.t.* Copy out; reproduce (shorthand etc.) in ordinary writing; (Mus.) adapt (composition) for voice or instrument other than that for which it was orig. written; **trä'nscript** (*or* -ah'-) *n.*, written copy; ~**i'ption** *n.* [L *transcribo* -*script*-]

**trä'nsdü'cer** (*or* -z-, -ah-) *n.* Device for changing the variations of a quantity (e.g. pressure) to those of another (e.g. voltage). [L (as DUCT)]

**trä'nsě'pt** (*or* -ah'-) *n.* Transverse part of cruciform church, either arm (**north, south,** ~) of this. [L (SEPTUM)]

**transfer. 1.** (trǎnsfěr', -ah-) *v.t.* & *i.* (-rr-). Convey, remove, hand over, (thing etc. *from* place or person *to* another); make over possession of (property, rights, etc., *to* person); convey (design etc.) from one surface to another; move (person) to, change or be moved to, another group; change (meaning) by extension or metaphor; go from one station, route, etc., to another in order to continue journey. **2.** (trä'nsfer, -ah'-) *n.* Transferring or being transferred; conveyance of property or right, document effecting this; design or picture (to be) conveyed from one surface to another. **3. trä'nsferable** (*or* -ah'-, -ěr'-) *a.*; **trä'nsferabi'litȳ** (*or*-ah-) *n.*; **trä'nsference** (*or* -ah'-) *n.*, action of transferring, (Psych.) redirection of desires etc. to new object. [F or L (*fero lat-* carry)]

**trä'nsfi'gure** (-ger; *or* -ah-) *v.t.* Change aspect of, make more spiritual or elevated; ~**ā'tion** *n.* (esp., *T*-, that of Christ, see Matt. 17: 2, celebrated on 6 Aug.). [F or L]

**trä'nsfi'x** (*or* -ah-) *v.t.* Pierce with lance etc.; (of horror etc.) paralyse faculties of (person). [L (FIX)]

**trä'nsfor'm** (*or* -ah-) *v.t.* Make (esp. considerable) change in form, appearance, character, disposition, etc., of; (Electr.) change voltage of (current); **trä'nsformā'tion** (*or* trah-) *n.*, transforming or being transformed; ~**er** *n.*, (esp.) apparatus for reducing or increasing voltage of alternating current. [F or L]

**tránsfū's|e** (-z; *or* -ah-) *v.t.* Cause (fluid, colour, influence, etc.) to permeate *into*, imbue (fluid, expanse, mind, institution, etc.) by such permeation *with*; (Med.) inject (blood or other liquid) into blood-vessel to replace that lost; **~ion** (-zhŏn) *n.* [L (FOUND²)]

**tránsgrĕ'ss** (*or* -z-, -ah-) *v.t.* Violate, infringe, go beyond bounds set by, (commandment, law, limitation, etc.); **~ion** (-shŏn) *n.*, (esp.) a sin; **~or** *n.*, (esp.) sinner. [F, or L *transgredior -gress-*]

**trá'nsiĕn|t** (*or* -z-, -ah-') *a.* Quickly passing away, fleeting; **~ce**, **~cў**, *ns.* [L (TRANCE)]

**tránsi'stor** (*or* -z-, -ah-) *n.* Semiconductor device with 3 electrodes and same functions as thermionic valve but smaller and consuming less power; **~** (**radio**), portable radio set equipped with transistors; **~ize** *v.t.*, design with transistors (rather than valves). [TRANS(FER), (RES)ISTOR]

**trá'nsĭt** (*or* -z-, -ah-') *n.* Going, conveying, being conveyed, across or over or through (*goods damaged in transit*; **~** **camp**, for temporary accommodation of soldiers, refugees, etc.; **~** **visa**, allowing only passage through (country); passage, route, (*the overland transit*); apparent passage of heavenly body across disc of another or meridian of place. [L (TRANCE)]

**tránsĭ'tion** (*or* -z-, -ah-) *n.* Passage or change from one state or action or subject or set of circumstances to another (*transition from high spirits to depression*); (Art) period during which one style develops into another (esp. Archit., from Norman to Early English); **~al** *a.* (**-lly**). [F or L (prec.)]

**trá'nsĭtive** (*or* -z-, -ah-') *a.* (Gram.) Taking direct object expressed or understood (e.g. *pick* in: *pick peas, pick till you are tired*; opp. to *intransitive* as in *picked at the hole to make it bigger*). [L (TRANSIT)]

**trá'nsĭtor|ў** (*or* -z-, -ah-') *a.* (**~ily**, **~iness**). Passing, not longlasting, merely temporary. [AF *transitorie* f. L (TRANSIT)]

**tránslā'te** (*or* -z-, trah-) *v.t.* Express the sense of (word, speech, book, etc., or *abs.*) in *or into* another

language, in or (*in*)to another form of representation (*translates emotion into music, speech into sign language*), in plainer words, etc.; infer or declare significance of, interpret, (signs, conduct, hint, etc.); move from one person, place, or condition to another, remove (bishop) to another see; **~ā'tion** *n.*, art or act or product of translating; **~ā'tor** *n.* [L (TRANSFER)]

**tránslĭ'ter|āte** (*or* -z-, trah-) *v.t.* Represent (word etc.) in more or less corresponding characters of another alphabet or language; **~ā'tion**, **~ātor**, *ns.* [L *littera* letter]

**tránslū'cen|t** (*or* -ah-, -z-, -ōō'-) *a.* Allowing light to pass through (esp. without being transparent); **~ce**, **~cў**, *ns.* [L (*luceo* shine)]

**trá'nsmĭgr|āte** (*or* -ĭ'g-, -z-, trah-) *v.i.* (Of soul) pass into different body; migrate; **~ā'tion** *n.* [L]

**tránsmĭ't** (*or* -z-, -ah-) *v.t.* (**-tt-**.) Pass on, hand on, transfer, communicate, (*will transmit the message, the parcel, the title, the disease*); allow to pass through, be a medium for, serve to communicate, (heat, light, sound, electricity, emotion, signal, news); **~ssĭble**, **~ttable**, *adjs.*; **~ssion** (-shŏn) *n.*, transmitting or being transmitted, broadcast programme, gear transmitting power from engine to axle in motor vehicle; **~tter** *n.*, equipment used to transmit message, (esp. broadcast) signal, etc. [L (*mitto miss-* send)]

**tránsmŏ'grĭf|ў** (*or* -z-, -ah-) *v.t.* (joc.) Transform esp. in magical or surprising manner; **~ĭcā'tion** *n.* [orig. unkn.]

**tránsmū't|e** (*or* -z-, -ah-) *v.t.* Change form or nature or substance of, convert into different thing; **~abĭ'lĭtў** *n.*; **~ā'tion** *n.* (**~ation** of metals, esp., turning of other metals into gold as alchemists' aim); **~atĭve** *a.* [L (*muto* change)]

**trá'nsŏm** *n.* (Window above) cross-beam, esp. lintel or horizontal bar in window. [F *traversin* (TRAVERSE)]

**tránspār'en|t** (*or* -ă'r-, trah-) *a.* That can be clearly seen through because allowing light to pass through without diffusion; (of disguise, pretext, etc.) easily seen through; evident, obvious, (*transparent sincerity*); easily understood, free from affectation or disguise; **~ce**

*n.*; **~cy̆** *n.*, being transparent, picture (esp. photograph) to be viewed by light passing through it. [F f. L (*pareo* appear)]

**transpīr'e** (*or* -ah-) *v.t. & i.* Emit (vapour, moisture) or pass off through pores of skin etc.; (of secret, fact, etc.) come to be known; (colloq.) occur, happen; **~ĭra'tion** *n.* [F or L (*spiro* breathe)]

**transplant** (-lah-; *or* trah-). **1.** (-lah'-) *v.t.* Uproot and replant elsewhere (often fig.); (Surg.) transfer (living tissue or organ) and implant in another part of body or in another (human or animal) body; **~ā'tion** (*or* -lă-) *n.* **2.** (trā'-, trah'-) *n.* Transplanting of tissue or organ, thing transplanted. [L]

**transport** (*or* -ah-). **1.** (-ôr'-) *v.t.* Cause (person, goods, etc.) to be carried from one place to another; (Hist.) deport (criminal) to penal colony; (esp. in *p.p.*) affect with strong emotion (*transported with joy*). **2.** (-ă'-, -ah'-) *n.* Transporting, means of conveyance (*the transport has arrived*; **~ café**, providing meals for drivers of esp. commercial motor vehicles); vessel employed to carry soldiers, stores, etc., to destination; vehement emotion (*in transports of delight*). **3.** **~abĭ'lĭty̆** *n.*; **transportā'tion** (*or* trah-) *n.*, (esp., Hist.) deporting of convicts; **transpôr'ter** (*or* -ah-) *n.* (esp. **~er bridge**, carrying vehicles across water on suspended platform). [L or F (PORT³)]

**trans|pō'se** (-z; *or* -ah-) *v.t.* Cause (two or more things) to change places; change position of (thing) in series; change natural or existing order or position of (words, a word) in sentence; (Mus.) write, play, in different key; **~posĭ'tion** (-zĭ'-) *n.* [F (POSE)]

**transsē'xūal** (-zs-; *or* trah-, -kshoō-) *a. & n.* (Person) having physical characteristics of one sex and psychological characteristics of the other; **~ĭsm** *n.* [TRANS-]

**trans-shī'p** (-nsh-, -ns-sh-, -nzsh-; *or* -ah-) *v.t.* (-pp-). Shift to or from another ship or conveyance; **~ment** *n.*

**transsubstă'ntĭ|āte** (-shĭ-; *or* trah-) *v.t.* Change into a different substance; **~ā'tion** (*or* -sĭ-) *n.*, (esp.) conversion of Eucharistic elements wholly into body and blood of Christ. [L (TRANS-, SUBSTANCE)]

**transūrā'nĭc** (*or* trah-) *a.* (Chem., of element) having higher atomic number than uranium. [TRANS-]

**transvĕr'se** (-z-; *or* -ah-, trā'-) *a.* Situated, arranged, acting, in crosswise direction. [L *transverto* -*vers*-turn across]

**transvĕ'st** (*or* -zv-, -ah-) *v.t.* (Psych.) Clothe (usu. one*self*) in other garments esp. those of opposite sex; **~ĭsm** *n.*; **~ĭte** *n.*, person given to transvestism. [L *vestio* clothe]

**trăp¹. 1.** *n.* Device, often baited, for catching animals; (fig.) trick betraying person into speech or act (*is this question a trap?*); arrangement to measure speed of vehicle and so detect infringement of speed limit; device for effecting sudden release e.g. of greyhound in race, of ball to be struck at, of clay pigeon to be shot at; curve in drain-pipe etc. serving when filled with liquid to seal it against return of gas; two-wheeled carriage (*pony and trap*); **= trapdoor**, (sl.) mouth (*shut your trap*); **~'door**, door flush with surface of floor or roof. **2.** *v.t.* (-pp-). Catch (animal, fig. person) in trap; furnish (place) with traps; stop and retain (as) in trap; **~'per** *n.*, person who traps wild animals esp. for furs. [E]

**trăp²** *n.* Kind of dark volcanic rock. [Sw.]

**trăp³. 1.** *v.t.* (-pp-). Furnish with trappings. **2.** *n.* (in *pl.*; colloq.) Baggage or belongings (usu. *pack up one's traps*). [obs. *trap* n. f. F *drap* cloth]

**trapē'z|e** *n.* Crossbar(s) suspended by cords as swing for acrobatics etc.; **~ĭum** *n.* (*pl.* **~ia**, **~iums**), ‖quadrilateral with (only) one pair of sides parallel, *trapezoid; **tră'pēzoid** *n.*, ‖quadrilateral with no sides parallel, *trapezium. [F f. L f. Gk *trapezion*]

**tră'ppings** (-z) *n.pl.* Harness of horse esp. when ornamental; (fig.) ornamental accessories (*of office* etc.). [TRAP³]

**Tră'ppist** *n.* Monk of an order noted for silence. [La *Trappe*, place]

**trăsh** *n.* Worthless or waste stuff, rubbish; worthless person(s); *~-can, dustbin; **~'y̆** *a.* (-ily, -iness). [orig. unkn.]

**trăttori'a** (-ē'a) *n.* Italian eating-house. [It.]

**trau'm|a** *n.* (*pl.* **~ata**, **~as**). Morbid condition of body caused by wound or external violence; emotional shock; ~ă'tĭc a., (esp., colloq.) unpleasant (a traumatic experience). [Gk, = wound]

trä'vail n., & v.i. (arch.) (Suffer) pangs of childbirth; (literary) (make) painful or laborious effort. [F travailler f. L trepalium]

trä'vel. 1. v.i. & t. (||-ll-||). Make journey(s) esp. of some length to distant countries, traverse (country, distance) thus, (ordered to travel for his health; has travelled the world); (colloq.) withstand long journey (wines that travel badly); act as COMMERCIAL traveller (for firm, in commodity); (of machine or part) move along bar etc., in groove etc.); pass esp. in deliberate or systematic manner from point to point (his eye travelled over the scene); move, proceed, in specified manner or at specified rate (travels at 600 m.p.h.; light travels faster than sound); (colloq.) move quickly; ~ling bag, small bag carried by hand, for traveller's requisites; ~ling clock, small clock in a case; ~ling crane (moving on esp. overhead support); *~ing salesman, commercial traveller. 2. n. (Spell of) travelling (has returned from his travels; likes reading travel books); range, rate, or mode of motion of part in machinery; ~ agency, agent, bureau, (making arrangements for travellers); ~-sick (ness), suffering from nausea induced by motion of vehicle etc.; ~-stained etc. (as result of travel). 3. ~led (-ld) a., experienced in travelling; ~ŏgue (-g) n., film or illustrated lecture with narrative of travel [after monologue]. [orig. = prec.]

||trä'veller, *-eler, n. Person who travels or is travelling; = COMMERCIAL traveller; gipsy; ~'s cheque, *check, (for fixed amount, encashable on signature in many countries); ~'s joy, wild clematis; ~'s tale, incredible and probably untrue story.

trä'verse (or trăvĕr's) v.t. & i. Travel or lie across (traversed the country; pit traversed by beam); (fig.) consider, discuss, whole extent of (subject); turn (large gun) horizontally; travĕr'sal n. [F (TRANSVERSE)]

trä'vĕstў. 1. n. Ridiculous and grotesque misrepresentation (of person or thing). 2. v.t. Make or be travesty of. [F (travestir disguise, f. It.)]

trawl. 1. n. ~(-net), large wide-mouthed fishing-net dragged by boat along bottom. 2. v.i. & t. Fish with trawl or seine; catch by trawling; ~'er n., (esp.) boat for use with trawl. [prob. Du. traghel drag-net]

tray n. Flat shallow vessel usu. with raised rim for carrying dishes etc. or containing small articles, papers, etc.; shallow lidless box forming compartment of trunk. [E]

trea'cher|ў (-ĕ'ch-) n. Violation of faith esp. by secret desertion of the cause to which one professes allegiance; ~ous a., guilty of or involving treachery, (of weather, ice, memory, etc.) not to be relied on, likely to fail or give way. [F f. trichier cheat (TRICK)]

trea'cl|e n. ||Uncrystallized syrup produced in refining sugar; molasses; ~ў a. [orig. = antidote for snake-bite (F f. L f. Gk)]

tread (-ĕd). 1. v.i. & t. (trod pr. -ŏd; tro'dden, trod). Set down one's foot, walk, step, (of foot) be set down, (~ lightly or warily, fig., deal cautiously with delicate subject; ~'mill, appliance for producing motion by stepping on movable steps on revolving cylinder esp. Hist. as prison punishment, fig. monotonous routine; ~ on air, feel elated; ~ on person's corns, toes, fig., offend his feelings or privileges); walk on, press or crush with the feet, (~ the boards, be an actor; ~ grapes, in making wine; ~ water, maintain upright position in water by moving feet and hands); perform by walking etc., make (hole etc.) by treading; (of male bird) copulate with (hen, or abs.). 2. n. Manner or sound of walking (his heavy tread); top surface of step or stair; part of wheel that touches ground or rails, part of rail that wheels touch, thick moulded part of vehicle tyre for gripping road, part of sole of boot etc. similarly moulded. 3. ~'le n., lever worked by foot and imparting motion to machine. [E]

trea'son (-z-) n. (High) ~, violation by subject of allegiance to sovereign or State punishable with death; breach of faith, disloyalty, (to cause, friend, etc.); ~able (-bly), ~ous, adjs., involving or guilty of treason. [AF *treisoun* f. L (TRADI-TION)]

**trea'sure** (-ĕ'zher). **1.** *n.* Precious metals or gems, hoard of these, accumulated wealth, (*buried treasure*; ~-**hunt,** search for treasure, game in which players seek hidden object(s); ~ **trove** [AF *trové* p.p. of TROVER], treasure of unknown ownership found hidden); thing valued for rarity, workmanship, associations, etc., (*art treasures*); (colloq.) beloved or highly valued person. **2.** *v.t.* Store (*up*) as valuable (lit., or fig. in memory); receive or regard as valuable. **3.** ~**r** *n.,* person in charge of funds of municipality, society, etc. [F f. L f. Gk *thēsauros*]

**trea'sury** (-ĕ'zherǐ) *n.* Place where treasure (lit. or fig.) is kept; funds or revenue of a State or institution or society; department managing public revenue of a country, offices and officers of this; T~ **bench,** (Parl.) front bench occupied by Prime Minister, Chancellor of Exchequer, etc.; ~ **bill,** bill of exchange issued by government to raise money for temporary needs. [F *tresorie* (prec.)]

**treat. 1.** *v.t.* & *i.* Act towards, behave to, (*treated me kindly, as if I were an idiot; better treat it as a joke*); deal with or apply process to (*treated him for sunstroke; treat it with acid*); manipulate, present, (subject) in literature or art; provide (person, or abs.) with food, drink, or entertainment at one's own expense (*to thing provided: treated us to a trip to the zoo; I'll treat myself to a cream bun*); negotiate (*with person*); give spoken or written exposition *of*. **2.** *n.* Thing that gives great pleasure (*what a treat it is not to have to get up early*); entertainment (e.g. picnic) designed to do this; treating of others to food etc. (*it's my treat;* STAND *treat*). **3.** ~**'ise** (*or* -z) *n.,* literary composition dealing esp. formally with subject; ~'**ment** *n.,* (mode of) dealing with or behaving towards person or thing, mode of treating subject in literature or art; ~'**ў** *n.,* formally concluded and ratified agreement between States, agreement between persons esp. for purchase of property. [F *traitier* f. L *tracto* handle]

**tre'ble** *a., n.,* & *v.* **1.** *a.* (-bly). Threefold, triple, 3 times as much or many (*treble the amount*); (of voice)

high-pitched; (Mus.) = SOPRANO (esp. ǁof boy's voice or boy, or of instrument; ~ **clef,** with G above middle C on second lowest line of staff). **2.** *n.* Treble quantity or thing; (Darts) hit on narrow ring between the two middle circles on the board, scoring treble; soprano; high-pitched voice. **3.** *v.t.* & *i.* Multiply, be multiplied, by 3 (*has trebled its value; its value has trebled*). [F f. L (TRIPLE)]

**tree. 1.** *n.* Perennial plant with single woody self-supporting stem (*trunk*) usu. unbranched for some distance above ground (*at the* TOP¹ *of the tree;* grow on ~**s,** fig., be plentifully available without effort); piece or frame of wood for various purposes e.g. BOOT²-*tree;* FAMILY *tree.* **2.** *v.t.* Force (animal, fig. person) to take refuge in tree. **3.** ~-**creeper,** small creeping bird feeding on insects in tree-bark; ~-**fern** (with large upright woody stem); ~-**ring** (in cross-section of tree, from one year's growth); ~ **surgeon,** one who treats decayed trees in order to preserve them. [E]

**tre'foil** *n.* Kind of plant with leaves of 3 leaflets (clover, shamrock, etc.); 3-lobed thing esp. ornamentation in tracery etc.; ~**ed** (-ld) *a.,* having such ornament. [AF (TRI-, FOIL¹)]

**trek.** (orig. S. Afr.) **1.** *v.i.* (-kk-). Migrate or journey with one's belongings in ox-wagons; travel arduously. **2.** *n.* Such journey, each stage of it; organized migration of body of persons. [Du., = draw]

**tre'llis** *n.* ~(-work), lattice or grating of light wooden or metal bars used esp. as support for fruit-trees or creepers and often fastened against wall. [F f. Rom. (TRI-, L *licium* warp-thread)]

**tre'matode** *n.* Kind of parasitic flatworm. [Gk (*trēma* hole)]

**tre'mble. 1.** *v.i.* Shake involuntarily with fear or excitement or weakness, (fig.) be in state of apprehension (*at danger, for* person *in danger, to think or at the thought of*); move in quivering manner (*leaves tremble in the breeze;* fig., of person's fate, life, etc., esp. ~ **in the balance,** have reached critical point, be in great danger); **tre'mblў** *a.* (colloq.) **2.** *n.* Trembling, quiver, (*a tremble in her voice*). [F f. Rom. f. L (as TREMOR)]

**tremē'ndous** *a.* Awe-inspiring,

overpowering, (colloq.) remarkable or considerable or excellent (*makes a tremendous difference*; *gave a tremendous performance*). [L *tremendus* to be trembled at (TREMOR)]

**tre′molō** *n.* (Mus.; *pl.* ∼s). Tremulous effect in singing or playing. [It. (TREMULOUS)]

**tre′mor** *n.* (Of leaf, part of body, voice, person) shaking, quivering; thrill (of fear, exultation, etc.); (earth) ∼, slight earthquake. [F or L (*tremo* tremble)]

**tre′mūlous** *a.* Trembling, quivering. [L *tremulus* (prec.)]

**trench. 1.** *v.t. & i.* Dig ditch(es) or esp. trench(es) in (ground), dig (soil, garden) thus so as to bring subsoil to the top; (arch.) encroach (*up*)*on* (person's rights, privacy, etc.), verge or border (*up*)*on* (heresy, vulgarity, etc.). **2.** *n.* Long narrow usu. deep ditch, esp. one dug by troops to stand in and be sheltered from enemy's fire, (in *pl.*) defensive system of these; ∼ **coat,** (soldier's) lined or padded waterproof coat; ∼ **mortar,** light simple mortar throwing bomb from one's own into enemy trenches. **3.** ∼′**ant** *a.,* (of style, language, etc.) incisive, terse, vigorous; ∼′**ancy̆** *n.*; ∼′**er** *n.,* (arch.) wooden platter for serving food (good ∼**erman,** one who eats much). [F *trenche, -ier* cut]

**trend. 1.** *v.i.* Bend or turn away in specified direction, (fig.) be chiefly directed, have general and continued tendency. **2.** *n.* General direction and tendency (esp. fig. of events, opinion, fashion, etc.); ∼-**setter,** person who leads the way in fashion etc.; ‖∼′y̆ *a.* (∼**ily,** ∼**iness**) & *n.,* (colloq., usu. derog.) fashionable (person). [E]

**trente-et-quarante** (trahṅtăkă-rah′ṅt) *n.* = ROUGE-*et-noir*. [F, = 30 and 40]

**trepă′n. 1.** *n.* Surgeon's cylindrical saw for removing part of skull. **2.** *v.t.* (-**nn**-). Perforate (skull) with trepan. [L f. Gk *trupanon* auger]

**trĕpĭdă′tion** *n.* Tremulous agitation, flurry; perturbation of mind. [L (*trepidus* flurried)]

**tre′spass. 1.** *v.i.* Make unlawful or unwarrantable intrusion (*on* or *upon* land, rights, etc., or abs.; ∼ **on** person's preserves, fig. meddle in a matter that he has made his own); make unwarrantable claims *on* (*shall trespass on your hospitality*); (literary or arch.) offend *against*

(*forgive them that trespass against us*). **2.** *n.* Transgression of law or right; (arch.) a sin or offence. [F f. L (TRANS-, PASS)]

**trĕss** *n.* Portion, lock, plait, of hair of human (esp. female) head; (in *pl.*) head of such hair. [F]

**tre′stle** (-sel) *n.* Supporting structure for table etc. consisting of bar supported by two divergent pairs of legs or of two frames fixed at an angle or hinged; ∼(-**table**), table of board(s) laid on trestles etc.; ∼(-**work**), open braced framework to support bridge etc. [F f. Rom. (L *transtrum* cross-beam)]

‖**trews** (-ōoz) *n.pl.* Close-fitting usu. tartan trousers. [Ir. & Gael. (TROUSER)]

**trey** (trā) *n.* 'Three' on dice or (arch.) cards. [F f. L *tres* three]

**T.R.H.** *abbr.* Their Royal Highnesses.

**tri- in** *comb.* Three (times); ‖∼′**căr** *n.,* 3-wheeled motor-car; ∼′**chŏrd** (-k-) *n.,* 3-stringed instrument; ∼**chrōmă′tĭc** (-k-) *a.,* 3-coloured, (of vision) having normal 3 colour-sensations (red, green, purple); ∼′**grăm** *n.,* figure of 3 lines; ∼**lă′teral** *a.,* having 3 sides, existing etc. between 3 parties; ∼**lĭ′ngual** (-nggw-) *a.,* of, in, using, 3 languages; ∼**mĕter** (trī′-) *n.,* (Pros.) verse of 3 measures; ∼**vă′lent** *a.,* (Chem.) having a valence of 3. [L & Gk]

**trī′ăd** (*or* -ăd) *n.* The number 3; group of 3 (esp. notes in chord); **triă′dĭc** *a.* (-**ically**). [F or L f. Gk]

**trī′al** *n.* Process or mode of testing qualities, experimental treatment, test, (*bicycle is hired, clerk employed,* **on** ∼, to be retained only if efficient; *will give you* or *it a* ∼, employ on trial; ∼ **and error,** repeated trials till one succeeds; ∼ (**match**), game of cricket, football, etc., played before selectors for an important team; *trial* HEAT; ∼ **run, trip,** of new vessel or vehicle to test performance); trying thing or experience or person (*old age has many trials*; *the boy next door is a trial*); judicial examination and determination of issues between parties by judge with or without jury (*on trial, stood trial, was brought to trial, for murder*; *trial* JURY). [AF (TRY)]

**trī′ăngle** (-nggel) *n.* Figure of 3 straight lines each meeting the others at different points, any 3 things not in a straight line, with the imaginary lines joining them (*a triangle of beacons*; **eternal** ~, two persons of one sex and one of the other with problems resulting from conflict of sexual attractions; implement etc. of this shape; (Mus.) instrument of steel rod bent into triangle sounded by striking with small steel rod; **triăˈngular** (-ngg-) *a.*, triangle-shaped (**triangular pyramid**, with 3-sided base), 3-cornered, (of contest, treaty, etc.) between 3 persons or parties; **triăˈngulāte** (-ngg-) *v.t.*, divide (area) into triangles for surveying purposes; **triāngulāˈtion** *n.* (-ngg-). [F, or L TRI-)]

**Triăˈssic** *a.* & *n.* (Of) earliest Mesozoic period or system. [TRIAD]

**tribe** *n.* Group of (primitive) families under recognized chief and usu. claiming common ancestor; any similar natural or political division; (usu. derog.) set or number of persons esp. of one profession etc. or family (*the whole tribe of them*, of *actors*); ~ˈsman, member of (one's own) tribe; **triˈbal** *a.* (-lly). [F or L *tribus*]

**tribŏˈlogy** *n.* Study of friction, wear, lubrication, and design of bearings. [Gk (*tribō* rub)]

**tribūlāˈtion** *n.* Great affliction. [F f. L (*tribulum* threshing-sledge)]

**tribūˈnal** *n.* Seat or bench for judge(s) or magistrate(s); court of justice (also fig.: *before the tribunal of public opinion*); board appointed to adjudicate in some matter. [F or L (foll.)]

**triˈbūn|e**[1] *n.* Popular leader or demagogue; (Rom. Hist.) ~e (**of the people**), officer chosen by the people to protect their liberties, **military** ~e, legionary officer; ~ate, ~eship (-nsh-), *ns.*, (tenure of) office of tribune; ~iˈcial, ~iˈcian, (-sha-) *adjs.* [L *tribunus* (TRIBE)]

**triˈbūne**[2] *n.* (Apse containing) bishop's throne in basilica; dais, rostrum. [F f. It. f. L *tribuna* (= TRIBUNAL)]

**triˈbūt|e** *n.* Payment made periodically by one State or ruler to another as sign of dependence, obligation to pay this (*was laid under tribute*); (fig.) contribution, esp. thing done, said, or given, as mark of respect, affection, etc., (*paid a tribute to him*; *floral tributes to actress, at*

*funeral*); ~arȳ, (*a.*; -ily, -iness) paying or subject to tribute, contributory, (of river) flowing into larger river or lake, (*n.*) tributary State, person, or stream. [L *tributum* (*tribuo* -*ut*- assign, orig. divide between TRIBES)]

**trice** *n.* In a ~, in an instant. [*trice* haul up, f. LDu.]

**triˈceps** *n.* Muscle (esp. in upper arm) with 3 points of attachment. [L (*caput* head)]

**trichˈinoˈsis** (-k-) *n.* Disease caused by hairlike worms in muscles; ~oˈlogy *n.*, study of hair; ~oˈlogist *n.* [Gk *thrix trikh-* hair)]

**trichŏˈtomy** (-k-) *n.* Division into, classification in, 3 parts (cf. DICHOTOMY). [Gk *trikha* threefold]

**trick. 1.** *n.* Fraudulent device or stratagem (*I suspect some trick*; *trick of the TRADE*), optical or other illusion (*a trick of the light*); feat of skill or dexterity, unusual action (e.g. begging) learned by animal, knack or way of doing things, (**a ~ worth two of that**, a better expedient; **do the** ~, sl., accomplish desired result; **how's** ~**s**?, sl., how are you?, how are things?; ~ **cyclist**, sl., psychiatrist); peculiar or characteristic habit (*has a trick of repeating himself*); mischievous, foolish, or discreditable act, practical joke, (*a mean, dirty, trick to play*; *~ **or treat**, Hallowe'en children's game of calling at houses with threat of pranks if sweets etc. are not given them; **up to** one's **~s**, misbehaving; **up to** person's **~s**, aware of mischief he is likely to cause); (Naut.) turn of duty at helm; (Cards) cards played in, the winning of, one round (ODD trick); (*attrib.*) done to deceive or mystify (*trick photography*). **2.** *v.t.* Deceive or cheat (person *out of* thing, *into* doing); (of thing) foil, baffle, take by surprise; ~ **out**, **up**, decorate esp. showily. **3.** ~ˈerȳ *n.*, (esp.) deceitful behaviour; ~ˈster *n.*, deceiver, rogue; ~ˈsȳ *a.*, full of tricks, playful; ~ˈȳ *a.* (-ily, -iness), crafty, deceitful, (of task etc.) requiring adroitness or avoidance of pitfalls. [F]

**triˈckle. 1.** *v.i.* & *t.* (Cause to) flow drop by drop (*out, down, along*, etc.); (fig.) come or go slowly or gradually (*information trickles out*). **2.** *n.* Trickling flow; ~ **charger**, accumulator-

-charger that works at steady slow rate from mains. [prob. imit.]

**tri´colour, \*-or,** (-ŭler) n. Flag of 3 colours, esp. French national flag of blue, white, and red. [F (TRI-)]

**tri´cŏt** (-kō; or trĕ´-) n. Knitted fabric. [F]

**tri´cўcl|e** n., & v.i. (Ride on) 3-wheeled pedal-driven vehicle; 3--wheeled motor vehicle for disabled driver; ~**ist** n. [CYCLE]

**tri´dent** n. Three-pronged implement e.g. fish-spear or gladiator's weapon; such spear or sceptre as attribute of Neptune or Britannia. [L (dens dent- tooth)]

**Trĭdĕ´ntine** a. Of traditional R.C. orthodoxy. [L Tridentum Trento, place of 16th-c. Council of Trent]

**trĭĕ´nnĭal** a. (~ly) Lasting, recurring every, 3 years. [L (annus year)]

**tri´er** n. Tester; one who perseveres in his attempts (a real trier). [TRY]

**tri´fle. 1.** n. Thing of slight value or importance, small amount esp. of money, (wastes time on trifles; was sold for a trifle; **a** ~ adv., somewhat: seems a trifle annoyed); ||confection of sponge--cake with custard, jelly, fruit, wine, cream, etc. **2.** v.i. Talk or act frivolously; ~ **with**, treat (person, thing, matter) with flippancy or derision, toy with (novel, cigarette, etc.). **3.** tri´fling a., (esp.) frivolous, unimportant, petty. [orig. trufle f. F = truf(f)e deceit]

**trĭfŏr´i|um** n. (pl. ~a). Arcade or gallery above nave and choir arches. [AL]

**tri´gger** (-g-). **1.** n. Movable device for releasing spring or catch and so setting mechanism (esp. that of gun) in motion; agent that sets off a chain reaction; **quick on the** ~, (fig.) quick to respond; ~**-happy**, apt to shoot on slight provocation. **2.** v.t. ~ (**off**), set in motion (as) by means of trigger, initiate or precipitate (process). [tricker f. Du. trekker (trekken pull)]

**trigon|ŏ´mĕtrў** n. Branch of mathematics dealing with relations of sides and angles of triangle, and with relevant functions of any angles; ~omĕ´trĭc(al) adjs. (-ally). [L f. Gk (trigōnon triangle)]

**trike** n., & v.i. (colloq.) Tricycle. [abbr.]

||**tri´lbў** n. ~ (**hat**), soft felt hat with narrow brim and lengthwise dent in crown. [character in novel]

**trĭll. 1.** n. Quavering or vibratory sound (e.g. quick alternation of notes in singing, bird's warbling, the letter r). **2.** v.t. & t. Produce trill, warble (song), pronounce (r etc.) with trill. [It.]

**trĭ´llion** (-lyon) n. (pl. ~, ~s; for pl. usage see HUNDRED). ||Million million millions; \*million millions; ~**th** a. & n. [F or It. (TRI-, MILLION, after billion)]

**tri´lobite** n. Kind of fossil arthropod. [L (TRI-, LOBE)]

**tri´logў** n. Group of 3 related literary or operatic works. [Gk (TRI-)]

**trĭm** a., v., & n. **1.** a. (-mm-). In good order, well arranged or equipped, neat, spruce. **2.** v.t. & i. (-mm-). Set in good order, make neat; remove irregular or untidy parts from (wick of lamp, hedge, beard, hair), remove (such parts; off, away); ornament (dress etc. with lace etc.); adjust balance of (ship, aircraft), arrange (sails) to suit wind; hold middle course in politics or opinion, attach oneself to temporarily prevailing views; (colloq.) rebuke sharply, thrash, worst in bargain etc. **3.** n. State of readiness or fitness (in good, perfect, fighting, trim); ornament or decorative material on dress, furniture, vehicle, etc.; trimming of hair etc. **4.** ~´mĭng n., (esp.) ornamentation of lace etc. on dress etc., (in pl., colloq.) usual accompaniments esp. of meat--joint etc. [E, =make firm]

**tri´marăn** n. Vessel like catamaran, with three hulls side by side. [CATAMARAN]

**trinĭtrotŏ´lŭene, -ŭŏl,** n. A high explosive. [NITRE, TOLUENE]

**tri´nitў** n. Being three, group of 3; **the** (**Holy**) **T~**, (Theol.) the 3 persons of the Godhead (Father, Son, Holy Spirit); **T~** (**Sunday**), Sunday next after Whit Sunday; ||**T~ House**, association concerned with licensing of pilots, erection and maintenance of lighthouses, etc.; ||**T~ term** (in university etc., beginning after Easter); **Trĭnĭtār´ian** n., believer in the Trinity. [F f. L trinitas (trinus threefold)]

**tri´nkĕt** n. Trifling ornament esp. one worn on the person. [orig. unkn.]

**trī'ō** (-ē'ō) n. (Mus.; pl. ~s). (Performers of) composition for 3 voices or instruments; middle part of minuet; set of 3. [F & It., f. L]

**trī'olèt** n. Eight-line poem with first line recurring as fourth and seventh, and second as eighth. [F (-LET)]

**trip. 1.** v.i. & t. (-pp-). Walk or dance with quick light steps, (fig. of rhythm etc.) run lightly; take a trip (*to* place, or colloq. with drugs); ~ (**up**), stumble (*on*, *over*, obstacle, difficulty, etc.), commit blunder or inaccuracy or moral lapse, cause (person) to stumble by entangling or suddenly catching his feet, (fig.) detect (person) in blunder; (Naut.) loose (anchor) from bottom; (Mech.) release (part of machine) suddenly by knocking aside catch etc. **2.** n. Journey, voyage, excursion esp. for pleasure; (colloq.) visionary experience caused by drug; nimble step; stumble (lit. or fig.), tripping or being tripped up; contrivance for tripping mechanism etc. **3.** ~-wire (stretched near ground to operate warning device, mine, etc., if disturbed). **4.** ||~'per n., person who goes on a trip esp. for a day's outing. [F f. Du. *trippen* skip, hop]

**tripär'tite** a. Consisting of 3 parts; shared by or involving 3 parties. [L (*partior* divide)]

**tripe** n. First or second stomach of ruminant, esp. ox, as food; (sl.) worthless or trashy thing, rubbish. [F]

**trī'ple** a., n., & v. **1.** a. (-ply). Threefold, consisting of 3 parts or involving 3 parties (~ **crown**, pope's tiara, winning of 3 important sporting events; ~ **jump**, = HOP[2], skip, and jump; ~ **time**, Mus., with 3 beats to bar); 3 times as great. **2.** n. Set of 3; number or amount 3 times another. **3.** v.t. & i. Multiply by three. **4. trī'plèt** n., set of 3 things esp. notes played in time of two or verses rhyming together, one of 3 children or animals born at a birth; **trī'plèx** a., triple, threefold; **trī'plicate**, (a.) having 3 corresponding parts, existing in 3 examples, tripled, (n.) state of being triplicate, (-ăt; v.) multiply by three, make in triplicate; **triplica'tion** n. [F or L *triplus* f. Gk]

**trī'pŏd** n. Stool, table, utensil, resting on 3 feet or legs; 3-legged

stand for camera etc.; ||**trī'pŏs** n., (Camb. Univ.) honours examination for B.A. degree. [L f. Gk, = three-footed]

||**trī'pper**. See TRIP.

**trī'ptych** (-k) n. Picture etc. of 3 panels hinged vertically together. [after DIPTYCH]

**trīr'ēme** n. Ancient warship with 3 banks of oars. [F or L (*remus* oar)]

**trisĕ'ct** v.t. Divide into 3 (usu. equal) parts; ~**ion** n. [L *seco sect-* cut]

**trīsў'll|able** n. Word or metrical foot of 3 syllables; ~**ǎ'bĭc** a. [TRI-]

**trīte** a. (Of sentiment, quotation, etc.) hackneyed, worn out by constant repetition. [L *tero trit-* rub]

**trī'tium** n. (Chem.) Heavy radioactive isotope of hydrogen with mass about 3 times that of ordinary hydrogen. [L f. Gk *tritos* third]

**Trī'ton** n. (Gk Myth.) Minor sea-god usu. represented as man with fish's tail and carrying trident and shell-trumpet. [L f. Gk]

**trī'tūrāt|e** v.t. Grind to powder or paste; ~**or** n. [L *trituro* grind corn (TRITE)]

**trī'umph. 1.** n. (Rom. Ant.) processional entry of victorious general into Rome; state of being victorious, great success or achievement, supreme example *of*, (*returned home in triumph*; *the triumph of good over evil*; *has achieved great triumphs*; *is a triumph of engineering*); joy at success, exultation, (*his triumph was short-lived*). **2.** v.i. (Rom. Ant.) ride in triumph; gain victory, be successful, prevail, (*over* enemy, obstacles, etc.), exult (*over*). **3. triŭ'mphal** a. (-lly), of, used in, celebrating, a triumph (*triumphal car, entry, arch*); **triŭ'mphant** a., victorious, successful, exultant. [F f. L]

**triŭ'mvir** n. (pl. ~s, ~i pr. -ī). Member of a government (esp. Rom. Hist.) or board of 3 men; ~**ate** n., such government or board. [L (*tres* three, *vir* man)]

**trī'ūne** a. Three in one (*triune God*). [TRI-, L *unus* one]

**trī'vèt** n. Iron tripod or bracket for cooking-pot or kettle to stand on; **as right** (orig. = steady) **as a** ~, (a. & adv., colloq.) in perfectly good state. [app. L TRIpes 3-footed]

**trī'via** n.pl. Trifles, trivialities. [mod. L, pl. of *trivium*, infl. by foll.]

**trī'vïal** a. (~ly). Of small value

or importance, trifling, (*trivial offence, loss*; *raised trivial objections*); (of person) concerned only with trivial things; (*arch.*) commonplace, humdrum, (*the trivial round of daily life*); **trivia'lity** *n*. [L *trivialis* commonplace (*trivium* 3-way street-corner)]

**tro'chee** (-kĭ) *n*. A metrical foot (- ˘); **trocha'ic** (-k-), (*a.*) of trochees, (*n.*, usu. in *pl.*) trochaic verse. [L f. Gk, = running]

**trŏd('den).** See TREAD.

**trŏ'glodyte** *n*. Cave-dweller. [L f. Gk *trōglē* cave)]

**troi'ka** *n*. (Russian vehicle with) team of 3 horses abreast; group of 3 persons esp. as administrative council. [Russ.]

**Trō'jan. 1.** *a.* Of ancient Troy in Asia Minor; ~ **War**, legendary struggle between Greeks and Trojans; ~ **Horse**, hollow wooden horse used by Greeks to enter Troy, (fig.) person or device insinuated to bring about enemy's downfall. **2.** *n.* Inhabitant of Troy; (fig.) person who works or fights or endures courageously (*like a Trojan*). [L (*Troia* Troy)]

**trŏll**[1] *v.t.* & *i.* Sing out in carefree jovial manner; fish by drawing bait along in water. [cf. F *troller* to quest)]

**trŏll**[2] *n*. (Scand. & Gmc Myth.) Supernatural being, giant or dwarf. [N]

**trŏ'lley, -llў,** *n*. ||Low truck running on rails; ||small table or stand on wheels or castors for serving food, transporting luggage, etc.; ~(-**wheel**), wheel attached to pole etc. for collecting current from overhead electric wire to drive vehicle (||~**bus**, electric bus using trolley). [dial., perh. f. TROLL[1]]

**trŏ'llop** *n*. Disreputable girl or woman. [cf. arch. *trull* prostitute]

**trŏmbō'ne** (*or* -ŏ'm-) *n*. Large brass wind instrument with sliding tube. [F or It. (*tromba* trumpet)]

**trompe-l'œil** (trŏmp lŭ'ē) *n*. & *a*. (Still-life painting etc.) designed to make spectator think objects represented are real. [F, lit. 'deceives the eye']

**-trŏn** *suf.* forming *ns.* denoting (accelerators for) elementary particles. [ELECTRON]

**trōop. 1.** *n*. Assembled company, assemblage of persons or animals, (*a troop of children, of antelopes*;

surrounded *by troops of friends*); (in *pl.*) soldiers, armed forces; cavalry unit commanded by captain; unit of artillery and armoured formation; group of 3 or more Scout patrols; ~-**carrier**, ~-**ship**, large aircraft *or armoured vehicle, ship, for transporting troops. **2.** *v.i.* & *t.* Come together or move in a troop (*along, in, out*, etc.); (colloq.) go, walk, *off or away*; ||~**ing the colour(s)**, ceremony of transferring flag(s) at public mounting of garrison guards. **3.** ~**er** *n.*, cavalry or armoured-unit private soldier (**swear like a ~er**, extensively or forcefully), cavalry horse, troop-ship, (Austral. Hist. & U.S.) mounted or motor-borne policeman. [F *troupe*]

**trōpe** *n*. Figurative use of a word. [L f. Gk *tropos* (*trepō* turn)]

**trŏ'phy** *n*. (Gk & Rom. Ant.) arms etc. of vanquished army set up as memorial of victory; thing kept as prize or memento of any contest or success; group of things arranged for ornamental display. [F f. L f. Gk *tropaion*]

**trŏ'pic. 1.** *n*. Parallel of latitude 23° 27′ north (~ **of Cancer**) or south (~ **of Capricorn**) of the equator (**the ~s**, region between these); corresponding circle on celestial sphere where sun appears to turn after reaching greatest declination. **2.** *a.* Tropical. **3.** ~**al** *a.* (-lly), of, peculiar to, suggestive of, the tropics (*tropical fish, plants, diseases, heat*), of trope(s), figurative. [L f. Gk (*tropē* turn)]

**trŏ'po|pause** (-z) *n*. Interface between troposphere and stratosphere; ~**sphere** *n.*, layer of atmospheric air extending about 7 miles upwards from earth's surface, in which temperature falls with increasing height (cf. STRATOSPHERE). [Gk *tropos* turn]

**troppo** (trŏ'pō) *adv.* (Mus.) Too; *andante* etc. **ma non ~**, but not too much so. [It.]

**trŏt. 1.** *v.i.* & *t.* (-tt-). (Of horse etc.) proceed at steady pace faster than walk lifting each diagonal pair of legs alternately, (of person) run at moderate pace esp. with short strides, traverse (distance) thus, cause (horse, person) to trot; (colloq.) walk, go; ~ **out**, cause (horse) to trot to show his paces, (fig.) produce or introduce (person, thing, information, subject) (as if) for inspection and approval. **2.** *n.* Action or exercise of trotting (*proceed at a trot; went for a trot*); **on the ~,** colloq., continually busy (*kept him on the trot*), in succession (*five weeks on the trot*); **the ~s,** (sl.) diarrhoea. **3.** **~'ter** *n.,* (esp.) horse bred or trained for trotting, (usu. in *pl.*) animal's foot as food, (joc.) human foot; **~'ting** *n.,* (esp.) harness racing for trotting horses. [F]

**tröth** *n.* (arch.). Truth (**by my ~, in ~,** truly, upon my word); faith, loyalty, (**pledge, plight,** one's **~,** pledge one's word esp. in marriage or betrothal). [E (TRUTH)]

**trou'badour** (-ōō'badoor) *n.* French medieval lyric poet singing of chivalry and gallantry. [F f. Prov. (*trobar* find, compose)]

**trou'ble** (trŭb-). **1.** *v.t.* & *i.* Agitate, disturb, be disturbed or worried (*don't let it trouble you, don't trouble about it; a troubled conscience*); afflict, cause pain etc. to, (*is troubled with headaches; how long has it been troubling you?*); subject, be subjected to, inconvenience or unpleasant exertion (*sorry to trouble you;* iron. *I'll trouble you to mind your own business*). **2.** *n.* Vexation, affliction, (*has been through much trouble; am having trouble with the ignition, with my teeth;* **ask, look, for ~,** colloq., meddle, be rash, etc.; **in ~,** subject to censure, punishment, etc., colloq. pregnant but unmarried; **make ~,** cause disturbance or disagreement); cause of annoyance (*the trouble with him is that he can't bear losing*); faulty condition or operation (*kidney, engine, trouble*), (in *pl.*) public disturbances; inconvenience, unpleasant exertion, bother, (*do not put yourself to any trouble; take the trouble to visit her, go to the trouble of visiting her*), cause of this (*the child is a great trouble to them;* **be no ~,** cause no inconvenience etc.); **~-maker,** troublesome person, esp. deliberate fomenter of disagreement; **~-shooter,** person who traces and corrects faults in machinery etc., mediator in dispute. **3.** **~some** (-bels-) *a.,* causing trouble, annoying; **trou'blous** (trŭb-) *a.,* (arch., literary) full of troubles, agitated, disturbed, (*troublous times*). [F f. L (TURBID)]

**trough** (-ŏf, -awf) *n.* Long narrow open receptacle for water, feed, etc.,

channel or hollow comparable to this; (Meteor.) elongated region of low barometric pressure. [E]

**trounce** *v.t.* Inflict severe punishment or defeat on. [orig. unkn.]

**troup|e** (-ōōp) *n.* Company of actors, acrobats, etc.; **~'er** *n.,* member of theatrical troupe, (fig.) staunch colleague. [F, = TROOP]

**trou'ser** (-z-) *n.* (**Pair of**) **~s,** two-legged outer garment reaching from waist usu. to ankles; WEAR *the trousers;* **~-suit,** woman's suit of trousers and jacket; **~ed** (-zerd) *a.* [in *pl.* after *drawers;* Ir. & Gael. *triubhas* trews]

**trousseau** (trōō'sō, trōōsō') *n.* (*pl.* **~s, ~x,** *pr.* -z). Bride's outfit. [F (TRUSS)]

**trout** *n.* (*pl.* usu. same). Fish related to salmon; (sl., derog.) *old etc.* woman. [E f. L *tructa*]

**tröve.** See TREASURE; **trö'ver** *n.,* (Law) action to recover value of goods wrongfully taken or detained. [AF *trover* find]

**trow** (or -ō) *v.t.* (arch.) Think, believe. [E, rel. to TRUCE]

**trow'el** *n.* Flat-bladed tool for spreading mortar or splitting bricks (LAY⁴ *it on with a trowel*); scoop for lifting small plants or earth. [F f. L *truella*]

**troy** *n.* **~** (**weight**), system of weights used for precious metals and gems, with pound of 12 ounces or 5760 grains. [*Troyes,* place]

**tru'an|t** (-ōō'-). **1.** *n.* Child who absents himself from school, (joc.) person missing from work etc., (**play ~t,** stay away thus). **2.** *a.* (Of person, conduct, thoughts, etc.) shirking, idle, wandering; **~cў** *n.* [F, prob. f. Celt.]

**truce** (-ōōs) *n.* (Agreement for) temporary cessation of hostilities (FLAG³ *of truce*). [orig. *trewes* pl.; E, = covenant (TRUE)]

**trŭck¹** *v.t.* & *i.,* & *n.* Barter, exchange, (arch.); **have no ~,** avoid dealing *with.* [F *troquer*]

**trŭck²** *n.* Strong vehicle for heavy goods; ‖open railway wagon; porter's barrow, hand-cart. [perh. f. foll.]

**trŭ'ckle. 1.** *n.* **~(-bed),** low bed on wheels that may be pushed under another, esp. as formerly used by servants etc. **2.** *v.i.* Submit obsequiously, cringe (*to*). [AF *trocle* f. L *trochlea* pulley f. Gk]

**trŭ'cŭlen|t** *a.* Fierce; aggressive,

savage; pugnacious; ∼**ce**, ∼**cў**, ns.
[L (*trux truc-* fierce)]

**trudge. 1.** *v.i.* & *t.* Go on foot esp.
laboriously, traverse (distance) thus.
**2.** *n.* Trudging walk. [orig. unkn.]

**true** (-ōō). **1.** *a.* (TRULY). In
accordance with fact or reality (*a
true story*; **come** ∼, be realized in
fact; (**it is**) ∼, certainly, admittedly:
*true, it would cost more*); genuine,
rightly or strictly so called, not
spurious or counterfeit etc., (*could
not form a true judgement*; *frog is not a
true reptile*; *the true heir*; ∼ **north**,
geographical, not magnetic; *true*
RIB); accurately conforming *to* (type
etc.; ∼ **to life**, accurately representing it); (of voice etc.) in good
tune; loyal or faithful or constant
(*to*); (of wheel, post, beam, etc.)
correctly positioned, balanced or
upright or level (opp. *out of true*);
∼ **bill**, (fig.) true assertion; ∼**-blue**
*a.* & *n.*, (person) of uncompromising
orthodoxy or loyalty; ∼**-love**, sweetheart; *true-*LOVE(*r's*) *knot*. **2.** *adv.*
Truly (*tell me true*); accurately (*aim
true*); without variation (*breed true*).
[E]

**truffle** *n.* Edible rich-flavoured
subterranean fungus; globular sweetmeat of chocolate mixture covered
with cocoa etc. [prob. Du. f. F]

‖**trug** *n.* Shallow oblong garden-
-basket usu. of wood strips. [perh.
dial. var. of TROUGH]

**truism** (-ōō'-) *n.* Statement too
obviously true or too hackneyed to
be worth making; proposition that
states nothing not already implied
in one of its terms (e.g. *I don't like my
tea too hot = I don't like it hotter than I
like it*). [TRUE]

**truly** (-ōō'-) *adv.* Sincerely,
genuinely, (*am truly grateful*; YOURS
*truly*); (usu. parenth.) really, indeed,
(*truly, I should never know what to say*);
faithfully, loyally, (*served him truly*);
accurately, truthfully, (*is not truly
depicted*); rightly, properly, (WELL[2]
*and truly*).

**trump**[1]. **1.** *n.* Playing-card of suit
temporarily ranking above others
(∼ **card**, card turned up to determine, or belonging to, trump suit,
fig. valuable resource; **play a** ∼,
fig., take a step that gives one an
advantage esp. by surprise; ‖**turn
up** ∼**s**, colloq., turn out better than
expected, have a stroke of luck);
(colloq.) person of great excellence.

**2.** *v.t.* & *i.* Defeat (card or its player)
with trump; ∼ **up**, fabricate, invent,
(story, excuse, accusation, etc.).
[corrupt. of TRIUMPH in same (now
obs.) sense]

**trump**[2] *n.* (arch., poet.) Trumpet-
blast (**the last** ∼, to wake the dead
on Judgement Day). [F *trompe*]

**trumpery. 1.** *n.* Worthless finery,
rubbish. **2.** *a.* Showy but worthless,
delusive, shallow. [F *tromperie* deceit]

**trumpet. 1.** *n.* Metal tubular or
conical wind instrument with flared
mouth and bright penetrating ringing
tone, used for military etc. signals,
by heralds, and in orchestral form
having valves etc. to give additional
notes (BLOW[1] one's *own* **trumpet**; ∼**-
-call**, fig., urgent summons to action;
∼**-major**, chief trumpeter of cavalry
regiment); trumpet-shaped thing
(EAR[1]-*trumpet*); sound (as) of trumpet. **2.** *v.i.* & *t.* Blow trumpet; (of
enraged elephant etc.) make loud
sound as of trumpet; proclaim
loudly, advertise, (person's or thing's
merit). **3.** ∼**er** *n.*, (esp.) cavalry
soldier giving signals with trumpet.
[F dim. (TRUMP[2])]

**truncate** *v.t.* Cut top or end from
(tree, body, cone, quotation, etc.);
∼**ion** *n.*; **truncheon** (-shŏn) *n.*,
short club carried by policeman,
staff or baton as symbol of authority.
[L (TRUNK)]

**trundle** *v.t.* & *i.* Roll, move on
wheel(s), esp. heavily or noisily,
(hoop, wheelbarrow, etc., *along*,
*down*, etc.). [var. of obs. or dial.
*trendle* (TREND)]

**trunk** *n.* Main stem of tree opp. to
branches and roots; person's or
animal's body apart from limbs and
head; main part of a structure;
elephant's elongated prehensile nose;
large luggage-box with hinged lid;
*boot of motor car; (in *pl.*) men's
close-fitting shorts worn for swimming, boxing, etc.; ∼**-call**, telephone
call on trunk-line with charges
according to distance; ∼**-line**, main
line of railway, telephone system,
etc.; ∼**-road**, important main road.
[F *tronc* f. L *truncus* cut short]

**truss. 1.** *n.* Supporting framework
of roof, bridge, etc.; surgical
appliance worn to support hernia;
compact cluster of flowers or fruit;
‖bundle of hay or straw. **2.** *v.t.*
Support (roof, bridge) etc. with
truss(es); tie up (fowl) compactly

for cooking; ~ **(up)**, tie (person) up with arms to sides. [F]

**trŭst. 1.** *n.* Firm belief that a person or thing may be relied on, state of being relied on, (**have, place, put,** ~ **in**, feel sure of the loyalty, reliability, etc., of; **in a position of** ~, having responsibility arising from others' confidence in one; **supply goods** etc. **on** ~, on credit; **take** assertion etc. **on** ~, accept it without evidence); thing or person committed to one's care, resulting obligation, (*have fulfilled my trust*); (Law) trusteeship, board of trustees, property committed to trustee(s), (*an estate held in trust*); association of several companies for purpose of united action to prevent competition; BRAINS *trust*; ~ **territory**, one under trusteeship of (State designated by) United Nations; ||UNIT *trust*. **2.** *v.t. & i.* Place trust in, believe in, rely on character or behaviour of, place reliance in, (~ **to**, place esp. undue reliance on; ~ person **with** thing, allow him to use it because one is confident that he will not misuse it); consign (thing *to* person etc.), place or leave (thing *with* person etc., *in* place etc.), without misgivings; allow credit to (customer *for* goods); hope earnestly (*that*, *to* hear etc.). **3.** ~**ee′** *n.*, person or member of board given possession of property with legal obligation to administer it solely for purposes specified, State made responsible for government of an area; ~**ee′ship** *n.*; ~**′ful** (**-lly**), ~**′ing** *adjs.*, not given to suspicion or apprehension, believing in others' honesty or in the kindness of providence; ~**′worthy** (-ẽrdhĭ) *a.* (**-iness**), deserving of trust, reliable; ~**′y̌**, (*a.*, arch.; ~**ily**, ~**iness**) trustworthy (*trusty steed*), (*n.*) well-behaved and privileged convict. [N]

**truth** (-ōō-) *n.* (*pl. pr.* -dhz, -ths). Quality or state of being true or truthful (*we doubt the truth of the rumour*; *there is some truth in what he says*); what is true (*tell us the whole truth*; *the truth is that I forgot*; HOME *truth*); **in** ~, (literary) truly, really, **to tell the** ~, ~ **to tell**, (introducing confession); ~**′ful** *a.* (**-lly**), habitually speaking the truth, (of story etc.) true. [E (TRŬE)]

**try̌. 1.** *v.t. & i.* Test (quality), test qualities of (person, thing) by

experiment, ascertain by experiment, make severe demands on (person etc.), (*try your strength*; *try the door, for* opening; *let us try whether it will break*; *my patience has been sorely tried*; *do not try your eyes with that small print*; ~ *one's* **hand**, see how skilful one is, esp. at first attempt; ~ **on**, put (clothes etc.) on to test fit, ||begin (*it, one's tricks*, etc., *with* person) experimentally to see how much will be tolerated: *no use trying it on with me*; ~**-on** *n.*, colloq., act of trying (it) on, attempt to deceive; ~ **out**, put to the test, test thoroughly; ~**-out** *n.*, experimental test), examine effectiveness or usefulness of for purpose (*try kicking it, soap and water, Harrods*); investigate and decide (case, issue) judicially, subject (person) to trial (*for* murder etc., *for his life*); attempt, endeavour, (to or to do; *better try something easier*; *do try to be on time*; *no use trying to mend it*; *tried my best or hardest*); ~ **and**, colloq. = *try to* do; ~ **for**, apply or compete for (appointment etc.), seek to reach or attain). **2.** *n.* Attempt (*at least have a try*); (Rugby Footb.) touching-down of ball by player behind goal-line, entitling his side to a kick at goal. **3.** ~**′ing** *a.*, (esp.) exhausting, endurable only with difficulty, exasperating. [orig. = separate, distinguish (F *trier* sift)]

**try̌′panosōme** *n.* Parasite infesting blood and often causing disease. [Gk *trupanon* borer, *sōma* body]

**tryst** *n.* (arch., literary). Time and place for (esp. lovers') meeting. [F]

**tsar, czar** (z-), *n.* (Hist.) Emperor of Russia. [Russ., ult. f. L *Caesar*]

**tsĕ′tsĕ** *n.* Afr. fly carrying disease (esp. sleeping sickness) to man and animals by biting. [Tswana]

**T.T.** *abbr.* Teetotal(ler); ||Tourist Trophy; tuberculin-tested.

**tŭb. 1.** *n.* Open flat-bottomed usu. round vessel (~**-thumper**, ranting preacher or orator); (||colloq.) bath (vessel or process); (derog. or joc.) clumsy slow boat. **2.** *v.t. & i.* (**-bb-**). Plant, bathe, wash, in tub. [prob. LDu.]

**tŭ′ba** *n.* Low-pitched brass wind instrument. [It., f. L, = trumpet]

**tŭ′bb|y̌** *a.* (~**ily**, ~**iness**). Tub-shaped, (of person) short and fat. [TUB]

**tūbe. 1.** *n.* Long hollow cylinder, natural or artificial structure having approximately this shape with open or closed ends and serving for passage of fluid etc. or as receptacle, (*a tube of toothpaste*; FALLOPIAN *tube*; TEST[1]--tube*); = INNER *tube* (*tubeless tyre*); cathode-ray tube, e.g. in television set (\*the ~, television), \*thermionic valve; (colloq.) underground electric railway running through cylindrical tunnels. 2. *v.t.* Furnish with, enclose in, tube(s). 3. **tū′bǐng** *n.*, indefinite length of tube or quantity of tubes. [F or L]

**tū′ber** *n.* Thick round root or underground stem of plant, freq. bearing buds, e.g. potato, dahlia; ~**ōse**, (*a.*) having tubers, (-z; *n.*) plant with fragrant creamy-white flowers; ~**ous** *a.* [L, = hump, swelling]

**tū′bercle** *n.* Small rounded swelling in plant or organ of body, esp. as characteristic of tuberculosis in lungs (~ **bacillus**, causing tuberculosis); **tūbĕr′cūlar** *a.*, (esp.) of the nature of tuberculosis; **tūbĕr′cūlin** *n.*, preparation from cultures of tubercle bacillus used for treatment and diagnosis of tuberculosis (**tuberculin-tested** *milk*, from cows shown by tuberculin test to be free of tuberculosis); **tūbĕrcūlō′sǐs** *n.*, infectious bacterial disease marked by tubercles, esp. in lungs; **tūbĕr′-cūlous** *a.* [L *tuberculum* dim. of prec.]

**tū′bǐng.** See TUBE.

**tū′bular** *a.* Tube-shaped, having or consisting of tubes, (of furniture etc.) made of tubular pieces; **tū′būle** *n.*, small tube. [L *tubulus* dim. as TUBE]

‖**T.U.C.** *abbr.* Trades Union Congress.

**tŭck. 1.** *n.* Flattened fold in garment etc. secured by stitching to make it shorter or close(r)-fitting or for ornament; ‖(sl.) eatables esp. cakes and sweets (~-**box**, ~-**shop**, where tuck is kept, esp. for school-children). **2.** *v.t.* Make tuck(s) in (garment, material); draw, thrust, roll, outer or end parts of (cloth, clothes, etc., *up*, *in*) close together or so as to be held (*tuck in the blankets*; *tuck up one's skirt*; *tuck trousers into boots*); draw together into small compass (*tucked his legs under him*; *bird tucks head under wing*); cover (person, one*self*) snugly and compactly *up* or *in* (*tucked up in bed*); stow away (thing *in* corner etc., *out of sight*,

etc.); ~ **in(to)**, (sl.) eat heartily; ~-*in* *n.*, large meal. **3.** ~**′er**, (*n.*) piece of lace etc. in or on woman's bodice (Hist. exc. in *best* BIB *and* tucker), (Austral., colloq.) food, \*(*v.t.*) ~**er** (**out**), (colloq.) tire, weary. [LDu.]

**-tŭde** *suf.* forming abstract *ns.* (*altitude*, *attitude*, *solitude*). [L]

**Tū′dor** *n. & a.* (Member) of royal family of England from Henry VII to Elizabeth I; ~ **rose**, conventional 5-lobed figure of rose; ~ **style** (late Perpendicular, or half-timbered elaborately decorated design of houses). [person]

**Tue(s).** *abbr.* Tuesday.

**Tū′esday** (tū′z-; *or* -dǐ). **1.** *n.* Day of week, following Monday; SHROVE[1] *Tuesday*. **2.** *adv.* (cf. FRIDAY 2). [E]

**tū′fa, tŭff,** *ns.* Kinds of coarse rock. [It. & F f. L *tofus*]

**tŭft** *n.* Bunch or collection of threads, grass, feathers, hair, etc., held or growing together at the base (also **tŭ′ffĕt**); ~**ў** *a.* [prob. F *tofe*]

**tŭg. 1.** *v.t. & i.* (-gg-). Pull hard, pull violently at; tow (vessel) by means of tugboat. **2.** *n.* Hard or violent or jerky pull (also fig.: *felt a great tug at parting*); ~(′**boat**), small powerful steam-vessel for towing others; ~ **of war**, trial of strength between two sides pulling opposite ways on a rope, (fig.) decisive or severe contest. [rel. to TOW[2]]

**tuï′tion** *n.* Teaching, instruction, esp. as thing to be paid for; fee for this. [F f. L (*tueor tuit-* look after)]

**tū′lip** *n.* (Flower of) bulbous spring-flowering plant with showy cup-shaped flowers; ~-**tree** (with tulip-like flowers). [L f. Turk. *tul(i)band* TURBAN (f. its shape) f. Pers.]

**tülle** *n.* Soft fine silk net for veils and dresses. [place]

**tŭm** *n.* (childish or joc.) Stomach (also ~′**tŭm**). [abbr. TUMMY]

**tŭm′ble. 1.** *v.i. & t.* Have a fall, suffer downfall, go sprawling; (of waves, sick person, etc.) roll, toss, to and fro; move, walk, run, in headlong or blundering fashion (*came tumbling along*; *tumbled up the stairs*; *tumbled out of bed*); fall rapidly in amount etc. (*prices of shares tumble*); perform acrobatic feats esp. somersaults; disarrange, rumple, (clothes, hair, etc.); overturn, fling or push (*down*, *out*, *in*, etc.) roughly or carelessly; ~ **to**, (sl.) grasp meaning of (idea etc.). **2.** *n.* Fall (*had a nasty tumble*); somersault or other acrobatic feat. **3.** ~**down**, falling or fallen into ruin, dilapidated; ~**r** *n.*, (esp.) acrobat, kind of pigeon that tumbles, flat-bottomed drinking-glass without handle or foot (orig. with rounded bottom so as not to stand upright), type of electrical switch, part of mechanism of lock or gun-lock; ~(**r**)-**drier**, machine for drying washing in heated rotating drum. [LG *tummelen*]

**tǔ′mbrel, -ǐl,** *n.* Open cart in which condemned persons were conveyed to guillotine during French Revolution. [F (*tomber* fall)]

**tǔm|ě′scent** *a.* Swelling; ~**ǐd** *a.*, swollen, inflated, (fig., of style etc.) inflated, bombastic; ~**ǐ′dǐtỹ** *n.* [L (as TUMOUR)]

**tǔ′mmỹ** *n.* (childish or colloq.) Stomach; ~**-button**, (colloq.) navel. [childish pr.]

**tǔ′mour, *-mor,** (*-er*) *n.* Abnormal or morbid swelling in the body. [L (*tumeo* swell)]

**tǔ′mult** *n.* Riot, angry demonstration of a mob; uproar or din e.g. of waves or crowd; conflict of emotions in the mind; **tǔmǔ′ltǔarỹ** *a.*, (esp.) riotous or undisciplined; **tǔmǔ′ltǔous** *a.*, (esp.) vehement, uproarious. [F or L (prec.)]

**tǔ′mǔl|us** *n.* (*pl.* ~**i** *pr.* -ī). Ancient sepulchral mound. [L (as TUMOUR)]

**tǔn** *n.* Large cask for wine; brewer's fermenting-vat. [E]

**tǔ′na** *n.* (*pl.* ~**s**, same). Tunny; ~(-**fish**), its flesh as food. [Amer. Sp.]

**tǔ′ndra** (*or* tŏŏ′-) *n.* Vast level treeless Arctic region where subsoil is frozen. [Lappish]

**tūne. 1.** *n.* Melody with or without harmony (**call the** ~, have control of events; see PIPER); correct pitch or intonation in singing or playing, adjustment of instrument to obtain this, (*sings in tune*; *piano is out of tune*); **in, out of,** ~ **with**, fig., harmonizing, clashing, with); **change** one's ~, **sing another** ~, change one's style of language or manner esp. from insolent to respectful tone; **to the** ~ (considerable or exorbitant amount) **of** £500 etc. **2.** *v.t.* Put (instrument) in tune, adjust (radio receiver etc.)

to particular wavelength of signals, adjust (engine etc.) to run smoothly and efficiently, (fig.) adjust or adapt (thing *to* purpose etc.); ~ **in**, set radio receiver to right wavelength to receive signal; ~ **up**, (of orchestra) bring instruments to proper or uniform pitch, begin to play or sing, bring to most efficient condition; **tuning-fork**, two-pronged steel fork giving particular note when struck. **3.** ~**ful** (-nf-) *a.* (-lly), melodious, musical; **tū′ner** *n.*, (esp.) person who tunes pianos etc. [TONE]

**tǔ′ngsten** *n.* Heavy refractory metallic element. [Sw., = heavy stone]

**tū′nǐc** *n.* Woman's or girl's loose often sleeveless garment (GYM-*tunic*); close-fitting short coat of police or military uniform. [F or L]

**tǔ′nnel. 1.** *n.* Artificial subterranean passage through hill etc. or under road, river, etc., esp. for railway; subterranean passage dug by burrowing animal; WIND-*tunnel*. **2.** *v.i.* & *t.* (||-ll-). Make tunnel through (hill etc.), make one's way *or* way so. [F dim. of *tonne* TUN]

**tǔ′nnỹ** *n.* Large edible sea-fish. [F *thon* f. Prov. f. L f. Gk *thunnos*]

**tǔp** *n.* Male sheep, ram. [orig. unkn.]

**Tu′pǐ** (tŏŏ′-) *n.* & *a.* (Member or language) of Amer. Ind. people in Amazon valley etc. [Tupi]

**‖tǔ′ppence, tǔ′ppennỹ.** = TWO*pence*, TWO*penny*. [phon. sp.]

**tu quoque** (tūkwŏ′kwī, tŏŏkwŏ′-kwā) *n.* The retort *So are* (or *did* etc.) *you.* [L, = you too]

**tū′ban** *n.* (Esp. Muslim or Sikh) man's head-dress of cotton or silk wound round cap; woman's head-dress or hat resembling this. [ult. f. Turk. f. Pers.; cf. TULIP]

**tū′b|ǐd** *a.* (Of liquid or colour, fig. of style etc.) muddy, thick, not clear or limpid or lucid; ~**ǐ′dǐtỹ** *n.* [L (*turba* crowd)]

**tū′b|ǐne** *n.* Rotary motor driven by flow of water or gas; ~**ō-** *comb. form*; ~**o-fan**, = FAN[1]-*jet*; ~**o-jet** (**engine**), (aircraft with) jet engine in which jet also operates turbine-driven air-compressor; ~**o-prop** (**engine**), (aircraft with) jet engine in which turbine is used as in turbo-jet and also to drive propeller. [F f. L *turbo -in-* spinning-top, whirlwind]

**tur′bot** *n.* Large Eur. flat-fish esteemed as food. [F f. Sw.]

**tur′bulen|t** *a.* Disturbed, in commotion; tumultuous; insubordinate, riotous; ~ce *n.*, (esp.) irregular variation of flow of air etc. [L (*turba* crowd)]

**Tur′co-, Tur′kō-,** *in comb.* Turkish (and). [L (TURK)]

**turd** *n.* (vulg.) Ball or lump of excrement; contemptible person. [E]

**tūree′n** *n.* Deep covered dish for soup. [orig. *terrine*; F (= earthenware dish) f. L (*terra* earth)]

**turf. 1.** *n.* (*pl.* ~s, turves *pr.* -vz.) Covering of grass etc. with earth and matted roots as surface layer of grassland, piece of this cut from ground, (the ~, the racecourse, horse-racing; ~ accountant, bookmaker); slab of peat for fuel; ~′y *a.* **2.** *v.t.* Plant (ground) with turf; (sl.) throw (person or thing) *out*. [E]

**tur′gid** *a.* Swollen, inflated, enlarged; (fig., of language) pompous, bombastic; ~ĕ′scent *a.*, becoming turgid; ~i′dity *n.* [L (*turgeo* swell)]

**Turk** *n.* Native of Turkey; member of Central Asian people from whom Ottomans derived, speaking Turkic languages; ferocious, wild, or unmanageable person; ~'s head, turban-like ornamental knot; ~′ı̆ *a.* & *n.*, (of) group of Ural-Altaic (incl. Turkish) languages and peoples, so ~′ı̆c *a.*; ~′ō- *comb. form.* (cf. TURCO-). [orig. unkn.]

**tur′key¹** *n.* Large (esp. domestic) orig. Amer. gallinaceous bird bred as food, its flesh (eaten esp. at ‖Christmas or *Thanksgiving); *TALK *turkey*; cold ~, (sl.) abrupt withdrawal of narcotics from addict, *(sl.) blunt statements; ~-cock, male turkey (red as a ~-cock, flushed with anger etc.), (fig.) pompous or self-important person. [TURKEY², whence bird was orig. supposed to have been imported]

**Tur′key²** *n.* ~ carpet (made of wool with thick pile and bold design); ~ red, (cotton cloth dyed with) scarlet pigment. [place]

**Tur′kish** *a.* & *n.* (Language) of Turkey or the Turks; of or in Turkish; ~ bath, hot-air or steam bath followed by washing, massage, etc., (in *sing.* or *pl.*) building for this; ~ carpet, = TURKEY² *carpet*; ~ coffee (black, strong, and very sweet); ~ delight, kind of gelatinous

sweetmeat; ~ towel (of cotton terry). [TURK]

**Tur′koman, Tur′kmen,** *n.* Member or language of any of various Turkic tribes in Turkmenistan etc. [Pers.]

**tur′meric** *n.* E. Ind. plant of ginger family; its aromatic root powdered as dyestuff, stimulant, or condiment. [perh. F *terre mérite*]

**tur′moil** *n.* Din and bustle and confusion. [orig. unkn.]

**turn. 1.** *v.t.* & *i.* Move round so as to keep at same distance from a centre, (cause to) receive such motion (*wheel turns*; *turn key in lock*); change from one side to another, invert, reverse, (*turn upside down, inside out, back to front*; fig., *turn an* HONEST *penny, turned the matter over and over in my mind*); perform (somersault); remake (garment) with former inner side out; make (profit); give new direction to, take new direction, adapt, have recourse to, (*turn your face this way*; *turn into a side--road*; *turned the hose on them, his attention to the matter*; *not know where, which way, to ~*, fig., what course to follow, how to proceed, where to seek help); divert (bullet); blunt (edge of knife etc.); move to other side of, go round; pass age or time of (*is or has turned 40, 4 o'clock*); cause to go, send, put, (*was turned loose, into a field*; *turn it out into a basin*); change in nature, form, condition, etc., change for the worse, (cause to) become, (*turned water into wine, prince into frog, beggar into millionaire*; *fear he will turn awkward*; *has turned traitor, Muslim*; *joy has turned to sorrow*; *my luck has turned at last*; *turned pale at the thought*; *the thought turns me pale*); (of leaves, hair) change colour; translate (*turn it into French*); make or become (milk) sour, (stomach) nauseated, (head) giddy; shape (object) in lathe; give (esp. elegant) form to (*well-turned compliment*). **2.** *n.* Act or fact or process of turning (*one turn of the handle*; *took a turn for the better or worse*; *do a hand's ~*, make slightest effort); turning of road; point of turning or change; change of tide (lit. or fig.) from ebb to flow or flow to ebb; tendency, formation, (*was of a mechanical turn of mind*; *do not like the turn of the sentence*); short walk (*take a turn in the garden*) or ride; short performance on stage, in circus, etc., opportunity, occasion, privilege, or obligation, that comes successively to each of several persons etc. (*it is your turn to go*; *your turn will come*; purpose (*will* SERVE *my turn*); service of specified kind (*did me a good turn*); one round in coil of rope etc.; (colloq.) momentary nervous shock (*gave me quite a turn*); (profit made by) difference between buying and selling prices of stocks etc.; (Mus.) ornament of principal note with those above and below it. **3. at every ~**, continually; **by ~s**, in rotation, alternately; **done to a ~**, cooked to exactly right degree; **in ~**, in succession; **in** one's **~**, when one's turn comes; *not turn a* HAIR; **on the ~**, just changing; **out of ~**, before or after one's turn, (fig.) at inappropriate moment; **take ~s**, work etc. alternately; **~ about**, face in new direction; *turn a* DEAF *ear*; **~ adrift**, give no further support etc. to; **~ against**, make or become hostile to; **(~ and) ~ about**, alternately; \***~ around**, turn round; **~ away**, refuse to look (at) or accept; **~ back**, begin or cause to retrace one's steps; *turn* one's BACK *on*; **~-buckle**, device for tightly connecting parts of metal rod or wire; **~'coat**, one who changes sides; **~ down**, fold down, fold down corner of sheet of (bed, page), place face downwards, reduce volume of (sound etc.) by turning knob etc., reduce flame of (gas, lamp, etc.) by turning tap etc., reject (proposal or its maker); *turn* one's HAND *to*; ~ person's **head**, fill him with vanity; **~ in**, fold or incline inwards, hand in, (colloq.) go to bed, (colloq.) abandon (plan etc.); *turn in* one's GRAVE[1]; **~'key**, gaoler; *turn* one's MIND *to*; **~ off**, enter side-road, stop flow or working of by means of tap etc., move (tap etc.) thus, (colloq.) cause to lose interest; **~-off** n., side-road; **~ of speed**, ability to go fast at need; **~ on**, start flow or working of by means of tap etc., move (tap etc.) thus, (colloq.) arouse emotions of (person sexually, with drugs, etc.), depend on, face hostilely; *turn on* one's HEEL[1]; **~ out**, expel, extinguish (electric light etc.), fold or incline outwards, equip, dress (*well turned out*), produce (manufactured goods etc.), empty of contents (*turn out this room*, *your pockets*) or expose thus, (colloq.) get

out of bed, (colloq.) go out of doors, (Mil.) call (guard) from guard-room, be found, prove to be the case, result, (*turns out to be true, that he was never there*; *see how things turn out*; *attempt turned out well*); **~out** n., turning out esp. for duty, number of persons who go to vote etc., equipage; **~ over**, (cause to) fall over, expose or bring uppermost the other side of (*~ over a new leaf*, improve one's conduct), cause (engine etc.) to revolve, consider thoroughly, transfer conduct of (thing *to* person); **~'over** n., turning over, pie or tart made by turning half of pastry over filling, amount of money taken in business, numbers of persons entering or leaving employment etc.; \***~'pike**, road on which toll is collected at gates; **~ round**, turn about, adopt new opinions or policy, unload and reload (ship etc.); **~'stile**, admission-gate with arms revolving on post; **~'table**, circular revolving platform for gramophone record being played or to reverse locomotive etc.; *turn* TAIL[1], *the* CORNER, *the* SCALE[2](*s*), TABLES, *the* TIDE; **~ to**, begin work, apply oneself to, go on to consider next; *turn to* ACCOUNT; *turn* TURTLE[2]; **~ up**, unearth, make one's appearance, (of opportunity etc.) present itself, (colloq.) cause to vomit, give upward turn to, place face up, increase volume of (sound etc.) by turning knob etc., increase flame of (gas, lamp, etc.) by turning tap etc.; **~-up** n., thing turned up, ‖esp. lower end of trouser leg, (colloq.) commotion, (colloq.) unexpected event; **~ upon**, turn on. **4. ~'er** n., (esp.) lathe-worker; **~'ery** n., objects made on, work with, lathe; **~'ing** n., (esp.) use of lathe, (in *pl.*) chips or shavings from this, place where roads meet, road meeting another; **~ing-circle**, smallest circle in which vehicle can turn; **~ing-point** (at which decisive change occurs). [E & F f. L *torno* (*tornus* lathe f. Gk)]

**tur'nip** n. (Plant with) globular root used as vegetable and fodder; **~-tops**, its leaves used as vegetable; **~y** a. [dial. *neep* (E f. L *napus*)]

**tur'pentine** n. Resin got from terebinth and other trees; (**oil of**) **~**, volatile pungent oil distilled from this, used in mixing paints and varnishes and in medicine. [F f. L (TEREBINTH)]

**tur′pitude** *n.* Baseness, depravity, wickedness. [F or L (*turpis* disgraceful)]

**turps** *n.* (colloq.) Oil of turpentine. [abbr.]

**tur′quoise** (-z; *or* -koiz, -kwahz) *n.* Precious stone, usu. opaque and greenish-blue. [F, = Turkish]

**tu′rret** *n.* Small tower esp. as decorative addition to building; low flat usu. revolving armoured tower for gun and gunners in ship or aircraft or fort or tank; rotating holder for tools in lathe etc. [F dim. (TOWER)]

**tur′tle**[1] *n.* (arch.) = ~-**dove**, wild dove noted for soft cooing and affection for its mate. [E f. L *turtur*]

**tur′tle**[2] *n.* Marine reptile with horny shell and flippers, its flesh used for soup (MOCK *turtle* soup); **turn ~**, capsize; ~-**neck**, high close-fitting neck of knitted garment. [alt. of earlier *tortue* (TORTOISE) after prec.]

**Tu′scan** *a.* & *n.* (Classical Italian language, inhabitant) of Tuscany; **~ order**, (Archit., least ornamented). [F f. L]

**tush** *int.* (arch.) expr. contempt or annoyance; ~′**ery** *n.*, (literary) use of archaisms such as *tush*. [imit.]

**tusk** *n.* Long pointed tooth esp. projecting from mouth as in elephant, walrus, or boar; ~′**er** *n.*, elephant with tusks developed. [E]

**tu′ssle** *n.*, & *v.i.* Struggle, scuffle, (*with* person, *for* thing). [orig. Sc. & N. Engl., perh. dim. of *touse* (TOUSLE)]

**tu′ssock** *n.* Clump of grass etc.; ~-**moth** (with tufted larvae); ~′**y** *a.* [perh. dial. *tusk* tuft]

**tu′ssore** *n.* Indian or Chinese silkworm yielding strong but coarse brown silk; ~(-**silk**), this silk. [Hindi]

**tut**(-**tŭt′**) *int.*, *n.*, & *v.* **1.** *int.* expr. impatience, contempt, or rebuke. **2.** *n.* Such exclamation. **3.** *v.i.* (-**tt**-). Exclaim thus. [imit.]

**tu′tor. 1.** *n.* Private teacher, esp. in general charge of person's education; ‖university teacher supervising studies and welfare of assigned undergraduates; ‖book of instruction in a subject. **2.** *v.t.* & *i.* Act as tutor to; work as tutor; restrain, discipline. **3.** **tu′telage** *n.*, (being under) guardianship, instruction, tuition; **tu′telary** *a.*, (of deity, care, etc.) giving protection; **tutor′ial**, (*a.*; -lly) of tutor, (*n.*) period of individual instruction given by college tutor; ~**ship** *n.* [F or L (*tueor tut*- watch)]

*tutti* (too′tē) *adv.* & *n.* (Mus.) All voices or instruments together; passage thus performed. [It., pl. of *tutto* all]

**tu′tu** (too′too) *n.* Ballet dancer's short skirt of stiffened frills. [F]

**tu-whit′** *or* **tu-whoo′** (too-) *n.*, & *v.i.* (Make) cry of owl. [imit.]

*****tuxe′do** *n.* (*pl.* ~s, ~es). Dinner-jacket. [place]

**T.V.** *abbr.* television (set).

**twa′ddle** (-ŏ′-) *v.i.*, & *n.* (Indulge in) useless or dull writing or talk. [earlier *twattle*, alt. of TATTLE]

**twain**, arch. form of *two* (*cut in twain*). [E, masc. of TWO]

**twăng. 1.** *n.* Sound made by plucked string of banjo, harp, bow, etc.; quality of voice compared to this (esp. *nasal twang*). **2.** *v.i.* & *t.* Emit twang, cause to twang. [imit.]

**'twas** (-z, -ŏz; arch., poet.) It was. [contr.]

**twăt** (*or* -ŏt) *n.* (vulg.) Female genitals; (derog.) person, esp. woman. [orig. unkn.]

**tweak. 1.** *v.t.* Pinch and twist or jerk. **2.** *n.* Such action. [prob. dial. *twick*, TWITCH]

‖**twee** *a.* (**tweer** *pr.* twē′er; **tweest** *pr.* twē′ĭst). (Esp. affectedly) dainty or quaint. [childish pr. of SWEET]

**tweed** *n.* Rough-surfaced woollen cloth freq. of mixed colours; (in *pl.*) suit of tweed; ~′**y** *a.*, (esp., fig.) heartily informal. [alt. *tweel* (Sc. var. of TWILL)]

**'tween** *prep.* Between; ‖**twee′nў** *n.*, (arch. colloq.) maid assisting two other servants. [BETWEEN]

**tweet** *n.*, & *v.i.* Chirp (of small bird); ~′**er** *n.*, loudspeaker for high frequencies. [imit.]

**twee′zers** (-z) *n.* (**Pair of**) ~, small pair of pincers for taking up small objects, plucking out hairs, etc. [orig. *tweezes* pl. of obs. *tweeze* case for small instruments]

**twĕlfth** *a.* & *n.* NUMERAL; ‖**the ~** (of August, as beginning of legal grouse-shooting); **~ man**, (Crick.) reserve; **T~night**, night of Epiphany, formerly a time of festivities. [E (foll.)]

**twĕlve** *a.* & *n.* NUMERAL; **the T~** (Apostles); ~′**month**, year; ~′**fold** (-vf-) *a.* & *adv.* [E]

**twĕ′ntў** *a.* & *n.* NUMERAL; (as large

number) told him twenty times; ~-**five,** (Rugby Footb. & Hockey) line drawn, ground within, 25 yds. from either goal; **twě'ntieth** a. & n.; ~**fōld** a. & adv. [E]

**'twere** (-er; arch., poet.) It were. [contr.]

**twěrp** n. (sl.) Stupid or objectionable person. [orig. unkn.]

**twice** adv. Two times, on two occasions, (twice 2 is 4; told him twice; THINK twice); in double degree or quantity (twice as good; is ~ **the man** he was, twice as strong etc.). [E (TWO)]

**twi'ddle. 1.** v.t. Twirl randomly or idly about (~ one's **thumbs,** make them rotate round each other esp. for want of anything to do). **2.** n. Act of twiddling; **twi'ddlӯ** a. [prob. imit.]

**twig**[1] n. Small shoot or branch of tree or shrub. [E]

**twig**[2] v.t. (colloq., -gg-). Understand, catch meaning or nature of, (person, words, plan, that etc., or abs.); perceive, observe. [orig. unkn.]

**twi'light** (-it) n. Light from sky when sun is below horizon in morning or (usu.) evening, period of this; faint light; (fig.) state of imperfect understanding; ~ **of the gods,** (Norse Myth.) conflict in which gods and giants destroy each other; ~ **zone,** decrepit urban area, area between others in position and character; **twi'lǐt** a., dimly illuminated (as) by twilight. [TWO, LIGHT[1]]

**twill. 1.** n. Fabric so woven as to have a surface of parallel ridges. **2.** v.t. (esp. in p.p.) Weave thus. [E, = two-thread]

**'twill** (arch., poet.) It will. [contr.]

**twin** n., a., & v. **1.** n. Each of a closely related or associated pair esp. of children or animals born at a birth (**the T~s,** sign of ZODIAC); exact counterpart of person or thing. **2.** a. Forming, or being one of, such a pair (twin brother(s); ~ **bed,** one of pair of single beds; ~~**engined,** having two engines; ~ **set,** woman's matching cardigan and jumper; ~ **towns,** two towns, usu. in different countries, establishing special links). **3.** v.t. & i. (-nn-). Join intimately together, pair, (with); bear twins. [E (TWO)]

**twine. 1.** n. Strong thread of strands of hemp, cotton, etc., twisted together; coil, twist. **2.** v.t. &

i. Make (string etc.) by twisting strands, weave (garland); garland (brow etc.) with; coil or wind (string, tendrils, itself, oneself, etc., or abs.) round or about something. [E]

**twinge** (-nj) n. Sharp momentary local pain (lit. or fig.; of toothache, conscience, etc.). [E]

**twi'nkl|e. 1.** v.i. & t. (Of light, star, etc.) shine with rapidly intermittent gleams; (of feet in dancing) move rapidly; (of eyes) sparkle; blink, wink, (one's eyes); emit (light) in quick gleams. **2.** n. Twitching of eyelid, blink; sparkle, gleam, of eyes; short rapid movement; slight flash of light. **3.** ~**ĭng** n.; **in a ~ing, in the ~ing of an eye,** in an instant. [E]

**twĭrl. 1.** v.t. Spin or swing or twist (dance-partner, umbrella, moustache, etc.) quickly and lightly round. **2.** n. Twirling motion, flourish made with pen. [imit.]

**twist. 1.** v.t. & i. Change the form of by rotating one end and not the other or the two ends opposite ways, undergo such change, make or become spiral, distort, warp, wrench, (twist round one's little FINGER); ~ person's **arm,** force his hand or wrist round as torture, fig. coerce him by moral pressure; ~ **off,** break off (piece) by twisting; ~ person's **words,** misrepresent him; ~**ed mind,** warped); wind (strands) about each other, make (rope, garland, etc.) thus; (of ball, river, etc.) take curved course, make its way in winding manner; ‖(colloq.) cheat. **2.** n. Twisting, twisted state (lit., or fig. of course of events etc.), dance with vigorous bodily contortions; peculiar tendency of mind, character, etc., (freq. derog.; **round the ~,** sl., crazy); thing made by twisting (e.g. kinds of thread and cord, twisted roll of bread or tobacco, curled piece of lemon etc. peel, ‖paper packet with screwed-up ends); (sl.) young esp. disreputable woman. **3.** ~**er** n., (esp.) swindler, *tornado; TONGUE-twister; ~'ӯ a. (~ily, ~iness), full of twists. [rel. to TWIN, TWINE]

**twit**[1] v.t. (-tt-). Reproach, taunt, (person with fault etc.). [E]

‖**twit**[2] n. (sl.) Foolish person. [orig. dial., perh. f. prec.]

**twitch. 1.** v.t. & i. Give short

sharp pull at or *at* (~ **off,** pull off thus); (of features, muscles, limbs) move or contract spasmodically. **2.** *n.* Sudden involuntary contraction or movement, sudden pull or jerk; (colloq.) state of nervousness. [E]

**twi′tter. 1.** *v.i.* & *t.* (Of bird, or fig. of person) utter succession of light tremulous sounds, utter or express thus. **2.** *n.* Twittering; (colloq.) tremulously excited state. [imit.]

**′twixt** *prep.* (poet., arch.) = BE-TWIXT. [abbr.]

**two** (tōō) *a.* & *n.* NUMERAL; **in** ~, in(to) two pieces; **put** ~ **and** ~ **together,** make inference from known facts; **that makes** ~ **of us,** (colloq.) that is true of myself also; *two a* PENNY; ~ **can play at that game** (threat of retaliation); ~**-dimensional,** having or appearing to have length and breadth but no depth; ~**-edged,** (fig.) = DOUBLE-edged; ~**-faced,** (fig.) insincere; ~**-handed,** used with both hands or by two persons; ǁ~**-pence** (tŭ′pens), sum of two pence, thing of little value (*don't care twopence*); ǁ~**penny** (tŭ′pĕnĭ), (fig.) cheap, worthless; ǁ~**penny-halfpenny** (tŭpnǐhā′pnǐ), contemptible, insignificant; ~**-piece,** suit of clothes or woman's bathing-suit comprising two separate parts; ~**-ply,** (wool etc.) of two strands, layers, or thicknesses; ~**-step,** ballroom dance in march or polka time; ~**-stroke,** (of internal combustion engine) having power cycle completed in one up-and-down movement of piston; ~**-time** *v.t.* (sl.) swindle, deceive (esp. by infidelity); ~**-way,** operating in two directions; ~**′fōld** *a.* & *adv.*; ~**′some** *a.* & *n.,* (game, dance, etc.) for two persons; pair or couple of persons. [E]

**′twould** (-ōōd) arch., poet.) It would. [contr.]

**-ty¹** *suf.* forming *ns.* denoting quality or condition (*cruelty, faculty, plenty, safety*); cf. -ITY. [F f. L *-tas -tatis*]

**-ty²** *suf.* = tens (*twenty, ninety*). [E]

**tycoo′n** *n.* (colloq.) Business magnate. [Jap., = great lord]

**ty′ing.** See TIE.

**tyke, tike,** *n.* Cur; ǁlow fellow; (Yorkshire) ~, Yorkshireman. [N]

**ty′mpan|um** *n.* (*pl.* ~**a,** ~**ums**). (Anat.) middle ear, ear-drum; space enclosed in pediment or between lintel and arch above. [L f. Gk *tumpanon* drum]

**Ty′nwald** (-ōld) *n.* Isle of Man annual assembly proclaiming newly enacted laws. [N, = assembly-field]

**type. 1.** *n.* Person, thing, event, serving as illustration, symbol, or characteristic specimen, of another or of a class; class of things having common characteristics (*dislike men of that type*); (as *suf.*) resembling, functioning as, (*ceramic-type materials; Cheddar-type cheese*); (colloq.) person (of specified character); object, conception, work of art serving as model for subsequent artists; piece of metal with raised letter or character on its upper surface for use in printing, a kind or size of such pieces, (collect. *sing.*) set or supply of these. **2.** *v.t.* & *i.* Be type or example of; assign to a type; write with typewriter. **3.** ~**-cast** *v.t.,* cast (actor) in role appropriate to his nature or previous theatrical successes; ~**-face,** (impression made by) inked part of types, set of types in one design; ~**′script,** typewritten document; ~**-setter,** compositor, composing-machine; ~**-setting,** setting of types in proper order for printing; ~**′writer,** keyed machine enabling user to produce printed characters instead of writing; ~**′written,** produced thus. [F, or L f. Gk, = impression]

**ty′phoid** *n.* ~ (**fever**), infectious bacterial fever attacking intestines. [TYPHUS]

**typhoo′n** *n.* Violent hurricane in E. Asian seas. [Chin., = great wind, & Arab.]

**ty′phus** *n.* An infectious fever. [Gk, = stupor]

**ty′pi|cal** *a.* Serving as type or characteristic example, representative, symbolical, (*a typical Scotsman, shingles rash*); characteristic of, serving to distinguish, a type (*typical markings, structure*); ~**fȳ** *v.t.,* represent by type, be type of; ~**fica′tion** *n.;* ~**pist** *n.,* (esp. professional) user of typewriter; **typo′graphy** *n.,* printing as an art, style and appearance of printed matter; **typogra′phic(al)** *adjs.* (-ically). [L (TYPE)]

**tyr′ant** *n.* Oppressive or cruel ruler, person exercising power arbitrarily or cruelly; (Gk Hist.) absolute ruler usurping power; **tyră′nnical** (-lly), **ty′rannous,** *adjs.,* given to or characteristic of tyranny; **tў'ran-nize** *v.i.* & *t.*, exercise tyranny (*over* person), rule (person etc.) despotically; **tў'rannў** *n.*, cruel and arbitrary use of authority, (period of) rule by tyrant, State thus ruled. [F f. L f. Gk *turannos*]

‖**tўre**, ***tīre**[1], *n.* Hollow inflated, or solid, rubber ring placed round wheel to prevent jarring. [TIRE[1]]

**Tў'rian** *a.* & *n.* (Native) of ancient Tyre; *Tyrian* PURPLE. [L (*Tyrus* Tyre, place)]

**tўr'ō.** See TIRO.

# U

**U**[1], **u**, (ū) *n.* (*pl.* **Us**, **U's**). Twenty-first letter; U-shaped object or curve; **U-boat**, German submarine [G *untersee* undersea]; **U-turn**, turning a vehicle to face in opposite direction without reversing (also fig. of policy etc.).

**U**[2] (ū) *a.* (colloq.) Upper-class; supposedly characteristic of upper class. [abbr.]

**ŭbi'quit|ous** *a.* Present everywhere or in several places simultaneously; often encountered; **~ў** *n.* [L (*ubique* everywhere)]

**ŭ'dder** *n.* Pendulous baggy milk-secreting organ of cow etc. [E]

**U.D.I.** *abbr.* unilateral declaration of independence.

**U.F.O.** *abbr.* unidentified flying object (esp. 'flying saucer').

**ugh** (ŭh, ŏŏh) *int.* expr. disgust or horror, or sound of cough or grunt. [imit.]

**ŭ'gli** *n.* Mottled green and yellow citrus fruit. [foll.]

**ŭ'gl|ў** *a.* (**~ily**, **~iness**). Unpleasing or repulsive to see or hear; morally repulsive, vile, discreditable; unpleasantly suggestive, threatening, dangerous; **~y customer**, unpleasantly formidable person; **~y duckling**, person who turns out to be more beautiful, talented, etc., than was at first expected; **~ifў** *v.t.*, make ugly. [N]

**U.H.F.** *abbr.* ultra-high frequency.
**U.K.** *abbr.* United Kingdom.
**ŭkā'se** *n.* Arbitrary command; (Hist.) edict of Russian government. [Russ.]

**Ukrai'nĭan** (ū-) *a.* & *n.* (Native, language) of the *Ukraine* in western U.S.S.R. [place]

**ŭkule'lĕ** (-ā'-) *n.* Small 4-stringed guitar. [Hawaiian]

**ŭ'lcer** *n.* Open sore on external or internal surface of body; (fig.) corroding or corrupting influence; **~āte** *v.i.* & *t.*, form ulcer (in or on); **~ā'tion** *n.*; **~ed** (-erd), **~ous**, *adjs.* [L *ulcus -cer-*]

**-ūle** *suf.* of dims. (*globule*, *granule*). [L]

**ŭ'lna** *n.* (*pl.* **~e**). Larger and thinner bone of forearm; corresponding bone in animal's foreleg or bird's wing; **~r** *a.* [L]

**ŭ'lster** *n.* Long loose overcoat of rough cloth; **U~man**, **U~woman**, native of Ulster. [place]

**ult.** *abbr.* ultimo.

**ŭltēr'ior** *a.* (Esp. of motive) situated in the background, not seen or avowed. [L, = further]

**ŭ'ltimate** *a.* Last, final, beyond which no other exists or is possible, fundamental, primary, unanalysable; *ultima Thule* (ŭltima thū'lē) *n.*, far-away unknown region [*Thule* L name of uttermost north]; **ŭltimā'-tum** *n.* (*pl.* **-tums**, **-ta**), final statement of terms, rejection of which by opposite party may lead to war or end of co-operation etc.; **ŭ'ltimō** *a.*, (Commerc.) of last month (*the 28th ultimo*). [L (*ultimus* last)]

**ŭ'ltra-** *pref.* Beyond; extreme(ly), excessive(ly), (*ultra-conservative*, *ultra-modern*); **~-high**, (of frequency) between 300 and 3000 megahertz; **~so'nic**, pitched above upper limit of human hearing; **~so'nics** *n.*; **~vi'olet**, of or using invisible rays (just) beyond violet end of spectrum. [L *ultra* beyond]

**ŭltramari'ne** (-ē'n) *a.* & *n.* Brilliant blue (pigment orig. from lapis lazuli). [It. & L, = beyond sea, whence lazuli was brought]

**ŭltramŏ'nt|āne** *a.* & *n.* Situated south of the Alps, Italian; (person) favourable to Pope's absolute authority in faith and discipline; **~anism, ~anist,** *ns.* [L (MOUNTAIN)]

*ultra vires* (ŭltra vīr´ēz, ōoltrah vēr´āz) *adv.* & *pred. a.* Beyond one's (legal) power or authority. [L]

**ŭ'lŭl|āte** *v.i.* Howl, wail; **~ā'tion** *n.* [L]

**ŭ'mbel** *n.* (Bot.) Inflorescence in which flower-stalks nearly equal in length spring from common centre and form flat or curved surface as in carrot; **~late, ~li'ferous,** *adjs.* [F, or L *umbella* sunshade]

**ŭ'mber** *n.* & *a.* (Of) colour or pigment like ochre but darker and browner (**burnt ~,** redder and deeper in colour). [F or It., f. L *umbra* shade]

**ŭmbi'lic|al** *a.* Of navel; **~al cord,** flexible structure attaching foetus to placenta, (fig.) essential connecting--line; **~us** *n.,* navel. [L]

**ŭ'mbr|a** *n.* (*pl.* **~ae, ~as**). Total shadow cast by moon or earth in eclipse (cf. PENUMBRA); **~age** *n.,* offence, sense of slight or injury, (take *umbrage at*); **~ā'geous** (-jŭs) *a.,* shady; **~al** *a.,* of umbra. [L, = shadow]

**umbrě'lla** *n.* Light portable device for protection against weather, consisting of collapsible usu. circular canopy of silk etc. mounted on central stick; (fig.) (means of) protection, co-ordinating agency; **~stand** (for holding closed umbrellas). [It. dim. (prec.)]

**u'mlaut** (ōo´mlowt) *n.* (Mark like diaeresis indicating) vowel-change (e.g. G *mann männer,* E *man men*). [G]

**ŭ'mpire. 1.** *n.* Person chosen to settle disputes and enforce rules, esp. in cricket and other games. **2.** *v.i.* & *t.* Act as umpire (in). [F *nonper* not equal (PEER²); for loss of *n-* cf. ADDER]

**ŭ'mpteen** (*or* -ē'n) *a.* (sl.) Many; an indefinite number of; **~th** *a.* (cf. NUMERAL). [-TEEN]

**'un** *pron.* (colloq.) One (*that's a good 'un*). [ONE]

**ŭn-** *pref.* Words with this prefix are listed in their alphabetical places with references to one of the 5 sections of this entry. The stress and inflexion are normally the same as for the word to which *un-* is prefixed. Where a word is not listed and defined in the section mentioned for it, its meaning is sufficiently explained by the introduction to that section. Many of the less common words of

obvious meaning are omitted altogether. Many *adjs.* belonging to section 4 and ending in *-able, -ed,* or *-ing* are identical in form with derivatives of verbs belonging to section 1; e.g., *an unbridled horse* may be one that has had its bridle removed, or one that has never worn a bridle; to such words is attached the reference 'see also UN- 1'.

**1.** Verbs formed from simple verbs and usu. denoting action contrary to or annulling that of the simple verb: **unbar** *v.t.,* remove bar from (gate etc.), unlock, open, (lit. or fig.); **unbend** *v.t.* & *i.,* change from bent position, straighten, relax (mind etc.) from strain or exertion or severity, become affable, (Naut.) unfasten (cable), untie (rope); **unblock** *v.t.,* remove obstruction from; **unbolt** *v.t.* (door etc.); **unbridle** *v.t.,* remove bridle from (horse, fig. tongue etc.); **unburden** *v.t.,* (esp.) relieve (oneself, conscience, etc.) by confession etc. (*to* person); **uncork** *v.t.,* draw cork from (bottle), (colloq.) give vent to (feelings); **uncouple** *v.t.,* release (dogs, wagons, etc.) from couples or coupling; **uncover** *v.t.* & *i.,* remove cover(ing) from, lay bare, disclose, doff one's hat or cap; **uncross** *v.t.,* remove (legs, knives, etc.) from crossed position; **undo** *v.t.,* annul (*cannot undo the past*), unfasten (coat, parcel, etc.), unfasten garment(s) of (person), ruin prospects or reputation or morals of; **undress** *v.t.* & *i.,* take off one's clothes, take off clothes of (person); **unfit** *v.t.,* make unsuitable (*for*); **unfold** *v.t.* & *i.,* open the folds of, spread out, reveal (thoughts etc.), become opened out, develop; **unfreeze** *v.t.* & *i.,* (cause to) thaw; **unfurl** *v.t.* & *i.,* spread out (sail etc.), become spread out; **unhang** *v.t.,* take down from hanging position; **unhook** *v.t.,* remove from hook(s), open (dress etc.) by releasing its hooks; **unlearn** *v.t.,* discard from one's memory, rid oneself of (false information, habit, etc.); **unload** *v.t.,* (ship etc.), load, gun, or abs.), (fig.) get rid of; **unlock** *v.t.,* release lock of (door etc., fig. mind etc.), (fig.) disclose (secret etc.); **unloose(n)** *v.t.,* loose; **unmake** *v.t.,* destroy, annul; **unmoor** *v.t.,* release moorings of (vessel etc., or abs.); **unnerve** *v.t.,* deprive of strength or resolution; **unpack** *v.t.*, open and remove contents of (luggage etc., or abs.), take (thing) out thus; **unpick** *v.t.*, undo (stitches, garment, etc.) by picking; **unquote** *v.i.*, terminate passage that is within quotation-marks; **unravel** *v.t.*, separate (threads etc.), separate threads of (material), disentangle (lit. & fig.); **unreel** *v.t.* & *i.*, unwind, become unwound, from reel; **unroll** *v.t.* & *i.*, open (roll of cloth etc.), (of roll) be opened, display, be displayed; **unsay** *v.t.*, retract (statement); **unscramble** *v.t.*, restore (esp. telephone conversation) from scrambled state; **unscrew** *v.t.*, unfasten by removing screws, loosen (screw); **unseat** *v.t.*, remove from seat, dislodge from horseback, depose (M.P. etc.) from seat; **unsettle** *v.t.*, disturb orderly arrangement of, discompose, disincline to routine etc. (*holidays unsettle me*), derange (intellect); **unship** *v.t.*, (esp.) remove (oar, mast) from place where it is fixed or fitted; **unsnarl** *v.t.*, disentangle; **unstick** *v.t.*, separate (thing stuck to another); *come unstuck*, (colloq.) fail; **unstitch** *v.t.*, undo stitches of; **unstop** *v.t.*, free from obstruction, remove stopper from; **unstring** *v.t.*, remove string(s) of, loosen string(s) of (bow, harp), take (beads etc.) off string, unnerve; **unthink** *v.t.*, retract in thought; **unthread** *v.t.*, take thread out of (needle); **untie** *v.t.*, undo (knot etc.), undo cords of (parcel etc.), liberate from bonds; **unwind** *v.t.* & *i.*, draw out at length (what is wound), become thus drawn out, (colloq.) relax; **unyoke** *v.t.* & *i.*, release (as) from yoke, (fig.) cease work; **unzip** *v.t.* & *i.*, undo zip-fastener of, allow such undoing.

**2.** Verbs actually or apparently formed from nouns and having the sense 'deprive of', 'divest (oneself) of', 'release from', 'displace from': **unbosom** *v.t.*, disclose (secrets etc.), relieve one*self* of or *of* secrets to or *to* person; **unearth** *v.t.*, discover by search or in course of digging or rummaging; **unfrock** *v.t.*, (esp.) deprive of ecclesiastical status; **unhand** *v.t.*, (rhet.) take one's hands off (person); **unhinge** *v.t.*, (esp., fig.) make (mind, person) crazy; **unhorse** *v.t.* (rider); **unleash** *v.t.* (dog, pursuers); **unmask** *v.t.* & *i.*, remove mask from, take off one's

mask, show up (villain, villainy); **unmuzzle** *v.t.*, (esp., fig.) relieve of obligation to remain silent; **unriddle** *v.t.*, solve (mystery etc.); **unseal** *v.t.*, open (letter, sealed receptacle); **unsex** *v.t.*, deprive of qualities of one's (esp. female) sex; **unveil** *v.t.* (esp.) reveal (secrets etc.), withdraw drapery from (new statue etc.) with ceremonies.

**3.** Transitive verbs formed from nouns and having the sense 'cause to be no longer', 'degrade from position of': **unman**, deprive of manly qualities, cause to weep etc.

**4.** Adjectives with their derivative nouns and adverbs; the sense of *un-* is either simply 'not' (as for most adjs. in *-able*, *-ed*, *-ing*, and a few others, e.g. **unofficial**), or more commonly, 'the reverse of', with implication of praise, blame, etc., (e.g. **unselfish**, **ungracious**). The sense of any adj. in *un-* not found below is that of the simple adj. preceded by 'not'. Most adjectives in this section can form adverbs in *-ly* and nouns in *-ness*. **unable**, not able (*to* do); **unaccompanied**, (esp., Mus.) without accompaniment; **unaccomplished**, (esp.) lacking accomplishments; **unaccountable**, that cannot be explained, strange, (of person) not responsible; **unaccounted for**, unexplained; **unaccustomed**, not accustomed (*to*), not usual (*his unaccustomed silence*); **unadopted**, (esp., ‖of road) not taken over for maintenance by local authority; **unaffected**, free from affectation, sincere, not affected (*by*); **unalloyed** (esp. of pleasure etc.); **un-American**, (esp.) not consistent with, or opposed to, American characteristics, ideas, traditions, etc.; **unanswerable**, that cannot be refuted; **unasked**, (esp.) spontaneously; **unassailable**, that cannot be attacked or questioned; **unassuming**, making little of one's own merits or status; **unattached**, (esp.) not (engaged or be) married, not belonging to any regiment or church or club or college; **unattended**, without attendance; **unavailing**, ineffectual; **unaware**, not aware (*of*, *that*); **unawares** (ŭnăwăr′z) *adv.*, unexpectedly, by surprise (*was taken unawares*); **unbacked**, not supported, having no backers (esp. in betting), having no back(ing); **unbalanced**, (esp., of the mind) disordered or unstable, (of person) deranged; **unbeaten,** not beaten, not surpassed (*unbeaten record*); **unbecoming,** indecorous, not befitting (person, *to* or *for* person), not suited to the wearer (*an unbecoming hat*); **unbeknown**(**st**), (ŭnbīnō'n-; colloq.), not known (esp. *unbeknown to*, without the knowledge of, *did it unbeknown to him*) **unbelieving,** (esp.) atheistic or agnostic, unduly incredulous; **unbending,** (esp.) inflexible, austere, (see also UN- 1, *unbend*); **unbiblical,** not in or authorized by the Bible; **unbidden,** not commanded, not invited; **unbirthday,** (joc., of present) given on a day other than a birthday; **unblushing,** shameless; **unbounded,** (esp.) infinite; **unbridled** (esp. fig.: *unbridled insolence, tongue*; see also UN- 1, *unbridle*); **unbroken,** not broken, not subdued, not interrupted (*unbroken slumber, peace*), not surpassed (*unbroken record*), not broken in (*unbroken horse*); **uncalled-for,** impertinently obtruded (*a quite uncalled-for remark*); **uncanny,** weird, mysterious; **uncared-for,** (of child, house, etc.) neglected; **unceremonious,** informal, familiar, abrupt in manner, lacking courtesy; **uncertain,** not certainly knowing or known (*am uncertain which he means; the result is uncertain*), not to be depended on (*is uncertain in his aim*), changeable (*uncertain temper, weather*); **uncharitable,** (esp.) censorious, severe in judgement; **unchristian,** contrary to Christian principles; **uncircumcised,** (fig.) heathen, unregenerate; **uncivil,** ill-mannered, rude; **unclean,** not clean, foul, unchaste, ceremonially impure; **uncoloured,** having no colour(s), not influenced *by*; **uncome-a′t-able,** (colloq.) not accessible or attainable; **uncommon,** unusual, remarkable; **uncommunicative,** reserved, taciturn; **uncompromising,** refusing compromise, decided, inflexible, unyielding; **unconcerned,** (esp.) easy in mind, free from anxiety or agitation; **unconditional,** not subject to conditions, absolute, (*unconditional surrender, refusal*); **unconsidered,** disregarded, not based on consideration; **unconstitutional,** (of measures, acts, etc.) opposed to a country's constitution; **unconventional,** not bound by convention or

custom, unusual; **uncovenanted,** not promised by or based on or subject to (esp. God's) covenant; **uncovered,** not covered by roof, clothing, hat, etc., (see also UN- 1, *uncover*); **uncritical,** disinclined or incompetent to criticize, not according to principles of criticism; **uncrossed,** not crossed, not thwarted (see also UN- 1, *uncross*); **uncrowned** (*uncrowned king*, esp., person having power but not title of king); **uncut,** (esp., of book) with full untrimmed margins, (of film) not censored, (of diamond) not shaped; **undaunted,** dauntless; **undecided,** not settled, irresolute; **undefended,** (esp., of lawsuit) in which no defence is put in; **undemonstrative,** not given to showing strong feelings, reserved; **undeniable,** that cannot be denied or disputed; **undescended,** (esp., of testicle) remaining in abdomen; **undetermined,** undecided; **undignified,** lacking or inconsistent with dignity; **undistinguished,** (esp.) not eminent; **undone,** not done (see also UN- 1, *undo*); **undreamed,** not dreamed or thought *of*; **undressed,** not dressed (see also UN- 1, *undress*); **undue,** excessive, disproportionate (*spoke with undue warmth*), improper (*undue influence*, e.g. exerted on sick or feeble testator); **undying,** immortal (*undying fame*); **unearned,** not earned (*unearned income*, from interest payments opp. wage or salary or fees; *unearned increment,* increase in value of land due to causes other than owner's labour or outlay); **unearthly,** supernatural, mysterious, (*unearthly cry, pallor*), (colloq.) absurdly early (*at this unearthly hour*); **uneasy,** disturbed or uncomfortable in body or mind (*you seem uneasy; passed an uneasy night*), disturbing (*had an uneasy suspicion*); **uneatable,** not able to be eaten, esp. because of its condition; **unemployable,** unfitted by character etc. for paid employment; **unemployed,** not used, lacking employment, temporarily out of work; **unencumbered,** (of estate) having no liabilities upon it; **unending,** having (apparently) no end; **un-English,** not (characteristic of) the English; **unequal,** not equal (*to*), of varying quality; **unequalled,** superior to all others; **unequivocal,** not ambiguous, plain, unmistakable; **unerring,** not erring or failing or missing the mark (*unerring wisdom, judgement, aim*); **unessential,** (*a.*) not essential, not of the first importance, (*n.*) unessential part or thing; **unethical,** (esp.) unscrupulous in professional conduct; **uneven,** not level or smooth, not uniform or equable (*makes uneven progress; has an uneven temper*); **unexampled,** without precedent; **unexceptionable,** with which no fault can be found; **unexceptional,** not out of the ordinary; **unfailing,** not failing, not running short (*unfailing supply*), not disappointing one's expectations (*unfailing resource, supporter,* etc.); **unfair,** not equitable or honest or impartial (*an unfair advantage; got by unfair means; unfair play*); **unfaithful,** (esp.) adulterous; **unfeeling,** lacking sensitivity, harsh, cruel; **unfit,** not fit (*to do, for* purpose); **unfitted,** not fit, not fitted, not furnished with fittings, (see also UN- 1, *unfit*); **unflappable,** (colloq.) imperturbable; **unfledged,** (fig., of person) undeveloped; **unformed,** not formed, shapeless; **unfortunate,** (*a.*) the reverse of fortunate, unlucky, unhappy, regrettable, (*n.*) unfortunate person; **unfounded,** without foundation (*unfounded hopes, rumour*), not yet founded; **unfurnished,** not supplied (*with*), without furniture (*unfurnished lodgings*); **unget-a′t-able,** (colloq.) inaccessible; **ungodly,** impious, wicked, (colloq.) outrageous; **ungovernable,** unruly, wild, violent (*ungovernable passions*); **ungracious,** not kindly or courteous (*ungracious reply, reception*); **ungrammatical,** contrary to rules of grammar; **ungrudging,** done or given with good will; **unguarded,** not guarded, incautious, thoughtless (*an unguarded expression, admission*); **unhallowed,** not consecrated, having evil associations, tainted with wickedness, (*unhallowed spot, gains*); **unhappy,** not happy, unlucky, wretched, unsuccessful; **unhealthy,** (esp., of place) harmful to health, (sl.) dangerous to life; **unheard-of,** unprecedented; **unhistoric(al),** (esp.) merely legendary; **unholy,** impious, wicked, (colloq.) frightful or outrageous; **unhuman,** not human, superhuman, inhuman; **un-idea'd,** having no ideas; **un-**

**impeachable,** giving no opportunity for censure; **uninformed,** (esp.) ignorant; **uninspired,** (esp., of oratory etc.) commonplace; **uninterested,** (esp.) unconcerned, indifferent; **uninviting,** unattractive, repellent; **unknowing,** not knowing, unconscious (*of*); **unknown,** (*a.*) not known (*he, his purpose, that district, was unknown to me; the Unknown Warrior* or *Soldier,* unidentified body of one killed in war selected for public burial with honours as symbolizing his country's sacrifice; *of unknown ingredients; x and y denote unknown quantities; we all dread the unknown*), (*n.*) unknown person or QUANTITY, (*adv.*) unknown *to,* without the knowledge of (*did it unknown to me*); **unlearned** (-ĭd), not well educated; **unlearned** (-nd), **unlearnt,** (of lesson etc.) not learnt (see also UN- 1, *unlearn*); **unlettered,** illiterate; **unlicked,** not licked into shape, unmannerly; **unlike** *a.* & *adv.,* not like (*is unlike both his parents; the two are unlike; unlike signs, +* and *−; plays quite unlike anyone I have heard before*); **unlikely,** improbable, unpromising, (*unlikely tale, errand*); **unlimited,** boundless, unrestricted, very great or numerous, (*has unlimited scope; unlimited expanse of sea; drinks unlimited coffee*); **unlined,** with no lines or lining; **unlisted,** not in published list, esp. of share prices or telephone numbers; **unlooked-for,** not expected; **unlovely,** not amiable or attractive; **unlucky,** not lucky or fortunate or successful, wretched, unsuccessful, bringing bad luck, ill-judged (*unlucky toss of coin; always unlucky at cards; unlucky fellow; begun in an unlucky hour; his unlucky efforts to please; unluckily, it is not true*); **unmanageable,** not (easily) to be managed or manipulated or controlled (*unmanageable child, material, situation*); **unmannerly,** rude, ill-bred; **unmarked,** not marked, not noticed; **unmeaning,** without meaning; **unmeant,** not intended; **unmentionable,** that cannot (properly) be mentioned; **unmerciful** (esp. of treatment); **unmerited** (esp. of hardships); **unmistakable,** that cannot be mistaken or doubted, clear; **unmitigated,** unqualified, absolute, (*unmitigated scoundrel, lie*); **unmoral,** non-moral; **unmoved,** not moved, not changed in purpose, not affected by emotion; **unmusical,** not pleasing to the ear, unskilled in or indifferent to music; **unnameable,** too bad to be named; **unnatural,** contrary or doing violence to nature, monstrous, (*unnatural vice*), lacking natural feelings (*unnatural parent, child*), artificial, forced, affected; **unnecessary,** not necessary, more than is necessary (*with unnecessary care*); **unoffending,** harmless, innocent; **unofficial,** not officially authorized or confirmed (*unofficial strike,* not formally approved by strikers' trade union); **unoriginal,** not possessing originality, derived; **unpaged,** with pages not numbered; **unpaid,** (of debt or person) not paid; **unparalleled,** having no parallel or equal; **unparliamentary,** contrary to parliamentary usage (*unparliamentary language,* oaths, abuse); **unplaced** (esp. in race or list); **unplayable** (esp. of ball in games); **unpleasant,** disagreeable; **unpointed,** having no point(s), not punctuated, without vowel points (in Hebrew), (of masonry) not pointed; **unpolitical,** not concerned with politics; **unpopular,** disliked by the public; **unpractical,** not practical, without practical skill; **unpractised,** not experienced or skilled, not put into practice; **unprecedented,** for which there is no precedent, unparalleled, novel; **unpremeditated,** not deliberately planned; **unpretending,** **unpretentious,** not given to display, making little show; **unpriced,** with the price not marked; **unprincipled,** lacking or not dictated by good moral principles; **unprintable,** (esp.) too blasphemous or indecent to be printed; **unprofessional,** not belonging to one's or a profession, contrary to professional etiquette; **unprofitable,** without profit, serving no purpose; **unprompted,** spontaneous; **unprovided,** not supplied with or *with* money etc.; **unprovoked,** without provocation; **unputdow'nable,** (colloq., of book) so engrossing that reader cannot put it down; **unqualified,** not competent, not legally or officially qualified, not modified, (*am unqualified to serve*; *an unqualified practitioner*; *gave his unqualified assent*); **unquestionable,** that cannot be questioned or doubted; **unquestioned,** not disputed or doubted, not interrogated; **unquestioning,** asking no questions (*unquestioning obedience,* yielded without asking questions); **unquiet,** restless, agitated, (*unquiet spirit, times*); **unread,** (of book etc.) not read, (of person) not well-read; **unreadable,** (esp.) too dull to be worth reading; **unready,** (esp.) not prompt in action; **unreal,** illusive, imaginary; **unreasonable,** exceeding the bounds of reason (*unreasonable demands, price*), not guided by or listening to reason; **unreciprocated** (esp. of affection); **unreflecting,** thoughtless; **unregenerate,** having had no moral awakening; **unrelieved,** (esp.) lacking the relief given by contrast or variation; **unremitting,** incessant (*unremitting care*); **unremunerative,** not (sufficiently) profitable; **unrequited** (esp. of affection); **unreserved,** not reserved, without reserve or reservation; **unreservedly** (-ĭdlĭ) *adv.,* without reservation; **unrighteous,** not upright or honest or just, evil, wicked; **unrivalled,** having no equal, peerless; **unruly,** lawless, refractory (*unruly* MEMBER); **unsaid,** not uttered (see also UN- 1, *unsay*); **unsaturated,** (esp., Chem.) able to combine with hydrogen to form a third substance by joining of molecules; **unsavoury,** uninviting, disgusting, (*an unsavoury dish, smell, theme*); **unscathed,** without suffering injury; **unscientific,** (esp.) transgressing scientific principles; **unscreened** (esp. of coal, unsieved); **unscripted,** (of speech etc.) delivered without prepared script; **unscriptural,** not in accordance with Scripture; **unscrupulous,** having no scruples, unprincipled; **unseeing,** (esp.) unobservant; **unseen** *a. & n.* (*unseen translation* or *unseen,* unprepared passage for translation); **unselfish,** regardful of others' interests rather than of one's own; **unsettled,** not settled, liable to change, open to further discussion, not paid (*unsettled bills*), (see also UN- 1, *unsettle*); **unshrinkable,** (of fabric etc.) that will not shrink; **unshrinking,** unhesitating, fearless; **unsighted,** not yet in sight, precluded from seeing; **unsightly,** repulsive to look at; **unsized,** not stiffened with size, not arranged according to size; **unskilled,** not having or needing special skill or training; **unsocial,** not social, not suitable for or seeking society; **unsophisticated,** artless, simple; **unsound,** not sound, unhealthy, rotten, ill-founded, erroneous, fallacious, unreliable, (*unsound lungs, fruit, doctrine, policy, argument*; *of unsound mind,* insane); **unsparing,** lavish (*unsparing praise, unsparing of* or *in praise, unsparing in his efforts*), merciless; **unspeakable,** that words cannot express, good or bad beyond description, (*unspeakable joys*; *an unspeakable bore*); **unspotted,** (fig.) not contaminated; **unstable** (esp. of disposition); **unstatutable,** not warranted by statute; **unsteady,** not steady or firm, shaking, reeling, changeable, fluctuating, of irregular habits, (*an unsteady hand*; *walked with unsteady steps*; *ladder is unsteady*; *was unsteady in his adherence*; *unsteady winds*); **unstrained,** not forced, not subjected to strain, not put through a strainer; **unstressed,** not subjected to or pronounced with stress; **unstructured,** (esp.) informal; **unstudied,** easy, natural, spontaneous, (*unstudied ease, eloquence*); **unsubstantial,** having little or no solidity or reality; **unsuited,** not fit (*for* purpose), not adapted (*to*); **unsung,** (esp.) not sung of; **unswerving,** steady, constant; **unsymmetrical,** lacking or not characterized by symmetry; **untaught,** not instructed or acquired by teaching; **unthinkable,** such as it is impossible even to form a notion of, (colloq.) highly unlikely or undesirable; **unthinking,** thoughtless; **untied,** not tied (see also **un-** 1, *untie*); **untimely** *a.* & *adv.,* inopportune(ly), (of death) premature(ly); **untold,** not told, not counted, beyond count (*untold wealth*); **untouchable,** (esp., *n.*) Hindu of group held to defile higher castes on contact; **untoward** (-tō-wŏr'd), perverse, awkward, unlucky, (*an untoward generation, accident*); **untravelled,** that has not (been) travelled; **untried,** (esp.) inexperienced; **untroubled,** tranquil; **untrue,** not true, contrary to the fact, not faithful or loyal (*to* person, principle, etc.), deviating from correct standard; **unusual,** not usual, remarkable; **unutterable,**

above or beyond description (*unutterable torment, joy,* etc.; *an unutterable fool*); **unvalued,** not esteemed or prized, not estimated or priced; **unvarnished,** not varnished or embellished (esp. *the unvarnished truth*); **unversed,** not experienced or skilled in; **unvoiced,** not spoken or uttered, (Phon.) not voiced; **unwarrantable, unwarranted,** unauthorized, unjustified; **unwashed** (*the great unwashed,* the rabble); **unwatered,** not watered or diluted or supplied with water; **unwearying,** (esp.) persistent (*unwearying efforts*); **unwell,** not in good health, indisposed; **unwilling,** not willing or inclined (*to do, for* thing *to be* done, *that,* or abs.); **unwinking,** (esp.) vigilant; **unwise,** foolish, imprudent; **unwished,** not wished (usu. *for*); **unworkable** (esp. of system etc.); **unworkmanlike,** amateurish; **unworldly,** not worldly, spiritual; **unworn,** that has not been worn or impaired by wear; **unworthy,** not worthy or befitting the character (*of*), discreditable, unseemly; **unwound,** not wound (see also **un-** 1, *unwind*); **unwritten** (*unwritten law,* resting originally on custom or judicial decision, not on written statutes etc.); **unwrung** (esp. WITHERS *unwrung*); **unyielding,** firm, obstinate.

**5.** Nouns formed from simple nouns and usu. having senses as in 4: **unbelief,** incredulity, disbelief esp. in divine revelation or in particular religion; **unconcern,** freedom from anxiety, indifference, apathy; **unconstraint,** freedom from constraint; **undress,** ordinary dress opposed to full dress or uniform, casual or informal dress; **unemployment,** lack of employment (*unemployment benefit,* payment made to unemployed worker); **unperson,** one whose name or existence is denied or ignored; **unreason,** lack of reason, nonsense, folly; **unreserve,** frankness; **unrest,** disturbed or agitated condition; **untruth,** being untrue, falsehood, lie, (*the manifest untruth of this statement*; *told me an untruth*); **unwisdom,** folly, imprudence. [E, of two origins, expressing (1) negation, (2) reversal]

**U.N.** *abbr.* United Nations.

**unabashed, -abated, -able, -abridged, -accommodating,**

-accompanied, -accomplished, -accountable, -accounted for, -accustomed, -acknowledged, -acquainted, -adopted, -adorned, -adulterated, -affected, -afraid, -aided, -alloyed, -alterable, -altered, -ambiguous, -ambitious, -American, -analysable, see UN- 4.

**ūnă′nĭmous** *a.* All of one mind, agreeing in opinion, (*we were unanimous in protesting*); (of opinion, vote, etc.) formed, held, given, etc., by general consent; **ūnani′mĭtȳ** *n.* [L (*unus* one, *animus* mind)]

unanswerable, -answered, -anticipated, -appetizing, -appreciative, -approachable, -arguable, -ashamed, -ashamedly *pr.* -ĭdlĭ, -asked, -assailable, -assuming, -attached, -attainable, -attended, -attractive, -authorized, -available, -availing, -avoidable, -aware(s), -backed, -balanced, see UN- 4; unbar, 1; unbearable, -beatable, -beaten, -becoming, -beknown(st), 4; unbelief, 5; unbelievable, unbeliever, 5; unbelieving, 4; unbend, 1; unbending, -bias(s)ed, -biblical, -bidden, 4; unbind, 1; unbirthday, -bleached, -blemished, -blinking, 4; unblock, 1; unblushing, 4; unbolt, 1; unborn, 4; unbosom, 2; unbound, -bounded, -breakable, 4; unbridle, 1; unbridled, -broken, 4; unbuckle, -burden, -button, 1; uncage, 2; uncalled-for, -canny, -cared-for, -caused, -ceasing, -ceremonious, -certain, 4; uncertainty, 5; uncertified, 4; unchain, 1; unchallengeable, -challenged, -changeable, -changed, -changing, -charitable, -charted, -chaste, 4; unchastity, 5; unchecked, -chivalrous, -christian, 4.

**ū′ncial** (-shăl). **1.** *a.* Of, written in, kind of writing with characters partly resembling modern capitals found in 4th–8th-cc. MSS. **2.** *n.* Uncial letter or MS. [L (*uncia* inch)]

uncircumcised, -civil, -civilized, -clad, -claimed, see UN- 4; unclasp, 1; unclassified, 4.

**ū′ncle** *n.* Parent's brother(-in-law); (children's *colloq.*) unrelated man friend; (*sl.*) pawnbroker; DUTCH[1] *uncle*; **U~ Sam**, (*colloq.*) U.S. government. [AF f. L *avunculus*]

unclean, see UN- 4; unclench,

-close, -clothe, 1; unclothed, -clouded, 4.

**ū′ncō** *adv.* (Sc.) Very, exceptionally. [UNCOUTH]

uncoil, see UN- 1; uncoloured, -combed, -come-at-able, -comfortable, -committed, -common, -communicative, -complaining, -complimentary, -compromising, -concealed, 4; unconcern, 5; unconcerned, -concernedly *pr.* -ĭdlĭ, -conditional, 4.

**ŭncondi′tioned** (-n-k-; -nd) *a.* Not subject to or determined by conditions; ~ **reflex**, instinctive response to stimulus. [UN- 4]

unconfined, -confirmed, -congenial, -connected, -conquerable, see UN- 4.

**ŭncŏ′nscionab|le** (-n-k-; -sho-) *a.* (~ly). Having no conscience; contrary to conscience; unreasonably excessive. [UN- 4, CONSCIENCE]

**ŭncŏ′nscious** (-n-k-; -shŭs). **1.** *a.* Not conscious (*was unconscious of any change*; *lay unconscious for some hours*). **2.** *n.* The part of the mind not normally accessible to consciousness. [UN- 4]

unconsidered, -constitutional, -constrained, see UN- 4; unconstraint, 5; uncontaminated, -contested, -controllable, -controlled, -controversial, -conventional, -converted, -convincing, -cooked, -co-operative, -coordinated, 4; uncork, 1; uncorroborated, -corrupted, -counted, 4; uncouple, 1.

**ŭncou′th** (-n-kōō′-) *a.* (Of appearance, manner, person) strikingly lacking in ease and polish. [E, = unknown]

uncovenanted, see UN- 4; uncover, 1; uncovered, -critical, 4; uncross, 1; uncrossed, -crowned, 4.

**UNCTAD** *abbr.* United Nations Conference on Trade and Development.

**ŭ′nct|ion** *n.* Anointing for medical or religious purposes (EXTREME *unction*); thing used in anointing, (fig.) soothing words or thought; fervent or sympathetic quality in words or tone caused by or causing deep emotion; pretence of this; **~ūous** *a.*, full of (esp. simulated) unction, greasy. [L (*ungo unct-* anoint)]

uncurl, see UN- 1; uncut, -damaged, -dated, -daunted, 4;

**undeceive,** 1 **; undecided, -defend-**
**ed, -defiled, -defined, -delivered,**
**-demanding, -democratic, -de-**
**monstrative, -deniable,** 4.

**ŭ'nder** *prep.*, *adv.*, & *a.* **1.** *prep.*
Below, in or to position lower than,
(*lay* or *fell under the table*; *tunnel under*
*the river*; ~ **the sun,** anywhere in the
world; ~ **water,** in and covered by
it); at foot of (high wall); within, on
the inside of, (surface etc.; ~
**separate cover,** in another
envelope); inferior to, less than, (*no*
*one under a bishop*; *did it in under an*
*hour*; *sums under £5*); at lower cost
than; in position or act of supporting
or sustaining, liable to, on condition
of, controlled or bound or commanded or ruled by, in accordance
with, in the form of, in the time of,
(*sank under the load*; *is now under repair*;
*accepted my ruling under protest*; *fought*
*under Wellington*; *prospered under his*
*rule*; *was under a vow, the impression*
*that*; *under the circumstances*; *is classified*
*under biology*); planted with (crop);
propelled by (*under* SAIL). **2.** *adv.* In
or to lower place or subordinate
condition; in(to) unconsciousness.
**3.** *a.* Lower (*under layers, surface*);
~**mŏst** *a.* [E]

**ŭ'nder-** *pref.* meaning: (1) under
(as prec. entry); (2) lower, inner;
(3) inferior, subordinate; (4) insuf-
ficient(ly), incomplete(ly), (among
the words given below, some are
without definitions; this implies
that *under-* adds merely the sense *not*
*enough*); ~**achie've,** do less than was
expected (esp. scholastically); ~**a'ct,**
act (role etc.), act role, with insufficient force; ~**arm** *a.* & *adv.*,
(Crick. etc.) with arm below
shoulder-level; ~**belly,** under surface of animal etc. esp. as vulnerable
to attack; ~**bi'd,** (*v.t.*) make lower
bid than, (Bridge) bid less on (one's
hand, or abs.) than its strength
warrants, (ŭ'-; *n.*) such bid; ~**bre'd,**
ill-bred, vulgar; ~**carriage,** supporting frame of vehicle, usu. retractable
structure under aircraft for support
during and after landing; ~**char'ge,**
charge too little for (thing) or to
(person), put too little (explosive,
electric, etc.) charge into; ~**cliff,**
terrace or lower cliff formed by
landslip; ~**clothes, -clothing,** (worn
under others, esp. next to skin);
~**coat,** coat of hair or layer of paint
under another; ~**co'ver,** surrep-

titious, spying esp. by working
among those observed; ~**croft,**
crypt [= obs. *croft* f. L]; ~**current,**
current below surface, (fig.) underlying (opposite) trend of influence or feeling; ~**cu't,** (*v.t.*)
strike (golf etc. ball) to make it rise
high, sell or work at lower price than,
(ŭ'n-; *n.*) ‖under-side of sirloin;
~**deve'loped,** (esp., of country etc.)
below its potential economic level;
~**dog,** (esp., fig.) person losing fight
or in state of inferiority or subjection;
~**do'ne,** not thoroughly done, esp.
lightly or insufficiently cooked;
~**e'mphasis** *n.*; ~**e'mphasize** *v.t.*;
~**employ'ed,** not fully occupied;
~**e'stimate** *v.t.*, & *n.*, (form) too low
an estimate (of); ~**expo'se** *v.t.*,
~**expo'sure** *n.*, (esp. Photog.);
~**fee'd** *v.t.*; ~**felt** (for laying under
carpet); ~**floor,** situated beneath
the floor; ~**foo't,** under one's feet,
on ground; ~**garment,** piece of
underclothing; ~**go',** be subjected
to, endure; ~**gra'duate,** member of
university who has not taken first
degree; ~**grou'nd,** (*adv.*) beneath
surface of ground, in(to) secrecy or
hiding, (ŭ'-; *a.* & *n.*) (railway)
situated underground, (fig.) secret
or hidden (group or activity), esp.
aiming at subversion; ~**growth,**
shrubs or small trees growing under
large ones; ~**hand,** secret, deceptive,
(Crick. etc.) underarm; ~**lay',** (*v.t.*)
lay thing under (another) to support
or raise, (ŭ'-; *n.*) thing laid under
another (esp. under carpet); ~**le't,**
sublet; ~**li'e,** lie under (stratum
etc., or abs.), (fig.) be basis of
(doctrine, conduct, etc., or abs.),
exist beneath superficial aspect of;
~**li'ne,** (*v.t.*) draw line under (word
etc.) to emphasize it, (fig.) emphasize, (ŭ'-; *n.*) line placed under word
or illustration; ~**ma'nned,** having
too few men as crew or staff;
‖~**me'ntioned,** mentioned at later
place in book etc.; ~**mi'ne,** make
excavation under, wear away base
of, injure (person etc.) by secret or
insidious means, weaken or wear out
(health etc.) imperceptibly; ~
**nou'rish(ment)** *v.t.*, & *n.*; ~**pants,**
undergarment for lower body and
part of legs; ~**-part,** lower or subordinate part; ~**pass,** road etc. passing
under another; ~**pay'** *v.t.*; ~**pi'n,**
place masonry etc. support under,
(fig.) support, strengthen; ~**pri'vi**

**leged**, less privileged than others, not enjoying normal living standard or rights; ~**proof**, containing less alcohol than proof spirit does; ~**ra'te**, have too low an opinion of; ~**scor'e** (or ŭ´-), underline; ~**sea**, below (surface of) sea; ~**seal**, seal under-part of (esp. motor vehicle against dirt etc.); ~**se'cretary**, secretary of government department where Minister is called Secretary; ~**se'll**, sell at lower price than (true value); ~**se'xed**, having less than normal sexual desire; ~**shirt**, undergarment worn under shirt, vest; ~**shoo't**, (of aircraft) land short of (runway etc.); ~**shot**, (of wheel) turned by water flowing under it, (of lower jaw) projecting beyond upper jaw; ~**side**, lower or under side or surface; ~**signed**, whose signature is appended; ~**sized**, of less than usual size; ~**skirt**, skirt worn under another, petticoat; ~**slung**, supported from above; ~**spe'nd** *v.t.* & *i.*; ~**sta'ffed**, having fewer staff than are necessary; ~**sta'te**, express in (unduly) restrained terms, represent as being less than it really is, (so ~*sta'tement* n.); ~**steer** *v.i.*, & *n.*, (of motor vehicle) (have) tendency to turn less sharply than was intended; ~**strapper**, underling; ~**study**, (*n.*) one who studies another's role or duties so as to act in his absence, (*v.t.*) study (role etc.) thus, act as understudy to (person); ~**tone**, subdued tone, underlying quality or feeling; ~**tow**, current below sea-surface in opposite direction to surface current; ~**trick**, (Bridge) trick by which one falls short of contract; ~**va'lue** *v.t.*; ~**vest**, vest (undergarment); ~**wa'ter** *a.* & *adv.*, (situated or done) under water; ~**wear**, underclothes; ~**weight**, (*n.*) insufficient weight, (-ā't; *a.*) below normal or suitable weight; ~**whe'lm**, (joc.) be far from overwhelming; ~**wood**, undergrowth; ~**world**, those who live by (organized) crime and immorality, (Myth.) abode of the dead under the earth; ~**write**, sign and accept liability under (insurance policy), accept (liability) thus, undertake to finance or support; ~**writer**, (esp.) marine insurer.

**ŭ'nderling** *n.* (usu. derog.) Subordinate. [-LING]

**ŭ'ndermŏst.** See UNDER 3.

**ŭndernea'th. 1.** *adv.* & *prep.* At or to lower place (than) (*underneath the trees*; *plate is dirty underneath*); on inside (of). **2.** *n.* Lower surface or part. [E (NETHER)]

**ŭnderstă'nd** *v.t.* & *i.* (-stoo'd). Perceive meaning of (words, person, language; ~ **each other**, know each other's views or feelings, be in agreement or collusion); perceive significance or explanation or cause or nature of, know how to deal with, (*do not understand why he came, the point of his remark*; *quite understand your difficulty*; *cannot understand him, his conduct*; *thoroughly understands children*); infer esp. from information received, take as implied or for granted, (*I understand that it begins at noon*; *but I understood that expenses were to be paid*; expr. uncertainty or surprise or indignation: *am I to understand that you refuse?*; GIVE person *to understand*); supply (word) mentally; have understanding in general or in particular; ~**ing** *n.*, (esp.) intelligence, power of apprehension, agreement, thing agreed upon, (*must come to an understanding with them*; *consented on the understanding that*). [E (STAND)]

**ŭndertă'k|e** *v.t.* (-too'k; -ta'ken). Agree to perform, make oneself responsible for, engage in; accept obligation (*to do*); guarantee, affirm, *that*; ~**er** *n.*, (esp., ŭ´-) one who makes arrangements for funerals; ~**ing** (or ŭ´-), (esp.) work etc. undertaken, enterprise, promise, management of funerals. [TAKE]

**undescended, -deserved, -deservedly** *pr.* -ĭdlĭ, **-deserving, -designed, -desirable** *a.* & *n.* (= undesirable person), **-detectable, -detected, -determined, -deterred, -developed,** see UN- 4.

**ŭ'ndies** (-ĭz) *n.pl.* (colloq.) (Esp. women's) underclothing. [abbr.]

**undignified, -diluted, -diminished,** see UN- 4.

**ŭ'ndine** (-ēn) *n.* Female waterspirit. [L (*unda* wave)]

**undiplomatic, -disciplined, -disclosed, -discoverable, -discovered, -discriminating, -disguised, -dismayed, -disputed, -dissolved, -distinguished, -disturbed, -divided,** see UN- 4; **undo, 1; undone, -doubted, -draped, -dreamed of, 4; undress** *n.*, 5;

undress v., 1; undressed, -drinkable, -due, 4.

**u'ndŭl|āte** v.i. Have wavy motion or look; ~ā'tion n., wavy motion or form, gentle rise and fall, a wave in these; ~ātorў a. [L (unda wave)]

unduly, -dying, -earned, see UN- 4; unearth, 2; unearthly, -easy, -eatable, -eaten, -economic, -economical, -edifying, -edited, -educated, -embarrassed, -emotional, -emphatic, -employable, -employed, 4; unemployment, 5; unenclosed, -encumbered, -ending, -English, -enlightened, -enterprising, -enthusiastic, -enviable, -equal, -equalled, -equivocal, -erring, 4.

**UNESCO** (ūně'skō) abbr. United Nations Educational, Scientific, & Cultural Organization.

unessential, -ethical, -even, -eventful, -exampled, -exceptionable, -exceptional, -expected, -expired, -explained, -explored, -exposed, -expressed, -expurgated, -fading, -failing, -fair, -faithful, -familiar, -fashionable, see UN- 4; unfasten, 1; unfastened, -fathomable, -favourable, -fed, -feeling, -feigned, -feminine, -fenced, -fermented, 4; unfetter, 1; unfinished, -fit a., 4; unfit v., 1; unfitted, -fitting, 4; unfix, 1; unfixed, -flappable, -flattering, -fledged, -flinching, 4; unfold, 1; unforeseen, -forgettable, -forgivable, -forgiving, -formed, -forthcoming, -fortified, -fortunate, -founded, 4; unfreeze, 1; unfrequented, -friendly, 4; unfrock, 2; unfruitful, -fulfilled, 4; unfurl, 1; unfurnished, 4.

**ŭngain'nlў** (-n-g-) a. (-iness). (Of person or animal or their movements) awkward-looking, clumsy. [obs. gain straight (N)]

ungallant, -garbled, -generous, -gentle(manly), -get-at-able, see UN- 4; ungird, 1; unglazed, -gloved, -godly, -governable, -gracious, -grammatical, -grateful, -grudging, -guarded, 4.

**ŭn'guent** (-nggw-) n. Soft substance used as ointment or for lubrication. [L (unguo anoint)]

**ŭn'gŭlate** (-ngg-) a. & n. Hoofed (mammal). [L (ungula hoof, claw)]

unhallowed, -hampered, see UN- 4; unhand, 2; unhang, 1; unhanged, -happy, -harmed, 4;

unharness, 1; unhealthy, -heard (-of), -heeded, -helpful, -hesitating, 4; unhinge, 2; unhistoric(al), 4; unhitch, 1; unholy, 4; unhook, 1; unhorse, -house (-z), 2; unhuman, -hung, -hurried, -hurt, 4.

**ū'ni-** in comb. (Having, consisting of) one; ~ca'meral a., with one (legislative) chamber; ~ce'llular, one-celled; ~la'teral, (of contract etc.) binding or done by one side only, (of vehicle-parking) restricted to one side of street; ~sex, (n.) tendency of each sex to adopt the other's habits, (a., of clothes) designed to be worn by either sex; ~se'xual, (Bot.) having pistils or stamens but not both; ~valent (-ĭ'-), having chem. valence of one; ~valve, (mollusc) with one valve. [L (unus one)]

**U'niat(e)** (ū'-) n. & a. (Member) of Church acknowledging Pope's supremacy but following Greek etc. ritual. [Russ. uniyat f. L unio UNION]

**UNICEF** (ū'nĭsěf) abbr. United Nations Children's Fund.

**ū'nicõrn** n. Mythical animal with horse's body and single straight horn. [F f. L (cornu horn)]

unidea'd, -identified, see UN- 4.

**ū'nifõrm. 1.** a. Not changing in form or character, unvarying; conforming to same standard or rule. **2.** n. Uniform distinctive dress worn by members of same body, e.g. soldiers, police, nurses, schoolchildren; ~ed (-md) a. **3.** ūnifõr'mĭtў n., being uniform, sameness, consistency. [F or L (FORM)]

**ū'nif|ȳ** v.t. Reduce to unity or uniformity; ~icā'tion n. [F or L (UNI-)]

unilluminated, -imaginable, -imaginative, -impaired, -impeachable, -impeded, -important, -impressive, -improved, -inflected, -influenced, -informed, -inhabitable, -inhabited, -initiated, -injured, -inspiring, -intelligent, -intelligible, -intentional, -interested, -interesting, -interrupted, -invited, -inviting, see UN- 4.

**ū'nion** (-yon) n. Uniting, being united, coalition, junction, (**the U~,** of England & Scotland in 1603 or 1707, or of Britain & Ireland in 1801); marriage; concord, agreement; a whole resulting from combination of parts or members, **esp.**

U.S. or U.K. or U.S.S.R.; = TRADE
*union*; (U~) general social club and
debating society at some universities;
part of flag with device symbolizing
union; U~ **Jack**, national ensign
of U.K. with combined crosses of 3
patron saints; ~**ist** *n.*, member of
trade union, advocate of trade
unions or of union esp. between
Britain and (N.) Ireland; ~**ism** *n.*;
~**ize** *v.t.*, bring under trade-union
organization or rules. [F or L (*unus*
one)]

**ŭni'que** (-ē'k) *a.* Being the only
one of its kind, having no like or
equal or parallel; (colloq.) unusual.
[F f. L *unicus* (*unus* one)]

**ū'nison** *n.* Coincidence in pitch;
combination of voices or instruments
at same pitch (**in** ~); agreement
(*acting in perfect unison*). [F or L (*sonus*
SOUND¹)]

**ū'nĭt** *n.* Individual thing or person
or group regarded as single and
complete; quantity chosen as
standard for expressing other
quantities; ‖smallest share in ~
**trust** (company investing in varied
stocks the combined contributions
from many persons); device with
specified function in complex
mechanism; piece of furniture for
fitting with others like it or made of
complementary parts; group with
special function in an organization;
~ **price** (charged for each unit of
goods supplied); ~ **volume** etc.
(taken as unit in calculating or
expressing other quantities); ~
**ār'ian** *n. & a.*, advocate of unity
or centralization, (U-) (member) of
religious body maintaining that God
is one person not Trinity; U~**ār'ianism** (ū-) *n.*; ~**arў** *a.*, of unit(s),
marked by unity or uniformity. [L
*unus* one]

**ūni'te** *v.t. & i.* Join together, make
or become one, combine, consoli-
date, amalgamate; agree, combine,
co-operate, (*in* sentiment, conduct,
do*ing*); U~d **Kingdom**, Great
Britain and N. Ireland; U~d **Nations**, international peace-seeking
organization; U~d **States** (of
**America**), republic in N. America.
[L *unio* -*it-* (*unus* one)]

**ū'nĭtў** *n.* Oneness, being one or
single or individual, being formed of
parts that constitute a whole, due
interconnection of parts; thing forming a complex whole; (Math.) the

number one; harmony between persons etc. [F f. L (*unus* one)]

**Univ.** *abbr.* University.

**ŭnĭvēr'sal** *a.* (~**ly**). Of or belonging to or done etc. by all persons or
things in the world or in the class
concerned, applicable to all cases
(*rule does not pretend to be universal*);
~ **coupling, joint**, (transmitting
power by a shaft at any selected
angle); ~ **language** (artificial, intended for use by all nations); ~**ĭtў**
(-ă'l-) *n.*; ~**ize** *v.t.*, treat as, make,
universal. [F or L (foll.)]

**ū'nivėrse** *n.* All existing things;
the whole creation (and the Creator);
the world, all mankind. [F f. L *uni-
versus* combined into one]

**ŭnivēr'sitў** *n.* Educational institution instructing or examining
students in all or many important
branches of learning, and conferring
degrees; members of this collectively;
team, crew, etc., representing a
university; **at** ~, studying there.
[F f. L (prec.)]

**unjust, -justifiable**, see UN- 4.

**ŭnkě'mpt** (-n-k-) *a.* Of rough or
uncared-for appearance. [= *un-
combed*]

**unkind**, see UN- 4; **unknit, -knot,**
1; **unknowable, -knowing,**
-known, -labelled, 4; **unlace,** 1;
**unladylike, -lamented,** 4; **unlatch,**
1; **unlawful,** 4; **unlearn,** 1; **unlearned, -learnt,** 4; **unleash,** 2;
**unleavened,** 4.

**unlě'ss** *conj.* If not, except when,
(*shall not go unless asked, unless I hear
from him*; *always walked unless I had a
bicycle*). [= *on less*]

**unlettered, -licensed, -licked,**
-lighted, -like, -likely, -limited,
-lined, see UN- 4; **unlink,** 1; **unlisted,** 4; **unload, -lock,** 1; **unlooked-for,** 4; **unloose(n),** 1; **un-
lovable, -lovely, -loving, -lucky,**
4; **unmake,** 1; **unman,** 3; **unmanageable, -manly, -mannerly,**
-marked, -marketable, -married,
4; **unmask,** 2; **unmatched,**
-meaning, -meant, -measurable,
-melodious, -mentionable, -mer-
ciful, -merited, -methodical,
-mindful, -mistakable, -miti-
gated, -mixed, -modified, -modu-
lated, 4; **unmoor,** 1; **unmoral,**
-mounted, -mourned, -moved,
-mown, -musical, 4; **unmuzzle,**
2; **unnameable, -named, -natural,**
-necessary, -neighbourly, 4; **un-**

nerve, 1; unnoticed, -numbered, 4.

**U.N.O.** *abbr.* United Nations Organization.

unobjectionable, -observant, -observed, -obtainable, -obtrusive, -occupied, -offending, -official, -opened, -opposed, -organized, -original, -orthodox, see UN- 4; unpack, 1; unpaged, -paid, -paired, -palatable, -paralleled, -pardonable, -parliamentary, -patriotic, 4; unperson, 5; unperturbed, 4; unpick, -pin, 1; unplaced, -planned, -playable, -pleasant, -pleasing, -plumbed, -pointed, -polished, -political, -popular, -practical, -practised, -precedented, -predictable, -prejudiced, -premeditated, -prepared, -prepossessing, -presentable, -pretending, -pretentious, -priced, -principled, -printable, -privileged, -productive, -professional, -profitable, -progressive, -promising, -prompted, -pronounceable, -propitious, -protected, -proved, -provided, -provoked, -published, -punctual, -punished, -putdownable, -qualified, -quenchable, -questionable, -questioned, -questioning, -quiet, -quotable, 4; unquote, -ravel, 1; unread, -readable, -ready, -real, -realistic, -realizable, 4; unreason, 5; unreasonable, -reasoned, -reasoning, -reciprocated, -recognizable, -recorded, -redeemed, 4; unreel, 1; unrefined, -reflecting, -reformed, -regenerate, -registered, -regretted, -regulated, -rehearsed, -related, -relenting, -reliable, -relieved, -remarkable, -remitting, -remunerative, -repentant, -representative, -represented, -requited, 4; unreserve, 5; unreserved(ly), -resisting, -resolved, -responsive, 4; unrest, 5; unrestrained, -restricted, -revised, -rewarded, 4; unriddle, 2; unrig, 1; unrighteous, -ripe, -rivalled, 4; unrobe, 2; unroll, 1; unromantic, 4; unroof, 2; unruffled, -ruly, 4; unsaddle, 2; unsafe, -said, -saleable, -salted, -satisfactory, -satisfied, -satisfying, -saturated, -savoury, 4; unsay, 1; unscarred, -scathed, -scheduled, -scholarly, -scientific, 4; unscramble, 1; unscreened,

4; unscrew, 1; unscripted, -scriptural, -scrupulous, 4; unseal, 2; unsealed, -seasonable, 4; unseat, 1; unseeded, -seeing, -seemly, -seen, -selfish, -sentimental, -serviceable, 4; unsettle, 1; unsettled, 4; unsex, 2; unshackle, 1; unshakeable, -shaven, 4; unsheathe, -ship, 1; unshockable, -shorn, -shrinkable, -shrinking, -sighted, -sightly, -signed, -sized, -skilful, -skilled, -smiling, -smoked, 4; unsnarl, 1; unsociable, -social, -soiled, -sold, 4; unsolder, 1; unsolicited, -solved, -sophisticated, -sorted, -sought, -sound, -sparing, -speakable, -specified, -spoiled, -spoken, -sporting, -sportsmanlike, -spotted, -stable, -stained, -stamped, -starched, -stated, -statutable, -steady, 4; unstick, -stitch, -stop, 1; unstoppable, 4; unstopper, 2; unstrained, -stressed, 4; unstring, 1; unstructured, -studied, -stuffy, -substantial, -substantiated, -successful, -suitable, -suited, -sullied, -sung, -sunned, -supported, -sure, -surpassed, -susceptible, -suspected, -suspecting, -suspicious, -sweetened, -swept, -swerving, -symmetrical, -sympathetic, -systematic, -tainted, -talented, -tameable, -tamed, 4; untangle, 1; untanned, -tapped, -tarnished, -tasted, -taught, -taxed, -teachable, -tenable, -tenanted, 4; untether, -think, 1; unthinkable, -thinking, 4; unthread, 1; untidy, 4; untie, 1; untied, 4.

**unti′l** *prep.* & *conj.* = TILL[1] (used esp. when its clause or phrase stands first, *until you told me I had no idea of it,* and in formal style, *resided there until his decease*). [N (TILL[1])]

untilled, -timely, -tiring, see UN- 4.

**u′nto** (-ŏŏ, -o) *prep.* (arch.) = TO (in all uses except with infinitive). [UNTIL, with *to* replacing *til*]

untold, -touchable, -touched, -toward, -traceable, -traced, -trained, -trammelled, -translatable, -travelled, -tried, -trodden, -troubled, -true, see UN- 4; untruss, 1; untrustworthy, 4; untruth, 5; untruthful, 4; untuck, 1; untuned, -turned, -tutored, 4; untwine, -twist, 1; unused, -usual, -utterable, -vaccinated,

-valued, -varied, -varnished, -varying, 4; unveil, 2; unventilated, -verified, -versed, -voiced, -wanted, -warrantable, -warranted, -wary, -washed, -watered, -wavering, -weaned, -wearable, -wearying, 4; unweave, 1; unwed(ded), -welcome, -well, -wholesome, 4.

ŭnwie'ld|y̆ a. (~ily, ~iness). Cumbersome or clumsy or hard to manage owing to size or shape. [WIELDy active]

unwilling, see UN- 4; unwind, 1; unwinking, 4; unwisdom, 5; unwise, -wished, 4.

ŭnwi'tting. a. Unaware of the state of the case, unintentional, (an unwitting offender, offence). [E (WIT)]

unwomanly, -wonted, -workable, -workmanlike, -worldly, -worn, -worthy, -wound, see UN- 4; unwrap, 1; unwritten, -wrought, -wrung, -yielding, 4; unyoke, -zip, 1.

ŭp adv., prep., a., n., & v. **1.** adv. Towards, at, or in high(er) place, position, degree, amount, value, etc., (high up in the air; water came up to his chin; 100 points up, scored or as side's lead; £5 up on the deal; roll your sleeves up; prices went up); ||to or in capital or university, to or in place farther north or regarded as high(er) or (more) important (went up to London, Balliol; up in or to Scotland); before magistrate etc.; (of jockey) in saddle; to place or time in question or where speaker etc. is (child came up to him; he's been good up till now); to or in erect, prepared, inflated, etc., position or condition (turn your collar up; wind up your watch; pump up the tyres; is he up yet?, out of bed); in progress (the hunt is up); (as int.) get, stand, etc., up; (of road etc.) being repaired; happening unusually (what's up?; **something is up**, something unusual is happening or being planned); completely or effectually (burn, eat, saw, speak, tear, use, up; **time is up**, exhausted); into compact or accumulated or secure state (pack, save, tie, up); **it is all up with** person, his case is hopeless; **up against**, close to, in(to) contact with, (colloq.) confronted with (up against it, in great difficulties); **up and about**, up and doing, arisen after sleep or illness, active; **up and down**, (fig.) to and fro; **up to**, until,

not more than, equal to, incumbent on, capable of, occupied or busy with; up to DATE², the MARK², the MINUTE¹; **up with** (person or thing, as int.) expr. wish for success of. **2.** prep. To or at higher or highest point of (climbed up the hill, ladder); along (walk up the street); **up and down**, (fig.) to and fro along; **up hill and down dale**, up and down in every direction; **up stage**, at or to back of theatre stage; up the POLE¹, the SPOUT. **3.** a. Directed upwards; **up-and-coming**, (colloq., of person) making good progress and likely to succeed; **up platform**, platform for departure or arrival of **up train** (going or coming to capital or place regarded as higher). **4.** n. On the **up-and-up**, (colloq.) steadily improving, honest(ly); **ups and downs**, rises and falls, alternate good and bad fortune. **5.** v.i. & t. (-pp-). (colloq.) Start (abruptly or unexpectedly) to say or do something (she ups and says); raise, esp. abruptly (they upped their prices). [E]

**ŭp-** pref. = UP. **1.** As adv. to vbs. and vbl derivs. = 'upwards'; **u'pbringing**, bringing up (of child), education; **u'pcurved**, curved upwards; **upda'te**, bring up to date; **up-e'nd**, set or rise up on end; **upgra'de**, raise in rank etc.; **uphea'val**, violent change or disruption; **upho'ld**, hold up, support, confirm (decision etc.); **u'pkeep**, (cost or means of) maintenance in good condition; **upli'ft**, (v.t.) raise, (ŭ'-; n.; colloq.) elevating influence; **upri'sing**, insurrection; **uproo't**, pull (plant etc.) up from ground, (fig.) displace (person) from accustomed location, eradicate; **u'prush**, upward rush; **upse't**, (v.t.) overturn, disturb composure or digestion of, (ŭ'-; n.) disturbance, surprising result; **u'pshot**, outcome, conclusion; **upsta'ge** (a. & adv.) nearer back of theatre stage, (fig.) snobbish(ly), (v.t.) move upstage from (actor) to make him face away from audience, (fig.) divert attention from (person) to oneself; **upsta'nding**, standing up, strong and healthy, honest; **u'pstart**, (person) who has risen suddenly to prominence or who behaves arrogantly; **u'pswept**, (of hair) combed to top of head; **u'pswing**, upward movement or trend; **u'ptake**, (colloq.) understanding (*quick, slow, in* or *on the uptake*, quick, slow, to understand); **u'ptight** (*or -i'-*), (colloq.) nervously tense, angry, rigidly conventional; **uptur'n**, (*v.t.*) turn up or upside-down, (ŭ'-; *n.*), upward trend, improvement. **2.** As *prep.* to *ns.* forming *advs.* and *adjs.*; **up-country**, inland; **u'pfield**, in or to position farther along field; **u'phill**, (*a.*) sloping up, ascending, (fig.) arduous, (-i'l; *adv.*) up a slope; **upstair's** *adv., a., & n.,* (to, on, of) upper floor of house etc.; \***u'pstate** *a. & n.,* (of) part of state remote from large cities, esp. northern part; **u'pstream** *a. & adv.,* (moving) against flow of stream etc.; \***u'p-town** *a., adv., & n.,* (in or of) residential part of town or city; **u'p-wind** *a. & adv.,* against the wind. **3.** As *a.* to *ns.*; **u'pbeat**, (*n.*; Mus.) unaccented beat, (*a.*) optimistic, cheerful; **u'pland** *a. & n.,* (of) higher part of country; **up-stroke** (made or written upwards). 

**upbrai'd** *v.t.* Chide, reproach, (person *with* or *for* fault etc.). [E (BRAID = brandish)]

**uphŏ'lster** (-p-h-) *v.t.* Provide (chair etc.) with textile covering, padding, springs, etc.; **~er** (by trade), **~erў**, *ns.* [obs. *upholster*, *upholder* ns. (*uphold* keep in repair)]

**upŏ'n** *prep.* = ON (*upon* is sometimes more formal, and is preferred in *once upon a time* and *upon my word*). [*up on*]

**ŭ'pper. 1.** *a.* Higher in place, situated above another part; higher in rank, dignity, etc., (*the upper class*); *upper* CASE²; **~ crust**, (colloq.) *the* aristocracy; **~-cut** *n.,* & *v.t.,* hit upwards with arm bent; **the ~ hand**, dominance, control; **U~ House**, (esp.) House of Lords; **~ regions**, sky. **2.** *n.* Upper part of boot or shoe; **on one's ~s**, (colloq.) extremely short of money. **3. ~mŏst**, (*a.*) highest, predominant, (*adv.*) at or to the highest or most prominent position; **u'ppish**, (colloq.) **u'ppitў**, *adjs.,* self-assertive, arrogant. [UP]

**u'pright** (-rīt). **1.** *a.* Erect, vertical, (*upright* PIANO²); (fig.) strictly honourable or honest. **2.** *n.* Post or rod fixed upright esp. as support to some structure; upright piano. [E]

**ŭ'proar** *n.* Tumult, violent disturbance; **ŭproar'ious** *a.* (of laughter etc.). [Du., == commotion]

**ŭpsĭde-dow'n** *adv. & a.* With upper part where lower part should be, inverted; in(to) total disorder. [*up-so-down* 'up as if down']

**ŭpsi'lon** (or ŏŏ-) *n.* Twentieth Gk letter (Υ, υ) = u. [Gk]

**ŭ'pward** *a. & adv.,* **ŭ'pwards** (-z) *adv.* (Moving or leading) towards higher place, level, etc.; **~(s) of**, more than (an amount). [E (UP-)]

**Ural-Altā'ĭc** (ūrală-) *a.* Of family of languages including Finnish and Turkish. [places]

**ūrā'nĭum** *n.* Radioactive heavy grey metallic element, capable of nuclear fission and used as source of nuclear energy; **ŭrā'nĭc**, **ūr'anous**, *adjs.* [foll.]

**Ur'anus** (ūr'-; or ūrā'-) *n.* Planet seventh in order from the sun. [Gk *ouranos* heaven]

**ŭr'ban** *a.* Of, living or situated in, a town or city; **~ guerrilla** (operating in cities etc. by kidnapping etc.); **ŭrbā'ne** *a.,* courteous, elegant; **ŭrbă'nitў** *n.,* urbane quality; **~īze** *v.t.,* render urban, remove rural character of (district); **~izā'tion** *n.* [L (*urbs* city)]

**ŭr'chĭn** *n.* Mischievous boy (**~ cut**, short hair-style for women); = SEA-*urchin*. [F f. L *ericius* hedgehog]

**Ur'du** (oor'dōō) *n.* Language allied to Hindī but with many Persian words, used esp. in Pakistan. [Hind.]

**-ure** *suf.* forming *ns.* of action (*censure*, *seizure*) or result (*creature*, *scripture*), and collective *ns.* (*legislature*, *nature*). [F & L]

**ūr'ĕa** (or -i'a) *n.* Soluble colourless crystalline compound contained esp. in urine; **ūrē'ter**, **ūrē'thra** (*pl.* -ae, -as), *ns.,* duct by which urine passes into, from, bladder. [L f. F *urée* f. Gk *ouron* urine]

**ūrge. 1.** *v.t.* Drive forcibly (*on*), hasten; encourage or entreat earnestly or persistently (person *to* action, *to* do); advocate (action, argument, etc.) emphatically (*on* or *upon* person), mention earnestly as reason or justification. **2.** *n.* Urging impulse or tendency; strong desire. **3. ŭr'gent** *a.,* requiring immediate action or attention, importunate; **ūr'gency** *n.* [L *urgeo*]

**ūr'ĭc** *a.* Of urine; **~ acid**, constituent of urine. [F *urique* (foll.)]

**ūr'ĭn|e** *n.* Fluid secreted by kidneys and discharged from bladder; **~al** (or -i'-) *n.,* place or receptacle for urination; ~**arў** *a.*, of or relating to urine; ~**āte** *v.i.*, discharge urine; ~**ā'tion** *n.*; ~**atorў** *a.*; **ūrogĕ'nĭtal** *a.*, of urinary and reproductive systems; **ūrŏ'logў** *n.*, study of urinary system. [F f. L *urina*]

**ûrn** *n.* Vase with foot and usu. rounded body, esp. for storing ashes of the dead or as vessel or measure; large vessel with tap, in which tea, coffee, etc., is made or kept hot. [L *urna*]

**Ur'sa** (ĕr'-) *n.* ~ **Major**, ~ **Minor**, the Great, Little, **BEAR**[1]; **ûr'sĭne** *a.*, of or like bear. [L, = bear]

**us.** See **WE**.

**U.S.** *abbr.* United States (of America); unserviceable.

**U.S.A.** *abbr.* United States of America.

**usable.** See **USE**[2].

**ū'sage** (*or* -z-) *n.* Manner of using or treating (*damaged by rough usage*); customary practice esp. in use of a language. [F (USE[1])]

**ūse**[1] *n.* Using, employment, (*taught him the use of maps*; *put it to good use*; *no longer in use*; **make ~ of**, use, benefit from); right or power of using (*lost the use of his right arm*); service-ability, utility, purpose for which thing can be used, (*a knife is of use, of no use, for this job*; **have no ~ for**, be unable to find a use for, fig. dislike, be contemptuous of; **no ~**, of no value or utility; custom, usage, (*long use has reconciled me to it*); ritual and liturgy of church etc. [F *us* f. L *usus* (foll.)]

**ūse**[2] (-z) *v.t. & i.* (**usable**). Cause to act or serve for a purpose, employ, (*use oil for frying*; *use the services of an agent*; *use your discretion*; ~ *person's* **name**, quote him as authority, reference, etc.); (in *p.p.*) second-hand; treat in specified manner (*has used me shamefully*); (in *past*, usu. *pr.* ūst; *neg.* **used not, did not use**, colloq. **use**(d)**n't** *pr.* ū'sᵊnt, or **didn't use**) had as one's or its constant or frequent practice or state (*to do, be,* etc.); (in *p.p.*, *pr.* ūst) familiar by habit, accustomed *to*; ~ **up**, consume, find use for (remainder). [F *user* f. frequent. of L *utor us-*]

**ū'seful** (-sf-) *a.* (~**ly**). Of use, serviceable, producing or able to produce good results, (**make oneself ~**, perform useful services); (sl.) creditable, efficient; **ū'selĕss**

(-sl-) *a.*, serving no purpose, unavailing. [USE[1]]

**ū'sher. 1.** *n.* Person who shows people to their seats in hall, theatre, etc.; door-keeper of court etc.; ||officer walking before person of rank; ~**ĕ'tte** *n.*, female usher esp. in cinema. **2.** *v.t.* Act as usher to; announce or show *in* etc. (lit. or fig.). [F f. L *ostium* door]

**U.S.S.R.** *abbr.* Union of Soviet Socialist Republics.

**ū'sual** (-zhōŏal) *a.* (~**ly**). Such as commonly occurs, customary, habitual; **as ~**, (joc.) **as per ~**, as commonly occurs; **my, the, ~** (drink, etc.). [F or L (USE[1])]

**usurer.** See **USURY**.

**ūsū'rp** (-z-) *v.t. & i.* Seize, assume, (throne, power, etc.) wrongfully; ~**ā'tion** (-zer-) *n.* [F f. L]

**ū'surў** (ū'zherĭ) *n.* (Lending of money at) exorbitant or illegal interest; ~**er** *n.*, one who lends money thus; **ūsū'rious** (-z-, -zh-) *a.* [AN or L (USE[1])]

**ŭtĕ'nsĭl** *n.* Instrument, implement, vessel, esp. for domestic use. [F f. L (USE[2])]

**ū'ter|us** *n.* (*pl.* ~**i** *pr.* -ī). Womb; ~**ĭne** *a.* [L]

**ūtī'lĭt|ў. 1.** *n.* Usefulness, profitableness; useful thing; = PUBLIC *utility*. **2.** *a.* Made or serving for utility; severely practical and (esp. in wartime) standardized; ~**y man**, actor of small parts. **3.** ~**ār'ian** *a. & n.*, of, based on, or confined to utility, (adherent) of utilitarianism; ~**ār'i-anĭsm** *n.*, doctrine that actions are right if they are useful or for benefit of majority; **ū'tĭlīze** *v.t.*, make use of, turn to account; **ūtĭlĭzā'tion** *n.* [F f. L (*utilis* useful f. as USE[2])]

**ŭ'tmŏst** (*or* -o-). **1.** *a.* Farthest, extreme, greatest. **2.** *n. The* utmost point, degree, etc.; **do one's ~** (all that one can). [E, = *outmost*]

**Utō'pĭa** (ū-) *n.* (Imagined) perfect place or state of things; ~**n, ū-,** *a.*, of Utopia, visionary, desirable but impracticable. [title of book 1516; L f. Gk *ou* not, *topos* place]

**ū'trĭcle** *n.* Cell or small cavity in animal or plant; **ūtrĭ'cūlar** *a.* [F or L dim. (*uter* bag)]

**ŭ'tter**[1] *attrib. a.* Complete, total, unqualified; ~**mŏst** *a.*, utmost. [E, compar. adj. of OUT]

**ŭ'tter**[2] *v.t.* Emit audibly (groan etc.); express (sentiment, lie, etc.) in words; put (esp. forged money) into circulation; ~**ance** *n.*, uttering, power or manner of speaking, thing spoken. [Du.]

**U.V.** *abbr.* ultraviolet.

**ū'vūla** *n.* (*pl.* ~e). Pendent fleshy part of soft palate; ~**r** *a.* [L dim. of *uva* grape]

**ŭxŏr'ĭous** *a.* (Excessively) fond of one's wife. [(L (*uxor* wife)]

# V

**V, v,** (vē) *n.* (*pl.* **Vs, V's**). Twenty-second letter; V-shaped thing; (as Roman numeral) 5; **V sign** (made by hand with fingers clenched except the first and second outspread in V shape, as gesture of victory, approval, or vulgar derision).

**V** *abbr.* volt(s).

**v.** *abbr.* verse; versus; very; *vide*.

**Va.** *abbr.* Virginia.

‖**văc** *n.* (colloq.) Vacation; vacuum cleaner. [abbr.]

**vă'can|t** *a.* Not filled or occupied (*house, post, is still vacant; will amuse your vacant hours*); not mentally active, showing no interest; ~**t possession** (of house etc. unoccupied); ~**cỹ** *n.*, (esp.) unoccupied post or place (*has a vacancy on his staff, in his hotel*); **vacā'te** (or vă'-) *v.t.*, leave vacant, cease to occupy (post, house, etc.); **vacā'tion,** (*n.*, esp.) fixed period of cessation from work esp. in ‖law-courts and universities, *holiday, (v.i.) *take holiday. [F f. L (*vaco* empty)]

**vă'ccĭn|āte** (-ks-) *v.t.* Inoculate with vaccine to procure immunity from smallpox or other diseases; ~**ā'tion,** ~**ātor,** *ns.*; ~**e** (or -ēn) *n.*, virus of cowpox used in vaccinating, any similar preparation used for inoculation. [*vaccine* f. L (*vacca* cow)]

**vă'cĭll|āte** *v.i.* Fluctuate in opinion or resolution; ~**ā'tion,** ~**ātor,** *ns.* [L]

**vă'cūum. 1.** *n.* (*pl.* -ua, -uums). Space entirely devoid of matter; space or vessel from which air has been (almost) removed by pump etc.; (fig.) absence of normal or previous content; (colloq.; *pl.* ~s) vacuum cleaner; ~ **brake,** train-brake worked by exhaustion of air; ~ **cleaner,** apparatus for removing dust etc. by suction; ‖~ **flask,** vessel with double wall enclosing vacuum so that liquid in inner receptacle

retains its temperature; ~ **tube** (with near-vacuum for free passage of electric current). **2.** *v.t.* & *i.* (colloq.) Use vacuum cleaner (on). **3. vă'cūous** *a.*, empty, unintelligent, expressionless; **vacū'ĭtỹ** *n.*, vacuousness. [L (*vacuus* empty)]

**V.A.D.** *abbr.* (Member of) Voluntary Aid Detachment.

**vādĕ-mē'cum** (or vahdĭmā'-) *n.* Handbook etc. carried constantly for use. [F f. L, = go with me]

**vă'gabŏnd. 1.** *a.* Having no fixed habitation; wandering. **2.** *n.* Wanderer, esp. idle one. **3.** ~**age,** ~**ĭsm,** *ns.*, vagabond state; **vă'garỹ** *n.*, caprice, freak. [F or L (*vagor* wander)]

**vagī'na** *n.* (*pl.* ~e, ~s). Canal between womb and vulva of female mammal; ~**l** *a.* [L, = sheath]

**vă'gran|t. 1.** *a.* Wandering, roving, (*vagrant musician, thoughts*); ~**cỹ** *n.* **2.** *n.* Person without settled home or regular work. [AF]

**vague** (-g) *a.* Of uncertain or ill-defined meaning or character (*vague proposals, answer; have not the vaguest notion what he means*); (of person or mind) imprecise, inexact in thought or expression or knowledge. [F, or L *vagus* wandering]

**vain** *a.* Empty, trivial, (*vain boasts, triumphs*); useless, followed by no good result, (*in the vain hope of dissuading him; all resistance, to resist, is vain*); **in** ~, without result or success: *we protested in vain; it was in vain that we protested;* TAKE *person's name in vain*); conceited (*of one's beauty* etc.); ~**glŏr'ỹ** (-n-g-) *n.*, boastfulness, extreme vanity; ~**glŏr'ĭous** (-n-g-) *a.* [F f. L *vanus*]

**vă'lance, -ence¹,** *n.* Short curtain round frame or canopy of bedstead or above window. [AF (*valer* descend)]

**vāle¹** *n.* (arch. or poet., exc. in

place-names). Valley. [F *val* f. L *vallis*]

**vā'lĕ²** (*or* vah'lā) *int.* & *n.* Farewell; **văledĭ'ction** *n.*, (words used in) bidding farewell; **vălĕdĭ'ctory** *a.* [L imper. of *valeo* be well]

**vā'lence²**, ‖**-ncў**, *n.* (Chem.) Combining or replacing power of an atom as compared with hydrogen atom. [L *valentia* power (VALE²)]

**vă'lentine** *n.* Sweetheart chosen on (St.) V∼'s day (14 Feb.); sentimental or comic often anonymous missive sent to person of opposite sex on this day. [persons]

**valēr'ian** *n.* One of various kinds of flowering herb. [F f. L]

**vă'lĕt** (*or* -lā). 1. *n.* Gentleman's personal attendant. 2. *v.t.* & *i.* Act as valet (to). [F *va(s)let*, rel. to VARLET, VASSAL]

**vălĕtūdĭnār'ian** *n.* & *a.* (Person who is) of infirm health or unduly anxious about his health; ∼**ĭsm** *n.* [L (VALE²)]

**vă'liant** (-lya-) *a.* (Of person or conduct) brave. [F f. L (VALE²)]

**vă'lĭd** *a.* (Of reason, objection, etc.) sound, defensible, (Law) executed with proper formalities, legally acceptable, (*valid contract, passport*); ∼**āte** *v.t.*, make valid, ratify; ∼**ā'tion** *n.*; **vali'dĭtў** *n.* [F or L (prec.)]

**vali'se** (-ē's, -ē'z) *n.* *Small portmanteau; kitbag. [F f. It.]

**vă'lley** *n.* Low area more or less enclosed by hills and usu. with stream. [F (VALE¹)]

**vă'lour**, *-lor, (-ler) *n.* (poet., formal, joc.) Courage esp. in battle; **vă'lorous** *a.* [F f. L (VALE²)]

**valse** (vah-, vaw-) *n.* Waltz. [F]

**vă'luab|le**. 1. *a.* (∼ly). Of great value or price or worth (*valuable property, information, assistance*). 2. *n.* (usu. in *pl.*) Valuable thing(s) (*deposited her valuables with the bank*). [foll.]

**vă'lūe**. 1. *n.* Worth, desirability, utility, qualities on which these depend, (*the value of fresh water, a friend, regular exercise*); worth as estimated (*sets a high value on his time*); amount of money or (Econ.) other commodities for which thing can be exchanged in open market; equivalent of a thing, what represents or is substituted for a thing, (*paid him the value of his lost property*); ability of a thing to serve a purpose or cause an effect

(*news value*); (in *pl.*) one's principles or standards, one's judgement of what is valuable or important in life; (Mus.) duration of sound signified by note; (Math.) amount denoted by algebraical term or expression; ∼**-a'dded tax**, tax on amount by which value of an article has been increased at each stage of its production; ∼ (**for money**), something well worth the money spent; ∼**-judgement**, subjective estimate of quality etc. 2. *v.t.* Estimate value of, appraise (professionally), (*value the whole at £2,000*); have high or specified opinion of, attach importance to, pride one*self* (*a valued friend*; *values himself on* or *for his conversational powers*). 3. **vălūā'tion** *n.*, estimation (esp. by professional valuer) of a thing's worth, worth so estimated; ‖∼**r** *n.*, (esp.) one who estimates or assesses values professionally. [F p.p. of *valoir* be worth f. L (VALE²)]

**vălv|e** *n.* Automatic or other device for controlling passage of fluid through pipe etc., usu. to allow movement in one direction only; ‖= THERMIONIC *valve*; (Anat., Zool.) membranous part of organ etc. allowing flow of blood etc. in one direction only; each of two shells of oyster, mussel, etc.; device to vary length of tube in trumpet etc.; ∼**'ūlar** *a.*, having (form or function of) valve(s). [L *valva* leaf of folding door]

***vamōō'se** *v.i.* (sl.) Depart hurriedly. [Sp. *vamos* let us go]

**vămp¹.** 1. *n.* Upper front part of boot or shoe. 2. *v.t.* & *i.* Repair, furbish usu. *up*; make *up* by patching or from odds and ends; improvise musical accompaniment (to). [AF (F *avantpié* front of the foot)]

**vămp².** (colloq.) 1. *n.* Unscrupulous flirt; woman who exploits men. 2. *v.t.* & *i.* Allure, exploit, (man); act as vamp. [abbr. foll.]

**vă'mpīre** *n.* Ghost or reanimated corpse supposed to suck blood of sleeping persons; person who preys ruthlessly on others; ∼ (**bat**), S. Amer. etc. bat (actually or supposedly) biting animals and persons and lapping their blood. [F or G f. Magyar]

**văn¹** *n.* Covered vehicle for conveying goods etc.; ‖railway carriage for luggage or for use of guard. [abbr. CARAVAN]

**văn²** n. Vanguard (lit. or fig.; *in the van of civilization*). [abbr.]

**vanā'dĭum** n. Hard grey metallic element used to strengthen steel. [L f. N *Vanadis*, name of the Scand. goddess Freyja]

**Vă'ndal** a. & n. (Member) of a Gmc people that in 4th-5th cc. ravaged Rome etc., destroying many books and works of art; (*v*~) wilful or ignorant destroyer or damager of works of art or other property; **v~ĭsm** n.; **v~īze** v.t., treat thus. [L f. Gmc]

**văndy'ke** n., a., & v. 1. n. Each of series of large points as border to lace, cloth, etc.; cape, collar, etc., with these. 2. a. (V~). In the style of dress, esp. with pointed borders, common in portraits by *Van Dyck*; **V~** (neat pointed) **beard**; **V~** (deep rich) **brown**. 3. v.t. Cut (cloth, edge of lawn, etc.) in vandykes. [person]

**vāne** n. Weathercock; blade of windmill, screw propeller, etc. [dial. var. of obs. *fane* banner]

**vă'nguard** (-n-gärd) n. Foremost part of army or fleet advancing or ready to do so; (fig.) leaders of movement, of opinion, etc. [F *avangarde* (*avant* before, GUARD)]

**vani'lla** n. Tropical climbing orchid with fragrant flowers; ~(- -pod), fruit of this; extract obtained from vanilla-pod or synthetically and used to flavour ices, chocolate, etc. [Sp. dim. (*vaina* pod)]

**vă'nish** v.i. Disappear suddenly or gradually; cease to exist; ~ing- -cream, emollient that leaves no visible trace when rubbed into skin; ~ing-point, point at which receding parallel lines viewed in perspective appear to meet, (fig.) stage of complete disappearance. [F f. L (VAIN)]

**Vă'nĭtory** n. Wash-basin surrounded by flat top as dressing- -table. [P]

**vă'nĭty** n. Futility, unsubstantiality, unreal thing, (*the vanity of human achievements*; *pomps and vanity of this wicked world*; **V~ Fair**, the world allegorized in Bunyan's *Pilgrim's Progress* as scene of vanity); ostentatious display; desire for admiration because of one's personal attainments or attractions; ~ **bag**, **case**, (carried by woman and containing small mirror, make-up, etc.). [F f. L (VAIN)]

**vă'nquĭsh** v.t. (literary). Conquer,

overcome, (lit. or fig.). [F *vencus* p.p. f. L *vinco*]

**va'ntage** (vah'-) n. = ADVANTAGE (esp. in Tennis); COIGN *of vantage*; ~-**ground**, advantageous position for defence or attack. [F (ADVANT- AGE)]

**vă'pĭd** a. Insipid, lacking interest, flat; **vapĭ'dĭty** n. [L *vapidus*]

**vă'pour**, *-por, (-per) n. Moisture or other substance diffused or suspended in air, e.g. mist, smoke; (Phys.) gaseous form of a normally liquid or solid substance; ~ **trail** (of condensed water from aircraft etc.); **vă'porīze** v.t. & i., convert or be converted into vapour; **vāporĭzā'tion** n.; **vă'porous** a., (esp.) in the form of or consisting of vapour; ~ў a., (esp.) resembling vapour. [F, or L *vapor* steam]

**vār'ĭ**‖**able. 1.** a. (**-bly**). That can be varied or adapted (*rod of variable length*; *the pressure is variable*); apt to vary, not constant, unsteady, (*variable mood, temper, fortune*); (Math., of quantity) indeterminate, able to assume different numerical values. **2.** n. Variable thing or quantity. **3.** ~**abi'lĭty** n.; ~**ance** n., difference of opinion, dispute, (*at variance among ourselves, with the authorities*), discrepancy; ~**ant**, (a.) differing in form or details from that named or considered, differing thus among themselves, (*a variant reading in some MSS.*; *40 variant types of pigeon*), (n.) variant form, spelling, type, etc.; ~**ā'tion** n., varying, (extent of) departure from a former or normal condition or action or amount or from a standard or type (*prices are subject to variation*), thing that varies from a type, (Mus.) tune or theme repeated in changed or elaborated form. [F f. L (VARY)]

**vă'rĭcose** a. (Of vein etc.) permanently and abnormally dilated. [L (*varix* varicose vein)]

**vār'ĭeg**‖**āted** (-rĭg-) a. Marked with irregular patches of different colours; ~**ā'tion** n. [L (VARIOUS)]

**varī'ety** n. Diversity, absence of uniformity, many-sidedness, (*has the charm of variety*; *the great variety of his accomplishments*); quantity or collection of different things (*for a variety of reasons*); (specimen or member of a) class of things differing in some common qualities from the rest of a larger class to which they belong;

different form *of* thing, quality, etc.; (Biol.) subspecies; ~ (**entertainment, show**), mixed series of dances, songs, comedy acts, etc. [F or L (foll.)]

**vār′ious** *a.* Different, diverse, several, (*for various reasons*; *too various to form a group*; *riots in various places*). [L *varius*]

**vār′let** *n.* (arch. or joc.) Menial, rascal. [F var. of *vaslet* VALET]

**vār′nish. 1.** *n.* Resinous solution used to give hard shiny transparent coating; other preparation for similar purpose; external appearance or display without underlying reality. **2.** *v.t.* Apply varnish to (lit. or fig.); gloss over (fact); ~**ing-day**, day before exhibition of pictures on which exhibitors may retouch and varnish their pictures already hung. [F *vernis* f. L or Gk]

**vār′sĭty** *n.* ‖(colloq., esp. w. ref. to sports). University. [abbr.]

**vār′y** *v.t.* & *i.* Make different, modify, diversify, (*can vary the pressure*; *never varies his style*; *a varied scene*); undergo change, be(come) different, be of different kinds, (*his mood varies*; *with varying success*; *opinions vary on the point*). [F, or L *vario* (VARIOUS)]

**văs** *n.* (Anat.) ~ **de′ferens**, spermatic duct of testicle. [L, = vessel]

**văs′cūlar** *a.* Of or containing vessels for conveying blood, sap, etc. [L (*vasculum* dim. of VAS)]

**vase** (vahz) *n.* Vessel, usu. tall and circular, used as ornament or container (*flower-vase*). [F f. L (VAS)]

**vasĕc′tomў** *n.* (Surg.) Removal of part of each vas deferens esp. for sterilization of patient. [VAS]

**Vă′selīne** (*or* -ēn) *n.* Type of petroleum jelly used in ointments etc. [P]

**văs′sal** *n.* (Hist.) holder of land by feudal tenure; (rhet.) humble dependant; ~**age** *n.*, vassal's condition. [F f. L f. Celt.]

**vast** (vah-) *a.* Immense, huge, very great, (*vast plain, difference*). [L]

**văt** *n.* Large tank or other vessel, esp. for holding liquids or something in liquid in process of brewing, tanning, dyeing, etc.; ~**ful** (-ool) *n.* [dial. var. of obs. *fat* f. E]

**V.A.T.** (*or* văt) *abbr.* value-added tax.

**vau′deville** (*or* vō′-) *n.* Variety entertainment; light stage-play with interspersed songs. [F]

**vault** (*or* vŏ-). **1.** *n.* Arched roof; vaultlike covering (*the vault of heaven*); arched apartment; underground chamber as place of storage, of interment beneath church or in cemetery, etc.; act of vaulting. **2.** *v.i.* & *t.* Leap, spring, esp. while resting on the hand(s) or with help of pole (~**ing horse**, gymnast's wooden block for use in vaulting); spring over (gate etc.) thus; (esp. in *p.p.*) make in form of, furnish with, vault(s); ~**′ing** *n.*, (esp.) arched work in vaulted roof or ceiling. [F f. Rom. (L *volvo* roll)]

**vaunt** *v.i.* & *t.*, & *n.* Boast. [F f. L (VAIN)]

**V.C.** *abbr.* Vice-Chairman; Vice-Chancellor; Victoria Cross.

**V.D.** *abbr.* venereal disease; Volunteer (Officer's) Decoration.

**'ve** *v.* (colloq., usu. after *prons.*) = HAVE. [abbr.]

**veal** *n.* Calf's flesh as food. [F f. L (*vitulus* calf)]

**vĕ′ctor** *n.* (Math.) quantity having direction as well as magnitude; carrier of disease; **vĕctŏr′ial** *a.* (-lly). [L (*veho vect-* carry)]

**Vē′d|a** (*or* vā′-) *n.* (in *sing.* or *pl.*) Ancient Hindu scriptures; ~**ĭc** *a.* [Skr., = knowledge]

**vee** *n.* (Thing shaped like) letter V. [name of letter]

**veer. 1.** *v.i.* Change direction esp. (of wind; cf. BACK) clockwise; (fig.) change in opinion or course. **2.** *n.* Change of direction. [F *virer*]

**vĕg** (-j) *n.* (colloq.) Vegetable(s). [abbr.]

**vē′gan** *n.* & *a.* (Person) eating no animals or animal products. [foll.]

**vē′gėt|able. 1.** *a.* Of (the nature of), derived from, concerned with, comprising, plants, esp. opp. *animal* or *mineral* (*vegetable* KINGDOM); (of life etc.) like that of vegetable, uneventful, monotonous. **2.** *n.* (Esp. herbaceous) plant or part of one used for food, e.g. cabbage, potato, turnip, bean; person living vegetable life through injury or lack of ambition. **3.** ~**al** *a.* (-lly), of (the nature of) plants; ~**ār′ian** *n.*, one who abstains from animal food, esp. that obtained by killing animals; ~**ār′ianĭsm** *n.*; ~**āte** *v.i.*, grow as plants do, (fig.) live uneventful or monotonous life; ~**ātĭve** *a.*; ~**ā′tion** *n.*, plants collectively, plant life, (*luxuriant vegetation*; *no sign of vegetation for miles round*). [F or L (*vegeto* animate)]

**vě″hěmen|t** (vē′ĭ-) *a.* Showing or caused by strong feeling, ardent, (*a vehement protest, desire*); **~ce** *n.* [F or L]

**vě″hĭcle** (vē′ĭ-) *n.* Carriage or conveyance used on land or in space; liquid etc. as medium for suspending pigments, drugs, etc.; thing or person used as medium for thought or feeling or action (*used the pulpit as a vehicle for his political opinions*); **věhĭ′cŭlar** *a.* [F or L (*veho* carry)]

**veil** (vāl). **1.** *n.* Piece of usu. more or less transparent material attached to woman's hat or otherwise forming part of head-dress, esp. to conceal face or protect against sun, dust, etc.; piece of linen etc. as part of nun's head-dress (**take the ~**, become nun); curtain, esp. that separating sanctuary in Jewish Temple, (**beyond the ~**, in the unknown state of after death); (fig.) disguise, pretext; **draw a ~ over**, avoid discussing or calling attention to. **2.** *v.t.* Cover (one's face, one*self*, or abs.) with veil; (fig.) partly conceal (*veiled threat, resentment*). [AF f. L *velum*]

**vein** (vān) *n.* Any of the tubes by which blood is conveyed to heart (cf. ARTERY); (pop.) any blood-vessel (*has royal blood in his veins*); rib of leaf or insect's wing; fissure in rock filled with ore; streak or stripe of different colour in wood, marble, cheese, etc.; distinctive character or tendency, mood, (*was of an imaginative vein*; *said this in a humorous vein*); **~ed** (-nd), **~′ỹ**, *adjs.* [F f. L *vena*]

**věld(t)** (or fělt) *n.* (S. Afr.) Open country. [Afrik. (FIELD)]

**vě″llum** *n.* Fine parchment orig. from skin of calf; manuscript on this; smooth writing-paper imitating vellum. [F *velin* (VEAL)]

**vělŏ′cĭtỹ** *n.* Speed, esp. in a given direction (usu. of inanimate things). [F or L *velox* swift)]

**velour(s)′** (-oor′) *n.* Plushlike woven fabric or felt; hat of such felt. [F]

**vě″lvět. 1.** *n.* Closely woven fabric with thick short pile on one side; furry skin on growing antler; **on ~**, in advantageous or prosperous position. **2.** *a.* Of, like, soft as, velvet; **~ glove**, outward gentleness cloaking inflexibility (*an iron hand in a velvet glove*). **3. ~ee′n** *n.*, cotton fabric with pile like velvet; **~ỹ** *a.* [F f. L (*villus* hair)]

**Ven.** *abbr.* Venerable (as title of archdeacon).

**vē″nal** *a.* (**~ly**). (Of person) that may be bribed; (of conduct etc.) characteristic of venal person; **věnă′lĭtỹ** *n.* [L (*venum* thing for sale)]

**věnd** *v.t.* (**~ible**). Offer (small wares) for sale (**~′ing-machine**, for automatic retail of small articles); **~′or** *n.*, (esp. Law) one who sells. [F or L (*vendo* sell)]

**věndě′tta** *n.* Blood feud; prolonged bitter hostility. [It. f. L (VINDICATE)]

**věneer′. 1.** *v.t.* Cover (wood) with thin coating of finer wood. **2.** *n.* Thin coating; superficial disguise. [obs. *fineer* f. G f. F (FURNISH)]

**vě″ner|able** *a.* Entitled to veneration on account of character, age, associations, etc., (*venerable priest, relics, beard, ruins*; in C.E. as title of archdeacon); **~āte** *v.t.*, regard with veneration; **~ā′tion** *n.*, deep respect, warm approbation; **~ātor** *n.* [F or L (*veneror* revere)]

**věněr′eal** *a.* (**~ly**). Of sexual desire or intercourse; relating to **~ disease** (contracted by sexual intercourse with person already infected). [L (VENUS *Vener-*)]

**Věnē′tian** (-shan). **1.** *a.* Of Venice; **v~ blind**, window-blind of adjustable horizontal slats. **2.** *n.* Native or dialect of Venice. [F or L (*Venetia* Venice)]

**vě″nge|ance** (-njans) *n.* Punishment inflicted or retribution exacted for wrong to oneself or to person etc. whose cause one supports; **with a ~ance**, in a higher degree than was expected or desired (*punctuality with a vengeance*); **~′ful** (-njf-) *a.* (**-lly**), disposed to revenge, vindictive. [F f. *venger* f. L (VINDICATE)]

**vě″nial** *a.* (**~ly**). (Of sin or fault) pardonable, excusable, (Theol.) not mortal; **věnĭă′lĭtỹ** *n.* [F f. L (*venia* forgiveness)]

**vě″nĭson** (or -z-, -ns-, -nz-) *n.* Deer's flesh as food. [F f. L *venatio* hunting)]

**vě″nom** *n.* Poisonous fluid of serpents, scorpions, etc.; (fig.) malignity, virulence, of feeling or language or conduct; **~ous** *a.* [F f. L *venenum*]

**vē″nous** *a.* Of, full of, contained in, veins. [L (VEIN)]

**věnt**[1]. **1.** *n.* ~(-hole), hole or opening allowing motion of air etc. out of or into confined space; anus esp. of lower animal; (fig.) outlet, free passage or play, (*gave vent to his indignation*; *impatience found a vent*). **2.** *v.t.* Make vent in (cask etc.); give vent or free expression to; ~ one's **spleen on,** scold or ill-treat without cause. [F f. L *ventus* wind]

**věnt**[2] *n.* Slit in garment, esp. in back of coat. [F *fente* f. L *findo* cleave]

**vě'ntĭl|āte** *v.t.* Cause air to circulate freely in (room etc.); submit (question, grievance) to public consideration and discussion; ~**ā'tion** *n.*; ~**ātor** *n.*, (esp.) appliance or aperture for ventilating room etc. [L *ventilo* blow, winnow (prec.)]

**vě'ntr|al** *a.* (Anat., Zool.). Of or on the abdomen; ~**ĭcle** *n.*, (Anat.) cavity in the body, hollow part of organ, esp. in brain or heart; ~**ĭ'cŭlar** *a.* of or shaped like ventricle; ~**ĭ'loquĭsm** *n.*, act or art of speaking or uttering sounds in such a manner that they appear not to come from the speaker [L *loquor* speak]; ~**ĭ'loquĭst** *n.*; ~**ĭ'loquĭze** *v.i.* [F or L (*venter* belly)]

**vě'nture. 1.** *n.* Undertaking of risk, commercial speculation, property risked, (*declined the venture*; *ready for any venture*; *one lucky venture made his fortune*; **at a ~,** at random, without previous consideration; **V~ Scout,** senior Scout. **2.** *v.t. & i.* Dare, not be afraid; dare to go etc. or to make or put forward, (*shall not venture out, an opinion, a step*); take risks, expose to risk, stake, (*nothing venture, nothing gain or have or win*); ~ (**up)on,** dare to engage in, to make, etc.; ~**some** (-chers-) *a.*, disposed to take risks, risky. [ADVENTURE]

**vě'nŭe** *n.* (Law) county etc. within which jury must be gathered and cause tried (**change the ~,** try case elsewhere to avoid riot, prejudiced jury, etc.); appointed meeting-place esp. for match, rendezvous. [F f. *venir* (L *venio* come)]

**Vē'nus** *n.* (Rom. Myth.) goddess of love; sexual love, amorous influences or desires; planet second from sun; ~'s **fly-trap,** plant with leaves that close on insects etc. [E f. L]

**verā'cious** (-sh*u*s) *a.* Speaking, disposed to speak, the truth; (of statement etc.) true, not (meant to be) false; **verā'cĭty** *n.* [L *verax* (*verus* true)]

**verā'nda(h)** (-*a*) *n.* Open portico along side of house. [Hindi f. Port. *varanda*]

**verb** *n.* (Gram.) Part of speech that predicates, word whose function is predication (e.g. italicized words in: Time *flies*; Salt *is* good; You *surprise* me); ~'**al** *a.* (-lly), of or concerned with words, oral not written, (of translation) literal, (Gram.) of (the nature of) a verb (~**al noun,** one derived from verb and partly sharing its constructions, e.g. nouns in -ING[1]); ~'**alĭsm** *n.*, minute attention to words; ~'**alĭze** *v.t. & i.*, express in words, be verbose; **verbā'tĭm** *adv. & a.*, in exactly the same words. [F, or L *verbum* word]

**verbē'na** *n.* Plant of a genus of herbs and small shrubs. [L]

**vēr'b|iage** *n.* Needless accumulation of words; ~**ō'se** *a.*, using or expressed in more words than are wanted; ~**ŏ'sĭtў** *n.* [F f. L (VERB)]

**vērb. săp.** *int.* expr. absence of need for further explicit statement. [abbr. L *verbum sapienti sat est* a word is enough for the wise]

**vēr'dan|t** *a.* (Of grass etc.) green, fresh-coloured; (of field etc.) covered with green grass etc.; (of person) unsophisticated, raw, green; ~**cў** *n.* [perh. F *verdeant* f. L (*viridis* green)]

**vēr'dĭct** *n.* Decision of jury on issue of fact in civil or criminal cause (*brought in a verdict of not guilty*; **open ~,** one affirming commission of crime but not specifying criminal, or occurrence of violent death but not specifying cause); decision, judgement. [AF *verdit* (*ver* true, *dit* p.p. of *dire* say)]

**vēr'dĭgrĭs** (*or* -ēs) *n.* Green deposit on copper or brass. [F, = green of Greece]

**vēr'dur|e** (-dyer) *n.* Green(ness of) vegetation; ~**ous** *a.* (poet.) [F (VERT)]

**verge**[1] *n.* Brink, border, (usu. fig.; *on the verge of destruction, tears, betraying his secret*); grass edging of flower-bed, road, etc.; **vēr'ger** *n.*, official in church who acts as attendant and caretaker, ‖officer who bears staff before bishop etc. [F f. L (*virga* rod)]

**verge**[2] *v.i.* Incline downwards or in specified direction; ~ **on,** border on, approach closely, (*path verges on* *the edge of a precipice; solemnity verging on the tragic).* [L *vergo* bend]

**vĕ′ri̇̄|fy̆** *v.t.* Establish truth or correctness of by examination or demonstration (*verify the statement, his figures*); (of event etc.) bear out, fulfil, (prediction, promise); **~fĭcā′tion, ~fiabĭ′lĭty̆,** *ns.;* **~ly̆** *adv.,* (arch.) really, truly. [F f. L (VERY¹)]

**vĕrĭsĭmĭ′litūde** *n.* Appearance of being true or real (*verisimilitude is not proof*). [L (as prec., SIMILAR)]

**vĕ′rit|able** *a.* (**-bly**) Real, rightly so called, (*a veritable boon*); **~y̆** *n.,* truth, true statement, esp. one of fundamental import. [F f. L (*veritas* truth)]

**vĕrmĭ′cĕllĭ** (*or* -chĕ′-) *n.* Pasta made in long slender threads; **~cĭde** *n.,* drug that kills worms; **~fŏrm** *a.,* worm-shaped (**~form appendix,** small blind tube extending from caecum in man and some other mammals). [It. dim. pl. f. L *vermis* worm]

**vĕrmĭ′lion** (-yon). **1.** *n.* (Brilliant red pigment made esp. from) cinnabar. **2.** *n. & a.* (Of) this colour. [F f. L *vermiculus* dim. (prec.)]

**vĕr′min** *n.* (usu. treated as *pl.*) Mammals and birds injurious to game, crops, etc., e.g. foxes, mice, owls; noxious or parasitic worms or insects; (fig.) vile persons; **~ous** *a.,* of the nature of or infested with vermin. [F f. L *vermis* worm]

**vĕr′mouth** (-ō̄oth, -uth) *n.* Wine flavoured with aromatic herbs. [F f. G (WORMWOOD)]

**vernā′cūlar. 1.** *a.* (Of language) of one's native country, not of foreign origin or of learned formation. **2.** *n.* Language or dialect of the country (*Latin gave place to the vernacular*); language of a particular class or group; homely speech. [L *vernaculus* native]

**vĕr′nal** *a.* (**~ly̆**) Of, in, or appropriate to spring (*vernal breezes,* EQUINOX, *migration, fancies*). [L (*ver* the spring)]

**vĕr′nier** *n.* Small movable graduated scale for obtaining fractional parts of subdivisions on fixed scale of barometer etc. [person]

**vĕ′ronal** *n.* Sedative drug. [G (*Verona,* place)]

**verō′nica** *n.* Speedwell. [person]

**vĕrru′ca** (-rōō′-) *n.* (*pl.* **~e** *pr.* -sē, **~s**). Wart(like protuberance). [L]

**vĕr′sat|ile** *a.* Turning easily or

readily from one subject or occupation to another, capable of dealing with many subjects; **~ĭ′lĭty̆** *n.* [F or L (*verto vers-* turn)]

**vĕrs|e** *n.* Metrical composition, metrical line complying with rules of prosody, stanza of such lines, (*in verse or prose; the first verse of the 'Iliad'; read the third line of the next verse*); each of the short numbered divisions in the Bible (CHAPTER *and verse*); **~ed** (-st) *a.,* experienced or skilled *in;* **~icle** *n.,* short sentence, esp. of each series in liturgy said or sung alternately by minister or priest and people; **~ĭfy̆** *v.t. & i.,* turn into or express in verse, compose verses; **~ĭfĭcā′tion** *n.;* **~ion** (-shŏn) *n.,* book etc. when translated into another language (AUTHORIZE*d,* REVISE*d, Version*), account of a matter from particular person's point of view (*now what is your version of the quarrel?*), particular variant *of.* [F *vers* f. L *versus* (prec.)]

**vers libre** (vārlē′br) *n.* Verse composition in which different metres are mingled, or prosodic restrictions disregarded, or variable rhythm substituted for definite metre; **versli′brist** (vārlē′-) *n.* [F]

**vĕr′sŏ** *n.* (*pl.* **~s**). Left-hand page of open book, back of leaf (cf. RECTO). [L, abl. p.p. of *verto* turn]

**vĕr′sus** *prep.* (esp. Law & Sport). Against (*Rex versus Crippen; Surrey v. Kent*). [L (VERSE)]

**vĕrt** *n. & a.* (Her.) Green. [F f. L *viridis*]

**vĕr′tĕbr|a** *n.* (*pl.* **~ae**). Each segment of backbone; **~al** *a.* (**-lly̆**); **~ate** (*or* -āt) *a. & n.,* (animal) having spinal column, esp. mammal, bird, reptile, amphibian, or fish. [L (*verto* turn)]

**vĕr′t|ĕx** *n.* (*pl.* **~ices** *pr.* -ĭsēz, **~exes**). Highest point, top, apex; (Geom.) each angular point of triangle, polygon, etc.; meeting-point of lines that form an angle; **~ical,** (*a.;* **-lly̆**) at right angles to plane of horizon (**~ical take-off,** directly upwards), in direction from top to bottom of picture etc., of or at the vertex, (*n.*) vertical line or plane. [L = whirlpool, crown of head (*verto* turn)]

**vĕr′tĭgŏ** (*or* vertĭ′-) *n.* (*pl.* **~s**). Dizziness; **vertĭ′ginous** *a.,* of or causing vertigo. [L, = whirling (prec.)]

**vĕr′vain** *n.* Herbaceous plant of

verbena genus esp. one with small blue, white, or purple flowers. [F f. L (VERBENA)]

**vĕrve** n. Enthusiasm, vigour, zest in artistic or literary work. [F]

**vĕ'rў¹. 1.** *attrib.a.* (arch.; VERILY). Real, true, that is such in the truest or fullest sense, (*the veriest simpleton knows that; in very truth*). **2.** the, this, his, etc., ~ (emphasizing identity, significance, or extreme degree; *this is the very spot where I found it; the very* SAME; *those were his very words; speaking in this very room; the very fact of his presence is enough; a needle is the very thing I want; a very little will do; at the very edge of the cliff*). **3.** *adv.* In the fullest sense (w. superl. *adjs.* or own) (*will do my very best; keep it for your very own*); (w. adjs.), adjectival participles, & *advs.*) in a high degree (*that is very easy, very easily done; a very trying time; very often fails; find very few instances; very much better, annoyed*); **not** ~, in a low degree, far from being; ~ **high frequency** (in range 30 to 300 megahertz); *Very* REVER-END; ~ **good,** ~ **well,** (formula of consent or approval). [F *verai* f. L *verus* true]

**Vĕ'rў²** (or vēr'ĭ) n. ~ **light,** flare projected from ~ **pistol** for temporarily illuminating part of battle-field etc. [person]

**vĕ'sĭcle** n. Small bladder or blister or bubble. [F or L]

**vĕ'sper** n. (Eccl., in *pl.*) Evening service; ~(-**bell**), bell that calls to vespers; ~**tĭne** a., of or occurring in the evening. [L, = evening]

**vĕ'ssel** n. Hollow receptacle esp. for liquid, e.g. cask, cup, pot, bottle, dish; ship, boat, esp. large one; (Bibl. or joc.) person viewed as recipient or exponent of a quality (**weaker** ~, woman); (Anat., Bot.) duct, canal, etc., holding or conveying BLOOD, sap, etc. [F f. L dim. (VAS)]

**vĕst. 1.** n. ||Knitted or woven under-garment worn on upper part of body; (||Commerc.) waistcoat; ~-**pocket,** of size suitable for the (waistcoat-) pocket. **2.** *v.t.* & *i.* Furnish (person *with* powers, property, etc.); ~ (property, powers) **in** (person), con-fer formally on him an immediate fixed right of present or future possession of; ~ **in,** (of property, rights, etc.) come into the possession of (person); ~**ed interests, rights,**

etc., (possession of which is estab-lished in a person by right or by long association); (poet.) clothe. [F f. It. f. L *vestis* garment]

**vĕ'stal** a. & n. ~ (**virgin**), (virgin) consecrated to Vesta and vowed to chastity, (fig.) chaste woman. [L *Vesta* Rom. goddess of hearth and home]

**vĕ'stĭbŭle** n. Antechamber, hall, lobby, next to outer door of house; *enclosed entrance to railway--carriage. [F or L]

**vĕ'stĭge** n. Trace, evidence, sign, (*found no vestige of his presence*); slight amount, particle, (*without a vestige of clothing*); (Biol.) part or organ now degenerate but well developed in ancestors; **vĕstī'gĭal** a. (esp. Biol.). [F f. L *vestigium* footprint]

**vĕ'st|ment** n. Garment, esp. official or state robe; any of the official garments of clergy, choristers, etc., worn during divine service; ~**rў** n., room or building attached to church for keeping vestments in, ||(Hist.) meeting of parishioners usu. in vestry for parochial business or body of parishioners meeting thus; ~**ure** (poet., rhet.), (n.) clothes, (v.t.) clothe. [F f. L (VEST)]

**vĕt.** (colloq.) **1.** n. Veterinary surgeon. **2.** *v.t.* (-tt-). Examine, treat, (animal); (fig.) make careful and critical examination of (scheme, work, candidate, etc.). [abbr.]

**vĕtch** n. Plant of pea family largely used for fodder; ~'**ling** n., an allied plant. [F f. L *vicia*]

**vĕ'teran** n. Person who has grown old in or had long experience of (esp. military) service or occupation (*a veteran of two world wars; a veteran golfer*); *ex-service man; ||~ **car** (made before 1916, or before 1905). [F or L (*vetus -er-* old)]

**vĕ'terĭnarў. 1.** a. Of or for (treatment of) diseases of farm and domestic animals; ~ **surgeon,** one skilled in such treatment. **2.** n. Veterinary surgeon (also **vĕterĭn-ār'ĭan**). [L (*veterinae* cattle)]

**vē'tō. 1.** n. (*pl.* ~es). Constitu-tional right to reject a legislative enactment, right of permanent member of U.N. Security Council to reject a resolution, (official message conveying) such rejection; prohi-bition (*put a or one's veto on*). **2.** *v.t.* Exercise veto against, forbid author-itatively. [L, = I forbid]

**věx** *v.t.* Anger by slight or petty annoyance, irritate, (*this would vex a saint; how vexing!*); (arch.) grieve, afflict; **a ~ed** (much discussed) **question**; **~ā'tion** *n.*, (esp.) annoying or distressing thing; **~ā'tious** (-shŭs) *a.*, such as to cause vexation, (Law) not having sufficient grounds for action and seeking only to annoy defendant. [F f. L *vexo* afflict]

**v.g.** *abbr.* very good.

**V.H.F.** *abbr.* very high frequency.

**vī'a** *prep.* By way of, through, (*London to Rome via Paris; sent it via his secretary*). [L, abl. of *via* way]

**vī'ab|le** *a.* Capable of living or existing or (of foetus etc.) maintaining life; (of plan etc.) feasible esp. from economic standpoint; **~i'lĭtỹ** *n.* [F *vie* life f. L *vita*)]

**vī'adŭct** *n.* Bridgelike structure esp. series of arches carrying railway or road across valley or dip in ground. [L *via* way, after *aquedust*]

**vī'al** *n.* Small (usu. cylindrical glass) vessel for holding liquid medicines etc. [PHIAL]

**vī'and** *n.* (usu. in *pl.*) Article(s) of food. [F f. L *vivo* live)]

**viā'tĭcum** *n.* Eucharist given to person (in danger of) dying. [L (*via* way)]

**vibes** (-bz) *n.pl.* (colloq.) Vibraphone; vibrations. [abbr.]

**vī'br|ant** *a.* Vibrating; thrilling *with* (action etc.); resonant; **~a-phōne** *n.*, percussion instrument of metal bars with motor-driven resonators and metal tubes giving vibrato effect; **~ā'te** *v.t. & i.*, move to and fro like pendulum, (cause to) oscillate, (of sound) throb (*on ear, in memory*, etc.), (Phys.) move unceasingly to and fro, esp. rapidly, quiver (*with* passion etc.); **~ā'tion** *n.*, vibrating, (in *pl.*) mental (esp. occult) influence; **~a'tō** (vēbrah'-) *n.* (*pl.* -os), (Mus.) tremulous effect in pitch of singing or of playing stringed or wind instrument; **~ā'tor** *n.*, (esp., Med.) electric or other instrument used in massage; **~atorỹ** *a.* [L *vibro* shake]

**Vic.** *abbr.* Victoria.

**vī'car** *n.* (In C.E.) incumbent of parish where tithes formerly belonged to chapter or religious house or layman (cf. RECTOR); **~ apostolic**, R.C. missionary or titular bishop; **~-general**, Anglican official assisting (arch)bishop in ecclesiastical causes etc., R.C. bishop's assistant in matters of jurisdiction etc.; **~ of Bray**, systematic turncoat [w. ref. to 18th-c. song]; **V~ of Christ**, the Pope; **~age** *n.*, vicar's house; **vĭcăr'ĭal** *a.* (-lly), of, or serving as, vicar; **vĭcăr'ĭous** *a.*, deputed, acting or done for another, experienced imaginatively through another person, (*vicarious authority, work, pleasure*). [AF f. L *vicarius* substitute (VICE³)]

**vice¹** *n.* Evil (esp. grossly immoral) habit or conduct, (particular form of) depravity, (*drunkenness is not among his vices; vice is duly punished and virtue rewarded in fifth act*); defect, blemish, (*of* character, literary style, etc.); fault(s) or bad habit(s) in horse etc.; **~ squad**, police department enforcing laws against prostitution etc. [F f. L *vitium*]

‖**vice²,** *vise,* *n.* Instrument with two jaws between which thing may be gripped so as to leave hands free to work on it. [F *vis* screw f. L *vitis* vine]

**vī'cè³** (or vĭs) *prep.* In the place of, in succession to. [L, abl. of (*vix*) *vicis* change]

**vice-** *pref.* forming *ns.* w. sense 'person acting or qualified to act in place of, or next in rank to'; *vice*-A'DMIRAL, *-chair'man;* **~-cha'ncellor**, deputy chancellor (esp. of university, discharging most administrative duties); *vice-co'nsul, -pre'sident, -pri'ncipal, -re'gent.*

**vicegè'rent** (-sj-; or -ēr'-) *a. & n.* (Person) exercising delegated power, deputy. [L (*gero* carry on)]

**vī'ce|roy** (-sr-) *n.* Ruler on behalf of sovereign in colony, province, etc.; **~rē'gal** *a.* (-lly); **~reine** (-ān) *n.*, viceroy's wife, woman viceroy; **~roy'altỹ** *n.*, office of viceroy. [F (VICE-, *roy* king)]

**vĭcè vēr'sa** *adv.* With order of terms changed, the other way round: *the man blames his wife and* **~** (*she blames him*); *calls black white and* **~** (*white black*). [L, = the position being reversed]

**Vichy** (vē'shĭ) *n.* **~ (water)**, effervescent mineral water from Vichy. [place]

**vī'cĭnage** *n.* Neighbourhood, surrounding district; relation of neighbours; **vĭcĭ'nĭtỹ** *n.*, surrounding district, nearness (*to*); **in the**

**vicinity (of)**, near. [F f. L *vicinus* (*vicus* district)]

**vi′cious** (-shus) *a.* Of the nature of or addicted to vice; (of language, reasoning, etc.) faulty or unsound; (of horse etc.) having vices; bad--tempered, spiteful, (*vicious dog, remark*); *vicious* CIRCLE, SPIRAL. [F f. L (VICE[1])]

**vici′ssitūde** *n.* Change of circumstances, esp. of fortune. [F or L (VICE[3])]

**vi′ctim** *n.* Living creature sacrificed to deity or in religious rite; person or thing injured or destroyed in pursuit of an object, in gratification of a passion etc., or as result of event or circumstance, (*the victims of his relentless ambition*; *fell a victim to his own avarice*; *the victims of disease, of a railway accident*); prey, dupe, (*the numerous victims of the confidence trick*); **~ize** *v.t.*, make (person etc.) a victim, make (striker etc.) suffer by dismissal or other exceptional treatment; **~izā′tion** *n.* [L]

**vi′ctor** *n.* Conqueror in battle or contest. [F or L (*vinco vict-* conquer)]

**victo′ria** *n.* Low light 4-wheeled carriage with collapsible top; **V~ Cross,** (holder of) decoration awarded for conspicuous bravery in armed services; **V~n** *a. & n.* (person, writer) of the time of Queen Victoria; ‖**Royal V~n Order** (awarded usu. for service to sovereign). [person]

**vi′ctory** *n.* Defeating one's enemy in battle or war or one's opponent in contest (lit. or fig.); **victo′rious** *a.*, conquering, triumphant, marked by victory. [AF f. L (VICTOR)]

**vi′ctual** (-ital; formal). **1.** *n.* (usu. in *pl.*) Food, provisions. **2.** *v.t. & i.* (‖-ll-). Supply with victuals; obtain stores; eat victuals. **3.** **~ler** (vi′tler) *n.*, one who furnishes victuals, ‖esp. **licensed ~ler,** innkeeper licensed to sell alcoholic liquor etc. [F f. L (*victus* food)]

**vicuña** (-kōō′nya, -na) *n.* S. Amer. mammal like llama, with fine silky wool; (imitation of) cloth made from its wool. [Sp. f. Quechua]

**vide** (vi′di, vī′dā) *v.t.* (*imper.*, in formal or joc. ref. to passage in book etc.) See, consult; **vidē′licĕt** *adv.,* = VIZ. [L *video* see, *licet* it is allowed]

**vi′dĕō** *a.* Relating to recording or broadcasting of photographic images; **~tape** *n.,* & *v.t.,* (make record of

with) magnetic tape suitable for records of television pictures and sound. [L, = I see]

**vie** *v.i.* (*vying pr.* vī′i-). Carry on rivalry (*with* another *in* quality, *in* doing). [prob. F (ENVY)]

**Viennē′se** (-z) *a. & n.* (*pl.* same). (Inhabitant) of *Vienna.* [place]

**Viĕtnamē′se** (-z) *a. & n.* (*pl.* same). (Native, language) of *Vietnam.* [place]

**view** (vū). **1.** *n.* Inspection by eye or mind, survey, (*of* surroundings, subject, etc.); power of seeing, range of vision, (*has a view of the sea from here*; *came into view*); what is seen, prospect, picture etc. representing this; manner of considering a subject, opinion, mental attitude, (*takes a different, a* DIM *or poor, view of her conduct*; *holds extreme views*; *take the* LONG[1] *view*); **in ~ of,** able to see, or to be seen by or from, having regard to, considering, in anticipation of; **on ~,** being shown (for inspection); **with a ~ to, with the** or **a ~ of,** for the purpose of, as a step towards; **with a ~ to,** with the aim of attaining; **have in ~,** have as one's object, bear (circumstance) in mind in forming judgement etc.; POINT *of view*; **~′finder,** part of camera showing extent of picture; **~ halloo,′** huntsman's shout on seeing fox break cover; **~′point,** point of view, standpoint. **2.** *v.t. & i.* Survey with eyes or mentally, form mental impression or judgement of, (*subject may be viewed in different ways*); *does not view the matter thus*); watch television. **3.** **~′er** *n.,* (esp.) television-watcher, device for looking at film transparencies etc. [AF f. L (*video* see)]

**vi′gil** *n.* Keeping awake during time usually given to sleep, watchfulness, (*keep vigil*); eve of a festival, esp. eve that is a fast; **~ance** *n.,* watchfulness, caution, (\***~ance committee,** self-appointed body for maintenance of order etc.); **~ant** *a.;* **~a′ntĕ** *n.,* member of vigilance committee or similar body. [F f. L *vigilia*]

**vignĕ′tte** (vēnyĕ′t) *n.* Illustration not in definite border; photograph etc. with background gradually shaded off; (fig.) character sketch, short description. [F dim. (VINE)]

**vi′gour, \*-gor,** (-ger) *n.* Active physical or mental strength or energy; healthy growth; trenchancy, animation; **vī′gorous** *a.* [F f. L (*vigeo* be lively)]

**Vī′king** *n.* Scandinavian trader and pirate of 8th–10th cc. [N]

**vīle** *a.* Morally base, depraved, disgusting; (colloq.) abominably bad (*vile weather*); **vī′lify** *v.t.*, defame, speak evil of; **vīlĭfĭcā′tion** *n.* [F f. L *vilis* worthless]

**vĭ′lla** *n.* Country residence; ‖(semi-)detached house in residential district; house for holiday-makers at seaside etc.; ∼**ge** *n.*, group of houses etc. larger than hamlet and smaller than town; ∼**ger** (-ĭj-) *n.*, inhabitant of village. [L & It.]

**vĭ′llain** (-ăn) *n.* Person guilty or capable of great wickedness; (colloq., playfully) rascal; ∼**ous** *a.*, worthy of a villain, (colloq.) abominably bad (*villainous weather*); ∼**ў** *n.*, villainous behaviour. [F f. L *villanus* (prec.)]

**vĭ′llein** (-ĭn) *n.* (Hist.) Feudal tenant entirely subject to lord or attached to manor; ∼**age** *n.*, tenure or status of villein. [var. VILLAIN]

**vĭm** *n.* (colloq.) Vigour. [perh. L, acc. of *vis* force]

**vĭnaigrĕ′tte** (-nĭg-) *n.* ∼ (sauce), salad dressing of oil and wine vinegar. [F dim. (VINEGAR)]

**vĭ′ndĭcāte** *v.t.* (∼**able**). Clear of suspicion etc.; establish existence or merits or justice of (one's courage, conduct, assertion); ∼**ā′tion**, ∼**ātor**, *ns.*; ∼**ātorў** *a.*; **vĭndĭ′ctĭve** *a.*, tending to seek revenge; ∼**tive damages** (exceeding simple compensation and awarded to punish defendant). [L *vindico* claim]

**vīne** *n.* Climbing or trailing woody-stemmed grape-bearing plant; slender trailing or climbing stem. [F *vi(g)ne* f. L *vinea* vineyard]

**vĭ′nĕgar** *n.* Sour liquid got from wine, cider, etc., by fermentation and used as condiment or for pickling; (fig.) sour behaviour or character; ∼**ў** *a.* [F, = sour wine (EAGER)]

**vĭ′nerў** *n.* Vine greenhouse; **vĭ′neyard** (-ny-) *n.*, plantation of grape-vines, esp. for wine-making. [VINE]

**vingt-et-un** (văntăĕr′n) *n.* Card-game in which object is to reach as nearly as possible 21 pips on one's cards and no more. [F, = 21]

**vin ordinaire** (văn ôrdĭnār′) *n.* Cheap (usu. red) wine. [F]

**vī′nous** *a.* Of, like, due to, addicted to, wine. [L (*vinum* wine)]

**vĭ′ntǀage. 1.** *n.* (Season of) gathering grapes for wine-making; (wine made from) season's produce of grapes, (fig.) (thing made etc. in) a particular year etc.; (poet., rhet.) wine; wine of high quality kept separate from others. **2.** *a.* Of high quality; of a past season; ∼**age car** (made 1917–1930). **3.** ∼**ner** *n.*, wine-merchant. [F *vendange* f. L (*vinum* wine)]

**vĭ′nŷl** *n.* One of group of plastics, made by polymerization, esp. POLY-vinyl chloride. [L *vinum* wine]

**vī′ol** *n.* Medieval stringed musical instrument, like violin but held vertically; **vīō′la**[1] *n.*, (player of) kind of large violin. [F f. Prov.]

**vĭō′la**[2] *n.* One of group of plants including violet and pansy. [L, = violet]

**vī′olǀate** *v.t.* (∼**able**). Disregard, fail to comply with, act against dictates or requirements of, (oath, treaty, law, conscience); treat profanely or with disrespect (sanctuary etc.); break in upon, disturb, (person's privacy etc.); rape; ∼**ā′tion**, ∼**ātor**, *ns.* [L *violo*]

**vī′olenǀt** *a.* Involving great physical force (*a violent storm; came into violent collision*; ∼**t death**, resulting from external force or from poison; cf. NATURAL); intense, vehement, (*violent pain, abuse, contrast, dislike*); ∼**ce** *n.*, being violent, violent conduct or treatment, unlawful use of force; **do** ∼**ce to**, act contrary to, outrage. [F f. L]

**vī′olet** *n.* & *a.* Plant with usu. blue, purple, or white flowers; (of) colour seen at end of spectrum opposite red, blue with slight admixture of red; violet pigment, clothes, or material. [F dim. of *viole* VIOLA[2]]

**viol|ĭ′n** *n.* Musical instrument with 4 strings of treble pitch played with bow (FIRST, SECOND, *violin*); its player (also ∼**ĭ′nĭst**); **vī′olĭst**[1] *n.*, viol-player; **vĭō′lĭst**[2] *n.*, viola-player; ∼**oncĕ′llō** (-chĕ′- *or* vĕ-) *n.* (*pl.* -os), bass instrument like very large violin, held upright on floor by seated player; ∼**oncĕ′llĭst** (-chĕ′- *or* vĕ-) *n.* [It. dim. (VIOL)]

**V.I.P.** *abbr.* very important person.

**vī′per** *n.* Venomous snake, esp. **common** ∼, or adder, the only poisonous snake in Gt. Britain; (fig.) malignant or treacherous person; ∼**ous** *a.* (fig.) [F or L]

**vĭrā′gō** (*or* -ah′-) *n.* (*pl.* ∼**s**).

Fierce or abusive woman. [E f. L, = female warrior]

**vīr′al.** See VIRUS.

**vir′gĭn.** 1. *n.* Person (esp. woman) who has had no sexual intercourse; **the (Blessed) V~ (Mary)**, mother of Christ; picture or statue of the Virgin; (*V~*) sign of ZODIAC. 2. *a.* Of or befitting or being a virgin; not yet used etc. 3. ~**al**, (*a.*; **-lly**) that is or befits a virgin, (*n.*) ~**al**, (**pair of**) ~**als**, legless spinet in box; **vǐr̄gǐ′nǐtў** *n.*, state of being a virgin. [F f. L *virgo -gins-*]

**Vǐr̄gǐ′nǐa** *n.* ~ **creeper**, vine cultivated for ornament. [place]

**Vǐr̄′gō** *n.* Sign of ZODIAC. [E f. L (VIRGIN)]

**vǐ′rīle** *a.* Of man as opp. to woman or child; of or having procreative power; (of character, literary style, etc.) having masculine vigour or strength; **vǐrǐ′lǐtў** *n.* [F or L (*vir* man)]

**vǐr̄′tūǀe** *n.* Goodness, uprightness, (particular) moral excellence, (*make a virtue of* NECESSITY; **the cardinal** ~**es**, justice, prudence, temperance, fortitude, faith, hope, and charity); chastity esp. of woman; good quality, efficacy, (*has the virtue of being adjustable; no virtue in such drugs*); **by** or **in** ~**e of**, on the strength of, on the ground of (*claims it in virtue of his long service*); ~**al** *a.* (**-lly**), that is such for practical purposes though not in name or according to strict definition (*is the virtual manager of the business; take this as a virtual promise*); ~**ō′sō** *n.* (*pl.* **-i** *pr.* **-ē**, **-os**), person skilled in technique of a fine art, esp. music; ~**ō′sǐtў** *n.*; ~**ous** *a.*, possessing or showing moral rectitude, chaste. [F f. L (as prec.)]

**vǐ′rūlenǀt** (*or* **-rōō-**) *a.* Poisonous; (of disease) malignant, violent; (fig.) malignant, bitter; ~**ce** *n.*; **vǐr̄′us** *n.*, any of numerous kinds of very simple organisms smaller than bacteria, able to cause diseases, (arch. or fig.) poison, source of disease; **vǐr̄′al** *a.* [L (*virus* poison)]

**vǐ′sa** (*vē′za*). 1. *n.* Endorsement on passport etc. esp. as permitting holder to enter or leave a country. 2. *v.t.* (~**ed**, ~**′d**, *pr.* **-ad**). Mark with visa. [F f. L, = seen]

**vǐ′sage** (**-z-**) *n.* (literary). Face, countenance; *vis-à-vis* (*vēzahvē′*), (*adv.*) facing one another, (*prep.*) opposite to, in relation to, (*n.*)

person or thing facing another. [F f. L *visus* face]

**Visc.** *abbr.* Viscount.

**vǐ′scera** *n.pl.* Internal organs of the body; ~**l** *a.* (**-lly**). [L]

**vǐ′scǐd** *a.* Glutinous, sticky. [L (as VISCOUS)]

**vǐ′scōse, vǐscǒ′sǐtў.** See VISCOUS.

**vǐ′scount** (*vī′k-*) *n.* British nobleman ranking between earl and baron; ~**ess** *n.*, viscount's wife or widow, woman with own rank of viscount; ~**cў**, ~**ў**, *ns.* [AF (VICE-, COUNT²)]

**vǐ′scǀous** *a.* Glutinous, sticky; semifluid; not flowing freely; ~**ōse** *n.*, cellulose in highly viscous state (for making into rayon etc.); ~**ǒ′sǐtў** *n.*, quality or degree of being viscous. [L (*viscum* birdlime)]

***vīse.** See VICE².

**vǐ′sǐbǀle** (**-z-**) *a.* (~**ly**). That can be seen by the eye or perceived or ascertained; (of exports etc.) consisting of actual goods (cf. INVISIBLE); ~**i′lǐtў** *n.*, (esp., Meteor. etc.) possibility of seeing, range of vision as determined by conditions of light and atmosphere. [F or L (as foll.)]

**vǐ′sion** (**-zhon**) *n.* Act or faculty of seeing, sight; thing or person seen in dream or trance; thing seen vividly in the imagination (*the romantic visions of youth*); person etc. of unusual beauty; imaginative insight; statesmanlike foresight, sagacity in planning; what is seen on television screen; ~**arў**, (*a.*) given to seeing visions or to indulging in fanciful theories, existing only in vision or in imagination, unpractical, (*n.*) visionary person. [F f. L (*video vis-* see)]

**vǐ′sǐt** (**-z-**). 1. *v.t.* & *i.* Go or come to see (person, place, etc., or abs.) as act of friendship or ceremony, on business or from interest, or for official inspection etc.; be visitor; (of disease, calamity, etc.) come upon, attack; (Bibl.) punish (person, sin), inflict punishment for (sin) *upon* person. 2. *n.* Act of visiting, temporary residence with person or at place, (*on a visit to some friends*; *paid him a long visit*); occasion of going *to* doctor etc.; formal or official call. 3. ~**ant** *n.*, (supernatural) visitor; ~**a′tion** *n.*, official visit of inspection etc. esp. by bishop, (colloq.) unduly protracted visit or social call, divine dispensation of punishment or reward, notable experience; *visiting*-CARD[2]; **~or** *n.*, one who visits person or place, migratory bird, ||college etc. official with right or duty of occasionally inspecting and reporting; **~ors' book** (in which visitors to hotel, church, etc., write their names and addresses and occas. remarks). [F f. L (as prec.)]

**vi′sor** (-z-), **-zor,** *n.* Shield at top of vehicle windscreen to protect eyes from bright sunshine; (Hist.) movable part of helmet covering face, mask. [AF *viser* (as VISAGE)]

**vi′sta** *n.* Long narrow view as between rows of trees; mental view of long succession of events. [It.]

**vi′sual** (-zhŏŏ-, -zyŏŏ-) *a.* (**~ly**). Of, concerned with, or used in, seeing; **~ aid,** film etc. as aid to learning; **~ize** *v.t.*, make visible esp. to one's mind (thing not visible to the eye); **~izā′tion** *n.* [L (*visus* sight)]

**vi′tal. 1.** *a.* (**~ly**). Of or concerned with or essential to organic life (*vital functions*; **~ power,** to sustain life); essential to existence of a thing or to the matter in hand (*question of vital importance*; *secrecy is vital to the success of the plan*); affecting life; fatal to life or to success etc. (*a vital error*); full of life or activity; **~ statistics,** number of births, marriages, deaths, etc., (colloq.) measurements of woman's bust, waist, and hips. **2.** *n.* (in *pl.*) Vital parts, e.g. lungs, heart, brain. **3. ~ism** *n.*, doctrine that life originates in a vital principle distinct from physical forces; **~ist** *n.*; **~i′stic** *a.* (-ically); **vitā′lity** *n.*, vital power, ability to sustain life, animation, liveliness; **~ize** *v.t.*, endow with life, infuse with vigour; **~izā′tion** *n.* [F f. L (*vita* life)]

**vi′tamin** *n.* Any of a number of substances present in many foodstuffs and essential to normal growth and nutrition; **~ C** (found in fruit and vegetables, preventing scurvy); **~ize** *v.t.*, introduce vitamin(s) into (food). [G f. L (prec.), AMINE]

**vi′ti|āte** (-shi-) *v.t.* Impair quality or efficiency of, debase; make invalid or ineffectual (*a single word may vitiate a contract*); **~ā′tion, ~ātor,** *ns.* [L (VICE[1])]

**vi′ticulture** *n.* Grape-growing. [L *vitis* vine]

**vi′tr|eous** *a.* Of (nature of) glass (*vitreous* HUMOUR); **~ify** *v.t.* & *i.*,

change into glass(y substance) esp. by heat; **~ifā′ction, ~ificā′tion,** *ns.* [L (*vitrum* glass)]

**vi′tri|ol** *n.* Sulphuric acid or a sulphate; (fig.) caustic speech or criticism; **~ŏ′lic** *a.* (-ically) (esp. of abuse etc.). [F or L (prec.)]

**vitū′per|āte** *v.t.* Revile, abuse; **~ā′tion, ~ātor,** *ns.*; **~ative** *a.* [L]

**viva**[1] (vē′va) *int.* & *n.* (The cry) 'long live' as salute etc. [It., = let live]

||**vi′va**[2] *n.*, & *v.t.* (**~ed, ~'d,** *pr. -ad*). (colloq.) = VIVA VOCE. [abbr.]

**vivā′cious** (-shus) *a.* Sprightly, lively, animated; **vivǎ′city** *n.* [L *vivax* (*vivo* live)]

**vivā′r|ium** *n.* (*pl.* -ia). Place artificially prepared for keeping animals in (nearly) their natural state. [L]

**viva vō′ce** (or -chī) *adv., a., n.,* & *v.* **1.** *adv.* & *a.* Oral(ly). **2.** *n.* Oral examination. **3.** *v.t.* (w. hyphen). Examine viva voce. [L, = with the living voice]

**vi′vi|d** *a.* (Of light or colour) strong, intense; (of mental faculty, description, impression) clear, lively, graphic; **~fy** *v.t.*, (esp. fig.) give life to, enliven, animate. [L]

**vivi′parous** *a.* (Zool.) Bringing forth young alive (cf. *ovi*parous). [L (*vivus* alive, *pario* produce)]

**vivisĕ′ction** *n.* Dissection or other painful treatment of living animals for scientific research; **vi′visĕct** *v.t.*, perform vivisection on; **~ist, vi′visĕctor,** *ns.* [L *vivus* living; DISSECTION]

**vi′xen** *n.* She-fox; spiteful woman. [E (FOX)]

**viz.** (or nā′mlĭ) *adv.* That is to say, in other words, namely, (usu. after wds that promise or need explanation etc.: *under the following conditions, viz. that* etc.). [abbr. VIDELICET; *z* = L symb. for abbr. of -*et*)]

**vizier′** (or vi′zier) *n.* High official in some Muslim countries. [ult. f. Arab.]

**vi′zor.** See VISOR.

**vō′cable** *n.* Word, esp. w. ref. to form not meaning; **vocǎ′bŭlary** *n.*, (list, arranged alphabetically with definitions or translations, of) words used by a language or book or branch of science or author, person's range of language (*his vocabulary is limited*), set of artistic or stylistic forms or techniques. [F or L (*voco* call)]

**vō′cal** *a.* (**~ly**). Of, concerned with,

uttered by, the voice (*vocal communication*; ~ **cords**, voice-producing part of larynx; ~ **music**, written for or produced by the voice); expressing one's feelings freely in speech (*was very vocal about her rights*); **vocă'lic** *a.*, of or consisting of vowel(s); ~**ĭst** *n.*, singer; ~**ĭze** *v.t. & i.*, form (sound) or utter (word) with voice, (joc.) speak, sing, etc.; ~**izā'tion** *n.* [L (VOICE)]

**vocā'tion** *n.* Divine call to, or sense of fitness for, a career or occupation, (*felt no vocation for the ministry; has never had the sense of vocation*); employment, trade, profession; ~**al** *a.* (-**lly**). [F or L (*voco* call)]

**vŏ'cative** *a. & n.* (Gram.) (Case or word) used in addressing or invoking person or thing.

**vocĭ'fer|āte** *v.t.* Utter noisily; shout, bawl; ~**ā'tion**, ~**ātor**, *ns.*; ~**ous** *a.*, noisy, clamorous, loud and insistent in speech. [L (VOICE, *fero* bear)]

**vŏ'dka** *n.* Alcoholic spirit distilled esp. in Russia from rye etc. [Russ.]

**vōgue** (vōg) *n.* The prevailing fashion; popular use or reception (*has had a great vogue*); **in ~**, in fashion, generally current; ~**-word**, word currently fashionable. [F f. It.]

**voice.** **1.** *n.* Sound formed in larynx etc. and uttered by mouth, esp. human utterance in speaking, shouting, singing, etc., (*heard a voice; spoke in a loud voice; the voice of the cuckoo*; **in good ~**, in proper vocal condition for singing or speaking), ability to produce this (*has laryngitis and has lost her voice*); use of voice, utterance esp. in spoken or (fig.) written words, opinion so expressed, right to express opinion, (*gave voice to his indignation; I have no voice in the matter*); agency by which opinion is expressed (**with one ~**, unanimously); (Gram.) set of verbal forms showing relation of subject to action (ACTIVE, MIDDLE, PASSIVE, *voice*). **2.** *v.t.* Give utterance to, express, (*am voicing the general opinion*); (Phon.) make sonant. **3.** ~**-over**, narration in film not accompanied by picture of speaker; ~'**lĕss** *a.*, (esp., Phon.) surd. [F f. L *vox voc-*]

**void** *a., n., & v.* **1.** *a.* Empty, vacant; (Law, of contract etc.) invalid, not binding; (*null and void*); ~ **of**, lacking, free from. **2.** *n.* Empty

space (*vanished into the void*; fig., *cannot fill the void left by his death*). **3.** *v.t.* Render void; evacuate (excrement etc.). [F]

**voile** (voil, vwahl) *n.* Thin semitransparent dress-material. [F, = VEIL]

**vol.** *abbr.* volume.

**vŏ'lat|īle** *a.* Evaporating rapidly; (fig.) lively, gay, changeable, (*volatile wit, writer, disposition*); ~**ĭ'lĭtў** *n.*; **volā'tilize** *v.t. & i.*, turn into vapour; **volătĭlizā'tion** *n.* [F or L (*volo* fly)]

**vŏl-au-vent** (-ō-vah'n̄, vŏ'-) *n.* (Usu. small) round case of puff pastry filled with savoury mixture. [F, lit. 'flight in the wind']

**vŏlcā'nō** (*pl.* ~**es**). Mountain or hill having opening(s) in earth's crust through which lava, steam, etc., are or have been expelled; (fig.) state of things likely to cause violent outburst; **vŏlcă'nĭc** *a.* (-**ically**), of, like, produced by, volcano. [It. f. L *Volcanus* Vulcan, Rom. god of fire]

**vōle** *n.* Small herbivorous rodent. [orig. *vole-mouse* f. Norw. *voll* field]

**volĭ'tion** *n.* Act or faculty of willing; ~**al** *a.* (-**lly**). [F or L (*volo* wish)]

**vŏ'lley.** **1.** *n.* Simultaneous discharge of a number of weapons; bullets etc. thus discharged at once; (fig.) noisy emission (*of* oaths etc.) in quick succession; (Lawn Tennis, Footb., etc.) playing of ball before it touches ground, (Crick.) full toss (**half-~**, ball so pitched that batsman may strike it as it bounces); ~**-ball**, game for two teams of 6 sending large ball by hand over net. **2.** *v.t.* Return or send by volley. [F *volée* f. L *volo* fly]

**vŏlt** *n.* Unit of electromotive force, difference of potential that would carry one ampere of current against one ohm resistance; ~'**age** *n.*, electromotive force expressed in volts; ~'**mēter** *n.*, instrument measuring electric potential in volts. [*Volta*, person]

**vŏlte-fa'ce** (-tfah's) *n.* Complete change of front in argument or opinion. [F f. It.]

**vŏ'lūb|le** *a.* (-**ly**). With vehement or incessant flow of words (*voluble excuses, spokesman*); ~**ĭ'lĭtў** *n.* [F or L (*volvo* roll)]

**vŏ'lūme** *n.* Set of printed sheets bound together usu. within cover and containing part of a book or one or more books (*issued in 3 volumes; an odd volume of 'Punch'; a library of 9,000 volumes;* SPEAK *volumes*); moving mass of water or smoke etc.; solid content, bulk, amount or quantity *of*; (Mus. etc.) quantity or power of sound; **vŏlŭmĕ'trĭc** *a.* (-ically), of measurement by volume; **volŭ'mĭnous** :(or -lōō'-) *a.*, (of book or writer) running to many volumes or great length, (of drapery etc.) loose or ample. [F f. L *volumen* (prec., ancient books being in roll form)]

**vŏ'luntar|y̆. 1.** *a.* (~ily, ~iness). Done, acting, able to act, of one's own free will, not constrained or compulsory, intentional, (*a voluntary gift; was a voluntary agent in the matter; voluntary service*); brought about by voluntary action, (of institution) supported by voluntary contributions; (of muscle, limb, movement) controlled by the will. **2.** *n.* Organ solo played before, during, or after church service; (arch.) piece of music played extempore. **3.** ~(y̆)**ism** *n.*, principle of relying on voluntary action rather than compulsion; **vŏlunteer'**, (*n.*) person who voluntarily undertakes task or enters military etc. service, (*v.i.* & *t.*) be volunteer, undertake, offer, (one's services, remark, etc.; *to do*) voluntarily. [F or L (*voluntas* will)]

**volŭ'ptŭ|ar̄y** *n.* Person given up to luxury and sensual pleasure; ~**ous** *a.*, of, tending to, occupied with, derived from, sensuous or sensual pleasure. [L (*voluptas* pleasure)]

**volŭ'te** *n.* (Archit.) Spiral scroll in stonework as ornament of esp. Ionic capital. [F or L (*volvo -ut-roll*)]

**vŏ'mĭt. 1.** *v.t.* Eject (matter, or abs.) from stomach through mouth; (fig., of volcano, chimney, etc.) eject violently, belch forth. **2.** *n.* Matter vomited from stomach. [F or L]

**vōō'dōō. 1.** *n.* Use of, belief in, religious witchcraft as practised among W. Ind. etc. Negroes. **2.** *v.t.* Affect by voodoo, bewitch. [Dahomey]

**vŏrā'cĭous** (-shus) *a.* Greedy in eating, ravenous, (lit. or fig.; *voracious schoolboy, reader*); **vŏrā'cĭty̆** *n.* [L *vorax* (*voro* devour)]

**vŏr'tĕx** *n.* (*pl.* ~ices *pr.* -ĭsĕz, ~exes). Whirlpool, whirlwind,

whirling motion or mass, (fig.) thing viewed as swallowing those who approach it (*the vortex of society*); ~**ĭcal** *a.* (-lly). [L (= VERTEX)]

**vŏ'tar|y̆** *n.* Person vowed or devoted to the service *of* a god or cult or pursuit; ~**èss** *n.* [L (foll.)]

**vōte. 1.** *n.* Formal expression of will or opinion in regard to election, passing of law or resolution, etc., signified by ballot, show of hands, voice, etc., (*shall give my vote to Smith;* **put to the ~**, decide thus); opinion expressed, ||money granted, by majority of votes (*a vote of confidence*); *the* collective votes given by party etc.; *the* right to vote; ticket etc. used for recording vote. **2.** *v.i.* & *t.* Give one's vote (*for, against*); enact, resolve, (*that*), grant (sum), by majority of votes; (colloq.) pronounce by general consent (*was voted a failure*), announce one's proposal (*that; I vote we go home*); ~ **down**, defeat (proposal etc.) by votes; ~ **in**, elect by votes; **vō'ter** *n.*, (esp.) person with right to vote at election. [L *votum* (*voveo vot-* vow)]

**vō'tĭve** *a.* Given or consecrated in fulfilment of vow (*votive offering*).

**vouch** *v.i.* Answer *for*, be surety *for*, (will vouch *for the truth of this, for him or his honesty*); ~'**er** *n.*, (esp.) document establishing payment of money or truth of accounts, document exchangeable for goods or services as token of payment made or promised; ~**sā'fe** *v.t.*, condescend to grant *or to do.* [F *vo*(*u*)*cher* (L *voco* call)]

**vow. 1.** *n.* Solemn promise esp. in form of oath to deity or saints (*under a vow;* **monastic ~**, taken by monk or nun). **2.** *v.t.* Promise solemnly (thing, conduct; *vow obedience, vengeance*); (arch.) declare, esp. solemnly. [F *vou*(*er*) (VOTE)]

**vow'el** *n.* Speech-sound made with vibration of vocal cords but without audible friction (cf. CONSONANT); letter(s) representing this, as *a, e, i, o, u, aw, ah*; **indeterminate, neutral, obscure, ~** (heard in '*a moment ago*'). [F f. L (VOCAL)]

**vox** (vŏks) *n.* **~ humana** (hūmah'na), organ-stop with tone supposed to resemble human voice; **~ populi** (pŏ'pūli, -ē), the people's voice (i.e. public opinion, general verdict, popular belief). [L, = voice]

**voy'age** n., & v.i. (Make) expedition to a distance, esp. by water or air or in space. [F f. L VIATICUM]

**voyeur'** (vwahyër') n. One who obtains sexual gratification from looking at others' sexual actions or organs; ~**ism** n. [F (voir see)]

**V.P.** abbr. Vice-President.

**vs.** abbr. versus.

‖**V.S.O.** abbr. Voluntary Service Overseas.

**Vt.** abbr. Vermont.

**V.T.O.(L.)** abbr. vertical take-off (and landing).

**Vŭ'lcan|ist** n. (Geol.) Holder of PLUTONIC theory; **v~ite** n., hard black vulcanized rubber; **v~ize** v.t., make (rubber etc.) stronger and more elastic by treating with sulphur at high temperature; **v~izā'tion** n.; **v~ŏ'logў** n., scientific study of volcanoes. [L (VOLCANO)]

**vŭ'lgar** a. Of or characteristic of the common people, coarse, (vulgar word, expression); in common use, generally prevalent, (~ **fraction**, expressed by numerator and denominator, not decimally); **the** ~ (national, vernacular) **tongue**; **vŭl-gār'ian** n., vulgar (esp. rich) person; ~**ism** n., word or expression in coarse or uneducated use, instance of coarse or uneducated behaviour; **vŭlgă'rĭtў** n.; ~**ize** v.t., affect with vulgarity, spoil by making too common or frequented or well known; ~**izā'tion** n.; **Vŭ'lgate** (or -āt) n., 4th-c. Latin version of Bible. [L (vulgus common people)]

**vŭ'lnerab|le** a. (~**ly**). That may be wounded (lit. or fig.); exposed to damage by weapon, criticism, etc.; (Contract Bridge) having won a game towards rubber and therefore liable to higher penalties; ~**ĭ'lĭtў** n. [L (vulnus -er- wound)]

**vŭ'lpine** a. Of (nature of) fox; crafty, cunning. [L (vulpes fox)]

**vŭ'lture** n. Large bird of prey feeding chiefly on carrion and reputed to gather with others in anticipation of a death; (fig.) rapacious person. [AF f. L]

**vŭ'lva** n. External female genitals. [L]

**vv.** abbr. verses; volumes.

**vў'ing**. See VIE.

# W

**W, w,** (dŭ'belyŏŏ) n. (pl. **Ws, W's**). Twenty-third letter.

**W.** abbr. watt(s); west(ern).

**w.** abbr. wicket(s); wide(s); with.

**W.A.** abbr. Western Australia.

**wă'ckў** a. & n. (sl.) Crazy (person). [orig. dial., = left-handed]

**wad** (wŏd). **1.** n. Lump of soft material to keep things apart or in place or to block hole; roll of bank-notes; ‖(sl.) bun, sandwich, etc. **2.** v.t. (-**dd**-) Fix or stuff with wad; stuff or line or protect with ~**'ding** n., soft material usu. of cotton or wool for stuffing quilts, packing fragile articles in, etc. [orig. uncert.]

**wa'ddle** (-ŏ'-) v.i. & n. (Walk with) short steps and swaying motion. [foll.]

**wāde. 1.** v.i. & t. Walk through water or some impeding medium, (fig.) progress slowly or with difficulty, (~ **in**, colloq., make vigorous intervention or attack; ~ **through** book, read in spite of dullness etc.); ford on foot. **2.** n. Spell of wading. **3. wā'der** n., (esp.) long-legged water-bird, (in pl.) high waterproof fishing-boots. [E]

**wa'dĭ** (-ah'-, -ŏ'-) n. Rocky water-course dry except in rainy season in N. Africa etc. [Arab.]

**wā'fer. 1.** n. Very thin crisp sweet biscuit; disc of unleavened bread used in Eucharist; disc of red paper stuck on law papers instead of seal; ~**-thin**, very thin. **2.** v.t. Fasten or seal with wafer. [AF wafre f. Gmc]

**wa'ffle**[1] (-ŏ'-) n. Small crisp batter cake baked in utensil called ~**-iron**. [Du.]

**wa'ffle**[2] (-ŏ'-) v.i., & n. (Indulge in) aimless verbose talk or writing. [dial., = yelp]

**waft** (-ah-, -ŏ-). **1.** v.t. Convey smoothly (as) through air or along water. **2.** n. Whiff of perfume etc.

[obs. *wafter* convoy (ship) f. LDu. *wachter* (*wachten* to guard)]

**wăg. 1.** *v.t.* & *i.* (**-gg-**). Shake or wave to and fro (*dog* ~**s tail**, shows pleasure; **tail** ~**s dog**, less important part has control; **tongues** ~, there is talk; **so the world** ~**s**, arch., such is the changing course of life); ~**'tail**, kind of small bird with long tail in frequent motion. **2.** *n.* Single wagging motion (*with a wag of his tail*); facetious person. [E]

**wāge. 1.** *n.* Workman's or servant's periodical pay (in *sing.* or *pl.*; **wages of £45 a week**; a LIVING¹ *wage*); ~**earner,** one who works for wages; ~ **freeze,** ban on wage-increases. **2.** *v.t.* Carry on (war); **wā'ger** *n.*, & *v.t.* & *i.*, bet. [AF f. Gmc; cf. GAGE¹]

**wă'gg|ery** (-g-) *n.* Facetiousness, a jest or practical joke; ~**ish** (-g-) *a.*, given to waggery, facetious; **wă'ggle** *v.i.* & *t.*, (colloq.) wag; ~**lў** *a.*, unsteady. [WAG]

**wă'gon,** ‖**wă'ggon,** *n.* Four-wheeled vehicle for heavy loads usu. drawn by two or more horses; tea-trolley; ‖open railway truck; **on the** (**water-**)~, (sl.) teetotal; ~**er** *n.*, driver of wagon; ~**ĕ'tte** *n.*, 4-wheeled open horse-drawn carriage with facing side-seats. [Du. (WAIN)]

**waif** *n.* (Law) ownerless object or animal; homeless and helpless person, esp. abandoned child; ~**s and strays,** odds and ends, homeless or neglected children. [AF; prob. Scand.]

**wail. 1.** *n.* Prolonged plaintive inarticulate loud high-pitched cry of pain, grief, etc.; sound resembling this. **2.** *v.i.* Utter wail or persistent or bitter lamentations or complaints. [N]

**wain** *n.* (poet., dial.) Wagon. [E]

**wai'nscot** *n.* Boarding or wooden panelling on lower part of room-wall; ~**ing** *n.*, wainscot, material for it. [LG *wagenschot* (*wagen* wagon)]

**waist** *n.* Part of human body below ribs and above hips, narrowness marking this; similar narrow part in middle of violin, wasp, etc.; part of garment corresponding to waist; part of garment between neck and waist; blouse, bodice; part of ship between forecastle and quarterdeck; *waist*BAND; ‖~**coat** (*or* -sk-), man's sleeveless upper garment worn between coat and shirt and showing in front when coat is open; ~**deep, -high,** up to waist (*in* water etc.); ~**'line,** outline or size of waist e.g. as showing fatness; (-)~**'ĕd** *a.* [E (WAX¹)]

**wait. 1.** *v.i.* & *t.* Defer action or departure until some expected event occurs (*for, till, to see,* (*for*) specified time); await (opportunity, one's turn, etc.); defer (meal) till another's arrival; act as waiter or attendant; *that can* ~, is not urgent; ~ **and see,** await progress of events; ~ (**up**)**on,** await convenience of, be attendant or respectful visitor to; ~ **up,** not go to bed (till another's arrival); **you** ~! (as threat of retribution). **2.** *n.* Act or time of waiting; watching for enemy (**lie in** ~, **lay** ~, be hidden and ready *for*); (in *pl.*) street singers of Christmas carols. **3.** ~**'er** *n.*, man who takes orders, brings food, etc., at hotel or restaurant tables; ~**'rĕss** *n.*; ~**'ing** *n.*, (esp.) (period of) official attendance at court; ~**ing game,** postponing action for greater effect; ~**ing-list** (of persons waiting for vacancy, next chance to obtain thing, etc.); ~**ing-room** (for persons to wait in esp. at railway station or surgery). [F f. Gmc (WAKE²)]

**waive** *v.t.* Refuse to insist on or use (right, plea, etc.); **wai'ver** *n.*, (Law) waiving. [AF *weyver* (WAIF)]

**wāke¹** *n.* Track left by moving ship on water (**in the ~ of,** following, as result or in imitation of); turbulent air left by moving aircraft. [LG f. N]

**wāke². 1.** *v.i.* & *t.* (woke *pr.* -ōk, ~d; ~d, wo'ken). Cease to sleep, cause to cease sleeping, (lit. or fig.; usu. ~ **up**); be awake (arch. exc. **waking**); disturb (silence, place) with noise, echo (echo); ~**robin,** wild arum. **2.** *n.* (Ir.) watch by corpse before burial, attendant lamentations and merry-making; (usu. in *pl.*) annual holiday in (industrial) N. England. **3.** ~**'ful** (-kf-) *a.* (**-lly**), unable to sleep, sleepless, vigilant; **wā'ken** *v.t.* & *i.*, make or become awake. [E]

**wāle** *n.* = WEAL¹; ridge on corduroy etc.; (Naut.) broad thick timber along ship's side. [E]

**walk** (wawk). **1.** *n.* Ordinary human gait with both feet never off ground at once; slowest gait of animal; person's action in walking;

spell or distance of walking; excursion on foot (*go for a walk*); place or track meant or fit for walking. **2.** *v.i.* & *t.* Go at a walk; travel or go on foot, take exercise thus; (of ghost) show itself; traverse (distance) in walking; tread floor or surface of; cause to walk with one. **3.** ∼ **about**, stroll; ∼'*about* n., informal stroll by royal person etc., Austral. Aboriginal's period of wandering; ∼ **away from**, easily outdistance; ∼ **away** or **off with**, (colloq.) steal, win easily; ∼ **into**, (sl.) attack, eat heartily; ∼ **person off his feet** or **legs**, exhaust him with walking; ∼ **of life**, one's occupation; ∼ **on air**, feel elated; ∼ **out**, depart suddenly or angrily (∼*-out* n., esp. as protest or strike), ‖ go for walks in courtship (*with*); ∼ **out on**, desert; ∼ **over**, traverse course as winner with little effort owing to competitor's absence or inferiority; ∼*-over* n., easy victory; *walk the* PLANK; ∼ **the streets**, (esp.) be prostitute; ∼ **up!** (showman's invitation to circus etc.); ∼'**way**, passage or path for walking along. **4.** ∼'**er** n., (also) framework for person unable to walk unaided; ∼'**ie-talkie** (-tawk-) n., small portable radio transmitting and receiving set; ∼'**ing** n. & a. (∼**ing dictionary** or **encyclopaedia**, person able to provide much miscellaneous information; ∼**ing-o'n part**, to appear on stage but not speak; ∼**ing-stick**, carried when walking). [E]

**wall** (wawl). **1.** n. Continuous narrow upright structure of stone, brick, etc., enclosing or protecting or separating a house or town or room or field etc., (**with** one's **back to the** ∼, at bay; **see through a brick** ∼, have miraculous insight; ∼**s have ears**, warning about eavesdroppers; **up the** ∼, colloq.) crazy, furious); thing like wall in appearance or effect; steep mountain-side; outermost layer of animal or plant organ, cell, etc.; side of road (*the weakest goes to the* ∼, is pushed aside, fares badly). **2.** *v.t.* Block up (aperture etc.) with wall; (esp. in *p.p.*) provide or protect with wall, shut in or *off* thus. **3.** ∼**-board** (made from wood-pulp etc. and used to cover walls); ∼'**flower**, yellow-flowered plant, (colloq.) partnerless woman at dance; ‖∼ **game**, Eton form of football played beside wall; ∼'**paper**

(for pasting on room-walls, often decoratively printed); W∼ **Street**, U.S. financial markets; ∼**-to-**∼, covering whole floor of room; ∼**-less** a. [E f. L *vallum* rampart]

**wa'llaby** (wǒ'-) n. Small species of kangaroo; (W∼; in *pl.*, colloq.) Australians, esp. Australian Rugby Union team. [Aboriginal]

**wa'llah** (wǒ'la) n. (orig. Anglo-Ind.) Person connected with a specified occupation or task; (colloq.) man, person. [Hindi]

**wa'llet** (-ŏ'-) n. Flat case for holding banknotes etc. [AF]

**wa'll-eye** (waw'lï) n. Eye with iris whitish or streaked, or with outward squint; ∼**d** a. [N]

**Walloo'n** **1.** n. Member or language of a people in Belgium and neighbouring part of France. **2.** a. Of the Walloons; in Walloon. [F f. L f. Gmc]

**wa'llop** (-ŏ'-) (sl.) **1.** *v.t.* Thrash, beat; (in *part.*) big. **2.** n. Heavy blow; beer. [F *waloper* f. Gmc; earlier senses 'boil', GALLOP]

**wa'llow** (wǒ'lō) **1.** *v.i.* Roll about in mud, sand, water, etc.; (fig.) take gross delight *in*. **2.** n. Act of wallowing; place where animals go to wallow. [E]

**wa'lnut** (waw'l-) n. Nut with kernel in pair of boat-shaped shells; tree bearing this, its timber used in cabinet-making. [E, = foreign nut]

**wa'lrus** (waw'-, wǒ'-) n. Long-tusked amphibious arctic mammal; ∼ **moustache** (long, thick, drooping). [Du.]

**waltz** (wawlts, wawls, wǒ-). **1.** n. (Music in triple time for) dance performed by couples swinging round and round as they progress with gliding steps. **2.** *v.i.* Dance waltz; dance *in*, *out*, *round*, etc., in joy etc.; move easily. [G *walzer*]

**wa'mpum** (wǒ'-) n. Strings of shell-beads formerly used by N. Amer. Indians for money or ornament. [Algonquin]

**wan** (wŏn) a. (∼'**ness** *pr.* -n-n-). Pale, colourless, weary-looking. [E, = dark]

**wand** (-ŏ-) n. Slender rod or staff carried as sign of office etc.; magician's or music conductor's baton. [N]

**wa'nder** (-ŏ'-) *v.i.* Go from place to place without settled route or aim (∼**ing Jew**, person always on the move [f. legend of Jew who insulted Christ and was condemned to remain on earth]); go aimlessly *in*, *off*, etc.; diverge from right way (lit. or fig.); talk or think irrelevantly or incoherently, be inattentive or delirious; **~ing** *n.*, (esp., in *pl.*) disjointed talk; **~lŭst** (*or* vah'nderlŏŏ-) *n.*, eager desire or fondness for travelling or wandering [G]. [E (WEND)]

**wāne. 1.** *v.i.* (Of moon, or transf.) decrease in (apparent) size or splendour, lose power or importance. **2.** *n.* Process of waning (**on the ~**, declining). [E]

**wă'ngle** (-ngg*e*l). (sl.) **1.** *v.t.* Secure (favour, desired result) by scheming or contrivance. **2.** *n.* Act of wangling. [orig. unkn.]

**Wă'nkel** (*or* v-) *n.* **~ engine** (with continuously rotating eccentric shaft). [person]

**want** (-ŏ-). **1.** *n.* Lack or deficiency *of* (took it for want of anything better); poverty; desire for something not possessed, thing so desired; **in ~ of**, needing. **2.** *v.t. & i.* Be without or insufficiently supplied with; be in want (*for*); require, need, (thing, do*ing*, to do or be done); have desire for, wish for possession or presence of, (*I want some sugar, to stay here, you to do it, it done*); *call me if I am wanted*); **do not ~ to**, be unwilling to, (colloq.) ought not to (*you don't want to overdo it*); **~ed (by the police)**, suspected to be criminal etc.; **~'ing** *a.*, lacking in quality or quantity, unequal to requirements, absent. [N]

**wa'nton** (-ŏ'-). *a., n., & v.* **1.** *a.* (**~ness** *pr.* -n-n-). Sportive, capricious, (*wanton child*, *wind*, *mood*); luxuriant, wild, (*wanton profusion*, *growth*); unchaste (*wanton woman*, *thoughts*); (of cruelty, damage, etc.) pu<sub></sub>poseless, unprovoked. **2.** *n.* Licentious person. **3.** *v.i.* Be sportive or capricious. [earlier *wantowen*, = undisciplined]

**wa'pĭtĭ** (wŏ'-) *n.* Large N. Amer. deer. [Cree]

**war** (wŏr). **1.** *n.* Strife usu. between nations conducted by force with suspension of ordinary relations, (period of) such suspension and the accompanying military or naval or air attacks; (fig.) hostility between persons, efforts against crime, disease, etc.; **at ~**, engaged in it (*with* enemy); CIVIL, COLD, *war*; **go to ~**,

begin hostile operations; **have been in the ~s**, (colloq.) show signs of injury; **holy ~** (in support of religious cause). **2.** *v.i.* (-rr-). Make war (arch.); (in *part.*) rival, antagonistic, (*warring factions*, *principles*). **3. ~-cry**, phrase or name shouted in battle, party catchword; **~-dance** (performed by primitive peoples before war or after victory); **~fare**, state of war, campaigning; **~'head**, explosive head of missile; **~-horse**, trooper's horse, (fig.) veteran soldier; **~ memorial**, monument to those killed in a war; **~'monger**, one who seeks to cause war; **~ of nerves**, attempt to wear down opponent by gradual destruction of morale; **~-paint** (put on body esp. by N. Amer. Indians before battle); **~-path**, march of N. Amer. Indians to make war (*on the ~-path*, fig., engaged in conflict, taking hostile attitude); **~'ship** (for use in war); **~'time**, period when war is being waged; **~ to the knife**, relentless struggle; **~'like** *a.*, martial, military, bellicose. [AF f. Gmc]

**War.** *abbr.* Warwickshire.

**war'ble**[1] (wŏr'-). **1.** *v.i. & t.* Sing (esp. of bird) or speak in gentle continuous trilling manner; **~r** *n.*, (esp.) kind of small bird. **2.** *n.* Warbling sound. [F *werble*(r) f. Gmc (WHIRL)]

**war'ble**[2] (wŏr'-) *n.* (Swelling on cattle etc. caused by) larva of **~-fly** beneath skin. [orig. uncert.]

**ward** (wŏrd). **1.** *n.* Guarding, defending, guardianship, (arch.; WATCH *and ward*); minor etc. under care of guardian or court; administrative division esp. for elections; separate room or division in hospital etc.; (in *pl.*) notches and projections in key and lock to prevent opening by wrong key. **2.** *v.t.* **~ (off)**, parry (blow), avert (danger etc.); (arch.) guard, defend. **3. ~'robe**, place (esp. large cupboard) where clothes are kept, person's stock of clothes; **~robe master**, *mistress*, one who has charge of actor's or company's costumes; **~robe trunk** (fitted with drawers etc. and able to stand on end as wardrobe); **~'room**, officers' quarters in warship. **4. ~'en** *n.*, president or governor (*of* some colleges, hospitals, and other institutions), official with supervisory duties; **~'er** *n.*, ||gaoler; **~'rĕss** *n.*; **~'shĭp** *n.*, tutelage. [E]

**-ward(s)** (-werd, -dz) *sufs.* added to *ns.* of place or destination and to *advs.* of direction and forming *advs.* (usu. in -*wards*) meaning 'towards the place etc.' (*backwards, homewards*), *adjs.* (usu. in -*ward*) meaning 'turned or tending towards' (*downward, onward*), and less commonly *ns.* meaning 'the region towards or about' (*look to the eastward*). [E]

**ware**[1] *n.* Articles made for sale, goods, esp. pottery, or in comb. (*hardware*); (in *pl.*) what one has for sale; ~**house,** (*n.*) building in which goods are stored or shown for sale, (*or* -z; *v.t.*) place or keep in warehouse. [E]

**ware**[2] (*or* wōr) *v.t.* (colloq., esp. in *imper.* as warning). Look out for or be careful of (*ware wire, hounds!*). [E]

**war'lock** (wôr'-) *n.* (arch.) Sorcerer. [E, = traitor]

**warm** (wôrm) *a., v.,* & *n.* **1.** *a.* Of or at fairly high temperature; (of person) at natural temperature, or with skin temperature raised by exercise or excitement or external heat; (of clothes) serving to keep one warm; (of feelings, behaviour, actions, agents, words, etc.) hearty or animated or affectionate or excited or passionate or susceptible; (of reception, welcome, etc.) heartily friendly, or vigorously hostile; (of position etc.) difficult or dangerous; (of colour) suggesting warmth esp. by presence of red or yellow; (of scent in hunting) fresh and strong; **getting** ~, near what is sought; ~**-blooded,** (of animals) having blood temperature well above that of environment, (fig.) ardent; ~**-hearted,** affectionate, sympathetic. **2.** *v.t.* & *i.* Make or become warm (lit. or fig.; often **up**); ~ **up,** reach temperature of efficient working, prepare for performance by exercise or practice; ~**-up** *n.;* ~**ed-up,** (of food) reheated, stale; ~**'ing-pan,** flat closed vessel holding live coals, formerly used for warming beds. **3.** *n.* Act of warming; warmth of atmosphere. **4.** (-)~**'er** *n.,* (esp.) device for warming; ~**th** *n.,* being warm. [E]

**warn** (wôrn) *v.t.* Put (person) on guard (*against* person or thing or doing), give (person) timely notice (*of* danger or consequences, *that* thing may happen or is happening); ~ **off,** tell (person) to keep away

(from); ~**'ing** *n.,* (esp.) what is said or done or occurs to warn person. [E]

**warp** (wôrp). **1.** *n.* Threads stretched in loom to be crossed by weft; contorted state of warped wood etc.; mental bias or obliquity; rope used in warping a ship. **2.** *v.t.* & *i.* Make or become crooked or twisted, change shape or change shape of (timber etc.), by uneven shrinkage or expansion; distort or permanently bias or fill with misconception (person's mind), suffer such distortion; (Naut.) haul (ship) along by rope fixed to external point. [E]

**wa'rrant** (-ŏ'-). **1.** *n.* Thing that authorizes an action; written authorization to receive or supply money or goods or services or to carry out arrest or search; certificate of service rank held by ~**-officer** (between commissioned officers and N.C.O.s). **2.** *v.t.* Serve as warrant for, justify; guarantee, answer for genuineness etc. of; **I(ʼll)** ~ **(you),** (usu. parenth.) I am certain, no doubt. **3.** ~**y** *n.,* authority or justification (*for* doing), vendor's undertaking that thing sold is his and fit for use etc., often accepting responsibility for repairs needed over a period. [F *warant* f. Gmc]

**wa'rren** (-ŏ'-) *n.* Rabbit colony; (fig.) densely populated or labyrinthine building or district. [AF *warenne* f. Celt.]

**wa'rrior** (-ŏ'-) *n.* Person famous or skilled in war (rhet.); fighting man (esp. of primitive peoples); (*attrib.,* of nation etc.) martial; UNKNOWN *Warrior.* [F dial. *werreior* (WAR)]

**wart** (wôrt) *n.* Small hardish roundish excrescence on skin (~**s and all,** without concealment of defects); protuberance on skin of animal, surface of plant, etc.; ~**-hog,** Afr. wild pig; ~**'y** *a.* [E]

**wār'|ly** *a.* (~**ily,** ~**iness**). (Habitually) on one's guard, circumspect; cautious *of* doing; showing caution. [WARE[2]]

**was.** See BE.

**wash** (wŏ-). **1.** *v.t.* & *i.* Cleanse with liquid esp. water; take (stain etc.) *out* or *off* or *away* thus; wash clothes or oneself or one's (face and) hands; (of fabric or dye) bear washing without damage (**won't** ~, colloq. of argument etc., fails when examined); (of stain etc.) be taken *off* or *out* by washing; moisten, (of river etc.) touch with its waters; (of moving liquid) carry in specified direction, go sweeping or splashing *along, over*, etc.; sift (ore) by action of water; brush thin coat of water--colour over. **2.** *n.* Washing, being washed; treatment at laundry (*send clothes to the wash*); **come out in the ~**, fig., eventually become satisfactory); quantity of clothes for washing; motion of agitated water or air esp. due to passage of vessel or aircraft; kitchen slops given to pigs; thin or weak or inferior or animals' liquid food; liquid to spread over surface to cleanse or heal or colour; thin coat of water-colour. **3.** **~-basin, -bowl,** (for washing one's hands etc.); *wash dirty* LINEN; **~-day** (on which clothes are washed); **~-down,** accompany or follow (food) *with* drink; **~ed out,** faded by washing, (fig.) limp, enfeebled; **~ed up,** (sl.) defeated, having failed; **~ one's hands,** decline responsibility *of*; **~-house,** (out)building where clothes are washed; **~-leather** (chamois or similar); **~ out,** clean inside of by washing, (colloq.) cancel; **~-out** *n.,* breach in railway or road caused by flood, (sl.) completely unsuccessful person or thing; **~-tub** (for washing clothes); **~ up,** wash (table utensils etc., or usu. abs.) after use, (of sea) carry on to shore. **4.** **~er** *n.,* (esp.) flat ring of leather, rubber, metal, etc., to tighten joint; **~'erwoman,** laundress; **~'ing** *n.,* (esp.) clothes to be washed (**get on with the ~ing,** sl., stop wasting time); **~ing-day,** = *wash-day*; **~ing--machine, -powder,** (for washing clothes); *washing-*SODA; ‖**~ing-u'p,** (washing of) table utensils after use; **~'y** *a.* (**-ily, -iness**), too watery or weak, lacking vigour. [E]

**Wash.** *abbr.* Washington.

**wasn't.** See BE.

**wasp** (wŏ-) *n.* Winged insect with formidable sting, slender waist, buzzing flight, yellow-and-black--barred colouring, and taste for fruit and sweets; **~-waist,** very slender waist; **~'ish** *a.,* irritable, snappish. [E]

**W.A.S.P.** (wŏsp) *abbr.* (usu. derog.) White Anglo-Saxon Protestant.

**wa'ssail** (wŏ'-; or -al; arch.) **1.** *n.*

Festive drinking. **2.** *v.i.* Hold wassail. [N *ves heill* be in good health (WHOLE)]

**wast.** See BE.

**wāste** *a., v.,* & *n.* **1.** *a.* Not inhabited or cultivated (**lay ~,** ravage; **~ land,** not used for cultivation or building); superfluous, no longer serving a purpose, (**~ paper,** spoiled or valueless; **~-(paper-)basket,** for temporary storage of this; **~ product,** useless by-product of organism or manufacture). **2.** *v.t.* & *i.* Lay waste; treat as waste; use to no purpose or for inadequate result or extravagantly; give (advice etc.) without effect (*on* person); wear gradually away, make or become weak. **3.** *n.* Waste region; diminution by use or wear; waste material; act of wasting (**go** or **run to ~,** be wasted); **~(-pipe),** pipe to carry off waste esp. from washing etc. **4.** **wā'stage** *n.,* amount wasted, loss by use or wear or leakage or by voluntary departure of employees; **~'ful** (-tf-) *a.* (**-lly**), extravagant, causing or showing waste; **wā'ster,** (esp., sl.) good-for-nothing person (also **wā'strel**). [F f. L (VAST)]

**watch** (wŏ-). **1.** *n.* State of being on the look-out, constant attention, (*keep watch*; **on the ~,** waiting for expected or feared occurrence); (Hist.) watchman or -men; (Naut.) 4-hour spell of duty, part of crew taking it; small portable usu. spring--driven timepiece for carrying on person. **2.** *v.i.* & *t.* Be on the watch, be vigilant, look *for* opportunity etc., exercise protecting care *over*; keep eyes fixed on, keep under observation, follow observantly; look out for, await (opportunity). **3. ~ and ward,** (emphat.) being watchful; **~-dog** (kept to guard property, or fig. rights); **~es of the night,** time when one lies awake; **~ing brief** (of barrister who follows case for client not directly concerned); **~ it,** (colloq.) = *watch* one's *step*; **~'man** (employed to look after empty building etc., or to patrol streets, esp. at night); **~-night,** (religious service on) last night of year; **~ out,** be on one's guard; **~ one's step** or (colloq.) oneself, take care; **~-tower** (for observation of approaching danger); **~'word,** phrase summarizing some party principle. **4. ~'ful** *a.* (**-lly**), accustomed to watching, on the watch. [E (WAKE[2])]

**wa'ter** (waw'-). **1.** *n.* Colourless transparent tasteless odourless liquid compound of oxygen and hydrogen; liquid consisting chiefly of this (in seas, rivers, rain, tears, saliva due to appetite, urine, etc.); sea, lake, or river; this liquid as supplied for domestic use; (in *pl.*) part of sea or river, mineral water at spa etc. (*take the waters*); state of tide (HIGH, LOW², *water*); solution of specified substance in water (*lavender water*); transparency and brilliance of diamond etc. (**of the first ~**, of finest or extreme quality); (*attrib.*) found in or near, used on, the water, of, for, worked by, made with, containing, using, or yielding water; **by ~**, using ship etc. for travel or transport; **in deep ~(s)**, in great difficulties or affliction; **like ~**, lavishly, recklessly; **make ~**, urinate, (of ship) leak; **on the ~**, (fig.) in ship etc. **2.** *v.t.* & *i.* Sprinkle or adulterate or dilute or supply with water, take in supply of water, (of mouth, eyes) secrete water (**makes one's mouth ~**, **is mouth~ing**, causes flow of saliva or fig. desire or envy); increase (nominal capital) by issuing new shares without adding assets; (in *p.p.*, of silk etc.) having irregular wavy gloss. **3.** **~bed**, rubber mattress filled with water; **~biscuit** (thin, unsweetened, made from flour and water); **~boatman**, aquatic bug swimming upside-down; **~-borne**, conveyed by water; **~buffalo**, common domestic Indian buffalo; **~ bus**, river or lake boat carrying passengers on regular run; **~-cannon**, device giving powerful water-jet to disperse crowd etc.; **W~-carrier**, sign of ZODIAC; **~-clock** (measuring time by flow of water); **~closet**, lavatory with means of flushing pan with water; **~-colour**, pigment diluted with water not oil, picture painted or art of painting with this; **~-cooled** (by circulating water); **~course**, (bed of) brook or stream, **~cress** (growing in springs etc., with pungent leaves used as salad); **~-cure**, hydropathy; **~-diviner**, dowser; **~ down**, dilute, make less forceful or horrifying; **~fall**, stream falling over precipice or down steep hill; **~fowl**, (usu. in *pl.*) water birds; **~front**, part of town adjoining river etc.; **~-glass**, solution of sodium or potassium silicate esp. for preserving eggs; **~-hammer**, percussion of water in pipe when tap is turned off; **~-hen**, kind of diving bird; **~-hole**, shallow depression in which water collects; **~-ice**, flavoured and frozen water and sugar; **~-jacket**, case filled with water and enclosing part of machine to be kept cool; **~-jump** (where horses in steeplechase etc. must jump over water); **~-level**, (height of) surface of water, water-table, level using water to determine horizontal; **~-lily**, aquatic plant with floating leaves and flowers; **~-line** (along which surface of water touches ship's side); **~-logged**, barely able to float from being saturated or filled with water, made useless by saturation with water; **~man**, boatman plying for hire, oarsman as regards skill in keeping boat balanced; **~mark**, (*n.*) faint design in paper to show maker etc., (*v.t.*) mark with this; **~meadow** (periodically flooded by stream); **~melon** (elliptical with smooth green skin, red pulp, and watery juice); **~mill** (worked by water-wheel); **~ on the brain** etc. (morbid accumulation of fluid); **~pistol**, toy pistol shooting jet of water etc.; **~ polo**, game played by swimmers with ball like football; **~power**, mechanical force from weight or motion of water; **~proof**, (*a.*) impervious to water, (*n.*) such garment or material, (*v.t.*) make waterproof; **~-rat**, water-vole; **~-rate**, charge for use of public water-supply; **~shed**, line between waters flowing to different river basins, (fig.) turning-point in affairs, [*shed* ridge]; **~side**, margin of sea, lake, or river; **~-ski** (on pair of which a person towed by motor boat can skim water-surface); **~s of forgetfulness**, oblivion, death; **~s of life**, spiritual enlightenment; **~-softener**, apparatus for softening hard water; **~-spaniel** (large kind used to retrieve waterfowl); **~-splash**, part of road submerged by stream; **~spout**, gyrating column of water and spray between sea and cloud; **~-table**, plane below which ground is saturated with water; **~tight**, closely fastened or fitted so as to prevent passage of water, (fig. of argument etc.) unassailable; **~ torture** (by exposing victim to incessant sound of dripping water); ~-**tower** (with elevated tank to give pressure for distributing water); ~ **under the bridge**, irrevocable past; ~-**vole** (ratlike aquatic kind); *water*-WAGON; ~-**way**, navigable channel; ~-**weed**, aquatic plant with no special use or beauty; ~-**wheel** (driven by water to work machinery, or used to raise water); ~-**wings**, inflated devices to support persons learning to swim; ~-**works**, establishment for managing water-supply, (sl.) shedding of tears, (sl.) urinary system. **4.** ~**ing** *n.*; ~**ing-can**, -**pot**, portable vessel for watering plants; ~**ing-place**, pool where animals drink, spa or seaside resort; ~**y** *a.* (~ily, ~iness), (consisting) of water, containing too much water, (fig.) vapid, uninteresting, (of colour) pale, (of sun, moon, sky) rainy-looking. [E]

**Waterloo'** (waw-) *n.* Decisive defeat or contest. [place]

**watt** (wŏt) *n.* Unit of electric power, one joule per second, rate of working in circuit when electromotive force is one volt and current one ampere; ~-**hour**, energy of one watt applied for one hour; ~'**age** *n.*, amount of electrical power expressed in watts. [person]

**wa'ttle**[1] (wŏ'-) *n.* Austral. acacia with pliant boughs and golden flowers used as national emblem; interlaced rods and twigs for fences etc.; ~ **and daub**, wickerwork plastered as building-material. [E]

**wa'ttle**[2] (wŏ'-) *n.* Fleshy appendage on head or throat of turkey etc. [orig. unkn.]

**wāve. 1.** *v.i.* & *t.* Show sinuous or sweeping motion as of flag or tree or cornfield in wind; give such motion to; move (hand etc.) to and fro in greeting or as signal; wave hand or held thing *to* person as signal or greeting; tell (person) thus to go *away, on,* etc., direct thus *to* do, express thus; give undulating form to (hair etc.), have such form; ~ **aside**, dismiss as intrusive or irrelevant; ~ **down**, wave to (vehicle or driver) as signal to stop. **2.** *n.* Ridge of water between two depressions; long body of water curling into arched form and breaking on shore; (in *sing.* or *pl.*, rhet.) the sea; body of persons coming in one of successive groups advancing like waves; (Phys.) disturbance of particles in fluid medium

to form ridges and troughs for propagation of motion, heat, light, sound, etc., single curve in this, (**long, medium, short,** ~, radio wave with length over 1 km, 1 to 0.1 km, 100 to 10 m); temporary increase of influence or condition (*wave of enthusiasm*; HEAT *wave*); undulating (out)line; gesture of waving; waving of hair; ~'**length**, distance between crests of successive waves, this as distinctive feature of radio waves from a transmitter or (fig.) a person's way of thinking; ~'**let** (-vl-) *n.*; **wā'vў** *a.* (-ily, -iness), having waves or alternate contrary curves. [E]

**wā'ver** *v.i.* Become unsteady, begin to give way; be irresolute; (of light) flicker. [N (prec.)]

**wăx**[1] *v.i.* Grow larger (usu. of moon in first two quarters, or as metaphor from this; ~ **and wane**, undergo alternate increases and decreases); (arch., poet.) pass into state or mood or tone specified by adjective (*wax fat, wroth, lyrical*). [E]

**wăx**[2] *n.* (sl.) Fit of anger. [orig. uncert.]

**wăx**[3]. **1.** *n.* Sticky plastic yellowish substance secreted by bees as material of honeycomb; this bleached and purified for candles, modelling, etc.; similar substance e.g. in ear or (colloq.) gramophone records; **be** ~ **in** person's **hands**, be entirely subservient to him; ~'**work**, (making of) objects modelled in wax, (in *pl.*) exhibition of lifelike wax dummies. **2.** *v.t.* Cover or treat with wax. **3.** ~'**en** *a.*, made of wax (arch.), smooth, pale, and translucent like wax. [E]

**wă'x|ў** *a.* (~ily, ~iness). Resembling wax in consistency or surface; (sl.) in a rage, easily enraged. [WAX[2,3]]

**way. 1.** *n.* Road or track for passing along (*across* or OVER *the way*); (best) course or route for reaching a place (*ask the* or *one's way to*); method or plan for attaining object; person's desired or chosen course of action; travelling-distance, length (to be) traversed; unimpeded opportunity to advance, space free of obstacles, region over which advance is desired or natural; advance in some direction, impetus, progress; being engaged, or time spent, in movement from place to place; specified direction (usu. in adv. phr. without prep.: *step this way*); chosen or desired or habitual behaviour; normal course of events (*that is always the way*); scope, range, line of occupation or business; specified condition or state (*things are in a bad way*); respect (*is satisfactory in one* or *a way, in some ways*); (in *pl.*) structure of timber etc. down which new ship is launched. **2.** *adv.* (colloq.) Far (*way off the target*). **3. all the ~**, the whole distance, completely; **by the ~**, (fig.) incidental(ly), irrelevant(ly); **by ~ of**, passing through, by means of, as a form or method of, habitually or ostensibly do*ing*; **clear the ~**, remove obstacles; **come** person's **~**, (fig.) become available to him; **either ~**, in either case; **get** or **have** or **have it** one's (**own**) **~**, get what one wants; **give ~**, not resist, yield under pressure, give precedence; *give ~ to*, be superseded by; **go** one's **~**, depart; *go* one's *own ~*, be independent; *go* person's *~*, (colloq.) accompany or favour him; *go out of* one's *~*, make special effort, act without compulsion; **in a ~**, not altogether; ‖*in a (great) ~*, (colloq.) agitated; *in a small ~*, on a small scale; *in its ~*, if regarded from a suitable standpoint; *in more ~s than one* (w. ref. to multiple meaning); *in the ~*, obstructing, inconvenient; **lead** or **show the ~**, act as guide or leader; **look the other ~**, ignore what one should notice; **lose** one's or **the ~**, go astray; **make ~ for**, allow to pass, be superseded by, advance (lit. or fig.); *make its* or one's *~*, go, prosper; **one ~ and another**, taking various aspects jointly; *one ~ or another*, by some means; **on the ~**, travelling, approaching, having progressed; *on the ~ out*, (colloq.) about to disappear; *on your ~!*, begone!; **out of the ~**, unusual, not obstructing, remote, disposed of; **pay its** or one's **~**, be profitable, not incur debt; **the other ~ round**, reversed; **under ~**, not anchored, in motion, in progress; **~ back**, (colloq.) long ago; **~-bill**, list of passengers or parcels conveyed; **~'farer, -faring**, traveller, travelling, esp. on foot; **~lay'**, lie in wait for, stop to rob or interview; **~-leave**, right of way rented to another; **~ of life**, principles or habits governing one's

actions; **Way** (= STATIONS) **of the Cross**; **~ of the world**, conduct no worse than is customary; *way of* THINKING; **~-out**, (colloq.) unusual, progressive, excellent; **~s and means**, methods of achieving something, (Parl.) means of providing money; **~'side**, (land at) side of road. **4. -ways** (-z) *suf.* forming *adjs.* & *advs.* of direction or manner (*sideways*). [E]

**way'ward** *a.* Childishly self-willed, capricious. [AWAY, -WARD]

**W.C.** *abbr.* water-closet; West Central.

**W/Cdr.** *abbr.* Wing Commander.

**wĕ** (or **wĭ**) *pron.* (*obj.* **us** *pr.* us or *emphat.* ŭs; *refl.* OURSELVES; *poss.* OUR, OURS). Pl. of I[2] (used also for *I* in royal proclamations etc. and by editorial writer in newspaper); I and you or others; **~ and they**, the groups including and opposed to us. [E]

**weak** *a.* Deficient in strength or power or number or cogency or resolution or vigour; **~ ending**, unstressed syllable in normally stressed place at end of verse-line; **~er brethren**, less able members of group; **~er sex**, women; *weaker* VESSEL; **~-kneed**, (esp.) lacking resolution; **~-minded**, (esp.) mentally deficient, lacking resolution; **~ moment**, time when one is unusually compliant or temptable; **~ point, spot**, place where defences are assailable, flaw in argument or character or resistance to temptation; **~ verb** (forming inflections by suffix not only by vowel-change); **~'en** *v.t.* & *i.*; **~'ling** *n.*, feeble person or animal; **~'lŷ** *a.* (-iness), sickly, not robust; **~'nĕss** *n.*, (esp.) weak point, self-indulgent liking *for*. [N]

**weal**[1] *n.*, & *v.t.* (Mark with) ridge raised on flesh by whip etc. [WALE]

**weal**[2] *n.* (literary). Welfare (*weal and woe*; *for the public weal*). [E]

**wealth** (wĕl-) *n.* Riches, being rich, rich people; abundance or a profusion *of*; **~'ŷ** *a.* (-ily, -iness), (esp.) having abundance of money.

**wean** *v.t.* Accustom (infant or other young mammal) to food other than milk; disengage *from* habit etc. by enforced discontinuance. [E, = accustom]

**wea'pon** (wĕ'p-) *n.* Thing designed

or used or usable for inflicting bodily harm (e.g. gun, bomb, dagger, poker, claw); means employed for getting the better in a conflict (e.g. logic, irony, tears, strike). [E]

**wear**[1] (wār). **1.** *v.t. & i.* (**wore**; **worn**). Be dressed in (*wear green, serge, shorts, two* HATS); have on, or as part of, one's person (*wear a beard, glasses, perfume,* one's *hair long, a sour look,* one's HEART *on* one's *sleeve*); (of ship) fly (flag); (colloq., usu. w. neg.) tolerate; injure surface of, partly obliterate or alter, by rubbing or stress or use, suffer such injury or change, rub or be rubbed or (fig.) pass *off* or *away* (*nap, novelty, soon wears off*); (of water etc.) make (hole etc.) by attrition; exhaust, put *down* by persistence; endure continued use or life *well* etc.; (of time) pass esp. tediously; ~ **out**, use or be used till no longer usable, tire or be tired out; ~ **thin**, (fig. of patience etc.) be over-used; (**well-**)**worn**, (of joke etc.) stale, (of clothes) damaged by much use. **2.** *n.* Wearing or being worn; thing(s) worn, fashionable or suitable apparel, (*sportswear, footwear*); ~ (**and tear**), damage from ordinary use (**the worse for** ~, damaged by use, fig. injured); ability to resist wear. [E]

**wear**[2] (wār) *v.t. & i.* (**wore**). Bring (ship) or come about by turning head off wind. [orig. unkn.]

**wear**|**y** (wēr). **1.** *a.* (~**ily**, ~**iness**). Unequal to or disinclined for further exertion or endurance; disgusted at continuing *of*; tiring, tedious. **2.** *v.t. & i.* Make or grow weary; ~**isome** *a.*, tedious, tiring by monotony or length. [E]

**wea´sel** (-z-) *n.* Small nimble ferocious carnivorous animal. [E]

**wea´ther** (wĕ´dh-). **1.** *n.* State of atmosphere at a place and time (as regards heat, cloudiness, dryness, sunshine, wind, rain); **make heavy** ~ **of,** find trying or needlessly difficult; **under the** ~, colloq., indisposed); (*attrib.*, Naut.) windward (**keep a** ~ **eye open,** be watchful). **2.** *v.t. & i.* Expose to or affect by atmospheric changes; be discoloured or worn thus; get to windward of (cape etc.); come safely through (storm, lit. or fig.). **3.** ~**-beaten**, exposed to storms, seasoned or injured thus; ~**-board,** sloping board at bottom of door to keep out rain,

horizontal board on wall, overlapping one next below it; ~**cock,** revolving pointer on church spire etc. to show direction of wind, (fig.) inconstant person; ~ **forecast**, prediction of weather for next few hours or longer; *weather* GAUGE; ~**proof,** resistant to rain and wind; ~**vane,** weathercock; ~**-wise,** able to forecast weather; ~**-worn,** damaged by storms. [E]

**weave**[1]. **1.** *v.t. & i.* (**wove**; **wo´ven**; *pr.* wō-). Form (fabric) by interlacing long threads in two directions, form (thread) into or make fabric thus; make (facts etc.) *into* story or connected whole, make (story etc.) thus; **wove paper** (with uniform surface; cf. *laid paper,* LAY[4]). **2.** *n.* Style of weaving. [E]

**weav**|**e**[2] *v.i.* Move repeatedly or deviously from side to side; **get** ~**ing,** (sl.) begin action immediately. [N (WAVE)]

**wea´ver** *n.* (Esp.) loom-worker; kind of tropical bird building elaborately interwoven nests. [WEAVE[1]]

**wĕb** *n.* Woven fabric, amount woven in one piece, (lit., or fig.: *a web of lies*); cobweb, gossamer, or similar product; membrane between toes of animal or swimming bird; large roll of paper for printing; thin flat connecting part in machinery; ~**-footed,** having toes connected by web; ~**bed** (-bd) *a.*; ~**bing** *n.*, strong narrow closely--woven fabric for belts etc. [E]

**wĕd** *v.t. & i.* (-**dd-**; *p.p.* occas. **wed**). Marry, (fig.) unite (quality *to* another often not accompanying it); (in *p.p.*) of marriage (*wedded life*), obstinately attached *to* a pursuit etc. [E, = pledge]

**Wed.** *abbr.* Wednesday.

**wĕ´dding** *n.* Marriage ceremony (**silver, golden, diamond,** ~, 25th, 50th, 60th or 75th, anniversary of wedding); ~ **breakfast,** meal etc. between wedding and departure for honeymoon; ~**-cake,** rich decorated cake distributed to guests and absent friends; ~**-ring** (used at wedding and worn on finger of married person). [E (WED)]

**wĕdge. 1.** *n.* Piece of wood or metal with sharp edge at one end, used esp. to split wood or widen aperture or tighten loose parts or adjust level by having the thin edge inserted and the thicker part forced to follow; sector-shaped area or volume, persons or things or substance filling this; golf club with wedge-shaped head; **the thin end of the ~**, a change that begins with small things but threatens or promises great extensions. 2. *v.t.* Force *open* or *apart*, fix firmly, with wedge; pack or thrust (thing, one*self*) tightly *in* or *into* or *between* or *together*. [E]

**Wĕ'dgwŏŏd** (-jw-) *n.* Kind of fine pottery esp. with white design; its characteristic blue colour. [person]

**wĕ'dlŏck** *n.* The married state (**born in, out of, ~**, of married, unmarried, parents). [E, = marriage vow]

**Wĕ'dnesday** (wĕ'nz-; *or* -dĭ). 1. *n.* Day of week, following Tuesday; Ash[2] *Wednesday*. 2. *adv.* (cf. Friday 2). [E]

**wee** *a.* (**~r** *pr.* wē'er, **~st** *pr.* wē'ĭst). Little (esp. childish or Sc. or Ir.); (colloq.) tiny. [E]

**weed.** 1. *n.* Wild herb growing where it is not wanted; lanky weakly horse or person; (arch.) tobacco; (sl.) marijuana; **~-killer**, substance used to destroy weeds. 2. *v.t.* & *i.* Rid of weeds or of inferior parts or members; destroy weeds; sort *out* (inferior parts etc.) for removal. [E]

**weeds** (-z) *n. pl.* Deep mourning worn by widow. [E, = garment]

**wee'dy̆** *a.* (**-ily, -iness**). Full of weeds; growing freely like a weed; lanky and weak. [WEED]

**week** *n.* Seven-day period reckoned usu. from Saturday midnight; any 7-day period; the 6 days between Sundays, the 5 days Monday-Friday, period of work then done (*35-hour week*); **a ~ (from) today,** *or* **today, Monday,** etc., **~,** 7 days after today etc.; **~'day** (other than Sunday); **~-end,** Sunday and (part of) Saturday (or longer period) for holiday or visit; **~'ly̆,** (*a.* & *adv.*) (produced or occurring) once every week, of or for a week, (*n.*) weekly newspaper or periodical. [E]

**wee'ny̆** *a.* (colloq.) Tiny. [WEE]

**weep.** 1. *v.i.* & *t.* (**wept**). Shed tears (*for, over*, person or thing; *at* event; *for* sorrow or joy); weep for, bewail; be covered with or send forth drops, come or send forth in drops, exude; (of tree, usu. in *part.*) having drooping branches; **~'y̆** *a.*, (colloq.)

inclined to weep, tearful. 2. *n.* Fit or spell of weeping. [E]

**wee'vil** *n.* Destructive granary--beetle. [LG]

**wee-wee.** (sl.) 1. *n.* Urination; urine. 2. *v.i.* Urinate. [orig. unkn.]

**w.e.f.** *abbr.* with effect from.

**wĕft.** *n.* Cross-threads of web; yarn for these; thing woven. [E (WEAVE[1])]

**weigh** (wā) *v.t.* & *i.* Find weight of; balance in hands (as if) to guess weight of; estimate relative value or importance or desirability of, compare *with* or *against*; be equal to (specified weight), have (specified) importance, exert influence, be heavy or burdensome; *weigh* ANCHOR, **~'bridge,** weighing-machine for vehicles on road; **~ down,** bring down by weight (lit. or fig.); **~ (heavy) on,** be burdensome or depressing to; **~ in,** be weighed (of boxer before contest, or jockey after race); **~ in with,** (colloq.) advance (argument etc.) confidently; **~ out,** take definite weight of, (of jockey) be weighed before race; **~ up,** (colloq.) form estimate of; **~ with,** be regarded as important by; **~ one's words,** choose those which precisely express one's meaning. [E, = carry]

**weight** (wāt). 1. *n.* Tendency of bodies to fall to earth, quantitative expression of a body's weight, a scale of such weights (*troy weight*), body of known weight for use in weighing, heavy body (*clock is worked by weights*), load or burden (*that's a weight off my mind*), amount of influence exercised by or importance attached to thing (CARRY *weight*); = SHOT[1] (in athletics); PULL one's *weight*; **throw** one's **~ about, around,** (colloq.) be self-assertive; **worth** one's **~ in gold,** exceedingly helpful; **~-lifting,** sport or exercise of lifting heavy objects. 2. *v.t.* Attach a weight to, hold down with a weight, impede or burden *with*; **~'ing** *n.*, (esp.) extra pay in special cases; **~'lĕss** *a.* (esp. in freely falling spacecraft etc.); **~'y̆** *a.* (**~ily, ~iness**), heavy, momentous, (of utterances etc.) deserving consideration or carrying weight, influential, authoritative. [E]

**weir** (wēr) *n.* Dam across river to retain water or regulate flow. [E]

**weird** (wērd) *a.* Connected with fate (**~ sisters,** Fates or witches);

unearthly, supernatural; (colloq.) queer, incomprehensible. [E,= destiny]

**welch.** See WELSH[2].

**we'lcome** int., n., v., & a. **1.** int. of greeting (often *welcome home, to England*, etc.). **2.** n. Saying 'welcome', kind or glad reception, (**bid** person ~, say 'welcome' to him; **outstay** one's ~, stay too long as visitor etc.). **3.** v.t. Receive (guest, arrival, news, gift, opportunity, event) with signs of pleasure. **4.** a. That one receives with pleasure (*welcome guest, rest, news*; **make** person ~, let him feel so); (*pred.*) ungrudgingly permitted *to* do or given right *to* thing, acquitted of obligation for favour etc., (*he is welcome to say what he pleases* or *to the use of it*; **you are** ~, there is no need of thanks). [E]

**weld. 1.** v.t. Hammer or press (pieces of iron etc. usu. heated but not melted) into one piece, join by fusion with electric arc etc., form by welding into some article, (fig.) fashion effectually *into* a whole. **2.** n. Welded joint. [alt. f. WELL[1] after p.p.]

**we'lfare** n. Good fortune, happiness, health and prosperity, (*of* person, community, etc.); maintenance of persons in such condition, money given for this purpose; W~ **State**, country ensuring welfare of all citizens by social service operated by government; ~ **work**, organized effort for welfare of class or group. [WELL[2], FARE]

**we'lkin** n. (literary). Sky. [E, = clouds]

**well[1]. 1.** n. Shaft sunk in ground to obtain water or oil; (arch.) water-spring; (in *pl.*) spa; (fig.) source *of*; enclosed space like well-shaft, e.g. in middle of building for stairs or lift, or light and air; ink-well; ‖railed space in lawcourt; ~**head, -spring,** source. **2.** v.i. (literary). Spring (*out, up*) as from fountain. [E]

**well[2]** adv., a., & int. **1.** adv. (BETTER[1], BEST). In right or satisfactory or thorough or adequate or kind way (*work is well done; is eating well now; polish it well; is well in the lead; treated me well*); with heartiness or approval (*speak well of*); probably, reasonably, (*you may well be right*; *cannot well refuse*); AS[1] *well* (*as*); DO[3] *well*; ~ **done!** etc. (cry of commendation). **2.** pred. a. In good health (also

*attrib.*); in satisfactory state or position; advisable (*it would be well to inquire*); **let** ~ **alone**, avoid needless change. **3.** int. expr. astonishment (*well, I* NEVER*!*; *well, well!*), relief (*well, that's over*), concession (*well, come if you like*), resumption of talk (*well, who was it?*), qualified acceptance (*well, but what about me?*), resignation (*well, it can't be helped*), etc. **4.** ~**-advi'sed,** prudent; ~ **and good** (accepting decision: *if you choose to ignore my advice, well and good*); ~ **and truly,** decisively (beaten etc.); ~**-appointed,** having all necessary equipment; ~ **away,** having made considerable progress; ~**-behaved,** having good manners; ~**-being,** welfare; ~**-born,** of noble family; ~**-bred,** having or showing good breeding or manners; ~**-connected,** related to good families; ~**-defined,** clearly shown; ~ **down,** near the bottom; ~ **earned,** fully deserved; ~ **founded,** ~ **grounded,** having foundation in fact or reason; ~**-groomed,** with carefully tended hair, clothes, etc.; ~**-heeled,** (colloq.) wealthy; ~**-informed,** having well-stored mind or access to reliable information; ~**-intentioned,** having or showing good intentions; ~**-judged,** opportunely or skilfully or discreetly done; ~**-knit,** (of human figure) compact; ~**-known,** known to many; ~**-made,** shapely; ~**-mannered,** having good manners; ~**-marked,** distinct; ~**-meaning,** ~ **meant,** well-intentioned (but ineffective); ~**'nigh,** (rhet.) almost; ~ **off,** fortunately situated, fairly rich; ~ **on,** at advanced stage; ~ **out of,** escaped from without disaster; ~**-read,** having read (and learned) much; ~**-rounded,** complete and symmetrical; ~ **set up,** (of human figure) compact; ~**-spo'ken,** ready or refined in speech; ~**-thought-out,** carefully devised; ~ **timed,** opportune; ~**-to-do,** prosperous; ~**-tried,** often tested with good results; ~**-trodden,** frequented; ~ **turned,** neatly expressed; ~ **up,** near the top; ~**-wisher,** person who wishes one well; ~**-worn,** (esp.) trite; ~ (certainly) **worth** do*ing*. [E]

**we'llingtons** (-z) *n. pl.* (colloq. abbr. **we'llies** *pr.* -ĭz). Waterproof rubber boots usu. reaching knees. [Duke of *Wellington*]

**Wĕlsh**[1]. **1.** *a.* Of Wales; in the Welsh language; **the ~**, Welsh people. **2.** *n.* The Welsh language; **~'man, ~'woman**, native of Wales; **~ rabbit**, (by folk etym.) **rarebit**, dish of melted cheese on toast. [E, = foreign]

**wĕlsh**[2], **-ch**, *v.i.* (Of loser of bet, esp. bookmaker) decamp without paying. [orig. unkn.]

**wĕlt. 1.** *n.* Leather rim sewn to shoe-upper for sole to be attached to; = WEAL[1]; heavy blow; ribbed or reinforced border of garment. **2.** *v.t.* Provide with welt; raise weals on, thrash.

**wĕl'ter**[1]. **1.** *v.i.* Roll or lie prostrate or be soaked *in*. **2.** *n.* General confusion; disorderly mixture or conflict. [LDu.]

**wĕl'ter**[2] *n.* Heavy rider or boxer; **~-weight** (see BOX). [orig. unkn.]

**wĕn** *n.* Benign tumour on skin esp. of scalp; **the great ~**, London. [E]

**wĕnch** *n.* (joc.) Girl or young woman. [abbr. *wenchel* (E, = child)]

**wĕnd** *v.t. & i.* (literary). **~** one's **way**, go (*to*). [E, = turn]

**wĕnt.** See GO[1]; **wĕpt**, see WEEP; **were(n't)**, see BE.

**wer(e)wolf** (wēr'wŏŏlf, wĕr'-) *n.* (*pl.* **~ves** *pr.* -vz). (Myth.) Human being turned into wolf. [E, perh. = man-wolf]

**wert.** See BE.

**Wĕs'leyan** (wĕz'lĭan, -s-) *a. & n.* (Hist.) (Member) of Methodist Church founded by John *Wesley*. [person]

**wĕst** *n., a., & adv.* **1.** *n.* Point of horizon where sun sets at equinoxes, compass point 90° to left of North (**to the ~ of**, in a westward direction from); (W~) part of world or country or town lying to the west (\*Middle W~, region adjoining northern Mississippi R.), European civilization, non-Communist States; **~-north-~, ~-south-~**, (compass point) midway between west and north-west, south-west. **2.** *a.* Towards, at, near, facing, west (W~ Country, S.W. England; ‖W~ End, fashionable part of London; *West* INDIAN, INDIES; \*W~ Side, western part of Manhattan; coming from west (*west wind*). **3.** *adv.* Towards, at, near, the west (*west* DUE *west*); *west* BY *north, south*; **~ of**, in a westward direction from; **go ~**, (sl.) be killed, lost, wrecked, etc. **4. ~'ering** *a.*, (of

sun) nearing the west; **~'erly** *a. & adv.*, in western position or direction, (of wind) blowing (nearly) from west; **~'ern**, (*a.*; *superl.* **~ernmost**), of or dwelling in the west (W~ern Church, acknowledging Pope), (*n.*) film or novel about cowboys in western N. America; **~'erner** *n.*, inhabitant of the west; **~'ward** *a.*, *adv.*, & *n.*; **~'wards** (-z) *adv.* [E]

‖**Wĕ'stmĭnster** *n.* (Houses of) Parliament in London. [place]

**wĕt** *a., v., & n.* **1.** *a.* (**-tt-**). Having water or other liquid permeating or forming the substance or spread on the surface, (of weather etc.) rainy, (*wet sponge, mist, plate, eyes, day*); **~ through, ~ to the skin**, with clothes soaked); (of paint etc.) not yet dried; used with water (*wet shampoo*); supplying, or not prohibiting sale of, alcoholic liquor; (sl.) mistaken, feeble. **2.** *v.t.* (**-tt-**; wet or we'tted). Make wet. **3.** *n.* Liquid that wets something; rainy weather; (sl.) a drink. **4.** *wet* BLANKET, **-BOB**[2]; **~ dream**, erotic dream with involuntary emission of semen; **~-nurse**, (*n.*) woman employed to suckle another's child, (*v.t.*) suckle thus, (fig.) treat as if helpless. [E]

**wĕ'ther** (-dh-) *n.* Castrated ram. [E]

**Wg. Cdr.** *abbr.* Wing Commander.

**whăck** *v.t., & n.* (colloq.) Hit esp. with stick (**have a ~ at**, sl., attempt); ‖(in *p.p.*) tired out; (sl.) share; **~'ing**, (*a.*) large, (*adv.*) very (*great* etc.). [imit.]

**whāle. 1.** *n.* (*pl.* **~s, ~**). Fishlike marine mammal, esp. large one hunted for oil, whalebone, etc.; **a ~ of**, (colloq.) an exceedingly (great); **a ~**, (colloq.) very good *at* or keen *on*. **2.** *v.i.* Hunt whales. **3. ~'bone**, elastic horny substance from upper jaw of some whales; **~-oil** (from blubber of whales); **whā'ler** *n.*, whaling ship or seaman. [E]

**whăm** *int.* expr. forcible impact. [imit.]

**wharf** (-ôrf). **1.** *n.* (*pl.* **-ves** *pr.* -vz, **~s**). Platform to which ship may be moored to load and unload. **2.** *v.t.* Moor (ship) at or store (goods) on wharf. **3. ~'age** *n.*, (fee for) accommodation at wharf; **~'inger** (-nj-) *n.*, owner or keeper of wharf. [E]

**what** (-ŏt) *a., pron., & adv.* **1.** *interrog. a.* asking for choice from indefinite or (colloq.) definite number or for statement of amount or number or kind (*what books have you read?*; colloq. *what book have you taken?*; *what money* or *men* or *news have you?*). **2. excl. a.** How great or remarkable (*what a fool you are!*; *what luck!*). **3. rel. a.** The or any . . . that (*lend me what money you can*). **4. interrog. pron.** What thing(s)? (*what is your name?*; *what did she talk about?*; *don't know what it was*); (in rhet. question) nothing (*what is the use of trying?*); = *what did you say?* (asking for remark to be repeated). **5. excl. pron.** How much (*what he must have suffered!*). **6. rel. pron.** That or those which, a or the or any thing that, (*what followed was worse*; *lend me what you can*; *tell me what you think of it*). **7. adv.** To what extent (*what does it matter?*). **8. so ~?**, that is irrelevant; **~ about,** what is the news of or your opinion of; **~-d'you-call-it** (substitute for name not recalled); **~e'ver,** = *what* rel. with emphasis on indefiniteness (*lend me whatever (money) you can*), though any(thing) (*we are safe whatever happens*), (w. neg. or interrog.) at all, of any kind (*there is no doubt whatever*); *what* EVER; **~ for?**, for what reason? (GIVE person *what for*); **~ good is it?**, what purpose does it serve?; **~ have you,** anything else similar; **~ ho!** (greeting or hailing); **~ (would result) if?**; *what* is MORE; **~ (does it) matter?**; *what*(*ever*) NEXT?; **~ not,** and many other similar things; **~ of,** = *what about*; **~ o'f it,** = *so* WHAT?; ||*what* PRICE?; **~'s-its-name,** = *what-d'you--call-it*; **~soe'ver,** = *whatever*; **~ (would happen) then?**; *what* THOUGH, TIME; **~ use is it?**, = *what good is it?*; **~ with,** because of (usu. several things). [E]

**wheat** *n.* (Grain of) a cereal plant bearing dense 4-sided seed-spikes, from which much bread is made; *wheat* GERM; ||**~meal,** (esp.) wholemeal. [E]

**whea′tear** *n.* Kind of small migratory bird. [WHITE, ARSE]

**whea′ten** *a.* Made of wheat. [E]

**whee′dle** *v.t.* Coax by flattery or endearments; cheat (person) *out of* thing or get (thing) *out of* person by wheedling. [orig. uncert.]

**wheel. 1.** *n.* Circular frame or disc arranged to revolve on axle and used to facilitate motion of vehicle or for

various mechanical purposes; = STEER[1]*ing-wheel*; wheel-like thing; motion as of wheel, (esp. Mil.) motion of line with one end as pivot; *go on* (oiled) **~s,** smoothly; **~s within ~s,** intricate machinery, (fig.) indirect or secret agencies. **2. v.t. & i.** Turn on axis or pivot, swing round in line with one end as pivot; **~ (round),** (cause to) change direction or face another way; push or pull (wheeled thing esp. barrow or bicycle or pram, or its load or occupant); go in circles or curves; \***~ and deal,** engage in political or commercial scheming. **3.** *wheel*-BARROW[2]; **~′base,** distance between axles of vehicle; **~′chair,** invalid's chair on wheels; **~-spin,** rotation of vehicle's wheels without traction; **~′wright,** maker of wheels. [E]

**wheez|e. 1.** *v.i.* Breathe with audible whistling sound. **2.** *n.* Sound of wheezing; (sl.) actor's interpolated joke etc., clever scheme; **~′y** *a.* (**~ily, ~iness**), wheezing or sounding like a wheeze. [N = hiss]

**whělk** *n.* Spiral-shelled marine mollusc. [E]

**whělm** *v.t.* (poet.) Engulf, crush with weight. [E]

**whělp. 1.** *n.* Pup or cub (arch.); ill-bred or unmannerly child or youth. **2.** *v.i.* Bring forth whelp(s) or (derog.) child. [E]

**whěn** *adv., conj., pron., & n.* **1. interrog. adv.** At what time?, on what occasion?, how soon?, (*when did, will, you see him?*; *don't know when it was*); (in rhet. question) never (*when did I suggest such a thing?*). **2. rel. adv.** (with *time* etc.) At or on which (*there are days when I could weep*). **3. conj.** At the or any time that, as soon as, (*come when you like*); ellipt. *come when ready, myself when young*); although (*walks when he could ride*); after which, and then, but just then (*I was about to reply when he interrupted*). **4. interrog. pron.** What time? (*till when can you stay?*). **5. rel. pron.** Which time (*since when it has been better*). **6. n.** Time, occasion, (*fixed the where and when*). **7. ~(so)e'ver** *conj. & adv.,* at whatever time, on whatever occasion, every time that. [E]

**whěnce** *adv., conj., & pron.* (arch. or literary). **1. interrog. adv.** From what place? **2. rel. adv.** (with *place* etc.) From which. **3. conj.** To the place from which (*return whence you came*); and thence (*whence it follows that*). **4.** *interrog. pron.* (*From*) what place? **5.** *rel. pron.* (*From*) which place. [E (prec.; cf. THENCE)]

**where** (-ār) *adv., conj., pron., & n.* **1.** *interrog. adv.* In or to what place or position?, in what direction or respect?, (*where is she?*; *where are you going?*; *showed me where it concerns us*); (in rhet. question) nowhere (*where is the sense of it?*). **2.** *rel. adv.* (with *place* etc.) In or to which (*places where they sing*). **3.** *conj.* In or to the or any place or direction or respect in which (*go where you like*; ellipt. *delete where inapplicable*); and there (*reached Crewe, where the car broke down*). **4.** *interrog. pron.* What place? (*where do you come from, are you going to?*). **5.** *n.* Place, scene of something, (cf. WHEN 6). **6.** ~**abou'ts**, (*adv.*) approximately where, (-ār´-; *n.*, as *sing.* or *pl.*) person's or thing's location roughly defined; ~**a's**, taking into consideration the fact that (esp. in legal preambles), in contrast or comparison with the fact that; ~**by'**, by what or which means; ~**'fore**, reason (*the whys and wherefores*); ~**i'n**, (formal) in what or which place or respect; ~**o'f**, (formal) of what or which; ~**soe'ver, where'ver**, *conj. & adv.*, in or to whatever place, in every place that; ~**upo'n**, immediately after which; ~**'withal**, (colloq.) money etc. needed for a purpose. [E]

**whe'rry** *n.* Light rowing-boat usu. for carrying passengers; ‖large light barge. [orig. unkn.]

**whet** *v.t.* (-**tt**-). Sharpen (scythe etc., appetite or desire); ~**'stone**, shaped stone for tool-sharpening. [E]

**whe'ther** (-dh-) *conj.* introducing each part or the first part (*a*) of an indirect question in which alternatives are expressed or implied (*I don't know whether he is here or whether he is at the office, whether he is here or at the office or at home, whether he is here or not, whether he is here; it is doubtful, it does not matter, the question, whether*); or (*b*) of a conditional clause containing alternatives (*whether we consent or whether we refuse or whether we compromise, we shall offend someone*; *stick to your story, whether it is true or false*; ~ **or no**, whether it is so or not. [E]

**whew** (hwū) *int.* expr. surprise, consternation, or relief. [imit.]

**whey** (wā) *n.* Watery liquid left when milk forms CURDS. [E]

**which** *a. & pron.* **1.** *interrog. a.* asking for choice from definite set of alternatives (*which Bob do you mean?*; *say which book you prefer*). **2.** *rel. a.* And or now or but or since or though this or these (*ten years, during which time he spoke to nobody*). **3.** *interrog. pron.* Which person(s) or thing(s)? (*which of you is responsible?*; *say which you prefer*); ~ **is** ~?, which of these things or persons corresponds to each of the given names etc.? **4.** *rel. pron.* (*poss.* **of** ~, **whose**), = *which thing(s)* or (arch.) *person(s)* (cf. sense 2): *the house, which is empty, has been damaged*; *Our Father, which art in Heaven*; (esp. after prep. or *that*) = THAT 4 (*there is the house in which I was born*; *hold fast that which is good*). **5.** ~**e'ver**, (arch.) ~**soe'ver**, *adjs. & prons.*, any which (*take whichever (book, books) you like*). [E]

**whiff** *n.* Puff of air or smoke or odour or (fig.) scandal etc.; small cigar. [imit.]

**Whig** *n.* (Hist.) Member of the British reforming and constitutional party succeeded in mid-19th c. by Liberals; ~**gery**, ~**gism**, (-g-) *ns.*; ~**gish** (-g-) *a.* [*whiggamores*, nickname of 17th-c. Sc. rebels]

**while** *n., v., adv., & conj.* **1.** *n.* Space of time, time spent in some action, (*happened a long while ago*; *have been waiting all this while*); BETWEEN *whiles*; **for a** ~, for some time; **in a** ~, soon; **once in a** ~, occasionally; **the** ~, during some other action; **worth** ~ or one's ~, worth the time spent on it. **2.** *v.t.* Pass (time etc.) away in interesting occupation. **3.** *rel. adv.* (with *time* etc.) During which. **4.** *conj.* During the time that, for as long as, at the same time as, (*while I was reading I heard a bang*; ellipt. *was drowned while bathing*); in spite of the fact that at the same time (*while I believe it is true, I cannot prove it*). **5.** **whi'lom**, (*a.*) former (*his whilom friend*), (*adv.*; arch.) formerly; **whilst** *adv. & conj.*, while. [E]

**whim** *n.* Sudden fancy, caprice. [orig. unkn.]

**whi'mper. 1.** *v.i.* Make feeble querulous or frightened sounds. **2.** *n.* Such sound. [imit.]

**whi'msy** (-zǐ) *n.* Whim; ~**ical** *a.*

(-lly), capricious, fantastic; **~ǐcǎ´-lǐtў** *n.* [orig. uncert.]

**whin** *n.* (in *sing.* or *pl.*) Furze; **~´chat**, a small song-bird. [Scand.]

**whine. 1.** *n.* Dog's or child's long--drawn wail; similar shrill prolonged sound; querulous tone or talk. **2.** *v.i.* Emit or utter whine. [E]

**whī´nny** *v.i.,* & *n.* (Give) gentle or joyful neigh. [imit.; cf. prec.]

**whĭp. 1.** *n.* Stick with lash attached for urging on or punishing; (also **~´per-in**) huntsman's assistant who manages hounds; ‖person appointed to control discipline and tactics of M.P.s in his party, his written notice requesting attendance at division etc. (variously underlined according to degree of urgency: *three-line ~*); food made with whipped cream etc. **2.** *v.t.* & *i.* (-pp-). Apply whip to, urge *on* or rouse *up* or bring (hounds) *in* etc. or set *up* thus (lit. or fig.), beat (cream or *eggs) into froth; (sl.) excel, defeat; bind with spirally wound twine; sew with overcast stitches; (w. *adv.* or *prep.*) move suddenly or unexpectedly or rapidly (*whipped behind the door*; *whip out a knife*). **3.** **~´cord**, tightly twisted cord; **~ hand** (that holds whip; *have the ~ hand*, be able to exercise control); **~´lash**, lash of whip (*~lash injury* to neck, caused by jerk of head in collision); **~´per-snap-per**, small child, insignificant but presumptuous person; **~´ping-boy**, (Hist.) boy educated with and chastised instead of young prince, (fig.) scapegoat; **~´ping-top** (kept spinning by blows of lash); ‖**~--round**, appeal for contributions from group to charitable cause; **~´stock**, handle of whip; **~´pў** *a.* (-iness), flexible, springy. [LDu.]

**whĭ´ppet** *n.* Cross-bred dog of greyhound type used for racing. [perh. *whippet* move briskly, f. *whip* it]

**whĭ´ppoorwill** *n.* N. Amer. night-jar. [imit.]

**whĭrl. 1.** *v.t.* & *i.* Swing round and round, revolve rapidly; send or travel swiftly in orbit or curve; convey or go rapidly *away* etc. in car etc.; (of brain, senses, etc.) seem to spin round. **2.** *n.* Whirling movement (lit. or fig.; *the social whirl*; *my thoughts are in a whirl*). **3.** **~´ĭgĭg** (-g-), spinning or whirling toy, merry-go--round; revolving motion; **~´pool**,

**~´wind**, circular eddy of water, of air (*attrib.*, very rapid: *whirlwind courtship*); **~´ybird**, (sl.) helicopter. [N & LDu.]

**whĭr(r)** *v.i.* (-rr-), & *n.* (Make) continuous rapid buzzing or softly clicking sound. [Scand.]

**whĭsk. 1.** *n.* Bunch of grass, twigs, bristles, etc., to remove dust or flies; utensil for beating up eggs or cream; whisking motion. **2.** *v.t.* & *i.* Brush *away* or *off* or beat up with whisk; take *away* or *off* with sudden motion; convey or go (esp. out of sight) lightly or quickly; wave or lightly brandish (tail, cane, etc.). **3.** **~´er** *n.* (usu. in *pl.*), hair of man's face esp. cheek, bristle(s) on face of cat etc., (colloq.) small distance (*within a whisker of*). [Scand.]

**whĭ´skў** (Ir. & U.S. **-key**) *n.* Spirit distilled esp. from malted barley. [abbr. of *usquebaugh*, Gael. = water of life]

**whĭ´sper. 1.** *v.i.* & *t.* Use breath instead of voice, talk or say in barely audible tone or secret or confidential way, (of leaves, wind, water) rustle or murmur; **it is ~ed**, there is a rumour. **2.** *n.* Whispering speech or sound, thing whispered. [E]

**whĭst** *n.* A card-game usu. for 4 players; **~ drive**, party for progressive whist. [alt. *whisk* w. ref. to the silence (*whist!*) usual in the game]

**whĭ´stle** (-sel). **1.** *n.* Clear shrill sound made by forcing breath through small hole between nearly closed lips; similar sound made by bird or wind or missile or instrument; instrument used to produce it as signal etc. (**penny** or **tin ~**, with 6 holes for different notes). **2.** *v.i.* & *t.* Emit whistle, give signal or express surprise or derision thus, summon or give signal to (dog etc.) thus, produce (tune) or produce tune thus, (**~ for**, colloq., vainly seek or desire); *~-stop, small unimportant town on railway (*~-stop speech*, election-eering speech made during brief pause on tour). [E]

**whĭt[1]** *n.* (arch., chiefly w. neg.) Particle, least possible amount. [app. = WIGHT]

**Whĭt[2], Whĭ´tsun,** *adjs.* Connected with, belonging to, or following **Whit Sunday,** 7th Sunday after Easter, commemorating Pentecost;

**Whitsuntide,** week-end or week including Whit Sunday. [E, = white]

**white** *a., n.,* & *v.* **1.** *a.* Reflecting all light, like milk or fresh snow, approaching this condition, pale esp. in face (~ **as a sheet,** in terror etc.; **bleed ~,** fig., drain of wealth etc.); albino (*white mouse*); (of hair) having lost its colour; (fig.) innocent, unstained; of the human group having light-coloured skin, of or reserved for such persons; (Polit.) opposed to red (= revolutionary). **2.** *n.* White colour, pigment, clothes or material (*dressed in white*), ball in billiards etc.; (player of) white men in chess etc.; translucent or white part round yolk of egg; visible part of eyeball round iris; white person. **3.** *v.t.* (arch.) Make white. **4.** *white* ADMIRAL; ~ **ant,** termite; ~**bait,** small silvery-white fish; ~ **bread** (of fine bolted flour); ~ **cell,** leucocyte; ‖~ **Christmas** (with snow); ‖~ **coffee** (with milk or cream); ~-**collar,** (of worker) not engaged in manual labour; ~ **corpuscle,** leucocyte; *white* CROW, CURRANT, ELEPHANT, ENSIGN, FEATHER, FLAG[3], FRIAR; ~ **frost** (with hoar-frost on grass etc.); ~-**headed boy,** highly favoured person; ~ **heat,** temperature at which metal is white, (fig.) state of intense passion or activity; ~ **hope,** person expected to achieve much; ~ **horses,** (fig.) white-crested sea-waves; ~-**hot,** at white heat; W~ **House,** U.S. president's official residence in Washington; *white* LEAD[2], LIE[1]; ~ **light** (colourless); ~-**livered,** cowardly; *white* MAGIC; ~ **man,** (fig., colloq.) honourable or well-bred person; ~ **matter,** fibrous part of brain and spinal cord; ~ **meat,** poultry, veal, rabbit, pork; ~ **metal,** white or silvery alloy; ~ **night** (sleepless); ‖W~ **Paper,** Government report giving information; *white* PEPPER; ~ **rose,** emblem of Yorkshire or Yorkists; W~ **Russian,** (native, language) of Belorussia in western U.S.S.R.; ~ **sale** (of household linen); *white* SAUCE; ~ **slave,** woman entrapped for prostitution; ~ **spirit,** light petroleum as solvent; ~ **sugar** (purified); ~**thorn,** hawthorn; ~ **tie,** man's white bow-tie in full evening dress; ~**wash,** (*n.*) solution of lime or whiting for whitening walls etc., (*v.t.*) cover with whitewash, (fig.) attempt to

clear reputation of; ~ **water** (shallow or foamy); ~ **whale,** northern cetacean, white when adult; ~ **wine** (of amber or golden colour); ~**wood** (light-coloured, esp. prepared for staining etc.). **5.** **whi′ten** *v.t.* & *i.;* **whi′ting** *n.,* small white-fleshed food-fish, (also **whi′tening** *pr.* -tn-) chalk prepared for use in whitewashing or plate-cleaning. [E]

‖**Whi′tehall** (-t-hawl) *n.* British Government or its offices or policy. [place]

**whi′ther** (-dh-) *adv.* & *conj.* (arch. or literary). **1.** *interrog. adv.* To what place or state? **2.** *rel. adv.* (with *place* etc.) To which. **3.** *conj.* To the or any place to which (*go whither you will*); and thither. **4.** ~**soe′ver,** to whatever place. [E]

**whi′ting.** See WHITE.

**whi′tlow** (-ō) *n.* Inflamed sore on finger. [orig. *white* FLAW[1]]

**Whi′tsun.** See WHIT[2].

**whi′ttle** *v.t.* & *i.* Pare (wood) with repeated slicings of knife, use knife thus (often *at* object); ~ (**away, down**), (fig.) reduce by repeated subtractions. [dial. *thwittle*]

**whiz(z).1.** *n.* Sound made by body moving through air at great speed. **2.** *v.i.* (-zz-). Move with or make a whiz; ~**kid,** (colloq.) brilliant or highly successful young person. [imit.]

**who** (hōō) *pron.* (*obj.* ~**m** *pr.* hōōm, colloq. ~; *poss.* ~**se** *pr.* hōōz). What or which person(s)? what sort of person(s)? (*who says so?; you know who it was; who am I to object?*); (in rhet. question) nobody (*who would have thought it?*); (person) that (*anyone who wishes can have it; the man whom,* colloq. *who, you saw*); and or but he, they, etc., (*gave it to Jim, who sold it to Tom*); *who* GO[1]*es there?;* ~ **is it** (substitute for name not recalled); ~**'s ~,** who or what each person is, list with facts about notable persons; ~(**so)e′ver,** the or any person(s) who (*whoever comes is welcome*), though anyone (*whoever else objects, I do not*). [E]

**W.H.O.** *abbr.* World Health Organization.

**whoa** *int.* used to stop horse etc. [HO]

**whodu′(n)nit** (hōō-) *n.* (colloq.) Detective or mystery story. [= *who done* (illiterate for *did*) *it?*]

**whoever.** See WHO.

**whole** (h-). **1.** *a.* In uninjured or unbroken or intact or undiminished state, not less than, all there is of, (*not a plate left whole; swallowed a plum whole; was talking the whole time; lasted three whole days; that is the whole truth*); (of blood, milk, etc.) with no part removed. **2.** *n.* Thing complete in itself; all there is of or *of* thing; all members etc. *of.* **3. as a ~**, as a unity, not as separate parts; **a ~ lot**, (colloq.) a great amount; **on the ~**, taking everything relevant into account; **~-hearted**, completely devoted, done with all possible effort or sincerity; **~-ho′gger**, one who goes the whole HOG; **~ life insurance** (with premiums payable throughout insured person's life); **~′meal** (not deprived of constituents by BOLT²-ing); **~ number** (got by adding units, without fractions, e.g. 1, 5, 63, not 1½); **~′sale**, (*n.*) selling of things in large quantities to be retailed by others, (*a. & adv.*) by wholesale, (fig.) on a large scale; **~′saler**, one who sells by wholesale; **~ wheat** (not separated into parts by BOLT²ing); **~′some** (-ls-) *a.*, promoting physical or moral health, prudent, not morbid, (*wholesome food, advice, respect, excitement*); **who′lly** (hō′l-lĭ) *adv.*, entirely, without limitation, purely. [E]

**whom.** See WHO.

**whoop** (or hōōp) *v.i.* & *n.* (Utter) loud cry (as) of excitement etc.; **~′ing cough**, infectious bacterial disease, esp. of children, with short violent cough followed by long sonorous inspiration; **~′ing crane, swan**, (species that make whooping or whistling sound); **~ it up**, (w-; colloq.) engage in revelry, *make a stir; **~s!** (wŏŏ-; colloq. apology for obvious mistake). [imit.]

**whoo′pee** (or -ē′). **1.** *int.* expr. exuberant joy. **2.** *n.* (colloq.) **Make ~**, rejoice noisily or hilariously.

**whop** *v.t.* (sl.; -pp-). Thrash, defeat; **~′per** *n.*, (sl.) big specimen, great lie; **~′ping** *a.*, (sl.) very big. [orig. unkn.]

**whore** (h-) *n.* Prostitute; immoral woman; **~-house**, brothel. [E]

**whorl** *n.* Ring of leaves round stem; one turn of spiral. [app. var. WHIRL]

**whor′tleberry** (wer′telb-) *n.* Bilberry. [orig. unkn.]

**whose.** See WHO, WHICH.

**whosoever.** See WHO.

**why** *adv., int., & n.* **1.** *adv.* For what reason or purpose? (*why did you do it?; why so¹?; don't know why you came*); (with *reason* etc.) for which. **2.** *int.* expr. surprised discovery or recognition (*why, it's Bill!*), impatience (*why, of course I do*), reflection (*why, yes, I think so*), objection (*why, what is wrong with it?*), etc. **3.** *n.* Reason (cf. WHEREfore). [E]

**W.I.** *abbr.* West Indies; ‖Women's Institute.

**wich-.** See WYCH-.

**wick** *n.* Strip or thread feeding flame with fuel. [E]

**wi′cked** *a.* Sinful, iniquitous, immoral; spiteful; playfully malicious; (colloq.) very bad. [orig. uncert.]

**wi′cker** *n.* Plaited osiers etc. as material of baskets etc.; **~work**, (things made of) wicker. [Scand.]

**wi′cket** *n.* Small door or gate esp. beside or in larger one or closing lower part only of doorway; (Crick.) 3 stumps with bails in position defended by batsman, (state of) ground between the two wickets, batsman's avoidance of being out (5 **~s down**, 5 men out); **win by 6 ~s**, with 7 batsmen not out); **keep ~**, be **~-keeper** (fieldsman stationed close behind batsman's wicket). [AN *wiket* = F *guichet*]

**widdershins.** See WITHERSHINS.

**wide** *a., adv., & n.* **1.** *a.* Having sides far apart, not tight or close or restricted, at or to or on distant points or subjects, open to full extent, far from the point aimed at, not within reasonable distance *of*, (appended to measurement) in width, (*wide road, angle, trousers, distribution, knowledge; 3 ft. wide*); (as *suf.*) extending to whole of (*nation-wide*). **2.** *adv.* Widely (FAR *and* wide); to full extent (*wide awake, open*); far from target etc. (*shot wide*). **3.** *n.* Wide ball; **to the ~**, completely. **4. ~ awake**, (colloq., fig.) wary, knowing; **~ ball** (Crick., judged by umpire to be beyond batsman's reach); *wide* BERTH; ‖**~ boy**, (sl.) man skilled in sharp practice; **~-eyed**, surprised, naïve; **~ of the mark**, (fig.) incorrect, irrelevant; **~ open**, (fig.) exposed (*to* attack etc.); **~′spread**, widely distributed; **the ~ world**, all the world great as it is. **5. wi′den** *v.t. & i.* [E]

**wi'(d)geon** (-jon) *n.* Kind of wild duck. [orig. uncert.]

**wi'dow** (-ō). **1.** *n.* Woman who has lost her husband by death and not married again; GRASS *widow*. **2.** *v.t.* Make into widow or widower, (in *p.p.*) bereft by death of husband or wife; ~'s **cruse**, ever renewed small supply (1 Kgs. 17); ~'s **mite**, humble contribution (Mark 12: 42); ~'s **peak**, V-shaped hair on forehead; ~er *n.*, man who has lost his wife by death and not married again, ~hŏŏd *n.* [E]

**width** *n.* Measurement from side to side; strip of material of full width; large extent; (fig.) liberality of views etc.; ~'ways (-z) *adv.* [WIDE]

**wield** *v.t.* (literary). Hold and use (*power, the sceptre, a formidable pen,* etc.). [E]

**Wie'ner** (vē'-) *a.* See SCHNITZEL. [G, = Viennese]

**wife** *n.* (*pl.* wives *pr.* -vz). Married woman esp. in relation to her husband (*my* etc. *wife*; *is a good wife*); (arch.) woman (**old wives' tale**, foolish tradition); HOUSEWIFE; MIDWIFE; ~**like,** ~**lȳ,** (-fl-) *adjs.*, befitting a wife. [E, = woman]

**wig**[1] *n.* Artificial head of hair. [abbr. PERIWIG]

**wig**[2] *v.t.* (colloq.; -gg-). Rebuke sharply (esp. *a wigging*). [orig. uncert.]

**wigeon.** See WIDGEON.

**wi'ggle.** (colloq.) **1.** *v.t.* & *i.* (Cause to) move from side to side. **2.** *n.* Act of wiggling. [LDu. *wiggelen*]

**wight** (wīt) *n.* (arch. or joc.) Person. [E, = creature, thing]

**wi'gwăm** *n.* N. Amer. Indian's hut or tent. [Ojibwa]

**wi'lcō** *int.* expr. compliance or agreement. [abbr. *will comply*]

**wild** *a., adv.,* & *n.* **1.** *a.* In original natural state, not civilized or domesticated or cultivated or populated (*wild plant, duck, scenery*); tempestuous, unrestrained, disorderly, uncontrolled, (*wild night, hair, confusion;* **run** ~, grow unchecked or undisciplined); intensely eager, frantic, (*wild delight, grief*); (colloq.) infuriated; haphazard, ill-aimed, rash, (*wild guess, shot, venture*). **2.** *adv.* In wild manner (*shooting wild*). **3.** *n.* Wild tract, desert; **in the** ~**s,** (colloq.) far from towns etc. **4.** ~ **about,** enthusiastically devoted to; ~ **and woolly,** lacking refinement;

~'**cat,** (*n.,* fig.) hot-tempered or violent person, (*a.*) reckless, financially unsound, (of strike) sudden and unofficial; ~'**fire,** (Hist.) combustible liquid used in war (*spread like* ~*fire*, with mysterious speed); ~'**fowl,** game-bird(s); ~-**goo'se chase,** foolish or hopeless quest; ~ **horses would not drag it from me,** I refuse to disclose the secret; ~'**life,** wild animals collectively; *wild* OATS; W~ **West,** western U.S. in time of lawlessness. [E]

**wi'ldèbeest** (*or* v-) *n.* Gnu. [Afrik. (prec., BEAST)]

**wi'ldernèss** *n.* Desert, uncultivated region, (**voice in the** ~, unheeded advocate of reform); confused assemblage *of.* [E (WILD, DEER)]

**wile. 1.** *n.* (usu. in *pl.*) Stratagem, trick. **2.** *v.t.* Lure *away, into,* etc. [perh. Scand.]

**wi'lful, \*-llf-,** *a.* (~ly). Committed intentionally and of free choice (*wilful murder, waste, disobedience*); obstinate, headstrong. [WILL]

**will** *v.* & *n.* **1.** *v. aux.* (*pres.* **will,** or '**ll** after pers. pron. or colloq., exc. 2 *sing.* arch. **wilt,** *neg.* **will not,** colloq. **won't** *pr.* wŏnt; *past* **would** *pr.* wŏŏd, wud, *or* '**d** after pers. pron. or colloq., exc. 2 *sing.* arch. **wouldst** *pr.* wŏŏdst, **wouldest** *pr.* wŏŏ'dĭst, *neg.* **would not** *or* '**d not,** colloq. **wouldn't** *pr.* wŏŏ'dent; no other parts used) expr. future or conditional statement or order or question (colloq. in 1st person; *you will,* colloq. *I will, regret this; you will leave at once; he would have been killed if he had gone*) or speaker's intention (*I will return soon*). **2.** *v.t.* Desire (thing; arch.); desire or choose to or consent or be persuaded or have constant tendency to be·accustomed or likely to (do; *I will have you know that; come when you will; would not go any farther; would you please pass the salt?; boys will be boys; will sit there for hours; don't know who it would be*). **3.** *v.t.* (with regular forms: ~ed etc.) Intend unconditionally, impel by willpower; bequeath by will. **4.** *n.* Faculty by which one decides what to do; ~(-**power**), control by deliberate purpose over impulse; fixed desire or intention (*will to live; did it against my* ~, under compulsion); (arch.) what is desired or ordained by person; arbitrary discretion (**at** ∼, whenever one wishes); disposition towards others (ILL *will*); usu. written directions in legal form for disposition of one's property after death. **5. a** ∼ **of** one's own, obstinacy; **free** ∼, power or inclination to determine one's own actions; **where there's a** ∼ **there's a way**, determination overcomes obstacles; ∼ **do**, (colloq.) I will do that; **with a** ∼, vigorously; **with the best** ∼ **in the world**, however good one's intentions; **would-be**, vainly aspiring to be; **I wouldn't know**, (colloq.) I do not know. **6.** *∼**ful**, see WILFUL; ∼**'ing**, (*n.*, esp.) cheerful intention (*show willing*), (*a.*, esp.) ready to consent or undertake, given etc. by willing person. [E]

**wi'llies** (-ĭz) *n. pl.* (sl.) Nervous discomfort (*gives me the willies*). [orig. unkn.]

**will-o'-the-wi'sp** (-dh-) *n.* = IGNIS FATUUS; elusive person. [= *William of the torch*]

**wi'llow** (-ō) *n.* Waterside tree with pliant branches yielding osiers and timber for cricket-bats; ∼**-herb**, plant with leaves like willow; ∼**-pattern**, conventional Chinese design of blue on white china etc.; ∼**y̆** *a.*, having willows, lithe and slender. [E]

**willy-ni'lly** *adv.* Whether one likes it or not. [= *will I, nill* (obs. for *will not*) *I*]

**wilt¹.** See WILL.

**wilt².** 1. *v.i.* & *t.* Wither, droop or make (flower etc.) droop. 2. *n.* Plant-disease causing wilting. [orig. dial.]

**Wilts.** *abbr.* Wiltshire.

**wi'l|y̆** *a.* (∼ily, ∼iness). Crafty, cunning. [WILE]

**wi'mple** *n.* Linen or silk head-dress covering neck and sides of face, worn now by nuns. [E]

**win. 1.** *v.t.* & *i.* (-**nn**-; won *pr.* wŭn). Secure as result of fight or contest or bet or effort, be victorious in (fight etc.), be the victor, make one's way or become (*free, through*, etc.) by successful effort; ∼ **over**, persuade, gain support of; **win** one's SPURS; ∼ **the day**, be victorious in battle (lit. or fig.); ∼ **through** or (colloq.) **out**, overcome obstacles; **you can't** ∼, (colloq.) there is no way to succeed; ∼**'ner** *n.*, (esp.) successful thing; ∼**'ning**, (*a.*, esp.) attractive, bringing victory, (*n.*, esp.,

in *pl.*) money won; ∼**ning-post** (marking end of race). **2.** *n.* Victory in game. [E, = toil]

**wince** *v.i.*, & *n.* (Show pain by) involuntary shrinking movement. [AF f. Gmc, rel. to WINK]

**wi'ncey** *n.* Lightweight fabric of wool and cotton or linen; ∼**ĕ'tte** *n.*, lightweight napped flannelette. [app. alt. *woolsey* in LINSEY-WOOLSEY]

**winch. 1.** *n.* Crank of wheel or axle; windlass. **2.** *v.t.* Lift with winch. [E]

**wind¹. 1.** *n.* Air in natural motion; smell carried by this as indicating presence; artificially produced air-current esp. for sounding a wind instrument, air (to be) so used, wind instruments in orchestra etc.; gas generated in bowels; breath as needed in exertion or speech, power of breathing without difficulty; point below centre of chest where blow temporarily paralyses breathing; empty talk. **2. before the** ∼, helped by it; **between** ∼ **and water**, at vulnerable point; BREAK *wind*; **cast** or **fling to the** ∼**s**, abandon all thought of or care for; **close to** or **near the** ∼, sailing as nearly against it as possible, (fig.) close to indecency or dishonesty; DOWN³ (*the*) *wind*; **get** ∼ **of**, begin to suspect; **get** or **have the** ∼ **up**, (sl.) become or be frightened; **how the** ∼ **blows**, the state of affairs or opinion; **in the** ∼, (fig.) about to happen; **in the** ∼**'s eye**, directly against it; **like the** ∼, swiftly; **on the** ∼, carried by it; **put the** ∼ **up**, (sl.) frighten; **second** ∼, recovery of regular breathing during continued exertion after breathlessness; **take the** ∼ **out of** person's **sails**, frustrate him by anticipation. **3.** ∼**'bag**, wordy orator; ∼**-break**, row of trees etc. to break force of wind; *∼**'breaker**, ‖∼**-cheater**, jacket as protection from cold wind; ∼**'fall**, fruit blown down, (fig.) unexpected good fortune, esp. legacy; ∼ **instrument** (sounded by blowing or air-current); ∼**-jammer**, merchant sailing-ship; ∼**'mill**, mill worked by wind acting on sails (*tilt at ∼mills*, attack imaginary enemy), toy of stick with revolving light card etc.; ∼ **of change**, tendency for reform; ∼**'pipe**, air-passage from throat to lungs; ‖∼**'screen**, *∼**'shield**, (of glass in front of motor-vehicle driver); **~-sock,** canvas cylinder or cone on mast to show direction of wind; **~-swept,** exposed to high winds; **~-tunnel,** tunnel-like device to produce air-stream past models of aircraft etc. for study of wind effects. **4.** *v.t.* Sound (bugle, call) by blowing (*pr.* wi-; *past* & *p.p.* also **wound**); detect presence of by scent; make breathe quick and deep by exercise; exhaust wind of by exertion or blow, renew wind of by rest. [E]

**wind**[2]. **1.** *v.i.* & *t.* (**wound**). Go in spiral or curved or crooked course; make one's or its *way* thus; coil, wrap closely, provide with coiled thread etc.; surround (as) with coil; wind up (clock etc.); **~ down,** unwind (lit. or fig.), lower by winding; **~ off,** unwind; **~ up,** coil whole of, tighten coiling or coiled spring of or fig. tension or intensity of, bring to a conclusion, end, arrange affairs of and dissolve (company), (colloq.) arrive finally. **2.** *n.* Bend or turn in course; single turn when winding. **3.** **~'ing** *n.*; **~ing-sheet** (in which corpse is wrapped for burial). [E]

**wi'ndlass** *n.* Machine with horizontal axle for hauling or hoisting. [AF f. N = winding-pole]

**wi'ndow** (-ō) *n.* Opening in wall etc. usu. with glass for admission of light etc.; space for display behind window of shop; window-like opening; **~-box** (placed outside window for cultivating ornamental plants); **~-dressing,** (art of) making the most of one's wares or merits; **~ envelope** (with opening or transparent part allowing address inside to show); **~-shopping,** gazing at goods displayed in shop-windows without buying anything. [N, = wind-eye]

**Wi'ndsor** (-nz-). House of **~,** British Royal Family since 1917. [place]

**wi'ndward** *a.*, *adv.*, & *n.* **1.** *a.* & *adv.* In the direction from which the wind is blowing. **2.** *n.* Windward direction (**get to ~ of,** place oneself there to avoid smell of or fig. gain advantage over). [WIND[1]]

**wi'ndy** *a.* (**-ily, -iness**). Exposed to or stormy with wind; generating, characterized by, flatulence; wordy; (sl.) nervous, frightened. [E (WIND[1])]

**wine. 1.** *n.* Fermented grape-juice as alcoholic drink, fermented drink resembling it made from other fruits etc., (**new ~ in old bottles,** new principle too powerful to be restrained by ancient forms; *cowslip, ginger, wine*); dark red colour of red wine. **2.** *v.i.* & *t.* Drink wine; entertain to wine. **3.** **~-bibber,** tippler; **~-cellar,** (contents of) cellar for storing wine; **~'glass** (of various shapes and sizes for drinking wine from); **~'press** (in which grapes are squeezed); **~'sap,** large red American winter apple; **~'skin,** whole skin of goat etc. sewn up and used to hold wine. [E]

**wing. 1.** *n.* One of the limbs or organs by which flying is effected; winglike supporting part of aircraft; projecting part of building or organ or structure or battle array; (in *pl.*) sides of theatre stage; ‖mudguard of motor vehicle; extreme section of political party; (Footb. etc.) player at either end of line (*wing forward*), outside part of playing-area; air-force unit of several ‖squadrons or *groups; **on the ~,** flying; **spread** one's **~s,** (fig.) develop powers fully; **take ~,** fly away; **take under** one's **~,** treat as protégé; **~-case,** horny cover of insect's wing; **~-chair** (with side-pieces at top of high back); **~-collar,** man's high stiff collar with turned-down corners; ‖**~ commander,** R.A.F. officer next below group captain; **~-nut** (with projections for fingers to turn it on screw); **~-span, -spread,** measurement right across wings; **~'er** *n.*, wing player. **2.** *v.t.* & *i.* Equip with wings, enable to fly, send in flight; wound in wing or arm; traverse or travel on wings. [N]

**wink. 1.** *v.t.* & *i.* Close and open (eye or eyes), wink eye(s), wink one eye to convey message to or *at* person; (of light) twinkle; **~ at,** purposely avoid seeing, pretend not to notice; **as easy as ~'ing,** very easy; **~'er** *n.*, (esp.) flashing indicator on motor vehicle. **2.** *n.* Act of winking (**tip person the ~,** give him information privately); short sleep (**not a ~,** no sleep at all). [E]

**wi'nkle. 1.** *n.* Small edible gastropod; **~-picker,** (sl.) long pointed shoe. **2.** *v.t.* **~ out,** extract or eject (as a winkle from its shell with a pin). [abbr. PERIWINKLE[2]]

**wi'nner, wi'nning.** See WIN.

**wi'nnow** (-ō) *v.t.* Blow (grain) free of chaff etc. by air-current, blow (chaff etc.) *out* or *away* or *from*, (often fig. of sifting evidence etc.). [E (WIND¹)]

**wi'nsome** *a.* (Of person or his or her looks or manner) winning, engaging. [E, = joyous]

**wi'nter** *n., a., & v.* **1.** *n.* Coldest and last season of year. **2.** *a.* Of or in winter; ~ **garden** (of plants flourishing in winter); ~**green**, kind of plant remaining green all winter; *winter* SOLSTICE; ~ **sports** (skiing, skating, etc.). **4.** **wi'ntry** *a.* (-iness), characteristic of winter, lacking warmth (lit. or fig.). [E]

**wi'ny** *a.* Wine-flavoured. [WINE]

**wipe. 1.** *v.t. & i.* Clean or dry surface of by rubbing esp. with absorbing cloth, rub *over* thus, get rid of (tears) or clear (stain, wet, etc.) *away* or *off* or soak (slops) *up* or clean (vessel) *out* or make *clean* etc. by wiping; ~ **off**, annul (debt); ~ **out**, avenge (insult etc.); ~ **out**, (sl.) ~ **the floor with**, utterly destroy or defeat. **2.** *n.* Act of wiping. **3.** **wi'per** *n.*, (esp.) device for keeping windscreen clear of rain etc. [E]

**wire. 1.** *n.* (Piece of) metal drawn out thin for use as barrier or frame or to work puppet or carry (e.g. telegraph) current; (colloq.) telegram; **get one's** ~**s crossed**, (fig.) become confused and misunderstand; **pull** ~**s**, = *pull* STRINGS. **2.** *v.t. & i.* Provide, fasten, strengthen, with wire; (colloq.) telegraph. **3.** ~**haired**, (esp. of dog) with stiff or wiry hair; ~ **netting** (of wire twisted into meshes); ~ **wool**, mass of fine wire for cleaning; ~**worm**, destructive larva of a beetle. ~**less**, (-ir'l-), (*a.*) without wires (~**less telegraphy**, radio), of radio, (*n.*) radio (‖receiving set), (*v.i. & t.*) radio; **wir'ing** *n.*, (esp.) electrical circuits in a building; **wir'y** *a.* (-ily, -iness), (esp.) tough and flexible as wire, sinewy, untiring. [E]

**Wis.** *abbr.* Wisconsin.

**Wisd.** *abbr.* Wisdom of Solomon (Apocrypha).

**wi'sdom** (-z-) *n.* Experience and knowledge together with sagacious judgement, expression of this esp. in sententious sayings; ~ **tooth**, hindmost molar usu. cut at age of about 20 (*cut* one's ~ *teeth*, gain discretion). [E (foll.)]

**wise¹** (-z) *a.* Having or showing or dictated by wisdom, having knowledge, aping wisdom or oracular, (*wise man, course, advice*; *it would not be wise to . . .*; *with a wise shake of the head*); **none the** ~**r**, knowing no more than before; ~ **after the event** (of one who explains but has failed to foresee); **be, get,** ~ **to,** (sl.) be, become, aware of; **put** ~ **(to),** (sl.) inform (of); ~'**crack,** (colloq.) (make) smart pithy remark; ~ **man,** wizard, esp. one of the Magi. [E]

**wise²** (-z) *n.* (arch.) Way or manner or degree (**in no** ~, not at all); **-wise** (-z), *suf.* freely appended to *ns.* to form *adjs. & advs.* meaning 'after the fashion of', 'arranged like', 'in conformity with', 'in respect of', (*crabwise, crosswise, clockwise, moneywise*). [E]

**wi'seacre** (-zāker) *n.* One who affects to be wise. [Du. *wijssegger* soothsayer]

**wish. 1.** *v.i. & t.* Have or express desire or aspiration *for*; regard as thing to be wished for (*wish I had never been born*; *wish person dead*); want or demand (*I wish to see him, it done* or *to be done*); be inclined *well* or *ill* to person; say one hopes for (specified fortune) to happen to person (*I* ~ *you joy of it,* iron., expect it will cause you trouble); (colloq.) foist (*up*)*on* person. **2.** *n.* (Expression of) desire or request; thing desired; **best** or **good** ~**es,** hopes felt or expressed for another's happiness etc. **3.** ~'**bone,** forked bone between neck and breast of bird, object of similar shape; ~**fulfilment,** tendency for subconscious desire to be satisfied in fantasy; ~'**ful** *a.* (-lly), desiring (*to* do); ~**ful thinking,** belief founded on wishes rather than facts. [E]

**wi'sh-wash** (-ŏsh) *n.* (sl.) Washy drink or talk; **wi'shy-washy** (-wŏ-) *a.*, (fig.) feeble in quality or character. [WASH]

**wisp** *n.* Small bundle or twist of or usu. *of* straw etc.; small separate quantity *of* smoke, hair, etc.; small thin person; ~'**y** *a.* [orig. uncert.]

**wist.** See WIT *v.*

**wistar'ia, -ēr'ia,** *n.* Climbing shrub with blue, purple, or white hanging flowers. [*Wistar,* person]

**wi'stful** *a.* (~ly). Yearningly or mournfully expectant or wishful.

[app. assim. of obs. *wistly* 'intently' to *wishful*]

**wit. 1.** *n.* Intelligence, understanding, (in *sing.* or *pl.*; *has quick wits, a nimble wit*; *is quick-witted*; **at one's ~'s** or **~s' end,** utterly at a loss; **have** or **keep** one's **~s about** one, be alert; LIVE[2] *by* one's *wits*; **out of** one's **~s,** mad); (power of giving pleasure by) unexpected combining or contrasting of ideas or expressions; person possessing such power. **2.** *v.t.* & *i.* (*sing. pres.* **wot**; *past* & *p.p.* **wist**; *part.* **witting**). Know (arch.); **to ~,** that is to say, namely. **3.** **~less** *a.*, (esp.) foolish, crazy; **~'tĭcĭsm** *n.*, (usu. derog.) witty remark; **~'tĭnglȳ** *adv.*, with knowledge of what one is doing; **~'tȳ** *a.* (**-ily, -iness**), showing verbal wit. [E]

**witch** *n.* Sorceress, woman supposed to have dealings with devil or evil spirits; old hag; fascinating girl or woman; **~'craft,** use of magic; **~-doctor,** MEDICINE-man; **~es' sabbath,** supposed midnight orgy of the Devil and witches; **~-hunt,** search for and persecution of supposed witches or persons suspected of unpopular or unorthodox views; **~'erȳ** *n.*, witchcraft, power exercised by beauty or eloquence or the like. [E]

**witch-.** See WYCH-.

**with** (-dh) *prep.* expr. antagonism (*quarrel with*), company and parting of company (*mix, compare, dealings, dispense, with*), agreement and disagreement (*sympathize, incompatible, with*), instrumentality (*cut with a knife*), cause (*shiver with fear*), possession (*man with red hair*), circumstances (*sleep with the window open*), manner (*behave with courage*), material (*laden, fill, with*), etc.; **in, on, out,** etc., **~,** take or send or put (him, it) in etc.; *with* CHILD, GOD; **~ it,** (colloq.) up to date, (capable of) understanding new ideas etc.; **~ that,** thereupon; *with* YOUNG. [E]

**witha'l** (-dhaw'l; arch.) **1.** *adv.* Moreover, as well. **2.** *prep.* (placed later than its expressed or omitted obj.) With (*what shall he fill his belly withal?*). [WITH, ALL]

**withdraw'** (-dh) *v.t.* & *i.* (**-drew'; -draw'n**). Pull aside or back, discontinue the giving or allowing or operation or stay or engagement of, retract or unsay, retire or go apart, (*withdraw curtain, privilege, coins from*

*circulation, child from school, horse from race, unparliamentary expression*; *after dinner the ladies withdrew*); (in *p.p.*) unsociable; **~al** *n.* [WITH = away]

**withe** (or **wĭdh**), **wi'thȳ** (-dhĭ), *n.* Tough flexible shoot used for tying bundle of wood etc. [E]

**wi'ther** (-dh-) *v.t.* & *i.* Make or become dry and shrivelled (*up*), deprive of or lose vigour or freshness (*away*), blight with scorn etc. [app. var. WEATHER]

**wi'thers** (-dherz) *n. pl.* Ridge between horse's shoulder-blades (**my ~ are unwrung,** imputation etc. does not affect me). [obs. *wither* against (the collar)]

**wi'thershĭns** (-dh-; -z), **wi'dder-,** *adv.* (esp. Sc.) Contrary to sun's course (and hence unlucky). [G, = contrary direction]

**withho'ld** (-dh-h-) *v.t.* (**-he'ld**). Hold back, restrain; refuse to give, grant, or allow, (*withhold supplies*, one's *consent*). [WITH = away]

**withi'n** (-dh-). **1.** *adv.* (arch., literary). Inside, indoors, (**pure ~,** in spirit). **2.** *prep.* Inside, not out of or beyond, not transgressing or exceeding, (*safe within the walls*; **~ reach, sight, of,** near enough to reach or be reached etc.; **~ a year, two miles, of,** at less than that time or distance from; **keep ~ the law,** avoid breaking it). [E (WITH, IN)]

**without'** (-dh-) *adv., prep.,* & *conj.* **1.** *adv.* (arch., literary). Outside, out-of-doors. **2.** *prep.* Not having or feeling or showing, with freedom from, in absence of, with neglect or avoidance of, (*without a thorn, difficulty, enthusiasm, friends, being discovered, your help, making provision, taking leave*; DO[3], GO[1], *without*; *goes without* SAYING); (arch., literary) outside. **3.** *conj.* (arch. or vulg.) Unless. [E (WITH, OUT)]

**withstă'nd** (-dh-) *v.t.* (**-stoo'd**). Oppose, hold out against. [E (WITH, STAND)]

**withy.** See WITHE; **wi'tless,** see WIT.

**wi'tness. 1.** *n.* Testimony, evidence, confirmation; person giving sworn testimony; person attesting another's signature to document; person present, spectator; person or thing whose existence etc. serves as testimony *to* or proof *of*; **bear ~ to** or **of,** attest truth of; **call to ~,**

appeal to for confirmation etc. **2.** *v.t. & i.* Be witness to authenticity of (document, signature); be spectator of; serve as evidence or indication of; be witness *against* or *for* or *to*; (arch.) state in evidence (thing, *that*), be a or the witness. **3.** ‖~**-box**, *-**stand**, enclosure in lawcourt from which witness gives evidence. [E (WIT)]

**wi′tticism, wi′ttingly, wi′tty.** See WIT; **wives,** see WIFE.

**wi′zard. 1.** *n.* Person of extraordinary powers, genius; magician, conjurer; ~**rỹ** *n.* **2.** *a.* (sl.) Wonderful. [WISE¹]

**wi′zened** (-nd) *a.* (Of person or his face etc.) shrivelled-looking. [E]

**W.M.O.** *abbr.* World Meteorological Organization.

**W.N.W.** *abbr.* west-north-west.

**W.O.** *abbr.* Warrant Officer.

**woad** *n.* (Plant yielding) a blue dye. [E]

**wŏ′bble. 1.** *v.i.* Sway from side to side, stand or go unsteadily, stagger; waver, vacillate. **2.** *n.* Wobbling motion; rocking movement. [cf. LG *wab(b)eln*]

**wŏe** *n.* (arch., literary, or joc.) Affliction, bitter grief, (in *pl.*) calamities, (*woe* BETIDE; ~ **is me**, alas); ~**′begone**, dismal-looking; ~**′ful** (wō′f-) *a.* (-**lly**), feeling affliction, afflicting, (joc.) very bad. [E; *begone* = surrounded]

**wŏg** *n.* (sl., derog.) Native of Middle East; foreigner. [orig. unkn.]

**wŏke(n).** See WAKE¹.

**wŏld** *n.* High open uncultivated or moorland tract. [E]

**wolf** (woŏ-). **1.** *n.* (*pl.* -ves *pr.* -vz). Wild animal allied to dog preying on sheep etc. and hunting in packs (**cry** ~, raise false alarm; **keep the** ~ **from the door**, avert starvation; **lone** ~, person who prefers to act alone; ~ **in sheep's clothing**, hypocrite); ~**′hound**, dog of kind used (orig.) to hunt wolves; ~**′sbane**, aconite; ~**-whistle** (by man sexually admiring woman). **2.** *v.t.* Devour greedily (*down*). **3.** **wo′lverine** (woŏ′lverēn) *n.*, Amer. glutton (animal). [E]

**wo′lfram** (woŏ′-) *n.* Tungsten (ore). [G]

**wo′man** (woŏ′-) *n.* (*pl.* **women** *pr.* wi′mǐn). Adult human female; the female sex; feminine emotions; (*attrib.*) female (*woman driver*); (as *suf.*) woman concerned or dealing or skilful with or describable as (*countrywoman, needlewoman, Welshwoman*); (colloq.) charwoman; ~**kind, wo′menkind,** women in general; *woman of the* WORLD; **wo′menfolk,** women in general, women in family; **Women's Lib (eration),** movement for release of women from domestic duties and subservient status; **women's rights,** position of legal and social equality with men; ~**hŏŏd** *n.*, female maturity, womanly instinct, womankind; ~**ish** *a.*, effeminate, unmanly; ~**īze** *v.i.*, consort illicitly with women; ~**lỹ** *a.* (-**iness**), having or showing qualities befitting a woman. [E]

**womb** (woōm) *n.* Organ of conception and gestation in woman and other female mammals. [E]

**wŏ′mbăt** *n.* Burrowing Australian marsupial. [Aboriginal]

**women.** See WOMAN; **won,** see WIN.

**wo′nder** (wŭ′-). **1.** *n.* Strange or remarkable thing or specimen or performance or event; emotion caused by what is unexpected or unfamiliar or inexplicable; **for a** ~, by way of welcome exception; **no** ~, **small** ~, **what** ~?, this event is quite natural; **seven** ~**s of the world,** 7 remarkable structures of antiquity; **work** or **do** ~**s,** do miracles, succeed remarkably; ~**land,** fairyland, land of surprises or marvels. **2.** *v.i. & t.* Be filled with wonder or great surprise; be surprised to find (*that*); desire to know (*wonder who it was*); **I** ~, (as excl.) I very much doubt it; **I shouldn't** ~ **if,** (colloq.) I think it likely that. **3.** ~**ful** *a.* (-**lly**), very remarkable or admirable; ~**ment** *n.*, surprise; **wo′ndrous** (wŭ′-) *a. & adv.*, (poet., rhet.) wonderful(ly). [E]

**wŏ′nkỹ** *a.* (sl.) Shaky, groggy, unreliable. [fanciful]

**wŏn't.** See WILL.

**wŏnt** *a., n.,* & *v.* (arch.) **1.** *pred. a.* Accustomed (*to* do). **2.** *n.* What is customary, one's habit, (**use and** ~, established custom). **3.** *v.i.* (3 *sing. pres.* **wonts, wont;** *past* **wonted, wont;** no *part.* or *inf.*) Be wont. [E]

**wŏ′ntĕd** *attrib. a.* Habitual, usual.

**woō** *v.t.* Court, seek the hand or love of, try to win (fame, fortune, etc.); coax or importune *to*. [E]

**woōd** *n.* Growing trees densely

occupying a tract of land (in *sing.* or *pl.*; **cannot see the ~ for the trees**, details impede general view; *don't* HALLOO *till you are out of the wood(s)*; **out of the ‖~ or *~s**, out of danger or difficulty); hard fibrous substance in trunks and branches of tree or shrub (growing, or cut for timber or fuel or artistic use), timber or fuel of this, (TOUCH *wood*); *the* cask (opp. bottles) for wine etc.; wooden--headed golf-club; = BOWL²; **wood** ANEMONE; **~'bine**, honeysuckle, *Virginia creeper; **~'chuck**, N. Amer. marmot; **~'cock**, game-bird allied to snipe; **~'cut**, (print from) relief cut on wood; **~'land**, wooded country, woods; **~-louse**, small many-legged land crustacean; **~'-man**, forester; **~-nymph**, dryad; **~'pecker**, bird tapping tree-trunks in search of insects; **~'pigeon**, ring-dove; **~'pile** (esp. for fuel); **~--pulp**, wood fibres prepared for paper-making; **~'ruff**, a white--flowered plant with fragrant leaves; *wood*-SCREW; **~-shed** (where wood is stored esp. for fuel); **~-wind**, orchestral wind instruments made (orig.) of wood; **~-wool**, fine wood--shavings for packing etc.; **~'work**, things made of wood; **~'worm**, beetle larva that bores in wood; **~'ėd** *a.*, having woods; **~'en** *a.* (-nness *pr.* -n-n-), made of wood, like wood, stiff or clumsy; **~en--headed**, stupid; *wooden* HORSE; **~en spoon**, (fig.) booby prize; **~'ў** *a.* (-iness), wooded, like or of wood; *woody* NIGHTSHADE. [E]

**woof¹** *n.* = WEFT. [E (WEB)]

**woof²** *n.*, & *v.i.* (Give) gruff bark of dog; **~'er** *n.*, loudspeaker for low frequencies. [imit.]

**wool** *n.* Fine soft wavy hair from fleece of sheep etc., woollen yarn or cloth or garments, wool-like substance, (**mineral ~**, made from molten slag for use as packing); DYEd *in the wool*; **pull the ~ over** person's **eyes**, deceive him; **~--gathering**, absent-minded(ness), dreamy (mood); **‖~'sack**, Lord Chancellor's wool-stuffed seat in House of Lords, his position; **~'len**, *~'en**, (*a.*) made (partly) of wool, (*n.*) woollen fabric, (in *pl.*) woollen garments; **~'lў**, (*a.*; **-iness**) bearing or like wool, (of sound) indistinct, (of thought) confused, (*n.*, colloq.) woollen (‖esp. knitted) garment;

**~-ly-bear**, large hairy caterpillar. [E]

*****Wŏp** *n.* (sl., derog.) South-European (esp. Italian) immigrant in U.S. [orig. unkn.]

**Worcester** (wŏo'ster) *n.* **~(shire) sauce**, a pungent sauce. [place]

**word** (wĕrd). **1.** *n.* Meaningful element of speech usu. shown with space on either side of it when written or printed; unit of expression in computer; speech esp. as opp. action; (in *sing.* or *pl.*) thing said, remark, conversation; (in *pl.*) text of song or actor's part, angry talk; news, message, (SEND *word*); command, password, motto; one's promise or assurance. **2.** *v.t.* Put into words, select words to express. **3. be as good as** one's **~**, do what one promised; **give** one's **~**, make promise; **have a ~**, converse briefly; **have ~s**, quarrel; **in a** or **one ~**, briefly; **in other**.**~s**, expressing the same thing differently; **in so many ~s**, explicitly, bluntly; **keep** one's **~**, do what one promised; LAST³ *word*; **not the ~ for it**, not an adequate description; **of few ~s**, taciturn; *man* **of his ~**, who keeps his promises; **put into ~s**, express (thought) in speech or writing; **say the ~**, give order etc.; **take my ~ for it**, accept my statement that it is so; **take** person **at his ~**, assume that he means what he says; **too** *funny* etc. **for ~s**, inexpressibly so; (**upon**) **my ~**, excl. at shocking or surprising thing; **~-blindness**, brain defect that prevents understanding of words seen; **~ for ~**, *repeat* in exactly the same words, *translate* literally; **~-game** (in which words are guessed etc.); **W~ (of God)**, the Bible; **~ of honour**, assurance given upon one's honour; **~ of mouth**, speech (only); **~-per'fect**, knowing one's part etc. by heart; **~s fail me**, I am too surprised to express my thoughts. **4. ~'ing** *n.*, (esp.) form of words used; **~'ў** *a.* (~ily, ~iness), using (too) many words, consisting of words. [E]

**wore.** See WEAR¹,².

**work** (wĕrk). **1.** *n.* Application of effort to a purpose, use of energy, (*all work and no play*); task (to be) undertaken, materials (to be) used in task; thing done or made by work, result of action, product *of*; piece of literary or musical composition, (in *pl.*) all such by an author, composer, etc.; (Theol., usu. in *pl.*) meritorious act; doings or experiences of specified kind (DIRTY *work*); employment esp. as means of earning money (*is out of work*); (usu. in *pl.* or *comb.*) defensive structure (EARTH*work*); (in *pl.*) operations of building etc. (**public ~s,** such operations by or for the State); (in *pl.*) operative part of clock etc., (sl.) all that is available (**give** person **the ~s,** give or tell him everything, esp. kill him); (in *pl.*, often treated as *sing.*) place of manufacture (GAS*works*); (articles with) ornamentation of specified kind (*embossed work*); things made of specified material or with specified tools etc. (IRON*work*, NEEDLE*work*). **2.** *v.i.* & *t.* (~ed, *or* wrought *pr.* rawt arch. exc. as below). Make efforts (*for or against*), engage in work (*at or on* thing), be craftsman *in* material, (often *wrought*); be in action, do appointed work, (*charm, drug, plan, scheme,* worked, *will not work*); put or keep in operation or at work (*worked to* DEATH; **~ the oracle,** fig., secretly influence result in one's favour), cause to toil; carry on, manage, control, (*work a mine; is worked by electricity*); have influence (*on, upon*; often *wrought*); produce as result (*work* WONDERS; often *wrought*); be in motion or agitated, ferment (lit. or fig.); make way, make (way etc.), cause to do this, slowly or with difficulty, (*out, in, through, round,* etc.), gradually become (*loose* etc.) by motion; knead, hammer, bring to desired shape or consistency (**wrought iron,** able to be forged or rolled, not cast); artificially excite (*worked himself into a rage*); do, make by, needlework etc.; solve (sum) by mathematics; purchase (one's PASSAGE etc.) with labour instead of money, obtain by labour the money for. **3.** *all in a* DAY's *work; at ~,* in action; **have** one's **~ cut out,** be faced with hard task; **make short ~ of,** quickly accomplish or dispose of; **set to ~,** (cause to) begin operations; **the ~ of** *a moment* etc., task occupying (specified time); ~'aday, ordinary, everyday, practical; ~'-basket (holding sewing materials); ~'day (on which work is usu. done); ~'-force, (number of) workers engaged or available; ~'house, (Hist.) public institution for paupers in

parish; **~ in,** find place for (illustration etc.) in composition or structure; ~'load, amount of work to be done; ~'man, man hired to do manual work, person *good* etc. at his job; ~'manlike, showing practised skill; ~'manship, degree of skill in doing task or of finish in product made; ~'mate, one engaged in same work as another; **~ of art,** fine picture, building, poem, etc.; **~ off,** get rid of by work or activity; **~ out,** solve (sum) or find (amount) by calculation, be calculated *at,* exhaust with work, attain with difficulty, have result (*plan did not work out well*), provide for all details of (*has worked out a scheme*); ~'out n., practice or test (esp. of boxer); **~ over,** examine thoroughly, (colloq.) treat with violence; ~'people (employed in labour for wages); ~'piece, thing worked on with tool or machine; ~'room (in which work is done); ~'sheet, paper for recording work (being) done; ~'-shop, room or building in which manufacture is done; ~'-shy, disinclined to work; **~ study,** system of measuring jobs so as to get best results for employees and employers; **~ to rule,** follow rules of one's occupation with pedantic precision to reduce efficiency, usu. as protest; ~-to-rule n.; **~ up,** bring gradually to efficient state, advance gradually *to* (climax), elaborate or excite by degrees, mingle (ingredients), learn (subject) by study. **4.** ~'able *a.* (-bly), that can be worked or will work or is worth working; ~abi'lity n.; ~'er n., (esp.) manual or industrial employee, neuter bee or ant; ~'ing, (n., esp.) mine or quarry (~ing capital, actually used in a business; ~ing day, workday, part of the day devoted to work; ~ing drawing, to scale, as guide in manufacture etc.; ~ing knowledge, adequate to work with; ~ing lunch etc., meal at which mainly business etc. is discussed; ~ing order, condition in which machine works), (*a.,* esp.) engaged in manual or industrial labour (*working man, class;* ~ing model, of machine etc., able to work though on small scale; ~ing party, ‖committee appointed to advise on some question). [E]

**world** (wẽr-) *n.* The universe, all that exists; the earth or a heavenly body like it; time or state or scene of human existence; secular interests and affairs; human affairs, active life; average or respectable people or their customs or opinions; all that concerns or all who belong to specified class or sphere of activity (the *world of sport*); vast amount (*of*); (*attrib.*) affecting many nations (*world politics*), of all nations (*world champion*); **all the ~,** everyone; **bring, come, into the ~,** give birth to, be born; **end of the ~,** cessation of all mortal life; **for all the ~,** precisely (*like, as if*); **would not do it for the ~,** *would give the ~ to* do or for, (anything no matter how great); **in the ~,** at all, that exists, of any possible kind (*what in the world is it?*); **man, woman, of the ~,** practical tolerant experienced person; **New W~,** America; **Old W~,** Europe, Asia, and Africa; **out of this ~,** (colloq.) incredibly good etc.; **round the ~,** travelling east or west until starting-point is reached again; TELL *the world;* **the best of both ~s,** benefit from two partly conflicting interests; **the next, the other, ~,** life after death; **the** or **this ~,** mortal life; **think the ~ of,** have highest possible regard for; **~-beater,** person or thing surpassing all others; **~-famous,** known throughout the world; **~ power,** nation having influence in world politics; **~'s end,** remotest point possible; **~ war** (involving many important nations); **~-wide,** covering, known in, all parts of the world; **~ without end,** for ever; **~'ly** *a.* (-iness), temporal, earthly, (*worldly goods*), engrossed in temporal affairs esp. pursuit of wealth and pleasure; **~ly-wise,** prudent as regards one's own interests. [E]

**worm** (wẽrm). **1.** *n.* Invertebrate limbless slender creeping or burrowing animal; blindworm or SLOW-WORM; (in *pl.*) intestinal parasites; larva of insect esp. in fruit or wood; abject or insignificant or contemptible person; spiral part of screw (esp. engaging with cog-wheel); **a ~ will turn,** there are things that even the meekest will not accept; **food for ~s,** dead; **~-cast,** convoluted tubular mass of earth from earthworm; **~-eaten,** full of worm-holes; **~-hole** (left by passage of worm); **~'s-eye view,** (joc.) view from

below or from humble position; **~'y** *a.* (-iness), full of worms, worm-eaten. **2.** *v.t.* & *i.* Insinuate one*self into* favour etc.; convey one*self* or progress with crawling motion; draw (secret etc.) by crafty persistence *out of,* or *from,* person. [E]

**wor'mwood** (wẽr-) *n.* A woody herb with bitter aromatic taste; (source of) bitter mortification (*the thought was wormwood to him*). [E; cf. VERMOUTH]

**wōrn.** See WEAR[1].

**wo'rr'|y** (wŭ'-). **1.** *v.t.* & *i.* (Of dog) shake or pull about with the teeth; harass, importune, be a trouble or anxiety to, deprive of peace and quiet; give way to anxiety; (in *p.p.*) uneasy; **I should ~y,** (colloq.) it doesn't trouble me at all; **not to ~y,** (colloq.) there is no need to worry; **~isome** *a.* **2.** *n.* Thing that causes anxiety or disturbs tranquillity; disturbed state of mind, anxiety; **~y beads,** string of beads manipulated with fingers to occupy or calm oneself. [E,= strangle]

**worse** (wẽrs) *a., adv.,* & *n.* **1.** *a.* More bad; (*pred.*) in or into worse health, in worse condition (*am none the worse for it*); *worse* LUCK; *the worse for* WEAR[1]. **2.** *adv.* More badly or ill. **3.** *n.* Worse thing(s) (*you might do worse than accept*); **from bad to ~,** into even worse state; **the ~,** worse condition (*a change for the worse*). **4. wor'sen** (wẽr-) *v.i.* & *t.* [E]

**wor'ship** (wẽr-). **1.** *n.* (Acts, rites, or ceremonies of) homage or service paid to God, adoration felt or shown for person or principle, (**public ~,** church services; **place of ~,** church etc.; **your, his, W~,** title of respect used to, of, certain magistrates etc.). **2.** *v.t.* & *i.* (‖-pp-). Adore as divine, honour with religious rites; idolize or regard with adoration; attend public worship; be full of adoration. **3. ~ful** *a.* (-lly), honourable or distinguished (arch., esp. in old titles of companies or officers). [E (WORTH, -SHIP)]

**worst** (wẽrst) *a., adv., n.,* & *v.* **1.** *a.* & *adv.* Most bad(ly). **2.** *n.* Worst part or possibility (*prepare for the worst*); **at its,** one's, **~,** in the worst state; **at (the) ~,** in the worst possible case; **get the ~ of it,** be defeated; **if the ~ comes to the ~,** if the worst happens; **do your ~**

(expr. defiance). **3.** *v.t.* Get the better of, defeat. [E (WORSE)]

**wor'stěd** (wŏŏ's-) *n.* (Fabric made from) fine woollen yarn. [place]

**wort** (wĕrt) *n.* Plant (arch. exc. in names, as *liverwort*); unfermented infusion of malt. [E]

**worth** (wĕr-). **1.** *pred. a.* (governing *n.* like *prep.*) Of value equivalent to, such as to justify or repay, having property amounting to, (*is worth £1, nothing, hearing, an effort; died worth a million*); **for all** one is ~, (colloq.) with utmost efforts; **for what it is** ~, without guarantee of its truth or value; WELL² *or* ~ **it**, (colloq.) worth while; ~ one's **salt**, having merit; *worth* (one's) WHILE; ~'**while**, that is worth while. **2.** *n.* What person or thing is worth, (high) merit; equivalent of money in commodity (*ten pounds' worth of petrol*); PENNY-*worth*); ~'**less** *a.*, without value or merit. [E]

**wor'thy** (wĕr'dhĭ). **1.** *a.* (-ily, -iness). Estimable or deserving respect, (of person) entitled to (condescending) recognition, deserving (*of*, to be or do), adequate, suitable to the dignity etc. *of*, (*lived a worthy life; a worthy old couple; worthy of praise, to be praised, to lead; a worthy reward; in words worthy of the occasion*); (as *suf.* forming *adjs.*) deserving of, suitable for, (*noteworthy, seaworthy*). **2.** *n.* Worthy person; person of some distinction in his country, time, etc.

**wŏt.** See WIT; **would(n't),** see WILL.

**wound¹** (wŏŏ-). **1.** *n.* Injury done to living tissue by cut or stab or blow or tear; injury to reputation or pain inflicted on feelings. **2.** *v.t.* Inflict wound on. [E]

**wound².** See WIND², WIND¹ 4; **wŏve(n),** see WEAVE¹.

**wow. 1.** *int.* expr. astonishment or admiration. **2.** *n.* (sl.) Sensational success. [imit.]

**w.p.b.** *abbr.* waste-paper basket.

**W.P.C.** *abbr.* woman police CONSTABLE.

**w.p.m.** *abbr.* words per minute.

‖**W.R.A.C.** *abbr.* Women's Royal Army Corps.

**wrăck** *n.* Seaweed cast up or growing on shore; = RACK². [LDu. *wrak*; cf. WRECK]

‖**W.R.A.F.** *abbr.* Women's Royal Air Force.

**wraith** *n.* Ghost; spectral appearance of living person supposed to portend his death. [orig. unkn.]

**wră'ngle** (ră'nggel) *n.*, & *v.i.* (Engage in) noisy argument or altercation or dispute; **wră'ngler** (-ngg-) *n.*, (esp., Camb. Univ.) first-classman in mathematical tripos. [LDu.]

**wrăp. 1.** *v.t.* & *i.* (-pp-). Envelop in folded or soft encircling material (often *up*), arrange or draw (pliant covering) *round* or *about* person etc., (of edges of garment or covering) overlap, (*wrap it in paper, cotton wool; hill, affair, is wrapped in mist, mystery*); ~ **up,** finish off (matter), protect oneself from cold with wraps; ~**ped up in,** engrossed in (beloved one, subject, one*self*, etc.). **2.** *n.* Shawl or scarf or other such addition to clothing; **under** ~s, (fig.) in secrecy. **3.** ~'**per** *n.*, (esp.) loose enveloping robe or gown, paper cover for sweet or book or posted newspaper; ~'**pǐng** *n.*, (esp., in *pl.*) wraps, enveloping garments. [orig. unkn.]

**wrässe** *n.* A bright-coloured sea-fish. [Corn. *wrach*]

**wrath** (rŏ-, raw-) *n.* (poet., rhet., joc.) Anger; ~'**ful** *a.* (-lly), angry. [E (WROTH)]

**wreak** *v.t.* Give play to (*vengeance*, one's *anger* etc., usu. *upon* enemy); cause (damage etc.). [E, = avenge]

**wreath** *n.* (*pl. pr.* -dhz, -ths). Flowers or leaves fastened in a ring esp. as ornament for head or buildings or for laying on grave etc.; curl or ring *of* smoke or cloud or soft fabric; ~**e** (-dh) *v.t.* & *i.*, encircle as or (as) with wreath (*face wreathed in smiles*), arrange as wreath, wind (one's arms etc.) *round* person etc., (of smoke etc.) move in wreaths. [E (WRITHE)]

**wrěck. 1.** *n.* Destruction or disablement esp. of ship; ship that has suffered wreck, greatly damaged or disabled building or thing or person; wretched remnant *of*. **2.** *v.t.* & *i.* Cause wreck of (ship, train, hopes, etc.); suffer wreck; (in *p.p.*) involved in wreck. **3.** ~'**age** *n.*, wrecked material, remnants of wreck; ~'**er** *n.*, (esp.) one who tries from shore to bring about shipwreck in order to plunder or profit by wreckage. [AF *wrec* f. Gmc]

**wren¹** *n.* Small short-winged usu. brown song-bird. [E]

‖**Wren²** *n.* Member of Women's

Royal Naval Service. [initials *W.R.N.S.*]

**wrench. 1.** *n.* Violent twist or oblique pull or tearing off, tool like spanner for gripping and turning nuts etc., (fig.) painful uprooting or parting. **2.** *v.t.* Inflict wrench on, pull (*off, away, round, open,* etc.) with wrench, distort (facts) to suit a theory etc. [E]

**wrest** *v.t.* Distort into accordance with one's interests or views; wrench away (weapon) or snatch (victory) or extract (consent) *from* opponent etc. [E]

**wre´stle** (-sel). **1.** *n.* Contest in which two opponents grapple and try to throw each other to the ground esp. as athletic sport under code of rules; hard struggle. **2.** *v.i. & t.* Take part in wrestle (with or *with*); struggle *with* or *against*, do one's utmost to deal *with*, (temptation, task, etc.); ~**er,** ~**ing,** (-sl-) *ns.* [E]

**wretch** *n.* Unfortunate or pitiable person; miscreant or conscienceless person (often as playful term of depreciation); ~**'ed** *a.,* unhappy or miserable, of bad quality or no merit, contemptible, unsatisfactory or displeasing, (*wretched health, horse, scribbler, weather, nuisance*). [E, = outcast]

||**wrick.** See RICK[2].

**wri´ggle. 1.** *v.i. & t.* (Of worm) twist about, go *along* etc. thus, (of person or animal) make wormlike motions, make way *through* etc. thus, (fig.) practise evasion (~ *out of an engagement* etc., avoid fulfilling on some pretext); move (one*self,* one's *hand,* etc.) with wriggling action. **2.** *n.* Act of wriggling. [LG *wriggelen*]

**wright** (rīt), *n.* Maker or builder (arch. exc. in *comb.; playwright, shipwright*). [E (WORK)]

**wring. 1.** *v.t.* (**wrung**). Squeeze tightly, squeeze and twist, break by twisting, torture, extract or extort by squeezing or pressure or importunity (*out, from, out of;* ~ *person's* **hand,** press it with emotion; ~ one's **hands,** clasp them as gesture of grief; ~ **out** or ~ *clothes* etc., squeeze out water by twisting them; ~ **neck of** *chicken* etc., kill it by twisting head; ~**'ing** (**wet**), so wet that water can be wrung out; ~**'er** *n.,* (esp.) device for wringing water from washed clothes etc. **2.** *n.* Act of wringing. [E]

**wri´nkl|e. 1.** *n.* Crease in skin such as is produced by age, similar mark in other flexible surface; (colloq.) piece of useful guidance; ~**y** *a.* **2.** *v.t. & i.* Make wrinkles in; form wrinkles. [E]

**wrist** *n.* Joint connecting hand with arm; part of garment covering this; ~**(-work),** working of hand without moving the arm; ~**-watch** (worn on strap etc. round wrist); ~**let** *n.,* band or ring to strengthen or guard or adorn wrist; ||~**let watch,** = *wrist-watch.* [E]

**write** *v.i. & t.* (**wrote** *pr.* rōt; **wri´tten,** arch. **writ,** *pr.* rĭt´-). Mark paper or other surface with symbols representing word(s); form or mark (such symbols); form or mark symbols of (word, sentence, document, etc.) thus; fill or complete (sheet, cheque, etc.) with writing; put (data) into computer store; (fig., esp. in *p.p.*) indicate (quality or condition) by appearance (*guilt was written all over her*); compose for written or printed reproduction or publication, be engaged in such literary composition; write and send letter (*to* person, *for* thing wanted), (U.S. or colloq.) write and send letter to (person); convey (news etc.) by letter; state in book etc.; ~ **down,** record in writing, write as if for inferiors, disparage in writing, reduce nominal value of (goods etc.); ~ **off,** write and send letter, cancel record of possession of (esp. bad debts, sum representing depreciation, lost property); ~**-off** *n.,* (esp.) vehicle so damaged as not to be worth repair; ~ **out,** write the whole of, exhaust one*self* by writing; ~ **up,** write full account of (so ~**-up** *n.*), praise in writing; **writ large,** in magnified or emphasized form; **writ** *n.,* form of written command to act or not act in some way; HOLY *Writ;* **wri´ter** *n.,* (esp.) author; ~**r's cramp,** muscular spasm due to excessive writing; W~**r to the Signet,** Sc. solicitor in Court of Session; **wri´ting** *n.,* (esp.) handwriting, written document, (in *pl.*) author's works; **in writing,** in written form; **writing-case** (holding materials for writing with); **the writing on the wall,** ominous event; **writing-paper** (esp. of size usual for letters). [E]

**writhe** (-dh) *v.i.* Twist or roll oneself about (as) in acute pain; suffer mental torture (*under* or *at* insult etc., *with* shame etc.). [E]

**wri´tten.** See WRITE.

‖**W.R.N.S.** *abbr.* Women's Royal Naval Service.

**wrŏng** *a., adv., n.,* & *v.* **1.** *a.* Out of order, in(to) bad or abnormal condition; contrary to law or morality; unsuitable, (more or most) undesirable; mistaken, in error; **get hold of the ~ end of the stick**, misunderstand completely; ~ **side**, worse or undesired or unusable (opp. RIGHT) side; ~ **side out**, inside out; ~ **´un**, (colloq.) person of bad character, googly; ~ **way round**, in opposite of normal orientation. **2.** *adv.* (usu. placed last). In wrong direction or manner, with incorrect result; **get person ~**, misunderstand him; **go** ~, take wrong path, cease virtuous behaviour, get out of working order. **3.** *n.* What is morally wrong, wrong or unjust action; **do** ~, **sin**; **do** ~ **to**, misjudge (person); **in the** ~, responsible for quarrel, mistake, or offence. **4.** *v.t.* Treat unjustly; mistakenly attribute bad motives to.

**5.** ~**´doer**, ~**´doing**, (person guilty of) breach of law or morality; ~**-headed**, perverse and obstinate; ~**´ful** *a.* (**-lly**), unwarranted, unjustified. [E]

**wrōte.** See WRITE.

**wrŏth** *pred. a.* (poet., rhet., joc.; no *adv.* in **-ly**). Angry. [E]

**wrought.** See WORK; **wrŭng**, see WRING.

‖**W.R.V.S.** *abbr.* Women's Royal Voluntary Service.

**wrȳ** *a.* (~**´er**, ~**´est**; ~**´ly**, ~**´ness**). Distorted, turned to one side, (~ **face, mouth**, grimace of disgust); ~**´neck**, small bird able to turn head over shoulder. [E]

**W.S.** *abbr.* Writer to the Signet.

**W.S.W.** *abbr.* west-south-west.

**wt.** *abbr.* weight.

**W.Va.** *abbr.* West Virginia.

**wȳch-, wĭ(t)ch-,** *pref.* in names of trees with pliant branches (~**-alder, -elm, -hazel**). [E, = bending]

**Wȳ´kehamĭst** (-kam-) *a.* & *n.* (Member) of Winchester College. [William of *Wykeham*, founder]

**Wyo.** *abbr.* Wyoming.

# X

**X, x,** (ĕks) *n.* (*pl.* **Xs, X's,** *pr.* ĕ´ksĭz). Twenty-fourth letter; (as Roman numeral) 10; (Alg.; *x*) first unknown quantity; cross-shaped symbol esp. used to indicate position (*X marks the spot*) or incorrectness or to symbolize kiss or vote, or as signature of person who cannot write; X-RAY.

**xĕnophō´bĭa** (z-) *n.* Morbid dislike of foreigners. [Gk *xenos* strange(r)]

**xēr┃o´graphy** (z-; *or* zĕr-) *n.* Dry copying process in which powder adheres to areas remaining electrically charged after exposure of surface to light from image of document to be copied; **X~´ŏx** *n.*, & *v.t.*, (reproduce by) a certain process of xerography, a copy so made, [P].

[Gk *xēros* dry]

**xī** (*or* gzī, zī) *n.* Fourteenth Gk letter (Ξ, ξ) = x. [Gk]

**-xion.** See -ION.

**Xmas** (krĭ´smas) *n.* = CHRISTMAS. [abbr., with X for initial chi of Gk *Khristos* Christ]

**X-ray** (ĕks-). **1.** *n.* (in *pl.*) Electromagnetic radiation of short wavelength, able to pass through opaque bodies; photograph made by X-rays, esp. showing position of bones etc. by their greater absorption of the rays. **2.** *v.t.* Photograph, examine, or treat with X-rays. [X, orig. w. ref. to unkn. nature]

**xȳ´lophŏn┃e** (z-) *n.* Musical instrument of graduated wooden bars struck with small wooden hammer(s) ~**ĭst** *n.* [Gk *xulon* wood]

# Y

**Y, y,** (wī) *n.* (*pl.* **Ys, Y's**). Twenty-fifth letter; (Alg.; *y*) second unknown quantity; Y-shaped thing.

**-y**[1] *suf.* forming *adjs.* f. *ns.* & *adjs.*, w. sense 'full of', 'having the quality of', 'addicted to', (*messy, slangy, browny-yellow, horsy*), & f. *vbs.* w. sense 'inclined to', 'apt to', (*runny, sticky*). [E]

**-y**[2], **-ie, -ey,** *suf.* forming dim. *ns.*, pet names, etc., (*granny, Sally, nightie, Mickey*). [orig. Sc.]

**yacht** (yŏt). **1.** *n.* Light sailing-vessel for racing (**ice-, sand-, ~,** similar vessel for use on land); larger usu. power-driven vessel used for private pleasure excursions, cruising, etc.; **~-club** (esp. for yacht-racing); **~'sman,** person who yachts. **2.** *v.i.* Race or cruise in yacht. [Du. (*jaghtschip*, lit. pursuit-ship)]

**yah** *int.* expr. derision or defiance. [imit.]

**yahoo'** (ya-h-) *n.* Bestial person. [race of brutes in *Gulliver's Travels*]

**Yah'veh, -weh.** See JEHOVAH.

**yăk** *n.* Long-haired Tibetan ox. [Tibetan]

**Yāle** *n.* **~ lock,** type of lock for doors etc., with revolving barrel. [person]

**yăm** *n.* (Edible starchy tuber of) tropical or subtropical climbing plant; *sweet POTATO. [Port. or Sp.]

**yă'mmer** *v.i.*, & *n.* (colloq. or dial.) Lament, wail, grumble; (utter) voluble talk. [E]

**yănk**[1] *v.t.*, & *n.* Pull with a jerk. [orig. unkn.]

**Yănk**[2] *n.* (colloq.) = foll. [abbr.]

**Yă'nkee** (-kǐ) *n.* ‖Inhabitant of U.S., American, (colloq.); *inhabitant of New England or of northern States. [perh. Du. *Janke* dim. of *Jan* John, used derisively; or repr. Amer. Ind. pronunc. of *English*]

**yăp. 1.** *v.i.* (**-pp-**). Bark shrilly or fussily; (colloq.) talk noisily or foolishly or complainingly. **2.** *n.* Sound of yapping. [imit.]

‖**yăpp** *n.* Bookbinding with projecting limp leather cover. [person]

**yăr'borough** (-rō) *n.* Whist or bridge hand with no card above a 9. [person]

**yărd**[1] *n.* Unit of linear measure (3 ft., 0·9144 metre), this length of material, (**by the ~,** fig., at great length; **~'stick,** rod a yard long usu. divided into inches etc., (fig.) standard of comparison); square or cubic yard; spar slung across mast for sail to hang from (**~-arm,** either end of this); **~'age** *n.,* number of yards of material etc. [E, = stick]

**yărd**[2] *n.* Piece of enclosed ground esp. attached to building(s) or used for particular purpose (CHURCH, COURT, DOCK[3], FARM, GRAVE[1], -yard; VINEYARD); *garden of house; ‖**the Y~,** (colloq.) SCOTLAND YARD. [E, = enclosure]

**yăr'mulka** *n.* Skull-cap worn by Jewish men. [Yiddish]

**yărn. 1.** *n.* Spun thread, esp. for knitting, weaving, etc.; (colloq.) story, traveller's tale, anecdote. **2.** *v.i.* (colloq.) Tell yarns. [E]

**yă'rrow** (-ō) *n.* Kind of perennial herb, esp. milfoil. [E]

**yă'shmak** *n.* Veil concealing face except eyes, worn by some Muslim women. [Arab.]

**yaw. 1.** *v.i.* (Of ship, aircraft, space-craft) fail to hold straight course, go unsteadily. **2.** *n.* Yawing of ship etc. from course. [orig. unkn.]

**yawl** *n.* Kind of ship's boat or sailing- or fishing-boat. [LDu. *jol(le)*]

**yawn. 1.** *v.i.* Open the mouth wide and inhale esp. in sleepiness or boredom; (of chasm etc.) gape, be wide open. **2.** *n.* Act of yawning. [E]

**yaws** (-z) *n.pl.* (usu. treated as *sing.*) Contagious tropical skin-disease with raspberry-like swellings. [orig. unkn.]

**yd(s).** *abbr.* yard(s).

**yē**[1] (*or* yǐ) *pron.* (forms as YOU; poet., arch., religious, dial., or joc.) Pl. of THOU[1] (*blessed are ye; ye mariners of England; how d'ye do?; ye GODS*). [E]

**yē**[2] (*or as* THE) *a.* (pseudo-arch.) =

THE (*ye olde tea-shoppe*). [f. old use of obs. *y*-shaped letter for *th*]

**yea** (yā; arch.) **1.** *adv.* Yes. **2.** *n.* The word 'yea'; ~**s and nays,** affirmative and negative votes; ~ **and nay,** shilly-shally. [E]

**yeah** (yĕă) *adv.* (colloq.) Yes; (oh) ~? (expr. incredulity). [casual pronunc. of YES]

**year** (or yĕr) *n.* Time occupied by the earth in one revolution round the sun, approx. 365¼ days (**astronomical, natural, solar,** etc., ~); period from 1 Jan. to 31 Dec. inclusive (**calendar, civil,** ~; LEAP *year*; ~ **of grace, of Our Lord,** date A.D.; ‖*year* DOT¹); period of same length as civil year commencing at any day (**academic, school,** ~, usu. reckoned from beginning of autumn term; **Christian, Church, ecclesiastical,** ~, round of sacred seasons reckoned from and to Advent; **financial, fiscal, tax,** ~, reckoned e.g. from 6 Apr. for taxing and accounting); group of students entering college etc. in same academic year; (in *pl.*) age, time of life, (**young for his** ~**s,** not showing much sign of his age); (usu. in *pl.*) very long time; ~**-book,** annual publication bringing information on some subject up to date; ~**'ling** *n.*, animal between 1 and 2 years old; ~**ly** *a. & adv.,* (produced or occurring) once every year, of or for a lasting a year. [E]

**yearn** (yĕrn) *v.i.* Be filled with longing or compassion or tenderness (*for* or *after* desired thing, to do, *to* or *towards* person etc.). [E]

**yeast** *n.* Greyish-yellow fungous substance got esp. from fermenting malt liquors and used as fermenting agent, to raise bread, etc.; ~**'ȳ** *a.* (**-ily, -iness**), frothy, in a ferment, working like yeast, (of talk etc.) light and superficial. [E]

**yell** *n.,* & *v.i. & t.* (Make, utter with) sharp loud cry of pain, anger, fright, derision, delight, or encouragement; shout. [E]

**yel'low** (-ō) *a., n., & v.* **1.** *a.* (~**er,** ~**est**). Of the colour of buttercups or lemons or yolks or gold; having yellow skin or complexion; (colloq.) cowardly. **2.** *n.* Yellow colour, pigment, clothes or material (*dressed in yellow*), or ball in snooker. **3.** *v.i. & t.* Turn yellow (*paper yellowed with age*; *the yellowing leaves*). **4.** ~ **fever,**

tropical virus disease with fever and jaundice; *yellow* FLAG³; ~**hammer,** bunting of which the male has yellow head, neck, and breast; ~ **pages,** section of telephone directory on yellow paper and listing business subscribers according to goods or services they offer; ~ **spot,** point of acutest vision in retina; ~ **streak,** trait of cowardice. [E]

**yelp** *v.i., & n.* (Utter) sharp shrill cry (as) of dog in pain or excitement. [E]

**yen¹** *n.* (*pl.* same). Japanese monetary unit. [Jap. f. Chin.]

**yen²** *v.i.* (**-nn-**), *& n.* (Feel) longing or yearning. [Chin.]

**yeo'man** (yō'-) *n.* (*pl.* **-men**). Man holding and cultivating small landed estate; ‖member of yeomanry force; ~**('s) service,** efficient or useful help in need; ‖**Y~ of the Guard,** member of sovereign's bodyguard; ~**lȳ** *a.;* ~**rȳ** *n.,* body of yeomen, ‖(Hist.) volunteer cavalry force raised from yeoman class. [E, prob. = young man]

**yes. 1.** *adv.* serving to indicate that the answer to the question is affirmative, the statement etc. made is correct, the request or command will be complied with, or the person summoned or addressed is present; ~?, indeed? is that so? what do you want?; ~, ~, (emphat.); ~ **and** (introducing stronger phr.: *would beat me, yes and you too*); **say** ~, grant request, confirm statement. **2.** *n.* The word *yes*; ~**-man,** (colloq.) weakly acquiescent person. [E, = YEA *let it be*]

**yester-** *in comb.* (poet., arch.) Of yesterday, that is last past, (*yester-eve, yestermorn*); ~**-year,** last year. [E]

**yes'terday** (or -dǐ) *n. & adv.* (On) the day before today (*arrived yesterday*; *yesterday was her birthday*); (in) the recent past (*not* BORN *yesterday*). [E (prec., DAY)]

**yet. 1.** *adv.* As late as or until now or then (*there is yet time; there's life in the old dog yet; his greatest achievement yet;* AS¹ *yet*); (w. neg. or interrog.) so soon as or by now or then (*it is not time yet; is he dead yet?; need you go just yet?*); again, in addition, (*more and yet more;* **nor** ~, and also not: *won't listen to me nor yet to her*); in the time that remains before the matter ends (*I will do it yet*); (w. compar.)

even (*a yet more difficult task*); nevertheless, and or but in spite of that, (*it is strange and yet it is true*). **2.** *conj.* But at the same time, but nevertheless, (*the work is done, yet what is the use of it all?*; *fragile-looking yet strong*). [E]

**yĕ'tĭ** *n.* = ABOMINABLE Snowman. [Tibetan]

**yew** *n.* Dark-leaved evergreen coniferous tree; its wood. [E]

**Yĭd** *n.* (sl., derog.) Jew. [back-form. f. foll.]

**Yĭ'ddĭsh** *a.* & *n.* (Of) language used by Jews in or from Europe, orig. a German dialect with words from Hebrew etc.; **∼er** *a.* & *n.* (person) speaking Yiddish. [G *jüdisch* Jewish]

**yield. 1.** *v.t.* & *i.* Produce or return as fruit or profit or result (*land yields good crops*; *investment yields 15%*); deliver over, surrender, resign, comply with demand for, concede, make submission *to*, respond as desired *to*, change one's course of action in deference *to*, be inferior or confess inferiority *to*, (*yield fortress, possession, place*; *yield oneself prisoner*; *town yielded*; *yield to superior force, persuasion*, etc.; *I yield to none in appreciation of his merits*); give right of way (*to* other traffic). **2.** *n.* Amount yielded or produced. [E, = pay]

**yĭ'ppee** *int.* expr. delight or excitement. [natural excl.]

**y'lăng-ylăng** (ē'l-; -ēl-) *n.* (Malayan tree with fragrant yellow flowers yielding) a perfume. [Tagalog]

**Y.M.C.A.** *abbr.* Young Men's Christian Association.

**yŏb('bō)** *n.* (sl.; *pl.* **∼s**). Lout, hooligan. [back sl. for BOY; cf. -O]

**yŏ'del. 1.** *v.t.* & *i.* (‖-ll-). Sing with melodious inarticulate sounds and frequent changes between falsetto and normal voice in manner of Swiss mountain-dwellers. **2.** *n.* Yodelling cry. [G]

**yŏ'ga** *n.* Hindu system of philosophic meditation and asceticism designed to effect reunion with the universal spirit; system of physical exercises and breathing control used in yoga; **yŏ'gĭ** (-gǐ) *n.*, devotee of yoga. [Hind. f. Skr., = union]

**yŏ'g(h)urt** (-gert) *n.* Semi-solid sourish food prepared from milk fermented by added bacteria. [Turk.]

**yogi.** See YOGA.

**yŏ'-heave-hō** *int.* & *n.* = HEAVE *ho*;

**yŏ-(hŏ-)hō'** *int.* used to attract attention, or = HEAVE *ho*. [natural excl.]

**yoicks** *int.* used by fox-hunter as halloo. [orig. unkn.]

**yōke. 1.** *n.* Wooden cross-piece fastened over necks of two oxen and attached to plough or wagon to be drawn; (fig.) sway or dominion or servitude (*submitted to his yoke*; *endure the yoke*); object like yoke in form or function, e.g. wooden shoulder-piece for carrying pair of pails, top part of dress, skirt, etc., from which the rest hangs; (fig.) bond of union esp. of marriage; pair *of* oxen etc. (*pl.* often same after numeral). **2.** *v.t.* & *i.* Put yoke on; couple or unite (pair); link (one to another); match or work together. [E]

**yō'kel** *n.* Rustic, country bumpkin. [perh. dial.]

**yōlk** (yōk) *n.* Yellow internal part of egg. [E (YELLOW)]

**Yŏm Kĭ'ppur** *n.* = *Day of* ATONEMENT. [Heb.]

**yŏn** (arch., poet., dial.). **1.** *a.* & *adv.* Yonder (**hither and ∼**, in various directions). **2.** *pron.* Yonder person or thing. [E]

**yŏ'nder** *a.* & *adv.* (literary). (Situated) over there, at some distance in that direction, in the place indicated by pointing etc.

**yoo'-hoo** *int.* expr. desire to attract person's attention. [natural excl.]

**yōre** *n.* (literary). **Of ∼**, formerly, in or of old days. [E, = long ago]

**York**[1] *n.* **∼ and Lancaster**, rival parties in Wars of the Roses; **House of ∼**, English kings from Edward IV to Richard III; **∼'ist** *a.* & *n.*, (adherent) of House of York esp. in Wars of the Roses. [person]

**yor'ker** *n.* (Crick.) Ball that pitches immediately under the bat; **york**[2] *v.t.*, bowl out with yorker. [prob. w. ref. to practice of Yorkshire cricketers]

**Yorks.** *abbr.* = foll.

**Yor'kshire** (-er, -ēr) *n.* **∼man**, **∼woman**, native of Yorkshire; **∼ pudding**, baked batter eaten with roast beef; **∼ terrier**, small shaggy blue and tan toy kind; *Yorkshire* TYKE. [place]

**you** (ū, yōō) *pron.* (*obj.* **you**; *refl.* YOURSELF, YOURSELVES; *poss.* YOUR, YOURS). Sing. and pl. *pron.* of 2nd pers.; the person(s) or thing(s) addressed; (as *voc.* w. *n.* in excl.

statement: *you fools!*; *you darling!*); *you and* YOURS; (in general statements) one, a person, anyone, everyone, (*you never can tell*; *it's bad at first, but you soon get used to it*). [E, orig. obj. case of YE¹]

**young** (yŭ-). **1.** *a.* (~ʹer, ~ʹest, *pr.* -ngg-). Not far advanced in life or development or existence, not yet old, immature, inexperienced, (*a young child, man, animal, plant, wine, institution*; ~ **love, ambition,** etc., felt in or characteristic of youth; Y~ **Liberals** etc., claiming to speak for young persons; **the** ~, young people; *young* and OLD); distinguishing son from father (*young Jones*; *the Young* PRETENDER) or (in compar.) one person from another of same name (*the younger Pitt*). **2.** *n.* (collect.) Offspring esp. of animals before or soon after birth (**with** ~, pregnant). **3.** one's ~ **day**(s), when one was young; ~ **lady** or **woman** or **man,** (colloq.) sweetheart, girl- or boy-friend; ~ **'un,** (colloq.) youngster. **4.** ~ʹ**ster** *n.*, child (esp. active or lively boy), young person. [E]

**your** (ūr, yŏr, *unemphat.* yer) *poss. pron. attrib.* Of you(rself or -selves) (for phrs. see HER², OUR); (colloq., usu. derog.) that we all know of (*none so fallible as your self-styled expert*; *your facetious bore is the worst of all*); ~**s** (ūrz, yŏrz) *poss. pron. pred.* (& abs.), of you (for phrs. see HERS), your letter, (**you and** ~**s,** you together with your family, property, etc.); ~**s,** yours EVER, FAITHFULLY, SINCEREly, truly, etc., formulae preceding signature of letter; ~**s truly,** joc., I (the speaker or writer); **what's** ~**s?,** colloq., what would you like to drink?; ~**sě'lf,** ~**sě'lves** (-vz), *prons.,* emph. & refl. forms of YOU sing. & pl. (for use cf. HER-

SELF; **how's** ~**self?,** sl., how are you?). [E gen. of YE¹]

**youth** (ūth) *n.* (*pl. pr.* ūdhz). Being young, (vigour or enthusiasm or inexperience or other characteristic of) period between childhood and adult age, (*an appearance of extreme youth*; *in my youth*; *the vague cynicism of youth*); **young man** (*a youth of 16*); (*as pl.*) young people collectively (*the youth of the country*; ~ **club,** place for young people's leisure activities; ~ **hostel,** place where (esp. young) holiday-makers, hikers, etc., (~ *hostellers*) can put up cheaply for the night); ~ʹ**ful** *a.* (-lly), young or (still) having the characteristics of youth. [E (YOUNG)]

**yowl** *n.,* & *v.i.* (Utter) loud wailing cry (as) of cat or dog in distress. [imit.]

**yŏ'-yō** *n.* (*pl.* ~s). Toy consisting of pair of discs with deep groove between them in which string is attached and wound, and which can be made to fall and rise. [orig. unkn.]

**yr.** *abbr.* year(s); younger; your.

**yrs.** *abbr.* years; yours.

**yŭ'cca** *n.* White-flowered garden plant. [Carib]

**Yu'goslav, Ju'goslav,** (ū'goslahv) *a.* & *n.* (Native) of Yugoslavia; hence ~ĭan (-ah'-) *a.* & *n.* [G f. Serb. *jug* south; SLAV]

**yule** (ūl) *n.* ~(-tide), (arch.) the Christmas festival; ~-**log** (large, burnt in hearth on Christmas Eve). [E]

**yŭ'mmy** *a.* (colloq.) Tasty, delicious; **yŭm-yŭ'm** *int.* expr. pleasure from (prospect of) eating. [natural excl.]

**Y.W.C.A.** *abbr.* Young Women's Christian Association.

# Z

**Z, z,** (zěd) *n.* (*pl.* Zs, Z's). Twenty-sixth letter; (Alg.; *z*) third unknown quantity.

**zabagliŏ'ne** (zahbahlyŏ'nā) *n.* Italian sweet of whipped and heated egg yolks, sugar, and wine. [It.]

**zā'nў. 1.** *n.* Buffoon, jester; (Hist.)

clown's attendant. **2.** *a.* Comically idiotic, crazily ridiculous. [F or It.]

**zăp** *v.t.* (sl.; -**pp**-). Hit, attack, kill. [imit.]

**Zarathustrian.** See ZOROASTRIAN.

**zeal** *n.* Earnestness or fervour in advancing a cause or rendering service; hearty persistent endeavour; ~**ous** (zĕ'l-) *a.*; ~**ot** (zĕ'l-) *n.*, extreme partisan, fanatic; ~**'otrў** (zĕ'l-) *n.* [L f. Gk *zēlos*]

**zĕ'bra** *n.* Striped Afr. quadruped allied to ass and horse; (*attrib.*) with alternate dark and pale stripes; ‖~ (**crossing**), striped street-crossing where pedestrians have precedence over vehicles. [It. or Port., f. Congolese]

**zē'bū** *n.* Humped ox of Asia and Africa. [F]

**Zech.** *abbr.* Zechariah (O.T.).

‖**zĕd**, *\*zee, n.* Letter Z. [F f. L f. Gk ZETA]

**Zĕn** *n.* Form of Buddhism emphasizing value of meditation and intuition. [Jap., = meditation]

**zĕna'na** (-ah'-) *n.* Part of house for seclusion of women of high-caste families in India and Iran. [Hind. f. Pers.]

**Zĕnd-Avĕ'sta** (*a*-) *n.* Zoroastrian scriptures of Avesta or text, and Zend or commentary. [Pers.]

**zĕ'nĭth** *n.* Point of heavens directly above observer (opp. NADIR); highest point (of power, prosperity, etc.; *is at his, its, the, zenith*); ~**al** *a.* [F or L f. Arab.]

**Zeph.** *abbr.* Zephaniah (O.T.).

**zĕ'phyr** *n.* Mild gentle breeze; fine cotton fabric; athlete's jersey. [F or L f. Gk, = west wind]

**Zĕ'ppelĭn** *n.* German large dirigible airship of early 20th c. [person]

**zēr'ō. 1.** *n.* (*pl.* ~**s**). Figure 0, nought; point on scale of thermometer etc. from which positive or negative quantity is reckoned; **absolute** ~, lowest possible temperature; GROUND[1] *zero*; ~(**-hour**), hour at which planned, esp. Mil. operation is timed to begin, crucial or decisive moment. **2.** *v.i.* ~ **in on**, take aim at, focus attention on. [F or It. f. Sp. f. Arab. (CIPHER)]

**zĕst** *n.* Piquancy, stimulating flavour, (esp. fig.; *adds a zest to*); keen enjoyment or interest, relish (*for*), gusto, (*entered into it with zest*); piece of orange or lemon peel as flavouring. [F]

**zē'ta** *n.* Sixth Gk letter (Z, ζ) = z. [Gk]

**zeu'gma** *n.* Figure of speech using verb or adjective with two nouns, to one of which it is strictly applicable while the word appropriate to the other is not used (*with weeping eyes and*

[sc. *grieving*] *hearts*); (loosely) = SYLLEPSIS. [L f. Gk, = a yoking (*zugon* yoke)]

**Zeus** *n.* (Gk Myth.) Supreme god of Olympus. [Gk]

**zĭ'ggurăt** *n.* Pyramidal tower in ancient Mesopotamia, surmounted by temple. [Assyr.]

**zĭ'gzăg** *n., a., adv., & v.* **1.** *n.* Succession of straight lines with abrupt alternate right and left turns; thing having such lines or sharp turns. **2.** *a.* Forming a zigzag (*zigzag line, road, flash of lightning*). **3.** *adv.* With zigzag course. **4.** *v.i.* (-**gg**-). Move in zigzag course. [F f. G]

*\***zĭ'llion** (-yon) *n.* Indefinite large number. [prob. after *million*]

**zĭnc. 1.** *n.* White metallic element used as component of brass and as coating for sheet iron (cf. GALVANIZE). **2.** *v.t.* (-**c-, -k-, -ck-,** *pr.* -k-). Coat or treat with zinc. [G *zink*]

**zĭng.** (colloq.) **1.** *n.* Vigour, energy. **2.** *v.i.* Move swiftly and shrilly. [imit.]

**zĭ'nnĭa** *n.* Garden plant with showy flowers. [*Zinn*, person]

**Zī'on** *n.* (Holy hill of) ancient Jerusalem; the Jewish religion; the Christian Church; the kingdom of Heaven; ~**ĭsm** *n.*, movement for the re-establishment and development of a Jewish nation in what is now Israel; ~**ĭst** *n.* [E f. L f. Heb.]

**zĭp. 1.** *n.* Light sharp sound; (fig.) energy, vigour; ~(**-fastener**), fastening device of two flexible strips with interlocking projections closed or opened by sliding clip pulled along them; *\****Zip code**, U.S. system of postal codes [*zone improvement plan*]. **2.** *v.t. & i.* (-**pp**-). Fasten (*up*) with zip-fastener; move with zip or at high speed; ~**'per** *n.*, zip-fastener. [imit.]

**zĭr'c|on** *n.* Zirconium silicate of which some translucent varieties are used as gems; ~**ō'nĭum** *n.*, a grey metallic element. [G *zirkon*, prob. ult. f. Arab.]

**zĭ'ther** (-dh-) *n.* Stringed instrument with flat sound-box, placed horizontally and played with fingers and plectrum. [G f. L (as GUITAR)]

**zō'dĭăc** *n.* Belt of the heavens including all apparent positions of sun, moon, and planets as known to the ancients, and divided into 12 equal parts called **signs of the** ~ (Aries or Ram, Taurus or Bull,

Gemini or Twins, Cancer or Crab, Leo or Lion, Virgo or Virgin, Libra or Balance or Scales, Scorpio or Scorpion, Sagittarius or Archer, Capricorn(us) or Goat, Aquarius or Water-carrier, Pisces or Fish(es)), used esp. in astrology; diagram of these signs; **zodi´acal** *a.*, of or in the zodiac. [F f. L f. Gk (*zōion* animal)]

**zo´mbie** *n.* Corpse said to be revived by witchcraft; (colloq.) dull or apathetic person. [W. Afr.]

**zone. 1.** *n.* Girdle or belt (arch.); encircling band of colour etc.; area between two concentric circles; any well-defined region of more or less beltlike form (**time ~**, range of longitudes where a common standard time is used); area having particular features, properties, purpose, or use, (*danger, erogenous, smokeless, zone*); **zo´nal** *a.* **2.** *v.t.* Encircle as or with zone; arrange or distribute by zones; assign to particular area. [F or L f. Gk *zōnē* girdle]

**zoo** *n.* Zoological garden. [abbr.]

**zoo´log|y̆** (*or* zōōō´-) *n.* Scientific

study of animals; **zoolo´gical** (*or* zōōō-) *a.* (**-lly**) **~ical garden(s)**, public garden or park with collection of animals for exhibition and study); **~ist** *n.* [f. L f. Gk *zōion* animal]

**zoom. 1.** *v.i.* Cause aeroplane to mount at high speed and steep angle; move quickly, esp. with buzzing sound; (of camera) change (esp. quickly) from long shot to close-up. **2.** *n.* Aeroplane's steep climb; **~ lens** (allowing camera to zoom by varying focus). [imit.]

**zo´ophyte** *n.* Plantlike animal, esp. coral, jellyfish, or sponge. [Gk (*zōion* animal, *phuton* plant)]

**Zoroä´strian, Zărathu´strian** (-ōō´-), *a.* & *n.* (Follower) of Zoroaster or Zarathustra, (adherent) of dualistic religious system taught by him; **~ism** *n.* [person]

**Zu´lu** (zōō´lōō) *n.* & *a.* (Member, language) of a S. Afr. Bantu people. [native name]

**zy´gŏte** *n.* (Biol.) Cell formed by union of two gametes. [Gk *zugōtos* yoked (ZEUGMA)]

**zymŏ´tic** *a.* Of fermentation. [Gk *zumē* leaven]

# ADDENDA

|| **A.C.A.S.** (ā´kăs) *abbr.* Advisory, Conciliation, and Arbitration Service.

**aficionado** (afĭsyonah´dō) *n.* (*pl.* **~s**). Devotee of sport (esp. bull-fighting). [Sp.]

**a.s.a.p.** *abbr.* as soon as possible.

**ayatŏ´llah** (ĭatŏ´la) *n.* Muslim religious leader esp. in Iran. [Pers.]

**banana.** || **go ~s**, (sl.) become crazy or angry.

**basket.** (Also) group or range (of comparable items).

**batter. 1. ~ed wife** (subjected to repeated violence by husband).

**bay[3].** (Also) area marked out for use when loading, parking, etc.

**B.B.C.** **~ English** (as spoken by B.B.C. announcers).

**bio´nic** *a.* (**~ally**). Relating to bionics; having mechanical body-parts or resulting superhuman powers; **~s** *n.*, study of mechanical systems behaving like living beings. [BIO-, ELECTRONICS]

**bi´orhy̆thm** (-rĭdhem, -them) *n.* Inherent biological process, recurring at regular intervals of about a month. [BIO-]

**bleep.** **~´er** *n.*, bleeping device, esp. for informing person sought.

**blow[1]. 3. ~-dry**, dry (hair) with hand-held source of hot air, styling hair at same time.

**bn.** *abbr.* billion.

**bomb. 2. ~er jacket** (reaching to waist, with tight waist and cuffs).

**boob[2].** (sl., in *pl.*) Woman's breasts. [prob. f. earlier *bub(by)*]

**bo´vver** *n.* (sl.) Deliberate trouble-making; **~ boots** (heavy, with metal capping); **~ boy**, violent hooligan. [Cockney pronunc. of BOTHER]

**cagou´le** (-gōō´l) *n.* Hooded thin windproof garment. [F]

**C.A.P.** *abbr.* Common Agricultural Policy (of E.E.C.).

**capital.** || **~ transfer tax** (on transfer of capital by gift etc.).

**cash. 1.** ~ **flow,** movement of money as affecting availability of cash.

**categ|ory.** ~**orize** v.t., place in category.

**chip. 2.** (Also) small square of semi-conductor to carry integrated circuit.

**chrome.** (Also) chromium-plated metal.

**Cŏ'mĕcŏn** abbr. Council for Mutual Economic Assistance (association of mainly E. Eur. countries).

**cruise. 1.** ~ **missile** (able to fly at low altitude and guide itself by reference to information about topography of region traversed).

**digital.** ~ **recording** (with information-content expressed in digits for more accurate transmission).

**direct. 1.** ~ **debit,** authorized transfer of money between bank accounts at request of recipient.

**equal. 1.** ~ **rights** (esp. for women relative to men's).

**E.T.A.** (ā'tah) n. Basque separatist movement. [abbr. of Basque wds, = freedom for Basque country]

**Euro-.** ~**communism,** Communism in European countries, seeking to be independent of Soviet Communists.

**eye. 1.** ~**s down,** start of bingo game.

**first. 4.** ~ **past the post,** winning an election with more votes than next candidate alone; || ~ **school** (for 5-to 9-year-olds).

**flight. 1.** ~ **bag** (with shoulder-strap and zip, suitable for taking into aircraft cabin).

**floppy.** ~ **disc** (of flexible material, for storage of information that can be read by computer).

**fob¹.** (Also) ornamental tab attached to key-ring.

**gay. 2.** n. (sl.) Homosexual person.

**G.D.P.** abbr. gross domestic product.

**granny.** ~ **bond,** form of index-linked investment available to persons over specified age; ~ **flat,** self-contained part of house as accommodation for relative.

**green. 4.** ~ **pound,** currency exchange unit for agricultural produce in E.E.C.

**gross. 1.** ~ **domestic product,** annual value of goods produced and services provided and received within a country.

**gun. 3.** ~'**ship,** armed helicopter.

**holocaust.** (Also, H~) mass murder of Jews by Nazis 1939–45.

**home. 4.** ~**land,** (also) Bantustan.

**hover. 3.** ~**port,** place for arrival and departure of hovercraft.

**hȳpĕrä'ctĭve** a. (Of person) morbidly over-active. [HYPER-]

**index. 1.** ~**-linked,** calculated in accordance with price index.

**industrial.** ~ **action,** strike etc. by employees in dispute with employer.

**inner. 1.** ~ **city,** overcrowded central part of city.

**interfer|e.** ~**ŏn** n., protein inhibiting development of virus in cell.

**job¹. 3.** || ~'**centre,** State office showing information about available jobs.

**jump. 2.** ~**-leads,** device for re-charging battery from another.

**keg.** ~ **beer** (supplied from metal container).

**knee.** ~'**capping,** shooting in legs as punishment; ~**s-up,** (colloq.) lively party with dancing.

**labour. 1.** ~ **camp,** place where prisoners must work as labourers.

**launder.** (Also) transfer (funds) so as to conceal their illegal origin.

**legionnaire.** ~**s' disease,** form of pneumonia, often fatal. [first identified after outbreak at meeting of American Legion 1976]

**liquid. 1.** ~ **crystal,** liquid in state approaching that of crystalline solid.

**look. 3.** *~**-alike,** person or thing closely resembling another.

**ma'chō** (mah'-) n. (pl. ~**s**) & a. (Man) asserting and displaying masculine vigour. [Sp., = male]

**martial.** ~ **arts,** fighting sports such as karate.

**melt.** ~'**down,** melting of (and consequent damage to) structure, e.g. overheated core of nuclear reactor.

**micro-.** ~**chip,** tiny piece of

semiconductor containing many electrical circuits; ∼**processor,** very small computer; ∼**wave oven** (heating food quickly by means of microwaves).

**middle. 1.** ∼ **school** (for 9- to 13--year-olds).

**minimum.** ∼ **lending rate,** announced minimum percentage for bill-discounting by central bank.

**mole².** (Also, colloq.) spy established deep within an organization; betrayer of confidential information.

**mountain.** (Also) large surplus stock of commodity.

**music.** ∼ **centre,** equipment combining radio, record-player, and tape-recorder.

**Mū′zăk** n. (System for transmitting) recorded music for playing in public place. [P]

**national. 1.** N∼ **Front,** U.K. organization with extreme views on immigration etc.

**no¹. 1. no-go′,** that cannot be entered (because of barricade, prohibition, etc.). **2. no can do,** (colloq.) I cannot do it.

**nut. 4.** ∼′**ter** n., (sl.) crazy person.

***Ostpolitik*** (ŏstpŏlĭtē′k) n. Politics of a Eur. country in relation to Communist countries. [G (*ost* east)]

\***păstra′mĭ** (-ah -) n. Seasoned smoked beef. [Yiddish]

**photo-. -fit,** picture like Identikit but made from photographs not drawings.

**plea.** ∼ **bargaining,** agreeing to drop a charge or give a lenient sentence in exchange for plea of 'guilty' on another charge.

**pole¹.** ∼ **position,** most favourable position at start of motor race [orig. next to fence].

**poly-.** ∼**unsa′turated,** (of fat or oil) not tending to form cholesterol.

**porridge.** (Also, sl.) imprisonment.

**poverty.** ∼ **trap,** inability to profit from increased pay, because of consequent loss of benefits given by the State.

**punk.** ∼ **rock,** simple vigorous but unpolished rock music.

**quă′ngō** (-nggō) n. (*pl.* ∼s). Semi--public body with some support

from Government. [*quasi-non-*governmental *o*rganization]

**quorum. quŏr′ate** a., constituting a quorum.

**rabbit. 2.** ∼ **on,** (sl.) talk pointlessly.

**Răstafăr′ian** a. & n. (Member) of Jamaican sect regarding Blacks as a chosen people. [*Ras Tafari*, title of Ethiopian emperor]

**Rĭ′chter** (-k-) n. ∼ **scale** (for stating magnitude of earthquakes). [person]

**riot.** ∼ **shield** (for use by police etc. in dealing with riots).

**self-.** ∼**ca′tering,** occupying rented accommodation on holiday etc. but providing own food.

**single. 1.** ∼ **parent** (bringing up family in absence of spouse).

**spoil. 1.** ∼′**er** n., device on vehicle to prevent it from being lifted off road at speed.

**tail¹. 3.** ∼**back,** queue of traffic unable to proceed freely.

**tă′ndoori** n. (Ind.) Food cooked over charcoal in clay oven. [Hind.]

**tax. 1.** ∼′**man,** inspector or collector of taxes.

**test¹. 3.** ∼ **drive** (to determine qualities of motor vehicle that one may buy).

**tug. 2.** ∼ **of love,** (colloq.) dispute over which member of family should be guardian of child.

**wănk** n., & v.i. (vulg.) (Engage in) masturbation; ∼′**er** n., (also) contemptible person. [orig. unkn.]

**welsh².** (Also) evade an obligation; ∼ **on,** fail to keep promise to (person), fail to act according to (obligation).

**wheel. 1.** ∼′**ies** (-ĭz) n., (colloq.) riding bicycle with one wheel off ground.

**word. 3.** ∼ **processor,** device for storing text entered from keyboard, incorporating corrections, and providing print-out.

**workahŏ′lic** (wĕrka-h-) n. Person who works compulsively. [WORK, ALCOHOLIC]

**yellow. 4.** ∼ **lines** (painted on road beside pavement to indicate restriction on parking of vehicles).

**zero. 1.** ∼**-rated,** on which no value-added tax is charged.

# NOTES

**NOTES**

**NOTES**

**NOTES**

**NOTES**

**NOTES**

**NOTES**